...to reality

If the Nautilus™ is a dream, here is the reality. B&W's Nautilus™801, flagship of a stunning new range, fuses the innovative Nautilus™ tube technology with a series of industry firsts: Fixed Suspension Transducer™, Kevlar® drive units, Matrix® cabinet bracing and Flowport™ technology. The result is an unprecedented purity of sound. The reason FMI's Abbey Road studios, along with the biggest and best in the recording industry, are now upgrading to the Nautilus™801. Listen and you'll see – at your nearest authorised Nautilus™ 800 Series dealer. For more information please contact B&W: 01903 750 750 or visit our website http://www.bwspeakers.com

LISTEN AND YOU'LL SEE

Alan Parsons is highly regarded in the recording industry. Principal engineer on Pink Floyd's 'Dark Side of the Moon', and producer of Al Stewart's 'Year of the Cat', Alan has worked with Paul McCartney, and has ten Grammy award nominations to his name. Himself a dedicated musician (The Alan Parsons Project), the former chief recording engineer at EMI's Abbey Road Studios says of the new loudspeakers: "The Nautilus™800 Series will undoubtedly make a major impact on the professional recording world, and influence loudspeaker technology well into the next millennium."

B&W

LISTEN AND YOU'LL SEE

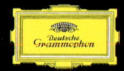

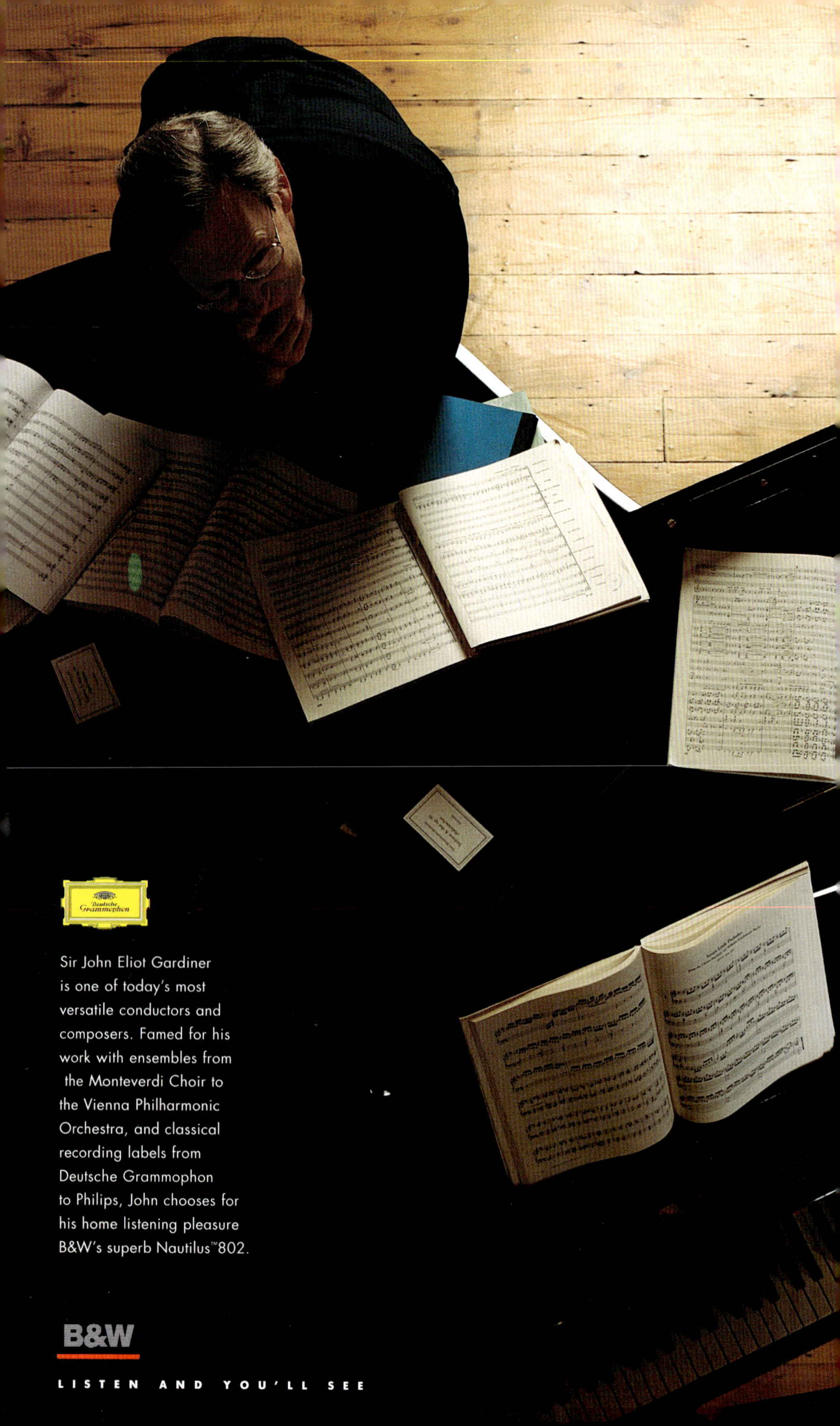
Deutsche Grammophon
Sir John Eliot Gardiner is one of today's most versatile conductors and composers. Famed for his work with ensembles from the Monteverdi Choir to the Vienna Philharmonic Orchestra, and classical recording labels from Deutsche Grammophon to Philips, John chooses for his home listening pleasure B&W's superb Nautilus™802.
B&W
LISTEN AND YOU'LL SEE

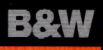

Sir John Eliot Gardiner, Composer

B&W Nautilus™ 802

Luz Vargas is a noted
Colombian architect who
now lives in London's
Notting Hill. Music is
as much a part of
her background as her
chosen profession; and
Luz understands the
importance of combining
design aesthetics with
musical performance.
Her choice is the
Nautilus™805 – the
perfect mix of
sculptural elegance
and audio power.

B&W

LISTEN AND YOU'LL SEE

Luz Vargas, Architect

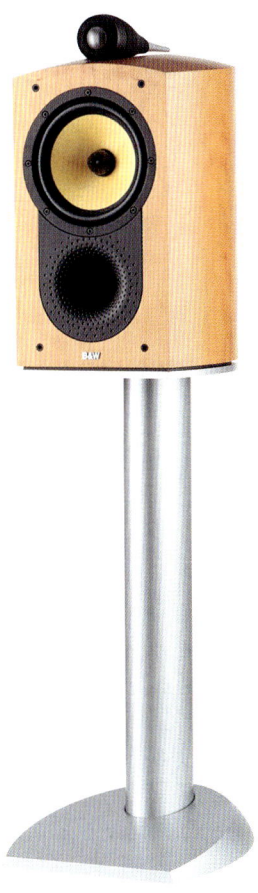

B&W Nautilus™*805*

Nautilus™ 800 Series

Nautilus™ 801

A new benchmark in loudspeaker design, the Nautilus™801 features B&W's radical Nautilus technology for tweeter and mid-range drivers. This professional studio monitor unleashes a titanic power, whilst retaining all the subtle dynamics so vital to the world's best recordings.

Nautilus™ 802

The Nautilus™802 offers all the virtues of B&W's flagship Nautilus™801 in a slimmer, curved cabinet. Performance is beyond question, delivering audio response that is as pure as it is powerful.

Nautilus™ 803

A floorstander that will grace any home with its purposeful beauty. Featuring Nautilus tweeter technology, the Nautilus™803 produces a class leading purity of sound which makes it ideal for any audiophile set-up or high-end surround sound.

Nautilus™ 805

Beautifully crafted and engineered to the same audiophile standards as the rest of the range, the Nautilus™805 is a compact monitor that will enhance any hi-fi or surround sound system. It can easily be used on a bookshelf or on the optional stand featured.

For more information contact
B&W Loudspeakers (UK) Ltd on: 01903 750 750
or visit our website http://www.bwspeakers.com

B&W

LISTEN AND YOU'LL SEE

Gramophone
Classical
Good CD Guide
2000

Gramophone magazine, founded by the novelist and writer Compton Mackenzie and the broadcaster Christopher Stone, has been published monthly since 1923. As one of the first magazines devoted to the discussion of recorded music, *Gramophone* has maintained its position as the most informed and influential publication of its kind. Calling on the wealth of talent of a panel of the world's leading writers on music, *Gramophone* is the record collector's bible and it is from these writers and in the tradition of *Gramophone* that this book is published. Each month the magazine carries over 200 reviews of music across a wide spectrum and talks to the leading performers of the day. We are once again delighted to be publishing the ***Good CD Guide*** in association with a fellow British company, B&W Loudspeakers, whose dedication to producing fine loudspeakers closely matches the ideals of *Gramophone* itself: expertise drawing on experience, consistency and an awareness of the requirements of the consumer.

Published by

Gramophone Publications Limited
135 Greenford Road
Sudbury Hill, Harrow
Middlesex HA1 3YD
Great Britain

© **Gramophone Publications Limited 1999**

UK ISBN 1-902274-05-9

US ISBN 1-902274-06-7

Recording companies reserve the right to withdraw any Compact Disc without giving prior notice, and although every effort is made to obtain the latest information for inclusion in this book, no guarantee can be given that all the discs listed are immediately available. Any difficulties should be referred to the issuing company concerned. When ordering, purchasers are advised to quote all the relevant information in addition to the disc numbers. The publishers cannot accept responsibility for the consequences of any error.

Sales and distribution

North America

Music Sales Corporation
257 Park Avenue South
New York, NY 10010 USA
Telephone (212) 254 2100
Fax (212) 254 2013

Record Trade (excluding North America)

Gramophone Publications Limited
135 Greenford Road
Sudbury Hill, Harrow
Middlesex HA1 3YD, Great Britain
Telephone +44 (0)181-422 4562
Fax +44 (0)181-869 8404

UK and Rest of World Book Trade

Music Sales
8/9 Frith Street
London W1V 5TZ, Great Britain
Telephone +44 (0)171-434 0066
Fax +44 (0)171-734 2246

Editor	**Máire Taylor**
Sub-editor	**Kathryn Wolfendale**
Editorial Assistants	**Abigail Frymann**
	Kathryn Maloney
Production	**Dermot Jones**

Contributors

**Andrew Achenbach · Nicholas Anderson
Mary Berry · Alan Blyth · Joan Chissell
Robert Cowan · Peter Dickinson
Duncan Druce · John Duarte
Adrian Edwards · Richard T. Fairman
David Fallows · David J. Fanning
Iain Fenlon · Hilary Finch · Fabrice Fitch
Jonathan Freeman-Attwood
Edward Greenfield · David S. Gutman
Stephen Johnson · Lindsay Kemp
Tess Knighton · Andrew Lamb
Robert Layton · Ivan March · Ivan Moody
Bryce Morrison · Patrick O'Connor
Michael Oliver · Richard Osborne
Tim Parry · Stephen Plaistow
Nicholas Rast · Guy Rickards
Marc Rochester · Julie-Anne Sadie
Stanley Sadie · Lionel Salter
Alan Sanders · Edward Seckerson
Robert Seeley · John Steane
Michael Stewart · Jonathan Swain
John Warrack · Arnold Whittall
Richard Wigmore**

Printed in England by William Clowes Limited,
Beccles, Suffolk NR34 9QE

Contents

Suggested Basic Library

10 CELLO CONCERTOS

Britten Cello Symphony
Dvořák Cello Concerto
Elgar Cello Concerto
Haydn Cello Concerto in C major
Prokofiev Symphony-Concerto
Saint-Saëns Cello Concerto No. 1
Schumann Cello Concerto
Shostakovich Cello Concerto No. 1
Tavener The Protecting Veil
Walton Cello Concerto

10 PIANO CONCERTOS

Beethoven Piano Concerto No. 4
Brahms Piano Concerto No. 1
Gershwin Rhapsody in Blue
Grieg Piano Concerto
Mozart Piano Concerto No. 2, K467
Prokofiev Piano Concerto No. 3
Rachmaninov Piano Concerto No. 3
Schumann Piano Concerto
Shostakovich Piano Concerto No. 2
Tchaikovsky Piano Concerto No. 1

10 VIOLIN CONCERTOS

Barber Violin Concerto
Bartók Violin Concerto No. 2
Beethoven Violin Concerto
Brahms Violin Concerto
Bruch Violin Concerto No. 1
Elgar Violin Concerto
Mendelssohn Violin Concerto
Mozart Violin Concerto No. 5
Sibelius Violin Concerto
Tchaikovsky Violin Concerto

10 WIND AND BRASS CONCERTOS

Copland Clarinet Concerto
Haydn Trumpet Concerto
Hindemith Horn Concerto
Hummel Trumpet Concerto
Mozart Clarinet Concerto
Mozart Horn Concerto No. 4
Nielsen Clarinet Concerto
R. Strauss Horn Concerto No. 1
Stravinsky Ebony Concerto
Weber Clarinet Concerto No. 1 in F minor

TEN CONCERTOS FOR MULTIPLE INSTRUMENTS

Vivaldi Concerto in G minor, RV577
Haydn Sinfonia concertante in
B flat major for violin, cello, oboe,
bassoon and orchestra

Bach Concerto for two violins
Mozart Sinfonia concertante for
violin and viola
Mozart Concerto for two pianos
Beethoven Concerto for violin,
cello and piano (Triple Concerto)
Brahms Concerto for violin and cello
(Double Concerto)
Poulenc Concerto for two pianos
Bruch Concerto for clarinet and viola
in E minor, Op. 88
Schnittke Concerto grosso No. 1 for
two violins, strings, harpsichord
and piano

20 SYMPHONIES

Beethoven Symphony No. 3, *Eroica*
Berlioz Symphonie fantastique
Bruckner Symphony No. 8
Copland Symphony No. 3
Dvořák Symphony No. 9,
From the New World
Elgar Symphony No. 2
Franck Symphony
Haydn Symphony No. 104, *London*
Mahler Symphony No. 5
Mendelssohn Symphony No. 4, *Italian*
Mozart Symphony No. 41, *Jupiter*
Prokofiev Symphony No. 5
Rachmaninov Symphony No. 2
Schubert Symphony No. 8, *Unfinished*
Schumann Symphony No. 3, *Rhenish*
Shostakovich Symphony No. 10
Sibelius Symphony No. 5
Tchaikovsky Symphony No. 6, *Pathétique*
Vaughan Williams Symphony No. 5
Walton Symphony No. 1

TEN BALLETS

Adam Giselle
Bartók The Miraculous Mandarin
Copland Appalachian Spring
Debussy Jeux
Poulenc Les biches
Prokofiev Romeo and Juliet
Rossini/Respighi Boutique fantasque
Stravinsky The Rite of Spring
Tchaikovsky The Sleeping Beauty
Tchaikovsky The Nutcracker

TEN TONE-POEMS

Debussy La mer
Dukas L'Apprenti sorcier
Elgar Falstaff
Gershwin An American in Paris

Liszt Mazeppa
Respighi Roman Trilogy
Sibelius Tapiola
Smetana Ma vlast
R. Strauss Also sprach Zarathustra
Tchaikovksy Romeo and Juliet

TEN STRING QUARTETS

Bartók String Quartet No. 6
Borodin String Quartet No. 2
Beethoven String Quartet in B flat major,
Op. 130 with *Grosse Fuge*, Op. 133
Debussy String Quartet
Dvořák String Quartet in F major, *American*
Haydn String Quartet in C major, Op. 76
No. 3, *Emperor*
Mozart String Quartet in C major, K465,
Dissonance
Ravel String Quartet
Schubert String Quartet in D minor, D804,
Death and the Maiden
Shostakovich String Quartet No. 10

TEN QUINTETS

Brahms Clarinet Quintet
Brahms Piano Quintet
Dvořák Piano Quintet in A major, B155
Mozart Clarinet Quintet
Mozart String Quintet in G minor
Nielsen Wind Quintet
Schubert Piano Quintet, *Trout*
Schubert String Quintet
Schumann Piano Quintet
Shostakovich Piano Quintet

TEN TRIOS

Beethoven Piano Trio in B flat major, Op. 97,
Archduke
Brahms Piano Trio No. 2 in C major,
Op. 87
Haydn Piano Trio in G major, HobXV/25,
Gipsy
Mendelssohn Piano Trio No. 1 in D minor
Mozart Kegelstatt Trio for piano,
clarinet/violin and viola
Tchaikovsky Piano Trio
Ravel Piano Trio
Schubert Piano Trio No. 2 in E flat major,
D929
Shostakovich Piano Trio No. 2 in E minor,
Op. 67
Smetana Piano Trio

TEN SETS OF VARIATIONS

Bach Goldberg Variations (keyboard)
Beethoven 32 Variations on an Original
Theme in C major on a Waltz by Diabelli (piano)

Beethoven 7 Variations on 'Bei männern,
welche Liebe fühlen' from Mozart's
Die Zauberflöte (cello and piano)
Brahms Variations on a Theme of Haydn,
St Antoni (orchestra)
Brahms Variations on a Theme of
Paganini (piano)
Dohnányi Variations on a Nursery Theme
(piano and orchestra)
Elgar Variations on an Original Theme,
Enigma (orchestra)
Rachmaninov Variations on a theme of
Corelli (piano)
Schoenberg Variations for Orchestra
Tchaikovsky Variations on a
Rococo Theme in A major (cello
and orchestra)

TEN PIANO SONATAS

Barber Piano Sonata, Op. 20
Beethoven Piano Sonata No. 23 in F minor,
Op. 57, *Appassionata*
Brahms Piano Sonata No. 3 in F minor
Chopin Piano Sonata No. 2,
Funeral March
Haydn Piano Sonata E flat major,
HobXVI/52
Liszt Piano Sonata
Mozart Piano Sonata No. 11 in A major,
K331
Prokofiev Piano Sonata No. 7
Rachmaninov Piano Sonata No. 2
Schubert Piano Sonata in B flat major,
D960

TEN SONATAS

Bartók Solo Violin Sonata
Beethoven Violin Sonata in A major,
Op. 47, *Kreutzer*
Brahms Cello Sonata No. 2 in F major, Op. 99
Debussy Violin Sonata
Fauré Violin Sonata No. 2
Franck Violin Sonata
Janáček Violin Sonata
Kodály Solo Cello Sonata
Schubert Sonata for Arpeggione
in A minor, D821
Shostakovich Cello Sonata

TEN SONGS-CYCLES

Beethoven An die ferne Geliebte
Berlioz Les nuits d'été
Britten Serenade for tenor, horn and strings
Mahler Kindertotenlieder
Mussorgsky Songs and Dances of Death
Poulenc Tel jour, telle nuit
Ravel Schéhérazade
Schubert Winterreise
Schumann Dichterliebe
Shostakovich Suite on Verses of
Michelangelo

Suggested Basic Library

TEN MASSES

Bach Mass in B minor
Beethoven Missa solemnis
Berlioz Grande Messe des Morts
Bruckner Mass in F minor
Brahms German Requiem
Fauré Requiem
Haydn Nelson Mass
Mozart Requiem Mass
Palestrina Missa Papae Marcelli
Verdi Messa da Requiem

TEN ORATORIOS

Bach St Matthew Passion
Berlioz L'enfance du Christ
Britten War Requiem
Elgar The Dream of Gerontius
Handel Messiah
Haydn The Creation
Mendelssohn Elijah
Prokofiev Alexander Nevsky
Tippett A Child of our Time
Walton Belshazzar's Feast

20 OPERAS

Beethoven Fidelio
Bellini Norma
Berg Wozzeck
Bizet Carmen
Britten Peter Grimes
Debussy Pelléas et Mélisande
Donizetti Lucia di Lammermoor
Gluck Orfeo ed Euridice
Handel Giulio Cesare
Janáček The Cunning Little Vixen
Leoncavallo Pagliacci
Monteverdi L'Incoronazione di Poppea
Mozart Le nozze di Figaro
Mussorgsky Boris Godunov
Puccini La boheme
Rossini Il barbiere di Siviglia
R. Strauss Elektra
Tchaikovsky Eugene Onegin
Verdi La traviata
Wagner Tristan und Isolde

Using the Guide

The presentation and design of this Guide is similar to that of its parent publication, *Gramophone*. Reviews of works generally appear in the following sequence: Orchestral, Chamber, Instrumental, Choral and Operatic (for ease of use, operas appear in alphabetical, as opposed to chronological, order). This edition has a new rating system of Recommended Recordings, indicated by the use of a symbol (see below). The rating is applied to releases which our reviewers consider to be recordings of particular distinction, having attained or deserving to attain classic status. Where there is more than one, or multiple reviews, of the same repertoire, we have indicated our top choice with the same symbol.

Generally, where more than three composers are represented on a single disc, the review appears in the Collections section which starts on page 1111 (the Index to Reviews is a quick route to the works reviewed in this section).

The title for each review contains the following information: Composer(s), work(s), artist(s), record company or label, price range, disc number and recording date, where available. *Gramophone* Award-winning discs from 1977 to 1998 are clearly indicated. The text within the brackets indicates the number of discs (if there is more than one), timing and mode of recording (AAD/ADD/DDD denote analogue or digital stages in the recording/editing or mixing/mastering or transcription processes in CD manufacture). The other symbols used in the titles are explained below.

Key to symbols

ⓕ   Full price £10 and over
Ⓜ   Medium price £7-£9·99
Ⓑ   Bargain price £5-£6·99
Ⓢ   Super bargain price £4·99 and below

🄷   denotes a Historic recording and generally applies to pre-1960 recordings. It can also be an indication that the recording quality may not be up to the highest standards.

🄿   denotes recordings where period instruments are used.

🅂   denotes those recordings which our listening panel has singled out as being particularly notable for their outstanding sound quality

🄴   *Gramophone* *Editor's choice* – in every issue of *Gramophone* ten outstanding discs are selected from the month's reviews.

🆁🆁   Where there is more than one, or multiple reviews, of the same repertoire, this symbol indicates our top choice. The rating is also applied to releases which have attained or deserve to attain classic status.

Although every effort is made to obtain the latest information for inclusion in this book, no guarantee can be given that all the discs listed are immediately available. Any queries concerning availability should be referred to the issuing company concerned. When ordering, purchasers are advised to quote all the relevant information in addition to the disc numbers.

Abbreviations

aas	all available separately	narr	narrator
alto	countertenor/male alto	oas	only available separately
anon.	anonymous	ob	oboe
arr	arranged	Op.	opus
attrib.	attributed	orig.	original
b	born	org	organ
bar	baritone	perc	percussion
bass-bar	bass-baritone	pf	piano
bn	bassoon	picc	piccolo
c	circa (about)	pub.	publisher/published
cl	clarinet	rec	recorder
clav	clavichord	rec.	recorded (date)
cont	continuo	rev.	revised
contr	contralto	sax	saxophone
cor ang	cor anglais	sngr	singer
cpsr	composer	sop	soprano
cpte(d)	complete(d)	spkr	speaker
d	died	stg	string
db	double bass	synth	synthesizer
dig pf	digital piano	tbn	trombone
dir	director	ten	tenor
ed.	edited (by)/edition	timp	timpani
exc	excerpt	tpt	trumpet
fl	flute	trad.	traditional
fl	flourished	trans.	transcribed
fp	fortepiano	treb	treble
gtr	guitar	va	viola
harm	harmonium	va da gamba	viola da gamba
hn	horn	vars.	variations
hp	harp	vc	cello
hpd	harpsichord	vib	vibraphone
keybd	keyboard	vn	violin
lte	lute	voc	vocal/vocalist
mez	mezzo-soprano	wds	words
mndl	mandolin		

The Reviews

Adolphe Adam

Le corsaire.
English Chamber Orchestra / Richard Bonynge.
Decca 430 286-2DH2 (two discs: 131 minutes: DDD). Recorded 1990. Ⓕ

Adam's *Le corsaire* was first heard in Paris during 1856 and was his last ballet score. Although eclipsed by the popularity of *Giselle*, it is superbly crafted and deserves to be more generally recognized. Predictably, the plot is convoluted, and occasionally absurd, but the approval of Parisian audiences secured 43 performances during 1856 alone. Richard Bonynge's realization is excellent in every respect, and includes later additions by Léo Delibes for the revival of 1867. Stylistically, his 'Pas de fleurs' *divertissement*, interpolated into the final act, hardly reveals an alien hand at work, and could easily pass as part of Adam's original score. The highlights are the splendid bacchanal of the pirate Conrad and his crew, and the 'Pas des éventails' from scene 2. The Second Act takes place at the Pasha's palace in Adrianople, as Conrad and his men, now disguised as pilgrims, plan to rescue the beautiful Medora from the harem. Due to the treachery of Conrad's henchman Birbanto, he is taken prisoner, and the final act recounts his efforts to escape, returning to his ship with Medora. Arguably the finest music is that portraying the lovers' premature rejoicing at their freedom, and the depiction of the storm which leaves them stranded together upon a rock following the destruction of the ship, reaching safety just as the final curtain falls. Bonynge draws the diverse threads of the score together with a degree of expertise acquired from a lifetime of involvement with music of this nature, enabling the listener to follow the plot without difficulty. He obtains notably superior playing throughout from the English Chamber Orchestra.

Giselle (complete).
Royal Opera House Orchestra, Covent Garden / Richard Bonynge.
Double Decca 452 185-2DF2 (two discs: 126 minutes: DDD). Recorded 1986. Ⓜ 🆁🆁

Adam's celebrated score has come in for some harsh words from the more superior music critics, but the public has rightly taken it to its collective heart for its atmospheric writing and its tender and haunting themes. The text used for this recording is Adam's complete original score, and Bonynge's desire to re-record it lies in matters of performance and interpretation. (His previous recording, also for Decca, was made with the Monte-Carlo Opera Orchestra in 1970.) Reviews of the previous version, on its original appearance and reissue, spoke of the limitations of the woodwind and brass and suggested that a little more rehearsal time might have brought benefits. Here the musicians of the Royal Opera House bring both a confidence of attack and a refinement that are not quite achieved by the Monte-Carlo players. Moreover, that same extra confidence of attack is displayed by Bonynge himself. Each of the discs of this issue is between one-and-a-half and two minutes longer than the older, but within that overall expansion the dramatic moments are more vigorously attacked and the slower ones more lovingly caressed – always to considerable effect. Add recorded sound that is warmer and more spacious, and there is no hesitation in acknowledging the superiority of this version over the old. There is no doubt that this represents the first-choice version of Adam's complete score.

Giselle (complete).
Slovak Radio Symphony Orchestra / Andrew Mogrelia.
Naxos 8 550755/6 (two discs: 114 minutes: DDD). Recorded 1994. Ⓢ

Naxos also offers the complete version of *Giselle* to challenge comparison with Bonynge's recording. Give or take some seeming slight variances in the Act finales, both offer essentially the same text, complete with traditional interpolations. In the ultimate comparison there can be little doubt that Bonynge gives more point to the contrasts in the score, and that the playing of the Covent Garden orchestra and Decca's recorded sound give just the edge over this set. Yet this is on any count a highly enjoyable alternative, with some especially rewarding passages such as the Act 1 'Pas seul'; many collectors will be more than happy to settle for it as a record of the complete text, and at super-bargain price too.

Giselle (abridged).
Royal Opera House Orchestra, Covent Garden / Mark Ermler.
Royal Opera House Records ROH007 (74 minutes: DDD). Recorded 1993. Ⓕ

The Royal Opera House, Covent Garden series of recordings includes an impressive collection of the classic popular ballet scores and this is well up to its usual standards. Mark Ermler brings a Bolshoi Ballet director's experience to bear on the score, and with the Royal Opera House Orchestra likewise playing music it has in its blood the results are consistently impressive. The brass are especially good in the important hunting music in Act 1 and the *galop* towards the end of the same Act goes off in lively fashion. Bradley Creswick's solo violin and the orchestra's woodwind section are shown to especially good effect in the Apparition and Scene of Myrthe in Act 2. Note, though, that the version of the score used here is that of Henri Busser, which means that there are some deviations of content and orchestration from other recordings. However, no ballet enthusiast should have any reason to be disappointed with this well-filled, opulently recorded and well-documented disc.

Le toréador.
Michel Trempont *bar* Don Belflor; **Sumi Jo** *sop* Coraline; **John Aler** *ten* Tracolin;
Welsh National Opera Orchestra / Richard Bonynge.
Decca 455 664-2DHO (77 minutes: DDD). Notes, text and translation included. Recorded 1996. Ⓕ

Richard Bonynge's ability to persuade Decca to record out-of-the-way nineteenth-century French stage works has been to our repeated benefit over the past 40 years. Yet few of the results have been more welcome than this delightful operatic soufflé. Despite the title, there is little specifically Spanish about the piece beyond the Barcelona setting and the cuckolded elderly husband who just happens to have been a toreador. The love interest is between the former opera-singer wife and her flautist admirer, and it is the important contribution of the flute (almost a fourth character, and admirably played by Jonathan Burgess) that accounts for much of the aforementioned incidental music. The admirer identifies himself by means of assorted operatic airs and grades the seriousness of the husband's infidelities by whether he plays a fandango or a cachucha. The score's most familiar number is a set of variations on *Ah, vous dirai-je, maman* (*Twinkle, twinkle, little star*, if you like); but there is much else that brings out Sumi Jo's crystal-clear, effortless coloratura to marvellous effect, as well as showing off John Aler's ardent, elegant tenor and Michel Trempont's well-practised comic baritone. This is a delightful recording.

John Adams

American 1947

Violin Concerto[a]. Shaker Loops[b].
Gidon Kremer *vn*
[a]**London Symphony Orchestra / Kent Nagano**; [b]**Orchestra of St Luke's / John Adams.**
Nonesuch 7559-79360-2 (59 minutes: DDD). Recorded 1995. Ⓕ

This superb CD displays two very different aspects of Adams's evolving art, *Shaker Loops* dancing to a minimalist pulse, lean, fidgety and cleverly designed, and the altogether deeper, more intimate Violin Concerto. The concerto brings Berg to mind – not his Violin Concerto, but *Wozzeck*, Act 3 scene 4, where an eerie 'drainage' effect symbolizes Wozzeck's drowning beneath a blood-red moon. This aural fluidity is common to both works (the scoring is similar, too), although Adams keeps up the momentum for the entire duration of his long first movement, shifting colours constantly until a brief solo passage marks a slowing down in preparation for the ensuing Chaconne. Adams floats his mysterious textures above a quietly undulating accompaniment. The Sibelius of *Tapiola* seems to hover somewhere around five minutes into the first movement (just as parts of *Shaker Loops* suggest an up-tempo *Lemminkäinen*) and the concerto ends with a fast, dancing Toccata. In the hands of Gidon Kremer – whose sinewy, lightly-bowed tone suits the piece perfectly – it is a compelling monologue. *Shaker Loops* is earlier, easier and rather less durable than the Violin Concerto. It started life as a string quartet (*Wavemaker*), then – beyond drastic recomposition – filled out to a septet which, suitably augmented, is how we hear it here. The term 'Shaker' refers to the frenzied dancing of a religious sect and Adams's four-part structure sets up a varied roster of tempos and textures. There have been other recordings of the work, but this is surely the best – agile, precise and extremely well balanced. The sound is excellent.

Chamber Symphony. Grand Pianola Music.
London Sinfonietta / John Adams.
Nonesuch 7559-79219-2 (53 minutes: DDD). Recorded 1993. Ⓕ

A loud bash on an old tin can, and they're off – yelping, tapping, chattering, chasing to and fro, like a barn-yard full of loopy professors. And to think that the prime mover for John Adams's madcap Chamber Symphony (1992) was its 'eponymous predecessor', Schoenberg's Op. 9. Even the instrumentation is similar, save that Adams has added synthesizer, jazz-style percussion, trumpet and trombone. It's a raw piece (Adams's minimal directions include 'coarse', 'intense', 'staccatissimo!'), with the merest suggestion of repose in the central 'Aria with Walking Brass' (initially sounding like a send-up of Bruckner's Fifth) and a 'Roadrunner' finale that includes a manic violin cadenza followed by an ingenious passage where synthesizer, bass clarinet, bassoon and horn crank up for the panic-stricken home straight. Granted, it might not be exactly rich in tunes (this is no New Age musical roller-coaster), but it is maddeningly moreish, a dazzling, high-speed comedy where all the characters are temporarily on holiday from their more serious selves. In complete contrast, the far gentler *Grand Pianola Music* (1971) provides a relatively 'easy' listen, what with its smooth-driving motor rhythms, sensual female voices, warming waves of brass tone and occasional bouts of thumping excitement. Clichés there certainly are, especially the 'big tune' that crowns the third section, 'On the Dominant Divide', and which is probably most effective when, towards the end of the work, it slims down to basic harmonic constituents. *Grand Pianola Music* is a sort of aural truck ride, with smooth tarmac, plenty of scenic incident, a glowing sunset on the far horizon and a closing cadence that recalls – rather unexpectedly – Sibelius. Both performances serve their respective works well. The recordings are superb.

Adams El Dorado.
Busoni Berceuse élégiaque, Op. 42 (arr. Adams)[a].
Liszt La lugubre gondola, S200 No. 1 (arr. Adams)[a].
Hallé Orchestra / Kent Nagano; [a]London Sinfonietta / John Adams.
Nonesuch 7559-79359-2 (47 minutes: DDD). Recorded 1993.   ⓕ **E**

El Dorado is a dramatic commentary on irreconcilable opposites: chromaticism versus pure modalities, malignancy versus rude health, and man's destructive impulses versus the unspoiled glory of unpopulated landscapes. Adams claims to have composed the second movement, 'Soledades' – the one 'without man' – in seven days. Indeed, the whole work appeared to him as a sort of apparition, 'alarmingly complete in its details, even before I wrote down a single sketch'. The first movement, 'A Dream of Gold' opens to sinister held chords, pensive shufflings and rising clouds of string tone. The last section charges forth like some maniacal spectre, racing out of control then stopping dead. By contrast, 'Soledades' weaves a delicate web of sound, at least initially, with unmistakably Sibelian undertones. While 'A Dream of Gold' suggests destructive intervention, 'Soledades' – which is no less exciting in its own way – is freer, brighter and lighter in tone. The ending, however, suggests a tranquil death.

The recording of *El Dorado* reproduces a dynamic sound curve. The performance itself is deft and well paced, very much on a par with Adams's own performances of his Busoni and Liszt arrangements. The *Berceuse élégiaque* is beautifully realized, with woodwinds breaking through the predominantly dark texture like rays of dying sunlight through a bank of cloud. The richly coloured orchestration of Liszt's late *La lugubre gondola* is in total contrast to other, more austere, readings. Adams rows Liszt's funeral gondola slowly and lovingly, using cellos and basses for oars. Winds and solo strings are used to sensitive effect and the playing is uniformly excellent.

Gnarly Buttons. John's Book of Alleged Dances.
Michael Collins *cl*
Kronos Quartet (David Harrington, John Sherba *vns* Hank Dutt *va* Joan Jeanrenaud *vc*)
London Sinfonietta / John Adams.
Nonesuch 7559-79465-2 (61 minutes: DDD). Recorded 1997.   ⓕ

It is fascinating to hear the way John Adams works the prepared piano into his *Book of Alleged Dances*. The original idea was to make a digitally sampled loop of the piano part which would then be triggered by one of the quartet members; but practical considerations necessitated recording the loops, which the quartet now performs live. *John's Book of Alleged Dances* (the equivocation in the title refers to dance steps that have yet to be invented) is prime-cut Adams, fidgety, tuneful, teeming with invention and all-but tactile in its aural variety. We start by following a streetcar from town to coast and back again, then visit 'Toot Nipple' with 'chainsaw triads on the cello'. There's a raw-edged 'Hoe-Down' for leader David Harrington, a 'Pavane' for cellist Joan Jeanrenaud and a doleful Habanera, 'a lament for a season without baseball' as Adams himself puts it. 'Hammer & Chisel' are contractor friends who construct to a knotty toccata; a slithery 'Alligator Escalator' employs reptilian harmonics and a chirpy 'Serenade' pays subtle homage to Beethoven and Schubert. These and more are kept on a high flame by the Kronos Quartet, whereas *Gnarly Buttons* (with oblique reference to walking sticks and Gertrude Stein) calls on the combined talents of Michael Collins and the London Sinfonietta. A more intense piece by far (rather less memorably, too), its dry but colourful demeanour occasionally recalls Schoenberg's similarly spice-flavoured Serenade. The first movement is based on a Protestant shape-note hymn; the second is a 'Mad-Cow' hoe-down (written for Adams's British friends and the principal point of speculative contact with the Schoenberg) and the third, a warming song with sure-fire 'hit' potential. Collins does Adams proud, and so does the London Sinfonietta. The recordings are first-rate.

Harmonielehre. The Chairman Dances.
Two Fanfares – Tromba lontana; Short Ride in a Fast Machine.
City of Birmingham Symphony Orchestra / Sir Simon Rattle.
EMI CDC5 55051-2 (62 minutes: DDD). Recorded 1993.   Ⓕ

Harmonielehre was inspired by a dream vision of a massive tanker that suddenly took flight, displaying a 'beautiful brownish-orange oxide on the bottom part of its hull'; the 'setting' was just off San Francisco Bay Bridge. 'Those pounding E minor chords are like a grinding of gears,' says John Adams of its violent, gunshot opening. Scored for a huge orchestra and structured in three contrasted sections, *Harmonielehre* is probably the nearest thing on offer to a minimalist symphony, and for that reason alone it could well appeal beyond the élite coterie of minimalist-fanciers. Rattle's recording has great heft and dynamic range, an informative balance and a vivid sense of aural perspective. The brass components of those opening chords have enormous weight and presence, and the ringing marimbas thereafter, a bright complexion. Adams's frequent requests for subtle tempo transitions are subtly honoured by the conductor. There are three fill-ups: the Copland-inspired *Short Ride in a Fast Machine* and *Tromba lontana*, and *The Chairman Dances*, a 'foxtrot for orchestra' that utilizes material from Adams's opera, *Nixon in China*. Rattle's view of Adams is recommended particularly to mainstream collectors who aren't yet sold on minimalism.

The Death of Klinghoffer.
Sanford Sylvan *bar* Leon Klinghoffer; **Stephanie Friedman** *mez* Omar; **James Maddalena** *bar* First Officer; **Thomas Hammons** *bar* First Officer; **Thomas Young** *sngr* Molqui; **Eugene Perry** *bar* Mamoud; **Sheila Nadler** *mez* Marilyn Klinghoffer;
London Opera Orchestra Chorus; Lyon Opera Orchestra / Kent Nagano.
Nonesuch 7559-79281-2 (two discs: 135 minutes: DDD). Notes and text included.
Recorded 1991.   Ⓕ

One wonders how many living composers would happily watch their scores lead a short life, relevant but finite. Not many; but John Adams might be one of them. First *Nixon in China*, then *The Death of Klinghoffer*: rarely before has a composer snatched subjects from yesterday's news and made operas out of them. They are works for instant consumption, for today rather than tomorrow. Admittedly themes of lasting significance lurk beneath this work's immediate surface: conflict between cultures and ideologies, rival claims to ancestral lands, human rights in general. Specifically, however, it takes us back no further than October 1985, when Palestinian terrorists hijacked the Italian cruise liner Achille Lauro, and murdered wheelchair-bound passenger Leon Klinghoffer. The opera guides us through those events, albeit in an oblique fashion. Whatever the long-term fate of the opera, Alice Goodman's libretto certainly deserves to be spared from falling into oblivion. It is eloquent and beautiful, compassionate and humanitarian, rich in imagery and spacious in its sentence-structure. Dialogue is virtually absent; it must surely rank as one of the least dramatic librettos ever devised. It is marvellous to read, but how can it possibly be the stuff of opera? Adams has been hard pressed to come up with a solution. If *The Death of Klinghoffer* finally disappoints, it is because the marriage of words and music is so fragile. For all that, the opera's musical language is firmly rooted in tradition, but it is doubtful if anyone will come away from *The Death of Klinghoffer* with a memorable lyric moment lodged in the mind. The recording uses the cast of the original production, and it contains no weak links. As one expects from Adams, the score has been superbly orchestrated, and it is done full justice by the Lyon Opera Orchestra. Least satisfactory is the chorus: Goodman entrusts it with her most purple passages, but little colour emerges from singing that is so carefully accurate and lifeless. (Listen to the opening Chorus of Exiled Palestinians and see what you can understand from it without turning to the booklet for help.)

Richard Addinsell   British 1904-1977

Film Music: Blithe Spirit – Prelude; Waltz. Encore – Miniature Overture. Gaslight – Prelude.
Parisienne – 1885. Southern Rhapsody. Waltz of the Toreadors – March; The General on Parade;
Waltz (all arr. Lane). Fire over England – Suite (arr. Zalva). Passionate Friends – Lover's Moon.
South Riding – Prelude (both arr. Isaacs). A Christmas Carol – Suite (arr. S. Bernstein).
WRNS March (arr. Douglas).
Robert Gibbs *vn* **Peter Lawson** *pf* **Royal Ballet Sinfonia / Kenneth Alwyn.**
ASV White Line CDWHL2115 (68 minutes: DDD). Recorded 1998.   Ⓜ

What delights this disc contains! Nobody should imagine that the *Warsaw Concerto* is all that is worth hearing from this fine composer. Addinsell obviously had an utterly natural feel for richly tuneful, romantic music in the very best tradition of British light music. The diverse subjects for which he was commissioned to provide music served to turn these gifts to contrasted musical styles, which together provide a rewardingly varied programme. The most immediately familiar music here for some readers will probably be the swaggering march and haunting waltz from the *Waltz of the Toreadors*. For others it may be the prelude and waltz from David Lean's film of *Blithe Spirit* or the suite from *A Christmas Carol*, starring Alistair Sim. Perennial favourites in this collection are the invigorating *WRNS March* (rewarding material for any military band), the delightfully mysterious prelude to the 1939 film of *Gaslight* and the waltz from the stage play *Parisienne*. This last has been given a splendid Glazunovian orchestration by compiler, producer, arranger and annotator Philip Lane, who again leaves us immensely in his debt, no less than conductor Kenneth Alwyn and the admirable Royal Ballet Sinfonia.

Thomas Adès British 1971

Arcadiana, Op. 12ᵃ. The Origin of the Harp, Op. 13ᵇ. Sonata da caccia, Op. 11ᶜ.
Living Toys, Op. 9ᵈ. Gefriolsae me, Op. 3bᵉ.
ᶜ**Michael Neisemann** *ob* ᶜ**Andrew Clark** *hn* ᶜ**Thomas Adès** *hpd*
ᵃ**Endellion Quartet** (Andrew Watkinson, Ralph de Souza *vns* Garfield Jackson *va*
David Waterman *vc*); ᵉ**King's College Choir, Cambridge / Stephen Cleobury;**
ᵇ**instrumental ensemble / Thomas Adès;** ᵈ**London Sinfonietta / Markus Stenz.**
EMI Debut CDZ5 72271-2 (64 minutes: DDD). Text and translation included. Recorded 1997.
Gramophone Award Winner 1998.   ⒷⒺ

This collection fully lives up to the excited expectations aroused by the first disc of Adès's music but does not suggest that he is yet at all ready to settle down into a predictable style. The five pieces here suggest a composer as delightedly surprised by his prodigal inventiveness as we are. *Arcadiana*, for example, is a seven-movement string quartet whose central and longest movement (four minutes) contains an extraordinary range of precisely imagined, highly original textures and yet in its penultimate section can settle to a serene and wonderfully beautiful *adagio* whose sound and mood can only be conveyed by the adjective 'Beethovenian'. Far more overtly, the engaging *Sonata da caccia* uses elements that are very directly derived from Couperin, but the sensibility is entirely modern, even when you strongly suspect that this or that phrase is a note-for-note quotation. However, as with Adès's first collection, his is an imagination that you can trust. *Living Toys* has a quite Birtwistle-like sense of ritual to it, though more lyrical, quite frequently with a tangible jazz element. *The Origin of the Harp* is a dark, dramatic chamber tone-poem. *Gefriolsae me*, for male voices and organ, is a brief but impressive motet to Middle English words. All five pieces are finely performed, all are further evidence of a rich, still developing but clearly exceptional talent. *Arcadiana*, with its exquisite textures and sheer melodic richness, is perhaps Adès's finest achievement so far, a work constantly aware of the musical past (including the string quartet's past) but renewing that past with astonishing freshness.

Catch, Op. 4. Darknesse visible. Still sorrowing, Op. 7. Under Hamelin Hill, Op. 6. Five Eliot
Landscapes, Op. 1. Traced overhead, Op. 15. Life story, Op. 8b.
Valdine Anderson, Mary Carewe *sops* **Lynsey Marsh** *cl* **Anthony Marwood** *vn*
Louise Hopkins *vc* **Thomas Adès** *pf/org* **David Goode, Stephen Farr** *orgs*
EMI Debut CDZ5 69699-2 (77 minutes: DDD). Texts included. Recorded 1996.   ⒷⒺ

Adès not only has the gift of seizing your attention with strange but ravishingly beautiful sonorities and then holding it with entrancingly mysterious inventions that allure the ear, he has the much rarer quality of inspiring utter confidence. His style cannot be defined by simply describing any one of these pieces. Each solves a new problem or investigates a new scenario with such adroitness and completeness that each work seems a quite new and delightful adventure. In *Still sorrowing* the starting point is a piano whose central register is muted with a strip of plastic adhesive. The effect on those pitches is obvious: they are dulled to a sort of subdued drumming, but by observing the new light that this casts on the un-damped upper and lower registers Adès – this is not too much of an exaggeration – invents an entirely new and alluring instrument, or rather three of them: a glittering, coruscating 'treble piano', a tolling, gently pounding 'bass piano' and in the middle a subtle sort of muted gamelan. And he plays all three (he is a pretty formidable pianist) with poetry and wonder. *Catch* is a game, in which a piano trio tempt and tease an off-stage clarinet; he eventually joins them in sober homophony, for this is a game with serious and lyrical substance as well as a jest. A similar but more ambiguous game is played in *Under Hamelin Hill*, where the piping toccata of one organist attracts two others to join him in co-operative apparent improvisation, but he is left alone for a shadowy soliloquy filled with shudders. *Darknesse visible* is a haunting meditation in which the presence of John Dowland is clearest where the music seems least like him: a magical illusion as well as a moving homage. In *Life story* the soprano is asked to imitate the manner of Billie Holiday in her wry reflection on a casual one-night encounter; it is the dark, searching piano that adds pity and bleakness to turn this into a riveting miniature opera. *Traced overhead* is filled with mysterious, glancing references to remembered piano music, but is grippingly coherent. And as if all this were not enough, in the Eliot settings that are his Op. 1, the 17-year-old Adès already proved himself a song-writer of rare talent. The performances are first-rate, as are the unobtrusively clean recordings.

Powder Her Face.
Jill Gomez sop Duchess; **Valdine Anderson** sop Maid, Confidante, Waitress, Mistress, Society Journalist, First Rubbernecker; **Niall Morris** ten Electrician, Lounge Lizard, Waiter, Delivery Boy, Second Rubbernecker; **Roger Bryson** bar Hotel Manager, Duke, Guest, Laundryman, Judge; **Almeida Ensemble / Thomas Adès.**
EMI CDS5 56649-2 (two discs: 116 minutes: DDD). Text included. Recorded 1996.   Ⓜ

Powder Her Face was written and had its first performances in 1995, when Thomas Adès was 24. It would be pretty remarkable, as the first opera by a composer of that age, if it demonstrated the fertility of invention and imaginative resource that erupted from the two discs of his shorter pieces (on EMI), combined with a promising but as yet understandably tentative gift for the stage. It does much more than that. The central character, though referred to in the cast-list simply as 'Duchess', is in fact Margaret, Duchess of Argyll, for many years a prominent figure in London society, who in 1963 was at the centre of a protracted and luridly sensational divorce case: the judge, in a verdict running to 65,000 words, described her sexual activities as 'disgusting' and her sexual appetite as 'debased'. Even after the divorce she counted the rich, the famous and the royal among her friends but died, penniless, in 1993.

Adès and librettist Philip Hensher imagine her as 'all cladding – powder, scent, painting, furs – nothing inside', and the risk of course is that she will appear either as an empty monster for whom we can feel little sympathy or as a glittering caricature whom we pity as the subject of the composer's and the librettist's mockery. Their wit is indeed dazzling. Hensher's libretto (*his* first work for the stage, too) is outstandingly good – economical, vivid, filled with the most adroit spurs to the composer's invention – and Adès's score is as satisfyingly rich, surprising and bizarre as his other works would lead one to hope and expect. He takes great risks – an aria and a duet that are sung simultaneously, a musical equivalent of the judge's interminable concluding speech – and they come off brilliantly. He cannot, of course, resist alluding to the music that would have furnished the Duchess's glamorous life – the score is pervaded with tangos – but he can use it to convey menace and desolation as well as picturesque period evocation. He uses chamber forces – an orchestra of 15, four singers enacting 16 roles – but draws astonishingly varied sounds and vivid dramaturgy from them. His highest achievement is his portrayal of the Duchess. From her first appearance, surprising a maid and an electrician sniggering at her grotesque reputation, she has iconic glamour and something like dignity. Although often off-stage – the 'second soprano' probably has more to sing – she dominates the opera effortlessly, and in the long final scene she achieves … not tragic stature, perhaps, but deep and genuine pathos: she is alone 'and there's no one to dress me, and no one to talk to me, and the only people who were ever good to me were paid for it'.

The opera gains enormously from a central performance as alluring and attention-riveting as Jill Gomez's, though all the other singers are very accomplished, Valdine Anderson standing out in a role like Zerbinetta with knobs on: composer and librettist envisaged her multiple roles for a 'Helden-Soubrette'. The score also makes huge demands of the orchestral players, many of them required to be virtuoso soloists, and they are very properly all named in the accompanying booklet. The recording is as vivid as it needs to be. A hugely enjoyable opera.

Jehan Alain   French 1911-1940

Suite. Climat. Prélude et Fugue. Choral dorien. Choral phrygien. Aria. Variations sur 'Lucis créator'. Berceuse sur deux notes qui cornent. Deux préludes profanes. Monodie. Ballade en mode phrygien. Choral cistercian pour une élévation. Variations sur un thème de Clément Janequin. Le jardin suspendu. Litanies. Fantasmagorie. Trois danses. Quatre pièces. Grave. Petite pièce. Intermezzo. Lamento. Première fantaisie. Deuxième fantaisie. Deux dances à Agni Yavishta. Cinque pièces faciles – Complainte à la mode ancienne; Fugue en mode de Fa; Verset-Choral; Berceuse. Postlude pour l'office de Complies. Page 21 du huitième cahier de notes de Jehan Alain.
Kevin Bowyer org
Nimbus NI5551/2 (two discs: 146 minutes: DDD). Recorded on the Marcussen Organ, Chapel of St Augustine, Tonbridge School, Kent in 1997.   Ⓟ Ⓔ ⓇⓇ

This is the most comprehensive and by far and away the most impressive recording yet of Alain's organ music. Bowyer offers nine pieces not included on Eric Lebrun's two-disc survey from Naxos. These may not be among the composer's most substantial creations, but Alain enthusiasts would not like to be without any of them, least of all the intensely moving page from one of Alain's notebooks setting out his musical reactions to the death, in a mountaineering accident, of his sister, Marie-Odile. Bowyer's performances are thought-provoking, stimulating and often inspired. His tempos are not especially quick although he does turn out the fastest performance ever recorded of the *Intermezzo*. Yet even here the choice of speed is symptomatic of Bowyer's whole approach; nobody could deny that when played so rapidly the work takes on an altogether new dimension. Nimbus achieves a near-perfect balance between clarity and atmosphere on the brand new Marcussen in Tonbridge School's recently rebuilt Chapel. When the disarming dialogue between a single reed and the flutes of the charming *Petite pièce* can be revealed in such detail nobody could realistically ask for a better setting for this magical music. Bowyer proves to be an unusually perceptive and persuasive advocate of Alain's music, and not only do these discs conclusively outstrip all present-day competition but one suspects it will be a long time before a serious contender to this outstanding release comes along.

Litanies. Petite pièce. Le jardin suspendu. Deuxième fantaisie. Variations sur un thème de Clément Janequin. Deux dances à Agni Yavishta. Deux préludes profanes. Choral cistercian pour une élévation. Climat. Monodie. Ballade en mode phrygien. Choral phrygien. Suite.
Eric Lebrun org
Naxos 8 553632 (64 minutes: DDD). ⑤

Trois danses. Intermezzo. Variations sur 'Lucis créator'. Berceuse. Grave. Lamento. Première fantaisie. Prélude et Fugue. Choral dorien. Aria. Postlude pour l'office de Complies.
Eric Lebrun org
Naxos 8 553633 (66 minutes: DDD). Both recorded on the organ of the Church of Saint-Antoine des Quinze-Vingts, Paris in 1995. ⑤

Whether it's the weirdly sombre *Lamento*, the captivating *Intermezzo*, evoking the movement of a spinning-wheel, the pseudo-archaic *Variations sur un thème de Clément Janequin* or the dramatically fervent *Litanies*, to have it all brought together under one roof, as it were, allows us to revel in that magical mix of mysticism, melancholy and modality which makes Alain's voice so distinctive. This splendid Cavaillé-Coll organ, set in a richly atmospheric acoustic, seems the perfect vehicle for Alain's music with its kaleidoscopic use of subtle colours and effects. It possesses glorious stops and seems fully equipped to deal with everything Alain's music demands of it. What a shame, then, that the recording itself misses the mark. An indistinct focus blurs much of the detail, while there just isn't enough of the church's ambience to compensate for this lack of clarity. There again Eric Lebrun is guilty of some pretty indistinct articulation himself, not least in a dreadful account of *Litanies*. Taken at breakneck speed and with heart-stopping lurches from section to section, you may be tempted to take the listening process no further.

But persevere, for much of his playing is outstanding. The best-known works verge on the controversial (*Le jardin suspendu*, for example, is superficial), but in the rarely heard *Suite* he produces playing of considerable conviction and magnetism. And with a deeply moving account of the *Postlude pour l'office de Complies*, which seems to hover on the very brink of eternity, he more than justifies Naxos's faith in him and in this important recording project. This valuable addition to the catalogue deserves a place on the shelves of all organ music devotees.

Isaac Albéniz
Spanish 1860-1909

Albéniz Iberia (arr. Gray) – El Albaicín; Triana; Rondeña.
Granados Valses poéticos (trans. Williams).
Rodrigo Invocación y Danza. En los trigales.
Anonymous (arr. Llobet). Ten Catalan Folk-songs.
John Williams gtr **London Symphony Orchestra / Paul Daniels.**
Sony Classical SK48480 (71 minutes: DDD). Recorded 1989-91. ⑤

The amalgam of technical guitaristic perfection in the face of daunting demands, fluid musicality and exemplary tone-production, caught in this exceptionally lifelike recording, represents a landmark in the instrument's march towards true parity with other instruments. Granados's *Valses* are unabridged, Rodrigo's moody *Invocación y Danza* comes in its original and more effective form, and two of the charming settings of Catalan folk-songs arranged by Llobet have no other recording. Nothing in Albéniz's virtuosic *Iberia* is accessible to the solo guitar, but with the aid of the London Symphony Orchestra and Gray's enchantingly evocative arrangements, Williams shows three of its movements in a new and colourful light. To anyone with the slightest interest in the guitar or Spanish romantic music this disc is a required purchase.

Albéniz (orch. Halffter). Rapsodia española, Op. 70.
Falla Noches en los jardines de España.
Turina Rapsodia sinfónica, Op. 66.
Alicia de Larrocha pf
London Philharmonic Orchestra / Rafael Frühbeck de Burgos.
Decca 410 289-2DH (52 minutes: DDD).   Ⓕ

The three magically beautiful nocturnes which make up Falla's *Nights in the gardens of Spain* express the feelings and emotions evoked by contrasted surroundings, whilst Albéniz's enjoyably colourful *Rapsodia española* is a loosely assembled sequence of Spanish dances such as the *jota* and the *malagueña*. Like Falla's *Nights* the work was conceived as a piano solo, but this disc contains a version with orchestra arranged by Cristóbal Halffter. The disc is completed by Turina's short, two-part work for piano and strings. All three pieces are excellently performed, but it is the Falla work which brings out the quality of Larrocha's artistry; her ability to evoke the colour of the Spanish atmosphere is remarkable. Frühbeck de Burgos supports her magnificently and persuades the LPO to produce some very Latin-sounding playing. The recording is suitably atmospheric.

Suite española, Op. 47. Cantos de España, Op. 232 – Córdoba (both orch. Frühbeck).
Iberia – Evocación; El Corpus en Sevilla; Triana (orch. Arbós).
Spanish National Orchestra / Rafael Frühbeck de Burgos.
Conifer Classics 75605 51326-2 (61 minutes: DDD). Recorded 1997.   Ⓕ

Despite going, at the age of 30, to study with Dukas and d'Indy, Albéniz was ill at ease in writing for the orchestra: his few works for that medium – the *Rapsodia cubana*, the *Rapsodia española* and the Piano Concerto – were all orchestrated by other hands from piano originals, and Dukas has always been suspected of having lent his assistance with *Catalonia*. But Albéniz's piano works are intrinsically so full of colour (and in the case of *Iberia* so bristling with pianistic technical demands) that it is not surprising that they have tempted others to clothe them in orchestral garb. Most expertly as this is done here by the two conductors responsible – Frühbeck was six years old when Arbós died in 1939 – a certain modification of character from the originals was inevitable. Pianists will continue to cherish Albéniz's Lisztian writing, but cannot but admire the ingenuity with which black-and-white has been transformed into Technicolor (which is likely to be of greater appeal to the public at large). Frühbeck takes 'Granada' extremely slowly, underlining the emotionalism (logically enough for a serenade); 'Sevilla' emerges very robustly, as does the final section of 'Asturias' (which Albéniz made more Moorish than Asturian); the *jota* of 'Aragon' is brilliantly vivid; and everywhere he adds interesting counterpoints and imitations. Only in 'Castille' and 'Cuba' do you feel that his orchestration over-eggs the pudding. The Spanish National Orchestra responds warmly to all these arrangements. The recording is first-class.

Iberia. Navarra (compl. de Séverac). Suite española, Op. 47.
Alicia de Larrocha pf
Decca 417 887-2DH2 (two discs: 126 minutes: DDD). Recorded 1986.   Ⓕ

Written during Albéniz's last three years, *Iberia* is his masterwork for the piano. The full extent of the journey he travelled in his all-too-brief life span of 49 years can't be fully appreciated by comparing these 12 richly colourful 'impressions' with the *Suite española*, generally accepted as his earliest serious foray into the nationalist field. Larrocha also gives us the bonus of the exuberant *Navarra* originally intended by the composer (before he rejected it as 'too plebeian') to end *Iberia*. Coming from such a distinguished specialist in the Spanish field, the album is as musically enjoyable as it is musicologically stimulating. Her playing has immediacy, subtlety and charm besides revealing fingers so magically able to conceal Albéniz's sometimes cruel technical demands. Compared to her old LP recording of *Iberia*, the clarity of colouring that Decca gives us now is like an old painting newly cleaned. But it's not just the recording that allows Larrocha's most recent *Iberia* to make a more vivid impact. Everything here carries just that little extra conviction even though overall differences of tempo are only marginal. Every tiny detail in Albéniz's multi-layered textures, every counter-strand, every fleck of colour, is always crystal-clear. As for Larrocha's range of colour, and the sheer sensuous beauty of her tone, that can only be described as a feast for the ear. She plays the *Suite española* with a spontaneous delight in their tunes, textures and rhythms; she enjoys them as the engaging *morceaux de salon* that, in comparison with what follows in *Iberia*, they undoubtedly are.

Albéniz Mallorca, Op. 202. Suite española, Op. 47. Cantos de España, Op. 232 – Córdoba.
Granados Cuentos de la juventud – Dedicatoria. 15 Tonadillas – El majo olvidado.
12 Danzas españolas, Op. 37 – Villanesca; Andaluza (Playera). 7 Valses poéticos.
Rodrigo Tres Piezas españolas.
Julian Bream *gtr*
RCA Navigator 74321 17903-2 (77 minutes: DDD). Recorded 1982-83. ⓢ

In 1982 Julian Bream recorded a solo recital of music by Albéniz and Granados in his favourite
recording venue, Wardour Chapel in Wiltshire. It offers playing of extraordinary magnetism and an
almost total illusion of the great guitarist seated in the room making music just beyond one's
loudspeakers; this effect is particularly striking in Albéniz's *Córdoba* and the *pianissimo* reprise of
the central section of the Granados *Danza española* No. 5, which is quite magical. The other works
included are all played with comparable spontaneity. RCA here reissue this disc at super-bargain
price on their enterprising Navigator label; moreover, they have added another 15 minutes of music
in the form of Rodrigo's *Tres Piezas españolas*, recorded a year later. The second of these, a
seven-minute 'Passacaglia', is quite masterly, while the final 'Zapateado' brings characteristically
chimerical virtuosity from the soloist. It is difficult to identify another recital of Spanish guitar
music that surpasses this, and it is now one of the great bargains in the Navigator catalogue.

Tomaso Albinoni
Italian 1671-1751

Concerti a cinque, Opp. 7 and 9.
Anthony Robson, Catherine Latham *obs*
Collegium Musicum 90 / Simon Standage *vn*
Op. 7 – No. 3 in B flat major; No. 6 in D major; No. 9 in F major; No. 12 in C major. Op. 9 – No. 2
in D minor; No. 5 in C major; No. 8 in G minor; No. 11 in B flat major.
Chandos Chaconne CHAN0579 (72 minutes: DDD). Recorded 1993 and 1996. Ⓕ Ⓟ 𝗥𝗥

Op. 7 – No. 1 in D major; No. 2 in C major; No. 4 in G major; No. 5 in C major. Op. 9 – No. 1
in B flat major; No. 3 in F major; No. 4 in A major; No. 6 in G major. Sinfonia in G minor.
Chandos Chaconne CHAN0602 (63 minutes: DDD). Recorded 1993 and 1996. Ⓕ Ⓟ 𝗥𝗥

Op. 7 – No. 7 in A major; No. 8 in D major; No. 10 in B flat major; No. 11 in C major;
Op. 9 – No. 7 in D major; No. 9 in C major; No. 10 in F major; No. 12 in D major.
Chandos Chaconne CHAN0610 (65 minutes: DDD). Recorded 1993 and 1996. Ⓕ Ⓟ 𝗥𝗥

Albinoni's Op. 7 and Op. 9 consist of four concertos *with* (rather than *for*, as the composer insisted)
one oboe, four with two oboes and four for strings only. Overall, the last show a strong family
resemblance, with vivacious outer movements and suave slow movements that tend to be more
chromatic; but the Op. 9 string concertos include a solo violin part, at times very elaborate. The first
volume contains the works for solo oboe and strings. Albinoni treats the oboe like a voice and the
slow movements have tunes that stay in the mind. The second volume contains the string and
double-oboe concertos. All are three-movement *da chiesa* works, with cheerful outer movements
and slow ones that often remind you that Albinoni wrote a good deal of vocal music. The two
oboes 'sing' together for the most part, either in thirds or in unison. The concertos on Vol. 3 for two
oboes display rather more individuality – the joyous finale of Op. 7 No. 11 intriguingly sharpens the
fourth of the scale, Op. 9 No. 9 allows the oboes more independence of each other, while in the
outer movements of Op. 9 No. 12 the oboes put up a good pretence at being trumpets. Anthony
Robson and Catherine Latham contribute deftly to the spirit of enjoyment that emanates from the
whole of this disc. Collegium Musicum 90 is one of the very best baroque bands around and here
the players are in their element. The recorded balance is just right, keeping soloists and strings in
equal perspective. In every positive sense these recordings bid strongly for a place on every shelf.

12 Concerti a cinque, Op. 9 – No. 2 in D minor; No. 3 in F major; No. 5 in C major; No. 8 in
G minor; No. 9 in C major; No. 11 in B flat major.
Anthony Camden, Julia Girdwood *obs* **The London Virtuosi / John Georgiadis.**
Naxos 8 550739 (64 minutes: DDD). Recorded 1992. ⓢ

Sinfonia in G major (arr. Camden). 12 Concerti a cinque, Op. 7 – No. 1 in D major; No. 2 in
C major; No. 3 in B flat major; No. 8 in D major; No. 9 in F major. Concerto in G major, Op. 9
No. 6.
Anthony Camden, Alison Alty *obs* **The London Virtuosi / John Georgiadis.**
Naxos 8 553002 (58 minutes: DDD). Recorded 1994. ⓢ

12 Concerti a cinque, Op. 7 – No. 4 in G major; No. 5 in C major; No. 6 in D major; No. 11 in C major; No. 12 in C major. Concerto in D major, Op. 9 No. 12.
Anthony Camden, Alison Alty obs **The London Virtuosi / John Georgiadis.**
Naxos 8 553035 (52 minutes: DDD). Recorded 1994.   Ⓢ

The oboe participates in, rather than dominates, these works in a chamber-music-like fashion. Albinoni had already experimented seven years earlier with the genre in his pioneering Concerti a cinque, Op. 7, the weaknesses in which were rectified in those of the more mature Op. 9. He was not in the business of springing harmonic surprises, but was a fluent writer of engaging tunes, particularly those in the *Adagios* – each of these works has one – and of elegant discourses between the soloist and the upper strings. Anthony Camden and Julia Girdwood produce liquid sounds from their modern instruments and are as meltingly expressive in the slow movements as they are light on their feet in the flanking ones. The London Virtuosi, also using modern strings, has a nice, clean air about it and gives the music neither more nor less than its due. The recording is bright and well balanced.

Volume 2 begins with a strings-only Sinfonia in G, to which Anthony Camden has added oboe parts; it is thematically related to the Concerto, Op. 7 No. 4 (given in its original form), but to appreciate this bit of auto-plagiary you will need Vol. 3. The three discs are better sampled than listened to from start to finish – unless you are an oboist or an insatiable 'baroque person'; there are some delectable pickings to be had, particularly among the slow movements. The performances and recording quality are of the same order as those of Vol. 1, 'couth, kempt and shevelled' – as is the graceful and amiable music itself. As an 'archive', the complete set is hard to resist at super-bargain price.

Six Sonate da chiesa, Op. 4. 12 Trattenimenti armonici per camera, Op. 6.
Locatelli Trio (Elizabeth Wallfisch vn Richard Tunnicliffe vc Paul Nicholson hpd/org).
Hyperion CDA66831/2 (two discs: 159 minutes: DDD). Recorded 1992.   Ⓕ Ⓟ

While Albinoni's concertos, and especially those for one and two oboes, have been reasonably well catered for by record companies, his chamber music has been largely overlooked. All the pieces on these discs are violin sonatas rather than trio sonatas but, sensibly, Paul Nicholson uses harpsichord for Op. 6 and organ for Op. 4, thereby providing the listener with variety in colour. This variety is maximized by a decision to intermingle the two sets. Each sonata is cast in the four movement slow-fast-slow-fast *da chiesa* pattern though, as with Corelli but to an even greater extent, Albinoni far from keeps to the *da chiesa* spirit, introducing a wealth of dance measures. Almost invariably the music is graceful in character, melodically appealing – above all, as so often with Albinoni – in the slow movements such as the *Adagio* of Op. 4 No. 6, and expressively restrained. These qualities are not lost on Elizabeth Wallfisch who affectingly captures the limpid, reflective content of slow movements, on the one hand, and the brilliance of the faster ones on the other. Richard Tunnicliffe gives her discreet and sensitive support throughout. Possibly a little more in the way of caprice in the sparkling *Allegros* would be nice. It is not that the playing lacks vitality but that a certain worthiness of approach is sensed; a dimension of playful virtuosity has not perhaps been fully realized. In all essentials, though, this is an enjoyable and very worthwhile release, illuminating less familiar aspects of Albinoni's music.

Hugo Alfvén   Swedish 1872-1960

Swedish Rhapsodies – No. 1, Op. 19, 'Midsummer Vigil'; No. 2, Op. 24, 'Upsala-rapsodi'; No. 3, 'Dalarapsodi'. A Legend of the Skerries, Op. 20. Gustav Adolf II, Op. 49 – Elegy.
Iceland Symphony Orchestra / Petri Sakari.
Chandos CHAN9313 (70 minutes: DDD). Recorded 1993.   Ⓕ

Petri Sakari gives us the most natural, unaffected and satisfying *Midsummer Vigil* to be heard on disc. He is light in touch, responsive to each passing mood and every dynamic nuance, self-effacing and completely at the service of the composer. Moreover in the *Upsala-rapsodi* and its later companion, he is fresher and more persuasive than any of his rivals on record. Even the Wagnerian-Straussian echoes from the skerries sound convincing. The only reservation concerns the *Elegy* from the incidental music to Ludwig Nordström's play about Gustav Adolf II, which might have benefited from greater reticence. Unusually for Sakari, he does not tell the tale simply or let the music speak for itself. The recorded sound is refreshingly free from analytical point-making; everything is there in the right perspective, though listeners whose first response is to find the recording recessed will find that a higher level of playback than usual will produce impressively natural results on high-grade equipment.

Charles-Valentin Alkan

Grand duo concertante in F sharp minor, Op. 21. Sonate de concert in E major, Op. 47.
Trio in G minor, Op. 30.
Trio Alkan (Kolja Lessing *vn* Bernhard Schwarz *vc* Rainer Klaas *pf*).
Marco Polo 8 223383 (75 minutes: DDD). Recorded 1991.   Ⓕ

As this disc so persuasively reveals, there are a number of Alkan's chamber works that are long
overdue for serious consideration. His violin sonata, the *Grand duo concertante*, for instance, is so
thoroughly original and masterly in invention that it should have acquired for itself a prominent
place in the French violin sonata repertoire. The somewhat unconventional tonal layout of the bold
and memorable first movement suggests, at times, the harmonic world of Berlioz, but perhaps more
strikingly looks forward, both here and in the final movement, to the melodic, Gallic charm of the
Fauré sonatas. The *Sonate de concert* for cello and piano is perhaps Alkan's finest and most
important contribution to chamber music. It's an expansive work of some 32 minutes in length.
Although clearly rooted in the classical tradition, it shouts Alkan from every page: the second
movement, in *siciliano* style, is a fine example of Alkan whimsy; in the slow movement, Alkan
draws musical inspiration from his Jewish faith to create a serene and somewhat mystical oasis of
calm before launching into the helter-skelter activity of the finale. The earlier Piano Trio of 1841 is
perhaps even more classical in design and utterance and is certainly more terse and economical in
its use of material. However, it's no easy ride for the performers. The *Scherzo* is strangely prophetic
of Tchaikovsky in places and is graced with a fiendishly difficult finale. The performances are quite
superb. Klaas copes admirably with all the keyboard pyrotechnics thrown at him, and Lessing and
Schwarz provide performances of dedication and great understanding. Recording is full-bodied and
close, though not uncomfortably so.

Alkan 25 Préludes dans les tons majeurs et mineurs, Op. 31.
Shostakovich 24 Preludes, Op. 34.
Olli Mustonen *pf*
Decca 433 055-2DH (76 minutes: DDD). Recorded 1990. *Gramophone* Award Winner 1992.   Ⓕ

It was brave of Decca to launch the career of its then newly-signed pianist with a disc of miniatures
few people actually know, since the *oeuvre* of Charles-Valentin Alkan is usually confined to
specialist labels and second-rate executants. The 25 Préludes are a reasonably benign introduction to
Alkan's idiosyncratic world – elusive and quirky to be sure but less ruthlessly barnstorming than
much of his output. They are by no means easy pieces to bring off, but you wouldn't know it from
Mustonen's exceptionally assured, brilliantly poised readings. Where rival versions are content to
offer the 25 Préludes without coupling, Mustonen adds deft and sparkling performances of
Shostakovich's not exactly insubstantial Op. 34 Preludes. Exceptional pianism, excellent, bright
recording and helpful notes.

Alkan Transcription de concert (Beethoven's Piano Concerto No. 3 in C minor, Op. 37 – first
movement). Three Etudes, Op. 76.
Busoni Sonatina No. 6 super Carmen (Kammerfantasie).
Chopin/Alkan Piano Concerto No. 1 in E minor, Op. 11 – Romanza.
Medtner Danza festiva, Op. 38 No. 3.
Marc-André Hamelin *pf*
Hyperion CDA66765 (72 minutes: DDD). Recorded live in 1994.   Ⓕ

The solo transcriptions on the first half of this disc are not intended as substitutes for the real
thing, at least not in the context of this disc, but are presented here as supreme examples of the art
of piano transcription in the late nineteenth century. In addition, they are superb display pieces,
revealing not only the subtleties of the transcriber's art and, in this case, the pianist's ability to
render them audible, but also Hamelin's extraordinary ability to make the pieces sound like
originals rather than transcriptions. Indeed, in the Alkan transcription of the first movement of
Beethoven's Third Piano Concerto, the absence of the orchestra never becomes a concern. The
principal glory of the disc, however, is Hamelin's account of Alkan's *Etudes*, Op. 76, for the hands
separately and reunited an exceptionally formidable opus, which here receives a formidable and
awe-inspiring performance. We also have the added *frisson* of knowing that what we hear is a
single take before a live audience; listen to the hair-raising final study, a blistering, unbroken
five-minute salvo of *prestissimo* semiquavers. The remaining items on the disc, a scintillating
account of Busoni's *Sonatina* No. 6 and Medtner's ebullient *Danza festiva* from Op. 38, provide
further evidence of Hamelin's skill. The recorded sound varies a little from piece to piece (they
were recorded over three evenings in the Wigmore Hall in London) but all are excellent in
quality.

12 Etudes dans les tons mineurs, Op. 39. Nocturne, Op. 22. Etude in F major, Op. 35 No. 5. Assez vivement, Op. 38 No. 1. Préludes, Op. 31 – No. 8, La chanson de la folle au bord de la mer; No. 12, Le temps qui n'est plus; No. 13, J'étais endormie, mais mon coeur veillait. Esquisses, Op. 63 – No. 2, La staccatissimo; No. 4, Les cloches; No. 11, Les soupirs; No. 48, En songe. Gros temps, Op. 74 No. 10. First Suite No. 2. Barcarolle, Op. 65 No. 6.
Jack Gibbons pf
ASV CDDCS227 (two discs: 155 minutes: DDD). Recorded 1995.   Ⓕ

There is an extremely generous two-CD set. 'Comme le vent' ('Like the wind'), the opening *Etude* from Op. 39, is a real baptism of fire for the pianist. Marked *prestissimamente*, it is an unrelenting deluge of notes which, if played at Alkan's specified metronome marking, travels at the rate of 160 bars per minute, or to put it another way, traverses 20 densely packed pages in just 4'30". Gibbons throws caution to the wind and completes the whirlwind in a staggering 4'38". Despite the odd occasion when he comes perilously close to tumbling into the abyss, this ranks among the most exhilarating feats of pianism to be heard on disc. If Gibbons's credentials as an Alkan pianist are not sealed in his performance of the first *Etude* then his reading of the following two *Etudes*, 'En rythme molossique' and 'Scherzo diabolico', surely confirm him as an Alkan interpreter of exceptional authority. Listening to these commanding and exceedingly sure-footed performances one is left with the feeling that Gibbons has grown with and nurtured these pieces for some time. The following four *Etudes* make up the *Symphony for Solo Piano*, and if anything Gibbons is even more impressive in his reading of this striking work.

Moving on to the *Concerto for Solo Piano*, *Etudes* Nos. 8-10, Gibbons gives a wildly romantic reading. More extraordinary feats of virtuosity await the listener in the twelfth *Etude* ('Le festin d'Esope') and the *Allegro barbaro* from the Op. 35 *Etudes*, but the delightful selection of miscellaneous pieces with which Gibbons fills the remainder of the set shows not only the more introverted side of Alkan's creativity but also allows Gibbons to display a less ostentatious and more directly poetic aspect of his playing. The simple *Nocturne* in B major, with its Chopinesque heartbeat, is beautifully rendered as are the 'Les soupirs' and 'En songe' from the *Esquisses*, Op. 63 and the *Barcarolle*, Op. 65 No. 6. However, the highlight of these miniatures comes with Gibbons's sensitive and effective delivery of the potently atmospheric 'La chanson de la folle au bord de la mer' ('Song of the mad woman on the seashore'), surely one of the most curious piano pieces to emerge from the nineteenth century. All in all, an exceptionally impressive issue that can be highly recommended to both Alkan devotees and newcomers alike. The recorded sound is excellent.

Grande sonate, Op. 33, 'Les quatre âges'. Sonatine, Op. 61. Barcarolle, Op. 65 No. 6. Etudes dans les tons mineurs, Op. 39 – No. 12, 'Le festin d'Esope'.
Marc-André Hamelin pf
Hyperion CDA66794 (70 minutes: DDD). Recorded 1994.   Ⓕ

Les quatre âges is an extraordinary piece in many respects, not least in its rather unconventional layout of four movements, each employing progressively slower tempos. Perhaps for this reason it has never attained a place in the repertoire – the extremely slow finale is hardly the sort of movement to ignite an overwhelming response from an audience at the close of the sonata, despite the feats of hair-raising bravura required in the first two movements. Hamelin's performance is everything one could wish for. The crispness and precision of his finger-work in the dazzling first movement is quite breathtaking and the sometimes superhuman feats of pianism demanded in the Faust-inspired second movement are executed with astounding ease. His reading of the third movement is beautifully poised and charmingly rendered whilst the tragic, Promethean finale is most effectively and powerfully projected. The Sonatine, Op. 61 is an entirely different matter, concise and concentrated in the extreme. Hamelin's direct, finely articulated no-nonsense reading brings out the clarity and economy of the writing, and he is quick, too, to underscore the work's more classical stance. A beautifully serene and hypnotic account of the seductive 'Barcarolle' follows, and the disc closes with a stunning display of pianistic gymnastics in the shape of 'Le festin d'Esope' from the Op. 39 *Etudes*. Recorded sound is excellent.

Gregorio Allegri
Italian c1582-1652

Allegri Miserere mei.
Palestrina Motets – Stabat mater a 8. Hodie beata virgo. Senex puerem portabat. Magnificat a 8. Litanie de Beata Virgine Maria I.
Roy Goodman treb **King's College Choir, Cambridge / Sir David Willcocks.**
Decca Legends 466 373-2DM (56 minutes: ADD). Recorded 1963-64.   Ⓜ ℝℝ

It is doubtful if any recording made by the choir of King's College, Cambridge, in the fertile Willcocks era, will prove more enduring than this celebrated performance of Allegri's *Miserere*. Admittedly there are more authentic versions in the catalogue, authentic not only in that they use the original Latin words where Willcocks opts for an English translation, but also in the sense that they search for a style less obviously redolent of choral evensong and the Anglican tradition. At the farthest extreme from King's, other versions strip Allegri's score of its various eighteenth- and nineteenth-century accretions – a nice piece of musical archaeology which, ironically, reveals the utter plainness of the *Miserere* when denied its familiar jewels, and sounds like an imposter when dressed up in even more garish baubles. For once, musicology seems doomed to failure; the richly communicative singing of King's remains for many an ideal impression of the piece, however far removed it may be from Allegri's intentions. On this compilation the *Miserere* is accompanied by some classic Palestrina performances, still as fresh as when they were recorded in 1964. Some tape hiss intrudes, but otherwise the sound is excellent. 'Fabulous' is the only word to describe this disc.

Miserere mei (two versions). Missa Vidi turbam magnam. De ore prudentis. Repleti sunt omnes. Cantate domino.
A Sei Voci / Bernard Fabre-Garrus with **Dominique Ferran** *org*
Auvidis Astrée E8524 (62 minutes: DDD). Texts and translations included. Recorded 1994.　　Ⓕ

Allegri's setting of the psalm *Miserere mei* is here presented in two versions. The first is sung with ornamentation added by the French musicologist, Jean Lionnet following seventeenth-century models, while the second presents the Burney-Alfieri version familiar from the classic 1963 Willcocks recording above. The curiously named group A Sei Voci (in fact there are ten of them) produces a rather varied sound, at times somewhat flat and white but at its best with an appropriate Italianate edge. For the most part the embellishments are negotiated with style and verve; just occasionally (in the first *Miserere*) they are fuzzy or insecure. *Miserere mei* apart, hardly any of Allegri's music is heard either liturgically or in the concert hall. By training a pupil of Nanino, a distinguished follower of Palestrina, his best music is confidently written in the High Renaissance contrapuntal manner. The six-voice *Missa Vidi turbam magnam*, composed on one of his own motets, is a fine work, and shows that the *stile antico*, far from being a mere academic exercise, could still be vividly sonorous and dramatic, qualities which are successfully brought out in this reading. The record is nicely rounded out with a selection of short continuo motets in the popular new manner, well established in Northern Italy, which was then becoming fashionable in Rome.

William Alwyn British 1905-1985

Piano Concerto No. 2. Symphony No. 5, 'Hydriotaphia'. Sinfonietta for Strings.
Howard Shelley *pf*
London Symphony Orchestra / Richard Hickox.
Chandos CHAN9196 (74 minutes: DDD). Recorded 1993.　　Ⓕ

The Second Piano Concerto opens heroically and contains a good deal of rhetoric, yet the string writing has a romantic sweep and the *Andante* proves to be the highlight of the piece. Howard Shelley plays with much bravura and an appealing sensitivity, and there is plenty of energy from the orchestra. The powerful Fifth Symphony is a cogent argument distilled into one movement with four sub-sections. The energetically kaleidoscopic first movement is sharply contrasted by a melancholy *Andante*. The violent *Scherzo* is followed by a curiously ambivalent finale which provides a moving and compelling, if equivocal, apotheosis for a succinctly argued work. The richly expansive *Sinfonietta for Strings,* almost twice as long as the symphony, is very much in the English tradition of string writing. It is vigorous in the first movement and hauntingly atmospheric in the beautiful but disconsolate *Adagio* – very touching in Hickox's tender performance. The unpredictable finale begins impulsively before the mood changes completely and becomes altogether more subdued and muted in feeling. The obviously dedicated LSO is particularly responsive in the *Sinfonietta*, a masterly work which ought to be in the concert repertoire.

Violin Concerto. Symphony No. 3.
Lydia Mordkovitch *vn*
London Symphony Orchestra / Richard Hickox.
Chandos CHAN9187 (75 minutes: DDD). Recorded 1993.　　Ⓕ

The Violin Concerto, although essentially threnodic and lyrical, opens confidently and the orchestra returns with regular bursts of energy. The end of the movement (the rapt *pianissimo* closing section) is exquisite: one is reminded here of the Vaughan Williams of *The lark ascending*, although as the second movement *Allegretto* opens, the melodic writing also brings hints of Elgar. The finale is fairly vigorous, but again the lyrical impulse is all important. The work is discursive, yet has moments of great intensity. The performance could not be bettered and Mordkovitch's *pianissimo* playing is touchingly beautiful. The Third Symphony is an outstanding example of Alwyn's earlier symphonic manner and is in three movements. The first combines driving rhythmic agitation with a powerful lyrical thrust. The *Adagio*, introduced by a peaceful horn theme, has an animated, brassy development, then ethereal strings restore the sense of repose, the horns returning glowingly. The finale restores the forward momentum with its rhythmic zest and has a powerful and satisfying resolution. Hickox's reading is truly convincing and the LSO responds committedly to a work that must be rewarding to play when the orchestration is so effective.

Symphonies – No. 1 in D major; No. 4.
London Philharmonic Orchestra / William Alwyn.
Lyrita SRCD227 (77 minutes: ADD). Recorded 1970s.   Ⓕ 🆁🆁

Symphony No. 4. Elizabethan Dances. Festival March.
London Symphony Orchestra / Richard Hickox.
Chandos CHAN8902 (65 minutes: DDD). Recorded 1992.   Ⓕ

It is interesting to compare William Alwyn's own recording (taped by Lyrita in the LP era), with Hickox's version of No. 4, an extraordinarily fine work. It would be normal received wisdom for us to suggest that the composer's performance has greater penetration and intensity – first recordings are usually special – but the impression is that this is not so. The two accounts are remarkably alike. Indeed, when one compares his phrasing of the long and beautiful string cantilena which opens the *Adagio e molto calmato* of the Passacaglia finale, its ebb and flow and dynamic gradations suggest either that Hickox has listened to the composer's LP or has a remarkable, instinctive feeling for the music (probably both). The *Scherzo* may have a bit more bite with Alwyn (as do the curiously plangent woodwind squawks at 7'22" of the opening movement of the Lyrita disc), but this is at least partly caused by the more leonine Lyrita sound. The centrepiece of the *Scherzo* brings a glorious blossoming from the violins which is equally thrilling in both performances, while at the very end of the symphony the final brass peroration has great forceful thrust from the composer. However, with the LSO and Hickox the slightly richer, more spacious Chandos recording adds to the weight of sonority. In short, these are both highly compelling performances of a remarkably diverse and well-argued symphony, bursting with lyrical ideas and melodic in the way traditional music is communicative, without being old-fashioned.

The couplings on Chandos are relatively slight. *The Elizabethan Dances* aren't very early Elizabethan, but the languid 'Waltz' (No. 2) is rather charming and the 'Poco Allegretto' (No. 5) is even more so; the vigorous numbers are more conventional. *The Festival March*, written for the 1951 Festival of Britain, is an agreeable occasional piece, although its big tune isn't as memorable as those of Walton or Elgar. Yet if you want a modern recording of the Fourth Symphony, these are acceptable makeweights. On the other hand, Lyrita offers the Symphony No. 1. It is a work teeming with ideas, and quite often reminds one of Alwyn's film music (which is not meant to be a pejorative remark). With its ample scoring the composer does go over the top a bit at times and this is not nearly so cogently argued a piece as the Fourth, although it has a rather appealing *Adagio*. It is splendidly played and the Lyrita recordings have been remastered most skilfully: the sound has body, weight, brilliance, and fine presence and clarity too.

Lyra Angelica. Autumn Legend. Pastoral Fantasia. Tragic Interlude.
Rachel Masters hp **Nicholas Daniel** cor ang **Stephen Tees** va
City of London Sinfonia / Richard Hickox.
Chandos CHAN9065 (64 minutes: DDD). Recorded 1991.   Ⓕ

Alwyn valued his *Lyra Angelica* concerto for harp above all his other music, and it is indeed very beautiful. It was premièred at the first night of the 1954 Proms and, not surprisingly, made an immediate impression. Alwyn is a master of texture as well as form and the textures here, delicately embroidered by the solo harp, are harmonically rich, and the effect on the listener is very moving. The concerto is played with a real feeling for the music's rapture, and the expansive recorded sound, with rich string timbres and a perfect balance with the solo harp is very fine indeed. The *Pastoral Fantasia* was written in 1939 and looks back nostalgically to a more peaceful England. The music opens like Delius, but the entry of the viola brings an immediate affinity with Vaughan Williams as the solo viola begins in rhapsodic soliloquy. The *Tragic Interlude* dates from 1936 when the composer's foreboding of the imminence of the war brought an eloquent protest at the waste of life. The piece opens passionately and gathers momentum, but after its climax, dissolves into a moving elegiac threnody. *Autumn Legend* is much later (1954). It has a particularly lovely opening, with shafts of sunlight on the strings piercing the clouds, and the music's disconsolate manner has an underlying romantic feeling, rather than conveying pessimism. Yet the dark-hued cor anglais line has a pervading melancholy. It is a fine if ambivalent piece, and Nicholas Daniel, the soloist, captures its mood persuasively, while Richard Hickox shows himself in complete affinity with Alwyn's world. The Chandos recording is outstandingly fine.

Miss Julie.
Jill Gomez *sop* Miss Julie; **Benjamin Luxon** *bar* Jean; **Della Jones** *mez* Kristin;
John Mitchinson *ten* Ulrik; **Philharmonia Orchestra / Vilem Tausky.**
Lyrita SRCD2218 (two discs: 118 minutes: ADD). Notes and text included. Recorded 1983.   Ⓕ **E**

In his colourful and confident adaptation of Strindberg's play, Alwyn consistently demonstrates his mastery of atmosphere and timing, bringing out the chilling intensity of this story of Miss Julie's sudden infatuation for her father's man-servant. He adapted the play himself, and understood far more than most librettists the need for economy over text. His principal modification of Strindberg is that to the play's three characters – Miss Julie, Jean the manservant and Kristin the cook – he adds the gamekeeper, Ulrik, who acts as a commentator. So in his drunken scene of Act 1 he makes explicit what is happening, to the embarrassment of both Miss Julie and Jean. He also shoots (off-stage) the lapdog which Miss Julie wants to take away with her on her elopement, a convenient but less horrific alternative to the slaughter of the pet finch in the original Strindberg. The idiom, harmonically rich and warmly lyrical, brings occasional Puccinian echoes which, along with reminiscences of other composers, add to the music's impact. By any reckoning this is a confidently red-blooded opera. Tausky's conducting is strong and forceful, with superb singing from all the principals. Jill Gomez is magnificent in the title-role, producing ravishing sounds. Benjamin Luxon gives a wonderfully swaggering portrait of the unscrupulous manservant, vocally firmer than on almost any of his other recordings. Della Jones is splendidly characterful too, relishing her venomous cry of 'Bitch!' when, at the very end of scene 1, she realizes Julie and Jean have gone off together. John Mitchinson is characterful too, in his drunken scene. The recording is excellent.

Anton Arensky

Russian 1861-1906

Arensky Piano Trios – No. 1 in D minor, Op. 32; No. 2 in F minor, Op. 73.
Beaux Arts Trio (Ida Kavafian *vn* Peter Wiley *vc* Menahem Pressler *pf*).
Philips 442 127-2PH (63 minutes: DDD). Recorded 1994.   Ⓕ

The presence of Tchaikovsky hovers benignly over Arensky in many pieces, not least in the First Trio: though Arensky does not have Tchaikovsky's felicity of invention, he can actually solve the problems of writing for piano and strings more steadily, and the work would surely have a more secure place in the repertory were it attached to a more famous name. Both are fine works, and the Beaux Arts Trio gives beautiful, perceptive performances. Again, comparisons with Tchaikovsky's Piano Trio are inevitable, and by no means odious. Arensky may not have Tchaikovsky's distinctive musical personality, but he can write at least as effectively for the difficult medium, sometimes more originally, and he never lapses into the mighty chordal piano textures with which Tchaikovsky can make problems for his players. Moreover, he has a melodic charm that is much in the manner of Tchaikovsky, who, with some reservations, was appreciative. The *Elegy* of the First Trio and the *Romanza* of the Second are beautiful inventions, and both *Scherzos* speed along delicately and wittily. Another influence for the good was Mendelssohn. It is important not to overplay the resemblances in performance, and indeed not to overplay at all: less makes more in this music, and does so in these admirable interpretations. Balance is very well managed throughout.

Thomas Arne

British 1710-1778

Artaxerxes.
Christopher Robson *counterten* Artaxerxes; **Ian Partridge** *ten* Artabanes; **Patricia Spence** *mez* Arbaces; **Richard Edgar-Wilson** *ten* Rimenes; **Catherine Bott** *sop* Mandane; **Philippa Hyde** *sop* Semira; **The Parley of Instruments / Roy Goodman.**
Hyperion CDA67051/2 (two discs: 140 minutes: DDD). Notes and text included.
Recorded 1995.   Ⓕ **P**

This is a work of great historical importance and musically fascinating. Thomas Arne, the leading English composer of his time for the theatre, wanted to write serious as well as comic English operas, and decided that Italian *opera seria* should serve, on the literary side, as his model; he chose the most famous of all the Metastasio librettos, *Artaserse*, as the basis for his first (and last) attempt at the genre. It is generally supposed that the translation was his own work. He performed the opera at Covent Garden in 1762 with considerable success and it remained a favourite for many years. He never followed up that success, and nor, regrettably, did anyone else. English vocal music of this period has quite a distinctive manner, tuneful, rather short-breathed, often with a faintly 'folky' flavour. It does not naturally reflect the exalted emotional manner of an *opera seria* text. Nevertheless, the music is enormously enjoyable, full of good melodies, richly orchestrated, never (unlike Italian operas of the time) long-winded. Several of its numbers became popular favourites in Arne's time, and for long after.

The story of *Artaxerxes* is a typical Metastasian one, with 'treasonous designs' and misunderstandings, and plenty of opportunity for the expression of strong and varied emotion. Much of the best and most deeply felt music goes to Arbaces, very finely and expressively sung by Patricia Spence. She uses more vibrato than anyone else in the cast but her warmth of tone and expressive power are ample justification. Mandane, Arbaces's beloved, composed for Arne's mistress Charlotte Brent, is another rewarding part and is finely sung here by Catherine Bott, bright in tone and true in pitch and scrupulous in her verbal articulation, who can encompass both the charming English ditties and the more Italianate virtuoso pieces. The opera begins with a duet for these two. Philippa Hyde sings very gracefully and charmingly in the role of Semira but does not always bring sufficient clarity to the words. As the conspiring Artabanes, Ian Partridge sings as clearly and intelligently as always. The role of Artaxerxes, the king, is taken by Christopher Robson, an excellent stylist, though this castrato part is bound to be testing for a countertenor and he is often covered by the orchestra. The smaller part of Rimenes, an insinuating traitor, is neatly sung and characterized by Richard Edgar-Wilson. Arne's orchestral style here is very rich, with much prominent wind writing; sometimes the singers – given less prominence by the engineers than one might expect – do not ride the full textures very comfortably. Roy Goodman's accompaniments are not generally very subtle or carefully shaded. The original score does not survive complete, a victim (like so many) of the frequent theatre fires of the time; Peter Holman has done a predictably unobtrusive and stylish job of reconstructing some of the lost recitatives for this recording. This is certainly a set that can be recommended warmly to anyone curious about this byway of eighteenth-century opera, and to anyone who is drawn to Arne's very individual and appealing melodic style.

Richard Arnell   British 1917

Arnell Punch and the Child – ballet.
Berners The Triumph of Neptune – ballet suite[a].
Delius Paris: The Song of a Great City.
[a]**Robert Grooters** bar
Royal Philharmonic Orchestra; [a]Philadelphia Orchestra / Sir Thomas Beecham.
Sony Classical Essential Classics SBK62748 (69 minutes: ADD). Recorded 1950-55.   Ⓑ🄷

Delians everywhere will rejoice at the reappearance of Beecham's 1955 recording of *Paris*. Comparison with this conductor's marvellous 1934 version shows his earlier offering to be the better co-ordinated of the two (both orchestrally and structurally), yet there are moments to treasure in this RPO performance and Beecham's poetic instincts do not desert him – witness his surpassingly lovely treatment of Delius's secondary lyrical material when it reappears at 15'21". Richard Arnell's ballet, *Punch and the Child*, dates from 1948, a commission for the American company, Ballet Caravan (later known as the New York City Ballet). Beecham conducted the English concert hall première in 1949 and recorded it the following year with the RPO in Kingsway Hall. It's an attractively rumbustious creation, reminiscent at times of Bliss in ballet mode, and delivered here with much gusto. Beecham twice recorded music from Lord Berners's 1926 ballet, *The Triumph of Neptune*. The present 1952 account of the Suite with the Philadelphia restores those two substantial numbers ('Cloudland' and 'The Frozen Forest') not found on Beecham's earlier 1937 LPO set. Again, good transfers, though in *Paris* the sound has not the extraordinary richness and depth that distinguishes Anthony Griffith's superb restoration of that earlier Columbia production.

Sir Malcolm Arnold   British 1921

Arnold Clarinet Concerto No. 2, Op. 115.
Copland Concerto for Clarinet and String Orchestra with Harp and Piano.
Hindemith Clarinet Concerto.
Martin Fröst cl **Malmö Symphony Orchestra / Lan Shui.**
BIS CD893 (57 minutes: DDD). Recorded 1997.   Ⓕ

All three of these concertos were written for Benny Goodman, but, not surprisingly, it is the Arnold work which most fully exploits his dedicatee's jazz background. The first movement is a typical Arnoldian *scherzando*, with an irrepressible *Tam O'Shanter/Beckus the Dandipratt* audacity. Fröst and Lan Shui clearly relish its verve and energy, and then bring a seductive richness to the main theme of the slow movement. Yet they do not miss the plangent emotional ambivalence later – for there are characteristic moments of Arnold-like darkness here too. The outrageous show-stopper finale, with its rooty-tooty clarinet tune and orchestral whoops, also has a surprise up its sleeve in its sudden lyrical interlude; but one and all let their hair down for the boisterous reprise. At the haunting opening of the Copland concerto, Martin Fröst's clarinet steals in magically on a half-tone. Lan Shui's sympathetic and flexible support contributes to a memorable performance of Copland's masterly first movement, with the coda gently fading into the cadenza (quite superbly done). The Hindemith concerto which follows produces a characteristic sinewy lyricism in the first of its four movements, with some nicely touched-in brass and woodwind comments. Again Fröst cajoles the ear with his pliable line and the effect is unexpectedly mellow. With extremely fine recording and marvellous solo playing, this triptych will be hard to surpass.

Flute Concertos – No. 1, Op. 45; No. 2, Op. 111. Three Shanties, Op. 4. Sonatina for Flute and Piano, Op. 19. Fantasia, Op. 89. Divertimento, Op. 37. Flute Sonata, Op. 121.
James Galway *fl*
James Galway Wind Quintet (Gareth Hulse *ob* Antony Pay *cl* Rachel Gough *bn*
Philip Eastop *hn*); **Philip Moll** *pf* **Academy of St Martin in the Fields / Sir Neville Marriner.**
RCA Victor Red Seal 09026 68860-2 (69 minutes: DDD). Recorded 1995. Ⓕ Ⓔ

In this expert, sweet-toned and affectionate music-making, these fine artists audibly enjoy themselves hugely, responding to Arnold's idiomatic and resourceful writing as to the manner born. Galway and friends are particularly enjoyable in the sparkling early *Three Shanties* for wind quintet and the delicious *Divertimento* for flute, oboe and clarinet. Cast in six pithy movements (and masterfully played here), the latter piece contains invention of great freshness and charm, with definite echoes of the *English Dances* from the same period. In the wistful central *Andante* of the First Flute Concerto, Sir Neville Marriner and his beautifully prepared Academy strings provide a poignant backdrop to Galway's ravishing playing, and this music's kinship with the great slow movement of Arnold's Second Symphony is most perceptively brought out. In fact, the performances of both concertos are probably the best we've ever had. Galway himself was, of course, the lucky recipient of the Flute Sonata (whose première he gave at the 1977 Cardiff Festival), and he and Philip Moll do full justice to this work's entrancing mix of lyricism (the lilting *Andantino* centrepiece boasts a particularly indelible main idea) and exhilarating virtuosity. Recording quality is nicely integrated, too, with Galway never overprominently balanced, though Moll's piano can sound just a touch rough in its lowest reaches. A delightful anthology all the same.

Arnold Guitar Concerto, Op. 67.
Rodrigo Concierto de Aranjuez.
Takemitsu To the Edge of Dream.
Julian Bream *gtr*
City of Birmingham Symphony Orchestra / Sir Simon Rattle.
EMI CDC7 54661-2 (58 minutes: DDD). Recorded 1991. Ⓕ

This is Bream's fourth recording of the Rodrigo, and his second version of the Arnold Concerto (his first, recorded in 1959, is available on various RCA reissues). His tempos in the outer movements are a mite slower than of yore but the differences are small and the energy, sparkle and clean delivery are undiminished. What differentiates these performances from others, including Bream's earlier ones, is the extraordinary accounts of their slow movements. Bream's views of the *sardana* and the smoky night club (respectively) come from within, to an extent that makes even the most expressive of others seem 'external', and they are conveyed with such wonderful fluidity of tone and phrasing that one might almost believe the feeling that one is hearing them for the first time. Takemitsu said of *To the Edge of Dream*: 'melodic fragments float in a transparent space like so many splinters of dream'; though they never quite coalesce into a stable, protracted melody, they give cohesion to the music. The work is scored for an unusually large orchestra but, as it most often alternates with, rather than opposes the guitar or is held to a breathless *pianissimo*, the guitar is always audible. It is a work of haunting beauty. And these are desert-island versions of the concertos, adding maturity to virtuosity.

Four Cornish Dances, Op. 91. English Dances, Op. 27; Op. 33. Irish Dances, Op. 126. Four Scottish Dances, Op. 59. Solitaire – Sarabande; Polka.
London Philharmonic Orchestra / Sir fMalcolm Arnold.
Lyrita SRCD201 (61 minutes: ADD/DDD). Ⓕ

A warm and well-deserved welcome was given to the *English*, *Scottish* and *Cornish Dances*, when these recordings, conducted by the composer, first appeared. Here, with the *Irish Dances* added, as well as the two movements which were written to go with the two sets of *English Dances* as the ballet, *Solitaire*, it is even more of a winner. The analogue sound is given a splendid transfer with plenty of presence and is full and brilliant. The newer items, in digital sound, very well recorded too, bring no feeling of inconsistency. Best-known of all is the first of the second set of *English Dances* with its jaunty piccolo theme, but one after another these little jewels first grab and then delight the ear with their brilliant pastiche of folk melodies. The first of the *Irish Dances*, written in 1986, opens with a rumbustious movement very much in the style of the earlier sets, with characteristic and attractive syncopations, but the other three dance dances are both sparer in instrumentation and darker in tone, effectively so. The two movements from *Solitaire* are equally valuable, particularly the superb, coolly atmospheric 'Sarabande', the longest and most ambitious movement of any here, again made weightier by Arnold's slow speed. Even if you don't want to play all 22 items at one go – and that is no penance at all – this is a wonderful box of delights.

Symphonies – No. 1, Op. 22; No. 2, Op. 40.
London Symphony Orchestra / Richard Hickox.
Chandos CHAN9335 (61 minutes: DDD). Recorded 1994.   Ⓕ

Here is an entirely appropriate coupling of the first two symphonies, superbly played by the LSO and given demonstration sound in what is surely an ideal acoustic for this music, with striking depth and amplitude and a wholly natural brilliance. The dynamic range is wide but the moments of spectacle, and there are quite a few, bring no discomfort. Richard Hickox shows himself thoroughly at home in both symphonies and the readings have a natural flow and urgency, with the two slow movements bringing haunting, atmospheric feeling. The First Symphony opens with thrusting confidence on strings and horns and at its climax, where the strings soar against angry brass ostinatos, the playing generates great intensity; then at the start of the slow movement the purity of the flute solo brings a calm serenity which returns at the close. There are only three movements and the plangent lyrical melancholia of the expansive march theme of the finale is filled out by some superb horn playing which is enormously compelling. The first movement of Symphony No. 2 brings a most winning clarinet solo (Arnold's fund of melodic ideas seems inexhaustible), there is an energetic, bustling *Scherzo* to follow, but again it is the slow movement which one remembers for its elegiac opening, its arresting climax and lovely epilogue-like close. Above all these are real performances without any of the inhibitions of 'studio' recording.

Symphonies – No. 3, Op. 63; No. 4, Op. 71.
London Symphony Orchestra / Richard Hickox.
Chandos CHAN9290 (74 minutes: DDD). Recorded 1993.   Ⓕ **RR**

These two Arnold symphonies share comparatively little of the amiable optimism which distinguishes so many of his shorter works. Instead they reflect his experience of life over a broader span, with disillusion and even tragedy as part of their symphonic ethos. As it happens the Third Symphony does have an exuberant, upbeat finale, but even here there is a last-minute change of mood in the coda with a sudden Holst-like, plangent rhythmic warning; nevertheless the final few bars are distinctly positive. The work, commissioned by the Royal Liverpool Philharmonic Society and first performed in 1957, produces a long, striking and expressively bleak string melody in the opening movement, while the despairing isolation of its *Lento* slow movement is similarly harrowing. The first movement of the Fourth Symphony is dominated by one of those entirely winning Arnoldian lyrical tunes even though there is jagged dissonance in the central episode, and it has been suggested that this ambivalence was prompted by the contemporary Notting Hill race-riots, which also may have brought the Caribbean percussion instruments into the orchestra. Richard Hickox has the full measure of both symphonies and the Chandos recording is superb, full of colour and atmosphere.

Symphonies Nos. 3 and 4.
National Symphony Orchestra of Ireland / Andrew Penny.
Naxos 8 553739 (69 minutes: DDD). Recorded 1996.   Ⓢ

These recordings of two of Arnold's finest symphonies carry the composer's imprimatur (he attended the sessions). Andrew Penny is clearly right inside every bar of the music and the orchestra plays with impressive ensemble and feeling, and above all great freshness and spontaneity. The Naxos recording's concert-hall ambience has been beautifully caught by Chris Craker who both produced and engineered this disc. One of the finest players in Dublin is the principal oboe and his solos often bring a specially plangent quality, particularly in the slow movement of No. 3 (at 4'55") where there is a real sense of desolation. The finale then lightens the mood with its kaleidoscope of wind and brass and a wispy string melody that soon becomes more fulsome. Penny's momentum and characterization here are superb, as is the orchestral response. Similarly the winningly scored opening of the Fourth Symphony flashes with colour: that marvellous tune (2'44") is played with captivating delicacy by the violins. The exquisitely fragile *Scherzo* is etched with gossamer lightness and the slow movement is shaped by Penny with fine lyrical feeling and the most subtle use of light and shade. Its romanticism is heart-warming, yet balanced by Arnold's underlying unease. The boisterous fugal finale brings some of the best playing of all.

Symphonies – No. 5, Op. 74; No. 6, Op. 95.
London Symphony Orchestra / Richard Hickox.
Chandos CHAN9385 (58 minutes: DDD). Recorded 1995.   Ⓕ

Arnold's Fifth Symphony is one of his most accessible and rewarding works. The inspiration for the symphony was the early deaths of several of the composer's friends and colleagues: Dennis Brain, Frederick Thurston, David Paltenghi and Gerard Hoffnung. They are all remembered in the first movement and Hoffnung's spirit clearly pops up in the third and fourth. The Chandos recording is richly resonant and reinforces the impression that in Hickox's hands the *Andante* has an added degree of acceptance in its elegiac close, while the last two movements are colourfully expansive. The Sixth Symphony is nothing like as comfortable as the Fifth, with a bleak unease in the unrelenting energy of the first movement, which becomes even more discomfiting in the desolate start to the *Lento*. This leads to a forlorn suggestion of a funeral march, which then ironically quickens in pace but is suddenly cut down; the drum strokes become menacingly powerful and the despairing mood of the movement's opening returns. Hickox handles this quite superbly and grips the listener in the music's pessimism, which then lifts completely with the energetic syncopated trumpet theme of the rondo finale. Although later there are moments of ambiguity, and dissonant reminders of the earlier music, these are eclipsed by the thrilling life-asserting coda. In both symphonies the splendidly expansive Chandos recording increases the weight and power of utterance.

Symphony No. 6. Fantasy on a Theme of John Field, Op. 116. Sweeney Todd, Op. 68a. Tam O'Shanter, Op. 51.
John Lill *pf* **Royal Philharmonic Orchestra / Vernon Handley.**
Conifer Classics 74321 16847-2 (78 minutes: DDD). Recorded 1993.   Ⓕ Ⓢ Ⓔ

Tam O'Shanter, with its vivid drunken carousing and a witches' sabbath complete with bagpipes, never fails to make an impact and its exuberant scoring is vividly conveyed here. The essentially good-natured, high-spirited music for the ballet, *Sweeney Todd*, is a far cry from the malignancy of Stephen Sondheim's musical. Arnold instead surely recalls Tod Slaughter's Victorian-styled melodrama, which toured the No. 2 Theatres during the inter-war years. 'I'll polish them off' was the old actor-impresario's punch line, articulated with guttural emphasis and a glare at the audience, as he wiped the tomato ketchup off his cut-throat razor. And Arnold's score has a genuine music-hall flavour, all brightly scored and most entertaining when presented with such spirited insouciance as it is here. The *Fantasy on a Theme of John Field* opens with a flourish, then the piano enters relatively unostentatiously to gently establish the *Nocturne* in C major. After various orchestral interruptions, the delightfully innocent melody asserts itself, first with the soloist and then warmly and tenderly on the lower strings. The powerful Sixth Symphony – even though it has an upbeat ending to its jovial rondo-like finale – is a work which broods a great deal. The composer has suggested that his writing carries an affinity with the jazz phrases of Charlie Parker, yet its character is essentially symphonic, the string lines both scurrying and angularly sonorous, matched by melancholy and energetic woodwind. The composer was present at the recording sessions and must have been impressed by the power, spontaneity and grip of all these performances, and certainly by John Lill's melting Irish delicacy in his *sotto voce* presentation of the *John Field Nocturne*. The recording, made in London's Henry Wood Hall, is in every way first-class.

Symphony No. 9, Op. 128.
National Symphony Orchestra of Ireland / Andrew Penny.
Naxos 8 553540 (57 minutes: DDD). Includes an interview between the composer and the conductor. Recorded 1995.   Ⓢ Ⓔ

This culmination to Arnold's symphonic series is both characteristic and distinctive. If at the start and elsewhere one is reminded of Shostakovich, the instrumentation is quite distinctive. The ear is regularly tweaked by the terracing of sounds, at extremes of register as well as of dynamic, culminating in the long slow finale, almost as long as the other three movements combined. With two poignant themes, the mood of tragedy and disillusion is clear. The parallel with the final *Adagio* of Mahler's Ninth Symphony comes obviously to mind. Yet unlike Mahler the music conveys no hint of neurosis or self-pity. The other three movements are just as direct, bald in their arguments but ever pointful, not facile, built on instantly memorable material. Andrew Penny draws not just a concentrated, consistently committed performance from the Irish players, but a warmly resonant one, with the strings sounding glorious and the woodwind and brass consistently brilliant. The recording is rich and full.

Thomas Ashwell
British c1478-after 1513

Ashwell Missa Jesu Christe.
Aston Missa Videte manus meas.
Choir of Christ Church Cathedral, Oxford / Stephen Darlington.
Metronome METCD1030/1 (two discs: 93 minutes: DDD). Recorded 1998.   Ⓕ

Wolsey would have rejoiced to hear these two great Easter Masses sung, as he may well have done, in his own College of Christ Church, which he had founded with such magnificence. His piety and sophistication would have revelled in their spaciousness, their spirit of unhurried contemplation. But he would have been amazed had he known that 470 years on they were both being sung again, in the same church, by a similar combination of young voices. Stephen Darlington has done us all a great service by bringing them back to life: their individual flavour fills a gap in the vocal repertoire of a period up to now mainly represented by Taverner, Cornysh and Ludford. Darlington lets the polyphony speak for itself. In Ashwell's Mass he adopts a very gentle *tactus* – a slow heart-beat – and underplays the dynamics, relying chiefly on the composer's different combinations of voices for variety and contrast. The trebles in the gymel sections (where one voice part divides into two) are true professionals. Hugh Aston's Mass *Videte manus meas*, based on an Easter Magnificat antiphon, is characterized by its sense of line, with fully developed melismata. The *Sanctus* is striking, with alternating trios and quartets and a strong homophonic 'Hosanna'. The opening of the *Agnus Dei* is powerful in its simplicity – an upward-striding scale. Darlington's straightforward approach brings all this easily into focus, the one criticism being that better balance could have been achieved by strengthening the entries of one or two rather quieter inner voices.

Daniel Asia
American 1953

Piano Concerto. Black Light. Gateways.
André-Michel Schub *pf*
New Zealand Symphony Orchestra / James Sedares.
Koch International Classics 37372-2 (52 minutes: DDD). Recorded 1996.   Ⓕ

Seattle-born Daniel Asia can number Jacob Druckman, Stephen Albert, Gunther Schuller and Isang Yun among his teachers. Since 1988, he has been a member of the Music Faculty at the University of Arizona and was the Phoenix Symphony's composer-in-residence from 1991-94. *Black Light* (1990) grew out of Asia's 1987 *Scherzo Sonata* for piano (five movements of which also eventually formed the basis for his First Symphony) and charts a course from evocative slumberings ('like the quiet time before daybreak', to quote the composer) to joyous clangour ('the fierceness of the appearance of the sun ... in all its glory, at that first instant of daybreak'). Aptly festive in demeanour, the five-minute overture *Gateways* (1993) was commissioned by the Cincinnati Symphony for their centenary and is pure Stravinsky from start to finish (Asia himself unashamedly admits to cribbing from *The Rite of Spring* at the close). However, by far the biggest offering is the Piano Concerto (1994), an approachable, strongly communicative 37-minute work, whose rhythmically invigorating outer movements frame a mellifluous (but not always untroubled) 20-minute meditation. The admirable André-Michel Schub produces a ravishing variety of tone colour throughout and he is excellently supported by James Sedares directing a meticulously prepared New Zealand SO. Impressive sound, too: spacious, transparent and expertly balanced.

Kurt Atterberg
Swedish 1887-1974

Symphonies Nos. 7 and 8.
Malmö Symphony Orchestra / Michail Jurowski.
Sterling CDS1026-2 (69 minutes: DDD). Recorded 1998.   Ⓕ

Although best known for his genial Sixth Symphony – the *Dollar* Symphony, so-called as it won a $10,000 prize in the Schubert Centenary Year – Atterberg's Seventh and Eighth Symphonies are both new to the catalogue. The Seventh was composed in 1941-42 and revised in 1972, two years before his death. It was conceived as a protest against the anti-romanticism of the day and reworks ideas which were first used in an opera, *Fanal*. When it received its première in Frankfurt under Abendroth during the war, there were four movements, but in the late 1960s the composer excised the finale and made a substantial cut in the first movement. The opening idea is very Straussian and none the worse for that; the *Andante* bears the colours and melancholy of the corresponding movement of the Sixth, and despite a certain *naïveté*, the folk-like third movement forms an effective finale. It is well fashioned even if at times overscored. The Eighth comes from 1944; folk ideas predominate but genuine symphonic coherence is not achieved. A lot of the music is overblown and there are stretches with more corn than gold. The finale is particularly vacuous and should have received the same treatment as No. 7. All the same, there are episodes, especially in the slow movement, that are imaginative and attractive. The Malmö orchestra is a very persuasive advocate and the recording is first-class.

Daniel-François-Esprit Auber

French 1782-1871

Le domino noir.
Sumi Jo *sop* Angèle d'Olivarès; **Isabelle Vernet** *sop* Brigitte de San Lucar; **Bruce Ford** *ten* Horace de Massarena; **Patrick Power** *ten* Count Juliano; **Martine Olmeda** *mez* Jacinthe; **Jules Bastin** *bass* Gil Perez; **Doris Lamprecht** *mez* Ursule; **Jocelyne Taillon** *mez* La tourière; **Gilles Cachemaille** *bar* Lord Elfort; **London Voices.**
Gustav III, ou Le bal masqué – Overture; Ballet Music.
English Chamber Orchestra / Richard Bonynge.
Decca 440 646-2DHO2 (two discs: 144 minutes: DDD). Notes, text and translation included. Ⓕ🅴
Recorded 1993-95.

Auber's operas were tremendously successful in the nineteenth century, but have hardly been performed in the twentieth at all. *Le domino noir* clocked up 1,200 performances in Paris alone, after its 1837 première, and was soon seen in London and in New Orleans. This spiffing recording is the surest blow yet to be struck for a revival of Auber's popularity in our time. The music is tuneful, danceable, constantly surprising in its form, and full of interesting orchestration. The story is a variation on the usual masked-ball romantic comedy. The heroine, Angèle, is confidently sung by Sumi Jo. As the young man in pursuit of the beautiful masked stranger, Bruce Ford sings with a good deal of elegance, taking the high notes in full voice, rather than the head tone which was probably customary in the 1830s. Both he and Sumi Jo deal pretty well with the French language – most of the rest of the cast consists of distinguished French singers: Isabelle Vernet as Angèle's confidante, Martine Olmeda splendid as the housekeeper, Jacinthe, and the veteran Jules Bastin as Gil Perez, porter at the convent. One of Auber's most successful tragic operas was another masked ball – *Gustav III*, the libretto of which, also by Scribe, later served for Verdi's *Un ballo in maschera*. As a fill-up on the second disc we get the ball scene from that opera, which is a ballet in itself. Bonynge conducts with his usual flair, keeping everything going at a sparkling pace and encouraging some really imaginative singing. Gilles Cachemaille has a cameo as one of those satirical English milords who were so much a part of nineteenth-century Parisian comedy. Auber and Scribe produced 50 operas together. No wonder the streets on either side of the Paris Opéra are named after them.

Carl Philipp Emanuel Bach

German 1714-1788

Cello Concertos – A minor, H432; B flat major, H436; A major, H439.
Bach Collegium Japan / Hidemi Suzuki *vc*
BIS CD807 (68 minutes: DDD). Recorded 1996. Ⓕ🅿🅴

Writing in the booklet for this release, Hidemi Suzuki wonders why it is that cellists who bemoan their lack of concerto repertory continue to neglect C.P.E. Bach's three essays in the genre. One can only agree with him that it is indeed a mystery, for these are excellent pieces, full of infectious nervous energy in their outer movements and tender lyricism in central ones. The Bach concertos are not unknown to the recording catalogues, however, not least because they also exist in alternative versions which the composer made for flute and harpsichord respectively. As Suzuki points out, there are times when the low-lying cello has difficulty making itself heard properly against the orchestra. Having said this he proceeds to make light of the matter with performances whose agility, lightness and textural clarity make those of Bylsma and the larger-sounding OAE sound heavy-handed by comparison. But while Suzuki – thanks to a generally thinner sound – is the more successful in the way he transmits the surface excitement and energy of the quick movements, he cannot match Bylsma's vocal inspiration in the eloquent poetry of the slow movement. Suzuki's, nevertheless, are refreshing and enlivening performances of attractive and substantial music.

Cello Concertos.
Anner Bylsma vc
Orchestra of the Age of Enlightenment / Gustav Leonhardt.
Virgin Classics Veritas VM5 61401-2 (70 minutes: DDD). Recorded 1998. Ⓜ🅿

However unlikely, circumstantially, that the cello versions came first, it is nevertheless that instrument which often seems to bring out the expressive qualities in this music most eloquently. This is, above all, the case in the slow movements where the cello captures that darkly shaded intensity of expression at which Bach excelled. The most striking of the three is the muted *Largo mesto* of the A major Concerto, which plunges the listener into a shadowy world whose wide-ranging imaginative content presages early German romanticism. None of this is lost on Anner Bylsma who is quite the most ardently persuasive advocate. His playing of all three slow movements is suffused with an intensity and rapt contemplation which draw in the listener, holding his concentration, as it were, spellbound. Fast outer movements, in contrast, dance along happily with lightly articulated solo passages, warm tone and eloquent projection. There are, admittedly, a few passages of shaky intonation, but taken in context with the performances as a whole, they are insignificant. Bylsma brings enormous warmth of spirit to the music, sometimes tender, sometimes quite fiercely passionate and always with sympathetic understanding of Bach's individual gestures. The cadenzas are Bylsma's own and very convincing they are too. The OAE provides strong support, Gustav Leonhardt's direction – from the podium rather than the harpsichord on this occasion – being characteristically sympathetic, bringing many insights to an elusive style. The recorded sound is admirably clear and ideally resonant.

Cello Concertos.
Timothy Hugh vc
Bournemouth Sinfonietta / Richard Studt.
Naxos 8 553298 (71 minutes: DDD). Recorded 1995. Ⓢ

Timothy Hugh's bow dances in the flanking movements and is matched by those of the Bournemouth Sinfonietta, alert to every nuance and disposed to throw their weight around only as much as is fitting. It is, however, the slow movements that are the heart of these works. They are all tinged with sadness but none more than the *Largo* of the A major Concerto, where Hugh's abated vibrato, attenuated lines and resistance to the excessive squeezing of *appoggiaturas* express a sadness that is held within, not spilt in salt tears. This is a recording to set alongside the two reviewed above and its bargain price may greatly twist the arm that reaches for the wallet.

Harpsichord Concertos – G minor, H409; A major, H411; D major, H421.
Miklós Spányi hpd
Concerto Armonico / Péter Szüts.
BIS CD767 (68 minutes: DDD). Recorded 1995. Ⓕ🅿

Whilst these particular concertos are not always consistently engaging, they nevertheless demonstrate the emerging inventiveness of C.P.E.'s musical personality within a growing trend towards public concerts in the mid-eighteenth century. In fits and starts there are those sparsely etched landscapes, complete with an unsettled weather front, which at their best can captivate us. If decorum sometimes gets overworked, Bach's originality is even more remarkable given that the ritornello structure inherited from his father's generation, with its alternating solo and string sections, is less easy to sustain in a relatively uncontrapuntal style. Contrast is therefore a key element and Bach needs a soloist who can discern how the relationship between the harpsichord and the orchestra can be manipulated to good effect. Miklós Spányi and Concerto Armonico, led by Péter Szüts, give wonderfully lucid, flexible and clearly articulated readings. Moreover, Spányi's cultivated asides are matched by a string ensemble which graciously responds to the soloist's discretion. The shading in the finale of the G minor and middle movement of the D major Concertos is also energized by a naturally discursive balance, a deft textural palette for which artist and engineer can take equal credit. With such eloquent and fresh playing, this volume of world première recordings will give the listener more than just an opportunity to refine his perspective on Bach's achievements. Much of this music gets under the skin in its own right, and more so on repeated listening. It deserves a welcoming audience.

Keyboard Concertos – D major, H414; E major, H417; A major, H422.
Concerto Armonico / Miklós Spányi *fp*
BIS CD785 (74 minutes: DDD). Recorded 1996.   Ⓕ🅟

With his fifth volume of C.P.E. Bach's complete keyboard concertos Miklós Spányi comes to three works composed in the mid-1740s, which he plays on a copy of a Silbermann fortepiano of that period – not only because such instruments existed at Frederick the Great's court, where Carl Philipp was employed, but because the keyboard layout is more suited to the fortepiano than the harpsichord, and because the A major work here – a first recording, like that of the D major – includes the marking *pianissimo* (impossible on the harpsichord). The present instrument is light and silvery in tone, which makes for some difficulties of proportion in the D major, which is performed with additional manuscript parts found in Brussels for trumpets and drums. The more embellished version of the A major Concerto is adopted here. The first movement displays some particularly athletic passagework for the piano. The second movement is striking in starting with a long unison melodic line over a rudimentary bass, with no internal harmonic filling: the attractive finale is characterized by a happy freshness. In the E major Concerto the instrumentation is augmented by horn parts found in a Berlin manuscript. Musically it is the most inventive and unusual, harmonically certainly the most adventurous, of the present three works – a splendid concerto that deserves to be better known. The recording has occasional problems with balance but the performances by Spányi and Concerto Armonico are praiseworthy.

Keyboard Concertos – E minor, H418; B flat major, H429; G minor, H442.
Miklós Spányi *fp*
Concerto Armonico / Péter Szüts *vn*
BIS CD786 (73 minutes: DDD). Recorded 1996.   Ⓕ🅟

On this recording Miklós Spányi has exchanged his previous harpsichord or fortepiano for a tangent piano: this was like a fortepiano but had the strings struck vertically by tangents (as in the clavichord) rather than at an angle by hammers; its tone could also be modified by raising the dampers completely or only in the treble, employing only one of each note's two strings (*una corda*), inserting a leather strip ('moderator') between tangents and strings, or creating a harp-like effect by damping the strings with small pieces of cloth. The boldness and unusual style of Emanuel's concertos took his contemporaries aback even though compelling their admiration, and even now they can surprise. The extrovert E minor work, for example, begins with dramatic energy but is interrupted by extraordinary, tentative-sounding broken phrases at the soloist's first entry before being allowed to continue on its way: the *Adagio*, which includes striking chromatic progressions, has imitative interplay between the solo instrument and the violins. The finale of the otherwise more 'normal' *galant* G minor Concerto (in whose central movement two flutes join the strings) generates very vehement chordal attacks – or are these being overdone in this performance? Spányi's playing throughout has vitality and neatness, although his lifting of the dampers in running passages inevitably causes them to become blurred.

C.P.E. Bach Sinfonias, H663-6 – No. 1 in D major; No. 2 in E flat major; No. 3 in F major; No. 4 in G major.
W.F. Bach Sinfonia in F major.
Salzburg Chamber Philharmonic Orchestra / Yoon K. Lee.
Naxos 8 553289 (52 minutes: DDD). Recorded 1994.   Ⓢ

The exhilarating C.P.E. Bach symphonies presented here are not the more frequently recorded, surprise-filled string symphonies of 1773 (H657-62), but the set of four for strings, flutes, oboes, bassoons and horns which Bach wrote a couple of years later. They are no less astonishing. Bewildering changes of direction, disorientating rhythmic games and unexpected solos all turn up in this nervous, excitable music, which for originality and sheer life-force could surely only have been matched in its day by that of Haydn. The Salzburg Chamber Philharmonic, under its founder Yoon K. Lee, turns in crisp, spirited and (the odd moment of slack tuning apart) disciplined performances which do the music full justice. They are not timid about making the most of Bach's strong contrasts, although they produce them more by the release of some thunderous *forte* passages than by the pursuit of too many unearthly *pianissimos*. The overall effect is wholly convincing, and only in the symphony by Emanuel's older brother Wilhelm Friedemann – more old-fashioned and less successful as a piece, though in its way just as determinedly unorthodox – does the use of modern instruments begin to get in the way of the spirit of music. This is an undeniably good buy.

Quartet for Keyboard, Flute, Viola and Continuo in D major, H538. Viola da gamba Sonata in G minor, Wq88 – Larghetto. Trio Sonatas – Two Violins and Continuo in C minor, H579; Flute, Violin and Continuo in C major, H571. Solo Flute Sonata in A minor, H562.
Florilegium (Ashley Solomon *fl* Rachel Podger *vn/va* Lucy Russell *vn* Daniel Yeadon *vc/va da gamba* Neal Peres da Costa *hpd/fp*).
Channel Classics CCS11197 (59 minutes: DDD). Recorded 1997.   Ⓕ🅿

Over half a century separates the earliest and the latest of the works here: the C major Trio Sonata was one of Bach's earliest compositions, written at the age of 17 more or less under his father's supervision, the D major Quartet in the last year of his life, while he was Music Director in Hamburg: the remaining items on this disc date from his time at the court of Frederick the Great. The youthful work is distinguished by an exhilaratingly sprightly finale and a remarkably fine, harmonically chromatic *Adagio*. The C minor Sonata is extraordinary, a programmatic work 'portraying a conversation between a Sanguineus and a Melancholicus' who disagree throughout the first two movements, but the former's outlook prevails in the finale. So for much of the sonata the musical phrases constantly alternate expressively between *lamentoso* or melancholy and high spirits. The talented Florilegium players bring out to the full the bewilderingly diverse character of this sonata, which is outstanding even for so strongly individual a composer as Carl Philipp. If the Sonata for unaccompanied flute was written for Frederick, as seems likely, he must have been quite skilled, able to cope not only with contrasting dynamics and the differentiation of the melodic line from suggestions of the bass and harmony, but with some fairly virtuosic passagework. Ashley Solomon's performance is most persuasive. How far Carl Philipp developed is shown by the late quartet, an attractive composition which, besides promoting the keyboard (fortepiano here) from a mere continuo to prominent solo status, is already in the style of the Viennese classics in form, and links the first two movements. The whole disc is strongly recommended.

Keyboard Sonatas – B minor, H35; E major, H39; F minor, H40; C major, H41; B flat major, H51.
Colin Booth *hpd*
Olympia OCD433 (78 minutes: DDD). Recorded 1992.   Ⓕ🅿

One interesting feature of these keyboard sonatas is the stylistic variety that is contained within individual movements. Recitative-like passages jostle with orchestrally conceived ideas, lyricism with more robust, challenging gestures, counterpoint with homophonic texture and baroque disciplines with *galant* phraseology. Rhythmic and harmonic uncertainties abound and all this is placed at the service of expression. Colin Booth plays with technical fluency and a ready awareness of all the little quirks and pitfalls in Bach's style which can be the undoing of players with a more prosaic outlook. He plays his own copy of a two-manual Mietke harpsichord. This is a recital well worth becoming acquainted with, above all for the music but also for the sympathetic playing and the distinctive sound of the harpsichord.

Organ Sonatas – F major, H84; A minor, H85; D major, H86; G minor, H87; A major, H133; B flat major, H134.
Marie-Claire Alain *org*
Erato 0630-14777-2 (70 minutes: DDD). Recorded on the organ of the Karlhorst-Kirche, Berlin. Recorded 1996.   Ⓕ🅿

Bach's sonatas for organ were originally written for Princess Anna Amalia; 'a princess who could not play the pedal or cope with difficulties, even though she had built for herself a beautiful organ with 2 manuals and pedal and liked to play on it'. It is on that very organ that these sonatas have here been recorded. The organ, built in 1755, makes a simply magical sound, beautifully captured in Erato's intimate, crystal-clear recording. The music may avoid the kind of technical demands with which Princess Anna could not cope and certainly does not require the kind of vast registration resource on which Alain seems to thrive – although she has taken the trouble to guide us through her registration – as usual, we can only marvel at the unending variety of sounds she has been able to conjure up from just 22 speaking stops. But these are endearing performances of undeniably charming music. Little hints of Mozart, maybe even of Bach *père* appear momentarily. For the most part, though, it is Bach's distinctive individual voice which comes through with an approach to the organ which owes nothing to his father other than the skill in writing music which suits the instrument to perfection.

Die Auferstehung und Himmelfahrt Jesu, H777.
Hillevi Martinpelto *sop* Christoph Prégardien *ten* Peter Harvey *bass* **Ghent Collegium Vocale Choir; Orchestra of the Age of Enlightenment / Philippe Herreweghe.**

Virgin Classics Veritas VC7 59069-2 (76 minutes: DDD). Text and translation included. ⓕⓟ
Recorded 1991.

Although frequently classified as an oratorio, *Die Auferstehung und Himmelfahrt Jesu* is really a cantata. C.P.E. considered it, in his own words as 'pre-eminent among all my vocal works in expression and in the composition'. The author of the text was Karl Wilhelm Ramler, an important poet of the German Enlightenment whose texts had earlier attracted Telemann. Ramler and Bach engaged in a close collaboration over the *Auferstehung*, entering into a lively correspondence concerning the details and shape of the cantata. The first performance took place in Hamburg in 1778 when it was warmly received. Many subsequent performances were given, culminating in three directed by Mozart in Vienna. There is a fine trio of soloists and The Orchestra of the Age of Enlightenment is notable for its warmth and refinement of sound. The recording is spacious and pleasing and the booklet includes Ramler's German text with English and French translations.

Johann Christian Bach   German 1735-1782

Harpsichord Concertos – D minor; B flat major; F minor.
Hanover Band / Anthony Halstead *hpd*
CPO CPO999 393-2 (57 minutes: DDD). Recorded 1995. ⓕⓟ

The works of J.C. Bach's Berlin years are almost indistinguishable from those of his brother, C.P.E., and anyone putting on this disc could be excused for thinking the first movement of the D minor Concerto – with its purposeful, energetic scales, its stark textures, its heavily used motifs, its rushing harpsichord writing, its sombre minor key and its total lack of lyricism – to be wholly C.P.E.'s work. It is in fact a very accomplished piece for a composer less than 20 years old and there are glimmerings of J.C.'s own voice in the *Adagio affettuoso* that follows; it still sounds like North German music, untouched by Italian softness and sunshine, but the harpsichord cantilena certainly has a more personal expressive character and so does some of the string writing in the ritornellos and accompaniment. The slow movements throughout seem the most individual and appealing in a sense that C.P.E.'s are not. The quick movements, especially in the B flat Concerto, contain gestures of the abrupt and musically violent kind that C.P.E. so often used. The finale of the D minor has a curious element of fantasy and an imaginative use of pizzicato behind the first solo entry. Halstead uses a small orchestra, strings only, 3.3.1.1.1, which is quite sufficient and very alert. The solo playing is extremely fluent and indeed brilliant; Halstead plays with ample energy and rhythmic precision and he realizes the elaborate melodic lines effectively. One may not be entirely convinced by some of his cadenzas, which seem to go harmonically too far afield too quickly; but this is a small blemish in an admirable disc which brings two virtually unknown works into the catalogue.

Symphonies concertantes – F major, T287 No. 2; B flat major, T287 No. 7; D major.
Anthony Robson *ob* **Jeremy Ward** *bn* **Graham Cracknell, Anna McDonald** *vns*
Sebastian Comberti *vc* **Hanover Band / Anthony Halstead.**
CPO CPO999 537-2 (52 minutes: DDD). Recorded 1997. ⓕⓟ

In the notes Ernest Warburton, the leading J.C. Bach scholar, draws a distinction between the baroque *concerto grosso* and the *symphonie concertante* form that became popular, especially in Paris, in the last three or four decades of the eighteenth century. The *symphonie concertante*, predominantly light-hearted, allotted a more prominent role to the solo instruments. The earliest of the present three works is that in F, and Warburton speculates that the choice of a solo oboe and bassoon suggests that it may have been written in 1761 for Naples, where Bach's opera *Catone in Utica* called for outstanding players of just these instruments. It is a cheerfully engaging two-movement work that constantly takes the bassoon up into the tenor register: its first movement is decidedly unorthodox in shape. The D major work, in three movements, likewise ends in a minuet, with a trio in the minor for a change. Overall, the writing markedly places more emphasis on virtuosity for the two soloists, and both in the energetic first movement and the more formal second there is a lengthy cadenza (found in the manuscript). The most notable *symphonie concertante* here, however, is that in B flat, for long considered lost and rediscovered only in 1996: this is, consequently, its first recording. Probably composed for J.C.'s London concerts in the late 1770s, it allows the orchestra greater say; the initial ritornellos in the first two movements, the former featuring clarinets, are unusually long. In the *Larghetto* the solo cello completely drops out, leaving the violin long, sweetly pungent cantilenas – a strikingly fine movement. Anthony Halstead secures neat performances of finesse of all three works, which also benefit from skilful soloists and well-balanced recording. Delightful.

Six Symphonies, Op. 6 – No. 1 in G major; No. 2 in D major; No. 3 in E flat major; No. 4 in B flat major; No. 5 in E flat major; No. 6 in G minor.
Hanover Band / Anthony Halstead.
CPO CPO999 298-2 (56 minutes: DDD). Recorded 1994.   Ⓕ Ⓟ

In the Op. 6 Symphonies, the frothy Italianate music of the composer's Italian and early London years was behind him; these pieces, dating from the late 1760s, though still of course Italian-influenced in their formal clarity and their melodic style, are sturdier music, more carefully composed, more symphonic in feeling. Both the E flat works in this set have something of the solidity and warmth associated with that key, and each has a C minor *Andante*; the G major's first movement has the confident ring and thematic contrasts of his mature music, and the D major contains Mannheim *crescendos* and some delightful textures, with flutes and divided violas, in its charming and slightly playful middle movement. The set ends with Bach's single minor-key symphony in G minor, very similar in spirit to Mozart's No. 25; this piece, often recorded before, shows an unfamiliar side to his musical personality. Anthony Halstead and his players convey the strength and the spirit of the music convincingly. The lively finales all go with a swing, and the opening movements have plenty of energy. The slow movements are not always quite so persuasive: the third C minor slow movement of the G minor Symphony is a little overdeliberate and becomes detached and modest in expressive impact. But generally these are strong and appealing performances of some attractive and unfamiliar music, clearly, slightly drily recorded, and admirers of the London Bach and his music need not hesitate.

Symphonies – Op. 9: No. 1 in B flat major; No. 2 in E flat major; No. 3 in B flat major; B flat major, Sieber No. 1; E flat major, Sieber No. 2; E flat major (ed. Warburton).
Hanover Band / Anthony Halstead.
CPO CPO999 487-2 (60 minutes: DDD). Recorded 1996.   Ⓕ Ⓟ

This disc offers the Op. 9 Symphonies published in The Hague in 1773, two of them in two versions, along with another symphony that is very little known. Ernest Warburton explains in his notes that the usual texts for these works, with oboes and horns, are in his view arrangements of originals calling for clarinets – still rarities in most European orchestras at the time these pieces were written – and bassoon, in which form one of them was published in Paris. Here, then, Op. 9 Nos. 1 and 2 are done twice over to allow listeners to compare the versions; and certainly they differ quite markedly in flavour with clarinets and bassoon – the E flat work, No. 2, one of Bach's finest and most vigorously argued symphonies, comes out particularly well, with quite a different ring to its tuttis. The other work here, an E flat Symphony, also has clarinets, though their parts lie in a lower-middle register that is rather uncharacteristic. It is an attractive work, with an eloquent violin line in the *Andante*, and a charming final gavotte. Of the works played twice, the B flat is lightish, probably originally an opera overture; the E flat has more substance and notably a C minor slow movement with a melody of a haunting, graceful beauty. The third Op. 9 Symphony is a brisk little piece which again started life as an overture. Halstead directs with his usual style and shapeliness.

Adriano in Siria – Overture. Six Grand Overtures, Op. 18 – No. 1 in E flat major; No. 4 in D major. Symphony in G minor, Op. 6 No. 6. Sinfonia concertante in C major, T289 No. 4 (ed. Maunder).
Academy of Ancient Music / Simon Standage *vn*
Chandos Chaconne CHAN0540 (65 minutes: DDD). Recorded 1993.   Ⓕ Ⓟ

The G minor Symphony is a magnificently fiery piece, similar in manner to Haydn's No. 39 and Mozart's No. 25; it is done here with plenty of *Sturm und Drang*, notably in the very forceful finale, and the fine, noble ideas of the slow movement are well caught too. The opening item is a three-movement D major Symphony, in effect, with a well-worked first movement and an *Andante* with rich wind writing. No other composer, besides of course Mozart, seems to have had as keen a feeling as J.C. Bach for the sensuous beauty of wind textures. The *Sinfonia concertante* isn't quite as successful a piece, being rather repetitive, but it is never less than charming and enjoyable music, again with some beautiful wind textures in the *Larghetto* and a delightful 'Two lovely black eyes' theme in the rondo. The solo playing is admirable. Recommended to anyone sympathetic to J.C. Bach's music.

Overtures – Gioas, re di Giuda; Adriano in Siria; Zanaida; Orione. La clemenza di Scipione – Overture; No. 5, March in G major; No. 22, March in E flat major. Carattaco – Overture; No. 20, March in B flat major; No. 26, March in G major. Symphony in D major, Schmitt Op. 18 No. 1.
Hanover Band / Anthony Halstead.
CPO CPO999 488-2 (58 minutes: DDD). Recorded 1996.   Ⓕ Ⓟ

Small-scale but elegantly fashioned, melodious and pleasurable music: it is no wonder that the London public in the 1760s and 1770s took Johann Christian to their hearts – though in their fickle way they then barely noticed his (in straitened circumstances) death in the following decade. Here we have the overtures to six works of his that were performed at the King's Theatre in the Haymarket – from his first opera there, *Orione* in 1763, to his last, *La clemenza di Scipione* in 1778, and the 1770 oratorio, *Gioas*, plus a symphony which is a *pasticcio* of the *Clemenza* overture with additional trumpets and drums and a revised version of the *Andante* from the overture to his only completed French opera, the 1779 *Amadis de Gaule*. With the exception of this last and of *Adriano in Siria*, all are either first recordings or the first in their original versions. The most striking feature about all these works, apart from their vigorous openings, is the freedom in the use of wind instruments: *Zanaida* has *soli* clarinets, and the trio of *Orione*'s minuet is for wind band only, as are passages in *Adriano*, the E flat March in *Clemenza* and the brilliant final *Presto* of *Carattaco*. The Hanover Band's playing is vital and fresh, rhythmically crisp and tonally clean-cut; the recording is first-rate.

Johann Sebastian Bach

German 1685-1750

Harpsichord Concertos – D minor, BWV1052; D major, BWV1054. Concerto for Flute, Violin, Harpsichord and Strings in A minor, BWV1044. Das wohltemperierte Klavier, BWV846-93 – Preludes and Fugues: F major, BWV880; B major, BWV892.
Le Concert Français / Pierre Hantaï *hpd*
Auvidis Astrée E8523 (70 minutes: DDD). Recorded 1993.   Ⓕ Ⓟ Ⓔ

The concertos come over well. Ensemble is tautly controlled and the string playing effectively articulated, though on occasion the first violin is a little too favoured in the recorded balance. However, the string playing is so unanimous in sound and purpose that there is little to worry about in this department. Hantaï himself is impressive for his wonderfully rhythmic playing, the clarity with which he interprets both his own keyboard textures and those which support and punctuate it, and not least for his supple, muscular concept of the music. These are extraordinarily invigorating performances, which draw the listener deep into the harmonic and contrapuntal complexities and conceits of Bach's art. Take for instance the elusive *Adagio* of BWV1052, where careful punctuation and sensitive interaction between solo and tutti make for a rewarding coherence. In the A minor Triple Concerto, Hantaï is joined by his flautist brother, Marc, and François Fernandez (violin), the leader of the ensemble. The work is a Leipzig arrangement of movements from earlier pieces not in concerto form, whose extent sources were almost certainly copied after Bach's death. The opening *Allegro* is a little too heavy, but the essentially three-part texture of the middle movement is realized with affection. Altogether a stimulating disc.

Oboe Concertos – F major, BWV1053; A major, BWV1055; D minor, BWV1059.
Chamber Orchestra of Europe / Douglas Boyd *ob/ob d'amore*
DG 429 225-2GH (46 minutes: DDD). Recorded 1989.   Ⓕ

Although Bach is not known to have written any concertos for the oboe he did entrust it with some beautiful *obbligato* parts, so he clearly did not underrate its expressive capacities. He did, however, rearrange many of his works for different instrumental media and there is musicological evidence that original oboe concertos were the (lost) sources from which other works were derived. The Harpsichord Concerto, BWV1055, is believed originally to have been written for the oboe d'amore, whilst the other two Oboe Concertos have been reassembled from movements found in various cantatas. Whatever the validity of the academic reasoning, the results sound very convincing. Douglas Boyd is a superb oboist, with a clear sound, and a fluency that belies the instrument's technical difficulty. He plays the faster, outer movements with winsome lightness, and with alertness to dynamic nuance; the slow ones, the hearts of these works, are given with sensitivity but without sentimentality – which can easily invade that of BWV1059, taken from Cantata No. 156, *Ich steh mit einem Fuss im Grabe*. The COE partners him to perfection in this crisp recording.

J.S. Bach Oboe d'amore Concerto in D major, BWV1053a (arr. Mehl). Cantata No. 156, 'Ich steh mit einem Fuss im Grabe' – Sinfonia. Trio in F major, BWV1040.
C.P.E. Bach Oboe Concertos – B flat major, H466; E flat major, H468.
Heinz Holliger *ob/ob d'amore* **Massimo Polidori** *vc* **Andreas Erisman** *hpd*
Berne Camerata / Thomas Zehetmair *vn*
Philips 454 450-2PH (63 minutes: DDD). Recorded 1996.   Ⓕ

It's nice to see J.S.'s music coupled with that of his second son, Carl Philipp Emanuel, an obvious enough idea, yet not one which is realized so very often. The J.S. pieces are the Oboe d'amore

Concerto reconstructed from the E major Harpsichord Concerto (and very convincingly so); the Sinfonia from Cantata No. 156, a sweetly lyrical piece for oboe and strings which also turns up as the slow movement of the F minor Harpsichord Concerto; and a tiny Trio which, in typical Bach fashion, makes light of the fact that it is canonic. The two C.P.E. concertos are both works of his late years in Berlin, expansive and varied as ever, and mixing polite *galanteries* with a more deeply felt, brooding changeableness, especially evident in the slow movements. The J.S. pieces receive the more convincing performance: Holliger's playing, as one might expect, shows superb technical control; he demonstrates a pleasing variety of articulation in the Concerto and the Trio (matched in the latter by the violin of Thomas Zehetmair), while the Sinfonia just oozes with all the gentle flow it demands. How odd then that, by comparison, the C.P.E. Bach performances should sound so old-fashioned, with more vibrato from the strings and a resultant slight loss of clarity and incisiveness. This is music which benefits more from the use of period instruments, but undoubtedly there are plenty who would disagree, and Holliger's musicianship cannot be faulted; there are few baroque oboists who could play with such fluidity. So unless you have an aversion to modern instruments, you can buy with confidence.

Violin Concertos – No. 1 in A minor, BWV1041; No. 2 in E major, BWV1042.

Violin Concertos Nos. 1 and 2. Double Concertos – C minor for Violin and Oboe, BWV1060[a]; D minor for Two Violins, BWV1043.
Arthur Grumiaux, Herman Krebbers *vns* **Heinz Holliger** *ob*
Les Solistes Romands; New Philharmonia Orchestra / Arpad Gerecz, [a]**Edo de Waart.**
Philips Silver Line 420 700-2PSL (61 minutes: ADD). Recorded 1970-78.　　　Ⓜ RR

In the old days, records of Bach violin concertos were adequately filled by the Concertos in A minor and E major, plus the Double Violin Concerto. On this disc these three works are played strongly by Arthur Grumiaux, who is joined in the Double Concerto by Herman Krebbers. Arpad Gerecz directs Les Solistes Romands and the 1970s recordings are vivid; some may even find it slightly strident. The fourth work (to fill the longer playing time available) is the Concerto for oboe and violin, BWV1060. Heinz Holliger plays beautifully in this work, and Grumiaux is utterly relaxed with the New Philharmonia Orchestra under Edo de Waart in a noticeably warm recording.

Violin Concertos Nos. 1 and 2. Double Violin Concertos – D minor, BWV1043; D minor, BWV1060.
Rachel Podger *vn* **Academy of Ancient Music / Andrew Manze** *vn*
Harmonia Mundi HMU90 7155 (57 minutes: DDD). Recorded 1996.　　　Ⓕ P

This recording contains not only the three well-known pieces, but also another D minor work (BWV1060), which is almost invariably heard nowadays in its putative version, sometimes in C minor, for violin and oboe. Here, it is treated as a double concerto for two violins. Manze's playing, and that of his partner in the double concertos, Rachel Podger, is engaging on a number of different levels. Welcome indeed, is the absence of intrusive mannerism, the offspring of too rigid an adherence to dogma. Instead these artists allow the poetry of Bach's music to unfold in a comfortably measured, lucidly punctuated and eloquently inflected way. Manze himself projects a highly developed sense of fantasy in his interpretations and, for the most part, it proves immensely effective here. The opening of the A minor Concerto is a particularly telling instance, but there are countless others to be found in the *ripieno* sections of each work. The two double concertos come over lyrically and with splendid rhythmic energy. The relationship between the two violins is not as close as that which exists in the other, great D minor work (BWV1043) but, as Manze remarks in his note, the poetic *Adagio* does come off uncommonly well on what one might be permitted to describe in these pages as a 'matched pair'. Here is a disc which is likely to have wide appeal. Everything is done with thought and affection for Bach's music as well as with a recognition of its expressive potential.

Double Concertos – D minor for Two Violins, BWV1043[a]; C minor for Violin and Oboe, BWV1060[b]; C minor for Two Harpsichords, BWV1060[c]; C minor for Two Harpsichords, BWV1062[c].
[a]**Jaap Schröder,** [a]**Christopher Hirons,** [b]**Catherine Mackintosh** *vns* [b]**Stephen Hammer** *ob*
[c]**Christophe Rousset** *hpd* **Academy of Ancient Music / Christopher Hogwood** [c]*hpd*
L'Oiseau-Lyre Florilegium 421 500-2OH (58 minutes: DDD).　　　Ⓕ P

The concept of a concerto with two or more soloists grew naturally out of the *concerto grosso*, and Bach was among those baroque composers who explored its possibilities. The Concerto in D minor, BWV1043, for two violins is perhaps the best known of his works in the *genre*, which Bach himself reworked as a Concerto for Two Harpsichords, BWV1062, in the key of C minor. No alternative version has survived in the case of the two-harpsichord Concerto BWV1060, also in C minor, but musicological evidence suggests that it was originally intended for two single-line instruments – two violins or one violin and an oboe. The work has thus been notionally reconstructed in the latter form. Baroque music never sounds better than when it is played on period instruments, in proper style, and by performers of the quality of those in this recording, not least the well-matched soloists. The famous slow movement of BWV1043 is taken a little faster than usual, convincingly stripped of the specious sentimentality with which it is often invested. The recording is of suitably high quality.

Brandenburg Concertos, BWV1046-51 – No. 1 in F major; No. 2 in F major; No. 3 in G major; No. 4 in G major; No. 5 in D major; No. 6 in B flat major.

Brandenburg Concertos Nos. 1-6. Orchestral Suites – No. 2 in B minor, BWV1066; No. 3 in D major, BWV1067.
Vienna Concentus Musicus / Nikolaus Harnoncourt.
Teldec 4509-95980-2 (two discs: 148 minutes: DDD). Recorded 1981-83.　Ⓜ️ⓅⓇⓇ

This is the second set of *Brandenburgs* directed by Nikolaus Harnoncourt, following his pioneering accounts of the 1960s. The later performances, in particular, have been favourites for reissue on a number of occasions since their original release in 1982, with the current and more attractive format of two orchestral suites making up this generously filled release: a brooding account of the B minor Suite and a gleeful No. 3. Packaging aside, a strong sense of reappraisal lies at the heart of these challenging performances of the *Brandenburgs*, plainly evident in the level of refinement and attention to detail, traits that have now become Harnoncourt's hallmark in later repertoire; the technical limitations of period instrumentalists from the first set are definitely a ghost laid to rest. Concerto No. 2, for instance, has a considered nonchalance and the trumpet playing is of a different order here: this is one of the most aristocratic and rounded performances on disc. While perhaps never totally succeeding in displacing the older (1967) version in many people's affections, the present one does have several strong points, not least among them the extraordinarily high quality of the recording itself. Where this set scores over the older one is in respect of the brass and woodwind playing. Great advances were made between the 1960s and the 1980s in rediscovering and developing techniques required to bring period horns, trumpets, oboes and flutes to life in a convincing way. The playing at its best is very good indeed. Such is the case with Alice Harnoncourt's solo violin playing in the Fourth Concerto of the set which, both from a technical and an interpretative viewpoint, is an outstanding feature of the set as a whole. The two string concertos (Nos. 3 and 6) also come over well. In summary, there is nothing here that is remotely dull and the level of execution is consistently high. Well worth becoming acquainted with.

Brandenburg Concertos Nos. 1-6.
Tafelmusik / Jeanne Lamon *vn*
Sony Classical Vivarte S2K66289 (two discs: 93 minutes: DDD).Recorded 1993-94.　ⒻⓅ

Tafelmusik's *Brandenburgs* come straight from the heart and as such they are performances which invite repeated listening and are furthermore both easy and enjoyable to live with. There are no startling novelties here and nothing which attempts to impede the natural course of musical flow. Tempos are sensibly chosen and, once chosen, consistently adhered to. That is not to say that there is an absence of affective gesture or a lack of rhetorical awareness. Everything in fact is punctuated in a way that allows the listener to follow the subtly shaded nuances of Bach's dialogue. Some readers may feel that these interpretations lack the stamp of a strong personality at the helm but any such fears of interpretative neutrality are largely dispelled by the sensibility of the players and their hitherto proven skill at reaching the heart of the music without the assistance either of pretension or muddled intellectual clutter. Reservations chiefly concern minutiae of tuning and to a much lesser extent, ensemble. Neither these weaknesses, nor the occasional blip or thwack, hindering the production of clean notes from oboe, horns or trumpet, spoil enjoyment of Nos. 1 and 2. It is a pity that the first movement of No. 3 is marred by indifferent tuning in the lower strands of the texture and, more disturbingly, by a marked acceleration in speed beginning at bar 84 (3'26"); but the second *Allegro* of the work is so well done that you are inclined to forgive them. Tafelmusik's account of this brilliant binary movement is not to be missed.

Brandenburg Concertos Nos. 1-3.
Boston Baroque / Martin Pearlman *hpd*
Telarc CD80368 (52 minutes: DDD). Recorded 1994.　ⒻⓅ

Brandenburg Concertos Nos. 4-6.
Boston Baroque / Martin Pearlman *hpd*
Telarc CD80354 (41 minutes: DDD). Recorded 1994.　ⒻⓅ

Boston Baroque is a close-knit group of highly accomplished and stylish instrumentalists. On their discs their enthusiasm is clear in the bustling outer movements; it's a wise leader who knows his team, in this case Martin Pearlman, who no doubt set the tempos. In the slow movements there is the breathing-space which is often found lacking. The soloists are first-class (though Friedemann Immer's trumpet trills in Concerto No. 2 sound a mite uncomfortable) and the multi-talented Daniel Stepner (violone piccolo in No. 2, violin soloist in Nos. 4 and 5, and viola soloist in No. 6) and Pearlman himself (harpsichord) are especially impressive. It is, however, the ensemble, supported by a finely balanced recording, that makes these accounts so outstanding, and those who are allergic to thin or nasal string sounds will find nothing to cringe from in the warmth of tone that characterizes these performances. The annotation states (but without explanation) that Concerto No. 6 'must remain a chamber piece with one player to a part': whether it must or not, the recording shows it to be wholly effective played in that way. We are also told that 'it includes the transparent sounds of gambas' and so it does, but we are left to guess who their players might be. There can be no clear 'best' in the *Brandenburgs*, but this set is likely to remain amongst those which will prove to be enduring.

Brandenburg Concertos Nos. 1-6. Orchestral Suites, BWV1066-69.
Adolf Busch Chamber Players / Adolf Busch.
EMI Références mono CHS7 64047-2 (three discs: 195 minutes: ADD). Recorded 1935-36. Ⓜ Ⓗ

This most celebrated of recordings of Bach's *Brandenburg* Concertos was made in 1935 and the four Orchestral Suites, also happily included in this three-disc set, a year later. When Adolf Busch performed and recorded the *Brandenburgs* during the 1930s there was already an awakening interest in the interpretation of baroque and pre-baroque music; these Bach discs therefore stand as an important landmark signposting much of what has subsequently taken place. Busch did not make concessions towards a growing awareness of period instruments; indeed, he could hardly have done so since he would not have been able to find a sufficient number of experienced players to draw from. And so in these *Brandenburgs* the violino piccolo part in Concerto No. 1 is played on a standard violin, flutes rather than recorders are used in the Second and Fourth Concertos, piano instead of harpsichord is both used as keyboard continuo throughout and as *concertante* instrument in Concerto No. 5 and in the Sixth Concerto cellos supplant the violas da gamba. All this may sound heretical to readers who have grown up with period-instrument performances; yet only the most prejudiced and insensitive ears could fail to respond to the enlightened musicianship which emerges from these interpretations. What Busch was obliged to forgo in respect of the tonal colours that Bach stipulated he compensated for in his almost visionary grasp of the essentially chamber character of the music. The most consistently convincing of Busch's *Brandenburgs* is, perhaps, the First Concerto. Tempos are well chosen – that is a feature of the set almost as a whole – and textures are transparently clear.

In Concerto No. 2 the trumpeter George Eskdale provides a shining example of restrained and beautifully phrased playing which, alas, has not always been emulated by succeeding generations of trumpeters. The Third Concerto is relaxed and crisply articulated though a little untidy in ensemble at times, while the Fourth features the flautists Marcel and Louis Moyse with Busch himself taking the virtuoso *concertante* violin part. This is a wonderfully animated performance with delicate continuo accompaniment by Rudolf Serkin. Serkin comes into his own, of course, in the Fifth Concerto, where he is joined by Busch and Marcel Moyse in a notably expressive account of the work. The Sixth Concerto is unquestionably the least successful. Busch certainly misjudged the character of this work and one can almost sense his bewilderment in the ponderous opening movement where he seems uncertain as to what the music is about. The *Adagio* fares better but is too slow and the finale is rather a scramble. The Orchestral Suites, though seldom uninteresting in these performances, are more variable in result. Some dance measures are effectively judged, though menuets are heavy-footed and too slow, and the overtures themselves likewise. Nevertheless, there are plenty of features in Busch's recording which lift it far above mere documentary significance, and no one interested in evolving styles, accomplished musicianship or indeed Bach's music itself should overlook this historical landmark. The remastering from 78s is astonishingly successful.

Orchestral Suites, BWV1066-69 – No. 1 in C major; No. 2 in B minor; No. 3 in D major; No. 4 in D major.

Orchestral Suites Nos. 1-4.
Wilbert Hazelzet *fl* Amsterdam Baroque Orchestra / Ton Koopman.
Deutsche Harmonia Mundi RD77864 (two discs: 79 minutes: DDD). Recorded 1988.
Gramophone Award Winner 1990. Ⓟ Ⓟ ℞℞

Bach's Orchestral Suites are deservedly well represented in the catalogue, with versions in plenty by orchestras of period and modern instruments alike. Koopman captures the contrasting colours and textures of these works with a sure feeling for orchestral sonority, but over and above that he is most persuasive in his gestures, graceful at times, ceremoniously pompous at others. Thus the Sarabande of the B minor Suite is one of the high-water marks of the entire set, exquisitely poised and lovingly articulated by the flautist, Wilbert Hazelzet, an artist of rare sensibility. Other dances in this suite fare equally well, with a Menuet redolent of courtly gesture and a Polonaise with an easy, carefree gait. As a general rule, Koopman favours rather slower tempos than many of his rival colleagues and he is to be applauded for doing so. The Rondeau of the B minor Suite is, comparatively speaking, slow yet avoiding monotony; the Forlane of the C major Suite is delightfully airy, as are the two Bourrées and the pleasingly leisurely Passepieds. Loveliest of all, perhaps, in this performance of the C major Suite, are the relaxed and affectingly articulated Courantes and the refined Menuets, whose kinetic energy is subtly realized under Koopman's direction. Koopman draws the strongest contrast between lighter textured dances and galanteries such as these, and the grandiose music contained in the two D major Suites. The Overtures in both instances are magnificent with commendably vibrant timpani and snarling trumpets which set the blood coursing through the veins. This is robust Bach playing but without a hint of vulgarity and in no sense lacking in appropriate restraint. This is a considerable achievement and if some listeners are mildly irked by Koopman's own brilliant but perhaps overbusy keyboard continuo realizations, they are unlikely to be able to resist the subtle inflexions and ravishing inner-part understanding of Suite No. 2; and, it should be added, the sheer exuberant spirit of occasion which shines through the performances of the other three suites. Splendid recorded sound.

Orchestral Suites Nos. 1-4; No. 5 in G minor, BWV1070 (attrib.).
Musica Antiqua Köln / Reinhard Goebel.
Archiv Produktion 415 671-2AH2 (two discs: 111 minutes: DDD). Recorded 1982-85.　　Ⓕ🅿

The spurious Suite in G minor was once in the possession of Bach's eldest son, Wilhelm Friedemann, who might also have been its composer. It has been handed down in copies of score and parts by Christian Friedrich Penzel who also copied Bach's Suites Nos. 2, 3 and 4. In an interesting insert-note, Reinhard Goebel explains that in the years between 1982 and the completion of the recordings in 1985, his ideas about how to perform the music changed. Taking an extreme view of his stance he considers the earlier essay in style as amongst the sins of his youth. Much of Goebel's newer thinking is influenced by the writings of the American musicologist, Frederick Neumann, in particular, those passages concerned with dotted rhythms. Some of the points are not presented clearly and these are truisms concerning 'authenticity', but in spite of an occasional feeling that Goebel is ousting one set of dogma for another, his essay comes over as thoughtful and constructive. All this might suggest that there are sweeping and irreconcilable differences between Musica Antiqua's performances and others which we have encountered in recent years. Not so, for whilst Goebel does largely put his ideas into practice it is in details of phrase and of articulation that his readings provide the most interesting comparisons with his competitors. In the B minor Suite, the phrases are beautifully shaped, the tempos nicely judged and the instrumental textures effectively clear. In the remaining three suites the string forces of the ensemble are considerably augmented with four first and four second violins, three violas, two cellos, a violone and two harpsichords. The solo and *ripieno* playing is of a very high order; and it needs to be since some of Goebel's tempos make what occasionally sound like ultimate demands on his wind players; the second *Bourrée* of Suite No. 4 provides an instance of a woodwind high-wire act during which one's heart is elevated to the mouth.

In its shaping of individual notes and of phrases these performances are probably more immaculate than any, yet that alone may not prove enough for you to switch your allegiance wholeheartedly to it. Lively, brisk, stylish and highly polished these readings certainly are; they afford many delightful and convincing views of Bach's music notably, perhaps, in the first two suites and in the lyrical account of the Air from the Third Suite. Nevertheless, at times you are conscious of a severity of outlook, a rigidity of temperament if not of interpretation which does not accord with the 'occasional' and often jubilant spirit of the music. Without wishing to dilute the virtues of this issue, which are considerable, we would sound a warning bell in earshot of anyone tempted to regard it as preferable to others based on comparable tenets of performing style merely on the grounds of its polished executancy. The recorded sound is clear and pleasantly resonant. All Bach's repeats are observed throughout this fascinating and stimulating release.

Orchestral Suites Nos. 1-4.
Orchestra of the Age of Enlightenment / Frans Brüggen.
Philips 442 151-2PH2 (two discs: 81 minutes: DDD). Recorded 1994.　　Ⓕ🅿

In Bach's hands the orchestral suite reached a peak of expressive refinement and it is this aspect of the music that Brüggen so effectively highlights, with discerningly applied *appoggiaturas*, gently swung rhythms and concern for eloquent turns of phrase. The Orchestra of the Age of Enlightenment responds well to his ideas and gives an alluringly intimate and relaxed performance of the First Suite in C major. The Second Suite, in B minor, is treated as pure chamber music, with single strings and a continuo of two lutes. This last-mentioned feature is a pleasing touch, and an effective one, too. The Third and Fourth Suites, both of them in D major, are of an entirely different character from the first two. Enter trumpets and drums to enrich the woodwind and string textures with a splendid sense of occasion. The Third Suite has long been the most popular of the four, chiefly on account of its celebrated 'Air on the G string', and the ebullient Gavottes which follow it. But the real jewel in the crown here is the Overture to the Fourth Suite. Its rich and subtle harmonies all contribute towards an exotic flavour which comes over uncommonly well. The only complaint is that in none of the Suites does Brüggen observe the second half repeats of the overtures themselves. A pity this, for they are supreme examples of the form. However, these performances are lightly delivered, with spirit, subtly shaded dynamics and, in general, a loving attention to every detail in the music. That's what it deserves and, in this instance, it has paid off, handsomely. A satisfying release, superbly recorded.

Bach Orchestral Suite No. 2. Brandenburg Concerto No. 1 in F major, BWV1046. Concerto for Flute, Violin, Harpsichord and Strings in A minor, BWV1044a.
Telemann Suite in A minor, TWV55:a2.
Michala Petri rec **Rainer Kussmaul** vn **Raphael Alpermann** hpd
Berlin Baroque Soloists.
RCA Red Seal 74321 57130-2 (71 minutes: DDD). Recorded 1998.   Ⓕ

This is not a selection you will encounter on one CD all that often, simply because it places a pair of genuine recorder pieces alongside two works borrowed from the flute repertoire. This is really something that might be made clear to potential purchasers on the outside of the box (indeed, it is barely admitted to inside), but in the end it does not matter very much, since both the music and the performances are of such high quality that it is hard to imagine anyone complaining for long. Michala Petri displays a mastery of her instrument which is breathtaking. Every line she plays is beautifully even, nimble and crisp. Other recorder players might bring out a little more of the playful side of the Telemann perhaps, and in the two Bach flute pieces – the Triple Concerto and Second Orchestral Suite – some of the warmth of the baroque flute is undoubtedly missing, but on the other hand there is an extra clarity of texture to be enjoyed here instead. The support Petri gains from the Berlin Baroque Soloists is first-class. There are times when even an experienced ear would have trouble detecting that these are modern strings: in his solos, leader Rainer Kussmaul draws from his violin a delicacy and flexibility of bowing and phrasing which one normally associates with a baroque instrument, and the string ensemble as a whole brings a consistent lightness and liveliness of touch. In short this is exemplary baroque-playing on modern instruments.

Bach Orchestral Suite No. 4. Concerto for Three Violins and Strings in D major, BWV1064. Cantata No. 42, Am Abend aber desselbigen Sabbats – Sinfonia.
Vivaldi Concertos – Strings in A major, RV158; Four Violins and Strings in B minor, Op. 3 No. 10. L'Olimpiade – Overture.
Freiburg Baroque Orchestra / Thomas Hengelbrock.
Deutsche Harmonia Mundi 05472 77289-2 (64 minutes: DDD). Recorded 1991-92.   ⒻⓅ

The Freiburg Baroque Orchestra scores ten out of ten for vitality in its pleasingly varied programme. Bach's Orchestral Suite No. 4 is heard in what is probably a pre-Leipzig version, which excludes trumpets and drums. That may not sound too promising for readers who like their 'fix' of brass and timpani, yet the immensely rewarding sonorities created by strings, three oboes and bassoon together with invigorating rhythmic patterns, provides wonderful mental and aural refreshment. However, the two Menuets in the Leipzig version are also missing. Of the two Vivaldi concertos, the A major piece for ripieno strings foreshadows the style of the early Mannheim symphonists, with its tremolos, breaks and short runs punctuated by trills in the outer movements, and the B minor, the tenth of the 12 which Vivaldi published under the title *L'estro armonico*, among the most inventive of the set. This enjoyable release is well recorded and helpfully documented.

The Art of Fugue, BWV1080.

The Art of Fugue. A Musical Offering, BWV1079. Canons, BWV1072-78; 1086-87.
Musica Antiqua Köln / Reinhard Goebel.
Archiv Produktion 413 642-2AH3 (three discs: 140 minutes: ADD). Recorded 1984.   ⓂⓅ**RR**

The great compilation of fugues, canons and a trio sonata which Bach dedicated to King Frederick the Great is one of the monuments of baroque instrumental music. Every contrapuntal device of canon at various intervals, augmentation, inversion, retrograde motion and so on is displayed here, and the performances are splendidly alive and authentic-sounding. It goes without saying that period instruments or modern replicas are used. The intellectually staggering *Art of Fugue* is a kind of testament to Bach's art and for this recording the instrumentation, unspecified by the composer, has been well chosen. The 14 miniature Canons which close this issue are for the most part a recent discovery and were written on a page of Bach's own copy of the *Goldberg Variations*; of curiosity value certainly but not much more than that. Excellent recording for these performances which have great authority.

Bach The Art of Fugue – Contrapuncti 1-11; Fuga.
Mozart Five Fugues, K405. Fugue in G minor, K401/K375e.
Phantasm (Laurence Dreyfus, Wendy Gillespie, Jonathan Manson, Markku Luolajan-Mikkola *viols*).
Simax PSC1135 (65 minutes: DDD). Recorded 1997. Ⓕℙ

Seeing that we enjoy Bach and Mozart on a modern piano – an instrument of course outside their time-frame – should we demur at their music being played on an equally anachronistic consort of viols? Leaving aside the argument advanced in Laurence Dreyfus's booklet-note that much viol consort music was fugal in texture anyway, the fact is that the contrapuntal lines here emerge with great clarity and with a subtlety of timbre, articulation and dynamics beyond even the ablest keyboard player, thanks to Phantasm's accomplished and expressive performances. The group offers the first 11 *contrapuncti*, without the canons or mirror fugues, but plus the final uncompleted *chef d'oeuvre* that was to have crowned the awesome project; Phantasm's playing offers new insights into Bach's prodigious mind. In his transcriptions for string quartet of fugues from the *48* (putting one a semitone down for convenience), Mozart – who, it is reported, constantly had Bach's volume lying open on his piano – made a few small adjustments to details of rhythm and part-writing; and the process also fired him to write several fugues of his own, including the one in G minor (for piano solo or duet) here. The Phantasm ensemble, despite a slight tendency to hurry, brings a smile to one's lips by its intonation, precision and, above all, musicality.

The Art of Fugue (string quartet version).
Juilliard Quartet (Robert Mann, Joel Smirnoff *vns* Samuel Rhodes *va* Joel Krosnick *vc*).
Sony Classical S2K45937 (two discs: 90 minutes: DDD). Ⓕ

Keller Quartet (András Keller, János Pilz *vns* Zoltán Gál *va* Ottó Kertész *vc*).
ECM New Series 457 849-2 (72 minutes: DDD). Recorded 1997. Ⓕ

Represented by versions respectively for orchestra, chamber orchestra, saxophone quartet, two pianos, solo piano, harpsichord, two harpsichords, organ and string quartet, *The Art of Fugue* graces the current catalogue in many guises. That is something of a paradox given that the work may not even have been intended for public performance. The Keller Quartet's highly recommendable recording for ECM comes into direct competition with an earlier string quartet version by the Juilliard Quartet, another fine production, spread across two warmly recorded Sony CDs and with the chorale *Vor deinen Thron tret' ich hiermit* added as a supplement – much as it was to the 1751 edition of the main work.

Comparisons are both instructive and rewarding in that while the Juilliard employs its full arsenal of expressive devices (pronounced vibrato being especially prominent), the Keller takes its lead from the early-music specialists, sometimes virtually abandoning vibrato altogether and opting for an often seamless *legato*, less emphatic accents and a more blended pooled tone, with subtle bulges at the centre of the note. Its tempos are usually quicker, too, and it opts for a different playing order: *Contrapuncti* Nos. 1-13, then the four canons and ending with No. 14; whereas the Juilliard chooses a sequence of *Contrapuncti* Nos. 1-11, followed by the four canons, then by Nos. 13, 12 and 14, with the chorale to close. Further contrast is occasioned by the Juilliard having commissioned (from Marten Cornellisen) a viola large enough to extend the instrument's normal range down by a fourth, thereby fleshing out its tone even more.

Those wishing to make 'quick-reference' comparisons should try track 1 (where the quartets' tonal credentials are stated more or less in full), then track 4 or track 6 ('in the French Style') where the Keller suggests courtly elegance and the Juilliard recalls the lustier, even old-fashioned interpretative manners of, say, Casals, Karl Richter or Sascha Schneider. Then again, comparing the two recordings in *Contrapunctus* No. 7 (track 7) reveals the Juilliard as having taken the livelier option. The Keller makes great play with Bach's ecstatically converging voices and offsets the potentially monotonous effect of unrelieved D minor by maximizing the potential for contrast between individual movements. That its performance is on one disc is another distinct advantage, and while the Juilliard probably remains the first choice, the Keller is so different, and so profoundly alive to every nuance and nerve-end in the music, that you may want both. Neither version offers a completion of Bach's last *Contrapunctus*. ECM's recording is spacious yet never overly resonant.

Flute Sonatas – No. 1 in B minor, BWV1030; No. 2 in E flat major, BWV1031; No. 3 in A major, BWV 1032; No. 4 in C major, BWV1033; No. 5 in E minor, BWV1034; No. 6 in E major, BWV1035.

Flute Sonatas Nos. 1, 2 and 4-6. Violin Sonata in G minor, BWV1020 (arr. fl).
James Galway *fl* **Sarah Cunningham** *va da gamba* **Philip Moll** *hpd*
RCA Victor Red Seal 09026 62555-2 (75 minutes: DDD). Recorded 1993.　　　　　　Ⓕ**E**

The basic six flute sonatas, BWV1030-35, can be accommodated on a single disc but Galway plays safe by keeping to what Bach (or someone else) actually wrote, omitting the unfinished A major Sonata, BWV1032, which other players have chosen to present in variously completed forms. There is, from the purist's point of view, still a 'risk' since it remains unproven that Bach was the composer of BWV1031, 1033 and 1020. However, their quality justifies their inclusion – if Bach didn't write them one doubts that he would have disowned them. Galway is at his warm, velvet-toned best, phrasing immaculately, caressing the slow movements and fleet of tongue in the quicker ones. His tempos are well chosen and he never allows virtuosity to get the better of his judgement. The 'supporting cast' are no less beyond reproach, but whilst the flute and viola da gamba are well balanced the harpsichord might profitably have been allowed a rather more equal say in BWV1030 and BWV1031, in which it has an obbligato role.

Flute Sonatas Nos. 1-6; C major, BWV1033 (solo version); Partita in A minor, BWV1013.
Janet See *fl* **Davitt Moroney** *hpd* **Mary Springfels** *va da gamba*
Harmonia Mundi HMU90 7024/5 (two discs: 114 minutes: DDD). Recorded 1990.　　　　Ⓕ**P**

The C major Sonata, BWV1033, originally a flute solo, to which Carl Philip Emanuel (the copyist) added a bass line, is presented here in both forms, solo and with continuo. The flute lines seem, when compared with those of BWV1013, less self-sufficient, and See's solo version does not quite convince you that they were originally meant to be unsupported. The mystery remains unsolved, but See/Moroney give everyone the chance to come to his/her own conclusion – if any. Bach's long lines are never more difficult than when they ride on the wind: See's long pauses for breath, some of them in curious places, interrupt the flow of the music in both solo works. No such intrusions disturb the flow in the accompanied sonatas, of which See gives excellent accounts. She has the style in her bloodstream. In the matter of ornamentation she is extremely cautious when it comes to adding any but the most clearly implied trills. She is splendidly supported by Moroney who is inventive in the with-continuo works. There are no complaints, either, regarding Springfels's gamba playing or the degree of its prominence. For period-instrument performances, See *et al* are a good choice, for their spontaneous expressiveness, the overall balance of the with-continuo sonatas, and for the provocative bonus of the solo version of BWV1033.

Flute Sonatas Nos. 1-6.
William Bennett *fl* **George Malcolm** *hpd* **Michael Evans** *vc*
ASV Quicksilva CDQS6108 (77 minutes: ADD). Recorded 1978.　　　　　　　　　　Ⓢ

There is something rather special about the Flute Sonatas and the more so when they are as well played as they are by William Bennett and George Malcolm. They were obviously written during a happy period in Bach's life for they are amiably inventive pieces, which is not to imply that they are slight, just very appealing. What matter if the E flat, BWV1031 (which has an engaging *Siciliano* slow movement), and the C major, BWV1033, are probably spurious – they still offer thoroughly worthwhile music. On this reissue, the first three sonatas (BWV1030-32) are played as a simple duet for flute and harpsichord; in the last three (BWV1033-35), written for flute and bass continuo, Michael Evans joins the ensemble and the balance – especially since his is not a baroque instrument – is quite perfect. As for that superb flautist Bennett, he too uses a modern instrument, yet is the soul of finesse as well as playing creatively and with consistently beautiful tone. The sound is forward but very convincing; and Malcolm's harpsichord is not over-amplified but admirably lifesize. This is a very good recording indeed and at super-bargain price should not be missed.

Trio Sonatas, BWV525-30 (arr. Palladian Ensemble) – No. 1 in E flat major; No. 3 in D minor; No. 5 in C major; No. 6 in G major. Four Duets, BWV802-05. 14 Verschiedene Canones, BWV1087.
Palladian Ensemble (Pamela Thorby *recs* Rachel Podger *vn* Susanna Heinrich *va da gamba* William Carter *gtr/archlte/theorbo*).
Linn Records CKD036 (75 minutes: DDD). Recorded 1994.　　　　　　　　　　　　Ⓕ**P**

The Palladian Ensemble consists of young early-music players whose fluent techniques have been directly developed on period instruments and who are well informed and imaginative. The Trio Sonatas are 'properly' transposed to keys more suited to the chosen instruments, and the Four Duets are given to the violin and viola da gamba. How do you bring a perpetual canon to an end? One way is by means of a fade-out, as happens with the fourteenth of the *Goldberg* canons, the colourful presentation of which as a whole drives a horse and cart through any notion that canons are just dry, academic exercises. Hairpin dynamics sometimes come close to sounding mannered and Rachel Podger does not always wash the tonal acid from her etched lines, but these are very tiny flies in the ointment of performances that are refreshingly committed and which stray from old paths in stimulating and revealing ways. Enjoy them, and feel compassion for anyone who is unable to do so.

Violin Sonatas, BWV1014-19 – No. 1 in B minor; No. 2 in A major; No. 3 in E major; No. 4 in C minor; No. 5 in F major; No. 6 in G major.

Violin Sonatas Nos. 1-6.
Fabio Biondi *vn* **Rinaldo Alessandrini** *hpd*
Opus 111 OPS30-127/8 (two discs: 90 minutes: DDD). Recorded 1995.   Ⓕ Ⓟ

Violin Sonatas Nos. 1-6.
Dimitry Sitkovetsky *vn* **Robert Hill** *hpd*
Hänssler Classic CD98 154 (76 minutes: DDD). Recorded 1996.   Ⓕ

Biondi and Alessandrini are probably the two most fêted members of Italy's growing early music community, but interest in them so far has depended a lot on the fact that they have been performing Italian music, in which, it is felt, caprice and a little bit of red-blooded passion have an important part to play. Such qualities are not so easy to apply to Bach, even if you wanted to; better here to play intelligently, in tune and with good articulation, and let Bach's robust notationally more complete music speak for itself. This is just what Biondi and Alessandrini do, though at the same time bringing a moving lyricism to slow movements, and above all a bold and biting energy to faster ones such as the last movement of BWV1014, the second movement of BWV1015 with its upward arpeggios, or the finale of the same sonata. Alessandrini, better known internationally as the Director of Concerto Italiano, is a crisp harpsichordist and shows considerable dexterity in the last movement of BWV1016, among others. The recording is fairly close for both instruments, which it needs to be for the harpsichord if it is to contribute much to the music's dialogue; but perhaps the violin could have been given a little more space, so that we do not have to hear Biondi breathing or the friction of his bow on the string. A very small complaint which does not detract from a warm recommendation.

There is still much to be said for having these wonderful works played on a (relatively) modern violin – especially by someone of Dimitry Sitkovetsky's stature. The tone is bright, intonation spot on, vibrato intelligently graded, the top line sweet but never saccharine and the phrasing subtly influenced by the 'period performance' school. Listeners averse to the astringent tones of a period violin will naturally gravitate to this recording. Robert Hill's harpsichord playing is pert and supple, often more prominent than the violin line (the harpsichord part in any case holds much of the musical interest) and very well recorded. Sitkovetsky presents the Sixth Sonata in its final version, which includes the delightful solo-harpsichord third movement *Allegro* and ends with a reprise of the heady *Presto* that opens the work. The closing *Allegro* quotes music from Bach's *Wedding* Cantata.

Six Keyboard Partitas, BWV825-30.

Six Keyboard Partitas. Italian Concerto in F major, BWV971. Overture in the French style in B minor, BWV831.
Andreas Staier *hpd*
Deutsche Harmonia Mundi 05472 77306-2 (three discs: 184 minutes: DDD). Recorded 1993.   Ⓕ Ⓟ

On which level these wonderfully rich pieces speak to us is, of course, largely in the hands of the performer. Andreas Staier is a performer with a keen understanding of decorum though it is the darkly imbued suites where he is especially penetrating. He takes a stark and disturbing view of the C minor Partita. The opening is remarkably powerful and rhetorical but the way he juxtaposes this with an almost ironically free-flowing *andante* before setting into an exacting and exhilarating *fugato* is musicianship of real conviction and flair. Staier's impeccable digital facility and steadiness is often at the root of the colourful devices which he imparts to the A minor Partita and before that a rounded and genial Sarabande, and finally a dreamy Gigue – a rare thing indeed! His performances are in the very top bracket, always thought-provoking and clearly argued, with moments of matchlessly vital and exquisite playing. The set also includes Part Two of the *Clavier-Übung*, an extra disc with the *Italian Concerto* and the B minor *Overture in the French style*, both beautifully played. Here, as elsewhere, his Keith Hill harpsichord after German examples gives a clearly defined attack and a focus which will have you on the edge of your seat.

Six Keyboard Partitas.
Angela Hewitt *pf*
Hyperion CDA67191/2 (two discs: 143 minutes: DDD). Recorded 1996-97.   Ⓕ🅴

After ages without any recordings of the Partitas on the piano, along comes Angela Hewitt and saves the situation, effortlessly eclipsing all competitors. If Bach is to be played on the piano, this is the kind of way to do it. Inherent in all her playing is a rhythmic vitality, always under control, that sweeps one along with its momentum, subtly varied articulation, dynamics that follow the natural rise or fall of phrases without exaggerations, an appreciation of Bach's harmonic tensions, an ability to differentiate between the strength of contrapuntal lines, and an unfailing clarity of texture. This is a sane and sensible interpretation, deeply musicianly and devoid of eccentricity. Her attitude, rather like Toscanini's, is to accept the text *com' è scritto* and then to make legitimate adjustments, so we get double-dotting and assimilation of rhythms. Technically she is immaculate, with the cleanest possible ornaments. In the great E minor Sarabande Hewitt is justifiably emotional, without becoming soggy: only in the first half of the A minor Allemande is there a hint of coyness. No, the whole disc gives unalloyed pleasure.

Keyboard Partitas – Nos. 2, 4 and 5.
Richard Goode *pf*
Nonesuch 7559-79483-2 (72 minutes: DDD). Recorded 1998.   Ⓕ🅴

Richard Goode approaches this music with the insights of a performer steeped in Mozart, Beethoven and classical culture in general. His Bach has a profound, self-communing quality, though his technical command of the notes – his sense of contrapuntal perspective – is second to none. He occasionally de-synchronizes chords to heighten a harmonic effect, but his pedalling is judicious and his employment of dynamics (as opposed to facile tone colouring) reveals a complete understanding of phrasal and contrapuntal relationships. He creates an objective, orderly space in these Partitas, a space pervaded with light and intelligence. The overture to the Fourth Partita, placed first on the recording, announces the artist's intentions: this is grand music for small rooms, music in which larger baroque gestures have been refined and simplified into a more intimate rhetoric. He grabs the listener's attention with a wonderful sleight of hand, by maintaining the overture's formal sweep, yet keeping it small and direct. These intimacies are sustained throughout the recording, which is deeply private without ever becoming agonizingly introspective. The emotional gravity is in the Sarabandes, and the Aria of the Partita No. 4, which all share a sweetly lyrical, *bel canto* sense of line, and a haunting vulnerability. There is something strikingly courteous about Goode's approach, the courtesy of honest, spontaneous expression tempered by textual fidelity and an impulse to underscore Bach's beauties without pedantry or vulgar highlighting of contrapuntal complexity. The 20 tracks that comprise this recording present a single and thoroughgoing vision of Bach's music; it has a robust honesty and it breathes clean, fresh air and that's enough to make it highly recommended.

Keyboard Partita No. 1. Five Preludes, BWV939-43. Prelude in C minor, BWV999. Fugue in C major, BWV953. Three Minuets, BWV841-43. French Suite No. 5 in G major, BWV816. Fughetta in C minor, BWV961. Clavier-Büchlein for W.F. Bach – Preludes: C major, BWV924; D major, BWV925; D minor, BWV926; F major, BWV927; F major, BWV928; G minor, BWV930. Concerto in F major, BWV971, 'Italian Concerto'. Anna Magdalena Notenbuch – Minuets: G major, BWVAnh114; G minor, BWVAnh115.
Richard Egarr *hpd*
EMI Debut CDZ5 69700-2 (78 minutes: DDD). Recorded 1995.   Ⓑ🅿🅴

Richard Egarr's programme is an attractive one in which three major solo harpsichord works – the Partita (BWV825), the *French Suite* (BWV816), and the *Italian Concerto* (BWV971) – are interspersed with Preludes, Minuets and two Fugues from the Kellner Collection, the *Clavier-Büchlein* for Wilhelm Friedemann Bach, 'the son I love, the one who fills me with joy', and the *Notenbuch* for Bach's second wife, Anna Magdalena. The character of Egarr's instrument, a copy by Joel Katzman of a 1638 Ruckers, has been effectively recorded, capturing its warm timbre in an intimate, domestic-sounding ambience. Egarr's B flat Partita is an unhurried affair, reflective in its Prelude and Allemande and rhythmically supple. Some readers may not at once respond to the extent to which he leans on notes, thereby breaking up that strict regularity of pulse that used to be the order of the day. His articulation and rhythmic flexibility are both illuminating and communicative. The music breathes, and with each breath comes a natural pause in the declamation allowing for rhetorical gesture and a feeling for scansion. Just occasionally in the Sarabande phrases are a little too clipped and skimped over, but such instances, both here and in the *French Suite*, are few and far between and certainly insufficiently intrusive to spoil your listening enjoyment. How refreshing, too, to hear minuets delivered in poised and eloquent terms. Each of the little Preludes and Minuets is lovingly shaped and played with affection for, and understanding of, the music's poetry. In short this is an outstanding disc, both for Egarr's technically accomplished playing and for his delicacy of feeling.

Keyboard Sonatas – D minor, BWV964; A minor, BWV965; C major, BWV966; G major, BWV968. Fugue in B flat major, BWV954.
Andreas Staier *hpd*
Teldec 3984-21461-2 (77 minutes: DDD). Recorded 1997.　　　　　　　　　　Ⓕ🅿

Some readers may be surprised to hear that Bach ever composed sonatas – not suites, but *sonatas* – for harpsichord. Well, actually he didn't. What he did do – if indeed it was he and not his eldest son – was transcribe his BWV1003 A minor Solo Violin Sonata (transposing it down a fifth) and the first movement of the BWV1005 C major (putting it down to G); and, more certainly, he himself adapted a number of movements from the *Hortus musicus* suites (for two violins, gamba and continuo) by Johann Adam Reincken, the aged master to whom, as a teenager, he had journeyed to Hamburg to hear. Taking his cue from Bach, Andreas Staier has transcribed the remaining movements of the C major Violin Sonata and added three movements to the C major Reincken adaptation – a suite, be it noted, not a sonata. Before purists throw up their hands in horror at Staier's temerity, let them listen to Bach's own startlingly audacious harpsichord version of BWV1005, with offbeat chords, surprising chromaticism and rolling left-hand arpeggios. In his own treatment of that work's Fuga, Staier, like his model in the BWV1003 fugue, is very free but most convincingly idiomatic: one would never guess that it was a transcription. Bach's arrangements of Reincken largely adhere to the originals but amplify the fugues by adding episodes, as is also the case in the A minor Gigue. Staier's playing (on a fine copy of an early eighteenth-century German instrument) is notable for the crispness and variety of his articulation and – except of course in the improvisatory Reincken preludes – the wonderfully invigorating vitality of his rhythmic drive. His Reincken C major Fuga is quite irresistible. A splendid disc.

The Art of Fugue, BWV1080.
Davitt Moroney *hpd*
Harmonia Mundi HMC90 1169/70 (two discs: 99 minutes: DDD). Recorded 1986.
Gramophone Award Winner 1986.　　　　　　　　　　Ⓑ🅿

Bach died before the process of engraving his last great work had been completed, thus leaving a number of issues concerning performance in some doubt. However, Davitt Moroney is a performer-scholar who has a mature understanding of the complexity of Bach's work; in a lucid essay in the booklet, he discusses the problems of presenting *The Art of Fugue* whilst at the same time explaining his approach to performing it. Certain aspects of this version will be of particular importance to prospective buyers: Moroney himself has completed Contrapunctus 14 but he also plays the same Contrapunctus in its unfinished state as a fugue on three subjects. He omits Bach's own reworkings for two harpsichords of Contrapunctus 13 on the grounds that they do not play a part in the composer's logically constructed fugue cycle; and he omits the Chorale Prelude in G major (BWV668a) which certainly had nothing to do with Bach's scheme but was added in the edition of 1751 so that the work should not end in an incomplete state. Moroney's performing technique is of a high order, placing emphasis on the beauty of the music which he reveals with passionate conviction. Exemplary presentation and an appropriate recorded sound enhance this fine achievement.

Bach/Busoni Chaconne in D minor.
Beethoven Rondo in G major, Op. 51 No. 2. Rondo a capriccio in G major, Op. 129.
Schumann Kreisleriana, Op. 16.
Evgeni Kissin *pf*
RCA Victor Red Seal 09026 68911-2 (63 minutes: DDD).　　　　　　　　　　Ⓕ🅴

This disc is pretty amazing – piano playing to startle, astonish and delight. Whether it's great Bach and Beethoven playing is less certain, and it is difficult to shake off reservations concerning the Schumann. The Bach/Busoni *Chaconne* is as remembered from when Kissin played it at London's Royal Festival Hall: grand, thrilling in its allure, full (nay, stentorian) in tone, the instrument taken to its limits, as if the requirement were to fill the Hollywood Bowl. There has been no modification of the scale of the operation here in the interests of the studio and the intimacy of domestic listening. Kissin might retort: why should there be? He could also fairly say, 'I am giving an account of what Busoni has done to Bach.' But his *Kreisleriana* is something to wonder at. It, too, is unremittingly sonorous, as if the concept of lightness were not something a pianist with his training and background could be expected to bother with; and although you may be no lover of wispy performances of this composer his version would be richer if it communicated a little more delight in those things that are unexpected and fleeting in Schumann. Nothing is left uncharacterized but what we have here is Schumann pressed at every moment, and in every voice of the texture, for the greatest weight of expression and power of effect. It is glorious, but the fantastic side of *Kreisleriana* is not always in focus. At the end of the seventh number, for example (track 12), when the dash and fury give way to the solace of a melody that floats in from heaven knows where, Kissin is oddly matter-of-fact, as if unable to account for something so surprising. Yet he then goes on to deliver the last of the eight pieces (track 13) with grace, colour, timing and character that are out of this world. The fifth (track 10) is similarly 'authentic' in conveying the essence of Schumann.

There is an edge of metal in his sound from time to time: all of a piece, one might say, with the searing nature of the experience. The recording suits Schumann better than Beethoven but is very decent. The Beethoven *Rondo a capriccio*, presented as a *tour de force*, is more enjoyable than the other *Rondo*, which could do with more tenderness in the outer sections and less hotting-up in the middle. The fact is that the acuteness of everything Kissin does will always make you react; no question of remaining indifferent. Really, you have to marvel at him all the time and he does keep drawing you back.

Sonatas and Partitas for Solo Violin, BWV1001-06: Sonatas – No. 1 in G minor; No. 2 in A minor; No. 3 in C major. Partitas – No. 1 in B minor; No. 2 in D minor; No. 3 in E major.

Sonatas Nos. 1-3. Partitas Nos. 1-3.
Arthur Grumiaux *vn*
Philips Duo 438 736-2PM2 (two discs: 113 minutes: ADD). Recorded 1960-61.　Ⓜ Ⓔ ⒭⒭

The totally innocent ear, deprived of any comparison, could be forgiven for judging Grumiaux's to be definitive performances of Bach's Partitas and Sonatas. There is little of the sweetness of a Heifetz, the passing whimsy of a Shumsky here. And yet they define, indeed, as few other performances do, the structural frame and rhythmic working-out of each movement with extraordinary determination and authority. The purity of intonation is absolute; the energy locked into the sheer sound of the instrument startling. *And* two discs, as they say, for the price of one! Those who know and love the artistry of Grumiaux will be thrilled to rediscover these Berlin recordings of the early 1960s, sharply remastered and sounding out in a roomy acoustic. The platinum gleam glancing off every moment of double-stopping, and the flinty brightness struck where contrapuntal voices meet ring out as never before. The arpeggios of the *Presto* of the G minor Sonata flash like light from a prism; and the same mesmeric steadiness of *moto perpetuo* makes for a heady finish to the C major Sonata. What dominates, though, is the rhythmic rigour of Grumiaux's playing. His perfectionism, fused with a real sense of struggle, brings sheer might to the fugues of the Sonatas: it is rather like watching a climber scaling a vast rock face, securing himself with a pick and leaping across the next crevasse.

Sonatas Nos. 1-3. Partitas Nos. 1-3.
Sigiswald Kuijken *vn*
Deutsche Harmonia Mundi Editio Classica GD77043 (two discs: 128 minutes: ADD).
Recorded 1981.　Ⓜ Ⓟ

Legion are the violinists who have sharpened their bows on these works; here we have a recording in which both player and instrument are 'period-adjusted'. The insert-booklet devotes over eight pages to a discussion of the music and its interpretation, and the instrumental tools and playing technique, after reading which the average listener may never again hear these works with quite the same ears. Given the benefit of such 'authenticity', what then might we expect? In-style readings, with unexceptionable ornaments? Yes – and so they are, though, as the annotator points out, the parameters of 'correctness' leave room for manoeuvre and within them it is a matter of 'you may', rather than 'you should (or must)'. A thin, scrapey sound? No – only from thin, scrapey players, of whom Kuijken is not one. There are abrasive moments, e.g. in the *Andante* of Sonata No. 2, but they are warmed by the heat of Kuijken's musicality. Overall the sound is clear, to the advantage of the contrapuntal textures, and not unduly thickened by vibrato. More compact and 'unanimous' three- and four-notes, thanks to the flatter string-profile and softer bow? There is little or no evidence of this: crisp chording, particularly in dance movements, seems due more to Kuijken's right-hand agility than to any mechanical advantage. Kuijken does little more of anything than the most adventurous of others. The slow movements of the Sonatas exchange something of their solemnity for a more urgently expressed eloquence. This is even more the case with the *Chaconne* (Partita No. 2), compressed with wonderful virtuosity into an incredible 11-and-a-bit minutes, but not allowed the space in which to unfold its majesty to the full. The Fugues, on the other hand, are taken at moderate tempos that do not exacerbate the technical problems, but aid the clear expression of their musical content. There are a few rough places but it is the overall effect that matters most. That said, this set represents a splendid, revelatory achievement, very well recorded.

Sonatas Nos. 1-3. Partitas Nos. 1-3.
Nathan Milstein *vn*
EMI mono ZDMB7 64793-2 (two discs: 114 minutes: AAD). Recorded 1950s.　Ⓜ️Ⓗ

Nathan Milstein was an assured, craftsman-like player with a silken tone, a superb technique and a stylish turn-of-phrase. His recording career began in the 1930s and spanned six decades. Technically and musically, Milstein always remained the stylish aristocrat, and to witness his traversal of Bach's Sonatas and Partitas is breathtaking. His natural brilliance, intelligence, sensitivity to inflexion and feeling for structure mark these mid-1950s solo Bach recordings as truly exceptional – and rather more assured (though less obviously flexible) than his 1971 re-makes for DG. Perhaps the high points are the B minor Partita and C major Sonata, the former with its judiciously phrased dance movements, the latter with a dazzlingly resilient fugue and a *Largo* that represents Milstein at his most deeply poetic. The transfers are excellent, and the annotation is informative and well written.

Sonatas Nos. 1-3. Partitas Nos. 1-3.
Oscar Shumsky *vn*
ASV CDDCD454 (two discs: 147 minutes).　Ⓕ

Oscar Shumsky has all the breadth of vision, the warmth and soaring vibrato of the best interpreters of this music. They are performances on a grand scale – which you either like or not – but they convey something more besides: a long-pondered, deeply assimilated study of the works. This puts movements like the *Chaconne* of the D minor Partita on to another plane. The sheer energy of response and assured sense of scope and span liberate the music from the instrument and compensate for the occasional overload in single-line counterpoint and in rubato. Shumsky, by the way, alternates Sonatas and Partitas, though he shuffles them around, departing from the usual chronological order.

Sonatas Nos. 1-3. Partitas Nos. 1-3 (arr. Galbraith).
Paul Galbraith *gtr*
Delos DE3232 (two discs: 119 minutes: DDD). Recorded 1997-98.　Ⓕ

This is a recording with several differences. Galbraith, who might be termed 'the thinking man's guitarist', uses an eight-string guitar which 'communicates with a floor-standing resonance box via a "Tortelier spike".' The Sonatas and Partitas are played in their original order, not divided into groups, and herein lies another novelty: Galbraith advances the plausible (but alas unprovable) proposition, that in their written order they form a triptych 'telling of the Birth, Passion and Resurrection of Christ'. Strange, that the Passion should be portrayed in a *da camera* work, with the *Chaconne* (here lasting an awed 20 minutes!) at its 'pivotal moment', but read his lucidly expressed arguments and make up your own mind about it all. No less contentious is his assertion that BWV1006a is 'an original lute version' of the Third Partita. Galbraith has transposed four of the works. He has quite properly made modifications to the original score, with some of which you may not feel entirely comfortable – the same applies to his articulation in a few passages – why, for instance, are the second-beat chords in the Chaconne not arpeggiated? But these are drops in the ocean of the total achievement. Galbraith's embellishments, notated and added, are impeccable. These are magnificently played, thoughtful and majestic performances. Beware: some of the track times given in the insert-booklet for BWV1006a defy belief! Strongly recommended, and not only to lovers of the guitar.

Solo Cello Suites, BWV1007-12 – No. 1 in G major; No. 2 in D minor; No. 3 in C major; No. 4 in E flat major; No. 5 in C minor; No. 6 in D major.

Solo Cello Suites Nos. 1-6.
Pierre Fournier *vc*
DG The Originals 449 711-2GOR2 (two discs: 139 minutes: ADD). Recorded 1961-63.　Ⓜ️ⒽⓇⓇ

Of all the great cellists over the years, either in the concert hall or in recordings of various kinds, Pierre Fournier came closer to the heart of the music than almost any other. Since he made these recordings, they have seldom been out of the catalogue. He seems to have possessed all the virtues of his fellow cellists without yielding to any of their self-indulgences; irrelevant personal idiosyncrasies are never allowed to intrude these finely sustained performances. He could be brilliant in execution – his technique was second to none, as he proves throughout this set – profound in utterance, aristocratic in poise and wonderfully coherent in his understanding of Bach's articulation and phrases. We need look no further than the *Prelude* of the First Suite in G major to find the supreme artistry which characterizes each and every moment of these performances. To be sure, there are very occasionally notes which fail to reach their centre but they are few and far between and certainly Fournier's intonation compares favourably with that of some of his virtuoso companions. Fournier's rubato is held tightly in rein and when he does apply it it is in the interests of enlivening aspects of Bach's formal writing. He can sparkle too, as he does in many of the faster dance-orientated movements such as courantes, gavottes, bourrées and so on; in the sarabandes, on the other hand, he invariably strikes a note of grandeur coupled with a concentration amounting at times almost to abstraction. Above all, Fournier's Bach playing is crowned with an eloquence, a lyricism and a grasp both of the formal and stylistic content of the music which will not easily be matched. All things considered, it is hardly surprising that these readings seem as fresh and as valid today as they did almost 40 years ago. Out and out purists, poor devils, may not be able to adjust to modern pitch, modern instrument and, in the case of Suites Nos. 5 and 6, the wrong instrument, but if that is so they are deserving more of compassion than censure. Fine recorded sound and strongly commended on virtually all counts.

Solo Cello Suites Nos. 1-6.
Pablo Casals *vc*
EMI Références mono CHS5 66215-2 (two discs: 130 minutes: ADD). Recorded 1936-39. Ⓜ Ⓗ

Young music-lovers today may find it difficult to believe that, 60 years ago, major works by Bach were considered to be of such specialized appeal that recordings could be obtained only in a limited 'Society' edition. The cello suites – nowadays available in dozens of versions – had never been recorded until Fred Gaisberg, after protracted efforts, finally persuaded Casals to play them for HMV. Casals had hesitated for 35 years before committing to disc these works – long regarded as unplayable, and never performed in their entirety – which he had discovered at the age of 13 and worked on for 12 years before playing them to an astonished public. To do so he had to evolve new techniques and, intellectually, to delve deeply into the character and inner structure of the music. He stressed the dance basis of the movements; and his vitality, rhythmic flexibility (to clarify the shape of phrases) and tonal nuance, and the vigour and variety of his bowing, still leap from the discs to impress the listener. EMI's term 'Références' could not be more apt, since these performances remain the classic yardstick by which all later ones must still be judged. The transfers from the original 78s, yielding an astonishingly clean ambience to the cello, represent a technical triumph for Keith Hardwick.

Solo Cello Suites Nos. 1-6.
Boris Pergamenschikov *vc*
Hänssler Edition Bachakademie 92 120 (two discs: 128 minutes: DDD). Recorded 1998. Ⓜ

Any worthy recording of Bach's solo cello compositions celebrates the balance of mind and body, prayer and dance, scholarship and unspoiled intuition. One of the most striking features of this set is the lavish way Pergamenschikov ornaments the musical line, usually in a repeat, but always with a convincing sense of style. He is equally adept at charting the precise mood of each movement, making free with the various preludes (usually at a fairly fast tempo), pointing courantes with a lively *staccato*, drawing expressive weight from the sarabandes without obscuring their rhythmic profile and dancing through the various minuets and gigues. His phrasing is supple, flexible and musically varied, his use of vibrato subtly expressive within the parameters of period style. There is a noticeable lilt to much of the phrasing, and an expressive *legato* that is unhampered by excessive vibrato. Pergamenschikov indulges a genuine sense of play and knows intuitively where to hold back, where to insert a tiny pause, and where to lean on the beginning of the bar. The recordings are excellent. Pergamenschikov should henceforth take his rightful place among the top modern recommendations of this exalted repertoire.

Solo Cello Suites Nos. 1-6.
Pieter Wispelwey *vc*
Channel Classics CCS12298 (two discs: 140 minutes: DDD). Recorded 1998. Ⓕ Ⓟ Ⓔ

Netherlands-born cellist, Pieter Wispelwey, is equally at home on baroque and modern instruments. These performances are carefully prepared, beautifully executed and most eloquently expressed. The instruments, too, sound well, Wispelwey having chosen an early eighteenth-century cello by Barak Norman for the first five Suites, and a five-stringed violoncello piccolo by an unidentified craftsman for the special requirements of the Sixth. Wispelwey is an imaginative player with a highly developed sense of fantasy. These qualities are as welcome in his performances of Bach as they are to be treated with circumspection in his almost entirely fanciful written introduction to the music. Preludes come across especially well since it is in these wonderfully varied opening movements, with their rhetorical diversity, that the performer can give rein most freely to his or her most natural conversational inflexions. And he makes the most of that thrilling climax at the peak of a chromatic accent through a full scale and a half. Sarabandes are profound and reflective without being weighty, and allemandes graceful and substantial. The *galanteries*, by contrast, are lightly bowed and redolent of playful and demonstrative gestures. That, to an extent, is true also of the courantes, while the gigues are firmly projected, full-toned and splendidly robust. Wispelwey's set of Bach's Cello Suites, then, is deserving of praise. If you are familiar with the gruff grandeur of Pablo Casals, or the aristocratic nobility of Fournier, then these performances will throw an entirely different light on the music, more conversational and with airier discourse. You may never want to be without the two earlier sets, but Wispelwey's version sits comfortably on the uppermost range of the period-instrument performance ladder.

Das wohltemperierte Klavier, Books 1 and 2 – 48 Preludes and Fugues, BWV846-93.

Das wohltemperierte Klavier, Books 1 and 2.
Kenneth Gilbert *hpd*
Archiv Produktion 413 439-2AH4 (four discs: 256 minutes: DDD). Recorded 1983.　　Ⓕ🅿🆁🆁

In Book 1 there are virtually no markings and so the performer carries heavy responsibility for phrasing and articulation. Gilbert's blend of scholarship and technique with artistic sensibility makes for notably convincing, often poetic playing. The D minor Prelude is one of many instances where his interpretation haunts the memory. Gilbert's vital rhythmic sense and love of refinement are qualities in his artistry which can be strongly felt throughout this vast project. Some readers may feel that he is comparatively unadventurous in his registration – others, for example, make a greater point of differentiation through instrumental colour – but it is one of the features of Gilbert's performance that is particularly praiseworthy, since he clearly and effectively achieves his contrasts through interpretation, renouncing the facility to emphasize them by more artificial means. In textural clarity he yields nothing to his competitors in this repertoire and, in short, arrives at a solution which is refined, lyrical and sometimes dazzlingly virtuosic, as in the Prelude in B flat, BWV866. The acoustic of the Musée de Chartres, where the *48* were recorded, is pleasantly resonant. Gilbert plays a seventeenth-century Flemish harpsichord enlarged first by Blanchet and then by Taskin in the following century. A satisfying achievement and an important issue.

Das wohltemperierte Klavier, Book 1.
Edwin Fischer *pf*
EMI Références mono CHS7 63188-2 (three discs: 237 minutes: ADD). Recorded 1933-36.　　Ⓜ🅷

'It would never sell', protested the HMV high-ups in the early 1930s when their music staff argued that it was time that Bach's *48*, one of the great pillars of the keyboard repertoire, was recorded in its entirety; though the musicians finally got their way, the records were issued only in a limited Bach Society edition – which was eagerly sought by music-lovers and quickly became famous. The choice of interpreter had fallen on the Swiss pianist and conductor Edwin Fischer, an intellectual musician known for his search for the 'inner experience of art' and for the beauty of his tone. His indeed remarkable control of tonal nuance is conspicuous everywhere in this historic set, and the lucidity of his part-playing, aware of every strand in Bach's textures, is illuminating. He employs the piano to the full as the instrument it is, taking advantage of contrasting *legato* and *staccato* articulation and of the use or non-use of the pedals; he does not hesitate to double octaves in the bass when he thinks it suitable, either to emphasize a subject or when he wants a special effect.

In today's musical climate his approach is bound to be regarded as too romantic. His treatment of fugues is of the 'hunt the slipper' school, every entry being highlighted, sometimes with excessive weight: useful as this may be in showing students how the wheels go round, not only is it an approach impracticable on the harpsichord, but the composer's aim was surely to absorb fugal entries into the texture as a whole. Fischer likes beginning some movements in an air of hushed mystery, often with the use of the left pedal, but – especially in Book 2 – he frequently drops the level quite unexpectedly in mid-stream to the velvety *pianissimo* which was his speciality, so producing a histrionic effect. Fischer was nervous in the recording studio, and it has to be said that he made a large number of fluffs (some just a wrong or missed note, others quite serious fumbles) which could not be cleaned up in editing, as such slips are today: the July 1936 sessions were particularly accident-prone. However, he mostly holds his speed admirably steady, with just an occasional lapse into hurrying or dragging. Keith Hardwick has done one of his usual splendid transfer jobs from the original 78s but could not totally eradicate some of the old surface scratch and swish (only really troublesome in the B flat Fugue of Book 2) and occasional moments of distortion. Despite the reservations mentioned, this set is well worth hearing for the profound musicality that shines through it all.

Das wohltemperierte Klavier, Book 1.
Angela Hewitt *pf*
Hyperion CDA67301/2 (two discs: 117 minutes: DDD). Recorded 1997.   Ⓕ

Admirers of Canadian pianist Angela Hewitt's lightly articulated and elegantly phrased Bach playing will not be disappointed by this recording. These qualities characterize the playing of each and every one of these profoundly didactic yet sublimely poetic pieces. In respect of her restrained use of the sustaining pedal, her consequently clearly spoken articulation, and the resultant lucidity of musical thought, Hewitt brings to mind those still controversial recorded performances of Edwin Fischer. Hewitt certainly sounds more comfortable in a studio than Fischer ever did, and her technique is more consistently disciplined than Fischer's was under these circumstances. Her reflective view of the more inwardly-looking Fugues, such as the lyrical one in E flat minor, is most attractive. Taut, but with a suppleness that is entirely devoid of stiffness, this is indeed cogent and gracefully beautiful playing of a high order. Some readers may sense, from time to time, an overtly intense element of subjective thought in her understanding of the music, a quality which seems to be endorsed by occasional references in her lively, illuminating and detailed introduction, to Bach's 'sense of inner peace', and so on. However, to conclude on a thoroughly positive and enthusiastic note, these are probably the first recorded performances by a pianist of Book 1 of the *48* that will make you want to hear them many times over and which sit most comfortably alongside Edwin Fischer. The recording and instrument sound well.

Six English Suites, BWV806-11.
Glenn Gould *pf*
Sony Classical Glenn Gould Edition SM2K52606 (two discs: 112 minutes: ADD).
Recorded 1971-73.   Ⓜ

No more original genius of the keyboard has existed than Glenn Gould, but this can lead to drawbacks as well as thrilling advantages. You may, for instance, sense how Gould can sacrifice depth of feeling for a relentless and quixotic sense of adventure. Yet love it or deride it, every bar of these lovingly remastered discs (the hiatus is explained in some riveting accompanying notes) tingles with *joie de vivre* and an unequalled force and vitality. Try the opening of the First Suite. Is such freedom glorious or maddening, or is the way the odd note is nonchalantly flicked in the following sustained argument a naughty alternative to Bach's intention? The pizzicato bass in the second Double from the same Suite is perhaps another instance of an idiosyncrasy bordering on whimsy, an enlivenment or rejuvenation that at least remains open to question. But listen to him in virtually any of the sarabandes from the Suites and you will find a tranquillity and equilibrium that can silence such criticism and even at his most piquant and outrageous his playing remains, mysteriously, all of a piece. The Gigue from the Second Suite is taken at a spanking *Presto* and the Prelude from the Third Suite is a gloriously true *vivace*, never rigid or merely metronomic. The fiercely chromatic, labyrinthine argument concluding the Fifth Suite is thrown off with a unique brio, one of those moments when you realize how Gould can lift Bach out of all possible time-warps and make him one of music's truest modernists. Sony's presentation is superb.

Six French Suites, BWV812-17.
Andrei Gavrilov *pf*
DG 445 840-2GH2 (two discs: 93 minutes: DDD). Recorded 1993.   Ⓕ

Bach compiled his *French Suites*, so-called – the composer himself did not give them this title – towards the end of his Cöthen period and at the beginning of his final appointment at Leipzig. Like others before him, Andrei Gavrilov acknowledges his debt to Glenn Gould, sensing a fellow spirit throwing down the gauntlet and challenging convention at every turn with his fearless mix of directness and idiosyncrasy. Yet as his performances so eloquently convey, there are depths and subtleties in these ever-fascinating cosmopolitan Suites which are often erased by Gould's manic determination to redefine the parameters of Bach interpretation. Gavrilov has a way, for instance, of casting light on even the simplest, least polyphonic of the composer's arguments. He may retain some of his former headstrong pugnacity yet in the sarabandes, which like pools of reflection form the nodal and expressive centre of each Suite, he finds an often glorious ease, repose and gently luminous sense of texture. Even those for whom such open-hearted espousal of the modern piano's resources ('the piano wins hands down' exclaims Gavrilov of arguments concerning harpsichord versus piano) is anachronistic will surely be touched and convinced. The DG sound quality is exemplary.

Six French Suites, BWV812-17. Sonata in D minor, BWV964. Five Preludes, BWV924-28. Prelude in G minor, BWV930. Six Preludes, BWV933-38. Five Preludes, BWV939-43. Prelude in C minor, BWV999. Prelude and Fugue in A minor, BWV894.
Angela Hewitt *pf*
Hyperion CDA67121/2 (two discs: 151 minutes: DDD). Recorded 1995.　　　　Ⓕ🅴

Even the most out-and-out purists who blench at the thought of Bach on so alien an instrument as the piano (as if Bach himself ever showed any reluctance at transferring his work from one instrument to another!) will find it hard not to be won over by Angela Hewitt's artistry. Eschewing all hieratic pretentiousness on the one hand and self-regarding eccentricities on the other, she gives us Bach performances that are not only admirable in style but marked by poise and what used to be called a 'quiet hand': 'chaste' might not be too fanciful a term, so long as that does not suggest any lack of vitality. There is intelligence in her carefully thought-out phrasing and subtle variety of articulation: gradations of sound are always alive without their becoming precious. The bulk of this recording is devoted to the *French Suites* (in which Hewitt includes a second Minuet in No. 2 and, more controversially, a Prelude and a vivacious second Gavotte in No. 4). Particularly enjoyable is the lightness of her treatment of the Airs of Nos. 2 and 4, the vigour of No. 5's Bourrée and the freshness of No. 6's Allemande; the extra decorations she adds in repeats everywhere sound properly spontaneous and are in the best of taste; ornaments are always cleanly played (though her mordants sometimes fall before, rather than on, the beat) and matched up in imitative voices.

Prelude and Fugue in A minor, BWV894. Chromatic Fantasia and Fugue in D minor, BWV903. Toccatas – C minor, BWV911; D major, BWV912. Prelude and Fugue in B minor on a theme of Albinoni, BWV923/951. Fantasia and Fugue in A minor, BWV944. Prelude in C minor, BWV999.
Pierre Hantaï *hpd*
Virgin Classics Veritas VC5 45322-2 (64 minutes: DDD). Recorded 1997.　　　Ⓕ🅿🅴

What connects this miscellany of pieces is that they are all early works of Bach's (though he later revised the *Chromatic Fantasia and Fugue*), none of which was published in his lifetime and of which no autograph manuscripts survive (while copies of them show numerous variants). The vitality and exuberant invention that bubble out of them go far to explain the bewilderment and shock felt by the burghers of Arnstadt and elsewhere at this headstrong and musically daring young man. It is difficult to imagine the effect on its first hearers of that *Chromatic Fantasia*, with its still astonishing key-shifts. Italian influence on Bach and his interest in his predecessors is exemplified in the B minor Fugue he borrowed from an Albinoni trio sonata, in the process extending it to nearly three times its original length; the multi-sectional Toccata in D curiously combines the improvisational with the fugal (the most organized of forms); and two of the present works were drawn upon for later compositions – the A minor Fugue, BWV944, became the basis for the BWV543 Fugue for organ, and the BWV894 Prelude and Fugue were lifted wholesale for the Triple Concerto for flute, violin and harpsichord. The fugue in this last is excitingly taken by Hantaï (playing on a copy of a Ruckers) at a breakneck pace, and elsewhere he underlines the young Bach's dashing style by the vigour and thrust of his rhythm. His dazzling runs, and the ferocious energy with which he attacks the *Chromatic Fantasia*, are absolutely electrifying: a performance to put nearly all others in the shade.

Goldberg Variations, BWV988.

Goldberg Variations.
Pierre Hantaï *hpd*
Opus 111 OPS30-84 (77 minutes: DDD). Recorded 1992.
Gramophone Award Winner 1994.　　　　Ⓕ🅿🅴🆁🆁

Pierre Hantaï's approach to the *Goldberg Variations* is tremendously spirited and energetic but also disciplined. What is most appealing about this playing, though, is that Hantaï clearly finds the music great fun to perform; some players have been too inclined to make heavy weather over this music. He makes each and every one of the canons a piece of entertainment while in no sense glossing over Bach's consummate formal mastery. Other movements, such as Var. 7 (gigue) and Var. 11, effervesce with energy and good humour and he is careful to avoid anything in the nature of superficiality. Not for a moment is the listener given the impression that his view of the music is merely skin deep. Indeed, there is a marked concentration of thought in canons such as that at the fourth interval (Var. 12). Elsewhere his feeling for the fantasy and poetry of Bach's music is effective and well placed (such as in Var. 13). The character of Bruce Kennedy's copy of an early eighteenth-century instrument by the Berlin craftsman, Michael Mietke is admirably captured by the effectively resonant recorded sound.

Goldberg Variations.
Glenn Gould *pf*
Sony Classical Glenn Gould Edition SMK52619 (51 minutes: DDD). Recorded 1981.   Ⓜ

This truly astonishing performance was recorded 26 years after Gould's legendary 1955 disc. Gould was not in the habit of re-recording but a growing unease with that earlier performance made him turn once again to a timeless masterpiece and try, via a radically altered outlook, for a more definitive account. By his own admission he had, during those intervening years, discovered 'slowness' or a meditative quality far removed from flashing fingers and pianistic glory. And it is this 'autumnal repose' that adds such a deeply imaginative dimension to Gould's unimpeded clarity and pin-point definition. The Aria is now mesmerically slow. The tremulous confidences of Variation 13 in the 1955 performance give way to something more forthright, more trenchantly and determinedly voiced, while Var. 19's previously light and dancing measures are humorously slow and precise. Var. 21 is painted in the boldest of oils, so to speak, and most importantly of all, Landowska's 'black pearl' (Var. 25) is far less romantically susceptible than before, has an almost confrontational assurance. The Aria's return, too, is overwhelming in its profound sense of solace and resolution. Although Gould devotees probably wouldn't want to be without any of Gould's recordings, it has to be said that this is surely the finest. The recording is superb.

Goldberg Variations.
Trevor Pinnock *hpd*
Archiv Produktion 415 130-2AH (61 minutes: ADD). Recorded 1980.   ⒻⓅ

Trevor Pinnock's reading is certainly one of the liveliest there has been of this great work, and effectively makes the point that veneration for Bach's genius does not have to be solemnly portentous: the sheer revelling in ingenuity and invention that bubbles out of this set is a welcome contrast to the hieratic attitudes of certain well-known Bach practitioners. One's initial reaction here may be that speeds are probably faster than Bach (or Goldberg) would have adopted; but Pinnock's apt articulation and pointing of detail never suffer thereby. You may feel that Var. 25 would be just as expressive without being so free rhythmically, and that taking the theme so slowly is at variance with the overall concept; but otherwise this recording – which captures every sound (musical and otherwise) of the Ruckers instrument with the utmost fidelity – is pure pleasure.

Goldberg Variations[a]. Das wohltemperierte Klavier, Book 2 – No. 33 in E major; No. 38 in F sharp minor.
Glenn Gould *pf*
Sony Glenn Gould Edition mono SMK52594 (46 minutes: ADD). Item marked [a] recorded 1955.   ⓂⒽ

Gould's pianistic skills have been universally and freely acknowledged, but his musical vision has elicited a range of critical response that has few parallels in this century. The view that Bach was a mere mathematical genius and little more has long passed, but it has its echoes in Gould's approach; he was fascinated by the structure of the music and was supremely skilful in showing the Jacquard-loom patterns woven by its contrapuntal threads. Every structural detail is exposed with crystal clarity but, switching metaphors, what is revealed is a marvellously designed and executed building, inhabited only by a caretaker. An overall time of 38 minutes does not seem unreasonable for the *Goldberg Variations* (here shorn of every repeat) but the statistic is misleading: many variations pass at breakneck speeds. As an exposition of the music's mechanism this is a remarkable performance but, despite occasional intrusions of sing-along – usually an indication of emotional involvement – and sparing use of the pedals (music first, pianism second), it says little of Bach's humanity. Two Fugues from the *48* extend the playing time to the lower limit of respectability. Neither is hurried and No. 33 proceeds with the solemnity that some others perceived to be its due. The sound quality of the recordings (the 'youngest' is 45 years old) is impressive, but overall this is probably of archival rather than definitive interest.

Fantasia in C minor, BWV906. 15 Two-Part Inventions, BWV772-86.
15 Three-Part Inventions, BWV787-801. Chromatic Fantasia and Fugue in D minor, BWV903.
Angela Hewitt *pf*
Hyperion CDA66746 (63 minutes: DDD). Recorded 1994.   ⒻⒺ

Angela Hewitt's approach may be gleaned from her refreshingly lucid annotation, or simply by listening to what she does. 'A skilful player can [bring out the different voices] with different colours' and 'To be capable of producing a true *legato* without using the pedal will serve a pianist well in any repertoire': Hewitt puts her fingers where her thoughts are, to signal effect. She never upsets the balance of the lines that it is in the nature of the harpsichord (Bach's chosen instrument) to yield, and her economy with the sustaining pedal helps to preserve their clarity. The two- and three-part *Inventions* are treated as music in their own right, not simply as the invaluable exercises they are; each is given its distinctive character, with a wonderful variety of sensitive touch and shapely rubato that never once threatens to become anachronistic. Her readings of the C minor *Fantasia* and the *Chromatic Fantasia and Fugue* are as eloquent and stimulating as any yet recorded by a harpsichordist.

Fantasias and Fugues – C minor, BWV537; G minor, BWV542; C minor, BWV562; G major, BWV572. Preludes and Fugues – D major, BWV532; F minor, BWV534; A major, BWV536; G major, BWV541; A minor, BWV543; B minor, BWV544; C major, BWV545; C minor, BWV546; C major, BWV547; E minor, BWV548, 'Wedge'; E flat major, BWV552, 'St Anne'.
Christopher Herrick *org*
Hyperion CDA66791/2. (two discs: 150 minutes: DDD). Recorded on the organ of the
Jesuitenkirche, Lucerne, Switzerland in 1993.   Ⓕ

These 15 works constitute some of the finest and most important music ever written for the organ. They are such mainstays of the repertory that no serious lover of organ music could consider a world without them. Herrick's performances are authoritative, scholarly and perceptive, but if that were all it would merely be putting Bach on a pedestal, making him accessible only to those who already possess the key to the door. Herrick's genius is in bringing the music vividly to life, injecting it with a sense of fun and a directness of appeal without for a moment compromising artistic integrity. Few could fail to be captivated by the wonderfully vibrant and smiling countenance of the great E flat Prelude while those of us who have laboured long and hard just to get our feet round that most ankle-twisting of all fugue subjects must surely surrender in the face of Herrick's effortless fluency in BWV542. The glorious Swiss instrument has been brilliantly recorded, portraying not just the instrument itself but its sumptuous aural setting.

Clavier-Übung III, BWV669-89. Prelude and Fugue in E flat major, BWV552, 'St Anne'. Fugue in G minor, BWV578. Passacaglia and Fugue in C minor, BWV582. Four Duets, BWV802-05. Concerto in G major, BWV973.
Kevin Bowyer *org*
Nimbus NI5561/2 (two discs: 119 minutes: DDD). Recorded on the Marcussen organ,
St Hans Kirke, Odense, Denmark in 1997.   Ⓜ

The music on this pair of discs encompasses almost every style in which Bach wrote for the organ. From the simple two-part *Duets* to the transcribed orchestral textures of a Vivaldi concerto; from the simple chorale prelude played by hands alone on a single four-foot stop (BWV677) to the complex double canon on two manuals and pedals of BWV678; from the transparent polyphony of a Trio (BWV676) to the immense contrapuntal complexity of the *Passacaglia*. Its value as a compact comprehensive compendium of Bach's organ writing is compounded by such uniformly good performances. Kevin Bowyer may not be at the cutting edge of Bach interpretation – but he does present unashamedly English performances. These are solid, reliable performances supported by a more than acceptable recording. Part 3 of the *Clavier-Übung* was never intended to be performed in one sitting by one organist on one organ so recordings such as this inevitably have about them an air of artificiality. Other organists have other approaches but Bowyer takes the broad view, treating it as one homogeneous whole. Not for him the desire to imitate two different instruments for the large and the *manualiter* preludes or to wrap them in a heady mix of varied registrations. Indeed Bowyer's registrations can best be described as sparing; even in the great C minor *Passacaglia and Fugue*, a work ripe for glittering registration effects, he rarely strays from a *pleno*. All in all, a most satisfactory release except for the largely unfathomable booklet-essay. Fledgling note writers would do well to study this booklet (preferably with a bottle of aspirin to hand) as an object-lesson in how to make the accessible inaccessible.

Preludes and Fugues – C major, BWV545; E flat major, BWV552, 'St Anne'. Trio Sonata in E minor, BWV528. Largo in A minor, BWV529. Fantasia in C minor, BWV562. Schübler Chorales, BWV645-50.
Piet Kee *org*
Chandos Chaconne CHAN0590 (66 minutes: DDD). Recorded on the Schnitger organ of
the Martinikerk, Groningen, The Netherlands in 1995.   Ⓕ

This is playing of heart-warming humanity and spiritual equilibrium, combining deep thought with complete spontaneity. Kee's control of the long, singing line goes hand in hand with a poetic command of baroque instrumental articulation. Dip anywhere into the Schübler Chorales or to either of the Trio Sonata slow movements and you can hear the separate melodic lines not only given individual character, shape and direction but combined with ease and gentle authority. Tempos in extrovert movements are unusually moderate, Bach's markings of *Vivace* and *Allegro* being taken by Kee as indications of mood rather than velocity, and yet the musical discourse is always involving and full of wit, helped by registrations that are both simple and wise. The disc is crowned by a magnificent performance of the Prelude and Fugue in E flat, one that fully exploits the vivid contrasts of theme and texture and yet binds the work into a structural unity without a hint of haste or stiffness. Rightly, the recording presents this refined, robust organ as heard within its natural acoustic habitat and Kee has subtly absorbed the church's acoustic into his interpretations.

Prelude and Fugue in E flat major, BWV552, 'St Anne'. Clavier-Übung III, BWV669-89. Four Duets, BWV802-05. Canonic variations on 'Vom Himmel hoch', BWV769a.
Ton Koopman *org*
Teldec 4509-98464-2 (two discs: 125 minutes: DDD). Recorded on the Silbermann organ of Freiburg Cathedral, Germany in 1996. Ⓕ

Three great joys await listeners to this pair of discs. First there is the sublime collection of chorale preludes, framed by one of the most majestic of all Bach's Preludes and Fugues, which forms the *Clavier-Übung III*. Then there is the glorious instrument, its unspeakably beautiful flutes, its delicate and subtle reeds, its invigorating full organ all captured magnificently in this vivid Teldec recording. And third there is the playing of Ton Koopman, who brings to his Bach a wealth of authority and perception flavoured with unflagging enthusiasm. He soothes those jagged double-dotted rhythms of the Prelude without losing one iota of the work's great stature. He imbues the 21 chorale preludes with an almost prayerful atmosphere, and to the four Duets he brings a lighter, more openly joyful nature, as if gently to relax the mood before the final, supremely celebratory Fugue. The overall effect is to re-create in purely musical terms the celebration of the Mass itself. He compares rather than contrasts the preludes with pedals with those for manuals alone, and thus achieves an unusually coherent sense of progress through the work, resulting in a refreshingly and convincingly unified performance. Throughout, ornamentation is not so much discreet as downright rare. His unusual reticence in this respect extends to a magnificent account of the *Canonic variations* where the clarity of the canonic lines is remarkably vivid. An immensely worthwhile issue.

Orgel-Büchlein, BWV599-644.
Christopher Herrick *org*
Hyperion CDA66756 (72 minutes: DDD). Recorded on the Metzler organ in the Stadtkirche, Rheinfelden, Switzerland in 1994. Ⓕ

With just two manuals and 32 speaking stops this wonderful organ is relatively small but still offers sufficient scope for Herrick to find a different registration for each of these 45 Preludes. The softer sounds used for *Herr Jesu Christ, dich zu uns wend* are preferable to the rather coarse *pleno* (*In dir ist Freude*) but it makes an undeniably ravishing sound. The *Orgel-Büchlein*'s 46 Chorale Preludes (here the almost identical pair on *Liebster Jesu* are merged, accounting for the disc's 45 tracks) are so brief that listening to them all in one sitting is the musical equivalent of eating salted peanuts one at a time in quick succession. In an attempt to make it all more palatable Herrick tries two tricks. First, he plays remarkably fast – which some people may not find particularly rewarding – *Der Tag, der ist so freudenreich* has as much of a relaxed air as an athletics track. Secondly, he revises the playing order, interspersing those Preludes based on 'general' themes between those for particular times in the church's year, and even mixing up the ones within each group. The booklet deserves paeans of praise. Robin Langley's notes are the perfect match for Herrick's playing: scholarly, erudite, infinitely rewarding and so easily communicative that one is barely aware one is absorbing some of the most complex and intellectually demanding ideas.

Orgel-Büchlein.
Ton Koopman *org*
Teldec Das Alte Werk 3984-21466-2 (70 minutes: DDD). Recorded in Ottobeuren Abbey, Bavaria in 1998. Ⓕ

These are short pieces, but brevity does not necessarily imply musical inconsequentiality – especially where Bach is concerned. Koopman is very impressive here, with sensitive, authoritative and perfectly gauged performances, imaginatively registered and stunningly recorded on the distinguished 1766 Riepp organ of Ottobeuren Abbey. Somehow he never lets the preludes sound short, treating each one as a gem to be lovingly nurtured so that, even when it survives barely 40 seconds, we feel we have lost an old and dear friend as it dies away in the Abbey's ambience. His sense of proportion is flawless, avoiding excessive sentimentality in *O Mensch, bewein' dein' Sünde gross* and creating the perfect balance between liveliness and majesty for *Komm, Gott Schöpfer, Heiliger Geist*. These are distinguished performances indeed, and if in places we hear signs of the instrument's great age, or its action impinges a little heavily on the ear, that serves only to enhance the sense of authority and stature this admirable release lends to some of Bach's briefest creations.

Fantasia and Fugue in G minor, BWV542. Trio Sonata No. 1 in E flat major, BWV525. Toccata and Fugue in D minor, BWV565. Pastorale in F major, BWV590. Organ Concerto No. 1 in G major, BWV592. Chorale Prelude – Erbarm' dich mein, O Herre Gott, BWV721. Organ Chorale – Aus tiefer Not schrei ich zu dir, BWV1099.
Kevin Bowyer *org*
Nimbus NI5280 (67 minutes: DDD). Recorded on the Marcussen organ of St Hans Kirke, Odense, Denmark in 1991. Ⓕ

This disc includes the best-known of all Bach's organ pieces – although some would dispute that it is an organ piece or even that Bach wrote it; Bowyer's account of the *Toccata and Fugue* in D minor is invigorating, exciting and very fast. It sets the scene for a CD of virtuoso performances and sound musicianship. The whole is a well-chosen, self-contained programme which also includes an indisputably 'great' organ work, a Trio Sonata, a transcription Bach made of an effervescent concerto by Ernst, a youthful chorale prelude as well as one from a collection only discovered in 1985 and one real oddity. Much thought has gone into the choice of organ and this instrument serves its purpose admirably; roaring magnificently in the *Fantasia* and emulating the tranquil sounds so characteristic of the *Pastorale*.

Toccatas – G minor, BWV915; G major, BWV916. Fugues on themes of Albinoni – A major, BWV950; B minor, BWV951. Fugue in C minor, BWV575. Preludes and Fugues – C major, BWV553; D minor, BWV554; E minor, BWV555; F major, BWV556; G major, BWV557; G minor, BWV558; A minor, BWV559; B flat major, BWV560. Fantasia con imitazione in B minor, BWV563.
Kevin Bowyer *org*
Nimbus NI5377 (74 minutes: DDD). Recorded on the Marcussen organ of St Hans Kirke, Odense, Denmark in 1992. Ⓕ

While critical opinion and academic argument may deter others, Bowyer is content to let the music speak for itself, whether it is 'by J.S. Bach, J.L. Krebs or A.N. Other'. On this disc the music speaks with absolute conviction. One thinks of the gloriously dramatic rhetoric Bowyer brings to the two Toccatas (BWV915 and 916). Harpsichordists may claim these as their own but who could deny this lovely Odense organ the opportunity to glitter with such flamboyant music? The eight 'short' Preludes and Fugues have a muscular, clean-shaven feel to them underlined by plain and simple registrations. While other recordings of such indefinable pieces seem like scraps from the cutting-room floor, Bowyer sets them firmly in the mainstream of high baroque organ music.

Toccata and Fugue in D minor, BWV565. Herzlich tut mich verlangen, BWV727. Fugue in G major, BWV577. Erbarm' dich mein, O Herre Gott, BWV721. Fugue on a theme by Corelli in B minor, BWV579. Prelude and Fugue in G major, BWV541. Pastorale in F major, BWV590. Clavier-Übung III, BWV669-89 – Wir glauben all' an einen Gott, BWV680. Orgel-Büchlein, BWV599-644 – O Mensch, bewein' dein' Sünde gross, BWV622. Passacaglia and Fugue in C minor, BWV582.
Peter Hurford *org*
EMI Eminence CD-EMX2218 (73 minutes: DDD). Recorded on the Schnitger organ of the Martinikerk, Groningen, The Netherlands in 1993. Ⓜ

'Peter Hurford playing organs of Bach's Time'. While Bach on 'authentic' instruments is no novelty, we certainly don't hear enough of the wondrous Ahrend organ which begins this series in such style. Ahrend? Builders of Bach's time? Well we're obviously going to have to take the title with a hefty pinch of salt. Although it dates back over 500 years, in its present form the organ dates back only as far as 1984. Bach never played it, and even if he had he certainly wouldn't recognize it now, but it sounds wonderful; Henry Mitton and Mark Nations have recorded it magnificently, closely focusing the sound within an aura of spaciousness. Splendid playing by Hurford too, of course. He begins (as everyone does) with the ubiquitous Toccata and Fugue in D minor. But what a performance! Everything else is given warmly communicative, unpretentious and immensely appealing performances. Hurford knows and loves his Bach, something which shines out of every note he plays.

Concerto in D minor after Vivaldi's Op. 3 No. 11, BWV596. Vater unser im Himmelreich, BWV737. Aria in F major, BWV587. Der Tag, der ist so freudenreich, BWV719. Trio Sonata No. 5 in C major, BWV529. Nun danket alle Gott, BWV657. Liebster Jesu, wir sind hier, BWV731. Fantasia super Valet will ich dir geben, BWV735. Nun freut euch, lieben Christen gemein, BWV734. Toccata, Adagio and Fugue in C major, BWV564.
Peter Hurford *org*
EMI Eminence CD-EMX2226 (66 minutes: DDD). Recorded on the Schnitger organ in the Ludgerikirche, Norden, Germany in 1993. Ⓜ

Given the virtues of the marvellous Schnitger organ at Norden (a clear, 'oakey' brilliance, imposing but not austere) it is perhaps a mite surprising that Hurford still occasionally shows a liking for frothy, high-pitched registrations which may be too neo-baroque for some tastes. But set against that, and far more important, is his ability to convey energy without haste. Indeed, his relaxed control (without any diminution of authority or personality) in quick movements results in performances that are, without exception mellow, humane and witty. And in terms of textual clarity they are exemplary. The close marriage of music and instrument is most fruitful in the chorale settings. Hurford knows exactly what he is about: with registrations carved from the meat of the instrument – solid choruses and reeds – these works are revealed as quintessential meditations for the Lutheran liturgy, dogma in music, patient, strong and assured. *Nun danket alle Gott*, in particular, is given an outstandingly trenchant performance. The engineering is first-rate, the slightly recessed pedal balance reflecting (but not distractingly so) the unusual layout of the instrument, which is fully explained in the insert-notes.

Fantasie and Fugue in G minor, BWV542. Six Preludes and Fugues – A minor, BWV543; B minor, BWV544; C major, BWV545; C minor, BWV546; C major, BWV547; E minor, BWV548 (all arr. Liszt).
Artur Pizarro *pf*
Collins Classics 1498-2 (73 minutes: DDD). Recorded 1996. Ⓕ

Whether paraphrasing operas, appropriating songs, or proselytizing great symphonic works, Liszt responded with imagination and resourceful variety to his chosen material for transcription. These are among Liszt's most straightforward and literal arrangements: his reverence for Bach, his devotion and fidelity to the spirit of his source, tempers the natural exuberance of his pianistic idiom. The G minor *Fantasie* has considerable grandeur and chromatic intensity, and Liszt accords it a suitably grand setting, creating the required mass of sound by fleshing out some of the textures. The *Six Preludes and Fugues*, on the other hand, are almost entirely literal re-castings, with Liszt using the piano's sustaining pedal to overcome the lack of the organ's pedal board. When one considers that these are early transcriptions (dating from the 1840s yet seemingly incongruous with Liszt's period of virtuosic glamour) one realizes how seriously he took his homage to Bach. Artur Pizarro approaches these works with a rigorous intensity, with refined sensitivity and impeccable judgement. In his hands the original Bach shines through every bar, and this is of course exactly how these transcriptions should sound – that they do is a tribute both to Pizarro and to Liszt. Tempos are well paced, ensuring a natural sense of flow and momentum. Everything is almost ideally shaped, and the sustaining pedal (absolutely essential in these transcriptions) is most sensitively deployed. Try the Preludes from BWV544 and 547 for an idea of Pizarro's beautifully crafted performances; with playing like this any questions of 'authenticity', of the validity of transcriptions, should become unimportant. The recording is excellent, even if occasionally one might like the sound to ring more resonantly.

Six Trio Sonatas, BWV525-30 – No. 1 in E flat major; No. 2 in C minor; No. 3 in D minor; No. 4 in E minor; No. 5 in C major; No. 6 in G major.

Trio Sonatas Nos. 1-6.
Christopher Herrick *org*
Hyperion CDA66390 (72 minutes: DDD). Recorded on the Metzler organ of the Parish Church of St Nikolaus, Bremgarten, Switzerland in 1989. Ⓕ

The common assumption is that Bach wrote his Six Trio Sonatas as training studies for his son Wilhelm Friedmann, and certainly to this day young organists regard the ability to play these pieces as a prerequisite in establishing proper organ technique. But if ever the notion that this music 'first to practise and secondly to admire' was shown to be false, this stunning disc presents an unanswerable argument. Christopher Herrick's performances are immense fun, brimming over with real affection for the music. He allows himself occasional displays of enthusiasm (adding a few exuberant *glissandos* in the last movement of the E flat major Sonata, for example) and he chooses his stops both to enhance the vitality of the quick movements and to underline the sheer beauty of the slower ones. Never has this music sounded less like a training study! The Hyperion recording of the sumptuous Swiss instrument makes this disc a worthwhile buy if only for its glorious sound; the organ speaks into a rich, opulent acoustic which treats each note as a priceless jewel, to be enhanced by its setting but not in any way to be obscured. A disc of rare beauty and a real gem in any collection.

Trio Sonatas Nos. 1-6.
Kay Johannsen *org*
Hänssler Classic 92 099 (78 minutes: DDD). Recorded on the Metzler organ of the Stadtkirche, Stein am Rhein, Germany in 1997. Ⓜ

Kay Johannsen is not a particularly familiar name outside her native Germany, but she has something distinctive to say in her Bach interpretations. Her performance is distinguished by uniformly stylish, immaculately tailored readings of the Trio Sonatas. At the beginning of the 1990s Herrick's Hyperion recording was perceived as the most persuasive, vivid and compelling performances ever of these sonatas. He has, at last, met his match. Johannsen has every bit as much verve, spirit and musical persuasiveness, the organ is ideal both for these sparkling performances and the transparency of the musical textures (like Herrick, Johannsen has chosen a glorious Swiss Metzler – this time the 1992 instrument in the municipal church of Stein am Rhein), and Hänssler Classic's recording has exceptional presence and clarity. What many may prefer is Johannsen's avoidance of those *glissandos* and exuberant over-the-top gestures which Herrick favours.

Allabreve in D major, BWV589. Aria in F major, BWV587. Canzona in D minor, BWV588. Four Duets, BWV802-05. Fantasias – A minor, BWV561; C major, BWV570. Fantasia con imitazione in B minor, BWV563. Fugues – C minor, BWV575; G major, BWV576; G major, BWV577, 'Jig Fugue'; G minor, BWV578. Pastorale in F major, BWV590. Preludes – A minor, BWV551; G major, BWV568; A minor, BWV569. Preludes and Fugues – E minor, BWV533; G minor, BWV535; D minor, BWV539; D minor, BWV549a; G major, BWV550. Toccata and Fugue in E major, BWV566. Trios – D minor, BWV583; C minor, BWV585; G major, BWV586. Trio Sonata in G major, BWV1027a (arr. cpsr). Musikalisches Opfer, BWV1079 – Ricercar a 3; Ricercar a 6.
Christopher Herrick *org*
Hyperion CDA67211/2 (two discs: 156 minutes: DDD). Recorded on the organ of the Stadtkirche, Rheinfelden, Switzerland in 1996. Ⓕ

Some might be tempted to describe what we have here as the 'scrapings from the barrel', for when you've taken out the chorale-based works, the trio sonatas, the concertos and the big preludes, fantasias, toccatas, passacaglias and fugues this is what's left. One could, however, be tempted almost to prefer these crumbs from the table of great genius to those stupendous musical feasts which are everybody's idea of the real J.S. Bach. And when you have those crumbs seasoned with such loving care, such elegance and such finesse as Christopher Herrick gives to, say, the G minor fugue (BWV578) or the enchanting Trio Sonata (BWV1027a), you realize that here is music every bit as worthy of close attention as anything Bach wrote for the organ. In matters of registration, tempo, articulation and phrasing, Herrick displays immaculate taste. This is playing of the very highest order. The modest two-manual Metzler, built in 1992, makes an enchanting sound, and the recording fully supports the superlative artistry of the playing.

Schübler Chorales, BWV645-50. Leipzig Chorales, BWV651-68. Chorales from Cantatas Nos. 36, 59, 62 and 180. Wenn wir in höchsten Nöten sein, BWV431. Du heiliger Brunst, süsser Trost, BWV226 No. 2. An Wasserflüssen Babylon, BWV267. Herr Jesus Christ, dich zu uns wend', BWV332. O Lamm Gottes, unschuldig, BWV401. Nun danket alle Gott, BWV386. Von Gott will ich nicht lassen, BWV418. Allein Gott in der Höh' sei Ehr', BWV260. Jesus Christus, unser Heiland, BWV363. Komm, Gott Schöpfer, heiliger Geist, BWV370.
Amsterdam Baroque Choir / Ton Koopman *org*
Teldec Das Alte Werk 4509-94459-2 (two discs: 142 minutes: DDD). Texts and translations included. Organ works recorded on the organ of the Grote Kerk, Leeuwarden in 1994. Ⓕ

Koopman's performances have a glorious sense of spontaneity born of the understanding that, with a cantata and a fistful of chorale preludes to compose and perform every week, Bach was hardly involved here in deep, painstaking creativity. Koopman seems totally attuned to the essential practicality of this music. As a result he can indulge in outrageously ebullient ornamentation, which from any other organist might seem merely bad taste, and maintain his light, dispassionate approach even through those Preludes usually afforded particular emotional significance, yet make it all sound stylistically convincing. A link between organ and cantata cycles is forged here by pairing each prelude with its chorale, sung by the choir with whom Koopman is currently working his way through the complete cantatas for Erato. The complete unity of approach between organist and singers is ingeniously underpinned by the use of organ accompaniment where unaccompanied singing might create a sense of dissociation. There is occasional variation but throughout, the singing of the Amsterdam Baroque Choir is an unalloyed joy. Koopman isn't going to be everybody's cup of tea every time, but with this beautifully recorded pair of discs any reservations are completely outweighed by the sheer musical integrity of what are truly wonderful performances.

Schübler Chorales. Leipzig Chorales. Kirnberger Chorales, BWV690-91 and BWV694-713.
Christopher Herrick *org*
Hyperion CDA67071/2 (two discs: 147 minutes: DDD). Recorded on the Metzler organ of the Jesuitenkirche, Lucerne, Switzerland in 1995. ⓕ

The Schübler Chorales are mostly drawn from cantata movements, the Leipzig, sometimes known as the '18' and sometimes as the 'great' due to their large stature (including in BWV652 the longest chorale prelude Bach wrote), and some miscellaneous chorale preludes which have absolutely nothing in common beyond the fact that Johann Philipp Kirnberger, a pupil and admirer of Bach, bundled them all together. Keenly aware of the artificiality of the situation – obviously no organist in Bach's day would have dreamt of playing 44 chorale preludes in one go – Herrick has approached the task with businesslike vigour. *Wachet auf* fizzes like champagne at a wedding – no wonder the sleepers seem so eager to waken with such a riotous wedding feast clearly already in full swing. But such unrelenting bubbliness can also seem misplaced: Schumann's description of *Schmücke dich, o liebe Seele* (BWV654) as 'priceless, deep and full of soul' hardly fits this dancing performance. Perhaps, then, not a recording from which to extract single preludes, but certainly one which can withstand repeated bouts of continuous listening. As ever, not only has Herrick found a simply ravishing Swiss organ which he uses with impeccable good taste (and his invariably sensitive registrations are all detailed in the booklet) but the Hyperion team have come up with a top-notch recording.

Cantatas
No. 4, Christ lag in Todesbanden
No. 5, Wo soll ich fliehen hin
No. 6, Bleib' bei uns, denn es will Abend werden
No. 7, Christ unser Herr zum Jordan kam
No. 8, Liebster Gott, wann werd' ich sterben
No. 11, Lobet Gott in seinen Reichen (Ascension Oratorio)
No. 13, Meine Seufzer, meine Tränen
No. 18, Gleich wie der Regen und Schnee
No. 19, Es erhub sich ein Streit
No. 21, Ich hatte viel Bekümmernis
No. 22, Jesus nahm zu sich die Zwölfe
No. 23, Du wahrer Gott und Davids Sohn
No. 24, Ein ungefärbt Gemüte
No. 25, Es ist nicht Gesundes an meinem Liebe
No. 26, Ach wie flüchtig, ach wie nichtig
No. 27, Wer weiss, wie nahe mir mein Ende!
No. 28, Gottlob! nun geht das Jahr zu Ende
No. 30, Freue dich, erlöste Schar
No. 31, Der Himmel lacht! die Erde jubilieret
No. 35, Geist und Seele wird verwirret
No. 39, Brich dem Hungrigen dein Brot
No. 40, Dazu ist erschienen der Sohn Gottes
No. 41, Jesu, nun sei gepreiset
No. 43, Gott fähret auf mit Jauchzen
No. 44, Sie werden euch in den Bann tun
No. 49, Ich gehe und suche mit Verlangen
No. 50, Nun ist das Heil und die Kraft
No. 51, Jauchzet Gott in allen Landen!
No. 54, Widerstehe doch der Sünde
No. 55, Ich armer Mensch, ich Sündenknecht
No. 58, Ach Gott, wie manches Herzeleid
No. 59, Wer mich liebet, der wird mein Wort halten
No. 61, Nun komm, der Heiden Heiland
No. 63, Christen, ätzet diesen Tag
No. 64, Sehet, welch eine Liebe
No. 65, Sie werden aus Saba alle kommen
No. 67, Halt im Gedächtnis Jesum Christ

No. 68, Also hat Gott die Welt geliebt
No. 69, Lobe den Herrn, meine Seele
No. 69a, Lobe den Herrn, meine Seele
No. 70, Wachet, betet, seid bereit allezeit
No. 71, Gott ist mein König
No. 73, Herr wie du willst, so schick's mit mir
No. 75, Die Elenden sollen essen
No. 76, Die Himmel erzählen die Ehre Gottes
No. 81, Jesus schläft, was soll ich hoffen?
No. 82, Ich habe genug
No. 84, Ich bin vergnügt mit meinem Glücke
No. 85, Ich bin ein guter Hirte
No. 93, Wer nur den lieben Gott lässt walten
No. 95, Christus, der ist mein Leben
No. 102, Herr, deine Augen sehen nach dem Glauben
No. 104, Du Hirte Israel, höre
No. 105, Herr, gehe nicht ins Gericht mit deinem Knecht
No. 106, Gottes Zeit ist die allerbeste Zeit
No. 107, Was willst du dich betrüben
No. 108, Es ist euch gut, dass ich hingehe
No. 111, Was mein Gott will, das g'scheh allzeit
No. 121, Christum wir sollen loben schon
No. 124, Meinen Jesum lass ich nicht
No. 125, Mit Fried und Freud ich fahr dahin
No. 127, Herr Jesu Christ, wahr' Mensch und Gott
No. 130, Herr Gott, dich loben alle wir
No. 131, Aus der Tiefen rufe ich, Herr, zu dir
No. 132, Bereitet die Wege, bereitet die Bahn
No. 136, Erforsche mich, Gott, und erfahre mein Herz
No. 138, Warum betrübst du dich, mein Herz?
No. 140, Wachet auf! Ruft uns die Stimme
No. 143, Lobe den Herrn, meine Seele
No. 144, Nimm, was dein ist, und gehe hin
No. 146, Wir müssen durch viel Trübsal
No. 147, Herz und Mund und Tat und Leben
No. 148, Bringet dem Herrn Ehre seines Namens
No. 149, Man singet mit Freuden vom Sieg
No. 152, Tritt auf die Glaubensbahn
No. 153, Schau, lieber Gott, wie meine Feind
No. 154, Mein liebster Jesus ist verloren
No. 155, Mein Gott, wie lang, ach lange
No. 158, Der Friede sei mit dir
No. 161, Komm, du süsse Todesstunde
No. 163, Nur jedem das Seine
No. 165, O heilges Geist- und Wasserbad
No. 167, Ihr Menschen, rühmet Gottes Liebe
No. 170, Vergnügte Ruh', beliebte Seelenlust
No. 171, Gott, wie dein Name, so ist auch dein Ruhm
No. 173, Erhöhtes Fleisch und Blut
No. 179, Siehe zu, dass deine Gottesfurcht
No. 180, Schmücke dich, o liebe Seele
No. 181, Leichtgesinnte Flattergeister
No. 182, Himmelskönig, sei willkommen
No. 184, Erwünschtes Freudenlicht
No. 185, Barmherziges Herze der ewigen Liebe
No. 186, Ärgre dich, o Seele, nicht
No. 190, Singet dem Herrn ein neues Lied!
No. 192, Nun danket alle Gott
No. 194, Höchsterwünschtes Freudenfest
No. 196, Der Herr denket an uns
No. 198, Lass, Fürstin, lass noch einen Strahl (Trauer Ode)
No. 199, Mein Herze schwimmt im Blut
No. 202, Weichet nur, betrübte Schatten
No. 207a, Auf, schmetternde Töne
No. 209, Non sa che sia dolore
No. 211, Schweigt stille, plaudert nicht, 'Coffee'
No. 212, Mer hahn en neue Oberkeet, 'Peasant'

Cantatas Nos. 4, 131 and 182.
Julianne Baird, Christine Brandes, Judith Nelson *sops* **Judith Malafronte** *mez* **Drew Minter,
Daniel Taylor** *altos* **Benjamin Butterfield** *ten* **Kurt-Owen Richards, James Weaver** *basses*
American Bach Soloists / Jeffrey Thomas *ten*
Koch International Classics 37235-2 (67 minutes: DDD). Texts and translations included.
Recorded 1994.   ⒡ⓟ

This programme contains three early works from Mühlhausen and Weimar. These are the cantatas
that benefit most from scaled-down forces since they are, in most cases, more closely related to the
Lutheran sacred concerto and motet of the late seventeenth century. Thomas, following in Joshua
Rifkin's steps, adheres strictly to the one-to-a-part principle. Judith Malafronte's beautifully
coloured voice has a timbre, clarity and understanding of Bach's melodic demands that make you
long to hear her in many more of Bach's cantatas. Sadly, she sings in only one work on the disc,
Bach's Annunciation/Palm Sunday Cantata, *Himmelskönig, sei willkommen* (No. 182). The
equivalent vocal range in the remaining two cantatas is served by countertenor Drew Minter who
also makes a fine contribution though a less satisfying one than Malafronte. There is in fact much
good singing throughout, James Weaver and Julianne Baird being but two whose expressive warmth
enhances the music. Thomas and his team apply a wealth of effective stylistic ideas. There is, for
instance, a wonderfully lyrical approach by the recorder player in the alto aria of No. 182; the
shaping of phrases is carefully thought out, he leans slightly on all the notes that call for it and
punctuates the music with all the skill of a seasoned rhetorician. Thomas himself, in the extended
declamatory tenor aria from the same work, has similarly persuasive ideas though occasionally
lacks the assured vocal technique to see him through. In summary, there is plenty of food for
thought here and much that is both stylistically apposite and emotionally satisfying. Some readers
will want a stronger vocal presence in the choral movements but overall the performances are
recommended. Good recorded sound.

Bach Cantatas: No. 5 – Ergeisse dich reichlich; No. 13 – Meine Seufzer, meine Tränen; No. 26 –
So schnell ein rauschend Wasser schiesst; No. 55; No. 102 – Erschrecke doch.
Hoffmann (attrib.) Meine Seele rühmt und preist.
Telemann Ich weiss, dass mein Erlöser lebt.
RIAS Chamber Choir, Berlin; C.P.E. Bach Chamber Orchestra / Peter Schreier *ten*
Philips 442 786-2PH (59 minutes: DDD). Texts and translations included.   ⒡

It was a good idea of Peter Schreier to include the two cantatas for solo tenor, once upon a time
thought to have been by Bach, but now known to be the product of other talents. Their removal
from the Bach canon leaves only one cantata for solo tenor as a genuine product of Bach's pen: *Ich
armer Mensch, ich Sündenknecht* (No. 55). This is a notoriously difficult work to bring off
successfully. The elaborate and often high-lying vocal writing makes huge demands upon the soloist.
Schreier offers a very fine account of the piece, revealing nuances in Bach's music which are left
undiscovered by many a rival. But it is the other two cantatas which make the disc particularly
interesting. The Telemann piece is seldom performed, while the other, attributed to Georg Melchoir
Hoffmann, has enjoyed a far less high profile than it deserves, since its erstwhile seemingly
impeccable pedigree was exposed a long time ago as fraudulent. Its opening aria, one of three, is
particularly alluring; but why substitute a transverse flute for the intended recorder, especially when
two recorders are available and used to effect in the aria from Cantata No. 13? Otherwise, the
performance of this lovely piece comes over well, as do the isolated arias from Bach's cantatas.
Schreier is on top form, bringing out the poetry in the music. The C.P.E. Bach Chamber Orchestra
gives sympathetic support to the voice and yields up some fine obbligatos, above all from the flute
in No. 55.

Cantatas Nos. 6, 41 and 68.
Barbara Schlick *sop* **Andreas Scholl** *counterten* **Christoph Prégardien** *ten* **Gotthold Schwarz**
bass **Accentus Chamber Choir; Limoges Baroque Ensemble / Christophe Coin** *vc*
Auvidis Astrée E8555 (63 minutes: DDD). Texts and translations included. Recorded 1995.   ⒡ⓟ

These three cantatas are Leipzig compositions dating from 1725. No. 41 is a New Year piece, No. 6
an Easter one, while No. 68 was written for Whitsun. Though belonging to the same year, these
cantatas are varied in structure, only No. 41 adhering to that unifying thematic pattern which was
such a distinctive feature of the chorale-based works of the 1724-25 annual cycle. The many
illuminating features of Coin's lively direction elsewhere ensure a high level of enjoyment; and his
own violoncello piccolo solos convey the poetry of the music with wonderfully intuitive expression
and grateful gesture. Happily, the four vocal soloists are outstanding and the small choir sound
well, on the whole, though they do not always make their presence sufficiently felt. The opening

chorus of No. 6, Schweitzer's 'masterpiece of poetry in music', is handled with extraordinary sensibility by Coin, who brings out details in Bach's scoring, such as the throbbing quavers of the upper and middle string parts, with loving tenderness. This gentleness of approach, together with a close identity and warm rapport with Bach's kaleidoscopic tonal palette, are virtues common to all three discs and sterling qualities that will survive the fickleness of changing fashion. And what is so refreshing about these recordings is the absence of intrusive mannerism. There are no empty gestures here, just total absorption in the music, and a disarming humility. A release of great distinction.

Cantatas Nos. 7, 11, 30, 68 and 104.
Hedy Graf, Emiko Iiyama, Agnes Giebel *sops* Barbara Scherler, Claudia Hellmann *mezzos* Georg Jelden, Kurt Huber, Theo Altmeyer *tens* Jakob Stämpfli, Bruce Abel, Erik Wenk *basses* Heinrich Schütz Choir, Heilbronn; Pforzheim Chamber Orchestra / Fritz Werner.
Erato 0630-12978-2 (two discs: 140 minutes: ADD). Texts and translations included.
Recorded 1964-70. Ⓜ

This reissue serves as evidence that Bach performance in the 1960s can boast qualities which have eluded many modern-day practitioners. As more 'historic' recordings come to light (and 1970 is historic given how quickly eighteenth-century performance practice has changed), it is easy to adopt a blanket perspective driven by the insatiable desire to reinvent the past. Indeed, not everything Werner did with Bach is as acceptable now as when the earliest of the cantatas in this set was recorded. Yet, above all, what these performances implore from the listener is that we distinguish between fashion and taste – what is a sign of its time and what transcends it, in the process begging a few questions on what constitutes 'the real thing' if we take the concept of authenticity to its logical conclusion. Most persuasive of all in Werner's Bach is the ingenuous reading of the musical line as dictated by the sentiments of the text. This is not merely a form of homogeneous vocalization but a sort of spontaneous connection between the composer's setting of words and an undistracted conviction to represent them.

We can witness this in the arias of No. 30, magnificently sung by Bruce Abel and Barbara Scherler, as well as the long-breathed direction in the gentle, pastoral lilt of the opening chorus of No. 104. There is fine singing on display: Kurt Huber is typical of the musicianly singer Werner seems to have attracted: sensitive and instinctively able to colour the music with memorable nuances (only Emiko Iiyama is disappointing). Better known is the quietly distinguished Jakob Stämpfli who comes up trumps every time, as indeed has the inimitable and gleaming voice of Agnes Giebel; No. 68, a fine Cantata for Pentecost, reveals a singer who transports the familiar sense of frolicking joy of 'Mein gläubiges Herze' ('My heart ever faithful') on to a new shining plateau, reinforced by the delightfully performed instrumental interlude which follows. There is much else to admire here including a notable Ascension Oratorio (No. 11) boasting a brilliant opening chorus. Werner's performance of No. 7 is still valid for its robust energy, even if there are details in continuo realization which are harder to reconcile in modern times. The sound transfers are outstanding – no less than these wonderful performances deserve.

Cantatas Nos. 8, 26, 43, 61, 85, 130 and 182.
Frederike Sailer, Ingeborg Reichelt *sops* Claudia Hellmann, Hertha Töpper *mezzos* Helmut Krebs *ten* Erik Wenk, Jakob Stämpfli, Franz Kelch *basses* Heinrich Schütz Choir, Heilbronn; Pforzheim Chamber Orchestra, ᵃSouth-West German Chamber Orchestra, / Fritz Werner.
Erato 4509-97407-2 (two discs: 147 minutes: ADD). Recorded 1959-61. ⓂⒽ

Fritz Werner, conductor and composer, championed Bach's cantatas in the 1960s and early 1970s with rare integrity and unaffected eloquence. The disc comprises reissues of seven cantatas, chosen from over 50 he recorded from 1958-74, and is skilfully conceived to cover all the important seasons of the church calendar. The Advent cantata is the magnificent *Nun komm, der Heiden Heiland* (No. 61), which is touchingly natural in its expression. The soloists here feature the sensitive singing of tenor, Helmut Krebs, who may not have an effortless vocal technique but his open-throated and committed performances are full of personality and his recitatives nobly delivered. Jakob Stämpfli, too, is a fine and highly consistent Bachian. The Heinrich Schütz Choir is also well suited to Werner's spontaneous and smooth transitions and classical pacing. How thrilling are the trumpets and drums in the bass aria of No. 130; no holds barred, crackling articulation and an inimitable moment when in the excitement of it all they get slightly out. And the free-flowing flute obbligato in the same cantata (again, with Krebs on top form) has a recognizable personality gently coaxed by a sympathetic, untyrannical director. No. 8, *Liebster Gott*, is another outstanding all-round performance. The opening chorus is instilled with compassion and radiant phrasing. The substantial *Himmelskönig, sei willkommen* for Palm Sunday (No. 182) is less consistent overall. This is a sobering release of near 'historical' (in its true sense) Bach cantatas, conceived by musicians whose innate perception of what they were doing relied principally on good artistry. Recorded sound transfers are good. Documentation is not up to scratch for such an important issue.

Cantatas Nos. 8, 125 and 138.
Deborah York *sop* **Ingeborg Danz** *mez* **Mark Padmore** *ten* **Peter Kooy** *bass*
Collegium Vocale / Philippe Herreweghe.
Harmonia Mundi HMC90 1659 (59 minutes: DDD). Texts and translations included.
Recorded 1998. Ⓕ Ⓟ

These recordings feature disciplined orchestral support for the voices and some very fine contributions indeed from solo vocalists and obbligato players. The programme itself contains three superb examples of Bach's craft in the sacred cantata medium. Nowhere is this more apparent than in the broad canvases of the choral fantasias with which each of the cantatas begins. The expressive range is vast, the assembly and deployment of varied and, at times, seemingly irreconcilable ideas almost breathtaking in their vitality, freshness, fluency and, in the case of 'Warum betrübst du dich, mein Herz?', deep complexity. But these particular pieces furthermore contain arias of outstanding beauty and contemplative depth. The group of soloists that Herreweghe has assembled for the disc could hardly be bettered. The burden is carried by Mark Padmore and Peter Kooy. Ingeborg Danz has one aria only (No. 125). It's a big piece and she sings it well. Deborah York is least well catered for with only a single recitative (No. 8) which she delivers with warmth and accuracy. Padmore's 'Was willst du dich' (No. 8) is splendid. He comfortably matches any of his rivals on disc. Kooy is seldom disappointing but here he seems to have risen even above his usual excellent form. His 'Doch weichet' (No. 8), one of Bach's most immediately captivating arias, is declamatory, supple and technically impeccable; and the 'Auf Gott steht meine Zuversicht' (No. 138), a notoriously difficult piece, succeeds where many another has faltered in the past. In conclusion, this is a rewarding issue. The oboist, Marcel Ponseele, makes an outstanding contribution. A considerable achievement all round.

Cantatas Nos. 11, 43 and 44.
Barbara Schlick *sop* **Catherine Patriasz** *contr* **Christoph Prégardien** *ten* **Peter Kooy** *bass*
Collegium Vocale / Philippe Herreweghe.
Harmonia Mundi HMC90 1479 (67 minutes: DDD). Texts and translations included.
Recorded 1993. Ⓕ Ⓟ

Gott fähret auf mit Jauchzen (No. 43) is resonant in its joyful celebration of Christ's Ascension to Heaven and the right hand of God the Father. The orchestra includes three trumpets, drums and two oboes, as well as the basic string band, and these all play a part in the majestic opening chorus. By comparison, *Sie werden euch in den Bann tun* (No. 44) is a modestly conceived piece. The Ascension 'Oratorio' (No. 11), though listed among Bach's cantatas, is an oratorio in more than just name, making use of a narrator who relates the events surrounding Christ's Ascension. Like Bach's two other oratorios, this one makes extensive use of music which had previously been written for other contexts. It also contains the music which eventually was to become the *Agnus Dei* of the B minor Mass. Herreweghe paces all three works with assurance and fluency and is supported by the excellence of his singers and instrumentalists. Fine recorded sound and an informative booklet complete an accomplished issue.

Cantatas Nos. 13, 28, 58, 61, 63, 64, 65, 81, 82, 111, 121, 124, 132 and 171.
Edith Mathis, Sheila Armstrong, Lotte Schädle *sops* **Anna Reynolds, Hertha Töpper** *mezzos*
Peter Schreier, Ernst Haefliger *tens* **Dietrich Fischer-Dieskau** *bar* **Theo Adam** *bass-bar*
Munich Bach Choir and Orchestra / Karl Richter.
Archiv Produktion 439 369-2AX4 (four discs: 278 minutes: ADD). Recorded 1960s-71. Ⓑ

It was only to be expected that, with the burgeoning interest in period instrument performances which took place in Europe and the USA during the 1970s, the more traditional and conservative approach of Karl Richter would be cast aside, for the time being. Yet, in the 1950s, when Richter made his earliest recordings of Bach's music his disciplined and vital approach was hailed as revelatory. Now, as period instruments have firmly established themselves in today's musical life, the climate has thankfully once more become conducive to a fuller and fairer integration of other styles of interpretation. Richter's involvement in Bach's Passions, oratorios and cantatas spanned a period of almost 30 years, from the early 1950s until his untimely death in 1981. This volume contains the cantatas for Advent, Christmas and Epiphany. The level of executancy is consistently high. Among the works that come off especially well are the Christmas cantata, *Christen, ätzet diesen Tag* (No. 63), the colourful Epiphany cantatas, *Sie werden aus Saba alle kommen* (No. 65) – still perhaps the most convincing version on disc – and *Was mein Gott will, das g'scheh allzeit* (No. 111). The tenor Ernst Haefliger is admirable in No. 65, Anna Reynolds and Peter Schreier superb in their surging, fervent G major duets, which steal the show in Nos. 63 and 111. The soprano, Edith Mathis is never less than dependable throughout the series and is often very much more than that, while Dietrich Fischer-Dieskau, sometimes sensitive (Nos. 61 and 82), sometimes boisterous almost to the point of caricature (No. 121), is never dull. Richter's Munich Bach Choir and Orchestra usually make a satisfying conjunction though the vocal forces are too large. Never mind, that is all part of his performance concept along with a style in organ continuo which is at times as strident in sound as it is inapposite in manner. The players are generally first-rate and this is a feature of the recordings which remains absolutely constant.

Cantatas Nos. 18, 143, 152, 155 and 161.
Midori Suzuki, Ingrid Schmithüsen sops **Yoshikazu Mera** counterten **Makoto Sakurada** ten
Peter Kooy bass **Bach Collegium Japan / Masaaki Suzuki** org
BIS CD841 (78 minutes: DDD) Texts and translations included. Recorded 1997. ⓅⓇⓈⒺ

The fifth volume of Bach's sacred cantatas performed by the Bach Collegium Japan continues their Weimar survey with five pieces written between c1713 and 1716. It begins with No. 18, performed in its Weimar version – Bach later revived it for Leipzig, adding two treble recorders to the purely string texture of the upper parts of the earlier composition. The scoring of No. 152 is more diverse, featuring in its opening Sinfonia a viola d'amore, viola da gamba, oboe and recorder.
A conspicuous feature of No. 155 is its melancholy duet for alto and tenor with bassoon obbligato. While the vocal writing sustains something of the character of a lament the wonderfully athletic, arpeggiated bassoon solo provides a magical third voice. The accompanying essay is confused here, emphasizing the importance of a solo oboe which in fact has no place at all in this work. No. 161 is a piece of sustained beauty, scored for a pair of treble recorders, obbligato organ, strings and continuo. Bach's authorship of No. 143 has sometimes been questioned. Much of it is indeed un-Bach-like, yet at times it is hard to envisage another composer's hand. The performances are of unmatched excellence. Masaaki Suzuki's direction never falters and his solo vocalists go from strength to strength as the series progresses. Suzuki makes a richly rewarding contribution with beautifully poised singing, a crystal-clear voice and an upper range that only very occasionally sounds at all threatened. Mera and Sakurada sustain a delicately balanced partnership in the elegiac duet of No. 155, the limpid bassoon-playing completing this trio of outstanding beauty. Kooy is a tower of strength, a sympathetic partner to Suzuki in the dance-like duet between Jesus and the Soul (No. 152), and resonantly affirmative in his aria from the same cantata. But the highest praise should go to Mera and Sakurada for their affecting performance in No. 161. All the elements of this superb cantata are thoroughly understood and deeply felt by all concerned. The disc is admirably recorded and, apart from the aforementioned confusion, painstakingly and informatively documented.

Cantatas Nos. 19, 40, 70, 140, 149 and 180.
Edith Selig, Ingeborg Reichelt, Agnes Giebel, Hedy Graf sops **Claudia Hellmann,**
Barbara Scherler mezzos **Georg Jelden, Helmut Krebs, Kurt Huber** tens **Jakob Stämpfli,**
Franz Kelch, Erik Wenk basses **Heinrich Schütz Choir, Heilbronn;**
Pforzheim Chamber Orchestra / Fritz Werner.
Erato 0630-11223-2 (two discs: 146 minutes: ADD). Texts and translations included. Ⓜ
Recorded 1964-70.

As with Richter, Leonhardt, Harnoncourt and others who have recorded a significant number of cantatas – a thin line divides supreme good judgement and lurking solecisms. This is the case with Erato's enlightened retrospective of Fritz Werner's distinguished legacy of Bach cantata recordings. The great advantage of reissuing single works from a larger project is the chance to select only the most accomplished performances, so long as the choice of what to include is governed by a discerning ear: we have enough of the original LPs to know that only Werner's most convincing accounts have seen the light of day. What he projects unlike anyone else is an inimitably gracious, free-breathing humanity; so often his Bach performances convey a sense of oblation without a sniff of self-importance – something to be treasured. This volume is another gem, though perhaps for slightly different reasons. There is that same direct, humble and profoundly spiritual response to Bach's musical 'gospel' but we experience here a greater chronological spread (1960-70). We forsake, except fleetingly, the touching strains of tenor Helmut Krebs and the shimmering intensity of Agnes Giebel but, instead, enjoy a greater range of Werner's evolution as a Bachian.

Nothing represents this more strikingly than the first track of the first disc, the opening chorus of *Es erhub sich ein Streit* (No. 19), where Werner's choir are rather more assured than in the earliest recordings – and they need to be. This is a symbolically confrontational choral *tour de force* between Heaven and Hell, as is appropriate for the Feast of St Michael. Bach's three cantatas for this feast seem to have inspired Werner greatly: his version of No. 130 in Vol. 1 is a testament to dangerous living, spontaneous and committed. Trumpets play their part in both pieces with memorable flair but Maurice André's playing is of a completely different order, epic in short: he acts as Werner's, Bach's and St Michael's first gunner, eager into battle supported by Werner's unforced rigour. Such momentum without neurosis also lies at the heart of *Wachet, betet* (No. 70), though overall this is even better; the extremes of fear, vigilance and fervour inspired by the Last Judgement are yet more pronounced. Again, André is in the thick of things with his subtly varied articulation, rhythmic buoyancy and easy lyricism, joined by singing of great understanding and commitment by Hedy Graf and Jakob Stämpfli, though there is no performance more moving than tenor Kurt Huber's innocent beauty in the aria at the start of Part 2.

Indeed, the quality of soloists seems generally to improve as the set proceeds. One wishes for Krebs's imaginative phrasing and colouring of words in No. 19 where Georg Jelden's technical limitations are too noticeable for comfort, though he is a different singer in his duet with Claudia Hellmann in the finely paced No. 149. Giebel's shimmering assurance in the same work, not surprisingly, puts Edith Selig's and Ingeborg Reichelt's honest and agreeable performances of the first two cantatas in the shade. Werner's meditative view of *Wachet auf* (No. 140) is one of Werner's earliest cantata recordings (1960); the two duets prey on a warm and lucid dialogue. *Schmücke dich* (No. 180) from ten years later is another accomplished achievement, its contemplative approach most convincing. To sum up: this is an important and exciting release, arguably Werner's best. One should not expect perfection in its modern sense. Werner does not wield the axe as many modern directors do, which can count against him in some choral movements, but what a small price for such rich illuminations of great music whose qualities transcend fickle taste. *Bravo!* The transfers are immediate with the odd touch of distortion.

Cantatas Nos. 21 and 31.
Monika Frimmer *sop* **Gerd Türk** *ten* **Peter Kooy** *bass*
Bach Collegium Japan / Masaaki Suzuki.
BIS CD851 (68 minutes: DDD). Texts and translations included. Recorded 1997. Ⓕ Ⓟ

Both of these are Weimar compositions, dating from *c*1713 and 1715 respectively, and both were later sung at Leipzig. Where No. 21 is concerned, the performance history is complex since Bach, who clearly and understandably set great store by this extended and profoundly expressive piece, made no fewer than four versions of it. Following what was probably its second Weimar performance, in 1714, Bach produced a new version which he used as a test-piece in Hamburg's Jacobikirche, when applying for an organist's post there in 1720. It is this version, for soprano and bass soloists only, in which the parts are transposed from C minor to D minor that forms the basis of the present recording. Suzuki offers listeners an opportunity, by way of an appendix, of hearing Bach's alternative thoughts on certain sections of the cantata. These are meticulously prepared and affectingly declaimed performances. Listen, for instance, to the beautifully articulated and delicately placed bassoon quavers in the poignant opening Sinfonia of No. 21. This is most sensitively done and an auspicious beginning to the work. String playing is not always quite as clean as it could be but the instrumental expertise is, nevertheless, impressive. The solo line-up is strong, with Monika Frimmer sustaining several demanding soprano arias with eloquence and tonal warmth. Gerd Türk and Peter Kooy are secure and expressive, and the singing of the 18-voice choir of women's and men's voices is impressive, though tenors sound strained in the first chorus of No. 21.

Cantatas Nos. 22, 23 and 75.
Midori Suzuki *sop* **Yoshikazu Mera** *counterten* **Gerd Türk** *ten* **Peter Kooy** *bass*
Bach Collegium Japan / Masaaki Suzuki *org*
BIS CD901 (64 minutes: DDD). Texts and translations included. Recorded 1998. Ⓕ Ⓟ

This eighth volume of Bach Collegium Japan's Bach cantata series bridges the period between Bach's departure from Cöthen and his arrival at Leipzig, early in 1723. *Du wahrer Gott und Davids Sohn* (No. 23) was mainly written at Cöthen, while *Jesus nahm zu sich die Zwölfe* (No. 22) must have been composed almost immediately on Bach's reaching Leipzig. The remaining cantata, *Die Elenden sollen essen* is on an altogether grander scale, in two parts, each of seven movements. The performances maintain the high standards of singing, playing and scholarship set by the previous issues in this series. There are little insecurities here and there – the oboes, which play a prominent role in each of the three pieces, are not always perfectly in agreement over tuning – but the careful thought given to the words, their significance and declamation, and the skill with which they are enlivened by the realization of Bach's expressive musical vocabulary, remain immensely satisfying. The disciplined, perceptively phrased and beautifully sustained singing of the two choral numbers of No. 23 illuminate the words at every turn, savouring the seemingly infinite expressive nuances of the music. As for No. 75, we can only imagine the astonishment with which Leipzig ears must have attuned to its music. In this absolutely superb piece Bach entertains us with a stylistic diversity that is breathtaking. Polyphony, fugue, chorale fantasia, *da capo* aria, instrumental sinfonia, varied recitative, wonderful oboe writing and a rhythmic *richesse* all contribute to the special distinction both of this cantata and No. 76. Lose no time in becoming acquainted with this one. It reaches, one might say, those parts which other performances do not. Fine recorded sound.

Cantatas Nos. 24, 25, 67, 95, 105, 136, 144, 147, 148, 173, 181 and 184.
Lisa Larsson *sop* **Bogna Bartosz, Elisabeth von Magnus** *mezzos* **Gerd Türk** *ten*
Klaus Mertens *bass* **Amsterdam Baroque Choir and Orchestra / Ton Koopman** *hpd/org*
Erato 3984-23141-2 (three discs: 214 minutes: DDD). Texts and translations included.
Recorded 1997.   Ⓕ Ⓟ

The seventh volume of Ton Koopman's projected complete cantata survey contains pieces which Bach performed at Leipzig in 1723 and 1724. Koopman's line-up of soloists has been taking a while to settle down and, in this volume, the alto solos are shared between Elisabeth von Magnus, one of the greatest strengths of the series, so far, and Bogna Bartosz. All the tenor arias are sung by Gerd Türk, and Lisa Larsson and Klaus Mertens provide their customarily stylish and warm-hearted performances as soprano and bass soloists respectively. As well as containing three superb examples of Bach's genius in the cantata medium – Nos. 67, 105 and 147 – Vol. 7 contains a handful of rarely heard pieces, of which No. 136, with its colourfully brilliant opening chorus, is perhaps the most immediately striking. This highly imaginative movement in A major was later to provide Bach with the 'In gloria Dei patris' of his Lutheran Mass in the same key. At the opposite end of the affective scale is the sombre, penitential chorus which determines the prevalent character of No. 25. This technically ingenious double fugue in E minor is difficult to carry off convincingly in performance but Koopman, with his clearly defined contrapuntal strands and responsive choir, succeeds better than any rival version. The gracefulness and fluency in his direction come together rewardingly in No. 95. This highly original cantata, with its syncopations, dissonances, bold key changes, and references to four hymns with their associated melodies, all in the opening chorus, is, quite simply, breathtaking. The music commands our attention at every turn, disturbing and pleasing our senses in equal measure. But perhaps it is the following two movements which most readily capture our imagination and win our hearts. Lisa Larsson sings the former with ingenuous charm while Gerd Türk, in the latter, seems to sustain Bach's mercilessly high vocal range with the greatest of ease.

With 12 cantatas under scrutiny it is impossible to discuss them all. But the overall picture of this set is mainly convincing, with some very fine playing and singing – only the occasionally over-assertive projection of countertenor voices from the choir fails to please. Any disappointment here, though, seems relatively slight beside the many excellent contributions of Koopman's artists. If, on balance, No. 105 is a shade lacking in strength of purpose, then such feelings are ameliorated by the wellnigh perfect partnership of Larsson and oboist, Marcel Ponseele, in its poignant soprano aria, certainly one of the highest peaks in a stimulating issue.

Cantatas Nos. 24, 76 and 167.
Midori Suzuki *sop* **Robin Blaze** *counterten* **Gerd Türk** *ten* **Chiyuki Urano** *bass*
Bach Collegium Japan / Masaaki Suzuki.
BIS CD931 (67 minutes: DDD). Texts and translations included. Recorded 1998.   Ⓕ Ⓟ

Bach Collegium Japan here tackles three pieces belonging to the composer's first weeks in office as Thomaskantor at Leipzig. Grandest in design by far, is the superb *Die Himmel erzählen die Ehre Gottes* which he performed on the Second Sunday after Trinity in 1723. In its terms of reference, musical variety and emotional impact this work complements, perhaps even surpasses No. 75, a cantata on a similarly expansive scale which he had presented to his Leipzig congregation a week earlier. For the most part the music comes over well in the hands of the Bach Collegium Japan, apart from a little disappointment in Chiyuki Urano. He doesn't settle comfortably into his recitatives and his declamatory aria, 'Fahr hin' lacks character and presence. But it should be added that in lesser company his performance would stand up well enough. Midori Suzuki sings her gently inflected aria with tonal warmth, clarity and assurance. Technically, she is unpredictable but, at her strongest, as here, she is well worth taking a chance with. Gerd Türk, rapidly becoming one of the major pillars of this enterprise, articulates his music with stylistic fluency, communicating textual content with declamatory fervour.

This is Robin Blaze's first involvement in this series. His voice is lightly coloured and unforced, and he should do well in the present company, as he ably demonstrates in the superb duet with Midori Suzuki. The remaining cantatas on the disc are for the Fourth Sunday after Trinity (No. 24) and St John's Day, both in 1723. Blaze gives a fine account of the joyful opening aria of No. 24. His phrasing is graceful and his articulation incisive, features which have so far been prominently to the fore in the instrumental playing of this series. No better example of its excellence can be found than in the trio sonata Sinfonia which introduces Part 2 of No. 76, scored for oboe d'amore, viola da gamba and continuo.

Cantatas Nos. 27, 158 and 198.
Rotraud Hansmann *sop* **Helen Watts** *contr* **Kurt Equiluz** *ten* **Max van Egmond** *bass*
Monteverdi Choir; Concerto Amsterdam / Jürgen Jürgens.
Teldec Das Alte Werk 4509-93687-2 (67 minutes: ADD). Texts and translations included.
Recorded 1966-67.   Ⓜ Ⓟ

This is a skilfully transferred account of Jürgen Jürgens's classic recording of the *Trauer Ode* (No. 198). Unlike many releases from yesteryear, this stands out as a beacon in early 'period performance' awareness of Bach's vocal music (the orchestra comprises Gustav Leonhardt as the continuo player, joined in the appropriate places by Anner Bylsma, Jaap Schröder and Wieland Kuijken), though its lasting qualities come from the same creative vessel as Richter's most successful recordings: incisive and perceptive response to texts and true musical conviction. Jürgens could hardly have chosen a more carefully assembled or densely argued work for his delectation than the *Trauer Ode*. This beautiful masterpiece was completed late in 1727 for the memorial ceremony of the Electress of Saxony, Queen Christiane Eberhardine. Heavily involved in the *St Matthew Passion* at the time (the 'mourning' *Affekt* in both pieces is strikingly similar), Bach appears to have been acutely aware of the atmospheric potential of 'soft' scorings, in this case with gambas, flutes, lutes and oboe d'amores depicting the bittersweet concoction of pain and consolation. The comprehension of how these unique figures find a meaningful context alongside all the other myriad interpretative considerations is where Jürgens succeeds whilst others fail, succeeding totally in creating sustained poignancy. He attends with typical thoughtfulness to two other cantatas, both of which maintain the theme of death and the hope of eternal life, No. 27 being the most substantial. Recommended to Bachians of all persuasions.

Cantatas Nos. 35, 54 and 170.
Andreas Scholl *counterten* **Collegium Vocale Orchestra / Philippe Herreweghe.**
Harmonia Mundi HMC90 1644 (59 minutes: DDD: 5/98). Texts and translations included.
Recorded 1997.   Ⓕ Ⓟ Ⓔ

Some 12 years separate the composition of the Weimar cantata, *Widerstehe doch der Sünde* (No. 54), from the Leipzig cantatas *Vergnügte Ruh'* (No. 170) and *Geist und Seele wird verwirret* (No. 35, written in 1726). All three are scored for a solo alto voice with strings and, in the case of the Leipzig pieces, various members of the oboe family and obbligato organ. Andreas Scholl is on top form in *Widerstehe doch der Sünde*, paying close attention to the relationship between text and music. *Vergnügte Ruh'* has long been a favourite piece with singers and audiences alike. Scholl sets an effectively contemplative tempo in the tender introductory aria and sounds comfortable with Bach's broadly spun melody. The remaining work, in two parts, is conceived on an ambitious scale, opening with an extended concerto movement for organ obbligato, oboe d'amore and strings, and containing another, similarly scored piece which serves as an introduction to Part Two. Organist Markus Märkl, with lively support from the orchestral players of the Collegium Vocale, gives a pleasingly jaunty, animated performance of these movements which together with the first aria may have belonged to a lost concerto. Scholl sings his music with warmth and technical fluency, generating a high level of interest for heart and mind alike.

Cantatas Nos. 39, 93 and 107.
Agnès Mellon *sop* **Charles Brett** *counterten* **Howard Crook** *ten* **Peter Kooy** *bass*
Collegium Vocale Chorus and Orchestra / Philippe Herreweghe.
Virgin Classics Veritas VC7 59320-2 (61 minutes: DDD). Texts and translations included.
Recorded 1991.   Ⓕ Ⓟ

The three pieces included here are mature examples of Bach's cantata writing; two of them, Nos. 93 and 107, were written in 1724 for the Fifth and Seventh Sundays after Trinity respectively, and thus belong to Bach's great second cycle in which he concentrated on a chorale-based scheme. The remaining cantata, No. 39, is a masterly work, above all in the concerto-like construction of the opening chorus, scored for voices with treble recorders, oboes and strings. Agnès Mellon is beguiling both in her three arias – one per cantata – and in her duo with Charles Brett. Both Crook and Kooy are on characteristically fine form. Enjoyable, too, are the contributions from the chorus and orchestra, and, as usual, the oboe playing of Marcel Ponseele is a constant pleasure, above all for his poetic phrasing and communicative articulation. Excellent recorded sound.

Cantatas Nos. 49, 58 and 82.
Nancy Argenta *sop* **Klaus Mertens** *bass* **La Petite Bande / Sigiswald Kuijken** *vn*
Accent ACC9395 (63 minutes: DDD). Texts and translations included. Recorded 1993.   ⓕ🅿

Few readers will be disappointed either by the music or the performances on this disc. It features
one of Bach's very finest cantatas, *Ich habe genug* (No. 82) for solo baritone, and two 'Dialogue'
cantatas for soprano and bass. Leaving out for the moment such issues as instrumental timbre,
Sigiswald Kuijken is among the most thoughtful of present-day practitioners of baroque music.
That is not to say that you will always like what he does but that he always has a good reason for
doing it and is prepared to defend it to the end. Here, there are no complaints whatsoever: tempos
are beautifully judged, the string sound is warmer than usual and the overall approach to the music
expressive and eloquently shaped. Klaus Mertens gives a fine performance of *Ich habe genug*, clearly
articulated and resonantly declaimed. Kuijken has opted for the first of several versions of this
cantata which Bach made subsequently for various voice pitches and with small instrumental
adjustments. In the two 'Dialogue' cantatas Mertens is joined by Nancy Argenta, an effective piece
of casting. Both voices are tonally well focused and project the music in a manner admirably free
from needless affectation or contrivance. An expressive peak is reached in Argenta's aria, 'Ich bin
herrlich, ich bin schön' (No. 49), a ravishing quartet movement with oboe d'amore and a violoncello
piccolo beautifully played by Hidemi Suzuki. Add to this a first-rate performance of the organ
obbligatos in the opening Sinfonia and final duo of the same cantata and you have a performance
of distinction. In short, this disc has the edge on several fine Bach cantata recordings currently
available. An outstanding achievement.

Cantatas Nos. 49, 115 and 180.
Barbara Schlick *sop* **Andreas Scholl** *counterten* **Christoph Prégardien** *ten*
Gotthold Schwarz *bass* **Concerto Vocale; Limoges Baroque Ensemble / Christophe Coin** *vc*
Auvidis Astrée E8530 (71 minutes: DDD). Texts and translations included. Recorded 1993.   ⓕ🅿

Three of Bach's Leipzig church cantatas form a characteristically well-thought-out programme
from the French gamba player, cellist and director, Christophe Coin. *Schmücke dich, o liebe Seele*
(No. 180) and *Mache dich, mein Geist, bereit* (No. 115) are among the most overlooked of the
cantatas, outside 'complete editions'; but they are towering masterpieces which deserve to be as
popular as, for instance, *Wachet auf!* (No. 140) or any of the others which find their way, albeit
infrequently, into concert programming. There is a more particular reason, however, beyond that of
sheer musical excellence, why Coin has chosen to perform these works: it is that in each of them
Bach has included a movement calling for the obbligato presence of a small, five-stringed cello, the
violoncello piccolo. Nine of Bach's cantatas contain a part for this distinctive-sounding instrument,
in each of which the composer employs it with telling effect. No. 180 is a delicately scored piece for
two recorders, oboe, oboe da caccia and strings, with an affecting undercurrent of elegy. Coin's
direction, his overall grasp of the musical idiom and his evident care over textual detail lead to the
heart of the piece. Not everything is refined – there are, for example, some rough moments in the
instrumental tuttis – but the spirit of the performance carries everything along with it. This much is
true for the remaining cantatas, too. No. 115 contains music of quite extraordinary inventive
richness and nowhere more so than in its two *da capo* arias for alto and soprano, respectively: the
second, in B minor, seems to lead us into almost uncharted emotional territory in its contemplative
profundity. This heart-rending trio for soprano, flute, violoncello piccolo and continuo is one of the
most astounding achievements in the entire canon; and it is beautifully sung by Barbara Schlick.
The Leipzig Concerto Vocale (a mixed choir of men's and women's voices), and the Limoges
Baroque Ensemble have gathered under Coin's direction in performances which probe far beyond
musical superficialities.

Cantatas Nos. 50, 50 (recons. Kleinbussink), 59, 69, 69*a*, 75, 76, 104, 179, 186, and 190.
Ruth Ziesak *sop* **Elisabeth von Magnus** *mez* **Paul Agnew** *ten* **Klaus Mertens** *bass* **Amsterdam
Baroque Choir and Orchestra / Ton Koopman** *org*
Erato 3984-21629-2 (three discs: 195 minutes: DDD). Texts and translations included.
Recorded 1997.   ⓕ🅿

This is the sixth volume in Ton Koopman's exhaustive series of Bach's complete cantatas. Koopman
is here engaged in the great Leipzig period from 1723. Bach's inaugural offering was a pair of
substantial bipartite cantatas, Nos. 75 and 76. Koopman gives us the second one initially,
Die Himmel erzählen die Ehre Gottes, in a muscular and assertive performance. The fine opening
chorus, with its swaggering trumpet obbligato, is zestfully negotiated and appropriately
full-blooded. The same commitment and character are plentiful in the formidably worked-out
contrapuntal edifice of No. 75 – a movement passionately declaiming the rewards of seeking God –

and the wonderfully evocative imagery in No. 104, *Du Hirte Israel, höre*. Memorable for different reasons is *Singet dem Herrn*, No. 190, a cantata whose opening two movements require major reconstruction. Koopman has completed the task with a dynamic scoring around the existing vocal parts. If a somewhat over-elaborate setting, it is nevertheless thrilling, and employs the sort of fervent Reformation-like unisons and belting brass which cannot fail to stir. Koopman has found in Ruth Ziesak a soprano who can get round the notes, sing consistently in tune (despite one under-par aria in No. 186) and express the meaning of the music with rhetorical personality. She dances around the lithe 'Ich nehme mein Leiden' from No. 75. This latter cantata abounds in arresting arias, none more so than the delicious 'Mein Jesus soll', a creation of such ingenious and agreeable melodic inflexion that Paul Agnew can but relish it devotedly. Both Agnew's and Klaus Mertens's singing throughout is a joy, a happy blend of technical security, musicianly shaping and tonal elegance. Elisabeth von Magnus is, in truth, the weak link. Her contribution to the stirring Part 2 of No. 76 is not especially undistinguished but her languid sound is repeatedly enervating, and too often the pitch dips unacceptably. In all other respects this is quite a turn-up for the books after the hits and misses of previous volumes. Bach was clearly intent on impressing his new employers with the most accomplished work he could produce; one only has to hear the richness of these scores (a bonanza here for those who like trumpets, and brilliantly played too) to suppose that Koopman has found similar inspiration at exactly the right time.

Cantatas Nos. 51, 202 and 209.
Agnes Giebel *sop*
Concerto Amsterdam / Jaap Schröder *vn* **Leonhardt Consort / Gustav Leonhardt** *hpd*
Teldec Das Alte Werk 3984-21711-2 (65 minutes: ADD). Texts and translations included.
Recorded 1966. Ⓜ Ⓗ Ⓟ

Followers of historical recordings of Bach's music admire Agnes Giebel for her impeccable delivery and shimmering control of line. She is a worthy mentor to current practitioners in that she communicates an utterly enraptured love of Bach and its expressive world. Whilst her voice may sound old-fashioned in its dignified restraint, that is merely the 'front'; as one can hear in the recitative and *arioso* of *Jauchzet Gott* (No. 51), she manipulates her heady control of the phrase with mesmerizing intensity. There is much consistently vintage Giebel in this welcome reissue. Stylish accompaniments from the early Dutch pioneers, Jaap Schröder and the Leonhardts, provide a tantalizing glimpse of how Giebel, had she been a generation younger, would have so ideally suited and relished the exciting possibilities of period instruments; the chamber-like *Non sa che sia dolore* (No. 209) has all the refinement and instinct for discerning gesture to render it a remarkably prescient document of its time: the aria, 'Partipur e con dolore' is a case in point and this really is vintage Giebel. No. 51 has been a favourite with technically capable sopranos in the post-war period. The opening is a touch pedestrian in the paucity of shaping in the ritornello arpeggios but Giebel's beady encirclement of the fiendish passagework as the piece unfolds is sheer joy. A precious disc of a great Bach singer.

Bach[a] Cantatas Nos. 54 and 170. Mass in B minor BWV232 – Agnus Dei.
Handel[b] Orlando Ah Stigie larve!. Jephtha, HWV70 – 'Tis Heaven's all-ruling pow'r. Theodora, HWV68 – Kind Heav'n, if Virtue be thy care, Sweet Rose, and Lilly, flow'ry Form.
Alfred Deller *counterten* [a]**Leonhardt Baroque Ensemble / Gustav Leonhardt** *org*
[b]**Handel Festival Orchestra / Sir Anthony Lewis.**
Vanguard Classics Alfred Deller Edition 08.5069.71 (59 minutes: ADD). Texts and translations included. Recorded [a]1953, [b]1960. Ⓜ Ⓟ Ⓗ

Of the many Vanguard reissues this one is, both musically and historically, perhaps the most remarkable. Not only does it contain in the two Bach cantatas and the *Agnus Dei* from the B minor Mass superlative performances by Alfred Deller, then at the height of his powers, but it also must be ranked among the earliest significant recordings to adopt period instruments. Made in 1953 and issued in America the following year, this is probably one of the first appearances on disc of the Leonhardt Baroque Ensemble, later to become the Leonhardt Consort. Many of its members have since played a leading role in the period-instrument revival and many are still going strong today: Michel Piguet (oboe), Edward Melkus and Marie Leonhardt (violins), Kurt Theiner and Alice Hoffelner (now Alice Harnoncourt) on violas, Nikolaus Harnoncourt (cello) and Gustav Leonhardt (organist and director). A redoubtable line-up. But, of course, it is Deller himself who immortalizes the performances with his unique voice and extraordinary musical sensibility.

The two cantatas are both for solo alto voice. They begin with arias of outstanding beauty to whose deeply contemplative, lyrical spirit Deller contributes his own, distinctively melancholic timbre. This conjunction of voice and music creates an atmosphere of sustained elegy which has not been equalled by any other performance. Of course, as we should expect, the period-instrumental playing then, as Purcell might have said, in its nonage, is still far from refined in all matters concerning tuning and ensemble. But it is so attentive to the contours of the voice and music that the issue pales into relative insignificance beside Deller's supreme artistry. All is stylishly performed. The *Agnus Dei* is on a comparable level with the cantatas in respect of performance, and the Handel pieces are also most enjoyable, though these were recorded several years later and accompanied by a modern instrumental ensemble conducted by Sir Anthony Lewis, a fine Handel exponent but one without much affection for the period-instrument revival. Hamor's "Tis Heaven's all-ruling pow'r' from Handel's last oratorio, *Jephtha*, is particularly affecting. Readers need no more exhortation from us. This is a release which must not be overlooked.

Cantatas Nos. 61, 63, 132 and No. 172.
Ingrid Schmithüsen *sop* **Yoshikazu Mera** *alto* **Makoto Sakurada** *ten* **Peter Kooy** *bass*
Bach Collegium Japan / Masaaki Suzuki *org*
BIS CD881 (78 minutes: DDD). Texts and translations included. Recorded 1997.   Ⓕ **P** **E**

Suzuki's gradual but assured journey through the complete Bach cantatas continues with the micro-series of works composed in Weimar between 1708 and 1717, the majority of which were written for performances at the castle chapel. That we have so many fine cantatas from this period is indeed thanks to the reigning duke's *diktat* that upon Bach's promotion to Kapellmeister in March 1714 he perform new works each month in the so-called 'Himmelsburg' chapel. Three of the cantatas here are works written for Advent and Christmas for 1714 and 1715 whilst *Erschallet* (No. 172) is a Pentecost cantata also from late on in Bach's tenure at Weimar. *Christen, ätzet diesen Tag* (No. 63) is both a resplendent and tender work, which juxtaposes grand, balletic framing choruses with closely-knit, reflective and limpid arias. It has received several fine performances on record over the years but surely none so delectably paced and naturally argued as this. If one could quibble with very occasional slips in wind intonation, the choruses here succumb delightfully, in the first of Bach's Christmas Day cantatas, to a placed *gravitas* in the articulation, simultaneously elevated by a focused choral sound; the words joyfully spin and leap out of this articulate ensemble, both here and in the equally thrilling opening movement of No. 172.

Yoshikazu Mera, whose countertenor voice displays a remarkable, shimmering beauty in the accompanied recitative of No. 63 and whose impressive control in 'Christi Glieder', from No. 132, is little like anything we have heard from him so far in this series. If Peter Kooy is a known quantity and acts as something of an *éminence grise*, he lightly and gracefully paves the way for the poised Ingrid Schmithüsen (she negotiates the high-pitched 'Bereitet die Wege' from No. 132 with unequivocal vitality) in the first of her two duets; the second in No. 172, 'Komm, lass mich' is a chorale-aria on *Veni Creator* which reveals the level of commitment and attention to detail which Suzuki derives from his singers. Some may find the well-known first version of *Nun komm, der Heiden Heiland* (No. 61) a touch lacking in human foreboding (despite a strong line in Advent-tide anticipation) but, as we have observed before, Suzuki is never less than unself-regarding in his approach, one where absence of mannerism and a freshness of enquiry (which belies deep understanding of each work), presents the listener with new 'texts' of rare thoughtfulness, serenity and sureness of touch. Apart from some careless documented listings, this recording can only be described as a triumph.

Cantatas Nos. 67, 108 and 127.
Antonia Fahberg *sop* **Lilian Benningsen** *contr* **Sir Peter Pears** *ten* **Kieth Engen** *bass*
Munich Bach Choir; Munich State Opera Orchestra / Karl Richter.
Teldec Das Alte Werk 9031-77614-2 (61 minutes: ADD). Texts and translations included.
Recorded 1958.   Ⓜ **H**

Collectors of Bach's choral music have strong views on Richter's performances, especially the church cantatas which represented the majority of his recorded output for Archiv. Most would agree that Richter's special affinity with Bach's music found its mark most persuasively in the 1960s before his mysterious adoption of the cloudy neo-romantic sound which did little to project his profound understanding of Bach's inner strength. Here we have a rarity from the late 1950s (a 'one-off' from Teldec not available in this country before) which forces us to revise our opinions about Richter's rigidity. These three cantatas were caught before the Munich Bach Orchestra had been formed though you would not know that they were not Bachians to the core; this is a state opera orchestra inspired by invigorating musical expression, blessed with an ignorance of self-conscious fashion. Certainly there are a few distracting mannerisms and a voice, notably Lilian Benningsen, which in hindsight seem somewhat out of place but they never detract from the prevailing conviction of the performances. In Cantata No. 67 the spirit of the text is directly and lucidly communicated by a spruce and well-balanced choral group, supported by the inimitable Peter Pears (a treasure or two here for his fans). The bass Kieth Engen is also a Bach singer out of the top drawer; the opening aria of Cantata No. 108 is lovingly sung and the legendary Edgar Shann delivers an obbligato oboe line which is worth the cost of the disc alone, even without the other priceless revelations here.

Cantatas Nos. 71, 106 and 131.
Midori Suzuki, Aki Yanagisawa *sops* **Yoshikazu Mera** *counterten* **Gerd Türk** *ten*
Peter Kooy *bass* **Bach Collegium Japan / Masaaki Suzuki.**
BIS CD781 (63 minutes: DDD). Texts and translations included. Recorded 1995. Ⓕ Ⓟ

These artists are abreast of current thinking concerning baroque style in this volume of church cantatas, yet sometimes you find yourself longing for a little more in the way of expression and a little less of fashionable orthodoxy. The three cantatas included here are among Bach's earliest essays in the form. Nos. 106 and 131 (*c*1707) belong to the Mühlhausen period, while No. 71 was written in 1708. By and large, Suzuki has chosen effective tempos, though there are notable exceptions. One of these affects the beautiful Sonatina for recorders and viola da gamba that introduces the *Actus tragicus* (No. 106), a funeral piece of startling intensity. Suzuki feels too slow here, adding a full 40 seconds on to performances by virtually all of his rivals. Elsewhere, and above all in his choice of soloists, Suzuki fields an exceptional team. We can feel this especially in the effortlessly projected singing of Midori Suzuki (Nos. 71 and 131) and Aki Yanagisawa (No. 106), the uncluttered declamation of Gerd Türk, and the resonant, stylish contributions by Peter Kooy. The countertenor here lacks either conviction or consistent aural charm. The Choir is well drilled and, as with the solo element, the voices respond urgently to the spirit of the text. Listen to the thrice supplicatory 'Israel' in the concluding chorus of No. 131 for one such example. The recorded sound is splendid.

Cantatas Nos. 73, 105 and 131.
Barbara Schlick *sop* **Gérard Lesne** *counterten* **Howard Crook** *ten* **Peter Kooy** *bass*
Ghent Collegium Vocale Chorus and Orchestra / Philippe Herreweghe.
Virgin Classics Veritas VC7 59237-2 (58 minutes: DDD). Texts and translations included.
Recorded 1990. Ⓕ Ⓟ

Philippe Herreweghe's choir consists of some 16 voices to which he has added four excellent soloists, all of whom are experienced artists in this repertoire. *Aus der Tiefen rufe ich* (No. 131) is one of Bach's earliest cantatas, dating back to 1707 or 1708. The text is a setting of Psalm 130, *De profundis* with additional verses from a Lenten hymn. Herreweghe conveys the sombre intensity of the piece and is especially well served by his soloists, choir and solo oboist, with a particularly lyrical contribution from Howard Crook. Harmonically, No. 73 is a work of considerable strength. The Gospel-based text underlines the contrasting states of human frailty on the one hand and God's omnipotence on the other. Counterpart and subtle instrumentation play a part in the work's dark climax, a bass recitative and aria in which Bach's extraordinary gifts at evoking musical-textual imagery are on display. Peter Kooy is resonant, declamatory and affecting and is well supported on the whole by the strings, though the violins are thin at times. The beautiful *Herr, gehe nicht ins Gericht* (No. 105) is masterly from start to finish. The text focuses on two themes, the parable of the unjust steward and St Paul's warning to the Corinthians against idolatry and pride. Barbara Schlick is on top form, making this perhaps the interpretative high point of the entire recording; Bach's musical concept, furthermore, is breathtakingly original. She is affectingly partnered by Marcel Ponseele whose delicately shaded oboe playing is all that one could wish for. Kooy declaims with firm control and a feeling for the poetry, and Crook is effective in his aria dispelling the emotional intensity of the earlier sections. Herreweghe manages all with tenderness and emotional restraint, achieving a sustained often deeply affecting performance. Three wonderful works, affectionately realized with solo contributions of distinction.

Cantatas Nos. 84, 202 and 209.
Nancy Argenta *sop* **Ensemble Sonnerie / Monica Huggett.**
Virgin Classics Veritas VC5 45059-2 (54 minutes: DDD). Texts and translations included.
Recorded 1993. Ⓕ Ⓟ

Of the three works on this disc, No. 84 is the only sacred cantata. Unlike the better-known *Ich habe genug* (No. 82), its two alternating recitatives and arias are followed by a four-part chorale set to a melody which occupies an important place in Bach's work, *Wer nur den lieben Gott lässt walten*. Nos. 202 and 209 are, respectively, a wedding cantata – though not one which is linked in any way to the marriage service – and a piece commemorating the departure on a journey of an unidentified friend, presumably of the composer, whoever he may have been, since Bach's authorship is also sometimes questioned. Bach or not, it is a very engaging work with an extended concerto movement for flute and strings in B minor in which Bach unquestionably must have had at least a hand. The performances are very good indeed. Both Nos. 84 and 202 are dominated by oboe writing rich in fantasy and this aspect is well understood by oboist Paul Goodwin, above all in the wonderfully expressive opening arias of each work. Argenta's youthful voice is well suited to all this music yet it is, perhaps, especially alluring in the Italian cantata, No. 209, in whose more galant idiom she sounds completely at home. This is a captivating performance in which Argenta is sensitively partnered by the limpid flute playing of Lisa Beznosiuk.

Cantatas: No. 140 – Wann kommst du, mein Heil?; Mein Freund ist mein!. No. 146 – Wie will ich mich freuen. No. 147 – Ich will von Jesu Wundern singen. No. 152 – Tritt auf die Glaubensbahn; Wie soll ich dich, Liebster der Seelen. No. 153 – Fürchte dich nicht, ich bin bei dir. No. 154 – Wisset ihr nicht. No. 185 – Das ist der Christen Kunst. No. 192 – Der ewig reiche Gott. No. 194 – Was des Höchsten Glanz erfüllt; O wie wohl ist uns geschehn. No. 196 – Der Herr segne euch.
Allan Bergius, Christoph Wegmann, Helmut Wittek, Stefan Gienger trebs **Kurt Equiluz** ten
Thomas Hampson bar **Vienna Concentus Musicus / Nikolaus Harnoncourt.**
Teldec 9031-74798-2 (55 minutes: DDD). Recorded 1983-87. Ⓕ🅿

This disc is both an alluring shop window for Teldec's complete series of Bach cantatas – though in no sense a substitute – and an attractive programme in its own right. Bach's sacred cantatas are richly endowed with vocal duets and the present issue offers only a selection from them. The common factor is the baritone, Thomas Hampson, who is partnered by some of the talented boy trebles who made such a distinctive contribution to the complete edition, and by the tenor, Kurt Equiluz. Hampson joined the team when the series was already two-thirds of the way through, so the earliest cantata to feature here is No. 140, *Wachet auf! ruft uns die Stimme*. That work, however, provides an auspicious starting-point since it contains two especially fine duets which are also among the most popular with audiences. Much else, though, will be comparatively unfamiliar to all but well-seasoned Bach cantata enthusiasts. In short, a very attractive compilation which, if it draws unsuspecting listeners into Bach's sacred dramatic wonderland will have more than fulfilled its purpose. Texts are not included, alas, but an accompanying note provides useful signposts to travellers in a strange land.

Cantatas Nos. 163, 165, 185 and 199.
Midori Suzuki, Aki Yanagisawa sops **Akira Tachikawa** counterten **Makoto Sakurada** ten
Stephan Schreckenberger bass **Bach Collegium Japan / Masaaki Suzuki.**
BIS CD801 (66 minutes: DDD). Texts and translations included. Recorded 1996. Ⓕ🅿

The level of vocal and instrumental artistry of the Bach Collegium Japan is consistently and fairly uniformly high, and the many editorial decisions that have to be made in a project such as this have been taken practically and sensibly. No. 199 is a generously proportioned work for solo soprano, obbligato oboe, viola and strings with continuo. Midori Suzuki's light, tonally pure and somewhat boyish timbre suits the music well, though some readers may find her at times expressively bland. Bach made provision, at different times and for different performances, for a variety of instruments to accompany the tenderly expressive choral movement preceding the concluding aria. Here a viola is preferred to the bass viol, violoncello piccolo or even perhaps standard cello which featured in subsequent performances. It works well and always strikes the ear as the happiest solution. The three remaining cantatas are all smaller in dimension than No. 199. For the most part they come over well though neither Yanagisawa nor Tachikawa perhaps quite match Suzuki in tonal allure. Sakurada and Schreckenberger both make strong contributions. It would be remiss to conclude without commending the excellence of oboist, Alfredo Bernardini, one of only two Europeans taking part in the enterprise, the fine continuo playing and the beautifully balanced one-to-a-part vocal ensemble comprising the soloists, which provides the chorale element. Deeply felt, sincerely expressed performances such as these deserve to win many friends.

Cantatas Nos. 207a and 212.
Christine Schäfer sop **Ingeborg Danz** mez **Stanford Olsen** ten **Michael Volle,**
Thomas Quasthoff bars **Gächinger Kantorei; Stuttgart Bach Collegium / Helmuth Rilling.**
Hänssler Classic CD98 163 (63 minutes: DDD). Texts and translations included.
Recorded 1994-95. Ⓕ

This volume in Rilling's series of Bach's secular cantatas gets off to a cracking start in No. 207a, a work in which Bach unashamedly presents, for its opening chorus, a splendid reworking of the third movement of *Brandenburg Concerto* No. 1. This movement and the majority of the others are drawn from an earlier secular cantata, *Vereinigte Zwietracht* (No. 207), which Bach composed in 1726 for a popular Leipzig professor of jurisprudence. Now, nearly ten years later, Bach revisited this splendid score for a performance celebrating the Elector of Saxony's name-day. It shows off Rilling at his best, for he infuses Bach's virtuoso vocal and instrumental lines with a golden-threaded flair, demonstrating exactly where his unyielding discipline can inspire, rather than enervate. The skittish and assured choral declamations in the outer choruses are brilliantly propelled by buoyed up trumpets and oboes who may exceed 'authentic' possibilities with excessive ornamentation – the oboes especially in the trio that follows the second aria – but whose attention to articulation is very stylish within its own parameters. The overall modern-instrument texture will inevitably have its detractors and there is no shortage of fine period-instrument performances.

Rilling's long career has witnessed an approach to Bach performance that has often appeared to British audiences, in particular, to be impressive if not always ultra-sympathetic. Yet, tellingly, Rilling appears not to have slipped one notch into a soft-edged opulence or to have dug his heels into a retrenched position: this performance, as with others in the current series, is extraordinarily well balanced, immediate and vitally conceived in characterization. If Rilling passes rather too hastily over the rustic symbolism in the *Peasant* Cantata, the work is clearly projected and led by a dazzling team of soloists. Christine Schäfer lends an intense, rarely comic, but richly coloured air to this charming comedy-homage. Rilling's gestures in the delicious 'Klein-Zschocher musse' are revealing and crisp but lack the mollifying, perfumed effect that this sensual creation demands alongside such bluff and bluster, especially with the eager *bonhomie* of the excellent Thomas Quasthoff in 'Dein Wachstum'. Rilling's agenda is carefully laid out here; yes, the interpretation is a touch clinical, as Rilling can be, but whether it's to your taste or not, this is an invigorating, technically outstanding and distinctive performance.

Cantatas Nos. 211 and 212.
Emma Kirkby *sop* **Rogers Covey-Crump** *ten* **David Thomas** *bass*
Academy of Ancient Music / Christopher Hogwood.
L'Oiseau-Lyre 417 621-2OH (52 minutes: DDD) Texts and translations included. ⒡ 🅿

These two most delightful of Bach's secular cantatas here receive sparkling performances fully alive to the humour and invention of the music. The *Coffee* Cantata illustrates a family altercation over a current enthusiasm, the drinking of coffee. A narrator tells the story whilst the soprano and bass soloists confront each other in a series of delightful arias. Thomas brings out the crabby dyspeptic side of Schlendrian's character imaginatively and Kirkby makes a charming minx-like Lieschen. Covey-Crump's sweet light tenor acts as a good foil. The *Peasant* Cantata also takes the form of a dialogue, here between a somewhat dull and simple young man and his sweetheart Mieke, a girl who intends to better herself. Through the 24 short movements Bach conjures up a wonderfully rustic picture with some vivid dance numbers and rumbustious ritornellos. The soloists' nicely rounded characterizations emerge with great humour and Hogwood directs with vitality and sprightly rhythmic control. The recording is excellent.

Motets – Singet dem Herren, BWV225; Der Geist hilft unsrer Schwachheit auf, BWV226; Jesu meine Freude, BWV227; Fürchte dich nicht, BWV228; Komm, Jesu, komm, BWV229; Lobet den Herren, BWV230.
Greta de Reyghere, Katelijne van Laetham *sops* **Martin van der Zeijst, Sytse Buwalda** *countertens* **Hans Hermann Jansen** *tens* **Johannes-Christoph Happel** *bar*
La Petite Bande Choir; La Petite Bande / Sigiswald Kuijken.
Accent ACC9287 (65 minutes: DDD). Texts and translations included. Recorded 1992. ⒡ 🅿

Motets, BWV225-30.
Netherlands Chamber Choir / Ton Koopman.
Philips 434 165-2PH (63 minutes: DDD). Texts and translations included. Recorded 1986-87. ⒡

These two approaches to Bach's Motets differ strongly from one another. Sigiswald Kuijken directs performances with *colla parte* instrumental support, that is to say with instruments doubling each of the vocal strands. Ton Koopman, on the other hand, prefers the vocal strands *a cappella* with instruments providing only the basso continuo. The choir in each version is made up of women sopranos and countertenors with the men's voices. Choosing between the versions is difficult and to a large extent must be a matter of which approach you prefer. Kuijken's performances are more relaxed than those of Koopman. He avoids anything in the nature of overdirection and, while neither singing nor playing is always quite as tidy as it might be, there is a lively spontaneity, especially rewarding in the radiant performance of *Singet dem Herren*. Koopman draws more sharply articulated singing than Kuijken from the Netherlands Chamber Choir though sometimes at the expense of natural declamation and spontaneity. But there is greater linear clarity here than in the other and it pays off handsomely in *Komm, Jesu, komm*. It is a pity that Koopman does not avail himself of the surviving instrumental parts for *Der Geist hilft* but, in other respects, the strengths and weaknesses of the two performances are fairly evenly distributed and both are highly recommended.

Bach Magnificat in D major, BWV243.
Vivaldi Ostro picta, RV642. Gloria in D major, RV589.
Emma Kirkby, Tessa Bonner *sops* **Michael Chance** *counterten* **John Mark Ainsley** *ten*
Stephen Varcoe *bar* **Collegium Musicum 90 Chorus and Orchestra / Richard Hickox.**
Chandos Chaconne CHAN0518 (64 minutes: DDD). Texts and translations included.
Recorded 1990. Ⓕ ℗ ℞℞

This issue was the first CD release featuring the then newly founded Collegium Musicum 90 under its directors Richard Hickox and Simon Standage. The Collegium embraces both choir and orchestra who are joined in this programme of Bach and Vivaldi by a comparably fine team of soloists. Hickox sets effective tempos in Bach's *Magnificat* and points up the many striking contrasts in colour and texture with which the piece abounds. From among the many successful features of the recording Stephen Varcoe's 'Quia fecit mihi magna' and the 'Et misericordia' sung by Michael Chance and John Mark Ainsley stand out. Vivaldi's *Gloria*, RV589 is the better known of two settings by the composer in D major. In this programme it is prefaced by an introductory motet *Ostro picta*, which may well in fact belong to the *Gloria* and is here sung with warmth and radiance by Emma Kirkby. Hickox's performance of this evergreen vocal masterpiece comes over with conviction. It is gracefully phrased, sensitively sung and affectingly paced with an admirable rapport between vocalists and instrumentalists. The recorded sound is first-rate.

Magnificat. Cantata No. 51.
Nancy Argenta, Patrizia Kwella, Emma Kirkby *sops* **Charles Brett** *counterten* **Anthony Rolfe Johnson** *ten* **David Thomas** *bass* **English Baroque Soloists / Sir John Eliot Gardiner.**
Philips 411 458-2PH (41 minutes: DDD). Texts and translations included. Ⓕ ℗

Bach's *Magnificat* is a work full of contrasts – contrasts of texture, of colour and of temperament – few of which escape the attention of Gardiner, his choir, orchestra and fine group of soloists. The choruses are sung with great vigour and precision; articulation is crisp and diction excellent. The solo singing is of a uniformly high standard with some outstanding contributions from Charles Brett, Anthony Rolfe Johnson and David Thomas. One thinks in particular of the 'Quia fecit', in which Thomas is admirably accompanied by a perfectly balanced continuo texture, and the 'Et misericordia' duet for alto and tenor, which is sung with great tenderness and restraint by these artists. Amongst the obbligato contributions we must single out that of the oboe d'amore in the 'Quia respexit' which is sensitively played and hauntingly beautiful. The cantata *Jauchzet Gott in allen Landen!* is one of three for solo soprano which Bach wrote at Leipzig during the 1730s. The spirit of the text, as its title implies, is one of rejoicing. It's a spirit which the soloist, Emma Kirkby, captures well. Her solo partner in the colourful opening movement and in the fugal 'Alleluia' at the close is Crispian Steele-Perkins who manages Bach's exacting trumpet parts with precision. Less enjoyable is the exaggerated acceleration in tempo for the 'Alleluia' section of the final movement, but it's a dazzling display without any doubt. These are fine performances of two of Bach's best-known church compositions, with admirably clear recordings.

Mass in B minor, BWV232.

Mass, BWV232.
Monteverdi Choir; English Baroque Soloists / Sir John Eliot Gardiner.
Archiv Produktion 415 514-2AH2 (two discs: 112 minutes: DDD).
Notes, text and translation included. Recorded 1985. Ⓕ ℗ ℞℞

There is much to be said for becoming acquainted with more than one version of Bach's B minor Mass. No single performance of a work of this distinction and stature, however perceptive, can embrace all its aspects. The argument for one singer to each vocal part has encouraged performers and audiences alike to think afresh about the forces best suited, above all, to the vocal element of the work. Gardiner opts for differentiation between soloists and a ripieno chorus. Gardiner bases his forces on the famous memorandum which Bach handed to the Leipzig town council in 1730 outlining the vocal and instrumental requirements for performances of his church music. This recording from Gardiner and his Monteverdi Choir and English Baroque Soloists is a fine achievement. Some listeners may feel the results would have been more satisfying if Gardiner had let the music unfold with greater natural freedom and not felt the need to tweak rhythms and tempos. Some may like that additional degree of excitement engendered by such methods but Bach, above all composers, perhaps, does not require 'whipping up' any more than his profound utterances benefit from exaggerated tempos in either direction in order to underline a point. The many strong points of Gardiner's direction, amongst which should be singled out a vital rhythmic understanding, a clear and positive sense of purpose, and a naturally affective response to Bach's music, combine in forming a concept of the work which not only explores its ineffable mysteries but also savours the magnificence of its architecture. The solo vocal line-up is a strong one and there are few weak moments. If we say that the crowning achievement of Gardiner's recording lies in the vitality, accuracy and homogeneity of the ripieno singing it is in no sense intended to underplay the considerable virtues of the soloists and the orchestra; but this, after all, is first a vocal work and foremost a choral one. The ripieno singing at its very best – as it is for example, in the 'Et resurrexit' – is thrilling and gives a fervent imprint to the entire work. There is a spontaneity about this singing to which few listeners could remain indifferent. Gardiner's choruses are immediately striking and handled with such skill and rigorous discipline that repeated hearing in no sense diminishes their impact. The pressings and presentation are exemplary.

Mass, BWV232.
Isabelle Poulenard sop **Guillemette Laurens** mez **René Jacobs** counterten **John Elwes** ten
Max van Egmond, Harry van der Kamp basses
Netherlands Bach Society Collegium Musicum; La Petite Bande / Gustav Leonhardt.
Deutsche Harmonia Mundi Editio Classica GD77040 (two discs: 111 minutes: ADD).
Notes, text and translation included. Recorded 1985.   Ⓜ️Ⓟ

This performance is a reissue of an LP previously released by EMI, when Deutsche Harmonia Mundi sheltered beneath that capacious umbrella. Gustav Leonhardt's achievement in conveying both a very strong sense of unity and a profound picture of the work's spiritual dimensions are remarkable. Tempos are, on the whole, slower than those favoured by other directors of performances employing period instruments, with pacing that takes into account dramatic features in the music without forcing them upon the listener. The soloists make up a strong team and there are some fine obbligato contributions, too. Sadly, the choir does not match up to the level of excellence maintained elsewhere. There is quite simply no comparison between the Netherlands Bach Society Choir, which sings in this recording, and the Monteverdi Choir for John Eliot Gardiner. One can only regret that Leonhardt did not have similar choral forces to Gardiner's at his disposal for this recording.

Masses – A major, BWV234; G minor, BWV235. Sanctus in D major, BWV238.
Agnès Mellon sop **Gérard Lesne** counterten **Christoph Prégardien** ten **Peter Kooy** bass
Ghent Collegium Vocale Chorus and Orchestra / Philippe Herreweghe.
Virgin Classics Veritas VC7 59587-2 (64 minutes: DDD). Texts and translations included.   Ⓕ Ⓟ
Recorded 1989.

Bach's four short Masses are a recycling of a few of his cantatas, and have excited little interest over the years. Few listeners today will be able to find much to object to in these charming pieces, in which Bach's personality shines through just as strongly as in any of his more reputable creations. And how many people *know* Cantata No. 187? Philippe Herreweghe's recordings of the Masses in G minor and A major – along with the sprightly (and original) D major Sanctus, BWV238 – should not, then, be of interest only to Bach enthusiasts. Both Masses share the same formal outline, the main contrast between them arising instead from their instrumental colouring, as Bach supplements the strings with oboes in BWV235, and flutes in BWV234. Herreweghe maximizes this gentle distinction by fixing his efforts on achieving a smooth blend and a rich, reverberant sound, in which he is undoubtedly helped by the echoing church acoustic of the Abbaye aux Dames in Saintes. If the sheer nobility and tenderness of Bach's church music appeals to you then you will have no problems with this disc.

Mass in F major, BWV233a. Cantatas Nos. 65 and 180. Sanctus in D major, BWV238.
Ann Monoyios sop **Angus Davidson** counterten **Charles Daniels** ten **Peter Harvey** bar
Gabrieli Consort and Players / Paul McCreesh.
Archiv Produktion 457 631-2AH2 (two discs: 160 minutes: DDD). Texts and translations included.
Includes readings, congregational hymns and organ works by Bach and Pachelbel.
Recorded 1997.   Ⓕ Ⓟ

This two-disc set contains four vocal works by Bach, set in the context of an Epiphany Mass 'as it might have been celebrated in St Thomas, Leipzig c1740'. Though several attempts have been made in the past to re-create the sequence of events at the two main services where Bach's cantatas were sung, the *Hauptgottesdienst*, in the morning, and the Vesper, in the afternoon, this is the first time that such a project has been committed to disc. You are very likely to be captivated by much of what Paul McCreesh and his musicians, with valuable help in liturgical canon from the scholar, Robin A. Leaver, have achieved. The sacred vocal works by Bach which have been chosen for this reconstruction of a *Hauptgottesdienst* for the *Dreikönigsfest* ('Feast of the Three Kings') are the F major Lutheran Mass, the *Sanctus* and two cantatas, *Sie werden aus Saba alle kommen*, a true Epiphany piece, and *Schmücke dich, o liebe Seele* which is foremost a Trinity piece but one which Bach may well have used on other occasions. McCreesh did well in securing the services of Ann Monoyios and Peter Harvey, but all involved make an impressive showing. The *Missa* comes over very well, Monoyios's 'Qui tollis peccata mundi' outstanding for its warmth of colour. An interesting experiment is carried out in the resonant Epiphany cantata, No. 65. Here the horns, which assume a prominent role in the opening chorus, are played an octave higher than usual, at trumpet pitch, with striking results. McCreesh emphasizes the lyrical character of this glorious movement, rather than its more readily captured processional grandeur.

The brisk tempo chosen for the superb chorale fantasy with which No. 180 begins is less convincing. The rhythm, admittedly, is that of a gigue and, taken at face value, this speed can be justified with complete propriety. But Bach's gently coloured, softly spoken consort of treble recorders, oboe, oboe da caccia and strings seems to tell a different story, evoking another aspect altogether of this tender, contemplative, yet radiant piece. The brilliant tenor aria with virtuoso flute obbligato which follows is, on the other hand, well considered in respect of tempo, and is furthermore beautifully articulated by flautist Jed Wentz. But it is Monoyios who, once more, steals the show with her affecting account of the lyrical elaboration with violoncello piccolo of a verse from the Communion hymn on which the cantata is based. And her subsequent aria is comparably fluent and secure. Much thought has gone into the solo organ elements of the Mass, not least by keyboard players James Johnstone, Timothy Roberts and James O'Donnell. Overall, this project, carefully conceived and put together, is likely to interest all lovers of Bach's music. The recorded sound, from Freiburg Cathedral and Brand-Erbisdorf in Saxony, is excellent.

St John Passion, BWV245.

St John Passion.
Gerd Türk *ten* Evangelist; **Chiyuki Urano** *bass* Jesus; **Ingrid Schmidthüsen, Yoshie Hida** *sops*
Yoshikazu Mera *counterten* **Makoto Sakurada** *ten* **Peter Kooy** *bass*
Bach Collegium Japan / Masaaki Suzuki.
BIS CD921/2 (two discs: 110 minutes: DDD). Text and translation included.
Recorded 1998. ⒻⓅⒺ🆁🆁

Bach seems to have performed his *St John Passion* on four Good Fridays during his tenure as Thomaskantor at Leipzig. However, he continued to make significant revisions right up to the last performance under his direction, on April 4th, 1749. Of the four versions, the second, dating from 1725, contains the most distinctive revisions, the first version (1724) and the last bearing close affinity with one another. Masaaki Suzuki and his talented Bach Collegium Japan have chosen Bach's latest version as their source. All has evidently been carefully prepared and deeply considered: what is refreshing about their approach is the importance afforded to the relationship between text and music, to the theological source of Bach's inspiration, and the emotional impact of the story and music on its audience. Some of their thoughts may strike readers as simplistic, even perhaps a shade sentimental, but on the strength of this fervent performance we can hardly question their sincerity.

The role of the Evangelist, crucial to the lyrical unfolding of the story, and traditionally a tenor role, is sung with clarity and lightness of inflexion by Gerd Türk. His performance is eloquently measured, his phrasing well shaped and his articulation engagingly varied. All of which makes him a riveting story-teller. The role of Jesus is taken by Chiyuki Urano, an artist with a warm-toned and resonant voice. From among the remaining soloists, Ingrid Schmidthüsen and Yoshikazu Mera make strongly appealing contributions in their respective arias and Peter Kooy (as Pontius Pilate and Peter) is satisfying and affecting. Excellent, too, are the contributions of the Collegium's choir of women's and men's voices. There is great textural clarity here, well balanced, furthermore, with the comparably lucid instrumental textures. Choral and instrumental articulation is incisive, propelling the rhythms with energy and urgency. The performance draws you into the drama from the start. This is a major recording event, and an eminently satisfying one.

St John Passion (sung in English).
Sir Peter Pears *ten* Evangelist; **Gwynne Howell** *bass* Jesus; **Heather Harper, Jenny Hill** *sops*
Alfreda Hodgson *contr* **Robert Tear, Russell Burgess, John Tobin, Adrian Thompson** *tens*
John Shirley-Quirk *bar*
Wandsworth School Boys' Choir; English Chamber Orchestra / Benjamin Britten.
Double Decca 443 859-2DF2 (two discs: 130 minutes: ADD). Recorded 1971. Ⓜ

Britten's recording of the *St John Passion* is very special indeed. He apparently preferred to perform this Bach choral work because of its natural potential for drama. With Sir Peter Pears a superb Evangelist (and you can hear every word!) this account takes over the listener completely. The soloists are all splendid, though one must single out the glorious contribution of Heather Harper, and the choral response is inspirational in its moments of sheer fervour. Britten's direction is both urgent and volatile, the Wandsworth School Boys' Choir sings out full-throatedly and the English Chamber Orchestra underpins the whole performance with gloriously rich string textures. (Listening to this unique recording one is tempted to conclude that the 'authentic' string sound, for all its clarity and bite, is less desirable than modern instruments in an expansive work of this kind.) Then there is the analogue recording itself which offers a demonstration of ambient fullness, vividness of detail and natural balance. In fact, one gets the impression that a live performance at The Maltings, Snape has been transported to the area just beyond one's speakers! As a bonus it is available at mid-price.

St Luke Passion, BWV246 (attrib.).
Mona Spägele *sop* **Christiane Iven** *contr* **Rufus Müller, Harry van Berne** *tens*
Stephan Schreckenberger, Marcus Sandmann *basses*
Alsfeld Vocal Ensemble; Bremen Baroque Orchestra / Wolfgang Helbich.
CPO CPO999 293-2 (two discs: 106 minutes: DDD). Text and translation included.
Recorded 1996.   Ⓕ Ⓟ

Those who love Bach will want to investigate the *St Luke Passion*; we know that Bach performed it at Leipzig at least twice, and evidently admired it for what it is: a succinct and highly competent blend of Lutheran *Kapellmeister* craft and a few fashionable *galant* nuances. In terms of scale, rhetorical intensity, structural and stylistic sophistication, musical invention and artistic ambition generally, this work finds no common ground with Bach's two extant passions. That said, Bach, whose hand appears at the start of the only existing source, judged that a simple, if austere, juxtaposition of chorus-(chorale)-recitative-chorus, with the occasional aria, could hold its own in the traditional deliberations of Leipzig's Holy Week. The modern listener will find much that is intimate and touching about this Passion setting. The meditative element comes less from contemplative arias than from a continuous and freshly fashioned narrative, although the arias, with their favoured wind obbligato parts, are often skilled and affecting.

Wolfgang Helbich and his Bremen forces pitch the dramatic climate just about right all the way through. Smoothly articulated, unmannered and technically accomplished, the chorales and *turba* scenes are especially well judged. The Evangelist, Rufus Müller, conveys the Gospel with soft-grained clarity and understated dignity and the other soloists do more than justice to the six arias. Indeed, for all the many qualities of the performance, especially the affectionate contribution of the Alsfeld Vocal Ensemble, this enterprising recording ever sharpens the distinction of Bach and his relatively functional role as Kantor with the parallel workings of his compositional mind. Whether this is Wolfgang Helbich's tacit intention, Bach's genius glows ever brighter.

St Matthew Passion, BWV244.

St Matthew Passion.
Anthony Rolfe Johnson *ten* Evangelist; **Andreas Schmidt** *bar* Jesus; **Barbara Bonney,**
Ann Monoyios *sops* **Anne Sofie von Otter** *mez* **Michael Chance** *counterten* **Howard Crook** *ten*
Olaf Bär *bar* **Cornelius Hauptmann** *bass* **London Oratory Junior Choir; Monteverdi Choir;**
English Baroque Soloists / Sir John Eliot Gardiner.
Archiv Produktion 427 648-2AH3 (three discs: 167 minutes: DDD). Text and translation included.
Recorded 1989. *Gramophone* Award Winner 1990.   Ⓕ Ⓟ ⓇⓇ

What makes John Eliot Gardiner's *St Matthew Passion* stand out in the face of stiff competition is perhaps more than anything his vivid sense of theatre. Bach's score is, after all, a sacred drama and Gardiner interprets this aspect of the work with lively and colourful conviction. That in itself, of course, is not sufficient to ensure a fine performance but here we have a first-rate group of solo voices, immediately responsive choral groups in the Monteverdi Choir and the London Oratory Junior Choir – a distinctive element this – and refined obbligato and orchestral playing from the English Baroque Soloists. Anthony Rolfe Johnson declaims the Evangelist's role with clarity, authority and the subtle inflexion of an accomplished story-teller. Ann Monoyios, Howard Crook and Olaf Bär also make strong contributions but it is Michael Chance's 'Erbarme dich', tenderly accompanied by the violin obbligato, which sets the seal of distinction on the performance. Singing and playing of this calibre deserve to win many friends and Gardiner's deeply-felt account of Bach's great Passion does the music considerable justice. Clear recorded sound.

St Matthew Passion.
Nico van der Meel *ten* Evangelist; **Kristinn Sigmundsson** *bass* Christus;
Maria Cristina Kiehr, Mona Julsrud *sops* **Claudia Schubert, Wilke te Brummelstroete** *contrs*
Ian Bostridge, Toby Spence *tens* **Peter Kooy, Harry van der Kamp** *basses*
**Boys' Choir of St Bavo's Cathedral, Haarlem; Netherlands Chamber Choir;
Orchestra of the Eighteenth Century / Frans Brüggen.**
Philips 454 434-2PH3 (three discs: 160 minutes: DDD). Text and translation included.
Recorded live in 1996. Ⓕ 🄿

This is a live recording with a good sense of drama and pace. Brüggen's orchestral forces offer
sturdy support and an apparent, effortlessly eloquent aural framework. His continuo groups are
impressive, with the sharply defined phrasing and articulation he requires from his players. A
weakness is the solo singing of the second soprano, Mona Julsrud. Her 'Blute nur, du liebes Herz' is
a sorry affair in which her technique and vocal range fall well short of what is required. Kristinn
Sigmundsson, who sings the role of Christ, has a very fine, resonant voice and his performance is
noble and at times awesome in the forthrightness of its declamation. Nico van der Meel's
performance is absolutely gripping – his tale is one of mystery, urgency and of commanding
importance. We are inescapably drawn in to his narrative which he declaims with sensibility and a
wide range of inflective nuance. His account of St Peter's denial is realized with consummate
artistry. In summary, this is a *St Matthew Passion* which should please many. Brüggen's
interpretation is eloquent, thoughtful in matters of style and expressive content, and it benefits from
a textural clarity which few competitors can rival.

Christmas Oratorio, BWV248

Christmas Oratorio.
Monika Frimmer *sop* **Yoshikazu Mera** *counterten* **Gerd Türk** *ten* **Peter Kooy** *bass*
Bach Collegium Japan / Masaaki Suzuki.
BIS CD941/2 (two discs: 145 minutes: DDD). Text and translation included.
Recorded 1998. Ⓕ 🄿 🄴 🆁🆁

The six cantatas that make up Bach's *Christmas Oratorio*, though each possessing its own musical
and expressive identity, are nevertheless part of a unified work celebrating not just Christmas itself
but also the New Year and Epiphany. Masaaki Suzuki faces plentiful if not invariably stiff
competition in this work. In fact, it outstrips most of its rivals, in respect both of vocal and
instrumental considerations. A notable quality in Masaaki Suzuki's direction is his feeling for
naturally expressive contours, allowing the music to breathe freely. Best of all, perhaps, is his refusal
to pay even lip service to the upheld beliefs concerning Bach's supposed predilection for fast
tempos. Everything here seems to be exceptionally well judged, which is not to say that the pace of
individual movements is necessarily slower than those in some competing versions, but rather that it
is more interrelated with a concept of each section as a whole, and perhaps more textually
conscious than some. In these respects the *Oratorio*'s underlying strength and unity of purpose is
wonderfully well served. The soloists are generally very good indeed. Yoshikazu Mera makes a
distinctive contribution and Gerd Türk is a communicative singer whose light articulation well suits
his partly narrative role. Peter Kooy never puts a foot wrong, while Monika Frimmer makes a
favourable impression in her duet with Kooy, 'Herr, dein Mitleid, dein Erbarmen' (Part 3).
Elsewhere, her freshly complexioned, somewhat boyish voice is seldom other than pleasing. A small,
well-balanced choir of technical agility and an accomplished quorum of instrumentalists set the
seal on an outstanding achievement. This is definitely the finest all-round performance of the
Christmas Oratorio on disc.

Christmas Oratorio.
Theo Altmeyer *ten* Evangelist and arias; **Hans Buchhierl** *treb* Andreas Stein *boy alto*
Barry McDaniel *bar* **Tölz Boys' Choir; Collegium Aureum / Gerhard Schmidt-Gaden.**
Deutsche Harmonia Mundi Editio Classica GD77046 (three discs: 163 minutes: ADD).
Notes, text and translation included. Recorded 1973. Ⓜ 🄿

This performance possesses radiance and spontaneity. It is not without its weaknesses, mainly in
passages of insecure instrumental playing; but these are outweighed by its merits chief among
which, perhaps, are the contributions, both solo and choral, of the Tölz Boys' Choir. All the
soprano and alto solos are sung by boys and in the choruses it is boys rather than countertenors
who sing the alto line. Gerhard Schmidt-Gaden effectively relaxes tempos which may at first sound
too leisurely to ears accustomed to the frenetic pace chosen by some rival versions. Occasionally, he
is a little too slow as, for instance, in the opening chorus of Part Four but for the most part he
directs a performance free from intrusive mannerisms which bedevil too many performances of

baroque music today. The treble, Hans Buchhierl and the alto, Andreas Stein, are outstanding, and the tenor Theo Altmeyer and the baritone, Barry McDaniel, are hardly less impressive. With its spirit of innocent joy and in its simple but sensitive response to the music this performance comes closer than most to the contemplative heart of Bach's Christmas masterpiece.

Easter Oratorio, BWV249. Cantata No. 11.
Monika Frimmer *sop* **Ralf Popken** *counterten* **Christoph Prégardien** *ten* **David Wilson-Johnson** *bar* **Choir and Orchestra of the Age of Enlightenment / Gustav Leonhardt.**
Philips 442 119-2PH (73 minutes: DDD). Texts and translations included. Recorded 1993.   ⓅⓅ

Of the two Bach oratorios on this generously filled disc, it is the *Easter Oratorio* which is the least performed today. It is a work of customary Bachian brilliance in the quality of individual movements, even if the whole is not entirely satisfying. It does, however, carry a unique flavour and one with which Leonhardt clearly feels a close affinity. This is evident in the way he handles the exuberant Sinfonia with knowing and stately bravura, also providing copious insights into the phrasing of the wonderful wind dialogues – all played with fastidious clarity and *élan* by the OAE. Whilst this movement sparkles, Leonhardt (or rather the oboist, Anthony Robson) gives more flesh to the subsequent *Adagio*; this is splendidly vocalized playing. Both here and in the *Ascension* Oratorio the chorus is fairly streamlined and although the quality of singing goes without saying, greater breadth to Bach's choruses in the second work would have been preferable. The soloists on the latter are variable. Only Ralf Popken in 'Saget, saget mir' is ideal. So where does that leave us? Despite some misgivings, Leonhardt's perceptive performances will always win friends and his recording of the *Easter Oratorio* still appeals more than its competitors. As for the *Ascension* Oratorio, although not a front-runner, this recording certainly has its revelatory moments.

Wilhelm Friedemann Bach
German 1710-1784

Sinfonias – D major, F64; D minor, F65; F major, F67, 'Dissonance'. Suite in G minor, BWV1070 (attrib.). Harpsichord Concerto in D major, F41.
Charlotte Nediger *hpd*
Tafelmusik / Jeanne Lamon *vn*
Sony Classical Vivarte SK62720 (72 minutes: DDD). Recorded 1996.   ⓅⓅ

W.F. Bach was a talented musician torn between the styles of the late baroque and early classical periods, so it is perhaps no surprise to find that there is considerable variety in the music on this disc. The opening Sinfonia in D major is one of those sunnily optimistic works that revel in the splendid new sound of the classical orchestra, but the D minor Sinfonia which follows is a highly serious piece for church use, containing a solemnly drooping fugue. There is also an Ouverture-Suite once attributed (pretty implausibly) to Johann Sebastian which, though undeniably attractive and individual, is now thought unlikely to be by Friedemann either; a quirkily expressive but perhaps rather rambling harpsichord concerto; and a by-now familiarly protean and surprise-filled Sinfonia in F major. Tafelmusik is the perfect ensemble to perform this music. Like much of it, they delight in sheer orchestral sound, enjoying the advantage themselves of being able to turn it out in particularly pleasing and well-finished form. Recommended to any lover of eighteenth-century orchestral music.

Cantatas – Lasset uns ablegen die Werke der Finsternis, F80. Es ist eine Stimme eines Predigers in der Wüste, F89.
Barbara Schlick *sop* **Claudia Schubert** *contr* **Wilfried Jochens** *ten*
Stephan Schreckenberger *bass* **Rheinische Kantorei; Das Kleine Konzert / Hermann Max.**
Capriccio 10 425 (54 minutes: DDD). Texts and translations included. Recorded 1991.   ⓅⓅ

Cantatas – Sinfonia in D major, F64. Dies ist der Tag, F85. Erzittert und fallet, F83.
Barbara Schlick *sop* **Claudia Schubert** *contr* **Wilfried Jochens** *ten*
Stephan Schreckenberger *bass* **Rheinische Kantorei; Das Kleine Konzert / Hermann Max.**
Capriccio 10 426 (60 minutes: DDD). Texts and translations included. Recorded 1991.   ⓅⓅ

These two discs of sacred cantatas make a valuable contribution towards a fuller understanding of this highly gifted but complex and somewhat enigmatic member of the Bach clan. In the mid-1740s Wilhelm Friedemann was appointed Director of Music and organist at the Marienkirche at Halle. He remained in the post for almost 20 years, a period which witnessed the composition and performance of all the cantatas represented here. Among the many delights to be found in this music are those occasioned by Friedemann's disparate, even opposing terms of reference. In other words the stylistic vocabulary is both rich and varied, often harking back to a strong paternal influence – what better one has there ever been? J.S. Bach's idiom, for instance, is startlingly apparent in the opening chorus of the Advent cantata, F80 ('Let us cast off the works of darkness'). Both the arias of this fine cantata are of high quality, the first, for soprano with obbligato flute ably demonstrating how carefully Friedemann thought out his declamation. This is a movement of real distinction, lyrical, poignant and admirably well sustained. The remaining three cantatas are rich in points of interest. The athletic trumpet and vocal writing of the opening chorus of the St John's Day cantata, F89 ('The voice of him that crieth in the wilderness') are immediately arresting; so too, is the wonderfully rhapsodic organ obbligato which accompanies the *galant*, virtuoso soprano aria of the same work.

The cantatas, F64 ('This is the day') and F83 ('Tremble and fall') probably date from the late-1750s and are less Janus-like in their musical stance. The Whitsun cantata, F85 is a particularly festive piece which is prefaced by a three-movement Sinfonia scored for horns, flutes, oboes, bassoon and strings. This in fact replaces the more usual elaborate choral movement, choral writing being confined to a simple concluding hymn verse. The two arias, one with limpid writing for two flutes, the other with horns, are beguiling and thoroughly in keeping with the developing style of early classicism. What of the performances? Well, for the most part they are excellent, discovering with eloquence and stylistic assurance the multifarious details and subtleties of Friedemann Bach's skill in this medium. The four soloists are first-rate with Barbara Schlick and Wilfried Jochens qualifying for special mention; and the singing of the Rheinische Kantorei is effective, too, though just occasionally its component 16 voices sounded under threat from Bach's sometimes exacting requirements. Das Kleine Konzert under Hermann Max is strongly supportive throughout and its obbligato players sensitive to the needs of its vocal partners. Imaginative programming and sympathetic performances add to this musical revelation. Full texts and informative notes set the seal on recordings of distinction.

Sir Edward Bairstow
British 1874-1946

Blessed City, heavenly Salem. The Lamentation. Jesu, the very thought of Thee. Lord, Thou has been our refuge. Let all mortal flesh keep silence. Lord, I call upon Thee. When Israel came out of Egypt. Jesu, grant me this I pray. Save us, O Lord. If the Lord had not helped me. A Blessed Virgin's Cradle Song. Evening Service in D major.
John Scott Whiteley *org*
York Minster Choir / Philip Moore.
Priory PRCD365 (62 minutes: DDD). Recorded 1991.   Ⓕ

'The Lord is the strength of my countenance': hearing Bairstow's vigorous setting of the line one thinks of the strength of his countenance. The wonder is that his music is characteristically so sweet-tempered, soft and tender in its touch. He could, of course, bring out the trumpets, quicken the pace and fret the Minster's echoes into a delirium of mimicry. But what seems most personal and individual in his music is the quiet mysticism of *Let all mortal flesh keep silence*, the modestly exercised skill of *Jesu, grant me this I pray* and the comfortable, judiciously sugared melodic and harmonic idiom of *Save us, O Lord*. This recital has an authenticity of place, coming from the great building where the composer did so much of his life's work, from 1913 till his death. The organ on which he must have played these very works is the one heard now, its bountiful resources imaginatively employed. The choir, under Philip Moore, has a particularly fine complement of trebles, and sings with sensitivity and, when required, considerable power. The recording also benefits from the grandeur of the York acoustic.

Mily Balakirev
Russian 1837-1910

Balakirev Piano Concertos – No. 1 in F sharp major, Op. 1; No. 2 in E flat major, Op. posth.
Rimsky-Korsakov Piano Concerto in C sharp minor, Op. 30.
Malcolm Binns *pf*
English Northern Philharmonia / David Lloyd-Jones.
Hyperion CDA66640 (61 minutes: DDD). Recorded 1992.   Ⓕ

'Op. 1' and 'Op. posth.' say a lot about Balakirev's two piano concertos. The First is a single movement only, composed at the age of 18 and massively indebted to the Chopin concertos. The Second was begun not long after, in 1861, but abandoned after the first movement; he was only persuaded to write the other movements down near the end of his life. At his death in 1910 the finale had to be completed by Lyapunov, which may be partly why it sounds so splendidly rambunctious, so close in places, to Gershwin. The concerto was certainly worth the efforts of all concerned; the first movement's fugal episodes and the slow movement's tinges of Russian Orthodox gloom stay in the mind, compensating for Balakirev's occasional recourse to inflating and overdecorating short sub-phrases. The First Concerto, too, has little flashes of individuality which keep you listening despite the obvious *naïveté* and derivative quality of the material. The Rimsky-Korsakov has come and gone from the catalogue over the years. It is in effect more of a folk-song fantasia than a concerto, but there is much post-Liszt-and-Griegian charm, as well as a striking foretaste of Rachmaninov's *Paganini* Rhapsody (Paganini's famous opening motif coincidentally also begins the second strain of Rimsky's chosen theme). These three works make an excellent programme, then. And Malcolm Binns, though not the most sparkling of soloists, plays with commendable solidity. The quality of the orchestra's contribution is high, and all in all this is an admirably conceived and executed disc.

Symphonies – No. 1 in C major[a]; No. 2 in D minor[b].
[a]**USSR State Symphony Orchestra / Evgeni Svetlanov;**
[b]**USSR State Radio and TV Grand Symphony Orchestra / Gennadi Rozhdestvensky.**
Revelation RV10038 (74 minutes: ADD). Item marked [a] recorded live in 1974, [b]1973.   Ⓜ

These recordings were made by Soviet Radio. Svetlanov was subsequently to re-record both symphonies in richer, more spacious sound for Hyperion, and there is no doubt that, both in terms of orchestral finesse and recorded sound, these later versions score higher marks. But when it comes to vitality and excitement the Soviet performances win hands down. Rhythms are crisp and well lifted and the readings have the urgency one expects of Russian music-making. The trumpets and trombones are blatant, but even that adds to the bite. At the gentle opening of the C major Symphony the violins shape their cantilena with allure, and when one comes to the *Andante* the listener is immediately transported to the exotically sinuous world of Rimsky-Korsakov. The effect is ravishing, with richly coloured wind solos following one another glowingly, and the strings hardly less enticing. The performance is unforgettable, both for its orchestral palette and heavy romanticism; the exotic woodwind return in the dancing finale, the oriental flavour becoming more and more insistent. The Second Symphony has been described as a paler copy of the First. Here the opening movement under Rozhdestvensky's baton generates much Slavic energy; tuttis are more noticeably brash, but they are certainly not dull. Both symphonies have a second movement scherzo; that in the Second is marked *alla cosacca* and Rozhdestvensky makes the most of its rumbustious character, whereas in the First, Svetlanov has sought out the movement's charm. In the repetitive *Polacca* finale the brazen Russian brass become a little wearing, although the performance retains a genial, spirited character. In short, both readings are strongly characterized and enjoyably full of life; the stereo is warm and vivid, if lacking something in amplitude; but one feels the composer himself would have been well pleased with the results.

Sir Granville Bantock   British 1868-1946

Pagan Symphony. Fifine at the Fair. Two Heroic Ballads.
Royal Philharmonic Orchestra / Vernon Handley.
Hyperion CDA66630 (80 minutes: DDD). Recorded 1992.   Ⓕ

This collection confirms Bantock as a composer of real achievement whose music has been undeservedly neglected. He was a superb technician, and his impressively large-scale structures (both of the principal works here are single movements lasting over half an hour) have a real urgency to them. Or perhaps we should say a real enjoyment. Despite the potentially tragic undertones of *Fifine at the Fair*, both works are almost untroubled, filled instead with the geniality of a craftsman joyfully exercising a craft of which he has become master. The cleverness of Bantock's thematic transformations can make you smile with pleasure once you've worked out what he's doing – and then smile again at the realization that the result of the transformation isn't an arid piece of technique for technique's sake, but another jolly good tune. And it is all very beautifully scored. Bantock was a master of the orchestra. Is there anything lacking? Is he just a bit too clever, for ever finding yet another ingenious and delightful thing that can be done with a scale-figure? Possibly, but on the other hand he is never dull. Is real emotional depth lacking, despite hints of it whenever the wronged wife appears in Fifine? Maybe; possibly he was more given to enjoying than to pondering. Horses for courses, Bantock for enjoyment. The performances are stunning, the recordings most sumptuous. Oh, and the two *Heroic Ballads*, for all that they're concerned with Cuchullan and his ilk, have not a shred of Irish Sea mist hanging around them: they are bold, colourful and stirring.

Atalanta in Calydon. Vanity of vanities.
BBC Singers / Simon Joly.
Albany TROY180 (66 minutes: DDD). Texts included. Recorded 1995. (F)

In 1911 Bantock embarked on the first of his two unaccompanied 'choral symphonies', a half-hour setting of texts from Swinburne's 1865 verse drama, *Atalanta in Calydon*. Written for the amateur Hallé Choir, it is an extraordinarily ambitious offering. Bantock's luxuriant 20-part writing (the composer envisaged 'not less than ten voices to each part') exhibits a prodigious technical facility allied to a remarkable fluency and poetic sensibility. By comparison, the 35-minute *Vanity of vanities* (based on Bantock's own selection of verses from the Book of Ecclesiastes) is a model of restraint, being laid out for a mere 12 parts. It was completed in September 1913. Again, the sounds created exhibit a ravishing variety of texture, colour and harmony, further testament to Bantock's fantastically vivid aural imagination. Both works impose great technical demands which are easily surmounted in these incisive, dedicated performances from the BBC Singers under Simon Joly, admirably captured by the recording team.

Samuel Barber   American 1910-1981

Violin Concerto, Op. 14.

Violin Concerto. Cello Concerto, Op. 22. Capricorn Concerto, Op. 21.
Kyoko Takezawa *vn* **Steven Isserlis** *vc* **Jacob Berg** *fl* **Peter Bowman** *ob* **Susan Slaughter** *tpt*
St Louis Symphony Orchestra / Leonard Slatkin.
RCA Victor Red Seal 09026 68283-2 (65 minutes: DDD). Recorded 1994-95. (F)

The Cello Concerto is a restless work touched through and through by the shock, uncertainty and fragile optimism of a world just coming out of war. Steven Isserlis is in many respects just the player for the piece. His agility is a boon in ensuring that it never becomes overly strenuous, that its capriciousness, its touches of irony (all those quizzical pizzicato *glissandos* and harmonics) are not lost in the shadows. The slow movement's cantilena really does warm to his personal touch, his long, canonic duet with oboe for once not a mismatch. Isserlis's cello is the lightest of Lieder baritones with the flexibility and imagination to fine-spin phrases as very few can and do. Listen to his withdrawal into the heart of the slow movement. Isserlis reflecting, Isserlis lost in thought, is always special. Kyoko Takezawa is not a player to keep much to herself. The casual opening page of the Violin Concerto, starting as it does mid-sentence through a shared confidence, is soon impatient to go public. Her sound – intense and focused – seems to reach way beyond the length of each phrase. She is mindful, too, of the fiercer contrasts, seeking always to maximize them. It's a very 'operatic' performance, the lyric and dramatic elements grippingly interacted. The big 'aria' – in which the first oboe gets to be the envy of all the surrounding players – comes, of course, with that ravishing principal subject of the slow movement, and when Takezawa does finally come to embrace it, the feeling of release, of fulfilment, is worth the wait. Slatkin responds with a full-throated tutti in the strings. All of which is wickedly offset by that mad highland fling of a finale, twirling woodwinds and fractured trumpet fanfares as belligerent as you could wish. Between the two main courses comes the sorbet. Barber's *Capricorn Concerto* (for flute, oboe, trumpet and strings) is a playful *concerto grosso* for the New World, a sharp take on baroque procedures, a streetwise *Brandenburg* No. 2.

Barber Violin Concerto.
Bloch Baal Shem.
Walton Violin Concerto in B minor.
Joshua Bell *vn*
Baltimore Symphony Orchestra / David Zinman.
Decca 452 851-2DH (68 minutes: DDD). Recorded 1996.
Gramophone Award Winner 1998. (F) (E) (RR)

Joshua Bell's coupling of the Barber Violin Concerto with Walton and Bloch brings together three highly romantic *concertante* works. In the Barber, Bell is placed less forward than in the rich-sounding recordings of Gil Shaham and Itzhak Perlman, but if anything the results are even more intense. In the central slow movement the opening oboe solo leads to a magically hushed first entry for the violin, and the balance of the soloist also allows a quicksilver lightness for the rushing triplets in the *moto perpetuo* finale. Shaham may find more humour in that brief movement, but Bell's view is equally valid. From an American perspective, Walton can well be seen as Barber's British counterpart. The playing of this American orchestra is warmly idiomatic, defying the idea that non-British orchestras find Walton difficult. Bell gives a commanding account of the solo part – his expansive treatment of the central cadenza of the first movement, making it more deeply reflective – is most appealing. Not just there but in many gentle moments the rapt intensity of his playing is magnetic. Bell's is among the finest versions ever, with Bloch's own 1939 orchestration of *Baal Shem* offering a fine, unusual makeweight.

Barber Violin Concerto.
Korngold Violin Concerto, Op. 35. Much ado about nothing, Op. 11 – The maiden in the bridal chamber; Dogberry and Verges; Intermezzo; Hornpipe.
Gil Shaham *vn*
London Symphony Orchestra / André Previn *pf*
DG 439 886-2GH (71 minutes: DDD). Recorded 1993.   Ⓕ 🄴

This performance of the Barber, warm and rich with the sound close and immediate, brings out above all the work's bolder side, allowing moments that are not too distant from the world of Hollywood music (no disparagement there) and aptly the Korngold emerges as a central work in that genre. There have been subtler readings of Barber's lovely concerto, with the soloist not always helped by the close balance, but it is good to have a sharp distinction drawn between the purposeful lyricism of the first movement, marked *Allegro*, and the tender lyricism of the heavenly *Andante*. In the finale Shaham brings out the fun behind the movement's manic energy, with Previn pointing the Waltonian wit. In the Korngold, Gil Shaham may not have quite the flair and panache of the dedicatee, Jascha Heifetz, in his incomparable reading (reviewed under Korngold), but he is warm and committed. What emerges again and again here is how electric the playing of the LSO is under Previn, rich and full as well as committed, echoing vintage Previn/LSO recordings of the 1970s. The recording helps, clear and immediate. The suite from Korngold's incidental music to *Much ado about nothing*, dating from his early precocious period in Vienna, provides a delightful and apt filler, with Previn, as pianist, just as understanding and imaginative an accompanist, and Shaham yearningly warm without sentimentality, clean and precise in attack.

Violin Concerto[a]. Piano Concerto, Op. 38[b]. Adagio for Strings, Op. 11[c]. Essay for Orchestra No. 2, Op. 17[d]. The School for Scandal Overture, Op. 5[d].
Isaac Stern *vn* **John Browning** *pf*
New York Philharmonic Orchestra / [a]**Leonard Bernstein,** [d]**Thomas Schippers;**
[b]**Cleveland Orchestra / George Szell;** [c]**Philadelphia Orchestra / Eugene Ormandy.**
Sony Classical Theta SMK60004 (74 minutes: ADD). Recorded 1964-65, item marked [c]1958.   Ⓜ 🄷

Isaac Stern's 1964 recording of the Barber Violin Concerto with Bernstein and the New York Philharmonic was the recording which belatedly gave this warmly expressive masterpiece the international currency it plainly deserved. It was written at very much the same period, just as the Second World War was beginning, as two British works with which it has clear links, the violin concertos of Walton and Britten, both also dating from 1939. The superb performance from Stern and Bernstein can stand comparison with any version since, easily fluent in the two lyrical movements, demonically intense in the *moto perpetuo* finale. That movement, initially disappointing as a resolution to the first two, may not match the finales of the Walton and Britten in weight, but it certainly makes a powerful conclusion here. The only reservation is that with close-up CBS sound for the soloist you rarely get a true *pianissimo*. Even more welcome, when it has long been unavailable, is John Browning's première recording of the Piano Concerto. This is an interpretation of the highest voltage, the more daring and bitingly intense for having been recorded after a long series of performances on tour, full of bravura, with recorded sound rather fuller and more clean than that of the Violin Concerto. Ormandy's resonant recording of the *Adagio*, taken at a flowing speed, and Schippers's dazzling, tautly controlled accounts of the *Essay* No. 2 and the Overture, also well transferred, make this an ideal disc for anyone wanting to investigate Barber at his finest.

Adagio for Strings, Op. 11.

Barber Adagio for Strings.
Bernstein Candide – Overture.
Copland Appalachian Spring – ballet.
W. Schuman American Festival Overture.
Los Angeles Philharmonic Orchestra / Leonard Bernstein.
DG Galleria 439 528-2GGA (54 minutes: DDD). Recorded live in 1982.   Ⓜ 🆁🆁

This is a beautiful collection of American music, lovingly and brilliantly performed. With Barber's lovely *Adagio* you might fear that Bernstein would 'do a Nimrod' and present it with exaggerated expressiveness. Although the tempo is very slow indeed, the extra hesitations are not excessive and the Los Angeles strings play with angelic refinement and sweetness, as they do also in the many hushed sequences of the Copland ballet. There the live recording made in San Francisco in a dryish acoustic brings a degree of constriction at heavy tuttis, but the advantages of digital recording in this beautiful score are obvious, not least at the climax of the haunting variations on the Shaker hymn, *Simple Gifts*. To the three favourite works here is added William Schuman's brazenly extrovert overture with its virtuoso opening section, its quiet *fugato*, ominously introduced, and a brazen conclusion to match the opening. It is a splendid work, almost as joyously inspired as Bernstein's *Candide* Overture, with the composer here adopting a fairly relaxed speed, though with a wild coda.

Adagio for Strings. Symphony No. 1, Op. 9. First Essay, Op. 12. Second Essay, Op. 17. Music for a Scene from Shelley, Op. 7. The School for Scandal Overture, Op. 5.
Baltimore Symphony Orchestra / David Zinman.
Argo 436 288-2ZH (64 minutes: DDD). Recorded 1991.⠀⠀⠀⠀⠀⠀⠀⠀Ⓕ

Zinman begins this striking set in quiet understatement with this most challenging of all sustained *legatos* – the *Adagio for Strings*. He and his Baltimore strings are calm, collected, resigned; the grief is contained; no wringing of hands at the climax, rather an intense transfiguration. The first of Barber's bite-size symphonies is rather more demonstrative in its tragedy, working up from the deep-set bass lines of an imposing *Andante sostenuto* to the most public of displays. And then there is the *Second Essay*, Barber rhetoric at its most biblical. The engineering throughout this disc is exceptionally vivid, but nowhere more so than here: the impact of timpani and bass drum is unnervingly realistic, the brass and tam-tam-laden climax comes at you full on. Add to that a pugnacious fugue with Baltimore woodwinds devilishly incisive, and you've an absolute winner. Zinman's account of the First Symphony is laudably coherent – whole. There is sweep and a strong sense of evolution about its development. Zinman's solo oboe and cellos are heart-breakers in the slow movement, the impassioned climax – like everything else here – magnificently inevitable. The *Music for a Scene from Shelley* is an early piece, but a highly accomplished one. It is an especially beguiling example of Barber's precocious lyric gifts. A sunburst of sound brings on one of Barber's most rapturous melodies, voluptuously scored, and there is an exquisite postlude where two horns briefly ruminate on what has been heard and scented, while the nocturnal murmurings of string and harp quickly evaporate to the barely audible.

Barber Adagio for Strings. Medea's Meditation and Dance of Vengeance, Op. 23.
Elgar Introduction and Allegro, Op. 47.
Tchaikovsky Serenade in C major, Op. 48.
Boston Symphony Orchestra / Charles Munch.
RCA Victor Gold Seal mono 09026 61424-2 (61 minutes: ADD). Recorded 1957.⠀⠀Ⓜ🄷

Munch's passionate reading of the *Adagio for Strings* was a one-time radio favourite, and rightly so: even now, with countless lustrous rivals readily to hand, its sustained expressive power easily activates the tear-ducts. It is hard to imagine that any alternative 'Dance of Vengeance' is more exciting than this – either for dramatic impact, or orchestral virtuosity. When it comes to Elgar's *Introduction and Allegro*, opinion is bound to be divided. It's definitely the view of a man who understands the general drift of the piece, but can't quite get the pacing right: Munch stands stiff as a board, like an over-respectful corporal before his sergeant. Otherwise, it's a bold, bracing performance, brilliantly played. With bulky, dry sound and fairly intense delivery, the Tchaikovsky sounds more like a string symphony than a string serenade: Munch drives hard, and his engineers seem unwilling to allow the Bostonians' soft playing to sound soft. But the 'Elegy' is sincerely heartfelt, and although – again – a conspicuous lack of genuine *piano* robs it of atmosphere, the performance works, as does the thrilling finale. Sound-wise, all goes reasonably well, but even within the first seconds of the *Serenade*, there's some evidence that the tapes aren't quite what they once were.

Barber Symphony No. 1, Op. 9. The School for Scandal Overture, Op. 5.
Beach Symphony in E minor, Op. 32, 'Gaelic'.
Detroit Symphony Orchestra / Neeme Järvi.
Chandos CHAN8958 (72 minutes: DDD). Recorded 1991.⠀⠀⠀⠀⠀⠀⠀⠀Ⓕ

Amy Beach's *Gaelic* Symphony (her only work in the genre) dates from 1896. Like Dvořák's *New World* Symphony, which had received its American première just a few years earlier, it draws its inspiration from folk material; though Beach's sources are drawn not from native America but rather from her Gaelic forebears. The writing reveals a remarkable degree of craftsmanship and maturity, and although the music contains perhaps more imitation than originality (Brahms,

Tchaikovsky and Parry spring to mind) there is nevertheless plenty of enjoyment to be had from this fresh and engaging work. Slatkin's account of Barber's First Symphony might in some ways be more satisfactory as his orchestra seems more comfortable, and the American conductor clearly has an innate grasp of the music's style. This one-movement, highly compact work deserves to be much better known as it contains some of Barber's most invigorating and memorable material. Stylistically it finds allegiance with the post-romanticism of symphonies such as Walton's First and Howard Hanson's Second (*Romantic*). The disc also includes Barber's equally engaging Overture to *The School for Scandal*. Committed performances.

Barber String Quartet, Op. 11.
Britten String Quartet No. 2 in C major, Op. 36.
Takemitsu A Way A Lone.
Tokyo Quartet (Peter Oundjian, Kikuei Ikeda *vns* Kazuhide Isomura *va* Sadao Harada *vc*).
RCA Victor Red Seal 09026 61387-2 (61 minutes: DDD). Recorded 1992.　　　　Ⓕ

Three very different minds grappling with the intricacies of four-way musical dialogue. Takemitsu, a habitual aesthete wandering in the thick of sensual Bergian textures; Barber, a compelling New World romantic revelling among memories of Dvořák and, perhaps, Nielsen; and then Britten, a bold, incandescent voice in prime condition, proclaiming during the year (1945) that also witnessed *Peter Grimes* and *The Holy Sonnets of John Donne*. All are summoned among the sonorous ranks of the Tokyo Quartet for performances that combine rigour, warmth and textual acuity. It's a compelling mix, the standard of playing is uniformly high, the recording pleasingly full-bodied and the programme itself well chosen, offering 'the responses of three composers to the challenge of tradition'.

Ballade, Op. 46. Excursions, Op. 20. Nocturne, Op. 33. Piano Sonata, Op. 26. Souvenirs, Op. 28.
Eric Parkin *pf*
Chandos CHAN9177 (63 minutes: DDD). Recorded 1992.　　　　Ⓕ

This is the complete published piano music, apart from *Three Sketches*, but there are quite a lot of unpublished pieces. None of this matters when the playing is as polished and sympathetic as Parkin's. He responds wonderfully to the nostalgic melancholia of Barber. The ballet score, *Souvenirs*, is available in the orchestral and piano-duet versions, but this solo piano treatment is just as engaging. Parkin knows exactly how to present this side of Barber and his treatment of the *Four Excursions* based on different popular idioms is equally convincing. A performer as well versed as Parkin in British post-romantics such as Ireland and Bax finds home ground again in Barber's *Nocturne* and the late *Ballade*. In Barber's classic, the Sonata, Parkin treats the work lyrically and never forces us to regard the finale, especially, as a hard-hitting block-buster in the way that so many young pianists do. He is transparent in the *Scherzo*, sings in the *Adagio*, and the final fugue subject has exactly the catchy, swinging quality that many players miss. At times there is a lack of brilliance, which the rather dull recording emphasizes, but this is a winning anthology of this major American romantic.

Hermit Songs, Op. 29[a]. Sleep now, Op. 10 No. 2[a]. The Daisies, Op. 2 No. 1[a]. Nocturne, Op. 13 No. 4[a]. Nuvoletta, Op. 25[a]. Knoxville: Summer of 1915, Op. 24[b]. Antony and Cleopatra[b] – Give me some music; Give me my robe.
Leontyne Price *sop* **Samuel Barber** *pf* [b]**New Philharmonia Orchestra / Thomas Schippers.**
RCA Victor Gold Seal 09026 61983-2 (63 minutes: ADD). Texts included. Items marked [a] recorded live in mono in 1953, [b]1968.　　　　Ⓜ Ⓗ

Leontyne Price's radiant performance of *Knoxville*, that hauntingly evocative cantata to words by James Agee, comes in a coupling with the heroine's arias from the opera, *Antony and Cleopatra*, the role she created at the Met in New York. More than ever it seems cruelly unjust that an over-involved stage production should have so undermined a fine opera, one that certainly didn't deserve to be counted a failure. Sadly, it affected Barber's creative confidence for far too long. In this collection of all Price's Barber recordings those items are splendidly rounded out by the private recordings made at the Library of Congress at the time of the very first performance in October 1953 of the *Hermit Songs*, also specifically written for her. Accompanied by the composer, she is rugged and intense; Barber, though a good pianist, is quite rough. That comes out even more clearly in the four separate songs, which include Barber's longest individual song, *Nuvoletta*, setting a passage, characteristically full of word-play, taken from James Joyce's *Finnegans Wake*. The other songs are taken quite fast, a typical sign of a composer's impatience in performing his own music – with the charming little setting of James Stephens's *The Daisies* made quite different in character, almost like an Irish folk-song at a speed half as fast again. The mono sound of 1953 is very limited, but conveys the atmosphere of a historic occasion. As on LP the 1968 stereo sound given to the orchestral items (recorded in London) is full and well focused, with the strings of the New Philharmonia under Thomas Schippers sounding pure and sweet.

Barber Twelfth Night, Op. 42 No. 1. To be sung on the water, Op. 42 No. 2. Reincarnations, Op. 16. Agnus Dei, Op. 11. Heaven-Haven. Sure on this shining night. The monk and his cat. The Virgin Martyrs, Op. 8 No. 1. Let down the bars, O Death, Op. 8 No. 2. God's Grandeur.
Schuman Perceptions. Mail Order Madrigals.
Anthony Saunders *pf* **The Joyful Company of Singers / Peter Broadbent.**
ASV CDDCA939 (66 minutes: DDD). Texts included. Recorded 1995.   Ⓕ

Newcomers should make haste to track 6 for a pleasant surprise. Here they will encounter Samuel Barber's indestructible *Adagio* in its alternative and mellifluous 1967 vocal guise, set to the text of the *Agnus Dei*. Peter Broadbent's Joyful Company of Singers acquit themselves extremely well. Elsewhere, one particularly relishes the exquisite Op. 42 pairing of *Twelfth Night* and *To be sung on the water*, the carefree lilt of *The monk and his cat* and, above all, the majestic, strikingly ambitious 1938 setting of Gerald Manley Hopkins's sonnet, *God's Grandeur* (perhaps the single most impressive achievement on the disc). Further delights are provided by Barber's countryman and contemporary, William Schuman. The concise, beautifully sculpted *Perceptions* (1982) are settings of choice aphorisms from the pen of Walt Whitman, while the *Mail Order Madrigals* (1972) wittily utilize the flowery prose drawn from advertisements contained within a Sears and Roebuck catalogue of 1897. A most attractive issue, in short, excellently produced and engineered.

A Slumber Song of the Madonna. There's Nae Lark. Love at the door. Serenades. Love's Caution. Night Wanderers. Oh that so sweet imprisonment. Strings in the Earth and Air. The Beggar's song. In the dark pinewood. Three Songs, Op. 2. Three Songs, Op. 10. Four Songs, Op. 13. Dover Beach, Op. 3. Two Songs, Op. 18. Nuvoletta, Op. 25. Mélodies passagères, Op. 27. Hermit Songs, Op. 29. Despite and Still, Op. 41. Three Songs, Op. 45.
Cheryl Studer *sop* **Thomas Hampson** *bar* **John Browning** *pf*
Emerson Quartet (Eugene Drucker, Philip Setzer *vns* Lawrence Dutton *va* David Finckel *vc*).
DG 435 867-2GH2 (two discs: 110 minutes: DDD). Notes and texts included. Recorded 1991-92.
Gramophone Award Winner 1994.   ⒻⒺ

Sung in chronological order these songs are almost an autobiography and the set provides a compelling argument for regarding Barber's songs as his art at its most complete. There's hardly a weak song in the collection. Hampson brings to this music a remarkable range of expression and colour, a subtle use of words and a conviction that not a few of these songs are masterpieces. Studer has a slightly cooler approach, but often provides the vocal glamour, the ability to sketch long curves and floated high notes, that Barber (singer himself and connoisseur of singing) so often demanded. And John Browning, to whose virtuosity Barber tailored his Piano Concerto, sounds not only like a man who has yearned to accompany these singers in these songs for a long while, but like a considerable accompanist indeed, matching Hampson's dynamic range and expressive flexibility and Studer's seamless line with resourceful sympathy. The recorded sound is flawless.

Jean Barraqué
French 1928-1973

Piano Sonata. Etude. Séquence. … au delà du hasard. Chant après chant. Le temps restitué. Concerto.
Rosemary Hardy, Julie Moffat, Claudia Barainsky *sops* **Christina Ascher** *mez*
Deborah Miles-Johnson *contr* **Bernhard Zachhuber, Ernesto Molinari** *cls*
Charlie Fischer *vib* **Stefan Litwin, Florian Müller** *pfs* **Jean Barraqué** *elec* **NOVA Vocal Ensemble; Klangforum Wien / Jürg Wyttenbach, Peter Rundel, Sylvain Cambreling.**
CPO CPO999 569-2 (three discs: 218 minutes: DDD). Texts and translations included. Recorded 1995-96.   Ⓕ

The music of Jean Barraqué, a self-confessed romantic who sought to emulate the expressive scope of Beethoven through an essentially modernist language, charts a course of fervent ambition and impressive failure. His first acknowledged piece, the Piano Sonata (1952), declares his position unequivocally. It is a fascinating if frustrating work, the attempt to re-create the sonata dynamic in the discontinuous medium of total serialism opening up a gap between conception and realization, which Litwin's scrupulous but literal reading only underlines. Apart from the brief but explosive electronic *Etude*, the only other composition of Barraqué's early maturity is *Séquence*, a darkly expressive song-cycle whose combination of voice with an ensemble rich in percussion was to be developed on a far more extensive scale in ... *au delà du hasard* (1958). This was the first of his works to draw its text from Hermann Broch's novel *The Death of Virgil*, a meditation on the relationship between creativity and destruction, henceforth to dominate his output (and seemingly his life too). In its epic grandeur and emotional intensity, ... *au delà* was to remain Barraqué's definitive statement and, in the context of mid-twentieth-century music, a significant one. *Chant après chant* suffers from the polarity between its expressive but fragile vocal line and a flamboyant but expressively inert percussion sextet. *Le temps restitué*, completed in 1968, is another all-embracing concept, but the text's urging towards a unity of time and knowledge is repeatedly undercut by the music's fatalistic, even defeatist tone. Surprising then that, in the same year, Barraqué realized a purely instrumental and immediately engaging work – the Concerto for clarinet, vibraphone and six instrumental groups. With its jazz-inflected, subtle and animated discourse, this work seems to offer a creative lifeline which the composer was unable to follow.

High points? Certainly the spine-chilling sequence in ... *au delà* (tracks 9 and 10) and the Concerto's closing five minutes, with its individual blend of humour and eloquence, demonstrate the emotional range of this music. Klangforum Wien, together with some excellent soloists, do it full justice, securing a strong recommendation for works that, while in no sense a comfortable listen, are compelling and at times moving.

Béla Bartók

Hungarian 1881-1945

Piano Concertos – No. 1, Sz83; No. 2, Sz95; No. 3, Sz119.

Piano Concertos Nos. 1-3.
Peter Donohoe *pf*
City of Birmingham Symphony Orchestra / Sir Simon Rattle.
EMI CDC7 54871-2 (77 minutes: DDD). Recorded 1990-92.   Ⓕ Ⓔ ⓡⓡ

Piano Concertos Nos. 1-3.
András Schiff *pf*
Budapest Festival Orchestra / Iván Fischer.
Teldec 0630-13158-2 (76 minutes: DDD). Recorded 1996.   Ⓕ

Making Bartók's First Piano Concerto sound fun must have taken some doing, but Donohoe and Rattle have certainly managed it. The recording blends the instrument in among the orchestra, so that Rattle's sensitivity to nuance, Donohoe's lightness of touch and the accommodating acoustic of Birmingham's Symphony Hall transform what we frequently hear as an angular confrontation into something genuinely palatable. The Second Concerto, in this impressively urgent account, could hold its own in any company, even though there are one or two passages where articulation momentarily falters. The rest is either pungent or evocative: the second movement's 'night music' *Adagio* sections are beautifully sustained and the finale has terrific *élan*. Taken overall, this is a marvellous trio of performances and serves as a fresh reminder of just how great these works are.

Although Schiff's free-flowing renditions are never too far from the written page, they rarely stick rigidly to the letter. The first solo statement in the Second Concerto, for example, is lilting and capricious, quite unlike the earnest pronouncements of Anda, Donohoe or Kocsis. True, his *Presto* isn't quite as nimble as Anda's but most readers will rejoice in the many subtle shifts in pace and dynamics that colour Schiff's performances. Fischer's Budapest Festival Orchestra are on great form; woodwind solos are characterful, brass choirs have immense force and the juggernaut big drums thrash thunder into the last movement of the Second Concerto. The First Concerto suggests a sense of play that rivals Donohoe and Rattle, especially in the first movement – although never letting you forget Donohoe's mesmerizing account of the *Andante*. The Third Concerto suits Schiff best of all: his tone is nicely rounded, his chords perfectly weighted and there's some nifty fingerwork. He virtually sings these concertos, which makes for a near-ideal Third but, in the case of the Second, prompts something of an uneven confrontation. Schiff's contribution to the Second is consistently bright, nimble, even a little coquettish, while Fischer's response is brazen and athletic. The same might be said of the First Concerto, except that there the sound is so astonishingly lifelike that it virtually amounts to an aural drama on its own terms.

Piano Concertos Nos. 1[a], 2[b] and 3[a].
Stephen Kovacevich *pf*
[a]**London Symphony Orchestra;** [b]**BBC Symphony Orchestra / Sir Colin Davis.**
Philips Silver Line 426 660-2PSL (77 minutes: ADD). Recorded [a]1975, [b]1968.   Ⓜ

For sheer value for money this mid-price CD takes some beating. These are readings which capture the rhythmic spring, the inner intensity, and the controlled fanaticism so crucial to the Bartók idiom. Kovacevich is a splendid soloist, in terms of sheer articulation often quite marvellous, his accentuation imaginative and his feeling for atmosphere acute. He and Davis make a fine team, and No. 1, by far the more difficult piece to come to terms with, is tough and exhilarating. Highly percussive, like much that Bartók wrote in the mid-1920s, it still is shaped with sensitivity. The finale is explosively energetic here, and something of this carries over into the equivalent movement of No. 3. The slow movements of Nos. 2 and 3 elicit a deeply poetic response from Kovacevich and Davis. The Third receives a large-scale performance, more aggressive than many that one hears. Davis is particularly searching in the *Adagio religioso*, and the LSO woodwind shines in the central section's 'insect music'. However, there are niggling faults, such as a few careless misreadings. However in its suppleness, mystery and fantasy, Kovacevich's account remains a distinguished one.

Piano Concertos Nos. 1-3.
Zoltán Kocsis *pf*
Budapest Festival Orchestra / Iván Fischer.
Philips 446 366-2PH (74 minutes: DDD). Recorded 1984-87.   Ⓕ

These performances represent a particular phase in the developing style of a great Bartók pianist. And as Bartók piano concerto cycles go, is certainly amongst the best available: playful in the First Concerto (though not as tautly argued as Donohoe's), riotous and atmospheric in the Second (without quite matching Anda and Frcisay for energy and elegance) and with an extremely fine account of the Third Concerto, one where Kocsis's nimble-fingered delivery climaxes in a particularly cogent reading of the closing *Allegro vivace*. At the time of recording, Iván Fischer's incisive though warmly shaded Budapest Festival accompaniments marked something of a dramatic upgrading in Hungarian performances of Bartók's orchestral music. These are excellent performances and the digital recordings have a pleasant tonal bloom.

Piano Concertos Nos. 1-3.
Géza Anda *pf*
Berlin Radio Symphony Orchestra / Ferenc Fricsay.
DG The Originals 447 399-2GOR (78 minutes: ADD). Recorded 1959-60.   Ⓜ Ⓗ

Much as one would like to tout the new as the best, there are some older recordings where a very special chemistry spells 'definitive', and that pose an almost impossible challenge to subsequent rivals. Such is this 1959 recording of Bartók's Second Piano Concerto, a tough, playful, pianistically aristocratic performance where dialogue is consistently keen and spontaneity is captured on the wing (even throughout numerous sessions). The first movement is relentless but never tires the ear; the second displays two very different levels of tension, one slow and mysterious, the other hectic but controlled; and although others might have thrown off the finale's octaves with even greater abandon, Anda's performance is the most successful in suggesting savage aggression barely held in check. The Third Concerto is again beautifully moulded and carefully thought-through. Moments such as the loving return from the second movement's chirpy central episode are quite unforgettable, while the finale is both nimble and full-toned. The First Concerto was the last to be recorded and is perhaps the least successful of the three: here ensemble is occasionally loose, and characterization less vivid than with, say, Donohoe and Rattle. Still, it is a fine performance and the current transfer has been lovingly effected.

Bartók Piano Concerto No. 3.
Prokofiev Piano Concertos – No. 1 in D flat major, Op. 10; No. 3 in C major, Op. 26.
Martha Argerich *pf*
Montreal Symphony Orchestra / Charles Dutoit.
EMI CDC5 56654-2 (70 minutes: DDD). Recorded 1998.   Ⓕ

As always with this most mercurial of virtuosos, Martha Argerich's playing is generated very much by the mood of the moment and many listeners may well be surprised at her relative geniality with Dutoit. Personal and vivacious throughout, she always allows the composer his own voice. This is particularly true in Bartók's Third Concerto where her rich experience in chamber music makes her often *primus inter pares*, a virtuoso who listens to her partners with the greatest care. In the *Adagio religioso* she achieves a poise that has sometimes eluded her in the past and her finale is specially characterful, her stealthy start to the concluding *Presto* allowing the final pages their full glory. Dutoit and the Montreal Symphony achieve a fine unity throughout, a sense of like-minded musicians at work. All true musicians will recognize performances of a special magic and integrity.

In the Prokofiev First Concerto, her opening is arguably more authentically *brioso* than ferocious, her overall view a refreshingly fanciful view of Prokofiev's youthful iconoclasm. The central *Andante assai* is inflected with an improvisatory freedom she would probably not have risked earlier in her career and in the *Allegro scherzando* she trips the light fantastic, reserving a suitably tigerish attack for the final octave bravura display. Her performance of the Third Concerto is less fleet or nimble-fingered than in her early days but is more delectably alive to passing caprice. Once more she is unusually sensitive in the central *Andantino*, to the fourth variation's plunge into Slavic melancholy and introspection. The recordings are clear and naturally balanced and only those in search of metallic thrills and rushes of blood to the head will feel disappointed.

Bartók Viola Concerto.
S. Albert Cello Concerto.
Bloch Schelomo.
Yo-Yo Ma *vc/alto vn*
Baltimore Symphony Orchestra / David Zinman.
Sony Classical SK57961 (78 minutes: DDD). Recorded 1993.   Ⓕ

The Stephen Albert Concerto is a gritty, Barber-style tussle, with its various participants scored on more or less equal terms; whereas Bartók's transparent dialogue has soloist and orchestra co-exist rather than interrelate, and Bloch's sumptuous evocation of King Solomon alternates candid incantation with huge, tonally complex orchestral tuttis. Yo-Yo Ma's decision to use a vertical viola, or alto violin ('a large viola fitted with a long endpin and held like a cello') in the Bartók Concerto stems from his apparent dissatisfaction with 'the registral displacement' of the authorized cello version. Using the alto violin also meant honouring the work's original pitch, although comparison with Wolfgang Christ's superb DG recording (currently out of the catalogue but until 1999 this guide's top recommendation for the Viola Concerto) may incline you towards the earlier performance, which is both richer in tone and more urgently communicated. You may also be somewhat taken aback when, at the beginning of the concerto, the prescribed cellos and double bass are replaced by timpani. The reason for this is that Ma and Zinman appear to have been working from a revision that incorporates certain re-interpretations of Bartók's original sketches and that does indeed substitute timpani for the low strings. It's a good performance, strongly accompanied and it 'fits' well – in programming terms, that is – between Albert and Bloch.

Albert composed a number of orchestral works, including two symphonies – the second of which lay unfinished at the time of his death. As it happens, this four-movement Cello Concerto (1990) is also conceived on a symphonic scale. Fairly cosmopolitan in overall style (audible influences include Sibelius and Bernstein), it opens with an intense, rhapsodizing solo, before a blast of brass and a flurry of strings make way for a Mahlerian rising figure on the woodwind and a good deal of agitated argument. Although initial encounters hardly suggest a revelatory masterpiece, the combination of Albert's inventive music, Ma's intense delivery and Zinman's alert conducting make for a pretty riveting experience. *Schelomo* wails or prays to theatrical effect, although some of Ma's scooping *portamentos* sound coyly affected rather than particularly expressive. Zinman, though, is quite magnificent, while his Baltimore players – who are superbly recorded – rise to survey Bloch's towering climaxes with a combination of bravura and finesse. An attractive and satisfying programme.

Violin Concerto No. 2, Sz112.

Violin Concerto. Rhapsodies – No. 1, Sz87; No. 2, Sz90.
Kyung-Wha Chung *vn*
City of Birmingham Symphony Orchestra / Sir Simon Rattle.
EMI CDC7 54211-2 (59 minutes: DDD). Recorded 1990-92.
Gramophone Award Winner 1994.   Ⓕ 🇷🇷

It is rare indeed to encounter a concerto recording where the critical honours can be evenly distributed, but this one really does suggest a strong team spirit. Heard purely for its own sake, Chung's playing is sinewy, agile and occasionally a mite brittle. Yet one soon realizes that every passage has been carefully thought through – the opening sequence, for example, which Chung traces as a continuous line of monologue. However, it is when soloist and conductor grapple in dialogue that the sparks really start to fly. Rattle and his players make the very most of Bartók's orchestral commentary: instrumental interplay is always alert, rhythms are keenly focused and his way of cushioning Chung, palpably convincing. The well-matched *Rhapsody* recordings are, again, revealing. The solo line is nicely attenuated, and the overall approach one of fine-tuned improvisation. Detail is legion (note how the solo violins and woodwinds intertwine at the beginning of the Second *Rhapsody*'s second movement), with Rattle compounding the rhapsodic idea by shaping his phrases with imaginatively applied rubato.

Bartók Violin Concerto.
Stravinsky Violin Concerto in D major.
Viktoria Mullova *vn*
Los Angeles Philharmonic Orchestra / Esa-Pekka Salonen.
Philips 456 542-2PH (57 minutes: DDD). Recorded 1997.   Ⓕ

This recording of these concerto masterpieces is forthright and confident, with energetic support
from Salonen and his orchestra. Mullova's playing is committed and intense, with a ripe tone and
some filigree passagework in the second-movement variations, where Salonen is careful to clarify
every bejewelled strand in Bartók's scoring. The first movement is well thought through, though the
timing exceeds Bartók's own by some three minutes. Still, most rivals are similarly expansive, and
the second movement is actually a few seconds faster than prescribed, which is perhaps one of the
reasons why it works so well. The finale is again clearly focused, but the big surprise comes with the
inclusion – or, rather, substitution – of Bartók's rarely heard original ending, where the soloist
retires and the orchestra alone shoulders the whole of the coda. The Stravinsky concerto is another
winner, with pert outer movements and a ravishing account of the second 'Aria'. Tempos are well
chosen, the sound is again first-rate. This performance of the Stravinsky ranks higher than any
digital rival. As to the Bartók, Mullova is on a par with the best.

Violin Concerto. Rhapsodies Nos. 1 and 2.
Gil Shaham *vn*
Chicago Symphony Orchestra / Pierre Boulez.
DG 459 639-2GH (65 minutes: DDD). Recorded 1998.   Ⓕ

The constituent parts of this carefully considered production include a velvet-toned solo line,
fastidious instrumental balancing, fine orchestral playing and considered articulation from all
concerned. Wherever the score quietens, the musical tension is well sustained and so is the rarefied
atmosphere created by Bartók's exquisite scoring. The playful banter between soloist and orchestra
works especially well. There are odd flashes of drama and also some magical details, a particular
favourite being at 5'41" into the second movement, where Shaham's passagework flutters within a
dark aural environment like a captive butterfly circulating Bluebeard's Castle. The one reservation
about this performance is a certain lack of temperament. Shaham's first entry is too urbane, too
carefully calculated. Sometimes his attack is strong, sometimes underpowered. Shaham, although
an extremely accomplished player, emerges as overly cool, excessively laid-back. He and Boulez
present a workable – and enjoyable – overview of the concerto, but sometimes fail to engage the
spirit. In the *Rhapsodies*, No. 2's first movement's entrancing recipe of solo violin, woodwinds and
gentle percussion make an unforgettable effect.

The Miraculous Mandarin, Sz73.

The Miraculous Mandarin. Hungarian Peasant Songs, Sz100. Hungarian Sketches, Sz97.
Romanian Folkdances, Sz68. Transylvanian Dances, Sz96. Romanian Dance, Sz47.
Hungarian Radio Chorus; Budapest Festival Orchestra / Iván Fischer.
Philips 454 430-2PH (67 minutes: DDD). Recorded 1996.
Gramophone Award Winner 1998.   Ⓕ Ⓔ ⓇⓇ

As *Mandarins* go, they don't come more miraculous than this – a vivid, no-holds-barred
performance. Everything tells – the flavour is right, the pacing too and the sound has a toughened,
raw-edged quality that is an essential constituent of Bartók's tonal language. Although lurid – even
seedy – in narrative detail, *The Miraculous Mandarin* is ultimately a tale of compassion, and Fischer
never forgets that fact. Observable detail – all of it musically significant – occurs virtually by the
minute. Delicacy trails bullish aggression, forcefulness alternates with an almost graphic
suggestiveness – and it's all there in the full score. Fischer never vulgarizes, brutalizes or overstates
the case and, what is most important, he underlines the quickly flickering, folkish elements in
Bartók's musical language that other, less intuitive conductors barely acknowledge. The strongly
individual character of the Budapest Festival Orchestra is delightful. The strings have a biting edge,
the woodwinds a gipsy-style reediness, while brass and percussion are forceful and incisive but never
raucous. All these qualities also come into their own in the five folk-music-inspired works. This is
Hungarian-grown Bartók that actually *sounds* Hungarian; it makes one wish that other European
orchestras would reclaim parallel levels of individuality.

The Miraculous Mandarin. Concerto for Orchestra.
City of Birmingham Symphony Chorus and Orchestra / Sir Simon Rattle.
EMI CDC5 55094-2 (70 minutes: DDD). Recorded 1992-93.   Ⓕ Ⓢ

Sir Simon Rattle's Bartókian credentials have never been better displayed on disc, with this particular version of *The Miraculous Mandarin* ballet. Tone and texture are securely on target, and those oddly elusive second and third trumpets at fig. 21 (which are curiously absent from many rivals) are here properly reinstated. The strings and winds project with impressive confidence throughout, the trumpets prior to 'The Chase' are more rhythmically secure than most, and the various dramatic incidents that succeed the closing pages of the Suite (and which include some of Bartók's most powerful music for the stage) are given with a genuine sense of pathos. The chorus is well balanced, the percussion too, while Rattle himself drives all with a combination of animal vigour and teeming imagination. However the disc's main claim to distinction is a live recording of the *Concerto for Orchestra* that, for sheer character and communicative power, virtually sweeps the board certainly as far as the digital field is concerned. Right from the opening *Andante non troppo*, it is clear that everyone is wholly engaged in the task in hand. The flight into *Allegro vivace* is especially exciting and the 'Elegia' is especially intense, with a positively outraged return of the first movement's initial *forte* idea – the dotted trumpet lending a genuinely Magyar tang to the proceedings. The closing minute or so of the 'Intermezzo' is more tender than any other in recent years, while the finale is full of witty incident – every little variation played for all its worth and the whole brimming over with life and energy. However, Rattle's most telling interpretative stroke occurs at 7'23", that mysterious, curiously elusive passage that most other conductors treat like some sort of hybrid interpolation marking time until the final pages arrive. Rattle, though, will have none of it: his reading betrays pin-point focusing, with intelligent phrasing, careful articulation and a sense of dramatic inevitability that lends the passage a new-found musical logic. The closing moments are thrilling, with a lacerating final chord tailed by a grateful but hardly ecstatic volley of applause. If it had been from the Proms, the cheers and shouts would doubtless have been deafening – and for good reason. Give this one a try: it certainly upstages all the modern competition.

Concerto for Orchestra, Sz116.

Concerto for Orchestra. Kossuth, Sz21. Village Scenes, Sz79.
Slovak Folk Ensemble Chorus; Budapest Festival Orchestra / Iván Fischer.
Philips 456 575-2PH (67 minutes: DDD). Recorded 1997. Ⓕ Ⓔ 🆁🆁

Bartók's youthful *Kossuth* is as enjoyable a tone-poem as any save for Strauss's or Liszt's best, lyrical and dramatic, especially in the eighth section, where perky bassoons prompt a head-on confrontation by poking fun at the Austrian national anthem. Fischer and his orchestra here steal a lead on all the recorded rivals, at virtually every juncture. Solos in all departments are highly distinctive, while tutti passages have an earthy, upfront quality that lends extra fibre to Bartók's textures. *Kossuth*'s musical effect relies almost entirely on the conviction of its interpreters, and in that respect alone Fischer wins hands down. Bartók completed his five *Village Scenes* (originally for voice and piano) in 1924, orchestrating three of them two years later at Koussevitzky's suggestion. Bartók places a doleful, slightly unsettling 'Lullaby' between a frisky 'Wedding' and a hyperactive 'Lad's Dance'. The Slovak Folk Ensemble Chorus (all ladies) squeal their hearts out for the wedding and Fischer keeps Bartók's hot-foot syncopations alive and kicking. A pity that Philips fails to include texts and translations. As to the *Concerto for Orchestra*, again it is the flavour of the performance that wins the day. Fischer is a dab hand at shaping and inflecting the musical line. He sails into the movement's 'brass chorale' trio without a hint of a pause and invests the 'Elegia' with the maximum respectable quota of passion. The finale is a riot of sunshine and swirling skirts, except for the mysterious – and notoriously tricky – *più presto* coda, with its rushing *sul ponticello* string choirs, which Fischer articulates with great care. One senses that the players are being driven to the very limits of their abilities, which only serves to intensify the excitement. Philips's dynamic sound frame works best in *Kossuth* and the *Village Scenes*, though most of the *Concerto* also sounds excellent. The only complaint is of a marginally flat brass chord in the finale and a quiet, short-lived low electronic hum in the same movement. Otherwise, a clear front runner in the full-price stakes.

Concerto for Orchestra. Music for Strings, Percussion and Celesta, Sz106. Hungarian Sketches, Sz97.
Chicago Symphony Orchestra / Fritz Reiner.
RCA Victor Living Stereo 09026 61504-2 (76 minutes: ADD). Recorded 1955. Ⓜ

Reiner's recordings were made in Chicago's Orchestra Hall in October 1955 (not that sampling reveals their age – quite the contrary). RCA's sound reportage of the *Concerto for Orchestra*'s quieter moments has uncanny realism and if the climaxes are occasionally reined in, the sheer fervour of Reiner's direction more than compensates. The 'Pair Play' is a very brisk 6'26", the finale taut and agile: compare the movement's opening with, say, Boulez's version, and Reiner's greater precision and control is immediately apparent. His couplings are excellent: a *Music for Strings, Percussion and Celesta* that goes all out for smooth transitions and fleet execution, and a stylishly turned set of *Hungarian Sketches* – with a substantially augmented percussion line in 'Bear Dance'. These too sound better than ever, the *Music for Strings, Percussion and Celesta* having lost a confusing layer of distortion that hampered some earlier LP editions.

Concerto for Orchestra. Kossuth.
San Francisco Symphony Orchestra / Herbert Blomstedt.
Decca 443 773-2DH (59 minutes: DDD). Recorded 1993.   Ⓕ

Blomstedt's cogently argued *Concerto for Orchestra*, although less overtly characterful than Rattle's and less virtuosic than Reiner's, boasts a clarity, intelligence and calm sense of purpose that lend the work an almost symphonic logic. The engineering, too, is usefully revealing. Don't expect a high-octane, tough-fisted *tour de force* (although the closing pages have plenty of impact), but those in search of a lively, keen-eyed and, particularly, a superbly recorded overview are unlikely to be disappointed. *Kossuth* was Bartók's first completed orchestral work. To be quite honest, it's a pretty weak piece, full of obvious derivations (Strauss, Wagner, Liszt and so on) although you do occasionally hear intimations of Bartók's own First Suite, and even *Bluebeard's Castle*. 'Good fun' might seem a rather half-hearted, even patronizing form of commendation, but the performance serves as a sobering reminder of a great composer's unpromising immaturity. A valuable, artistically accomplished coupling.

Concerto for Orchestra[a]. Dance Suite, Sz77. Two Portraits, Sz37. Mikrokosmos, Sz107
(orch. Serly): Book 4 – Bourrée; Book 6, Sz107 – From the diary of a fly.
[a]**London Symphony Orchestra; Philharmonia Hungarica / Antál Dorati.**
Mercury Living Presence 432 017-2MM (72 minutes: ADD). Recorded [a]1962, 1958.   Ⓜ Ⓗ

Dorati's recording of *Concerto for Orchestra* is probably the finest recording of all on this label from the early 1960s. It certainly emerges with remarkable vividness and clarity on CD. For bite, intensity and vibrant idiomatic feeling the performance has not been surpassed, and the wit of 'Giuoco delle coppie' and the touching poise of the 'Elegia' match up attractively to the bravura thrills of the outer movements. Here there is tremendous attack from strings and brass alike. The sound is characteristically clean in definition, boldly coloured and firmly placed, but there is a touch of shrillness on top. On the rest of the disc Dorati conducts the Philharmonia Hungarica and we are offered equally distinguished and vital accounts of the *Dance Suite*, the *Two Portraits* (with Erwin Ramor, the glowingly ardent violin soloist in the first) and as an encore, two engaging excerpts from Tibor Serly's free orchestrations of *Mikrokosmos*. The second, 'From the diary of a fly', energetically buzzes around with sharply focused precision of orchestral detail, until the poor thing is swotted at the end!

The Wooden Prince, Sz60. Cantata profana, Sz94.
John Aler *ten* **John Tomlinson** *bass*
Chicago Symphony Chorus and Orchestra / Pierre Boulez.
DG 435 863-2GH (73 minutes: DDD). Recorded 1991.   Ⓕ

Bartók's parable of fathers, sons and fleeing the nest, his 1930 *Cantata profana*, is a mesmerizing, symmetrically designed masterpiece, where words and music are forged into an action-packed 18 minutes. Boulez provides what is by far the best studio recording the work has ever had (also the first to be digitally recorded), and truly state-of-the-art in terms of sound. Boulez is able to command a shimmering, hushed *pp* yet the battle-hardy *Allegro molto* with its hectoring syncopations and warlike percussion is full of grit and muscle. John Aler is wonderfully adroit with Bartók's high-flying solo tenor line, John Tomlinson sounds like an authentic Magyar, and the Chicago Symphony Chorus eggs the proceedings on with tireless zeal. Turn then to *The Wooden Prince* and you confront the final flowering of Bartók's post-romantic phase; it's an effulgent, exotic piece, full of wistful, melancholy wind solos (clarinet and saxophone figure prominently) and billowing, heavily-scored climaxes. How astonishing to reflect that it was written *after* the composer's trail-blazing opera, *Bluebeard's Castle*. Again, the soft music is wonderfully atmospheric: the *ppp* muted violins in the Prelude have a ghostly pallor that is so typical of this orchestra's quiet string playing, yet when all are engaged at full throttle, the effect is shattering. Detail is legion throughout: the basses, brass and drums have immense presence.

Bartók Divertimento, Sz113. Romanian Folkdances, Sz68 (arr. Willner).
Rózsa Concerto for String Orchestra, Op. 17.
Virtuosi di Kuhmo / Peter Csaba.
Ondine ODE919-2 (60 minutes: DDD). Recorded 1998.   Ⓕ

An interesting programme, with Miklos Rózsa's powerful *Concerto for String Orchestra* as its principal attraction. Rózsa composed the work in 1943, three years after he left his native Hungary for American shores. Stylistically, the *Concerto* more resembles Kodály than Bartók, though the first movement's darkly contrapuntal exposition is highly individual and its strongly motorized development creates an imposing sense of musical tension. Virtuosi di Kuhmo invests all three works with a notable degree of dynamism. The *Divertimento*'s outer movements are vigorous and supple, but it is the *Molto adagio* that comes off best, with its hushed *pianissimos* and feline *portamentos*. Peter Csaba and his players connect fully with Bartók's nightmare vision and the hilarious, mock-classical *pizzicato* Minuet that appears towards the end of the finale lands with a hefty wallop (especially among the cellos and basses). The *Romanian Folkdances* are played in Arthur Willner's sensitive string-band arrangement. The 'Pe loc' and 'Buciumeana' (slow Third and Fourth Dances) are expressively sustained, while the fast closing sequence sounds suitably rustic. Ondine's recordings have an impressive tonal bloom.

String Quartets – No. 1, Sz40; No. 2, Sz67; No. 3, Sz85; No. 4, Sz91; No. 5, Sz102; No. 6, Sz114.

String Quartets Nos. 1-6.
Takács Quartet (Edward Dusinberre, Károly Schranz *vns* Roger Tapping *va* András Fejér *vc*). Decca 455 297-2DH2 (two discs: 152 minutes: DDD). Recorded 1996.
Gramophone Award Winner 1998. Ⓕ 🅂 🅴 🆁🆁

These performances provide more impressive sampling points than one could hope to enumerate in a single review. The First Quartet's oscillating tempo-shifts work wonderfully well, all with total naturalness. Characterization is equally strong elsewhere, not least the first movement of the Second Quartet where Debussian arpeggios engage the senses, and the second movement where Fejér races back into the rustic opening subject. The nightmare climax in the last movement has rarely sounded more prophetic of the great *Divertimento*'s central movement. The middle quartets work very well, with prominent inner voices in the Third and plenty of swagger in the Fourth. The high spots of No. 4 are Fejér's improvisational cello solo in the third movement and a finale where the violent opening is a hefty *legato* to compare with the sharper, more Stravinskian attack of, say, the Tokyo Quartet. Likewise, the sudden dance-like episode in the first movement of the Fifth Quartet, savage music played from the pit of the stomach, while the third movement's bleary-eyed viola melody over teeming violin triplets suggests peasants in caricature.

The Takács are especially responsive to Bartók's sardonic humour – the 'barrel-organ' episode at the end of the Fifth Quartet, and the corny 'Burletta' in the third movement of the Sixth. The Sixth itself features some of the saddest, wildest and wisest music written in the last 100 years: the opening viola solo recalls Mahler's Tenth and the close fades to a mysterious question. Throughout the cycle, Bartók's metronome markings are treated more as guidelines than as literal commands. The playing communicates Bartók's all-embracing humanity, and if the greatest string quartets after Beethoven are still unknown to you, then this Takács set may well prove the musical journey of a lifetime. The recording here has ambient, full-bodied sound that is more reminiscent of the concert hall than of the studio.

String Quartets Nos. 1-6.
Emerson Quartet (Eugene Drucker, Philip Setzer *vns* Lawrence Dutton *va* David Finckel *vc*). DG 423 657-2GH2 (two discs: 149 minutes: DDD). Recorded 1988.
Gramophone Award Winner 1989. Ⓕ

Any cycle of Bartók quartets has to be pretty special if it is to stand out against the competition. The Emerson Quartet's is, and it does: powerful and refined, paying close attention to the letter of the score, and excelling in virtuoso teamwork. The impression one gains from these recordings is of massive tonal projection and superlative clarity, each textural strand coloured and made audible to a degree possibly unrivalled in the recorded history of these works. DG's close brightly-lit, yet never oppressive recording quality must share some of the credit for that, of course. Combine this with controlled vehemence, headlong velocity and razor-sharp unanimity (any fast movement from quartets two to five can serve as illustration) and you have a formidable alliance of virtues. Well recorded, when this set first appeared it was hailed as one of the most exciting chamber music recordings for many years.

String Quartets Nos. 1-6.
Tokyo Quartet (Koichiro Harada, Kikuei Ikeda *vns* Kazuhide Isomura *va* Sadao Harada *vc*). DG 20th Century Classics 445 241-2GC3 (three discs: 159 minutes: ADD). Recorded 1979.
Gramophone Award Winner 1981. Ⓜ

String Quartets Nos. 1-6.
Novák Quartet (Antonín Novák, Dušan Pandula *vns* Josef Podjukl *va* Jaroslav Chovanec *vc*).
Philips Duo 442 284-2PM2 (two discs: 158 minutes: ADD). Recorded 1965.   Ⓜ

Both these reissued sets outclass many of their more recent digital rivals, and yet initial
comparisons between the two reveal a number of telling differences: the Novák Quartet's mellow
reserve, for example, is in marked contrast to the Tokyo's febrile, acutely responsive attack; while
Philips's warm-textured sound is quite unlike the harder profile and sharper focusing favoured by
DG. Sometimes you feel that the Novák rather dulls the cutting edge of Bartók's more acerbic
writing (in the Third and Fourth Quartets, particularly), but then the last two quartets are
wonderfully communicative: the Fifth with its shimmering *Adagio* and *Andante*, the Sixth with its
sorrowful predominance of *Mesto* ('sad'). Not that the Tokyo lacks heart. In fact, of the two
quartet leaders, Koichiro Harada has the more vibrant tone, and his contribution to the Sixth
Quartet in particular wrings every ounce of emotion from the score. And when it comes to the
work's closing *pizzicato* chords, his players are the more lovingly attentive, arpeggiating the phrase
so as to highlight its relationship to crucial episodes earlier on in the movement.

In the Third and Fourth Quartets, the Tokyo again scores by dint of superior ensemble, keener
accents and a winning *élan*; they are also more alert to the music's delicate textures and rhythmic
complexities, whereas the more laid-back Novák tends to underplay *sforzatos* and occasionally
allows the tension to flag. And yet its very suppleness pays its own special dividends – in the
Fourth's *Allegretto pizzicato*, for example, where relative ease of delivery makes for impressive
textural and stereophonic clarity. The first two quartets find the Novák strong on mystery, the
Tokyo on dynamic inflexion. Still, when the cards are down and a final reckoning to hand, the
Tokyo has the edge: its searing intensity, acute sense of colour and total commitment to each score
combine for maximum impact which, if you don't already know the music, can't fail to win you
over. If you do, then the Novák's manifold insights should make for an enlightening extension of
your experience. The DG recordings were taped at various locations but have been fairly well
matched, whereas Philips's (excellent) engineering is more wholly consistent. Both sets represent, in
their very different ways, superb value for money, although it is a pity that DG didn't follow
Philips's lead and issue the six works on two CDs.

Violin Sonata No. 1, Sz75. Solo Violin Sonata, Sz117.
Isabelle Faust *vn* **Ewa Kupiec** *pf*
Harmonia Mundi Les Nouveaux Interprètes HMN91 1623 (69 minutes: DDD). Recorded 1996.
***Gramophone* Award Winner 1997.**   Ⓑ🄴

Bartók's First Violin Sonata is notoriously reluctant to yield its secrets: many have braved its pages
and although most available recordings convey the scale of the movement, none is more
comprehensively perceptive than this recording by the young violinist Isabelle Faust. Harmonia
Mundi counts Faust among the 'cream of the new generation of musicians' and, on the evidence
presented here, no one could rightly counter that claim. Ewa Kupiec provides Faust with motivated
support. Faust favours a sensual approach that draws active – and unexpected – parallels with the
music of Berg. She ventures deep among the first movement's more mysterious episodes. This is
truly empathetic playing, candid, full of temperament and always focused securely on the note's
centre. The *crescendo*ing processional that sits at the heart of the second movement is charged with
suspense and the steely finale suggests an almost savage resolve. Faust and Kupiec visit corners and
perspectives in this score that others merely gloss over, and the recording supports them all the way.
The Solo Sonata is virtually as impressive. Here Faust approaches the music from a Bachian axis:
her tone is pure, her double-stopping immaculate and her sense of timing acute. Faust is a
persuasive narrator; she and her piano partner break down barriers in the First Sonata that, for
some readers, will mean the difference between approachability and continuing bafflement. Do give
them a try.

Violin Sonatas – No. 1, Sz75; No. 2, Sz76. Contrasts, Sz111.
Kálmán Berkes *cl* **György Pauk** *vn* **Jenö Jandó** *pf*
Naxos 8 550749 (75 minutes: DDD).   Ⓢ🄴

Readers who habitually fight shy of Bartók's provocatively astringent piano writing might initially
find these endlessly fascinating works rather unpalatable, the First Sonata especially. But careful
scrutiny reveals manifold beauties which, once absorbed, tend to haunt one's memory and prompt
repeated listening. Jenö Jandó's piano playing is fairly forthright yet without the naked agression of,
say, Sviatoslav Richter. Furthermore, it provides an effective foil for György Pauk's warm tone and
fluid solo line, especially in the First Sonata, where ungainly tone production could so easily

compound one's discomfort. Here, however, the interpretation is at once thoughtful and well shaped, and fully appreciative of the mysterious 'night music' that sits at the heart of the *Adagio*. The Second Sonata is both gentler and more improvisatory, its language and structure – although still pretty formidable – somewhat in the manner of a rhapsody. Pauk and Jandó again hit the target, and the full-bodied recording makes for a homogeneous sound picture. To have a spirited performance of the multi-faceted *Contrasts* (with Kálmán Berkes on clarinet) as a bonus certainly helps promote this well-annotated CD to the front line of competition. A confident mainstream recommendation, then, and superb value for money.

Violin Sonata in E minor, Op. posth. Andante. Slovak Folk Songs (arr. Móži). Burlesques, Sz47 – A Bit Tipsy (arr. Urai). For Children, Sz42 – Ten Pieces (arr. Zathureczky). Contrasts, Sz111.
Susanne Stanzeleit *vn* **Michael Collins** *cl* **Gusztáv Fenyö** *pf*
ASV CDDCA982 (65 minutes: DDD). Recorded 1995.   Ⓕ

An interesting case of 'before and after', with the early E minor Sonata representing Bartók in 'czardas' mode and the late *Contrasts* echoing the earthy tang of genuine Hungarian folk music. Susanne Stanzeleit brings a wide range of gipsy-style inflexions to the various short pieces and the tipsy *Burlesque* finds her wisely avoiding a sober straight line. A touch of ruggedness suits the *Contrasts*, though there the real star of the show is clarinettist Michael Collins. True, Fenyö and Stanzeleit set the scene, but Collins's witty, lightly inflected solo has immense colour and personality. The little *Andante* for violin and piano (it lasts for just 3'18" in this performance) was written for Adila Arányi as a 'thank you' for a house party, but wasn't actually premièred until 1955. It's a pleasant but fairly uncharacteristic piece, whereas the half-hour Sonata of 1903 that precedes it contains many auguries of the mature Bartók. Strauss is an audible influence and so is Wagner: the very opening rises out of post-romantic mists, gently brushed by arpeggiated pizzicatos. Although not a masterpiece to compare with the two mature violin sonatas, the E minor Sonata is attractive, memorable and well worth bringing into the repertoire. ASV's recordings are very nicely balanced.

Contrasts, Sz111. Rhapsodies – No. 1, Sz86; No. 2, Sz89. Six Romanian Folk Dances, Sz56 (arr. Székely). Solo Violin Sonata, Sz117.
Michael Collins *cl* **Krysia Osostowicz** *vn* **Susan Tomes** *pf*
Hyperion CDA66415 (72 minutes: DDD). Recorded 1990.   Ⓕ

Unusually for a composer who wrote so much fine chamber music Bartók was not himself a string player. But he did enjoy close artistic understanding with a succession of prominent violin virtuosos, including the Hungarians Jelly d'Arányi, Joseph Szigeti and Zoltán Székely, and, towards the end of his life, Yehudi Menuhin. It was Menuhin who commissioned the Sonata for solo violin, but Bartók died before he could hear him play it – Menuhin was unhappy with the occasional passages in quarter-tones and the composer had reserved judgement on his proposal to omit them. It was Menuhin's edition which was later printed and which has been most often played and recorded; but Krysia Osostowicz returns to the original and, more importantly, plays the whole work with intelligence, imaginative flair and consummate skill. The Sonata is the most substantial work on this disc, but the rest of the programme is no less thoughtfully prepared or idiomatically delivered. There is the additional attraction of an extremely well balanced and natural-sounding recording. As a complement to the string quartets, which are at the very heart of Bartók's output, this is a most recommendable disc.

---

44 Duos for Two Violins, Sz98.
Sándor Végh, Albert Lysy *vns*
Auvidis Astrée E7720 (50 minutes: ADD).   Ⓕ

Like all the finest teaching material, Bartók's violin duos are accessible to virtually all levels of technical accomplishment yet conceal meanings which only the finest artists can bring out. Végh and Lysy are certainly in this category, and listening to all 44 pieces in one go, although not something one would often choose to do, is no hardship when the playing is of this order. This is partly a tribute to their care in devising a satisfying sequence of pieces, with variety of pace, dynamic and technical difficulty, but avoiding constant arbitrary fluctuation (Bartók stated that the published order was for pedagogic purposes only and not to be followed in performance). One particularly revealing conjunction is of Nos. 43, 22 and 36, which might all be taken as studies for the Fourth or Fifth String Quartets (the composition of the Duos falls between those two masterpieces). Intelligent planning is actually less important to the success of the disc than the sheer pungency of the violin playing. The resiny attack, the physical contact of horsehair on gut and steel, is vividly captured in a close-miked recording, and it lends an unmistakably idiomatic quality to all the varied moods. Végh and Lysy sound ideally matched in temperament – no trace of the compromise or struggle for supremacy which such enterprises can produce. If you buy this CD to fill a gap or out of curiosity you will probably get a far richer experience than you bargained for.

For Children, Sz42. The First Term at the Piano, Sz53. 15 Hungarian Peasant Songs, Sz71. Three Hungarian Folksongs from the Csík District, Sz35*a*. Hungarian Folktunes, Sz66. Eight Improvisations on Hungarian Peasant Songs, Sz74. Three Rondos on (Slovak) Folktunes, Sz84. Romanian Christmas Carols, Sz57. Six Romanian Folkdances, Sz56. Two Romanian Dances, Sz43. Suite, Sz62, with original Andante. Piano Sonata, Sz80. Sonatina, Sz55. 14 Bagatelles, Sz38. Four Dirges, Sz45. Petite Suite, Sz105. Violin Duos, Sz98 (arr. Sándor) – No. 1, Teasing Song; No. 17, Marching Song; No. 35, Ruthenian kolomejka; No. 42, Arabian Song; No. 44, Transylvanian Dance. 10 Easy Pieces, Sz39. Allegro barbaro, Sz49. Out of doors, Sz81. Seven Sketches, Sz44. Two Elegies, Sz41. Three Burlesques, Sz47. Nine Little Pieces, Sz82. Three Studies, Sz72.
György Sándor *pf*
Sony Classical SX4K68275 (four discs: 287 minutes: DDD). Recorded 1993-95. Ⓜ

There can't be many pianists on the current circuit whose fund of experience extends to working with a major twentieth-century master; but of those still recording, György Sándor must surely take pride of place. Sándor prepared Bartók's first two piano concertos under the composer's guidance and gave the world premières of the Third Concerto and the piano version of the *Dance Suite*. The present collection is Sándor's second survey of Bartók's piano music and he programmes all the major works apart from *Mikrokosmos*. Many of these performances are exceptionally fine, even though the passage of time has witnessed something of a reduction in Sándor's pianistic powers, mostly where maximum stamina and high velocity fingerwork are required (as in the first *Burlesque*). However, you may be astonished at the heft, energy and puckish humour of Sándor's 1994 recording of the Piano Sonata, a more characterful rendition than its predecessor, with a particularly brilliant account of the folkish *Allegro molto* finale. The *Allegro barbaro* is similarly 'on the beam', while Sándor brings a cordial warmth to the various collections of ethnic pieces, the *Romanian Christmas Carols* especially. His phrasing, rubato, expressive nuancing, attention to counterpoint and command of tone suggest the touch of a master, while his imagination relishes the exploratory nature of the *Improvisations, Bagatelles* and *Miraculous Mandarin*-style *Studies*. Sándor connects with all the music's abundant qualities: harmonic or rhythmic innovation, powerful emotion, humour, introspection, ethnic variety and the sheer scope and complexity of Bartók's piano writing in general. Intuitive interpreters, especially those who knew and understand the composers they perform, are becoming an increasingly rare breed. In that respect alone, György Sándor's Bartók deserves an honoured place in every serious CD collection of twentieth-century piano music.

---

14 Bagatelles, Sz38. Two Elegies, Sz41. Sonatine, Sz55. Six Romanian Folk Dances, Sz56. Three Hungarian Folktunes, Sz66.
Zoltán Kocsis *pf*
Philips 434 104-2PH (54 minutes: DDD). Recorded 1991. Ⓕ

Bartók himself admitted that his *Bagatelles* (1908) were largely experimental, and indeed at least half-a-dozen of them could easily have fallen from a jazz-pianist's copybook (Nos. 7, 11 and 12, particularly), their sensual harmonies and capricious rhythmic computations prophetic of so much that was to happen in that world. Debussy, too, is much in evidence (No. 3), as is Bartók's love of folk-song (Nos. 4 and 5). The *Elegies* would sit nicely among the shorter works of Busoni. These virtuosic effusions recall the moon-flecked world of late Liszt, albeit flushed with a Hungarian rather than a gipsy complexion. Folk-song proper informs Kocsis's last three selections: the familiar *Six Romanian Folk Dances*, the cheerful and ingenious *Sonatine* and the relatively dense *Hungarian Folktunes*, Sz66 – the last bringing us to the far edge of the Great War. It's a cliffhanger of a finale, and has us eager for more. Kocsis's readings are absolutely on target. A peach of a disc.

Piano Sonata, Sz80. Out of doors, Sz81. Nine Little Pieces, Sz82. Petite Suite, Sz105.
Zoltán Kocsis *pf*
Philips 446 369-2PH (49 minutes: DDD). Recorded 1996. ⒻⓈ

Kocsis's mastery of tone, rhythm and articulation, allied to his painstaking attention to important source material, make for a level of pianistic distinction that is fairly unique in this repertory. To say that with Kocsis 'less is more' is to suggest executive reticence, which is certainly not the case. The first movements of the Sonata and *Out of doors* (both works dating from 1926) hit hard without hammering, the former displaying a multitude of tiny inflexional gestures and pulse changes, the latter, a quick-boiling final chase of great intensity. Playing of this calibre takes us back to the days of 78s – playing where so much rhythmic flexibility is achieved within such a disciplined interpretative framework. In *Out of doors*, Kocsis's ability to command differing colours simultaneously heightens the musical effect, especially in the 'Barcarolla' and what is surely the most exquisitely tooled performance of 'The Night's Music' ever recorded. 'The Chase' is pin-sharp, its every gear-change expertly negotiated, while Kocsis makes maximum capital out of the rich harmonic world in 'Musettes'. The *Nine Little Pieces* transcend their brevity, 'Menuetto' recalling the second movement of the First Piano Concerto (another product of 1926), the closing 'Preludio – All'Ungherese' providing a little mini-suite all on its own. The disc closes with the *Petite Suite*, a tuneful half-dozen ingeniously refashioned from the *44 Duos* for two violins. This production is of superb quality and although 49 minutes is short measure for a full-price, solo piano CD, this is unquestionably one of the great piano records of the post-war period.

Two Romanian Dances, Sz43. Three Hungarian folksongs from the Csík district, Sz35a. Allegro barbaro, Sz49. Four Dirges, Sz45. Suite, Sz62. Romanian Christmas Carols, Sz57. Three Studies, Sz72. Three Rondos on Folktunes, Sz84. The first term at the piano, Sz53.
Zoltán Kocsis *pf*
Philips 442 016-2PH (71 minutes: DDD). Recorded 1993. ⓕ Ⓔ

Zoltán Kocsis's Bartók series is the first major interpretative project to call on the substantial evidence of Bartók's own recordings. There was a spontaneity in Bartók's own recorded performances, a quality that Kocsis achieves in his own playing. He also displays an ecstatic involvement in Bartók's harmonic writing, most particularly in the delicious, eloquently voiced *Three Hungarian folksongs from the Csík district* (how the second song seems a natural continuation of the first) and the exploratory *Three Studies*, the first as violent as the Miraculous Mandarin's murder, the third, a shifting sequence of computations that anticipates the player-piano studies of Conlon Nancarrow. Kocsis tackles all three *Studies* with absolute confidence. In any case, Kocsis's performances are never mere replications of Bartók's own; rather, they take the composer's lead in generating energy without aggression, poetry without indulgence and accuracy without pedantry.

The rest of the programme is as varied as the incidents within each individual opus. The *Two Romanian Dances*, both of them rich in novel variation, are thrust forwards in heady excitement, the first breaking half-way for a darkly rhapsodic central section, the second, a sort of mad-cap burlesque. The *Allegro barbaro* discards its customary metallic sheen and, instead, assumes more authentically Hungarian characteristics. Then there are the deeply expressive *Four Dirges*, the varied and instantly memorable *Romanian Christmas Carols*, the masterly Suite, Op. 14 and, to end on a simplistic note, *The first term at the piano* – attractive teaching material, similar in concept to the first books of *Mikrokosmos*, but strictly for completists. This is a superb CD. The music itself is of exceptionally high quality, the disc contents are imaginatively varied, the interpretations beyond criticism, the recordings superb (warm, close and lifelike, as per Philips's 'house' style) and the documentation highly informative. No other survey of music from the last decade of the twentieth century has so many claims to overall excellence.

Piano works.
Béla Bartók *pf*
Pearl mono GEMMCD9166 (69 minutes: ADD). Recorded 1929-42. Ⓜ Ⓗ

The Bartók scholar László Somfai observed how Bartók's manner of playing was 'fortified with his rich experiences of Classical interpretation and adopted very carefully the truly personal "accentuations" of his own music'. In most instances, Bartók didn't so much transcend his own rules as allow himself maximum freedom within them: time and again one notices minute adjustments in matters of rhythm, dynamics or inflexion, none of which disrupts the flow or distorts the character of the music. This compilation, the most comprehensive available on a single disc, offers full-bodied transfers of some fascinating commercial recordings, not least of Liszt's 'Sursum corda' (*Années de pèlerinage – Troisième année*) which sounds like a spontaneous transcription of an orchestral piece – such is its rugged grandeur. The next track (17) finds Bartók unsteady at the start of *Mikrokosmos*'s 'Staccato', but how thrilling are the hungry, almost Schnabelian 'snatched' phrases of the succeeding 'Ostinato' and the wicked caprices of that underrated masterpiece, *Improvisations on Hungarian Peasant Songs* (which Bartók recorded only in excerpt). There are 38 tracks in all on this disc, with the Suite, Op. 14, and the First *Romanian Dance* taking pride of place as Bartók's finest solo recordings. The *Allegro barbaro* is also good, though nowhere near as barbaric as some – a significant fact given a plethora of fierce-fisted Bartókians, all of whom should make an effort to hear this invaluable CD.

Five Songs, Sz61. Five Songs, Sz63. Hungarian Folksongs, Sz64 – Black is the earth; My God, my God; Wives, let me be one of your company; So much sorrow; If I climb the rocky mountains. Five Songs, Sz61 (orch. Kodály). Five Hungarian Folksongs, Sz101.
Júlia Hamari contr **Ilona Prunyi** pf **Hungarian State Orchestra / János Kovács.**
Hungaroton HCD31535 (67 minutes: DDD). Texts and translations included. Recorded 1992.　　Ⓕ

Kodály's rose-tinted orchestrations of Bartók's uncompromisingly erotic Op. 15 (Sz61) make for pleasant listening, but they sidetrack the real heart of the matter. The 34-year-old Bartók had a year-long relationship with the 15-year-old Klára Gombossy, and three of the songs are based on her poetry; the fourth sets a poem by the daughter of Klára's piano teacher, while the remaining 'In Vivid Dreams' is a re-working of another poem by Klára, added later. Heard in its original form for voice and piano, Op. 15 is a bold, harmonically far-reaching cycle (countless passages anticipate the harsher Bartók of the 1920s), often angular in design but, within its tough framework, passionately suggestive. Kodály's orchestrations date from 1961 and soften the music's contours in a way that Bartók himself would not have countenanced – at least not in 1915, the year in which the songs were composed. The *Five Songs*, Op. 16 (to poems by Endre Ady) consolidate the dark, introspective language of Op. 15, while the ten folk-song settings – Bartók's clearly-focused orchestrations (Sz101) and the five for voice and piano (Sz64) – are rather more outgoing and varied. All this music is so absorbing that one tends temporarily to forget the performers – which wouldn't be possible were they less than good. Júlia Hamari projects a secure, strong body of tone and fully comprehends the potent love images of Op. 15, while her accompanist, Ilona Prunyi, etches Bartók's vivid piano writing with a sure hand and much imagination. The orchestral items are patchily dealt with (winds are good, strings not), but the impressionistic nature of the writing (Kodály's especially) responds better to Kovács's soft-centred approach than, say, the *Village Scenes* would have done. The recordings are perfectly adequate. Recommended to all Bartókians and Lieder *aficionados*.

Duke Bluebeard's Castle.
Walter Berry bass-bar Bluebeard; **Christa Ludwig** mez Judith;
London Symphony Orchestra / István Kertész.
Decca The Classic Sound 443 571-2DCS (59 minutes: ADD). Notes, text and translation included. Recorded 1965.　　ⓂⓇⓇ

Duke Bluebeard's Castle.
John Tomlinson bass Bluebeard; **Anne Sofie von Otter** mez Judith; **Sandor Elès** spkr
Berlin Philharmonic Orchestra / Bernard Haitink.
EMI CDC5 56162-2 (63 minutes: DDD). Notes, text and translation included.
Recorded live in 1995.　　ⒻⒺ

Bernard Haitink's poetic axis is vividly anticipated in the rarely recorded spoken prologue where Sandor Elès bids us search beneath the story's surface. Elès's timing and his sensitivity to word-colouring and the rhythmic inflexions of his native language greet the Gothic imagery of Bartók's solemn opening bars. The main protagonists soon establish very definite personalities, Bluebeard/Tomlinson as commanding, inscrutable and just a little arrogant, von Otter/Judith as profoundly frightened but filled with curiosity. Haitink and the Berlin Philharmonic paint a rich aural backdrop that is neither too slow nor overly lugubrious and that shows due appreciation of Bartók's seamless scoring, especially in terms of the woodwind. The disembodied sighs that greet Judith's violent hammering on the first door mark a momentary retreat from the Philharmonie's ambient acoustic (or so it seems) and in so doing suggest – quite appropriately – a chilling 'world beyond'. Judith's shock as she recoils in horror is conveyed in clipped, halting tones by von Otter (note too how seductively she manipulates Bluebeard into opening the first door).

Beyond the expansive introduction come the doors themselves, and here too Haitink balances the 'outer' and 'inner' aspects of Bartók's score to perfection – whether in the torture chamber, the glowing textures of 'The Secret Garden' or the Brucknerian expanses of the fifth door, 'Bluebeard's Kingdom' (the opera's structural apex), launched here on a series of epic *crescendos*. Von Otter's stunned responses suggest lonely disorientation within a vast space, whereas the sullenness of the 'Lake of Tears' prompts an exquisite blending of instrumental timbres, most particularly between brass and woodwind. Haitink draws an aching curve to the string writing, but when Judith rushes panic-stricken towards the seventh door, fearful of Bluebeard's secret murders, he effects a gradual but cumulatively thrilling *accelerando*. The internment itself is devastating, while Bluebeard's helpless retreat marks a slow journey back to the questioning void. Recording live can have its pitfalls, but here the atmosphere is electric, the grasp of Bartók's sombre tone-painting – whether sung or played – absolute. EMI's engineering favours a full sound stage rather than picking out specific instrumental details, but the overall effect remains comprehensively satisfying.

Kertész, on the other hand, favours a far richer sound stage, with softer contours (his armoury suggests more weight than glinting steel, his torture chamber, anxiety rather than cruelty) and a passionate swell to the string writing. Kertész represents the opera's compassionate core. When it comes to the husband-and-wife team of Walter Berry and Christa Ludwig, one senses more a woman discovering sinister aspects of the man she loves than an inquisitive shrew intent on plundering Bluebeard's every secret. Here, Judith seems perpetually poised to take Bluebeard's arm and linger lovingly about him, while Berry's assumption of the title-role – which is beautifully, if not terribly idiomatically, sung – suggests neither *Angst* nor impatience. Ludwig, too, was in wonderful voice at the time of this recording, and instances of her eloquence are far too numerous to list individually. The transfer is superb, with a thunderous organ beyond the fifth door and merely the odd rogue edit or spot of tape hiss to betray the passing years.

Sir Arnold Bax
British 1883-1953

Symphonies – No. 1 in E flat major[a]; No. 7[b].
London Philharmonic Orchestra / [a]**Myer Fredman,** [b]**Raymond Leppard.**
Lyrita SRCD232 (78 minutes: ADD). Recorded [a]1970, [b]1974.   Ⓕ

Few English composers have expressed such intense and fiercely passionate emotions as Bax has in the first two movements of his First Symphony. Such rage and grief as can be found there seem to suggest a psycho-drama being played out, and when we learn that at the time of its composition (1921) Bax may still have been coming to terms with the aftermath of the Great War, the loss of friends in the Easter Rising in Ireland and the irretrievable breakdown of his marriage, it is tempting to imagine that the symphony is indeed exercising some kind of personal exorcism on these events. Bax himself, however, was always reluctant to admit the existence of such a 'programme' behind the symphony, and in many ways he was probably right to do so. Whatever personal experiences Bax had poured into it, the end result is unquestionably a powerful, cogent symphony of universal appeal. The Seventh and last of Bax's symphonies makes an intelligent and well-contrasted coupling. The first movement, though not without tension and some storm-tossed passages (very much a Baxian seascape this), has a prevailing mood of hope and expectation – as though embarking on some adventurous seaward journey to new lands, whilst the second movement finds Bax in wistful 'legendary' mood so evocative of the early tone-poems. The last movement begins by echoing the optimism of the first movement, but finally gives way, in the long and beautiful epilogue, to a mood of autumnal nostalgia and sad farewell. These are classic Lyrita recordings, with exceptionally fine performances and superb digital transfers.

Symphony No. 2 in E minor/C. November Woods.
Royal Scottish National Orchestra / David Lloyd-Jones.
Naxos 8 554093 (57 minutes: DDD). Recorded 1995.   Ⓢ🅴

From the grinding dissonances at the outset right through to the inconsolable coda, David Lloyd-Jones and his Scottish band bring out the unremitting toughness of Bax's uncompromising, breathtakingly scored Second Symphony; even the gorgeous secondary material in the first movement offers just an occasional shaft of pale, wintry sunlight. It helps, too, that Lloyd-Jones has clearly thought long and hard about the task in hand. How lucidly, for example, he expounds the arresting introduction, where the symphony's main building-blocks are laid out before us, and how well he brings out the distinctive tenor of Bax's highly imaginative writing for low wind and brass. The Scottish brass have a field-day (spectacularly clean-limbed trumpets in the finale especially). Lloyd-Jones proves an equally clear-sighted navigator through the storm-buffeted landscape of *November Woods*, for many people, Bax's greatest tone-poem. Thoroughly refreshing in its enthusiasm and exhilarating sense of orchestral spectacle, this recording has a physical impact and emotional involvement that genuinely compel. Overall, then, a veritable blockbuster, unmissable at the price.

Octet. String Quintet. Concerto. Threnody and Scherzo. In Memoriam.
Margaret Fingerhut *pf* **Academy of St Martin in the Fields Chamber Ensemble.**
Chandos CHAN9602 (72 minutes: DDD). Recorded 1997.   Ⓕ🅴

This is a beautiful and enterprising collection of works by Bax. *In Memoriam* for cor anglais, harp and string quartet probably dates from 1917. Subtitled 'An Irish Elegy', and like the *Elegiac Trio* from the same period, its poignant mood reflects Bax's despair at the tragic events of the Easter Rising. In the single-movement String Quintet (completed in January 1933) Bax draws some luscious, almost orchestral sonorities from his chosen forces. Scored for horn, piano and string sextet, the 1934 Octet (labelled 'Serenade' on the short score) is a two-movement work of strong appeal and engaging charm: the magically evocative opening brings with it echoes of those unforgettable horn solos in the Third Symphony's central *Lento*, while the icy glitter of the piano part from 1'53" in the second-movement *Scherzo* momentarily conjures up the far-Northern landscape of *Winter Legends*. The *Threnody and Scherzo* for bassoon, harp and string sextet of 1936 is perhaps less immediately striking. The writing is as fluent and accomplished as ever but the melodic material isn't quite as fresh as one might have wished. By contrast, the Concerto for flute, oboe, harp and string quartet now stands revealed as one of Bax's most likeable chamber offerings. This is a captivating transcription for septet of a Sonata for flute and harp from 1928 and proves to be an exquisite gem, its deft and joyous outer movements framing a lovely central 'Cavatina'. The dedicated, sensitive performances have been accorded warm, transparent sound.

Nonet. Oboe Quintet. Elegiac Trio. Clarinet Sonata. Harp Quintet.
Nash Ensemble (Philippa Davies *fl* Gareth Hulse *ob* Michael Collins *cl* Marcia Crayford, Iris Juda, Elizabeth Wexler *vns* Roger Chase *va* Christopher van Kampen *vc* Duncan McTier *db* Skaila Kanga *hp* Ian Brown *pf*).
Hyperion CDA66807 (73 minutes: DDD). Recorded 1995. Ⓕ 🄴

A truly first-rate modern recording of Bax's Nonet. What a bewitching creation it is, overflowing with beguiling invention and breathtakingly imaginative in its instrumental resource (the sounds created are often almost orchestral). Bax worked on the Nonet at the same time (1929-30) as he was composing his Third Symphony and there are striking similarities between the two works. The Nash Ensemble (under the direction of Ian Brown) gives a masterly, infinitely subtle reading. The remainder of the disc brings comparable pleasure. The delightful Oboe Quintet (written for Leon Goossens in 1922) receives immensely characterful treatment, especially the jaunty, Irish-jig finale (such sparkling, richly communicative playing). The same is true of the lovely Harp Quintet, which is essayed here with a rapt intensity and delicious poise. In the hands of these stylish artists, the *Elegiac Trio* possesses a delicacy and gentle poignancy that are really quite captivating. That just leaves the engaging Clarinet Sonata, a work that has fared well in the recording studio over the last few years. Suffice to report, Michael Collins and Ian Brown are compelling advocates, and theirs is a performance to set beside (if not supersede) all rivals. Beautiful sound throughout.

David Bedford
British 1937

Symphony No. 1[a]. Recorder Concerto[b]. Alleluia Timpanis[c]. Twelve Hours of Sunset[d].
Piers Adams *recs* **Crouch End Festival Chorus;**
BBC Symphony Orchestra / [acd]**Jac van Steen,** [b]**Martyn Brabbins.**
NMCD049 (79 minutes: DDD). Text included. Recorded 1997. Ⓕ

These substantial works by David Bedford comprise a very mixed bag. By the mid-1970s, when *Alleluia Timpanis* and *Twelve Hours of Sunset* were written, he was exploring an expansive, backward-looking idiom that is still the most striking feature in the Recorder Concerto. *Alleluia Timpanis* makes an excellent case for this eclectic style. Imposing, dramatic, a terrific workout for a youth orchestra, abrasive and witty in its treatment of 'found' material (the *Alleluia psallat*) and not inclined to outstay its welcome. By contrast, *Twelve Hours of Sunset* rambles interminably, with less interesting material and a less convincing structure. The grand climax is very grand indeed in its speaker-rattling way, but 30 minutes is too long to wait for it. An even more powerful build-up occurs in the altogether more cogent and engaging music of the Symphony No. 1 (1985). You may well be reminded of Percy Grainger, another composer whose liking for happy endings and boldly sculptured designs dispenses the freshest of musical air. The freshness of Bedford's Recorder Concerto is somewhat tainted by the relatively routine nature of the material, engaging though it is, and brilliantly played. There can be nothing but praise for either the recordings or performances on this disc, and two of the works, at least, will make it clear why Bedford's music deserves to be heard.

Ludwig van Beethoven
German 1770-1827

Piano Concertos – No. 1 in C major, Op. 15; No. 2 in B flat major, Op. 19; No. 3 in C minor, Op. 37; No. 4 in G major, Op. 58; No. 5 in E flat major, Op. 73, 'Emperor'.

Piano Concertos Nos. 1-5. Piano Sonata in C minor, Op. 111.
Wilhelm Kempff *pf*
Berlin Philharmonic Orchestra / Ferdinand Leitner.
DG 427 237-2GX3 (three discs: 195 minutes: ADD). Recorded 1960s. Ⓜ 🆁🆁

Kempff was never a heavyweight among Beethoven pianists. What he had was intellect and imagination in perfect balance, a fabulous touch, great rhythmic *élan*, and a kind of improvisatory zeal that – translated into other terms – can best be described as a true and abiding sense of wonder. And how beautifully Leitner and the Berlin Philharmonic accompany Kempff. This was the new young Berlin Philharmonic of the early 1960s, poet-musicians to a man, trained to listen and respond and then, in performance, take wing into precisely those areas of mind and imagination that were Kempff's own natural habitat. Kempff's recording of the first two concertos dates from the early 1960s, but the sound quality is pleasingly open and full-bodied, so that the soloist's pearly, immaculate tone quality is heard to good effect. Kempff and Leitner enjoy what is obviously a close rapport and their aristocratic, Olympian but poetic music-making suits both works admirably.

His cadenzas, his own in the first four concertos, will infuriate some as much as they will delight those of us – people who like steam trains and still refer to the wireless – who occasionally tire of all the regimentation and ratiocination of modern music-making. His account of the *Emperor* remains a classic recording that sounds very well in DG's remastering of the 1962 originals which often bring out previously unnoticed orchestral details with remarkable immediacy. This applies to the set as a whole, which is a very tempting proposition, quirky cadenzas and all. In the Fourth Piano Concerto (1961) you may be less than happy with his decision to use his own cadenzas, but the performance as a whole is such a joy, so light-filled, that even that qualification tends to fade into insignificance. It sounds especially radiant in these transfers. Despite a touch of gruffness in some of the orchestral tuttis in the *Emperor* it, too, generally comes up with glistening clarity. In many ways these are the liveliest performances of all the complete sets available, physically and intellectually, since Schnabel's pre-war set (available on Arkadia) with a matchless, if paradoxical, blend of rigour, energy, delight, and inspired whimsy.

Piano Concertos Nos. 1-5.
Claudio Arrau *pf*
Staatskapelle Dresden / Sir Colin Davis.
Philips 422 149-2PH3 (three discs: 189 minutes: DDD). Recorded 1986-88.   Ⓕ

With its sometimes diffuse structuring and recurrent strain of fantasy, Beethoven's C minor Piano Concerto is tricky to bring off, though in a good performance a larger coherence will generally emerge, not least because of Beethoven's long-term exploitation of a pun on the schizoid G sharp/A flat. Initially, the *Largo*'s E major tonality seems merely bleakly to confront the prevailing C minor and E flat major; but all is revealed at the point of transition into the finale when the violins' G sharp in the *Largo*'s final chord is swiftly contradicted and reaffirmed by the piano at the start of the *Rondo*. After that it's a case of 'watch this space'. This seemingly abstruse detail is mentioned because the moment implies the kind of segue that Beethoven will make mandatory in the lead to the finales of his last two piano concertos. You may well experience horror, then, when you find that Philips has split the C minor Concerto across two discs, with the break coming, believe it or not, between the Concerto's slow movement and finale. This was Arrau's fourth recording of the C minor Concerto and it is far removed in style from the rather more extrovert and brilliant 1947 recording with the Philadelphia Orchestra under Ormandy (once available on Columbia), the accompaniment bright but sometimes slovenly in rhythm. This performance is far better accompanied and is touched with a host of fresh insights conveyed in phrasing and tone-colouring of a rare and settled beauty. Arrau, at best, gives us music-making of rare depth and breeding, but the performances are perhaps best taken singly, the *Emperor* first, followed by the readings of the G major and C major Concertos.

Piano Concertos Nos. 1-5. Choral Fantasia C minor, Op. 80.
Daniel Barenboim *pf*
John Alldis Choir; New Philharmonia Orchestra / Otto Klemperer.
EMI CMS7 63360-2 (three discs: 211 minutes: ADD). Recorded 1967.   Ⓜ

Klemperer had done concert cycles, perhaps most memorably in London in the 1950s with Claudio Arrau but his decision to record the piano concertos at the age of 82 came as a result of his admiration for the most precociously talented of all young Beethoven pianists at the time, Daniel Barenboim. Barenboim was 25 and about to embark on what was to be an exceptionally fine cycle of the Beethoven piano sonatas. He was steeped in Beethoven and perhaps peculiarly well suited to the concertos which, we should not forget, are essentially a young man's music. It was a fascinating pairing, Klemperer and Barenboim contrasted in age and to some extent in temperament but at the same time symbiotically at one musically. Had this not been the case, Barenboim would have been swamped, lost in the wash of Klemperer's accompaniments which deliver the orchestral argument and the orchestral detail with an articulacy and authority unique in the history of these works on record. The performance of the B flat Concerto, the first historically if not numerically, is a typical joy, full of fire and grace and unstoppably vital. Given Klemperer's propensity for taking slow tempos in Beethoven, you might imagine him being taken for a ride by the young Barenboim in the B flat and C major finales. But not a bit of it. It is Klemperer, as much as his youthful soloist, who seems to be the driving force here. Rarely on record has the slow movement of the C major Concerto been played with so natural a sense of concentrated calm, the whole thing profoundly collected on the spiritual plane. One of the joys of the Barenboim/Klemperer cycle is its occasional unpredictability: rock-solid readings that none the less incorporate a sense of 'today we try it this way'.

Ensemble is mostly first-rate during the cycle. The tricky coda of the first movement of the C minor Concerto is both rapt and dramatic. But in the coda of the first movement of the G major there is little doubt that Klemperer drags the pulse. And elsewhere there are some occasionally awkward adjustments to be made between soloist and orchestra. At the time of its initial appearance, the *Emperor* performance was generally adjudged a success. It is again broadly conceived. At first the finale seems a little staid; but later the 6/8 rhythms are made to dance and the performance has a burning energy by the end. So does the account of the *Choral Fantasia*, always one of the set's rarer delights. Barenboim manages to be both imposing and playful in the piano preface. Given Klemperer's magisterial style and authority, this set could have emerged as five symphonies with piano obbligato. In fact, it is a set of rare authority and spontaneity, and given the slightly unconventional idea of the soloist as *primus inter pares*, it is probably unique.

Piano Concertos Nos. 1-5.
Alfred Brendel *pf*
Vienna Philharmonic Orchestra / Sir Simon Rattle.
Philips 462 782-2PH3 (three discs: 178 minutes: DDD). Recorded 1998.　　　　　Ⓕ

Happily, Alfred Brendel's fourth recorded cycle of the Beethoven piano concertos shares with the previous three qualities of energy, sensibility, intellectual rigour and high pianistic finish which made the earlier recordings so interesting to contemplate. There has never been anything less than first-rate about the recording partners he has worked with in these concertos and all the cycles have their moments of inspired togetherness. For example, Brendel has always played all five slow movements supremely well, drawing the orchestra around him like a celebrant at the communion table (here we have even finer performances than we have previously had).

In the two early concertos the Vienna Philharmonic's playing has a sweetness and allure, in the grander, later works a black-browed power, that is specially its own. Brendel's playing in the early concertos recalls his fine recordings of the early sonatas and the early and late *Bagatelles*, but it is as a private person impatient with the conventions and frock-coated formalities of the concertos as 'public' works. (It is not for nothing that the cadenzas shine so brightly out, particularly the astonishing and anachronistically late third cadenza Brendel uses in the first movement of the First Concerto.) With the Third Concerto we move into a different world. This is a marvellous performance from all three partners, purposeful and robust, the tonic C minor the cue for a reading which is full of darkness and menace, basses to the fore, drums at the ready. The finale is particularly ominous (relieved only by a gloriously lustrous clarinet solo) after an account of the slow movement, full-toned yet deeply quiet, the like of which one might dream of but rarely hope to hear. The C minor Concerto's heroic antitype, the *Emperor* in E flat, fares less well. Not the slow movement or finale, but the first movement which is slower than heretofore, to no very good effect. Perhaps it is that interpreters nowadays are less happy than their predecessors were with Beethoven's heroic persona. Back in the private world of the Fourth Concerto, where charmed magic casements open on the foam of perilous seas in faerie lands forlorn, soloist, orchestra and conductor are at their inspired best. Brendel's glittering, wonderfully propelled account of the solo part is superbly backed by playing of real fire and sensitivity. It is a powerful performance, too. The recordings are first-rate and have been generally well assembled.

Piano Concertos Nos. 1-5. Rondos, Op. 51.
Wilhelm Kempff *pf*
Berlin Philharmonic Orchestra / Paul van Kempen.
DG Dokumente mono 435 744-2GDO3 (three discs: 189 minutes: ADD). Recorded 1953.　　Ⓜ🄷

Kempff's Berlin cycle with Paul van Kempen has long been a collectors' item, often preferred to the Leitner set reviewed above. Apart from Kempff's whimsical though not ineffective line in home-grown cadenzas, these are exemplary performances in matters of style and execution. Yet they are something more. The cycle gives an extraordinary sense of the imaginative dimension of the first four concertos. As the eighteenth century turned into the nineteenth so the mists of romanticism began to drift across the landscape. The 1960s stereo set has an equally fine First Concerto and a better recorded *Emperor*. There is generally more glitter and dash. But the Second, Third and Fourth Concertos are all more revealingly realized in 1953. The mono recordings have been strikingly refocused. What on LP sounded recessed here takes on a startlingly physical immediacy. Whether this is an advance is debatable. At first it seems to be all gain: the slightly dim sounding ritornellos given a new weight and presence. On the other hand, the recordings are now rather more wearing on the ear. In the *Emperor* Concerto, for example, the mono recording sounds – and makes the piano sound – much coarser than one had remembered. However, with suitable doctoring of filters you will be able to come up with a tolerable mix of new-found immediacy and old-fashioned clarity and warmth. A marvellous set, none the less.

Piano Concertos Nos. 1-4[a]. Two Romances – No. 1 in G major, Op. 40; No. 2 in F major, Op. 50[b].
Stephen Kovacevich *pf* **Arthur Grumiaux** *vn*
[a]**BBC Symphony Orchestra / Sir Colin Davis;** [b]**Concertgebouw Orchestra / Bernard Haitink.**
Philips Duo 442 577-2PM2 (two discs: 152 minutes: ADD). Recorded 1970-74.   Ⓜ

The Beethoven concerto cycle that Stephen Bishop-Kovacevich (as he then was) and Sir Colin Davis recorded for Philips in London in the early 1970s blazed across the sky like a meteor. Kovacevich's own playing, and the orchestral work, individually and collectively, was fiery and refined. They were serious readings, intellectually rigorous; but they were also readings which left us in no doubt that the music in question is combustible stuff. You could say they are young men's readings, an emanation of the excited mood of the late 1960s: 'Bliss was it in that dawn to be alive/But to be young was very heaven!' Davis conducted a very different cycle for Arrau in the 1980s (see above), more profound, more inward-looking; Davis the Sage of Highbury rather than the white-jacketed whizz-kid of the Promenade. But this earlier set still sounds extraordinarily vivid, musically as well as technically.

Piano Concertos Nos. 1-5.
Maurizio Pollini *pf*
Berlin Philharmonic Orchestra / Claudio Abbado.
DG 439 770-2GH3 (three discs: 174 minutes: DDD). Recorded live in 1992-93.   Ⓕ

There may be more individual and idiosyncratic interpreters of the music than Maurizio Pollini but there is none whose command, at best, is sovereign. The Fourth Concerto has a keenly felt sense of the evolving drama, and a slow movement where the dialogue between piano and orchestra is spellbinding in its intensity. Maybe Pollini is not yet entirely reconciled to Beethoven's prankish first concerto, the Concerto No. 2 in B flat. In the outer movements, he can seem brusque: ill-at-ease with Beethoven in his rumbustious, amorous, Hooray Henry mood. By contrast, the performance of the Third is a joy from start to finish. Abbado and Pollini are hand-in-glove, which gives this cycle a cohesiveness which Pollini's previous sets with Jochum and Böhm (both for DG) rather obviously lacked, though the Berliners don't play the first movement of the *Emperor* Concerto as commandingly as Böhm and the Vienna Philharmonic on the earlier recording. But the slow movement goes well, and the finale is more jovial than before. Musically, though, there are evident gains – in these live recordings – moments where the tension is palpable in a way that it rarely is in the recording studio. The sound is full-bodied and immediate, with applauses, a few squeaks, bumps and ill-timed coughs.

Piano Concertos Nos. 1 and 2.
Lars Vogt *pf*
City of Birmingham Symphony Orchestra / Sir Simon Rattle.
EMI CDC5 56266-2 (66 minutes: DDD). Includes a bonus disc of Piano Concerto No. 1 with Glenn Gould's cadenzas. Recorded 1995.   Ⓕ Ⓔ ⓇⓇ

This is a remarkable disc, as fine a recorded account of these two concertos as we had in the 1990s. Alongside these performances, most rivals sound unduly one-dimensional. Vogt's playing in the two slow movements is wonderfully pellucid, but deep too. One thinks of Kempff, here and in the exquisite shaping of the lyric meditation midway through the Second Concerto's first movement. The CBSO's playing is also a miracle of finely wrought colours and despite the fact that these performances have evidently been worked out with great care, they remain spontaneously alive in a way that is rare on record. In the B flat Concerto, the dialogue between soloist and orchestra in the first movement has a Haydnesque alertness. The slow movement is exquisitely done; the finale is an almost perfect re-enactment of Beethoven's impish game of musical hide-and-seek. Vogt is a great admirer of Glenn Gould. So much so that we have here a rather strange 'bonus'. The performance of the First Concerto is reprinted on a separate CD not with Beethoven's cadenzas (Vogt uses the big third cadenza in the first movement of the main performance) but with Gould's. Although it would probably not sway you one way or another in deciding whether or not to buy this disc, who needs further persuasion when faced with performances of this order of delight?

Piano Concertos Nos. 1 and 2.
Murray Perahia *pf*
Concertgebouw Orchestra / Bernard Haitink.
Sony Classical SK42177 (70 minutes: DDD). Recorded 1986. Ⓕ

It is a pleasure here to salute such all-round excellence: a very remarkable soloist, superb orchestral playing and direction, and a recording which gets everything right, offering the kind of sound picture and natural perspective of solo piano with orchestra as we might experience them from a good seat in the Concertgebouw itself where these performances were recorded. Precision, clarity of expression, variety of character, beauty of sound: these are the qualities which Haitink and Perahia sustain and through which their readings gain an illuminating force. And it's perhaps in the slow movements that the illumination brings the most distinguished results. Their raptness and distinctive colouring are established from the first notes, and the inward quality of the expression takes breath as if there was nothing to the business of delineating these great set-pieces, so special among the achievements of Beethoven's first maturity, except to sing them through. Perahia has the gift of reducing his voice to the quietest level and still remaining eloquent. The poise of the playing is classical, the authority of the soloist unblemished by any hint of exaggeration or false emphasis.

Piano Concertos Nos. 1 and 2. Rondo in B flat major, WoO6.
Robert Levin *fp*
Orchestre Révolutionnaire et Romantique / Sir John Eliot Gardiner.
Archiv Produktion 453 438-2AH (75 minutes: DDD). Recorded 1996. ⒻⓅ

What is striking about Levin's Beethoven concertos is not so much the distinctive sound world of his chosen instruments and orchestral accompaniment, as the subtlety of imaginative insight, vigour of intellect and sheer delight expressed in his music-making. This reaches boiling-point in his thrillingly improvised lead-ins and cadenzas where instinct so vibrantly recharges understanding. The period instruments of the ORR and the carefully chosen fortepianos are simply the highly efficient tools with which the musicians' vision is shaped. And the tension of newly assured, propulsive energy coiled within the first movement of the Concerto No. 1 in C surely re-creates about as convincingly as possible Beethoven's sheer excitement and struggle in working with both a developing language and fast-evolving instruments. But first things first. The dancing dotted rhythms of the opening of the Concerto No. 2 point to where this music came from as much as where it is going to. As Levin writes in his penetrating booklet-notes, in matters of rhetoric and thematic development Beethoven looked to Haydn; but his rhythmic and harmonic vocabulary was Mozart's. Levin's deep study of both enriches his voyage into Beethoven. The silvery treble of this fortepiano makes this movement far from earthbound; and the more luminous voice of the instrument chosen for the C major Concerto guides the articulation and breathing of its second movement in such a way that its pulse seems to find new, steady health. This disc also generously offers a revealing reconstruction of Beethoven's discarded and as yet unpublished *Rondo* in B flat.

Piano Concertos Nos. 1 and 2.
Martha Argerich *pf*
Philharmonia Orchestra / Giuseppe Sinopoli.
DG Masters Series 445 504-2GMA (65 minutes: DDD). Recorded 1985. Ⓜ

Argerich is an exceptionally brilliant pianist, but she needs to be if she is to master a world in which great issues are often rumbustiously addressed. Some works in the Beethoven canon have been tellingly illuminated by pianists like Clara Haskil and Dame Myra Hess but women who can take on Beethoven in his most bullish mood are few and far between. Argerich has something of the necessary dauntlessness; she has also studied with some of the most distinguished as well as the most radical of post-war Beethoven pianists, including Gulda, Michelangeli, and Kempff who as long ago as 1970 singled out Argerich for special praise. She is, of course, a brilliant technician; but there is also a fantastic streak in her make-up, a capacity for creative fantasy, which is needed if areas of these remarkable works are to be brought fully and vividly to life. In both these early concertos, her touch is light and expert. It is difficult to fault Argerich although her performance will unsettle the concentration of some collectors who may be happier with Kempff's performances with Leitner (reviewed above). Sinopoli is at once attentive and unobtrusive in the C major Concerto, a perfect foil to Argerich. In the B flat Concerto, both Argerich and Sinopoli seem intent on personal point-making. There is room for private improvisation in this concerto as Kempff has amply demonstrated, but it is the pianist who must give the lead here. DG's recording is very agreeable, the ampleness of the orchestral acoustic offset by a certain distance and depth of perspective.

Piano Concertos Nos. 1 and 5.
Michael Roll *pf*
Royal Philharmonic Orchestra / Howard Shelley.
Tring International Royal Philharmonic Collection TRP075 (70 minutes: DDD). Recorded 1995.　Ⓢ

This is a fresh, festive and properly assertive account of the *Emperor* Concerto, coupled with a performance of the C major Concerto (an unusual pairing but a shrewd one) in which the earlier work reveals its own imperial ambitions. Such faults as there are, are usually faults in the right direction. The finale of the C major Concerto is here very fast and fierce: quicker than Beethoven's *Rondo-Allegro*, and not especially *scherzando*. What comes out is the aggressive, iconoclastic side of Beethoven's personality. It is also a big-boned performance, deploying a substantial orchestra in a lively acoustic. This suits the *Emperor* but could be thought to give the earlier work a slightly bloated feel. If, in the final analysis, it does not, it is because the performance itself has an all-redeeming urgency and spontaneity about it. In the end, what marks these performances out from their more run-of-the-mill rivals is the musicianly accord that exists between Michael Roll and his pianist-conductor, Howard Shelley. The performance of the *Emperor* is strong and grammatical but it is no mere hammer-and-tongs affair; the visionary side of the work is caught in a host of fine shadings and quiet accommodations of rhythm and sound between piano and orchestra.

Piano Concertos Nos. 2 and 5.
Evgeni Kissin *pf*
Philharmonia Orchestra / James Levine.
Sony Classical SK62926 (69 minutes: DDD). Recorded 1996.　Ⓕ🄴

From his very first entry, in the B flat Concerto, Kissin is revealed as a Beethoven player of great articulacy, brilliance and sensitivity after the manner of such pianists as Kempff, Solomon, and Gilels. The playing is vital and fluent, the technique awesome, not least in the way Kissin is able to refine his tone and taper dynamics in the high-lying coloratura passages where Beethoven's writing is at its most inspired and rarefied. The recitative at the end of the slow movement is predictably beautiful: intense and otherworldly. Levine draws from the Philharmonia playing that is both spirited and engaged. The recorded sound is admirable, too: strong and clean yet appropriately intimate. The performance of the *Emperor* Concerto is also very fine. If you take the view that this is essentially a symphony with piano obbligato, you may hanker after a grander kind of musical theatre than that provided by Levine. He directs with decision and accompanies superbly. Kissin, too, plays with great flair and technical security. If there is a problem here it is with the articulation of the simple-seeming lyric statements where a degree of self-consciousness occasionally creeps in: where the flow is arrested and music suddenly seems to be walking on stilts. There is an element of this in the slow movement, though Kissin's playing of the bleak, trailing 24-bar-long *diminuendo* close is masterly. Kissin takes a rather dashing view of the finale. This is very much a young man's view of the music, but weighty too, such is the power of his technique.

Piano Concertos Nos. 3 and 4.
Murray Perahia *pf*
Concertgebouw Orchestra / Bernard Haitink.
Sony Classical SK39814 (70 minutes: DDD). Recorded 1986.
Gramophone Award Winner 1986.　Ⓕ🆁🆁

These performances have rightly been described as exceptional. They were directly compared to Alfred Brendel's accounts with James Levine (on Philips) but in the event, there is little to choose between these two distinguished soloists. The first movements are brilliantly and sensitively etched (Perahia uses Beethoven's bigger first cadenza in the first movement of the G major Concerto). Tempos are steady but with a fine degree of forward projection. Once past the daunting opening solo, Perahia plays the C minor's slow movement with great sureness and subtlety of touch; and with Haitink as his partner the exchanges in the G major Concerto's slow movement are memorably brought off. Note the superior quality of the Sony recordings and the wonderfully judicious accompaniments prepared for Perahia by the Concertgebouw Orchestra under Haitink. If there is little to choose between Perahia and Brendel as soloists, there is a great gulf between Haitink, who is exemplary, and Levine who is unexceptional. This CD reissue confirms the high quality of the recording whilst at the same time giving complete stability to the sound image.

Piano Concertos Nos. 3 and 4.
Mitsuko Uchida *pf*
Royal Concertgebouw Orchestra / Kurt Sanderling.
Philips 446 082-2PH (72 minutes: DDD). Recorded 1994 (No. 3 recorded live).   Ⓕ

The playing on this formidable pairing of works is at once brilliant and sensitive, rigorous and free-spirited. Of the two performances, that of the Fourth Concerto is perhaps the more memorable. Uchida re-creates the solo part with flair and imagination, and dazzling technique. And what a wonderful voyage of discovery the slow movement is here. If the performance seems a touch mellower and more confiding than that of the C minor Concerto, it is perhaps because it was being played live to an audience in the Concertgebouw, a hall whose famous acoustic can be a shade severe when empty. What we have here in the Fourth Concerto is a first-rate concert-hall perspective (with the applause edited out). Some might argue that the C minor Concerto is a severe piece. Certainly, this generally appears to be Sanderling's and Uchida's view of the first movement. The performance is wonderfully alive, which is more than can be said for 75 per cent of extant recordings of this music, but there are pianists – Kempff for example – who have made the music of the first movement move a shade more gracefully and songfully than Uchida does here. The slow movement, by contrast, emerges as a wonderfully rapt soliloquy for the solo pianist, the orchestra doing little more than make simple acts of obeisance before the soloist. (Rather stiff acts of obeisance: throughout the C minor Concerto Sanderling is inclined to make the orchestra sit rather heavily on down-beats and *sforzandos*.) The recording of the C minor Concerto is best heard at a safe distance. Played too loud or heard too close it can seem unduly fierce and odd blemishes show up.

Piano Concerto No. 3. Piano Trio in B flat major, Op. 97, 'Archduke'.
Solomon *pf* **Henry Holst** *vn* **Anthony Pini** *vc*
BBC Symphony Orchestra / Sir Adrian Boult.
Dutton Laboratories mono CDLX7015 (71 minutes: ADD). Recorded 1944.   Ⓑ🄷

These performances remind us of Solomon's classic stature; the outer sobriety yet inner strength and radiance of his interpretations. By apparently saying so little, he often said everything. Such quality is surely demonstrated to perfection in the *Archduke* Trio, where he transcends the problems created by the sad lack of assurance of his colleagues. His subdued opening to the finale could well seem shy or hesitant in the case of lesser artists, yet such discretion surely stems from an innate musical assurance. And in the final pages he achieves a truly ineffable sense of calm and transparency. In the Concerto you may miss something of, say, Kempff's irrepressible wit and sparkle. Solomon, as it were, takes a middle course, emphasizing rather than negating Beethoven's connection with Mozart; the Apollonian as well as Dionysian side of his genius. You may find his way of making Beethoven's drama, his C minor of life, almost too civilized, though there is a dancing rhythmic lightness in the final pages absent from other more strenuously and energetically pointed performances. He also opts for Clara Schumann's richly eventful cadenza. Throughout, Solomon is at his greatest in the slow movements of these works, where he somehow creates the musical equivalent of great pools of quiet and light. Both an indomitable and speculative presence, this great artist always allowed his listeners their own space. Indeed, his performances are like a firm but gentle rebuke to all who have the temerity to thrust their own personalities to the fore. Dutton's transfer is very successful.

Beethoven Piano Concerto No. 4[a].
Saint-Saëns Piano Concerto No. 2 in G minor, Op. 22[b].
Artur Rubinstein *pf*
[a]**Royal Philharmonic Orchestra / Sir Thomas Beecham;**
[b]**Paris Conservatoire Orchestra / Philippe Gaubert.**
Testament mono SBT1154 (53 minutes: ADD). Recorded 1947 and 1939.   Ⓕ🄷

Rubinstein was unhappy with Gaubert's partnership and the recorded sound in this performance of Saint-Saëns's Second Concerto and he withdrew his permission for release, with the result that this corruscating performance lay entombed and forgotten in the EMI archives. True, Gaubert finds it hard to keep pace with Rubinstein's exuberance which takes virtuosity to the very edge. The closing pages in particular degenerate into an approximate rough-and-tumble. Although Saint-Saëns marks the first-movement development *Un poco animato*, Rubinstein is off like the proverbial hare, scattering all before him. Yet listen to his magically inflected opening or the instantly recognizable depth of his *cantabile* in the elegantly side-stepping second subject and you are in the presence of a master pianist. His *Scherzo* is a riot of high-jinks; a ripple of laughter here, a sly wink there (Saint-Saëns's Second was always among Rubinstein's popular successes).

Beethoven's Fourth may seem an odd bed-fellow for the Saint-Saëns, a linking of Teutonic poetry with Gallic levity. And yet, with both in Rubinstein's hands, you are made to sense a spiritual kinship and never more so than when he chooses Saint-Saëns's gloriously anachronistic cadenzas, spun off with all of his unique virtuoso relish. Elsewhere it is very much a case of full steam ahead. The central climax's anguish is played down and there are times in the finale where Rubinstein's outgoing nature makes the music fall into predictable pattern-making rather than express musical significance. The partnership with Sir Thomas is, however, infinitely superior to Gaubert's in the Saint-Saëns and the 1947 recording is a clear advance on 1939. Whether you prefer this or that pianist in either of these concertos is oddly beside the point. Rubinstein is, after all, Rubinstein, and both these performances tell you that with a mere flick of his wrist he could play most other pianists under the table.

Piano Concertos Nos. 4 and 5.
Emil Gilels *pf*
Philharmonia Orchestra / Leopold Ludwig.
Testament SBT1095 (73 minutes: ADD). Recorded 1957.　　　　　　　Ⓕ🅗

This is one of the – perhaps *the* most – perfect accounts of the Fourth Concerto ever recorded. Here poetry and virtuosity are held in perfect poise, with Ludwig and the Philharmonia providing a near-ideal accompaniment. The recording is also very fine, though be sure to gauge the levels correctly by first sampling one of the tuttis. If the volume is set too high at the start, you will miss the stealing magic of Gilels's and the orchestra's initial entries and you will be further discomfited by tape hiss that, with the disc played at a properly judged level, is more or less inaudible. The recording of the *Emperor* Concerto is also pretty good, not quite on a par with that of the Fourth Concerto. Ludwig and the orchestra tend to follow Gilels rather than always integrate with him and there are times, too, especially in the slow movement, when Gilels's playing borders on the self-indulgent. This is not, however, sufficient reason for overlooking this fine and important Testament reissue.

Piano Concertos Nos. 4 and 5.
Maurizio Pollini *pf*
Vienna Philharmonic Orchestra / Karl Böhm.
DG Classikon 439 483-2GCL (71 minutes: ADD). Recorded 1976.　　　　　　　Ⓑ

This is an outstanding coupling of Pollini's earlier recordings of these works (the complete set of his later recordings with Abbado is reviewed above). The present performances are, arguably, more spontaneous and the recording (especially of the piano) more natural, with the VPO expanding warmly within the ambience of the Grosser Saal of the Vienna Musikverein. These readings are freshly individual, with poise and poetry nicely balanced in both works, and with Böhm providing admirable accompaniments (the interchange in the slow movement of the G major is memorable). And Pollini is suitably magisterial in the *Emperor*. Most enjoyable, and stimulating too.

Piano Concerto No. 4. Triple Concerto in C major, Op. 56.
Michael Roll *pf* **Jean-Jacques Kantorow** *vn* **Raphael Wallfisch** *vc*
Royal Philharmonic Orchestra / Howard Shelley.
Tring International Royal Philharmonic Collection TRP077 (66 minutes: DDD). Recorded 1995. Ⓢ🄴

These excellent performance are beautifully conducted throughout and Michael Roll is an extremely alert and sensitive soloist in the Fourth Piano Concerto. Equally, a team of soloists has been assembled for the Triple Concerto that really is a team, musically distinguished but modest too, no mere aggregation of stars. The playing is fresh, alert, sensitive and full of joy. And the recording? That too is superb. So, are there no drawbacks? Perhaps one could point to an occasional roughness of intonation in Kantorow's playing in the Triple Concerto and the occasional moment of stiffness in Roll's detailing of some of the stellar passagework of the first movement of the Fourth Concerto, but that would be to set up a Council of Perfection into which other things in both performances (including much of Wallfisch's contribution) would be openly admitted. This is a super bargain in every way, a disc you will want to return to for the high finish of its musicianship and its irresistible freshness.

Piano Concerto No. 5.
Murray Perahia *pf*
Concertgebouw Orchestra / Bernard Haitink.
Sony Classical Masterworks SK42330 (39 minutes: DDD).　　　　　　　Ⓕ🆁🆁

This is an excellent *Emperor*, on a level with the best. Comparisons with other pianists, at this level, can be rather futile. It is a splendidly engineered recording, with a natural concert-hall type of balance, and there is good presence to the sound and depth to the perspective. The presentation of the orchestral detail allows one to delight in it, and perhaps to discover new subtleties, without a moment of unease as to whether anything has been forced into the wrong kind of relief. Perahia's performance has the freshness and natural authority one has now come to expect of him in Beethoven. His reading might be described as uncomplicated if that didn't risk implying that it is in some way lightweight, or that he plays like a child of nature. The weight is certainly there, in sound (when he wants it) as in expression. Perahia himself has spoken of the happy experience of making this Beethoven cycle with Haitink (the other concertos are reviewed above). It has indeed been a successful collaboration, and a joyous quality about the music-making communicates itself quite strongly from the beginning.

Piano Concerto No. 5.
Arturo Benedetti Michelangeli *pf*
Vienna Symphony Orchestra / Carlo Maria Giulini.
DG 419 249-2GH (42 minutes: ADD). Recorded live in 1979.   Ⓕ

There has, over the years, been mixed reactions to Michelangeli's Beethoven. He was a most perplexing artist, perplexing because he liked to keep his musical personality well hidden – or at any rate mysterious – behind the armour-plated magnificence of his playing; disconcerting too because it is hard to arrive at a reasoned assessment of readings of classical music by someone who is evidently not a man of balance. To interpret texts of the classical masters in a way which will give them the most vivid life does not seem to be his principal concern. There could be an intellectual *froideur* about his playing of Beethoven which verges on the disdainful and which was sometimes more than off-putting. Not here though. This performance was recorded at a public performance in the Musikverein. He drives the opening flourishes hard, and thereafter responds keenly to Giulini's exposition, grand but always moving forward, matching it with a purpose that seems to derive from just that long-range musical thinking which is so often missing in his accounts of the other concertos. There is spaciousness, and time for everything, and always that rock-like strength of rhythm. The detailing could hardly be bettered but isn't allowed to deflect attention from our perception of the form. The security of the technique is enough to make most other pianists attempting an Olympian view of the concerto seem clumsy; but it does not draw attention to itself. Since the depth of his sonority is perfectly matched to the orchestra's, it makes for some especially exciting listening in the finale. Great playing, then, by a great pianist.

Piano Concerto No. 5. Triple Concerto in C major, Op. 56[a].
Leon Fleisher, Eugene Istomin *pfs* **Isaac Stern** *vn* **Leonard Rose** *vc*
Cleveland Orchestra / George Szell; [a]**Philadelphia Orchestra / Eugene Ormandy.**
Sony Classical Essential Classics SBK46549 (74 minutes: ADD). Recorded 1961, [a]1964.   Ⓜ

Leon Fleisher's recording of the *Emperor* is very powerful indeed. He was relatively young at the time and obviously George Szell had a considerable influence on the reading, but the solo playing is remarkably fresh and its pianistic authority is striking. That great octave passage in the first movement, just before the recapitulation, is enormously commanding, and Fleisher's lyrical playing, in the slow movement especially, has striking poise. Szell keeps the voltage high throughout, but for all its excitement this is by no means a hard-driven, unfeeling interpretation. The Cleveland Orchestra plays with fervour and there is a joyously buoyant rhythmic lift in the main theme of the finale. The recording is bright, bold and forward in the CBS 1960s manner, and the Severance Hall acoustic prevents any ugliness. A splendid *Emperor*, then, but what makes this disc even more enticing is the inclusion of an equally distinguished version of the Triple Concerto, recorded in Philadelphia Town Hall (a much more successful venue than many used over the years for this great orchestra). The very gentle opening by the orchestra is full of anticipatory tension, and at the beginning of the slow movement Ormandy's preparation for Rose's glorious cello solo demonstrates what a superb accompanist he is. Indeed, this is no mere accompaniment, but a complete partnership. Although Stern's personality dominates marginally, the three soloists play together like a chamber-music team, without in any way submerging their individuality. The sound is very good for its time. This entire disc is a prime example where Sony's sobriquet 'Essential Classics' is justly appended.

Piano Concerto No. 5. Choral Fantasia in C minor, Op. 80.
Melvyn Tan *fp*
Schütz Choir of London; London Classical Players / Sir Roger Norrington.
EMI Reflexe CDC7 49965-2 (52 minutes: DDD). Text and translation included.
Recorded 1989.   ⒻⓅ

The opening, threefold flourish of the *Emperor* Concerto has always seemed to be the herald of a work of huge, and self-aware, grandeur; that is certainly how it is generally played, with due weight, deliberation and sense of rhetoric. Beethoven's *espressivo* markings towards the end of the first two parts of the flourish certainly seem to demand something of the kind. In this extraordinarily fine and highly provocative performance on period instruments it is simply a flourish, brilliant, to be sure, but with no special implications about what is to follow. And perhaps that is right, because what follows is not the *Emperor* we are used to but a work expressively much leaner. The tempos, of course, are quickish, in Roger Norrington's usual manner. The performance is very much of a piece, and it is no surprise that the arrival of the recapitulation, usually so big a moment, carries very little rhetorical weight here; the same goes for the tutti preceding the cadenza. You will be content to trade some of this for the thrilling sound of the fortepiano with period orchestral instruments, which reveals so much that is sometimes lost. Tan's kind of pianism tends to emphasize the closeness of Beethoven not only to Mozart but also to Chopin, and this may strike listeners particularly in the *Adagio*, with the high piano writing and floating lines. There is little dawdling, and gentle pathos rather than profound contemplation. The finale has plenty of exuberance and brilliance and Tan plays it commandingly, but if you expect grandeur and mystery you may feel slightly short-changed. The sheer keyboard mastery of Tan and the razor-keen playing of Norrington's group are in a class by themselves, and enormously exciting simply for what they are. The filler, the *Choral Fantasia*, receives as convincing a performance as any, done with a fine swing to the rhythms, cleanly played by Tan and well sung. In all a very attractive and stimulating disc.

Piano Concerto No. 5. Choral Fantasia in C minor, Op. 80.
Robert Levin *fp*
Monteverdi Choir; Orchestre Révolutionnaire et Romantique / Sir John Eliot Gardiner.
Archiv Produktion 447 771-2AH (60 minutes: DDD). Text and translation included.
Recorded 1995.   Ⓕ Ⓟ

You may find the very opening of the *Emperor* more disconcerting than Tan's rival period version, not only because Gardiner's orchestra is fuller-bodied, underlining the discrepancy of scale, but because of the instrument Robert Levin has chosen. This 1812 fortepiano by Salvatore Lagrassa has body enough in the lower registers, but at the top there is a disconcertingly twangy, almost harp-like area leading at the very top to notes so unresonant that they sound like a xylophone. However, quickly enough your ears will adjust to the idiosyncrasies of the solo instrument, and you will appreciate the fine, positive qualities of a reading in which the soloist, matching Gardiner himself, takes a more freely expressive view than Tan, playing with a greater element of bravura. It would have been better if the disc had started with the *Choral Fantasia*, for there with the opening improvisation one has ample time to adjust to the scale and the individual sound of the fortepiano before the orchestra enters. The whole performance, too, has tremendous panache. Gardiner, not surprisingly, crowns the performance with a superb choral section, in which soloists and full chorus are cleanly contrasted. As a supplement Levin offers on separate tracks two alternative improvisations of his own, easily interchangeable with the one Beethoven published years after the first performance. There is similar exuberance to that of the *Fantasia* in the finale of the *Emperor*, with crystal-clear passagework from the soloist. In the two earlier movements Levin's speeds are slower than those of Tan (who is consistently fast, notably in the central *Adagio*). You may find it a help to play the disc at a relatively high volume, when the oddities of the fortepiano are less distracting. Though interpretatively this is probably the first choice for a period-performance *Emperor*, would-be purchasers should sample both discs first.

Violin Concerto in D major, Op. 61.

Beethoven Violin Concerto.
Bernstein Serenade.
Hilary Hahn *vn*
Baltimore Symphony Orchestra / David Zinman.
Sony Classical SK60584 (75 minutes: DDD). Recorded 1998.   Ⓕ Ⓔ ⒭⒭

At first glance, this would seem a pretty strange coupling, yet by trailing the most Olympian of classical violin concertos with a semi-concerto based on a Platonic dialogue Hilary Hahn and Sony suggest their own quaint form of programming logic. Hahn employs her sweet-centred tone with the utmost finesse and David Zinman's Baltimore accompaniment is smooth, unhurried and clear-thinking. Hahn opts for Kreisler's cadenza and makes a special feature of the simultaneous projection of themes, broadening the pace then re-entering into the movement, as if caught in a trance. Her approach is lyrical and unindulgent, though most definitely post-romantic. She is an immaculate technician who favours a calculated though richly expressive approach to phrasing. She breathes considerable warmth into the *Larghetto* (again, sensitively accompanied under Zinman) and offers a crisp account of the finale. Of its kind, this performance looks unbeatable. One of

Bernstein's most enduring works, the lovable 1954 *Serenade*, draws on ideas from Plato's *The Symposium*, principally those concerning love, and includes a gorgeous three-part song and a finale that looks sideways at *On the Waterfront* and forwards to *West Side Story*. Hahn's tender-hearted rendition lays claim to being the finest interpretation ever, aided and abetted by Zinman's firmly focused conducting. Both works are beautifully recorded.

Violin Concerto. Romances – No. 1 in G major, Op. 40; No. 2 in F major, Op. 50.
Gidon Kremer *vn*
Chamber Orchestra of Europe / Nikolaus Harnoncourt.
Teldec 9031-74881-2 (57 minutes: DDD). Recorded live in 1992.　　　　　　Ⓕ

Gidon Kremer offers one of his most commanding performances, both polished and full of flair, magnetically spontaneous from first to last. Rarely do you hear such consistently pure tone in this work and the orchestral writing too is superbly realized, with magical sounds in the slow movement in particular. It has become customary to treat the long first movement as expansively as possible but Kremer takes a much more urgent view, and after his thoughtful and dedicated, slightly understated reading of the slow movement, he and Harnoncourt round the performance off magically with a finale that skips along the more infectiously thanks to light, clean articulation and textures. Traditional performances seem heavyweight by comparison. The controversial point for some will be the cadenza in the first movement where he uses a transcription of the big cadenza which Beethoven wrote for his piano arrangement of the work. However, this is altogether one of the most refreshing versions of the concerto ever committed to record, backed up by crisp, unsentimental readings of the two *Romances*.

Violin Concerto. Romance No. 2.
Oscar Shumsky *vn*
Philharmonia Orchestra / Sir Andrew Davis.
ASV Quicksilva CDQS6080 (54 minutes: DDD). Recorded 1988.　　　　　　Ⓑ

Oscar Shumsky's recording of the Violin Concerto is one of the finest in the catalogue and was strongly recommended at premium price. In this reissue it is a bargain *par excellence*. The reading is relaxed and assured and has a serene purity of line, notably so in the memorable *Larghetto*, which is quite beautifully played. Sir Andrew Davis provides his soloist with admirable support and the orchestral contribution is highly sympathetic. The sound balance favours the soloist with something of a spotlight, but otherwise the recording is very good: those wanting a bargain-price version of this work could hardly better this, especially as the *Romance* in F major is given as an encore.

Violin Concerto. Romances Nos. 1 and 2.
Thomas Zehetmair *vn*
Orchestra of the Eighteenth Century / Frans Brüggen.
Philips 462 123-2PH (54 minutes: DDD). Recorded live in 1997.　　　　　　ⒻⓅ

This is a great performance, one that simply has to be heard. The first movement is built on a tug of war between dynamic extremes and, for once, it actually sounds like a concerto, and a brilliant one at that. The more familiar average playing time of around 25 minutes (Zehetmair's lasts a mere 22) tends, for all its beautiful effect, to compromise on forward momentum. Here, the use of period instruments adds extra fibre to the aural mix, and Brüggen's conducting has a pressing urgency about it that, again, intensifies the drama. The *Larghetto* is full of subtle nuances and telling inflexions, and the Rondo has great rhythmic verve. Two recording venues are used, the excellent Muziekcentrum at Enschede for the two *Romances* and the rather cavernous Vredenburg, Utrecht for the concerto. The former yields the more sympathetic acoustic (Zehetmair and Brüggen offer limpidly flowing performances of both pieces), but it is unlikely that the slightly rougher-edged concerto recording will give much cause for complaint. This is one of *the* recordings of Beethoven's Violin Concerto, and is to be strongly recommended.

Beethoven Violin Concerto[a].
Mendelssohn Violin Concerto in E minor, Op. 64[b].
Yehudi Menuhin *vn*
[a]**Philharmonia Orchestra,** [b]**Berlin Philharmonic Orchestra / Wilhelm Furtwängler.**
EMI mono CDM5 66990-2 (71 minutes: ADD). Recorded 1952-53.　　　　　　ⓂⒽ

Furtwängler and Menuhin enjoyed a long artistic partnership, and Menuhin's support for his older colleague was no small factor in Furtwängler's musical rehabilitation during the late 1940s after he had remained active in Nazi Germany. They recorded the Beethoven Concerto on two occasions, and this second version, made in 1953, has an extraordinary quality of spirituality and profundity. At once Furtwängler's conducting of the opening tutti has a magnificently arresting, weighty quality, and Menuhin's response, profound and rich in re-creative imagination shows the two great artists in perfect accord. Their account of this movement is on the largest scale, yet they convey Beethoven's vision in a very humane, approachable fashion. The slow movement has a highly concentrated yet serene character, with Menuhin's rapt, singing tone achieving rare eloquence, and the finale is superbly balanced, with an affecting sense of a shared, joyful experience. The recording sounds quite similar to the original LP issue, and is none the worse for that, for the quality is quite acceptable. The Mendelssohn was recorded a year earlier, and here remastering has brought a slight roughening in an orchestral sound which was never very ingratiating, though the defect is still not serious. Menuhin and Furtwängler float the first movement in an unhurriedly serene, elegantly shaped fashion. In the slow movement they achieve a touchingly tender, almost innocent quality and the finale, taken at a moderate tempo, has lightness and an appealingly eager character. Two very different works are here illuminated in appropriately contrasting fashion by two great artists.

Triple Concerto in C major, Op. 56.

Beethoven Triple Concerto[a].
Brahms Double Concerto in A minor, Op. 102[b].
David Oistrakh *vn* **Mstislav Rostropovich** *vc* **Sviatoslav Richter** *pf*
[a]Berlin Philharmonic Orchestra / Herbert von Karajan; [b]Cleveland Orchestra / George Szell.
EMI CDM5 66954-2 (70 minutes: ADD). Recorded 1969.　　　　　　　　Ⓜ🔲🔲

These are illustrious performances and make a splendid coupling. EMI planned for a long time to assemble this starry line-up of soloists, conductor and orchestra for Beethoven's Triple Concerto, and the artists do not disappoint, bringing sweetness as well as strength to a work which in lesser hands can sound clumsy and long-winded. The recording, made in a Berlin church in 1969, is warm, spacious and well balanced, placing the soloists in a gentle spotlight. Indeed, the sound need make no apology for its age, and since we also hear playing of effortless mastery this disc would be worth the money for this work alone. As it is, we also have the same great violinist and cellist playing another masterpiece with another superb orchestra and conductor of the time (the recording is also from 1969), this time in Cleveland. This account of Brahms's Double Concerto is perhaps the most powerful recorded performance since the days of Heifetz and Feuermann or Thibaud and Casals. The recording has come up extremely well in this remastering: although one cannot deny that the sound is not as smooth as can be achieved nowadays, one soon forgets that and is caught up in the magnificent music-making.

Triple Concerto. Choral Fantasia in C minor, Op. 80.
Beaux Arts Trio (Ida Kavafian *vn* Peter Wiley *vc* Menahem Pressler *pf*);
Mid-German Radio Chorus; Leipzig Gewandhaus Orchestra / Kurt Masur.
Philips 438 005-2PH (52 minutes: DDD). Recorded 1992-93.　　　　　　　　Ⓕ

Kurt Masur has rarely conducted more electrifying Beethoven performances on disc. The opening tutti of the concerto establishes a speed markedly faster than usual, and if the three soloists modify it slightly, the characteristic which marks this performance is its urgency. But there is no feeling of breathlessness, simply exhilaration. The evenness and clarity of Pressler's articulation in scales and passagework is a delight. As for the brief central meditation, led – like most main themes in this work – by the cello, it flows very warmly and naturally, with Peter Wiley just as rich and positive an artist as Pressler. This now stands as one of the very finest versions of a work which at last looks like being appreciated, not as a rarity, but as a pillar of the Beethoven canon. The *Choral Fantasia* is hardly likely to establish itself in a comparable niche, but this performance is most persuasive. The variations on the corny main theme are regularly pointed with engaging wit, not just by Pressler but by the wind soloists, and the brass sound is glorious. It is rather like having the choral finale of the Ninth anticipated with tongue-in-cheek. Balances are always difficult, not just in this work but notoriously in the Triple Concerto. The soloists are well focused and the orchestral sound is warm and full.

Triple Concerto. Choral Fantasia in C minor, Op. 80.
Itzhak Perlman *vn* **Yo-Yo Ma** *vc*
Chorus of the Deutsche Oper, Berlin; Berlin Philharmonic Orchestra / Daniel Barenboim *pf*
EMI CDC5 55516-2 (55 minutes: DDD). Text and translation included. Recorded live in 1995.　　Ⓕ

Though EMI's Berlin sound for Barenboim is warm with plenty of presence, and the soloists are justly balanced not too far in front, the textures grow opaque in tuttis. There is also an edge on the solo violin and cello tone, particularly the former, which is occasionally distracting. Even so, anyone responding to the zestful, infectiously sprung Berlin performance is unlikely to be overcritical of the sound, and the brass is very well caught. In this concerto the cellist is the leader, and Yo-Yo Ma's cello tone here is not as ample as, for example, Rostropovich's in an earlier EMI recording (reviewed above). Yet Ma's sound brings positive advantage in the tender, hushed intensity of his big opening solo in the slow movement. Unlike many so-called 'live performances' put on disc, these Berlin readings keep a few seconds of applause at the end of each work. If that for the *Fantasia* is markedly more enthusiastic than for the Concerto, the larger forces with chorus may partly account for that, as well as Barenboim's Furtwängler-like whipping up of speed in the final coda, an endearing touch.

Overtures – Coriolan, Op. 62; Die Geschöpfe des Prometheus, Op. 43; Die Ruinen von Athen, Op. 113; Fidelio, Op. 72; Leonore No. 1, Op. 138; No. 2, Op. 72; No. 3, Op. 72; Egmont, Op. 84.
Chamber Orchestra of Europe / Nikolaus Harnoncourt.
Teldec 0630-13140-2 (76 minutes: DDD). Recorded 1993-96. Ⓜ Ｅ

Harnoncourt's Beethoven overtures are highly eventful affairs that will have your critical faculties working overtime. Surprises emerge virtually by the bar. For example, the orchestral sonority is 'heated' not by the strings, but by the woodwind section. Here, the COE's string tone is sinewy and chaste, with lightly brushed bowing and agile phrasing, while the woodwinds sound far mellower than on most rival discs. Harnoncourt's preference for limpid, baleful woodwind phrasing is familiar from his recordings of baroque music and the option works well in this context. *Coriolan* features a mobile though never overprominent cello line, the coda more suggesting recollected tragedy than the torture of Coriolan's plight. *Prometheus* opens to thunderclap chords, then busies along excitedly with much animated banter between woodwinds. *Die Ruinen von Athen* is neon-lit and keenly attenuated and the *Fidelio* 'foursome' – the opera's overture plus the three *Leonores* – is delivered with a dramatic impetus that occasionally borders on abruptness. *Fidelio* itself features a majestic introduction and a leisurely, open-plan *Allegro* where individual voices take the lead and where the opening motive gallops back with tremendous vigour. *Leonore* No. 1 goes with a swing, the introduction to *Leonore* No. 2 suggests intimations of Berlioz and the way Harnoncourt tiers the accumulating woodwind lines is very impressive. A natural ebb and flow is common to both of these 'bigger' *Leonore* overtures; both feature a first-rate off-stage trumpet, and both have fiery codas (*Leonore* No. 3's 'last blast' climaxes with colossal power). The disc ends with a fairly forceful *Egmont* overture. All the recordings except *Coriolan* are live and convey a luminous, dynamic and realistically three-dimensional sound stage. Purchase will be mandatory for those without preconceptions.

Symphonies – No. 1 in C major, Op. 21; No. 2 in D major, Op. 36; No. 3 in E flat major, Op. 55, 'Eroica'; No. 4 in B flat major, Op. 60; No. 5 in C minor, Op. 67; No. 6 in F major, Op. 68, 'Pastoral'; No. 7 in A major, Op. 92; No. 8 in F major, Op. 93; No. 9 in D minor, Op. 125, 'Choral'.

Symphonies Nos. 1-9.
Edith Wiens *sop* **Hildegard Hartwig** *contr* **Keith Lewis** *ten* **Roland Hermann** *bar*
Chorus of the Hamburg State Opera; North German Radio Chorus;
North German Radio Symphony Orchestra / Günter Wand.
RCA Victor Symphony Edition 74321 20277-2 (five discs: 356 minutes: DDD).
Recorded 1985-88. Ⓑ 🆁🆁

In RCA's series of budget-price box-sets of major symphonies, this one stands out. Günter Wand's performances are inspired; he is a conductor who never imposes his own ego and never does anything for the sake of effect, resulting in performances that are honest, direct and unpretentious. His tempos are superbly judged; brisk, but not hurried, allowing the pristine articulation of the strings to come shining through (this needs to be heard to be believed; orchestral playing such as this is rare indeed). The orchestral balance is ideal, with woodwind textures nicely integrated into the orchestral sound, and this is supported by the excellent recorded sound which approaches demonstration quality. The First Symphony sets the pattern: strikingly fresh with keenly articulated, vigorous *allegros* and a degree of expressive warmth in the slow movement that is very satisfying. The *Eroica* is a strong reading, yet with an appealing underlying lyricism; and there is some splendid horn playing in the *Scherzo* and finale. The Fifth makes a powerful statement and the *Pastoral* is steadily paced yet has no lack of forward movement; here the recording misses something in the deep bass end, although the cellos sing warmly and the finale is radiant. Wand is generous with repeats and especially so in the Seventh, which is not pressed forward frenetically.

The Eighth is admirably spirited and the *Choral* provides a splendid culmination. Here the transparency of the recording is particularly striking at the very opening, and the slow movement is deeply eloquent. The soloists make a first-rate team in the last movement, notably the ardour of Keith Lewis and the firmness of Edith Wiens. The combined choruses sing with weight and fervour, and following Wand's broadening of the tempo at the movement's centre, the excitement of the closing section is rendered the more telling with an impressive balance adding to the impact. In short, it is hard to think of a relatively modern series of Beethoven symphonies which is better recorded or more rewarding to live with. It is the consistency of this set that is one of its prime virtues.

Symphonies Nos. 1-9.
Charlotte Margiono sop **Birgit Remmert** mez **Rudolf Schasching** ten **Robert Holl** bass
Arnold Schoenberg Choir; Chamber Orchestra of Europe / Nikolaus Harnoncourt.
Teldec 2292-46452-2 (five discs: 358 minutes: DDD). Recorded live in 1990-91.
Gramophone Award Winner 1992.   Ⓕ

Brimful of intrepid character and interpretative incident, Nikolaus Harnoncourt and the splendid Chamber Orchestra of Europe give us what is surely one of the most stimulating Beethoven symphony cycles of recent times. As Harnoncourt himself states in a lively interview for the accompanying booklet to this set: 'It has always been my conviction that music is not there to soothe people's nerves ... but rather to open their eyes, to give them a good shaking, even to frighten them.' So it transpires that there's a re-creative daring about his conducting – in essence an embracement of recent scholarly developments and Harnoncourt's own pungent sense of characterization – which is consistently illuminating, thus leaving the listener with the uncanny sensation that he or she is in fact encountering this great music for the very first time. In all of this Harnoncourt is backed to the hilt by some superbly responsive, miraculously assured playing from the COE: their personable, unforced assimilation of Harnoncourt's specific demands (complete with period-style lean-textured strings and bracingly cutting brass and timpani), allied to this conductor's intimate knowledge of the inner workings of these scores, make for wonderfully fresh, punchy results. In this respect Symphonies Nos. 6-8 in particular prove immensely rewarding, but the *Eroica* and (especially) the Fourth, too, are little short of superb. In sum, it's a cycle which excitingly reaffirms the life-enhancing mastery of Beethoven's vision for the 1990s and into the next century beyond.

Symphonies Nos. 1-9. Egmont Overture, Op. 84.
Lucia Popp sop **Carolyn Watkinson** contr **Peter Schreier** ten **Robert Holl** bass
Netherlands Radio Chorus; Concertgebouw Orchestra / Bernard Haitink.
Philips Bernard Haitink Symphony Edition 442 073-2PB5 (five discs: 365 minutes: DDD).
Recorded 1987.   Ⓑ

Haitink's second Beethoven cycle was greeted warmly when it first appeared; his virtues of textural rhythmic clarity well in evidence. He is often at his most impressive in the allegedly 'lighter' symphonies; Nos. 1, 8 and especially No. 4 are very enjoyable – vital, flexible, elegantly shaped and balanced, and thoroughly civilized. Perhaps the problem with the *Eroica*, Fifth, Seventh and *Choral* Symphonies is that they are a degree *too* civilized. This is no vision of a Beethoven – as one critic put it – 'storming heaven with his boots on'. Still, there is more than one way of approaching any great work, and for most of the set the phrase 'intensely agreeable' seems a good, bite-sized summary. Tempos almost always seem well chosen – except perhaps the slowish *Scherzos* of Nos. 2 and 4 – and it's good to find Haitink taking a less extreme view of scherzo-trio contrasts in No. 7 (and observing all the repeats in the *Scherzo*). The recordings have lost none of their virtues – breadth, depth, clarity, warmth of tone – in the transfers.

Symphonies Nos. 1-9.
Luba Orgonasova sop **Anne Sofie von Otter** mez **Anthony Rolfe Johnson** ten
Gilles Cachemaille bar
Monteverdi Choir; Orchestre Révolutionnaire et Romantique / Sir John Eliot Gardiner.
Archiv Produktion 439 900-2AH5 (five discs: 328 minutes: DDD). Recorded 1993-94.   Ⓕ ⓅⒺ

This set conducted by John Eliot Gardiner is remarkable and we suspect many will rate it as Mr Knightley rates Emma Woodhouse 'faultless in spite of her faults'. The tone is set by Peter Czorny's booklet essay 'In the Spirit of Rediscovery'. The recordings are offered, he tells us, in the hope of transporting the listener back 'to that moment when this music burst forth into a world of heroes, wars and revolution, creating its own world of the sublime and ineffable'. It is a theme that is developed by Gardiner himself in a characteristically robust and contentious 20-minute talk on the project that comes free on a sixth CD. Gardiner's opinion that Beethoven wanted his musicians to live dangerously has some peculiar consequences.

Symphony No. 1: The opening is superbly judged. Gardiner doesn't overplay the *Adagio molto*, and the *Allegro con brio*, always something of an awkward customer and often played with a fatal languor by members of the old German School, is pretty quick. After his absurdly brisk reading of the second movement, Gardiner goes on to conduct dazzlingly successful accounts of the *Scherzo* and finale. **Symphony No. 2:** This was the first symphony to be recorded and is very fine throughout. By following the written tempo markings and his own musical instincts Gardiner produces a perfomance of the first movement that, if anything, opens out the drama most compellingly. **Symphony No. 3:** More *révolutionnaire* than *romantique*. A very fast first movement gets within spitting distance of an impossible metronome mark. That and keen texturing undoubtedly make for a tremendous sense of dramatic urgency. Unfortunately, there is also too little accommodation *en route* of the rich cargo of ideas that Beethoven has shipped into this movement. In their haste to get to the recapitulation itself, Gardiner and his players are decidedly unpoised. He is superb in the last two movements; but these are considerably less than half the story where the *Eroica* is concerned. **Symphony No. 4:** An unusually quick introductory and brisk *Allegro vivace*. Gardiner treats the pivotal drum entry before the recapitulation atmospherically. Glorious slow movement, impossibly quick finale.

Symphony No. 5: Here is the stuff of which revolutions are made. Gardiner plays the piece pretty straight, and at white heat. The orchestra is superb, helped by the Francophone bias of its sound base. That said, the *Scherzo* (which has its repeat) is surely too fast. It starts briskly and not especially quietly (Berlioz said the opening should 'fascinate like the gaze of a mesmerizer'). The pace drops back for the Trio, which is just as well since the strings are hard-pressed to articulate clearly. The finale is also very fast, again ahead of what is generally regarded as a good metronome. There is a grandeur to the Scherzo-cum-finale, over which Beethoven laboured so long, that could be seen to reflect a vision (Hegelian, to be precise) that transcends the politics of revolution. Still, for its *éclat terrible*, this is unbeatable. The slow movement is also superbly shaped and directed. **Symphony No. 6:** Despite some lovely playing in the slow movement and a general air of brisk efficiency, this is a rather joyless account of the *Pastoral*. Nor is it at all a spiritually uplifting one. The *Scherzo* – 'A merry gathering of country folk' – is a very high-speed affair. At such a pace the various amusing false entries rather lose their point; to play in this village band you would need to be a virtuoso, and teetotal to boot.

Symphony No. 7: A glorious performance. The introduction sets the scene with an ideal blend of weight and anticipation. The *Vivace* has a splendid dance feel and a power that is utterly unforced. *Scherzo* and finale are also superbly paced. The *Allegretto* is eloquent with a sense of barely sublimated grieving. Marvellous brooding basses and fine, veiled colourings. The recording is magnificent. **Symphony No. 8:** In general, the symphony thrives on the Gardiner approach, though in the finale the emphasis is again on high-speed locomotion. Metronome chasing merely fazes the players and foreshortens the listener's perspective on the movement's huge architectural reach. **Symphony No. 9:** The first movement has never been dispatched as rapidly as it is here, not even by Toscanini. This is another example of a dubious metronome being preferred to a very specific tempo marking. In fact, Gardiner doesn't get the bit between the teeth until bar 51, so the celebrated introduction has room to breathe. Of course, he isn't entirely inflexible and he and his players show remarkable skill in making busy detail 'tell'. Yet a lot does go by the board. The slow movement is also played very quickly. However, Gardiner's finale is superb. Tempos are unerringly chosen, the choral singing is beyond criticism, and there is a rare expressive quality to the singing of the solo quartet. Still, superb as Gardiner's account of the finale is, neither can he be said to conduct a wholly satisfactory Ninth.

High quality playing from the Orchestre Révolutionnaire et Romantique and often exceptional Archiv sound. At best, the physical and intellectual vitality of this music-making brings us close to the *Ding an sich*, the inexplicably wonderful 'thing-in-itself'. It is a best that occurs only intermittently in this set. That it occurs at all is perhaps a sufficient miracle.

Symphonies Nos. 1-9. Leonore Overture No. 3, Op. 72a.
Eileen Farrell *sop* **Nan Merriman** *mez* **Jan Peerce** *ten* **Norman Scott** *bass*
NBC Symphony Orchestra; Robert Shaw Chorale / Arturo Toscanini.
RCA Victor Gold Seal mono GD60324 (five discs: 337 minutes: ADD). Recorded 1939-51.   Ⓜ 🄷

Toscanini recorded seven of the symphonies on more than one occasion, but he left only one complete cycle. In all but the case of the overture, then, we have examples of Toscanini at a very late stage in his career, when he was between the ages of 82 and 85 and had been conducting for well over 60 years. We can never hear how he conducted Beethoven in the earlier part of his career, of course, but even in the 1930s, when he first recorded complete symphonies, it is apparent that his Beethoven had greater flexibility, poise and lyricism than in his last years, when he had a tendency to drive the music very hard. These are old arguments but they should be aired for the benefit of those approaching Toscanini's Beethoven for the first time. Although taped in New York's Carnegie Hall there is to a greater or lesser extent a somewhat close, harsh quality in the sound, which has little tonal bloom or sense of space. However the transfers seem very faithful, clear and forward, and they preserve, despite the foregoing, some remarkable music-making. There isn't a single bar throughout all nine symphonies which is unconsidered or routine. Toscanini's passionate, urgent desire is to convey Beethoven's genius in as perfect a way as is humanly possible. These are immensely strong, lean, direct performances.

Nowhere is Toscanini's genius more apparent than in Nos. 1 and 2. He brings an incomparable sense of discovery and freshness to No. 1. The first movement, lithe, taut and superbly balanced, makes an enormous impact, as does the wonderfully lyrical, beautifully drawn slow movement, the virile *Scherzo*, and the fast, urgent, yet finely poised finale. Similar qualities inform the Second Symphony, which is given another searching, exemplary reading. The *Eroica*'s first movement is highly assertive, followed by a deeply expressive slow movement, a fast *Scherzo* and a tense, precisely articulated finale. There is altogether more tension and less mystery in the Fourth and by and large his performance is fairly hard-driven, though impressively so, but ensemble at the beginning of the last movement is badly awry, a rare lapse. The Fifth is similarly tough, and those who like a swift-moving though by no means hard-hearted *Pastoral* will warm to Toscanini's attractive interpretation. The Seventh fitted Toscanini's highly developed sense of rhythm to perfection. It is an enormously powerful, deeply impressive reading. A strong, straightforward, somewhat serious account of the Eighth offers rather less reward, but in the Ninth, Toscanini achieves great heights. The first movement occasionally finds him impatiently rough-riding his basic rhythmic pulse, but the *Scherzo* is tremendously virile, the slow movement exquisitely tender and powerful in turn, and the finale, with a good group of soloists and an excellent chorus, fervent and uplifting. Toscanini's Beethoven lives on in good health.

Symphonies Nos. 1 and 2.
Zurich Tonhalle Orchestra / David Zinman.
Arte Nova Classics 74321 63645-2 (54 minutes: DDD). Recorded 1998. Ⓢ **RR**

True to form, David Zinman here takes the latest Beethoven scholarship on board, which in this case includes some novel emendations to the opening of the Second Symphony. A few textual details are worth pondering, all concerning trills. At bar four of the slow introduction (0'13"), a trill is added to the woodwind line; the trilling triplets at 0'30" are freshly articulated, and at bar 29 (at 1'59"), the trills that alternate between flute and first violins are given fuller note value. Throughout the work, woodwind lines enjoy occasional embellishment and the stinging attack of valveless horns adds fibre to the tonal mix. In the *Scherzo*'s rollicking trio, the second string chord of the second section (at 1'54" and again at 2'17") is played as the prescribed *sforzando*, something that very few other conductors think to do. Both performances are swift, taut and texturally luminous – punchy but never punch-drunk. Other versions might offer parallel interpretative virtues (though none are on sale at Arte Nova's modest price point), but if you fancy Zinman's light touch and direct manner of interpretation, then you can hardly go wrong.

Symphonies Nos. 1 and 4. Egmont Overture, Op. 84ª.
Berlin Philharmonic Orchestra / Herbert von Karajan.
DG Galleria 419 048-2GGA (64 minutes: ADD). Recorded ª1969, 1975-76. Ⓜ **RR**

The opening of the First, perfectly timed and chorded, announces playing of rare pedigree, though the *Allegro* itself, taken at a gently ruminative pace, is a surprise. The autumnal side of Karajan's make-up is one we don't often see. It is a beautifully shaped reading, with glorious wind playing and a nobly sustained through-rhythm. The mellow *Andante*, like the Minuet and Trio, emerges as a miracle of instrumental ensemble, reminding one how summer by summer Karajan encouraged his players to make chamber music together on vacation. After so gentle a start, the finale seems strangely quick. Orchestrally, it is the finest quick Beethoven playing imaginable and for all the aerial excitement the final *ff* peaks are compelling placed. Karajan's instinctively dynamic approach to Beethoven is modified in the Fourth by a contrasted but equally strong feel for the German symphonic tradition. The performance strikes deepest at the points of stasis midway through each of the first three movements. Indeed, the sonority of the performance is remarkable throughout, with great use made of bass and cello colourings (something which the BPO had perfected by this time) and a huge dynamic range – implicit in the score from massive tutti chords down to the most perfectly regulated quiet drum rolls. Thus it is, in playing as subtle as it is creatively alive, that the flame of Beethoven's genius can be seen to burn brightly on. The *Egmont* Overture, played superbly and surprisingly swiftly, makes a welcome filler. The transfers are excellent.

Symphonies Nos. 1 and 6. Die Geschöpfe des Prometheus, Op. 43.
London Classical Players / Sir Roger Norrington.
Virgin Veritas VM5 61374-2 (75 minutes: DDD). Recorded 1987.   Ⓜ𝐏

Norrington's reading of the finale of the First Symphony is as lithe and witty as you could wish for. The first movement is more difficult to bring off and it is a measure of the competence and confidence of the London Classical Players that the difficult slow introduction is brought off with superb aplomb and that the *Allegro con brio* is reasonably quick but with space in the lyrical subjects and the most ferocious account of the coda on record, the period brass snarling viciously in the tuttis and the timpani roaring menacingly on the final page. Other conductors have played the *Andante cantabile con moto* reasonably swiftly but Norrington is very brisk, the tone nicely sec, the whole thing playful and witty in a delightfully brittle way. Again, the articulation of the London Classical Players is first-rate, giving the performance real presence style, and individuality. Indeed, this must be counted one of the best accounts of the First Symphony.

The *Pastoral* is also a revelation. Norrington adopts a swift tempo in the joyous first movement but there's no hint of that relentless, driven quality which we have sometimes had on record. He is fully up to tempo in the vibrant tuttis; elsewhere he's most careful to allow the music to expand and dance and breathe, the transitions always most sensitively moulded. It is also a joy to hear this, of all the Beethoven symphonies, on period instruments. The instrumental timbres will come as a revelation to many listeners; equally, they are obviously a source of real joy and fascination to the players. This *Pastoral* is a real voyage of aural discovery. Sometimes the wind tuning is not 100 per cent true, at others it is simply a matter of Norrington teasing us with the timing of a trill's release or pointing up dissonances that usually get smoothed over. The sound is wonderfully clear and trenchant. How marvellous it is at the start of the last movement of the *Pastoral* to have such clean, honest string sound and to have it spread right across the orchestral spectrum as the first and second violins answer one another antiphonally across the landscape. Norrington adds *The Creatures of Prometheus* Overture for good measure.

Symphonies Nos. 2 and 4.
Philharmonia Orchestra / Otto Klemperer.
EMI Studio CDM7 63355-2 (73 minutes: ADD). Recorded 1957.   Ⓜ𝐇

In the autumn of 1957, Klemperer and the Philharmonia took all nine Beethoven symphonies into the concert hall. And whilst the concerts were being prepared and performed the symphonies were recorded in the Kingsway Hall. Some critics at the time thought the performance of the slow movement of the Second Symphony rather severe and the finale somewhat 'avuncular', but the performance is of a piece and the first movement is superb, a reading that leaves us in no doubt whatsoever about the sheer presence and creative energy of the young Beethoven. It is coupled with the Fourth Symphony which receives from Klemperer and the Philharmonia as spacious, finely considered and as inwardly vital a reading as you will find anywhere on record. There have been fierier readings, and more romantically charged ones, but none more effortlessly true to itself than this. This coupling should be in every Beethoven collection.

Symphonies Nos. 2 and 8.
Royal Philharmonic Orchestra / James Lockhart.
Tring International Royal Philharmonic Collection TRP039 (62 minutes: DDD). Recorded 1994.   Ⓢ

These were two of Sir Thomas Beecham's favourite symphonies, and you can well imagine him cocking an approving ear towards these performances, from his eyrie on Mount Olympus. Note for note this is probably – dare we say it? – a better played performance than Beecham's own 1951 recording of the Eighth which was so diligently assembled over a period of several months in two separate halls. (The Beecham Edition CD reissue is, alas, no longer available.) James Lockhart's conducting is proof of the old adage that there is no better place to learn the conductor's craft than in the opera house. Not only are these finely articulated performances, they also have the merit of being wonderfully well phrased and timed. They are performances you could probably choreograph and certainly sing to, the music's symphonic and dramatic elements held in the nicest possible poise. Tempos are always broad enough to allow the music time to breathe, urgent enough to activate its potential as musical theatre. The recording has air around it, yet every section of the orchestra presents itself to us with admirable directness and immediacy. Once or twice the merest hint of a disrupted pulse suggests a slightly chancy mixing of takes. In most respects, though, this could be counted a worthwhile disc at a far higher price than the one currently being asked.

Symphonies Nos. 2 and 8. Overtures – Coriolan, Op. 62; Egmont, Op. 84.
London Classical Players / Sir Roger Norrington.
Virgin Veritas VM5 61375-2 (73 minutes: DDD). Recorded 1986.
Gramophone Award Winner 1987.   Ⓜ️🅿️

Norrington's way with Beethoven – which is recognizably Toscaninian in some of its aspects – is, in
his own words, his aim of recapturing much of 'the exhilaration and sheer disturbance that his
music certainly generated in his day'. Like Toscanini, Erich Kleiber, and others before him,
Norrington achieves this not by the imposition on the music of some world view but by taking up
its immediate intellectual and physical challenges. Norrington is not unduly preoccupied by matters
of orchestral size but sound interests him a good deal. Throughout, the contributions of horns,
trumpets and drums most rivet the attention (the introduction to the Second Symphony's first
movement is glorious). What really fascinates Norrington, though, is rhythm and pulse and their
determining agencies: eighteenth-century performing styles, instrumental articulacy (most notably,
bowing methods), and Beethoven's own metronome markings. In the Second Symphony Norrington
makes the music smile and dance without any significant loss of forward momentum, and he treats
the metronome marks more consistently than Karajan (who spins out the symphony's
introduction), whilst sharing with him a belief in a really forward-moving pulse in the *Larghetto*
(again an approach to the printed metronome if not the thing itself). The recordings are warm and
vivid and generally well balanced. The *fff* climax of the development of the Eighth Symphony's
first movement is slightly underpowered, which is odd when the horns and trumpets are elsewhere
so thrillingly caught; perhaps, in the Eighth, the recording could have been a shade tighter and drier
in order better to define the playing of the London Classical Players. None the less, when it first
appeared, it was hailed as the most interesting and enjoyable new record of a Beethoven symphony
recorded for some considerable time. This reissue also includes vigorous accounts of the *Coriolan*
and *Egmont* Overtures.

Symphony No. 3. Grosse Fuge in B flat major, Op. 133.
Philharmonia Orchestra / Otto Klemperer.
EMI Studio mono CDM7 63356-2 (70 minutes: ADD). Recorded 1959 and 1956.   Ⓜ️🅷️🆁🆁

Klemperer recorded the *Eroica* for the second time in the autumn of 1959 and even critics who
didn't normally think of themselves as Klemperer fans – Deryck Cooke, for instance – admitted to
being bowled over by it. Though there are times when it has been thought to be decidedly lacking in
Schwung, there are other occasions when the sheer grandeur and titanic reach of the reading is what
appears most pertinent. Coupled now with the intensely compelling and eloquently played 1956
recording of the *Grosse Fuge*, it makes a fine CD's worth, the more so as EMI has managed to do a
certain amount of discreet renovation of the apparently flawed 1956 tapes.

Symphony No. 3. Overtures – Leonore Nos. 2 and 3.
Philharmonia Orchestra / Otto Klemperer.
EMI mono CDM7 63855-2 (76 minutes: ADD). Recorded 1954-55.   Ⓜ️🅷️

In 1955 the Philharmonia Orchestra was at the peak of its powers. And what cogency there is
sustaining and feeding the drama. Where other orchestras and conductors whip themselves into a
terrible lather at the start of the finale, Klemperer and the Philharmonia sail majestically on. This is
a great performance, steady yet purposeful, with textures that seem hewn out of granite. (Once or
twice they cause a slight buzz of distortion for which EMI apologizes in the booklet.) There is no
exposition repeat, and the trumpets blaze out illicitly in the first movement coda, but this is still one
of the great *Eroicas* on record. As Karajan announced to Klemperer after flying in to a concert
performance around this time: 'I have come only to thank you, and say that I hope I shall live to
conduct the Funeral March as well as you have done'. In the *Leonore* Overtures, recorded in 1954,
the playing is a bit more rough-edged.

Symphony No. 3. Overture – Leonore No. 3, Op. 72a.
North German Radio Symphony Orchestra / Günter Wand.
RCA Victor RD60755 (65 minutes: DDD). Recorded live in 1989 and 1990.   Ⓕ

In many ways Wand stands as a legitimate successor to Klemperer as one of the holders of the
great Teutonic tradition of interpreting Beethoven in terms of struggle and triumph. Certainly he
launches into the symphony with tremendous vigour and power and he sustains these
characteristics throughout. Following an opening movement in which the tension never relaxes at
all, Wand leads a reading of the Funeral March which is deeply felt but without self-indulgence.

The *Scherzo* and trio provide well-pointed relief prior to an epic reading of the triumphant final movement, which carries all before it. The fill-up, an equally powerful reading of the *Leonore* Overture No. 3, precedes the performance of the *Eroica* and acts as an excellent curtain-raiser and introduction to Wand's interpretative style: genuine and powerful and wholly without self-indulgence. The North German Radio recording is excellent, capturing the involved atmosphere of a live performance without any of the distractions normally to be expected from such venues.

Symphony No. 3. Overture – Coriolan, Op. 62.
Le Concert des Nations / Jordi Savall.
Auvidis Fontalis ES8557 (52 minutes: DDD). Recorded 1994. ⒡ 🄿

There is a real sense of burgeoning excitement at the start of Savall's performance; and the sound of the orchestra really does conjure up the sense of one being transported back to some dusky Viennese concert room *c*1805 where the musicians are as dangerous a crew as the militias roaming the mud-filled streets outside. Yet as the musical arguments begin to multiply and deepen, so the performance gets slightly garbled. For all Savall's skill in moulding and modifying the pulse, there's a jauntiness about parts of the first movement development section which muddles and trivializes the music. In the *Marcia funèbre*, the performance is astonishing for the mood it conjures. The drum (calf skin head, hard sticks) is fierce and seductive, an instrument of war that suggests also the soft thud of death. Savall's brass are similarly remarkable, at once brazen and mellow-sounding. The horn section alone – Thomas Muller, Raul Diaz and Javier Bonet – deserves an award for the way the players colour and characterize this astonishing music. There is no disguising the fact that Savall's thinking about tempo is controversial. It is all very modern: post-modern, even. (After Savall, conductors like Norrington sound distressingly 'safe'.) It is typical of Savall that though he conducts very quick, very earthy, very exciting accounts of the *Eroica*'s *Scherzo* (those horns again!) and finale, he still slows up pretty massively for the finale's oboe-led *Poco andante* at bar 348. It is a performance, none the less, that you will want for the sonic profile alone. The Auvidis recording is first-rate: warm and immediate.

Symphonies Nos. 1 and 3. Fidelio – Overture.
NBC Symphony Orchestra / Arturo Toscanini.
Naxos Historical mono 8 110802/3 (two discs: 91 minutes: ADD). Recorded live in 1939. ⒮ 🄷

Symphony No. 3.
Vienna Philharmonic Orchestra / Wilhelm Furtwängler.
Tahra mono FURT1031 (53 minutes: ADD). Recorded 1944. ⒡ 🄷

These two *Eroicas* confound critical clichés about their respective conductor. Furtwängler's recording is swifter than you might imagine, certainly in the first movement and Toscanini's forceful 1939 radio broadcast is among the most songful, most flexibly phrased interpretations on disc. They both lay claim to being the best of various alternatives under the same conductors, and both have been reissued many times before; but while Naxos's transfer is only moderately successful, Tahra's is among the finest around. There have been various unofficial transfers – both on CD and LP – in better-focused sound, that run this rather rough-edged Naxos transfer pretty close. Furtwängler's first movement is distinguished above all by warmly arched string phrasing. The second subject slows less perceptibly than in Toscanini's performance. Toscanini keeps the same passage very much in tempo and while his handling of the coda is incandescently intense, Furtwängler draws greater attention to the *crescendo*ing repeated string figures that lead up to it. In the *Marcia funèbre*, Furtwängler is broadly paced and loose-jointed, with mellow lower strings and impressive weight of tone, while Toscanini is anxious, candid and desperately expressive. Furtwängler slows the closing bars so dramatically that the fragmented theme all but disintegrates. Toscanini, on the other hand, holds fast to the lyrical line, and the effect is hardly less devastating. Toscanini's *Scherzo* is fleet and furious, whereas Furtwängler's gentler manner breaks the *Marcia*'s spell like a lone dove fluttering against a stormy sky. Both finales work well, though Toscanini 'holds the plot' with a firmer grip.

You end up being equally well disposed towards both Toscanini and Furtwängler, although not everyone will want Toscanini's hard-driven account, let alone the ephemeral spoken commentaries that surround it. Still, in the *Eroica*, both conductors offer a singular musical experience: gripping, inspired and always worth the effort needed to 'listen through' old sound. The further we journey from these venerable old masters, the more we treasure their individuality and commitment. True, opposing camps will lock horns over who best realizes the composer's intentions (as if we could ever know), but those listeners sensible enough to keep an open mind on the matter cannot fail to perceive that both routes lead to the same life-enhancing destination. Which is surely what great music-making is all about.

Symphonies Nos. 3 and 4.
Zurich Tonhalle Orchestra / David Zinman.
Arte Nova Classics 74321 59214-2 (75 minutes: DDD). Recorded 1998. Ⓢ Ⓔ 🆁🆁

David Zinman's account of the Fourth Symphony is fleet and mercurial, as compelling a case as we
have for honouring Beethoven's fast metronome markings and, in the finale, bursting with unforced
vitality. We are told that this is the first modern-instrument recording of the new Bärenreiter text,
which, presumably, is why the clarinet line is embellished from about six minutes into the *Adagio*.
Elsewhere in the Fourth, things remain much as we already know them. Few Beethoven Fourths tell
a happier tale, and there is none at budget price that even begins to compete with this one. Viewed
as a whole, Zinman's *Eroica* levels with various up-tempo period-instrument alternatives, though its
many distinguishing features include a notably animated and quick-witted first-movement
development section. Taking on board various minor novelties of phrase and nuance, Zinman
parades a lean, sprightly, incisively articulated *Eroica*, 'late classical' rather than 'early romantic' in
style (very roughly speaking) and a joyous alternative to the grand though heavy artillery favoured
by earlier generations of conductors. Of course, you wouldn't want to miss out on them, either; but
Zinman helps adjust our ears for a new perspective – without dropping the pitch or inflicting
enfeebled string sonorities on us. For the money – and, happily, not much of it is needed – his is
the most palatably performed presentation of the Beethoven symphony as perceived by modern
scholarship. The recordings are generally first-rate.

Symphonies Nos. 3 and 8.
North German Radio Symphony Orchestra / Günter Wand.
RCA Symphony Edition 74321 20280-2 (DDD). Recorded 1985-87. Ⓜ 🆁🆁

The traditionalist-classicist approach to Beethoven is in abundant health. This *Eroica* is a very
special release. Wand finds the melodic thread that pulls all the sharply defined short phrases in the
opening *Allegro con brio* together, while at the same time homing in on expressive or colouristic
details – it's a performance that seems alive on many levels at once. Everything moves at a measured
tread, except for a few telling moments where the pace seems briefly to falter, and it's this very
tension between control and deep feeling that makes the performance so memorable. Purposefulness
intensifies in the finale, until the glorious opening out at the *poco andante*. In Wand's hands this is
the symphony's true apotheosis, radiant at first, then recalling the *Marcia funèbre* in the broken
woodwind-strings exchanges just before the tumultuous final *presto*. The notes are so familiar, and
yet the experience Wand draws from them is one of continual discovery. The performance of the
Eighth begins with the right kind of snapping wit and ends with a measured and not always entirely
tidy account of the finale. Only once or twice do you feel that Wand is overworking the orchestra,
gingering it up at climaxes in a way that is ultimately counter-productive. The central sections of the
first movement seem somewhat stage-managed after Wand's spontaneous-seeming way with the
work's opening. All in all, however, this is an admirably spirited reading.

Symphonies Nos. 4 and 5.
La Scala Philharmonic Orchestra, Milan / Carlo Maria Giulini.
Sony Classical SK58921 (73 minutes: DDD). Recorded 1993. Ⓕ

Giulini's Fifth, which ends with a piccolo singing high in the stratosphere as C major sounds
majestically beneath, is not a performance in the histrionic (or historic) sense of the word. Rather, it
is a meditation on the work's informing vision, what Goethe called 'the Fall upwards', the transition
from dark to light, the seeds of spiritual regeneration planted in the very ground of despair. And
that is not an elaborately circuitous way of saying that the performance is a bit dull, that the old
boy is not quite what he was. Giulini's desire is to give the music time to breathe and be heard. And
he is absolutely the master of how best to bring that about. You hear this in the time he allots to the
opening fermatas (and in the fineness of their sound, rich and unforced); you hear it in the slight
'lift' he imparts to the rhythm, the time they are given to dance; and you hear it in the steady,
unflustered pulse of the whole. The final two movements are treated as a seamless robe. Logically –
since there is no repeat of the *Scherzo*'s first half – Giulini omits the finale's exposition repeat. The
music is thus allowed to move forward with a simple momentum of its own. Climaxes are finely
judged, and rarely has the *Scherzo*'s unexpected return within the finale seemed so fine an invention
as it does here. The symphony's slow movement, incidentally, is played as though it is first cousin to
Schubert's *Unfinished* Symphony. Giulini has never previously recorded the Fourth Symphony and
coming to it late has its risks. The slow introduction, the slow movement and the still points of the
Allegro vivace's turning world are wonderfully well reimagined and realized. The word *vivace*,
though, implies a slightly more spirited gait than Giulini allows. But if parts of the first movement
seem a touch lumpy, the finale is a miracle of unforced motion, the La Scala playing relaxed, the

mood gamesome as it invariably is when the conductor takes note of Beethoven's written instruction: *Allegro ma non troppo*. (Klemperer was always very persuasive in this movement.) Sony's Milan recordings place the orchestra a shade distantly, giving a slightly veiled quality to the string tone, but since this is consonant with the sound Giulini draws from the orchestra it is hardly a matter of great concern.

Symphonies Nos. 4 and 7.
London Classical Players / Sir Roger Norrington.
Virgin Veritas VM5 61376-2 (69 minutes: DDD). Recorded 1988. Ⓜ️ 🅿️

Norrington's opening to the Fourth is subdued, but the tension lies beneath the surface and facilitates a striking contrast with the *allegro*, which is light in feeling, with a very brisk tempo indeed. Norrington presses the *Adagio* forward but it is light and songful. His briskness continues in the *Scherzo* but is slightly tempered by the relatively mellow acoustic. The London Classical Players articulate the bustling finale with great panache. In this splendid version of the Seventh, Norrington's allegiance to Beethoven's metronome markings is particularly convincing, and not only in the second movement *Allegretto*. His sharp pointing of the accents of the introduction is immediately arresting, and the dance rhythms in the main theme of the first movement and again in the finale bring joyously buoyant articulation to match the sparkle of the *Scherzo* (the swiftly rippling low-register pedal duplets from the second horn which build up to the bold restatement of the Trio are a memorable touch). In the finale the hammering of the timpani is unforgettable and at the close the horns sing out as they do at the triumphant ending of the first movement. Like the pairing of Nos. 2 and 8, Norrington's coupling of Nos. 4 and 7 is well worth seeking out.

Symphonies Nos. 5 and 7.
Vienna Philharmonic Orchestra / Carlos Kleiber.
DG The Originals 447 400-2GOR (72 minutes: ADD). Recorded 1974. Ⓜ️ 🆁🆁

The recording of the Fifth, always very fine, comes up superbly in this transfer. What, though, of the Seventh Symphony, an equally distinguished performance though always perceptibly greyer-sounding on LP, and on CD? Well, it too is superb. What the Original-Image Bit-Processing has done to it, heaven only knows, but the result is a performance of genius that now speaks to us freely and openly for the first time. In some ways this is a more important document than the famous Fifth. Great recordings of the Seventh, greatly played and greatly conducted, but with first and second violins divided left and right, are as rare as gold-dust. Freshly refurbished, this Kleiber Seventh would go right to the top of any short list of recommendable Sevenths. It is wonderful to have these two legendary performances so expertly restored and placed together on one disc for the first time.

Symphonies Nos. 5 and 6.
Zurich Tonhalle Orchestra / David Zinman.
Arte Nova Classics 74321 49695-2 (74 minutes: DDD). Recorded 1997. Ⓢ Ⓔ

This production, 'according to the new Bärenreiter Edition', parades a good number of textual novelties. Both scores are visited by all manner of dynamic *crescendos, diminuendos* and other emphases (mostly applied to short phrases) and the sum effect is notably refreshing. Tempos are very fast, phrasing trimly tailored (sometimes even a trifle abrupt) and rubato kept well in check. In the Fifth Symphony, Zinman plays all three repeats (first movement, *Scherzo* and finale) and his handling of the *Scherzo*'s double-bass Trio deserves a round of applause. The *Pastoral*'s proto-minimalist first-movement development section flies off at a fair lick and the slimline peasants make merry with energy to spare. This disc is particularly recommended to readers who know their Klemperers, Toscaninis and Furtwänglers backwards and who fancy investigating some scholarly emendations but who dislike period-instrument sonorities. Zinman's performances offer a peach of a bargain, and the sound quality is truly state-of-the-art.

Symphonies Nos. 5 and 6.
North German Radio Symphony Orchestra / Günter Wand.
RCA Victor Red Seal 09026 61930-2 (79 minutes: DDD). Recorded live in 1992. Ⓕ

To judge from this live performance of the Fifth Symphony, Wand has the trick of keeping something back for the performance itself; a remarkable skill in repertory as familiar as this after so much detailed preparation. In matters of rhythm and phrasing and the balancing of lines, Wand is difficult to fault. Indeed, you will hear things in these performances – from the basses and bassoons, and, in the Fifth Symphony, from the trombones – which are all too often glossed over. Apart from a curiously measured *Scherzo*, the Fifth Symphony goes exceptionally well. The first movement is not overdriven, yet the finale has real *élan*, the reading – for want of a better word – suddenly and surprisingly rather Furtwänglerish. In the *Pastoral* Symphony it is Wand's exemplary account of the Scene by the Brook that most obviously stands out. Here he has the knack of marrying the music's necessary forward movement with the murmurous beauty of its inner detailing. Wand's *Pastoral* gives profound pleasure at every level.

Symphony No. 6. Overtures – Coriolan, Op. 62; Egmont, Op. 84.
La Scala Philharmonic Orchestra, Milan / Carlo Maria Giulini.
Sony Classical SK53974 (65 minutes: DDD). Recorded 1993.   Ⓕ🄴

This is Giulini's third recording of the Sixth and, by some distance, his finest. Superbly sustained and expressively moulded, this is a performance in which every sentence is gloriously phrased and where individual string lines are always richly distinct; not a note is extraneous to Beethoven's purpose. The whole performance is wonderfully at odds with the hell-for-leather spirit of an agnostic age. It is, in the end, a deeply *spiritual* performance of a work which was conceived by Beethoven, first and last, as an essentially spiritual experience. The disc begins with a profoundly satisfying *Coriolan* Overture and the dramatic opening of the *Egmont* Overture is played with a near-ideal blend of trenchancy and *espressivo* intensity. As for the coda, the so-called 'Victory Symphony', few have brought out as vividly as Giulini its musical and moral sure-footedness.

Symphonies Nos. 5 and 6.
London Classical Players / Sir Roger Norrington.
Virgin Veritas VM5 61377-2 (74 minutes: DDD). Recorded 1988.   Ⓜ🄿

Norrington conducts an enjoyable, memorable account of the Fifth. He throws off the introduction to the first movement with crisp brilliance, and the *Allegro* conveys enormous underlying energy. His *Andante* is beautifully phrased and flows most delicately; in the bustling double-bass theme at the centre of the *Scherzo* the bowing is light, the effect refined and offering easy virtuosity. Norrington's finale is strongly accented, his horns in the secondary idea broadly sonorous, partly as a result of the resonant EMI sound. The *Pastoral* brings a similarly fast pace in the opening movement, with subtle shading of dynamics. The contributions of horns and woodwinds produce an attractive exuberance. The slow movement, however, is less convincing, the phrasing curiously choppy. Many will like the warm Abbey Road acoustic, but (apart from the braying horns) the *Scherzo* lacks refined detail. The extra resonance means that the timpani thunderbolts are less effective than they might be. The finale seldom fails, and here the expansive EMI sound adds to the fullness: the lower strings resonate richly and the climax is radiant.

Beethoven Symphony No. 6
Schubert Symphony No. 5 in B flat major, D485.
Vienna Philharmonic Orchestra / Karl Böhm.
DG The Originals 447 433-2GOR (74 minutes: ADD). Recorded 1971 and 1979.   Ⓜ🆁🆁

Karl Böhm's Beethoven is a compound of earth and fire. His VPO recording of Beethoven's Sixth of 1971 dominated the LP catalogue for over a decade, and has done pretty well on CD on its various appearances. His reading is generally glorious and it remains one of the finest accounts of the work ever recorded. It still sounds well (perhaps the bass is a bit lighter than on LP) and the performance (with the first movement exposition repeat included) has an unfolding naturalness and a balance between form and lyrical impulse that is totally satisfying. The brook flows untroubled and the finale is quite lovely, with a wonderfully expansive climax. The Schubert dates from the end of Böhm's recording career. It is a superb version of this lovely symphony, another work that suited Böhm especially well. The reading is weighty but graceful, with a most beautifully phrased *Andante* (worthy of a Furtwängler), a bold Minuet and a thrilling finale. The recording is splendid. If you admire Böhm this is a worthy way to remember his special gifts.

Symphonies Nos. 6-8. Overtures[a] – Fidelio, Op. 72; Leonore No. 3, Op. 72a.
Vienna Philharmonic Orchestra; [a]**Staatskapelle Dresden / Karl Böhm.**
DG Double 437 928-2GX2 (two discs: 130 minutes: ADD). Recorded 1971.   Ⓜ

This coupling of the Sixth, Seventh and Eighth symphonies is eminently recommendable. At best, not many conductors began to match the kind of trenchancy and articulacy we have here from Böhm and the Vienna Philharmonic, recordings made in splendidly clear and explicit sound. At worst, you might think him merely dogged (the finale of the Eighth Symphony, for example), but even there the grammar and the diction give the music-making its own special habitation and character: more Austrian, perhaps, than Flemish but none the worse for that. Böhm's Seventh is generally glorious, and his account of the *Pastoral* is the finest account of the work available (this is the same recording as the one reviewed above – our top recommendation for the Sixth). The two *Fidelio*-derived overtures in this collection were recorded with the Staatskapelle Dresden. Both have moments of sudden scything ferocity that may or may not have been there in the performance of *Fidelio* that so affected Ingmar Bergman who once said of a performance of *Fidelio* conducted by Böhm: 'Everything looked simple, the notes in place, no remarkable tricks, nothing astonishing, the tempi never heard. The interpretation was what the Germans with light irony call *werktreu* [faithful to the work]. The miracle was nevertheless a fact.'

Symphonies Nos. 7 and 8.
Zurich Tonhalle Orchestra / David Zinman.
Arte Nova Classics 74321 56341-2 (61 minutes: DDD). Recorded 1997.　　　　Ⓢ

No one who relates to Toscanini's Beethoven on the one hand or Gardiner's on the other will take issue with David Zinman's 'short ride in a fast machine' approach to the Eighth Symphony (with apologies to John Adams). Zinman's recording, 'according to the new Bärenreiter Edition', packs a fair punch and the Eighth is exhilarating in the extreme. Every strand of argument bristles with life and Zinman's view of it makes for essential listening. His Seventh is slightly more problematic in that while similar virtues pertain, a certain levelling of dynamics does rather compromise important dramatic episodes. Horns ring out in the *Scherzo*'s Trio (played very fast and with minimal vibrato from the strings) and the swirling finale, which is performed with tremendous dynamism, suggests disco-style momentum: Wagner's epithet of an 'apotheosis of the dance' has rarely been more apt in contemporary terms. All repeats are played in both symphonies; the recordings are excellent and if your current library preference is for one of the modern-instrument 'greats', Zinman at super-budget price will prove both instructive and refreshing.

Symphony No. 9.
Anna Tomowa-Sintow *sop* **Agnes Baltsa** *mez* **Peter Schreier** *ten* **José van Dam** *bass-bar*
Vienna Singverein; Berlin Philharmonic Orchestra / Herbert von Karajan.
DG Galleria 415 832-2GGA (67 minutes: ADD). Text and translation included.
Recorded 1976.　　　　Ⓜ **RR**

All collections need Beethoven's *Choral* Symphony as one of the works at the very core of the nineteenth-century romantic movement. Within its remarkable span, Beethoven celebrates both the breadth and power of man's conception of his position in relation to the Universe; his sense of spirituality – especially in the great slow movement – and in the finale the essential life-enhancing optimism emerges, which makes human existence philosophically possible against all odds. Karajan lived alongside the Beethoven symphonies throughout his long and very distinguished recording career, and he recorded the Ninth three times in stereo. His 1976 version is the best of the three. The slow movement has great intensity, and the finale brings a surge of incandescent energy and exuberance which is hard to resist. All four soloists are excellent individually and they also make a good team. The reading as a whole has the inevitability of greatness and the recording is vivid, full and clear. At mid-price this is very recommendable indeed.

Symphony No. 9
Alessandra Marc *sop* **Iris Vermillion** *mez* **Siegfried Jerusalem** *ten* **Falk Struckmann** *bar*
Berlin State Opera Chorus; Berlin Staatskapelle / Daniel Barenboim.
Erato 4509-94353-2 (74 minutes: DDD). Text and translation included. Recorded 1992.　　　　Ⓕ

Barenboim's is an important recording in that it re-establishes – in its own way and with a telling eloquence that is specially its own – that the Ninth is a work of the new romanticism, a prophetic work that cannot be adequately dealt with by so-called 'authenticists' desirous of tethering it either to the letter of the written text or to performance practice in Beethoven's own lifetime. The literalists and authenticists have had some powerful advocates on record – Toscanini, for example, not easily gainsaid. Barenboim's Ninth starts deep in the *Urwald*, far away, wreathed in the mists of time. Yet it is a measure of his mastery that the reading never appears to meander or hold fire. On the contrary, the development and recapitulation blaze quietly, from within. 'Quietly' because the Erato recording, made in Berlin's Jesus-Christus Kirche, is rather soft-grained. Important solo voicings, human or instrumental, are neither obscured nor specifically 'lit'. In the finale, words sound clearly enough whilst at the same time being part of the performance's general euphony. The extreme inwardness of Barenboim's reading at key points – the symphony's opening bars, most of the slow movement, the very slow *molto pianissimo* start of the first instrumental statement of the 'Joy' theme – is complemented by considerable ebullience in the *Scherzo* and in the later stages of the finale. The soloists are generally reliable, the choir first-rate, the orchestra more than adequate to the considerable task in hand.

Symphony No. 9.
Gillian Webster *sop* **Catherine Wyn-Rogers** *contr* **Martyn Hill** *ten* **Robert Hayward** *bar*
Ambrosian Singers; Royal Philharmonic Orchestra / Raymond Leppard.
Tring Royal Philharmonic Collection TRP051 (70 minutes: DDD). Recorded 1994.   Ⓢ

It is possible to be too much in awe of the Ninth Symphony. Self-belief and a touch of flamboyance, such as we have here from Raymond Leppard, never did anyone any harm. After all, one of the finest of all recorded post-war Ninths came from Stokowski, no less (once available on Decca in the 1970s). Leppard's direction of the difficult first movement is particularly impressive, strong yet songful, urgent yet happy to accommodate the frequent fluctuations of pace the music asks for and the score demands. It is also a ripe-toned performance, something of a *sine qua non* when fashioning the special sound world and the very obviously post-classical harmonic style of this extraordinary work. But, then, even as an early pioneer of the revival of interest in pre-classical repertory, Leppard was never a member of the rope-sandal-and-metronome school of interpretation. The *Scherzo*, taken more slowly than usual, also goes very well. There is a nice spring to the rhythm and the structure is beautifully pointed. The slow movement, somewhat surprisingly, is given a slightly restless performance, as though Leppard distrusts the Germanic soulfulness of the movement's opening paragraphs. There is a strong team of soloists and some robust singing from the choir; though, deliberately or otherwise, a note of coarseness creeps into the performance in the finale. The recording may have something to do with this. Bold and clear in the earlier movements, it takes on a slightly brasher, rather more manipulated feel in the finale. Still, it is difficult to think of a better super-bargain Ninth than this.

Symphony No. 9.
Dame Elisabeth Schwarzkopf *sop* **Elisabeth Höngen** *mez* **Hans Hopf** *ten* **Otto Edelmann** *bass*
Bayreuth Festival Chorus and Orchestra / Wilhelm Furtwängler.
EMI mono CDM5 66953-2 (75 minutes: ADD). Recorded live in 1951.   Ⓜ Ⓗ

This performance has become a legendary one, as much for the occasion of its happening as for the music-making itself. The reopening of Wagner's Festival Theatre in Bayreuth in 1951 after the catastrophe of war was nothing if not symbolic. If anything could lay the ghost of Bayreuth's immediate past, the years from 1930 to 1944 when the theatre was run by the English-born, Nazi-worshipping Winifred Wagner, it might be a performance of the Ninth Symphony under the most celebrated of the German conductors who had lived through Nazi rule without being, in any real sense, morally or artistically party to it. Certainly, it is not difficult to think of the slow movement's second subject, unfolded here in a way that has never been bettered, as an atonement and a benediction. However, not everyone will respond to this vision of the Ninth: as an interpretation it is broadly based, with some slow tempos and some quirky adjustments of pace; though beneath everything – beneath the gear changes and failures in ensemble – a great current massively flows. The solo vocal and choral work in the finale is electric after the *fugato* but is breezily, bumpily Teutonic before that; Hans Hopf is his usual restless, hectic self. The CD transfer provides some added clarity of image for the generally excellent mono recording; and it also provides an all-important continuity. Instrumental bass frequencies are rather wooden but the recording reproduces higher frequency string, wind, and vocal sound more smoothly than was often the case at this time. Many collectors will be looking to a stereo, digital recording of the Ninth as a CD library acquisition; yet we would be prepared to argue that this performance has a prior, if not absolute, claim on collectors' attention.

Symphony No. 9.
Dame Elisabeth Schwarzkopf *sop* **Elsa Cavelti** *mez* **Ernst Haefliger** *ten* **Otto Edelmann** *bass*
Lucerne Festival Chorus; Philharmonia Orchestra / Wilhelm Furtwängler.
Tahra mono FURT1003 (78 minutes: ADD). Recorded live in 1954.
Gramophone Award Winner 1995.   Ⓕ Ⓗ

The fortieth anniversary of Furtwängler's death on November 30th, 1954 brought forth a rich crop of reissues and remasterings, most notably on the French label Tahra, which secured the rights to publish limited editions of some of Furtwängler's most important (and, it must be said, most frequently pirated) live recordings. Some of Furtwängler's finest performances of Beethoven's music were given in the last months of his life, an odd paradox given his failing health and, by November, the apparent extinction of his will to live. Yet this Lucerne Ninth is a seismic utterance, the final heroic regrouping of musical and psychic powers that in certain works of the repertory have this gangling figure towering over all his rivals. This is arguably the greatest of all Furtwängler's recordings of the symphony. Walter Legge wanted to acquire the performance as EMI's official replacement for the momentous 1951 Bayreuth account, but it wasn't to be. Since then, there have been various 'unofficial' editions. The Tahra differs in being 'official', well transferred, and further enhanced by a few introductory remarks from Furtwängler himself.

Here, the most significant section is that in which Furtwängler sees the problem of interpreting the Ninth as one that effectively post-dates the performing culture into which it was born. Furtwängler understood the Ninth as well as any conductor in the twentieth century. You can argue this way or that over the pacing of the slow movement (though we defy anyone to say that his performance is anything other than deeply eloquent) or the leisurely speed of the second movement Trio. In the all-important first movement, though, there is no doubt that Beethoven's written tempo markings and frequent subsequent modifications clearly presuppose the kind of uniquely singing, flexible, harmonically searching (but by no means over-slow) reading Furtwängler invariably gave us.

Choral Fantasia in C minor, Op. 80. Piano Concerto No. 5.
Alfred Brendel *pf*
London Philharmonic Choir and Orchestra / Bernard Haitink.
Philips Insignia 434 148-2PM (61 minutes: ADD). Recorded 1976-77.　Ⓜ️🆁🆁

Philips Insignia has an impressive back catalogue to drawn upon. Philips achieves consistent success with digital remastering, adding a presence and firmness of focus that seldom produce unwanted edginess. This certainly applies to Alfred Brendel's recording of the Fifth Concerto, coupled with his even more impressive *Choral Fantasia*. This latter is unforgettable, he and Haitink making something especially dazzling of this work. No one plays the big opening cadenza with more power and authority than Brendel and a similar magisterial breadth informs the *Emperor*; even though the first movement perhaps sounds a little too controlled, this is still a very satisfying performance. The choral contribution to the *Fantasia* is quite splendid. The recording combines orchestral weight with brilliance, and a most believable piano image.

Beethoven Piano Quintet in E flat major, Op. 16.
Mozart Piano Quintet in E flat major, K452. Sinfonia concertante in E flat major, K297*b*.
Walter Gieseking *pf* **Philharmonia Wind Quartet** (Sidney Sutcliffe *ob* Bernard Walton *cl*
Dennis Brain *hn* Cecil James *bn*); **Philharmonia Orchestra / Herbert von Karajan.**
Testament mono SBT1091 (80 minutes: ADD). Recorded 1955.　Ⓕ🅷🆁🆁

There have never been any doubts about these performances. The horn playing in the *Sinfonia concertante* is unsurpassable and in the quintets Gieseking's lightness and clarity and sense of style is beyond praise. The tempos are on the slow side in the first movement of the Mozart and the finale of the Beethoven but somehow with Gieseking, slow tempos have a way of seeming just about right. Richard Osborne's excellent notes quote a letter from Sidney Sutcliffe of touching modesty. Speaking of their run-through of the Mozart, he says, 'On reaching the *Allegro moderato*, the great man played two bars at an absolutely perfect tempo and then stopped and asked in the most gentle and hesitant manner, "Will that be all right for you?" So it was a most happy occasion although I found it a grave responsibility matching the artistry of my colleagues when Bernard [Walton], Cecil [James] and Dennis [Brain] were producing sounds of breath-taking beauty'. Breathtaking is just the right word for all concerned on what is, after all, one of the great chamber music records of the LP era. Great pains have been taken with the transfers, which sound fresher and more full-bodied than on any earlier LP transfers.

Beethoven Piano Quintet. Horn Sonata in F major, Op. 17.
Mozart Piano Quintet in E flat major, K452.
Robert Levin *fp* **Academy of Ancient Music Chamber Ensemble**
(Frank de Bruine *ob* Antony Pay *cl* Danny Bond *bn* Anthony Halstead *hn*)
Decca L'Oiseau-Lyre 455 994-2OH (67 minutes: DDD). Recorded 1996.　Ⓕ🅿️

A captivating record. To be sure, if you like the Viennese classics to sound suave and demure, it may not be for you: there's plenty of mellifluous playing, but the dominant impression is of rhythmic energy, drama and colour – with the characters of all five instruments vividly projected. Robert Levin is an unusually creative performer – not just in the way he searches for the right sound and style for every passage, but in his ability to add happily conceived extra ornamentation and short cadenzas, in the Mozart especially, where he starts to elaborate the text as early as the third bar. The wind players catch the mood and make appropriate decorations, too, particularly during repeated sections. Some may feel that this sort of thing has no place on a recording which may be played many times. The counter-argument is that a recording can never be more than one performance, that the ornamentation, wonderfully stylish, really does add something to the music, and that it's impossible to imagine that Mozart himself would have always stuck to the written text. And the disc would be well worth acquiring just for the Horn Sonata; Levin and Halstead give it a touch of extravagance and bravado that seems to capture the essence of early Beethoven. The recorded sound is admirably clear, with a pleasingly intimate quality.

Beethoven Septet in E flat major, Op. 20.
Mendelssohn Octet in E flat major, Op. 20.
members of the **Vienna Octet.**
Decca 421 093-2DM (74 minutes: ADD). Recorded 1959 and 1972.   Ⓜ

After its triumphant first performance in 1800, Beethoven's Septet went on to become not only one of the most popular but also one of the most influential chamber works of the period. The composer himself grew to dislike the piece, but it remains one of the most treasured products of the classical era. There are many fine performances of the Septet available. Curiously, compared to the 1972 Mendelssohn coupling, the 1959 sound in the Septet seems sweeter and more natural, to complement a performance which is an utter delight. Here is that old-fashioned, spontaneous yet relaxed Viennese style, with ample, beautifully-shaped phrasing and an engaging, slightly rustic quality in the clarinet tone which, alas, seems to have gone out of fashion. In the Mendelssohn Octet, the playing has a delicious buoyancy of spirit and an abundance of charm. The *Andante*, in particular, has an affecting, wistful delicacy and there is total clarity in the *fugato* which launches a strongly-played finale. The recording is clean and well balanced.

Septet in E flat major, Op. 20. Piano Quintet in E flat major, Op. 16. Sextet in E flat major, Op. 81*b*.
Ottó Rácz *ob* **József Balogh** *cl* **József Vajda** *bn* **Jenö Keveházi, János Keveházi,
Sándor Berki** *hns* **Ildikó Hegyi, Péter Popa** *vns* **Gyözö Máthé** *va* **Peter Szabó** *vc*
István Toth *db*
Naxos 8 553090 (74 minutes: DDD). Recorded 1994.   Ⓢ

These talented Hungarian players offer a fluent, responsive account of the Septet that highlights the music's intimate chamber character – delight in the music's elegance and perfect balance of instrumental forces. In the present instance, vivid recording creates a clear, natural ambience for this alert, sensitively blended ensemble. In the Sextet, horn players, Jenö and János Keveházi play with subtlety and panache as required, their tone spontaneous and free. This excellent, value-for-money Naxos disc also offers an elegant, well-turned performance of Beethoven's E flat Quintet.

Sextet in E flat major, Op. 71. March in B flat major, WoO29. Octet in E flat major, Op. 103.
Rondino in E flat major, WoO25. Duets, WoO27 – No. 1 in C major.
Charles Neidich *cl* **Mozzafiato** (Gerard Reuter, Marc Schachman *obs* Charles Neidich,
Ayako Oshima *cls* Dennis Godburn, Michael O'Donovan *bns* William Purvis, Stewart Rose *hns*).
Sony Classical Vivarte SK53367 (65 minutes: DDD). Recorded 1992-93.   ⒻⓅ

Beethoven composed the Octet, Op. 103, and *Rondino*, WoO25, some time around 1792 and, although it was published separately, there is evidence to suggest that the *Rondino* was originally intended as the fourth movement of a five-movement work. Mozzafiato plays the *Rondino* after the Octet, suggesting that the *Presto* finale was written to replace the *Rondino*. Its full-bodied tone-quality creates a warm, broadly conceived result: the oboe and bassoon solos which open the *Andante* second movement sound heavenly; the Minuet and Trio is cheerfully witty; a more flexible approach to the *Presto* finale produces a heightened dramatic effect and, in the *Rondino*, they deliciously reveal the music's textural diversity. In the Sextet, Op. 71, Neidich's clarinet playing is stupendous and his mellifluous virtuosity, especially in the faster outer movements, is well matched by the other performers to demonstrate this group's fine soloistic skills as well as their strong corporate identity. Enchanting performances of the March, WoO29, and the Duo for clarinet and bassoon, WoO27 No. 1, complete a delightful and immensely enjoyable concert.

Beethoven Piano Quartet in E flat major, Op. 16.
Schumann Piano Quartet in E flat major, Op. 47.
Isaac Stern *vn* **Jaime Laredo** *va* **Yo-Yo Ma** *vc* **Emanuel Ax** *pf*
Sony Classical SK53339 (65 minutes: DDD). Recorded 1992.   Ⓕ

There are numerous recordings of Beethoven's Op. 16 in its original Mozart-inspired quintet version for piano and wind against only a few for the piano quartet arrangement in which it rapidly re-emerged. But this 1992 performance of the quartet from Isaac Stern and his eminent younger colleagues makes it hard to believe that it was conceived for any other combination than theirs – and what higher praise than that? The *Andante cantabile*, with its delicately embellished melodic strands, surely gains in expressive eloquence from the more personal inflexions of caressing strings. And with their bold dynamic contrasts and piquant accentuation, what drama all four players draw from the opening movement. As a brilliant pianist himself, Beethoven entrusted the pianist with a load of responsibility, at once arrestingly and effortlessly discharged here by Emanuel Ax. As for Schumann's Piano Quartet, no longer is it dwarfed in popularity by its immediate predecessor in the same key, the Piano Quintet. This recording will surely win it a host of new friends – and not only for the mercurial lightness and grace of the Mendelssohnian sprites in the *Scherzo* and the glowing but essentially unsentimentalized intimacy of the *Andante cantabile* (as dedicated a love-song as Schumann ever wrote). The performers' impulse in the two flanking movements is unflagging and the overall impression is of spontaneous enjoyment – friends making music together for their own delight rather than as just another professional engagement. The sound is as vibrant as the playing.

Piano Quartets, WoO36 – No. 1 in E flat major; No. 2 in D major; No. 3 in C major. E flat major, Op. 16.
Raphael Oleg *vn* **Miguel da Silva** *va* **Marc Coppey** *vc* **Philippe Cassard** *pf*
Auvidis Valois V4715 (two discs: 88 minutes: DDD). Recorded 1994. Ⓕ

This issue of the three piano quartets Beethoven completed at the age of 15 but subsequently suppressed, in double harness with the 26-year-old composer's piano quartet arrangement of his Op. 16 Quintet for piano and wind, is more than welcome – despite its shortish playing time. Indebted to the still youthful Mozart the teenage Beethoven may well (and should) have been, as also tempted to entrust too much to the piano. But the unpredictability of even immature genius is striking. Never can you for a second foretell what surprise, whether of key, harmony, rhythm or scoring, lies just around the corner. His fluent, confident craftsmanship makes you marvel no less. Even when borrowing the three-movement sequence of Mozart's G major Violin Sonata (K397) for his own E flat major work, Beethoven gives his chromatically intensified opening *Adagio assai*, his stormy minor-key *Allegro* and even the beguiling variations, an unmistakable stamp of his own. The playing itself of course contributes to the pleasure, with first praise to Philippe Cassard for never allowing the keyboard to dominate. But all four Paris Conservatoire-trained colleagues are artists of taste and finesse. Their characterization is most sensitively attuned to the music's own true scale. Never does point-making sound self-consciously inflated. The recording itself has a pleasingly soft-grained intimacy.

String Quartets – No. 1 in F major, Op. 18 No. 1; No. 2 in G major, Op. 18 No. 2; No. 3 in D major, Op. 18 No. 3; No. 4 in C minor, Op. 18 No. 4; No. 5 in A major, Op. 18 No. 5; No. 6 in B flat major, Op. 18 No. 6; No. 7 in F major, Op. 59 No. 1, 'Rasumovsky'; No. 8 in E minor, Op. 59 No. 2, 'Rasumovsky'; No. 9 in C major, Op. 59 No. 3, 'Rasumovsky'; No. 10 in E flat major, Op. 74, 'Harp'; No. 11 in F minor, Op. 95, 'Serioso'; No. 12 in E flat major, Op. 127; No. 13 in B flat major, Op. 130; No. 14 in C sharp minor, Op. 131; No. 15 in A minor, Op. 132; No. 16 in F major, Op. 135.

Quartets Nos. 1-16. Grosse Fuge in B flat major, Op. 133.
Quartetto Italiano (Paolo Borciani, Elisa Pegreffi *vns* Piero Farulli *va* Franco Rossi *vc*)
Philips 454 062-2PB10 (ten discs: 544 minutes: ADD). Recorded 1967-75.
Also available separately:
426 046-2PM3 – Nos. 1-6. 420 797-2PM3 – Nos. 7-11. 426 050-2PM4 – Nos. 12-16.
Grosse Fuge in B flat major, Op. 133. Ⓜ

It goes without saying that no one ensemble can unlock all the secrets contained in these quartets. The Quartetto Italiano recordings have assumed a variety of formats since their first appearance. The quartets now comprise ten CDs but Philips wisely offers the performances at a highly competitive price in three separate sets and it is as separate entities they should be considered. Their claims are strongest in the Op. 18 Quartets. The Quartetto Italiano offers eminently civilized, thoughtful and aristocratic readings. Their approach is reticent but they also convey a strong sense of making music in domestic surroundings. Quite frankly, one could not do very much better than this set. Turning to the middle-period quartets the Italians are hardly less distinguished, even though there are times when the Végh offers even deeper insights: one thinks in particular of the slow movement of Op. 59 No. 1, which means more in their hands. Taken in isolation, however, the Quartetto Italiano remains eminently satisfying both musically and as recorded sound. As far as sound quality is concerned, it is rich and warm. In Opp. 74 and 95, the Quartetto Italiano more than holds its own against all comers. These are finely proportioned readings, poised and articulate.

The gain in clarity because of the remastering entails a very slight loss of warmth in the middle register, but as recordings the late quartets, made between 1967 and 1969, can hold their own against their modern rivals. Take care of the sense and the sound takes care of itself: the sonority that the Quartetto Italiano produces is well blended and has a great variety of tone colour and generally speaking, they give each musical point more time to register. Not all of these received universal acclaim at the time of their first release. The opening fugue of No. 14 is too slow at four-in-the-bar and far more *espressivo* than it should be but, overall, these performances still strike a finely judged balance between beauty and truth, and are ultimately more satisfying and searching than most of their rivals. The musical merits seem to well withstand the test of time.

String Quartets Nos. 1-9.
Végh Quartet (Sándor Végh, Sándor Zöldy *vns* Georges Janzer *va* Paul Szábo *vc*).
Auvidis Valois V4401/4 (four discs, oas: 57, 71, 66, 71 minutes). Recorded 1974.　　　Ⓕ **RR**
V4401 – Nos. 1 and 5. V4402 – Nos. 2, 3 and 4. V4403 – Nos. 6 and 7. V4404 – Nos. 8 and 9.

The Végh's classic accounts of the String Quartets are in a completely different league from any of their rivals: there is no cultivation of surface polish but there is no lack of elegance and finesse. Above all, there is no attempt to glamorize their sound. In No. 1 they find the *tempo giusto* right at the beginning and they find more depth in the slow movement than anyone else on record. Végh himself floats the melodic line in this movement in a most imaginative way and is wonderfully supported. In the civilized exchanges that open No. 2 the Végh brings an altogether light touch to bear and has an elegance and wit that is almost unmatched and, of course, great refinement of tone. At the time of its appearance on LP, there were complaints of the bottom-heavy recording and it is less transparent and lifelike than more modern recordings.

The *Rasumovsky* set is admirable for its alertness of articulation, rhythmic grasp and flexibility and its subtle range of tone-colour. The effortlessness with which the dialogue proceeds silences criticism. The Végh brings special insights to this inexhaustible music. The style and the quality of perception seem so remarkable and so well sustained here that any deficiencies can be overlooked. There are lapses in tone and intonation, most of them on the part of the leader, yet what a musician he is, and what a remarkable guide to the visionary content of these quartets. Where the music demands most in such matters he is never wanting. To sum up, though these are neither the most 'perfect' nor the most sumptuously recorded performances in the catalogue, they are the deepest and most searching. When listening to them you are conscious only of Beethoven's own voice. The transfers give a slightly firmer focus and sharper detail though the slight bottom-heaviness of which various critics have complained still remains.

String Quartets Nos. 3 and 7.
Orpheus Quartet (Charles-André Linale, Emilian Piediçuta *vns* Emile Cantor *va*
Laurentiu Sbarcea *vc*).
Channel Classics CCS6094 (68 minutes: DDD). Recorded 1993.　　　　　　　　　Ⓕ

The Orpheus Quartet does not use this music as a vehicle for its virtuosity or prowess; and they do not draw attention to their spot-on ensemble, immaculate intonation and tonal finesse, though they possess all these qualities in no small measure. Take the *Presto* finale of the D major: we are not presented with the headlong rush favoured by many ensembles. The sense of pace is in harmony with the horse-drawn rather than the jet-driven; every note speaks, every phrase tells and the overall effect is all the more exhilarating. Generally speaking, the Orpheus find the *tempo giusto* throughout. They remain attuned to the sensibility of the period and relate their pace to a dance movement in a manner that their rivals have lost. There is something very natural about the players' music-making. They are inside these scores and convey their involvement; no auto pilot, no *ersatz* feeling, no exaggerated or mechanized *sforzatos*. What a relief! The recording is bright and clean, and enhances the claims of this impressive issue.

String Quartets Nos. 4 and 15.
Petersen Quartet (Conrad Muck, Gernot Süssmuth *vns* Friedemann Weigle *va*
Hans-Jakob Eschenburg *vc*).
Capriccio 10 722 (63 minutes: DDD). Recorded 1995.　　　　　　　　　　　　　Ⓕ

The Petersen Quartet possesses impeccable technical address, immaculate ensemble, flawless intonation and tonal finesse. Tempos are judged with real musicianship, and dynamic markings are observed without being exaggerated. The C minor Quartet, Op. 18 No. 4, has dramatic tension without loss of lyrical fervour and the *Scherzo* has wit. When we move to the first movement of the A minor Quartet the sound world changes as if youth has given way to wisdom and experience.

They hardly put a foot wrong here and their *Heiliger Dankgesang* is rapt and inward-looking. They press ahead fractionally in one or two places – on the reprise of the main section in the second movement and when the main theme returns in the finale. But one or two minor reservations apart, theirs is quite simply the most satisfying late Beethoven to have appeared in recent years. Above all the Petersen do not invite you to admire their prowess. They appear to be untouched by the three 'g's (Gloss, Glamour and Glitz) and their concern is with truth rather than beauty.

String Quartets Nos. 5 and 6.
Quatuor Mosaïques (Erich Höbarth, Andrea Bischof *vns* Anita Mitterer *va* Christophe Coin *vc*).
Auvidis Astrée E8541 (58 minutes: DDD). Recorded 1994. Ⓕ🅿Ⓔ

Of the Op. 18 works the A major probably has most to gain from a responsive performance on period instruments. Its light textures and air of amiable elegance are particularly resistant to the brilliance of certain modern-instrument ensembles; and the Mosaïques, most imaginative and penetrating of 'original' quartets, give an almost ideal reading. The imitative interplay of the finale gains particularly from the textural clarity easier to achieve on period instruments played with sparing vibrato. The tempo, characteristically, is on the broad side here. But few ensembles have brought such wit and grace, such a subtle variety of colour and bowing, to the quicksilver instrumental dialogues. Yet the Mosaïques' delicacy and intimacy do not preclude an authentic Beethovenian trenchancy in the development, bows biting deeply into gut strings in those vehement *fortissimo* exchanges. The *Andante* variations can often outstay their welcome; but these players bring an unusual grave eloquence to the theme itself. In the B flat Quartet they are hardly less persuasive. The epigrammatic opening *Allegro* is as spring-heeled and quick-witted as you could wish, yet avoids the clipped, relentlessly sportive approach heard in many performances. In the *Adagio ma non troppo* Erich Höbarth brings a rare sense of fantasy to the conventional-looking violin *fioriture*; and the protracted ending is, for once, witty rather than tedious. For musical insight the Mosaïques' beautifully recorded readings of these quartets hold their own with any of the modern-instrument versions in the catalogue.

String Quartets Nos. 7-9.
The Lindsays (Peter Cropper, Ronald Birks *vns* Roger Bigley *va* Bernard Gregor-Smith *vc*).
ASV CDDCS207 (two discs: 115 minutes: DDD). Ⓜ

In the few years that separate the Op. 18 from the Op. 59 quartets, Beethoven's world was shattered by the oncoming approach of deafness and the threat of growing isolation. The Op. 59 consequently inhabit a totally different plane, one in which the boundaries of sensibility had been extended in much the same way as the map of Europe was being redrawn. Each of the three quartets alludes to a Russian theme by way of compliment to Count Rasumovsky, who had commissioned the set. The immediate impression the F major Quartet conveys is of great space, breadth and vision; this is to the quartet what the *Eroica* is to the symphony. Although the Lindsays may be rivalled (and even surpassed) in some of their insights by the Végh, taken by and large, they are second to none and superior to most. In each movement of the E minor they find the *tempo giusto* and all that they do as a result has the ring of complete conviction. The development and reprise of the first movement are repeated as well as the exposition and how imaginatively they play it too! The C major is not quite in the same class though the opening has real mystery and awe and some listeners might legitimately feel that the whole movement could do with a little more momentum. On the other hand, they move the second movement on rather too smartly. Yet how splendidly they convey the pent-up torrent of energy unleashed in this fugal onrush. Even if it does not command quite the same elevation of feeling or quality of inspiration that distinguishes their F major and E minor quartets, it is still pretty impressive.

String Quartets Nos. 8 and 13.
Talich Quartet (Petr Messiereur, Jan Kvapil *vns* Jan Talich *va* Evzen Rattai *vc*).
Calliope CAL9637 (73 minutes: ADD). Ⓕ

The advantage of this Talich recording is that it couples a masterpiece from Beethoven's middle period, the great E minor Quartet, with one of the greatest of his last years. The B flat was the third of the late quartets to be composed and at its first performance in 1826 its last movement, the *Grosse Fuge*, baffled his contemporaries. Later that same year, he substituted the present finale, publishing the *Grosse Fuge* separately. The Talich Quartet has a no less impressive technical command than other ensembles but theirs are essentially private performances, which one is privileged to overhear rather than the overprojected 'public' accounts we so often hear on record nowadays. At 73 minutes this is marvellous value too.

String Quartets Nos. 11 and 15.
Végh Quartet (Sándor Végh, Sándor Zöldy *vns* Georges Janzer *va* Paul Szabó *vc*).
Auvidis Valois V4406 (68 minutes: ADD). Ⓕ **RR**

String Quartets Nos. 15 and 16.
Talich Quartet (Petr Messiereur, Jan Kvapil *vns* Jan Talich *va* Evzen Rattai *vc*).
Calliope CAL9639 (68 minutes: ADD). Ⓕ

After the expansive canvas of the Op. 59 Quartets and the *Eroica*, Beethoven's F minor Quartet, Op. 95, displays musical thinking of the utmost compression. The first movement is a highly concentrated sonata design, which encompasses in its four minutes almost as much drama as a full-scale opera. With it comes one of the greatest masterpieces of his last years, the A minor, Op. 132. The isolation wrought first by his deafness and secondly, by the change in fashion of which he complained in the early 1820s, forced Beethoven in on himself. Opus 132 with its other-worldly *Heiliger Dankgesang*, written on his recovery from an illness, is music neither of the 1820s nor of Vienna, it belongs to that art which transcends time and place. Though other performances may be technically more perfect, these are interpretations that come closer to the spirit of this great music than any other on CD. Collectors need have no doubts as to the depth and intelligence of the Talich Quartet's readings for they bring a total dedication to this music: their performances are innocent of artifice and completely selfless. There is no attempt to impress the listener with their own virtuosity or to draw attention to themselves in any way. The recordings are eminently faithful and natural, not 'hi-fi' or overbright but the overall effect is thoroughly pleasing.

String Quartets Nos. 10 and 12.
Végh Quartet (Sándor Végh, Sándor Zöldy *vns* Georges Janzer *va* Paul Szabó *vc*).
Auvidis Valois V4405 (71 minutes: ADD). Ⓕ **RR**

String Quartets Nos. 14 and 16.
Végh Quartet
Auvidis Valois V4408 (66 minutes: ADD). Ⓕ **RR**

Beethoven stepped both outside and beyond his period nowhere more so than in the late quartets and the last five piano sonatas. The Op. 127 has been called Beethoven's 'crowning monument to lyricism', whilst the Op. 131 is more inward-looking. Every ensemble brings a different set of insights to this great music so that it is not possible to hail any single quartet as offering the whole truth – yet these are as near to the whole truth as we are ever likely to come. The Végh give us music-making that has a profundity and spirituality that completely outweigh any tiny blemishes of intonation or ensemble. One does not get the feeling of four professional quartet players performing publicly for an audience but four thoughtful musicians sharing their thoughts about this music in the privacy of their own home. They bring us closer to this music than do any of their high-powered rivals.

String Quartets Nos. 13 and 16. Grosse Fuge in B flat major, Op. 133.
Juilliard Quartet (Robert Mann, Joel Smirnoff *vns* Samuel Rhodes *va* Joel Krosnick *vc*).
Sony Classical SK62792 (76 minutes: DDD). Recorded 1996. Ⓕ

The Juilliard take Op. 130's long first-movement repeat then play the *Grosse Fuge* as its rightful finale, relegating the lighter-hearted 'rewrite' to encore status at the very end of the piece. Hearing the fugue as a structural summation rather than a disembodied torso makes good musical sense (its replacement turns most of Op. 130 into a sort of elevated divertimento), and the Juilliard's concentration more than justifies their decision. The performance itself is full of subtle beauties, not least in the first movement, at the point near the onset of the development (around 8'29") where *Allegro* fragments prompt *espressivo Adagio* responses and where the players gauge the music's oscillating moods with characteristic perception. Similarly, there is a sense of infinite sadness at 5'16" into the *Andante con moto* third movement, whereas the *Presto* and *Alla danza tedesca* are, by turns, fleeting and elegant; the *Grosse Fuge* struts, sings and swings, and the 'second' finale dances to a pointed *staccato*. This is profound, deeply pondered music-making, the sort that would be impossible to achieve in less than half a lifetime. Op. 135 is similarly persuasive, with a playfully disruptive *Vivace*, a heart-rending *Lento assai* and, most significantly, an account of the finale that includes the important – though rarely played – second repeat. Sony's recordings are warm.

String Quartets Nos. 14 and 16 (both orch. Mitropoulos/Bernstein).
Vienna Philharmonic Orchestra / Leonard Bernstein.
DG 435 779-2GH (77 minutes: ADD / DDD). Recorded live in 1977 and 1989. Ⓕ

When the young Leonard Bernstein was a student at Harvard University he went to Dimitri Mitropoulos's first concert with the Boston Symphony Orchestra in 1936, which included his own arrangement for string orchestra of Beethoven's longest, most complex and – in the composer's own opinion – finest string quartet: No. 14, whose seven movements are meant to be played consecutively, without pauses in between. Bernstein borrowed Mitropoulos's copy of the Eulenburg miniature score, made his own adjustments to the latter's editing, and performed the work several times with his first orchestra, the New York City Symphony, and once, later, with the New York Philharmonic. DG's recording was an amalgamation of takes from several live performances with the strings of the Vienna Philharmonic Orchestra ('the perfect people to do this', Bernstein said) both at the Salzburg Festival and in Vienna, with no 'touch-up' session in the studio afterwards. The virtuosity and unanimity of the VPO strings command the highest respect. The grave opening fugue, the brilliant *Scherzo* and the impassioned finale sound terrific; right or wrong, this is a performance that takes you by the throat. No. 14 is prefaced with Beethoven's last Quartet, No. 16, recorded in what were presumably comparable circumstances in the Musikverein in Vienna in 1989, less than a year before Bernstein's death. It could be argued that this in many ways more intimate music responds less well to performance by an orchestral string section; but listen to the VPO playing the *Scherzo* and the *Lento* which follows it and see if you are not persuaded otherwise. This is a fabulous disc.

String Quartets Nos. 15 and 16.
Cleveland Quartet (William Preucil, Peter Salaff *vns* James Dunham *va* Paul Katz *vc*).
Telarc CD80427 (69 minutes: DDD). Recorded 1995.   Ⓕ

The members of the Cleveland Quartet are upholders of tradition, rather than seekers after new truths. One of this ensemble's most notable characteristics is its rich, warm tone, well captured here. The first movement of the A minor Quartet has a level of emotional commitment that's quite compelling – all the details of this complex music fall into place and contribute to the overall effect. If the rest of the quartet isn't quite so outstanding it's still very good, with a lovely swinging rhythm to the second movement, and delightfully sprightly accounts of the *Andante* episodes in the slow movement – absolutely 'feeling new strength', as Beethoven's caption puts it. Their Op. 135 is also very impressive. The *Lento* is deeply felt, their rich sound really coming into its own. And the finale must be one of the best versions on record – spirited, touching, playful, as the music's mood demands.

Piano Trios – E flat major, Op. 1 No. 1; G major, Op. 1 No. 2; C minor, Op. 1 No. 3;
B flat major, Op. 11; D major, Op. 70 No. 1, 'Ghost'; E flat major, Op. 70 No. 2; B flat major,
Op. 97, 'Archduke'; B flat major, WoO39; E flat major, WoO38; E flat major, Op. 44; G major,
Op. 121*a*.
Beaux Arts Trio (Daniel Guilet *vn* Bernard Greenhouse *vc* Menahem Pressler *pf*).
Philips The Early Years 438 948-2PM3 (three discs: 235 minutes: ADD). Recorded 1965.   Ⓜ **RR**

It's the immediacy and freshness, the wholehearted commitment of the playing by the Beaux Arts Trio that holds you spellbound in almost every context. To begin with, in the *joie de vivre* of the E flat and G major Op. 1 Trios, it's so good to be reminded that a colossus like Beethoven was once so young at heart – in the persuasive lyricism of slower tempos no less than the teasing, devil-may-care sparkle and wit of their finales (taken at a breathless pace without for a moment sounding gabbled). The crowning performance is nevertheless the *Archduke*. The players' expansive yet warmly human nobility in the opening *Allegro moderato*, their urgent, mercurial response to the undertones of the *Scherzo*, their raptness in the visionary serenity of the slow movement and their pungency in the finale convince you that no greater piano trio has ever been written. Here, too, you're given the fullest chance to enjoy the silken beauty of Guilet's violin and the velvet richness of Greenhouse's now legendary 1707 Stradivari cello; also the wonderful blend of tone achieved by all three in contexts like the *pizzicato/staccato* of the first movement's development, or the eerie chromatic start to the trio of the *Scherzo*. Hailed in the booklet as 'the soul of the entire ensemble', Pressler himself achieves many miracles of delicacy and fleetness.

Piano Trios – B flat major, Op. 11; B flat major, Op. 97, 'Archduke'.
Chung Trio (Kyung-Wha Chung *vn* Myung-Wha Chung *vc* Myung-Whun Chung *pf*).
EMI CDC5 55187-2 (61 minutes: DDD). Recorded 1992.   Ⓕ

The playing of Kyung-Wha Chung – sweet, sentient and sharply defined – almost persuades you again of the violin's adapted and adopted role in the Op. 11 Trio. And what the modern piano loses in the immediacy of its own voice and its empathy with the others is generously compensated by Myung-Whun's nimble, light-filled playing. This piano's warmer resonance comes into its own in the long distances of the rolling *crescendos* and *decrescendos* which form the heart of the *Adagio*, and lift it into the major. The real wonder of this disc, though, is the Chungs' performance of the Op. 97. Beethoven dedicated it 'in deep reverence' to Austria's Archduke – and Myung-Whun never forgets it, whether in his awed, reverential opening, or in the simplicity of the wonderfully hushed frame of his slow movement theme. Violin and cello merely brush, rather than gush, against it, and lead it into a dream sequence of variations. The Chungs' gentle unfolding and nourishing of this opening movement – everything is done within a veiled undertone – leave plenty of fuel unburned for the *Scherzo*, which starts on tiptoe, and whose dark chromatic shadows in the trio are never overbriskly dissipated by what can often be an overassertive waltz. This is chamber-music-making at its most perceptive and rewarding.

String Trio in E flat major, Op. 3; Serenade in D major, Op. 8.
Leopold String Trio (Marianne Thorsen *vn* Sarah-Jane Bradley *va* Kate Gould *vc*).
Hyperion CDA67253 (73 minutes: DDD). Recorded 1998.

Ⓕ **E**

String Trios, Op. 9 – No. 1 in G major, No. 2 in D major, No. 3 in C minor.
Leopold String Trio.
Hyperion CDA67254 (77 minutes: DDD). Recorded 1998.

Ⓕ **E**

The Leopold String Trio is a group with the kind of virtues that come from long study together: polished ensemble, excellent intonation and notably consistent and well-thought out interpretations. Just occasionally the viola is swamped by the outer voices, but this is only an infrequent problem; overall it's a particularly well-balanced and recorded set. They show that a restrained style can bring out the inward aspect to the music. On the fourth track of Op. 8, where Beethoven alternates a sombre *Adagio* with a facetiously jolly *Scherzo*, the stark yet gentle Leopold playing of the slow music expresses more pathos and melancholy than the intensity of other versions. And the Leopold's care and respect for the text also tips the balance in its favour – in Op. 3's second Minuet, for example, Marianne Thorsen's beautiful and exact interpretation is utterly winning. In Op. 9 No. 1's *Scherzo*, another splendidly poised and spirited reading, there's a special bonus – a second Trio, omitted from most editions. It's an attractive bit of music and gives the movement a new dimension. For the Op. 9 Trios, L'Archibudelli (below) has some advantages over this recording: the luminous tone of its period instruments, and a daring approach to musical characterization. Its tempos for the *Adagios* are markedly faster than the Leopold's; this may be correct for the 1790s, but the breadth and serenity of the Leopold String Trio is more persuasive.

String Trios, Op. 9 – Nos. 1-3.
L'Archibudelli (Vera Beths *vn* Jürgen Kussmaul *va* Anner Bylsma *vc*).
Sony Classical Vivarte SK48190 (68 minutes: DDD). Recorded 1991.

Ⓕ **P**

A group with 'a special love for historical stringed instruments' is how L'Archibudelli is described, as might be gleaned from its name (an Italian compilation of bows and strings), plus the fact that Anner Bylsma plays a 1835 Gianfrancesco Pressenda cello, Vera Beths a 1727 Stradivari violin and Jürgen Kussmaul a 1785 William Forster viola. But though striving for a special period quality of sound they are anything but antiquarian in their approach to these works, all of them striking enough to have placed Beethoven among the immortals even if he had written nothing else. With their brisk tempo, strong dynamic contrast and piquant accentuation, they leave no doubt of the urgency inherent in the key of C minor for this composer. The other two Trios in major keys are equally imaginatively characterized and contrasted. Some listeners might even feel the players are overvolatile in their response to every detailed innuendo, at the expense of firmly drawn, classical line. But their relish of the music wins the day. Once or twice busy figuration in the lower strings emerges a bit bottom-heavy. The recording is most realistic.

Cello Sonatas – No. 1 in F major, Op. 5 No. 1; No. 2 in G minor, Op. 5 No. 2; No. 3 in A major, Op. 69; No. 4 in C major, Op. 102 No. 1; No. 5 in D major, Op. 105 No. 2.

Beethoven Cello Sonatas Nos. 1-5.
Brahms Cello Sonata No. 2 in F major, Op. 99.
Pablo Casals *vc* Mieczyslaw Horszowski, Otto Schulhof *pfs*
EMI Références mono CHS5 65185-2 (two discs: 136 minutes: ADD). Recorded 1930-39.

Ⓜ **H**

Sensitive phrasing was the very hub of Pablo Casals's art, and these CDs are more revealing than many of how this most communicative of cellists could mould and energize a musical line, reducing his tone to a soulful tenor then thrusting a powerful *sforzando* for maximum dynamic contrast. The Beethoven sonatas are endlessly rewarding in this respect, but even they must bow to the marginal supremacy of Casals's 1936 account of the Brahms F major Sonata, one of the truly great cello recordings. No one since has projected the work's heroic opening with as much confidence (the repeat is observed, by the way), nor brought greater suppleness or tonal variety to the *Adagio affettuoso*. Note, too, how both Casals and Horszowski explore the winding musical thickets of the *Allegro passionato* and make play with the closing *Allegro molto*. The Beethoven sonatas are equally indelible, the Op. 5 works sounding very much their innovatory selves, and those of Op. 102 more probing and explosive than most. Both players invest Op. 102 No. 2's searching *Adagio con molto sentimento d'affetto* with an intriguing sense of the numinous, then dig deep into the succeeding *Allegro fugato* – a gritty debate on the preceding mystery. Casals recorded the Op. 69 Sonata some nine years before Opp. 5 and 102, not with Horszowski, but with the stylish and facilitating Otto Schulhof. It differs from its companions in being more songful than soulful and with a *bel canto* solo line that extends to the charming Menuet makeweight. Recordings of this unique quality deserve painstaking restoration, and Andrew Walters's transfers are excellent. Surface levels are low, the solo cello sounds clean and immediate, and the piano is more recognizably itself than on some 78s from the 1930s.

Cello Sonatas Nos. 1 and 2. 12 Variations in F major on 'Ein Mädchen oder Weibchen' from 'Die Zauberflöte', Op. 66. Seven Variations in E flat major on Mozart's 'Bei Männern, welche Liebe fühlen' from 'Die Zauberflöte', WoO46.
Mischa Maisky *vc* **Martha Argerich** *pf*
DG 431 801-2GH (66 minutes DDD). Recorded 1990.   Ⓕ

The two sets of variations flank the two sonatas. All four works are early, the sonatas and first variation set were written in 1796, the other piece in 1801. In these circumstances, we rightly expect to hear Beethoven in youthful vein. The courtly and conventional gestures of the genial *Mädchen* Variations are a bit too predictable despite a degree of Beethovenian humour that is evident in some bouncy rhythms and dynamics (the slow F minor music towards the end goes deeper, too). But the music is attractive in its own right and is played with ample wit, agility and impeccable ensemble. The same may be said of the other variation set (a more imaginative piece as perhaps befitting its more tender and lilting theme), which is presented with considerable grace. Both the *Mädchen* Variations and the First Cello Sonata are in F major, but so vivid is the playing that you do not feel any sameness. It is alert and crisp, while still offering a proper degree of cello warmth. As always, Argerich's attack is most sharply focused but her tone isn't hard. The recording is satisfying, with a good dynamic range. The two artists manage the varying moods and tempo changes skilfully in these unusually shaped sonatas, in which slow and fast speeds both find their place in big first movements (complete with exposition repeats) which are then followed by rondo finales. Few artists in this repertoire can match the special electricity that Maisky and Argerich give us.

Cello Sonatas Nos. 2, 3 and 5.
David Watkin *vc* **Howard Moody** *fp*
Chandos Chaconne CHAN0561 (70 minutes: DDD). Recorded 1994.   Ⓕ **P**

If you're not sure about the advantages of original-instrument performance of classical chamber music, try this disc! Watkin and Moody demonstrate that 'authentic' Beethoven need not in any way diminish the grandeur and emotional depth of his music. David Watkin, very correctly, uses vibrato discreetly and selectively, and is most imaginative in finding just the right bow-stroke for each musical nuance – his urgent phrasing of the G minor Sonata's first *Allegro*, and the way he breathes the phrases at the start of the D major's slow movement are two examples of many memorable details. Howard Moody plays two original period instruments – a Rosenberger fortepiano of *c*1800 for the G minor Sonata, and an 1826 Graf for the two later works – and seems always able to find reserves of sonority to encompass Beethoven's most dramatic moments. The climactic codas of the A major Sonata's outer movements are especially exciting. The 'big' feeling of these performances is partly due to the lively, intimate recording – the sound is not diluted in any large spaces and we can also hear quite a bit of mechanical noise from the piano, and sniffs from the players.

Violin Sonatas – No. 1 in D major, Op. 12 No. 1; No. 2 in A major, Op. 12 No. 2; No. 3 in E flat major, Op. 12 No. 3; No. 4 in A minor, Op. 23; No. 5 in F major, Op. 24, 'Spring'; No. 6 in A major, Op. 30 No. 1; No. 7 in C minor, Op. 30 No. 2; No. 8 in G major, Op. 30 No. 3; No. 9 in A major, Op. 47, 'Kreutzer'; No. 10 in G major, Op. 96.

Violin Sonatas Nos. 1-10.
Itzhak Perlman *vn* **Vladimir Ashkenazy** *pf*
Decca Ovation 421 453-2DM4 (four discs: 239 minutes: ADD). Recorded 1973-75.   Ⓜ **RR**

Although Beethoven designated these works as 'for piano and violin', following Mozart's example, it is unlikely that he thought of the piano as leading the proceedings, or the violin either, for that matter: both instruments are equal partners and in that sense this is true chamber music. Perlman and Ashkenazy are artists of the first rank and there is much pleasure to be derived from their set. Such an imaginative musician as Ashkenazy brings great subtlety to these works composed by a supreme pianist-composer. And the better the pianist is in this music, the better does the violinist play. Discernment is matched by spontaneity and the whole series is remarkably fine, while their celebrated performance of the *Kreutzer* Sonata has quite superb eloquence and vitality. The recording boasts unusually truthful violin sound capturing all the colour of Perlman's playing – and that is saying something. Ashkenazy's vivid attack is always faithful to the Beethoven idiom.

Violin Sonatas Nos. 1-4.
Jascha Heifetz *vn* **Emmanuel Bay** *pf*
RCA Victor Gold Seal mono GD87704 (69 minutes: ADD). Recorded 1947-52. Ⓜ Ⓗ

Violin Sonatas Nos. 5-7.
Jascha Heifetz *vn* **Emmanuel Bay** *pf*
RCA Victor Gold Seal mono GD87705 (63 minutes: ADD). Recorded 1950-52. Ⓜ Ⓗ

Violin Sonatas Nos. 8-10.
Jascha Heifetz *vn* **Emmanuel Bay, Brooks Smith** *pfs*
RCA Victor Gold Seal mono GD87706 (72 minutes: ADD). Recorded 1952-60. Ⓜ Ⓗ

There is a distinct danger that our ears may well be killed with kindness by these reissues of all the sonatas played by Heifetz. Each volume gives over an hour of generous playing time and, unless one is rigorously self-disciplined, the temptation to listen to far too much at once is almost impossible to resist. The transfers are of the highest quality, revealing the very essence of Heifetz's art. In the three early Op. 12 Sonatas, we hear that flinty intonation which fusing with the mere caress of the bow, creates unique finesse for the brio of the opening of No. 1 and the gleeful quick changes of register in the first movement of No. 3. One is reminded, too, that unlike so many of his Juilliard-trained successors to virtuosity, there is never any concession to the primacy of polished sound alone: it is always the nature of the instrument itself, the grain of its wood, the pliability of its strings, the tension of the horsehair, which is brought to bear on the nature of the interpretation itself. No. 3 points to the happiness of Heifetz's partnership with his pianist, Emmanuel Bay. Overriding the slight and inevitable dryness of recording, there is a sweetness, a simplicity, a quicksilver response which at times achieves the rare feat of enabling the ear to apprehend both players' contributions simultaneously. In the slow movement Heifetz, as if acknowledging where Beethoven's heart lay in this Sonata, is cool, almost distanced from the piano's dominant role.

Heifetz as miniaturist makes himself known in the Fourth Sonata and in the very last one (No. 10). In No. 7, he refuses the temptation to don the tragic mask, leaning almost nonchalantly on the accents and upbeats of the first movement, and treating the *Andante scherzoso* with a piquant near-minimalism. The two big sonatas, on the other hand, are boldly characterized. No. 5 is, typically, one of the fastest in the business: this is a true driving *Allegro*, with the sap rising fast through Heifetz's intense vibrato and his firm, heavy pressure on the down-bow. He makes it clear that *molto espressivo* does not mean *molto adagio* in the slow movement: this, too, is marked by a steady sense of direction, with each carefully shaded sustained note carrying through the momentum of the whole. Brooks Smith is a generally less characterful, more self-effacing pianist in the *Kreutzer* (No. 9). But Heifetz redoubles the attack, never letting us forget that this is the spirit as well as the letter of a true *Presto*. Stark, biting passages of bowing suddenly draw back to moments of smoky half-voice before the cool air of the slow movement. The theme is penny-plain in its unfolding, the better to offset the electric signals with which Heifetz responds to the piano in the first variation, the audaciously driven *moto perpetuo* of the second, and the remarkable trills of the fourth.

Violin Sonatas Nos. 6-8.
Gidon Kremer *vn* **Martha Argerich** *pf*
DG 445 652-2GH (64 minutes: DDD). Recorded 1993. Ⓕ Ⓔ

Beethoven's Op. 30 Violin Sonatas are three irresistibly lively and individual spirits in the hands and imaginations of Martha Argerich and Gidon Kremer. The first, in A major, has that particular quality of blithe and elusive joy reminiscent of the *Spring* Sonata, and created here by the lightest and truest touch on string and key, fused with bright rhythmic clarity. The slow movement is a tremulous song of long-forgotten, far-off things, in which violin and piano find an intimate balance of tone. The second sonata of the group is here less an heroically clenched C minor fist, more the unfolding of a gripping and tense *Märchen*: a dark children's fairy-tale told through the rapid tapering of a phrase-ending on the violin, the gutsy ebb and flow of a piano *crescendo*, the sudden *pianissimo* picking up after the loud chords of a second theme. At the start of the development,

Argerich even seems to be asking if her listeners are sitting comfortably – and rather hoping they are not. The G major Sonata's centrepiece is its Minuet and Trio, which Argerich and Kremer cunningly tease and charm into revealing its archaic qualities: a dance glimpsed through a lace veil. It is framed by two fast movements that would identify their performers anywhere, with their high-voltage velocity and wittily imaginative anticipation of each other's every move.

---

12 Variations on Handel's 'See the conqu'ring hero comes', WoO45. 12 Variations on Mozart's 'Ein Mädchen oder Weibchen', Op. 66. Seven Variations on Mozart's 'Bei Männern, welche Liebe fühlen', WoO46. Horn Sonata, Op. 17 (arr. vc).
Pieter Wispelwey vc **Lois Shapiro** fp
Channel Classics CCS6494 (45 minutes: DDD). Recorded 1994.   Ⓕ ℗

There may be only 45 minutes of it, but this recital of Beethoven variations teems with fresh insights in the irresistible serendipity of its playing. Lois Shapiro partners Pieter Wispelwey's 1701 cello on a 1780 Viennese fortepiano whose wiry energies she unleashes without more ado in an attention-grabbing opening theme for Handel's *See the conqu'ring hero comes*. Her bright-eyed first variation glints as phrases dart from dynamic shadow to light and back again. Then the cello's lean, slightly astringent voice makes itself felt in no uncertain terms before the keyboard gets its own back in mercurial scale passages. The players' delight in teasing, sparring and debating with each other comes into its own in the variations on *Ein Mädchen oder Weibchen*. The theme itself struts forward cheekily, only to peck its way through the first variation, before the cello makes the most of the wry harmonic subtext of the second. In the seventh, one half of a shared phrase caresses and preens the other; the tenth casts the shadow of Papageno's noose. Each player's imagination and technique is tested to the full in an absorbing account of the more abstracted *Bei Männern* variations. The world of *Singspiel* is not far away, either, in this performance of the Sonata in F major, Op. 17: Wispelwey and Shapiro summon up the nascent world of Marzelline and Jacquino in their quick, ardent responses to the music and to each other's playing.

Beethoven Andante favori in F major, WoO57.
Chopin Waltzes, Op. 34 – No. 2 in A flat major; No. 3 in A minor; No. 4 in F major. Scherzo No. 2 in B flat minor, Op. 31. Barcarolle in F sharp major, Op. 60.
Debussy Suite bergamasque. Estampes.
Sviatoslav Richter pf
Orfeo d'Or C491981B (75 minutes: ADD). Recorded live in 1977.   Ⓜ

This live Richter recital from Salzburg must go close to the top of the priority list. Unlike some of his other live recordings, it's superbly recorded, with plenty of air in the sound and an instrument capable of withstanding fairly imperious *fortissimos* without losing its tonal bloom or firmness of tuning. The *Andante favori* is a gem of a performance, tonally ravishing yet unerringly responsive to the structural flow. In the Chopin group Richter not only displays his customary authority but revels in the music and the occasion. Abandon without indiscipline is the key, and the result is a tremendous sense of *élan*, bordering on exaltation; the applause and bravos between each piece seem only fitting. Debussy's *Suite bergamasque* goes like a dream, with a 'Clair de lune' hypnotically slow yet never in danger of becoming merely prosaic, thanks to sheer beauty of sonority and hypersensitive weighting of harmony. Richter's concentration wavers a little more in *Estampes*, but what a treasurable recital this is otherwise.

Bagatelles – Op. 33; Op. 119; Op. 126; A minor, WoO59, 'Für Elise'ᵃ; B flat major, WoO60. Rondo in C major, Op. 51 No. 1. Allegretto in C minor, WoO53.
Alfred Brendel pf
Philips 456 031-2PH (77 minutes: DDD). Recorded 1996, item marked ᵃ1984.   Ⓕ

Listening to Beethoven's *Bagatelles* can be like looking over the composer's shoulder as he works. A scrap of a theme, a repeated chord, a formulaic accompanying figure – suddenly blossoms into something rich and strange; the one-dimensional turns magically into the three-dimensional. An unassuming little *Andante con moto* tune dissolves into a cadenza, then emerges transfigured in ecstatic counterpoint (Op. 126 No. 1); an innocent, almost plain folk-melody reappears floating on high, a voice from another world (Op. 119 No. 11). And so often in the *Bagatelles* humour is at the core. If there's such a thing as profound levity, this is it. Brendel, who has written so effectively about humour in Beethoven, plainly revels in this aspect of the *Bagatelles*. The quirkiness, the delight in pulling the rug from under the listener's feet – he seems to have made it all his own. One could argue with the approach here or there – Op. 119 No. 5 strikes one as more laboured than *Risoluto*; the strange half-pedal at the end of Op. 119 No. 3 produces a momentarily metallic aura around the notes – but much more often, character and texture are calculated to a nicety. And could any merely human pianist be expected to please in all of these hugely contrasted miniatures? He also conveys a sense of Op. 126 as – in Beethoven's own words – a 'cycle of *Bagatelles*', the extraordinary No. 11 (a gorgeous *Andante amabile* framed by music-hall fanfares) making a very thought-provoking finale.

33 Variations on a Waltz by Diabelli, Op. 120.

Diabelli Variations.
Stephen Kovacevich *pf*
Philips Concert Classics 422 969-2PCC (54 minutes: ADD). Recorded 1969.   ⑧ **RR**

Diabelli Variations.
Alfred Brendel *pf*
Philips 426 232-2PH (53 minutes: DDD). Recorded 1988.   ⑤

Here is a treat, indeed; for in Brendel and Kovacevich we have two of the gramophone's finest interpreters of the *Diabelli* Variations. Brendel has now recorded the work three times. His live 1977 recording of the work, made by Philips in collaboration with the BBC (available on a five-CD set), is still something of a landmark. The piano itself may sound a trifle battle-weary by the end, but the performance is a *tour de force*, a finely thought-out reading seemingly improvised into life with astonishing fire and intellectual acumen. By contrast, this 1988 recording is a calmer affair and this relates not so much to tempos but the general mood. We are off the hustings and back in the study. This version is more measured as befits a reading that works its way slightly more circumspectly to the newly poised expressiveness of the final variations, the concluding Minuet now an even more sophisticated essay in sublime gracefulness.

The reissue of Kovacevich's famous recording does, however, present a considerable challenge to Brendel. The reissue is at bargain-price and though the booklet is bereft of notes, the CD has the full range of cueing points and the sound has almost as much clarity and bloom as the 1988 rival. Kovacevich was a pupil of Dame Myra Hess and his performance has a clarity, poise and vitality that has commended itself to more than one generation of collectors over the past 30 years. It is a performance that avoids other people's mistakes – whilst teaching us to relish uncomplicated skill. Try the Variations Nos. 25 to 27 and you will find playing that is sensitive and exciting but quite unselfregarding; and even where Kovacevich adopts slow tempos, as in Var. 14, there is always light in the texture and the rhythms are cleanly sculpted. Where the *Diabelli* is concerned one version can never be enough but Kovacevich remains the safest 'library' recommendation.

Diabelli Variations. 32 Variations on an Original Theme in C minor, WoO80.
Benjamin Frith *pf*
ASV Quicksilva CDQS6155 (62 minutes: DDD). Recorded 1990.   ⑤

This bargain on ASV's super-budget Quicksilva label offers a currently almost unbeatable coupling of the *Diabelli* Variations and the *32 Variations on an Original Theme*. Benjamin Frith is one of those artists whose musical perceptions are not to be doubted, and whose playing is almost never troubled by technical blemishes, and certainly not here. In short, both performances are masterly, the interpretations clearly thought through, concentrated in tension and feeling. With excellent recording this disc is unsurpassed, even by Brendel who, of course, has his own insights to offer in the *Diabelli*. But then so has Frith, and very impressive they are too.

Beethoven Six Variations in F major on an Original Theme, Op. 34. Six Variations in D major, Op. 76. 15 Variations and a Fugue on an Original Theme in E flat major, Op. 35, 'Eroica'.
Schumann Etudes symphoniques, Opp. 13 and posth.
Sviatoslav Richter *pf*
Olympia OCD339 (77 minutes: ADD). Recorded 1970-77.   ⑤

Remarkably well recorded considering the source, one performance after another here is so memorable as to rank among the best versions around of the piece in question. There is such richness in the Beethoven Variations that it seems pointless and unfair to highlight any one in particular. Nevertheless, the *Eroica* Variations end with Richter playing most pianists under the table. His Schumann has always been dazzling, because he has a temperament that convincingly responds to the extreme swings in mood. The reading of the *Etudes symphoniques* is an overwhelming experience. The fourth of the supplementary variations emerges as an exotic lament of ravishing beauty and the pianist's very large hands enable him to attack the chords of the finale with ferocious confidence. Well chosen and excellent in sound, these performances should not be missed.

Piano Sonatas – **No. 1** in F minor, Op. 2 No. 1; **No. 2** in A major, Op. 2 No. 2; **No. 3** in C major, Op. 2 No. 3; **No. 4** in E flat major, Op. 7; **No. 5** in C minor, Op. 10 No. 1; **No. 6** in F major, Op. 10 No. 2; **No. 7** in D major, Op. 10 No. 3; **No. 8** in C minor, Op. 13, 'Pathétique'; **No. 9** in E major, Op. 14 No. 1; **No. 10** in G major, Op. 14 No. 2; **No. 11** in B flat major, Op. 22; **No. 12** in A flat major, Op. 26; **No. 13** in E flat major, Op. 27 No. 1, 'quasi una fantasia'; **No. 14** in C sharp minor, Op. 27 No. 2, 'Moonlight'; **No. 15** in D major, Op. 28, 'Pastoral'; **No. 16** in G major, Op. 31 No. 1; **No. 17** in D minor, Op. 31 No. 2 'Tempest'; **No. 18** in E flat major, Op. 31 No. 3; **No. 19** in G minor, Op. 49 No. 1; **No. 20** in G major, Op. 49 No. 2; **No. 21** in C minor, Op. 53, 'Waldstein'; **No. 22** in F major, Op. 54; **No. 23** in F minor, Op. 57 'Appassionata'; **No. 24** in F sharp major, Op. 78; **No. 25** in G major, Op. 79; **No. 26** in E flat major, Op. 81a, 'Les adieux'; **No. 27** in E minor, Op 90; **No. 28** in A major, Op. 101; **No. 29** in B flat major, Op. 106, 'Hammerklavier'; **No. 30** in E major, Op. 109; **No. 31** in A flat major, Op. 110; **No. 32** in C minor, Op. 111.

Piano Sonatas Nos. 1-32.
Richard Goode pf
Nonesuch 7559-79328-2 (ten discs: 608 minutes: DDD). Recorded 1990s.　　　　Ⓕ 🆁🆁

Until the last few years Richard Goode was active principally as an ensemble player in chamber music, a field in which he excels. There is some unevenness of achievement in his playing but the level, in general, is wonderfully high, with no lapses from grace. Everything demands assessment in the company of the best there is. The interpretation of the A major Sonata, Op. 101, is one of the finest ever put on record. Reservations? You may have a doubt as to whether all the playing represents everything Goode is capable of: sometimes he disappoints, slightly, by appearing to hold back from the listener the boldness and fullness of communication the greatest players achieve. One might say that, for all their insight and illumination, some of the performances lack the final leap and a degree of transcendence. A quality often to be observed in Goode is allure. Maybe that is why his playing is so very likeable: the finish of his playing, technical and musical, is immaculate but on top of that he is exciting. His sound always makes you listen. His feeling for it and for fine gradations of sound from one end of his wide dynamic range to the other are those of a virtuoso and inform everything he does. And when he's more obviously on virtuoso territory, as in the *Waldstein* and *Appassionata*, he responds to their demands for brilliance and thrilling projection as to the manner born. He is constantly inside the music, not on the outside looking in, and what a lively, cultivated, lucid and stimulating guide he is. There is nothing diffident or half-hearted about the way he makes this cycle of Beethoven resound wonderfully, the earlier sonatas appearing as no less masterly or characteristic of their composer than the later.

Piano Sonatas Nos. 1-32.
Artur Schnabel pf
EMI Références mono CHS7 63765-2 (eight discs: 605 minutes: ADD). Recorded 1932-38.　　Ⓜ 🄷

Artur Schnabel was almost ideologically committed to extreme tempos; something you might say Beethoven's music thrives on, always provided the interpreter can bring it off. By and large Schnabel did. There are some famous gabbles in this sonata cycle, notably at the start of the *Hammerklavier*, with him going for broke. In fact, Schnabel also held that 'It is a mistake to imagine that all notes should be played with equal intensity or even be clearly audible. In order to clarify the music it is often necessary to make certain notes obscure.' If it is true, as some contemporary witnesses aver, that Schnabel was a flawless wizard in the period pre-1930, there is still plenty of wizardry left in these post-1930 Beethoven recordings. They are virtuoso readings that demonstrate a blazing intensity of interpretative vision as well as breathtaking manner of execution. Even when a dazzlingly articulate reading like that of the *Waldstein* is home and dry, the abiding impression in its aftermath is one of Schnabel's (and Beethoven's) astonishing physical and imaginative daring. And if this suggests recklessness, well, in many other instances the facts are quite other, for Schnabel has a great sense of decorum. He can, in many of the smaller sonatas and some of the late ones, be impeccably mannered, stylish and urbane. Equally he can (within the parameters of the finished work of art) be devilish or coarse. At the other extreme, Schnabel is indubitably the master of the genuinely slow movement. Listen to the way that from the earliest sonatas to the final movement of No. 32, Schnabel is able to reconcile a calm and concentrated slowness with a breathing pulse and stirring inner life that is beyond the wit of most latter-day imitators. For the recorded sound, CD is a godsend. There is nothing that can be done about the occasional patch of wow or discoloration but, in general, the old recordings come up very freshly indeed.

Piano Sonatas Nos. 1-32.
Wilhelm Kempff pf
DG Dokumente mono 447 966-2GDO8 (eight discs: 511 minutes: ADD). Includes bonus disc, 'Wilhelm Kempff – An All-Round Musician'. Recorded 1951-56.　　　　Ⓜ 🄷

Wilhelm Kempff was the most inspirational of Beethoven pianists. Those who have cherished his earlier stereo cycle for its magical spontaneity will find Kempff's qualities even more intensely conveyed in this mono set, recorded between 1951 and 1956. Amazingly the sound has more body and warmth than the stereo, with Kempff's unmatched transparency and clarity of articulation even more vividly caught, both in sparkling *Allegros* and in deeply dedicated slow movements. If in places he is even more personal, some might say wilful, regularly surprising you with a new revelation, the magnetism is even more intense, as in the great *Adagio* of the *Hammerklavier* or the final variations of Op. 111, at once more rapt and more impulsive, flowing more freely. The bonus disc, entitled 'An All-Round Musician', celebrates Kempff's achievement in words and music, on the organ in Bach, on the piano in Brahms and Chopin as well as in a Bachian improvisation, all sounding exceptionally transparent and lyrical. Fascinatingly, his pre-war recordings of the Beethoven sonatas on 78s are represented too. Here we have his 1936 recording of the *Pathétique*, with the central *Adagio* markedly broader and more heavily pointed than in the mono LP version of 20 years later.

Piano Sonatas – Nos. 1-32; E flat major, WoO47 No. 1; F minor, WoO47 No. 2; D major, WoO47 No. 3. Andante favori in F major, WoO57.
Malcolm Bilson, Tom Beghin, David Breitman, Bart van Oort,
Ursula Dütschler, Zvi Meniker, Andrew Willis *fps*
Claves CD50-9707/10 (ten discs: 689 minutes: DDD). Recorded 1996.   ⑧℗

It is easy to point out the fortepiano's shortcomings, especially in the middle to late works of Beethoven. It isn't simply that the tone – somewhere between a small upright piano and a harpsichord – takes a lot of getting used to. There's the limited sustaining power – pitifully limited in the singing high notes of the first-movement *Allegro* of *Les adieux*, or the lilting Menuetto of No. 7. Could this really be the sound Beethoven heard in his head, or was his imagination already straining ahead of its time? But the instruments included in this set were the kind of pianos at which Beethoven played and composed. He knew their capabilities and limitations better than we do. There may be good reasons for preferring the modern concert grand, but reject the fortepiano utterly and you miss revelations. For a start, some passages sound surprisingly beautiful: the ethereal trills and pulsations in the finale of No. 32; the ecstatic final climax (again trill-dominated) of No. 30. The players – respectively Tom Beghin and Malcolm Bilson – deserve a lot of the credit, of course, but these moments do show how responsive fortepianos can be, even in late Beethoven.

Then there are passages where Beethoven's instrument actually scores above the modern piano. Textures like the racing left-hand quavers in the *Scherzo* of No. 12 can be transformed – rarely before has this sounded so incisive and gripping. Then there's the so-called *una corda* ('one string') pedal, which turns the usual percussive brightness into something duller and more mysterious. Beethoven clearly asks for this in the slow movement of No. 28, requesting a gradual return to full strings in the slow cadenza writing at the end. And all credit to Bilson for bravely taking Beethoven's instructions in the first movement of the *Moonlight* (No. 14) at face value ('*pianissimo* throughout and with raised dampers') – the result is, well, at least interesting. The performances most notable for character or musical intelligence turn out to be by Malcolm Bilson. Tom Beghin and Ursula Dütschler are also consistently impressive. Certainly they're never dull; and however quirky Bilson can be on occasion, he avoids the affected rubato of some of his colleagues, which tends to sound as though the players might just be trying to compensate for the instrument's expressive shortcomings. Recording tone varies, suggesting very mixed venues, from relatively spacious rooms to intimate salons. Fortunately, none of the recordings is too close to the instrument – the last thing one wants is to have the sound of the mechanism enhanced. Not a Beethoven sonata set to treasure for all time maybe, but one that offers unique illuminations.

Piano Sonatas Nos. 1-3.
Alfredo Perl *pf*
Arte Nova Classics 74321-27762-2 (73 minutes: DDD).   Ⓢ

Piano Sonatas Nos. 4, 13, 14 and 24.
Alfredo Perl *pf*
Arte Nova Classics 74321-30459-2 (73 minutes: DDD).   Ⓢ

Piano Sonatas Nos. 5-7 and 26.
Alfredo Perl *pf*
Arte Nova Classics 74321-30460-2 (72 minutes: DDD).   Ⓢ

Piano Sonatas Nos. 8, 12, 27 and 28.
Alfredo Perl *pf*
Arte Nova Classics 74321-27764-2 (74 minutes: DDD).   Ⓢ

Alfredo Perl does not follow the sonatas strictly in sequence: this may irritate some collectors, but it does allow each disc to stand as an independent 'recital' while also forming just one part of the complete journey. There is an enormous amount to celebrate in these performances. The rhythmic power of these works is communicated with a genuine sense of enjoyment, and one of the most striking features of Perl's playing, particularly in the outer movements, is that he never shies away from the *sforzandos* or the *subito piano*s which are so important to Beethoven's style. Indeed, he attacks these dynamic accents and contrasts with such dramatic rigour that certain movements – the finale to the *Moonlight*, for example – are animated with a rare vitality. It is in the more highly charged movements where Perl is most compelling (the outer movements of the *Pathétique*, the opening movement of Op. 10 No. 1, and the finales of Op. 2 No. 1 and Op. 10 No. 2). The A major Sonata, Op. 101, receives a tremendous performance, both musically and technically, and the second movement in particular is a marvel of understated virtuosity. In the movements of more lyrical simplicity Perl can be less convincing. In the second movement of Op. 90, for example, he does not make the piano sing, and his tone can occasionally sound a little bland. His *fortes*, too, can be rather hard-edged, although the bright recording does not help him here. Perl's tempos have been the cause of some debate: he favours extremes, juxtaposing especially rapid fast movements with protracted slow movements. In Op. 101, for example, he follows the march-like second movement, taken dangerously fast, with a particularly drawn-out *Adagio*. If you wish to sample just one disc from this series to get a flavour of Perl's playing, then try Vol. 4 (ranging from the *Pathétique* to Op. 101). Perl has entered a hugely competitive field, but once his cycle is complete it could be one of the finest versions by a young pianist to have emerged in recent years.

Piano Sonatas Nos. 1-3.
Alfred Brendel *pf*
Philips 442 124-2PH (70 minutes: DDD). Recorded 1994.   Ⓕ

Brendel reminds us here that, in their different ways, these works of Beethoven's first maturity are as finished and as characteristic as the later ones, and it's a measure of his artistry that he makes us aware of the Op. 2 trilogy as three 'highly profiled individuals' – the description in the notes – and not just as generalized 'early' Beethoven. You need to play this disc at a reasonably high level to savour the full range of Brendel's dynamics and colouring. Perhaps not everything is communicated here as vividly as Brendel habitually achieves in the concert hall. The playing conveys a total vision and is musically alive as few can rival, but one is inclined to regret that no place had been found for a passing breeze of impetuosity. The spellbinding inner worlds of the great slow movements in the A major and C major Sonatas of Op. 2 are as demanding for the player as any. The piano has to be transcended. Brendel treats the *Largo appassionato* of the A major as a processional, and keeps it nicely on the move; even finer is his control of nuance and movement in the E major *Adagio* of Op. 2 No. 3 – the end is marvellous. His simpler, sculpted eloquence in the slow movement of the F minor Sonata is also touching, and in general, he allows himself plenty of time for reflectiveness and quasi-improvisatory exploration. The first movement of the A major Sonata is a particularly interesting journey: *Allegro vivace* certainly, two in a bar, but never a rush, so one can be all the more aware of the teeming incident on the way. The radiant finale of this Sonata is another high spot, clearly hugely enjoyed by him in this affectionate account of it. This is fresh, youthful Beethoven in which there is room for caprice and laughter and good humour as well as profundity and the shocks of the new.

Piano Sonatas Nos. 4, 15 and 20.
Alfred Brendel *pf*
Philips 446 624-2PH (65 minutes: DDD). Recorded 1994.   Ⓕ Ⓔ

Brendel's interpretation of the *Pastoral* has changed – and its status has stratospherically soared – in two interrelated respects. In the first place, the two outer movements are both slower than on either the 1960s Turnabout recording or the 1970s Philips version. What we have here is not some amiable musical ramble; rather, it is a multi-layered music-drama in which the pianist's relish in debating the issues the music is already asking itself makes for the most exhilarating kind of listening. And what a debate it is, substantial and charged with feeling. The lead back to the recapitulation – the lurch into B major, the sudden silence, the restatement in B minor, a further silence, the unresolved question on the home dominant – is realized with quite heart-stopping intensity. But, then, intensity is very much the order of the day in this latest cycle of recordings, a throwing open of the gates, with a far greater use of declamatory effects and rhetorical tropes than was the case in either of his two earlier cycles. Not that Brendel has thrown overboard any of his wryness, wit or natural sense of balance. He plays the two inner movements of the *Pastoral* Sonata every bit as elegantly as before. And yet here again one notices sudden deepenings and new-found beauties. The performance of the E flat Sonata, Op. 7, is similarly grand, open and free-spirited. And here a word needs to be said about the recordings, which are thrillingly loyal to the music-making. The sound, like the playing, can be both grand and awesomely quiet. Above all, it offers a persistently clear view of the rich ensemble of inner voices that is so vital to Brendel's purpose. The engagingly brief G major Sonata makes a delightful postlude.

Piano Sonatas Nos. 5-7.
Alfred Brendel *pf*
Philips 446 664-2PH (59 minutes: DDD). Recorded 1995. Nos. 5 and 6 recorded live.   Ⓟ Ⓔ

The two shorter sonatas, each in its own right a miracle of concentrated wit and musical daring, thrive not only on the acumen of Brendel's playing but on the clear sense there is here of the music being played *for* someone. (After which, in No. 7, one rather misses – or, rather, one senses Brendel may be missing – the generally unobtrusive Frankfurt audience.) The one movement in the two shorter sonatas which Brendel would appear to have thought and rethought down the years is the F major Sonata's central minor-key *Allegretto* and its awed D flat major Trio, the music's strangeness and hushed inward mood wonderfully gathered in only to be, as it were, played out again. It is the art of the public expression of private emotion brought to its highest level of sophistication. The much grander D major Sonata also has its fair share of wit. As to the great slow movement, D minor *Largo e mesto*, here Brendel has always treated the opening eight-bar threnody slowly and rather formally, allowing the note of tragic dejection to sound only at the appearance of the lovely *cantabile* transition theme. Others have seen the music differently, but Brendel's playing of the concluding eight bars, by contrast, is as telling as anyone's. To adapt Malcolm's tribute to the Thane of Cawdor, nothing in the movement becomes Brendel like the leaving of it. Brendel stands apart in a class of his own.

Piano Sonatas Nos. 5 and 32. 32 Variations on an Original Theme in C minor, WoO80.
Lars Vogt *pf*
EMI CDC5 56136-2 (55 minutes: DDD). Recorded 1995.   Ⓕ

Beethoven in C minor (No. 5): now here's a subject worthy of cogitation. Vogt constructs such a journey here, opting to see Beethoven through the prism of three essays in C minor taken from different periods of the composer's career, before, in the concluding measures of Op. 111 (No. 32), he arrives at what Browning famously called 'my resting-place', 'The C major of this life'. As a concept, this disc is both fascinating and delightful, not least because it allows one to set speculation and a spirit of musical and psychological enquiry over 'interpretation' and the tyranny of comparisons. Here, it is enough to hear and enjoy the disc *through*, for its own sake. As befits a programme of variations and sonata-form movements in C minor and related keys, the playing is brilliant in tempo and tone (the execution more or less flawless), severe yet 'fine' when needs be: as in the hauntingly beautiful phrases in rising sequence shortly after the start of the slow movement of the Fifth Sonata. The playing in the outer movements of this sonata is not, in itself, especially witty, but the rapidity and precision of his delivery of Beethoven's lines constitute a form of pleasure in their own right. The EMI recording is very brilliant, a touch light-headed perhaps, though with a very respectable bass presence. This isn't soul music – at least, not until the concluding movement of No. 32. Its principal aim is to divert, challenge, and delight; and in that it succeeds magnificently.

Piano Sonatas Nos. 8-11.
Stephen Kovacevich *pf*
EMI CDC5 56586-2 (70 minutes: DDD). Recorded 1997.   Ⓕ

There are performances that take you through a familiar work as though you were hearing it for the first time. Stephen Kovacevich's version of Beethoven's *Pathétique* is one of those. It's hard to analyse what it is that makes it so fresh. On the face of it, nothing about his interpretation is strikingly or provocatively 'new' – no unusual tempos or articulation of phrases. But there's so much life, evident in crisp, muscular rhythms, *crescendos* that draw you forward in your seat, and tender, confidential lyricism. The recording helps, bringing out the power and brilliance, without losing sense of the subtlety of the playing in more intimate passages. There are similar qualities in the other three sonatas – though not always so consistently. Energy and humour in the *Andante* variations and *Scherzo* finale of Op. 14 No. 2 seems just right; but the opening *Allegro* could perhaps be a little lighter and more intimate. The Rondo finale of Op. 11 starts a little soberly – but wit and the lighter touch aren't absent for long. The rest of the performance (especially the first two movements) makes one wonder why this sonata so rarely turns up in concert programmes. Perhaps someone should give it a title. There were no causes for critical doubt in Op. 14 No. 1, only pleasure, and renewed wonder at Beethoven's brilliance and originality. That's typical of Kovacevich's playing. He's no pianistic egoist, using Beethoven's ideas as a medium to demonstrate his own genius. He wants you to love and appreciate the music as he does. When combined with such refinement of technique, energy, sense of colour and imagination, it's an attitude that is particularly compelling.

Beethoven Piano Sonatas Nos. 8, 23 and 31.
Handel Keyboard Suite in D minor, HWV428 – Prelude; Air and Variations; Presto. Chaconne and Variations in G major, HWV435.
Edwin Fischer *pf*
APR Signature mono APR5502 (72 minutes: AAD). Recorded 1931-38.   Ⓜ 🄷

On this invaluable disc are some of Fischer's finest and most legendary performances. His very first published recording (1931) of the Handel Chaconne, for example, was made at a time when his matchless *leggiero* and radiant tone were unimpeded by obvious blemishes or erratic pianism. Both this performance and that of the pieces from the Suite No. 3 have an improvisatory magic, a strength and grace and supreme assurance. Fischer commences the *Pathétique* with a scrupulous adherence to Beethoven's *fp* marking, a sudden shift of sound that is fascinatingly modernist or prophetic. The *Allegro di molto e con brio* is exactly that, dancing with an irrepressible lightness and urgency; and if one listens to the slow octave descent just before the final outburst one will hear a rapt 'all-passion-spent' quality, something Fischer could achieve with supreme naturalness, without even a hint of artifice or calculated effect. All past vicissitudes are finally resolved in Op. 110 in a blaze of heroic glory, and time and again he makes you pause to consider key points and details that somehow elude others. There is here a richness and humanity that was uniquely Fischer's.

Piano Sonatas Nos. 8, 14, 15, 17, 21, 23 and 26.
Alfred Brendel *pf*
Philips Duo 438 730-2PM2 (152 minutes: ADD). Recorded 1970-77.   Ⓜ

Piano Sonatas Nos. 8 and 23. Choral Fantasia in C minor, Op. 80. Bagatelles – Op. 33 Nos. 3 and 5; Op. 119 Nos. 2, 7 and 9; Op. 126 Nos. 1, 4 and 6.
Sviatoslav Richter *pf*
Russian State Academic Choir; Moscow Radio Symphony Orchestra / Kurt Sanderling.
Melodiya mono 74321 29462-2 (80 minutes: ADD). Recorded 1952-60.   Ⓜ 🄷

The Philips reissue, containing seven of Beethoven's most popular named sonatas admirably played by Alfred Brendel, is in every way an outstanding bargain, well worth obtaining, even if duplication is involved. All the performances are authoritative and offer consistently distinguished playing, while the recording is very realistic indeed. The *Tempest* resonates in the memory and the central movements of the *Pastoral* are most beautifully shaped. The *Pathétique, Moonlight* and *Appassionata* all bring deeply satisfying readings that are compellingly conceived and freshly executed. This set can be recommended without any reservations whatsoever. The booklet-notes with the Melodiya reissue claim that Richter's live 1960 Moscow *Appassionata* is his favourite among his recorded performances of the work, and from the elemental power it unleashes one can well believe it. The *Pathétique* is magnificently implacable, while the *Choral Fantasia* is a remarkable curiosity – cavernous acoustic, fierce recording, the text in Russian, sung with intimidating gusto. The mono sound is acceptable.

Beethoven Piano Sonatas Nos. 9, 11, 12[a] and 27[a].
Haydn Keyboard Sonatas[a] – No. 39 in D major, HobXVI/24; No. 62 in E flat major, HobXVI/52.
Weber Piano Sonata No. 3 in D minor, J206[a].
Sviatoslav Richter *pf*
Philips 438 617-2PH2 (two discs: 131 minutes: ADD/DDD). Recorded 1963-64, items marked [a]1994.   Ⓕ

In Haydn's E flat Piano Sonata, Richter's extreme sensitivity to detail produces a captivating performance of great delicacy and charm. Haydn's D major Sonata provides further evidence of Richter's wholly unselfconscious approach: the opening movement is expressed with transparent clarity; the *cantabile Adagio* is beautifully judged, and the finale has an engaging ethnic gait. In the Beethoven sonatas from 1963 there is a noticeably drier quality to the sound and the performances have retained a remarkable freshness of resonance. The dramatic intensity of the E major work, for example, is heightened by Richter's tendency to controversial extremes of tempo in both directions. Specifically, Richter rejects the *Allegretto* marking for the second movement in favour of a speed that is closer to *Adagio* to which the finale provides a scintillating conclusion. His wide dynamic and expressive range in both of these sonatas creates effects that are quite simply miraculous. The versions of the Sonatas, Op. 26 and Op. 90, are digital recordings, but there are no signs that

Richter has lost any of his interpretative power or originality. His command of broad structural relationships is as assured as ever, as is his scrupulous attention to the music's harmonic and motivic detail. His comprehensive exploitation of the music's intrinsic possibilities generates great energy and pace as a means of intensifying its natural warmth and expressiveness. The set concludes with a startling performance of Weber's Third Piano Sonata. The first movement, marked *Allegro feroce*, contrasts a powerfully driven opening with music of simple melodic charm which, after a richly diverse variation slow movement, culminates in a bravura finale of breathtaking virtuosity. As is so often the case with Richter's performances, then, these are landmarks in piano playing.

Beethoven Piano Sonata No. 14.
Brahms Variations on a Theme by Paganini, Op. 35.
Franck Prélude, choral et fugue.
Evgeni Kissin pf
RCA Victor Red Seal 09026 68910-2 (57 minutes: DDD). Recorded 1997.　　　Ⓕ E

Strange how many top-flight pianists find it difficult to achieve a natural delivery in the opening movement of the *Moonlight*. With some it's a case of exaggerated hesitation on the upbeats; with Kissin it's a tendency to place the melody fractionally before the left-hand octaves, the reverse of the old left-before-right mannerism. This is vaguely unsettling at first, then positively distracting once you realize the cause. The young Russian does little to temper his strongly projected sound for the intimacy of the recording studio; occasionally climaxes have more metal in the tone than some may like, even in a relatively undemonstrative piece such as the second movement of the Beethoven. Nor does he make concessions as regards sustained intensity of phrasing or ostentatiously grand rubato, especially in the Franck. Yet how much richness of experience you'd be missing if you resist Kissin's manner. And who would want to resist it anyway, when the sense of intellectual, emotional and pianistic identity with the music is so strong? Listen to the lonely arching-up of the lines in Beethoven's first movement as they win temporary freedom from the opening broken chords; or their long-term destination in the defiant arpeggios in the finale, here wonderfully articulate and full of tensile strength; or the sensitivity to each cross-current in Franck's chromatic maelstrom; or the solidity and authority of every one of the Brahms *Variations*; or the staggering dexterity of the notorious seventh and eleventh variations from Book Two. Listen to these and then say that this is anything other than a wonderful disc. If you do, it can only be that you are allergic to the forcefully projected piano tone. To which one can only say that there are others just as forceful, but very few who have comparable musical insights to project. This is modern piano playing at its finest. The recording quality is of the finest too, combining clarity and impact with perspective and bloom.

Piano Sonatas Nos. 14-18. Variations on an Original Theme in F major, Op. 34.
Seven Bagatelles, Op. 33.
Artur Schnabel pf
Pearl mono GEMMCDS9123 (two discs: 141 minutes: AAD). Recorded 1933.　　　Ⓜ H

Heavy background hiss is a small price to pay for Schnabel's immediacy and quality, and both of these discs, the original material transferred with a courageous candour and honesty, do much to convince one that Beethoven and Schnabel are, indeed, synonymous. How characteristic is that gruff but musicianly refusal in No. 14 of all undue solemnity, all notion of romantic, moonlit effusion. Such robust eloquence will hardly appeal to those who long for a prolonged gaze into the infinite (the first movement is over almost before you realize it), but the balance of sense and sensibility provides a superbly authoritative alternative. Of course, there are moments when Schnabel's impetuosity, his embattled rather than fluent resolution of purely pianistic problems, can cause momentary confusion. Yet the odd snatched phrase or telescoped rhythm pales into oblivion when you consider Schnabel's overall achievement, his salty brio and the profound eloquence of his slow movements (has anyone played the central *Adagio* of No. 17 so directly yet so speculatively?). His technique, while undeniably erratic, was brilliant; and every page pulses with a vividness and rough-hewn vitality that are somehow pure Schnabel, pure Beethoven. Time and again he wears his immense learning lightly and in, say, the dazzling wit and repartee of No. 16 the dust of ages seems to fall away before one's very eyes and ears. The Op. 33 *Bagatelles* – diamond-chippings from the master's workshop – also prove that Schnabel was as much at home in concentrated aphorism as in lengthy working-out. So, true Beethoven lovers will treasure these discs, even when they turn to a different sort of enlightenment from Wilhelm Kempff, Schnabel's nominated heir. But then Schnabel and Kempff are like North and South Poles of interpretation, and both are indispensable.

Piano Sonatas Nos. 16-18.
Stephen Kovacevich pf
EMI CDC5 55226-2 (64 minutes: DDD). Recorded 1994.　　　Ⓕ E

The Op. 31 Sonatas offer a wonderful way into the Beethoven sonatas, not least because they have done unusually well on record. And what to buy? Well, this offering from Stephen Kovacevich from his Beethoven sonata cycle is very brilliant, an exceptional record in every way. There is stiff competition from Brendel and Richard Goode, to name just two, but Kovacevich finds a middle way that seems effortlessly right. His tempo in the E flat Sonata's *Menuetto* is more or less exactly what one imagines a *moderato e grazioso* should be, and it serves Minuet and Trio equally well. The preceding *Scherzo* is a touch fiercer than Goode's or Brendel's, the finale a show-stopping *Presto con fuoco*. In the *Tempest*, Kovacevich's playing can be as angry as his rivals but it is always terrifically focused. EMI has been obliged to take on board some pretty ferocious playing. The recording occasionally threatens to fray at the edges but never quite does. War-weary and battle-hardened, it bears these marvellous performances triumphantly home.

Piano Sonatas Nos. 19, 20, 22, 23, 30, 31 and 32.
Sviatoslav Richter *pf*
Philips 438 486-2PH2 (two discs: 122 minutes: DDD). Recorded 1992.　　　　　　　Ⓕ

Piano Sonatas Nos. 18 and 28. Two Rondos, Op. 51. Piano Trio in B flat major, Op. 97, 'Archduke'[a]. Quintet for Piano and Wind in E flat major, Op. 16[b].
Sviatoslav Richter *pf* [a]members of the **Borodin Quartet;** [b]members of the **Moraguès Quintet.**
Philips 438 624-2PH2 (two discs: 131 minutes: DDD). Recorded 1986-92.　　　　　　Ⓕ

There are times in a reviewer's working life when he or she folds away the notebook, discards the score, and just listens – the performance demands it. This was one such event. Those whose chief pleasure as critics is to pounce on minute blemishes (preferably blemishes no one else has noticed) would no doubt have a joyous time here – Richter is no chromium-plated perfectionist. But to go glitch-hunting in the face of playing of this quality would surely require a heroic degree of insensitivity. Granted, Richter would hardly be Richter if there wasn't something bizarre to pick out, and there is one detail that does call for comment. In the Quintet for piano and wind, Op. 16, Richter and the four members of the Moraguès Quintet repeat not only the first movement exposition, but the exposition plus the slow introduction. For those who listen for structural signposts it is disorientating; and yet it is all so wonderfully played – the colour, the vitality, the sense of creative give-and-take between the players are all you could wish for in this sunny, in every sense young piece. Throughout these two sets the sheer aliveness of the playing can be breathtaking – no exaggeration. It doesn't matter whether the territory is the most searching late Beethoven or an early, 'easy' sonata (Beethoven's own description) such as the G minor, Op. 49 No. 1. One could make endless lists of favourite details – little touches that show how thorough Richter's understanding is, but what finally distinguishes Richter's Beethoven is a quality … the word is 'improvisatory': it is as though you were hearing the music not merely played, but composed. This is what holds the attention even when Richter's conscious decisions go against what you expect of the music – the slow tempos in the *Scherzo* and Fugue of Op. 110, for instance. These four discs form another valuable counterweight to the modern nostalgists' claim that great playing – and especially great Beethoven playing – is a thing of the remote past. The transfers serve Richter excellently: intrusive audience noise is minimal, in fact in Op. 111 you might only realize that there is an audience at all when the clapping and cheering thunders in at the end. The engineering is good.

Piano Sonatas Nos. 21, 24 and 31.
Stephen Kovacevich *pf*
EMI CDC7 54896-2 (53 minutes: DDD). Recorded 1992.　　　　　　　　　　　　　Ⓕ

Few pianists today – not Brendel, not Ashkenazy, not Serkin – can free themselves of self-awareness enough to find the tender simplicity of the opening *Moderato cantabile* of Beethoven's Op. 110. Kovacevich can, and he goes on to fill each moment of figuration and trilling with light. His finale has a mesmeric inwardness generated by the seemingly infinite nuances he can find in a single repeated note. A steadiness of purpose in the *Arioso* leads naturally into the quiet self-assurance of the effortless building of the Fuga. The coupling – with the little Op. 78 and the *Waldstein* – makes for a sensitively built recital in its own right. Again, Kovacevich's skill at drawing the listener in marks the Op. 78 Sonata, with its effervescent figurework and spontaneous major-minor changes. The same nimble fingerwork, over a thrumming bass, makes the *Waldstein* positively tingle with life: Kovacevich's joy in the physical excitement and momentum of the writing is equalled by his strength in delineating the song at its heart.

Piano Sonatas Nos. 21, 23 and 26.
Emil Gilels *pf*
DG 419 162-2GH (ADD). Recorded 1970s.　　　　　　　　　　　　　　　　　Ⓕ

This reissue couples the *Waldstein*, the *Appassionata*, and *Les adieux*, and immediately establishes a claim to being one of the most desirable of all Beethoven piano sonata reissues. Perhaps there is something rather chilly and understated about Gilels's reading of the *Waldstein*'s brief slow movement (by contrast, his playing of the slow movement of *Les adieux* is ravishing), but Beethoven must take some of the blame here, too. Throughout these three sonatas Gilels plays the music with an architect's sense of structure, great technical brilliance, and that uncanny blend of intellectual attack and intellectual distance which give his recordings their peculiar force and distinction. The digital transfers are brilliant and true. The opening of *Les adieux* sounds a trifle muted and there is some tape background, but the ear dismisses this as rapidly as, initially, it picks it up.

Piano Sonatas Nos. 26ᵃ and 29ᵇ.
Alfred Brendel *pf*
Philips 446 093-2PH (62 minutes: DDD). Item marked ᵃ recorded 1994, ᵇlive in 1995.   Ⓕ

Brendel has said that this is the last recording of the *Hammerklavier* Sonata we shall have from him. He felt that this one, given in Vienna in the Musikverein, was good enough to be 'a decent way of leaving the piece'. Surely there can't be any doubt about that for Brendel is at his very best. At the start, applause fades and off he goes, at ease with his timing and the scale and rhetoric and, it would seem, completely confident of how the work is to be seen through to the finish. As listeners, the reassurance is excellent to have: we know straight away that he is going to be not just a reliable guide but an inspiring one. Having embarked on the huge journey – likened in the excellent booklet essay to a 'progression of heroic struggle and suffering leading to a rebirth of creative possibilities' – we sense the musical experience is to prove supremely satisfying, even if discomfiting in the course of it. (But one doesn't turn to the *Hammerklavier* Sonata for solace.) Brendel has played this mighty work for more than 40 years and commands it. The fusion of sound and sense is thrilling. The *Hammerklavier* Sonata realized only in the interpreter's head is not much good and the pianism here is marvellous, an object-lesson in how technique, at this level, is above all a matter of knowing what you're doing and of fortune favouring the brave. Hats off! The recording is credited to the Austrian Radio. It's a good one: we are in the Musikverein but also of course at home, and the distance from the sound is just right, with a wide dynamic range defined at all levels just as one would have experienced it there. The production is impeccable too, with applause fore and aft but no extraneous noise to irritate in between; and the pauses between movements have been correctly judged as part of the performance. Brendel in the E flat Sonata – less agitated, warmer and more relaxed than many players – is very enjoyable, but this is a disc you buy for his *Hammerklavier*.

Piano Sonatas Nos. 27-32.
Solomon *pf*
EMI Références mono/stereo CHS7 64708-2 (two discs: 141 minutes: ADD). Recorded 1951-56.   Ⓜ🄷🄴.

Solomon's 1952 recording of the *Hammerklavier* Sonata is one of the great recordings of the century. At the heart of his performance there is as calm and searching an account of the slow movement as you are likely to hear this side of the Great Divide. And the outer movements are also wonderfully well done. Music that is so easy to muddle and arrest is here fierily played; Solomon at his lucid, quick-witted best. The CD transfer is astonishing. It is as though previously we have merely been eavesdropping on the performance; now, decades later, we are finally in the presence of the thing itself. It is all profoundly moving. What's more, EMI has retained the juxtaposition of the 1969 LP reissue: Solomon's glorious account of the A major Sonata, Op. 101 as the *Hammerklavier*'s proud harbinger. We must be grateful that Solomon had completed his recording of these six late sonatas before his career was abruptly ended by a stroke in the latter part of 1956. The Sonatas, Op. 90 and Op. 110, were recorded in August 1956. The warning signs were – in retrospect – already there; yet listening to these edited tapes one would hardly know anything was amiss. There is the odd fumble in the *Scherzo* of Op. 110; but, if anything, the playing has even greater resolve, both in Op. 110 and in a songful (but never sentimental) account of Op. 90. The recordings of Opp. 109 and 111 date from 1951. Sonata, Op. 109, is very fine; Op. 111 is – by Solomon's standards – a shade wooden in places, both as a performance and as a recording. Still, this is a wonderful set, very much a collectors' item.

Piano Sonatas Nos. 27ᵃ, 28ᵇ and 29ᶜ.
Sviatoslav Richter *pf*
Praga CMX354003 (75 minutes: ADD). Item marked ᵃ recorded 1965, ᵇ1986, ᶜ1975.   Ⓑ

These entirely unedited performances feel not only live but somehow extraordinarily real. Not that Richter ever gives the impression of playing for the microphone, and his vision of musical structures remains constant whether he is in the studio or the concert hall. Nevertheless the atmosphere within which that vision is realized differs from venue to venue, and in Prague it seems to have been extraordinarily conducive. This is outstanding Beethoven playing, though frustratingly the 1965 *Hammerklavier* has a little memory black-out at 8'20" in the first movement, without which it might have grown into something even more extraordinary.

Piano Sonatas Nos. 28-32.
Maurizio Pollini *pf*
DG The Originals 449 740-2GOR2 (two discs: 126 minutes: ADD). Recorded 1975-77.
Gramophone Award Winner 1977.   Ⓜ

This reissued DG Originals set makes an exceptionally neat package. Consistent praise has been heaped on these recordings since they won the Instrumental Record Award way back in 1977. One of Pollini's greatest strengths is his ability to stand up to the accumulated momentum of Beethoven's structure, but he can also build on it so as to leave the impression of one huge exhalation of creative breath. In the first movement of the *Hammerklavier* the astonishing technical assurance has you on the edge of your seat with excitement. His controlled vehemence is without rival in the outer movements, and though he does not get right to the bottom of No. 29's poetry, his far-sighted phrasing and paragraphing is again remarkable (hear the build-up to the finale recapitulation and resist it if you can!). In the last three sonatas there are others who stop to peer deeper into some of the psychic chasms, but Pollini's mastery of integration and continuous growth, and his ability to hold potentially conflicting musical demands in balance, are again sources of wonder. In terms of the qualities just mentioned, who is Pollini's equal? Other than small touches of pre-echo in Op. 111, nothing distracts from the exalted quality of the music and the playing.

Piano Sonata No. 29.
Emil Gilels *pf*
DG 410 527-2GH (49 minutes: DDD). Recorded 1983. *Gramophone* Award Winner 1984.   Ⓕ

The great Soviet pianist Emil Gilels died in 1986, not many months before his seventieth birthday, and left behind him a major legacy of recorded performances. This account of the *Hammerklavier* is a fine memorial. The work is very long and exceedingly taxing technically and the pianist must plumb its often turbulent emotional depth, not least in the enormous 20-minute slow movement which requires deep concentration from player and listener alike. After the recording was made, the pianist told his producer: 'I feel that the weight has been lifted, but I feel very empty'. Gilels manages to give it more tonal beauty and warmth than most pianists, without any loss of strength or momentum. His is measured and beautiful playing, and finely recorded too.

Piano Sonatas Nos. 30-32.
Alfred Brendel *pf*
Philips 446 701-2PH (66 minutes: DDD). Recorded 1995.   Ⓕ

Since it is the critic's job to pontificate, what does one do about a performance so satisfying that, after it, even a single well-honed sentence seems an irrelevance? Retire, possibly, and devote oneself to a more useful and benign trade such as growing vegetables. So much, then for Brendel's performance of the E major Sonata, Op. 109. Op. 111 is a brute of a thing interpretatively. Mismanaged, it can sound more like an imposition than a work of art. Fortunately, Brendel has always been one of its most lucid exponents, neither stalling the introduction, which he plays with a well-nigh ideal blend of grandeur and impetus, nor mismanaging the shifting pulses of the subsequent *Allegro con brio ed appassionato*. Nowadays, he delivers the theme of the second movement less as an *Arietta*, more as an aria, more *Adagio*, less *semplice*. In the opening of Op. 110 there is a noble, grieving air that openly anticipates the journey to come: the 'Passion music' (Brendel's phrase) of the great complex of movements – recitative, *arioso* and fugue – that makes up the sonata's latter half. Brendel plays the whole sonata superbly. Again, it is a 'big' sound but the sounding of recitative and *arioso* is masterly and the fugue is finely paced and elucidated both on its initial appearance and on the return. Brendel's playing here is lucidity itself, in a way that seems at once natural, moving, and true to the letter of Beethoven's text.

Egmont – incidental music, Op. 84.
Pilar Lorengar *sop* **Klaus-Jürgen Wussow** *spkr*
Vienna Philharmonic Orchestra / George Szell.
Decca The Classic Sound 448 593-2DCS (48 minutes: ADD). Text and translation included.
Recorded 1969.   Ⓜ

As a simple demonstration of what it is to conduct a great orchestra properly, George Szell and the Vienna Philharmonic in the *Egmont* music will do very nicely – at the moment of Egmont's execution, this uniquely imaginative man could create an entire drama, not out of the music, but out of the silence. It is, indeed, a classic set that is likely even now to remain unsurpassed for many years to come. Some may object to short measure but it will appeal to the tidy-minded library builder. In any case, why should a great recording have to rub shoulders with some distracting fill-up? The original 1969 recording was indeed in 'classic sound' – sound, that is, which comes from a great orchestra directed and balanced *at source* by a great conductor (not by the engineers) in a hall that is entirely sympathetic to the matter in hand. In the circumstances, there is little Decca's engineers can usefully do to 'improve' the sound, apart, that is, from reassert and redefine once and for all the peerless quality of the original. This they have done. The result: perfection. And all this lavished on words and music which – the overture apart – might not be given the time of day were the name of Beethoven not associated with it. Here, though, it makes compelling listening from first to last.

Sechs Gellert Lieder, Op. 48. Lieder – Op. 52: No. 3, Das Liedchen von der Ruhe; No. 4, Mailied; Op. 75: No. 2, Neue Liebe, neues Leben; No. 3, Aus Goethes Faust; Op. 83: No. 1, Wonne der Wehmut; No. 2, Sehnsucht. Adelaide, Op. 46. An die Hoffnung, Op. 94. An die ferne Geliebte, Op. 98. Klage, WoO113. Der Liebende, WoO139. An die Geliebte, WoO140.
Stephan Genz *bar* **Roger Vignoles** *pf*
Hyperion CDA67055 (69 minutes: DDD). Texts and translations included. Recorded 1998.　　　Ⓕ

The young baritone Stephan Genz is in the first bloom of his youthful prime. Beethoven's setting of Goethe's 'Mailied' (Op. 52 No. 4), with its lightly breathed, springing words, could have been written with Genz in mind. Roger Vignoles, Genz's regular accompanist, contributes an irresistible bounding energy and even a sense of mischief to one of Beethoven's most spontaneous yet subtle settings, 'Neue Liebe, neues Leben'; and an elusive sense of yearning is created as the voice tugs against the piano line in 'Sehnsucht'. The six *Gellert Lieder* form the centrepiece of this recital: Beethoven's song-cycle, *An die ferne Geliebte*, its grand finale. The intensity of Genz's cry 'Is there a God?' in *An die Hoffnung*, at the start of the disc, gives some indication of the *gravitas* he brings to his firmly enunciated 'spiritual songs' of Gellert. Genz and Vignoles have here reinstated a number of the original verses omitted by Beethoven in the first printed edition, creating a greater sense of balance and proportion within the set. The concluding song-cycle is quite simply one of the best performances currently available. Fresh and bright of tone, awe-filled and beautifully paced and scaled, Genz's singing is modulated exquisitely from song to song by Vignoles's sentient piano accompaniment.

Cantata on the death of the Emperor Joseph II, WoO87. Cantata on the accession of the Emperor Leopold II, WoO88. Opferlied, Op. 121*b*. Meeresstille und glückliche Fahrt, Op. 112.
Janice Watson, Judith Howarth *sops* **Jean Rigby** *mez* **John Mark Ainsley** *ten*
José van Dam *bass-bar* **Corydon Singers and Orchestra / Matthew Best.**
Hyperion CDA66880 (80 minutes: DDD). Texts and translations included. Recorded 1996.　　ⒻⒺ

Beethoven was only 19 when in Bonn he was commissioned to write this 40-minute cantata on the Emperor's death. It was never performed, the musicians claiming it was too difficult, and remained buried for almost a century. Arguably Beethoven's first major masterpiece, it was one of his few early unpublished works of which the master approved. When he came to write *Fidelio*, he used the soaring theme from the first of the soprano arias here, 'Da stiegen die Menschen an's Licht', for Leonore's sublime moment in the finale, 'O Gott! Welch' ein Augenblick'. The tragic C minor power of the choruses framing the work is equally memorable. Dramatic tension is then kept taut through all seven sections, with recitatives clearly indicating the young composer's thirst to write opera. Matthew Best conducts a superb performance, at once fresh, incisive and deeply moving, with excellent soloists as well as a fine chorus. In this first cantata the solo quartet simply contribute to the opening and closing choruses.

The second cantata, only a little more than half the length of the first, was written soon after, when Leopold II had succeeded as Emperor. It is apt to have the two works presented successively, when one seems to develop out of the other. This second work is less ambitious, expressing less deep emotions, yet it brings fascinating anticipation of later masterpieces. Much more specific is the way that the finale of the cantata, 'Heil! Stürzet nieder, Millionen', clearly anticipates the choral finale of the Ninth Symphony (even with the word 'Millionen'), a point reinforced by the key of D major. The two shorter pieces, both dating from Beethoven's difficult interim period between middle and late, with Jean Rigby as soloist in the *Opferlied*, make a generous fill-up, performed with equal dedication. With plenty of air round the chorus, the recording has ample weight yet is transparent enough to clarify even the heaviest textures. A revelatory issue.

Mass in D major, Op. 123, 'Missa solemnis'.

Missa solemnis.
Charlotte Margiono sop **Catherine Robbin** mez **William Kendall** ten **Alastair Miles** bass
Monteverdi Choir; English Baroque Soloists / Sir John Eliot Gardiner.
Archiv Produktion 429 779-2AH (72 minutes: DDD). Text and translation included. Recorded 1989.
Gramophone Award Winner 1991. ⒻⓅ🆁🆁

The *Missa solemnis* is generally agreed to be one of the supreme masterpieces of the nineteenth century, but attempts to record a genuinely great performance have over many years run into difficulties. Usually the greatness itself is flawed, perhaps in the quality of the solo singers or in some particular passages where the conductor's approach is too idiosyncratic or momentarily not up to the challenge of Beethoven's inspiration (an example is Klemperer's heavy-handedness in the fugues). The strain upon the choir, especially its sopranos, is notorious; similarly the technical problems of balance by producer and engineers. This performance combines discipline and spontaneous creativity, the rhythms are magically alive and the intricate texture of sound is made wonderfully clear. The great fugues of the *Gloria* and *Credo* achieve at the right points their proper Dionysiac sense of exalted liberation. Gardiner uses a choir of 36 and an orchestra of 60 playing on period instruments, aiming at a 'leaner and fitter' sound. With Gardiner, the exceptional clarity of his smaller body of singers and players, their meticulous responsiveness to direction and concentrated attention to detail is as impressive as ever; yet one is very aware of it *as* a performance. Sometimes, as in the first sounding of drums and trumpets signifying war, Gardiner's extra intensity brings a real gain.

Missa solemnis. Choral Fantasia in C major, Op. 80.
Elisabeth Söderström sop **Marga Höffgen** contr **Waldemar Kmentt** ten **Martti Talvela** bass
Daniel Barenboim pf **New Philharmonia Chorus and Orchestra;**
John Alldis Choir / Otto Klemperer.
EMI CMS7 69538-2 (two discs: 100 minutes: ADD). Texts and translations included.
Recorded 1960s. Ⓜ

Suspicions began to dawn in the very first bars that this might be not just a good but a rather great performance. The growth of the sustained theme-note in the *Kyrie* tells of power and purpose, and the measured development of the movement induces confidence that all is in safe hands. Doubts begin to creep in somewhere about the middle of the *Gloria*. Isn't the 'Qui tollis' section too ... perhaps 'plodding' overstates, and 'syllabic' isn't quite right either, but too much a matter of advance note-by-note? Then 'plod' becomes the inescapable word when Klemperer starts the 'In gloria Dei' fugue in such ponderous style and at such a laboured tempo that one goes back again to Gardiner. Perhaps it is the old notion of fugue as an 'academic' form, meaning that it is weightily serious to start with and can only get more so. This is the pattern for the great fugues of the *Credo* in Klemperer's recording, and the stern majesty thus established generally seems to chide away with almost puritan severity any suggestion of dance-movement in the 'Et ascendit'. Other matters come into question, such as the use of the soloists in the *Sanctus* 'Osanna', and indeed the actual choice of soloists, for Söderström and Höffgen in their different ways both have wrong sorts of vibrancy for this, while Kmentt lacks power for the 'Et homo factus est', and Talvela, good in the *Agnus*, has the wrong voice for the *Benedictus*. So criticisms mount up. But greatness remains, and above all, this is felt in the work of the chorus. The disc is a marvellous monument to its great trainer, Wilhelm Pitz. No doubt at all that Klemperer and the sense of occasion fired the chorus to give this recording its enduring life. However, it's doubtful whether the chorus would make this impression if it was recorded today for in nearly all modern recordings of such works the choir is too recessed for it to be the vivid, immediate human presence it is here. The *Choral Fantasia*, included on the second disc, is a well-chosen fill-up. Sadly, it's a performance without humour. Sound, fine in the *Fantasia*, is rather less comfortable in the *Missa*: sometimes a little harsh, and a little furry in soft passages. The vivid presence of that choir more than compensates.

Missa solemnis.
Eva Mei sop **Marjana Lipovšek** contr **Anthony Rolfe Johnson** ten **Robert Holl** bass
Arnold Schönberg Choir; Chamber Orchestra of Europe / Nikolaus Harnoncourt.
Teldec Ultima 0630-18945-2 (two discs: 81 minutes: DDD). Text and translation included.
Recorded live in 1992. ⒷⓅ

There are many marvellous performances in the catalogue of Beethoven's great Mass. Gardiner catches the greatness, rises to it with his uncanny freshness of perception, and secures a performance produced virtually without fault. Levine on DG, with what we would probably still call 'conventional' forces (but of totally unconventional magnificence), presents a large-scale performance, not universally liked, but one which impresses you almost unequivocally on every hearing. And here is Harnoncourt: very different from either of the others, but having at least equally upon it the stamp of devotion and of high attainment. Choir and orchestra achieve wonderful precision and clarity of articulation; they are sensitive to the needs of shading, to the ever-shifting balance of the parts, and to the purpose of cross-rhythms which at first may look like anarchy. The soloists, all of them meeting their immense individual challenges, also work intelligently as a quartet. It might be good simply to stop there and say, 'Enjoy it'. But once comparisons start, such simplicity begins to melt. There is no doubt that Gardiner's performance is more brightly, sharply, recorded. Returning to Harnoncourt after listening to a few minutes of that is to feel a relative remoteness of contact with the sound. Moving then to Levine, there is again a more immediate presence in the sound. Yet Harnoncourt in this three-way comparison emerges as a kind of halfway-house between Gardiner and Levine, and not quite as colourful as either. It may well be that an undecided reader may opt for Gardiner finally for the much more mundane reason that his performance is confined to a single disc (and after all it was *Gramophone* Record of the Year in 1991). Yet, listening again to the *Credo*, there is something almost military in the way Gardiner's people march along, and, as Harnoncourt stresses, the whole Mass is above all 'an appeal for peace'. Harnoncourt's is a performance of great integrity: that is, it is a complete, consistent whole, and all its parts are sound.

Missa solemnis.
Cheryl Studer, Jessye Norman *sops* **Plácido Domingo** *ten* **Kurt Moll** *bass*
Leipzig Radio Chorus; Swedish Radio Chorus; Eric Ericson Chamber Choir;
Vienna Philharmonic Orchestra / James Levine.
DG 435 770-2GH2 (two discs: 83 minutes: DDD). Text and translation included.
Recorded live in 1991.   Ⓕ

James Levine's performance from the 1991 Salzburg Festival is on a large scale. Where Gardiner trimmed both choir and orchestra so as to gain maximum precision and clarity, there are here three choirs (exceptionally accomplished) and the full opulence of one of the world's great orchestras. Then for the soloists: Gardiner's are good individually and well matched as a quartet, but not chosen from among the élite company of 'great names' as these so conspicuously and with such a lavish hand have been. There is also the difference of circumstances, in that this from Salzburg is a live recording, so that while the precision of attack would be improved under studio conditions (and in this respect Gardiner is demonstrably preferable), the more general 'feel' of the performance (which matters a great deal where the *Missa solemnis* is concerned) may fire the imagination and exalt the spirits beyond anything that comes within the scope of analytical criticism. In style, the conducting encourages breadth, warmth, nobility: so that, for example, the final pages of the *Kyrie* have that suggestion of Mahler, perhaps even Elgar, and the 'In gloriam Dei Patris' fugue has the kind of weight which momentarily and with due modification recalls the tradition represented by Klemperer. But there is mobility and excitement too, and the lightness of heart in the lilt of the 'Dona nobis pacem' has rarely conveyed its benediction more happily than here. As for the great ones whose names alone are sufficient to make this, as the blurb says, 'the most luxurious *Missa solemnis* of our time', they bring a splendour which is not the mere glamour of their stardom. Norman produces the richest contralto tone ever recorded in this music, Domingo sings with superb definition and intensity, Moll excels in the *Agnus Dei*. Studer makes too free with the *portamentos*, but she also meets the fearsome challenges of her part resourcefully. The fifth soloist is the Vienna Philharmonic's leader, the violinist, Gerhart Hetzel, with regard to whom the occasion has a particular preciousness and poignancy, for he has since died following a climbing accident. On the *Benedictus* he plays with a sweetness and grace worthy of a Kreisler.

Mass in C major, Op. 86. Ah! perfido, Op. 65. Meeresstille und glückliche Fahrt, Op. 112.
Charlotte Margiono *sop* **Catherine Robbin** *mez* **William Kendall** *ten* **Alastair Miles** *bar*
Monteverdi Choir; Orchestre Révolutionnaire et Romantique / Sir John Eliot Gardiner.
Archiv Produktion 435 391-2AH (62 minutes: DDD). Recorded 1989-91.   Ⓕ Ⓟ

Gardiner's genius – for that is what his capacity for renewal amounts to – is plentifully in evidence here. Of course it is true that the opening movement, the *Kyrie eleison*, is a plea for mercy. But its opening bars speak of comfort: there is almost the simple good faith of a quiet, very Germanic carol about them. Gardiner sets a mood of deliberate seriousness, with lowered period, pitch and a tempo rather slower than that suggested by Beethoven's direction: *Andante con moto, assai vivace, quasi allegretto ma non troppo*. He also appears to have encouraged the soloists, especially the soprano, to shape and shade the phrases, so intensifying the feeling of seriousness and deliberation. Happily, this policy prevails for only a short time, and to some extent the music itself goes out to meet it. As the second *Kyrie* (following the *Christe*) moves towards its climax, the *fortissimo* brings suspensions where the alto part grinds against the soprano, and then come sudden *fortissimos* with intense modulations and momentary discords, all of which are particularly vivid in this performance. What follows has the same exhilarating quality as that which was so applauded in Gardiner's *Missa solemnis* and, just as he did there, Gardiner is constantly illuminating detail while maintaining an apparently easy natural rightness throughout. Again, an outstanding contribution is made by the Monteverdi Choir. Splendidly athletic, for instance, are the leaps of a seventh in the fugal 'Hosanna'. The tone-painting of *Meeresstille* finds them marvellously alert and vivid in articulation. *Ah! perfido* brings a similar sense of renewal: there is not even a momentary suspicion of concert routine, but rather as though it is part of an exceptionally intense performance of *Fidelio*. Charlotte Margiono sings the angry passages with the concentration of a Schwarzkopf, and brings to those that are gentler-toned a special beauty of her own. The other soloists in the Mass sing well if without distinction. Distinction is certainly a word to use of the disc as a whole.

Fidelio.
Birgit Nilsson *sop* Leonore; **James McCracken** *ten* Florestan; **Tom Krause** *bar* Pizarro; **Kurt Böhme** *bass* Rocco; **Graziella Sciutti** *sop* Marzelline; **Donald Grobe** *ten* Jaquino; **Hermann Prey** *bar* Don Fernando; **Kurt Equiluz** *ten* First Prisoner; **Gunter Adam** *bass* Second Prisoner;
Vienna State Opera Concert Choir; Vienna Philharmonic Orchestra / Lorin Maazel.
Double Decca 448 104-2DF2 (two discs: 119 minutes: ADD). Recorded 1964.   Ⓜ 🅁🅁

With the exception of doubts about James McCracken's Florestan, this set was given a cordial welcome when it first appeared, but it was generally and inevitably given second place to the then all-conquering Klemperer version. Maazel has a clear-eyed, piercingly vivid view of the work, Toscanini-like in its fierce accents, insistent rhythms, refusal to linger in the cause of sentiment, not as aware of a metaphysical dimension as other conductors. The Vienna Philharmonic's playing faithfully seconds its conductor's view. In 1964 Decca made one of their most elaborate attempts at 'staging'. Characters can be heard approaching, receding, moving about the spectrum in the John Culshaw tradition (Erik Smith was the producer), and, controversially, an echo effect was used to suggest the dungeon. It is not unduly disturbing since, apart from Florestan's opening 'Gott', which sounds artificially contrived, the echo is confined to the dialogue (here greatly foreshortened), but as a whole the sound has little of the warmth found on the Harnoncourt set (Teldec). Birgit Nilsson seems something of a paragon in her effortless vocalization, but there's not only the gleaming voice to admire. Her well-thought-through characterization, though not quite as moving as Ludwig's (Klemperer), combines heroic resolve with womanly vulnerability. McCracken's Florestan seems to have been underrated. His vibrant, heroic tenor is equal to all the demands placed on it and if he occasionally over-emotes he never sentimentalizes his role as Klemperer's Vickers is inclined to do. Krause is an incisive, boldly sung Pizarro. Böhme is a paragon of a Rocco. Sciutti makes an appealing Marzelline but one not always able to sustain a line to the end of a phrase. Grobe is a decent Jaquino. Prey makes much of little as Don Fernando; that is even truer of Kurt Equiluz who offers a touching cameo of the First Prisoner. The Pitz-trained chorus excels itself. No praise, however, for the omission of text and translation.

Fidelio.
Christa Ludwig *mez* Leonore; **Jon Vickers** *ten* Florestan; **Walter Berry** *bass* Don Pizarro; **Gottlob Frick** *bass* Rocco; **Ingeborg Hallstein** *sop* Marzelline; **Gerhard Unger** *ten* Jaquino; **Franz Crass** *bass* Don Fernando; **Kurt Wehofschitz** *ten* First Prisoner; **Raymond Wolansky** *bar* Second Prisoner;
Philharmonia Chorus and Orchestra / Otto Klemperer.
EMI CDS5 56211-2 (two discs: 128 minutes: ADD). Notes, text and translation included. Recorded 1962.   Ⓕ

Klemperer's set has been a classic since it first appeared. The performance draws its strength from his conducting: he shapes the whole work with a granite-like strength and a sense of forward movement that is unerring, while paying very deliberate attention to instrumental detail, particularly as regards the contribution of the woodwind. With the authoritative help of producer Walter Legge, the balance between voices and orchestra is faultlessly managed. The cumulative effect of the whole reading is something to wonder at and shows great dedication on all sides. Most remarkable among the singers is the humanity and intensity of Christa Ludwig's Leonore. In her dialogue as much as in her singing she conveys the single-minded conviction in her mission of rescuing her beleaguered and much-loved husband. As her Florestan, Jon Vickers convincingly conveys the anguish of his predicament. One or two moments of exaggeration apart this is another memorable assumption. Walter Berry, as Pizarro, suggests a small man given too much power. Gottlob Frick is a warm, touching Rocco, Ingeborg Hallstein a fresh, eager Marzelline, Gerhard Unger a youthful Jaquino and Franz Crass a noble Don Fernando. This is a set that should be in any worthwhile opera collection.

Fidelio.
Charlotte Margiono *sop* Leonore; **Peter Seiffert** *ten* Florestan; **Sergei Leiferkus** *bar* Pizarro;
László Polgár *bass* Rocco; **Barbara Bonney** *sop* Marzelline; **Deon van der Walt** *ten* Jaquino;
Boje Skovhus *bar* Don Fernando; **Reinaldo Macias** *ten* First Prisoner; **Robert Florianschütz**
bass Second Prisoner;
Arnold Schoenberg Choir; Chamber Orchestra of Europe / Nikolaus Harnoncourt.
Teldec 4509-94560-2 (two discs: 119 minutes: DDD). Notes, text and translation included.
Recorded 1994. Ⓕ

Everything Harnoncourt touches leaves one with a sense of a country rediscovered: we listen to the
piece in hand with new ears. So it is again here. Beethoven's sole but intractable opera has seldom
emerged from the recording studio, or indeed the theatre, with such clarity of texture, such
promptness of rhythm, such unity of purpose on all sides. This is a reading that gives full play to
winds and horns, making one aware, whether it's in the Overture, Pizarro's aria, Leonore's big scena
or the Prelude to Act 2, just how important they are both to the structure and character of each
movement. Where tempos are concerned, Harnoncourt is almost bound to be controversial
somewhere. If many speeds are to their advantage just on the measured side of the customary, as in
the Dungeon quartet, allowing us for once to hear every strand of the argument, that for 'O
namenlose Freude' is uncommonly moderate. At this pace, Leonore and Florestan seem to be
conducting a gentle exchange of deeply felt emotions on an interior level rather than allowing their
pent-up emotions to burst forth in an explosion of joy, as is more usual.

The dialogue is delivered – it must be intentionally – in an understated fashion. Two vocal
interpretations stand out for excellent singing and pungent characterization. Once Leiferkus's
Pizarro takes centre-stage the action lifts on to a new, more tense plane. This vicious little dictator
with his incisive diction, spoken and sung, and his biting, vital voice is a commanding presence. But
Evil is up against an equally arresting advocate of Good in Margiono's gloriously sung and read
Leonore. Hers isn't the quasi-dramatic soprano usually associated with the part, but she never
sounds either strained or overparted in the context of a more lyrical, smaller-scale performance.
Seiffert fills Florestan with more refulgent tone than any other tenor on recent recordings – the high
tessitura of his aria's close causes him no distress at all – but one has to admit that there is little of the
Schmerz in the tone found, quite differently, in the recording of Vickers (Klemperer). In that sense,
though, he fits into Harnoncourt's well-ordered scheme of things. Polgár turns in a well-rounded but
not very individual Rocco. Bonney is her customary stylish self as Marzelline but a trifle cool in
expression. Van der Walt is a more than adequate Jaquino. There has, however, been a major piece of
miscasting where Don Fernando is concerned. A role that needs a solid bass with strong low notes has
been cast with a high baritone who sounds anything but authoritative. Harnoncourt has opted for a
professional chamber choir to second the superb Chamber Orchestra of Europe. The fact has to be
faced that until this recording, this opera hadn't received a really satisfying recording for at least 20
or so years and the old favourites are beginning to show their age. By the side of the superb Teldec
recording, the Klemperer and Maazel sound less than immediate.

Leonore.
Hillevi Martinpelto *sop* Leonore; **Kim Begley** *ten* Florestan; **Matthew Best** *bass* Pizarro;
Franz Hawlata *bass* Rocco; **Christiane Oelze** *sop* Marzelline; **Michael Schade** *ten* Jaquino;
Alastair Miles *bass* Don Fernando; **Robert Burt** *ten* First Prisoner; **Colin Campbell** *bar*
Second Prisoner;
Monteverdi Choir; Orchestre Révolutionnaire et Romantique / Sir John Eliot Gardiner.
Archiv Produktion 453 461-2AH2 (two discs: 138 minutes: DDD). Notes, text and translation
included. Recorded 1996. Ⓕ Ⓟ

Romain Rolland, writing specifically of Beethoven's *Leonore*, described the work as 'a monument of
the anguish of the period, of the oppressed soul and its appeal to liberty'. John Eliot Gardiner, in
the first complete recording of *Fidelio*'s predecessor for more than two decades, reveals both
musically and verbally how the early, more radical opera has worked its spell on him, too. This, he
says, is Beethoven struggling to recover the revolutionary fervour of his Bonn years; this is the score
where the direct expression of spontaneous emotion, rather than the nobility of philosophical
abstraction, is really to be found. This recording brings in its wake both a reappraisal of all the
available source material, and insights aplenty gathered from the touring production which preceded
it. The slower musical pace of *Leonore* is counterbalanced by a stronger narrative thrust and the
actor, Christoph Bantzer, contributes a sprightly narration which interleaves, deftly and movingly,
brief asides from the likes of Wordsworth, Goethe and Hölderlin.

And then, of course, there is the music. The *Leonore* No. 2 Overture is distinguished by the telling
contrasts Gardiner draws between brooding strata of strings and the pearly light of the woodwind;

and a reversal of the first two numbers gives Christiane Oelze a head start as a radiant Marzelline. The trio (Rocco, Marzelline and Jaquino) which prepares the Quartet, 'Mir ist so wunderbar', does tend to impede the momentum but it has a telling effect on the beat of the work's human heart, and Gardiner's sensitivity to its pulse throughout makes good any shortfall in dramatic impetus. The D major March which introduces Act 2 is here restored to its original place for the first time since the première. With brass and timpani making menacing circumstance out of what can be mere pomp, it makes the entry of Don Pizarro darker still. Matthew Best is, in articulation if not in range, one of the most blood-curdling Pizarros on disc, just as Alastair Miles is one of the noblest Don Fernandos. 'Komm, Hoffnung' reveals the resilience and steady, gleaming core of Hillevi Martinpelto's Leonore. There are times when one craves a fiercer edge of passion; but, with the equally sharply focused tenor of Kim Begley, it is a joy to hear 'O namenlose Freude' perfectly paced, and really *sung*. This Florestan sings his great aria without *Fidelio*'s vision of an 'Engel Leonore': Begley, no Heldentenor after all, is particularly well suited to the constant, dark minor key of this 'Lebens Frühlingstagen', which presages Gardiner's triumphant – and often surprising – finale.

Vincenzo Bellini
Italian 1801-1835

I Capuleti ed i Montecchi.
Edita Gruberová *sop* Giulietta; **Agnes Baltsa** *mez* Romeo; **Dano Raffanti** *ten* Tebaldo; **Gwynne Howell** *bass* Capellio; **John Tomlinson** *bass* Lorenzo; **Royal Opera House Chorus and Orchestra, Covent Garden / Riccardo Muti.** EMI CMS7 64846-2 (two discs: 130 minutes: DDD). Text and translation included. Recorded live in 1984. Ⓜ

Muti and his two principals, caught at white heat on the stage of Covent Garden, offer a rendition of Bellini's supple, eloquent score that gives the work a new definition and standing in the Bellini canon. Away from the limbo of studio recording, the music lives at a heightened level of emotion and the sound reflects a true opera-house balance. Muti persuades his singers and the Royal Opera House players to noble utterance. Baltsa's Romeo has a Callas-like conviction of phrase and diction: here is a Romeo who will go to his death for the love of his Juliet. Who wouldn't do that when that role is sung so delicately and affectingly as by Gruberová, then at the absolute height of her powers, as indeed was Baltsa? Raffanti's open-throated Italian tenor is just right for Tebaldo's bold incursions. Gwynne Howell and John Tomlinson both contribute effectively to what is a wholly engrossing performance.

Norma.
Maria Callas *sop* Norma; **Christa Ludwig** *mez* Adalgisa; **Franco Corelli** *ten* Pollione; **Nicola Zaccaria** *bass* Oroveso; **Piero De Palma** *ten* Flavio; **Edda Vincenzi** *sop* Clotilde; **Chorus and Orchestra of La Scala, Milan / Tullio Serafin.** EMI CMS7 63000-2 (three discs: 161 minutes: ADD). Notes, text and translation included. Recorded 1960. Ⓜ 🆁🆁

Norma.
Maria Callas *sop* Norma; **Ebe Stignani** *mez* Adalgisa; **Mario Filippeschi** *ten* Pollione; **Nicola Rossi-Lemeni** *bass* Oroveso; **Paolo Caroli** *ten* Flavio; **Rina Cavallari** *sop* Clotilde; **Chorus and Orchestra of La Scala, Milan / Tullio Serafin.** EMI Callas Edition mono CDS5 56271-2 (three discs: 160 minutes: ADD). Notes, text and translation included. Recorded 1954. Ⓕ 🄷

Norma may be considered the most potent of Bellini's operas, both in terms of its subject – the secret love of a Druid priestess for a Roman general – and its musical content. It has some of the most eloquent music ever written for the soprano voice. The title-role has always been coveted by dramatic sopranos, but there have been few in the history of the opera who have completely fulfilled its considerable vocal and histrionic demands: in recent times the leading exponent has been Maria Callas. Is the 1960 recording better or worse than the 1954 recording? The answer cannot be put in a word. But those who heard Callas sing Norma at Covent Garden in 1953-54, and then again, slim, in 1957, will know the difference. The facts are that in 1954 the voice above the stave was fuller, more solid and more certain, but that in 1960 the middle timbres were more beautiful and more expressive; and, further, that an interpretation which was always magnificent had deepened in finesse, flexibility and dramatic poignancy. The emphasis you give to these facts must be a matter of personal opinion. Certainly Callas's voice lets her down again and again, often when she essays some of her most beautiful effects. The F wobbles when it should crown a heart-rending 'Oh rimembranza'; the G wobbles in an exquisitely conceived 'Son io' (the unforgettable moment when Norma removes her wreath, declares her own guilt) – and yet how much more moving it is than the simpler, if steadier *messa di voce* of the earlier set. There are people who have a kind of tone-deafness to the timbres of Callas's later voice, who don't respond to one of the most affecting and eloquent of all sounds. They will stick to the earlier set. But ardent Callas collectors will probably find that it is the later one to which they will be listening again and again, not unaware of, not even unflinching from, its faults, but still more keenly responsive to its beauties.

'Casta Diva', by the way, is sung in F, as in 1954 – not in the original G, as in the Covent Garden performances of June 1953. (There is no point in fussing about Bellini's keys; the composer's favourite Amina, Malibran, used to put 'Ah non giunge' down a full fourth.) The big duet with Adalgisa is again down a tone, 'Deh! con te' in B flat, 'Mira, o Norma' in E flat, and the change is once again effected in the recitative phrase 'nel romano campo'. Callas does not decorate the music. Adalgisa, a soprano role, is as usual taken by a mezzo. Ludwig blends beautifully with Callas in the low-key 'Mira, o Norma' (though her downward scales are as ill-defined as her colleague's). She is no veteran Adalgisa, but youthful and impetuous except when (for example in her verse of 'Deh! con te') she lets the rhythm get heavy, and Serafin does nothing to correct her. On the earlier set, Stignani is a worthy partner whilst Filippeschi is rough but quite effective. On both sets, Serafin restores the beautiful quiet coda to the 'Guerra' chorus, and on both sets, Callas disappointingly does not float over the close of that slow rising *arpeggio*. It is a pity that Serafin did not restore the second statement (solo cello and woodwinds) of the *con dolore* melody that opens Act 2 – even though Bellini was right to cut it for the theatre. In the later set, the conducting is spacious, unhurried, elevated and eloquent. Only in his handling of the mounting tension and the two great climaxes and releases of the finale, might you decisively prefer the earlier version. The La Scala playing is superlative, and the recording is excellent.

La sonnambula.
Maria Callas *sop* Amina; **Nicola Monti** *ten* Elvino; **Nicola Zaccaria** *bass* Count Rodolfo; **Fiorenza Cossotto** *mez* Teresa; **Eugenia Ratti** *sop* Lisa; **Giuseppe Morresi** *bass* Alessio; **Franco Ricciardi** *ten* Notary. **Chorus and Orchestra of La Scala, Milan / Antonino Votto.**
EMI Callas Edition mono CDS5 56278-2 (two discs: 121 minutes: ADD). Notes text and translation included. Recorded 1957. Ⓕ Ⓗ RR

La sonnambula, first performed in Milan in 1831, was once the most popular opera in England. Dramatically this opera is a tepid mix which might be subtitled *The mistakes of a night* if that did not suggest something more amusing than what actually takes place. Musically, the promise of a brilliant finale keeps most people in their seats until the end, and there are half-a-dozen charming, sometimes exquisite items on the way. But it is all a little insubstantial, and much depends upon the performance, especially that of the soprano. The name of Maria Callas is sufficient to guarantee that there will be a particular interest in the work of the heroine. As usual, her individuality is apparent from the moment of her arrival. Immediately a character is established, not an insipid little miss but a woman with a potential for tragedy. This is the pattern throughout and much has exceptional beauty of voice and spirit. Nicola Monti has all the sweetness of the traditional lyric tenor. Nicola Zaccaria sings the bass aria gracefully, and carrying off her small role with distinction is Fiorenza Cossotto, at the start of her career. The orchestral playing is neat, the conducting sensible and the recording clear.

La sonnambula.
Dame Joan Sutherland *sop* Amina; **Nicola Monti** *ten* Elvino; **Fernando Corena** *bass* Count Rodolfo; **Margreta Elkins** *mez* Teresa; **Sylvia Stahlman** *sop* Lisa; **Giovanni Foiani** *bass* Alessio; **Angelo Mercuriali** *ten* Notary; **Chorus and Orchestra of the Maggio Musicale Fiorentino / Richard Bonynge.**
Decca Grand Opera 448 966-2DMO2 (two discs: 136 minutes: ADD). Notes, text and translation included. Recorded 1962. Ⓜ

La sonnambula was Bonynge's and Sutherland's first Bellini recording. Sutherland's Amina in the early 1960s was sung with extraordinary freedom and exuberance. It is difficult to describe her in the role: it is felt. She does not touch a thrilling nerve of passion as Callas can; but in the final scene – a wonderfully sustained and imaginative piece of dramatic, as well as delicate and brilliant singing – she is very moving. Far more so, in fact, than Callas, who overloaded 'Ah! non credea' and made 'Ah non giunge' too artful. It's no good comparing Sutherland with Callas at this late stage – but it is inevitable where this is concerned, especially as the Elvino, Nicola Monti, sings the role on both sets. No Sutherland admirer is going to convert to Callas in this opera, but it is fascinating to find one's remembered reactions sometimes wrong. Callas does superb things in the coloratura of 'Sovra il sen', Sutherland is full of dramatic fire in the scene in the inn – the tone, the note-shaping is again and again simply exquisite. Bonynge excels in conducting the choruses.

Georg Benda

Romeo und Julie.
Christian M. Immler *bar* Capellet; **Heidrun Kordes** *sop* Julie; **Hermann Treusch** *spkr* Lorenzo; **Claron McFadden** *sop* Laura; **Scot Weir** *ten* Romeo Montecchi; **Christoph Tomanek** *spkr* Francesco; **Ralf Emge** *bar* Mourner; **Simone Brähler** *sop* Maiden; **Bremen Vocal Ensemble for Ancient Music; La Stagione Frankfurt / Michael Schneider.**
CPO CPO999 496-2 two discs: (91 minutes: DDD). Notes, text and translation included. Recorded 1997.
Ⓜ Ⓟ

This seems to be the first of Benda's operas to be recorded. Described in the booklet as a *Singspiel*, which is usually taken to imply a lightweight work, it was called *Ernsthafte Oper* – serious opera – by the composer, and that it certainly is. Written in 1776, it draws on Shakespeare (unlike several later operatic versions, notably Bellini's), but begins after the marriage of the lovers, and it ends happily, with Juliet awakening before Romeo has had time to kill himself, and her father ready to welcome Romeo into the family and end the feud (the drama of family reconciliation was a standard type in German theatre). The ending isn't in fact entirely persuasive, not simply because it violates Shakespeare and our expectations but mainly because Benda didn't provide music sufficiently powerful or sustained to make the reconciliation convincing. The first two acts include some very fine, extended numbers, among them a beautiful, solemn opening scene for Juliet and an intense group of numbers at the end of Act 2, a duet for Juliet and her confidante Laura and an impassioned pair of arias for her in the tomb scene (she is the protagonist: Romeo's role is much smaller). There is also a very fine, Gluckian funeral chorus. Benda had command of a considerable range of emotion, particularly sombre emotion. Anyone familiar with his melodramas will recognize the same musical personality here, in the extended accompanied recitatives as well as the arias.

Michael Schneider directs an intense and persuasive performance with his Frankfurt group. Heidrun Kordes has a warm, gleaming voice, with an excellent and well-controlled top register. She sings strongly and vividly. Claron McFadden, a little lighter in tone, sings Laura's music commandingly. Romeo is sung by Scot Weir, an American tenor with a lightish heroic voice, fluent and eloquent in his Act 1 aria and especially in the one he sings in Act 3 over Juliet's supposed tomb when he believes her dead. Christian Immler's pleasing baritone serves well for Capulet (here Capellet) without making him too severe and retaining Benda's characterization of a man of keen sensibility. The playing time is short (the second disc is only 26'37") – hence its release at mid-price – but there is a good booklet with a complete text and translation.

Sir Richard Rodney Bennett

Bennett Guitar Concerto[a].
Arnold Guitar Concerto, Op. 67[b].
Rodrigo Concierto de Aranjuez[c].
Julian Bream *gtr*
Melos Ensemble / [c]**Sir Colin Davis.**
RCA Julian Bream Edition 09026 61598-2 (62 minutes: ADD). Item marked [a] recorded in 1972, [b]1959, [c]1963.
Ⓕ

This is an enjoyable demonstration both of Julian Bream's skills and of how he has stimulated composers to extend the guitar's repertoire. Sir Richard Rodney Bennett's Guitar Concerto was written in 1970 and Bream was its dedicatee. The problems of combining the guitar with an orchestra are fairly obvious, and Bennett sensibly uses a chamber ensemble whose scope for intimacy matches that of the guitar itself. Over its 20-minute length, it contains many flexible dialogues between solo instrument and ensemble, passages in which the former accompanies the latter, some especially good woodwind and percussion scoring, all carried through with this composer's usual technical skill. Besides inventive textures, there is a good variety of moods, and the guitar even finds a place in some boisterous outbursts during the work's later stages. The music deserves the fine performance it receives and the performance deserves the excellent recording. Sir Malcolm Arnold's Concerto was written for Bream in 1957. Bream made his record in partnership with the composer – directing the Melos Ensemble – two years later and the results are in every way definitive. The recording was made for RCA by Decca engineers and is beautifully balanced and strikingly warm and atmospheric. The other coupling is Bream's first stereo recording of the Rodrigo *Concierto de Aranjuez* with Sir Colin Davis in charge of the accompaniment (he went on to record it several more times). There are many, many versions of the Rodrigo available and, whilst some may cheerfully be passed over, it has long been both difficult and pointless to nominate any of the remaining ones as 'the best'. This, however, can certainly be included in their number.

Alban Berg

Berg Violin Concerto.
Stravinsky Violin Concerto in D major.
Ravel Tzigane[a].
Itzhak Perlman *vn*
Boston Symphony Orchestra / Seiji Ozawa;
[a]New York Philharmonic Orchestra / Zubin Mehta.
DG The Originals 447 445-2GOR (57 minutes: ADD/[a]DDD). Recorded 1978. Ⓜ 🔳🔳

Perlman's account of the Berg Violin Concerto with the Boston orchestra under Ozawa has long occupied a respected place in the catalogue. The original reviewer in *Gramophone* in March 1980 was completely convinced by Perlman's 'commanding purposefulness'. As to the recording, he wrote that 'though Perlman's violin – beautifully caught – is closer than some will like, there is no question of crude spotlighting'. Twenty years later and in a different competitive climate, his verdict ('These are both performances to put with the very finest') still holds good. Perlman is also a little too close in the *Tzigane*, the recording of which sets him very firmly front-stage again. All the same, this is playing of stature and still among the best available versions. There are, however, more desirable recordings now available of the Stravinsky Concerto.

Berg Violin Concerto.
Rihm Gesungene Zeit.
Anne-Sophie Mutter *vn*
Chicago Symphony Orchestra / James Levine.
DG 437 093-2GH (52 minutes: DDD). Recorded 1992. Ⓕ 🔳

One of the very few 12-note pieces to have retained a place in the repertory, Berg's Violin Concerto is in fact a work on many levels. Behind the complex intellectual façade of the construction is a poignant sense of loss, ostensibly for Alma Mahler's daughter, Manon Gropius, but also for Berg's own youth; and behind that is a thoroughly disconcerting mixture of styles which resists interpretation as straightforward Romantic consolation. Not that performers need to go out of their way to project these layers; given a soloist as comprehensively equipped as Anne-Sophie Mutter and orchestral support as vivid as the Chicago Symphony's they simply cannot fail to register. Their recording, then, makes a fine demonstration-quality recording alternative to the even more idiomatically insightful historic version of Krasner and Webern.

Violin Concerto. Lyric Suite (original version).
Louis Krasner *vn*
Galimir Quartet (Felix Galimir, Adrienne Galimir *vns* Renee Galimir *va* Marguerite Galimir *vc*); BBC
Symphony Orchestra / Anton Webern.
Testament mono SBT1004 (57 minutes: ADD). Recorded 1936.
Gramophone Award winner 1991. Ⓕ 🔳

This is an extraordinary issue of more than mere documentary interest. Krasner commissioned the Violin Concerto and had just given the first performance at the 1936 ISCM Festival in Barcelona (with Hermann Scherchen conducting) only three months after Berg's death. Webern was to have conducted on this occasion but withdrew at the last moment much to the consternation of the BBC who had booked him for the following month with (it would seem) some misgivings. Fortunately adequate rehearsal time had been allotted and the players of the BBC Symphony Orchestra proved more expert in coping with the score than their Barcelona colleagues. The latter, for all their dedication and enthusiasm, must have been under some strain since the Civil War was on the point of breaking out. Webern had appeared on a number of occasions with the BBC orchestra, but no recording of him survives in the BBC Archives. Berg's death had shocked the musical world, though not as much as the death of the 18-year-old Manon Gropius had shaken the composer, who wrote the concerto as a memorial to her. The disc is exceptionally well documented and includes interesting notes by Krasner himself.

What strikes one most of all about this performance is what can only be described as its glowing intensity. There is no sense of the bar-line or of the music ever being 'moved on'; time seems to stand still and yet there is also a natural sense of musical phrase. The surface noise on this recording, made before an invited audience in the Concert Hall of Broadcasting House, London, cannot disguise the care with which the textures are balanced and the finesse of the wind players. This was only the work's second performance and yet the players sound as if they had lived with the music all their lives. It has all the anguish and poignancy this music demands and Krasner is an eloquent exponent. The opening bars suffer from some minor audience coughs and the surface noise and moments of distortion call for a tolerance that is well worth extending. The Galimir Quartet specialized in contemporary music and its playing has commendable ensemble and dedication. Unfortunately its pioneering account of the *Lyric Suite*, recorded shortly before the performance of the Violin Concerto took place, was hampered by a very dry acoustic and this must have deterred many other listeners. It was the only version for many years and in spite of its musical excellence cannot have made many new friends for the work. The dry sound is worrying, but that should not deter collectors from investigating this remarkable issue.

String Quartet, Op. 3. Lyric Suite (original version).
Alban Berg Quartet (Günther Pichler, Gerhard Schulz *vns* Thomas Kakuska *va* Valentin Erben *vc*). EMI CDC5 55190-2 (46 minutes: DDD). Recorded 1991-92. Ⓕ

This disc brings into focus Berg's two masterpieces for the medium. EMI offers a broad perspective, the four players very forward and distinct. Details may at times seem too intrusive for the good of an integrated interpretation, and the concern to make every emotional nuance tell risks spilling the music over into melodrama. The Berg Quartet probes the extremes of the music determinedly, and their unfailingly bright sound can sometimes seem larger than life. However, there's no doubting the emotional power of the recording.

Berg Piano Sonata, Op. 1.
Liszt Piano Sonata in B minor, S178. Nuages gris, S199. R.W. – Venezia, S201. Schlaflos, Frage und Antwort, S203. Elegie No. 2, S197.
Webern Variations, Op. 27.
Barry Douglas *pf*
RCA Victor Red Seal 09026 61221-2 (61 minutes: DDD). Recorded 1991. Ⓕ

Liszt's Piano Sonata leads something of a double life in the musical world. First of all it is a calling card for virtually every young virtuoso seeking to make a big impression; secondly it is recognized as one of the great path-breaking achievements in terms of compositional innovation, since its four-movements-in-one structure is a source of inspiration for the early works of Schoenberg. Even more strikingly, the near-atonal intensity of the late piano works prepares for the harmonic explorations of Schoenberg, Berg and Webern. So Barry Douglas has been extremely astute in planning this recital. Berg's single-movement Sonata shares its home tonality with the Liszt Sonata and its main motif with that of *Nuages gris*, while the Webern *Variations* show the distant consequences of essentially the same line of thought. The outstanding performance is of the Berg, where Douglas is more responsive to the expressive ebb and flow than any current rival. His Liszt Sonata does not approach the heights of a Zimerman or a Brendel, but it is still an impressive achievement and the other works give much satisfaction too. The warm acoustic of Watford Town Hall lends a welcome glow to the recorded sound.

Three Orchestral Pieces, Op. 6. Seven Early Songs. Der Wein.
Anne Sofie von Otter *mez* **Vienna Philharmonic Orchestra / Claudio Abbado.**
DG 445 846-2GH (49 minutes: DDD). Texts and translations included. Recorded 1992-93. Ⓕ

Anne Sofie von Otter included the *Seven Early Songs* on a recital disc, a programme glowing in the sunset of German romanticism. Singing with orchestra, von Otter naturally works on a larger scale. The words are more firmly bound into the vocal line; there is not the detailed give-and-take that is possible with a pianist. But the outline of her interpretation remains that of a true Lieder singer, always lighting upon unexpected subtleties of colour and emphasis to inflect the poetry. In all this Abbado is an equal partner. Von Otter needs careful accompaniment in the concert hall if she is to dominate an orchestra and Abbado, in co-operation with DG's technical team, has produced a balance that never drowns her, but still sounds fairly natural. In *Der Wein*, Berg's late concert aria, von Otter and Abbado catch the lilt of the jazz rhythms. In the *Seven Early Songs* are they a touch too cool? Perhaps, but in the final song, 'Sommertage', they throw caution to the winds and end the cycle on a passionate high.

Abbado has recorded the *Three Orchestral Pieces* before and his 1970s recording has long been one of the standard versions of this work. The opportunity to see how his thoughts have developed since then brings more surprises than one might have expected. In short, his outlook is progressing from the Italianate to the Germanic. No doubt the influence of the Vienna Philharmonic Orchestra has much to do with this and their marvellously eloquent playing is one of the prime attractions of the disc. In their company Abbado finds more depth and complexity in the music than before, although that does mean that the March loses the Bartókian attack and driving rhythms that made his first version so exciting.

Berg Fünf Orchesterlieder nach Ansichtskartentexten von Peter Altenberg, Op. 4.
Lyric Suite (arr. cpsr; originally for string quartet). Lulu – Symphonie.
Juliane Banse sop **Vienna Philharmonic Orchestra / Claudio Abbado.**
DG 447 749-2GH (54 minutes: DDD). Texts and translations included. Recorded 1994.   Ⓕ

Claudio Abbado's account of *Lulu* is ravishingly beautiful, with a warmly poetic ardour to Alwa's music that so few real-life singers can give it (the 'Hymne', too, is genuinely hymn-like). The concluding scene has a dark, passionate vehemence and pity that are deeply moving. Any suspicion that he might be overbeautifying the music (and there are hints of him doing just that in the opening movement of the *Lyric Suite*) is erased by the hectic, almost garish drama of the second movement ostinato and the sober gravity that both he and Juliane Banse bring to the 'Lied der Lulu'. Banse is admirable in the *Altenberg* Lieder, too: expressive, unhampered by the range of the vocal line, and bringing to the last song a wide-spanning lyricism that seems almost a foretaste of Geschwitz's death-song in *Lulu*. Aside from a slightly blunted edge, even a slight loss of wit, in its opening movement, the *Lyric Suite* has the same admirable combination of richness and orchestral detail as the *Altenberg* Lieder – in the central movement Abbado demonstrates that clarity and a marking of *misterioso* are not incompatible – and the third movement, as it should be, is the Suite's emotional nub: the Vienna Philharmonic's strings respond with glowing passion. One can say no better of the recording than it sounds as though Abbado did his own balancing.

Berg Seven Early Songs.
Korngold Liebesbriefchen, Op. 9 No. 4; Sterbelied, Op. 14 No. 1; Gefasster Abschied, Op. 14 No. 4; Drei Lieder, Op. 18; Glückwunsch, Op. 38 No. 1; Alt-spanisch, Op. 38 No. 3; Sonett für Wien, Op. 41.
R. Strauss Wie sollten wir geheim sie halten, Op. 19 No. 4; Ich trage meine Minne, Op. 32 No. 1; Der Rosenband, Op. 36 No. 1; Hat gesagt – bleibt's nicht dabei, Op. 36 No. 3; Meinem Kinde, Op. 37 No. 3; Befreit, Op. 39 No. 4; Die sieben Siegel, Op. 46 No. 3.
Anne Sofie von Otter mez **Bengt Forsberg** pf
DG 437 515-2GH (64 minutes: DDD). Texts and translations included. Recorded 1991-93.   Ⓕ Ⓔ

The chosen Strauss songs here are characteristically gentle and affectionate, a mood in which von Otter is often at her best. Not that, having captured a mood, she is content to let it lie dully over as much as a verse or a line. In *Der Rosenband* she is always sensitive to the modulations; in *Ich trage meine Minne* the voice darkens with the change of tonality in verse two; in *Wie sollten wir geheim sie halten* she captures the subdued excitement of the opening as she does the frank exultation of the close. For lightness of touch, the Op. 38 songs endear themselves among the Korngold group: *Glückwunsch* has an unaffected, comfortable way with it (a little adaptation could turn it neatly into Roger Quilter or even Jerome Kern), and *Alt-spanisch* (with its reminiscence of 'On yonder hill there stands a maiden') is a charmer. At the centre of the recital are the *Seven Early Songs* of Alban Berg. The first, 'Nacht', which is also the longest and most readily memorable, is taken rather more slowly than usual, but gaining in its subtler evocations of the mists and then the silvered mountain paths. Von Otter's draining the voice of all vibrato also helps create the sense of watchful stillness, just as in the sixth song, 'Liebesode', it makes for an almost other-worldly dreaminess, deepening to a full-bodied passion as the rose scent is borne to the love-bed. Always the mezzo-soprano voice is resourcefully used, able to colour deeply at such points, to float a pure head-tone in 'Traumgekrönt' or launch a radiant high A in 'Die Nachtigall'.

Lulu (orchestration of Act 3 completed by Friedrich Cerha).
Teresa Stratas sop Lulu; **Franz Mazura** bar Dr Schön, Jack; **Kenneth Riegel** ten Alwa;
Yvonne Minton mez Countess Geschwitz; **Robert Tear** ten The Painter, A Negro;
Toni Blankenheim bar Schigolch, Professor of Medicine, The Police Officer; **Gerd Nienstedt** bass An Animal-tamer, Rodrigo; **Helmut Pampuch** ten The Prince, The Manservant, The Marquis;
Jules Bastin bass The Theatre Manager, The Banker; **Hanna Schwarz** mez A Dresser in the theatre, High School Boy, A Groom; **Jane Manning** sop A 15-year-old girl; **Ursula Boese** mez Her Mother; **Anna Ringart** mez A Lady Artist; **Claude Meloni** bar A Journalist;
Pierre-Yves Le Maigat bass A Manservant; **Paris Opéra Orchestra / Pierre Boulez.**
DG 415 489-2GH3 (three discs: 172 minutes: ADD). Notes, text and translation included.
Recorded 1979. *Gramophone* Award Winner 1986.   Ⓕ ⚫⚫

Now here's a masterpiece that fulfils all the requirements needed for a commercial smash hit – it's sexy, violent, cunning, sophisticated, hopelessly complicated and leaves you emotionally drained. *Lulu* was Berg's second opera and easily matches his first – *Wozzeck* – for pathos and dramatic impact. The meaningful but gloriously over-the-top story-line, after two tragedies by Frank Wedekind, deserves acknowledgement. Lulu, mistress of Dr Schön, is married to a medical professor. An artist also has the hots for her, but just as his passion gets interestingly out of hand, her husband walks in, catches them approaching the act and dies of shock. She marries the artist, who learns about Dr Schön and kills himself; then she marries the jealous Dr Schön, and eventually kills *him*. Smuggled out of prison by an adoring lesbian, she sets up home in Paris with Schön's son, gets blackmailed and ends up in London as one of Jack the Ripper's victims! And that's not the half of it – but we'll spare you the rest.

What matters is that Berg's music is magnificent, romantic enough to engage the passions of listeners normally repelled by 12-tone music, and cerebral enough to keep eggheads fully employed. It's opulent yet subtle (saxophone and piano lend the score a hint of jazz-tinted decadence), with countless telling thematic inter-relations and much vivid tonal character-painting. Berg left it incomplete (only 390 of the Third Act's 1,326 bars were orchestrated by him), but Friedrich Cerha's painstaking reconstruction is a major achievement, especially considering the complicated web of Berg's musical tapestry. This particular recording first opened our ears to the 'real' Lulu in 1979, and has transferred extremely well to CD. The booklet contains a superb essay by Boulez which in itself is enough to stimulate the interest of a potential listener. Performance-wise, it is highly distinguished. Teresa Stratas is an insinuating yet vulnerable Lulu, Yvonne Minton a sensuous Gräfin Geschwitz and Robert Tear an ardent artist. Dr Schön is tellingly portrayed by Franz Mazura (who also turns up as Jack the Ripper), Kenneth Riegel is highly creditable as Schön's son and that Boulez himself is both watchful of detail and responsive to the drama, hardly needs saying. It's not an easy listen, but it'll certainly keep you on your toes for a stimulating, even exasperating evening.

Wozzeck.
Franz Grundheber *bar* Wozzeck; **Hildegard Behrens** *sop* Marie; **Heinz Zednik** *ten* Captain; **Aage Haugland** *bass* Doctor; **Philip Langridge** *ten* Andres; **Walter Raffeiner** *ten* Drum-Major; **Anna Gonda** *mez* Margret; **Alfred Sramek** *bass* First Apprentice; **Alexander Maly** *bar* Second Apprentice; **Peter Jelosits** *ten* Idiot; **Vienna Boys' Choir; Vienna State Opera Chorus; Vienna Philharmonic Orchestra / Claudio Abbado.**
DG 423 587-2GH2 (two discs: 89 minutes: DDD). Notes, text and translation included. Recorded live in 1987. Ⓕ **RR**

A live recording, in every sense of the word. The cast is uniformly excellent, with Grundheber, good both at the wretched pathos of Wozzeck's predicament and his helpless bitterness, and Behrens as an outstandingly intelligent and involving Marie, even the occasional touch of strain in her voice heightening her characterization. The Vienna Philharmonic responds superbly to Abbado's ferociously close-to-the-edge direction. It is a live recording with a bit of a difference, mark you: the perspectives are those of a theatre, not a recording studio. The orchestra is laid out as it would be in an opera-house pit and the movement of singers on stage means that voices are occasionally overwhelmed. The result is effective: the crowded inn-scenes, the arrival and departure of the military band, the sense of characters actually reacting to each other, not to a microphone, makes for a grippingly theatrical experience. Audiences no longer think of *Wozzeck* as a 'difficult' work, but recordings have sometimes treated it as one, with a clinical precision either to the performance or the recorded perspective. This version has a raw urgency, a sense of bitter protest and angry pity that are quite compelling and uncomfortably eloquent.

Wozzeck.
Eberhard Waechter *bar* Wozzeck; **Anja Silja** *sop* Marie; **Heinz Zednik** *ten* Captain; **Alexander Malta** *bass* Doctor; **Horst Laubenthal** *ten* Andres; **Hermann Winkler** *ten* Drum-Major; **Gertrude Jahn** *mez* Margret; **Alfred Sramek** *bass* First Apprentice; **Franz Waechter** *bar* Second Apprentice; **Walter Wendig** *ten* Idiot; **Vienna State Opera Chorus; Vienna Philharmonic Orchestra / Christoph von Dohnányi.**
Schoenberg Erwartung, Op. 17.
Anja Silja *sop* **Vienna Philharmonic Orchestra / Christoph von Dohnányi.**
Decca 417 348-2DH2 (two discs: 123 minutes: DDD). Notes, texts and translations included. Recorded 1979. Ⓕ

Wozzeck is an expressionist score, not a late romantic one; there is a danger that once the hideous difficulties of playing it have been mastered, an orchestra (especially if that orchestra be the Vienna Philharmonic, perhaps) will be tempted by the obvious, just-under-the-surface kinships with Mahler to play it as though it were Mahler. Dohnányi's outstanding performance falls into this trap once in a while. Dohnányi's version is more beautiful in orchestral texture, more sophisticated in recording technique, at times more subtle in its pacing than Abbado's rawly urgent account, but both his principal singers sound strained, Waechter severely so. Dohnányi's *Wozzeck* is easier to listen to than Abbado, and it is refreshing to return to it whenever you want a more comfortable perspective or a more Straussian view of the work (and the inclusion of a reliably decent but not outstandingly vivid account of Schoenberg's *Erwartung* makes it better value than its other rivals), but compared to the Abbado it is studio-bound, with all the singers in word-enhancing, but illusion-shattering, close-up.

Luciano Berio
Italian 1925

Rendering. Concerto II, 'Echoing Curves'. Quattro versioni originali della 'Ritirata notturna di Madrid'.
Andrea Lucchesini *pf*
London Symphony Orchestra / Luciano Berio.
RCA Victor Red Seal 09026 68894-2 (68 minutes: DDD). Recorded 1995.　　　　　Ⓕ

Reworking takes many different forms with Berio. The simplest kind is to be heard here in the maddeningly repetitive but gloriously witty fusing together of Boccherini's four versions of his successful pot-boiler, *Ritirata notturna di Madrid*. On a much grander scale comes *Rendering*, which works around Berio's orchestration of the sketches for Schubert's Tenth Symphony. At 35 minutes this is a big piece – the composer's own reading is phrased throughout with special sensitivity, and relishes the gentle and strange discontinuities between Schubert and Berio with absorbing delicacy. Berio is at his best, and most distinctive, when the composer he reworks is Luciano Berio. *Concerto II, 'Echoing Curves'*, from 1988-89, is a rich, complex elaboration of a work for piano and ensemble called *Points on the curve to find ... from* 1974. More Boulezian than much Berio in its slow-moving tissue of clusters, trills and *tremolandos*, its shimmering textures conjure up a remarkable blend of density and luminosity, and the music is perfectly shaped to prepare a finely graded 'dying fall'. The performances have absolute authorial conviction, and the 'big hall' sound is plushy without excessive resonance.

Cinque Variazioni; Wasserklavier; Sequenza IV; Rounds; Erdenklavier; Luftklavier; Feuerklavier; Brin; Leaf; Petite Suite.
David Arden *pf*
New Albion NA089CD (49 minutes: DDD). Recorded 1996.　　　　　Ⓕ

Given that line is as important to Berio as to Bellini, it's not surprising that he has written relatively little solo piano music. Even including a rather bland student effort, the *Petite Suite*, this disc can muster less than 50 minutes of material. Despite the short measure, however, the music is characteristically probing in the way it seeks out new approaches to keyboard sonority. The attractions of the disc are also enhanced by the well-controlled, never over-incisive playing of David Arden, recorded in dryish but decently realistic sound. After the early *Variations*, which demonstrate Berio's personal brand of expressionism with a turbulence that never strays into congestion, tempered as it is by moments of Dallapiccola-like lyricism, Berio waited a full decade before composing what remains his most extended solo piano piece, *Sequenza IV* (1965-66). The texture, woven from a tissue of clusters and brief linear flourishes, may derive from the fixed explosions of Stockhausen's seminal *Piano Piece X*, but there is a more relaxed volatility to Berio's coherent disconnections, and to the way he articulates a form through varied degrees of action and repose. All the other pieces are much shorter, but they contain such gems as *Wasserklavier*, an early example of Berio's liking for wry allusions to tonal music (here Schubert and Brahms) and the two memorial pieces from 1990, *Brin* ('Wisp') and *Leaf*, which offer potent distillations of procedures and ideas explored more fully in other works. A pity about the price-tag, then, but this is an essential addition to the Berio discography.

Coro.
Cologne Radio Chorus and Symphony Orchestra / Luciano Berio.
DG 20th Century Classics 423 902-2GC (57 minutes: ADD). Recorded 1980.　　　　　Ⓜ

The entire concept of *Coro* depends on pairings, which can emphasize both the differences and the similarities between each member of the pair. Thus each of the 40 choral singers is paired with an instrumentalist (they sit together in performance), while the text pairs 'folk' poetry – the 'tribal' expression of concern with such universals as love and death – with 'art' poetry – the individual expression of a single poet, Neruda, who turns poetry towards an explicitly political content. *Coro* returns regularly to several of its texts, but most persistently to Neruda's line 'Come and see blood in the Streets'. Whether or not Berio intends to preach a sermon on the need for individuals to engage in collective action, the music is undeniably forceful, and also well varied. The opening, in the composer's most lyric vein, shows how important repetition will be, and also reveals the kind of melodic patterns which increasingly evoke Stravinsky's *Les noces* as the work proceeds. *Les noces* also comes to mind during the more dance-like episodes, and in the denser, more impassioned sections Berio's own post-Stravinskian 'ritualism' is evident.The texture of *Coro* may seem overloaded in places, and the text itself is often submerged by the sheer complexity of the competing musical lines. But the work avoids the episodic diffuseness of some of Berio's other large-scale compositions, and is hampered neither by a spoken narration nor an electronic tape. Its diverse elements are skilfully integrated, and the result is a highly personal, yet urgently communicative statement, persuasively performed and well recorded. In fact, *Coro* emerges as one of Berio's best and most ambitious works of synthesis.

Berio Recital I for Cathy[a]. 11 Folk Songs[b].
Weill (arr. Berio. Sung in English) Die Dreigroschenoper – Ballade von der sexuellen Hörigkeit. Marie Galante – Le grand Lustucru. Happy End – Surabaya-Johnny.
Cathy Berberian *mez*
[a]**London Sinfonietta;** [b]**Juilliard Ensemble / Luciano Berio.**
RCA Victor Gold Seal 09026 62540-2 (65 minutes: ADD). Texts included. Recorded 1972. Ⓜ

These are classic recordings that no contemporary music enthusiast or Berberian/Berio admirer will want to be without. This disc could be regarded as a fitting tribute to Cathy Berberian and her inimitable vocal genius. As an artist she was unique. As a champion of contemporary music (particularly music by her one-time husband Luciano Berio) she was second to none – not only for her interpretative prowess but also the inspirational quality of her highly individual style; many composers (including Stravinsky) wrote music specifically with her voice in mind. The recordings gathered together here were all composed, or arranged for her, by Luciano Berio. The two principal items are perhaps among the most famous of the Berberian/Berio collaborations. *Recital I for Cathy* makes use of Berberian's dramatic training in a composition in which the vocalist, frustrated by the non-appearance of her pianist, struggles through the programme whilst simultaneously sharing a Beckett-like stream-of-consciousness monologue with her audience. Berberian's performance here is a monumental *tour de force*. Another example of the extraordinary qualities of Berberian's voice can be found in the celebrated *Folk Songs* of 1964. The three songs by Kurt Weill reveal Berberian as a natural Weill interpreter (perhaps the best since Lotte Lenya). They are something of a find, this being their first ever release on disc. All in all, this is a wonderful tribute to a phenomenal talent.

Sequenzas – I-VIII, IX*a*, IX*b* and X-XIII, 'Chanson'.
Luisa Castellani *sop* **Sophie Cherrier** *fl* **Lazlo Hadady** *ob* **Alain Damiens** *cl* **Pascal Gallois** *bn* **Christian Wirth** *alto sax* **Gabriele Cassone** *tpt* **Benny Sluchin** *tbn* **Jeanne-Marie Conquer** *vn* **Christophe Desjardins** *va* **Frédérique Cambreling** *hp* **Elliot Fisk** *gtr* **Florent Boffard** *pf* **Teodoro Anzellotti** *accordion*
DG 20/21 457 038-2GH3 (three discs: 158 minutes: DDD). Recorded 1964-67. Ⓕ

Berio's ongoing sequence of solo compositions complements his larger-scale vocal and orchestral works in various productive ways. That does not make the *Sequenzas* 'miniatures', however: one of the most recent, No. 12 for bassoon (1995), is at 18 minutes also the longest, and even the shortest (No. 1, for flute, at just over six minutes) offers a distillation which, for all its elegance, is far from lightweight. It's also inappropriate to call these pieces 'monodies', when the essence of what they offer is the image of a single voice, or line, opening out into a series of dialogues. Berio has come a long way since 1958, when No. 1 was written, yet the flexible eloquence with which he imbues some relatively ordinary avant-garde gestures in that piece is early evidence of a distinctive quality of thought which was to mature and intensify in the years ahead. Five years on, in No. 2 for harp (1963), the instrument's conventionally genteel image is transformed into vivid confrontations between the seductive and the aggressive, and this formula is developed still more radically in No. 3 for female voice (1965). No. 4 (1966) is also highly expressionistic, concentrating on the brittle, dense textures of which the piano is capable, rather than seeking to spin a long, connected line. No. 5 for trombone (1965), by contrast, is a haunting exploration of the instrument's 'voice', as well as of the voice of the player, the use of long, slow *glissandos* a model for the more elaborate treatment of the device in the bassoon *Sequenza* 30 years later.

That all the performers on these discs – most of them members of the Ensemble InterContemporain – are on top of challenging material goes without saying. They might not always stick to the letter of dynamic markings, but the spirit of the music is always vividly conveyed, and the recordings are good – possibly, as with No. 2, a little too close and resonant, but with an engagingly 'live' atmosphere. Of the later *Sequenzas*, none is finer than the staggeringly virtuosic No. 6 for viola (1967) charting Berio's complex response to the Paganinian romantic heritage, and No. 8 for violin (1976) where Bach replaces Paganini as model in a piece with enough of the grandeur and sense of inevitability of Bach's great Chaconne to justify the comparison. With the short No. 7 for oboe (1967) Berio hit on the strategy of placing the instrument's intensely volatile line against a single sustained tone (off-stage or electronic), and a comparable effect is used in No. 10. Here the trumpet occasionally plays into an open grand piano, which (with pedal and silently sustained chords) catches and transforms the resonance to create ethereal echo-effects. No. 9 from 1980 (for clarinet, and also for saxophone) is to some extent an experiment in constraint, limiting the melodic materials and developing dialogues between varied repetitions, while No. 11 (1988) for guitar wittily explores the ways in which the instrument's own limitations can be both exploited and challenged. With No. 12's superbly long-drawn out but never monotonous bassoon lament, and No. 13 for accordion (also 1995) revealing the instrument's capacity for delicate and poetic, as well as brusque, even sinister utterance, it is clear that Berio's interest in putting single instruments under the spotlight was as strong in the mid-1990s as it had been nearly 40 years before. These discs are a wonderful reminder of why Berio's music matters, and a definitive document of a very special twentieth-century achievement.

Sinfonia. Eindrücke.
Regis Pasquier *vn*
New Swingle Singers; French National Orchestra / Pierre Boulez.
Erato MusiFrance 2292-45228-2 (45 minutes: DDD). Recorded 1980s. Ⓕ

This was the first complete recording of Berio's *Sinfonia*. Until this, this absorbing and bewilderingly complex work was available only in the four-movement version that Berio himself prepared in 1969 for the first performance with the Swingle Singers and the New York Philharmonic Orchestra (once available on CBS); less than happily coupled with Bartók's *Music for strings, percussion and celesta*). Within a few months, Berio had completed a fifth and final movement which, though ostensibly an appendix, arguably stands as the apotheosis of the entire work; for it is genuinely a 'sounding together' (sinfonia) of the preceding movements, a rich sequence of reminiscences, just as the celebrated third movement leads us through memories of the standard orchestral repertoire in a kind of stream of subconsciousness. To hear the work in its completed form is nothing short of a revelation, and for this reason alone Boulez's performance must be said to supersede Berio's own. To complete the disc he has chosen one of Berio's less-familiar orchestral works, *Eindrücke* ('Impressions') of 1973-74. This is a complete contrast: a vast monody, projected by the string orchestra against the stuttering interjections and lingering trills of the wind and percussion, a stark and uncompromising conception. Again, the reading is a powerful one. This is a most important issue, far too good to miss.

Sir Lennox Berkeley

British 1903-1989

Piano Sonata, Op. 20. Six Preludes, Op. 23. Five Short Pieces, Op. 4. Palm Court Waltz, Op. 81 No. 2ª. Sonatina for Piano Duet, Op. 39ª. Theme and Variations, Op. 73ª.
Raphael Terroni, ªNorman Beedie *pfs*
British Music Society BMS416CD (58 minutes: DDD). Recorded 1993. Ⓕ

This is some of the finest British piano music of the century. If you find Bax turgid, Ireland too sweet, Tippett gawky or repetitive, Britten and Walton virtually non-existent in the solo repertoire, then Sir Lennox Berkeley's consistently melodic piano writing should be a real discovery. Terroni really understands the Berkeley style. The outer movements of the Sonata demand a special feeling for flow to give quite diverse material continuity, and Terroni achieves this. The finale is excellent, and the overwhelming impression confirms Malcolm Williamson's description: 'a flawless masterpiece'. There are real delights, too, in the rest of his offering. His *Six Preludes* are just right, musically dedicated and unidiosyncratic. The *Five Short Pieces* are a microcosm of Berkeley's style in the 1930s, as are the *Preludes* for the 1940s. Terroni gauges them beautifully – the balance of melody and accompaniment in No. 4 is sheer perfection. And his duo with Norman Beedie is everything one could ask for in the *Sonatina* and *Theme and Variations*, exquisite piano duets in the great tradition of Schubert, Fauré or Satie.

Berkeley Five Poems, Op. 53. Night covers up the rigid land, Op. 14 No. 2. Lay your sleeping head, my love, Op. 14 No. 2b.
Britten On this Island, Op. 11. Fish in the unruffled lakes. Night covers up the rigid land. To lie flat on the back. The sun shines down. What's on your mind? Underneath the abject willow (two versions). When you're feeling like expressing your affection. Four Cabaret Songs.
Della Jones *mez* **Philip Langridge** *ten* **Steuart Bedford** *pf*
Collins Classics 1490-2 (61 minutes: DDD). Texts included. Recorded 1995-97. Ⓕ

The treasure-trove of previously undiscovered Britten songs is still growing. Langridge and Bedford give us three enjoyable additions to the canon: the somewhat cynical *The sun shines down*, the flighty *What's on your mind?* and the love-song *Underneath the abject willow*. They are among the highlights of this cornucopia of Britten's, and Berkeley's, settings of Auden, of which the centrepiece is the well-known early cycle, *On this Island*, which the partnership sing with their flair for going to the heart of the matter. We are consoled for the fact that Langridge's tone now judders uncomfortably when it comes under pressure by the imagination he brings to his word-painting. He also offers three settings, *Fish in the unruffled lakes*, *Night covers up the rigid land* and *To lie flat on the back*: the readings are admirable.

Night covers up the rigid land was also set by Berkeley, at the time friend of the poet and his fellow composer, and the two pieces offer a nice contrast in style, Britten's the more economical, Berkeley's the more haunting and direct. Langridge sings them both with a fine line and inner understanding. Britten was intending to set the erotic *Lay your sleeping head, my love*, but in the event Berkeley musicked it, a song of seductive beauty. His later Op. 53 set of *Five Poems* doesn't have quite such an individual quality but it's well worth hearing. Della Jones gives the *Cabaret Songs* everything she's got. It's strong stuff, but only faint hearts will wilt at her wholly involving style. Then Jones and Langridge come together for the earlier setting of *Underneath the abject willow*, meltingly sung by Langridge. Bedford's playing is an asset throughout. The recordings of all bar the too-resonant *Cabaret Songs* are excellent.

Hector Berlioz French 1803-1869

Overtures – Les francs-juges, Op. 3. Waverley, Op. 1. King Lear, Op. 4. Le carnaval romain, Op. 9. Béatrice et Bénédict. Le corsaire, Op. 21. Benvenuto Cellini.
Staatskapelle Dresden / Sir Colin Davis.
RCA Victor Red Seal 09026 68790-2 (74 minutes: DDD). Recorded 1997.   Ⓕ

Berlioz's seven overtures fit comfortably into an hour and a quarter, in performances that reflect Sir Colin's long absorption with music that remains difficult, original, surprising. The most extrovert, the Ball Scene in *Le carnaval romain*, is exhilaratingly played, but done so without the strenuous attempts after excitement at all costs, through speed and volume, which are all too familiar. The music is more interesting than that, its tensions more dramatic. What are perhaps the two hardest overtures to play successfully, *Waverley* and *King Lear*, benefit from some understatement, especially in the quieter sections when, particularly in *Lear*, a sense of trouble animates the music. As elsewhere, Berlioz's melodies made out of awkward rhythms and uneven metres call for a skilled hand: nowhere is this more evident than at the opening of *Benvenuto Cellini*, whose oddity does not immediately strike the listener but whose 'rightness' is proved by its wonderful verve. Davis handles this superbly, as in different vein he does the soft music answering the opening of *Le carnaval romain*, in which he is given some beautiful playing (especially from the cor anglais) by the Dresden orchestra. It responds to his understanding of the different levels of tension and expression, as well as different dynamic levels, at which Berlioz can make his effects, such as at the start of *Les francs-juges*. Sometimes a slight emphasis in the accompaniment, even the touch of warmth on a single note, can illuminate much in the melody. It is all beautifully done.

Harold in Italy, Op. 16. Tristia, Op. 18.

Harold in Italy. Tristia. Les Troyens à Carthage – Act 2, Prelude.
Nobuko Imai *va* **John Alldis Choir; London Symphony Orchestra / Sir Colin Davis.**
Philips 416 431-2PH (70 minutes: ADD). Texts and translations included.
Recorded 1969-80.   Ⓕ 🅡🅡

Berlioz was much influenced by the British romantic poet, Byron, and his travels in Italy – where he went in 1831 as the winner of the Prix de Rome – led him to conceive a big orchestral work based on one of Byron's most popular works, *Childe Harold's Pilgrimage*. Like Berlioz's earlier *Symphonie fantastique*, *Harold in Italy* was not only a programme work but brilliantly unconventional and imaginative in its structure and argument. A commission from the great virtuoso, Paganini, led him to conceive a big viola concerto, but the idea of a Byronic symphony got in the way of that. Though there is an important viola solo in the symphony as we know it – richly and warmly played on Davis's recording by Nobuko Imai – it is far from being the vehicle for solo display that Paganini was wanting. Sir Colin Davis's 1975 performance, beautifully transferred to CD, emphasizes the symphonic strength of the writing without losing the bite of the story-telling. The shorter works are also all valuable in illustrating Berlioz's extraordinary imagination. Excellent sound on all the different vintage recordings.

Harold in Italy. Tristia.
Gérard Caussé *va* **Monteverdi Choir; Orchestre Révolutionnaire et Romantique / Sir John Eliot Gardiner.**
Philips 446 676-2PH (60 minutes: DDD). Text and translation included. Recorded 1994. ©ⓅⓈⒺ

It is to Gardiner's credit that, like Davis, he conveys that element of wildness without ever slackening control. With Gardiner dynamic contrasts are extreme, far more strikingly so than in most period-instrument performances, and some of the *pianissimos* from the ORR strings are ravishing. The central *Canto religioso* of the second movement of the Pilgrims' hymn provides a remarkable instance, with the arpeggios *sul ponticello* of the solo viola far more eerie than usual. Gardiner's soloist, Gérard Caussé, uses vibrato sparingly. Yet for the smooth phrases of Harold's theme, the work's motto, Caussé consciously produces warm tone. It is a fine solo performance, but not so dominant that one feels the lack of a soloist in the last three-quarters of the finale. It is there that Gardiner's reading, intense from the start, reaches white heat, and it is worth noting that there, as in the rest of the performance, his speeds are never excessively fast. Altogether a thrilling performance, highly recommendable to those who would not normally consider a version with period instruments. In the three movements of *Tristia* Gardiner, using his own Monteverdi Choir, gives equally refreshing performances, and here the dynamic contrasts are more extreme than in Davis's analogue recording. So the epilogue to the 'Hamlet Funeral March', the third of the three movements, is the more chilling and broken in mood for the extreme hush of the *pianissimo*.

Berlioz Le carnaval romain, Op. 9. Béatrice et Bénédict – Overture. Le corsaire, Op. 21. Les Troyens – Royal Hunt and Storm. Benvenuto Cellini – Overture. Roméo et Juliette, Op. 17 – Queen Mab scherzo.
Saint-Saëns Le rouet d'Omphale in A major, Op. 31.
Boston Symphony Orchestra / Charles Munch.
RCA Victor Gold Seal 09026-61400-2 (61 minutes: ADD). Recorded 1957-61. ⓂⒽ

This particular Berlioz concert has long enjoyed classic status. Munch secures an electrifying response from his great Boston orchestra, whose playing is virtuosic and tender by turns. Highlights include truly exhilarating renderings of *Le corsaire* and *Benvenuto Cellini* as well as a quite riveting Royal Hunt and Storm, which attains a breathtaking poetry in the horn-led moments of repose. The bonus item, Saint-Saëns's colourful tone-poem, *Le rouet d'Omphale*, is also superbly managed here: its central climax has surely never sounded more gripping. Recordings are a bit thin in the treble, but not enough to take the shine off what is an irresistible mid-price anthology.

Symphonie fantastique, Op. 14

Symphonie fantastique[a]. Roméo et Juliette, Op. 17[b] – Love scene; Queen Mab scherzo.
[a]**Concertgebouw Orchestra;** [b]**London Symphony Orchestra / Sir Colin Davis.**
Philips Solo 446 202-2PM (80 minutes: ADD). Recorded 1974 and 1968. Ⓜ🆁🆁

This classic performance comes up well again on CD, the sound a little hard at times but everything clear and in place. With what appears to be well over 50 versions of the work available, choice is certainly wide, though there are a good many, some of them by famous names, that pay more attention to the names in question than to Berlioz's still astonishing romantic vision. Davis remains among those conductors who can seek out the individualities in Berlioz with unerring judgement: the telling emphasis that troubles a 'normal' cadence, the lean on a phrase that corrupts it, the crack of a rhythm that makes this March one which ends on the scaffold. The orchestra is, of course, modern, that is to say not 'period' in any form (it does, incidentally, include the extra part for the cornet which Berlioz added, not, in many opinions, much to the music's advantage). Those who prefer period instruments, which can indeed reveal colours something near to those heard by Berlioz, deeply influencing the music's actual invention, will prefer the fine performance by John Eliot Gardiner (below); others can feel themselves as safe in Davis's hands as any – or rather, as skilfully led on a dangerous experience.

Berlioz Symphonie fantastique.
Dutilleux Métaboles.
Paris Opéra-Bastille Orchestra / Myung-Whun Chung.
DG 445 878-2GH (67 minutes: DDD). Recorded 1993. Ⓕ

Not many versions of the *Symphonie fantastique* rival Myung-Whun Chung's in conveying the nervously impulsive inspiration of a young composer, the hints of hysteria, the overtones of nightmare in Berlioz's programme. He makes one register it afresh as genuinely fantastic; the volatile element in this perennially modern piece is something which Chung brings out to a degree rarely known before, and that establishes his as a very individual, sharply characterized version with unusually strong claims. Such an approach as Chung's might easily have sounded fussy or self-indulgent, but the rapport between the conductor and the Bastille orchestra is so complete that all the subtleties of expression, the highly complex rubato, sound natural and spontaneous, regularly making one register this – despite the nationality of the conductor – as a very French performance. Only at the start of the finale does tension momentarily slacken, and Chung's fast tempo for the clarinet's grotesque version of the motto theme challenges the players to the limit, again conveying wildness. The conclusion brings all the expected thrills in its impulsiveness, with the bass drum vividly caught. The coupling is original, the set of five brief and brilliant pieces which Dutilleux wrote for Szell and the Cleveland Orchestra in 1964. Chung's view is both poetic and atmospheric, bringing out the subtly contrasting timbres in each piece, with the different sections of the orchestra brought together in the final *Presto*, where Chung relishes the marking 'Flamboyant', underlining jazzy syncopations in fractional anticipation to make this an exciting and volatile reading. This is a makeweight to welcome, for it is sure to surprise and delight.

Symphonie fantastique.
Orchestre Révolutionnaire et Romantique / Sir John Eliot Gardiner.
Philips 434 402-2PH (53 minutes: DDD). Recorded 1991.   Ⓕ Ⓟ

In his preface, Gardiner sets out the issues again, and claims to 'recreate as closely as the available documentation permits the sound and atmosphere of the first performance'. Even if we have here only an approximation to the sounds of the first performance, that is a good starting point. Gardiner's performance is in some ways sharper than Roger Norrington's (whose own ground-breaking performance is available on EMI), and more insistent on detail. This can lead to over-phrasing, though he does almost nothing that cannot be justified from Berlioz's intricately, often oddly, marked score. Both performances are of endless fascination and enjoyment. Norrington is, in general, more concerned to use his recovered instrumental sounds to shape a performance of the kind with which we are familiar, cleaning everything up and presenting it afresh. Gardiner is perhaps more interested in the kind of performance with which Berlioz might have startled his audience that December night in 1830. So he plays the music with an extra emphasis on sudden flicks of phrasing, an extra abruptness in the stamp of a rhythm or the snap of an interrupting chord, a concern for the extreme. Who can tell what the instruments really sounded like? What matters is that we have, to set beside other well-loved performances with a modern orchestra, this one that takes us very close to the sound world out of which Berlioz created a completely new kind of music.

Les nuits d'été, Op. 7.

Les nuits d'été. Herminie.
Mireille Delunsch *sop* **Brigitte Balleys** *mez*
Orchestre des Champs-Elysées, Paris / Philippe Herreweghe.
Harmonia Mundi HMC90 1522 (54 minutes: DDD). Texts and translations included.
Recorded 1994.   Ⓕ RR

It is not fanciful to hear decided pre-echoes in *Herminie* of Cassandra's fateful, searing music (quite apart from the very obvious dry-run for the *Symphonie fantastique*'s main motif). This extraordinary work of 1828, almost as arresting as its near-contemporary *Cléopâtre*, receives a grand rendering from Mireille Delunsch, who sings it in a compact, direct manner. Her tone is narrow and focused, her French diction clear. Herreweghe and his orchestra adopt a lean sound, surely close to that of Berlioz's time. Delunsch enters into the inner agony of the distraught, frustrated Herminie with a will. All in all, her interpretation is absorbing from start to finish. The recording imparts a slight glare to her tone as it does to that of Balleys in the much more familiar *Nuits d'été*, but that is hardly enough to detract from what is an idiomatic, unfussy reading. Her voice does not luxuriate in the more sensual moments of the cycle as does Régine Crespin's in her famous version (reviewed in the Collections section) but it has a clarity of profile and a definition of phrase and, where strength of feeling is called for, Balleys provides it, as in 'Au cimitière' and 'Absence'. This makes a sensible pairing with the cantata. What may also influence your choice is, again, Herreweghe's lean, well-pointed support which often emphasizes, rightly, the striking originality of Berlioz's scoring.

Les nuits d'été[a]. La mort de Cléopâtre[b]. Les Troyens – Act 5, scenes 2 and 3[c].
Dame Janet Baker *mez* [c]**Bernadette Greevy** *contr* [c]**Keith Erwen** *ten* [c]**Gwynne Howell** *bass*
[c]**Ambrosian Opera Chorus;** [a]**New Philharmonia Orchestra / Sir John Barbirolli;**
[bc]**London Symphony Orchestra / Sir Alexander Gibson.**
EMI Studio CDM7 69544-2 (78 minutes: ADD). Recorded 1967-69.   Ⓜ

Crespin's *Nuits d'été* has always been the interpretation by which others have been assessed and there is still no reason to challenge the verdict. Both in terms of idiomatic and natural French, languorous tone and understanding of the poetry's and the music's meaning, it stands above all other versions. Even Dame Janet Baker's appreciable reading sounds a trifle affected in its vocal grammar besides Crespin's. However, overall, the Baker disc is just as recommendable, and at 78 minutes provides more than generous fare. Her account of that remarkable cantata, *La mort de Cléopâtre*, has definitely not been surpassed. In *Les Troyens* she portrays the death-haunted queen with deep feeling and firm resolution. Her essays way above the stave disclose her at the absolute peak of her powers in 1969; her accomplishment of this role a few months earlier on stage is suitably remembered in the closing scenes of the work: she encompasses both the private and public side of Dido's tragedy unerringly. The declamation is vital, the pathos moving. The recordings need little indulgence from the listener. EMI – reprehensibly – provides no texts or translations, and they are really essential for the listener. In spite of that, admirers of this much-loved artist and of this music are urged to acquire this disc.

Les nuits d'été. Benvenuto Cellini – Tra la la ... Mais qu'ai-je donc?. Les Troyens – Je vais mourir ... Adieu, fière cité. Béatrice et Bénédict – Dieu! Que vien-je d'entendre? ... Il m'en souvient. La damnation de Faust – D'amour l'ardente flamme.
Susan Graham *mez* **Royal Opera House Orchestra, Covent Garden / John Nelson.**
Sony Classical SK62730 (61 minutes: DDD). Texts and translations included.
Recorded 1996-97.   Ⓕ ▣

It would be hard to imagine a more inspiriting and rewarding display of Berlioz singing than this from a singer who has the composer's style in her voice and heart. Running the gamut of Berlioz's writing for the female voice Graham manages to explore and deliver the soul of each of her chosen pieces, her voice – firm yet vibrant, clear yet warm – responding interpretatively and technically to the appreciable demands placed on it by this programme. In *Les nuits d'été*, she faces the greatest challenge from revered favourites and meets it head on, catching in almost every respect the varied moods of each song. Her French pronunciation is excellent and she uses the language to evoke the atmosphere of each song without a hint of exaggeration. Marguérite's nobly impassioned solo from *Damnation* is confidently voiced, managing in the studio to conjure up all the heroine's longing, quite arrestingly so at 'Je suis à ma fenêtre'. Throughout the piece Graham maintains a wonderfully secure tone and a long line. The noble dignity of her account of Dido's farewell, in particular at the recollection of the love duet, is deeply moving, and Béatrice's equivocal thoughts about her lover are another triumph, the touch of the martial at 'Les Mores triomphaient' nicely contrasted with the sensual tone of the repeated 'Il m'en souvient'. The fleeter, lighter side of Graham's art is caught in the rapturous cabaletta to Béatrice's aria and in Ascanio's excitable aria from *Benvenuto Cellini*, both dispatched securely. Nelson and the LSO provide idiomatic support, and the recording catches the full colour of the singer's performances. Here is a disc as thoughtfully planned as it is executed.

L'enfance du Christ, Op. 25

L'enfance du Christ[a]. Tristia, Op. 18 – Méditation religieuse; La mort d'Ophélie. Sara la baigneuse, Op. 11. La mort de Cléopâtre.
Elsie Morison, Anne Pashley *sops* **Sir Peter Pears, Edgar Fleet** *tens* **John Cameron** *bar*
John Frost, Joseph Rouleau *basses*
St Anthony Singers; [a]Goldsbrough Orchestra; English Chamber Orchestra / Sir Colin Davis.
Double Decca 443 461-2DF2 (two discs: 142 minutes: ADD). Recorded [a]1960 and 1967.   Ⓜ ▣▣

Despite advances in recording since 1960, highly commended performances by other conductors of *L'enfance du Christ*, and another by Colin Davis himself 16 years later, many Berliozians still retain a special affection for his original version, now 40 years old. At the time of the recording he had only recently shot into the limelight as a conductor and was in the first flush of a youthful enthusiasm for Berlioz, of whom he became an outstanding interpreter. There is an electric excitement in the scene of Herod and the soothsayers, the Goldsbrough Orchestra (which was shortly to be reborn as the English Chamber Orchestra) responding alertly, under Davis's guidance, to the drama of the situation; and even before that, there is a sense of veiled mystery in the Roman soldiers' nocturnal rounds. But he was also fortunate in his cast: Peter Pears as a most expressive narrator, adapting his tone to each aspect of the story, Elsie Morison with her light soprano, perfectly suggesting Mary's youthful purity and innocence, John Cameron as a solicitous Joseph, and Joseph Rouleau skilfully changing his timbre to double as the tormented Herod and the kindly Ishmaelite father. One or two reservations remain: the duet between Mary and Joseph in Part 1 is not well balanced, the baritone swamping the soprano; and choral intonation is not always as exact as we have come to expect from present-day chorus standards. But overall this is, as has always been recognized, a fine reading.

Criticism must be made, however, of the fact that no texts are provided for any of the works here. These pieces appear only rarely in the catalogue; *La mort de Cléopâtre* has had some distinguished later interpreters, including Dame Janet Baker and Yvonne Minton – Jessye Norman, luscious as is her voice, does not really 'get inside' the work – but Anne Pashley, an artist who disappeared far too quickly from the catalogue, has a fine sense of the dramatic, and is superbly backed up by Davis and the orchestra.

L'enfance du Christ.
Jean Rigby *mez* **John Aler, Peter Evans** *tens* **Gerald Finley, Robert Poulton** *bars*
Alastair Miles, Gwynne Howell *basses* **St Paul's Cathedral Choir;**
Corydon Singers and Orchestra / Matthew Best.
Hyperion CDA66991/2 (two discs: 101 minutes: DDD). Text and translation included.
Recorded 1994.   Ⓕ Ⓢ

Best treats *L'enfance du Christ* as overtly operatic, not so much by cast movements or varied microphone placings as by his pacing of the action and by encouraging his artists to throw themselves wholeheartedly into the emotions of the story. He gets off to a tremendous start with a superb reading by a black-voiced Alastair Miles as a Herod haunted by his dream and startled into belligerent wakefulness by the arrival of Polydorus. Later, there is desperate urgency in the appeals for shelter by Joseph (an otherwise gently lyrical Gerald Finley), harshly rebuffed by the chorus. And, throughout, there are spatial perspectives – the soldiers' patrol advancing (from practically inaudible pizzicatos) to centre stage and going off again; a beautifully hushed and atmospheric faraway 'Amen' at the end. The angels' warning to the Holy Family in Part 1, however, is miscalculated by the voices being too distantly placed for their words to be audible. Balance in general is excellent, a notable passage being the duet in the tender scene at the manger. The clear enunciation (in very good French) of nearly everyone is a plus point: only Jean Rigby, sweet-toned and radiating innocence as Mary, might have given her words greater precision. The chorus's response to the mood and meaning of words is always alert and sensitive, matched by the nuanced orchestral playing. The scurrying of the Ishmaelite family to help, played really *pianissimo*, is vividly graphic; and their home entertainment on two flutes and a harp, which sometimes marks a drop in the interest, here has great charm. But overall it is Best's pacing which makes this recording distinctive. This recording of Berlioz's appealing work well stands comparison with its much-praised predecessors.

L'enfance du Christ.
Véronique Gens *sop* **Paul Agnew** *ten* **Olivier Lallouette** *bar* **Laurent Naouri, Frédéric Caton**
basses **La Chapelle Royale; Collegium Vocale;**
Orchestre des Champs-Elysées / Philippe Herreweghe.
Harmonia Mundi HMC90 1632/3 (two discs: 95 minutes: DDD). Text and translation included.
Recorded live in 1997.   Ⓕ Ⓔ

Herreweghe paces his performance perceptively, and if it cannot quite match the impact that Colin Davis's 1960 recording made at the time, it makes a strong claim to figure among the most recommendable present-day interpretations. Though recorded at public performances, the sound is extraordinarily clean and fresh, and the balance deserves much praise for the technicians as well as the artists. Care is taken over dynamics; the distance of the angels' warning to the Holy Family has been well judged, the result being better in focus than for Best; the orchestra's soft scurrying for the bustle in the Ishmaelite house is atmospheric; and the forward sound for the flutes-and-harp trio lends illumination to the spirited central episode. The chorus is admirable – flexible and alert, their words not merely clear but sensitively coloured. Of the soloists, chief honours go to Paul Agnew as the narrator and to Véronique Gens in her touchingly tender portrayal of Mary. Frédéric Caton exudes kindly sympathy as the benevolent Ishmaelite father; Olivier Lallouette makes more of an impression as Polydorus than in voicing Joseph's increasing despair in Saïs, though his duet with Mary at the crib is treated with sensitivity.

Roméo et Juliette.

Roméo et Juliette.
Olga Borodina *mez* **Thomas Moser** *ten* **Alastair Miles** *bass*
Bavarian Radio Chorus; Vienna Philharmonic Orchestra / Sir Colin Davis.
Philips 442 134-2PH2 (two discs: 96 minutes: DDD). Text and translation included.
Recorded 1993.   Ⓕ

Davis's return to Berlioz's highly demanding dramatic symphony is more than welcome (he first recorded it in 1968, also for Philips). He has not substantially rethought what was by some way the finest recorded performance, but he has lived through the music again and been allowed by the recording to clarify what was before in places obscure. But the gains are also musically more positive. Thomas Moser sings the vocal version of 'Queen Mab' with a verve and wit that make it all sound easy, which it is not. Olga Borodina is excellent in the 'Strophes', phrasing with a long but internally detailed line which is essentially Berliozian, and adding just the right throb of vibrato when he lovingly asks for it at the sacred word 'Shakespeare'. Alastair Miles has more difficulty with the problematic role of Friar Laurence, and his French is less secure than that of the others, but this cantata finale, never the strongest part of the work, stands up well and he leads it firmly, supported by the excellent chorus. Davis himself makes of this as good a case as possible for a reconciliatory conclusion to a whole symphonic experience, one whose variety as well as quasi-symphonic cohesion he understands better than any other conductor.

Roméo et Juliette.
Catherine Robbin *mez* **Jean-Paul Fouchécourt** *ten* **Gilles Cachemaille** *bar*
Monteverdi Choir; Orchestre Révolutionnaire et Romantique / Sir John Eliot Gardiner.
Philips 454 454-2PH2 (two discs: 136 minutes: DDD). Text and translation included. Includes earlier variants. Recorded 1995. Ⓕ **E**

If not exactly a 'variorum' edition, Gardiner's is one that adds to the standard version much of the discarded music that has been rescued (often from under *collettes*, glued-on pieces of paper). Track programming will allow listeners to chart their preferred course through the work, 'standard' or so-called 'original' or Gardiner's own mixture of the two. Briefly, the main differences are as follows. Berlioz expanded the original Prologue so as to bring in more glimpses of music later to be heard and the revised 'Queen Mab' *Scherzo* has a more strongly composed ending. This Second Prologue seems not to have been orchestrated, and it is, here, by Oliver Knussen with a quick Berliozian ear. The finale had the most alterations; they are mostly to do with shortening Friar Laurence's sermon which is the better for it. This often maligned finale is more than justified in Gardiner's performance.

Gilles Cachemaille's voice is a little light for Père Laurence but he has an intelligent perception of the part, and sings with an affecting ruefulness as well as firmness. The 'Strophes' are attractively sung by Catherine Robbin, a light contralto such as Berlioz would have known. Jean-Paul Fouchécourt throws off the difficult Queen Mab *Scherzetto* with the panache he might bring to a comic opera aria. Robbin is probably using more vibrato than singers of the day would have done. The question of how much vibrato would have been used by a Paris orchestra of the time is arguable; Gardiner is almost certainly right to discourage it. Yet he also appears to discourage *portamento*, which was coming in as an expressive device. It may partly account for him pressing the music rather hard in consequence, where Davis can allow the great rapturous phrases to unfold more naturally. Gardiner also presses the 'Queen Mab' *Scherzo* hard, where Davis floats the phrases on the light, speeding tempo. But he gives 'Romeo in the Tomb of the Capulets' a brilliantly eloquent account and his reading of the Ball is vigorous and exuberant, even if it lacks the whiff of foreboding which Davis scents in it. No one with a care for Berlioz will want to be without Gardiner's remarkable set. Sir Colin's recordings are more devoted to the inward emotions, and touch more eloquently on the tragedy of young love destined never to flourish, but never to fade. There is room for both views of a wonderful work.

Grande messe des morts, Op. 5.

Grande messe des morts[a]. Symphonie funèbre et triomphale[b].
Ronald Dowd *ten* [a]**Wandsworth School Boys' Choir;**
[b]**John Alldis Choir; London Symphony Chorus**[a] **and Orchestra / Sir Colin Davis.**
Philips 416 283-2PH2 (two discs: 127 minutes: ADD). Notes, texts and translations included. Ⓕ

Berlioz's Requiem is not a liturgical work, any more than the *Symphonie funèbre* is really for the concert hall; but both are pieces of high originality, composed as ceremonials for the fallen, and standing as two of the noblest musical monuments to the French ideal of a *gloire*. The Requiem is most famous for its apocalyptic moment when, after screwing the key up stage by stage, Berlioz's four brass bands blaze forth 'at the round earth's imagin'd corners'; this has challenged the engineers of various companies, but the Philips recording for Sir Colin Davis remains as fine as any, not least since Davis directs the bands with such a strong sense of character. He also gives the troubled rhythms of the *Lacrymosa* a stronger, more disturbing emphasis than any other conductor, and time and again finds out the expressive counterpoint, the emphatic rhythm, the telling few notes within the texture, that reveal so much about Berlioz's intentions. The notorious flute and trombone chords of the *Hostias* work admirably. Ronald Dowd is a little strained in the *Sanctus*, but the whole performance continues to stand the test of time and of other competing versions. The same is true of the *Symphonie funèbre et triomphale*, which moves at a magisterial tread and is given a recording that does well by its difficult textures. A fine coupling of two remarkable works.

Grande messe des morts.
Richard Lewis *ten* **Royal Philharmonic Chorus and Orchestra / Sir Thomas Beecham.**
BBC Music Legends mono BBCL4011-2 (78 minutes: ADD). Text and translation included.
Recorded live in 1959. Ⓜ Ⓗ

Almost 60 years to the day since his first Berlioz performance, Beecham conducted the *Grande
messe des morts* in the Albert Hall. Though the *Dies irae* thunders out tremendously, and the
'Lacrymosa' has a wonderful snap on the off-beat chords, it is the quieter movements that
characterize what is, after all, a Requiem Mass. Beecham's response to them is with a lifetime's
devotion to one of the composers who had been closest to his heart. The 'Quid sum miser' has an
enchanting clarity (with some lovely cor anglais playing); the long, hushed end of the 'Offertoire',
as Berlioz lingers over the gently alternating notes that suffuse the invention, is finely judged; the
Sanctus is eloquently sung by Lewis and the splendid chorus; the return of the opening 'Te decet
hymnus', near the close of the whole work, is sublime. Such things are not achieved without the
attention to detail with which Beecham used to complain people did not credit him. How wrong.
His orchestral parts were always covered with powerful blue pencil marks and the signature 'TB', so
that it was impossible to mistake intentions which players would then shape for him in rehearsal (and
which he was capable of nerve-rackingly contradicting in performance). Here, the detail is exquisite,
always natural. Occasionally he takes his own view, not Berlioz's, about phrasing; and the orchestra
contains not a whiff of an ophicleide. No matter. This is a recording of a great occasion – remarkably
full in recording, scarcely bothered by audience noise – but also of a marvellous performance.

Messe solennelle (also includes revised version of Resurrexit).
Donna Brown *sop* **Jean-Luc Viala** *ten* **Gilles Cachemaille** *bar*
Monteverdi Choir; Orchestre Révolutionnaire et Romantique / Sir John Eliot Gardiner.
Philips 442 137-2PH (61 minutes: DDD). Text and translation included. Recorded live in 1993. Ⓕ Ⓟ

The reappearance of Berlioz's lost Mass of 1824 is the most exciting musical discovery of modern
times. To an incredulous meeting of the New Berlioz Edition in 1992 the General Editor, Hugh
Macdonald, announced that a Belgian choirmaster, Frans Moors, had made contact with news of
an improbable find in an Antwerp organ loft. A few days later, Prof Macdonald reported back from
Antwerp that this was indeed the *Messe solennelle* which Berlioz alleged that he had burnt after a
couple of performances: in fact, he had given a copy to a Belgian friend, going on to use some of
the music elsewhere. John Eliot Gardiner with his Monteverdi Choir and Orchestre Révolutionnaire
et Romantique gave performances in Bremen, Vienna, Madrid, Rome and Westminster Cathedral.
This is a live recording of that last, thrilling occasion.

Why did Berlioz abandon the work? Only the *Resurrexit* was retained, though it was rewritten: both
versions are included here. Some of it, but not much, is dull: the *Offertory* and *Sanctus* sit rather
stolidly with the rest. He was unfair on what he denounced in an angry scribble on the MS as an
'execrable' fugue. Some is disconcertingly awkward, and Gardiner tells in the notes to this record of
his and the singers' and players' confusion – until they all came together and suddenly the music
made sense. The best of the work is superb: among this one may count the *Incarnatus*, the
O Salutaris and the lovely *Agnus Dei*. The latter was too good to lose, and survives in another form
in the *Te Deum*. So do other ideas: it was at first disconcerting to hear the chorus singing
'Laudamus te. Benedicimus te' to the Carnival music from *Benvenuto Cellini*, more so than to hear
the slow movement of the *Symphonie fantastique* in the beautiful *Gratias*. Once these and other
associations are overcome, the work coheres remarkably well. Yet perhaps it did not do so well
enough for Berlioz, and perhaps he was dissatisfied with the conjunction of some rather academic
music with ideas that were too original, indeed too beautiful, to make a satisfying whole. All the
same, no wonder the precocious 20-year-old was embraced after the first performance by his
teacher, old Le Sueur, with the promise that he would be a great composer. Who knows whether he
might have been made to think twice about abandoning the work had he heard a performance such
as this. This applies to the wonderful Monteverdi Choir, to the orchestra, and above all to Gardiner
himself. There will doubtless be more performances, even if it is not likely to be a repertory work.
In any case, this is a recording of a great musical event, not to be missed.

Béatrice et Bénédict.
Susan Graham *sop* Béatrice; **Jean-Luc Viala** *ten* Bénédict; **Sylvia McNair** *sop* Héro;
Catherine Robbin *mez* Ursule; **Gilles Cachemaille** *bar* Claudio; **Gabriel Bacquier** *bar*
Somarone; **Vincent Le Texier** *bass* Don Pedro; **Philippe Magnant** *spkr* Léonato;
Lyon Opera Chorus and Orchestra / John Nelson.
Erato MusiFrance 2292-45773-2 (two discs: 111 minutes: DDD). Notes, text and translation
included. Recorded 1991. Ⓕ

We have to note that the title is not a French version of *Much Ado about Nothing*, but that it takes the two principal characters of Shakespeare's play and constructs an opera around them. The comedy centres on the trick which is played upon the protagonists by their friends, producing love out of apparent antipathy. Much of the charm lies in the more incidental matters of choruses, dances, the magical 'Nocturne' duet for Béatrice and Héro, and the curious addition of the character Somarone, a music-master who rehearses the choir in one of his own compositions. There is also a good deal of spoken dialogue. Perhaps surprisingly, the extra dialogue is a point in its favour, for it is done very effectively by good French actors and it makes for a cohesive, Shakespearian entertainment. John Nelson secures a well-pointed performance of the score, and with excellent playing by the Lyon Orchestra. Susan Graham and Jean-Luc Viala are attractively vivid and nimble in style, and Sylvia McNair makes a lovely impression in Héro's big solo. The veteran Gabriel Bacquier plays the music-master with genuine panache and without overmuch clownage. There is good work by the supporting cast and the chorus and the recording is finely produced and well recorded.

La damnation de Faust, Op. 24.
Susan Graham *sop* **Thomas Moser** *ten* **José van Dam** *bass-bar* **Frédéric Caton** *bass*
Chorus and Orchestra of Opéra de Lyon / Kent Nagano.
Erato 0630-10692-2 (two discs: 122 minutes: DDD). Text and translation included.
Recorded 1994. ⓕ

New versions of *Faust* appear regularly, but it is rare to encounter one as good as Kent Nagano's. At its centre is a perception of Berlioz's extraordinary vision, in all its colour and variety and humour and pessimism, and the ability to realize this in a broad downward sweep while setting every detail sharply in place. *La damnation* is a work about the steady failure of consolations in a romantic world rejecting God, until all Faust's sensations are numbed and Mephistopheles has him trapped in the hell of no feeling. Every stage of the progress is mercilessly depicted here. The chorus is brilliant in all its roles, offering in turn the lively charms of peasant life, raptures of faith in the Easter Hymn, beery roistering in Auerbach's Cellar that grows as foul as a drunken party, cheerful student Latin bawls (those were the days); later they sing with delicacy as Mephistopheles's spirits of temptation and finally become a vicious pack of demons. Nagano takes the Hungarian March at a pace that grows hectic as the dream of military glory turns hollow. It is all brilliantly realized.

There is the same care for orchestral detail. Nagano seems to be conducting from the New Berlioz Edition score, and he uses his imagination with it. He has an unerring sense of tempo, balancing weight of tone against speed, and he can light upon the telling contrapuntal line, or point a detail of instrumental colour (like the viola tremolo that 'betrays' the will-o'-the-wisps as the devil's creatures) or even a single note (like the snarl in the Ride to the Abyss), elements that give Berlioz's marvellous orchestration its expressive quality. José van Dam is an outstanding Mephistopheles, curling his voice round phrases with hideous elegance, relishing the mock-jollity of the Serenade and the Song of the Flea, taunting Faust with lulling sweetness on the banks of the Elbe, yet also disclosing the sadness of the fallen spirit. Thomas Moser sings gravely and reflectively as he is first discovered on the plains of Hungary, and rises nobly to the challenge of the Invocation to Nature (*très large et très sombre*, as Berlioz wanted), but is almost at his finest in the many recitative passages as he twists and turns in Mephistopheles's tightening grasp. Susan Graham does not match these two superb performances, but she sings her two arias simply and well. This version sets Nagano among the outstanding Berlioz conductors of the day.

Les Troyens.
Josephine Veasey *mez* Dido; **Jon Vickers** *ten* Aeneas; **Berit Lindholm**.*sop* Cassandra;
Peter Glossop *bar* Corebus, Corebus's ghost; **Heather Begg** *sop* Anna; **Roger Soyer** *bar*
Narbal, Spirit of Hector; **Anthony Raffell** *bass* Panthus; **Anne Howells** *mez* Ascanius;
Ian Partridge *ten* Iopas; **Pierre Thau** *bass* Priam, Mercury, Trojan Soldier; **Elizabeth Bainbridge**
mez Hecuba, Cassandra's ghost; **Ryland Davies** *ten* Hylas; **Raimund Herincx** *bar* Priam's ghost,
First Sentry; **Dennis Wicks** *bar* Hector's ghost, Second Sentry; **David Lennox** *ten* Helenus;
**Wandsworth School Boys' Choir; Chorus and Orchestra of the Royal Opera House,
Covent Garden / Sir Colin Davis.**
Philips 416 432-2PH4 (four discs: 241 minutes: ADD). Notes, text and translation included.
Recorded 1969. ⓕ **RR**

This is basically the original Covent Garden cast and players, and Colin Davis here asserts his eminence as the greatest Berlioz conductor of his day. His command of the score has never seemed more complete. A splendid rhythmic impetus lies at the heart of Davis's interpretation, matching the nervous intensity of the meters and the constant sense of unrest. He builds his large structures upon a closely observed rhythmic detail, down to the crisp beat of the *constructeurs* and the witty trudge of the two soldiers and up to the hectic, despairing thrust of Cassandra's 'Non, je ne verrai pas' and the inexorable tread of the *Marche et Hymne* (No. 4). For once, the prophetic vision of Rome really does seem to crown the work.

Veasey's Dido is womanly, touching, decided and sung with great musical intelligence. Vickers is at his finest in the heroic scenes: his first irruption into Troy is thrilling, and he never loses his grip on Aeneas's sense of mission. Only in the duet does he slip into the habit of allowing phrases to distort under tonal pressure: but his aria 'Ah! quand viendra l'instant' is affectingly done. He pairs Veasey intelligently, though there are times when the balance seems to favour him. As Cassandra, Berit Lindholm characterizes the unhappy priestess superbly, conveying a sense of constant, unremitting tragedy without ever allowing her voice to slip into the lachrymose, and carrying an extraordinary weight of suffering in her bitter phrase, 'mon inutile vie'. She leads her doomed Trojan women with a fine spirit and a glistening top B. The smaller parts are no less carefully cast. Heather Begg supports Veasey almost too discreetly, though Anna is not an easy role to distinguish without self-assertion; Ian Partridge sings Iopas beautifully, with a ravishing soft A flat and C at the end of his song, where most tenors cannot resist ruining the piece for the sake of their own effect; Roger Soyer descends unruffled to a low F in his noble, sombre performance of Narbal; Anne Howells is a touching Ascanius. The chorus, despite less than excellent French, sings magnificently. The recording itself is worthy of the whole enterprise, the 1969 sound superbly focused, giving a vivid sense of presence.

Les Troyens.
Françoise Pollet *sop* Dido; **Gary Lakes** *ten* Aeneas; **Deborah Voigt** *sop* Cassandra; **Gino Quilico** *bar* Corebus; **Hélène Perraguin** *mez* Anna; **Jean-Philippe Courtis** *bass* Narbal; **Michel Philippe** *bass* Pantheus; **Catherine Dubosc** *sop* Ascanius; **Jean-Luc Maurette** *ten* Iopas; **René Shirrer** *bar* Priam's ghost, First Soldier; **Claudine Carlson** *mez* Hecuba; **John Mark Ainsley** *ten* Hylas; **Marc Belleau** *bass* Hector's ghost, Second Soldier, Greek Captain; **Gregory Cross** *ten* Sinon; **Michel Beuachemin** *bass* Mercury; **Montreal Symphony Chorus and Orchestra / Charles Dutoit.**
Decca 443 693-2DH4 (four discs: 238 minutes: DDD). Notes, text and translation included. ⓕⓈⒺ
Recorded 1993.

It is a tribute to the quality of Davis's *Les Troyens* that it remained unchallenged by any rival on record for a quarter of a century. Then came Dutoit and the Montreal Symphony Orchestra, who have established themselves as second to none in the French repertory. Add to that a largely French-speaking cast, on balance even more sensitive and tonally more beautiful than Davis's, plus two minor but valuable textual additions, and the advantage of the new over the old is clear. Interpretatively, the contrasts between Dutoit and Davis are quickly established at the very start. Dutoit launches in at high voltage, more volatile than Davis, conveying exuberance consistently preferring faster speeds. Davis may be marginally less exciting, but he often compensates in the extra crispness and clarity of the playing of the Covent Garden orchestra. The advantage of Dutoit's faster speeds comes not just in thrilling *Allegros*, but in flowing *Andantes*. So Cassandra's first solo is more persuasively moulded at a flowing speed, with Deborah Voigt far warmer than Berit Lindholm for Davis, both in her beauty of tone and in her *espressivo* phrasing. In 'La prise de Troie' such a moment as the clash of arms within the Trojan horse comes over more dramatically with Dutoit thanks to his timing, and there is more mystery before the arrival of Hector's ghost at the beginning of Act 2. For completeness Dutoit includes the brief prelude that Berlioz wrote for the garbled 1863 performances of the second part of the opera, but not intended to be given in the full five-act version. In sequence here, one immediately registers the drop in inspiration, but on CD the track is easily programmed out.

The other textual addition comes in Act 1. After the Andromache scene – with a clarinet solo of breathtaking gentleness from the Montreal player – there is an extra scene lasting six minutes which the Berlioz scholar, Hugh Macdonald, editor of the Barenreiter score, has orchestrated from the surviving piano score. In what he describes as 'a somewhat breathless episode' Sinon, a Greek spy, convinces King Priam that the horse is a gift to Pallas Athene and must be brought inside the city. Not only does the scene give an individual role to King Priam, it provides a motivation for the disastrous decision to take in the horse. Berlioz ripped the scene out of the full score at a late stage, simply to shorten Act 1, which as we now appreciate was not needed. The minor disadvantage is that the entry of Aeneas with his dire news of Laocoon and the serpents is not so dramatic when it follows another busy scene rather than the stillness of the Andromache scene. The role of Cassandra's lover, Corebus, is taken by Gino Quilico, in rich, firm voice. As Aeneas Gary Lakes may not have so richly heroic a voice as Jon Vickers for Davis, being rather more easily stressed at the top, but among today's tenors he is the most experienced of all in this role, having sung it many times. His big advantage over Vickers, most of all in the great love scene with Dido in Act 3, is that he shades his voice far more subtly. Though the role of Dido very often goes to a mezzo, here Decca firmly opts for a soprano, Françoise Pollet. Very much attuned to the idiom, she sings

Berlioz Opera

consistently with full, even tone, so that, matching Dutoit's expressiveness and the richness of the Montreal sound, she brings out the feminine sensuousness of the role more than a mezzo normally would. Anna is very well taken by another French singer, Hélène Perraguin, with her firm rich mezzo providing a clear contrast with Pollet.

Throughout the opera Dutoit's degree of rhythmic freedom, notably in heavily syncopated passages, intensifies the controlled frenzy behind much of the most dramatic writing, and here Dido's hysteria, like Cassandra's earlier on, is most tellingly conveyed. There is barely a weak link in the rest of the huge cast. Catherine Dubosc makes a breathily boyish Ascanius, and Gregory Cross sings with sharp clarity in the tenor role of the spy, Sinon. John Mark Ainsley, though not quite so free of tone as usual on top, makes a sensitive Hylas in the sailor song of Act 5; and the high tessitura of the other tenor role of Iopas strains Jean-Luc Maurette uncomfortably at the top, bringing unsteadiness. As recorded, Michel Philippe as Pantheus sounds unsteady too, but that is very much the exception. As for the chorus, though on balance the Covent Garden Chorus for Davis sings with even crisper ensemble, the passionate commitment of the Montreal Chorus matches the fire of Dutoit's whole reading. This is a thrilling set to have one marvelling afresh at the electric vitality of Berlioz's inspiration, and marvelling too that the formidable problems of recording so massive a work have been accomplished so confidently.

Lord Gerald Berners
British 1883-1950

The Triumph of Neptune. L'uomo dai baffi. Valses bourgeoises. Polka (both orch. Lane).
English Northern Philharmonia, Royal Ballet Sinfonia / David Lloyd-Jones.
Marco Polo 8 223711 (69 minutes: DDD). Recorded 1996.   Ⓕ

A biography of Berners arrived at last in 1998 (Mark Amory, *Lord Berners: The Last Eccentric*; Chatto & Windus). Unfortunately the emphasis on his eccentricity caused several uninformed reviewers to regard that as the main thing rather than his music – a problem Satie understood. The present release is the complete version of Berners's first ballet, *The Triumph of Neptune*, so it breaks new ground and unlike the Suite (Beecham recorded it twice – see his second version on Sony, reviewed under Arnell), where the numbers were reordered, it allows us to follow the original sequence of dances. *The Triumph of Neptune* is certainly Berners's best-known orchestral work – parts of it fitted well into the Last Night of the Proms in 1993 – and the Suite scintillates with the infectious enjoyment of all his theatre scores. It is well worth having the full version now, even if some of the scoring sounds heavy and the orchestral playing is not always as clean as it should be. *L'uomo dai baffi* ('The man with a moustache') was a ballet for puppets put on in Rome, where Berners lived, in 1918. It looks as if his friend and colleague, Alfredo Casella, may have scored five of Berners's early piano pieces for chamber group and so Philip Lane has added the remaining two. This makes a convincing set and brings these established documents of avant-garde piano music into another medium, although there are odd disagreements between the piano scores and the chamber versions. Lane has also orchestrated the only one of Berners's three sets of piano duets he didn't score himself – the enchanting *Valses bourgeoises* of 1919 – and a solo piece, the *Polka*, which was used in the Cavalcanti film, *Champagne Charlie*. It is a joy to hear these old favourites in full orchestral colour and Lane has done an excellent job. These performances with the Royal Ballet Sinfonia are some of the most lively on the CD, which opens up further aspects of Berners's music in the most attractive way.

Leonard Bernstein
American 1918-1990

Symphonies – No. 1, 'Jeremiah'; No. 2, 'The Age of Anxiety'; No. 3, 'Kaddish'. Chichester Psalms. Serenade after Plato's Symposium. Prelude, Fugue and Riffs.
Jennie Tourel *mez* **John Bogart** *counterten* **Felicia Montealegre** *spkr* **Zino Francescatti** *vn*
Benny Goodman *cl* **Philippe Entremont** *pf* **Camerata Singers; Columbus Boy Choir;**
New York Philharmonic Orchestra; Columbia Jazz Combo / Leonard Bernstein.
Sony Classical SM3K47162 (three discs: 162 minutes: ADD). Recorded 1960s.   Ⓜ

Leonard Bernstein's recordings of his own music occupy an important place in his discography. He was commissioned by the Dean of Chichester to compose settings of some psalms for performance at the July 1965 meeting of the Southern Cathedral Festivals which takes place successively in Winchester, Salisbury and Chichester – the three choirs of these cathedrals coming together to sing the liturgy and to give two evening concerts. You may be surprised not to be able to distinguish any of the words, until it transpires that the Hebrew version is used. *The Chichester Psalms* are an amalgam of just about every sort of music that touched Bernstein. In this excellent performance and recording, they are hugely enjoyable (there is also, incidentally, a very impressive recording of *The Chichester Psalms* by Matthew Best and the Corydon singers; see the review under Copland). Bernstein's own version of *Prelude, Fugue and Riffs* succeeds precisely because he eschews unnecessary vulgarity and insists on rhythmic stringency. Bernstein's heroically implausible determination to emancipate the vernacular – to embrace the world in true, post-Mahlerian style – was a continuing preoccupation right up until his death. The *Jeremiah* Symphony differs somewhat in this respect. Despite elements culled from Jewish liturgy, it remains formally circumspect, is by no means incorrigibly urban and certainly seems less effortful than much of Bernstein's subsequent output. The opening is symptomatic, breathing a cooler (New England?) air, more redolent of Roy Harris than Aaron Copland. The soloist in the *Jeremiah*'s third movement 'Lamentation' is that remarkable mezzo Jennie Tourel, featured in the 1944 première and by the time of this recording a slightly threadbare *grande dame*. (Her age, like her country of origin, used to be shrouded in mystery, but it seems she was well into her sixties at the time of this recording.)

There are genuine problems with Bernstein's No. 2, *The Age of Anxiety*. This is not absolute music, and it is to some extent the programmatic scheme drawn from Auden's poem which dictates the dangerous eclecticism of the music. Hence the last section's rejoicing is supposed to sound Hollywood-hollow, after the manner of the finale of Shostakovich's Fifth. The *Kaddish* has always been a problem for Bernstein's admirers. Though its attempt to reach out beyond orthodox Judaism for some 'ebullient, renewed will to survive the apocalyptic' is scarcely unprecedented in his work, Bernstein's perennial, spiritual concerns are allowed to run rampant as never before. The piece can seem as much a hysterical lecture to a recalcitrant deity (with background music) as a genuinely 'symphonic' *entrée*. This is particularly so in the 1963 version recorded here, where the embarrassing narration runs to its original heavenly length. Jennie Tourel is in better voice here than for No. 1, aptly matriarchal in her 'Kaddish 2' lullaby. The New York Philharmonic tears into the third movement's Coplandish 'big tune' with considerable aplomb (and palpable relief). The one disappointment of this collection is Zino Francescatti's *Serenade after Plato's Symposium*. Airily described in the note as 'sunny' and 'lyrical', this persistently underrated work is both hauntingly melodic and tautly constructed – if only he'd called it just plain 'Violin Concerto'. The New York Philharmonic of 1965 plays superbly, even if the digital remastering does not always flatter its sound.

Candide – Overture. West Side Story – Symphonic Dances. On the Waterfront – Symphonic Suite. Fancy Free.
New York Philharmonic Orchestra / Leonard Bernstein.
Sony Classical Bernstein Century SMK63085 (69 minutes: ADD). Recorded 1960-63.　　Ⓜ

When Bernstein died, there was a widespread feeling that he had tried to do too much, and yet, in these days of crossover and musical pluralism, his reckless eclecticism might best be seen as prophetic: his film- and show-derived concert music is more popular than ever and these performances have long been considered definitive. All but *Fancy Free* were taped in New York's Manhattan Center in the early 1960s, a problematic venue in which the original sound engineers sought to reconcile the close-miking of individual sections and sometimes individual players with a substantial reverberation period. The results have a synthetic, larger-than-life quality which suits most of the music here. The exception is the Overture to *Candide*, a more driven sort of reading, the brashness of Broadway insufficiently tempered by the rapid figurations of Rossini, the academicism of Brahms, the *joie de vivre* of Offenbach: subtler details tend to disappear into a fog of resonance. In the Symphonic Dances from *West Side Story*, the players eschew the customary shouts in the 'Mambo' but it is doubtful whether there will ever be a more idiomatic reading of what was then essentially 'new music'. The score, by no means a straightforward 'greatest hits' selection, had only recently been unveiled, with Lukas Foss conducting, at a gala concert intended to raise funds for the New York Philharmonic pension fund. Here certainly was the 'aura of show business' which so irked Harold Schonberg, the influential music critic of the *New York Times*: Bernstein's own recording from March 6th has the quality of an unanswerable rejoinder. *On the Waterfront* is if anything even more intense, its lyrical core dispatched with an overwhelming ardour. Last up is what is almost the best of all possible *Fancy Free*s. It was originally sung in inimitable style by Billie Holiday.

Songfest[a]. Chichester Psalms[b].
[a]**Clamma Dale** *sop* [a]**Rosalind Elias,** [a]**Nancy Williams** *mezzos* [a]**Neil Rosenshein** *ten*
[a]**John Reardon** *bar* [a]**Donald Gramm** *bass* [b]soloists from the **Vienna Boys' Choir;**
[b]**Vienna Jeunesse Choir;** [a]**National Symphony Orchestra of Washington,**
[b]**Israel Philharmonic Orchestra / Leonard Bernstein.**
DG 415 965-2GH (62 minutes: ADD). Texts and, where appropriate, translations included.
Recorded 1977.　　Ⓕ

'I, too, am America', is the message of Leonard Bernstein's orchestral song-cycle *Songfest*. The subject of the work is the American artist's emotional, spiritual and intellectual response to life in an essentially Puritan society, and, more specifically, to the eclecticism of American society and its many problems of social integration (blacks, women, homosexuals and expatriates). As expected from a composer/conductor equally at home on Broadway or in Vienna's Musikverein, the styles range widely. The scoring is colourful, occasionally pungent, always tuneful. Bernstein's soloists are well chosen and sing with feeling. This vivid live recording of the *Chichester Psalms* offers the full orchestral version and the performers all give their utmost.

Candide (1988 final version).
Jerry Hadley *ten* Candide; **June Anderson** *sop* Cunegonde; **Adolph Green** *ten* Dr Pangloss, Martin; **Christa Ludwig** *mez* Old lady; **Nicolai Gedda** *ten* Governor, Vanderdendur, Ragotski; **Della Jones** *mez* Paquette; **Kurt Ollmann** *bar* Maximilian, Captain, Jesuit father; **Neil Jenkins** *ten* Merchant, Inquisitor, Prince Charles Edward; **Richard Suart** *bass* Junkman, Inquisitor, King Hermann Augustus; **John Treleaven** *ten* Alchemist, Inquisitor, Sultan Achmet, Crook; **Lindsay Benson** *bar* Doctor, Inquisitor, King Stanislaus; **Clive Bayley** *bar* Bear-Keeper, Inquisitor, Tsar Ivan; **London Symphony Chorus and Orchestra / Leonard Bernstein.**
DG 429 734-2GH2 (two discs: 112 minutes: DDD). Notes and text included. Recorded 1989.
Gramophone Award Winner 1992. Ⓕ

Here it is – all of it – musical comedy, grand opera, operetta, satire, melodrama, all rolled into one. We can thank John Mauceri for much of the restoration work: his 1988 Scottish Opera production was the spur for this recording and prompted exhaustive reappraisal. Numbers like 'We Are Women', 'Martin's Laughing Song' and 'Nothing More Than This' have rarely been heard, if at all. The last mentioned, Candide's 'aria of disillusionment', is one of the enduring glories of the score, reinstated where Bernstein always wanted it (but where no producer would have it), near the very end of the show. Bernstein called it his 'Puccini aria', and that it is – bittersweet, long-breathed, supported, enriched and ennobled by its inspiring string counterpoint. And this is but one of many forgotten gems.

It was an inspiration on someone's part (probably Bernstein's) to persuade the great and versatile Christa Ludwig and Nicolai Gedda (in his sixties and still hurling out the top Bs) to fill the principal character roles. To say they do so ripely is to do them scant justice. Bernstein's old sparring partner Adolph Green braves the tongue-twisting and many-hatted Dr Pangloss with his own highly individual form of *Sprechstimme*, Jerry Hadley sings the title role most beautifully, *con amore*, and June Anderson has all the notes, and more, for the faithless, air-headed Cunegonde. It is just a pity that someone didn't tell her that discretion is the better part of comedy. 'Glitter and Be Gay' is much funnier for being played straighter, odd as it may sound. Otherwise, the supporting roles are all well taken and the London Symphony Chorus has a field-day in each of its collective guises. Having waited so long to commit every last note (or thereabouts) of his cherished score to disc, there are moments here where Bernstein seems almost reluctant to move on. His tempos are measured, to say the least, the score fleshier now in every respect: even that raciest of Overtures has now acquired a more deliberate gait, a more opulent tone. But Bernstein would be Bernstein, and there are moments where one is more than grateful for his indulgence: the grandiose chorales, the panoramic orchestra-scapes (sumptuously recorded), and of course, that thrilling finale – the best of all possible Bernstein anthems at the slowest of all possible speeds – and why not (prepare to hold your breath at the choral *a cappella*).

On the Town.
Frederica von Stade *mez* Claire; **Tyne Daly** *sngr* Hildy; **Marie McLaughlin** *sop* Ivy; **Thomas Hampson** *bass* Gabey; **Kurt Ollmann** *bar* Chip; **David Garrison** *sngr* Ozzie; **Samuel Ramey** *bass* Pitkin; **Evelyn Lear** *sop* Madame Dilly; **Cleo Laine** *sngr* Nightclub singer; **London Voices; London Symphony Orchestra / Michael Tilson Thomas.**
DG 437 516-2GH (75 minutes: DDD). Notes and text included. Recorded 1992. Ⓕ
Gramophone Award Winner 1994.

On the Town is a peach of a show, a show which positively hums along on the heat of its inspiration, a show rejoicing in the race of time, but regretful of its passing, a show which lovingly encapsulates those transitory moments seized and then lost amidst the impatient, pulsating heart and soul of the lonely city – the Big Apple. On two amazing nights Michael Tilson Thomas and this starry cast brought New York City to the Barbican in London. Recording this semi-staged performance live must have been a living nightmare for DG's engineers, but one wonders if they might not have pulled off a more up-front balance for the voices. Only Cleo Laine gets to be really intimate with her bluesy nightclub song 'Ain't got no tears left'. You'll hang on every breath Laine takes. Many of the notes are threadbare, but who needs the notes when you've got instincts like hers? The major roles are happily well cast. Samuel Ramey was an inspired choice for Claire's monumentally boring boyfriend, Pitkin. His 'Song', a masterpiece of arch formality, is very funny indeed. In performance, Tyne Daly's cab-driving Hildy knocked 'em in the aisles with her huggable personality, and the three sailors, Gabey, Chip, Ozzie – Thomas Hampson, Kurt Ollmann, David Garrison – are just perfect. Not only are they well matched vocally, but you could put them on any stage and never look back. Hampson's two big numbers – 'Lonely Town' and 'Lucky to be Me' – are handsomely sung with careful avoidance of that peculiarly 'operatic' articulation. The real heroes of this dizzy enterprise are Tilson Thomas and the London Symphony Orchestra, every last player a character, an individual. John Harle's soaring, throaty sax and rhythms are so hot, tight and idiomatic that you'd never credit this wasn't an American band. The playing here is stunning; there's no other word for it.

West Side Story.
Dame Kiri Te Kanawa *sop* Maria (Nina Bernstein); **José Carreras** *ten* Tony (Alexander Bernstein); **Tatiana Troyanos** *mez* Anita; **Kurt Ollmann** *bar* Riff; **Marilyn Horne** *mez* Off-stage voice; **composite chorus and orchestra from 'on and off' Broadway;** ªIsrael Philharmonic Orchestra / Leonard Bernstein.
DG 457 199-2GH2 (two discs: 98 minutes: DDD). Notes and texts included.
Recorded 1984.   Ⓕ **RR**

If the job of a 'crossover' record is to shatter preconceptions on both sides of any musical fence, then this is the greatest ever. Not all the *aficionados* of Broadway musicals are going to warm to *de facto* operatic treatment of West Side Story: not all opera-lovers or devotees of Leonard Bernstein as star-conductor are going to rate *West Side Story* as an equivalent to opera. But any listener on whichever side of the fence who keeps any sort of open mind, forgetting the constriction of barriers, must recognize this historic set as superb entertainment and great music-making on every level, with an emotional impact closely akin to that of a Puccini opera and an intensity of excitement to match anything from disco to *The Rite of Spring*. That of course is the doing of Leonard Bernstein as conductor as well as composer. It is astonishing that before this recording he had never conducted his most famous work. Interviewed by John Rockwell of the *New York Times* during the sessions, Bernstein noted how difficult it was to cast *West Side Story*, and explained that in a recording 'I decided to go for sound'.

Dame Kiri Te Kanawa may not be a soprano one would ever cast as Maria on stage, yet the beauty of the voice, its combination of richness, delicacy and purity, consistently brings out the musical strengths of Bernstein's inspiration. Similarly, with José Carreras as Tony, it is self-evident to point out how such a voice brings out the pure beauty of the big melodies like 'Maria' or 'Tonight', but even a sharp number like his first solo, 'Something's coming', with floated *pianissimos* and subtly-graded *crescendos* allied to sharp rhythms, makes it more clearly a question-mark song, full of expectation, more than just a point number. Marilyn Horne is in glorious voice, while Tatiana Troyanos will surprise you as Anita with the way that she could switch her naturally beautiful operatic voice into a New York throaty snarl, rather like an Italian mezzo switching into a chest voice. Troyanos, it appears, was brought up in exactly the area of the West Side, where the story is supposed to be set, which makes her natural affinity with the idiom less surprising. Kurt Ollmann, American too, as Riff equally finds a very confident balance between the traditions of opera and those of the musical. Diction may not always be so clear as with less rich-toned singers, but after coaching Carreras has managed a very passable american accent and Dame Kiri a creditable Spanish-American one. The speed with which the whole piece moves is astounding, not just as a superb entertainment but as a Shakespearean tragedy modernized and intensified.

West Side Story.
Tinuke Olafimihan Maria; **Paul Manuel** Tony; **Caroline O'Connor** Anita; **Sally Burgess** Off-stage voice; **Nicholas Warnford** Riff; **Julie Paton** Rosalia; **Elinor Stephenson** Consuela; **Nicole Carty** Francisca; **Kieran Daniels** Action; **Mark Michaels** Diesel; **Adrian Sarple** Baby John; **Adrian Edmeads** A-rab; **Garry Stevens** Snowboy; **Nick Ferranti** Bernardo; **chorus and National Symphony Orchestra / John Owen Edwards.**
TER CDTER2 1197 (two discs: 101 minutes: DDD). Recorded 1993.   Ⓕ

This recording of *West Side Story* is something of an achievement. The set starts with the major advantage of being inspired by a production at the Haymarket, Leicester, so that many of the cast are really inside their roles. They have youth on their side, too. Paul Manuel from that company may not have a large voice, but his sympathetic portrayal of Tony, both in his solos and duets with Maria, makes one feel that he identifies totally with the part. Moreover, the way in which he can float a high note, as at the end of the alternative film version of 'Something's Coming' puts him on a par with Carreras (for Bernstein). His Maria, Tinuke Olafimihan, is a gem. Her ability to interact with him and to express the laughter and the tragedy of the heroine is very real. At the heart of the 'Somewhere' ballet, Sally Burgess voices the lovers' plea for peace with a magnificent rendition of its famous soaring tune. Nicholas Warnford as leader of the Jets gives no less than his rival in the tricky 'Cool' sequence and Jet song. John Owen Edwards directs Bernstein's score as if he believes in every note of it. Moreover, he has imparted to his players the very pulse that sets this music ticking.

Franz Adolf Berwald

Swedish 1796-1868

Symphonies – No. 1 in G minor, 'Sinfonie sérieuse'; No. 2 in D major, 'Sinfonie capricieuse'; No. 3 in C major, 'Sinfonie singulière'; No. 4 in E flat major. Konzertstück for Bassoon and Orchestra.
Christian Davidsson bn **Malmö Symphony Orchestra / Sixten Ehrling.**
BIS CD795/6 (two discs: 131 minutes: DDD). Recorded 1996.   Ⓕ

As one would expect, given Sixten Ehrling's excellent account of the *Singulière* and the E flat Symphonies with the LSO for Decca way back in the late 1960s and his no less impressive 1970 Swedish Radio version of the *Sérieuse*, the performances are *echt*-Berwald. Ehrling gives us plenty of space without ever lingering too lovingly. Even apart from the *tempo giusto*, one feels rather more comfortable with Ehrling's handling of phrasing and balance. He is very attentive to dynamic markings and sometimes, as at the beginning of the *Sinfonie singulière*, pianissimo becomes *pianopiano-pianissimo*! The recording reproduces these dynamic extremes flawlessly. The Malmö Concert Hall where this set was made has a good acoustic. Generally speaking the recordings are excellent, though there seems to be more back-to-front perspective and air around the players in the *Singulière* and E flat Symphonies than in the *Sérieuse*. Generally speaking, the recording is truthful and vivid, and the soloist in the *Konzertstück* is excellently balanced. One has to conclude that Ehrling and his fine players bring us closer to the spirit of this music than do any of the current rivals.

Piano Trio No. 2 in F minor. Quartet for Piano and Wind in E flat major. Grand Septet in B flat major.
Gaudier Ensemble (Richard Hosford cl Robin O'Neill bn Jonathan Williams hn Marieke Blankestijn vn Iris Juda va Christoph Marks vc Stephen Williams db Susan Tomes pf).
Hyperion CDA66834 (67 minutes: DDD). Recorded 1995.   Ⓕ Ⓔ

The Septet is innovative and anticipates the *Sinfonie singulière*, in enfolding the *Scherzo* into the body of the slow movement, and its invention is delightfully fresh. The Gaudier Ensemble brings elegance and finesse not only to the Septet but also to its companions. The early E flat Quartet for piano and wind of 1819 is more conventional in its formal layout and is musically less interesting, but at the same time there are touches of that intelligence and wit that illumine all Berwald's music and the piece shines in the Gaudier's hands. The much later F minor Piano Trio of 1851 is more substantial and an unqualified delight. The writing is full of original touches and rhythmic vitality. Its placid surface is disturbed by all sorts of characteristic flourishes: in the theme of the slow movement there is one of those sudden and unexpected modulations for which Berwald's contemporaries were always berating him. Susan Tomes handles the demanding piano part with exemplary skill and taste. It is all hugely enjoyable and well recorded too, with very present and finely detailed sound.

Heinrich Biber

Bohemian 1644-1704

Arias a 4 in A major. Ballettae a 4 violettae. Balletti a 6 in C major. Balletti lamentabili a 4 in E minor. Harmonia Romana. Trombet undt musicalischer Taffeldienst.
Ars Antiqua Austria / Gunar Letzbor vn
Symphonia SY95143 (75 minutes: DDD). Recorded 1995.   Ⓕ

The baroque palace of Kromeriz or, in German, Kremsier was the summer residence of Prince-Bishop Karl Liechtenstein-Kastelkorn of Olmütz. He was an ardent music lover and during his rule, which lasted from 1664 to 1695, the palace library acquired what is now recognized as an extremely important, precious collection of manuscripts. This programme features some of the ensemble music by Biber from the Kremsier source, though the authenticity of the *Harmonia Romana* anthology, some of whose dances are played on the disc, has not been established. Never mind, the sequence put together by violinist and director, Gunar Letzbor, is entertaining and very well executed by the members of Ars Antiqua Austria. Most of the music is for strings but there are contributions from variously sized recorders, too, as well as some splendidly gruff, earthy and inebriate interjections from bass, Michael Oman, as the Nightwatchman. Nowadays, he'd be 'taken in' for making that kind of racket in public.

Letzbor has built his programme around an idea of a Carnival Feast at the Bishop's court. It goes something like this: the Bishop enters to a fanfare – dance music greets the guests – a nightwatchman passes by – table music during dinner – dancing – the nightwatchman passes by once more, this time drunk – peasant dancing – midnight, the end of Carnival and the beginning of Lent. The revelry is concluded by the 12 strokes of midnight sounded on what sounds like a school bell. The notion comes off well, for Letzbor's scheme allows for a degree of musical contrast, both of sound and, above all, of mood. Biber's dances are enchanting for the fullness of their character and for their rhythmic bite, and Ars Antiqua brings them to life with vigour, imagination and an apposite sense of style. In short, the group offers us well over an hour of first-class entertainment in which only the Bishop's festive board and the contents of his cellar are not shared with us. The disc is superbly recorded and the music played with fire and enthusiasm, not least by Letzbor himself.

Biber Battalia a 10 in D major[c]. Passacaglia in C minor[a].
Sonata violino solo representativa in A[c]. Harmonia artificiosa – Partita in C minor[c].
Locke Canon 4 in 2[c]. The Tempest[c].
Zelenka Fanfare in D[b].
[a]Luca Pianca *lte* [b]**Innsbruck Trumpet Consort;** [c]**Il Giardino Armonico / Giovanni Antonini** *rec*
Teldec 3984-21464-2 (68 minutes: DDD). Recorded 1998.   Ⓕ

Biber's *Battalia* has arguably become the most celebrated programmatic suite of the seventeenth century with its easy Bohemian juxtaposition of poignant airs and almost choreographic stage music. Too often we hear each implicit detail exaggerated to death; here, Il Giardino Armonico conveys each movement within the bounds of courtly decorum. The group's leader, Enrico Onofri, provides a memorable and effective gimmick in the March as he walks from right to left and disappears into the distance. His playing in the *Sonata violono solo representativa* is impressive and acutely characterized: the Cuckoo is positively charming, the Frog leaps in a spontaneous counterpoint of improvised special effects and the Hen and the Cock fly by the seats of their pants with a stirring full-throttled sound and thrilling technical precision. Such qualities are also apparent in the remarkable *Harmonia artificiosa* of 1696. Composed for two violas d'amore, this is a beguiling work.

Il Giardino Armonico generates a ringing, almost orchestral palette – darkened by a tenor chalumeau – upon which float these soft-grained viole. Less agreeable is the Allemande which is fussily handled and never quite allowed to bed down into its natural harmonic rhythm; the 'Aria variata' that ends the suite has reflective sobriety nonchalantly sacrificed for Mediterranean effervescence. This is both the strength and weakness of Il Giardino in northern and central European repertoire, exemplified in Locke's music for *The Tempest*, from which a majestic orchestral suite can be wrought. The musical ideas are impressive (the famous Curtain Tune with its force-ten wind finds a natural home here), but too often miscast with ill-suited outbursts imposed on such temperate dances. Overall though, this is a dynamic and distinctive programme with some brilliant performances.

Eight Sonatas for Violin and Continuo (1681). Sonata violino solo representativa in A major.
Sonata, 'La Pastorella'. Passacaglia for Solo Lute. Mystery Sonatas – Passacaglia in G minor.
Romanesca (Andrew Manze *vn* Nigel North *lte/theorbo* John Toll *hpd/org*).
Harmonia Mundi HMU90 7134/5 (two discs: 127 minutes: DDD). Recorded 1993-94.
Gramophone Award Winner 1995.   Ⓕ**P****S****E**

Whilst the more famous *Mystery Sonatas* have quickly found friends, the 1681 set is still largely unknown amongst players and listeners alike. Yet what is immediately noticeable from this première recording of the sonatas is that Biber is not only a legendary virtuoso, probably never bettered in the seventeenth or eighteenth centuries, but one of the most inventive composers of his age: bold and exciting, certainly but also elusive, mercurial and mysterious. The majority of the works comprise preludes, arias and variations of an unregulated nature: improvisatory preludes over naked pedals and lucid arias juxtaposing effortlessly with eccentric rhetorical conceits are mixed up in an unpredictable phantasm of contrast, and yet at its best it all adds up to a unified structure of considerable potency. Whatever the philosophical key to Biber's intangible and unstable world may be, Andrew Manze is the protagonist *par excellence* for music which requires a notable degree of considered response to complement the adventurous spirit of the virtuoso. In short, this is masterful playing in which Manze has enough confidence in his subject not to overcharacterize Biber's volatile temperament. Hence the preludes are sweet and restrained and yet there is also a held-back, almost smouldering quality, which is skilfully pitched against the free-wheeling energy of the fast music.

Sonatae tam aris quam aulis servientes.
Rare Fruits Council / Manfredo Kraemer *vn*
Auvidis Astrée E8630 (67 minutes: DDD). Recorded 1997. Ⓕ

A more radiant and gratifyingly robust collection of baroque instrumental works would be hard to imagine. These 12 sonatas (which broadly translate as 'sonatas suitable for altar or court') juxtapose pieces for a rich five- or six-part string palette – pursuing an exhilarating, intensely-wrought, sophisticated and unpredictable musical rhetoric – with quasi-concerted and swaggering trumpets. Unlike some of the other printed collections, in which boxes of tricks can sometimes over-prevail, this one comprises highly compelling and accessible music: the satisfying textural surety and tunefulness of Sonata IV is a case in point and so too is the noble ecclesiastical *alla breve* conclusion to Sonata VI (marvellously shaped here). The secret for performers is to let the antiquated contrapuntal dance-infused music ring, to allow it to unfold as if each contrasted section meant something greater than its mere existence. The emotive, almost physical impact of Biber in his best colours is lavishly exuded in the Rare Fruits Council's strongly projected account. It takes a glowing, colourful and uncomplicated approach, espousing a textural breadth and rhythmic thrust underpinned by a deep violone (8ft bass), theorbo and harp. The playing is often dazzling here – the trumpet sound is peerless, round and coppery – and the total concept unfussy (though this occasionally applies to tuning also).

Mystery Sonatas.
John Holloway *vn* **Davitt Moroney** *org/hpd* **Tragicomedia**
(Stephen Stubbs *lte/chitarrone* Erin Headley *va da gamba/lirone* Andrew Lawrence-King *hp/regal*).
Virgin Classics Veritas VCD7 59551-2 (two discs: 131 minutes: DDD). Recorded 1989.
Gramophone Award Winner 1991. ⒻⓅ

Biber was among the most talented musicians of the late seventeenth century. He was a renowned violinist and his compositions, above all for the violin, are technically advanced and strikingly individual. The 15 *Mystery Sonatas* with their additional *Passacaglia* for unaccompanied violin were written in about 1678 and dedicated to Biber's employer, the Archbishop of Salzburg. Each Sonata is inspired by a section of the Rosary devotion of the Catholic Church which offered a system of meditation on 15 Mysteries from the lives of Jesus and His mother. The music is not, strictly speaking, programmatic though often vividly illustrative of events which took place in the life of Christ. All but two of the 16 pieces require *scordatura* or retuning of the violin strings; in this way Biber not only facilitated some of the fingerings but also achieved sounds otherwise unavailable to him. The Sonatas are disposed into three groups of five: Joyful, Sorrowful and Glorious Mysteries whose contrasting states are affectingly evoked in music ranging from a spirit reflecting South German baroque exuberance to one of profound contemplation. John Holloway plays with imaginative sensibility and he is supported by a first-rate continuo group whose instruments include baroque lute, chitarrone, viola da gamba, a 15-string lirone, double harp and regal.

Biber Litaniae de Sancto Josepho. Sonata Sancti Polycarpi. Fidicinium sacro-profanum – Sonata XI.
Bertali Sonata a 13. Sonata Sancti Placidi.
Muffat Missa in labore requies.
Cantus Cölln; Concerto Palatino / Konrad Junghänel.
Harmonia Mundi HMC90 1667 (69 minutes: DDD). Texts and translations included.
Recorded 1998. ⒻⓅⒺ

Cantus Cölln's main priority has always been to promote largely unexplored vocal repertoire of the seventeenth century from the German lands and central Europe. The mainstay of this disc is two substantial works probably composed for special feasts in the luxurious recesses of Salzburg Cathedral during the 1670s and 1680s. Both are rarities to the catalogue. Biber's *Litaniae de Sancto Josepho* were written in 1677 for the founding of the Fraternity of St Joseph, a well-heeled group of local worthies, by all accounts. Textural imagination is built around contrasted solo and tutti vocal dispositions emboldened by trumpet obbligatos. Cantus Cölln and the pre-eminent cornett and sackbutters, Concerto Palatino, are plainly in their element, blazing a thrilling trail of dynamic declamation, yet the seamless shaping in the solo litany, 'present at Nativity and servant of Christ', provides the essential lyrical contrast to extended full-throttled opulence. Muffat's 24-part Mass of multiphonic strings, cornetts, trombones and trumpets perhaps hangs less convincingly, both as a work and in performance. The Mass was long thought to have been written by another (it is Muffat's only surviving vocal work) but the 'Et incarnatus' has the hallmark of the composer's control of harmonic direction and tightly wrought inner-part writing. The 'Crucifixus' is really extraordinary, almost Viennese at the end of the next century (Haydn actually owned the autograph for a while). As with so much seventeenth-century innovation, one wishes it went on a little longer. Again, the performances here want for little. One could quibble with the occasionally limited dynamic range (Biber's *Sonata Sancti Polycarpi* for eight trumpets is too smoothed out at the edges and lacks the raw nobility of brass on their 'uppers' before battle) but this is a stunning achievement by any standards. The fragrant instrumental pieces relieve the danger of homogeneous overkill and leave the listener relishing the next irresistible mosaic.

Biber Requiem a 15 in A major.
Steffani Stabat mater.
Marta Almajano, Mieke van der Sluis *sops* **John Elwes, Mark Padmore** *tens*
Frans Huijts *bar* **Harry van der Kamp** *bass*
Chorus and Baroque Orchestra of the Dutch Bach Association / Gustav Leonhardt.
Deutsche Harmonia Mundi 05472 77344-2 (64 minutes: DDD). Texts and translations included. Recorded 1994. ⒠🄟

This Requiem may well have been performed at the funeral in 1687 of Biber's employer, Max Gandolph von Khuenberg, Archbishop of Salzburg. It is sonorous, stirring and noble and these qualities are at once encountered in the work's richly colourful opening, 'Requiem aeternam dona eis' and to an even greater extent in the wrathful 'Dies irae'. This is a splendid section which inspires Leonhardt and his musicians to deliver it with fearful fervour. But the piece as a whole has clearly captured his imagination and he makes much of the drama. The occasions which prompted grand, ceremonial gestures of the kind which we encounter here must have been quite awe-inspiring since much of the music is redolent of processional solemnity highlighted by dashes of brilliant colour – the scoring includes trumpets and three trombones as well as the standard woodwind and strings. The companion piece on the disc is of an altogether different hue. In his intimate and contemplative setting of the *Stabat mater*, Biber's Italian contemporary Steffani matches the text with grief-stricken vocal declamation and agonized string suspensions. The scoring, as we should expect, is much more modest and subdued than that required for the Requiem. Comparatively small in scale it may be, but its emotional content is at least as affecting as Biber's more public demonstration of the Catholic faith. Leonhardt has picked a fine ensemble of vocalists, notably Marta Almajano and Mieke van der Sluis. The Chorus and Baroque Orchestra of the Dutch Bach Association perform well throughout and the programme, offering two starkly different baroque visions of heaven, is a richly rewarding one.

Gilles Binchois

French c1400-1460

Triste plaisir et douleureuse joie. Amours merchi de restout mon pooir. Je me recommande humblement. En regardant vostre tres doulx maintiens. Se la belle n'a le voloir. Je vous salue. Adieu mes tres belles amours. De plus en plus. Lune tres belles. Les tres doulx yeux. Amoureux suy et me vient toute joye. Adieu, adieu, mon joieulx souvenir. Jamais tant. Adieu, m'amour et ma maistresse. Dueil angoisseus. Pour prison ne pour maladie. Filles à marier.
Ensemble Gilles Binchois / Dominique Vellard *ten*
Virgin Classics Veritas VC5 45285-2 (60 minutes: DDD). Texts and translations included.
Recorded 1996-97. ⒠

Binchois's songs have rarely appeared in any quantity on CD, yet the booklet-notes to this timely offering set out an objective case for considering Binchois a more significant song composer than his more famous contemporary, Dufay. If one turns to the music, the reasons for Dufay's greater popularity are equally obvious: Binchois's songs yield their secrets more slowly, and operate within a more limited expressive ambit. They demand repeated listening, whereas Dufay's songs tend to make their impact at first hearing. True, Binchois's surface charm is most beguiling, broken as it is by the occasional disconcerting dissonance or quirk of line; but so too is the sense of extreme stylization. Some characteristic turns of phrase recur between pieces. It is all the more important for recordings of his music to bear repeated listening as well. This one certainly fulfils that requirement, and there is sufficient variety of scoring to sustain interest from song to song. Perhaps the crux of interpreting Binchois is whether to match his fabled restraint in performance, or to coax the songs' expressivity to the surface. Dominique Vellard seems to prefer the former approach, which relies for its effectiveness on the innate vocal qualities of his singers. For the most part, they respond admirably. The special artistry of Lena Susanne Norin, whose increasing involvement in this repertory (as here, in *Adieu, adieu* and especially *Je vous salue*) is a cause for celebration;

Anne-Marie Lablaude's contributions (such as *Pour prison*) are lighter in tone, but graceful and supple, yet you do wonder whether a more impassioned delivery of the text might not be appropriate – particularly in *Dueil angoisseus*, surely one of the finest poems set to music in the fifteenth century. And it continues to be puzzling that certain stanzas are shorn of their text to allow for instrumental participation (especially with texts of this quality). The Binchois discography makes up in quality for what it lacks in quantity, and notwithstanding these reservations, this disc sits comfortably in a distinguished niche of the repertory.

Sir Harrison Birtwistle
British 1934

The Triumph of Time. Gawain's Journey.
Philharmonia Orchestra / Elgar Howarth.
Collins Classics 1387-2 (55 minutes: DDD). Recorded 1993.
Ⓕ

Gawain's Journey offers a substantial set of extracts from Birtwistle's opera *Gawain* (vocal lines allotted to instruments) which forms a convincing whole and reinforces the impression that this is one of the weightiest dramatic scores of this or any other age. It has the immediate, unmeditated forcefulness so typical of Birtwistle. It may verge on the unremitting, but there's no mistaking the visceral theatrical power. In no sense is *The Triumph of Time* operatic, but its structure and material (which Birtwistle linked to the Bruegel engraving) is vividly dramatic, the sure-footed skill and economy of its gradual accumulation of tension and density still unsurpassed in Birtwistle's output – this triumphant return to the catalogue of a 1970s masterwork is cause for jubilation.

Gawain.
Marie Angel *sop* Morgan Le Fay; **Anne Howells** *mez* Lady de Hautdesert; **Richard Greager** *ten* Arthur; **Penelope Walmsley-Clark** *sop* Guinevere; **Omar Ebrahim** *bar* Fool; **Alan Ewing** *bass* Agravain; **John Marsden** *ten* Ywain; **François Le Roux** *bar* Gawain; **Kevin Smith** *counterten* Baldwin; **John Tomlinson** *bass* Green Knight, Bertilak;
Chorus and Orchestra of the Royal Opera House, Covent Garden / Elgar Howarth.
Collins Classics 7041-2 (two discs: 136 minutes: DDD). Notes and text included. Recorded live in 1994. *Gramophone* Award Winner 1996.
Ⓕ Ⓢ Ⓔ

Gawain is Birtwistle's finest dramatic work so far, an opera of compelling power and grandeur. Its magnificent opening gesture immediately promises that it will be an epic one. The First Act ends with the characteristic Birtwistle device of a fivefold cycle of the seasons, symbolically portraying Gawain's preparation for his confrontation with the Green Knight, while Act 2 turns on a threefold cycle of lullabies, hunting scenes and seductions in which he learns how few of the knightly virtues for which he is famed he in fact possesses. These cyclical structures are not mere machines, nor is the plot a mere pretext for them, as it arguably was in Birtwistle's earlier work, *The Mask of Orpheus*. Although none of the characters in this fable is a rounded personality – *Gawain* is no *verismo* opera – each of them is boldly and tellingly portrayed. Morgan is unchanging, venom personified. Arthur, too, does not change: an old soldier, bored with peace but unwilling to emerge from the cosy myth of Camelot. But Gawain matures, from arrogance to bitter self-awareness. Most strikingly of all the Green Knight, the opera's real and profoundly mysterious central character, has music of true lyrical strength and pride at his first challenge, denunciatory eloquence when he spares Gawain's life at their second encounter, telling him that mere cowardice is too small a sin to die for.

It is an opera whose drama often takes place in the wonderfully rich and strange sounds of Birtwistle's orchestra: massive, striding bass-lines, whooping brass, the prominent cimbalom at times almost as central as it once was in Stravinsky's imagination. The solo singers must achieve extremes of intensity to stand out in relief. Among them John Tomlinson is in outstandingly noble voice as the Green Knight and François Le Roux, when not obliged to force, is moving in the title-role. Marie Angel is fearless though often bitingly shrill as Morgan, Anne Howells a voluptuous Lady de Hautdesert. The recording brings the voices forward, which helps comprehension of the text, but does not diminish Elgar Howarth's masterly control of the score's burnished splendours. The whole enterprise is a huge achievement, a worthy and commendably prompt recording of one of the most powerful operas of the late twentieth century.

The Mask of Orpheus.
Jon Garrison *ten* Orpheus: Man; **Peter Bronder** *ten* Orpheus: Myth, Hades; **Jean Rigby** *mez* Euridice: Woman; **Anne-Marie Owens** *mez* Euridice: Myth, Persephone; **Alan Opie** *bar* Aristaeus: Man; **Omar Ebrahim** *bar* Aristaeus: Myth, Charon; **Marie Angel** *sop* Aristeus: Oracle of the Dead, Hecate; **Arwel Huw Morgan** *bar* Caller; **Stephen Allen** *ten* Priest, First Judge; **Nicholas Folwell**

bar Priest, Second Judge; **Stephen Richardson** *bass* Priest, Third Judge; **Juliet Booth** *sop*
Woman, First Fury; **Philippa Dames-Longworth** *sop* Woman, Second Fury;
Elizabeth McCormack *mez* Woman, Third Fury; **Ian Dearden** *sound diffusion*
BBC Singers; BBC Symphony Orchestra / Sir Andrew Davis, Martyn Brabbins.
NMC NMCD050 (three discs: 162 minutes: DDD). Notes and text included. Recorded 1996.
Gramophone Award Winner 1998.   Ⓜ

Birtwistle's opera is about the Orpheus myth, but the familiar story has been fragmented, several
different versions of its main events being presented, sometimes simultaneously, often
non-chronologically. Each of the principal characters is represented by two singers and a (silent)
dancer, and much of what happens is not directly described in the libretto. Without following the
libretto you will not be able to follow all of what is being sung; at times very little (the text is
sometimes broken up; some passages, including much of Act 3, are sung in an invented language).
Rituals are often at their most powerful when they appeal to the imagination rather than to reason,
and here the sense of ritual is awesomely powerful: solemn and often gravely beautiful in Act 1,
much tougher and more complex but at the same time hugely exciting in Act 2 and with a
formidable, gathering sense of culmination in Act 3. It is an extraordinarily patterned opera, with
many varied repetitions, all meticulously labelled ('First Structure of Decision', 'Second Time Shift'
and so on) in the score. The ritual repetitions, the elaborate patternings and allegorical structures
make their own effect. In the boldest of these, the 17 'arches' over which Orpheus passes in his
quest for Euridice in Act 2, Birtwistle aids comprehension by quite extensive use of speech. But the
music says far more than the sometimes enigmatic words, and the ceremonial retelling of the whole
story in Act 3, would perhaps have less impact if the words of the song verses were comprehensible.
Birtwistle communicates his refracted but gripping myth with, above all, orchestral colour: an
orchestra of wind, percussion and plucked instruments (plus tape, sampler and a small chorus) used
with vivid mastery. The sheer sound of this opera is quite haunting and, not least at the end when
the myth dissolves, moving. *The Mask of Orpheus* is a masterpiece, and this performance is fully
worthy of it. There are no weak links at all in the extremely fine cast. Although it is unfair to single
out any singer for special mention, Jon Garrison's portrayal of Orpheus the Man is outstanding.
The recording, direct and pungent but by no means lacking in atmosphere (the electronic tape is
pervasive in the right sense: it is the voice of Apollo), leaves nothing to be desired.

Georges Bizet   French 1838-1875

Symphony in C major. Overture in A major (ed. d'Almeida). Patrie, Op. 19. La jolie fille
de Perth – Suite.
Montreal Symphony Orchestra / Charles Dutoit.
Decca 452 102-2DH (72 minutes: DDD). Recorded 1995.   Ⓕ

The early Overture in A minor/major is a rarity; it is an oddly proportioned work in four sections,
the second a sudden brief theatrical storm, the substantial third an expressive Italian *Andante*
(which Dutoit shapes most lovingly): it ends in an energetic but more conventional finale. The work
was never heard in Bizet's lifetime. The same fate befell his Symphony, written in the same year: in
fact, it was not performed until 80 years later. It is hard to resist the delicately exotic *Adagio*, the
fresh, vigorous *Scherzo*, or the compelling vivacity of the finale, with its Schubertian key-shifts. One
of its themes was to reappear in the sparkling opera buffa *Don Procopio* composed five years later:
that in turn furnished the *Serenade* borrowed for *La jolie fille de Perth*, the orchestral suite from
which was put together by Bizet's publishers after the composer's death. The title of *Scènes
bohémiennes* springs from the fourth movement, which anticipates the gipsy dance in *Carmen*.
Splendidly vivid playing throughout, and recording too (at times even too bright).

Bizet Symphony. Jeux d'enfants – petite suite.
Debussy Danse sacrée et danse profane.
Vera Badings *hp* **Concertgebouw Orchestra / Bernard Haitink.**
Philips 416 437-2PH (50 minutes: ADD). Recorded 1979.   Ⓕ

Symphony[a]. L'Arlésienne[b] – Suites Nos. 1 and 2.
[a]**French National Radio Symphony Orchestra;**
[b]**Royal Philharmonic Orchestra / Sir Thomas Beecham.**
EMI CDC7 47794-2 (65 minutes: ADD). Recorded 1956-59.   Ⓕ Ⓗ

Comparing these two CDs is a joy. They are both desirable and certainly distinguished in different
ways, and to choose one as a best buy is almost impossible. On grounds of recorded sound,
however, there is a clear first choice. Haitink's Philips coupling of the Symphony with a deliciously

sparkling *Jeux d'enfants* was regarded as a demonstration disc in its LP days and this aspect of the analogue recording's excellence remains, particularly in the translucently vivid textures of *Jeux d'enfants*, a work which matches the Symphony in its charm. Within the warm Amsterdam Concertgebouw acoustics the Symphony is made to sound particularly spacious, the slow movement serene, with the most lovely playing from all concerned. The fill-up of Debussy's *Danses sacrée et profane* is also radiantly beautiful. Of course in Beecham's hands the Symphony is made to sound wonderfully songful and although the French orchestral playing is less than ideally polished (at the beginning and end of the *Adagio* intonation is not quite secure), the *joie de vivre* of Beecham's performance is irresistible. What makes the Beecham disc doubly desirable are the marvellous RPO wind solos (and, of course, the haunting strings in the *Adagietto*) in *L'Arlésienne*. The performances of these two suites stand head and shoulders above present CD competition, their loving finesse combines evocative magic (the 'Intermezzo' of No. 2) with wonderful rhythmic vivacity and sparkle (the closing 'Farandole'). The refurbishing of the recordings is remarkably successful, especially *L'Arlésienne*.

Carmen.
Teresa Berganza *sop* Carmen; **Plácido Domingo** *ten* Don José; **Ileana Cotrubas** *sop* Micaëla; **Sherrill Milnes** *bar* Escamillo; **Yvonne Kenny** *sop* Frasquita; **Alicia Nafé** *mez* Mercédès; **Robert Lloyd** *bass* Zuniga; **Stuart Harling** *bar* Moralès; **Gordon Sandison** *bar* Dancaïre; **Geoffrey Pogson** *ten* Remendado;
Ambrosian Singers; London Symphony Orchestra / Claudio Abbado.
DG 427 885-2GX3 (three discs: 157 minutes: ADD). Notes, text and translation included.
Recorded 1977. Ⓜ ℞℞

This notable recording followed immediately on the famous Faggioni production at the 1977 Edinburgh Festival, a staging finely observed enough to still remain in the minds of those who were there. In it Berganza declared her aim of rescuing the role from bad traditions and from its insults to Spanish womanhood. Her reading was restrained, haughty, but no less attractive and haunting for that. She developed the character, as she does on the recording, from carefree gipsy to tragic woman and, in doing so, is scrupulous in her obedience to Bizet's notes, rhythms and dynamics. Nothing is exaggerated yet nothing is left out in this sensuous yet never overtly sensual portrayal, bewitchingly sung. Maybe you don't feel quite the full engagement of her emotions in her entanglement with José, but better a slight reticence than overacting. Migenes, on the Maazel set, is more immediately seductive, and occasionally more varied in tonal colouring, but Berganza is the more subtle artist. She works in keen rapport with Abbado, who brings clarity of texture, Mediterranean fire, and intense concentration to the score. You may find more elegance, more Gallic wit in, say, Beecham's famous EMI set, but only Maazel of other conductors comes near Abbado's emphasis on close-knit ensemble and histrionic strength – and both their sets come as the result of experience of 'real' performances. Domingo benefits here, as on the Maazel in the same way, being more involved in affairs. Like his Carmen, he sometimes lacks variety of colour in his singing, but its sheer musicality and, in the last two acts, power, count for much. Sherrill Milnes is at once virile and fatuous as Escamillo should be. Cotrubas makes a vulnerable, touching Micaëla. Robert Lloyd, the Zuniga speaks and sings in excellent French, and is the most engaging of the supporting cast. The dialogue is heavily foreshortened as compared with rival sets. Abbado chooses some of the questionable Oeser alternatives, but – apart from the one in the finale – they are not disturbing. The recording is absolutely first-rate.

Carmen.
Julia Migenes *mez* Carmen; **Plácido Domingo** *ten* Don José; **Faith Esham** *sop* Micaëla; **Ruggero Raimondi** *bass* Escamillo; **Lilian Watson** *sop* Frasquita; **Susan Daniel** *mez* Mercédès; **Jean-Philippe Lafont** *bar* Dancaïre; **Gérard Garino** *ten* Remendado; **François Le Roux** *bar* Moralès; **John Paul Bogart** *bass* Zuniga; **French Radio Chorus;**
French Radio Children's Chorus; French National Orchestra / Lorin Maazel.
Erato 2292-45207-2 (three discs: 151 minutes: DDD). Notes, text and translation included.
Recorded 1992. Ⓕ

Too many recordings of *Carmen* have blown up the work to proportions beyond its author's intentions but here Maazel adopts a brisk, lightweight approach that seems to come close to what Bizet wanted. Similarly Julia Migenes approaches the title part in an immediate, vivid way, exuding the gipsy's allure in a performance that suggests Carmen's fierce temper and smouldering eroticism, and she develops the character intelligently into the fatalistic person of the card scene and finale. Her singing isn't conventionally smooth but it is compelling from start to finish. Plácido Domingo has made the part of Don José very much his own, and here he sings with unstinting involvement and a good deal of finesse. Ruggero Raimondi is a macho Toreador though Faith Esham is a somewhat pallid Micaëla.

Carmen.
Béatrice Uria-Monzon *mez* Carmen; **Christian Papis** *ten* Don José; **Leontina Vaduva** *sop*
Micaëla; **Vincent le Texier** *bass-bar* Escamillo; **Maryse Castets** *sop* Frasquita; **Martine Olmeda**
mez Mercédès; **Franck Leguérinel** *bar* Dancaïre; **Thierry Trégan** *ten* Remendado;
Olivier Lallouette *bass* Moralès; **Lionel Sarrazin** *bass* Zuniga; **Paul Renard** *spkr* Lillas Pastia;
Bordeaux CNR Children's Choir; Bordeaux Theatre Chorus;
Bordeaux Aquitaine Orchestra / Alain Lombard.
Auvidis Valois V4734 (two discs: 142 minutes: DDD). Notes, text and translation included.
Recorded 1994.   Ⓕ

Having a French singer in the title-role is one of the advantages of this set. Béatrice Uria-Monzon
is a full-bodied Mediterranean mezzo: her Carmen is bold and earthy, with thrilling contralto-like
tone for such important moments as the 'Tra-la-la' replies to her interrogators in Act 1. She handles
the dialogue with Don José very well, before the Séguidille, in which she pretends that, like him, she
is from Navarre (this is usually cut). This weight of voice rather tells against her where charm is
concerned, with the 'Chanson bohème' sounding haughty rather than festive. The version of
Carmen used here reverts to spoken dialogue rather than the spurious recitatives. Leontina Vaduva
is a good Micaëla but Christian Papis's Don José isn't really a match for either of his leading ladies.
In 'Parle-moi de ma mère' he exhibits an unfortunate beat in the voice that makes it all sound too
tragic – after all he should really just seem nostalgic and quite happy to be talking to his young
visitor, although he can produce effective, soft notes, as at the end of 'Là bas, là bas'. One has
nothing but sympathy for Carmen's preference for Vincent le Texier's Escamillo whose performance
is the best among the other principals. This is a well-recorded, authentically French *Carmen*,
conducted with flair by Alain Lombard.

Carmen.
Victoria de los Angeles *sop* Carmen; **Nicolai Gedda** *ten* Don José; **Janine Micheau** *sop*
Micaëla; **Ernest Blanc** *bar* Escamillo; **Denise Monteil** *sop* Frasquita; **Marcelle Croisier, Monique**
Linval *sops* Mercédès; **Jean-Christophe Benoit** *bar* Dancaïre; **Michel Hamel** *ten* Remendado;
Bernard Plantey *bar* Moralès; **Xavier Depraz** *bass* Zuniga; **Les Petits Chanteurs de Versailles;**
French National Radio Chorus and Orchestra / Sir Thomas Beecham.
EMI CDS5 56214-2 (three discs: 161 minutes: ADD). Notes, text and translation included.
Recorded 1958-59.   Ⓕ 🅷

This Beecham set should be in every collection. It breathes French elegance, wit and charm in a way
still not equalled elsewhere, while not neglecting the passion and tragedy when they are called for.
In brief, Beecham is the complete *Carmen* conductor – listen to the entr'actes, if nothing else, if you
are in doubt. The only way he sins is in preferring the Guiraud recitatives on which he was nurtured
rather than the more authentic dialogue. When it first appeared it was hailed as a milestone in the
history of *Carmen* on record, not least because of Victoria de los Angeles – her sense of humour in
Act 1, the *élan*, the seductiveness of Act 2, the fatal acceptance of the card scene, the proud dignity
of the finale. While missing nothing in verbal clarity or of subtle interpretation, she actually sings
the role as musically as one would want. Berganza (for Abbado) is her peer in that respect but
sounds a little detached by comparison with her Spanish predecessor. Indeed, los Angeles captures
virtually every facet of the consistently fascinating part, if she is not quite so immediately alluring
as Migenes (Maazel). Gedda turned in one of his most persuasive performances as José, one full of
good singing but wanting only the sense of dark, doomed intensity for the last two acts that
Domingo manages (for Abbado and Maazel – where he's at his very best), but nobody achieves the
natural flow of the Flower song so easily as Gedda. Blanc is as idiomatic as any Escamillo, Micheau
is also authentic in timbre, but somewhat dry of tone at this stage of her career. A change of
Mercédès was needed as the first singer of the role unfortunately died in the 15 months intervening
between the two series of sessions. EMI honestly point this out in an accompanying note, which
also suggests that on CD the change in recorded quality is marked. It will not detract much from
your enjoyment in this admirable set which has a perfect balance between voice and orchestra.

Les pêcheurs de perles.
Barbara Hendricks *sop* Leïla; **John Aler** *ten* Nadir; **Gino Quilico** *bar* Zurga;
Jean-Philippe Courtis *bass* Nourabad;
Toulouse Capitole Chorus and Orchestra / Michel Plasson.
EMI CDS7 49837-2 (two discs: 127 minutes: DDD). Notes, text and translation included.
Recorded 1989.   Ⓕ

Let a tenor and a baritone signify that they are willing to oblige with a duet, and the cry will go up
for *The Pearl Fishers*. It's highly unlikely that many of the company present will know what the duet

is about – it recalls the past, proclaims eternal friendship and nearly ends up in a quarrel – but the melody and the sound of two fine voices blending in its harmonies will be quite sufficient. In fact there is much more to the opera than the duet, or even than the three or four solos which are sometimes sung in isolation; and the EMI recording goes further than previous versions in giving a complete account of a score remarkable for its unity as well as for the attractiveness of individual numbers. It is a lyrical opera, and the voices need to be young and graceful. Barbara Hendricks and John Aler certainly fulfil those requirements, she with a light, silvery timbre, he with a high tenor admirably suited to the tessitura of his solos. The third main character, the baritone whose role is central to the drama, assumes his rightful place here: Gino Quilico brings genuine distinction to the part, and his aria in Act 3 is one of the highlights. Though Plasson's direction at first is rather square, the performance grows in responsiveness act by act. It is a pity that the accompanying notes are not stronger in textual detail, for the full score given here stimulates interest in its history. One of the changes made in the original score of 1863 concerns the celebrated duet itself, the first version of which is given in an appendix. It ends in a style that one would swear owed much to the 'friendship' duet in Verdi's *Don Carlos* – except that Bizet came first.

Boris Blacher

German 1903-1975

Concertante Musik, Op. 10. Fürstin Tarakanowa – suite, Op. 19*a*. Two Inventions, Op. 46. Music for Cleveland, Op. 53. Clarinet Concerto.
Dmitri Ashkenazy *cl*
Deutsches Symphony Orchestra, Berlin / Vladimir Ashkenazy.
Ondine ODE912-2 (55 minutes: DDD). Recorded 1997.   Ⓕ 🄴

The chances are that if you had telephoned Boris Blacher, whistled a couple of notes and asked him to make a satisfying piece of music from permutations of them he would have done it. The second (and final) movement of his Clarinet Concerto is a set of variations on a not particularly complex chord. Like much of Blacher's music it is fast, rhythmically alert and light on its feet. His very restricted material leads not to monotony but to fertile fantasy until the music reaches a slower middle section, lyrical and quiet, the soloist almost unaccompanied, in which there is a real sense that every note has meaning, purpose and a reason for being there. This absorbingly planned disc demonstrates how he arrived at that point of masterly economy (the Concerto, written in 1971, counts as a fairly late work). The *Concertante Musik*, from 1937, was his first success, and was once widely played. No wonder: redolent both of neo-classicism and of jazz, it has strong, syncopated rhythm and clean textures; it is catchy and is scored with exuberant brilliance. The Suite from the opera, *Princess Tarakanowa* (premièred, amazingly, in Germany in 1941, when Blacher was a known anti-Nazi and an acknowledged admirer of such 'degenerates' as Stravinsky, Bartók and Berg) adds a rather Shostakovich-like astringency (a strutting, menacing march) and touches of melodic grace and of an appealing expressiveness that was not obvious in the *Concertante Musik*. With the post-war works Blacher's preoccupation with extreme economy, making endlessly resourceful use of brief motifs, is obvious in the rather bony *Two Inventions*, more impressive and more entertaining still in the *Music for Cleveland*, in which great variety of texture, including a lot of vividly brilliant brass-writing, is drawn from and palindromically retreats to a deliberately un-theme-like 12-note cell. His music is open, even bare in texture, but it is anything but arid. The Clarinet Concerto, in particular, is an entrancingly inventive work by a composer who clearly hated using ten notes when one perfectly placed one would be at least as effective. Both Ashkenazys, father and son, have clearly fallen for this lean, clean and invigorating music: those adjectives would do very well for these performances, which have been no less cleanly recorded.

William Blezard

British 1921

Sonatinas Nos. 1-3. Preludes, Book 1. The Circle of Time. Jeux d'esprit. October Dance. Central Park West. Fast Forward. Jonathan's Scherzo. On Reflection.
Eric Parkin *pf*
Priory PRCD617 (67 minutes: DDD). Recorded 1997.   Ⓕ

Blezard has had to wait until his later seventies to reach the CD catalogue and these are first recordings of music that he says he has barely heard in the concert hall. As a pianist he reached a wide public as Joyce Grenfell's accompanist and his Second *Sonatina* is dedicated to another comedian, Donald Swann. At times Blezard's music has this kind of wry, understated English humour. His muse is modest, introspective, gently neo-classical and there is nothing monumental here: the longest movement lasts less than five minutes in these sets of pieces composed during periods between the 1960s and 1998. *The Circle of Time* is nicely devised around the seasons and

Parkin sports a neat finger-technique in the rapid 'Spring'. Written specially for Parkin just before the recording sessions, the piece called *On Reflection* is quite a discovery, since it goes much deeper than the rather pallid slow movements elsewhere – a nice tribute. The jazzy qualities of the outer movements in the set called *Jeux d'esprit* and in the Third *Sonatina* are also appealing. Parkin, well recorded, delivers these with his usual infectious rhythmic zest and shows himself to be a firm advocate of Blezard throughout.

Sir Arthur Bliss

British 1891-1975

Cello Concerto, T120. Music for Strings, T54. Two Studies, T16.
Tim Hugh *vc*
English Northern Philharmonia / David Lloyd-Jones.
Naxos 8 553383 (64 minutes: DDD). Recorded 1995.

Ⓢ🄴

This is a first-rate performance of Bliss's Cello Concerto from Tim Hugh, stylishly and sympathetically partnered by David Lloyd-Jones and the English Northern Philharmonia. The work is a delightful creation, ideally proportioned, impeccably crafted and full of the most beguiling invention. Hugh plays with commanding assurance, great beauty of tone and rapt commitment throughout, and the accompaniment is sprightly and sensitive to match. What makes this release indispensable to all Bliss admirers is the inclusion of the *Two Studies*. These date from 1921 and were believed lost until they turned up in the composer's papers after his death in 1975. The first is a memorably chaste, coolly serene affair, scored with delicious poise, whereas the second is an energetic, good-humoured and occasionally face-pulling romp. That just leaves the tremendous *Music for Strings*, and here, alas, is where reservations have to be raised. This superb score displays and demands a formidable technical facility and Bliss's exhilaratingly well-judged writing would surely test any string section in the world. It would be idle to pretend that the hard-working strings of the English Northern Philharmonia are ideally secure protagonists. Lloyd-Jones's clear-headed, expressive interpretation serves the work well but in the finale's crucial introductory bars do you feel that his approach is oddly perfunctory, and rather lacking the necessary tingling expectancy. The Cello Concerto and the *Two Studies* alone though, will probably be enticement enough for many readers. The recorded sound is excitingly realistic.

Bliss Checkmate – suite.
Lambert Horoscope – suite.
Walton Façade – Suites Nos. 1 and 2.
English Northern Philharmonia / David Lloyd-Jones.
Hyperion CDA66436 (74 minutes: DDD).

Ⓕ🅂

What a joy to welcome on CD, a major British ballet score (comparable in appeal to Walton's *Façade* with which, happily, it is coupled). Constant Lambert's *Horoscope* is a highly individual score that is somehow very English. It is played here with striking freshness and expansiveness and is easy to enjoy. Lloyd-Jones responds to Bliss's lyricism very warmly. What makes this disc particularly enticing is the inclusion of the two *Façade* suites, welcome (for once) away from the spoken poems. This is music that in a witty performance can really make one smile and even chuckle. So it is here, especially the 'Tango Pasodoble' with a delicious lilt for 'I do like to be beside the seaside' contrasting with its Offenbachian gusto, the 'Swiss Yodelling Song' with its droll Rossini quotation and refined mock-melancholy, and the irresistibly humorous 'Polka' that just manages not to be vulgar. All are quite ideally paced and the solo wind playing is a constant delight. The recording with its bloom and clarity is near perfect.

A Colour Symphony. Adam Zero.
English Northern Philharmonia / David Lloyd-Jones.
Naxos 8 553460 (74 minutes: DDD). Recorded 1995.

Ⓢ🅂🄴

David Lloyd-Jones's exciting and idiomatic account of *A Colour Symphony* proves easily more than a match for all current competition, including the composer's own 1955 recording so spectacularly transferred by Dutton Laboratories. Speeds are judged to perfection – nicely flowing for the first and third movements, not too hectic for the flashing *Scherzo* – and countless details in Bliss's stunning orchestral canvas are most deftly attended to. Phrasing is sensitive and ideally affectionate, solo work is consistently excellent (the slow movement's delicate woodwind arabesques are exquisitely voiced), and tuttis open out superbly in what is technically the finest recording to date from Naxos (magnificently keen-voiced horns throughout). Whereas *A Colour Symphony* was inspired by the heraldic associations of four different colours (one for each movement), the theme of *Adam Zero* is the inexorable life-cycle of humankind. In its entirety, this 1946 ballet score does admittedly have its occasional *longueurs*, but for the most part Bliss's invention is of commendably high quality. Certainly, the vivid exuberance and theatrical swagger of numbers like 'Dance of Spring' and 'Dance of Summer' have strong appeal. Equally, the limpid beauty of both the 'Love Dance' and the hieratic 'Bridal Ceremony' which immediately ensues is not easily banished, while the darkly insistent 'Dance with Death' distils a gentle poignancy which is most haunting.

Ernest Bloch   Swiss/American 1880-1959

America. Concerto grosso No. 1.
Patricia Michaelian *pf* **Seattle Symphony Chorale and Orchestra / Gerard Schwarz.**
Delos DE3135 (61 minutes: DDD). Text included. Recorded 1993.   Ⓕ

Ernest Bloch's 'Epic Rhapsody for Orchestra', *America,* is a warming musical flight across the history of the United States, and uses the anthem of the same name as a leitmotif that helps bind English, American Indian and Jewish-style themes into a homogeneous and hugely accessible whole. There are three variegated movements, each a dramatic tone-poem reflecting such universal ideas as 'Struggle and Hardships' or 'Hours of Joy – Hours of Sorrow' (the second movement's subtitle), with the third visiting the world of jazz and culminating in a full-throated choral celebration of the anthem itself. However, Bloch's 'programme' is fairly specific. *America* might be best described as a great film score that never was, a highly emotive thanksgiving from a man who had himself only recently arrived in his new home, with tender references to such perennial favourites as *John Brown's Body* and *Dixie*. There are also veiled references to other of Bloch's works, including *Schelomo* and the delightful *Concerto grosso* that Gerard Schwarz programmes as *America*'s coupling. Demonstration standard sound.

Symphony in C sharp minor. Schelomo.
Torleif Thedéen *vc* **Malmö Symphony Orchestra / Lev Markiz.**
BIS CD576 (78 minutes: DDD). Recorded 1990-92.   ⒻⒺ

Bloch's early symphony is an endearing and at times impressive showcase for a young composer (he was 23) endowed by nature and nurture with all the gifts save individuality (though there are hints in the later movements that that too is on the way). He can write impressively strong, expansive melodies, develop them with real ingenuity and build them into monumental climaxes. Climax-building, indeed, is what young Bloch seems most interested in at this stage of his career, that and a love for all the rich contrasts of colour and texture that a big orchestra, imaginatively used, can provide. He is so very good at his craft, so adept at pulling out still more stops when you thought there could hardly be any left, so sheerly and likeably clever that one is scarcely ever made impatient by the occasional feeling that this or that movement could have ended two or three minutes earlier. It's a pleasure, too, to listen for fulfilled echoes of that youthful exuberance in the mature 'biblical rhapsody' *Schelomo*. Just as Lev Markiz adroitly avoids any impression of overpadded grossness in the symphony, so he and his fine soloist find more than richly embroidered oriental voluptuousness in this portrait of King Solomon; there is gravity and even poignancy to the music as well, and Thedéen's subtle variety of tone colour gives the work shadow and delicacy as well as richness. The recording is excellent.

John Blow   British 1649-1708

God spake sometime in visions. How doth the city sit solitary. The Lord is my shepherd. God is our hope and strength. I beheld and lo! a great multitude. Turn thee unto me, O Lord. Blessed is the man. Lift up your heads. O Lord I have sinned. O give thanks unto the Lord. O Lord, thou hast searched me out. Cry aloud and spare not. Lord, who shall dwell in thy tabernacle. I said in the cutting off of my days.
Robin Blaze *counterten* **Joseph Cornwell, William Kendall** *tens* **Stephen Varcoe,**
Stephen Alder *bars* **Winchester Cathedral Choir / David Hill;**
The Parley of Instruments / Peter Holman.
Hyperion CDA67031/2 (two discs: 116 minutes: DDD). Texts included. Recorded 1995.   ⒻⓅ

In choosing a range of Blow's best and most representative anthems, Peter Holman and David Hill have had quite a task on their hands: Blow was even more prolific than Purcell in this domain. They have sensibly cast their critical eyes over those works written in the 'golden' age of Charles II, several of whose reputations go before them. The dignity and sobriety of the fine coronation anthem *God spake sometime in visions* is a joy to behold, and it is given a grand and spacious reading here. David Hill, ever the choral director to sustain and shape a line, is peerless in the opening paragraph. Here, as in other distinguished works like *I beheld and lo!*, the success of these performances is determined by deft recognition of the structural strengths and solecisms of Blow's music. He is helped by a pleasing integration between soloists, choir and instruments. Blow's particular attraction is a disarming tunefulness and an idiomatic simplicity of expression. *O Lord I have sinned* has a distinctive Purcellian flavour with its chromatic inflexions and unpredictable contrapuntal movement, yet it fails to plumb the depths as in the similar type of piece which became something of a Purcell speciality. Indeed, for all Blow's quality there are several works here that just miss the mark despite their distinctive place in English Restoration musical life. Whether or not such a state of affairs warrants two discs is arguable, but there is no doubt that this is an important addition to Hyperion's English Orpheus series.

Blow I was glad when they said unto me.
Boyce Lord, thou hast been our refuge.
Handel Utrecht Te Deum and Jubilate, HWV278-79.
Julia Gooding, Sophie Daneman *sops* Edward Burrowes, Timothy Burtt, Alastair Cook *trebs*
Robin Blaze, Ashley Stafford *altos* Rogers Covey-Crump, Mark Le Brocq *tens*
Andrew Dale Forbes *bass*
St Paul's Cathedral Choir; The Parley of Instruments / John Scott.
Hyperion CDA67009 (74 minutes: DDD). Texts included. Recorded 1997.   Ⓕ

Anyone who has tried to listen to music in St Paul's Cathedral might be forgiven for hesitating before buying a recording made there: however, by some magic the Hyperion engineers have succeeded in producing a recording that is a model of clear sound, even in the fullest tuttis, while at the same time capturing something of the cathedral ambience. This CD happily celebrates the tercentenary, which fell in 1997, of the official opening of the cathedral, offering three of the finest pieces written for performance there. The Blow anthem was written for the opening event and also to give thanks for the Peace of Ryswick. It is an attractive work, including a countertenor duet, exquisitely done here by Robin Blaze and Ashley Stafford, and a tenor solo sung fluently and with much refined detail by Rogers Covey-Crump, supported by a pair of obbligato trumpets. The Boyce anthem was written in 1755 for the Festival for the Sons of the Clergy, still held annually at St Paul's; again, there is distinguished solo singing from Covey-Crump in the expressive 'Yea, like as a father pitieth his own children', and from Blaze in 'The eyes of all wait upon thee'; but perhaps the most appealing number is the trio sung here, in very accomplished style, by three of the boys. And there are rousing choral Hallelujahs to end with.

However, the main item is Handel's *Te Deum and Jubilate* for the Peace of Utrecht, given at St Paul's in 1713 and Handel's first serious venture into Anglican church music. Although modelled on Purcell and Croft, it has something of the freshness and vitality of the church music Handel had recently composed in Italy, even if the constraints of the English anthem manner caused him to work on a rather smaller canvas – few of the individual movements run much over two minutes or so. It is a colourful piece, full of original ideas, and it is done here under John Scott, the incumbent St Paul's organist, with great vitality, with breadth, with excellent discipline and with clear verbal articulation. The St Paul's boys seem to sing in a fresher, less inhibited style than some, with a distinctive edge to their tone. Sopranos are used for the solos here rather than boys, with Julia Gooding and Sophie Daneman singing with much delicacy, and the other soloists, plus the bass Andrew Dale Forbes, shine again. A disc well worthy of its subject.

Venus and Adonis.
Rosemary Joshua *sop* Venus; **Gerald Finley** *bar* Adonis; **Robin Blaze** *counterten* Cupid, Second Grace; **Maria Cristina Kiehr** *sop* Shepherdess, First Grace; **Christopher Josey** *counterten* Huntsman, First Shepherd; **John Bowen** *ten* Second Shepherd; **Jonathan Brown** *bass* Third Shepherd, Third Grace.
Clare College Choir, Cambridge; Orchestra of the Age of Enlightenment / René Jacobs.
Harmonia Mundi HMC90 1684 (51 minutes: DDD). Texts included.   ⒻⓅ

Historically in the shadow of Purcell's *Dido*, *Venus and Adonis* is fast becoming a recognized masterpiece of small-scale baroque drama. Blow draws considerable inspiration from French chamber opera both in matters of constitution and balance, though *Venus and Adonis* is still a distinctly English work with its poised, understated dialogue and an emotional denouement where Adonis's death from the tusks of a boar is touchingly tender in its measured, if demonstrative grief; the effect is not far removed from Dido's lament, though Purcell's tragic vein is ultimately untouchable. There are, however, some superb examples of indigenous word-setting and declamatory *arioso* which put Blow in the Purcell bracket in several instances, not least in Cupid's forthright scene-setting, sung with increasing assurance by Robin Blaze. Indeed, René Jacobs surrounds himself with many fine singers here, all of whom he marshals in lively and responsive performances. Rosemary Joshua is an irresistable Venus, who wastes not a word either in colourful representation or vocal suppleness, and Gerald Finlay's reflective longing accords with Jacobs's elegant and full-flavoured direction. There is a nobility in the initial exchanges between the protagonists which, although it constitutes little more than spouting the other's name, is elevated by a doleful shimmer of recorders, which under Jacobs augurs much in its funereal symbolism. These responsive instrumental interjections from the OAE are even more effective in 'Hark, hark the rural music sounds'. This admirable recording puts the work on another footing entirely.

Luigi Boccherini
Italian 1743-1805

Cello Concertos – No. 3 in D major, G476; No. 7 in G major, G480; No. 9 in B flat major, G482. Concert aria – Se d'un amor tiranno, G557.
Marta Almajano *sop* **Limoges Baroque Ensemble / Christophe Coin** *vc*
Auvidis Astrée E8517 (62 minutes: DDD). Recorded 1993.   Ⓕ Ⓟ

Christophe Coin throws off in the deftest fashion the typical Boccherinian filigree figuration, the little ornamental flourishes perfectly placed and timed, the numerous stratospheric excursions above the treble stave sweet-toned and delicate. And with it he shows a command of Boccherini's style, affectionately graceful, sometimes with a faintly quizzical air. The tone of Coin's instrument is light and translucent, and with this small orchestra the sound in the solos, which are anyway lightly accompanied, is particularly sweet: in the first movement of G482 (the concerto known from the Grützmacher version) the unassuming handling of the virtuoso writing has a special kind of charm and the rather grander manner called for in the D major work G476 is also very happily caught, not without a hint of the romantic at times, for Coin is no austere stylist. The aria that completes his disc is a large-scale duet for cello, in its full concerto manner, and soprano; the lines are full of eloquent appoggiaturas and there is some beguiling duetting for the voice and the instrument. Marta Almajano has a big, clear top register and plenty of drama to her singing.

Simply Baroque
Boccherini Cello Concertos – No. 5 in D major, G478; No. 7 in G major, G480.
Bach Cantatas: No. 22, Jesus nahm zu sich die Zwölfe: Choral – Ertöt' uns durch dein' Güte; No. 136, Erforsche mich, Gott, und erfahre mein Herz: Choral – Dein Blut, der edle Saft; No. 147, Herz und Mund und Tat und Leben: Choral – Jesu bleibet meine Freude; No. 163, Nur jedem das Seine: Aria – Lass mein Herz die Münze sein; No. 167, Ihr Menschen, rühmet Gottes Liebe: Choral – Sei Lob und Preis mit Ehren. St Matthew Passion, BWV244 – Erbarme dich. Orgel-Büchlein – Ich ruf' zu dir, BWV639. Schübler Chorales – Kommst du nun, Jesu, von Himmel herunter, BWV650. Orchestral Suite No. 3 in D major, BWV1068 – Air (all arr. Koopman).
Yo-Yo Ma *vc* **Amsterdam Baroque Orchestra / Ton Koopman** *hpd/org*
Sony Classical SK60680 (69 minutes: DDD). Recorded 1998.   Ⓕ Ⓟ Ⓔ

Sony's title to this disc 'Simply Baroque' suggests yet another addition to the stacks of such compilations that are currently on the CD market. And yet if you stop to think for a moment or two, you will probably suss that neither Yo-Yo Ma nor Ton Koopman would be likely to collaborate for a mere 'greatest hits' CD. In fact, this musically appealing compilation is extremely imaginative: nine movements from Bach sensitively arranged for cello and chamber orchestra, plus an attractive pair of Boccherini cello concertos. Ma's Stradivarius was altered for the occasion by luthier Charles Beare (using a baroque bridge, a tail-piece in place of an end-pin and gut strings), and Ma himself uses a baroque bow. As superior 'light' listening goes, it is difficult to think of a happier 70 minutes' worth. It also provides an ideal 'soft-option' introduction to the sound of period instruments.

The *St Matthew Passion*'s 'Erbarme dich' might seem like a bizarre place to start, and yet Bach's heart-rending aria becomes a cleverly worked duet for violin and cello, always flowing and discreet, aided by responsive strings and a tactile lute continuo. Koopman's harpsichord brushes *Jesu Joy of Man's Desiring* into action with a flourish, answered by a mellifluous mix of solo cello, strings and winds. Bassoon and cello join forces for a swaggering 'Lass mein Herz die Münze sein', before the brief chorale 'Dein Blut, der edle Saft' (decorously embellished by a recorder). Last comes the inevitable 'Air' from the Third Orchestral Suite, tellingly arranged (as a duet for cellos) and superbly played. In fact, Koopman's 'second' cello – his lead cellist Jaap ter Linden – is every bit as eloquent as the star act. Listening to the two Boccherini works on this marvellous CD remind you again of Ma's uncanny technical facility, at once elegant and unselfconsciously virtuosic. Ton Koopman provides the cadenzas and the performances are pure delight.

Symphonies, Op. 37 – No. 1 in C major, G515; No. 3 in D minor, G517; No. 4 in A major, G518.
Academia Montis Regalis / Luigi Mangiocavallo.
Opus 111 OPS30-168 (55 minutes: DDD). Recorded 1996.   Ⓕ**P****E**

'Sinfonie a grande orchestra', says Boccherini's own catalogue, in description of his Op. 37, a set of
four symphonies written in 1786-87 (only the three recorded here survive). Here they are played by
a rather *piccola* orchestra yet the performance is brilliant and effective, with its very light and
translucent textures conveying the detail with remarkable clarity. All the music sparkles with life –
specially effective movements are the finale of the C major, with its curiously fragmented textures,
and the *Andante* of the A major, one of Boccherini's loveliest orchestral slow movements, with the
gentle and graceful melancholy of its oboe theme. There are attractive minuets here too – listen to
the exquisitely played bassoon solo in the Trio of the D minor work or the oddly ambiguous
rhythms in the C major. The conductor paces the music well and brings plenty of spirit and vivacity
to the quick movements. In general this is an outstanding disc.

Symphonies – No. 4 in D minor, G506 (Op. 12), 'La casa del diavolo'; No. 4 in F major, G512
(Op. 12); C minor, G519 (Op. 41).
Academy of Ancient Music / Christopher Hogwood.
L'Oiseau-Lyre 436 993-2OH (58 minutes: DDD). Recorded 1992.   Ⓕ**P**

In this issue the incisive edge of the orchestra's period instruments offers a vivid expression of
the music's dramatic content. In *La casa del diavolo*, for example, the AAM brings out the radiance
of the opening *Allegro* and gentle pathos of the second movement, but crisper, clearer textures in
the finale create a more chilling representation of the music's diabolical character. The AAM's
stylish response to Boccherini's imaginative rhythms and inventively varied textures is delightfully
apparent in the F major Symphony, where the finale's sudden diversion into a minuet is deftly
handled. The four-movement C minor Symphony is the most expansive and truly 'symphonic' of
the three works recorded here. The AAM's taut control of the opening movement's dialogue between
various instrumental groupings, the engagingly pastoral tone in the *Lentarello*, the suitably rustic
Minuet and Trio and astonishing brilliance in the tarantella-like finale, produce a genuinely
compelling result. These fresh, vigorous accounts are attractively presented in resonant sound.

String Quintets, Op. 11 – No. 4 in F minor, G274; No. 5 in E major, G275; No. 6 in D major, G276.
Smithsonian Chamber Players (Marilyn MacDonald, Jorie Garrigue *vns* Anthony Martin *va*
Anner Bylsma, Kenneth Slowik *vcs*).
Deutsche Harmonia Mundi RD77159 (67 minutes: DDD). Recorded 1988.   Ⓕ**P**

Boccherini was a virtuoso cellist and often played together with a family string quartet in Madrid
and the experience was obviously a very pleasant one, for he wrote 100 quintets for two violins,
viola and two cellos. He was never at a loss for ideas: the quintets are richly varied in form and
texture, the latter enhanced by Boccherini's intimate knowledge of the techniques and sound-
qualities of the bowed-string instruments. Many of us know the famous Minuet – but how many
are familiar with the work from which it comes? The Quintet in E, the fifth of the six Quintets of
his Op. 11 (1775), of which it is the third movement, is one of those in this recording. The bucolic
Quintet in D, *dello l'ucceleria*, ('The aviary') is a cyclic work with bird-song, shepherd's pipes and
hunting sounds. If Boccherini was, as Giuseppe Pupo described him, 'the wife of Haydn', his music
has the charm, grace and poise of the best wives, and there is nothing wrong with that! The
Smithsonian Players play like good Italians, which none of them is, and are superbly recorded in
this irresistibly attractive album. They all use Stradivarius instruments, producing clear sounds and
textures such as may have been heard in Boccherini's time.

Cello Sonatas – No. 2 in C minor, G2b[b]; No. 4 in A major, G4[a]; No. 10 in E flat major, G10[a];
No. 17 in C major, G17[a]; No. 23 in B flat major, G565[b].
Richard Lester *vc* [a]**David Watkin** *vc continuo* [b]**Chi-Chi Nwanoku** *db*
Hyperion CDA66719 (67 minutes: DDD).   Ⓕ

Richard Lester's slightly impetuous playing of these sonatas seems to capture very happily their
character: their somewhat wayward invention, their sense of being formalized versions of a cellist's
improvisations. The momentary hesitancies hint at the player-composer who is deciding as he goes
which of the ideas in his mind to try out next. Yet beneath it is a strong rhythm and a very sure
compositional technique. The music is very high lying: the cellist has prolonged spells in high
thumb positions with quite rapid passagework, and these Lester executes with great brilliance and
crispness. The opening movement of the C major sonata is a particularly fine piece, with its pensive

moments and its sudden flights of fancy; there is an eloquent central *Largo* and a dashing, witty finale. The E flat work has jaunty syncopations, the A major a first movement of particular brilliance and again there is an intensely expressive slow movement. The final sonata here is the B flat work that was evidently the model for the outer movements of the famous Boccherini-Grützmacher Concerto. Lester's bowing is vigorous, his tone warm and sharply defined with very little vibrato. Usually these sonatas are accompanied by a keyboard but here the practice, undoubtedly very common in Boccherini's day, of using another string instrument is preferred. In two sonatas a double-bass is used: the effect is a bit gruff, with something of a chasm between top and bottom when the cello is in its upper reaches. The two cellos are much more persuasive, especially when the second is as supportively played as it is here.

Joseph Bodin de Boismortier
French 1689-1755

Six Concertos, Op. 15 – No. 1 in G major; No. 2 in A minor; No. 3 in D major; No. 4 in B minor; No. 5 in A major; No. 6 in E minor.
Soloists of Le Concert Spirituel (Jocelyn Daubigney, Anne Savignat, Jan de Winne, Vincent Touzet, Jacques-Antoine Bresch *fls*).
Naxos 8 553639 (50 minutes: DDD). Recorded 1995.   ⓈⓅ

Five solo flutes is not a sound you hear every day, and when those flutes are mellow-toned baroque-style instruments, all copies of a single Flemish model dating from the 1720s, then you really do have something to make you sit up and take notice. Boismortier may have written over 100 opus numbers, but only one of them was devoted to this unusual instrumental combination, and we may speculate that whatever it was that inspired him to such innovation was also enough to prevent him from falling victim to the facility for which he was, and still is, so often criticized. And in any case in Op. 15, published in 1727, he was a man with a mission. These were the first works by a Frenchman to carry the Italian appellation 'concerto', and indeed their style, though French in its surface details, clearly derives from the Vivaldian style of ritornello concerto. The soloists of Le Concert Spirituel are fine interpreters of this music, with a polished sense of style and, for the most part, a commendable uniformity of intonation and ensemble (the unison passages are particularly remarkable in this respect). As usual with recordings of complete opus numbers, you probably would not want to listen to this one from beginning to end; but this is pleasantly melodious music and, linked as it is to a strange and beautiful sound, it certainly deserves repeated listening.

Arrigo Boito
Italian 1842-1918

Mefistofele.
Cesare Siepi *bass* Mefistofele; **Mario del Monaco** *ten* Faust; **Renata Tebaldi** *sop* Margherita; **Floriana Cavalli** *sop* Elena; **Lucia Danieli** *mez* Marta, Pantalis; **Piero De Palma** *ten* Wagner, Nereo; **Chorus and Orchestra of the Santa Cecilia Academy / Tullio Serafin.**
Decca Grand Opera 440 054-2DMO2 (two discs: 141 minutes: ADD). Notes, text and translation included. Recorded 1958.   ⓂⒽ

This recording has in Siepi a real Italian bass with a fine sense of line and a genuine enjoyment of Boito's words. Phrases that are often merely snarled are here truly sung, and Siepi's is the only devil to suggest in the quartet that he is trying to seduce Martha, and that he will very probably succeed. There is incisiveness and grain there, too, to add menace to his suavity. Tebaldi gives one of the best accounts of 'L'altra notte' on record, strongly sung and very touching in its suggestion of grieving guilt. Del Monaco sings 'Dai campi, dai prati' without the slightest acknowledgement of its poetry, but the splendour of the sound and his instinctive feeling for *legato* have their own allure, and they give nobility to his finely phrased 'Giunto sul passo estremo'. The recording doesn't allow Serafin to make a sonic spectacular of the outer scenes, but his care for Boito's often rather old-fashioned *cantabile,* his quirky rhythms and orchestral colours is scrupulous throughout.

Alexander Borodin
Russian 1833-1887

Symphonies – No. 1 in E flat major; No. 2 in B minor; No. 3 in A minor. Prince Igor – Overture; Dance of the Polovtsian Maidens; Polovtsian Dances. String Quartet No. 2 in D major – Notturno (orch. N. Tcherepnin). In the Steppes of Central Asia. Petite Suite (orch. Glazunov).
Torgny Sporsén *bass* Gothenburg Symphony Chorus and Orchestra / Neeme Järvi.
DG 435 757-2GH2 (two discs: 148 minutes: DDD). Recorded 1989-91.   Ⓕ

While it is possible to imagine performances of even greater power and finesse in this strangely unfashionable repertoire, Järvi's Borodin set is arguably the best to have apeared in recent years. The extravagant layout means we get not just the symphonies but a rich supplement of orchestral works, including even the *Petite Suite* as arranged by Glazunov. Another rarity, Nikolay Tcherepnin's orchestration of the famous *Notturno* will astonish those familiar with the chaste original: Tcherepnin transforms it into an exotic Scriabin-like tableau, almost as remote from Borodin as its kitschy *Kismet* mutation. The more recognizable *Steppes* are negotiated with ample eloquence and the *Prince Igor* excerpts include a brief contribution from the great Khan himself, reminding us of the music's original operatic context. The main works are equally persuasive. Järvi plays the First Symphony for all its worth, with DG's big, resonant sound boosting the work's symphonic credentials. The unfinished Third is also tougher and more dramatic than usual, no mere pastoral reverie in Järvi's interventionist view. The Second Symphony is rather different, suitably epic and yet unusually long-drawn and thoughtful. Thus, the *Scherzo* is bubbling but sensibly articulate, while the *Andante* is daringly broad with a superbly sensitive horn solo.

Symphony No. 2 in B minor. In the Steppes of Central Asia. Prince Igor – Overture;
Polovtsian Dances; Polovtsian March.
Royal Philharmonic Orchestra / Ole Schmidt.
Tring International TRP104 (65 minutes: DDD). Recorded 1996. ⑤ **E**

This is an excellent version of the Second Symphony, beautifully played and recorded, and with an ideal coupling, at super-budget price, making it an outstanding bargain. In the first movement of the Symphony Schmidt avoids the pitfall of adopting too slow a speed, avoiding any ponderousness, while giving the music an idiomatically earthy tang. So, the flurries at the opening have a fiercely Slavonic bite, heightened by the way that Schmidt slightly exaggerates the pauses between them, and from then on rhythms are delectably strong. After that brisk first movement Schmidt takes a relatively relaxed view of the *Scherzo*. At a nicely flowing tempo the great horn solo of the slow movement is gloriously played by the RPO's longtime principal, Jeffrey Bryant. In the finale Schmidt springs rhythms so infectiously that the music is given panache rather than fierceness or urgency, with the second subject melody emerging with extra warmth. The rich, open orchestral sound is just as impressive in the fill-ups. The *Prince Igor* Overture brings more glorious horn-playing, while the Polovtsian Dances and March show off the brilliance of the RPO wind soloists. Percussion is superbly caught too, as it is in the Symphony, and at a broad, flowing speed *In the Steppes of Central Asia* could hardly be more evocative, highlighting its thematic links to *Prince Igor*.

String Quartet No. 2 in A major.

Borodin String Quartet No. 2[a].
Shostakovich String Quartet No. 8 in C minor, Op. 110[a].
Tchaikovsky String Quartet No. 1 in D major, Op. 11[b].
[a]**Borodin Quartet** (Rostislav Dubinsky, Jaroslav Alexandrov *vns* Dmitri Shebalin *va* Valentin Berlinsk, *vc*);
[b]**Gabrieli Quartet** (Kenneth Sillito, Brendan O'Reilly *vns* Ian Jewel *va* Keith Harvey *vc*).
Decca 425 541-2DM (76 minutes: ADD). Recorded [a]1962 and [b]1976. Ⓜ **RR**

A slightly curious compilation (two Russian performances dating from 1962, one English from 1976) but an attractive one, and very good value. The Borodin Quartet plays its eponymous composer's affectionate tribute to his wife with a charming demureness shading the ardour, and in the sharply characterized finale manages even to hint that Shostakovich (and in C minor – after all this D major!) will be the next composer on the programme. He is, and its reading of his Eighth Quartet is nobly expressive as well as exhaustingly virtuoso. As a tiny bonus for Shostakovich scholars there is even an interesting variant reading towards the end of the third movement. If you have not heard the Gabrieli's Tchaikovsky before, you will probably like it a great deal: properly chamber-scale, in colour as well as tone of voice, and nice underlining of the lyricism even in Tchaikovsky's most exuberant pages. The recordings still sound very well, slightly close but very clean for the Gabrieli, a little more open for the Borodin.

String Quartet No. 2. String Quintet in F minor. Serenata alla spagnola.
Alexander Gotthelf *vc* **Moscow String Quartet** (Alexander Detisov, Alexander Gelfat *vns* Igor Suliga *va* Alexander Osokin *vc*).
CdM Russian Season RUS288 142 (60 minutes: DDD). Recorded 1995-96. Ⓕ

Formed in 1970, the Moscow Quartet comprises four members of Vladimir Spivakov's Moscow Virtuosi. Theirs is an eminently recommendable (and truthfully engineered) reading of the gorgeous Second Quartet, though admiration for the Borodin Quartet's Decca recording is certainly not diminished. The brief but delectable *Serenata alla spagnola* (1886) was Borodin's contribution to a Quartet co-written with Glazunov, Liadov and Rimsky-Korsakov for their patron Mitrofan Belayev, whereas the fluent, undemanding String Quintet is extremely early, probably dating from the second half of the 1850s. Both receive persuasive treatment here.

Borodin Song of the dark forest. The sleeping princess. The pretty girl no longer loves me. The fishermaiden. Listen to my song, little friend. For the shores of thy far native land. Pride. Arabian melody. The magic garden. Those folk. The sea princess.
Dargomïzhsky Elegy (Deep down). I am in love, my maiden, my beauty. The worm. It is both tedious and sad. The night zephyr stirs the air. I am sad. The Miller. Lullaby. The Titular Councillor. It's all the same to me. Eastern romance. The Old Corporal.
Sergei Leiferkus bar **Leonid Gorokhov** vc **Semion Skigin** pf
Conifer Classics 75605 51275-2 (63 minutes: DDD). Texts and translations included.
Recorded 1996.　　　　　　　　　　　　　　　　　　　　　　　　　　Ⓕ

This is beautiful and original music. Leiferkus includes about two-thirds of Borodin's total output, and makes out a good case for their range by skilfully modifying tone and manner to each of their various needs. Perhaps he is rather overemphatic with *Song of the dark forest*, but it does help to set in contrast his charmingly tender handling of *The sleeping princess* and the warmth he brings to *For the shores of thy far native land*, skilfully invoking the richness of Schumann. *The pretty girl no longer loves me* is ruefully not tragically sung, with a sly tinge of irony. Dargomïzhsky, more of a Slavophile than Borodin, had the realism and the sharp wit to turn various poems into little dramatic sketches that depend more on sharp observation than on forms. *The Titular Councillor* who gets rejected paces away from the girl with an awkward dignity exactly caught in Semion Skigin's stiff rhythms and Leiferkus's mock dignity. Pushkin's miller, drunkenly muddling his boots with a pair of buckets, lurches with a good deal less security. *The worm* who allows the Count's attentions to his wife attracts a brilliant sarcasm. And nothing in this whole recital is more affecting than the handling of what is perhaps Dargomïzhsky's masterpiece among his songs, the scena in which the old corporal who has insulted a young popinjay of an officer stiffens up his comrades' resolve and sets the pace as they march to where he must be shot. A last puff at his pipe, an angry rejection of a blindfold, and he wishes them a safe journey home. Leiferkus's refusal of sentimentality, and Skigin's quiet delivery of the very short postlude, say all that need be said.

Prince Igor.
Mikhail Kit bar Igor; **Galina Gorchakova** sop Yaroslavna; **Gegam Grigorian** ten Vladimir; **Vladimir Ognovenko** bass Prince Galitzky; **Bulat Minjelkiev** bass Khan Kontchak; **Olga Borodina** mez Kontchakovna; **Nikolai Gassiev** ten Ovlour; **Georgy Selezniev** bass Skula; **Konstantin Pluzhnikov** ten Eroshka; **Evgenia Perlasova** mez Nurse; **Tatyana Novikova** sop Polovtsian Maiden; **Kirov Opera Chorus and Orchestra / Valery Gergiev.**
Philips 442 537-2PH3 (three discs: 209 minutes: DDD). Notes, text and translation included.
Recorded 1993.　　　　　　　　　　　　　　　　　　　　　　　　　　Ⓕ Ⓢ

Prince Igor, even after 18 years of work, remained unfinished at Borodin's death in 1887, and it was finally completed by Rimsky-Korsakov and Glazunov. Borodin's main problem with *Prince Igor* was the daunting task of turning what was principally an undramatic subject into a convincing stage work. In many ways he never really succeeded in this and the end result comes over more as a series of epic scenes rather than a musical drama. Despite this, however, one is nevertheless left with an impression of a rounded whole, and it contains some of Borodin's most poignant and moving music, rich in oriental imagery and full of vitality. Curious things happen long before the official surprises of this vitally fresh *Prince Igor*, not least in the Overture, where Gergiev takes the horn's beautiful melody at a very slow pace. Gergiev is anxious to prepare us for the weighty events which follow and his particular point with the theme is to relate it to its place in the opera as the heart of Igor's great aria. There, in league with the bass-baritonal timbre of Gergiev's prince, Mikhail Kit, it solemnly underlines the fact that this is an aria of potency frustrated, sung by a hero who spends most of the opera in captivity; and that is further emphasized by a second aria which no listener will ever have heard before. It is the most significant of the passages discovered among Borodin's papers, rejected by Rimsky-Korsakov in his otherwise sensitive tribute to Borodin's memory but specially orchestrated for this recording by Yuri Faliek.

The other problem with the *Prince Igor* we already know is the way that Act 3 rather weakly follows its much more imposing Polovtsian predecessor. Gergiev obviates both that, and the problem of too much time initially spent in Igor's home town of Putivl, by referring to a structural outline of Borodin's dating from 1883 which proposes alternating the Russian and Polovtsian acts. In the theatre, we might still want the famous Polovtsian *divertissement* as a centrepiece; but on the recording the new order works splendidly, not least because Gergiev is at his fluent best in the scenes of Galitzky's dissipation and Yaroslavna's despair, now making up the opera's Second Act. While Borodina executes Kontchakovna's seductive chromaticisms with astonishing breath control and focus of tone, Bulat Minjelkiev's Kontchak is a little too free and easy, at least in comparison with Ognovenko's perfectly gauged Galitzky, a rogue who needs the extra rebellion music of the more recent version to show more threatening colours. There's just the right degree of relaxation, too, about his drunken supporters Skula and Eroshka. It takes two Russian character-singers to make sense of this pair – 'with our wine and our cunning we will never die in Russia', they tell us truthfully – and their comical capitulation on Igor's return wins respect for Borodin's daring happy-end transition here. It's beautifully paced by Pluzhnikov, Selezniev and their conductor, and crowned by a choral cry of joy which brings a marvellous rush of tearful adrenalin. That leaves us with Gorchakova, so touching in Yaroslavna's first aria but not always projecting the text very vividly and clearly not at her best in the big scena of the last act. Still, in terms of long-term vision, orchestral detail and strength of ensemble, Gergiev is ahead of the competition.

Daniel Börtz

Swedish 1943

Marie Antoinette.
Olle Persson bar Axel von Fersen; **Mikael Axelsson** bass Silfversparre, Judge/Executioner; **Rolf Lindqvist** sngr Bartolin; **Ulf Lundmark** bar Lambert; **Katarina Nilsson** sop Marie Antoinette; **Fredrik Zetterström** bar Louis XVI; **Ann Hallenberg** mez Princess Lamballe; **Ellen Andreassen** mez Countess Polignac; **Malin Gjörup** sop Page; **Marianne Eklöf** mez Madame de la Motte; **Stephen Smith** ten Rohan; **Bo Rosenkull** bar Saint-Priest; **Olle Sköld** bass Orléans; **Erling Larsen** ten Gustav III, Surgeon, Guard;
Swedish Folk Opera Chorus and Orchestra / Kerstin Nerbe.
Caprice CAP22047 (three discs: 152 minutes: DDD). Notes and text included. Recorded live in 1998. Ⓜ

Marie Antoinette, came straight to the 1998 Brighton Festival and then, commendably hot on its heels, came the recording. Thanks to its fine quality – acoustic depth matched by spatial breadth and vividly distributed detail – the ecstasies and the agonies of Marie Antoinette's love for the Swedish Count Axel von Fersen in a time of revolution are focused compellingly for private listening. Until this and his *Bacchae* opera (*Baccanterna*), Börtz had been best known for essentially small-scale chamber and solo works. And it is this co-existence of a broad dramatic canvas, characteristically stretching across shifting time-scales, and a fine eye for detail and imaginatively spare use of full orchestral resources which now distinguishes Börtz as a composer of music drama. For that is what *Marie Antoinette* must be called. As Börtz time-travels between the Paris of 1789 and the Stockholm of 1810, where Marie Antoinette and Axel meet their respective deaths at the hands of a revolutionary mob, the shifting levels of recession between past and future, dream and reality, art (Purcell and Gluck) and life, are expressed through a virtuoso range of vocal expression.

Chamber-musical textures express what words cannot: in the first love duet, a solo violin gives coherent voice to what Marie and Axel express only haltingly. And a miniature concerto for orchestra brings an austere, almost ritualized tone to Marie Antoinette's trial scene. Her solo melismas soar above its verbosity, and lead to a final, beautifully declaimed prayer for forgiveness; Axel's last moments are met by the dry bones of a dance of death, and a final superimposition of lenses as the mob's laughter, Börtz's characteristic orchestral tone clusters, and strains of rococo music merge. One appreciates to the full Börtz's shifting kaleidoscope of minor characters, sympathizing, gossiping, intriguing. The casting provides a vivid palette of characters, from Malin Gjörup's piping Page and Erling Larsen's versatile Surgeon/Gustav III/Guard to Marie Antoinette herself. The title-role is splendidly created by the young soprano, Katarina Nilsson, whose wide and brilliantly focused range incarnates the sentient, the sensual and the noble in the beleaguered Queen. Sweden's great Iago and Don Giovanni, Olle Persson, is the powerful and many-faceted Axel; mezzo-soprano Marianne Eklöf the sinister and scheming Madame de la Motte. Those who already declare an interest in Franco-Swedish history and/or contemporary Nordic music drama will pounce on this recording: those who don't should hasten to discover what they're missing.

Rutland Boughton

British 1878-1960

The Immortal Hour.
Roderick Kennedy bass Dalua; **Anne Dawson** sop Etain; **David Wilson-Johnson** bar Eochaidh; **Maldwyn Davies** ten Midir;
Geoffrey Mitchell Choir; English Chamber Orchestra / Alan G. Melville.
Hyperion CDD22040 (two discs: 125 minutes: DDD). Notes and text included. Recorded 1983. Ⓜ

Boughton Opera

The Immortal Hour is part of theatrical folklore: in London in the early 1920s it ran, unprecedentedly, for 216 consecutive performances and, shortly afterwards, for a further 160 at the first of several revivals; within a decade it had been played a thousand times. Many in those audiences returned repeatedly, fascinated by the other-worldly mystery of the plot (it concerns the love of a mortal king, Eochaidh, for the faery princess Etain and the destruction of their happiness by her nostalgic longing for the Land of the Ever Young, removed from her memory though it has been by a magic spell) and by the gentle, lyrical simplicity of its music. In the bleak aftermath of 1918, with civil war in Ireland, political instability at home and the names of Hitler, Mussolini and Stalin already emerging from obscurity into the headlines, what blessed escapism this blend of Celtic myth and folk-tinged pentatonic sweetness must have offered.

Legends cannot always withstand revisiting, but Boughton's score still has the power to evoke that world, immediately and effortlessly. The libretto by 'Fiona McLeod' (the *nom de plume* of William Sharp) is post-Rossetti high kitsch, often veering into bathos or becoming embarrassingly over-heated, but it does grope towards something uncomfortably deep in the human psyche, the potentially schizoid fracture-zone between physical and spiritual. It is quiet, sweet music, muted in colour and softly plaintive in utterance, and whenever the plot demands more than this the opera sags. Midir, the visitant from the Land of the Ever Young who lures Etain away from the mortal world, really needs music of dangerously heady, Dionysiac incandescence – something like that Strauss gave to Bacchus in *Ariadne auf Naxos*, perhaps – but Boughton's vocabulary can run to nothing more transported than the prettily lilting Faery Song and to some pages of folksy lyricism with a few showy high notes for emphasis. No less seriously the music has little dramatic grip. Despite all this, and the consequent evocation of a mythology that is at times a lot closer to Never-Never-Land than to Tir-na-n'Og, *The Immortal Hour* does have a quality, difficult to define, that is genuinely alluring. It is there in the touching purity of Etain's music, as she sings of a beauty she can no longer recall but whose loss is an inassuageable ache (and how movingly Anne Dawson sings the role). It is there in the moments of true darkness that the music achieves: Dalua, the tormented Lord of Shadow conjures up something of the sombre shudder of the supernatural world. The performance could hardly speak more eloquently for the opera. Alan G. Melville allows the music to emerge from and retreat into shadowy silences, all the principal singers are accomplished and the excellent chorus has been placed so as to evoke a sense of space. The recording seldom suggests the studio: it is easy to imagine oneself in the 'dark and mysterious wood' at the world's end where the drama takes place.

Pierre Boulez
French 1925

Répons. Dialogue de l'ombre double[a].
[a]**Alain Damiens** *cl* **Frédérique Cambreling** *hp* **Vincent Bauer** *vib* **Daniel Ciampolini**, **Michel Cerutti** *perc* **Dimitri Vassilakis, Florent Boffard** *pfs*
Ensemble InterContemporain / Pierre Boulez.
DG 20/21 457 605-2GH (61 minutes: DDD). Recorded 1996.   Ⓕ

When it first appeared in 1981, *Répons* was hailed as a breakthrough in the integration of instruments and electronics in a dynamic sound continuum. It is thus not only groundbreaking but also supremely relevant as a model of what it is possible to do creatively with sound in the late twentieth century. The version here is the third, from 1984 although, as so often with Boulez, further expansions are always possible. A 24-piece ensemble is enclosed by the audience, who are in turn surrounded by six instrumental soloists, a physical immersion in sound startlingly conveyed here by the *spatialisateur* computer programme. Only the soloists are electronically transformed, and it is these 'real time' processes that make the musical textures as sensuous as they are complex. Within this convincing overall trajectory, two sections – track 5, with the piano accumulating layers of sound at a relentless rate, and track 10, where the soloists' spiralling resonances carry their own expressive current – are as satisfying musically as anything Boulez has achieved. *Dialogue de l'ombre double* introduces a theatrical dimension, the clarinet's electronic double gradually becoming more mobile and more 'real' than the actual soloist.

Piano Sonatas Nos. 1-3.
Idil Biret *pf*
Naxos 8 553353 (64 minutes: DDD). Recorded 1995.   Ⓢ

It sometimes seems as if Boulez has spent a lifetime paying the penalty for having found composition so easy as a young man. The first two piano sonatas, works of his early twenties, are formidably assured in technique and tremendously rich in ideas. Those sections of the Third Sonata released for performance sound cold and tentative by comparison. Or is it that the Third Sonata's much more extreme rejection of tradition is itself a triumph, an authentic modernity that stands out the more prominently for its individualism? Such thoughts are inspired by Idil Biret's absorbing disc. In the first movement of the First Sonata the broader picture proves to be well fleshed-out, the argument kept on the move, the young composer's impatience and arrogance palpable in Biret's steely touch and the rather dry but never merely harsh recorded sound. The Second Sonata is no less confidently played. Is it in the Second Sonata's diverse finale that premonitions of the Third Sonata's rejections of continuity begin to appear? Quite possibly – and yet the power of the Second Sonata as a whole suggests why such experiments as No. 3 represents could never be a last word for Boulez. This disc is not the first to bring us the three sonatas together, but Biret's musical persuasiveness, and the up-to-date sound, earn this Naxos issue a strong recommendation.

Pli selon pli.
Phyllis Bryn-Julson sop
BBC Symphony Orchestra / Pierre Boulez.
Erato 2292-45376-2 (68 minutes: DDD). Recorded 1981. *Gramophone* Award Winner 1983.　Ⓕ

Pli selon pli, composed between 1957-62, is one of the great pillars of post-war musical modernism. If that proclamation merely makes it sound forbidding, then it could scarcely be less appropriate. 'Pillar' it may be, but as exciting in its moment-to-moment shifts of colour and contour, and as compelling in its command of large-scale dramatic design as anything composed since the great years of Schoenberg and Stravinsky. Easy, no: enthralling and rewarding – yes. This is no grand, single-minded work in the great Germanic symphonic tradition, but a sequence of distinct yet balanced responses to aspects of the great symbolist poet Mallarmé. On his second recording of the piece, Boulez is prepared to let the music expand and resonate, the two large orchestral tapestries enclosing three 'Improvisations', smaller-scale vocal movements in which the authority and expressiveness of Phyllis Bryn-Julson is heard to great advantage. The sound is brilliantly wide-ranging and well balanced, and while the contrast between delicacy and almost delirious density embodied in *Pli selon pli* does take some getting used to, to miss it is to miss one of modern music's most original masterworks. His first version has a special historical status as embodying the composer's view of the work near the time of its actual completion, when forcefulness, and even ferocity, seemed to count for more as foils to the music's moments of relative restraint than the sustained densities so strongly emphasized in the Erato recording.

William Boyce
British 1711-1779

Eight Symphonies, Op. 2.
Academy of Ancient Music / Christopher Hogwood.
L'Oiseau-Lyre 436 761-2OH (61 minutes: DDD). Recorded 1992.　ⒻⓅ

The Boyce *Eight Symphonys* (as he himself spelt the title) are one of the treasures of English eighteenth-century music, cheerful, unassuming and confident, full of good tunes, and typically English in style – their quirky lines, their refusal to follow the regular procedures, their mixture of baroque and classical features, with their fugues declining to remain fugal, their very un-French French overtures: all this is part of their particular charm. Hogwood catches the eccentric character of the music well and gives a great deal of attention to the textural depth of the music and its inner detail. All the fugal movements go well, done with vitality and a feeling for their logic.

Peleus and Thetis. Corydon and Miranda. Incidental music – Florizel and Perdita;
Romeo and Juliet.
Julia Gooding, Philippa Hyde sops **Robin Blaze** counterten **Joseph Cornwell** ten
Andrew Dale Forbes bass **Jilly Bond, Jack Edwards** spkrs
Opera Restor'd / Peter Holman hpd
Hyperion CDA66935 (68 minutes: DDD). Texts included. Recorded 1996.　ⒻⓅ

Boyce was in his time one of the leading theatre composers. *Peleus and Thetis* is a short masque, based on a simple story reminiscent of *Acis and Galatea*, except that here the jealous Jupiter resigns his amorous claims on Thetis on learning that her son would outshine his father (he was of course Achilles). Among the best moments are Peleus's spirited song of defiance, Jupiter's fine, richly contrapuntal one of renunciation and the lovers' duet at the end. Boyce's music has a flavour all its own, and at its best a very appealing one; Peter Holman conducts the piece in lively fashion, and uses singers with a good command of the style. Two of the other items are incidental music to Shakespeare productions. The little amorous competition of Mopsa and Dorcas for *The Winter's Tale* (in *Florizel and Perdita*) will remind the listener of Purcell. It is sung here in something of a brogue, which would probably be more persuasive on stage than on a recording. Then there is a dirge for Romeo and Juliet, a touching, richly harmonized setting of words as Juliet's body is carried across the stage. The 'Pastoral interlude', *Corydon and Miranda*, in which a shepherd chooses between rival claimants for his love, consists of four airs, mostly in a simple, melodious style, but a final fiery one for the girl who loses, linked by recitative, and a final chorus. It isn't great music, but it is tuneful, in a characteristically English way, and it shows sensitivity to the words and their sense. A very agreeable disc.

Joly Braga Santos

Portuguese 1924-1988

Symphonies Nos. 1 and 5.
Portuguese Symphony Orchestra / Alvaro Cassuto.
Marco Polo 8 223879 (67 minutes: DDD). Recorded 1997.   Ⓕ **S**

Portugal has never figured large in our musical consciousness in England, and until very recently the name of Joly Braga Santos had been all but unrepresented in the catalogue here. His output was considerable and the disc suggests that a symphonist of some stature has been overlooked. His First Symphony, created in 1946 at the age of 22 in memory of those fallen in the Second World War, is couched in a largely modal idiom with some kinship to Sibelius and, more particularly, Vaughan Williams, and reveals a gift for structure, highly effective orchestration and for the writing of long, flowing melodic lines. But the Fifth Symphony of 20 years later (which won a UNESCO prize) – of which there *was* once a Decca LP recording – is a totally different matter. Scored for a huge orchestra including a percussion section of 12 who in the fascinating second movement handle an absolute forest of marimbas, it colourfully reflects the composer's visit to Mozambique (then a Portuguese colony) and is written in a wilder, completely atonal but not dodecaphonic idiom – though it ends unexpectedly on a chord of F major. The composer's close friend Alvaro Cassuto, director since its foundation in 1993 of the Portuguese Symphony Orchestra, has moulded it into a body of international quality: its deeply committed performances here impressively make us aware of Braga Santos. Fantastic recorded sound, especially in the Fifth's massive, cataclysmic finale.

Symphonies – No. 3; No. 6ᵃ.
ᵃ**Ana Ester Neves** *sop*
ᵃ**São Carlos National Theatre Chorus; Portuguese Symphony Orchestra / Alvaro Cassuto.**
Marco Polo 8 225087 (65 minutes: DDD). Text and translation included. Recorded 1997.   Ⓕ **S**

Here we have one work from each of Brago Santos's two contrasting compositional periods. Symphony No. 3 (written in 1949) is bound together by a number of common motifs: it is a closely reasoned, strikingly scored work of modal tendencies (occasionally bringing Vaughan Williams to mind); the *Allegro* section of its finale is centred on a brilliant double fugue. A strong, virile symphony whose stature can be ranked with Sibelius – absolutely not to be missed! His Sixth (and last) symphony (1972) is in one movement but several sections, and is curiously disparate in character and idiom. For two-thirds of its length it is purely orchestral, aggressively atonal and disjunctive, with numerous angry outbursts; then it suddenly changes tack to a more consonant choral section and a peaceful, entirely tonal movement for soprano, both settings (in the Galician tongue) of poems by the sixteenth-century Camões. In both works, performance and recording are first-rate.

Johannes Brahms

German 1833-1897

Violin Concerto in D major, Op. 77.

Violin Concerto. Violin Sonata No. 3 in D minor, Op. 108.
Maxim Vengerov *vn*
Chicago Symphony Orchestra / Daniel Barenboim *pf*
Teldec 0630-17144-2 (62 minutes: DDD). Recorded live in 1997-98.   Ⓕ **E** **RR**

Until this recording, Maxim Vengerov's success had rested largely on the Russian romantic and twentieth-century repertory, but here he tackles one of the most formidable war-horses of the central repertory, and emerges equally triumphant. It is a live recording, and it has the feel of one in its tension, the sense of immediate and spontaneous expression, the magnetism, the excitement. It is a performance of extremes, just as felicitous in bravura as in lyrical purity, with wide tonal contrasts. It adds to the feeling of freshness and new discovery that Vengerov uses a formidable cadenza he has written himself. In the slow movement he is light and flexibly songful, with rubato sounding completely natural, never self-conscious, and the finale, taken fast, has a joyful swagger, with a little agogic hesitation before the accented chord each time in the third phrase of the theme, which underlines its folk-like quality. The coupling is an inspired one too, with Barenboim in a double role, freely spontaneous. As for Vengerov, he brings out the mystery in the sonata, as well as the power. The recording of both works is clear and full, with the violin not unduly spotlit.

Brahms Violin Concerto.
Sibelius Violin Concerto in D minor, Op. 47.
Tasmin Little *vn*
Royal Liverpool Philharmonic Orchestra / Vernon Handley.
EMI Eminence CD-EMX2203 (72 minutes: DDD). Recorded 1991.　　　　Ⓜ

Tasmin Little admits that she prefers not to commit her interpretations to disc until she has 'something to say and the means with which to say it'. That is certainly the case with the Brahms Concerto, a clear, considered reading (much aided in the slow movement by Jonathan Small's excellent oboe solo), quite without mannerism and beautifully accompanied by Vernon Handley and the Royal Liverpool Philharmonic. The Sibelius has even more character, and here Little adds to an impressive roster of the work's many great female interpreters (Neveu, Wicks, Bustabo, Ignatius, etc). Handley is an impressive Sibelian whose feel for the idiom is apparent in every bar, and both recordings are excellent. As a coupling the two performances are irresistible.

Brahms Violin Concerto.
Schumann Violin Concerto in D minor, Op. posth.
Joshua Bell *vn*
Cleveland Orchestra / Christoph von Dohnányi.
Decca 444 811-2DH (68 minutes: DDD). Recorded 1994.　　　　Ⓕ

Bell's first entry in the Brahms instantly demonstrates the soloist's love of bravura display, his gift for turning a phrase individually in a way that catches the ear, always sounding spontaneous, never self-conscious. Regularly one registers moments of new magic, not least when, in the most delicate half-tones, *pianissimos* seem to convey an inner communion, after which the impact of bravura *fortissimos* is all the more dramatic. He rounds off the movement with his own big cadenza and a magically hushed link into the coda, rapt and intense. The slow movement, sweet and songful, gains too from Bell's love of playing really softly, not least in stratospheric registers. In the finale the vein of fantasy is less apparent. Next to others this can seem a little plain. Dohnányi and the Cleveland Orchestra provide weighty and sympathetic support and the generous Schumann coupling in another commanding performance adds to the attractions of the disc. There too Dohnányi and the Cleveland Orchestra add to the weight and dramatic impact of a performance that defies the old idea of this as an impossibly flawed piece, with Bell bringing out charm as well as power. The central slow movement has a rapt intensity rarely matched, and the dance-rhythms of the finale have fantasy as well as jauntiness and jollity, with Bell again revelling in the bravura writing. The recording is full-bodied and well balanced.

Violin Concerto. Double Concerto in A minor, Op. 102.
Gidon Kremer *vn* **Clemens Hagen** *vc*
Royal Concertgebouw Orchestra / Nikolaus Harnoncourt.
Teldec 0630-13137-2 (69 minutes: DDD). Recorded live in 1996-97.　　　　Ⓕ

A radical rethink of two great concertos and as good a justification as any for repertoire duplication. These captivating performances illustrate Harnoncourt's habitual fondness for tapered phrase-shaping and pin-sharp articulation. Kremer's first entry in the Violin Concerto is bold and forceful, and yet listen to his sensitive handling of the triplets at 4'43" or his knowing interpretation of Brahms's prescribed *piano lusingando* at 14'50" and the degree of his perception soon registers. He plays a startlingly original 1903 cadenza by Enescu and takes a swift view of the *Andante*, albeit one that is both lissom and flexible. The finale, on the other hand, suggests the impulsive gaiety of a Hungarian dance (the charming 'hiccup' that characterizes the opening theme is fairly typical), with fast speeds and rugged textures. Generally speaking, it is a more daring, less overtly 'virtuoso' Violin Concerto than other versions. In the Double Concerto Clemens Hagen employs a subtle, variegated tonal palette and Harnoncourt underlines the concerto's symphonic dimensions (especially in the first movement). The *Andante* second movement moves on, lasting 6'06", and the effect suggests parallels with the piano *Intermezzos* or even the middle movements of the Third Symphony. Intimate interludes abound but time and again one senses, above all, great strength of purpose, particularly in the return of the first theme. Harnoncourt, Kremer, Hagen and the orchestra invest both concertos with a wealth of insights, leaving nothing to chance but within a highly spontaneous interpretative framework. Like Harnoncourt's Brahms symphonies, they will usefully supplement – if not always challenge – other fine (perhaps sweeter-toned) recordings. The sound is pleasingly ambient, with precious few coughs or extraneous noises and no applause.

Brahms Violin Concerto.
Tchaikovsky Violin Concerto in D major, Op. 35.
Jascha Heifetz vn
Chicago Symphony Orchestra / Fritz Reiner.
RCA Victor Living Stereo 09026 61495-2 (64 minutes: ADD). Recorded 1955 and 1957.   Ⓜ 🅷

This combination appears unbeatable. You may think that Reiner starts the opening tutti at an extraordinarily quick speed – until you remember that he is going to accompany no less a virtuoso than Heifetz, so he is merely taking it to match his soloist's performance. You will like this if you think that this concerto is too often played in the kind of 'autumnal' manner often attributed to Brahms's compositions but which really should not apply to many of them. With Heifetz it is played with respect but without any kind of reverent hushed awe. The slow movement is lovely and the finale is a winner, the playing of an exuberant young man, yet Heifetz was over 50 when he made this record. Reiner conducts the fast movement with a fiery rhythmic impetus that incandescently matches the exhilarating, yet unforced bravura of his great soloist. It is entirely confident throughout – and just listen to his real *staccato*, a rare thing from violinists. The RCA recording comes up extraordinarily well – although the soloist is balanced forwardly, he is naturally focused and the Chicago acoustic ensures a convincing concert-hall balance. If anything, the remastering of the Tchaikovsky is even more remarkable, considering that originally Heifetz was apparently placed right up against the microphone. One soon adapts to the closeness when the fiddle-playing is so peerless; and Heifetz colours Tchaikovsky's melodies ravishingly. The gentle Russian melancholy of the *Canzonetta* is perfectly caught, too.

Piano Concertos – No. 1 in D minor, Op. 15; No. 2 in B flat major, Op. 83.

Piano Concertos Nos. 1 and 2. Seven Piano Pieces, Op. 116.
Emil Gilels pf
Berlin Philharmonic Orchestra / Eugen Jochum.
DG The Originals 447 446-2GOR2 (two discs: 125 minutes: ADD). Recorded 1972-75.   Ⓜ 🆁🆁

The booklet-notes make reference to the original *Gramophone* review, in which Gilels and Jochum were praised for 'a rapt songfulness that in no way detracts from Brahms's heroism, and so comes closer to that unique and complex combination of attitudes that for me is Brahms more than any other performances of these concertos I have ever heard, on records or otherwise'. One might add that Jochum and the Berlin Philharmonic make plain sailing where others struggle with choppy cross-currents (admittedly sometimes to Brahms's advantage) and that the recordings don't sound their age. Other interpreters have perhaps probed a little deeper here and there; neither concerto rests content with a single interpretation, the Second especially. As for the Seven Piano Pieces, Gilels viewed the opus as a single piece, a musical novella in several chapters.

Piano Concertos[a] Nos. 1 and 2. Scherzo in E flat minor, Op. 4. Four Ballades, Op. 10.
Eight Pieces, Op. 76.
Stephen Kovacevich pf
London Symphony Orchestra / Sir Colin Davis.
Philips 442 109-2PM2 (two discs: 141 minutes: ADD/DDD). Recorded [a]1979 and 1983.   Ⓜ

This performance of the First is extremely fine. Stephen Kovacevich brings to it a vast amount of eloquence, tenderness and lyrical feeling and he is more poetic and imaginative than most of his rivals. In the slow movement there is much inwardness of feeling, without any attempt either to over- or understate the leonine, combative side of the solo part. Sir Colin Davis and the LSO give him sympathetic support and it is only a pity that although the balance between soloist and orchestra is well judged, the overall sound is opaque. If the recording had been as distinguished as the solo playing, this would have been a truly outstanding reading. But for those who are prepared to make allowances for the sound recording, this No. 1 offers huge musical rewards. However, the Second must be numbered among the very finest available, and the recording is far more successful. This is every bit as well balanced as its companion but detail is infinitely more transparent. The performance combines poetic feeling and intellectual strength in no small measure. The first movement unfolds without any false urgency and momentum; it is spacious, autumnal, reflective as well as majestic. The second movement is sparkling and fresh and it is difficult to recall a more beautiful account of the slow movement. In the *Più adagio* section he is quite magical, and in the bars that precede this, he is rapt and poetic without going over the top. There is wit, delicacy and poetry in the finale, too. Some may feel that it is almost too relaxed and smiling, but he captures the lambent qualities of texture. As with the First Concerto, Sir Colin provides impeccable support throughout and the unnamed cellist in the slow movement plays with both tenderness and nobility.

In the E flat minor *Scherzo* and the *Ballades* Kovacevich's playing reminds you strongly that this was the music of a pianist-composer, writing for the instrument with a keener ear for texture and tone colour than he is often given credit for. The *Scherzo*, for instance, is not just big and burly all the way through, but sufficiently lithe and crystalline in the recurrent main theme to bring home the full contrast of the sumptuously sustained second trio. He is just as keen in response to the exploratory textures of the *Ballades*. The eight pieces of Op. 76 already pre-echo the intimate keyboard confessions of Brahms's last years – especially No. 3 which Kovacevich plays with exquisite delicacy and tenderness. Throughout the solo works Kovacevich stresses the composer's impressionability more than his intensity. But as imagination is coupled with the most scrupulous regard for the letter of the text, the musical results are always refreshing. The recorded sound is clear.

Brahms Piano Concerto No. 1[a].
Franck Symphonic Variations[b].
Litolff Concerto symphonique No. 4 in D minor, Op. 102 – Scherzo[b].
Sir Clifford Curzon *pf*
[a]London Symphony Orchestra / George Szell;
[b]London Philharmonic Orchestra / Sir Adrian Boult.
Decca Legends 466 376-2DM (74 minutes: ADD). Recorded [a]1962, [b]1955. Ⓜ Ⓗ ℝℝ

It is debatable as to whether there is any other recording of the D minor Concerto that so instantly takes fire and which burns thereafter with so pure and steady a flame. To all outward appearances, Curzon and Szell were an oddly contrasted couple; yet they worked wonderfully well together, in Mozart and here in Brahms. The 1962 recording still comes up phenomenally well, despite some occasional muzzling of the orchestra's bass texturing. A merciful muzzling, you might think, given the frequency with which Szell detects and detonates the small arsenal of explosive devices Brahms has hidden in the undergrowth. We obviously don't lack great recordings of this concerto but this 1962 Decca version remains as collectable as any. The fill-ups to this repackaged CD are also welcome. The Franck is beginning to sound its age technically but the performance is charming. As for the Litolff, it is irresistible, a gem of a performance, well recorded.

Piano Concerto No. 1. Zwei Gesänge, Op. 91.
Stephen Kovacevich *pf*
Ann Murray *mez* **Nobuko Imai** *va*
London Philharmonic Orchestra / Wolfgang Sawallisch.
EMI CDC7 54578-2 (59 minutes: DDD). Texts and translations included.
Gramophone Award Winner 1993. Ⓕ Ⓢ

This is an altogether exceptional account of this leonine, beautiful, but often elusive work. It is one of those profoundly musical performances, thought out in a myriad small details, that at the same time flows freely and spontaneously from the minds and imaginations of musicians for whom the work is no longer a thing to be mastered but an experience to be wonderingly relived. The disc also offers the most imaginative and raptly performed fill-ups imaginable on a Brahms concerto record. The concerto over, Kovacevich is joined by mezzo-soprano Ann Murray and viola player Nobuko Imai for two of Brahms's greatest songs: his setting of Rückert's beautiful eventide poem *Gestillte Sehnsucht* and the sublime *Geistliches Wiegenlied*, a lullaby to the Christ child that bleakly foreshadows the agony that is to come. How wonderfully this song casts its shadow back over the concerto, making us ponder afresh the spiritual meaning of its great slow movement. As for that slow movement, it has rarely been more sensitively played or recorded than it is here. Kovacevich performs the music with astonishing fine-toned inwardness – the playing fabulously underpinned by the LPO's awed and extraordinarily hushed accompaniment.

Piano Concerto No. 1. Three Piano Pieces, Op. 117.
Leif Ove Andsnes *pf*
City of Birmingham Symphony Orchestra / Sir Simon Rattle.
EMI CDC5 56583-2 (64 minutes: DDD). Recorded 1998. Ⓕ

Rattle's CBSO players match desk for desk the leading rivals in this formidable, thrilling and superbly directed account of the D minor Concerto. The sonorities are full and dark, the string sound centred in the violas and cellos. The timpani playing is also outstanding, with magnificent articulation of the hallmark trills, themselves flawlessly matched to the huge answering trills of soloist and full orchestra. It is an expressive performance which also has tremendous drive and contrapuntal clarity, the agogic shifts never drawing attention to themselves. The *pianissimo* string playing in the slow movement has to be heard to be believed, intensely quiet yet with a 'nerve' in it (as Pavarotti once said of Karajan's *pianissimo*). The performance is not in any way in thrall to urbanity and polish. True, it is not as self-evidently weighty as that older generation of players – Arrau and Backhaus, for example – whose phrasing of a Brahms melody, as it were, takes you by the elbow. You notice this more in Andsnes's fill-up, the Op. 117 *Intermezzos*, where No. 2 is exquisitely done, a hauntingly lovely reverie, but where No. 1 is inclined to be mannered (the opening sentence fractured by odd phrasing and too marked a *ritardando* at the end) and the opening of No. 3 is not at all ominous. The performance of the concerto, however, is certainly not lacking in *gravitas* or power. Indeed, the more you hear it the more aware you are of just how formidable Andsnes's playing is technically, and how mature emotionally. The recording is magnificent, of demonstration quality. Aided by that superb recording, the Concerto has about it a true sense of 'occasion', with beauties, excitements and moments of torrential splendour that are distinctively and thrillingly its own.

Brahms Piano Concerto No. 1[a].
Mozart Piano Concerto No. 23 in A major, K488[b].
Sir Clifford Curzon *pf*
National Symphony Orchestra / [a]**Enrique Jordá,** [b]**Boyd Neel.**
Dutton Laboratories Essential Archive mono CDEA5507 (72 minutes: ADD). Recorded 1945. ⑧🄷

Since Sir Clifford Curzon's recorded output is a slim volume of finely crafted work, there is nothing here that is not germane. The Brahms gets prime billing on the CD cover which initially may not seem like a good idea. Jordá's conducting is sensitive and sure-footed but workmanlike rather than inspired, the playing of the National Symphony Orchestra (already being plundered by Legge and Beecham) marvellous in places but not 100 per cent reliable. (The horns are specially fallible.) Yet, for all that, you will find yourself listening spellbound to Curzon's playing. This is the Curzon who, at the age of 39, was only emerging into the full light of an international career after a long and inspiring apprenticeship with such teachers as Artur Schnabel and Nadia Boulanger. Indeed, it is that very *emergent* quality which gives his performance a freshness and shy-voiced eloquence which has the effect of setting the young Brahms vividly and appealingly before us. It is the Mozart, though, which ravishes sense. This is a performance of rare lucidity and grace which has about it all the clarity and radiance of a revealed truth. It is also marvellously well accompanied. Boyd Neel was a master of clear texturing and balanced tempos. This isn't the Boyd Neel Orchestra itself, but it sounds like it. No doubt it contained many old friends. At the time there were stern things said about surface noise and extraneous whines on the original 78s of the Brahms. Dutton's flawless transfers suggest that Mike Dutton is either a miracle-worker or has had access to better copies. The Mozart seems to have been in pretty good sound from the very start. Happily so, since, in the last resort, the recording of the Brahms *is* a period relic. The Mozart, by contrast, is timeless. Which is why this is a performance to be treasured as well as enjoyed.

Piano Concerto No. 2. Four Ballades, Op. 10.
Emil Gilels *pf*
Berlin Philharmonic Orchestra / Eugen Jochum.
DG Classikon 439 466-2GCL (77 minutes: ADD). Recorded 1972. ⑧🆁🆁

This has excitement, breadth of vision, warmth and humanity in perfect balance. Gilels and Jochum bring such warmth and humanity to the score as well as a magisterial authority that they carry all before them. But Gilels can also be tender and delicate as well, as the slow movement and finale shows: the prevailing calm of the slow movement is exquisite and the Berlin solo cello contributes a good deal to its effect, while much of the playing in the finale is of the utmost delicacy. This is a great bargain and if you have not acquired Gilels's Second already, it is a 'must', whatever other versions you may already have. The digital remastering for CD has been entirely beneficial. The overall sound is fresher, the bass resonance very slightly modulated, but the rich Brahmsian textures remain satisfyingly full and the piano timbre is well focused and natural. Moreover, we have extra bounty in Gilels's recordings of the *Ballades*, again with good sound quality.

Piano Concerto No. 2.
Maurizio Pollini *pf*
Berlin Philharmonic Orchestra / Claudio Abbado.
DG 453 505-2GH (49 minutes: DDD). Recorded live in 1995. ⑤

Pollini's and Abbado's Second is among the most formidably single-minded on record. This does not mean a chilling exclusivity, one that, humanly speaking, omits too much in its quest for a crystalline perfection. On the contrary, the sense is of a granitic reading stripped of all surplus gesture, preening mannerism or overt display, intent only on the unveiling of a musical or moral truth. Again, this is hardly the sort of performance which allows you to savour this or that pianistic luxury, to delight in spectacular octaves here or a ravishing *dolce* there, and there will be listeners who, more in love with pianism than with great music-making, will turn away awed but unmoved, ultimately feeling short-changed. Their opening at once suggests a promise of the epic journey to come and in that moment when, as Tovey once put it, 'the air seems full of whispering and the beating of mighty wings' their performance achieves a rare sense of transcendence, of an inspiration above and beyond the printed page. Again, in the *Scherzo* or *Allegro appassionato* Brahms's octave and double-note play at 5'00" is less an opportunity for technical wizardry than a scarifying musical commentary. It is also doubtful whether many artists have achieved such sublimity in the *Andante* (not forgetting the Berlin Philharmonic's most eloquent but unsung cellist) where they combine, most notably in the *Più adagio*, to create an astonishing sense of 'the still centre of the turning world'. Their way, too, with Brahms's 'great and child-like finale' (Tovey again) has a tensile strength that forbids all dalliance. This recording is a memento of a grand and almost palpable occasion that clearly stunned its audience – there is never a sneeze or sniffle – into submission. Here, surely, is a performance above the vagaries of changing taste and fashion; one which could achieve a timeless validity.

Piano Concerto No. 2. Lieder, Op. 105.
Stephen Kovacevich *pf* **Ann Murray** *mez*
London Philharmonic Orchestra / Wolfgang Sawallisch.
EMI CDC5 55218-2 (62 minutes: DDD). Texts and translations included.   Ⓕ **S**

Brahms's song of the dying girl, 'Immer leiser wird mein Schlummer', recalls with tender pathos the ghostly half-remembered outline of the theme of the slow movement of the Second Piano Concerto. It is one of five songs that make up his Op. 105 Lieder and it is marvellous to have not only this song so sympathetically performed by Ann Murray and Stephen Kovacevich but the whole group. Three of the songs are decently represented on record – 'Immer leiser', the thrilling 'Auf dem Kirchhofe' and the soaringly lovely 'Wie Melodien zieht es mir'. But until this you would have sought in vain the group as a group. This is a pity when the third song, the folksy 'Klage', makes so delightful a foil to its immediate neighbours, and when the final song, 'Verrat', is such a splendid example of a ballad about homicide, treated by the mature Brahms with a subtlety we don't always find in some of his more bloodcurdlingly dramatic earlier settings.

The rest of the performance is very fine, yet that isn't to say this disc has it all its own way. In the first place, there is still formidable competition from Kovacevich's own 1979 recording. The impression is that at times the newer performance is cooler and more detached than the LSO/Davis version. This may, in part, be an impression fostered by the EMI recording which seems thinner-toned and marginally more distant than the Philips. (Always a risk with a pianist whose skills include the ability to play with an extraordinary inner fineness of timbre and dynamic.) But it is also the conducting. True, No. 2 doesn't begin with the furnace fully stoked. That said, there's a touch of coolness about the orchestral playing in the all-important first-movement exposition and development (things get better in the re-exposition). The fact is, though, that Sawallisch produces a less full-bodied, less emotionally weighty reading of the orchestral part than Davis. The slow movement is here noticeably quicker. Since Brahms marks it *Andante* and since Kovacevich's playing has an even more musing feel to it, you could judge this an advantage. Gilels and Kovacevich with Davis are all slower and more intense. The finale is also quicker by a hair's breadth; but this can tip the scales between success and failure. Kovacevich again plays it with great buoyancy, brilliance and charm. It is playing after the manner of Solomon; and it just about works, despite Sawallisch pushing Brahms's *Allegretto* marking to its limit.

Double Concerto in A minor, Op. 102.

Brahms Double Concerto[a].
Beethoven Triple Concerto in C major, Op. 56[b].
David Oistrakh *vn* **Mstislav Rostropovich** *vc* [b]**Sviatoslav Richter** *pf*
[a]**Cleveland Orchestra / George Szell;** [b]**Berlin Philharmonic Orchestra / Herbert von Karajan.**
EMI Studio Plus CDM7 64744-2 (70 minutes: ADD). Recorded 1969.   Ⓜ **RR**

These are illustrious performances and make a splendid coupling at mid-price. EMI planned for a long time to assemble this starry line-up of soloists, conductor and orchestra for Beethoven's Triple Concerto, and the artists do not disappoint, bringing sweetness as well as strength to a work which in lesser hands can sound clumsy and long-winded. The recording, made in a Berlin church, is warm, spacious and well balanced, placing the soloists in a gentle spotlight. Indeed, the sound need make no apology for its age, and since we also hear playing of effortless mastery this disc would be worth the money for this work alone. As it is, we also have the same great violinist and cellist playing another masterpiece with another superb orchestra and conductor of the time, this time in Cleveland. This account of Brahms's Double Concerto is perhaps the most powerful recorded performance since the days of Heifetz and Feuermann or Thibaud and Casals. The recording has come up extremely well in this remastering: although one cannot deny that the sound is not as smooth as can be achieved nowadays, one soon forgets that and is caught up in the magnificent music-making. Collectors not already possessing these performances may be confidently urged to acquire this disc.

Double Concerto. Piano Quartet No. 3 in C minor, Op. 60.
Isaac Stern *vn* **Jaime Laredo** *va* **Yo-Yo Ma** *vc* **Emanuel Ax** *pf*
Chicago Symphony Orchestra / Claudio Abbado.
CBS Masterworks MK42387 (68 minutes: DDD).   Ⓕ

The grave, declamatory utterances at the beginning of the Double Concerto tell us much about the nature of what will follow. They can also reveal a great deal about the two soloists who enter in turn with solo cadenzas separated by thematic orchestral material. Perhaps surprisingly, it is the much younger man, Yo-Yo Ma, who brings out most strongly the noble gravity of the composer's inspiration, while the relatively veteran Isaac Stern is more melodious and spontaneous-sounding. The music's steady but unhurried paragraphs are very well handled by Claudio Abbado and the excellent Chicago Symphony Orchestra is responsive and pretty faithfully balanced with the soloists. This is a performance to satisfy rather than to thrill, perhaps, but satisfy it does. The recording is rich and rather reverberant, notably in orchestral tuttis. The powerful C minor Piano Quartet is also well played and provides a substantial partner to the concerto. Apparently Brahms once said that it had the mood of a man thinking of suicide, but one hastens to say that it is nothing like as gloomy as that would suggest.

Brahms Double Concerto.
Schumann Cello Concerto in A minor, Op. 129.
Ilya Kaler *vn* **Maria Kliegel** *vc*
National Symphony Orchestra of Ireland / Andrew Constantine.
Naxos 8 550938 (59 minutes: DDD).   Ⓢ Ⓔ

The Brahms and Schumann concertos make an excellent and apt coupling, here on Naxos given warmly spontaneous-sounding performances, very well recorded. The violinist, Ilya Kaler, is as clean in attack and intonation as Maria Kliegel. Kliegel in her opening cadenza allows herself full freedom, but any feeling that this is to be an easygoing, small-scale reading is dispelled in the main *Allegro*, which is clean and fresh, sharp in attack, helped by full-bodied sound. Kaler and Kliegel make the second subject tenderly expressive without having to use exaggerated rubato. Similarly there is no self-indulgence in the soaring main melody of the central *Andante*, but no lack of warmth or tenderness either. The finale is then unhurried but has dance-rhythms so beautifully sprung and such delicate pointing of phrases that any lack of animal excitement is amply replaced by wit and a sense of fun. In the Schumann Kliegel takes a spacious, lyrical view of the first movement, using a soft-grained tone at the start with wide vibrato. She then builds up the power of the performance, and with Constantine providing sympathetic accompaniment, the spontaneous expression is most compelling. So, too, is the simple, dedicated playing in the central *Langsam*, and, as in the Brahms, Kliegel brings witty pointing to the finale, not least in the second subject. The balance of the soloists is good.

---

21 Hungarian Dances.
Stuttgart Radio Symphony Orchestra / Georges Prêtre.
Forlane UCD16770 (57 minutes: DDD). Recorded 1997.   Ⓕ

Georges Prêtre has been honorary guest conductor of the Stuttgart Radio Symphony Orchestra since 1995 and he brings a touch of Gallic flamboyance to these delightful, variously orchestrated dances. The playing is mostly spirited and responsive, and the recording pleasantly blended save that the brass are sometimes a mite recessed. The First *Hungarian Dance* is bouncy and keenly accented; the Fourth features a novel 'question-and-answer' effect between the two halves of the principal melody; the Fifth is more elegant than rustic; the Tenth pleasingly vivacious; the Fourteenth broad and bold (almost like a majestic fragment from one of Brahms's larger orchestral works); the Sixteenth warmly impassioned (with some of the best string-playing on the disc) and the Twentieth employs some telling rubato. There is also a 'CD-ROM/extra multimedia' rehearsal and concert track – six minutes' worth – for use with your PC. This is an enjoyable disc and a fine sampling of a highly competent radio orchestra on good form.

Serenades – No. 1 in D major, Op. 11; No. 2 in A major, Op. 16.
West German Sinfonia / Dirk Joeres.
Carlton Classics 30367 0142-2 (79 minutes: DDD). Recorded 1992.   Ⓜ

If the term serenade suggests something which is open-hearted and uncomplicated then Brahms's two compositions in this form follow classical conventions up to a point. Each work has an appealing geniality and mellow warmth, but Brahms had a perpetually serious side to his nature, and there's always a nearby cloud threatening to move over the sun. Such mixed characteristics are particularly evident in the Second Serenade, which is scored without violins, and lacks the brightness which upper strings bring to orchestral textures. It is no easy task for a conductor to balance the opposing elements in either work, but Dirk Joeres manages this very successfully. He has at his disposal a very fine body of players, who are given clear, high-quality recordings. In the faster, more outgoing sections of each score he points the rhythms very skilfully, and he shapes the slower, more inward movements in a highly sympathetic, attentive fashion. Even the First Serenade's long *Adagio non troppo* movement, which so easily loses direction, is kept on course through Joeres's subtle use of phrase and pulse.

Symphonies – No. 1 in C minor, Op. 68; No. 2 in D major, Op. 73; No. 3 in F major, Op. 90; No. 4 in E minor, Op. 98.

Symphonies Nos. 1-4.
Staatskapelle Dresden / Kurt Sanderling.
RCA Victor Classical Navigator 74321 30367-2 (three discs, aas: 197 minutes: ADD).
Recorded 1971-72.   Ⓑ 🆁🆁
74321 21285-2: No. 1. Tragic Overture, Op. 81. 74321 17894-2: Nos. 2 and 3.
74321 24206-2: No. 4. Variations on a Theme by Haydn, Op. 56a, 'St Antoni Chorale'.

Kurt Sanderling has recorded the Brahms symphonies twice (his first set, with the Berlin Symphony Orchestra, is available on Capriccio), but what started out as solid, patient and well built broadened significantly, and in doing so stressed the epic element that was always implicit in the first recordings: the first movement of the later First Symphony is slower than its predecessor by over two minutes. Sanderling's great strength is in the way he handles Brahms's choppy, obdurate string writing, whether in the First Symphony's strutting first movement *Allegro* or the opening *Allegro non troppo* of the Fourth. Tempos are consistently held firm, the lyrical passages allowed their due only within a solid structural frame (the Third Symphony's middle movement, for example) and first-movement repeats omitted. As ever, it's the Third Symphony that underlines specific interpretative differences between conductors – the first movement especially, a vigorous *Allegro con brio* that, for some reason or other, defeats even the greatest maestros. Sanderling takes a majestic, even marmoreal option that seems misguided: the gestures are grand, certainly, but the music remains rooted to earth. And if ever a piece said 'come fly with me', it is the first movement of Brahms's Third Symphony. So, summing up, Sanderling is sturdy, intelligently phrased, warmly played, fairly well recorded (the strings are a little grainy) and supplemented by equally well-considered accounts of the *Haydn* Variations and *Tragic Overture*.

Symphonies Nos. 1-4. Variations on a Theme by Haydn. Tragic Overture, Op. 81. Academic Festival Overture, Op. 80. Hungarian Dances – No. 1 in G minor; No. 3 in F major; No. 10 in F major. Serenades – No. 1 in D major, Op. 11; No. 2 in A major, Op. 16.
Concertgebouw Orchestra / Bernard Haitink.
Philips Bernard Haitink Symphony Edition 442 068-2PB4 (four discs: 291 minutes: ADD).
Recorded 1970-80.   Ⓑ

Concertgebouw standards at the time of Haitink's survey (1970-80) left little to be desired. Perhaps the clarinets don't always overcome reservations about their tone and intonation with the sensitivity of their phrasing; but the horns invariably do, and more often than not Brahms's favourite instrument is a source of joy in these recordings, blazing gloriously at appropriate moments (especially in the Fourth Symphony), or opening up and sustaining huge vistas in the 'dawn' of the First's finale. As to the strings, Haitink's insistence on firmly defined (though never over-emphatic) rhythms from the bass-lines up is altogether exceptional; there are countless examples, but most memorable of all is the cellos' and basses' ostinato that sees the Second Symphony's finale in the home straight. What an articulate, integrated Brahms sound this is, too; a case of conductor and engineers easily achieving their aims working in a familiar acoustic. Nor is that acoustic to be taken for granted; how unappealing is the equally informative but stark sound of Klemperer's

Philharmonia and Toscanini's NBC tapings in comparison. There is a degree of tape hiss, most noticeable in the Third Symphony where there is also a trace of hardness, and a chill to the string tone in parts of the Second Symphony, but none of this is serious. The only movement you may initially find overly sober is the first of the Third Symphony, taken very broadly, though it is determined and imposing, and the launching of the coda is stupendously powerful. All in all, there is no better way of getting to know the Brahms orchestral works on a budget.

Symphonies Nos. 1-4. Variations on a Theme by Haydn. Academic Festival Overture.
Tragic Overture.
Berlin Philharmonic Orchestra / Nikolaus Harnoncourt.
Teldec 0630-13136-2 (three discs: 214 minutes: DDD). Recorded live in 1996-97.   Ⓕ🅔

Any fears that Nikolaus Harnoncourt's Brahms will be quirky, provocative or abrasive can be dispelled. There are interpretative novelties (freshly considered articulation and clarified counterpoint) and the Berlin strings project a smooth, curvaceous profile. Harnoncourt makes a beeline for the brass, and the horns in particular. The live recordings have remarkable presence and are mostly cough-free. The *Haydn* Variations serves as a useful sampler for Harnoncourt's Brahms style as a whole, with an unforced vitality and many salient details subtly underlined. The First Symphony's opening *Un poco sostenuto* seems a trifle soft-grained but the pounding basses from bar 25 are beautifully caught and the first-movement *Allegro* is both powerful and broadly paced. The *Andante sostenuto* slow movement is both limpid and conversational, with trance-like dialogue between oboe and clarinet and sparing use of vibrato among the strings. Harnoncourt makes real chamber music of the third movement, though he drives the trio section to a fierce climax, and the finale's first accelerating pizzicatos are truly *stringendo poco a poco* – the excitement certainly mounts, but only gradually. The main body of the movement generates considerable tension and moments are overwhelmingly exciting.

The Second Symphony's first movement is relatively restrained. Harnoncourt's strategy is to deliver a sombre exposition and a toughened development. Again, the slow movement is fluid and intimate, with some tender string playing. The third movement's rustling trio is disarmingly delicate and the finale, tightly held, keenly inflected and heavily accented: the coda threatens to break free and the effect is thrilling. First impressions of Harnoncourt's Third suggest a marginal drop in intensity, yet the first movement's peroration is so powerful, so insistent, that one retrospectively suspects that everything prior to it was mere preparation. The middle movements work well but it is the rough-hewn, flexibly-phrased finale that really 'makes' the performance. Like the Third, the Fourth opens with less import than some of its older rivals, yet the development intensifies perceptibly, the recapitulation's hushed *piano dolce* opening bars are held on the edge of a breath and the coda is recklessly headstrong. The slow movement has some heartfelt moments, the top-gear *Scherzo* is quite exhilarating and the finale, forged with the noble inevitability of a baroque passacaglia. Ultimately, Harnoncourt delivers a fine and tragic Fourth. The two overtures are hardly less absorbing. Harnoncourt's Brahms is the perfect antidote to routine, predictability and interpretative complacency.

Symphonies Nos. 1-4.
South West German Radio Symphony Orchestra / Sergiu Celibidache.
DG 459 635-2GH3 (three discs: 166 minutes: ADD). Includes bonus disc of rehearsal of
Symphony No 4. Recorded live in 1974-76.   Ⓕ

Most performances conducted by Sergiu Celibidache (or Celi as he was popularly known) harbour at least one incomparable 'Celi moment', and this set includes plenty. The man was undoubtedly a phenomenon: he could galvanize, mesmerize, enrapture and insinuate even the most bizarre interpretative ideas into your consciousness. As a musical magician, he was peerless; but as an exponent of the Classics, he constantly courted controversy. He abandoned the recording studio soon after the war, and it is only thanks to his son and family that the flood of pirate Celi CDs can at last be challenged by superior authorized alternatives. This particular set is better played and better produced than anything that preceded it. The recorded balance is excellent. Textures are transparent (the woodwinds especially), instrumental perspectives are unusually true and the incredible force of fully scored passages is never compromised. The First Symphony is awe-inspiring. Although the coda is broad, it never drags and the slow movement is something of a minor miracle. It is another one of those moments, but there are more in store, notably in the finale, where slowly interweaving violin desks achieve a perfect *diminuendo*. Another occurs around the famous horn episode, where horns answer each other with incredible power. The celebrated string melody is leisurely and serene, but the tempo soon picks up and the rest of the movement is pure joy. All in all, this must be counted among the most imposing Brahms Firsts currently available.

Celi frequently alters Brahms's written dynamics. For example, near the beginning of the Second Symphony, where the strings take the lead, the horns remain much in evidence. The slow movement builds to an epic climax at 8'47" where full winds and brass declaim above a slow-moving tide of first-violin semiquavers (another of those unforgettable moments), and the finale's accelerating coda is immensely exciting. Indeed, the whole score enjoys an unusually cogent interpretation. By contrast, parts of the Third Symphony sound decidedly odd, yet there are some wonderful moments: the quieter episodes in the central development, the fire of the string playing in the recapitulation and the delicate balance of forces elsewhere. The Third's principal 'Celi moment' happens at 7'46" into the second movement, at the point where the strings draw a broad expressive arch, played here with the greatest intensity and mesmerizing control. The finale receives a relatively straightforward reading, often at white heat and again with some first-rate string playing. But, viewed as a whole, this is not a Brahms Third to live with.

For the Fourth Symphony, in addition to the complete performance, we are treated to a full rehearsal of the opening *Allegro non troppo* where a fully 'fired-up' Celi takes the greatest pains over matters of rhythm and articulation. The slow, sweet centre of the movement is addressed in almost mystical terms, far more effectively in concert than in the rehearsal. Cumulatively, the Fourth Symphony is taut, intimate, transparent and rich in incident, and only sometimes deprived of the 'long' view. Remarkable, inspiring, exasperating – Celibidache was all of these, and more. And if the overall approach was sometimes excessively interventionist, you learn so much from listening that eccentricities soon cease to register. These discs enshrine the work of a man who obviously loved every note of Brahms's symphonies (although he omits all three first-movement repeats) and was not afraid to express that love in interpretative terms.

Symphonies Nos. 1-4. Double Concerto in A minor, Op. 102 (with **Mischa Mischakoff** *vn* **Frank Miller** *vc*). Variations on a Theme by Haydn. Tragic Overture. Academic Festival Overture. Hungarian Dances – No. 1 in G minor; No. 17 in F sharp minor; No. 20 in E minor; No. 21 in E minor. Gesang der Parzen, Op. 89 (**Robert Shaw Chorale**). Liebeslieder-Walzer, Op. 52 (chorus; **Artur Balsam, Joseph Kahn** *pfs*).
NBC Symphony Orchestra / Arturo Toscanini.
RCA Victor Gold Seal mono GD60325 (four discs: 267 minutes: ADD). Texts and translations included. Recorded 1948-53.   Ⓜ Ⓗ

Despite many reissues, technical tinkerings, and critical re-evaluations, the recordings of the great Italian maestro Arturo Toscanini still stand head and shoulders above those which have the unenviable task of rivalling his genius as conductor and interpreter. This generous Brahms set is an excellent example of why Toscanini's recordings are still essential. The readings of the four symphonies must stand as benchmarks against which others are compared, and generally are found wanting. Toscanini's command of this music is total: his sense of architecture is unfailing, his control of tempos and rubato are masterly, and his ability to persuade the NBC Symphony Orchestra to play with extraordinary dynamic variety and tonal beauty is proof of his genius. In addition to the symphonies the set contains a fiery performance of the Double Concerto with the orchestra's principals as eloquent, if occasionally overshadowed, soloists and excellent readings of the essential shorter works of Brahms: the *Haydn* Variations, *Academic* and *Tragic* Overtures and *Hungarian Dances*. And to round off the set there are good, if not perfect, performances of two choral works, the rarely performed *Gesang der Parzen*, or 'Song of the Fates', and the *Liebeslieder Waltzes,* Op. 52. The transfer to CD of the original tapes has been handled particularly well: the worst tonal excesses have been successfully tamed, and there is a fine sense of balance throughout. With such a giant as Toscanini recommendation really becomes superfluous. Suffice it to say that these recordings are testimony to the genius of one of the greatest conductors this century has ever known.

Brahms Symphonies Nos. 1[a] and 2-4[b]. Variations on a Theme by Haydn[a]. Hungarian Dances[a] – No. 1 in G minor; No. 3 in F major; No. 10 in F major.
Beethoven Overtures – Coriolan, Op. 62[a]; Leonore No. 2, Op. 72[b].
[a]**Vienna Philharmonic Orchestra**; [b]**Berlin Philharmonic Orchestra / Wilhelm Furtwängler.**
EMI Références mono CHS5 65513-2 (three discs: ADD). Recorded 1948-56.   Ⓜ Ⓗ

These are extraordinary performances, the Third and Fourth Symphonies especially. In the Fourth it is almost as though Furtwängler, to a Berlin audience in 1948, were saying 'You *still* don't believe that this symphony is an appalling tragedy? Listen!' It is desperately serious from the very beginning: austere, big-phrased, with sober grace amidst the intensity, but also suspense, troubled anxiety. The coda is wildly turbulent, and ends in blackness. The slow movement begins in an unearthly hush, soon giving way to expressive warmth, but the rejoinder of the strings is unutterably poignant: the movement is a mourning procession, relieved only by vain defiance. And the *Scherzo*, which Brahms marked *giocoso*? More like grim determination, and although there are moments of relaxation the very fast tempo maintains uneasy tension through them. The finale is baleful, the strings returning to their intense eloquence, the chorale subdued and prayer-like, the fierce conflict terribly urgent, ending in bleak despair. You might find the Third Symphony, often portrayed as Brahms's most genial, even more disturbing. Furtwängler notices all the music's hushed shadows; he explores them, lingers in them, and on emerging you realize that the *Andante*'s serenity is not untroubled, that clouds are often apt to fall across the music's warm colours. The finale has a funereal tread, the noble string theme is determined, not relaxed or exuberant; there is a feverish quality that leaves the coda hushed, haunted.

In the First Symphony there is a palpable sense of Brahms confronting the shade of Beethoven. The theme of the finale is not radiant at its first appearance: after an almost distraught slow movement and a strangely unstable *Scherzo* (the whole symphony takes up where the *first* movement of Beethoven's Ninth left off, not its fourth) that theme will have to struggle for its victory. And thus, Furtwängler seems to say, the forest horns at the outset of the Second Symphony, the huge energy of its first movement, the intense, impulsive romanticism of its *Adagio*; hence the exuberant robustness of the finale: Brahms has earned this romantic richness by what he achieved in the First Symphony. Subjective? Of course, and anyone who objects to interpretations so subjective that they can rule out alternative views may dislike them very much indeed. But if one of a conductor's functions is to reveal the composer's intentions, another is to convince you that those intentions matter. Furtwängler's Third has the power to make you question whether it is as ripely autumnal as most commentators seem to think; his Fourth could keep you awake at night; all four symphonies have a visionary urgency that can sweep you along with it. They are all live recordings, with some audience noise; the strings are a bit acid at times, the climaxes occasionally dense (not often: the clarity of detail is extraordinary), but you would probably gladly put up with far worse for performances as toweringly eloquent as these.

Brahms Symphony No. 1.
Schumann Symphony No. 1 in B flat major, Op. 38, 'Spring'.
Berlin Philharmonic Orchestra / Herbert von Karajan.
DG The Originals 447 408-2GOR (76 minutes: ADD). Recorded 1964 and 1971.　　　　Ⓜ🔲🔲

The first of Karajan's three Berlin Brahms cycles was, by general consent, his finest for DG. As to which was Karajan's finest 'phase' in general (if such a thing is calculable), only time will tell. Few would deny that this Brahms C minor Symphony has a 'halcyon days' feel. It is certainly present in the first two movements, the drive established in the main *Allegro* of the first (no repeat) allowing Karajan to relax for the second theme without loss of purpose – Brahms both poet and powerful symphonic thinker handsomely served. The second movement, ideally mobile, evolves freely and seamlessly, with masterfully graded wide dynamic contrasts felt rather than fashioned. Here, as elsewhere, this orchestra's tone production is even, rich and rounded. So far, so good. In the third movement, bar-by-bar dynamic contrasts are smoothed out, with the route to the Trio's climax taken as one very gradual *crescendo*. The finale's 'daybreak' is broad and awe-inspiring (with horn pitching that may be deemed not quite true). Karajan here has gauged tempo, dynamics and accentuation in order that the strings can articulate without strain; all very impressive, but his *Allegro*'s progress is thus relatively short on attack, energy and the ability to fly. The more you hear Karajan's Schumann First Symphony, the more convinced you may be that it is spring cultivated and monitored under laboratory conditions. The most unsettling of those conditions is an 'effect' common to a number of his 1970s DG Berlin recordings, namely, for a fairly closely balanced orchestra (particularly the strings, which are not entirely glare-free), as dynamic levels drop, to walk off several paces into a glowing Berlin sunset. The 'effect' also exaggerates the conductor's own contrasts, neither exactly redolent of the vitality and freshness of spring: the resolutely robust and measured delivery of the rustic *forte*, and the carefully crafted confection of his *dolce* piano.

Symphony No. 1. Gesang der Parzen, Op. 89.
Berlin Radio Chorus; Berlin Philharmonic Orchestra / Claudio Abbado.
DG 431 790-2GH (58 minutes: DDD). Recorded 1990.　　　　　　Ⓕ

Abbado's tempos are generally broad: his first movement (without its repeat) boldly emphatic but he never stints on affection, and few would find fault with his warm, lyrical handling of the beautiful *Andante*, 'sostenuto', indeed! Abbado ventures between the score's little nooks and crannies, highlighting small details without impeding the music's flow or weakening the performance's overall structure. When the finale breaks from *Più andante* to *Allegro non troppo, ma con brio* (not *too* fast, but with plenty of spirit), Abbado really goes for the burn, very much as Furtwängler did before him. It's a truly inspired reading, grand but never grandiose; appreciative of Brahms's thick-set orchestration, but never stodgy. The fill-up is of enormous import, and opens with one of the composer's most inspired musical gestures: a bold, burgeoning *Maestoso*, anticipating the words 'The gods should be feared/by the human race ...'. *Gesang der Parzen* is a setting of a particularly unsettling poem by Goethe, one that warns how the uplifted have particular reason to fear the gods, those who 'turn their beneficent eyes away from whole races.' Abbado surely sensed the terrible truth of that prophecy, and his reading of Op. 89 breathes a deeply disquieting air.

Brahms Symphony No. 1.
Wagner Siegfried Idyll. Siegfried – Siegfried's horn-call.
Dennis Brain *hn* **Philharmonia Orchestra / Guido Cantelli.**
Testament mono SBT1012 (62 minutes: ADD). Recorded 1947-53.   Ⓕ Ⓗ

Cantelli conducts an interpretation of the Symphony which is free of any idiosyncrasy. Yet there is an extraordinary electricity in his conducting, a sense of concentration and conviction which lifts the performance into one of the greatest ever set down on record. The fiery young Italian makes the vintage Philharmonia play in an inspired fashion, and the 1953 mono recording is very acceptable. A slightly edgy string sound betrays the 1951 origin of the *Siegfried Idyll* recording, but the performance has a tenderness, warmth and eloquence which has never been surpassed. Dennis Brain's exuberant horn-call completes a very desirable Testament disc.

Symphonies Nos. 1[a] and 3[b].
[a]**London Symphony Orchestra / Hermann Abendroth;**
[b]**Vienna Philharmonic Orchestra / Clemens Krauss.**
Biddulph WHL052 (75 minutes: ADD). Recorded [a]1928, [b]1930.   Ⓜ Ⓗ

Symphonies Nos. 2[a] and 3[b].
[a]**New York Symphony Orchestra / Walter Damrosch;**
[b]**London Symphony Orchestra / Hermann Abendroth.**
Biddulph WHL053 (79 minutes: ADD). Recorded [a]1928, [b]1927.   Ⓜ Ⓗ

Thank heavens for such independent labels as Biddulph and others like it, for were it not for their sterling efforts, performances such as these would be lost with the passage of time. And what valuable recordings they are. Much as we prize the Brahms of Furtwängler, Toscanini, Klemperer and Walter, anyone with active critical faculties – and the ability to listen 'through' old sound – is likely to enjoy Krauss, Abendroth or Damrosch virtually as much. All three conductors reflect a performing style that might well have been recognized by the composer himself. Flexibility is a constant attribute, though the three orchestras featured produce very different pooled sonorities. A good many of Abendroth's post-war East German recordings have latterly found their way on to CD, but most collectors will have first encountered the conductor through these Brahms 78s with the LSO. The original sound quality – although generally well balanced – is cramped and mono-dimensional, but the transfers make the best of a difficult job. The First Symphony opens magisterially. The main body of the first movement is pliable but energetic, whereas the *Andante sostenuto* second movement flows nicely and the finale generates considerable visceral excitement. Abendroth leans on the initial upbeat of the big string tune then pushes forwards. Just occasionally the tempo seems too fast for comfort, but the sum effect of Abendroth's approach is rugged and impulsive. The LSO's strings are more expressive than its rather acid woodwinds, the cellos being especially fine – most notably in the glorious melody that sits at the centre of the Fourth Symphony's *Andante moderato*. Again, as in the First Symphony, wide tempo fluctuations are conspicuous but convincing, save perhaps in the Passacaglia where the flow is sometimes impeded. Most of Brahms's dynamics are faithfully observed and Abendroth's treatment of the interrelationship of the movements is as perceptive as one would expect from a skilled opera conductor.

Clemens Krauss was even more celebrated as an opera conductor than Abendroth, and his symphonic records are few and far between. This Vienna Philharmonic account of the Third is distinguished by taut string playing, glorious contributions from the horn section and an unselfconscious approach to rubato. You could easily imagine that anyone who learned the *Andante* from this recording will have found all subsequent versions pallid and unconvincing. Krauss's handling of the opening bars – where violas, cellos and basses answer woodwinds and horns – suggests the intimacy of chamber music. Rarely has the writing breathed more naturally, or the underlying sentiment been more precisely gauged. Although some of the finale's faster passages are a little unco-ordinated, the driving force of Krauss's approach marks a telling contrast with the symphony's reflective coda. Among Walter Damrosch's many claims to musical fame are the first American performances of Brahms's Third and Fourth Symphonies, and his New York recording of the Second is in some respects the most interesting of the set. The second subject is very broadly paced, but the highlight of the performance is surely the *Adagio non troppo* slow movement, a minutely observed reading full of tender incident. On the debit side, violins tend to lack body at anything above *mezzo-forte* and some will question the finale's very fast speeds (especially later on in the movement). But viewed as a whole, Damrosch's Brahms 2 is both lyrical and lively, a quietly individual reading that repays close scrutiny. With fine transfers and expert annotation, these two CDs provide an invaluable historical supplement to existing Brahms symphony recommendations. You may not always agree with what you hear, and yet all four performances should significantly extend your knowledge of these wonderful works.

Symphonies Nos. 2 and 3.
Columbia Symphony Orchestra / Bruno Walter.
Sony Classical Bruno Walter Edition SMK64471 (75 minutes: ADD). Recorded 1960.　　　Ⓜ🆁🆁

Bruno Walter (1876-1962) was, quite simply, a lovely man, gentle and kind beyond the ordinary (though his kindness did not extend to anything that compromised his artistic standards). He was always a fine interpreter of Brahms's music, which seemed so suited to his temperament, for Brahms, too, was also a deeply human person. So there was an empathy between the two and Walter responded to the music with his whole heart. In an interview shortly before his death, he gave an account of how the character of Brahms interpretations had changed during his lifetime. Performances seemed to him to have become warmer, more expansive: the Brahms of his youth had been muscular, firmly classical, even a little acerbic. This statement may be of more value for what it tells us about Walter's own development than about Brahms interpretations in general, and certainly these recordings tend to confirm this viewpoint. Whatever Walter's conception of the work as a whole, song-themes are always allowed to open out with glorious effect. There is something almost pianistic about Walter's subtle flexibility of tempo: this, one imagines, is how Brahms might have envisaged it as he played through these works on the piano.

Phrasing too has a marvellous feeling of controlled freedom about it: dynamics may rise and fall considerably during a short phrase, and yet Walter's shaping of longer lines is always masterly. The whole second group of the Second Symphony is like one huge, continually evolving tune with one point of climax and one final resolution. Perhaps there could be more tautness and inner tension in some of the *allegros*, but the generosity and sensitivity of Walter's readings more than compensate: emphasis is upon the lyrical continuity of the music – Brahms the Schubertian rather than Brahms the Beethovenian – and it is none the worse for that. The recordings have come up marvellously in their digital remastering, gaining clarity and depth. Unfortunately the treble frequencies still sound harsh but that's the problem with technology – it has a habit of revealing the naked truth!

Symphony No. 2. Tragic Overture.
Boston Symphony Orchestra / Bernard Haitink.
Philips 432 094-2PH (62 minutes: DDD). Recorded 1990.　　　Ⓕ

Brahms's Second Symphony is the warmest, most lyrical of the four, and Haitink's performance brings out those qualities to the full. His reading is very straightforward and unselfconscious: he allows the first movement to blossom attractively, but ensures that this process is achieved within a strong framework – one is always aware that detail has its secure place within the musical argument. The second movement's basic pulse is on the slow side, but Haitink's affectionate, watchful conducting ensures that the music flows naturally. The third movement is brought to life quite gently too, but accents are light and rhythms are sharp enough to ensure that the mood is still outgoing. In the finale Haitink sets a fast initial tempo, but he allows the music to breathe through the use of subtle inflexions and changes of pulse. There's plenty of excitement, but nothing is too hectic. In the Overture his basic tempo is quite measured, but again accents are sharp, and the score's dramatic element is well brought out. The playing of the Boston Symphony Orchestra is superlative, and the recording is excellent, apart from an occasional moment of slightly acid string tone.

Symphony No. 2. Academic Festival Overture.
New York Philharmonic Orchestra / Kurt Masur.
Teldec 9031-77291-2 (50 minutes: DDD). Recorded 1992.　　　Ⓕ

Masur brings warmth and affection to the symphony. In the first movement he maintains a strong sense of line, and paces the music more objectively than Haitink. The structure is clearer, but there's also a natural, unforced lyricism. The *Adagio* has a natural ebb and flow, and once again Masur makes the listener aware of the music's shape and argument very clearly. After a neatly pointed *Allegretto* the finale is given a beautifully balanced, strongly argued reading which eschews

superficial excitement, but satisfies through the feeling of a symphonic argument brought to a
logical conclusion. To sum up, Haitink caresses the music with more subjective warmth than Masur,
whose reading by no means lacks affection, but is more architectural and objective. The New York
Philharmonic responds to Masur with highly sensitive, very accomplished playing, and Teldec's
attractively warm but clearly recorded disc is completed by a genial, uplifting *Academic Festival
Overture*.

Symphony No. 2. Alto Rhapsody, Op. 53.
Marjana Lipovšek *contr* **Ernst Senff Choir; Berlin Philharmonic Orchestra / Claudio Abbado.**
DG 427 643-2GH (60 minutes: DDD). Recorded 1988.　　　　　　　　　　　　　　　　Ⓕ

These sessions took place before the BPO elected Abbado as its Chief Conductor, but the
orchestra responds with unmistakable enthusiasm to the Italian conductor. The BPO's sound under
Abbado is different from the Karajan sound. It still has a wonderful depth and sonority, but
whereas Karajan encouraged a homogeneous, ultra-refined quality Abbado persuades the orchestra
to play with more separated, slightly lighter textures, and a greater translucency. In the symphony's
first movement Abbado opts for a good, spacious middle-of-the-road tempo, and lets the music
unfold easily and lyrically, but with affectionate care. The music-making is quite unidiosyncratic
and direct, but develops genuine fire and passion at climaxes. In the second movement the basic
tempo is even a little on the slow side, but there is still an appealing lightness and a quiet, glowing
quality in the orchestral sound. Abbado gently but firmly persuades the music on, maintaining an
adroit balance between warmth of expression and clarity. The third movement has good balance
and clarity, too, and if the middle section lacks its customary eager, crisp quality there is still plenty
of vitality in the movement overall. There is just a slightly tame feel to the finale, and the climax
doesn't quite have its usual impact. But in general it's a most satisfying performance of the
symphony, very well recorded, adorned by Lipovšek's singing in the *Alto Rhapsody*. This has good
tone and good sense – perhaps a slightly dry-eyed quality too – and Abbado's characterful
conducting is impressive.

Symphony No. 2. Alto Rhapsody.
Christa Ludwig *mez* **Philharmonia Chorus and Orchestra / Otto Klemperer.**
EMI Studio CDM7 69650-2 (51 minutes: ADD). Recorded 1956 and 1962.　　　　Ⓜ Ⓗ

Klemperer recorded just one Brahms symphony cycle, which was made near the beginning of his
association with the Philharmonia Orchestra, in 1956-57, at a time when the great conductor was at
the height of his Indian summer. In fact this was exactly the right time, since it was just late enough
for all the symphonies to be recorded in stereo. Fortunately the sound is everywhere more than
acceptable; not particularly seductive, but clear and immediate, with wind instruments to the fore,
as was his norm. Klemperer is in lyrical mood, as befits the nature of the work. There are some
changes of pulse in the first movement, and moments of real warmth and tenderness. The slow
movement, too, has considerable depth of expression, as well as underlying strength, and there is no
lack of tenderness in the *Allegretto*. The finale has plenty of energy and excitement, but a superb
sense of proportion. Overall this is a gloriously ripe, experienced reading. Ludwig sings the *Alto
Rhapsody* superbly, and her interpretation is more overtly expressive than that of many other
famous singers in this work.

Symphony No. 3. Tragic Overture, Op. 81. Schicksalslied, Op. 54.
Ernst-Senff Choir; Berlin Philharmonic Orchestra / Claudio Abbado.
DG 429 765-2GH (68 minutes: DDD).　　　　　　　　　　　　　　　　　　　　Ⓕ

This disc is gloriously programmed for straight-through listening. He gets off to a cracking start
with an urgently impassioned *Tragic Overture* in which the credentials of the Berlin Philharmonic to
make a richly idiomatic, Brahmsian sound – already well accepted – are substantially reaffirmed.
A wide-eyed, breathtaking account of the *Schicksalslied* ('Song of Destiny') follows to provide
sound contrast before the wonders of the Third Symphony are freshly explored. This is a reading of
the Symphony to be savoured; it is underpinned throughout by a rhythmic vitality which binds the
four movements together with a forward thrust, making the end inevitable right from the opening
bars. Even in the moments of repose and, especially, the warmly-felt *Andante*, Abbado never lets
the music forget its ultimate goal. Despite this, there are many moments of wonderful solo and
orchestral playing along the way in which there is time to delight, and Abbado seems to bring out
that affable, Bohemian-woods, Dvořák-like element in Brahms's music to a peculiar degree in this
performance. The Symphony is recorded with a particular richness and some may find the heady
waltz of the third movement done too lushly, emphasized by Abbado's lingering tempo.
Nevertheless, this is splendid stuff, and not to be missed.

Brahms Symphony No. 3.
Schubert Symphony No. 5 in B flat major, D485.
Mendelssohn The Hebrides, Op. 26.
Chicago Symphony Orchestra / Fritz Reiner.
RCA Victor Gold Seal 09026 61793-2 (69 minutes: ADD). Recorded 1956-60.　　　Ⓜ🅷

Perhaps the very opening of the Brahms is unexceptional; it's not very passionate; maybe there is a little too much of what Reiner called his 'self-controlled control'. However, slowly but surely, the benefits of that control make themselves felt. The first movement is tautly drawn; no undue roaming in the pre-recapitulation gloaming. Speaking of control and pivotal points, as we turn into this movement's coda, the reins are loosened and the ride is fabulously exciting. The slow movement's mellow (here, very autumnal) pastoral takes its time, and is wonderfully phrased and shaded. The concentration is so intense you can almost sense the falcon eye surveying the scene. And this is how to record Brahms: forget the over-ripe textures and fudged balances of many a modern Brahms symphony recording; here one-and-all is for all to hear (with, admittedly, a moderate amount of tape hiss). No small thanks to Reiner, this is a lean, athletic, supremely articulate, eloquent and well-tempered Brahms sound.

With slimmed-down strings, the Schubert is as light on its feet, as perfectly balanced, as poised and as stylishly pointed as any period-instrument or chamber-orchestra performance, and very few of them are as immaculately precise. As in the Brahms, there are no repeats, except in the Minuet and Trio, where the repeats are subtly varied and the *ritardandos* consummately handled. The whole is suave and sleek, but shaped, savoured and illumined by the hand of an epicure. As to *The Hebrides*, the way Reiner holds on to the long notes in those wind calls about a third of the way in is very striking indeed, as is the timpani playing, superbly forthright (and very clear) but always musical. Drawbacks? Well, it's as Reiner commented on receipt of the news that he and his orchestra had become box office: 'One must take the good with the good'.

Symphonies Nos. 3 and 4.
London Classical Players / Sir Roger Norrington.
EMI CDC5 56118-2 (73 minutes: DDD). Recorded 1995.　　　Ⓕ🅿

This Third is a trail-blazing performance, rather than an interpretation that's had time to mature, and not everything is fully convincing: the transition to the first movement's more relaxed second group could certainly have been more flexible. But on the whole Norrington is far from rigidly metronomic; the contrast between dramatic, urgent *allegro* and the more reflective *un poco sostenuto* passage at the heart of the movement is particularly telling. And as the symphony progresses the insights seem to come more and more frequently. The *Andante* second movement is refreshingly expressive. There are similar fine things in the third movement; not least the horn solo in the recapitulation: Norrington uses nineteenth-century valve horns, but the tone is appreciably different from what we expect today – warmer, less penetrating, and with an indefinable woodland character as the horn sounds through softly rustling leaves. It is this sylvan stillness (not quite serenity) that returns in the symphony's closing pages.

The opening out of the orchestral sound in the Fourth Symphony is reminiscent, startlingly in places, of the marvellously alive 1935 Toscanini/BBC Symphony Orchestra recording on EMI. Norrington's version is nowhere near as compelling (the relaxed pace at the opening was surprising), but it is full of fine things: the pungent sound of the woodwind choir announcing the slow movement, the warm, confidential tone of the wooden flute at the heart of the finale, and those rasping, but never over-powering trombones. So, not perfection – but surely that was never Norrington's aim. As in all his best performances and recordings he has thrown down a gauntlet. Are we going to go on deferring to tradition – and at the same time grumbling about how uninspiring most modern Brahms orchestral performances are? Or are we going to face up to the possibility that a composer's scores and recorded remarks, and the testimonies of his contemporaries, could be an even more valuable source of insight into the music than even the greatest recordings of the past? Listen to these recordings without prejudice and your idea of The Brahms Sound will never be quite the same again.

Symphonies Nos. 3 and 4.
Philharmonia Orchestra / Otto Klemperer.
EMI Studio CDM7 69649-2 (76 minutes: ADD). Recorded 1956-57.　　　Ⓜ🅷

In the Fourth Symphony Klemperer is on his best form, providing a powerful, very expressive account of the first movement, a beautifully balanced, eloquent slow movement and a third where, despite the insertion of some unmarked commas, there is strong, rugged impetus. The last movement was surely made for Klemperer's objective, architectural style, and he holds the episodes together magnificently in pointing the way to a glorious climax. The Third Symphony is a comparative disappointment. It is the only Brahms symphony in which Klemperer takes the first movement repeat. But there's a hint of reserve in his conducting, and tempos by and large seem to be just a little on the slow side. It's a good, sound performance, but he seems less than at ease throughout the work. But this disc is worth acquiring for the Fourth which has real stature and unmistakable greatness.

Symphony No. 4.
Vienna Philharmonic Orchestra / Carlos Kleiber.
DG The Originals 457 706-2GOR (40 minutes: DDD). Recorded 1981.　　　　Ⓜ️🆁🆁

Carlos Kleiber's charismatic 1981 Vienna recording – a classic of sorts and still sounding exceptionally well – continues to stand its ground. Significantly, Kleiber's recording marked the 100th reissue in DG's Originals series and a crossing at the technological divide between analogue and digital. The CD comes handsomely packaged with a 112-page, full-colour 'Compactotheque' résumé of the whole series, complete with 'quotes from the critics'. But, to return to the music. From the beginning, Kleiber keeps the speed fairly steady. In the first movement's coda, he scores over many of his rivals with prominent horns and a particularly exciting conclusion. He opens the second movement in a rather perfunctory manner, but the Vienna cellos make a beautiful sound in the *piano dolce* second subject. In the *Scherzo*, Kleiber pulls back for the two accented notes that dominate the first theme, an interesting gesture that lends the music an appropriately swaggering gait. This, arguably, is his finest movement – also from 4'48", where he keeps the timpani's triplets crystal-clear (accentuating the first beat of the bar), then pushes his horns very much to the fore. Overall, Kleiber in the Fourth is the knight with shining breast-plate, bold, handsome (beautifully played), outgoing, relatively straightforward and (this will doubtless court controversy) perhaps just a little superficial.

Symphony No. 4. Variations on a Theme by Haydn.
Boston Symphony Orchestra / Bernard Haitink.
Philips 434 991-2PH (62 minutes: DDD). Recorded 1992.　　　　Ⓕ

There is a little more separation of timbre in the sound of Haitink's Boston Brahms Fourth and *Haydn* Variations than in his previous 1972-73 Amsterdam recordings; perhaps marginally less ambient warmth in tuttis, though certainly more than in Kleiber's. However, the 20 years that separate Haitink's accounts have brought some much more marked musical changes, not only in his overall view – he adds a minute to each of the symphony's first two movements – but in a more acute moment-by-moment control (comparable, at times to Kleiber's), pliant pacing and communicative phrasing. The first movement is now not so much an older man's Brahms as an older Brahms, more poignantly reflective, more given to mysterious depths, less heroic and purposeful in overall cast though still able to bestir himself mightily, and when the coda arrives, to declaim with the terrifying rage of age. The second movement (smoother clarinet tone in Boston), now serene and very slow indeed has a timeless Brucknerian tread. The *Scherzo* is quite as fearsomely jocular as before, though with more interesting shadings. This is Brahms playing, conducting and recording of real stature.

Symphony No. 4ᵃ. Warum ist das Licht gegeben, Op. 74 No. 1. Fest- und Gedenksprüche, Op. 109. Three Motets, Op. 110.
Leipzig Radio Men's Chorus; ᵃLeipzig Gewandhaus Orchestra / Herbert Blomstedt.
Decca 455 510-2DH (71 minutes: DDD). Texts and translations included. Recorded 1996.　　Ⓕ

Herbert Blomstedt homes in on relative subtleties and the small print, as sympathetic a Brahmsian as any. As early as the ninth bar, he pushes both the tempo and the volume. He is utterly responsive to Brahms's finer dynamics – for example the mysterious *pianissimo* string figurations at 5'23". He treats the first movement as a structure viewed from within and the second movement – with a telling *legato* – effects a subtle transition to *pianissimo* winds. Blomstedt plays by the book, though his finale is more flexible than many – and rather less dramatic, certainly in the *forte* opening chords. He broadens the tempo more for the flute solo at 97 (not necessarily a virtue) and his re-entrance to 'tempo 1' later on is less of a jolt, tempo-wise, though he is by then noticeably faster than at the beginning of the movement. The final reckoning is easily summed up: Blomstedt excels in the lyrical, equivocal sides of the score, thinking through each passage with great sensitivity though always with an ear for structure. The couplings are some of Brahms's finest *a cappella* choruses. Indeed, it was something of an inspiration to tail an 'act that no one could follow' (the catastrophic ending of the Fourth Symphony) with a chorus based on Job's despair. The harmonically 'old world' *Fest- und Gedenksprüche* remind us of Brahms's interest in early music, and the opening verse of the last of the Motets, Op. 110 – 'When we are in direst need and know not where to turn' – has a meaningful harmonic complexity that is light years ahead of its time. It marks a beautifully sung conclusion to an extremely fine disc, one that enjoys the added advantage of excellent sound and that includes a performance of the Fourth Symphony that stands its ground even in comparison with the exalted benchmark versions reviewed elsewhere in this section.

Brahms (orch. Schoenberg) Piano Quartet No. 1 in G minor, Op. 25.
Bach (orch. Schoenberg) Prelude and Fugue in E flat major, BWV552, 'St Anne'. Schmücke dich, o liebe Seele, BWV654. Komm, Gott Schöpfer, BWV631.
Houston Symphony Orchestra / Christoph Eschenbach.
RCA Victor Red Seal 09026 68658-2 (70 minutes: DDD). Recorded 1995.　　　　　Ⓕ

In terms of style, the Schoenberg Piano Quartet orchestration is rather like a private conversation re-scripted for the theatre. Only the most sensitive Brahms conductors can make it work and this is an excellent performance from Eschenbach and the Houston orchestra. Tempos are generally quite broad although the 'Intermezzo' second movement is both keenly accented and properly pensive. Eschenbach grants considerable weight to the brass lines, while in the *Andante con moto*, burbling woodwinds are extraordinarily clear. Only the *Rondo alla zingarese* third movement seems to be marginally underpowered, although it, too, is crystal clear. Certainly Schoenberg's desire 'once to hear everything in the piece' is vividly realized and the recording captures the whole dazzling spectacle, from glittering high percussion, through tactile *col legno* strings to sonorous low brass. The couplings are both highly appropriate and superbly performed. Best is *Schmücke dich* which, although heavily modified contrapuntally, has a mellow grandeur that is inherent in the original. *Komm, Gott*, with its bony textures and filled out harmonies, is both rugged and celebratory and the *St Anne* Prelude and Fugue's principal glory is its variously orchestrated triple fugue. Still, Eschenbach and his players do all four transcriptions proud and, viewed as a whole, this excellent CD can be recommended virtually without reservation.

String Sextets – No. 1 in B flat major, Op. 18; No. 2 in G major, Op. 36.

String Sextets Nos. 1 and 2.
Raphael Ensemble (James Clark, Elizabeth Wexler *vns* Sally Beamish, Roger Tapping *vas* Andrea Hess, Rhydian Shaxson *vcs*).
Hyperion CDA66276 (74 minutes: DDD). Recorded 1988.　　　　　Ⓕ

Completed after the First Piano Concerto, but still comparatively early works, the Sextets are typified by lush textures, ardent emotion, and wonderfully memorable melodic lines. The first is the warmer, more heart-on-the-sleeve piece, balancing with complete naturalness a splendidly lyrical first movement, an urgent, dark set of intricate variations, a lively rustic dance of a *Scherzo*, and a placidly flowing finale. The Second Sextet inhabits at first a more mysterious world of half-shadows, occasionally rent by glorious moments of sunlight. The finale, however, casts off doubt and ends with affirmation. Both works are very susceptible to differing modes of interpretation, and the Raphael Ensemble has established very distinctive views of each, allowing the richness of the texture its head without obscuring the lines, and selecting characteristically distinct tone qualities to typify the two works. The recording is clear and analytic without robbing the sound of its warmth and depth. Altogether an impressive recording début for this ensemble.

String Sextet No. 1. Piano Trio No. 1 in B major, Op. 8.
Pablo Casals, Madeline Foley *vcs*
Isaac Stern, Alexander Schneider *vns* **Milton Katims, Milton Thomas** *vas* **Dame Myra Hess** *pf*
Sony Classical Casals Edition mono SMK58994 (77 minutes: ADD). Recorded 1952.　　　　Ⓜ Ⓗ

Casals is, of course, the lynch-pin. A charismatic presence, he embraces each work with the passion of a devoted horticulturist tending his most precious flowers, and that his love extended beyond the realms of music to mankind itself surely enriched his art even further. Being a proud and unhypocritical humanitarian, Casals had long refused to step foot in Franco's Spain, and it was Alexander Schneider who coaxed him from self-imposed retirement for a series of music festivals in the French town of Prades – hence these recordings. This is a majestic, big-boned account of the early B flat Trio and a sublime version of the sun-soaked B flat Sextet, one of the glories of the Casals Edition. If you need a prime sampling of the Casals manner at its most inspired, then try the Sextet's second movement and note the sullen, ghostly tone of the master himself at 8'32" – like some ancient bard relaying a solemn but wise message.

Clarinet Quintet in B minor, Op. 115.

Brahms Clarinet Quintet.
Mozart Clarinet Quintet in A major, K581.
Alessandro Carbonare *cl* **Luc Héry, Florence Binder** *vns* **Nicolas Bône** *va* **Muriel Pouzenc** *vc*
Harmonia Mundi Les Nouveaux Interprètes HMN91 1691 (70 minutes: DDD).
Recorded 1997.
ⒷⒺ🆁🆁

The coupling of these two supreme masterpieces among clarinet quintets is surprisingly rare, coming as a rule in reissues of vintage recordings. Here, by contrast, we have a recording of talented young performers in Harmonia Mundi's budget-price series, Les Nouveaux Interprètes. The Italian, Alessandro Carbonare, produces exceptionally beautiful, liquid tone colours over the widest dynamic range, evidently a result of the development work he has undertaken with the clarinet manufacturers, Selmer. What is specially striking is Carbonare's ability to produce extreme, ear-catching *pianissimos*, making the slow movements of both works the high points, and with his entries in all the movements of the Brahms magically gentle. In the Mozart *Larghetto* he very tastefully elaborates the main melody on its reprise without diminishing the tenderness of his playing. The four string players are not quite so distinctive, but provide sympathetic support, though the recording at times gives an edge to the violin tone, which then tends to sound thin next to the clarinet. The one slight irritation is that the recording from time to time picks up the clicking of Carbonare's keys. A most desirable coupling.

Clarinet Quintet. String Quartet No. 2 in A minor, Op. 51 No. 2.
Karl Leister *cl* **Leipzig Quartet** (Andreas Seidel, Tilman Büning *vns* Ivo Bauer *va*
Matthias Moosdorf *vc*).
Dabringhaus und Grimm MDG307 0719-2 (71 minutes: DDD).
Ⓕ

One of the most attractive qualities of this version of a well-loved quintet is the skill with which the artists, abetted by the record producer, have integrated the clarinet into the string textures. Having listened more creatively than any other composer to Mozart's example, Brahms allows the clarinet to become part of the tone colour in the string ensemble; and he has also followed the implications, as not all his interpreters seem to understand. Here, the little falling third theme, one of his lifelong obsessions, moves in and out of the musical texture with wonderful subtlety, so that the return of the opening figure at the very end needs no special emphasis but is a natural conclusion. Leister is an artist of long skill and experience, and also of great musical intelligence; the qualities tell. They also mean that there is no need to confer upon the performance anything approaching the sentimentality which can afflict it, in the name of 'nostalgia' as the old composer looks affectionately back upon his life's work. This is quite a robust performance, clearly appreciated by the enthusiastic young string quartet, who give a suitably matching account of the Op. 51 work. There are, of course, any number of performances of the quintet, but this is a unique one.

Clarinet Quintet. Trio for Horn, Violin and Piano in E flat major, Op. 40.
Reginald Kell *cl* **Aubrey Brain** *hn* **Rudolf Serkin** *pf*
Busch Quartet (Adolf Busch, Gosta Andreasson *vns* Karl Doktor *va* Hermann Busch *vc*).
Pearl mono GEM0007 (63 minutes: ADD). Recorded 1937 and 1933.
Ⓜ🅗

There is no need, at this remove of time, for further praise to be lavished on these performances. This account of the Horn Trio remains at, or very near, the top of any list of recorded rivals. HMV's recording of this somewhat idiosyncratic combination of instruments survives well and has been cleanly, honestly transferred. However, the performance of the Clarinet Quintet will give you even deeper pleasure. Where nowadays do we hear playing of such emotional range, such probing intensity? Here the Busch Quartet and Reginald Kell out-sing and out-search most rivals in the work's autumnal aspect but manage to make everything seem alive and doubly intense with their fierce and intense response to the music's wild mood-swings. It helps to have a clarinettist who can coo like a dove and exult like a gipsy; but, in the end, the performance's genius rests in the players' profound and unflinching sense of identification with Brahms's shifting moods.

Clarinet Quintet. Clarinet Trio in A minor, Op. 114.
Thea King *cl* **Karina Georgian** *vc* **Clifford Benson** *pf*
Gabrieli Quartet (Kenneth Sillito, Brendan O'Reilly *vns* Ian Jewel *va* Keith Harvey *vc*).
Hyperion CDA66107 (65 minutes: DDD).
Ⓕ

These players' tempo in the Clarinet Quintet is more leisurely than most of their rivals. In the faster flanking movements of the trio, a stronger forward drive might not have come amiss. On the other hand, the group allows itself time to savour every bar to the full. The first thing that strikes you about both these performances is the warmth of heart underlying them. You will respond easily to their quality of good-natured, unforced civility. The ensemble is excellent, with the clarinet very much one of the team, never assuming the role of soloist in a quasi-chamber concerto. Thea King's phrasing is unfailingly perceptive and stylish, and her undemonstrative, wise artistry in both works is most appealing. In the Trio, the sumptuous-sounding cello is impressive, which at times makes you feel that Brahms could just as well have called the work a cello trio. This is a disc which will bear frequent repetition. Playing such as this, committed and serious, yet at the same time relaxed and spontaneous, is not easy to contrive in the recording studio, and Hyperion has done well to capture these interpretations on the wing. The sound is very good indeed, mellow and natural.

Clarinet Quintet. Clarinet Trio in A minor, Op. 114.
József Balogh *cl* **Csaba Onczay** *vn* **Danubius Quartet** (Judit Tóth, Adél Miklós, *vns* Cecilia Bodolai *va* Ilona Wibli *vc*); **Jenö Jandó** *pf*
Naxos 8 550391 (59 minutes: DDD). Recorded 1991. ⑤

Brahms's late music invariably has a sense of space and often an autumnal quality as well, partially indicated by the minor keys of the two works here. The Quintet is, of course, the better-known work, but there have always been those who think the Trio even finer; as it is, both are masterpieces and have considerable beauty despite their predominantly sombre emotional colour. These are strong performances from artists clearly in sympathy with the music, not least the cellist, whose dark eloquence is so telling here – not forgetting, of course, the central role played by the clarinet, who must be velvety and authoritative by turns and is always given compelling music. The recording quality suits the music pretty well in that it has plenty of the necessary body, and although it could have a crisper focus, it is perfectly serviceable. The Trio's first movement unfolds in an unhurried yet purposeful way, and its unquietude, rightly, is allowed to spill over into the one that follows, a movement whose agitation belies its *Adagio* designation – this is hardly music 'at ease' with itself. All in all, this is a fine performance. That of the Clarinet Quintet is also very pleasing but here the sound is too rich and deprives the music of intimacy. For this reason, a more satisfying version of these two clarinet works is the sensitive yet vivid one by Thea King and various colleagues on Hyperion. However, this is still quite a bargain.

Clarinet Quintet. Horn Trio in E flat major, Op. 40.
Reginald Kell *cl* **Aubrey Brain** *hn* **Rudolf Serkin** *pf* **Busch Quartet** (Adolf Busch, Gösta Andreasson *vns* Karl Doktor *va* Hermann Busch *vc*).
Testament mono SBT1001 (65 minutes: AAD). Recorded 1938 and 1933. ⑤ Ⓗ

In the musical climate of today it is hard to believe the upheaval and opposition aroused in the mid-1930s by Reginald Kell's adoption of vibrato for the clarinet, which was customarily played 'straight' and rather pale in colour. But his warm, sensuous tone won the approbation of Furtwängler and other conductors and wind players, and soon of the public also; and his approach became largely accepted as the norm. It is difficult to describe the impact of that Clarinet Quintet when it was first heard in 1938, with Kell's first *dolce arpeggio* rising like a benison. That performance, with Kell and the Busch Quartet beautifully integrated and balanced, and with infinitely subtle gradations of tone, became a classic at once. With most, if not quite all, the surface sound now eliminated, it entrances all over again. The disc also contains the Horn Trio with Aubrey Brain (a distinguished and influential player later overshadowed by the fame of his son Dennis) who, as always with him, employed the narrow-bore French horn – he regarded the German-type instrument now universal as 'too euphonium-like': though the former was more risky to play, Aubrey was uncommonly sure-footed and rarely split a note (never in this recording). This performance starts rather stiffly and cautiously, and the first movement takes wing only intermittently (with Adolf Busch as the vitalizing force); and keen ears will not be happy with the tuning of the piano nor the horn's accommodation to it. The *Adagio*, too, lacks convincing continuity; but the performance is just saved from being merely an interesting piece of historical documentation by the tremendous verve of the finale.

Piano Quintet in F minor, Op. 34.

Piano Quintet.
Maurizio Pollini *pf* **Quartetto Italiano** (Paolo Borciani, Elisa Pegreffi *vns* Dino Asciolla *va* Franco Rossi *vc*).
DG 419 673-2GH (43 minutes: AAD). *Gramophone* Award winner 1980. Ⓕ 🆁🆁

Most Brahms enthusiasts would agree that the Piano Quintet is his most exciting chamber work, and when it is supported by a quite unusually exciting performance it really does carry all before it.

In this recording you will find an exceptional degree of inspiration in both the music and in the way it is played. If you'll forgive the cliché, Pollini will sweep you off your feet. The combination of such notable musicians arouses high hopes, and this is indeed a fascinating performance. Pollini is very much in the driving seat. He dominates this Piano Quintet, at times perhaps a little more than he should, but this does give the performance a special quality. This is partly due to the rather variable balance which quite often makes the piano sound close and the strings a long way off. When Pollini is letting fly you cannot always hear the lower strings; too often you feel that he is a soloist, the strings the accompaniment. The slow movement is marvellous. Most of it sounds like a piano solo because it is written that way (and how beautifully Pollini plays it). The admirable Quartetto Italiano contributes to the full, notably in the *Scherzo* which receives the most exuberant and thrilling performance imaginable. And what an absolutely stunning movement it is when played like this! But all four movements have an almost mesmeric tension, a positively creative musicality; your attention is gripped, your absorption demanded as of right. The sound is splendidly rounded and full, especially the piano tone.

Piano Quintet. String Quartet No. 2 in A minor, Op. 51.
Elizo Virzaladze *pf* **Borodin Quartet** (Mikhail Kopelman, Andrei Abramenkov *vns*
Dimitri Shebalin *va* Valentin Berlinsky *vc*).
Teldec 4509-97461-2 (77 minutes: DDD). Recorded 1990. Ⓕ

These were recorded at The Maltings, Snape, which provides warm, reverberant reproduction very much in keeping with these players' vision of the well-nourished composer in middle age, a Brahms aglow yet at the same time more traditionally Germanic than Viennese. With the incisive Elizo Virzaladze at the keyboard, the Piano Quintet emerges with magisterial strength and breadth. Not even an earthquake could disrupt the rhythmic stability underpinning each movement (and not least the *Scherzo*), or shake the absolute certainty of each player's conviction. If the Brahms as guardian of classical tradition looms larger than the romanticist, there are still memorable reminders of the vulnerable heart behind it all – as, notably, in the stabbing intensity they bring to the finale's *poco sostenuto* introduction and temperamental coda.

Brahms Piano Quintet.
Henze Piano Quintet.
Peter Serkin *pf* **Guarneri Quartet** (Arnold Steinhardt, John Dalley *vns* Michael Tree *va*
David Soyer *vc*).
Philips 446 710-2PH (66 minutes: DDD). Recorded 1995. Ⓕ

Henze's Piano Quintet, in three relatively compact movements, develops a dialogue that is often dense but avoids the tendency to diffuseness sometimes found in his larger compositions. The piano shares ideas with the strings as well as standing apart from them, and, as with all Henze's best work, emotional intensity leads directly to troubled, never-quite-serene lyricism. Even though there are occasional moments of rhetorical overemphasis, moods of uneasy nostalgia and unquiet agitation are much more characteristic, especially in the urgently flowing, almost triumphantly assertive finale, with its satisfyingly abrupt ending. Henze's Quintet is given a fine performance by its dedicatees, and the conviction with which its rapidly shifting moods and textures are realized creates some regret that more Henze, or another twentieth-century piano quintet, was not included on the disc. Not that the performance of the Brahms is likely to disappoint. But there are so many other recommendable versions available. Both the Brahms and the Henze are recorded in a way which favours breadth of perspective over intimacy, but this seems right, given the grand style of the playing.

Brahms Piano Quintet.
Schubert Piano Quintet in A major, D667, 'Trout'.
Sir Clifford Curzon *pf* **Amadeus Quartet** (Norbert Brainin, Siegmund Nissel *vns* Peter Schidlof *va*
Martin Lovett *vc*); **James Edward Merrett** *db*
BBC Legends BBCL4009-2 (two discs: 82 minutes: ADD). Recorded live in 1974 and 1971. Ⓜ

If you put this set on at the end of a long day you will feel as if a new day has begun. Such is the power of great music-making … and these performances are indeed 'great'. Granted, the 1971 recording of the Schubert sounds marginally better than the 1974 Brahms, but the visceral excitement generated by the Brahms Quintet has to be heard to be believed. It would be fairly easy to imagine a tidier performance, but not one that is more spontaneous or inspired. Sir Clifford Curzon's grand vision registers within a few bars of the opening movement and heats to near-boiling point by the start of the recapitulation (from about ten minutes in). The emotional temperature rises even higher for the second movement. The distinction of the performance resides not so much in individual contributions as in the co-operation of all five players, which reaches unprecedented heights in the finale. No wonder the audience explodes: it is doubtful that anyone present has heard a finer performance since. Both Quintets include their important first-movement repeats.

The *Trout*'s repeated exposition is even more exciting than its first statement, and there is some gentle tempo acceleration during the development section. True, the strings make a fractionally late entrance at the beginning of the *Andante*, but the vitality of the *Scherzo* would be hard to beat, while the Theme and Variations features some notable playing from Lovett. There's an amusing spot of premature congratulation when applause momentarily breaks in at the end of the *Allegro giusto*'s exposition, but it soon withers to silence for a joyous finale. Here the recording rather favours the strings (there's a lifelike buzz to the double-bass), but better that than have the piano drown everyone else out. Wonderful stuff, all of it.

String Quintets – No. 1 in F major, Op. 88; No. 2 in G major, Op. 111.

String Quintets Nos. 1 and 2.
Walter Trampler *va* **Juilliard Quartet** (Robert Mann, Joel Smirnoff *vns* Samuel Rhodes *va* Joel Krosnick *vc*).
Sony Classical SK68476 (59 minutes: DDD). Recorded 1995. Ⓕ

What playing! Listen to how the Juilliard Quartet tackles the Second Quintet's opening: the pulse is vibrant, articulation is clean but never exaggerated, chords are properly weighted and when we reach the development's shimmering first bars at 5'54" – absolute rapture – there's simply no other word for it. The *Adagio*'s sombre outer sections are both expressive and transparent and one has to cite the opening bars of the *Un poco Allegretto* third movement as among the most perfect examples of instrumental voicing ever heard on a chamber music record: *everything* tells, and yet the phrasing remains mobile and expressive. The First Quintet is virtually as good, with a warmly cosseted account of the first movement's waltz-like second set and an impressive build-up of tension from, say, 6'41" – one of the most Dvořákian passages in all of Brahms. Readers who only know the Juilliard Quartet from its lean, intense and tonally fragile RCA/CBS recordings of the late 1950s and early 1960s will find these performances far warmer and more 'European' in tone – although a binding intelligence is common to virtually all of the group's recordings (even through various changes of personnel).

String Quintets Nos. 1 and 2.
Gérard Caussé *va* **Hagen Quartet** (Lukas Hagen, Rainer Schmidt *vns* Veronika Hagen *va* Clemens Hagen *vc*).
DG 453 420-2GH (59 minutes: DDD). Recorded 1996. Ⓕ

The affirmative *Allegro* that launches the Second String Quintet on its course is exhilarating and the recording by the augmented Hagen Quartet greets the air like an unexpected sunbeam. This particular recording combines clarity and substance; nothing is left to chance and the end result is notably colourful, both in tone and in feeling. The First Quintet is crisply pointed, with crystalline textures, a pleasantly laid-back account of the first movement's lovely second set and a finely tensed development section. Furthermore, the heavily contrapuntal finale is played with great precision and rhythmic *élan*. Both performances include first-movement exposition repeats and both represent the Hagens' 'stylistic grid' at its most convincing, in other words, with vividly attenuated dynamics, occasional volatility, a consistent sense of line, impressive internal clarity, equal distribution of voices and a remarkable degree of concentration. Very well recorded and expertly annotated.

Piano Quartets – No. 1 in G minor, Op. 25; No. 2 in A major, Op. 26; No. 3 in C minor, Op. 60.
Isaac Stern *vn* **Jaime Laredo** *va* **Yo-Yo Ma** *vc* **Emanuel Ax** *pf*
Sony Classical S2K45846 (two discs: 128 minutes: DDD). Recorded 1986-89.
Gramophone Award Winner 1991. ⒻⓈ

The piano quartets belong to the middle of Brahms's life. They have all the power and lyricism that we associate with his music; but alongside a wealth of melodic and harmonic invention there are some shadows: all we know of Brahms's life suggests that he was never a happy man. Even if this is reflected in the music, and especially the C minor Quartet, all is kept in proportion and there is no overt soul-bearing. These quartets are big pieces which often employ a grand manner, though less so in No. 2 than the others. For this reason, the present performances with their exuberant sweep are particularly telling, and although no detail is missed the players offer an overall strength. Top soloists in their own right, they combine their individual gifts with the ability to play as a well-integrated team. The recording is close but not overwhelmingly so.

Piano Quartet No. 1. Four Ballades, Op. 10.
Emil Gilels *pf* members of the **Amadeus Quartet** (Norbert Brainin *vn* Peter Schidlof *va* Martin Lovett *vc*).
DG The Originals 447 407-2GOR (65 minutes: ADD). Recorded 1970 and 1975.   Ⓜ

This is an outstanding performance of Brahms's G minor Piano Quartet, unforgettable for its spontaneity and uninhibited romantic warmth and verve. The booklet reminds us that this 1971 recording made history since 'a contract between an artist from the Soviet Union and a Western label was a sensational event in cultural diplomacy'. Reproduced with respect for the sound quality of its time, the playing has a glowing strength and intensity throughout. Only in the first movement's opulent textures does the keyboard occasionally dominate. From Gilels we're also given a maturely unhurried, essentially 'inward' recording (made some five years later) of Brahms's four youthful *Ballades*, with their strange, almost supernatural undertones. A bargain. (Incidentally this is the same recording of the Ballades as the one reviewed with Gilels's recording of Concerto No. 2 earlier.)

String Quartets – No. 1 in C minor, Op. 51 No. 1; No. 2 in A minor, Op. 51; No. 3 in B flat major, Op. 67.

String Quartets Nos. 1 and 3.
Borodin Quartet (Mikhail Kopelman, Andrei Abramenkov *vns* Dimitri Shebalin *va* Valentin Berlinsky *vc*).
Teldec 4509-90889-2 (69 minutes: DDD). Recorded 1993.   Ⓕ

It's essentially the mature, middle-aged composer that the Borodin Quartet evokes in this full-bodied, spacious and firmly-contoured performance of the C minor Quartet. Compared with the Alban Berg Quartet (see below), the first and most obvious difference is the Borodin's more deliberate tempo for the powerful flanking movements in the home key. It prefers breadth to its rivals' urgency. In the *Romanze*, richly romantic from both teams, the Borodin favours a riper sound world, warmly fortified by their viola and cello, as against the Berg's more translucent sonority, with its ethereal *pianissimo* often evoking the rapt magic of moonlight. Differences in the B flat Quartet are less marked: both readings are vividly characterful. But again – and perhaps most of all in the finale – the overriding impression is of more traditionally Germanic romanticism from the Russians, whereas from the Viennese team we meet a more minutely impressionable as well as a more highly-strung composer. The Teldec recording, made in this company's Berlin studio, is as full, warm and open as the playing. Whichever group you choose, you will not be disappointed.

String Quartets Nos. 1-3.
Alban Berg Quartet (Günter Pichler, Gerhard Schulz *vns* Thomas Kakuska *va* Valentin Erben *vc*).
EMI CDS7 54829-2 (two discs: 102 minutes: DDD). Recorded 1991.   Ⓕ

Whereas the C minor and B flat major Quartets were recorded at sessions in a Swiss church, the A minor Quartet is a live concert performance, as applause confirms. All three works emerge not only with the technical fluency and finish for which this Viennese team has long been renowned but also with quite exceptional immediacy and vividness. The first and last movements of No. 1 spring at you with all the drama Brahms invariably drew from C minor. Yet the music's cajoling lyricism is very lovingly cherished too. The players' wide dynamic range is faithfully reproduced right down to the most intimate confidence – and of course the ensuing *Romanze*, very tenderly and delicately interwoven, brings still stronger proof of their awareness of the eloquence of *pianissimo* in all its variations of colour and character. In the B flat Quartet (No. 3), which shares the first disc, they at once capture its carefree rustic verve with their bold dynamic contrasts and relish of the composer's rhythmic teasing. For the *Andante*'s confident F major song Pichler finds a glowing fervour. The A minor Quartet, recorded at St Petersburg's Palais Yusopov, monopolizes the second disc – some might think a little extravagantly since the playing time is only just 35 minutes. Tonal production is no less clear and true, even if just a shade less vibrant and lustrous than in that resonant Swiss church. Or maybe this impression can be attributed to the players themselves in their desire to convey the work's retreat into a more elusive, wistful world, a world they evoke with such effortless fluency, fluidity and grace. In sum, a strongly recommended issue for anyone wanting a keen-edged reminder of this composer's warm and vulnerable romantic heart.

String Quartets Nos. 1 and 2.
Cleveland Quartet (William Preucil, Peter Salaff *vns* James Dunham *va* Paul Katz *vc*).
Telarc CD80346 (68 minutes: DDD). Recorded 1993.   Ⓕ

Though the Cleveland Quartet has changed both its leader and viola player in recent years, all the old tonal opulence is still very much there. So is all the old fire, and equally, the determination to wring the last drop of expression from even the most intimate confession. In short, you would be unlikely to meet a more overtly romantic composer than the Brahms you meet here. In the C minor Quartet's *Romanze* some listeners might in fact prefer the very mellow but more emotionally reticent Borodin Quartet, or the Alban Berg with their ethereally withdrawn *pianissimo*. In the bolder flanking movements it is as compulsive as the highly-strung, impressionable Alban Berg while often finding a broader, suaver, melodic sweep. The venue was its favoured Mechanics Hall at Worcester, Massachusetts, a warmly reverberant building – as the sheer fullness of the sound makes plain.

Brahms String Quartet No. 3.
Schubert String Quintet in C major, D956.
Miloš Sádlo *vc* **Smetana Quartet** (Jiří Novák, Lubomír Kostecký *vns* Milan Skampa *va* Antonín Kohout *vc*).
Testament SBT1120 (75 minutes: ADD). Recorded 1965 and 1973.   Ⓕ

This documents the prime of a fine ensemble that sprang to life in wartime Prague and retired from active service as recently as 1989. The beauty of tone, balancing of chords, dynamic shading, precision of ensemble and matching vibrato were, for most of the time, as much in evidence in the 1960s and early 1970s as in the 1950s. There is no doubt whatever that this disc exhibits some supremely distinguished string quartet playing, but whether readers will unanimously warm to each featured interpretation is another matter. The Schubert Quintet has many admirable virtues, including absolute internal clarity, genial characterization of the first movement's second subject and the whole of the finale, rhythmic stability and excellent sound quality. But the original producer had insisted that the players employ a single swift tempo for both the inner and the outer sections of the *Adagio*, an option that will strike some as needlessly pedantic. No tempo alteration is marked in the score and although the results are quite refreshing, the actual phrasing seems a trifle bland. The Brahms Op. 67 coupling is less controversial, though no less musical: inner voices are crystal-clear and the first movement is nearer to a genuine *Vivace* than in many better-known performances. Only the *Andante*'s opening is rather foursquare. Sound quality tends to vary between sessions but the transfers are truly state-of-the-art.

Brahms Clarinet Trio in A minor, Op. 114.
Holbrooke Clarinet Quintet No. 1 in G major, Op. 27 No. 1.
Weber Clarinet Concertino in E flat major, J109.
Reginald Kell *cl* **Anthony Pini** *vc* **Louis Kentner** *pf* **Willoughby Quartet** (Louis Willoughby, Kenneth Skeaping *vns* Aubrey Appleton *va* Vivian Joseph *vc*); **orchestra / Walter Goehr**.
Testament mono SBT1002 (54 minutes: ADD). Recorded 1941.   Ⓕ Ⓗ

In the rapturous love-duet between clarinet and cello in the *Adagio* of the Clarinet Trio, Reginald Kell's tonal warmth and beauty seem more than ever appropriate. Elsewhere in this work, though, despite his liquid sound and finesse of dynamics he is all but outshone by the eloquent lyricism and passion of that superb player Anthony Pini (listen to his statement of the *Allegro*'s second subject). Together with Kentner's understanding collaboration, never over-assertive but always supportive, an admirably cohesive team is formed, always alive to Brahms's interplay of interest and changes of mood. Kell is unquestionably the star of the Quintet by Josef Holbrooke which has fallen into total neglect, and frankly the present diffuse work (concocted out of previous compositions in the most extraordinary way) will not prompt much revaluation of his status. Nevertheless, it offers great opportunities for *cantabile* clarinet playing in the central Canzonet and for fluent virtuosity in the finale, and Kell excels in both (though the latter finds weaknesses in the Willoughby Quartet). Not unexpectedly the Weber *Concertino*, every clarinettist's party-piece, finds Kell displaying, besides an easy technical brilliance, beauty of tone, a charming sense of phrase and sensitive dynamic nuances. Walter Goehr's orchestral accompaniment is clean and fully alert throughout.

Horn Trio in E flat major, Op. 40. Piano Quintet.
Nash Ensemble (Marcia Crayford, Elizabeth Layton *vns* Roger Chase *va* Christopher van Kampen *vc* Frank Lloyd *hn* Ian Brown *pf*).
CRD CRD3489 (73 minutes: DDD). Recorded 1991.   Ⓕ

It would be hard to imagine more amiable performances of these two strongly characterized Brahms works. The Nash Ensemble's comfortable approach is intense as well as warm, plainly derived from long experience performing this music in concert. The speeds in both works are markedly slower than on other versions, and the ensemble is a degree less polished, but in their expressive warmth they are just as magnetic, with a sense of continuity that the higher-powered readings do not always convey. The romanticism of the Nash approach comes out particularly strongly in the opening *Andante* of the Horn Trio, with the horn soloist, Frank Lloyd, producing an exceptionally rich, braying tone, reminiscent of Dennis Brain. After relaxed accounts of the first three movements the galloping finale is then given with great panache. Thanks partly to the CRD recording, the Nash performances are made to sound satisfyingly beefy, almost orchestral, though some may find the full-bodied sound a degree too reverberant, with the piano rather in front of the strings. The disc can be strongly recommended, particularly as this is the only available coupling of these two works.

Piano Trios – No. 1 in B major, Op. 8; No. 2 in C major, Op. 87; No. 3 in C minor, Op. 101.

Piano Trios Nos. 1-3. Horn Trio in E flat major, Op. 40. Clarinet Trio in A minor, Op. 114.
Richard Hosford *cl* **Stephen Stirling** *hn* **Florestan Trio** (Anthony Marwood *vn* Richard Lester *vc* Susan Tomes *pf*).
Hyperion CDA67251/2 (two discs: 137 minutes: DDD). Recorded 1997.   Ⓕ

Aided by an especially clear, vivid, yet spacious recording, the Florestan Trio and their two colleagues allow us to hear far more of this music than usual – the elaborate decoration of Op. 114's *Adagio*, or the sinister detail of the more delicate passages in Op. 8's *Scherzo*. Much of the credit for this goes to Susan Tomes; her playing is an object-lesson in sensitivity and in matching the other voices. Balance and blend are a special feature of these performances. Anthony Marwood and Richard Lester match their sounds perfectly for the lovely duet passages in the slow movements of Op. 8 and Op. 101. What is less expected, and less usual, is the matching of violin and horn, cello and clarinet. But perhaps the single outstanding feature of all the performances is the way the music is shaped. It's not only that the phrases are projected clearly and expressively – the approach moves outwards to encompass the music's larger paragraphs and, indeed, whole movements. These are very desirable recordings, then. Pires, Dumay and Wang (DG) offer big-toned performances on the grand scale of Opp. 8 and 87, splendidly recorded. It's not easy to choose between them and the wholehearted, but more intimate approach of the Florestan.

Brahms Piano Trio No. 1.
Mendelssohn Piano Trio No. 1 in D minor, Op. 49.
Chung Trio (Kyung-Wha Chung *vn* Myung-Wha Chung *vc* Myung-Whun Chung *pf*).
Decca 421 425-2DH (65 minutes: DDD). Recorded 1987.   ⒻⓇⓇ

These are real connoisseur performances. It is the streamlining, the new clarity and economy of idea and structure in Brahms's revision of the Op. 8 which the Chungs uniquely reveal. As timbres blend gently at each confluence, it is the journey rather than the destination which really matters to them in the first movement. The care with which the piano feels its way into the second subject prepares for the subtlest nuances of detail and variation in the development, so that the first idea resurfaces in its final form under bright, new light. The *Scherzo* is one of the sharpest on disc; the clarity of the *Adagio*'s quiet playing as much credit to Christopher Raeburn's direction as to the performers' sensitivity. The Mendelssohn *Molto allegro agitato* restrains its tendency to romp ahead too early: the Chungs' antennae focus on the underlying melancholy within the music's dark wash, built up by the cello's introduction of both first and second subjects. They give space and time enough for the maximum clarity of articulation of shorter note values, and create a substantial head of steam for their first joint statement. The restrained tempo means that Myung-Whun's piano can glory in its strength of direction, and in the quiet beauty of its linking passages, while Kyung-Wha's violin can sing its heart out. The slow movement follows as a continuing though becalmed song. And the *Scherzo*, Ariel-like, drinks the air before it and, in turn, influences the finale whose dactylic dance barely touches the ground.

Piano Trios Nos. 1 and 2.
Augustin Dumay *vn* **Jian Wang** *vc* **Maria João Pires** *pf*
DG 447 055-2GH (67 minutes: DDD). Recorded 1995.   Ⓕ

In the Chinese cellist Jian Wang, the duo of Augustin Dumay and Maria João Pires have found themselves a true soul mate as this, their first disc of piano trios together, engagingly shows. The B major Trio doesn't quite topple the Chungs' recording, still at the very top of the list; but it comes pretty near it. The *Scherzo*'s trio, likewise, pulls back to form a slow, soupy centrepiece. Here the rubato is a little mannered, lacking perhaps the instinctive lilt of other versions. Everything, though, can be traded in for the sheer wonder of this *Adagio*. As slow as any on disc, it reveals the real empathy between Dumay and Wang in moments of great beauty where the Milstein legacy in Dumay's playing is wonderfully apparent. For the C major Trio, Dumay, Pires and Wang offer a generally broad and spacious performance, and a suppleness of repartee in the slow movement's variations which matches their fluency of invention. The *Scherzo*'s niggling is as compact and securely balanced as any, before the players glide, then stride, into the bright sunlight of the Trio.

Cello Sonatas – No. 1 in E minor, Op. 38; No. 2 in F major, Op. 99.

Cello Sonatas Nos. 1 and 2.
Heinrich Schiff vc **Gerhard Oppitz** pf
Philips 456 402-2PH (55 minutes: DDD). Recorded 1996.   Ⓕ **RR**

Brahms's cello sonatas make for an ideal coupling, and not merely because there are only two of them. The differences between them are significant, both in terms of tone and character – the First being fairly mellow and soft-spoken, the Second full of bold contrasts. Oppitz is already well known for some excellent Brahms recordings, primarily the solo works, and his subtlety follows through in this recording. Schiff and Oppitz enjoy a warm, intimate acoustic (at Reinstadl, Neumarkt in Germany) that suits the fastidiously articulated profile of their performances. In the Second Sonata's *Allegro vivace* first movement their handling of the eerie F sharp minor development is particularly fine, and Schiff's vibrant pizzicatos near the start of the *Adagio affettuoso* create precisely the sort of sound world that Brahms must have envisaged. Schiff and Oppitz are also enjoyable in the First Sonata's elegant *Allegretto quasi Menuetto* and in the way they slowly edge into the third movement of the Second Sonata. This is a delicate partnership, sensitive to nuance and attentive to phrasal minutiae. Schiff's refined performance readily connects with the music's song-like, musing qualities. This coupling is a delight; comely music-making much enhanced by a fine balance of head and heart.

Cello Sonatas Nos. 1 and 2.
Mstislav Rostropovich vc **Rudolf Serkin** pf
DG 410 510-2GH (58 minutes: DDD). Recorded 1982.   Ⓕ

Our younger generation of cello soloists seems to favour a tone production which balances a refined upper range (which at times might be mistaken for a viola, or even a violin) with a middle and lower register that is strong and well focused, rather than expansively rich and resonant. Readers will not need to be told that Rostropovich's solo image is definitely not of this ilk: his musical personality is in every sense larger than life and in this magnificent coupling of the cello sonatas, in partnership with Rudolf Serkin, the very forward balance of the recording exaggerates this impression in the most vivid way. By comparison the piano image – to the right of and behind the cello – is more reticent in timbre and seldom matches Rostropovich's rich flood of sound, which is not, of course, to suggest that Serkin fails to project the music, merely that the microphone placing makes Rostropovich very much the dominating artist. This passionately warm-hearted and ripely Brahmsian music-making almost overwhelms the listener in its sheer impact. But with playing of this calibre, with both artists wonderfully attuned to each other's responses, every nuance tells and Brahms's bold melodic lines soar out from the speakers (and the cello seems only just inside them) to capture the listener's imagination, and provide an enthralling musical experience in each and every work.

Cello Sonatas Nos. 1 and 2.
Peter Bruns vc **Olga Tverskaya** fp
Opus 111 OPS30-144 (52 minutes: DDD). Recorded 1996.   Ⓕ **P**

This highly accomplished pair opt for the kind of sound that Brahms himself would have envisaged when writing for these two instruments. The German cellist, Peter Bruns, plays a Venetian Tononi of 1730 in partnership with the Erard grand piano, built at their London factory around 1850, chosen by the Russian-born Olga Tverskaya. It's not hard to understand why this Tononi was Casals's favourite concert instrument (according to the booklet) for 12 years: its glorious tonal plangency would melt a stone. The Erard has a clear-cut translucency that yet never seems undernourished or edgy throughout a very considerable range. The artists themselves cannot be overpraised for their finely attuned balance throughout both sonatas: not even in the low-lying string line in the finale of the earlier, more classically conceived E minor work, or the richer keyboard textures of its successor, is the cello overpowered. Nor is any detail in Brahms's closely interwoven dialogue overlooked: your ear is always where it ought to be thanks to their intimate give and take. Have no fear that concern for period sound in any way cools their approach. What ultimately makes this very truthfully recorded disc so enjoyable is the immediacy and intensity of their personal response to the composer's warm romantic heart. Every note speaks in a way that can scarcely fail to touch your own.

Brahms Viola Sonatas – No. 1 in F minor, Op. 120 No. 1; No. 2 in E flat major, Op. 120 No. 2.
Schumann Märchenbilder, Op. 113.
Lars Anders Tomter *va* **Leif Ove Andsnes** *pf*
Virgin Classics VC7 59309-2 (60 minutes: DDD). Recorded 1991.   Ⓕ

Although the last piece of Schumann's *Märchenbilder* has generally been regarded as a little gem,
the first three – and especially the two faster middle movements – have been criticized for
repetitively patterned figuration that can sometimes sound obsessive. But such is the imaginative
vitality of these two Norwegian artists that there's no such danger here. There's an irresistible
buoyancy in the springy dotted rhythms of No. 2 as well as true urgency in the scurrying
semiquaver triplets of No. 3, while the regret-tinged opening reflection and the heart-easing, lullaby-
like 'Abschied' are both phrased with loving tenderness. Thanks to Schumann's comparatively light
keyboard texture Tomter and Andsnes achieve a more subtly balanced partnership here than in the
two Brahms sonatas. Though unfailingly attentive to softer confidences in these, the young Andsnes
nevertheless often strikes you as more assertive in response to louder dynamic markings than the
pleasingly incandescent but not outsize-toned Tomter, as his forceful *marcato* in the fifth (*allegro*)
variation of the E flat Sonata's finale makes very clear. At moments of heightened challenge he's
inclined to forget that the low-voiced viola has not quite the tonal penetration of the clarinet which
inspired these works. That said, there's infinitely more to praise than to question in these works too.
Fundamentally, both players are discerning musicians, keenly anxious to convey the ageing Brahms's
autumnal nostalgia, a lifetime's emotion so eloquently 'recollected in tranquillity'. The recording is
clear and truthful, even picking up intakes of breath as proof of the viola's involvement.

Violin Sonatas – No. 1 in G major, Op. 78; No. 2 in A major, Op. 100; No. 3 in D minor, Op. 108.

Violin Sonatas Nos. 1-3.
Itzhak Perlman *vn* **Vladimir Ashkenazy** *pf*
EMI CDM5 66945-2 (70 minutes: DDD). Recorded 1983.   Ⓜ 🅁🅁

If anyone doubts that these three sonatas represent Brahms at his most blissfully lyrical, then this is
an essential set to hear. The trouble-free happiness of these mellow inspirations, all written after the
main body of Brahms's orchestral music had been completed, comes over richly and seductively in
these fine performances. In their sureness and flawless confidence, they carry you along cocooned in
rich sound. Perlman consistently produces rich, full-bodied tone, an excellent illustration being the
way that he evokes a happy, trouble-free mood in the melody which opens the second movement
Adagio of No. 3. The obverse of this is that with such consistent richness and warmth, the three
sonatas come to sound more alike than they usually do, or maybe should, a point which comes out
the more from playing them in sequence. It is true that Perlman does quite often play softly, but for
some tastes he is placed too close to the microphone, and the actual dynamic level remains rather
high, however gently he is playing. This is not to say that with sharp imagination and with superbly
clean articulation from the pianist, these performances lack range of expression, and one thinks
especially of the rhythmic pointing, which gives a Hungarian or a Slavonic tang to such passages as
the first contrasting episode in the 'raindrop' finale of No. 1 or the contrasting *Vivace* passages in
the second movement of No. 2, where the last pizzicato reprise is made totally delectable. These
performances are both distinctive and authoritative. The recording is bright, with a good sense of
atmosphere to give bite to the piano tone without diminishing the warmth of Perlman's violin.

Violin Sonatas Nos. 1-3.
Pamela Frank *vn* **Peter Serkin** *pf*
Decca 455 643-2DH (69 minutes: DDD). Recorded 1996.   Ⓕ

Pamela Frank's free-spirited, lean, lightly bowed and subtly variegated tone production is
thoroughly eventful and thought-provoking. Both she and Peter Serkin make a nutritious meal out
of the First Sonata's opening *Vivace ma non troppo*, supple and low-key but action-packed, with
Serkin's quiet trills meaningfully mirroring Frank's shuddering double-stopped arpeggios. The
Adagio is delicate, limpid and sensitively set up by Serkin; note, too, Frank's meticulously graded
chords and her chaste playing of the finale's opening theme. The first page of the Second Sonata
finds her adapting her lean but strong tone to the music's mellower sound world, with Serkin
offering her colourfully pedalled support. True, Serkin's pedalling sometimes registers on the
recording as mechanical action (i.e. as a sort of distant thunder), but you soon get used to it. In the
Third Sonata, the balance of power shifts from Frank to Serkin. But there is delicacy aplenty, too –
not least in the *Scherzo*. The *Adagio* is very slow indeed, effectively so for most of its duration
though some might feel that the more flowing tempo chosen by some of Frank's best rivals is
musically more appropriate. Decca's recordings are both intimate and realistic and, of modern
digital, single-disc recordings of this repertoire, this is one of the best.

Violin Sonatas Nos. 1-3.
Augustin Dumay *vn* **Maria João Pires** *pf*
DG 435 800-2GH (72 minutes: DDD).   Ⓕ

Of the numerous recordings of the violin sonatas available, Dumay and Pires easily deserve to be
considered amongst the best, for their playing is consistently mature, stylistically homogeneous and,
above all, refined. They never waste a note of the music, and yet it is always allowed to unfurl
naturally. A reflective eloquence at the opening of the G major Sonata sets the mood for the entire
CD. Pires contributes many lovely delicate touches and there is great breadth to her phrasing when
this is required. The first movement of the A major work may be slightly slack in its cohesiveness,
but in the *Andante tranquillo* that follows one realizes that the duo sees Brahms above all else as a
lyrical dreamer. Only in the D minor Sonata does one feel the darkly intense aspect of the
composer's character and here the *Presto agitato* finale is everything it should be in terms of tempo
and storminess. The recorded sound is pleasant on the ear, without being ideal. The piano tone is a
bit muffled and wanting in colour; this is especially apparent when the two instruments are playing
together. But overall this is a release of considerable distinction.

Two Rhapsodies, Op. 79. Three Intermezzos, Op. 117. Six Piano Pieces, Op. 118. Four Piano
Pieces, Op. 119.
Radu Lupu *pf*
Decca 417 599-2DH (71 minutes: ADD). Recorded 1970s.   Ⓕ **RR**

Here are 71 minutes of the finest Brahms piano music, played by one of the outstanding Brahms
exponents of our day. What is most treasurable about it is the quiet rapture of some of the most
quintessentially Brahmsian moments; for example, the way Lupu sleepwalks into the last section of
Op. 117 No. 3 and the revelation in Op. 118 No. 2 that the inversion of the theme is even more
beautiful than its original statement. The Op. 79 *Rhapsodies* are perhaps a fraction less memorable.
Decca's recording sounds a little bottom-heavy, in the manner of certain Ashkenazy records of this
vintage, and in the heavier textures of the *Rhapsodies* Lupu compounds the problem by reinforcing
the bass with octaves and even fifths. Still, this remains as fine a selection of Brahms's piano works
as you are likely to find on one disc.

Brahms Variations on a Theme by Paganini, Op. 35.
Schumann Arabeske in C major, Op. 18. Etudes symphoniques, Opp. 13 and posth.
Jean-Yves Thibaudet *pf*
Decca 444 338-2DH (65 minutes: DDD).   Ⓕ

This is a refreshingly individual, though never quirky, display of imaginative vitality in the two most
virtuosic works for solo piano that Schumann and Brahms ever wrote. Predictably the technical
challenges of Brahms's notorious *Paganini* Variations hold few fears for Thibaudet. Even Horowitz
once admitted that in Liszt's *Faust* Waltz he'd heard Thibaudet's fingers do things that his own
couldn't in dexterity, clarity of articulation and general command. But virtuosity is never an end in
itself. What surprises and pleases most is Thibaudet's readiness to relax and revel in the romance,
the mystery, the lyrical charm and the sheer tonal seductiveness of the less demonstrative, the more
personally expressive, variations. Some listeners may of course find his whole approach too
fancifully Gallic, insufficiently Germanic for interpretations of works by these composers. But more
than one road leads to Rome, and arguably even Brahms himself would succumb to the spring-like
allure of this one. Schumann's *Arabeske*, delectably liquid (despite its overhasty second A minor
episode), brings brief respite before the *Etudes symphoniques*, which, like nearly everyone today,
Thibaudet plays in the posthumously published 1861 edition (reinstating the two numbers excluded
by Schumann in his own 1852 revision though retaining its tautened finale). His leisurely unfolding
of the theme, followed by an uncommonly brisk first variation (marked only *un poco più vivo*)
typifies his immediacy of response to every changing mood, which once more, as in the Brahms,
results in a reading perhaps more memorable for variety than continuity. But again his fingers sing
as finely as they sparkle. He wisely plays the five posthumously published, rejected early variations
as a separate group at the end of the work, rightly reserving his most intimately poetic revelations
for the last two, both beautifully done. Sound reproduction throughout is at once natural and never
too forward for comfort in your own room.

Variations on a Theme by Paganini, Op. 35. Variations and Fugue on a Theme by Handel, Op. 24.
Four Ballades, Op. 10. Variations on a Theme by Schumann, Op. 9. Variations on an Original
Theme, Op. 21 No. 1. Variations on a Hungarian Song, Op. 21 No. 2. Waltzes, Op. 39.
Two Rhapsodies, Op. 79. Piano Sonatas – No. 1 in C major, Op. 1; No. 2 in F sharp minor, Op. 2;

No. 3 in F minor, Op. 5. Scherzo in E flat minor, Op. 4. Piano Pieces – Op. 76; Op. 116; Op. 117; Op. 118; Op. 119. Hungarian Dances (with Jean-Pierre Marty *pf*).
Julius Katchen *pf*
Decca 430 053-2DM6 (six discs: 388 minutes: ADD). Recorded 1962-66.   Ⓜ

The American pianist Julius Katchen made his name in the early 1950s and died in 1969, but although one thinks of him as a distinguished figure from the last generation, it is salutary to realize that he would probably be performing today if his career had not ended when he was only 42. Even so, his legacy of recordings reminds us of his gifts and the breadth of his repertory, and the present Brahms cycle has distinction. It begins with an account of the *Paganini* Variations that gives ample proof of his splendidly assured technique: the playing tells us at once that the challenging variations in sixths (Nos. 1 and 2 in Book 1) held no terrors for him, and the athleticism here is matched by a fluency in the *leggiero* writing of the variation that follows. In general, though, he makes one more aware of a keyboard virtuoso in this work, rather than a poet; there are other performances which balance these two qualities more finely. Tempos tend to rapidity, too, and the piano sound tends to have a hardish brilliance. However, he does bring a gentler quality to the three other sets of variations here, not least in his freer use of rubato and tonal nuance, as witness (say) the serene Variations Nos. 11-12 in the big *Handel* set, where the recording from three years earlier is easier on the ear too. Here, as elsewhere, there is a little tape hiss, but it is not enough to distract.

If praise over the *Paganini* Variations seems a touch grudging, it should be said at once that poetry is to be found in good measure in Katchen's playing of the *Four Ballades*, Op. 10. These pieces belie the composer's youth in their deep introspection, though the pianist takes a brisk view of the *Andante con moto* tempo in No. 4. The 16 Waltzes of Op. 39 are attractive too in their crispness and charm, and the early *Scherzo* in E flat minor has the right dour vigour. The three sonatas are also impressive in their strong, energetic interpretative grasp, though one could wish that the first-movement repeat of No. 1 had been observed. Also, slow movements could have a still more inward quality to convey that brooding self-communion which is so characteristic of this composer (though that of Sonata No. 3 in F minor is pretty near it). But the great F minor Sonata is spacious and thoughtful as well as leonine, and this is a noble performance, well recorded in 1966. The shorter pieces are finely done also. Katchen is in his element in the Two Rhapsodies of Op. 79, balancing their stormy and lyrical qualities to perfection. The *Fantasias*, Op. 116, are not so well recorded (the sound is a bit muffled, as if the engineers wished to tame the pianist's attack). However, the playing is masterly and Katchen's sympathy for the idiom is evident, with tenderness, tragedy, twilight mystery and storm and stress fully playing their part and giving a golden glow to such pieces as the lovely E major *Intermezzo* which is No. 6 of the set and the A major *Intermezzo*, Op. 118 No. 2. Possibly more sensuous gipsy charm could be found in, say, the B minor *Capriccio* of Op. 76, but it is very attractive playing and the playful C major *Intermezzo* in Op. 119 is delightful, as is the tender lullaby that begins Op. 117. Only the first 10 of the 21 Hungarian Dances exist in the composer's own (extremely difficult) version for piano solo, and in the others, written for piano duet, Katchen is joined by Jean-Pierre Marty; there's plenty of fire here and much to enjoy. Altogether, this Brahms set is a fine memorial to Katchen and a worthy issue; purchasers will not be disappointed.

Piano Sonata No. 3 in F minor, Op. 5.

Brahms Piano Sonata No. 3. Intermezzos[a] – E flat major, Op. 117 No. 1; C major, Op. 119 No. 3.
Schubert Piano Sonata No. 21 in B flat major, D960[a].
Sir Clifford Curzon *pf*
Decca The Classic Sound 448 578-2DCS (77 minutes: ADD). Recorded 1962, [a]1972.   Ⓜ

It took wild horses to drag Curzon into the studio, at least in his last years, and he was a record company's nightmare when it came to agreeing what might be issued. One could say that Curzon was not a natural pianist, yet he developed a technique which admirably served the force of his will: and when the two were in harness and in good shape the transcendental aspects of his playing could produce an indelible musical experience. These recordings have lost none of their freshness. The little holes and imperfections are quite unimportant because at every moment Curzon is conveying an exactitude of character and sense. His sound 'speaks' and persuades you to listen to something precise. Nothing is generalized. Yet the overview is there as well as the detail, particularly in the Schubert. As with every great pianist, the quality of his sound is distinctive: tightly focused, crystalline, refulgent. With his sovereign control of line and timing, the pianism seems at all times to be perfectly weighted and to have everything within its sights. You could say that about other great interpreters, no doubt, but there is a special attractiveness about Curzon's ability to delight the senses while penetrating to the heart of the matter. When he was on form he could talk of the most serious things while singing at you like a nightingale. How crude most performances of the Brahms F minor Sonata seem when compared with his. All the climaxes well up from within (and how they glow), yet its scale and range are thrillingly made manifest. This is terrific value at mid-price. The sound is fair to good in both the big pieces – and only slightly inferior in the earlier recording. The two Brahms *Intermezzos* are in a very dry acoustic as if Curzon had recorded them at home (perhaps he did?); but so they were on the original LP.

Brahms Piano Sonata No. 3.
Liszt La leggierezza, S144 No. 2ª. Années de pèlerinage, Première Année, S160, 'Suisse' – Au bord d'une sourceª. Hungarian Rhapsody No. 15 in A minor, S244ᵇ.
Schumann Carnaval, Op. 9.
Solomon *pf*
Testament mono SBT1084 (79 minutes: ADD). Recorded 1952; item marked ª recorded
1930, ᵇ1932.   Ⓕ🄷

Solomon's 1952 recordings of Schumann's *Carnaval* and the Brahms Sonata in F minor are essential for the desert island, so this well-produced Testament compilation, generously filled out with Liszt, recommends itself. If you've heard tell of Solomon's reputation but don't know his work, or perhaps know only his Beethoven, snap it up. The sound has come up astonishingly well, also in the Liszt pieces which were made in 1930 and 1932. Solomon's performance of 'Au bord d'une source' is a match for Liszt's poetic inspiration, as few recordings of it are. Technical address and refinement on this level constitute a small miracle.

---

16 Waltzes, Op. 39. Ten Hungarian Dances.
Idil Biret *pf*
Naxos 8 550355 (52 minutes: DDD). Recorded 1992.   Ⓢ

Both the *Waltzes* and the *Hungarian Dances* are extremely demanding in their two-hand form, and in the latter collection one could often believe that the 20 fingers of two duettists must be involved, so many notes are being played in all registers (for an example, try No. 8 in A minor). However, the technical problems evidently hold no terrors for this pianist and her performances are both convincing and attractive. What more need be said about this playing of music in which Brahms portrayed, in turn, sophisticated Vienna and untamed Hungary? Well, not a great deal. The quicker *Waltzes* have plenty of vivacity, and the slower ones are lyrical in an aptly Viennese manner. Tempos, textures, phrasing, rubato and pedalling are well managed and the playing has a very convincing blend of subtlety and simplicity. She treats these 16 pieces as a sequence, as Brahms's key structure allows, and leaves relatively little gap between them. The *Hungarian Dances* have a darkly surging Magyar energy and sound that are very pleasing: indeed, Biret seems totally at home in this music. The recording is a bit larger than life, but perfectly acceptable.

Two Rhapsodies, Op. 79 – No. 1 in B minor; No. 2 in G minor. 16 Waltzes, Op. 39.

Two Rhapsodies, Op. 79. 16 Waltzes, Op. 39. Six Piano Pieces, Op. 118.
Stephen Kovacevich *pf*
Philips 420 750-2PH (53 minutes: DDD).   Ⓕ

The Op. 79 *Rhapsodies* have been described as the 'most temperamental' of all Brahms's later keyboard works. It would certainly be hard to imagine more vehement performances than those given by Kovacevich, thanks to his robust tone, trenchant attack and urgent tempos – perhaps even a shade too fast for the *Molto passionato, ma non troppo allegro* of the Second. But the pleading second subject of No. 1 in B minor brings all the requisite lyrical contrast. The Waltzes, too, have their tenderer moments of *Ländler*-like sentiment and charm. However, they emerge faster and more excitable than usual, as if Kovacevich were trying to remind us of Brahms's old love of Hungary no less than his new love of Vienna. 'It is wonderful how he combines passion and tenderness in the smallest of spaces' was Clara Schumann's comment on the miniatures, and the phrase fits Kovacevich's warmly responsive account of the Op. 118 set just as well. The piano is faithfully and fearlessly reproduced in what sounds like a ripely reverberant venue.

Two Rhapsodies, Op. 79. 16 Waltzes, Op. 39. Eight Piano Pieces, Op. 76.
Mikhail Rudy *pf*
EMI CDC7 54233-2 (59 minutes: DDD). Recorded 1991-92.   Ⓕ

Mikhail Rudy's account of the Two *Rhapsodies* and the 16 Waltzes makes a pleasing alternative to Stephen Kovacevich's disc. For a start, the younger pianist has been exceptionally well recorded in the Salle Wagram in Paris, and he also plays a fine instrument that is in perfect condition. Of course that is not all: Rudy brings great character to the Eight Pieces, Op. 76, with each one fully (but not exaggeratedly) characterized, not least in matters of texture, dynamics and pedalling.

Similarly, this pianist effortlessly encompasses the blend of passion and gentler poetry that we find in the *Rhapsodies*. As for the Waltzes, this golden chain of Viennese melody and lilting charm comes across with affection and panache, as well as idiomatic rubato, not least in the famous A flat major Waltz which is the penultimate number. Repeats, too, are never mechanical, but often reveal something subtly new about the music which we could not have with a single playing. Finally, the frequent difficulty of Brahms's idiosyncratic piano writing, both here and in the other pieces, presents no more than a pleasing challenge to this intelligent and sensitive artist and all proceeds fluently, though never in a routine way.

Two Motets, Op. 74. Fest- und Gedenksprüche, Op. 109. Three Motets, Op. 110.
Missa Canonica. Two Motets, Op. 29.
RIAS Chamber Choir, Berlin / Marcus Creed.
Harmonia Mundi HMC90 1591 (61 minutes: DDD). Texts and translations included.
Recorded 1994-95.   Ⓕ

These are wonderful pieces, which, hearing, you would suppose to be all heart, looking at, you think must be all brain, and in fact are compounded of both, the one feeding upon and stimulating the other. In no other department of his work is Brahms quite so conscious of his heritage. Writing in the midday of romanticism, he finds the great formal, contrapuntal tradition not a weight upon him but a refreshment. He draws upon Schütz as upon Bach, and from the Italian polyphonists and masters of the double choir as well as from his own German background. The innocent ear would never suspect the mathematical intricacies, the sheer musical logic, and yet it tells, even without conscious recognition: one senses the workmanship, and the emotion which would in any case go out to greet such strong, vivid word-setting is immeasurably enhanced. A striking example is provided by the three movements, all that survive, from the *Missa Canonica*, undertaken in 1856. The *Sanctus* is set in deeply reverential mood and, like the flowing triple-time *Benedictus*, betrays nothing of its origin as an academic exercise. The *Agnus Dei* is overtly polyphonic, yet that too gives way to a gently lyrical mode, in the 'Dona nobis pacem'. They were published in 1984 and this is their first recording. The motets, of course, have been recorded many times and very well too, yet, on balance, no more satisfyingly than they are here. The RIAS Chamber Choir produces a fine quality of homogeneous tone and, under Marcus Creed, shows itself fully responsive to both words and music. This disc carries a strong recommendation, especially for its inclusion of the surviving *Missa Canonica* fragments.

Gesänge – Op. 17; Op. 42; Op. 104. Sieben Lieder, Op. 62. Deutsche Volkslieder, WoO33 – In stiller Nacht.
Stefan Jezierski, Manfred Klier hns [a]**Marie-Pierre Langlamet** hp
RIAS Chamber Choir, Berlin / Marcus Creed.
Harmonia Mundi HMC90 1592 (62 minutes: DDD). Texts and translations included.
Recorded 1995-96.   Ⓕ

The RIAS Chamber Choir's blend of voices is impeccable and the tone-quality perfectly lovely. They are sensitive to word and phrase, responding all as one to their conductor's shading and shaping. Their performances give pleasure enough for one to ask nothing further. The sheer beauty of sound preserves the gentle, romantic qualities of the music faithfully; and there is never any question of dullness, for text and music are both lovingly tendered. The pieces themselves always have more to them than one at first thinks, and the sureness of Brahms's feeling for choral sound impresses immediately. All are unaccompanied save Op. 17, where the harp and horns bring a delightful enrichment. This is quiet, late-night listening, of the kind that helps to ease the day into retrospective contentment.

Liebeslieder, Op. 52. Neue Liebeslieder, Op. 65. Three Quartets, Op. 64.
Edith Mathis sop **Brigitte Fassbaender** mez **Peter Schreier** ten **Dietrich Fischer-Dieskau** bar
Karl Engel, Wolfgang Sawallisch pfs
DG 423 133-2GH (55 minutes: DDD). Texts and translations included. Recorded 1982.   Ⓕ

These delightful works will be eagerly snapped up by lovers of these seemingly simple but, in fact, quite complex settings for one, two or four voices. The performances are thoroughly idiomatic, both as regards the singers and pianists, with full value given to the words and their meaning. It is not merely a question of fine singing, which with this quartet one may more or less take for granted: the subtlety and charm of the interpretations makes what can all too often be a dreary sequence of three-four numbers into a poetic response to the nature of the waltz. There is an intelligent give-and-take between the soloists, so that voices move in and out of the limelight, as the skilful recording allows, and an extra dimension of the music is disclosed here that is too often obscured.

The immediate sound is here a great advantage. This is a very worthwhile and welcome reissue of a most attractive individual record.

Brahms Liebeslieder, Op. 52.
Rossini Soirées musicales – La promessa; La partenza; La regata veneziana; La pesca.
Tchaikovsky Duets, Op. 46 – No. 1, Evening; No. 3, Tears; No. 4, In the garden; No. 6, Dawn.
Heather Harper *sop* Dame Janet Baker *mez* Sir Peter Pears *ten* Thomas Hemsley *bar*
Claudio Arrau, Benjamin Britten *pfs*
BBC Music Legends/IMG Artists Britten the Performer BBCB8001-2 (62 minutes: ADD).
Recorded 1968-71. Ⓜ

Another archive treasure mined from the catacombs of Broadcasting House comes blinking into the sunlight. A reminder, on this occasion, of the old Aldeburgh where the concert hall became a drawing-room peopled with genius and we, the far-flung radio audience, eavesdropped for a precious hour or so in the privacy of our own homes. The programme is odd, but a joy: the product of taste and knowledge, and a profound pleasure in music-making. First, Brahms's *Liebeslieder* with Claudio Arrau, no less, partnering Britten at the keyboard. It had not been planned as such; cancellations had caused the hosts to shuffle the musical house guests. The result is a performance of great strength and spontaneity, the two pianists – the engine-room of this thoroughly 'instrumental' work – playing with a singleness and singularity of spirit that takes the breath away. Brahms occasionally allows solo voices to shine. Here the tones of Baker and Pears shine characteristically through. In the end, though, it is (as it should be) the power and charm of the whole ensemble that provides the pleasure.

The Tchaikovsky songs, four of the six duets, Op. 46, he wrote for his niece, Tatyana Davïdova, are sung in English and are thus as accessible as 'Come into the garden, Maud'. Heather Harper and Dame Janet Baker, accompanied by Britten, sing them grandly, without inhibition, but it is the piano writing that tends to catch the imagination. Finally, there is Rossini, four of *Les soirées musicales*. Should the singing be quite so declamatory? Perhaps not, until one realizes just how grand and funny something like the performance of 'La partenza' really is; Baker imperiously parodying the heroic style, Britten's playing of the 22-second postlude a model of enigmatic humour. At one level, this, and the performance of 'La regata veneziana' which concludes the programme, are high parody. It is in the mordant postlude to 'La partenza', however, that we have 'Essence de Rossini', distilled to a recipe of the composer's own making by Britten himself in another of those acts of musical empathy which made him one of the wonders of the musical world.

Lieder.
Dame Margaret Price *sop* **Graham Johnson** *pf*
Op. 96 – No. 1, Der Tod, das ist die kühle Nacht; No. 3, Es schauen die Blumen; No. 4, Meerfahrt. Op. 85 – No. 1, Sommerabend; No. 2, Mondenschein. Es liebt sich so lieblich im Lenze!, Op. 71 No. 1. Op. 14 – No. 1, Vor dem Fenster; No. 2, Vom vernundeten Knaben; No. 7, Ständchen; No. 8, Sehnsucht. Mädchenfluch, Op. 69 No. 9. Klage, Op. 105 No. 3. Op. 148 – No. 4, Gold überwiegt die Liebe; No. 6, Vergangen ist mir Glück und Heil. Op. 84 – No. 4, Vergebliches Ständchen; No. 5, Spannung. Deutsche Volkslieder, WoO33 – No. 6, Da unten im Tale; No. 15, Schwesterlein, Schwesterlein; No. 37, Du mein einzig Licht. Op. 97 – Dort in den Weiden, No. 4. Zigeunerlieder, Op. 103 – No. 1, He, Zigeuner, greife; No. 2, Hochgetürmte Rimaflut; No. 3, Wisst ihr, wann mein Kindchen; No. 4, Leiber Gott, du weisst; No. 5, Brauner Bursche führt zum Tanze; No. 6, Röslein dreie in der Reihe; No. 7, Kommt dir manchmal; No. 11, Rote Abendwoken ziehn.
RCA Victor Red Seal 09026 60901-2 (61 minutes: DDD). Notes, texts and translations included.
Recorded 1992. Ⓕ

With Graham Johnson to devise intelligent, logical programmes and Dame Margaret Price and himself to interpret them, a remarkable unanimity of thought and confidence of manner is being achieved, the delights there for the taking. Here we begin with six contrasted settings of Heine, all reasonably familiar songs, each given with a nice balance between breadth of phrasing and warmth of feeling. The account of *Mondenschein* fully realizes its autumnal melancholy in phrases that seem to linger endlessly in the air. The judicious choice of *Volkslieder* settings once more indicates Brahms's deep understanding of the originals and just how to clothe them in appropriate harmonies, as in the antique Dorian mode of *Sehnsucht* and *Vergangen ist mir Glück und Heil*, both sung and played here with an exquisite sense of longing. Finally, the partnership lavish a winningly uninhibited *élan* on the *Zigeunerlieder*. If we are occasionally aware of a momentary strain on Price's present resources, we are consoled by the passionate spontaneity of the results. The intimate recording is ideally balanced.

Brahms Die Trauernde, Op. 7 No. 5. Sehnsucht, Op. 14 No. 8. Mädchenfluch, Op. 69 No. 3. Mädchenlied, Op. 85 No. 3. Lieder, Op. 95 – No. 5, Vor schneller Schwur; No. 6, Mädchenlied. Lieder, Op. 107 – No. 3, Das Mädchen spricht; No. 5, Mädchenlied. Deutsche Volkslieder, WoO33 – No. 34, Wie komm'ich denn zur Tür herein?; No. 41, Es steht ein Lind; No. 42, In stiller Nacht, zur ersten Wacht. Regenlied.
Mahler Lieder und Gesänge – No. 1, Frühlingsmorgen; No. 2, Erinnerung; No. 3, Hans und Gretche; No. 6, Um schlimme Kinder artig zu machen; No. 7, Ich ging mit Lust durch einen grünen Wald; No. 9, Starke Einbildungskraft; No. 11, Ablösung im Sommer; No. 12, Scheiden und Meiden; No. 13, Nicht wiedersehen!.
Lucia Popp sop **Geoffrey Parsons** pf
Arts Music 47367-2 (47 minutes: DDD). Texts included. Recorded 1983.   Ⓢ

Here is treasure indeed to add to our precious storehouse of Popp recordings. Recorded in Munich in 1983, this recital catches the well-remembered soprano in fine voice and at the top of her interpretative form in an intelligent programme devoted to folk-settings or quasi folk-songs by Brahms and Mahler. To these pieces the singer and that other late, lamented performer, Geoffrey Parsons, bring just the right balance between the artless and the sophisticated: in other words they bring all their considered artistry to bear on basically unassuming pieces without ever overloading them with too much conscious interpretation. Though she is predictably charming in the lighter, teasing songs, Popp is particularly affecting in the sad songs of loss and/or yearning as regards the loved one, where her peculiarly plaintive timbre comes very much into its own. In the Brahms settings such as 'Sehnsucht' or 'Es steht ein Lind' you sense the inner feelings of the bereft protagonist, and in two of Mahler's most affecting early songs, 'Nicht wiedersehen!' and 'Erinnerung', Popp emphasizes key phrases with an added tranche of intensity, in the final couplet of the first, and at 'Die Liebe immer wieder!' in the second. The recording is full and clear. The quality and the super-budget price console you for the short measure.

Lieder.
Anne Sofie von Otter mez **Bengt Forsberg** pf
Zigeunerlieder, Op. 103 – Nos. 1-7 and 11. Dort in den Weiden, Op. 97 No. 4. Vergebliches Ständchen, Op. 84 No. 4. Die Mainacht, Op. 43 No. 2. Ach, wende diesen Blick, Op. 57 No. 4. O kühler Wald, Op. 72 No. 3. Von ewiger Liebe, Op. 43 No. 1. Junge Lieder I, Op. 63 No. 5. Wie rafft' ich mich auf in der Nacht, Op. 32 No. 1. Unbewegte laue Luft, Op. 57 No. 8. Heimweh II, Op. 63 No. 8. Mädchenlied, Op. 107 No. 5. Ständchen, Op. 106 No. 1. Sonntag, Op. 47 No. 3. Wiegenlied, Op. 49 No. 4. Zwei Gesänge, Op. 91 (with Nils-Erik Sparf va).
DG 429 727-2GH (61 minutes: DDD). Texts and translations included. Recorded 1989.   Ⓕ

Many of the Lieder here are but meagrely represented in current catalogues, so that this recital is all the more welcome, particularly in view of the perceptive musicality of both singer and pianist. They show a fine free (but unanimous!) flexibility in the *Zigeunerlieder*, with a dashing 'Brauner Bursche' and 'Röslein dreie' and a passionate 'Rote Abendwolken'; but there is also lightness, happy in 'Wisst ihr, wann mein Kindchen', troubled in 'Lieber Gott, du weisst'; and von Otter's coolly tender tone in 'Kommt dir manchmal in den Sinn' touches the heart. Also deeply moving are the profound yearning and the loving but anxious lullaby in the two songs with viola obbligato (most sensitively played). Elsewhere, connoisseurs of vocal technique will admire von Otter's command of colour and *legato* line in the gravity of *O kühler Wald*, the stillness of *Die Mainacht* and the intensity of *Von ewiger Liebe*, and her lovely *mezza voce* in the *Wiegenlied* and the partly repressed fervour of *Unbewegte laue Luft*; but to any listener her remarkable control, her responsiveness to words and, not least, the sheer beauty of her voice make this a most rewarding disc, aided as she is by Forsberg's characterful playing.

Ein deutsches Requiem, Op. 45.

Ein deutsches Requiem.
Elisabeth Schwarzkopf sop **Dietrich Fischer-Dieskau** bar
Philharmonia Chorus and Orchestra / Otto Klemperer.
EMI CDM5 66955-2 (69 minutes: ADD). Notes, text and translation included.
Recorded 1961.   Ⓕ **RR**

Brahm's *German Requiem*, a work of great concentration and spiritual intensity, is rather surprisingly, the creation of a man barely 30 years old. Klemperer's reading of this mighty work has long been famous: rugged, at times surprisingly fleet and with a juggernaut power. The superb Philharmonia is joined by its excellent chorus and two magnificent soloists – Schwarzkopf offering comfort in an endless stream of pure tone and the superb solo contribution from Fischer-Dieskau, still unequalled, taking us closer to the work's emotional, theological and musical sources than any other. Digital remastering has not entirely eliminated tape noise, but the engineers appear to have encountered few problems with the original tapes (some tight editing apart). It remains a uniquely revealing account of the work.

Ein deutsches Requiem.
Margaret Price sop **Samuel Ramey** bar
Royal Philharmonic Orchestra; Ambrosian Singers / André Previn.
Teldec Digital Experience 9031-75862-2 (75 minutes: DDD). Notes, text and translation included. Recorded 1986. Ⓜ

Those seeking a more up-to-date recording would be well advised to investigate Previn's recording. He may not be so electrifying at nodal points as Klemperer but his performance comes from the heart, with love and understanding. It is cast from strength (Price and Ramey are perhaps the finest soloists since Schwarzkopf and Fischer-Dieskau), with a first-rate choir (the Ambrosian Singers vying, again, with Klemperer's Philharmonia Chorus), and eloquent orchestral playing from the RPO. It is evident from his pacing and phrasing of the music that Previn knows the score from within and knows the pitfalls it presents. Nowhere is the music overdriven or overindulged. Previn's careful handling of the orchestral writing brings instrumental parallels to mind time and time again. The recording was made in All Saint's, Tooting, in an acoustic that sheds a mellow light over string and wind detailing whilst giving a pleasing depth, not inconsistent with inner clarity, to the choir's distinguished contribution. Price, singing with heavenly assurance in 'Ihr habt nun Traurigkeit', has a slight edge about her tone but the recording is generally free of unattractive sibilance.

Ein deutsches Requiem.
Charlotte Margiono sop **Rodney Gilfry** bar
Monteverdi Choir; Orchestre Révolutionnaire et Romantique / Sir John Eliot Gardiner.
Philips 432 140-2PH (66 minutes: DDD). Text and translation included. Recorded 1990. Ⓕ Ⓟ

Gardiner's performance is notable for its intensity and fervour and for the superb singing of his choir: splendidly firm and secure attacks and phrasing, always with fine tonal quality, meticulous attention to dynamic nuances, and alertness to verbal meaning and nuance. The solo baritone is a real find: an admirably focused voice with cleanly projected words and sensitive tonal gradations: if the soprano, pure-voiced and consoling, seems slightly less distinguished, it may be that she is set a trifle too far from the microphone. Pains have been taken throughout to bring out contrapuntal strands with clarity, both in the chorus and in the orchestra; and here the employment of period instruments (particularly noticeable in the case of the oboes and horns, and with the hard sticks adding extra menace to the timpani's triplets in the second movement) and of selective string vibrato proves to make a significant contribution. In the past Gardiner has sometimes been accused of minimizing the spiritual quality of religious works: that can certainly not be said of this outstanding performance.

Havergal Brian

British 1876-1972

Symphony No. 1, 'Gothic'.
Eva Jenisová sop **Dagmar Pecková** contr **Vladimir Dolezal** ten **Peter Mikulás** bass
Slovak Philharmonic Choir; Slovak National Theatre Opera Chorus;
Slovak Folk Ensemble Chorus; Lucnica Chorus; Bratislava Chamber Choir;
Bratislava Children's Choir; Youth Echo Choir; Czechoslovak Radio Symphony Orchestra, Bratislava; Slovak Philharmonic Orchestra / Ondrej Lenard.
Marco Polo 8 223280/1 (two discs: 111 minutes: DDD). Text and translation included. Recorded 1989. Ⓕ

The *Gothic* (1927) is legendary for its length, for its everything-but-the-kitchen-sink scoring and for having been left unperformed for decades. The tiny handful of hearings it has had since its belated première have not wholly dispelled that image; indeed they have fuelled dismissal of Brian as an incompetent visionary, a self-taught composer whose reach far exceeded his grasp and who, creating in a vacuum of non-performance (the accusation rubs off on to his 31 subsequent symphonies), was unable to check his impractical imaginings with his ear. Admiration for Brian's boldness and inventive daring was mingled with exasperation that his teeming textures and wildly complex proliferations seemed self-defeating, that at his most exultant or would-be mystical the plethora of lines and instrumental colours simply congealed into a grey opacity. And there was the sheer barnstorming quality of the piece, too: the piling of climax upon climax, especially in the gigantic setting of the *Te Deum* which forms the Symphony's Part 2 (Part 1, for orchestra alone, is almost conventionally scored; it is Part 2 that requires triple chorus, soloists, four brass bands and practically everything else you can think of, from pedal clarinet to thunder-machine).

But in a performance as good as this one the real reasons for the Symphony's long neglect soon become apparent. The choral writing is almost unbelievably difficult, but with choral singing as splendidly prepared as that of the seven choirs assembled here, the remarkable precision of Brian's ear is unarguably demonstrated. In a sympathetic performance the huge choral climaxes are not simply repetitive; they chart the successive emotions of the text, from jubilance, through panic dread, to a moving expression of trust, humble and chastened. Hence the title. Yes, it is a fine performance, fine enough to dispose of two other possible reservations about the piece: that it is simply too long, and in any case falls apart in the middle. The performance, indeed, has one of the Symphony's own characteristics: it is sure enough and strong enough for the occasional slack page and the evident fact that Brian was learning his mastery as he went along (the first movement is less assured than the others) to matter hardly at all. And how hugely the Slovak singers, to say nothing of the virtuoso first trumpet and the entire, splendid brass section, enjoy this not wholly unaccustomed idiom. A towering achievement; recorded, a touch of acidity aside, with a commendable combination of clarity and spaciousness.

Symphony No. 2 in E minor. Festival Fanfare.
Moscow Symphony Orchestra / Tony Rowe.
Marco Polo 8 223790 (55 minutes: DDD). Recorded 1996. Ⓕ

Built over a resourcefully deployed group of ostinato figures and upon the pounding of three sets of timpani and two pianos, the *Scherzo* of Brian's Second Symphony rises to a climax of extraordinary ferocity dominated by bellowing, stereophonically-placed horns. He wanted 16 of them; here he gets eight, and the effect is very nearly as overwhelming as he had planned. This is followed by a 20-minute slow finale, constructed from a sequence of sombre and striking phrases: a grandiose and epic funeral march in effect, but incorporating within it moments of noble, Sibelius-like darkness, a superb central lament for richly sonorous strings and, after a vast, triple climax, an epilogue of frozen poignancy. It is a movement that would convince even those most dubious of Brian's gifts that he was a composer touched by genius. If you are less convinced by the first two movements this may be partly due to Brian's habit, characteristic of this stage of his career, of writing extremely dense counterpoint, in which the primacy of a particular theme isn't always immediately obvious on first hearing. You sense, too, that the orchestra and conductor on this disc, so obviously bowled over by and committed to the third and fourth movements, were perplexed by the first and second. Lines that you sense should be presented with real eloquence emerge here rather half-heartedly, squarish of rhythm; once or twice they have difficulty in emerging at all from Brian's luxurious textures. Nor is the recording, which in the symphony is on the dull, flat side, much of a help. But the latter half of this symphony is so superb that it is likely to convince you that the first half is worth persevering with. The ceremonious *Fanfare*, late Brian and thus terse, non-repetitive but cumulative, provides a further, rousing inducement.

Frank Bridge

British 1879-1941

The Sea, H100. Summer, H116. Cherry Ripe, H119*b*. Enter Spring, H174. Lament, H117.
Royal Liverpool Philharmonic Orchestra / Sir Charles Groves.
EMI British Composers CDM5 66855-2 (60 minutes: ADD). Recorded 1975. Ⓜ

An ideal introduction to the music of Frank Bridge, this much-loved programme was always one of the highlights of Sir Charles Groves's Liverpool tenure, and its reappearance is more than welcome. Although a handful of individual performances – most notably Vernon Handley and the Ulster Orchestra in a stunningly engineered account of *The Sea* (on Chandos) – may have surpassed them in terms of poetic rapture and beguiling finish, Groves's clear-headed, stirringly sympathetic *Enter Spring*, though at times a little too sturdy on its pins, easily outranks the competition. The transfer is the same as that used for an earlier mid-price EMI Studio offering from 1989, and the finished article sounds as resplendent and full-bodied as ever (if, perhaps, with a touch less background hiss than before). Don't miss this reissue.

Suite, H93. There is a willow grows aslant a brook, H174. The Two Hunchbacks, H95. Threads, H151. Rosemary, H68*b*. Canzonetta, H169. Berceuse, H8. Serenade, H23.
Britten Sinfonia / Nicholas Cleobury.
Conifer Classics 75605 51327-2 (63 minutes: DDD). Recorded 1997. Ⓕ 🅴

Nicholas Cleobury and the admirable Britten Sinfonia give what is, on balance, the most shapely and unaffectedly eloquent realization of Frank Bridge's delectable Suite for strings (1908) yet committed to disc. Not only are these fine artists scrupulously faithful to both the letter and spirit of the score, their perceptive treatment of the haunting third movement in particular distils a fragrant, other-worldly atmosphere that looks forward to the first of Bridge's *Two Poems* (after Richard Jefferies) of seven years later. Similarly impressive is Cleobury's acutely sensitive rendering of that miniature masterpiece, *There is a willow grows aslant a brook* (1927). Cleobury not only brings out the human anguish in this extraordinary essay, but there's a refinement of texture and suppleness of expression about this dedicated music-making that is deeply moving. Conifer also gives us two specimens of Bridge's incidental music. He employs Belgian folk melodies to match the setting of *The Two Hunchbacks* (based on Emile Cammaerts's fairy-tale play) and the results are very endearing. Likewise the two intermezzos from Frank Stoyton's three-act comedy entitled *Threads* (1921). Four miniatures round off the proceedings, including the *Two Entr'actes*, published in 1939, otherwise known as *Rosemary* (originally the second of the *Three Sketches* for piano from 1906) and *Canzonetta* (first conceived for piano under the title of *Happy South* following a Mediterranean holiday in 1926). A first-rate Bridge anthology, ripely recorded.

Bridge String Sextet in E flat major, H107.
Goossens Concertino, Op. 47. Phantasy Sextet, Op. 37.
Academy of St Martin in the Fields Chamber Ensemble (Kenneth Sillito, Malcolm Latchem, Rita Manning, Robert Heard *vns* Robert Smissen, Stephen Tees *vas* Stephen Orton, Roger Smith *vcs*).
Chandos CHAN9472 (59 minutes: DDD). Recorded 1995. Ⓕ

This admirable programme presents three fine chamber offerings, excellently realized. Goossens's high-quality invention and effortless craft are strikingly evident in the *Concertino*, here performed in its original 1928 guise for string octet and also the elegantly structured *Phantasy Sextet* of 1923. Scored for three violins, one viola and two cellos, this impressive composition is consistently fertile, tightly knit and confidently conceived for the medium. Bridge's Sextet is laid out for the more traditional line-up comprising pairs of each instrument, and is at once the most ambitious and sumptuous of the composer's early chamber offerings. Perhaps the most striking music can be found in the central *Andante con moto*, a wistfully lilting threnody which itself frames a brief *Scherzo* of nervy propulsion. As usual with Bridge, the elegant formal design, captivating lyrical flow and satisfying cogency yield enormous pleasure. The playing is splendid and the sound and balance are impeccable.

String Quartets – No. 2 in G minor, H115; No. 3, H175.
Bridge Quartet (Catherine Schofield, Kaye Barker *vns* Michael Schofield *va* Lucy Wilding *vc*).
Meridian CDE84311 (58 minutes: DDD). Recorded 1996. Ⓕ

The string quartets of Frank Bridge are some of the most rewarding in the repertoire and here the composer is, on the whole, eminently well served by this eponymous group. In the glorious Second Quartet of 1915, the Bridge Quartet acquit themselves well. Theirs is a thoughtful rendering which, in its comparatively restrained manner, will undoubtedly give pleasure. By the time we reach the superb Third Quartet of 1926, Bridge's command of the medium is total. This score is one of his most searching, deeply felt utterances. The musicians impress it with the honest and hard-working integrity of their playing; however, you may feel that they fight rather too shy of the darker emotional undertow of Bridge's expressionist vision – the intellectual sinew and questing harmonic scope of this marvellous creation are perhaps not as comprehensively conveyed here as one would wish. A most pleasing coupling, however, boasting very good recorded sound.

Bridge Cello Sonata in D minor H125.
Schubert Sonata for Arpeggione and Piano in A minor, D821.
Mstislav Rostropovich *vc* **Benjamin Britten** *pf*
Decca The Classic Sound 443 575-2DCS (52 minutes: ADD). Recorded 1968. Ⓜ 🄍🄍

The Maltings, Snape, July 1968: Britten was greeting two of his dearest musical friends and mentors; Rostropovich was making two important discoveries. This reissue is a major historic document reminding some listeners of, and revealing to others for the first time, the special nature of the musical relationship between composer, cellist and the music which they were performing. Rostropovich's is certainly the dominant voice at the start of the Frank Bridge Sonata, though both cello and piano go on to flex the work's Bergian muscles to the full in a recording which eavesdrops on every movement of the finger, every breath in the body. Schubert's *Arpeggione* Sonata was new to Rostropovich. In the broad, exploratory charting of its territory, both Britten and Rostropovich enjoy many a moment of – if not drooling – then licking their lips over its more delectable turns of melody and harmonic contours. And why not? They make us stand and stare at much we might have missed: every time its opening melody recurs, it seems reinvented, and Britten's delight in peeping out when least expected from the 'cradle' Rostropovich said that he had created for him, throws many an idea into bright new relief. Britten as Lieder accompanist comes to the fore, of course, in the slow movement. Here Rostropovich does make a meal of it, and it will be something of a relief to most listeners, one suspects, to move into the clearer air of the finale. Even here, though, the bite as well as the bark of the *furiant* episodes is something else.

Bridge Cello Sonata. Four Short Pieces, H104 – Spring Song. Melodie, H99. Scherzo, H19a.
Britten Cello Sonata, Op. 65.
Steven Doane *vc* **Barry Snyder** *pf*
Bridge BCD9056 (52 minutes: DDD). Recorded 1994.   Ⓕ

Bridge's two-movement Cello Sonata of 1917 is very English in its rich eloquence, although there is an affinity with Fauré, a composer with whom Bridge shared qualities of quietly glowing passion and unerring craftsmanship. The sonata's deeply emotional second movement is masterly, and this performance by the American duo of Steven Doane and Barry Snyder is warmly sympathetic and thoroughly enjoyable. The Bridge miniatures that accompany it are equally effective. Britten's Sonata, written for Rostropovich, is equally unconventional in having five movements, of which Nos. 2, 4 and 5 each last less than three minutes but are none the less characterful and telling. This duo also responds keenly to the younger man's crisper invention and here is another strong yet sensitive performance. If you want these two sonatas together this attractive disc provides a safe recommendation. The recording favours the cello, but is otherwise faithful and pleasing.

Benjamin Britten   British 1913-1976

Piano Concerto in D major, Op. 13. Violin Concerto, Op. 15.
Mark Lubotsky *vn* **Sviatoslav Richter** *pf*
English Chamber Orchestra / Benjamin Britten.
Decca London 417 308-2LM (67 minutes: ADD). Recorded 1970.   Ⓜ

Just after Britten's performances were released on LP in 1971, the composer admitted with some pride that Sviatoslav Richter had learned his Piano Concerto 'entirely off his own bat', and had revealed a Russianness that was in the score. Britten was attracted to Shostakovich during the late 1930s, when it was written, and the bravado, brittleness and flashy virtuosity of the writing, in the march-like finale most of all, at first caused many people (including Lennox Berkeley, to whom it is dedicated) to be wary of it, even to think it somehow outside the composer's style. Now we know his music better, it is easier to accept, particularly in this sparkling yet sensitive performance. The Violin Concerto dates from the following year, 1939, when Britten was in Canada, and it, too, has its self-conscious virtuosity, but it is its rich nostalgic lyricism which strikes to the heart and the quiet elegiac ending is unforgettable. Compared to Richter in the other work, Mark Lubotsky is not always the master of its hair-raising difficulties, notably in the *Scherzo*, which has passages of double artificial harmonics that even Heifetz wanted simplified before he would play it (Britten refused), but this is still a lovely account. Fine recordings, made at The Maltings at Snape.

Piano Concerto. Soirées musicales, Op. 9. Matinées musicales, Op. 24.
Ralf Gothóni *pf*
Helsingborg Symphony Orchestra / Okko Kamu.
Ondine ODE825-2 (71 minutes: DDD). Recorded 1994.   Ⓕ🅴

Here is a perceptive, at times daring, always thought-provoking account of Britten's Piano Concerto. Indeed, pungent characterization is the order of the day, especially in the two middle movements. Here the 'Waltz' is teased out with sly seduction by Okko Kamu and his excellent Swedish group, yet at the same time the ominous undertones of this music – its elements of ghostly burlesque and bitter irony – have never been more unnervingly projected. Even more distinctive is Ralf Gothóni's provocatively expansive way with the opening of the 'Impromptu'. Britten's theme here emerges like some ravishingly intimate meditation, its quasi-improvisatory air (as the movement's title suggests) compellingly conveyed. Yet such is the magnetic concentration of Gothóni's playing that the line never falters, and the rest of the movement is again memorably realized. We are also offered the concerto's original slow movement, a sharply inventive, highly capricious 'Recitative and Aria' (which Britten withdrew in 1945, seven years after the work's première). No complaints about the fizz and bravura on show in the opening 'Toccata', nor about the mock-banal finale, whose *largamente* climax struts forth in superbly grim fashion here. Welcome contrast comes with the two Rossini-inspired suites, and Kamu does them both proud. The orchestral playing in Helsingborg has all the necessary poise, affection and wealth of tender expression in the two most reflective numbers (namely the 'Canzonetta' from *Soirées* and 'Nocturne' from *Matinées*). Ondine's sound throughout is simply first-rate.

Britten Cello Symphony.
Walton Cello Concerto.
Julian Lloyd Webber vc
Academy of St Martin in the Fields / Sir Neville Marriner.
Philips 454 442-2PH (71 minutes: DDD). Recorded 1996.   Ⓕ Ⓔ

This is an inspired coupling of two works, closely parallel in the careers of their composers, each reflecting the mastery of a great Russian cellist (respectively Rostropovich and Piatigorsky), but which could hardly be more sharply contrasted. Julian Lloyd Webber in an illuminating note makes that very point, and the passionate commitment of his playing in both works confirms his views. Not only is the power of each piece fully laid out, the beauty – not just in the lusciously romantic Walton Concerto, but in the grittily taxing Britten piece too – is presented as never before on disc, helped by sumptuous, beautifully balanced sound. On any count this is the finest, most formidable disc that Julian Lloyd Webber has yet given us. Anyone wanting this unique coupling need not hesitate. In the Britten it almost goes without saying that, like his rivals on disc, Lloyd Webber cannot quite command the power and thrust of Rostropovich. That said, Lloyd Webber and Sir Neville Marriner, helped by the far greater dynamic range of the recording, not only convey the extraordinary originality of Britten's scoring in a way beyond any rival, but find an extra warmth.

In the Walton, Lloyd Webber is individual and imaginative in his phrasing – he is outstanding in the deeply meditative statement of the theme in the variation finale – and the sumptuousness of the Philips sound makes this exceptionally warm, while the sparky complexity of the central *Scherzo* is thrillingly clear and transparent. This is a performance which fully confirms this post-war work as vintage Walton, the equal of his pre-war concerto masterpieces for viola and violin. In both the Walton and the Britten Lloyd Webber makes light of the formidable technical difficulties. Plainly this has been a project that has involved him deeply, and he has been wonderfully well served by his collaborators.

Simple Symphony, Op. 4. Temporal Variations. A Charm of Lullabies, Op. 41 (both orch. C. Matthews). Lachrymae, Op. 48a. Suite on English Folk Tunes, 'A time there was ...', Op. 90.
Catherine Wyn-Rogers contr **Nicholas Daniel** ob **Philip Dukes** va
Northern Sinfonia / Steuart Bedford.
Collins Classics 1526-2 (72 minutes: DDD). Text included.   Ⓕ

Steuart Bedford brings a keen perception and rare intelligence to every item in this attractive, chronologically wide-spanning programme, and he draws some beautifully polished playing from his ever-responsive Tyneside band. Only the *Simple Symphony* will raise any eyebrows. Bedford's is a distinctive conception, more athletically trim than playful in the 'Frolicsome Finale', a touch stern, perhaps, in the 'Boisterous Bourrée', and poised rather than especially affectionate in the 'Sentimental Sarabande'. Some will understandably prefer more in the way of easy charm and communicative warmth, but elsewhere Bedford's wonderfully clear-sighted direction makes for riveting results, not least in the *Suite on English Folk Tunes*, given here with a bracing acuity and affecting restraint that come close to the ideal. As heard in Colin Matthews's wonderfully idiomatic accompaniment for string orchestra, the sparky *Temporal Variations* of 1936 (originally scored for oboe and piano) now seem but a mere step away from the astounding achievement of the *Variations on a Theme of Frank Bridge* completed the following summer. Nicholas Daniel is an immaculate, characterful soloist, and those adjectives equally apply to violist Philip Dukes's contribution in *Lachrymae*, utterly compelling in his fastidious sensitivity and unremitting concentration. Throw in Catherine Wyn-Rogers's vividly sympathetic rendering of *A Charm of Lullabies* in (again) Colin Matthews's orchestral guise (and, like the *Temporal Variations*, another world première recording), and it all adds up to a very recommendable disc. The recording is clean and beautifully balanced.

Prelude and Fugue, Op. 29. Lachrymae, Op. 48a. Elegy. Simple Symphony, Op. 4. Variations on a theme of Frank Bridge, Op. 10.
Lars Anders Tomter va **Norwegian Chamber Orchestra / Iona Brown.**
Virgin Classics VC5 45121-2 (78 minutes: DDD). Recorded 1988-91.   Ⓕ Ⓔ

The *Frank Bridge* Variations are finely disciplined, strongly characterized and benefit from sumptuous engineering. The hushed intensity achieved in such variations as the 'Adagio' and 'Chant' recalls Britten's own remarkable interpretation – and there can be no higher praise than that! In the *Simple Symphony* the infectious 'Playful Pizzicato' could perhaps have been given with a greater sense of fun; elsewhere, though, there can be no complaints about the outer movements (both wonderfully crisp and vital), whilst the lovely 'Sentimental Sarabande' has surely seldom enjoyed such tenderly expressive advocacy. The *Prelude and Fugue* is brought off with exhilarating poise and panache, and it is difficult to imagine a more eloquent contribution than that of violist Lars Anders Tomter in the early solo *Elegy* and haunting, Dowland-inspired *Lachrymae*. Consistently superior sound, Michael Oliver's admirable booklet-notes and an uncommonly generous playing time add to the considerable attractions of this release.

Britten Temporal Variations. Six Metamorphoses after Ovid, Op. 49. Two Insect Pieces. Phantasy, Op. 2.
Poulenc Oboe Sonata. Trio for Oboe, Bassoon and Piano.
François Leleux *ob* **Jean-François Duquesnoy** *bn* **Guillaume Sutre** *vn* **Miguel da Silva** *va* **Marc Coppey** *vc* **Emmanuel Strosser** *pf*
Harmonia Mundi Les Nouveaux Interprètes HMN91 1556 (76 minutes: DDD). Recorded 1995.   Ⓑ

The pairing of these composers is apt, for they were friends and their musical high spirits – frequent in the Parisian, less so in the uneasy East Anglian – often have a darker side. The oboist here possesses an excellent technique and is a deeply sensitive artist. Both qualities quickly become evident in the flowing, quietly poignant opening melody of Poulenc's Sonata, where Leleux's tone is not only beautiful but also admirably responsive to the subtle dynamic shading and rhythmic flexibility. Yet this is far from the whole story, and the *grotesquerie* of the passage starting at 2'16" shows that there is more to his playing than gentleness – as does the mercurial *Scherzo*, delivered with delightful point and relish. The final *Déploration* of this sonata, as played here, is infinitely moving and nothing less than superb. Fortunately Leleux and his pianist partner, who is equally attuned to Poulenc's world, have been extremely well recorded. This performance and that of the bouncy Trio both give keen pleasure. So do the Britten pieces, three of them early (the characterful *Six Metamorphoses* being the exception) and edgy. Performed as vividly as this, they are undoubtedly worth having. A fine, generously filled disc.

Britten The Young Person's Guide to the Orchestra, Op. 34. Simple Symphony, Op. 4ᵃ.
A Spring Symphony, Op. 44 – Spring, the sweet spring. Noyes Fluddeᵇ – Noye, Noye, take thou thy company ... Sir! heare are lions. Serenade for Tenor, Horn and Strings, Op. 31 – Nocturne. Folk Songs – The Plough Boy; Early One Morning. Billy Budd – Interlude and Sea Shanties. A Ceremony of Carols, Op. 28 – Adam lay i-bounden. A Hymn to the Virgin. War Requiem – Lacrimosa. Peter Grimes – Interlude (Dawn).
Sir Peter Pears *ten* **Barry Tuckwell** *hn* **various soloists; choirs, choruses and orchestras, London Symphony Orchestra**, ᵃᵇ**English Chamber Orchestra / Benjamin Britten** *pf* ᵇ**Norman Del Mar.**
Decca 436 990-2DWO (74 minutes: ADD). Recorded 1963-68.   Ⓜ RR

This reissue includes the composer's own 1963 recording of *The Young Person's Guide to the Orchestra* with the LSO and his complete 1968 ECO version of the *Simple Symphony*. The latter is delightfully fresh and is unforgettable for the joyful bounce of the 'Playful Pizzicato', helped by the resonant acoustic of The Maltings, Snape. In *The Young Person's Guide*, without the now rather dated text, he adopts quick tempos that must have been demanding even for the LSO players, with more spacious ones for the more introspective sections. This is beautiful playing, possessing wit and brilliance, with all kinds of memorable touches. If this transfer is a little dry in sonority this disc is invaluable for these two performances alone. As a bonus we also get ten short excerpts from other major Britten works, including *Billy Budd*, the *War Requiem*, *Peter Grimes* and the haunting, echoing 'Nocturne' from the *Serenade* (sung by Peter Pears with Barry Tuckwell playing the horn obbligato). We also get Pears's singing of Britten's arrangements of *Early One Morning* and *The Plough Boy* (with the boisterous whistling refrain heard in the upper register of the piano accompaniment). The only curious inclusion here is the exuberant excerpt from Norman Del Mar's *Noyes Fludde*.

String Quartets – No. 2 in C major, Op. 36; D major; F major.
Sorrel Quartet (Gina McCormack, Catherine Yates *vns* Vicci Wardman *va* Helen Thatcher *vc*).
Chandos CHAN9664 (74 minutes: DDD). Recorded 1998.   Ⓕ

The Sorrel Quartet can claim a significant 'first' in its account of the recently resurrected F major Quartet from 1928. At 15, Britten was nothing if not precocious, and although the ideas in this substantial piece offer few hints of his mature style, he was already using the medium to excellent effect. Three years later, in the D major Quartet which has been a repertory item since Britten revised it in 1974, there are signs of a more individual voice; this is an attractive performance, well shaped and effectively characterized. Nevertheless, it is on the interpretation of the Quartet No. 2 that the disc must be judged. The Sorrel's naturalness and feeling for line are much in evidence. Tempos for the first movement are broader than most rivals, but they serve an approach which makes a virtue of reticence, and still manages to be quite gripping. It has just about the best sound currently available (with The Maltings, Snape, providing an ideal acoustic – quite closely focused yet satisfyingly rich and spacious), and the otherwise unrecorded F major Quartet adds strength to the recommendation.

Solo Cello Suites – No. 1, Op. 72; No. 2, Op. 80; No. 3, Op. 87.

Solo Cello Suites Nos. 1 and 2. Cello Sonata, Op. 65.
Mstislav Rostropovich vc **Benjamin Britten** pf
Decca London 421 859-2LM (68 minutes: ADD). Recorded 1961-69. Ⓜ 🆁🆁

This is a classic recording of the Cello Sonata, with Rostropovich and the composer playing with an authority impossible to surpass, and is here coupled with the unaccompanied First and Second Cello Suites. The suggestive, often biting humour, masks darker feelings. However, Britten manages, just, to keep his devil under control. Rostropovich's and Britten's characterization in the opening *Dialogo* is stunning and their subdued humour in the *Scherzo-pizzicato* also works well. In the *Elegia* and the final *Moto perpetuo*, again, no one quite approaches the passion and energy of Rostropovich. This work, like the two Suites, was written for him and he still remains the real heavyweight in all three pieces. Their transfer to CD is remarkably successful; it is difficult to believe that these recordings were made in the 1960s.

Solo Cello Suites Nos. 1-3.
Jean-Guihen Queyras vc
Harmonia Mundi Les Nouveaux Interprètes HMN91 1670 (65 minutes: DDD). Recorded 1998. Ⓑ

Britten's three Cello Suites have all the strength of musical character needed to sustain a permanent place in the repertory. Inspired by the personality, and technique, of Mstislav Rostropovich, they are remarkable for the way in which they acknowledge yet at the same time distance themselves from the great precedent of Bach's Cello Suites. The best performers (like Rostropovich himself, though he has never recorded No. 3) are equally at ease with the music's Bach-like contrapuntal ingenuity and its lyric intensity, where Britten's own most personal voice is heard. Queyras has such a fine sense of phrase that his slower speeds do not sound unconvincing, and his playing – technically superb – has an impressive consistency of style. The quality of the recording is another plus, with the close focus needed to ensure that all the details tell, and the occasional tap of the bow and other non-musical noise an acceptable intrusion. The only disappointment came in the final track, with the Russian Prayer for the Dead that ends Suite No. 3. Here, of all places, Queyras is simply too fast. Nevertheless, this lapse is not so great as to deprive the disc of a place in this guide.

Britten Solo Cello Suite No. 3.
Tavener The Protecting Veil. Thrinos.
Steven Isserlis vc
London Symphony Orchestra / Gennadi Rozhdestvensky.
Virgin Classics VC7 59052-2 (74 minutes: DDD). *Gramophone* Award Winner 1992. Ⓕ

First impressions of *The Protecting Veil* are of a consonant, major-key sweetness that could portend a pastoral after the style of Samuel Barber. Yet it soon becomes evident that this is not neo-romantic music. Nor, despite the often static harmony, is it in the vein of English minimalism. The religious aura of this Hymn to the Mother of God explains its style – moving between simple contemplativeness and heartfelt lament – but not the enthusiasm with which audiences have greeted it. One suspects that its most telling effect – the return of the opening idea with heightened eloquence at the end, which then dissolves into potent images of grief – is one major reason for its impact. Many listeners will also welcome Tavener's total rejection of contemporary complexity, though there is a price to pay for this in occasional passages where the musical thought grows dangerously desultory. But this performance, well recorded, is ideal in every way, with a soloist who shapes the long, simple lines effortlessly, and a conductor who is never tempted to push the music on beyond its natural pace. Steven Isserlis also plays Britten's *Third Suite* with free expression and superfine control. After the Tavener this is the music of a troubled, doubting mind, and a feeling of dramatic tension replaces his meditative ritual. There is nevertheless a touching sense of humanity in Tavener's short, unaccompanied *Thrinos*, a lament for a close friend, whose simple chant is clouded by the colours of a vivid sorrow. As with *The Protecting Veil*, the recordings of the Britten and of *Thrinos* are superbly natural and immediate.

Cello Symphony, Op. 68[a]. Sinfonia da Requiem, Op. 20[b]. Cantata misericordium, Op. 69[c].
Mstislav Rostropovich *vc* **Sir Peter Pears** *ten* **Dietrich Fischer-Dieskau** *bar*
[a]**English Chamber Orchestra,** [b]**New Philharmonia Orchestra,** [c]**London Symphony Chorus and Orchestra / Benjamin Britten.**
Decca London 425 100-2LM (75 minutes: ADD). Text and translation included. Recorded 1964. Ⓜ

This disc offers two of Britten's finest works, the *Cello Symphony* and the *Sinfonia da Requiem*. The latter was written in 1940 and is one of the composer's most powerful orchestral works, harnessing opposing forces in a frighteningly intense way. From the opening drumbeat the *Sinfonia* employs a sonata form with dramatic power, though the tone is never fierce or savage; it has an implacable tread and momentum. The central movement, 'Dies irae', however, has a real sense of fury, satirical in its biting comment – the flutter-tongued wind writing rattling its defiance. The closing 'Requiem aeternam' is a movement of restrained beauty. On this recording from 1964 the New Philharmonia play superbly. The Cello Symphony, written in 1963 as part of a series for the great Russian cellist Mstislav Rostropovich, was the first major sonata-form work written since the *Sinfonia*. The idea of a struggle between soloist and orchestra, implicit in the traditional concerto, has no part here; it is a conversation between the two. Rostropovich plays with a depth of feeling that has never quite been equalled in other recordings and the playing of the ECO has great bite. The recording too is extraordinarily fine for its years. The *Cantata misericordium*, one of Britten's lesser-known works, was written in 1962 as a commission from the Red Cross. It takes the story of the Good Samaritan and is scored for tenor and baritone soloists, chorus, string quartet and orchestra. It is a universal plea for charity and here receives a powerful reading. This is a must for any Britten enthusiast.

Britten Four Cabaret Songs. When you're feeling like expressing your affection. On this Island – As it is, plenty. Blues (arr. Runswick) – The Spider and the Fly; Blues; The clock on the wall; Boogie-Woogie.
Porter Paris – Let's do it. Gay Divorce – Night and Day. Leave it to Me – My heart belongs to daddy. Miss Otis Regrets. Nymph Errant – The Physician.
Jill Gomez *sop* **Martin Jones** *pf* **instrumental ensemble** (David Roach *cl/sax* Graham Ashton *tpt* Beverley Davison *vn* Chris Lawrence *db* John Constable *pf* Gregory Knowles *perc*).
Unicorn-Kanchana DKPCD9138 (52 minutes: DDD). Texts included. Recorded 1992.   Ⓕ **E**

Britten's cabaret songs were written for the singing actress Hedli Anderson; there were more than four, but these are the only ones to have seen publication so far. The texts by Auden are full of the spirit that William Coldstream described, writing about one of Anderson's performances, 'teaching of carefree lucidity and the non-avoidance of banality'. *When you're feeling like expressing your affection* which is published and performed here for the first time is one of the results of Auden and Britten's work for the GPO in the 1930s. Apart from the references to 'any telephone kiosk' and 'Press button A' it would still serve well as an encouragement to make use of the telephone. 'As it is, plenty', the last song from *On this Island*, being also in the ironic popular-music style, rounds off the group nicely. Jill Gomez's performances are perfect in every nuance, her beautiful tone, clear diction and just hinted-at irony, never overdoing it, give the songs the exact weight they need. The Cole Porter encores and Daryl Runswick's arrangements of four *Blues* by Britten complete a quite delicious record.

A Spring Symphony, Op. 44[a]. Cantata Academica, Op. 62[b]. Hymn to St Cecilia, Op. 27[c].
Jennifer Vyvyan *sop* **Norma Procter, Helen Watts** *contrs* **Sir Peter Pears** *ten*
Owen Brannigan *bass* [a]**Emanuel School Boys' Choir;** [a]**Chorus and Orchestra of the Royal Opera House, Covent Garden / Benjamin Britten;**
London Symphony [bc]**Chorus and** [c]**Orchestra / George Malcolm.**
Decca London 436 396-2LM (74 minutes: ADD). Texts and translation included.
Recorded 1960-61.   Ⓜ **H**

Britten's performance of the *Spring Symphony* fairly leaps out of one's loudspeakers, and the 1960 sound is as crisp and alive as the performance and the work itself. In the last two pieces George Malcolm's direction is as vivid as Britten's elsewhere. The *Cantata Academica* (1959) is one of Britten's happiest pieces, bubbling over with warmth, jollity and good fellowship. Indeed the Latin title is only one of mock-solemnity. Try 'Tema seriale con fuga' to hear how this composer could make living music out of the most perniciously academic device of our troubled century. Further high points are Owen Brannigan's marvellously pompous bass aria and the boisterous 'Canone ed ostinato'. The performance of the *Hymn to St Cecilia* is skilful, idiomatic and touching.

A Spring Symphony[a]. Hymn to St Cecilia. Five Flower Songs, Op. 47.
Alison Hagley sop **Catherine Robbin** mez **John Mark Ainsley** ten [a]**Choristers of Salisbury Cathedral; Monteverdi Choir;** [a]**Philharmonia Orchestra / Sir John Eliot Gardiner.**
DG 453 433-2GH (62 minutes: DDD). Texts included.   Ⓕ Ⓢ

John Eliot Gardiner directs a memorable and thoroughly invigorating account of Britten's vernal paean. Right from the start, one registers the exceptional refinement and transparency of his approach, to say nothing of the exciting realism of DG's sound. No praise can be too high for the marvellously nimble and extremely well-focused contribution of the Monteverdi Choir or the Philharmonia's superbly disciplined response throughout. The Choristers of Salisbury Cathedral also emerge with great credit. High-spots abound: the smiling, easy sway of 'Spring, the sweet Spring' (whose bird-call cadenzas are delightfully attended to); an exceptionally perceptive 'Waters above', whose truly *pppp diminuendo* conclusion leads magically into 'Out on the lawn I lie in bed'; the terrific bounce and clean-limbed swagger of the triptych comprising Part 3 (both 'Fair and fair' and 'Sound the flute' come close to perfection); and, of course, the joyous, bank holiday clangour of the finale (splendidly dapper and affirmative on this occasion), with its heart-stopping appearance of 'Sumer is icumen in' – a moment which never fails to send shivers down the spine (though the four horns might perhaps have cut through the orchestral fabric just a touch more than they do here?). Gardiner's soloists are very good, if perhaps not quite a match for the finest. Ainsley stands out for his honeyed tone, and the intelligence of his word-painting always catches the attention, as does the warmth and projection of Alison Hagley's soprano. Overall, then, while not displacing the composer's classic recording, Gardiner's version can hold its own against all-comers and should give much pleasure to seasoned Brittenites. Both *a cappella* fill-ups are also a treat: an exquisitely poised and supremely touching *Hymn to St Cecilia*, followed by the delicious *Five Flower Songs*.

Hymn to St Cecilia. A Ceremony of Carols, Op. 28. Rejoice in the Lamb, Op. 30.
Missa brevis in D major, Op. 63. Sacred and Profane, Op. 91. A Hymn to the Virgin.
Frances Kelly hp **Christopher Allsop** org **Trinity College Choir, Cambridge / Richard Marlow.**
Conifer Classics 75605 51287-2 (79 minutes: DDD). Texts included. Recorded 1996.   Ⓕ

Britten's genius as a writer of choral music in his early years is laid before us in this attractive, vividly performed programme: the extraordinary variety of these settings shows unerringly his response to the needs of the text in hand and/or for the specific occasion for which the music was written. Marlow and his famed Trinity College Choir have assembled a logical programme and sing with confidence, *élan* and, above all, awareness of Britten's needs. Their accounts, for instance, of *A Ceremony of Carols* and *Rejoice in the Lamb* are well disciplined and responsive to the texts. Marlow seems aware of the fact that Britten eschewed cathedral tradition. While his choir's readings don't altogether replace the composer's classic versions (the more distanced recording means diction is often occluded), they have a life and vigour of their own that is most exhilarating. Marlow includes a subtle performance of the early *Hymn to St Cecilia* as well as the wondrous *Missa brevis*, with its many touches of Brittenesque inspiration and its pre-echoes, particularly in the 'Benedictus', of the *War Requiem*. He ends with the late *Sacred and Profane*, where the composer's settings of medieval texts shows that he had lost none of his skills in the last years of his life.

Britten Folk-song Arrangements[a]. Folk-song Arrangements – orchestral versions[b]. King Herod and the Cock[c]. The Twelve Apostles[d]. The Holly and the Ivy[e].
Felicity Lott sop **Philip Langridge** ten **Thomas Allen** bar **Carlos Bonell** gtr
Osian Ellis hp **Christopher van Kampen** vc [a]**Graham Johnson,** [cd]**David Owen Norris** pfs
[cd]**Wenhaston Boys' Choir / Christopher Barnett;** [e]**BBC Singers / Simon Joly;**
[b]**Northern Sinfonia / Steuart Bedford.**
Collins Classics 7039-2 (three discs: 199 minutes: DDD). Texts included.   Ⓕ

Those who bought the attractive Hyperion set of Britten's 'complete' folk-song arrangements probably thought that they had at least one area in their collection which was complete and need not be reconsidered. Now comes another set, on three CDs rather than two. So the questions run: 'What is the extra material?', 'How good is it?' and 'How do the performances compare?' Eight unpublished settings for solo or duet, one for choir and tenor and one unidentified folk-song setting plus 14 of the published songs rearranged for voice and orchestra: that is the tally. Additions to the voice-and-piano repertoire include *Greensleeves* and *The Crocodile* (the song of a sailor who spins a yarn for landsmen gullible enough to swallow the 500-mile length of croc with attendant wonders). *I wonder as I wander*, a favourite encore in Sir Peter Pears's concerts, is here on record for the first time. These and two light-hearted duets all give pleasure, though perhaps not so acute as to make the purchase imperative. More unexpected, perhaps, is the setting which goes under the title of *The Stream in the Valley* and which turns out to be *Da unten im Tale*, best known today in the arrangement by Brahms. In this Britten introduces to very lovely effect a part for cello. Interest, then, begins to add up. The orchestrations may not add much more, though it is striking to find that the remoteness of tonality in *Fileuse* and to some extent *Eho* (Vol. 2) seems increased.

The choral settings are fun (perhaps more than that), and the great discovery among them is the unfinished, comparatively large-scale arrangement of *The Bitter Withy*, a fascinating piece and apparently going so well that it is astonishing to find Britten putting it aside and never returning to it. Certainly for first-time buyers this is the set to have. As to the performances, much in a Britten collection of this kind depends on the tenor, and Philip Langridge quickly establishes himself as a worthy successor to Pears, a singer of intelligence and bold, distinctive character. In most of the volumes he shares with Felicity Lott, who is comparably sensitive to modulations and underlying feeling. Thomas Allen makes only a brief appearance, but it is good to hear his warm tone and fine *legato* in the version of *The Salley Gardens* with strings. Fine playing by Osian Ellis and the guitarist Carlos Bonell and a strong contribution from the Wenhaston Boys' Choir are further attractions. Graham Johnson's playing is uniformly excellent. The set is well recorded, the Collins engineers skilfully aligning the acoustics of their five different locations.

Harmonia Sacra – Lord! I have sinned; Hymn to God the Father; A Hymn on Divine Musick. This way to the Tomb – Evening; Morning; Night. Night covers up the rigid land. Fish in the unruffled lakes. To lie flat on the back with the knees flexed. A poison tree. When you're feeling like expressing your affection. Not even summer yet. The red cockatoo. Wild with passion. If thou wilt ease thine heart. Cradle song for Eleanor. Birthday song for Erwin. Um Mitternacht. The Holy Sonnets of John Donne, Op. 35.
Ian Bostridge *ten* **Graham Johnson** *pf*
Hyperion CDA66823 (65 minutes: DDD). Texts included. Recorded 1995. Ⓕ🄴

Bostridge is in the royal line of Britten's tenor interpreters. Indeed his imaginative response to words and music may come closer than any to Pears himself. He is heard here in a veritable cornucopia of by and large unfamiliar and even unknown songs (the Donne cycle apart), mostly from the earliest period of Britten's song-writing career when his inspiration was perhaps at its most free and spontaneous. The three settings from Ronald Duncan's *This way to the Tomb* nicely match that poet's florid, vocabulary-rich style as Britten was to do again two years later in *Lucretia*, with 'Night', based on a B minor ground bass, a particularly arresting piece. The Auden settings, roughly contemporaneous with *On this Island*, all reflect Britten's empathy with the poet at that time. The third, *To lie flat on the back*, evinces Britten's gift for writing in racy mode, as does *When you're feeling like expressing your affection*, very much in the style of *Cabaret Songs*. Much deeper emotions are stirred by the two superb Beddoes settings (*Wild with passion* and *If thou wilt ease thine heart*), written when the composer and Pears were on a ship returning home in 1942. *The red cockatoo* itself is an early setting of Waley to whom Britten returned in *Songs from the Chinese*. All these revelatory songs are performed with full understanding and innate beauty by Bostridge and Johnson, who obviously have a close artistic rapport. They form a lengthy and rewarding prelude to their shattering account of the Donne Sonnets. They are as demanding on singer and pianist as anything Britten wrote, hence their previously small representation in the catalogue. Both artists pierce to the core of these electrifying songs, written after, and affected by, Britten's visit to Belsen with Menuhin in 1945 shortly after the war's end. The recording which catches the immediacy of these riveting performances complete one's pleasure in this richly satisfying issue.

Serenade for Tenor, Horn and Strings, Op. 60.

Serenade. Nocturne, Op. 60. Les illuminations, Op. 18.
John Mark Ainsley *ten* **David Pyatt** *hn* **Britten Sinfonia / Nicholas Cleobury.**
EMI Eminence CD-EMX2247 (73 minutes: DDD). Texts and translations included.
Recorded 1995. Ⓜ🄴 🅁🅁

John Mark Ainsley is representative of the third generation of Britten interpreters with fewer of the inhibitions that inevitably afflicted those tenors who lived in the immediate shadow of the composer. Which is not to say that, in these absorbing performances, he is in any way flouting tradition: these are mainstream interpretations, but ones with their own validity. He is most compelling in *Nocturne*, arguably the most difficult of the three to encompass. Here he has nothing to fear in comparisons with Pears. In his liquid tone, response to the texts and technical accomplishment of the challenging line, he is well-nigh faultless. More important still in this cycle, he catches the individual mood of each setting through finding the right timbre for each. With Cleobury and the highly skilled soloists of the Britten Sinfonia lending ideal support, this is a reading to savour. Apart from too many aspirates in the runs of 'Hymn', the *Serenade* is almost on a par with *Nocturne*, the many facets of this still-amazing cycle fully realized both in terms of vocal refinement and textual acuity. He is helped by the most thrilling account yet of the horn solo from young David Pyatt. His playing is nothing short of masterly and magical. In *Les illuminations*, although the delicacy of 'Phrase' and the sensuous erotic touch essential for 'Antique' are admirable, you may be less happy with a too hectic pace for 'Villes', though Ainsley has no difficulty coping with the fast tempo; you are conscious that the smile Pears gets into his tone throughout was generally absent. Ainsley's French, though not wholly idiomatic, is clearly articulated. However, if you want these three works together on a single CD in modern sound, you need not hesitate, especially as the price is fair.

Serenade[a]. Les illuminations[b]. Nocturne, Op. 60[c].
Sir Peter Pears *ten* **Alexander Murray** *fl* **Roger Lord** *cor ang* **Gervase de Peyer** *cl*
William Waterhouse *bn* **Barry Tuckwell** *hn* **Dennis Blyth** *timp* **Osian Ellis** *hp* [ac]strings of the
London Symphony Orchestra; [b]**English Chamber Orchestra /** [abc]**Benjamin Britten.**
Decca London 436 395-2LM (73 minutes: ADD). Texts included. Recorded 1959-66.   Ⓜ Ⓗ

No other instrument was more important to Britten than the human voice and, inspired by the musicianship and superb vocal craftsmanship of his closest friend, Peter Pears, he produced an unbroken stream of vocal works of a quality akin to those of Purcell. Three of his most haunting vocal pieces are featured on this wonderful CD. The performances date from between 1959 and 1966 with Pears in penetratingly musical form, even if the voice itself was by now a little thin and occasionally unsteady. The ECO and LSO are superb in every way and of course Britten was his own ideal interpreter. The recordings are vintage Decca and excellent for their time. This welcome mid-price reissue is strongly recommended.

Serenade[a]. Our Hunting Fathers, Op. 8. Folk-song arrangements – Oliver Cromwell; O waly waly.
Ian Bostridge *ten* [a]**Marie Luise Neunecker** *hn*
Britten Sinfonia / Daniel Harding; [a]**Bamberg Symphony Orchestra / Ingo Metzmacher.**
EMI CDC5 56871-2 (58 minutes: DDD). Texts and translations included. Recorded 1996-97.   Ⓕ

On each hearing, Britten's *Serenade* still has the power to astonish anew for its amazingly apt setting of the diligently chosen poems and for the deftly woven, dazzling horn part written for Dennis Brain. There is something inevitable and predestined about these pieces, as though they existed for all time, an impression enhanced by this performance. Bostridge is spontaneous and immediate in his responses to text and music. He sounds fresh and eager, his interpretation suggesting the work had just been conceived. One small reservation concerns a weakness in the lower register in the Keats Sonnet, 'Oh soft embalmer of the still night'. In the horn contribution, Neunecker is as lithe and full-toned as any that has gone before. Metzmacher follows tradition in tempo matters and his players are alive to every nuance of the diaphanous scoring. This compilation also offers an interesting conspectus of the composer when young and culminates in the early, quirky masterpiece, *Our Hunting Fathers*, written in 1936 under the influence of Auden and echoes of terrible events in Germany. Ian Bostridge's well-known affinity with the composer's music and his virtue of verbal illumination are amply demonstrated here. The folk-song settings receive pertinent readings, the first plangent, the second skittish, as is appropriate to their texts.

Seven Sonnets of Michelangelo, Op. 22. The Holy Sonnets of John Donne, Op. 35.
Winter Words, Op. 52.
Justin Lavender *ten* **Julian Milford** *pf*
Carlton Classics 30366 0056-2 (66 minutes: DDD). Texts and translations included.
Recorded 1996.   Ⓜ

The highlight of this recording is the *Donne* Sonnets, where Lavender has the advantage, over other Britten tenor interpreters to date, of an Italianate metal in his tone, just what these dramatic, even heroic settings call for. He also has the range and technique to make them sound less intractable, vocally speaking, than they often seem, which is not to imply that he is unable to fine away his tone to a silvery line as required by that great Schubert-like song, 'Since she whom I lov'd'. Together with Milford's eager response to the stringent challenge to his technical resources, this is a convincing reading. That Italianate sound also serves Lavender well in the more extrovert *Michelangelo* Sonnets. These are sung with a fine feeling for line and verbal colouring. In *Winter Words*, intelligently as he enters into the quirky, intense world of this wonderful cycle, he doesn't quite match Philip Langridge on Collins in tonal management or verbal acuity, but the difference is slight and, with Milford again a resourceful and vital partner, this is an interpretation to cherish. The recording ambience sometimes lends a slight edge to the singer's tone, but as a whole this issue is recommendable on every count.

Phaedra, Op. 93. Lachrymae, Op. 48a. Sinfonietta, Op. 1. The Sword in the Stone. Movement for Wind Sextet. Night Mail – End sequence.
Jean Rigby *mez* **Nigel Hawthorne** *narr* **Roger Chase** *va* **Nash Ensemble / Lionel Friend.**
Hyperion CDA66845 (65 minutes: DDD). Text included. Recorded 1995.   Ⓕ

A chronologically wide-ranging Britten programme performed with unerring sensitivity and much quiet insight. The *Movement* for wind sextet (here receiving its première recording) dates from 1930. Britten composed it during his last term at Gresham's School and annotator Philip Reed suggests that a hearing of Janáček's identically scored *Mládí* may have acted as a possible spur. The *Sinfonietta*, which Britten completed two years later while still a student at the Royal College of Music, represents a remarkable achievement for one so young. Amazingly inventive and concise, it bears a dedication to his mentor, Frank Bridge, whose tangily pastoral idiom can be discerned in the rapt central *Andante*. The Nash Ensemble's account could hardly be bettered: in this same movement, for example, how perceptively Friend and his colleagues gauge (and sustain) the mood of gentle rapture, and how effortlessly they handle the almost Sibelian transition into the 'Tarantella' finale. Britten's and Auden's unforgettable collaboration for the end sequence from the documentary *Night Mail* dates from 1936 when both artists were briefly employed by the GPO Film Unit. Remarkably, this is its first commercial recording – and a marvellous one it is, too, with Nigel Hawthorne the exemplary reciter. Three years later, Britten was approached by the BBC to write the incidental music for an adaptation of T. H. White's *The Sword in the Stone*. Scored for a small ensemble, the suite abounds in witty motivic borrowings fromWagner's *Ring*. The disc opens with a persuasive rendering of *Phaedra* from Jean Rigby. Eloquently though she responds (and the final climax certainly rises to a memorable pitch of intensity), her contribution overall is perhaps not quite as characterful or involving as that of, say, Dame Janet Baker (the work's dedicatee) or Felicity Palmer. With first-rate sound and balance throughout this is an excellent anthology.

An American Overture, Op. 27. King Arthur – Suite (arr. Hindmarsh). The World of the Spirit (arr. Hindmarsh).
Susan Chilcott *sop* **Pamela Helen Stephen** *mez* **Martyn Hill** *ten* **Stephen Varcoe** *bar*
Hannah Gordon, Cormac Rigby *spkrs*
Britten Singers; BBC Philharmonic Orchestra / Richard Hickox.
Chandos CHAN9487 (79 minutes: DDD). Text included.   Ⓕ **Ｅ**

The performance of the Coplandesque *An American Overture* by Hickox and the excellent BBC Philharmonic has exemplary polish, commitment and dash. The remaining items owe their revival to the considerable efforts of Paul Hindmarsh. Britten wrote his incidental music for a BBC radio dramatization of the King Arthur legend in 1937. It was the first of his 28 radio commissions and contains much high-quality invention. Hindmarsh has fashioned the 23-year-old composer's inventive inspiration into a terrific four-movement orchestral suite lasting some 25 minutes, which Hickox and the BBC PO duly devour with audible relish. The 'radio cantata' *The World of the Spirit* dates from May 1938. Commissioned by the BBC as a successor to *The Company of Heaven* (1937), it intersperses sung and spoken texts chosen by R. Ellis Roberts. Once again, Britten's fertile compositional powers are very much in evidence. Indeed, the work contains a whole string of memorable numbers, from the lilting barcarolle-like treatment of Emily Brontë's 'With wide-embracing love', via the joyful strut and swagger of Part 2's concluding 'The Spirit of the Lord' with its unmistakable echoes of Walton's *Belshazzar's Feast*, to a strikingly imaginative setting of Gerard Manley Hopkins's *God's Grandeur*, a poem which also features in Britten's unaccompanied choral suite of a year later entitled *A. M. D. G.*. Framing the whole 42-minute edifice are two radiant settings of the Whitsuntide plainsong, *Veni Creator Spiritus* – an idea possibly inspired by a recent encounter with Mahler's Eighth Symphony at the Queen's Hall in a performance under Sir Henry Wood. Superbly wide-ranging, realistic recording.

A Ceremony of Carols, Op. 28. Missa brevis in D major, Op. 63. A Hymn to the Virgin. A Hymn of St Columba, 'Regis regum rectissimi'. Jubilate Deo in E flat major. Deus in adjutorum meum.
Sioned Williams *hp* **Westminster Cathedral Choir / David Hill** with **James O'Donnell** *org*
Hyperion CDA66220 (49 minutes: DDD). Texts included.   Ⓕ

A Ceremony of Carols sets nine medieval and sixteenth-century poems between the 'Hodie' of the plainsong Vespers. The sole accompanying instrument is a harp, but given the right acoustic, sensitive attention to the words and fine rhythmic control the piece has a remarkable richness and depth. The Westminster Cathedral Choir performs this work beautifully; diction is immaculate and the acoustic halo surrounding the voices gives a festive glow to the performance. A fascinating *Jubilate* and *A Hymn to the Virgin*, whilst lacking the invention and subtlety of *A Ceremony*, intrigue with some particularly felicitous use of harmony and rhythm. *Deus in adjutorum meum* employs the choir without accompaniment and has an initial purity that gradually builds up in texture as the psalm (No. 70) gathers momentum. The *Missa brevis* was written for this very choir and George Malcolm's nurturing of a tonal brightness in the choir allowed Britten to use the voices in a more flexible and instrumental manner than usual. The effect is glorious. St Columba founded the monastery on the Scottish island of Iona and Britten's hymn sets his simple and forthright prayer with deceptive simplicity and directness. The choir sings this music beautifully and the recording is first-rate.

Hymn to St Peter, Op. 56a. A Hymn of St Columba, 'Regis regum rectissimi'. A Hymn to the Virgin. Hymn to St Cecilia, Op. 27. Rejoice in the Lamb, Op. 30. Choral Dances from 'Gloriana'. A.M.D.G.
Finzi Singers / Paul Spicer with **Andrew Lumsden** *org*
Chandos CHAN9511 (67 minutes: DDD). Texts included.   Ⓕ

The four hymns which open this recital cause one to marvel afresh at this creativity which made everything new and individual yet totally of the composer's unmistakable substance. Each is a small masterpiece, not least the *Hymn of St Columba* (1962), less than three minutes long, and the *Hymn to the Virgin* (1930) written with unfaltering taste and clarity of purpose at the age of 16. Of the other works included here, *Rejoice in the Lamb* (1943) must be the most often recorded, and *A.M.D.G.* the least. A set of seven poems by Gerard Manley Hopkins, it dates from 1939 when the outbreak of war prevented the scheduled première. Shortly afterwards Britten withdrew it, still unpublished, and it remained unheard till 1984, eight years after his death. It commands attention and gains an admiration that one can't quite see growing into affection. By contrast, the remaining work here, the *Choral Dances from 'Gloriana'*, inspired love on first meeting and have continued to move and delight ever since. This is the first volume of a projected series, a Britten Choral Edition, with the Finzi Singers taking part throughout. An expert choir, successfully directed, with Andrew Lumsden constantly bringing out something in colour or rhythm that adds flavour and distinction.

War Requiem, Op. 66

War Requiem[a]. Sinfonia da Requiem, Op. 20. Ballad of Heroes, Op. 14[b].
Heather Harper *sop* [a]**Philip Langridge,** [b]**Martyn Hill** *tens* **John Shirley-Quirk** *bar*
[a]**St Paul's Cathedral Choir; London Symphony Chorus and Orchestra / Richard Hickox.**
Chandos CHAN8983/4 (two discs: 125 minutes: DDD). Texts and translations included. *Gramophone* Award Winner 1992.   ⒻⓈ🆁🆁

Britten's *War Requiem* is the composer's most public statement of his pacifism. The work is cast in six movements and calls for massive forces: full chorus, soprano soloist and full orchestra evoke mourning, supplication and guilty apprehension; boys' voices with chamber organ, the passive calm of a liturgy which points beyond death; tenor and baritone soloists with chamber orchestra, the passionate outcry of the doomed victims of war. The most recent challenger to the composer's classic Decca version offers up-to-date recording, excellently managed to suggest the various perspectives of the vast work, and possibly the most convincing execution of the choral writing to date under the direction of a conductor, Richard Hickox, who is a past master at obtaining the best from a choir in terms of dynamic contrast and vocal emphasis. Add to that his empathy with all that the work has to say and you have a cogent reason for acquiring this version even before you come to the excellent work of the soloists. In her recording swan-song, Harper at last commits to disc a part she created. It is right that her special accents and impeccable shaping of the soprano's contribution have been preserved for posterity. Shirley-Quirk, always closely associated with the piece, sings the three baritone solos and duets with rugged strength and dedicated intensity. He is matched by Langridge's compelling and insightful reading, with his notes and words more dramatic than Pears's approach. The inclusion of two additional pieces, neither of them short, gives this version an added advantage even if the *Ballad of Heroes* is one of Britten's slighter works.

War Requiem.
Galina Vishnevskaya *sop* **Sir Peter Pears** *ten* **Dietrich Fischer-Dieskau** *bar*
Simon Preston *org* **Bach Choir; Highgate School Choir; Melos Ensemble;**
London Symphony Orchestra / Benjamin Britten.
Decca 414 383-2DH2 (132 minutes: DDD). Texts and translations included.
Includes rehearsal sequence. Recorded 1963.   Ⓕ

Decca has used the most recent digital and Cedar technology to improve the original sound, under the overall supervision of veteran technician James Lock. This is one of the great performances of recording history. As an imaginative bonus, Decca – with the approval of the Britten Estate – gives us the first issue of a long rehearsal tape. This was made by the producer John Culshaw without

Britten's approval. When Culshaw presented it to the composer on his 50th birthday, Britten was 'appalled', considering it a betrayal of trust and 'an unauthorised invasion of a territory exclusively his own and his performers', as Donald Mitchell relates in the booklet. Now Mitchell believes that we should be allowed 'to assess the tape as a contribution to our knowledge of him [Britten] as a performer and interpreter of his own music and to our understanding of the *War Requiem* itself.' Throughout this fascinating aural document you hear evidence of Britten's vision of his own music, his astonishing ear for timbre and intimate details, above all his wonderful encouragement of all his forces, culminating in his heart-warming words of thanks at the end of the sessions, not to mention his nice, tension-breaking sense of humour and a couple of sharp comments from Vishnevskaya, who remains unsurpassed as soprano soloist. The merit of this ground-breaking performance and recording is that it so arrestingly conveys Britten's intentions. We are lucky now to have not only the composer's personal and irreplaceable reading refurbished, but also his commentary on it suggested by the rehearsal sequences.

The Rescue of Penelope. Phaedra, Op. 93ª.
ªᴸorraine Hunt *mez* **Alison Hagley** *sop* Athene; **Catherine Wyn-Rogers** *mez* Artemis;
John Mark Ainsley *ten* Hermes; **William Dazeley** *bass* Apollo; **Dame Janet Baker** *narr*
Hallé Orchestra / Kent Nagano.
Erato 0630 12713-2 (52 minutes: DDD). Notes and text included.   Ⓕ

Soon after his return from America, at the height of the war in 1943, Britten wrote the incidental music for a radio play by Edward Sackville-West on the Homeric subject of Odysseus's return to Penelope. Drawn from the complete score with barely any amendment of the original, and compressed into a 36-minute cantata, with Chris de Souza tailoring the text and Colin Matthews, Britten's last amanuensis, most tactfully editing the music, the result is extraordinarily powerful. The most important role is that of the narrator, here masterfully taken by Dame Janet Baker, who brings the story vividly to life despite the stylized classical language (e.g. 'Odysseus, Lord of sea-girt Ithaca' or 'His fair wife, white-armed Penelope'). Rather confusingly Athene also appears as a soprano, with the radiant Alison Hagley sounding totally unlike Dame Janet. She is one of a godly quartet of singers who contribute Greek-style commentaries – vocal passages which regularly add to the atmospheric beauty of the piece. The surprise is that the idiom is not for the most part very Britten-like, except in the vitality of the writing. Here with a bigger orchestra than was usual for him, he allows himself far richer sounds, with the strings in particular often sounding like Walton. The result is hugely enjoyable, and for all the unexpected echoes – not just of Walton's film music but also of Elgar and Wagner – the more one listens, the more one identifies Britten. This is music which is not just illustrative but strong and purposeful in heightening the drama, in bringing home emotions. It is a welcome addition to the Britten *oeuvre*. It is apt that another encapsulated classical drama should provide the coupling, particularly one inspired by the singing of Dame Janet Baker. *Phaedra* was Britten's last vocal work, and after the richness of the early work the spareness of the writing hits one the more sharply. Lorraine Hunt's performance may not quite match that of Dame Janet in conveying the heroine's agony, but there is comparable intensity, with vocal colouring of similarly grave beauty and variety; with Hunt this is above all the portrait of a deranged woman, chillingly powerful. In both works Kent Nagano draws strongly committed playing from the Hallé, with some fine solo work, instrumental as well as vocal. Though, reasonably enough, Dame Janet's narration is rather close in the bigger work, the sound is full and well balanced.

Albert Herring.
Sir Peter Pears *ten* Albert Herring; **Sylvia Fisher** *sop* Lady Billows; **Johanna Peters** *contr*
Florence Pike; **John Noble** *bar* Mr George; **Owen Brannigan** *bass* Mr Budd; **Edgar Evans** *ten*
Mr Upford; **April Cantelo** *sop* Mrs Wordsworth; **Sheila Rex** *mez* Mrs Herring; **Joseph Ward** *ten*
Sid; **Catherine Wilson** *mez* Nancy; **English Chamber Orchestra / Benjamin Britten.**
Decca London 421 849-2LH2 (two discs: 138 minutes: ADD). Notes and text included.
Recorded 1964.   Ⓕ 🆁🆁

Albert Herring.
Christopher Gillett *ten* Albert Herring; **Dame Josephine Barstow** *sop* Lady Billows;
Felicity Palmer *mez* Florence Pike; **Peter Savidge** *bar* Mr George; **Robert Lloyd** *bass* Mr Budd;
Stuart Kale *ten* Mr Upford; **Susan Gritton** *sop* Mrs Wordsworth; **Della Jones** *mez* Mrs Herring;
Gerald Finley *bar* Sid; **Ann Taylor** *mez* Nancy; **Northern Sinfonia / Steuart Bedford.**
Collins Classics 7042-2 (two discs: 142 minutes: DDD). Text included. Recorded 1996.   Ⓕ 🆂

As in all his recordings, Britten is a hard act to follow. Yet when his version of *Albert Herring* appeared in 1964 (17 years after the première) there were plenty who found Sylvia Fisher's classic portrayal of Lady Billows not really up to their memories of Joan Cross, nor April Cantelo as deliciously funny a Miss Wordsworth as her creator, Margaret Ritchie, or her peerless successor

Jennifer Vyvyan. Cantelo's is an enchanting portrayal, and those who have grown up with it may find Susan Gritton not *quite* her equal ... and so on: it is that sort of opera. Its superbly varied recitative and its pungent, thumbnail-sketch 'arias' provide resourceful singer-actors with the juiciest chances imaginable to become obstinately memorable. Gritton seizes those chances with both hands, sounding at times uncannily like Vyvyan. Felicity Palmer is a splendid Florence, relishing gossip, moral outrage and her authority as Lady Billows's ADC. Of course Christopher Gillett cannot erase memories of Pears in the title-role. But there is more sense of a worm turning in his performance, less of a feeling that no one so irredeemably daft and downtrodden could possibly escape from Mum's apron-strings, firmly tied though they are by Della Jones. Ann Taylor and Gerald Finley are admirable, believable both as lovers and as baker's girl and butcher's boy respectively. The village worthies are all sharply done, with Robert Lloyd especially good as an irascible Superintendent Budd. The one reservation concerns Josephine Barstow's Lady Billows. She is formidably authoritative, at her best when she loses her notes in mid-speech but improvises with magnificent clichés ('Cleanliness is next to ... God for England and Saint ... Keep your powder dry and leave the rest to nature!'). But, at least as recorded here, her voice has a very sharp edge to it, all the more apparent since she almost never sings quietly. Of course the newer recording cannot supersede Britten's own, but Bedford is worthy of the opera and as good as Britten at making clear that *Albert Herring* is as central to the Britten canon as any of his other operas.

Billy Budd.
Peter Glossop *bar* Billy Budd; **Sir Peter Pears** *ten* Captain Vere; **Michael Langdon** *bass*
John Claggart; **John Shirley-Quirk** *bar* Mr Redburn; **Bryan Drake** *bar* Mr Flint;
David Kelly *bass* Mr Ratcliffe; **Gregory Dempsey** *ten* Red Whiskers; **David Bowman** *bar*
Donald; **Owen Brannigan** *bass* Dansker; **Robert Tear** *ten* Novice; **Robert Bowman** *ten* Squeak;
Delme Bryn-Jones *bar* Bosun; **Eric Garrett** *bar* First Mate; **Nigel Rogers** *ten* Maintop;
Benjamin Luxon *bar* Novice's Friend; **Geoffrey Coleby** *bar* Arthur Jones;
Ambrosian Opera Chorus; London Symphony Orchestra / Benjamin Britten.
The Holy Sonnets of John Donne, Op. 35. Songs and Proverbs of William Blake, Op. 74.
Sir Peter Pears *ten* **Dietrich Fischer-Dieskau** *bar* **Benjamin Britten** *pf*
Decca London 417 428-2LH3 (three discs: 205 minutes: ADD). Notes and text included.
Recorded 1961.   Ⓕ **RR**

Billy Budd is remarkable in having been composed for male voices, yet not once is there any lack of colour or variety. Britten marvellously supports the tenor, baritone and bass protagonists with extraordinary flair in the use of brass and woodwind. This was the last operatic recording John Culshaw produced for Decca and he again showed himself unsurpassed at creating a theatrical atmosphere in the studio. Although there have been several striking and brilliant stage productions of this opera in recent years, not to mention Nagano's recording, it must also be said that both technically and interpretatively this Britten/Culshaw collaboration represents the touchstone for any that follows it, particularly in the matter of Britten's conducting. Where Britten is superb is in the dramatic tautness with which he unfolds the score and his unobtrusive highlighting of such poignant detail as the use of the saxophone after the flogging. His conducting of the choral scenes, particularly when the crew are heard singing below decks while Captain Vere and his officers are talking in his cabin, is profoundly satisfying and moving. Most of all, he focuses with absolute clarity on the intimate human drama against the background of life aboard the ship.

And what a cast he had, headed by Peter Pears as Vere, conveying a natural authoritarianism which makes his unwilling but dutiful role as 'the messenger of death' more understandable, if no more agreeable. Peter Glossop's Billy Budd is a virile performance, with nothing of the 'goody-goody' about him. Nor does one feel any particular homo-eroticism about his relationship with Michael Langdon's black-voiced Claggart: it is a straight conflict between good and evil, and all the more horrifying for its stark simplicity. Add to these principals John Shirley-Quirk, Bryan Drake and David Kelly as the officers, Owen Brannigan as Dansker and Robert Tear and Benjamin Luxon in the small roles of the novice and his friend, and one can apply the adjective 'classic' to this recording with a clear conscience. Also on the discs are two of Britten's most sombre song-cycles, the *Donne Sonnets* and the *Blake Songs and Proverbs*, the former with Pears, the latter with Fischer-Dieskau, and both incomparably accompanied by Britten. They make ideal complements to *Billy Budd*. This is a vintage set.

Billy Budd (four-act version).
Thomas Hampson *bar* Billy Budd; **Anthony Rolfe Johnson** *ten* Captain Vere; **Eric Halfvarson** *bass-bar* John Claggart; **Russell Smythe** *bar* Mr Redburn; **Gidon Saks** *bass* Mr Flint; **Simon Wilding** *bass* Mr Ratcliffe; **Martyn Hill** *ten* Red Whiskers; **Christopher Maltman** *bar* Donald; **Richard Van Allan** *bass* Dansker; **Andrew Burden** *ten* Novice; **Christopher Gillett** *ten* Squeak; **Matthew Hargreaves** *bass* Bosun; **Ashley Holland** *bass* First Mate; **Simon Thorpe** *bar* Second

Mate, Arthur Jones; **Robert Johnston** *ten* Maintop; **William Dazeley** *bar* Novice's Friend;
Manchester Boys' Choir; Northern Voices; Hallé Choir and Orchestra / Kent Nagano.
Erato 3984-21631-2 (two discs: 148 minutes: DDD). Notes and text included. Recorded live in
1997.
Ⓕ

This recording is an exciting achievement; it restores to circulation the original, four-act version of
the score. The crucial difference between this and Britten's two-act revision is a scene at the close of
what is here Act 1, in which 'Starry' Vere addresses his crew and is hailed by them as the sailors'
champion, thus establishing the relationship between captain and foretopman. It is thus an
important scene though musically not particularly distinguished. One can quite see why Britten
wanted a tauter two-act drama. Nagano gives us a wonderfully full-bodied, accurate and detailed
account of the many-faceted score. There are electrifying moments, not least the battle scene, where
the listener feels very much in the middle of things, and the end of Act 3 where those tremendous
and ominous series of chords represent Vere telling Budd of the sentence of death. Britten, in his
studio recording, prefers a leaner sound and a slightly tauter approach all-round – in his hands you
feel the tension of the personal relationships even more sharply than with Nagano. Hampson is
very good, singing with all his customary beauty of voice and intelligence of style, though he
imparts a touch of self-consciousness that goes against the grain of the writing. Halfvarson, as
Budd's antagonist, the evil Claggart, gives us a mighty presence, singing with power and bite,
though not always a steady tone. Rolfe Johnson sings his heart out as he presents Vere's tormented
soul. For the rest, Gidon Saks makes a dominant Mr Flint, the sailing-master, Richard Van Allan,
is here, predictably, a characterful Dansker, and Andrew Burden stands out as a properly scared
Novice, far preferable to Tear's placid reading on Decca. The sum here is greater than the parts, and
this set can be heartily recommended. In Manchester's Bridgewater Hall, where the recording was
made (though, to judge by the absence of background noise, there must have been sessions without
an audience), the orchestral contribution was, apparently, exceptionally clear. That has been carried
over into the amazingly wide spectrum of sound on the recording: indeed sometimes the orchestra
is simply too loud.

Curlew River.
Sir Peter Pears *ten* Madwoman; **John Shirley-Quirk** *bar* Ferryman; **Harold Blackburn**
bass Abbot; **Bryan Drake** *bar* Traveller; **Bruce Webb** *treb* Voice of the Spirit;
English Opera Group / Benjamin Britten and Viola Tunnard.
Decca London 421 858-2LM (69 minutes: ADD). Text included. Recorded 1965.
Ⓜ **RR**

Curlew River captured completely the composer's fascination with the Japanese Noh play on which
it was based. It was an inspired idea to locate the action in East Anglia, so one has the clash and
intermingling of East and West with an immediacy that reflects the keenness of Britten's response
to both. The recording, produced by John Culshaw, was made in Orford Church (is there an aircraft
overhead near the start?). The atmosphere of thus unforgettable occasion is preserved. The
procession of monks at the beginning and end comes towards us and recedes, just as if we were
sitting in a pew. Peter Pears's performance as the Madwoman is one of his finest and most
touching, while John Shirley-Quirk and Bryan Drake are equally authoritative as the Ferryman and
Traveller. The voice of the Madwoman's dead son is devoid of the sentimentality that might have
been a peril if any treble other than Bruce Webb had sung it, and the inventive and beguiling
orchestral score is marvellously played. With the composer and Viola Tunnard directing the
performance, it is in a class of its own.

Curlew River.
Philip Langridge *ten* Madwoman; **Thomas Allen** *bar* Ferryman; **Gidon Saks** *bass* Abbot;
Simon Keenlyside *bar* Traveller; **Charles Richardson** *treb* Voice of the Spirit;
London Voices; Academy of St Martin in the Fields / Sir Neville Marriner.
Philips 454 469-2PH (70 minutes: DDD). Notes and text included.
Ⓕ

Until now, nobody has wanted to challenge the hegemony of Britten's magical performance, but the
newer performance is given almost as much presence and perspective by Erik Smith as John
Culshaw achieved in the Decca version. Marriner and his hand-picked team of instrumentalists
follow in the tradition of the Britten-led performance, exposing the extreme originality of the
composer's reworking of the Japanese play, the results as mesmeric and concentrated as they should
be. The spare beauty of the scoring and the subtlety of the interaction between voices and
instruments is as convincing as one could wish, so there's little to choose here between the two
readings. Because the Madwoman was undoubtedly one of Pears's greatest achievements and fitted
his voice like the proverbial glove, his interpretation remains, as it always will, *hors concours*.
Langridge is a perceptive enough artist not to ape Pears. He treats the part in an inward, dreamy
manner, more intimate and personal than Pears's hieratical approach, just as valid in its way and,

needless to say, finely executed. As the strong-willed Ferryman, Thomas Allen almost but not quite matches Shirley-Quirk's firm, acutely enunciated portrayal: there is just that much more youthful sap in Shirley-Quirk's voice. On the other hand Keenlyside far surpasses his predecessor as the more ruminative Traveller, singing with the strong, vibrant tone and sharply etched *legato* for which he has become famed. Gidon Saks is a suitably grave Abbot, and the London Voices sing securely and solemnly as the Monks. The newer recording obviously has a greater range than the old one; both are sensitively directed to capture the work's very special ethos. Those who have the old one can probably remain satisfied, but newcomers and those seeking another view of the piece, should certainly consider this invaluable, carefully crafted and eloquent newcomer.

Death in Venice.
Sir Peter Pears *ten* Gustav von Aschenbach; **John Shirley-Quirk** *bar* Traveller, Elderly Fop, Old Gondolier, Hotel Manager, Hotel Barber, Leader of the Players, Voice of Dionysus; **James Bowman** *countertenor* Voice of Apollo; **Kenneth Bowen** *ten* Hotel Porter; **Peter Leeming** *bass* Travel Clerk; **Neville Williams** *bass-bar* **Penelope MacKay** *sop* Strolling Players; **Iris Saunders** *sop* Strawberry-seller; **English Opera Group Chorus; English Chamber Orchestra / Steuart Bedford.** Decca London 425 669-2LH2 (two discs: 145 minutes: ADD). Notes and text included. Recorded 1973.   Ⓕ

In his insert-notes, Christopher Palmer has pertinent things to say about the sexual climate of Britten's last opera, *Death in Venice*; but these seem to become of less consequence as one listens to the music. Its potency and inventiveness create this opera's disturbing and intense atmosphere, each episode heightened dramatically by instrumental colouring. Steuart Bedford's conducting avoids any tendency towards the episodic as a result of the quick succession of scenes: under his direction each scene is fully integrated into a fluent and convincing whole. This recording was made while Britten was very ill; it omits Aschenbach's first recitative ('I have always kept a close watch over my development as a writer ... '), given as an optional cut in the vocal score, which was published after the recording was made, by which time Britten had changed his mind about this cut and wished it had been included in the recording. Pears's Aschenbach, a very English conception, is a masterly performance, matched by John Shirley-Quirk's assumption of the six characters who are Aschenbach's messengers of death and the Voice of Dionysus.

Gloriana.
Dame Josephine Barstow *sop* Queen Elizabeth I; **Philip Langridge** *ten* Earl of Essex; **Della Jones** *mez* Lady Essex; **Jonathan Summers** *bar* Lord Mountjoy; **Alan Opie** *bar* Sir Robert Cecil; **Yvonne Kenny** *sop* Penelope; **Richard Van Allan** *bass* Sir Walter Raleigh; **Bryn Terfel** *bass-bar* Henry Cuffe; **Janice Watson** *sop* Lady-in-waiting; **Willard White** *bass* Blind ballad-singer; **John Shirley-Quirk** *bar* Recorder of Norwich; **John Mark Ainsley** *ten* Spirit of the Masque; **Peter Hoare** *ten* Master of Ceremonies; **Welsh National Opera Chorus and Orchestra / Sir Charles Mackerras.** Argo 440 213-2ZHO2 (two discs: 148 minutes: DDD). Notes and text included. Recorded 1992. *Gramophone* Award Winner 1994.   ⒻⒺ

Four decades on from the ill-fated première of Britten's Coronation opera where, instead of the staid pageant expected by the bejewelled and stiff audience assembled for a royal gala, they were given an intimate study of the ageing Queen's torment as she copes with the conflict of private emotions in the midst of public pomp, *Gloriana* has now at last been given a complete recording on CD. Sir Charles Mackerras presents it here with the utmost conviction, drawing together the motivic strands of the score into a coherent whole (not an altogether easy task), appreciating the contrast of the public and private scenes, exposing the sinews of the writing for the two principal characters, and drawing superb playing from his own WNO Orchestra. Josephine Barstow crowns her career with her performance as Queen Elizabeth, commanding the opera by her vocal presence, her imposing, vibrant tone, her vital treatment of the text, and her attention to detail. Philip Langridge projects all the vehement impetuosity of Essex but also, in the famous lute songs, the poetic ardour of the handsome if unruly Earl. There is much discerning interpretation elsewhere and the recording is worthy of the performance. Any small reservations are as nothing before the triumph of the achievement as a whole.

A Midsummer Night's Dream.
Alfred Deller *counterten* Oberon; **Elizabeth Harwood** *sop* Tytania; **Sir Peter Pears** *ten* Lysander; **Thomas Hemsley** *bar* Demetrius; **Josephine Veasey** *mez* Hermia; **Heather Harper** *sop* Helena; **John Shirley-Quirk** *bar* Theseus; **Helen Watts** *contr* Hippolyta; **Owen Brannigan** *bass* Bottom; **Norman Lumsden** *bass* Quince; **Kenneth Macdonald** *ten* Flute; **David Kelly** *bass* Snug;

Robert Tear *ten* Snout; **Keith Raggett** *ten* Starveling; **Richard Dakin** *treb* Cobweb;
John Prior *treb* Peaseblossom; **Ian Wodehouse** *treb* Mustardseed; **Gordon Clark** *treb* Moth;
Stephen Terry *spkr* Puck;
Choirs of Downside and Emanuel Schools; London Symphony Orchestra / Benjamin Britten.
Decca London 425 663-2LH2 (two discs: 144 minutes: ADD). Notes and text included.
Recorded 1966.   Ⓕ **RR**

A Midsummer Night's Dream.
Brian Asawa *counterten* Oberon; **Sylvia McNair** *sop* Tytania; **John Mark Ainsley** *ten* Lysander;
Paul Whelan *bar* Demetrius; **Ruby Philogene** *mez* Hermia; **Janice Watson** *sop* Helena;
Brian Bannatyne-Scott *bass* Theseus; **Hilary Summers** *contr* Hippolyta; **Robert Lloyd** *bass*
Bottom; **Gwynne Howell** *bass* Quince; **Ian Bostridge** *ten* Flute; **Stephen Richardson** *bar* Snug;
Mark Tucker *ten* Snout; **Neal Davies** *bar* Starveling; **David Newman** *treb* Cobweb;
Claudia Conway *sop* Peaseblossom; **Sara Rey** *sop* Mustardseed; **Matthew Long** *treb* Moth;
Carl Ferguson *spkr* Puck;
New London Children's Choir; London Symphony Orchestra / Sir Colin Davis.
Philips 454 122-2PH2 (two discs: 148 minutes: DDD). Notes and text included.
Recorded 1995.   Ⓕ **S**

The Philips set is in almost every respect immediate and present, almost to a fault, yet there are few
if any attempts at suggesting the perspectives you hear on the 34-year-old Decca set for the
composer. For instance, on Decca, Puck seems to be everywhere, yet on the newer version you are
in the front stalls listening to an enjoyable concert with little attempt to simulate a stage. That may
have influenced the often leisurely pacing of Davis's reading. Everything is heard with great clarity,
the sensuousness of Britten's ravishing score, with all its mysterious harmonies and sonorities, is
fully realized, action and reaction among the singers are keenly heard, yet something of the
midsummer magic of Britten's direction eludes Davis and his team. On Decca we hear this music
fresh-minted, unadorned; in Davis's hands the work is viewed through a tougher, more modern
prism, something that those who know the original set will need to become accustomed to. One
wonders if any members of the LSO today were in the orchestra under the composer back in 1966:
they are certainly as acute if not more so in their playing than their predecessors. As for pacing, if
you try either Oberon's 'I know a bank' or Tytania's solo 'Come, now a roundel and a fairy song'
you will immediately hear how much tauter is Britten's approach, Davis allowing his singers more
licence. In the case of McNair this gives her space to develop what is a knowingly sophisticated
approach to her role, even more evident in her sensual account of the Act 2 solo 'Hail, mortal, hail'.
Her singing is in itself lovely, but it is an earthly reading where Elizabeth Harwood for Britten
suggests a more other-worldly Queen of the Fairies.

Similarly the luscious, vibrant voice of the American countertenor Brian Asawa is very different
from Deller's ethereal delicacies. Like McNair's singing, Asawa's, taken on its own terms, is most
seductive, certainly a new look at the familiar, but disconcerting at first hearing. Puck is also
upfront, not so much puckish as rough-hewn. With Bottom we meet another thought-provoking
interpretation. Lloyd makes the weaver sound more high-born than his predecessor. This is almost a
noble craftsman, with no hint of the rustic portrayed unforgettably by Owen Brannigan, the role's
creator, who savours the text so lovingly. Lloyd scores with his splendidly resonant account of
'O grin-look'd night' in the play. One thing is sure: there has never been a more amusing Flute than
Ian Bostridge (hilarious as Thisbe) or a better sung Quince than Gwynne Howell. Another plus for
Davis is the casting of the lovers with young singers in their early prime, a small advance on the
Britten set. In particular, Philogene's ripe mezzo as Hermia and Ainsley's ardent tenor as Lysander
stand out as ideal interpretations. Neither Hippolyta nor Theseus matches the regal authority of
Helen Watts and Shirley-Quirk on the composer's set. You will derive a great deal of pleasure from
the newcomer with its exemplary recording and careful preparation on all sides. It is now the prime
recommendation for a modern set. But the Decca remains as fresh and inspired as the day it was
made; Britten's taut, disciplined yet magical reading unsurpassed.

Noye's Fludde.
Owen Brannigan *bass* Noye; **Sheila Rex** *mez* Mrs Noye; **David Pinto** *treb* Sem;
Darian Angadi *treb* Ham; **Stephen Alexander** *treb* Jaffett; **Trevor Anthony** *spkr*
The Voice of God; **Caroline Clack** *sop* Mrs Sem; **Maria-Thérèse Pinto** *sop* Mrs Ham;
Eileen O'Donnovan *sop* Mrs Jaffett; **chorus; English Opera Group Orchestra;**
An East Suffolk Children's Orchestra / Norman Del Mar.
The Golden Vanity, Op. 78.
Mark Emney *treb* Captain; **John Wojciechowski** *treb* Bosun; **Barnaby Jago** *treb* Cabin-boy;
Adrian Thompson *treb* Captain; **Terry Lovell** *treb* Bosun; **Benjamin Britten** *pf*
Wandsworth School Boys' Choir / Russell Burgess.
Decca London 436 397-2LM (66 minutes: ADD). Texts included. Recorded 1961 and 1966.   Ⓕ

Britten wrote these two works for children, yet one must not imagine that they are cosy and (in the pejorative sense) childish. Many of Britten's friends thought that there remained much of the child in him, and this clearly comes out in the boisterous high spirits of some of this music. By and large, *Noye's Fludde* and *The Golden Vanity* are happy works. *Noye's Fludde* makes invigorating listening. This 1961 performance, recorded in Orford Church where it had its première three years before (at the 1958 Aldeburgh Festival), is immensely vivid and one responds to the enthusiasm of the young singers and instrumentalists. All of the children of East Suffolk seem to be involved in the enterprise: consorts of recorders, bands of bugles, peals of handbell-ringers, plenty of violins, a few lower strings, seven percussion players, child soloists, and a choir as big as you like, enough to give full representation to the 49 different species of animal mentioned in the text. Then three grown-ups, and the English Chamber Orchestra. The skill and imaginative power with which Britten has used these forces defy adequate description. There are inevitably rough edges in the singing and playing, but the spirit is there in abundance. The same is true of *The Golden Vanity*, and although there's more conscious vocal skill in the singing of the Wandsworth School Boys' Choir, in this performance with Britten at the piano it never gets in the way of the presentation, which bubbles with life.

Peter Grimes.
Sir Peter Pears *ten* Peter Grimes; **Claire Watson** *sop* Ellen Orford; **James Pease** *bass* Captain Balstrode; **Jean Watson** *contr* Auntie; **Raymond Nilsson** *ten* Bob Boles; **Owen Brannigan** *bass* Swallow; **Lauris Elms** *mez* Mrs Sedley; **Sir Geraint Evans** *bar* Ned Keene; **John Lanigan** *ten* Rector; **David Kelly** *bass* Hobson; **Marion Studholme** *sop* First Niece; **Iris Kells** *sop* Second Niece;
Chorus and Orchestra of the Royal Opera House, Covent Garden / Benjamin Britten.
Decca 414 577-2DH3 (three discs: 144 minutes: ADD). Notes and text included.
Recorded 1958. Recorded 1958. *Gramophone* Award Winner 1986.   Ⓟ Ⓗ

Peter Grimes.
Philip Langridge *ten* Grimes; **Janice Watson** *sop* Ellen Orford; **Alan Opie** *bar* Captain Balstrode; **Ameral Gunson** *mez* Auntie; **John Graham-Hall** *ten* Bob Boles; **John Connell** *bass* Swallow; **Anne Collins** *contr* Mrs Sedley; **Roderick Williams** *bar* Ned Keene; **John Fryatt** *ten* Rector; **Matthew Best** *bass* Hobson; **Yvonne Barclay** *sop* First Niece; **Pamela Helen Stephen** *mez* Second Niece; **London Symphony Chorus; City of London Sinfonia / Richard Hickox.**
Chandos CHAN9447/8 (two discs: 147 minutes: DDD).
Notes and text included. Recorded 1995.   Ⓟ Ⓢ Ⓔ ⓇⓇ

The Decca set has long been regarded as the definitive recording which, in 1958, introduced this opera to many listeners and one which has never been superseded in its refinement or insight. Britten's conducting, lithe, lucid and as inexorable as 'the tide that waits for no man', reveals his work as the complex, ambiguous drama that it is. Sir Peter Pears, in the title-role which was written for him, brings unsurpassed detail of nuance to Grimes's words while never losing sight of the essential plainness of the man's speech. The rest of the cast form a vivid portrait gallery of characters. The recording is as live and clear as if it had been made yesterday and takes the listener right on to the stage. The bustle of activity and sound effects realize nicely Britten's own masterly painting of dramatic foreground and background. For Hickox on Chandos there is Langridge's tense, sinewy, sensitive Grimes. Predictably he rises to the challenge of the Mad scene; this is a man hugely to be pitied, yet there is a touch of resignation, of finding some sort of peace at last, after all the agony of the soul. His portrayal is tense and immediate and a match for that of Pears in personal identification – listen to the eager touch at 'We strained in the wind'.

The next composite heroes are the members of the chorus. Electrifying as their rivals are, the LSO singers, trained by Stephen Westrop, seem just that much more arresting, not least in the hue-and-cry of Act 3, quite terrifying in its immediacy as recorded by Chandos. Hickox's whole interpretation has little to fear from the distinguished competition. Many details are placed with special care, particularly in the Interludes and the parodistic dances in Act 3, and whole episodes, such as the Grimes/Balstrode dispute in Act 1, have seldom sounded so dramatic. Once or twice one would have liked a firmer forward movement, as in the fifth Interlude (Britten's own direction of this Passacaglia is that bit more urgent), but the sense of total music-theatre is present throughout and it's excitingly laid before us by the City of London Sinfonia and the recording. Of the other soloists, the one comparative disappointment is Janice Watson's Ellen Orford. She sings the part with tone as lovely as any of her rivals on disc and with carefully wrought phrasing and is very much part of a convincing team but doesn't have the experience to stand out from the village regulars and sound important, as Ellen should. Britten's set remains *hors concours* (the composer's own taut conducting is unsurpassed), but that recording stretches over three CDs. Hickox is the finest of the modern recordings: as sound it is quite spectacular, vast in range, with well-managed perspectives and just enough hints of stage action to be convincing.

The Turn of the Screw.
Sir Peter Pears ten Prologue, Quint; **Jennifer Vyvyan** sop Governess; **David Hemmings** treb
Miles; **Olive Dyer** sop Flora; **Joan Cross** sop Mrs Grose; **Arda Mandikian** sop Miss Jessel;
English Opera Group Orchestra / Benjamin Britten.
Decca London mono 425 672-2LH2 (two discs: 105 minutes: ADD). Notes and text included.
Recorded 1955. Ⓔ **H** **RR**

As Sir Colin Davis has shown on Philips, there is room for an alternative interpretation of this
remarkable work, but this superb first recording will remain as documentary-historical evidence of
the highest importance and value. Will there ever be a better performance, let alone recording, of
The Turn of the Screw than this by the original cast, recorded less than four months after the 1954
Venice première? Christopher Palmer contributes a stimulating essay to the booklet with this
reissue, in which he faces squarely all the implications of this choice of subject by Britten as far as
what Palmer calls his 'intellectual paedophilia' is concerned. It is a valid and provocative comment,
and was a useful contribution to the growing body of Britten criticism. This score is Britten at his
greatest, expressing good and evil with equal ambivalence, evoking the tense and sinister
atmosphere of Bly by inspired use of the chamber orchestra and imparting vivid and truthful life to
every character in the story. As one listens, transfixed, all that matters is Britten's genius as a
composer. Jennifer Vyvyan's portrayal of the Governess is a classic characterization, her vocal
subtleties illuminating every facet of the role and she has the perfect foil in Joan Cross's motherly
and uncomplicated Mrs Grose. The glittering malevolence of Pears's Quint, luring David
Hemmings's incomparable Miles to destruction; the tragic tones of Arda Mandikian's Miss Jessel;
Olive Dyer's spiteful Flora – how fortunate we are that these performances are preserved. As with
all of the Decca/Britten reissues, the transfer is a triumph.

The Turn of the Screw.
Philip Langridge ten Prologue; **Robert Tear** ten Quint; **Helen Donath** sop Governess;
Michael Ginn treb Miles; **Lilian Watson** sop Flora; **Ava June** sop Mrs Grose; **Heather Harper**
sop Miss Jessel; **Orchestra of the Royal Opera House, Covent Garden / Sir Colin Davis.**
Philips 446 325-2PH2 (two discs: 108 minutes: ADD). Notes and text included.
Recorded 1981. Ⓕ

Davis yields little if anything to the composer in realizing the taut, claustrophobic feeling of the
score. The players of the ROH Orchestra are quite as alert as Britten's chamber ensembles to the
minutiae of the fastidious instrumentation, bringing out the genius of Britten's variation form.
Davis unerringly pinpoints the change from the lyrical euphony of some of the earlier scenes and
the sinister, otherworldly suggestions of the later ones. The cast stands comparison with its rivals –
though Tear, for all his competence, cannot quite match the peculiarly haunting quality of Pears's
tone as Quint in a role specifically tailored to Britten's partner. Tear doesn't attempt to double with
the Prologue, here sung with predictable intelligence and refined poetic expectancy by the young
Langridge. Donath very properly lets a note of nervous agitation enter into her tone and evinces
full understanding of the Governess's predicament, 'Lost in my labyrinth' rightly given as a
whispered, interior monologue, though she doesn't build all the tensions as unerringly as Vyvyan
(Britten). Heather Harper, herself an erstwhile Governess, is a rightly hard-bitten Miss Jessel. Ava
June is even more articulate than her teacher Joan Cross as Mrs Grose. Lilian Watson makes a vivid
Flora, but Michael Ginn, accomplished treble though he is, doesn't suggest the paradox of evil in
innocence as David Hemmings so amazingly does on Decca. The years make one newly aware of
the historic importance of Britten's own reading but each version is wholly worthy of this score.

Sébastien de Brossard   French 1655-1730

In Convertendo Dominus. Miserere mei, Deus. Canticum eucharisticum pro pace.
Delphine Collot, Catherine Padaut sops **Jean-Paul Fouchécourt, Gilles Ragon** tens
Olivier Lallouette, Jérôme Corréas basses
Accentus Chamber Choir; Limoges Baroque Ensemble / Christophe Coin.
Auvidis Astrée E8607 (76 minutes: DDD). Texts and translations included. Recorded 1995. Ⓕ

The name of Sébastien de Brossard usually appears in music history books only when its owner is
being quoted in his capacity as a revealing theorist and lexicographer. As a composer, mainly of
church music, his achievements are less often considered next to those of notable contemporaries
such as Charpentier and Lalande, but in 1995 the Centre de Musique Baroque de Versailles devoted
one of its annual short festivals to him, and this recording arises from that occasion. The three
grands motets – large-scale pieces for choir, soloists and orchestra – are surprisingly eventful music,

seemingly conceived more for entertainment than for liturgical edification. *Canticum eucharisticum pro pace*, a 40-minute show-piece written to celebrate the joining of Strasbourg to France, depicts God/Louis XIV as both angry war hero and generous peacemaker, and even includes a dramatic solo for a singer representing the voice of God. The other two motets, too, contain interesting contrasts and a few good descriptive moments of their own. The performances are refined and attractive, even if the choir is occasionally a little unfocused.

Max Bruch
German 1838-1920

Violin Concertos – No. 1 in G minor, Op. 26; No. 2 in D minor, Op. 44; No. 3 in D minor, Op. 58.

Violin Concertos Nos. 1-3. Scottish Fantasy, Op. 46. Serenade in A minor, Op. 75. Konzertstück in F sharp minor, Op. 84. Adagio appassionato, Op. 57. In memoriam, Op. 65. Romance in A minor, Op. 41.
Salvatore Accardo *vn*
Leipzig Gewandhaus Orchestra / Kurt Masur.
Philips Silver Line 432 282-2PSL3 (three discs: 214 minutes: ADD). Recorded 1977. Ⓜ

This three-disc set contains all the major *concertante* works for violin and orchestra. They are quite marvellously played by Salvatore Accardo, admirably accompanied by the Leipzig Gewandhaus Orchestra under Kurt Masur. The G minor Concerto is clearly the most concentrated in its inspiration but there are plenty of attractive ideas elsewhere in this anthology. Certainly the Second and Third Concertos prove to have many memorable pages, especially when the advocacy is so persuasive. Bruch originally intended to use the description 'concerto' for both the *Konzertstück* and the relatively lightweight but charming *Serenade*, but thought better of it. The very enjoyable *Allegro appassionato* and *Romanze* are both admirably described by their titles, while *In memoriam*, which Bruch considered the finest of all these works, is undoubtedly inspired. We all know the *Scottish Fantasy* is brimming with engaging invention and Accardo's acount is full of warmth and colour. The only snag – and it should not deter the enthusiastic collector – is that this issue proves an exception to the usual excellence of the Philips sound balance. Possibly because of the resonant acoustics of the Leipzig Gewandhaus, the engineers have been tempted to place their microphones too close to the soloist. With remastering, this creates a dominating effect (which you may well not mind) and brings a degree of shrillness at times to the solo timbre. It can be mitigated by a roll-off treble control; otherwise it is best to play these recordings at not too high a level. Then the poetry of the solo playing and the rich orchestral tapestry combine to captivate the ear in this lovely music.

Bruch Violin Concerto No. 1[a].
Beethoven Violin Concerto in D major, Op. 61[b].
Kyung Wha Chung *vn*
[a]**Royal Concertgebouw Orchestra;** [b]**London Philharmonic Orchestra / Klaus Tennstedt.**
EMI CDC7 54072-2 (70 minutes: DDD). [b]Recorded live in 1989. ⒻⓇⓇ

Kyung Wha Chung has recorded both of these central concertos before, but in this generous and attractive coupling these EMI performances not only have the benefit of more modern sound but are more spontaneous in their expressive warmth. The Bruch was recorded in the studio and reflects Chung's growing ease in a recording environment. Notoriously, she dislikes the constraints of recording, when she is so essentially spontaneous in her expressiveness. Here her expressive rubato is freer, so that in the first movement the opening theme is more impulsive, and her freedom in the second subject vividly conveys the sort of magic you find in her live performances. The slow movement brings extreme contrasts of dynamic and expression from orchestra as well as soloist, and the finale is again impulsive in its bravura. The Beethoven is a live recording. Chung sustains spacious speeds very persuasively indeed. She is freely flexible in her approach to Beethoven, as Tennstedt is too, but magnetically keeping an overall command. The element of vulnerability in Chung's reading adds to the emotional weight, above all in the slow movement, which in its wistful tenderness is among the most beautiful on disc. As for the outer movements, they are full of flair, with a live event bringing few if any penalties in flaws of ensemble or other blemishes. This release is an exceptionally attractive one, and essential listening for this much-loved violinist's admirers.

Bruch Violin Concerto No. 1.
Mendelssohn Violin Concerto in E minor, Op. 64.
Maxim Vengerov *vn*
Leipzig Gewandhaus Orchestra / Kurt Masur.
Teldec 4509-90875-2 (51 minutes: DDD). Recorded 1993. ⒻⒺ

As one might expect with Mendelssohn's own orchestra, the Leipzig Gewandhaus, under Kurt Masur, there is a freshness and clarity in the Mendelssohn which ideally matches the soloist's playing, at once keenly felt and expressive but clean and direct, with articulation of diamond precision and fine tonal shading. If anyone has ever thought this work at all sentimental, this shatters any such idea, and characteristically Masur encourages a flowing speed in the central *Andante*, which brings out the songfulness of the main theme. It is consistent with this approach that in his expressiveness Maxim Vengerov is more inclined to press ahead than to hold back, so that with a dashingly fast speed for the finale one is left breathless at the end. The slow movement of the Bruch gains from being taken at a flowing speed, and Vengerov finds a rare depth of expressiveness, which makes the movement a meditation rather than simply a lyrical interlude. With outstanding recorded sound, warm yet clear and detailed, there is now no more recommendable disc of this coupling.

Violin Concerto No. 1. Scottish Fantasy.
Cho-Liang Lin *vn*
Chicago Symphony Orchestra / Leonard Slatkin.
CBS Masterworks SK42315 (53 minutes: DDD). ⓕ Ⓢ

This is a radiantly beautiful violin recording, ravishing in the combination of passion and purity, strength and dark, hushed intensity. There are quite a number of virtuoso violinists with a special affection for Bruch's *Scottish Fantasy* and Lin's warm and committed performance plainly indicates comparable involvement. He is prepared to play with the gentlest possible *pianissimo* and the engineers provide a balance which allows you fully to appreciate this, the natural balance being particularly welcome. The orchestral sound is warm and atmospheric in CBS's Chicago manner, slightly diffused but with the solo instrument nicely distinct. Although Lin may be a fraction less volatile, not quite so fierily individual in freely expressive phrasing, he is even more firmly positive in bravura passages, producing double-stopping of astonishing purity and precision, with the cleanest possible articulation in dazzling passagework. He actually makes the *Scottish Fantasy* seem compact. This is a work that is not only rather diffuse in its four-movement construction, it lasts a full half-hour, but this performance make you want to hear it again at once, so many moments of delight does it bring. If Lin scores a distinct point or two over his rivals, it is most clearly in the dashing finale, not least when at the end its bravura fades into a dreamy cadenza which Lin plays with a celestial purity and repose. Leonard Slatkin's and the Chicago Symphony Orchestra's accompaniments are outstanding.

Violin Concerto No. 1. Scottish Fantasy.
Yuzuko Horigome *vn*
Royal Philharmonic Orchestra / Yuri Simonov.
Tring International TRP108 (56 minutes: DDD). Recorded 1996. Ⓢ

This coupling of Bruch's two most popular *concertante* works, very well played and recorded, makes an excellent super-budget recommendation. Yuzuko Horigome plays here with rich, pure tone, using an aptly wide dynamic range, taking a relatively expansive view of both works. If there is a point on which this version fails quite to match the other outstanding accounts reviewed here, it lies largely in the way that Horigome's expressiveness – matched by the RPO's accompaniment under Yuri Simonov – tends at times to sound too deliberate, rarely surging forward from a relatively broad basic speed. The rival versions are a degree more impulsive, with more sparkle and more fantasy. Equally, Chung and Lin more readily convey a tender intensity in reflective melodies, where Horigome is a degree plainer, less individual, less subtle in tonal shading, but on any count these are warmly enjoyable performances and the recording is full and immediate, with the important harp part in the *Scottish Fantasy* given appropriate prominence.

Bruch Violin Concerto No. 2.
Goldmark Violin Concerto No. 1 in A minor, Op. 28.
Nai-Yuan Hu *vn*
Seattle Symphony Orchestra / Gerard Schwarz.
Delos DE3156 (60 minutes: DDD). Recorded 1993-94. ⓕ

Hu is a virtuoso in the best sense of that word, with uncommon lyrical gifts, who can shape phrases with a sense of gentle rapture and coax his violin to produce the most lovely sounds. Even though the Bruch was specifically written for Sarasate, neither of these warm-hearted concertos impresses primarily by its brilliance. Here both gain from the understanding partnership attained by Hu with Schwarz and his excellent Seattle orchestra within a kindly acoustic. Having attended the première of Bruch's Second Concerto, Brahms wrote to Simrock: 'Hopefully a law will not be necessary to prevent any more first movements being written as an *Adagio*. That is intolerable for normal people.' Bruch's riposte was, 'If I meet with Brahms in heaven, I shall have myself transferred to Hell'. He could not understand why the popularity of the First Concerto precluded performance of the others, 'which are just as good if not better'. Certainly Hu's superb reading here bears out the composer's evaluation of the D minor Concerto. The ardently simple presentation of the glorious main theme of that maligned *Adagio* goes right to the heart.

Clarinet and Viola Concerto in E minor, Op. 88. Romance, Op. 85. Eight Pieces, Op. 83.
Paul Meyer *cl* **Gérard Caussé** *va* **François-René Duchâble** *pf*
Orchestra of the Opéra National de Lyon / Kent Nagano.
Erato 2292-45483-2 (65 minutes: DDD). Recorded 1988.   Ⓕ

The Double Concerto and the Eight Pieces both stem from Bruch's later years as a composer, by which time he was ill and tiring, also embittered and resentful of the successes being enjoyed by Strauss and Debussy (the latter 'an unqualified scribbler'). His Concerto is not only a backward-looking and inward-looking work: it is the music of a weary composer with little more to say but the habit of a lifetime in saying it. The technique does not fail, though the last movement is thinly stretched; the manner is still lyrical, and makes graceful use both of the solo instruments and of the accompaniments. This is unusually disposed so that the chamber orchestra of the first movement gradually swells in numbers until it is virtually a full symphony orchestra for the finale. Some problems ensue for the viola, which is in any case cast in a secondary role to the clarinet. Parity is restored with the *Eight Pieces*, though Bruch wrote them for the talents of his son Max Felix, a gifted clarinettist whose performance of these pieces earned him favourable comparison with the great Richard Mühlfeld from the conductor Fritz Steinbach. They are pleasant pieces, sometimes drawing on the tonal companionship which Mozart discovered the instruments to have in his *Kegelstatt* Trio, sometimes contrasting them with opposing kinds of music.

Bruch Scottish Fantasy.
Lalo Symphonie espagnole, Op. 21.
Tasmin Little *vn*
Royal Scottish National Orchestra / Vernon Handley.
HMV Classics HMV5 73041-2 (68 minutes: DDD). Recorded 1996.   Ⓑ

It is an excellent idea to couple Bruch's evocation of Scotland with Lalo's of Spain, both works in unconventional five-movement *concertante* form. Tasmin Little takes a ripe, robust and passionate view of both works, projecting them strongly, as she would in the concert hall, but neither is she lacking in poetry. Her leisurely speeds give her freedom to point rhythms infectiously and play with an extra degree of individuality in her phrasing, daringly using *portamentos* or agogic hesitations in a way that adds to the character of the reading. Little has the gift of sounding totally spontaneous on disc, with no feeling of strict studio manners. In this she is here greatly helped by the splendid, keenly polished playing of the Scottish orchestra under Vernon Handley, a most sympathetic partner. Handley is also excellent in pointing the rhythms of the fast movements of the Lalo, matching his soloist, and the recording is superb, with brass in particular vividly caught.

Symphonies – No. 1 in E flat major, Op. 28; No. 2 in F minor, Op. 36; No. 3 in E major, Op. 51.
Cologne Gürzenich Orchestra / James Conlon.
EMI CDS5 55046-2 (two discs: 103 minutes: DDD). Recorded 1992-93.   Ⓕ

Bruch's three symphonies are works whose rather reticent melodic style, at times dense scoring and formal stiffness, need affectionate help if their genuine qualities are to emerge and outweigh their flaws. Carefully handled there is real romantic charm (and some agreeably brusque sturdiness) to the first movement of the Third Symphony; its *Adagio* has sonorous solemnity and an ardent climax, and its *Scherzo* some fire. The Second Symphony, its over-extended finale apart, is stronger still. Conlon and his Cologne players cannot always disguise passages of awkwardly coarse scoring, but their sound, though full, is lean and that is in itself an advantage. Conlon is also able to relax into Bruch's genial melodies, to linger and shape them with affectionate rubato. For anyone wanting all the symphonies of this neglected but likeable composer, his set is a pretty safe recommendation.

Anton Bruckner   Austrian 1824-1896

Symphonies – No. 0 in D minor, 'Die Nullte'; No. 1 in C minor; No. 2 in C minor; No. 3 in D minor; No. 4 in E flat major, 'Romantic'; No. 5 in B flat major; No. 6 in A major; No. 7 in E major; No. 8 in C minor; No. 9 in D minor.

Symphonies – Nos. 1 (Linz version), 2, 3 (1889 version, ed. Nowak.), 4-7, 8 (ed. Haas.) and 9.
Berlin Philharmonic Orchestra / Herbert von Karajan.
DG Karajan Symphony Edition 429 648-2GSE9 (nine discs: 520 minutes: ADD/DDD).
Recorded 1975-81. Ⓜ **RR**

It is often said that the essence of good Bruckner conducting is a firm grasp of structure. In fact that is only a half-truth. Of course one must understand how Bruckner's massive statements and counterstatements are fused together, but a performance that was nothing but architecture would be a pretty depressing experience. Karajan's understanding of the slow but powerful currents that flow beneath the surfaces of symphonies like the Fifth or Nos. 7-9 has never been bettered, but at the same time he shows how much more there is to be reckoned with: strong emotions, a deep poetic sensitivity (a Bruckner symphony can evoke landscapes as vividly as Mahler or Vaughan Williams) and a gift for singing melody that at times rivals even Schubert. It hardly needs saying that there's no such thing as a perfect record cycle, and Karajan's collection of the numbered Bruckner symphonies (unfortunately he never recorded 'No. 0') has its weaknesses. The early First and Second Symphonies can be a little heavy-footed and, as with so many Bruckner sets, there's a suspicion that more time might have been spent getting to know the fine but elusive Sixth. However, none of these performances is without its major insights, and in the best of them – particularly Nos. 3, 5, 7, 8 and 9 – those who haven't stopped their ears to Karajan will find that whatever else he may have been, there was a side to him that could only be described as 'visionary'. As for the recordings: climaxes can sound a touch overblown in some of the earlier symphonies, but on the whole the image is well focused and atmospheric. A valuable set, and a landmark in the history of Bruckner recording.

Symphonies Nos. 0-9.
Concertgebouw Orchestra / Bernard Haitink.
Philips Bernard Haitink Symphony Edition 442 040-2PB9 (nine discs: 592 minutes: ADD).
Recorded 1963-72. Ⓑ

Right from the start of Haitink's cycle, you sense here is a man who briefed his team, read the map and is raring to go. The cycle began in 1963 with Symphony No. 3. The playing is alert, rousing even, though inclined to edginess. This is partly to do with the sound of the post-war Concertgebouw (marginally more Francophone in those days), partly a matter of an as yet not-quite-symbiotic bond between Haitink and the players. The Fourth Symphony followed in 1965. This suggests some deepening and refining of the bond between conductor and orchestra and is a very fine performance. The *Scherzo* is particularly exciting. The Ninth Symphony (also 1965) came surprisingly early in the cycle. The performance explains why. Both conductor and orchestra play the symphony as if in the grip of a deep compulsion. The orchestral response alone has a terrific explicitness and immediacy. As for Haitink, he plays the work very dramatically, as a symphonic psycho-drama, 'a vastation', as thinkers and theologians of Bruckner's time often termed breakdown and purgation of the spirit.

When it comes to the great central tetralogy, Symphonies Nos. 5-8, there are some problems. Most problematic is the Eighth Symphony. The Seventh has a quick first movement; but it survives. Not so the Eighth. The first movement just about hangs together, thanks to some finely concentrated playing at critical junctions. But the *Scherzo* is absurdly quick, as is the finale. Haitink's account of the Sixth Symphony is less of a problem than it is with some rivals. The recording is exceptionally fine – everything thrillingly immediate, finely 'terraced'. The *Adagio* always sounded well and so it remains, the keening Dutch oboe and bright trumpets the perfect foil for the Rembrandt-colourings of the strings and lower brass. Symphonies Nos. 1, 2, 5 and 6 were the last to be recorded. (Haitink actually ended with this rousing account of No. 1.) They are all very fine. This is one of the best Fifths ever made; dramatic where Karajan is epic but fascinatingly alive and well integrated. The Second Symphony also receives an exceptional performance (the text, as elsewhere in the cycle, is Haas). Philips's CD remastering realizes just how vivid and astonishingly natural these Concertgebouw-played, Concertgebouw-made recordings are. You will need a supplementary account of the Eighth; but is this too much to ask when the set as a whole is being offered, new-minted, at a knock-down price?

Symphonies Nos. 3-9. Choral Works.
Munich Philharmonic Orchestra / Sergiu Celibidache.
EMI Celibidache Edition CDS5 56688-2 (12 discs: 712 minutes: ADD/DDD). Texts and translation included. Also available separately. Recorded live 1982-95. Ⓟ **E**
CDC5 56689-2 (66 minutes): No. 3 (ed. Nowak).
CDC5 56690-2 (79 minutes): No. 4 (ed. Haas).

CDS5 56691-2 (two discs: 90 minutes): No. 5 (ed. Haas).
CDC5 56694-2 (66 minutes): No. 6 (ed. Haas).
CDS5 56695-2 (two discs: 114 minutes): No. 7 (ed. Haas); Te Deum (**Dame Margaret Price** *sop*
Christel Borchers *contr* **Claes H. Ahnsjö** *ten* **Karl Helm** *bass* **Munich Philharmonic Chorus;
Munich Bach Choir**).
CDS5 56696-2 (two discs: 104 minutes): No. 8 (ed. Nowak).
CDS5 56699-2 (two discs: 113 minutes): No. 9 (ed. Nowak). Rehearsal sequences.
CDC5 56702-2 (77 minutes): Mass No. 3 in F minor (**Price**; **Doris Soffel** *mez* **Peter Straka** *ten*
Matthias Hölle *bass* **Munich Philharmonic Chorus**).

As a thinker, Celibidache was part genius, part crank. (This Bruckner set reveals both aspects.) A
bizarre aggregation of musical, spiritual and quasi-scientific ideas led him to believe that because of
what he called 'epiphenomena' – the need for each note to sound, resonate and return – it was
necessary to place round the music an inordinate amount of space: 'The richer the music, the slower
the tempo.' It is Celibidache's overriding preoccupation with slowness, with temporal space, which
helps conjure forth what has got to be one of the greatest Bruckner performances ever recorded –
this 1987 account of the Fourth Symphony, a truly towering act of the re-creative imagination –
and several that are well-nigh interminable. His initial tempos are often quite sprightly. It is when he
gets to the second and third subjects – to the great *Gesangsperiode* in each movement – that he
drops down many more gears than most Bruckner conductors would dare imagine. What
Celibidache gives us, in effect, is a sequence of slow movements within the symphonic continuum.
In each case, the slow movement itself is the crown (what a revelation his reading of the slow
movement of the Sixth Symphony is!), the dark sun at the centre of the Bruckner universe around
which the *adagio* sections of the opening and closing movements (and the third movement Trio)
slowly circle.

The problems come in the Seventh, Eighth and Ninth Symphonies where the adage 'the richer the
music, the slower the tempo' causes broadenings that render entirely otiose the idea of the
symphony as dramatic discourse. The Haas edition of the Eighth Symphony (Celibidache uses the
slightly shorter Nowak edition) gives an estimated playing time of 78 minutes. Many conductors are
quicker than this. Some are slower. But even these are as the flash of a swallow's wing alongside the
dinosaur flap of Celibidache's record-breaking 104 minutes. The performance of the Seventh
Symphony is almost as odd. Here Haas gives an estimated playing time of 68 minutes. Par for the
course is nearer 62 or 63 minutes. Celibidache takes nigh on 80. Since the symphonies and the
F minor Mass are available separately, the performances to acquire are those of the Fourth and
Sixth Symphonies. The Fifth, too, if you don't already have one of Jochum's performances or
Karajan's 1975 Berlin recording to which the Celibidache is surprisingly close in tempo and style,
even though the manner of the music-making is a good deal earthier.

The ensemble playing, even in the best performances, is not faultless. Celibidache occasionally has
trouble getting woodwind and brass in together; the solo flute can play like a seraph but the flutes
en masse are tentative, and the clarinet playing is chancy. The brass playing is generally first-rate,
but it is the strings that one comes back to. The recordings have weight, warmth and immediacy,
with enough air around them to avoid a sense of incipient or actual claustrophobia. The choral
works, though, fare less well; in the *Te Deum*, the choir is a misty irrelevance and although you hear
more of it in the F minor Mass, neither the recording nor the choral or solo singing is in the top
flight. Despite Celibidache's occasional flashes of insight, there are better versions of both works to
be had elsewhere. The transfers have been well done. Applause (rarely instantaneous, Celibidache
clearly had his public well trained) is separately banded, and the pauses between movements are
'live', and feel right in context. Thus we have the best of all worlds, live music-making sensitively
preserved on record. For, whatever Celibidache himself might have thought or argued, recordings
give us privacy and time: time to hear these deeply contemplative and astonishingly long-drawn
readings on occasions of our choosing, alone or in company, away from the bustle and discomfort
of the concert hall.

Symphony No. 1 (Linz version).
Chicago Symphony Orchestra / Sir Georg Solti.
Decca 448 898-2DH (47 minutes: DDD). Recorded 1995.

In its original 1866 Linz version, Bruckner's First Symphony is something of a cheeky chappy
among the nine, a delightful romp of a symphony but also tender and affecting and rich in
intimations of things to come. There have been times in the past when Solti has seemed a restless
Brucknerian, inclined to harry the music or drive it too hard. Here there is a thrilling sense of
forward propulsion, apt to a young man's work, yet nothing is forced or gratuitously aggressive.
This is even true of the *Scherzo* which Solti takes extremely briskly. It is also a very sensitive
performance and a very observant one. The Chicago players are on superb form. It is difficult to

imagine the symphony being better played than it is here. Solti's reading has a vibrancy and beauty about it, a quality of flawless yet unassuming virtuosity that is the mark of an élite orchestra at the very height of its powers. The many difficult, high-lying violin passages are played not only with confidence, but with imagination. The playing of the violas and cellos is consummate in its eloquence. In the circumstances, it would be difficult for the engineers to go wrong. But the recording, too, is of a piece with the rest. As Bruckner recordings go, it is of demonstration quality, ripe yet clear, immediate yet rich in atmosphere.

Symphony No. 1 (Linz version). Te Deum.
Jessye Norman sop **Yvonne Minton** mez **David Rendall** ten **Samuel Ramey** bass
Chicago Symphony Chorus and Orchestra / Daniel Barenboim.
DG Galleria 435 068-2GGA (70 minutes: DDD). Text and translation included. Recorded 1980.　Ⓜ

There is still a relative lack of choice when it comes to single CDs of the boisterous First Symphony in its original Linz version, so the reissue of this Chicago recording under Barenboim is a most attractive choice, particularly if you don't mind adding to your collection a superb – eloquently sung, expertly played, exceptionally well-recorded – account of Bruckner's mighty *Te Deum*. In the symphony, Barenboim is witty, affectionate and vital and the Chicago playing is sumptuous without in any way being bland or suffocating. Here and there one might long for the countrified tread of Eugen Jochum, a German Bruckner conductor of the old school, but one can understand DG's desire to give the best of this Barenboim Bruckner cycle another airing. Warmly recommended if the coupling suits.

Symphony No. 2 (ed. Carragan).
National Symphony Orchestra of Ireland / Georg Tintner.
Naxos 8 554006 (71 minutes: DDD). Recorded 1996.　ⓈⓇⓇ

This exceptional recording by veteran Austrian conductor Georg Tintner is in a league of its own. It is a beautifully shaped performance, characterfully played and vividly recorded. What's more, it is, in effect, a gramophone 'first', for though the original, 1872 version of Bruckner's Second Symphony has been recorded elsewhere this is the first to reach a wider market. Not that the differences between editions are hugely significant. What the earlier 1872 version principally offers is the reversal of the order of the two inner movements (the *Scherzo* now comes before the *Andante*), a full clutch of repeats in the *Scherzo* and Trio, a rather longer development section in the finale, various small changes to the orchestration and the absence of some of the more meretricious tempo markings. What is appealing about the 'full monty' is the feeling it gives of the symphony's Schubertian pedigree: heavenly length joining hands with a deep sense of melancholy and melodic *Angst*. Which brings us to Tintner's reading of the symphony, which is shrewd and affectionate, tellingly phrased and beautifully paced, the moves away from and back to the basic pulse nicely handled. This is Bruckner conducting of the old school. There is also something reassuringly old-fashioned about the playing of the National Symphony Orchestra of Ireland. It is a first-rate ensemble. The entire orchestra has the character of a well-to-do country cousin who is blessedly innocent of the more tiresome aspects of metropolitan life. This is an exceptional recording.

Symphony No. 2 (ed. Haas).
Saarbrücken Radio Symphony Orchestra / Hiroshi Wakasugi.
Arte Nova Classics 74321 27770-2 (61 minutes: DDD). Recorded 1992.　Ⓢ

Budget-price Bruckner is something of a rarity in the record catalogues; super-budget Bruckner more or less unheard of. Hiroshi Wakasugi's performance of the Second Symphony is a delight. He plays the complete text and plays it with fluency and affection. He has a keen eye for the letter of the score, a keen ear for its Schubertian sonorities, and an even keener instinct for the flow and continuity of its rhythms and the logic of the whole. This couldn't replace the Karajan but anyone happening upon this recording is likely to find a friend for life, in both the music and its performance.

Symphony No. 3 (1877 version).
Vienna Philharmonic Orchestra / Bernard Haitink.
Philips 422 411-2PH (62 minutes: DDD).　ⒻⓇⓇ

This is the least perfect of the nine symphonies, though not the least magnificent. As a symphonic project it is both magnificent and characteristic. Unfortunately, the sweep of the musical vision outdistanced Bruckner's ability to control it structurally; in 1889 he returned to the text and radically revised it. For most Bruckner scholars, however, the 1877 text is the ideal. 'It is stylistically purer,' Robert Simpson has written 'and though its construction leaves much to be desired, its weaknesses are exacerbated, not propped, by the crude remedies of the later version.' The 1877 is the version to collect. The finale's polka subject, which has a certain sly wit and grace in Haitink's Concertgebouw recording, retains a certain slyness and grace but with the Vienna Philharmonic it is more the slyness and grace some of us associate with that old darling of Chancery Lane, Mr Horace Rumpole. This newer recording, like the playing, is immensely forceful. Haitink, dedicated Brucknerian that he is, makes a wonderful job of the work without resort to all those unseemly cuts, revisions and re-orchestrations that most of his rivals rely on. He is a Brucknerian bold and true, and the Vienna Philharmonic, the brass in particular, plays gloriously, with particular thrust, spontaneity, and weight of tone in the much disputed finale.

Symphonies – No. 3 (1889 version); No. 4 (both ed. Nowak).
Vienna Philharmonic Orchestra / Karl Böhm.
Double Decca 448 098-2DF2 (two discs: 125 minutes: ADD). Recorded 1970 and 1973.　Ⓜ️ 🆁🆁

The 1973 Böhm Bruckner Fourth is a classic, widely praised and much reissued, but the 1970 recording of the Third Symphony (the tidied-up 1889 edition) is every bit as fine. Some slightly dusty, quiet string tone apart, the recording verges on the spectacular, as does the playing, sophisticated and folksy by turns. The VPO responds splendidly throughout (Bruckner's rustic trio section is inimitably Viennese in its earthy gait). There is something mountainously grand in their response in full cry under Böhm. They also have it game, set and match over their competitors in the Austrian dance subjects of the *Scherzo* and finale. The exemplary focus and spectacular dynamic range of this Sofiensaal production really does take one's breath away. As for the Fourth Symphony, this has been more or less *hors concours* for a generation.

Symphony No. 4.
Vienna Philharmonic Orchestra / Karl Böhm.
Decca Legends 466 374-2DM (68 minutes: ADD). Recorded 1973.　Ⓜ️ 🆁🆁

As discussed above, Böhm's VPO account of the Fourth Symphony has the unmistakable stamp of greatness. It was made in the Sofiensaal in Vienna with its helpful acoustic; for though one can detect a whisper of tape-hiss if you put your ear against the loudspeaker, in almost every other way the sound is realistic and warm. There is a roundness in the brass tone with plenty of bite and fullness but no unwanted rasp – especially important in this symphony. Böhm's Fourth is at the head of the field irrespective of price. The warmth as well as the mystery of Bruckner are far more compellingly conveyed in Böhm's spacious view than with any other conductor.

Symphony No. 4.
Berlin Philharmonic Orchestra / Günter Wand.
RCA Victor Red Seal 09026 68839-2 (69 minutes: DDD). Recorded live in 1997.　Ⓕ

The pacing of each movement is majestic, not too fast, in the first movement; a slow, contemplative tread in the second; animated, but capable of opening out into something more leisurely in the *Scherzo*; varied, but with the sense of an underlying slow pulse in the finale. Wand allows himself some fairly generous rubato from time to time, halting slightly on the high unaccompanied cello phrase in the first movement second subject. From the start there's something about Wand's performance that puts it in a different league from rival recordings. There's the depth and richness of the string sound in the opening *tremolo*. A few seconds later the Berlin Philharmonic's principal horn intones the opening phrases so magically and majestically that it's hard to believe one isn't listening to a real voice – a superhuman larynx, not just a contraption of brass and valves. Of course the sound is, to some extent, the orchestra's own, but there is a feeling that the players are giving extra for Wand, something with more inner life; and the unaffected eloquence and shapeliness of the phrasing is all Wand. It carries you along even when the rubato ought to jar, as it does sometimes in other versions. This is a concert performance, and it feels like one. Things that work in concert – the once-off live inspiration – aren't always ideal solutions on a repeatable commercial recording. Take Wand's big *ritardando* at the fleeting reference to Brünnhilde's Magic Sleep motif in the finale – the effect might pall after a couple of playings. But then he does ease very effectively into the weird *pianissimo* cello and bass figures that follow, triplet quavers gradually *becoming* triplet crotchets. The sound quality is excellent.

Symphony No. 4.
Philadelphia Orchestra / Wolfgang Sawallisch.
EMI CDC5 55119-2 (67 minutes: DDD). Recorded 1993.　Ⓕ

The Philadelphians have always had their special sound, nurtured and lovingly preserved down the years by Stokowski, Ormandy and Muti; and to judge by this fine Bruckner Fourth it is something that Sawallisch will not willingly forgo. Indeed, the genius of this particular reading lies in its protean quality, the very way the sound is so interestingly adapted and applied. The Fourth is an odd work. Popular, certainly, but popular for certain specific moments: the mistily romantic opening, the fine hunting *Scherzo* and the finale's magnificent peroration. The finale does not so much round off the work as propose the kind of grounds on which it might originally have been built. Which is where Sawallisch's reading, and the Philadelphians' realization of it, is so interesting. Apart from one passage midway through the slow movement, where the mood darkens and the music mysteriously broods, the first two movements can have an almost straightforwardly classical feel. This seems to be Sawallisch's view, and the Philadelphia playing here is lucid and eloquent. How different is the finale! Here we are deep in the Wagnerian forest – the dramatic change of mood graphically registered. What sounded at first light like just another Bruckner Fourth has proved to be anything but. The recording is glorious.

Symphony No. 4.
Royal Concertgebouw Orchestra / Nikolaus Harnoncourt.
Teldec 0630-17126-2 (65 minutes: DDD). Recorded live in 1997.　　　　　　　　　　Ⓕ

If you're expecting something controversial – something to fulminate against – you'll probably be disappointed. Harnoncourt's Bruckner Fourth is nothing like as provocative as his Beethoven. It is relatively fast, but not startlingly so. If Harnoncourt's first movement is more gripping, more like a symphonic drama than usual, that has more to do with the crisp, clear rhythmic articulation than with the number of crotchets per minute. The solo woodwind and horn playing that follows is lovely, expansive enough; what else would one expect from the Concertgebouw in Bruckner? This is an unusually compelling Bruckner Fourth – exciting throughout the first movement and *Scherzo*, and in passages like the problematical Brucknerian Ride of the Valkyries that erupts after the finale's bucolic second theme. In many more traditional Bruckner performances the bass often seems to move in sustained, undifferentiated pedal points. In Harnoncourt's version one is often aware of a deep pulsation – like the throbbing repeated notes that open the finale – continuing, however discreetly, while the tunes unfold above. To hear the finale's second theme in this version is to be reminded that Bruckner was an excellent dancer, light on his feet until he was nearly 70. Of course one shouldn't confuse the man with the musical personality, but why should Bruckner always sound heavy, sedentary, as though slowly digesting a gigantic meal? Harnoncourt gives us the light-footedness, while allowing the music to unfold at its own speed, to take time. No question, Nikolaus Harnoncourt must be considered a serious contender in Bruckner.

Symphony No. 4 (ed. Haas).
Berlin Philharmonic Orchestra / Herbert von Karajan.
EMI Karajan Edition CDM5 66094-2 (70 minutes: ADD). Recorded 1970-71.　　　　　　Ⓜ

There was always something very special about the EMI recordings of the Fourth and Seventh Symphonies by Karajan and the Berlin Philharmonic which were coupled originally on a three-LP set. Both works had, of course, been in Karajan's repertory for many years, though it was not until 1970 that he made his first recordings of either work. The recording of the Fourth Symphony is one of the finest ever made in Berlin's Jesus-Christus Kirche, the church's clear but spacious acoustic allowing the Berlin playing to be heard in all its multicoloured, multi-dimensional splendour.

Symphony No. 5 (ed. Nowak).
London Philharmonic Orchestra / Franz Welser-Möst.
EMI CDC5 55125-2 (70 minutes: DDD). Recorded live in 1993.　　　　　　　　　Ⓕ **RR**

Welser-Möst has looked, listened, and decided 'enough is enough'. Enough pussy-footing around the Fifth as though it were some sacred monolith, enough of circumspection. This is a sensual and exciting performance, certainly not for those of a nervous disposition or those who genuinely seek the longer view such as Karajan provides. Welser-Möst's reading is more in the Jochum style where analysis doesn't drive out passion, where what is contemplated in the study doesn't entirely predetermine what is experienced in performance. Welser-Möst takes risks with the finale, where the fugue is driven fiercely on, and in the *Adagio* where his observation of the *alla breve* marking gives a generous pendulum-swing to the crotchet-triplet accompaniment. This can make for a reading that is unconsidered and overquick, but not here. The play of two against three is beautifully realized as the basis for one of the most richly expressive of all recorded accounts of this movement. In general, Welser-Möst favours an almost Beethoven-like drive and directness. Yet there is plenty of space around the lyric subjects and chorales. In the first movement the gearing of the transitions whereby this is achieved is especially elaborate. He is most obviously himself, the boy from Linz, in the *Scherzo* and Trio. It begins fiercely, as Bruckner requires, but then opens out in a wonderfully broad lolloping Upper Austrian dance. The London Philharmonic plays gloriously throughout and the engineers get superb results from the Vienna Konzerthaus auditorium.

Symphony No. 5.
Cleveland Orchestra / Christoph von Dohnányi.
Decca 433 318-2DH (74 minutes: DDD). Recorded 1991. Ⓕ E

Rarely can Bruckner's Fifth Symphony have seemed as gaunt, as dramatic, as fiercely concentrated as it does here in this awesome and exacting recording by Dohnányi and the Cleveland Orchestra. Awesome because this is not a reading that falsifies the logic of Bruckner's argument with arbitrary or upbeat tempos in the way that some performances do nowadays. There has rarely been a Bruckner performance that, in the last resort, is more physically exciting than this; yet the source of the excitement is not in the tempos as such. In the finale, for example, Dohnányi takes a relatively measured view of the music. The *Allegro moderato* is perfectly judged, neither too lumbering nor too quick; but its effect is made electric by the skilful way Dohnányi holds successive subjects within the gravitational pull of that enunciatory pulse. Dohnányi binds the fabric of the symphony together with hoops of finely tempered steel. Yet, at the same time, the whole thing exults and blazes. It is evident from the fascinatingly voiced wind tuttis near the start of the symphony that this is a performance that has been scrupulously prepared. What we have here is the Cleveland Orchestra at its exacting best, and a uniquely exciting account of the Fifth Symphony.

Bruckner Symphony No. 6 (ed. Haas).
Wagner Wesendonk Lieder.
Christa Ludwig *mez*
New Philharmonia Orchestra / Otto Klemperer.
EMI CDM5 67037-2 (77 minutes: ADD). Recorded 1964 and 1968. Ⓜ RR

Alleluias are in order. This is the finest – nay, the only wholly acceptable – account of Bruckner's Sixth Symphony on record. Quite why this terse, searching and exhilarating symphony has so eluded interpreters is difficult to establish; suffice it to say that Klemperer's performance, made in London's Kingsway Hall over eight sessions in November 1964, is masterly from first note to last. It is a performance by turns lofty tender and serene, but it is, above all, a structurally cogent performance and within the compass of its steady-treading tempos an intensely exciting one. Back in 1965, it was hailed as glorious – the Klemperer Bruckner style majestic, magisterial, magnificently architectural – at its very finest, and time has dimmed neither the performance nor EMI's superbly articulate recording which reproduces with clarity and immediacy the marvellously transparent textures of Klemperer's reading, the fabulous string traceries and the stark beauty of woodwind and brass playing. All this comes up very vividly on this reissue. Walter Legge disbanded the Philharmonia in 1964 and eight months on, one senses the players – every jot of their former expertise in place – in doubly determined mood. The performance has immense backbone, yet in the *Scherzo* and the fantastic echoing Trio section the playing marries clarity with immense subtlety. Here and in the slow movement, Klemperer and his players demonstrate that you don't have to be effete to be tender, sensitive or profound. This is a performance that no Brucknerian can afford to miss. This latest CD reissue also has historical significance, the Ludwig/Klemperer *Wesendonk* interpretation having something of a classic status. Surprisingly, Klemperer's speeds are on the fast side, and he is occasionally perfunctory, but Ludwig's singing is dark and meaningful, the tone refulgent. Her account is illuminating, even if on the heavy side, but it is compelling in its urgency and elevation, with correspondingly warm support from conductor and orchestra.

Bruckner Symphony No. 6.
Bach (orch. Webern) Musikalisches Opfer, BWV1079 – Fuga ricercarta a 6.
Cleveland Orchestra / Christoph von Dohnányi.
Decca 436 153-2DH (63 minutes: DDD). Recorded 1991-93. Ⓕ

Recording after recording of the Sixth has come apart at the seams as a result of the conductor's inability to gauge the pulse of the two outer movements. Bruckner's tempo indications and his bowing marks both imply a certain breadth of utterance that has to be reconciled none the less with pulsing rhythms and demystified textures. Dohnányi sets a very good basic tempo in the first movement, which he then proceeds to modify in ways that don't always accord with Bruckner's carefully documented wishes; and quite a good tempo in the finale. The flux is not always Bruckner's. However, as Eugen Jochum often proved, a living response to Bruckner can be mightily effective. Dohnányi's reading of the two inner movements deserves nothing but praise. He allows the *Adagio* the space it needs. The quality of the Cleveland sound in the grieving C minor funeral lament is such as to make one want to rank this slow movement alongside those of the better-known Seventh and Eighth Symphonies. And how beautifully the slow movement's coda is handled and characterized. This is pure *Meistersinger*, Bruckner dressed in Sachs's garb. The slowish, minor-key *Scherzo* is also perfectly judged. Rarely can the trio's sweet academic debate between horns, woodwinds and strings have sounded more irresistible or affecting than it does here. After so fabulously played a Bruckner Sixth, the finale all complexity and clamour, the sudden dip into the cooler waters of Webern's hallucinatorily beautiful orchestration of the Ricercar from Bach's *Musical Offering* is as welcome as a solitary stroll at eventide.

Symphony No. 7.
Concertgebouw Orchestra / Bernard Haitink.
Philips Solo 446 580-2PM (65 minutes: ADD). Recorded 1979.   Ⓜ **RR**

Bernard Haitink's 1979 Concertgebouw account of Bruckner's Seventh Symphony was both a change from and an advance on his 1966 Concertgebouw recording. Broader in pace and warmer-toned, it retained much of the earlier reading's classical integrity whilst at the same time paying more attention to the music's Schubertian aspect. Haitink does not go as far down that particular road as Karajan does in his deeply reflective, pantheistically charged 1971 Berlin Philharmonic version. The velvet sonorities of the Berlin performance (quite different from the Concertgebouw's sharper-edged way even in *sostenuto* passages) will not please everyone, of course, though it has to be said that the Berliners' quiet, affective glow of colour is part and parcel of a reading which is deeply thought through and of a piece with itself. (The *Adagio* is especially fine, more *innig* than the Haitink and more of a piece.) But the return of this later Haitink recording to the catalogues is both timely and welcome for those in search of a fine, middle-of-the-road, mid-price recording of the symphony.

Symphony No. 7 (ed. Haas).
Berlin Philharmonic Orchestra / Herbert von Karajan.
EMI Karajan Edition CDM5 66095-2 (68 minutes: ADD). Recorded 1970-71.   Ⓜ

'Glowing' is an apt word with which to describe this account of the Seventh. Very much *sui generis*, this is arguably the most purely beautiful account of the symphony there has ever been on record. Other readings may surge and carol more than this but none captures so intense a sense of spiritual longing within the context of a calm yet unerringly sure articulation of the symphonic structure. Oddly, the recording has moments of slightly wispy string sound which sound wispier here than they did on EMI's earlier less spacious, less full-bodied – digital remastering. That, though, is not enough to undermine the recommendation as such.

Symphony No. 7 (ed. Haas).
Vienna Philharmonic Orchestra / Herbert von Karajan.
DG Karajan Gold 439 037-2GHS (66 minutes: DDD). Recorded 1989.   Ⓕ

The Vienna Philharmonic features on what was Karajan's last recording, an idiomatic account of the Seventh Symphony, lighter and more classical in feel than either of his two Berlin recordings yet loftier, too. As for the Original-image bit-processing you need go no further than the first fluttered violin *tremolando* and the cellos' rapt entry in the third bar to realize how ravishingly 'present' the performance is in this reprocessing. Or go to the end of the symphony and hear how the great E major peroration is even more transparent than before, the octave drop of bass trombone and bass tuba 13 bars from home the kind of delightfully euphoric detail that in 1989 only the more assiduous score-reader would have been conscious of hearing. This remastered Bruckner Seventh is definitely pure gold.

Symphony No. 7.
Royal Scottish National Orchestra / Georg Tintner.
Naxos 8 554269 (66 minutes: DDD). Recorded 1997.   Ⓢ

Since there are no recommendable budget, let alone super-budget recordings of Bruckner's Seventh Symphony, this will do nicely. It is a finely schooled performance, chaste and discreet, with a notable reading of the *Adagio* which lies at the heart of the work. Tintner sees this very much as a piece, the first (G major) climax finely achieved, the later, greater climax splendidly 'placed'. The coda, Bruckner's lament for the dead Wagner, is played relatively swiftly, touchingly and without bombast. In general, his reading of the score is loyal without being in any sense dull or hidebound.

In an ideal world, the playing of the first violins would be more consistently secure *in alt*. In particular, you have the feeling that both the players and the engineers (the engineering is generally excellent) would have benefited from a chance to refine and tidy parts of the performance of the first movement. A notable bargain, none the less.

Symphony No. 8 (ed. Haas).
Vienna Philharmonic Orchestra / Herbert von Karajan.
DG 427 611-2GH2 (two discs: 83 minutes: DDD). Recorded 1988.　　　　Ⓕ**S**🅁🅁

As if by some strange act of providence, great conductors have often been remembered by the immediate posthumous release of some fine and representative recording. With Karajan it is the Eighth Symphony of Bruckner, perhaps the symphony he loved and revered above all others. It is the sense of the music being in the hearts and minds and collective unconscious of Karajan and every one of the one hundred and more players of the Vienna Philharmonic that gives this performance its particular charisma and appeal. It is a wonderful reading, every bit as authoritative as its many predecessors and every bit as well played but somehow more profound, more humane, more lovable if that is a permissible attribute of an interpretation of this Everest among symphonies. The end of the work, always astonishing and uplifting, is especially fine here and very moving. Fortunately, it has been recorded with plenty of weight and space and warmth and clarity, with the additional benefit of the added vibrancy of the Viennese playing. The sessions were obviously sufficiently happy for there to shine through moments of spontaneous eloquence that were commonplace in the concert hall in Karajan's later years, but which recordings can't always be relied upon to catch.

Symphony No. 8 (ed. Nowak).
Vienna Philharmonic Orchestra / Carlo Maria Giulini.
DG Masters 445 529-2GMA2 (two discs: 88 minutes: DDD). Recorded 1984.　　　　Ⓜ

Giulini's performance of the Eighth can confidently be claimed as also being among one of the great Bruckner recordings of the age. It is an immensely long-breathed performance, yet it is of a piece with itself and the music it serves. It is a reading that is suffused from start to finish with its own immutable logic, cast and voiced, you might say, like a great tenor bell. The playing of the Vienna Philharmonic is similarly whole: luminous as though lit from within, immensely strong, yet flawless in every aspect of tone and touch. You might argue that Giulini's case is helped by his use of the tidied Nowak text; that Karajan, in his last and greatest recording, goes one stage further by conjuring from the fuller Haas edition a performance of even greater grandeur and sweep. But the two are not in contention. Both are miracles sufficient unto themselves; the Karajan a shade earthier, perhaps, a shade rougher-hewn than the Giulini which glows, in this magnificent transfer, like Carrara marble lit by the evening sun.

Symphony No. 9.
Berlin Philharmonic Orchestra / Daniel Barenboim.
Teldec 9031-72140-2 (63 minutes: DDD). Recorded live in 1990.　　　　Ⓕ🅁🅁

This is an outstanding version of Bruckner's Ninth Symphony – and no surprise, given Barenboim's evident sympathy for the work in concert performances over the past three decades. Like Karajan's reading on DG, it is essentially a 'central' account of the score that attempts neither extreme breadth of utterance nor sharp-edged drama. Rather it is a reading that combines long lines, flowing but astutely nuanced, and sonorities that are full-bodied yet always finely balanced. The outer movements have great rhetorical and emotional power; the *Scherzo* is thunderous and glinting by turns. The *Adagio* begins very slowly but, for once, Barenboim gets away with it, the movement growing organically rather than remaining still-born near the start. This is a live performance and, as you would expect, it is superbly executed, the playing every bit as fine as it is on the Karajan recording. But even that doesn't compete with the natural splendours of the Teldec. This is superb Bruckner sound, spacious and clear, with strings, woodwind and brass at once unerringly 'placed' and finely matched. Given good engineering and the kind of astute playing we have from Barenboim and the Berliners, the Philharmonie is far from being the acoustic lemon it is sometimes said to be. This is currently a front-runner where this symphony is concerned.

Symphony No. 9.
Vienna Philharmonic Orchestra / Carlo Maria Giulini.
DG 427 345-2GH (68 minutes: DDD). Recorded 1988.　　　　Ⓕ

Giulini's Ninth is an idiosyncratic reading – nearly seven minutes longer than Karajan's – but it has about it a kind of immutable breadth and boldness of utterance that is not to be gainsaid. Despite the slowness, there is very much the sense of his being the master of his own brief. As a concept it is quite different from the musically dynamic readings of others. In the first movement's main *Gesangsperiode* it can seem dangerously broad with the Vienna strings rather tensely following the contours of Giulini's protracted beat. Here the wary score-watcher may notice some unevenness in ensemble though, that said, this is a reading which should be patiently heard rather than proof-read. The *Scherzo* is very effective, with drive and dynamism. After that, the orchestra is at its finest in the concluding *Adagio*, not only the Viennese horns, but the entire ensemble in the difficult broad transitions and in the literally terrific C sharp minor climax. The recording is magnificent.

Symphony No. 9.
Berlin Philharmonic Orchestra / Herbert von Karajan.
DG Galleria 429 904-2GGA (62 minutes: ADD). Recorded 1976.   Ⓕ

Karajan's 1976 recording has long been something of a classic, capturing the conductor and the Berlin Philharmonic on top form. From the opening of the titanic first movement to the final grinding dissonance of the lofty *Adagio* Karajan's control of phrase lengths, tempo and rhythmic swing are gloriously apparent. This beautifully recorded performance seems refreshingly urgent, cohesive and properly threatening. Exceptionally vivid, it was sometimes difficult to tame on LP, but the CD version gives unalloyed pleasure.

String Quintet in F major. Intermezzo in D minor. Rondo in C minor. String Quartet in C minor.
L'Archibudelli (Vera Beths, Lisa Rautenberg *vns* Jürgen Kussmaul, Guus Jeukendrup *vas* Anner Bylsma *vc*).
Sony Classical Vivarte SK66251 (76 minutes: DDD). Recorded 1994.   Ⓕ🄿

'Bruckner is long, he takes time,' remarked Anner Bylsma in a **Gramophone** interview in March 1995; not exactly controversial, but it is important in understanding his, and his ensemble's, approach to the Quintet. The first movement in particular is more spacious than any other version. But there is more to it than tempo. What matters here is the subtlety of phrasing and fineness of the shading, giving vitality and inner intensity to patterns that can easily sound repetitive, especially at this speed. Much of the Quintet is marked *p*, *pp* or *ppp*; L'Archibudelli shows how magically suggestive so many of the quiet passages can be and how important it is to respect those dynamic gradings. They also make the work as a whole sound as unified and sublimely purposeful as the best of the symphonies. As for coupling, the 22-minute student Quartet, with its hints of Mendelssohn and rather more obvious debt to Haydn, is beautifully played, and there is more than one pre-echo of greater things to come. The spaciousness of the Sony sound suits the Quintet especially well, the more obviously 'chamber' textures of the Quartet perhaps less so.

Masses – No. 1 in D minor; No. 2 in E minor; No. 3 in F minor.

Masses – Nos. 1ª, 2 and 3ᵇ.
ªEdith Mathis, ᵇMaria Stader *sops* ªMarga Schiml, ᵇClaudia Hellmann *mezzos*
ªWiesław Ochman, ᵇErnst Haefliger *tens* ªKarl Ridderbusch, ᵇKim Borg *basses*
Bavarian Radio Chorus and Symphony Orchestra / Eugen Jochum.
DG The Originals 447 409-2GOR2 (two discs: 148 minutes: ADD). Text and translation included. Ⓜ

Like Bruckner, Eugen Jochum came from a devout Catholic family and began his musical life as a church organist. He would have known the Mass texts more or less inside out, which explains why his readings focus not on the sung parts – which, for the most part, present the text in a relatively foursquare fashion – but on the orchestral writing which, given the gloriously full-bodied playing of the Bavarian orchestra, so lusciously illuminates familiar words. He approaches the Masses with many of the same ideas he so eloquently propounds in his recordings of the symphonies and the music unfolds with a measured, almost relaxed pace which creates a sense of vast spaciousness. This can have its drawbacks: one is so entranced by the beautifully moulded orchestral introduction to the *Benedictus* from the D minor Mass that the entry of a rather full-throated Marga Schiml comes as a rude interruption. DG's transfers are extraordinarily good – they really seem to have produced a sound which combines the warmth of the original LP with the clarity of detail we expect from CD.

Mass No. 1. Te Deum in C major.
Joan Rodgers *sop* **Catherine Wyn-Rogers** *contr* **Keith Lewis** *ten* **Alastair Miles** *bass*
Corydon Singers and Orchestra / Matthew Best with **James O'Donnell** *org*
Hyperion CDA66650 (67 minutes: DDD). Texts and translations included. Recorded 1993.   Ⓕ🄴

Earth-shaking is the only way to describe Bruckner's great *Te Deum* – literally as well as metaphorically with, on this disc, the thundering Westminster Cathedral organ (sensitively superimposed). The considerably enlarged Corydon Singers sing with consummate skill, rooting out all the subtleties and nuances of Bruckner's magnificent score yet always faithful to Matthew Best's thrusting, athletic direction. It is followed with a performance of the D minor Mass of extraordinary power and strength. From the dazzling orchestral colour and the electrically charged climaxes piling in one on top of the other, to the opulent writing for voices encompassing a vast array of human emotions, Bruckner's debt to Wagner is everywhere apparent. This is very much Bruckner the symphonist – the orchestra certainly dominates the work – and this orchestra produces playing of the very highest calibre.

Mass No. 2. Afferentur regi. Ave Maria in F major (1861). Ave Maria (1882, with **Peter King** *org*). Ecce sacerdos magnus. Locus iste. Aequali for Three Trombones, Nos. 1 and 2.
Anne-Marie Owens *mez* **City of Birmingham Symphony Chorus; Birmingham Symphony Orchestra Wind Ensemble / Simon Halsey.**
Conifer Classics CDCF192 (64 minutes: DDD). Texts and translations included. Recorded 1990. Ⓕ

Bruckner's religious works require for their full realization an elusive combination of classical restraint and romantic fervour. In this excellent recording this style is captured perfectly. Under conductor Simon Halsey the chorus's finely tuned singing and rich tone are ideally suited both to the E minor Mass of 1866 and the four brief but intense motets which provide an excellent makeweight. The CBSO Wind Ensemble's accompaniment in the Mass, and solo playing in the two *Aequali* for three trombones, is well balanced and sonorous, qualities which are also shared by Conifer's atmospheric recorded sound. These choral works display a more personal side to Bruckner's character than the mighty symphonies, and so help to round out in a unique way the musical portrait of this great composer. Thus this finely prepared CD, completed by the first-ever recording of the *Ave Maria,* is an essential complement to the more well-known, and more public, works.

Mass No. 3. Psalm 150 in C major.
Juliet Booth *sop* **Jean Rigby** *mez* **John Mark Ainsley** *ten* **Gwynne Howell** *bass*
Corydon Singers and Orchestra / Matthew Best.
Hyperion CDA66599 (68 minutes: DDD). Texts and translations included. Recorded 1992. Ⓕ

The F minor Mass can certainly be regarded as being among the finest music Bruckner ever created. The intensity of religious feeling is heightened rather than diminished by the sumptuous orchestral support, and the soaring melodies and opulent harmonies are somehow purified and enriched by the devotional character of these familiar texts. Matthew Best's performance, by understating the music's abundant richness, gives tremendous point to the inner conviction of Bruckner's faith. His orchestra, brought together for this recording but sounding as if it has been playing this music all its days, plays with commendable discretion, balancing admirably with a relatively small choral body. As with everything the Corydon Singers and Best turn their hands to, it is an impeccable performance, infused with real artistry and sensitive musicianship. Enhanced by the glorious solo voices from a high-powered team this is a CD of rare depth and conviction.

Mass No. 3 (ed. Nowak). Te Deum.
Jane Eaglen *sop* **Birgit Remmert** *contr* **Deon van der Walt** *ten* **Alfred Muff** *bass*
Linz Mozart Choir; London Philharmonic Orchestra / Franz Welser-Möst.
EMI CDC5 56168-2 (79 minutes: DDD). Texts and translations included. Recorded 1995. ⒻⒷ

Welser-Möst's quartet of soloists, for all their manifest strengths, give the impression of trying a little too hard for their own good. Yet the sheer, almost operatic, spectacle of Welser-Möst's riveting performance of the Mass should not be missed. Raw excitement on an almost primeval level sets the scene for the exhilarating *Te Deum.* Here again Welser-Möst goes at it with all guns blazing. Joakim Svenhedren treats us to a ravishing solo violin obbligato in the 'Aeterna fac' but this is only the briefest of respites in a performance which sweeps all before it in a consuming whirlwind of energy. Best and the Corydons find a greater depth to this music than Welser-Möst and his team. But if it's sheer, unbridled excitement you want nothing beats the outstanding EMI disc.

Bruckner Te Deum.
Verdi Messa da Requiem.
Leontyne Price, Leonie Rysanek *sops* **Hilde Rössl-Majdan, Christa Ludwig** *mezzos*
Fritz Wunderlich, Giuseppe Zampieri *tens* **Walter Berry** *bass-bar* **Cesare Siepi** *bass*

Vienna Singverein; Vienna Philharmonic Orchestra / Herbert von Karajan.
EMI Salzburg Festival Edition mono CMS5 66880-2 (two discs: 107 minutes: ADD).
Recorded live in 1960 and 1958.   Ⓜ Ⓗ

Karajan recorded these works more than once in the studio, in better sound, yet these live
recordings made at Salzburg have their own validity in the vast Karajan discography because they
catch performances undoctored in any way by the conductor or others, and recorded, obviously, at
a single stretch. The Verdi was recorded in the Felsenreitschule. In spite of Karajan's many better-
recorded versions, we would recommend listening to this one because you will be rewarded with a
more immediate experience than with those recorded in the studio (the 1967 film done at La Scala
apart). Everything here seems that much more vivid, more spontaneously felt than in the studio. It
is true there are a few noises off, including one incident that sounds like a member of the audience
falling off their perch, and some questionable intonation among the soloists, but these are worth
tolerating for Karajan's visionary reading, one also strong on orchestral detail. His Vienna forces
are on tremendous form, alive to the nuances Karajan wants us to hear and to his overview of the
work's structure.

Heading the solo team is Rysanek, her only recording of this piece. After a tentative start she soon
finds her most responsive form, with the arching phrases of 'Salva me' finely taken, a beautifully
floated entry at 'Huic ergo' and an even more ethereal one at 'Sed' in the 'Domine Jesu Christe'
movement. She may lack some of the dramatic bite needed for the 'Libera me' but compensates
with warmth and sensitivity in the reflective moments. Ludwig is as ever strength personified in the
mezzo solos. Zampieri – Vienna's tame Italian tenor at the time and a favourite with the conductor
– sings with vibrant tone and great feeling, although his dynamic range is limited. Siepi is his firm
sympathetic self on the bass line. The Verdi is complemented by the 1960 Bruckner recorded in the
new Festspielhaus, a performance of breadth and conviction, adorned by the singing of Price and
the youthful Wunderlich. The sound of the Verdi is reasonable, of the Bruckner very good, albeit
still mono. The notes offer contemporary reviews. Gottfried Kraus, as always in these archive sets
from Austria, places everything in context.

Ignaz Brüll   Austrian 1846-1907

Piano Concertos – No. 1 in F major, Op. 10; No. 2 in C major, Op. 24.
Andante and Allegro, Op. 88.
Martin Roscoe *pf*
BBC Scottish Symphony Orchestra / Martyn Brabbins.
Hyperion CDA67069 (73 minutes: DDD). Recorded 1998.   Ⓕ Ⓔ

Ignaz Brüll is remembered today for two things: first his hugely successful opera *Das goldene
Kreuz*, and secondly, for being a member of Brahms's circle in Vienna. His association with
Brahms has to some extent militated against an independent evaluation of his work, something
this recording should go some way towards redressing. Brüll was an early developer (the booklet
contains a photograph of him aged 24 with a six-inch beard!) and his two piano concertos are
youthful works. The first was written when he was just 14, and it shows an incredible fertility
of ideas and maturity of formal and orchestral handling. The first movement is bold and
passionate, and the finale is witty and brilliant, but it is the powerful central *Andante* that
most impresses. The Second Concerto, written when Brüll was 22, is a more accomplished work,
with a stronger melodic vein and more varied and imaginative orchestral writing. The *Andante
and Allegro*, Op. 88 (1902), is a more mature work, the lyrical first section (based on an earlier
unpublished song) offset by a sparkling finale. The performances are exemplary, full of warmth
and character from soloist and orchestra. Roscoe's muscularity and authoritative firmness of
style are complemented by his delicacy and range of colour. And the BBC Scottish Symphony
Orchestra offers tonal refinement and some lovely woodwind playing. All this is helped by
the full and clean recorded sound – the clarity, balance and tonal blending really are
magnificent.

Gavin Bryars   British 1943

Cello Concerto, 'Farewell to Philosophy'. One Last Bar, Then Joe Can Sing. By the Vaar.
Julian Lloyd Webber *vc* **Charlie Haden** *db*
Nexus (Bob Becker, Bill Cahn, Robin Engelman, Russell Hartenberger, John Wyre *perc*);
English Chamber Orchestra / James Judd.
Point Music 454 126-2PTH (75 minutes: DDD). Recorded 1995.   Ⓕ Ⓔ

Rather like Sibelius's *Swan of Tuonela*, Gavin Bryars's 1995 Cello Concerto (or *Farewell to Philosophy*, to quote its Haydn-inspired subtitle) emerges from among shadows, its solo line climbing sadly and patiently until the long first section takes its leave among *Parsifal*-style string figurations. Section two is more animated, at least initially (timpani set the scene), until the mood darkens again; the fifth recalls the orchestration of Haydn's *Philosopher* Symphony ('pairs of English and French horns playing alternating *legato* phrases, muted violins and unmuted lower strings accompanying with *staccato* quavers'), and the sixth, blurring dissonances and a softly chiming bell. The *Farewell* connection, again after Haydn, greets the tender final section with its progressive reduction of forces, a haunting twentieth-century parallel to the various *fin de siècle* swan-songs of Franz Liszt. Lloyd Webber's tone seems perfectly suited to the job, being full-bodied and expressive but relaxed enough to blend with the components of a predominantly dark accompaniment.

One Last Bar, Then Joe Can Sing (1994) was an Arts Council commission for the percussion quintet Nexus and, to quote Bryars himself, 'is a reflexion on aspects of percussion history, both personal and musical'. The work's opening takes as its starting-point the last bar at the end of the first part of Bryars's opera *Medea*, then calls on varieties of tuned percussion (the glow of marimbas in contrast to the glitter of high bells), prompts some haunting modulations and fades to a tranquil coda. *By the Vaar* (a river in Flanders and the scene of another Bryars opera) was written for – and is performed by – jazz bass-player Charlie Haden, whose specific sound (he uses gut strings) inspired a husky, mellow 'extended *adagio*'. Much of the solo work is played pizzicato which of course underlines the jazz element, while bass clarinet, percussion and strings set up a warming backdrop. It's a nice piece, but the Cello Concerto is rather more than that, and *One Last Bar, Then Joe Can Sing*, more still.

Cadman Requiem. Adnan Songbook. Wonderlawn – Epilogue.
Valdine Anderson *sop*
The Hilliard Ensemble; Fretwork; Gavin Bryars Ensemble / Dave Smith.
Point Music 462 511-2 (61 minutes: DDD). Texts included. Recorded 1997.   Ⓕ

Gavin Bryars is primarily concerned to let instruments and voices sound naturally, irrespective of the historical associations that these sounds may sometimes carry. When his music is as well performed and recorded as on this disc, it achieves a sense of power and inevitability that is rare in new music. The voice seems to suit Gavin Bryars's compositional approach. The very presence of a singer accords a subjective intensity that nicely complements the unwavering, dry-eyed clarity of Bryars's instrumental writing. Bryars says he attempts to write vocal material that will highlight the unique character of each singer's voice and that all the vocal works are being performed on this recording by the specific singers he had in mind. His writing for The Hilliard Ensemble does indeed reconstitute the characteristic four-part sound, but they are also given every opportunity to be appreciated as soloists. In composing the *Adnan Songbook* for the young British soprano Valdine Anderson, Bryars could almost have used Richard Strauss as a model, so expressive is his treatment of her highest tessitura. On the other hand, the blunt, even artless handling of the text and instrumental accompaniment is entirely typical of Bryars. It is this oblique mixture of understatement and expressive warmth that makes the work so original in conception. *Cadman Requiem*, which opens the album, is also very impressive. Dedicated to the sound engineer Bill Cadman, who died in the Lockerbie aircrash in 1988, the piece was recorded with its two ensembles, Fretwork and The Hilliard Ensemble, facing each other. The resulting rich blend of timbres, well captured by the recording, makes for arresting listening. To sum up, a hauntingly beautiful album that provides compelling evidence of the recent resurgence in Gavin Bryars's work.

Ferruccio Busoni   Italian/German 1866-1924

Piano Concerto, Op. 39.
Garrick Ohlsson *pf*
Men's voices of the **Cleveland Orchestra Chorus;**
Cleveland Orchestra / Christoph von Dohnányi.
Telarc CD80207 (72 minutes: DDD). Recorded 1989.   Ⓕ

Busoni's Concerto is a thundering vehicle for virtuosity and one doubts whether the concerto has ever been performed as outstandingly as this, by the conductor and his players as well as the soloist. The second *Scherzo* is so infectiously exciting that one feels tempted to cheat and play it all over again before proceeding to the finale, and the enormous central movement has a formidable sense of scale and pacing, to which Ohlsson's sonorous pianism is a bonus as well as a contributing factor. The orchestral sound is outstandingly beautiful and transparent and the piano produces crags of grandiose tone without ever seeming to approach its limit or to have been helped by the engineers.

Busoni Turandot – Suite, Op. 41.
Casella Paganiniana, Op. 65.
Martucci Nocturne in G flat major, Op. 70 No. 1. Novelletta, Op. 82 No. 2. Giga, Op. 61 No. 3.
La Scala Philharmonic Orchestra, Milan / Riccardo Muti.
Sony Classical SK53280 (59 minutes: DDD). Recorded 1992.   Ⓕ

Riccardo Muti takes time out here to present some of the lesser-known, rarely heard orchestral scores of his fellow countrymen, and a superbly played, enjoyable concert it is too. Proceedings commence with a fine and spirited performance of Alfredo Casella's divertimento *Paganiniana* – not a great piece by any means but a work possessing plenty of charm and humour nevertheless; the outer movements are a bit of a romp (very *opera buffa*) and must have been as much fun to write as they clearly are for the La Scala Philharmonic to play. The tone and temperature rise a few degrees in Martucci's gorgeously lyrical *Nocturne*, Op. 70 No. 1 – a sort of Mahler-meets-Puccini-meets-Respighi love song – and this is nicely contrasted with the affable if somewhat lightweight musings of his *Novelletta* and *Giga*. The high point of the disc, though, must surely be Muti's account of Busoni's *Turandot* Suite, Op. 41, the work that, after several tinkerings, finally ended up forming the basis of his 1917 opera. The recording is exceptionally clear and well focused, if at times a little dry.

Fantasia contrappuntistica. Fantasia nach J.S. Bach. Toccata.
John Ogdon *pf*
Continuum CCD1006 (60 minutes: AAD).   Ⓕ

Busoni's *Fantasia contrappuntistica* is of legendary difficulty, density and length, and pianists are understandably very reluctant to learn it. John Ogdon plays it with consummate virtuosity, clarity and sustained concentration, and alongside the technical assurance there is in evidence a firm intellectual grasp of Busoni's prodigious structure and a lofty eloquence in expressing his faith. It is a formidable feat of musicianship as well as pianism. The two other pieces are more personal and many readers may find them even more moving. The *Fantasia nach J.S. Bach* is freer in structure than the *Fantasia contrappuntistica* and with its dedication to his father's memory it is as though Busoni has chosen particularly beloved and appropriate pages for his tribute, adding his own meditations on them. The very late *Toccata* is a resurgence of the Faustian vein that runs throughout Busoni's work, but now dark and pessimistic. The three works add up to a sort of triple self-portrait and Ogdon characterizes them finely. Busoni's piano-writing demands a huge range of sonority as well as endurance and sheer dexterity; in these performances (and this superb recording) Busoni's piano is rendered full-size.

Arlecchino.
Robert Wörle *ten* Arlecchino (Peter Matič *spkr*) Leandro; **Marcia Bellamy** *mez* Colombina (Katharina Koschny *spkr*); **René Pape** *bass* Ser Matteo del Sarto; **Siegfried Lorenz** *bar* Abbate Cospicuo; **Peter Lika** *bass* Dottor Bombasto;
Berlin Radio Symphony Orchestra / Gerd Albrecht.
Capriccio 60 038 (67 minutes: DDD). Notes and synopsis included. Recorded 1992.   Ⓕ

Albrecht's *Arlecchino* is one of the finest readings of a Busoni opera yet committed to disc. He projects a great feeling of drama and dramatic pace (as well as the *commedia dell'arte* aspects of the opera) and seems to have absorbed the Busoni spirit successfully; the presence of Busoni's final masterpiece, *Doktor Faust*, is exceptionally strong. Marcia Bellamy is well suited to the role of Colombina, and there are some exceptionally good performances from René Pape, Siegfried Lorenz and Peter Lika in the roles of Matteo, Abbate Cospicuo and Dottor Bombasto. The master-stroke, however, is the casting of Robert Wörle in both the Arlecchino and Leandro roles, an inspired idea and one which is delivered with great aplomb and panache. Albrecht draws superb orchestral playing from the Berlin Radio Symphony Orchestra (especially in the wind and brass departments), and the recording is well balanced and atmospheric.

George Butterworth   British 1885-1916

Butterworth Bredon Hill and other songs. A Shropshire Lad.
Finzi Let us garlands bring, Op. 18.
Ireland Sea Fever. The Vagabond. The Bells of San Marie.
Vaughan Williams Songs of Travel.
Bryn Terfel *bass-bar* **Malcolm Martineau** *pf*
DG 445 946-2GH (77 minutes: DDD). Texts included. Recorded 1995.   Ⓕ **E**

As in all the best singing of songs, whatever the nationality, there is strong, vivid communication: Terfel will sometimes sing so softly that if he had secured anything less than total involvement he would lose us. There is breadth of phrase, variety of tone, alertness of rhythm, all the musical virtues are there; and yet that seems to go only a little way towards accounting for what is special. One after another, these songs are brought to a full life with intelligence and the genuine flash of inspiration. Malcolm Martineau's playing is also a delight: his touch, in its way, is as sure and illuminating as the singer's. From the recording you might prefer less hall-reverberance around the voice. From the songs themselves you could not possibly wish for anything more: hearing them performed like this you probably won't swap them for half the German song repertoire or the whole of the French.

Dietrich Buxtehude

German *c*1637-1707

Nimm von uns, Herr, BuxWV78. Jesu, meines Lebens Leben, BuxWV62. Mit Fried und Freud, ich fahr dahin, BuxWV76. Führwahr, er trug unsere Krankheit, BuxWV31. Herzlich lieb, hab' ich dich o Herr, BuxWV41. Der Herr ist mit mir, BuxWV15.
Claron McFadden *sop* **Franciska Dukel** *mez* **Jonathan Peter Kenny** *counterten*
Marius van Altena *ten* **Stephan MacLeod** *bass*
Collegium Vocale; The Royal Consort; Anima Eterna Orchestra / Jos van Immerseel.
Channel Classics CCS7895 (65 minutes: DDD). Texts included. Recorded 1994. Ⓕ 🄴

The North German middle ground between chorale *concertato* and the early cantatas of Bach is an interesting one, especially in the hands of composers of Buxtehude's stature. In these cantatas the disparate textual elements of bible passage, hymn and devotional poetry, typical of the time, are complemented by the composer's skill in drawing together the comparably disparate musical ones of sonata, concertato principles, aria and chorale. That in itself might give these cantatas only an ephemeral charm, but Buxtehude was a musician who was gifted in the art of word-painting and, above all, in the expression of deep, often grief-stricken emotions. He could be brilliant, too, in his lyrical approach to texts, but it is an all-pervading melancholy which seems to characterize most strongly much that is most profound in his sacred vocal music. These six works demonstrate Buxtehude's formal versatility with two large-scale chorale cantatas; a beautiful ostinato-based strophic aria, with an almost startling dissonance; the famous, austere and highly contrapuntal *Canticum Simeonis* ('*Mit Fried und Freud*') which Buxtehude performed at his father's funeral in 1674; and two *concertante* pieces, one consisting of a sinfonia and multisectional aria, the other of a sinfonia, aria and alleluia. The performances respond to the highly charged emotional outpouring of these works but occasionally lack polish. However, the music is first-rate (the ostinato- and chaconne-based movements make particularly strong appeal) and Immerseel's direction is stylish and sensitive. The cantata texts are in German only but there is a translation of Immerseel's interesting introductory essay.

Membra Jesu nostri, BuxWV75.
Bach Collegium Japan / Masaaki Suzuki.
BIS CD871 (59 minutes: DDD). Text and translation included. Recorded 1997. Ⓕ

Buxtehude's *Membra Jesu nostri patientis sanctissima* is a cycle of seven cantatas, each one of which is an address to a different Member of the Body of Christ crucified, implicit in the work's title. It has been well represented in the catalogue but this recording offers an impressive addition. Indeed, in respect of ensemble and expressive *gravitas* it is, perhaps, the most convincing of them all, but the pleasure of this deeply felt reading, for some readers, may be diluted by too reverberant an acoustic. If you were present in such a building and able to sense other aspects of its ambience you might feel differently. But in the context of a CD, one would like to hear more detail, above all from the string instruments. Even so, there is no mistaking the technical skill and sensibility with which these artists have realized the tender, agonized suspensions and expressive power of these beautiful pieces. Only the intimacy of the music suffers. The solo vocal contributions are almost uniformly strong, and there are electrifying moments in the ensemble singing as, for example, in the limpid, perfectly balanced textures of the 'Ad ubera portabimini' which concludes the second cantata of the cycle. Notwithstanding reservations, this version is on balance the first recommendation.

William Byrd

British 1543-1623

Byrd Fantasia a 6. Pavan and Galliard – Kinbourough Good, MB32. The Queen's Alman, MB20, 'Hugh Ashton's Ground'. Pavan and Galliard a 6. Pavan and Galliard, MB14. Browning. Pavan a 5.

The Carman's Whistle, MB36. The Irish March, MB94. My Lord of Oxenford's Maske. Pavan, MB17. A Fancie, MB25. Praeludium and Ground. Pavan and Galliard, MB60.
Anonymous Pavans – Mille regretz; Belle qui tiens ma vie.
Capriccio Stravagante / Skip Sempé hpd
Auvidis Astrée E8611 (73 minutes: DDD). Recorded 1997. Ⓕ🅿🅔

This is technically superb and musically distinctive. Skip Sempé and his musicians grab hold of each piece and play it in a way that leaves no doubt why it was chosen; that is, they have something new and interesting to say musically about each work. The sound is also wonderful: Sempé plays on a Skowroneck harpsichord that he enthusiastically describes as 'one of the first truly admirable harpsichords of the 20th century'; the viols and the recorder group are beautifully recorded, with every detail of the dense polyphony clear. So this is the kind of disc you could play to almost any music-lover as a way of explaining that Byrd is not just a great composer but one of the greatest. On the other hand, those who know the music may well feel a touch uncomfortable. While Sempé plays with often truly dazzling skill and virtuosity, many may wish that his pavans were a touch steadier. He also has a slightly mannered way of overdotting cadential bass figurations. The ensemble pieces are sometimes heavily orchestrated: the great six-part *Fantasia* that opens the disc, for example, has recorders and continuo instruments added to the viols as though to underline contrasts that some would think were already there in the music. Caveats apart, this is an invigorating disc which gives you a new understanding of some of the finest masterpieces of English music.

Byrd Fantasia a 5, BE17/8. Browning a 5, BE17/10. Fantasias a 6, BE17/13-14. In Nomines a 5, BE17/19-22.
Mico Fancies a 4 Nos. 4a, 5-7, 9, 10, 14, 18 and 19. Pavans a 4 Nos. 2-4.
Phantasm (Laurence Dreyfus, Wendy Gillespie, Jonathan Manson, Markku Luolajan-Mikkola, *viols*) with **Martha McGaughey, Alison McGillivray** viols
Simax PSC1143 (60 minutes: DDD). Recorded 1996. Ⓕ

The odd juxtaposition of Byrd's very finest chamber music with pieces by Richard Mico may seem rather like pairing late Beethoven with Vanhal; but it works extremely well here. Though Mico has been little regarded, much of his music shows absolute mastery (his Pavan No. 4 is in some ways one of the most perfect and beautiful examples of the simple eight-bar pavane); it was eminently worth devoting half a disc to this obscure but lovely composer and bringing it to the public by associating it with Byrd. The Mico selection includes two pieces that are by no means certainly his (*Fancies* Nos. 18 and 19); but they are still glorious pieces and all the more welcome for that. The Mico works are intriguingly organized into little 'sets' according to their key-centres. Phantasm plays this music with immaculate control and balance, finding many telling details that might elude less careful musicians. Some listeners may be a touch less happy with the Byrd, feeling that the honeyed sounds cover certain details, that the speed of *Browning* loses the work's harmonic and contrapuntal magic, that the myriad changes in the grand six-voice *fantasias* could benefit from greater lightness of touch. But that would be like saying that only the English can perform Elgar idiomatically. What Phantasm brings to this music is a clear and unusual view of the music. Moreover, they present what is absolutely the best of Byrd's consort work, omitting the troublesome first *In Nomine* and the less perfect first six-part *Fantasia*. The four *Fantasias* and the four *In Nomines* on this disc are the core of Byrd's claim to stand among the world's greatest composers of chamber music. The performances convincingly support that claim.

Masses – Three Voices; Four Voices; Five Voices. Motet – Ave verum corpus a 4.
The Tallis Scholars / Peter Phillips.
Gimell 454 945-2PH (67 minutes: DDD). Ⓕ🅿

Byrd was a fervently committed Roman Catholic and he helped enormously to enrich the music of the English Church. His Mass settings were made for the many recusant Catholic worshippers who held services in private. They were published between 1593 and 1595 and are creations of great feeling. The contrapuntal writing has a much closer texture and fibre than the Masses of Palestrina and there is an austerity and rigour that is allowed to blossom and expand with the text. The beautifully restrained and mellow recording, made in Merton College Chapel, Oxford, fully captures the measure of the music and restores the awe and mystery of music that familiarity can dim.

Mass for Five Voices (with Propers for the Feast of Corpus Christi). Gradualia ac cantiones sacrae: Part 2 – Corpus Christi. Gradualia seu cantionum sacrarum, liber secundus: Votive Mass for the Blessed Sacrament – Ab ortu solis; Alleluia: Cognoverunt discipuli.
Winchester Cathedral Choir / David Hill.
Hyperion CDA66837 (73 minutes: DDD). Texts and translations included. Recorded 1995. Ⓕ

On this CD the five movements of Byrd's Mass for five voices are interspersed with the five pieces of the Proper for the Feast of Corpus Christi. We can therefore transport ourselves back in time to the end of the sixteenth and beginning of the seventeenth century, and imagine their being performed, in early summer, at a live celebration of Mass in one of the great houses of the Catholic nobility. Winchester Cathedral Choir has purposely sought out an enclosed space in the great cathedral to make this recording, so that the sound captures something of the immediacy of singers performing in a small hidden room. One is particularly struck by the quality of the trebles – the slight edge to the gentle tone of very young singers – and also by the teamwork of the whole choir. The secret of this recording lies in its unity of theme and in its understanding of Byrd's triumphant statements of belief, expressed in music of great tenderness as well as strength.

Gradualia – Volume 1/i: Saturday Lady Masses in Advent. Domine quis habitabit. Omni tempore benedic Deum. Christe redemptor omnium. Sermone blando a 3. Miserere. Ne perdas cum implis. Lamentations of Jeremiah. Christe, qui lux es a 5. Christe qui lux es a 4. Sanctus. Audivi vocem de caelo. Vide Dominum quoniam tribulor. Peccavi super numerum (all ed. Skinner).
The Cardinall's Musick; Frideswide Consort (Caroline Kershaw, Jane Downer, Christine Garratt, Jean McCreery *recs*) **/ Andrew Carwood.**
ASV Gaudeamus CDGAU170 (70 minutes: DDD). Texts and translations included.
Recorded 1996.   Ⓕ

This is a great start to The Cardinall's Musick's project to record Byrd's complete output. On the disc, some of the shorter motets are entrusted to The Cardinall's' habitual instrumental accomplices, the Frideswide Consort. A full list of sources is given for each piece, along with appropriate editorial commentary. Since Byrd set certain texts a number of times, such precision seems only sensible. Much of this music is new to the CD catalogue, and even in this selection of largely unpublished motets, there are impressive finds (the nine-voice *Domine quis habitabit*, for instance). This repertory is the mother's-milk of English choristers, and of the younger generation of English vocal ensembles The Cardinall's Musick remains perhaps the closest to that tradition outside of actual choral establishments. So they respond to Byrd with a suavity and confidence born of longstanding acquaintance. The expansive penitential pieces, such as the early *Lamentations*, are far removed from the small-scale forms of the *Gradualia*. The Cardinall's respond effectively to these different functions and moods, and the recording complements them admirably.

Gradualia – Volume 2: Nativity of our Lord Jesus Christ – Puer natus est; Viderunt ... omnes fines terrae; Dies sanctificatus; Tui sunt coeli; Viderunt omnes fines terrae; Hodie Christus natus est; O admirabile commercium; O magnum mysterium. Ave regina caelorum. O salutaris hostia. Confitemini Domino. In exitu Israel (with Sheppard and Mundy). Laudate pueri Dominum. Decantabat populus. Deus in adjutorium. Ad Dominum cum tribularer (all ed. Skinner).
The Cardinall's Musick / Andrew Carwood.
ASV Gaudeamus CDGAU178 (73 minutes: DDD). Texts and translations included.   ⒻⒺ

This second volume of The Cardinall's Musick's Byrd edition is, if anything, more impressive than the first. It may be a matter of programming, for the works recorded here seem to be of a higher overall calibre: even an obviously experimental piece such as *O salutaris hostia* could have been included on merit alone – yet this appears to be its first recording. Complete surveys sometimes turn up items of lesser interest, yet they also allow one to hear pieces that might have difficulty in finding a home elsewhere: witness the responsory, *In exitu Israel*, an intriguing collaborative effort by Byrd and his contemporaries, Mundy and Sheppard. Finally, one can judge for oneself the authenticity of works that modern scholarship has deemed doubtful (such as the opening *Ave regina caelorum*). Most of the pieces here involve male altos on the top line. The centrepiece is a collection of Propers from the *Gradualia* of 1607, this time for the Nativity. As on their first set, Skinner's and Carwood's decision to structure each volume around a set of Propers proves an astute piece of programming, integrating shorter items as it does (such as the various *Alleluia* settings) within a framework that allows them their own space. The singers are on very fine form indeed. It takes confidence to carry off *O salutaris hostia*, whose fierce false relations could so easily have sounded merely wilful. Only in the final, extended settings does the pace flag: the disc's last moments are rather ponderous. That aside, this is a disc to delight Byrd-lovers everywhere.

Gradualia – The Marian Masses: Mass Propers – Feasts of the Purification of the BVM, the Nativity of the BVM, the Annunciation of the BVM, the Assumption of the BVM; Votive Masses of the BVM: Advent, Christmas to the Purification, Purification to Easter, Easter to Pentecost and Pentecost to Advent.
William Byrd Choir / Gavin Turner.
Hyperion CDA66451 (80 minutes: DDD). Texts and translations included. Recorded 1990.   ⒻⓅ

This useful recording explores the cycle of motets Byrd composed for English Roman Catholics to sing in their clandestine services. He began the project soon after writing the three Masses (which date from the mid-1590s), and took ten years to bring it to completion. Like so much of Byrd's late music, the *Gradualia* motets are compact and economical in expression: miniature masterpieces that glow with the warmth of the composer's personal religious convictions, and miraculously balance exquisite musical design with the most intelligent word-setting. Their chamber-music scale is nicely captured in these performances by the William Byrd Choir, headed by a superb team of five solo voices. Everything on the disc belongs to feasts of the Blessed Virgin, many of which share texts with one another. Byrd economized by setting each text once only, and to play them in their correct liturgical order the various tracks of the CD have to be pre-selected. This is great fun to do; but the disc also makes perfectly satisfying listening when played straight through from start to finish.

Cantiones Sacrae (1575) – Tribue, Domine. Siderum rector. Domine secundum. Fantasias – C major; D major. Attollite portas. Miserere mihi. Aspice Domine. Peccantem me quotidie. Salvator mundi I. O lux, beata Trinitas.
New College Choir, Oxford / Edward Higginbottom with **Timothy Morris** *org*
CRD CRD3492 (64 minutes: DDD). Texts and translations included. Recorded 1994. Ⓕ

There is so much wonderful six-part writing in this attractive selection from the 1575 *Cantiones Sacrae* that such a medium appears in a new light, particularly when performed by the choir and in the acoustic of New College Chapel – where, as Edward Higginbottom reminds us, they 'have been rehearsing for 500 years'. The beauty and balance of the musical architecture is constantly conveyed to the listener, particularly in the six-part writing. It doesn't matter whether these compositions were intended for liturgical or domestic use, or as a noble offering to the Queen: from a purely musical point of view they are superb. To give a single example, the little Vespers hymn *O lux, beata Trinitas* displays consummate craftsmanship through the ingenious use of the number three – three high, then three low voices, three diverse voices, a canon three-in-one, three strophes, triple time, and so on, building up to a tremendous final 'Amen'. The point made by this recording is that it all sounds natural, uncontrived, magnificent. The three organ pieces are a welcome addition: with their brilliant fingerwork and gentle registrations they present a charming and lively contrast to the vocal settings.

O Lord, within thy tabernacle. Quis me statim. With Lilies White. Wretched Albinus. Blame I Confess. Ye Sacred Muse. Rejoice unto the Lord. Fair Britain Isle. In Nomines a 5, BE17 Nos. 18-22. Browning a 5, BE17 No. 10. Fantasia a 5, BE17 No. 8. Praeludium and Ground a 5.
Gérard Lesne *counterten* **Ensemble Orlando Gibbons** (Wieland Kuijken, Kaori Uemura, Anne-Marie Lasla, Sylvie Moquet, Jérôme Hantaï *viols*).
Virgin Classics Veritas VC5 45264-2 (65 minutes: DDD). Ⓕ

The five *In Nomines* reveal the growing maturity and control over form of the inventive fledgling Byrd, though you will need to shuffle tracks to follow it in sequence. This is the only CD where the *In Nomines* are coupled with Byrd's consort songs. Of the other instrumental items, the *Praeludium and Ground* are treated with winsome lightness but the 20 remarkable variations on *Browning* hang more heavily than is suggested by the words of either version of the tune (the other is *The leaves be green*). Solemnity is the prevailing mood of the consort songs, four of them laments. *Wretched Albinus* refers to the disgracing of the Earl of Essex, attributed to a 'silly woman' – the same Queen Elizabeth whose protection of Byrd from anti-Catholic laws is obliquely celebrated in *Rejoice unto the Lord*, the only cheerful oasis in this desert of sorrow. Fortunately the sorrow is expressed in magnificent music of which *Ye Sacred Muse*, Byrd's tribute to the recently deceased Tallis, is the jewel in the crown. Magnificent vocal music calls for a matching singer and Gérard Lesne fills that need to the full. First-class recording and excellent booklet-notes are additional reasons for acquiring this disc.

All in a garden green. La volta No. 1 in G major, 'Lady Morley'. O mistress mine I must. Wolsey's Wild. O Lord, how vain are all our delights. Psalms, Sonets and Songs – Who likes to love; My mind to me a kingdom is; Farewell, false love. Triumph with pleasant melody. Truth at the First. Ad Dominum cum tribularer. Cantiones sacrae – Attollite portas; Da mihi auxilium; Domine secundum actum meum; Miserere mihi, Domine.
Sophie Yates *virg* **I Fagiolini / Robert Hollingworth; Fretwork.**
Chandos Chaconne CHAN0578 (73 minutes: DDD). Texts and translations included. Recorded 1994. ⒻⓅ

This disc adopts an imaginative approach to programming Byrd's music by presenting works in different genres grouped together to demonstrate a single stage in his development. It includes Latin motets, keyboard dances and variations on popular songs of the day, and sacred and secular songs (and a dialogue) with viols. There is so much here that wins our admiration: the dazzling contrapuntal elaboration of *Attollite portas*, the close-knit texture of *Da mihi auxilium* and the massive *Ad Dominum cum tribularer*; the exuberant variations on *O mistress mine* (neatly played by Sophie Yates) and Byrd's melodic gift in the strophic *O Lord, how vain*. The singers' adoption of period pronunciation of English – so that, for example, 'rejoice' emerges as 'rejwace' – affects the tuning and the musical sound, it is claimed here, but without rather clearer enunciation the point remains not proven. Probably more upsetting to many will be the Anglicized pronunciation of Latin. The viol consort gives quiet, stylish support and is well balanced, the Fagiolini sopranos occasionally 'catch the mike' on high notes (e.g. in the passionate pleas of *Miserere mihi, Domine*), and the recorded level of the virginals might have been a little higher without falsifying its tone. But these are very minor criticisms of a most rewarding disc.

Juan Cabanilles

Cabanilles Tientos – de falsas II; lleno secondo tono; de falsas ottavo punto alto; XXIII por A la me re; I ple; XVII de Pange Lingua, quinto tono punto alto; IX de contres. Passacalles I and IV. Corrente Italiana (Obertura).
Kerll Batalla Imperial.
Hespèrion XX / Jordi Savall *va da gamba*
Alia Vox AV9801 (62 minutes: DDD). Recorded 1996. Ⓕ

What is on offer here are consort performances of contrapuntal organ pieces by the instrument's greatest Spanish exponent during the second half of the seventeenth century, Valencia Cathedral organist, Juan Cabanilles. They are sufficiently convincing as consort pieces; their contrapuntal emphasis gives them more of a renaissance flavour than a baroque one, but there are plenty of baroque-style virtuosic divisions, decorations and, in the two *tientos falsas*, anguished chromaticism. Savall has assembled for them a mixed ensemble of viols and assorted winds, plus a chamber organ and a harp, and through imaginative mixing and matching achieved the kind of textural contrasts and balances Cabanilles would presumably have had in mind for the organ. The difference, however, is that these performances have none of the harsh attack or unforgiving sound of the organ, bringing to the music instead a vocal warmth and flexibility, while losing nothing in instrumental agility when it comes to florid passagework. In short these are beautiful and gentle performances, carefully modulated, lovingly balanced and well thought out from beginning to end.

John Cage

Sonatas and Interludes.
Aleck Karis *prepared pf*
Bridge BCD9081A/B (65 minutes: DDD). Recorded 1997.
Includes bonus disc of Cage reading his lecture 'Composition in Retrospect'. Ⓜ

There are now numerous recordings of Cage's 1948 classic in the current British catalogue, a situation unthinkable even a decade ago. Now pianists yearn to record Cage's *Sonatas and Interludes* the way actors were supposed to want to play Hamlet. What emerges is that prepared pianos can sound very different. The latest contender, the American Aleck Karis, plays the opening Sonata more briskly than most and overall has a lively rhythmic sense – and these are American rhythms after all. Some pianists have had trouble with Cage's calligraphy and get the exposed third note of the Fourth Sonata wrong. Karis is right with an A – not a B – in this fully notated work. His sense of swing is again utterly idiomatic in the Fifth Sonata, and the Eighth, which starts with such a poetic figure, is lovely and dreamy. When it comes to the spacious opening of the Twelfth Sonata, one of Karis's preparations is twanging and feels in danger of working loose. But these are details, and Karis's performance of the cycle is as attractive as any. With its mid-price and Cage's 1982 lecture added as a free bonus disc, this is a good buy.

Music for Piano – 1; 2; 3; 4-19; 20; 21-36; 37-52; 53-68; 69-84; 85. Music for ... Two Pianos I/II; Three Pianos; Four Pianos; Five Pianos. Electronic Music for Two Pianos.
Steffen Schleiermacher *pf*
Dabringhaus und Grimm MDG613 0784-2 (two discs: 153 minutes: DDD). Recorded 1996. Ⓕ

This set is devoted to the *Music for Piano* series almost entirely written in the 1950s. Schleiermacher's recording of the *Sonatas and Interludes* for prepared piano is one of many currently obtainable but the whole *Music for Piano* series is neglected and mostly unavailable. One can see why performers have found these pieces less attractive. After Cage's crisis year of 1952, which saw him produce the so-called silent piece 4'33", he was obsessed with removing his own tastes and desires from his compositions. Before he became fully committed to the I Ching's random numbers he marked out blotches and imperfections in the manuscript paper he was using as a way of getting the notes. Cage said he looked at his paper and suddenly realized that all the music was there. This procedure also settled the density of notes on the page. In the whole series the performer is left to decide dynamics and pace in a continuity dominated by single notes.

If this sounds austere, we are reckoning without the ingenuities of Schleiermacher. Cage specifies various types of sound production, apart from the use of the keys: primarily plucking the strings from inside or muting them. As in Schleiermacher's prepared piano recordings, the quality of sound has been most carefully considered. A muted low note or a single plucked string can be marvellously evocative in conjunction with conventionally produced pitches. The ambience of the prepared piano is not far away. Further, instead of simply going through the entire series, Schleiermacher avails himself of Cage's provision for several of these pieces to be played together, which he does at intervals in the series. Since we have heard the same pieces solo, the superimposed versions bring back familiar material in a fascinating way. There are discoveries too, since *Music for Piano 85* is not listed in *Grove*, and *Electronic Music for Two Pianos* extends the palette refreshingly at the end of the second CD. Schleiermacher's realization uses several levels of sound input, including some attractive bird-song. Fastidiously researched and performed, Schleiermacher says he has taken the pieces seriously. This shows, and as a result he has begun a new chapter of virtually unknown Cage.

Litany for the Whale. Aria No. 2. Five. The Wonderful Widow of Eighteen Springs. Solo No. 22. Experiences No. 2. Thirty-six Mesostics re and not re Marcel Duchamp. Aria (arr. Hillier). The Year Begins to Be Ripe.
Theatre of Voices (Paul Elliott, Andrea Fullington, Allison Zelles, Terry Riley *vocs* Alan Bennett *voc/closed pf* Shabda Owens *voc/electronics*) / **Paul Hillier** *voc*
Harmonia Mundi HMU90 7187 (72 minutes: DDD). Texts included. Recorded 1995. Ⓕ

This is a landmark for Cage, Paul Hillier's group and everyone else. Hillier says he has been interested in Cage for years – as a composer and not just an influence – and here his own considerable advocacy has turned Cage into a troubadour of our global village. The Theatre of Voices' collection jumps right in at the deep end with *Litany for the Whale* (1980), a 25-minute monody with two uncannily similar voices (Alan Bennett and Paul Elliott) using only five notes in antiphonal phrases. Shut your eyes and this ritual could almost be Gregorian chant, austere and liturgical, since there are powerful associations with these voices in early-music repertoire. The scope narrows to three notes in *The Wonderful Widow*, where the closed piano part is slightly subdued, and the same three recur in *Thirty-six Mesostics* (organized like an acrostic but down the middle), spoken by American minimalist Terry Riley and sung by Hillier.

Cage's *Aria* (1958), for Cathy Berberian, has always been associated with one voice but this realization for seven voices and electronic sounds is thoroughly idiomatic. *Experiences* No. 2, another monody to a poem by e. e. cummings (who said Cage couldn't write a tune?), is beautifully sung by Andrea Fullington, but the precisely notated pauses are not always accurate. The realization of *Aria* No. 2 is a fastidious mix of extended vocal techniques by Alan Bennett with weather sounds. Cage convinces us of the musical beauty of rainfall, water and thunder. *Five* is a vocal version of one of Cage's late number pieces. This type of sustained writing is ideal for voices and there are recognizable meditative qualities in all these performances. The close-microphone breathing in *Solo* No. 22 is, like everything else here, artistic and well engineered.

Antonio Caldara
Italian *c*1670-1736

Maddalena ai piedi di Cristo.
Maria-Cristina Kiehr, Rosa Dominguez *sops* **Bernarda Fink** *contr* **Andreas Scholl** *counterten* **Gerd Türk** *ten* **Ulrich Messthaler** *bass* **Schola Cantorum Basiliensis** / **René Jacobs**.
Harmonia Mundi HMC90 5221/2 (two discs: 126 minutes: DDD). Notes, text and translation included. Recorded 1995. *Gramophone* Award Winner 1997. ⒻⒺ

Caldara was the most prolific and famous oratorio composer of his day and this one, written around 1700, is wonderfully rich in fresh and attractive invention. Practically devoid of external action, it is dramatically tense and concentrates on the continuous struggle between the forces of good and evil, the sinner Magdalen being urged towards penitence by her sister Martha; the roles of

Christ and a Pharisee are considerably smaller. The work opens in immediately arresting fashion, with an agitated sinfonia followed by the hypnotic aria 'Dormi, o cara': then come another 27 brief *da capo* arias with their associated recitatives. There is no lack of variety: some arias are accompanied only by a continuo instrument; others are furnished with different usages of the five-part strings. René Jacobs furthers the dramatic impact by his pacing, of the recitatives in particular; and his casting is flawless. He has the highly effective idea of differentiating the parts of Earthly and Celestial Love by allocating the former to a mezzo and the latter to a countertenor. Both are excellent, but so are all the participants in this performance. It seems almost invidious to single out highlights but one must cite the aria 'Diletti' for Magdalen (Kiehr) and the succeeding ornate 'Vattene' for Martha (Dominguez) and, even more, two florid arias from Scholl rejoicing in the eventual triumph of good and two, delivered passionately by Fink, of fury by evil at its overthrow. You are urged to acquire this disc.

Joseph Canteloube
French 1879-1957

Canteloube Chants d'Auvergne – La pastoura als camps; Baïlèro; L'ïo de rotso; Ound' onorèn gorda; Obal, din lou Limouzi; Pastourelle; L'Antouèno; La pastrouletta è lo chibaliè; La delíssádo; N'aï pas iéu de mio; Lo calhé; Lo fiolaïré; Passo pel prat; Lou boussu; Brezairola; Maluros qu'o uno fenno. Jou l'pount d'o Mirabel; Oï, ayaï; Pour l'enfant; Chut, chut; Pastorale; Lou coucut; Postouro sé tu m'aymo; Quand z-éyro petituono; Té, l'co tèl; Uno jionto postouro; Hél beyla-z-y-dau fél; Obal, din lo combuèlo; Là-haut, sur le rocher; Lou diziou bé.
Villa-Lobos Bachianas brasileiras No. 5.
Dame Kiri Te Kanawa *sop* **English Chamber Orchestra / Jeffrey Tate.**
Double Decca 444 995-2DF2 (two discs: 111 minutes: DDD). Notes, text and translation included. Recorded 1982-83. Ⓜ

Dame Kiri Te Kanawa's richly sensuous approach to these delightful songs is undoubtedly very seductive, especially when the accompaniments by Jeffrey Tate and the ECO are so warmly supportive and the sound so opulent. Her account of the most famous number, 'Baïlèro', must be the most relaxed on record, yet she sustains its repetitions with a sensuous, gentle beauty of line, supported by lovely wind playing from the orchestra which seems to float in the air. There is a resonance given to the sound, which means that certain of the brighter, more obviously folksy numbers, lose a little of their rustic sharpness. However, there is no question that the overall effect is very appealing, particularly when Dame Kiri's voice (recorded in the early 1980s) is so young and fresh and the sound so lustrously beautiful. As an encore we are offered the Villa-Lobos *Bachianas brasileiras* No. 5, an 'Aria' for soprano and cellos. She sings this in Portuguese and the result is ravishing, almost decadent at its softly intoned reprise. An enticing disc.

Canteloube Chants d'Auvergne, Volume 2 – La pastoura als camps; Baïlèro; L'ïo dè rotso; Ound' onorèn gorda; Obal, din lou Limouzi; L'Antouèno; La pastrouletta è lo chibaliè; N'aï pas iéu de mio; Lo calhé; Maluros qu'o uno fenno; Pour l'enfant; Quand z-éyro petituono; Hél beyla-z-y-dau fél; Là-haut, sur le rocher; Lou diziou bé.
Emmanuel Chansons bourguignonnes du Pays de Beaune, Op. 15 – Quand j'ai sôti de mon villaige; Il était une fille, une fille d'honneur; Le pommier d'Août; Noël; Complainte de Notre Dame; Aidieu, bargeire!.
Dawn Upshaw *sop* **Orchestra of the Opéra de Lyon / Kent Nagano.**
Erato 0630-17577-2 (63 minutes: DDD). Texts and translations included. Recorded 1996. Ⓕ

Canteloube Chants d'Auvergne – Baïlèro; L'ïo dè rotso; Ound' onorèn gorda; Obal, din lou Limouzi; L'Antouèno; La delíssádo; N'aï pas iéu de mio; Lo calhé; Lo fiolaïré; Passo pel prat; Brezairola; Oï, ayaï; Pour l'enfant; Chut, chut; Lou coucut; Tè, l'co, tèl!; Uno jionto postouro; La pastoura als camps; Pastourelle; La pastrouletta è lo chibaliè; Lou boussu; Malurous qu'o uno fenno; Jou l'pount d'o Mirabel; Pastorale.
Frederica von Stade *mez* **Royal Philharmonic Orchestra / Antonio de Almeida.**
Sony Classical Essential Classics SBK63063 (73 minutes: DDD). Recorded 1980s. Ⓑ

Maurice Emmanuel's arrangements of his local Burgundian folk-songs are obvious antecedents to what Canteloube was to do a decade or two later. Although none of these songs seems destined to become a popular hit, the pithier style does have its attractions. This is the second disc that Dawn Upshaw has devoted primarily to Canteloube's *Songs of the Auvergne*. Upshaw and Nagano seem to have taken a conscious decision to re-establish a link with the music's folk texts and banish as much sentimentality as they can. Their 'Baïlèro' is keenly dramatized and positively refuses to wallow. The simple 'Pour l'enfant' is bright-eyed with detail; and 'L'ïo dè rotso' is given a more sarcastic edge than usual. In general, there is a grittiness to the performances here that sets them apart from most other recordings, thanks to Upshaw's determination to put across the words and Nagano's restraint in the orchestra, encouraging cool strings to let the bright Lyon wind section pipe through clearly. Perhaps we do scent more of the smells of the countryside in this version. The Sony selection with Frederica von Stade is an old friend. Two sets of recordings have been combined and all the best-known songs are here in more conventional performances than are found on the Erato disc. Von Stade varies her tone according to the sense of each song, but the overall mood is less sharp, more comfortable if you like, than with Upshaw. The Royal Philharmonic Orchestra sounds a lot richer than its Lyon counterpart and, at generally slower speeds, Antonio de Almeida provides big-orchestra accompaniments, where Nagano prefers chamber-music detail. The record-buying public will probably find that the consoling romanticism of the *Songs of the Auvergne*, as they appear on this tried-and-trusted disc, is more what they had in mind.

Vincenzo Capirola Italian 1474-after 1548

Capirola Lutebook – Ricercare I; Padoana alla francesca I; De tous biens pleine; Et in terra; Qui tollis.
Milano Ricercars Nos. 9, 12, 34, 84 and 88. Fantasias Nos. 28, 31, 33 and 36. Las je m'y plains. De mon triste desplaisir.
Spinacino Three Recercares. Malor me bat. Adieu mes amours.
Christopher Wilson *lte*
Metronome METCD1025 (50 minutes: DDD). Recorded 1987.   (F)

When this recording was first issued on Hyperion in 1987 Italian lute music was an area far less generally known than it is today, but the disc remains an outstanding one. The staples of the lute's repertory are those of dances, solo versions of and variations on songs, intabulations (arrangements) of vocal music (chansons, motets and the like) and fantasias or ricercars. This recording focuses on the last two of these, interrupted by only one dance. The ricercar or fantasia (the terms are virtually synonymous) grew out of the improvised prelude or *tastar de corde*, as a contrapuntal piece marked by imitative voices. The point (opening motif) was sometimes taken from a work by another composer (Richafort's chanson *De mon triste desplaisir* appears here as both Milano's intabulation and the Fantasia he developed from its opening), but in most cases it was original. The fantasia/ricercar was the first of all purely instrumental forms, independent of the song or dance. All three composers are among the earliest known lutenist-composers: 1997 was the quincentenary of Milano's birth; Capirola's music survives only in a lovingly hand-written manuscript by one of his pupils – a remarkable rarity, and Spinacino's *Intabulatura de lauto* (1507) is the earliest known printed book of lute music. The importance of this repertory is both historical and musical, and no more sensitive, intelligent and persuasive recording of it than this one has yet been made.

André Caplet French 1878-1925

Caplet Suite persane – Nihavend. Légende pour orchestre. Marche triomphale et pompière.
Debussy (orch. Caplet) Children's Corner. Pagodes. Suite bergamasque – Clair de lune.
Rheinland-Pfalz State Philharmonic Orchestra / Leif Segerstam.
Marco Polo 8 223751 (56 minutes: DDD). Recorded 1987.   (F)

The valuable services that André Caplet rendered his friend Debussy – besides the pieces orchestrated here he also completed *Gigues* and *Boîte à joujoux*, scored the *Martyre de Saint-Sébastien* and conducted its first performance – have overshadowed his own gifts as a composer. Colour plays a large part in Caplet's early (1901) *Nihavend*, despite its having originally been scored only for double wind quintet: it is a kind of Rimskian passacaglia or set of variations on a simple, and apparently authentic, Persian melody. The *Légende* of four years later is also an orchestral expansion, from a nonet: a solo saxophone has a prominent role in both versions. Highly charged emotionally and clearly structured, it is disquieting in mood: like the previous piece, it has nothing Debussian about it. The Debussy items are well done, especially *Pagodes*, which culminates in a shimmering web of exotic sound with its combination of celesta, string trills and *glissandos* in contrary motion from two harps.

Conte fantastique. Les prières[a]. Deux divertissements. Deux sonnets[b]. Septet à cordes vocales et instrumentales. Septet.
[a]**Sharon Coste,** [b]**Sandrine Piau** *sops* **Sylvie Deguy** *mez* **Laurence Cabel** *hp*
Ensemble Musique Oblique.
Harmonia Mundi Musique d'abord HMA190 1417 (55 minutes: DDD). Recorded 1992.   (B)

Caplet Choral and song

The music of André Caplet is particularly haunting, and surely few listeners will fail to respond to the evocative opening of the chamber version of his *Conte fantastique* for harp and strings based on Poe's *Masque of the Red Death*. It is dramatic too, but far from lurid in its menace, with the harp itself chiming to represent Death. The other three major works on this disc are even more appealing and often quite ravishing. The composer makes a memorable success of the combination of voices, harp and string quartet, helped by lovely singing, sensitive playing, and warmly atmospheric sound. Two solo *Divertissements* for harp make a central interlude. If you enjoy Ravel's chamber music, you are bound to respond to this captivating Caplet anthology.

Manuel Cardoso Portuguese 1566-1650

Missa Miserere mihi Domine. Magnificat Secundi Toni.
Ensemble Vocal Européen / Philippe Herreweghe.
Harmonia Mundi HMC90 1543 (52 minutes: DDD). Texts and translations included.
Recorded 1994. Ⓕ🄴

One wonders what the seventeenth-century Portuguese composer Manuel Cardoso, for most of his life a monk at a Carmelite monastery in Lisbon, would have made of the idea that his music would enjoy a revival in the 1990s. This recording of his *Missa Miserere mihi Domine* (a first) from the Ensemble Vocal Européen is a further – and very welcome – contribution to our knowledge and appreciation of the flowering of sacred polyphony in Portugal in the first half of the seventeenth century, music that, seen in a wider European context, seems 'out of phase with its time' (to quote the accompanying notes). With music as fine as this, however, any latter-day perception of an unbroken line of musical progress seems completely irrelevant. Cardoso's setting, highly reminiscent of Victoria with its never-ending sequence of suspensions, is up there with the best. Only the more straightforward, five-voice *Magnificat* lightens the tone of a disc that otherwise wallows in glorious misery. The choir sings superbly, responding sensitively to the words and creating a full and sonorous sound that well suits Cardoso's music. Full credit, too, to Herreweghe – and the Harmonia Mundi technicians – for achieving such an exceptionally satisfactory balance between the voice parts.

Elliott Carter American 1908

Piano Concerto. Concerto for Orchestra. Three Occasions.
Ursula Oppens *pf*
South West German Radio Symphony Orchestra / Michael Gielen.
Arte Nova Classics 74321 27773-2 (62 minutes: DDD). Recorded 1992. Ⓢ

Oppens and Gielen have collaborated in a recording of the Piano Concerto before, and their long familiarity with the work brings an air of confidence to an account which is admirable in its feeling for the essential character as well as the formal logic of a score whose shoals of notes will defeat all but the most dedicated of interpreters. Gielen's ability to bring a convincing sense of shape and a persuasive expressive profile to complex music is no less apparent in an admirable reading of the *Concerto for Orchestra*. Again and again, the solo lines marked in the score are brought out, although the recording isn't able to give ideal clarity to the highly detailed string writing (a compositional problem, perhaps). But Gielen's is as compelling a presentation of this turbulent yet strangely affirmative music as one could hope to hear. In *Three Occasions* Gielen (in what appears to be a public performance, though the booklet makes no mention of it) is weighty, perhaps to excess in the often delicate third piece. Nevertheless, the interpretation is full of character, and the orchestra confirms its excellence in this demanding repertory. Recommended, despite the inadequate insert-notes.

Wind Quintet. Eight Etudes and a Fantasy. Quartet-Sonata. Esprit rude/Esprit doux.
Enchanted Preludes.
Ensemble Contrasts (Michael Faust *fl* Christian Hommel *ob* David Smeyers *cl* Dag Jensen *bn* Volker Grewel *hn* Johannes Wohlmacher Georg Faust *vcs* Ilton Wjuniski *hpd*).
CPO CPO999 453-2 (55 minutes: DDD). Recorded 1995.

This disc underlines the differences between the earlier and later Carter: the neo-classical disciple of Nadia Boulanger in the Wind Quintet and wind quartet *Etudes*, the senior expressionist in the two short duos. But there's also an in-between Carter, and the most substantial and rewarding work here is the Sonata for flute, oboe, cello and harpsichord, written in 1952 immediately after the visionary

First String Quartet in which Carter renounced easygoing neo-classicism, while reinforcing those virtues of control and clarity which he had learned from Boulanger. The *Quartet-Sonata*, as it's known, is a marvellous piece, brimming with musical energy and offering that unmistakable Carterian blend of toughness and refinement. It is rarely heard in the concert hall, and this performance does the work justice. The recording solves most of its tricky balance problems, even though the wind instruments seem rather too closely miked, and the harpsichord has all the necessary features, as meticulously notated in the score. The early pieces for wind ensemble are more lightweight, their rhythmic procedures more interesting than melody or harmony. Indeed, the Quintet from 1948 is not a million miles from the civilized pattern-making of a Jean Françaix: nothing wrong with that, but it's just not Carter! The rewards of his rejection of such traditional thinking are abundantly evident in *Esprit rude/Esprit doux* (1984) and *Enchanted Preludes* (1988). Other excellent recordings of these works can be found, but the inclusion of the *Quartet-Sonata* makes this a particularly valuable disc.

String Quartet No. 5. Duo. Cello Sonata. Fragment. Figment. 90+.
Ursula Oppens *pf* **Arditti Quartet** (Irvine Arditti, Graeme Jennings *vns* Garth Knox *va* Rohan de Saram *vc*).
Auvidis Montaigne MO782091 (76 minutes: DDD). Recorded 1996.   Ⓕ

There is a 47-year time-span for the compositions on this hugely rewarding disc, and comparison of the earliest and most recent works underlines that, for Carter, there has been no turning back. While casting a few glances over its shoulder at the fast-disappearing world of neo-classicism, the Cello Sonata (1948) is well on the way to Carter's own personal brand of modernism, and the Fifth String Quartet (1994-95) is a notably intense distillation of that arrestingly personal style. The quartet is by some way the toughest item included, a lattice of eloquently shaped, persistently diverse fragments, whose moments of continuity are the more telling for their rarity. This is the kind of musical discourse in which silence can be as highly charged as sound, and there's little of the kind of loquacious yet never incoherent exuberance that makes the Cello Sonata such a joy, and which is realized to admiration in this superbly characterized performance by Rohan de Saram and Ursula Oppens. An even more powerful shaping of dialogue in terms of a constantly shifting kaleidoscope of similarities and differences can be heard in the *Duo* for violin and piano (1973-74). Irvine Arditti and Ursula Oppens ensure that the music's epic voyage grips as strongly as ever, even though the dryish recording makes their reading sound almost superhumanly effortless. With three of Carter's typically resourceful late miniatures, rather clinically but very clearly recorded, and all played with outstanding sympathy and technical skill, this is an indispensable addition to the Carter discography.

Dario Castello   Italian 1590-1644

Castello Sonate concertate, in stil moderno, libro secondo – Nos. 5, 8, 10, 11, 13, 14 and 17.
Picchi Canzoni da sonar con ogni sorte d'istromenti – Canzoni XIV, XV, XVII, XVIII and XIX.
Toccata. Ballo Ungaro. Padoana ditta la Ongara.
His Majestys Sagbutts and Cornetts.
Hyperion CDA67013 (75 minutes: DDD). Recorded 1997.   Ⓕ

The title of this disc, 'The Floating City', seems ironic at a time when the Adriatic tides seem to be washing ever more alarmingly over the Piazza San Marco. If Venice sinks, we shall at least have a legacy of fine instrumental music. The music by Dario Castello and Giovanni Picchi broadly represents new and old respectively. Castello is self-consciously modern; the title of the main publication, *Sonate concertate, in stil moderno* (1629), leaves you in no doubt of his fashionable intentions. On the other hand, Picchi's *Canzoni da sonar con ogni sorte d'istromenti*, which appeared in print four years earlier, are altogether more Gabrielian in vein, exploiting contrasting instrumental groups in impressive full-textured sonority. The juxtaposition of the two constitutes a convincing programme (delightfully thrown off by Picchi's wild Frescobaldi-like *Toccata*, magically played by harpsichordist Timothy Roberts).

The considerable strengths of this disc as a whole range from the poised and instinctive ensemble of the sackbuts to the sweet timbral properties of the cornetto-playing which consistently presents a dialogue of irresistible *élan*. This is playing of a high order, reinforced by the expressive coloration, virtuosity and rhythmic verve that keeps the sectionalized Castello on the straight and narrow. The energy in his Sonata No. 11 *a 3* (this enigmatic figure was remarkably specific in choosing instrumental dispositions) for violins is also a high point, not always flawless but notably risk-orientated. Most strikingly, the players supremely judge the quixotic essence of Castello – the last track is a gem – and bring suitable authority to the larger consorts.

Mario Castelnuovo-Tedesco

Italian/American 1895-1968

Castelnuovo-Tedesco Guitar Concerto No. 1 in D major, Op. 99.
Rodrigo Concierto de Aranjuez.
Villa-Lobos Guitar Concerto.
Norbert Kraft *gtr*
Northern Chamber Orchestra / Nicholas Ward.
Naxos 8 550729 (60 minutes: DDD). Recorded 1992. Ⓢ

The time has long passed when it was possible to point to any one recording of any of these concertos (the Rodrigo in particular) as 'The Best'; as with players, one can only discern a 'top bracket' within which choice depends finally on personal preference – or allegiance to one's favourite performer, or indeed with the other works on the disc. Norbert Kraft's accounts of these concertos takes its place therein. In this recording Kraft is placed forwardly enough for every detail to be heard, but not to create an impression of artificiality. The Northern Chamber Orchestra plays with freshness and is alert to every detail and the beautifully clear recording catches it faithfully. At super-budget price this disc is an exceptional bargain.

Castelnuovo-Tedesco Violin Concerto No. 2, 'I profeti'.
Ferguson Violin Sonata No. 1, Op. 2.
Françaix String Trio in C major.
K. Khachaturian Violin Sonata in G minor, Op. 1.
Jascha Heifetz *vn* Joseph de Pasquale *va* Gregor Piatigorsky *vc* Lilian Steuber *pf*
Los Angeles Philharmonic Orchestra / Alfred Wallenstein.
RCA Victor Gold Seal GD87872 (69 minutes: ADD). Recorded 1954-66. ⓂⒽ

Heifetz's recorded legacy is particularly rewarding for reasons other than the simple fact that he was a great violinist. He obviously liked to get away from standard repertoire and explore the byways of violin literature. He gave much attention to music of his own time – nothing too 'modern', mark you; and he clearly enjoyed the experience of playing chamber works with other great artists. Castelnuovo-Tedesco's Second Violin Concerto, written for Heifetz in 1933, is a very colourful, immediately enjoyable work. Sub-titled *I profeti* ('The Prophets'), the names of Isaiah, Jeremiah and Elijah head its three movements. Heifetz clearly relishes the score's attractive lyricism, and Wallenstein's conducting is full of personality too. The 1954 stereo recording is more than adequate. Howard Ferguson wrote his First Violin Sonata in 1931, when he was 23. This is a gently flowing, somewhat reflective piece, apart from a brief central *Allegro furioso* movement, to which Heifetz responds with alacrity. Elsewhere his rather sharp-toned, virtuoso approach tends to be somewhat at odds with the work's nature, and a rather close recording does not help. He is more suited to the early Sonata of Karen Khachaturian, who is Aram Khachaturian's nephew. On the evidence of this work, like his uncle, Karen writes in an outgoing, vigorous, uncomplicated style, which Heifetz plays in a cheerful, extrovert fashion. The recording was made at the same sessions as the Ferguson sonata (in 1966). Françaix's String Trio is a typically brief, slight, but cleverly written piece, and here Heifetz and his two colleagues relax to give a delightfully spry, pithy performance, which is matched with a good 1964 recording. The noise of tuning between two movements may come as a surprise here!

Emmanuel Chabrier

French 1841-1894

Suite pastorale. Habanera. España. Larghetto. Prélude pastoral. Joyeuse marche.
Gwendoline – Overture. Le roi malgré lui – Fête polonaise.
Ronald Janezic *vn* **Vienna Philharmonic Orchestra / Sir John Eliot Gardiner.**
DG 447 751-2GH (66 minutes: DDD). Recorded 1995. ⒻⓈⒺ ⓇⓇ

For more than 40 years the Detroit SO/Paray recording on Mercury has held top place in our affections when Chabrier's orchestral music is wanted. Now Gardiner has entered the orchestral fray, and aided by superbly responsive playing by the Vienna Philharmonic and first-class recording that, while warm, leaves all detail clear, sweeps the board with a set of outstanding, exuberant performances. The early *Larghetto* for horn and orchestra is the least characteristic of the composer, being a long-breathed, lyrical piece in the romantic tradition: it is played with quiet mastery by Ronald Janezic. But the *Suite pastorale* of five years later is quintessential Chabrier. Poulenc described the 'Idylle' as being as heady as one's first kiss; and light-footed as the 'Danse villageoise' is here, with telling cross-accents and a splendidly rowdy end, and spruce the 'Scherzo-valse', given subtle rhythmic flexibility, it is 'Sous bois', lush in tone, which is utterly enchanting. *España*, that ever-fresh centrepiece, is enormously ebullient; but for all its verve, its internal balance is excellent throughout, the brass brilliant but never drowning out the ornamental subsidiary phrases. In contrast, the *Habanera* is suitably languorous. The Overture to *Gwendoline* – the nearest Chabrier came to Wagnerism – has one clinging to the edge of one's seat in the agitated urgency of the opening and the blazing ferocity of its final pages; and Gardiner brings well-managed rubato to the noisy orgy of the *Roi malgré lui* scene. Judging by the speed at which he takes it, he seems to have had French *chasseurs* in mind for the brash *Joyeuse marche*, which the orchestra obviously enjoyed. Altogether an exhilarating disc.

Chabrier España. Suite pastorale. Joyeuse marche. Bourrée fantasque. Le roi malgré lui – Fête polonaise; Danse slave. Gwendoline – Overture.
Roussel Suite in F major, Op. 33.
Detroit Symphony Orchestra / Paul Paray.
Mercury 434 303-2MM (68 minutes: ADD). Recorded 1957-60.   Ⓜ H

Paray's classic Chabrier collection radiates a truly life-enhancing spontaneity, an all-too-rare commodity in this day and age. His *España* has to be one of the most twinklingly good-humoured ever committed to disc – an account overflowing with rhythmic panache and unbuttoned exuberance – whilst the adorable *Suite pastorale* has rarely sounded so fresh-faced and sheerly disarming, even though Paray's very swift 'Sous bois' does admittedly take some getting use to. The excerpts from *Le roi malgré lui* are dispatched with memorable theatrical charisma and huge gusto, qualities which extend to a blistering rendition of the remarkable, almost feverish overture to *Gwendoline*. But Paray reserves perhaps his finest achievement for the uproarious *Joyeuse marche* and *Bourrée fantasque* (an astonishingly quick-witted, vital conception). The orchestra respond with irrepressible spirit and characteristic Gallic poise, and the Mercury engineering astonishes in its intrepidly wide range of dynamic and full-blooded brilliance (just sample those wonderfully hefty bass-drum thwacks towards the end of *España*). All this and Roussel's bustling, neo-classical *Suite* too! An irresistible confection.

Dix Pièces pittoresques. Pièces posthumes. Impromptu in C major. Trois valses romantiques[a].
Kathryn Stott, [a]Elizabeth Burley *pfs*
Unicorn-Kanchana DKPCD9158 (74 minutes: DDD). Recorded 1994.   Ⓕ

Listening to these delectable performances of piano pieces by Chabrier it is easy to see why alert musical minds like Ravel and Poulenc held him in such admiration. Cortot declared that his style of piano writing was unique; this may have been partly due to Chabrier's brilliance in keyboard improvisation, a talent which he was delighted to show off, and whose sometimes unstructured nature is illustrated in No. 8 of the *Pièces pittoresques* and, more particularly, in his early *Impromptu* in C major (described by Poulenc as 'ravishing') and also in the 'Caprice' of the *Pièces posthumes*. Throughout the disc Kathryn Stott is at her most sparkling and subtle best, with ebullient gaiety in the 'Scherzo-valse', fragile delicacy in the gentle 'Sous bois', rhythmic gusto in the 'Danse villageoise', quiet lyricism in 'Idylle' (all from the *Pièces pittoresques*), and wistful charm in 'Feuillet d'album' and enchanting lightness in 'Ballabile' (from the *Pièces posthumes*): there is freshness and imaginative nuance in evidence everywhere. She is joined by Elizabeth Burley in neat, scintillatingly spirited performances of the two-piano *Trois valses romantiques* – only the third of which really lives up to its title (with playful filigree decoration): the Second is coquettishly lyrical, the First just sheer fun. Aided by first-class recording, this is an immensely enjoyable disc.

Cécile Chaminade   French 1857-1944

Piano Sonata in C minor, Op. 21. Rigaudon, Op. 55 No. 6. Les Sylvains, Op. 60. Arabesque, Op. 61. Prelude in D minor, Op. 84 No. 3. Troisième valse brillante, Op. 80. Inquiétude, Op. 87 No. 3. Quatrième valse, Op. 91. Valse-Ballet, Op. 112. Album des enfants – Book 1, Op. 123: No. 4, Rondeau; No. 5, Gavotte; No. 9, Orientale; No. 10, Tarantelle; Book 2, Op. 126: No. 1, Idylle; No. 2, Aubade; No. 9, Patrouille; No. 10, Villanelle. Le passé, Op. 127 No. 3. Cortège (Fragment), Op. 143. Sérénade espagnole, Op. 150.
Peter Jacobs *pf*
Hyperion CDA66846 (74 minutes: DDD). Recorded 1995.   Ⓕ

Cécile Chaminade's craftsmanship, talent for graceful melodic inventiveness, easy natural charm and effective keyboard writing are indisputable even by those whose tastes are for more elaborate or more solid fare. This volume from Peter Jacobs offers eight of her children's pieces of Opp. 123 and 126 – small but far from the conventional pap so often palmed off on children, as is shown by the scintillating *Tarantelle* (which is not all that easy!). There are more substantial concert works here too: the emotional *Le passé*, the once very popular *Sérénade espagnole* which Kreisler took up, and the immensely engaging *Troisième valse brillante*. Since Chaminade is usually thought of as a miniaturist, however, the big eye-opener here is a relatively early C minor Sonata which, if not a masterpiece, reveals that as well as knowing her Chopin and Schumann she had a firm sense of form and an enviable abundance of ideas; the lyrical *Andante* is unexpectedly thoughtful, and the spirited finale goes well beyond Norman Demuth's rather patronizing remark that she was 'nearly a genius who knew what and how to write for pianists of moderate ability' – which perhaps is best exemplified here in a brilliant D minor *Prelude* that sounds harder than it is. As before, Peter Jacobs shows himself to be fluent, clean-fingered, elegantly delicate where required, and able to invest the music with fine nuances of tone and pace – an ideal interpreter of Chaminade.

Gustave Charpentier French 1860-1956

Louise.
Berthe Monmart *sop* Louise; **André Laroze** *ten* Julien; **Louis Musy** *bar* Father;
Solange Michel *mez* Mother;
Paris Opéra-Comique Chorus and Orchestra / Jean Fournet.
Philips mono 442 082-2PM3 (three discs: 163 minutes: ADD). Notes, text and translation
included. Recorded 1956. Ⓜ Ⓗ

This recording has an air of authority and authenticity throughout. All the principals were members of the company at the Opéra-Comique during the 1950s, when Jean Fournet was its Music Director. Berthe Monmart may not be the soprano of one's dreams, but her singing is full of charm, and she achieves complete conviction. All the singers have well-nigh perfect diction – essential in this supreme example of French *verismo*. What genius Charpentier mustered for this one work. When the Father makes his entrance in Act 1, to his 'tired' music and asks if the soup is ready, the psychological portrait is completed – mother/father/daughter, caught in this early picture of youth in rebellion. Musy's career had begun in the 1920s, and he had sung the entire baritone repertory at the Opéra-Comique before becoming its director of productions. André Laroze is the real thing – a French tenor. In the duet that follows 'Depuis le jour' he and Monmart get up steam in fine ecstatic fashion. Fournet's pacing of the score achieves excitement at the climactic moments, the lovers' duets, Louise's almost hysterical apostrophe to Paris in the closing scene, while making the faintly mystical opening of Act 2 a miniature poem, with its street cries and little ripples of *chanson*. The mono sound is amazingly vivid – you are swept along by its fresh sense of theatricality and by the true *opéra-comique* style of all concerned.

Louise (abridged version).
Ninon Vallin *sop* Louise; **Georges Thill** *ten* Julien **André Pernet** *bass* Father;
Aimée Lecouvreur *mez* Mother; **Christiane Gaudel** *mez* Irma;
Rougel Chorus; Orchestra / Eugène Bigot.
Nimbus Prima Voce mono NI7829 (69 minutes: ADD). Recorded 1935. Ⓜ Ⓗ Ⓔ

The première of *Louise* took place at the Opéra-Comique in April 1900 and it now seems to be coming back into fashion for its centenary in 2000. With this in mind, this reissue of Nimbus's transfer of this beloved 'abridged version' made by the composer in 1935 is timely. At the very first moment, the spell works, with Georges Thill's clarion voice calling up the hill in Montmartre for his lover. As can be seen in Abel Gance's famous film of the opera, made in 1938, Thill was a trifle stiff as an actor, visually, but the power and passion of his vocal acting is heart-stopping. Until you've heard him you don't know just how heroic French tenors can be like. Vallin's voice was sometimes described as mezzo-soprano and her version of 'Depuis le jour' is robust, with more urgency about it than many modern sopranos put into it. The scenes chosen here concentrate on Louise, Julien and Louise's father – her mother and all those extras and crowds don't get much of a hearing. The final scene, the terrible family row between Louise and her father – the first resounding blow struck for modern feminism in a modern opera – is the greatest moment in this recording, Vallin and André Pernet generating enough electricity to light up the Eiffel Tower. The sound is very well reproduced. This adorable opera is heard to great advantage in Fournet's complete recording, but this historic glimpse of the opera, under the supervision of the composer, is one of the most delightful and important of all historic recordings.

Marc-Antoine Charpentier French 1643-1704

Concert pour quatre parties de violes, H545. Il faut rire et chanter: Dispute de bergers, H484. La pierre philosophale, H501. Airs – Ah! Qu'ils sont courts les beaux jours, H442. Ah qu'on est

malheureux, H443. Ah, laissez-moi rêver, H441. Auprès du feu l'on fait l'amour, H446. Ayant bu du vin claret, H447. Charmantes fleurs naissez, H449b. En vain rivaux assidus, H452. Fenchon, la gentile Fenchon, H454. Non, non je ne l'aime plus, H455. Quoi! Je ne verrai plus, H461. Quoi! rien ne peut vous arrêter, H462. Rentrez, trop indescrets soupirs, H464. Sans frayeur dans ce bois – Chaconne, H467. Tristes déserts, sombre retraîte, H469.
Sophie Daneman, Adèle Eikenes, Patricia Petibon *sops* **Paul Agnew, Andrew Sinclair, François Piolino** *tens* **David le Monnier** *bar* **Alan Ewing** *bass*
Ensemble Orlando Gibbons; Les Arts Florissants / William Christie.
Erato 3984-25485-2 (74 minutes: DDD). Texts and translations included.   Ⓕ ℗ 🄴

Here is a delightfully constructed programme, of which only the tenderly expressive *Concert pour quatre parties de violes* has made previous appearances on disc. But it is the way in which William Christie has dispersed its six movements irregularly within a longer sequence of mainly continuo airs for one and two solo voices that lends particular charm to the programme, ensuring at the same time a consistently high and diverting musical interest. The four-strand string *Concert* is a piece of outstanding merit, beautifully crafted and affectingly expressive. Ensemble Orlando Gibbons plays with tonal warmth, rhythmic suppleness and insight into the subtle inflective nuances present in each and every section of the piece. The texture is light and transparent, which it needs to be in order to disclose the sheer beauty of the harmonies and phrase contours. After the *Concert* it is the *airs sérieux*, all but one of which are supported solely by continuo, that most readily engage your interest. The odd one out is *Charmantes fleurs naissez* for two sopranos and, in this performance, sporting two recorders. It's a ravishing piece, sung with sensibility by Sophie Daneman and Adèle Eikenes. Daneman's performance of it is accomplished, her subtle blend of theatre and chamber styles paying off handsomely. Paul Agnew has four solo airs which he sings with declamatory elegance and a feeling for their expressive intensity. The *à boire* element is represented by three lively airs for two- and three-voice ensembles. The remaining components in the programme are *La pierre philosophale*, a short *divertissement*, and a single *scène pastorale*, *Il faut rire et chanter: Dispute de bergers*. They date from the 1680s and both are musically delightful. *La pierre philosophale* is a comedy by Thomas Corneille and Donneau de Visée, for which Charpentier provided music for one of its five acts. If we mention a Menuet for a little gnome, and a chorus, during which another rises out of the ground, you will quickly get an idea of the high seriousness of the spectacle. Charpentier's contribution probably saved the day. Living up to its name, there is much laughter and singing in the *Dispute de bergers*. The story-line is Indian paper-thin, but Charpentier's score, in 11 short sections, is characteristically animated and entertaining. Christie brings it to life with all his customary flair and the performance is captivating from start to finish. In short, this disc is a winner.

Leçons de Ténèbres du Vendredi Saint.
Agnès Mellon *sop* **Ian Honeyman** *ten* **Jacques Bona** *bar*
Il Seminario Musicale / Gérard Lesne *counterten*
Virgin Classics Veritas VC7 59295-2 (71 minutes: DDD). Texts and translations included.
Recorded 1994.   Ⓕ ℗

Charpentier wrote many settings of the *Tenebrae*, or *Leçons de Ténèbres* as they were known in France, and they invariably inspired him to great heights of expressive intensity. Their texts come from the *Lamentations of Jeremiah the Prophet*, but are interspersed with affective, ornamental, melismatic phrases inspired by letters of the Hebrew alphabet. In addition to the *Leçons* the sequence includes Antiphons and Responses as well as plainchants with their faburdens for the Psalms, and occasional instrumental ritornellos. Not quite all of this music is by Charpentier. There are, for instance, pieces by Nivers, one of the greatest French organists of the time, included in the sequence; but though most of the assembled chants with their harmonizing faburdens were common property of the Catholic Church throughout Europe, one faburden at least is by Charpentier (H156). The French baroque *Leçons de Ténèbres* are deeply moving, with their distinctive blend of Italian monodic *lamentazioni* and French *airs de cour*. The idiom allows for dramatically highly charged effects and, in the hands of Charpentier, such effects are often realized with thrilling suspensions, dissonances and impassioned declamation. Indeed, with Charpentier one often senses the composer's love for, and experience in writing for, the stage in the many theatrical gestures and in his vividly pictorial handling of the texts. Certainly this highly emotive blend of sacred and secular ingredients resulted in music of extraordinary intensity, none of which is lost on Gérard Lesne and his ensemble, Il Seminario Musicale. They are sensible to the myriad expressive nuances suggested by the texts and realized in music of reflective intensity.

Te Deum, H147. Mass, H1. Precatio pro filio regis, H166. Panis quem ego dabo, H275. Canticum Zachariae, H345, 'Benedictus Dominus Deus'.
Le Concert Spirituel / Hervé Niquet.
Naxos 8'553175 (57 minutes: DDD). Texts and translations included. Recorded 1996.   Ⓢ 🄴

This early Mass is a beautiful piece, intimately scored for voices with two melody instruments and continuo. Charpentier's vocal requirements consist of pairs of sopranos, alto, tenor and bass soloists, with a four-part chorus that splits into two four-part entities for the 'Pleni sunt coeli ... Hosanna' of the *Sanctus*. The Mass is harmonically richly inventive with passages of characteristically vivid word-painting. Taken as a whole the work is perhaps less immediately arresting than the larger-scale Masses that were to follow; yet it is generously endowed with subtle inflexions, a pervasive element of contemplation, and effectively varied rhythmic juxtapositions which enliven the text and hold our attention. Conductor Hervé Niquet has appropriately included an Offertory, *Precatio pro filio regis*, and an Elevation, *Panis quem ego dabo*, to conform with standard practice. The *Te Deum*, for four soloists, four-part choir and *colla parte* instruments, is not that one for which Charpentier is renowned but a smaller, later piece belonging to the last years of his life. Modest in scale it may be but musically it is impressive and emotionally satisfying. The choir and instrumentalists of Le Concert Spirituel are on their usual lively form. Some of the solo vocal contributions are more focused than others but the choir maintains a high standard of vocal blend and secure intonation almost throughout. The recorded sound is very good indeed and all is directed with stylistic assurance by Niquet.

Charpentier Beatus vir, H221. Laudate pueri, H149. Laetatus sum, H216. Nisi Dominus, H150. Lauda Jerusalem, H210. Ave maris stella, H60. Magnificat, H72. Salve regina, H24.
Nivers Antiphonarium Monasticum, Antiennes I-VI.
Le Concert Spirituel / Hervé Niquet.
Naxos 8 553174 (61 minutes: DDD). Texts and translations included. Recorded 1995.   Ⓢ

This release offers a liturgical reconstruction of the Vespers office. The five Vesper psalms and *Magnificat* belong to different periods in Charpentier's life and the six antiphons are not by him at all but by his organist-composer contemporary, Nivers. The reconstruction works well and Le Concert Spirituel, under Hervé Niquet's direction, here demonstrates its rapport with Charpentier's music. The vocal sound is fresh and the wide range of musical *Affekt* shows off a greater diversity of tonal colour. Tenors and basses incline towards a roughness of timbre here and there yet, overall, the bright and full-blooded choral sound is pleasing and vital. Some readers may feel that the recording balance of the psalms and canticle is a fraction too close, creating the atmosphere of a drawing-room Vespers rather than one in more spacious, ecclesiastical surroundings. The antiphons fare much better in this respect, being given a deeper aural perspective. In summary, this is a richly rewarding programme of music which never disappoints.

Actéon.
Dominique Visse *counterten* Actéon; **Agnès Mellon** *sop* Diane; **Guillemette Laurens** *mez* Junon; **Jill Feldman** *sop* Arthébuze; **Françoise Paut** *sop* Hyale;
Les Arts Florissants Vocal Ensemble
La Comtesse d'Escarbagnas/Le Mariage Forcé – Ouverture.
Michel Laplénie *ten* Philippe Cantor *ten*
Les Arts Florissants Instrumental Ensemble / William Christie.
Harmonia Mundi Musique d'abord HMA190 1095 (47 minutes: ADD).
Gramophone Award Winner 1982-83.   Ⓕ

One always feels rather sorry for poor old Actaeon; if you remember, he was caught hiding in the bushes while the Goddess Diana and her followers were bathing. Without being given much of an opportunity to explain himself, Diana turns him into a stag, whereupon he is torn to pieces by his own hounds. Charpentier's little *vignette* opera is an astonishingly rich score containing most, if not all, the ingredients of a *tragédie-lyrique*. There is a profusion of fine choruses and dances but an overture which departs somewhat from the standard Lullian pattern. *Actéon* is made up of six short scenes well contrasted with one another. William Christie directs the work from beginning to end with conviction and assurance. The action is well paced and there is an intensity of expression, a fervour, which gives a touching emphasis to the drama.

Médée.
Lorraine Hunt *sop* Médée; **Bernard Deletré** *bass* Créon; **Monique Zanetti** *sop* Créuse;
Mark Padmore *ten* Jason; **Jean-Marc Salzmann** *bar* Oronte; **Noémi Rime** *sop* Nérine;
Les Arts Florissants / William Christie.
Erato 4509-96558-2 (three discs: 195 minutes: DDD). Texts and translations included.
Recorded 1994.   ⒻⓅ

Lorraine Hunt's Medea is something of a *tour de force*. She invests every word with meaning and produces the widest range of colour to express all the emotional nuances in Medea's complex character – jealousy, indignation, tenderness, sorrow, fury, malignity and outright barbarism: she is especially outstanding in Act 3, one of the most superb acts in all baroque opera, in which she has no fewer than four great monologues, the first with affecting chromatic harmonies, the second accompanied by feverish rushing strings, the third the sombre 'Noires filles du Styx' with its eerie modulations, the fourth with dark orchestral colours. Charpentier's orchestration and texture, indeed, are wonderfully effective: string writing varies between extreme delicacy (beautifully played here) and savage agitation; the cool sound of the recorders is refreshing and the many dances featuring recorders and oboes are enchanting. As Jason, Mark Padmore, a real *haute-contre*, sings with admirable ease and intelligence and the tragic Creusa, poisoned by the vengeful Medea is the light-voiced Monique Zanetti, the very embodiment of youthful innocence and charm: her death scene, still protesting her love for Jason, is most moving. A notable detail in all the principals, incidentally, is their absorption of *agréments*, with Hunt showing special mastery in this regard. There is a large cast for the numerous minor roles, all well taken; and the chorus sings cleanly and with evident commitment. All told, a considerable achievement, and a triumph for Christie.

Ernest Chausson French 1855-1899

Symphony in B flat major, Op. 20. Viviane, Op. 5. Soir de fête, Op. 32. La têmpete – Air de danse; Danse rustique.
BBC Philharmonic Orchestra / Yan Pascal Tortelier.
Chandos CHAN9650 (67 minutes: DDD). Recorded 1997. Ⓕ

There are at least two misconceptions to put right about Franck's arguably most gifted pupil. The first, which this disc dispels admirably, is that the majority of Chausson's music, in the manner of his *Poème*, is endlessly melancholic or elegiac. And the second, which Tortelier's disc doesn't dispel quite so well, is that in his orchestral writing Chausson never managed to free himself from Wagner's embrace. Never *entirely* perhaps, but by the time the 43-year-old composer came to write his last orchestral piece, the nocturnal *Soir de fête* included here, his escape from Wagner was well underway, and who knows where it might have led, had it not been for his tragically early death the following year? The outer sections of *Soir de fête* have something about them of 'the vibrating, dancing rhythms of the atmosphere' of Debussy's later *Fêtes*. The programme as a whole, the overall richness of the orchestral process – whether Wagnerian, Franckian, Straussian (as in the Arthurian sorcerer Merlin's final enchantment by Viviane) or Chaussonian – is well served by the full-bodied sound of Tortelier's BBC Philharmonic. The Symphony, like Franck's, is cyclical, but not otherwise as indebted to the older composer as is often suggested. There are none of Franck's organ-loft sonorities anywhere in Chausson's wonderfully variegated, open-air orchestration. Tortelier here gives us the finest modern recording of the Symphony now available. Each movement is superbly built, and Chandos's recording is truly impressive although in the pastoral pleasures derived from Chausson's incidental music for *The Tempest*, the sound is perhaps a little bulky.

Poème, Op. 25 (arr. cpsr.). Piano Trio in G minor, Op. 3. Andante et Allegro. Pièce, Op. 39.
Charles Neidich *cl* **Philippe Graffin** *vn* **Gary Hoffman** *vc* **Pascal Devoyon** *pf*
Chilingirian Quartet (Levon Chilingirian, Charles Sewart *vns* Asdis Valdimarsdottir *va*
Philip de Groote *vc*).
Hyperion CDA67028 (62 minutes: DDD). Recorded 1997. Ⓕ

The opulent sound of this disc is ideal for Chausson; it especially suits the impassioned early Trio. Devoyon plays the demanding piano part in the grand style, yet the strings are never swamped. In particular, Philippe Graffin's sensuous, unforced tone sails above the texture without any of the strenuous feeling we experience in other performances. All three players sound completely at home, whether in the rhetorical gestures of the work's big moments, or the poised delicacy of the second movement. This Trio, though an early work, is already fully characteristic of Chausson – the way the carefree, day-in-the-country atmosphere at the start of the finale is gradually overtaken by tragic portents very strongly shows his melancholic nature. The *Andante et Allegro* is less individual, but here, too, the performance rises to the occasion – and beyond. Neidich's playing is quite remarkable for its breadth of expression in the *Andante* as well as for the extraordinarily brilliantly articulated *Allegro*. Hoffman and Devoyon are equally convincing in the beautiful, dreamy *Pièce* for cello and piano. The most novel aspect of the disc, paradoxically, concerns the most familiar music: this is the first recording of a newly rediscovered version of the *Poème*, with string quartet and piano accompaniment. As a chamber work, the music's essentially intimate tone is felt more strongly, and Graffin gives a plangent account of the solo part, with something of that sense of freedom that Ysaÿe, the work's sponsor, would certainly have conveyed. The only trouble with the arrangement is the loss of perspective between the soloist and an 'orchestra' led by another solo violin. But the Chilingirian and Devoyon play the sustained 'tutti' music beautifully.

Luigi Cherubini

Italian 1760-1842

Overtures – Ali-Baba; Les Abencérages; Les deux journées; Lodoïska; Médée; Anacréon; Faniska; L'hôtellerie portugaise.
City of Birmingham Symphony Orchestra / Lawrence Foster.
Claves CD50-9513 (70 minutes: DDD). Recorded 1995.   Ⓕ

Cherubini was a musician whom Beethoven regarded as the greatest living composer (when asked to leave himself out of consideration), whom Berlioz vilified in his writings and passionately admired in his music, and is not to be dismissed as a footnote to history. Revivals of *Médée* have demonstrated his mastery of the stage and of instrumental colour, among much else, and many more of his operas, represented here by their overtures, well merit revival. For the curious, this is a good introduction to Cherubini's style. There is the brilliant use of instruments, especially the capacity for individualizing them so that the actual sound bears dramatic expression: this is the true beginning of romantic orchestration, profoundly influential on Weber and thence on Berlioz. There is the rhythmic *élan*, the charge of energy that inspired Beethoven's admiration. There is the shrewd sense of structure, and of using this to encapsulate the drama to come. There is gaiety and brightness. There is, not least, a passion in the invention that seems at odds with the crabbed countenance of the portraits and the tales of the dry contrapuntalist ferociously disciplining his Conservatoire students. Cherubini was a man of contradictions, a composer of, if something short of genius, certainly profound and exciting talent. The enthusiastic performances here are enjoyable in their own right, and suggest his variety and range; they also keep alive hopes that more of his operas may yet be recorded.

Mass No. 1 in C minor. Marche funèbre.
Corydon Singers; Corydon Orchestra / Matthew Best.
Hyperion CDA66805 (54 minutes: DDD). Text and translation included. Recorded 1995.   Ⓕ

It would be an oversimplification to suggest that Matthew Best emphasizes the Beethoven rather than the Berlioz aspect of the main work here; but he does seem less interested in the fascinating use of colour as an element in the actual invention than in the rugged moral strength and the force of the statements. The recording reflects this emphasis, and is firm and clear without being especially subtle over orchestral detail. The choir delivers the *Dies irae* powerfully, and much dramatic vigour is recalled in the fugue traditionally reserved for 'Quam olim Abrahae'. Berlioz, however, was satirical about Cherubini's fugues, and saved his admiration for the wonderful long *decrescendo* that ends the *Agnus Dei*. This is beautifully controlled here. Best includes the tremendous *Marche funèbre*, inspiration here again for Berlioz (especially in his *Hamlet* funeral march). Best handles this superbly, opening with a merciless percussion crash and sustaining the pace and mood unrelentingly. In his hands, it sounds more original than ever, a funeral march that, rather than mourn or honour, rages against the dying of the light.

William Child

British 1606/7-1697

Sing we merrily. O Lord God, the heathen. O bone Jesu. O God, wherefore art thou absent. Jubilate Deo. Psalm Settings – Blessed is the man; O Lord, rebuke me not; I will give thanks unto thee; In the Lord I put my trust; The fool hath said in his heart; Save me O God. Turn thou us, O good Lord. Magnificat and Nunc dimittis. Behold how good and joyful. The earth is the Lord's. O Lord, rebuke me not. Glory be to God on high. Holy, holy, holy. O Lord, grant the King a long life.
Rachel Platt, Rebecca Outram sops **William Towers** counterten **Timothy Mirfin** bass
Gonville and Caius College Choir, Cambridge / Geoffrey Webber
with **Andrew Arthur, Jeremy Bines** orgs
ASV Gaudeamus CDGAU182 (65 minutes: DDD). Texts included. Recorded 1997.   Ⓕ

Remembered principally (or exclusively) for his verse-anthem 'at the Restauration', *O Lord, grant the King a long life*, Dr William Child was certainly granted a good long life for himself, dying at the age of 92. The seventeenth was an interesting century for a church musician to span. Child was a chorister at Bristol Cathedral, graduated from Oxford and was appointed to St George's, Windsor, whence to the Chapel Royal. This of course closed for the duration of the Commonwealth, and Child's anthem, *O Lord God, the heathen are come into thine inheritance*, shows clearly what he thought of that: the words 'Lord, how long?' are made to stand out, and no doubt there was great rejoicing when the year 1660 proclaimed an answer. The selection of works here gives pleasure from beginning to end. The style looks back to the Tudors, forward to Purcell, and takes in a flash of colour from Italy. Child is good with words, occasionally adding a pictorial flourish, as for the flight of a bird or the altitude of God's glory. Fertile in rhythm and harmony, the eight-part writing is finely woven and vigorously sustained. He has a good ear for the combination of voices, the trio for basses in *The earth is the Lord's* being particularly effective and unusual. Likeable too is the Evening Service 'for four means' with its impressive *Gloria* for full choir. All is well performed. The choir sings with fresh tone and clean style. Among the soloists, William Towers and Timothy Mirfin deserve special mention. The accompaniments are neatly played and the acoustic of Jesus College Chapel proves ideal.

Fryderyk Chopin
Polish 1810-1849

Piano Concertos – No. 1 in E minor, Op. 11; No. 2 in F minor, Op. 21.

Piano Concertos Nos. 1 and 2.
Martha Argerich *pf*
Montreal Symphony Orchestra / Charles Dutoit.
EMI CDC5 56798-2 (69 minutes: DDD). Recorded 1998.   Ⓕ **E** **RR**

Martha Argerich's first commercially released recordings of the Chopin concertos were for DG; No. 1 in 1968, No. 2 in 1978. Here she revisits both concertos and offers an act of re-creative daring, of an alternating reverie and passion that flashes fire with a thousand different lights. Indeed, her earlier performances are infinitely less witty, personal and eruptive, less inclined to explore, albeit with the most spontaneous caprice and insouciance, so many new facets, angles and possibilities. Now, everything is accomplished without a care for studios and microphones and with a degree of involvement that suggests an increase rather than a diminution of her love for these works. The recordings, when you stop to notice them, are impressively natural (very much as you would hear these concertos in the concert hall), and if Dutoit occasionally seems awed if not cowed into anonymity by his soloist (the opening tuttis to the slow movements of both concertos are less memorable than they should be) he sets off Argerich's charisma to an exceptional degree. Argerich's light burns brighter than ever. Rarely in their entire history have the Chopin concertos received performances of a more teasing allure, brilliance and idiosyncrasy.

Piano Concertos Nos. 1 and 2. Mazurkas – F minor, Op. 63 No. 2; F minor, Op. 68 No. 4. Waltz in E minor, Op. posth.
Evgeni Kissin *pf*
Moscow Philharmonic Orchestra / Dmitri Kitaienko.
RCA Victor Red Seal 09026 68378-2 (71 minutes: ADD). Recorded live in 1984.   Ⓜ

Here is a living rather than fabricated example of just what is possible from a 12-year-old genius. It is no exaggeration to say that these performances, taken from a 1984 Moscow concert, are among the most phenomenally assured and meteoric of any on record. Every page blazes with youthful confidence and a stylistic know-how that would be astonishing from a pianist twice Kissin's age. Even at that age he possessed the peculiar attributes of Russian pianism at its greatest, with flawless, even strength and the most full-bodied *cantabile*. True, there are moments (the opening of the F minor Concerto's central *Larghetto*) where he sounds too relentlessly upfront, too aggressively thrusting, and doubtless when he comes to re-record these concertos in his maturity he will find an even wider spectrum of colour and nuance; a greater subtlety. However, it is doubtful whether he will ever surpass the infallible and propulsive brilliance of these performances. The sound is immaculate.

Piano Concertos Nos. 1 and 2.
Murray Perahia *pf*
Israel Philharmonic Orchestra / Zubin Mehta.
Sony Classical SK44922 (76 minutes: DDD). Recorded live in 1989.   Ⓕ

Despite the attendant hazards, Perahia has never made any secret of his liking for the 'inspirational heat-of-the-moment' of a live performance as opposed to a studio recording, where 'sometimes things get tame'. As enthusiastic audience applause (albeit discreetly rationed on the disc) makes plain, these two concertos were in fact recorded live at Tel Aviv's Mann Auditorium. Whether they were subsequently 'doctored' we don't know, but the finished product brings us a Perahia miraculously combining exceptional finesse with an equally exceptional urgency. In all but the finale of No. 1 (where Pollini on EMI beats him by a minute) his timings throughout both works are considerably faster than most of his rivals on disc. Was this prompted by 'inspirational heat-of-the-moment'? Or was it a deliberate attempt to come closer than others do to the surprisingly briskish metronome markings printed in the Eulenburg scores? The two slow movements are distinguished *by* exquisitely limpid *cantabile* and superfine delicacy of decorative detail while again conveying more urgent undercurrents than we often hear. But in a guessing-game perhaps it would be the two finales that would most betray the identity of the soloist. Not only are they faster, but also of a more scintillating, *scherzando*-like lightness. The recording is first-rate – not too close, and with ideal balance between the rich-sounding but clearly reproduced Israel Philharmonic and Perahia's glistening piano.

Piano Concertos Nos. 1 and 2.
Krystian Zimerman *pf*
Los Angeles Philharmonic Orchestra / Carlo Maria Giulini.
DG 415 970-2GH (72 minutes: ADD). Recorded 1978. Ⓕ

There's plenty in these youthful Zimerman reissues to explain why he won the 1975 Chopin Contest when still in his teens. Zimerman's light, translucent semiquaver figuration (and sometimes his willingness to stand back and merely accompany – as in certain episodes in the Second Concerto's finale) often conjures up visions of Chopin himself at the keyboard; Chopin was often criticized for insufficiently strong projection. In No. 1 there is a flowing *Romanze* and a propulsive finale. But in both concertos, he is always spirited and characterful. Throughout, Giulini extracts an exceptionally rich *cantabile* from his American orchestra. The recording has a close, ripe sonority, with Zimerman's piano quite forwardly placed.

Piano Concertos Nos. 1ᵃ and 2ᵇ.
Noel Mewton-Wood *pf*
ᵃ**Netherlands Philharmonic Orchestra,** ᵇ**Zurich Symphony Orchestra / Walter Goehr.**
Dante Historical Piano Collection HPC105 (69 minutes: ADD). Recorded *c*1951 and 1948. Ⓕ Ⓗ

Inconsolable after the death of his partner Bill Fredricks, Noel Mewton-Wood (1922-53) committed suicide and robbed the world of a musical genius. Born in Melbourne, he included, in his London-based career, work with Schnabel, a début (in Beethoven's Third Concerto) with Sir Thomas Beecham, the frequent replacement of Benjamin Britten as Peter Pears's musical collaborator and, mercifully for the present generation, the making of several recordings taken from his eclectic and enterprising repertoire. Amazingly, in his incomparably sensitive and robust hands, the Chopin concertos seem as though heard for the first time, their passions and intimacies virtually re-created on the spot. Who of today's pianists would or could risk such candour or phrase and articulate Chopin's early intricacy with such alternating strength and delicacy? The sympathetic insert-notes (in French only) suggest parallels with Solomon, Anatole Kitain and Murray Perahia, yet as with all truly great artists, Mewton-Wood's playing defies comparison, however exalted. No more vital or individual performances exist on record. The orchestra is hardly a model of precision or refinement, but the recordings have come up remarkably well.

Piano Concerto No. 1. Ballade in G minor, Op. 23 . Nocturnes, Op. 15 – No. 1 in F major ; No. 2 in F sharp minor. Nocturnes, Op. 27 – No. 1 in C sharp minor; No. 2 in D flat major. Polonaise No. 6 in A flat major, Op. 53, 'Heroic'.
Maurizio Pollini *pf*
Philharmonia Orchestra / Paul Kletzki.
EMI Studio Plus CDM5 66221-2 (73 minutes: ADD). Recorded 1960-68. Ⓜ

This disc is a classic. The concerto was recorded shortly after the 18-year-old pianist's victory at the Warsaw competition in 1959. Nowadays we might expect a wider dynamic range to allow greater power in the first movement's tuttis, but in all other respects the recording completely belies its age, with a near perfect balance between soloist and orchestra. This is, of course, very much Pollini's disc, just as the First Concerto is very much the soloist's show, but effacing as the accompaniment is, Pollini's keyboard miracles of poetry and refinement could not have been achieved without one of the most characterful and responsive accounts of that accompaniment ever committed to tape. The expressive range of the Philharmonia on top form under Kletzki is at once, and throughout, exceptional, as is the accord between soloist and conductor in matters of phrasing and shading. The solo items are a further reminder of Pollini's effortless bravura and aristocratic poise.

Piano Concerto No. 2. Preludes, Op. 28.
Maria João Pires *pf*
Royal Philharmonic Orchestra / André Previn.
DG 437 817-2GH (74 minutes: DDD). Recorded 1992. Ⓕ

Here, beautifully and responsibly partnered by Previn and the Royal Philharmonic, and recorded with the greatest warmth and clarity, Pires gets the treatment she deserves. What gloriously imposing breadth as well as knife-edged clarity she brings to each phrase and note; absolutely nothing is taken for granted. The intricacy and stylishness of her rubato remind us that the inspiration behind the F minor Concerto was Constantia Gladkowska, a young singer and Chopin's first love. Listen to Pires's *fioritura* in the heavenly *Larghetto* or her way of edging into the finale's scintillating coda and you will gasp at such pianism and originality. Indeed, the opening of her finale may surprise you with its dreaminess (*Allegro vivace*?) but as with all great pianists, even her most extreme ideas are carried through with unshakeable conviction and authority. Pires's 24 Preludes, too, remind us that she is the possessor of one of the most crystalline of all techniques. More importantly, her way with the more interior numbers among Chopin's teeming and disparate moods is of exceptional drama and intensity. Understatement plays little part in her conception and those who prefer the more classically biased playing of artists such as Pollini are in for some surprises. You will rarely hear Chopin playing of greater mastery or calibre. In her own scrupulously modern way she surely embodies the spirit of the great pianists of the past; of Kempff, Edwin Fischer and, most of all, Cortot.

Piano Concertos Nos. 1 and 2 (chamber versions).
Fumiko Shiraga *pf*
Jan-Inge Haukås *db* **Yggdrasil Quartet** (Fredrik Paulsson, Per Oman *vns* Robert Westlund *va* Per Nyström *vc*).
BIS CD847 (72 minutes: DDD). Recorded 1996.   Ⓕ

This is one of the most exciting Chopin recordings in recent years because it confronts and deepens the uneasiness that Chopin lovers have with his concertos. They are more comfortable as chamber works, the chamber works he never succeeded in writing when he confronted that form head on. If you find Chopin's ideas inflated when cast in orchestral form, this recording will remove the last traces of doubt. Pianist Fumiko Shiraga has reduced the scope of the music, and wisely so. The heroism and grandeur is of the sort one finds in Schumann's piano-chamber context, the dynamic and expressive extremes that Shiraga achieves are no less compelling than a pianist unleashed against a large orchestra. Shiraga doubles in some tutti passages – a surprise at first, but again a wise decision. She adds gravity and fullness to the Yggdrasil Quartet's excellent accompaniment while remaining hidden, diligently underscoring but never overbearing.

Piano Trio in G minor, Op. 8. Cello Sonata in G minor, Op. 65. Introduction and Polonaise brillant in C major, Op. 3 (versions for pf, vc and pf, arr. Feuermann).
Pamela Frank *vn* **Yo-Yo Ma** *vc* **Emanuel Ax, Eva Osinska** *pfs*
Sony Classical SK53112 (72 minutes: DDD). Recorded 1989-92.   Ⓕ

This most welcome reminder of the 'chamber music' Chopin starts with his G minor Piano Trio (1828-29) dedicated to his compatriot, the music-loving would-be composer-cum-cellist, Prince Radziwill. Rarely has it enjoyed what might be termed 'bigger-named' rescue on disc. For even if Chopin's beloved piano gets the best of it, a performance as imaginatively characterized as this makes you salute the teenage work anew. Despite the procrustean (for Chopin) demands of sonata-form, the minor-key challenges of the opening *Allegro con fuoco* are conveyed with appealing urgency before the amiable grace of the *Scherzo*, the smouldering romance of the *Adagio sostenuto* and the dance-like gaiety of the finale. Shortly after accepting the Trio's dedication, Prince Radziwill invited Chopin to stay at his country estate – hence the Op. 3 *Polonaise brillant* in C (the slow introduction came later) for the Prince to play with his bewitching 17-year-old pianist daughter. Here, Yo-Yo Ma chooses Emanuel Feuermann's reworking of the cello part – as Chopin himself might well have enhanced it with decorative *fioriture* had the Prince's fingers been as agile as his daughter's. More importantly, the disc offers what is thought to be the first recording of this work in a solo-piano version, recently discovered by the Polish pianist-musicologist Jan Weber. It is played here with spirited affection by Weber's pupil, Eva Osinska. The mature Cello Sonata receives a tactfully balanced, persuasively fluid performance from Yo-Yo Ma and Emanuel Ax that ranks with the best of its rivals. The recording is vivid and true.

Cello Sonata in G minor, Op. 65. Polonaise brillante in C major, Op. 3 (ed. Feuermann). Grande duo concertante in E major on themes from Meyerbeer's 'Robert le Diable'. Nocturne in C sharp minor, Op. posth. (arr. Piatigorsky). Etude in E minor, Op. 25 No. 7 (arr. Glazunov). Waltz in A minor, Op. 34 No. 2 (arr. Ginzburg). Etude in D minor, Op. 10 No. 6 (arr. Glazunov).
Maria Kliegel *vc* **Bernd Glemser** *pf*
Naxos 8 553159 (64 minutes: DDD). Recorded 1994.   Ⓢ

Here are Chopin's complete works for cello and piano complemented by an intriguing garland of encores. Performed with a relish inseparable from youth, impressively balanced and recorded, this is a notable offering, particularly at Naxos's super-bargain price. Clearly, Kliegel and Glemser have few reservations concerning the sonata's surprisingly Germanic overtones. Recognizably Chopin in virtually every bar there remains an oddly Schumannesque bias, particularly in the finale's tortuous argument – an irony when you consider that Chopin had so little time for his adoring colleague. Yet this awkward and courageous reaching out towards a terser form of expression is resolved by both artists with great vitality and, throughout, they create an infectious sense of a live rather than studio performance. Kliegel and Glemser are no less uninhibited in Chopin's earlier show-pieces, written at a time when the composer had a passing passion for grand opera and for what he himself dismissed as 'glittering trifles'. Their additions (transcriptions by Glazunov, Piatigorsky and Ginzburg) remind us how singers, violinists and cellists beg, borrow or steal Chopin from pianists at their peril. As Chopin put it, 'the piano is my solid ground; on that I stand the straightest', and his muse has proved oddly and, indeed, magically resistant to change or transcription. Still, even though the selection often suggests an alien opacity, the performances are, again, most warmly committed.

Four Ballades – No. 1 in G minor, Op. 23; No. 2 in F major, Op. 38; No. 3 in A flat major, Op. 47; No. 4 in F minor, Op. 52.

Ballades Nos. 1-4. Mazurkas – No. 7 in F minor, Op. 7 No. 3; No. 13 in A minor, Op. 17 No. 4; No. 23 in D major, Op. 33 No. 2. Waltzes – No. 1 in E flat major, Op. 18; No. 5 in A flat major, Op. 42; No. 7 in C sharp minor, Op. 64 No. 2. Etudes, Op. 10 – No. 3 in E major; No. 4 in C sharp minor. Nocturne No. 1 in F minor, Op. 15.
Murray Perahia *pf*
Sony Classical SK64399 (61 minutes: DDD). Recorded 1994.
Gramophone Award Winner 1995.   Ⓕ**S**|**E**|**RR**

This is surely the greatest, certainly the richest, of Perahia's many exemplary recordings. Once again his performances are graced with rare and classic attributes and now, to supreme clarity, tonal elegance and musical perspective, he adds an even stronger poetic profile, a surer sense of the inflammatory rhetoric underpinning Chopin's surface equilibrium. In other words the vividness and immediacy are as remarkable as the finesse. And here, arguably, is the oblique but telling influence of Horowitz whom Perahia befriended during the last months of the old wizard's life. Listen to the First *Ballade*'s second subject and you will hear rubato like the most subtle pulsing or musical breathing. Try the opening of the Third and you will note an ideal poise and lucidity, something rarely achieved in these outwardly insouciant pages. From Perahia the waltzes are marvels of liquid brilliance and urbanity. Even Lipatti hardly achieved such an enchanting lilt or buoyancy, such a beguiling sense of light and shade. In the mazurkas, too, Perahia's tiptoe delicacy and tonal irridescence (particularly in Op. 7 No. 3 in F minor) make the music dance and spin as if caught in some magical hallucinatory haze. Finally, two contrasting *Etudes*, and whether in ardent lyricism (Op. 10 No. 3) or shot-from-guns virtuosity (Op. 10 No. 4) Perahia's playing is sheer perfection. The recording beautifully captures his instantly recognizable, glistening sound world.

Ballades Nos. 1-4. Barcarolle in F sharp major, Op. 60. Berceuse in D flat major, Op. 57. Scherzo No. 4 in E major, Op. 54.
Evgeni Kissin *pf*
RCA Red Seal 09026 63259-2 (62 minutes: DDD).   Ⓕ**E**

Kissin plays Chopin with a rhetorical drama, intensity and power that few could equal, an astonishing achievement which shines like a beacon of light. His technique is of an obliterating command, enough to make even his strongest competitors throw up their hands in despair, and yet everything is at the service of a deeply ardent and poetic nature. Listen to his slow and pensive *Andantino* in the Second *Ballade*, its rhythm or thought-pattern constantly halted and checked, the following *presto* storms of such pulverizing force that they will make even the least susceptible hackles rise and fists clench as Jove's thunder roars across the universe. The first subject of the First *Ballade* is daringly slow and inward-looking, the start of the glorious Fourth evoking the feelings of a blind man when first granted the gift of sight, while the *Berceuse* is seen through an opalescent pedal haze that creates its own hallucinatory and rarified atmosphere. The final page of the *Barcarolle* – always among music's most magical homecomings – is given with an imaginative brio known to very few, and the Fourth *Scherzo* is among the most Puckish and highly coloured on record. The recordings are less than ideally beautiful but more than adequate.

Ballades Nos. 1-4. Barcarolle. Fantaisie in F minor, Op. 49.
Krystian Zimerman *pf*
DG 423 090-2GH (60 minutes: DDD).   Ⓕ

With Zimerman there is total surrender to the impulse of the moment. Each piece comes up with all the immediacy of a brand-new discovery. His is musical story-telling at its most arrestingly dramatic, reproduced with a richness and warmth of sonority to match the playing. In the First *Ballade* the way he sustains a feeling of self-evolving growth is admirable. The intensity of his involvement is apparent (even in his breathing) right from the start, but as in all four he holds so very much in reserve for impassioned outbursts to come. No. 2 allows him to give full rein to his liking for the boldest contrasts of both dynamics and tempo, though its two great storms are all the more powerful for not being rushed. And how beautifully he dissolves tumult into the last, plaintive minor-key recall of the opening theme – even if allowing himself a little license in achieving his ends. In the A flat *Ballade* his delight in the unexpected C major tonality in bars 29 to 35 is wholly irresistible, as indeed is his very simple, quiet opening. In the F minor *Ballade* he surely overdoes the pause on that G flat melody note (which Chopin marks only with a *tenuto*) in bar 56. But he plays almost as if composing the music as he goes along. His *Barcarolle* is richly sensuous and passionate. As for the *Fantasie*, rarely will you hear this music given stronger undertones of patriotic protest, pride, and even prayer. The introduction is surely too slow, and here Zimerman reacts too literally to the score's every dot and rest. But though slightly affected in effect, its ominous spirit accords with his disturbed conception of the work as a whole.

Ballades Nos. 1-4. Berceuse. Impromptu No. 2 in F sharp major, Op. 36. Etude in A flat major, Op. 25 No. 1. 24 Preludes, Op. 28.
Alfred Cortot *pf*
Music & Arts mono CD871 (77 minutes: ADD). Recorded 1925-29.   Ⓕ **H**

Here you will find yourself marvelling at playing of a unique, elemental fire and poetic verve. For Cortot, music was always an exalted language above and beyond the commonplaces of day-to-day discourse; a supreme glorification of both intellect and emotion. You may wave a disapproving finger at his frequent inaccuracy (the wildly flailing left-hand octaves in the *Impromptu*'s central march, for example), or raise an eyebrow at what can sometimes seem like rhetorical violence or excess. But you can hardly deny that every bar quivers with a spine-tingling *joie de vivre*, colour and vibrancy. Cortot unquestionably saw sheer ecstasy as the prime requisite of great music-making. Listen to his freely elasticated rubato in the First *Ballade*, tugging and stretching the music to the very edge (and in the opening of the Fourth, arguably, beyond), to that sobbing, quasi-operatic declamation. The Second's *Presto* storms (complete with Cortot's opening chordal reinforcement) blaze with heroic defiance, and the vertiginous semiquaver flights in the Third can rarely have cascaded with such dazzling virtuoso aplomb. No more rhapsodic account of the Fourth *Ballade* exists, one unforgettably coloured by the haunting sweetness of Cortot's *cantabile*, and the melody of the A flat Etude floats on a seeming air-cushion of harmony. Today, such breathless ardour would be laughed out of court in both the exam room and on the competition circuit. But the loss would be ours, for Cortot had an elegance and vivacity that can make more 'tasteful', accurate and executive-style pianism seem small beer indeed. A few flaws notwithstanding, the transfers have been excellently managed.

Etudes, Opp. 10 and 25.
Maurizio Pollini *pf*
DG 413 794-2GH (56 minutes: ADD).   Ⓕ **RR**

The 24 *Etudes* of Chopin's Opp. 10 and 25, although dating from his twenties, remain among the most perfect specimens of the genre ever known, with all technical challenges – and they are formidable – dissolved into the purest poetry. With his own transcendental technique (and there are few living pianists who can rival it) Pollini makes you unaware that problems even exist – as for instance in Op. 10 No. 10 in A flat, where the listener is swept along in an effortless stream of melody. The first and last of the same set in C major and C minor have an imperious strength and drive, likewise the last three impassioned outpourings of Op. 25. Lifelong dislike of a heart worn on the sleeve makes him less than intimately confiding in more personal contexts such as No. 3 in E major and No. 6 in E flat minor from Op. 10, or the nostalgic middle section of No. 5 in E minor and the searing No. 7 in C sharp minor from Op. 25. Like the playing, so the recording itself could profitably be a little warmer at times, but it is a princely disc all the same.

Etudes, Opp. 10 and 25.
Vladimir Ashkenazy *pf*
Decca 414 127-2DH (63 minutes: ADD). Recorded 1975.   Ⓕ

These are excellent performances of these two dozen pieces, offering a feast of beautiful playing, and with very realistic sound. Hear the controlled impulsiveness with which Ashkenazy throws off

Op. 10 No. 9, or his perfect wedding of the stormy inner and lyrical outer sections of Op. 10 No. 3. Other notable points include the finely judged flow of Op. 25 No. 1, the elegant celerity of Op. 25 No. 9 and his lovely singing of the left-hand melodies of Op. 25 Nos. 5 and 7. They have been digitally remastered from analogue originals but the sound quality is always up to Decca's consistently high standard.

Fantasie in F minor, Op. 49. Waltzes – No. 2 in A flat major, Op. 34 No. 1; No. 3 in A minor, Op. 34 No. 2; No. 5 in A flat major, Op. 42. Polonaise No. 5 in F sharp minor, Op. 44. Nocturnes – No. 1 in C sharp minor, Op. 27 No. 1; No. 2 in D flat major, Op. 27 No. 2; No. 10 in A flat major, Op. 32 No. 2. Scherzo No. 2 in B flat minor, Op. 31.
Evgeni Kissin pf
RCA Victor Red Seal 09026 60445-2 (67 minutes: DDD). Recorded live in 1993.   ℗ 🄴

Evgeni Kissin's playing at 21 (when these performances were recorded) quite easily outmatches that of the young Ashkenazy and Pollini – and most particularly in terms of the maturity of his musicianship. The programme launches off with a reading of the great F minor *Fantasie*, which, though a bit measured, is integrated to perfection. The power and determination of the performance certainly make one sit up and listen, but at the same time it would be difficult not to be moved by the heartfelt lyricism of the melodic passages. Although Kissin may be a little unsmiling in the three waltzes, at least he has admirable sophistication in being able to add interest to the interpretations. His control in the tricky A flat, Op. 42, is quite amazing. The *Nocturne* in C sharp minor is a jewel. This reading is amongst the most darkly imaginative and pianistically refined on disc. The release is rounded off by a powerfully glittering performance of the Second *Scherzo*.

Mazurkas – Nos. 1-63: Op. 6 Nos. 1-4; Op. 7 Nos. 1-5 (5-9); Op. 17 Nos. 1-4 (10-13); Op. 24 Nos. 1-4 (14-17); Op. 30 Nos. 1-4 (18-21); Op. 33 Nos. 1-4 (22-25); Op. 41 Nos. 1-4 (26-29); Op. 50 Nos. 1-3 (30-32); Op. 56 Nos. 1-3 (33-35); Op. 59 Nos. 1-3 (36-38); Op. 63 Nos. 1-3 (39-41); Op. 67 Nos. 1-4 (42-45); Op. 68 Nos. 1-4 (46-49); Nos. 50-63: Op. posth.

Mazurkas Nos. 1-51.
Artur Rubinstein pf
RCA Victor Red Seal RD85171 (two discs: 140 minutes: ADD). Recorded 1960s.   ℗ 🄷 🆁🆁

Recording in the studio, rather than at a live concert, quite naturally leads to a safe and uniform approach, which does not really serve the inspired inventiveness of the music. In some ways these recordings suffer from this. If one compares Rubinstein's readings here with those that he recorded on 78rpm records in 1938-39 (reviewed opposite), one immediately notices that an element of fantasy and caprice has given way to a more sober view of the music. The *Mazurkas* are so intricate in their variety of moods that the successful pianist has to be able to treat each one as a definite entity, contrasting the emotional content within the context of that particular piece. Rubinstein, with his serious approach, lends the music more weight than is usual and he wholly avoids trivializing it with over-snappy rhythms. With him many of the lesser-known *Mazurkas* come to life, such as the E flat minor, Op. 6 No. 4, with its insistent little motif that pervades the whole piece. His phrasing is free and flexible and he has utter appreciation of the delicacy of Chopin's ideas. He does not, however, take an improvisatory approach. Rubinstein judges to perfection which details to bring out so as to give each piece a special character. He convinces one that he has made this music his own. When you hear Rubinstein tackle the C sharp minor Mazurka, Op. 53, No. 3, you at once know that he fully comprehends the depth of this, perhaps the greatest of all of them. He ranges from the pathos of the opening to a persuasive tonal grandeur in the more assertive parts, and yet is able to relate the two. The recording has a number of blemishes: the piano is too closely recorded, the loud passages are hollow-toned, especially in the bass, and there is very little sparkle to the sound.

Mazurkas – Nos. 1-63.
Vladimir Ashkenazy pf
Double Decca 448 086-2DF2 (143 minutes: DDD/ADD). Recorded 1976-85.   🄑

Vladimir Ashkenazy made his integral set of the *Mazurkas* over a decade. He has always played outstandingly. He does so again here, giving complete satisfaction. The set includes all those published posthumously and the revised version of Op. 68 No. 4; so his is the most comprehensive survey in the current catalogue. Ashkenazy memorably catches their volatile character, and their essential sadness. Consider, for example, the delicacy and apparently untrammelled spontaneity with which he approaches these works. He shows the most exquisite sensibility, each item strongly, though never insistently characterized. His accounts of the *Mazurkas*, Op. 6 and Op. 7, for instance, offer a genuine alternative to Rubinstein. Nine pieces in all, they were Chopin's first published sets and their piquancy, the richness of their ideas, is here made very apparent. One is given a sense of something completely new having entered music. Although there are fine things in all the groups, Op. 24 is the first *Mazurka* set of uniformly high quality and No. 4 is Chopin's first great work in the genre. On hearing them together like this one appreciates the cumulative effect which the composer obviously intended, and Ashkenazy makes a hypersensitive response to their quickly changing moods. The recorded sound throughout has the warmth, fullness and immediacy typical of this series, with a nice bloom to the piano tone. About two-thirds are digital and all are believably natural in balance and timbre.

Mazurkas Nos. 1-51. Waltz in A flat major, Op. 34 No. 1. Scherzos Nos. 1-4. Barcarolle. Berceuse. Polonaises Nos. 1-7. Andante spianato and Grand polonaise in E flat major, Op. 22.
Artur Rubinstein *pf*
EMI Références mono CHS7 64697-2 (three discs: 233 minutes: ADD). Recorded 1938-39.　Ⓕ🄷

When Artur Rubinstein plays Chopin you are taken into another world. Who else has ever played Chopin with such patrician ease, such fire and elegance? These recordings, first on 78rpm then on LP, and here (superbly remastered) on CD, have always been among the most deeply cherished possessions of avid piano-music collectors. From Rubinstein, the robust and interior qualities of the *Mazurkas* as they evolve from relatively humble beginnings to the subtle psychological and emotional ambivalence of, say, Op. 59, are caught with the rarest stylistic consistency and acuteness. His ravishing sonority and seamless *legato* and, above all, his rubato – his musical breathing, his minute easings and accelerations within a fundamental if always elusive pulse – such things lie at the very centre of his art. The *Scherzos*, on the other hand, show Rubinstein's virtuosity at its most trail-blazing and unbuttoned. Who cares about the near shipwreck at 5'25" in the Second, when the preceding *leggiero* quaver-work is spun off with an agility virtually unknown today? Both here, in the *Polonaises* and perhaps most of all in the *Barcarolle*, Rubinstein's flashing impulse occasionally gets the better of him. But even then one's sense is of the overspill of a prodigious facility and poetic exultance rather than other more rash or intemperate qualities. The solitary Waltz opening the first disc, too, demonstrates Rubinstein's nonchalant disregard for safety nets and his heart-stopping, reeling brilliance is light years away from the work of today's more cautious and 'serious' practitioners. These then are among the greatest of all Chopin recordings. And, countering popular belief that Rubinstein played better as he got older, they conclusively show that it is the early Rubinstein that matters supremely, his time of unparalleled exuberance and poetic impulse.

Nocturnes – No. 1 in B flat minor, Op. 9; No. 2 in E flat major, Op. 9; No. 3 in B major, Op. 9; No. 4 in F major, Op. 15; No. 5 in F sharp major, Op. 15; No. 6 in G minor, Op. 15; No. 7 in C sharp minor, Op. 27; No. 8 in D flat major, Op. 27; No. 9 in B flat major, Op. 32; No. 10 in A flat major, Op. 32; No. 11 in G minor, Op. 37; No. 12 in G major, Op. 37; No. 13 in C minor, Op. 48; No. 14 in F sharp minor, Op. 48; No. 15 in F minor, Op. 55; No. 16 in E flat major, Op. 55; No. 17 in B flat major, Op. 62; No. 18 in E major, Op. 62; No. 19 in E minor, Op. 72; No. 20 in C sharp minor, Op. posth.; No. 21 in C minor, Op. posth.

Nocturnes Nos. 1-19.
Maria João Pires *pf*
DG 447 096-2GH2 (two discs: 109 minutes: DDD). Recorded 1996.　Ⓕ🄴🅁🅁

Passion rather than insouciance is Pires's keynote. Here is no soft, moonlit option but an intensity and drama that scorn all complacent salon or drawing-room expectations. How she relishes Chopin's central storms, creating a vivid and spectacular yet unhistrionic contrast with all surrounding serenity or 'embalmed darkness'. The *con fuoco* of Op. 15 No. 1 erupts in a fine fury and in the first *Nocturne*, Op. 9 No. 1, Pires's sharp observance of Chopin's *appassionato* marking comes like a prophecy of the coda's sudden blaze. Chopin, she informs us in no uncertain terms, was no sentimentalist. More intimately, in Op. 15 No. 3 (where the music's wavering sense of irresolution led to the sobriquet 'the Hamlet Nocturne') Pires makes you hang on to every note in the coda's curious, echoing chimes, and in the *dolcissimo* conclusion to No. 8 (Op. 27 No. 2) there is an unforgettable sense of 'all passion spent', of gradually ebbing emotion. Pires with her burning clarity has reinforced our sense of Chopin's stature and created a new range of possibilities (showing us that there is life after Rubinstein). Naturally, Rubinstein's legendary cycles possess a graciousness, an ease and elegance reflecting, perhaps, a long-vanished *belle époque*. Yet moving ahead, as we all must, one has no hesitation in declaring Maria João Pires – a pianist without a trace of narcissism – among the most eloquent master-musicians of our time.

Nocturnes Nos. 1-21. Fantaisie-impromptu in C sharp minor, Op. 66. Barcarolle.
Kathryn Stott *pf*
Unicorn-Kanchana DKPCD9147/8 (two discs: 124 minutes: DDD). Recorded 1992.　Ⓕ

Stott not only includes the two posthumously published *Nocturnes* in C sharp minor and C minor after the usual 19, but also launches her two discs with the C sharp minor *Fantaisie-impromptu* as well as ending with what has been described as the finest nocturne of all, otherwise the *Barcarolle*. She never for a moment allows you to forget that Chopin totally transformed the nocturne, as a genre, from the sphere of the drawing-room aquarelle into something infinitely more personal and potent. Right from the start she opens your ears to the mystery of shadowland and night. Her playing is both deeply felt and sensitive, and always with melody beguilingly sung. But such is her essential seriousness of approach, with few, if any, yieldings to the impulse of the moment, that you are aware of how much she chooses to emphasize Chopin's slow tempo markings throughout. You occasionally miss the full variety of mood so miraculously to be found in Rubinstein's legendary recordings. However, in the great C sharp minor (Op. 27 No. 1) and C minor (Op. 48 No. 1) *Nocturnes*, both in the nature of laden tone-poems, she compensates for exceptionally held-back starts with her fervour in their later climaxes. The climaxes of the *Barcarolle* are equally eager and ardent, even if that in the reprise is not achieved without momentary sacrifice of this composer's aristocratic elegance. Unflagging in impulse, the *Fantaisie-impromptu* brings vivid contrasts of restlessly surging minor-key semiquavers (where she achieves an excellent compromise between Chopin's long-held pedals and clarity of detail) and glowing major-key song. It has rarely been more enjoyable. And it's good to be able to add that the recording itself is pleasingly ripe and true.

Nocturnes Nos. 1-19. Waltz in C sharp minor, Op. 64 No. 2. Piano Concertos Nos. 1 and 2.
Artur Rubinstein *pf*
London Symphony Orchestra / Sir John Barbirolli.
EMI Références mono CHS7 64491-2 (two discs: 161 minutes: ADD). Recorded 1931-37. Ⓜ **H**

Rubinstein's 1936-37 cycle of the *Nocturnes* still serves as a yardstick for all subsequent rivals. Listening to just two, namely Op. 37 No. 2 and Op. 48 No. 1, is enough to arouse excitement. The former has a unique finesse and drama, especially where Rubinstein returns from a stormy and heroic central section without as much as a hair out of place, while the latter is full of the most natural and telling rubato, aided by perfect timing and inimitable refinement of tone. Although his later versions could boast virtually as much composure, they hadn't quite this degree of ardour and inner tension. The First Concerto is similarly stylish, its outer movements full of brilliant but often subtle fingerwork, its *Romanze* coolly poetic. The Second is perhaps less wholly satisfying; although undeniably a virtuoso, the Rubinstein of 1931 hadn't quite balanced impulse and control with the precision timing that he achieved a few years later. There's an extra, too – an elegant performance of the C sharp minor Waltz, clean-fingered and particularly winning, and although earlier than any other recording in the set, somehow more prophetic than its companions of the 'aristocratic' Rubinstein of post-war years. It just goes to show that chronology isn't always a reliable gauge for artistic development. The transfers are superb, but some 78 surfaces are more pronounced than others.

Polonaises – No. 1 in C sharp minor, Op. 26; No. 2 in E flat minor, Op. 26; No. 3 in A major, Op. 40, 'Military'; No. 4 in C minor, Op. 40; No. 5 in F sharp minor, Op. 44; No. 6 in A flat major, Op. 53, 'Heroic'; No. 7 in A flat major, Op. 61, 'Polonaise-fantaisie'; No. 8 in D minor, Op. 71; No. 9 in B flat, Op. 71; No. 10 in F minor, Op. 71; No. 11 in B flat minor; No. 12 in G flat major; No. 13 in G minor; No. 14 in B flat major; No. 15 in A flat major; No. 16 in G sharp minor.

Polonaises Nos. 1-16. Allegro de concert in A major, Op. 46. Etudes – F minor, Op. posth.; A flat major, Op. posth.; D flat major, Op. posth. Tarantelle in A flat major, Op. 43. Fugue in A minor. Albumleaf in E major. Polish Songs, Op. 74 – Spring. Galop marquis. Berceuse. Barcarolle. Two Bourrées.
Vladimir Ashkenazy *pf*
Double Decca 452 167-2DF2 (two discs: 145 minutes: DDD/ADD). Recorded 1974-84. Ⓑ **RR**

Ashkenazy's Chopin hardly needs any further advocacy. His distinguished and virtually complete survey rests alongside the Rubinstein recordings in general esteem. The 16 *Polonaises* were not recorded in sets but individually, or in small groups, which is one reason why they sound so fresh, with Ashkenazy striking a sensitive artistic balance between poetic feeling and the commanding bravura that one takes for granted in the more extrovert pieces, with their Polish patriotic style. The recordings (even within groupings of opus numbers) vary between analogue and digital, and the recording venues are as different as the Kingsway Hall, St John's, Smith Square, and All Saints, Petersham; but the realism of the piano sound is remarkably consistent. A series of shorter pieces is included on the second disc and the playing is always distinguished. Among the major items, the gentle *Berceuse* is quite melting, while both the *Allegro de concert* and *Barcarolle* are hardly less memorable.

Polonaises Nos. 1-7.
Maurizio Pollini *pf*
DG The Originals 457 711-2GOR (62 minutes: ADD). Recorded 1975.   Ⓜ

Here is Pollini in all his early glory, in expertly transferred performances. Shorn of all virtuoso compromise or indulgence, the majestic force of his command is indissolubly integrated with the seriousness of his heroic impulse. Rarely will you be compelled into such awareness of the underlying malaise beneath the outward and nationalist defiance of the *Polonaises*. The tension and menace at the start of No. 2 are almost palpable, its storming and disconsolate continuation made a true mirror of Poland's clouded history. The C minor *Polonaise*'s denouement, too, emerges with a chilling sense of finality, and Pollini's way with the pounding audacity commencing at 3'00" in the epic F sharp minor *Polonaise* is like some ruthless prophecy of every percussive, anti-lyrical gesture to come. At 7'59" Chopin's flame-throwing interjections are volcanic indeed, and if there is ample poetic delicacy and compensation (notably in the *Polonaise-fantaisie*, always among Chopin's most profoundly speculative masterpieces), it is the more elemental side of his genius, his 'canons' rather than 'flowers' that are made to sear and haunt the memory. Other pianists may be more outwardly beguiling, but Pollini's magnificently unsettling Chopin can be as imperious and unarguable as any on record. That his performances are also deeply moving is a tribute to his unique status.

Preludes: Op. 28: No. 1 in C major; No. 2 in A minor; No. 3 in G major; No. 4 in E minor; No. 5 in D major; No. 6 in B minor; No. 7 in A major; No. 8 in F sharp minor; No. 9 in E major; No. 10 in C sharp minor; No. 11 in B major; No. 12 in G sharp minor; No. 13 in F sharp major; No. 14 in E flat minor; No. 15 in D flat major; No. 16 in B flat minor; No. 17 in A flat major; No. 18 in F minor; No. 19 in E flat major; No. 20 in C minor; No. 21 in B flat major; No. 22 in G minor; No. 23 in F major; No. 24 in D minor; No. 25 in C sharp minor; Op. 45; No. 26 in A flat major, Op. posth.

Preludes Nos. 1-26[a]. Barcarolle[b]. Polonaise No. 6[c]. Scherzo No. 2 in B flat minor, Op. 31[d].
Martha Argerich *pf*
DG Galleria 415 836-2GGA (62 minutes: ADD). Recorded [a]1977, [b]1961, [c]1967, [d]1975.   Ⓜ **RR**

Professor Zurawlew, the founder of the Chopin Competition in Warsaw, was once asked which one of the prize-winners he would pick as having been his favourite. The answer came back immediately: 'Martha Argerich'. This disc could explain why. There are very few recordings of the 24 Preludes that have such a perfect combination of temperamental virtuosity and compelling artistic insight. Argerich has the technical equipment to do whatever she wishes with the music. Whether it is in the haunting, dark melancholy of No. 2 in A minor or the lightning turmoil of No. 16 in B flat minor, she is profoundly impressive. It is these sharp changes of mood that make her performance scintillatingly unpredictable. In the *Barcarolle* there is no relaxed base on which the melodies of the right hand are constructed, as is conventional, but more the piece emerges as a stormy odyssey through life, with moments of visionary awareness. Argerich is on firmer ground in the *Polonaise*, where her power and technical security reign triumphant. The CD ends with a rippling and yet slightly aggressive reading of the second *Scherzo*. This is very much the playing of a pianist who lives in the 'fast lane' of life. The sound quality is a bit reverberant, an effect heightened by the fact that Argerich has a tendency to overpedal.

Preludes Nos. 1-24. Scherzo No. 2 in B flat minor, Op. 31. Mazurkas Nos. 13, 15 and 25. Polonaise No. 5.
Seta Tanyel *pf*
Collins Classics 1330-2 (69 minutes: DDD). Recorded 1992-93.   Ⓕ

Avoiding all overtly self-conscious point-making in pursuit of expression, Seta Tanyel gets to the heart of the matter with a stylish simplicity. And how beautifully she makes the piano sing within a sound world that is wholly Chopinesque in its translucency. That said, there is certainly no lack of strength, either of motivation or sheer tonal weight, as the more demonstratively disturbed of the 24 Preludes make very clear. However stormy the outburst or complex the figuration, she nevertheless always manages to reveal a hidden melodic thread. Slower numbers carry their weight of sentiment without being allowed to drag. Nothing in the first half of the recital is more pleasing than the three *Mazurkas*. Each tells its own personal tale while – with a spring-like tonal delicacy and freshness – never allowing you to forget its origin in the dance. In the flanking B minor *Scherzo* and F sharp minor *Polonaise*, darker undertones of disquiet and defiance are conveyed with an urgent nervous energy far more telling than bombast. And what beguiling *cantabile* she draws from her instrument in the gracious mazurka-like trio of the *Polonaise*. The Abbey Road reproduction is pleasing enough.

Scherzos – No. 1 in B minor, Op. 20; No. 2 in B flat minor, Op. 31; No. 3 in C sharp minor, Op. 39; No. 4 in E major, Op. 54.

Chopin Scherzos Nos. 1-4.
Schumann Bunte Blätter, Op. 99.
Sviatoslav Richter *pf*
Olympia OCD338 (75 minutes: ADD). Recorded 1970-77.   Ⓔ **RR**

Remarkably well recorded considering the source, one performance after another here is so memorable as to rank among the best versions around of the piece in question. There is nothing amidst all the glorious playing here that will not keep your attention galvanized to the music. Richter is not usually thought of as a very credible Chopin player, and yet he strides through the four *Scherzos* with an abundance of technique and deftly coloured textures that make this version a definite front-runner. His Chopin is finely controlled, spaciousness being the watchword rather than overt passion. His Schumann, on the other hand, has always been dazzling, because he has a temperament that convincingly responds to the extreme swings in mood. Many of the *Bunte Blätter* are amazingly fast and unnerving. These performances should not be missed by those attracted to this repertoire.

Scherzos Nos. 1-4.
Ivo Pogorelich *pf*
DG 439 947-2GH (42 minutes: DDD). Recorded 1995.   Ⓕ

Love him or hate him, Pogorelich guarantees a response. Chopin for the faint-hearted this is not; original, provocative, challenging, daring, it emphatically is. As piano playing this disc is simply phenomenal, and yet in its straining for extremes of contrast and its saturation of musical and pianistic incident it may arouse controversy. Nevertheless, while recognizing that Pogorelich's most unconventional ideas approach wilful eccentricity, or will incite accusations of pianistic self-glorification, the rewards far outweigh any reservations. True, if they weren't reinforced by such transcendental pianism Pogorelich's interpretations wouldn't carry nearly the same authority or conviction; but it is precisely the marrying of his imaginative scope with his extraordinary technical resource that opens up such startling expressive possibilities. The first and second *Scherzos* show the juxtaposition of extremes at its most intense, stretching the limits of the musically viable. Predictably, the outer sections of the B minor *Scherzo* are incredibly fast, possessed with an almost demonic drive, while the central Polish carol (*Sleep, little Jesus*) is unusually slow and luxuriously sustained. But such extremes, of character as much as tempo, place enormous tension on the musical structure, and this is most evident in the B flat minor *Scherzo*. Make no mistake, Pogorelich's playing is astounding, from the imperious opening to the lingering and ravishing middle section, where his sublime lyrical simplicity is of the deepest inward poetry. The contrasts inherent in the Third *Scherzo* are surprisingly underplayed, the showers of descending arpeggios taken quite slowly, eschewing the element of virtuosity. In the more elusive E major *Scherzo* Pogorelich captures the capricious mood perfectly, and sings the central arabesque with a finely spun melodic line.

To sum up a recording like this is not easy. For all the hugely seductive pianistic allure, some may find Pogorelich's probing individualism too overwhelming. There are more ideas crammed into under 42 minutes than on many discs almost twice the length, although most collectors will still feel short-changed by the playing time. This may not be Chopin for every day, but the force of Pogorelich's musical personality subtly and irrevocably shapes one's view of the music. He has also been given a wonderfully clear and immediate recorded presence. A truly extraordinary disc.

Scherzo No. 1. Polonaises Nos. 1 and 6. Waltzes Nos. 1 and 2. Mazurka No. 1. Fantasie in F minor, Op. 49. Nocturnes Nos. 1 and 2.
Ronan O'Hora *pf*
Tring International Royal Philharmonic Collection TRP086 (62 minutes: DDD). Recorded 1995.   Ⓢ

Here is Chopin playing to ravish the senses while maintaining an unerring sense of perspective, allowing the music's innate quality to surface without fuss or impediment. O'Hora tempers valour with discretion and is never led into neurosis by the composer's fire and fury. You may have heard a more trenchant, heart-stopping call to arms in the *Polonaise*. Yet, again, you will find yourself compelled to return to playing of such unforced eloquence and inner strength. In the C sharp minor *Polonaise* O'Hora's pensiveness reminds you, most unusually, that the seeds of the *Polonaise-fantaisie* were already sown and his delicacy and translucency in the elegiac C sharp minor *Waltz* weave their entirely unindulgent spell. All these performances are of an exquisite musical civility and the recordings are a great advance on Tring's sometimes overly resonant earlier offerings. More Chopin from this artist is imperative.

Waltzes – No. 1 in E flat major, Op. 18; No. 2 in A flat major, Op. 34 No. 1; No. 3 in A minor, Op. 34 No. 2; No. 4 in F major, Op. 34 No. 3; No. 5 in A flat major, Op. 42; No. 6 in D flat major, Op. 64 No. 1; No. 7 in C sharp minor, Op. 64 No. 2; No. 8 in A flat major, Op. 64 No. 3; No. 9 in A flat major, Op. 69 No. 1; No. 10 in E minor, Op. 69 No. 2; No. 11 in G flat major, Op. 70 No. 1; No. 12 in F minor, Op. 70 No. 2; No. 13 in D flat major, Op. 70 No. 3; No. 14 in E minor, Op. posth.; No. 15 in E major, Op. posth.; No. 16 in A flat major, Op. posth.; No. 17 in E flat major, Op. posth.; No. 18 in E flat major, Op. posth.; No. 19 in A minor, Op. posth.

Waltzes Nos. 1-14.
Artur Rubinstein *pf*
RCA Red Seal RD89564 (50 minutes: ADD). Recorded 1960s. Ⓔ 🄁🄁

There has in recent years been a tendency to take Rubinstein's imposing series of Chopin recordings from the mid-1960s for granted, but to hear them digitally refurbished soon puts a stop to that. His tone does not have much luxuriance, being quite chiselled; yet a finely-tuned sensibility is evident throughout. This is at once demonstrated by his direct interpretation of Op. 18, its elegance explicit. His reading of Op. 34 No. 1 is *brillante*, as per Chopin's title. In Op. 34 No. 2 Rubinstein judges everything faultlessly, distilling the sorrowful yet cannily varied grace of this piece. The two finest are Opp. 42 and 64 No. 2, and with the former Rubinstein excels in the unification of its diverse elements, its rises and falls of intensity, its hurryings forward and holdings back. This is also true of his reading of Op. 64 No. 2, the yearning of whose brief *più lento* section is memorable indeed. The sole fault of this issue is that conventional programming leads to the mature Waltzes, published by Chopin himself, coming first, the lesser, posthumously printed, items last. Not all of these latter are early but they have less substance than Opp. 18-64, and should come first.

Waltzes Nos. 1-17. Polonaises – G minor, Op. posth.; B flat major, Op. posth.
Allan Schiller *pf*
ASV Quicksilva CDQS6149 (60 minutes: DDD). Recorded 1994. Ⓢ

Allan Schiller's playing has a wholesomely musical, straightforward directness that could be described as quintessentially English. Far more sparing than his rivals in resorting to cajoling rubato, he avoids personal idiosyncrasies of all kinds so that the music, as printed, can tell its own tale. The recording itself has a similar unforced naturalness. That said, sometimes Schiller's well-trained, obedient fingers are a little too impersonal in more nostalgic moods – Op. 64 No. 2 in C sharp minor, Op. 69 No. 1 in A flat (inspired by a youthful love, Maria Wodzinska) and even Op. 69 No. 2 in B minor. In several more agile contexts a little more light-fingered fancy and charm would not have come amiss. However, in both contexts Schiller's imagination seems to be given freer rein as the set progresses. And he certainly comes close to the truth in the spirited Op. 70 No. 1 in G flat, likewise in the warmly benign posthumous E flat major Waltz with which he concludes. Both *Polonaises* are played with an engaging youthful purity of sound and sentiment.

Waltzes Nos. 1-14. Mazurka in C sharp minor, Op. 50 No. 3. Barcarolle. Nocturne in D flat major, Op. 27 No. 2.
Dinu Lipatti *pf*
EMI mono CDM5 66956-2 (65 minutes: ADD). Recorded 1947-50. Ⓜ 🄷

As an erstwhile pupil of Cortot, it was perhaps not surprising that Lipatti always kept a special place in his heart for Chopin. And thanks, primarily, to the 14 Waltzes, played in a non-chronological sequence of his own choosing, it is doubtful if the disc will ever find itself long absent from the catalogue. Like the solitary *Mazurka*, they were recorded in Geneva during his remarkable renewal of strength in the summer of 1950. The *Nocturne* and *Barcarolle* date back to visits to EMI's Abbey Road studio in 1947 and 1948 respectively. Just once or twice in the Waltzes you might question his sharp tempo changes for mood contrast within one and the same piece – as for instance in No. 9 in A flat, Op. 69 No. 1. But for the most part his mercurial lightness, fleetness and charm are pure delight. His *Nocturne* in D flat has long been hailed as one of the finest available. And even though we know he himself (one of the greatest perfectionists ever) was not completely happy about the *Barcarolle*, for the rest of us this glowing performance has a strength of direction and shapeliness all its own. In fuller contexts there is just a trace of plumminess in the recorded sound.

Waltzes Nos. 1-19.
Vladimir Ashkenazy *pf*
Decca 414 600-2DH (56 minutes: AAD/ADD). Ⓕ

No one has served Chopin's cause more faithfully than Ashkenazy. He always preferred miscellaneous programmes which, while wholly understandable from his own point of view, occasionally posed problems for the collector wanting conveniently packaged sets of this or that genre in its entirety. So hats off to Decca for this reissue. All 19 known waltzes are here, including the last six posthumous publications. Rubinstein and Lipatti have long been the heroes in the sphere of the waltz. Ashkenazy must now join their number. From all three of these outstanding artists the waltzes emerge as true 'dance poems'. Ashkenazy also finds the ideal, translucent sound world for this composer, without excessive weight in the bass or injudicious use of the right pedal. What lessons he can teach certain younger contenders about exaggerated point-making (especially in the spotlighting of inner parts), and whirlwind spontaneity in faster numbers achieved without loss of grace or finesse. There is no need to be worried by any suggestion of inconsistency arising from date, level or system of recording.

Piano Sonatas – No. 1 in C minor, Op. 4; No. 2 in B flat minor, Op. 35; No. 3 in B minor, Op. 58.

Piano Sonatas Nos. 2 and 3. Etudes – Op. 10 Nos. 1-12 (two versions); Op. 25 Nos. 1-12 (two versions). Waltzes Nos. 1-14. Ballades Nos. 1-4. Preludes Nos. 1-24. Impromptus Nos. 1-3. Nocturnes Nos. 2, 4, 5, 7, 15 and 16. Polonaise No. 6. Berceuse (two versions). Fantasie in F minor, Op. 49. Tarantelle in A flat major, Op. 43. Barcarolle. Chants polonais, Op. 74 – No. 2, Spring (trans. Liszt); No. 12, My darling; No. 14, The ring. Piano Concerto No. 2.
Alfred Cortot *pf*
orchestra / Sir John Barbirolli.
EMI mono CZS7 67359-2 (six discs: 429 minutes: ADD). Recorded 1920-43.   Ⓜ 🄷

Has there ever been a more bewitching or endearing virtuoso than Alfred Cortot? His touch (an old-fashioned word but one inseparable from the man) was of a crystalline clarity, his coloration alive with myriad tints and hues. Combined with a poetic passion that knew no limits, such qualities created an idiosyncrasy and style that usually survived a fallible and bewilderingly confused keyboard mechanism. The truth is that Cortot had neither the time nor the inclination to polish his performances to a high degree of perfection. His hyperactive life (conductor, teacher, editor, writer and, more darkly, politician) made systematic practice a luxury. This, together with a gremlin who mischievously deflected his fingers away from the right notes – often at crucial if surprisingly undemanding points in the musical argument – added piquant harmonies and dissonances undreamed of by his composers. Cortot's left hand in particular had a way of drifting in and out of focus and leading a wayward and disobedient life of its own. Such famous errors surely resulted not from incompetence, but from Cortot's nervous, high-pitched intensity; a sheer involvement that could easily cloud his composure or unsettle his equilibrium. Yet for the greater part Chopin's elusive essence emerged unscathed from so much inaccuracy and caprice.

Here on six glorious CDs is Cortot's Chopin at last in all its infinite richness and variety. The transfers are outstanding, with no attempt made to mask the glitter of his brilliance in the interests of silent surfaces or to remove other acoustical hiccups. Although not everything is included, the selection is wonderfully enterprising and judicious, with several alternative performances of the same work shown for perusal. The only quibble is the preference shown for the 1942 set of the *Preludes* when the earlier 1933 recording seems to be infinitely superior. The 1931 B minor Sonata is far superior to a later version from 1933. Cortot's 1933 B flat minor Sonata is also a far cry from one made in 1953, where his powers failed him almost totally and is, indeed, of a dizzying aplomb and brio.

There is elaboration in the Second *Ballade*, the volcanic interjections ablaze with added notes, and in the opening of the last and glorious Fourth *Ballade* there is a convulsive leap across the rhythm. However, the gem is surely the Third *Ballade* with the opening pages played as if improvised on the spot, the figuration foaming and cascading with a freedom and liberality unknown to most players. The F minor *Fantasie* also suggests that Cortot never compromised where his intensity of vision was concerned. Cortot's *Barcarolle* is as insinuating as it is blisteringly intense, even though the hectic rush through the final pages shows him at his least eloquent. In the *Etudes* (the 1934 is preferable to the 1942 set; both are included) he reaches out far beyond mere pedagogical concerns. The final and awe inspiring Op. 25 No. 12, too, is not the *cantus firmus* of a traditional view but an elemental declamation and upheaval.

In the Waltzes there is a near operatic freedom in the melody of Op. 42 with its cunning mix of duple and triple rhythm, a charming decorative aside at bar 20 in the E flat, Op. 18 (only in the 1943 version), and a puckish mercurial touch throughout that banishes all possible monotony from so many pieces in three time. There is a comically confused start to the A flat, Op. 64 No. 3, and an unholy muddle at the end of the final Waltz in E minor. The Second Concerto, heard in Cortot's own arrangement or refurbishment with some marginal re-texturing here and there, shows him at his most excitingly rhetorical. Barbirolli's accompaniment may be rumbustious rather than subtle, yet the music sounds as if newly minted, alive in all its first audacious ardour and novelty. Six *Nocturnes* are included in the set and while hardly examples of the stylistic purity to which we have become accustomed in the post-Cortot era, are brilliantly alive with his own heady alternative. You will not easily find a more absorbing box-set of piano discs.

Piano Sonatas Nos. 2[a] and 3[b]. Scherzo No. 3 in C sharp minor, Op. 39[c].
Martha Argerich pf
DG 419 055-2GGA (56 minutes: ADD). Recorded [a]1975, [b]1967, [c]1961.　　　Ⓜ 🎵🎵

This consolidates and confirms (if confirmation were necessary) our sense of a unique vision and virtuosity. Here, simply and assuredly, is one of the most magisterial talents in the entire history of piano playing. She is hardly a comfortable companion, confirming your preconceptions. Indeed, she sets your heart and mind reeling so that you positively cry out for respite from her dazzling and super-sensitive enquiry. But again, in the final resort, she is surely a great musician first and a great pianist second. From her, Chopin is hardly the most balanced or classically biased of the romantics. Argerich can tear all complacency aside. How she keeps you on the *qui vivre* in the Second and Third Sonatas. Is the Funeral March too brisk, an expression of sadness for the death of a distant relative rather than grief for a nation? Is the delicate rhythmic play at the heart of the Third Sonata's *Scherzo* virtually spun out of existence? Such qualms or queries tend to be whirled into extinction by more significant felicities. Who but Argerich, with her subtle half-pedalling, could conjure so baleful and macabre a picture of 'winds whistling over graveyards' in the Second Sonata's finale, or achieve such heart-stopping exultance in the final pages of the Third Sonata (this performance is early Argerich with a vengeance, alive with a nervous brio). And if her free spirit leaves us tantalized, thirsting for Chopin's First, Second and Fourth as well as his Third *Scherzos*, for example, she has also left us overwhelmingly enriched, for ever in her debt.

Piano Sonatas Nos. 1-3.
Vladimir Ashkenazy pf
Decca Ovation 448 123-2DM (76 minutes: ADD). Recorded 1976-81.　　　Ⓜ

Ashkenazy's grouping of the three sonatas is particularly valuable as he makes such a good case for the early (1827) C minor Sonata, and his account of No. 3 is undoubtedly very fine, with an excitingly spontaneous account of the last movement. But it is the 'Funeral March' Sonata that one especially remembers. He obviously identifies with the music profoundly and after the concentration of the first two movements the dazzling finale seems the more mercurial. The analogue piano recording is very real and vivid.

Piano Sonatas Nos. 2 and 3.
Maurizio Pollini pf
DG 415 346-2GH (52 minutes: DDD). Recorded 1986.　　　Ⓕ 🎵🎵

These two magnificent romantic sonatas are Chopin's longest works for solo piano. The passion of the B flat minor Sonata is evident throughout, as is its compression (despite the overall length) – for example, the urgent first subject of its first movement is omitted in the recapitulation. As for its mysterious finale, once likened to 'a pursuit in utter darkness', it puzzled Chopin's contemporaries but now seems totally right. The B minor Sonata is more glowing and spacious, with a wonderful *Largo* third movement, but its finale is even more exhilarating than that of the B flat minor, and on a bigger scale. Pollini plays this music with overwhelming power and depth of feeling; the expressive intensity is rightly often disturbing. Magisterial technique is evident throughout and the recording is sharp-edged but thrilling.

Piano Sonatas Nos. 2 and 3.
Murray Perahia pf
Sony MK76242 (50 minutes: ADD). Recorded 1974.　　　Ⓕ

Listening to Murray Perahia's Chopin Sonatas, you have the impression of an unusually searching mind at work behind the fine fingers. The catalogue has long offered more urgently-driven performances but with his deliberate tempo and his very lightly pedalled texture, Perahia draws attention to a host of hidden subtleties – harmonic and rhythmic, as well as inner voices – often merely glossed over. Just now and again you might feel that pursuit of detail encourages shorter-lapped phrasing than we often hear, that it breaks the music's broader sweep. But if so, that is a small price to pay for revelations of such beauty. Chopin specialists will find much of interest in the text he uses for the *Largo* (or rather its central *sostenuto* section) of the B minor Sonata, incidentally one of the loveliest things on the disc. The CD transfer is good enough even if the acoustic lacks ideal spaciousness.

Piano Sonatas Nos. 2 and 3. Fantasie in F minor, Op. 49.
Artur Rubinstein pf
RCA Red Seal RD89812 (61 minutes: ADD). Recorded 1960s.   Ⓕ

In the Chopin sonatas it is difficult to think of which performance to choose as the greatest. Aside from the Funeral March itself, Rubinstein's account of the Second Sonata is a bit too imperious; the Third is much more thrilling, with considerable technical risks being taken both in the first movement and the finale. His feeling for quiet nuances in the *Largo* of this work is superb, and here too Pollini on DG achieves an innocence that is disarming. Pollini's disc is the most perfect, both in terms of the pianist's technical accomplishment and the lucid piano sound, with nothing that offends the ear. The middle treble range in Rubinstein's piano sound has a hollow resonance. Rubinstein tackles the F minor *Fantasie* in rather a heavy-handed manner, with more power than searching drama. To sum up, if you want your Chopin sonatas balanced and formally cohesive, Rubinstein is for you.

Piano Sonata No. 2. Nocturnes Nos. 5, 13, 18 and 20. Barcarolle. Scherzo No. 2.
Mikhail Pletnev pf
Virgin Classics VC5 45076-2 (68 minutes: DDD). Recorded 1988.   Ⓕ Ⓢ

These are superb and audacious performances. Love them or hate them you will never – not for a minute, not for a second – remain indifferent. Is his *Barcarolle* daringly free or scrupulously true to both the music's outer and inner manifestation? Dare one mention a glaring rhythmic distortion in the closing octaves, a vulgarization of Chopin's nobility in the second bar of the C minor *Nocturne*, or question the *forte* rather than *pianissimo* start to the *doppio movimento* in the same *Nocturne*? Such questions are asked in a spirit of awe rather than impertinence and are, in any case, invariably silenced by Pletnev's technical and musical imperiousness. The Second Sonata will have experts (and particularly Polish experts) locked in furious debate when not mesmerized by the spine-tingling drama Pletnev achieves at the start of the first-movement development, the sinister underlying waltz rhythm he finds in the *Scherzo*, the chillingly exact 'timpani' rolls in the Funeral March and, most of all, the terrifying miasma emanating from the finale. Rarely, too, has the *Nocturnes'* erotic undertow surfaced so tellingly through their civilized veneer. In short, not since Michelangeli's heyday has Chopin been played with such compulsive brilliance, individuality and pianistic mastery. The recordings capture Pletnev's sound world to perfection and are of optimum range and clarity.

Piano Sonata No. 2. Polonaises Nos. 5 and 6. Impromptu No. 3 in G flat major, Op. 51. Nocturne No. 2. Barcarolle. Etudes – Op. 10: No. 4 in C sharp minor; No. 5 in G flat major; Op. 25: No. 1 in A flat major; No. 5 in E minor. Waltzes – Op. 34: Nos. 1 and 2.
Artur Rubinstein pf
Revelation RV10013 (78 minutes: ADD). Recorded live in 1964.   Ⓜ

After a prolonged absence Rubinstein returned to Russia in 1964, gave one of his greatest recitals, and set musical Moscow by the ears. The intention is unmistakable in every blazing and heroic bar. Dazzled and, possibly, chastened, the Russians listened in awe to the confirmation of a legend. Here is the pianist who changed the parameters of Chopin for ever, freeing him of all neurosis and salon sentimentality and sending his spirit soaring with an overwhelming force and fantasy. Beckmessers will, of course, note how in the heat of the moment (and the temperature is white-hot) assorted *piano* and *pianissimo* markings turn into *fortissimos*, and eyebrows will also be raised over a wrong turning that wreaks momentary havoc with the *Scherzo* from the Second Sonata. Then there is the way the A flat *Polonaise*'s central equestrian gallop is launched with a blistering inaccuracy. Yet such things are somehow part and parcel of the total experience and it is difficult to imagine this recital without them. Even a hint of playing or recording for safety and the overwhelming intensity would have been lost. As it is, the Second Sonata's opening *Grave* and *doppio movimento* become virtually one and the same thing, and who but Rubinstein could declaim the climax of the first movement's development with such rhetorical defiance? In the second movement, too, where Chopin hurls blocks of sound in all directions simultaneously, Rubinstein creates a true Mephisto scherzo. But it is in Chopin's more intimate and confiding pages in, say, the D flat *Nocturne* or A minor *Waltz* that Rubinstein shows his most aristocratic and cardinal quality. Here, pulse and vocal 'line' never fail, yet the fluctuations within that pulse are like some infinite and sophisticated poetic play. Such charisma is, perhaps, more familiar to great singers than pianists and, again, in the *Barcarolle*, Rubinstein's largesse, his supreme generosity of spirit, illuminates every bar. Rubinstein could play the aristocrat to the hilt, but he was also a force of nature transcending all carefully prescribed notions of neatness, musical taste or decorum. To a greater extent than any other pianist he set Chopin's turbulent genius free to charm and intimidate, to sing and resonate across the universe.

Piano Sonata No. 3. Mazurkas Nos. 36-38. Nocturne No. 4. Polonaise No. 6. Scherzo No. 3.
Martha Argerich *pf*
EMI CDC5 56805-2 (52 minutes: ADD). Recorded 1965.   Ⓕ

Argerich's pianism is notable for its remarkable combination of seemingly effortless technical resource and temperamental volatility. For all the combustibility of the mixture, however, the vehemence of Argerich's playing is seldom exploited to the disadvantage of the extraordinary subtleties of her art. Moreover, despite the self-imposed limits she places on the repertory she performs, such is the spontaneity of her approach that each of her interpretations, no matter how familiar in broad outline, is characterized by a profusion of contrasting details beneath the surface. In the B minor Sonata she omits the first-movement repeats. Such a formal contraction can, of course, contribute to the momentum with which the movement unfolds. Ironically, however, Argerich seems to some extent to rein in the propulsive power for which she has been renowned, even at this stage in her career, appearing instead to be seeking at every turn to exploit a deeply-felt exprssive lyricism to offset the febrile intensity of the most energetic figurational devices. This has the virtue of allowing us a less hectic view of subsidiary elements within the music, which elsewhere can too often be overwhelmed by the sheer turbulence of the action. Some of the most satisfying playing on the disc comes in her account of the Op. 59 *Mazurkas*. There is a vulnerability as well as an affecting wistfulness about the playing which captures the elusiveness of the idiom, with its harmonic ambiguities, with rare acuity. At the other end of the scale, the excitement she generates in the A flat *Polonaise* is of an order that goes far beyond mere effect. Given the extraordinarily convoluted machinations behind the scenes which preceded the final release of these performances, we should be doubly grateful that they are now available. If they do not necessarily outstrip her other recordings, they nevertheless offer an intriguing insight into ongoing 'work in progress' from a pianistic giant whose artistry continues to fascinate, and perplex, more than 30 years later.

Piano Sonata No. 3. Mazurkas – A minor, Op. 17 No. 4; B flat minor, Op. 24 No. 4; D flat major, Op. 30 No. 3; D major, Op. 33 No. 2; C sharp minor, Op. 50 No. 3; C major, Op. 56 No. 2; F sharp minor, Op. 59 No. 3; B major, Op. 63 No. 1; F minor, Op. 63 No. 2; C sharp minor, Op. 63 No. 3; F minor, Op. 68 No. 4.
Evgeni Kissin *pf*
RCA Victor Red Seal 09026 62542-2 (65 minutes: DDD). Recorded live in 1993.   Ⓕ **∃**

Kissin is unquestionably among the master-pianists of our time, and in their poise and maturity all these performances seem light-years away from colleagues twice his age. What magnificence and assertion he finds in the B minor Sonata's opening (for once truly *maestoso*), what menace in the following uprush of chromatic scales, his deliberate pedal haze capturing one of Chopin's most truly modernist moments. Kissin may relish left-hand counter-melody in the return of the second subject and elsewhere, yet such detail is always offered within the context of the whole, within the most bracing and invigorating sense of propulsion. A momentary failure of concentration at 1'04" in the *Scherzo*'s central section comes as reassuring evidence of human fallibility but elsewhere one can only marvel at a manner so trenchant, musicianly and resolutely unsentimental. The equestrian finale is among the most lucid on record and concludes in a controlled triumph that has the audience cheering to the heavens. The 12 *Mazurkas* are no less remarkable for their strength and discretion. Nothing is rushed, everything is unfolded with complete naturalness and authority. Kissin's rubato is beautifully idiomatic yet so stylishly applied that you are only aware of a musical 'breathing', of the finest fluctuations of pulse and emotion. Few other pianists have gone to the heart of the matter with such assurance (always excepting Artur Rubinstein). The recording captures Kissin's clear, unnarcissistic sonority admirably and audience noise is kept to a minimum.

Piano Sonata No. 3. Polonaise-Fantaisie in A flat major, Op. 61. Nocturne No. 1. Scherzo No. 4. Barcarolle. Ballade No. 4.
Nelson Goerner *pf*
EMI Debut CDZ5 69701-2 (77 minutes: DDD). Recorded 1996.   Ⓑ

Nelson Goerner is Argentinian, a student of Maria Tipo, and devotes his most personal and inflammatory recital to Chopin's later masterpieces. How fearlessly he launches the B minor Sonata's imperious opening, never using Chopin's *maestoso* instruction as an excuse for undue rhetoric or inflation. Even the startling sense of hiatus contained in the first movement repeat (can this really be authentic?) makes sense given such voltage and intensity. His second movement *Scherzo* is as colourful as it is volatile and in the *Largo* the playing is, again, gloriously free-spirited and keenly felt. His transition out of the *Polonaise-Fantaisie*'s central *Più lento*, back to Chopin's principal idea, shows a compelling sense of the composer's depth and introspection, and if his choice of the Fourth *Scherzo* is surprising, given such seriousness, he is once more brilliantly attuned to one of Chopin's most elusive and mercurial major-key flights of fancy. The C minor *Nocturne* pulses with a profound sense of elegy, its central octaves fired off like so many ceremonial cannons, and Goerner makes something very special out of the Fourth *Ballade*'s coda, tempering Chopin's bravura with a fine sense of melodic intricacy. Finally, EMI has provided this most personal and distinctive artist with an impressively bold and spacious recording.

Francesco Cilea
Italian 1866-1950

Adriana Lecouvreur.
Renata Scotto *sop* Adriana Lecouvreur; **Plácido Domingo** *ten* Maurizio; **Sherrill Milnes** *bar* Michonnet; **Elena Obraztsova** *mez* Princesse de Bouillon; **Giancarlo Luccardi** *bass* Prince de Bouillon; **Florindo Andreolli** *ten* Abbé de Chazeuil; **Lillian Watson** *sop* Jouvenot; **Ann Murray** *mez* Dangeville; **Paul Crook** *ten* Poisson; Major-domo; **Paul Hudson** *bass* Quinault; **Ambrosian Opera Chorus; Philharmonia Orchestra / James Levine.**
Sony M2K79310 (two discs: 135 minutes: ADD). Notes, text and translation included.
Recorded 1977.   Ⓕ

Adriana Lecouvreur is an archetypal prima donna vehicle. Look at the plot coldly, without reference to the music, and it is costumed hokum of an improbability that takes the breath away but it is still ... well, hokum with some damned good tunes. But Cilea wrote his opera in the full knowledge that an essential five per cent of its appeal would be added by the prima donna. Not with faultless vocalism, though that's a prerequisite too, but with the sort of allure of vocal personality that elsewhere would be called 'star quality'. With that extra five per cent, arguments about the artifice of the plot and the occasional thinness of the score fall away as the irrelevancies that they are. And you can tell very soon whether the soprano in question has that quality: after Cilea's brief but evocative scene-setting (telling us that we're back-stage at the Comédie Française in the eighteenth century, a world of glamour and intrigue), she enters, a prima donna portraying a prima donna, and tells us, to a sumptuous melody, that star though she is she's but the humble handmaid of her art. Scotto has that magic quality, in abundance. That Domingo is an ardent hero, Milnes a touching elderly admirer, Obraztsova a baleful rival and Levine an enthusiastic exponent of the subtleties and ingenuities of a composer often despised for having written prima donna vehicles is all bonus, making this a performance that you can return to again and again. But the centre of its allure, its *raison d'être*, is Renata Scotto. Her entrance is electrifying, her death moving and everything between is more than life-size.

Domenico Cimarosa
Italian 1749-1801

Il matrimonio segreto.
Arleen Auger *sop* Carolina; **Julia Varady** *sop* Elisetta; **Dietrich Fischer-Dieskau** *bar* Geronimo; **Júlia Hamari** *contr* Fidalma; **Ryland Davies** *ten* Paolino; **Alberto Rinaldi** *bar* Count Robinson; **English Chamber Orchestra / Daniel Barenboim.**
DG 437 696-2GX3 (three discs: 165 minutes: ADD). Text and translation included.
Recorded 1975.   Ⓜ Ⓔ

The music may not have the more adventurous harmony or contrapuntal dexterity of Mozart, but it abounds in delightfully fresh melodic invention and rhythmic vitality – its bubbling patter-work too is worthy of Rossini at his best. Together with its construction, with as many ensembles as solo arias and with skilfully planned finales, and its scoring, primarily aimed at supporting the singers but giving the orchestra some independent interest, it marks not merely an expert craftsman but a composer of distinction whose wide popularity at the time is understandable. Barenboim makes the music dance along with the utmost sparkle, and he is fortunate in having a splendid cast, in whom it is almost invidious to praise Ryland Davies (with free tone-production, fine breath-control and native-sounding Italian) and the silver-voiced Arleen Auger as the young couple at the centre of the plot. But Alberto Rinaldi also brings a real sense of character to the blustering Count Robinson, who sets his heart on the clandestinely married Caroline and ends up, most improbably, marrying her shrewish elder sister whom he had previously declared he would rather die than wed; and Julia Varady gives a stunning performance of that character's big florid aria in the last act. An issue not to be missed.

Muzio Clementi

Piano Sonatas – B flat major, Op. 24 No. 2; F sharp minor, Op. 25 No. 5; B minor, Op. 40 No. 2; D major, Op. 40 No. 3.
Nikolai Demidenko *pf*
Hyperion CDA66808 (69 minutes: DDD). Recorded 1994. Ⓕ

Several recent excellent releases – on period and modern instruments – have done much to counter Mozart's evaluation of Clementi as a 'mere mechanicus'. For those who remain unconvinced, Demidenko's issue of Clementi sonatas (on a modern piano) provides a comprehensive demonstration of the composer's skill and imagination that should ensure an enthusiastic following. The B flat Sonata, Op. 24 No. 2, which Clementi played at Joseph II's court in December 1781, is an exuberant exhibition piece. Demidenko's spontaneous keyboard virtuosity and delightful variety of touch underlines the music's surprising diversity. Indeed, the soft lighting of his performances in general heightens the emotional impact of his interpretations. Two of the Op. 40 Sonatas offer remarkable illustrations of Clementi's dramatic and expressive power. Demidenko's performance of the dazzling D major Sonata reveals its potent cocktail of Beethovenian boldness and Mozartian *dolce* in the first movement, and luxuriates in its poignant, improvisatory melody and rich harmony in the second. However, Demidenko's tonal range, technical polish and musical intelligence are even more impressive in the B minor Sonata. Here, his apt characterization of the first movement's turbulent mix of icy reserve and fiery bravura, and deft handling of the second movement's fusion of *adagio* and finale, compellingly evoke the music's spirit of fantasy.

Louis-Nicolas Clérambault

La mort d'Hercule. Poliphème. Sonatas – No. 2, 'La félicité'; No. 5, 'Chaconne'; No. 6, 'L'impromptu'; No. 7, 'La magnifique'.
Luc Coadou *bass* **Les Solistes du Concert Spirituel** (Jocelyn Daubigney *fl*
Patrick Cohën-Akenine, Hilary Metzger *vns* Blandine Rannou *hpd*).
Naxos 8 553743 (66 minutes: DDD). Texts and translations included. Recorded 1996. Ⓢ

Les Solistes du Concert Spirituel perform two of Clérambault's chamber cantatas for bass, interspersed with instrumental compositions. Luc Coadou has chosen from two of Clérambault's five anthologies, published between 1710 and 1726. *Poliphème* comes from the First Book, and *La mort d'Hercule* from the Third. He is responsive to the many expressive details of text and music and has a fluent understanding of the ornaments and inflexions that characterize French music of the time. But his voice does not always settle comfortably in the centre of his notes, and the pervading tonality is established more by implication than precision. Strikingly declamatory though the *Hercules* piece is, it is not, perhaps, one of Clérambault's most inspired cantatas, and certainly not among the most immediately accessible of them. The imagery contained in the *Polyphemus* text seems to have sparked off Clérambault's imagination, and, indeed, that of Coadou, more than the other. The giant, tormented by Galatea's beauty, takes his revenge upon her beloved Acis, with harsh and hopeless consequences. Clérambault paints a touching picture of the Cyclops's despair in an 'Air fort et tendre', gently accompanied by a flute which perfectly mirrors his melancholy. The remaining pieces are instrumental 'Simphonies', some of them with fanciful, allusive titles.

Orphée. Léandre et Héro. Harpsichord Suite No. 2 in C minor. Sonata prima in G major, 'Anonima'. Simphonie à cinq in G minor.
Sandrine Piau *sop* **Les Solistes du Concert Spirituel** (Jocelyn Daubigney *fl*
Patrick Cohën-Akenine, Martha Moore *vns* Alix Verzier *va da gamba* Catherine Arnoux *viol*
Blandine Rannou *hpd*)
Naxos 8 553744 (62 minutes: DDD). Texts and translations included. Recorded 1996. ⓈⒺ

These chamber cantatas, *Orphée* and *Léandre et Héro*, are captivating pieces which reveal Clérambault's sensitivity in setting texts and endorse his reputation as, perhaps, *the* master of the *cantate française*. *Orphée*, contained in the First of his five anthologies of cantatas, is often regarded as Clérambault's masterpiece, but *Léandre et Héro*, from the Second Book, at times hardly seems inferior. Sandrine Piau is no stranger to this subtly inflected repertoire and sings with passion and a lively sense of style. Her voice is clear, lightly textured and attractive, and she pays close attention to textural detail. *Léandre et Héro*, inspired by the touching love-story of Hero and Leander, is similarly scored to *Orphée*, that is, for high voice with violin, flute and continuo. Perhaps Clérambault, notwithstanding a splendidly vigorous *air de tempête*, never quite achieves the expressive variety of *Orphée*, but *Léandre* is graced throughout by music of strong character, admirably realized by Piau. The remaining items are instrumental and contribute to a satisfying programme, very well performed.

Eric Coates

Saxo-Rhapsody. Wood Nymphs. Music Everywhere (Rediffusion March). From Meadow to Mayfair.
The Dam Busters – march; London. Cinderella – Phantasy. London Again.
Royal Liverpool Philharmonic Orchestra / Sir Charles Groves;
The Merrymakers – Miniature Overture. Summer Days – At the dance. By the Sleepy Lagoon.
The Three Men – Man from the sea. The Three Bears – Phantasy.
London Symphony Orchestra / Sir Charles Mackerras;
Calling all Workers – March. The Three Elizabeths.
City of Birmingham Symphony Orchestra / Reginald Kilbey.
HMV Classics HMV5 72327-2 (two discs: 129 minutes: ADD). Recorded 1956-71.   ⊕ Ⓗ

Eric Coates reached a vast public through the use of his music as signature tunes for radio
programmes, and the cinema furthered the cause with the huge success of *The Dam Busters* march.
There is much more to his music, though, than mere hit themes. Suites such as *London, London
Again*, *From Meadow to Mayfair* and *The Three Elizabeths* offer a wealth of delights and are all the
better for the juxtaposition of their contrasted movements. The two tone-poems for children,
Cinderella and *The Three Bears*, are splendidly apt pieces of programme music – simple to follow,
ever charming, never trite. The miniature overture *The Merrymakers* and the elegant waltz 'At the
dance' are other superb pieces of light music, whilst the *Saxo-Rhapsody* shows Coates in somewhat
more serious mood. Throughout there is a rich vein of melody, and an elegance and grace of
orchestration that makes this music to listen to over and over again with ever increasing admiration.
The three conductors and orchestras featured adopt a no-nonsense approach that modestly
suggests that his music should not be lingered over, never taken too seriously. Considering that
the Mackerras items were first issued in 1956 (the rest being from 1968-71), the sound is of
astonishingly good and remarkably uniform quality. This is a veritable feast of delightful music
and, at its low price, a remarkable bargain.

Sweet Seventeen. Summer Afternoon. Impressions of a Princess[a]. Salute the Soldier.
Two Light Syncopated Pieces. For Your Delight. The Unknown Singer[a]. I Sing to You. Coquette.
Over to You. Idyll. Under the Stars. By the Tamarisk. Mirage. Last Love. The Green Land.
[a]**Peter Hughes** *sax* **BBC Concert Orchestra / John Wilson.**
ASV White Line CDWHL2107 (79 minutes: DDD). Recorded 1996.   Ⓜ

The title of these pieces won't ring much of a bell with any but the most avid Coates fans.
Indeed, none of them seems to have been recorded in the LP or CD era, and four pieces are here
recorded for the first time ever. But what delights there are! It goes without saying that Coates's
craftsmanship is in evidence from start to finish. Yet so often, one wonders just *why* a particular
piece never quite made it in the way his most popular works did. Isn't *Summer Afternoon* every bit
as delightful as *By the Sleepy Lagoon*? And wouldn't *Salute the Soldier* have served just as well as
other marches as a radio signature tune? Most simply, aren't *Under the Stars*, *For Your Delight* and
others just simply such utter charmers? The BBC Concert Orchestra plays beautifully, and the
conductor seems thoroughly imbued with the Coates style. The recorded sound is crisp and clean,
too. Readers are urged to sample the pleasures of this splendid collection.

Songs – Rise up and reach the stars; At vesper bell; The young lover; The grenadier; Four old
English songs; Because I miss you so; Sigh no more, ladies; Tell me where is fancy bred; The fairy
tales of Ireland; Music of the night; Betty and Johnny; The mill o' dreams; When I am dead;
The little green balcony; Ship of dream; The outlaw's song; Your name; Beautiful lady moon;
Princess of the dawn. First meeting.
Richard Edgar-Wilson *ten* **Michael Ponder** *va* **Eugene Asti** *pf*
Marco Polo 8 223806 (69 minutes: DDD). Texts included. Recorded 1994.   Ⓕ

Richard Edgar-Wilson has a delightfully natural, free-ranging and expressive tenor voice, his words
coming through with complete clarity, while Eugene Asti clearly revels in Coates's luxurious
accompaniments. Such is the consistency of Coates's luxurious accompaniments. Such, moreover, is
the consistency of Coates's inspiration and musicianship that, though these are not his best-known
songs, the selection here is still immensely enjoyable. At the most obviously popular end of the
spectrum *The grenadier* has one of those rousing Fred Weatherly lyrics after the fashion of
Stonecracker John, while at the more ambitious end are some delightfully fresh Shakespeare settings,
as well as the short song-cycle *The mill o' dreams*. The songs *because I miss you so*, *The fairy tales of
Ireland* and *Music of the night* are particularly lovely compositions. By way of variety the collection
also includes a piece for viola and piano that Coates composed for his teacher Lionel Tertis. This
gives producer Michael Ponder a chance to step into the limelight, which he richly deserves for this
utterly diverting collection.

Edward Confrey

African Suite. Amazonia. Blue Tornado. Coaxing the Piano. Dizzy Fingers. Fourth Dimension.
Jay Walk. Kitten on the Keys. Meandering. Moods of a New Yorker. Rhythm Venture. Sparkling
Waters. Stumbling. Three Little Oddities. Wise Cracker Suite.
Eteri Andjaparidze *pf*
Marco Polo 8 223826 (63 minutes: DDD). Recorded 1995. Ⓝ

This diverting disc celebrates the art of Edward 'Zez' Confrey whose limited but infectious flair first
lit the American music scene in 1921. Later, at the peak of his fame, Confrey achieved top billing
(above Gershwin) when, in 1924, he shared a concert featuring his own novelty numbers and
Gershwin's *Rhapsody in Blue*. Confrey's many admirers included Aaron Copland who clearly saw
him as the occupant of a small but brilliantly lit space in the history of Americana. Georgian-born
but American-based, Eteri Andjaparidze is gloriously equal to the occasion. Everything goes with a
swing and a sparkle and whether she eases you out of *Amazonia*'s perky start into a seductive
rumba, remembers the final whirl of Gershwin's immortal *Rhapsody in Blue* in *Fourth Dimension* or
finds just the right degree of response in 'Relaxation' (No. 3 in *Moods of a New Yorker*), her playing
is imperiously brilliant and idiomatic. She is scarcely less agile and uninhibited in *Kitten on the Keys*
which may, understandably, be your ear-catching favourite. And you only have to try a few bars of,
say, *Coaxing the Piano* and, of course, *Kitten on the Keys* to want to hear more of this disc. The
sound is vivid and immediate.

Aaron Copland

Clarinet Concerto. Connotations. El salón México. Music for the Theatre.
Stanley Drucker *cl* **New York Philharmonic Orchestra / Leonard Bernstein.**
DG 431 672-2GH (74 minutes: DDD). Recorded live in 1989. Ⓝ

This is a real scoop for Copland enthusiasts. These recordings reveal Bernstein and the NYPO on
top form in the kind of music they find absolutely natural. The least familiar piece, *Connotations*,
may be the place to start since Bernstein brings it off splendidly. It was commissioned for the
opening of the Lincoln Center in 1962 and Copland may have been disappointed that the piece
failed to win friends. This recording makes an extremely eloquent plea for Copland's most extended
serial work on orchestral scale. The language is unrelievedly dissonant, harking back to the 1920s in
New York. There is even a near quotation from Copland's Piano Variations and a solo piano enters
with glacial chords like ice-blocks followed by rapt strings and some gentle groans from Bernstein.
The rest of this generous disc is just as rewarding and all in Copland's popular manner. *Music for
the Theatre* (1925) brilliantly sets the style for much of later Copland – and gave Bernstein some
ideas too. The style is absolutely right and so is *El salón México* which Bernstein knew from making
the piano arrangement shortly after it was composed. Both these performances are as good as any
available and well recorded too. The Clarinet Concerto is another bonus in Stanley Drucker's
interpretation. Perhaps Bernstein overdoes the Mahler aspects of the first movement but not
seriously. Drucker throws in a few bends; the balance at 6'14" nearly loses the soloist; but the drive
towards the end is really exciting. In view of the riches of the CD as a whole, this is probably the
performance of the Clarinet Concerto to have, along with excellent performances of the three other
works.

Piano Concerto. Orchestral Variations. Short Symphony. Symphonic Ode.
Garrick Ohlsson *pf*
San Francisco Symphony Orchestra / Michael Tilson Thomas.
RCA Victor Red Seal 09026 68541-2 (66 minutes: DDD). Recorded 1996. Ⓝ**S**

According to Virgil Thomson, jazz was Aaron Copland's 'one wild oat'. Page after page of *Music
for the Theatre* and its first cousin, the 1926 Piano Concerto, featured here, read like the blueprints
for symphonic dance to come. A bold proclamation passes between trumpets and trombones, a
'fanfare for ...'; but before you can finish the sentence, a dramatic cut to the wide shot: a glorious
lyric effusion, its sights set on yet another gleaming skyline. Brave new world or lonely town?
The quizzical solo piano isn't entirely sure, but the yearning grows: rhapsody in blue. Garrick
Ohlsson kicks into this rhythm-bending mood-swing with terrific aplomb, and the San Francisco
Symphony stretches every sinew to get its long limbs co-ordinated. Tilson Thomas has the players
well blooded in the ways of this music: it's slick, it's tight, but it still retains that sense of wilful
precariousness. It's hard to imagine that the *Orchestral Variations* were ever laid down in anything
but orchestral terms, their sonority and harmony stretched from top to bottom of the score in
spare, spacey chords. And then you remember that in its ground-breaking piano original it was as if

the keyboard itself had been surrealistically elongated. It has the look of a modern metropolis in sound, this music: lean, clean, oblique. *Symphonic Ode* – Copland's first big orchestral piece after the Piano Concerto – proceeds onwards and upwards in sky-scraping, octave-leaping tower blocks of sound. It's so very much a young man's America, alternately monolithic and toughly contrapuntal. A jazzy hint of misbegotten adolescence, a reflective heart and a tremendous conclusion as proud and implacable as the US Constitution itself. The performance *knows* just how good it is – and that's a fact. Deep-set, blockbusting recording. A winner.

Concert Suites – The Red Pony; Our Town; Music for Movies. The Heiress – Prelude; Finale. Prairie Journal (Music for Radio).
St Louis Symphony Orchestra / Leonard Slatkin.
RCA Victor Red Seal 09026 61699-2 (67 minutes: DDD). Recorded 1991-92.   Ⓕ

Though the front cover bears the title 'Music for Films', the earliest offering here was written in 1936 following a commission from the CBS radio network. *Music for Radio* (also known as *Saga of the Prairies* or *Prairie Journal*) was one of Copland's first conscious efforts to attain a greater simplicity of utterance and stronger melodic appeal, and its clean-cut, out-of-doors demeanour is relished to the full by these performers. Copland wrote eight film scores in all, the first three of which – *The City* (1939), *Of Mice and Men* (1939) and *Our Town* (1940) – formed the basis for his 1943 concert suite, *Music for Movies*. Slatkin gauges the differing moods of each of the five tableaux with unerring perception. Perhaps Copland's most enduring achievement in this particular field remains his 1948 score for *The Red Pony*. Again, the performance is all one could wish and there's real swagger in the joyous 'Happy Ending' number. In addition, Slatkin gives us the heart-warmingly evocative concert suite Copland compiled from his score for *Our Town*, as well as a first commercial recording for Arnold Freed's idiomatic 1990 reconstruction of Copland's Academy Award-winning 1948 score for *The Heiress*, which happily restores the 'Prelude' that director William Wyler rejected for the final print. With excitingly full-bodied sound, this is an unmissable Copland collection.

El salón México[a]. Danzón cubano[b]. An Outdoor Overture[b]. Quiet City[b]. Our Town[b]. Las agachadas[a]. Fanfare for the Common Man[b]. Lincoln Portrait[b]. Appalachian Spring – suite[b]. Rodeo – Four Dance Episodes[b]. Billy the Kid – orchestral suite[b]. Music for Movies[c]. Letter from Home[b]. John Henry[b]. Symphony No. 3[c]. Clarinet Concerto[d].
Benny Goodman *cl* **Henry Fonda** *narr*
[a]**New England Conservatory Chorus;** [b]**London Symphony Orchestra;**
[c]**New Philharmonia Orchestra;** [d]**Columbia Symphony Orchestra / Aaron Copland.**
Sony Classical SM3K46559 (three discs: 226 minutes: ADD). Recorded 1963-76.   Ⓜ 🆁🆁

These are all reissues, mostly from the 1970s, and a welcome gathering together of a lot of Copland's own performances. Only *Las agachadas* ('The shake-down song') for unaccompanied chorus is new to the British catalogue, although several other pieces are making their return. This is a rather lame performance of a choral piece that should be a sparkling example of Copland's Latin-American output, so nobody would buy the three-CD set for that. The oldest recording is the Clarinet Concerto with Benny Goodman – the second of the two he made under Copland. *Lincoln Portrait* with Henry Fonda is disappointing, but apart from earlier recordings in Spanish and Portuguese, this one, made in 1968, is the only one under Copland's baton. He was surprisingly modest about interpretation and wrote (in *Copland on Music*; New York: 1960): 'Composers rarely can be depended upon to know the correct tempi at which their music should proceed'. And he tried to prove the point by saying – 'A composer listening to a performance of his music when the pacing is inept is a sorry spectacle indeed! He may be unable to set the right speed but he certainly can recognise the wrong one.' All the same it is a pleasure to have Copland as both composer and interpreter in some of his most delightful shorter works such as *Letter from Home*, *John Henry*, *Quiet City* and *An Outdoor Overture*. And at an average of over 75 minutes for each of the three CDs, mostly remastered with acceptable results, this is an economical way to build up a collection of Copland's own performances which provide such an insight into his whole personality.

El salón México. Dance Symphony. Fanfare for the Common Man. Rodeo – Four Dance Episodes. Appalachian Spring – suite.
Detroit Symphony Orchestra / Antál Dorati.
Decca Ovation 430 705-2DM (74 minutes: DDD). Recorded 1980s.   Ⓜ

This glorious disc shows how well Antál Dorati assimilated the music of Aaron Copland. The big-boned swagger of 'Buckaroo Holiday' from *Rodeo* with its vision of open spaces and clear blue skies is established straightaway in Dorati's performance with keen rhythmic drive and fine orchestral articulation. The 'Hoe Down' is properly exciting while the other two dance episodes are wonderfully expressive. In the 1945 suite of *Appalachian Spring* Dorati secures marvellous phrasing and dynamics but tends to understate the poetic elements of the score. Decca's sound quality is exemplary and is of demonstration standard in *Fanfare for the Common Man*, as it is in the enjoyable curtain-raiser, the sturdy, big-hearted *El salón México*. Dorati's vast experience as an interpreter of Stravinsky and Bartók pays fine dividends in Copland's gruesome *Dance Symphony*, music inspired by the vampire film fantasy, *Nosferatu*. This survey of Copland's most popular orchestral works is a welcome addition to the mid-price catalogue.

Organ Symphony. Short Symphony. Dance Symphony. Orchestral Variations.
Simon Preston *org*
St Louis Symphony Orchestra / Leonard Slatkin.
RCA Victor Red Seal 09026 68292-2 (67 minutes: DDD). Recorded 1993-95.   Ⓕ

Copland's *Organ Symphony* is an oddly eclectic mix born of oddly eclectic elements. Russian immigrant parents, a French teacher, jazz – the new national identity: all have a hand in the composition. But still the voice which emerges most strongly is American. Something stirs in the great outdoors but, as yet, it's untamed and more than a little unpredictable. In the *Dance Symphony* young Copland taps once more into his French connections, to indulge himself, to bring on the cornets and two harps, to lend a Berlioz-like enchantment to the solo bassoon; the second movement's shadowy waltz is the one that never made it into the *Symphonie fantastique*. The fact is that the real Copland only fully emerges with the *Short Symphony* (No. 2) of 1932-3. The Stravinsky factor is strong, of course (wiry, angular, busy neo-classical tone and a folkloric homespun quality), but the true grit is entirely Copland's own. The rhythmic bounce and the sometimes belligerent syncopations are all his, too. Slatkin and his band are as spry as can be in that respect. The most exciting item on the disc, however, comes last in the chronology. Nearly three decades after Copland famously got tough with his *Piano Variations* (1930), he laid them out for orchestra – they came up sounding like a brand-new piece. This is Copland outreaching himself, theoretical ingenuity allied to vision. And rather like this sharp, smart, punchy performance, the overriding impression is of evolution – onwards and upwards.

Violin Sonata. Duo for Flute and Piano. Rodeo – suite (arr. cpsr). Piano Quartet.
Jeanne Baxtresser *fl* **Glenn Dicterow, Charles Rex** *vns* **Rebecca Young** *va*
Alan Stepansky *vc* **Israela Margalit** *pf*
EMI Anglo-American Chamber Music CDC5 55405-2 (77 minutes: DDD). Recorded 1995.   Ⓕ Ⓔ

Experienced NYPO concert-master Glenn Dicterow invests the memorably serene and sinewy melodic lines of the Violin Sonata (1942-43) with great imaginative intensity and flair, and his partnership with pianist Israela Margalit must be deemed a great artistic success. Margalit then teams up with the NYPO's principal flautist, Jeanne Baxtresser, for a stylish rendering of the *Duo* (1971), an ingratiating, witty offering based on thematic ideas from Copland's sketch-books from the 1940s. Margalit also makes a decent showing in the 1962 *Rodeo* excerpts for solo piano, and the challenging Piano Quartet of 1950, a work of purpose and substance, is here given a performance which does full justice to its striking integrity and admirable ambition.

Copland In the Beginning. Four Motets – Help us, O Lord; Have mercy on us, O my Lord; Sing ye praises to our King.
Barber Agnus Dei, Op. 11.
Bernstein Chichester Psalms.
Dominic Martelli *treb* **Catherine Denley** *mez* **Rachel Masters** *hp* **Gary Kettel** *perc*
Thomas Trotter *org* **Corydon Singers / Matthew Best.**
Hyperion CDA66219 (54 minutes). Texts included.   Ⓕ

Half of this programme is devoted to unaccompanied choral music by Copland: *In the Beginning*, a striking 15-minute 'Creation' for mixed four-part chorus and solo mezzo (eloquently done by Catherine Denley) written in 1947, and three of four short motets he composed in 1921, while studying with Nadia Boulanger in Paris. The performance of the *Chichester Psalms* recorded here uses Bernstein's own reduced (but very effective) instrumentation of organ, harp and percussion, but follows the composer's New York precedent in employing a mixed chorus – although the illusion of a cathedral choir is persuasively conveyed. It is very impressive. The singing of the Corydon Singers under Matthew Best is very fine, and Hyperion's vivid recording, which gives the voices a pleasant bloom while avoiding the resonance of King's College Chapel, reproduces the instrumental accompaniment, notably the percussion, with electrifying impact. Matthew Best's soloist is Dominic Martelli, and very sweetly he sings too. The disc is completed by Barber's setting of the *Agnus Dei* which dates from 1967 and is an arrangement of the famous *Adagio for Strings* which made his name when Toscanini performed it in New York in 1938. This is an imaginative and enterprising programme, with a nice balance between the familiar and the obscure, extremely well sung and vividly recorded.

Arcangelo Corelli   Italian 1653-1713

12 Concerti grossi, Op. 6 – No. 1 in D major; No. 2 in F major; No. 3 in C minor; No. 4 in D major; No. 5 in B flat major; No. 6 in F major; No. 7 in D major; No. 8 in G minor; No. 9 in F major; No. 10 in C major; No. 11 in B flat major; No. 12 in F major.
The English Concert / Trevor Pinnock.
Archiv Produktion 423 626-2AH2 (two discs: 130 minutes: DDD). Recorded 1988.
Gramophone Award Winner 1989.   Ⓕ Ⓟ

In his working life of about 40 years Corelli must have produced a great deal of orchestral music, yet the 12 *Concerti grossi*, Op. 6, form the bulk of what is known to have survived. Their original forms are mostly lost but we know that those in which they were published in Amsterdam by Estienne Roger had been carefully polished and revised by the composer – and that they were assembled from movements that had been written at various times. The first eight are in *da chiesa* form, the last four in *da camera* form – without and with named dance movements respectively, and the number of their movements varies from four to seven. Each features the interplay of a group of soloists, the *concertino* (two violins and a cello) and the orchestra, the *ripieno*, the size of which Corelli stated to be flexible. These are masterpieces of their genre, one that was later developed by, notably, Bach and Handel, and they are rich in variety. The scores leave scope for embellishment, and the players of The English Concert take full advantage of them.

Trio Sonatas, Op. 3ᵃ – F major; D major; B flat major; B minor; D minor; G major.
Trio Sonatas, Op. 4ᵇ – C major; G minor; A major; D major; A minor; E major.
Jakob Lindberg *theorbo* **Purcell Quartet** (Catherine Mackintosh, ᵃElizabeth Wallfisch, ᵇCatherine Weiss *vns* Richard Boothby *vc*); **Robert Woolley** ᵃ*hpd*/ᵇ*org*
Chandos Chaconne CHAN0526 (76 minutes: DDD). Recorded 1990s.   Ⓕ Ⓟ

Corelli's chamber music was reprinted 84 times during his lifetime and 31 more during the rest of the eighteenth century, a record that most composers would find enviable even today. The Sonatas of Op. 3 are *da chiesa*, those of Op. 4 are *da camera* (with dance-titled movements); the recording contains the first six of each set – the remaining ones are on another disc (Chandos CHAN0532), should you (as is probable) be tempted to add them to your collection. They are small gems: most have four movements and their durations range from five-and-a-half to seven-and-a-half minutes, within which they pack a wealth of invention, pure beauty and variety of pace and mood. Surviving evidence suggests that they were played at a much lower pitch than today's standard, the lower string tension adding warmth and opulence to the sound. Catherine Mackintosh takes full advantage of the works' opportunities for pliant phrasing and added embellishments; Elizabeth Wallfisch 'converses' with her in her own characteristic way, whilst Catherine Weiss follows her example more closely. The Purcell Quartet's oneness of thought and timing is a joy to hear and the recording is superb in all respects.

John Corigliano   American 1938

Symphony No. 1. Of Rage and Remembrance.
Michael Accinno *treb* **Michelle DeYoung** *mez* **Washington Oratorio Society;**
Washington Choral Arts Society; National Symphony Orchestra / Leonard Slatkin.
RCA Victor Red Seal 09026 68450-2 (53 minutes: DDD). Text and translation included.
Recorded live 1990s.   Ⓕ

Corigliano's First Symphony is an elegy in memory of the composer's friends who have died of AIDS. The violent first movement expresses fury over this plague, leading to the first of three elegies for particular friends, with the Albéniz *Tango* in Godowsky's piano arrangement poignantly heard from off-stage. The 'Tarantella' *Scherzo* of the second movement then builds on a trivial piano piece that Corigliano had written for a pianist friend – anger expressed in distortions of triviality. As a culmination the long third movement, 'Giulio's Song', is both a chaconne on a 12-note theme and an elegy for a cellist friend, whose improvisation Corigliano found on a tape after his death, and here uses in the most moving section of all, with solo cellos interweaving. In a brief epilogue the composer simply refers back to each of the previous movements in turn, and closes the work peacefully. What makes this disc even more recommendable is the inclusion as a prelude to the symphony of the related choral work, *Of Rage and Remembrance*. This is substantially a reworking of 'Giulio's Song' with the words filled in. Corigliano built the later part of 'Giulio's Song' on a poem by William M. Hoffman, librettist of his opera, *The Ghosts of Versailles*, with references by name to the friends commemorated. Corigliano then left out the words, using instruments alone. The choral work – with the central mezzo soprano part superbly sung by Michelle DeYoung – restores the words, leading to a section involving free, spoken chant, with chorus members individually naming those they have lost.

Peter Cornelius

German 1824-1874

Stabat mater. Requiem.
Danielle Borst *sop* **Jacqueline Mayeur** *contr* **Jean-Luc Viala** *ten* **Frédéric Vassar** *bass*
Cannes-Provence-Alpes-Côte d'Azur Chorus and Orchestra / Michel Piquemal.
Harmonia Mundi HMA190 5206 (53 minutes: ADD). Texts and translations included.
Recorded 1989. Ⓕ

Requiem. Requiem aeternam. Absolve Domine animas. Drei Psalmlieder, Op. 13.
Drei Liebe, Op. 18. So weich und warm. Trost in Tränen, Op. 14. Die Vätergruft, Op. 19.
Drei Chorgesänge, Op. 11.
Carl-Heinz Müller *bar* **Andras Lust** *ten* **North German Figural Choir / Jörg Straube.**
Thorofon Capella CTH2033 (49 minutes: DDD). Recorded 1988. Ⓕ

Peter Cornelius's *Stabat mater* is a fine work that could well find a home in the choral repertory, and more than deserves its revival on this recording. In it many of Cornelius's gifts come together – his lyrical charm, his gift for chromatic harmony, his vivid response to pious texts, his fine ear for choral textures. There is much less Wagner than might be expected from this gentle, likeable man who sat at Wagner's feet but managed to avoid being trampled under them. Cornelius has individual ideas, and controls them well; and his division of the poem's 20 verses into ten sections works well dramatically. Neither soloists nor chorus are in general outstanding, and are indeed somewhat overtaxed in places, while the recording is rather murky of texture. Never mind: Michel Piquemal's enthusiastic and sympathetic conducting does well for a work more than meriting his care. He is rather less successful with the Requiem based on Hebbel's *Seele, vergiss sie nicht* than Straube is with the German choir, which takes it more easily and thus much more effectively. This is an odd work for Cornelius to have set, but presumably his deep affection and admiration for Hebbel led him to accept such a strongly agnostic text in the poet's memory. It is remarkable not only for the beautifully sensitive choral writing, but for a skilful use of chromatic harmony to lend key words an acute tinge of meaning and then turn in a new expressive direction. The remainder of Straube's disc consists of a good selection of Cornelius's shorter choral pieces, among them the ingenious Psalm Songs which he wrote using the music of three Bach keyboard pieces as his material. The selection includes the fine setting of Goethe's *Trost in Tränen* and the version of Uhland's *Die Vätergruft* which he wrote in the last year of his life. Despite the cheese-paring lack of texts and translations, it is a good introduction to this amiable, intelligent composer, but the Harmonia Mundi disc, in the *Stabat mater*, includes something not far short of a masterpiece.

William Cornysh

British 1468-1523

Salve regina. Ave Maria, mater Dei. Gaude virgo mater Christi. Magnificat. Ah, Robin.
Adieu, adieu, my heartes lust. Adieu courage. Woefully arrayed. Stabat mater.
The Tallis Scholars / Peter Phillips.
Gimell 454 914-2PH (65 minutes: DDD). Texts and translations included. Recorded 1988. Ⓕ

Cornysh's music is a riot of abundant, often seemingly wild melody, constantly in search of wanton, abstract, dare-devil ideas. Take, for example, the extraordinary conclusion to the five-part *Magnificat*, where pairs of voices, rising in turn from the lowest in the choir to the highest, are challenged with music of gradually increasing complexity, peaking in an exchange of quite hair-raising virtuosity between the sopranos – and all this just for the words 'and ever shall be, world without end'! As far as the sacred works are concerned, The Tallis Scholars respond magnificently to Cornysh's audacious imagination. Theirs is a majestic and glorious sound, to be relished in full in the *Stabat mater*, a huge piece that survives incomplete and for which the late Frank Harrison composed treble parts that may even trump Cornysh himself in their sheer bravura. Marginally less striking in The Tallis Scholars' performances are the short part-songs and the carol *Woefully arrayed*, robbed as they are here of some of their latent expressiveness and strength by being sung (admittedly very beautifully) in an inappropriately resonant building, and in rounded modern English vowels rather than their brighter, more robust Tudor equivalents. But judged as a whole this disc must be reckoned an outstanding success.

François Couperin
French 1668-1733

Premier livre de pièces de clavecin – Premier ordre. Concerts royaux – No. 1 in G major; No. 2 in D major.
Laurence Cummings *hpd* **Reiko Ichise** *viol/viol da gamba*
Naxos 8 550961 (71 minutes: DDD). Recorded 1994.   ⑤ⓅⒺ

On this disc Cummings presents the *Concerts royaux* in the harpsichord version authorized by the composer (here calling on the services of a viol for the extra part in the last number of each *Concert*). Cummings, besides being an exceptionally clean player, with intelligent phrasing, the neatest possible ornaments unobtrusively incorporated into the textural lines, splendidly rhythmic yet not at all inflexible, is a persuasive stylist: all his performances are marked by a vitality that is most appealing. In the *Premier ordre*, with its several references to the Duke and Duchess of Maine's circle, he captures the tender expressiveness of 'Les Sentimens', the pomposity of 'La Majesteuse' and the delicacy of 'Les Abeilles'; and in the *Concerts royaux* his Allemandes are particularly exhilarating, while 'Les échos' is very effective. The harpsichord is recorded with striking fidelity.

Deuxième livre de pièces de clavecin – huitième ordre. Concerts royaux – No. 3 in A major; No. 4 in E minor.
Laurence Cummings *hpd* **Reiko Ichise** *va da gamba*
Naxos 8 550962 (67 minutes: DDD). Recorded 1994.   ⑤Ⓟ

This disc of Couperin's solo harpsichord music contains the composer's masterly Eighth *Ordre*, or suite, with its celebrated 'Passacaille'. In addition, Cummings plays the Third and Fourth *Concerts royaux*. He is a neat and fastidious player, and one who enjoys a comfortable relationship with the profuse ornamentation, the observance and precise execution of which, in the composer's own words, are 'absolutely indispensable to the correct performance of my pieces.' These are rhythmic performances, eloquent and warmly communicative. There are pieces of great stature in this recital, notably the allemande 'La Raphaéle', with which the Eighth *Ordre* begins, and the previously mentioned 'Passacaille', whose noble theme and eight succeeding *couplets* explore a wide range of techniques and emotions. None of this is lost on Cummings who, at the same time, manages to convey something of his own ardour and affection for the repertoire.

L'art de toucher le clavecin – Prelude No. 6 in B minor. Troisième livre de pièces de clavecin – Treizième ordre; Quatorzième ordre; Quinzième ordre.
Robert Kohnen *hpd* **Barthold Kuijken** *fl*
Accent ACC9399D (64 minutes: DDD). Recorded 1993.   ⑤Ⓟ

Kohnen's playing is rhythmically incisive, fastidious in detail – Couperin was hot on that – and full of character. If, on first acquaintance, his realization of Couperin's vignette 'Les lis naissans' (*Ordre* No. 13) seems a shade spiky then his lyrical approach to the flowing 6/8 melody of the rondeau 'Les rozeaux', which follows, reassures us that Kohnen does have the poetry of the music at heart, and intends that it should be so. Less appealing are Kohnen's somewhat intrusive vocal introductions to 'Les folies françoises'. This information is provided in the booklet so it hardly needs to be reiterated. In a concert recital such snatches of actuality can be effective; on a disc, after repeated listening, they become an unwelcome interruption. Occasional departures from the norm in the following two *ordres* are of an altogether more agreeable nature. In 'Le rossignol-en-amour' (*Ordre* No. 14) Kohnen takes Couperin up on his suggestion to use a transverse flute, played here with a beautifully rounded tone by Barthold Kuijken. Likewise, in the jaunty rondeau, 'La Julliet', the trio texture is realized by flute and harpsichord rather than the more usual two-harpsichord texture. This piece is beautifully done, as is the subtly bell-like 'Carillon de Cithère' which follows it. In short, a stylish and entertaining release – apart from the aforementioned spoken prefaces – which is as likely as any to draw the cautious listener into Couperin's refined, allusory and metaphor-laden idiom.

Quatrième livre de pièces de clavecin.
Christophe Rousset *hpd*
Harmonia Mundi HMC90 1445/6 (two discs: 152 minutes: DDD). Recorded 1993.   ⑤Ⓟ

Couperin's Fourth Book of harpsichord pieces, his last, published in Paris in 1730 though completed around three years earlier does not, perhaps, contain as many masterpieces as the First and Second Books, but a high proportion of them possess a character nevertheless poignant and sometimes enigmatic which both stimulates the imagination and haunts the memory. This anthology is deeply rewarding. Rousset is fastidious in matters of ornament – for that he would have gained Couperin's wholehearted approval – and has a lively response to the many and varied musical gestures, some of them of enormous subtlety. He has, furthermore, the technique to implement Couperin's requirements with absolute fluency, and the sense to eschew exaggerated or misplaced mannerisms.

Trois Leçons de Ténèbres. Quatre Versets du Motet.
Sophie Daneman, Patricia Petibon sops **Les Arts Florissants** (Marc Hantaï, Charles Zebley fls Monica Huggett, Emilia Benjamin vns Anne-Marie Lasla bass viol) / **William Christie** hpd
Erato 0630-17067-2 (47 minutes: DDD). Texts and translations included. Recorded 1996. ℗℗

All three of Couperin's Lessons for the Wednesday of Holy Week – the first two for a single voice, the third for a pair – represent the composer at his most heart-rendingly intense, underlining the character of the text by chromaticisms, expressive appoggiaturas and ornaments (on the interpretation of which he set great store). Each verse of these Lamentations of Jeremiah is preceded by an elaborate melisma on a successive letter of the Hebrew alphabet, like an illuminated capital in a medieval manuscript. On this disc the gamba continuo line is filled out only by harpsichord. The singers are intelligent and stylish, well matched (as they need to be) in the singularly beautiful intertwining lines of the introductory letters. Sweet-voiced and gentle, they are particularly touching in the First Lesson's 'plorans ploravit' and the Third's 'desolatam'. Unusually, Daneman and Petibon adopt a Gallic pronunciation of the Latin, with French nasal vowels in words like 'princeps' and 'gentes'.

Messe à l'usage ordinaire des paroisses (with plainchant).
Marie-Claire Alain org **Les Chantres de la Chapelle de Versailles / Emmanuel Mandrin.**
Erato 0630-17581-2 (66 minutes: DDD). Text and translation included. Recorded on the Clicquot organ of Cathédrale St Pierre de Poitiers, France in 1996. ℗

Couperin's two Organ Masses are his earliest known compositions. Marie-Claire Alain here plays the larger of the two, the parish Mass, which is spaciously laid out and was designed for the liturgy on the principal church feast days. Couperin supplied details of organ registration for both Organ Masses, though left matters concerning ornamentation and phrasing to the discretion of the performer. An effective feature of this recording is the placing of the music in an appropriate context. Thus the various sections of Couperin's Mass are integrated with an irregularly alternating pattern of Gregorian chant. This is sung by Les Chantres de la Chapelle de Versailles under the direction of Emmanuel Mandrin. He has chosen ornamented versions of the plainsong melodies based on those which were in use at the end of the seventeenth century. The contrasting colours of Couperin's Organ Masses, whether merely the product of his highly imaginative registration or of textual affinity, are among their most glorious features. Intimacy, exuberance, grandiose declamation and the quiet fervour of prayer all take their turn in a work of great nobility. The late-eighteenth-century Clicquot organ of Poitiers Cathedral is well known to organ music specialists and sounds splendid in the context of this music. In summary, this is a satisfying, sometimes thrilling recital.

Louis Couperin
French c1626-1661

Harpsichord Suites – C major; C minor; F major; E minor; A major; F major; C major; D minor; A minor; B minor; D minor; A minor; D major; G minor; C major; A minor; G major. Pavanne in F sharp minor. Prelude and Chaconne in G minor. Two Pieces in B flat major. Three Pieces in G minor. Four Pieces in G major.
Davitt Moroney hpd
Harmonia Mundi Musique d'abord HMA190 1124/7 (four discs: 315 minutes: ADD).
Recorded 1983. ⑧℗

Louis Couperin was a pupil of Chambonnières, generally recognized as founder of the great French harpsichord school. After his nephew 'François Le grand', Louis Couperin was undoubtedly the most gifted member of a musically illustrious family. His harpsichord music amounts to somewhat over 130 pieces, all of which Davitt Moroney has included in this impressive and largely satisfying survey. This repertory is striking for its invention, variety of character and on frequent occasions its elegiac content. This last quality can be found time and again in the chaconnes whose pervasive melancholy is irresistible, indeed perhaps the irresistible feature of his style; but it is also present in many of the sarabandes, préludes and more consciously, of course, in his single essay in that peculiarly French musical-poetic form, the 'tombeau'. Couperin's tombeau commemorates the lutenist Blancrocher who fell downstairs to his death after imbibing to excess. Moroney has lavished his musical expertise, scholastic and practical, on this giant project and has matched the fine craftsmanship and noble gestures of the composer with performances that are stylish and affectionate. He invests the music with colour and graceful gesture. These are not discs which should necessarily be listened to from beginning to end all in one sitting; Couperin grouped his pieces according to keys, leaving the performer to make up his own suites. Richly inventive and extended pieces such as the F sharp minor Pavanne deserve to be listened to on their own. Three different harpsichords are featured in the recording. The earliest, built in Antwerp in 1671, subsequently passed through the workshops of two great French harpsichord makers of the following century, Messrs Blanchet and Taskin. The other two are eighteenth-century instruments. The instruments come over clearly and resonantly and the booklet is carefully documented by Moroney himself.

George Crumb American 1929

Crumb Quest[a].
Ruders Psalmodies[b].
J.A. Lennon Zingari[c].
David Starobin *gtr*
[ab]Speculum Musicae / [a]William Purvis, [b]Donald Palma;
[c]SMU Meadows Symphony Orchestra / David Milnes.
Bridge BCD9071 (72 minutes: DDD). Recorded [a]1995, [b]1992, [c]1993.   Ⓕ

It is important for the guitar's absorption into mainstream music-making, that the gap between lone recitalist and concerto soloist should be bridged; the two works by Crumb and Ruders, in which the guitar plays a *concertante* role, make a valuable contribution to that end. Crumb's work is an eight-movement sextet in which he uses a remarkable variety of instruments to produce haunting sounds. His 'quest', prompted by quotations from Dante and Lorca, is 'a long tortuous journey towards an ecstatic and transfigured feeling of arrival', in which interjected phrases from *Amazing Grace* have a moving effect akin to that of the Bach chorales in Berg's Violin Concerto and Takemitsu's *Folios*. The title of Ruders's 11-movement *Psalmodies* has 'no specific religious content or aim'; he compares its message with that of his First Symphony, *Of Joy and Grief; of Worship and Oblivion*. He uses more conventional forces than Crumb but does so to equally arresting effect: 'Solo for two', for guitar and cello, left hands only, is one of many instrumental *tours de force*. Here, then, are two of the most remarkable twentieth-century ensemble works ever written for the guitar, albeit not for the faint-hearted. John Anthony Lennon pays tribute to gipsy culture and the spontaneity of its music. He describes *Zingari* as 'a suite of [five] concert arias rather than a concerto in the classic form'. Here the 'conventional' listener will find the most familiar ground. Only a guitarist of the highest technical skill and musical insight could play and empathize with these works: Starobin is a model of the ilk, teamed with other players of similar calibre. This is a remarkable and magnificently recorded disc, nothing less than a milestone in the progress of the twentieth-century guitar.

Bernhard Crusell Finnish 1775-1839

Crusell Clarinet Concerto No. 2 in F minor, 'Grand'.
Baermann Adagio in D flat major.
Rossini Introduction and Variations in C minor.
Weber Concerto Concertino in C minor, J109.
Emma Johnson *cl*
English Chamber Orchestra / Sir Charles Groves.
ASV CDDCA559 (55 minutes: DDD).   Ⓕ

It was this Crusell Grand Concerto which Emma Johnson played when she won the BBC Young Musician of the Year competition in 1984. That occasion was the first time she had ever played a concerto with a full symphony orchestra, and her special affection for the piece, her total joy in each of the three movements, comes over vividly in this recorded performance. The uninhibited spontaneity of her playing, exactly matching a live performance, brings an extra compulsion and immediacy of expression. Emma Johnson in each movement translates the notes with very personal phrasing and expression, always taking risks and bringing them off. This is a daring performance, naughtily lilting in the outer movements, happily songful in the *Andante pastorale* of the slow movement. In the three delightful shorter pieces Johnson may not have quite the same technical perfection, but the free expressiveness could not be more winning. Her moulding of *legato* melodies in the Weber and Rossini works, as well as the Baermann, brings warm expressiveness, with free rubato and sharp contrasts of tone and dynamic. The orchestral sound is full and bright, with Groves a lively and sympathetic accompanist.

Luigi Dallapiccola
Italian 1904-1975

Canti di Prigionia. Cinque frammenti di Saffo. Due Liriche di Anacreonte. Sex Carmina Alcaei. Tempus destruendi – Tempus aedificandi.
Due Cori di Michelangelo Buonarroti il Giovane; Julie Moffat *sop*
New London Chamber Choir / James Wood; Ensemble InterContemporain / Hans Zender.
Erato 4509-98509-2 (72 minutes: DDD). Texts included. Recorded 1992.　　　Ⓕ

This disc charts Dallapiccola's 40-year journey as a vocal composer from 1933 to 1971. It is a fascinating, thought-provoking odyssey, as the rather easygoing flow of the early style yields to more turbulent lines which seem to resist assimilation into conventionally balanced structures. The music that comes between these extremes confirms that Dallapiccola was at his best when his personal, Italianate lyricism was contained by small-scale forms and refined yet rigorous contrapuntal textures of the kind he so admired in Webern. On a larger scale, as in the *Canti di Prigionia* for chorus with pianos, harps and percussion (1938-41), whose ritualistic style has links with middle-period Stravinsky, his strongly expressive melodic lines do not always sustain a convincing sense of purpose, and the members of the New London Chamber Choir sound less at home here than in the *a cappella* works. The contrast between the restrained, reflective idiom of the *Canti di Prigionia* and the intense yet eloquent cycles for solo voice and instruments from the 1940s which follow are striking. It is in the *Sappho Fragments*, the *Anacreon Lyrics* and the *Alcaeus Songs* that Dallapiccola found his true musical identity, absorbing Webernian austerities into his own warmer and more rhythmically flexible idiom. These performances are generally excellent, though the recordings opt for atmosphere at the expense of the fullest clarity of texture.

Jean-François Dandrieu
French c1682-1738

Dandrieu Premier livre d'orgue – Mass and Vespers for Easter Sunday.
Gregorian Chant Mass and Vespers for Easter Sunday.
Paris Gregorian Choir / Jaan-Eik Tulve with **Jean-Patrice Brosse** *org*
Pierre Verany PV794034 (59 minutes: DDD). Texts and translations included. Recorded on the organ of St Bertrand-de-Comminges, France in 1993.　　　Ⓕ

A peculiarly French recording, this. Jean-Patrice Brosse plays Dandrieu's organ music for Easter Day Mass on the splendid instrument at St Bertrand-de-Comminges (the town where Herod Antipas is supposed to have spent his last years), and the chant is supplied by the Paris Gregorian Choir. Dandrieu's music is – while naturally more restrained than his harpsichord works – colourful and inventive, though not as memorable as Couperin's Organ Masses, and is extremely well played by Brosse. What makes the recording interesting is the liturgical context in which Dandrieu's music is placed. Bells are rung, the choir sounds suitably monkish, and there is a sense of connection between the chant and the organ music which is of course essential (for example, in the *Kyrie* or the *Sanctus*), but in practice extremely difficult to achieve on a recording. The sound quality itself is excellent.

Jan Yves Daniel-Lesur
French 1908

Daniel-Lesur Le cantique des cantiques.
Jolivet Epithalame.
Messiaen Cinq Rechants.
The Sixteen / Harry Christophers.
Collins Classics 1480-2 (60 minutes: DDD). Texts and translations included. Recorded 1996.　　　Ⓕ

All these works concentrate on the erotic, and both Jolivet and Messiaen employ musical devices drawn from non-western sources (the second part of Jolivet's *Epithalame* is clearly heavily influenced by Chinese music). Messiaen's *Cinq Rechants* is based on the legend of Tristan and Isolde, and as such forms part of a trilogy dating from the late 1940s (the other parts being *Harawi* and the *Turangalîla* Symphony), while Jolivet sets his own poem dedicated to his wife on their twentieth wedding anniversary in a piece almost too full of disparate ideas and diverse musical idioms. Jean Yves Daniel-Lesur has turned to that most erotic of all writing, the *Song of Songs*, and been inspired to compose music which is gloriously lavish and luxuriant. Recordings of twentieth-century *a cappella* music have invariably turned up outstanding performances. This is no exception. The Sixteen produce some of the most brilliant and technically accomplished singing imaginable. The lavish tone colours in the Messiaen are all the more astonishing since here The Sixteen are reduced to just 12 voices, while despite doubling that number for Daniel-Lesur's opulent textures Harry Christophers can still draw from his singers such immaculate precision and uniformity of expression. The recording is gloriously full-blooded.

Richard Danielpour American 1956

Danielpour Cello Concerto.
Kirchner Music for Cello and Orchestra.
Rouse Cello Concerto.
Yo-Yo Ma *vc*
Philadelphia Orchestra / David Zinman.
Sony Classical SK66299 (79 minutes: DDD). Recorded 1996. Ⓕ**SE**

All these works were commissioned for Yo-Yo Ma which makes the performances definitive in at least one sense. David Zinman secures committed playing from the Philadelphia Orchestra and the sensitive recording team makes a positive contribution. The most straightforward music is provided by the youngest of the three men, Richard Danielpour. His music and even his movement titles are derivative of Leonard Bernstein's but you may think that no bad thing. Danielpour is a shameless eclectic who wants his music to have 'an immediate, visceral impact' and so it does. What one misses is memorable melodic invention. Leon Kirchner, Ma's sometime teacher at Harvard, places greater stress on internal logic and intellectual consistency even if he has moved away from the world of Arnold Schoenberg (his own teacher) to forge a personal style of 'euphonious dissonance'. There is here a rich, loving, almost Korngoldian lyricism, at first suppressed, at length permitted to flower. Christopher Rouse is one of the more genuinely individual composers working in America today and his neglect in the UK is a puzzle. His mode of address is both boldly communicative and formally coherent, rarely lapsing into the obvious paths of professorial post-expressionism and/or workmanlike nostalgia. If his Cello Concerto is less effective than some of his other pieces that may be because it does not quite measure up to its stated programme as 'a meditation upon death'. Rouse is good at the noisy accumulation of rhythmic energy, less original in the contemplative, static processional of his second movement. Concluding with a death rattle – one last reprise of the hissing and rattling percussion idea from the first movement – this *Adagiati* encompasses references to other people's death pieces – Monteverdi, Schumann and, seemingly, Pärt's *Cantus* in memory of Benjamin Britten, although that section might also be said to constitute an unravelling of the rather banal ascending idea that opens the concerto.

Louis-Claude Daquin French 1694-1772

Nouveau livre de noëls, Op. 2.
Christopher Herrick *org*
Hyperion CDA66816 (65 minutes: DDD). Recorded on the organ of St Rémy, Dieppe in 1995. Ⓕ**E**

Le coucou is probably the only thing many people know of Daquin, Louis XV's prized court organist, hailed by contemporaries such as Marchand as a supreme virtuoso and recognized even by Rameau as the finest improviser of his day. His only organ compositions to have survived are the present 12 *Noëls* – treatments of traditional Christmas carols – a genre dating from Lebègue's collection about 60 years earlier. Daquin's *Noëls*, written around 1740, employ a technique of variations of ever-increasing brilliance: they extend from the swaggering boldness of No. 1, the bucolic No. 3 over a long drone bass and the briskly breezy No. 4 to the charmingly naïve No. 9 (on flutes), the aggressively cheerful No. 10 and the stunningly exultant No. 12. This is something all organ lovers will want to have. The splendid instrument, almost exactly contemporary with the work presented (much rebuilt but in 1992 restored on historical lines), allows Christopher Herrick to display both his own virtuosity and the organ's rich range of colours (the specification is provided) with vividness – he has fun with multiple echo effects in Nos. 6 and 10 – and the recording is wonderfully fresh in sound. Smashing!

Claude Debussy

Images. Berceuse héroïque[a]. Danse sacrée et danse profane[b]. Jeux. Nocturnes. Marche écossaise sur un thème populaire. Prélude à l'après-midi d'un faune. La mer. Première rapsodie[c].
[b]**Vera Badings** *hp* [c]**George Pieterson** *cl*
Concertgebouw Orchestra / [a]**Eduard van Beinum, Bernard Haitink.**
Philips Duo 438 742-2PM2 (two discs: 141 minutes: ADD). Recorded [b]1957, 1976-79.
Gramophone Award Winner 1980. Ⓜ ℞℞

Philips has repackaged Haitink's late-1970s recordings on two CDs for the price of one. Space has also been found for Debussy's last orchestral work, the short *Berceuse héroïque* conducted by Eduard van Beinum (in excellent 1957 stereo). In every respect this package is a genuine bargain. In *La mer*, like the 1964 Karajan on DG Galleria, there is a concern for refinement and fluidity of gesture, for a subtle illumination of texture; and both display a colourist's knowledge and use of an individually apt variety of orchestral tone and timbre. It is the wind playing that you remember in Haitink's *Images*: the melancholy and disconsolate oboe d'amore in 'Gigues'; and from 'Ibéria', the gorgeous oboe solo in 'Les parfums de la nuit', and the carousing clarinets and raucous trumpets in the succeeding holiday festivities. And here, as elsewhere in the set, the Concertgebouw acoustic plays a vital role. Haitink's *Jeux* is slower and freer than average, and possessed of a near miraculous precision, definition and delicacy. The jewel in this set, for many, will be the *Nocturnes*, principally for the purity of the strings in 'Nuages'; the dazzling richness and majesty of the central procession in 'Fêtes'; and the cool beauty and composure of 'Sirènes'. Haitink opts for an ethereal distance; there may be passages where you are unsure if they are singing or not, but the effect is magical.

Debussy Images.
Ravel Boléro. La valse. Rapsodie espagnole.
Boston Symphony Orchestra / Charles Munch.
RCA Victor Living Stereo 09026 61956-2 (74 minutes: ADD). Recorded 1955-57. Ⓜ Ⓗ

Munch, as one writer put it, 'preferred "taking-off" at concerts instead of nit-picking at rehearsals'. Though he didn't generally live as dangerously in his studio recordings, you are unlikely to hear a more bracing 'Rondes de Printemps'. And his 'Gigues' most certainly does 'take-off' as soon as the opportunity arises, after perhaps the most atmospheric opening on disc (whose secret is in the barely audible muted trumpet – what control! – and the flute vibrato). No matter what Munch does, he seems to be able to rely on an orchestra who move with him, with grace, at the speed of light, and with not a musical hair out of place. Brass playing in particular is truly 'legendary'; in other words, faultless, but expressive, not merely ostentatious. And was there ever a more hauntingly distant horn solo in the slow movement of 'Ibéria', or a conductor and leader who drew more humour from the (here, delightfully tipsy) strolling fiddler in its last movement? There is marginally more fantasy, flair and fun in Munch's *Images* than any other. Boston's orchestra and its hall have rarely, if ever, had a more natural stereo showing on disc. Compared with other remakes, these older recordings have more detail, a more convincing balance, livelier timbres and more of the hall's acoustic. *Boléro* starts at Ravel's surprisingly fast marking, and gradually gets faster; and *La valse* finds Munch and the orchestra at their greatest (trumpets in a spin in the final bars – once heard never forgotten). There isn't today's dynamic range, of course (though the *Images* come very close).

Debussy La mer. Prélude à l'après-midi d'un faune.
Ravel Daphnis et Chloé – Suite No. 2. Boléro.
Berlin Philharmonic Orchestra / Herbert von Karajan.
DG Galleria 427 250-2GGA (64 minutes: ADD). Recorded 1964-65. Ⓜ ℞℞

Karajan never concealed his passion for French music and these supreme and most frequently performed masterpieces of French orchestral music are masterly (and rightly celebrated); beautifully recorded too. Controlled and aristocratic, they show a scrupulous regard for the composers' wishes. The sound of the Berlin strings is sumptuous, with detail well placed and in a generally natural perspective. It is a joy to relish the beauty of the playing in such clear, well-defined sound. It has that indefinable quality that one can more readily recognize than describe, a magic that makes one forget the performer and transports one directly into the composer's world. You can either be seduced by some of the most sheerly beautiful orchestral sound ever recorded, or appreciate it for its wide-ranging imagery and its properly mobile pacing; but whichever way you look at it, it is one of the great recorded *La mer*s and one of the classics of the gramophone. Karajan's interpretation of *Prélude à l'après-midi d'un faune* remains one of the most beautiful readings ever committed to record – the first flute, Karlheinz Zöller, plays like a wizard. *Boléro* is slow and steady (but Karajan risks floating the early solos). This is also a ravishing account of the Second Suite from *Daphnis et Chloé*.

La mer. Nocturnes. Première rapsodie. Jeux.
Franklin Cohen cl **Cleveland Chorus and Orchestra / Pierre Boulez.**
DG 439 896-2GH (71 minutes: DDD). Recorded 1991-93.　　　　　　　　　Ⓕ▪

No one, we would submit, is the equal of Karajan in 1964 as a colourist in *La mer*, although few have had the Berlin Philharmonic's rich and varied palette to deploy on it. And very few are Karajan's equal in relating Debussy's detailed tempo indications. Boulez's speed for 'Jeux de vagues' was, and still is, too leisurely by half, and the orchestra seems to be here – untypically – on auto-pilot. Boulez does at least forge ahead in the middle of the second half's gathering wave. But for the remaining 56 minutes of music-making on this disc, there is nothing but praise. Boulez conducts *Jeux* with obvious authority and passionate urgency, without lingering unduly in its moments of fantasy and sophisticated sensuality. In the clarinet *Rapsodie* and *Nocturnes* there is a quite fabulous subtlety and variety of pace, texture and colour. From the latter, 'Nuages' is more mobile than is common and 'Fêtes' is rather more gentle than usual (with a perfectly judged distance for the trumpets at the start of the central procession). Boulez greatly varies the vowels from phrase to phrase in the chorus's *vocalise* in 'Sirènes', sometimes within a phrase, in a manner that is both haunting and hypnotic, and which is entirely consistent with the music's dynamic. The Cleveland ladies' pitching is beyond criticism, as is Franklin Cohen's clarinet-playing. There is also a grace and poise about this singing and playing and the 20-odd years of Boulez's experience with the work show, too, in his now more moderate slowings and suspensions. The sound is warm and full.

Nocturnes – Nuages; Fêtes. Prélude à l'après-midi d'un faune. Le martyre de Saint-Sébastien – symphonic fragments. La mer.
Philharmonia Orchestra / Guido Cantelli.
Testament mono SBT1011 (67 minutes: ADD). Recorded 1954-55.　　　　　　　Ⓕ▣

The death of Guido Cantelli in an air crash at the age of 36 in 1956 was a terrible loss. In a career lasting just 13 years he made his way right to the top of his profession, although at the end of his life he was still developing and maturing, and would surely have been one of the most important artists of our time. Fortunately he made a number of superlative recordings over a period of seven years and this disc, which contains all his Debussy, shows clearly why concert audiences in the 1950s were bowled over by him. It is a pity that he never conducted all three *Nocturnes*, for 'Nuages' flows beautifully and expressively and he chooses just the right tempo for 'Fêtes'. He does not press this piece too hard as most conductors do, and its colour and piquant personality thus flower freshly and easily. *L'après-midi* is also given plenty of room to breathe: the playing cool, elegant, beautifully poised, yet very eloquent. In *La mer* Cantelli avoids the ham-fisted, overdramatic approach of so many conductors, and instead we have a performance with clear, gleaming textures. The first movement ebbs and flows in a movingly poetic fashion: every detail makes its effect and everything is perfectly in scale. The middle movement is taken quite briskly, but phrasing is hypersensitive and appropriately fluid. In the last movement there is plenty of drama and excitement, although climaxes are kept within bounds in a way which paradoxically makes for a greater effect than if they were given Brucknerian proportions, as they often are. During Cantelli's lifetime *Le martyre de Saint-Sébastien* was strangely regarded as a tired, feeble work, yet he conducted the 'Symphonic fragments' quite frequently. His approach is very much of the concert hall in that he gives the four pieces a life of their own rather than relating them to the unfolding drama. Nevertheless, he still captures the music's peculiarly fervent, religious-cum-exotic flavour very effectively. The Philharmonia plays with extraordinary subtlety, and the recordings sound very well indeed.

Printemps. La boîte à joujoux. Children's Corner. La plus que lente.
Montreal Symphony Orchestra / Charles Dutoit.
Decca 444 386-2DH (69 minutes: DDD). Recorded 1992-94.　　　　　　　　　Ⓕ

Children's Corner and the main work here – the ballet *La boîte à joujoux* – are variously linked. Both were intended for Debussy's daughter ChouChou, whose toys were the inspiration for most of the portraits of the former and also for the latter's 'pantomime' (as Debussy originally called it) and both were (very idiomatically) orchestrated by André Caplet. *La boîte à joujoux*, to quote David Cox, 'has not the sustained musical invention of *Children's Corner*, though with the interest focused on the stage action it could undoubtedly be an attractive entertainment for children and adults alike'. And indeed it would be for the listener at home, if a full printed scenario and linked tracking (or indexing) points were provided. Yet Decca's notes (otherwise excellent) give us little more than an outline of the story. Still, even without moment-by-moment knowledge of the stage action, many will surely respond to the gentle humour, whimsy, parody and the touching tenderness of the piece. Performance and recording are generally up to Decca/Montreal standards – the very slow and dream-like 'Jimbo's lullaby' from *Children's Corner* is especially effective.

Debussy Khamma.
Ravel Daphnis et Chloé.
Het Groot Omroepkoor; Royal Concertgebouw Orchestra / Riccardo Chailly.
Decca 443 934-2DH (74 minutes: DDD). Recorded 1994.   Ⓕ

You would expect this *Daphnis* to sound superb, and, of course, it does. In the Concertgebouw acoustic the full flood of choral tone at the climax of Chailly's 'Daybreak' has to be heard to be believed (Chailly's timing of this sunburst is masterly), and it hardly needs saying that this disc's ability to astonish with decibels at climaxes is greater than Decca's previous Dutoit or Monteux recordings of works by Ravel. Possibly the wind machine is cranked with excessive enthusiasm, and the strange lights scenes of *Daphnis* do not seem to be enjoyed or exploited for the strangeness that can result from even the ordinary (i.e. musical) instruments being asked to play or phrase in unusual ways. Chailly is faster, too, in the dance scenes where, if you are Sir Simon Rattle (on EMI), lingering leads to marvels of characterization, which is not to say that Chailly is bland. And blandness is emphatically the last word to use in describing Chailly's way with Debussy's *Khamma*. This immediately pre-*Jeux* (conceptually speaking) ballet is a sort of Egyptian *Salome*-cum-*Rite of Spring*, in as much as Khamma dances herself to death for the Sun God Amun-Ra that he might be persuaded to save the city from siege. The ominous opening pages here are immediately gripping: a Nibelheim-like family of lower woodwind slithering around, marvellously focused drum, and trumpet fanfares that genuinely do 'give one the shivers' as Debussy once asserted. In general, Chailly, Decca and these superb musicians realize more of the score's 'discoveries of harmonic chemistry' and sheer theatre than one dared imagine possible.

Debussy Images – Ibéria.
Ravel Rapsodie espagnole. Pavane pour une infante défunte. Valses nobles et sentimentales. Alborada del gracioso.
Chicago Symphony Orchestra / Fritz Reiner.
RCA Victor Gold Seal GD60179 (68 minutes: ADD). Recorded 1956-57.   Ⓜ Ⓗ

These performances are seldom less than mesmeric. The extremes of tempo and dynamics are exploited to the full in the Spanish night/day pieces: has any other conductor managed the gradual transition from *Ibéria*'s 'perfumes of the night' to the gathering brilliance of the succeeding morning's holiday festivities, with such a delicate, yet precisely focused tracery of sounds? This is the very stuff of a waking dream. And the disc opens with what has to be the slowest, most languid account of the 'Prélude' from the *Rapsodie espagnole* ever recorded; the resulting total concentration of the players on their conductor for control of rhythm and dynamics can be felt in every bar; it's not just a musical stunt, it creates a unique tension and atmosphere. Just listen to the finesse of the playing throughout, particularly the percussion, and marvel at how Reiner balances the textures in even the most riotous outbursts of the *Rapsodie*'s explosive 'Feria'. And the sound? It is difficult to think of any modern recording that renders the spectacle, colour and refinement of these scores with more clarity and atmosphere.

Debussy String Quartet in G minor, Op. 10.
Ravel String Quartet in F major.
Webern String Quartet (1905).
Hagen Quartet (Lukas Hagen, Rainer Schmidt *vns* Veronika Hagen *va* Clemens Hagen *vc*).
DG 437 836-2GH (70 minutes: DDD). Recorded 1992-93.   Ⓕ ⓇⓇ

The first movement of the Debussy is taken fastish, but its passionate urgency convinces and it is not forced tonally or tempo-wise. Indeed, the playing is beautifully polished, and this fine ensemble also fully understands the emotional world of the music, the slow movement (again more flowing than usual) offering an acid test which they pass easily. The finale is thrilling. In the Ravel, the playing is sensitive and skilful. Webern's one-movement Quartet was inspired by a painting entitled 'Evolving, Being, Passing Away', and the music begins with a motif akin to Beethoven's 'Muss es sein?' figure in his String Quartet, Op. 135. The scenario here is predictable: youthfully Germanic heart-searching and struggle, but with little that is memorable, and ultimately somewhat constipated. Still, this performance is persuasive, and the work deserves to be heard when played as well as this. The recording deserves praise: the sound is excellent, not least for viola and cello.

Debussy String Quartet in G minor, Op. 10.
Ravel String Quartet in F major.
Quartetto Italiano (Paolo Borciani, Elisa Pegreffi *vns* Piero Farulli *va* Franco Rossi *vc*).
Philips Silver Line 420 894-2PSL (57 minutes: ADD). Recorded 1968.   Ⓜ

Coupling the Debussy and Ravel String Quartets has become a cliché of the record industry, but as someone has said, a cliché is only a great truth made stale by repetition, and these two wonderful pieces do make a satisfying pair. The account of them by the Quartetto Italiano is over 30 years old but none the worse for that. They are marvellously vital performances in which intensity of feeling does not preclude refinement. The only quibble is about the high-level transfer to CD which may send you reluctantly to the volume control of your amplifier. But when the necessary adjustment is made, the result as sound is satisfactory and the playing good enough to make this Philips issue a first choice at medium price in these works despite its age.

Debussy String Quartet in G minor, Op. 10
Fauré String Quartet in E minor, Op. 121
Ravel String Quartet in F major.
Pro Arte Quartet (Alphonse Onnou, Laurent Halleux *vns* Germain Prévost *va* Robert Maas *vc*).
Biddulph mono LAB105 (78 minutes: ADD). Recorded 1933.   Ⓜ Ⓗ

When the Pro Arte Quartet made these recordings in the 1930s (yes, all of them, including the Fauré, though this wasn't released until later), it was at the height of its powers and had just been appointed quartet to the court of Belgium. Listening to these remarkably well-transferred discs, it seems clear that the Pro Arte was indeed a great quartet. The Debussy is very cleanly recorded, with surface noise intrusive only in some quiet passages. There is an agitated urgency about the first movement – *animé et très décidé* indeed – and great delicacy in the murmurings of the second movement. One or two small imperfections of intonation scarcely affect the overall persuasiveness of this reading. The team is perhaps heard at its best in the adorable Ravel Quartet, where the silky, sweet tone, sensitive dynamic nuances and firm rhythm are immediately striking: the players produce a fine rhythmic bite in the finale, and in the second movement (where the cello splendidly helps the cross-rhythms) the balance where the two themes are combined is judged to a nicety. Fauré's Quartet, completed only a few days before his death, starts impressively here, with elegant long lines that develop in intensity, and with carefully judged interplay of voices; and the shifting sands of its finale are negotiated with finesse; but the enigmatic long *Andante* proves somewhat elusive, and the off-beat chords under the first violin's cantilena are too heavy. But no one in this world is perfect.

Debussy Violin Sonata.
Poulenc Violin Sonata.
Ravel Violin Sonata. Tzigane.
Tasmin Little *vn* **Piers Lane** *pf*
EMI Eminence CD-EMX2244 (61 minutes: DDD). Recorded 1990s.   Ⓜ Ⓔ ⓇⓇ

Even by today's high standards this disc is outstanding, perfectly recorded by Andrew Keener and Mike Hatch. It begins with Ravel's Sonata, of which the first movement is played with a crisp coolness that may be off-putting to ears expecting cajolery but rightly emphasizes the titillating acidity of the world-weary 1920s idiom. Indeed, the playing has great subtlety and there can be nothing but praise for Tasmin Little's acutely judged sonority as well as the actual beauty of her tone. Piers Lane is no less admirable: listen, for example, how he shapes and textures the elegantly edgy phrases of the (finally) flagellatory central Blues. The duo bring the same insight, unselfishness and sheer affection to the very different worlds of Debussy and Poulenc. Debussy's wonderful but fragile Sonata again comes alive in a quite extraordinary way. Nothing is routine, and yet nothing is out of place. Little and Lane have all the virtues of sensitivity and virtuosity of Dumay and Pires plus an extra flair and intensity which puts them in a class of their own.

Debussy Violin Sonata.
Franck Violin Sonata in A major.
Ravel Berceuse sur le nom de Gabriel Fauré. Pièce en forme de habanera. Tzigane.
Augustin Dumay *vn* **Maria João Pires** *pf*
DG 445 880-2GH (56 minutes: DDD). Recorded 1993.   Ⓕ

There is a spacious, eloquent view here of Franck's Sonata, in which Dumay's essentially sweet tone also has the requisite strength; as for Pires, she accompanies where necessary and yet can offer a partner's contribution too, as well as being equal to the composer's considerable pianistic demands, not least in terms of large stretches. Although the recorded balance favours the violinist, the brilliant second movement is very effective, and so is the flowing canonic finale, in which the players rightly think in long phrases. Debussy's emotionally fragile world fares even better: this playing has the right flexibility of time and tone, and the rapidly shifting moods of this essentially sad music, so different from Franck's with its emotional assurance, are unerringly captured; and the sound is excellent here. Dumay and Pires are also at home in Ravel's music with its characteristic delicate tenderness and – in *Tzigane* at least – glittering virtuosity.

Debussy Cello Sonata in D minor.
Britten Cello Sonata, Op. 65.
Schumann Fünf Stücke im Volkston, Op. 102.
Mstislav Rostropovich *vc* **Benjamin Britten** *pf*
Decca The Classic Sound 452 895-2DCS (51 minutes: ADD). Recorded 1961.　Ⓜ️**RR**

Rostropovich was second only to Sir Peter Pears as a Britten catalyst, inspiring some of his finest instrumental works as well as some of his most memorable accompanying. Or should we say partnering, for soloist and accompanist are so well matched, and respect each other so much, that the rigid role-play of leader and follower is joyously over-ruled, turning chamber music into a dramatic experience which suggests the dialogue of two actors. This is particularly evident in the temperamental caprice of the Debussy Sonata, where the range of colour drawn by Britten from the keyboard, in response to Rostropovich's own, has to be heard to be believed. Their spontaneously attuned rubato throughout, as well as their rhythmic vitality in the finale, are further sources of delight.

Rostropovich and Britten are also indisputable winners in Schumann's five folk-style pieces (even though No. 2, marked *langsam*, is questionably fast), much more at one with each other as well as with the rustic simplicity and strength of the music itself. Regardless of more recent recordings, Rostropovich remains the real heavyweight in the Britten Sonata – it's a classic. Rostropovich's and Britten's characterization in the opening 'Dialogo' is probably unsurpassable. It's difficult to believe the recording is nearly 40 years old. This disc can confidently be hailed as a collector's piece, likely to survive in the gramophone archives for all time.

Debussy Cello Sonata.
Bridge Cello Sonata in D minor, H125. Four Short Pieces, H104 – Meditation; Spring song.
Dohnányi Cello Sonata in B flat minor, Op. 8.
Bernard Gregor-Smith *vc* **Yolande Wrigley** *pf*
ASV CDDCA796 (68 minutes: DDD).　　　　　　　　　　Ⓕ

The *commedia dell'arte* inspiration of the Debussy Cello Sonata can be readily appreciated on minimal acquaintance, but the highly individual formal structure of the work and its extraordinary variety of mood and content present huge challenges which are not easily met in live performance; and the Sonata can seem even more unattainable on disc. Bernard Gregor-Smith and Yolande Wrigley take up the challenge in this very fine performance of lyrical elegance, and not a little rococo irony and wit. Speeds are admittedly on the fast side, but there is no lack of refinement and flexibility in the playing, with superb bravura displays from Gregor-Smith in the finale. Whilst the performance of the Debussy is generally excellent, the centrepiece, and arguably the major triumph of this recital disc, is the fervent and frequently heroic account of the Sonata in B flat by Ernö Dohnányi. The work is seldom performed, and Gregor-Smith's fine-toned and dexterous reading deserves high praise indeed; it is to be hoped that more cellists might be prompted to take it up and certainly the performance is self-recommending.

The Frank Bridge Cello Sonata is a personal expression of grief and outrage, dating from the final year of the First World War, and shares a common tonality with the Debussy. Its broad paragraphs dictate the interpretative approach to a greater and more obvious extent, but the work receives a fluent and idiomatic reading, reserving the last degree of energy for the poignantly rhetorical closing pages of the piece. The disc also includes two characteristic Bridge miniatures, again eloquently played by this expert husband-and-wife duo. They have been faithfully, if not excessively brilliantly recorded. As for the playing, however, the skill of execution is matched by a refined insight into each work, lending a rare sense of equilibrium to an altogether superb recital of unusual perception and eloquence.

En blanc et noir. Petite suite. Nocturnes (arr. Ravel) – Nuages; Fêtes. Six épigraphes antiques. Lindaraja.
Katia and **Marielle Labèque** *pf duet/pfs*
Philips 454 471-2PH (58 minutes: DDD). Recorded 1996.　　　　Ⓕ

Katia and Marielle Labèque give us here a Debussy programme which is stylish and scintillating. Whatever sparkles and delights is here in superabundance. Playing with a fierce, recognizably French clarity and verve they make you doubly aware of the extraordinary force of nature that consumed Debussy during his final years. Faced with the outbreak of war, the possible destruction of his beloved France and his own terminal illness, he composed, among other masterpieces, his *En blanc et noir*, a wild dreamscape containing some of his most startling and original music. And if the Labèques play with an electrifying bravura, they are no less enviably refined, registering every detail of the score with scrupulous precision and sensitivity (and never more so than in the finale's flickering play of light and shade). They are no less dazzling in the more openly endearing *Petite suite* and if 'Fêtes' (from the *Nocturnes*) explodes in an orgy of brilliance, such open display is poetically balanced in *Epigraphes antiques*, where the duo are hauntingly memorably. Time and again they show how the finest insights are only available to pianists liberated from all difficulty, who are free to concentrate on a purely musical discourse. The recordings are immaculate and combined with the Labèque sisters' verve and pianistic aplomb provide a special, crystalline experience.

Complete Piano Works.
Walter Gieseking *pf*
Hessian Radio Orchestra, Frankfurt / Kurt Schröder.
Préludes, Books 1 and 2. Pour le piano. Estampes. Images, Sets 1 and 2. Children's Corner.
12 Etudes. D'un cahier d'esquisses. Rêverie. Valse romantique. Masques. L'isle joyeuse.
La plus que lente. Le petit nègre. Berceuse héroïque. Hommage à Haydn. Danse bohémienne.
Mazurka. Deux Arabesques. Nocturne. Tarantelle styrienne. Ballade. Suite bergamasque.
Fantaisie (recorded live).
HMV Classics mono HMVD5 73192-2 (four discs: 276 minutes: ADD). Recorded 1951-55.
Gramophone Award Winner 1996. Ⓜ Ⓗ

Gieseking's insight and iridescence in Debussy are so compelling and hypnotic that they prompt either a book or a blank page – an unsatisfactory state where criticism or assessment is concerned! First and foremost, there is Gieseking's sonority, one of such delicacy and variety that it can complement Debussy's witty and ironic desire to write music 'for an instrument without hammers', for a pantheistic art sufficiently suggestive to evoke and transcend the play of the elements themselves ('the wind, the sky, the sea ...'). Lack of meticulousness seems a small price to pay for such an elemental uproar in 'Ce qu'a vu le vent d'ouest', and Puck's elfin pulse and chatter (*pp aérian*) are caught with an uncanny deftness and precision. The final Debussian magic may not lie in a literal observance of the score, in the unfailing dotting and crossing of every objective and picturesque instruction, yet it is surely the start or foundation of a great performance. More domestically, no one (not even Cortot) has ever captured the sense in *Children's Corner* of a lost and enchanted land, of childhood re-experienced through adult tears and laughter. 'Pour les tierces', from the *Etudes*, may get off to a shaky start but, again, in Debussy's final masterpiece, where pragmatism is resolved into a fantasy undreamed of even by Chopin, Gieseking's artistry tugs at and haunts the imagination. Try 'Pour les sonorités opposées', the expressive centre of the *Etudes*, and you may well wonder when you have heard playing more subtly gauged or articulated, or the sort of interaction with a composer's spirit that can make modern alternatives seem so parsimonious by comparison. So here is that peerless palette of colour and texture, of a light and shade used with a nonchalantly deployed but precise expertise to illuminate every facet of Debussy's teeming and insinuating imagination. An added bonus, a 1951 performance of the *Fantaisie* for piano and orchestra (an ecstatic and scintillating work, played here with a life-affirming chiaroscuro), completes an incomparable set of discs. The transfers are a triumph, with an immediacy much less obvious in the originals. These records should be in every musician's library, be they singer or conductor, violinist or pianist.

Préludes – Books 1 and 2.
Krystian Zimerman *pf*
DG 435 773-2GH2 (two discs: 84 minutes: DDD). Recorded 1991.
Gramophone Award Winner 1994. Ⓜ Ⓔ ⓇⓇ

Two discs, retailing at a high mid-price and playing for a total of 84 minutes? The playing and the recording had better be in the luxury class. Fortunately they are. Zimerman is the very model of a modern virtuoso. His overriding aim is vivid projection of character. His quasi-orchestral range of dynamic and attack, based on close attention to textual detail (there are countless felicities in his observation of phrase-markings) and maximum clarity of articulation, is the means to that end. As a result, he draws out the many connections in this music with the romantic tradition, especially in pianistic *tours de force* such as 'Les collines d'Anacapri', 'Ce qu'a vu le vent d'ouest' and 'Feux d'artifice', which are treated to a dazzling Lisztian *élan*. The instrument he has selected is itself something of a star and DG's recording combines opulence with razor-sharp clarity. At the other extreme Zimerman displays an exquisite refinement of touch that makes the quieter pieces both evocative and touching. Such sensitively conceived and wonderfully executed Debussy playing stands, at the very least, on a level with a classic recording such as Gieseking's.

Préludes – Books 1 and 2ª. Images. Children's Corner.
Arturo Benedetti Michelangeli *pf*
DG 449 438-2GH2 (two discs: 128 minutes: ADD/ªDDD). Recorded 1971-88.　　Ⓕ

Of Debussy playing his own music Alfredo Casella said 'he made the impression of playing directly on the strings of the instrument with no intermediate mechanism – the effect was a miracle of poetry'. This is not Michelangeli's way. He can certainly be poetic and produce miracles but his manner is not ingratiating. Generalized 'atmosphere' doesn't interest him. His superfine control is put at the service of line and movement, above all, and the projection of perspectives. He gives you a sense not just of foreground and background but of many planes in between. Michelangeli was capable of a transcendental virtuosity, not always noticed, that had nothing to do with playing fast and loud and everything to do with refinement, and it is very much in evidence here – in many *Préludes* and especially in the first two *Images* of the Second Book; also, less expectedly, in 'The snow is dancing' from *Children's Corner*. The clarity of texture and the laser-like delineation can sometimes be disconcerting if you're accustomed to a softer, more ethereal style, but they have a way of making Debussy's modernism apparent and thrilling. He sounds here as if he has had nothing to do with the nineteenth century. The *Images* and *Children's Corner* are among the finest versions ever recorded. But in some of the *Préludes*, particularly in Book 1, the sound is rather close and dry – maybe how Michelangeli wanted it. He uses as little pedal as he can get away with. There are people who regard Gieseking as unparalleled in this music, but after a quarter of a century the best of Michelangeli, similarly, will run and run. Today's generation of Debussy pianists will be expected to work from a less corrupt text, quite rightly, but they will have far to go before they can rival the penetrating qualities of Michelangeli's Debussy at its best. He could take your breath away and he was illuminating in this repertoire in a rare way.

Préludes – Books 1 and 2.
Walter Gieseking *pf*
EMI Références mono CDH7 61004-2 (70 minutes: ADD). Recorded 1953-54.　　ⓂⒽ

This disc reveals keyboard artistry undimmed by the intervening years. The instrument really does appear to dissolve into something illusory and magical, just as Debussy intended – take 'Le vent dans la plaine', as one of a dozen possible examples. And if that seems surprising from a 15-stone, six-foot-three German pianist, perhaps even more so are the delightful humour of 'La danse de Puck' and 'Hommage à S. Pickwick Esq., PPMPC' and the sheer naughtiness of 'Minstrels'. Two aspects of Gieseking's art have not stood the test of time quite so well. Reports of his technical perfection sit uneasily alongside his scrambling through the virtuosic preludes, such as 'Les collines d'Anacapri' and 'Ce qu'a vu le vent d'ouest' which suggests that he actually needed to practise rather more than he thought he did (though 'Feux d'artifice' shows the technique in impressive shape). And Gieseking's much-vaunted fidelity to the text is surely a bit of a fiction. He can be as cavalier over dynamics as the next man – 'Ce qu'a vu' works up a good stormy *forte* long before Debussy cancels the initial *piano*, for example – and in any case he was clearly working from editions which we now know to be serious misrepresentations. Far more important though is the precision of artistic image imparted to each piece – even when Gieseking casts caution and dozens of notes to the winds, this imaginative strength carries him through. And it is worth pondering on the fact that despite the impression of spaciousness, this must be one of the fastest Debussy *Préludes* on record. Background hiss is roughly what one would expect, but if there are any other signs of age in the recording quality Gieseking's artistry conquers them with ease.

Suite bergamasque. Images oubliées. Pour le piano. Estampes.
Zoltán Kocsis *pf*
Philips 412 118-2PH (55 minutes: DDD).　　ⒻⓈ

Images – Sets 1 and 2. D'un cahier d'esquisses. L'isle joyeuse. Deux arabesques. Hommage à Haydn. Rêverie. Page d'album. Berceuse héroïque.
Zoltán Kocsis *pf*
Philips 422 404-2PH (62 minutes: DDD). Recorded 1988. *Gramophone* Award Winner 1990.　　Ⓕ

Zoltán Kocsis stands out as an especially idiomatic exponent of Debussy's piano style. On the first disc here, he plays four relatively early sets of pieces of which all but the *Suite bergamasque* are in the composer's favourite triptych form that he also used in *La mer*. The rarity here is the *Images oubliées*, pieces dating from 1894 that Debussy left unpublished, doubtless because he reworked material from them in the *Estampes* and very obviously in the Sarabande of *Pour le piano*, but they are fine in their own right and here we can compare the different treatments of the similar ideas. The second recital also offsets the familiar with the less known. It also brings playing not only of exceptional finesse, but at times of exceptional brilliance and fire. The main work is of course *Images*, its two sets completed in 1905 and 1907 respectively, by which time the composer was already master of that impressionistic style of keyboard writing so different from anything known before. For superfine sensitivity to details of textural shading Kocsis is at his most spellbinding in the first two numbers of the second set, 'Cloches à travers les feuilles' and 'Et la lune descend sur le temple qui fût'. He is equally successful in reminding us of Debussy's wish to 'forget that the piano has hammers' in the atmospheric washes of sound that he conjures (through his pedalling no less than his fingers) in *D'un cahier d'esquisses*. The sharp clear daylight world of *L'îsle joyeuse* reveals a Kocsis exulting in his own virtuosity and strength as he also does in the last piece of each set of *Images*, and even in the second of the two familiar, early *Arabesques*, neither of them mere vapid drawing-room charmers here. The recording is first rate. Both discs are highly recommendable. Zoltán Kocsis brings refinement and brilliance to all this music and the piano sound is exceptionally rich and faithful.

Deux Arabesques. Suite bergamasque – Clair de lune; Passepied. Rêverie. Children's Corner – The little shepherd; Golliwog's cakewalk. Préludes, Book 1 – Voiles; Les sons et les parfums; La fille aux cheveux de lin; La cathédrale engloutie; Minstrels. Images – Hommage à Rameau. L'îsle joyeuse.
Ronan O'Hora *pf*
Tring International TRP068 (65 minutes: DDD). Recorded 1995.   Ⓢ

Even in a crowded market-place this recital takes its place among the most distinguished Debussy recordings. Nothing is taken for granted, everything is recreated with such care and affection that a largely popular selection at once seems fresh and unfamiliar. How many pianists can set the stage in 'La cathédrale engloutie' with such understated skill, ideally capturing Debussy's direction, *profondément calme, dans une brume doucement sonore* or, later, make such a subtle differentiation between *forte, più forte* and *fortissimo*? The 'Passepied' (from the *Suite bergamasque*) is kept briskly on the move yet there is ample time for the most judicious pointing and colouring, and 'Hommage à Rameau' (from *Images*, Book 1) seems exemplary in its lucidity, its avoidance of the sort of brittleness or affectation common to pianists anxious to make their mark at any price. Finally, you may have heard or seen more joyous islands (*L'îsle joyeuse*), yet O'Hora's performance beautifully captures the spirit of romance and there is no lack of animation in the exultant close. Everything is given time to register, to weave its spell, and although the resonant recordings cast a haze over the sound the ear quickly adjusts, particularly when the performances are so distinguished.

Etudes – Books 1 and 2.
Mitsuko Uchida *pf*
Philips 422 412-2PH (47 minutes: DDD). Recorded 1989.   Ⓕ

The harmonic language and continuity of the *Etudes* is elusive even by Debussy's standards, and it takes an artist of rare gifts to play them 'from within', at the same time as negotiating their finger-knotting intricacies. Mitsuko Uchida is such an artist. On first hearing perhaps rather hyperactive, her playing wins you over by its bravura and sheer relish, eventually disarming criticism altogether. This is not just the finest-ever recorded version of the *Etudes*; it is also one of the finest examples of recorded piano playing in modern times, matched by sound quality of outstanding clarity.

Le martyre de Saint-Sébastien.
Sylvia McNair *sop* **Ann Murray** *mez* **Nathalie Stutzmann** *contr* **Leslie Caron** *narr*
London Symphony Chorus and Orchestra / Michael Tilson Thomas.
Sony Classical SK48240 (66 minutes: DDD). Text and translation included. Recorded 1991.
Gramophone Award Winner 1993.   ⒻⓈ

'Archers aim closely, I am the target; whoever wounds me the most deeply, loves me the most. From the depths I call forth your terrible love … again … again! … AGAIN!' cries the Saint in ecstasy. What Oscar Wilde did to the story of Salome, so the Italian writer D'Annunzio did to the story of Saint Sebastian (a young Roman officer ordered to be killed by his own archers because of his sympathy for persecuted Christians). This was the first modern recording, not of the complete play (which lasted five hours!), but of an intelligent and effective reduction of the written text using the Saint as narrator, and incorporating all of an hour's worth of Debussy's incidental music. And it must be deemed a triumph. Leslie Caron's Saint is quietly intense and a model of restraint; Sylvia McNair's *vox coelestis* is just that, a gift from God; and the chorus and orchestra respond with total conviction to what is evidently, from Tilson Thomas, direction with a mission. The sheer sorcery of Debussy's music, as strongly imbued as his *Pelléas* with Wagner's *Parsifal*, benefits enormously from the acoustic of, appropriately, All Saints Church in Tooting, London.

La damoiselle élue[a]. Prélude à l'après-midi d'un faune. Images – Ibéria.
[a]**Maria Ewing** *sop* Damoiselle; [a]**Brigitte Balleys** *contr* Narrator;
London Symphony [a]**Chorus and Orchestra / Claudio Abbado.**
DG 423 103-2GH (49 minutes: DDD). Text and translation included. ⒻⓈ🆁🆁

The London Symphony Orchestra has rarely sounded so sensuously beautiful on record as in this Debussy collection, bringing together two favourite works with the exotic early cantata *La damoiselle élue* inspired by Rosetti's Blessed Damozel. That early work takes pride of place on the disc, and rightly so when it brings the most distinctive performance. The recording was made in All Saints, Tooting, and the church resonance greatly adds to the evocative beauty of the writing, not least in the singing of the chorus, set at a fair distance. The two solo voices too are beautifully caught, so that the touch of rawness on some of Brigitte Balleys's notes have an attractive freshness, and Maria Ewing has never sounded sweeter. Abbado's reading of the work is poised and spacious. The *Prélude à l'après-midi d'un faune* and *Ibéria*, on the other hand, bring relatively compelling and impulsive performances. The sound is very vivid and full, the performances fast and urgent, yet still sound evocative and unrushed with rubato very persuasive. Peter Lloyd plays the flute solo in the *Prélude* quite ravishingly. Although it would have been good to have had all three of the *Images*, not just 'Ibéria', this makes a fine celebration of Abbado's long and fruitful period with the LSO.

Pelléas et Mélisande.
Jacques Jansen *bar* Pelléas; **Irène Joachim** *sop* Mélisande; **Henri Etcheverry** *bar* Golaud;
Paul Cabanel *bass* Arkel; **Germaine Cernay** *mez* Geneviève; **Leila ben Sedira** *sop* Yniold;
Emile Rousseau *bass* Shepherd; **Armand Narçon** *bass* Doctor;
Yvonne Gouverné Choir; symphony orchestra / Roger Desormière.
EMI Références mono CHS7 61038-2 (three discs: 196 minutes: ADD). Booklet with translation
included. Recorded 1941. Ⓜ🄷🆁🆁

The strength of the performance owed much to the fact that Irène Joachim, Jacques Jansen and Henri Etcheverry had already sung the work many times under Desormière at the Opéra-Comique. Irène Joachim had studied the role of Mélisande with its creator, Mary Garden; and both she and Jansen had been coached by Georges Viseur, who with Messager had been the *répétiteur* for the opera's first performance. Jansen with his free, youthful-toned production and Joachim with her silvery voice and intelligent response to every verbal nuance, set standards for the doomed lovers that, though nearly equalled, have never been surpassed; but even more impressive is Etcheverry's interpretation of Golaud, a role in which, arguably, he has yet to be rivalled. Leila ben Sedira gives one of the most convincing portrayals ever heard of the child Yniold; and Germaine Cernay and Paul Cabanel (who alone is just a trifle free with the text in places) fill the parts of the older characters with distinction. In this recording, the placing of the voices is such that every single word is crystal-clear. More important every word is invested with meaning by a native French cast – in other versions allowances sometimes need to be made for non-French singers – which had immersed itself totally in the emotional nuances and overtones of the text. Every shade of expression is caught, but nevertheless the overall feeling is of subtle Gallic understatement – with Golaud's self-tormenting jealousy and Pelléas's final inability to resist declaring his love for his brother's mysterious, fey wife creating the great emotional climaxes. Keith Hardwick's alchemy in transforming these old recordings into sound of improved quality (and with only minimal vestiges of the 78rpm surfaces) is nothing short of amazing. He has not, of course, been able to correct the thin 1941 recording of the woodwind, but one soon comes to terms with the dated instrumental sound because of Desormière's inspired pacing and moulding of the score, the committed orchestral playing, and the well-nigh perfect casting.

Pelléas et Mélisande.
François Le Roux *bar* Pelléas; **Maria Ewing** *sop* Mélisande; **José van Dam** *bar* Golaud;
Jean-Philippe Courtis *bass* Arkel, Shepherd; **Christa Ludwig** *mez* Geneviève;
Patrizia Pace *sop* Yniold; **Rudolf Mazzola** *bass* Doctor;
Vienna State Opera Chorus; Vienna Philharmonic Orchestra / Claudio Abbado.
DG 435 344-2GH2 (two discs: 148 minutes: DDD). Notes, text and translation included.
Recorded 1991. Ⓕ

This is a superb issue that challenges the finest. The warmth of the VPO strings in the very first bars holds out a promise that is never disappointed: the orchestra, always subtle but positively glowing, is responsive to every one of Debussy's dynamics and rises to the most intense of climaxes in the emotional high spots of Act 4. Abbado directs a sensitive and flexible reading, rather faster than usual in some places – impelled by the dramatic situation, he pushes ahead when Golaud flares up on hearing that Mélisande has lost his ring, and in that terrible scene when little Yniold is made to spy on his stepmother. José van Dam is an artist who, in whatever he undertakes, leaves one reaching for superlatives: in this performance his Golaud is a character on a dangerously short fuse, heavy with menace in his first warning to Pelléas, quickly losing control with Yniold, and lashing himself into a frenzy at the 'grande innocence' of Mélisande's eyes, leading him to seize her by her long hair. Maria Ewing makes the hapless heroine less of a wimp than she is sometimes represented, and in a remarkable way nuances and colours her every word with meaning. She is tender to Golaud when he suffers a slight wound, sweet but very erotic in the Act 3 soliloquy as she combs her hair, and bursts out in suddenly awakened passion at the fatal nocturnal parting from Pelléas. Or is it so sudden? We notice that her words to him at the end of Act 1, 'Oh! Pourquoi partez-vous?', are delivered not ingenuously, as with some interpreters of the part, but already with a vague yearning.

Le Roux's Pelléas sounds young, fresh and ardent, his singing is always refined, his words are meaningful, and he conveys Pelléas's unease in the sinister scene with Golaud in the cavern. (The only slight shortcoming in the whole recording, unfortunately, is when his eventual declaration of love is almost lost under orchestral reverberation.) For some reason the casting of the aged Arkel has often been a weakness in the past: either he is not entirely accurate or he emerges as just dull. Here the intelligence of Courtis makes of him a figure akin to wise old Gurnemanz in *Parsifal*, an opera much in Debussy's mind (despite his professed dislike of Wagner). Patrizia Pace makes a very credible child, and that no pains were spared in the production is suggested by the fact that no less an artist than Christa Ludwig takes the tiny part of Geneviève. Even those readers with one or other of the other recommended recordings of the opera are urged not to miss this one.

Pelléas et Mélisande.
Claude Dormoy ten Pelléas; **Michèle Command** sop Mélisande; **Gabriel Bacquier** bar Golaud; **Roger Soyer** bass Arkel; **Jocelyne Taillon** mez Geneviève; **Monique Pouradier-Duteil** sop Yniold; **Xavier Tamalet** bass Doctor, Shepherd;
Burgundian Chorus; Orchestra of the Opéra de Lyon / Serge Baudo.
RCA Opera 74321 32225-2 (two discs: 147 minutes: ADD). Synopsis and text included. Recorded 1978. Ⓑ

There have been many fine historic recordings of *Pelléas et Mélisande*: reissues have included Desormière's of 1941 and Cluytens's of 1956. The excellence of this performance from Baudo leaves one wondering why it took the best part of 20 years to reappear. Baudo produces a warm sound from the Lyon orchestra, knows how to shape Debussy's subtle phrases, and is notably good at making use of silences. He is fortunate to have a cast without a single weak member. It is often the case that the central figure of Golaud, tortured by blind jealousy, steals the show, but Gabriel Bacquier is superb, capturing every nuance from tenderness to abrupt anger (at the news of the loss of the ring) or agonized frustration beside Mélisande's deathbed. Michèle Command, here at an early stage of her career, and entirely free from the undue weightiness that has sometimes characterized her work since, makes a shy, fey Mélisande who remains an enigmatic figure; she invests the famous solo about her long hair with a sense of melancholy. The big surprise of this set is the Pelléas, a sensitive singer who seems, inexplicably, to have appeared in only one other recording (*The Merry Wives of Windsor*), made in the year before this – in a bass role! Listed here as a tenor, he is more a high baritone (which is appropriate for the part), just occasionally sounding a trifle stretched on a high note. The part of Arkel is given nobility by Roger Soyer; and the Yniold sounds convincingly childlike. Care has been taken in the production, as can be heard in the hollower acoustic of the scene in the vaults; only the perspective of the sailors on the unseen ship – always a problem in recordings – is a little uncertain. Make no mistake: this is a very rewarding version of this masterpiece, and as a two-disc bargain-price issue is a real snip.

Rodrigue et Chimène (recons. Langham Smith and orch. Denisov).
Laurence Dale ten Rodrigue; **Donna Brown** sop Chimène; **Hélène Jossoud** mez Iñez; **Gilles Ragon** ten Hernan; **Jean-Paul Fouchécourt** ten Bermudo; **José van Dam** bass-bar Don Diègue; **Jules Bastin** bass Don Gomez; **Vincent le Texier** bass-bar King; **Jean-Louis Meunier** ten Don Juan d'Arcos; **Jean Delescluse** ten Don Pèdre de Teruel; **Chorus and Orchestra of the Opéra de Lyon / Kent Nagano.**
Erato 4509-98508-2 (two discs: 109 minutes: DDD). Notes, text and translation included. Recorded 1993-94. ⒻⒺ

It may come as a surprise to many who treasure the unique magic of *Pelléas et Mélisande* that Debussy toyed with some 30 other plans for operas, and two years before *Pelléas* had all but completed his first operatic venture. Debussy very soon realized that the libretto's blustering tone was alien to his ideals of half-hinted action in short scenes, and became increasingly restive, finally abandoning it and claiming that it had been accidentally destroyed. In reality it survived complete in a sketch in short score, though some pages have since been lost. Richard Langham Smith reconstructed the work from the manuscripts in the Piermont Morgan Library in New York, it was completed and orchestrated, with a remarkable insight into Debussian style, by Edison Denisov, and in 1993 it was presented by the Opéra de Lyon to mark the opening of its new house. Inconsistencies of style reveal something of Debussy's uncertainties and doubts over a subject inappropriate for him. There is little in Act 3 that would lead anyone to identify him as the composer, and virtually the only sections of the work with a harmonic idiom that was later to become characteristic of him are Rodrigue's and Chimène's mutual declaration of love at the start of Act 1 (after a reflective modal prelude with a tinge of Russian influence), the orchestral prelude to Act 2 and the unexpected quiet interlude that precedes Rodrigue's mortal challenge to his beloved's father Don Gomez, who had shamed his own father. Debussy is less at home with the choral scene leading up to the angry conflict between the two initially friendly houses, the heroic and warlike atmosphere of much of Act 2, and the bombastic assembling of the royal court; but all these are tackled, if not with individuality, at least with vigour. Don Gomez's death scene is affecting, and the unaccompanied choral requiem for him makes an effective close to Act 2.

Unlike *Pelléas*, there are a number of extended set pieces for the singers, including Rodrigue's dutiful dilemma, Don Diègue's hymn to the concept of honour, Chimène's lament for her father and her final anguish as she is torn between love and hate for Rodrigue. As a performance and recording, this is in the highest class. Nagano's orchestra plays for him with finesse, and the work is cast from strength. Laurence Dale is a near-perfect Rodrigue – youthful, ardent, sensitive to changes of mood, and with a free vocal production that is a constant pleasure to hear; Donna Brown makes a passionate Chimène, though occasionally just too close to the microphone for sudden outbursts and José van Dam is his always reliable self, with nobility in his voice. Clarity of enunciation throughout (except, at times, from the chorus) is to be applauded.

Léo Delibes
French 1836-1891

Coppélia.
Orchestra of the Opéra de Lyon / Kent Nagano.
Erato 4509-91730-2 (two discs: 99 minutes: DDD). Recorded 1993.   Ⓕ🄴

Though the text played absolutely complete may be straightforward Delibes, the interpretation instantly announces itself as being anything but straightforward. Every phrase, every accent, every nuance seems to be newly considered, without losing the feel for the action that is taking place on the stage. The overriding impression here is of the rightness and naturalness of Nagano's whole reading. The rare quality of the performance is evident at once from the way the music lights up at the *cantando* section in the twelfth bar of the Prelude. Later, in Act 2, the Boléro has a rare dash and brio, while the opening March of Act 3 has a similarly compelling onward momentum. The sequence of speciality dances that makes up most of the final Act is delightfully turned, with a quite heavenly viola solo in 'La Paix' and a thrilling final Galop. It is unfortunate that the recording is spread over two CDs, but anyone who loves this music should make a point of hearing Nagano's outstanding reading.

Coppélia[a]. Sylvia.
London Symphony Orchestra / Anatole Fistoulari;
[a]**Minneapolis Symphony Orchestra / Antál Dorati.**
Mercury Living Presence 434 313-2MM3 (three discs: 173 minutes: ADD).
Recorded 1957-58.   Ⓜ🄷

The quality of sound in these reissues really is astonishing in that in recordings over 40 years old, brass and percussion can burst forth with such vividness, or that instrumental detail can be so clear and faithful as they are here in *Sylvia* (*Coppélia* is not quite of the same standard). Nor, of course, do the attractions by any means stop at the quality of recorded sound. These always were highly regarded performances of two of the most attractively tuneful ballets ever composed. Moreover, both conductors here had a great deal of experience in, and feeling for, the ballet style and this is immediately evident in their handling of the scores. Both extract playing that is for the most part gracious and brilliant in turn, if just occasionally lacking the final degree of finesse, and in such passages as Fistoulari's vigorous 'Les chasseresses' or Dorati's 'Musique des automates' one can scarcely fail to be won over. It is only fair to mention that this recording of *Sylvia* is itself not absolutely complete, since it lacks the 'Pas des esclaves' and 'Variation-Valse' from the Act 3 'Divertissement'. On its own terms though, the reissue represents a most compelling offering.

Lakmé.

Natalie Dessay *sop* Lakmé; **Gregory Kunde** *ten* Gérald; **José van Dam** *bass-bar* Nilakantha;
Delphine Haidan *mez* Mallika; **Franck Leguérinel** *bar* Frédéric; **Patricia Petibon** *sop* Ellen;
Xenia Konsek *sop* Rose; **Bernadette Antoine** *sop* Mistress Bentson; **Charles Burles** *ten* Hadji;
Toulouse Capitole Chorus and Orchestra / Michel Plasson.
EMI CDS5 56569-2 (two discs: 144 minutes: DDD). Text and translation included.　　　　Ⓕ

Opera audiences in nineteenth-century Paris may never have visited India, but they loved to dream
about it. After the successes enjoyed by *Les pêcheurs de perles* and *Le roi de Lahore* Delibes knew
what he was doing when he chose to set an adaptation of Pierre Loti's exotic Indian novel *Rarahu*
and duly scored a hit with his opera *Lakmé* at the Opéra-Comique in 1883. Today most of these
French essays in exoticism seem to have lost their appeal in the opera house. Also, *Lakmé* invites a
few surreptitious giggles at its un-PC attitudes towards the colonial era, portraying the local
population as colourful oddities and the British as stuck-up prigs. But it would be a shame if that
deterred anybody from exploring an opera that is pure enchantment, filled with sensuous music of
the kind that only French composers ever seem able to write.

The opera is nothing without a star in the title-role. Natalie Dessay is certainly that and yet she
never fails to remember that Delibes's heroine must be a fragile and sensitive young creature. Her
Bell Song, brilliantly sung, is also intent on telling a story. Her singing of the death scene, with its
delicate *fil de voce* perfectly poised each time the high A comes round, is heartfelt and leaves no
doubt that this is a Lakmé who deserves to go to heaven. EMI found a worthy tenor to partner her.
Gregory Kunde, as Gérald, is at ease at the top of his voice. At the first entrance of the colonial
Brits, Frédéric describes Gérald as a poet and Kunde lives up to the promise by phrasing his
opening solo, 'Fantaisie aux divins mensonges', with a nice poetic sensibility. In the duets he and
Dessay are tender young love personified. The supporting cast is a decent one. José van Dam sings
the vengeful Nilakantha with complete authority. Patricia Petibon and Franck Leguérinel make an
attractive couple as Ellen and Frédéric; Bernadette Antoine is aware she has to make a character
out of the pompous governess Mistress Bentson. Delphine Haidan's Mallika gets to sing the
favourite in-flight *Lakmé* duet, made popular by British Airways, but does not blend ideally with
Dessay. Michel Plasson gives the music room to breathe and is able to conjure a dreamy atmosphere
in the scenes of romance set among the jasmine and roses. His Toulouse orchestra is adequate, if
not exceptional, and the recording is of a good standard. What reason is there to resist?

Delibes Sylvia.
Saint-Saëns Henry VIII – Ballet-divertissement.
Razumovsky Sinfonia / Andrew Mogrelia.
Naxos 8 553338/9 (two discs: 114 minutes: DDD). Recorded 1995.　　　　ⓈⒺ

Of Delibes's two full-length ballets, *Coppélia* is the more obviously popular, the one with the bigger
tunes and the greater number of recordings. However, *Sylvia* is also a superbly crafted score, full of
haunting melodies. Andrew Mogrelia's Naxos series is one to be collected and treasured: there is
loving care applied to selection of tempos, shaping of phrases, orchestral balance and refinement of
instrumental detail. Here you thrill to *Sylvia*'s Act 1 Fanfare, marvel at the control of tempo and
refinement of instrumental detail in the 'Valse lente' and 'Entrée du sorcier', and revel in the sheer
ebullience of Sylvia's return in Act 2. The inclusion of the ballet music from Saint-Saëns's
Henry VIII was an admirably enterprising move, even though it doesn't amount to anything major
apart from the 'Danse de la gitane', being essentially a collection of mock 'Olde Britishe' dances.
All the same, a quite remarkable bargain.

Frederick Delius　　　　British 1862-1934

Double Concerto. Cello Concerto. Paris: The Song of a Great City.
Tasmin Little *vn* **Raphael Wallfisch** *vc*
Royal Liverpool Philharmonic Orchestra / Sir Charles Mackerras.
EMI Eminence CD-EMX2185 (64 minutes: DDD). Recorded 1991.　　　　Ⓜ

Paris is an extravagant nocturnal impression of the city where 'Le grand anglais', as Delius was
known to his friends, spent a decade of his life, during which he developed, as Eric Fenby put it, 'a
painter's sense of orchestral colour'. Premièred in 1901, it shows Delius relishing the full palette of
his Straussian-sized orchestra to conjure an intoxicating merry-go-round of the city's night-life.
Mackerras's performance is very physical, propelling the dancing to wild, whirling climaxes, and his
balance engineers place us firmly among the excitement. In the Cello Concerto, a personal favourite

of Delius's, Raphael Wallfisch and Mackerras seek out the contrasts inherent in the score, and, for the first time on disc, its pervasive dreaminess is offset by faster decorative passages, and a genuine playfulness. In short, it dances as well as sings. They are joined by Tasmin Little for an account of the Double Concerto that has never before received teamwork of such confidence, security and unanimity of purpose. An essential acquisition for all Delians, especially at the modest asking price.

Brigg Fair. In a Summer Garden. Paris: The Song of a Great City. On Hearing the First Cuckoo in Spring. Summer Night on the River. A Village Romeo and Juliet – The Walk to the Paradise Garden.
BBC Symphony Orchestra / Sir Andrew Davis.
Teldec British Line 4509-90845-2 (77 minutes: DDD). Recorded 1992.　　　　　　Ⓕ 🄴 🆁🆁

This *Brigg Fair* is unique. What a lovely surprise to hear real London sparrows sharing the air space of St Augustine's Church with Delius's translated Lincolnshire larks (flute and clarinet) in the opening minutes of the work, albeit much more distantly. Very effective too are those almost still pools of string sound (early morning mists?), given the extended boundaries of this acoustic, and the familiar warmth and depth of tone Davis draws from the orchestra's strings. In the final magnificently broad climax (pealing bells, for once, very clear), you cannot fail to be impressed by the depth, coherence and articulacy of the sound – hallmarks, indeed, of the entire disc. Davis's strings come into their own in the *Walk to the Paradise Garden*. For *In a Summer Garden*, Davis mutes his strings more often than Delius asks; but the reading's delicacy of texture and hazy, suffusing warmth are difficult to resist.

Over the Hills and Far Away. North Country Sketches[a]. Eventyr. Koanga – Closing scene.
BBC Chorus; Royal Philharmonic Orchestra / Sir Thomas Beecham.
Sony Classical British Pageant mono SBK62747 (64 minutes: ADD). Recorded 1949-51,
[a]1959.　　　　　　Ⓑ 🄷

No one, it seems, could quite 'magick' the music of Frederick Delius the way that Sir Thomas Beecham did. Listen, if you will, to 'Autumn, the wind soughs in the trees', the first of the wonderfully atmospheric, seldom-heard *North Country Sketches*: one doubts whether the desolate beauty of the Yorkshire uplands has ever been more hauntingly evoked, whilst in the closing bars time really does seem to stand still. Indeed, all this music-making undoubtedly distils a very real sense of enchantment: *Eventyr* has never been given with more poetry and *Over the Hills and Far Away* is simply captivating, a performance which far outstrips Beecham's later stereo-remake in fantasy, joyful vigour and spontaneity. Transfers have been expertly managed, with one irritating exception – the very start of 'The March of Spring' (the last of the *North Country Sketches*) has been fractionally clipped. In sum, a collection that should be in every self-respecting Delian's library, for none of this music has ever been surveyed with greater imagination and rapture than here.

Fantastic Dance. A Dance Rhapsody No. 1[a]. A Dance Rhapsody No. 2. A Song of the High Hills. Three Preludes. Zum Carnival.
Maryetta Midgley *sop* **Vernon Midgley** *ten* **Eric Parkin** *pf* **Ambrosian Singers; Royal Philharmonic Orchestra / Eric Fenby, [a]Norman Del Mar.**
Unicorn-Kanchana Souvenir UKCD2071 (65 minutes: DDD). Recorded 1981-90.　　Ⓜ

Irmelin Prelude. A Song of Summer. A Late Lark. Piano Concerto in C minor[a]. Violin Concerto[b].
Anthony Rolfe Johnson *ten* **Ralph Holmes** *vn* **Philip Fowke** *pf*
Royal Philharmonic Orchestra / Eric Fenby, [a]Norman Del Mar, [b]Vernon Handley.
Unicorn-Kanchana Souvenir UKCD2072 (71 minutes: DDD). Recorded 1981-90.　　Ⓜ

Koanga – La Calinda (arr. Fenby). Idyll: Once I passed through a populous city. Songs of Sunset. A Village Romeo and Juliet – The Walk to the Paradise Garden[a].
Felicity Lott *sop* **Sarah Walker** *mez* **Thomas Allen** *bar* **Ambrosian Singers; Royal Philharmonic Orchestra / Eric Fenby, [a]Norman Del Mar.**
Unicorn-Kanchana Souvenir UKCD2073 (73 minutes: DDD). Recorded 1981-90.　　Ⓜ

The unique insight that the late Eric Fenby would bring as an interpreter of Delius was the reason for many of these Unicorn recordings, but we owe the idea and its realization to their producer, the late Christopher Palmer. As well as providing Delians with some of the most illuminating and inspiring text on the music (in books and sleeve-notes), Palmer, in the studio, and especially in a work like *A Song of the High Hills*, was able to put his understanding (and Fenby's, of course) into practice. You don't need the score of *A Song of the High Hills* to tell you that the passage from 9'54" represents 'The wide far distance, the great solitude'. That to which you are listening – totally spellbound – could be nothing else (and by nobody else). Ralph Holmes's recording of the Violin Concerto (with Vernon Handley) is a warm, leisurely reading. The Piano Concerto, as recorded here, is a grand showstopper in the best romantic piano concerto tradition, yet Fowke and Del Mar alert you to all the Delian reverie in the making (the dynamic range of Fowke's piano is colossal). But the outlay for Vol. 2 is justified by Anthony Rolfe Johnson alone, in the all too brief six minute-long *A Late Lark* ('one of Delius's works that is surely entirely without flaw, a most moving farewell', as Trevor Harvey put it in his original review).

In Vol. 3, Fenby's control in *Songs of Sunset* does not always match his insight (choral work is often sloppy and too distantly recorded); the recent Hickox, or the 1957 Beecham is to be preferred. But without Fenby in the recording studio (or at Grez!), we would never have had *Idyll*: Whitman texts combined with a late reworking of music from an earlyish opera, *Margot la Rouge*, to provide a reflective then rapturous love duet that looks back to Delius's Paris as well as to his *Paris* – this makes Vol. 3 indispensable, especially as sung and played here. And a very considerable bonus to be found in Vol. 3 is Del Mar's previously unissued *Walk to the Paradise Garden*. This is not the Beecham version for reduced orchestra, as stated in the otherwise excellent notes, though it incorporates many of Beecham's dynamics and tempo indications. It is, most assuredly, a *Walk* on the grandest (11'00" to Beecham's 8'38"), most passionate scale (there's not a bar-line in earshot, either), and turns out to be yet another of these three discs' memorials to inspired Delians who died in our, but before their, time.

Over the Hills and Far Away (ed. Beecham). Sleigh Ride. Irmelin – Prelude. Dance Rhapsody No. 2. Summer Evening (ed. and arr. Beecham). Brigg Fair. On Hearing the First Cuckoo in Spring. Summer Night on the River. A Song Before Sunrise. Marche-caprice. Florida Suite (ed. and arr. Beecham). Songs of Sunset[a]. Fennimore and Gerda – Intermezzo (ed. and arr. Beecham).
[a]**Maureen Forrester** *contr* [a]**John Cameron** *bar* [a]**Beecham Choral Society;**
Royal Philharmonic Orchestra / Sir Thomas Beecham.
EMI CDS7 47509-8 (two discs: 147 minutes). Recorded 1956.
Gramophone Award Winner 1987.   Ⓜ H RR

Many collectors waited impatiently for years for this anthology to appear on CD – the greatest recordings made in stereo by our greatest British conductor, at the peak of his career in the last few years of his life. Those who heard Beecham live will remember vividly how he could totally transform the sounds an orchestra made. Beecham's understanding and mastery of Delius showed an incandescent creativity rarely caught in the recording studio. The total spontaneity of his music-making was aided by his ability almost to mesmerize his players and lift them up on the inspiration of the moment. It is perhaps a pity that EMI chose not to open this anthology with *Brigg Fair*, Delius's masterpiece among his shorter orchestral works, which is so superlatively played here. There is a feeling of complete rapture at the opening, the RPO wind elysian, the plaintive reediness of the oboe solo contrasting with the soft pliability of the flute. Everything is so perfectly balanced and when, later, the long-breathed string melody arrives, it is given a sensuous, lazy somnambulance that perfectly encapsulates a warm English summer afternoon. The actual string sound here (as in the gentle syncopated dance of the third movement of the *Florida Suite*) has a hazy almost unfocused shimmer that is unique to Beecham and is beautifully caught by the recording engineers.

One has not space to mention the many other moments of magic, but the radiant, veiled strings and luminous woodwind at the opening of *On Hearing the First Cuckoo in Spring*, the textural delicacy of *Summer Night on the River*, glowing like a French painting, or the free flexibility of tempo in *Summer Evening* must all receive a special mention. The CD transfers make the very most of the recordings, opening up the textures and limiting the background noise to inconsequential proportions. At *piano*, *pianissimo* and *mezzo forte* levels the orchestral quality is warm and lustrous, and while tuttis harden (the dynamic range is remarkably wide) and the massed violins at *forte* tend to thin out, one can readily adjust, for the sparkle of the upper range adds piquancy to the opening of the *Sleigh Ride* and increases the feeling of gaiety when 'La Calinda' appears in the *Florida Suite*. As can be seen above, playing time is very generous indeed and if the forward balance of the vocal soloists remains unattractive in *Songs of Sunset*, this is integral to the master tape and the inclusion of this work is welcome. But with the freedom possible with CD banding, you may well find yourself spending most time with *Brigg Fair* and the shorter orchestral evocations, while the opening of the early (1897) *Over the Hills and Far Away*, which comes first, immediately demonstrates the Beecham/Delius evocation at its most poetent, even if there is some melodrama later in the work.

Delius Cello Sonata. Caprice and Elegy. Hassan – Serenade (arr. Fenby). Romance.
Grieg Cello Sonata in A minor, Op. 36. Intermezzo in A minor, CW118.
Julian Lloyd Webber *vc* **Bengt Forsberg** *pf*
Philips 454 458-2PH (66 minutes: DDD). Recorded 1996.   Ⓕ

The links, both musical and personal, between Grieg and Delius are many, which makes this a very apt and attractive coupling, bringing together all the works each composer wrote for this medium. This is Julian Lloyd Webber's second recording of the Delius Cello Sonata. The overall duration this time is almost two minutes shorter, and the easier flow goes with a lighter manner and a less forward balance for the cello. The result in this freely lyrical single-movement structure is more persuasive, less effortful, with greater light and shade, and with just as much warmth in the playing. Bengt Forsberg's variety of expression and idiomatic feeling for rubato consistently match those of his partner. The *Caprice and Elegy* of 1930, originally dictated to Eric Fenby, much slighter pieces with obsessively repetitious phrases, inspire equally free and spontaneous performances, and it is particularly good to have the tuneful *Romance* of 1898, which inexplicably remained neglected for 80 years till Lloyd Webber revived it. The Grieg Sonata, too, among the most inspired and intense of his longer works, prompts magnetic playing, again with more light and shade than is common, helped by not having the cello spotlit, in a natural recording acoustic. The lyrical *Intermezzo* provides an attractive makeweight. Though a very high proportion of the music here is reflective, the meditative intensity of the playing sustains it well.

Violin Sonatas Nos. 1-3. Cello Sonata.
Ralph Holmes *vn* **Julian Lloyd Webber** *vc* **Eric Fenby** *pf*
Unicorn-Kanchana Souvenir UKCD2074 (65 minutes: ADD/DDD). Recorded 1972-81.   Ⓜ

This is selfless, utterly dedicated music-making, always spontaneous-sounding yet never losing the organic thread of Delius's remarkable, free-flowing inspiration. There is a slight fragility to Holmes's distinctive, silvery tone that is extremely moving, and Fenby, though no virtuoso practitioner, accompanies with intuitive sympathy. The recording of the piano (the instrument used is the three-quarter Ibach grand left to Fenby by Delius himself) remains a touch boxy and wanting in bloom, though the balance is otherwise natural and the overall effect nicely intimate. In the Cello Sonata Lloyd Webber and Fenby adopt a mellow, notably ruminative approach. Dedicatee Beatrice Harrison's 1926 recording with Harold Craxton (available on a Symposium reissue) should be sought out by all discerning Delians, for through the surface crackle emerge a rapt wonder, generous flexibility and instinctive sense of line that are something special. A small textual observation of note: Lloyd Webber (like Harrison before him) eschews the cello's final D major chord.

Violin Sonatas – B major; Nos. 1-3.
Tasmin Little *vn* **Piers Lane** *pf*
Conifer Classics 75605 51315-2 (77 minutes: DDD). Recorded 1997.   Ⓕ

Tasmin Little's Delian instincts are formidable indeed, here amply confirmed by Conifer's rewarding coupling. The wonderful First Sonata receives big-hearted, confident advocacy here. These marvellously sensitive performers strike a near-ideal balance between flexibility and purposeful concentration, even by the standards of Holmes and Fenby. Little and Lane are not out of place in such august company. Likewise, the Second Sonata is given a commandingly articulate, thoughtful interpretation that never once threatens to hang fire. In the Third Sonata Little's playing positively glows with fervour and understanding. Moreover, she and Lane see to it that the fine Sonata in B major (1892) emerges in infinitely convincing fashion. To both outer movements they bring fiery propulsion as well as a firm sense of direction, while the haunting central processional of the lovely *Andante molto tranquillo* (which so impressed Grieg) really captures the imagination. The recording is full-bodied, though the piano focus could be sharper within a church acoustic that is surely too expansive for such intimate repertoire. The sessions (as Little relates in her touching booklet-notes) were lent an extra poignancy by the news of Eric Fenby's death on the first day of recording.

Sea Drift. Songs of Sunset. Songs of Farewell.
Sally Burgess *mez* **Bryn Terfel** *bass-bar* **Waynflete Singers; Southern Voices; Bournemouth Symphony Chorus and Orchestra / Richard Hickox.**
Chandos CHAN9214 (77 minutes: DDD). Texts included. Recorded 1993.
Gramophone Award Winner 1994.   Ⓕ 🅱

Sea Drift is a sublime conjunction of Whitman's poetry and Delius's music describing love, loss and unhappy resignation, with the sea (as Christopher Palmer put it) as 'symbol and agent of parting'. Written in 1903-04 (the same years as Debussy's *La mer*), it is surely Delius's masterpiece; right from the swaying opening bars its spell is enduring and hypnotic. Hickox in his second recording of the work now gives us the finest recorded post-Beecham *Sea Drift*. The shaping of the opening falling woodwind figures at a slow tempo more than usually (and very beautifully) portends the sad turn of events; and the climax is broad and superbly co-ordinated. Terfel's bar-by-bar characterization (and glorious voice), conveys the full expressive range of the role from impassioned appeal to gentle call without artifice; and the choral singing is superb. The whole is recorded with warmth, spaciousness, depth and clarity. A strongly recommended recording.

Five Partsongs (1887). Her ute skal gildet staa. Irmelin Rose (arr. Lubin). On Craig Dhu. Wanderer's Song. Midsummer Song. The splendour falls on castle walls. Two Songs for Children. To be sung of a summer night on the water. A Village Romeo and Juliet – The dream of Sali and Vrenchen (arr. Fenby). Appalachia – Oh, Honey, I am going down the river (arr. Suchoff). Irmelin – Away; far away to the woods. Hassan – Chorus behind the scenes; Chorus of Beggars and Dancing Girls.
Joanna Nolan sop **Stephen Douse** ten **Andrew Ball** pf **Mark Brafield** org
Elysian Singers of London / Matthew Greenall.
Somm Recordings SOMMCD210 (50 minutes: DDD). Texts and translations included.
Recorded 1992.   Ⓕ

Delius had a special relationship with the collective human voice, and the songs here are presented chronologically, which allows us to follow pleasurably the development of his style. The extracts from *A Village Romeo and Juliet* and *Appalachia* prolong what would otherwise be a rather brief encounter and their accompaniments also provide contrast of timbre, but they do need to be heard in context to 'take off'. The 'essential' Delius comes with *On Craig Dhu* – experience of nature not so much tinged by melancholy as perceived through it; a haunting evocation in grey; and the setting of Tennyson's *The splendour falls on castle walls*, as characteristically Delius as Britten's setting of it, in his *Serenade*, is Britten. Though the singing itself deserves a generally warm welcome, not all Delius's chromatic wanderings are as confidently charted as they might be. The sopranos seem the strongest contingent, and the ones most often in the expressive spotlight (maybe they also excite more resonance, and with it prominence, from the generously reverberant location). Nor are the soloists ideal, the tenor sounding unhappy in the higher regions of the second of the two songs, *To be sung of a summer night on the water*. And on occasions, as in the first of those two songs, one might have wished for more varied pacing and dynamic shading from the conductor. But the world of Delius performance is one where devotees are used to taking the roundabouts with the swings, and this is the only all-Delius collection of its kind on the market.

A Mass of Life[a]. Requiem[b].
[a]**Joan Rodgers,** [b]**Rebecca Evans** sops **Jean Rigby** mez **Nigel Robson** ten
Peter Coleman-Wright bar **Waynflete Singers;**
Bournemouth Symphony Chorus and Orchestra / Richard Hickox.
Chandos CHAN9515 (two discs: 129 minutes: DDD). Texts and translations included.
Recorded 1996.   Ⓕ

This is only the third commercial recording of *A Mass of Life*. The previous two recordings were the 1952 Beecham (no longer available) and the 1971 Groves on EMI. You might imagine modern recording would best place this vast canvas between your loudspeakers. And yes, Hickox's dynamic peaks are marginally higher, his perspectives marginally wider and deeper. Actually, some of this has as much to do with Hickox's own pacing and shading as the engineering. In general, this 'idealized' light- and air-filled sound brings a sharper, bright presence for the chorus, and such things as the piccolo trilling atop the final 'Hymn to Joy'. What it doesn't bring is the sense of performers in a specific acoustic space. But the chorus shines in the prominent role which the Chandos balance gives them, with ringing attack for all entries where it is needed, and singing as confident as it is sensitive, even if one has to make the odd allowance for not quite perfect pitching on high (Delius's demands are extreme) and moments where they are too loud. The soloists are fine; Hickox's baritone, Peter Coleman-Wright, has a good line in stirring, virile address, though little of Benjamin Luxon's nobility, inwardness and true *legato*. What makes the Hickox *Mass* preferable to the Groves (but only just) is the conductor's inspired handling of each part's central dance panels. Hickox makes you believe in them, with a judicious drive, lift to the rhythms, and really incisive, eager singing and playing. As a coupling, Hickox has only the second-ever commercial recording of the Requiem: more Nietzsche, but this time dogma not poetry, all the more unpalatable/ embarrassing (regardless of your faith) for being in English, but containing much unique Delius.

Ernö Dohnányi   Hungarian 1877-1960

Dohnányi Violin Concerto No. 2 in C minor, Op. 43.
Bartók Violin Concerto No. 2, Sz112.
Mark Kaplan vn
Barcelona Symphony Orchestra / Lawrence Foster.
Koch International Classics 37387-2 (70 minutes: DDD). Recorded 1996.   Ⓕ

Throughout Dohnányi's immensely likeable Second Violin Concerto, the general idea is to keep the solo line as busy and as prominent as possible, even to the extent of dispensing with orchestral violins. The first movement features a furious *fugato*, Straussian tutti passages and Kreislerian solo writing (especially when double-stopped). The *Scherzo* recalls Reger at his most mischievous, and the slow movement has a warmth reminiscent of Brahms. A spirited finale features a novel cadenza with solo horn and the overall effect of the concerto is of spontaneous invention bursting at the seams. Mark Kaplan's idiomatically luscious performance is given alert support from Lawrence Foster's Barcelona orchestra, and the recording is more than acceptable. Kaplan's Bartók is equally forceful and the partnership with Foster works particularly well when soloist and orchestra indulge in vigorous banter. This is a strong, spontaneous and warmly felt reading, flexible in gesture and with the added interest of Bartók's brassy original coda – a more powerful ending than the revision, albeit without any contribution from the soloist. It provides an enjoyable coupling for the more-ish Dohnányi concerto.

Symphony No. 1 in D minor, Op. 9. American Rhapsody, Op. 47.
BBC Philharmonic Orchestra / Matthias Bamert.
Chandos CHAN9647 (67 minutes: DDD). Recorded 1998.   (F)

The First Symphony is a fascinating if uneven work. Sundry influences spontaneously spring to mind: Tchaikovsky, Brahms and Richard Strauss. The five-movement structure has its obvious models in Beethoven and Berlioz, but the scoring, although tending towards Wagnerian sonorities, is frequently individual, and so is the 23-year-old Dohnányi's command of symphonic argument. Bamert offers a broad reading, with much drama, most notably at the beginning of the *Scherzo* and the furious *fugato* passage 12'00" into the finale, where the BBC lower strings 'dig in' with a vengeance. Bamert and Chandos also offer us an excellent performance of the much later *American Rhapsody* (1950 as opposed to 1900 for the Symphony). Here, Dohnányi's sound world recalls the Delius of *Appalachia* and the *Florida* suite and his use of American traditional tunes are reminiscent of Charles Ives's Second Symphony. If all this sounds as if Dohnányi didn't have an original idea in his head, it is certainly not meant to. The references are intended to focus superficial similarities but should not mask the fact that Dohnányi had plenty to say, and said it well. The recording is in the demonstration class.

Dohnányi Variations on a Nursery Theme, Op. 25.
Brahms Piano Concerto No. 1 in D minor, Op. 15.
Mark Anderson *pf*
Hungarian State Symphony Orchestra / Adám Fischer.
Nimbus NI5349 (75 minutes: DDD). Recorded 1994.   (F)

Mark Anderson gives a glittering performance of the Dohnányi, and a spontaneous one; he is superbly accompanied by Adám Fischer and the Hungarian State SO. Nimbus's recording is admirable in everything but the backward placing of the woodwind in general and the bassoons in particular. One thing the Dohnányi *Variations* share with the D minor Brahms Concerto is a passionate minor key opening. Again Fischer and his Hungarian orchestra are superb, the playing incisive and gloweringly vivid. It is a measure, too, of the accord that exists between conductor and soloist that the pianist enters the fray with the perfectly groomed musical manners of a soloist in a baroque concerto. And it is the logic of Anderson's playing, his sweet reasonableness, that holds the attention, even though Brahmsians may find Anderson a shade light-toned in bravura passages. The Brahms obviously faces tough competition, but the Dohnányi is a very fine performance in its own right.

Dohnányi Sextet in C major, Op. 37[a].
Fibich Quintet in D major, Op. 42.
Endymion Ensemble (Mark van de Wiel *cl* Stephen Stirling *hn* Krysia Osostowicz *vn* [a]Iris Juda *va* Jane Salmon *vc* Michael Dussek *pf*)
ASV CDDCA943 (66 minutes: DDD). Recorded 1995.   (F)

Both composers employ their chosen resources with great expertise, Dohnányi in a richly harmonized Sextet that opens among the clouds and ends in a mood of dance-like exuberance, Fibich with a more conventional structure and a genial stream of melody. Each work owes something to Brahms although in the case of Fibich's Quintet, Schumann seems as much in evidence, not only through the score's specific melodic complexion, but in a *Scherzo* that features two contrasting trios. Smetana is another possible point of reference, especially at the start of the finale, although – as Jan Smaczny usefully points out in his excellent booklet-note – the younger Fibich 'often anticipated the achievements of the elder composer'. Dohnányi's Sextet is a far darker piece, opening as it does among rolling string arpeggios and toughening for a fairly tense development. The 'Intermezzo' second movement suggests (at least initially) Brahms as siphoned through the imagination of Schoenberg, whereas the eventful third movement suddenly breaks into a rhythmically upbeat finale that sounds as much Afro-Caribbean as Hungarian, albeit with a luscious 'big' tune to offset the fun. The Endymion Ensemble does both Fibich and Dohnányi proud and the recordings are excellent.

Piano Quintets[a] – No. 1 in C minor, Op. 1; No. 2 in E flat minor, Op. 26. Suite in the Old Style, Op. 24.
[a]**Vanbrugh Quartet** (Gregory Ellis, Elizabeth Charleson *vns* Simon Aspell *va* Christopher Marwood *vc*); **Martin Roscoe** *pf*
ASV CDDCA915 (70 minutes: DDD). Recorded 1994.   Ⓕ

Dohnányi's First Piano Quintet, Op. 1, written when the composer was only 18, is a work of abounding confidence and energy that is played here with suitable verve and exuberance. Roscoe and the Vanbrugh Quartet luxuriate in lush, romantic textures in the first movement, and delight in the melodic exchanges of the warmly expressive *Adagio*. Moreover, their expression of Hungarian flavour, evident in the *Scherzo*'s jaunty cross-rhythms and the engagingly dance-like finale, has considerable charm. The Second Quintet, written some 19 years later, shows a striking advance in technique. Sensitive evocation of atmosphere in the first movement by Roscoe and the Vanbrugh Quartet highlights both Dohnányi's more searching harmonic language and his remarkably fresh and imaginative approach to form. The performers deftly blend the *Intermezzo*'s faintly Viennese character with the flamboyant toccata material, and the final movement's fusion of slow movement and finale is ingeniously turned from sombre minor to radiant major. Both the quintets display Dohnányi's considerable pianistic skills; the *Suite in the Old Style* provides further evidence with a highly effective display of the composer's parody of baroque keyboard techniques. Roscoe's evident sympathy for Dohnányi's music contributes to this arrestingly persuasive account, which fully exploits the work's rich variety of style and technique. Newcomers to Dohnányi's music will find much to enjoy in this disc of repertoire that clearly deserves to be much better known.

Dohnányi String Quartets – No. 2 in D flat major, Op. 15; No. 3 in A minor, Op. 33.
Kodály Intermezzo.
Lyric Quartet (Patricia Calnan, Harriet Davies *vns* Nick Barr *va* David Daniels *vc*).
ASV CDDCA985 (60 minutes: DDD). Recorded 1996.   Ⓕ

Dohnányi's output is nothing if not rich in contrasts: both slow movements of these appealing quartets are visited by animated, mood-changing faster sections, stormy and passionate in the Second Quartet and skittish in the Third. The earlier quartet is the more wholesomely romantic of the two, with a *Presto acciacato* second movement that recalls the orchestral storm sequence at the beginning of Wagner's *Die Walküre*. The Second Quartet's heart is in its poignant slow movement finale which incorporates references to previous movements. Dohnányi's musical language suggests something of Strauss, Brahms and Mendelssohn, with the Third Quartet's cynically argumentative first movement providing the grittiest musical activity on the disc. The earliest work programmed is by Kodály, a pleasant but uncharacteristic *Intermezzo* from 1905 that the Lyric Quartet performs – like everything else – with gusto and warmth.

Gaetano Donizetti   Italian 1797-1848

Sinfonia in G minor (recons. Päuler). Sonata in C minor (orch. Hoffmann). Oboe Sonata in F major (orch. Hoffmann). Concerto for Violin, Cello and Orchestra in D minor (recons. Wojciechowski). Cor Anglais Concerto in G major. Clarinet Concertino in B flat major (recons. Meylan). Sinfonia in D minor (recons. Andreae).
Budapest Camerata / László Kovács.
Marco Polo 8 223701 (64 minutes: DDD). Recorded 1994.   Ⓕ

This is an intriguing issue of instrumental concertos, recorded for the first time. As in his string quartets, Donizetti's dramatic flair and imaginative instrumentation provide the main points of interest, while the G major Concerto for cor anglais – a theme and variations – provides an opportunity to sample Donizetti's formal ingenuity and thematic invention. After a crisp performance of the buoyant G minor *Sinfonia*, the Budapest Camerata offers a group of solo concertos featuring a variety of instruments. The C minor flute *Concertino* and F major oboe *Concertino* – originally intended as instrumental sonatas – are presented in Wolfgang Hoffmann's sensitive orchestrations. Contrasts (textural, dramatic and dynamic) are well defined, with admirably clear recording. The infectiously exuberant *allegros* are not especially profound, but Donizetti's slow movements are often most effective. The D minor Concerto for violin, cello and orchestra is the longest and most impressive work here. The Budapest Camerata balances solo and ensemble forces with subtle refinement throughout this charming piece, whose brief *Andante* has genuine pathos, and smiling finale has engaging wit.

Anna Bolena.
Maria Callas *sop* Anna Bolena; **Nicola Rossi-Lemeni** *bass* Enrico VIII;
Giulietta Simionato *mez* Giovanna Seymour; **Gianni Raimondi** *ten* Riccardo Percy;
Plinio Clabassi *bass* Rochefort; **Gabriella Carturan** *mez* Smeton; **Luigi Rumbo** *ten* Hervey;
Chorus and Orchestra of La Scala, Milan / Gianandrea Gavazzeni.
EMI mono CMS5 66471-2 (two discs: 140 minutes: ADD). Notes, text and translation included.
Recorded live in 1957.   Ⓜ 🄷

One of Callas's unique qualities was to inspire an audience with the sense of a great occasion, and to key-up a sympathetic conductor into the production of something to match her own intensity and the public's expectations. Here she gives one of her finest performances. The first impression is essentially a vocal one, in the sense of the sheer beauty of sound. Then, in the first solo, 'Come innocente giovane', addressing Jane Seymour, she is so clean in the cut of the voice and the style of its usage, delicate in her *fioriture*, often exquisite in her shading, that anyone, ignorant of the Callas legend, would know immediately that this is an artist of patrician status. There are marvellous incidental moments, and magnificent *crescendos*, into, for instance, 'per pietà delmio spavento' and 'segnata è la mia sorte', culminating in the Tower scene. Unfortunately, the singers at her side hardly measure up. Simionato has a splendid voice that nevertheless bumps as it goes into the low register and is not reliably steady in many passages, while the manner is too imperious and unresponsive in expression. The tenor role, of the ineffectual lover Percy, has been reduced by Gavazzeni's cuts (of which there are several), but Gianni Raimondi makes limited impression in what remains; and, as the King, Rossi-Lemeni produces that big but somewhat woolly tone that became increasingly characteristic. Even so, the great ensembles still prove worthy of the event, and the recording, which is clear without harshness or other distortion, conveys the special quality of this memorable evening at the opera with remarkable vividness and fidelity. For those who insist on a modern recording, there is an imaginatively conducted 1994 performance on Nightingale Classics by Elio Boncompagni, with Edita Gruberová in the title-role. But this Callas/Gavazzeni set is in a different class altogether.

Don Pasquale.
Renato Bruson *bar* Don Pasquale; **Eva Mei** *sop* Norina; **Frank Lopardo** *ten* Ernesto;
Thomas Allen *bar* Malatesta; **Alfredo Giacomotti** *bass* Notary;
Bavarian Radio Chorus; Munich Radio Orchestra / Roberto Abbado.
RCA Victor Red Seal 09026 61924-2 (two discs: 120 minutes: DDD). Notes, text and translation
included. Recorded 1993.   Ⓕ

Roberto Abbado balances equably the witty and more serious sides of this score, finding a gratifying lightness in the 'A quel vecchio' section of the Act 1 finale and creating a delightful sense of expectancy as Pasquale preens himself while awaiting his intended bride. Abbado plays the score complete and respects Donizetti's intentions. This set has many strengths and few weaknesses: indeed it would be hard to cast the piece more successfully today. Pasquale is usually assigned to a veteran singer and with Bruson you hear a voice hardly touched by time and a technique still in perfect repair. Apart from weak low notes, he sings and acts the part with real face, and his vital diction, particularly in recitatives, is a pleasure to hear. He works well with Thomas Allen's nimble, wily Malatesta, an unexpected piece of casting that proves to be inspired. Like Bruson, Allen sings every note truly and relishes his words, evincing a sense of comedy as he prepares, cruel to be kind, to gull his friend. Eva Mei's Norina is an ebullient creature with a smile in her tone. The edge to her voice seems just right for Norina though others may find it tends towards the acerbic under pressure. Her skills in coloratura are as exemplary as you would expect from a reigning Queen of Night. Lopardo is that rare thing, a tenor who can sing in an exquisite half-voice, yet has the metal in his tone to suggest something heroic in 'E se fia', the cabaletta to 'Cercherò lontana terra', which in turn is sung in a plangent, loving way, just right. The recording here is exemplary.

L'elisir d'amore.
Angela Gheorghiu *sop* Adina; **Roberto Alagna** *ten* Nemorino; **Roberto Scaltriti** *bar* Belcore;
Simone Alaimo *bar* Dulcamara; **Elena Dan** *sop* Giannetta;
Chorus and Orchestra of the Opéra National de Lyon / Evelino Pidò.
Decca 455 691-2DHO2 (two discs: 123 minutes: DDD). Notes, text and translation included.
Recorded 1996.   Ⓕ 🆁🆁

This work, ideally combining the needs of comedy and sentiment, has always been a favourite of opera goers. This set catches these contrasting moods to perfection under Pidò's alert and affectionate conducting, not least because the recording is based on live performances at the Lyon Opera. The main interest is undoubtedly on how our most sought-after operatic pairing fare in the central roles. Gheorghiu presented her credentials as Adina at Covent Garden prior to this recording; some found her dramatically a shade shrewish in the part, but Adina is a feisty, temperamental girl, and a touch of steel doesn't seem inappropriate. It makes her capitulation when she realizes the true depth of Nemorino's feelings that much more moving. She provides plenty of flirtatious fire in the early scenes and turns Nemorino away with determination, making her intentions clear in pointed attack in the recitative, but her concern for him is never far below the surface and comes to the fore in her colloquy with Dulcamara. All this is conveyed in singing that matches warmth with pointed diction and fleet technique, something essential at Pidò's sometimes racy speeds. Alagna's Nemorino is almost on the same level. He obviously enjoys himself greatly as the lovelorn yokel, one with a vulnerable soul as he shows at his moment of greatest heartbreak, 'Adina, credimi' in the Act 1 finale. His sense of fun is obvious in the bottle-shaking episode when he thinks he has found the elixir of the title. The two Italians in the lower roles are admirable. Scaltriti may not be as preening as some Belcores but he sings the part with a firmness that older singers miss and he is fully in character. Alaimo is a naturally witty Dulcamara and never indulges in unwanted *buffo* mugging. The Erato set, at mid-price, presents formidable opposition. Devia is a less wilful, less vivid Adina than Gheorghiu, but her style is, if possible, even more idiomatic. There's not much to choose between the other roles, but as a whole the Decca sounds, not surprisingly, the more lifelike reading, worth every penny of the asking price. Decca has provided an ideally balanced sound picture which has plenty of natural presence.

L'elisir d'amore.
Mariella Devia *sop* Adina; **Roberto Alagna** *ten* Nemorino; **Pietro Spagnoli** *bar* Belcore;
Bruno Praticò *bar* Dulcamara; **Francesca Provvisionato** *mez* Giannetta;
Tallis Chamber Choir; English Chamber Orchestra / Marcello Viotti.
Erato 0630-17787-2 (two discs: 129 minutes: DDD). Notes, text and translation included.
Recorded 1992.   Ⓜ Ⓔ

This set is a delight from start to finish, making one fall in love all over again with this delightful comedy of pastoral life. Roberto Alagna, disciple of Pavarotti, sings Nemorino with all his mentor's charm and a rather lighter tone appropriate to the role. He also evinces just the right sense of vulnerability and false bravado that lies at the heart of Nemorino's predicament. He is partnered by Mariella Devia who has every characteristic needed for the role of Adina. With a fine sense of buoyant rhythm, she sings fleetly and uses the coloratura to enhance her reading. She can spin a long, elegiac line where that is needed, and her pure yet full tone blends well with that of her colleagues. She also suggests all Adina's high spirits and flirtatious nature. The other principals, though not as amusing in their interpretations as some of their more experienced predecessors, enter into the ensemble feeling of the performance. All are helped by the lively but controlled conducting of Viotti and by the ideal recording.

La favorita.
Fiorenza Cossotto *mez* Leonora; **Luciano Pavarotti** *ten* Fernando;
Gabriel Bacquier *bar* Alfonso; **Nicolai Ghiaurov** *bass* Baldassare;
Ileana Cotrubas *sop* Ines; **Piero de Palma** *ten* Don Gasparo;
Chorus and Orchestra of the Teatro Comunale, Bologna / Richard Bonynge.
Decca Grand Opera 430 038-2DM3 (three discs: 168 minutes: ADD). Text and translation
included. Recorded 1974.   Ⓜ

La favorita's lack of popularity has been attributed to the lack of an important soprano role, which is a pity, for it really is a very fine opera. Though there are passages where it fails to rise to the situation, and unfortunately the final duet is one of them, it has much in it that goes to the heart within the drama, and it is richly supplied with melody and opportunities for fine singing. The opportunities are well taken here. The recording has Pavarotti in freshest voice. That understates it: his singing is phenomenal. Wherever you care to test it, it responds. Of the two best-known solos, 'Una vergine' in Act 1 is sung with graceful feeling for line and the shape of the verses; the voice is evenly produced, of beautifully pure quality and with an excitingly resonant top C sharp. Throughout the opera he gives himself sincerely to the role dramatically as well as vocally. Cossotto, who in her absolute prime was one of the most exciting singers ever heard, is just fractionally on the other side of it here; she still gives a magnificent performance, gentle as well as powerful, in a part she made very much her own at La Scala. The role of Alfonso attracted all the great baritones in the time when the opera was heard regularly. Here, Gabriel Bacquier sings with a somewhat colourless tone. Yet Alfonso emerges as a credible character, a man of feeling, whose

'A tanto amor' has, in context, a moving generosity of spirit and refinement of style. Ghiaurov brings sonority, Cotrubas sweetness, Piero de Palma character. The chorus is poorly recorded but that may be to its advantage. The orchestra does well under Bonynge, especially in the 20-minute stretch of ballet music which would be ten too many if less well played. Recorded sound is fine; the booklet contains a brief note, synopsis and text with a not unamusing translation.

La fille du régiment.
Dame Joan Sutherland sop Marie; **Luciano Pavarotti** ten Tonio; **Spiro Malas** bass Sulpice;
Monica Sinclair contr Marquise; **Edith Coates** contr Duchess; **Jules Bruyère** bass Hortensius;
Eric Garrett bar Corporal; **Alan Jones** ten Peasant;
Chorus and Orchestra of the Royal Opera House, Covent Garden / Richard Bonynge.
Decca 414 520-2DH2 (two discs: 107 minutes: ADD). Notes, text and translation included.
Recorded 1968.   Ⓕ

Even Dame Joan Sutherland has rarely, if ever, made an opera recording so totally enjoyable and involving as this. With the same cast (including chorus and orchestra) as at Covent Garden, it was recorded immediately after a series of live performances in the Royal Opera House, and both the comedy and the pathos come over with an intensity born of communication with live audiences. That impression is the more vivid on this superb CD transfer. As with some of Decca's early CD transfers, you could do with more bands to separate items and it strikes one as odd not to indicate separately the most spectacular of Luciano Pavarotti's contributions, his brief but important solo in the finale to Act 1, which was the specific piece which prompted the much-advertised boast 'King of the High Cs'. For those who want to find it, it comes at 2'58" in band 13 of the first disc. Dazzling as the young Pavarotti's singing is, it is Sutherland's performance which, above all, gives glamour to the set, for here in the tomboy Marie she found a character through whom she could at once display her vocal brilliance, her ability to convey pathos and equally her sense of fun. The reunion of Marie with the men of her regiment and later with Tonio makes one of the most heartwarming operatic scenes on record, at once a moment for laughing and crying, magically captured here. The recording is one of Decca's most brilliant, not perhaps quite so clear on inner detail as some, but equivalently more atmospheric. Though there are one or two deliberately comic touches – such as Edith Coates's last cry of 'Quelle scandale' – that get near the limit of vulgarity, the production is generally admirable. The sound at once takes one to the theatre, without any feeling of a cold, empty studio.

Linda di Chamounix.
Mariella Devia sop Linda; **Luca Canonici** ten Carlo; **Alfonso Antoniozzi** bar Marquis
de Boisfleury; **Petteri Salomaa** bass Antonio; **Sonia Ganassi** mez Pierotto; **Donato di Stefano**
bar Prefect; **Francesca Provvisionato** mez Maddalena; **Boguslaw Fiksinski** ten Intendant;
Koor van de Nationale Reisopera; Orchestra of Eastern Netherlands / Gabriele Bellini.
Arts Music 47151-2 (three discs: 177 minutes: DDD). Italian text included. Recorded 1992.   Ⓢ

For a newcomer to *Linda di Chamounix*, it may be helpful to think of it as Donizetti's *Luisa Miller*. There are similarities in subject – a strong father-and-daughter relationship, a simple family and communal life threatened by the high-and-mighty. More than that, both operas evoke a strong sense of compassion. Donizetti's is lighter, with a comic element, a happy ending, and reassurance from the start in that the 'villain' is only the *buffo* bass-baritone whom operatic convention will not allow to win. Still, tragedy looms and the situations involve heartache of various kinds, of which the separation of soprano-and-tenor lovers is not the only one. Musically, it suffers at first hearing from having its best and most famous number (Linda's 'O luce di quest'anima') at the start. There is also a homeliness about the melodies and their harmonies that makes it seem all rather tame. Yet the proof, or at any rate evidence, that this is far from the whole story lies in the way that this opera has of deepening its impression on each encounter over the years. *Linda di Chamounix* is generally thought of as 'the soprano's opera', and obviously much depends upon her. Mariella Devia sings with purity of tone and brilliancy of range and technique; she presents a fully human Linda and no mere coloratura-singing doll. In the main supporting roles, Petteri Salomaa is outstanding, and the 'trousers' role of Pierotto is sung by the rather fruitily vibrant Sonia Ganassi. Ensemble, chorus work and orchestral playing are fine.

Lucia di Lammermoor.
Maria Callas sop Lucia; **Ferruccio Tagliavini** ten Edgardo; **Piero Cappuccilli** bar Enrico;
Bernard Ladysz bass Raimondo; **Leonard del Ferro** ten Arturo; **Margreta Elkins** mez Alisa;
Renzo Casellato ten Normanno;
Philharmonia Chorus and Orchestra / Tullio Serafin.
EMI Callas Edition CDS5 56284-2 (two discs: 142 minutes). Notes, text and translation included.
Recorded 1959.   ⒻⒽⓇⓇ

Callas was certainly more fallible here than in her first Lucia for Serafin in 1953, but the subtleties of interpretation are much greater; she is the very epitome of Scott's gentle, yet ardently intense heroine, and the special way she inflects words and notes lifts every passage in which she is concerned out of the ordinary gamut of soprano singing. In that sense she is unique, and this is certainly one of the first offerings to give to an innocent ear or a doubter to help convince them of Callas's greatness. The earlier part of the Mad scene provides the most convincing evidence of all. Then the pathos of 'Alfin son tua', even more that of 'Del ciel clemente' are here incredibly eloquent, and the coloratura is finer than it was in 1953, if not always so secure at the top. Tagliavini, after a rocky start, offers a secure, pleasing, involving Edgardo. Cappuccilli, then in his early prime, is a forceful but not insensitive Enrico, Bernard Ladysz a sound Raimondo. Serafin is a far more thoughtful, expressive Donizettian than his rivals on other sets, confirming this as the most persuasive account of the opera ever recorded.

Lucia di Lammermoor.
Cheryl Studer sop Lucia; **Plácido Domingo** ten Edgardo; **Juan Pons** bar Enrico; **Samuel Ramey** bass Raimondo; **Jennifer Larmore** mez Alisa; **Fernando de la Mora** ten Arturo; **Anthony Laciura** ten Normanno; **Ambrosian Opera Chorus; London Symphony Orchestra / Ion Marin.**
DG 435 309-2GH2 (two discs: 138 minutes: DDD). Notes, text and translation included.
Recorded 1990. Ⓕ

With Studer and Domingo in the leading roles, this version is certainly fit as a whole to stand alongside its eminent predecessors. The fine deep colours of the orchestra, the sturdy dramatic cohesion and well-wrought climaxes, are well brought out; passages traditionally omitted are in place (and deserve to be). The role of Lucia's confidante is sung with distinction by Jennifer Larmore, and though Juan Pons could do with more bite to his tone and Samuel Ramey with more expressiveness in his vocal acting these have their strengths too. Studer combines beautiful tone, technical accomplishment and touching pathos. Details include an extended cadenza in the Mad scene, which ends on a not too exposed high E flat (D being the ceiling elsewhere). Domingo triumphantly overcomes the difficulties such a role must pose at this stage of his career: Edgardo di Ravenswood in this recording is as firmly at the centre of the opera as is its eponymous heroine.

Maria Stuarda (sung in English).
Dame Janet Baker mez Maria Stuarda; **Rosalind Plowright** sop Elisabetta; **David Rendall** ten Leicester; **John Tomlinson** bass Talbot; **Alan Opie** bar Cecil; **Angela Bostock** sop Anna; **English National Opera Chorus and Orchestra / Sir Charles Mackerras.**
Chandos Opera in English Series CHAN3017 (two discs: 136 minutes: ADD).
Notes and English text included. Recorded live in 1982. Ⓜ

This revival celebrates the association of Dame Janet Baker and Sir Charles Mackerras within the context of the ENO company and one of its most memorable productions. For those who saw this, the set will call the stage back to mind with wonderful vividness; but the appeal goes well beyond that, preserving a performance stamped with the strong individuality that confers the status of a gramophone classic. This brought a personal triumph for Dame Janet and it impresses afresh by the distinctiveness of her vocal characterization. It is not every singer who reflects, or re-creates, the distinctive identities through vocal colour and 'registration'. Everyone who was there will remember the 'Royal bastard!' in confrontation with Elizabeth, but equally powerful, and more regal, is her command – 'Be silent! Leave me!' – to the Lord Chancellor of England who brings to Fotheringay news of her condemnation to death. By contrast, the quieter moments can be immensely moving, as, for instance, in the line in which she acknowledges an unexpected generosity in her great opponent. In that role, Rosalind Plowright gives what surely must have been one of the supreme performances of her career. The writing for Elizabeth makes immense demands of the singer, and in these fearsome opening solos the technical challenges are triumphantly met, the voice thrillingly ample, the quality in full bloom.

John Tomlinson's massive bass commands attention (which it does not then always reward with evenness of production). The male soloists have not the most grateful of roles, but Alan Opie's Cecil shows its quality in the duet with Elizabeth, and David Rendall endows the ineffectual Leicester with plenty of Italianate ardour. The chorus has limited opportunities, and has certainly been heard to better advantage on other occasions. A word of warning must be added concerning texts which involve cuts and adaptations. The transpositions are defended as standard practice when an exceptional mezzo-soprano (such as Malibran) took a soprano role, in the present instance merely conforming to the lower orchestral pitch of Donizetti's time. However, it is unlikely that at this date the set would be bought or rejected with this kind of consideration foremost. What remains are the strong positives, most notably the vitality of Mackerras's conducting and the glory of Baker's singing. Also, of course, for those to whom this is a priority, the opera is given in clear English.

Poliuto.
Franco Corelli *ten* Poliuto; **Maria Callas** *sop* Paolina; **Ettore Bastianini** *bar* Severo;
Nicola Zaccaria *bass* Callistene; **Piero de Palma** *ten* Nearco; **Rinaldo Pelizzoni** *ten* Felice;
Virgilio Carbonari, Giuseppe Morresi *basses* Christians;
Chorus and Orchestra of La Scala, Milan / Antonino Votto.
EMI mono CMS5 65448-2 (two discs: 111 minutes: ADD). Notes, text and translation included. Ⓜ🄷
Recorded live in 1960.

This is the first appearance of this recording in the official canon, by incorporation into EMI's
Callas Edition; and the quality is certainly an improvement on the previous 'unofficial' incarnation.
The sound is clear and faithful to the timbre of the voices, which are slightly favoured in the
balance at the expense of the orchestra. With it comes unforgettable testimony to what was clearly a
great night at La Scala. Its place in the Callas history owes less to the importance of this new role
in her repertory than to the triumph of her return to the house she had left in high dudgeon in
1958. The part of Paolina in this Roman tragedy is restricted in opportunities and leaves the centre
of the stage to the tenor. In other ways it suits her remarkably well, the Second Act in particular
involving the heroine in grievous emotional stress with music that here runs deep enough to give it
validity. There is a big part for the chorus, which sings with fine Italian sonority. Nicola Zaccaria,
La Scala's leading *basso cantabile*, has not quite the sumptuous quality of his predecessors, Pasero
and Pinza, but is still in their tradition. Ettore Bastianini is rapturously received and, though
wanting in polish and variety of expression, uses his firm and resonant voice to exciting effect. The
tenor *comprimario*, Piero de Palma cuts a by no means inadequate vocal figure by the side of
Corelli, who, for the most part, is stupendous: it is not just the ring and range of voice that impress,
but a genuinely responsive art, his aria 'Lasciando la terra' in Act 3 providing a fine example. It is
for his part in the opera, quite as much as for Callas's, that the recording will be valued.

Rosmonda d'Inghilterra.
Renée Fleming *sop* Rosmonda; **Bruce Ford** *ten* Enrico II; **Nelly Miricioiu** *sop*
Leonora di Guienna; **Alastair Miles** *bass* Gualtiero Clifford; **Diana Montague** *mez* Arturo;
Geoffrey Mitchell Choir; Philharmonia Orchestra / David Parry.
Opera Rara ORC13 (two discs: 150 minutes: DDD). Notes, text and translation included.
Recorded 1994. Ⓕ

By the criteria appropriate to its kind, *Rosmonda d'Inghilterra* is a very good opera, inferior to
Lucia di Lammermoor but not annihilatingly so. To say that score and libretto are highly
workmanlike may register as a kind of belittlement, though it should not do so, and it needs saying
since we know that Donizetti worked fast and turned out operas by the dozen and so are inclined to
assume that he must have been slipshod. In fact, this, his forty-first, shows the confident mastery of
form that can make useful, unselfconscious innovations, and there is scarcely more than a single
item in which he seems not to be writing with genuine creativity. The performance could hardly be
improved. David Parry conducts with what feels like a natural rightness. More than that, the
playing of the Philharmonia is of unvaryingly high quality – the Overture is one of Donizetti's best,
and the orchestral score shares interest on equable terms with the voice-parts. These include two
virtuoso roles for sopranos, who in the final scene confront each other in duet. As Rosmonda, the
immured and misled mistress, Renée Fleming shows once again that not only has she one of the
most lovely voices to be heard in our time but that she is also a highly accomplished technician and
a sympathetic stylist. Nelly Miricioiu is the older woman, the Queen whose music encompasses a
wide range of emotions with an adaptable vocal character to match. Whether by design or by the
condition of her voice in the different recording sessions, she fits the Second Act more happily than
the First, where for much of the time the tone appears to have lost its familiar incisive thrust. Bruce
Ford is an excellent, incisive Enrico, and Alastair Miles makes an authoritative father and
councillor as Clifford. The *travesto* role of Arturo is taken by the ever welcome Diana Montague,
and it is good to find that a solo has been dutifully included for 'him' in Act 2, even if it is a less
than inspired piece of music. The only complaint with the recording concerns balance, which
sometimes accords prominence and recession in a somewhat arbitrary way. The opera and
performance, however, are strong enough to take that on board.

John Dowland British *c*1563-1626

Lachrimae, or Seaven Teares.
Christopher Wilson *lte* **Fretwork** (Wendy Gillespie, Richard Campbell, Julia Hodgson,
William Hunt, Richard Boothby *viols*).
Virgin Classics Veritas VC5 45005-2 (60 minutes: DDD). Recorded 1987-89. Ⓕ🄿

Dowland Chamber

Did Dowland ever expect this collection to be played in its entirety, at one sitting? If so, in what order? Whatever your own 'answers' to these unanswerable questions may be, you can (if you feel strongly about it) easily impose them on any of the various integral versions on CD. Fretwork's reissue presents them as an entirety, with the dances in their original published order – the whole book 'as is'. The performances are laudable in their characterization (of the pavans in particular), discreet embellishment of the dances, clarity of detail (the product of pleasantly dry string sound and acoustic) and overall balance, in which the lute is neither forced into the background nor obtrusive. Christopher Wilson adds a firmly propulsive edge to the dances. This is the best available version of Dowland's monumental work, graced with Peter Holman's splendid notes and blessed with superbly engineered recording.

The First Booke of Songes or Ayres – If my complaints could passions moue; Can she excuse my wrongs with vertues cloake; Deare if you change ile neuer chuse againe; Go Cristall teares; Sleepe wayward thoughts; All ye whom loue or fortune hath betraide; Come againe: sweet loue doth now enuite; Awake sweet loue thou art returnd.
The Second Booke of Songs or Ayres – I saw my Lady weepe; Flow my teares fall from your springs; Sorrow sorrow stay, lend true repentant teares; Tymes eldest sonne, old age the heire of ease; Then sit thee down, and say thy 'Nunc Dimitis'; When others sings 'Venite exultemus'; If fluds of tears could clense my follies past; Fine knacks for Ladies, cheap, choise, braue and new; Come ye heauie states of night; Shall I sue, shall I seeke for grace.
Paul Agnew *ten* **Christopher Wilson** *lte*
Metronome METCD1010 (59 minutes: DDD). Texts included. Recorded 1995.　　　Ⓕ

Lovesongs and Sonnets of John Donne and Sir Philip Sidney
Paul Agnew *ten* **Christopher Wilson** *lte*
G. Tessier In a grove most rich of shade. **Dowland** O sweet woods, the delight of solitarie-nesse. Sweete stay a while, why will you? Preludium. **Morley** Who is it that this darke night. **Coprario** Send home my long strayde eies to mee. **A. Ferrabosco II** So breake off this last lamenting kisse. **Corkine** The Fire to see my woes for anger burneth. 'Tis true, 'tis day, what though it be?. **Hilton II** A Hymne to God the Father. **Anonymous** Come live with me. So breake off this last lamenting kisse. Goe my flocke, goe get you hence. Goe and catch a fallinge star. O deere life when shall it be. Sir Philip Sidney's Lamentacion. Dearest love I doe not goe.
Metronome METCD1006 (62 minutes: DDD). Texts included. Recorded 1994.　　　Ⓕ

In the Dowland, Paul Agnew is light of step in the quicker songs, and he languishes longer than most over the variously sorrowful ones; it says much for his artistry, that in 'Flow my teares' and 'I saw my Lady weepe' he protesteth neither too much nor too long. Many of his choices now enjoy 'pop' status, but his inclusion of the beautiful trilogy of which 'Tymes eldest sonne' is the first part, commonly neglected in mixed programmes such as this, is particularly welcome. He receives the most sensitive of support from Wilson clearly articulated, warm in tone, and perfectly complementary in completing the contrapuntal textures – neither intrusively nor coyly balanced with the voice. Dowland's lute songs have generated many fine recordings, as they richly deserve, and here is one more, beautifully presented, with a booklet containing first-class annotation and all the texts. Love is a familiar peg on which to hang a song recital, and if there is a further focus it is usually on the composer of the music; Agnew and Wilson turn the tables, for once, by spotlighting the writers of the texts, namely Sir Philip Sidney and John Donne. Sidney's sonnets *Astrophel and Stella*, written between 1581 and 1583, may have been addressed to the daughter of the Earl of Essex but she was unwillingly married to Lord Rich in 1581, so Sidney may have had in mind the daughter of Sir Francis Walsingham, whom he married in 1583. The emotional range of Donne's *Songs and Sonets* may also mirror the fluctuating fortunes of his own, basically happy marriage. In both cases the operative word is 'may'. To the good features of the recording of the Dowland songs are to be added notably clearer diction and some graceful embellishments (trippingly lithe in *Dearest love I doe not goe*) from Agnew, and two well-chosen lute solos by way of interludes from Wilson.

The First Booke of Songes or Ayres.
The Consort of Musicke / Anthony Rooley.
L'Oiseau-Lyre 421 653-2OH (76 minutes: ADD). Texts included. Recorded 1976.　　　ⒻⓅ

This is the recording that launched The Consort of Musicke's series devoted to the complete works of John Dowland. It deserves a permanent place in the lists and the sympathetic performances have much to commend them. When the record was first released, the idea of performing all 21 songs in strict order of Dowland's 1597 publication struck the critics as admirably scholarly but perhaps lacking variety, despite the fact that The Consort of Musicke explores all the possible permutations of scoring that Dowland builds into these flexible pieces: voice and solo lute, voices alone, or any combination of voices, lute and viols. But it is precisely the all-inclusiveness of the project that is important – those looking for Dowland anthologies are well served elsewhere. If a slight monotony does occasionally creep in, this can be attributed to the fact that not all the singing is as witty, charming or seductive as it might have been. Even Emma Kirkby seems reticent, and there's a distinct shortage of magic in the songs that Martyn Hill has to himself. But the performances scored for fuller consorts are unfailingly exquisite, and they demonstrate the richness of Dowland's counterpoint more fully than the standard voice-plus-lute combination can do. A disc for connoisseurs, and a most welcome reissue.

The Second Booke of Songes.
The Consort of Musicke / Anthony Rooley *lte*
L'Oiseau-Lyre 425 889-2OH (70 minutes: ADD). Texts included. Recorded 1976. Ⓕ Ⓟ

The 'Second Booke of Songes' dates from 1600 and contains two of Dowland's most famous compositions, *Flow my teares* and *I saw my Lady weepe*, though here these are presented unusually (and not entirely convincingly) as vocal duets. In fact there is a surprisingly wide variety of vocal and instrumental combinations throughout the disc, from consort song to four-part vocal to the more familiar sound of solo voice and lute, all of which were suggested as performance possibilities by Dowland himself. It is partly as a result of this that the recording retains its freshness in spite of its age, but it would be wrong to ignore the contribution made by the intelligent and sensitive singing of Emma Kirkby and Martyn Hill, both of whom sound completely in their element.

Preludium, P98. Fantasias – P6; P71. Pavans – Lachrimae, P15; The Lady Russell's Pavan, P17; Pavana Johan Douland, P94; La mia Barbara, P95. Galliards – Frog Galliard, P23; Galliard (upon a galliard by Dan Bachelar), P28; The Lord Viscount Lisle, his Galliard, P38; The Earl of Essex, his Galliard, P42a; Galliard to Lachrimae, P46; A Galliard, P82; Galliard on 'Awake sweet love', P92. An Almand, P96. My Lord Willoughby's Welcome Home, P66a. Loth to departe, P69. The Shoemakers Wife, a Toy, P58. Coranto, P100. Come away, P60.
Paul O'Dette *lte*
Harmonia Mundi HMU90 7163 (64 minutes: DDD). Recorded 1995. Ⓕ Ⓟ

Cadential trills played on one string are a recurrent problem for performers; the less well equipped use a *rallentando* or slurr them, whilst guitarists tend to play them across two strings. No one is more adept at delivering them cleanly and in tempo than O'Dette, whose technical armoury shows no weak spot. It is in the suppleness of his phrasing, clarity of his contrapuntal lines and close attention to the functional purpose of every note, that O'Dette is pre-eminent – and has the edge over Lindberg. This disc has all the virtues of its predecessors, and though it is doubtful that the Earl of Essex would have been happy to dance his galliard at O'Dette's (and others') pace, you can share the sentiment of its last track – you will be loath to leave it.

A fancy, P73. Pavana Dowlandi Angli. Doulands rounde battell galyarde, P39. The Erle of Darbies galiard, P44. Mistris Norrishis delight, P77. A jig, P78. Galliard, P76. Une jeune fillette, P93. Gagliarda, P103. Squires galliard. A fancy, P72. Sir Henry Umptons funerall. Captayne Pipers galliard, P88. A fantasie, P1.
Paul O'Dette *lte*
Harmonia Mundi HMU90 7164 (73 minutes: DDD). Recorded 1996. Ⓕ
Bacheler (arr.?) The Earl of Essex galliard, P89. **Moritz, Landgrave of Hessen** (arr. Dowland?) Pavin. **Joachim Van Den Hove** Pavana Lachrimae. **Holborne** Hasellwoods galliard.
R. Dowland Sir Thomas Monson, his Pavin and Galliard. Almande.

Given the odd transmission of John Dowland's lute music, any 'complete' recording of it is inevitably going to include a fair number of works that can have had little to do with him. Paul O'Dette has boldly put most of these together in his fifth and last volume, adding for good measure the three surviving works of the master's son, Robert Dowland. O'Dette is engagingly candid in expressing his views about the various works and their various degrees of authenticity. The only works he seems to think authentic are the *Sir Thomas Monson* pavan and galliard that survive only under the name of Robert Dowland. The collection is none the less fascinating for all that. They are nearly all thoroughly worthwhile pieces, some of them very good indeed (including the one now agreed to be by Holborne and the one O'Dette thinks likely to be by Daniel Bacheler); and he ends with what he considers a late adaptation of one of Dowland's most famous fantasies. O'Dette continues to show that in terms of sheer freedom of technique he is hard to challenge among today's lutenists: the often complicated counterpoint is always crystal clear; and he invariably conveys the strongest possible feeling for the formal design of the works. He plays with a thoughtfulness and control that are always invigorating. Anyone who is fascinated by the work of the prince of lutenists will want to have this disc.

Almains – Sir John Smith his Almain, P47; My Lady Hunsdons Puffe, P54. Ballads and Other Popular Tunes – Fortune, P62; Go from my Window, P64; My Lord Willoughby's Welcome Home, P66a; Walsingham, P67; Robin, P70. Fantaisies – Fantasie, P1a; Forlorne Hope Fancye, P2. Galliards – Captaine Digorie his Galliard, P19; Frog Galliard, P23a; Melancholy Galliard, P25; Mignarde, P34; The King of Denmarke his Galliard, P40; The most sacred Queene Elizabeth, her Galliard, P41a; Can she excuse, P42; Galliard to Lachrimae, P46. Jigs, Corantos, Toys – Mistris Winters Jumpe, P55; Mrs Vauxe's Gigge, P57; The Shomakers Wife, P58. Pavans – Piper's Pavan, P8; Semper Dowland Semper Dolens, P9; Lachrimae, P15. Preludium, P98.
Nigel North *lte*
Arcana A36 (72 minutes: DDD). Recorded 1995. ⓕⓅ

The disc contains 24 items, but of the 42 in Robert Dowland's anthology of 1610 Dowland contributed only seven, not all of which are included here. If this disappoints anyone who might expect a direct connection between the album's title, 'Lute Lessons' and that of Robert Dowland's book, there is more than ample compensation in the marvellous quality of playing on this disc, and in the appearance of 'Volume 1' on the cover, suggesting that it may herald yet another integral set of Dowland's lute works. If this should be the case we should have a clear market-leader in the field. The present disc is quite simply superb. Whilst North's fingers are always ready to dance to Dowland's more joyous tunes, they sometimes take a little longer to allow the more contemplative music plenty of breathing space, as in *Semper Dowland* and *Forlorne Hope Fancye*, delivered with the utmost eloquence. His readiness to embellish is unequalled in quantity, quality and the smoothness with which it blends into the lines. Nor does anyone put rubato to more telling use. In his *Musick's monument* (1674) Thomas Mace describes the 'sting' – vibrato – as an ornament, and though there is no evidence that the resource was used in earlier times, North's application of it is so effective that it is hard to believe that it was not; added to his beautiful tone, it is a potent aid to expressiveness.

Antonio Draghi   Italian 1635-1700

La vita nella morte.
Roberta Invernizzi, Cristiana Presutti, Elena Cecchi Fedi *sops* **Olga Gurkovska** *contr*
Rodrigo del Pozo *ten* **Fulvio Bettini** *bar* **Antonio Abete** *bass*
Limoges Baroque Ensemble / Christophe Coin *vc*
Auvidis Astrée E8616 (71 minutes: DDD). Text and translation included. Recorded 1997. ⓕⓅ

Antonio Draghi spent 20 years as Kapellmeister at the Viennese court, yet of his music we scarcely hear a note. *La vita nella morte* ('Life in Death') is a *sepolcro*, a type of sacred oratorio popular at the Habsburg Court and designed to be performed in costume during Holy Week, in this case on Good Friday 1688. The libretto abounds with allegorical figures, and shows Humanity moving from grief and repentance following the Fall, to redemption through hope and trust in God and, of course, Christ's sacrifice on the Cross. If that sounds more worthy than exciting, more sententious than sensuous, then fear not because the music has all the qualities of emotiveness and dramatic life that you are entitled to expect from a man who composed over 120 operas. It is also, in some places, extraordinarily beautiful. The orchestra is a lush-textured, typically Austrian ensemble of three violas, three violas da gamba and continuo, and there is one aria for Mary Magdalene which has an enchanting accompaniment for baryton. The performance is first-rate. Christophe Coin draws a loving sound from his instrumentalists, while the singers all show a keen declamatory sense in recitative and sensitive musicality in their short arias. The star is undoubtedly Rodrigo del Pozo as Humanity, a tenor with a light and agile voice, but with an exquisite and affecting quality of his own. Quite a discovery then, this work, and well worth exploring.

Guillaume Dufay   French c1400-1474

Complete secular music.
Timothy Penrose *counterten* **Rogers Covey-Crump, John Elwes, Paul Elliott** *tens* **Paul Hillier, Michael George** *bars* **Medieval Ensemble of London / Peter Davies** and **Timothy Davies.**
L'Oiseau-Lyre 452 557-2OC5 (five discs: 321 minutes: ADD). Texts and translations included. Recorded 1980. ⓑ

The passage of time has not diminished the grandeur of the achievement of the Medieval Ensemble of London. The opportunity of hearing the entire corpus of Dufay's songs from the same interpretative perspective is irreplaceable – it is doubtful that any record company today would be willing to undertake such an ambitious project. More than just the scope of Dufay's invention (that is hardly surprising in a career that spanned nearly 60 years), it is its astonishing consistency that strikes the listener – nearly every song has something to delight, to intrigue, to teach. The rough chronology, traced from first to last, is a programme in itself, beginning with the jaunty, seemingly effortless songs of his youth, catchy and dazzling by turns, to the increasingly involving works of maturity, culminating in the sublime poise of his last years.. Although the ensemble doesn't always match Dufay's phenomenal consistency, it's hard to argue with a line-up that includes Paul Elliott, Rogers Covey-Crump and John Elwes, all of them in their prime. And yes, one can disagree with the odd phrase here, spot a fluffed note among the instrumentalists (or, rather more rarely, the singers), or wonder at some surprising glitches in the CD transfer but with the last song, the beautiful, canonic *Les doleurs* lingering in the mind's ear, one accepts the series's limitations as its many virtues endure. Every serious collector should have this.

Missa S Jacobi. Rite majorem Jacobum canamus. Balsamus et munda cera. Gloria 'Resurrexit dominus' and Credo 'Dic Maria'. Apostolo glorioso.
The Binchois Consort (Mark Chambers, David Gould, Fergus McLusky, Robin Tyson *countertens* James Gilchrist, Chris Watson, Andrew Carwood, Edwin Simpson *tens*) / **Andrew Kirkman.**
Hyperion CDA66997 (67 minutes: DDD). Texts and translations included. Recorded 1997.　Ⓟ🅴

In what is only their second CD, The Binchois Consort shows absolute mastery of Dufay's difficult early style, with immaculate balance, wonderfully free phrasing, and crystalline clarity. Moreover in the *Missa S Jacobi* Andrew Kirkman shows an uncanny ability to set the perfect tempo every time, so that the music emerges with its full force. The *Missa S Jacobi* is an odd but supremely important work. It is one of two early Dufay Mass cycles that have rarely been recorded, partly because they are less obviously part of the grand tradition than his later four-voice cantus firmus Masses. And this one is particularly difficult because its many different textures and styles present a severe challenge if it is not to seem fragmented and incoherent. Here it stands as a glorious masterpiece, its nine movements spanning over 40 minutes, with the various styles acting as necessary contrast and culminating in the famous Communion that Heinrich Besseler many years ago argued was the earliest example of *Fauxbourdon* writing. Strangely, two of the motets work less well: both the earlier *Rite majorem* and the later *Balsamus* seem to go too fast for the details to have their full effect, perhaps because they are so strikingly different in style from the other works performed here. And it seems a touch perverse to use the now fashionable 'old French' pronunciation of Latin, particularly in a motet composed for a papal ceremony (even if the original singers would have been Franco-Flemish): in all his early motets the text seems centrally important, and this kind of pronunciation loses too many of the consonants. But the Italian-texted *Apostolo glorioso* is again quite superb, as is the astonishing *Gloria* and *Credo* pair. Briefly, then, this is as close to a perfect Dufay CD as any available.

Missa 'Se la face ay pale'. Gloria ad modum tubae. Chanson 'Se la face ay pale'.
Early Music Consort of London / David Munrow.
Virgin Veritas Edition VER5 61283-2 (45 minutes: ADD). Texts and translations included. Recorded 1973.　Ⓜ

A good number of Munrow's first performances remain unsurpassed. One would single out Dufay's Mass *Se la face ay pale* in this regard. Nowadays, tempos might be slightly brisker, and voices used in preference to instruments on the lower parts; but only compare the serene tranquillity of the *Kyrie I* with the exhilaration at the end of the *Credo*: here are poetry and variety in abundance. For this, one of the most significant performances of fifteenth-century Mass cycles, there is still no convincing alternative performance on CD. The earlier more 'medieval' *Gloria ad modum tubae* is performed here with tenor sackbuts on the lower lines, and two countertenors (Bowman and Brett) descanting above in cheerful canon; quite the most convincing account of the piece available, and a good beginning to the disc. The disc concludes with the chanson *Se la face ay pale* in its original three-part version.

Nuper rosarum flores. Alma redemptoris mater II. Letabundus. Ecclesie militantis. Magnificat sexti toni. Benedicamus Domino II. Recollectio Festorum Beate Marie Virginis: Plainchant for Vespers I.
Pomerium / Alexander Blachly.
Archiv Produktion 447 773-2AH (60 minutes: DDD). Texts and translations included. Recorded 1995-96.　Ⓕ

Pomerium here presents a new addition to our knowledge of Dufay's music, the set of plainchants he wrote for a new feast, the Recollection of the Feasts of the Virgin Mary, composed in 1458. The work is fascinating in many ways: as one of the very few cases of liturgical chant by a named composer, let alone the greatest composer of his age; as an example of Dufay's work in his full maturity (he was perhaps 60 years old at the time), and entirely different from what we know of his late polyphony; and as a case of unambiguously dated chant composition. Pomerium performs only the music for the First Vespers, a mere fragment of the whole feast. Perhaps there could have been more than four singers for these chants: elegant though the performance is, it hardly sounds like a cathedral *schola*. But the longer pieces are particularly persuasive: the hymn *Gaude redempta* and the Responsory *Surge propera*. For the rest, they add two of Dufay's most famous motets and a group of very rarely heard polyphonic liturgical works, particularly the glorious *Letabundus* setting and the *Magnificat* in the sixth tone, sung with superb lucidity. Pomerium sings with men and women, showing an attractive vibrant energy, everything neatly controlled. The sound in the Grotto Church of Notre Dame, New York, is well captured.

Paul Dukas

French 1865-1935

L'apprenti sorcier. Symphony in C major. La péri.
French National Orchestra / Leonard Slatkin.
RCA Red Seal 09026 68802-2 (71 minutes: DDD). Recorded 1996.　　　　Ⓕ E RR

In the best Franckian tradition, Dukas's three-movement Symphony is as abstract as his *Sorcerer's Apprentice* is vividly narrative. Both works are from the mid-1890s. And from over a decade later, the ballet *La péri* is something else again. A *poème dansée* in which glittering Russian Nationalist orientalism, and later Salome's Dance, merge with French late romantic impressionism, the end result hinting at, among other things, Ravel's *La valse* to come. The orchestration is a wonder; Dukas himself said he wanted it to be like 'a kind of dazzling, translucent enamel'. Here, as always in Slatkin's best work, structure is powerfully attended to, the texture has a beautiful sheen, and the whole disc confirms him as an exceptional stylist. In the weighting and scale of the orchestral sound, and the way lines and surface detail are projected, accentuated and articulated, Slatkin sounds marginally more French than Tortelier (below), the textures and timbres a degree more vibrant and varied. His orchestra is French, of course, and his recording is also less reverberant. And all of these elements enhance appreciation of the Symphony's brilliantly active, flaring orchestration and its fundamentally classical stance. While Tortelier's perspectives may be deeper in the shimmering landscapes and poetic melancholy of the slow movement, Slatkin's performance on the whole is slightly better geared and 'gathered'.

Dukas L'apprenti sorcier.
Saint-Saëns Symphony No. 3 in C minor, Op. 78, 'Organ'.
Simon Preston *org*
Berlin Philharmonic Orchestra / James Levine.
DG 419 617-2GH (47 minutes: DDD).　　　　Ⓕ

James Levine and the BPO, on cracking form, offer a performance of Saint-Saëns's Third Symphony which is still among the best available. The balance between the orchestra and organ, here played powerfully by Simon Preston, is well judged and the overall acoustic very convincing. Levine directs a grippingly individual reading, full of drama and with a consistently imaginative response to the score's detail. The organ entry in the finale is quite magnificent, the excitement of Preston thundering out the main theme physical in its impact. The music expands and blossoms magnificently, helped by the spectacular dynamic range of the recording. Levine's choice of coupling is a happy one, especially as his account of Dukas's masterpiece is still the best in the catalogue. Levine chooses a fast basic tempo, but justifies his speed by the lightness of his touch and, of course, the clean articulation and rhythmic bounce of the Berlin Philharmonic playing help considerably. The climax is thrilling, but Levine reserves something for the moment when the sorcerer returns to quell the flood. Levine must have Disney's imagery in his mind in the closing pages of the story, for the picture of the crestfallen Mickey handing back the broom to his master springs readily to mind. A marvellous finish to an exhilarating listening experience.

Symphony in C major. Polyeucte – overture.
BBC Philharmonic Orchestra / Yan Pascal Tortelier.
Chandos CHAN9225 (56 minutes: DDD). Recorded 1993.　　　　Ⓕ S

Before *L'apprenti sorcier*, the tradition Dukas was following was that of Franck, and he was also heavily influenced by the Wagnerianism then holding French composers in thrall. Both models can be discerned in the overture *Polyeucte*: nevertheless, and despite extensive Wagnerian use of the brass, there is a clarity (even delicacy in the third of its five sections) and an imaginative sense of colour which are individual to him. The finely crafted Symphony composed four years later, in 1896 – daringly in C major at a time when tonality was undergoing such general buffeting – shows Dukas as essentially a classicist, although the middle section of the central movement reveals that Nature romanticism had not passed him by. The eloquent performance here gives the vigorous first movement a splendid *élan* while also luxuriating in the Franckian secondary subjects, there is lovely warm, lyrical playing and sensitive nuance in the second movement, and the finale (even more Franckian in its harmonic thinking) bubbles over with nervous energy. Exemplary recording quality.

Dukas L'apprenti sorcier (arr. Rabinovitch).
Ravel La valse (arr. cpsr).
R. Strauss Symphonia domestica, Op. 53 (arr. Singer).
Martha Argerich, Alexandre Rabinovitch *pfs*
Teldec 4509-96435-2 (62 minutes: DDD). Recorded 1995.   ⓕ **E**

Dukas's *L'apprenti sorcier* and Ravel's *La valse* both inhabit worlds of exuberant nightmare, and although one can marvel at the concentrated wit and verve of Argerich and Rabinovitch, it is their uncanny evocation of unsettled states where all equilibrium is lost and the 'ceremony of innocence' is well and truly drowned that forms the most lasting impression. Such vividness brings parts of *La valse* to a near standstill before accelerating away and achieving an effect not unlike suddenly applied centrifugal force. The opening quivers with unease, the commencement of a vision where even the most opulent Viennese gaiety and extravagance is menacingly clouded and distorted. The Dukas, too, develops from sinister hints to a situation diabolically out of control yet one sustained by both players with an iron grip all the more remarkable when you consider the immense virtuoso resources involved. Otto Singer's skilful version of Strauss's *Symphonia domestica* hardly transcends its orchestral origin yet it is illuminated at every point – whether in rhetorical uproar or flickering, Lisztian half-lights – by playing of an overwhelming brio and crystalline clarity. If anything Argerich's blow-torch incandescence has increased rather than diminished over the years. The recordings are close but unconfined, capturing faithfully the dazzling impact of these performances.

Dukas Piano Sonata in E flat minor.
Dutilleux Piano Sonata.
Schmitt Deux mirages.
John Ogdon *pf*
EMI Matrix CDM5 65996-2 (79 minutes: ADD). Recorded 1972.   Ⓜ

The first of Schmitt's *Mirages*, written in 1920 and published in memory of Debussy, is a haunting, elaborately textured elegy; the second, a ferocious rendering of the story of Mazeppa's tragic ride, was dedicated to Cortot. One wonders whether he would ever have had the technique to play it: Ogdon, however, revels in its enormous demands. His fluency and limpid clarity are to be admired, too, in the Dutilleux Sonata, whose spiky first movement veers from fragile delicacy to pounding *fortissimo* chords; its slow movement (headed 'Lied') is deeply moving in its intensity; and rather more diatonicism marks the final massive chorale, with its brilliant ensuing variations. The main work here, however, is the big Dukas Sonata, written at the turn of the century, and advanced for its time. It has always been hailed by French critics as a masterpiece, but despite that it is not often performed, at least in this country. The sonata's Franckian harmonic and melodic traits are combined with a pianistic exuberance which suits Ogdon's temperament admirably, as does the demonic *Scherzo*, but this is balanced by his air of mystery in its trio section and by his tonal purity in the quiet slow movement. This disc brings home to us just how outstanding a pianist we lost.

Henri Dumont   French 1610-1684

Dumont Pavane. Two Preludes. Litanies de la Vierge. Allemande Gravis. Antienne de St Cecile. O Sponse mi. Symfonia. Domine salvum fac, Regem.
Anonymous Veni sponsa mea. Pater noster. Egredimini Filiae Sion. O veneranda Trinitas.
Ensemble Dumont / Peter Bennett *org*
Linn Records CKD067 (65 minutes: DDD). Texts and translations included. Recorded 1997. ⓕ **P** **E**

For most people, the achievements of Henri Dumont have been obscured by the more famous figures of Lully and Lalande. For Peter Bennett, however, he 'can justifiably be seen as the foundation on which French sacred music would stand for the next half-century', a composer who had a modernizing effect on a repertoire whose style in the 1650s lagged behind that of other countries in Europe. This beautifully recorded and enterprisingly programmed disc reconstructs a sacred concert as it might have been heard in the Parisian household of Louis's pious brother (and

Dumont's employer), Philippe of Anjou, mixing some of the composer's sacred works for two to five voices and continuo with pieces for small viol consort. There are also four anonymous works which seem to be old-style unaccompanied vocal pieces to which continuo parts were added during the 1750s. This is music which is quietly rather urgently expressive but it is almost unremittingly beautiful, and Ensemble Dumont's singing and viol-playing have a grace and refined sound which serve the pieces rather well. Quite simply, this is a gorgeous disc that you will never regret buying.

John Dunstable
British c1390-1453

Descendi in ortum meum. Ave maris stella. Gloria in canon. Speciosa facta es. Sub tuam protectionem. Veni, Sancte spiritus/Veni creator spiritus. Albanus roseo rutilat/Quoque ferundus eras/Albanus domini laudus. Specialis virgo. Preco preheminencie/Precursor premittitur/textless/Inter natos mulierum. O crux gloriosa. Salve regina mater mire. Missa Rex seculorum.
Orlando Consort.
Metronome METCD1009 (74 minutes: DDD). Texts and translations included. Recorded 1995.
Gramophone Award Winner 1996. Ⓕ **E**

This disc contains three of Dunstable's well-known motets – *Preco preheminencie*, *Veni veni* and *Albanus* – but the rest are rarely performed. For some of the delicious antiphons, it is hard to see why: *Salve regina mater mire* is particularly striking – one of those pieces that sounds far more impressive than it looks on the page. There are also some total novelties. The canonic *Gloria* was discovered in Russia: it is a massively inventive work that adds a substantial new dimension to our knowledge of Dunstable. And *Descendi in ortum meum*, though discovered and published a quarter of a century ago, surely stands as the latest known work of its composer: a magnificent piece that builds an entirely new kind of edifice with the materials of his characteristic style. Most impressive of all, though, is the Mass, *Rex seculorum*, which ends the disc. This may or may not be by Dunstable – which is probably why it has never been recorded. Whoever the composer, though, it is a key work in the history of the polyphonic mass cycle, brimming with invention. The Orlando Consort has a wonderfully forward style that beautifully matches the music and helps the listener to understand why Dunstable achieved such an enormous reputation on the continental mainland. If they are occasionally a touch rough, these are classic performances that will be hard to challenge.

Henri Duparc
French 1848-1933

L'invitation au voyage. Sérénade florentine. Extase. Chanson triste. Le manoir de Rosemonde. Lamento. Au pays où se fait la guerre. La fuite. La vague et la cloche. Sérénade. Testament. Phidylé. Romance de Mignon. Elégie. Le galop. Soupir. La vie antérieure.
Danielle Borst *sop* **François Le Roux** *bar* **Jeff Cohen** *pf*
REM REM311049 (63 minutes: DDD). Texts and translations included. Recorded 1987. Ⓕ **RR**

If you consider Duparc's songs the most rewarding in the French language you will rejoice at this issue. Without hesitation, we would say Le Roux's are the most successful performances of these masterpieces in miniature since the war. In his foreword to this issue the veteran composer Henri Sauguet comments: 'The interpretations of François Le Roux and Danielle Borst are remarkable, not just for their vocal qualities and their emotional commitment but also for their exemplary use of words, which illustrates perfectly the profound unity of poetry and music.' That almost says all that needs to be said, at any rate about Le Roux who has the lion's share of the burden. His voice can sometimes take on a rough edge but his understanding of the Duparc idiom is second to none, rivalling that of Panzéra and Bernac in the distant past, precisely because he realizes what French can convey when it is sung with a scrupulous care over diction. Added to that he and his admirable pianist, Jeff Cohen, seem almost always to find exactly the right tempo for each *mélodie*, not indulging in the excessively slow speeds adopted by some non-Francophone singers today. Le Roux is partnered in *La fuite* by Borst, another dedicated Duparcian who catches some of its trance-like beauty. She also offers the *Romance de Mignon*, not in the official canon and perhaps Duparc's weakest song. The recorded sound is ideal, the voice very present in a way that is entirely suited to this repertory. A 'must' for anyone interested in great performances of *mélodies*.

L'invitation au voyage. Sérénade florentine. La vague et la cloche. Extase. Phidylé. Le manoir de Rosemonde. Lamento. Testament. Chanson triste. Elégie. Soupir. La vie antérieure. Le galop. Sérénade. Au pays où se fait la guerre. Romance de Mignon. La fuite.
José van Dam *bass-bar* **Florence Bonnafous** *sop* **Maciej Pikulski** *pf*
Forlane UCD16692 (67 minutes: DDD). Texts and translations included. Recorded 1993. Ⓕ

These songs may justly be held to represent the peak of development of the French *mélodie* in their sensitivity, intensity, scope of expression and unfaltering taste. Influences may be seen of his teacher César Franck in his emotionalism and chromatic texture, of Gounod in the rippling piano part of a song like *Chanson triste*, and particularly of Wagner in the harmonic colouring of *Soupir* and the almost Tristanesque *Extase*; but it has been well observed that the sinister drama of *Le manoir de Rosemonde*, with its insistent rhythm, is worthy of Hugo Wolf, and that the bleak tints of *Lamento* foreshadow Ravel's *Le gibet*. Despite all this, however, Duparc is very much an individual genius; and the breadth of his stylistic range, from the passionate lyricism of *L'invitation au voyage* or the haunting sensuousness of *Phidylé* to the simple heartbreak of *Au pays où se fait la guerre*, makes any *intégrale* of his songs riveting. Particularly so when sung with such insight, commitment and verbal intensity as by José van Dam here. He is expertly partnered by a responsively musical accompanist.

Marcel Dupré French 1886-1971

Prelude and Fugue in F minor, Op. 7 No. 2. Cortège et Litanie, Op. 19 No. 2. Symphonie-Passion, Op. 23. Symphony No. 2 in C sharp minor, Op. 26. Evocation, Op. 37 – Allegro deciso.
John Scott *org*
Hyperion CDA67047 (71 minutes: DDD). Recorded on the organ of St Paul's Cathedral, London in 1998.   Ⓕ

This is an impressive release on every account. As we have come to expect from John Scott, the playing is superb – that perfect combination of technical virtuosity and intense musicianship which is so rare among organists – and numerous Hyperion recordings from the cavernous St Paul's over the past 15 years have fine-tuned its engineering to such an extent that we no longer admire the sound, *per se*, but find that the acoustic positively enhances it. That awesome echo, as the final chord of Scott's vehement account of the *Symphonie-Passion* is cast adrift to fend for itself in the cathedral's vastness, adds a tangible sense of presence. Yet the clarity is there; the precision of Scott's fingerwork is captured in microscopic detail in his stunning performance of the Second Symphony's 'Preludio' and 'Toccata' movements. The Prelude and Fugue receives a richly atmospheric performance which makes you wonder why it is that this deeply moving piece, with its strong melodic ties with the popular Requiem, has been so overshadowed by its companions. Musically, technically and emotionally these are truly distinguished recordings.

Francesco Durante Italian 1684-1755

Durante Magnificat in B flat major.
Astorga Stabat mater.
Pergolesi Confitebor tibi Domine.
Ann Monoyios *sop*
Balthasar Neumann Choir; Freiburg Baroque Orchestra / Thomas Hengelbrock.
Deutsche Harmonia Mundi 05472 77369-2 (59 minutes: DDD). Texts and translations included. Recorded 1995.   Ⓕ Ⓟ

The common factor in this programme is the adherence of its three composers to what is generally called the Neapolitan style. Durante was one of its most important representatives during the first half of the eighteenth century, and Pergolesi his most celebrated pupil. Astorga was a Spaniard whose family had settled in Italy, though he himself eventually returned to Spain and Portugal. The *Magnificat* in B flat by Durante, is an immediately appealing, expressively vital piece, concise, tautly constructed and tonally radiant. Both its opening and concluding sections are closely linked by the quotation of its psalm tone, *cantus firmus*, similarly treated in each instance. Altogether, this is a warmly satisfying setting of the canticle with sumptuous choral homophony colouring the short but effective 'Gloria patri'. Astorga's *Stabat mater* in C minor is of a very different expressive hue. It's an extended piece with a spacious opening chorus in which occasional unexpected modulations colour the musical rhetoric. The remainder of the work is shared between solo voices, vocal ensembles and choruses. Pergolesi's psalm setting, *Confitebor tibi Domine*, is close in spirit and in style to the *Magnificat* of his teacher, Durante.

Pergolesi introduces a larger solo element with only four choral sections as opposed to Durante's six. Pergolesi was foremost an opera composer, Durante, exceptionally among Neapolitan composers, was not, and it is in this respect that the two works reveal the most interesting contrasts. The performances are very good indeed. The Balthasar Neumann Choir consists of 14 voices from which various soloists in various groupings emerge as required. Over and above these, however, are the valuable contributions from Ann Monoyios. Her 'Sancta mater' in the Astorga is beautifully sung, as are the remaining five solos apportioned to her in that work and the Pergolesi psalm.

Sebastián Durón

Durón Tono a la Pasión de Christo, 'Quando muere el Sol'. Lamentación segunda, del Viernes Santo.
Navas Tono di Miserere, 'Si mis hierros os tienen pendiente'.
Torres Miserere. Lamentación segunda, del Jueves Santo.
Al Ayre Español / Eduardo López Banzo.
Deutsche Harmonia Mundi 05472 77376-2 (66 minutes: DDD). Texts and translations included.
Recorded 1996.   Ⓕ ⓟ Ⓔ

This CD, part of Al Ayre Español's 'Barroco Español' series, focuses on Latin-texted sacred music from the Royal Chapel in Madrid in the years before and just after 1700. The music, all of a penitential nature, is of a consistently high quality, and the performances from Al Ayre Español represent their most polished yet. An excellent quartet of Spanish soloists is given superb support by the more international team of instrumentalists, and Eduardo López Banzo, as usual, takes the music by the scruff of the neck and shakes off the accumulated dust of centuries in interpretations of real fervour and vitality. The two settings of the Lamentations – one by José de Torres, the other by Sebastián Durón – are brilliantly conceived, the string accompaniments constantly shifting in texture and *Affekt*, providing the perfect foil to the vocal lines. This is particularly the case in the Durón Lamentations, where the writing for three violins is really quite remarkable, while the solo part is sung with consummate mastery and beauty of tone by the young countertenor, Carlos Mena – Spain's answer to Michael Chance? A minor reservation: the plucked strings (chitarrone and theorbo) are excellently and imaginatively played, but where is the harp, so characteristic of the continuo in Spanish sacred music of this period? Overall, however, these are outstanding performances which bring out the intensity and drama inherent in this music.

Maurice Duruflé

Duruflé Requiem, Op. 9[a].
Fauré Requiem, Op. 48[b].
[a]**Ann Murray** *mez* [a]**Thomas Allen** *bar* [b]**Mary Seers** *sop* [b]**Michael George** *bass* [b]**John Scott** *org*
Corydon Singers; English Chamber Orchestra / Matthew Best.
Hyperion CDA67070 (78 minutes: DDD). Text and translation included. Recorded 1985-87.   Ⓕ ⒭⒭

Matthew Best favours Duruflé's compromise version of his Requiem (with strings, harp and trumpets). The combination of chamber ensemble with solo organ lines (sometimes not entirely convincing) makes for some problems of balance – there is a lack of bass in parts of the *Domine Jesu Christe*, the trumpets' plainchant is overloud in the *Kyrie*, and the first 'Hosanna' in the *Sanctus* is inaudible; but for the performance itself there can be nothing but praise – soloists, chorus, orchestra and organ are all first-class – the Corydon Singers offer expressive singing, with a wide dynamic range and remarkably clear words; and Best shapes the work expressively and sensitively. In Fauré's Requiem Best uses either John Rutter's reconstruction of the pre-publication state of Fauré's score, or something very closely resembling it, but the resulting performance sounds quite different to Rutter's own (reviewed under Fauré). He chooses slightly but perceptibly slower speeds for a start (save in the *In Paradisum*, which is a little faster than Rutter's). More significantly, he uses a larger, warmer, less grainy string force which together with a spacious acoustic and exceptionally refined choral singing gives a honeyed glow to the music which many will find a very acceptable compromise between the slightly austere leanness of Rutter's own presentation of his edition and the somewhat cumbrous opacity of the 1900 score.

Duruflé Requiem. Prélude et Fugue sur le nom d'Alain, Op. 7. Quatre Motets sur des thèmes grégoriens, Op. 10.
Fauré Requiem, Op. 48. Cantique de Jean Racine, Op. 11. Messe basse.
Poulenc Mass in G major. Salve Regina. Exultate Deo. Litanies à la vierge noire.
Jonathon Bond, Andrew Brunt, Robert King *trebs* **Benjamin Luxon** *bar*
Christopher Keyte *bass* **St John's College Choir, Cambridge; Academy of St Martin in the Fields / George Guest** with **Stephen Cleobury** *org*
Double Decca 436 486-2DF2 (two discs: 149 minutes: ADD). Recorded 1969-76.   Ⓜ

Here is almost two-and-a-half hours of bliss. These are recordings to set aside for the time when, as the prayer says, 'the busy world is hushed'. Asked to characterize Fauré's and Duruflé's Requiems as compared with others, we might suggest words such as 'delicate', 'restrained', 'meditative', 'undramatic'; but that last would be a mistake. These performances certainly do not go out of their way to 'be' dramatic or anything else other than faithful to the music, but one is struck by the power exercised by those rare moments that rise to a *forte* and above. The choir is surely at its best, the trebles with their fine clear-cut, distinctive tone, the tenors (so important in the Fauré) graceful and refined without being precious, the altos exceptionally good, and only the basses just occasionally and briefly plummy or obtrusive in some way. The Poulenc works further test a choir's virtuosity yet in the extremely difficult Mass, the choir seems secure, and in the *Salve Regina* they catch the necessary tenderness. The treble soloists sing beautifully, Christopher Keyte dramatizes almost too convincingly in Duruflé's 'tremens factus', and Benjamin Luxon, his production less even, builds finely in Fauré's *Libera me*. Stephen Cleobury, the organist throughout, contributes an admirably played solo written by Duruflé as a tribute to the young organist Jehan Alain, killed early in the war. These recordings have a vividness, certainly in the choral sound, that modern recordings generally lack.

Duruflé Requiem[a].
Fauré Requiem, Op. 48[b].
[a]Dame Kiri Te Kanawa, [b]Lucia Popp *sops* Siegmund Nimsgern *bass-bar*
Ambrosian Singers; [a]Desborough School Choir;
[a]New Philharmonia Orchestra, [b]Philharmonia Orchestra / Sir Andrew Davis.
Sony Classical Essential Classics SBK67182 (79 minutes: ADD). Recorded 1977.   Ⓑ

These recordings, made within six months of each other with substantially the same forces and in the same church, were issued separately but obviously go together. Both had outstandingly good reviews in *Gramophone* and although textural matters have arisen to enrich the choice and complicate the issue, if what were then regarded as the standard versions (in full orchestral score) are required, then the recommendations can remain. Davis's superiority over more recent versions is especially apparent in the Duruflé. His way with the opening is typical: the flow, the gentle wave-like motion, is beautifully caught and in the 'Libera me' he discovers the full richness of Duruflé's colours. Dame Kiri Te Kanawa sings with feeling and is incomparably lovely in sheer sound. There may be a few misgivings about the sound produced in remastering, but it settles down (or one's ears do).

Pascal Dusapin   French 1955

Dusapin Extenso. Apex. La melancholia[a].
Nan Christie *sop* Cécile Eloir *mez* Timothy Greacen *counterten* Martyn Hill *ten*
Lyon National [a]Chorus and Orchestra / Emmanuel Krivine, [a]David Robertson.
Auvidis Montaigne MO782073 (59 minutes: DDD). Recorded 1995-96.   Ⓕ

The three works on this CD make abundantly clear that Pascal Dusapin's music merits serious attention. The 'opératorio' *La melancholia* (1991) establishes a mood that is maintained in the two later works as well, with a kaleidoscopic text, printed in full in the booklet but set in a way that makes it difficult to follow in performance. The solo vocal writing is often uncompromisingly direct in its rhetoric – no Gallic reticence here – and this forthrightness is, understandably, one of Dusapin's most admired characteristics. He is strong on lament, favouring a broodingly sustained music which normally moves at a very deliberate pace yet can generate waves of turbulence without ever quite dispelling the suspicion that the effect is more static than is good for it. The character of all three pieces – *Extenso* dates from 1994, *Apex* from 1995 – leaves something to be desired in comparison with stronger creative personalities such as Xenakis, Scelsi, Richard Barrett or James Dillon. Nevertheless, if you enjoy sustained demonstrations of louring menace, kitted out in fascinatingly diverse sonic outfits, these admirable performances, recorded with no-less admirable clarity, are well worth investigating.

Henri Dutilleux   French 1916

Cello Concerto, 'Tout un monde lointain'. Métaboles. Mystère de l'instant.
Boris Pergamenschikov *vc*
BBC Philharmonic Orchestra / Yan Pascal Tortelier.
Chandos CHAN9565 (60 minutes: DDD). Recorded 1997.   Ⓕ Ⓢ

Dutilleux Orchestral

This is the third issue in the Chandos Dutilleux series with the BBC Philharmonic and Yan Pascal Tortelier. The virtues of those earlier issues remain evident here, with meticulously prepared, well-played performances, and recordings carefully adapted to the coloristic subtlety and textural delicacy of the music. *Métaboles* is particularly tricky to bring off, but this version is admirable in the way it builds through some dangerously episodic writing to underline the power of the principal climaxes, although a more sharply delineated sound picture could have reinforced these contrasts even more appropriately. Boris Pergamenschikov is an eloquent soloist in the Cello Concerto. Tortelier's account of *Mystère de l'instant* – using a full orchestral complement of strings – is excellently done. As with *Métaboles*, the structure is shaped with great flexibility and feeling for its ebb and flow, and as a result this emerges as a highly dramatic score, despite the inherent reticence of Dutilleux's style.

Dutilleux Violin Concerto, 'L'arbre des songes'. Timbres, espace, mouvement. Deux Sonnets de Jean Cassou (orch. cpsr).
Alain (orch. Dutilleux) Prière pour nous autres charnels.
Martyn Hill *ten* **Neal Davies** *bar* **Olivier Charlier** *vn*
BBC Philharmonic Orchestra / Yan Pascal Tortelier.
Chandos CHAN9504 (58 minutes: DDD). Texts and translations included. Recorded 1996.　Ⓕ🅁🅁

Timbres, espace, mouvement (1978, revised 1991) can be counted as Dutilleux's best orchestral composition, at once rooted in tradition yet persistently sceptical about conventional 'symphonic' values. It's a tricky score to bring off, and Tortelier is entirely successful in negotiating its twists and turns of form. In the Violin Concerto (1985) Tortelier again favours a symphonic approach, and very effective it is too, with a soloist who is authoritative without any hint of counterproductive self-assertiveness. In the rival Decca recording (reviewed below) Pierre Amoyal is more intense in tone, with a volatility from which all sense of effort has not been completely purged. Is the Charlier/Tortelier version too staid, or does this richly perfumed music demand a response that keeps its more flamboyant qualities under firmer control than that provided by the Decca team? Amoyal and Dutoit make the more immediate impact, but it could well be that Charlier and Tortelier prove more satisfying in the longer run. The Chandos disc also includes Dutilleux's orchestral arrangement of his Cassou settings, and also his orchestration, made in 1944, of Jehan Alain's touching prayer. Well-characterized contributions from Martyn Hill and Neal Davies complete this valuable release.

Violin Concerto, 'L'arbre des songes'. Cello Concerto.
Pierre Amoyal *vn* **Lynn Harrell** *vc*
French National Orchestra / Charles Dutoit.
Decca 444 398-2DH (51 minutes: DDD). Recorded 1993.　Ⓕ🆂

The Cello Concerto, first performed in 1970, was written for Rostropovich, and Lynn Harrell boldly confronts this formidable precedent; there is certainly no sense of undue reticence or constraint in his playing. The many technical challenges present no problems: more significantly, Harrell the interpreter has the full measure of the music's tricky blend of boldness and delicacy. From the start of the 'very free and flexible' first movement the undertones of mystery and menace which reflect the music's source in Baudelaire's poetry are fully in evidence, and Harrell has the advantage of first-class recorded sound. The cello is placed well forward, but the orchestra is never recessed to compensate. The Violin Concerto builds on the sultry, surreal Baudelairean spirit of the Cello Concerto – the 'tree' of the title seems tropical, the 'dreams' mainly unquiet – and Pierre Amoyal, with admirable support from Dutoit and the FNO, succeeds brilliantly in shaping the rhapsodic solo line with a mixture of intensity and fantasy, so that the piece works well as both structure and expression. Here, too, the production team has ensured that the concerto's rich textures can be heard without strain or artificiality. The whole enterprise can be warmly recommended.

Symphonies – No. 1; No. 2, 'Le double'.
BBC Philharmonic Orchestra / Yan Pascal Tortelier.
Chandos CHAN9194 (60 minutes: DDD). Recorded 1993.
Gramophone Award Winner 1994.　Ⓕ🆂

This pair of relatively early works by Henri Dutilleux, completed in 1951 and 1959 respectively, show him poised to inherit the Honegger/Martinů strand of the symphonic tradition. Yet, while an almost Simpsonian *élan* in the first movement of No. 2 promises a rich vein for further exploration, the Stravinskian strategies of the finale, ending with a virtual recomposition of the chorale that concludes the *Symphonies of Wind Instruments*, reveals a more modernist tendency, and leads away from the well-made, tonally-resolving symphony altogether. With their broad thematic vistas and persuasive adaptations of traditional forms, Dutilleux's symphonies offer considerable rewards to interpreters and listeners alike. Yan Pascal Tortelier and the BBC Philharmonic allow the music all the space it needs in strongly characterized, rhythmically well-sprung performances with uniformly excellent solo playing in No. 2, and the Chandos sound is rich and natural.

The Shadows of Time.
Joel Esher, Rachael Plotkin, Jordan Swaim *trebs*
Boston Symphony Orchestra / Seiji Ozawa.
Erato (special price) 3984-22830-2 (22 minutes: DDD). Recorded live in 1998.

Boldly, Erato gambled that the interest and appeal of the first substantial work by Henri Dutilleux for almost a decade would justify this issue of a CD single. We can only commend the enterprise and the finely engineered recording. *The Shadows of Time* is an unambiguously emotional, even angry work, and may well stand as the musical testament of a composer who, while seeking to celebrate 'the unity of time and place' (as his brief note accompanying the disc puts it), can only do so from the basis of considerable pessimism about the ability of the real world to achieve the kind of harmonious, classical ideals to which he, as an artist, aspires. Pessimism and anger are most explicit in the way the first and last sections depict the inexorable passage of time, and in the increasing density and urgency of the orchestral lament which explodes out of a central episode in which childrens' voices repeat the questions, 'Why us? Why the star?'. This is a reference to Anne Frank and 'all the innocent children of the world', Dutilleux declares, yet there is nothing mawkish here, rather an almost *Wozzeck*-like pathos in the way the music searches for consolation without, in the end, quite achieving it. By the time of these performances Ozawa, his orchestra and the three assured young singers, had achieved absolute authority in this often testing music. The result is a moving and memorable document of a very special occasion, and a very special work.

Antonin Dvořák

Bohemian 1841-1904

Cello Concerto in B minor, B191.

Dvořák Cello Concerto.
Tchaikovsky Variations on a Rococo Theme, Op. 33.
Mstislav Rostropovich *vc*
Berlin Philharmonic Orchestra / Herbert von Karajan.
DG The Originals 447 413-2GOR (60 minutes: ADD). Recorded 1968. ⓂⓇⓇ

This splendid disc offers a coupling that has justifiably held its place in the catalogue at full price (both on LP and CD) for over 30 years. The upper surface of the CD itself is made to look like a miniature reproduction of the original yellow label LP – complete with light reflecting off the simulated black vinyl surface. There have been a number of outstanding recordings of the Dvořák Concerto since this DG record was made, but none to match it for the warmth of lyrical feeling, the sheer strength of personality of the cello playing and the distinction of the partnership between Karajan and Rostropovich. Any moments of romantic licence from the latter, who is obviously deeply in love with the music, are set against Karajan's overall grip on the proceedings. The orchestral playing is superb.

You have only to listen to the beautiful introduction of the secondary theme of the first movement by the Principal Horn to realize that the Berlin Philharmonic is going to match its illustrious soloist in eloquence, while Rostropovich's many moments of poetic introspection never for a moment interfere with the sense of a spontaneous forward flow. The recording is as near perfect as any made by DG in that vintage analogue era. The CD transfer has freshened the original and gives the cello a highly realistic presence, and if the passionate *fortissimo* violins lose just a fraction in fullness, and there seems to be, comparably, just a slight loss of resonance in the bass, the sound picture has an impressively clear and vivid focus. In the coupled Tchaikovsky *Rococo* Variations, Rostropovich uses the published score rather than the original version. However, he plays with such a masterly combination of Russian fervour and elegance that any criticism is disarmed. The music itself continually demonstrates Tchaikovsky's astonishing lyrical fecundity, as one tune leads to another, all growing organically from the charming 'rococo' theme. The recording here is marvellously refined and the illusion of the artists sitting out beyond one's speakers is very real indeed. The description 'legendary' is not a whit too strong for a mid-price reissue of this calibre.

Cello Concerto. Silent woods, B173. Rondo in G minor, B171. Slavonic Dance in A flat major, B147 No. 8.
Heinrich Schiff *vc*
Vienna Philharmonic Orchestra / André Previn *pf*
Philips 434 914-2PH (54 minutes: DDD). Recorded 1992.   Ⓕ

Schiff's cello is recorded in a more natural balance than is common in this concerto, so that the solo instrument's first entry does not give the impression of a super-cello, as most recordings do, but the concentration and tension bear witness to the scale and power of the interpretation. When it comes to the great second subject melody Schiff's hushed *pianissimo* is ravishingly gentle, and unlike almost every rival he avoids drawing the tempo out, observing Dvořák's *In tempo* marking at a very marginally broader speed. The result has a touching simplicity and tenderness. André Previn is a fresh and understanding partner, pointing rhythms even more crisply, and the Vienna Philharmonic brings out the Slavonic tang in the score. The bright detailed recording helps, with the Vienna horns – so important in this work from the opening tutti on – sounding glorious. Schiff's flowing speed in the slow movement again brings out the freshness of folk-based ideas. Only in the finale does the cello balance make for a less biting result. Few versions come near to matching this. The coupling is apt. These are not the usual orchestral arrangements but have Previn as a sparkling piano partner.

Dvořák Cello Concerto.
Herbert Cello Concerto No. 2 in E minor, Op. 30.
Yo-Yo Ma *vc*
New York Philharmonic Orchestra / Kurt Masur.
Sony Classical SK67173 (61 minutes: DDD). Recorded 1995.   Ⓕ

Ma's and Masur's version of the Dvořák is among the very finest, matched by few and outshining most, including Ma's own previous version with Maazel and the Berlin Philharmonic (also available on Sony Classical). It is fascinating to compare Ma's two versions side by side, the newer one more readily conveying weight of expression despite the less spotlit placing of the soloist, more disciplined yet more spontaneous-sounding. This time Ma's expressiveness is simpler and more noble, and the recording (made in Avery Fisher Hall, New York), once a trouble-spot for engineers, is fuller and more open than the Berlin one, cleaner in tuttis, with only a touch of unwanted dryness on high violins. Ma and Masur together encompass the work's astonishingly full expressive range, making it the more bitingly dramatic with high dynamic contrasts. The Victor Herbert Concerto here receives a high-powered performance, but one which does not overload the romantic element with sentiment, whether in the brilliant and vigorous outer movements or in the warmly lyrical slow movement. Ma's use of rubato is perfectly judged, with the slow movement made the more tender at a flowing speed. The finale is then given a quicksilver performance, both brilliant and urgent. Herbert's concerto, first given in 1894, was almost certainly what prompted Dvořák to write his own concerto later that same year, triumphantly demonstrating the viability of the genre.

Dvořák Cello Concerto[a].
Bruch Kol nidrei, Op. 47[b].
Elgar Cello Concerto in E minor, Op. 85[c].
Pablo Casals *vc*
[a]**Czech Philharmonic Orchestra / George Szell;** [b]**London Symphony Orchestra / Sir Landon Ronald;** [c]**BBC Symphony Orchestra / Sir Adrian Boult.**
EMI Références mono CDH7 63498-2 (75 minutes: ADD). Recorded 1936-45.   Ⓜ Ⓗ

It scarcely seems necessary to write anything further about Casals's famous recordings of the Dvořák and Elgar concertos, which have long been recognized as classics of the recorded repertoire. The former, destined to mark a standard for generations, and seemingly played with a sword rather than a bow, still exercises a powerful effect: the incandescent solo playing is so mesmeric that one can accept the rather harsh and dry orchestral sound which betrays its age (from 1937). Some of Casals's passionate quality may have been due to his decision to break out of his self-imposed restricted activities caused by the Spanish civil war: the astute Fred Gaisberg, hearing that he had consented to appear with Szell in Prague, swung into action and talked them into making a recording the day after the concert. *Kol nidrei* is a quietly eloquent, broad reading of this meditation, adroitly accompanied by Sir Landon Ronald.

About Casals's Elgar there has always been controversy: his reading was heavily criticized as over-emotional ('un-English') when he first played it in London before the war, but when he returned in 1945 and performed it, according to Boult, in exactly the same way, it was said that 'in the deeply meditative sections ... it reached an Elgarian mood of wistfulness that few artists understand'. In the light of subsequent performances by other famous cellists this raises an interesting point for discussion, from which we here prudently excuse ourselves. (These same performances of the Elgar and Bruch, incidentally, are also available on a Biddulph set, reviewed in the Collections section – refer to the Index.)

Dvořák Violin Concerto in A minor, Op. 53.
Bruch Violin Concerto No. 1 in G minor, Op. 26.
Tasmin Little *vn*
Royal Liverpool Philharmonic Orchestra / Vernon Handley.
Classics for Pleasure CD-CFP4566 (60 minutes: DDD). Recorded 1989.   Ⓑ

This rare coupling of Dvořák and Bruch delivers performances of a positive assurance to stand comparison with any. In quality of recording as well as artistry this is in every way a match for full-price rival recordings, with on balance the best sound of all. Little brings to Dvořák an open freshness and sweetness, very apt for this composer, that is equally winning. The firm richness of her sound, totally secure on intonation up to the topmost register, goes with an unflustered ease of manner, bringing little or no spotlighting of the soloist. She establishes her place firmly with sound that co-ordinates the soloist along with the orchestra. She is particularly successful in the finale and plays the syncopations of the dance-like main theme with a happy lilt. In the Bruch the movement where Little's individuality comes out most clearly is the central *Adagio*, raptly done, with a deceptive simplicity of phrasing; totally unselfconscious, matching the purity of her sound. Her speeds in the outer movements are broad and although the finale may not have quite the thrusting excitement of some of her rivals, the clarity and precision of her playing are fair compensation, along with the fuller, more faithful sound. At full price this would be highly recommended; at Classic for Pleasure's modest price it is a quite outstanding bargain.

Czech Suite, B93. Festival March, B88. The Hero's Song, B199. Hussite, B132.
Polish National Radio Symphony Orchestra / Antoni Wit.
Naxos 8 553005 (65 minutes: DDD). Recorded 1993-94.   Ⓢ

Wit's achievement, especially in the case of *The Hero's Song*, is considerable. This colourful, rather sprawling tone-poem was Dvořák's last orchestral work and is not an easy piece to bring off. Wit finds genuine nobility in it, while his gentle, mellow way with the lovely *Czech Suite* also gives much pleasure. The opening 'Praeludium' is just a touch sleepy, but there is no want of lyrical affection or rhythmic bounce elsewhere and the whole performance radiates an idiomatic, old-world charm that really is most appealing. As for the *Hussite* overture, Wit's clear-headed reading impressively combines dignity and excitement. Given such finely disciplined orchestral playing, the results are once again both eloquent and characterful. All of which just leaves the rousing *Festival March* of 1879, splendidly done here, with the excellent Katowice brass sounding quite resplendent in their introductory call-to-arms. Recordings throughout possess a most agreeable bloom and transparency.

The water goblin, B195. The golden spinning-wheel, B197. The noon witch, B196. The wild dove, B198. The Hero's Song, B199. My home Overture, B125*a*.
Scottish National Orchestra / Neeme Järvi.
Chandos CHAN8798/9 (two discs: 111 minutes: DDD). Recorded 1986-87.   Ⓕ

Originally issued as 'fillers' (what a demeaning expression that is!) to Järvi's symphony cycle, the four tone-poems that Dvořák wrote after his return from America, based on Karl Jaromir Erben's collection of gruesome folk ballads, are here framed by the much earlier *My home* Overture and his last orchestral work, *The Hero's Song*. Received wisdom has taught us to be patronizing about these late works – ignore it! Janáček was fascinated enough by the four Erben poems to publish a detailed analysis of them. Indeed, in the central section of *The golden spinning-wheel*, where the wheel and assorted paraphernalia are offered to the false queen in return for the various dismembered portions of our heroine's body, the ostinatos on muted strings sound like pure Janáček. The descriptive range and imagination of Dvořák's orchestration are a consistent joy throughout this set, even if his fiends seem imagined from the warm interior of a Victorian nursery – one shudders to think what Janáček himself might have made of them. The orchestral colourings are firmly rooted in the late romantic tradition – the 'forest murmurs' of the water goblin's domain, for example. And yet, there are prophetic moments too: the exquisite closing pages of *The wild dove* could be the best thing Dvořák ever wrote. Järvi's performances are wholly recommendable. Chandos's wide-screen, superbly balanced sound adds greatly to the atmospheric strains of these works, and the informative notes enable you to pinpoint every incidental delight. A musical feast!

Slavonic Dances, B83 and B147.

Slavonic Dances.
Cleveland Orchestra / George Szell.
Sony Classical Essential Classics SBK48161 (74 minutes: ADD). Recorded 1963-65. Ⓑ 🆁🆁

This reissue is something of a revelation. Both discs have been lovingly remastered and the quality is an amazing improvement over the old LPs. The remastering engineers seem to have discovered a whole 'bottom octave' in the sound, which before had appeared to lack richness and weight to support the brilliant upper range. The *Slavonic Dances* are offered as Szell recorded them, with no repeats cut, so the phenomenal orchestral virtuosity is revealed in all its glory. There is much evidence of the conductor's many captivatingly affectionate touches of rubato and, throughout, this large orchestra follows Szell's every whim, with playing full of lyrical fervour and subtlety of nuance, wonderful precision and a lilting rhythmic pulse. The recordings were made within the acoustics of Cleveland's Severance Hall, usually a pair of dances at a time. The result is infectiously spontaneous and we cannot recommend this disc too highly; even if the close balance prevents any real *pianissimos* to register, the dynamic range of the music-making is still conveyed.

Slavonic Dances.
Vienna Philharmonic Orchestra / André Previn.
Philips 442 125-2PH (71 minutes: DDD). Recorded 1993. Ⓕ

Previn, with his rhythmic flair, brings out the playfulness of the *Slavonic Dances* as few others do. One is regularly reminded of the proximity of Dvořák's Bohemia to Vienna, when in the warm Musikverein acoustic, these dances become first cousins to the waltzes and polkas of the Strauss family. Previn also brings out the many warm cello descants which normally go unnoticed, but which here surge up in rich, yet transparent, textures. The energetic dances, too, regularly bring a rush of adrenalin at the climaxes, such as one gets from this orchestra every New Year's Day. In his different way Szell with the Cleveland Orchestra on peak form is fiercer than Previn in such *Furiant* dances as Nos. 1 and 8, with his recording adding weight of sound. Yet helped by the acoustic, Previn has more light and shade, and sounds just as easily idiomatic.

Slavonic Dances.
Russian National Orchestra / Mikhail Pletnev.
DG 447 056-2GH (72 minutes: DDD). Recorded 1994. Ⓕ 🆂

Though Pletnev has Slavonic musicians, the results are not quite traditionally Czech, with refinement and crispness of ensemble the keynotes rather than earthier qualities. His is a distinctive and highly enjoyable version of Dvořák's colourful dances. These are, after all, works which for all their lack of pretension are open to all kinds of subtleties of interpretation, with different views totally valid. At times with such refined playing one might even dub Pletnev's approach as Mozartian, with elegance a regular element, and with even the wildest *furiants* kept under control. The crispness of ensemble and clarity of texture give a sharpness of focus that avoids any idea that these are performances lacking in bite, though after the Previn one might well feel they are on the cool side, with the extrovert joy of the music rather underplayed. So the *Dumka* lament of the second dance is lighter and cooler than with Previn, charming rather than warmly expressive. Dynamic contrasts are sharply defined through all the dances, and Pletnev and his Russian players consistently make one marvel at the beauty of the instrumentation.

Symphonies – No. 1 in C minor, B9, 'The Bells of Zlonice'; No. 2 in B flat major, B12; No. 3 in E flat major, B34; No. 4 in D minor, B41; No. 5 in F major, B54; No. 6 in D major, B112; No. 7 in D minor, B141; No. 8 in G major, B163; No. 9 in E minor, B178, 'From the New World'.

Symphonies Nos. 1-9. Scherzo capriccioso, B131. Overtures – In nature's realm, B168; Carnival, B169; My home, B125a.
London Symphony Orchestra / István Kertész.
Decca 430 046-2DC6 (six discs: 431 minutes: ADD). Recorded 1963-66. Ⓑ 🆁🆁

István Kertész recorded the Dvořák symphonies during the mid-1960s and his integral cycle was quick to achieve classic status, with his exhilarating and vital account of the Eighth Symphony rapidly becoming a special landmark in the catalogue. The original LPs, with their distinctive Bruegel reproduction sleeves are now collectors' items in their own right, but these magnificent interpretations became available again in 1992, in glitteringly refined digitally remastered sound, and it is a tribute to the memory of this tragically short-lived conductor that this cycle continues to set the standard by which all others are judged. Kertész was the first conductor to attract serious collectors to the early Dvořák symphonies which, even today are not performed as often as they should be; and his jubilant advocacy of the unfamiliar First Symphony, composed in the composer's twenty-fourth year, has never been superseded. This work offers surprising insights into the development of Dvořák's mature style, as does the Second Symphony. Kertész shows that Symphonies Nos. 3 and 4 have much more earthy resilience than many commentators might have us believe, insisting that Dvořák's preoccupation with the music of Wagner and Liszt had reached its zenith during this period. The challenging rhetoric of the Fourth has never found a more glorious resolution than here, with Kertész drawing playing of gripping intensity from the London Symphony Orchestra.

The Fifth Symphony, and to a still greater extent, its glorious successor, Symphony No. 6, both reveal Dvořák's clear affinity with the music of Brahms. Kertész's superb reading of the Sixth, however, shows just how individual and naturally expressive this underrated work actually is, whilst the playing in the great climax of the opening movement and the vigorous final peroration remains tremendously exciting, even almost 30 years after the recording first appeared. In the great final trilogy, Kertész triumphs nobly with the craggy resilience of the Seventh Symphony, and his buoyant ardour brings a dynamic thrust and momentum to the Eighth Symphony, whereas his *New World* is by turns indomitable and searchingly lyrical. The six-disc set also offers assertive and brilliant readings of the Overtures *Carnival*, *In nature's realm* and the rarely heard *My home*, together with a lucid and heroic account of the *Scherzo capriccioso*. These definitive performances have been skilfully reprocessed, the sound is astonishingly good, even by modern standards, and the playing of the London Symphony Orchestra is often daringly brilliant under the charismatic direction of one of this century's masters of the podium.

Symphonies Nos. 3 and 7.
Vienna Philharmonic Orchestra / Myung-Whun Chung.
DG 449 207-2GH (71 minutes: DDD). Recorded 1995.   ℗ **E**

An impressive coupling. Myung-Whun Chung takes an affectionately fleet-of-foot view of the Third Symphony. With the Vienna Philharmonic on their toes throughout (and audibly enjoying themselves), Chung's reading is notable for its newly minted freshness and intelligent sense of proportion. So we find that the opening *Allegro moderato* emerges in shapely, sensitive fashion, yet with no lack of cumulative intensity at its close. In the ideally flowing slow movement Chung locates both dignity and drama. Again, phrasing is always imaginative and thoughtful, while the stately central processional has never sounded more luminously refined. The performance of the Seventh is an interpretation of red-blooded fervour and rugged contrasts, whose dramatic impact is greatly heightened by the burnished glow of the VPO's contribution, to say nothing of DG's enormously ripe close-knit sound. In Chung's pungently characterful, ever flexible hands, the first movement progresses with pleasing dignity and purpose, nowhere more striking than in the coda where his decision not to press ahead too soon pays handsome dividends. Equally, Chung sees to it that the sublime second subject really takes wing both times round, the Viennese warmth and charm much in evidence. The succeeding *Poco adagio* is distinctive, possessing an almost Brucknerian hush and concentration. Whatever Chung's *Scherzo* slightly lacks in home-grown, idiomatic lilt, the arresting vigour and clean-limbed transparency of the playing provide fair compensation. What's more, the anxious Trio is voiced with unusual clarity, its many subtle details set in bold relief. The storm-tossed finale is magnificent, a conception of irresistible rigour and muscular conviction.

Symphony No. 5. Othello, B174. Scherzo capriccioso.
Oslo Philharmonic Orchestra / Mariss Jansons.
EMI CDC7 49995-2 (64 minutes: DDD). Recorded 1989.   ℗ **RR**

Of all the romantic composers, it is probably Dvořák who best evokes a sunlit, unspoiled and relatively untroubled picture of nineteenth-century country life. Light and warmth radiate from his Fifth Symphony, composed in just six weeks when he was in his early thirties. It has been called his 'Pastoral Symphony', and it is easy to see why, especially in a performance as fresh and sunny as this one. Mariss Jansons brings out all the expressiveness and heart of the music without exaggerating the good spirits and playful humour that are so characteristic of the composer, and one would single out for praise the fine wind playing of the Oslo Philharmonic Orchestra (and not least its golden-toned horns) were it not for the fact that the strings are no less satisfying. The lyrical *Andante con moto* brings out the fine interplay of the instrumental writing, the bouncy *Scherzo* is uninhibited without going over the top and the exciting finale has plenty of momentum. The other two pieces are nicely done, the *Scherzo capriccioso* having both lilt and vigour and the rarely played *Othello* overture (a late work) being a suitably dramatic response to Shakespeare's tragedy. The recording is warm and clear.

Symphony No. 6. The wild dove.
Czech Philharmonic Orchestra / Jiří Bělohlávek.
Chandos CHAN9170 (63 minutes: DDD). Recorded 1992.　　　　　　　　　　Ⓕ **RR**

Bělohlávek has referred to his Czech orchestra's 'singing art of playing' and its 'mellow sound' and it is indeed Bohemia's woods, fields and wildlife, rather than energetic village green festivities, that linger in the memory here. Perhaps you shouldn't expect a Czech Philharmonic performance to 'go' or leap about excitedly in the manner of Kertész's with the LSO; in these days of high adrenalin, high contrast and high definition, there's a lot to be said for a less assertive and vigorous approach, always artlessly sung, and for this orchestra's Old World timbres a Brahmsian fireside glow, for example, to the Symphony's first movement second subject on cellos and horns (beautifully eased in by Bělohlávek). These horns, always more rounded in tone than their rasping counterparts in London (Kertész), bear an obvious family resemblance to the woodwind, not only in timbre, but also in the use of vibrato (again, that 'singing art of playing'). And the 'silver moon' flute is one of this disc's principal joys. Bělohlávek also projects the drama of *The wild dove* with relish. Chandos, as ever, guarantees a sepia-toned warmth throughout.

Symphonies[a] Nos. 7-9. Symphonic Variations, B70[b].
[a]**Concertgebouw Orchestra;** [b]**London Symphony Orchestra / Sir Colin Davis.**
Philips Duo 438 347-2PM2 (two discs: 139 minutes: ADD). Recorded [a]1977-78, [b]1968.　　Ⓜ **RR**

Sir Colin Davis's magnificent Amsterdam Dvořák Seventh remains one of the most compellingly taut available: gloriously played and paced to perfection, it has a dark, searing intensity wholly apt for this, the Czech master's most tragic utterance; certainly, only a select handful of rivals on disc have matched this performance's irresistible symphonic drive. The Eighth is excellent, too: it is notable for its keen vigour, textural transparency and unfailing sense of purpose – only a little more nudging affection might not have gone amiss. Davis's finely-sculpted *New World* (first-movement repeat included) is another powerful, involving affair – the sublimely articulate orchestral response alone ensures enormous pleasure. Although not as endearingly flexible or evocative a reading as some would prefer, Davis's directness is always refreshing and never brusque. The result: an impressively cogent, concentrated conception. Apart from some distractingly close balancing in the finale of No. 8, all three symphonies are blessed with Philips engineering of the highest analogue quality. Davis's 1968 version of the masterly *Symphonic Variations* is very fine: sounding admirably fresh still, it's an effective and unfussy rendering.

Symphony No. 7. Nocturne in B major, B47. The water goblin.
Czech Philharmonic Orchestra / Jiří Bělohlávek.
Chandos CHAN9391 (69 minutes: DDD). Recorded 1992.　　　　　　　　　　　　　Ⓕ

Bělohlávek is a lucid, sure-footed guide through Dvořák's mightiest symphonic utterance, and his sympathetic direction combines both warm-hearted naturalness as well as total fidelity to the score (dynamics are scrupulously attended to throughout). If it sounds just a little under-energized next to other vividly dramatic accounts, the sheer unforced eloquence and lyrical fervour of the playing always give enormous pleasure. Certainly, the first movement's secondary material glows with affectionate warmth, whilst the sublime *Poco adagio* emerges seamlessly, its songful rapture and nostalgic vein captured as to the manner born by this great orchestra (listen out for some gorgeous work from the principal flute, clarinet and horn). The *Scherzo* trips along with an infectious, rhythmic spring, as well as an engaging poise and clarity; moreover, the dark-hued unsettling Trio (a casualty in so many rival performances) is handled with equal perception. The finale, too, is immensely pleasing, marrying symphonic thrust with weighty rhetoric rather in the manner of Sir Colin Davis's distinguished Amsterdam account. The closing bars are very broad and imposing indeed. All in all, a performance of considerable dignity and no mean stature, benefiting from characteristically vibrant Chandos engineering. The symphony is followed by a long-breathed, slumbering account of the *Nocturne* (gloriously played by the Czech PO strings) and the disc concludes with a fine *Water goblin*. Again, the orchestral response is as disciplined and poised as you could hope to hear.

Symphonies Nos. 7 and 8.
Oslo Philharmonic Orchestra / Mariss Jansons.
EMI CDC7 54663-2 (74 minutes: DDD). Recorded 1992.　　　　　　　　　　　　Ⓕ **E**

Mariss Jansons's popular pairing makes most agreeable listening. With clean-cut playing from the fine Oslo orchestra and natural, unexaggerated sonics, these are engagingly alive, refreshingly energetic readings, if not quite as warm-hearted or openly affectionate as some Dvořákians might like. Jansons's sophisticated sense of texture impresses throughout, however, and the outer movements of No. 8 in particular emerge with genuinely vivid freshness. Jansons's clean-heeled direction brings with it a certain endearing spontaneity and rhythmic resilience that will undoubtedly give pleasure.

Symphonies Nos. 7 and 9.
London Philharmonic Orchestra / Sir Charles Mackerras.
EMI Eminence CD-EMX2202 (79 minutes: DDD). Recorded 1991.   Ⓜ

Sir Charles Mackerras's longstanding authority in the Czech repertoire is of course well known by now, so his thoughts are not to be dismissed lightly, especially when, at nearly 80 minutes, Nos. 7 and 9 make a terrifically generous pairing. In the tragic Seventh, Mackerras concentrates largely on the more endearingly lyrical side of Dvořák's invention; in this respect both inner movements are particularly memorable in their open-hearted grace and charm. However, those who (rightly) crave a greater degree of intensity and symphonic rigour in the two great flanking outer movements such as one encounters with rival interpreters will perhaps come away not quite so satisfied. Similarly, this *New World* is an affectingly unfussy traversal. The slow movement glows ravishingly at an exceptionally broad tempo, and in the finale Mackerras draws Dvořák's structural threads together with undemonstrative cogency. His are warmly affectionate readings, superbly played and resplendently recorded.

Symphony No. 8. The wood dove.
Scottish National Orchestra / Neeme Järvi.
Chandos CHAN8666 (57 minutes: DDD). Recorded 1987.   Ⓕ 🆁🆁

Neeme Järvi and the SNO's account of the Eighth Symphony underlines the expressive warmth of the piece, the rhapsodic freedom of invention rather than any symphonic tautness. That the result seems so warm and natural is due above all to the responsiveness of the SNO players who here, even more strikingly than usual, seem to feel Järvi's wonderfully free rubato and affectionate moulding of phrase with collective spontaneity. It is a joy to have the sort of rubato that you expect from a solo performer so freshly transferred to the orchestra, with such precision and without any feeling of mannerism, not even of the kind that Karajan's comparable moulding with the Berlin Philharmonic sometimes induces. The score, of course, to take an obvious example, is marked *allegro con brio* from the first bar, and anyone wanting a more firmly structured reading will be happier with a version such as the Davis/Philips. But Järvi is here doing no more than follow a long-established performing tradition, and one which in a performance such as his – always purposeful, marked by strong dramatic contrasts – hardly sounds wayward, persuasive rather. Though he allows himself fair breadth, Järvi's speeds are never eccentric. The finale is marginally slower than usual, but Järvi's relaxation goes with a control of tension that almost suggests the telling of a story, easy and natural in its sharp changes of mood. In all four movements the incidental delights are many, with charm a regular ingredient.

The wood dove, which comes as a valuable fillup, was the fourth and last of the symphonic poems which Dvořák based on a collection of folk ballads by Karl Jaromir Erben, *The garland*. There, as in the symphony, Järvi's feeling for the rhapsodic side of Dvořák's invention makes for a persuasive performance, warm and colourful. The Chandos sound has a characteristic bloom.

Symphony No. 8. Symphonic Variations.
London Philharmonic Orchestra / Sir Charles Mackerras.
EMI Eminence CD-EMX2216 (60 minutes: DDD). Recorded 1992.   Ⓜ

This is an unmissable account of the Eighth Symphony. Mackerras realizes all the score's indications of shading, pointing and phrasing, or to put it another way, all its elegance and bittersweet ambiguity. He has a spirited and willing LPO in the palm of his guiding, illuminating hand. Articulation and emphases are consistently light, and not only in the energetic tuttis. In the flute solo some 40 seconds into the first movement the LPO principal, without disturbing the tranquillity of the scene, animates the solo to suggest bird-song (all the solo and ensemble flute work on the Mackerras disc is outstanding). It is this wide range of pictorial suggestion and emotion, and an orchestra audibly fired up by the occasion, that mark Mackerras's performance of the Symphony as an example of great Dvořák conducting. Mackerras relaxes in the *Symphonic Variations* but keeps the work flowing along and gives as fine a performance of this work as you are likely to hear. The Eminence sound for Mackerras (from London's Henry Wood Hall) is immediate and lively, with a wider dynamic range.

Symphonies Nos. 8 and 9.
Berlin Philharmonic Orchestra / Rafael Kubelík.
DG The Originals 447 412-2GOR (73 minutes: ADD). Recorded 1972. Ⓜ 🆁🆁

These accounts are quite magnificent and their claims on the allegiance of collectors remain strong. They have the kind of freshness and vigour that remind one of what it was like to hear these symphonies for the first time. The atmosphere is authentic in feeling and the sense of nature seems to be uncommonly acute. Kubelík has captured the enthusiasm of his players here and generates a sense of excitement and poetry. The playing of the Berlin Philharmonic is marvellously eloquent throughout and, as is so often the case, a joy in itself. The woodwinds phrase with great poetic feeling and imagination though, come to that, all the departments of this great orchestra respond with sensitivity and virtuosity. The recording has great dynamic range and encompasses the most featherweight string *pianissimos* to the fullest orchestral tutti without discomfort. The listener is placed well back in the hall so that the woodwind, though they blend beautifully, may seem a little too recessed for some tastes, though it should be said that there is no lack of vividness, power or impact. The balance and the timbre of each instrument is natural and truthful; nothing is made larger than life and Kubelík has a natural warmth and flexibility. This will always remain high on any list of recommendations for it has a vernal freshness that is wholly reviving.

Symphony No. 9[a]. American Suite[b].
[a]**Vienna Philharmonic Orchestra / Kyrill Kondrashin;**
[b]**Royal Philharmonic Orchestra / Antál Dorati.**
Decca 430 702-2DM (63 minutes: DDD). Recorded 1979-83. Ⓜ

Kondrashin's *New World* caused something of a sensation when originally transferred to CD. Here was a supreme example of the clear advantages of the new medium over the old and the metaphor of a veil being drawn back between listener and performers could almost be extended to a curtain: the impact and definition of the sound is really quite remarkable and the acoustics of the Sofiensaal in Vienna are presented as ideal for this score. The upper strings have brilliance without edginess, the brass – with characteristically bright VPO trumpets – has fine sonority as well as great presence, the bass is firm, full and rich and the ambience brings luminosity and bloom to the woodwind without clouding.

Piano Quintet in A major, B155. String Quintet in G major, B49.
Gaudier Ensemble (Marieke Blankestijn, Lesley Hatfield *vns* Iris Juda *va* Christoph Marks *vc* Stephen William *db* Susan Tomes *pf*)
Hyperion CDA66796 (66 minutes: DDD). Recorded 1995. Ⓕ

The pianist here is Susan Tomes, who matches even Pressler in imagination, encouraging a performance lighter than that for DG, full of mercurial contrasts that seem entirely apt. For example, in the second movement *Dumka* there is more light and shade, and the *Scherzo* sparkles even more, leading to a jaunty, exuberant finale. The G major String Quintet, the earliest of the two which Dvořák wrote, the one with extra double-bass, is similarly lighter than the Chilingirian Quartet on Chandos. The Chilingirian is just as strongly characterized as the Gaudier, with a firmer, fuller tone. Marieke Blankestijn's violin is thinner than Levon Chilingirian's, but it can be just as beautiful, as in the lovely high-floating second subject of the slow movement. Altogether a fine disc.

Piano Quintet[a]. Piano Quartet No. 2 in E flat major, B162.
Menahem Pressler *pf*
Emerson Quartet (Eugene Drucker, [a]Philip Setzer *vns* Lawrence Dutton *va* David Finckel *vc*).
DG 439 868-2GH (75 minutes: DDD). Recorded 1993. Ⓕ

If the Piano Quintet with its wealth of memorable melody is by far the better-known, Pressler and the Emersons demonstrate how the Piano Quartet, sketched immediately after the other work and completed two years later in 1889, is just as rich in invention and in some ways even more distinctive in its thematic material. If there is one movement that above all proves a revelation, it is the *Lento* of the Quartet. Opening with a duet for cello and piano, it is here played with a rapt, hushed concentration to put it among the very finest of Dvořák inspirations. The performance of the Quintet, too, is comparably positive in its characterization. Many will prefer the easier, even warmer reading from Domus in the Piano Quartet (reviewed opposite), which is neatly if not so generously coupled with the much earlier Piano Quartet in D, B53. In this music it is not always the high-powered reading that makes its mark most persuasively, and the Hyperion sound for Domus is far warmer than the DG New York recording for this disc, which gives an unpleasant edge to high violins, making the full ensemble rather abrasive. None the less, if the volume is curbed, one can readily enjoy these passionate and intense accounts of two of Dvořák's most striking chamber works.

String Quintets – G major, B49; E flat major, B180. Intermezzo in B major, B49.
Chilingirian Quartet (Levon Chilingirian, Mark Butler *vns* Louise Williams *va* Philip De Groote *vc*); **Simon Rowland-Jones** *va* **Duncan McTier** *db*
Chandos CHAN9046 (69 minutes: DDD). Recorded 1990-91.   (F)

Dvořák's G major String Quintet is a thoroughly engaging affair. Originally in five movements, Dvořák subsequently removed the 'Intermezzo' second movement, revising and publishing it separately eight years later as the haunting *Nocturne* for string orchestra. Enterprisingly, this Chandos disc includes that 'Intermezzo' in its original string quintet garb. The E flat Quintet from 1893, on the other hand, is a wholly mature masterpiece. Completed in just over two months during Dvořák's American sojourn, it replaces the double-bass of the earlier Quintet with the infinitely more subtle option of a second viola. Brimful of the most delightfully fresh, tuneful invention, the score also shares many melodic and harmonic traits with the popular *American* Quartet – its immediate predecessor. The Chilingirian Quartet, ideally abetted by double-bassist Duncan McTier and violist Simon Rowland-Jones, are enthusiastic, big-hearted proponents of all this lovely material, and the excellent Chandos recording offers both a realistic perspective and beguiling warmth.

Piano Quartets – No. 1 in D major, B53; No. 2 in E flat major, B162.
Domus (Krysia Osostowicz *vn* Timothy Boulton *va* Richard Lester *vc* Susan Tomes *pf*).
Hyperion CDA66287 (70 minutes: DDD). Recorded 1987.   (F)

These are two very enjoyable works. Hans Keller's description of the opening pages of the E flat Quartet as 'childish' is staggering – this from the leading campaigner against 'posthumous critical torture'! Childlike would be much more suitable, and this appealing characteristic is well brought out by the members of Domus: Susan Tomes's descent from incisive *fortissimo* clarity to *pianissimo* mystery in the opening bars is a delight, and fully prophetic of the kind of musicianship we're to hear. Two other unforgettable moments from this performance: the lovely return of the first movement second subject, with its heart-easing B major/E flat major modulation – very sensitive use of rubato here – and cellist Richard Lester's richly expressive solos at the beginning of the *Lento*. The D major Quartet is a delightful, if not fully mature piece – it does tend to rely rather heavily on sequence and repetition. Domus makes sure we don't miss any of its virtues, but it doesn't force anything: the timing in the magical opening shift from D major to B major is finely judged, and Dvořák's wonderfully effortless melodies are affectionately shaped and shaded; admirable too the way Susan Tomes finds so much beauty in what often looks like conventionally decorative piano writing. In general the sound is very pleasing, intimate enough to draw one right into the performances without being intimidating, even in the somewhat histrionic second theme of the E flat Quartet's *Lento*. A richly rewarding disc.

String Quartets – No. 1 in A major, B8; No. 2 in B flat major, B17; No. 3 in D major, B18; No. 4 in E minor, B19; No. 5 in F minor, B37; No. 6 in A minor, B40; No. 7 in A minor, B45; No. 8 in E major, B57; No. 9 in D minor, B75; No. 10 in E flat major, B92; No. 11 in C major, B121; No. 12 in F major, B179, 'American'; No. 13 in G major, B192; No. 14 in A flat major, B193.

String Quartets Nos. 1-14; F major, B120 (Fragment). Cypresses, B152. Quartettsatz.
Two Waltzes, B105.
Prague Quartet (Břetislav Novotný, Karel Přibyl *vns* Lubomír Malý *va* Jan Sírc *vc*).
DG 429 193-2GCM9 (nine discs: 589 minutes: ADD). Recorded 1975-77.   (B) **RR**

Like Schubert, Dvořák turned to the string quartet early in his career. The three complete quartets included in Vol. 1 (Nos. 1-3) show considerable facility in writing for strings (after all, Dvořák was a violinist), but it took him some time to arrive at a fully idiomatic quartet style: the first movement of No. 2 for instance wouldn't lose much by being orchestrated. Dvořák also had to learn to rein in his natural expansiveness: the Third Quartet spins out its modest material to an astonishing 70 minutes – the first movement alone is longer than the whole American Quartet! The outer movements of the No. 4 in E minor (Vol. 2) show him concentrating admirably, though the later shortened version of the central *Andante religioso* is a considerable improvement. So the interest of Vol. 1 (three discs) is largely musicological. Despite this, with playing so fresh and authoritative even the impossibly long-winded Third Quartet has rewards to offer. Each performance has a strong sense of purpose, but that doesn't mean an inability to enjoy all those charming Dvořákian byways. Technically the playing is admirable, though you may be surprised at the scrunch at the climax of No. 1's slow movement – very untypical.

Nevertheless, the enjoyment increases strongly through Vol. 2. The violin cavatina in the *Andante* of the Fifth Quartet has just the right gentle lilt – recommended to the unconverted. Listening to the Prague in the fine first movement of No. 7 one realizes how what looks on the page like very simple music can come glowingly to life in the right hands – and the way they handle the slightly tricky *poco più mosso* at the second subject is very impressive. The finest work in Vol. 2 (discs 4-6) is undoubtedly the D minor Quartet, No. 9. Volume 3 contains three gems: the E flat Quartet (No. 10), the *American* and No. 13 in G major – the outstanding work of the collection. The Prague are very sensitive to dynamic contrast (Dvořák's markings are often surprisingly detailed). Another good sample extract might be the opening of the G major's slow movement; strong, intense playing here, and fine command of long phrasing – and what marvellous music! So don't let the size of this set put you off. There's plenty of fine music on these nine well-filled discs, all of it more than well performed and the recordings are generally creditable.

Dvořák String Quartet No. 12. Cypresses, B152 – Nos. 1, 2, 5, 9 and 11.
Kodály String Quartet No. 2, Op. 10.
Hagen Quartet (Lukas Hagen, Annette Bik *vns* Veronika Hagen *va* Clemens Hagen *vc*).
DG 419 601-2GH (61 minutes: DDD).   Ⓟ **RR**

The Hagen Quartet never exaggerates, and there are moments (like the lead back to the first subject in the first movement of the *American*) where the beauty and poise of the playing really do take the breath away. There's astonishing elegance and subtlety here (not to mention technical precision), but the playing may strike you as rather too cosmopolitan in manner to allow any expression of purely national feeling. And it isn't just a question of mood: there are places where the Hagen's concern to emphasize folk characteristics is evident (the little 'blue' appoggiatura which leader Lukas Hagen appends to the recitative theme of Kodály's second movement for instance), but it somehow sounds a little studied. Quite simply, the playing may strike you as over-refined: rough edges are smoothed down: abrupt transitions are, where possible, delicately eased into. The *Scherzo* of the *American* Quartet is full of sudden changes in dynamics and texture: the Hagen has a tendency to cushion the surprise by making a rapid but perceptible *crescendo* or *decrescendo*. Effectively this puts a distance between the listener and the music – all very civilized of course, but ultimately perhaps muffling the sharpness of human contact. The Hagen plays down the accents in the finale theme of the Dvořák (obviously not wanting to spoil the effect of that wonderfully rarefied *pianissimo*). You would never suspect that Dvořák's dynamic contrasts are actually quite extreme. But the playing is winning, and the coupling is interesting. Over-cultivated it may be, but it has plenty to tell us about this music. Even so, CD buyers who are looking for one authoritative recording of Dvořák's most popular quartet have yet to receive a wholly satisfying recording.

String Quartets Nos. 12 and 13.
Vlach Quartet, Prague (Jana Vlachová, Ondřej Kukal *vns* Petr Verner *va* Mikael Ericsson *vc*).
Naxos 8 553371 (69 minutes: DDD). Recorded 1995.   Ⓢ

On the face of it, the credentials of the Vlach Quartet of Prague would seem to be impeccable – the group's leader, Jana Vlachová, is the daughter of the great Josef Vlach – and, indeed, the players make a most pleasing impression on this vividly recorded Naxos coupling. They certainly produce a beguilingly rich, beautifully blended sound and bring to this music a big-hearted, songful fervour as well as textural mastery. What is more, Dvořák's characteristic, chugging cross-rhythms are handled with particular felicity. Interpretatively, their approach contrasts strongly with other readings in that the Vlach team adopt a coaxing, lyrically expressive stance (with the gorgeous slow movement of the *American* a highlight). In the case of the masterly G major Quartet, these gifted newcomers show fresh insights (they are especially perceptive in those wistful reminiscences at the heart of the finale).

Piano Trios – No. 3 in F minor, B130; No. 4 in E minor, B166, 'Dumky'.
Florestan Trio (Anthony Marwood *vn* Richard Lester *vc* Susan Tomes *pf*).
Hyperion CDA66895 (68 minutes: DDD). Recorded 1996.   Ⓟ **E**

A favourite and appropriate pairing – Dvořák's most passionate chamber work in harness with one of his most genial. The F minor Piano Trio (1883) was contemporaneous with the death of Dvořák's mother; it anticipates something of the storm and stress that characterizes the great D minor Seventh Symphony (1884-5) and the Florestan Trio serves it well. All three players allow themselves plenty of expressive leeway and yet the musical line is neither distorted nor stretched too far. The second movement *Allegretto* is truly *grazioso* and the qualifying *meno mosso* perfectly judged. The finale is buoyant rather than especially rustic, whereas the more overtly colourful *Dumky* Trio inspires a sense of play and a vivid suggestion of local colour – 2'45" into the third movement, for example, or 1'25" into the fourth. Throughout the performance, the manifest 'song and dance' elements of the score (heartfelt melodies alternating with folk-style faster music) are keenly projected. The recordings are first-rate, as are the insert-notes. If you're after a subtle, musically perceptive coupling of these two works, then you could hardly do better.

Violin Sonata in F major, B106. Ballad in D minor, B139. Four Romantic Pieces, B150.
Violin Sonatina in G major, B183. Nocturne in B major, B48a (arr. cpsr).
Anthony Marwood vn **Susan Tomes** pf
Hyperion CDA66934 (67 minutes: DDD). Recorded 1997.   Ⓕ

This delectable release enshrines music-making of sensitivity and eloquence. Marwood may not produce as luscious a sound as that of some of his rivals, but his subtly variegated tone colouring more than compensates; Tomes, too, displays the deftest touch throughout. The F major Sonata receives a wonderfully pliable reading, full of imaginative touches. You will especially warm to their unhurried, yet purposeful way with the opening movement (Dvořák's *ma non troppo* marking ideally judged). The beautiful ensuing *Poco sostenuto* has both Brahmsian warmth and hushed intimacy; the finale is joyous and articulate. Marwood's and Tomes's account of the captivating *Sonatina* is less 'glamorous' and high-powered than the Gil and Orli Shahams' 1995 account on DG – and altogether more personable as a result. Try from the *Scherzo* (track 3) to hear Marwood and Tomes at their sparkling best. Similarly, the second of the *Four Romantic Pieces* has an earthy tang reminiscent of Janáček, while the *Allegro appassionato* third movement unfolds with just the right flowing ardour. Hyperion also offers the haunting *Nocturne* in B major and a sombre, vividly characterized *Ballad* in D minor from 1884 (written just before the Seventh Symphony). This anthology must now take the palm, not least in view of the marvellously realistic and impeccably balanced recording.

Requiem Mass, B165. Mass in D major, B153.
Pilar Lorengar sop **Neil Ritchie** treb **Erzesébet Komlóssy** contr **Andrew Giles** counterten
Robert Ilosfalvy, Alan Byers tens **Tom Krause** bar **Robert Morton** bass **Nicholas Cleobury** org
Ambrosian Singers; Christ Church Cathedral Choir, Oxford / Simon Preston;
London Symphony Orchestra / István Kertész.
Double Decca 448 089-2DF2 (two discs: 138 minutes: ADD). Texts and translations included.
Recorded 1968.   Ⓜ

Kertész's Requiem dates from 1968 and on all counts but one, it surpasses Karel Ančerl's classic 1959 set, reissued on DG in 1995 and coupled with Fischer-Dieskau's 1960 set of Dvořák's *Biblical Songs* with Jörg Demus. The exception is the rather too soft-grained singing of Pilar Lorengar as compared with the clear, more vibrant soprano of Maria Stader. But Lorengar's singing is particularly sensitive and appealing in the quieter passages. The lovely quality of Robert Ilosfalvy's voice tells beautifully in 'Liber scriptus proferetur' and in the opening section of the quartet, 'Recordare, Jesu pie'. Dvořák distributes short passages among the soloists impartially. They combine beautifully in the quartet, and the chorus with them in 'Pie Jesu Domine', perhaps the loveliest movement in the work. The hero of the occasion is Kertész. He gets choral singing and orchestral playing of the finest quality. It is abundantly evident that he cherishes a great love for this work. The Mass in D (which is sung in the original version with organ) sits well with the Requiem; Simon Preston produces a fine, well-balanced performance, with the Christ Church choristers on excellent form.

Stabat mater. Psalm 149.
Lívia Aghová sop **Marga Schiml** contr **Aldo Baldin** ten **Luděk Vele** bass
Prague Children's Choir; Prague Philharmonic Choir;
Czech Philharmonic Orchestra / Jiří Bělohlávek.
Chandos CHAN8985/6 (two discs: 96 minutes: DDD). Notes, texts and translations included.
Recorded 1991.   Ⓕ

The ten sections of the *Stabat mater* are well laid out for the different vocal and instrumental forces and so avoid the monotony which might seem inherent in this contemplative and deeply sombre text. This performance was recorded in Prague Castle, and in it we feel the full dignity and drama of the work, an oratorio in all but name. The four solo singers convey genuine fervour and one feels that their sound, which is quite unlike that of British singers, must be akin to what the composer originally imagined. If they are a touch operatic, that doesn't sound misplaced and they perform well together, as in the second verse quartet 'Quis est homo'. The choral singing is no less impressive, and indeed the whole performance under Bělohlávek gets the balance right between reverent simplicity and intensity of feeling. Psalm 149 is a setting of 'Sing unto the Lord a new song' for chorus and orchestra and its celebratory mood provides a fine complement to the other work.

Dvořák Mass in D major, Op. 86.
Eben Prague Te Deum 1989.
Janáček Our Father.
Dagmar Masková *sop* Marta Benacková *mez* Walter Coppola *ten* Peter Mikulás *bass*
Lydie Härtelová *hp* Josef Ksica *org*
Prague Chamber Choir / Josef Pancík.
ECM New Series 449 508-2 (59 minutes: DDD). Texts and translations included.
Recorded 1993.   Ⓕ

This imaginative coupling brings together three fine pieces of Czech church music in skilled and
sympathetic interpretations. Dvořák's Mass, the best known of them, has received a number of
good recorded performances; this one, in the original 1887 version with organ, has a very well-
matched quartet of soloists who blend smoothly with each other and with the chamber choir. It
is a work of particular intimacy and charm, and these qualities mark this performance. Janáček's
setting of the Lord's Prayer dates from 1906, and is in turn a meditative piece, not without vivid
illustrative touches appropriate to a work originally designed to accompany a sequence of
devotional pictures; and Petr Eben's *Prague Te Deum* coincided, in 1969, with a moment of
apparent release from political oppression. It has something of Janáček's suddenness in the
invention, and a graceful melodic manner. Each of these works is in its way inward, personal and
reflective, but they all share a Czech character; and this is well related to Czech history by Antonín
Pešek in an exceptionally interesting, long essay setting the country's church music in its historical
and religious context.

Rusalka.
Renée Fleming *sop* Rusalka; **Ben Heppner** *ten* Prince; **Franz Hawlata** *bass* Watergnome;
Dolora Zajick *mez* Witch; **Eva Urbanová** *sop* Foreign Princess; **Iván Kusnjer** *bar* Hunter,
Gamekeeper; **Zdena Kloubová** *sop* Turnspit; **Lívia Aghová** *sop* First Woodsprite;
Dana Burešová *mez* Second Woodsprite; **Hana Minutillo** *contr* Third Woodsprite;
Kühn Mixed Choir; Czech Philharmonic Orchestra / Sir Charles Mackerras.
Decca 460 568-2DHO3 (three discs: 163 minutes: DDD). Notes, text and translation included.
Recorded 1998.   Ⓕ 🇷🇷

Renée Fleming's tender and heart-warming account of Rusalka's Invocation to the Moon reflects
the fact that the role of the lovelorn water-nymph, taken by her in a highly successful production at
the Met in New York, has become one of her favourites, the one she has now performed more often
than any other in her repertory apart from the Countess in *Figaro*. Ben Heppner also has a special
relationship with the opera, for the role of the Prince was the first he ever studied in depth as a
student. He has sung it repeatedly since then, often opposite Renée Fleming, and both he and
Sir Charles Mackerras have long harboured the ambition to make a complete recording. The joy of
this magnificent set is that in almost every way it fulfils every expectation and more, offering a
recording with glowing sound that more than ever before reveals the richness and subtlety of
Dvořák's score.

As interpreted by Fleming and Mackerras, Rusalka's big aria at the start of Act 3, when having
been rejected by the Prince, she seeks consolation in returning to the water, is as poignantly
beautiful as the more celebrated Invocation to the Moon in Act 1, when she laments over loving a
human. In addition, the climactic moments bring glorious top-notes, firm and true up to B flat and
B. Heppner, like Fleming, conveys his special affection for this music, unstrained up to top C,
combining heroic power with lyric beauty. Dolora Zajick as the Witch, Jezibaba, is characterful and
fruity. Franz Hawlata as the Watergnome, Rusalka's father, is satisfyingly firm and dark, bringing a
Wagnerian weight to the role, in places drawing parallels with Wotan or even Hans Sachs. The
engineers also thrillingly capture the off-stage effects so important in this opera, with the
Watergnome balefully calling from the waters of the lake. Even the smaller roles have been cast
from strength, all of them fresh, true and idiomatic. The clear-toned First Woodsprite, Lívia
Aghová, is a leading soloist in the Prague National Theatre, as is Eva Urbanová, the firmly focused
mezzo who takes the role of the Foreign Princess. Similarly, Iván Kusnjer (Gamekeeper and
Hunter) is a noted Simon Boccanegra. What is striking is that there is not a hint of a Slavonic
wobble from any of the singers. In the orchestra, too, the Czech horns are consistently rich and
firm. And if anyone is worried about having four non-Czech principals, they are as idiomatic as any
rivals, with three of them – Fleming, Zajick and Hawlata – helped by having Czech forebears.

The final glory of the set lies in the warmly understanding conducting of Sir Charles Mackerras. It
may seem surprising that such a specialist in Czech music is only now tackling his first complete
Dvořák opera recording, but in every way this matches and even outshines his supreme achievement
in the Decca series of Janáček operas. In those you had the Vienna Philharmonic, but here the

Czech Philharmonic is both a degree more idiomatic and just as opulent in tone, with superb solo work. The strings produce ravishing sounds, refined and transparent in the lovely evocations of water, often with instruments muted. He is helped there by the rich Decca recording, giving a keen sense of presence. The balance between voices and orchestra is well managed, with voices never drowned, though one oddity of the recording – which will not trouble everyone – is that characters tend to emerge on the scene with an initial phrase or two heard from off-stage.

Rusalka.
Milada Subrtová *sop* Rusalka; **Eduard Haken** *bass* Watergnome; **Marie Ovčačíková** *contr* Witch; **Ivo Zídek** *ten* Prince; **Alena Míková** *mez* Foreign Princess; **Jadwiga Wysoczanská** *sop* First Woodsprite; **Eva Hlobilová** *sop* Second Woodsprite; **Věra Krilová** *contr* Third Woodsprite; **Ivana Mixová** *sop* Turnspit; **Václav Bednář** *bar* Hunter, Gamekeeper;
Prague National Theatre Chorus and Orchestra / Zdeněk Chalabala.
Supraphon SU0013-2 (two discs: 149 minutes: ADD). Notes, text and translation included.
Recorded 1961. Ⓕ

This excellent set boasts Eduard Haken, one of the great interpreters of the Watergnome, in robust voice, infusing the somewhat enigmatic character with a rueful gentleness as well as a firmness of utterance. Ivo Zídek as the Prince was in his mid-thirties and in his prime at the time of this recording, singing ardently and tenderly and with a grace of phrasing that matches him well to Milada Subrtová's Rusalka. Hers is a beautiful performance, sensitive to the character's charm as well as to her fragility and pathos. The Slavonic tradition of the old watersprite legend places her in the line of the suffering heroine and it is a measure of Dvořák's success that her delicate appeal holds throughout quite a long opera, and her sinuous but never oversensual lines and the piercing harmony associated with her give her a unique appeal. Subrtová sings the part with unfaltering sensitivity. Zdeněk Chalabala, who died only a couple of months after completing this recording, handles the score with great tenderness and an affection that shines through every bar. He was sometimes underrated as a conductor: this is a beautiful performance. The recording comes up remarkably well; and the booklet includes full text and translations into French, German, and – one or two unfortunate turns of phrase apart – quite reasonable English.

The Jacobin.
Václav Zítek *bar* Bohuš; **Vilém Přibyl** *ten* Jiří; **Daniela Sounová** *sop* Terinka; **Karel Průša** *bass* Count Vilém; **René Tuček** *bar* Adolf; **Marcela Machotková** *sop* Julie; **Karel Berman** *bass* Filip; **Beno Blachut** *ten* Benda; **Ivana Mixová** *mez* Lotinka;
Kantilena Children's Chorus; Kühn Chorus; Brno State Philharmonic Orchestra / Jiří Pinkas.
Supraphon 11 2190-2 (two discs: 155 minutes: ADD). Notes, text and translation included.
Recorded 1977. Ⓕ

This was the first (and, so far, only) recording of Dvořák's charming village comedy – for the Jacobin of the title is not here a political activist but a young man, Bohuš, returning from exile in Paris to his stuffy old father, Count Vilém. The sub-plots include all manner of misunderstandings, and set in the middle of them is the touching figure of Benda, the fussy, rather pedantic but wholly moving music-master. Dvořák is known to have had in mind his own boyhood teacher, Antonín Liehmann, whose daughter gives her name, Terinka, to Benda's daughter. Beno Blachut celebrated his sixty-fourth birthday during the making of this set. His was a long career, as well as one of great distinction; he is still well able to get round the lines of this part, and gives an affecting picture of the old musician, never more so than in the rehearsing of the welcome ode. This is an idea that has cropped up in opera before, but it is charmingly handled here. Václav Zítek sings Bohuš pleasantly and Marcela Machotková trips away lightly as Julie. Vilém Přibyl sounds less than his most energetic, though his voice is in good fettle; and there is some lack of drive from Jiří Pinkas, who might have done more to bring out the often witty touches in Dvořák's scoring. Never mind: this revived version of a delightful piece can be safely recommended. There is a full libretto, with translations into French, German and rather stilted English.

Kate and the Devil.
Anna Barová *contr* Kate; **Richard Novák** *bass* Devil Marbuel; **Miloš Ježil** *ten* Shepherd Jirka; **Daniela Suryová** *contr* Kate's mother; **Jaroslav Horáček** *bass* Lucifer; **Jan Hladík** *bass* Devil the Gate-keeper; **Aleš Stáva** *bass* Devil the Guard; **Brigita Sulcová** *sop* Princess; **Natália Romanová** *sop* Chambermaid; **Pavel Kamas** *bass* Marshall; **Oldřich Polášek** *ten* Musician;
Brno Janáček Opera Chorus and Orchestra / Jiří Pinkas.
Supraphon 11 1800-2 (two discs: 119 minutes: AAD). Notes, text and translation included.
Recorded 1979. Ⓕ

Though this was never one of the best Supraphon recordings, it is perfectly serviceable. The plot is complicated, and broadly speaking concerns the bossy Kate who, finding herself a wallflower at the village hop, angrily declares that she would dance with the Devil himself. Up there duly pops a junior devil, Marbuel, who carries her off to hell, where her ceaseless chatter wearies Lucifer himself. The diabolical company is only too happy to allow the shepherd Jirka to remove her again. Jirka, attractively sung by Miloš Ježil, also manages to help the wicked but later repentant Princess to escape the Devil's clutches, and all ends well. The work has a proper coherence, and much good humour besides. Anna Barová's Kate is strong and full of character, but manages not to exclude the charm that should underlie her rantings at Marbuel, who is handsomely sung by Richard Novák. Brigita Sulcová similarly makes much of the not very sympathetic Princess. Jaroslav Horáček enjoys himself hugely as Lucifer and Jiří Pinkas accompanies them well.

Sir George Dyson
British 1883-1964

The Canterbury Pilgrims. In Honour of the City. At the Tabard Inn.
Yvonne Kenny sop **Robert Tear** ten **Stephen Roberts** bar
London Symphony Chorus and Orchestra / Richard Hickox.
Chandos CHAN9531 (two discs: 118 minutes: DDD). Texts included. Recorded 1996.
Gramophone Award Winner 1997.
Ⓕ Ⓔ

It seems extraordinary that Dyson's *Canterbury Pilgrims* had to wait so long for a première recording. This superb offering from Hickox of this full-length cantata based on the Prologue to Chaucer's *Canterbury Tales* bears out its reputation as Dyson's masterpiece. This is a fresh, openly tuneful work, aptly exuberant in its celebration of Chaucer. Following the scheme of Chaucer's Prologue, Dyson in his 12 movements, plus Envoi, presents a sequence of portraits, deftly varying the forces used, with the three soloists well contrasted in their characterizations and with the chorus acting as both narrator and commentator, providing an emotional focus for the whole work in two heightened sequences, the sixth and twelfth movements, moving and noble portraits of the two characters who aroused Dyson's deepest sympathy, the Clerk of Oxenford and the Poor Parson of a Town. If the idiom is undemanding, with occasional echoes of Vaughan Williams's *A Sea Symphony* and with passages reminiscent of Rachmaninov's *The bells*, the cantata sustains its length well.

Sensibly, *At the Tabard Inn*, the concert overture which Dyson wrote in 1943, basing it on themes from the cantata, is given first. Outstanding among the soloists is Robert Tear who not only characterizes brilliantly but sings with admirable fullness and warmth. The beautiful, fading close, when Tear as the Knight begins the first tale, moving slowly off-stage, is most atmospherically done. Yvonne Kenny and Stephen Roberts sing well too, but are less distinctive both in timbre and expression. The London Symphony Chorus sings with incandescent tone, superbly recorded, and with the orchestra under Hickox – an ideal advocate – brings out the clarity and colourfulness of Dyson's instrumentation. *In Honour of the City* provides the perfect fill-up. Like the main work, it uses a modern-language version of a middle-English text. The idiom is very similar to that of the Chaucer work, music designed for a good amateur chorus, fresh, direct and tuneful, again with Hickox drawing glowing sounds from chorus and orchestra.

Hanns Eisler
German 1898-1962

Suites for Orchestra – No. 2, Op. 24, 'Niemandsland'; No. 3, Op. 26, 'Kuhle Wampe'; No. 4, Op. 30, 'Die Jugend hat das Wort'; No. 5, Op. 34, 'Dans les rues'. Balladen – Op. 18: Ballade vom Nigger Jima; Op. 22: Ballade von der Wohltätigkeit; Ballade von der Säckeschmeissern; Op. 41: Das Lied vom SA-Mann. Die Rundköpfe und die Spitzköpfe, Op. 45 – Lied von der belebenden Wirkung des Geldes; Die Ballade vom Wasserrad. Ideal und Wirklichkeit.
Ensemble Modern / Heinz Karl Gruber bar
RCA Victor Red Seal 74321 56882-2 (70 minutes: DDD). Texts and translations included. Recorded 1998.
Ⓕ

This is Hanns Eisler conveying anger, derision or fierce joviality at the top of his voice, and very enjoyable it is, if perhaps a little exhausting after 70 minutes. Bourgeois greed, capitalist market-manipulation, American colour prejudice, the Nazis' betrayal of their own supporters – these are the subjects of his songs, delivered by Gruber with the sort of raucous relish that Eisler so much appreciated in Ernst Busch, his close collaborator in the 1930s, when all these songs were written. So were many of Eisler's film scores, from which the four suites derive. They are scored, like the songs, for an ensemble of wind and percussion, with piano, banjo, two cellos and double-bass, closely resembling what would have been termed a 'jazz band' in the Germany of that period. And much of the music uses jazz elements, too, chosen for its energy and stridency, but also setting Eisler's grave or sober, often strikingly economical lyricism in sharp contrast. It is good amidst all the hectic energy to be reminded of that element, so central to Eisler's output as a whole. The very last piece here is irresistible. It dates from 1956, and is a world-weary song about how everyone ends up with second best, if that ('You fancy a tall, slim one, but what you get is short and fat. C'est la vie! In the days of the Emperor we imagined a republic. And now we've got one ...'). Gruber has encouraged his players (though from the sound of it they hardly needed urging) to produce sounds that are as far from the gentility of the concert hall as his own voice is remote from that of a Lieder recital: clarinets wail, saxophones leer, trombones rasp, and all are recorded with maximum, in-your-face directness.

In den Weiden. Frühling. Speisekammer 1942. Auf der Flucht. Über den Selbstmord. Die Flucht. Gedenktafel für 4000 Soldaten. Epitaph. Spruch. Ostersonntag. Der Kirschdieb. Hotelzimmer 1942. Die Maske des Bösen. Zwei Pascal Lieder. Die letzte Elegie. Winterspruch. Fünf Elegien. Nightmare. Hollywood-Elegie No. 7. Der Schatzgräber. Panzerschlacht. L'automne californien. Fünf Anakreontische Fragmente. Erinnerung an Eichendorff und Schumann. Sechs Hölderlin-Fragmente. Der Mensch. Vom Sprengen des Gartens. Die Heimkehr. Die Landschaft des Exils. Der Sohn. An den kleinen Radioapparat.
Matthias Goerne *bar* **Eric Schneider** *pf*
Decca 460 582-2DH (70 minutes: DDD). Texts and translations included. Recorded 1998.

This is a hugely impressive issue of major importance. Goerne has obviously been smitten by these wonderful, neglected songs: he calls them 'the 20th century *Winterreise*', and in performances as gripping as these it is hard to contradict him. They are Eisler's songs of exile, written in Hollywood while the Germany for which he felt both passionate revulsion and deep nostalgia sank into the abyss. Most of the 46 short songs are settings of poems by Brecht, some written specifically for Eisler, but they also incorporate 'mini-cycles' to texts by Mörike and Eichendorff, two poems by Blaise Pascal (set in English) and one or two others including a single poem by Eisler himself. The songs are not here sung in the order in which Eisler eventually published them, but the sequence chosen makes poignant dramatic sense, chronicling Brecht's and Eisler's horror at what was happening in Germany, their flight and exile, their reaction to the alien world of Hollywood and meditations on Germany's vanished past, hideous present and uncertain future. As performed here, the cycle ends with a loving homage to Schubert, 'On Watering the Garden', followed by the haunting and moving 'Homecoming', a vision of Berlin obliterated by bombardment, and by the intense and characteristically Eislerian lyricism of 'Landscape of Exile'.

These works demand a prodigious expressive range from any singer who undertakes them. Goerne can sing 'On Suicide' with a mere thread of sound without ever losing the quality of his voice but can then swell in an instant to a formidable *fff* for the last syllable of the terrifying final line ('People just throw their unbearable lives away'). The sheer beauty of his voice is just what those many homages to the Lied tradition need. His English is pretty good, his diction immaculate, and he makes a memorably sinister thing of the seventh *Hollywood Elegy* (set in English; Brecht's German original is lost), that horrifying image of a man sinking in a swamp with a 'ghastly, blissful smile'. Goerne's is a masterly and profoundly moving achievement. Eric Schneider's accompaniment is first-class and the recording is excellent.

Edward Elgar
British 1857-1934

Cello Concerto in E minor, Op. 85.

Cello Concerto. Sea Pictures, Op. 37.
Jacqueline du Pré *vc* **Dame Janet Baker** *mez*
London Symphony Orchestra / Sir John Barbirolli.
EMI CDC5 56219-2 (54 minutes: ADD). Recorded 1965.

Issued in 1965 and one of EMI's best-sellers ever since, these Elgar recordings make the most cherishable of couplings. Though both Jacqueline du Pré and Dame Janet Baker were already well established and widely appreciated in 1965, this disc marked a turning point for both of them in their recording careers. With Barbirolli so warm-hearted and understanding an accompanist to each, these are both in every sense classic performances that can never be replaced. Jacqueline du Pré's Elgar has been all the more appreciated since her tragic illness took her away. In principle her *espressivo* may be too freely romantic, but the slow movement and epilogue remain supreme in their intensity, conveying in whispered *pianissimos* of daring delicacy an inner communion, while the bravura of the brilliant passages remains astonishing from an artist who was still only 20. Equally, the young Janet Baker translated the work into something greater than had been appreciated before. Until this recording, *Sea Pictures* had tended to be underprized even among Elgarians; but the passion, intensity and sheer beauty of this performance with each of the five songs sharply distinct rebutted any idea that – in reflection of verse of varying quality – it had anything of sub-standard Elgar in it. It is a work which you will probably never be able to listen to again without hearing in your mind Dame Janet's deeply individual phrasing on this disc. What strikes you more than anything else is the central relevance to Dame Janet's whole career of the last stanza in 'Sabbath morning at sea', a radiant climax. 'He shall assist me to look higher' says the Barrett Browning poem, and the thrust of meaning as Dame Janet sings it invariably conveys a *frisson* such as you rarely get on record. The CD transfer is valuable for clarifying the sound, but it adds little to the original LP. The sound in the Cello Concerto exactly matches the LP sound, and the precise placing makes the soloist all the more vivid. The precision of CD makes more apparent the slight discrepancy between the sides, with *Sea Pictures* a degree fresher and fuller and with more bloom on the sound. The slight sibilant emphasis is not the fault of the transfer, but also comes on the LP.

Elgar Cello Concerto.
Bloch Schelomo.
Steven Isserlis vc
London Symphony Orchestra / Richard Hickox.
Virgin Classics Ultraviolet CUV5 61125-2 (51 minutes: DDD). Recorded 1988. Ⓜ Ⓢ

Cellists are apt to 'come of age' in recordings of the Elgar. Isserlis was no exception. This is a wonderful account of the Concerto – brave, imaginative, individual – indeed, quite the most personal in its perception of the piece since the treasurable Du Pré on EMI. And that, you will appreciate, is saying something though not, we hasten to add, that the two readings are in any outward sense similar. Far from it. With Isserlis, the emotional tug is considerably less overt, the emphasis more on shadow and subtext than open heartache. Yet the inner-light is no less intense, the phrasing no less rhapsodic in manner than Du Pré. On the contrary. This is free-range Elgar alright, and like Du Pré it comes totally without affectation. Both Isserlis and Du Pré take an appropriately generous line on the first movement's sorrowful song, with Isserlis the more reposeful, the more inclined to open out and savour key cadences. The *Scherzo* itself is quite simply better played than on any previous recording; the articulation and definition of the semiquaver 'fours' would, we are sure, have astonished even the composer himself. From a technical point of view Isserlis is easily the equal, and more, of any player currently before us. And if you still feel that Du Pré really did have the last word where the epilogue is concerned, listen to Isserlis sinking with heavy heart into those pages preceding the return of the opening declamation. He achieves a mesmerizing fragility in the bars marked *lento* – one last backward glance, as it were – and the inwardness of the final *diminuendo* is something to be heard and remembered. Hickox and the LSO prove model collaborators and it almost goes without saying that they bring all their well-oiled skills to bear on the outrageous biblical climaxes of Bloch's soulful *Schelomo*; trumpets and horns positively outreach themselves. Isserlis does not stint himself either, pouring forth his darkest and most impassioned colours. Thanks also to an impeccably balanced recording, the integration, the give and take between soloist and orchestra in one of Elgar's most perfectly crafted scores, is seamless. Don't on any account miss these performances.

Cello Concerto[a]. Violin Concerto[b].
[b]**Albert Sammons** vn **Pablo Casals** vc
[a]**BBC Symphony Orchestra / Sir Adrian Boult;**
[b]**New Queen's Hall Orchestra / Sir Henry Wood.**
Avid Master Series AMSC587 (72 minutes: ADD). Recorded [a]1945, [b]1929. Ⓜ Ⓗ

Two legendary performances indeed, both among the very finest versions of either work. The Casals/Boult Cello Concerto has an irresistible fervour and a whole-hearted impulsiveness that have always courted controversy. You find yourself overlooking Casals's occasional waywardness and fallibility (not to mention his clearly audible grunts and groans) in the face of the enormous emotional impact his playing generates. Boult's accompaniment, too, is a model of scrupulous flexibility and dedication. Likewise, the 1929 Sammons/Wood account of the Violin Concerto must be deemed a veritable classic of the gramophone, for it possesses a fire, poetry and nobility that have rarely been matched, and certainly not surpassed. This enticing pairing from Avid shows a marked sonic improvement over some previous transfers from this source. The Sammons/Wood was never the most vividly recorded affair, but the Avid engineers have done well to extract so much body from the original shellacs. They achieve tolerable enough results with the Cello Concerto, but, again, there is a want of tonal lustre. None the less, the disc does offer newcomers the chance to acquaint themselves with two inimitable Elgar interpretations for comparatively little outlay.

Violin Concerto in B minor, Op. 61.

Elgar Violin Concerto.
Vaughan Williams The lark ascending.
Kennedy *vn*
City of Birmingham Symphony Orchestra / Sir Simon Rattle.
EMI CDC5 56413-2 (72 minutes: ADD). Recorded 1997.   Ⓕ **RR**

Astonishingly, in the case of the first two movements at least, this release, recorded during the week following a live concert at Birmingham's Symphony Hall in July 1997, fully re-creates the heady excitement of that memorable event. From every conceivable point of view – authority, panache, intelligence, intuitive poetry, tonal beauty and emotional maturity – Kennedy surpasses his 1985 *Gramophone* Award-winning EMI Eminence recording (now on HMV Classics). The first movement is a magnificent achievement all round, with tension levels extraordinarily high for a studio project. Rattle launches the proceedings in exemplary fashion, his direction passionate, ideally flexible and texturally lucid (the antiphonally divided violins help). The CBSO, too, is on top form. But it's Kennedy who rivets the attention from his commanding initial entry onwards. There's no hiding in this of all scores and Kennedy penetrates to the very essence of 'the soul enshrined within' in his melting presentation of the 'Windflower' theme – Elgar's *dolce semplice* realized to tear-spilling perfection. The slow movement is almost as fine. What poise and dedication these artists bring to this rapt meditation. Only the finale oddly dissatisfies. Not in terms of technical address or co-ordination (both of which are stunning); rather, for all the supreme accomplishment on show, the results are not terribly moving. Despite any lingering doubts about this last movement we are still left with an enormously stimulating and marvellously well-engineered display. The fill-up is a provocative account of *The lark ascending*, which Kennedy (whose tone is ravishing) and Rattle spin out to a (surely unprecedented?) 17-and-a-half minutes.

Violin Concerto[a]. Cello Concerto[b].
Yehudi Menuhin *vn* **Beatrice Harrison** *vc*
[a]**London Symphony Orchestra,** [b]**New Symphony Orchestra / Sir Edward Elgar.**
EMI Great Recordings of the Century mono CDH7 69786-2 (75 minutes: AAD).
Recorded 1932 and 1928.   Ⓜ **H**

Elgar's conducting for Menuhin in the Violin Concerto's opening orchestral tutti is quite magnificent, as is his solicitous, attentive accompaniment throughout the work. Menuhin's youthful, wonderfully intuitive musicianship in fact needed little 'instruction', as is well known, and the success of the recording may be judged from the fact that there have been few periods in the years since it was first issued when it has not been available in some shape or form. Beatrice Harrison first studied the Cello Concerto for an abridged, pre-electric recording with Elgar conducting. So impressed was the composer then that he insisted that Harrison should be the soloist whenever he conducted the work again. Their authoritative performance is deeply felt and highly expressive, but it has a quality of nobility and stoicism which comes as a refreshing change from some overindulgent modern performances. After EMI had made the first LP transfer of the Menuhin Violin Concerto for the composer's centenary in 1957 the original matrices were destroyed. When Anthony Griffith made a fresh transfer in the early 1970s using improved technology the results were at the same time better and worse, for Griffith was obliged to work with commercial pressings. In going back to the 1957 tape for this transfer EMI's engineers have on balance made the right decision, for although the 1957 engineers did not quite capture all the body of the originals there is an impressive clarity in their transfer, now brightened a little more for CD. Griffith's 1970s transfer of the Harrison/Elgar Cello Concerto was impressively managed, and this reissue has given still more presence to the sound without any sense of falsification.

Falstaff, Op. 68. Froissart, Op. 19. Grania and Diarmid, Op. 42 – Incidental Music; Funeral March. Romance, Op. 62.
Graham Sheen *bn*
BBC Symphony Orchestra / Sir Andrew Davis.
Teldec The British Line 4509-98436-2 (66 minutes: DDD). Recorded 1995.   Ⓕ **SE**

This version of *Falstaff* takes a little time to get into its stride. Don't fret, though: it isn't long before Sir Andrew Davis's formidable Elgarian instincts make themselves evident. One only has to sample his shaping of the imploring theme that appears shortly into the first Boar's Head Tavern episode, the tingling expectancy before the Gadshill double-ambush, or the thrilling grit and muscular purpose of those *con fuoco martellato* strings in the struggle which ensues. That final lump-in-the-throat appearance of Hal's theme brings with it a poignancy not found on most other versions. Listen out, too, for the strings' gentle, unutterably wistful 'stab': a moment cherishable beyond words. Aided by glowing, indeed demonstration-worthy sound quality, Davis draws a meticulously observant, warm-hearted response from his forces. Not only does his interpretation evince a compelling long-term rigour, an unerring feel for the grand scheme of Elgar's masterpiece, it is also consistently involving in its spontaneity, winning depth of characterization and (most crucially) tender vulnerability. Davis's reading is one to set beside both the composer's own and Barbirolli's at (or very near) the top of the pile. Some readers may think Davis's *Froissart* too loose-limbed a conception. However, what it may marginally lack in glinting swagger, is more than compensated for by Davis's palpable affection for Elgar's at times touchingly naïve inspiration as well as his meltingly lovely handling of the exquisite secondary material: sheer magic (Davis has an exceptional gift for communicating the introspective hush so characteristic of this composer). Teldec also gives us a hauntingly atmospheric *Grania and Diarmid* diptych, while the BBC SO's principal bassoon, Graham Sheen (such an engaging personality in the main work), makes a similarly fresh-faced showing in the little-heard Op. 62 *Romance*. Altogether a highly desirable Elgar collection.

Falstaff[a]. Introduction and Allegro, Op. 47[b]. Serenade for Strings in E minor, Op. 20[b].
[a]**London Symphony Orchestra,** [b]**New Symphony Orchestra / Anthony Collins.**
Beulah mono 1PD15 (59 minutes: ADD). Recorded 1952-54.   Ⓜ Ⓗ

Even among the many recordings of *Falstaff*, few match Collins in the way his timing helps you to visualize the story behind each incident. The reading is strong and purposeful yet not at all rushed, with each section sharply characterized and with linking passages leading the ear on. Though the LSO of 1954 was rather in the doldrums, the crisp ensemble would have done credit to the orchestra as reconstituted later in the decade, not just in the woodwind and brass sections but in the strings too. Plainly Collins inspired the players, who may well have been rediscovering the work, for that was a period when Elgar's music, rather like the orchestra, was out of favour. The Beulah transfer does not quite capture the full vividness of Decca's recording at the time, but there is a fair body in the sound and the bite of the brass is splendid. What is irritating, however, is that there is only a single track for the 34-minute work, with no sections separately indexed. In the *Serenade* and the *Introduction and Allegro* Collins equally reveals his natural understanding of Elgarian timing and rubato. However, the playing from what was then called the New Symphony Orchestra is not nearly as polished as in *Falstaff* and the string sound tends to be fizzy. None the less, this is an invaluable offering, reminding us of the mastery of a conductor whose achievement was never fully appreciated in his lifetime.

Variations on an Original Theme, Op. 36, 'Enigma'.

Enigma Variations. Cockaigne Overture, Op. 40. Introduction and Allegro, Op. 47.
Serenade for Strings.
BBC Symphony Orchestra / Sir Andrew Davis.
Teldec British Line 9031-73279-2 (74 minutes: DDD). Recorded 1991.   Ⓕ ℝℝ

These are four of the best Elgar performances on disc available. First, the recording is superb, with near-perfect balance and a really natural sound (listen to the brass in the final climax of 'Nimrod' on track 15). Second, the playing of the BBC Symphony Orchestra is first-rate. Andrew Davis's conducting of all four works is inspired, as if he had forgotten all preconceived notions and other interpretations, gone back to the scores and given us what he found there. In *Cockaigne*, for example, the subtle use of *ritardando*, sanctioned in the score, gives the music that elasticity which Elgar considered to be an ideal requisite for interpreting his works. The poetry and wit of this masterpiece emerge with renewed freshness. As for the *Enigma* Variations, instead of wondering why another recording was thought necessary, you will find yourself rejoicing that such a fine performance has been preserved to be set alongside other treasured versions. Each of the 'friends pictured within' is strongly characterized by Davis, but without exaggeration or interpretative quirks. Tempos are just right and the orchestral playing captures the authentic Elgarian sound in a manner Boult would have recognized. Similarly, in the *Introduction and Allegro*, how beautifully the string quartet is recorded, how magical are the gentle and so eloquent pizzicatos which punctuate the flow of the great melody. The fugue is played with real zest and enjoyment. This is music on a large scale and is played and conducted in that way, whereas the early *Serenade* is intimate and dewy-eyed and that is how it sounds here.

Enigma Variations. Falstaff. Grania and Diarmid – Incidental Music; Funeral March.
City of Birmingham Symphony Orchestra / Sir Simon Rattle.
EMI British Composers CDC5 55001-2 (79 minutes: DDD). Recorded 1992-93.   Ⓕ

Rattle gives us perhaps the most meticulously prepared and subtly blended *Falstaff* ever committed to disc. This conductor's keen intellect and almost fanatical fidelity to the letter of the score team up to produce the most invigorating, wittily observant results. It is, however, a bit like viewing a pristinely restored portrait of Shakespeare's fat knight, whereas Barbirolli presents us with the lovable, vulnerable creature of flesh and blood himself – his epilogue really does touch to the marrow every time. In *Enigma* the results are always enjoyable and refreshing, with myriad details in Elgar's lovingly-woven, orchestral canvas adroitly pinpointed. A fine, deeply-felt performance. The most completely successful item here is the glorious *Grania and Diarmid* incidental music: the magnificent 'Funeral March' is one of Elgar's most inspired creations and Rattle gauges its brooding melancholy most eloquently. Balance is impeccable (and the transfer level comparatively low) in all three works, though the quality in *Falstaff* isn't quite as rich and glowing as elsewhere. An exceedingly stimulating release.

Enigma Variations[a]. Falstaff[b].
[a]**Philharmonia Orchestra,** [b]**Hallé Orchestra / Sir John Barbirolli.**
EMI Studio CDM7 69185-2 (65 minutes: ADD). Recorded 1962 and 1964.   Ⓜ

This disc restores to the catalogue at a very reasonable price two key Elgar recordings of works which Sir John Barbirolli made very much his own. Barbirolli brought a flair and ripeness of feeling to the *Enigma* with which Elgar himself would surely have identified. Everything about his performance seems exactly right. The very opening theme is phrased with an appealing combination of warmth and subtlety, and variation after variation has a special kind of individuality, whilst for the finale Barbirolli draws all the threads together most satisfyingly. *Falstaff* is a continuous, closely integrated structure and again Barbirolli's response to the music's scenic characterization is magical while he controls the overall piece, with its many changes of mood, with a naturally understanding flair. The original recordings perhaps sounded more sumptuous but on CD there is more refined detail and greater range and impact to the sound.

Enigma Variations[a]. Pomp and Circumstance Marches, Op. 39[b].
[a]**London Symphony Orchestra,** [b]**London Philharmonic Orchestra / Sir Adrian Boult.**
EMI CDM7 64015-2 (55 minutes: ADD). Recorded 1970 and 1976.   Ⓜ

As one might expect, Sir Adrian Boult's 1970 recording of the *Enigma* Variations offers similar riches to those of Barbirolli with the additional bonus of a slightly superior recorded sound. Boult's account has authority, freshness and a beautiful sense of spontaneity so that each variation emerges from the preceding one with a natural feeling of flow and progression. There is warmth and affection too coupled with an air of nobility and poise, and at all times the listener is acutely aware that this is a performance by a great conductor who has lived a lifetime with the music. One need only sample the passionate stirrings of Variation 1 (the composer's wife), the athletic and boisterous 'Troyte' variation, or the autumnal, elegiac glow that Boult brings to the famous 'Nimrod' variation to realize that this is a very special document indeed. The LSO, on top form, plays with superlative skill and poetry and the excellent recording has been exceptionally well transferred to CD. The *Pomp and Circumstance* Marches, recorded six years later with the London Philharmonic Orchestra, are invigoratingly fresh and direct – indeed the performances are so full of energy and good humour that it is hard to believe that Boult was in his late eighties at the time of recording! A classic.

Symphonies – No. 1 in A flat major, Op. 55; No. 2 in E flat major; No. 3 in C minor, Op. 88.

Elgar Symphonies Nos. 1 and 2. Falstaff. The Dream of Gerontius, Op. 38 – Prelude; Kyrie eleison; Rescue him, O Lord; Go in the name of Angels; Praise to the Holiest; And now the threshold ... Praise to the Holiest; Jesu! by that shuddering dread; Take me away (with **Margaret Balfour** *contr* **Steuart Wilson** *ten* **Herbert Heyner** *bass* **Royal Choral Society**). The Dream of Gerontius – So pray for me, my friends; O Jesu, help!; Jesu! by that shuddering dread; Take me away (**Balfour, Tudor Davies** *ten* **Horace Stevens** *bass* **Three Choirs Festival Chorus**). The Music Makers, Op. 69 – We are the music makers; With wonderful deathless ditties; A breath of our inspiration; For we are afar with the dawning (**Three Choirs Festival Chorus**). Civic Fanfare. **Anonymous** (arr. Elgar) The National Anthem (**Three Choirs Festival Chorus**).
London Symphony Orchestra, Royal Albert Hall Orchestra / Sir Edward Elgar.
EMI mono CDS7 54560-2 (three discs: 211 minutes: ADD). Texts included.
Recorded 1927-32.   Ⓕ Ⓗ

In 1957 HMV issued three LPs containing Elgar's recordings as part of his birthday centenary celebrations. Then in the early 1970s Pearl World Records and HMV undertook systematic reissues of the composer's performances. At one point, in fact, everything he had recorded, both acoustically and electrically, could be obtained on LP. This was a crucial time. On the one hand some traditional Elgarians reacted to the reissues in a puzzled and worried fashion through being accustomed to second-generation performances by eminent English conductors. These succeeded in bringing out the noble, Edwardian character of the music, but failed to convey adequately its restless, questioning and sometimes despairing elements – as Elgar's performances did so clearly. Some musicians who should have known better suggested that Elgar's readings were influenced by 78rpm recording techniques, others showed points of detail where he ignored markings in his own scores.

On the other hand, Elgar's greatness as a composer was becoming increasingly recognized. There were more and more performances of his works, and his own interpretations were influencing changes in styles of performance. This was precisely the most important function of a composer recording. Would-be interpreters studying the music could not only see Elgar's intentions in the printed score, but could follow the creative process a stage further – to the ultimate stage, in fact, and hear the creator realize his work in its natural medium, that of sound. And so the multi-faceted style of Elgar's own readings was absorbed directly or indirectly by a new generation of interpreters – many of them non-British – and the way they painted the music in all its aspects struck a new chord with modern listeners. Elgar's music had begun to mirror our own times.

These transfers, using up-to-date technology, yield an astonishingly vivid quality of sound. All the clarity and detail is there, but there is also body and warmth which one remembers from the original 78s. Never before has such a large degree of surface noise been eliminated without any loss of recording information. There are imperfections, of course. Some of the recordings have inherent distortion which could not be eliminated. There are also, for instance, patches in the First Symphony's second movement where the sound becomes momentarily unfocused. And there are mains hums and background noises which could not be suppressed. But overall the achievement is very remarkable. Elgar's recordings from first to last have a notable consistency of style. He had the ability to phrase his long melodies in a particularly intense and poignant fashion, asking the violins to use bows which were 'ten foot long'. Sir Adrian Boult wrote of his 'nervous, electric beat' which he used in faster music to great effect in creating tension and variations of pulse. It is these pulse variations which are the secret of Elgar's music-making. In none of his performances will you find any foursquare rhythms. There is always an ebb and flow, an inner energy used to enhance mood and expression. His accounts of the two symphonies and *Falstaff* have all these qualities in full measure, and yet the symphonies' every movement's structure is clearly conveyed. The LSO at this period was not the greatest instrument, and Elgar sometimes drives the players beyond their real capabilities, but goodness, how they play their hearts out for him.

In his illuminating notes for these CDs, Gerald Northrop-Moore aptly refers to the live choral recordings as 'snapshots'. Here are brief extracts from public Elgar performances caught on the wing. The solo and choral singing seems dated now, and is variable in quality, but how vividly the tension and atmosphere of a live performance is preserved. Elgar's conducting of the *Gerontius* Prelude has particular beauty and depth of feeling. Hopefully, the fact that the discs are at full price will not deter too many collectors, for they deserve the widest possible circulation.

Symphony No. 1. Serenade for Strings. Chanson de nuit, Op. 15 No. 1.
Chanson de matin, Op. 15 No. 2.
London Philharmonic Orchestra / Sir Adrian Boult.
EMI CDM7 64013-2 (70 minutes: DDD). Recorded 1968-76.
Gramophone Award Winner 1977.   Ⓜ RR

Boult in Elgar on CD: the combination is irresistible, particularly when in addition to the symphony it comes with substantial and valuable makeweights. The 1976 recording of the symphony is among the last that Boult made of Elgar, a noble, unforced reading with no hint of extreme speeds in either direction. In Boult's view the flow of the music is kept free and direct, with *rallentandos* and *tenutos* reduced to the minimum in the links between sections. The sound in this digital transfer is first-rate, every bit as fine as the original LP. The brass is gloriously full, which with Elgar is one of the main necessities. On the fill-ups, more than in the symphony, the analogue original is revealed in the degree of tape-hiss, noticeable but not distracting, and if anything the 1973 recording of the Serenade brings sound even more vivid in its sense of presence than that of the bigger ensemble. Without a hint of over-expressiveness Boult so naturally conveys the tenderness and delicacy of the inspiration, and so it is too in the two shorter pieces from 1968 with violin tone noticeably less full and rounded but still sweet enough. The couplings will for many be irresistible.

Symphony No. 1. In the South, Op. 50, 'Alassio'.
London Philharmonic Orchestra / Leonard Slatkin.
RCA Victor Red Seal RD60380 (74 minutes: DDD). Recorded 1989.   Ⓕ

Elgar's First Symphony was one of those rare pieces of music that seemed to attain full stature and admiration from the very first public hearing. At its première in Manchester in 1908 it caused a sensation. Its popularity has never waned and it still holds a special place in the affections of the public today. Leonard Slatkin is a conductor whose passion for British music has become something of a crusade, and a listener hearing him play Elgar's First Symphony without knowing the artists could well think that this was a performance under a conductor such as Sir Adrian Boult. Slatkin's understanding of this composer is abundantly clear throughout. There is no trace of sentimentality in the mighty first movement, for here is real grandeur and not just grandiose utterance while the noble sadness of the coda has special beauty. The other movements are hardly less fine, for the richly textured *Adagio* is most eloquently done and the finale is thrilling. Elgar's massive though subtle scoring can present problems for engineers; here they are magnificently solved and the sound is rich yet detailed with excellent bass. The Overture *In the South* which begins the disc is brilliantly vivid and dramatic.

Symphony No. 2. In the South.
BBC Symphony Orchestra / Sir Andrew Davis.
Teldec 9031-74885-2 (70 minutes: DDD). Recorded 1992. ⒷⓈ🆁🆁

In what is unquestionably his finest achievement on record to date, Andrew Davis penetrates right to the dark inner core of this great symphony. In the opening *Allegro vivace e nobilmente*, for example, how well he and his acutely responsive players gauge the varying moods of Elgar's glorious inspiration: be it in the exhilarating surge of that leaping introductory paragraph or the spectral, twilight world at the heart of this wonderful movement, no one is found wanting. In fact, Davis's unerring structural sense never once deserts him, and the BBC Symphony Orchestra simply plays its heart out. Above all, though, it's in the many more reflective moments that Davis proves himself an outstandingly perceptive Elgarian, uncovering a vein of intimate anguish that touches to the very marrow; in this respect, his account of the slow movement is quite heart-rendingly poignant – undoubtedly the finest since Boult's incomparable 1944 performance with this very same orchestra – whilst the radiant sunset of the symphony's coda glows with luminous beauty. Prefaced by an equally idiomatic, stirring *In the South* (and aided throughout by some sumptuously natural engineering), this is an Elgar Second to set beside the very greatest. In every way a treasurable release.

Symphony No. 2.
BBC Philharmonic Orchestra / Sir Edward Downes.
Naxos 8 550635 (56 minutes: DDD). Recorded 1993. Ⓢ

Here is further proof that Sir Edward Downes is an Elgarian to be reckoned with. This account of the Second Symphony is up there with the very best. In the first movement, Downes steers a gloriously clear-sighted course: here is the same unexaggerated, splendidly authoritative conception heard from this conductor in the concert hall. Unlike some rivals on record, Downes resists the temptation to give too much too soon, and this feeling of power in reserve lends an extra cumulative intensity to the proceedings; indeed, the coda here is absolutely thrilling. The ensuing *Larghetto* sees Downes striking a near-perfect balance between introspection and heart-warming passion. Both the *Rondo* and finale are ideally paced – the former not too hectic, the latter flowing to perfection, culminating in an epilogue of rare delicacy. Throughout, the BBC Philharmonic plays outstandingly for its former chief: the orchestra's golden-toned cello section must be singled out for special praise. Just a touch more clarity in tuttis, and the recording would have been ideal. In sum, a deeply sympathetic Elgar Second, definitely the preferred budget version, possessing qualities to match any rival. At Naxos price, it's surely a must for all Elgarians.

Elgar/Payne Symphony No. 3.
BBC Symphony Orchestra / Sir Andrew Davis.
NMC NMCD053 (56 minutes: DDD). Recorded 1997. ⒻⓈⒺ

Symphony No. 3 – sketches and commentary by Anthony Payne.
Robert Gibbs *vn* **David Owen Norris** *pf*
BBC Symphony Orchestra / Sir Andrew Davis.
NMC NMCD052 (70 minutes: DDD). Recorded 1997. Ⓜ

Elgar left 130 pages of sketches for his Third Symphony and they have haunted the composer, author and critic, Anthony Payne, ever since he first gained access to them back in 1972. Longstanding opinion was that the ideas for the symphony (which occupied Elgar during 1933, the last full year of his life) showed a sad waning of his powers. Yet Payne utterly disproves this theory.

The sweeping, almost grimly defiant opening paragraph with its gaunt parallel open fifths (the first 17 bars of which Elgar actually left in full score) is hard to dislodge from one's mind, as is the sublimely wistful second subject. After an unexpected exposition repeat (Elgar's, not Payne's, in case you were wondering), the development is launched with a magical new idea, whose incense-laden mystery and penetrating harmonic scope seem to cast a wistful glance back to the world of the oratorios. From a series of seemingly unpromising fragments, Payne proceeds to fashion a movement of great power and immensely satisfying proportions, while his idiomatic orchestration will surely win him many plaudits. The winsome main idea is drawn from Elgar's 1923 incidental score for Laurence Binyon's drama, *Arthur*. There are also two contrasting episodes, the second of which features a delectable little tune in A major. By contrast, the *Adagio solenne* slow movement wears a nobly tragic, world-weary demeanour. The mournful, daringly harmonized introduction immediately grips with its pain and anguish, yet the rapt D major second subject seems to offer new hope. Between these two themes comes another one of those visionary ideas which, as Payne asserts, 'positively demands the sound of muted strings'. The close could hardly be more chilling, a single solo viola note hanging in the air; it was this phrase, marked *fine*, that the dying composer gave to his dear friend, the violinist W.H. Reed, uttering the famous words: 'Billy, this is the end.' The finale begins with a rousing fanfare (in Elgar's scoring) and struts out in bustling fashion. All the same, the thematic invention is not quite on the same level as in the remainder (much of it is again drawn from the *Arthur* music), though the second subject has a *Cockaigne*-like swagger about it. Payne's resolution is intriguing, ingenious and, naturally, very personal. It is perhaps not terribly satisfying, but everyone will form their own view – and anyway, there is so much in the preceding 55 minutes for which to be exceedingly thankful.

All praise to Sir Andrew Davis and the BBC SO for such an eloquent, profoundly involving performance and to the production team for obtaining such handsome sound. The companion issue is also beautifully realized, with over 50 musical examples, including the sketches for violin and piano that Elgar would play through on the piano with Billy Reed. There are excellent contributions here from David Owen Norris and Robert Gibbs (the latter uses Reed's own instrument). A fascinating and, above all, deeply rewarding pair of CDs which no Elgarian will want to miss.

Introduction and Allegro. Chanson de nuit (arr. Fraser). Chanson de matin (arr. Fraser). Three Characteristic Pieces – No. 1, Mazurka, Op. 10. Serenade for Strings. Salut d'amour, Op. 12 (arr. Fraser). Elegy, Op. 58.
José-Luis Garcia, Mary Eade *vns* **Quentin Ballardie** *va* **Olga Hegedus** *vc*
English Chamber Orchestra / Yehudi Menuhin.
Arabesque Z6563 (45 minutes: DDD). Recorded 1982.   Ⓕ

Elgar's pieces for string orchestra contain some of his greatest music and certainly the *Introduction and Allegro, Serenade* and *Elegy* included in this delightful programme embody quintessential Elgar. Yehudi Menuhin's readings dig deep into the hearts of these works, drawing out the nostalgia and inner tragedy that underpins even some of the most seemingly high-spirited of Elgar's music. The lighter pieces allow relief from the intensity of the major works, thus making that intensity all the more effective. The English Chamber Orchestra is more than capable of providing first-rate soloists from its own ranks, and the quartet extracted for the *Introduction and Allegro* is suitably virtuosic. Both performers and engineers have produced an ideal integration of this solo group with the main string body, and the generally effervescent sound suits the celebratory nature of the piece.

String Quartet in E minor, Op. 83. Canto popolare. Piano Quintet in A minor, Op. 84.
Piers Lane *pf* **Vellinger Quartet** (Stephanie Gonley, Harvey de Sousa *vns* James Boyd *va* Sally Pendlebury *vc*).
EMI Eminence CD-EMX2229 (65 minutes: DDD). Recorded 1994.   Ⓜ

The Vellinger Quartet brings enormous heart, effortless technical accomplishment and (most importantly) genuine freshness of new discovery to the Quartet. In both outer movements their playing ideally combines propulsive excitement with passionate flexibility, yet, at the same time, they do not miss out on the vein of wistfulness and vulnerability coursing through Elgar's glorious inspiration. For the Piano Quintet they are joined by the excellent Piers Lane. Again, the emotional temperature is high, with these young performers extracting maximum drama from the opening movement in particular. The central *Adagio*, stately and very intense, could perhaps do with greater intimacy of feeling; their account of the finale generates all the edge-of-seat thrust of a live concert. Some Elgarians may baulk at the sheer physicality and unrelenting wholeheartedness of it all but their fervour has its place too. As a further appealing bonus, Lane partners the Vellinger's violist, James Boyd, for a generously sung rendering of *In Moonlight*, more familiar as the gloriously long-breathed *Canto popolare* theme from the central portion of *In the South*. Excellent recording.

Romance in C minor, Op. 1. Pieces, Op. 4 – No. 1, Idylle; No. 3, Virelai. Mazurka in C minor, Op. 10 No. 1. Salut d'amour. Bizarrerie in G minor, Op. 13 No. 2. Chanson de nuit. Chanson de matin. La capricieuse, Op. 17. Gavotte in A major. Etude-Caprice (cpted Reed). Serenade. May Song. In Hammersbach. Carissima. Adieu. Etudes characteristiques.
Marat Bisengaliev vn **Benjamin Frith** pf
Black Box BBM1016 (67 minutes: DDD). Recorded 1998. Ⓕ

Born in 1962, Marat Bisengaliev originally hails from Kazakhstan and is a prize-winning graduate from the Moscow Conservatory. On the evidence of this most enjoyable anthology he is a violinist of great technical accomplishment and communicative warmth, and he generates a really fine rapport with the admirable Benjamin Frith. As the opening *Romance* (with its striking echoes of the finale from Schumann's Fourth Symphony) immediately reveals, these artists bring an affectingly uncloying, totally unforced naturalness of expression to this charming repertoire. Even such well-worn nuggets as the two *Chansons* and *Salut d'amour* emerge with a new-minted freshness. Only in *La capricieuse* do you feel that the rubato lacks the last ounce of spontaneity. Elsewhere, Black Box's programme very usefully plugs a number of gaps in the current Elgar discography, not least the delectable *Bizarrerie*, Op. 13 No. 2 (companion piece to *Mot d'amour*), *Virelai* (a particularly fetching morsel from 1884) and a cheeky *Gavotte* from the following year. The winsome *In Hammersbach* will be more familiar as the second of the *Three Bavarian Dances* (though it actually began life as the third of six part-songs that went to make up the 1895 *Scenes from the Bavarian Highlands*).

Eagle-eyed enthusiasts will also have spotted two world-première recordings in the contents listed above: it was left to violinist W.H. Reed to complete the *Etude-Caprice* that Elgar first sketched as long ago as 1877 (the composer handed his dear friend the unfinished manuscript in 1918), while the ferocious difficulty of the five solo *Etudes characteristiques* of 1878 has long put off any potential champions on disc (and Bisengaliev rises to the challenge with fearless aplomb). Piano tone seems a touch metallic at the outset (and Bisengaliev's occasional sniffing may prove distracting to some listeners), but the ear soon adjusts, and balance within the generous church acoustic is generally excellent.

The Black Knight, Op. 25. Scenes from the Bavarian Highlands, Op. 27.
London Symphony Chorus and Orchestra / Richard Hickox.
Chandos CHAN9436 (61 minutes: DDD). Texts included. Recorded 1995. ⒻⓈ

The Black Knight is a large-scale, red-blooded choral setting of Longfellow's translation of a German poem by Ludwig Uhland. Elgar completed it in 1893 and it provided him with his first big success – especially in the Midlands, where it was gratefully taken up by many choral societies. The text tells of a sinister, unnamed 'Prince of mighty sway', whose appearance at the King's court during the feast of Pentecost has disastrous consequences. Elgar's score boasts much attractive invention, some of it strikingly eloquent and prescient of greater offerings to come. The choral writing is always effective, the orchestration already vivid and assured. Richard Hickox and his combined London Symphony forces are dab hands at this kind of fare and their performance has great bloom and spaciousness. Similarly, in the tuneful, vernally fresh *Scenes from the Bavarian Highlands* (given here with the orchestral accompaniment Elgar supplied in 1896), Hickox and his colleagues respond with commendable spirit and pleasing polish. Typical of Chandos, the recording is bright and clear, tonally beyond reproach and with just the right balance between choir and orchestra.

The Light of Life (Lux Christi), Op. 29.
Judith Howarth sop **Linda Finnie** mez **Arthur Davies** ten **John Shirley-Quirk** bar
London Symphony Chorus and Orchestra / Richard Hickox.
Chandos CHAN9208 (63 minutes: DDD). Text included. Recorded 1993. Ⓕ

In the glorious orchestral 'Meditation' Hickox's conducting demonstrates a noble flexibility, sensitivity to dynamic nuance and feeling for climax. Equally the engineering, sumptuous yet detailed, comes close to the ideal. The LSO and Chorus contribute to proceedings in exemplary, disciplined fashion. As The Blind Man, Arthur Davies could hardly be more ardent, but his slightly tremulous timbre will not be to all tastes. John Shirley-Quirk, so eloquent and firm-toned a Jesus for Groves (on EMI) back in 1980, now shows signs of unsteadiness in the same part. On the other hand, Linda Finnie and Judith Howarth make a creditable showing. Hickox's reading excels in precisely the areas where the Groves was deficient, and vice versa. If you already have the Groves reissue, hang on to it, for it is by no means outclassed by the Hickox. However, for anyone coming to this underrated score for the first time, Hickox's must now be the preferred version.

The Music Makers. Dream children, Op. 43. Elegy, Op. 58. Sursum corda, Op. 11. Sospiri,
Op. 70. Chanson de matin. Chanson de nuit. Salut d'amour.
Jean Rigby *mez* **BBC Symphony Chorus and Orchestra / Sir Andrew Davis.**
Teldec British Line 4509-92374-2 (76 minutes: DDD). Text included. Recorded 1993.　　　Ⓕ🄴

Davis strikes right to the heart of *The Music Makers* and the results are profoundly idiomatic and
enchanting. Indeed, 'special' moments abound in this performance: note the chilling hush of Elgar's
prescribed *ppp* marking at the words 'In the buried past of the earth' (7'24"); the ravishing tone
Davis draws from his excellent choir for 'A breath of our inspiration' (11'43"); and how touching is
his handling of that sublime passage beginning at 25'52" ('O men! it must ever be/That we dwell, in
our dreaming and singing,/A little apart from ye'), with its poignant intertwining of themes from
the *Enigma* Variations and the Violin Concerto. Davis underlines the intensely personal nature of
Elgar's inspiration, whilst at the same time doing full justice to this underrated score's dreams and
aspirations. The predominantly wistful atmosphere of the main work carries over into the two
exquisite miniatures which comprise *Dream children*; Davis and the BBC orchestra capture their
nostalgic mood to perfection, and prove to be no less affectionate advocates of the two *Chansons*
and *Salut d'amour*. Similarly, both the *Elegy* and *Sospiri* find the BBC strings at their very finest.
The sound is sumptuous.

Sea Pictures, Op. 37. The Music Makers.
Felicity Palmer *mez* **London Symphony Chorus and Orchestra / Richard Hickox.**
EMI British Composers CDM5 65126-2 (62 minutes: DDD). Texts included. Recorded 1986.　　Ⓜ

These idiomatic Elgar performances from Richard Hickox well merit their mid-price resuscitation
within EMI's British Composers series. Hickox's admirable London Symphony Chorus impresses in
matters of intonation and diction. Felicity Palmer sings commandingly, though her contribution in
The Music Makers doesn't always generate the tear-laden intensity the part requires. However,
Hickox doesn't quite match Sir Andrew Davis's Teldec account – he in particular evinces a personal
identification with Elgar's inspiration that is rather special. In the *Sea Pictures*, however, Hickox
and Palmer form an intelligent, distinctive partnership, less endearing, perhaps, than many would
like in 'In Haven' and 'Where corals lie', yet tough and dramatic in 'Sabbath morning at sea' and
'The swimmer'. It is a thrusting, unsentimental view which is most refreshing. The orchestral
playing is excellent.

The Dream of Gerontius, Op. 38[a]. Sea Pictures[b].
Dame Janet Baker *mez* [a]**Richard Lewis** *ten* [a]**Kim Borg** *bass*
[a]**Hallé Choir;** [a]**Sheffield Philharmonic Chorus;** [a]**Ambrosian Singers;**
[a]**Hallé Orchestra,** [b]**London Symphony Orchestra / Sir John Barbirolli.**
EMI Studio CMS7 63185-2 (two discs: 122 minutes: ADD). Texts included.
Recorded 1964-65.　　Ⓜ🅁🅁

This *Gerontius* very much belongs to the Angel of Dame Janet Baker and the conducting of Sir
John Barbirolli here giving another example of that instinctive rapport which filled the few precious
recordings they made together. Barbirolli penetrated to the core of the work's spirituality. In
showing his affection for it, he was liable to embark on slow tempos and unmarked *ritardandos*.
Whether one accepts these or finds them self-indulgent rather depends on one's mood. The Prelude
at once announces the intensity of feeling Sir John brings to the whole work. He is superb with his
choir. Though it may not be as impressive a body as that on some other sets, it sings with perhaps
the greatest character and conviction of all, especially as hissing Demons and ecstatic Angelicals.
Thank goodness it's given a forward recording, something of a lesson to more recent contestants
in this field. The Hallé is a superb instrument in Barbirolli's hands and Dame Janet is superb. We
hear all the tenderness and eloquence one expects from an Angel, and a radiance balanced by
other-worldliness. Her skill with the text is unrivalled. It comes to the fore in the description of
St Frands's stigmata and in the whole dialogue with Gerontius. The farewell is the very epitome of
serene consolation. Richard Lewis declaims 'Take me away' with the proper terror and utters a quite
beautiful 'Novissima hora est' but elsewhere is less communicative and shows less spontaneity than
for Sargent ten years earlier. The cold from which he was said to be suffering seems occasionally
evident. Perhaps it accounts for the very audible cough at the start of the 'Be merciful' chorus, just
after he has stopped singing. If Kim Borg's Priest and Angel of the Agony are an acquired taste
because of his peculiar accenting of the English language it's one worth acquiring. He has all the
authority for the first role, the supple expression for the second. Many, many years ago this set
found its way into many people's hearts, as it deserves, and they will be delighted to have it so
arrestingly refurbished. Like so many other accounts of this piece, it is its own justification because
everyone concerned was obviously inspired by the glorious music to give of his and her very best.

The Dream of Gerontius[a]. Cello Concerto[b].
Gladys Ripley contr **Heddle Nash** ten **Dennis Noble** bar **Norman Walker** bass **Paul Tortelier** vc
Huddersfield Choral Society; [b]**BBC Symphony Orchestra,**
[a]**Liverpool Philharmonic Orchestra / Sir Malcolm Sargent.**
Testament mono SBT2025 (two discs: 120 minutes: ADD). Text included. Recorded 1945-53. ℗ 🅷

This pioneering set of *Gerontius* has come up newly minted in these superbly engineered transfers taken from 78rpm masters. That only enhances the incandescence and fervour of the reading itself, in virtually all respects the most convincing the work has received. Sargent's conducting, influenced by Elgar's, is direct, vital and urgently crafted with an inborn feeling for the work's ebb and flow and an overall picture that comprehends the piece's spiritual meaning while realizing its dramatic leanness and force. Heddle Nash's Gerontius is unrivalled in its conviction and inwardness. He was encouraged by Elgar in 1930 to take the part and sang it under the composer's baton in 1932 to his satisfaction. By 1945 the work was in Nash's being; he sang it from memory and had mastered every facet of interpreting it. Such phrases as 'Mary pray for me', 'Novissima hora est' and 'My soul is in my hand, I have no fear' come from and go to the heart. 'Take me away' is like a searing cry of pain from the depth of the singer's soul. Gladys Ripley is a natural and communicative Angel throughout, her flexible and appealing tone always a pleasure to hear. The Liverpool Philharmonic lives up to its reputation at the time as the country's leading orchestra (in particular the sonorous string section) and the members of the Huddersfield Choral Society sing as if their lives depended on the outcome. Tortelier's Cello Concerto presents the classical approach as compared with the romantic one of Du Pré, and is the best of Tortelier's readings of the work on disc, with his tone and phrasing at their firmest and most telling. A considered and unaffected reading among the best ever committed to disc.

The Spirit of England, Op. 80. Give unto the Lord, Op. 74. O hearken thou, Op. 64. The Snow, Op. 26 No. 1. Land of Hope and Glory (arr. Fagge).
Dame Felicity Lott sop **London Symphony Chorus; Northern Sinfonia / Richard Hickox.**
EMI British Composers CDM5 65586-2 (52 minutes: DDD). Texts included. Recorded 1987.   Ⓜ

Hickox adopts a purposeful approach to the great wartime cantata, *The Spirit of England*. Many collectors got to know this compassionate and moving score through Sir Alexander Gibson's extremely fine 1976 recording (originally made for RCA, now reissued at mid-price on Chandos). Gibson's spacious and eloquent interpretation enshrined one of his very finest achievements in the studio, and possibly this EMI rival doesn't match it in sheer depth of feeling. That said, Hickox draws some magnificent singing from the London Symphony Chorus, and his mobile reading compensates with a fervour to which many will positively respond. The fillers are all worth having, especially the sublime coronation Offertory from 1911, *O hearken thou*. The production lacks nothing in transparency and amplitude, though in *The Spirit of England* one ideally craves a more expansive acoustic.

Elgar's Interpreters on Record, Volume 1.
Crown of India – March of the Mogul Emperors[a]. The Dream of Gerontius[b] – My work is done; I see not those false spirits; We now have passed the gate; Softly and gently; My work is done; It is because then thou didst fear. The Saga of King Olaf, Op. 30 – And King Olaf heard the cry![d]. The Apostles, Op. 49 – By the Wayside[e]. Caractacus, Op. 35[f] – Leap, leap to light; O my warriors. O hearken thou, Op. 64[g]. The Starlight Express[h] – O children, open your arms to me; There is a fairy hides in the beautiful eyes; I'm everywhere; My Old Tunes; Dustman, Laugher's Song. Songs (arr. Haydn Wood)[i] – Like to the damask rose; Queen Mary's song; Shepherd's Song, Op. 16 No. 1; Rondel, Op. 16 No. 3. The shower, Op. 71 No. 1[j].
[e]**Dora Labbette,** [h]**Alice Moxon** sops [b]**Dame Clara Butt,** [c]**Kathleen Ferrier** contrs
[b]**Maurice d'Oisly,** [d]**Tudor Davies,** [e]**Hubert Eisdell** tens [e]**Dennis Noble,** [e]**Harold Williams,**
[h]**Stuart Robertson** bars [f]**Peter Dawson** bass-bar [e]**Robert Easton** bass [c]**Gerald Moore** pf
[a]**Black Diamonds Band;** [b]**New Queen's Hall Orchestra / Sir Henry Wood;**
[d]**Symphony Orchestra / Sir Eugene Goossens;** [e]**Hallé Orchestra / Sir Hamilton Harty;**
[f]**orchestra / Sir John Barbirolli;** [g]**St George's Chapel Choir, Windsor / Sir Walford Davies;**
[i]**Light Symphony Orchestra / Haydn Wood;** [j]**Glasgow Orpheus Choir / Sir Hugh Roberton.**
Dutton Laboratories Elgar Society mono CDAX8019 (76 minutes: ADD). Recorded 1912-48.   Ⓜ 🅷

The great composers, we know, are for all time, but there is still something special about them in their own era, especially if it should be close to that of the listener. This wonderful collection of recordings, made for the most part in Elgar's own lifetime, has not only authenticity of period; for those born into that time it is something to be played and savoured where no absurdity of unmeasured response will be wondered at, or, ever so kindly, derided. The voices of the soloists, for instance. A snigger at Dame Clara Butt's Angel in *The Dream of Gerontius* would incite thoughts of murder. Those five who sing the Beatitudes and commentary in *The Apostles*, they too are so wonderfully of their period, and fine singers too. Tudor Davies, fiery as a Welsh Martinelli in his declamation of Olaf's saga, or Peter Dawson, exponent of 'singing that *was* singing' in *Caractacus*: these also are part of the sacred book. Kathleen Ferrier's test recording is movingly lovely to hear again, as, for that matter, is the Glasgow Orpheus Choir. In fact, not forgetting some of the less likely contents, this is an anthological treasure. Wondrously clean transfers have been mastered by Dutton Laboratories. Just hear that first track, the *Crown of India* March, and make a guess, without looking, at the date; or, listening with perfect clarity to that record from *The Apostles*, recall how the light blue label whizzed round amid the gunge and dust bequeathed by the second-hand shop whence it came. But everything is for congratulations here, including the admirable booklet-notes by John Knowles.

George Enescu Romanian 1881-1955

Symphonies – No. 1 in E flat major, Op. 13; No. 2 in A major, Op. 17.
Monte Carlo Philharmonic Orchestra / Lawrence Foster.
EMI CDC7 54763-2 (78 minutes: DDD). Recorded 1990-92.   Ⓕ🅔

Brahmsian in colour the First Symphony may very well be, but the rhythmic vigour of its outer movements is quite unlike Brahms. Wagner? Well, any 24-year-old in 1905 writing a slow movement with moments of romantic yearning to it may be permitted to veer towards *Tristan*. Strauss may be the first name which springs to mind when listening to the Second Symphony, but by then Enescu's orchestration, highly individual and remarkably refined, had matured: 'Strauss', here, is merely a metaphor for richness of incident and colour. There is a flavour of Rachmaninov to the Second Symphony's slow movement, and an apparent kinship with Mahler, audible in the tense, martial finale, an apparent reaction to the outbreak of the First World War. Apart from the vividly imaginative orchestration, Enescu's own voice is heard most clearly in his extremely detailed and complex working of what is often basically bold and clear-cut melodic material. The symphonies are accomplished, immaculately crafted, and add up to distinctly more than the sum of their sometimes only apparent influences. Lawrence Foster's direction is brilliantly successful in ensuring that the wood is not obscured by all its luxuriant foliage; the recording is natural but very clear.

Pedro de Escobar Portuguese c1465-1535

Escobar Missa pro defunctis.
Peñalosa Inter vestibulum et altare. Adoro te, Domine Iesu Christe.
Anchieta Libera me, Domine.
Ensemble Gilles Binchois (Akira Tachikawa, Carlos Mena *countertens* Eric Trémolières,
Christophe Einhorn, Hervé Lamy *tens* Philipps Balloy, Jacques Bona *basses*) **/**
Dominique Vellard *ten*
Virgin Classics Veritas VC5 45328-2 (58 minutes: DDD). Texts and translations included.
Recorded 1998.   Ⓕ

Pedro de Escobar's polyphonic setting of the Requiem Mass is the earliest extant from the Iberian peninsula, and among the very few versions from the whole of Europe that may have been composed before 1500. It is thus a very important 'document' for the music historian, yet it remains an enigma: we do not know the occasion for which it was composed, nor for which institution. Certain factors – as yet unprovable – point to the death of Prince Juan, only son of Ferdinand and Isabella, and heir to the kingdoms of Aragon and Castile until his untimely, and much lamented, death in 1497. Escobar was, at that time, a singer in the Castilian royal chapel. A major study by Grayson Wagstaff of the Iberian Requiem in the sixteenth century has shed much light on other puzzling aspects of Escobar's setting, both in terms of the texts set and the chants used, but to date the piece has refused to yield up all its secrets. This recording by Ensemble Gilles Binchois does, however, take advantage of chant research by the Catalan scholar, Marius Bernardó, who also devised the reconstruction presented here (which includes pieces by Escobar's contemporaries, Juan de Anchieta and Francisco de Peñalosa). Ensemble Gilles Binchois, with two voices per part (except in the Tract), are quite measured, adopting generally slow tempos and stressing the solemnity of the music with its unadorned chant in the upper voice fleshed out by the lower vocal lines which often move – albeit in general independently – in a similarly sustained fashion. The overall effect is appropriately lugubrious and austere despite the rich sonority achieved by the singers, who are aided by a resonant acoustic. These performances convince you of the high quality of Escobar's music which looks unpromising on the page but which in performance reveals its true worth.

Manuel de Falla

Harpsichord Concerto. El sombrero de tres picos.
Maria Lluisa Muntada *sop* **Tony Millan** *hpd*
Jaime Martin *fl* **Manuel Angulo** *ob* **Joan-Enric Lluna** *cl* **Santiago Juan** *vn* **Jorge Pozas** *vc*
Spanish National Youth Orchestra / Edmon Colomer.
Auvidis Valois V4642 (56 minutes: DDD). Recorded 1989.   Ⓕ

Falla's *El sombrero de tres picos* ('The three-cornered hat') started life as a 'mimed farce', but
Diaghilev then persuaded the composer to revise and enlarge it as a one-act ballet for his company
which had its première in London in 1919. Besides the orchestra, it features a soprano solo warning
wives to resist temptation and cries of 'Olé' from men's voices representing a bullring crowd. Much
of the score consists of dances such as the fandango and seguidilla, while the finale is a jota. This
performance by Maria Lluisa Muntada and the Spanish National Youth Orchestra, playing under
the direction of its founder Edmon Colomer, brings to us all the vivid colours, intense melodies and
vigorous rhythms that together evoke that southernmost province of Spain which is Andalusia.
These artists clearly love and understand this music and they bring tremendous gusto to the famous
'Miller's Dance' (the longest single number) with its chunky chords getting louder and faster. The
Harpsichord Concerto, completed in 1926, shows us another side of Falla and was among the first
twentieth-century compositions for the instrument. It is less obviously Spanish in style and instead
more neo-classical – indeed, Stravinsky was probably the chief model – although we may detect an
Iberian element in its directness and even toughness. With just five instruments playing alongside
the soloist, it is really a chamber work, but the writing is so powerful that the composer's title is
doubtless justified. Here, too, the playing is fine and the recording of both these works is full-
blooded and atmospheric.

Falla El amor brujo – ballet (complete)[a]. Noches en los jardines de España[b].
Rodrigo Concierto de Aranjuez[c].
Huguette Tourangeau *mez* **Carlos Bonnell** *gtr* **Alicia de Larrocha** *pf*
[ac]**Montreal Symphony Orchestra / Charles Dutoit;**
[b]**London Philharmonic Orchestra / Rafael Frühbeck de Burgos.**
Decca Ovation 430 703-2DM (71 minutes: DDD). Recorded 1980-83.   Ⓜ

Decca's hugely enjoyable disc of Spanish music includes Rodrigo's most famous work, the *Concierto
de Aranjuez* which has never lost its popularity since its Barcelona première in 1940. Here Carlos
Bonnell imparts a wistful, intimate feeling to the work, aided by a thoughtful accompaniment from
Charles Dutoit's stylish Montreal Orchestra. The famous string tune in the *Adagio* enjoys a fulsome
rendition. Dutoit's beautifully played interpretation of *El amor brujo* captures the wide range of
emotions that this fiery, mysterious piece requires and his performance of the famous 'Ritual Fire
Dance' must be among the best in the catalogue. A cooler mood is captured in *Nights in the gardens
of Spain* with Alicia de Larrocha as the distinguished soloist. Her smooth, effortless playing matches
the mood of the piece exactly and de Burgos's accompaniment with the London Philharmonic is
equally sympathetic, with ripe tone colour and careful dynamics. Those unfamiliar with these great
Spanish works will be hard pressed to find a better introduction than this superbly recorded disc.

Falla Quatre pièces espagnoles. Fantasía bética. La vida breve – Danse espagnole No. 1.
Serenata andaluza. El retablo de Maese Pedro – Sinfonia.
Montsalvatge Divagación. Three divertimentos on themes of forgotten composers.
Si, à Mompou. Berceuse a la memoria de Oscar Esplá. Sonatine pour Yvette.
Alicia de Larrocha *pf*
RCA Victor Red Seal 09026 61389-2 (70 minutes: DDD). Recorded 1992.   Ⓕ

It is odd of RCA to label this disc 'Serenata andaluza' when half of it is occupied by music by a
Catalan composer with nothing Andalusian about him. The popularity of Montsalvatge's
Canciones negras has misled some commentators into exaggerating the West Indian calypso
influence on his output: a truer perspective on his style is offered by this selection of his piano
music. From the *Divertimentos* of 1942 only the habanera, with its echoes of Milhaud's *Saudades do
Brasil*, falls into the West Indian category. These pieces were dedicated to Alicia de Larrocha and
the cheerful *Divagación* was a wedding present to her. The *Sonatine* was written in 1962 for his then
ten-year-old daughter, obviously not for her to play (unless she was the most extraordinary child
super-virtuoso of all time) but as a musical portrait of her vivacious and temperamental moods.
Larrocha takes the first movement gently and quietly and the second with impassioned depth: the
entertaining finale (which quotes the most famous of nursery tunes) is as brilliant as ever. It then
comes as a surprise to find a very different, tougher idiom in the two *in memoriam* pieces (for left
hand only) for older contemporaries. In the Falla works Larrocha has surpassed herself. In the

austere, penetrating and incisive *Fantasía bética*, so elusive to bring off in performance, she displays great tonal imagination throughout, confirming her status as the foremost interpreter today of Spanish keyboard music.

Atlántida (arr. E. Halffter)[a]. El sombrero de tres picos[b].
[a]**Enriqueta Tarrés**, [b]**Victoria de los Angeles** *sops* **Anna Ricci** *mez*
Eduardo Giménez *ten* **Vincente Sardinero** *bar*
[a]**Children's Chorus of Our Lady of Remembrance**; [a]**Spanish National Chorus and Orchestra**;
[b]**Philharmonia Orchestra / Rafael Frühbeck de Burgos.**
EMI Matrix CMS5 65997-2 (two discs: 146 minutes: DDD). Texts and translations included.
Recorded 1963-77.   Ⓜ

Not even the devoted efforts of Falla's pupil Ernesto Halffter could succeed in making a convincing whole of the oratorio his master left in a jumble of disorganized fragments. Both textually and musically it remains a disparate collection of ideas that the composer, through ill-health and the depression caused by the cumulative effects of the Spanish civil war, an unhappy refuge in Argentina and then the great European war, was for over two decades unable to muster into order. Yet it was conceived with the most elevated of aims – a mystic 're-emergence' of submerged Atlantis signifying a celebration of Spain's extending the bounds of Christianity. There is much splendid music in the widest diversity of styles, particularly for the chorus who, with a baritone narrator, carries the main weight of the work. Sardinero is a noble-voiced narrator, Ricci brings pathos to her solo as the dying Queen Pyrene; in the charmingly folk-like 'Isabella's dream' a steadier line than Tarrés produces would have been preferable. The chorus, which has some of the most impressive sections, is mostly good, and the orchestra provides useful support. In view of its troubled genesis, the work is inevitably flawed, and some people might prefer merely a suite of its finest sections; but the full Halffter reconstruction, now accepted as definitive, gives us a glimpse of the masterpiece *Atlántida* might have been. There have been other excellent performances of the ever-fresh *Three-cornered hat*, but none better than this imaginative and scintillating reading by Frühbeck and the Philharmonia. So vivacious and idiomatic is the playing, so flexible and alive to all the score's sly, witty allusions, and so subtle are the nuances, that the stage-pictures seem to be conjured up before our eyes. The recording is as vivid as the performance. Terrific!

Falla El retablo de Maese Pedro.
Matthew Best *bass* Don Quijote; **Adrian Thompson** *ten* Maese Pedro; **Samuel Linay** *treb*
El Trujamán; **Maggie Cole** *hpd*
Milhaud Les malheurs d'Orphée.
Malcolm Walker *bar* Orphée; **Anna Steiger** *sop* Eurydice; **Paul Harrhy** *ten* Maréchal,
Le sanglier; **Patrick Donnelly** *bass* Le charron; **Matthew Best** *bass* Le vannier, L'ours;
Gaynor Morgan *sop* Le renard, La soeur Jumelle; **Patricia Bardon** *sop* Le loup, La soeur aînée;
Susan Bickley *mez* La soeur cadette.
Stravinsky Renard.
Hugh Hetherington, Paul Harrhy *tens* **Patrick Donnelly, Nicolas Cavallier** *basses*
Christopher Bradley *cimbalom* **Matrix Ensemble / Robert Ziegler.**
ASV CDDCA758 (77 minutes: DDD). Texts and translations included.   Ⓕ

The performances here by Robert Ziegler and his Matrix Ensemble are full of flair and his chosen singers for the three works sound at home in Spanish, French and Russian in turn. As presented here, Falla's puppet-opera is full of Iberian colour and verve, and although Milhaud's piece on the Orpheus legend is not so striking or dramatic it still has beauty and is elegantly and expressively sung and played. But the best music comes in Stravinsky's magnificently earthy and vivid 'barnyard fable' *Renard*, not a long work but a dazzling one, where this performance of great panache simply bursts out of one's loudspeakers to transport us instantly to a farmyard of old Russia. There's excellent cimbalom playing here from Christopher Bradley. The libretto of all three works is usefully provided in the booklet, together with an English translation. The recording is first class, being both immediate and atmospheric.

Ernest Farrar   British 1885-1918

Rhapsody No. 1, 'The Open Road', Op. 9. Variations on an Old British Sea Song, Op. 25. The Forsaken Merman, Op. 20. Heroic Elegy, Op. 36. English Pastoral Impressions, Op. 26.
Howard Shelley *pf*
Philharmonia Orchestra / Alasdair Mitchell.
Chandos CHAN9586 (72 minutes: DDD). Recorded 1996.   Ⓕ

A victim of the First World War, Ernest Farrar studied under Stanford at the RCM (where he distinguished himself greatly, winning a number of prizes). After spells in Dresden and South Shields, he settled in Harrogate where, in 1912, he was appointed organist of Christ Church. His name will perhaps be more familiar as the dedicatee of Frank Bridge's magnificent Piano Sonata, while Gerald Finzi inscribed his *Requiem da camera* 'in memory of E.B.F.' (he had been a composition pupil of Farrar). Of the five offerings gathered together on this long-overdue anthology, only the *English Pastoral Impressions* (which had been published within the prestigious Carnegie Edition) were available with printed parts. Now, thanks to the pioneering efforts of conductor Alasdair Mitchell and the RVW Trust (who prepared performing materials from the manuscript scores held within the Bodleian Library), a major reassessment of Farrar's achievement can begin.

From the bagpipe drone which greets the dawn of the 1908 orchestral rhapsody, *The Open Road*, to the jaunty gait of the third (and last) of the *English Pastoral Impressions* from 1915, this 72-minute collection spells firm enjoyment. Especially striking is *The Forsaken Merman* (1914), an extremely well-made and colourful 27-minute tone-poem, which contains not only plenty of memorable ideas but also ample evidence of a most impressive, budding orchestral resource. Granted, the shadow of *Gerontius* looms large over Farrar's stylistic landscape (there are even one or two near-cribs), but it's a stirring, immensely likeable creation for all that, and enthusiastically performed here. A similarly deft touch illuminates both the charming 1914 *Variations on an Old British Sea Song* for piano and orchestra (with Howard Shelley a stylish and affectionate soloist) and the *English Pastoral Impressions*. In the latter's opening movement, 'Spring Morning', with its attractive incorporation of *Sumer is icumen in* and the *Angelus*, annotator Bernard Benoliel finds Farrar's inspiration 'so delicate and atmospheric [that] it is almost felt rather than heard', an observation that extends to the poignantly evocative outer portions of the ensuing 'Bredon Hill'. The concluding 'Over the Hills and Far Away' has a Grainger-like perkiness and harmonic tang. Last but not least, we have the *Heroic Elegy* of 1918, a deeply moving processional, incorporating 'the fine old English "Song of Agincourt"' (to quote the composer's own words). It was Farrar's last orchestral work and he returned from France on leave to lead its Harrogate première in July 1918; ten weeks later, he fell in the Battle of Epéhy Ronssoy. Mitchell and the Philharmonia do Farrar proud, and Chandos's sound is glowingly realistic to match.

Gabriel Fauré
French 1845-1924

Pelléas et Mélisande, Op. 80 (with Chanson de Mélisande – orch. Koechlin). Three Songs, Op. 7 – Après un rêve (arr. vc/orch. Dubenskij). Pavane, Op. 50. Elégie, Op. 24. Dolly Suite, Op. 56 (orch. Rabaud).
Lorraine Hunt *sop* **Jules Eskin** *vc*
Tanglewood Festival Chorus; Boston Symphony Orchestra / Seiji Ozawa.
DG 423 089-2GH (56 minutes: DDD). Texts and translations included. Recorded 1986.   Ⓕ

Fauré's music for Maeterlinck's play *Pelléas et Mélisande* was commissioned by Mrs Patrick Campbell and to the usual four-movement suite Ozawa has added the 'Chanson de Mélisande', superbly sung here by Lorraine Hunt. Ozawa conducts a sensitive, sympathetic account of the score, and Jules Eskin plays beautifully in both the arrangement of the early song, *Après un rêve*, and the *Elégie*, which survived from an abandoned cello sonata. The grave *Pavane* is performed here in the choral version of 1901. *Dolly* began life as a piano duet, but was later orchestrated by the composer and conductor Henri Rabaud. Ozawa gives a pleasing account of this delightful score and the recording is excellent.

Masques et bergamasques, Op. 112. Ballade, Op. 19. Pavane, Op. 50. Fantaisie, Op. 79. Pénélope – Overture. Elégie, Op. 24. Dolly Suite (orch. Rabaud).
Richard Davis *fl* **Peter Dixon** *vc* **Kathryn Stott** *pf*
BBC Philharmonic Orchestra / Yan Pascal Tortelier.
Chandos CHAN9416 (72 minutes: DDD). Recorded 1995.   Ⓕ

The biggest *concertante* work here, the *Ballade* of 1881, is Fauré's orchestration of his piano piece of the same name; it is gentle music that persuades and cajoles in a very Gallic way. Though not an overtly virtuoso utterance, it makes its own exacting technical demands on the soloist, among them being complete control of touch and pedalling. The highly-regarded Fauréan Kathryn Stott meets these with consistent success. *Masques et bergamasques*, which takes its title from Verlaine's sad, mysterious poem *Clair de lune*, is a late stage work that the composer himself described as melancholy and nostalgic, but it is hardly romantic, being instead pointedly neo-classical in character and shape, recalling Bizet's youthful C major Symphony and Grieg's *Holberg Suite*. The playing here under Yan Pascal Tortelier is very satisfying, as are the elegant flute solos of the exquisitely delicate *Pavane*, performed here without the optional chorus, and in *Dolly*. The rarely heard Overture to the opera *Pénélope* is also effectively presented here. There's little rhetoric and no bombast in Fauré's art, but how civilized he was, and what sympathetic interpreters serve him here! The recording is warm yet delicate.

Fauré Ballade, Op. 19.
Franck Symphonic Variations, Op. 46.
d'Indy Symphonie sur un chant montagnard français in G major, Op. 25.
François-Joël Thiollier *pf*
National Symphony Orchestra of Ireland / Antonio de Almeida.
Naxos 8 550754 (55 minutes: DDD). Recorded 1993.   ⑤ **E**

The renamed RTE Symphony Orchestra, a match for its more recorded counterpart in Ulster, taped this programme in their Dublin concert hall (acoustically clean, bright and airy, but warm, if this disc's sound is representative). François-Joël Thiollier's playing is individual, often impulsive but always idiomatic, helped by the sensitive, guiding hand of a conductor obviously well acquainted with the music. A more high-profile production would probably have retaken those passages where piano and orchestra co-ordination is occasionally fractionally awry, such as in the last variation of the Franck, but it might also have seemed less spontaneous. Thiollier's rubato is always distinctive and attractive; the style, particularly and crucially in the Fauré, properly fluid. Both the piano and the orchestra's woodwind are discreetly prominent, but internal balances are generally excellent. There are no budget-price competitors in this repertoire that reproduce with such beauty of tone.

Piano Quintets – No. 1 in D minor, Op. 89; No. 2 in C minor, Op. 115.
Domus (Krysia Osostowicz *vn* Timothy Boulton *va* Richard Lester *vc* Susan Tomes *pf*);
Anthony Marwood *vn*
Hyperion CDA66766 (60 minutes: DDD). Recorded 1994. *Gramophone* Award Winner 1995.   ⑤

This is not music that yields up its secrets easily. Indeed, despite pages pulsing with all of Fauré's sustained radiance and energy the abiding impression is of music of such profound introspection that the listener often feels like an interloper stumbling into an essentially private conversation. But perseverance reaps the richest rewards and moments like the opening of the D minor Quintet where Fauré achieves what is referred to in the insert-notes as a 'rapt weightlessness', or the closing pages of the C minor Quintet's *Andante moderato* send out resonances that finally embrace the entire work. The other-worldly dance commencing the finale of the First Quintet, the wild catch-as-catch-can opening and elfin close of the C minor Quintet's *Allegro vivo* or the grave serenity of the following *Andante moderato*; all these are surely at the heart of Fauré's simultaneously conservative and radical genius. Simply as a person Fauré remained conscious of an elusiveness that baffled and tantalized even his closest friends, companions who felt themselves gently but firmly excluded from his complex interior world. Domus fully suggests this enigma yet plays with such ardour and *élan* that the composer himself would surely have been delighted ('people play me as if the blinds were down'). The recordings are superb.

Piano Quartets – No. 1 in C minor, Op. 15; No. 2 in G minor, Op. 45.
Domus (Krysia Osostowicz *vn* Robin Ireland *va* Timothy Hugh *vc* Susan Tomes *pf*).
Hyperion CDA66166 (62 minutes: DDD). *Gramophone* Award Winner 1986.   ⑤

The First Piano Quartet reveals Fauré's debt to an earlier generation of composers, particularly Mendelssohn. Yet already it has the refined sensuality, the elegance and the craftsmanship which were always to be hallmarks of his style and it is a thoroughly assured, highly enjoyable work which could come from no other composer's pen. The Second Quartet is a more complex, darker work, but much less ready to yield its secrets. The comparatively agitated, quicksilver *Scherzo* impresses at once, however, and repeated hearings of the complete work reveal it to possess considerable poetry and stature. Just occasionally one could wish that the members of Domus had a slightly more aristocratic, commanding approach to these scores, but overall the achievement is highly impressive, for their playing is both idiomatic and technically impeccable. The recording has an appropriately intimate feel to it and is faithful and well balanced.

Romance in A major, Op. 69. Elégie, Op. 24. Cello Sonatas – No. 1 in D minor, Op. 109; No. 2 in G minor, Op. 117. Allegretto moderato[a]. Sérénade, Op. 98. Sicilienne, Op. 78. Papillon, Op. 77. Andante.
Steven Isserlis, [a]**David Waterman** *vcs* **Pascal Devoyon** *pf* **Francis Grier** *org*
RCA Victor Red Seal 09026 68049-2 (62 minutes: DDD). Recorded 1993-94.   ⑤

This, surely, is the most 'complete' of Fauré's complete works for cello yet to appear. Isserlis has unearthed the original version of the *Romance*, Op. 69 (entitled *Andante*), with a sustained, chordal accompaniment for organ in place of the piano's broken chordal semiquavers, and a gracious flourish from the cello itself by way of adieu. Mystically accompanied by Francis Grier at the organ of Eton College Chapel, the cello's song, restored to the church, seems to acquire more depth. But let it be said at once that in the familiar version of this work, as throughout the disc, Pascal Devoyon is a partner in a thousand, keenly aware of Isserlis's respect for the 'discretion, reticence and restraint' once hailed as the hallmarks of Fauré's style. In fact only in the noble *Elégie* do we discover the full breadth and richness of this cello's (a 1745 Guadagnini) tonal range.

A world war, plus the private trauma of incipient deafness, helps to explain the yawning gulf between the miniatures and the two sonatas of 1918 and 1922. Skipping through the score of the First you notice that only once does Fauré use a dynamic marking above a *forte*, relying on the word *espressivo* to elicit just that little extra intensity at moments of climax. This is appreciated by both artists, most movingly in the central *Andante*. In the first movement, however, it is Devoyon's piquant accentuation that brings home the music's menace. The urgency and *Elégie*-evoking heart-throb of the G minor work again benefit from the immediacy of keyboard characterization, and the variety of keyboard colour, underpinning this poetically introspective cellist's fine-spun line.

Violin Sonatas – No. 1 in A major, Op. 13; No. 2 in E minor, Op. 108.

Fauré Violin Sonatas Nos. 1 and 2.
Franck Violin Sonata in A major[a].
Arthur Grumiaux *vn* **Paul Crossley**, [a]**György Sebok** *pfs*
Philips Musica da Camera 426 384-2PC (73 minutes: ADD). Recorded 1979. Ⓜ 🆁🆁

Those Fauré-lovers who long prayed for a CD reissue of the two sonatas from Grumiaux and Paul Crossley won't be disappointed. The sound itself is pleasing – better, even, than it was on LP. And there is a radiance in the playing suggesting an unerring understanding of structure and style that somehow goes hand in hand with the joyous spontaneity of new discovery. The hyper-sensitive suppleness of Grumiaux's shading and phrasing is a particular delight, as is his awareness that just as much of the musical message comes from the piano – particularly in the Second Sonata. As for Crossley, not for nothing has he come to be recognized as one of this country's most dedicated Fauré specialists. It would certainly be difficult to over-praise the subtlety of the two artists' interplay in both works. Incidentally, their immediacy of response often finds outlet in a slightly faster tempo than most of their rivals, not least in both slow movements, where they rise more urgently to moments of heightened excitement (perhaps even too urgently in the *Andante* of the Second Sonata). Despite the slightly plummier-sounding reproduction of György Sebok's piano, there is also much pleasure to be found in the open-hearted warmth brought by both artists to the Franck Sonata, where you have the impression that Grumiaux himself might have put aside a silken Strad in favour of a throatier Guarnerius.

Violin Sonatas Nos. 1 and 2. Morceau de concours. Andante in B flat major, Op. 75. Romance in B flat major, Op. 28. Berceuse, Op. 16.
Pierre Amoyal *vn* **Pascal Rogé** *pf*
Decca 436 866-2DH (65 minutes: DDD). Recorded 1992. Ⓕ 🅴

These radiant early and late masterpieces are unforgettable reflections of Fauré's first romantic ardour and his subsequent, deeply courageous journey through the most remote and interior regions of both soul and mind. Amoyal and Rogé are superbly challenging and authentic at every level. The opening *Allegro molto* from the First Sonata becomes a tumultuous rush of events, a committed alternative to more 'classical' or staid readings, while the *Andante* is kept firmly on the move. Yet how stellar is Rogé's way with the *a tempo* and *dolcissimo* at 2'36", and what an Elysium both players find as the music sinks to its final resting place. The *Allegro vivo*, on the other hand, could hardly be more nimble, a true catch-as-catch-can with a delightful relishing of Fauré's constantly shifting and mischievously altered phrase lengths. Again, in the Second Sonata, both violinist and pianist play with rare individuality and unanimity, Amoyal's sweet and slightly nasal tone complemented by Rogé's greater fullness. Their *Andante* is, again, coolly paced but elsewhere there is a powerful recognition of Fauré's strength and delicacy and the way his ceaseless flow of ideas is so often tinged with irony and unease. For their encores Amoyal and Rogé give us three miniatures in which salon clichés are effortlessly and, indeed, magically transformed. Even the *Berceuse*'s passing resemblance to the *Eton Boating Song* seems sublime rather than unfortunate. The recordings are excellent and the entire recital should do much to erase notions (sadly, still current) of Fauré as a poor country cousin of Ravel and Debussy.

Five Impromptus. Impromptu, Op. 86. Thème et Variations in C sharp minor, Op. 73. Romances sans paroles, Op. 17. Quatre valses-caprices. 13 Barcarolles. Ballade in F sharp major, Op. 19. 13 Nocturnes. Souvenirs de Bayreuth[a]. Pièces brèves, Op. 84. Dolly, Op. 56[a]. Nine Préludes, Op. 103. Mazurka in B flat major, Op. 32.
Kathryn Stott, [a]Martin Roscoe *pfs*
Hyperion CDA66911/4 (four discs: 297 minutes: DDD). Recorded 1994.　　　Ⓜ🄴

Fauré's piano works are among the most subtly daunting in all keyboard literature. Contradicting his diffidence ('it seems that I repeat myself constantly'), they possess, on the contrary, an astonishing scope. Encompassing Fauré's entire creative life, they range through an early, finely wrought eroticism via sporting with an aerial virtuosity as teasing and light as the elements themselves (the *Valses-caprices*) to the final desolation of Fauré's last years. There, in his most powerful works (*Barcarolles* Nos. 7-11, *Nocturnes* Nos. 11-13), he faithfully mirrors a pain that 'scintillates in full consciousness', a romantic agony prompted by increasing deafness and a lack of recognition that often seemed close to oblivion. Few compositions have reflected a darker night of the soul, and Fauré's anguish, expressed in both numbing resignation and unbridled anger, could surely only be exorcized by the articulation of such profound and disturbing emotional complexity. The task for the pianist, then, is immense, but in Kathryn Stott Fauré has a subtle and fearless champion.

How thrilled Fauré would have been by the sheer immediacy of Stott's responses. Time and again she throws convention to the winds, and although it would be surprising if all her performances were consistent successes, disappointments are rare. Sometimes her rubato and luxuriant pedalling soften the outlines of Fauré's starkest, most austere utterances. The Twelfth and Thirteenth *Nocturnes*, for example, are surely too loosely controlled to achieve their fullest drama and focus. But such quibbles remain quibbles. How Stott relishes a modern Steinway's opulent transformation of the harp's thin and glittering textures in the Sixth *Impromptu*, and the *Mazurka* has rarely been spun off with such a truly virtuoso insouciance. The Fourth *Nocturne* is gloriously supple, and the 13 *Barcarolles* show Stott acutely responsive to passion and finesse alike. The *Pièces brèves*, too, are played with rare affection. A true and dedicated Francophile (though with an exceptionally wide repertoire), Stott is among the more stylish and intriguing of the younger generation of pianists. For *Souvenirs de Bayreuth* and *Dolly* she is robustly partnered by Martin Roscoe.

L'absent, Op. 5 No. 3. Après un rêve, Op. 7 No. 1. Au cimetière, Op. 51 No. 2. Les berceaux, Op. 23 No. 1. Cantique de Jean Racine, Op. 11. La chanson du pêcheur, Op. 4 No. 1. Les Djinns, Op. 12. Madrigal, Op. 35. La naissance de Vénus, Op. 29. Pavane, Op. 50. Pleurs d'or, Op. 72. Puisqu'ici-bas, Op. 10 No. 1. Le ruisseau, Op. 22. Le secret, Op. 23 No. 3. Sérénade toscane, Op. 3 No. 2. Tarentelle, Op. 10 No. 2.
Isabelle Eschenbrenner, Brigitte Lafon, Sylvie Pons *sops* **Anna Holroyd** *contr*
Adrian Brand, Bruno Ranc *tens* **Jacques Bona** *bass* **Bo Yuan** *db* **Jean-Claude Pennetier** *pf*
Louis Robilliard *org* **Ravel Quartet** (Giovanni Battista Fabris, Reiko Kitahama *vns*
Zoltán Tóth *va* Jean-Michel Fonteneau *vc*);
Solistes de Lyon-Bernard Tétu / Bernard Tétu.
EMI CDC5 56728-2 (74 minutes: DDD). Texts and translations included. Recorded 1998.　　Ⓕ

La naissance de Vénus, the 'scène mythologique' that gives this CD its title, was composed by Fauré for an amateur choral society. The piece is in one movement lasting nearly 23 minutes, including parts for soprano, alto, tenor and bass soloists. The opening immediately reminds you of Fauré's piano writing at its finest, a beautiful slow melody that acts as a prelude to the first choral section. In this the scene is set with a glowing dawn which seems to onlookers to herald some divine occurrence. Another piano interlude, in a barcarolle rhythm, precedes the appearance of Venus from the waves. The bass announces that Jupiter himself is there to greet his daughter. It's a surprise to find Jupiter cast as a tenor – perhaps the original group dictated who should be assigned which role. Jupiter's catalogue of all the delights Venus will bestow on the world forms the centre of the cantata. The choir re-enter to cry 'Salut à toi' – they are on 'tu-toi' terms with the goddess immediately. She answers with a soaring phrase over the chorus, assuring them that 'the sad life of the most humble being can become the most enviable'. This is a real discovery and Bernard Tétu and his chorus with Jean-Claude Pennetier at the piano give a reading which suggests all the lost charm of private small-scale choral singing that belongs to the world of the late nineteenth-century Paris salons. Bruno Ranc, who is Jupiter, also sings four of Fauré's best-known *mélodies* in the ensuing recital. There are many more sophisticated performances on disc of *Après un rêve* and *Au cimetière* but there is a freshness and simplicity about this whole CD, juxtaposing choral items (including *Les Djinns*, a Victor Hugo poem evoking a nightmare of howling and wailing) with duets and solo numbers. *La naissance de Vénus*, which has never before been recorded, is a must for Fauré collectors, and others will find this a charming, gentle and haunting disc.

Le papillon et la fleur, Op. 1 No. 1. Op. 3 – No. 1, Seule!; No. 2, Sérénade toscane. L'absent, Op. 5 No. 3. Op. 8 – No. 1, Au bord de l'eau; No. 3, Ici-bas. Op. 10 – No. 1, Puisqu'ici-bas; No. 2, Tarentelle. La fée aux chansons, Op. 27 No. 2. Op. 39 – No. 2, Fleur jetée; No. 3, Le pays des rêves; No. 4, Les roses d'Ispahan. Nocturne, Op. 43 No. 2. Clair de lune, Op. 46 No. 2. Op. 51 – No. 1, Larmes; No. 2, Au cimetière. Arpège, Op. 76 No. 2. Accompagnement, Op. 85 No. 3. Le plus doux chemin, Op. 87 No. 1. Le don silencieux, Op. 92. Chanson, Op. 94. C'est la paix!, Op. 114. Vocalise-étude. Pelléas et Mélisande – Chanson de Mélisande.
Sarah Walker *mez* **Malcolm Martineau** *pf*
CRD CRD3477 (68 minutes: DDD). Texts and translations included. Recorded 1991.   Ⓕ

Starting with an early song, and a charmer, *Le papillon et la fleur* has the young Fauré with (so it seems) a head full of Schubert, as the piano enters with a ripple of *Die Forelle* and waltzes away into something more like *Seligkeit*. Here, that rather crusty quality in Sarah Walker's louder tones is something of a liability. Still, if this is the initial reaction it is not one that prevails for long. It is hard to imagine the *Nocturne* and *Au bord de l'eau* more beautifully sung, the first entering a very private world, the second catching perfectly the relaxed, reflective mood, and both benefiting from the softened, warmed tone of the singer and her excellent accompanist. The programme follows no chronological order. This has the advantage that the best-known songs can be distributed fairly evenly, with *Clair de lune*, *Les roses d'Ispahan* and *Aurore* mingled here with some from the 1870s and others that extend into the twentieth century. These include the frank emotion of the postwar *C'est la paix!* and *Le don silencieux* which Sarah Walker sings so affectionately to the haunting accompaniment of those wistfully unfulfilled harmonies. Most haunting of all, perhaps, is Mélisande's song, in English, written for Mrs Patrick Campbell in 1889.

Requiem, Op. 48.

Requiem[a]. Pavane, Op. 50.
[a]**Robert Chilcott** *treb* [a]**John Carol Case** *bar* ·
[a]**King's College Choir Cambridge; New Philharmonia Orchestra / Sir David Willcocks.**
EMI CDM7 64715-2 (42 minutes: ADD). Text and translation included. Recorded 1967.   Ⓜ🅁🅁

This is the Fauré Requiem to come home to. It is tempting to describe it as a recording as near as can be to absolute perfection from start to finish. It has still not been overtaken on its own ground. The textual dimension of course is new since then, and if an earlier version of the score is wanted, the smaller orchestra being in some ways preferable, then the recording by the Cambridge Singers under the text's editor, John Rutter, might be tried instead. But for what we used to mean by the Fauré Requiem in days when ignorance (of textual complications) was bliss, then this is still the best. Willcocks neither sentimentalizes nor hurries; the choir (especially in respect of its tenors) is on top form; Robert Chilcott sings the *Pie Jesu* with the most touchingly beautiful purity and control, and John Carol Case brings to his solos a style that exactly matches that of the famous choir. If anything, time has enhanced appreciation, for the recorded sound compares so favourably, giving due prominence to the choir and obtaining an immediacy of sound that these days is exceptional. The only matter for regret is that the *Pavane* was not performed in its choral version, but as it is such an exquisite composition in either form the regret is short-lived.

Requiem (original version – ed. Rutter). Motets – Ave verum corpus; Tantum ergo; Ave Maria; Maria, Mater gratiae. Cantique de Jean Racine, Op. 11 (orch. Rutter). Messe basse.
Caroline Ashton, Ruth Holton *sops* **Stephen Varcoe** *bar* **Simon Standage** *vn* **John Scott** *org*
Cambridge Singers; City of London Sinfonia / John Rutter.
Collegium COLCD109 (63 minutes: ADD/DDD). Texts and translations included. Recorded 1984.
Gramophone Award Winner 1985.   Ⓕ

Fauré began his Requiem in 1885, under the impact of the death of his father, but the work did not take on the form in which we now know it until 15 years later. The familiar 1900 score, therefore, cannot really be regarded as 'definitive'; it is a compromise, rather, between Fauré's original conception and what his publisher no doubt saw as the practicalities of concert performance. It is Fauré uncompromised that John Rutter has sought to restore in his edition of the seven-movement 1892 version, and his performance of it, using a chamber orchestra, a small choir and, in the 'Pie Jesu', a soprano who could easily be mistaken for a treble (Fauré's own early performances used a boy soloist) is a most convincing argument for accepting this score as more 'authentic' than the customary 1900 version.The differences are audibly obvious, and most are no less obviously improvements. The almost omnipresent organ (John Scott's registrations are beautifully clean and transparent) now sounds more like a continuo instrument than (as can easily happen with the 1900 score) an unwelcome thickening of an already dark orchestra. Above all, one is more aware than in any other recording that the sound in Fauré's head when he conceived the work was not that of a conventional orchestra but the rich, dark graininess of divided violas and cellos, the radiant luminosity of the work provided not by violins or woodwind but by the voices. It is thus more unified than the later revision as well as being more intimate. Rutter's chorus is a fine one, immaculate of diction and pure of line; Stephen Varcoe's light and unforced baritone could well be just what Fauré had in mind and Caroline Ashton's absolute purity in her brief solo is most moving. The recording is excellent. The *Messe basse* and four motets were added to this reissue to make quite a generous CD coupling. If you listen to these in sequence (including his blandly dozy account of the *Cantique*) you may well find it a slow and sweetly sad *diminuendo* from the Requiem: more of the same but not quite so good.

Fauré Requiem[a]. Messe basse[b]. Cantique de Jean Racine[b].
Vierne Pièces de fantaisie. Suite No. 1, Op. 51 – Andantino[c].
Séverac Tantum ergo[d].
[a]Lisa Beckley *sop* [a]Nicholas Gedge *bass-bass* [abd]Oxford Schola Cantorum;
[a]Oxford Camerata / Jeremy Summerly with [abc]Colm Carey *org*
Naxos 8 550765 (60 minutes: DDD). Texts and translations included. Recorded 1993.   Ⓢ

One could say at once that this is a highly competitive recording of the Fauré Requiem but in fact it stands on its own because of the version it presents and the edition it uses. Most of the available recordings are of the final 1900 version. This one is of an edition by Denis Arnold (1983) based on the original version but incorporating the two additional movements. On first impulse, the word arising is 'austere'. Certainly the flashes of gold and scarlet made by the few but highly effective brass entries in the familiar versions are missed; the harp is notably absent from the *Sanctus*, and that wispy, high solo violin (1894) is now a less other-worldly presence at normal on-the-stave pitch. The instrumental colours are dark*ish*, yet not sombre, and are lightened by the sunlight stippling of the organ in the *In Paradisum*. With the voices added, the effect is of a subtler beauty, still more distinctively itself than even the 1894 score. The performance of the Requiem and the *Messe basse* is admirable, with excellent playing by Jeremy Summerly's Oxford Camerata, and fresh-voiced, sensitively attuned choral singing from Oxford Schola Cantorum. Authenticity extends now to French pronunciation of the Latin ('luceat eis' very French indeed). The rather flaccid organ solo by Vierne, written as a sight-reading exercise for his pupils, is finely played by Colm Carey. The *Tantum ergo* by Séverac is a haunting, carol-like little piece, beautifully sung, and Fauré's *Cantique de Jean Racine* makes a perfect conclusion.

Robert Fayrfax

British 1464-1521

Magnificat, 'O Bone Ihesu'. Missa, O Bone Ihesu. Salve regina. Most clere of colour.
I love, loved and loved wolde I be. Benedicite! What dreamed I? (all ed. Skinner).
The Cardinall's Musick / Andrew Carwood.
ASV Gaudeamus CDGAU184 (76 minutes: DDD). Texts and translations included.
Recorded 1996.   Ⓕ Ⓔ

The Cardinall's Musick put the focus here around Fayrfax's Mass *O bone Ihesu*. Tragically, only a single voice survives of the antiphon that was probably its model, so in that respect their recording cannot be complete, unless David Skinner is prepared to indulge in the massive and quixotic task of reconstruction for this and other fragmentary survivals. But fascinatingly we do have a glorious *Magnificat* built on the same materials, one of the most widely distributed of all early Tudor works. By far the most commanding performance here is of that *Magnificat*: wonderfully controlled and perfectly tuned. The group is slightly rougher in the Mass and in the *Salve regina* – a work that, as David Skinner's useful note points out, stands rather apart from the style we otherwise know from Fayrfax and which may be one of his earliest surviving works. Intriguingly, this is the piece that seems to show the strongest debts to composers from the continental mainland (especially Brumel), giving important insights into the evolution of his music. Similarly, the three songs presented here, in performances that are skilled but slightly wooden, show a remarkable affinity with other mainland music, particularly that of Alexander Agricola. These little three-voice works, with their beautifully evocative texts, are among the glories of early Tudor music.

Fayrfax (ed. Skinner) Missa O quam Glorifica. Ave Dei patris filia. Somewhat musing. To complayne me, alas.
Anonymous That was my joy. Sarum Chant: Kyrie Orbis factor; O quam Glori fica.
The Cardinall's Musick / Andrew Carwood.
ASV Gaudeamus CDGAU142 (74 minutes: DDD). Texts and translations included.   Ⓕ Ⓟ
Recorded 1994. *Gramophone* Award Winner 1995.

The centrepiece here is the Mass *O quam Glorifica*, a setting composed by Fayrfax for the taking of his doctorate in music from Cambridge University in 1504. He would also have been expected to write an antiphon for the occasion, but this does not appear to have survived. There is always something intriguing about an occasional piece; given that it was composed for a particular event, there is always that possibility of being able to reconstruct the forces used and, from contemporary descriptions and such like, something of the ambience of the original occasion. In this case, as David Skinner points out in the insert-notes, Fayrfax would have been expected to display his technical prowess as a composer, and it is likely that in its original version the *Missa O quam Glorifica* presented an intellectual challenge to the singers through the use of the most complicated notational devices. But this setting is much more than an academic exercise. To the ear it is a rich, sonorous piece of contrapuntal writing, with hints of rhythmic complexities that generate an exciting sense of momentum.

The Cardinall's Musick give a committed and polished performance of the Mass. They produce a well-nourished and sustained sound which adds a ceremonial touch to the performance, and yet the rhythmic intricacies are always clearly and tautly projected. All in all, this is a substantial piece, and a very welcome addition to the catalogue. The antiphon *Ave Dei patris filia* might well have been sung in the recording venue: the Fitzalan Chapel in Arundel Castle in West Sussex – although it was also very widely disseminated, the text being popular among English sixteenth-century composers. It certainly is a more reflective work which exploits the contrast between chordal and contrapuntal textures in a more continental way. The Cardinall's Musick's performance takes account of the more contemplative style. Finally, the secular songs – *Somewhat musing* and *To complayne me, alas* – emphasize Fayrfax's versatility as a composer; here the chapel acoustic is less appropriate and these are perhaps the least successful items on the disc.

Philip Feeney
British 1954

The Hunchback of Notre Dame.
Miranda Bevin *sop*
Opera North Chorus; Northern Ballet Theatre Orchestra / John Pryce-Jones.
Black Box BBP1009 (74 minutes: DDD). Recorded 1998.   Ⓕ

This recording gives us extended passages from Feeney's ballet score, a setting of Victor Hugo's *The Hunchback of Notre Dame*. It's a suitably raw-boned score, full of bold, dramatic splashes of colour to evoke the stark grandeur of Paris's great cathedral and the human tragedy taking place around and above it. The choral finale to Act 2 is especially powerful, notable for the boldness of its invention. The music is closely geared to the action, but the commendably detailed, well-cued synopsis helps the listener get the best out of the work. It is a generous, superbly executed souvenir for those with the good fortune to experience the ballet in the theatre.

Morton Feldman
American 1926-1987

Coptic Light. Cello and Orchestra. Piano and Orchestra.
Robert Cohen *vc* **Alan Feinberg** *pf*
New World Symphony Orchestra / Michael Tilson Thomas.
Argo 448 513-2ZH (74 minutes: DDD). Recorded 1995.   Ⓕ

Tilson Thomas has been quoted as saying he thought Feldman's music was still greatly underestimated given it was so beautiful and important. *Piano and Orchestra* (1975) is a single contemplative span, a kind of anti-concerto, with just one brief aggressive outburst somewhat anticipated by menacing *crescendos* to which the piano remains impervious. It is all poetically done – with luscious orchestral sound too. *Cello and Orchestra* (1972) uncannily anticipates Tavener's hit *The Protecting Veil* with its high sustained writing for the cello. A not dissimilar spiritual atmosphere pervades the work and we are reminded that Feldman at this time said he regarded his music as elegiac, symbolizing a state of mourning – for the Holocaust, civilization or Western culture. The continuity is beautifully imagined with cello melisma periodically obliterated by gentle clusters. There is a loud brass chord at 9'38" and the ending settles down to oscillations between two chords and finally single notes. *Coptic Light* (1986), a New York Philharmonic commission written in Feldman's last year, owes its title to his fascination with the patterning of oriental carpets. Listening, you can imagine this multicoloured source and so this late piece is more static: the patterns barely vary for long stretches. With these scrupulous, well-recorded performances Tilson Thomas helps to ensure that Feldman is no longer underestimated.

Feldman Palais de Mari.
Wuorinen Piano Sonata No. 3. Bagatelle. Capriccio.
Alan Feinberg pf
Koch International Classics 37308-2 (65 minutes: DDD). Recorded 1994. (F)

Alan Feinberg is an exemplary type of late-twentieth-century, usually American, pianist who can swing the best *Kitten on the Keys* in the business. The Wuorinen works, all from the 1980s, are in the tough New York dialect of the post-Webern school but, with playing like this from Alan Feinberg, and so vividly recorded, they provide some scintillating listening. Whatever the music, Feinberg brings his own kind of commitment and panache to bear – a winning combination. You can imagine his fans wanting to buy anything he records because of this powerful impact. The often cataclysmic Sonata No. 3 was written for Feinberg but the *Bagatelle*, if you can imagine anything by Wuorinen being a mere bagatelle, at least starts in poetic mode, quietly. So does the *Capriccio*, which starts with a Brahmsian expressiveness, albeit via Schoenberg: by the end the piano sounds under attack.

The very late Feldman piece is a bonus, a relentlessly quiet oasis thrown into sharp relief in such a welter of hyperactivity. *Palais de Mari* was commissioned by Bunita Marcus, but it is only a third the length of *For Bunita Marcus* written in the previous year. Feinberg's performance of *Palais* has every detail of the score in place and he brings his unique qualities to this mesmerizingly rapt meditation, where events take the form of the occasional dry chord in a liquid landscape. This disc comes strongly recommended to Feldman enthusiasts.

Zdenék Fibich

Bohemian 1850-1900

Piano Quartet in E minor, Op. 11. Piano Quintet in D major, Op. 42.
Ensemble Villa Musica (Ulf Rodenhäuser *cl* Radovan Vlatkovič *hn* Ida Bieler *vn*
Enrique Santiago *va* Martin Ostertag *vc* Kalle Randalu *pf*)
Dabringhaus und Grimm MDG304 0775-2 (69 minutes: DDD). Recorded 1997. (F)

Fibich's chamber music is not usually rated as highly by his compatriots as are his operas or orchestral music. As far as the Piano Quartet is concerned, this may well be to do with the fact that he had not then, in 1874 at the age of 23, grown away from the German training he received at the Leipzig Conservatoire. Yet the piece is well worth hearing. It has the melodic richness that characterizes him, together with a skill in presenting his ideas that may owe much to Brahms and Schumann, in particular, but that has a warmth and fluency all his own. However, the Quintet is the more original work. Fibich makes this sound so easy and natural as to awake surprise that it has not been more often attempted; but clearly the choice of contrasted and blending wind and string sonorities around the keyboard, and the manner in which the music is conceived, has a particular relevance. It is a very attractive work, sympathetically played here, without affectation but with much devotion, and the recording makes the most of the timbres.

Moods, Impressions and Reminiscences, Op. 41 – 40 excerpts.
William Howard pf
Chandos CHAN9381 (71 minutes: DDD). Recorded 1993. (F)

Fibich's Op. 41 is the sequence of short piano pieces, most of them lasting somewhere between two and three minutes, written in response to his love for Anežka. In all, 376 survive, and an unknown number more of them are thought to have been lost or destroyed, while some were absorbed into other works, including operas, from which clues can be found to their original association. Though a good many of the pieces are either mysteriously titled or left without allusion, they chart, in music of warmth, charm and emotional delight, his deep love for a woman who gave him a movingly complete emotional, physical and intellectual devotion. The moods include not only delight but jealousy and regret at having caused her pain; the impressions often have highly erotic associations; the reminiscences refer to shared experiences through which their lives grew and deepened. However, it is as a loose suite of short, impressionistic pieces that such a programme is best heard, Schumannesque in nature and sometimes in manner.

William Howard plays them with a careful attention to detail, to the deft manner in which a memorable idea can be created in only a page, and with affectionate phrasing of their warm melodies. Fibich is, here, a romantic miniaturist to set beside Schumann and perhaps even more Tchaikovsky, whose short piano pieces can be as apt in their creation of a mood. Touchingly, the sequence of pieces has unity as well as diversity. Anežka must indeed have been a fascinating woman.

John Field

Piano Concertos – No. 1 in E flat major, H27; No. 3 in E flat major, H32.
Benjamin Frith *pf*
Northern Sinfonia / David Haslam.
Naxos 8 553770 (52 minutes: DDD). Recorded 1996.   Ⓢ

Benjamin Frith presents a very formidable challenge to rival versions, at super-budget price. Both works are played with effortless fluency, plus all the immediacy and freshness of new discovery. In No. 1 Frith is acutely responsive to the delicate charm of the Scottish-inspired (*'Twas within a mile of Edinboro' Town*) slow movement. He makes one aware of Field's teasing delight in the unexpected in the smiling outer movements, to which he brings a wide range of tone, and piquant accentuation in the last. There is warm, sympathetic support from the Northern Sinfonia under David Haslam. The performers revel in the composer's surprises of modulation, rhythm and orchestral colouring, while from the soloist there is not a trace of the perfunctory in passagework. The recording (in a resonant venue) might be thought overforward and full, but it remains a true bargain.

Nocturnes – No. 1 in E flat major, H24; No. 2 in C minor, H25; No. 3 in A flat major, H26; No. 4 in A major, H36; No. 5 in B flat major, H37; No. 6 in F major, H40; No. 7 in C major, H45; No. 8 in A major, H14E; No. 9 in E flat major, H30; No. 10 in E minor, H46B; No. 11 in E flat major, H56A; No. 12 in G major, H58D; No. 13 in D minor, H59; No. 14 in C major; No. 15 in C major, H61; No. 16 in F major, H62A.

Nocturnes Nos. 1-15.
Roberto Mamou *pf*
Pavane ADW7110 (64 minutes: DDD).   Ⓕ

Nocturnes Nos. 1-16.
Joanna Leach *fp*
Athene ATHCD1 (76 minutes: DDD). Recorded 1990-91.   Ⓕ 🅿

The Tunisian-born pianist Roberto Mamou achieves an often exemplary middle course between drama and understatement and he stresses Field's closeness to, rather than his remoteness from, Chopin. The recordings are satisfactory and this is an appealing issue. Joanna Leach performs on square pianos by Stodart, Broadwood and Thomas D'Almaine dating from 1823 to 1835 and, most persuasively, suggests an intimacy and transparency hard to parallel on more modern, brilliant and forceful instruments. The ear is quickly attuned to the sound, to the radically different pedalling Leach refers to in her excellent notes, and to a cloudy but appropriate and often hypnotic resonance. Melody and accompaniment (at the very heart of this music) are more closely entwined than on today's instruments, offering a greater sense of Field's harmonic subtlety. There are some extraneous noises, inseparable from period instruments, but so far from distracting attention they somehow add to the potent atmosphere of these performances. A fascinating pair of issues.

Michael Finnissy

Traum des Sängers. WAM. Enek. Mars + Venus.
Charles Mutter *vn* **Ixion / Michael Finnissy.**
NMC NMCD043 (54 minutes: DDD). Recorded 1996.   Ⓕ

These are works for ensemble that Michael Finnissy has written since 1990. He continues to plunder Eastern European music for its gestural and intervallic vocabulary. Even so, only the wistful *Enek* for solo violin adopts it as an explicit foreground feature and, interestingly enough, this is the oldest piece on the CD. The other three pieces take their inspiration instead from the Western European cultural mainstream. The titles of *Traum des Sängers* and *Mars + Venus* are drawn from paintings by Caspar David Friedrich and Rubens, while the gleeful *WAM* seizes upon fragments from Mozart's early symphonies, piano concertos and *divertimentos*, with subversive intent. The Mozart fragments are scattered liberally between three totally unsynchronized parts for piano, flute and clarinet. The NMC recording manages wonderfully well to dramatize the successive departures of the flautist and clarinettist off-stage without compromising the overall balance of the ensemble. The idea of separate musical elements co-existing alongside each other is explored in *Traum des Sängers*, too, but in a less explosive way. Lines from two ensembles gradually meld together to create a dream-like atmosphere in which the foreground focus of attention is always left open to question, only for this reverie to be broken at the end by a number of pauses. The most haunting music, however, is to be heard in *Enek* and in the title-piece, *Mars + Venus*, which concludes the CD.

Both pieces feature extended string solos. Charles Mutter gives a truly authoritative performance of *Enek*, bringing considerable lyrical feeling to the work; and Bridget Carey plays her long obbligato viola solo in *Mars + Venus* with harrowing intensity against the shell-shocked, sustained backdrop of the rest of the ensemble. Indeed, all the performances here from Ixion could be said to be definitive. This CD is the best possible introduction to the music of one of Britain's most distinctive compositional talents.

Gerald Finzi

British 1901-1956

Clarinet Concerto in C minor, Op. 31. Five Bagatelles, Op. 23 (orch. Ashmore). Love's Labour's Lost – Soliloquies Nos. 1-3. A Severn Rhapsody in D minor, Op. 3. Romance in E flat major, Op. 11. Introit in F major, Op. 6.
Robert Plane *cl* **Lesley Hatfield** *vn*
Northern Sinfonia / Howard Griffiths.
Naxos 8 553566 (71 minutes: DDD). Recorded 1995.   Ⓢ Ⓔ

This is a highly accomplished, indeed commanding performance of Finzi's gorgeous Clarinet Concerto from Northern Sinfonia principal, Robert Plane. With his bright, singing tone and effortless technical mastery, there's no shortage of intuitive poetry from Plane in the sublime central *Adagio*. Howard Griffiths's conducting is exemplary. We also get an atmospheric account of Lawrence Ashmore's idiomatic orchestration of the *Five Bagatelles* (with the poignant 'Romance' a highlight), as well as exquisitely drawn renderings of both the *Romance* for strings and 'Three Soliloquies' from Finzi's incidental music for a 1946 BBC production of *Love's Labour's Lost*. The fragrant, very early *Severn Rhapsody* (1923) makes a welcome return to the catalogue under Griffiths's deeply felt advocacy, and Lesley Hatfield makes a touching soloist in the radiant *Introit* (the slow movement of a withdrawn Violin Concerto from 1925-27). The sound and balance are extremely truthful, though the acoustic may be a little over-resonant for some tastes. Really helpful presentation too. All in all, a remarkable bargain.

Finzi Eclogue, Op. 10.
Delius Piano Concerto in C minor.
Vaughan Williams Piano Concerto in C major.
Piers Lane *pf*
Royal Liverpool Philharmonic Orchestra / Vernon Handley.
EMI Eminence CD-EMX2239 (61 minutes: DDD). Recorded 1994.   Ⓜ

Piers Lane brings an exhilarating dash and bravura to Vaughan Williams's craggy concerto and the results are both clean-cut and refreshing. The balance obtained on EMI Eminence does not lack anything in naturalness, and the dynamic range is certainly satisfyingly wide (that brazen orchestral tutti towards the end of the *Fuga chromatica* opens out rivetingly), but the overall effect is perhaps just a little too distant. In the lovely Finzi *Eclogue*, Handley's accompaniment positively glows. In the Delius Concerto, however, Lane's big-hearted gusto and genuine poetic insights prove something of a revelation. A memorable concentration and flexibility inform every bar of the central *Largo*, where Lane effortlessly sustains his measured initial tempo. Handley and the RLPO are exemplary partners in all of this (memorable solo contributions throughout); indeed, Handley's wonderfully clear-sighted conception makes for a glorious sense of home-coming at the close, with the clinching climax unerringly resolved. The piano sound, too, seems marginally more full-blooded than it was in the VW Concerto. All in all, the most rewarding version of Delius's endearing work available.

Love's Labour's Lost – Suite, Op. 28. Clarinet Concerto in C minor, Op. 31. Prelude in F minor, Op. 25. Romance in E flat major, Op. 11.
Alan Hacker *cl*
English String Orchestra / William Boughton.
Nimbus NI5101 (65 minutes: DDD). Recorded 1987.   Ⓕ

There are several other Finzi issues available which include the Clarinet Concerto. Alan Hacker, however, encompasses all his colleagues' virtues, providing special insights and revelling in the brilliant writing. He also adds something extra – an almost mystical realization of the music's poetic vision which is deeply moving. This is in spite of the fact that the string-playing sometimes lacks polish and precision. Finzi wrote incidental music for a BBC production of *Love's Labour's Lost* and expanded it for a later open-air production. It is tuneful, graceful music, but one cannot feel that the stage was Finzi's world. The disc is completed by two interesting early pieces for strings, the *Prelude* and *Romance*, both wholly characteristic of the composer and very well played.

Dies natalis, Op. 8. Intimations of Immortality, Op. 29.
John Mark Ainsley *ten* **Corydon Singers and Orchestra / Matthew Best.**
Hyperion CDA66876 (67 minutes: DDD). Texts included. Recorded 1996.   Ⓕ

What is central, and essential, is the capacity of Finzi's music to grow in the listener's mind over long years, deepening in appeal, strengthening in the conviction of its purpose. Moreover, these performances are marvellously good at clarifying the strengths. Rather more than their predecessors, they clarify structure and texture. The soloist is more distinctly focused in the recording-balance, and this makes an important difference when the poet's words are as vital an element as they are here. Ainsley sings with grace and clarity. The small choir conveys a restrained presence in the *Intimations*; but for much of the time this kind of halo over the sound is appropriate, and in certain important passages the fewer numbers help to compensate with clearer definition. Highly recommended.

All this night, Op. 33. Let us now praise famous men, Op. 35. Lo, the full, final sacrifice, Op. 26. Magnificat, Op. 36. Seven Part-songs, Op. 17. Though did'st delight my eyes, Op. 32. Three Anthems, Op. 27. Three Short Elegies, Op. 5. White-flowering days, Op. 37.
Finzi Singers / Paul Spicer with **Harry Bicket** *org*
Chandos CHAN8936 (79 minutes: DDD). Texts included. Recorded 1990.   Ⓕ

To the listener who seeks music in which the fastidious limitation of its means is itself some guarantee of the depth of its purposes, Finzi will always be rewarding. This is true of all the works collected here. Some, such as the first and last, *God is gone up* and *Lo, the full, final sacrifice*, are relatively well known, though not necessarily the most satisfying. There are some fine shorter pieces including the unaccompanied *Seven Poems of Bridges* and the *Three Drummond Elegies* that delight as word-settings. 'White-flowering days', to words by Edmund Blunden, comes from *A Garland for the Queen*, the Coronation gift of ten composers in 1953, none happier than this in catching the fresh hopefulness of the time. Best of all perhaps is the *Magnificat*, which also had its first British performance in that year. It is heard here in its original version with organ, beautifully played on this disc and providing a more spiritual association than the orchestral accompaniment added later. The Finzi Singers are sensitive, assured and accurate; their tone is uniformly good, and they convey a sense of personal involvement in the music. The sound and presentation are well up to the rest.

César Franck   Belgian/French 1822-1890

Franck Symphony in D minor[a].
Berlioz Béatrice et Bénédict – Overture[b].
d'Indy Symphonie sur un chant montagnard français in G major, Op. 25[c].
[c]**Nicole Henriot-Schweitzer** *pf* [a]**Chicago Symphony Orchestra / Pierre Monteux;**
[bc]**Boston Symphony Orchestra / Charles Munch.**
RCA Victor Papillon GD86805 (72 minutes: ADD). Recorded 1960-64.   Ⓜ ⒽⓇⓇ

Monteux's celebrated 1961 Chicago Franck Symphony must be in the collection of anyone who loves this work. But regardless of that imperative, this is a very enjoyable coupling. Monteux demonstrates that urgency, ardour, even impetuousness, are not at all foreign to Franck's nature, and that Berlioz was one of his ancestors. There is no lack of solemnity or gravity, but the music is kept firmly moving (tempo relationships, especially in the tricky first movement, are very precisely judged) and he sees the chorale in the finale as joyously affirmative, and is not tempted to turn it into an earnest oration. He allows the brass to blare proudly at climaxes and the very clear woodwind detail gives sinew to the orchestral texture throughout. Munch's account of d'Indy's exuberant hike through the Cévennes is invigorating, too, the theme phrased with tender freshness at the outset, the climaxes exultantly brassy and the jovial dance-finale (the bit everyone goes home whistling afterwards) going with a swing. The Berlioz is good as well, not harmed in the slightest by a less than headlong tempo at the outset, and with wonderfully eloquent string playing. The recordings are a bit raw (adding a by no means disagreeable touch of brashness to all three works) but they still sound very well for their age.

Franck Symphony in D minor.
d'Indy Symphonie sur un chant montagnard français.
Jean-Yves Thibaudet *pf*
Montreal Symphony Orchestra / Charles Dutoit.
Decca 430 278-2DH (67 minutes: DDD). Recorded 1989.   Ⓕ

Franck Orchestral

These two French masterpieces of the 1880s complement each other perfectly. The Franck is very much in the Austro-German symphonic tradition. Its language calls to mind the vaulted splendours and gothic interiors of many a Bruckner Symphony. D'Indy's Symphony is in reality more of a piano concerto. Definitely outdoors music this, and far more recognizably French; indeed, with its echoes of Berlioz to its pre-echoes of Debussy and even 'Les Six', it occupies a central position in a century of French music. Dutoit's elegant, flowing way with the Franck (marvellously refined *espressivo* playing from the Montreal violins, and shining, incisive brass) is ideal for those who shy away from the Brucknerian monumentalism of the work; and Jean-Yves Thibaudet's eloquent solo-playing in the d'Indy is matched by exquisitely drawn instrumental solos from within the orchestra. Decca's spacious Montreal sound, too, proves just as apt for the organ-like timbres of the Franck, as for the d'Indy.

Psyché. Le chasseur maudit.
BBC Welsh Chorus; BBC National Orchestra of Wales / Tadaaki Otaka.
Chandos CHAN9342 (65 minutes: DDD). Texts and translations included. Recorded 1994. Ⓕ

The symphonic poem about the Rhenish Count who goes hunting on the Sabbath and is punished for his sacrilege by a curse which condemns him to be pursued for all time by the flames and demons of Hell is worthy of Liszt (Franck's model), and as performed by the Welsh orchestra is vividly programmatic. The breadth of dynamic contrasts is a feature of the recording – as it also is of *Psyché*, the opening of which is almost on the edge of sound. The sensual nature of the music can scarcely be missed, particularly in the section depicting the union of Psyche and Eros (in which the cellos shine) and in the final pardoning of Psyche for disobeying the order not to look at her lover. When, in the first of the choral passages (which are most often omitted from performance), the words run 'Do you not feel a sweet desire unfolding in your agitated breast?', this is surely the emotional cry of the composer himself, who was then violently in love with his pupil Augusta Holmès. Tadaaki Otaka shapes the orchestral playing with tenderness and passion, and the chorus contributes sympathetic tone and clear articulation of the words.

Franck Symphonic Variations, Op. 46[a].
Grieg Piano Concerto in A minor, Op. 16[b].
Schumann Piano Concerto in A minor, Op. 54[c].
[ab]**Sir Clifford Curzon,** [c]**Friedrich Gulda** *pfs*
[b]**London Symphony Orchestra / Øivin Fjeldstad;** [a]**London Philharmonic Orchestra /
Sir Adrian Boult;** [c]**Vienna Philharmonic Orchestra / Volkmar Andreae.**
Decca Headline Classics 433 628-2DSP (76 minutes: ADD). Recorded 1955-59. Ⓑ Ⓗ

Since the advent of the LP the Grieg and Schumann concertos have been ideally paired, and here we have Sir Clifford Curzon's classic account of the Grieg from 1959 where he is sympathetically and idiomatically accompanied by Øivin Fjeldstad and the LSO. Curzon was at his finest in romantic piano concertos, and his playing achieves an exceptional balance between poetry and strength. This is a performance which clearly stakes a claim for the concerto as a work of genius. These same characteristics are also to the fore in the Franck *Symphonic Variations*, this time with Sir Adrian Boult conducting. Probably the finest performance of this popular work, it is imaginative and romantic with a perfect sense of style, and excellent rapport between conductor and soloist. As if these riches were not enough, and at bargain price, it is rounded off with another masterly reading of the Schumann Concerto by Friedrich Gulda, dating from 1956 and with Volkmar Andreae leading the Vienna Philharmonic. This reading is right in the centre of the authentic romantic style: extremely personal and authoritative. Decca's recorded sound for all three performances is more than acceptable, with true piano tone throughout. This is probably one of the finest bargain issues currently available.

Franck Violin Sonata in A major.
Debussy Violin Sonata. Sonata for Flute, Viola and Harp.
Ravel Introduction and Allegro.
Kyung-Wha Chung *vn* **Osian Ellis** *hp* **Radu Lupu** *pf* **Melos Ensemble.**
Decca 421 154-2DM (67 minutes: ADD). Recorded 1962-77. Ⓜ ⓇⓇ

Here we have masterpieces from the French tradition in excellent performances that have won the status of recording classics. Kyung-Wha Chung and Radu Lupu are a fine duo who capture and convey the delicacy and poetry of the Franck Sonata as well as its rapturous grandeur, and never can the strict canonic treatment of the great tune in the finale have sounded more spontaneous and joyful. They are no less successful in the different world of the elusive Sonata which was Debussy's last work, with its smiles through tears and, in the finale, its echoes of a Neapolitan tarantella. The

1977 recording is beautifully balanced, with a natural sound given to both the violin and piano. The Melos Ensemble recorded the Ravel *Introduction and Allegro* 15 years before, but here too the recording is a fine one for which no allowances have to be made even by ears accustomed to good digital sound; as for the work itself, this has an ethereal beauty that is nothing short of magical and Osian Ellis and his colleagues give it the most skilful and loving performance. To talk about this disc as one for every collection savours of cliché, but anyone who does not have it may safely be urged to make its acquisition.

Prélude, choral et fugue. Prélude, aria et final. Grand caprice. Les plaintes d'une poupée. Danse lente. Choral No. 3 in A minor (arr. Hough).
Stephen Hough *pf*
Hyperion CDA66918 (68 minutes: DDD). Recorded 1996.   Ⓕ**S**Ⓔ

Hough has a dream-ticket combination of virtues – astonishing agility, a faultless ear for texture, fine-tuned stylistic sensibility and an exceptional understanding of harmonic and structural tensions. He acknowledges all Franck's nuances, notated and implied, without ever disturbing the broader flow; he gives full rein to the heroic Lisztian cascades, without ever tipping over into melodrama. The only hint of a nit to be picked would be that the *fortissimo* arpeggiations in the 'Choral' don't ring as resonantly as they might. One can't imagine the calm at the end of the 'Aria' being better judged. In their very different ways the almost comical bravura of the *Grand caprice* and the salon charm of the *Danse lente* and *Les plaintes d'une poupée* are extremely difficult to bring off. Yet anyone who has followed Hough's recording career will know that this sort of thing is meat and drink to him. As for his own transcription of the A minor *Chorale*, the unavoidable adjective is 'awesome'.

Pièce héroïque in B minor. Cantabile in B major. Fantaisie in A major. Grande pièce symphonique in F sharp minor, Op. 17. Pastorale in E major, Op. 19. Fantaisie in C major, Op. 16. Prélude, fugue et variation in B minor, Op. 18. Trois chorales – No. 1 in E major; No. 2 in B minor; No. 3 in A minor. Prière in C sharp minor, Op. 20. Final in B flat major, Op. 21.
Marie-Claire Alain *org*
Erato 0630-12706-2 (two discs: 152 minutes: DDD). Recorded on the Cavaillé-Coll organ, Saint-Etienne, Caen, France in 1995.   Ⓕ

Alain is a completely involved communicator. More than anyone else she delves into the very soul of these works. Thus we have an intensely prayerful *Prière*, a majestically statuesque *Grande pièce symphonique* while the *Chorales* are delivered with an unexpected degree of fervour; perhaps the Third is a shade overfervent since some of the semiquaver figurations lack absolute clarity – something which after one or two hearings serves to heighten the excitement but which might, after repeated listening, become irritating. This is a highly authoritative release not just in terms of playing but also in Alain's accompanying notes. The Caen organ is a particularly fine specimen of a Cavaillé-Coll, dating from 1884 – 25 years after the St Clotilde organ for which Franck wrote much of this music. The recording captures it, and the church's atmosphere, effectively.

Les béatitudes.
Diana Montague, Ingeborg Danz *mezzos* **Cornelia Kallisch** *contr* **Keith Lewis, Scot Weir** *tens*
Gilles Cachemaille *bar* **John Cheek, Juan Vasle, Reinhard Hagen** *basses*
Stuttgart Gächinger Kantorei and Radio Symphony Orchestra / Helmuth Rilling.
Hänssler Classic 98 964 (two discs: 131 minutes: DDD). Text and translation included.
Recorded 1990.   Ⓕ

Vincent d'Indy said of *Les béatitudes* that 'this musical epic is undoubtedly the greatest work for a very long time in the development of the art'; Dukas in similar vein spoke of it being 'exclusively concerned with shedding light on the most profound meaning of the divine word'; and even a non-disciple like Debussy, while criticizing the 'large number of images and truisms which force even the most determined to beat a retreat', admitted that 'only the healthy and stable-minded genius of a César Franck could forge his way successfully through this'. The texture is rich and the orchestration highly effective: more controversial is Franck's restless chromatic harmony (the snarls of the Seventh *Béatitude* presage a figure in the Symphony a decade later), and he makes overmuch use of a device (common also in Berlioz and Gounod) of rabbeting a figure a semitone or tone upwards or downwards (as in Nos. 1 and 3 and the final Hosannas). Helmuth Rilling, though perhaps a bit inclined to exaggerate *ritardandos*, is nevertheless responsible for a remarkably fine performance. He has at his disposal a first-class chorus, firm-toned, precise in intonation and clean in articulation (with very good French). The orchestra is equally good. It's not made clear which of the soloists sings what, but the mellifluous tenor of Keith Lewis and the radiant tone of Diana

Montague are unmistakable. Gilles Cachemaille, in his attempt to make the words of Christ sound measured and calm, seems cautious, and his deliberation somewhat impedes the musical flow; and John Cheek with his incisive, black-toned voice succeeds in imparting a menace to the words of Satan which Franck's music itself, it has to be said, fails to supply. The recording team has done an excellent job.

Benjamin Frankel American 1906-1973

Violin Concerto, Op. 24[a]. Viola Concerto, Op. 45. Serenata concertante, Op. 37[b].
[a]Ulf Hoelscher, [b]Alan Smith vns Brett Dean va David Lale vc Stephen Emmerson pf
Queensland Symphony Orchestra, Brisbane / Werner Andreas Albert.
CPO CPO999 422-2 (66 minutes: DDD). Recorded 1990s.   Ⓕ🄴

The Violin Concerto, which made Benjamin Frankel's name with the concert public when it was premièred in 1951 (he was already well known as a film composer), is inscribed 'In memory of the six million'; it is 'about' the Holocaust. The slow movement of the concerto is a moving elegy, expressing deep sadness with beautiful lyricism, but there is nothing of horror or bitterness. There is an edge to the brilliant and witty, rather Walton-like *Scherzo* and something of sobriety to the expressive first movement, and it is difficult to listen to the finale, in which a violin line of lovely, hovering grace turns into a light-hearted, even high-spirited waltz, without smiling. It is a work with a grieving centre, but not a Requiem. The Viola Concerto of 1967 is possibly even finer. It begins even more arrestingly than the earlier work with a long, lyrical melody over a lapping accompaniment and a deeper pulse. This theme is never literally repeated but it is recalled twice, after more angular music, and its last appearance is quite haunting. The serene slow movement is of similar form; so is the exuberant rondo finale, but Frankel was by now a past master at his own individual, highly tonal and melodious adaptation of serialism, and it gives the whole piece an audible logic and unity that is quite absorbing. You realize that a beautiful idea in the finale is a transformed variant of a spiky one from the first movement, and you want to play the whole work again to find out how it was done.

Something similar happens in the delightful *Serenata concertante*. It is almost light music (Frankel described it as a 'street scene' in which passing traffic, a distant jazz band, lovers dancing and all manner of other things could be heard) but strictly ordered, all the episodes derived from a single 12-note row. For listeners who have never been able to get on with serialism the strange experience will not be discovering a serial work that is as engagingly tuneful as this one, but discovering that Frankel's manipulation of his row is perfectly audible. All three performances are fine, and the recordings very pleasing. If you still haven't tried Frankel's music this coupling is an ideal introduction to him.

Girolamo Frescobaldi Italian 1583-1643

Il primo libro di madrigali.
Concerto Italiano / Rinaldo Alessandrini.
Opus 111 OPS30-133 (53 minutes: DDD). Texts and translations included.   Ⓕ🄿🄴
Recorded 1995.

Frescobaldi, in Antwerp with his Roman patron in 1608, was commissioned by a local printer to produce his first and indeed only book of madrigals. The collection seems to have had little impact on contemporaries. It was never reprinted and in our own times its existence gradually became submerged under the weight of Frescobaldi's reputation as a composer for the keyboard. Those interested in pursuing the matter discovered that the only known surviving copy lacks one of its voice-parts. Frescobaldi's *Primo libro* seemed set fair to remain a footnote in the textbooks rather than a musical reality. All that changed with the discovery of a complete set of partbooks, then in a private library, a challenge that Rinaldo Alessandrini has now taken up by both editing and recording the music. The distinctive sound and approach of his Concerto Italiano will be familiar to all enthusiasts for Italian music of the Monteverdi period, and their many admirers will not be disappointed with the result. Their instinctive feel for the diction, sound and sense of the Italian language married to a sophisticated and dynamic interpretational approach brings out all the rhetorical subtleties of Frescobaldi's extraordinary music, with its obvious parentage in the madrigals of Gesualdo and Monteverdi. This is virtuoso madrigal singing at its most exhilarating, all the more effective for being sometimes imaginatively underpinned by continuo instruments. The real revelation here is not so much the Concerto Italiano, whose powerful performances we have come to expect, but Frescobaldi's madrigals; no one with a soul should miss them.

Robert Fuchs

Piano Sonata No. 3 in D flat major, Op. 109. Jugendklänge, Op. 32. 12 Waltzes, Op. 110.
Daniel Blumenthal *pf*
Marco Polo 8 223474 (68 minutes: DDD). Recorded 1991-92.   Ⓕ

This disc offers a tantalizing mix of tradition and novelty. The Third Sonata is not without
incidental felicities yet it really does suggest reject-Brahms or at any rate music he might have put
on ice for later consideration. Even those who live and breathe the atmosphere of late nineteenth-
century Vienna will find the finale hard going and agree that the Sonata as a whole is apt to
collapse under its own weight. The 12 *Waltzes*, on the other hand, show a strong Schubertian bias,
though you will only hear a few of the subtleties – the poetic light and shade – of Schubert's
incomparable dance sequences. No, the real treat is the *Jugendklänge*, music glowing with all sorts
of affectionate surprises. 'Bogey Man' is an Alkanesque oddity and 'The Rain Drizzles' is an
intriguing foretaste of impressionism. But 'Butterfly in the Meadow' and 'Merry Month of May'
are irresistible; the first an evocation of some long-past summer idyll, the second a Schumannesque,
harmonically piquant re-telling of custom and ceremony. Seekers after unusual encores need look
no further. Yet nothing is without interest in this recital, particularly the revelation that Fuchs
comes into his own in miniatures rather than epics. No grumbles about the vivid recording, and
Daniel Blumenthal is a warmly assured and dependable pianist.

Giovanni Gabrieli

G. Gabrieli Symphoniae sacrae (1615) – Jubilate Deo a 10; Misericordia tua a 12; Suscipe
clementissime a 12; In ecclesiis a 14; Buccinate in neomenia a 19. Intonazioni – del nono tono;
duodecimo tono. Canzoni et Sonate – Canzon XIV a 10; Sonata XVIII a 14; Sonata XIX a 15;
Sonata XX a 22; Sonata XXI per tre violini. Timor et tremor a 6. Magnificat a 33 (arr. Keyte).
Domine Deus meus a 6.
Barbarino Audi, dulcis amica mea. Ardens est cor meum.
Timothy Roberts *org* **Gabrieli Consort and Players / Paul McCreesh.**
Archiv Produktion 449 180-2AH (78 minutes: DDD). Texts and translations included.
Recorded 1995.   Ⓕ🅴

The words 'Venice' and 'splendour' were simply made to go together and are certainly brought
together in this recording entitled 'Music for San Rocco'. Paul McCreesh and his team of advisers
have taken Thomas Coryat's description, *Coryats Crudities*, of the 1608 festivities in honour of
St Roch as the starting-point for this concert programme, which was performed in the magnificent
Scuola Grande di San Rocco, famous for its sequence of paintings by Tintoretto. The programme
explores a wide range of works by Gabrieli, from the more intimate motets with organ
accompaniment right through the spectrum to the extraordinary 33-part *Magnificat* reconstructed
for the occasion by Hugh Keyte. The sheer magnificence of the sound of massed cornetts and
sackbuts, blending so harmoniously with the voices, clearly struck Coryat, and is equally irresistible
the best part of four centuries later. This is where the Gabrieli Consort and Players came in some
years ago when one could only wonder at McCreesh's logistical abilities in bringing together the
required number of chamber organs and so on. The group has, of course, gone from strength to
strength, exploring a wide range of repertory, but they clearly retain a strong affinity with Gabrieli's
music. The singing and playing are quite superb, securely and compellingly flamboyant. It's difficult
to single out individuals but one must mention David Hurley who sings the remarkable solo motets
by Barbarino with great poise. For the sheer splendour of the music, and the excellence of the
performances, this recording is a must.

The 16 Sonatas and Canzonas from Sacrae symphoniae. Toccata quinti toni. Three Toccatas.
Intonatione del noni toni.
His Majesties Sagbutts and Cornetts / Timothy Roberts *org*
Hyperion CDA66908 (75 minutes: DDD). Recorded 1997.   Ⓕ🅿🅴

Giovanni Gabrieli is arguably the earliest composer to write a significant body of instrumental
music to a formula which can be said to be truly idiomatic and timelessly palatable. The *Sacrae
symphoniae* publication of 1597 is a mixed set of vocal and instrumental pieces and, in its grand
design, preserves a glorious heyday of textural opulence, intimate and playful dialogue between
galleries and unashamedly ostentatious virtuosity. His Majesties Sagbutts and Cornetts have
augmented their chamber consort to form, as cornettist David Staff proudly proclaims, 'the largest
group of cornett and sagbutt players to have been assembled from one city since the 17th century'.
These wonderful 16 canzonas and sonatas make up the complete instrumental music of the 1597

collection. In essence it is the extensive juxtaposition between sombre blocks and glittering small-scale exchanges which gives the music its seminal quality of moving both inevitably and eventfully towards a self-assured resolution, befitting its aristocratic gait. Having a 'moderator' (in this case the fine keyboardist, Timothy Roberts), as opposed to an artistic director, is pragmatic and democratic but there is the odd moment where a strong artistic presence at the helm would have, ironically perhaps, empowered the musicians towards a more flexible and varied approach to articulation and colour. That said, there are some glorious and majestic sounds here: you can fly to the buzzing *Canzon duodecimi toni a 10*, bathe in the fragrant harmonic mosaic of the three-choir *Canzon quarti toni a 15* and relish elsewhere the peculiarly delicate and sweet sounds of this ensemble. Overall, a notable and distinctive achievement. Recommended to a broad listenership.

Niels Gade
Danish 1817-1890

Symphony No. 1 in C minor, Op. 5. Hamlet Overture, Op. 37. Echoes from Ossian, Op. 1.
Danish National Radio Symphony Orchestra / Dmitri Kitaienko.
Chandos CHAN9422 (61 minutes: DDD). Recorded 1992-93.　　　　Ⓕ

Gade's First Symphony, which was turned down by the Copenhagen Music Society but accepted and championed in Leipzig by Mendelssohn, launched him on his long and successful career. Its subtitle, *On Sjøland's fair plains*, alludes to one of the folk-songs collected and published by his teacher Andreas Peter Berggreen though it is not the only folk-song to figure in the score. The First Symphony comes from 1842 and is eminently civilized, well-schooled music which deserves a place in the repertory. The performance is both vital and sensitive and the recording is splendidly natural, with a good perspective and front-to-back depth and no want of detail or presence. The *Echoes from Ossian* Overture is Gade's first opus, which he composed two years earlier. Like the symphony it is one of his most frequently recorded pieces, and its second group has a charm that is difficult to resist. This performance, incidentally, has appeared before on the Chandos issue of *The Elf-king's Daughter*. The *Hamlet Overture* was written 21 years later under the influence of what Jens Cornelius calls 'Leipzig-inspired ideals'. It is beautifully crafted and fresh in its inspiration.

The Elf-king's Daughter, Op. 30[a]. Spring Fantasy, Op. 23[b].
[a]**Susanne Elmark,** [b]**Anne Margrethe Dahl** *sops* **Kirsten Dolberg** *mez* [b]**Gert Henning-Jensen** *ten* [a]**Guido Paëvatalu** *bar* [b]**Sten Byriel** *bass-bar* **Elisabeth Westenholz** *pf*
Tivoli Concert Choir and Symphony Orchestra / Michael Schønwandt.
Da Capo 8 224051 (63 minutes: DDD). Texts and translations included. Recorded 1996.　　　Ⓕ

Michael Schønwandt gives a brisk, fresh account of *The Elf-king's Daughter*, an impression aided, perhaps, by the forward recording balance. The singers are admirable, particularly Kirsten Dolberg. The *Spring Fantasy* was written in 1852 after Gade's return from Leipzig, where he had briefly succeeded Mendelssohn as conductor of the Gewandhaus Orchestra. By this time Gade was in his early thirties and held several key positions in Copenhagen both as a conductor and organist, and had just been knighted. So he felt secure enough to marry Sophie, the daughter of Denmark's senior composer, J.P.E. Hartmann. The *Spring Fantasy* was a betrothal gift for his fiancée. An atmosphere of spring and happiness pervades this and is one of the composer's sunniest works. All four soloists here are excellent and there is a prominent part for the piano, expertly played here by Elisabeth Westenholz. It is a lovely work, its Mendelssohnian opening with clarinet and piano almost misleading one into thinking one has wandered into the wrong piece!

String Quartet in F major, 'Willkommen und Abschied'. Allegro in A minor. Andante and Allegro molto in F minor[a]. Octet in F major, Op. 17.
Kontra Quartet (Anton Kontra, Boris Samsing *vns* Peter Fabricius *va* Morten Zeuthen *vc)*
Anne Egendal, Per Lund Madsen *vns* **Sune Ranmo** *va* [a]**Hans Nygaard** *vc*
BIS CD545 (76 minutes: DDD). Recorded 1992.　　　Ⓕ

All these works come from 1836-48; the *Allegro* in A minor for string quartet from 1836, when Gade was 19; the F minor *Andante and Allegro molto* for string quintet from the following year; the F major Quartet *Wilkommen und Abschied* from 1840 and the Octet from 1848 towards the end of his Leipzig period. All this music is fluent, urbane, civilized and inventive. In some ways its musical ideas are fresher than in Gade's mature pieces. The F minor Quintet is particularly delightful. But all this music has charm and is expertly and persuasively played by the members of the Kontra Quartet and their musicianly colleagues. The recording is very acceptable, though there is a slight edge in tuttis. A useful supplement to the three mature Gade quartets already available and in some ways more enjoyable.

Francesco Geminiani

Italian 1687-1762

Concerti grossi, Op. 2 – No. 1 in C minor; No. 2 in C minor; No. 3 in D minor; No. 4 in D major; No. 5 in D minor; No. 6 in A major. Concerti grossi after Corelli's Op. 5 – No. 3 in C major; No. 5 in G minor.
Tafelmusik / Jeanne Lamon vn
Sony Classical Vivarte SK48043 (59 minutes: DDD). Recorded 1990.   Ⓕ🅿

Imagine the scene. The year is 1715 and Francesco Geminiani is playing his violin for King George I, accompanied on the harpsichord by none other than Handel. But Geminiani had not always enjoyed the absolute favour of his colleagues; it is said that in Italy complaints were voiced regarding his excessive use of rubato – a very unexpected phenomenon, especially when seen in the light of our own attitudes to period performance. So, he left his workplace in Naples (where he was Concert Master), came to London – his new 'base', so to speak – and additionally went on to work in Dublin and Paris. The individual works in Geminiani's concerto-style Op. 2 set are forged in the *sonata da chiesa* (slow-fast-slow-fast) format and contain much beautiful music, especially where, in chordal passages, there is an overlapping of string lines. The faster movements set out on dancing feet – an aspect of the music that Tafelmusik indulges with obvious relish – and the slower ones have a mildly sensuous character. Nowhere, however, will you find as much as a hint of the wayward rubato about which Geminiani's colleagues complained! Similar positive qualities apply to the performances of the two Corelli violin sonata transcriptions, the second of which is particularly appealing. The recordings, too, are warm and immediate, with plenty of space around them and impressive definition.

Roberto Gerhard

Spanish/British 1896-1970

Symphony No. 2. Concerto for Orchestra.
BBC Symphony Orchestra / Matthias Bamert.
Chandos CHAN9694 (55 minutes: DDD). Recorded 1997.   Ⓕ

Although the avowed purpose of Gerhard's *Concerto for Orchestra* (1965) was to highlight the orchestra as an entity rather than its constituent sections or instruments, and while it may not have the immediate universal appeal of, say, Kodály's or Bartók's works with the same title (written in a very different idiom some 20 or so years earlier), it has never been surpassed for its imaginative handling of instrumental sonorities or for its virtuoso demands on the players. It has to be said right away that this is a stunning performance: not merely does the BBC SO rise spectacularly to the work's demands, but Bamert shows himself exceptionally skilful at securing internal balances. It is worth quoting Gerhard's own words: 'My favourite listener is one who does not read explanatory programme notes ... I stand by the *sound* of my music, and it is the sound that must make the sense ... a work of music takes shape only in the mind of the listener.' Gerhard's Second Symphony has been represented on disc only by the revised version (*Metamorphosis*) which had had to be completed by Alan Boustead (available on Auvidis Montaigne); although Gerhard may have felt the original too cerebral, it was at least all his, and tough going as it undoubtedly is, it is very welcome to all interested in the mental processes of this exceptional musician. The opening of the work's second section, with its clicking percussion, is hauntingly mysterious, and the final nightmare palindrome *Scherzo* (of which only a fraction exists in the Boustead version) is one of his most astonishing creations. With first-class recording throughout, this is an essential disc for all admirers of Gerhard.

Piano Trio. Cello Sonata. Chaconne. Gemini.
Cantamen (Caroline Balding vn Jo Cole vc Timothy Lissimore pf).
Metier MSVCD92012 (77 minutes: DDD). Recorded 1995.   Ⓕ

Between Gerhard's Piano Trio, written in 1918 at the age of 22, and *Gemini*, composed nearly half a century later, yawns a stylistic gulf that almost defies credence; but of the genuineness of his convictions in each case there is no question. The sensuous warmth of the Trio demonstrates the influence of Ravel, with clear reminiscences of the Frenchman's String Quartet in the finale. The second movement is exquisitely seductive, and Cantamen plays the whole work with tenderness and sympathy. Five years later, everything was to change when Gerhard went to study in Vienna with Schoenberg; but his perpetually enquiring mind and ultra-sensitive ear, along with his strong sense of Catalan identity, led him to temper the dodecaphonic system, so that later works broke free of serial dogma and frequently incorporated references to Spanish turns of phrase. This is so in the 1956 Cello Sonata which, for all the trenchant energy of its outer movements, is never less than euphonious: its deeply lyrical slow movement is beautifully shaped by Jo Cole. The *Chaconne* for

Gerhard Chamber

solo violin is rather more uncompromising in idiom but Caroline Balding fulfils its virtuosic demands with distinction. *Gemini*, with its plucked piano strings and keyboard clusters, its violin scurries and its frenetic outbursts, shows Gerhard's love of experimentation in sonorities and the two instruments are presented as antagonists rather than partners. The performance has real fire and conviction.

Sir Edward German

British 1862-1936

Richard III – Overture. Theme and Six Diversions. The Seasons.
RTE Concert Orchestra / Andrew Penny.
Marco Polo 8 223695 (65 minutes: DDD). Recorded 1994.   Ⓕ

This is a well-planned and impressively executed collection. Of course German could not match the passion or genius of Elgar; but the collection here proves that his music does not deserve the neglect that has been its lot. From the dark, brooding opening of the *Richard III* Overture this is music of real character, meticulously worked out, imaginatively scored, and more than once showing its Elgarian kinship. There may be something a little saccharine about the theme upon which German based the *Theme and Six Diversions* (1919) but the way he builds upon it shows his skills at their best, with some striking contrapuntal writing and a swirling waltz section. Perhaps best of all is the symphonic suite *The Seasons* (1899), in which the restful yearning of the 'Autumn' movement is especially striking. Andrew Penny conducts the programme with a fine feel for the music's shape and dynamics, and he coaxes from the RTE Concert Orchestra the impression that this is music they have come to know and love. Listeners may do so too.

George Gershwin

American 1898-1937

Piano Concerto in F major. Porgy and Bess – symphonic suite. Second Rhapsody.
Aalborg Symphony Orchestra / Wayne Marshall *pf*
Virgin Classics VM5 61243-2 (72 minutes: DDD). Recorded 1995.   Ⓜ

Wayne Marshall makes his first entry in the Piano Concerto and, in the space of a bar or two, you hear a quick wit and a cool head, the ability to convey (just as Gershwin strove to do) the jazzman's freewheeling, rhapsodic manner alongside a concert pianist's formality. Where Gershwin sits back in the wee small hours spinning yet another of his blue tunes, Marshall is in no hurry to go anywhere. And yet there's a very real sense of the imperative, too, a 'something's coming' kind of feeling. When it comes, it's a special moment. So, too, is Gershwin's grandiose recapitulation (and Marshall goes all the way with that). Generally speaking, the Aalborg Symphony is well up on the style – no mean achievement when the orchestra can so easily sound like a dead-weight in this piece. But then, Marshall's 'Jack-be-nimble' approach is plainly infectious, encouraging reflexes from his band that are as quick and sparky as his own. The pulse of the Roaring Twenties was racy and capricious. But there was always time to dream. That's the tenor of Marshall's performance. The same is true of his dashing account of the *Second Rhapsody*. Again the contrasts are strong, the manner spontaneous – impulsive, Manhattan-brash to a degree – though Marshall never lets us forget that these are luxury goods. Gershwin's shot-silk climaxes (Hollywood dreams indeed), with all their audacious modulations and fruity horn counterpoints (nobody played with wrong-note harmonies like Gershwin), are played for all they're worth. There's also a spirited account of the Robert Russell Bennett *Porgy and Bess* Suite, as felicitous (real delicacy of atmosphere as 'Clara' emerges from the opening street cries) as it is robust (that's quite a hurricane that blows through Catfish Row).

Gershwin An American in Paris. Rhapsody in Blue.
Bernstein Candide – Overture. West Side Story – symphonic dances.
New York Philharmonic Orchestra / Leonard Bernstein *pf*
Sony Classical SMK47529 (60 minutes: ADD). Recorded 1958-59.   Ⓜ ⒽⓇⓇ

Bernstein conducted and played the music of Gershwin with the same naturalness as he brought to his own music. Here, *An American in Paris* swings by with an instinctive sense of its origins in popular and film music; no stilted rhythms or four-squareness delay the work's progress, and where ripe schmaltz is wanted, ripe schmaltz is what we get, devoid of all embarrassment. *Rhapsody in Blue* is playful and teasing, constantly daring us to try to categorize its style, and then confounding our conclusions. Although the solo passages from individual players are beautifully taken, the orchestra captures the authentic flavour of Gershwin's and Bernstein's idiom, and Bernstein pushes them to transcend the printed scores. His own playing in the *Rhapsody* is tantalizingly unpredictable. The recording is clear and bright, perhaps a touch hard-edged, and a little of the richness of the original LP issue might have been preferred by some, especially as the editing is now made more obvious.

Fantasy on Porgy and Bess (arr. Courage). Three Preludes (arr. Heifetz). A Damsel in Distress – Nice work if you can get it. Girl Crazy – But not for me (both arr. Tunick); Embraceable you; I got rhythm. Show Girl – Liza. Tip-Toes – Sweet and low-down[a]. Goldwyn Follies – Love is here to stay (all arr. Brohn).
Joshua Bell vn George Gershwin pf **London Symphony Orchestra / John Williams** pf
Sony Classical SK60659 (55 minutes: DDD). Recorded 1997. Item marked [a] incorporates composer's 1926 piano roll.   Ⓕ Ⓔ

In the 1920s George Gershwin used to encounter Jascha Heifetz at smart New York parties, and the two sometimes improvised violin-piano duets. Heifetz urged Gershwin to compose a major concert work for him, but Gershwin never got around to it. After the composer's death, Heifetz himself arranged five songs from *Porgy and Bess* as well as Gershwin's three Preludes for piano. These transcriptions and arrangements are the springboard for this CD. John Williams has arranged eight songs from *Porgy* into a 20-minute *Fantasy*. It comes as something of a surprise to hear 'Bess, you is my woman now' in such a high key, and Joshua Bell takes on the wailing 'My man's gone now' and of course 'Summertime' to make a very convincing virtuoso effect. Heifetz's transcriptions of the Preludes sound so natural that one would believe that Gershwin had composed them that way, whereas Williams's arrangements of some other show- and film-tunes seem to look forward more to the style of Grappelli. This is a light-hearted, sunny disc, which makes huge demands on Bell as soloist but none at all on the listener – it's sheer pleasure.

Gershwin Piano Rolls, Volume 2.
Gershwin La La Lucille – From Now On[a]. Rialto Ripples[a]. **Frey** Havanola[a]. **Conrad** Singin' the Blues ('till My Daddy Comes Home)[a]. **Akst** Jaz-o-mine[a]. **Various** Greenwich Village Follies of 1920 – Just Snap Your Fingers at Care[a]. **Kern** Zip Goes a Million – Whip-Poor-Will[a]. **Pinkard** Waitin' for Me[a]. **P. Wendling** Buzzin' the Bee[a]. **Schonberg** Darling[ab]. **Berlin** For Your Country and My Country[ac]. **M. Morris** Kangaroo Hop[a]. **Matthews** Pastime Rag No. 3[e]. **O. Gardner** Chinese Blues[d]. **Schonberger** Whispering[a]. **B. Grant** Arrah Go On I'm Gonna Go Back to Oregon[a].
[a]George Gershwin, [b]Cliff Hess, [c]Rudy Erlebach, [d]Bert Wynn, [e]Fred Murtha pfs
Nonesuch 7559-79370-2 (42 minutes: DDD). Derived from piano rolls cut between 1916 and 1921. Recorded 1992-93.   Ⓕ

There are some curiosities here but only two numbers are by Gershwin himself. The first of these is *Rialto Ripples*, a catchy rag Gershwin wrote in collaboration with Will Donaldson and put on to a roll in September 1916. It is fascinating to compare Gershwin's own 1916 performance with the sheet music published a year later. The roll has much more of the ragtime idiom in oom-pah left-hand chords and even reveals a few misprints in the score. Another ragtime connection is the 1916 roll, under one of Gershwin's pseudonyms (Fred Murtha), of *Pastime Rag No. 3*, one of only five polished rags in different styles by black composer Artie Matthews. Again there are interesting differences between the sheet music published in the same year and Gershwin's roll – he doesn't play repeats but he returns to the A strain at the end. He doesn't seem to know what to do with the 'stoptime' effect (1'21") in Strain C and just holds the pedal down. The rest of the song arrangements, which sometimes employ two players, show the ragtime background of this piano style, especially in the earlier rolls. These are also good examples of the techniques of the roll arrangers, who hyped it all up by adding notes to create the effect of a whole team of pianists.

Gershwin Cuban Overture (arr. Stone). Rhapsody in Blue. Second Rhapsody. An American in Paris (all arr. cpsr).
Grainger Fantasy on George Gershwin's 'Porgy and Bess'.
Peter Donohoe, Martin Roscoe pfs
Carlton Classics 30366 0068-2 (77 minutes: DDD). Recorded 1994.   Ⓜ Ⓔ

This is two-piano playing of superlative accomplishment and breathtaking bravura: the infectious zest and affectionate swagger of this music-making really do seem to leap out of the speakers. Thus the *Cuban Overture* has all the glitter and panache one could wish for, and much the same applies to *An American in Paris*. In the latter, note also the melting fantasy this partnership brings to that gorgeous episode where Gershwin prepares us for the arrival of that indelible trumpet tune. The wittily flexible and superbly co-ordinated realization of *Rhapsody in Blue* is another delight. It's not all barnstorming virtuosity, mind you. Donohoe and Roscoe lend thoughtful, exquisitely moulded advocacy to Percy Grainger's *Fantasy on George Gershwin's 'Porgy and Bess'* and the hugely underrated *Second Rhapsody* blossoms in their poetic hands. The sound is rich and refined.

Three Preludes. Sleepless Night. Rubato. Novelette in Fourths. Fragment. Blue Monday Suite. Three-quarter blues. Impromptu in two keys. Three Note Waltz. Romantic. Machinery Going Mad. Sleepless Night. Sutton Place. Rhapsody in Blue (all ed. Zizzo).
Alicia Zizzo pf
Carlton Classics 30366 0005-2 (56 minutes: DDD). Recorded 1995.   Ⓜ

Revisionism has hit Gershwin, whose manuscript affairs have needed sorting out ever since his death. Unscrupulous editors took a hand in preparing his scores for publication and he was always too busy to bother. So was everybody else until now. At last Alicia Zizzo has gained access to what material survives, or has recently been discovered, and she has made new editions of the music, which she performs here. This disc contains unknown short pieces which everyone interested in Gershwin will need to possess. It has always been known that there were more than the three published Preludes. No. 5 is the nifty 1919 *Novelette in Fourths*, anticipating both Confrey and Mayerl, which surfaced in the CD transfer of Gershwin's own piano-roll performances which makes Zizzo's treatment seem tame. No. 7 is negligible since it is only a 25-second fragment but both Nos. 2 and 3, like most of the other short pieces, are really charming discoveries. Some are already familiar. As played by Zizzo the original manuscript of the *Irish waltz* (also known as *Three-quarter blues*) simply goes round its tune twice and so does the *Impromptu in two keys* – now in the higher key of E flat and a vast improvement on the 1973 score. Both have detailed rhythmic differences. The *Blue Monday Suite* is based on Gershwin's piano score for the unsuccessful 1922 one-act opera which is often regarded as a study for *Rhapsody in Blue* and *Porgy and Bess*. Although almost half the length of the opera, the suite provides further access to some characteristic Gershwin full of pre-echoes of things to come, including 'The man I love'.

Of Thee I Sing – Prelude[a]; Jilted. Second Rhapsody[a]. The Shocking Miss Pilgrim – For you, for me, for evermore. Cuban Overture[a]. Pardon My English – Isn't it a pity? Variations on 'I got rhythm'[a]. Catfish Row[a]. Shall we dance? – Let's call the whole thing off[a]; They can't take that away from me[a]. Goldwyn Follies – Our love is here to stay.
Jack Gibbons pf
ASV White Line CDWHL2082 (77 minutes: DDD). Items marked [a] arr. Gibbons.
Recorded 1992-93.   Ⓜ

This disc is mostly comprised of Gibbons's own arrangements, based on Gershwin's film music, two-piano pieces, and in the case of the 'Catfish Row' *Porgy and Bess* suite, his orchestrations. The longest work is the *Second Rhapsody*, composed for a scene in the Gershwins' first Hollywood movie, *Delicious* (from which the best-known song is 'Blah, blah, blah'). The film starred Janet Gaynor and Charles Farrell, and in this sequence the heroine wanders frightened through Manhattan – it might be rechristened *A Scotswoman in New York*. George Gershwin referred to the main tune as his 'Brahmsian theme' but today no one would mistake it for anything but Gershwin. 'For you, for me', one of the melodies salvaged from their files by Ira Gershwin and used ten years after George's death, emerged in the 1947 film *The Shocking Miss Pilgrim*. Ira and Kay Swift hoped it would be a gold-mine and rated the tune higher than any among Gershwin's unpublished songs. The solo version of the *Cuban Overture* is Gibbons's own adaptation of Gershwin's four-hand arrangement; like the 'Catfish Row' suite it makes formidable demands on the pianist and Gibbons gives them both virtuoso performances. The recital ends with three of the standards Gershwin wrote in Hollywood during the last months of his life. 'They can't take that away from me' must be a strong contender for the great songs of the twentieth century, and no one hearing 'Our love is here to stay' can doubt that a premonition of death lingered somewhere in the composer's heart in the autumn of 1936.

Porgy and Bess.
Willard White bass Porgy; **Cynthia Haymon** sop Bess; **Harolyn Blackwell** sop Clara;
Cynthia Clarey sop Serena; **Damon Evans** bar Sportin' Life; **Marietta Simpson** mez Maria;
Gregg Baker bar Crown;
Glyndebourne Chorus; London Philharmonic Orchestra / Sir Simon Rattle.
EMI CDS5 56220-2 (three discs: 189 minutes: DDD). Notes and text included. Recorded 1988.
Gramophone Award Winner 1989.   Ⓕ 🆁🆁

The company, orchestra and conductor from the outstanding 1986 Glyndebourne production re-create once more a very real sense of Gershwin's 'Catfish Row' community on this complete recording. Such is the atmosphere and theatricality of this recording, we might easily be back on the Glyndebourne stage. From the very first bar it's clear just how instinctively attuned Simon Rattle and this orchestra are to every aspect of a multi-faceted score. The cast, too, are so *right*, so much a part of their roles, and so well integrated into the whole, that one almost takes the excellence of their contributions for granted. Here is one beautiful voice after another, beginning in style with Harolyn Blackwell's radiant 'Summertime', which at Rattle's gorgeously lazy tempo, is just about as beguiling as one could wish. Willard White conveys both the simple honesty and inner-strength of Porgy without milking the sentiment and Haymon's passionately sung Bess will go wherever a little flattery and encouragement take her. As Sportin' Life, Damon Evans not only relishes the burlesque elements of the role but he really *sings* what's written a lot more than is customary. But the entire cast deliver throughout with all the unstinting fervour of a Sunday revivalist meeting. Sample for yourself the final moments of the piece – 'Oh Lawd, I'm on my way' – if that doesn't stir you, nothing will.

Carlo Gesualdo
Italian c1561-1613

Ahi, disperata vita. Sospirava il mio cor. O malnati messaggi. Non t'amo, o voce ingrata. Luci serene e chiare. Sparge la morte al mio Signor nel viso. Arde il mio cor. Occhi del mio cor vita. Mercè grido piangendo. Asciugate i begli ochi. Se la mia morte brami. Io parto. Ardita Zanzaretta. Ardo per te, mio bene. Instrumental items – Canzon francese. Io tacerò. Corrente, amanti.
Les Arts Florissants / William Christie.
Harmonia Mundi HMC90 1268 (55 minutes: DDD). Texts and translations included.   ©℗

To many, Gesualdo is known above all for the *crime passionnel* which left his wife and her lover impaled on the same sword, but the notion that his highly-charged music is the product of a tortured and unstable mind is, no doubt, over-romanticized. For this foray into the schizophrenic world of Gesualdo's five-voice madrigals, Les Arts Florissants have selected their programme from the last three books, pieces in which the highly-mannered and exaggerated aspects of the composer's style reach their most extreme expression. Nevertheless, we should not think of all these works being undifferentiated in style, and one of the fascinations of this disc, which has been very carefully planned, is the insight it offers into the gradual emergence and sharpening of the features which characterize Gesualdo's late madrigalian manner. Some of those elements can already be heard in *Sospirava il mio cor* from the Third Book, and by the last tracks they are present, with all their compositional distortions in full dress.

William Christie and Les Arts Florissants are no strangers to the aesthetic of the Italian madrigal in its last decades. This recording, like so many of their productions, is full of surprises on both the large and small scales. The first, of a general kind, is the decision to add continuo accompaniments *avant la lettre*. This is certainly justifiable on historical grounds, though less certain is the precise way it has been done with some passages within a piece still left *a cappella*. What is certainly less justifiable, if only on artistic grounds, is the performance of two madrigals on instruments alone (*Io tacerò* and *Corrente, amanti*); it makes little sense to attempt such highly-charged word-driven music in this way. What will also surprise some is the rather understated, almost classically-pure character of the interpretations, though it is a relief that the calculatedly neurotic and deliberately out-of-tune manner so often turned out for Gesualdo has here been eschewed. These are technically very fine and dramatically convincing and coherent readings which are certainly preferable to any other recordings of Gesualdo's madrigals currently available.

Orlando Gibbons
British 1583-1625

Preludes – A minor, MBXX/1; G major, MBXX/2. Fancy, MBXX/3. Fantasias – G major, MBXX/6; D minor, MBXX/8; G minor, MBXX/9. Pavan, MBXX/15. Pavins – MBXX/16; MBXX/17. Pavan and Galliard in A minor, 'Lord Salisbury', MBXX/18-19. Galliard, MBXX/22. Galljardo, MBXX/23. Ground in A minor, MBXX/26. Whoope, doe me no harm, good man, MBXX/31. French Ayre, MBXX/32. Almayne, MBXX/33. Alman, 'The King's Jewel', MBXX/3. Allmaine, MBXX/37. French Coranto, MBXX/38. French Allmaine, MBXX/41. The Wellcome, MBXX/42.
Richard Egarr *hpd/virg*
Globe GLO5168 (63 minutes: DDD). Recorded 1997.   ©℗

Gibbons was described by contemporaries as having 'the best hand in England'. Nevertheless, his considerable output for the keyboard is under-represented on disc as compared with that of his older contemporary, Byrd. Could this be because his virtuosity, unlike that of the exhibitionist John Bull, is less a matter of finger dexterity than of compositional technique (exploiting imitative counterpoint) and emotional depth – qualities less immediately captivating to the casual listener?

The severe style of two substantial Fantasias here reflects Gibbons's austere nature – even his galliards are cast in a minor key; but all the pavans are remarkable for their expressive depth. A lighter vein, however, is struck in a group of French-inspired pieces, *The King's Jewel* and the brief variations on the popular tune *Whoope, doe me no harm, good man*. Presenting half this programme on a sweet-toned muselar (a Flemish virginal for domestic use) and half on a harpsichord – both Dutch copies of Ruckers instruments of 1640 – Egarr vigorously abjures the 'sterile, metronomic approach of our time' and instead opts for flexible phrasing that responds to the music's inner stresses. In so doing he brings out admirably the individual character of a composer, the exploration of whom is richly rewarding to the thoughtful music-lover.

O clap your hands. Great Lord of Lords. Hosanna to the Son of David. Prelude in G major[a]. Out of the deep. See, see, the Word is incarnate. Preludes – No. 3 in D minor, MBXX/3[a]. Lift up your heads. Almighty and everlasting God. First (Short) Service – No. 6, Magnificat; No. 7, Nunc dimittis. Second Service – No. 3, Magnificat; No. 4, Nunc dimittis. Fantazia of four parts[a]. O God, the king of glory. O Lord, in Thy wrath rebuke me not.
Oxford Camerata / Jeremy Summerly with [a]**Laurence Cummings** org
Naxos 8 553130 (65 minutes: DDD). Texts included. Recorded 1994. Ⓢᴱ

The Oxford Camerata provides us here with a representative selection of choral works by Orlando Gibbons, together with three of his organ pieces. The programme is introduced by a bright and busy performance of the eight-part *O clap your hands*, followed by the noble verse anthem *Great Lord of Lords* – and it is pleasing to hear in this piece, and in the other verse-anthems, the rich timbre of the countertenor Robin Blaze, a welcome acquisition for the Camerata. In fact the group has a great deal of vocal talent in its make-up and they are strengthening their reputation all the time. They tackle the gently moving *See, see, the Word is incarnate* with great confidence, together with the First and Second Services and the quiet collects with all the knowledge and aplomb of cathedral lay clerks or choral scholars from Oxford and Cambridge. Laurence Cummings plays two short preludes, the one in G major – a real test of agility – from *Parthenia* and that in D minor from Benjamin Cosyn's *Virginal Book*. The *Fantazia of four parts* is a most extraordinary work, quite hard to steady and control. Nevertheless, it is a welcome addition to the programme.

Pavan and Galliard a 6. Fantasia a 2 No. 1. Go from my window. Fantasias a 6 – Nos. 3 and 5. Fantasia a 4 No. 1 'for the great double bass'. Galliard a 3. In Nomine a 4. Pavan and Galliard in A minor, 'Lord Salisbury'. Prelude in G major. Masks – Lincoln's Inn mask; The Fairest Nymph. Alman in G major. Behold, thou hast made my days. Glorious and powerful God. The First Set of Madrigals and Mottets – Daintie fine bird; Faire is the rose; I weigh not fortune's frown; I see ambition never pleased; I feign not friendship where I hate; The silver swanne.
Tessa Bonner sop **Timothy Roberts** keybds **Red Byrd; Rose Consort of Viols.**
Naxos 8 550603 (68 minutes: DDD). Recorded 1992. Ⓢ

Beautifully performed and finely recorded, this selection of Gibbons's music is especially attractive on account of the variety of its programme. At its richest it presents writing for voice and viols combined, five parts to each, or for viols alone, sometimes in six parts. In lightest, most transparent texture there is a charming piece for two viols. Three keyboard instruments are used for solos: virginals, harpsichord and organ. A soprano also sings solos to viol accompaniment. Moods and styles vary correspondingly. The *Masks* and *Alman* for virginals have a high-spirited, almost popular manner; the Fifth *Fantasia* includes some unusual chromaticism and harmonic developments that for a while almost anticipate Purcell. Tessa Bonner sings with unvibrant purity; but what will probably be found the most striking feature of the singing here is the pronunciation. It is one of the distinguishing marks of this curiously named group, Red Byrd, that they sing such music with vowel-sounds modified to fit theories about the English in which it would originally have been sung. Thus the 'daintie fine bird' tells 'oi sing and doy', and the 'u' acquires a sort of umlaut in *I weigh not fortune's frown*, 'weigh' and 'frown' also having a measure of rusticity. Perhaps it is a good idea, but it does increase the desirability of printed texts in the booklet. The instrumental music is all finely played, the viols avoiding any imputation of belonging to the squeeze-and-scrape school, and Timothy Roberts's keyboard solos are particularly skilful, both in *legato* and fluent passagework.

Second Service (ed. Higginbottom) – Te Deum Laudamus; Jubilate Deo; Magnificat; Nunc dimittis. Anthems – O Lord, in Thy wrath rebuke me not. O God, the king of glory. Glorious and powerful God. Sing unto the Lord. O clap your handsr. See, see, the Word is incarnate.
Organ works – Fantasia of four parts. A Fancy in A major. A Fancy for a double organ.
David Burchell org **New College Choir, Oxford / Edward Higginbottom.**
CRD CRD3451 (66 minutes: DDD). Texts included. Recorded 1987. Ⓕ

Of all the English composers of the Shakespearian age, Gibbons is in many ways the easiest to love. But he can also be the easiest to destroy by taking too solemn an approach to his delicate lines. So the New College Choir offers what seems to be the ideal sound quality. All the voices are mellow and light – which may well surprise and initially disconcert those who are accustomed to a more stentorian reading of the bass solo that opens *Glorious and powerful God*, for example. To match this, Edward Higginbottom prefers dancing tempos, occasionally perhaps thereby covering a much-treasured detail, but in general stressing the range of colours and rhythms that are so vital to this music. His organist, David Burchell, adds to the effect with his limpid and stylish playing. Higginbottom also gives us an important treat in reconstructing the incomplete *Te Deum* and *Jubilate* of the large Second Service. This is impressive and wonderful music; but, more than that, the complete Second Service is, at some 24 minutes, the longest and grandest conception that survives from Gibbons. It is very good to have; and it is doubly good to hear the massive and varied *Te Deum* moulded so sensitively.

Alberto Ginastera
Argentinian 1916-1983

Ginastera Harp Concerto, Op. 25.
Glière Harp Concerto, Op. 74. Concerto for Coloratura Soprano and Orchestra, Op. 82.
Eileen Hulse *sop* **Rachel Masters** *hp*
City of London Sinfonia / Richard Hickox.
Chandos CHAN9094 (65 minutes: DDD). Recorded 1992.   Ⓕ

Glière was among the comparatively few front-rank Russian composers who stayed on in their homeland after the 1917 Revolution. The music he composed there adopted a middle-of-the-road conservative style which helped him to steer clear of the more viscous controversies of the 1920s and 1930s. The Concertos for harp and coloratura soprano date from 1938 and 1942 respectively, and are unashamedly ingratiating, high-grade mood-music, here played and recorded in a manner that those with a sweet tooth should find absolutely irresistible. The Harp Concerto by Ginastera is made of sterner stuff, but only slightly – it's Bartókian acerbities are tempered by an engaging Latin American swing. Once again the performance is crisp and bouncy, although in this instance the reverberant recording takes something of the edge off the rhythmic bite.

Panambí. Estancia.
Luis Gaeta *bass-bar* **London Symphony Orchestra / Gisèle Ben-Dor.**
Conifer Classics 75605 51336-2 (72 minutes: DDD). Recorded 1997.   ⒻⒺ

Panambí, a ballet on a supernatural legend of the Guaraní Indians, was the first work that Ginastera acknowledged (dismissing earlier efforts), and it made the 21-year-old's name, immediately winning a well-merited national prize and stimulating the choreographer Lincoln Kirstein to commission another ballet (*Estancia*) from him. The theme in this case was a day on a ranch, with the traditional figure of the gaucho as its focus. Recordings of extracts from *Estancia*, and the concert suite from *Panambí*, have been available, but here for the first time are the complete ballets. With typical youthful abandon, Ginastera demanded a huge orchestra (including quadruple woodwind, piano, celesta and two harps, besides masses of percussion with no fewer than three bass-drums) for *Panambí*, but used it with a remarkably imaginative sense of elaborately exotic colour – as the introductory movement at once reveals. Stylistically the music ranges from the primitive violence of the 'Warriors' dance' and the *Sacre*-influenced 'Invocation to the spirits of power' to the scintillating brilliance of 'The water sprites' and to a luscious lyricism that offers opportunities to several orchestral soloists. The 'Dawn' finale is worthy to stand beside Ravel's. *Estancia* calls for a normal-size orchestra (though again with a large percussion contingent) but is no less vigorous: gaucho existence is clearly extremely macho. It is a score of heady excitement (as in the frenetic final 'Malambo'), with occasional lyrical sections like 'Afternoon' and 'Twilight idyll', but in general it is rather less inventive, relying perhaps overmuch on repetitive patterns (as in the 'Rodeo'). Luis Gaeta is a histrionic narrator but a firm-voiced singer. Strikingly virtuosic playing throughout by the LSO, and spectacular recording.

Umberto Giordano
Italian 1867-1948

Andrea Chénier.
Luciano Pavarotti *ten* Andrea Chénier; **Leo Nucci** *bar* Gerard; **Montserrat Caballé** *sop* Maddalena; **Kathleen Kuhlmann** *mez* Bersi; **Astrid Varnay** *sop* Countess di Coigny; **Christa Ludwig** *mez* Madelon; **Tom Krause** *bar* Roucher; **Hugues Cuénod** *ten* Fleville;

Giordano Opera

Neil Howlett bar Fouquier-Tinville, Major-domo; **Giorgio Tadeo** bass Mathieu;
Piero De Palma ten Incredible; **Florindo Andreolli** ten Abate; **Giuseppe Morresi** bass Schmidt;
Ralph Hamer bass Dumas;
Welsh National Opera Chorus; National Philharmonic Orchestra / Riccardo Chailly.
Decca 410 117-2DH2 (two discs: 107 minutes: DDD). Notes, text and translation included.
Recorded 1982-84.   Ⓕ

Whatever else, this is undoubtedly the best-recorded and probably the best-conducted *Chénier* yet.
Chailly overconducts the score, drawing attention to himself rather than to Giordano, but by and
large he is sympathetic to both the score and his singers. *Chénier* isn't easy to interpret; it bustles
along busily all the time, but not always with much distinction or to any very strong purpose.
Chailly almost convinces us that the story and the music, especially where Gérard is concerned, is
about something more than merely contrivance and cardboard, and he and the National
Philharmonic bring out the work's colour and melodrama, both vividly presented. For the many
and important small roles, Decca has assembled half a dozen old faithfuls in various states of vocal
health. Varnay goes rather over the top as the old Countess in Act 1. The three *comprimario* tenors,
whose combined ages must be more than 200, all make the mark with Piero De Palma the most
potent as the spy Incredible, an object-lesson in acting with the voice. Giorgio Tadeo, a *buffo* bass
of distinction, here turns himself into the nasty Mathieu. Krause is an honourable Roucher. But
Christa Ludwig is better than any, making old Madelon's brief appearance into a moving vignette.
Of the younger singers, Kathleen Kuhlmann is a rather anonymous Bersi, Neil Howlett a snarling
Fouquier-Tinville.

But *Chénier* stands or falls by its three principals. All three here perform eloquently. Pavarotti tends
to rasp his way through the Improvviso, but improves no end in his first love duet with Maddalena,
and defies the court in Act 3 with real heroism. But it is in the final act that his tone recaptures its
old refulgence in his poetic musings and his death-going duet. Again and again a phrase will set
Caballé apart as a uniquely subtle artist. There are occasionally those self-regarding mannerisms
that she indulges in, also a want of sheer tonal weight, but you will warm to her portrayal. Nucci's
Gérard is excellent, delivered with a nice balance between line and punch. Pavarotti and Caballé
enthusiasts will need to have this set; others should perhaps endeavour to hear the pros and cons of
Levine.

Andrea Chénier.
Plácido Domingo ten Andrea Chénier; **Renata Scotto** sop Maddalena;
Sherrill Milnes bar Carlo Gérard; **Michael Sénéchal** ten Incredible; **Maria Ewing** mez Bersi;
Gwendolyn Killebrew mez Madelon; **Jean Kraft** mez Countess; **Allan Monk** bar Roucher;
Terence Sharpe bar Fléville; **Stuart Harling** bass Fouquier-Tinville; **Isser Bushkin** bass Schmidt;
Malcolm King bass Dumas; **Piero De Palma** ten Abate; **Nigel Beavan** bass-bar
Maestro di casa; **Enzo Dara** bar Mathieu;
John Alldis Choir; National Philharmonic Orchestra / James Levine.
RCA 74321 39499-2 (two discs: 114 minutes: ADD). Notes, text and translation included.
Recorded 1976.   Ⓜ

Choosing between these two recordings, it might seem sensible to start with the tenor in the
title-role, and here a strong inclination would be to plump for RCA and Domingo: he is in
splendid voice, with a touch of nobility to his manner that makes for a convincing portrayal
of a poet. Pavarotti (Chailly) begins with a rather leather-lunged Improvviso, but he later finds
poetry in the role as well, especially when responding to his soprano, Caballé, who is rather
stretched by the more exhausting reaches of her role and sounds audibly grateful for the
occasional opportunities he gives her to float rather than belt a high-lying phrase. However,
Pavarotti is an *Italian* tenor, and his Italianate sense of line adds one per cent or so of elegance to
some phrases that even Domingo cannot match. Caballé does many things beautifully, and her fine-
spun *pianissimos* and subtle shadings only occasionally sound mannered, but the role is undeniably
half-a-size too big for her. So it is for Scotto, you might say, and a hint of strain is audible once or
twice, in her timbre rather than her phrasing. It is her phrasing, indeed, that tips the balance back
to RCA: Scotto is as subtle a vocalist as Caballé, but she gives meaning and eloquence to every
phrase without ever breaking the long line, which one cannot always say of the Spanish soprano.
Matters are about even as far as the baritones are concerned: Milnes acts admirably, but refrains
from over-acting, and the voice is rich and characterful. In the supporting cast, but RCA's striking
Bersi, vividly characterized Incredible, and their Roucher, too, are not outmatched (only their
Madelon, both fruity and acid – a grapefruit of a voice – is disappointing). A lot of people will
enjoy the huge energy and bustle of Levine's direction. It is vividly characterful, but a shade
exhausting and overassertive. The flow of the music seems more natural in Chailly's hands, and
orchestral detail is clearer. The Decca recording, too, is warmer than the RCA, which has a slight
edge to it.

Giordano Fedora.
Magda Olivero *sop* Fedora; **Mario del Monaco** *ten* Loris; **Tito Gobbi** *bar* de Siriex;
Leonardo Monreale *bass* Lorek, Nicola; **Lucia Cappellino** *sop* Olga;
Virgilio Carbonari *bass* Borov; **Silvio Maionica** *bass* Grech; **Piero de Palma** *ten* Rouvel;
Peter Binder *bar* Kiril; **Dame Kiri Te Kanawa** *sop* Dmitri; **Riccardo Cassinelli** *ten* Desire;
Athos Cesarini *ten* Sergio; **Pascal Rogé** *pf* Boleslao Lazinski;
Monte-Carlo Opera Chorus and Orchestra / Lamberto Gardelli.
Zandonai Francesca da Rimini: Act 2 – E ancora sgombro il campo del comune? ... Date il
segno, Paolo, date ... Un'erba io m'avea, per sanare ... Onta et orrore sopra[abde]. Act 3 – No,
Smadragedi, no! ... Paolo, datemi pace! ... Ah la parola chi i miei occhi incontrano[ab]. Act 4 – Ora
andate ... E così, vada s'è pur mio destino[abc].
[a]**Magda Oliviero** *sop* Francesca; [b]**Mario del Monaco** *ten* Paolo; [c]**Annamaria Gasparini** *mez*
Biancofiore; [d]**Virgilio Carbonari** *bass* Man-at-arms; [e]**Athos Cesarini** *ten* Archer;
Monte-Carlo Opera Orchestra / Nicola Rescigno.
Decca Grand Opera 433 033-2DM2 (two discs: 132 minutes: ADD). Notes, texts and translations
included. Recorded 1969. Ⓜ

Fedora has some Trivial Pursuits claim to be the first opera to feature bicycles in the plot! The
music is richly textured orchestrally and finely written for the voices, and this recording made in
1969 is notable for the singing of Magda Olivero and Mario del Monaco, who, despite being in
their mid-fifties, bring tremendous verve, vocal resource and dramatic skill to their roles. Tito
Gobbi has less to do as the diplomat de Siriex, but gives him character, and another plus is the
playing of Pascal Rogé, who performs the non-singing role of the Polish pianist and spy Boleslao
Lazinski in Act 2 who, while performing, eavesdrops on a dialogue between Loris and Fedora. This
exchange is a marvellous example of verismo writing and singing, and so is their final scene with
her death. The set opens with excerpts from another opera, Zandonai's *Francesca da Rimini* with
the same two excellent principals. The recordings are as clear and fresh-sounding as they were on
the original releases.

Mauro Giuliani
Italian 1781-1829

Giuliani Guitar Concerto No. 1 in A major, Op. 30.
Schubert Sonata for Arpeggione and Piano in A minor, D821 (arr. Williams).
John Williams *gtr*
Australian Chamber Orchestra.
Sony Classical SK63385 (52 minutes: DDD). Recorded 1998. Ⓕ

The guitar has played a part in several adaptations of the Schubert A minor Sonata, substituting
for either the arpeggione or the piano, but never before with a string orchestra in the supporting
role, reversing the bowed/percussive relationship. Good arranging does not consist of literal
adherence to the original score but, as here, in making small changes to take advantage of the new
instrumentation. Rarely has such a transmutation been accomplished with greater conviction. Put
any doubts or prejudices you may have on the back burner and prepare to enjoy familiar beauty in
new clothing. The Giuliani is familiar in every respect – except that of interpretation. What we have
in this recording is the recognition of the relationship between instrumental and vocal music in
Giuliani's work; it is apparent in his (and others') frequent adaptation of operatic music for the
guitar, but has more or less escaped the attention of guitarists on record. The vocal quality of the
writing is fully realized here, producing what might even be regarded as the first stylistically faithful
recording of the First Concerto. The performances are exemplary and praise should also extend to
the engineers who recorded them with such clarity and ideal balance. If you already have these
works, don't let it deter you from adding this revelatory one to your collection.

Choix de mes fleurs chéries, Op. 46 – Le jasmin; Le rosmarin; La rose. Etude in E minor, Op. 100
No. 13. Grande ouverture, Op. 61. Leçons progressives, Op. 51 Nos. 3, 7 and 14. Minuetto,
Op. 73 No. 9. Preludes, Op. 83 Nos. 5 and 6. Rondeaux progressives, Op. 14 Nos. 1 and 5.
Six variations, Op. 20. Variazioni sulla cavatina favorita, Op. 101, 'De calma oh ciel'.
David Starobin *gtr*
Bridge BCD9029 (48 minutes: DDD). Recorded 1990. Ⓕ

Giuliani was born and died in Italy, in between which he lived for many years in Vienna, where he
achieved great success in salon-music circles with his guitar virtuosity and counted many
distinguished musicians amongst his friends and colleagues. He was in a sense the rival of Sor for
the guitar's nineteenth-century crown but the two were 'chalk and cheese'. Giuliani the more

volatile, ebullient and (as a composer) loquacious – with over 200 works as against Sor's less than 70. Giuliani's incessant desire to please his public (and to make much-needed money in the process) led to the presence of much treadmill dross amongst the gold of his best works, a thing that has contributed to his chronic undervaluation. David Starobin, playing a nineteenth-century guitar, greatly helps to redress the balance in his unfailingly musical and technically fluent playing of a selection of Giuliani's best works. Some testify to Giuliani's contribution to the student literature, the titles of others reflect the salon tastes at which they were aimed; all show that, when he took the trouble, Giuliani could be charming, polished and ingenious, all at the same time. This is a disc to charm the ear without bruising the emotions, in the nicest possible way.

Philip Glass

American 1937

Symphony No. 2. Orphée – Interlude. Concerto for Saxophone Quartet and Orchestra.
Raschèr Saxophone Quartet (Carina Raschèr *sop sax* Harry Kinross White *alto sax* Bruce Weinberger *ten sax* Kenneth Coon *bass sax*)
Vienna Radio Symphony Orchestra, Stuttgart Chamber Orchestra / Dennis Russell Davies.
Nonesuch 7559-79496-2 (69 minutes: DDD). Recorded 1996. (F)

Glass is not a symphonist in the conventional sense, but then nor was Messiaen. Glass himself has indicated that his large-scale orchestral works are conceived with their probable role in the conventions of concert programming (and, presumably, recording) in mind. This sounds outrageously manipulative when stated explicitly, but is of course no more than a description of the context of the symphonic form since its inception, which conveniently returns us to square one. Glass has also said that he devoted his earlier career to subtracting elements from his music and is now deciding what to put back in. In the case of this symphony, the specified element is polytonality, the presence of which in much twentieth-century music (Glass cites Honegger, Milhaud and Villa-Lobos in his booklet-note) is perhaps taken for granted. However, when it is added into this stripped-down, austere idiom, the results are quite striking. The opening movement recalls the prelude to *Akhnaten*, the third and final movement reprises the chattering arpeggios of the composer's earlier works, closing with an exciting – indeed, viscera-loosening – *crescendo*. After recovering during the snippet from *Orphée*, we come to the marvellous Concerto. Conceived for performance either as a quartet or in this quartet-plus-orchestra version, this is a gloriously animated work, almost Coplandesque, yet remaining true to Glass's own vision. Despite being presented as the secondary work on this disc, its presence makes the whole recommendable.

The Canyon. Itaipú[a].
Atlanta Symphony [a]**Chorus and Orchestra / Robert Shaw.**
Sony Classical SK46352 (56 minutes: DDD). (F)

Space is central to the work of most composers who have cultivated minimalist techniques: Reich Górecki, Kancheli, MacMillan, Bryars and Glass all employ it as an essential creative constituent, and all have in some way managed to reclaim it for our own claustrophobic imaginations. The idea of spacious natural vistas has always been central to the work of Glass. *Itaipú* and *The Canyon* are the second and third of his 'portraits of nature', the former being a commission from the Atlanta Symphony Orchestra and Chorus, while the latter was composed specifically for the Rotterdam Philharmonic. Itaipú is located on the Paraná River, which in turn forms the border between Brazil and Paraguay. It is the location of a massive hydro-electric dam with individual generators large enough to house a full symphony orchestra. So it's little wonder that Itaipú provided Glass with instant inspiration. The score itself is divided into four separate sections and calls on substantial orchestral and choral forces. Although consistent with Glass's other work, *Itaipú* has an especially dark, rugged tonal profile. The hub of the work – 'The Dam' itself – is in the third movement, where brass and winds abet a pounding ostinato and a series of modulations redolent of such scenically aware late-romantics as Sibelius, Bruckner and Roy Harris. It's one of the most arresting passages in Glass's output and gives a vivid impression of the dam's overwhelming physical presence.

Itaipú sets Guarani Indian texts, although Glass intended that the words support the music, rather than vice versa. *The Canyon* is purely orchestral, and much shorter. It's built around two basic ideas, with a jagged middle section that heats up for a powerful climax. Less heavily scored than *Itaipú*, *The Canyon* utilizes a large array of percussion, which Glass exploits with his usual ear for nuance. But *Itaipú* is definitely the disc's main 'event' – a patient, cumulatively powerful essay, easily assimilated and well enough crafted to repay repeated listening. Those who find certain other of Glass's works monotonous and uneventful would do well to sample it. The recordings are cleanly balanced, the performances neat. Recommended, especially to those not normally 'behind Glass'.

La Belle et la Bête.
Janice Felty *mez* La Belle; **Gregory Purnhagen** *bar* La Bête, Avenant, Ardent, Port Official;
John Kuether *bass* Father, Usurer; **Ana Maria Martinez** *sop* Felicie; **Hallie Neill** *sop* Adelaide;
Zheng Zhou *bar* Ludovic;
Philip Glass Ensemble / Michael Riesman.
Nonesuch 7559-79347-2 (two discs: 89 minutes: DDD). Notes, text and translation included.
Recorded 1994. Ⓕ

This is one of Philip Glass's most innovative and impressive works. It isn't exactly an opera, nor is it film music; cantata is the nearest term, but even that won't really convey the idea. What Glass has done is to make a setting of the script for Jean Cocteau's 1946 film *La Belle et la Bête*, using every word as it is spoken in the film, but having it sung, the whole thing designed to be performed in concert, with a print of the film being projected silently. Of all Cocteau's movies, *La Belle et la Bête* is visually the most stylized, with its images of the Beast's castle, and the Vermeeresque settings for the family home of the merchant whose search for a rose to give to his youngest daughter sets off the nightmarish story. Cocteau described his film as 'the illustration of the border that separates one world from the other'. For all its surreal photography and extravagant décor by Christian Bérard (the apparently living, arms-bearing candelabra, poking out from the wall, have influenced hundreds of interior decorators), the dialogue in the film is delivered in a naturalistic way. The words are sung in an ethereal, other-worldly way, and the music trembles with typical Glass motifs. *La Belle et la Bête* hovers somewhere between genteel beat music and Messiaen-influenced *mélodie* and defies categorization. As Beauty, Janice Felty's voice matches the image of Josette Day in the film, but Gregory Purnhagen's light baritone would never suggest Jean Marais, whose smoky tones were such an inspiration to Cocteau. Most people prefer the Beast with his hairy face and claws to the rather effete-looking Prince Charming who emerges at the end, and Glass's music seems to make an ironic commentary on this transformation. Well worth investigating.

Alexander Glazunov Russian/USSR 1865-1936
Violin Concerto in A minor, Op. 82.

Glazunov Violin Concerto.
Dvořák Violin Concerto in A minor, B108.
Frank Peter Zimmermann *vn*
London Philharmonic Orchestra / Franz Welser-Möst.
EMI CDC7 54872-2 (52 minutes: DDD). Recorded 1993. Ⓕ

It is characteristic of Frank Peter Zimmermann that, even in two Slavonic blockbusters among violin concertos, he draws out the lighter qualities, tackling the most formidable passagework with quicksilver agility and precision, and finding tenderness and poetry in the big melodies rather than juicy romanticism. If at first you find such a relatively lightweight approach leaves you short on panache and bravura, you should quickly come to enjoy the freshness of Zimmermann's view. His very assurance, too, with clean, seemingly effortless articulation and intonation even in the most formidable passages of double-stopping, may rob the performances of something in sheer excitement, but the purely musical qualities provide ample compensation. Zimmermann, for all his emotional restraint and his refusal to use a big fat tone in the main lyrical themes, is hardly too cool for the music. With Welser-Möst and the LPO providing clean, sympathetic accompaniments to match the soloist, his rubato is free and natural without self-indulgence. Zimmermann's observance of *pianissimo* markings, normally disregarded, brings magical moments.

One catches the breath when the *Tranquillo* theme returns in the Glazunov, and the whole of the slow movement of the Dvořák is intensely beautiful. In the latter's finale, it makes up in its sense of fun for any lack of flamboyance. The marking is, after all, *Allegro giocoso*, and his similar avoidance of vulgarity in the finale of the Glazunov equally results in a carefree, lilting performance, with admirably clear triplets in the closing passage. So although these performances – with the soloist balanced naturally, not spotlit – may not please traditionalists looking for blockbusting qualities, anyone fancying this apt but unusual coupling should certainly investigate.

Glazunov Violin Concerto.
Kabalevsky Violin Concerto in C major, Op. 48.
Tchaikovsky Valse-scherzo in C major, Op. 34. Souvenir d'un lieu cher, Op. 42 (orch. Glazunov).
Gil Shaham *vn*
Russian National Orchestra / Mikhail Pletnev.
DG 457 064-2GH (62 minutes: DDD). Recorded 1996. Ⓕ

Easily the most substantial work in this enjoyably light-hearted programme is the Glazunov Violin Concerto, still generally undervalued because of its conservative idiom. Not that Shaham's account is in any way radical. After Maxim Vengerov's intense and penetrating Teldec version, Shaham's sounds relaxed and smoochy, his warm-toned instrument set somewhat closer than the orchestra in the wide open spaces of the Great Hall of the Moscow Conservatory. The generous romantic manner almost but not quite conceals a few moments of suspect intonation that Jascha Heifetz would never have passed. Unlike the Glazunov, Kabalevsky's work is in three separate, small-scale movements. One of his 'youth' concertos, it dates from 1948, the year in which most of his peer group faced ideological censure. It isn't great music, and yet there is a natural, unforced quality about its invention that stands up well enough. The slow movement is memorable and the watered-down Prokofiev of the rest is by no means unattractive. The orchestral playing here is impressively clean and often radiantly beautiful. The Tchaikovsky *Souvenir d'un lieu cher* is heard in Glazunov's orchestration and the *Valse-scherzo* wraps things up in skittering, suitably dazzling fashion. Heard live, such a performance would bring the house down.

Glazunov Violin Concerto.
Tchaikovsky Violin Concerto in D major, Op. 35.
Maxim Vengerov *vn*
Berlin Philharmonic Orchestra / Claudio Abbado.
Teldec 4509-90881-2 (55 minutes: DDD). Recorded 1995.   Ⓕ**Ⓔ**

This seems to be the only disc coupling what might reasonably be counted as the two greatest romantic Russian violin concertos: if Vengerov's reading of the Tchaikovsky emerges clearly as a leading contender among many superb versions, in the Glazunov he turns this warhorse concerto from a display piece into a work of far wider-ranging emotions. This Tchaikovsky immediately establishes itself as a big performance in the manner and in the range of dynamic of the playing. For all his power, and his youthfully eager love of brilliance, Vengerov is never reluctant to play really softly, and how magical that often is. Each theme in turn is sharply characterized, with dynamic contrasts cleanly established. The central Canzonetta is full of Russian temperament, with Vengerov freer in his rubato than most rivals, but conveying such natural unforced expressiveness there is nothing self-conscious about it. The finale is fast, light and sparkling, with articulation breathtakingly clean to match the transparency of the orchestral textures as controlled by Abbado. Vengerov rounds the performance off with an explosion of excitement such as one might expect in the concert hall but not often in the recording studio. The Glazunov is if anything even more remarkable, with Vengerov making you appreciate afresh what a wonderful and varied sequence of melodies Glazunov offers. It is characteristic of Vengerov how he shades and contrasts his tone colours. He reserves his big, romantic tone for the third theme, where most rivals let loose sooner with less subtle results. As in the Tchaikovsky, rubato is free but always spontaneous-sounding, and the lolloping fourth section brings some delicious *portamento*. Predictably the dashing final section is spectacular in its brilliance, with orchestral textures fresh and clean.

Glazunov The Seasons – ballet, Op. 67.
Tchaikovsky The Nutcracker – ballet, Op. 71[a].
[a]**Finchley Children's Music Group; Royal Phiharmonic Orchestra / Vladimir Ashkenazy.**
Decca 433 000-2DH2 (two discs: 131 minutes: DDD). Recorded 1989-90.   Ⓕ**Ⓢ**

One cannot think of a happier coupling than Glazunov's complete *Seasons* – perhaps his finest and most successful score – with Tchaikovsky's *Nutcracker*. Glazunov's delightful ballet, with even the winter's 'Frost', 'Hail', 'Ice' and 'Snow', glamorously presented, and the bitterness of a Russian winter quite forgotten are, like the scenario of the *Nutcracker*, part of a child's fantasy world. Glazunov's twinklingly dainty scoring of the picturesque snowy characters is contrasted with the glowing summer warmth of the 'Waltz of the cornflowers and poppies', and the vigorously thrusting tune (perhaps the most memorable theme he ever wrote) of the Autumn 'Bacchanale'. Tchaikovsky's ballet is beautifully played by the RPO; there is much finesse and sparkle, and the lightest and most graceful rhythmic touch from Ashkenazy. The conductor's affection for the score and his feeling for Tchaikovsky's multi-hued orchestral palette is a constant delight to the ear. Yet the big *Pas de deux* brings a climax of Russian fervour. The recording is properly expansive here; made at Walthamstow, it sets everything within a glowing acoustic ambience. The aural richness and glowing woodwind detail of the recording of *The Seasons* is most impressive.

Four Preludes and Fugues, Op. 101. Prelude and Fugue in D minor, Op. 62. Prelude and Fugue in E minor (1926).
Stephen Coombs *pf*
Hyperion CDA66855 (60 minutes: DDD). Recorded 1995.   Ⓕ

Piano Sonata No. 2 in E minor, Op. 75. Prelude and Two Mazurkas, Op. 25. Two Impromptus, Op. 54. Idylle, Op. 103. Barcarolle sur les touches noires. Song of the Volga Boatmen, Op. 97 (arr. Siloti). In modo religioso, Op. 38. Triumphal March, Op. 40 (with **Holst Singers / Stephen Layton**). Pas de caractère, Op. 68 (all arr. cpsr).
Stephen Coombs pf
Hyperion CDA66866 (70 minutes: DDD). Recorded 1995.   Ⓕ

The third disc in Stephen Coombs's series is devoted to Glazunov's six essays in the form of the prelude and fugue. It begins and ends with intricately wrought homages to Bach – the first, of 1899, darker and much more chromatic than the last, a wholesome specimen revealing none of the problems of the composer's declining years. The Op. 101 set is both freer and more fantastical in its fugal treatments. Taken as a whole, it seems to be Glazunov's towering achievement in any field, working its way from the restless A minor No. 1, with its hyper-Elgarian sequences, and the capricious No. 2, to the C minor Prelude and Fugue – swooning Tchaikovskian romanticism within the perspectives of Bach and Chopin – and on to a thoroughly diatonic C major celebration – hard-earned victory indeed. Coombs meets the challenge unflinchingly; there's a little too much use of the sustaining pedal in the earlier chromatic welters, but the later stages are appropriately lucid and bright.

The fugue at the heart of the Second Sonata's finale does give us an extra taste of his contrapuntal genius, and it's all the more welcome in a sea of romantic rodomontade. That, though, is clearly what Glazunov felt the piano sonata was all about – and he does it with style: the E major transformation of the scherzo theme towards the end of this exhaustingly busy Second Sonata is a fine stroke. The rest of Vol. 4 either ties up loose ends, following Glazunov along the road of whimsical, radiant Chopin stylization, or throws in some enjoyable novelties. Coombs's orchestral thunder comes in useful for the weighty transcription of a *Triumphal March* for the Chicago Columbian Exposition; when the Holst Singers enter with their 'Slava, Columbus's, it's probably just as well that the recording presents them as a solid backdrop to the busy piano part, not a wall in front of it. Glazunov's handling of *John Brown's Body* here shows a surprising wit and spirit, and the serious transcription of the *Song of the Volga Boatmen* that follows, with its shades of Mussorgsky's 'Bydlo', makes a surprising contrast – one of many that will surely raise this composer's status immeasurably.

Reyngol'd Glière   Ukraine/USSR 1875-1956

Symphony No. 2 in C minor, Op. 25. The Red Poppy – Ballet Suite, Op. 70.
New Jersey Symphony Orchestra / Zdenek Macal.
Delos DE3178 (73 minutes: DDD). Recorded 1995.   Ⓕ

This performance of Glière's colourful late-romantic Second Symphony is extremely satisfying, with a fine blend of transparency and warmth. Glière never puts a foot wrong, but that's because he's going along trails blazed for him by others long before 1908. Although the romantic parts of *Firebird* are audibly just round the corner, here the magic is tamed and the amount of repetition can even become slightly irksome. The New Jersey cor anglais plays with peerless refinement in the slow movement, and Macal coaxes suave phrasing from his musicians. Delos could have made its disc indispensable by choosing something less well known than the *Red Poppy* Suite as a filler; but for newcomers to the composer this is certainly a necessary work. Delos makes a big pitch about their 'Virtual Reality' recording quality. Ultimately destined for Surround Sound Home Theatre reproduction, it involves, amongst other things, a careful choice of venue, slightly more than usual spatial separation of the players in the hall, and a pragmatic approach to multi-miking.

Symphony No. 3 in B minor, Op. 42, 'Il'ya Mouromets'.
Royal Philharmonic Orchestra / Harold Farberman.
Unicorn-Kanchana Souvenir UKCD2014/5 (two discs: 93 minutes: DDD). Recorded 1978.   Ⓜ

Glière's Third Symphony of 1912 is his undoubted masterpiece. It is a supremely late-romantic Technicolor score, extreme but never uncontrolled in its excess, and always directed towards vividness of narrative rather than self-display. Now usually performed without the once-standard cuts, its four movements are fairly protracted, the more so when taken at exceptionally spacious tempos as they are here by Harold Farberman. But the spaciousness proves the making of the piece, giving the dimensions a truly epic feel and developing an unstoppable slow momentum. The recording quality no longer quite seems to justify the 'demonstration-class' praise originally accorded it, but it is still impressive enough.

Mikhail Glinka

Russian 1804-1857

Ruslan and Lyudmila.
Vladimir Ognovienko *bass-bar* Ruslan; **Anna Netrebko** *sop* Lyudmila; **Mikhail Kit** *bar* Svetozar;
Larissa Diadkova *mez* Ratmir; **Gennadi Bezzubenkov** *bass* Farlaf; **Galina Gorchakova** *sop*
Gorislava; **Konstantin Pluzhnikov** *ten* Finn; **Irina Bogachova** *mez* Naina; **Yuri Marusin** *ten*
Bayan; **Chorus and Orchestra of the Kirov Theatre / Valery Gergiev.**
Philips 446 746-2PH3 (three discs: 202 minutes: DDD). Notes, text and translation included.
Recorded live in 1995.   Ⓕ

With Gergiev, the playing rises well above the reliability of long-practised routine; indeed, the
Overture, always a winner, has quite exceptional brilliance and exhilaration. Later, the performance
is just as remarkable for its refinement of detail and for sensitivity in the meditative, tender passages
which enrich the musical score as they do the humanity of this operatic fairy-tale. The principals
act with the professionalism of those brought up in a rigid school; they know their job and proceed
accordingly. The Ruslan (Ognovienko) is an ample bass-baritone, the Farlaf (Bezzubenkov) a sturdy
bass with a neat capacity for patter, Bayan (Marusin) a tenor with tense tone, slightly flat
intonation, especially memorable as the bardic figure who holds in thrall an audience with a longer
attention-span than might be counted on today. Larissa Diadkova's Ratmir made a strong
impression in the 1995 Edinburgh Festival and it is good to hear her here. Gorchakova brings
glamour of voice to her role of Gorislava, and the Lyudmila of Netrebko is outstanding.

Christoph Gluck

Bohemian 1714-1787

Gluck Paride ed Elena – O del mio dolce ardor. Orfeo ed Euridice – Che puro ciel!; Che farò
senza Euridice. Alceste – Non vi turbate.
Haydn Il mondo della luna – Una donna come me. Orlando Paladino – Ad un sguardo, a un
cenno solo. La fedeltà premiata – Deh soccorri un'infelice.
Mozart Le nozze di Figaro – Voi che sapete. Don Giovanni – Batti, batti; Vedrai, carino; In quali
eccessi ... Mi tradì quell'alma ingrata. Lucio Silla – Dunque sperar ... Il tenero momento. La finta
giardiniera – Dolce d'amor compagna. La clemenza di Tito – Ecco il punto, oh Vitellia ... Non più di
fiori.
Anne Sofie von Otter *mez* **The English Concert / Trevor Pinnock** *hpd*
Archiv Produktion 449 206-2AH (71 minutes: DDD). Texts and translations included.
Recorded 1995.   ⒻⓅ

For the sake of both vocal and family well-being, Anne Sofie von Otter has always followed the
wise course of self-rationing in opera. This disc, an entirely personal selection of arias from the
Viennese classical period, means all the more to her including, as it does, arias sung by dramatic
and passionate women 'most of whom', von Otter admits in the accompanying notes, 'I have never
performed on stage and, alas, probably never will'. They include *La clemenza di Tito*'s Vitellia whom
von Otter has irresistibly observed in her own role as Sesto: here she at last voices her guilt at
implicating Sesto in her crime of passion, and expresses that unique fusion of sadness and
desperation of 'Non più di fiori' in the eloquent company of Colin Lawson's basset-horn, followed
by Gluck's Alceste, again keenly observed by von Otter in a *comprimario* role. Her lyric mezzo is
perfectly suited to that grave Gluckian passion of 'Non vi turbate'. Gluck's Orfeo is, of course,
familiar to von Otter at first hand, and here The English Concert's introduction to the accompanied
recitative which precedes 'Che farò' creates exquisitely the 'nuova serena luce' of the Elysian fields
against which von Otter's grief, affectingly ornamented, is the darker, the more plangent.

The Mozart arias evoke memorable stage and concert performances by von Otter: a Cherubino
whose phrasing combines with that of the wind soloists to create the warm breath of tender
burgeoning sensuality in 'Voi che sapete'; a Cecilio (*Lucio Silla*) whose coloratura captures the
thrilled anticipation of that 'tenero momento'; and a moustachioed Ramiro (*La finta giardiniera*)
who pays ecstatic *cantabile* tribute to the power of love.

Armide.
Mireille Delunsch *sop* Armide; **Charles Workman** *ten* Renaud; **Laurent Naouri** *bar* Hidraot;
Ewa Podles *mez* Hate; **Françoise Masset** *sop* Phénice, Mélisse; **Nicole Heaston** *sop* Sidonie,
Shepherdess, Lucinde; **Yann Beuron** *ten* Artémidore, Danish Knight; **Brett Polegato** *bar* Ubalde;
Vincent le Texier *bar* Aronte; **Magdalena Kožená** *mez* Pleasure; **Valérie Gabail** *sop* Naiad;
Choeur des Musiciens du Louvre; Les Musiciens du Louvre / Marc Minkowski.
Archiv Produktion 459 616-2AH2 (two discs: 139 minutes: DDD). Notes, text and translation
included. Recorded live in 1996.   ⒻⓅ

'Perhaps the best of all my works', said Gluck of his *Armide*. But this, the fifth of his seven 'reform operas', has never quite captured the public interest as have *Orfeo*, *Alceste*, the two *Iphigénies* and even *Paride ed Elena*. Its plot is thinnish, concerned only with the love of the pagan sorceress Armide, princess of Damascus, for the Christian knight and hero Renaud, and his enchantment, disenchantment and finally his abandonment of her; the secondary characters have no real life. But *Armide* has two features that set it apart. One is the extraordinary soft, sensuous tone of the music; Gluck said that it was meant 'to produce a voluptuous sensation', and that if he were to suffer damnation it would be for the passionate love duet in Act 5. And certainly his orchestral writing here has a warmth, a colour and a richness going far beyond anything in his other reform operas (apart from parts of *Paride ed Elena*). Secondly, there are several great solo dramatic scenes, two of them for Armide herself: the opera's closing scene, in which she rails furiously at Renaud's treachery, and one at the end of Act 2, where, discovering him asleep and torn between love and hatred of her enemy, she cannot bring herself to kill him.

The success of *Armide*, then, depends critically on the Armide herself. Here it goes to Mireille Delunsch, who brings to it a good deal of intensity where it is needed but does not have command of a wide range of tone, and does not seem to make much use of her words. Her voice is perhaps a high mezzo rather than a true soprano, which is by no means inappropriate (imagine what Dame Janet Baker might have done with this role!). There is some graceful singing in the softer music and the scene where she cannot bring herself to kill Renaud is finely done, with a firm line, clear detail and a degree of passion, but neither here nor in the invocation of Hate is there a great deal of agitation or emotional tension. The closing scene is of course powerfully done, and is also conducted with plenty of fire. This is a very adequate performance by Delunsch though a little short of a thrilling one. Renaud is sung by Charles Workman, in a strong tenor, sounding almost baritonal in his opening scene with Artémidore but then singing the sleep song, 'Plus j'observe ces lieux', with soft, sweet tone and much delicacy. The lovers' duet in Act 5 is sung gently and with much charm. Among the other singers, Ewa Podles of course makes a strong impression as Hate with her large and steady voice – and some remarkable music to sing. Françoise Masset and Nicole Heaston sing Armide's confidantes and various smaller roles; Heaston in particular sings with delicacy and allure. Laurent Naouri shows a pleasant, firm baritone as Hidraot, and Yann Beuron (whose lyrical high tenor and clarity of diction give especial pleasure) and Brett Polegato sing the two lesser male roles.

Marc Minkowski makes much of the score's colour and flow. He uses a substantial orchestra which, however, plays lightly and flexibly and with rhythmic spring, and there is some excellent solo woodwind playing (notably the flute solos, from Kate Clark). He tends towards quickish tempos: here and there, and especially in some of the dances (of which a few are omitted), he could have given the music a little more space. But he certainly keeps the score moving along well, is attentive to the accompanying figures and to the characterization of individual numbers – there are jolly and lively pieces here as well as impassioned ones – and he draws alert, spirited singing from the chorus.

Iphigénie en Aulide.
Lynne Dawson *sop* Iphigénie; **José van Dam** *bass* Agamemnon; **Anne Sofie von Otter** *mez* Clytemnestre; **John Aler** *ten* Achille; **Bernard Deletré** *bass* Patrocle; **Gilles Cachemaille** *bass* Calchas; **René Schirrer** *bass* Arcas; **Guillemette Laurens** *mez* Diane; **Ann Monoyios** *sop* First Greek woman, Slave; **Isabelle Eschenbrenner** *sop* Second Greek woman; **Monteverdi Choir; Lyon Opéra Orchestra / Sir John Eliot Gardiner.**
Erato 2292-45003-2 (two discs: 132 minutes: DDD). Notes, text and translation included.
Recorded 1987. Ⓕ

Gluck's first reform opera for Paris has tended to be overshadowed by his other *Iphigénie*, the *Tauride* one. But it does contain some superb things, of which perhaps the finest are the great monologues for Agamemnon. On this recording, José van Dam starts a little coolly; but this only adds force to his big moment at the end of the Second Act where he tussles with himself over the sacrifice of his daughter and – contemplating her death and the screams of the vengeful Eumenides – decides to flout the gods and face the consequences. To this he rises in noble fashion, fully conveying the agonies Agamemnon suffers. The cast in general is strong. Lynne Dawson brings depth of expressive feeling to all she does and her Iphigénie, marked by a slightly grainy sound and much intensity, is very moving. John Aler's Achille too is very fine, touching off the lover and the hero with equal success, singing both with ardour and vitality. There is great force too in the singing of Anne Sofie von Otter as Clytemnestre, especially in her outburst 'Ma fille!' as she imagines her daughter on the sacrificial altar. John Eliot Gardiner's Monteverdi Choir sings with polish, perhaps seeming a little genteel for a crowd of angry Greek soldiers baying for Iphigénie's blood. But Gardiner gives a duly urgent account of the score, pressing it forward eagerly and keeping the tension at a high level even in the dance music. A period-instrument orchestra might have added a certain edge and vitality but this performance wants nothing in authority. Securely recommended.

Orfeo ed Euridice.
Derek Lee Ragin *counterten* Orfeo; **Sylvia McNair** *sop* Euridice; **Cyndia Sieden** *sop* Amore;
Monteverdi Choir; English Baroque Soloists / Sir John Eliot Gardiner.
Philips 434 093-2PH2 (two discs: 89 minutes: DDD). Notes, text and translation included.
Recorded 1991.   ⓅⒺⓇⓇ

This version of *Orfeo*, played on period instruments and following the original text, has a degree of
spiritual force to which other recordings scarcely aspire, and that is to the credit primarily of the
conductor, John Eliot Gardiner. It begins with a taut, almost explosive account of the overture,
moves to a deeply sombre opening chorus and then a *ballo* of intense expressiveness, finely and
carefully moulded phrases (but plenty of air between them) and a lovely translucent orchestral
sound. Every one of the numerous dances in this set, in fact, is the subject of thoughtful musical
characterization, shapely execution and refined timing of detail. Derek Lee Ragin excels himself as
Orpheus; the sound is often very beautiful, the phrasing quite extraordinarily supple and responsive
for a countertenor voice. Eurydice is sung clearly and truly, and with due passion, by Sylvia McNair
– she delivers 'Che fiero momento' and some of the recitative, with considerable force – and the
casting of Cyndia Sieden, with her rather pert, forward voice, as Amore is very successful.

Orfeo ed Euridice (abridged recording).
Kathleen Ferrier *contr* Orfeo; **Ann Ayars** *sop* Euridice; **Zoë Vlachopoulos** *sop* Amore;
Glyndebourne Festival Chorus; Southern Philharmonic Orchestra / Fritz Stiedry.
Dutton Laboratories Essential Archive mono CDEA5015 (63 minutes: ADD). Recorded 1947.   ⒷⒽ

Nothing like comparisons for putting things in perspective. 'What a horrible sound!' you may think
at the beginning of this, and then, if you try the 1992 reissue in Decca's Ovation series, you may
decide that it is relatively Elysian after all. The Decca is edgy, acid and crackly. Dutton has
eliminated the crackles and to some extent rounded the edginess; the acid tone of the violins is
presumably beyond remedy unless through a top-cut of the kind that would draw scandalized
condemnation from practically every reviewer except this one. However, the sound remains
unpleasing though it is certainly a great deal better than its predecessor. Dutton improves on the
previous version also by including everything in the original set. Missing on Ovation are the dance
at the start of Act 2, the flute solo ('Dance of the Blessed Spirits'), Euridice's 'Quest'asilo dolce e
beato', and the first, concerted, 'Trionfi, amore' passage in the finale. The omissions are pointless
and the restorations entirely to be welcomed.

Towards the performance itself you cannot fail to warm. The text is the hybrid Ricordi version that
was most commonly in use at the time and which is now usually disowned in favour of either
Vienna, Paris or Berlioz. In these excerpts it coheres, and the effect of the abridgement is
concentrated and moving. Stiedry's speeds, especially the urgent 'Che farò', are likely (as Alan Blyth
says in his notes) now to seem 'right', far more than they did at the time. The beauty of Ferrier's
singing will often go straight to the heart – in 'Euridice non è più ed io respiro ancor' for instance.
Her Italian is clear and serviceable but unmistakably English, with a slight tendency ('Millay
paynay') towards diphthong. Her colleagues are better in this respect and indeed sing very agreeably
throughout. The chorus has a less impersonal sound than is usual nowadays, but is not all that well
recorded. These of course are minor matters. The set goes into the library, and stays there, for its
noble and intensely human Orfeo.

Leopold Godowsky   Polish/American 1870-1938

Godowsky Studies on Chopin Etudes – No. 44, Nouvelle étude No. 1 in F minor; No. 45,
Nouvelle étude No. 2 in E major; No. 45a, Nouvelle étude No. 2 in D flat major (left hand); No. 46,
Nouvelle étude No. 3 in G major, 'Menuetto'; No. 47 in G flat major, 'Badinage'; No. 48 in F major.
Passacaglia – 44 variations, cadenza and fugue on the opening of Schubert's Unfinished
Symphony.
Chopin (arr. Godowsky) Waltzes – No. 8 in A flat major, Op. 64 No. 3; No. 9 in A flat major,
Op. 69 No. 1; No. 12 in F minor, Op. 70 No. 2; No. 13 in D flat major, Op. 70 No. 3.
Carlo Grante *pf*
Altarus AIR-CD9094 (54 minutes: DDD). Recorded 1996.   Ⓕ

Disarming to the last, Godowsky denies any wish to gild the lily, saying, 'the author would strongly
condemn any artist for tampering ever so little with such works as those of Chopin. The original
Chopin studies remain as intact now as they were before any arrangements of them were even
published; in fact the author claims that after assiduously studying the present versions, many hidden

beauties in the original studies will reveal themselves even to the less observant listener.' This is shrewdly put. And yet Godowsky's decadent and perverse ingenuity, his lubricious ornament and harmony would surely have sent Chopin, had he lived to witness such an 'arrangement', into an apoplectic rage. However, for those of us with less sense of innocence deflowered or of *parti pris*, there is a mischievous delight in confronting such musical wickedness and, for virtuoso fanciers in particular, an almost narcotic addiction to such teeming and lavish inventiveness. To say that Carlo Grante is equal to the occasion would be to deal in understatement. Remarkably, even the most outrageous or overladen difficulty is resolved in purest poetry. His way with the *Passacaglia* hardly suggests the chill that must settle over even the most intrepid virtuoso when he confronts such multi-layered demands (Horowitz confessed he needed six hands to play it). In the *Waltz* paraphrases he makes something civilized, even courtly, out of their cloyingly rich and perfumed overload, a tribute to his unfailing artistry. The recordings are warm if not ideally focused and Grante's achievement will prove a hard act to follow.

Alexander Goehr
British 1932

Arianna.
Ruby Philogene *sop* Arianna; **Angela Hickey** *mez* Venus, Dorilla; **Juliet Schiemann** *sop* Cupid;
Lawrence Zazzo *counterten* Bacchus; **Timothy Dawkins** *bass* Jupiter, First Messenger;
Philip Sheffield *ten* Theseus; **Jeremy Huw Williams** *bar* Counsellor; **Andrew Hewitt** *ten* Herald;
Stephen Rooke *ten* Second Messenger;
Arianna Ensemble / William Lacey.
NMC NMCD054 (two discs: 132 minutes: DDD). Recorded live in 1996.　　　　　　　Ⓕ

The title-page of *Arianna* describes it as a 'lost opera by Monteverdi, composed again by Alexander Goehr'. Precisely. At its heart is Ariadne's lament, all that survives of Monteverdi's score, some of its phrases lightly modified, richly and movingly sung by Ruby Philogene. The vocal line is embedded in an elaborate instrumental texture in Goehr's own manner, in which the modernism he grew up with (his father, the conductor Walter Goehr, was a pupil of Schoenberg) is enriched with a modality that owes a lot to Goehr's own teacher, Olivier Messiaen, but a good deal also to Monteverdi himself. Whether Monteverdi ever set these lines we may never know. Goehr has set them effectively and very beautifully, in Monteverdi's manner: a reminder that although Schoenberg watched over Goehr's cradle, so did Monteverdi – Walter Goehr, who both edited and performed his works, was one of the pioneers of the Monteverdi revival. Indeed, at times, it is as though Goehr and Monteverdi had collaborated on this opera, the vocal lines, brilliant toccatas and madrigalesque choruses often sounding very much like the earlier composer, even the instrumentation suggesting that Claudio Monteverdi has been so deeply excited by the sound of the modern keyed flute, the soprano saxophone and bass clarinet that he cannot resist using them. Often you sense the two composers absorbedly recognizing affinities. Goehr's score is at once a loving homage, an entrancing game, and a vivid evocation for the 1990s of how dazzling, fast-moving and emotionally hard-hitting Monteverdi's lost original must have been to its first audiences in 1608. But it could only have been written in our time and only, you conclude, by Alexander Goehr. The soloists are almost without exception excellent. Philip Sheffield's eloquent Theseus, Jeremy Huw Williams's Counsellor, and the Messengers of Timothy Dawkins and Stephen Rooke stand out, even in the company of Ruby Philogene's tremendous Ariadne, and William Lacey is clearly a conductor of real gifts. The live recording is admirable.

Johann Goldberg
German 1727-1756

Trio Sonatas – F minor (attrib. Quantz); B flat major; A minor; G minor; C major (attrib. Bach, BWV1037). Sonata in C minor for Two Violins, Viola and Continuo. Keyboard Polonaises –
C major; C minor; D minor; E flat major; F major; G major.
Bernward Lohr *hpd* **Musica Alta Ripa.**
Dabringhaus und Grimm MDG309 0709-2 (77 minutes: DDD). Recorded 1996.　　　　　　　Ⓕ

Being remembered on the one hand for music you did not write, while at the same time the only piece of yours that *is* heard is attributed to someone else, is probably not what every composer would wish for. Nevertheless, Johann Gottlieb Goldberg's ghost is probably not complaining too much that his name is for ever linked with Bach's great set of keyboard variations. Whether he really was the player for which that work was intended is open to doubt (although an excellent harpsichordist, he was only 14 years old at the time), but it is no use pretending that his music or name would be as familiar to us today without it, or indeed without the C major Trio Sonata whose style so closely resembles that of his teacher, Bach, that it was long attributed to him and given a

BWV number. The good news to emerge from this disc, however, is that Goldberg is a composer who does deserve recognition on his own merits. These five trio sonatas and a quartet for two violins, viola and continuo show a happy mix of solid compositional skill, with a strong musical personality characterized by rhythmic vigour and muscular harmony. The performances by the Hanover-based Musica Alta Ripa are first-class. The string-players trace a detailed course around the music as if they have always loved it, producing a rich and tactile sounde, and the group's harpsichordist Bernward Lohr does all that could be asked of him with the *Polonaises*. The recording is pleasingly natural.

Károly Goldmark
Austrian/Hungarian 1830-1915

Goldmark Violin Concerto No. 1 in A minor, Op. 28[a].
Lalo Symphonie espagnole, Op. 21[b].
Nathan Milstein *vn*
[a]**Philharmonia Orchestra / Harry Blech;**
[b]**St Louis Symphony Orchestra / Vladimir Golschmann.**
Testament [a]stereo/[b]mono SBT1047 (71 minutes: ADD). Recorded 1954-57.   Ⓕ Ⓗ

The Goldmark A minor Concerto inspired what was surely Nathan Milstein's finest hour in the recording studio, a reading of the utmost refinement: warm, effortlessly brilliant and displaying that unmistakably suave, silken tone. The work itself recalls both Reger and Dvořák, with wistful melodies, lilting rhythms and much busy counterpoint. How delightful, therefore, to have – by way of a bonus – a quarter-of-an-hour's worth of unpublished session takes, where Milstein exhibits the utmost patience (and technical consistency) in playing and replaying even the most taxing passages. Harry Blech directs a beautifully turned accompaniment, and one can only echo the sentiments of Hugh Bean who, reminiscing about these sessions in the context of Testament's excellent booklet, confesses 'that if a visitor from an alien planet asked me, "What does a violin sound like?", I would want him to hear the second theme of the first movement – the innocence, the freshness and purity, the sheer simplicity that takes a lifetime to achieve.' That 'innocence, freshness and purity' are equally apparent in the 1954 *Symphonie espagnole*, in spite of dry, NBC-style sound and an excessively close-up solo image. Vladimir Golschmann's conducting is every bit as distinctive as Blech's, especially in the *Andante*, where the St Louis strings exhibit impressive tonal lustre. This was Milstein's second recording of the piece and, like its predecessor, omits the work's tangy 'Intermezzo'. As a performance it has real sparkle and provides a worthy companion for the superb Goldmark Concerto.

Berthold Goldschmidt
German 1903-1996

Clarinet Concerto[a]. Violin Concerto[b]. Cello Concerto[c].
Sabine Meyer *cl* **Chantal Juillet** *vn* **Yo-Yo Ma** *vc*
[a]**Berlin Komische Opera Orchestra / Yakov Kreizberg;** [b]**Philharmonia Orchestra / Berthold Goldschmidt;** [c]**Montreal Symphony Orchestra / Charles Dutoit.**
Decca Entartete Musik 455 586-2DH (67 minutes: DDD). Recorded 1990s.   Ⓕ

The oblivion into which these three concertos fell after their premières in the 1950s is puzzling. Their style, even by the standards of 40-odd years ago, is not 'advanced', but they make highly original use of traditional forms. The first movement of the Cello Concerto, for example, has half a dozen themes instead of the expected two, but the ideas are subtly related so that the overall impression is of a richly fertile but disciplined invention: there is not the slightest hint of garrulity, nor any sense that the music is derived from Hindemith, whom at a few moments it superficially resembles. In the corresponding movement of the Clarinet Concerto each idea grows out of its predecessor, all of them flowering from a gently lyrical opening which repeatedly returns, sounding beautifully different at each recurrence. It is partly this shrewd and practised but quite unobtrusive craftsmanship that gives these pieces their unmistakably personal flavour, their ability to encompass a wide range of mood and texture within a short movement.

The finale of the Clarinet Concerto includes nimbly pattering scherzo material, gracious lyricism, athletic energy and jovial exuberance, but they are unified, not merely juxtaposed. Goldschmidt's lyricism is firm and strong, and a fast movement does not have to relax to incorporate it. The slow movement of the Violin Concerto is marked *Andante amoroso*, but its beauty is grave and ample, not languishing. All three of these concertos, in fact, are strong and rich enough to repay repeated listening. The Violin Concerto was recorded after a series of performances by Chantal Juillet that so impressed Goldschmidt that he dedicated the neglected 40-year-old work to her. Although he did not live to see the release of that recording he had the satisfaction of knowing that it was being delayed until it could be coupled with his other two concertos. Juillet's reading of 'her' concerto is a splendid one, but the others here are no less fine, and all three are admirably recorded.

Nicolas Gombert
Flemish c1495-c1560

Missa Tempore paschali. Magnificat octavi toni. Adonai, Domine Iesu Christe. In illo tempore loquente Jesu. O Rex gloriae.
Henry's Eight / Jonathan Brown.
Hyperion CDA66943 (65 minutes: DDD). Texts and translations included. Recorded 1996.　　Ⓕ

This disc reinforces the impression of Gombert as the most involving composer of his generation; the booklet-note aptly describes his music as a cross between the imitative processes of Josquin's generation and the seamless style of Ockeghem. The *Missa Tempore paschali* is thought to be a fairly early work, whereas the *Magnificat* is one of a set that probably dates from Gombert's last years. The Mass is most ambitious, culminating in a 12-voice *Agnus Dei* modelled on Brumel's Mass, *Et ecce terrae motus*. The singing is confident and assured, with a good grasp of large-scale form in the *Credo*. The final *Agnus Dei* seems to crown the Mass in a more credible manner. An added feature is the more inventive, and highly convincing, use of false relations in the readings prepared for Henry's Eight by John O'Donnell. The result contains invigorating harmonic incident throughout. The Mass is complemented by some of the composer's most well-known works; the motet, *In illo tempore* is particularly lovely and Henry's Eight respond with some particularly sensitive singing. Those already familiar with their very English, yet full-bodied sound won't be disappointed; those who aren't can start here. In Henry's Eight Gombert has found worthy champions.

Henryk Górecki
Polish 1933

Symphony No. 3, Op. 36, 'Symphony of Sorrowful Songs'.
Dawn Upshaw *sop* **London Sinfonietta / David Zinman.**
Elektra Nonesuch 7559-79282-2 (54 minutes: DDD). Recorded 1991.
Gramophone Award Winner 1993.　　Ⓕ **RR**

Górecki's Third Symphony has become legend. Composed in 1976, it has always had its champions and admirers within the contemporary music world, but in 1993 it found a new audience of undreamt-of proportions. A few weeks after its release, this Elektra Nonesuch release not only entered the classical top-ten charts, but was also riding high in the UK Pop Album charts. It has since become the biggest selling disc of music by a contemporary classical composer. The Symphony, subtitled *Symphony of Sorrowful, Songs* was composed during a period when Górecki's musical style was undergoing a radical change from avant-garde serialism to a more accessible style firmly anchored to tonal traditions. The Symphony's three elegiac movements (or 'songs') form a triptych of laments for all the innocent victims of World War Two and are a reflection upon man's inhumanity to man in general. The songs – including a poignant setting of an inscription scratched by a girl prisoner on the wall of her cell in a Gestapo prison – are beautifully and ethereally sung by Dawn Upshaw, and David Zinman and the London Sinfonietta provide an intense and committed performance of the shimmering orchestral writing. The recording quality is excellent.

Kleines Requiem für eine Polka, Op. 66ª. Harpsichord Concerto, Op. 40ᵇ. Good Night, 'In memoriam Michael Vyner', Op. 63.
Dawn Upshaw *sop* **Sebastian Bell** *fl* **John Constable** *pf* **Elisabeth Chojnacka** *hpd*
David Hockings *perc*
London Sinfonietta / ªDavid Zinman, ᵇMarkus Stenz.
Nonesuch 7559-79362-2 (59 minutes: DDD). Recorded 1993-94.　　Ⓕ **E**

Like a small café huddled within the shadow of some ancient church, Górecki's *Kleines Requiem für eine Polka* (1993) evokes feelings of paradox. The work's ground-springs are inscrutably personal, yet the sum effect is one of overwhelming intensity. The opening movement suggests distracted tranquillity. This is followed by a grating *Allegro* which approximates, at least in overall effect, the sort of vicious 'knees-up' that Shostakovich penned whenever he bared his teeth at empty celebration. Later, we are back within the tranquil interior of Górecki's imagination – and it's there that we stay until the work ends. The *Kleines Requiem für eine Polka* displays a characteristic profundity expressed via the simplest means. It is therefore a pity that the Harpsichord Concerto breaks the mood so quickly: one's initial impression is of a further violent 'episode' from the first work, although the stylistic contrast breaks the illusion soon enough. This is probably the most famous twentieth-century harpsichord concerto after Falla's, and the most popular of Górecki's pieces after the Third Symphony. Bach served as its creative prime mover, while Elisabeth Chojnacka is both its dedicatee and its most celebrated interpreter. Here she revels in the piece's playful aggression. It's an unrelenting display and in total contrast to *Good Night*, Górecki's deeply felt memorial to one of his staunchest supporters, the late Michael Vyner. The language is sombre, but never merely mournful. Mostly quiet and contemplative, *Good Night* is scored for alto flute, piano and tam-tam with Dawn Upshaw intoning Hamlet's 'flights of angels' in the closing movement. The work ends in a spirit of veiled ritual with a sequence of quiet gong strokes. The performance and recording are consistently fine.

Miserere, Op. 44[a]. Amen, Op. 35[a]. Euntes ibant et flebant, Op. 32[a]. My Vistula, grey Vistula, Op. 46[b]. Broad waters, Op. 39[b].
[a]**Chicago Symphony Chorus;** [a]**Chicago Lyric Opera Chorus / John Nelson;**
[b]**Lira Chamber Chorus / Lucy Ding.**
Elektra Nonesuch 7559-79348-2 (67 minutes: DDD). Texts and translations included.
Recorded 1994.   Ⓕ

Miserere is an intensely spiritual, imploringly prayerful work in which Górecki responds with heartfelt passion to the political events of 1981 (a sit-in by members of Rural Solidarity which ultimately led to the democratization of Poland). This is as intellectually demanding and emotionally compelling as anything by Górecki yet released on disc. Lovers of the Third Symphony will fall under its spell straight away, but it should gain respect from those less easily swayed by the opulent orchestral textures of that work, for here Górecki is using what is probably his favourite medium, the unaccompanied choir. The voices enter in a series of layered thirds until all ten parts commence an electrifying ascent through the word 'Domine' to the work's climax which, with the first statement of 'Miserere', suddenly bathes us in a quiet chord of A minor – a moment as devastatingly effective as an orchestra full of banging drums and crashing cymbals. John Nelson directs a hypnotic performance which wants for nothing in its impact, his choral forces both emotionally committed and technically excellent. The recording itself is certainly not technically excellent – there are a number of persistent background rattles and bangs. The church where the recording was made suffers from a cloudy acoustic and there is a haze of surface noise. In the end, though, it only serves to reinforce this grainy aural picture of those dark, frightening times in Poland's recent history.

Górecki Totus tuus, Op. 60. Amen, Op. 34.
Pärt Magnificat. The Beatitudes.
Tavener Magnificat. Nunc dimittis. Funeral Ikos. Plainchant – Alma redemptoris mater.
Ave Maria. Regina caeli laetare. Alleluia, venite ad me. Beati mundo corde. Requiem aeternam.
Ego sum resurrectio et vita. In paradisum.
[a]**David Goode** org **Choir of King's College, Cambridge / Stephen Cleobury.**
EMI CDC5 55096-2 (59 minutes: DDD). Texts and translations included.
Recorded 1994.   Ⓕ

This disc links the music of these three composers in an illuminating way. The contemporary pieces are separated by soberly sung plainchant which acts as a kind of sorbet to cleanse the palate between the various dishes. The performances of Górecki's *Totus tuus* and *Amen* are technically superb, and can rarely have been sung with such absolute control: similarly Tavener's *Funeral Ikos* is performed with perfect pacing and tuning. Yet there is something missing: these three pieces do not have that sense of spontaneity they need. They are too polite, perhaps, so that the Górecki works never quite catch fire, and the Tavener never really moves one. The response is more convincing in the Tavener *Collegium Regale* canticles, sung with virtuoso flair and the Pärt *Magnificat* and *The Beatitudes*. Here the performances have just that element of flexibility which is lacking in the other pieces, for all their beauty of sound. Pärt's intimate austerity is well served indeed in the care with which his melodies are shaped and the dynamic levels maintained.

François-Joseph Gossec   Belgian/French 1734-1829

Symphonies – Op. 5: No. 2 in E flat major, B26; No. 3 in D major, B27, 'Pastorella'; Op. 12: No. 5 in E flat major, B58; No. 6 in F major, B59; D major, B86.
London Mozart Players / Matthias Bamert.
Chandos CHAN9661 (67 minutes: DDD). Recorded 1997.   Ⓕ

François-Joseph Gossec, born in what is now Belgium, was the leading instrumental composer in Paris during the second half of the eighteenth century. He wrote some 50 symphonies, much admired in their time, and very attractive they are too. The two symphonies from his Op. 5, of the early 1760s, are lively, Italianate pieces in four movements; there is a charming if inventively slightly ordinary *Romanza* in one of them, and a particularly jolly Minuet and a spirited, well worked out finale in the other. But some of the musical ideas seem static and anonymous. The later compositions, two from his Op. 12 of 1769 and one from the mid-1770s, are in three movements, and altogether more interestingly written. The *Andantino* of the one in F has some very poetic writing and rich textures; the E flat work has a solemn, elevated slow introduction and an *Andante* with real pathos; while the one in D is a big piece with trumpets, a martial first movement and a sombre second, then a cheerful finale – all most appealing. Matthias Bamert directs the performances with energy and commitment. Anyone interested in the byways of the classical or late pre-classical era should give this disc a hearing.

Louis Moreau Gottschalk American 1829-1869

O ma charmante, épargnez-moi, RO182. Grande fantaisie triomphale sur l'hymne national brésilien, RO108. Melody in D flat major. Bamboula, RO20. The Dying Poet, RO75. Grande étude de concert, RO116, 'Hercule'. The last hope, RO133. Murmures éoliens, RO176. Symphony No. 1, RO5, 'La nuit des tropiques' – Andante (arr. Napoleão). La chute des feuilles, RO55. Tournament Galop, RO264.
Philip Martin *pf*
Hyperion CDA66915 (73 minutes: DDD). Recorded 1996. ⓕ

It is not only the playing here which gives such satisfaction, but the whole package is stylishly produced – Rousseau on the booklet cover and fine notes from Jeremy Nicholas. The piano sound from the fastidious Hyperion team is absolutely flawless. Martin, operating in a context where some pianists can hardly play softly at all, has a really ravishing *pianissimo*. This makes *O ma charmante* and the perennial – but highly original – *The last hope* simply enchanting. Gottschalk is a real melodist. Martin understands the intimacies of the salon but he also lacks nothing in his transcendental virtuosity. The more flamboyant numbers, such as *Tournament Galop* prove this. About ten years after Gottschalk's death, his pianist colleague, Artur Napoleão, made a piano arrangement of the first movement of Symphony No. 1 (*Night in the tropics*) which Martin includes here. It is slightly drab compared with the orchestral version and soon feels repetitive. But don't let that put you off this outstanding continuation of Martin's Gottschalk series.

Charles François Gounod French 1818-1893

Symphonies – No. 1 in D major; No. 2 in E flat major.
Orchestra of St John's, Smith Square / John Lubbock.
ASV CDDCA981 (65 minutes: DDD). Recorded 1996 and 1993. ⓕ

Gounod's symphonies are certainly not brow-furrowing and do not represent any advance in symphonic thought beyond Schumann and Mendelssohn, but they reveal Gounod in the Gallic tradition of elegantly crafted works with a light touch rather than in his familiar sentimental, sanctimonious image. The melodious, classically built and even witty First Symphony, with its delicate second-movement fugue and vivacious finale, is not to be peremptorily brushed aside. The longer Second Symphony makes an attempt to sound more serious, especially in the first movement and the dramatic *Scherzo* – the cantilena of the *Larghetto* is beautifully shaped here – but high spirits return in the finale. John Lubbock and his St John's orchestra are adept at the crisply neat treatment that this music demands. His wind section is outstanding, but in the finale of No. 1 the violins too show real virtuosity. A warm but clean recorded sound adds to our pleasure.

Où voulez-vous aller? Le soir. Venise. Ave Maria. Sérénade. Chanson de printemps. Au rossignol. Ce que je suis sans toi. Envoi de fleurs. La pâquerette. Boléro. Mignon. Rêverie. Ma belle amie est morte. Loin du pays. Clos ta paupière. Prière. L'absent. Le temps des roses. Biondina. The Worker. A lay of the early spring. My true love hath my heart. Oh happy home! Oh blessed flower! The fountain mingles with the river. Maid of Athens. Beware! The Arrow and the Song. Ilala: stances à la mémoire de Livingston. If thou art sleeping, maiden.
Dame Felicity Lott *sop* **Ann Murray** *mez* **Anthony Rolfe Johnson** *ten* **Graham Johnson** *pf*
Hyperion CDA66801/02 (two discs: 136 minutes: DDD). Texts and translations included. Recorded 1993. ⓕ

Gounod Choral and song

This well-filled two-CD set is surely the most wide-ranging single issue ever devoted to Gounod's *mélodies*. The first of the discs confirms the commonly held view of Gounod. Almost without exception the songs are pleasing and sentimental, a sweetly-scented posy of hymns to flowers, of reveries and serenades. The selection includes two settings of poems that Berlioz had used in *Les nuits d'été*, plumbing the depths of the poetry, where Gounod is content to skim across the surface. Arranged in chronological order, the songs show how little Gounod's music deepened, but also how evergreen was his inspiration in melody and harmony. To turn to the second disc is to have all one's prejudices overturned. This comprises non-French settings, for which Gounod dons first Italian garb for the song-cycle *Biondina*, and then English for a group of ten songs written during his stay in London in the 1870s. The Italian cycle is a delight. It would be impossible to guess the composer, as Gounod exchanges his customary flowing themes and rippling arpeggios for an ardent, Tosti-like vocal line over dry *staccato* chords. Anthony Rolfe Johnson catches its mix of sunny lyricism and Gallic sensitivity to perfection. The English songs are even more unusual, ranging from the Victorian ballad style of *The Worker* to a bizarre musical tribute to Livingstone, entitled *Ilala*. All three singers are on their best form here, with Rolfe Johnson bringing an air of intimate seductiveness to Byron's *Maid of Athens*.

Faust.
Richard Leech *ten* Faust; **Cheryl Studer** *sop* Marguerite; **José van Dam** *bar* Méphistophélès; **Thomas Hampson** *bass* Valentin; **Martine Mahé** *mez* Siébel; **Nadine Denize** *sop* Marthe; **Marc Barrard** *bar* Wagner
French Army Chorus; Toulouse Capitole Choir and Orchestra / Michel Plasson.
EMI CDS5 56224-2 (three discs: 204 minutes: DDD). Notes, text and translation included. Recorded 1991. Ⓕ 🆁🆁

Richard Leech as the eponymous hero sings his part with the fresh, eager tone, the easy *legato*, the sense of French style that it has so badly been wanting all these years, certainly since Nicolai Gedda essayed the role on the now rather aged Cluytens/EMI sets from 1953 and 1958. Gedda's voice may be more lyrical, more liquid in the role, but Leech encompasses it with less effort, and creates a real character. It is extremely distinguished singing. Beside him he has an equally impressive loved one in Studer and antagonist van Dam. Studer finds herself another amenable *métier* in Gounod; her Marguérite is not only sung with her customary attributes of innate musicality, firm tone and expressive phrasing but also with a deep understanding of this style of French music in terms of nuance and the lighter touch.

The Jewel song is a treasure; the King of Thulé, even more, the sad solo in Marguerite's chamber are touching. In the latter this Marguérite really captures the sense of hopelessness combined with longing for the absent lover. To add to one's satisfaction her French seems faultless. Van Dam achieves so much more by subtlety of accent and by care over note values that have basses, mostly from eastern Europe in modern times, by over-egging the pudding. Here is a resolute, implacable Devil with a firm, even tone to second the insinuating characterization. His voice may have dried out a little, but he remains a paragon of a stylist in all he attempts. The three French-speaking singers excel in subsidiary roles. Thomas Hampson is in places overextended as Valentin, a role that needs experience and perfect French. Plasson almost but not quite kills the score with kindness. He so loves the piece that his tempos, especially in the more reflective moments, such as the start of the Garden scene, become much slower than the score predicates and demands. Against that must be set his respect for the minutiae of Gounod's often inspired writing for orchestra and a general warmth that lights the score from within. It was an inspired stroke to invite the French Army Chorus to sing the Soldiers' Chorus, delivered with such verve as to make it seem unhackneyed.

Faust.
Jerry Hadley *ten* Faust; **Cecilia Gasdia** *sop* Marguerite; **Samuel Ramey** *bass* Méphistophélès; **Alexander Agache** *bar* Valentin; **Susanne Mentzer** *mez* Siébel; **Brigitte Fassbaender** *mez* Marthe; **Philippe Fourcade** *bass* Wagner;
Welsh National Opera Chorus and Orchestra / Carlo Rizzi.
Teldec 4509-90872-2 (three discs: 211 minutes: DDD). Notes, text and translation included. Recorded 1993. Ⓕ

Where Gounod is at his most inspired this version of his most popular work is more than commendable. Most notable are the solos for Marguerite and Faust, the Garden scene, the vignette in Marguerite's room that used to be regularly cut, and the Prison scene. The tender, sweet-toned and idiomatically French singing and style of Gasdia and Hadley quite exceed expectations in these days of homogenized and uniform interpretation. These two principals step outside those predictable parameters to give us readings of high individuality, favouring their grateful music with delicately etched line, varied dynamics and real involvement in their characters' predicaments –

Faust's vain search for the elixir of renewal, Marguerite for the ideal man. Both their happiness and later remorse are eloquently expressed. Gasdia gives a well-nigh faultless performance – light-hearted, elated in the Jewel song, ardent in the Garden duet, ecstatic in the bedtime solo that follows, ineffably sad in her 'Il ne revient pas'. How can this exquisite solo have ever been omitted, we think, when Gasdia moves us so deeply? She is no less touching when she has lost her reason. Subtle timbres, poised high notes inform all her singing.

Hadley, with the ideal weight of voice for Faust, has done nothing better. 'Je t'aime' at the first meeting with Marguerite is whispered in wonder. In the love duet he sings to her as a gentle lover, never bawling, caressing his music, and Gasdia replies in kind. The good news continues with Mentzer. She sings both Siébel's regular solos with vibrant, properly virile tone, the quick vibrato attractive. It's a real coup to have Fassbaender as Marthe, making so much of little. Ramey is the one singer to give a standardized performance. His Méphisto is as soundly and resolutely sung as one would expect from this sturdy bass, but it doesn't have the Francophone smoothness and subtlety of other interpretations. The only drawback is the often lax conducting. Rizzi conducts an often alarmingly slow account of the score and in compensation the more exciting passages are given rather too much verve. However, he is always aware of the sensuous nature of Gounod's scoring and the WNO Chorus and Orchestra are excellent. The recording is by and large open, full of presence and well balanced.

Faust (sung in English).
Paul Charles Clarke ten Faust; **Mary Plazas** sop Marguerite; **Alastair Miles** bass Méphistophélès; **Gary Magee** bar Valentin; **Diana Montague** mez Siébel; **Sarah Walker** mez Marthe; **Matthew Hargreaves** bass Wagner;
Geoffrey Mitchell Choir; Philharmonia Orchestra / David Parry.
Chandos Opera in English Series CHAN3014 (three discs: 208 minutes: DDD). Notes and text included. Recorded 1998. Ⓕ

After listening to this *Faust*, straight through from beginning to end, one can feel something very like awe. The structure is massive, the workmanship infinitely thorough, the boldness of stroke (dramatic and musical) almost breath-taking. And of course the winning numbers come up as in some dream-world lottery. No doubt the performance contributes to the awe. That is because it is in many ways a very good one, and partly because it underlines seriousness and grandeur. But it appears that David Parry has joined the swelling ranks of the slowcoaches. The Church scene and Faust's solo in the garden, for instance, are probably the slowest on record, and in the Ballet music the second dance (marked *adagio* but not *lento*) goes half as slow again as the metronome marking. Happily, there is nothing boring about it. This recording and its production keep the stage in view, and it is particularly good to have the chorus in such clear focus. The principals, too, form a strongly gifted team. Paul Charles Clarke, the Faust, is an interesting tenor, thrustful both in tone and manner yet capable of gentleness and delicacy. He never lets us forget that this is *his* story; when he is singing there are no throwaway lines, everything counts. By comparison, Alastair Miles's Méphistophélès seems a mild-mannered type with reserves of authority and a magnificent voice. Vocally he is very impressive indeed, the fine texture of his voice showing up to great advantage, his production admirably firm and even, his style unfailingly musical. The absence of overt devilry may pass as a virtue, but the absence of character is surely taking the disguise too far. Gounod's Mephisto is a joker, a man of the world and an exhibitionist; this one, rarely in the spotlight, loses it entirely when Marthe enters the garden in the person of Sarah Walker.

The Valentin, Gary Magee, has a fine, vibrant baritone and rises well both to his high notes and his big moments. Diana Montague is an excellent Siébel (and how effectively she rises to hers). The Marguerite, Mary Plazas, is totally likeable, ingenuous but not winsomely so, touchingly sincere in her love and her loss, clean in the scale-work of her Jewel song, a little underpowered in the grand melody of the Church scene, but having a powerful high C in reserve. The English version by Christopher Cowell reads well, sounds natural and does not affect the artless colloquialism that can be an embarrassing feature of modern translations.

Roméo et Juliette.
Plácido Domingo ten Roméo; **Ruth Ann Swenson** sop Juliette; **Alastair Miles** bass Frère Laurent; **Kurt Ollmann** bar Mercutio; **Susan Graham** sop Stephano; **Alain Vernhes** bar Capulet; **Sarah Walker** mez Gertrude; **Paul Charles Clarke** ten Tybalt; **Christopher Maltman** bar Paris; **Erik Freulon** bar Gregorio; **Toby Spence** ten Benvolio; **David Pittman-Jennings** bar Duc; **Dankwart Siegele** bass Frère Jean;
Bavarian Radio Chorus; Munich Radio Orchestra / Leonard Slatkin.
RCA Victor Red Seal 09026 68440-2 (two discs: 156 minutes: DDD). Notes, text and translation included. Recorded 1995. Ⓕ 🄴

Thanks to the advocacy of Leonard Slatkin and his team, Gounod's romantic work, *Roméo et Juliette*, seems the epitome of the well-made French nineteenth-century opera. Swenson shows a true empathy for the shape and feeling of a Gounod phrase. At the start, in the famous Waltz song, she announces her gifts. Besides singing this showpiece with technical confidence, a full, rounded tone and refined delicacy in coloratura, she shows an understanding of the girl's youthful vivacity yet tempers that with inner feeling in the 'Loin d'hiver' passage. The fear at having to enter the tomb of Tybalt in the solo at the end of Act 4, so often omitted in the opera house, is graphically expressed; as are the last, desperate utterances as she eagerly grasps the *poignard* to join her beloved in Elysium. Her French, though not perfect, is well learnt, and quite adequate to support her impressive portrayal. She seems to have inspired Domingo back to almost his best, youthful form. Roméo's famous aria is sung with growing ardour and full resonance. The outburst against Tybalt when he has killed Mercutio is heroic to a fault. But the golden tenor is still able to soften in the duets in response to this Juliette. Only once or twice the strain on high betrays the advancing years.

Two principals of such calibre deserve and, by and large, get worthy support and all are brought together into a firm ensemble by Slatkin's loving yet never lingering direction. He brings all the bitter-sweetness out of the Entr'actes by which Gounod obviously set so much store, cares for the composer's refined orchestration and shapes the set pieces with an unerring ear for matching tempos. What more can you ask for? Well, a chorus and orchestra that respond with a like mind, and that's what we have here. Most of the original 1873 score is in place, except for the first three movements of the Wedding tableau, often omitted. To complete our pleasure the recording is well-nigh faultless. The voices are up-front where they should be, but never to the detriment of the orchestra.

Percy Grainger American/Australian 1882-1961

Grainger The Warriors.
Holst The Planets, H125[a].
[a]women's voices of the **Monteverdi Choir; Philharmonia Orchestra / Sir John Eliot Gardiner.**
DG 445 860-2GH (68 minutes: DDD). Recorded 1994. Ⓕ

Grainger's *magnum opus*, *The Warriors*, was the 'music for an imaginary ballet', a commission set up by Sir Thomas Beecham for Diaghilev's Ballets Russes, but one which failed to materialize. Grainger wrote it anyway, of course, his imagination running riot with visions of a great tribal pageant, a 'wild sexual concert', the ghostly clans of all humankind spirited together in celebration of life's prime. *The Warriors* was his corrective, a symphony of dissolution. It is excessive, vulgar, as strange as it is beautiful. Above all, it's the rhythmic excitement of the piece that is so totally irresistible. Gardiner's classical and pre-classical explorations have, by necessity of style, set great store by rhythmic matters, and what a boon they are in *The Planets*. It's Gardiner's insistence upon precise articulations that keeps fleet-footed 'Mercury' so airborne, that brings the opening of 'Jupiter' into such sharp relief, making it shine all the brighter. There are other moments where a little more theatrical rhetoric would not have gone amiss: is the controlled fury of 'Mars' perhaps a shade too controlled? But the marmoreal beauty of 'Venus' and 'Neptune' (a ravishing texture descending from the gleam of celeste to an organ pedal sunk too deep to fathom), the sensitivity of the Philharmonia's playing, duly leave their impression. The recorded sound is superb.

Grainger In a Nutshell. Train Music (ed. Rathburn). The Warriors. Lincolnshire Posy. Country Gardens, BFMS22 (rev. 1950).
Debussy (orch. Grainger) Pagodes.
Ravel (orch. Grainger) La vallée des cloches[a].
City of Birmingham Symphony Orchestra / Sir Simon Rattle.
EMI CDC5 56412-2 (70 minutes: DDD). Recorded [a]1990 and 1996. ⒻⒺ

This is a marvellous Grainger anthology. Rattle surpasses Richard Hickox's commendable account of *In a Nutshell* in terms of rhythmic point and bracing character and makes us even more aware of the startling originality of Grainger's vision. *The Warriors* is handsomely served on CD by Geoffrey Simon and John Eliot Gardiner (see above). Rattle's stunning version of *The Warriors* possesses a mastery of texture and irresistible choreographic flair to remind us of the piece's ballet origins. *Country Gardens* is quirkily scored, harmonically eventful and hugely entertaining. The delectable arrangements of Ravel's *La vallée des cloches* and Debussy's *Pagodes* are quite captivating in their imaginative sonorities and both receive exquisite treatment here. *Train Music* is an intriguing torso, dating from 1901, which the ambitious teenage composer began to score for an orchestra of about 150 players. It's heard here in a reduced orchestration by the American Grainger authority, Eldon Rathburn. Finally, we are given an exceptionally perceptive *Lincolnshire Posy*. Not only do the fabulous blend and immaculate intonation of the CBSO's wind and brass really take the breath away, but Rattle's interpretation is also full of insight. Most remarkable of all is 'Rufford Park Poachers', full of tragic grandeur; 'Lord Melbourne', too, is memorable, acquiring a fierce, hard-edged intensity. Both the recording and presentation are immaculate.

Youthful Suite. Molly on the Shore, BFMS1. Irish Tune from County Derry, BFMS15. Shepherd's Hey, BFMS16. Country Gardens. Early one Morning, BFMS unnum. Handel in the Strand, RMTB2. Mock Morris, RMTB1. Dreamery (ed. Ould). The Warriors (ed. Servadei).
BBC Philharmonic Orchestra / Richard Hickox.
Chandos Grainger Edition CHAN9584 (75 minutes: DDD). Recorded 1997.   Ⓕ

Featuring some ripe, beautifully clean-cut sonics, this collection represents a great success for all involved. As the opening, chest-swelling 'Northern March' of the *Youthful Suite* immediately demonstrates, Hickox draws playing of infectious swagger from the ever-excellent BBC Philharmonic (marvellous brass sounds especially). The suite boasts some really striking invention, not least in the central 'Nordic Dirge' (a hauntingly eloquent processional, incorporating plenty of 'tuneful percussion') and a winsome, at times almost Ivesian 'English Waltz'. There follow seven of Grainger's most popular miniatures in the orchestrations Gershwin made for Leopold Stokowski. Hickox gives us Grainger's original thoughts and a delectable sequence they comprise, full of truly kaleidoscopic textural and harmonic variety. By the side of Rattle's CBSO version, Hickox's *Country Gardens* is perhaps marginally lacking in twinkling good humour and entrancing lightness of touch, but his infectious energy and evident affection more than compensate. *Dreamery*, described by Grainger as 'Slow Tween-Play' (an epithet which, as annotator Barry Peter Ould suggests, 'could be construed as his particular term for an intermezzo'), appears here in the extended orchestral version. For *The Warriors*, Hickox uses a new critical edition prepared by the Australian Grainger authority, Alessandro Servadei. Grainger's orchestral palette has never sounded more gloriously extravagant than here. Then again, this impression is just as much a tribute to Hickox's performance, which is breathtaking in its virtuosic brilliance and stunning co-ordination.

Piano music for four hands, Volume 2.
Children's March (Over the Hills and Far Away), RMTB4. Shepherd's Hey, BFMS16. Hill Song No. 1. Handel in the Strand, RMTB2. Harvest Hymn. The Widow's Party, KS7. The Lonely Desert Man Sees the Tents of the Happy Tribes. The Rival Brothers. Warriors II. Two Musical Relics of My Mother. Let's Dance Gay in Green Meadow, Fl. Blithe Bells. Pritteling, Pratteling, Pretty Poll Parrot.
Penelope Thwaites, John Lavender *pfs*
Pearl SHECD9623 (66 minutes: DDD). Recorded 1989-91.   Ⓕ

Piano Music for four hands, Volume 3.
Rondo. Crew of the Long Dragon. Fantasy on George Gershwin's 'Porgy and Bess'. Ye Banks and Braes, BFMS32. Tiger-Tiger, KS4/JBC9. Walking Tune, RMTB3. **C. Scott** Three Symphonic Dances. **Delius** A Dance Rhapsody No. 1, RTVI/18. **Grieg** Knut Lurasens Halling II. **Addinsell** Festival. **Le Jeune** La Bel'aronde. **Gershwin** Girl Crazy – Embraceable you (all trans. Grainger).
Penelope Thwaites, John Lavender *pfs*
Pearl SHECD9631 (78 minutes: DDD). Recorded 1989-1991.   Ⓕ

Grainger's 'dishings-up' of his music for keyboard is often more satisfying than the better-known orchestral versions. Quite frequently his arrangements for two pianists are his last thoughts about music that has often gone through as many as half a dozen rethinkings already, so Vol. 2 of this highly accomplished series is something more than an anthology of pieces that many Graingerites will already have. *Shepherd's Hey*, for example, is equipped with a particularly exuberant new coda, and the bafflingly titled *Pritteling, Pratteling, Pretty Poll Parrot* turns out to be our old friend the *Gum-suckers' March* with an entirely new middle section and some affectionate sidelong glances at (apparently) Erik Satie. There is literally new music as well, most substantially *Warriors II*, which has little connection with the strange 'imaginary ballet' that we might now call *Warriors I*. Reconstructed from Grainger's sketches by no fewer than four hands it is one of his stronger pieces: ardently melodious, at times very close to Rachmaninov, big gestured and with more urgency than some of his works of this length. Volume 3 contains shorter original Grainger compositions and a number of his transcriptions. These latter are fascinating in their combination of scrupulous fidelity and creative rethinking for an entirely different medium. You wouldn't think that a transcription, even for *two* pianos, of Delius's First *Dance Rhapsody* could possibly work. In fact, it works so well that some may prefer Grainger's version to the original. In the *Porgy and Bess* Fantasy he treats the tunes with loving respect, but as a pianist can't help seeing different ways of presenting them: the very big gestures surrounding 'My man's gone now'; a searching little prelude to 'It ain't necessarily so' implying all sorts of interesting things Grainger could have done with that slithery little tune if he weren't obliged to play it straight – which he then does, with sparkling enjoyment.

Grainger Jutish Medley, DFMS8. Colonial Song, S1. Molly on the Shore, BFMS1. Harvest Hymn. Spoon River, AFMS1. Country Gardens, BFMS22. Walking Tune, RMTB3. Mock Morris, RMTB1. Ramble on Themes from Richard Strauss's 'Der Rosenkavalier'. Shepherd's Hey, BFMS4. Irish Tune from County Derry, BFMS6. Handel in the Strand, RMTB2. The Hunter in his career, OEPM4. Scotch Strathspey and Reel, BFMS37. In a Nutshell Suite – No. 4, The Gum-suckers March. The Merry King, BFMS38. In Dahomey.
Stanford (arr. Grainger) Four Irish Dances, Op. 89 – No. 1, A March-Jig; No. 4, A Reel.
Marc-André Hamelin *pf*
Hyperion CDA66884 (73 minutes: DDD). Recorded 1996. Ⓕ **E**

This is perhaps one of the most riveting and satisfying anthologies of Grainger's music. Hamelin's superb control and artistry just about sweep the board if you're looking for a disc that not only brings you all the old favourites but also explores some of the less familiar music, such as Grainger's arrangements of two of Stanford's *Irish Dances*, the Cakewalk Smasher, *In Dahomey* or some of the less familiar folk-music settings such as *The Merry King* – the latter a delightful discovery. The deceptive ease with which Hamelin presents these pieces is quite breathtaking. The *Irish Tune from County Derry*, for instance, contains some exacting problems which call on the pianist to play *ppp* in the outer fingers and *mf* with the middle in order to bring out the melody which Grainger places almost entirely in the middle register of the piano, and yet Hamelin makes it sound incredibly natural. His subtle control of melodic voicing can also be heard in, among others, the marvellous *Scotch Strathspey and Reel* and the *Jutish Medley* and in the gorgeous *Ramble on Themes from Richard Strauss's 'Der Rosenkavalier'*, Hamelin's mastery of the pedal (especially the seldom used middle pedal) is a real delight. All in all a very desirable Grainger anthology.

The Power of Rome and the Christian Heart. Children's March: Over the Hills and Far Away, RMTB4. Bell Piece. Blithe Bells. The Immovable Do. Hill Songs – No. 1; No. 2. County Derry Air, BFMS29. Marching Song of Democracy.
James Gilchrist *ten*
Royal Northern College of Music Wind Orchestra / Timothy Reynish, Clark Rundell.
Chandos Grainger Edition CHAN9630 (65 minutes: DDD). Recorded 1992-97. Ⓕ

Rundell's compelling realization of the extraordinary *Hill Song* No. 1 – regarded by Grainger as one of his finest achievements and performed here in its original guise for (wait for it!) two piccolos, six oboes, six cors anglais, six bassoons and double-bassoon – was actually made by BBC Manchester back in 1992; the remaining items date from 1997 and benefit from the typically splendid sound and balance achieved by the Chandos recording team. As well as the *Hill Song* No. 1, we get the 1929 scoring of its pithier successor from 1907. Another of Grainger's most striking wind-band compositions opens the disc, namely the 12-minute *The Power of Rome and the Christian Heart*. Its central section will be familiar as the six-and-a-half-minute orchestral piece, *Dreamery* (both works were completed in 1943), while its closing measures utilize material from the first movement ('The Power of Love') of the *Danish Folk-song Suite*. Both the *Children's March* and *Bell Piece* feature some unexpected vocal contributions. In the latter – a charming 'ramble' on John Dowland's *Now, O now I needs must part* – Grainger incorporates a bell part specially written for his wife, Ella. The delightfully piquant arrangements of *Blithe Bells* and *The Immovable Do* date from March 1931 and November/December 1939 respectively. These fine players equally revel in the 'scrunchy' harmonies of the eventful version of *Irish Tune from County Derry* (made in 1920 for military band and pipe-organ). That just leaves the boisterous *Marching Song of Democracy* (in a transcription from July 1948), which Rundell again directs as to the manner born. All in all, a most entertaining and stimulating release.

Rudyard Kipling Settings – Dedication, KS1; Dedication II; Anchor Song; The Widow's Party, KS7; Soldier, Soldier; The Sea-wife; Ganges Pilot; The First Chantey; The Young British Soldier. Three Settings of Robert Burns. Songs of the North – Fair Young Mary, SON7; The Woman are a Gane Wud, SON9; My Faithful Fond One, SON10; O'er the Moor, SON12. The Power of Love, DFMS4. The Twa Corbies. A Reiver's Neck-Verse. Lord Maxwell's Goodnight, BFMS14.
Martyn Hill *ten* **Penelope Thwaites, John Lavender** *pfs*
Chandos Grainger Edition CHAN9610 (69 minutes: DDD). Texts included. Ⓕ **E**

Grainger cared for neither rules nor forms; he wrote what he wanted and for whom he wanted, and one sees him flinging down collar and tie to do it. A singer probably needs to shed a few inhibitions in coping with these songs, and if Martyn Hill had any to start with he has got rid of them like the discarded collar and tie. He gives magnificent performances, and is matched by Penelope Thwaites who seems unerringly to make sense of the idiosyncratic piano parts. Some are folk-songs or settings of Burns, and in at least one of these – *Afton Water* – a comparison with Britten's way with folk-song inevitably comes to mind, Grainger being similarly determined and single-minded in working out his concept, but exquisite in the delicacy of his murmurous water-colouring. Then in others he stands almost in reproach of Britten, for the traditional melody so 'takes' him that he wants little more than to present it, lovingly, almost reverently, in its own unadorned beauty. As for the eight poems of Kipling – one of them set twice – they inspire him with strange, fierce compassion and unquenchable energy: 'ballads' as they are, surely too close to brutally humorous reality to be acceptable in the drawing-room 'ballad' musical-evenings of the age.

The song with two settings is *Dedication*, or 'Mother o' mine', a poem in passionately bad taste that must have meant something special to Grainger (with that mother o' his). Martyn Hill sings with fine abandon, especially in the first version with its desperately high-lying phrases at the start and its ultimate abasement. To the 'character' songs – *The Widow's Party* and the relentless *Young British Soldier* for instance – he brings an unfailingly right touch, directed by a sense of passionate, imaginative conviction. His voice is not now beautiful, at any rate not above a *mezzo-forte*; but it is pliant and resourceful, and at times (as in the folk-song *Fair Young Mary*) capable of most lovely 'pure' singing. He has made many good recordings, but this, surely, is his masterpiece.

The Power of Love, DFMS4. Early one morning. Scherzo. Random Round, RMTB8. O Gin I Were Where Gadie Rins, SON13. Skye Boat Song, SON3. Danny Deever, KS12. Irish Tune from County Derry (all ed. Ould). Mock Morris, RMTB1. Died For Love, BFMS10 (ed. Perna). Love Verses from 'The Song of Solomon'. Shepherd's Hey, RMTB3.The Three Ravens, BFMS41. Youthful Rapture. The Merry King, BFMS39 (ed. Rogers). Dollar and a Half a Day, SCS2. Molly on the shore, BFMS1.
Susan Gritton sop **Pamela Helen Stephen** mez **Mark Tucker** ten
Stephen Varcoe bar **Tim Hugh** vc
Joyful Company of Singers; City of London Sinfonia / Richard Hickox.
Chandos Grainger Edition CHAN9653 (62 minutes: DDD). Texts included. Recorded 1998.   Ⓕ E

Once considered the musical equivalents of Betjeman's 'chintzy chintzy cheeriness', *Molly on the shore*, *Mock Morris* and *Shepherd's Hey* now raise a delighted smile in appreciation of their energy, wit, skill, grace and joy. Like most of the items here, they are short pieces, and it would be unthinkable to call any of them 'major works'. But in each instance, for the space of three or four minutes, Grainger is the Jupiter of composers: the unfeigned, unforced, Bringer of Jollity. He is other things as well. In all of his folk-song arrangements there is scarcely one which at some moment does not make the heart jump, as (for instance) he feels his way towards the secretive beauty of the *Brigg Fair* tune in *Died For Love* or as he commits himself with unstinting sympathy and inflamed musical imagination to the protest of *Dollar and a Half*. His *Random Round*, meant for improvisation but eventually (in 1943) written out, begins as casual fun and ends in something very like ecstasy. Among the soloists, Susan Gritton brings a deliciously pure tone and a ready understanding, and Stephen Varcoe leads a haunting performance of *The Three Ravens*. The Joyful Company of Singers deserves to remain so, and with its conductor, Richard Hickox, the City of London Sinfonia sounds as though playing for pleasure too. With fine sound and a good booklet, the disc is a stayer.

I'm Seventeen Come Sunday, BFMS8. Brigg Fair, BFMS7. Love Verses from 'The Song of Solomon'. The Merry Wedding. Shallow Brown, SCS3. Father and Daughter. My Dark-Haired Maid, 'Mo Nighean Dhu'. The Bride's Tragedy. Irish Tune from County Derry, BFMS5. Scotch Strathspey and Reel, BFMS28. The Lost Lady Found, BFMS33. The Three Ravens, BFMS41. Danny Deever. Tribute to Foster.
Monteverdi Choir; English Country Gardiner Orchestra / Sir John Eliot Gardiner.
Philips 446 657-2PH (75 minutes: DDD). Texts included. Recorded 1994-95.
Gramophone Award Winner 1996.   Ⓕ

The really startling thing about all these settings is the way in which Grainger unlocks the *inner* life of each text, each melody. He'll digest it, understand it, respect it, and then in his response – which is nothing if not personal – he'll elaborate, creating as little or as much subtext as is appropriate. Like Britten, in his folk-song settings, Grainger knew how and when to get out of the way. The plaintive *Brigg Fair* is no more, no less than the tenor solo and chiefly wordless chorus will allow us – a tune so precious to Grainger that even the harmony is almost an intrusion. Then there is the classic *Londonderry Air* – no words, just voices – a harmony that is so rich, so expressive, so integrated, that it always shrouds the melody in the imagination. Then what, you may ask, could be more extraordinary than the *Love Verses from 'The Song of Solomon'*? Well, *Shallow Brown* for a start, which is astounding. A sea shanty with the reach of a spiritual, it is set as the sailors will have yelled it, the vocal line stretching and distorting, straining to be heard over furious oceanic *tremolandos* in guitars and strings. This is a fabulous disc. John Eliot Gardiner may well have inherited some of his joy in this music from his great-uncle, Balfour Gardiner (one of the 'Frankfurt Gang', which included Grainger). He is characteristically hot in his response to its rhythmic zest as are his wonderfully articulate, impeccably tuned, Monteverdi singers and players. The singing is, by turns, fleet, spry, fireside-cosy cathedral-rich – or plain raucous. Brilliant, revealing recorded sound.

Enrique Granados
Spanish 1867-1916

---

12 Danzas españolas, Op. 37. 7 Valses poéticos.
Alicia de Larrocha *pf*
RCA Victor Red Seal 09026 68184-2 (68 minutes: DDD). Recorded 1994.   Ⓕ

Alicia de Larrocha, that incomparable interpreter of the Spanish repertoire, is here revisiting many of her favourite musical haunts. And if some of her former edge and fire, her tonal and stylistic luxuriance are now replaced by more 'contained' and reflective qualities, her warmth and affection remain undimmed. Her rubato, while less lavishly deployed than before, is potent and alluring, as instantly recognizable as ever, and each and every dance is played with rare naturalness, ease and authority. But if a touch of sobriety occasionally blunts the fullest impact of these fascinating, most aristocratic idealizations of local Spanish life and colour, the actual playing is never less than masterly. The *Valses poéticos* are offered as an engaging encore. The recordings have much less range and reverberance than her previous ones on Decca; however, all lovers of this still misunderstood and neglected repertoire, played by one of the great pianists of our time, will want to add this to their collection.

Goyescas.

Granados Goyescas.
Albéniz Iberia. Navarra.
Alicia de Larrocha *pf*
Double Decca 448 191-2DF2 (two discs: 141 minutes: ADD). Recorded 1972-76.   Ⓜ 🟥🟥

Alicia de Larrocha has been playing these works, the greatest in the repertoire of Spanish piano music, all her life. Complete technical assurance in these extremely demanding works has now become taken for granted, and Larrocha is not unique in mastering their terrors; but though there have been other distinguished interpreters, her readings have consistently remained a touchstone. She employs plenty of subtle rubato but possesses the ability to make it sound as natural as breathing. In the true sense of that much-misused word, this is classical playing, free from any superimposed striving for effect but responding fully to the music's sense of colour; and even in the densest of textures she is able to control conflicting tonal levels. *Goyescas*, which can tempt the unwary into exaggerated 'expressiveness', brings forth a wealth of poetic nuance, without losing shape – as for instance in the splendid 'El amor y la muerte'. The recorded quality throughout always was good and here emerges as fresh as ever. Anyone who does not already possess these recordings in one of their previous issues should not hesitate to acquire them now – all the more since the two discs together cost the same as one full-price one.

Goyescas. El pelele.
Eric Parkin *pf*
Chandos CHAN9412 (61 minutes: DDD). Recorded 1993.   Ⓕ

The Granados *Goyescas* are profoundly Spanish in feeling, but the folk influence is more of court music than of the flamenco or *cante hondo* styles which reflect gipsy and Moorish influence. A direction in the score at the beginning of the *Goyescas* is *con garbo y donaire* ('with charm and elegance'). The description aptly fits Parkin's performances. His readings have an element of free rubato about them, but this is not allowed to become excessive, and it serves to underline the essentially improvisatory nature of these pieces. Aided by a clean technique in this sometimes complex texture he gives persuasive performances that also contain much poetry. He captures the dignified flamboyance of the traditional dance in the 'Fandango by candlelight', carefully observing the direction *avec beaucoup de rythme*. Two of the hardest tests for a pianist in this collection of Goyesque studies are the preservation of coherence in the long 'Serenata del espectro' and the avoidance of mawkishness in 'La maja y el ruiseñor': Parkin emerges successfully from both. A piano with particularly bright top octaves was perhaps not the ideal instrument for this recording, but there is no lack of colour or nuance from the performer.

Alexandr Grechaninov

Piano Trios – No. 1 in C minor, Op. 38; No. 2 in G major, Op. 128.
Bekova Sisters (Elvira Bekova *vn* Alfia Bekova *vc* Eleonora Bekova *pf*).
Chandos CHAN9461 (53 minutes: DDD). Recorded 1996.　　　　　Ⓕ

Composed in 1906, Grechaninov's First Piano Trio is a typical product of Russia's 'Silver Age': typical in its expert, school-of-Rimsky craftsmanship, typical in its languishing lyricism, typical in its fundamental complacency. The first movement draws heavily on the figurations from Tchaikovsky's Fourth Symphony but divests them of all emotional immediacy or dangerous intensity. This makes for a pleasant, undemanding listening experience, and throws into relief the achievements of Rachmaninov, Scriabin and Stravinsky. But don't expect any more than that. Grechaninov is one of several candidates for the label of 'the Russian Brahms'. That fits him as unsatisfactorily as it does Taneyev or Glazunov or anyone else it has been applied to, but the finale of his Second Trio at least shows why it sticks. This playful, yet sturdy and always well-crafted music has a feel of 1881 rather than 1931. Composed in California, at two removes from the Russia its composer had left once and for all six years earlier, its childlike escapism is undoubtedly touching, and its sounds agreeable and rewarding to play. Strong, enjoyable, upfront performances from the talented Bekova sisters; Chandos's recording is well lubricated with resonance, but not absurdly so.

Edvard Grieg

Piano Concerto in A minor, Op. 16.

Grieg Piano Concerto[a]. Piano Sonata in E minor, Op. 7[b].
Schumann Piano Concerto in A minor, Op. 54[a].
[a]**Stephen Kovacevich**, [b]**Zoltán Kocsis** *pfs*
BBC Symphony Orchestra / Sir Colin Davis.
Philips Solo 446 192-2PM (78 minutes: [a]ADD/[b]DDD).　　Ⓜ 🆁🆁

Stephen Kovacevich's wholly natural, intimately poetic phrasing, his delicately glistening fingerwork and his bravura and rhythmic virility, too, when required (as in Grieg's finale) must of course be noted first. Yet it is difficult to recall any other performance in which pianist, conductor and orchestra are in closer or more subtly balanced and shaded accord than in this classic account. Each and every participant sounds as personally involved as they would in chamber music-making. The sound quality has not the forward brightness of present-day reproduction: you may need to turn up your volume control a little higher than usual. But its old-world mellowness seems just right for performances as loving as these. For good measure we're even given an encore – though curiously there is no mention of it in the accompanying booklet-notes – and from a totally different pianist. But Zoltán Kocsis's account of Grieg's early E minor Sonata is certainly sufficiently incisive and characterful to justify resurgence.

Grieg Piano Concerto.
Schumann Piano Concerto in A minor, Op. 54.
Lars Vogt *pf*
City of Birmingham Symphony Orchestra / Sir Simon Rattle.
EMI CDC7 54746-2 (62 minutes: DDD). Recorded 1992.　　　　Ⓕ

Lars Vogt and Simon Rattle with his Birmingham orchestra are up against stiff competition. These celebrated performances are spot on target stylistically, but there are others nearly as fine. Even if you do have other versions, this disc is worth investigating. Vogt and Rattle begin with the Schumann, and play it more forcefully than some: as they see it, this is passionate music as well as offering cosier moments of romantic warmth. Their account of the first movement is a bit too urgent and the Intermezzo that follows a touch over-brisk, but that is better than weakening it with Hollywood-style sentimentality. For a sample of Vogt's artistry, try the cadenza at the 12-minute mark. The recording has faithful piano sound and a natural balance. In the Grieg, the artists are again more forceful than some and pay small heed to the composer's cautionary addition of *molto moderato* to his *Allegro* marking for the first movement. Although they don't altogether overlook the spaciousness of the invention and the second subject is gracefully played, it lacks the sense of wonder that Kovacevich and Davis give us, and the same is true of the magical F major interlude in the finale (beginning with the flute solo) which in the finest performances evokes a pure and serene vision of a Norwegian fjord at morning. Ultimately, you may find that these admirably assured performances leave some poetry unrealized. Still, try to hear these artists if you think that your own view of the works may be closer to theirs.

Grieg Piano Concerto.
Schumann Piano Concerto in A minor, Op. 54.
Murray Perahia *pf*
Bavarian Radio Symphony Orchestra / Sir Colin Davis.
Sony Classical SK44899 (60 minutes: DDD). Recorded live in 1987 and 1988.   Ⓕ

Albeit conceding the existence of attendant hazards, Murray Perahia has admitted to a delight in
the inspirational heat-of-the-moment of a live recording. Though there are no claps, coughs or
shuffles to confirm the presence of an audience, we're told on the label that both concertos were in
fact recorded live at Munich's Philharmonie Gasteig. Of the two works, the Grieg is better served
by the immediacy and warmth of Perahia's response, whether through rhythmic bite in livelier
dance tempo or total surrender to lyrical nostalgia elsewhere. Never is there the slightest sacrifice of
his customary artistic sensitivity or keyboard finesse. You will be delighted to discover that someone
so dedicated to Mozart, Beethoven and the light-fingered Mendelssohn in the concerto field could
so patently revel in Grieg's unabashed sentiment and bravura too. His Schumann is no less ardent.
In the spirited finale, as throughout the Grieg, any collector would be just as happy with this
performance as that of the much praised Kovacevich for Philips. But in the first two movements,
where Schumann speaks more personally, it is Kovacevich who finds a simpler, more confiding note
– as well as more artfully weaving the piano into the comparatively light texture as if it were just
part of the orchestra instead of a spot-lit outsider. Davis, needless to say, goes all the way in both
works to uphold Perahia in his open-hearted point-making, and the Bavarian Radio Symphony
Orchestra gives him all he asks of it. The sound is more arrestingly clear-cut than the old Philips,
which nevertheless is still as pleasing as ever for its mellowness and subtle balance.

Grieg Piano Concerto[a]. Lyric Pieces – French Serenade, Op. 62 No. 3;
Cradle song, Op. 68 No. 5.
Franck Symphonic Variations[b].
Liszt Piano Concerto No. 1 in E flat major, S124[b].
Walter Gieseking *pf*
[a]**Berlin State Opera Orchestra / Hans Rosbaud;**
[b]**London Philharmonic Orchestra / Sir Henry Wood.**
APR mono APR5513 (63 minutes: ADD). Recorded 1931-37.   Ⓜ Ⓗ

Gieseking's Grieg from 1937 is fascinating. There are moments where Gieseking's refusal to
transform this delicate concerto into a romantic war-horse leads him into rushing phrases that
another pianist might have lingered over, but in the first movement his subtle rubato seeks out veins
of fantasy, impulsive urgency and intimate quietness that are often missed. His determined,
headlong rush at the first movement cadenza and, still more so, at the flourishes before the finale's
coda are endearing: 'Do I have to?' he seems to be saying; 'Oh well, if you insist', and he abruptly
transforms himself – just this once, mind – into a keyboard tiger. Gieseking the classical stylist in
Liszt? In fact his account of Liszt's First Concerto is one of the most illuminating here. It is, in a
word, Gallic: strong where necessary, but with such delicacy and purity of line, such a scrupulous
refusal to rant that one soon discovers unexpected qualities of charm, delicacy, even (in the third
movement) humour. Here and in the Franck there are ample gestures but little rhetoric, and
Gieseking the French-born German finds Gallic clarity in Franck, too. The partnership with Wood
is fascinating, especially when compared with the rather warmer sound of the Berlin orchestra.
Wood's robustness, his almost rough exuberance in the finale of the Liszt is an admirable foil to
Gieseking's ebullience, and both of them obviously enjoyed the collaboration. The sound
throughout is even better than on some post-war concerto recordings, the Grieg charmingly
intimate and the transfers seem immaculate.

Grieg Peer Gynt – Suites Nos. 1 and 2, Opp. 46 and 55. Holberg Suite, Op. 40.
Sibelius Legends, Op. 22 – No. 2, The Swan of Tuonela. Kuolema – Valse triste, Op. 44.
Finlandia, Op. 26.
Berlin Philharmonic Orchestra / Herbert von Karajan.
DG Karajan Gold 439 010-2GHS (78 minutes: DDD). Recorded 1981-84.   Ⓜ 🆁🆁

Very impressive indeed. Comparing the LP and CD formats and the greater definition and presence
of the latter tells, particularly at the bass end of the spectrum. Somehow one feels that one could
stretch out and touch the players, so vivid is the sound. In the *Peer Gynt* movements, there is much
greater range and separation. *Peer Gynt* is most beautifully done. At times you might think the wind
could have been a shade more distant, particularly in the 'By the seashore' movement but there is
no want of atmosphere here – quite the contrary! Not to put too fine a point on it, this is a
marvellous recording. In the *Holberg Suite*, the sound has marvellous clarity and definition as well

as exemplary range. For some tastes it may be a little too sophisticated but one's admiration for it remains undimmed. The playing throughout is beautifully cultured and there is wonderful lightness and delicacy. The present issue is Karajan's third account of 'The Swan of Tuonela' and it is regrettable that he never committed to disc the four *Legends* in their entirety. It is as powerful and atmospheric an account as ever recorded, and the remaining two pieces, 'Valse triste' and *Finlandia*, reinforce one's feeling that this partnership has never been equalled. The stirring account of *Finlandia* is incredibly wide-ranging – the orchestral playing is really in a class of its own.

Holberg Suite. Two Elegiac Melodies, Op. 34. Peer Gynt – Suites Nos. 1 and 2. Two Lyric Pieces.
Academy of St Martin in the Fields / Sir Neville Marriner.
Hänssler Classic 98 995 (66 minutes: DDD). Recorded 1994.   Ⓕ

The clean ruggedness of Grieg's music comes across well here. Indeed, there is much to praise: the sheer zest of the opening *Allegro vivace* of the *Holberg Suite* and, in the same five-movement work, the way Marriner and his players convey the necessary 'period' quality. The *Two Elegiac Melodies* are also fine; the second of them is the poignant 'Last spring' and features some movingly hushed playing from the violins. The incidental music to *Peer Gynt*, which follows, has a similarly attractive freshness. One gets the impression that this is the kind of music that the ASMF can play beautifully at the drop of a hat, but beautiful playing it remains, with nothing routine about it. Even the well-worn 'Morning' in Suite No. 1 sounds as fresh as if it were the morning of the world, and one could not ask for a more loving account of 'Solveig's Song'. The two transcriptions of the *Lyric Pieces* are also evocative, with fine oboe playing in the first, 'Evening in the mountains'. The recording is richly reverberant but permits detail to emerge.

Norwegian Dances, Op. 35. Lyric Suite, Op. 54. Symphonic Dances, Op. 64.
Gothenburg Symphony Orchestra / Neeme Järvi.
DG 419 431-2GH (68 minutes: DDD).   Ⓕ

Grieg's music has that rare quality of eternal youth: however often one hears it, its complexion retains its bloom, the smile its radiance and the youthful sparkle remains undimmed. Though he is essentially a miniaturist, who absorbed the speech rhythms and inflections of Norwegian folk melody into his bloodstream, Grieg's world is well defined. Both the *Norwegian Dances* and the *Symphonic Dances* were originally piano duets, which Grieg subsequently scored: Järvi conducts both with enthusiasm and sensitivity. In the *Lyric Suite* he restores 'Klokkeklang' ('Bell-ringing'), which Grieg omitted from the final score: it is remarkably atmospheric and evocative, and serves to show how forward-looking Grieg became in his late years. The recording is exceptionally fine and of wide dynamic range; the sound is very natural and the perspective true to life.

Grieg String Quartets – No. 1 in G minor, Op. 27; No. 2 in F major, CW146.
Schumann String Quartet No. 1 in A minor, Op. 41 No. 1.
Petersen Quartet (Conrad Muck, Gernot Süssmuth *vns* Friedemann Weigle *va*
Hans-Jakob Eschenburg *vc*).
Capriccio 10 476 (75 minutes: DDD). Recorded 1993.   Ⓕ

Grieg String Quartet No. 1 in G minor, Op. 27.
Mendelssohn String Quartet No. 2 in A minor, Op. 13.
Shanghai Quartet (WeiGang Li, HongGang Li *vns* Zheng Wang *va* James Wilson *vc*).
Delos DE3153 (64 minutes: DDD). Recorded 1993.   Ⓕ

Since Grieg owed much to Schumann, coupling their quartets seems a good idea. These G minor and A minor Quartets were written when the composers were in their thirties, although Grieg was a few years older. Yet it is his work that sounds more youthfully passionate, while the Schumann is a rather self-conscious homage to his friend Mendelssohn and classical models. The Petersens invest the Grieg G minor Quartet with *gravitas* and are skilful in linking together the disparate sections of its structure. Their recording has a very natural balance and an impressively wide dynamic range with real *pianissimo*; it also copes well with Grieg's forceful, semi-orchestral string writing. The whole performance has vigour and tenderness in good proportion, and a truly Scandinavian feeling. The unfinished F major Quartet is another sensitively moulded performance and the work sounds no more incomplete than Schubert's *Unfinished* Symphony. The Schumann is no less enjoyable; the artists are fully inside his idiom and make a consistently beautiful and meaningful sound. The Shanghai Quartet's brightly-lit account of the Mendelssohn suggests a rich store of interpretative potential. Theirs is a sizzling, multi-coloured performance. The Grieg coupling is, if anything, even finer, with an *Allegro molto* first movement that truly is *ed agitato*, a warming *Romanze* and a superbly characterized *Intermezzo*. It is arguably the most compelling performance of this endearing score since the original Budapest Quartet's trail-blazing HMV 78s from 1937. It is richly recorded.

Grieg Cello Sonata in A minor, Op. 36.
Liszt Romance oubliée, S132. Elégies – No. 1, S130; No. 2, S131. Die Zelle in Nonnenwerth, S382. La lugubre gondola, S134.
Rubinstein Cello Sonata No. 1 in D major, Op. 18.
Steven Isserlis *vc* **Stephen Hough** *pf*
RCA Victor Red Seal 09026 68290-2 (76 minutes: DDD). Recorded 1994.   Ⓕ

With Steven Isserlis and Stephen Hough an inspired duo, natural recording artists both, it would be a pity if the sentimental title, 'Forgotten Romance', a translation of the shortest and least ambitious piece in the collection, deterred any serious listener from investigating it. The logic of the grouping is that the five cello pieces of Liszt, all of them brief and all adapted from earlier works, are used to frame the high romantic cello sonatas, by Grieg and Rubinstein, that are in danger of neglect. With performances like these, as sharply disciplined as they are passionate, all the emotion is very well founded, with sentimentality firmly kept at bay. The magnificent Grieg Sonata was written when he was considering composing a second piano concerto and its material and manner very much reflect the A minor Concerto, with the composer at his most richly distinctive. Isserlis and Hough are light and imaginative, choosing speeds that flow easily and naturally. Paradoxically that makes the result more moving than any underlining of expression. One could say the same about all these performances. The two *Elégies* – with Isserlis most persuasive in the improvisation-like passages – lead to the Rubinstein First Sonata. It has the lyrical directness and honest four-square construction which make the Mendelssohn cello sonatas so attractive. The disc is rounded off by two Liszt pieces slightly more substantial than the others – *Die Zelle in Nonnenwerth* ('The Cell in Nonnenwerth') – a late adaptation of an early song, spare in texture, and Liszt's tribute to Wagner after his death, *La lugubre gondola*, one of many different adaptations.

Violin Sonatas – No. 1 in F major, Op. 8; No. 2 in G major, Op. 13; No. 3 in C minor, Op. 45.
Augustin Dumay *vn* **Maria João Pires** *pf*
DG 437 525-2GH (70 minutes: DDD). Recorded 1993.   Ⓕ **RR**

Grieg's violin sonatas span his creative life, the first two dating from his early twenties, before his Piano Concerto, and the Third Sonata of 1887 belonging to the last decade of his life. Augustin Dumay brings to this music a youthful *seigneur*, manifest in the impetuosity, charm and command of his playing. He and Maria João Pires are at their considerable best in the G major Sonata, with its vivid first movement, lilting *Allegretto* and triumphant finale – whose conclusion they lift to the skies. The recording does full justice to Dumay's silky and resourceful tone. Pires is rightly an equal partner, and both artists bring an infectiously fresh response to the music. The finale of the C minor Sonata, music that anticipates Sibelius in its urgency and elemental force, is compellingly played.

Violin Sonatas Nos. 1-3.
Henning Kraggerud *vn* **Helge Kjekshus** *pf*
Naxos 8 553904 (67 minutes: DDD). Recorded 1996.   Ⓢ

This disc gives us consistently enjoyable performances. The two young Norwegians play with idiomatic style, and give the impression of absorbing and expressing every aspect of the music. The eagerness with which they set off at the start of Op. 8's first *Allegro* sets the tone; the *doloroso* opening of Op. 13, the delicacy and serenity of the E major section of that sonata's middle movement, and the exciting 'Hall of the Mountain King' atmosphere they generate in the finale of Op. 45 – these are just a few of the places where Kraggerud and Kjekshus convince us they've found exactly the right sound and manner of expression. Dumay and Pires on DG are magnificently recorded, causing one to regret the slight lack of brilliance in the Naxos recording and wish that the violin in particular had been given a more glamorous presence. They are as deeply involved as the Norwegians but play with far greater freedom and a wonderfully uninhibited range of expression. However, Kraggerud's account of the 'big tune' in the last movement of Op. 45, respecting all Grieg's marks of expression and phrasing, has a nobility that Dumay, more heart-on-sleeve and cavalier about dynamics and slurs, misses. The Naxos disc is, in short, highly recommendable – as a contrast to Dumay/Pires or simply as an excellent bargain.

Piano Works, Volume 1.
Piano Sonata in E minor, Op. 7. Funeral March for Rikard Nordraak, CW117. Melodies of Norway – The sirens' enticement. Stimmungen, Op. 73. Transcriptions of Original Songs I, Op. 41 – No. 3, I love thee. Four Humoresques, Op. 6. Four Piano Pieces, Op. 1.
Einar Steen-Nøkleberg *pf*
Naxos 8 550881 (72 minutes: DDD). Recorded 1993.   Ⓢ

Piano Works, Volume 2.
Two Improvisations on Norwegian Folksongs, Op. 29. Melodies of Norway – A Ballad to
Saint Olaf. 25 Norwegian Folksongs and Dances, Op. 17. Transcriptions of Original Songs II,
Op. 52 – No. 2, The first meeting. 19 Norwegian Folksongs, Op. 66.
Einar Steen-Nøkleberg *pf*
Naxos 8 550882 (70 minutes: DDD). Recorded 1993. ⑤ 🄴

Piano Works, Volume 3.
Four Album Leaves, Op. 28. Six Poetic Tone-pictures, Op. 3. Melodies of Norway – Iceland. Three
Pictures from life in the country, Op. 19. Three Pieces from 'Sigurd Jorsalfar', Op. 56 – Prelude.
Ballade in G minor, Op. 24, 'in the form of variations on a Norwegian melody'.
Einar Steen-Nøkleberg *pf*
Naxos 8 550883 (64 minutes: DDD). Recorded 1993. ⑤

Piano Works, Volume 4.
Holberg Suite, Op. 40. Melodies of Norway – I went to bed so late. Six Norwegian Mountain
Melodies, CW134. Peer Gynt Suite No. 1, Op. 46 – Morning. 17 Norwegian Peasant Dances,
Op. 72.
Einar Steen-Nøkleberg *pf*
Naxos 8 550884 (71 minutes: DDD). Recorded 1993. ⑤

These are the first four volumes of a complete Grieg cycle which stretches to no fewer than
14 discs. Since all of them are at super-budget price they make a very competitive alternative to
other complete or near-complete surveys. Einar Steen-Nøkleberg came into prominence in the 1970s
and won numerous Norwegian and other prizes. He was professor of the piano at the Hanover
Musikhochschule for some years and is the author of a monograph on Grieg's piano music and its
interpretation.

8 550881: The first disc juxtaposes early pieces, the Sonata, Op. 7, the Op. 6 *Humoresques* and the
Funeral March for Rikard Nordraak, all written in the mid-1890s with his very last piano work,
Stimmungen (or 'Moods'), Op. 73. He plays these bold and original pieces with great flair and
understanding. Whatever its limitations there is much greater range in Grieg's piano music than is
commonly realized and Steen-Nøkleberg is attuned to the whole spectrum it covers, whether in the
Bartókian 'Mountaineer's Song' from the Op. 73 to the charm and innocence of the *Allegretto con
grazia*, the third of the *Humoresques*, Op. 6. *8 550882:* The *19 Norwegian Folksongs* (1896) are
remarkable pieces as Grieg himself knew. He wrote to the Dutch composer, Julius Röntgen, of
having 'put some hair-raising chromatic chords on paper. The excuse is that they originated not on
the piano but in my mind.' Readers will recognize No. 14 as the source of the theme for Delius's *On
hearing the first cuckoo in spring*. Steen-Nøkleberg plays them with great tonal finesse and
consummate artistry. *8 550883:* The most substantial work on this disc is the *Ballade* which Grieg
wrote on the death of his parents. This recording can hold its own with the best in this healthy area
of the catalogue – even if there are moments where Steen-Nøkleberg seems too discursive. Yet what
an imaginative colour he produces in the *Adagio* variation when the music suddenly melts
pianissimo. *8 550884:* The *Norwegian Peasant Dances* are amazing pieces for their period, and
though their audacity and dissonance were later overtaken by Bartók, they still retain their capacity
to surprise. The playing conveys the extraordinary character and originality of these pieces as do
few others. The smaller pieces on this disc – and on its companions – are full of rewards.

Piano Sonata in E minor, Op. 7. Six Poetic Tone-pictures, Op. 3 – Nos. 4-6. Four Album Leaves,
Op. 28 – No. 1 in A flat major; No. 4 in C sharp minor. Agitato. Lyric Pieces – Book 3, Op. 43;
Book 5, Op. 54.
Leif Ove Andsnes *pf*
Virgin Classics VC7 59300-2 (72 minutes: DDD). Recorded 1992. Ⓕ

Andsnes was 22 when he recorded Grieg's Sonata – exactly the composer's age when he wrote it.
Despite the heroic opening, Andsnes does not save the first movement from sounding repetitive. It is
the two inner movements that display real character and imagination and the pianist rises to the
occasion in both. The finale is stunningly played. He is to be heard at his very best in the *Lyric
Pieces*, Op. 43, which is the most familiar set of all. One relishes the glinting colours in 'Butterfly',
the simple heartfelt yearnings of 'Solitary Wanderer' and the delightful twittering energy of the
'Little Bird'. Here is a pianist with sufficient insight and subtlety not to feel the need to prettify the
music. This well-crafted CD has pleasant piano sound, not overclose in impact.

Lyric Pieces – Arietta, Op. 12 No. 1. Berceuse, Op. 38 No. 1. Butterfly, Op. 43 No. 1. Solitary
Traveller, Op. 43 No. 2. Album Leaf, Op. 47 No. 2. Melody, Op. 47 No. 3. Norwegian Dance,

'Halling', Op. 47 No. 4. Nocturne, Op. 54 No. 4. Scherzo, Op. 54 No. 5. Homesickness, Op. 57 No. 6. Brooklet, Op. 62 No. 4. Homeward, Op. 62 No. 6. In ballad vein, Op. 65 No. 5. Grandmother's Minuet, Op. 68 No. 2. At your feet, Op. 68 No. 3. Cradle Song, Op. 68 No. 5. Once upon a time, Op. 71 No. 1. Puck, Op. 71 No. 3. Gone, Op. 71 No. 6. Remembrances, Op. 71 No. 7.
Emil Gilels *pf*
DG The Originals 449 721-2GOR (56 minutes: ADD). Recorded 1974.   Ⓜ

Here, surely, is a classic recording, one of calibre and status for all time. Rarely can a great artist have declared his love with such touching candour. By his own admission Gilels discovered in Grieg's *Lyric Pieces* a 'whole world of intimate feeling' and at the sessions where these were recorded fought tirelessly to capture their intricate mix of innocence and experience. The results are of an unblemished purity, grace and contained eloquence. He brings the same insight and concentration to these apparent trifles as he did to towering masterpieces of the classic repertoire. The programme proceeds chronologically and one can appreciate the gradual but marked development in Grieg's harmonic and expressive language – from the folk-song inspired early works to the more progressive and adventurous later ones. Gilels's fingerwork is exquisite and the sense of total involvement with the music almost religious in feeling. Never can Debussy's sniping estimate of Grieg', 'a pink bonbon filled with snow' (or DG's dreary accompanying notes), have seemed wider of the mark. The recordings remain as impeccable as the playing. This is a disc for everyone's desert island.

Peer Gynt – The Bridal March passes by; Prelude; In the Hall of the Mountain King; Solveig's Song; Prelude; Arab Dance; Anitra's Dance; Prelude; Solveig's Cradle Song. Symphonic Dance, Op. 64 – Allegretto grazioso. In Autumn, Op. 11. Old Norwegian Romance with Variations, Op. 51.
Ilse Hollweg *sop*
Beecham Choral Society; Royal Philharmonic Orchestra / Sir Thomas Beecham.
EMI Great Recordings of the Century CDM5 66914-2 (77 minutes: ADD). Recorded 1957.   Ⓜ Ⓗ

Grieg's incidental music was an important integral part of Ibsen's *Peer Gynt* and from this score Grieg later extracted the two familiar suites. This recording of excerpts from *Peer Gynt* goes back to 1957 but still sounds well and is most stylishly played. Included is the best known ('Anitra's Dance' is a delicate gem here) together with 'Solveig's Song' and 'Solveig's Cradle Song'. Sir Thomas uses Ilse Hollweg to advantage, her voice suggesting the innocence of the virtuous and faithful peasant heroine. There is also an effective use of the choral voices which are almost inevitably omitted in ordinary performances of the two well-known orchestral suites: the male chorus of trolls in the 'Hall of the Mountain King' are thrilling, and the women in the 'Arab Dance' are charming. The other two pieces are well worth having too; *Symphonic Dances* is a later, freshly pastoral work, while the overture *In Autumn* is an orchestral second version of an early piece for piano duet. This reissue is further enhanced by the first release in stereo of the *Old Norwegian Romance*.

Haugtussa, Op. 67. Two brown eyes, Op. 5 No. 1. I love but thee, Op. 5 No. 3. A swan, Op. 25 No. 2. With a waterlily, Op. 25 No. 4. Hope, Op. 26 No. 1. Spring, Op. 33 No. 2. Beside the stream, Op. 33 No. 5. From Monte Pincio, Op. 39 No. 1. Six Songs, Op. 48. Spring showers, Op. 49 No. 6. While I wait, Op. 60 No. 3. Farmyard Song, Op. 61 No. 3.
Anne Sofie von Otter *mez* **Bengt Forsberg** *pf*
DG Grieg Anniversary Edition 437 521-2GH (68 minutes: DDD). Texts and translations included. Recorded 1992. *Gramophone* Award Winner 1993.   Ⓕ Ⓢ Ⓔ

With performances like this, Grieg in his celebratory year emerged as a first-rank composer in this genre. Anne Sofie von Otter is at the peak of her powers, glorying in this repertoire which she obviously loves and knows intimately. Take the *Haugtussa* cycle, which Grieg considered his greatest achievement in this sphere of writing. Von Otter projects her imagination of the visionary herd-girl with absolute conviction. She is no less successful in the German settings that follow. The sad depths of *One day, my thought* from Six Songs, Op. 48, also set memorably by Wolf in his *Spanish Songbook*, the hopelessness of Goethe's *The time of roses* (Op. 48 No. 5), a setting of great beauty, are encompassed with unfettered ease, but so are the lighter pleasures of *Lauf der Welt*. Even the familiar *A dream* (Op. 48 No. 6) emerges as new in von Otter's daringly big-boned reading. Throughout, her readings are immeasurably enhanced by the imaginative playing of Bengt Forsberg. They breathe fresh life into *A swan* and in the almost as familiar *With a waterlily*, another superb Ibsen setting, the questing spirit expressed in the music is marvellously captured by the performers. And there are more pleasures to come. A superb account of *Hope*, a wistful, sweetly voiced and played account of *Spring*, the charming, teasing *While I wait* and a deeply poetic reading of the justly renowned *From Monte Pincio* are just three more definitive interpretations. This should be regarded as a 'must' for any collector of songs, indeed a collector of any kind.

Sofia Gubaidulina

Gubaidulina String Quartet No. 2.
Kurtág String Quartet No. 1, Op. 1. Hommage à Milhály András, Op. 13. Officium breve in memoriam Andreae Szervánzky, Op. 28.
Lutosławski String Quartet.
Arditti Quartet (Irvine Arditti, David Alberman *vns* Levine Andrade *va* Rohan de Saram *vc*).
Auvidis Montaigne MO789007 (72 minutes: DDD). Recorded 1990.   Ⓕ

The need for a personal tone of voice is a quality all three of these eastern European composers well understand. Lutosławski's quartet (1964) came at a crucial time in his development, as the first work to relate his new technique of aleatory counterpoint (in which the pitches but not necessarily the rhythms are prescribed) to a traditional, abstract genre. Compared to the best of his later works the quartet is perhaps too long-drawn-out, but this highly expressive and strongly disciplined performance makes an excellent case for it. Alongside the Lutosławski the three works by György Kurtág sound remarkably intense and concentrated, yet with a lyricism that prevents their evident austerity from growing merely arid, and which makes the reference to a tonal melody in the *Officium breve* seem natural as well as touching. The world of consonant harmony is also evoked by Gubaidulina, not as an expression of regret for the irretrievable past but as a way of extending her own essentially modern language. There is a special sense of personal certainty and confidence about all the music on this well-recorded disc. It needs no special pleading, but the commanding authority of the Arditti Quartet's performance is still something to marvel at.

Francisco Guerrero

Missa Sancta et immaculata. Hei mihi, Domine. Trahe me post te, Virgo Maria. Magnificat septimi toni. Vexilla Regis. O lux beata Trinitas. Lauda mater ecclesia.
Westminster Cathedral Choir / James O'Donnell.
Hyperion CDA66910 (65 minutes: DDD). Texts and translations included. Recorded 1997.   Ⓕ

Quite why Guerrero has had to wait so long in the wings of musical history is a complicated story, having partly to do with the inaccessibility of editions and partly the reputation with which he was left, until recently, by music historians. This disc should help to introduce Guerrero as composer whose music is exhilarating, full of variety and spiritually uplifting. The *Missa Sancta et immaculata*, based as it is on Morales's sublime motet of that name, is magnificent. The motet's melodic contours determine the character of the Mass, Guerrero finding infinitely subtle ways to vary and embellish his model and fully exploiting his grasp of vocal colour. The two motets, *Hei mihi, Domine* and *Trahe me post te*, show a more intimate, contemplative aspect of Guerrero, but what really brings one up with a jolt are the three hymns, *Vexilla Regis*, *O lux beata Trinitas* and *Lauda mater ecclesia*, which have been provided with the appropriate *alternatim* chants and which reveal themselves to be absolutely wonderful music. *Vexilla Regis* is a miniature drama running the gamut of emotions and lasting nearly 11 minutes. *Lauda mater ecclesia*, a magnificent text for the Feast of St Mary Magdalen, is a flash of lightning. Westminster Cathedral Choir is on its very best form, incisive and thrilling.

Alexandre Guilmant

Guilmant Organ Symphony No. 1 in D minor, Op. 42.
Poulenc Organ Concerto in G minor.
Widor Organ Symphony No. 5 in F minor, Op. 42 No. 1.
Ian Tracey *org*
BBC Philharmonic Orchestra / Yan Pascal Tortelier.
Chandos CHAN9271 (80 minutes: DDD). Recorded on the organ of Liverpool Cathedral in 1993. Ⓕ

As horoscope writers in some magazines might put it, with Yan Pascal Tortelier and the BBC Philharmonic in conjunction with Ian Tracey and the Liverpool Cathedral organ within the orbit of Chandos the earth is bound to move for you. And so it does. The Guilmant is one of those great spectaculars which thrives in just such a steamy acoustic environment, but Tortelier with his incisive, thrusting direction ensures that while there is vivid aural spectacle, musical integrity is preserved with quite remarkable clarity and co-ordination. The BBC Philharmonic is magnificent and Tracey plays this great hulking brute of an organ with a surety of touch which comes not only from years of intimate experience, but from a deep understanding of what is needed. As for the Poulenc, this is a splendid performance, combining high drama with spiritual intensity, but misplaced in these gargantuan Liverpudlian cavities. The sound is just too beefy and Poulenc's lightning changes of mood are largely masked by an all-enveloping acoustic. Tracey's true colours are shown off to the full in the Widor – and what an inspired piece of programme planning to include this famous solo organ symphony as the meat in the sandwich between works for organ and orchestra.

Pavel Haas Czechoslovakian 1899-1944

P. Haas String Quartets – No. 2, Op. 7, 'From the Monkey Mountains'; No. 3, Op. 15.
Krása String Quartet.
Hawthorne Quartet (Ronan Lefkowitz, Si-Jing Huang *vns* Mark Ludwig *va* Sato Knudsen *vc*).
Decca 440 853-2DH (76 minutes: DDD). Recorded 1993. *Gramophone* Award Winner 1995. Ⓕ Ⓔ

Like Hans Krása, Haas was influenced by the modern movement, including neo-classicism, jazz and 'the new tonality', and both entered Theresienstadt in 1941 to travel to their deaths (on the same day) three years later in the gas chambers of Auschwitz. Of all Janáček's pupils it was Haas who absorbed rather than merely imitated his ideas. Something of the master's aphoristic, questing manner remains, but other than that the Quartet represents the mature Haas. An air of tension pervades the three movements, alternating passages of lyricism with tightly intertwining parts of harmonic complexity. Krása's Quartet also reveals a voice of exceptional talent. As a product of his studies with Zemlinsky its harmonic world leans more towards *fin de siècle* Vienna than his homeland. The central movement contains a marvellous section of burlesque on a theme from the overture to Smetana's *The Bartered Bride*, whilst the slow finale opens up a magical, almost mystical, twilight world that Zemlinsky himself would have been proud to have penned. Excellent performances and superb recording.

The Charlatan.
Vladimír Chmelo *bar* Doctor Pustrpalk; **Anda-Louise Bogza** *sngr* Rozina;
Miroslav Svejda *ten* Bakalář; **Leo Marian Vodička** *ten* Kyška; **Ladislav Mlejnek** *sngr* Pavučina;
Jitka Svobodová *sop* Amaranta; **Jiri Kubik** *ten* Jochimus;
Prague Philharmonic Choir; Prague State Opera Orchestra / Israel Yinon.
Decca Entartete Musik 460 042-2DHO2 (two discs: 128 minutes: DDD). Notes, text and
translation included. Recorded live in 1997. Ⓕ

The idiom of *The Charlatan* ('Sarlatán') is firmly rooted in that of Janáček, his teacher. Haas may have refashioned his harmonic language to acknowledge his Jewish roots in the incomplete Symphony of 1940-42, but the folksiness of his opera, premièred in Brno in April 1938, is recognizably Czech. As in Janáček's *Cunning Little Vixen*, the choppy, naturalistic declamation of the text does not preclude an emotive, melodic dimension. Heard on disc, the opera persuades musically rather than dramatically (the tragi-comic libretto describing the life and loves of a fairground healer is the composer's own). Trailing its quack-hero from one bit of chicanery to the next, it offers many incidental delights. Indeed, given the circumstances of its composition, the score shows Haas in engagingly cosmopolitan mood, embracing Parisian attributes such as one finds in the music of Prokofiev and Martinů. The piquant sonorities remind one of Milhaud or even Weill and give the music a sufficiently distinctive profile to suggest that, had he lived, Haas might have turned Czech opera away from Janáček's aggressive Slavophilia towards a more mainstream, consciously European style. There are bigger questions too. Could all this 'lost' tonal music have sustained a more bracing challenge to the rising tide of serialism, curbing the post-war tendency to wipe the slate clean?

Decca's recording has been edited together from Prague concert performances given in June 1997 to what was reportedly a poor house. The singing is committed, with Vladimír Chmelo a firmly projected Doctor Pustrpalk, and the wind playing is certainly characterful enough. Only the strings can sound thin and under-rehearsed and Haas's rhythmic irregularities might be expected to make for a few rough edges, but enthusiasts should not be put off. The approach is affectionate, sometimes ardent, the sound bright and immediate, the documentation excellent. Like the rest of Haas's small *oeuvre*, this is magical music well worth getting to know.

Reynaldo Hahn Venezuelan/French 1875-1947

A Chloris. Le rossignol des lilas. L'enamourée. Trois jours de vendange. Etudes latines – Lydé;
Tyndaris; Phyllis. Les fontaines. Automne. Infidélité. Dans la nuit. D'une prison. Quand la nuit n'est

pas étoilée. Fumée. Le printemps. Je me souviens. Quand je fus pris au pavillon. Paysage. Fêtes galantes. Nocturne. Mai. L'heure exquise. Offrande. Si mes vers avaient des ailes.
Susan Graham *sop* **Roger Vignoles** *pf*
Sony Classical SK60168 (62 minutes: DDD). Texts and translations included. Recorded 1998. Ⓕ▣

A pupil of Massenet and Saint-Saëns, Hahn wrote over 30 stage works, as well as orchestral and chamber compositions and a first-class book on the interpretation of French song. He also conducted Mozart at Salzburg, was music critic of *Le Figaro*, and after the Second World War directed the Paris Opéra. But the record catalogue at least has done him proud, not least with this pleasurable collection. Susan Graham brings to it a voice of lovely quality, excellent French and – in keeping with Hahn's own insistence – gives overriding importance to clarity of enunciation, the verbal meaning governing the vocal colour. It is certainly better to savour these songs a few at a time, but the programme has been well put together to show Hahn's range, from the Bachian pastiche of *A Chloris* or the antique simplicity of *Lydé* to the adventurous harmonic progressions of *Fumée*, *Le printemps* or *Je me souviens*, from the despairing pathos of *D'une prison* to the light-heartedness of *Quand je fus pris au pavillon*, from the quiet rapture of *Nocturne* to the passion of *Dans la nuit* (a splendid miniature). His outstanding gift for lyricism is evident throughout; *Le rossignol des lilas*, for example, is enchanting. Susan Graham perfectly captures these songs' elegant intimacy with a wealth of nuance, from the gentle tone of *L'enamourée* to the fullness of *L'automne*; and the way she floats the words 'l'heure exquise' is haunting. Roger Vignoles provides most sensitive partnership throughout: he has more scope in songs like *Les fontaines* or *Dans la nuit*, but equally noteworthy is his subtle treatment of the repeated pattern of *Infidélité*.

Douze rondels. Etudes latines. Si mes vers avaient des ailes. Paysage. Rêverie. Offrande. Mai. Infidélité. Seule. Les cygnes. Nocturne. Trois jours de vendange. D'une prison. Séraphine. L'heure exquise. Fêtes galantes. Quand la nuit n'est pas étoilée. Le plus beau présent. Sur l'eau. Le rossignol des lilas. A Chloris. Ma jeunesse. Puisque j'ai mis ma lèvre. La nymphe de la source. Au rossignol. Je me souviens. Mozart – Air de la lettre. O mon bel inconnu – C'est très vilain d'être infidèle. Ciboulette – C'est sa banlieue; Nous avons fait un beau voyage. Une revue – La dernière valse.
Dame Felicity Lott *sop* **Susan Bickley** *mez* **Ian Bostridge** *ten* **Stephen Varcoe** *bar*
Graham Johnson, Chris Gould *pfs* **London Schubert Chorale / Stephen Layton.**
Hyperion CDA67141/2 (two discs: 134 minutes: DDD). Texts and translations included. Recorded 1995. Ⓕ

The two cycles, *Douze rondels* and *Etudes latines*, are linked by a common fascination with the past. The *Douze rondels* were composed to poems in a medieval metre, which allowed Hahn to try his hand at pastiche madrigals and courtly ballads. The *Etudes latines* cast their gaze back still further in time to classical antiquity. For Hahn, as for Debussy in his *Bilitis* songs and Ravel in *Daphnis et Chloé*, that era seemed to represent the ultimate in purity and sensuality rolled into one. This collection of ten songs is a real discovery and rivals late Fauré, both in its refinement and mesmerizing simplicity of utterance. The three main singers divide the songs between them. Apart from a few moments when one would like a more substantial tone, Stephen Varcoe's light baritone suits Hahn very well and he is a refreshingly unaffected interpreter, who sings with grace and feeling. Susan Bickley is better at the larger canvas of a piece like *Quand la nuit n'est pas étoilée* than the more intimate songs but the most celebrated pair of all Hahn's *mélodies* goes to Dame Felicity Lott, whose sympathy for the French style could have no happier outlet. Both *Si mes vers avaient des ailes* and *L'heure exquise* are included here, the latter if not an hour, then at least two-and-a-half minutes that are truly exquisite. They are both beautifully sung and are undisturbed by the discomfort around the top of the stave that sometimes mars Lott's singing elsewhere. At the end, she offers four operetta solos as an encore. Graham Johnson's accompaniments are as sensitive as ever. The piano could have been placed a little closer, but the voices have been well captured.

George Frederic Handel German/British 1685-1759

Concerti grossi, Op. 3, HWV312-17. Concerti grossi, Op. 6, HWV319-30.

Concerti grossi, Opp. 3 and 6.
Vienna Concentus Musicus / Nikolaus Harnoncourt.
Teldec 4509-95500-2 (four discs: 237 minutes: ADD/DDD). Recorded 1982-85. Ⓑ🆁🆁

The somewhat perfunctory look of these recoupled reissues (there are no insert-notes and precious little information of any sort about the recordings) masks just what extraordinary music-making lies within. It took a long time for Harnoncourt's prodigious musical personality to be recognized for what it is. And it is true that these recordings come from a time when even Harnoncourt's supporters, for all the admiration they could muster, were finding him a little too eccentric to handle. But listening now to these searching, unceasingly imaginative performances of Handel's finest instrumental music, you can't help feeling that Harnoncourt was (as he has been so often) simply ahead of his time. Here he shows the very creative freshness and insight that have characterized his Beethoven. If Handel were as much a part of the general music press's view of things as Beethoven is, then perhaps these recordings would have been treated to the same level of scrutiny and indulgence as Harnoncourt's more recent ones have, and we could all have celebrated a radical talent about a decade earlier. The fact is that there is ferocious creativity in every bar. Every opening slow movement is the prelude to a drama, every fugue a precisely related episode. You can find imposing examples of the former in Op. 6 No. 5 (its opening solo violin notes are like being tickled under the nose with a feather) or Op. 6 No. 6 (like the start of some great operatic scena), and stunning demonstrations of the latter in Op. 3 No. 3 or Op. 6 No. 1 (both broadly painted but leading to very different types of climax). There is hardly a place where Handel's music is allowed to lie down or just play itself; Harnoncourt is everywhere busy with thunderous dynamic contrasts, stomping dance rhythms or the sort of vivid articulation that at one moment has us enthralled by a grippingly minimal *staccato*, at another swept up by the warm embrace of a sudden but grandly *legato* phrase (quite a Harnoncourt trademark, this).

The Vienna Concentus Musicus plays for the most part with a virtuosity and precision that is well highlighted by the slightly dry but transparent acoustic in which they are recorded, and that is so typical of Teldec's 1980s Das Alte Werk recordings. There are a few places where the basic pulse seems oddly uncertain (most off-puttingly, perhaps, at the very beginning of the whole set, in the opening bars of Op. 3 No. 1), but elsewhere Harnoncourt's control of every aspect of the music is tight, his involvement total. To him this is big music, and these are big performances. Of course, there is no denying that they sound eccentric, even now. Certainly not everything works and we would hesitate to recommend them as one's only encounter with this music. But their consistent and often audacious probing at the music's meaning is a spirit-reviving antidote to what by comparison seems like bland cautiousness on the part of some of Harnoncourt's rivals. Whether you actually like it or not (and we certainly can't guarantee that you will), this re-release performs the double and timely favour of reminding us that this man was always a genius of some kind, and of putting before us more convincingly than ever a Handel we can associate with Beethoven's judgement of him as 'the greatest of composers'.

Concerti grossi, Op. 3.
Tafelmusik / Jeanne Lamon.
Sony Classical Vivarte SK52553 (60 minutes: DDD). Recorded 1991. Ⓕ ℗ Ⓔ

This is a fine issue impressive both for its stylistic fluency and its infectious response to Handel's music which could not conceivably disappoint anyone. Tafelmusik plays only the six concertos of which Handel's authorship is undisputed. This version, in respect of finesse and vitality, has the edge over all the competition. Where Tafelmusik scores is in the sheer virtuosity of its playing and the easy gracefulness of its phrasing. Strong accents are not overemphasized and, though vigorous, there is nothing aggressive in this approach to the music. Tafelmusik includes a plucked string instrument among the continuo colloquium; they have large reinforcements at the top and bottom of the string texture and the performances have great radiance. The disc is beautifully recorded.

Concerti grossi, Op. 6 Nos. 1-4.
The English Concert / Trevor Pinnock.
Archiv Produktion 410 897-2AH (42 minutes: DDD). Ⓕ ℗ ℞℞

Nos. 5-8.
The English Concert / Trevor Pinnock.
Archiv Produktion 410 898-2AH (61 minutes: DDD). Ⓕ ℗ ℞℞

Nos. 9-12.
The English Concert / Trevor Pinnock.
Archiv Produktion 410 899-2AH (58 minutes: DDD). Ⓕ ℗ ℞℞

Trevor Pinnock's accounts contain much that is satisfying: polished ensemble, effectively judged tempos, a natural feeling for phrase, and a buoyancy of spirit which serves Handel's own robust musical language very well. Crisp attack, a judicious application of appoggiaturas and tasteful embellishment further enhance these lively performances. Pinnock varies the continuo colour by using organ and harpsichord and also includes Handel's autograph (though not printed) oboe parts for Concertos Nos. 1, 2, 5 and 6; where they occur a bassoon is sensibly added to fulfil the customary three-part wind texture of the period. Recorded sound is clear and captures well the warm sonorities of the instruments.

Concerti grossi, Op. 6 Nos. 1-5.
Collegium Musicum 90 / Simon Standage *vn*
Chandos Chaconne CHAN0600 (62 minutes: DDD). Recorded 1996.　　　　　ⒻⓅⒺ

Concerti grossi, Op. 6 Nos. 6-9.
Collegium Musicum 90 / Simon Standage *vn*
Chandos Chaconne CHAN0616 (58 minutes: DDD). Recorded 1997.　　　　　ⒻⓅ

Concerti grossi – Op. 6 Nos. 10-12; C major, HWV318, 'Alexander's Feast'.
Collegium Musicum 90 / Simon Standage *vn*
Chandos Chaconne CHAN0622 (56 minutes: DDD). Recorded 1997.　　　　　ⒻⓅ

The first disc of the ever-fresh Op. 6 *Concerti grossi* includes the oboe parts that Handel later added to Nos. 1, 2, 5 and 6. The performances are brimful of vitality, and the clean articulation and light, predominantly detached style give the music buoyancy and help to bring out Handel's often mischievous twinkle in the eye. Speeds are generally brisk, with boldly vigorous playing, but Standage's team can also spin a tranquil broad line. Dynamics, throughout, are subtly graded and natural-sounding, and except in one final cadence ornamentation is confined to small cadential trills. On the second disc, except, rightly, in the sombre colours in the splendid Sixth (G minor) Concerto – here with oboe and the agreeable addition of a theorbo to the continuo – there is a general air of cheerfulness about the performances that is most engaging. The fugue in No. 7 is wittily buoyant, the *Allegro* in No. 9 borrowed from the *Cuckoo and the nightingale* Organ Concerto could scarcely be more high-spirited, the final Passepied of No. 6 and the Hornpipe of No. 7 are spring-toed; and Standage's feeling for convincing tempos is nowhere better shown than in the long Musette of No. 6, which too often, in other hands, can drag. Phrasing everywhere is shapely, and the surprise chords that interrupt the flow of No. 8's Allemande are admirably 'placed'. A thoroughly enjoyable disc, cleanly recorded.

On the final disc the playing is always on its toes – positively twinkling in dance movements such as the concluding fugal gigue of No. 12. The final two concertos, No. 11 in particular, also give Simon Standage an opportunity to shine as a soloist; his *ad lib* sections are tastefully done, without excesses, and his semiquavers in the variants of the A major *Andante* are feather-light. Dynamics everywhere are well contrasted in a natural way (no suspicion of being imposed from without), and tempos are nicely judged; a slightly faster repeat of the first half of No. 10's fifth movement suggests the splicing of a different take. As a fill-up to the series there is the *Alexander's Feast* Concerto grosso, for which the string group is joined by oboes and bassoon. The excellent concertino of two violins and cello is thrown into high relief, and the *Allegro* movements are delightfully springy.

---

12 Concerti grossi, Op. 6.
Academy of Ancient Music / Andrew Manze *vn*
Harmonia Mundi HMU90 7228/9 (two discs: 157 minutes: DDD). Recorded 1997.　　　　　ⒻⓅⒺ

With one stride, Harmonia Mundi has stolen a march on Chandos Chaconne's rival set of Handel's Op. 6 with Simon Standage's Collegium Musicum 90; by juggling with the order, the 12 concertos have been accommodated on only two CDs. The AAM is on sparkling form, clearly enjoying itself under Andrew Manze's leadership. Performances are invigoratingly alert, splendidly neat (all those semiquaver figurations absolutely precise) and strongly rhythmical but not inflexible, with much dynamic gradation which ensures that phrases are always tonally alive and sound completely natural (even if more subtly nuanced than Handel's players ever dreamt of). Manze's basically light-footed approach is particularly appealing, and he sees to it that inner-part imitations are given due weight. Speeds are nearly all fast, occasionally questionably so (though exhilarating), as in the first *Allegro* of No. 1, the big *Allegro* of No. 6 and the *Allegro* in No. 9. But Manze successfully brings out the character of all the movements, and you can't fail to love the vigorous kick of his No. 7 hornpipe. He is mostly sparing in embellishing solo lines except in Nos. 6 and 11. Altogether this is an issue of joyous vitality, to which you will find yourself returning with pleasure.

Organ Concertos, Op. 4 – No. 1 in G minor; No. 2 in B flat major; No. 3 in G minor; No. 4 in F major; No. 5 in F major; Op. 7 – No. 1 in B flat major; No. 2 in A major; No. 3 in B flat major; No. 4 in D minor; No. 5 in G minor; No. 6 in B flat major. Harp Concerto in B flat major, Op. 4 No. 6.

Paul Nicholson *org* Frances Kelly *hp*
The Brandenburg Consort / Roy Goodman *hpd*
Hyperion CDA67291/2 (two discs: 154 minutes: DDD). Recorded 1996.   Ⓕ Ⓟ

This recording was made at St Lawrence Whitchurch on the organ which Handel must certainly have played and which has recently been admirably restored. Under Paul Nicholson's hands, the organ sounds well. There is plenty of brightly glittering passagework – in the second movement of Op. 4 No. 1, for example, or the *Allegro* of Op. 4 No. 2 – and rich diapason sound in such movements as the passacaglia-like first of Op. 7 No. 1; while the softer side of the instrument is particularly appealing in Op. 4 No. 5, where Nicholson, doubtless conscious that this is a transcription of a recorder sonata, draws from it some very sweet sounds. It has of course a mechanical action, and here and there the incidental noise may be rather disconcerting. Still, it is authentic, so possibly we should be grateful to have it so clearly reproduced. There is some very lively and at times virtuoso playing from Nicholson in the quick movements, with sturdy rhythms, and some of the dance movements too go with a good swing. Nicholson gives good, precise accounts of the various solo fugues and the transcriptions and improvisatory movements used here when Handel offered merely an ad lib. He is a thoughtful player; his added ornamentation is always musical and intelligent, and stylish too, and his treatment of the natural caesuras in the music is always dictated by the structure. In several movements, however, overdeliberate orchestral phrasing or accentuation can be damaging. This happens quite often and it sometimes affects Nicholson's playing. Op. 4 No. 6 is played on the harp, with some very delicate timing from Frances Kelly. The recording is bright and clear, capturing happily the acoustic of this moderate-sized church.

Music for the Royal Fireworks, HWV351. Water Music, HWV348-50.

Music for the Royal Fireworks. Water Music.
Le Concert des Nations / Jordi Savall.
Auvidis Astrée E8512 (74 minutes: DDD). Recorded 1993.   Ⓕ Ⓟ Ⓔ ⓇⓇ

Of the period-instrument couplings of these two 'elemental' suites, particularly the *Fireworks Music*, Savall's must be placed at the top of the list. It is, however, strange that though the booklet-notes acknowledge that the *Water Music* falls into 'three suites' and that the Suite in G major was probably played during supper, the recorded performance ends with that in F major (described as 'Suite II') preceded by the rest ('Suite I') – neither the published nor the 'logical' order. The movements from the earlier Concerto in F are not included and there is also the familiar retitling and juggling with the order of movements. What splendid performances these are though, spirited, clean-edged and elegantly embellished – by a solo trumpet in the *Adagio* of the Overture of the *Fireworks Music*, where the preceding section is repeated as marked. The orchestral force is substantial, and the comparatively high-level recording and generous acoustic give a deliberate sense of being close to the performers – just as, on the Thames, King George I may have been in a barge adjacent to the musicians – rather than of hearing them from the riverside.

Music for the Royal Fireworks. Concertos – F major, HWV331; D major, HWV335*a*. Passacaille, Gigue and Minuet in G major. Occasional Suite in D major (both arr. Pinnock).
The English Concert / Trevor Pinnock *hpd*
Archiv Produktion 453 451-2AH (60 minutes: DDD). Recorded 1996.   Ⓕ Ⓟ

Trevor Pinnock uses George II's preferred scoring rather than Handel's – that is, just wind and percussion. What we know about the first performances of the work seems to indicate that Handel had his way and strings were used, along with a massed wind; probably the wind version was never heard in Handel's day. Well, here it is, with 24 oboes, 12 bassoons, double bassoon, nine each of trumpets and horns and six percussion. It's certainly rousing stuff, and a noble noise. With his direct and unaffected rhythm, Pinnock sets up a sturdy momentum for the Overture and the effect is grand and imposing. The dances too receive straightforward performances, with plenty of spirit and energy. This disc offers some welcome rarities. The F major Concerto is made up of versions of two movements from the D major part of the *Water Music*, here in F major; one is the movement generally labelled in the eighteenth century 'Mr Handel's Water Peice', again, with some interesting and very characteristic differences from the familiar version and the other is the *Alla Hornpipe*. In between Pinnock plays, as a slow movement, an *Adagio* from Op. 3 No. 5. The D major Concerto consists of what are probably early versions – less purposefully shaped, but again with some highly characteristic touches – of two movements from the *Fireworks Music* with a version of a movement from a violin sonata, on the organ, in between. The Passacaille, Gigue and Minuet come from a trio sonata and the *Occasional Suite* draws on the *Occasional Oratorio* overture, the *Ariodante* ballet and music composed for *Joshua* and *Alessandro Severo*. It all works pretty well, although some of the music in this last is not the most distinguished of Handel. But the concertos especially are well worth having, and certainly George II's vision of the *Fireworks Music* is to be relished in its way.

Music for the Royal Fireworks. Concerti a due cori – No. 1 in B flat major, HWV332; No. 2 in F major, HWV333; No. 3 in F major, HWV334.
Tafelmusik / Jeanne Lamon *vn*
Sony Classical Vivarte SK63073 (66 minutes: DDD). Recorded 1997.   Ⓕ **P**

It hasn't been done before, but it makes excellent sense to devote a CD to the three *Concerti a due cori* and the *Music for the Royal Fireworks*. Here the *Fireworks Music* is done in the form, with strings as well as wind, that Handel preferred. The less familiar *Concerti a due cori* were composed in the late 1740s for use in the intervals of oratorio performances. They borrow freely from other works – in particular *Messiah* (at the time scarcely known to London audiences) and *Belshazzar* – and some of the movements seem a little odd in shape because the structure is dictated, in the originals, by the texts; but they are cheerful, outgoing pieces and make very attractive listening, undemanding but, typically, touching here and there on deeper feeling. These performances are splendidly spirited and enjoyable on every plane. Tafelmusik tends to favour speedy tempos in Handel. In the *Fireworks Music* 'La paix' is taken steadily but it is all very nicely judged, and the jauntiness they bring to the main *Allegro* of the overture is particularly likeable, making it a shade more detached than usual to good effect. Handel's directions for the repeats in the dance movements are decidedly ambiguous, and Tafelmusik makes sensible decisions of its own which don't always quite accord with the instructions but work perfectly well. Once or twice there is a stylish lilt, almost a hint of *inégalité*, in the dances. The band sounds a big one, but the strings are only 5.6.3.3.2, with a fair number of wind – six oboes, three bassoons, four horns and three trumpets, with percussion (their collective intonation is as good as one has any right to expect). In the concertos, there is some first-rate wind playing and there is a fine, earthy ring from the horns throughout. One or two tempos may strike you as quickish; no one would think of singing 'And the glory of the Lord' as fast as Tafelmusik plays Handel's transcription of it, but after all there's no reason why it shouldn't be done this way on instruments.

Water Music.
Simon Standage, Elizabeth Wilcock *vns* **The English Concert / Trevor Pinnock** *hpd*
Archiv Produktion 410 525-2AH (54 minutes: DDD). Recorded 1983.   Ⓕ **P RR**

Whatever the circumstances were which prompted Handel to write his *Water Music*, it is highly unlikely that George I ever witnessed performances matching up to this one. These are sparkling performances of the three groups of movements which comprise the *Water Music*. Tempos are well judged and there is a truly majestic sweep to the opening F major French overture; that gets things off to a fine start but what follows is no less compelling with some notably fine woodwind playing, so often the disappointing element in performances on period instruments. In the D major music it is the brass department which steals the show and here, horns and trumpets acquit themselves with distinction. Archiv Produktion has achieved a particularly satisfying sound in which all strands of the orchestral texture can be heard with clarity. In this suite the ceremonial atmosphere comes over particularly well with some resonant brass playing complemented by crisply articulated oboes. The G major pieces are quite different from those in the previous groups, being lighter in texture and more closely dance-orientated in character. They are amongst the most engaging in the *Water Music* and especially, perhaps, the two little 'country dances', the boisterous character of which Pinnock captures nicely. Pinnock's is still quite the best performance of the *Water Music* on the market.

Water Music. Music for the Royal Fireworks.
Scottish Chamber Orchestra / Nicholas McGegan.
Classic fM The Full Works 75605 57044-2 (68 minutes: DDD). Recorded 1998.   Ⓜ

Classic fM has introduced the 'layman' to a great deal of accessible art music, often in the form of detached movements; any fear that extension of the process via The Full Works series might involve a measure of 'dumbing down' is dispersed by this recording. The only punch that is pulled here is that modern instruments and pitch are used, but Nicholas McGegan is too wise and experienced to allow that to count for much. He places Handel's *Water Music* Suites in the order usually accepted as appropriate to a single excursion along the Thames – F major on the outward journey, D major on the way back, and the gentler G major during supper – one that is equally effective in a recording. Identifying the movements by their titles provides the usual occupation for a relaxed winter's evening, but no matter – the music is magnificent in whatever order it is played, and by whatever titles it bears. The flanking Suites are recorded in a more spacious acoustic, as befits the postulated outdoor location of their original performances. The beginning and end of the *Music for the Royal Fireworks* are ablaze with the brilliant sounds of the trumpets and drums that the King loved. Authentic or not, these beautifully balanced performances are most enjoyable.

Water Music. Il pastor fido – Suite, HWV8c.
Tafelmusik / Jeanne Lamon vn
Sony Classical Vivarte SK68257 (76 minutes: DDD). Recorded 1995.　　　　　ⒻⓅⒺ

The jubilant spirit of the *Water Music* is splendidly captured here. This Canadian group has a good grasp of Handelian style, and lots of energy; there is plenty of vigour to its playing but no roughness. There are many nicely and unobtrusively managed details of timing and accent, yet always perfectly natural and justified from within. The tempos in the main are on the quick side but not hurried. The flowing *Andante* for the famous Air, which so readily becomes sticky if done slowly, is particularly likeable; here it sounds just right and no less expressive than usual. Only the D major *Lentement* seems heavy and ponderous, and perhaps the *Bourrée* that follows is also a little clumsily done. The horn playing, recorded well forward, is particularly impressive – clean and clear, with a fine ring; it would have sounded well across the Thames. The movements are done here with the F major music first, then the D major and G major mixed, an unusual arrangement these days but one that probably has Handel's authority: and it works well. Tafelmusik gets through the *Water Music* in some 52 minutes, and there is room for a substantial suite of dances from the second version of *Il pastor fido*, when Handel added ballet music for the French dancer Marie Sallé and her troupe. These are charming and lively pieces and the final Chaconne, with its inventive textures, is particularly appealing. The sound here is a shade middle- and bottom-heavy, rather more so than in *The Water Music*, but again the playing is splendidly fresh and spirited.

Trio Sonatas, Op. 5, HWV396-402 – No. 1 in A major; No. 2 in D major; No. 3 in E minor; No. 4 in G major; No. 5 in G minor; No. 6 in F major; No. 7 in B flat major.
London Baroque
Harmonia Mundi HMC90 1389 (69 minutes: DDD). Recorded 1991.　　　　　ⒻⓅ

Handel's publisher, Walsh, printed the six Trio Sonatas, Op. 2, in about 1730, following them up in 1739 with seven further trios which he published as the composer's Op. 5. In each set Handel offered a choice of melody instruments though the writing suggests that he had violins foremost in mind. The performances by London Baroque are poised, well shaped and susceptible to the subtle nuances of Handel's part-writing. Ingrid Seifert and Richard Gwilt are partners of long standing and their even dialogue, sometimes grave, sometimes lively and at other times playful, serves the music effectively. Tempos are well judged and phrases are eloquently shaped and articulately spoken. In all this the violinists are sympathetically supported by the continuo players who make their own vital contribution to clear textures and overall balance. Recorded sound is appropriately intimate, serving the sound character of the instruments themselves and evoking a chamber music ambience. The music, it hardly need be said, maintains a high level of craftsmanship and interest which will surely delight listeners.

Trio Sonatas – Op. 2 No. 5 in G minor, HWV390; Op. 5 Nos. 4 and 7. Tra le fiamme, HWV170. Notte placida e cheta, HWV142.
Catherine Bott sop **Caroline Kershaw, Jane Downer** recs/obs **Nigel Amherst** violone
Jonathan Manson vc **Purcell Quartet** (Catherine Mackintosh, Catherine Weiss vns
Richard Boothby va da gamba/vc Robert Woolley hpd).
Chandos Chaconne CHAN0620 (70 minutes: DDD). Texts and translations included.
Recorded 1997.　　　　　ⒻⓅ

The idea of alternating trio sonatas with cantatas is a happy one, based perhaps on the idea that people play CDs for pleasure and not simply for reference. The two cantatas presented here are rarities on record. *Tra le fiamme* is a spectacularly scored piece, its textures enriched by a viola da gamba obbligato (probably composed for a visiting virtuoso) and wind instruments (recorders in some numbers, oboes in another) as well as strings. *Notte placida e cheta* is a delightful evocation of night, sleep and amorous reflection, with its opening aria full of sinuous, voluptuous interweaving violin lines and its soft, gently accompanied recitatives; it ends – a slightly rude awakening, perhaps, to chime with the words – with a fugal aria in which the singer takes one of the four contrapuntal parts along with the violins and the bass. Catherine Bott sings them very responsively, both to the words and to the sense of Handel's lines, with neatly placed detail and some attractively floated phrases. The viol obbligato is done in accomplished style by Richard Boothby who supplies much of the continuo harmony with multiple stops.

In the Trio Sonatas there is some splendidly athletic playing from the violins of the Purcell Quartet, which plays with its usual spruce rhythms and conversational give and take; in several movements, such as the second and the fourth of Op. 2 No. 5 or the second of Op. 5 No. 7, the cello joins in on equal terms (its rushing semiquavers come out rather prominently in the recording). There is some gently eloquent playing in the *Adagio* of the Op. 2 Sonata and the Purcellian *Passacaille* in Op. 5 No. 4, and nicely sprung rhythms in the dances in the Op. 5 pieces. These are probably the most appealing performances available of these works.

Sonatas for Recorder and Continuo – No. 1 in G minor, HWV360; No. 2 in A minor, HWV362; No. 3 in C major, HWV365; No. 5 in F major, HWV369; No. 6 in B flat major, HWV377. Sonata for Flute and Continuo No. 3 in B minor, HWV367b.
Marion Verbruggen *rec/fl* **Jaap ter Linden** *vc* **Ton Koopman** *hpd/org*
Harmonia Mundi HMU90 7151 (58 minutes: DDD). Recorded 1994.   Ⓕ 🄿

These are very lively and musically intelligent performances. The recorder playing is outstandingly fine, sweet in tone, pointed in articulation, perfectly tuned, technically very fluent, and informed by a really good understanding of the art of ornamentation. Add to that the fact that Marion Verbruggen has a real command of Handel's language and you will realize that this CD is out of the ordinary. Some of Ton Koopman's accompaniments are a little busy (half are on the organ, half on the harpsichord), but it's all part of the sense of lively music-making that runs through this attractive disc.

Flute Sonatas – No. 1 in E minor, HWV359b; No. 2 in G major, HWV363b; No. 3 in B minor, HWV367b; No. 4 in A minor, HWV374; No. 5 in E minor, HWV375; No. 6 in B minor, HWV376; No. 7 in D major, HWV378; No. 8 in E minor, HWV379.
Barthold Kuijken *fl* **Wieland Kuijken** *va da gamba* **Robert Kohnen** *hpd*
Accent ACC9180 (73 minutes: DDD). Recorded 1991.   Ⓕ 🄿

In this recording of solo flute sonatas Barthold Kuijken plays pieces unquestionably by Handel as well as others over which doubt concerning his authorship has been cast in varying degrees. Certainly not all of the pieces here were conceived for transverse flute – there are earlier versions of HWV363b and 367b, for example, for oboe and treble recorder, respectively; but we can well imagine that in Handel's day most, if not all, of these delightful sonatas were regarded among instrumentalists as more-or-less common property. Barthold Kuijken, with his eldest brother Wieland and Robert Kohnen, gives characteristically graceful and stylish performances of the music. Kuijken is skilful in matters of ornamentation and is often adventurous, though invariably within the bounds of good taste. Dance movements are brisk and sprightly though he is careful to preserve their poise, and phrases are crisply articulated. This is of especial benefit to movements such as the lively *Vivace* of the B minor Sonata (HWV367b) which can proceed rather aimlessly when too *legato* an approach is favoured; and the virtuosity of these players pays off in the *Presto (Furioso)* movement that follows. In short, a delightful disc which should please both Handelians and most lovers of baroque chamber music.

Keyboard Suites: HWV426-33 – No. 1 in A major; No. 2 in F major; No. 3 in D minor; No. 4 in E minor; No. 5 in E major; No. 6 in F sharp minor; No. 7 in G minor; No. 8 in F minor. HWV434; HWV436-41 – No. 1 in G minor; No. 2 in D minor; No. 3 in D minor; No. 4 in E minor; No. 5 in B flat major; No. 6 in G major; No. 7 in D minor; No. 8 in G minor.

Handel Keyboard Suites, HWV426-33 Nos. 2, 3 and 5. Chaconne in G major, HWV435.
D. Scarlatti Keyboard Sonatas – B minor, Kk27; D major, Kk29; E major, Kk206; A major, Kk212; C sharp minor, Kk247; D major, Kk491; A major, Kk537.
Murray Perahia *pf*
Sony Classical SK62785 (69 minutes: DDD). Recorded 1996.
Gramophone Award Winner 1997.   Ⓕ 🅂 🄴

In his projection of line, mass and colour Perahia makes intelligent acknowledgement of the fact that none of this is piano music, but when it comes to communicating the forceful effects and the brilliance and readiness of finger for which these two great player-composers were renowned, inhibitions are thrown to the wind. Good! Nothing a pianist does in the *Harmonious Blacksmith* Variations in Handel's E major Suite, or the Air and Variations of the D minor Suite could surpass in vivacity and cumulative excitement what the expert harpsichordist commands, and you could say the same of Scarlatti's D major Sonata, Kk29; but Perahia is extraordinarily successful in translating these with the daredevil 'edge' they must have. Faster and yet faster! In the Handel (more than in the Scarlatti) his velocity may strike you as overdone; but one can see the sense of it. It is quite big playing throughout, yet not inflated. Admirable is the way the piano is addressed, with the keys touched rather than struck, and a sense conveyed that the music is coming to us through the tips of the fingers rather than the hammers of the instrument. While producing streams of beautifully moulded and inflected sound Perahia is a wizard at making you forget the percussive nature of the apparatus. There are movements in the Handel where the musical qualities are dependent on instrumental sound, or contrasts of sound, which the piano just can't convincingly imitate. And in some of the Scarlatti one might have reservations about Perahia's tendency to idealize, to soften outlines (hard to avoid, given the piano's capacity for nuance) and to make the bite less incisive. You could of course raise a more fundamental objection and say that it begs the question: why do it on the piano at all? If you can't bear to hear it on anything other than the harpsichord this record won't be for you. But Perahia is an artist, not just a pianist, and if you don't rule out of court the prospect of these composers *transcribed* for the piano, he has an experience to offer that is vivid and musically considered at the highest level – and not at all second-best. The virtuosity is special indeed, and there is not a note that hasn't been savoured.

Handel Keyboard Suites, HWV426-33 Nos. 1[b], 2-3[a], 4[b], 5[a], 6-7[b] and 8[a].
[a]**Sviatoslav Richter,** [b]**Andrei Gavrilov** *pfs*
EMI Forte CZS5 69337-2 (two discs: 119 minutes: ADD). Recorded live in 1979.   (M)

Handel Keyboard Suites, HWV434; HWV436-41 Nos. 1[a], 2-3[b], 4[a], 5[b], 6[a], 7[b] and 8[a].
Beethoven Piano Sonata No. 17 in D minor, Op. 31 No. 2, 'Tempest'[a].
[a]**Sviatoslav Richter,** [b]**Andrei Gavrilov** *pfs*
EMI Forte CZS5 69340-2 (two discs: 119 minutes: ADD). Recorded live in 1979.   (M)

Even by Sviatoslav Richter's Tours Festival standards, 1979 was a red-letter year. Then, partnered by his dazzling young compatriot Andrei Gavrilov, he played Handel's 16 Suites, offering performances of such quality that long-familiar reservations concerning their provenance and overall success evaporated as if by magic. From Richter and Gavrilov these baroque chains of dances emerge with an unforgettable wit and vitality. Listen to Gavrilov in the First Suite's opening Prelude and you will hear an authentic as well as spirited emulation of the extempore style. Yet it is in the slow movements that Gavrilov achieves his greatest effect. In such hands, the Sarabande from the Seventh Suite becomes Handel's 'black pearl', if you like, and in the same grave and ceremonial dances from Suites Nos. 11 and 13, the music emerges like great mysterious pools of light. Richter's genius has rarely sounded more imperturbable and, whether he is playful and resilient in, say, the Fifth Suite's Gigue or poised and tonally translucent – a model of sense and sensibility – in the *Air con Variazione* (the famous *Harmonious Blacksmith* Variations), you are always aware of the musical artist first and the transcendental pianist second. Tempos are judicious rather than extreme, and even the most determined Beckmesser will surely find himself abandoning pencil and paper and succumbing to the spell of such serenity and affection. Finally, as a further reminder of Richter's unique stature there is his legendary 1961 disc of Beethoven's D minor Sonata, Op. 31 No. 2. Rarely can Beethoven's suggestion that we should read Shakespeare's *The Tempest* (a metaphysical fantasy concerned with the mystery of death and rebirth) have seemed more teasing or obtuse. In any event, from Richter the music retains its mystery, its eloquence 'contained' to the point of enigma. Richter 'does' so little and the result is hauntingly pure and distilled. The recordings, though occasionally showing their age, have been beautifully transferred.

Keyboard Suites, HWV426-33 – Nos. 1 and 7; HWV438 – No. 4 in D minor. Chaconne in G major, HWV435. Prelude in D minor. The Lady's Banquet – Sonata in C major; Capriccio in F major, HWV481; Preludio ed Allegro in G minor, HWV574; Fantaisie in C major, HWV490.
Olivier Baumont *hpd*
Erato 0630-14886-2 (63 minutes: DDD). Recorded 1995.   (F)(P)

A splendid disc, imbued with freshness and vitality. Employing three different instruments – a Flemish harpsichord (1652) by Couchet, a shallower, 'dustier'-toned anonymous Italian instrument of 1677, and a wonderfully rich 1707 French instrument by Dumont – all tuned to a pitch a whole tone lower than that of today, Olivier Baumont presents two of Handel's 1720 'grand suites', the D minor Suite from the 1733 collection, which is seldom heard, the great C major Chaconne (one of Handel's own favourites), which Baumont plays with every variant repeated, and a handful of very early shorter pieces. Two things in particular are striking about these performances – Baumont's stylishness and spontaneous-sounding skilful free decorations of Handel's text (not only in repeats but, for example, in the minor-key variants of the Chaconne). Definitely a disc to raise one's spirits.

Chandos Anthems – No. 4a, HWV249a, 'O sing unto the Lord'; No. 6, HWV251, 'As pants the hart'; No. 11, HWV256, 'Let God arise'.
Ensemble William Byrd; Académie Sainte-Cécile / Graham O'Reilly.
L'Empreinte Digitale ED13072 (57 minutes: DDD). Texts included.   (F)

Graham O'Reilly is clearly a fine musician with a keen and true feeling for this music. He uses very small forces, modelled on those Handel is likely to have had available to him; the Académie

Sainte-Cécile has five violins, no violas, two cellos and a double-bass, with one oboe and one bassoon, with just the solo singers (soprano, tenor and bass in two of the anthems, with an extra tenor in the other). This produces not only lucid and well-balanced textures – it's a real advantage to hear the instruments so well in the choruses – but also an intimacy of atmosphere that the more traditional type of choral performances rules out. It also allows O'Reilly to phrase the music sensitively. Listen for example to the opening Sonata of *O sing unto the Lord*, with its slightly detached articulation and its gently sprung rhythms, or to the vigorous but poised Sonata beginning *As pants the hart*. The sound in the first chorus here has an almost sensuous quality, with its rich suspensions and chromaticisms; and later, in 'Why so full of grief', taken at a nicely measured tempo, the effect is of highly expressive, devotional chamber music. In *Let God arise* there is some happy interplay between soprano and oboe in 'Let the righteous be glad', and spirited ensemble singing in the closing items. The recording is beautifully clear, with a good, firm bass.

Alcina – Mi lusinga il dolce affetto; Verdi prati, selve amene; Stà nell'Ircana. Ariodante – E vivo ancora? ... Scherza infida; Dopa notte. Giulio Cesare – Va tacito e nascosto; Se in fiorito ameno prato; Piangerò, la sorte mia; Dall' ondoso periglio ... Aure, deh, per pietà. Serse – Fronde tenere e belle ... Ombra mai fù; Se bramate d'amar, chi vi sdegna; Crude furie degl'orrido abissi.
Ann Murray *mez* **Orchestra of the Age of Enlightenment / Sir Charles Mackerras.**
Forlane UCD16738 (75 minutes: DDD). Texts and translations included. Recorded 1994.　　ⒻⓅ

The cautious tread of the watchful huntsman, with the lovely dialogue of voice and basset-horn in Caesar's first aria, makes a delightful beginning, and as the recital proceeds one realizes afresh what variety of mood and manner will be found in almost any collection of arias by Handel. These range from the simple ease and beneficence of 'Verdi prati' to the florid outburst of the frustrated Xerxes in 'Crude furie'. In between are Cleopatra's lament, Caesar's love song, Ariodante's sadness and his new-found joy. The musical interest is unfailing wherever one likes to look for it, in rhythm, in harmonic poignancy, or in the scoring – the solo violin as woodbird in 'Se in fiorito ameno prato' or in the basset-horn of 'Va tacito'. Handel and Sir Charles have long been associated, and with the Orchestra of the Age of Enlightenment he provides the singer with a stylish accompaniment that is never assertive or doctrinaire but scrupulous in its care for phrasing and texture. Ann Murray responds with singing which has not only her customary expressiveness and energy but also a generally well-preserved beauty of tone that has not always been so characteristic. Occasionally a harsher, less firmly placed tone threatens to emerge, as at the start and *da capo* of 'Stà nell' Ircana', but such moments are short-lived and instead she encourages a mellower, warmer sound which also has the advantage of being precise in its focus. The voice is quite closely recorded.

Armida abbandonata, HWV105. Agrippina condotta a morire, HWV110. La Lucrezia, HWV32.
Véronique Gens *sop* **François Fernandez, Mira Glodeanu** *vns* **Les Basses Réunies**
(Bruno Cocset *vc* Pascal Monteilhet *theorbo* Blandine Rannou *hpd* Richard Myron *db*).
Virgin Classics Veritas VC5 45283-2 (53 minutes: DDD). Texts and translations included.
Recorded 1996.　　Ⓕ

Composed during Handel's youthful years in Italy, these cantatas contain some of the boldest and most adventurous music he ever wrote, and certainly amongst the most passionate. They are not set to the pastoral, amorous texts that were widely favoured: two of them deal with tragic episodes in Roman history (the rape of Lucretia and the condemnation to death of Agrippina by her son Nero), the other, after Tasso, with the betrayal of Armida. These performances by Véronique Gens amply capture this passionate character. She brings to them a full, warm, large voice, not entirely without hints of vibrato, but handled with real feeling for style; she uses the words and their sound effectively, phrases expressively and sometimes subtly, varies her colour a good deal, and brings particular emotional energy to the recitatives. *Lucrezia* draws some remarkably intense singing from her, in the highly chromatic F minor aria and in the lament-like 'Alla salma infedel'. In this lament, the main continuo accompaniment is assigned to the theorbo, which emphasizes the intimate tone of the music. The violin playing in *Armida* is also particularly enjoyable – brilliant in the *furioso* recitative, stylish and sweet-toned in 'Venti, fermate', which is not dashed off at excessive speed. They play with admirable spirit and rhythmic spring in the lively second aria of *Agrippina*, too, where again Gens sings commandingly, impassioned in the first aria ('Orrida, oscura'), with lightness in the second and then with much intensity in the beautiful 'Come, o Dio!' (again with the theorbo aptly prominent) and also in the concluding recitatives. Les Basses Réunies supplies excellent continuo support. Altogether highly impressive performances of some superlative music.

Ariodante – E vivo ancora ... Scherza infida in grembo al drudo. Giulio Cesare – Cara speme, questo core; Va tacito e nascosto; L'angue offeso mai riposa; Al lampo dell'armi; Dall' ondoso periglio ... Aure, deh, per pietà. Rinaldo – Cara sposa; Venti, turbini, prestate. Rodelinda –

Pompe vane di morte! ... Dove sei?; Vivi tiranno!. Serse – Fronde tenere ... Ombra mai fù.
Tamerlano – A dispetto.
David Daniels *counterten* **Orchestra of the Age of Enlightenment / Sir Roger Norrington.**
Virgin Classics Veritas VC5 45326-2 (69 minutes: DDD). Texts and translations included.
Recorded 1998.   Ⓕ🇪

The ever-increasing popularity of Handel and his contemporaries, and their employment of alto
castratos, has encouraged the development of countertenors capable of similar vocal feats to the
original interpreters of the heroic roles in these works. Among these David Daniels is a leading
contender. He displays and deploys his talent here in a wide range of arias reflective and dramatic.
His amazing technique runs through Tamerlano's virtuoso 'A dispetto' and Bertarido's 'Vivi
tiranno!' without a blemish in the sound and with every division in its place yet part of a
confidently delivered whole: by and large Daniels's runs and embellishments are smoothly
accomplished. In more reflective pieces such as Giulio Cesare's 'Aure, deh, per pietà' (he also tackles
Sesto's 'Cara speme' from *Giulio Cesare*, a particularly liquid, subtle piece of singing), Bertarido's
'Dove sei?' and Ariodante's sad lament, 'Scherza infida', written for the great Senesino, he uses his
impeccable Italian to express wide-ranging emotions. In all the pieces Norrington and the OAE give
excellent support. The recording is blameless so there's every reason to try this fine exposition of
the countertenor's art.

Judas Maccabaeus – I feel the Deity within ... Arm, arm, ye brave!. Te Deum in D major,
'Dettingen' – Vouchsafe, O Lord. Samson – Honour and arms scorn such a foe. Berenice – Si, tra i
ceppi e le ritorte. Alcina – Verdi prati, selve amene. Orlando – O voi del mio poter ... Sorge infausta
una procella. Acis and Galatea – I rage, I melt, I burn! ... O ruddier than the cherry. Semele –
Where'er you walk. Alexander's Feast – Revenge, revenge, Timotheus cries ... Behold a ghastly
band. Giulio Cesare – Va tacito e nascosto. Serse – Fronde tenere ... Ombra mai fù. Messiah –
Thus saith the Lord ... But who may abide?; Why do the nations?; Behold I tell you a mystery ...
The trumpet shall sound.
Bryn Terfel *bass-bar* **Scottish Chamber Orchestra / Sir Charles Mackerras.**
DG 453 480-2GH (73 minutes: DDD). Texts and translations included. Recorded 1995.   Ⓕ

'I feel', sings Terfel with assurance in his voice matching the solemnly, expectantly, ceremonious
opening bars; and then, the second time, 'I feel', but now with the awed conviction of one who has
experienced 'the Deity within'. The adjustment, the change of expression, is small, and no doubt
when described sounds obvious enough; but it is typical of the imaginative intelligence Terfel
brings. Comparing recordings, one hears authority in early versions, something more mystical in
recent ones, but never such alertness as in Terfel. And what of his singing, his voice-production, his
care for *legato*? As to the latter, conflict always lurks as expressive emphasis, shading and verbal
naturalism assert their rights in the face of pure beauty and the evenness of the singing-line. Terfel
is one in whom the rival claims work their way to a compromise, though if one side has to win it
will generally be the expressive element. A good example of the compromise is the second track, the
'Vouchsafe, O Lord', quietly and simply sung, preserving the movement's unity and yet with a
power of feeling that, at 'let thy mercy lighten upon us', is as overtly emotional as an operatic aria.
The adapted arias, 'Where'er you walk', 'Verdi prati' and 'Ombra mai fù', justify their inclusion
readily enough, and it is good to hear Terfel in the solos from *Messiah*. The singing here
incorporates a good deal of embellishment, some of it of Sir Charles Mackerras's devising. He is an
excellent conductor for Terfel, sharing with him an appreciation of the zest in Handel. The Scottish
Chamber Orchestra appears to share it too, and the recording, though made in the resonant Usher
Hall, is vivid and clean.

Alexander Balus, HWV65.
Lynne Dawson, Claron McFadden *sops* **Catherine Denley** *mez* **Charles Daniels** *ten*
Michael George *bass*
New College Choir, Oxford; The King's Consort and Choir / Robert King.
Hyperion CDA67241/2 (two discs: 156 minutes: DDD). Notes and text included.
Recorded 1997.   Ⓕ🇵

Alexander Balus has never been one of Handel's more popular oratorios. That is mainly because its
plot is by modern standards lacking in drama and motivation, and accordingly does not call forth
the vein of his music that nowadays has the strongest appeal. It tells a tale of treachery by
Ptolomee, King of Egypt, against Alexander, King of Syria and the husband of his daughter
Cleopatra (no relation to the famous one), who is allied to the Jews, under Jonathan. *Alexander
Balus* is essentially a sentimental drama, one in which the interest centres on the various characters'
emotional reactions to their situations, amatory, political and religious, and these are rather static in
the first two acts but much more powerful in the more eventful third with the deaths of both

Alexander and Ptolomee. To an eighteenth-century audience it would have had resonances in terms of contemporary politics and religion, and in particular it explains, by analogy with English Protestantism, the seemingly smug attitude taken up by the Jews: everything would have been all right if only they had the right religion. Understanding its background helps you to understand why the music is as it is, so it is a pity that the otherwise informative note here touches on none of this. Here we have a very capable, idiomatic, sensibly cast performance under Robert King. The choruses are especially accomplished. The New College Choir, supported by men from The King's Consort Choir, is confident, bright-toned and vigorous, clean in line and well balanced. Lynne Dawson sings beautifully in her firm and resonant soprano and her usual poised and unaffected style. Her singing of the lamenting music in the final act is particularly moving. Cleopatra has a couple of duets, one with some attractive interplay with the secondary character Aspasia, sung with much assurance by Claron McFadden. As Alexander, Catherine Denley sings with much confidence and directness in music that isn't all of special individuality. Jonathan is sung fluently and warmly, but very plainly, by Charles Daniels. Lastly there is Michael George, ideally suited to the villainous Ptolomee, with his forceful (but always musical) manner and the touch of blackness in his tone. The orchestral playing is accomplished, often rather carefully shaped. The recitative moves at a steady but natural pace; ornamentation is generally modest. All Handelians will want this set, and others should not be put off by the indifferent press *Alexander Balus* has had from time to time.

Alexander's Feast, HWV75. Concerto grosso in C major, HWV318, 'Alexander's Feast'.
Donna Brown sop **Carolyn Watkinson** contr **Ashley Stafford** counterten
Nigel Robson ten **Stephen Varcoe** bar
Monteverdi Choir; English Baroque Soloists / Sir John Eliot Gardiner.
Philips 422 053-2PH2 (two discs: 98 minutes: DDD). Text included. Recorded live in 1987. Ⓕ ℗

Alexander's Feast was the first work Handel had set by a major English poet (Dryden) and it was also the first time he allotted the principal male part to a tenor instead of the castrato heroes of his Italian operas. These two factors, combined with much fine music, scored with great brilliance and imagination, ensured the immediate success of *Alexander's Feast*. It is strange that nowadays it is seldom performed so this recording would have been very welcome even had it not been so full of vitality and so stylishly performed (though perhaps with more sophisticated detail than the eighteenth century would have managed). The Monteverdi Choir and the soloists are all Gardiner regulars, and the English Baroque Soloists have ample opportunities to shine – especially the violins, although the natural horns' lusty entry in the bucolic 'Bacchus, ever fair and young' is exhilarating.

L'Allegro, il Penseroso ed il Moderato, HWV55.
Patrizia Kwella, Marie McLaughlin, Jennifer Smith sops **Michael Ginn** treb
Maldwyn Davies, Martyn Hill tens **Stephen Varcoe** bar
Monteverdi Choir; English Baroque Soloists / Sir John Eliot Gardiner.
Erato 2292-45377-2 (two discs: 116 minutes: ADD). Notes, text and translation included.
Recorded 1980. *Gramophone* Award Winner 1987. Ⓕ ℗

The score of *L'Allegro, il Penseroso ed il Moderato* is presented virtually complete. The soprano aria 'But O, sad virgin' is omitted, which if you look at the marvellous opening for two cellos, seems savage indeed, but the music does rather lose its way in the long decorative passages for both voice and instruments, and its absence need not be regretted. The band is small and so is the superbly alert chorus. Playing and singing constantly delight by their delicacy. The three soprano soloists sound poised and clean-cut. Jennifer Smith's high notes are an especial joy. Handel wanted a boy treble for two arias and presumably knew that their words were never very clear; this one produces some pretty sounds. The succession of charming miniatures is interrupted in the middle of Part 2 by more substantial items and a blaze of brilliant coloratura from several soloists. Martyn Hill's 'These delights' is triumphantly good, and the choral singing here is excitingly precise. The final chorus in Part 2, a fugue with four subjects, is sublime, but he did not bother himself unduly with the final chorus in Part 3. But in general this is very likeable music, its charm, conciseness and emphasis on word-painting unlike anything else in Handel. The quality of the sound is very good.

Apollo e Dafne, HWV122, 'La terra e liberata'. Crudel tiranno amor, HWV97.
Nancy Argenta sop **Michael George** bass **Collegium Musicum 90 / Simon Standage.**
Chandos Chaconne CHAN0583 (58 minutes: DDD). Texts and translations included.
Recorded 1994. Ⓕ ℗

Handel's *Apollo e Dafne* is a difficult work to put in context. Completed in Hanover in 1710 but possibly begun in Italy, its purpose is not clear, while as secular cantatas go it is long (40 minutes) and ambitiously scored for two soloists and an orchestra of strings, oboes, flute, bassoon and continuo. But this is not just a chunk of operatic experimentation: it sets its own, faster pace than the leisurely unfolding of a full-length baroque stage-work, yet its simple Ovidian episode, in which Apollo's pursuit of the nymph Dafne results in her transformation into a tree, is drawn with all the subtlety and skill of the instinctive dramatic genius that Handel was. This recording features the by-now familiar expert Handelian voices of Nancy Argenta and Michael George, and both convey their roles convincingly. Argenta's hard, clear tone seems just the thing for the nymph, who is not required to be especially alluring but who does have to sound quick to anger and (literally) untouchable; and George strikes the right note as Apollo, bragging loudly at the opening of his superior skill in archery to Cupid before succumbing more gently, and in the end extremely touchingly, to Cupid's arts. The orchestra is bright and efficient (though without ever creating a very big sound), and the pacing of the work seems just right. This is superb Handel then, and as if that were not enough there is a bonus in the form of a shorter cantata for soprano and strings, *Crudel tiranno amor*. It is a beautiful piece indeed, and Argenta performs it perfectly.

Clori, mia bella Clori, HWV92. Armida abbandonata, HWV105. Il delirio amoroso, HWV99.
Ann Murray *mez* **Symphony of Harmony and Invention / Harry Christophers.**
Collins Classics 1503-2 (67 minutes: DDD). Texts and translations included. Recorded 1997. Ⓕ Ⓟ

Clori, mia bella Clori, is the most orthodox work here, consisting simply of four arias each preceded by a recitative – but very fine arias, especially the truly gorgeous third one, an E flat miniature which gives Ann Murray opportunity for particular eloquence. *Armida abbandonata* strikes a highly original note right from the start, with its opening recitative accompanied not by continuo but by brilliant violin arpeggios, leading into 'Ah! crudele', an *Adagio* aria with just continuo support (but very richly accompanied here by Alistair Ross) and sung with great intensity. Then comes a hectic *furioso* recitative as she calls on the elements to destroy her betrayer – but contradicts herself by trying to call them off in the desperate aria that follows. Possibly even more remarkable is *Delirio amoroso*, one of the largest in scale of all Handel's solo cantatas, with extended orchestral ritornellos. The first number, though a setting of tragic words, is a spacious piece in A major with demanding violin solos (finely done by Walter Reiter) and a virtuoso solo line too, with a darker-toned middle section in F sharp minor. Then the second is a lament for her beloved, with solo cello, the third a gentle aria with solo flute, evoking the zephyr that bears him down the Acheron to Hades. Ann Murray makes no pretensions to period-style singing and brings to this music a wide expressive range, from the drama of the first aria to the grief of the second, while the third and the closing Minuets are done with gentle resignation. Harry Christophers paces the music well and secures some excellent playing from his band.

Deborah, HWV51.
Yvonne Kenny, Susan Gritton *sops* **Catherine Denley** *mez* **James Bowman** *counterten*
Michael George *bass*
New College Choir, Oxford; Salisbury Cathedral Choristers; The King's Consort / Robert King.
Hyperion CDA66841/2 (two discs: 140 minutes: DDD). Text included. Recorded 1993. Ⓕ Ⓟ

Deborah, written in 1733, was the first oratorio composed for the entertainment of London theatre audiences. It is also a compound of numerous earlier works, including the Chandos and Coronation Anthems, the *Brockes Passion* and the *Ode for the Birthday of Queen Anne*, and in putting *Deborah* together in this manner, Handel was less successful than he usually was in creating a unified work – though the librettist and indeed the Bible itself have to be assigned some of the blame. It is, however, worth revival. It begins with an overture different from the one usually heard: a fine, stirring D major trumpety piece, with a concluding minuet that was to find a place in the *Fireworks* Music. There are some noble choruses, several of which are in five or even eight voices, giving Handel the opportunity for grand effects. The chief interest rests with the choruses. Here they are very well sung by the combined forces of 32 trebles, eight countertenors, six tenors and eight basses, who produce a lot more sound than you might expect. Robert King's control of this group and the polish he imparts to the choral singing, with its clearly projected lines and its firmness of tone is admirable, as is Michael George's warm and resonant contribution as Abinoam and Catherine Denley's firm, direct and stylish singing of the music of the unfortunate Sisera. The orchestral playing is polished; the recorded sound is more reverberant than might be ideal.

Dixit Dominus, HWV232[a]. Nisi Dominus, HWV238[b]. Salve Regina, HWV241[c].
[ac]**Arleen Auger,** [a]**Lynne Dawson** *sops* [ab]**Diana Montague** *mez* [a]**Leigh Nixon,**
[b]**John Mark Ainsley** *tens* [ab]**Simon Birchall** *bass*
Choir and Orchestra of Westminster Abbey / Simon Preston.
Archiv Produktion 423 594-2AH (56 minutes: DDD). Texts and translations included. Ⓕ Ⓟ

Although *Dixit Dominus* is the earliest surviving large scale work by Handel (he was only 22 at the time of its composition in 1707) it displays a remarkable degree of competence and invention and also looks forward to the mature style to come. The vocal writing for both chorus and soloists is extremely ornate and embellished and requires a considerable amount of expertise and flair in order to do full justice to the music. Fortunately, Simon Preston and his team possess all the necessary requirements – indeed, this is one of the most energetic, exhilarating and purposeful performances of this work ever recorded. One need only single out the rhythmically incisive performances of the opening 'Dixit Dominus Domineo meo' or the 'Judicabit in nationibus' and the superbly crisp and articulate performances from the Orchestra of Westminster Abbey to realize that it is a very special recording indeed. The well thought out coupling of *Nisi Dominus* and *Salve Regina* are no less impressive, with the latter offering the listener another chance to sample the beautiful solo contributions of Arleen Auger. The recorded sound is also outstandingly fine. A delightful disc.

Israel in Egypt, HWV54.
Nancy Argenta, Emily Van Evera *sops* **Timothy Wilson** *counterten*
Anthony Rolfe Johnson *ten* **David Thomas, Jeremy White** *basses*
Taverner Choir and Players / Andrew Parrott.
Virgin Classics Veritas VMD5 61350-2 (two discs: 135 minutes: DDD). Text included. Recorded 1989. Ⓜ️Ⓟ

Israel in Egypt, of all Handel's works, is the choral one *par excellence* – so much so, in fact, that it was something of a failure in Handel's own time because solo singing was much preferred to choral by the audiences. Andrew Parrott gives a complete performance of the work, in its original form: that is to say, prefaced by the noble funeral anthem for Queen Caroline, as adapted by Handel to serve as a song of mourning by the captive Israelites. This first part is predominantly slow, grave music, powerfully elegiac; the Taverner Choir shows itself, in what is testing music to sing, to be firm and clean of line, well focused and strongly sustained. The chorus has its chance to be more energetic in the second part, with the famous and vivid Plague choruses – in which the orchestra too plays its part in the pictorial effects, with the fiddles illustrating in turn frogs, flies and hailstones. And last, in the third part, there is a generous supply of the stirring C major music in which Handel has the Israelites give their thanks to God, in some degree symbolizing the English giving thanks for the Hanoverian monarchy and the Protestant succession. Be that as it may, the effect is splendid. The solo work is first-rate, too, with Nancy Argenta radiant in Miriam's music in the final scene and distinguished contributions from David Thomas and Anthony Rolfe Johnson.

Jephtha, HWV70.
Lynne Dawson, Ruth Holton *sops* **Anne Sofie von Otter** *mez* **Michael Chance** *counterten*
Nigel Robson *ten* **Stephen Varcoe** *bar* **Alastair Ross** *hpd* **Paul Nicholson** *org*
Monteverdi Choir; English Baroque Soloists / Sir John Eliot Gardiner.
Philips 422 351-2PH3 (three discs: 158 minutes: DDD). Text included. Recorded live in 1988.
Gramophone Award Winner 1989. Ⓕ Ⓟ

Jephtha has the same basic story as several eastern Mediterranean myths familiar to the opera-goer (in *Idomeneo* and *Iphigénie en Aulide*, for example), of the father compelled to sacrifice his child. Jephtha's daughter Iphis is not in the event sacrificed: when Abraham-like, her father has shown himself willing to perform God's will, and she has shown herself ready to accept it, an angel happily intervenes and commutes her sentence to perpetual virginity. But not before the tragic situation has provoked some of the noblest music Handel wrote. From the moment that Jephtha sees that it is his daughter who has to fall victim to his improvident oath, the music, hitherto on a good but not outstanding level, acquires a new depth, above all in the sequence at the end of Act 2. This recording does the work full justice. It could scarcely have been better cast. Nigel Robson seems ideal as Jephtha. He has due weight as well as vigour, style as well as expressive force. Lynne Dawson's Iphis is also a real success. Sometimes this role is done in a girlishly 'innocent' vein; she does more than that, establishing the character in the appealing love duet in Part 1. Her firm, well-focused, unaffected singing is just right for this role. The other outstanding contribution comes from Michael Chance as Hamor, her unfortunate betrothed. His first song, 'Dull delay', is beautifully measured and delicately shaped, and indeed all his singing is impeccably musicianly, attentive to the words too: his declamation of the recitative is a model.

Stephen Varcoe sings Zebul's music with due resonance and spirit, and Anne Sofie von Otter makes a distinguished contribution in Storgè's music: 'Scenes of horror' has a splendid attack and depth of tone, and 'Let other creatures die!' is spat out with rare power. Ruth Holton makes a pleasantly warm and mellifluous angel. The Monteverdi Choir is in fine voice: vigorous in attack, precise in ensemble, firm in tone at all dynamic levels, responsive to all that Gardiner asks of them. Here and there one might cavil at some of the dynamic shaping in the choruses, for example in 'Doubtful fear' in Act 3; and the Overture can be a trifle fussy in detail. But the broad vision of the work, the rhythmic energy that runs through it and the sheer excellence of the choral and orchestral contributions speak for themselves. Cuts are very few, and amply justified by authentic precedent. This recording is firmly recommended as likely to be the standard version of this great work.

Joseph and his Brethren, HWV59.
Yvonne Kenny sop **Catherine Denley** mez **Connor Burrowes** treb
James Bowman counterten **John Mark Ainsley** ten **Michael George** bass
New College Choir, Oxford; The King's Consort Choir; The King's Consort / Robert King.
Hyperion CDA67171/3 (three discs: 164 minutes: DDD). Text included. Recorded 1996. Ⓕ Ⓟ

There has never been a complete, professional recording of *Joseph and his Brethren*, a neglect grotesquely out of proportion to the merits of its music. It is full of good and characteristic things, and there are several scenes, including the extended denouement in the last act, that are very moving. The work begins splendidly, with an unusual overture heralding a fine and deeply felt opening scene for Joseph, languishing in an Egyptian prison. The setting of his prophecy is effective, with seven bars of darting arpeggios for the years of plenty and seven of sparse harmonic writing, *adagio*, for the famine years. The rest of Act 1 is a celebration of Joseph's foresight, preferment and marriage to Asenath, Pharaoh's daughter. The highlights of Act 2 include a prison scene for Simeon, an agonized G minor accompanied recitative and aria, a beautiful, nostalgic pastoral idyll for Joseph, and scenes for Joseph with his brothers which incorporate a splendid outburst from Simeon, an aria from Benjamin and a moving chorus from the brothers, a sustained prayer and a richly worked fugue. The soloists dispatch all this music with spirit and accuracy. Of course, the central figure is James Bowman in the very demanding title-role. He is in excellent voice, as full and rich as ever and duly agile in the rapid music. *Joseph* is well suited to Robert King's way of conducting Handel. This is not a specially dramatic performance, but carefully moulded, well balanced, intelligently paced. The choir produces a sound that is bright and firm and the singing is resolute, although the attack is soft-edged rather than incisive. King is particularly good at shaping the dynamics in a natural and unanimous way.

Messiah, HWV56.

Messiah.
Dorothea Röschmann, Susan Gritton sops **Bernarda Fink** contr
Charles Daniels ten **Neal Davies** bass
Gabrieli Consort and Players / Paul McCreesh.
Archiv Produktion 453 464-2AH2 (two discs: 132 minutes: DDD). Text included.
Recorded 1996. Ⓕ Ⓟ Ⓢ Ⓔ ⓇⓇ

The Gabrieli Consort and Players are as responsive and professional a group as you will find these days. McCreesh has fastidiously assembled solo singers with broad mainstream experience and Handel's choruses encapsulate all the vitality and litheness of the modern English vocal consort at its best. More than that, McCreesh is a natural dramatist and all his singers respond magnificently to the evangelical fervour which Jennens, if one senses not always Handel, envisioned. McCreesh's expression is candid and immediate, if not imparted with the unfolding spirituality of Suzuki, or fragrancy of Christie; his is a particular type of musicianship which reaches out, quite Sargent-like in the robust swagger of 'And the Glory', the grand leisurely 'Amen' and almost elegiac enunciation in 'Comfort ye' – perhaps too static for some but Charles Daniels's supreme control has us holding our breath. McCreesh, in employing, for the most part, the Foundling Hospital version of 1754, treats us to a second soprano. His casting serves him well with two incandescent performances: Susan Gritton is suitably unmollifiable in 'a refiner's fire' though she turns on the intensity, if not exactly sweetness in 'I know that my Redeemer liveth'. Dorothea Röschmann provides a similarly bright edge and in both cases, we are treated to singing of considerable technical finesse. Bernarda Fink's heady and rasping contralto may not appeal to everyone but 'He was despised' leaves one in little doubt of Jennens's starkest sentiments. Neal Davies is sure-footed and impressive. The energy and focused proclamation of this reading will surely win many friends: whilst tempos may appear hard-pushed, there is a consistency and rooted concentration to proceedings, always thoroughly engaged. Recorded sound is resonant but also close, and fairly compressed in its livelier moments.

Messiah.
Arleen Auger sop **Anne Sofie von Otter** mez **Michael Chance** counterten
Howard Crook ten **John Tomlinson** bass
The Choir of the English Concert; The English Concert / Trevor Pinnock.
Archiv Produktion 423 630-2AH2 (two discs: 150 minutes: DDD). Text included.
Recorded 1988. Ⓕ Ⓟ

How authentic is authentic? Trevor Pinnock and The English Concert, while using period instruments, are guaranteed to appeal very widely to traditional lovers of Handel's masterpiece, who might as a rule opt for a performance using modern instruments. Pinnock gets the best of both worlds. One of the most distinctive points is that, even more than his rivals, he brings out the impact of timpani and trumpets, above all in the 'Hallelujah' and 'Amen' choruses. In that he stirs the blood in a way that even Sargent would have envied. Another distinctive point is that a genuine, dark, firm, bass soloist has been chosen, John Tomlinson, who is ripely resonant here. Traditionalists who lament the lack of dark bass tone and the predominance of baritonal shades in Handel today will doubtless raise a cheer, and if it comes to authenticity, Handel must surely have been thinking of just such a voice, rather than anything thinner or more discreet. Not only Tomlinson but Arleen Auger too will delight listeners of all Handelian persuasions. She has one of the sweetest, most ravishing soprano sounds on any of the current versions, and the warmth of expressiveness, whether strictly authentic or not, brings many of the most memorable moments in the whole performance. Try the close of 'I know that my Redeemer liveth', where the dramatic contrasts of dynamic are extreme and masterfully controlled, without a hint of sentimentality. The male alto, Michael Chance, also outshines his direct rivals in artistry and beauty of tone, but he is given only a proportion of the alto numbers. The majority are given to Anne Sofie von Otter. Hers is another beautiful voice, finely controlled. The Archiv recording is one of the finest available, with plenty of bloom and with inner clarity never making textures sound thin or overanalytical.

Messiah.
Dame Isobel Baillie sop **Gladys Ripley** contr **James Johnston** ten **Norman Walker** bass
Huddersfield Choral Society; Liverpool Philharmonic Orchestra / Sir Malcolm Sargent.
Dutton Laboratories Essential Archive mono 2CDEA5010 (two discs: 146 minutes: ADD).
Recorded 1946.   ⓑⓗ

From the 1940s until the early 1960s one of the greatest of regular British musical events (every bit as important as the Proms) was Sir Malcolm Sargent's *Messiah*. He conducted it up and down the country, always to packed houses; and indeed for one to be able to attend the performance at Huddersfield Town Hall needed very special connections (ideally with a member of the choir), for tickets were scarcer than an invitation to Buckingham Palace! It was easier to go to the final London performance with the Royal Choral Society on Good Friday, which was unabridged, and involved both afternoon and evening sessions! Otherwise Sargent usually omitted – as he does on this recording – three numbers from Part 2 and four from Part 4. Even then, the performance time was two-and-a-half hours without the interval. Apart from spacious tempos, Sargent had his own ideas about Handelian style. Today we usually listen to a quite different kind of *Messiah*, brisker, often exchanging grandeur for exhilaration; so it is heart-warming to have the opportunity to return to a great tradition that Sargent kept alive for so many years.

This is made possible by one of Dutton Laboratories' most miraculous 78rpm transfers – the finest ever heard taken from 78s of any music – of Sargent's extraordinarily vivid and expansive recording (the most spontaneous of the three he made). The four splendid soloists – that queen of oratorio sopranos, Dame Isobel Baillie; the rich-voiced Gladys Ripley; the warmly lyrical James Johnson; and the vibrant Norman Walker are right inside their parts. But the star of the performance is undoubtedly Isobel Baillie. Her first entry in 'There were shepherds' is a truly ravishing moment, while her gloriously beautiful 'I know that my Redeemer liveth' has never been surpassed on record. Sargent opens the work with a sumptuous presentation of the Overture, while his tempos for the choruses now sound very slow to ears used to 'authenticity'. Sargent believed deeply in this music and he carried the listener with him. The hushed close of 'All we like sheep' almost brings tears to the eyes. The sound itself is truly astounding! In its original 78rpm format this set sold over 120,000 copies in America alone, and it cost a great deal of money in those days. At bargain price it is an ideal investment for anyone who relishes an old-fashioned, large-scale approach to Handel's Messiah.

The Occasional Oratorio, HWV62.
Susan Gritton, Lisa Milne sops **James Bowman** counterten
John Mark Ainsley ten **Michael George** bass
New College Choir, Oxford; The King's Consort / Robert King.
Hyperion CDA66961/2 (two discs: 144 minutes: DDD). Text included. Recorded 1994.   ⓕⓟ

The occasion that called forth this work was the Jacobite rising of 1745 and its impending defeat. The Duke of Cumberland's victory at Culloden was yet to come. Handel, anticipating it, hit off the mood of the moment with a rousing piece full of appeals to patriotic feeling, partly through the traditional identification between the English Protestant culture of Hanoverian times with that of the biblical Hebrews. Much of the music comes from existing works, notably *Israel in Egypt*. The 'plot' pursues the familiar route of Anxiety-Prayer-Victory-Jubilation, but the work lacks the unity of theme and purpose of the great dramatic oratorios; if, however, you value Handel primarily because the music is so splendid you will find a lot to relish here. King rises to the challenge of this sturdier side of Handel's muse and produces playing and singing full of punch and energy, and with that command of the broad Handelian paragraph without which the music lacks its proper stature. The grand eight-part choruses, with the choir properly spaced, antiphonally, over the stereo span, make their due effect. King has a distinguished solo team. John Mark Ainsley's singing is particularly touching in the highly original 'Jehovah is my shield', where the rocking figures in the orchestra eventually turn out to symbolize sleep. Also very enjoyable is Susan Gritton's soprano, a sharply focused voice with a fine ring and due agility in the lively music and handled with taste and a keen feeling for the shape of phrases in the contemplative airs. A fine set.

Samson, HWV57.
Lynne Dawson, Lynda Russell *sops* **Catherine Wyn-Rogers** *contr* **Mark Padmore,**
Thomas Randle, Matthew Vine *tens* **Jonathan Best, Michael George** *basses*
The Sixteen; Symphony of Harmony and Invention / Harry Christophers.
Collins Classics 7038-2 (three discs: 205 minutes: DDD). Text included. Recorded 1996. Ⓕ P

This complete recording of *Samson* gives a straightforward account of the work, in tune with styles of Handel performance favoured today, except for one in particular – the choice of tempos. This is a decidedly leisurely reading of the work; clearly Christophers has a sense of its magnitude, of the big issues with which it is involved and the nobility of its utterance, and he will not let himself be hurried. He has an excellent cast. Thomas Randle is well equipped for Samson, a firm, strong tenor, with a hint of baritonal quality in his middle and lower registers. There is no bombast here. 'Total eclipse' has much of pathos but no heroics. 'Why does the God of Israel sleep' is done with some power, and the renunciation of Dalila ('Your charms to ruin') is weightily sung; and there is plenty of fire in his rejection of the Philistine braggart, Harapha, but never at the cost of musical singing. Samson's father, Manoah, is sung with characteristic warmth and depth of tone and feeling by Michael George; his bass contrasts aptly with the tauter, more focused one of Jonathan Best's Harapha. Mark Padmore contributes some well-placed singing as both the Israelite and the Philistine man. Lynne Dawson does the same as the woman from both camps; she contributes a vigorous 'Let the bright seraphim' (which here has a brief choral section at the end, surviving in Handel's manuscript but probably never heard before). Lynda Russell's soft, seductive Dalila, a modest role, confined to Act 2, is enjoyable; but perhaps above all Catherine Wyn-Rogers excels as Micah, with beautifully intense singing and concentrated tone in all her music – her phrasing in 'Then long eternity'', for example, is quite outstanding. Stylistically the performance is cautious, with only modest added ornamentation and brief cadenzas, but of course the requisite appoggiaturas in the recitative. The Sixteen provide clear and spirited choral singing throughout, suitably jolly in the Philistine music, duly noble in that for the Hebrews, achieving unusual clarity of texture.

Saul, HWV53.
Lynne Dawson, Donna Brown *sops* **Derek Lee Ragin** *counterten* **John Mark Ainsley,**
Neil Mackie, Philip Salmon, Philip Slane *tens* **Alastair Miles, Richard Savage** *basses*
Monteverdi Choir; English Baroque Soloists / Sir John Eliot Gardiner.
Philips 426 265-2PH3 (three discs: 159 minutes: DDD). Recorded live in 1989. Ⓕ P

Saul is considered by many to be one of the most arresting music dramas in the English language, even though it is officially classed as an oratorio. In it Handel explores in some psychological depth the motivation of his characters, most notably that of the eponymous anti-hero, whose tantrums caused by envy and his searching for supernatural intervention are all vividly delineated; as is the friendship of David and Jonathan and the different characters of Saul's daughters, Merab and Michal. In yet another compelling performance of Handel under his baton, John Eliot Gardiner – in this live recording made at the Göttingen Handel Festival in Germany – fulfils every aspect of this varied and adventurous score, eliciting execution of refined and biting calibre from his choir and orchestra. Alastair Miles captures Saul in all his moods. John Mark Ainsley and Derek Lee Ragin are both affecting as Jonathan and David; so are Lynne Dawson and Donna Brown as Michal and Merab. There are a few cuts, but not serious enough to prevent a firm recommendation.

Solomon, HWV67.
Andreas Scholl *counterten* **Inger Dam-Jensen, Susan Gritton, Alison Hagley** *sops*
Susan Bickley *mez* **Paul Agnew** *ten* **Peter Harvey** *bass*
Gabrieli Consort and Players / Paul McCreesh.
Archiv Produktion 459 688-2AH3 (three discs: 161 minutes: DDD). Notes and text included.
Recorded 1998. Ⓕ P

Solomon is universally recognized as one of Handel's finest masterpieces, not only with magnificent choruses, but more importantly containing rapturous love music, nature imagery, affecting emotion and, in Part 2, the vividly portrayed dramatic scene of Solomon's famous judgement over the disputed infant. This is in fact the only dramatic part of the oratorio; and each of the female characters appears in only one of the work's three parts. Paul McCreesh, responsive to the work's stature, employs an orchestra of about 60 (including a serpent as the bass of the wind group, and incidentally instructing the horns to play with their bells up to produce a more pungent tone) and presents the oratorio in the original 1749 version, full and uncut. It has been argued that even in so splendid a work Handel was fallibly human enough to include some dead wood. McCreesh, however, stoutly defends Handel's original structural balance. In one respect, nevertheless, he does depart from Handel's intentions. By the time *Solomon* was written, Handel was using no castratos in his oratorios, and the title-role in this case was deliberately designed for a mezzo-soprano; but here the opportunity for securing the pre-eminent countertenor Andreas Scholl proved irresistible. The colour of Handel's predominantly female vocal casting (only Zadok and the smaller-part Levite being exceptions) is thus slightly modified. This historical infidelity is one of the few reservations that could be made about the set as a whole, which is a notable achievement.

McCreesh is fortunate in his cast, too. Predictably, Scholl becomes the central focus by his beauty of voice (conspicuously in 'When the sun o'er yonder hills'), calm authority, charm ('What though I trace') and intelligent musicianship throughout. Inger Dam-Jensen, as Solomon's queen, sounds suitably ecstatic in the florid 'Blessed the day' and amorous in 'With thee th'unsheltered moor', and her duet with Solomon flows with easy grace. The confrontation between the two harlots in Part 2 is brilliantly characterized by Alison Hagley as the tenderly maternal one (her 'Can I see my infant gored?' is most moving) and Susan Bickley as the inhumanly vengeful one. And to Susan Gritton falls the sublime 'Will the sun forget to streak', with its wonderful unison oboe-and-flute obbligato. As the high priest Zadok, Paul Agnew shines in the ornate 'See the tall palm'. A more positive and audible keyboard continuo would have been welcome but this is a minor shortcoming, and the effect of the performance as a whole is deeply impressive, with such things as 'Will the sun', the grave interlude to 'With pious heart' and the elegiac chorus 'Draw the tear from hopeless love' haunting one's mind.

Susanna, HWV66.
Lorraine Hunt, Jill Feldman *sops* **Drew Minter** *counterten* **Jeffrey Thomas** *ten*
William Parker *bar* **David Thomas** *bass*
Chamber Chorus of the University of California, Berkeley;
Philharmonia Baroque Orchestra / Nicholas McGegan.
Harmonia Mundi HMU90 7030/2 (three discs: 178 minutes: DDD). Notes and text included.
Recorded live in 1989. *Gramophone* Award Winner 1991.　　ⒻⓅ

Here is a case of the most astonishing neglect by the record companies. *Susanna* was neglected even by Handel himself, who revived it only once, in his last year, after the première performances of 1749. *Susanna* tells the tale from the Apocrypha of the two Elders who, espying a beautiful and virtuous woman about to bathe, decide when she rejects their advances to denounce her as an adultress; she is sentenced to death and saved only when Daniel, deftly overturning their testimony, comes to judgement and restores her to her loving husband. This performance leaves one in no doubt that it is a deeply serious work, with no more than a flicker of comedy in the representation of the Elders. In a long opening scene the marital happiness of Susanna and Joacim is firmly established, to provide a context for Susanna's virtue and morality, and there is music of great warmth and consequence too for Chelsias, Susanna's father. When Joacim departs, Susanna is struck with a sense of foreboding, marvellously expressed in an accompanied recitative and an aria, in B minor with rich, five-part strings, in which a new tone enters, grave yet glowing and steadfast: 'Bending to the throne of glory' is one of Handel's noblest utterances, as sung here by Lorraine Hunt. Then enter the Elders, artfully characterized by Handel: a tenor, capable of a graceful paean to love and nature ('Ye verdant hills'), and eager to woo Susanna; and a bass, whose music is more fiery and whose inclinations are more violent. These are cleverly cast: Jeffrey Thomas is brilliantly successful at infusing the tenor music with a kind of insinuating sensuality that perfectly catches the character's lasciviousness, while David Thomas sings the bass's music with a sharpness of line and a graphic expression of the music and its sense that seem truly menacing.

Drew Minter makes a musical Joacim, gentle in tone and phrasing, perfectly tuned; the part is perhaps a shade high-lying for him. His tone lacks the firm centre that might be ideal here, especially for the fiery aria at the end of the Second Act, but the delicate control of his singing does give pleasure. He and the Susanna, Lorraine Hunt, match extraordinarily well. Her soprano may not be the most beguiling as such, but her singing achieves great power and tonal concentration in the great expressive arias that are the heart of the work, to which she truly rises – and her bathing aria at the beginning of Part 2 has an apt touch of languor, too. Jill Feldman's singing of the

Attendant's arias, and later of Daniel's, is duly fresh and stylish, possibly a shade shrill in sound though apt enough for these youthful roles. There is some first-rate choral singing, marked by strong and direct rhythms and clear, firm lines, very telling in the vigorous fugal movements. The Philharmonia Baroque Orchestra produces a sound warmer and less scrawny than many baroque bands but with welcomely little of surface gloss; they are excellently disciplined and their articulation is pleasantly incisive. Nicholas McGegan's feeling for tempo and for the sense of the music seems to be unerring, and the power and the springiness of the rhythms he sets in the big choral numbers lends them true grandeur. An excellent recording, a first-rate accompanying booklet: you are guaranteed to obtain immense pleasure from this set.

Theodora, HWV68.
Lorraine Hunt sop **Jennifer Lane** mez **Drew Minter** counterten **Jeffrey Thomas** ten
Nigel Rogers ten **David Thomas** bass
Chamber Chorus of the University of California, Berkeley;
Philharmonia Baroque Orchestra / Nicholas McGegan.
Harmonia Mundi HMU90 7060/2 (three discs: 170 minutes: DDD). Text included.
Recorded 1991.   ⒻⓅ

If contemporary audiences were put off by the theme of martyrdom, we should be grateful that the self-righteous piety of Morell's libretto inspired some of Handel's finest music here, with the added bonus of both the original and revised versions of 'Symphony of Soft Musick'. This recording can be wholeheartedly recommended. David Thomas as Valens, the Roman governor, opens the proceedings with a firm and resolute tone and later gives the bloodthirsty 'Racks, gibbets, sword and fire' much menace. Lorraine Hunt was an inspired choice for the taxing title-role: the top notes of 'Angels ever bright and fair' are celestially floated, while she finds great intensity in 'With darkness deep', the emotional centre of the work. Drew Minter gives a mellifluous and characterful account of Didymus, a Roman officer recently converted to Christianity who attempts to save Theodora. Listen to their duet, 'To Thee, Thou glorious Son', to hear how winningly they blend their voices. Praise too for Jeffrey Thomas as Septimius, particularly in his elegant ornamentation in the virtuoso aria 'Dread the fruits of Christian folly', only occasionally showing strain in the wide leaps in 'From virtue springs'. Jennifer Lane is also impressive as Irene (described in the libretto simply as 'A Christian') – despite being burdened with some of Morell's most trite utterances. Nicholas McGegan has at his command a highly skilled orchestra and excellent choir, chooses tempos which are unfailingly apt, supporting and giving weight to the vocal lines.

Alessandro – Overture; Sinfonia; Che vidi?; No, più soffrir; Placa l'alma; Solitudine amate ... Aure, fonti; Pur troppo veggio ... Che tirannia d'Amor; Svanisci, oh reo timore ... Dica il falso. Admeto, Re di Tessaglia – Il ritratto d'Admeto; La sorte mia vacilla; Quest'è dunque la fede ... Vedrò fra poco. Riccardo Primo, re di Inghilterra – Morte vieni ... A me nel mio rossore ... Quando non vede. Siroe, re di Persia – A costei, che dirò?; L'aura non sempre; Si diversi sembianti ... Non vi piacque, ingiusti dei. Tolomeo, re di Egitto – E dove, e dove mai ... Fonti amiche; Ti pentirai, crudel.
Catherine Bott, Emma Kirkby sops **Brandenburg Consort / Roy Goodman.**
Hyperion CDA66950 (76 minutes: DDD). Texts and translations included. Recorded 1997. ⒻⓅⒺ

It was a happy idea to assemble a selection of Handel's arias written for the two sopranos whose famous rivalry coloured the last years of the first Royal Academy. Francesca Cuzzoni – impersonated here by Catherine Bott – was Handel's principal soprano from 1723, creating among other roles Cleopatra and Rodelinda. Faustina Bordoni – her roles here go to Emma Kirkby – arrived in 1726 and the two sang together in several operas including five new ones by Handel, all represented on this recording. Both were superlative singers and each had a characteristic style. Cuzzoni was praised for her clear and sweet high notes, her use of rubato, her control of volume and above all for her affecting expression. Bordoni, whose voice lay slightly lower, was admired for her fine articulation, her flexibility in divisions and ornamentation, and her passion and expression in slow arias. In his music composed for them, Handel clearly differentiated between their capacities, as this disc illustrates. The 'rival queens' first sang together in *Alessandro*, which is the opera most fully represented here. There are two of Cuzzoni's arias, one brilliant piece with rapid divisions, which Bott throws off in splendidly free fashion, and a pathetic one, a typical F minor *siciliano*, taken very slowly here, allowing plenty of time for some expressive (but restrained) elaboration in the *da capo*. Of Faustina's music we have the exquisite *scena* that opens Act 2, including the aria, 'Aure, fonti', and the lively one with which the act closes. The aria typifies, in the way it demands and rewards precisely detailed singing, Handel's writing for her, and Kirkby's refinement of detail is remarkable. There is beautifully managed interplay between the singers in the *Alessandro* duet; they seem to feed one another with opportunities. The programme is imaginatively put together and Roy Goodman is a prompt and stylish accompanist.

Acis and Galatea, HWV49b.
Norma Burrowes *sop* Galatea; **Anthony Rolfe Johnson** *ten* Acis; **Martyn Hill** *ten* Damon;
Willard White *bass* Polyphemus; **Paul Elliot** *ten*
English Baroque Soloists / Sir John Eliot Gardiner.
Archiv Produktion 423 406-2AH2 (two discs: 95 minutes: ADD). Notes, text and translation
included. Recorded 1978. *Gramophone* Award Winner 1978.

This lively performance of *Acis and Galatea* was issued on LP over 20 years ago. It received a warm welcome though not an unqualified one. John Eliot Gardiner's direction is stylish and affectionate but these were comparatively early days in the British revival of period instruments and even the most casual of listeners will detect both ensemble and intonation problems in various departments, vocal and instrumental. Some of the oboe playing suffers particularly in this latter respect but considered in context with the many delightful features of the performance we should not worry overmuch. The solo team who, with an additional tenor, Paul Elliot, also sing the choruses, are, by and large a strong one with fine contributions especially from Norma Burrowes and Anthony Rolfe Johnson. Martyn Hill makes a fine Damon and gives an excellent account of his aria, 'Shepherd, what art thou pursuing'. His diction is excellent and his sensibility to the text a pleasure to listen to. Willard White is a fairly convincing Polyphemus but he does not really capture the humour of the role, which is a pity, nor does he make much of the contrasting sides of the giant's character. This is the only real disappointment in an otherwise enjoyable performance. Clear but not outstanding recorded sound, and full texts are provided.

Admeto, Re di Tessaglia.
René Jacobs *counterten* Admeto; **Rachel Yakar** *sop* Alceste; **Ulrik Cold** *bass* Ercole, Apollo;
Rita Dams *mez* Orindo; **James Bowman** *counterten* Trasimede; **Jill Gomez** *sop* Antigona;
Max van Egmond *bar* Meraspe, A Voice;
Il Complesso Barocco / Alan Curtis.
Virgin Classics Veritas VMT5 61369-2 (three discs: 217 minutes: ADD). Notes, text and translation
included. Recorded 1979.

This reissue is the first *Admeto* on CD. It is full of fine things, particularly in its music for the two women – Alceste, the nobly self-sacrificing wife of King Admetus, and Antigona, the princess he had once wooed but then rejected, who now returns after the supposed death of Alceste. The plot, then, is akin to the familiar one of Gluck's *Alceste*, but with an extra sub-plot that allows for touches of wit and irony (it was based on a Venetian libretto) and insights into human character. When it was first released, the recording was something of a pioneer as regards the use of period instruments and performing conventions. Things have moved on, of course: it seems a bit dated now, heavier in manner than most Handel opera recordings of recent years – for example, the recitatives are slowish, and the bows spend more time on the strings than is customary now. And some of the cast are not wholly at home in a baroque style where little vibrato is wanted. One thinks in particular of Rachel Yakar, but although her articulation and attack are not always ideally clean she does bring a good deal of spirit to some of the arias, for example her Act 3 'Là dove gli occhi io giro'. Jill Gomez's lighter, bell-like voice is, however, more convincingly Handelian: she sings Antigona's music charmingly and with due agility, and expressively too in the beautiful Act 2 *siciliana*. James Bowman is in his best voice as Trasimede, Admetus's brother who loves Antigona. René Jacobs, however, lacks the heroic tones and the incisiveness that the role demands. Ulrik Cold makes a strong Ercole, with appropriately sturdy, masculine tone, and Meraspe is neatly and very stylishly sung by Max van Egmond. Alan Curtis's direction is attentive to matters of style, but he sometimes lets the bass-line plod. Even so, Handelians need not hesitate.

Agrippina.
Della Jones *mez* Agrippina; **Derek Lee Ragin** *counterten* Nero; **Donna Brown** *sop* Poppea;
Alastair Miles *bass* Claudius; **Michael Chance** *counterten* Otho; **George Mosley** *bar* Pallas;
Jonathan Peter Kenny *counterten* Narcissus; **Julian Clarkson** *bass* Lesbo;
Anne Sofie von Otter *mez* Juno;
English Baroque Soloists / Sir John Eliot Gardiner.
Philips 438 009-2PH3 (three discs: 217 minutes: DDD). Notes, text and translation included.
Recorded 1991-92.

Agrippina is Handel's Venetian opera, composed in 1709 for the S. Giovanni Gristostomo theatre, where it was evidently and deservedly a great success. Handel drew on its music, but he never revived it: its scheme, with a large number of short and lightly accompanied arias, is very much of its time and its place. Yet *Agrippina* is a very effective piece, if directed with due vitality (as it certainly is here), and it is full of appealing music in a wide variety of moods. Any admirer of countertenor singing should be prepared to buy the set for Michael Chance's singing alone. But in fact there are two other countertenors here who are well worth hearing, especially Derek Lee Ragin, whose high-lying voice and sensitive, thoughtful phrasing serve Nero's music admirably. His last aria, a brilliant piece with colourful instrumental writing, as he renounces Poppea in expectation of the imperial crown, is breathtakingly done, fiery singing with very precise execution of the divisions. The third of the countertenors is Jonathan Peter Kenny as Narcissus, rather softer in tone and line, who provides some particularly musical singing in his Act 2 aria.

Della Jones gives a masterful performance in the title-role. Her music is very varied in mood: there are several brief and catchy little pieces, which she throws off with spirit, but also some larger-scale numbers, such as the marvellous C minor aria near the end of Act 1 (although totally insincere in sentiment), which is done with great vigour, and the noble, invocation-like 'Pensieri, voi mi tormentate', another of the opera's high points, to which she brings much intensity. Donna Brown as Poppea makes the most of a role with much lively and appealing music. Alastair Miles's full and resonant bass – the part goes down to cello C – brings due weight of authority to the emperor Claudius; Pallas is done by a clean, lightish but nicely firm baritone, George Mosley, and Julian Clarkson contributes some very neat singing in the role of Lesbo. Anne Sofie von Otter comes in as a *dea ex machina* at the every end, not to rescue the situation but to honour the marriage of Poppea and Otho – which of course she does in style. John Eliot Gardiner is a fine and very experienced conductor of Handel and he has a sure feeling for tempo and for the character of each movement. The orchestral playing is beyond reproach. The text followed is that of the Chrysander edition. This recording is comfortably among the half-dozen finest recordings of Handel operas.

Alcina.
Arleen Auger *sop* Alcina; **Eiddwen Harrhy** *sop* Morgana; **Kathleen Kuhlmann** *mez* Bradamante; **Della Jones** *mez* Ruggiero; **Patrizia Kwella** *sop* Oberto; **Maldwyn Davies** *ten* Oronte; **John Tomlinson** *bass* Melisso;
Opera Stage Chorus; City of London Baroque Sinfonia / Richard Hickox.
EMI CDS7 49771-2 (three discs: 217 minutes: DDD). Notes, text and translation included. Recorded 1985.　Ⓕ Ⓟ

Alcina, musically and dramatically, is among the finest of Handel's operas. This set must certainly have a strong claim to be reckoned one of the best sung of Handel opera recordings. There is no member of the cast who is not a Handelian of high quality and natural sense of style. What Arleen Auger loses in sheer brilliance of tone or technique she makes up by the sweetness and musicality of her voice. Her big central aria in Act 2, 'Ah! mio cor!', is best of all, for its intensely musical singing and purity of tone. Auger is at her best in the early part of the opera, lacking in the later part the edge that can give full force to the scorned sorceress's angry music. Della Jones in the *primo uomo* role of Ruggiero, excels in the incisive music, like her two arias in Act 1 and the one in Act 3, though this last is rushed and becomes a shade hectic in feeling (and there is some wild ornamentation). She gives a fine performance too of the lovely 'Mi lusinga', well focused in tone, strongly expressed yet always stylish. But the sensuous beauty of castrato tone needed for the finest of her arias, the incomparable 'Verdi prati', perhaps understandably, eludes her; it is, however, well done, if marred at the end by the solecism of a large, romantic *rallentando*. For Kathleen Kuhlmann, the Bradamante, there can be nothing but warm praise. She has a splendid natural sense of how to give direction to the music, she throws off the semiquaver passages with clarity and fire, and conveys the character's qualities admirably with her firm line and heroic manner. The smaller roles are taken by established British Handel singers of the middle generation. The choral numbers are also well done, if with what sounds like a larger group than is appropriate for the music. The orchestral playing is generally very capable. There are, however, reservations about the direction, especially on matters of tempo. One sometimes feels that Richard Hickox hasn't got a very dependable instinct for tempo in Handel – the slower music is often exaggeratedly slow, the fast sometimes driven – or that he characterizes the music very effectively. In sum, then, a recording with many merits, principally vocal ones. The recorded quality is a little variable: sometimes the acoustic seems hugely spacious, at other times more conventional. There is an excellent booklet. As a whole there can be little doubt that this *Alcina*, in its style and its completeness, comfortably surpasses its recorded predecessors.

Ariodante.
Lorraine Hunt *sop* Ariodante; **Juliana Gondek** *sop* Ginevra; **Lisa Saffer** *sop* Dalinda; **Jennifer Lane** *mez* Polinesso; **Rufus Müller** *ten* Lurcanio; **Nicolas Cavallier** *bass* King of Scotland; **Jörn Lindemann** *ten* Odoardo; **Wilhelmshaven Vocal Ensemble; Freiburg Baroque Orchestra / Nicholas McGegan.**
Harmonia Mundi HMU90 7146/8 (three discs: 202 minutes: DDD). Notes, text and translation included. Recorded 1995. *Gramophone* Award Winner 1996.　Ⓕ Ⓟ Ⓔ ⓇⓇ

This recording, made with the cast from the Göttingen Festival in 1995 (largely American singers who have collaborated with McGegan in his Californian performances), seems at least the equal of the best he has done before. The quality of the music is of course a factor: *Ariodante* is one of the richest of the Handel operas. It begins with a flood of fine numbers, mostly love music for the betrothed pair, Ariodante and the Scottish princess Ginevra – she is introduced in a wonderfully carefree aria, he in a gentle, exquisite slow arietta; then they have a very individual and beautiful love duet, and each goes on to a more jubilant aria. But the plot thickens and the music darkens with Polinesso's machinations, designed to impugn her fidelity: thus Act 2 contains music of vengeance and grief (above all the magnificent 'Scherza infida!' for Ariodante, a G minor aria with muted upper and pizzicato lower strings, and soft bassoons), while the final act shows all the characters *in extremis*, until the plot is uncovered and equilibrium restored. This is also one of Handel's few operas with extensive ballet; each act includes some splendid and ingeniously tuneful dance music. McGegan directs in his usual spirited style. There is a real theatrical sense to his conducting: this is one of those opera sets where, after the overture, you find your spine tingling in expectation of the drama. Lorraine Hunt's soprano seems warm and full for a castrato part, but her line is always well defined and she has a delightfully musical voice. A fine set.

Ariodante.
Anne Sofie von Otter *mez* Ariodante; **Lynne Dawson** *sop* Ginevra;
Veronica Cangemi *sop* Dalinda; **Ewa Podleś** *mez* Polinesso; **Richard Croft** *ten* Lurcanio;
Denis Sedov *bass* King of Scotland; **Luc Coadou** *ten* Odoardo;
Choeur des Musiciens du Louvre; Les Musiciens du Louvre / Marc Minkowski.
Archiv Produktion 457 271-2AH3 (three discs: 178 minutes: DDD). Text and translation included.
Recorded 1997. ⒻⓅ

Lynne Dawson is the star of this show – and perhaps the leading Handel opera soprano today. In Act 2, where Ginevra finds herself inexplicably rejected and condemned by everyone, Dawson brings real depth of tone and feeling to her E minor lament, 'Il mio crudel martoro'; in the final act she shines in the desolate miniature 'Io ti bacio' and brings much fire to the outburst 'Sì, morro'. But she never transgresses the canons of baroque style. Von Otter, too, has much marvellous music – the aria 'Scherza infida' is one of Handel's greatest expressions of grief – and she sings it beautifully, but she is not really at one with this idiom and seems to lack a natural feeling for the amplitude of Handel's lines. She tries, perhaps, to do too much with them in terms of shaping and detailed expression. Yet of course there is much to enjoy here too, the beauty of the actual sound, the immaculate control, the many telling and musicianly touches of phrasing. But the noble, climactic triumphant aria, 'Dopo notte' doesn't have quite the effect it should. For that, however, Minkowski is partly to blame. Carried away, it almost seems, by the passion of the music, he is often inclined to go at it baldheaded, too fast and with a ferocity of accent, especially in the bass lines, that seems foreign to the style and dangerously close to ugly. This happens in several of Ariodante's numbers, including this last aria, but also in the scene that opens Act 3, first in the dark-toned D minor Sinfonia and then, particularly, in the extraordinary C minor aria, 'Cieca notte', with its extravagant leaps in the violin part and its jerky rhythms.

Veronica Cangemi makes a charming Dalinda, light, spirited and duly agile, with some gently pathetic expression in the delightful *siciliana* song early in Act 2. Ewa Podleś brings her large, resonant voice to Polinesso's music; the Lurcanio, Richard Croft, is a sturdy tenor, rather heavy in tone and at times almost baritonal. The King of Scotland's fatherly music is done with due fullness and warmth by Denis Sedov, who covers the two-octave range with comfort and resonance and brings due nobility to his *siciliana* aria in Act 2. Despite the driven quality of Minkowski's performance, especially in the high dramatic music of the latter part of the opera, the sheer passion of this set does give it claims to be considered first choice. The admirable McGegan performance is possibly a safer buy, and in some respects it is a more stylish performance, but the singing here, Lynne Dawson's above all, is on balance superior.

Athalia.
Dame Joan Sutherland *sop* Athalia; **Emma Kirkby** *sop* Josabeth; **Aled Jones** *treb* Joas;
James Bowman *counterten* Joad; **Anthony Rolfe Johnson** *ten* Mathan;
David Thomas *bass* Abner;
New College Choir, Oxford; Academy of Ancient Music / Christopher Hogwood.
L'Oiseau-Lyre 417 126-2OH2 (two discs: 122 minutes: DDD). Notes and text included.
Recorded 1985. *Gramophone* Award Winner 1987. ⒻⓅ

Athalia, composed for Oxford in 1733 to a libretto that draws on Racine's play, tells the story of the usurping, apostate Jewish queen, Athalia, and her overthrow when the prophet Joad and his wife Josabeth bring the true heir, the boy Joas, to the throne. The action is pretty feebly handled by

Handel's librettist, Samuel Humphreys (in particular it is never made clear what actually happens to Athalia in the end, or why); but several of the characters are quite strong and Handel grasps the opportunities offered him for striking music. Athalia herself fares best of all, musically, as one would expect; and it was a brilliant stroke of imagination to ask Dame Joan Sutherland to take this role in the present recording. She is of course a great Handelian, but is scarcely a figure one expects to see in early-music circles. In the event, the slight disparity of approach between her and the other members of the cast serves ideally to symbolize the separation of Athalia from her fellow-Israelites, putting her, as it were, on a different plane. Dame Joan uses more vibrato than the others in the cast, but the singing is truly magnificent in its grandeur and its clear, bell-like, perfectly focused tone. Athalia's part is not in fact a large one, with only two full-length arias; the second, 'My vengeance awakes me', is an energetic piece which she throws off with enormous spirit.

Among the rest, Emma Kirkby is on her very best form, singing coolly, with poised musicianship, and with quite astonishing technical command at times. Listen to 'Through the land', in Act 2, where the voice is beautifully balanced with two recorders and violins, the passagework perfectly placed, the oddly shaped phrases pitched with absolute sureness, the thrilling a delight. Her Act 1 aria 'Faithful cares' is finely done too, in spite of a hint of clumsiness in the accompaniment once or twice. James Bowman, as Joad, has his moments, and always sounds well. David Thomas is dependable in the often very vigorous music for the priest, Abner; and as Athalia's priest, Mathan, Anthony Rolfe Johnson sings in shapely fashion. The boy Joas is sung, as it should be, by a boy, in this case Aled Jones, who gives a very controlled, very exact performance, perhaps rather careful but of intense tonal beauty. The choral singing is a little variable. At its best, for example in the chorus that opens the Second Act, it is first-rate, spirited, forthright and accurate, but in certain of the others there is an air of the routine. There is much good, crisp orchestral playing, though some of the AAM's less positive characteristics are in evidence: an occasional moment of unsure ensemble, and a lack of broad shaping. These are however small, perfectionist quibbles: as a whole these two discs, excellently recorded, give an admirable and often striking realization of a choice work.

Flavio.
Jeffrey Gall *counterten* Flavio; **Derek Lee Ragin** *counterten* Guido; **Lena Lootens** *sop* Emilia; **Bernarda Fink** *contr* Teodata; **Christina Högman** *sop* Vitige; **Gianpaolo Fagotto** *ten* Ugone; **Ulrich Messthaler** *bass* Lotario;
Ensemble 415 / René Jacobs.
Harmonia Mundi HMC90 1312/3 (two discs: 156 minutes: DDD). Notes, text and translation included. Recorded 1989. ⓕⓅ

Flavio is one of the most delectable of Handel's operas. Although it comes from his 'heroic' period, it is rather an ironic tragedy with a good many comic elements. Does that sound confusing? – well, so it is, for you never know quite where you are when King Flavio of Lombardy starts falling in love with the wrong woman; this starts as an amusing idle fancy but develops into something near-tragic, since he imperils everyone else's happiness, ultimately causing the death of one counsellor and the dishonour of another. The delicately drawn amorous feeling is like nothing else in Handel, and in its subtle growth towards real passion and grief is handled with consummate skill. The opera, in short, is full of fine and exceptionally varied music, and it is enhanced here by a performance under René Jacobs that, although it takes a number of modest liberties, catches the moods of the music surely and attractively, with shapely, alert and refined playing from the admirable Ensemble 415. And the cast is strong. The central roles, composed for two of Handel's greatest singers, Cuzzoni and Senesino, eighteenth-century superstars, are sung by Lena Lootens, a delightfully natural and expressive soprano with a firm, clear technique, and the countertenor Derek Lee Ragin, who dispatches his brilliant music with aplomb and excels in the final aria, a superb minor-key expression of passion. The singers also include Bernarda Fink as the lightly amorous Teodata and Christina Högman, both fiery and subtle in the music for her lover, and the capable Jeffrey Gall as the wayward monarch. Altogether a highly enjoyable set, not flawless but certainly among the best Handel opera recordings.

Giulio Cesare.
Jennifer Larmore *mez* Giulio Cesare; **Barbara Schlick** *sop* Cleopatra; **Bernarda Fink** *mez* Cornelia; **Marianne Rørholm** *mez* Sextus; **Derek Lee Ragin** *counterten* Ptolemy;
Furio Zanasi *bass* Achillas; **Olivier Lallouette** *bar* Curio; **Dominique Visse** *alto* Nirenus;
Concerto Cologne / René Jacobs.
Harmonia Mundi HMC90 1385/7 (three discs: 243 minutes: DDD). Notes, text and translation included. Recorded 1991. *Gramophone* Award Winner 1992. ⓕⓅ RR

Handel's greatest heroic opera sports no fewer than eight principal characters and one of the largest orchestras he ever used. Undoubtedly this, and the singing of Francesca Cuzzoni (Cleopatra) and

Senesino (Caesar), helped to launch *Giulio Cesare* into the enduring popularity that it enjoys to this day. But it is primarily the quality of the music, with barely a weak number in four hours of entertainment, that has made it such a favourite with musicians and audiences. Here the period instruments are an immediate advantage in giving extra 'bite' to the many moments of high drama without threatening to drown the singers in *forte* passages. This performance is a particularly fine one with an excellent cast; Caesar, originally sung by a castrato, is here taken by the young mezzo, Jennifer Larmore. She brings weight and a sense of integrity to the role (which surely couldn't be matched by a countertenor), seemingly untroubled by the demands of the final triumphant aria, 'Qual torrente'. Occasionally her vibrato becomes intrusive, particularly near the beginning of the opera, but that is a minor quibble in a performance of this stature. Handel could just as well have called his opera 'Cleopatra' as it is she who is the pivotal element in the drama, a role taken here by Barbara Schlick. One of Handel's most vividly developed characters, this many faceted woman is represented by Schlick with acuity and imagination, ranging from the haunting pathos of 'Piangerò', where she occasionally seems stretched on the top notes, to the exuberant virtuosity of 'Da tempeste' in the final act. If Cleopatra represents strength in a woman, then Cornelia is surely the tragic figure, at the mercy of events. Her first aria, 'Priva son', here taken very slowly, shows Bernarda Fink to be more than equal to the role, admirable in her steady tone and dignity of character. Derek Lee Ragin's treacherous Ptolemy is also memorable, venom and fire injected into his agile voice. A first-rate cast is supported by René Jacobs and Concerto Cologne on fine form, though the continuo line is sometimes less than ideally clear. The recording is excellent.

Giulio Cesare (sung in English: ed. Mackerras).
Dame Janet Baker *mez* Giulio Cesare; **Valerie Masterson** *sop* Cleopatra;
Sarah Walker *mez* Cornelia; **Della Jones** *mez* Sextus; **James Bowman** *counterten* Ptolemy;
John Tomlinson *bass* Achilles; **Christopher Booth-Jones** *bar* Curio;
David James *counterten* Nirenus;
English National Opera Chorus and Orchestra / Sir Charles Mackerras.
Chandos Opera in English Series CHAN3019 (three discs: 183 minutes: DDD).
Notes and English text included. Recorded 1984.   Ⓕ

This opera was a personal triumph for Dame Janet. As Caesar, she arms the voice with an impregnable firmness, outgoing and adventurous. Valerie Masterson shares the honours with Dame Janet, a Cleopatra whose bright voice gains humanity through ordeal. The tinkle of surface-wear clears delightfully in her later arias, sung with a pure tone and high accomplishment. As a total production, *Julius Caesar* was an outstanding achievement in ENO's history. Strongly cast, it had a noble Cornelia in Sarah Walker, a high-spirited Sesto in Della Jones, and in James Bowman a Ptolemy whose only fault was that his voice lacked meanness of timbre appropriate to the odious character. John Tomlinson's massive bass also commands attention. At the time of this recording the cuts and adaptations in the texts were severely condemned in some quarters. Mackerras's conducting is impeccable and the opera is given in clear, creditable English.

Orlando.
Patricia Bardon *mez* Orlando; **Rosemary Joshua** *sop* Angelica; **Hilary Summers** *contr* Medoro;
Rosa Mannion *sop* Dorinda; **Harry van der Kamp** *bass* Zoroastro;
Les Arts Florissants / William Christie.
Erato 0630-14636-2 (three discs: 168 minutes: DDD). Notes, text and translation included.
Recorded 1996.   Ⓕ Ⓟ

Christie is very much concerned with a smooth and generally rich texture and with delicacy of rhythmic shaping. His management of the recitative could hardly be bettered and moments of urgency or of other kinds of emotional stress are tellingly handled. Sometimes he favours a rather sustained style in the arias, making the textures seem airless and heavy, and the lines within them too smooth. However, to set against it there is his exceptional delicacy of timing, his careful but always natural-sounding moulding of cadences and other critical moments in the score. Not many Handel interpreters show this kind of regard for such matters and it is certainly a delight to hear Handel's music so lovingly nurtured; also, of course, it helps the singers to convey meaning. The cast is very strong. The title-role is taken by a mezzo, Patricia Bardon, who draws a very firm and often slender line, with that gleam in her tone that can so enliven the impact of a lowish mezzo – the famous Mad scene is magnificent. The Sleep scene, with very sweet, soft-toned playing of the *violette marine*, is lovely. Hilary Summers offers a very sensitively sung Medoro, pure and shapely in line. Harry van der Kamp makes a finely weighty Zoroastro, with plenty of resonance in his lower register; the last aria in particular is done in rousing fashion. As Angelica, Rosemary Joshua's musicianship comes through in her attractive phrasing and timing. Rosa Mannion's Dorinda is no less full of delights, catching the character to perfection. Hogwood's lighter orchestral textures are appealing but the refinement of detail in the newer set is equally admirable.

Radamisto.
Ralf Popken *counterten* Radamisto; **Juliana Gondek** *sop* Zenobia;
Lisa Saffer *sop* Polissena; **Dana Hanchard** *sop* Tigrane; **Monika Frimmer** *sop* Fraarte;
Michael Dean *bass-bar* Tiridate; **Nicolas Cavallier** *bass* Farasmane;
Freiburg Baroque Orchestra / Nicholas McGegan *hpd*
Harmonia Mundi HMU90 7111/3 (three discs: 190 minutes: DDD). Notes, text and translation
included. Recorded 1993. ⒻⱣⒺ

Radamisto was Handel's first opera for the Royal Academy of Music, the company set up in 1719
under his musical directorship to put London opera on a secure basis (as optimistic a notion then
as now). It is a tale of dynastic doings in post-classical Thrace, with King Tiridate of Armenia
forsaking his wife Polissena because he becomes enamoured of Zenobia, Radamisto's queen;
Radamisto and Zenobia go through various trials, but 'after various Accidents, it comes to pass,
that he recovers both Her and his Kingdom'. It is easy enough to poke fun at plots such as these,
but the score of *Radamisto*, one of Handel's richest, is its justification. Handel certainly knew
how to 'wow' the London audiences on these big occasions. In the Second Act particularly, one
arresting number follows another; Radamisto's 'Ombra cara', which has been claimed (not without
justice) as the finest aria Handel ever wrote, falls early in the act, and towards the end there is a
wonderful sequence, chiefly of minor-key numbers, as the emotional tensions mount, culminating
in a duet for the apparently doomed lovers. The Third Act, although dramatically less powerful, is
also full of colourful and characterful music, including a noble quartet which Handel clearly
remembered 30 years later when composing *Jephtha*. Any Handelian will relish the constantly
alert playing, the strong dramatic pacing and the weight given to the orchestral textures, and the
excellent cast.

Rodelinda.
Sophie Daneman *sop* Rodelinda; **Daniel Taylor** *counterten* Bertarido;
Adrian Thompson *ten* Grimoaldo; **Catherine Robbin** *mez* Eduige;
Robin Blaze *counterten* Unulfo; **Christopher Purves** *bass* Garibaldo;
Raglan Baroque Players / Nicholas Kraemer *hpd*
Virgin Classics Veritas VCT5 45277-2 (three discs: 173 minutes: DDD). Notes, text and
translation included. Recorded 1996. ⒻⱣ

Composed just after *Giulio Cesare* and *Tamerlano*, *Rodelinda* must rank in many people's top
half-dozen of the Handel operas, with its complex plot of dynastic intrigue revolving around
the powerful, steadfast love of Bertarido (the ousted king of Milan) and his queen Rodelinda:
just the kind that unfailingly drew strong music from Handel. Nicholas Kraemer gives a very
direct and unaffected reading of this score. The pacing is sensible, if anything slightly on the
slow side (at least by recent standards of Handel opera conducting), especially perhaps in the
recitative; the playing of the Raglan Baroque Players is alive and rhythmically well sprung, with
a firmly defined bass-line. There is some modest ornamentation in the *da capo* sections of the
arias. What you don't get very strongly is much sense of urgency or boldness, of an unfolding
drama, or indeed of the musical characterization of individual numbers. There is just a hint here
of the 'concert in costume'. Its star is undoubtedly Sophie Daneman. The voice is bright and
intense, very firm in focus, dead sure in pitch, with only the faintest and most discriminatingly used
hint of vibrato. It is ideally suited to Rodelinda's character, as the poignant singing of her lovely,
elegiac opening aria makes clear – and that is immediately followed by a defiant one, vigorously
thrown off. Adrian Thompson is also particularly enjoyable as the would-be usurper Grimoaldo.
Thompson's easy and natural delivery, his natural feeling for the shape of Handel's phrases and his
elegant manner make all his music a pleasure to listen to, and perhaps especially his final aria,
which is a delight.

Catherine Robbin sings Eduige's music with spirit and rhythmic life. The two castrato roles,
Bertarido and Unulfo, are both taken by countertenors. Daniel Taylor is a very accomplished singer,
even-toned and accurate, well able to realize the pathos of Bertarido's prison scene (a B flat minor
aria, *Largo*; though he doesn't quite rise to the drama of the accompanied recitative that follows),
and the famous 'Dove sei' is touchingly done. But this role was written for Senesino, one of the
great expressive singers of his day, and Taylor (or indeed the countertenor voice) isn't quite capable
of conveying emotion on the scale the music demands. Unulfo's rather smaller part is neatly and
clearly done – and some exceedingly awkward passagework is surely negotiated in his Act 1 aria –
by Robin Blaze, although the general effect is rather bland and sober. Christopher Purves takes
the role of the villainous Garibaldo capably but is rather strident at the top. This may not be the
most dramatic of Handel opera recordings, but it does give an excellent account of the music
and there is some first-rate singing – and in one of the very finest and most compelling of the
Handel operas.

Serse.
Judith Malafronte *mez* Serse; **Jennifer Smith** *sop* Romilda; **Brian Asawa** *counterten* Arsamene;
Susan Bickley *mez* Amastre; **Lisa Milne** *sop* Atalanta; **Dean Ely** *bar* Ariodate;
David Thomas *bass* Elviro;
Hanover Band and Chorus / Nicholas McGegan.
Conifer Classics 75605 51312-2 (three discs: 177 minutes: DDD). Notes, text and translation
included. Recorded 1997. Ⓕ Ⓟ

Handel's *Serse* has proved to be one of the most popular of his operas over recent years – certainly
in England. Wit may not be a part of most people's image of Handel's operas, and rightly: but from
time to time, and especially when he was using a libretto of Venetian origins, Handel and his
London librettists permitted themselves touches of ironic humour and sometimes rather more than
that – *Serse* has one truly comic character, a servant, and King Xerxes himself is in some degree
made a figure of fun by his unruly amorous whims. But as in all the best comedy, the situations give
rise to serious emotion too, and in Act 2 of *Serse*, when events provoke first Xerxes, then Romilda
(whom he thinks he loves) and then Amastre (who loves him) into forceful expressions of passion,
touchingly followed by a gentle aria from Xerxes's brother Arsamene (Romilda's true lover), the
music springs into real life and enters more than a purely entertaining plane. Otherwise, however, it
is inclined to be elegant, thin-textured and short-breathed. Although the cast here isn't obviously
starry it is evenly accomplished and the performance holds together very well under Nicholas
McGegan's assured direction. His own personal touch is unmistakable – the light textures, the
quickish tempos, the spruce rhythms, the dapper cadences, the generally faintly ironic tone – and it
works well for this opera, perhaps better than it does for a big heroic piece. Since all of the soloists
are exemplary – in both its direction and its singing this set must surely be the choice for anyone
wanting a stylish version of this lively and appealing work.

Teseo.
Eirian James *mez* Teseo; **Julia Gooding** *sop* Agilea; **Della Jones** *mez* Medea:
Derek Lee Ragin *counterten* Egeo; **Catherine Napoli** *sop* Clizia; **Jeffrey Gall** *counterten* Arcane;
François Bazola *bar* Sacerdote di Minerva;
Les Musiciens du Louvre / Marc Minkowski.
Erato 2292-45806-2 (two discs: 148 minutes: DDD). Texts and translations included.
Recorded 1992. Ⓕ Ⓟ

Teseo was Handel's third opera for London, given at the beginning of 1713. Exceptionally, its
libretto was based on a French original, written by Quinault for Lully; it is a spectacular piece, in
five acts, with Medea (after the events of *Médée*) and Theseus (before the events of *Hippolyte* or the
Ariadne operas) as its central characters. It is Medea who, as slighted lover and jealous sorceress,
provides the principal musical thrills; but the score is, in any case, an unusually rich and inventive
one, with much colourful orchestral writing even before she turns up at the beginning of Act 2.
When she does, she introduces herself with a *Largo* aria, 'Dolce riposo', of a kind unique to Handel
in its depth of poetic feeling, with a vocal line full of bold leaps above throbbing strings and an
oboe obbligato; but, lest we should think her docile, Medea hints at her true colours in the ensuing
C minor aria, and by the end of the act she is singing furious recitative and fiery, incisive lines – real
sorceress music. Her biggest scene comes at the start of the final act, a *Presto* vengeance aria,
packed with raging rapid semiquavers. Handel scored the opera for a more varied orchestra than
usual; there are recorders, flutes, oboes, bassoons and trumpets called for. The arias themselves tend
to be rather shorter than usual for Handel. The work needs first-rate singing, and by and large
receives it here. The role of Medea falls to Della Jones, a singer with a superb technique and a
remarkable ability to identify with the role; she truly lives Medea's part and brings to it great
resources of spirit and technique. Except when allowed to play too fast, too loudly or too coarsely,
the Musiciens du Louvre are impressive. Several numbers are accompanied with only a continuo
instrument, to good effect. The recitative always moves well, and appoggiaturas are duly observed.

Howard Hanson American 1896-1981

Symphonies – No. 2, Op. 30, 'Romantic'; No. 4, Op. 34, 'The Requiem'. Elegy in memory of
Serge Koussevitzky.
Jena Philharmonic Orchestra / David Montgomery.
Arte Nova Classics 74321 43306-2 (60 minutes: DDD). Recorded 1996. Ⓢ

Here is enticingly off-the-beaten-track repertory from this new super-budget label. The Fourth
(*Requiem*) was apparently Hanson's own favourite of his seven symphonies. Inscribed 'in memory of

my beloved father', it is a darkly intense, neo-Sibelian outpouring which won the composer the first Pulitzer Prize ever given to music in 1944. The tuneful, opulently scored *Romantic* (No. 2) has understandably remained a firm favourite with American orchestras and audiences since its première in November 1930 under Serge Koussevitzky. More recently, its use on the soundtrack of the 1979 feature-film *Alien* won Hanson an entirely new band of admirers. The *Elegy* (1956) is a supremely touching memorial to a close friend and great conductor to whom American music this century owes an incontestably profound debt of gratitude. Performances are capable and shapely, and the sound is very good too. The orchestra responds with plenty of enthusiasm to David Montgomery who obviously knows his way round these scores. That said, there is nothing here which poses a serious challenge to Gerard Schwarz and the splendid Seattle Symphony in terms of orchestral finesse or interpretative insight: Montgomery's provincial band inevitably don't possess the ingratiating tonal lustre and sheer muscle of their American counterparts, while Schwarz's direction displays just that little bit of extra commitment to the cause. None the less, at its absurdly low price, this issue will find many new friends for Hanson's ripely romantic vision.

Symphonies – Nos. 2, 4 and 6; No. 7, 'A Sea Symphony'. Fantasy Variations on a Theme of Youth. Elegy in memory of Serge Koussevitzky. Serenade, Op. 36. Mosaics.
Carol Rosenberger *pf* **New York Chamber Symphony Orchestra;**
Seattle Symphony Chorale and Orchestra / Gerard Schwarz.
Delos DE3705 (two discs: 136 minutes: DDD). Recorded 1988-92.　Ⓜ

Gerard Schwarz's red-blooded 1988 account of the Second Symphony (*Romantic*) remains a match for any rival. Schwarz and his excellent Seattle band do full justice to its dark opulence, concision and organic power. Similarly, there's no missing the communicative ardour and clean-limbed security of Schwarz's lucid reading of the Sixth. Commissioned in 1967 by the New York Philharmonic for their 185th anniversary season, it boasts a formidable thematic economy and intriguing formal scheme of which Hanson himself was justifiably proud. Its successor, *A Sea Symphony* from 1977, sets texts from Walt Whitman's *Leaves of Grass*. In the unashamedly jubilant finale Hanson fleetingly quotes from his *Romantic* Symphony of more than four decades earlier: it is a spine-tingling moment in a score of consummate assurance and stirring aspiration. Schwarz's traversal finds the Seattle Symphony Chorale on rousing form. We also get exemplary renderings of the pretty 1945 Serenade for flute, harp and strings (a gift for Hanson's wife-to-be, Margaret Elizabeth Nelson) and characteristically inventive *Fantasy Variations on a Theme of Youth* from 1951 (with Carol Rosenberger a deft soloist), both these featuring Schwarz directing the New York Chamber Symphony. The present warm-hearted accounts of both the *Elegy in memory of Serge Koussevitzky* and *Mosaics* (a highly appealing set of variations written in 1957 for Szell and the Cleveland Orchestra) need not fear comparison with the composer's own Mercury recordings. Engineering is wonderfully ripe.

Merry Mount.
Lawrence Tibbett *bar* Wrestling Bradford; **Göta Ljungberg** *sop* Lady Marigold Sandys;
Gladys Swarthout *mez* Plentiful Tewke; **Edward Johnson** *ten* Sir Gower Lackland;
Alfredo Gandolfi *bar* Myles Brodrib; **Giordano Paltrinieri** *ten* Jonathan Banks;
Arnold Gabor *bar* Faint-not-Tinker; **James Wolfe** *sngr* Samoset; **Irra Petina** *mez* Desire Annable;
Louis d'Angelo *bar* Praise-God-Tewke;
Chorus and Orchestra of the Metropolitan Opera, New York / Tullio Serafin.
Naxos Historical mono 8 110024/5 (two discs: 126 minutes: ADD). Recorded live in 1934.　ⓈⒽ

Hanson's only opera was a considerable success when first given. It provided a major role for Tibbett (Wrestling Bradford) and included other luminaries of the international opera scene. This is the first opportunity to register the impact of the entire opera. The recording itself is a lucky scoop taken from 78rpm acetate and metal discs of the broadcast originally in the possession of Tibbett. No doubt technical wonders have been worked on the original sound but the result is still patchy, although, with announcements, commentary and applause included, the recording has a powerful sense of occasion. The story started with a grisly episode in New England history (about 1625) concerning feuding Puritan and Cavalier colonists. This was made the basis of a slender short story by Nathaniel Hawthorne and considerably embroidered in a libretto by Richard L. Stokes, which was published separately before the opera had even been staged. The crowd scenes gave Hanson the opportunity to write some magnificent choruses, and the dances before the maypole in Act 2 (scene 1) were so exciting at this première that they stopped the show. When Bradford gives his soul to the devil (scene 3) the choral and orchestral panoply is as vivid as anything in the Shakespeare film scores of Walton, and similar in style. Tibbett is magisterial in conveying all the horrors of repressive Puritanism souring into devil-worship but Ljungberg (Marigold/Astoreth) is resplendent in her lyrical role, specially the climactic Act 3 lament (track 14). Their joint immolation must have made a convincing peroration on stage, judging by reports of 50 curtain calls. What is remarkable is that a composer with so little experience in the theatre could deliver such an operatic grand opera. It has everything opera houses normally – like star roles, crowd scenes, violence and spectacle. This is a very worthwhile release and let's hope it leads to a revival.

Lou Harrison
American 1917

Symphony No. 3. Grand Duo.
Romuald Tecco vn **Cabrillo Music Festival Orchestra / Dennis Russell Davies** pf
MusicMasters 7073-2 (68 minutes: DDD). Ⓕ

The Third Symphony (1982) is a work of some substance and no little potential for widespread appeal. The boldly striding outer paragraphs of the opening *Allegro moderato* frame a more contemplative, raptly lyrical central section (with some beautiful writing for solo strings). Next follow three linked, nicely contrasted dance episodes, the first of which, a bouncy, good-natured 'Reel in Honor of Henry Cowell' (one of Harrison's teachers), is particularly infectious. The slow movement comprises a gently swaying *Largo ostinato* of great dignity and slumbering power, whilst the finale is a joyous, finely-sustained *Allegro* of deceptive rigour and satisfying proportions. The *Grand Duo* for violin and piano from 1988 perhaps makes less consistently compelling listening, though its five movements also contain much characterful invention. Both the 'Stampadé' and 'Polka' offer plenty of opportunities (gratefully seized here) for vigorous violin double-stopping and piano cluster-chords, whereas a simple, trance-like euphony illuminates the tender, central 'A Round'. Moreover, Harrison's eloquent sense of dialogue similarly distinguishes the thoughtful extended slow movement and more declamatory initial 'Prelude'. Both works were commissioned by the Cabrillo Music Festival in California, whose eponymous orchestra performs with admirable discipline and total dedication under the ever-sympathetic guidance of Dennis Russell Davies. In the *Grand Duo*, he partners Romuald Tecco with equally idiomatic, wonderfully assured results.

Symphony No. 4, 'Last Symphony'. Solstice – excerpts. Concerto in slendro. Elegy, to the Memory of Calvin Simmons. Double Music.
Al Jarreau sngr **Maria Bachmann** vn
California Symphony / Barry Jekowsky
Argo 455 590-2ZH (79 minutes: DDD). Text included. Recorded 1997. Ⓕ Ⓔ

Commissioned by the Brooklyn PO and Brooklyn Academy of Music, the *Last Symphony* was premièred in November 1990, since when Harrison has revised the work no fewer than four times; the (final) version recorded here dates from 1995. Like its predecessors, the *Last Symphony* draws its curious compulsion from Harrison's unique stylistic synthesis of Eastern and Western traditions spanning many centuries. The resulting timelessness lends his music a strongly communicative serenity (as exemplified by the *Largo* third movement), yet there's also a trance-like concentration and fine craft which ensure that one's attention rarely wavers. Of the symphony's four movements, the last is the most immediately striking, featuring as it does a vocalist (here a characterful Al Jarreau) narrating three native-American (or Navajo, to be precise) 'Coyote Stories' against a background of gamelan-like percussion sonorities. A similarly luminous, tintinnabulatory backcloth courses through the opening *Largo*, whereas the outer portions of the ensuing 'Stampede' exhibit a pungent rhythmic ingenuity that can be traced back over 50 years to Harrison's *Double Music* for percussion quartet (an exhilarating collaboration with John Cage dating from 1941, and the final item here). Elsewhere, we are treated to six numbers from *Solstice* (one of a clutch of dance works Harrison completed whilst living in New York from 1943-51), which imaginatively deploys an ensemble of flute, oboe, trumpet, two cellos, double-bass, piano and celesta. The *Concerto in slendro* (1961) for violin, two tack-pianos, celesta and percussion was composed aboard a freighter bound for Tokyo and takes its name from a five-tone Indonesian mode. The collection kicks off with a touching *Elegy* written in just three days in 1982 – inscribed to the memory of Calvin Simmons, the young conductor of the Oakland Symphony, and premièred a couple of days later at the Cabrillo Music Festival. The performances and recording are beyond reproach.

Karl Amadeus Hartmann
German 1905-1963

Symphonies – Nos. 1[a], 2 – Adagio[b], 3[c], 4-6[b], 7 (1957-58)[d], 8[b]. Gesangsszene (1963).
Doris Soffel contr **Dietrich Fischer-Dieskau** bar
Bavarian Radio Symphony Orchestra / [a]**Fritz Rieger,** [b]**Rafael Kubelík,** [c]**Ferdinand Leitner,**
[d]**Zdenek Macal**.
Wergo WER60187-50 (four discs: 225 minutes: ADD). Ⓕ

In the 1930s Hartmann was beginning to establish a reputation, but was forced to withdraw himself and his works from public musical life as a known opponent of the Nazi regime. During the war he destroyed or radically revised most of his output up till then, and these eight symphonies (five of which are based on, or are revisions of, earlier works) appeared between 1946 and his death in 1963. Together they show his broad sympathies with the twentieth-century masters. You can hear the presence of Bruckner in the monumental sense of structure, of Reger in the densely chromatic counterpoint and an intense, tortured lyricism derived from Berg. There is a tribute to the neo-classical Stravinsky in the Fifth Symphony, and more than a hint of Bartók in the irresistible momentum of the fugues that conclude the Sixth. Mahler is present in the Whitman settings of the First Symphony, significantly entitled *Attempt at a Requiem* and in the upheavals of the first movement of the Eighth. The spectral Funeral March in Webern's *Pieces*, Op. 6, haunts sections of the First, Third and Eighth Symphonies. Whether, with Hartmann's synthesis of his models, he managed to forge a demonstrably personal idiom is open to question. What is indisputable is the power of Hartmann's music to communicate, and its capacity to fascinate as sheer sound. On the debit side, not all the vigorously contrapuntal sections of the later works avoid sounding academic. The dates of these live recordings are not given, but they are all naturally balanced, with excellent clarity – Hartmann's torrents of tuned percussion are thrillingly captured. The Bavarian Radio Symphony Orchestra plays with polish and evident conviction.

Jonathan Harvey British 1939

I love the Lord. Carols. Lauds (with **Paul Watkins** *vc*). Sobre un éxtasis alte contemplación. Come, Holy Ghost. O Jesu, nomen dulce. Two Fragments. The Angels. Forms of Emptiness.
The Joyful Company of Singers / Peter Broadbent.
ASV CDDCA917 (63 minutes: DDD). Texts and translations included. Recorded 1994.   Ⓕ

Compare Jonathan Harvey's *Come, Holy Ghost* with one of his large-scale instrumental works and you might suspect that they are the work of different Jonathan Harveys, one providing short pieces for cathedral choirs, the other active on the avant-garde concert scene. So it is a particular virtue of this disc that by providing such a generous cross-section of Harvey's choral music it makes it easier to hear how the two Harveys are in fact one far-from-inconsistent composer. Since Harvey himself has progressed from choir school to electronic studio it is not so surprising that his music can relate to both worlds so effectively, and most of the compositions here take a fresh look at aspects of the English cathedral tradition without attempting to force those aspects into an unholy alliance with modernist techniques, and technologies. From the early *Fragments* (1966) to *The Angels* (1994) we can hear versions of the kind of contemplative intensity that informs some of Harvey's finest concert works (for example, *Bhakti*), and these choral pieces are never poor relations. The short *Sobre un éxtasis alte contemplación* works within its own essential sounds, and in exploring speech as well as song develops the more dramatic dialogue to be found in the larger-scale *Forms of Emptiness* (1986) and *Lauds* (1987). In such compositions, with their highly diverse textures, spiritual and sensual elements are brought into purposeful conjunction. The Joyful Company of Singers are the ideal interpreters to project all facets of this often challenging music.

Johann Hasse German 1699-1783

Overtures – Cleofide; Asteria. Salve regina in A major. Chori angelici laetantes. Fugue and Grave in G minor. Salve regina in E flat major.
Barbara Bonney *sop* **Bernarda Fink** *contr* **Musica Antiqua Köln / Reinhard Goebel** *vn*
Archiv Produktion 453 435-2AH (72 minutes: DDD). Texts and translations included. Recorded 1996.   Ⓕ Ⓟ

The greater part of the vocal music here is for mezzo-soprano or contralto, in this instance Bernarda Fink. These are full-bodied performances, vocally and instrumentally, and both the aural luxuriance of Fink's warm, rounded tone and the richness of the accompanying string textures are enjoyable. The motet, *Chori angelici laetantes* is a joyful, spirited and virtuoso composition with an accompaniment of strings and continuo. Fink is on superb form here, attentive to the words of the text and effortless in the delivery of her bravura passages. The motet is hugely appealing both for its warmth of sentiment and, as so often with Hasse, for its ravishing melodies. The E flat *Salve regina* is no less captivating, with a pair of oboes and a bassoon added to the string texture. Bonney and Fink are evenly matched and blend together pleasingly in music which few will be able to resist. A delightful programme, thoughtfully put together and very well executed.

Quel vago seno, ò Fille. Fille dolce, mio bene. La conversione di Sant' Agostino – Ah Dio, ritornate. Four Venetian ballads. Trio Sonata in B minor, Op. 2 No. 6. Keyboard Sonata in C minor, Op. 7 No. 6.

Julianne Baird *sop* **Nancy Hadden** *fl* **Erin Headley** *va da gamba* **Malcolm Proud** *hpd*
CRD CRD3488 (75 minutes: DDD). Texts and translations included. Recorded 1991. Ⓕ **E**

Though chiefly celebrated in his own day, as an opera composer, Hasse wrote a significant quantity of sacred pieces and much delightful chamber music for voices and instruments. The two cantatas provide the greatest substance here. They are expertly crafted pieces, each consisting of two pairs of alternating recitatives and arias. Hasse seems often to have gone in for unusually extended da capo arias; one of them – the captivating *Quel vago seno, ò Fille* – lasts for almost nine minutes, while two others are of almost equally impressive proportions. But they are skilfully written and hold our attention with their engaging melodic contours and effective accompaniments. Julianne Baird is a stylish and thoughtful interpreter of baroque and early classical music; and the conjunction of an agile technique with an alluring vocal timbre gives considerable strength to her performances. The instrumental items, too, are enjoyable. Malcolm Proud, who provides first-rate continuo realizations throughout, also gives us a favourable impression of Hasse's solo keyboard skill in a fine Sonata in C minor for harpsichord. The outstanding movement here is the third one, a deeply felt, darkly coloured *Adagio* which Proud plays with unhurried and affecting intensity. The flautist Nancy Hadden gives a lively account of a B minor Sonata, while Erin Headley plays the composer's own alternative version for viola da gamba of an aria from Hasse's last cantata, *La conversione di Sant' Agostino*. Like Proud, both Hadden and Headley contribute excellent obbligatos and continuo, respectively, elsewhere in the programme. A delightful disc, well performed and intimately recorded.

Josef Hauer

Austrian 1883-1959

Salambo.
Susan Roberts *sop* Salambo; **Diane Elias** *mez* Taanach; **Claes Hakon Ahnsjö** *ten* Spendius; **Rudolf Constantin** *bar* Matho; **Friedemann Hanke** *bass* Gisko; Schahabarim; **Austrian Radio Chorus; Vienna Radio Symphony Orchestra / Lothar Zagrosek.**
Orfeo Musica Rediviva C493981A (60 minutes: DDD). Notes, text and translation included. Recorded live in 1983. Ⓕ

Josef Matthias Hauer, even to those who have never heard a note of his music, is known as the man who invented a 12-note system before Schoenberg did, and quite independently of him. He seems also to have coined the word 'atonal'. However, Hauer's music does not sound even slightly like Schoenberg. It doesn't sound at all like late Stravinsky either. In fact, his music is very easy to follow and easy to describe as 'melodious', if not, perhaps, as 'tuneful', though no less so than, again, the minimalists. It is far more eventful than that of, say, Philip Glass, because his rate of change or permutation is much faster, and because Hauer's scoring is so richly textured and so colourful. His vocal lines are on the whole grateful (and they are conspicuously well sung), but his word-setting is not: rather often a word or phrase seems to receive a particular pattern of notes not because it 'expresses' those words but because of a beaverish working out of the permutational process. His rhythmic language is also, at times, monotonous, though where the savage and picturesque plot demands it he can build up quite a head of excitement, feverish energy or dancing vigour. *Salambo* is dramatically ambitious: although barely an hour long it is divided into seven scenes, each requiring a different stage picture, several also involving dances or elaborate ceremonies – the stage directions to Scene 7 are much longer than its sung text. Hauer's 'system' may seem mechanical (it extends to all aspects of his work, harmony and part-writing as well as ordering of pitch), and he himself compared it to a children's game. But here its outcome, combined with his often gorgeous, brocaded colours, is an oddly effective medium for Flaubert's elaborately exotic myth. In a performance as good as this, and it is very decently recorded, you can imagine it being quite gripping on stage.

Joseph Haydn

Austrian 1732-1809

Cello Concertos – No. 1 in C major, HobVII*b*/1; No. 2 in D major, HobVII*b*/2.

Cello Concertos Nos. 1 and 2.
Truls Mørk *vc*
Norwegian Chamber Orchestra / Iona Brown.
Virgin Classics VC5 45014-2 (50 minutes: DDD). Recorded 1991. Ⓕ **RR**

Playing a rare early eighteenth-century Domenico Montagnana cello, Truls Mørk brings an unusual lyrical tenderness to these perennially popular concertos. He can certainly produce a big, gutsy tone where appropriate, as in his imposing initial entry in the C major work; and the agility of his bowing is never in question, as you can hear in the finale of the same concerto, where he responds eagerly to the dramatic and comic potential of Haydn's bravura episodes, with their wide leaps and *staccato* repeated notes. But what lingers in the mind is the delicacy and suppleness of Mørk's *cantabile* phrasing and his beautiful range of colour in piano dynamics. Listen, for instance, to his veiled, dusky tone in the first-movement development of the C major, his sudden withdrawn *pianissimo* in the slow movement, the bow barely brushing the string, or his gravely eloquent shaping of the D major's *Adagio*. The very leisurely first movement, with its (for Haydn) unusually slow harmonic rhythms, mingles elegance, animation and just the right degree of expressive freedom (rubato acutely judged, here as elsewhere) while the finale, which can be a lumbering bore, dances with a lithe, airy grace. The expert Norwegian Chamber Orchestra accompanies crisply and attentively, though oboes and horns get a slightly raw deal in the resonant church acoustic. Among the rival versions of these concertos, several are outstanding, but Mørk can hold his own; and in some moods you might well prefer his fresh, sweet-toned, uncommonly gracious performances before all others.

Haydn Cello Concertos Nos. 1 and 2.
A. Kraft Cello Concerto in C major, Op. 4.
Anner Bylsma *vc*
Tafelmusik / Jeanne Lamon.
Deutsche Harmonia Mundi RD77757 (67 minutes: DDD). Recorded 1989.   Ⓕ Ⓟ

At best, an 'authentic' performance can only aspire to return to the spirit, rather than the letter of the period it strives to re-create, and yet the fine Dutch cellist Anner Bylsma comes as near as anyone to convincing us that this is indeed the way Haydn might have wished these sunny, yet highly sophisticated concertos, to be played. Haydn composed these works for the virtuoso cellist of the Esterházy court orchestra, Anton Kraft, and the bold and adventurous solo writing reflects his fabled technical prowess and musical sensitivity. Bylsma offers a lithe, yet scrupulously classical and poised account of the C major Concerto, with a romantically inflected central *Adagio* followed by a dashingly brilliant, yet suitably witty finale. His rapid passagework in higher registers is astonishing, while he reveals the stately dignity of the D major work (long attributed to Kraft) in a cultured and attractively proportioned reading of rich intensity and variety. Bylsma includes his own revisions of period cadenzas, which are never less than apposite, and deftly executed.

The real discovery here, though, is the Cello Concerto by Kraft himself, which combines the expected brilliant pyrotechnics with some effective melodic writing in a work which anticipates the styles developed during the early nineteenth century. In fact, Kraft advised Beethoven on the cello part of his Triple Concerto, and his compositions exercised great influence in the genesis of modern cello technique. Bylsma is superbly supported by the excellent Tafelmusik, and the recording is first-rate. A stunning collection.

Cello Concertos Nos. 1 and 2. Sinfonia concertante in B flat, Hobl/105. Symphony No. 13 in D major – Adagio cantabile.
Steven Isserlis *vc* **Douglas Boyd** *ob* **Matthew Wilkie** *bn* **Marieke Blankestijn** *vn*
Chamber Orchestra of Europe / Sir Roger Norrington.
RCA Victor Red Seal 09026 68578-2 (75 minutes: DDD). Recorded 1996.   Ⓕ Ⓔ

What a versatile artist Steven Isserlis is. Having made his name as a sympathetic interpreter of a wide variety of romantic and modern music, here he shows he can be just as persuasive in eighteenth-century repertoire. His stylistic awareness is evident in beautiful, elegant phrasing, selective use of vibrato and varied articulation, giving an expressive range that never conflicts with the music's natural language. In the cello concertos he is helped by an extremely sensitive accompaniment, stressing the chamber musical aspects of Haydn's pre-London orchestral writing. The *Adagios* are taken at a flowing speed, but Isserlis's relaxed approach means they never sound hurried. The *Allegro molto* finale of the C major Concerto, on the other hand, sounds poised rather than the helter-skelter we often hear. Mørk's vivacious, imaginative performances characterize the music very strongly, but some may prefer Isserlis's and Norrington's lighter touch and greater refinement. And this is not taking into account the extras – the lovely symphony movement (a cello solo throughout) and what many may find the highlight of the disc – the *Sinfonia concertante*. The first movement's tuttis have excessively prominent added dynamics that detract from the music's vigour and grandeur, but the serenade-like *Andante*, the robust and witty finale and, throughout, the conversational exchanges of the four soloists, are an unalloyed delight.

Cello Concertos Nos. 1 and 2.
Academy of St Martin in the Fields / Mstislav Rostropovich *vc*
EMI CDC7 49305-2 (49 minutes: ADD). Recorded 1975.   Ⓕ

This deserves a place on any collector's shelf. With Rostropovich directing from the bow the ASMF sounds a little less sturdy than usual, a little more lithe in the First Concerto. The scale of its first movement is little short of perfection: everything a *Moderato* should be, with Rostropovich humming along nonchalantly with the lightest of breaths in its second theme. He is leisurely in the *Adagio*, playing it as an extended meditation which exists almost outside time altogether. Without ever losing the life of the melodic line, Rostropovich progresses as slowly as it is humanly possible to do without total stasis; and, to wonderfully joyful effect, breaks all records for speed in the finale. Every note, every sequential phrase is there in its place, secured by glintingly true intonation and needle-sharp dramatic timing. The almost complete absence of physical stick and finger sound which Rostropovich and his engineers manage between them makes the latter two movements of the Second Concerto a most pleasing experience. Rostropovich takes deep, long breaths: the surface of his slow movement is glassy, every fragment of bowing and phrasing given the microscopic hair-pin treatment. For his deep, instinctive understanding of scale, and for Britten's cadenzas, many collectors' preferences in these concertos will remain with Rostropovich.

Haydn Horn Concerto No. 1 in D major, HobVIId/3.
Danzi Horn Concerto in E major.
Rosetti Horn Concerto in D minor.
Hermann Baumann *hn*
Concerto Amsterdam / Jaap Schröder.
Teldec Das Alte Werk 0630-12324-2 (52 minutes: ADD). Recorded 1968.   Ⓜ

Hermann Baumann has always been one of the most impressive performers on the eighteenth-century hand horn, and in his late 1960s recording of Haydn's splendid First Horn Concerto the characterful smoothness of his playing brings virtually no indications of the problems of hand 'stopping', and his intonation is absolutely true. The *Adagio* soars and there are also some wonderfully resonant low notes. The coupled Danzi Concerto is also appealing and brings ready bravura in its flowing opening movement, which is followed by a mellifluous central 'Romance' and a perky finale. The third work here, a fine Bohemian Concerto by Antonio Rosetti, is *galant* in style, but with hints of high drama. The first movement is slightly reminiscent of Hummel's E major Trumpet Concerto and the slow movement is operatically romantic, the finale jolly. Jaap Schröder and his Concerto Amsterdam provide stylish accompaniments which maintain a firm late-eighteenth-century flavour, and the sound, fresh, warm and clear, is excellent.

Keyboard Concertos – F major, HobXVIII/3; G major, HobXVIII/4; D major, HobXVIII/11.
Franz Liszt Chamber Orchestra / Emanuel Ax *pf*
Sony Classical SK48383 (59 minutes: DDD). Recorded 1992.   Ⓕ

Whilst none of the works recorded here could claim to add to the development of the concerto form in the way that those of Mozart did, all three possess great charm: take for example the *Largo cantabile* of the early F major work to hear Haydn's melodic gift at its most endearing. The *Presto* finale of the same concerto recalls some of his later piano sonatas in its juxtaposition of knockabout comedy and theatrical minor-key drama. The G major, supposedly written for the blind pianist, composer and singer Maria Theresia von Paradis boasts an extended *Grave* slow movement. But it is the D major with its larger orchestra (horns and oboes added to strings) that works best and the *Rondo all'Ungarese* finale, with its myriad key changes and sparkling good humour, is predictably the highlight of the disc. Emanuel Ax (directing from the keyboard) gives performances of the utmost finesse and affection: if any performance were to help to restore the fortunes of these works then this is surely it. His playing throughout is deeply felt: graceful in the slow movements and dexterous in the outer ones. In addition, he plays his own charming cadenzas in the F and G major works. Sony's sound is spacious, with the piano forwardly placed.

Trumpet Concerto in E flat major, HobVIIe/1[a]. Cello Concerto in D major, HobVIIb/2[b].
Violin Concerto No. 1 in C major, HobVII[c].
Wynton Marsalis *tpt* **Cho-Liang Lin** *vn* **Yo-Yo Ma** *vc*
[a]**National Philharmonic Orchestra / Raymond Leppard;**
[b]**English Chamber Orchestra / José Luis Garcia;** [c]**Minnesota Orchestra / Sir Neville Marriner.**
CBS Masterworks MK39310 (59 minutes: DDD).   Ⓕ 🆁🆁

Haydn Orchestral

The American trumpeter Wynton Marsalis has all the fluency one could wish for and an instrument allowing a full three octaves to be displayed in his own cadenza to the first movement. Although this is an efficient performance, it in no way approaches the class of the next one. The cellist Yo-Yo Ma is very different as a performer: though equally a master of his instrument, and indeed a virtuoso who seems incapable of producing an ugly sound or playing out of tune, one feels a deep emotional involvement in all he does. In addition, the recording in the D major Cello Concerto is unusually faithful in blending the cello well into the ensemble without ever covering it. Ma is supported by the excellent English Chamber Orchestra and the qualities of integration and ensemble under their leader's direction are all that one could wish for. In the C major Violin Concerto the skilful Cho-Liang Lin has the benefit of a most sympathetic conductor in Sir Neville Marriner, but he cannot match Ma's subtlety and commitment.

Overtures – Acide e Galatea; Lo speziale; Le pescatrici; L'infedeltà delusa; Philemon und Baucis; Der Götterrath; Il ritorno di Tobia; Der Feuersbrunst; L'incontro improvviso; Il mondo della luna.
Vienna Haydn Sinfonietta / Manfred Huss.
Koch Schwann 317232 (61 minutes: DDD). Recorded 1994. Ⓕ Ⓟ

The Haydn Sinfonietta's stylish, vigorous approach – enhanced by period instruments and exemplary recording – creates striking portrayals of the repertoire under review. Here, listeners are given the opportunity to sample overtures from Haydn's theatrical music composed between 1762 and 1777 in an absorbing illustration of life at Esterházy. The Sinfonietta's arresting vitality in *Acide e Galatea, Le pescatrici, Lo speziale* and *Il mondo della luna*, underlines this music's originally festive purpose; while suitably majestic performances of *L'infedeltà delusa* and *Philemon und Baucis* attest to their presentation before the Empress Maria Theresia. Increased intensity in minor-key pieces such as *Der Götterrath*, with its grand depiction of the 'Council of the Gods' (an allegory for the Hapsburg family), and *Il ritorno di Tobia* highlight Haydn's overtly dramatic writing. Brighter, more startling colours are brilliantly projected by these musicians in an aptly fiery account of *Der Feuersbrunst* and the exotic *L'incontro improvviso* which conjures up vivid images of a Turkish harem. With potent contrast between rhythmically taut energy in the fast movements and elegant sensitivity in the imaginatively scored slow ones, this disc is surely a winner.

Six Scherzandos, HobII/33-38.
Vienna Haydn Sinfonietta / Manfred Huss.
Koch Schwann 314432 (52 minutes: DDD). Recorded 1993. Ⓕ

The *Six Scherzandos* which Haydn wrote in 1761 to impress his new patron, Prince Paul Anton Esterházy, exhibit all the typical characteristics of the composer's mature style. Each of these miniature symphonies presents the four movements of the classical symphony with a degree of thematic and formal concentration associated with Beethoven's Op. 126 *Bagatelles* and, ultimately, with the works of Anton Webern. Moreover, their sequence here creates a compelling musical cycle. The abounding vitality and subtle sensitivity with which Manfred Huss and the Vienna Haydn Sinfonietta perform this music emphasizes its remarkable formal and instrumental variety, highlighting the startling emotional intensity created by its sudden changes of mood. Sample the vivacious opening *allegros*, the rugged minuets, the affecting *adagios*, and the brief, energetic finales. Ensemble is impeccably balanced throughout, and the recorded sound is vividly clear and natural.

Symphonies: No. 1 in D major; **No. 2** in C major; **No. 3** in G major; **No. 4** in D major; **No. 5** in A major; **No. 6** in D major, 'Le matin'; **No. 7** in C major, 'Le midi'; **No. 8** in G major, 'Le soir'; **No. 9** in C major; **No. 10** in D major; **No. 11** in E flat major; **No. 12** in E major; **No. 13** in D major; **No. 14** in A major; **No. 15** in D major; **No. 16** in B flat major; **No. 17** in F major; **No. 18** in G major; **No. 19** in D major; **No. 20** in C major; **No. 21** in A major; **No. 22** in E flat major, 'Philosopher'; **No. 23** in G major; **No. 24** in D major; **No. 25** in C major; **No. 26** in D minor, 'Lamentatione'; **No. 27** in G major; **No. 28** in A major; **No. 29** in E major; **No. 30** in C major, 'Alleluja'; **No. 31** in D major, 'Hornsignal'; **No. 32** in C major; **No. 33** in C major; **No. 34** in D minor; **No. 35** in B flat major; **No. 36** in E flat major; **No. 37** in C major; **No. 38** in C major; **No. 39** in G minor; **No. 40** in F major; **No. 41** in C major; **No. 42** in D major; **No. 43** in E flat major, 'Mercury'; **No. 44** in E minor, 'Trauersinfonie'; **No. 45** in F sharp minor, 'Farewell'; **No. 46** in B major; **No. 47** in G major, 'Palindrome'; **No. 48** in C major, 'Maria Theresia'; **No. 49** in F minor, 'La passione'; **No. 50** in C major; **No. 51** in B flat major; **No. 52** in C minor; **No. 53** in D major, 'Imperial'; **No. 54** in G major; **No. 55** in E flat major, 'Schoolmaster'; **No. 56** in C major; **No. 57** in D major; **No. 58** in F major; **No. 59** in A major, 'Fire'; **No. 60** in C major, 'Il distratto'; **No. 61** in D major; **No. 62** in D major; **No. 63** in C major, 'La Roxelane'; **No. 64** in A major, 'Tempora mutantur'; **No. 65** in A major; **No. 66** in B flat major; **No. 67** in F major; **No. 68** in B flat major; **No. 69** in C major, 'Loudon'; **No. 70** in D major; **No. 71** in B flat major; **No. 72** in D major; **No. 73** in D major, 'La chasse'; **No. 74** in E flat major; **No. 75** in D major; **No. 76** in

E flat major; **No. 77** in B flat major; **No. 78** in C minor; **No. 79** in F major; **No. 80** in D minor; **No. 81** in G major; **No. 82** in C major, 'L'ours'; **No. 83** in G minor, 'La poule'; **No. 84** in E flat major; **No. 85** in B flat major, 'La reine'; **No. 86** in D major; **No. 87** in A major; **No. 88** in G major, 'Letter V'; **No. 89** in F major; **No. 90** in C major; **No. 91** in E flat major; **No. 92** in G major, 'Oxford'; **No. 93** in D major; **No. 94** in G major, 'Surprise'; **No. 95** in C minor; **No. 96** in D major, 'Miracle'; **No. 97** in C major; **No. 98** in B flat major; **No. 99** in E flat major; **No. 100** in G major, 'Military'; **No. 101** in D major, 'Clock'; **No. 102** in B flat major; **No. 103** in E flat major, 'Drumroll'; **No. 104** in D major, 'London'.

Symphonies – Nos. 1-104; 'A' in B flat major; 'B' in B flat major. Sinfonia concertante in B flat major, HobI/105, 'No. 105'.
Philharmonia Hungarica / Antál Dorati.
Decca 448 531-2LC33 (33 discs: ADD). Recorded 1969-73. Ⓑ

Dorati's famous integral recording of all 104 of the published Symphonies now returns in a Decca bargain box containing 33 CDs. It still holds its place in the catalogue as the only complete set to contain everything Haydn wrote in this medium, including the Symphonies 'A' and 'B', omitted from the original numbering scheme simply because at one time they were not thought to be symphonies at all. The survey also encompasses additional alternative movements for certain works (notably Nos. 53 and 103) and alternative complete versions of the *Philosopher* Symphony and No. 63, which are fascinating. The remastering confirms the excellence of the vintage Decca sound. No more needs to be said, except that the one minus point in these very convincing modern-instrument performances is Dorati's insistence on measured, often rustic tempos for the minuets. For those who can run to the complete series this bargain box is self-recommending – a source of inexhaustible pleasure.

Symphonies Nos. 1, 2, 4, 5, 10, 11, 18, 27, 32, 37 and 107.
Academy of Ancient Music / Christopher Hogwood.
L'Oiseau-Lyre 436 428-2OH3 (three discs: 172 minutes: DDD). Recorded 1990-91. ⒻⓅ

These very early symphonies, composed before Haydn moved to the Eszterházy court in 1761, may all too easily blur together in the mind: driving *allegros*, long on physical energy but short on memorable ideas, sparse-textured 'walking' *andantes* and breezy *buffo* finales. Superficially some of the opening movements and finales can seem virtually interchangeable. But even here there is more variety than you might at first suspect; and there is a world of difference between, say, the opening movement of No. 1, all quivering nervous energy, and that of No. 2, with its surprising amplitude and contrapuntal weight. If some of the slow movements are dull and arid, there is a melancholy, neo-baroque D minor *Andante* in No. 4 and a delicately expressive *Adagio, ma non troppo* in No. 32, probably the first in Haydn's long line of ceremonial C major symphonies with trumpets and timpani. But the two richest slow movements, both in texture and expression, stand at the head of works cast in church-sonata form (a sequence of slow, fast, minuet, fast): that in No. 5, with its high-lying *concertante* writing for horns; and the noble, processional *Adagio cantabile* of No. 11, whose eloquent violin writing foreshadows the well-known *Adagio* of No. 44. Hogwood's performances are pretty persuasive: crisp, precise, lightly and elegantly articulated, rhythmically spruce and almost invariably well tuned, with clear recorded sound.

Symphonies Nos. 6-8.
Northern Chamber Orchestra / Nicholas Ward.
Naxos 8 550722 (59 minutes: DDD). Recorded 1993. ⓈRR

Although this disc doesn't offer any revelations, there's quite a lot to enjoy in the popular Times of Day trilogy, with their colourful and entertaining *concertante* writing. The Northern Chamber Orchestra is a lively, responsive group, and fields a personable bunch of soloists – deft work from flute and violin, for instance, in the finales of Nos. 6 and 7, an eloquent cello in the *Andante* of No. 8, and nicely turned cameos from the double-bass in the Trios of *Le midi* and *Le soir*. The minuets could move with a nimbler spring, and the slow movements, especially that of *Le matin*, are sometimes short on delicacy and fantasy, with a dearth of truly soft playing. But *Allegros* are bright-eyed and propulsive, with ample verve and virtuosity in the finales. The horns are sometimes unduly discreet, but in general the full, immediate recording is very acceptable. No one staking a fiver on this disc could possibly be disappointed.

Symphonies Nos. 6-8.
The English Concert / Trevor Pinnock *hpd*
Archiv Produktion 423 098-2AH (65 minutes: DDD). ⒻⓅ

Haydn took the opportunityx to give his new colleagues in the princely band something interesting to do here, for there are numerous solos, not only for the wind instruments but for the section leaders, such as the *Adagio* of No. 6, with solo violin and prominent flutes and cello, a delectable piece of writing. Inventively, the music is uneven; the concerto-like style was not wholly harmonious with Haydn's symphonic thinking. But there is plenty of spirited and cheerful music here, and that is well caught in these vivacious performances by Pinnock and his band, with their brisk tempos and light textures; the playing is duly agile, and the period instruments give a bright edge to the sound.

Symphonies Nos. 17-21.
Hanover Band / Roy Goodman.
Hyperion CDA66533 (79 minutes: DDD). Recorded 1993.   Ⓕ Ⓟ

The symphonies numbered 17-20 were among Haydn's very first; and while none is especially riveting in its invention they are all compact in design, with lean, economical orchestration and a characteristically high quota of nervous energy. The most colourful and ambitious work in this group, and the only one in four movements, is the ceremonial C major, No. 20, with its panoply of trumpets, timpani and horns. Symphony No. 21, the final work on the disc, dates from several years later (1764) and sounds it: the ideas in the fast movements are more striking in themselves and more tautly developed, while the opening *Adagio* is perhaps the most lyrically intense movement in all Haydn's early symphonies. Goodman allows the *Adagio* plenty of space, shaping the music sympathetically, with a firm sense of harmonic direction. Faster movements are rhythmically vital yet never overdriven, with Haydn's contrasts of colour and dynamics vividly realized (thrilling brass sonorities in No. 20). The Minuets in Nos. 20 and 21 are neatly phrased, light on their feet. Delightful performances, stylish, spirited and deftly executed.

Symphonies Nos. 21-24, 28-31 and 34.
Academy of Ancient Music / Christopher Hogwood.
L'Oiseau-Lyre 430 082-2OH3 (three discs: 190 minutes: DDD). Recorded 1988-89.   Ⓕ Ⓟ

The Academy of Ancient Music is usually a small orchestral body, supporting the contention expressed by Joseph Webster that Haydn's orchestra in 1764-65 was of about 13 to 16 players and that there was no keyboard continuo. In other words, there is no harpsichord to fill out textures, but although some listeners may miss it initially the playing soon convinces. As usual with Haydn, even these relatively unfamiliar pieces are inventive and often beautiful. The playing has zest, but however brisk the tempo chosen for quick movements they never degenerate into mere bustle. There are real discoveries to be made here, including the nervous, dramatic finale to Symphony No. 21 and minuets such as the enigmatic ones to Nos. 28 and 29. Similarly, slow movements have dignity, grace and often a quiet humour too, while phrasing is intelligent and affectionate and textures well balanced. Indeed, Hogwood's wind and string players alike are precise and stylish. Repeats are faithfully observed. Finally, the recording is clear and atmospheric.

Symphonies Nos. 22, 29 and 60.
Northern Chamber Orchestra / Nicholas Ward.
Naxos 8 550724 (60 minutes: DDD). Recorded 1992-93.   Ⓢ

In the *Philosopher*, Nicholas Ward and the Northern Chamber Orchestra (using modern instruments) present a spacious, elegantly phrased account of the title-character's personality. Ward's idiomatic feeling for Haydn's style produces a subtly balanced, appealingly smooth-lined performance. The E major Symphony, No. 29, offers Ward and the NCO the opportunity to explore Haydn's attractive variety of instrumental forces and powerful opposition of major and minor. The programme culminates with No. 60 (*Il distratto*). Here, Ward controls his orchestra with customary deftness to make the music's overtly descriptive elements especially telling. Haydn's comic depiction of the protagonist's absent-mindedness is vividly portrayed in the two outer movements, and distinctive thematic characterization effectively heightens the dramatic contrasts in the Minuet and *Adagio*, in a winning performance that fully captures the composer's infectious wit.

Symphonies Nos. 22, 86 and 102.
City of Birmingham Symphony Orchestra / Sir Simon Rattle.
EMI CDC5 55509-2 (68 minutes: DDD). Recorded 1994.   Ⓕ

Rattle establishes a middle path between traditional and period styles of performance. In addition, the idea of coupling symphonies from different periods of Haydn's career – not new but relatively rare – is refreshing, and has here produced an issue that one can warmly recommend to anyone simply wanting a representative Haydn symphony disc. The limited vibrato and light phrasing used by the strings throughout these performances set them apart from most others using modern instruments, giving them extra freshness and transparency. So in the *Adagio* of No. 102, elegant at a flowing speed, the solo cello is clearly defined, and the Minuet brings the strongest contrast of all with modern-instrument rivals, exuberantly turned into a scherzo at one-in-a-bar. No. 86, the fifth of the 'Paris Symphonies', less appreciated only for lack of a nickname, is similarly refreshing, and here too Rattle refuses to rush his first movement in the name of authenticity. The main *Allegro* is marginally more relaxed than that of Dorati (on Decca). By contrast Rattle's *Presto* for the finale is hectic, and one marvels at the agility of the Birmingham horns in their repeated triplets. In the square rhythms of the opening *Adagio* of No. 22, Rattle manages to achieve elegance without sacrificing the chunky strength of the chorale on cor anglais, and this symphony, unlike the later ones, finds Rattle using harpsichord continuo. The helpful acoustic of Symphony Hall, Birmingham, sets the seal on the disc's success with warm, clear sound.

Symphonies Nos. 26, 35, 38, 39, 41-52, 58, 59 and 65.
Orchestra of the Age of Enlightenment / Frans Brüggen.
Philips 462 117-2PH5 (five discs: 389 minutes: DDD). Recorded 1996. Ⓜ Ⓟ

Although increasingly rejected by scholars, the label *Sturm und Drang* is still widely used to describe the symphonies Haydn wrote during the late 1760s and early 1770s. Storm and stress is, of course, most evident in the half-dozen minor-key symphonies of this period. Several of the major-key works here also have their share of turbulence, above all No. 46, in the (for late-eighteenth-century audiences) bizarre key of B major. Others, though, employ the fundamentally cheerful, Italianate musical language of the day with a new force, originality and, as in movements like the 'limping' Minuet of No. 58, comic eccentricity. No. 42 in D has an unprecedented amplitude and harmonic breadth, No. 43 a mingled fire and reflective lyricism, while No. 48, the erroneously named *Maria Theresia*, is one of the noblest and most imposing in a line of eighteenth-century C major ceremonial symphonies. Stormy, majestic or playful, virtually every work here reflects Haydn's restless exploration of the symphony's expressive and intellectual potential during these years.

Some or all of these symphonies have been well served by previous period-instrument recordings, but this set – 19 works on five discs – more than holds its own with the competition. Brüggen is certainly the most 'romantic' of the conductors in this repertoire: and he has little truck with the smart tempos and clean-cut phrasing favoured by Hogwood and Weil, in particular. Outer movements are often surprisingly broad and Brüggen phrases the lyrical music as expressively as any traditional conductor, and reveals a strong control of cumulative symphonic tensions. Slow movements are shaped with all the refinement and chamber-musical delicacy heard on Pinnock's recordings, and often with a degree more affection. In one or two of the faster movements Brüggen's tempo is arguably a notch too expansive, above all in the first movement of the C major, No. 41. He also shows an intermittent fondness for shading away at cadences, notably in the opening movement of the *Lamentatione*, No. 26. Equally controversial is his speeding up for the trios of several of the minuets, most blatantly in that of *La Passione*, though his tempos for the minuets themselves are thoughtfully chosen, ranging from the measured, elegiac No. 26 (an unusual and effective reading) to the stinging one-in-a-bar quasi-*Scherzo* of No. 52. The beautiful, melancholy Minuet of No. 46 is much broader than on any rival period version, to its advantage; and Brüggen hilariously heightens the 'limping' effect in the Minuet of No. 58 with outrageous unmarked *sforzandos*. Brüggen eschews a harpsichord continuo – not strictly necessary in these works – though he rightly reinforces the bass-line with a clearly audible bassoon. And he omits second-time repeats in all but a few sonata movements, a small price to pay for an average of nearly four symphonies per disc. Brüggen's performances, though occasionally questionable, are the most individual in their shaping and characterization. The playing of the OAE is both brilliant and refined (it was criminal not to name the superlative horn players), and the recording is natural, detailed and atmospheric. If you're still undecided, this set – five well-filled discs for the price of four – offers a serious price advantage over the other contenders.

Symphonies Nos. 50, 54-57 and 60.
Academy of Ancient Music / Christopher Hogwood.
L'Oiseau-Lyre 443 781-2OH3 (three discs: 179 minutes: DDD). Ⓕ Ⓟ

All six symphonies on these discs date from 1773-74, when the intensity of Haydn's musical language during the preceding years was being tempered with a new urbanity and a deliberately calculated popular appeal. The older style is represented by the *Adagios* of Nos. 54 and 56, with their spacious lines and rarefied atmosphere. Typical of the newer, more 'accessible' manner is the obscurely nicknamed *Schoolmaster*, No. 55, with its droll, *faux-naïf* variation slow movement and its catchy finale, a deft and witty amalgam of variation, rondo and sonata forms. The little-known

No. 57 also aims frankly at popular effect in its theme-and-variation slow movement, its stomping *Ländler*-Minuet and its *Prestissimo* finale suggesting a riotous comic opera imbroglio. The spirit of *opera buffa*, in fact, permeates several movements here, including the opening *Presto* of No. 54, a symphony Hogwood opts to perform in its original version – that is, without the slow introduction and the enhanced scoring for flutes, trumpets and timpani. Two of the other symphonies, both in C major with high horns, trumpets and timpani, have overt theatrical connections: No. 50 probably started life as the introduction to *Der Götterrath*, the lost prologue to the marionette opera *Philemon und Baucis*, while the burlesque six-movement *Il distratto*, No. 60, originated as incidental music to a farce centring on an 'absent-minded' hero – hence the music's frequent air of distractedness and comic inconsequentiality. Hogwood is not a conductor to impose a strikingly individual stamp on the music, but, as ever, there are no affectations, no eccentricities. Hogwood has thought carefully about the precise character of each movement, chooses his tempos shrewdly and is always alive to felicitous details of wind colour or inner string writing. Abetted by marvellously lithe, incisive playing from the Academy of Ancient Music, he gives a viscerally exciting reading of No. 56, the finale dispatched with phenomenal panache at the fastest possible tempo. Here, and in Nos. 50 and 60, brass and timpani rasp and thunder to thrilling effect. The finale of No. 57 is likewise breathtaking, not only in its accuracy at high speed but also in its delicacy and point. Aided by notably sweet, refined string playing, the filigree writing in Nos. 54 and 57 is exquisitely realized. The recording is clean, immediate and well balanced.

Symphonies Nos. 45-47.
Tafelmusik / Bruno Weil.
Sony Classical Vivarte SK53986 (68 minutes: DDD). Recorded 1993.   Ⓕ Ⓟ

Symphonies Nos. 50, 64 and 65.
Tafelmusik / Bruno Weil.
Sony Classical Vivarte SK53985 (50 minutes: DDD). Recorded 1993.   Ⓕ Ⓟ

Whatever the numberings may suggest, the six symphonies on these discs cover a short chronological span, probably all composed in 1772-73. As H.C. Robbins Landon points out in his notes, No. 65, with its quirky, disjointed *Andante* and stomping, Brueghelian Minuet, may have originally been composed as incidental music. He also proposes a theatrical connection – probably less likely – with the enigmatically titled No. 64, an altogether more searching, introspective work, with strange, almost Schubertian harmonic deflexions in the opening movement and a *Largo* of rare gravity and eloquence. The performances by the Toronto-based period-instrument orchestra under Bruno Weil offer playing of verve, flair and finesse allied to vital, decisive characterization and enhanced by unusually close attention to the composer's markings. Weil eschews a harpsichord continuo. Captured in vivid, immediate sound, he has a strong feeling for long-range symphonic tensions, and conveys most consistently the reach and dramatic power of the sonata allegros, above all in his searing reading of the much-recorded *Farewell*.

Symphonies Nos. 82-84.
Tafelmusik / Bruno Weil.
Sony Classical Vivarte SK66295 (73 minutes: DDD). Recorded 1994.   Ⓕ Ⓟ ℞℞

Symphonies Nos. 85-87.
Tafelmusik / Bruno Weil.
Sony Classical Vivarte SK66296 (71 minutes: DDD). Recorded 1994.   Ⓕ Ⓟ

Written in 1785-86 for the ample forces of the Concert de la Loge Olympique, Haydn's *Paris* symphonies were his grandest and most imposing works in the form to date. Bruno Weil and his brilliant period orchestra bring to the *Paris* Symphonies the same flair and finesse that distinguished the previous discs in their ongoing complete cycle. The blazing, far-reaching opening movement of *L'ours*, No. 82, augurs well: an urgent, though never rushed, tempo, keen texturing – some details more tellingly etched than ever heard before on disc – and lithe, vital rhythms. In the *Allegretto*, Weil evokes the spirit of the corresponding movement of Beethoven's Eighth; and the finale, full of razor-sharp instrumental detailing, combines dancing grace with an exhilarating drive. Only in the Minuet does one have reservations: Weil's very purposeful tempo here does underestimate the element of *ancien régime* opulence in this music. In the opening movement of *La poule* Weil brings a real bite and trenchancy to the pervasive dotted rhythms and an exciting dramatic sweep to the development. The *Andante*, more flowingly paced than in the rival versions, is elegantly shaped, with long-breathed lyrical phrasing and beautifully poised woodwind playing. In the finale Weil drives rather fiercely. In the opening *Allegro* of No. 84 Weil phrases graciously and shapes the repeated-note bass lines with a strong sense of direction. The beautiful *Andante* is ideally paced and full of subtle, delicately placed detail.

On the second disc Weil and his players are aggressively brisk in the *Adagio* introduction of No. 85. But they shape the main theme of the *Vivace* alluringly and bring plenty of fire to the tuttis, pointing Haydn's nervous, syncopated inner parts and ramming home the *sforzando* offbeat accents. Again, the trio of the Minuet is short on wit and affection. But the finale is as spirited and gamesome as you could wish, and works up a fine lather in the central development; and there is lightness and elegant ease in the *Allegretto* variations. No. 86, the most imposing of the *Paris* Symphonies, seems less successful. The slow introduction is, again, uncomfortably brisk, while for all the eager athleticism of the playing the *Allegro spiritoso* rather lacks grandeur. In the *Capriccio* second movement Weil plays up Haydn's violent rhetorical outbursts; but at his controversially swift tempo the music's grave, majestic tread and intense, brooding harmonies go for comparatively little. The finale, on the other hand, combines ample symphonic breadth with terrific élan; and Weil brings a nice deadpan wit in the Rossini-ish second theme. No. 87 is vividly done and Weil scores both in his attention to detail and in his control of long-term tensions. In the *Adagio* he encourages warm, gracious phrasing, and shapes the violin sextuplets eloquently. These Sony discs come out marginally ahead of period rivals, and score decisively in their more transparent recorded sound.

Symphonies Nos. 90-92.
Orchestra of the Eighteenth Century / Frans Brüggen.
Philips 446 677-2PH (76 minutes: DDD). Recorded live in 1984-95.　　　　Ⓕ🅿

All three performances display Brüggen's familiar hallmarks in this repertoire: colourful textures, strong, resilient rhythms, thoughtful, detailed phrasing and a vivid feeling for the music's drama and glorious unpredictability. There are occasional slight reservations about Brüggen's idiosyncrasies, but these are small provisos to set against music-making of real imagination and panache. He creates a marvellous sense of quizzical expectancy in the introduction of the *Oxford*, for instance, and, at a cracking tempo, gives a thrilling account of the finale. In the *Andante* of No. 90 Brüggen phrases expressively, making much of the chromaticism in the second half of the theme and the poetic turn to D flat in the coda. In the corresponding movement of No. 91, he really lets rip in the raucous series of trills towards the end. The finale of this symphony is a touch fierce and driven, missing the mellow gaiety characteristic of Haydn in E flat. However, at a spacious tempo Brüggen captures both the lyrical grace and the taut symphonic drama of the opening movement and he gives a specially delightful reading of the trio, pointing the 'oompah' accompaniment and relishing the rude off-beat *sforzandos* from the horns. The recordings are very acceptable; the close recording in Nos. 91 and 92 catches a fair amount of animated sniffing and teeth-sucking from the conductor.

Symphonies Nos. 95, 97 and 101.
Philharmonia Orchestra / Leonard Slatkin.
RCA Victor Red Seal 09026 68426-2 (73 minutes: DDD). Recorded 1993-94.　　　　Ⓕ

This disc confirms Slatkin's credentials as an urbane and attentive Haydn interpreter. No. 95, the least favoured of the set, and No. 97 come off particularly well. With no hint of ponderousness, Slatkin brings an imposing breadth and weight to the first movement and Minuet of No. 95, while the brilliant contrapuntal sallies in the finale gain much from the division of the violins left and right. The aggressively extrovert *Vivace* that opens No. 97 has a fine snap and thrust to its rhythms, the mounting tensions of the development powerfully realized; and Slatkin clearly relishes the strut and swagger of the Minuet and the comic bravado of the finale. Here and elsewhere the playing of the Philharmonia is alert and refined, with delectable work from the woodwind. In the slow movements of both these symphonies Slatkin phrases warmly and graciously, bringing out the felicities of Haydn's part-writing. Purists, though, may raise an eyebrow at the romantic liberties he occasionally takes with tempo. The *Clock* is also enjoyable. However, abetted by a recording that gives a more incisive edge to brass and timpani, Davis and the Concertgebouw (below) bring a shade more élan and excitement to the faster movements. Slatkin again scores, notably in the first and second movements (the latter taken at a crisp, high-stepping *Andante*), by placing the violins on opposite sides. But if he yields to Davis in the *Clock*, there is little to choose between the two conductors in Nos. 95 and 97, where some may prefer Slatkin's rather more expansive, *espressivo* treatment of the slow movements. RCA's recordings combine clarity with ample body and presence.

Symphonies Nos. 93, 94, 97 and 99-101.
Concertgebouw Orchestra / Sir Colin Davis.
Philips Duo 442 614-2PM2 (two discs: ADD/DDD). Recorded 1975-81.　　　　Ⓜ🆁🆁

Symphonies Nos. 95, 96, 98 and 102-104.
Concertgebouw Orchestra / Sir Colin Davis.
Philips Duo 442 611-2PM2 (two discs: ADD/DDD). Recorded 1975-81.　　　　Ⓜ🆁🆁

A superb achievement all round – indeed, it's nigh-on impossible to imagine better 'big-band' Haydn than one encounters here on Sir Colin Davis's four exceedingly well-filled CDs. His direction has exemplary sparkle (try the superb opening movement of the *Miracle* Symphony) and sensitivity (witness his eloquent moulding of No. 98's great *Adagio*). Minuets are never allowed to plod, outer movements have an ideal combination of infectious zip and real poise, and the humour (a commodity, of course, that is never absent for too long in Haydn's music) is always conveyed with a genial twinkle in the eye. Quite marvellous, wonderfully unanimous playing from the great Amsterdam orchestra, too (the woodwind contributions are particularly distinguished), with never a trace of routine to betray the six-year recording span of this critically acclaimed project. The Philips engineering, whether analogue or digital, is of the very highest quality throughout, offering a totally natural perspective, gloriously full-bodied tone and consistently sparkling textures within the sumptuous Concertgebouw acoustic. Invest in this set: it will yield enormous rewards for many years to come.

Symphonies Nos. 103 and 104.
La Petite Bande / Sigiswald Kuijken.
Deutsche Harmonia Mundi 05472-77362-2 (57 minutes: DDD). Recorded 1995. Ⓕ Ⓟ

In the slow movements of these symphonies Kuijken is more gracious and reflective than his rivals, with affectionate touches of timing; and he leaves you in no doubt that the central *minore* section is the most awesome, physically powerful music in any eighteenth-century symphonic slow movement. Kuijken's grave, steady tread in the C minor-major theme and variations of No. 103 is also appealing, he brings a swaggering grandeur to the final C major variation and shapes with tenderness the quiet string phrases that usher in the coda – a sudden and magical change of atmosphere. In the minuets, conversely, Kuijken is appreciably faster than most, especially in No. 103, where at his headlong tempo the flicking 'Scotch snap' figures tend to be blurred. He is genial and gamesome in the opening *Allegro con spirito* of No. 103 and broad yet thrilling in the finale. No. 104 opens with a magnificently imposing, portentous introduction, and both the first *Allegro* and the finale are strong and spirited, the urgent drama of the developments powerfully limned. The recorded sound has an attractive spaciousness and bloom, if not total clarity: inner string parts are not always ideally defined and both horns and bassoons at times seem underbalanced. Kuijken's interpretations, vividly realized by his 35-strong orchestra (particularly delectable work from first flute and first oboe), can be recommended to anyone seeking these symphonies in period performances that do ample justice to the music's boldness and imaginative reach.

Otte Notturni, HobII/25-32.
Marten Root *fl* **Michael Niesemann** *ob* **Mozzafiato** (Charles Neidich, Ayako Oshima *cls* William Purvis, Stewart Rose *hns* Marji Danilow *db*) **L'Archibudelli** (Vera Beths, Lucy van Dael *vns* Jürgen Kussmaul, Guus Jeukendrup *vas* Anner Bylsma *vc*).
Sony Classical Vivarte SK62878 (77 minutes: DDD). Recorded 1996. Ⓕ Ⓟ

Between 1788 and 1790 Haydn was commissioned to write a set of *Notturni* for a curious and complex instrument, the *lira organizzata*, a kind of hurdy-gurdy with an inbuilt miniature organ. On the rare occasions when these works are aired today, the two *lire* parts are taken by flute and oboe, following Haydn's own practice in his London concerts. In six of the *notturni* the *lire* are complemented by clarinets, horns, violas, cello and double-bass, while in two (Hob Nos. 27 and 28) clarinets are replaced by violins. All of them are on a miniature scale, with, usually, three brief movements (fast-slow-fast). Haydn was incapable of turning out a dull piece: the *Notturni*, for all their brevity and lightness of touch, are beautifully crafted, often sophisticated in their harmony and motivic development and exquisitely scored, with kaleidoscopically varied colours that at times recall Mozart's wind serenades. Most of the finales are racy rondos, full of quick-fire instrumental interplay; an exception is that of No. 29, one of Haydn's ingenious amalgams of fugue and sonata form. Slow movements are often pastoral in feeling, with touches of sensuous chromaticism; one or two, though, touch a deeper vein, above all the brooding, darkly coloured *Adagio* of No. 27, probably reflecting Haydn's increasing melancholy and loneliness in his final year at Esterháza in 1790. This *Adagio* is taken very flowingly here. The players' technical finesse is matched by their pointed, shapely phrasing, their care for blend and dovetailing and their palpable delight in Haydn's witty raillery. Here and there the horns could have brayed out more rudely; but otherwise balance is excellent, and the recorded sound vivid and immediate.

Divertimentos – G major, HobII/1; D major, HobII/D22 Add; G major, HobII/9.
Vienna Haydn Sinfonietta / Manfred Huss.
Koch Schwann 312862 (57 minutes: DDD). Recorded 1994. Ⓕ Ⓟ

This programme exemplifies Haydn's exploitation of the orchestra's instrumentalists most impressively. Thus, in this set of *Divertimentos*, Manfred Huss appropriately takes every opportunity to highlight the Vienna Haydn Sinfonietta's excellent soloist and ensemble skills in performances of abounding vitality. The period-instrument sound – emphasized by a full, bright recording – does have the occasional rough edge, but this only adds power and piquancy to these compelling accounts. Huss and his team vividly bring out the striking baroque colours in the G major *Divertimento* (HobII/1), conveying the music's startling array of expressive moods with elegant phrasing in the slow movements, and further underlining the score's rich stylistic diversity in the theme and variations of the finale. In the D major *Divertimento*, on the other hand, Huss deftly balances bravura horn writing and strings to reveal the full sparkle and textural variety of this engagingly robust piece. Listen to the enchanting discourse between the horns in the slow movement, or the dazzling virtuosity from everyone in the finale. Until recently, the unfortunate state of the sources for the G major *Divertimento* (HobII/9) had made modern performances impossible. However, with the discovery of new material, Huss and the Haydn Sinfonietta here display the work's infectious vivacity with exquisite playing all round, thus restoring this splendid music to the repertory. Serene poise in the slow movement evocatively contrasts *cantabile* melody and pizzicato accompaniment, and the piece culminates in a finale of arresting vigour.

Cassation in F major, HobII/20. Divertissement in B flat major, HobII/B4. Flute Quartet in A major, HobII/A4. Notturno No. 1 in C major, HobII/25.
Linos Ensemble.
Capriccio 10 719 (68 minutes: DDD). Recorded 1994.   Ⓕ

The Linos Ensemble's highly polished, enthusiastic performances generate a compelling immediacy that is hard to resist. Moreover, the attractively diverse choice of pieces provides plenty of opportunity to demonstrate both the excellent soloistic skills of Linos's members and its deftly balanced ensemble, while suitably close recording throughout presents this group's eloquence and fresh vitality in fine, clear detail. The delightful, open-air qualities of this repertoire are exemplified by the F major *Cassation*, whose amiable good humour is captured with buoyant, cheerful vigour in the opening *Allegro*; with stately elegance in the two minuets, affecting melodiousness in the *Adagio*, and an engaging swing in the final rondo. The extrovert B flat *Divertissement* offers a charming display of fluent, conversational playing, a style which the Linos exploits to particular effect in the lively alternation of different instrumental groupings in the elegant A major Quartet for flute and strings. Ultimately, the infectiously high-spirited, effervescent exchanges between flute and oboe in the witty C major *Notturno* (originally for *lira organizzata*) sum up the allure of this entertaining issue.

String Quartets: Op. 1 – No. 1 in B flat major, 'La chasse'; **No. 2** in E flat major; **No. 3** in D major; **No. 4** in G major; **No. 5** in E flat major; **No. 6** in C major. **Op. 9 – No. 1** in C major; **No. 2** in E flat major; **No. 3** in G major; **No. 4** in D minor; **No. 5** in B flat major; **No. 6** in A major. **Op. 20, 'Sun' – No. 1** in E flat major; **No. 2** in C major; **No. 3** in G minor; **No. 4** in D major; **No. 5** in F minor; **No. 6** in A major. **Op. 33 – No. 1** in B minor; **No. 2** in E flat major, 'Joke'; **No. 3** in C major, 'Bird'; **No. 4** in B flat major; **No. 5** in G major; **No. 6** in D major. **Op. 42** in D major. **Op. 50 – No. 1** in B flat major; **No. 2** in C major; **No. 3** in E flat major; **No. 4** in F sharp minor; **No. 5** in F major, 'The Dream'; **No. 6** in D major, 'Frog'. **Op. 54 – No. 1** in G major; **No. 2** in C major; **No. 3** in E major. **Op. 55 – No. 1** in A major; **No. 2** in F minor; **No. 3** in B flat major. **Op. 64 – No. 1** in C major; **No. 2** in B minor; **No. 3** in B flat major; **No. 4** in G major; **No. 5** in D major, 'The Lark'; **No. 6** in E flat major. **Op. 71** – No. 1 in B flat major; **No. 2** in D major; **No. 3** in E flat major. **Op. 74 – No. 1** in C major; **No. 2** in F major; **No. 3** in G minor, 'Rider'. **Op. 76 – No. 2** in D minor, 'Fifths'; **No. 3** in C major, 'Emperor'; **No. 4** in B flat major, 'Sunrise'. **Op. 77 – No. 1** in G major; **No. 2** in F major.

String Quartets: Op. 1 No. 1. Op. 20 Nos. 2 and 5. Op. 50 No. 3. Op. 54 Nos. 1-3. Op. 64 Nos. 3 and 4. Op. 74 No. 3. Op. 76 Nos. 3 and 4. Op. 77 No. 2.
Pro Arte Quartet (Alphonse Onnou, Laurent Halleux *vns* Germain Prévost *va* Robert Maas *vc*).
Testament mono SBT3055 (three discs: 229 minutes: ADD). Recorded 1931-38.   ⒻⒽ

String Quartets: Op. 1 No. 6. Op. 20 Nos. 1 and 4. Op. 33 Nos. 2, 3 and 6. Op. 50 No. 6. Op. 55 Nos. 1 and 3. Op. 64 No. 6. Op. 71 No. 1. Op. 74 Nos. 1 and 2. Op. 77 No. 1.
Hoffstetter String Quartets, Op. 3 – No. 4 in B flat major; No. 5 in F major.
Pro Arte Quartet (Alphonse Onnou, Laurent Halleux *vns* Germain Prévost *va* Robert Maas *vc*).
Testament mono SBT4056 (four discs: 243 minutes: ADD). Recorded 1931-38.   ⒻⒽ

The Pro Arte Quartet's first London appearance in 1925 prompted *The Times* to declare, 'One has never heard it surpassed, and rarely equalled, in volume and beauty of tone, in accuracy of intonation and in perfection of balance between the parts' – and that could well be the verdict on these sets. The musicians' tempos invariably seem just right and their phrasing has an inner life that is extraordinarily potent. Alphonse Onnou and Laurent Halleux were superbly matched, and Halleux often led in their early days. Such virtuosity as the quartet exhibits is effortless and totally lacking in ostentation. Of course, the actual sound is dated – the string tone is wanting in bloom and freshness, particularly in some of the earlier recordings – but the ear soon adjusts, though one might wish that these transfers could have given us a little more space between movements.

String Quartets, Op. 1 Nos. 1-6.
Petersen Quartet (Conrad Muck, Gernot Sussmuth *vns* Friedemann Weigle *va*
Hans-Jakob Eschenburg *vc*).
Capriccio 10 786/7 (two discs: 99 minutes: DDD). Recorded 1995-96.　　　　　　　　Ⓕ

The history of the string quartet in effect began with these cheerful, compact *Divertimenti a quattro*, as the composer titled them; and though they contain only spasmodic hints of future glories, their freshness and exuberance make for highly pleasurable listening. All are in five movements, with two contrasted Minuets placed second and fourth, the former a leisurely *Minuetto galante*, the latter brisker and earthier, with the *sansculotte* two-part writing and octave doublings found in Haydn's later minuets right through to the Op. 76 Quartets. As in the early piano sonatas, the trios usually turn to the comic minor, often with striking effect – for example in the violins' canonic imitations in the fourth movement of No. 4, or the eloquent chromaticism in the second movement of No. 5. The slow movements are all accompanied arias for the first violin, often touching in their innocence and candour, while the ebullient *Presto* outer movements delight in quirkily irregular phrase-lengths, quick-fire repartee and sudden contrasts of texture and register – the kind of music that led po-faced North German critics to accuse Haydn of debasing the art with 'comic fooling'. The Petersen Quartet responds vividly to the music's youthful verve, with polished ensemble, keen attack and a wide spectrum of colour and dynamics. Purists may raise an eyebrow at the special effects the players deploy in repeats, especially in minuets – added touches of imitation, pizzicato and even *col legno*, a technique Haydn asks for once in a symphony (No. 67) but never in the quartets. But the young Haydn, famed for his mischievous humour, may well have enjoyed these liberties. No complaints about the recording, which combines clarity with an attractive church resonance.

String Quartets, Op. 9 Nos. 1, 3 and 4.
Kodály Quartet (Attila Falváy, Tamás Szabó *vns* Gábor Fias *va* János Devich *vc*).
Naxos 8 550786 (52 minutes: DDD). Recorded 1993.　　　　　　　　　　　　　　Ⓢ

String Quartets, Op. 9 Nos. 2, 5 and 6.
Kodály Quartet (Attila Falváy, Tamás Szabó *vns* Gábor Fias *va* János Devich *vc*).
Naxos 8 550787 (58 minutes: DDD). Recorded 1993.　　　　　　　　　　　　　　Ⓢ

Overshadowed by four dozen later masterpieces, Haydn's Op. 9 has usually received short shrift from both players and commentators. Least neglected of the set is the D minor, No. 4, described by Hans Keller as 'the first great string quartet in the history of music'. The minor mode at this period (1769-70) invariably drew something special from Haydn, and this work stands apart from the others for its intensity of expression, its mastery of texture and development and the sheer character of its ideas. The opening *Allegro moderato* could well have been at the back of Mozart's mind when he came to write his own great D minor Quartet, K421. Of Nos. 1-5 it is true that there are *longueurs*, nowhere more so than in the stiff, gawky opening movements of Nos. 1-3, and the routine set of variations that opens No. 5. But there are compensations elsewhere: in the terse, resourceful and (especially in No. 3) witty finales; in the varied minuets, ranging from the high-stepping No. 5, with its alfresco octave doublings, to the suave, chromatically subtle No. 2; and in several of the slow movements. The Kodály Quartet is, as ever, a sympathetic Haydn exponent, impressing with its slightly old-fashioned warmth of sonority, the natural musicality of its phrasing and its care for blend, balance and intonation, though the boomy church acoustic hardly helps.

String Quartets, Op. 20 Nos. 1-6.
Quatuor Mosaïques (Erich Höbarth, Andrea Bischof *vns* Anita Mitterer *va* Christophe Coin *vc*).
Auvidis Astrée E8784 (two discs: 147 minutes: DDD). Recorded 1990.
Gramophone Award Winner 1993.　　　　　　　　　　　　　　Ⓕ🅿Ⓔ🆁🆁
Also available separately: E8785 – Nos. 1, 5 and 6. E8786 – Nos. 2-4.

The Op. 20 String Quartets date from the composer's so-called *Sturm und Drang* period, though Haydn's increasingly frequent use of the more dramatic and 'serious' minor mode in these pieces can perhaps be attributed just as much to the fruitful influence of the three operatic projects he had been working on just a few years previously between 1766 and 1769. Moreover, these quartets also reveal a greater preoccupation with counterpoint than any of his music to that date, and the great fugal finales of Nos. 2, 5 and 6 clearly herald the arrival of the consummate craftsman so overwhelmingly displayed in the mature quartets to come. Incidentally, the Op. 20 set's nickname *Sun* derives from the illustration on the handsome title-page of the Hummel edition of this music, at the top of which peers out the sun-god's head. These wonderfully flexible performances display an altogether breathtaking refinement, sensitivity and illumination. Indeed, in terms of expressive subtlety, imaginative intensity and sheer depth of feeling, the Mosaïques' achievement in these marvellous works is unmatched.

String Quartets, Op. 20 Nos. 1, 3 and 4.
The Lindsays (Peter Cropper, Ronald Birks *vns* Robin Ireland *va* Bernard Gregor-Smith *vc*).
ASV CDDCA1027 (79 minutes: DDD). Recorded 1997.　　　　　　　　　　　　　　Ⓕ🅴

The Lindsays are Haydn interpreters of rare understanding and communicative flair. Their characterization is bold and decisive, enhanced by a scrupulous observation of the composer's expression and dynamic markings. Faster movements tend to be more urgent, less ruminative, than those from the Quatuor Mosaïques. The *zingarese* cross-rhythms of No. 4's Minuet have an abrasive edge, and the *Presto e scherzando* finale is no mere frolic in The Lindsays' hands – its wit can scathe and sting, and the closing theme, with its gipsy *acciaccaturas*, has an almost manic insistence. Elsewhere The Lindsays bring an ideal warmth and lyricism to the opening movement of No. 1, characteristically phrasing in long, eloquent spans, and a quixotic energy to the outer movements of the G minor, No. 3, where the Quatuor Mosaïques is broader and tougher. In the Minuet of No. 3 The Lindsays' singing line and flexibility of pulse realize to the full Haydn's searching harmonic progressions; and the lulling E flat Trio is exquisitely floated, with the players venturing an even more hushed, absorbed tone colour on the repeat. Each of the slow movements reveals dedication and profound identification. The players vindicate their dangerously slow tempo in the sublime *Affettuoso e sostenuto* of No. 1 with the breadth and intensity of their phrasing, their subtlety of colour and their feeling for harmonic flux. Conversely, the slow movements of No. 3 and, especially, No. 4 are more flowing than with the Quatuor Mosaïques yet no less moving. As ever, the occasional moment of impure intonation and marginally imprecise ensemble is a small price to pay for performances of such colour, character and spontaneity. The Lindsays observe all the important marked repeats and the recording is vivid and truthful, though the close balance picks up a fair bit of sniffing.

String Quartets: Op. 33 – No. 1 in B minor; No. 2 in E flat major, 'Joke'; No. 3 in C major, 'Bird'; No. 4 in B flat major; No. 5 in G major; No. 6 in D major.

String Quartets, Op. 33 Nos. 1, 2 and 4.
The Lindsays (Peter Cropper, Ronald Birks *vns* Robin Ireland *va* Bernard Gregor-Smith *vc*).
ASV CDDCA937 (62 minutes: DDD). Recorded 1994.　　　　　　　　　　　　　　Ⓕ🅴

The Lindsays' is chamber-music-making of unusual re-creative flair, untouched by the faintest hint of routine. In their uncommonly grave, inward readings of the slow movements of the E flat and B flat Quartets they sustain a daringly slow tempo magnificently, phrasing in long, arching spans, always acutely sensitive to harmonic movement, as in their subtle colouring of Haydn's breathtaking tonal excursions in No. 4. Beethoven is evoked in The Lindsays' swift, mordant reading of No. 1's epigrammatic *Scherzo*: rarely have the waspish part-writing and the abrupt, disconcerting contrasts in dynamics and articulation been so vividly realized. Typically, it makes the most of the complete change of mood and texture in the major-key Trio, finding an almost Viennese sweetness of tone and phrase, complete with touches of *portamento*. The finale, fast, fierce, utterly uncomical, has a distinct whiff of the Hungarian *puszta* here, both in the wild gipsy figuration from 0'10" and the mounting passion of the sequence in the development. The Lindsays bring an ideal spaciousness and flexibility to the urbane, quietly spoken first movement of the E flat Quartet, No. 2, taking due note of Haydn's *cantabile* marking. In the finales of this Quartet and No. 4 they enter fully into the music's spirit with vital, inventively varied phrasing, palpably relishing Haydn's exuberance and comic sleight of hand. Here, as occasionally elsewhere, it's easy to overlook the odd moment of rhythmic unsteadiness or impure intonation for the sake of such involved and characterful music-making.

String Quartets, Op. 33 Nos. 1, 4 and 6.
Quatuor Mosaïques (Erich Höbarth, Andrea Bischof *vns* Anita Mitterer *va* Christophe Coin *vc*).
Auvidis Astrée E8570 (60 minutes: DDD). Recorded 1996.　　　　　　　　　　　Ⓕ🅿

From the teasingly timed initial upbeat of the D major Quartet, No. 6, the Quatuor Mosaïques' performances have all the familiar hallmarks: inventive phrasing, subtly varied colour, a sure sense of organic growth and a spontaneous-sounding delight in Haydn's inspired unpredictability. Tempo and manner in the opening *Vivace assai* of No. 6 are, typically, gentler than that of the equally imaginative Lindsays, the articulation lighter and more delicate, as you would expect from period strings. It catches ideally the music's glancing *scherzando* spirit, with a delightfully eager, quick-witted give-and-take between the instruments. Like The Lindsays, the Mosaïques vividly plays up the contrast between the perky, high-stepping D major theme and alternating D minor melody. But, characteristically, the Mosaïques flexes the tempo more freely and plays with the length of Haydn's upbeats, to witty or pathetic effect. In the *Andante* of the B minor Quartet the Mosaïques arguably overdoes the whimsical hesitations. However, its unusually reflective way with this movement, and the sense of remoteness it brings to the strange, spare second theme, the tone blanched, the octave doublings perfectly in tune, is very appealing. As for the undervalued B flat Quartet, it is a delight throughout, from the puckish opening movement, with its quasi-improvisatory freedom (The Lindsays are fiercer and more brittle here) to the comic exuberance of the finale; the vitality and point of the inner voices' semiquavers in the finale's G minor episode are typical of the character the Mosaïques brings to seemingly routine accompanying figuration throughout these performances. In sum, this disc represents yet another winner from this period-instrument quartet. The recording has an attractive ambient warmth.

String Quartets, Op. 33 Nos. 2, 3 and 5.
Quatuor Mosaïques (Erich Höbarth, Andrea Bischof *vns* Anita Mitterer *va* Christophe Coin *vc*). Auvidis Astrée E8569 (61 minutes: DDD). Recorded 1995.
Gramophone Award Winner 1996. ⓔⓟⒺ

The Mosaïques, at a rather slower tempo than usual, find in the theme-and-variation finale of the G major Quartet, No. 5, an unsuspected reflective tenderness. The theme itself is played with a characteristic touch of flexibility and a gentle lift to the dotted rhythms; in the first variation Erich Höbarth shapes his decorative semiquavers *fioriture* with apparently spontaneous fantasy; the luminous, high-lying textures of the second are exquisitely realized; and even the *Presto* send-off has a delicacy and whimsy in keeping with what has gone before. The Mosaïques' readings of the slow movements in the so-called *Joke* (No. 2) and *Bird* (No. 3) Quartets are again outstanding in their grave tenderness, their sensitivity to harmonic flux and the improvisatory freedom Erich Höbarth brings to his ornamental figuration. The *Bird*, in particular, receives as searching a performance as ever heard: in the first movement the players steal in almost imperceptibly, respond vividly to the music's richness and wit, and bring a spectral *pianissimo* to the mysterious lull in the development. The Slavonic finale, one of several movements to benefit from the lighter, more flexible period bows, goes with terrific fire and panache. In the opening *Allegro* of the *Joke* they take to heart Haydn's *moderato e cantabile* qualification, phrasing fluidly and expansively, with a vital and delicate interplay between the voices. The finale, like that of No. 5, is unusually graceful, with the notorious ending deliciously managed. In sum, this truthfully recorded disc has playing that marries uncommon style, technical finesse (tuning, blend and balance suffering little by comparison with the finest modern-instrument quartets) and re-creative flair.

String Quartets, Op. 33 Nos. 3, 5 and 6.
The Lindsays (Peter Cropper, Ronald Birks *vns* Robin Ireland *va* Bernard Gregor-Smith *vc*). ASV CDDCA938 (61 minutes: DDD). Recorded 1995. Ⓕ

The Lindsays eclipse all-comers in range of colour, vital, creative phrasing and emotional penetration. They respond gleefully to the subversive comedy that pervades each of the three works – most overtly in the Slavonic-influenced finale of *The Bird* (No. 3), and in the outrageous *Scherzo* of No. 5, where with explosive *sforzandos* and sly touches of timing it relishes to the full Haydn's rhythmic and dynamic mayhem. But time and again in this music wit is suddenly suffused with poetry; and The Lindsays bring a glancing delicacy and grace of interplay to, say, the startling tonal deflexions in the opening *Vivace assai* of No. 6. With The Lindsays' slower-than-usual tempo and wonderfully tender, contained *sotto voce*, the second movement of No. 3, where Haydn transmutes the Minuet-scherzo into a hymn, becomes the expressive core of the quartet. The variation finales of Nos. 5 and 6 can easily seem anticlimactic. Here, though, the players' rhythmic point and inventively varied phrasing and dynamics (repeats are never mere repetitions) make the music consistently compelling. The Lindsays play from the Henle Urtext edition, which corrects tempo markings and numerous details of phrasing in the unreliable Peters and Eulenburg editions; and it observes both repeats in sonata movements – particularly important in the first movement of *The Bird*, where the four-bar lead-back to the development adds yet another point of harmonic subtlety. The Lindsays constantly provoke you to respond afresh to Haydn; to his wit and comic exuberance, his inexhaustible inventiveness and his often unsuspected profundity.

Haydn String Quartet, Op. 42.
Schumann String Quartet No. 3 in A major, Op. 41 No. 3.
Shostakovich String Quartet No. 3 in F major, Op. 73.
Allegri Quartet (Peter Carter, David Roth *vns* Jonathan Barritt *va* Bruno Schrecker *vc*).
Naim Audio NAIMCD016 (73 minutes: DDD). Recorded 1996.   Ⓕ

The beauty of these readings is that they mean what they say. There is no hint of any
over-earnestness and the programme has been very carefully chosen. Haydn's exquisite Op. 42 is
given an especially winning rendition, the *Andante ed innocentemente* first movement donning a
degree of understatement that reflects its equivocal personality. Following Haydn's Op. 42 with
Shostakovich's Op. 73 was an inspired idea: the former ends quietly and the latter opens with a sort
of distracted innocence, marking time before the real drama starts. The argument suddenly
intensifies, playfully, provocatively, though characterization is cleverly differentiated. In the second
movement, Prokofiev is an obvious point of reference and there has rarely been a more delicately
pointed account of the weird, tiptoe *staccato* passage that emerges out of the first idea. The third
movement is a striking precursor of the Tenth Symphony's violent 'Stalin' *Scherzo*, the slow
movement redolent of the Twelfth Symphony's noble opening and the long finale ending in a mood
of veiled mystery. Above all, this is profoundly natural playing and the recordings maintain a
realistic 'small concert-hall' ambience throughout. The disc ends with an affectionate, flexible
performance of Schumann's loveliest string quartet. The opening *Andante espressivo* sets the mood
while the ensuing second set (1'19") is limpid and rapturous, and the finale – which in some hands
can seem repetitive – is given precisely the right degree of rhythmic emphasis. Again one senses
wholehearted identification between the repertoire and its interpreters – and while one may question
the wisdom of mixed-repertory CD programmes, this one is so well planned and well played, that it
can be recommended even to those readers who already own recordings within cycles.

String Quartets, Op. 54 Nos. 1-3.
The Lindsays (Peter Cropper, Ronald Birks *vns* Robin Ireland *va* Bernard Gregor-Smith *vc*).
ASV CDDCA582 (66 minutes: DDD).   Ⓕ

All three quartets are in the usual four-movement form but with many surprises: in No. 1, the false
recapitulation in the first movement, the dark modulations in the following sonata-form *Allegretto*
and the Hungarian gipsy flavour (anticipated in the Minuet) and mischievousness of the final
rondo. No. 2 has a rhapsodic fiddler in its second movement, a nostalgic minuet with an
extraordinarily anguished trio, and an *Adagio* finale in which a *Presto* section turns out to be no
more than an episode. A notable feature of No. 3 is its ternary-form *Largo cantabile*, the centre of
which is more like a mini-concerto for the first violin; 'Scotch snaps' pervade the Minuet, and pedal
points the finale. The performances (and the recording) are superb, marked by unanimity, fine tone,
suppleness of phrasing, and acute dynamic shaping; in the second movement of No. 1 there are
hushed passages whose homogeneity and quality of sound are quite remarkable. This recording is
irresistible.

String Quartets, Op. 55 Nos. 1-3.
The Lindsays (Peter Cropper, Ronald Birks *vns* Robin Ireland *va* Bernard Gregor-Smith *vc*).
ASV CDDCA906 (64 minutes: DDD). Recorded 1994.   Ⓕ🅴

Most immediately striking of the trilogy is the F minor work, No. 2, with its searching double
variations on related minor and major themes (a favourite form in Haydn's later music), spiky,
rebarbative second movement *Allegro* and strangely spare contrapuntal Minuet. The A major,
No. 1, has much of this key's traditional brilliance, with ample scope for the leader's creative
virtuosity in the outer movements and the stratospheric trio of the minuet; in contrast the noble,
wonderfully scored *Adagio cantabile* prefigures the profound slow movements of Haydn's final
years. The more inward-looking No. 3 in B flat is specially remarkable for the varied recapitulations
in the flanking movements, astonishingly free and inventive even for Haydn, and the subtle
chromatic colouring in all four movements which may just owe something to the quartets Mozart
had dedicated to Haydn three years earlier. Here and there The Lindsays' intonation is less than
true, especially from the leader, but as so often with this group, this is a small price to pay for
performances of such colour and penetration. The balance, as with many recent quartet recordings,
is a shade closer than ideal but the overall sound picture is very acceptable.

String Quartets, Op. 64 Nos. 1-3.
Kodály Quartet (Attila Falvay, Tamás Szabo *vns* Gábor Fias *va* János Devich *vc*).
Naxos 8 550673 (64 minutes: DDD). Recorded 1992.   Ⓢ🅴🆁🆁

String Quartets, Op. 64 Nos. 4-6.
Kodály Quartet (Attila Falvay, Tamás Szabo *vns* Gábor Fias *va* János Devich *vc*).
Naxos 8 550674 (65 minutes: DDD). Recorded 1992.　　　　　　　Ⓢ**E**　**RR**

The so-called *Lark* (No. 5), with its soaring opening melody and *moto perpetuo* finale, is perhaps the most immediately fetching of all Haydn's quartets. But No. 6 is at least as fine, with its intimate and intensely argued opening movement, its poignant, exquisitely textured *Andante* and a finale full of instrumental fooling and insouciant contrapuntal virtuosity. Of the other works, No. 2 is one of Haydn's most astringent pieces, from its tonally deceptive opening to the mordant, unsettling humour of the finale. Quartets Nos. 3 and 4 return to a more familiar vein of sociable wit. Both are endlessly subtle and surprising in their arguments, with *cantabile* slow movements of peculiar candour and eloquence. Quartet No. 1, the least favoured of the six is certainly the plainest in its thematic ideas. But it is an absorbing, immensely sophisticated piece, exploring an astonishing range of textures; the recapitulation of the leisurely first movement opens up marvellous new harmonic vistas, while the central development of the finale is a canonic *tour de force*. The Kodály Quartet has rightly won plaudits for its wonderfully civilized playing; mellow and lyrical, far removed from the highly-strung brilliance cultivated by many modern quartets. Ensemble and intonation are first-class, tempos generally spacious, with broad, natural and beautifully matched phrasing. It is at its very finest where Haydn is at his most searching; and the Quartets Nos. 2, 5 and 6 each receive outstanding, deeply considered performances. In one or two movements the Kodály's penchant for slowish tempos leads to a slight dourness. Against that, it brings a deliciously lazy *Ländler* lilt, enhanced by the first violin's *portamentos*, to the Trio of No. 6, and a grave, inward intensity to each of Haydn's slow movements. The recording, made in a Budapest church, is resonant and less intimate than is ideal in this music.

Op. 64 – No. 1 in C major; No. 2 in B minor; No. 3 in B flat major; No. 4 in G major; No. 5 in D major, 'The Lark'; No. 6 in E flat major.

String Quartets, Op. 64 Nos. 1-3.
Salomon Quartet (Simon Standage, Micaela Comberti *vns* Trevor Jones *va*
Jennifer Ward Clarke *vc*).
Hyperion CDA67011 (69 minutes: DDD). Recorded 1995.　　　　　　Ⓕ**P**

String Quartets, Op. 64 Nos. 4-6.
Salomon Quartet (Simon Standage, Micaela Comberti *vns* Trevor Jones *va*
Jennifer Ward Clarke *vc*).
Hyperion CDA67012 (60 minutes: DDD). Recorded 1995.　　　　　　Ⓕ**P**

These are predictably stylish, clean-limbed readings of the quartets Haydn composed in his final months at Eszterházy, just before his first visit to London. As Peter Holman points out in his informative note, the Op. 64 works are generally less demonstrative, less 'public' in tone than the quartets that precede and follow them. The Salomon brings to them an aptly relaxed, intimate manner, with the familiar hallmarks of lucid textures, vital phrasing and a natural feeling for the music's conversational interplay. Tempos in the outer movements tend to be quite spacious, allowing the Salomon ample room for manoeuvre. They are particularly enjoyable in No. 5, where Simon Standage shows an inventive variety of inflexion in the first movement's *Lark* theme – there's a beautiful sense of lyrical repose, for instance, when the theme appears for the only time in a full *legato* texture near the start of the development; and the unhurried tempo in the finale allows for much more meaningful phrasing than in the slick, virtuoso performances one often hears – again, the players' light, airy articulation is a delight here. The Salomon's observant, sympathetic readings, beautifully recorded, make a highly persuasive case for all these works.

String Quartets, Op. 71 Nos. 1-3.
Kodály Quartet (Attila Falvay, Tamás Szabo *vns* Gábor Fias *va* János Devich *vc*).
Naxos 8 550394 (62 minutes: DDD). Recorded 1989.　　　　　　　　Ⓢ

String Quartets, Op. 74 Nos. 1-3.
Kodály Quartet (Attila Falvay, Tamás Szabo *vns* Gábor Fias *va* János Devich *vc*).
Naxos 8 550396 (63 minutes: DDD). Recorded 1989.　　　　　　　　Ⓢ

The Kodály Quartet plays with self-evident joy in the music and an easy neatness of ensemble. There is never a hint of routine and the intercommunication is matched by enormous care for detail and clean ensemble. In short it plays as one, and projects this wonderful music with enormous dedication. Just sample the elegant *Andante* with variations which form the slow movement of Op. 71 No. 3, or the witty Minuet which follows, or any of the consistently inspired Op. 74 set. The hushed intensity of playing in the *Largo assai* of Op. 74 No. 3 is unforgettable. The recordings are wholly natural and balanced within a well-judged acoustic; the sound is of the highest quality and documentation is excellent. At their modest price this pair of CDs is irresistible.

String Quartets, Op. 76 Nos. 1-6.
Tátrai Quartet (Vilmos Tátrai, Mihály Szücs *vns* György Konrád *va* Ede Banda *vc*).
Hungaroton HCD12812/3-2 (two discs: 128 minutes: ADD). Recorded 1964-65. Ⓕ 🄷 🆁🆁

Your immediate reaction to this receiving our top recommendation may be, for heaven's sake, why not a modern recording in stereo? Not until you have played them will you know the answer. The performances are breathtaking – for each player's individual sensitivity and brilliance, for their intimately interwoven ensemble and, most of all, for their revelatory characterization. Even the recording itself is remarkable for its age. When writing these six works in his mid-sixties (his last essays in the quartet genre but for two) Haydn was at the very peak of his powers. You will be totally bowled over as much by their unfailingly unpredictable ingenuity of craftsmanship as by their startling range and variety of experience – extending from Croatian merrymaking on the village green to visionary regions scarcely explored more searchingly and personally by Beethoven. It would be difficult to remain unstirred by such music. The Tátrai's musical response is very immediate. This finds outlet in readiness to risk fast tempos for livelier movements (always with a touch of virtuoso brilliance when required) as well as great intensity in slow movements – not least as exemplified in the unforgettable revelations of the last three. Pungency of accentuation and clarity of articulation also contribute to its youthful vividness of characterization, as does, even more, its wide range of dynamics (with some real *pianissimo*) and colour – so arrestingly demonstrated in the dramatic opening movement of No. 2. Though the sound quality may not compare with the best on offer today, its clarity is admirable: microphones seem less close than on many modern recordings, permitting everything to emerge in better perspective. But in the final resort it's Haydn's genius that overwhelms you, and just as Haydn's own imagination seems progressively to take wing in the course of the six works, so does the players' own commitment.

String Quartets, Op. 76 Nos. 2-4.
Alban Berg Quartet (Günter Pichler, Gerhard Schulz *vns* Thomas Kakuska *va* Valentin Erben *vc*).
EMI CDC5 56166-2 (66 minutes: DDD). Recorded 1993-94. Ⓕ

This disc is uncommonly fine, above all the performance of the D minor, No. 2. The Berg takes both outer movements more spaciously than most of its rivals. The opening *Allegro* is tough and austere, the players thinking and phrasing, as ever, in long spans, bringing an urgent sweep to the development and a true sense of climax to the coda, where the lower instruments' syncopated cross-rhythms scythe through the texture. And with its broader tempo the Berg realizes tellingly details like the repeated hairpin *crescendos* on the sequence of tied notes in the second group. In the Berg's hands the Hungarian-tinged finale has great trenchancy and symphonic weight, with an imaginative variety of colour and accent. The *Emperor* and the *Sunrise* are hardly less fine, marrying an impressive formal control with a vivid sense of character and felicity of detail: listen, for instance, to the subtle timing and hushed, veiled tone at the sudden dip to E flat in the first movement of No. 3; the rapt tenderness and breadth of phrase in the sublime *Adagio* of the *Sunrise*, the melody unfolding in a single unbroken span; or the deft management of the progressive speed increases in the finale of the same work. The leader's very fluid, ruminative phrasing in the Quartet's opening (from which it gets its nickname) makes it seem even more than usual like a slow introduction, with the first phrase stealing in magically from nowhere. At its best, and especially in No. 2, the Berg brings a rare imaginative insight to this ever-astonishing, inexhaustible music. EMI's recording, despite a slight bias towards the first violin, is clear and sympathetic.

String Quartets – Op. 77 Nos. 1 and 2; Op. 103 in D minor (unfinished).
Quatuor Mosaïques (Erich Höbarth, Andrea Bischof *vns* Anita Mitterer *va* Christophe Coin *vc*).
Auvidis Astrée E8799 (62 minutes: DDD). Ⓕ 🄿

Anyone who thinks that period-instrument performance means austerity and coolness should listen to this disc. Here is playing full of expressive warmth and vigour. The opening of Op. 77 No. 1 is done duly gracefully, but with a sturdy underlying rhythm and the *Scherzo* is as crisp and alive as one could ask for. Then the first movement of the F major work is very beautifully done, with many sensitive details; and the lovely second movement is ideally leisurely, so that the players have ample room for manoeuvre and the leader makes much of his opportunities for delicate playing in the filigree-like high music. The players show a real grasp of the structure and they know when to illuminate the key moments, with a touch of extra deliberation or a little additional weight of tone. These performances, clearly recorded, are competitive ones not merely within the protected world of 'early music' but in the bigger, 'real' world too!

Seven Last Words, Op. 51.
The Lindsays (Peter Cropper, Ronald Birks *vns* Robin Ireland *va* Bernard Gregor-Smith *vc*).
ASV CDDCA853 (71 minutes: DDD).   Ⓕ

This performance by The Lindsays is magical. There are few groups who could sustain these seven slow movements, each lasting about ten minutes, and yet give them such variety of intensity, colour and mood. Haydn revealed himself as a visionary composer in the way he set about creating these seven miniature tone-poems for string quartet. The work is divided into nine sections comprising the seven slow movements each describing one of the final utterances of Christ on the Cross together with a slow introduction and a final *Presto con tutta la forza* which depicts the earthquake which occurred when 'the veil of the temple was rent in twain'. Some people may not find it a disc to be listened to from beginning to end; they may need substantial breaks between one movement and the next.

Piano Trios: Hob XV – **No. 1** in G minor; **No. 2** in F major; **No. 5** in G major; **No. 6** in F major; **No. 7** in D major; **No. 8** in B flat major; **No. 9** in A major; **No. 10** in E flat major; **No. 11** in F minor; **No. 12** in E minor; **No. 13** in C minor; **No. 14** in A flat major; **No. 15** in G major; **No. 16** in D major; **No. 17** in F major; **No. 18** in A major; **No. 19** in G minor; **No. 20** in B flat major; **No. 21** in C major; **No. 22** in E flat major; **No. 23** in D minor; **No. 24** in D major; **No. 25** in G major, 'Gipsy Trio'; **No. 26** in F sharp minor; **No. 27** in C major; **No. 28** in E major; **No. 29** in E flat major; **No. 30** in E flat major; **No. 31** in E flat minor; **No. 32** in G major; **No. 34** in E major; **No. 35** in A major; **No. 36** in E flat major; **No. 37** in F major; **No. 38** in B flat major; **No. 39** in F major; **No. 40** in F major; **No. 41** in G major; **No. C1** in C major; **No. f1** in E flat major.

Piano Trios: HobXIV – No. 6 in G major; No. C1 in C major; HobXV – Nos. 1-2, 5-32, 34-41, C1 and f1. Hob XVI – No. 6 in G major. Hob*deest* – D major.
Beaux Arts Trio (Isidore Cohen *vn* Bernard Greenhouse *vc* Menahem Pressler *pf*).
Philips 454 098-2PB9 (nine discs: 394 minutes: ADD). Recorded 1970-79.
Gramophone Award Winner 1979.   Ⓑ

Haydn's trios are essentially accompanied keyboard sonatas, with the cello wedded to the keyboard bass almost throughout; this lack of cello independence has deterred many groups from investigating their undoubted musical riches. Not, fortunately, the Beaux Arts, whose acclaimed complete cycle accumulated by stealth during the 1970s (when it was finally completed it received almost universal accolades, including *Gramophone*'s Record of the Year Award) and has now reappeared on nine mid-price discs. A dozen of the works date from the 1760s, or even earlier, and offer little more than rococo charm, though the G minor (No. 1 in Hoboken's catalogue), with its neo-baroque severity, is a notable exception. But the majority of the trios date from the 1780s and 1790s and contain some of Haydn's most imaginative, lyrical and harmonically adventurous music. Two outstanding works from the 1780s are the E minor, No. 12, with its passionate, closely worked opening *Allegro*, and No. 14 in A flat, with its exquisitely tender *Adagio* in a remote E major that leads without a break into one of Haydn's most hilariously quixotic finales.

The 14 magnificent trios of the 1790s range from relaxed, intimate pieces like the E flat, No. 29, through the sombre, almost tragic F sharp minor, No. 26, to the C major, No. 27, unsurpassed in the whole series for its intellectual and virtuoso brilliance. Finest of all, perhaps, are the E major, No. 28, with its radiant outer movements and its astonishing central E minor *passacaglia*; and the E flat, No. 30, with its noble, lyrically expansive first movement, its deep-toned, often richly chromatic *Andante* and its glorious German-dance finale. The Beaux Arts' playing throughout is vital, refined, and sharply responsive to the music's teeming richness and variety. The early trios were conceived for harpsichord, though such is the deftness and delicacy of Menahem Pressler's touch here that there is no question of the music being overpowered by the modern Steinway; and among individual delights in the group's performances of these early works mention should be made of their gentle, affectionate way with the central minuets, underlining their dual function as dances and surrogate slow movements. In the later trios they catch beautifully the leisurely, almost improvisatory feel of many of the opening movements, and bring a ruminative intensity, and a wonderful quality of soft playing to the great slow movements, while the finales have immense brio, wit and virtuosity, with ideally clean, crisp articulation from Pressler. Occasionally in the earlier works the Beaux Arts sounds a touch oversophisticated for this guileless music – the opening violin solo in No. 2 is a case in point. And there are a few disappointments in the later trios – the first movement of the great F sharp minor, No. 26, sounds too lightweight, even skittish while, conversely, in the *passacaglia* of No. 28 they take a surprisingly ponderous view of Haydn's *Allegretto*. But there's a feast of superlative, little-known music here, most of the playing is extraordinarily felicitous, and the recording has Philips's customary warmth and refinement. £70 or so may seem a lot to fork out all at once, but no one is likely to regret the investment – this set will last a lifetime.

Piano Trios: HobXV – Nos. 14, 27, 29 and 31.
Yuuko Shiokawa *vn* **Boris Pergamenschikov** *vc* **András Schiff** *pf*
Decca 444 862-2DH (69 minutes: DDD). Recorded 1994.   Ⓕ

This disc gathers together four of Haydn's most inventive late keyboard trios, each one astonishing
in its physical and intellectual energy, formal freedom and harmonic vision. The pianist is, of
course, the motivating force in these works, above all in the C major Trio, which contains the most
virtuosic keyboard writing in all Haydn. Schiff and his colleagues relish the wit, brilliance and sheer
speed of Haydn's thoughts in the outer movements, with their comic off-beat accents, sudden
changes of register and breathtaking harmonic scope. Rapid keyboard passagework is always
imaginatively shaped and directed; and the pellucid, subtly coloured sonorities Schiff draws from
his Bösendorfer are a constant source of delight. So, too, is the sharply etched cello of Boris
Pergamenschikov, palpably relishing the mobility and vitality of Haydn's bass-lines. The *Andante*, in
the third-related key of A major, is swift and light with a *siciliano* lilt – though there is plenty of
weight and intensity in the A minor central section which breaks in rudely on Haydn's pastoral idyll.
Occasionally, in this movement and elsewhere, Yuuko Shiokawa's tuning is slightly sour. And her
phrasing of the soaring solo in the first movement of No. 31 is rather chilly. However, she takes her
chances in the German dance-style finale, where keyboard virtuosity is balanced by an unusually
elaborate, high lying violin part. Here Shiokawa and Schiff really strike sparks off each other; and
sudden moments of poetry are exquisitely handled. The far more riotous German dance that closes
No. 29 goes with a terrific swing. Decca's recording is intimate and finely balanced, with just the
right degree of ambient warmth.

Piano Trios: HobXV – Nos. 18, 24, 25 and 29.
Vienna Piano Trio (Wolfgang Redik *vn* Marcus Trefny *vc* Stefan Mendl *pf*).
Nimbus NI5535 (60 minutes: DDD). Recorded 1997.   Ⓕ Ⓔ

The *Gipsy* Trio, No. 25, may have been written in and for London, but this ensemble's short, snappy
bowing, stomping piano accents and, above all, uniquely instinctive fluctuations of tempo and pulse
in the finale, locate the work unmistakably in the grape-treading, Romany heart of the Burgenland.
The steps of the dance shape and pervade the E flat Trio, too, in the jauntily sprung rhythms of the
opening *Allegretto*, and the splendidly boisterous and cross-accented Allemande of its finale.
Among countless other delights in these bold and addictive performances is the sensitivity to the
power of silence, and the short, hushed half-tones within the long-breathed lines of the *Andante* of
the A major Trio. And, not least, the perceptive understanding and judgement of the shifting
qualities of an *Allegro* which so well supports the structure of the outer movements of the D major,
as well as enabling many a clearly articulated yet fanciful variation in the *Gipsy* Trio. These
recordings are close, sometimes breathy, but always thrillingly true.

Piano Trios: HobXV – Nos. 27-30.
Vera Beths *vn* **Anner Bylsma** *vc* **Robert Levin** *fp*
Sony Classical Vivarte SK53120 (74 minutes: DDD). Recorded 1992.   Ⓕ Ⓟ

These are truly magnificent pieces, full of ideas of startling originality, and conceived on a grand
scale – not simply long (though No. 42 certainly is that) but composed with a remarkable
spaciousness to their ideas and their working-out. These performances do them ample justice, with
their very brilliant and stylish pianism and a beautifully held instrumental balance: clearly Bylsma
doesn't see Haydn's cello parts as routine stuff. Robert Levin, using a McNulty copy of a 1780
piano by J.A. Stein, produces playing of great vitality and delightful crispness, and puts across
powerfully the intellectual force and the argumentative character of the music. Outstandingly keen
and vital musicianship, excellently recorded.

Piano Sonatas Nos. 1-62, Hob XVI.

Piano Sonatas Nos. 1-62. HobIX – No. 8, Seven Menuets from 'Kleine Tänze für die Jugend'.
HobXVII – No. 1, Capriccio in G major; No. 2, 20 Variations in A major; No. 3, 12 Variations in
E flat major; No. 4, Fantasia in C major; No. 5, Six Variations in C major; No. 6, Variations in
F minor; No. 7, Five Variations in D major; No. 9, Adagio in F major. Seven Last Words.
John McCabe *pf*
Decca London 443 785-2LC12 (12 discs: 873 minutes: ADD). Recorded 1974-77.   Ⓑ

McCabe's recordings of Haydn's piano sonatas represent one of the great recorded monuments of
the keyboard repertoire. Sample any one of the discs in this budget-price set and you will
immediately become aware of the immense treasures on offer. The special qualities McCabe brings

to his performances benefit from a composer's awareness of musical content, pursuing the structural argument with acute perceptions. Thus, assisted by the rich resonance and tonal subtlety of the modern piano, McCabe provides a consistently stylish view of Haydn's developing musical persona that comprehensively exploits this repertoire's inherent expressive potential. Spare textures and astonishing formal concentration in the earliest works establish a perfect balance between structure and content, and McCabe's crisp, beautifully poised playing enables the music to make its own potently expressive impact. The middle-period sonatas demonstrate Haydn's further experimentation and consolidation of style and technique. Harpsichord textures, reminiscent of Scarlatti, are still apparent in works such as the A flat Sonata (No. 31), but so, too, are new influences. For instance, McCabe luxuriates in the *Sturm und Drang* characteristics of the G minor Sonata (No. 32), penetrating to the core of the musical fabric to release the full power of the score's passionate centre.

Haydn's piano sonatas reach a supreme level of refinement in the late works, and McCabe responds with suitably spacious playing, sensitive to the music's richer 'orchestral' colours. He brings a connoisseur's touch to the impressionistic harmonic effects in the first movement of the C major Sonata (No. 60); his sinuous phrasing underlines the Schubertian flavour of the opening *Andante* to the D major Sonata (No. 61); he charmingly points the Beethovenian syncopation in the same work's *Scherzo* and ultimately achieves the perfect balance between content and design in the magisterial E flat Sonata (No. 62). McCabe's consummate poise between foreground motivic activity and structural background is equally remarkable in the separate keyboard pieces, which add to the appeal of this set. His outstanding performances of both *Seven Last Words* and the ingeniously constructed F minor Variations are obvious highlights; but try, also, the enchanting *Adagio*, and the charming selection of dances, which provide further evidence of Haydn's mastery of miniature forms. The vividly clear 1970s recordings have retained all the clarity for which they are justly renowned and, as for comparisons, McCabe's performances here set the standards against which others will be judged.

Piano Sonatas: HobXVI – No. 20 in C minor; No. 49 in E flat major; No. 34 in E minor; No. 32 in B minor; No. 42 in D major; No. 48 in C major; No. 51 in D major; No. 50 in C major; No. 52 in E flat major; No. 40 in G major; No. 37 in D major. No. 4, Fantasia in C major. No. 6, Variations in F minor. No. 9, Adagio in F major.
Alfred Brendel *pf*
Philips 416 643-2PH4 (four discs: 205 minutes: ADD/DDD). Booklet included.
Gramophone Award Winner 1987.   Ⓕ **RR**

The sonatas collected in this set are some magnificent creations, wonderfully well played by Alfred Brendel. Within the order and scale of these works Haydn explores a rich diversity of musical languages, a wit and broadness of expression that quickly repays attentive listening. It is the capriciousness as much as the poetry that Brendel so perfectly attends to; his playing, ever alive to the vitality and subtleties, makes these discs a delight. The sophistication innate in the simple dance rhythms, the rusticity that emerges, but above all, the sheer *joie de vivre* are gladly embraced. Brendel's continual illumination of the musical ideas through intense study pays huge dividends. The recording quality varies enormously between the different works and though the close acoustic on some of the later discs could be faulted for allowing one to hear too much of the keyboard action, it certainly brings one into vivid contact with the music.

Piano Sonatas: HobXVI – G minor, No. 44; C minor, No. 20; E minor, No. 34; G major, No. 40; C major, No. 48; E flat major, No. 49; C major, No. 50;D major, No. 51; E flat major, No. 52. HobXVII – No. 4, Fantasia in C major.
András Schiff *pf*
Teldec 0630-17141-2 (two discs: 147 minutes: DDD). Recorded 1997.   Ⓕ

András Schiff has consistently championed Haydn, not only the sonatas but also the glorious late piano trios. He has, though, long delayed recording any of the sonatas, but this two-disc set, offering the last five sonatas plus four of the finest earlier ones, has been worth the wait. If his way with Haydn tends to be more intimate, less robust and less gleefully subversive than Alfred Brendel's (on his four-disc *Gramophone* Award-winning Philips set), Schiff is equally acute in his responses to the music's drama, wit and poetry, and in his control of narrative line. His 'centred' tone and limpid, subtly coloured soft playing are a constant delight, as is his variety of articulation and nuance. He plays all the marked repeats, embellishing and dramatizing them as appropriate; and he is keenly alive to Haydn's manipulations of silence, timing pauses and fermatas with an ear for their exact comic or dramatic significance. As for the great C minor Sonata, Schiff's is one of the most searching readings on record: the outer movements combine his characteristic refinement of detail with bold dramatic contrasts and a terrific overall sweep. The finale, a notch slower than Brendel's, is also more impassioned and disturbing, rising (especially in the repeat) to a final climax of desperate intensity. Schiff's virtuoso technique – and his understanding of Haydn's silences – pays special dividends in a dazzling performance of the C major *Fantasia*. And he wonderfully realizes the richness and sophistication of the final three sonatas. In the first movement of the C major, where Haydn conjures miracles from his initial vision of dry bones, Schiff's playing is as crisp and as vividly orchestrated as Brendel's. Schiff is also more spacious in the E flat sonata, a magnificent, probing reading which realizes the music's reach, poetry and harmonic daring as completely as any. The recording faithfully capture the beautiful, luminous sonorities of his Bösendorfer, and provide just the right amount of space around the sound.

Piano Sonatas: HobXVI – A major, No. 26; B minor, No. 32; C sharp minor, No. 36; D major, No. 37; E flat major, No. 49.
Leif Ove Andsnes *pf*
EMI CDC5 56756-2 (58 minutes: DDD). Recorded 1997. ⓕ

This disc offers delectable performances of five shrewdly contrasted works: two troubled, trenchant minor-key sonatas from the 1770s juxtaposed with a pair of lightweight pieces from the same period and culminating in the great E flat Sonata. Andsnes is eagerly responsive to the individual character of these sonatas, to their richness and variety of incident, and their sheer unpredictablility. With his wide spectrum of colour and dynamics he makes no apologies for using a modern Steinway. But his playing, founded on a pellucid *cantabile* touch and diamantine passagework, marries classical refinement and clarity with a spontaneous exuberance, a sense that the next phrase is yet to be created. Repeats are never merely repetitions, and Andsnes is always ready to add stylish and witty touches of embellishment. The opening movements of both minor-key sonatas have a lithe, sinewy urgency, above all in the vehement sequences of their developments, together with a rare delicacy of nuance: and here, as elsewhere, you notice how alive and concentrated is his *piano* and *pianissimo* playing. Andsnes brings a bright, buoyant yet lyrical approach to the E flat Sonata's outer movements, to the wonderful *Adagio* a limpid line, a subtly flexed pulse and, in the B flat minor central episode, a true sense of passion. With few provisos this is just the sort of playing – joyous, imaginative, involving – to win Haydn's sonatas a wider following. The recording of the E flat, made in a church in Oslo, has slightly more ambient warmth than that of the remaining sonatas, recorded at EMI's Abbey Road studios. But throughout, the piano sound is natural and present without being too closely miked.

Haydn Piano Sonatas: HobXVI – A major, No. 30; E flat major, No. 52.
Schubert Piano Sonata No. 14 in A minor, D784. Marche militaire No. 1 in D major, D733 (arr. Tausig).
Evgeni Kissin *pf*
Sony Classical SK64538 (62 minutes: DDD). Recorded 1994. ⓕ🅴

Enormously enjoyable! This is Haydn playing of high style and verve – also affectionate, articulate, colourful and expressive – and its vitality seems authentic even when Kissin asks you to admire the means with which he achieves it. This is not wilful or eccentric playing. By the end of the A major work, an engaging and (even by Haydn's standards) unconventional sonata, you feel its stature has been enhanced, which is just as it should be. Kissin meets the greater challenge of Haydn's last Sonata equally well. The breadth as well as the brilliance of the first movement is there, and its warmth; his tempo may be a little brisker than usual but it still allows for weight. The last movement *Presto* really is breakneck, at a speed which would be unwise, not to say unrealistic, for most others; once again, the impression is of allure allied to perfectly judged dramatic tension and articulate speech. Maybe he sustains the phrases of the *Adagio* with less success: they tend to emerge a bar at a time instead of as an arching span. How difficult this is to do when tone on the piano dies so quickly. But it is precisely this kind of growth and building through sentences and long paragraphs – and through silences – that he manages so well in the first movement of the Schubert sonata. Admire here what you will: the unforced, perfectly scaled range of dynamics and attacks; the motivating force of the left hand, so often neglected by those who see interest only in the right; the sensitivity to harmonic movement, again, and to the smallest shifts of colour and weight; the infallible timing and marvellous sense of rhythm in all aspects; the voicing and vitality of the texture from top to bottom. Above all, there is a commanding vision of the whole. The finale is equally fine. The recording balance is not too close and the sound is pleasingly open and natural.

Piano Sonatas: HobXVI – B minor, No. 32; E minor, No. 34; G minor, No. 44; E flat major, No. 49.
Emanuel Ax *pf*
Sony Classical SK53635 (61 minutes: DDD). Recorded 1993. ⓕ

Emanuel Ax's choice of piano sonatas focuses on the remarkable influence of C.P.E. Bach in this repertoire. Of the three minor-key sonatas recorded here, the two-movement G minor work makes the influences the most poignantly apparent. Ax's performance is finely proportioned, and his elegant, sensitively shaped phrasing creates an arresting expression of the music's homogeneity and dramatic intensity. Ax includes all repeats, which, in the finale of the one in B minor, for example, produces startling results. In the finale of the E minor Sonata, by comparison, Ax's distinctive handling of different textures, which enhances the contrast between sections, vividly reveals the movement's fusion of rondo and variation forms. Ax ends his programme with the E flat major Sonata. Haydn himself was especially proud of the *Adagio*, and Ax's performance of this movement's passionate minor-mode middle section makes a dramatic impact. However, after panache and brilliance in the finale, Ax's breathtakingly beautiful, gentle final cadence leaves the deepest impression. Ax's penetrating insights into the *Sturm und Drang* characteristics of these sonatas make an outstanding contribution to the appreciation of this aspect of the composer's keyboard sonata output.

Piano Sonatas: HobXVI – C major, No. 35; C sharp minor, No. 36; D major, No. 37; E flat major, No. 38; G major, No. 39.
Jenö Jandó *pf*
Naxos 8 553128 (62 minutes: DDD). Recorded 1993.   Ⓢ

The exquisite, classical balance evident in these six keyboard sonatas makes them especially rewarding examples of the composer's exploitation of the piano's broad expressive range and rich textural variety. This volume in Jenö Jandó's complete edition presents these pieces in a compelling, modern-instrument version. For example, there is brilliance and sparkle in the opening movements of the D major and E flat Sonatas; warmth and dramatic intensity in the slow movements (most notably in the baroque echoes of the Sonatas in C major and D major), and an appealing blend of wit and elegance in finales such as the third movement of the D major Sonata, or the minuets which conclude the C sharp minor and E flat major Sonatas. Most remarkable, though, is the G major Sonata, where Jandó's customary precision and his sensitive balance of the music's linear and harmonic dimensions powerfully convey the work's concerto character and Haydn's imaginative approach to form. Try Jandó's engaging account of the opening *Allegro*, his deft balance of the slow movement's effective blend of major and minor, and his exuberant virtuosity in the finale.

Piano Sonatas: HobXVI – E flat major, No. 49; C major, No. 50; D major, No. 51; E flat major, No. 52.
Jenö Jandó *pf*
Naxos 8 550657 (62 minutes: DDD). Recorded 1992.   Ⓢ

The keyboard sonatas which Haydn originally intended for piano, such as the four considered here, show the composer's exploration of the instrument's capacity for greater dynamic variation. Jandó is sensitive to the relationship between motif and dynamics which is particularly evident in the E flat and D major Sonatas respectively. Aided by clear recorded sound, Jandó's satisfying warmth in the lyrical passages provides an effective dramatic contrast to his crisp, positive approach in the livelier music. Jandó's glittering technique has a high profile in the other two sonatas in the programme. Jandó's stylistically well-turned readings are uncontroversial, but they lack nothing in excitement. Sample the finale of the E flat Sonata, where the wealth of expressive detail at an extremely fast tempo is breathtaking.

Missa Sancti Bernardi de Offida in B flat major, HobXXII/10, 'Heiligmesse'. Mare Clausum, HobXXIVa/9. Insanae et vanae curae. Motetti de Venerabili Sacramento, HobXXIIIc/5a-d. Te Deum in C major, HobXXIIIc/2.
Jörg Hering *ten* **Harry van der Kamp** *bass* **Tölz Boys' Choir; Tafelmusik / Bruno Weil.**
Sony Classical SK66260 (63 minutes: DDD). Texts and translations included. Recorded 1994. Ⓕ℗

A special attraction for Haydn lovers is the first-ever recording of the unfinished ode *Mare Clausum*, commissioned in 1794 by Haydn's colourful English friend Lord Abingdon, and evidently abandoned when the nobleman was imprisoned for libel. The gauche, crudely chauvinistic verses, trumpeting England's sovereignty of the sea, should make the most hardened Europhobe blush. But the two numbers Haydn completed are worthy of his ripest style: a noble F major bass aria with rich, inventive writing for woodwind, authoritatively sung by Harry van der Kamp, and a D major chorus whose verve and contrapuntal power presage the late Masses and oratorios. Under Bruno Weil's spirited direction both the Tölz Boys' Choir, with their bright-edged, slightly breathy tone, and the period orchestra, Tafelmusik, is on first-rate form here and throughout this enterprisingly planned disc. It includes the thrilling, majestic, late *Te Deum* and the motet *Insanae et vanae curae*, adapted from a 'storm' chorus in the oratorio *Il ritorno di Tobia*. Weil's reading is eagerly responsive to the music's drama, with taut rhythms, sharp dynamic contrasts and keen instrumental detailing; and he maintains the initial pulse through the tranquil D major section. Between these masterpieces the four little *Motetti de Venerabili* from the 1750s (another recorded first) inevitably sound tame, for all their easy tunefulness and skilful marshalling of rococo cliché. The largest work on the disc is, of course, the so-called *Heiligmesse*, first of the six magnificent Mass settings of Haydn's old age. Like the shorter pieces, this receives an energetic, uplifting reading, with brisk tempos, fresh, incisive choral work and strongly etched orchestral colours. In one or two sections Weil can drive too hard and Harry van der Kamp sometimes overwhelms the excellent boy soloists. But there is no doubting the vigour and joyfulness of Weil's reading, nor the skill and commitment of his forces. Quite apart from its pioneering value, this is an inspiring Haydn collection whose appeal is enhanced by vivid sound.

Mass No. 1, Missa Sunt bona mixta malis, HobXXII/2 – Kyrie; part of Gloria. Non nobis, Domine, HobXXIIIa/1. Ave regina in A major, HobXXIIIb/3. Responsoria de Venerabilis, HobXXIIIc/4a-d. Responsorium ad absolutionem in D minor, HobXXIIb/1. Salve regina in E major, HobXXIIIb/1. Mass No. 7 in B flat major, HobXXII/7, Missa brevis Sancti Johannis de Deo ('Little Organ Mass').
Marie-Claude Vallin, Ann Monoyios *sops* **Tölz Boys' Choir; L'Archibudelli** (with **Anner Bylsma** *vc* **Anthony Woodrow** *db* **Bob van Asperen** *org*); **Tafelmusik / Bruno Weil.**
Sony Classical Vivarte SK53368 (60 minutes: DDD). Texts and translations included.
Recorded 1992-93.   ⒡ ℗

This is the first appearance on disc of two recent Haydn discoveries, the brief Offertorium *Non nobis, Domine* and fragments (the *Kyrie* and part of the *Gloria*) of a Mass *Sunt bona mixta malis*. But its real charms lie in two works for solo soprano, choir and orchestra composed to mark the entry into convent life of Therese Keller whom Robbins Landon suggests was Haydn's great love. Be that as it may, what seeps out of every pore is a warmth and sincerity, something akin to profound inner happiness, which makes one wonder just how deep Haydn's love was for the devout Therese Keller. Marie-Claude Vallin's captivating performance perfectly captures the essential innocence of the *Ave regina*. Her voice has a naive, almost childlike quality, although in her ethereally soaring high notes and fluent trills there is no doubting her technical command. Ann Monoyios has an altogether fuller, more mature quality as befits the more intense *Salve regina* although, again, if this is Haydn heartbroken, he must have had superhuman powers of recuperation. Bruno Weil's support for these two delightful singers is as unobtrusive as it is sympathetic. His excellent team of musicians (not forgetting the splendid work from the Vivarte recording team) are allowed to relax in performances which seem almost to float on air, so graceful and effortless does it all sound. Add to this a performance of the *Little Organ Mass* (No. 7) of rare poise and elegance and you have a disc of real beauty.

Masses – No. 1a in G major, HobXXII/3, 'Missal rorate coeli desuper'; No. 13 in B flat major, HobXXII/13, 'Schöpfungsmesse' (with alternative setting of the Gloria).
Susan Gritton *sop* **Pamela Helen Stephen** *mez* **Mark Padmore** *ten* **Stephen Varcoe** *bar* **Collegium Musicum 90 Chorus; Collegium Musicum 90 / Richard Hickox.**
Chandos Chaconne CHAN0599 (62 minutes: DDD). Texts and translations included.
Recorded 1995.   ⒡ ℗ ⒠

The *Creation* Mass is no less resplendent or searching than, say, the *Nelson* Mass or the *Harmoniemesse*, a glorious affirmation of Haydn's reverent, optimistic yet by no means naive faith. Even by Haydn's standards, the work is startling in its exploitation of colourful and dramatic key contrasts, as in the sudden swerve from F major to an apocalyptic *fortissimo* D flat at 'Judicare vivos'; the *Benedictus*, characteristically, moves from serene pastoral innocence (shades of 'With verdure clad' from *The Creation*) to urgent intensity in its central development; and the sublime G major *Agnus Dei* has a profound supplicatory fervour extraordinary even among the composer's many memorable settings of this text. This reading eclipses previous recordings both in the quality of its choir and soloists, the subtlety of Hickox's direction and the vividness and transparency of the recorded sound. In faster movements like the *Kyrie* and the openings of the *Gloria* and *Credo* Hickox strikes just the right balance between dignity and happy, pulsing energy, relishing each of Haydn's dramatic *coups*; and he brings a marvellous clarity and verve, and a sure sense of climax, to the chromatically inflected fugues in the *Gloria* and at 'Dona nobis pacem'. Abetted by his first-rate orchestra, Hickox is always alive to the felicities of Haydn's scoring, while the 24-strong professional choir is superbly responsive throughout, firm and fresh of tone, maintaining a beautiful, even line in *piano* and *pianissimo*. We also get the alternative version of the *Gloria*, and the ultra-compressed (6'49") and instantly forgettable *Missa rorate coeli desuper*, which David Wyn Jones, in his excellent note, wryly describes as 'a reminder of how perfunctory church music in eighteenth-century Austria could be'. It is neatly dispatched by Hickox and his forces, but inevitably comes as an anticlimax.

Masses – Mass No. 7 in B flat major, HobXXII/7, Missa brevis Sancti Johannis de Deo ('Little Organ Mass'); No. 12 in B flat major, HobXXII/12, 'Theresienmesse'.
Janice Watson *sop* **Pamela Helen Stephen** *mez* **Mark Padmore** *ten* **Stephen Varcoe** *bar*
Collegium Musicum 90 Chorus; Collegium Musicum 90 / Richard Hickox.
Chandos CHAN0592 (60 minutes: DDD). Texts and translations included. Recorded 1995. ⓕⓅⒺ

Hickox generates the physical and spiritual elation essential to this music, calling to mind Haydn's own much-quoted remark that whenever he praised God his heart leapt with joy. In the glorious *Theresienmesse* of 1799 Hickox's manner is particularly fine in the exultant, springing *Gloria* and the rough-hewn vigour of the *Credo*. He understands, too, the Mass's dramatic and symphonic impetus, bringing a powerful cumulative momentum to the sonata-form 'Dona nobis pacem' and thrillingly tightening the screws in the closing pages. The choir is placed forward, though never at the expense of orchestral detail, keenly observed by Hickox. His uncommonly well-integrated solo quartet framed by the sweet-toned Janice Watson and the gentle, mellifluous Stephen Varcoe, sings with a chamber-musical grace and refinement in the 'Et incarnatus est' and the *Benedictus*. And their supplicatory tenderness in the 'Dona nobis pacem' contrasts arrestingly with the choir's urgent demands for peace. Hickox also captures the peculiar serenity and innocence of the much earlier *Missa brevis Sancti Johannis de Deo*, or *Little Organ Mass*, its intimacy enhanced here by the use of solo strings. A disc guaranteed to refresh the spirit.

Mass No. 10 in C major, HobXXII/9, 'Missa in tempore belli'. Salve regina in G minor, HobXXIIIb/2.
Dorothea Röschmann *sop* **Elisabeth von Magnus** *contr*
Herbert Lippert *ten* **Oliver Widmer** *bar*
Arnold Schoenberg Choir; Vienna Concentus Musicus / Nikolaus Harnoncourt.
Teldec Das Alte Werk 0630-13146-2 (58 minutes: DDD). Texts and translations included.
Recorded 1996. ⓕⓅ

Harnoncourt's *Missa in tempore belli* is an urgent, dramatic, fiercely accented reading, playing up Haydn's aggressive, brassy sonorities. Moments like the 'Pleni sunt coeli' in the *Sanctus* – an unusually troubled setting of this text – erupt with startling vehemence and the famous *Agnus Dei* which gives the work its other nickname of 'Kettledrum Mass' grows from a hushed, awed opening. He shapes both vocal and instrumental lines with an eye to maximum dramatic and rhetorical effect. Here and there you may find his phrasing mannered; and while his tempos are on the whole shrewdly chosen, balancing breadth with a strong forward momentum, the *Allegro moderato* of the *Kyrie* is unduly ponderous in its efforts to banish any hint of levity. He is splendidly served by his orchestra and his responsive, firm-toned choir, though the recording favours the orchestra over the chorus. The soloists phrase and balance sensitively in the 'Benedictus', where they and Harnoncourt catch both the music's gentle dance lilt and its underlying gravity and unease. Harnoncourt's reading, for all its occasional self-consciousness and over-calculation, scores consistently over several recordings in breadth, intensity and physical power. His performance of the much earlier *Salve regina*, with its touching chromatic pathos, is likewise dramatic and varied in expression. The soloists here are admirable both individually and in ensemble, with notably sweet, gleaming tone from Dorothea Röschmann.

Mass No. 10 in C major, HobXXII/9, 'Missa in tempore belli'. Te Deum in C major, HobXXIIIc/1. Te Deum in C major, HobXXIIIc/2. Alfred, König der Angelsachsen, HobXXX/5 – Aria des Schutzgeistes; Chor der Dänen.
Nancy Argenta *sop* **Catherine Denley** *mez* **Mark Padmore** *ten* **Stephen Varcoe** *bar*
Jacqueline Fox *spkr* **Collegium Musicum 90 Chorus and Orchestra / Richard Hickox.**
Chandos Chaconne CHAN0633 (64 minutes: DDD). Texts and translations included.
Recorded 1997. ⓕ

Few other conductors on disc convey so happily the mingled drama, symphonic power and spiritual exhilaration of these glorious works than Richard Hickox. He is fully alive to the ominous unease that permeates the great *Mass in Time of War*, but while others consciously strive for maximum dramatic and rhetorical effect, Hickox directs the Mass with a natural, unforced sense of phrase and pace. His tempos in the *Kyrie* and the opening of the *Gloria* are animated, yet never at the expense of dignity; and at the end of the *Credo* the prospect of the life to come rouses Hickox and his forces to a blaze of dancing jubilation. The playing of Collegium Musicum 90, led by Simon Standage, is predictably polished and athletic, with detail sharply etched, while the chorus sings with its accustomed fresh tone and incisive attack. The four soloists are well matched in the anxious C minor *Benedictus*; elsewhere Nancy Argenta brings a pure, slender tone, and a graceful sense of phrase to the *Kyrie*, while in the 'Qui tollis' Stephen Varcoe deploys his mellow baritone with real sensitivity to the meaning of the text, abetted by the eloquent solo cello of Richard Tunnicliffe.

The fill-ups, all but one sharing the Mass's C major, trumpet-and-drum sonorities, are imaginatively chosen. The two *Te Deum* settings epitomize the immense distance Haydn travelled during his long career, the rococo exuberance and strict species counterpoint of the little-known early work contrasting with the grandeur, sweep and massive, rough-hewn energy of the 1799 setting. The two numbers of incidental music Haydn completed for the play *King Alfred* in 1796, shortly before embarking on the Mass, are a real collectors' item. Argenta sings the first hymn-like E flat aria with chaste elegance, while choir and orchestra palpably enjoy themselves in the following number, a rollicking, brassy celebration of the Danes' victory over the Anglo-Saxons. In sum, a winner of a disc: enterprising planning, invigorating performances and first-class recorded sound, with an ideally judged balance between chorus and orchestra.

Mass No. 11 in D minor, HobXXII/11, 'Nelson'. Te Deum in C major, HobXXIIIc/2.
Dame Felicity Lott sop **Carolyn Watkinson** contr **Maldwyn Davies** ten
David Wilson-Johnson bar
The English Concert and Choir / Trevor Pinnock.
Archiv Produktion 423 097-2AH (50 minutes: ADD). Texts and translations included.
Gramophone Award Winner 1988.　　　　　　　　　　　　　　　　　　　　ⒻⓅ

The British Admiral had ousted the Napoleonic fleet at the Battle of the Nile just as Haydn was in the middle of writing his *Nelson* Mass. Although the news could not have reached him until after its completion, Haydn's awareness of the international situation was expressed in the work's subtitle, 'Missa in Augustiis', or 'Mass in times of fear'. With its rattle of timpani, its pungent trumpet calls, and its highly-strung harmonic structure, there is no work of Haydn's which cries out so loudly for recording on period instruments; and it is the distinctive sonority and highly charged tempos of this performance which set it apart from its competitors. The dry, hard timpani and long trumpets bite into the dissonance of the opening *Kyrie*, and the near vibrato-less string playing is mordant and urgent. The fast-slow-fast triptych of the *Gloria* is set out in nervously contrasted speeds, and the *Credo* bounces with affirmation. Just as the choral singing is meticulously balanced with instrumental inflexion, so the soloists have been chosen to highlight the colours in Pinnock's palette.

Mass No. 14 in B flat major, HobXXII/14, 'Harmoniemesse'. Salve regina in E major, HobXXIIIb/1.
Nancy Argenta sop **Pamela Helen Stephen** mez **Mark Padmore** ten **Stephen Varcoe** bar
Collegium Musicum 90 Chorus; Collegium Musicum 90 / Richard Hickox.
Chandos Chaconne CHAN0612 (59 minutes: DDD). Texts and translations included.
Recorded 1996.　　　　　　　　　　　　　　　　　　　　　　　　　　ⒻⒺ

Haydn's first major work, the *Salve regina* of 1756, is here juxtaposed with his last, the *Harmoniemesse* of 1802, so-called because of its exceptionally full scoring for woodwind. The gulf between the two works, in sophistication, mastery and emotional range, is predictably vast. Yet, in their very different ways, both reconcile the formal liturgical conventions of their era with the expression of Haydn's own life-affirming religious faith. Hickox and his forces ideally capture this sense of celebratory spiritual energy. Tempos are lively yet never overdriven, rhythms alert and vital. In the Mass Hickox generates an exhilarating symphonic momentum in, say, the opening sections of the *Gloria* and *Credo*, and, aided by an outstandingly clear, well-balanced recording, realizes to the full such dramatic *coups* as the sudden swerve into A flat in the recapitulation of the 'Benedictus' and the martial fanfares that slew the music from D major to B flat at the start of the 'Dona nobis pacem'. The steely-edged valveless trumpets are thrilling here; and elsewhere the wind players do rich justice to Haydn's glorious, inventive writing, nicely balancing rusticity and refinement. Nancy Argenta's innocent, bell-like tones and graceful sense of line are heard to touching effect in the 'Et incarnatus est' of the Mass. In the *Salve regina*, placed last on the disc but better taken as an aperitif, she also reveals her deft, fluent coloratura technique. No great depths in this youthful work, of course: but Haydn's setting of the Marian antiphon is elegant and affecting, with a command of shapely, Italianate melody and a feeling for dramatic contrast. This is certainly the most memorable work of Haydn's from the 1750s and aptly complements Hickox's fervent, inspiring reading of the *Harmoniemesse*.

Die Jahreszeiten (The Seasons), HobXXI/3.
Barbara Bonney sop **Anthony Rolfe Johnson** ten **Andreas Schmidt** bar
Monteverdi Choir; English Baroque Soloists / Sir John Eliot Gardiner.
Archiv Produktion 431 818-2AH2 (two discs: 127 minutes: DDD). Text and translation included.
Recorded 1990.　　　　　　　　　　　　　　　　　　　　　　　　　ⒻⓅ ⓇⓇ

The comparative unpopularity of Haydn's *The Seasons* when considered against his other great oratorio, *The Creation*, is understandable perhaps, but it is not really all that well deserved. Less exalted its subject and libretto may be, but its depiction of the progress of the year amid the scenes and occupations of the Austrian countryside drew from its composer – then in his late sixties – music of unfailing invention, benign warmth and constant musical-pictoral delights. It is charming music written with great affection, and as such it is not only quintessentially Haydnesque, but also virtually guaranteed to raise a smile. As usual, John Eliot Gardiner and his forces turn in disciplined, meticulously professional performances, though the orchestra is slightly larger – and consequently a tiny bit less lucid – than the sort you might nowadays find playing a classical symphony. The choir, however, performs with great clarity and accuracy, and brings, too, an enjoyable sense of characterization to their various corporate roles. The soloists all perform with notable poise and intelligence: Barbara Bonney's voice is pure and even, Anthony Rolfe Johnson sounds entirely at ease with the music, and Andreas Schmidt is gentle-voiced but certainly not lacking in substance. Perhaps in the end this is a performance which just lacks that last inch of necessary warmth to make it unbeatable, but it's a first-rate recommendation none the less.

Die Schöpfung (The Creation), HobXXI/2.
Sylvia McNair, Donna Brown *sops* **Michael Schade** *ten* **Rodney Gilfry, Gerald Finley** *bars*
Monteverdi Choir; English Baroque Soloists / Sir John Eliot Gardiner.
Archiv Produktion 449 217-2AH2 (two discs: 101 minutes: DDD). Text included. Recorded 1995.
Gramophone Award Winner 1997. Ⓕ Ⓟ Ⓔ 🆁🆁

With Gardiner's first down-beat it is obvious that Chaos's days are numbered. Not that 'days' (strictly speaking) are in question till the mighty words have been spoken, and then, in this performance, what an instantaneous blaze! No premonitory intimation (of pre-echo in the old days whereas now even the faintest stirring in the ranks of the choir will do it), but a single-handed switching-on of the cosmic power-grid and a magnificently sustained C major chord to flood the universe with light. This is one of the great characteristics here: the superbly confident, precise attack of choir and orchestra. Enthusiasm, then, in plenty; but how about the *mystery* of Creation? It is certainly part of the aim to capture this, for the bass soloist's 'Im Anfange' ('In the beginning') with *pianissimo* chorus has rarely been so softly and so spaciously taken: the Spirit that moved upon the face of the waters is a veiled, flesh-creeping presence, felt again in the first sunrise and the 'softer beams with milder light' of the first moon. Even so, others have incorporated this element more naturally. Gardiner has an excellent Raphael in Gerald Finley, and gains from having extra singers for Adam and Eve, especially as the Eve, Donna Brown, brings a forthright style doubly welcome after the somewhat shrinking-violet manner and breathy tone of Sylvia McNair's Gabriel. On the whole, Gardiner is sound: yet his is a fun *Creation* and a real enrichment of the library. Against others of comparable kind, Gardiner stands firm as an easy first choice: a re-creator of vision, a great invigorator and life-enhancer.

Die Schöpfung (The Creation).
Ann Monoyios *sop* **Jörg Hering** *ten* **Harry van der Kamp** *bass*
Tölz Boys' Choir; Tafelmusik / Bruno Weil.
Sony Classical Vivarte SX2K57965 (two discs: 91 minutes: DDD). Text and translation included.
Recorded 1993. Ⓕ Ⓟ

Bruno Weil's reading, using a period orchestra of up to 45 players and an all-male choir of similar strength, is above all a luminous, joyous affair, with generally fleet tempos, nimble, dancing rhythms and a richly communicated sense of delight in the work's sublime, pre-lapsarian innocence. Tafelmusik equals and sometimes surpasses rival period orchestras in the point and relish of its playing, and the Tölz Boys' Choir sings with brio, accuracy and characteristically fresh, bright-edged tone; textures in the great contrapuntal choruses are lucidly sifted, yet the climaxes pack a proper punch. Weil's direction mingles a sense of spontaneous discovery with a strong feeling for shape and structure and a sharp ear for Haydn's wonderful orchestral detail. Weil's eager, vital pacing and judgement of tempo relationships almost invariably feel right, though occasionally you long for a deeper sense of mystery and reverence. The three soloists are all stylish singers, clean of line and tone (vibrato used quite sparingly) and notably flexible in coloratura. They make their mark in recitative and aria, and blend and balance unusually well in ensemble. If Ann Monoyios's soprano lacks the hint of tonal depth ideally required by the central part of 'Nun beut die Flur', her purity, freshness and shapely sense of phrase are delectable. And like her male colleagues, she ornaments tastefully at fermatas and cadences. Jörg Hering is a compact, elegant tenor with no hint of bleat or strain. The best-known of the solo trio, Harry van der Kamp, can become parched at the top of his compass, and occasionally spoils his *legato* through verbal over-emphasis. But he has amply resonant low notes. To sum up, Weil conveys most infectiously the work's unique joy and exhilaration. The recording has a fine depth of perspective and an almost ideal balance between voices and orchestra.

Armida.
Jessye Norman *sop* Armida; **Claes Hakon Ahnsjö** *ten* Rinaldo; **Norma Burrowes** *sop* Zelmira;
Samuel Ramey *bass* Idreno; **Robin Leggate** *ten* Ubaldo; **Anthony Rolfe Johnson** *ten* Clotarco;
Lausanne Chamber Orchestra / Antál Dorati.
Philips 432 438-2PH2 (two discs: 140 minutes: ADD). Recorded 1978.   Ⓕ

Armida, widely considered Haydn's finest opera, is based on a familiar literary classic adopted for
opera by numerous other composers: what is surprising is that in his setting Haydn reverted to
opera seria style, with no *buffo* characters, very few ensembles and extensive *secco* recitatives.
Dramatic action is minimal: for three acts Rinaldo lingers under the spell of the enchantress
Armida despite all the efforts of fellow-Crusaders to recall him to his mission. The work's static
nature, however, casts the emphasis on its musical qualities, and in this regard *Armida* is of the
highest standard. The enchantress herself, personified by the redoubtable Jessye Norman, has the
widest range of emotions to portray, from tenderness to rage; Ahnsjö as Rinaldo produces a fine
legato and very accurate florid passagework, but his low register rather lets him down; Ramey
shows laudable firmness and flexibility; and Burrowes's fresh youthful charm is very appealing.
Another strength is the alert orchestral playing. The most notable features of the opera are three
long through-composed sequences and imaginative scoring: the scene in the magic forest, where
Rinaldo at last, to Armida's fury, breaks free from her spell, is masterly, and in itself is sufficient to
compel a revision of the too common neglect of Haydn as an operatic composer.

L'anima del filosofo, ossia Orfeo et Euridice.
Uwe Heilmann *ten* Orfeo; **Cecilia Bartoli** *mez* Euridice, Genio; **Ildebrando d'Arcangelo** *bass*
Creonte; **Andrea Silvestrelli** *bass* Pluto; **Angela Kazimierczuk** *sop* Baccante; **Roberto Scaltriti**
bar First Chorus; **Jose Fardilha** *bass* Second Chorus; **Colin Campbell** *bar* Third Chorus;
James Oxley *ten* Fourth Chorus;
Chorus and Orchestra of the Academy of Ancient Music / Christopher Hogwood.
L'Oiseau-Lyre 452 668-2OHO2 (two discs: 124 minutes: DDD). Notes, text and translation
included. Recorded 1996.   Ⓕ ℙ

Christopher Hogwood here builds his band on the model of those prevalent in late-eighteenth-
century London theatres. Not only does his phrasing and articulation discover no end of both witty
and poignant nuances, but the grave austerity of the string playing, and the plangency of the early
woodwind instruments are eloquent advocates of an opera whose uncompromisingly tragic ending
(even the seductive Bacchantes perish) owes more to Ovid and Milton than to operatic tradition.
Hogwood also remembers that Haydn was writing for a Handelian London choral tradition: his
chorus, be they cast as Cupids, Shades or Furies, have robust presence and sculpt their lines with
firm muscle. Cecilia Bartoli takes the role of Euridice. In her very first aria, 'Filomena
abbandonata', she understands and eagerly re-creates the type of coloratura writing which
simultaneously fleshes out the central nightingale simile and incarnates the single word 'crudeltà'.
Her unmistakable, melting half-voice comes into its own as emotion first clouds reason, only to
create the fatal emotional extremes to which she gives voice so thrillingly. Uwe Heilmann is just the
tenor of rare agility and wide vocal range vital for this particular Orfeo. The minor parts are
strongly profiled: Ildebrando d'Arcangelo is a stern, noble Creonte, Andrea Silvestrelli a fearsome,
stentorian Pluto – and there's even a convincing *strepito ostile* off-stage as Euridice's abduction is
attempted in Act 2. Beyond the detail, it is above all the unique poignancy of the musical drama at
the heart of this strange, grave *Orfeo* which Hogwood discovers and reveals with such sympathetic
and compelling imaginative insight.

L'isola disabitata.
Ying Huang *sop* Silvia; **Susanne Mentzer** *mez* Costanza; **John Aler** *ten* Gernando;
Christopher Schaldenbrand *bar* Enrico; **Padova Chamber Orchestra / David Golub.**
Arianna a Naxos, HobXXVIb/2.
Susanne Mentzer *mez* **David Golub** *pf*
Arabesque Z6717-2 (two discs: 121 minutes: DDD). Notes, texts and translations included.
Recorded 1997.   Ⓕ

L'isola disabitata is probably the least viable of all Haydn's operas in the theatre. But if
characterization is limited and dramatic action minimal, it contains some memorable, richly worked
music, not least the strenuous, impassioned G minor Overture. The heroine, Costanza, a latter-day
Ariadne, has two eloquent *Adagio* arias, though their tone is grave and dignified rather than, as
their texts suggest, truly tragic. The music for Costanza's husband, Gernando, abducted by pirates
13 years earlier and now returned to the desert island to rescue his wife and her sister, is also
predominantly slow and soulful, though his one extended aria, 'Non turbar' (Act 2), provides the

emotional climax of the opera. Costanza's younger sister Silvia, who has grown up on the island as an ingenuous child of nature, is charmingly portrayed in her opening number; and Gernando's companion Enrico, with whom Silvia inevitably falls in love at first meeting, expresses his devotion to his friend in a sturdy, confident aria with ringing high horns. The opera's most obviously attractive number is the splendid – if overexpansive – final quartet, with elaborate *concertante* parts for violin, cello, flute and bassoon symbolizing each of the four characters.

David Golub secures decent rather than specially keen or pointed playing from the Padova Chamber Orchestra, which admittedly is not helped by the cavernous acoustic, but his soloists are uniformly excellent. As Costanza Susanne Mentzer sings with intense, burnished tone and a fine breadth of phrase; Ying Huang, a lyric soprano of rare quality, sings quite beautifully, with pure, sweet tone, naturally graceful phrasing and a surprising fullness in the lower register. John Aler's personable tenor has plenty of sap as Alva, though his *fioriture* in 'Non turbar' are less than ideally fluent; and the young American baritone Christopher Schaldenbrand makes a notable recording début as Enrico, warm and deep of tone and elegant of line. Arabesque adds the great tragic cantata *Arianna a Naxos*, paradoxically more dramatic than anything in the opera. If other singers have brought to the music more vivid colours and a greater sense of vulnerability and desperation, Susanne Mentzer sings very impressively, with a grandeur and nobility of mien that never let you forget that Ariadne was the daughter of Minos.

Michael Haydn
Austrian 1737-1806

Symphonies – B flat major, MH82 (P9); A major, MH152 (P6); G major, MH334 (P16); E flat major, MH473 (P26); F major, MH507 (P32).
London Mozart Players / Matthias Bamert.
Chandos CHAN9352 (69 minutes: DDD). Recorded 1994.   Ⓕ

Michael Haydn joined the orchestra of Oradea Cathedral as a violinist in 1757, before becoming *Kapellmeister* there. The first three movements of his A major Symphony (P6) began life as a ballet, while its finale comes from music previously used in the ballet-pantomime *Hermann*. Nevertheless, this tasteful reading by Bamert and the LMP presents a convincing structural unit. They offer great finesse and precision of ensemble in bright, fresher recordings. Dynamics and instrumental forces are strikingly opposed in the first movement, as are the major/minor contrasts in the Minuet. The slow movement has an appropriately mannered stateliness, and the finale is engagingly vivacious. Like the A major Symphony, the B flat work (P9) has as its finale a later addition; but once again, the LMP's stylish playing, in a naturally lit recording, sounds thoroughly satisfying. The spacious acoustic, moreover, effectively highlights the ceremonial character of the G major Symphony, recalling its initial conception as part of the cantata for Nikolaus Hoffmann's installation as Abbot of Michaelbeuern.

Christopher Headington
British 1930-1996

Piano Concerto. The Healing Fountain (In Memoriam Benjamin Britten). Cello Serenade.
Andrew Carwood *ten* **Alexander Baillie** *vc* **Gordon Fergus-Thompson** *pf*
Britten Sinfonia / Nicholas Cleobury.
ASV CDDCA969 (60 minutes: DDD). Texts included. Recorded 1996.   Ⓕ

The tragic death in a skiing accident of *Gramophone* contributor, Christopher Headington, robbed 'British music of one of its most versatile and engaging talents of the post-war era' (to quote Terry Barfoot's sympathetic annotation). Apart from his reviewing commitments, Headington successfully combined a career as a composer, pianist, author, broadcaster, examiner and lecturer. The fastidious craft, lyrical restraint and pleasing proportions of the Piano Concerto attest to lessons well learnt from Headington's days as a composition student at the RAM under Sir Lennox Berkeley. As with the earlier Violin Concerto, the predominant influence is that of Britten (with whom Headington had briefly studied as a young man and whose music he admired enormously). Not surprisingly, given Headington's own considerable gifts as a pianist, the solo writing is always deft and idiomatic. The work as a whole exerts a ready appeal and never threatens to outstay its welcome. Written in 1978 as a direct response to Britten's death, *The Healing Fountain (In Memoriam Benjamin Britten)*, for high voice and chamber orchestra, welds eight settings of poems by Siegfried Sassoon, W.H. Auden, John Masefield, Wilfred Owen, Thomas Moore and Shelley into a deeply felt, 26-minute sequence. Headington's word-painting skills and compositional facility are not in doubt, though as one listens one can't help but draw unflattering comparisons with Britten's genius for this sort of thing – an impression which

the work's sprinkling of quotations from *Peter Grimes*, *Death in Venice*, *Nocturne* and
A Midsummer Night's Dream merely tends to reinforce. Commissioned by Julian Lloyd Webber
and premièred by him in January 1995, the *Serenade* for cello and strings is cast in a single
movement: not only is the writing civilized and resourceful, there's a luminosity and variety of
texture that is really most beguiling. Performances and recording are exemplary; a worthy
memento of a fine musician and composer.

Johann Heinichen

German 1683-1729

Concertos – C major, S211; G major, S213; G major, S214, 'Darmstadt'; G major, S214, Venezia';
G major, S215; G major, S217; F major, S226; F major, S231; F major, S232; F major, S233;
F major, S234; F major, S235. Serenata di Moritzburg in F major, S204. Sonata in A major, S208.
Movement in C minor, S240.
Musica Antiqua Köln / Reinhard Goebel.
Archiv Produktion 437 549-2AH2 (two discs: 137 minutes: DDD). Recorded 1992.
Gramophone Award Winner 1993.   Ⓕ ℗ 🄴

Johann David Heinichen was a contemporary of Bach and one of an important group of musicians
employed by the Dresden court during the 1720s and 1730s. As well as being an inventive composer,
Heinichen was also a noted theorist and his treatise on the continuo bass was widely admired. All
the music collected here was probably written for the excellent Dresden court orchestra and most of
it falls into that rewarding category in which north and central German composers were pre-
eminent. Vivaldi had provided effective models but the predilection for drawing upon other
influences, too, gives the concertos of the Germans greater diversity. Heinichen admittedly does not
so readily venture into the Polish regions whose folk-music gives such a piquancy to Telemann's
concertos and suites, but the wonderful variety of instrumental colour and deployment of
alternating 'choirs' is every bit as skilful. Your attention will be held from start to finish. Much of
the credit for this must go to Reinhard Goebel and his impeccably drilled Musica Antiqua Köln.
Some of these pieces might well seem less entertaining in the hands of less imaginative musicians
and it would be untruthful to claim that everything here is of uniform interest; there is an element
of routine passagework, especially in the wind writing from time to time, but by far the greater
amount of this music is of high interest and very entertaining. Each concerto fields its own
distinctive wind group drawing variously upon recorders, flutes, oboes, bassoons and horns, the
latter always in pairs, in addition to *concertante* parts in many of them for one or more violins and
cellos. There is little need to say more. The recorded sound is first-rate, and Goebel's painstaking
essay is fascinating to read.

Peter Heise

Danish 1830-1879

Heise When the swan dreaming. Springsong in Autumn. Springsong of the young lark.
Summersong. Poems from the Middle Ages – Your father shall not scold. Love's Philosophy.
The dreams of the Sleeping Beauty. The songs of Dyveke.
Lange-Müller Three Songs, Op. 4. Songs, Op. 6 – Sulamite's song in the Queen's garden.
Folk-songs, Op. 18 – No. 4, Shine out, clear sunshine; No. 6, The willow bends. Spanish Students
– The sun shines now (Juana's first song); Rose bushes! (Juana's second song). The shepherd
pulls on his cape, Op. 34 No. 8. Cosmos Songs, Op. 57 – No. 3, The sun comes out like a rose;
No. 4, I am singing of a King's son. Songs, Op. 64 – Vol. 2: No. 2, Oh, I own such lovely little
fingers; No. 6, Speak quietly, young nightingale; Vol. 3: No. 2, Little birds are twittering in the sun.
Inger Dam-Jensen *sop* **Christen Stubbe Teglbjerg** *pf*
Da Capo 8 224065 (65 minutes: DDD). Texts and translations included. Recorded 1996.   Ⓕ

Peter Heise and Peter Erasmus Lange-Müller represent the rapturous spring and the melancholy
autumn of Danish romantic song. Heise, who wrote 300 songs in his short lifetime, is the real
standard-bearer of Danish song and this disc represents the best of his output: his exultant
Springsong in Autumn and the *Springsong of the young lark* – a rippling paean of praise to the great
Nordic thaw. Heise's seven *Songs of Dyveke* of 1879 – a brightly coloured pre-Raphaelite tapestry
of Holger Drachmann's ballads about the ups and downs of falling in love with royalty
(King Christian II in this case) – is a thrilling, inexplicably neglected cycle of constantly
self-renewing melodic invention. Inger Dam-Jensen and her imaginative accompanist Christen
Stubbe Teglbjerg show how superbly Heise writes for the voice. This disc also offers some of
Lange-Müller's sympathetic and poignant settings of his friend, Thor Lange's translations of
Russian, Czech and Serbian poetry. It is a natural selection for the collector and reinstates this
neglected music into the recital repertoire.

Piers Hellawell

Sound Carvings from the Water's Edge. Truth or Consequences. Sound Carvings from the Ice Wall. Memorial Cairns. Sound Carvings from Rano Raraku.
BT Scottish Ensemble / Piers Hellawell; Psappha / Paul MacAlindin.
Metronome METCD1029 (70 minutes: DDD). Recorded 1997.   Ⓕ

Piers Hellawell teaches composition at the Queen's University of Belfast and is fast emerging as one of the leading composers of his generation. This disc juxtaposes two works for string orchestra, *Sound Carvings from the Water's Edge* and *Memorial Cairns*, with three works for chamber groups of differing sizes. Three of these pieces are what Hellawell calls 'Sound Carvings', where individual sections stand apart from each other almost like sculptural objects to be appreciated on their own terms. He takes palpable delight in bright and open textures, and in gritty gestures inspired by Irish folk music and the Balinese gamelan. It is possible to trace echoes of Messiaen and Steve Reich in some of the works on this disc, but Hellawell has a fine feeling for the 'grain' of instrumental sound that leads him, in a pleasing way, to shift the focus of the music at a moment when you are least expecting it. The fine balance he strikes between stasis and change perhaps accounts for his music's special sense of poise.

Hellawell tends to build textures out of heterogeneous elements as in Balinese gamelan. An individual section may place on top of each other a tapped percussive rhythm, an unfolding chord sequence and a solo melismatic line in such a way that their precise rhythmic relationship cannot be analysed by the listener but can still be felt. You would expect such an idea to be less easy to realize for a homogeneous grouping such as a string orchestra, but the scoring is well judged, if a little harsh and thick in places. Nevertheless, the BT Scottish Ensemble clearly relishes the variety of textures and colours in *Sound Carvings from the Water's Edge* and gives a moving account of the elegiac second half to the earlier *Memorial Cairns*. In the smaller of the chamber pieces, *Truth or Consequences* and *Sound Carvings from Rano Raraku*, the exposed nature of the writing for each instrument seems to allow Hellawell more space to explore different types of texture, with the players of Psappha responding well to every light and shade of this multifaceted music. All credit to Metronome for this useful introduction to the music of a composer who promises much for the future.

Adolf von Henselt

Henselt Piano Concerto in F minor, Op. 16. Variations de concert, Op. 11, on 'Quand je quittai la Normandie' from Meyerbeer's 'Robert le diable'.
Alkan Concerti da camera, Op. 10 – No. 1 in A minor; No. 2 in C sharp minor.
Marc-André Hamelin *pf*
BBC Scottish Symphony Orchestra / Martyn Brabbins.
Hyperion CDA66717 (70 minutes: DDD). Recorded 1993.   Ⓕ 🄴

Much of the credit for this disc must go to the phenomenal playing and superb musicianship of Marc-André Hamelin. The main work of the disc, both in terms of quality and length, is the Henselt F minor Concerto, which, although once an active participant in the repertoire of most top league pianists during the late nineteenth century, dropped out of sight in the early part of this century until revived by Raymond Lewenthal and Michael Ponti. As a concerto it is particularly 'giving' to the listener and very *un*forgiving to the pianist, as the extreme technical difficulties are concealed in such a way that they become almost transparent to the ear – which probably accounts for its disappearance from the repertoire. Musically the concerto owes allegiance to Chopin (in the *Larghetto*) and Thalberg and Mendelssohn in the outer movements, but generally the overall Henseltian style has its own peculiar flavour which should win many friends through Hamelin's highly persuasive and thoroughly committed performance. The slightly earlier *Variations de concert* (on a theme from Meyerbeer's *Robert le diable*) is admittedly slighter fare but is nevertheless an attractive and enjoyable work which hails from the same stable as Chopin's *Là ci darem* Variations.

The remainder of the disc consists of two 'mini' concertos by Henselt's exact contemporary and fellow 'reticent' Charles-Valentin Alkan (Henselt, like Alkan, gave very few public concerts due to stage-fright that bordered on the pathological). The two early *Concerti da camera* (the only surviving *concertante* pieces by Alkan) are not, it has to be said, 'major' Alkan works, but they are original in invention and full of melodic appeal, with more than a hint or two of the Alkan of later years. Hamelin, who has already proved himself a formidable Alkan exponent, delivers them with astonishing dexterity and panache and, as in the Henselt pieces, he is given equally committed support from the BBC Scottish Symphony Orchestra under the direction of Martyn Brabbins. A thoroughly enjoyable disc, well worth exploring.

Hans Werner Henze

Symphony No. 9.
Berlin Radio Chorus; Berlin Philharmonic Orchestra / Ingo Metzmacher.
EMI CDC5 56513-2 (56 minutes: DDD). Text and translation included. Recorded live in 1997.   Ⓕ

Henze's Ninth Symphony deals with his experience of Nazi Germany and it is dedicated 'to the heroes and martyrs of German anti-Fascism'. All seven of its movements are choral, settings of poems by Hans-Ulrich Treichel, themselves based on the novel by Anna Seghers, *The Seventh Cross*. The novel tells of seven prisoners, condemned to be crucified, who escape from a concentration camp. Six are recaptured; after a series of horrifying experiences the seventh manages to reach freedom by boarding a Dutch ship on the Rhine. The first movement, 'The Escape', is not an exciting action scene but a portrayal of abject, pitiful terror; in its successor, 'Among the Dead', the delirious prisoner finds himself in a no man's land of shadows. There is a brief, savage portrayal of the persecutors, then the trees from which the crosses will be made sing lyrically of their own beauty before they are ruthlessly hacked down. Now the fate of one of the other prisoners is described; he is an artist, and as he dies, 'I ... the wounded eagle, spread my wings and fly once more over the only land I have'. At this point what is marked in the score as a *gran canto*, a grave, plangent string melody, rises with poignant eloquence in the strings. The penultimate movement, much the longest of the seven, is a hideous nightmare drama set in a cathedral, where the exhausted prisoner has hidden at night. Christ will not reply to his prayers; all he can hear is the voices of the dead (12 soloists, placed at the opposite end of the hall from the orchestra and choir), raptly and horribly praising the voluptuous pleasures of torture and martyrdom. 'The Rescue', finally, provides the huge contrast of rich, calm, multilayered polyphony, but though the prisoner has survived, the horror remains. The extremest of emotions are explored and extremes are needed to express them. The lines are often tortuous or angular, the textures often dense.

This is a live recording of the first performance. The chorus is not large and is placed well behind the main body of the orchestra. The recording balance does not always compensate for this, and at times it is difficult to follow both the choral counterpoint and the words, even with the text in front of you. Despite this the cumulative impact is shockingly powerful. It is a piece that one senses Henze has been steeling himself to write for years, and its eloquence catches you by the throat.

Undine.
London Sinfonietta / Oliver Knussen with **Peter Donohoe** *pf*
DG 453 467-2GH2 (two discs: 103 minutes: DDD). Recorded 1996.   ⒻⓈⒺ

Henze's *Undine* (or *Ondine*, as Frederick Ashton's ballet for which it was written is called) is easily his most approachable score, filled with melody, magically delicate evocation and humour. When the ballet first appeared, in October 1958, the music was dismissed by some critics as an eclectic and derivative mish-mash, and indeed it makes no effort to disguise its indebtedness to, in particular, the neo-classical Stravinsky (the *Symphony in Three Movements* is briefly but almost literally quoted on more than one occasion). What we have been missing all these years, this enthusiastically committed performance demonstrates, is a score that pays homage to the whole tradition of classical dance and the music written for it, a score whose richness is out of all proportion to the chamber orchestra it uses. That richness ranges from a quite magnificently sonorous evocation of the sea, via the stately wedding music in Act 2, to the deliciously tongue-in-cheek miniature piano concerto that accompanies the quite irrelevant but entertaining *divertissement* in Act 3. The second *divertissement*, that is: disastrously for the otherwise poetic scenario about a water-nymph's fatal love for a human, Ashton insisted on two of them. But the heart of the ballet is the subtle, quietly iridescent music associated with Ondine herself. Ashton's ballet was described as a 'concerto' for Margot Fonteyn who was its inspiration, and much of Henze's score is a sort of portrait of 'the radiant centre of the whole ballet ... this wonder floating, almost, above the ground', as Henze described her at the time. It is his achievement that the concluding passacaglia, even after those interpolations, is so moving as Ondine, knowing that her kiss will kill her beloved, is nevertheless irresistibly drawn to embrace him. Knussen's performance is so good that you can almost imagine your own staging, and it is superbly recorded.

Louis Hérold

La fille mal gardée – excerpts (arr. Lanchbery).
Orchestra of the Royal Opera House, Covent Garden / John Lanchbery.
Decca Ovation 430 196-2DM (51 minutes: ADD). Recorded 1962.   Ⓜ

Hérold Orchestral

The Royal Ballet's *La fille mal gardée* remains a source of perpetual delight, not least for the music that John Lanchbery arranged largely from Hérold's patchwork score for the 1828 version. The Clog dance is the obvious highlight of the score; but there are felicitous moments throughout, with snatches of Rossini, Donizetti *et al* cropping up all over the place. This recording is the original one that Lanchbery conducted when the ballet proved such a success in the Royal Ballet's repertoire in 1960. More recently he has recorded the score complete; and ballet lovers will doubtless consider this fuller version essential. However, others will undoubtedly find that the complete score rather outstays its welcome by comparison with this constantly uplifting selection. At medium price and wearing its 30-odd years lightly, it makes a most compelling recommendation.

Hildegard of Bingen

German 1098-1179

Favus distillans. Et ideo puelle. O tu illustrata. O vos angeli. Studium divinitatis. O ignee Spiritus. O rubor sanguinis. O orzchis Ecclesia. O gloriosissimi lux vivens angeli. Rex noster promptus est. Deus enim in prima muliere. De patria. Sed diabolus in invidia. Nunc gaudeant materna viscera Ecclesia.
Sinfonye (Jocelyn West, Vivien Ellis, Stevie Wishart, Emily Levy, Vickie Couper, Julie Murphy); **members of the Oxford Girls' Choir.**
Celestial Harmonies 13127-2 (62 minutes: DDD). Texts and translations included. ⓕ Ⓔ

Stevie Wishart succeeds in putting Hildegard's music across chiefly by her imaginative choice of singers, which includes quite young girls. The tuneful, unsophisticated timbre of the youngest voices – as, for example, that of Vickie Couper in *Deus enim in prima muliere* – acts as a foil to the sturdy chest voices of the older women – which have a quality of their own, somewhat akin to that of Hungarian folk singers. Such contrasts seem to be typical of the whole Hildegardian picture. Hildegard herself was made up of contrasts: she is ecstatic and at the same time quietly tender; she can be passionate while maintaining a sense of decorum; she is erotic but also chaste. One could do without the hurdy-gurdy and dispense with the drones and the improvised organum. What is left is an understanding, a penetration of Hildegard's music, which rarely comes through in other interpretations. One thinks particularly of the composer's portrayal of the mystery of the Incarnation in *O tu illustrata* and also, particularly, of the remarkably sustained lines of ecstasy in *O vos angeli* – this extraordinary outpouring ranging over two octaves, but which yet has shape and structure for all Hildegard's protestations that she had never studied her art formally.

A Feather on the Breath of God
Columba aspexit. Ave, generosa. O ignis spiritus Paracliti. O Jerusalem. O Euchari, in leta vita. O viridissima virga. O presul vere civitatis. O Ecclesia.
Gothic Voices / Christopher Page with **Doreen Muskett** *symphony* **Robert White** *reed drones*
Hyperion CDA66039 (44 minutes: DDD). Recorded 1981. *Gramophone* Award Winner 1982-83. ⓕ

This remarkable record contains a collection of choice gems from one of the greatest creative personalities of the Middle Ages. Admittedly, we have limited means of assessing how these inspired pieces were actually performed during the lifetime of Hildegard herself. But the refreshingly unsophisticated timbre of the four sopranos and the reedy, almost boyish, vocal quality of the contralto are convincing enough to transport the listener right back to the unpolluted atmosphere of Hildegard's cloister. Most to be savoured are the unaccompanied items, amounting to 50 per cent of the total. Indeed, since the notes go out of their way to tell us that 'distractions such as the intrusion of instrumental decorations' were to be avoided, why did the producer go out of his way to introduce symphony and reed drones in the performance of the other 50 per cent? However, this is a delightful recording. When it was first released it sparked new interest in the music of the Middle Ages by a broader audience and it remains a jewel in Hyperion's crown.

Ordo Virtutum (arr. Thornton/Gaver). Symphoniae – O quam magnum miraculum; O felix anima; O quam mirabilis.
Sequentia Vocal and Instrumental Ensembles / Barbara Thornton, Benjamin Bagby *vocs* **Elizabeth Gaver** *vn*
Deutsche Harmonia Mundi 05472 77395-2 (two discs: 92 minutes: DDD).
Notes, texts and translations included. Recorded 1997. ⓕ Ⓟ

This masterly production, undoubtedly the fruit of maturity and experience, strikes the listener at once by its note of calm self-confidence. Peter Dronke's assertion that the likeliest occasion for the original performance was the consecration of Hildegard's new monastery on the Rupertsberg in the spring of 1152 is made with conviction. There would have been a part to sing for each of the 20 nuns that made up Hildegard's community of *moniales*. Dronke defends the introduction of instruments (in this recording three medieval fiddles, flute and organistrum) by quoting a letter from the impassioned pen of Hildegard herself. He suggests that the characters may have been costumed in garments resembling those depicted in the illuminations of Hildegard's other theological work, *Scivias*. The subject-matter – the strife experienced by the Soul (Anima) assailed by the devil but strengthened and finally victorious through recourse to the Virtues – would not have been unfamiliar to nuns who, once clothed in the robes of their Profession, followed the Rule of St Benedict, enrolled in his 'school of sanctity'. The recording, therefore, is faced with the task of attempting to reproduce a festive occasion of much solemnity and depth of meaning, not a mere medieval jollity. The achievement is total. The singing is open and fluid and the rhythmic interpretation convincingly flexible. The instrumental interludes do not disturb the onward flow of the drama: they broadly punctuate the text. A recording worthy indeed to mark the 900th anniversary of the birth of Hildegard!

Vespers – Deus in adjutorium meum intende; O aeterne Deus; Spiritus Sanctus vivificans vita; O magne Pater; Caritas abundat in omnia; Lesung; O vis aeternitatis; O ignis Spiritus Paracliti; O quam mirabilis – Magnificat; Kyrie and Pater noster; O presul vere civitatis; O Jerusalem, aure civitas.
Scholars of St Hildegard, Eibingen / Johannes Berchmans Göschl, Sr Christiane Rath, OSB.
Ars Musici AM1203-2 (69 minutes: DDD). Texts and translations included. Recorded 1997.　　Ⓕ

Here is Hildegard sung by Benedictine *moniales*! They're from St Hildegard's Abbey, Eibingen, a modern abbey, founded around 1900, above the site of Hildegard's own monastery. These nuns are living the same life as that of Hildegard's community, singing daily the same Benedictine Office, breathing the same air and trying to capture the spirit of their great twelfth-century predecessor. This is more than a mere anthology. It cannot properly be described as a reconstructed office. The structure of Vespers is used here to place a somewhat random selection of pieces in a plausible context. The chosen antiphons do, in fact, look as if they are intended to be sung with psalmody: they appear in the sources with their corresponding *evovae* (psalm-tone ending) – not always, let it be whispered, the most correct or appropriate ending – and they represent really lovely, rather unusual tones, beautifully sung by these Benedictines, who chant office psalms regularly and with understanding. As for their interpretation of Hildegard's music, this is influenced, but not unduly so, by some of the findings of semiology.

Paul Hindemith　　German 1895-1963

Cello Concerto. The Four Temperaments.
Raphael Wallfisch *vc* **Howard Shelley** *pf*
BBC Philharmonic Orchestra / Yan Pascal Tortelier.
Chandos CHAN9124 (52 minutes: DDD). Recorded 1992.　　Ⓕ

These two concertos, both from Hindemith's maturity (1940), make a good pairing. The outwardly conventional Cello Concerto contrasts a relatively small voice (the cello) which carries the work's lyrical message, with a large orchestra used initially for active statements delivered with great power. Hindemith's plan would seem to be gradually to reconcile these apparently contradictory modes of address. *The Four Temperaments* is a concerto for piano and string orchestra, a much more evenly balanced combination, using theme and variations form to integrate and relate the contrasted 'humours'. Hindemith's treatment of his material appears to argue that all temperaments, whatever the dominant disposition, are closely related. His portraiture, in fact, reveals characterization of great depth and dimension. Performances are superbly accomplished, indeed this is the finest of many currently available recordings of *The Four Temperaments*. And Chandos has resisted the temptation to move in on the soloist in the Cello Concerto. The sound is open and spacious.

Clarinet Concerto. Horn Concerto. Concerto for Trumpet, Bassoon and Strings. Concerto for Flute, Oboe, Clarinet, Bassoon, Harp and Orchestra.
Walter Buchsel *fl* **Liviu Varcol** *ob* **Ulrich Mehlhart** *cl* **Carsten Wilkening** *bn* **Reinhold Friedrich** *tpt* **Marie Luise Neunecker** *hn* **Charlotte Cassedanne** *hp* **Brigitte Goebel** *spkr*
Frankfurt Radio Symphony Orchestra / Werner Andreas Albert.
CPO CPO999 142-2 (70 minutes: DDD). Recorded 1990-93.　　Ⓕ

Hindemith's four wind concertos (1947-49) have never enjoyed the success of the *Kammermusik* concertos with which they have much in common; that for clarinet came first, to a commission from

Benny Goodman and its lack of overt display may have militated against its popularity. Ulrich Mehlhart's performance more than bears comparison with any rivals, and is served by the best sound. The 1949 Horn Concerto was written for Dennis Brain. If not quite in Brain's class, Marie Luise Neunecker's is a fine, highly musical account. The declamation of Hindemith's poem in praise of the horn, inscribed over its wordless setting, may be thought intrusive. The other two concertos (both 1949) are rarities indeed, not until now commercially available in the UK. In them, Hindemith most nearly approaches his 1920s manner, for instance in the woodwinds and harp Concerto with the finale's quotations from Mendelssohn's *Wedding March*, occasioned by his silver anniversary. In the Clarinet and Horn Concertos, Albert's tempos are brisker than the composer's own; in all four works the soloists and Frankfurt orchestra prove committed advocates.

Violin Concerto[a]. Symphonic Metamorphosis on Themes of Carl Maria von Weber[b].
Mathis der Maler[c].
David Oistrakh *vn* [ab]**London Symphony Orchestra /** [a]**Paul Hindemith,** [b]**Claudio Abbado;** [c]**Suisse Romande Orchestra / Paul Kletzki.**
Decca Enterprise 433 081-2DM (77 minutes: ADD). Recorded 1962 and 1968.   Ⓜ

Hindemithians who can afford to be choosy about the *Mathis der Maler* Symphony and the *Symphonic Metamorphosis* will immediately recognize the superiority of the full-price Blomstedt readings (reviewed below). Consistently spectacular 1960s Decca sound adds allure to the merely proficient performances on offer here. What makes this medium-price disc indispensable is the 30-minute Violin Concerto with Oistrakh at his legendary best and the composer conducting. The late Deryck Cooke, in his original **Gramophone** review, wrote of Oistrakh as 'superbly poised and eloquent ... and as performed here the Concerto shows that behind Hindemith's stony neo-classical facade beats a romantic German heart'. Listening to this recording it's hard to understand the concerto's relative neglect but easy to imagine current star violinists finding Oistrakh's an impossible act to follow. The 1962 sound gives Oistrakh a discreet dominance, and the engineers flatten out the slow movement's central climax, but thankfully no other allowances need be made for this preservation of a classic recording.

Mathis der Maler. Trauermusik[a]. Symphonic Metamorphosis on Themes of Carl Maria von Weber.
[a]**Geraldine Walther** *va*
San Francisco Symphony Orchestra / Herbert Blomstedt.
Decca 421 523-2DH (55 minutes: DDD). Recorded 1987.   Ⓕ ⓇⓇ

The charge sometimes levelled against Hindemith of being dry and cerebral utterly collapses in the face of Blomstedt's disc. Masterly craftsmanship and virtuosity there is in plenty; but the powerful emotions of *Mathis der Maler* and the festive high spirits of the *Symphonic Metamorphosis* could not be denied except by those who wilfully close their ears. Each of the three movements of the *Mathis* Symphony is based on a panel of Grünewald's great Isenheim altar. The eventual glorious illumination of 'The angels' folk-tune, the poignant slow movement and the blazing triumphant Alleluias after the desperate struggle with the demons in the finale have a searing intensity in Blomstedt's performance, which also presents Hindemith's elaborate web of counterpoints with the utmost lucidity. For brilliant and joyously ebullient orchestral writing few works can match that based on Weber's piano duets and his *Turandot* overture: here the San Francisco woodwind and brass have a field day. In addition, this warmly recommended disc contains a heartfelt performance of the very moving and beautiful elegy on the death of King George V, *Trauermusik*. It is tenderly played, with Geraldine Walther as a sweet-toned soloist and a full, rich sonority from the San Francisco strings.

Symphonic Metamorphosis on Themes of Carl Maria von Weber. Mathis der Maler.
Nobilissima Visione.
Philadelphia Orchestra / Wolfgang Sawallisch.
EMI CDC5 55230-2 (71 minutes: DDD). Recorded 1994.   Ⓕ

The Philadelphia players for Sawallisch give taut performances that simply outclass much of the competition. Another plus point is the unusual running order that achieves a better musical balance, starting with the most brilliant piece, the *Symphonic Metamorphosis*, and increasing in weight to the resounding brass Alleluias at the climax of the *Mathis* Symphony. Sawallisch's interpretations rank with Blomstedt in the *Mathis* Symphony and *Symphonic Metamorphosis*. Though many will prefer the leaner sound of the San Francisco Orchestra, EMI's sound for Sawallisch is relatively recessed. Given the spacious acoustic of Memorial Hall and the conductor's largeness of vision this is entirely apposite, with no loss of detail.

Konzertmusik for strings and brass, Op. 50. Mathis der Maler. Symphonic Metamorphosis on Themes of Carl Maria von Weber.
Israel Philharmonic Orchestra / Leonard Bernstein.
DG 429 404-2GH (67 minutes: DDD). Recorded live in 1989.   Ⓕ

This is the finest version of the *Konzertmusik* to have appeared on disc. The command from the podium is total; the attention to dynamics, articulation and attack are unrivalled and Bernstein is, of course, in his element for the big band and blues allusions of the second movement. He takes his time over the rapt 'Once upon a time' opening bars of the *Mathis* Symphony, and the 'Angelic concert' is gentle and relaxed. The heart is firmly on the sleeve for the second movement, 'Entombment', and here the open, assertive tones of the Israel woodwind and brass are poignant but rather understated. Come the finale, though, and all reservations are swept aside. The opening is magnificent with its confident contouring of those twisting string recitatives, answered here by razor-sharp brass snapping like the jaws of Hell – nobody has delivered St Anthony's torments with such explicit force. And the mounting excitement and gloriously broad *ritardando* before the final alleluias are the most supreme example of Bernstein, the climax builder.

The closing pages of the *Symphonic Metamorphosis* offer a more humorous but equally joyous release – the hat-hurling elation as the March swings into top gear and the staggering precision of the final pay-off are a living testament to his own inspired brand of live music-making. Blomstedt and his elegant San Franciscans offer a lighter, more quicksilver wit throughout, but you will not hear a modern version of the *Turandot Scherzo* where the orchestra has so obviously relished all those trills and the engineering has allowed you to hear them. And the central brass *fugato* –well, Bernstein was born to conduct that (expectations are certainly fulfilled). The sound is co-ordinated, clear and has an alarming physical impact. In all, a fine tribute to the rapport Bernstein had with this orchestra, to the level of excellence they were able to achieve together, and a disc to play to anyone who thinks that they don't like Hindemith.

Kammermusiken – No. 1, Op. 24 No. 1; No. 2; No. 3, Op. 36 No. 2; No. 4, Op. 36 No. 3; No. 5, Op. 36 No. 4; No. 6, Op. 46 No. 1; No. 7, Op. 46 No. 2. Kleine Kammermusik No. 1 for Wind Quintet, Op. 24 No. 2.
Konstanty Kulka *vn* **Kim Kashkashian** *va* **Norbert Blume** *va d'amore* **Lynn Harrell** *vc* **Ronald Brautigam** *pf* **Leo van Doeselaar** *org* **Royal Concertgebouw Orchestra / Riccardo Chailly.**
Decca 433 816-2DH2 (two discs: 138 minutes: DDD). Recorded 1990.
Gramophone Award Winner 1993.   Ⓕ 🆁🆁

Even were the performances and recordings not outstanding (and they most certainly are) this would be an extremely valuable set. Hindemith's series of *Kammermusik* ('Chamber Music') began in 1921 as an iconoclastic response to the hyper-intense emotionalism of German 'Expressionist' music over the previous 15 years. It continued until 1927, at which point he began to rationalize both the harmonic and the expressive foundations of his style. This, then, is neo-classicism with a German accent and as such it was to be a vital force in sweeping away the cobwebs of musty late romanticism; Walton, Prokofiev, Shostakovich and Britten were among those who, however indirectly, would feel the benefit. The music is also immensely enjoyable in its own right. Hindemith cheekily throws together disparate idioms and sheer force of personality is all that guards against total anarchy. All this is done with more than half an eye on the performers' own enjoyment of recreation, and the fine array of artists assembled by Chailly savour every detail. Recording quality is exemplary.

Kammermusiken – Nos. 1, 4 and 5.
Kolja Blacher *vn* **Wolfram Christ** *va* **Berlin Philharmonic Orchestra / Claudio Abbado.**
EMI CDC5 56160-2 (55 minutes: DDD). Recorded 1996.   Ⓕ

First impressions do not always prove reliable; when you first listen to these performances you may be underwhelmed. The opening chords seem not nearly grotesque enough, the tempo too relaxed. Persistence, though, has its rewards: by the end you will be won round – the performances are really excellent. Where the *Gramophone* Award-winning Chailly underlines the music's 1920s radicalism, Abbado takes a broader line, rather as the composer might have done in, say, the 1940s. He is well served by his band and soloists – violinist Kolja Blacher especially has the edge over any of his rivals – as well as the sound which varies its focus for each work. For example, No. 1 (1922), scored for 12 instruments with no soloist, is closely miked to give a real chamber feel, while Nos. 4 and 5 (1924-25) sound more like orchestral works. For those readers already in possession of the Chailly (reviewed above), this disc may be redundant; if the thought of all seven at once is too daunting, then this is the place to start. Recommended with enthusiasm.

Hindemith String Quartet No. 3, Op. 22.
Prokofiev String Quartet No. 2 in F major, Op. 92.
Walton String Quartet in A minor.
Hollywood Quartet (Felix Slatkin, Paul Shure *vns* Paul Robyn *va* Eleanor Aller *vc*).
Testament mono SBT1052 (74 minutes: ADD). Recorded 1951.   Ⓕ 🅷

Although numerous accounts of the Prokofiev have appeared over the years, none has approached, let alone surpassed, the Hollywood version of the Second Quartet. The same would no doubt apply to the Hindemith but for the fact that there have been fewer challengers. What a wonderful feeling for line these players had, what an incredible, perfectly matched and blended ensemble they produced – and how well these transfers sound! That goes for the Walton, too: there is no other account of the piece that makes so positive a case for it.

Violin Sonatas – E flat major, Op. 11 No. 1; D major, Op. 11 No. 2; E major (1935); C major (1939).
Ulf Wallin *vn* **Roland Pöntinen** *pf*
BIS CD761 (56 minutes: DDD). Recorded 1995.   Ⓕ

The E major Sonata of 1935 is brief (under 10 minutes long – as is Op. 11 No. 1) and not complex (it is more of a *sonatina*), yet it is familiar Hindemith from first note to last. The C major work (1939) is more complex and grave, and probably the finest of them. The longest sonata – and most conservative in idiom – is that in D major. Both Op. 11 works were written in 1918 while Hindemith was on active service, and are remarkable for bearing few traces of either the grimness of the Great War or Hindemith's personal voice. Both deserve wider currency. This issue is also welcome in including the fragmentary abandoned finale of Op. 11 No. 1, a rustic dance not in keeping with the symmetry of the whole. The sweet-toned Ulf Wallin is fully attuned to Hindemith's wavelength and Pöntinen provides exemplary support. The recording is typical BIS (i.e. excellent). A splendid disc.

Viola Sonatas – F major, Op. 11 No. 4; Op. 25 No. 4; C major (1939).
Nobilissima visione – Meditation. Trauermusik.
Paul Cortese *va* **Jordi Vilaprinyó** *pf* **Philharmonia Orchestra / Martyn Brabbins.**
ASV CDDCA978 (70 minutes: DDD). Recorded 1993.   Ⓕ

The late-romantic lyricism of the early F major Sonata, Op. 11 No. 4, comes over as slightly saccharine, with a tendency for the extremes to be evened out – a common problem with works from Hindemith's most radical decade. But in the more acerbic Second, Op. 25 No. 4 (1922), Cortese's warmth is very persuasive. He is at his best in No. 3 (1939), giving a performance of real depth that edges out even the composer's own, revelatory though that is, from the top spot – though some might prefer a quicker pace. On balance, this can be recommended as first choice in the sonatas and *Meditation* (from *Nobilissima visione*). The *Trauermusik* is a bonus, though it does not supplant the Walther-Blomstedt version (reviewed on page 472).

Hindemith Ludus tonalis.
Prokofiev Visions fugitives, Op. 22.
Olli Mustonen *pf*
Decca 444 803-2DH (68 minutes: DDD). Recorded 1994.   Ⓕ

Ludus tonalis is not an easy work for either audience or artist: its contrapuntal, angular and unforgiving textures pose demanding interpretative problems for the pianist, and at 50 minutes' duration its knotty sound world can be difficult to digest for even the most enthusiastic of listeners. In Mustonen's reading there is a real sense of journey as he traverses the 25 studies and there is great tonal variation, expressive range and playfulness in his playing, which helps the listener to feel more involved in this music. He is extremely persuasive in the way he sheds new light on this music, making it more accessible – ideal for winning new admirers to the work. Mustonen adds Prokofiev's *Visions fugitives* which makes an effective contrast. There's strong competition here but Mustonen acquits himself well, giving a fluid and beautifully shaped account of these 'fleeting thoughts', and the recordings for both works are excellent.

Mass. Six Chansons. Eine lichte Mitternacht. Du musst dir Alles geben. Der Tod. Nun da der Tag.
Zwölf Madrigale – Mitwelt; Tauche deine Furcht in schwarzen Wein; Trink aus!; Frühling;
Judaskuss; Du Zweifel an dem Sinn der Welt.
Netherlands Chamber Choir / Uwe Gronostay.
Globe GLO5125 (57 minutes: DDD). Texts and translations included. Recorded 1994.   Ⓕ

Mass. Zwölf Madrigale – Eines Narren, eines Künstlers Leben; An eine Tote; An einen Schmetterling; Magisches Rezept; Es bleibt wohl, was gesagt wird; Kraft fand zu Form. Lieder nach alten Texten, Op. 33.
Danish National Radio Choir / Uwe Gronostay.
Chandos CHAN9413 (52 minutes: DDD). Texts and translations included. Recorded 1995. Ⓕ

Hindemith's tardiness in composing a Mass can partly be explained by his view that Palestrina had had the last word with the Mass as a musical form. What is more important is the quality of the music, irrespective of why he wrote it. If not quite capturing the spirit of the missal, the Mass is still an evocative, exploratory setting, proving that he was far from being a spent force. Uwe Gronostay obviously has an affection for this work in particular, given that he has recorded it twice in as many years for two separate companies. There is little to choose between the performances, both being beautifully sung and shaped, qualities that are evident in the rest of each programme. Nor, indeed, are the couplings much help in the selection process, since the Mass is the sole duplication. Both discs contain six of the 12 deeply felt Madrigals Hindemith composed in 1958. The early *Lieder nach alten Texten* (1923) on Chandos are not really a sufficient makeweight, delightful though they are. Globe offers more in the lovely Rilke *Chansons* (1939) and the four male choruses, written between 1929 and 1939 to words by Whitman, Gottfried Benn, Hölderlin and Nietzsche. Chandos's sound is fuller, but Globe's is still very good. If you want just one disc of Hindemith's *a cappella* choral music, then go for Globe; but the Mass is worth having twice for its own sake, let alone in completing the Madrigal set.

When Lilacs Last in the Door-yard Bloom'd (Requiem for those we love).
Jan DeGaetani *mez* **William Stone** *bar*
Atlanta Symphony Chorus and Orchestra / Robert Shaw.
Telarc CD80132 (62 minutes: DDD). Text included. Recorded 1986. Ⓕ

Hindemith's Requiem is a setting of Whitman's poem – the lilacs piled on President Lincoln's coffin as it was taken across the country after his assassination just as the Civil War was over, the thrush ('voice of uttermost woe') symbolizing his own mourning, and the then fallen Western star (hailed at Lincoln's inauguration as a good omen) – further layers of association were added when, 80 years later almost to the day, President Roosevelt died as the Second World War was coming to an end. It includes a tragedy-laden sinfonia, arias, recitatives, marches, a massive double fugue and a passacaglia. It is not, however, the great technical virtuosity – in places as close-packed as Whitman's verse – which leaves the most lasting impression, but the haunting beauty of much of the setting. Robert Shaw gives a superlative and deeply moving performance of the work and receives an outstandingly vivid recording. He, of course, knows the work perhaps more intimately than anyone (having commissioned it from Hindemith in 1945 for his Collegiate Chorale in New York), and he makes the most of every expressive nuance, every shade of dynamics, every verbal inflexion, though without losing the overall shape. There is greater subtlety in the playing of the prelude than ever before; the big brass chords have weight and fullness without stridency (a splendid outburst at 'the tolling bells' perpetual clang'), and the orchestral playing generally is first-rate; it would scarcely be possible to find a more sympathetic baritone than William Stone, an unforced lyrical singer with clean technique and exemplary enunciation, or a sweeter or purer-voiced mezzo than Jan DeGaetani; and the chorus is wonderfully alert to the words and has a fine command of tone colour. Add all these factors together and you will understand why this disc should be added to your collection.

Das Unaufhörliche.
Ulrike Sonntag *sop* **Robert Wörle** *ten* **Siegfried Lorenz** *bar*
Berlin Radio Children's Choir;
Berlin Radio Chorus and Symphony Orchestra / Lothar Zagrosek.
Wergo WER6603-2 (two discs: 95 minutes: DDD). Text and translation included. Recorded 1995. Ⓕ

The oratorio *Das Unaufhörliche* ('The One Perpetual'), setting a poem by Gottfried Benn, was Hindemith's longest concert work. It never established itself in the repertoire (although Boult conducted the UK première as early as 1933). *Das Unaufhörliche* is cast in three parts, the first describing the 'one perpetual' itself, the second its effect on diverse areas of activity (including art, science and love), the third Humankind's reaction away from it and final acquiescence: 'Ever expansion and eternal change'. How closely Hindemith accorded with Benn's viewpoint – they later fell out over Benn's Nazi sympathies – is a matter for conjecture, but his evanescent score matched the poem's expansiveness of theme and nobility of utterance. In this alone it pointed the way to *Mathis der Maler*, for there is nothing here akin to the *Kammermusiken* or *Neues vom Tage* (a smash-hit in Berlin at the time). This is the work's first recording and the performance is a fine one with good sound. Flies in the ointment? Soprano Ulrike Sonntag, who seems too often to be straining for her notes and whose intonation is not always secure, and Wergo's failure to provide a translation of Benn's spoken introduction, recorded in 1932 and included as the final track. These are minor quibbles, however, and should not deter anyone from investing in this important release.

Sancta Susanna.
Susan Bullock *sop* Susanna; **Della Jones** *mez* Clementia; **Ameral Gunson** *mez* Old Nun;
Mark Rowlinson *spkr* Farmhand; **Maria Treedaway** *spkr* Maid;
Leeds Festival Chorus.
Drei Gesänge, Op. 9. Das Nusch-Nuschi, Op. 20 – Dances. Tuttifäntchen – Suite.
Susan Bullock *sop*
BBC Philharmonic Orchestra / Yan Pascal Tortelier.
Chandos CHAN9620 (70 minutes: DDD). Notes, text and translations included. Recorded 1997. Ⓕ

Sancta Susanna is one of the three early stage works Hindemith composed in the wake of the First World War, its companions being *Mörder, Hoffnung der Frauen* (1919) and *Das Nusch-Nuschi* (1920), based on a play for Burmese marionettes and represented here by its dances. Hindemith earned a living in the Frankfurt Opera during this period and so it is natural that he nurtured operatic ambitions. *Sancta Susanna* enjoyed a certain notoriety during its time. Fritz Busch refused to conduct its première on account of its blasphemous plot. It tells briefly of a young nun, Susanna, inflamed by the legend she hears from Sister Clementia, of a girl coming naked to the altar to embrace the lifesize figure of Christ on the Cross. For this blasphemy she is buried alive. Aroused and undeterred Susanna strips off and rips the covering from Christ's torso. She is terrified when a huge spider falls on to her head from the crucifix and, horrified by her deed, begs the nuns to wall her up. A drastic cure for arachnophobia or blasphemy! The opera is short, concentrated, highly imaginative and resourceful in its use of sonority; and its expressionist musical language is so powerful that one feels at the end of its barely 23 minutes that one has heard a much longer piece. It is superbly done here. No praise can be too high for the singers and for the delicacy, eloquence and power of the playing that Yan Pascal Tortelier draws from his orchestra. The recorded sound is of demonstration quality in its unforced naturalness. The gorgeous Straussian *Drei Gesänge*, Op. 9, are very vehement and passionate and at times wildly over the top but their assured craft and confident ambition is breathtaking. Susan Bullock performs them with thrilling panache. They are written for a large orchestra and there is little of what we think of as Hindemith in them. Nor is there much in *Tuttifäntchen*, a children's pantomime first performed in Darmstadt in 1922. The dances from *Nusch-Nuschi* are expertly done. There is some quite extraordinary music here and *Sancta Susanna* is a great find.

Mathis der Maler.
Roland Hermann *bar* Mathis; **Josef Protschka** *ten* Albrecht; **Gabriele Rossmanith** *sop* Regina;
Sabine Hass *sop* Ursula; **Harald Stamm** *bass* Riedinger; **Heinz Kruse** *ten* Hans Schwalb;
Victor von Halem *bass* Lorenz von Pommersfelden; **Hermann Winkler** *ten* Wolfgang Capito;
Ulrich Hielscher *bass* Truchsess von Waldberg; **Ulrich Ress** *ten* Sylvester von Schaumberg;
John Cogram *ten* Der Pfeiffer des Grafen von Helfenstein; **Marilyn Schmiege** *mez* Helfenstein;
North German Radio Chorus;
Cologne Radio Chorus and Symphony Orchestra / Gerd Albrecht.
Wergo WER6255-2 (three discs: 166 minutes: DDD). Notes and text included. Recorded 1990. Ⓕ

The masterpiece, *Mathis der Maler,* is one of the pinnacles of twentieth-century German opera. It has become axiomatic to see in it a parable of the times, with Hindemith using the turbulent world of sixteenth-century Germany to mirror the Nazi Reich and his place in it. But in reality *Mathis* is a spiritual and historical opera, not a political one, even in the handling of the artist's relationship to the society around him. Rudolf Stephan in his essay for Wergo plays down the political angle; if Hitler had not risen to power until, say, 1936, one doubts that *Mathis* would have turned out much different. Gerd Albrecht's acquaintance with Hindemith's music, particularly the operas, goes back to the early 1960s, before the composer's death. Hindemith even sanctioned some retouching of the orchestration in *Mathis* made by Albrecht for a festival performance, though it is not made clear whether Albrecht has applied this here, nor to what extent. Rarely have Hindemith's often heavy textures sounded so clear. As to the music, is not the brief concluding 'Alleluia' duet that crowns the sixth tableau one of *the* great moments in twentieth-century opera? You will be convinced from your very first hearing of it. There are fine moments aplenty in Albrecht's reading, not least where familiar passages from the *Mathis* Symphony surface and precipitate some of the most intense music of the opera. Roland Hermann is, perhaps, a shade stolid in places as the painter (though his world-weariness in the final scene is just right); Josef Protschka makes a most authoritative Cardinal, acting as a perfect foil to Hermann's Mathis. They head a fine cast, supported by some lusty singing and playing from the combined forces of Cologne and North German Radios.

Mathis der Maler.
Dietrich Fischer-Dieskau *bar* Mathis; **James King** *ten* Albrecht; **Gerd Feldhoff** *bass* Lorenz von Pommersfelden; **Manfred Schmidt** *ten* Capito; **Peter Meven** *bass* Riedinger; **William Cochran** *ten* Schwalb; **Alexander Malta** *bass* Truchsess von Waldburg; **Donald Grobe** *ten* Sylvester von Schaumberg; **Rose Wagmann** *mez* Ursula; **Urszula Koszut** *sop* Regina; **Trudeliese Schmidt** *mez* Countess Helfenstein; **Bavarian Radio Chorus and Symphony Orchestra / Rafael Kubelík.**
EMI CDS5 55237-2 (three discs: 183 minutes: ADD). Notes, text and translation included.
Recorded 1977.   (F)

Comparing Albrecht with Kubelík's reissued version shows that honours are fairly even; choosing between them would depend largely on one's keenness for individual names. There is little to choose between the two versions; neither is perfect, but both are very fine. Albrecht, who makes one or two minor but noticeable cuts, has the benefit of more modern sound, but EMI's for Kubelík has transferred well. The choruses in particular are excellent, although Albrecht's seem tame in the famous 'Temptation of St Antony' scene when set next to Kubelík's devilish-sounding Bavarians. Comparison of the casts yields a mixed picture; many readers will prefer Fischer-Dieskau as Mathis to the rather raw-voiced Hermann (except, as mentioned oppositee, in the final tableau); for many this will be the crucial criterion, but Wergo does have the better of some other principals. The roles of Schwalb and his daughter encapsulate the predicament: for EMI, William Cochran is more imposing than Heinz Kruse as the peasant leader but Wergo's Gabriele Rossmanith is sweeter and younger-toned as Regina. For Albrecht, their first appearance seems to be a mid-afternoon stroll and not the convincing escape from pursuit that Kubelík effects here (first disc, track 4). Despite the urgings of sentiment, neither set outclasses the other. For most, choice will rest on preferences for specific cast members. Those who love this score will want both.

Alun Hoddinott   British 1929

Symphonies – No. 2, Op. 29[a]; No. 3, Op. 61[b]; No. 5, Op. 81[c].
[ab]**London Symphony Orchestra** / [a]**Norman Del Mar,** [b]**David Atherton;**
[c]**Royal Philharmonic Orchestra** / **Sir Andrew Davis.**
Lyrita SRCD331 (74 minutes: ADD). Recorded 1967-73.   (F)

Alun Hoddinott is one of the best and most resourceful of living British symphonists, and the return to the catalogue of three demonstrations of that fact is welcome. What is meant by 'resourceful' is well illustrated by this coupling. The Second Symphony, from 1962, is apparently in a conventional four-movement layout, but in fact the outer movements investigate the arch-like or palindromic forms that Hoddinott was to make much use of later. Its successor is in two movements, but both are in two parts, with opening and closing *adagios* reflecting each other across the two intervening quick sections. The Fifth Symphony, most striking of all, has a finale of six panels, each slow section having a faster 'pair'. Its first movement (again there are only two) is described by the composer as an 'interrupted passacaglia'; the effect is of craggy, splendidly stormy music continually encroaching upon lyricism. The performances are excellent, the recordings for the most part decent.

Leopold Hofmann   Austrian 1738-1793

Cello Concertos – D major, B:D3; C major, B:C3; D major, B:D1; C major, B:C1.
Northern Sinfonia / Tim Hugh *vc*
Naxos 8 553853 (68 minutes: DDD). Recorded 1996.   (S)

The supremacy of Haydn and Mozart has always cast a shadow over the other Viennese composers of their time. In his day Leopold Hofmann, Kapellmeister at St Stephan's Cathedral from 1772, was one of the most eminent among them, as a composer of church music, symphonies, concertos and chamber works. His cello concertos – there are eight in all – belong to the 1760s or early 1770s, much the time of the Haydn C major Concerto, which they closely resemble in style. They are attractive, agreeable pieces, technically and formally assured if without very much individuality. The longest of the four concertos here, the one catalogued as D3, is clearly more mature in style than the others (listen to the well-argued development of the first movement) and also makes greater demands on the soloist. Tim Hugh's advocacy certainly makes the revival of these concertos worthwhile. He brings a very sound modern technique to the music, throwing off the rapid passages with evident ease, and there is a breadth to his phrasing that gives some amplitude to Hofmann's writing. His intonation is faultless, his tone full and warm, and he brings a keen feeling for *galant* expression to the slow movements. And there is vivacity in the quick movements too. The Northern Sinfonia plays responsively. Anyone who relishes good cello playing, should try this disc.

Violin Concertos – B flat major, B:Bb1; A major, B:A2. Concerto for Violin, Cello and Strings in G major, B:G1.
Lorraine McAslan *vn* **Tim Hugh** *vc*
Northern Chamber Orchestra / Nicholas Ward.
Naxos 8 554233 (60 minutes: DDD). Recorded 1997.   Ⓢ

For a composer long represented in the catalogue only by a concerto that masqueraded for a time as Haydn's (Hob VII*f*:D1), this is a most welcome issue of some of Leopold Hofmann's orchestral works, admirably edited and presented by the New Zealand scholar Allan Badley. These Viennese concertos, probably from the 1760s, are *galant* works, with quite florid solo parts and elaborate lines, a leisurely harmonic pace and a good deal of sequence, but they are shapely and effective music, with a good deal of tenderness in the slow movements – and also wit: the finale of the B flat Concerto is especially ingenious and beguiling. Then there is the double concerto, for violin and cello, which has much attractive dialogue and duetting, rather in the manner of the Mozart violin-viola *Sinfonia concertante* (although of course on a different level). The *Adagio* here is also particularly eloquent. The performances are excellent, with clean, perfectly tuned and expressive violin playing from the silver-toned Lorraine McAslan. Tim Hugh plays equally securely and with a keen sense of style. Tempos are well chosen by Nicholas Ward who obtains spruce accompaniments from the Northern Chamber Orchestra.

Robin Holloway   British 1943

Second Concerto for Orchestra, Op. 40.
BBC Symphony Orchestra / Oliver Knussen.
NMC (Special price) NMCD015 (34 minutes: DDD). Recorded 1993.
Gramophone Award Winner 1994.   Ⓔ

A North African holiday was the initial stimulus for Robin Holloway's *Second Concerto for Orchestra*. The extremes of contrast, he tells us – 'opulence and austerity, richness and drabness, brilliant light and dense shadow ... And above all, the noises ... the polyphony of hammering, tapping, thudding, tinkling, bashing ...' – haunted him and were soon demanding to be turned into music. At the same time, the experience seems to have set him off on a more enigmatic, private voyage through his, and our musical past. We hear a few particularly aching bars from Act 2 of *Tristan* and rather more of Chopin's F sharp major *Barcarolle*; while a strange, broken tune on muted trombone metamorphoses neatly into Parry's *Jerusalem*. It's bewildering, but gripping at the same time. Holloway can swerve from lush, late romanticism to strident modernism and back again with the alarming quickness of an opium dream; but as with any really revelatory dream, the more you probe it, the more lucid it seems. There are few contemporary orchestral works about which you will feel, on reaching the end, that you want to go back and soak in the experience all over again, and then go away somewhere and ponder its riddles. The members of the BBC Symphony Orchestra play as though each one of them were engaged on his or her own voyage of discovery – this is the kind of piece that will expose weakness or lack of conviction in every section of an orchestra. Oliver Knussen's triumph in pulling it all together, and then shaping and shading it so lovingly, is just one of the technically miraculous aspects of this disc; another is that the production team have somehow turned BBC Maida Vale Studio No. 1 into a fine, spacious acoustic, with teeming details beautifully focused. It adds up to a fascinating disc.

Third Concerto for Orchestra, Op. 76.
London Symphony Orchestra / Michael Tilson Thomas.
NMC NMCD039 (45 minutes: DDD). Recorded live in 1996.   Ⓕ

The first ideas for No. 3 came during a trip through South America – sound pictures of Lake Titicaca, riotous New Year's Day celebrations in the Bay of Bahia, the slow train-crossing of the Great Brazilian Swamp and the huge, satanic slag heap at the Potosi Silver Mine. Holloway jotted them all down on the spot: then his notebook was stolen, and it took another 13 years to recall them and finish the piece. By then, of course, the alchemical processes of memory had transformed the original musical impressions into something quite different. What might have been simply a descriptive tone-poem finally emerged as a powerful and unusual musical argument – a huge slow movement, with a moderately fast dance-like finale, which evolves from tiny scraps of motifs (hardly a 'theme' in sight). And yet much of the original 'illustrative' character remains. String and woodwind textures recall dense, overripe rain forest foliage; the dark, 'sluggish' first movement suggests the movement of a vast, slow, muddy river; extravagant sensuousness contrasts with clangorous bells or craggy brass. This recording, based on its 1996 première, is quite an achievement. It is rare for a conductor and an orchestra to show such a compelling grasp of the shape and atmosphere of a work at its first performance. Technically the sound has none of the usual problems of live recording – virtually no intrusive noise, good balance, warm tone.

Holloway Fantasy-Pieces on the Heine 'Liederkreis' of Schumann, Op. 16. Serenade in C, Op. 41*b*.
Schumann Liederkreis, Op. 24.
Toby Spence *ten* **Ian Brown** *pf*
Nash Ensemble / Martyn Brabbins.
Hyperion CDA66930 (75 minutes: DDD). Text and translation included. Recorded 1996. Ⓕ **E**

A contemporary composer takes a nineteenth-century classic – Schumann's song-cycle *Liederkreis* – and sets it in a musical frame of his own devising: a short, astringent 'Praeludium' and four extended movements, the style hovering between pure homage and what the composer calls 'phantasmagorical collage'. Certainly sufficient to cause hackles to rise! But the result, entitled *Fantasy-Pieces on the Heine 'Liederkreis' of Schumann* is uniquely fascinating, haunting and increasingly rewarding the more one goes back to it. Brief though it is, the 'Praeludium' is just enough to tell the ear that the performance of *Liederkreis* that follows (very persuasive in this recording) is not going to be the whole story. Holloway picks up magically on Schumann's ending, in a short movement, 'Half asleep' (what follows is, at times, intensely dream-like). Then come an *Adagio*, a *Scherzo* and a finale – on one level, symphonic, on another, an intricate series of references and cross-references based on Schumann's songs (not all from *Liederkreis*). The manner drifts between masterful irony and fleeting moments of intense self-revelation. *Liederkreis* remains *Liederkreis*, and yet something profound and (in the wider sense) modern is added. The Serenade in C is a kind of post-modern *divertimento*. Scored for the same forces as Schubert's Octet, it alternates, charmingly and teasingly, between sensuous Viennese cosiness, something closer to the salon Elgar, and delightful, end-of-the-pier vulgarity – though with a more acerbic harmonic colouring from time to time. Play a short extract to a musical friend and he/she might well date it before the First World War. But nothing is ever what it seems for very long; the disruptive subtlety of *Fantasy-Pieces* is here too, despite the seeming holiday feeling. Splendid performances from the Nash Ensemble – colourful, precise and sensitive to Holloway's kaleidoscopic shifts in mood. The recordings are excellent: the change in perspective for the Schumann songs makes perfect aural sense.

Vagn Holmboe

Danish 1909-1996

Chamber Concertos – No. 7 for Oboe and Chamber Orchestra, Op. 37; No. 8 for Orchestra, Op. 38, 'Sinfonia concertante'; No. 9 for Violin, Viola and Orchestra, Op. 39.
Max Artved *ob* **Mikkel Futtrup** *vn* **Tim Frederiksen** *va*
Danish Radio Sinfonietta / Hannu Koivula.
Da Capo 8 224086 (62 minutes: DDD). Recorded 1997. Ⓕ

While Holmboe remained audibly the same composer, Holmboe the concerto writer had a very different agenda from Holmboe the symphonist, and nowhere does that become more apparent than in No. 8 (1945), subtitled *Sinfonia concertante*, a splendid chamber-orchestral concerto yet also a direct precursor of the magnificent *First Chamber Symphony* (1953). Internal cohesion seems to be No. 8's *raison d'être*, not the interplay of soloist(s) and tutti found in, for instance, Nos. 7 (1944-45) and 9 (1945-46). The Eighth also stands a little apart from its companions by virtue of its more Hindemithian aspect. The arch-form first movement of No. 7, for oboe, has in its outermost sections distinct pre-echoes of the humane luminosity that infuses so much of the music of Holmboe's last three decades, and – as does the second of No. 8 – nimbly synthesizes elements of multiple movements within a single span as do several of the symphonies. No. 9 is more conventional, a delightful two-part invention in three movements for violin and viola, with orchestral accompaniment in the outer spans only. The performances are exemplary, the sound clear if very slightly studio-bound. A definite must-buy for Holmboe enthusiasts.

Chamber Concertos – No. 10 for Orchestra, Op. 40; No. 11 for Trumpet and Orchestra, Op. 44; No. 12 for Trombone and Orchestra, Op. 52; No. 13 for Oboe, Viola and Orchestra, Op. 67.
Max Artved *ob* **Ole Edward Antonsen** *tpt* **Jacques Mauger** *tbn* **Tim Frederiksen** *va*
Danish Radio Sinfonietta / Hannu Koivula.
Da Capo 8 224087 (75 minutes: DDD). Recorded 1997. Ⓕ

Holmboe Orchestral

Chamber Concerto No. 10 (1945-46) is a bracing early example of Holmboe's metamorphosis technique, its nine sections acting like variations within a traditional concerto format: the sections in pairs respectively form an introduction and three 'movements', with the last acting as coda. The concerto is described on the back of the jewel-case as being 'for wood-brass-gut and orchestra': in the official Hanson catalogue, 'Wood-brass-gut' – in Danish *Trae-messing-tarm* – is the subtitle, the concerto being listed as the composer's second (of three) for orchestra. Nos. 11-13 (1948, 1950 and 1955-56) are conventional in layout. The gem of the disc is No. 13, for the unusual combination of oboe and viola (for the most part playing as a pair in intertwining lines). This is music suffused by that wonderful Nordic light so prevalent in Holmboe's later works, utterly beguiling and beautifully played. For Holmboe enthusiasts this disc is self-recommending. Although Da Capo's recording is a mite studio-bound, this is, nevertheless, a fine disc.

Concertos – No. 11 for Trumpet and Orchestra, Op. 44; No. 12 for Trombone and Orchestra, Op. 52; Tuba and Orchestra, Op. 127. Intermezzo concertante, Op. 171.
Håkan Hardenberger *tpt* **Christian Lindberg** *tbn* **Jens Bjørn-Larsen** *tuba*
Aalborg Symphony Orchestra / Owain Arwel Hughes.
BIS CD802 (55 minutes: DDD). Recorded 1995.   Ⓕ

The Trumpet Concerto has a leanness of texture and neo-classical air that will surprise those familiar with Holmboe's symphonies. Hardenberger's first entry creates an electricity that is maintained throughout the work – indeed, the disc as a whole. No. 11's tripartite design recurs, condensed into a single movement, in No. 12: a brief, expressively crucial slow section framed by a large-boned *Allegro* (rather grave in character in the trombone work), and a good-humoured, rollicking finale. The Tuba Concerto (1976), by contrast, requires a full orchestral complement, its one integrated span bearing little semblance of traditional three-movement form. It is the most dramatic and exploratory work here, both in mood and sonority, the demands of which on tuba virtuosos over the years have occasioned it to be played in slightly differing versions, especially with regard to the taxing cadenza. The short *Intermezzo concertante* reaffirms that, however ungainly it may seem, the tuba really can sing. Wonderful music, wonderfully performed and recorded.

Symphonies – No. 11, Op. 144; No. 12, Op. 175; No. 13, Op. 192.
Aarhus Symphony Orchestra / Owain Arwel Hughes.
BIS CD728 (63 minutes: DDD). Recorded 1994.   Ⓕ

Few who have invested in this series so far can have been left in any doubt that these are among the most commanding symphonies to have emerged in post-war Europe. Some might even argue that they are *the* finest since Sibelius and Nielsen. All credit to Owain Arwel Hughes and the Aarhus orchestra for their committed advocacy and to BIS for recording them in such vivid, naturally balanced sound. The Eleventh, composed in 1980, is quintessential Holmboe, and its atmosphere resonates in the mind long after you have heard it. To quote Knud Ketting's notes, 'the symphony's climax in dynamic and emotional terms comes in the second movement and it then slowly retreats within itself ... [it] is cast as a strong arch, which impresses at first hearing, and commands increasing admiration on closer acquaintance'. The arabesque that opens the symphony seems to come from another world and the transparent, luminous textures communicate the sense of a spiritual quest that one rarely encounters in modern music. The Twelfth is a taut, well-argued piece, and is, like its two companions on this disc, in three movements. No one listening to the Thirteenth, written at the instigation of Owain Arwel Hughes, would think that it was the work of an 85-year-old. Of course, there have been other octogenarian symphonies but none that sounds quite so youthful or highly charged as this one.

Symphonic Metamorphoses – No. 1, Op. 68, 'Epitaph'; No. 2, Op. 76, 'Monolith'; No. 3, Op. 80, 'Epilog'; No. 4, Op. 108, 'Tempo variabile'.
Aalborg Symphony Orchestra / Owain Arwel Hughes.
BIS CD852 (75 minutes: DDD). Recorded 1996.   Ⓕ

In form the symphonic metamorphosis is an offshoot of the symphonic fantasia (but of a radically different ilk to Sibelius's *Pohjola's Daughter*), each of these four completely different from its companions. The vigour and luminous orchestration of the symphonies are present, as many of the internal developmental processes, but not the level of integration. Holmboe's priorities here are unlike those of many others of his pieces, yet the music coheres perfectly on its own terms. Hughes is fully inside Holmboe's idiom, whether in the single-minded determination of *Monolith* or in the magnificent and visionary *Epilog*, one of the composer's most searching utterances, prefiguring both the Ninth Symphony (1969) and *Requiem for Nietzsche*. This is extraordinary music: everyone with an ounce of inquisitiveness is urged to try it and be won over.

String Quartets – No. 10, Op. 102; No. 11, Op. 111; No. 12, Op. 116.
Kontra Quartet (Anton Kontra, Boris Samsing *vns* Peter Fabricius *va* Morten Zeuthen *vc*).
Da Capo 8 224101 (67 minutes: DDD). Recorded 1997.   Ⓕ

These works are worthy of comparison with the best in twentieth-century cycles, namely those of
Bartók, Shostakovich and Simpson. True, Holmboe's idiom was less overtly pioneering or
sensational (in the best sense of the word) than such peers, yet his quartets are no less visionary or
searching. The crucial difference was his uncommon humanity, which refracts through his music
like light through a prism, with no place for Shostakovich-type desolation. The Tenth Quartet
(1969) is serious, high-minded even, in tone but always positive in spirit. Cast as a diptych, the
constituent sections (fast-slow-fast, and slow-fast) together form a five-movement arch design to
which he would often return later – as in No. 12 (1973). The Tenth is typically subtle and seems to
grow and develop with each re-hearing. The same is true of No. 11 (1972). Do not be fooled by its
comparative brevity (just over 18 minutes), the subtitle (*Quartetto rustico*) or the light, bird-like
twitterings of the opening *Allegro leggiero* into believing it a relaxation or something merely
diverting: it is just as purposeful as any of its fellows, even if it smiles throughout. No. 11's *Andante
tranquillo* third movement is yet another of Holmboe's wonderful creations combining Nordic light
with sublime counterpoint. The Twelfth has two such spans, and is one of his finest quartets. The
opening *Allegro robusto* has a Bartókian air reminding us that eastern European folk music was a
lasting influence, while the work's final bars, unusually, resolve on a question mark. The Kontra
Quartet has the idiom under its skin; though the clear recording is not exactly spacious. Still, a fine
disc of excellent music.

Gustav Holst   British 1874-1934

A Somerset Rhapsody, H87. Beni Mora, H107. Invocation, H75. A Fugal Overture, H151.
Egdon Heath, H172. Hammersmith, H178.
Tim Hugh *vc* **Royal Scottish National Orchestra / David Lloyd-Jones.**
Naxos 8 553696 (69 minutes: DDD). Recorded 1996.   Ⓢ🄴

This superb recording was made in the Henry Wood Hall in Glasgow. Lloyd-Jones has as his two
weightiest items the Hardy-inspired *Egdon Heath*, arguably Holst's finest work, as well as the
prelude and fugue, *Hammersmith*, comparably dark and intense. In the latter he chooses the wind-
band version, achieving a subtlety of shading in phrasing and dynamic amply to justify that striking
choice. The Naxos sound is vividly atmospheric while letting one hear inner detail, particularly
important in the fugue. Lloyd-Jones generally adopts flowing speeds and is objective in his
interpretation while bringing out to the full the tenderness and refinement of the writing.
Particularly beautiful is the performance of *A Somerset Rhapsody* which opens the disc, with the
cor anglais solo ravishingly played. The six works are neatly balanced, three dating from before the
climactic period of *The Planets* and *The Hymn of Jesus*, and three after. Particularly valuable is the
atmospheric *Invocation* for cello and orchestra of 1911, rather dismissed by Imogen Holst, but here
given a yearningly intense, deeply thoughtful performance with Tim Hugh as soloist. This is a
highly recommendable offering, whether for the dedicated Holstian or the newcomer wanting to
investigate this composer's more characteristic work outside *The Planets*.

The Planets, H125.

Holst The Planets[a].
Elgar Variations on an Original Theme, Op. 36, 'Enigma'[b].
[a]**Geoffrey Mitchell Choir;** [a]**London Philharmonic Orchestra,**
[b]**London Symphony Orchestra / Sir Adrian Boult.**
EMI Studio Plus CDM7 64748-2 (78 minutes: ADD). Recorded [a]1978, [b]1970.   Ⓜ🆁🆁

Sir Adrian Boult's long association with *The Planets* is well known (since the famous first run-
through – for it can scarcely have been more – at the Queen's Hall in 1919). This splendid set from
1978 has been admirably remastered. Boult, in the composer's words, 'first made the *Planets* shine'
and he always had something special to say about the music on all his recordings. Apart from public
performances, he made five recordings of the work, and this is considered by many to have been the
finest. Sir Adrian's interpretation varied very little throughout his long association with the work,
only being temporarily shaken when he heard the reissue of Holst's own very different 1926
performance. However, he stuck to his own view which the composer thoroughly approved of. The
actual performance has an indefinable 'rightness' about it, a supreme authority that makes it
difficult to imagine the score being interpreted in any other way. Has 'Mars' ever resounded with
more terrifying ferocity since? We very much doubt it. In 'Venus' the playing has a translucent

beauty, while the impish 'Mercury' really sparkles. 'Jupiter' has marvellous exuberance and sparkle, its big tune lent enormous dignity and humanity. 'Saturn', too, is paced to perfection (the central climax has a massive inevitability about it), and 'Uranus' goes about his mischievous antics with terrific swagger. In 'Neptune' one notes again the exquisite poise of the orchestral response, and the choir contributes admirably. If you've never heard Boult's *Planets*, we urge immediate investigation of this set! Plenty of *Enigma* recordings have been added to the catalogue since 1970 when this recording was made, but none has surpassed it in authority and fidelity. Just listen to the clarity of detail – nothing overdone, but so many little touches that give this familiar music a freshness that projects its originality. There is also a slightly elegiac feel to the phrasing here as if Boult, no sentimentalist, was nevertheless aware that his *Enigma* days must inevitably be numbered. Yet the faster variations have the vitality and brio that one might expect from a younger conductor. The LSO's performance is excellent and the recording too.

The Planets.
Women's voices of the **Montreal Symphony Chorus and Orchestra / Charles Dutoit.**
Decca 417 553-2DH (53 minutes: DDD). Recorded 1986. *Gramophone* Award Winner 1987.　Ⓕ

Holst's brilliantly coloured orchestral suite, *The Planets*, is undoubtedly his most famous work and its success is surely deserved. The musical characterization is as striking as its originality of conception: the association of 'Saturn' with old age, for instance, is as unexpected as it is perceptive. Bax introduced Holst to astrology and while he wrote the music he became fascinated with horoscopes, so it is the astrological associations that are paramount, although the linking of 'Mars' (with its enormously powerful 5/4 rhythms) and war also reflects the time of composition. Throughout, the work's invention is as memorable as its vivid orchestration is full of infinite detail. No recording can reveal it all but this one comes the closest to doing so. Dutoit's individual performance is in a long line of outstanding recordings.

The Planets. Egdon Heath, H172.
BBC Symphony Chorus and Orchestra / Sir Andrew Davis.
Teldec British Line 4509-94541-2 (64 minutes: DDD). Recorded 1993.　ⒻⓈ

This is a mightily impressive account of *The Planets*. The high spot of Sir Andrew Davis's reading is undoubtedly 'Saturn', whose remorseless tread has rarely seemed more implacable. Aided by orchestral playing that is both memorably concentrated and rapt, Holst's textures in the closing section acquire a breathtaking translucency, and how memorably the BBC SO brass thrusts home the terrifying central climax at 5'34". 'Neptune', too, is exceptionally successful: ethereally delicate *tremolando* harps set the scene for a tone picture of exquisite beauty, graced by choral work of notable purity from the women of the BBC Symphony Chorus. Elsewhere, 'Mercury' darts hither and thither in suitably impish fashion. 'Venus' is cool and chaste: if the BBC violins can't quite command the bloom and sheen of the very finest groups, the liquidity and poise of the woodwind are most striking. The burst of energy at the close of 'Jupiter' is genuinely exhilarating. The spectacularly ample sound certainly makes the mischievous antics of 'Uranus' a feast for the ears, and Davis handles the coda superbly, plunging the listener into a world which is truly unnerving in its bleakness. Davis shows comparable perception in the similarly remote terrain of *Egdon Heath*. He succeeds in conveying much of the sombre intensity of Holst's cloud-hung evocation.

The Hymn of Jesus, H140[a]. First Choral Symphony, H155[b].
[b]**Felicity Palmer** *sop* [a]**St Paul's Cathedral Choir;** [a]**London Symphony Chorus;**
London Philharmonic [b]**Choir and Orchestra /** [a]**Sir Charles Groves,** [b]**Sir Adrian Boult.**
EMI British Composers CDM5 65128-2 (72 minutes: ADD). Texts included. Recorded 1974 and 1977.　Ⓜ

When it first appeared in 1978, Groves's account of *The Hymn of Jesus* was generally rated a finer effort than Boult's 1961 Decca recording. The authority and honesty of the former's direction is impressive. True, orchestral discipline could at times be tighter, but the choral singing is never less than very commendable. It should, however, be pointed out that Groves's achievement has since been outshone by Richard Hickox (reviewed below), who in turn cannot quite match the extraordinary fervour and intensity of Sir Malcolm Sargent in his pioneering 1944 account (available on a Dutton Laboratories compilation CD). The really good news here, though, is Boult's powerful 1974 première recording of the awesome *Choral Symphony*. This was one of Holst's most ambitious, imaginative and questing creations, still under-appreciated to this day. It contains pages that are amongst the most original he ever conceived, not least the opening 'Invocation to Pan' and extraordinarily intense setting of the *Ode on a Grecian Urn*. The sound in both items remains satisfyingly full and immediate.

Seven Partsongs, H162. A Choral Fantasia, H177. A Dirge for Two Veterans, H121.
Ode to Death, H144.
Patricia Rozario *sop* **London Symphony Chorus; Joyful Company of Singers;**
City of London Sinfonia / Richard Hickox.
Chandos CHAN9437 (59 minutes: DDD). Texts included. Recorded 1994.   Ⓕ

It is the First World War that is the unnamed, ever-felt presence here. 'I float this carol with joy,
with joy to thee O Death', chants Walt Whitman with that willed mystical intoxication that proved
so surprisingly attractive to both Holst and Vaughan Williams, composers who could face reality
soberly enough and in Holst's case often with a bleak, spare beauty of sound that takes and
bestows only a hard-won comfort. Listening even to the relatively 'light' and partially happy Bridges
settings (the *Seven Partsongs*), one becomes aware of a hollow, half-anxious feeling, located in that
mysterious area of midriff wherein these undefined apprehensions take their dwelling. With it
comes a musician's cherishing of silence, as though the music which intrudes upon it must be most
finely attuned if it is to justify the presumption. Death emerges from its temporary hiding place in
the seventh ('Assemble, all ye maidens') and then, for the rest of the recital, comes into its kingdom.
Most explicitly, the *Dirge for Two Veterans* takes up the 'full-keyed bugles' of war, and that was
written in the last months of 1914. In the *Ode to Death* (1931) and even the partsongs for women's
voices, it is surely the dreadful sadness of that war which fills the hollow places and so, for comfort,
enhances the apprehension of beauty in music. The programme has a very special value, and the
performances are worthy of it.

The Cloud Messenger, H111. The Hymn of Jesus, H140.
Della Jones *mez* **London Symphony Chorus and Orchestra / Richard Hickox.**
Chandos CHAN8901 (66 minutes: DDD). Texts included. Recorded 1990.   Ⓕ

When this CD was first released, the great talking point was *The Cloud Messenger*, a 43-minute
work of considerable imaginative power, virtually forgotten since its disastrous première under the
baton of Holst himself in 1913. It shows the composer already working on an epic scale –
something which casts light on the subsequent eruption of *The Planets*. It is marvellous to have the
work on disc, though it is, as you might expect, uneven. Those who admire the ascetic rigour of
Holst's later music may share the reservations of Imogen Holst and find the score disappointingly
'backward'. There are certainly echoes of Vaughan Williams's *A Sea Symphony* and several older
models. On the other hand, the glittering approach to the sacred city on Mount Kailasa and the
stylized orientalism of the climactic dance are new to British music; another world, the world of
'Venus', is foreshadowed in the closing pages. The text is Holst's own translation from the Sanskrit.
One of the few incontrovertible masterpieces in Holst's output, the familiar *Hymn of Jesus* has
seldom received a better performance on disc, although the grand acoustics of London's St Jude's
impart a certain warm imprecision – the choral singing itself is splendidly crisp – which can blunt
the impact of Holst's acerbic harmonies.

Arthur Honegger   Franch/Swiss 1892-1955

Symphonies – No. 1 in C major; No. 2 for Strings and Trumpet obbligato in D major, H153;
No. 3, H186, 'Liturgique'; No. 5 in D major, H202, 'Di tre re'.

Symphonies Nos. 1-5. Three Symphonic Movements – No. 1, H53; 'Pacific 231';
No. 2, H67, 'Rugby, H67.
Bavarian Radio Symphony Orchestra / Charles Dutoit.
Erato Ultima 3984-21340-2 (two discs: 141 minutes: DDD). Recorded 1982-84.   ⑧ 🅢

Although a pupil of d'Indy, and someone who may have both learned too much from 1920s
Stravinsky and Prokofiev, Honegger is very obviously next generation, musically, and in his
response to not one, but two world wars. The music is harmonically daring (plenty of writing in two
keys at once), dealing in sometimes consecutive, at others simultaneous, but always very bold and
often very moving contrasts – gesturally graphic grim realities and possible deliverance or almost
escapism – all within a neo-classical framework. Dutoit is perhaps rather better at the often seraphic
beauty of the deliverance and escapism – for example, the haven of the Fourth Symphony is the
single most successful performance here – than he is with the music's muscular driving force and
dark power. Nevertheless his cycle is a considerable achievement, and the Munich recordings,
though not as vividly present as some, are faultlessly balanced and satisfyingly natural. In short, at
the price, an attractive starting-point for the Honegger symphonies. Minimal insert-notes, as you'd
expect from these Ultima reissues.

Honegger Symphonies Nos. 2 and 3.
Stravinsky Concerto in D.
Berlin Philharmonic Orchestra / Herbert von Karajan.
DG The Originals 447 435-2GOR (72 minutes: ADD). Recorded 1969. Ⓜ **RR**

Karajan's performances of these Honegger symphonies enjoy legendary status – and rightly so. This recording remains in a class of its own for sheer beauty of sound and flawless ensemble. The French critic, Bernard Gavoty, once spoke rather flightily of Karajan 'transcending emotions and imparting to them that furnace heat that makes a work of genius give off light if brought to the desired temperature' – but it's true! There is a luminous quality and an incandescence about these performances. The Stravinsky Concerto in D major was written within a year of the *Symphonie liturgique* and may perhaps be a little too 'cultured' and not spiky enough for some tastes. The lightness of touch, sprightliness of rhythm and flawless ensemble of the Berlin Philharmonic are a joy in themselves.

Symphony No. 2, H153. Three Symphonic Movements Nos. 1-3. Pastorale d'été, H31. Monopartita, H204.
Zurich Tonhalle Orchestra / David Zinman.
Decca 455 352-2DH (70 minutes: DDD). Recorded 1998. Ⓕ

With the Symphony for strings David Zinman gives us a handful of shorter orchestral pieces ranging from the well-known to a comparative rarity, the *Monopartita*. This was Honegger's very last orchestral work and has even been referred to as a Sixth Symphony which has imploded. It finds the composer at his most resourceful: one of its episodes hints at the slow movement of the *Deliciae basiliensis* Symphony. The Tonhalle does not offer string playing that can match Karajan's Berlin Philharmonic, but Zinman can more than hold his own against most comers. He gets responsive and sensitive playing from the orchestra. A finely characterized *Pastoral d'été* and a *Pacific 231* that sounds as if it is definitely coming in on time, and very good Decca sound – well detailed, spacious and with plenty of impact – enhances the attractions of this issue.

Symphonies Nos. 3 and 5. Three Symphonic Movements – No. 1.
Danish National Radio Symphony Orchestra / Neeme Järvi.
Chandos CHAN9176 (57 minutes: DDD). Recorded 1992. Ⓕ

There is a resemblance in the Fifth to the opening bars (with their triads in contrary motion) to Milhaud's *Moses* and one wonders whether it was a deliberate tribute or merely fortuitous. Be that as it may, the Fifth remains one of Honegger's most individual scores, and this recording serves it well. There is nothing restrained here and even if the finale does not quite match the sheer exhilaration and gusto of Serge Baudo's wonderful Supraphon account from the early 1960s (which now sounds far more full bodied in its new transfer), the Järvi is not far behind: moreover it is very well recorded. So, too, is the rest of the programme and although the playing of the Danish orchestra for Järvi in the Third does not outshine that of the Berlin Philharmonic for Karajan this is a thoroughly convincing and compelling account. The *Pacific 231* also thunders mightily along the track.

Jeanne d'Arc au bûcher.
Françoise Pollet, Michèle Command *sops* **Nathalie Stutzman** *contr* **John Aler** *ten*
Marthe Keller, Georges Wilson, Pierre-Marie Escourrou, Paola Lenzi *narrs*
Chorus and Children's Voices of French Radio; French National Orchestra / Seiji Ozawa.
DG 429 412-2GH (69 minutes: DDD). Text and translations included. Recorded live in 1989. Ⓕ **S**

Honegger described *Joan of Arc at the stake* as a 'dramatic oratorio', but it is a work almost impossible to categorize, the two chief characters – Joan and Brother Dominc – being speaking parts, but with a chorus, a children's chorus, and a curiously constituted orchestra including saxophones instead of horns, two pianos and, most notably, an ondes martenot which, with its banshee shriek, bloodcurdlingly reinforces the climax as Joan breaks her earthly chains. The action is partly realistic, partly symbolic, unfolding in quasi-cinematic flashbacks. The musical techniques and styles employed by Honegger are extraordinarily varied, with humming and shouting besides singing, and with elements of polyphony, folk-song, baroque dances and jazz rhythms; yet all is fused together in a remarkable way to produce a work of gripping power and, in the final scenes, almost intolerable emotional intensity: the beatific *envoi* 'Greater love hath no man ...' is a passage that catches the throat and haunts the mind. Ozawa fully captured the work's dramatic forces in this public performance, which has been skilfully served by the recording engineers; Marthe Keller vividly portrays Joan's bewilderment, fervour and agony, John Aler makes a swaggering Procus, and Françoise Pollet is radiant-voiced as the Virgin. Even more than *Le roi David*, this is Honegger's masterpiece.

Jacques Hotteterre

French 1674-1763

L'art de préluder – D major; G major; B minor; C major; C minor; G minor. Première livre – Suite No. 3 in G major. Deuxième livre – Suite No. 1 in G minor; Suite No. 2 in C minor. Airs et Brunettes – Rochers, je ne veux point que votre eco fidelle; J'ay passé deux jours sans vous voir; Dans ces deserts paisibles; Pourquoy, doux rossignol; Le beau berger Tircis.
Wilbert Hazelzet *fl* **Jaap ter Linden** *va da gamba* **Konrad Junghänel** *theorbo*
Jacques Ogg *hpd*
Glossa GCD920801 (76 minutes: DDD). Recorded 1996. ⓔⓟ

With musicianship which is refined and thoughtful, Wilbert Hazelzet here treats us to an enjoyable programme of *préludes*, suites and song arrangements from a spread of Hotteterre's publications, ranging from 1708 to 1723. Hazelzet plays on a copy of a flute made by a member of the Hotteterre family itself, and its unusually dark and fruity sound is well matched to the music which, though it offers its fair share of lively moments, often shows in addition a melancholy side which can be deeply moving. Hazelzet's eloquent, unshowy playing does the music nothing less than excellent service, and he is helped by discreet and nicely varied continuo accompaniments. This is an exquisite and surprising release, which also happens to be most attractively packaged.

Alan Hovhaness

American 1911

Khrimian Hairig, Op. 49. The Holy City, Op. 218. Psalm and Fugue, Op. 40a. Kohar, Op. 66. Symphony No. 17, Op. 203, 'Symphony for Metal Orchestra'.
Chris Gekker *tpt* **Manhattan Chamber Orchestra / Richard Auldon Clark.**
Koch International Classics 37289-2 (53 minutes: DDD). Recorded 1995. ⓕ

The lengthiest offering here (at just over 20 minutes) is the *Symphony for Metal Orchestra* (the seventeenth of Hovhaness's 67 symphonies to date) which was composed in 1963 shortly after a visit to Japan. Scored for the singular combination of six flutes, three trombones and metallic percussion, its four contemplative movements incorporate elements of Japanese *gagaku* music together with sounds inspired by the Shó (a Japanese mouth-organ, here imitated by the flutes). Rather more rewarding is *The Holy City*, a highly evocative, nine-and-a-half-minute essay for trumpet, harp, chimes and strings dating from 1967 and full of atmospheric sonorities.
Chris Gekker is the superb trumpet soloist both here and in the serene, yet deceptively purposeful *Khrimian Hairig* (composed in 1944 and revised four years later), which takes its name from 'a heroic Armenian priest'. The glowing string textures in the *Psalm and Fugue* (1941) cast quite a spell, as do the hypnotic, mantra-like melodic lines of *Kohar* (1946), another Armenian-inspired creation, scored for flute, cor anglais, timpani and strings. Richard Auldon Clark and his New York group give outstandingly sympathetic performances. Really excellent sound, too.

Hovhaness Symphony No. 2, Op. 132, 'Mysterious Mountain'.
Prokofiev Lieutenant Kijé – Suite, Op. 60.
Stravinsky Divertimento from 'La baiser de la fée'.
Chicago Symphony Orchestra / Fritz Reiner.
RCA Victor Living Stereo 09026 61957-2 (64 minutes: ADD). Recorded 1957-58. ⓜⒽ

Reiner's mastery is everywhere in evidence, from the hymn-like cadences of Hovhaness's wholesome, though skilfully crafted, Symphony to the fairy-tale excitement of *Kijé*'s 'Troika'. The Chicago Symphony plays like a generously augmented chamber ensemble, with delicately tapered strings, sweet-toned woodwinds, impeccable brass and a rhythmically alert but never overzealous percussion section. Reiner's Straussian credentials are particularly telling wherever musical lines converge, while the *Fairy's Kiss* 'Divertimento' has a positively Mozartian elegance. Try Stravinsky's 'Scherzo' and 'Pas de deux'; or, if you've ever doubted Reiner's capacity for tenderness, put on the closing half-minute of *Kijé*'s 'Romance'. There's impressive virtuosity, too – especially in the Nielsenesque string flurries that open Hovhaness's hectic *Allegro vivo*. Musically, this is a superb programme and the performance of *Mysterious Mountain* – an American 'classic' – is unmissable. Similarly, the Stravinsky is in a class of its own and *Lieutenant Kijé* is superbly executed. This transfer is fairly good, save for a momentary tape glitch 0'47" into Hovhaness's opening *Andante* and a fair degree of tape noise. The overall sound is more hollow than one remembers from the old LPs, but there's ample clarity and impressive channel separation. All in all, a priceless CD – certainly from a musical stand-point.

Hovhaness Four Bagatelles, Op. 30. String Quartets – No. 1, Op. 8, 'Jupiter'; No. 3, Op. 208 No. 1, 'Reflections on my Childhood'; No. 4, Op. 208 No. 2, 'The Ancient Tree'. Suite from String Quartet No. 2 – Gamelan in Sosi Style; Spirit Murmur; Hymn.
Z. Long Song of the Ch'in.
Shanghai Quartet (WeiGang Li, HongGang Li *vns* Zheng Wang *va* James Wilson *vc*).
Delos DE3162 (69 minutes: DDD). Recorded 1994.   Ⓕ

The likeable First Quartet of 1936 boasts, like Mozart's *Jupiter* Symphony, a four-part fugue of impressive rigour (hence the work's subtitle). Next come three out of the seven pithy movements that comprise the Second Quartet from 1952: the concluding 'Hymn' is a particularly affecting creation. The Third and Fourth Quartets were inspired by childhood memories. The former basks in a soothing, supplicatory glow, with occasional touches of Eastern promise (aural reminders of the composer's Armenian roots), whereas its more nostalgic companion is a sweetly lyrical essay of beguiling euphony and striking resonance. Delos's collection begins with the haunting, perfectly crafted *Four Bagatelles* (delightful miniatures, these) and ends with *Song of the Ch'in* by the Chinese composer, Zhou Long: the 'ch'in' is a traditional Chinese zither and this imaginative, fastidiously conceived piece from 1985 attempts to convey the piquant sounds of that ancient instrument through the 'modern' medium of the string quartet. These are consistently pure-toned, beautifully rapt performances from the talented young Shanghai Quartet, and Delos's sound is warm and true to match.

Herbert Howells

British 1892-1983

Howells Organ Sonata No. 2. Six Pieces (1940-45).
Graham Barber *org*
Priory PRCD524 (67 minutes: DDD). Recorded on the organ of Hereford Cathedral in 1995.   Ⓕ

These are powerful and authoritative performances which ooze the spirit of Howells – that odd mixture of emotional detachment with a hint of deep personal passion, an undercurrent of tragedy and an almost improvisatory fluidity of structure. The Sonata has a formal structure which makes it easy to follow while the *Six Pieces* present such a kaleidoscopic array of organ colours that the ear is continually enchanted. The Hereford organ is a lovely instrument. Certainly Priory has, in focusing the microphones on the organ, expunged much of the building's aural ambience, but the sound is an utter delight to the ear.

Hymnus Paradisi[a]. An English Mass.
[a]**Julie Kennard** *sop* [a]**John Mark Ainsley** *ten*
Royal Liverpool Philharmonic Choir and Orchestra / Vernon Handley.
Hyperion CDA66488 (80 minutes: DDD). Texts included. Recorded 1991.   Ⓕ

An axiom in the aesthetics of eschatology has it that Hell is good value and Paradise rather a liability. Perhaps that puts it crudely. Hell, evidently, is an absolute (we all know how dreadful it would be to exist for ever in a concentration camp), but Heaven is relative (eternal happiness being imaginable only with at the very least the injection of some painful memory to convince us that it isn't bland). First encounters with *Hymnus Paradisi* tend to call the axiom to mind. It is music awash with ecstasy, and the listener may resist becoming part of this swimmingly coloured dream. Now, further listening proves this is not so: that is, the better you know it, the more you see in it of form, energy and pain. The pain is real enough, as biographical facts attest. Howells wrote it as a method of escape from 'the crippling numbness of loss,' as he described the effect upon him of his son's death from polio at the age of ten. The work was so full of the emotion of that time that for many years it had to remain private, and it was only with the approach of the fifteenth anniversary of the death that he showed it to Vaughan Williams and arrangements were made for its inclusion in the Three Choirs Festival of 1950. A work of art should stand on its own, no doubt (and this one does), but, knowing its human cause, one can see more readily the purpose, and hence the form and structure, of its lingering over the single sentence of 'Requiem aeternam'.

A strong performance helps and this it gets from Vernon Handley. There is a feeling for the dramatic quality in the score, the crises and relaxations, without losing sight of the essential lyricism. Handley brings to it an intensity and clarity of structure and orchestral detail. The soloists sing with sensitivity and pleasing tone. In many ways, the English Mass has a natural kinship here. Written in 1955 for Harold Darke and his St Michael's Singers, it is richly scored (the optional instruments being included) and is probably too expansive for liturgical use. As a symphonic structure, the Anglican placing of the *Gloria* at the end, instead of following the Creed, is far more satisfying, and the work balances well its elements of prayer and praise. Again the performance carries conviction.

Howells Requiem. Take him, earth, for cherishing.
Martin Mass for Double Chorus.
Sally Barber *sop* Julia Field *mez* Mark Johnstone *ten* Andrew Angus *bass*
Vasari / Jeremy Backhouse.
Cala United CACD88033 (56 minutes: DDD). Recorded 1994.   Ⓕ

Both pieces here are private works, not really intended for performance. Howells wrote the Requiem to exorcize his grief at the death of his son, and only at the very end of his life allowed it to be published. Martin described his Mass as 'something between God and myself, and of no concern to anyone else' and he kept it to himself for close on 40 years. Both now look like crucial works in each composer's development. Howells's Requiem is not only the source of his masterpiece, the *Hymnus Paradisi*, but also of much that is characteristic in his later music, its radiance (sometimes shadowed) and its long expressive lines. Martin's Mass is not only a research laboratory into the problems of setting religious texts (how he enjoys 'dramatizing' the various sections of the *Credo*, using elaborate choral coloratura in the *Gloria*, inventing a surprising but effective *staccato* imagery to convey a heaven and earth filled with dazzling glory in the *Sanctus*!) but also into the neo-classical element that seasoned his later serialism. Although they make a fascinating coupling, they demand quite different types of singing; so again does Howells's much later motet, with its more public gestures and its broader span. Vasari succeeds admirably. The difficulties of the Howells Requiem are exemplified in the image of light (a wonderful Howells chord, needing absolutely precise pitching and balance) and the expressive intensification of line that follows it in the fifth movement. It is beautifully done, but the singers also have the athletic virtuosity for Martin's twining melismas, the hurtling excitement of his 'et resurrexit'. This is choral singing of a high order, given a very spacious and natural recording.

Johann Hummel   Austrian 1778-1837

Piano Concerto No. 4 in E major, Op. 110. Double Concerto in G major, Op. 17.
Hagai Shaham *vn* **London Mozart Players / Howard Shelley** *pf*
Chandos CHAN9687 (63 minutes: DDD). Recorded 1998.   Ⓕ

Shelley is outstanding in this music, synthesizing the classical and romantic elements perfectly. These two concertos are wonderfully infectious. The E major Concerto occupies a kind of bridge between Mozart and Chopin, although Mozart's depth and subtlety are in a rather different vein. Hummel is more of a show-off, and his music almost smiles at you, its charm and sparkle eschewing any hint of pretentiousness – no false grandeur here. Throughout, Shelley communicates the music's *joie de vivre*, revelling in the figurative passagework. The Double Concerto may have been inspired by Mozart's *Sinfonia concertante*, K365; it doesn't have the same harmonic or lyrical variety as the E major Concerto, but it is a charming work, especially when so persuasively played. Shelley's well-proportioned piano part is perfectly complemented by Hagai Shaham's sweet-toned violin. Shelley fulfils his dual role admirably, and the London Mozart Players respond well to his playing and conducting. The recorded sound is first-rate. A lovely disc.

Concertino in G major, Op. 73. Piano Concerto No. 5 in A flat major, Op. 113. Gesellschafts Rondo in D major, Op. 117.
London Mozart Players / Howard Shelley *pf*
Chandos CHAN9558 (59 minutes: DDD). Recorded 1997.   Ⓕ

These are decorous rarities played with an assured brilliance and affection. Hummel's Mozartian rather than Chopinesque bias declares itself most obviously in his Op. 73 *Concertino*, though even here the figuration has a recognizably Hummelian froth and sparkle. Too charming to be vacuous, such surface brio has little in common with Mozart's depth and subtlety, and for music of greater romantic range and ambition we turn to the A flat major Concerto, with its fuller scoring and lavishly decorated solo part. Lovers of a finespun, operatic cantilena will warm to the central 'Romanze'. The *Gesellschafts Rondo* (offered here in a première recording) commences in solemn *Adagio* vein before turning to a more typically bustling and ceremonious *Vivace*. It may be that

Hummel 'puffed, blew and perspired' when he played but he won the admiration of Chopin (a hard master to please and one who turned Hummel's animation to rare poetic advantage) and his sheer style is infectious when projected with such unfailing expertise by Howard Shelley in his dual role as pianist and conductor. The recordings are exceptionally well balanced.

Piano Concertos – No. 2 in A minor, Op. 85; No. 3 in B minor, Op. 89.
Stephen Hough *pf*
English Chamber Orchestra / Bryden Thomson.
Chandos CHAN8507 (66 minutes: DDD). *Gramophone* Award Winner 1987. ⓕ

This is a staggering disc of Hummel's piano concertos played by Stephen Hough. The most obvious comparison is with the piano concertos of Chopin, but whereas those works rely on the grace and panache of the piano line to redeem an often lacklustre orchestral role, the Hummel works have finely conceived orchestral writing and certainly no shortage of original ideas. The piano part is formidable, combining virtuosity of a very high order indeed with a vigour and athleticism that does much to redress Hummel's somewhat tarnished reputation. The A minor Concerto is probably the better known of the two works here, with a thrilling rondo finale, but the B minor is no less inventive with some breath-taking writing in the piano's upper registers. This disc makes strong demands to be heard: inventive and exciting music, a masterly contribution from Stephen Hough, fine orchestral support from the ever sympathetic ECO under Thomson and, last but not least, a magnificent Chandos recording.

Piano Trios – E flat major, Op. 12; G major, Op. 35; G major, Op. 65; E flat major, Op. 96.
Beaux Arts Trio (Ida Kavafian *vn* Peter Wiley *vc* Menahem Pressler *pf*).
Philips 446 077-2PH (69 minutes: DDD). Recorded 1996. ⓕ 🄴

These are delightful, intelligent and witty performances of some very attractive music. The Op. 12 work is fresh and untroubled, taking delight in the easy mastery of counterpart that was one of Hummel's qualities, and the Beaux Arts Trio plays it with a lively sense of enjoyment that suits it ideally. Hummel was not a profound composer, but he was an immensely talented one and the variety of his invention is remarkable. He never forgot Mozart, as can be heard in the G major Trio of 1811, and he kept an ear on current developments without changing his essentially classical approach to music. Romantic ideas were accommodated rather than imitated or seriously taken up. The Beaux Arts players understand the balance well, and do excellent justice to all these works. There is much pleasure to be had from these engaging performances of this charming music.

Englebert Humperdinck
German 1854-1921

Hänsel und Gretel.
Elisabeth Grümmer *sop* Hänsel; **Dame Elisabeth Schwarzkopf** *sop* Gretel;
Maria von Ilosvay *mez* Mother; **Josef Metternich** *bar* Father;
Anny Felbermayer *sop* Sandman, Dew Fairy; **Else Schürhoff** *mez* Witch;
Loughton High School for Girls' Choir; Bancroft's School Choir;
Philharmonia Orchestra / Herbert von Karajan.
EMI mono CMS5 67061-2 (two discs: 103 minutes: ADD). Recorded 1953. Ⓜ 🄷 🇷🇷

This classic performance has never been surpassed. We have come near to perfection before, but never so close as in this recording of Humperdinck's exquisite fairy-tale opera. It is a tribute not just to Karajan and his supreme cast, but to Walter Legge as producer. The scene in the forest is sung and played and recorded with a sensitive regard for the atmosphere the music can create that has never been equalled. The stage direction tells us that on the rise of the curtain to this scene 'Gretel is humming quietly to herself' the folk-song, 'There stands a little man in the wood alone'. Elisabeth Schwarzkopf produces the illusion perfectly, and the orchestra responds in like manner, on the plane of absolute quietness. We are with the lost children in the dark forest. The tender intimacy of performance and recording are something to marvel at – it could not have been better cast.

The two Elisabeths sound always like the delightful children they are supposed to be and avoid all suspicion of archness: and both sing beautifully throughout. Josef Metternich and Marie von Ilosvay are equally good as the parents and Else Schürhoff produces an amazing variety of sinister sounds as the witch. Her 'hocus-pocus' is really frightening. Anny Felbermayer's pretty voice is brought forward as the Dew Fairy and this differentiates her sufficiently from the Sandman. The fresh and enthusiastic singing of the school choirs is pure delight: and the moment when principals and chorus sing the last words in the opera, to Humperdinck's inspired melody, 'When past bearing is our grief, God the Lord will send relief', is incredibly moving. Karajan never puts a baton wrong, so to speak, in this recording. There is not a moment when he overplays the brilliantly scored sections. The themes are woven together with a *Meistersinger*-like richness, but the counterpoint is always made beautifully clear. The Witch's Ride (she is perhaps a sort of fallen Valkyrie!) is vividly done and the gradual transition to the quietness of the forest scene is managed with much skill. Karajan is in affectionate accord with the score throughout. The recording of the orchestra, which plays like the angels of the dream tableau, is really superb and the high string tone comes out with almost unbelievable beauty. With the extra clarity of the latest remastering now sharpening the sense of presence, you would be forgiven for thinking the recording was in stereo. However, for all its extra clarity, the CD transfer is at a relatively low level, tending to give the impression that the sound has too little body. You can boost it with the volume control, but that brings up the hiss, which is relatively high but not objectionable. Whatever the reservations about the transfer, this remains a gorgeous performance.

Hänsel und Gretel.
Jennifer Larmore *mez* Hänsel; **Ruth Ziesak** *sop* Gretel; **Hildegard Behrens** *sop* Mother; **Bernd Weikl** *bar* Father; **Rosemary Joshua** *sop* Sandman; **Christine Schäfer** *sop* Dew Fairy; **Hanna Schwarz** *mez* Witch;
Tölz Boys' Choir; Bavarian Radio Symphony Orchestra / Donald Runnicles.
Teldec 4509-94549-2 (two discs: 103 minutes: DDD). Notes, text and translation included. Ⓕ
Recorded 1994.

Donald Runnicles here makes a very impressive recording début in a major opera set. He has a light touch, regularly favouring faster speeds than other conductors. The lightness and refinement of the playing brings transparent textures and the most delicate *pianissimos*, with gentler markings observed more closely than usual, a point that comes out at the very start of the Overture. Far from reducing the impact of the performance, the lightness goes with an element of fantasy delightfully in keeping with the fairy-tale atmosphere. Ruth Ziesak as Gretel and Jennifer Larmore as Hänsel are, above all, natural-sounding, with little or no feeling of mature opera-singers pretending to be children. Hanna Schwarz's Witch is sharply sinister without being too frightening. Hildegard Behrens is strong and characterful as the Mother, with Bernd Weikl firm and dark as the Father, while young voices are chosen for the two incidental roles of the Sandman and Dew Fairy. This Teldec set brings, incidentally, a fascinating supplement in a brief orchestral coda, just over a minute long, which Humperdinck wrote in 1894 for a production of the opera in Dessau with Cosima Wagner as director. Ingeniously he has the Dessau national anthem set in counterpoint against various themes from the work, with toy trumpets providing a commentary.

Jacques Ibert

French 1890-1962

Ibert Divertissement.
Milhaud Le boeuf sur le toit, Op. 58. La création du monde, Op. 81.
Poulenc Les biches – Suite.
Ulster Orchestra / Yan Pascal Tortelier.
Chandos CHAN9023 (68 minutes: DDD). Recorded 1991. Ⓕ

Here is 1920s French music directed by a conductor who is completely in the spirit of it, and plenty of spirit there is, too. Except for Ibert's *Divertissement*, this is ballet music, and that work too originated in the theatre as incidental music for Eugène Labiche's farce *The Italian Straw Hat.* Poulenc's suite from *Les biches*, written for Diaghilev's ballet company and first heard in Monte Carlo, is unfailingly fresh and bouncy and stylishly played here, although Chandos's warm recording, good though it is, takes some edge off the trumpet tone; the genial nature of it all makes us forget that it is a unique mix of eighteenth-century *galanterie*, Tchaikovskian lilt and Poulenc's own inimitable street-Parisian sophistication and charm. As for Ibert's piece, this is uproariously funny in an unbuttoned way, and the gorgeously vulgar trombone in the Waltz and frantic police whistle in the finale are calculated to make you laugh out loud. Milhaud's *Le boeuf sur le toit* also has Parisian chic and was originally a kind of music-hall piece, composed to a scenario by Cocteau. It was while attending a performance of it in London in 1920 that the composer first heard the American jazz orchestra that, together with a later experience of New Orleans jazzmen playing 'from the darkest corners of the Negro soul' (as he later expressed it), prompted him to compose his masterly ballet *La création du monde*, in which a deep-rooted African voice seems to speak through western instruments. Tortelier and his orchestra understand this strangely powerful music no less than the other pieces. This is a most desirable disc.

Six pièces. Deux mouvements. Jeux. Le jardinier de Samos. Française. Aria. Trois pièces brèves.
Pastoral. Paraboles. Cinq pièces en trio.
Kees Hülsmann *vn* **Eleonore Pameijer** *fl* **Pauline Oostenrijk** *ob* **Hans Colbers** *cl*
Peter Gaasterland *bn* **Herman Jeurissen** *hn* **Peter Masseurs** *tpt* **Olga Franssen,**
Helenus de Rijke *gtrs* **Ernestine Stoop** *hp* **Arnold Marinissen** *perc/pipes* **Sepp Grotenhuis** *pf*
Olympia OCD468 (80 minutes: DDD). Recorded 1991-96.   Ⓕ

Entr'acte. Ariette. L'âge d'or. Pièce. String Quartet. Trio. Deux interludes. Etude-caprice pour
un tombeau de Chopin. Ghirlarzana. Caprilena. Impromptu. Carignane.
Eleonore Pameijer *fl* **Peter Gaasterland** *bn* **Peter Masseurs** *tpt* **Arno Bornkamp** *sax*
Olga Franssen *gtr* **Ernestine Stoop** *hp* **Menno van Delft** *hpd* **Sepp Grotenhuis** *pf*
New Netherlands Quartet (Kees Hülsmann, Mieke Biesta *vns* Gerrit Oldeman *va*
Marien van Staalen *vc*).
Olympia OCD469 (79 minutes: DDD). Recorded 1991-96.   Ⓕ

Apart from the *Trois pièces brèves* for wind quintet, justly famous for their wit, Ibert's chamber
music is little known and most of this repertoire is new to the catalogue. Because so much of it is
very attractive indeed, this pair of CDs is to be warmly welcomed. The playing of these Dutch
musicians is appealingly idiomatic. In addition to the *Pièces brèves* (1930), which are delightfully
presented, the Trio for violin, cello and harp on the second disc, written 14 years later, is especially
appealing. The *scherzando* finale in particular really fizzes!

The second of the *Deux interludes* (1946) brings an unexpected Spanish gipsy flavour from the
violin and then a ravishing flute solo. Less surprisingly, Spanish influences are also found in the
music featuring the guitar, notably the *Entr'acte* for flute and guitar (1935), which even has some
flamenco strumming. The two programmes are presented in order of composition, and the first CD
begins with the *Six pièces* (1916-17) for solo harp, of which the second ('Scherzetto') is the best
known. These compositions are aural balm if not entirely characteristic; but the *Deux mouvements*
(1921) for wind quartet certainly are representative, opening with trills before the flute takes flight
like a bird, followed by a pleasing oboe solo. *Jeux* could hardly be more deliciously French, and the
start of *Le jardinier de Samos* (1924) reminds one a little of *Les biches*. The *Cinq pièces en trio*
(1935) have a more pastoral flavour than the *Pièces brèves* and are most winning.

The French write for the saxophone with special understanding, seldom allowing it to sound vulgar,
and the melody of *L'âge d'or* (1935-36) has something of the character of a solemn chorale. The
pieces for solo stringed instruments are full of character, and the jolly trumpet *Impromptu* (1950)
has a nice hint of jazz inflexion. Perhaps the key work on the second disc is the String Quartet
(1937-42), which looks back to Ravel, especially in its pizzicato *Scherzo*. The work is most
impressively presented and the recording is very naturally balanced with the acoustic. To sum up,
over two-and-a-half hours of delightful entertainment.

Sigismondo d'India   Italian *c*1582-1629

Il terzo libro de madrigali.
La Venexiana (Rossana Bertini, Nadia Ragni *sops* Giuseppe Maletto, Sandro Naglia *tens*
Daniele Carnovich *bass* Paul Beie *lte* Franco Pavan *theorbo* Fabio Bonizzoni *hpd*) /
Claudio Cavina *counterten*
Glossa GCD920903 (57 minutes: DDD). Texts and translations included. Recorded 1997.   Ⓕ

D'India's *Terzo libro* closely resembles Monteverdi's Fifth Book. Both contain a number of pieces
incorporating a *basso continuo* (something of a novelty at this date), and both close with a series
of madrigals in which the independent bass plays an essential rather than a merely decorative role.
In these, the most forward-looking pieces in both collections, the bass becomes the foundation of
a structure characterized by that polarity between lower and upper voices that is the hallmark of
the new seventeenth-century manner. There are other similarities too, such as in the choice of texts,
with both composers showing a keen interest in Tasso and Guarini, while d'India's *Canzone
di lontananza* strongly recalls Monteverdi's *Lamento d'Arianna*. Monteverdi apart, d'India's most
obvious stylistic debts are to the music of the Neapolitan school, and above all to the late madrigals
of Gesualdo. Like many of those pieces, the language of most of the madrigals in d'India's Third
Book is highly rhetorical and discontinuous even to the point of fragmentation, with sudden shifts
of mood and colour. La Venexiana has a full-blooded and appropriately mosaic-like approach
which maintains its intensity even across the frequent silences in the narrative. D'India's is a vivid
language of gesture, made up of individual pristine moments, and the ensemble's carefully shaded
punctuation of the architecture of the whole is telling and dramatic.

Vincent d'Indy

d'Indy Concerto for Piano, Flute, Cello and Strings, Op. 89.
Fumet La nuit.
Honegger Le dit des jeux du monde.
Patrick Dechorgnat *pf* **Jean Ferrandis** *fl* **Hervé Noël** *tpt* **Jean-Jacques Wiederker** *vc*
Jean-Jacques Wiederker Chamber Orchestra / Frédéric Bouaniche.
Koch Schwann 310652 (56 minutes: DDD). Recorded 1992. (F)

The name of Fumet is probably unfamiliar to most people. A pupil of Franck, his radical politics seem to have hindered his career, although d'Indy supported his work. His symphonic poem for strings, *La nuit*, is atmospheric and the performance sensitive, although the rich textures are not fully served by the relatively small sound of this orchestra. Fumet reflects the more hothouse fervour of his teacher, and there is also some affinity with Szymanowski; if ultimately this music offers more sensuality than substance or shape, it has some interest and receives a committed performance. D'Indy's Concerto is surprisingly neo-classical, with little of the Franckian richness that one might expect, and this work of 1927 was his last orchestral piece. This again receives a sympathetic performance, although the music lacks weight and fails to make a strong impression. But admirers of this composer should snap up this disc while they can. The same applies to *aficionados* of Honegger, whose early (1918) incidental music to a mystery play called *Le dit des jeux du monde* receives its first recording in the form of a suite of six pieces. They are scored for 14 instruments including a bouteillophone (tuned bottles), and the third piece, 'Mountain and Stones', is for percussion only. This suite is the most interesting music here and the performance is a strong one. The recording is clear, though not very atmospheric.

Symphony No. 2 in B flat major, Op. 57. Souvenirs, Op. 62.
Monte Carlo Philharmonic Orchestra / James DePreist.
Koch International Classics 37280-2 (64 minutes: DDD). Recorded 1994. (F)

D'Indy's Second Symphony (1902-03) is a mighty utterance, epic in ambition and scale, yet tightly knit too. However, for all the intellectual strength of the writing, there is also plenty of tenderness and nobility on display (the first movement's secondary material has an almost Elgarian glow about it). D'Indy's scoring, too, is rich and colourful. This is, in short, a most imposing and rewarding piece, and any reader who has ever fallen under the spell of the symphonies of, say, Chausson, Dukas or Magnard should hasten to make its acquaintance. The coupling on this Koch disc is *Souvenirs*, an eloquent and moving poem for orchestra from 1906 which d'Indy dedicated to the memory of his wife Isabelle, who had died the previous year. James DePreist presides over a finely prepared, characterful pair of performances and the Monte Carlo Philharmonic, though not of the first rank, responds with striking commitment and evident understanding throughout, while the recording has great warmth and naturalness.

Symphony No. 3, Op. 70, 'de bello gallico'. Saugefleurie, Op. 21. Souvenirs, Op. 62.
Strasbourg Philharmonic Orchestra / Theodore Guschlbauer.
Auvidis Valois V4686 (72 minutes: DDD). Recorded 1992. (F)

Souvenirs is a haunting, imaginatively scored tone-poem that starts with what sounds like a ghostly premonition of Shostakovich's Eleventh Symphony, then proceeds to varieties of chromatic lyricism that recall the Debussy of *Pelléas* and the lone Symphony of Ernest Chausson. The Third Symphony, a highly inventive commentary on aspects of the Great War, suggests a specific programme and is an ambiguous, loosely constructed piece that effectively extends one's limited experience of its composer. Theodore Guschlbauer's broadly sympathetic readings are more appreciative of the music's *lent et calm* than its *vif et agité*. Essential listening for all incurable romantics.

John Ireland

Ireland Piano Concerto in E flat major.
Moeran Symphony in G minor.
Eileen Joyce *pf*
Hallé Orchestra / Leslie Heward.
Dutton Laboratories mono CDAX8001 (67 minutes: ADD). Recorded 1942. (M) [H]

In 1942 the British Council decided to sponsor recordings of British music, and Moeran's Symphony was the first work to be chosen. Leslie Heward had conducted the first performance in

1938, but at the age of 45 he was now mortally ill with tuberculosis, and time was running short if his authoritative interpretation was to be preserved. At the autumn recording sessions in Manchester both Moeran and the producer Walter Legge were alarmed by Heward's poor physical condition, but somehow he fought off pain and fatigue to create a performance which deeply impressed the composer. It became the most important recording left by a highly sensitive musician. Legge admired Heward greatly, describing him as 'musically speaking, the most satisfying conductor this country has had since Beecham'. Here is a wonderfully vital and heartfelt performance of a fine symphony. Large-scale recordings had retreated to the provinces in the face of the enemy bombing of London, and whilst it is true that the Hallé was no longer quite the body it had been under Harty, it plays its heart out for Heward. The original recording was dry and lacking in range, but Michael Dutton has opened up the sound in a remarkable fashion. There is now increased tonal depth, more warmth in the strings and a new solidity in the bass. Here is a case of new technology being put to very best artistic use. Eileen Joyce was an excellent pianist at her best, and her vivacious but thoughtful performance of the Ireland Concerto is richly satisfying. She is sympathetically supported by Heward, and once more Dutton has drawn startlingly vivid sound from commercial pressings. Notes and presentation are first-class.

A Downland Suite (arr. Ireland and Bush). Orchestral Poem in A minor. Concertino pastorale.
Two Symphonic Studies (arr. Bush).
City of London Sinfonia / Richard Hickox.
Chandos CHAN9376 (64 minutes: DDD). Recorded 1994.   Ⓕ

Hickox gives a sensitive account of the *Downland Suite* and extracts great expressive intensity from the glorious second movement 'Elegy'. The *Concertino pastorale* is another fine work, boasting a most eloquent opening 'Eclogue' and tenderly poignant 'Threnody', towards the end of which Ireland seems to allow himself a momentary recollection of the haunting opening phrase of his much earlier orchestral prelude, *The Forgotten Rite*. In 1969 Ireland's pupil, Geoffrey Bush, arranged two sections of the score for the 1946 film *The Overlanders* which were not incorporated into the 1971 concert suite compiled by Sir Charles Mackerras. The resulting, finely wrought *Two Symphonic Studies* were recorded many years ago by Sir Adrian Boult for Lyrita – no longer available – and Hickox proves just as sympathetic an interpreter, whereas the *Orchestral Poem* in A minor is here receiving its recorded début. This is a youthful essay, completed in 1904, some three years after Ireland's studies with Stanford. It is a worthy rather than especially inspiring effort, with hardly a glimpse of the mature manner to come, save for some particularly beautiful string writing. Hickox makes out a decent enough case for it. However, with rich, refined Chandos sound, this is most enjoyable.

Violin Sonatas – No. 1 in D minor; No. 2 in A minor. Bagatelle. Berceuse. Cavatina.
The Holy Boy (arr. cpsr).
Paul Barritt *vn* **Catherine Edwards** *pf*
Hyperion CDA66853 (66 minutes: DDD). Recorded 1995.   Ⓕ

After many years of neglect by the record companies, Ireland's glorious Second Violin Sonata of 1917 at last appears to be coming into its own once again. Here is a satisfying, passionate, superbly disciplined reading which communicates strongly, especially in the lovely *Poco lento quasi adagio* slow movement. Barritt and Edwards put not a foot wrong in the ambitious 1909 Cobbett Prize-winning First Violin Sonata. The rest of the disc is filled out with all the four pieces which comprise the remainder of Ireland's output for violin and piano. The good-humoured *Bagatelle* (1911) bears a dedication to Marjorie Hayward, who participated in the belated 1913 première of the First Sonata (with Ireland himself at the piano). Both the *Berceuse* (1902) and *Cavatina* (1904) are early miniatures – tuneful, pretty and unpretentious offerings. Finally, *The Holy Boy* receives radiant advocacy. Recording quality is clean and intimate; balance seems eminently well judged.

Sarnia. London Pieces. In Those Days. Prelude in E flat major. Ballade. Columbine. Month's Mind.
John Lenehan *pf*
Naxos 8 553700 (60 minutes: DDD). Recorded 1995.   Ⓢ

The pleasures here are many. John Lenehan is a very accomplished performer: not only is his technical address impeccable, but he also possesses a strikingly wide dynamic range and sophisticated variety of tone colour, both of which he uses to marvellously poetic (and never remotely self-conscious) effect throughout. That Lenehan has a considerable affinity for Ireland's muse is immediately evident from his raptly intimate delivery of the gentle opening diptych, *In Those Days*. Similarly, in the extraordinarily imaginative, harmonically questing *Ballade* of 1929 Lenehan rises superbly to the elemental fury of the remarkable central portion, with its brooding echoes of the 'Northern' Bax from the same period. Elsewhere, *Columbine* is a treat, as is the ravishing *Month's Mind* and the haunting Prelude in E flat. Lenehan's supremely affectionate and wonderfully articulate advocacy will surely win Ireland many new friends and this finely engineered Naxos release clearly represents exceptional value for money.

Charles Ives
American 1874-1954

Symphony No. 2. The Gong on the Hook and Ladder. Tone Roads – No. 1. A Set of Three Short Pieces – Largo cantabile, Hymn. Hallowe'en. Central Park in the Dark. The Unanswered Question.
New York Philharmonic Orchestra / Leonard Bernstein.
DG 429 220-2GH (68 minutes: DDD). Recorded 1987-88.   Ⓕ

Although Bernstein thought of Ives as a primitive composer, these recordings reveal that he had an undeniably deep affinity for, and understanding of, his music. The Second Symphony (written in 1902 and first performed in 1951) is a glorious work, still strongly rooted in the nineteenth century yet showing those clear signs of Ives's individual voice that are largely missing from the charming but lightweight First Symphony. Bernstein brings out all its richness and warmth without wallowing in its romantic elements, and he handles with utter conviction the multi-textures and the allusions to popular tunes and snatches from Bach, Brahms and Dvořák, to name but a few. The standard of playing he exacts from the NYPO, both here and in the disc's series of technically demanding shorter pieces, is remarkably high with the depth of string tone at a premium – and the engineers retain this to a degree unusual in a live recording. An essential disc for any collection.

Ives Piano Sonata No. 1.
Barber Piano Sonata in E flat major, Op. 26. Excursions, Op. 20.
Joanna MacGregor *pf*
Collins Classics 1107-2 (68 minutes: DDD). Recorded 1990.   Ⓕ

There are many fine recordings of the Barber Sonata since it is a work which has attracted well-equipped players right from the start. MacGregor stands up well, but the greater attraction is her Ives Sonata No. 1. The work, which waited 45 years for a first performance, is just as characteristic of Ives as the Second Sonata, and in some ways its mixture of hymn-tunes and ragtime makes a more coherent impact. The ragtime aspects are based on what Ives heard improvised or played that way himself: he went to a lot of trouble to catch the difference between playing the dots and swinging away. This informality is superbly caught, MacGregor risking all in truly Ivesian fashion in one or two places. She thoroughly understands the driving rhythms as well as the transcendental calm. By comparison anything by Barber is more polite. But the four *Excursions* come off well and show a different approach to popular idioms – more that of a tourist than an insider. But both composers know how to make use of sonata form in these two American classics, vividly played and recorded.

Piano Sonata No. 2, 'Concord, Mass., 1840-60'. Three Quarter-tone Pieces[a].
Alexei Lubimov, [a]Pierre-Laurent Aimard *pfs*
Erato 0630-14638-2 (60 minutes: DDD). Recorded 1995.   Ⓕ

Lubimov here is utterly idiomatic, and the pacing of the four movements, each based on a different New England sage, is unexceptional. Perhaps the first movement, 'Emerson', is a little wearing to listen to in the slightly tight and close piano sound favoured by Erato. But the echo passages in 'Hawthorne' are magical. Here and elsewhere Lubimov seems sensibly aware of the recordings by the original performer, John Kirkpatrick – all now sadly deleted. The simpler textures of 'The Alcotts' are phrased immaculately and the more wayward last movement, 'Thoreau', has all the atmosphere of its mystical setting at Walden Pond as well as a lovely flute solo. Lubimov has absolute fluency in delivering everything from the massed sonorities of 'Emerson' through the rags in 'Hawthorne' to the transcendental calm of 'Thoreau'. There are other recordings of this repertoire but the field is open to Lubimov as an all-Ives first choice. The significant bonus is the *Three Quarter-tone Pieces* for two pianos, which juxtaposes ragtime figures from the song *The Seer* in different tunings. This is hilarious Ives in a new idiom. The recorded sound here is very good. An essential Ives release.

Psalms – No. 54, Save me, O God, by Thy name; No. 67, God be merciful to us; No. 90, O Lord, Thou hast been our refuge; No. 135. Easter Carol. Crossing the Bar. The Celestial Country.
instrumental soloists; Duke Quartet; BBC Singers / Stephen Cleobury.
Collins Classics 1479-2 (68 minutes: DDD). Texts included. Recorded 1995.   Ⓕ

Some of the church works here are very early: Ives, at the age of about 17 in 1891, could have been the first American to set Tennyson's classic, *Crossing the Bar*. This is a remarkably mature response from a teenager to a poem about death, utterly sincere. Unfortunately, in this performance, the recorded balance distances the sopranos when we need to hear their juicy melodies in low register. Something similar happens in Psalm 67, where the first soprano is lost in the second bar and the jubilation of the middle section is uninspiring. This is the exploratory Ives, a study in bitonality written when he was about 20. Psalm 90 is the absolute core of Ives, a deeply spiritual meditation with organ and bells that Ives worked on well into the 1920s when he had more or less stopped composing. It comes off well here, although the voices could have been softer and more mystical in the last section. *Easter Carol* is another piece of teenage Victoriana, conventional but fluent in style. The most extended piece is *The Celestial Country*, a 47-minute cantata premièred at Central Presbyterian Church in New York, where Ives was organist. Its occasional departures from the accepted idiom of Victorian church music indicate the growing tensions Ives felt between his own visions and the rights of his congregation. Cleobury's interpretation is sensibly free of excesses, perhaps lacking exhilaration in the bigger moments. The recording is not particularly flattering but, details apart, this is an essential recording to see Ives in all dimensions.

Jacquet de la Guerre

French 1666/67-1729

Premier livre de pièces de clavecin. Pièces de clavecin.
Carole Cerasi *hpd*
Metronome METCD1026 (79 minutes: DDD). Recorded 1997. Ⓕ Ⓟ

Elisabeth Jacquet was a remarkable girl. A member of a family of musicians, at the age of only five she attracted the benevolent attention of Louis XIV by her harpsichord playing, and subsequently was taken under the wing of his favourite, Mme de Montespan. At 18 she married the organist Marin de la Guerre and became famous for the concerts she gave at her home, in which her powers of improvisation were greatly admired. She wrote trio sonatas, an opera (the first one by a woman to be produced in France), violin sonatas, and two books of *Cantates françaises* on Old Testament subjects. Her first book of harpsichord pieces was published as early as 1687 – even before Lebègue's – and contains in its four suites, apart from partly unmeasured Louis Couperin-like preludes, sequences of dances that have considerable individuality and feeling for expressive harmony, a very unusual *Tocade* (to open the F major Suite) and a couple of chaconnes. Twenty years later, after a tragic series of family deaths, she produced two more harpsichord suites 'that can be played on the violin'. All this music is performed with flair, vitality, panache and character by the Swedish-born harpsichordist Carole Cerasi. Her playing on a rich-toned Ruckers instrument (originally single-manual but with a *ravalement* to two manuals by Hemsch in 1763) is deeply impressive and rewarding, and a model of clarity.

Leos Janáček

Moravian 1854-1928

Janáček Sinfonietta, Op. 60[a]. Taras Bulba[a].
Shostakovich The Age of Gold – Suite, Op. 22a[b].
[a]Vienna Philharmonic Orchestra / Sir Charles Mackerras;
[b]London Philharmonic Orchestra / Bernard Haitink.
Decca Ovation 430 727-2DM (66 minutes: DDD). Recorded 1980 and 1979. Ⓜ ℞℞

The Janáček items on this disc have long been a favourite coupling and in these thoroughly idiomatic performances the effect is truly spectacular. Of course these are far more than just orchestral show-pieces. Both works were fired by patriotic fervour – *Taras Bulba* by Czechoslovakia's struggle towards independence, the *Sinfonietta* by the city of Brno, the composer's adopted home town. Both works display a deep-seated passion for the basic elements of music and yield unprecedented levels of excitement. To get the most out of *Taras Bulba* you really need all its gory programmatic details (of battles, betrayal, torture and murder) to hand. The *Sinfonietta* on the other hand needs no such props; its impact is as irresistible and physically direct as a massive adrenalin injection. If the listener is to fully revel in this music a corresponding sense of abandon in the playing is even more important than attention to precision. The Vienna Philharmonic Orchestra here supplies a good measure of both these and Sir Charles Mackerras's commitment and understanding of the music are second to none, while the high-level recording captures every detail in a vivid close-up sound image. Bernard Haitink's highly disciplined if somewhat straitlaced London Philharmonic Orchestra account of Shostakovich's *Age of Gold* suite is the coupling.

Janáček Taras Bulba. The Cunning Little Vixen – Suite.
V. Novák Slovak Suite, Op. 32.
Czech Philharmonic Orchestra / Václav Talich.
Supraphon Historical mono 11 1905-2 (71 minutes: AAD). Recorded 1953-54. Ⓜ H RR

Talich's *Taras Bulba* is hugely imposing. Aided by playing of brazen fervour from the Czech PO, his reading has a rare dignity, culminating in an apotheosis of overwhelming grandeur and majesty (magnificent brass sounds). Not that there's any want of energy and momentum: in Talich's hands, the battle scenes of the first two tableaux possess thrilling snap and vigour. Some might crave a leaner, harder-edged orchestral sonority, but the impact and stature of this music-making is not in question. It's followed by the affectionate orchestral suite from *The Cunning Little Vixen* which Talich himself compiled in 1937. Of course, not all Janáčekians will approve of the great conductor's 'sensualizing' of the original instrumentation, but many collectors will be grateful to have this classic 1954 recording restored to circulation at long last, and its sense of enchantment and magical atmosphere remain utterly intoxicating. The Novák coupling is an unmitigated delight. Talich's wonderful conception has all the tangy affection and lithe, rhythmic punch one could wish for, but he also locates and taps into a vein of tangible, old-world nostalgia that is extremely moving. If you don't already know these lovely scores, we urge immediate investigation, for you won't ever hear better performances than these.

Pohádka. Presto in E minor. Violin Sonata. Capriccio. Concertino.
Pierre Amoyal *vn* **Gary Hoffman** *vc* **Mikhail Rudy** *pf*
members of **L'Orchestre de l'Opéra National de Paris / Sir Charles Mackerras.**
EMI CDC5 55585-2 (72 minutes: DDD). Recorded 1995. Ⓕ

This is an odd assemblage of Janáček's late chamber music, but the music itself is capable of an oddity which does not dim with time. Mikhail Rudy contrasts well the eccentricity of the left-hand *Capriccio*, never losing sight of its contained lyricism, with the more approachable lyricism of the *Concertino*. In this he is ideally supported by Sir Charles Mackerras, whose expert judgement of the weight and pace and contrasts of the music never falters. Much of the secret in bringing off this difficult, haunting music lies in a sense of timing, together with something more, a long-acquired skill in contrasting textures dramatically, which has itself something to do with timing, at any rate with a sense of dramatic cut and thrust. The violin and cello works, themselves very different in their more romantic natures, are finely handled by Amoyal and Hoffman, with Rudy a sympathetic and supportive partner. There are now many different versions of each of these works, none in this exact compilation. It is certainly one that can be strongly recommended.

String Quartets – No. 1, 'Kreutzer Sonata'; No. 2, 'Intimate Letters'.
Along an Overgrown Path (1906-08) – Suite No. 1.
Radoslav Kvapil *pf*
Talich Quartet (Petr Messiereur, Jan Kvapil *vns* Jan Talich *va* Evzen Rattai *vc*).
Calliope CAL9699 (73 minutes: DDD). Recorded 1986. Ⓕ RR

This recording does not give a true balance, and in places the sound itself is rather grey. At first blush, too, the Talich Quartet's manner can seem tentative. Yet this is exactly what is right. The music is sudden, questing, unpredictable, by turns mysterious, vehement in its emotions, passionately lyrical. The whole programme of the Second Quartet, with its reference in the title to secret affections, indicates the extraordinariness of the emotion for the younger woman that overcame Janáček; and its exceptional and impossible nature finds ideal expression in the idiom of Janáček's astonishing final years. The Talich Quartet suggests secrecy, fear even, in the quick shifts between musical gestures; yet it can allow Janáček's beautiful phrases declaring his full heart to find passionate expression. It is a more restrained manner of playing than that adopted by other groups, and it can make its effect by skilful understatement; but repeated hearings increasingly find it to yield subtle and true performances of both works. Room is also found for the First Suite of *Along an Overgrown Path*. Kvapil is direct and eloquent in his approach to Janáček's oblique statements and half-hidden memories, both passionate and tragic; but he never overstates, and his allusive manner is very effective.

Janáček String Quartets Nos. 1 and 2.
Dvořák String Quartet No. 10 in E flat major, B92.
Vanbrugh Quartet (Gregory Ellis, Elizabeth Charleson *vns* Simon Aspell *va*
Christopher Marwood *vc*).
Collins Classics 1381-2 (73 minutes: DDD). Recorded 1992. Ⓕ

These are tense and lively performances of Janáček's quartets embodying two aspects of love. On the whole, the players' style is more suited to the First Quartet. The prancing seducer, the succumbing woman, all the sharply juxtaposed impressions that are of the essence of Janáček's style are here neatly characterized; and if the recording is a little shrill, it is also vivid and does no harm to the clarity of the music. The Second Quartet is another matter, and in its heartfelt, touching devotion to Kamila Stösslová is one of the most moving of all love-letters. The tension is here, again, in this performance; but there is missing an element of warmth, even of sadness, as well as the frantic passion. The moment described in the letters when 'the earth trembled with joy', and celebrated in this quartet, has been played with more rapture; and Kamila's swiftly changing moods have been characterized with more affection. Nevertheless, this is an intelligent, perceptive and urgent performance. Had the players felt that the warmth they discover in Dvořák's Quartet No. 10, also included here, could have infused it more fully, more might have been released.

Janáček Pohádka.
Kodály Cello Sonata, Op. 4.
Liszt Elégies – No. 1, S130; No. 2, S131. La lugubre gondola, S134.
Anne Gastinel vc **Pierre-Laurent Aimard** pf
Auvidis Valois V4748 (50 minutes: DDD). Recorded 1995.   Ⓕ

This is an imaginative piece of programme planning, with arrangements of Liszt's *Elégies* and *La lugubre gondola* separated by Kodály's Sonata and Janáček's *Pohádka*. Liszt, writing in the 1870s and early 1880s, sounds as modern as either of the two composers writing in 1910; and indeed there is much in his augmented-chord harmony and his fondness for unusual scales that influenced Kodály, while Janáček also admired him and used his religious music for teaching purposes. This is romantic music outside the mainstream of European musical romanticism. Gastinel and Aimard give performances as intelligent as these juxtapositions suggest, oblique and dark in the linking figure of Liszt, especially with *La lugubre gondola*, one of the most extraordinary late piano pieces. Kodály's sonata is played with a quiet intensity, rhapsodic in manner but in fact strongly held together by the clarity of emphasis on the motto theme and its musical implications. Janáček's pieces can sound sharper and quirkier than here, and in such performances make their point more strongly; but this playing is of a piece with the whole approach. Gastinel has a clean, resinous tone, and a strong sense of line; she is well partnered by Aimard, and the recording is clear and well balanced.

Piano Sonata 1.X.1905, 'From the Street'. Along an Overgrown Path. In the Mists. Thema con variazioni, 'Zdenka'.
Rudolf Firkušný pf
DG 20th Century Classics 429 857-2GC (79 minutes: ADD). Recorded 1971.   Ⓜ

Janáček's only piano sonata has a history almost as dramatic as the events which inspired it. Its subtitle, *From the Street*, commemorates a student demonstration in which a 20-year-old worker was killed, an event which so outraged Janáček that he wrote a three-movement sonata as an expression of his feelings. Before the première in 1906 he burnt the third movement and after a private performance in Prague he threw the remaining movements into a river. It is only thanks to the pianist, Ludmil Tučkova, who had copied out the first two movements, that the work survives. The underlying theme of Firkušný's approach to this work (who may claim historical authenticity as he studied with Janáček) is anger, turning the first movement into a defiant roar of fury whilst the slow movement has an inherent restlessness, bitterness never far below the surface. Much of the same characteristics can be found in the other works – *Along an Overgrown Path* and the masterly *In the Mists* – although he occasionally overloads these delicate little pieces with dramatic power. The early Theme and Variations are conventionally romantic but impeccably played. This disc represents playing of the highest class with full notes and tracking details.

Diary of one who disappeared (two versions).
[a]**Nicolai Gedda**, [b]**Beno Blachut** tens [a]**Véra Soukupová**, [b]**Stěpánka Stěpánová** mezzos
[a]**Prague Radio Chamber Chorus**; [b]**Czech Singers Chamber Chorus**; [ab]**Josef Páleniček** pf
Supraphon [a]stereo/[b]mono SU0022-2 (73 minutes: DDD/AAD). Text and translation included.
Recorded 1956 and 1984.   Ⓜ Ⓗ

Here is a highly interesting enterprise: two parallel performances of Janáček's song-cycle, both recorded in Prague, but one being the classic version with Beno Blachut made in 1956, the other hitherto unknown in this country and made in 1984 by Nicolai Gedda. Blachut, who despite his heroic use of his voice kept it in good order throughout a long career, was then in his early forties, and in his prime; Gedda, another singer who has preserved his voice carefully, was in his sixtieth year. Any lover of Janáček's music is strongly urged to acquire this striking record. The commentary, by the distinguished scholar Jiří Vysloužil, makes no bones about preferring Blachut, observing that 'what may have displeased some critics, including even those abroad, was the operatic style of Gedda's interpretation'. It is easy enough to see what he means: for instance, in No. 6, translated as 'Hey there my tawny oxen', as the young man ploughing has his head set afire by a glimpse of the gipsy girl in the bushes, Gedda gives the climactic phrase 'v jednom je plameni' an Italianate fervour where Blachut develops the song's passion more steadily towards the phrase, which can therefore be less strenuously emphasized. Nevertheless, Gedda's vocal elegance and eloquence have their own appeal; and his Russian background has long helped him towards a deep understanding of music in the Slavonic repertory. His is a superb performance of a work that can well sustain a new approach, whatever loyalties there may be to Blachut's identification with the work. Listeners have a unique opportunity here for getting, literally, two for the price of one and enjoying the comparisons. A lynch-pin of both performances, as he so often was, is Josef Páleníček.

Janáček Glagolitic Mass.
Korngold Passover Psalm, Op. 30.
Zemlinsky Psalm LXXXIII.
Eva Urbanová sop **Marta Beňačková** mez **Vladimir Bogachev** ten **Richard Novák** bass
Thomas Trotter org **Slovak Philharmonic Chorus;**
Vienna Philharmonic Orchestra / Riccardo Chailly.
Decca 460 213-2DH (62 minutes: DDD). Texts and translations included. Recorded 1997. Ⓟ 🆁🆁

Riccardo Chailly's Slovak Philharmonic Choir – idiomatic to the last cry – gives his impassioned and beautifully recorded account of Janáček's *Glagolitic Mass* a significant advantage over other modern recordings of the piece. Their declamation, acclamation, exclamation – for that is the nature of the writing – carries with it an innate understanding, a fervour, a confidence that easily surmounts the work's difficulties. There is passion and precision in their singing. Although Eva Urbanová doesn't always convey the sheer exultancy of her lines, the colour and cast of her voice is well disposed to the character of the writing. Vladimir Bogachev's Slavic Otello of a voice scythes into the *Slava* (*Gloria*) as if true belief were a demand. The mad 'amens' which carry us breathlessly toward the *Veruju* (*Credo*) protest too much. There is about them an element of delirium – a need-to-know – that is just right. The repetition of that one word 'Veruju' ('I believe') takes us to the very heart of the piece, and it is here that Chailly really shines. Only when the cellos duly find consolation (and how gloriously the Vienna Philharmonic attends that moment) does a lasting faith seem possible. Therein lies Janáček's metaphor. There's a great deal of food for agnostic thinking in this piece. The only reservation about the performance is the orchestral sound. Play any other account and Janáček's startlingly unvarnished colours sound hewn as opposed to honed. Stark, exposed, unlovely. Abrasive sonorities are somewhat compromised by the luxuriant homogeneity of the Vienna Philharmonic. No question, though, that Chailly and Decca offer a more 'finished' product. Play it at healthy volume to maximize impact and bring out those fine resonant bass lines. There's the additional incentive of Chailly's bonuses, Zemlinsky and Korngold, teacher and pupil – except that Zemlinsky's is the youthful work and Korngold's the product of a mature benevolence. In Zemlinsky's setting of Psalm 83 the fire and brimstone of the words is writ large with determination. Korngold's lovely *Passover Psalm* exudes contentment (and more than a pinch of Hollywood sweetener).

Glagolitic Mass[a]. Sinfonietta, Op. 60[b].
Felicity Palmer sop **Ameral Gunson** mez **John Mitchinson** ten **Malcolm King** bass
Jane Parker-Smith org
[a]**City of Birmingham Chorus and Orchestra;** [b]**Philharmonia Orchestra / Sir Simon Rattle.**
EMI CDM5 66980-2 (62 minutes: DDD). Text and translation included. Recorded 1980s. Ⓜ

'I am not an old man, and I am not a believer – until I see for myself.' Thus Janáček replied angrily to a critic after the première of his *Glagolitic Mass*. This is a gritty, masterful performance of a jagged, uncomfortable masterpiece. Its unusual title stems from the script of the ancient Slavonic text (*Glagol*) which Janáček set to music. Rattle's is a full-blooded, urgent view of the work, with particularly fine solo contributions from Felicity Palmer and John Mitchinson. That the language is an unfamiliar one is occasionally evident in the chorus, though they, like the orchestra, give totally committed performances under Rattle's inspired leadership. Also included on this disc is the *Sinfonietta* (originally entitled 'Military Sinfonietta', reflecting in the brass-heavy scoring of the work). It is as much a study in orchestration as form with the melody of the fourth movement appearing unaltered no less than 14 times, changed only in orchestral colour. It is brilliantly played here, with the 12 trumpets coming up gleaming in the final climax. An enticing proposition!

Janáček (ed. Wingfield) Glagolitic Mass (original version).
Kodály Psalmus Hungaricus, Op. 13[a].
Tina Kiberg *sop* **Randi Stene** *contr* **Peter Svensson** *ten* **Ulrik Cold** *bass* **Per Salo** *org*
[a]**Copenhagen Boys' Choir; Danish National Radio Choir and Symphony Orchestra /**
Sir Charles Mackerras.
Chandos CHAN9310 (63 minutes: DDD). Texts and translations included. Recorded 1994.   Ⓕ

Mackerras's version of the *Glagolitic Mass* is of particular interest as it embodies one of the
reconstructions that have been painstakingly made of Janáček's original intentions in different
works as his stature has drawn greater scholarly interest. This one has been made by Paul
Wingfield. He has gone into the nature of his restorations in great detail in his excellent monograph
on the work in the Cambridge Music Handbooks series (CUP: 1992), and summarizes them in his
note to this recording. Briefly, they involve the playing of the Intrada at the beginning and the end,
in the Introduction a very complex rhythmic pattern and in the 'Gospodi pomiluj' ('Kyrie') use of
quintuple metre instead of the familiar four-in-a-bar (both far more effectively), and fierce timpani
interjections in the wild organ solo. There are other points; but in any case, most interested listeners
will care less for them in detail than for the heightened force and impact of the music. This it
certainly now (or once again) has. These matters make it the more regrettable that, despite
marvellous handling of the work by Mackerras, there are problems with a quartet of soloists that is
less than exciting, and a recording that even with the most modern techniques can obscure the
detail of the music and the clarity of the words. This should not detract from the interest of the
disc, which every lover of the work will surely want to hear. Those who acquire it will have the
additional benefit of a fine performance of Kodály's *Psalmus Hungaricus*, though the restored Mass
is naturally the occasion here for recommendation and choice.

Moravian folk poetry in songs.
Zdena Kloubová *sop* **Leo Marián Vodička** *ten* **Radoslav Kvapil** *pf*
Unicorn-Kanchana DKPCD9154 (70 minutes: DDD). Texts and translations included.
Recorded 1994.   Ⓕ

Janáček reckoned that he collected over 3,000 folk-songs as a young man tramping across Moravia
with his friend František Bartos and scribbling down notes of the instrumentation as well as the
actual tunes. It may well seem that 42 in a row is asking a lot of listeners' patience, but it works out
interestingly. There being two voices helps, and the singers have the manner in their blood, so does
Radoslav Kvapil, with his very sharp piano accompaniments: he not only has the bounce and kick,
the lilt and sudden swerve of the rhythms at his fingertips, but can pick up the instrumental
implications, for instance with *The Musicians* and their skirling fiddle, trilling cimbalom and
thumping bass. But this might not be enough. The contrast in the sequence is good, so that there is
an alternation, sometimes an accumulation, of mood between the lively, witty folk vignettes, and on
the other hand more serious numbers such as the grim song of Jano, who has killed his girl and
must ride off to the gallows field, and the last song, a brigand's funeral. Time and again there is the
stuff of a Janáček phrase, as we know his lyrical line from the operas and still more from *The diary
of one who disappeared*, for of course these tiny folk-songs and romances and dirges are the roots of
his art. One need not be a Janáček specialist to enjoy this disc: it is graphic and refreshing. There
are texts and clear translations into English and French.

The Cunning Little Vixen. The Cunning Little Vixen – orchestral suite (arr. V. Talich).
Lucia Popp *sop* Vixen, Young vixen; **Dalibor Jedlička** *bass* Forester; **Eva Randová** *mez* Fox;
Eva Zikmundová *mez* Forester's wife, Owl; **Vladimir Krejčik** *ten* Schoolmaster, Gnat; **Richard
Novák** *ten* Priest, Badger; **Václav Zítek** *bar* Harašta; **Beno Blachut** *ten* Pásek; **Ivana Mixová**
mez Pásek's wife, Woodpecker, Hen; **Libuše Marová** *contr* Dog; **Gertrude Jahn** *mez* Cock, Jay;
Eva Hríbiková *sop* Frantik; **Zuzana Hudecová** *sop* Pepik; **Peter Saray** *treb* Frog, Grasshopper;
Miriam Ondrášková *sop* Cricket; **Vienna State Opera Chorus; Bratislava Children's Choir;
Vienna Philharmonic Orchestra / Sir Charles Mackerras.**
Decca 417 129-2DH2 (two discs: 109 minutes: DDD). Notes, text and translation included.
Recorded 1981. *Gramophone* Award Winner 1983.   Ⓕ 🆁🆁

Janáček used the most unlikely material for his operas. For *The Cunning Little Vixen* his source was
a newspaper series of drawings, with accompanying text, about the adventures of a vixen cub and
her escape from the gamekeeper who raised her. The music is a fascinating blend of vocal and
orchestral sound – at times ludicrously romantic, at others raw and violent. Sir Charles Mackerras's
Czech training has given him a rare insight into Janáček's music and he presents a version faithful
to the composer's individual requirements. In the title-role, Lucia Popp gives full weight to the text
while displaying all the richness and beauty of her voice. There is a well-chosen supporting cast of

largely Czech singers, with the Vienna Philharmonic to add the ultimate touch of orchestral refinement. Decca's sound is of demonstration quality, bringing out all the violent detail of Janáček's exciting vocal and orchestral effects.

Jenůfa.
Elisabeth Söderström *sop* Jenůfa; **Wieslaw Ochman** *ten* Laca; **Eva Randová** *mez* Kostelnička; **Petr Dvorskü** *ten* Steva; **Lucia Popp** *sop* Karolka; **Marie Mrazová** *contr* Stařenka; **Václav Zitek** *bar* Stárek; **Dalibor Jedlička** *bass* Rychtar; **Ivana Mixová** *mez* Rychtarka; **Vera Soukopová** *mez* Pastuchyňa, Tetka; **Jindra Pokorná** *mez* Barena; **Jana Janasová** *sop* Jano; **Vienna State Opera Chorus; Vienna Philharmonic Orchestra / Sir Charles Mackerras.**
Decca 414 483-2DH2 (two discs: 130 minutes: DDD). Recorded 1982.
Gramophone Award Winner 1984.   ℗**RR**

Janáček's first operatic masterpiece is a towering work which blends searing intensity with heart-stopping lyricism. It tells of Jenůfa and the appalling treatment she receives as she is caught between the man she loves and another who eventually comes to love her. But dominating the story is the Kostelnička, a figure of enormous strength, pride and inner resource who rules Jenůfa's life and ultimately kills her baby. Randová's characterization of the role of the Kostelnička is frightening in its intensity but also has a very human core. The two men are well cast and act as fine foils to Söderström's deeply impressive Jenůfa. The Vienna Philharmonic plays beautifully and Mackerras directs magnificently. The recording is all one could wish for and the booklet is a mine of informed scholarship.

Kátá Kabanová. Capriccio[a]. Concertino[a].
Elisabeth Söderström *sop* Kátá Kabanová; **Petr Dvorský** *ten* Boris; **Naděžda Kniplová** *contr* Kabanicha; **Vladimír Krejčík** *ten* Tichon; **Libuše Márová** *mez* Varvara; **Dalibor Jedlička** *bass* Dikoj; **Zdeněk Svehla** *ten* Kudrjáš; **Jaroslav Souček** *bar* Kuligin; **Jitka Pavlová** *sop* Glaša; **Gertrude Jahn** *mez* Fekluša; **Vienna State Opera Chorus; Vienna Philharmonic Orchestra / Sir Charles Mackerras;** [a]**Paul Crossley** *pf* [a]**London Sinfonietta / David Atherton.**
Decca 421 852-2DH2 (two discs: 140 minutes: ADD). Notes, text and translation included.
Recorded 1976-78. *Gramophone* Award Winner 1977.   ℗**RR**

Kátá, a free spirit, is imprisoned by marriage into, and domicile with, a family in a provincial Russian town on the Volga. The family is manipulated by her mother-in-law, a widow whose sole, obsessive concern is her status (familial and social). The only son (Kátá's husband) is understandably spineless, and Kátá looks for escape in love. She finds the love, but true escape only in suicide. Janáček focuses on his heroine, giving her at least two of the most moving scenes in opera: the first where, to music of shimmering, seraphic beauty she describes her childhood imagination given free rein by pillars of sunlight streaming through the dome in church; and the second in the last scene where, after her confession of adultery, she concludes that 'not even God's own sunlight' gives her pleasure any more. Söderström has the intelligence and a voice which guarantees total credibility; and of the superb all-Czech supporting cast one might only have wished for a slightly younger-sounding sister-in-law. Mackerras obtains the finest playing from the Vienna Philharmonic; and Decca, true to its best operatic traditions, reproduces the whole with clarity, atmosphere, ideal perspectives and discernible stage movement – only a detectable levelling of the score's few extreme *fortissimos* points to the recording's vintage. As a bonus, Decca adds the late chamber concertos, both excellently performed and engineered, and equally essential Janáček.

John Jenkins   British 1592-1678

Fantasias a 5 – No. 7 in C minor; No. 8 in C minor; No. 16 in D major. Fantasias a 4 – No. 5 in F major; No. 6 in F major; No. 12 in D major. Fantasias a 6 – No. 3 in C minor; No. 8 in A minor. Two In Nomines a 6. Pavan a 6 No. 2 in F major. Fantasia-Suite a 4 No. 4 in C major. Fantasia-Suite a 4 No. 7 in D minor. Divisions in D major. Pavan in A minor. Three Pieces for Lyra Viol.
Paul Nicholson *org* **Fretwork** (Wendy Gillespie, Richard Campbell, Richard Boothby, William Hunter, Julia Hodgson, Susanna Pell *viols*).
Virgin Classics Veritas VC5 45230-2 (78 minutes: DDD). Recorded 1995.   ℗**P**

Jenkins may be neither as dramatically striking nor as melodically individual as William Lawes but his infectious lyricism, and control of broad spans of subtly inflected polyphony, is often masterful in the very best of English traditions. Not all the works played here reach the peaks of which Jenkins was capable (lyra viol solos really are best heard behind closed doors) but this is none the less an astutely compiled programme reflecting the composer's versatility within fairly arcane idioms which Fretwork makes accessible to a wide audience. We now take Fretwork's keen ensemble and technical virtuosity for granted but the players clearly identify closely with Jenkins's undemonstrative and equable geniality. The sound is often dispassionately soft-grained, sweet and fresh but still capable of an earthy warmth such as can be heard in the *Pavan a 6*. The price of such reserve is that when Jenkins hauls a melodic idea over the coals, we are often left wanting a more primal and broadly selected investigation by the player: a recognition of an association through a darkening of the sound, an articulation re-articulated and time taken to accentuate a particularly 'connected' dialogue. Such things are often just a matter of taste and in this case should not detract from a disc which is one of Fretwork's finest achievements.

André Jolivet
French 1905-1974

Alla rustica. Chant de Linos. Pastorale de Noël. Flute Concerto. Suite en concert.
Fantaisie-caprice. Cabrioles.
Manuela Wiesler *fl* **Christian Davidsson** *bn* **Erica Goodman** *hp* **Patrik Swedrup** *vn*
Håkan Olsson *va* **Helena Nilsson** *vc* **Roland Pöntinen** *pf* **Kroumata Percussion Ensemble;**
Tapiola Sinfonietta / Paavo Järvi.
BIS CD739 (64 minutes: DDD). Recorded 1992-95. Ⓕ

This wide-ranging collection contains short items for flute and piano or harp (the *Fantaisie-caprice*, *Cabrioles* – 'Capers' – both written around 1953, and *Alla rustica* from ten years later), two ensemble pieces from the mid-1940s involving the harp (*Chant de Linos* and *Pastorale de Noël*), plus the two concertos: the first with string orchestra (1949), and the second, *Suite en concert*, with percussion (1965). Fine as are the rival readings, Manuela Wiesler is arguably preferable. This may be due partly to her remarkable and commendable width of repertoire, but mainly to her wonderfully intuitive way with Jolivet's music itself. Somehow she makes it sound just that bit more natural than anyone else, and let's not forget that he is still a 'difficult' composer for many listeners. The BIS sound is splendid, though it cannot hide the disparities in dates, venues and internal balance of the pieces recorded, so volume adjustment between pieces is necessary for optimum playback.

Sidney Jones
British 1861-1946

The Geisha.
Lilian Watson *sop* O Mimosa San; **Sarah Walker** *mez* Miss Molly Seamore;
Christopher Maltman *bar* Lieutenant Reginald Fairfax; **Michael Fitchew** *bar* Marquis Imari;
Jozik Koc *bar* Lieutenant Dick Cunningham; **Richard Suart** *bass* Wun hi;
New London Light Opera Chorus and Orchestra / Ronald Corp.
Hyperion CDA67006 (77 minutes: DDD). Text included. Recorded 1998. ⒻⒺ

This is a riotous, and in its day daring and improper, parody of the story of the Geisha and the visiting naval officer. Sidney Jones's 'musical play' was one of the greatest successes of late-Victorian London. It opened at Daly's Theatre in April 1896 where it ran for 760 performances. It reached New York the same year and was taken up in Berlin, Vienna, Budapest, Paris and elsewhere. Military bands featured its famous songs – and they were *very* famous – at least until the 1920s: 'Chin-Chin-Chinaman', 'The amorous goldfish', 'Chon Kina', 'Star of my soul' and 'A Geisha's life'. To listeners with no previous experience of turn-of-the-century musical comedy, it may sound just like a parody of *The Mikado*, and the pseudo-Japanesy rhythms and 'quaint' words may jar on those with politically correct notions. A few minutes in, though, and one is swept along, not so much by nostalgia for a vigorous and uninhibited era in the British theatre, but with simple enjoyment for a score bristling with good tunes, performed here with sincerity and panache, and thank goodness, no sense of condescension. The cast is led by Lilian Watson as O Mimosa San, the Geisha who attracts the attention of Reginald Fairfax, sung by Christopher Maltman. They both dispatch the famous songs with clear diction and a nice sense of operetta style. It falls to Richard Suart as the teahouse owner, Wun hi, and Sarah Walker as the 'other woman', Molly Seamore, to demonstrate a more subtle understanding of the almost imperceptible method of 'putting over' the songs. It's a trick of giving the sense of improvisation, of abandoning themselves to the moment. Walker sings 'Chon Kina' – where she is dressing up as a Geisha – 'The toy monkey' and 'The interfering parrot' with all her familiar sense of fun. Ronald Corp conducts everything with a bounce and lilt – perhaps the New London Orchestra sounds a shade too precise – the theatre bands of the 1890s had a raunchier sound. *The Geisha* belongs to a group of works with their own distinct musical qualities. This disc makes you long to hear more of them.

Joseph Jongen

Symphonie concertante, Op. 81ª. Suite, Op. 48ᵇ. Allegro appassionato, Op. 79ᵇ.
Hubert Schoonbroodt *org* **Therese-Marie Gilissen** *va*
ᵃ**Liège Symphony Orchestra / René Defossez;** ᵇ**RTBF Symphony Orchestra / Brian Priestman.**
Koch Schwann 315 012 (70 minutes: DDD). Recorded 1975-85. Ⓕ

Joseph Jongen is known primarily to organists. The strong aroma of Ravel and Debussy is understandable since Jongen had close associations with Parisian musical life. Clear glimpses of Holst and especially Bax appear through the swirling atmospheric mists of the Suite's ravishing 'Poème élégiaque' – again understandable since Jongen was living in England at the time. It is hard to understand why the works for viola and orchestra are virtually unknown. Jongen's *Symphonie concertante* is a spectacular showpiece for organ and large orchestra, full of thrilling effects, unforgettable tunes, spine-tingling climaxes and flashes of great beauty. Written in 1926 its rare performances today belie its sheer crowd-pulling potential, so it's very good to have the work readily available on CD. Having said that, what makes this a 'Good CD' are the two works for viola and orchestra. The viola has little worthwhile concert repertory yet here is some wonderful music (especially the ravishing 'Poème élégiaque' from the *Suite*) which has been allowed to wallow in obscurity for the best part of a century. Gilissen puts her all into this music, summoning up a vast array of emotions in the *Suite* and producing the kind of virtuoso playing in the *Allegro appassionato* more usually associated with the violin.

Scott Joplin

Joplin The Entertainer. Maple Leaf Rag. The Easy Winners. Bethena. Magnetic Rag. Elite Syncopations. Gladiolus Rag. Treemonisha – A Real Slow Drag (all arr. Roberts).
Roberts Everything's Cool. Hidden Hues. From Rags to Riches. Play What You Hear. Play What's Written. The Joy of Joplin. Before the Party Begins. After the Party is Over.
Marcus Roberts *pf*
Sony Classical SK60554 (58 minutes: DDD). Recorded 1998. Ⓕ

As a jazz musician Roberts sees his roots in the tradition of the great pianists – J.P. Johnson, Jelly Roll Morton and Thelonious Monk. His ragtime derivations even suggest his namesake Luckey Roberts. This is not really Joplin, but Joplin as a basis for taking off. Roberts admits that Joplin would probably not have approved but jazz musicians have always helped themselves and, after all, Joplin survives elsewhere. These Joplin arrangements are riotous celebrations of the spirit of ragtime. The familiar rags are hilariously varied with stop-go patterns, extra beats thrown in and, in *Bethena* and *Gladiolus Rag*, cack-handed deliberate wrong notes and bits of bitonality *à la* Milhaud in *The Entertainer*. It's rather like what happened when Cow Cow Davenport, who couldn't read music, played Carey Morgan's *Trilby Rag* from memory years later. The knowing way that Roberts does this constitutes his comic keyboard personality – a touch of Fats Waller? – which is also expressed in his own music. Roberts's own pieces are much less interesting. It's one thing to take off in a witty way on Joplin but quite another to be self-sufficient. These tracks have less sustained personality and are prone to fall into the pointless clichés of casual improvisation. But they make a good foil to the Joplin arrangements in a lightweight fun collection.

Maple Leaf Rag. The Entertainer. The Ragtime dance. Gladiolus Rag. Fig Leaf Rag. New Rag. Euphonic Sounds. Elite Syncopations. Bethena. Paragon Rag. Solace. Pine Apple Rag. Weeping Willow. The Cascades. Country Club. Stoptime Rag. Magnetic Rag.
Joshua Rifkin *pf*
Nonesuch 7559-79449-2 (71 minutes: ADD). Recorded 1970s. Ⓜ

Joshua Rifkin based his whole approach on Joplin as a notated music in the classical tradition and not merely raw material for jazz musicians to knock about like any standard. After all, Joplin stated on most of his printed scores that it was 'never right to play ragtime fast' and he clearly wanted to hear more or less what he wrote, as his own piano rolls show. Rifkin's approach is now totally vindicated. He brought the critical acumen of a musicologist to bear and it gave him the right answers. This collection of 17 rags is carefully balanced and invariably as musically conscientious as if he were playing Mozart. These performances of Rifkin's have stood repetition for some 25 years, whereas many more idiosyncratic treatments have become tiresome. *The Entertainer*, for example, sounds just as fresh here as when it was written. There are times when Rifkin's rare ornamentation in repeats seems slightly stilted, but he always respects the style of the period. There are other recordings of this repertoire but for the real thing – on the piano – there is no substitute for Rifkin, who provides the authentic Joplin experience. This is essentially the best buy now.

Josquin Desprez

French c1440-1521

Josquin Desprez Missa de beata virgine.
Mouton Nesciens mater. Ave Maria virgo serena. Ave sanctissima Maria. O Maria piissima.
Ave Maria gemma virginum.
Theatre of Voices / Paul Hillier.
Harmonia Mundi HMU90 7136 (53 minutes: DDD). Texts and translations included.
Recorded 1993.   Ⓕ

Among the group of glorious composers who make the years around 1500 one of the richest eras in the history of music, Jean Mouton was one of the most successful; and he was the one who, in the eyes of sixteenth-century musicians, most successfully challenged the peerless Josquin Desprez. So it was a good idea to assemble a programme that juxtaposes the two composers: for Josquin it is his most successful Mass; and for Mouton a group of motets on the same theme – varied but all of them luscious and exhilarating. Effectively Paul Hillier divides up the Mass, as it would have been divided in a celebration, and puts Mouton's motets into the gaps. This works particularly well, the constant juxtaposition of the two similar yet contrasting styles clarifying one's perception of both composers. The music is also superbly performed. The 15 singers of the Theatre of Voices are effortlessly clear, wonderfully in tune and beautifully balanced. You hear the lines and spaces of Josquin just as you hear the immaculately modulated colours of Mouton; and that is partly because the singers have such good control of a range of vocal timbre. But beyond that there is an energy in the performances that keeps everything marvellously alive: even if you occasionally feel that Hillier takes the music a touch briskly, there is constant delight in the shapes that result. This is an issue of enormous distinction.

Missa Gaudeamus. Recordare virgo Mater. Regina caeli. Missa Ave maris stella. Virgo salutiferi/Ave Maria.
A Sei Voci; Maîtrise des Pays de Loire / Bernard Fabre-Garrus bass
Auvidis Astrée E8612 (68 minutes: DDD). Texts and translations included. Recorded 1997.   Ⓕ

Bernard Fabre-Garrus has long been experimenting with different ways of performing renaissance polyphony. It seems that each of his recordings offers a new sound; and in this particular case his novelty is to use the children of the Maîtrise des Pays de Loire – both boys and girls – to sing the top line of Josquin's Mass *Gaudeamus*. This is one of Josquin's most rhythmically intricate works, so there is a major challenge here; just occasionally the rhythms slip a little. But to compensate for that there is a stirring energy to their singing; and part of the elegance of Fabre-Garrus performances has always been in his fluid, linear approach to polyphony, which works splendidly here. Moreover, with just six singers on the three lower lines, he always manages to produce a beautifully clear and balanced texture. This is a very successful and exciting performance of one of Josquin's most stunning masterpieces. His astonishingly varied treatment of the *Gaudeamus* melody ranges from straight imitation through unusually long-held tenor notes (that have a stunning effect on the work's harmonic rhythm), via bravura exercises in ostinato, to the heart-stopping modulations of the final *Agnus Dei*. The plainchants are sung with an unusual lucidity and energy. The motets include the rarely heard *Recordare virgo Mater*, which gives a special opportunity for the children to sing in three parts; and they end with a superlatively eloquent and clear performance of one of Josquin's most famous five-voice motets, *Virgo salutiferi*.

Josquin Desprez Missa L'homme armé super voces musicales. Missa L'homme armé sexti toni.
Anonymous L'homme armé.
The Tallis Scholars / Peter Phillips.
Gimell 454 919-2PH (74 minutes: DDD). Text and translation included.   Ⓕ

Towards the end of the Middle Ages it became customary to use popular secular melodies instead of the usual plainchant themes as the basis for composing polyphonic Masses. One such was the fifteenth-century melody *L'homme armé* ('Beware of the armed man'), a melody that may have originated as a crusader song. These settings would provide endless opportunities for a composer to demonstrate his contrapuntal skills. In the first of Josquin's two settings, *Super voces musicales*, he uses the tune over and over again, beginning each time on successive ascending degrees of the six-note scale *Ut re mi fa sol la*, so that it rises higher and higher as the Mass progresses. Sometimes the melody appears back to front from halfway through the piece on to the end. In the *Sexti toni* Mass the tune is transposed so that F rather than G is the final note. The listener's enjoyment is in no way lessened by all this contrapuntal ingenuity. The music flows along with unsurpassed ease and beauty, displaying that unique quality of seeming inevitability which characterizes all great music. It is well matched by the expertise and enthusiasm of The Tallis Scholars and the first-class recording.

Missa Pange lingua. Missa La sol fa re mi.
The Tallis Scholars / Peter Phillips.
Gimell 454 909-2PH (62 minutes: DDD). *Gramophone* Award Winner 1987. Ⓕ

This is absolutely superb. We must accept, of course, that Josquin is unlikely to have heard this
music with two ladies on the top line, but they do it so well that only a fundamentalist would mark
the disc down for that. It should also be said that the least successful performance on the entire disc
is in the opening *Kyrie* of this Mass where there is a certain brutality in the approach; and although
The Tallis Scholars make much of the 'Benedictus' and the last *Agnus Dei*, there may still be better
ways of doing it. On the other hand, as just one example among many, these were the first
musicians to make the 'Osanna' truly successful and understand why Josquin should have chosen to
compose it that way. But actually they sing even better in the Mass, *La sol fa re mi*. Again and again
in the singing one has the feeling that Josquin's lines are projected with an understanding and
clarity that have rarely been heard before. The *La sol fa re mi* of the title denotes (among other
things) the melodic passage which appears over 200 times in the course of the work with its
intervals unchanged – which may not seem a recipe for the kind of music one would want to hear.
But Josquin treats his material with such astonishing sophistication that you are rarely aware of the
melodic fragment as such; and Phillips is scrupulously careful never to emphasize the melody except
in places – such as the end of the second 'Osanna' – where it is clearly intended to work as an
ostinato. This performance shows that the *La sol fa re mi* belongs with the greatest works of its era.

Dmitry Kabalevsky
Russian/USSR 1904-1987

Kabalevsky Cello Concerto No. 2 in G major, Op. 77.
Khachaturian Cello Concerto.
Rachmaninov (trans. Rose) Vocalise, Op. 34 No. 14.
Mats Lidström *vc*
Gothenburg Symphony Orchestra / Vladimir Ashkenazy *pf*
BIS CD719 (65 minutes: DDD). Recorded live in 1995. Ⓕ

This BIS coupling provides performances of two works which, if not masterpieces, are still
sufficiently rewarding to be in the regular concert repertory. Ashkenazy creates an evocative
opening atmosphere for the first movement of the Kabalevsky, when after mysterious string
pizzicatos the soloist steals in with a gentle, singing tone. The soliloquy continues, for the work's
unusual structure, with its three unbroken sections linked by cadenzas, invites an improvisational
approach well understood by Mats Lidström. The Khachaturian Concerto opens with a
flamboyantly coloured orchestral declamation before the cello sails off with vigorous animation.
This is followed by a sinuous Armenian theme from the wind which the cello takes up ruminatively,
with well-judged *espressivo*. Yet it is the energetic main theme that dominates and the soloist is
carried along on its impetus, while ardently recalling the secondary material, finally leading to an
exciting sequential coda. The finale offers the busy, rumbustious Khachaturian we know so well
from the Violin Concerto. This composer's major works (with the exception of the Violin Concerto)
can seem rather inflated, but here the combined concentration of Lidström and Ashkenazy
minimizes this impression. As an encore we are given a beautiful, restrained account of
Rachmaninov's *Vocalise*. The recording is of high quality and well balanced, but a shade over-
resonant, although the ear adjusts.

Mauricio Kagel
Argentinian 1931

Auftakte, sechshändig. Phantasiestück. Serenade. Transición II.
L'Art Pour l'Art (Astrid Schmeling *fl* Michael Schräder *gtr* Hartmut Leistritz *pf*
Nils Grammersdorf, Matthias Kaul *perc*)
CPO CPO999 577-2 (67 minutes: DDD). Recorded 1997. Ⓕ

This refreshingly different disc enables collectors to catch up with Kagel, increasingly valued for his
humane and unaggressive occupation of those more progressive, even experimental, regions of
musical activity which often seem to be the sole preserve of the solemn and the pretentious. At the
same time, there's much more to Kagel's music than skittishness and satire. *Transición II* for piano,
percussion and tape (1958-59) takes up the idea of 'modulating' between live and recorded sound in
textures of continuous discontinuity. Though Kagel could easily devise the kind of expressionistic
flurries of activity that were the avant-garde calling-card of the late 1950s, there is already an
unusually playful quality to the sound manipulation. The music may be dry, but it is also bracing,

and this essential sprightliness, allied to wry good humour (sometimes indistinguishable from dead-pan seriousness), come to the fore in his later, more personal works. In *Phantasiestück* for flute and piano (1987-88), Kagel shows his willingness to flirt with instrumental cliché without sliding into inconsequence, and moments of Gallic winsomeness are offset by more sardonic sound effects. In the *Serenade* for flute, guitar and percussion (1994-95) the expressive range is even wider. The whole piece (lasting a substantial 24 minutes) is held together by intricate, beguiling displays of ingenuity, and there's a fine-tuned feeling for textural subtlety which never flags, even if some of the more basic ideas outstay their welcome. Finally, *Auftakte, sechshändig* for piano and percussion (1996) offers a more concentrated narrative in which pitched and unpitched materials wrestle to dominate the enthralling course of events. It's difficult to imagine more persuasive performances, and all the recordings are good.

Giya Kancheli

Georgian 1935

Liturgy for Viola and Orchestra, 'Mourned by the Wind'. Bright Sorrow.
Ian Ford, Oliver Hayes *trebs* **France Springuel** *vc*
Cantate Domino Chorus; I Fiamminghi / Rudolf Werthen.
Telarc CD80455 (72 minutes: DDD). Recorded 1996.   Ⓕ

Givi Ordzhonikidze, the editor of a well-known book on Shostakovich, was one of Kancheli's closest friends and staunchest supporters, and it was the sense of loss after his death in 1984 that prompted the composition of the heart-rendingly beautiful *Liturgy* (subtitled *Mourned by the Wind*). The other inspiration was Yuri Bashmet, for this four-movement lament was originally a Viola Concerto. It goes superbly on the cello too, thanks to France Springuel's passionate advocacy, and in this form it inevitably invites comparisons with Tavener's *The Protecting Veil*. A common feature of these two pieces is that they can seem almost unbearably moving if they catch you in the right mood and yet almost unbearably protracted if they don't. Yet for all the obvious gestures of lamentation and assuaging, *Liturgy* is not a tear-jerking piece. In fact the texture is for the most part quite transparent, and Kancheli constantly steers away from potentially manipulative clichés on to stonier paths. The more intense the urge towards consolation the more the sense of inconsolability grows; as a result the blind rage which erupts in the second and fourth movements is painfully intense. The Flemish orchestra gives a wonderfully controlled performance and Telarc's recording quality is superb.

Bright Sorrow again draws from the bottomless well of lamentation which is the ex-USSR composer's special curse and privilege. It bears the dedication, 'To children, the victims of war', hence the choice of two boy soloists to intone phrases from Goethe, Shakespeare, Pushkin and the contemporary Georgian poet, Galaktion Tabidze, symbolizing the innocent victims of the last world war addressing themselves to the present-day generation. The soloists sing only slow, fragmented lines, marvellously conveying the fragility of innocence. The overall concept of polyglot texting and the fusion of pacifism and religiosity reflects a conscious admiration for Britten's *War Requiem*. The second half of the work seems to be gaining strength and optimism, but these are soon obliterated, leaving behind only a heart-broken crippled waltz. Highly recommended, whether or not you already have the Kancheli 'bug'.

... à la Duduki. Trauerfarbenes Land.
Vienna Radio Symphony Orchestra / Dennis Russell Davies.
ECM New Series 457 850-2 (57 minutes: DDD). Recorded 1997.   Ⓕ ⑤Ⓔ

... *à la Duduki* (a 'duduki' is a Georgian folk-reed instrument) should prove the ideal introduction to Kancheli's current style. And while a momentary encounter might suggest familiar territories revisited (vast terrains sparsely but dramatically populated), the musical material is more immediately striking, the scoring more texturally variegated, and the time sequences – even the rhetorical uses of silence – somehow quite different from those in Kancheli's other recent work. Furthermore, echoes of modern jazz frequently fall within earshot. *Trauerfarbenes Land* ('Country the Colour of Mourning') employs a large orchestra and is different again (though both scores employ big drums to impressive effect), being nearly twice as long as ... *à la Duduki* and darker in tone. The opening has solo piano and *fortissimo* trombones hammer what sounds like a recollection of Carl Ruggles before six significant quavers (which turn up again later, in different hues and keys) mark a dramatic dynamic contrast. Time and again Kancheli's penchant for 'cliff-hanger' climaxes bring us to the edge of a towering aural precipice. This is the music of personal displacement: desolate, spacious, occasionally cryptic, and with sudden pangs of sweetened nostalgia that flutter across the canvas like torn diary jottings tossed by the wind. Dennis Russell Davies and producer Manfred Eicher conjure between them a precision-tooled sound picture where every grade of nuance is meticulously reported. Performance standards are unusually high throughout, so much so that it's hard to imagine either work being better played. An exceptional release, featuring some extraordinarily powerful music.

Johann Kapsberger

Libro IV d'intavolatura di chitarrone. Libro I d'intavolatura di chitarrone – Toccata arpeggiata.
Rolf Lislevand *theorbo* **Eduardo Eguez** *gtr* **Brian Feehan** *chitarrone* **Guido Morini** *org/hpd*
Lorentz Duftschmid *violone* **Pedro Estevan** *perc*
Auvidis Astrée E8515 (60 minutes: DDD). Recorded 1993. (F)(P)

Rolf Lislevand is one of the most interesting lutenists active today. He has dazzling technique, an extraordinarily wide dynamic range, an effortlessly infectious rhythmic style, and he grasps hold of the music in a way that makes each piece very much his own. Briefly, he projects with uncanny ease, and everything here sizzles with life. Kapsberger generally has a reputation as an extremely interesting bad composer – a reputation enthusiastically endorsed in Lislevand's quirky insert-note. But the performances here bring the music very much to life. Taking his lead from Agazzari's treatise, Lislevand uses a five-man continuo group to back the solos: a wonderfully flexible and exciting group. And, drawing hints from some of the titles and styles as well as from the international ambience of Kapsberger's Venice, he makes much use of oriental sources, not least in the colourful percussion playing of the virtuosic Pedro Estevan: there is very sophisticated drumming here, and for the 'Canario' he creates an uncanny imitation of a canary. The only faint criticism is that there could have been a little more documentation. Details of who is playing what would help the ear to understand the myriad sounds.

Albert Ketèlbey

In a Monastery Garden[a]. The Adventurers. Chal Romano. Suite romantique. Caprice pianistique. The Clock and the Dresden Figures. Cockney Suite – No. 3, At the Palais de Danse; No. 5, Bank Holiday. In the Moonlight. Wedgwood Blue. Bells across the meadows. Phantom melody. In a Persian Market[a].
[a]**Slovak Philharmonic Male Chorus; Bratislava Radio Symphony Orchestra / Adrian Leaper.**
Marco Polo 8 223442 (74 minutes: DDD). Recorded 1992. (F)

What a splendid CD! The obvious favourites (*In a Monastery Garden, In a Persian Market, Bells across the meadows*) are played with a grace and sensitivity that never invites unfavourable comparison with earlier recordings of the same pieces. If others in the same somewhat maudlin vein (*In the Mystic Land of Egypt, In a Chinese Temple Garden, Sanctuary of the Heart*) are missing, it is to give us the opportunity to hear some of Ketèlbey's unjustly overshadowed compositions. And what delights there are! Over-exposure to Ketèlbey's more stereotyped, highly perfumed compositions has disguised what varied and inventive music he composed. Once you acquaint yourself with the charms of *The Clock and the Dresden Figures, In the Moonlight* and the invigorating open-air spirit of *Chal Romano*, you will want to hear them again and again. Not to mention the equally invigorating overture *The Adventurers*, the elegant *Suite romantique* and the sparkling *Caprice pianistique* – and what a pity we are restricted to just two movements of the *Cockney Suite*. It is a pity, too, that the generally excellent notes should perpetuate the myth that 'Ketèlbey' was a pseudonym. But, no matter. With playing, conducting and recording of a high standard, this is a collection that absolutely demands to be heard.

Aram Khachaturian

Piano Concerto. Dance Suite. Five Pieces for Wind Band – Waltz; Polka.
Dora Serviarian-Kuhn *pf*
Armenian Philharmonic Orchestra / Loris Tjeknavorian.
ASV CDDCA964 (59 minutes: DDD). Recorded 1995. (F)

In the Piano Concerto Dora Serviarian-Kuhn and her Armenian compatriot, Loris Tjeknavorian, are in every way first-class: both identify naturally with the sinuous oriental flavour of the melodic lines and understand that the outer movements need above all to convey thrusting vitality; here there is plenty of drive and rhythmic lift. But what primarily makes this performance memorable is Serviarian-Kuhn's sense of fantasy, so that her various cadential passages, for all their brilliance, are charismatically quixotic rather than merely bravura displays. The other works on the disc are small beer. The 'Waltz' for wind band has an engaging carousel flavour; the somewhat vulgar 'Polka' which follows roisterously suggests the circus. The *Dance Suite* goes through the usual Khachaturian routines with which he likes to clothe his agreeable but at times rather insubstantial Armenian folk ideas. Easily the most memorable movement is the first and much the longer of the two Uzbek dances, which opens gently and touchingly: the reprise, with its haunting cor anglais solo, has a genial Nordic feeling. The closing 'Lezghinka', too, is rather jolly, but repetitive. Excellent performances, vividly recorded.

Khachaturian Violin Concerto in D minor.
Tchaikovsky (arr. Glazunov) Méditation, Op. 42 No. 1.
Itzhak Perlman *vn*
Israel Philharmonic Orchestra / Zubin Mehta.
EMI CDC7 47087-2 (46 minutes: DDD). Recorded 1983. Ⓕ

Khachaturian's concerto is a work of considerable charm, beautifully written. Shostakovich once pointed out that a 'natural and folk idiom' was evident in everything his friend wrote, and Khachaturian's Armenian origin is agreeably evident in the melodic and harmonic contours of the lilting second theme in the first movement and the *Andante sostenuto* that follows. It goes without saying that Itzhak Perlman plays this work with total technical command and persuasive feeling, and the result is most enjoyable, even if one feels in some places, such as the first movement's long cadenza, that musical inspiration is being spread rather thin. The finale, however, is predictably exciting. The Tchaikovsky *Méditation* coupling is well worth having, both for its intrinsic quality and also because it was originally planned as the slow movement of his own Violin Concerto. There is good accompaniment from Mehta and the Israel Philharmonic Orchestra and a bright recording.

Masquerade – Waltz; Nocturne; Mazurka. Violin Concerto in D minor. Gayaneh – Sabre Dance; Ayesha's Dance; Dance of the Rose Maidens; Lullaby; Lezghinka; Gayaneh's Adagio; Lyrical duo; Dance of the old people.
David Oistrakh *vn* **Philharmonia Orchestra / Aram Khachaturian.**
EMI Composers in Person mono CDC5 55035-2 (79 minutes: ADD). Recorded 1954. Ⓕ Ⓗ

The 1954 mono sound is not exactly state-of-the-art for its time, despite the expert attention of the remastering engineer, but it is more than good enough to convey the superb quality of the Philharmonia's playing at a vintage period in its existence. Khachaturian was a vigorous, effective conductor and the players respond to his uncomplicated, outgoing style as a composer with obvious enthusiasm. The recordings were sandwiched between Beethoven sessions with Klemperer and must have made a pleasant contrast. The Violin Concerto was written for Oistrakh in 1940 and he plays it with effortless, cheerful virtuosity in the outer movements and responds to the warmth of the central *Andante* in a particularly expressive, eloquent fashion. The three attractively romantic *Masquerade* pieces are very charmingly played, while in the seven numbers from *Gayaneh* the Philharmonia tears into the faster items with great gusto, and produces a particularly beautiful quality of string tone in the *Adagio*. None of the music on this disc is exactly first-rate, but it all comes to life very vividly and enjoyably through being played with such expertise and authority.

Khachaturian The Widow of Valencia – Suite. Gayaneh – Suite No. 2.
Tjeknavorian Danses fantastiques.
Armenian Philharmonic Orchestra / Loris Tjeknavorian.
ASV CDDCA884 (65 minutes: DDD). Ⓕ

Khachaturian's *The Widow of Valencia* is an early work (1940), yet already reveals the composer's fund of good tunes. He admitted its lack of authentic Spanishness and while the 'Introduction' opens with flashing southern Mediterranean gusto, it soon makes way for a sultry Armenian melody of best local vintage. However, why worry? Altogether this is a most winning suite, without a dull bar, piquantly scored and brilliantly presented by an orchestra which is completely at home and clearly enjoying themselves. They also give us another suite, comprising six indelible numbers – for the most part little known – from Khachaturian's masterpiece, *Gayaneh*. Tjeknavorian's own *Danses fantastiques* frequently burst with energy and the gentler dances have that Armenian flavour so familiar in *Gayaneh*. Brilliant playing in glittering yet spacious sound.

Spartacus – Ballet suites Nos. 1-3.
Royal Scottish National Orchestra / Neeme Järvi.
Chandos CHAN8927 (63 minutes: DDD). Recorded 1990. Ⓕ

Khachaturian's ballet, *Spartacus*, first produced in 1956, was a judicious, and in the event a highly successful artistic response to the demands of Soviet populist realism. For its dramatic narrative of a Roman slave rebelling against his captors, eventually to be betrayed and killed, the composer created a score of striking vitality, at once full-blooded and crude, passionate and tuneful, and yet undoubtedly individual. The ballet's most famous number, the 'Adagio of Phrygia and Spartacus', with its sweeping string tune, is justly popular and the theme returns nostalgically at the end in Phrygia's parting scene. Elsewhere there are many expressions of joyous extroversion and scenes of wild revelry, in which the music erupts with great physical energy, for example the 'Entrance of the Merchants' and the wild 'Dance of the Pirates', both in Suite No. 2. The scene of 'The Market' which opens Suite No. 3 has enormous bustle. The romantic side of the score is full of languid sensuality: the Gaditanian Maidens (in the First Suite) are deliciously and decadently alluring, and the 'Dance of the Egyptian Girl' is hardly less seductive in its sentient atmosphere. Those who enjoy the 'Sabre Dance' from *Gayaneh* will respond to the vigorous 'Dance of a Greek Slave' with its fiery rhythmic bite. Järvi and his Scottish players respond exuberantly to the near vulgarity of the unbuttoned animation and obviously revel in the lusher evocations. The resonant acoustics of the Henry Wood Hall, Glasgow, cast a rich ambient glow over Khachaturian's vivid primary colours and prevent the cruder climaxes from sounding too aggressive.

Gideon Klein

Czechoslovakian 1919-1945

Klein String Trio. Fantasie a Fuga. Piano Sonata. String Quartet, Op. 2.
Ullmann String Quartet No. 3, Op. 43.
Hawthorne Quartet (Roman Lefkowitz, Si Jing Huang *vns* Mark Ludwig *va* Sato Knudsen *vc*);
Virginia Eskin *pf*
Channel Classics CCS1691 (68 minutes: DDD). Recorded 1991.   Ⓕ

This CD is devoted to music by two Jewish musicians incarcerated in the Theresienstadt ghetto camp established by the Nazis in November 1941. Gideon Klein and Viktor Ullmann were substantial figures whose music needs no special pleading. In stylistic terms, Ullmann is perhaps the more predictable of the two. His Third Quartet shows him remaining true to Schoenbergian expressionism within a tonal context. Klein, deported to the camp at the age of 21, was by all accounts an astonishingly accomplished musician. His own music shows clear signs of potential greatness even if the major influences – including Schoenberg, Janáček and Bartók – are not fully assimilated. The invigorating String Trio, completed only nine days before Klein's disappearance, receives a magnificent performance from members of the Hawthorne Quartet, a group drawn from the Boston Symphony Orchestra. Virginia Eskin gives a powerful account of the Piano Sonata, humming along discreetly as she plays. High praise also for these ideally balanced recordings which document a form of spiritual resistance of an isolated and terrorized community which we can barely begin to comprehend.

Oliver Knussen

British 1952

Flourish with Fireworks, Op. 22. The Way to Castle Yonder, Op. 21a. Two Organa, Op. 27.
Horn Concerto, Op. 28. Music for a Puppet Court, Op. 11. Whitman Settings, Op. 25.
'... upon one note', Fantazia after Purcell.
Lucy Shelton *sop* **Barry Tuckwell** *hn*
London Sinfonietta / Oliver Knussen.
DG 449 572-2GH (45 minutes: DDD). Text included. Recorded 1995.   Ⓕ ⓈⒺ

This is a sample of what Knussen has written since his two one-act operas *Where the Wild Things are* (1984) and *Higglety Pigglety Pop!* (1985), a period during which, he says, he has come to prefer being 'bewitched for a few minutes than hypnotized for an hour'. Bewitching these short pieces certainly are. The *Flourish* has lyrical substance as well as the appropriate 'occasional' brilliance. *The Way to Castle Yonder* is a very brief suite from *Higglety Pigglety Pop!*, but also a vivid orchestral tone-poem in its own right. The *Organa* are fine examples of his love of fantasy, ingenious pieces that use a twelfth-century technique to modern ends with such audible logic and lucid instrumentation that you want to hear both again immediately. Something similar happens in *Music for a Puppet Court*, two solutions to puzzle-canons by the Tudor composer John Lloyd flanking further developments of the same material. The lengthiest works here are both in a sense dreams. '... *upon one note*' is a day-dream from which Knussen is awoken by Purcell. The Horn Concerto is a beautiful, allusive dream about all the worlds that the solo horn can evoke, from woodland poetry to dark menace. Knussen is a masterly orchestrator. This disc will give unalloyed pleasure.

Zoltán Kodály

Symphony in C major. Summer Evening. Magyar Rondo.
Christopher Warren-Green *vn* **Philharmonia Orchestra / Yondani Butt.**
ASV CDDCA924 (54 minutes: DDD). Recorded 1994.   Ⓕ

Kodály's only Symphony has an engagingly pastoral quality, with mild but memorable thematic material, lively – even somewhat overwrought – musical arguments and notably scenic orchestration. Yondani Butt presents a volatile view of the piece, with weighty textures and a fairly intense delivery, especially in the first movement's emphatic development section. The slow movement, an elegiac *Andante* based on folk-style motives, is appealingly atmospheric, while the fresh-faced finale generates plenty of rustic excitement. *Summer Evening* underlines the music's alternation of dance and reverie, whereas Butt's invigorating performance of the rarely heard but strangely more-ish *Magyar Rondo* (shades of Bartók's *Romanian Folk Dances*) has the Philharmonia playing like a generously augmented gipsy band, with stylish solo work from Christopher Warren-Green. Enthusiasm and sincerity are much in evidence throughout this well-recorded concert, while the odd spot of executive ruggedness is fairly appropriate to the music's outdoor character.

Háry János – concert suite. Dances of Marosszék. Variations on a Hungarian folksong,
'The Peacock'. Dances from Galánta.
Montreal Symphony Orchestra / Charles Dutoit.
Decca 444 322-2DH (77 minutes: DDD). Recorded 1994.   Ⓕ

Dutoit presents a warmly persuasive reading of *Háry János*. In the fifth movement, 'Intermezzo', the big *tenutos* in this very nationalistic piece are winningly timed. The instrumental solos are imaginatively played by the Montreal principals, as is, for example, the saxophone in the final Funeral March section of the fourth movement, the 'Battle and Defeat of Napoleon'. The *Peacock* Variations benefit even more than *Háry János* from the opulence of the Montreal sound, most of all in the glorious climax of the finale, which with Dutoit has tremendous panache. In the two sets of *Dances* Dutoit is warmly sympathetic in his springing of rhythms and moulding of phrases. For this apt and generous coupling of Kodály's four most popular orchestral pieces Dutoit stands as a clear first choice.

Solo Cello Sonata, Op. 8. Cello Sonata, Op. 4. Three Chorale Preludes (after Bach).
Maria Kliegel *vc* **Jenö Jandó** *pf*
Naxos 8 553160 (64 minutes: DDD). Recorded 1994-95.   Ⓢ

Maria Kliegel rises to the challenge of Kodály's Solo Sonata with considerable gusto: harmonics, *glissandos* (sometimes plucked with vibrato, as on a guitar), *sul ponticello*, fiery arpeggios – all are expertly employed and delivered via a nicely rounded tone. Kliegel's lustrous account of the *Adagio* (to be played *con grand espressiono*) underlines harmonic similarities with late Liszt and the folky, one-man-band finale has plenty of panache. The appreciative booklet-note relates Bartók's enthusiasm for the Solo Sonata's 'unusual and original style ... [and] surprising vocal effects'. In fact, no other work by Kodály is so profoundly Bartókian in spirit (propulsive rhythms, novel tonalities, declamatory gestures, and so on). The Sonata, Op. 4, is a far milder piece, though forthright expressive declamation sits at the centre of the first movement and the second is infused with the spirit of folk music. Kliegel and Jenö Jandó are in obvious musical accord, and the recording is very good – although if you listen to the 'Bach-Kodály' tracks and wait for the Solo Sonata to start, you'll note a huge expansion in the cello's recorded profile. The three *Chorale Preludes* that open the programme are 'attributed Bach' and enjoy the rich trimmings of a thunderous piano part (Busoni-cum-Liszt, with a snatch of Bartók added for good measure) and a warm flood of tone from Kliegel. A fine bargain, then, and a well-planned coupling.

Háry János, Op. 15ᵃ.
Erzesébet Komlóssy *contr* Orzse; **László Palócz** *bass-bar* Marczi; **György Melis** *bar*
Háry János, Napoleon; **Zsolt Bende** *bar* Bombazine; **Olga Szönyi** *sop* Marie-Louise;
Margit László *sop* Empress; **Sir Peter Ustinov** *narr*

Variations on a Hungarian folksong, 'The Peacock'ᵇ. The Peacockᶜ. Psalmus Hungaricus, Op. 13ᵈ.
Lajos Kozma *ten*
ᵃ**Edinburgh Festival Chorus;** ᵈ**Brighton Festival Chorus;** ᵃᵈ**Wandsworth School Boys' Choir;**
London Symphony ᶜ**Chorus and** ᵃᵇᵈ**Orchestra / István Kertész.**
Double Decca 443 488-2DF2 (two discs: 153 minutes: ADD). Recorded 1968-70.   Ⓜ

An absolute must for children young and old, and certainly for all lovers of the Suite that Kodály extracted from his delightful musical-cum-opera-cum-pantomime. Peter Ustinov's dazzling, occasionally Goon-like characterizations of the entire speaking cast are inexhaustibly entertaining, and yet the kindly moral theme that underpins the libretto of *Háry János* – Hungarian nationalism benevolently respected by the Austrians – emerges intact. And if you're wondering whether the complete score harbours much in the way of worthwhile music that lovers of the Suite don't already know, then the answer is a resounding 'yes' – gipsy tunes, Hussar songs, colourful extensions of familiar material (the 'Intermezzo', especially) and a substantial finale based on the Suite's 'Song'. Kertész's extrovert conducting is quite beyond criticism and Decca's 1968 recording is an experience in itself, with sundry sound effects (galloping steeds, gurgling liquids, crowd scenes, and so on) and a thrillingly aggressive presentation of brass and percussion. Decca's transfer is admirably up-front, and the odd audible edit or spot of rumble (tape or traffic, or both) hardly amount to adequate grounds for complaint. The fill-ups are both welcome and musically substantial. It was a good idea to preface the *Peacock* Variations with Kodály's choral arrangement of the original folk-song (a fine performance by the London Symphony Chorus), while the Variations themselves are given with considerable gusto and feeling for atmosphere. The *Psalmus Hungaricus* (arguably Kodály's masterpiece) receives a bright and forceful performance under Kertész, dramatically sung by tenor Lajos Kozma. This is a remarkably well-filled and well-planned set, although readers are warned that the otherwise excellent annotation includes neither texts nor translations.

Charles Koechlin

French 1867-1950

Koechlin Cello Sonata, Op. 66. 12 Chansons bretonnes sur d'anciennes chansons populaires, Op. 115.
Pierné Cello Sonata in F sharp minor, Op. 46.
Mats Lidström *vc* **Bengt Forsberg** *pf*
Hyperion CDA66979 (67 minutes: DDD). Recorded 1997.   Ⓕ

These two near-contemporaries, born in the 1860s, were pupils of Massenet. Koechlin is represented by two attractive works – a set of Breton folk-song arrangements – which allow Lidström to display his tonal range from robust ('Le vin des Gaulois') to a thread of sound ('Le seigneur Nann et la fée'), and a short sonata from over a decade earlier, written in 1917. Despite being written in wartime, for much of the work the prevailing mood is one of contemplative tranquillity (which calls forth some ravishing soft playing from the cellist), though the central movement has an extremely complex piano part in a free atonality that continues into the agitated finale. Pierné's big sonata is a rhapsodic, largely ecstatic work in one continuous movement that nevertheless divides into four sections, the material of the long slow first returning after a yearningly sensual *Animez*: the sonata culminates in an imaginative finale with moments of brilliance. The performance here is an eloquent one by both players, and the recording is strikingly truthful.

Le livre de la jungle – Poèmes, Op. 18. La course de printemps, Op. 95. La méditation de Purun Bhagat, Op. 159. La loi de la jungle, Op. 175. Les Bandar-Log, Op. 176.
Iris Vermillion *mez* **Johan Botha** *ten* **Ralf Lukas** *bass* **Berlin Radio Chamber Choir;**
Berlin Radio Symphony Orchestra / David Zinman.
RCA Victor Red Seal 09026 61955-2 (Special price) (two discs: 90 minutes: DDD). Texts and translations included. Recorded 1993. *Gramophone* Award Winner 1994.

For 40 years, from his mid-thirties onwards, Koechlin, when he wasn't day-dreaming about goddesses of the cinema screen, was obsessed with Kipling's two *Jungle Books*. This eventually materialized in a large canvas of four symphonic poems, preceded by three songs (with chorus) that he then orchestrated. The complete sequence, called *The Jungle Book*, appears for the first time here; the inclusion of the Op. 18 songs necessitates spreading to two discs, (though priced as a single disc). The first song, the lushly scored 'Seal lullaby', is seductively beautiful, well sung as it is by Iris Vermillion. Of the symphonic poems, only *The Bandar-Log* is at all known here. The title refers to the noisy, empty-headed race of monkeys which gives Koechlin an opportunity to pillory parallelism, dodecaphony and the sterile 'Back to Bach' movement then topical (in a *fugato* with each voice in a different key), all in a dazzlingly virtuoso piece of scoring for a huge orchestra. Much the longest of the orchestral pieces is *La course de printemps*, another virtuoso score, which falls into four sections – mysticism as spring slowly stirs in the forest, Mowgli's urge finally to leave the animal companions with whom he has lived and return to mankind, the painful following of unsettling 'new trails' and 'time of new talk' (another metaphor for the world of musical composition), and night falling again (mainly an immensely long monodic line over a pedal-note). Do not miss these remarkable scores. The orchestra rises fully to the occasion and the sound is clear and vivid.

Erich Wolfgang Korngold

Austro/Hungarian 1897-1957

Korngold Violin Concerto, Op. 35. Much Ado about Nothing, Op. 11 – Maiden in the Bridal Chamber; Dogberry and Verges; Intermezzo; Hornpipe.
Barber Violin Concerto, Op. 14.
Gil Shaham vn
London Symphony Orchestra / André Previn pf
DG 439 886-2GH (71 minutes: DDD). Recorded 1993.　　　　　　　　Ⓕ 𝐑𝐑

Though the conjunction of Barber and Korngold might not seem pointful, it works splendidly here. The performance of the Barber, warm and rich with the sound close and immediate, brings out above all the work's bolder side, allowing moments that are not too distant from the world of Hollywood music (no disparagement there) and aptly the Korngold emerges as a central work in that genre. There have been subtler readings of Barber's lovely concerto, with the soloist not always helped by the close balance, but it is good to have a sharp distinction drawn between the purposeful lyricism of the first movement, marked *Allegro*, and the tender lyricism of the heavenly *Andante*. In the *moto perpetuo* finale Shaham brings out the fun behind the movement's manic energy, with Previn pointing the Waltonian wit. In the Korngold, Gil Shaham may not have quite the flair and panache of the dedicatee, Jascha Heifetz, in his incomparable reading, but what emerges here again and again is how electric the playing of the LSO is under Previn. The recording helps, though the balance of the soloist is quite close. Shaham and Previn together consistently bring out the work's sensuous warmth without making the result soupy. Previn gives a rhythmic lift to the dashing *moto perpetuo* of the finale, relishing the Waltonian cross-rhythms. The suite from Korngold's incidental music to *Much Ado about Nothing*, dating from his early precocious period in Vienna, provides a delightful and apt makeweight, with Previn, as pianist, just as understanding and imaginative an accompanist, and Shaham yearningly warm without sentimentality, clean and precise in attack. The four strongly contrasted movements draw on the most open and lyrical side of the composer, again often sensuous in beauty, but with sharply rhythmic contrasts as in the Hornpipe finale.

Korngold Violin Concerto[a].
Rózsa Violin Concerto, Op. 24[b]. Tema con variazioni, Op. 29a[b].
Waxman Fantasy on Bizet's 'Carmen'[c].
Jascha Heifetz vn Gregor Piatigorsky vc
[b]**Chamber Orchestra;** [a]**Los Angeles Philharmonic Orchestra / Alfred Wallenstein;**
[b]**Dallas Symphony Orchestra / Walter Hendl;**
[c]**RCA Victor Symphony Orchestra / Donald Voorhees.**
RCA Victor Gold Seal [ac]mono/[b]stereo GD87963 (70 minutes: ADD). Recorded 1946-63.　　Ⓜ 𝐇

Heifetz's legendary recording of the Korngold Concerto serves a double purpose: as an effective introduction to Korngold's seductive musical style, and as the best possible example of Heifetz's violin artistry. The work itself was written at the suggestion of Bronislaw Huberman, but it was Heifetz who gave the première in 1947. It calls on material that Korngold had also used in three of his film scores (he was at the time composing for Hollywood), although the way he welds the themes into a three-movement structure is masterly enough to suggest that the concerto came to him 'of a piece'. The very opening would be enough to seduce most listeners, unless – that is – they have an aversion to the film music of the period. Miklós Rózsa's Concerto has its roots in the composer's Hungarian soil, and echoes of Bartók are rarely absent. But whereas Korngold's score is taken from movie music, Rózsa's (or parts of it) became a film score – namely, *The Private Life of Sherlock Holmes*. Rózsa's self-possessed, skilfully written *Tema con variazoni* was taken, in 1962, from a much larger work then in progress, but Heifetz and Piatigorsky play it in a reduced orchestration. As to the *Carmen Fantasy* by Franz Waxman (another notable film composer), its luscious tunes and frightening technical challenges were written with the great violinist very much in mind. It's a stunning piece of playing, and wears its years lightly. The other recordings sound far better, and the Rózsa items are in stereo. Marvellous stuff!

Symphony in F sharp major, Op. 40. Einfache Lieder, Op. 9 – No. 1, Schneeglöckchen; No. 3, Ständchen; No. 4, Liebesbriefchen; No. 6, Sommer. Die tote Stadt – Glück, das mir verblieb.
Barbara Hendricks sop **Philadelphia Orchestra / Franz Welser-Möst.**
EMI CDC5 56169-2 (63 minutes: DDD). Recorded 1995.　　　　　　　　Ⓕ 𝐄

Franz Welser-Möst's view of Korngold's magnificent Symphony is less expansive than other interpretations, especially in the weighty *Adagio* slow movement, but he is no less impressive for that. His account is curvaceous and 'filmic', but one has less of an image of Errol Flynn sailing the high seas when that wonderful horn theme appears in the *Scherzo*. The sombre *Adagio* is superbly controlled and beautifully crafted. Elsewhere, he generates a huge degree of rhythmic incisiveness from his players – the fleet-footed *Scherzo* for instance, or the daring-do finale. Although not wearing its heart on its sleeve, Welser-Möst's reading is not lacking in passion. Barbara Hendricks's ravishing accounts of four of the six *Einfache Lieder* and the famous Marietta's Lied from *Die tote Stadt* make an excellent foil to the symphony.

Korngold Suite, Op. 23.
Schmidt Piano Quintet in G major.
Joseph Silverstein, Joel Smirnoff *vns* **Michael Tree** *va* **Yo-Yo Ma** *vc* **Leon Fleisher** *pf*
Sony Classical SK48253 (75 minutes: DDD). Recorded 1991 and 1993.   Ⓕ🄴

Paul Wittgenstein's many commissions for piano left-hand (he lost his right arm during the First World War) significantly enriched the twentieth-century's musical repertoire, and Sony's superb CD bears witness to two of the finest. Both date from the inter-war years, Korngold's Suite being a product of 1930 and Schmidt's Quintet – one of three that he composed for Wittgenstein – from 1926. It is of course easy, with hindsight, to appreciate the abundant virtues of both pieces, even though back in the 1930s Nazi ideology drew a spurious racial barrier between Korngold's supposed 'degeneracy' and Schmidt's 'healthy' inheritance of the Brahms-Reger tradition. This ludicrous mock-crisis is tellingly exemplified by listening first to Korngold's sensual 'Lied' (the Suite's fourth movement), the musical equivalent of death by chocolate, then to the homely tones – no less lovely in their way – of Schmidt's *Adagio*. Both tug insistently at the heart-strings, but they are very different. Korngold also gives us a purple-hued waltz and a pungent 'Groteske' with a buttermilk centre. His is a music ripe to bursting point, though it is also wickedly subtle and immensely clever.

Schmidt's first movement has a second set that could easily have strayed from an undiscovered Brahms sextet, with piano writing that is unexpectedly prophetic of Bartók's Third Concerto. His third movement opens like a Brahms piano miniature, and continues in the manner of Reger. Both works feature delightful finales, Korngold's being a set of variations on a tender theme. Sony's stellar line-up gives Schmidt's Quintet the outing of its life: you will wait impatiently to replay the two middle movements. Fleisher's beautifully graded playing is granted affectionate support from Silverstein and his colleagues, supple but sweet-centred and very well balanced. A hugely enjoyable coupling.

Suite, Op. 23. Piano Quintet in E major, Op. 15.
Claire McFarlane, Jan Peter Schmolck *vns* **Schubert Ensemble of London**
(Simon Blendis *vn* Douglas Paterson *va* Jane Salmon *vc* William Howard *pf*).
ASV CDDCA1047 (69 minutes: DDD). Recorded 1997.   Ⓕ

This supremely stylish interpretation of Korngold's Op. 23 Suite (1930) has a very great deal to commend it, occupying a satisfying middle ground between the Czech Trio's endearingly homely view and the far more grandly virtuosic (and, in the heavenly fourth-movement 'Lied', self-consciously protracted) approach espoused by Sony's starry team. Not for the first time on disc, William Howard's decidedly superior brand of pianism is a very real boon, and the whole performance radiates an affection and gentle purposefulness that are genuinely appealing. Anyway, Korngoldians will surely want to acquire this ASV coupling for the marvellous Piano Quintet, which here receives a reading that marries refreshing spontaneity to notable architectural elegance. Dating from 1921 and composed just after *Die tote Stadt*, it's an exuberantly confident offering cast in three movements. These artists audibly revel in Korngold's taxing, yet sumptuously rewarding writing, and the recording is handsome and true.

Piano Trio in D major, Op. 1. Suite, Op. 23.
Jana Vlachová *vn*
Czech Piano Trio (Dana Vlachová *vn* Jan Páleníček *vc* Milan Langer *pf*)
Supraphon SU3347-2 (62 minutes: DDD). Recorded 1997.   Ⓕ

Supraphon's well-recorded version of the Suite is remarkably fast. Where this Czech team scores over recorded rivals is in the 'Lied', which Korngold asks to be played *Nicht zu langsam*. Their timing is a nifty 3'09". The coupling is Korngold's outrageously precocious – and utterly unmissable – Op. 1 Piano Trio. No other musical 12-year-old could have penned such a memorable – and meaningful – opening theme (a sure premonition of Korngold's film scores), not to mention the *Scherzo*'s Trio and the brief *Larghetto* third movement. Astonishing! It is no surprise that, following the Trio's New York première, W. J. Henderson wrote (in the New York *Sun*), 'if we had a little boy of 12 who preferred writing this sort of music to hearing a good folk tune or going and out and playing in the park, we should consult a specialist.' Fortunate for us, folk tunes and football took second place to chronicling some marvellous musical ideas.

Märchenbilder, Op. 3. Vier kleine Karikaturen für Kinder, Op. 19. Much Ado about Nothing, Op. 11 – Maiden in the Bridal Chamber; Dogberry and Verges: March of the Watch; Masquerade. Die tote Stadt – Mein Sehnen, mein Wähnen, 'Pierrotlied'. Four Waltzes. Don Quixote: Six Characteristic Pieces. Geschichten von Strauss, Op. 21.
Ingrid Jacoby *pf*
Carlton Classics 30366 01102 (66 minutes: DDD). Recorded 1997.   Ⓜ

The most striking thing about Korngold's *Märchenbilder*, Op. 3, is that it is the work of a 13-year-old. Korngold was surely one of the most remarkable of all child prodigy composers. He drew on literary sources one would have thought beyond his years: the *Don Quixote* pieces were written when he was 11, and although they are not so richly expressive, the resourcefulness and imagery are extraordinary. The musical and technical sophistication of the *Vier kleine Karikaturen für Kinder*, Op. 19, suggests that Korngold had some difficulty identifying with children of more normal talents. Some works repay repeated listening more than others, of course, but little is without interest. Ingrid Jacoby is superbly responsive to Korngold's vivid imagination, and plays with style and character. Her clear sense of line, the clarity and warmth of her tone and her feeling for orchestral colouring are all admirable. She can also be suitably coquettish when necessary, and seems firmly committed to whatever she is playing. The recorded sound is slightly distant, the perspective rather like sitting towards the back of an empty hall; a more closely focused sound would have done the performances better justice.

Die Kathrin.
Melanie Diener *sop* Kathrin; **David Rendall** *ten* François; **Robert Hayward** *bass-bar* Malignac; **Lilian Watson** *sop* Chou-Chou; **Della Jones** *mez* Monique;
BBC Singers; BBC Concert Orchestra / Martyn Brabbins.
CPO CPO999 602-2 (three discs: 162 minutes: DDD). Notes, text and translation included.
Recorded 1997.   Ⓕ

In the mid-1970s, when the revival of Korngold's music got underway, not even the most ardent enthusiast can have imagined that one day all of his operas would be given commercial recordings. That, however, is what has been achieved with this, the first modern performance and recording of his last stage work. *Die Kathrin* is separated by ten years from its predecessor, *Das Wunder der Heliane*. Between *Heliane* and *Die Kathrin*, Korngold's career had changed. From being the wunderkind of the 1910s, he had developed into the film composer and arranger of large-scale operettas. If *Heliane* is the most grandiose of his operas, *Die Kathrin* is the most unpretentious; Korngold had thought of labelling it a folk-opera. The story is simple. The hero, François, is a singer who has been conscripted into the army. He falls in love with Kathrin, leaving her pregnant. She loses her job, follows him to Marseilles, where in a vaguely *Tosca*-like plot-twist François is implicated in the murder of the villain, who has actually been shot by one of the cabaret girls. Five years pass, François returns to find Kathrin and his child. The opera ends with a rapturous love duet. The music is full of typically lush Korngold scoring. In the night-club scene, obligatory in any 1930s opera, there are two catchy numbers, and Korngold brings in such fashionably jazzy instruments as a trio of saxophones and a banjo. The cast is exceptionally strong. Diener has just the right weight of voice for Kathrin, and Rendall makes François into a very positive hero. In the night-club scene, Watson and Jones are suitably exotic as the good-time girls, while Hayward conveys the nasty side of things as Malignac. Brabbins brings out the essentially Puccinian side of the score; in its structure the opera resembles *La rondine* more than a little: *verismo* didn't die with *Turandot*. Devotees of Korngold's music won't need any encouragement. Those with a taste for tuneful, romantic opera, sometimes bordering on operetta, should give it a chance.

Hans Krása   Czechoslovakian 1899-1944

Verlobung im Traum.
Jane Henschel *contr* Marja Alexandrowna; **Juanita Lascarro** *sop* Sina; **Charlotte Hellekant** *mez* Nastassja; **Albert Dohmen** *bar* The Prince; **Robert Wörle** *ten* Paul; **Michael Kraus** *ten* Archivist of Mordasov; **Bogna Bartosz** *sngr* Barbara; **Christiane Berggold** *mez* Sofja Petrowna;
Ernst Senff Chamber Chorus; Deutsches Symphony Orchestra, Berlin / Lothar Zagrosek.

Symphony.
Brigitte Balleys *mez*
Deutsches Symphony Orchestra, Berlin / Vladimir Ashkenazy.
Decca Entartete Musik 455 587-2DHO2 (two discs: 119 minutes: DDD). Notes, text and translation included. Recorded 1996.   Ⓕ 🄴

Think in terms of Mahler's Seventh or Ninth (that is, the 'Rondo burlesque'), and you will have at least some idea of what to expect from Krása's pungent orchestral palette. Throughout *Verlobung im Traum* Krása makes imaginative – and frequently ironic – use of the solo violin, while his vocal writing favours conversational naturalness. Had Krása lived, he would almost certainly have amounted to a major force in modern music. Above all, he had the requisite creative originality and strength of musical character, and his mastery of the orchestra is beyond doubt. *Verlobung im Traum* dates from the late 1920s and is based on a Dostoevsky story which deals, roughly speaking, with the amatory dilemma of one Sina, who is pressured away from her true love into a loveless marriage. The dramatic denouement is unexpectedly tragic and yet there is humour aplenty and copious opportunities for Krása to indulge his skill as a miniaturist tone painter. The principal action is flanked either end by a prologue – which precedes even the brief overture – and epilogue (both magnificently sung by Michael Kraus), whereas the orchestral interludes trace escalating tensions with a degree of emotional exactitude that words couldn't hope to emulate. Significant musical asides leap off the page, whether as thematic references or pointers towards a specific mood or dramatic solution. Lothar Zagrosek directs an intensely committed performance, pertly phrased and consistently on-the-ball, with fine instrumental solos and a uniformly first-rate cast. Juanita Lascarro's Sina and Charlotte Hellekant's Nastassja deserve special mention, and so does Albert Dohmen's Prince; but the overall effect more suggests strong teamwork than a showcase for individual singers. As with the opera, Krása's 16-minute Symphony – a somewhat earlier piece – teems with musical incident, although the scoring (for small orchestra) is generally leaner and more transparent. Each multi-faceted movement features telling shifts in colour and tempo and the vocal finale – here with the excellent Brigitte Balleys as soloist – sets a playfully erotic poem by Arthur Rimbaud about two sisters who cleanse a boy's scalp of 'the torments hot and red' of lice. Vladimir Ashkenazy's performance is full of personality and the recording is superb.

Fritz Kreisler

Austrian 1875-1962

Kreisler Original Compositions and Arrangements – works by **Kreisler** and arrangements of works by **Bach, Brandl, Dvořák, Falla, Glazunov, Heuberger, Poldini, Rimsky-Korsakov, Schubert, Scott, Tchaikovsky** and **Weber**.
Fritz Kreisler *vn* with various artists.
EMI Références mono CDH7 64701-2 (78 minutes: ADD). Recorded 1930-38. Ⓜ Ⓗ

Kreisler Praeludium and Allegro in the style of Pugnani. Schön Rosmarin. Tambourin chinois, Op. 3. Caprice viennois, Op. 2. Précieuse in the style of Couperin. Liebesfreud. Liebesleid. La Gitana. Berceuse romantique, Op. 9. Polichinelle. Rondino on a theme by Beethoven. Tempo di Menuetto in the style of Pugnani. Toy Soldier's March. Allegretto in the style of Boccherini. Marche miniature viennoise. Aucassin and Nicolette, 'Canzonetta medievale'. Menuet in the style of Porpora. Siciliano and Rigaudon in the style of Francoeur. Syncopation.
Joshua Bell *vn* **Paul Coker** *pf*
Decca 444 409-2DH (63 minutes: DDD). Recorded 1995. Ⓕ

Years of 'encore' employment have guaranteed the cult longevity of Kreisler's music – certainly among violinists. The repertoire on Kreisler's disc consists of his own pieces and a large number of arrangements. Some of the latter are pretty feeble musically, yet the great violinist's unique artistry and magical tone-quality shine through. Sometimes he does not land right in the middle of a note, but as always plays with the timing and phrasing of a great singer. Nothing is ever routine or set in his playing, which has a continual feeling of discovery and freshness. The transfers are excellent. Joshua Bell learned Kreisler from his teacher, the late Josef Gingold, and yet his approach is anything but 'old school'. He habitually avoids the pitfalls of imitation, flashiness and patronizing overkill, preferring instead to revisit the music with modern ears. His *Caprice viennois* is light years removed from the composer's own, a fresh-faced, strongly characterized reading that trades sentimentality for just a hint of jazz. And of course there's that inseparable twosome, *Liebesfreud* and *Liebesleid*, the latter in particular displaying Bell's tone at its most alluring. The longest piece on the disc is the *Praeludium and Allegro in the style of Pugnani* which Bell gives 'the full treatment', deftly pointing the *Allegro*, relishing passagework and double-stopping with impressive accuracy. Some pieces seem indivisible from Kreisler's own very individual tone and phrasing, *Polichinelle*, for example, and *Marche miniature viennoise*, both of which paraded the sort of personalized rubato, timing and tone-production that have for so long seemed part of the music's very essence. Here and in a few other instances, Bell's brighter, more overtly virtuosic approach doesn't quite catch the music's period charm and yet a mini-masterpiece like the rarely heard *Berceuse romantique* (a sort of Fauré-Korngold synthesis) displays ample style, subtlety and affection of phrasing. Bell's smooth, witty and keenly inflected readings make for elevated entertainment: they may not replace the composer's own, but they do provide a youthful and in many ways illuminating alternative. The recordings are excellent, but Coker's excellent accompaniments occasionally seem overprominent.

Ernst Krenek

Austro/American 1900-1991

O Lacrymosa, Op. 48. Stella's Monolog, Op. 57. Die Nachtigall, Op. 68. Fünf Lieder, Op. 82. Four Songs, Op. 112. The Flea, Op. 175. Wechselrahmen, Op. 189.
Christine Schäfer sop **Axel Bauni** pf
Orfeo Musica Rediviva C373951A (67 minutes: DDD). Texts and translations included. Recorded 1994.   (F)

In this entertaining recital, the chronological arrangement of the songs affords a fair view of Krenek's stylistic development across nearly 40 years (1926-65). And quite a development it was, too, from the radiant *O Lacrymosa*, three further musings by Rilke on the Virgin Mary, to the near-volcanic *Wechselrahmen* ('Changing Settings'), to poems by Emil Barth. In terms of musical style, *O Lacrymosa* is clearly suggestive of Hindemith's *Das Marienleben*. More individual is *Stella's Monolog* (1928), on lines from Goethe's play *Stella*. Cast as a dramatic scena, this compositional *tour de force* has a wide range of moods, some of *buffa*-like airiness at odds with the text's romantic ardour, suggesting a send-up. When in 1937 Krenek came to set five brief stanzas by Kafka, he had finally embraced Schoenberg's 12-note method. The Kafka songs, Op. 82, as well as those of Op. 112 (1946-47, setting Gerard Manley Hopkins) show a concomitant spareness of texture, but his setting of Donne's *The Flea* (1960) is wonderfully exuberant, while *Wechselrahmen*'s extremity of expression is entirely apposite given Krenek's tirelessly adventurous spirit. Christine Schäfer is a sympathetic interpreter; a touch shrill in the topmost registers, her voice is big enough to cope with these songs' widely varying demands. Axel Bauni gives first-class support and the recording sounds bright and truthful. A must for anyone remotely interested in Lieder, of the twentieth century or any other.

Johann Kuhnau

German 1660-1722

Ihr Himmel jubilirt von oben. Weicht ihr Sorgen aus dem Hertzen. Gott, sei mir gnädig nach deiner Güte. Wie schön leuchtet der Morgenstern. Tristis est anima mea. O heilige Zeit.
Deborah York sop **Gary Cooper** org
The King's Consort Choir; The King's Consort / Robert King.
Hyperion CDA67059 (75 minutes: DDD). Texts and translations included. Recorded 1998.   (F)

Johann Kuhnau was Cantor at St Thomas's, Leipzig until his death, crossing paths with Bach and inspiring the younger man to borrow the title *Clavier-Übung* for the prime repository for Bach's published keyboard works. Out of Bach's shadow, Kuhnau stands tall as a polymath of a sort that had almost ceased to exist in the pragmatic social climate of the seventeenth-century musician: lawyer, novelist, philosopher, theorist, linguist and musician. This splendid and varied cross-section of his choral music leaves us in no doubt that Kuhnau is far more than merely a confident practitioner who followed the plot of changing fashion. Through a keen sense of assimilation comes a singular, mainly sober, yet highly accomplished church composer. *Gott, sei mir gnädig* is a fine, evocative work full of rhetorical detail and inference, whilst in *Wie schön leuchtet der Morgenstern* the declamation straddles the concentrated world of the Bach motet, *Komm, Jesu, komm*, yet punctuated by the secular ostentation and chuckling horns of another world. Robert King and his consort of singers and players highlight the multi-layered references in Kuhnau's cantatas, from the graceful Bach-aria lilt of *Weicht ihr Sorgen*, with the sympathetic colouring, if questionable diction, of Deborah York offset by an affectionate and responsive band of strings and unison oboes, to the decidedly pietist world of the *accompagnato* recitative in *Wie schön leuchtet*. The beguiling and antiquated *Tristis est anima mea* is worth its weight in gold. Vocally colourful (all the soloists are on fine form, but especially Robin Blaze and Peter Harvey) and instrumentally outstanding, this is an important recording of a woefully neglected figure whose music has real stature.

György Kurtág

Romanian 1926

Aus der Ferne III. Officium breve, Op. 28. Ligatura, Op. 31*b*. String Quartet, Op. 1. Hommage à Mihály András (12 Microludes), Op. 13.
Keller Quartet (András Keller, János Pilz vns Zoltán Gál va Ottó Kertész vc);
Miklós Perényi vc **György Kurtág** celesta
ECM New Series 453 258-2 (49 minutes: DDD). Recorded 1995.   (F)

This disc, devoted exclusively to Kurtág's music for string quartet, is of great significance, and both performance and recording are equal to the enterprise. The Keller Quartet has secure technique as well as emotional commitment, while ECM has provided a warm yet spacious acoustic for this expressive music. The journey begins with Kurtág's Op. 1 of 1959, in a world, dominated by expressionistic fragmentation, of which he is clearly the master. Eighteen years later, in the Op. 13 *Microludes*, Kurtág has perfected his own personal style, in which small, separate forms are linked together, and the music's allusions – to Bartók and Webern, in particular – are subsumed into a lyrical, dramatic discourse. The fruits of Kurtág's long apprenticeship are most evident here in the superb *Officium breve* of 1988-89, a miracle of textural imagination and musical thought whose richly varied language is distilled further into the two miniatures – *Ligatura* (also 1989) and *Aus der Ferne* (1991). By now Kurtág's music is characterized by a concentrated homogeneity, and by a harmony whose tensions, and stability, are the result of bringing convergence and divergence into confrontation. The result is memorable, and these fine recordings are immensely rewarding.

Játékok – excerpts from Books 1-5 and 8. Transcriptions from Machaut to Bach – No. 46, Gottes Zeit ist die allerbeste Zeit (Bach: BWV106); No. 48, Aus tiefer Not (Bach: BWV687); No. 50, Trio Sonata in E flat major (Bach: BWV525/1); No. 52, O Lamm Gottes unschuldig (Bach: BWV*deest*).
György Kurtág, Márta Kurtág *pf duet*
ECM New Series 453 511-2 (50 minutes: DDD). Recorded 1996.   Ⓕ

If any contemporary composer can persuade the musical world that compositions of between 30 seconds and four minutes in length are the natural vehicle for progressive post-tonal music, and therefore for the music of the future, that composer is Kurtág. This sequence of compositions, the longest of which lasts just over five minutes, offers a very special experience. The disc contains a selection from Kurtág's ongoing sequence of 'games' (*Játékok*) for solo piano and piano duet. They are a mixture of studies and tributes, not explicitly pedagogic in *Mikrokosmos* mode, but ranging widely in technical demands and style, from fugitive fragments, in which even the smallest element tells, to the extraordinary flamboyance of a *Perpetuum mobile* containing nothing but *glissandos*. Most are sombre in tone, and even the more humorous items, like the furiously constrained 'Beating – Quarrelling', have a bitter side to them. For access to another musical world, Kurtág has included four of his Bach transcriptions, music whose serenity and confidence speaks immediately of utter remoteness from the real present. Yet there is no nostalgia: Bach was then, Kurtág is now. The performances risk overprojection but they are supremely characterful, and the close-up recording reinforces the impression of music that is mesmerically persuasive in its imagination and expressiveness. If only even more of these pieces had been included!

Pierre de La Rue   Flanders c1460-1518

Missa de feria. Missa Sancta Dei genitrix. O domine, Jesu Christe. Pater de caelis.
Regina caeli. Salve regina.
Gothic Voices (Catherine King *alto* Steven Harrold, Julian Podger, Leigh Nixon *tens*
Stephen Charlesworth, Donald Greig *bars*) / **Christopher Page** with **Shirley Rumsey,
Christopher Wilson** *ltes*
Hyperion CDA67010 (66 minutes: DDD). Texts and translations included. Recorded 1997.   Ⓕ

Pierre de la Rue comes across as an inherently serious composer, his music reminiscent of the weightier Trappist ales of his homeland (the term 'specific gravity' describes it very well). This holds not only for works that are richly scored (the five-voice *Missa de feria* and the six-voice *Pater de caelis*, a jewel among renaissance motets) but also for those having the more usual four-voice layout, like the Mass *Sancta Dei genitrix*. Of the composers of his generation, La Rue comes perhaps closest to incorporating the qualities of textural and formal 'seamlessness' associated with Ockeghem in the previous generation, and with Gombert in the next. Christopher Page observes in his sensitive annotations that La Rue's music 'does not buzz with the open fifths and octaves so familiar to the singers of Gothic Voices from medieval music'. Here, the group sounds less brittle than it sometimes does, although tempos are still comparatively brisk in relation to many recordings of Franco-Flemish polyphony. The determination to adapt its sound to the needs of the music marks Gothic Voices out from many ensembles for early polyphony, and cannot be overpraised; yet on this recording there are signs that its careful search for the 'right' sound in this repertory has not quite reached equilibrium. One suspects that Gothic Voices' treble-dominated sound, appropriate to so much medieval music (especially that in which it has specialized), is not quite so suited to early renaissance polyphony in which all voices have equal prominence. Above all, the ebb and flow of La Rue's music (so masterfully in evidence in *Pater de caelis*) does not elicit the same measure of give-and-take from the singers. It is as though they were (collectively) still feeling their way into an unfamiliar idiom. But what price intellectual curiosity, or the thrill of new discoveries? Gothic Voices' risk-taking has been praised before, and if the results are not quite as satisfying here, they may represent the first stage of a new exploration. Meanwhile, the beauty and integrity of La Rue's music warrant a strong recommendation.

Michel-Richard de Lalande

French 1657-1726

Lalande Trois Leçons de Ténèbres et le Miserere.
L. Couperin Tombeau de Monsieur de Blancrocher.
Marais Pièces de viole, Deuxième livre – Tombeau pour Monsieur de Lully;
Tombeau de Monsieur de Sainte-Colombe.
Visée Tombeau des Mesdemoiselles de Visée.
Isabelle Desrochers *sop* **Mauricio Buraglia** *theorbo* **Nima Ben David** *va da gamba*
Pierre Trocellier *hpd/org*
Auvidis Astrée E8592 (73 minutes: DDD). Texts and translations included. Recorded 1996. Ⓕ🅟🅔

With Lalande's handsome settings of texts from the Lamentations of Jeremiah interspersed with
eloquent instrumental *tombeaux* by Marais, Robert de Visée and Louis Couperin, this is an
exquisite and deftly planned programme. Lalande left only three *Leçons de Ténèbres* out of the
possible nine scored for solo voices and continuo. Though they resemble the better-known Couperin
settings in many ways, they probably predate them by several years. Compared to those of
Couperin, Lalande's *Leçons* are more energetic and rhythmic; Lalande was a keen observer of text
in his sacred music, and where Couperin achieves an aching but rather objective beauty, he is more
gestural and in places more impassioned. It is an approach which is matched by the intelligent and
expressive singing of Isabelle Desrochers, a soprano whose voice is pretty if slightly hard, but who
really touches the heart with her ardent yet controlled delivery of this music. She is not always the
most fluid or accurate of singers, but the urgency with which she implores Jerusalem to 'turn to the
Lord thy God' at the end of the third *Leçon* is not easily forgotten. The accompaniment is nicely
varied throughout, and the instrumental items are well played. This is basically a beautiful,
life-enhancing disc.

Edouard Lalo

French 1823-1892

Lalo Cello Concerto in D minor[a].
Saint-Saëns Cello Concerto in A minor, Op. 33[b].
Schumann Cello Concerto in A minor, Op. 129[a].
János Starker *vc*
London Symphony Orchestra / [a]Stanislaw Skrowaczewski, [b]Antál Dorati.
Mercury 432 010-2MM (65 minutes: ADD). Recorded 1962-64. Ⓜ🆁🆁

Starker's playing is exemplified by a highly individual blend of intensity and specialized musical
intelligence which has, on occasions, been misconstrued as cool detachment, rather than
interpretative integrity. His formidable intellectual, as well as technical assimilation of the
Schumann Cello Concerto, presents it with rare *ipso facto* cogency. This work reflects the
composer's almost Byronic heroism in the face of mounting paranoia, having been completed in a
mere six days of mental torment during 1854. Starker's reading has an elemental pulse and fearless
zeal; despite his dubious insertion of a cadenza, this remains a truly valiant performance. Lalo's
Cello Concerto receives a similarly massive reading, and few recorded accounts can approach
Starker's emphatic gravity in the opening *Allegro maestoso*, but the prelude, marked *Lento*, is simply
over-dramatized. There is the expected relaxation in the second subject, but the relentless dynamism
of this turbulent movement is fearlessly maintained. There are some fine woodwind contributions,
too, in the central Intermezzo, and Starker moderates his vibrato to great effect in the dream-like
Andantino sections, while his quicksilver brilliance in the finale could not offer greater contrast.
Starker's reading of Saint-Saëns's First Concerto dates from 1964, and is in many ways exemplary
in its studied clarity. The gripping urgency of the opening is well sustained, with only marginal
repose found in the lyrical secondary theme, whilst the soloist's effortless facility in the difficult
double-stopped passage later is also noteworthy. Starker succeeds in making this work sound a good
deal more substantial than it really is! Here, then, are some highly individual, occasionally
provocative, and yet never less than totally valid, accounts of three seminal works of the cello
literature. That these performances are now almost 40 years old seems scarcely credible, given the
transparency and range of the sound, whilst from a historical standpoint they form a vivid
document of one of the great cellists of the century, heard at the height of his powers.

Lalo Cello Concerto.
Massenet Fantaisie.
Saint-Saëns Cello Concerto No. 1 in A minor, Op. 33.
Sophie Rolland *vc*
BBC Philharmonic Orchestra / Gilbert Varga.
ASV CDDCA867 (65 minutes: DDD). Recorded 1993. Ⓕ🅔

Sophie Rolland's performance of the Lalo Concerto is surely as fine as any recorded. It opens with great character, thanks to Gilbert Varga's strong accompaniment, and the solo playing is wonderfully songful. But Rolland is heard at her very finest as she plays her introduction to the finale with commanding improvisatory spontaneity. The orchestra bursts in splendidly and she shows her technical mettle with some lovely bouncing bowing in the attractive closing Rondo. The Saint-Saëns Concerto brings similar felicities. Massenet's *Fantaisie* opens dramatically and is rhythmically vital, flowing onwards boldly to produce a winningly sentimental yearning melody which the soloist clearly relishes. A cadenza then leads to a charming, very French Gavotte (which has a flavour of *Manon*) and the piece ends jubilantly. It really is a find, and it could hardly be presented more persuasively. The recording is as near perfect as one could wish.

Lalo Symphonie espagnole, Op. 21[a].
Vieuxtemps Violin Concerto No. 5 in A minor, Op. 37[b].
Sarah Chang vn
[a]**Royal Concertgebouw Orchestra,** [b]**Philharmonia Orchestra / Charles Dutoit.**
EMI CDC5 55292-2 (52 minutes: DDD). Recorded [a]live in 1995, [b]1994.   ⓔ🅔🆁🆁

Vieuxtemps's Fifth Violin Concerto opens disarmingly, but the tutti gathers strength in Dutoit's hands before Chang steals in silkily and proceeds to dominate the performance with her warm lyricism and natural, flowing rubato. In a performance like this it remains a small-scale work to cherish, for it hasn't a dull bar in it. The recording is warm and full, the balance treating the relationship between the violin and the excellent Philharmonia Orchestra as an equal partnership. The *Symphonie espagnole* is altogether more ambitious, as befitting its portentous title, but Lalo's inventive Spanishry holds up well throughout the five movements. How attractive is the Concertgebouw acoustic for the fanfare-like opening – giving it weight as well as point. Again Dutoit's approach is full of impetus so that when the malagueña secondary theme arrives, presented with a special feminine allure, it makes a shimmering contrast. The delicious piping woodwind *crescendo* and *decrescendo* which begins the finale sets the scene for scintillating salterello fireworks from the soloist, with Dutoit's spirited orchestral interjections adding to the fun, and the solo lyrical interludes as seductive as ever. The dash into the home straight brings vociferous applause, which makes one realize that the concentration and spontaneity of the performance has been helped by the presence of an audience, who aren't apparent until this point. Certainly the splendidly resonant Concertgebouw sound and perfect balance would never have given the game away.

Lalo Symphonie espagnole.
Saint-Saëns Violin Concerto No. 3 in B minor, Op. 61.
Chee-Yun vn
London Philharmonic Orchestra / Jésus López-Cobos.
Denon CO-18017 (61 minutes: DDD). Recorded 1996.   ⓕ

Chee-Yun is yet another of the formidable string-players to have emerged from South Korea in recent years. This disc bears witness to her artistry, built on a flawless technique, with immaculate intonation and exceptional sweetness of tone. Plainly she is a violinist to be judged by the highest standards. In her winning account of the Saint-Saëns the freshness and sweet lyricism mean that there is not the slightest hint of sentimentality or self-indulgence, with bright, clean attack in the first movement, purity in the interlude of the barcarolle-like slow movement and sparkle in the tarantella of the finale. For all the relative lightness there is no lack of bravura in the Lalo either, but in this colourful five-movement work you are more aware of understatement. Curiously, it is the very point on which one would have expected a Spanish conductor to shine that underlies that impression of understatement, for the LPO players seem reluctant to point Lalo's Spanish dance rhythms with quite the lift and emphasis they plainly require. Here the results sound a degree too literal, not sufficiently flexible, though that is hardly a criticism of the soloist, whose playing is as responsive here as in the Saint-Saëns. The cleanly focused recording is well suited to these readings.

Lalo Symphonie espagnole.
Dvořák Violin Concerto in A minor, B108.
Christian Tetzlaff vn
Czech Philharmonic Orchestra / Libor Pešek.
Virgin Classics VC5 45022-2 (63 minutes: DDD). Recorded 1992-93.   ⓕ

This is a unique and generous coupling, and if Virgin Classics' decision to record Tetzlaff in Prague was dictated by the obvious advantage in having Dvořák's compatriots accompanying in his Violin Concerto, the Czech Philharmonic's playing under Pešek proves just as idiomatic in the Spanish dance rhythms of Lalo as in Czech dances, with crisp ensemble and rhythm deliciously sprung.

What is especially remarkable about Tetzlaff's performances of the *Symphonie espagnole* as well as the Violin Concerto, is the quicksilver lightness of the passagework, which brings out the element of fantasy; in that he is helped by a recording balance which does not spotlight the soloist as sharply as in most other versions. In both works, each more episodic than most and hard to hold together, Tetzlaff's concentration makes for a sense of spontaneity, leading one on magnetically. Tetzlaff's sense of fantasy consistently marks him out, so that with delectable pointing of rhythm and phrase he makes the Lalo more subtly winning than it often is, helped by the extra transparency of textures.

Constant Lambert
British 1905-1951

Tiresias. Pomona.
English Northern Philharmonia / David Lloyd-Jones with ᵃ**Michael Cleaver** *pf*
Hyperion CDA67049 (72 minutes: DDD). Recorded 1998.   Ⓕ Ⓔ

Constant Lambert's *Tiresias* was commissioned for the Festival of Britain in 1951 and the subject was one which had been preoccupying the composer for over 20 years. In the event, Lambert (not by then in the best of health) struggled to meet his July deadline and called upon the assistance of colleagues like Robert Irving, Alan Rawsthorne, Elisabeth Lutyens, Gordon Jacob, Denis Apivor, Humphrey Searle and Christian Darnton to help him finish the orchestration. Lambert himself directed eight performances in all, but the work was coolly received and he died the following month, just two days short of his 46th birthday. Boldly, the instrumentation of *Tiresias* calls for neither violins nor violas and features a notably varied battery of percussion as well as an important role for piano obbligato (brilliantly played here by Michael Cleaver). The music has a dark-hued intimacy and at times starkly ritualistic demeanour which probably baffled that glitzy first-night audience. However, Lambert's achievement is surely ripe for reassessment, and David Lloyd-Jones's meticulously prepared realization allows us to revel anew in the score's many effective set-pieces. Both Stravinsky and Ravel are prime influences throughout, but the work as a whole is suffused with that distinctive mix of keen brilliance and bleak melancholy so characteristic of its creator. The present account is all one could wish for. *Pomona* (1927) is much earlier and altogether lighter in tone, the product of a prodigiously gifted 22-year-old. Deftly scored for a chamber orchestra of 34 instrumentalists, *Pomona* comprises eight delightfully inventive numbers whose neo-classical spirit breathes very much the same air as that of Stravinsky and Les Six from the same period. Again, the performance is first rate and the sound quite admirable.

Peter Lange-Müller
Danish 1850-1926

Fantasy, Op. 66. Soft Melodies, Op. 68. In Memoriam. Seven Woodland Pieces, Op. 56.
Morten Mogensen *pf*
Kontrapunkt 32228 (70 minutes: DDD). Recorded 1995.   Ⓕ

This often touching and occasionally robust Danish composer was a conservative only in a subtle and inclusive sense. The booklet writer aptly evokes Fauré to define the intricate harmonic life of many of these works; also their elusive and recondite nature. The *Fantasy*, for example, is subtitled 'Autumn' and a similarly seasonal haze hangs over *Soft Melodies*. *In Memoriam*, as its title declares, is a funeral elegy, while the *Seven Woodland Pieces* return us not so much to Schumann's *Waldszenen* as to Grieg's *Lyric Pieces*. Yet despite the evocation of such names, Lange-Müller's writing has a distinctive flavour and character. His *Fantasy* is a large-scale offering from a composer who clearly delighted in the miniature or lyric, and the title of Op. 68 is misleading when you consider the set's frequent blossoming into breadth and complexity. A Nordic introspection envelops the *Woodland Pieces* and it is sad to think of the composer's despair when he considered such music too tame and unadventurous to appeal to the taste of his time. Yet Lange-Müller yields up riches and secrets on repeated hearings. One can imagine performances of greater pianistic colour and freedom (too often melody and accompaniment become one and the same thing) yet they have a cool authority. They are also finely recorded.

Rued Langgaard
Danish 1893-1952

Music of the Spheres. Four Tone Pictures.
Gitta-Maria Sjöberg *sop*
Danish National Radio Choir and Symphony Orchestra / Gennadi Rozhdestvensky.
Chandos CHAN9517 (53 minutes: DDD). Recorded 1996.   Ⓕ

With Rozhdestvensky at the helm, Chandos presents what is probably this composer's most important – certainly most original – work, *Music of the Spheres* (1916-18). So radical did its sonic experiments seem even in the late-1960s that Ligeti no less, when inspecting the score, quipped that he had merely been a 'Langgaard imitator' all along. The manipulation of blocks of sound rather than conventional thematic development does have much in common with trends in post-Second World War avant-garde composition (though stemming from impressionism), but other contemporaries of Langgaard's, such as Schoenberg and Scriabin, had traversed similar terrain at least in part. The main difference between Langgaard and Ligeti lies in the former's reliance on a fundamentally tonal language, however eccentrically deployed, and *Music of the Spheres* seems in hindsight to be a bridge between two other highly virtuosic scores with celestial connotations: Holst's *The Planets* and Ligeti's *Atmosphères*. The *Tone Pictures* (1917) were written alongside this extraordinary work, yet possess none of its stature: four charming songs, they seem effusive and outmoded by comparison. Chandos's sound is of demonstration quality.

Libby Larsen

American 1950

Symphonies – No. 1, 'Water Music'; No. 3, 'Lyric'. Parachute Dancing. Ring of Fire.
London Symphony Orchestra / Joel Revzen.
Koch International Classics 37370-2 (57 minutes: DDD). Recorded 1996.   Ⓕ🄴

This is a terrific disc. Right from the very first bars of the invigorating *Water Music* Symphony (1984), one is drawn irresistibly into Larsen's sound world and left in no doubt that here is a composer who has made the art of symphonic writing very much her own. On the evidence of the present collection, her principal musical antecedents seem to be Sibelius, Stravinsky and the American symphonic composers of the mid-twentieth century (such as Schuman and Harris). But there is much more that is distinctively her own, and the result is a muse full of zest and vim. True, *Water Music* is more a sinfonietta than a symphony, but it is very accomplished none the less. One can almost 'hear liquid', as it were, and this is the finest water music since Respighi's *Fountains*. The Third Symphony (1991) is an electric score. *Ring of Fire* (1995) is no less involving, a brilliant tone-poem inspired by lines from T.S. Eliot's *Little Gidding*. The performances from the LSO – on top form – take wing, with everyone clearly at home with the idiom.

Orlando Lassus

Franco/Flemish 1532-1594

Libro de villanelle, moresche, e altre canzoni. Madrigals – Tutto 'l dì piango; Sol'e pensoso i più deserti campi; O Lucia miau; Madonna mia pietà.
Concerto Italiano / Rinaldo Alessandrini.
Opus 111 OPS30-94 (59 minutes: DDD). Texts and translations included.
Recorded 1994.   Ⓕ

This wickedly funny disc was released to coincide with the commemoration of the quincentenary of Lassus's death. Here Concerto Italiano gets a chance to let its hair down: the result is as hilarious as one could have hoped. The singers get inside both the meaning *and* the sound of the words, transfiguring musical texts that are (at times) purposefully naive. They also capture the incipient, slightly worrying hysteria that pervades many of these pieces, and of which the French songs usually steer clear. Psychologically, this is well judged: as Lassus's letters show, Italian is the language of his manic phases, just as French corresponds to his depressive ones. This disc, then, completes the picture of the composer in his more unbuttoned moments. Apart from some indispensable anthology numbers such as 'Matona mia cara' from the *Libro de villanelle* (performed with all the parody that the text demands), the most convincing performances are those of the *moresche*. A few more serious items are thrown in for the sake of contrast. These are the only disappointing pieces in the set, too slow for comfort by some margin – but then again, the rather archaic madrigal, *Madonna mia pietà* is delivered with real passion. The humour here is more often allusive than explicit, and as often lavatorial as genuinely bawdy. Those familiar with French *chanson* texts will probably have seen worse. Besides, one cannot help but respond to Lassus's evident relish at setting these dubious gems. Do follow the composer's and the singers' example, and let your hair down as well.

Lagrime di San Pietro.
Ensemble Vocal Européen / Philippe Herreweghe.
Harmonia Mundi HMC90 1483 (60 minutes: DDD). Texts and translations included.
Recorded 1993.   Ⓕ

Lassus completed his swan-song days before his death in 1594. The decision to set 20 stanzas from Luigi Tansillo's unfinished meditation on 'the tears of St Peter' must have been a highly personal one. The poet's portrayal of a man driven nearly insane with remorse allowed Lassus to exorcize the mental illness that engulfed him in his last years. The result is perhaps his most moving work, for there is in these *madrigali spirituali* a sense of distilled mannerism that calls to mind the understated passion of late-period Brahms. Philippe Herreweghe captures the detached expression of pain that makes this music so haunting. This is partly a matter of vocal timbre: individually the singers' tone is a shade cool, but collectively they sound full-bodied. Their interpretative acuteness is best illustrated by their approach to rubato: Herreweghe ever so slightly *stretches* the pulse when the voices achieve a poignant inflexion or come to a standstill. Such moments acquire an intensity that clearly identifies them as the key moments in a psychological drama, making the cycle as a whole compulsive listening. Quite simply, Herreweghe's singers achieve something very, very special indeed.

Missa Entre vous filles. Missa Susanne un jour. Infelix ego.
Oxford Camerata / Jeremy Summerly.
Naxos 8 550842 (68 minutes: DDD). Text and translation of *Infelix ego* included. Recorded 1993.   Ⓢ

The Masses *Entre vous filles* and *Susanne un jour* show Lassus at his best, full of variety and invention, music of an immediate impact; in fact, they display exactly the same qualities as the better-known motets. The Oxford Camerata has understood this well, taking considerable care with the nuances of the text and really enjoying the music's rich sonorities. Sometimes a slight imprecision in the playing of chords is detectable, but this is more than outweighed by the sense of melodic contour and the powerful, somewhat dark and austere sound which conveys so well the spirit of the music. With over 68 minutes of some of the finest sixteenth-century polyphony available at such a low price, no one should hesitate to buy this disc.

William Lawes   British 1602-1645

Royall Consorts – No. 2 in D minor; No. 4 in D major; No. 5 in D major; No. 8 in C major; No. 10 in B flat major.
The Greate Consort (Anne Schumann *vn* Emilia Benjamin, Reiko Ichise *va da gambas* Elizabeth Kenny, William Carter *theorbos*) **/ Monica Huggett** *vn*
ASV Gaudeamus CDGAU147 (68 minutes: DDD). Recorded 1996.   ⒻⓅ

These formalized dances give us a less familiar view of this composer: the broody cavalier reflecting, in exquisitely fashioned thematic strains, the unequivocal decorum of musical conceits in Charles I's cultivated time-bomb of a court. The soft-grained and unforced string timbre of The Greate Consort is underpinned by delightfully subtle and undemonstrative theorbo playing. For some, the characterization in, say, the Aires of Consort No. 4 will seem a touch under-explored but given the Pavan's wonderful concentration of seamless allusions, gently passed back and forth, the sense of an integral suite is strongly and vitally projected. Monica Huggett leads by example with tonal sweetness and exemplary musicianship. Rare qualities indeed, and treasure from which she has effected chamber music playing of the very highest quality.

Gaspard Le Roux   French second half of 17th century-1705/7

Pièces de clavessin (arr. Meyerson and Crawford).
Mitzi Meyerson, Lisa Crawford *hpds*
Harmonia Mundi HMC90 1660 (72 minutes: DDD). Recorded 1994-96.   ⒻⓅ

We know hardly anything about this shadowy figure in French musical life, but in his own time Le Roux was evidently quite a prominent musician, and the fact that Bach's pupil, Krebs, had copied one of Le Roux's suites is some indication of his standing further afield. Le Roux's suites – there are seven of them – were published in Paris in 1705, and were not exclusively designed as harpsichord music. In fact Le Roux wrote out the parts in such a way that the pieces could be played by two melody instruments and figured bass, by a solo harpsichord or by two harpsichords. It is this last realization that has been chosen by Mitzi Meyerson and Lisa Crawford, who play two mid-eighteenth-century French harpsichords. These highly adaptable *Pièces de clavessin* offer in such performances wonderful opportunities for resonant sonority and imaginative elaboration. None of this is lost on Meyerson and Crawford, whose rhythmic playing and vital responses to

Le Roux's inventive talent make for engaging entertainment. Two of the suites seem worthy of special mention, that belonging to the Sixth Suite, variously recalling both Couperin and Rameau, and another belonging to the Third Suite, eloquent, flowing, and with some deliciously dissonant moments, highlighted by the equally delicious, but astringent tuning that gives a bite to much else in the programme. A stylish performance, with supple body, though in no way lacking in sensibility.

Jean-Marie Leclair   French 1697-1764

Flute Concerto No. 3 in C major, Op. 7. Violin Concertos – Op. 7: No. 4 in F major;
No. 6 in A major. No. 2 in A major, Op. 10.
Rachel Brown *fl*
Collegium Musicum 90 / Simon Standage *vn*
Chandos Chaconne CHAN0564 (65 minutes: DDD). Recorded 1994.   Ⓕ**P**

Of the violin concertos here, Op. 10 No. 2 is the richest harmonically. The solo instrument in Op. 7 No. 3 is Leclair's stated alternative of flute, the only one of his 12 violin concertos to be so designed. Accordingly, it lacks the double-stopping so much favoured by this greatly admired violinist-composer. Otherwise it exploits the graceful sequential passagework found in the other concertos, though here with a fuller accompanying texture, with more movement in inner parts. Rachel Brown's playing throughout is deliciously cool and poised. Virtuoso violin fireworks abound in the vigorous first movements of the other two Op. 7 concertos here and the ebullient finale of the A major (the start of whose first movement has a Vivaldian resonance): as expected, Simon Standage throws off their difficulties with panache and an apparent ease that allows him also to add stylish embellishments of his own. The extensive multiple-stopping on which the elegant minuet-like Aria of Op. 7 No. 6 relies is performed with well-nigh impeccable intonation.

Violin Concertos – Op. 7: No. 1 in D minor. Op. 10: No. 3 in D major; No. 4 in F major;
No. 6 in G minor.
Collegium Musicum 90 / Simon Standage *vn*
Chandos Chaconne CHAN0589 (59 minutes: DDD). Recorded 1995.   Ⓕ**PE**

This disc contains Leclair's most vivacious and attractive works, played with great élan, sensitivity and neatness, and recorded with exemplary clarity and balance. The concertos represent a high-water mark in eighteenth-century violin technique, with extensive double-stopping, an extended range that soars up to heights scarcely ventured previously, rapid scales and flying arpeggios, and elaborate figurations of all kinds. To all of this Standage brings a seasoned virtuosity which he places completely at the service of the music's grace: his bowing in particular commands admiration. From the stylistic viewpoint these concertos are interesting for their mingling of French and Italian elements. There are Vivaldian unisons, but French dance forms for the middle movements – a pair of minuets in the D minor, minuets *en rondeau* in the G minor, a pair of gavottes with unusual interplay between solo and tutti in the F major, and an ornate solo line over supporting reiterated chords in the D major. Standage adds spontaneous embellishments of his own on repeats.

Violin Sonatas, Op. 1 – No. 1 in A minor; No. 3 in B flat major; No. 8 in G major; No. 9 in A major.
François Fernandez *vn* **Pierre Hantaï** *hpd* **Philippe Pierlot** *va da gamba*
Auvidis Astrée E8662 (64 minutes: DDD). Recorded 1995.   Ⓕ**PE**

Leclair's Op. 1 set was so successful when it was first published in 1723 that it had to be reprinted four times. Though the technical demands it makes on the violinist are considerable, the composer himself was at pains not to employ virtuosity as an end in itself and to condemn the 'trivialisation' of players who exaggerated the speed of quick movements. Leclair also, like Couperin, was insistent that performers should not add ornamentation of their own – though in the four sonatas here only the initial *Adagio* of No. 3 is much decorated. Rather did he place emphasis on 'le beau chant' – expressive *cantabile*, which is well exemplified in the first movements of Nos. 1, 8 and 9. The crisp *Allegro*, with its rapid dipping across strings, and the *Largo* of No. 3 make play with multiple stopping, including double trills, and there is vigorous cross-string work too in the ebullient Giga of No. 1. Leclair shows himself fond of the rondeau form with long episodes, and the Sarabande of No. 9 is a set of variations. This last has an athletic gamba line, as does the whole of the G major Sonata; and the alert and positive continuo playing here (from both gamba and harpsichord) is a special pleasure. But naturally the main spotlight falls on François Fernandez, whose lively, pointed bowing, delicate and sprightly fast movements and graceful slow ones (like the gentle G major Musette) do full justice to Leclair's attractive invention.

Franz Lehár

Gold und Silber, Op. 79. Wiener Frauen – overture. Der Graf von Luxemburg – Waltz;
Waltz Intermezzo. Zigeunerliebe – overture. Eva – Wär' es auch nichts als ein Traum von Glück;
Waltz Scene. Das Land des Lächelns – overture. Die lustige Witwe – concert overture.
Zurich Tonhalle Orchestra / Franz Lehár.
Beulah mono 1PD16 (58 minutes: ADD). Recorded 1947.   Ⓕ Ⓗ

These were the 77-year-old composer's last recordings. Most were reissued on LP (latterly on the
Eclipse label), but here they are for the first time complete. Mostly the selections represent obvious
items from Lehár's melodic output. However, the inclusion of the *Wiener Frauen* overture is an
especial joy, representing Lehár at his less familiar but most melodic and inventive. The operetta's
principal character was a piano tuner, and the overture includes an ingenious passage where one
hears the piano being tuned up before launching into one of Lehár's most luxuriant and beautiful
waltzes. In his excellent notes Malcolm Walker aptly describes these recordings as, in a sense,
Lehár's last will and testament. Slower and more indulgent than his earlier recordings they may be;
but never for a moment the slightest bit ponderous. Rather they are full of nostalgia, wonder and
joyful pride – lovingly caressed performances by a master melodist, master orchestrator and master
conductor. The transfers have been excellently done from original shellac discs. Filtering may be
required to minimize hiss; but it is more than worthwhile for uniquely beautiful recordings of some
of the most heavenly melodies ever created.

Tatjana – Prelude, Act 1; Prelude, Act 2; Prelude, Act 3; Russian Dances. Fieber. Il guado.
Concertino for Violin and Orchestra in B flat minor. Eine Vision: meine Jugendzeit. Donaulegenden,
'An der grauen Donau'.
Robert Gambill *ten* **Latica Honda-Rosenberg** *vn* **Volker Banfield** *pf*
North German Radio Philharmonic Orchestra / Klauspeter Seibel.
CPO CPO999 423-2 (70 minutes: DDD). Texts and translations included. Recorded 1996-97.   Ⓕ

This splendidly produced collection will surprise and delight. Lehár's mastery of the orchestra has
never been in doubt; and here is further evidence of his technical accomplishment. Such touches of
the operetta composer as are here are of the more ambitious operetta scores such as *Zigeunerliebe*.
More often it is Wagner, Richard Strauss and Korngold who come to mind. Throughout, the music
is tastefully and evocatively written, and with a supreme confidence in the handling of a large
orchestra. *Tatjana* was an early operatic attempt of which Lehár was especially fond, and its
preludes and dances capture the starkness of its Siberian setting. *Il guado* ('The ford') and the
concert overture *Eine Vision* are works from the *Lustige Witwe* years, when Lehár was still seeking
to determine in which direction his future lay. The former is a symphonic poem with some
attractively rippling writing for the piano, the latter a recollection of the Bohemian countryside of
his youth. The elegant *Concertino* for violin and orchestra, which has been recorded previously, is a
student work that demonstrates his affection for his own instrument. *Fieber* is the starkest piece in
the collection – a bitter First World War portrayal of a soldier in the throes of a deadly fever.
Donaulegenden gives glimpses of the familiar waltz-time Lehár, but a Lehár looking back sadly at a
bygone age. What other operetta or waltz composer could have written music as powerful, gripping
and spine-tingling as this? Do try it!

Aus längst vergang'ner Zeit. Sieben Karst-Lieder. Reiterlied 1914. Nur einer. Erste Liebe. Der
Thräne Silberthau! Sehnsucht, heimliches Verlangen. Die du mein alles bist. Das lockende Lied.
Schau mich an, sei mir gut. Schillernder Falter. Ich liebe dich! Frauenherz, du bist ein kleiner
Schmetterling! Wenn eine schöne Frau befiehlt. Liebesglück. Geträumt! Die ganze Welt dreht sich
um die Liebe.
Gabriele Rossmanith, Heidi Wolf *sops* **Iris Vermillion** *mez* **Jürgen Sacher** *ten*
Jens-Peter Maintz *vc* **Cord Garben** *pf*
CPO CPO999 432-2 (62 minutes: DDD). Texts and translations included. Recorded 1996.   Ⓕ

This collection of songs is a revelation. It is proof that, though Lehár found fame in operetta, he
could readily have succeeded in more serious fields. Those serious ambitions are shown in the
earliest items here – in *Aus längst vergang'ner Zeit*, an emotional song about faded youth, or in the
Karst-Lieder, songs that evoke the Croatian landscape where he was stationed as bandmaster in the
early 1890s. That Lehár's serious ambitions outlasted his early operetta successes is exemplified by
the wartime laments, *Reiterlied 1914* and *Nur einer*. Though he thereafter concentrated on more
popular, sentimental numbers, he never lowered his standards of musicianship. *Das lockende Lied* is
a taxing coloratura test-piece, but in *Wenn eine schöne Frau befiehlt*, written for Richard Tauber,
there is a delicious touch of syncopation. The sheer variety of these songs is astonishing. There are
glorious melodies, too, in the entrancing *Erste Liebe*, in the slow waltz *Ich liebe dich!*, with its

haunting solo cello part, and in *Frauenherz, du bist ein kleiner Schmetterling!*, a capricious little number finished at 4.30 one morning just before the première of his *Paganini*. That, for all its diversity, the collection never seems less than an entity is a tribute to accompanist Cord Garben and his refreshingly youthful team of singers. This really is quite irresistible!

Giuditta (sung in English).
Deborah Riedel *sop* Giuditta; **Jerry Hadley** *ten* Octavio; **Jeffrey Carl** *bar* Manuele Biffi, Antonio;
Andrew Busher *spkr* Duke; **Naomi Itami** *sop* Anita; **Lynton Atkinson** *ten* Pierrino;
William Dieghan *ten* Sebastiano;
English Chamber Orchestra / Richard Bonynge.
Telarc CD80436 (78 minutes: DDD). Text included. Recorded 1996.   Ⓕ

Giuditta was Lehár's last stage work and the peak of his compositional development. Written for the Vienna State Opera, it is a highly ambitious score, containing some fiendishly difficult vocal writing and using a large orchestra featuring mandolin and other exotic instruments. For this recording some two hours of music have been compressed into 78 minutes by means of snips here and there and the omission of a couple of subsidiary numbers. The piece has a *Carmen*-like story, about the disenchanted wife of an innkeeper who persuades a soldier to desert, before eventually abandoning and ruining him as she goes from lover to lover. The best-known number is Giuditta's 'On my lips every kiss is like wine', here gloriously sung by Deborah Riedel; the leading male role was written for Tauber, and there are some marvellous and demanding tenor solos, equally superbly sung by the ever impressive Jerry Hadley. Despite writing for the opera house, Lehár remained faithful to his formula of interspersing the music for the principal couple with sprightly dance numbers for a comedy pair, here in the hands of Naomi Itami and Lynton Atkinson. Assisted by Richard Bonynge's lilting conducting, these contribute richly to the appeal of the recording.

Das Land des Lächelns.
Anneliese Rothenberger *sop* Lisa; **Harry Friedauer** *ten* Gustl; **Nicolai Gedda** *ten* Sou-Chong;
Renate Holm *sop* Mi; **Jobst Moeller** *bar* Tschang;
Bavarian Radio Chorus; Graunke Symphony Orchestra / Willy Mattes.
EMI CMS5 65372-2 (two discs: 87 minutes: ADD). Recorded 1967.   Ⓜ

The great glory of this *Das Land des Lächelns*, Lehár's portrayal of the clash of western and eastern cultures, is the singing of Nicolai Gedda, who brings off 'Dein ist mein ganzes Herz' and the other Richard Tauber favourites to splendid effect. Anneliese Rothenberger is on excellent form vocally and full of charm, and she and Gedda make an excellent partnership. Renate Holm is a smiling Mi and the other principals, chorus and orchestra all play their full parts. Willy Mattes is an experienced and sympathetic conductor of operetta. The score here is, of course, not identical with that given in London when the operetta was first produced there in 1931. Apparently, Tauber was in and out of the cast every other day, providing his understudy, Robert Naylor, with plenty of opportunities. The show only had a short run in London on its first appearance. It seems that it was Tauber rather than Lehár that people wanted to hear. This reissue should be in every Viennese operetta collection.

Die lustige Witwe.
Cheryl Studer *sop* Hanna; **Boje Skovhus** *bar* Danilo; **Bryn Terfel** *bass-bar* Zeta;
Rainer Trost *ten* Camille; **Barbara Bonney** *sop* Valencienne; **Uwe Peper** *ten* Raoul;
Karl-Magnus Fredriksson *bar* Cascada; **Heinz Zednik** *ten* Njegus;
Richard Savage *bar* Bogdanowitsch; **Lynette Alcantara** *sop* Sylviane;
Philip Salmon *ten* Kromow; **Constanze Backes** *mez* Olga; **Julian Clarkson** *bass* Pritschitsch;
Angela Kazimierczuk *sop* Praškowia;
Wiener Tschuschenkapelle; Vienna Philharmonic Orchestra / Sir John Eliot Gardiner.
DG 439 911-2GH (80 minutes: DDD). Notes, text and translation included.
Recorded 1994.   Ⓕ Ⓔ RR

This is one of those great operetta interpretations that is committed to record once in a generation if one is lucky. Gardiner's approach is on an altogether more inspired plane than his rivals. In the Viennese rhythms, he shows himself utterly at home – as in the Act 2 Dance scene, where he eases the orchestra irresistibly into the famous waltz. But there are also countless instances where Gardiner provides a deliciously fresh inflexion to the score. The cast of singers is uniformly impressive. If Cheryl Studer's 'Vilja' isn't quite as assured as some others, her captivatingly playful 'Dummer, dummer Reitersmann' is typical of a well-characterized performance. As Danilo, Boje Skovhus acquits himself well with a polished performance and he offers a natural, more human characterization than his rivals, while Barbara Bonney is superb. Not the least inspired piece of casting comes with Bryn Terfel, who transforms himself outstandingly well into the bluff Pontevedran ambassador. As for Gardiner's personally selected chorus, they make Monteverdi to Montenegro and Pontevedra seem the most natural transition in the world. DG's recorded sound has an astonishing clarity and immediacy, as in the way the piccolos shriek out at the Widow's Act 1 entrance or in the beautiful *pianissimo* accompaniment to the 'Vilja-Lied'.

Die lustige Witwe.
Dame Elisabeth Schwarzkopf *sop* Hanna; **Erich Kunz** *bar* Danilo; **Anton Niessner** *bar* Zeta; **Nicolai Gedda** *ten* Camille; **Emmy Loose** *sop* Valencienne; **Josef Schmidinger** *bass* Raoul; **Ottakar Kraus** *bar* Cascada;
Philharmonia Orchestra and Chorus / Otto Ackermann.
EMI mono CDH7 69520-2 (72 minutes: ADD). Recorded 1953.   Ⓕ Ⓗ

In this star-studded performance from the previous generation to Gardiner's, the music emerged as one of the great classics of light opera. Emmy Loose has exactly the right appealing kind of voice for the 'dutiful wife' who plays with fire, and Nicolai Gedda is a superb Camille, sounding extraordinarily like Tito Schipa at his best. His high notes ring out finely and his caressing lyrical tones would upset a far better-balanced woman than the susceptible Valencienne. These two sing their duets beautifully, both excelling in the second act duet, in which Gedda has the lion's share. Nothing in this recording, except Schwarzkopf's 'Vilja', is so ravishing as his soft tone in the second half of the duet ('Love in my heart is waking'), which begins 'Sieh' dort den kleinen Pavillon' ('See over there the little pavilion') which is perhaps the loveliest in the score. Erich Kunz has not the charm but more voice and a perfect command of the style the music requires; and he is very taking in the celebrated Maxim's song. He speaks the middle section of the little song about the Königskinder possibly because the vocal part lies uncomfortably high for him; and perhaps his rich laughter would not be considered quite the thing in the diplomatic service. But his is, in most ways, a very attractive and lively performance. The Baron's part was probably much written up for George Graves but here what little he has to do is done well by Anton Niessner.

Elisabeth Schwarzkopf sings Hanna radiantly and exquisitely. She commands the ensembles in no uncertain manner and makes it clear that the 20-million-francs widow would be a personage even if she had only 20 centimes. It is a grand performance, crowned with the sensuous, tender singing of the celebrated waltz in Act 3. The chorus singing is first-rate and its Viennese abandon sounds absolutely authentic, whatever its address. Otto Ackermann conducts with complete understanding, and notable sympathy for the singers, and the members of the Philharmonia Orchestra play like angels for him. The recording is as good as one can reasonably expect and, very important in such a score, the string tone is lovely throughout. The balance between orchestra and voices, also, could not be better.

Kenneth Leighton   British 1929-1988

God's Grandeur. What love is this of thine?. Give me wings of faith[a]. Crucifixus pro nobis, Op. 38[a]. Lully, lulla, thou little tiny child, Op. 25b. Mass, Op. 44[a]. Laudate pueri, Op. 68.
Finzi Singers / Paul Spicer with [a]**Andrew Lumsden** *org*
Chandos CHAN9485 (71 minutes: DDD). Texts and translations included. Recorded 1993.   Ⓕ

There is a fine unease in Kenneth Leighton, a sense that fulfilment, musical and spiritual, must be striven for, that nothing worthwhile is gained without what Hardy called 'a full look at the worst'. Every new phrase in these choral settings sounds like the outcome of innumerable rejections: nothing is facile. In several of them, comfort is found – in *God's Grandeur* 'There lives the dearest freshness', in *What love is this of thine?* 'Oh, that thy love might overflow my heart' – and with it a sweetness that means so much more when hard won out of bleakness. He is a composer for the pilgrimage – not joyless by any means, but serious. In this excellent programme never does anything (not even of a bar's length) compromise this integrity. In date the works range from a student composition, his fine, independent setting of the Coventry Carol, to the anthem, *What love is this of thine?*, written not very long before his death. In style, rhythm, melody, harmony, counterpoint and the expert management of choral sound, all contribute, taking turn as a principal source of life and interest. The performances have all that could be desired in textual responsiveness and technical control. Somewhere among the sopranos is a voice (or it may be two voices) which at a *forte* has a worn or otherwise obtrusive edge; but clearly all members are valuable singers, as is shown by the ample supply of soloists from the ranks. Most of the works here are sung *a cappella*, those that are not being accompanied with clarity and discretion by Andrew Lumsden. The acoustic of All Saints', Tooting, is resonant but not excessively so for such a programme as this. This disc is a most welcome addition to the catalogue.

Ruggiero Leoncavallo

Leoncavallo Pagliacci.
Carlo Bergonzi *ten* Canio; **Joan Carlyle** *sop* Nedda; **Giuseppe Taddei** *bar* Tonio;
Rolando Panerai *bar* Silvio; **Ugo Benelli** *ten* Beppe.

Mascagni Cavalleria rusticana.
Fiorenza Cossotto *mez* Santuzza; **Carlo Bergonzi** *ten* Turiddu; **Giangiacomo Guelfi** *bar* Alfio;
Adriane Martino *mez* Lola; **Maria Gracia Allegri** *contr* Lucia;
Chorus and Orchestra of La Scala, Milan / Herbert von Karajan.

Opera Intermezzos.
Berlin Philharmonic Orchestra / Herbert von Karajan.
DG 419 257-2GH3 (three discs: 198 minutes: ADD). Notes, texts and translations included.
Recorded 1965. ⓕ**RR**
Pagliacci is also available on a single disc: DG The Originals 449 727-2GOR (78 minutes: ADD). Ⓜ
Opera Intermezzos: **Verdi** La traviata – Prelude, Act 3. **Puccini** Manon Lescaut – Intermezzo.
Suor Angelica – Intermezzo. **Schmidt** Notre Dame – Intermezzo. **Massenet** Thaïs – Méditation
(with Michel Schwalbé *vn*). **Giordano** Fedora – Intermezzo. **Cilea** Adriana Lecouvreur –
Intermezzo. **Wolf-Ferrari** I gioiello della Madonna – Intermezzo. **Mascagni** L'amico Fritz –
Intermezzo

Cav and Pag, as they are usually known, have been bedfellows for many years. Lasting for about
75 minutes each, both operas have certain similarities. Each work concerns the passions,
jealousies and hatred of two tightly-knit communities – the inhabitants of a Sicilian town and
the players in a travelling troupe of actors. *Cavalleria rusticana* ('Rustic chivalry') concerns the
triangular relationship of mother, son and his rejected lover. Played against a rich musical tapestry,
sumptuously orchestrated, the action is played out during the course of an Easter day. Bergonzi is a
stylish, ardent Turiddu whose virile charms glitter in his every phrase and Fiorenza Cossotto makes
a thrilling Santuzza motivated and driven by a palpable conviction; her contribution to the well-
known Easter hymn scene is gripping. But the real hero of the opera is Karajan, whose direction of
this powerful work is magnificent. Conviction and insight also instil *Pagliacci* with excitement and
real drama. A troupe of actors arrives to give a performance of a *commedia dell'arte* play. The
illustration of real love, life and hatred is portrayed in the interplay of Tonio, Silvio, Nedda and her
husband Canio. As the two rivals, Caro Bergonzi and Giuseppe Taddei are superb. Taddei's sinister,
hunch-backed clown, gently forcing the play-within-the-play closer to reality until it finally bursts
out violently is a masterly assumption, and Karajan controls the slow build-up of tension with a
grasp that few conductors could hope to equal. The Milan La Scala forces respond wholeheartedly
and the 1965 recording sounds well. The third disc is filled by a selection of very rich, very
soft-centred opera intermezzos.

Leoncavallo Pagliacci.
Giuseppe di Stefano *ten* Canio; **Maria Callas** *sop* Nedda; **Tito Gobbi** *bar* Tonio; **Rolando
Panerai** *bar* Silvio; **Nicola Monti** *ten* Beppe.

Mascagni Cavalleria rusticana.
Maria Callas *sop* Santuzza; **Giuseppe di Stefano** *ten* Turiddu; **Rolando Panerai** *bar* Alfio;
Anna Maria Canali *mez* Lola; **Ebe Ticozzi** *contr* Lucia.
Chorus and Orchestra of La Scala, Milan / Tullio Serafin.
EMI mono CDS5 56287-2 (two discs: 141 minutes): ADD. Notes, texts and translations included.
Recorded 1954. ⓕ**H**

The sound here is much more confined than on the Karajan set, though rather more immediate.
Serafin conducts swifter-moving performances, yet ones quite as notable as Karajan's for pointing
up relevant detail. All four interpretations carry with them a real sense of the theatre and are quite
free from studio routine. It is difficult to choose between the casts on these two sets. Callas lives the
characters more vividly than anyone. The sadness and anguish she brings to Santuzza's unhappy
plight are at their most compelling at 'io piango' in 'Voi lo sapete' and at 'Turiddu mi tolse' in her
encounter with Alfio, where the pain in Santuzza's heart is expressed in almost unbearable terms.
As Nedda, she differentiates marvellously between the pensiveness of her aria, the passion of her
duet with Silvio, and the playfulness of her *commedia dell'arte* acting. One unforgettable moment
among many is when her tone shivers on the word 'lurido' as she sees Tonio leaving, then becomes
all smiling a moment later as she greets her love with 'Silvio!' Her partner in both operas is di
Stefano. They work up a huge lather of passion in the big *Cavalleria* duet, and the tenor is wholly
believable as the caddish Turiddu. In the immediacy of emotion of his Canio, it is the tenor's turn
to evoke pity and display anguish. Di Stefano does it as well as any Canio on record without quite

having the heroic tone for the latter part of the opera. Panerai is a strong Alfio on the Serafin set, but Guelfi, with his huge voice, is possibly better suited to this macho part. It is impossible to choose between the two Tonios, both pertinently cast. Taddei plays the part a little more comically, Gobbi more menacingly. Callas or Karajan enthusiasts will have no difficulty making their choice. Others may be guided by quality of sound. With either you will be ensured hours of memorable listening.

Pagliacci (sung in English).
Dennis O'Neill *ten* Canio; **Rosa Mannion** *sop* Nedda; **Alan Opie** *bar* Tonio;
William Dazeley *bar* Silvio; **Peter Bronder** *ten* Beppe; **Geoffrey Mitchell Choir;**
Peter Kay Children's Choir; London Philharmonic Orchestra / David Parry.
Chandos Opera in English Series CHAN3003 (80 minutes: DDD). Notes and text included.
Recorded 1997. Ⓕ

'Hello … Hello' is the neat rendition of 'Si può … si può', presumably unthinkable in the days which produced 'A word allow me' as its translation. 'A slice of life as we live it' replaces 'life with its laughter and sorrow', 'Will ye hear then the story?' becomes 'Now you know what we're here for', and 'Ring up the curtain' (can't do much about that) is now 'Bring up the curtain'. Two others: at the point in the Nedda-Silvio duet which inspired Fred Weatherly's couplet 'For such a passion/The whip's the fashion', Edmund Tracey wisely renounces rhyme in favour of 'I tamed him nicely ... I gave him a beating', and 'Put on your costume' (this is almost like rewriting *The Book of Common Prayer*) does for 'On with the motley'. The text is one thing, the performance another. Opera singers are trained to pronounce their words in a very pure English which nowadays sounds more upper-class than it did not so long ago when all 'official' pronunciation was 'pure' in this sense. The 'slice of life' involves travelling players and villagers, but they all sound like ladies and gentlemen: it takes some of the verity out of *verismo*. Dennis O'Neill's Canio is fine as to vocal resource and avoidance of cheapness; but 'Un tal gioco' wants ironical bite, 'Vesti la giubba' more sense of occasion, 'No, Pagliaccio non son' more tension, bitterness and (at one point) sweetness. Rosa Mannion is an admirable Nedda, and both baritones do well, Alan Opie excellent in the Prologue, William Dazeley showing himself a lyric baritone of pleasing quality and tasteful style. The off-stage serenade is nicely sung by Peter Bronder, and the chorus is fine. Over the years, David Parry's conducting has grown steadily in authority, and in the climax (menace in the accompaniment to 'No, Pagliaccio' for instance) more than fulfils expectations. With effective work by producer and sound engineers, this is a *Pagliacci* which will much enhance appreciation of the opera.

Anatoli Liadov Russian 1855-1914

Liadov The Enchanted Lake, Op. 62.
Mussorgsky Boris Godunov – I am sick at heart[a].
Tchaikovsky Marche slave, Op. 31. Capriccio italien, Op. 45. Eugene Onegin – Waltz; Polonaise.
Kirov Theatre [a]**Chorus and Orchestra / Valery Gergiev.**
Philips 442 775-2PH (54 minutes: DDD). Recorded 1993. This set includes a bonus sampler
CD of previous recordings from the Kirov Theatre forces conducted by Gergiev. Ⓕ

Liadov's orchestral pieces have always had a tenuous hold on the repertory, and afford glimpses of an exceptional talent. In the shifting harmonies and dissolving textures of *The Enchanted Lake*, which shimmers atmospherically, there is not only acknowledgement of *Siegfried*'s Forest Murmurs but anticipation of Scriabin and even Schoenberg. It was a novel idea to have the Kirov orchestra's 'Russian Spectacular', the title of this disc, open to the rich aural canvas of *Boris Godunov*'s 'Coronation Scene' as refashioned by Shostakovich, complete with tolling bells, weighty brass and generous cymbal spray. The sound is big and generalized, the conducting more majestic than excitable – which usefully serves to minimize the contrast with *Marche slave*, a comparatively lyrical statement with a notably sad-eyed account of the principal theme and lightweight, almost balletic sequences thereafter. Gergiev never drives too hard, while his artful shaping of *Eugene Onegin*'s 'Polonaise' incorporates particularly sensitive handling of the central section. Likewise in the Waltz, where the cello line is affectionately moulded. *Capriccio italien* is thoughtfully held together, with much deft passagework in the closing tarantella.

There's a bonus CD too, made up of snippets from Gergiev's various Russian stage work recordings for Philips – nothing earth-shattering, but a nice cross-section to whet the appetite for more. This is a good, well-planned (if hardly generous) programme, warmly recorded and fairly representative of Gergiev's sympathetic and often dramatic conducting style.

Gyorgy Ligeti

Violin Concerto[a]. Cello Concerto[b]. Piano Concerto[c].
[a]**Saschko Gawriloff** vn [b]**Jean-Guihen Queyras** vc [c]**Pierre-Laurent Aimard** pf
Ensemble InterContemporain / Pierre Boulez.
DG 439 808-2GH (67 minutes: DDD). Recorded 1992-93. *Gramophone* Award Winner 1995. Ⓕ

The Violin Concerto (1992) is music by a composer fascinated with Shakespeare's *The Tempest*:
indeed, it might even prove to be a substitute for Ligeti's long-mooted operatic version of the play.
There are plenty of 'strange noises', the result not just of Ligeti's latter-day predilection for
ocarinas, but of his remarkable ability to play off natural and artificial tunings against each other.
This work is superior to the Piano Concerto because the solo violin is so much more volatile and
poetic as a protagonist, an animator who 'fires up' the orchestra, functioning as a leader at odds
with the led. Saschko Gawriloff is a brilliantly effective soloist, and well served by a sharply defined
yet expressive accompaniment – Boulez at his most incisive – and a totally convincing recording.
The other works are played and recorded with similar success. The Cello Concerto (1966) is a
particularly powerful reminder of the strengths of the earlier Ligeti, where simple, basic elements
generate anything but minimal consequences.

Horn Trio[a]. Six Bagatelles[b]. Ten Pieces[b]. Sonata for Solo Viola[c].
[a]**Marie Luise Neunecker** hn [a]**Saschko Gawriloff** vn [c]**Tabea Zimmermann** va
[a]**Pierre-Laurent Aimard** pf [b]**London Winds** (Philippa Davies fl Gareth Hulse ob Michael Collins cl
Robin O'Neill bn Richard Watkins hn).
Sony Classical SK62309 (71 minutes: DDD). Recorded 1994-96. Ⓕ

This issue presents music from the 1950s and 1960s (*Ten Pieces*, *Bagatelles*) to the 1980s and 1990s
(Horn Trio, Viola Sonata). Those looking for a specific reason to buy this disc need look no further
than the account of the Horn Trio, Ligeti's homage to Brahms, a work which has become a classic
of its kind. What distinguishes this version is the astonishing horn-playing of Marie Luise
Neunecker – the impression of near-effortlessness and breadth of dynamic range she conveys are
hardly likely to be bettered. As to her companions, they have both recorded the Trio before, and
their experience is audible. This interpretation is especially effective at projecting the music's
multiple levels and layers. As to its expressive power, even those who find Ligeti's later music
problematic can hardly deny the poignant, tragic beauty of the concluding *Lamento*.

The two sets of wind pieces are given polished, bravura performances by London Winds. The
Bagatelles are among the composer's most convincing music from his pre-Western period; as to the
Ten Pieces, they plough the same furrow as those two masterpieces from the same year (1968), the
Second String Quartet and *Continuum* for harpsichord (and the *Chamber Concerto*, begun the
following year); but they are altogether more lightweight, their brevity almost provocative when
heard against the broader canvas of those other works. Provocative in a very different way is the
Viola Sonata, completed in 1994. Listen to Tabea Zimmermann's commanding and expressive
playing, and hear a composer for whom confounding the critics' expectations has always been
second nature.

Etudes – Book 1; Book 2; Book 3. Musica ricercata.
Pierre-Laurent Aimard pf
Sony Classical SK62308 (65 minutes: DDD). Recorded 1995. *Gramophone* Award Winner 1997. Ⓕ

Let us salute Pierre-Laurent Aimard first – not just a modern music specialist but an artist of
phenomenal gifts, and excellently recorded here. First impressions of the music are likely to be of its
immediacy. The complexities are a problem only for the pianist – whatever the sources of Ligeti's
inspiration, his ideas serve only a musical/poetic purpose. Central to these dazzling pieces is his
longstanding interest in composing with layers of material in different metres or different tempos
and in producing what he calls 'an illusion of rhythm'; evident, too, are his more recent
preoccupations with modern mathematics, in particular the young science of dynamical systems
which seeks to explain the precarious balance between pattern and chaos, order and disorder.
Ligeti's powerful imagination is fuelled by many things, but there is no question of having to have a
special key to enter his world. The music is enough. There are 15 *Etudes* so far, in two books plus
the beginning of a third, and as with the collections of Chopin and Debussy there is a good deal to
be gained from hearing each book in sequence. The example of Liszt might also come to mind, who
opened up a world of sound on the piano as Chopin before him had done, and as Debussy was to
do. When we reach the end of Ligeti's Book 2, apparently at the limits of pianistic possibilities and
expression, there can be no doubt that Ligeti's *Etudes* belong with the greatest piano music of this
or any other century. They are amazing.

Le grand macabre.
Sibylle Ehlert *sop* Venus, Gepopo; **Laura Claycomb** *sop* Amanda; **Charlotte Hellekant** *mez*
Amando; **Derek Lee Ragin** *counterten* Prince Go-Go; **Jard van Nes** *contr* Mescalina;
Graham Clark *ten* Piet the Pot; **Willard White** *bass* Nekrotzar; **Frode Olsen** *bass* Astradamors;
Martin Winkler *bar* Ruffiak; **Marc Campbell-Griffiths** *bar* Schobiak; **Michael Lessiter** *bar*
Schabernack; **Steven Cole** *ten* White Minister; **Richard Suart** *bass* Black Minister;
London Sinfonietta Voices; Philharmonia Orchestra / Esa-Pekka Salonen.
Sony Classical Ligeti Edition S2K62312 (two discs: 102 minutes: DDD).
Text and translation included. Recorded live in 1998.   Ⓕ

Le grand macabre, a comedy about the end of the world, an elaborate game of musical time-travel,
an ambiguous dance on the brink of an abyss, looks more and more like the key opera of the end
of the twentieth century. Direct comparison between this version and Elgar Howarth's splendid
1987 Wergo performance is difficult, because Ligeti extensively revised the score in 1996, and it is
that 'final version', as he calls it, that is recorded here. He has made a number of cuts, a great deal
of what was originally spoken dialogue is now sung and there have been many changes to the
scoring, making it more practical but also thinning it out. The reduction of spoken dialogue and
the lightening of the orchestral texture make life a little easier for the singers (though not for the
soprano singing Gepopo, which Ligeti has described as an attempt to out-Zerbinetta Zerbinetta)
and for the players. The whole performance is rather more assured than Howarth's (his was
recorded at a concert, Salonen's during a series of staged performances with presumably much
longer rehearsal time) and the score's beauties are more lovingly polished. It now sounds rather
closer to a 'normal' opera and, perhaps inevitably, lacks a degree of Howarth's alarming impact.
Interestingly enough, it is Salonen's performance, sung in English to a French audience (Howarth's
was in German, his audience Austrian), that draws more laughs at the jokes. As Gepopo Sibylle
Ehlert is spectacularly virtuoso and Willard White's gravity is effective in the role of Nekrotzar.
Graham Clark is hugely exuberant as Piet the Pot, and Steven Cole and Richard Suart make a
splendid double-act of the two Ministers. Jard van Nes and Frode Olsen are perhaps inhibited by
the English language from making Mescalina and Astradamors as grotesque as they can be, though
both sing well, as does every other member of the cast. The recording, like the performance, is a
little more comfortable, rather less in-your-face, than Howarth's. This version is the one to have –
Ligeti's revisions are all improvements, and the performance is a fine one – but the older one has a
shade more of the quality that Ligeti says he has hoped for in stage productions of the opera, that
of 'demoniacal farce'.

Thomas Linley II   British 1756-1778

The Song of Moses. Let God Arise.
Julia Gooding, Sophie Daneman *sops* **Robin Blaze** *counterten*
Andrew King *ten* **Andrew Dale Forbes** *bass*
Holst Singers; The Parley of Instruments / Peter Holman *hpd*
Hyperion CDA67038 (67 minutes: DDD). Text included. Recorded 1997.   Ⓕ

There is no doubting that English music in the second half of the eighteenth century did not quite
know where to go. In one direction lay the Handelian oratorio tradition, already a seemingly
immovable feature of the nation's musical landscape, while in the other there was the unstoppable
force of the new, continental *galant* style, as introduced to the country by J.C. Bach. The kind of
synthesis of these two which Haydn and Mozart achieved may have lain beyond the capabilities of
most composers, but in England many were in any case happy simply to place them side by side in
the same work and leave it at that. That is just what Thomas Linley junior's did in his oratorio, *The
Song of Moses*, composed in 1777 for the Drury Lane Theatre, and here recorded for the first time.
As the title suggests, it sets out along a Handelian path, with imposing and dramatic choruses,
fugues and Hallelujahs not in any way uninfluenced by *Israel in Egypt*, yet in its arias and duets the
style is wholly up to date and in a charmingly tuneful English way at that. More striking still,
however, is the ease with which both styles are handled by their 21-year-old composer, whose death
by drowning a year later was a genuine loss to English music. The performance (which Peter
Holman claims as probably the first since 1778) does it full justice. Sophie Daneman seems
technically the more comfortable of the two excellent female soloists, but Julia Gooding's charming
vocal quality also somehow sounds just right in this English repertoire. The stars of the show,
however, are the Holst Singers; true, there are occasional weaknesses in the inner parts, but on the
whole the choir is well drilled and impressively resounding in its descriptions of the Egyptians'
misfortunes. The anthem, *Let God Arise*, composed for the 1773 Three Choirs Festival, is a more
frankly Handelian piece and also a less interesting one. In *The Song of Moses*, on the other hand,
we have a real find.

Franz Liszt

Piano Concertos – No. 1 in E flat major, S124; No. 2 in A major, S125.

Piano Concertos Nos. 1 and 2. Piano Sonata in B minor, S178[a].
Sviatoslav Richter *pf* **London Symphony Orchestra / Kyrill Kondrashin.**
Philips Solo 446 200-2PM (69 minutes: ADD). Recorded 1961 and [a]1988. Ⓜ️ 🅡🅡

A bargain in a million, albeit one that reflects two very different aspects of Richter's art. The concertos (from 1961) are strong, clear-headed, brilliantly executed and superbly accompanied. Philips confesses Mercury engineering, and Wilma Cozart-Fine has herself remastered the original three-track tapes – which means that what started out as a clean-cut, judiciously balanced production, now sounds fuller, brighter and keener-edged than ever. The improvements are particularly telling where Kondrashin and the LSO are concerned: everything tells with more presence than before which, given the lofty standard of orchestral playing, is a real boon. As to Richter, his *pianissimos* are rapt, his running passages crystal-clear and the stormier elements in both concertos are given with immense force. The Sonata, a concert performance, was recorded in 1988 on a somewhat less well-tuned instrument. However, the mind behind the notes has lost none of its grip and the notes themselves, although occasionally blurred or botched, spring to life as in no other performance. The *Allegro energico* and final peroration rage mercilessly, while the closing *Lento assai* can rarely have sounded so calmly inevitable. In terms of sound, things aren't as well managed as in the concertos: there's the odd thump or cough and the piano tone is a mite shallow, but the performance is so compelling that you soon forget any sonic inadequacies.

Piano Concertos Nos. 1 and 2. Totentanz, S126.
Krystian Zimerman *pf*
Boston Symphony Orchestra / Seiji Ozawa.
DG 423 571-2GH (56 minutes: DDD). Ⓕ

This is playing in the grand manner. From the start of First Concerto you are aware of a consciously leonine approach. This is no bad thing either; for the music really calls for it. Zimerman even deliberately takes risks in a few technically perilous places where some of his colleagues, at least in the studio, play safe; and indeed his octaves in the opening cadenza are an example. The result sounds spontaneous and, yes, even brave. Ozawa and the orchestra are behind the soloist in all this. Not only do lyrical sections sing with subtlety, the big passages also are shapely. There is plenty of drive in this Concerto. In the Second Concerto Zimerman adopts a different approach; he evidently considers it a more poetic piece and the playing style, strong though it is, is to match. Finely though he handles the gentler music, there are odd sniffs and hums in the *molto espressivo* passage following the D flat major cello solo, and also in the last of the work's quiet sections. In the gorgeously grisly *Totentanz*, both music and playing should make your hair stand on end. The sound has a depth that suits the music and the piano is especially impressive. Zimerman's freshness (he reminds us that this is a young man's music), and the coupling, makes this disc most desirable.

Piano Concertos Nos. 1 and 2. Totentanz.
Alfred Brendel *pf*
London Philharmonic Orchestra / Bernard Haitink.
Philips Silver Line 426 637-2PSL (56 minutes: ADD). Recorded 1976. Ⓜ

Few pianists have made a more persuasive case for Liszt than Brendel. He penetrates far below the surface of the composer's emotional vortex and surface rhetoric. This set shows him at his very finest and Bernard Haitink conducts the LPO with comparable distinction; indeed it is orchestral playing of the highest calibre. The disc opens with the Second Piano Concerto, sounding wonderful from the very first bar, and the coupling, the E flat Concerto and the rarer *Totentanz*, are hardly less memorable, combining brilliance with warmth and subtlety of keyboard colouring. The recording, too, is very good, if not quite so richly textured as more modern recordings.

Liszt Piano Concerto No. 1.
Chopin Piano Concerto No. 1 in E minor, Op. 11.
Martha Argerich *pf*
London Symphony Orchestra / Claudio Abbado.
DG The Originals 449 719-2GOR (56 minutes: ADD). Recorded 1968. Ⓜ

These performances, in DG's beautifully refurbished sound, remain as fanciful and coruscating as the day they were made. Argerich's fluency and re-creative spark dazzle and dumbfound to a unique degree but, given her reputation for fire-eating virtuosity, it is perhaps necessary to say that both performances quiver with rare sensitivity as well as drama. Time and again she provides a telling and haunting poetic counterpoint to her, arguably, more familiar way of trailing clouds of virtuoso glory. Abbado partners his mercurial soloist as to the manner born, finding (in the Chopin in particular) a burgeoning sense of wonder where others sound dry and foursquare.

The Tchaikovsky International Competition, Volume 1.
Liszt Piano Concerto No. 1[a]. Mephisto Waltz No. 1, S514[a].
Tchaikovsky Piano Concerto No. 1 in B flat minor, Op. 23[b]. Dumka, Op. 59[b].
[a]**John Ogdon**, [b]**Vladimir Ashkenazy** pfs
USSR State Symphony Orchestra / Victor Dubrovsky, Konstantin Ivanov.
Melodiya mono/stereo 74321 33219-2 (71 minutes: ADD). Recorded 1962.   Ⓜ Ⓗ

This recording (made after rather than during the 1962 occasion) is the first in a series celebrating Moscow's International Tchaikovsky Competition, and is dramatically called 'The Draw' on Melodiya's jewel-case. 1962 was an exceptional year in competition history, confirming and expanding Ogdon's and Ashkenazy's already formidable reputations. Ashkenazy may have entered the competition under duress, increasingly resentful of his use as a puppet in his country's musical-political schemes and tiring of a romantic virtuoso repertoire that hardly allowed him his fullest scope and musical quality. Yet with a magnificent resurgence of his early aplomb he gives us Tchaikovsky as to the manner born, expansive and individual yet without even a hint of self-conscious display or point-making. His style had broadened considerably since his glittering triumphs in Warsaw (1955) and Brussels (1956), already a rich prophecy of greatness to come. The *Dumka*, too, is as red-blooded as even the most ardent Russian romantic could wish, yet of these two virtuosos John Ogdon is surely the more heroic and scintillating, the more arrestingly characterful. In Liszt's First Concerto nothing is taken for granted and everything is rekindled with a spine-tingling verve and poetry. Ogdon's pianism may be less 'perfect', less foolproof than Ashkenazy's yet there are few of those technical flaws and gaucheries that plagued him during his later troubled years and pages of a brilliance which set the entire keyboard ablaze. Here, surely, is the sort of electricity only a born virtuoso could generate. The recordings are more than adequate to the occasion.

A Dante Symphony, S109[a]. Années de pèlerinage – deuxième année, S161, 'Italie' – No. 7, Après une lecture du Dante (fantasia quasi sonata)[b].
Berlin Radio Women's Chorus; Berlin Philharmonic Orchestra / Daniel Barenboim pf
Teldec 9031-77340-2 (67 minutes: DDD). Item marked [a] recorded live in 1992.   Ⓕ Ⓔ

This disc proves conclusively that the *Dante Symphony* (a contemporary of the *Faust Symphony*) is no longer one that needs its apologists. Tone, full and rounded, firm and true, and rock-steady pacing elevate the symphony's opening beyond its all too familiar resemblance to a third-rate horror-film soundtrack. As the symphony progresses, together with the countless examples of Berlin tone and artistry filling out, refining or shaping gestures in often revelatory ways, you become aware of Barenboim's skill in maintaining the large-scale tension he has created. And that is a very real achievement. As for the final choral Magnificat, if Liszt owed Wagner a debt of gratitude for persuading him to conclude the symphony with the 'noble and softly soaring' bars that precede a more noisily affirmative appended coda, in Barenboim's Magnificat (and much else in the symphony), it is Wagner's debt to Liszt that is more readily apparent; the *Parsifal*ian radiance of these final pages is unmistakable. More importantly, for once they sound convincingly conclusive. The *Dante* Sonata was recorded with the kind of risk-taking abandon and occasionally less than perfect execution that you might expect from a live event. Improvisatory, impulsive and full of extreme contrasts, Barenboim's *Dante* Sonata is vividly pictorial (with almost orchestral colourings). The instrument itself (closely miked and widely spaced) sounds larger than life. This recording is, in a word, riveting. The recording of the symphony is spacious, focused and expertly balanced.

A Faust Symphony, S108.
Hans-Peter Blochwitz ten **Hungarian Radio Chorus;**
Budapest Festival Orchestra / Iván Fischer.
Philips 454 460-2PH (74 minutes: DDD). Text and translation included. Recorded 1996.   Ⓕ ⎡RR⎤

Iván Fischer here realizes the full breadth of Liszt's vision, focusing to near-perfection Faust's anguish, Gretchen's tender modulations and the cynical thematic transformations that keep Mephistopheles alive and kicking. It is, above all, a profoundly authentic – or should one say authentically 'lived' – production, consistently animated, vividly recorded and with heavily scored tutti passages granted maximum impact. Flutes and clarinets at the outset of Gretchen suggest a chaste, winsome maiden and the *Tristan*esque passage, where the strings exchange affections over a fluid woodwind accompaniment, is beautifully phrased. As to Mephistopheles, no other performance experience projects the devilish, quick-witted variants of Faust's principal themes with as much keenness of attack as Fischer does here. The Budapest woodwinds are outstanding, and the strings have real bite. Select string *portamentos* sweeten the texture and there is no hint of the glutinous, excessively homogenized 'sound blanket' that evades the musical issue on so many modern recordings. Furthermore, Iván Fischer affords us the rare opportunity of hearing Liszt's first (purely orchestral) ending, which Wagner so admired for its lack of 'forced excitement or arousal of attention'. It is impossible not to heartily agree with Wagner, though lovers of the better-known – and more extended – 'Chorus mysticus' have the chance to enjoy that, too. Hans-Peter Blochwitz sings well, and so does the Hungarian Radio Chorus.

A Faust Symphony.
Kenneth Riegel *ten* **Tanglewood Festival Chorus;**
Boston Symphony Orchestra / Leonard Bernstein.
DG The Originals 447 449-2GOR (77 minutes: ADD). Recorded 1976.   Ⓜ

David Gutman's absorbing booklet-note for the Leonard Bernstein release informs us that at a particular Tanglewood concert in 1941 (August 8th) Bernstein scored a triumph in modern American repertoire and Serge Koussevitzky conducted the first two movements of *A Faust Symphony*. Some 20 years later Bernstein himself made a distinguished recording of the work, faster than this superb 1976 Boston remake by almost five minutes yet ultimately less involving. The passage of time witnessed not only an easing of tempo but a heightened response to individual characters, be it Faust's swings in mood and attitude, Gretchen's tender entreaties or the unpredictable shadow-play of 'Mephistopheles'. Orchestral execution is first-rate, the strings in particular really showing their mettle (such biting incisiveness), while Bernstein's pacing, although often slower than average, invariably fits the mood. The sound too is far warmer and more lifelike than its rather opaque New York predecessor, although when it comes to the tenor soloist in the closing chorus, Kenneth Riegel is rather strident.

A Faust Symphony.
András Molnár *ten* **Hungarian State Choir;**
Orchestra of the Franz Liszt Academy / András Ligeti.
Naxos 8 553304 (73 minutes: DDD). Recorded 1994.   Ⓢ

There's a lot right with this performance, not least being its outspoken acknowledgement of Faust's stormy character. Liszt's first-movement portrait receives zestful advocacy (with a real *Allegro agitato ed appassionato*), less polished than some, perhaps, but fired by immense gusto. The recording, too, has plenty of body, while András Ligeti's vocal promptings vie with Toscanini's in *La bohème*! Gretchen is quite comely and Ligeti effectively traces both her darker moods and those passages associated with Faust's yearning. Mephistopheles is more angry than 'ironico' and if you want confirmation of Ligeti's Lisztian mettle, then try from 5'49" through the following minute or so: it really is thrilling. True, woodwind pointing isn't as vivid as under, say, Bernstein, but there's certainly no lack of enthusiasm. The Orchestra of the Franz Liszt Academy gives its all and the Hungarian State Choir makes noble music of the final chorus, even though András Molnár's wobbly tenor is something of a distraction. It's a compelling if flawed production, less carefully prepared than its best rivals but more spontaneous than most.

Hungarian Rhapsodies, S359 – No. 1 in F minor (arr. cpsr/Doppler);
No. 2 in D minor (arr. Doppler); No. 3 in D (arr. cpsr/Doppler);
No. 4 in D minor. No. 5 in E minor; No. 6 in D (all arr. cpsr).
Budapest Festival Orchestra / Iván Fischer.
Philips 456 570-2PH (60 minutes: DDD). Recorded 1997.   Ⓕ

Fischer's idiomatic foray into this well-worn repertoire is distinguished by tonal lustre and high spirits, with the authentic gipsy violin of József 'Csócsi' Lendvay lending a touch of added spice to No. 3 (i.e. the piano No. 6) and a tangy cimbalom much in evidence throughout. Rubato is legion, though more improvisatory than schmaltzy. Even if you have never particularly liked Doppler's version of the Second, Fischer's performance is so vivid, so imaginative of phrasing, that you may well be won over. Charm is in generous supply everywhere. There is plenty of power, too, with meaty brass and growling *crescendos* at the start of No. 4, and a riot of colour to close No. 6. Fischer's *Hungarian Rhapsodies* are as frisky as foals and as flavoursome as goulash, as dashing and as dancing as anyone might want. They are further aided by excellent, full-bodied sound.

Ce qu'on entend sur la montagne, S95. Tasso, S96. Les Préludes, S97. Orpheus, S98.
Prometheus, S99. Festklänge, S101. Mazeppa, S100.
London Philharmonic Orchestra / Bernard Haitink.
Philips 438 751-2PM2 (two discs: 127 minutes: ADD). Recorded 1968-71.   Ⓜ

Héroïde funèbre, S102. Die Ideale, S106. Mephisto Waltz No. 1, S514, 'Der Tanz in der
Dorfschenke'; No. 2, S110. Hungaria, S103. Hamlet, S104. Hunnenschlacht, S105.
Von der Wiege bis zum Grabe, S107.
London Philharmonic Orchestra / Bernard Haitink.
Philips 438 754-2PM2 (two discs: 131 minutes: ADD). Recorded 1968-71.   Ⓜ

The 12 'numbered' symphonic poems date from Liszt's rich maturity, with the lean, near-
expressionist *Von der Wiege bis zum Grabe* ('From the Cradle to the Grave') following on after a
period of some 25 years. Haitink's readings have an abundance of personality. In *Héroïde funèbre*,
for example, his dangerously slow tempo exceeds Liszt's prescribed timing by some seven minutes: it
is a terrifying vision, superbly sustained and beautifully played. He also copes manfully with the
more explosive aspects of *Hamlet, Prometheus* and *Hunnenschlacht*, and his way with the scores'
many reflective episodes is entirely winning. Elsewhere, he sorts through the complexities of Liszt's
colourful orchestration with a cool head and a warm heart, etching the frequent examples of
'nature music' much as he does Wagner's and keeping abreast of each tone-poem's narrative trail.
True, some of Liszt's *marcatos, impetuosos, appassionatos* and *agitatos* are occasionally brought to
heel, but then others aren't – and we have Liszt's blessing for flexibility in what he himself terms
'the degree of sympathy' that conductors employ for his work. What matters is that Haitink has us
enter Liszt's world direct, rather than through the distorting mirror of the conductor's own ego.
It is a volatile sequence, yes, and not without its *longueurs*, but it remains an essential musical
confrontation for all students of the romantic orchestra and an accurate pointer to where
Tchaikovsky, Smetana and countless others found significant musical sustenance. With excellent
sound and commonsense documentation, these two sets will provide hours of aural adventure.

Tasso, S96. Trois Odes funèbres, S112.
Berlin Radio Men's Chorus; Berlin Radio Symphony Orchestra / Karl Anton Rickenbacher.
Koch Schwann 317682 (57 minutes: DDD). Recorded 1994.   Ⓕ

Rickenbacher's is a strong, sombre reading of *Tasso* that responds to the powerful opening – much
the best music in a very uneven work – and does well with the minuet passage and with the later
pages in which Liszt is at his most assertive and least creative. Nevertheless, the record has a claim
on Lisztians for the inclusion, as what appears to be a first recording, of three very fine works that
have lain neglected. Two are personal elegies, moving laments on the death of his son Daniel and
his eldest daughter Blandine. 'Les morts', a so-called Oration for Orchestra for Daniel, makes use of
a chorus to intone, during the work, words by the Christian thinker who at one stage profoundly
affected Liszt, the Abbé Lammenais. 'La notte', for Blandine, is based on *Il penseroso*, from the
Italian book of the *Années de pèlerinage*, but also includes some haunting Hungarian reminiscences.
He asked for these two works to be played at his funeral. Dying half-ignored in Bayreuth, he went
to his grave without any proper music. The *Odes* were not performed until 1912. The third is a kind
of pendant to *Tasso*, and uses some of its themes. The *Odes* are strong, moving works, perhaps
difficult to programme in concerts even individually. To have them available at last, in an ideal
recording, in very sympathetic performances, is a cause for gratitude.

Piano Sonata in B minor, S178.

Liszt Piano Sonata. Hungarian Rhapsody No. 6.
Brahms Two Rhapsodies, Op. 79.
Schumann Piano Sonata No. 2 in G minor, Op. 22.
Martha Argerich pf
DG Galleria 437 252-2GGA (64 minutes: ADD). Recorded 1963-72.   Ⓜ 🅁🅁

No one could accuse Martha Argerich of unstructured reverie or dalliance and her legendary DG
performance of the Liszt Sonata from 1972 suggests a unique level of both technical and musical
achievement. Her prodigious fluency unites with a trail-blazing temperament, and Valhalla itself
never ignited to such effect as at the central *Andante*'s central climax. Both here and in the final
Prestissimo there are reminders that Argerich has always played octaves like single notes, displaying
a technique that few if any could equal. There are times when she becomes virtually engulfed in her
own virtuosity yet this is a performance to make other pianists turn pale and ask, how is it possible
to play like this? Argerich's Schumann, too, is among her most meteoric, headlong flights. In terms
of sheer brilliance she leaves all others standing yet, amazingly, still allows us fleeting glimpses of

Eusebius (the poetic dreamer in Schumann, and one of his most dearly cherished fictions). The Brahms and Liszt *Rhapsodies*, taken from Argerich's very first 1963 DG disc, are among the most incandescent yet refined on record. The sound, when you bother to notice it, is excellent. (The Liszt and Brahms works, incidentally, are also included in a compilation disc reviewed in the Collections section; refer to the Index.)

Piano Sonata. Nuages gris, S199ᵃ. Unstern: sinistre, disastro, S208. La lugubre gondola, S200, No. 1ᵃ. R. W. – Venezia, S201ᵃ.
Maurizio Pollini *pf*
DG 427 322-2GH (46 minutes: DDD). Items marked ᵃ recorded live in 1988.   Ⓕ

No prizes for predicting that this Liszt B minor Sonata is technically flawless and beautifully structured. What may come as more of a shock (though not to those who have followed Pollini's career closely) is its sheer passion. To say that he plays as if his life depended on it is an understatement, and those who regularly accuse him of coolness should sit down in a quiet room with this recording, a decent hi-fi system and a large plateful of their own words. The opening creates a sense of coiled expectancy, without recourse to a mannered delivery, and Pollini's superior fingerwork is soon evident. His virtuosity gains an extra dimension from his ability at the same time to convey resistance to it – the double octaves are demonstrably a fraction slower than usual and yet somehow feel faster, or at least more urgent. There is tensed steel in the very fabric of the playing. By the two-minute mark so much passion has been unleashed one is bound to wonder if it has not all happened too soon. But that is to underestimate Pollini's unerring grasp of the dramatic structure and its psychological progression from paragraph to paragraph; it is also to underestimate his capacity to find extra technical resources when it would seem beyond the power of flesh and blood to do so. Another contributing factor, which for some listeners may take more adjusting to, is his determination to maintain the flow in lyrical paragraphs, at tempos slightly more forward-looking and with breathing-spaces slightly less conspicuous than usual. Throughout the performance floods of feeling and dams of intellectual will-power vie with one another to extraordinarily compelling effect. The final page is pure mastery, a fitting conclusion to a spell-binding performance. It seems not so much that Pollini has got inside the soul of the music but that the music has got inside him and used him, without mercy, for its own ends. In Pollini's hands *Unstern* certainly has a fine inexorable tread and *La lugubre gondola* and *R. W. – Venezia* are both beautifully weighted. The audience (a rather restive one) adds nothing to the sense of involvement in any of the three live recordings. The background ambience changes suddenly in *La lugubre gondola*. Still, after such a classic account of the Sonata, anything would have been an anti-climax.

Piano Sonata. Two Légendes, S175. Scherzo and March, S177.
Nikolai Demidenko *pf*
Hyperion CDA66616 (67 minutes: DDD). Recorded 1992.   Ⓕ

Even in an impossibly competitive field Demidenko's Liszt Sonata stands out among the most imperious and articulate. His opening is precisely judged and once the Sonata is under its inflammatory way his virtuosity is of a kind to which few other pianists could pretend. The combination of punishing weight and a skittering, light-fingered agility makes for a compulsive vividness yet his economy in the first *cantando espressivo*, sung without a trace of luxuriance or indulgence, is no less typical. There are admittedly times when he holds affection at arm's length, but just as you are wondering why he commences the central *Andante* so loudly he at once withdraws into a wholly apposite remoteness or reticence. Earlier, his pedalling is deeply imaginative. Predictably, the fugue is razor-sharp and in the storming pages just before the retrospective coda the sense of concentration becomes almost palpable. The final climax, too, is snapped off not only with a stunning sense of Lisztian drama but with an even truer sense of Liszt's score and instructions. Demidenko's couplings are no less autocratic and refined, with a capacity to make seemingly arbitrary ideas sound unarguable. His *Légendes* are far from benign or, indeed, Franciscan, yet his tautness and graphic sense of their poetic power carry their own authority. Finally, Demidenko is in his element in the *Scherzo* and March's diablerie, music which coming after the two *Légendes*, affects one like an upside-down crucifix, or some dark necromancy. The recording is outstanding and Demidenko's intimidating dynamic range emerges without even a trace of distortion.

Piano Sonata. Années de pèlerinage – Deuxième année, Italie, S161: Après une lecture du Dante (fantasia quasi sonata). Harmonies poétiques et réligieuses, S173 No. 7, Funérailles. Gnomenreigen, S145 No. 2.
Mikhail Pletnev *pf*
DG 457 629-2GH (67 minutes: DDD). Recorded 1997.   Ⓕ🅴

Pletnev's is a seasoned and nuanced reading of the great B minor Sonata. There is throughout a great sense of ease and luxury, amply displaying his congenial affection for the music's intimate voices. The *Dante* Sonata is, on the whole, less successful. The *Dante* Sonata works by accumulation of sound-mass, and Pletnev's occasionally brittle tone works against the music's almost geological accumulation of force. A touch more evenness to the *tremolo* playing would also give the performance a luminescence it lacks in the upper range. A quirky reading of *Gnomenreigen*, giving it a strangely grim humour, and a powerful traversal of the 'Funérailles', fills out the recording. Dedicated Lisztians will be happier with more conventionally romantic performances but fans of Pletnev's sinewy keyboard determination will find much to please them.

---

12 Etudes d'exécution transcendante, S139.
Jenö Jandó *pf*
Naxos 8 553119 (64 minutes: DDD). Recorded 1994. ⓢ

The 12 *Transcendental Etudes* are the ultimate test of quasi-orchestral virtuosity and of the capacity to achieve nobility and true eloquence. Jandó perhaps lacks diabolic *frisson* in the more ferocious numbers but his performances, overall, are not disfigured by wilful, sensational attributes or hysteria. No. 1 is dramatically pointed, an impressive curtain-raiser, and he can hell-raise with assurance in 'Mazeppa'. His 'Feux follets' hardly sparks with the brilliance of, say, some of the full-blooded accounts of certain Russian artists, but even when it hardly modulates from study to tone-poem it is still more than capable (higher praise than you might think where such intricacy is concerned). He flashes an impressive rapier at the start of 'Eroica' and there is plenty of swagger and facility in the so-called 'Appassionata' *étude*. 'Chasse-neige', too, proceeds with a fine sense of its menacing start to a howling, elemental uproar before returning to distant thunder. Jandó is less assured in introspection, yet it has to be said that all-encompassing versions of the *Transcendental Etudes* are hard to come by. Jandó is impressively recorded.

Impromptu in F sharp major, S191. Nuages gris, S199. La lugubre gondola, S200 Nos. 1 and 2. Unstern: sinistre, disastro, S208. Totentanz, S525. Danse macabre (Saint-Saëns), S555. Réminiscences des Huguenots (Meyerbeer), S412.
Arnaldo Cohen *pf*
Naxos 8 553852 (71 minutes: DDD). Recorded 1996. ⓢ

Arnaldo Cohen is as poetically and imaginatively intrepid as he is technically coruscating, and all these performances offer refinement and ferocity in equal proportion. Few pianists could identify or engage so closely with music which hovers on the edge of silence or extinction (*Nuages gris*, *La lugubre gondola* Nos. 1 and 2), or which sparks and sports with a truly devilish intent (*Danse macabre*, *Totentanz* and so on). In the *Danse macabre* the music emerges from Cohen's fingers supercharged with malevolence. On the other hand he can send the F sharp *Impromptu* spiralling into a true sense of its ecstasy, or momentarily inflect *Nuages gris* in a manner that accentuates rather than detracts from its abstraction and economy. He makes something frighteningly bleak out of *Unstern* (or 'Evil Star'), with its savagely dissonant climax and unresolved hymnal solace, yet is no less at home in *Réminiscences des Huguenots*, dismissing ambuscades of treacherous skips, octaves and every other technical terror with a telling mix of verve and nonchalance. These, then, are performances of rare lucidity, virtuoso voltage and trenchancy, and all excellently recorded.

Funérailles, S173 No. 7. Gnomenreigen, S145 No. 2. Liebesträume, S541 – No. 2 in E major; No. 3 in A flat major. Valses oubliées, S215 – Nos. 1-3. Mephisto Waltz No. 1, 'Der Tanz in der Dorfschenke', S514. Troisième Année de pèlerinage, S163 – Aux cyprès de la Villa d'Este. Etudes d'exécution transcendante, S139 – No. 5, Feux follets. Hungarian Rhapsody No. 17.
Sviatoslav Richter *pf*
Revelation mono RV10011 (59 minutes: ADD). Recorded live in 1958. Ⓜ🄷

The pianism on this disc is very special. The recital was recorded in concert in 1958, before Richter had made his breakthrough in the West and at a time when his playing had a raw energy and a sense of abandon that has become increasingly tempered over the years. There are places where the sheer electricity and bravura carries one away (and occasionally – in the *Mephisto Waltz* No. 1, for example – nearly carries Richter himself over the edge). However, equally awe-inspiring is the magical *pianissimo* playing, where it is easy to forget that such sounds are being coaxed from an essentially percussive instrument. In the monumental *Funérailles* one marvels at how Richter maintains such intensity in playing seemingly so straightforward and understated. Pianism of such concentration and inwardness draws the listener wholly into the artist's world. The recorded sound is variable and generally rather claustrophobic (particularly at louder dynamics) and the endings of some tracks have been faded out rather prematurely, presumably to omit the audience applause.

Liszt Fantasia on two themes from Mozart's 'Le nozze di Figaro', S697. Réminiscences de Don Juan (Mozart), S418. Réminiscences de Norma (Bellini), S394. Rigoletto (Verdi) – paraphrase, S434. Faust (Gounod) – Waltz, S407.
Rossini/Ginsburg Il barbiere di Siviglia – Largo al factotum.
Grigory Ginsburg *pf*
Melodiya mono 74321 33210-2 (70 minutes: ADD). Recorded 1948-58. Ⓜ 🄷

What can be said of Grigory Ginsburg's Liszt transcriptions? They are already well known to piano buffs, if only by reputation, since the LP versions have long been like gold-dust. From the stable of Goldenweiser, and a longtime colleague of his at the Moscow Conservatoire, Ginsburg possessed a jaw-dropping facility and lightness of touch which recall the piano rolls of Lhevinne and Rosenthal. It's the kind of playing that sets you wondering if he was equally phenomenal in live performance and whether such playing could perhaps only be achieved on light-touch instruments. Whatever the case, his seemingly spontaneous eloquence and wit, heard at their most breathtaking in his own *Barber of Seville* transcription, shine through the very shabby sound quality. This is about as 'must-have' as a must-have can be for collectors of great piano recordings.

19 Hungarian Rhapsodies, S244 – No. 1 in C sharp minor; No. 2 in C sharp minor; No. 3 in B flat major; No. 4 in E flat major; No. 5 in E minor, 'Héroïde-Elégiaque'; No. 6 in D flat major; No. 7 in D minor; No. 8 in F sharp minor, 'Capriccio'; No. 9 in E flat major, 'Carnival in Pest'; No. 10 in E major; No. 11 in A minor; No. 12 in C sharp minor; No. 13 in A minor; No. 14 in F minor; No. 15 in A minor 'Rákóczy'; No. 16 in A minor, 'For the Munkascy festivities in Budapest'; No. 17 in D minor; No. 18 in F sharp minor, 'On the occasion of the Hungarian Exposition in Budapest'; No. 19 in D minor.

Hungarian Rhapsodies Nos. 1-19. Rhapsodie espagnole, S254.
Roberto Szidon *pf*
DG 453 034-2GTA2 (two discs: 156 minutes: ADD). Recorded 1972. Ⓜ 🆁🆁

This well-known set has been in and out of the catalogue a number of times in various formats, always to considerable acclaim. And the performances are every bit as good as everybody has always said. Although individual readings of isolated *Rhapsodies* may surpass Szidon's, taken as a whole this is certainly the most pleasurable set available. Szidon's technique is especially geared towards clarity of passagework and rhythmic precision and he also possesses a convincingly dreamy temperament that enables the slow passages to emerge with a rare distinction. His technical mastery is in no doubt and this is playing of great flair, with a natural idiomatic feeling for rubato. The *Rapsodie espagnole* is a welcome bonus. The recorded sound is acoustically sympathetic and vivid.

Hungarian Rhapsodies Nos. 2 and 9. Ballade No. 2 in B minor, S171. Bénédiction de Dieu dans la solitude, S173 No. 3. Berceuse, S174. Polonaise in C minor, S223 No. 1. Scherzo and March, S177.
Louis Kentner *pf*
APR mono APR5514 (79 minutes: ADD). Recorded 1937-41. Ⓜ 🄷

This glorious recital is a timely reminder of Louis Kentner's greatness, his richness and enterprise during his heyday. Here is playing which in its life-affirming sweep and opulence makes accusations concerning Liszt's theatricality doubly misleading. What expansiveness, what true *molto espressivo* Kentner achieves in the Second *Hungarian Rhapsody*, what poetic warmth and freedom in the more heartfelt, soaring melodies of the First *Polonaise* and Second *Ballade*. True, some may find him more luxuriant than devotional in the *Bénédiction* (a reminder, perhaps, that the temporal and spiritual aspects of Liszt's life were opposite sides of the same coin) but the personal charisma and magnetism are in any case a far cry from our own age where one pianist is so easily mistaken for another. In the *Scherzo and March*, where Liszt sardonically raises hell-fire, Kentner's mastery is unassailable, and his elegance in the ravishing *Berceuse* (so closely modelled on Chopin yet so far from his classic economy) again evokes a time when pianists were indeed kings of the keyboard. Above all, these performances show a patrician ease that makes you sit back and marvel, and forget a later period in Kentner's life when his playing so sadly became a parody of its former quality. Superb transfers.

Années de pèlerinage – Première année, S160, 'Suisse'; Deuxième année, S161, 'Italie'; Troisième année, S163.

Années de pèlerinage – Première année; Deuxième année; Troisième année. Venezia e Napoli, S162.
Lazar Berman *pf*
DG 437 206-2GX3 (three discs: 176 minutes: ADD). Recorded 1977. Ⓜ 🆁🆁

Liszt's three volumes of *Années de pèlerinage* are rarely recorded complete, largely because many pianists remain baffled by the dark-hued prophecy and romanticism of the third and final book. Berman's resource here is remarkable and his performance of the entire book is hauntingly inward and sympathetic to both the radiance of 'Les jeux d'eau à la Villa d'Este' and to Liszt's truly dark night of the soul (*lamentoso, doloroso* and so on), and to his desolate lack of spiritual solace elsewhere. He is hardly less persuasive in the first two books. 'Chapelle de Guillaume Tell' is a true celebration of Switzerland's republican hero with alpine horns ringing through the mountains, while in 'Au lac de Wallenstadt' Berman's gently undulating traversal is truly *pianissimo* and *dolcissimo egualamente*. His 'Orage' is predictably breathtaking, and in the gloomy Byronic 'Vallée d'Obermann' the severest critic will find himself mesmerized by Berman's free-wheeling eloquence. These superb recordings have been finely remastered.

Années de pèlerinage – Première année.
Jorge Bolet *pf*
Decca 410 160-2DH (50 minutes: DDD). Recorded 1983.   Ⓕ

Bolet places these works in the context Liszt intended and it thus makes an impact which in retrospect is experienced as being more complex. He uses pale colours but they are subtly differentiated, and his control of textures, as of phrasing, displays the most exceptional sensitivity. Although the Obermann piece is his major essay, one finds in the other eight pieces, also, the new qualities that Liszt brought to music, the extraordinarily fresh perceptions which they embody. As that freshness survives we may glimpse how disconcertingly original this music must have sounded when new. Yet some of these pieces, such as 'Au lac de Wallenstadt' or 'Eglogue', are remarkably simple. Bolet plays these, and 'Au bord d'une source', limpidly, with a pearl-like tone. They are a series of pastorals and, in this haunting interpretation, a series of enchantments, above all perhaps, in the case of 'Les cloches de Genève'. He is as imaginatively evocative in 'Chapelle de Guillaume Tell', and it is in keeping with everything else on this absolutely outstanding, and finely recorded disc that 'Orage', the most *étude*-like piece, with its profuse octaves, is shown to be a purely musical emanation. 'Le mal du pays' is as original as 'Vallée d'Obermann', and receives another performance of surpassing beauty.

Années de pèlerinage – Deuxième année.
Jorge Bolet *pf*
Decca 410 161-2DH (51 minutes: DDD). Recorded 1982.   Ⓕ

The exceptionally wide dynamic range Bolet uses in this work is most faithfully conveyed. So, too, is the lovely sound he produces throughout. There is necessarily much pedalling in, for example, his ardent reading of 'Sposalizio', yet clarity is always complete. Also here are a beautiful, dark-toned realization of 'Il penseroso', and a piquant one of 'Canzonetta del Salvator Rosa'. The piano truly sings in the 'Sonetti', and all three receive ideal performances – hear the last page of No. 104, for instance. Bolet's long-drawn-out, though never excessive, sweetness in these pieces sets off the acrid *Dante* Sonata, of which an almost alarmingly vivid performance is given. As well as embodying a fresh response to a wide range of moods this is obviously a great feat of pianism.

Complete Solo Piano Music, Volume 15 – Song transcriptions.
Adelaïde, S466. Sechs geistliche Lieder, S467. An die ferne Geliebte, S469. Lieder von Goethe, S468 (Beethoven). Lieder, S547 (Mendelssohn). Lieder, S485 (Dessauer). Er ist gekommen in Sturm und Regen, S488. Lieder, S489 (Franz). Two songs, S554 (Rubinstein). Lieder von Robert und Clara Schumann, S569. Provenzalisches Lied, S570. Two songs, S567. Frühlingsnacht, S568. Widmung, S566 (Schumann).
Leslie Howard *pf*
Hyperion CDA66481/2 (two discs: 147 minutes: DDD). Recorded 1990.   Ⓕ

Few composers have ever shown a more insatiable interest in the music of others than Liszt, or devoted more time to transcribing it for the piano. Here Howard plays 60 of Liszt's 100 or so song transcriptions, including several by the lesser-known Dessauer, Franz and (as composers) Anton Rubinstein and Clara Schumann, alongside Beethoven, Mendelssohn and Robert Schumann. The selection at once reveals Liszt's variety of approach as a transcriber no less than his unpredictability of choice. Sometimes, as most notably in Beethoven's concert aria, *Adelaïde*, the keyboard virtuoso takes over: he links its two sections with a concerto-like cadenza as well as carrying bravura into an amplified coda. Mendelssohn's *On wings of song* brings imitative subtleties all his own, while the fullness of heart of Schumann's *Dedication* and *Spring Night* is likewise allowed to expand and overflow. But after the dazzling pyrotechnics of many of his operatic arrangements, the surprise here is the self-effacing simplicity of so much included. The five songs from Schumann's *Liederalbum für die Jugend* are literal enough to be played by young children. Even his later (1880) fantasy-type transcriptions of Rubinstein's exotic *The Asra* has the same potent economy of means, characterizing his own original keyboard music in advancing years. Howard responds keenly to mood and atmosphere, and never fails, pianistically, to emphasize the 'singer' in each song – in response to the actual verbal text that Liszt was nearly always conscientious enough to write into his scores. The recording is clean and true.

Complete Solo Piano Music, Volume 21.
Soirées musicales, S424. Soirées italiennes, S411. Nuits d'été à Pausilippe, S399. Tre sonetti del Petrarca, S158. Venezia e Napoli, S159. La serenata e L'orgia (Grande fantaisie sur des motifs des Soirées musicales), S422. La pastorella dell'Alpi e Li marinari (Deuxième fantaisie sur des motifs des Soirées musicales), S423.
Leslie Howard *pf*
Hyperion CDA66661/2 (two discs: 157 minutes: DDD). Recorded 1991-92.   Ⓕ

The two discs comprising Vol. 21 of Howard's enormous cycle remind us of the young Liszt's love affair with Italy, the spotlight now falling primarily – though not exclusively – on frolics with Rossini, Mercadante and Donizetti in lighter, lyrical vein. The special interest of the two original sets of pieces included, i.e. the three *Sonetti del Petrarca* and the four *Venezia e Napoli*, is that Howard introduces them as first written (*c*1839 and 1840 respectively) before Liszt's characteristically painstaking later revisions. There is much to enjoy in the playing itself, especially in simpler contexts when gondolas glide through calm waters, or lovers dream, or shepherds dance. Melody, so important throughout, is nicely sung. And whether in filigree delicacy or exuberant zest (as in excitable Venetian regattas)

Complete Solo Piano Music, Volume 29.
Hungarian Themes and Rhapsodies, S242.
Leslie Howard *pf*
Hyperion CDA66851/2 (two discs: 159 minutes: DDD). Recorded 1993.   Ⓕ

When listening to these 22 pieces, officially entitled *Magyar Dalok* and *Magyar Rapszódiák*, you at once realize you've heard many a snatch of them before. And not surprisingly, for they are in fact the source of most of what eventually emerged as Liszt's world-wide best-sellers, the *Hungarian Rhapsodies*. The composer revels in the lavishly decorative, cimbalom-coloured, improvisational style of the gipsies, in the process making demands on the pianist variously described by Leslie Howard in his insert-notes as 'devil-may-care, frighteningly difficult, frenetic, hand-splitting' and so on. Whether due to Liszt's own waning interest in platform pyrotechnics, or the fact that only he could really bring them off, simplification and formal condensation seem to have been primary aims when recasting these first flings as *Hungarian Rhapsodies*. But as Howard reveals, there are losses as well as gains in the maturer Liszt. Despite moments of protracted rodomontade there is a vast amount to enjoy.

Complete Solo Piano Music, Volume 30.
Oberon – Overture, S574 (Weber). Fantasia on themes from Le nozze di Figaro and Don Giovanni, S697 (Mozart). Ernani Paraphrase, S432. Miserere du Trovatore, S433. Rigoletto Paraphrase, S434. Réminiscences de Boccanegra, S438 (Verdi). Valse de concert sur deux motifs du Lucia et Parisina, S214/3 (Donizetti). Réminiscences de Robert le diable (Meyerbeer) – Cavatine; Valse infernale, S413. Les Adieux – Rêverie sur un motif de Roméo et Juliette, S409 (Gounod). Schwanengesang and Marsch from Hunyadi László, S405 (Erkel). Lohengrin – Elsa's Bridal Procession, S445/2; Two Pieces, S446. Fantasy on themes from Rienzi, S439 (Wagner).
Leslie Howard *pf*
Hyperion CDA66861/2 (two discs: 153 minutes: DDD). Recorded 1993.   Ⓕ

Liszt's operatic outings range from literal transcriptions, such as the opening *Oberon* Overture, to the most free fantasias, like that on motives from *Rienzi* at the end of the disc. The sequence is artfully planned to provide the maximum contrast between Liszt as lion and dove, with four of the 16 items earmarked as 'first recordings'. Of these, the Gounod *Roméo et Juliette* Rêverie is a tender, nocturne-like idyll that not for a second outstays its welcome. Liszt scholars may nevertheless be still more grateful for Howard's rescue of the other three, and first and foremost the nearly 22-minute long Fantasia on themes from *Le nozze di Figaro and Don Giovanni*, the 'almost-complete' manuscript of which Howard has now himself completed for performance and publication. Though self-indulgently protracted (as Busoni surely realized when preparing his own shortened version), its thematic interweavings *en route* still take your breath away. With Verdi and

Wagner we are on more familiar ground, where it goes without saying that Howard has formidable CD rivals. But throughout the disc there is a spaciousness in his characterization that far more often than not compensates for momentary technical strain or loss of finesse. His tonal range is certainly wide, ranging from the deep, dark, brooding intensity he finds for the *Ernani* and *Il trovatore* excerpts to his translucent delicacy in the upper reaches of Gounod's Rêverie. Apart from a slightly metallic touch above a certain dynamic level in the treble, the recorded sound quality can best be described in a nutshell as ripe.

Complete Solo Piano Music, Volume 34.
Douze Grandes Etudes, S137. Morceau de salon, S142.
Leslie Howard *pf*
Hyperion CDA66973 (76 minutes: DDD). Recorded 1994.   Ⓕ

In this first recording of the concert version of the *Douze Grandes Etudes* (1837), Leslie Howard brings his customary technical wizardry to bear on this outrageously difficult music in an arresting virtuoso display that demonstrates Liszt's consummate skill at transforming musical material. Moreover, despite Liszt's exhortation that only the later revisions of the studies should be played, there is a great deal to recommend the 1837 set, as these performances attest. The extreme technical demands of these pieces have led to critical scorn, but the challenges they contain are not designed merely for display, but are the result of the composer's comprehensive exploitation of the piano's expressive capabilities. Saint-Saëns said that 'in Art a difficulty overcome is a thing of beauty' and, in the present instance, Howard's triumph over the monumental difficulties posed by these pieces compellingly reveals the astonishing beauty of Liszt's 'orchestral' use of tone colour and sparkling virtuosity.

Opera Transcriptions – Rigoletto (Verdi) – Paraphrase, S434. Lucia et Parisina (Donizetti) – Valse à capriccio, S401. Faust (Gounod) – Waltz, S407. Eugene Onegin (Tchaikovsky) – Polonaise, S429. Der Fliegende Holländer (Wagner) – Spinning Chorus, S440. Tannhäuser (Wagner) – Rezitativ und Romanze, S444. Lohengrin (Wagner) – Verweis an Elsa, S446. Tristan und Isolde (Wagner) – Liebestod, S447. Le nozze di Figaro (Mozart) – Fantasia, S697.
Jean-Yves Thibaudet *pf*
Decca 436 736-2DH (69 minutes: DDD). Recorded 1992.   Ⓕ

In these operatic transcriptions Jean-Yves Thibaudet artfully contrasts five of the more demonstrative kind with four in which faithfulness to the original text was Liszt's main concern – these latter, significantly, drawn from the music of his formidable son-in-law to be, Richard Wagner. The filigree delicacy of Thibaudet's effortlessly brilliant finger-work is very impressive, not least in the decorative flights of the first three Verdi, Donizetti and Gounod items. Sometimes it suggests the trickles of scintillating fairy lights in the sky after the bursting of a rocket, sometimes the liquidity of water itself though still with each note retaining its own pinpoint glisten. In the earlier Wagner items Thibaudet matches Wagner's comparative simplicity with a similar concern for the unadorned truth, again, with his light pedalling, drawing sounds of ear-catching translucency from the keyboard's upper reaches. He finds the full, close-woven intensity of the 'Liebestod' harder to sustain but the piece is finely shaped as a whole. The recital ends heartily with the less frequently heard *Figaro* Fantasia completed in 1912 by no less a man than Busoni.

Excelsior!, S666. Am Grabe Richard Wagners, S267. Harmonies poétiques et réligieuses, S173 – Funérailles (trans. Kynaston). Two Recital Pieces, S268 – No. 2, Trauerode. Orpheus, S98. Fantasia and Fugue, S259, 'Ad nos, ad salutarem undam'.
Nicolas Kynaston *org*
IMP Masters 30366 0003-2 (75 minutes: DDD). Played on the Klais organ of Ingolstadt, Münster, Germany. Recorded 1994.   Ⓕ Ⓢ Ⓔ

As one of the wonders of the organ world the Ingolstadt Klais has frequently been the focus of record producers' attention. This disc is a true colossus among organ recordings. The instrument's vast dynamic range positively luxuriates in a sumptuous acoustic, vividly captured by a recording of true demonstration quality. Here's one to impress neighbours and friends with, whether or not they (or you, for that matter) enjoy organ music. Sometimes the Liszt of seemingly endless transcriptions and small programmatic organ pieces can pall, but it's in these very pieces – not least Kynaston's own perceptive transcription of 'Funérailles' – that the real strengths of this disc lie and there is a thrilling account of the great *Ad nos, ad salutarem undam*. Kynaston handles the organ with matchless sensitivity, continually conjuring up ravishing sounds and making these performances intensely pleasurable. His astute interpretative insight reveals every bar of music with utter conviction.

Ave Maria, S20 No. 1. Die Seligkeiten (Seligpreisungen), S25. Via crucis, S53. Pater noster, S41
No. 1. Pater noster, S29.
Antonella Balducci *sop* **Dorothee Labusch** *mez* **Furio Zanasi** *bar* **Ulrich Rausch** *bass*
Paolo Crivellaro *org* **Lugano Radio Choir / Diego Fasolis** *pf*
Naxos 8 553786 (62 minutes: DDD). Texts and translations included. Recorded 1993.   Ⓢ

With 27 voices the Lugano Radio Choir is intimate enough to capture the innocent simplicity of the
Pater noster and the essential prayerfulness of *Ave Maria*, in which Antonella Balducci is a simply
divine soloist. Yet it has enough substance and maturity to produce the kind of quasi-operatic drama
demanded by the 15 short but passion-filled movements of *Via crucis*, a curious work in which Liszt
the devout Catholic collides head on with Liszt the great romantic. The singers successfully run the
gauntlet of a huge dynamic and expressive range but they are cast into a shadow by Diego Fasolis
who unleashes vast reserves of passion on to quite the most booming-toned piano imaginable.
Liszt's odd mixture of experimental harmonies, distorted plainsong (the *Vexilla regis* crops up in
barely recognizable guises) and Lutheran chorale ('Santa Veronica' is, after an unrelated piano
introduction, the Passion Chorale from the *St Matthew Passion*) results in a somewhat disjunct
work. But this is an immensely rewarding performance and is matched by an outstanding recording.

Ihr Glocken von Marling, S328. Im Rhein, im schönen Strome, S272. Bist du!, S277. Vergiftet sind
meine Lieder, S289. Jugendglück, S323. Freudvoll und leidvoll, S280. Wilhelm Tell, S292 –
Der Fischerknabe; Der Hirt, Der Alpenjäger. Die drei Zigeuner, S320. Der Glückliche, S334. Kling
leise, mein Lied, S301. Die Macht der Musik, S302. Wer nie sein Brot mit Tranen ass, S297. Ich
möchte hingehn, S296. Die Vätergruft, S281. Ich scheide, S319. Über allen Gipfeln ist Ruh, S306
(Wanderers Nachtlied II).
Philip Langridge *ten* **John Constable** *pf*
Unicorn-Kanchana DKPCD9162 (71 minutes: DDD). Recorded 1995.   Ⓕ

Liszt's songs, a much underrated part of his output, find a most sympathetic interpreter in Philip
Langridge. He has the intelligence and poetic sensibility to appreciate their very varied nature, and
indeed without such qualities no singer is likely to make very much of them. There is much here
that is well chosen from quite a long list, and Langridge shows a striking ability to enter the world
of each song and think it through with real perception. He can colour the graceful melodies of *Bist
du!* and *Kling leise* with a sweetness of tone that is exactly judged to match his smooth line; he can,
appropriately, seem to poison this for *Vergiftet sind meine Lieder* and darken it for *Die Vätergruft*;
he can characterize the three gipsies colourfully (with Constable strutting out the proud Hungarian
cadences); he can produce a remarkable burst of power for *Jugendglück*. Only in *Der Alpenjäger*
does he seem rather overwhelmed, careful as Constable is at all times to do justice to Liszt's piano
sonorities without unleashing too much sheer volume. Theirs is a sensitive partnership, and
Constable is scrupulous in judging when the piano is supportive and when independent.

Christus, S3.
Henriette Bonde-Hansen *sop* **Iris Vermillion** *mez* **Michael Schade** *ten* **Andreas Schmidt** *bar*
Cracow Chamber Choir; Stuttgart Gächinger Kantorei;
Stuttgart Radio Symphony Orchestra / Helmuth Rilling.
Hänssler Classic Exclusive Series CD98 121 (three discs: 162 minutes: DDD). Text and translation
included. Recorded live in 1997.   Ⓕ

Christus is essentially a contemplative work and so could really be said to exist in a different time-
scale to most music. Much of the opening part, the 'Christmas Oratorio', uses very simple melody
and harmony, and is studiously undramatic. Helmuth Rilling does well not to charge it with too
much colour, and, if listened to as meditation rather than drama, what can seem static takes on a
positive atmosphere as a group of long reflections on the Christmas events. This is a far cry from
the sensational Liszt of the early virtuoso years, even from the creative ventures of the previous
decade, not yet reaching the terse, inward pieces of the last years. There is greater drama in the
middle part, 'After Epiphany', especially in the superb scene of Christ walking on the water.
Although there is still the suggestion that a wonder is being contemplated, Liszt stirs up a terrific
storm. This part also includes the beautiful setting of the Beatitudes, sung by Andreas Schmidt with
a degree of uncertainty which he entirely sheds when he comes to pronounce the sentences in Part 3
('Passion and Resurrection') for the scene of the Agony in the Garden. Liszt here turns to his most
intense chromatic idiom. The long *Stabat mater* is beautifully controlled by Rilling. His soloists
support him well, though Iris Vermillion can seem rather operatic; Henriette Bonde-Hansen sings
with a beautiful, clear tone. The recording does excellent justice to Liszt's wide-ranging
orchestration, especially considering its live performances. *Christus* is not a work for every day, nor
for every conductor. It is done justice in this sympathetic, patient performance.

Antonio Literes

Los elementos.
Marta Almajano *sop* El Ayre, La Aurora; **Lola Casariego** *mez* La Tierra;
Anne Grimm *sop* El Agua; **Xenia Meijer** *mez* El Fuego; **Jordi Ricart** *bar* El Tiempo;
Al Ayre Español / Eduardo López Banzo.
Deutsche Harmonia Mundi 05472 77385-2 (61 minutes: DDD). Notes, text and translation
included. Recorded 1997.   Ⓕ

This disc is fascinating for the insight it affords into this little-explored territory of the Spanish
baroque, *Los elementos* by the court composer Antonio de Literes. Subtitled 'opera armonica al
estilo ytaliano', the work is not really an opera, more perhaps an extended prologue, or *loa*, that
possibly originally introduced another theatrical entertainment, whether an opera proper or a play
with or without music. So little is known about the origins of *Los elementos* that it is difficult to
categorize or contextualize at present. What is absolutely clear is the influence of the Italian style
that pervaded the Spanish court towards the end of the seventeenth century. The succession of
recitatives and arias in *Los elementos* is occasionally disrupted by the introduction of the
indigenous verse-and-refrain form of *estribillo* and *coplas*; even here the musical style is
wholeheartedly Italian, which makes the use of castanets (for the most part in the tutti sections)
seem totally anachronistic. Apart from this quibble, however, the performance is generally excellent
with a strong line-up of Spanish singers. The roles of the four elements are taken by four female
voices, while the figure of Tiempo (Time) is here sung by the Catalan baritone Jordi Ricart.
Literes gives his soloists plenty of opportunity to shine, seemingly quite at home with the virtuoso
aria as well as with the lyrical style of recitative characteristic of music for the Spanish theatre.
In the first part of the piece the properties of the four elements – air, earth, fire and water – are
described, giving the composer plenty of scope for contrast, while the portrayal of the gradual
arrival of dawn – and the ways in which each of the elements is affected – is equally vividly
drawn. Literes proves himself to be a composer of imagination and secure technique and Eduardo
López Banzo's choice of tempos is on the whole convincing. The playing is fine (the continuo
occasionally over-exuberant), and the overall sound is very good. This disc is particularly
recommended to anyone with an interest in baroque music (and not just Spanish music) for the
quality of the work and the contribution this recording makes to a richer and fuller picture of the
musical past.

George Lloyd

Iernin.
Marilyn Hill Smith *sop* Iernin; **Geoffrey Pogson** *ten* Gerent; **Henry Herford** *bar* Edryn;
Malcolm Rivers *bass-bar* Bedwyr; **Jonathon Robarts** *bass* Priest; **Jeremy White** *bass*
Saxon Thane; **Stephen Jackson** *bar* Huntsman; **Claire Powell** *mez* Cunaide;
BBC Singers and Concert Orchestra / George Lloyd.
Albany TROY121/3 (three discs: 173 minutes: ADD). Notes and text included. Also includes an
interview with George Lloyd. Recorded 1985.   Ⓜ

At the London première in 1935 *The Times* found the opera 'spontaneous in invention and almost
consistently effective ... the only exception [being] the choral writing which, conceived along
unusual lines and largely unisonous, does not quite achieve the composer's intentions and might
well be revised'. Whether the hint was taken we are not told, but the score has not been revised for
this performance, and most of the choral writing (not all that 'unisonous') works well. More
important is the writing for soloists, and on the whole this seems instinctively expert: for instance,
the high notes are sparingly required, so that when they occur they have maximum effect. The
heroine's role wants a coloratura soprano who also has a substantial middle and lower-middle
register. That should not be too much to ask, but one can only guess at the kind of Italianate full-
bodied sound that was probably in the composer's ear when he wrote the work. Marilyn Hill-Smith
is more successful with the higher, more agile and less dramatic parts of the role. All the male
principals have splendidly singable music, but the best performance comes from Claire Powell,
sumptuous of voice and noble of manner.

Jonathan Lloyd

Symphony No. 4.
BBC Symphony Orchestra / Martyn Brabbins.
NMC D046M (32 minutes: DDD). Recorded 1996.   Ⓜ

This recording is a revelation. It is not difficult to see why. Although Lloyd's work has much in common with the polystylism and neo-romanticism of composers such as Robin Holloway, Schnittke and Del Tredici, his very particular sensibility shies away from hyperbole and grand statement in favour of something more oblique. Like his more famous contemporaries, Lloyd orientates his music around motifs that come with a past, in this case a veiled suggestion of Elgar, skiffle band or close harmony. The precise instrumental garb in which they come is crucial to the whole effect, but even more impressive is the way that Lloyd maintains their tension throughout the half-hour span of this work by constantly undercutting them, reharmonizing them and placing them in unexpectedly new contexts. The way Lloyd subverts your expectations in terms of harmony, texture and, above all, timing is absolutely masterly. Structural downbeats are hinted at, only to be avoided altogether. At the moment the music gathers momentum, it is in fact spiralling out of the reach of the listener, at a tangent to any feeling you might have developed about the work's structure. Brabbins and the BBC Symphony Orchestra acquit themselves magnificently. Anyone interested in new music is urged to hear this disc.

William Lloyd Webber

British 1914-1982

Viola Sonatina. Nocturne. Two Pieces for Cello and Piano. Badinage de Noël. Song Without Words. Scherzo in G minor. Arabesque. Presto for Perseus. Romantic Evening. Explanation. Five Songs. Missa Sanctae Mariae Magdalenae.
John Graham-Hall ten **Philip Dukes** va **Julian Lloyd Webber** vc **Sophia Rahman, John Lill, Philip Ledger** pfs **Ian Watson** org
Richard Hickox Singers / Richard Hickox.
ASV CDDCA961 (59 minutes: DDD). Texts included. Recorded 1995. Ⓕ

The fluent *Sonatina* has three pithy, beautifully crafted movements which contain much resourceful, attractively idiomatic writing. The wistful *Nocturne* for cello and piano derives from Lloyd Webber's 1948 oratorio *St Francis of Assisi*, while the (undated) piano miniature entitled *Explanation* has a similar, innocent charm (it certainly fits very happily into the sequence of piano pieces here). The five songs are really very pretty indeed (suggesting comparisons with Roger Quilter), as, indeed, are the two other cello and piano offerings, 'In the half-light' and the 'Air varié' (based on César Franck's *Tantum ergo*). That just leaves the immensely assured, five-movement *Missa Sanctae Mariae Magdalenae*, a substantial late work dating from 1979. Performances and recordings are excellent.

Alonso Lobo

Spanish c1555-1617

Lobo Missa Maria Magdalene. O quam suavis est, Domine. Quam pulchri sunt. Ave regina caelorum. Versa est in luctum. Credo quod Redemptor. Vivo ego, dicit Dominus. Ave Maria.
Guerrero Maria Magdalene.
The Tallis Scholars / Peter Phillips.
Gimell 454 931-2PH (63 minutes: DDD). Texts and translations included. Ⓕ Ⓔ

Alonso Lobo has mainly become known for one work, his setting of the funerary *Versa est in luctum*. This is undoubtedly a masterpiece of its kind but to have it placed alongside other pieces from Lobo's 1602 collection (one of the six Masses in the volume, and all seven motets) affords a welcome chance to assess his composition skills more fully. Lobo's music is sonorous in a manner that is direct and unfussy in effect, though often highly expressive, and always structured with the utmost technical control. Take, for example, Lobo's *Ave Maria*, an 8-in-4 canon (in other words, four more voices are generated from the original quartet) which emanates a sense of absolute serenity. In fact, each of the motets explores a different aspect of the compositional techniques brought to the genre, and the Mass is equally fine, Lobo making the spacious textures of the motet, *Maria Magdalene* by his teacher Guerrero a distinguishing feature of his own setting of the Ordinary. The Tallis Scholars are on superb form, the overall sound vibrant and immediate with solo sections providing contrast through a more introspective approach. Even if you've never bought a CD of late-Renaissance polyphony before, try this one – you'll be bowled over.

Pietro Locatelli

Italian 1695-1764

10 Sonatas, Op. 8.
Locatelli Trio (Elizabeth Wallfisch vn Richard Tunnicliffe vc Paul Nicholson hpd); **Rachel Isserlis** vn
Hyperion CDA67021/2 (two discs: 116 minutes: DDD). Recorded 1994. Ⓕ Ⓟ

There is a sense of the decadent about the music of Locatelli. But decadence, we all know, can be quite fun, and it would be an austere spirit that took little pleasure in these sonatas and especially the playing of them here. This two-disc set of his Op. 8 (published in 1744) contains six violin sonatas and four trio sonatas, three for two violins and continuo and one using the much less common combination of violin, cello and continuo. A number of them have a slowish movement and most end with a quick triple-metre piece, again in brilliant violinistic style. The most attractive is No. 5, with its interesting gestures and hints of wit in the second movement. The most demanding is No. 6 with its final minuet with variations, quite breathtaking (and improbably set in E flat, a perverse gesture): here Elizabeth Wallfisch clambers unruffled through the technical thickets, which include an extraordinary variation with trills on one string and moving parts on another and dashes from one end of the compass to the other and back again, and much more besides. This is amazing violin playing of a kind of virtuosity rarely heard from a period instrument player. The three trio sonatas for two violins are not of course virtuoso music in quite the same way, and musically not generally very inventive. The performances are altogether admirable; no one who admires good violin playing will want to miss Wallfisch's crisp, rhythmic playing on this disc.

Matthew Locke

British 1621-1677

Consort of Fower Parts. Duos – No. 1 in D major; No. 2 in C major.
Fretwork (Wendy Gillespie, Richard Campbell, William Hunt, Julia Hodgson, Susanna Pell, Richard Boothby *viols*); **Nigel North** *lte* **Paul Nicholson** *org/spinet*
Virgin Classics Veritas VC5 45142-2 (67 minutes: DDD). Recorded 1990. Ⓕ🅿

Locke is capable of some exquisite music and Fretwork here are loving advocates. Experienced as they are in the performance of so much of the finest English consort music of the seventeenth century from Byrd to Purcell, Fretwork are particularly well placed to discriminate between the elusive properties in an age of subtle, abstract ideals. In the Ayre of No. 4 and the equivalent in Suites Nos. 2 and 6, there is a simplicity of utterance entirely appropriate to Locke's delightful tunefulness, as does the disarming warmth of expression in the opening movements of the major-key works. Fretwork's intonation is perfect. There is a considered and deft use of a variety of continuo instruments, not to mention two attractive *Duos* for bass viols, which break up the prevalent quartet texture. Locke's special language shines as brightly here as one can remember.

Carl Loewe

German 1796-1869

Die drei Lieder, Op. 3 No. 3. Elvershöh, Op. 118 No. 2. Der Woywode, Op. 49 No. 1. Die nächtliche Heerschau, Op. 23. Der letzte Ritter, Op. 124. Tom der Reimer, Op. 135. Odins Meeresritt, Op. 118. Waffenweihe Kaiser Heinrich's IV, Op. 122.
Andreas Schmidt *bar* **Cord Garben** *pf*
CPO CPO999 253-2 (65 minutes: DDD). Recorded 1994. Ⓕ

This opening volume in CPO's Loewe Edition contains only one really well-known ballad, *Tom der Reimer*, sung here with a devotion to the words and to their dramatic import. This is an essential quality for these ballads, and Andreas Schmidt's control of the portrayal of character and of the often sensational unfolding of events is superb. He and his pianist, Cord Garben (sometimes set rather far back and not sufficiently clear in articulation), have a sure instinct for Loewe's structures, for the movement from one section or tempo into another, for the telling surprise modulation, for the decorative touches in the melody, so that these fine works are not merely a string of events but a dramatic experience. Apart from the spooky ballads, such as *Elvershöh* and others which were said to have gripped Loewe's listeners as he sang them himself at the piano, a strong vein which he explored was the historical narrative. There is a chilling delivery of the ballad embodying that popular nineteenth-century image, the dead troops reviewed by their dead general – in this case, Napoleon. This is an excellent beginning to a major enterprise.

Kleiner Haushalt, Op. 71. Die Heinzelmännchen, Op. 83. Heinrich der Vogler, Op. 56 No. 1. Das Vaterland, Op. 125 No. 2. Der Nöck, Op. 129 No. 2. Fünf Lieder, Op. 145. Prinz Eugen, der edle Ritter, Op. 92. Archibald Douglas, Op. 128.
Kurt Moll *bass* **Cord Garben** *pf*
CPO CPO999 306-2 (58 minutes: DDD). Texts and translations included. Recorded 1994. Ⓕ

Kurt Moll has all the attributes that go to make a fine Loewe singer, not only the splendidly flexible bass voice that can darken the grim songs (plunging to a strong low E), brighten the cheerful ones and colour all the detail of the ballads vividly, but nimbleness of wit as well as gravity, a sense of comedy as well as dignity, a sense of being on stage. The delightful Rückert *Kleiner Haushalt* is a real comic *tour de force*; at the other end of his recital, *Archibald Douglas* has an impetus that is dramatic but adroitly skirts the melodramatic. He makes a compelling narrative of *Heinrich der Vogler*, changing tone and manner for the lyrical songs that make up the *Fünf Lieder*, Op. 145 and in 'Der Feind' deftly sketching the animals who all shy away from their common enemy approaching through the wood – a man.

Drei Balladen, Op. 1 – Edward; Erlkönig. Drei Balladen, Op. 2 – Herr Oluf. Drei Balladen, Op. 3 – Elvershöh; Die drei Lieder. Lieder, Gesänge, Romanzen und Balladen, Op. 9 – Book 1: Wandrers Nachtlied; Book 3: Ich denke dein; Book 8: Türmwachter Lynkeus zu den Füssen der Helena; Lynkeus, der Türmer, auf Fausts Sternwarte singend; Gutmann und Gutweib. Drei Balladen, Op. 20. Die Gruft der Liebenden, Op. 21. Zehn Geistliche Gesänge, Op. 22 – Book 1: Gottes ist der Orient!. Drei Balladen, Op. 44 – Der getreue Eckart; Der Totentanz. Drei Balladen, Op. 56 – Heinrich der Vogler. Drei Balladen, Op. 59 – Der Schatzgräber. Zwölf Gedichte, Op. 62 – Book 1: Süsses Begräbnis; Hinkende Jamben. Kleiner Haushalt, Op. 71. Vier Legenden, Op. 75 – Der heilige Franziskus. Sechs Gesänge, Op. 79 – Frühzeitiger Frühling. Fünf Lieder, Op. 81 – In Vorübergehen. Prince Eugen, Op. 92 Drei Balladen, Op. 97 – Der Mohrenfürst auf der Messe. Odins Meeresritt, Op. 118. Drei Gesänge, Op. 123 – Trommelständchen; Die Uhr. Archibald Douglas, Op. 128. Drei Balladen, Op. 129 – Der Nöck. Tom der Reimer, Op. 135a. Fünf Lieder, Op. 145 – Meeresleuchten. Canzonette. Freibeuter. Wenn der Blüten Frühlingsregen.
Dietrich Fischer-Dieskau bar **Jörg Demus** pf
DG 449 516-2GX2 (two discs: 156 minutes: ADD). Texts and translations included. Recorded 1968-79. Ⓜ

All the best-known ballads are included here, magnificently sung by a great artist at the height of his powers. *Edward, Herr Oluf, Heinrich der Vogler, Prince Eugen, Der Zauberlehrling*: these and others are sung with a wonderful sense of the graphic, conveyed through an appreciation of the colour of the words that never descends into overemphasis and that is beautifully attuned to Loewe's illustrative manner. Fischer-Dieskau and Demus are ideal partners, Demus responding quickly and with an ear for the sinister that often marks the piano writing and its subtle use of motive. Not just a composer of ballads, Loewe was also a Lieder writer in the great German tradition, and this is too often overlooked, but not by Fischer-Dieskau. Two songs alone, from this magisterial collection, are witness to Loewe's stature. They are settings of the wonderful poems from the second part of *Faust* in which Lynceus, the lynx-eyed watcher on the tower, sees the magical appearance, of Helen of Troy herself. He, incarnating the gift of the perception of visual beauty, after a life of watching from his tower can conceive of nothing that could surpass this wonder; and, in the second song, hymns his gratitude to the gift of sight. Loewe's two settings are beautiful responses to the poetry of a great artist with the gift of an ideal simplicity. These two songs alone should persuade the responsive listener to make the exploration.

Op. 1 – No. 1, Edward; No. 3, Erlkönig. Alles ist eitel, Op. 4 No. 4. Op. 9 – Book 1: No. 3, Über allen Gipfeln ist Ruh; No. 4, Der du von dem Himmel bist; Book 8: No. 1, Turmwächter Lynceus zu den Füssen der Helena; No. 2, Lynceus der Helena seine Schätze darbeitend; No. 3, Lynceus auf Fausts Sternwarte singend. Hochzeitlied, Op. 20 No. 1. Der Bergmann, Op. 39. Die Begegnung am Meeresstrande, Op. 120. Der Asra, Op. 133. Findlay. Wandrers Nachtlied.
Christoph Prégardien ten **Cord Garben** pf
CPO CPO999 417-2 (66 minutes: DDD). Texts and translations included. Recorded 1997. Ⓕ

Christoph Prégardien has many of the qualities called for by Loewe's songs and ballads, and awareness of the demands made by a composer with a far wider range than is sometimes allowed. He can be eerie in the blood-curdling *Edward* and again in *Erlkönig* (songs that thrilled Wagner), especially by his sensitive and discreet articulation of the words within the melodic line. *Edward* is powerfully impelled towards the realization of the murder with softly anguished calls of the repeated 'O!'. The Erl-King's threat of force is the more sinister for the underemphasis of the key word, 'Gewalt'; and the whole uneasy alternation between major and minor, as spirit and human worlds contest, is delicately balanced until the final, terrible triumph of the Erl-King's major third in the climactic discord. These are superb performances. The amiable cycle of five songs about a miner, *Der Bergmann*, is lightly and touchingly handled, with a lively contribution from Cord Garben. Prégardien uses his eloquence of line to fine effect in the Goethe songs. The two *Wandrers Nachtlied* settings, beautifully sung here, are as remarkable as any in the repertory. Still more could be said of the *Lynceus* triptych. Dazzled by his glimpse of Helen of Troy, in the last of the songs the watcher on the high tower gives thanks for the gift of sight that has brought him so many marvels. Far-ranging arpeggios spread the world beneath him, and the rapt melodic line, wonderingly enunciated by Prégardien, is a prayer of thanks. Here is one of the great German Lieder.

Paolo Lorenzani

Italian 1640-1713

Antienne à la Vierge. Motet pour l'élévation. Motet pour tous les temps. Dialogue entre Jésus et l'Ame. Motet pour les confesseurs. Litanies à la Vierge.
Le Concert Spirituel / Hervé Niquet.
Naxos 8 553648 (63 minutes: DDD). Texts and translations included. Recorded 1997. Ⓢ

Paolo Lorenzani was a Roman-born composer who towards the end of the seventeenth century spent 16 years in France, where he tried to raise the profile of Italian music. In this he had little success, especially as in doing so he inevitably came up against the machinations of the tyrannical Lully; indeed their rivalry – hardly an equal one considering Lully's power and influence – seems to have become quite acrimonious, and eventually Lorenzani returned to Italy to finish his days as director of the Cappella Giulia at the Vatican. This rarity to the catalogue offers five of the *grands motets* for soloists, choir, violins and continuo which he published in Paris in 1693, plus a *Litany of Our Lady* for voices and continuo which he probably wrote when back in Rome. The lack of success the *motets* enjoyed at the time – for all that the King liked them and that they were very much in the French style – no doubt hastened Lorenzani's departure, but listening to them now, musico-political distractions put aside, it is hard to understand why they should have failed; this is highly attractive music, easily on a par with that of some of the better-known *grand motet* composers of the time, and there is some clever responsiveness to text as well. The performances, too, are very enjoyable. Hervé Niquet's experience in this type of music pays off in a well-balanced and lithe ensemble, good stand-out solos, and an intelligent, quick-witted approach to the music's interpretation. Lorenzani may not be a forgotten genius exactly, but his music is well worth unearthing. Lully has plenty to answer for.

Antonio Lotti

Italian c1667-1740

Duetti, terzetti e madrigali a più voci, Op. 1 – Inganni dell'umanità; Lamento di tre amanti; La vita caduca; Moralità d'una per la; Incostanza femminile; Lontananza insopportabile; Funerale della speranza; Crudeltà rimproverata; Giuramento amorosa; Querela amorosa; Incostanza della sorte Scherzo d'amore; Capriccio; Supplica ad amore.
Il Complesso Barocco / Alan Curtis *hpd*
Virgin Classics Veritas VC5 45221-2 (78 minutes: DDD). Texts and translations included. Recorded 1996. Ⓕ

A Venetian contemporary of Vivaldi, Lotti's association with St Mark's lasted all of his working life, nearly 60 years. In addition, his music was performed and published all over Europe, arousing the enthusiasm of no less a patron than the Emperor Leopold I. The madrigal enjoyed a revival at the turn of the eighteenth century; what fascinates here is the music's hybrid nature and its flexibility. The texture is largely imitative, with each text-line having its own melodic point; but alongside this convention are Lotti's very contemporary-sounding harmonic touches. They are a source of unexpected delight, especially in this vivacious and spirited interpretation. This is music of high vocal virtuosity, requiring the utmost agility in execution and deftness of characterization: on that count Il Complesso Barocco can hardly be faulted, though admittedly the higher voices are perhaps slightly less sure-footed in their extreme registers. The continuo, spearheaded by Curtis himself, is equally natural and unfussy (though in the more richly scored pieces, as in *La vita caduca*, the organ may be a touch too obtrusive). There can be few better opportunities to broaden (or to make) one's acquaintance with Lotti.

Jean-Baptiste Lully

Italian/French 1632-1687

Acis et Galatée.
Jean-Paul Fouchécourt *ten* Acis; **Véronique Gens** *sop* Galatée; **Monique Simon** *sop* Diane, Second Naiad; **Jean-Louis Meunier** *ten* Comus; **Howard Crook** *ten* Apollon, Télème, Priest of Juno; **Françoise Masset** *sop* Scylla, Dryad; **Rodrigo del Pozo** *counterten* Tircis; **Mireille Delunsch** *sop* Aminte, Abundance; First Naiad; **Laurent Naouri** *bar* Polyphème; **Thierry Félix** *bar* Neptune, Sylvan; **Choeur des Musiciens du Louvre; Les Musiciens du Louvre / Marc Minkowski.**
Archiv Produktion 453 497-2AH2 (two discs: 107 minutes: DDD). Notes, text and translation included. Recorded 1996. Ⓕ 🅿 🅴

Acis et Galatée was Lully's last completed opera, and one of his greatest. A *pastoral héroïque* performed in 1686 to entertain the Dauphin during a hunting party at the Duc de Vendôme's château, it employs many features of his *tragédies en musique* – vocal ensembles, instrumental movements and an enhanced use of the orchestra in general; and each act contains a *divertissement* with choruses and dances. One of the glories of the score is the concluding *passacaille*, which with instrumental sections builds up from single voices to chorus. There is also a small but affecting chaconne for Galatea in Act 2; but another glorious moment is the lengthy scene in which she discovers the body of her lover and calls on her father, Neptune, who guarantees Acis immortality by transforming him into a river. The opera is prefaced by a prologue in which various gods and a personification of Abundance flatter the king and his son: points of special interest are the riches of the scoring at Apollo's entrance and the charm of the dances – in fact the whole prologue is permeated by dance rhythms. The classical story of the cyclops destroying his young rival was given a typically French slant and topical moral by making Galatea initially play hard to get, in contrast to the simple, unaffected love of shepherds and shepherdesses (though the haughty Scylla is an exception). In the main body of the opera Lully ensures vitality by constantly, and extremely effectively, changing metre. Marc Minkowski brings out all the drama of the work by thoughtful treatment of the verbal text, intelligent pacing and varied instrumental articulation and weight: especially striking are the rough sonorities of the march in which Polyphemus first appears, and the intensity of the lovers' angry confrontation in Act 2. Jean-Paul Fouchécourt projecting the image of an ardent youthful lover, and Véronique Gens that of a passionate goddess, are both excellently cast, but Laurent Naouri almost steals the scene from them with his fearsomely powerful Polyphemus: Howard Crook contributes valuably in various roles, though he is ill at ease in the very highest register. There is considerable finesse in the chorus singing, and the theorbo continuo, working overtime, is admirable. An altogether splendid performance of a masterpiece.

Hans Christian Lumbye   Danish 1810-1874

Salute to August Bournonville Galop. Queen Louise's Waltz. Berlin Vauxhall Polka. King Christian IX's March of Honour. Copenhagen Steam Railway Galop. Summer Night on the Møn Cliffs. Caecilie Waltz. Columbine Polka-Mazurka. Britta Polka. Cannon Galop. Amélie Waltz. Dagmar Polka. Deborah Polka-Mazurka. Artist Dreams. Otto Allin's Drum Polka. Champagne Galop.
Tivoli Symphony Orchestra / Giordano Bellincampi.
Marco Polo 8 223743 (69 minutes: DDD). Recorded 1997.   Ⓕ

This disc is devoted to the works of the 'Nordic Strauss', Hans Christian Lumbye. His music has an enduring freshness, with melodic appeal linked to simplicity and utter lack of pretension. There is a fair chunk here of his most familiar compositions. The three or four pieces that have not previously been recorded on CD match up well to the general standard of Lumbye's invention. Those unfamiliar with Lumbye can therefore happily obtain this collection for representation of him at his best. The use of Lumbye's own Tivoli Symphony Orchestra ensures the utmost authenticity and charm in the performances, since this repertory is as much in the blood of the Danes as that of the Stausses is in the Viennese. The admirable documentation by Knud Arne Jürgensen is not the least attraction of this appetizing release.

Witold Lutosławski   Polish 1913-1994

Cello Concerto. Livre pour orchestre. Novelette. Chain 3.
Andrzej Bauer *vc*
Polish National Radio Symphony Orchestra / Antoni Wit.
Naxos 8 553625 (73 minutes: DDD). Recorded 1995.   Ⓢ

This is an excellent disc; fine music, well played and recorded, and all at the special Naxos price. The earliest composition, *Livre* (1968), was the first work completed by Lutosławski after the Second Symphony, and it shows him at his freshest and boldest, as if relieved to be free (if only temporarily) from the burden of one of music's weightiest traditions. With its well-nigh surreal juxtapositions of strongly contrasted materials, and the unusual ferocity of its tone – the 'book' in question must have been of the blood and thunder variety – *Livre* reveals a Lutosławski quite different from the relatively benign, ironic master of the later works. Coming immediately after *Livre*, the Cello Concerto has an even wider expressive range: indeed, in the balance it achieves between lamenting melodic lines and mercurial scherzo-like writing, coupled with a tendency to home in on crucial pitch-centres, it sets out the basic elements of the composer's later style. This performance owes a great deal to Antoni Wit's skilful shaping of the music's alternations between relatively free and precise notation, and this skill is even more evident in the remaining orchestral scores. *Novelette*, completed in 1979, is Lutosławski's response to his first American commission; it is far more cogent and concentrated than its title might lead you to expect. *Chain 3* (1986) is one of the best later works, let down only by some rather perfunctory quasi-tonal harmony near the end. But this does not undermine the impression the disc as a whole conveys of some of the most characterful and individual music of the last 30 years.

Concerto for Orchestra. Jeux vénitiens. Livre pour Orchestre. Mi-parti.
Polish National Radio Symphony Orchestra / Witold Lutosławski.
EMI Matrix CDM5 65305-2 (78 minutes: ADD). Recorded 1976-77. Ⓜ **RR**

A note with this reissue proclaims the 'particular significance' of these works for Lutosławski. Their most immediate significance for the listener is in offering convincing performances of works which illustrate Lutosławski's progress from relatively traditional to relatively radical styles – two modes of expression which he employed with equal conviction and finesse. The *Concerto for Orchestra* fully deserves to stand alongside Bartók's slightly earlier, similarly exuberant essay in the genre, and this performance, by turns punchy and passionate, proves that Lutosławski was not always an overly reticent conductor of his own scores. The playing and recording lack some of the refinement of Barenboim's Chicago version, but it has an attractively raw energy, the composer contemplating 'youthful' excesses with enjoyment rather than embarrassment. Hearing *Jeux vénitiens* immediately after the concerto supports the argument that Lutosławski's change of direction, around 1960, risked losing much that was most substantial in his earlier music. The aleatory jam sessions of *Jeux vénitiens* seem especially dated in this rather cluttered, airless recording, but at least the performance doesn't attempt to add spurious solemnity to a liberating *jeu d'esprit*. *Livre* and *Mi-parti* are both much finer works, and the blend of formal mastery with vivid, well-contrasted materials – especially in *Mi-parti* – offers one of the most satisfying and distinctive musical experiences of recent times. The remastered recordings can't eliminate the artificialities and imbalances of the analogue originals, but neither do they interfere with the impact of these authoritative and engaging performances.

Concerto for Orchestra. Funeral Music. Mi-parti.
BBC Philharmonic Orchestra / Yan Pascal Tortelier.
Chandos CHAN9421 (55 minutes: DDD). Recorded 1993. Ⓕ **S**

Tortelier's virtues as a conductor – expressive warmth allied to a special rhythmic buoyancy – are generously apparent in a sizzling account of the *Concerto for Orchestra*. The musical flow is firmly controlled, yet the effect is never inflexible, and the technical precision and alertness of the playing throughout is something for the listener to revel in. The sound is bright, well differentiated dynamically, and even if the BBC's Manchester studio lacks some of the depth and atmosphere of Chicago's Orchestra Hall, as caught in Barenboim's version, this recording is generally more vivid, in keeping with a performance which has precisely the kind of bite and energy that the score demands. It is good that Chandos and Tortelier chose *Mi-parti* to complete the disc, since of all Lutosławski's later instrumental works this one makes out the best possible case for his radical change of technique around 1960.

Concerto for Orchestra. Symphony No. 3.
Chicago Symphony Orchestra / Daniel Barenboim.
Erato 4509-91711-2 (58 minutes: DDD). Recorded live in 1992. Ⓕ **E**

Lutosławski's Third Symphony was commissioned by the Chicago SO and first performed by them under Sir Georg Solti in 1983, but only nine years later did the orchestra record the work. None of the versions made in the interim can equal Barenboim's blend of refined detail and cumulative power, and the Erato recording is also more faithful to the dynamics marked in the score. The *Concerto for Orchestra*, completed almost 30 years before the symphony, is comparatively conservative in style, but it has ample substance to match its panache. It also remains a formidable challenge to an orchestra. As with the symphony, Barenboim's strength is the large-scale creation and sustaining of tension, and the Erato recording contains the heavy climaxes without draining them of clarity or impact.

Symphonies – No. 1; No. 2. Symphonic Variations. Funeral music.
Polish National Radio Symphony Orchestra / Witold Lutosławski.
EMI Matrix CDM5 65076-2 (71 minutes: ADD). Recorded 1976-77. Ⓜ

All four works included on this superbly refurbished CD share an acute sense of texture, with the *Symphonic Variations* (1938) serving as a sort of changing room where the composer busily experiments with all manner of musical dress. The *Funeral music* for Bartók (1956-58) is a powerful synthesis of original thought and active homage, with plentiful reminders of the master himself – especially of his *Divertimento* for strings. The real ground-breaker, however, is the Second Symphony, a seething, structured mass in two parts: the first, nervous and diffuse (with strikingly original passagework for piano and percussion), the second – which arrives without a break – initially dense, but ultimately ethereal. All in all, this must surely count as *the* introduction to Lutosławski's symphonic world, and helpful notes offer the uninitiated plenty of useful musical signposts.

Chantefleurs et Chantefables. Preludes and Fugue. Five Songs. Chain 1.
Solveig Kringelborn *sop* **Norwegian Chamber Orchestra / Daniel Harding.**
Virgin Classics VC5 45275-2 (73 minutes: DDD). Texts and translations included.   Ⓕ

Chantefleurs et Chantefables, Lutosławski's penultimate work, was heard as a late and exquisite flowering of lyricism, prompted in part by the French language, in part by the delicately fresh evocations of childhood wonder that he found in Robert Desnos's poems. It was by no means unheralded: it has obvious ancestors in the *Five Songs* to Polish texts that Lutosławski wrote over 30 years earlier but which have seldom been heard since, no doubt because of their language. They are very beautiful, with gratefully lyrical vocal lines over strikingly evocative orchestral textures (strings, two harps, piano, timpani and percussion) that are complex in technique but lucidly 'readable' to the ear. Solveig Kringelborn, who gave the first performance of *Chantefleurs et Chantefables* under the composer's direction, sounds just as much at home in Polish as in French. The two purely instrumental works here are quite as absorbingly coupled. The seven Preludes are played in the order in which they are printed in the score, but for all the disparate material they contain it is obvious that Lutosławski composed them with great care so that they would make equal but different sense played in any order. The extended 'Fugue' (quotation marks inserted because although it isn't really a fugue it has the feeling of one), a remarkable work from 1972, is clearly an ancestor of the three *Chains* that followed in the 1980s. *Chain 1*, for 14 instruments, progresses from a sequence of crisp, lively, at times almost neo-classical 'events' to a climax of density (ultimately a 12-note chord) in which until the very last moment every line is clearly distinguishable. These are quite admirable performances and recordings, the Norwegian Chamber Orchestra responding with enthusiasm and warmth to Lutosławski's implicit demands that they should play like an ensemble of soloists. Daniel Harding's love for this music is apparent in his care for balance, vivid sonority and the sheer range (from eloquent intensity to touching tenderness) of Lutosławski's lyricism.

David Lyon
British 1938

Ballet. Concerto for Horn and Strings. Country Lanes. Fairytale Suite.
Fantasia on a Nursery Song. Farnham Suite. Overture to a Comic Opera. Waltz.
Michael Thompson *hn*
Royal Ballet Sinfonia / David Lloyd-Jones.
Marco Polo British Light Music 8 225039 (61 minutes: DDD). Recorded 1997.   Ⓕ

David Lyon claims Benjamin Britten as a major influence. This indebtedness (and perhaps also that to Elgar) is evident especially in the extensive representation here of pieces for strings. Of the works for full orchestra, perhaps the most melodic are the charming short *Country Lanes* (a representation of pony and cart meandering through the countryside) and the delightful *Fairytale Suite*, which includes a 'Snow Scene' reminiscent of Prokofiev and a delightful waltz. There is also an intriguing set of variations on *Nick Nack Paddiwack* that evokes other composers in various ways. The most complex writing is to be found in the final *Ballet*, which impressively exploits the capabilities of the various sections of the orchestra. Even the annotator admits, though, that this last may not comply with everyone's definition of 'light classical' music. This is therefore a collection that may interest enthusiasts for more serious British music as well as the lighter kind. It is, at all events, a feather in the cap of the excellent Royal Ballet Sinfonia, which is making something of a speciality of more approachable modern music of this sort.

Edward MacDowell
American 1860-1908

Piano Sonata No. 4 in E minor, Op. 59, 'Keltic'. Forgotten Fairy Tales, Op. 4. Six Poems after Heine, Op. 31. 12 Virtuoso Etudes, Op. 46.
James Barbagallo *pf*
Marco Polo 8 223633 (65 minutes: DDD).   Ⓕ

Edward MacDowell's star may have faded to near oblivion over the years. Yet even when his very personal and oddly touching voice seems stifled by deference to outmoded European ideals he provides enough poetic and psychological interest to make James Barbagallo's affectionate tribute more than worthwhile. The rough-and-tumble of academic life, with its hard-nosed jockeying for position, was ill-suited to MacDowell's gentle nature and his professorship at Columbia was short-lived. The gems of this disc are surely the six Op. 31 *Poems after Heine*, their charm and piquancy evoking Scottish castles, nightingales and a shepherd boy 'crowned with golden sunshine'. The *Forgotten Fairy Tales*, too, have their moments but the 12 *Virtuoso Etudes* are less interesting than their title implies: the 'Polonaise' is truly awful and the 'Valse triste' an unengaging mixture of whimsy and complacency. But 'Wilde Jagd', with its sinister chromatic undertow, is effective and there is much homely lyricism elsewhere. Although the *Keltic* Sonata urges us on with instructions such as 'with tragic pathos', the music is overwhelmed by Grieg's influence and by too many tub-thumping, inflated gestures. Overall, Barbagallo is more persuasive in intimacy than in brilliance. However, he is unfailingly warm-hearted in his approach.

Sir John McEwen

British 1868-1948

Hymn on the Morning of Christ's Nativity.
Janice Watson *sop*
Brighton Festival Chorus; London Philharmonic Orchestra / Alasdair Mitchell.
Chandos CHAN9669 (60 minutes: DDD). Text included. Recorded 1997.   Ⓕ

Here is comfort for composers who feel (as probably most do) that they have been neglected in their lifetime. Fifty years after his death, a major work is edited, performed and recorded, and the name of John Blackwood McEwen is heard again in the land. Written over a long period (from 1901 to 1905), we are told, it is 'major' in scope and length. The 11 movements and their interrelationships are conceived symphonically; the choral and orchestral forces envisaged are quite large, and the idiom is European rather than distinctively British. The opening of the fifth movement ('The shepherds on the lawn') does indeed strike a pastoral note, so that one thinks momentarily of the English 'pastoral' school; but it passes and settles into something much more opulent, with suggestions of the Russian ballet. The inspired verses beginning 'Ring out, ye crystal spheres' are set with a certain panoply of splendour but without rejoicing. And in the quiet conclusion to the whole work, McEwen takes rather abrupt leave as though too promptly accepting the hint in Milton's 'Time is our tedious song should here have ending.' Brought back to life by a good performance, it has life in it. Chorus and orchestra work with conviction, Janice Watson sings with freshness and clarity, and Alasdair Mitchell can justifiably feel that he has done his fellow countryman good service. And Chandos has gained another première recording to its credit.

Guillaume de Machaut

French *c*1300-1377

Messe de Nostre Dame. Je ne cesse de prier (Lai 'de la fonteinne'). Ma fin est mon commencement.
Hilliard Ensemble / Paul Hillier.
Hyperion CDA66358 (54 minutes: DDD). Texts and translations included.   Ⓕ

Machaut's *Messe de Nostre Dame* is the earliest known setting of the Ordinary Mass by a single composer. Paul Hillier avoids a full reconstruction: his deference to 'authenticity' restricts itself to the usage of fourteenth-century French pronunciation of the Latin. His ensemble sings two to a part, with prominent countertenors. It is arguable whether the musicians sing the chant at too fast a tempo but they are smooth and flexible and the performance as a whole is fluid and light in texture. Also included are two French compositions. The wonderful *Lai 'de la fonteinne'* is admirably sung by three tenors and is pure delight – food for the heart as well as the intellect. The more familiar *Ma fin est mon commencement,* with its retrograde canon, completes this admirable disc.

Tant doucement me sens emprisonnes. Comment puet on. De Fortune. Mors sui se je ne vous voy. Se quanque amours. Je ne cuit pas qu'onques. Liement me deport. Je puis trop bien. Certes mon oueil. En amer a douce vie. Hé dame de valour. Une vipere. Ma fin est mon commencement. De toutes flours.
Orlando Consort (Robert Harre-Jones *counterten* Charles Daniels, Angus Smith *tens* Donald Greig *bar*).
Archiv Produktion 457 618-2AH (78 minutes: DDD). Texts and translations included. Recorded 1997.   Ⓕ

This is unique: a disc devoted entirely to Machaut's songs, all performed with voices alone. Only the texted line in the manuscripts is sung with text; the rest are vocalized. While this has been the accepted orthodoxy in many circles for some years, nobody has previously quite had the courage to do it for an entire 78 minutes. It works very well, not least because the sheer skill of the Orlando Consort leaves one speechless: everything is immaculately tuned, balanced and phrased; the music is flawlessly edited; absolutely nothing seems to impede the flow of the music. What some listeners may feel is that the texts are not quite sufficiently projected. Particularly in the four-voice pieces you need to listen carefully to distinguish the texted line, which is after all the 'main' voice in any of these songs. But that becomes a lot easier if you follow the texts in the booklet: suddenly the ear can focus on the texted line. And that seems important. The choice of works is also excellent, with an emphasis on pieces that are rarely heard.

Sir Alexander Mackenzie

Mackenzie Scottish Concerto, Op. 55.
Tovey Piano Concerto in A major, Op. 15.
Steven Osborne *pf*
BBC Scottish Symphony Orchestra / Martyn Brabbins.
Hyperion CDA67023 (62 minutes: DDD). Recorded 1998.   Ⓕ

From the horns' call-to-arms at the outset to the irrepressible merrymaking of the closing pages, Edinburgh-born Sir Alexander Mackenzie's *Scottish Concerto* (1897) spells firm enjoyment, and it is astonishing that it is only here receiving its first recording. Cast in three movements, each of which employs a traditional Scottish melody, it is a thoroughly endearing, beautifully crafted work which wears its native colours without any hint of stale cliché or cloying sentimentality; indeed, the canny wit, genuine freshness and fertile imagination with which Mackenzie treats his material are evident throughout. By contrast, Edinburgh-based Sir Donald Tovey's Piano Concerto (1903) exhibits a rather more formal demeanour, its three movements brimful of youthful ambition and possessing a very Brahmsian solidity and dignity. Certainly, there's plenty to admire in the imposing, lucidly structured first movement, which boasts a development section of impressive emotional scope and satisfying rigour. Tovey's idiomatically assured writing is not always entirely untouched by a certain academic earnestness, but on the whole any unwanted stuffiness is deftly kept at bay. In fact, repeated hearings only strengthens one's admiration for this work. No praise can be too high for Steven Osborne's contribution, while the excellent Martyn Brabbins draws a splendidly stylish and alert response from his fine BBC group. Sound and balance are excellent too.

James MacMillan

Cello Concerto[a]. The World's Ransoming[b].
[b]**Christine Pendrill** *cor ang* [a]**Raphael Wallfisch** *vc*
BBC Scottish Symphony Orchestra / Osmo Vänskä.
BIS CD989 (61 minutes: DDD). Recorded 1997.   Ⓕ

Symphony, 'Vigil'.
Fine Arts Brass Ensemble; BBC Scottish Symphony Orchestra / Osmo Vänskä.
BIS CD990 (49 minutes: DDD). Recorded 1997.   Ⓕ

The three works on these two CDs comprise James MacMillian's Easter triptych *Triduum* (1996-97) – a believer's response to the biblical story of Christ's betrayal, crucifixion and resurrection. This is Passion music at the opposite extreme from the austere choral rituals of an Arvo Pärt, and music far more directly engaged with the European symphonic tradition than any of Messiaen's large-scale treatments of sacred themes. MacMillan does not shy away from the melodramatic, building his extended structures around tensions that, at their most powerful, bring very different types of music into opposition. There are places in all three of these compositions where MacMillan seems to run the risk of making his quotations or parodies of chants and chorales rather more memorable than the more personal material alongside them; you need to be in tune with his spiritual objectives and convictions to appreciate fully the musical processes at work. If you are, then this Easter triptych is undoubtedly an absorbing as well as an ambitious enterprise.

The World's Ransoming is a single-movement concert piece for cor anglais and orchestra, its prevailing tone of meditative lament moving beyond the purely liturgical associations of an extended chant line towards a musical drama in which the lament is subject to bombastic assaults from generically opposed materials. The BIS recording of this is excellent in the way the solo line, played with exemplary control and sensitivity by Christine Pendrill, survives the batterings aimed at it by the spacious orchestral textures. In the Cello Concerto, which continues the drama of conflict between a suffering individual and an oppressive society on a much larger scale, Raphael Wallfisch has a harder time in asserting a suitably charismatic presence, and might have benefited from a slightly more forward placement. As it is, MacMillan's imaginative orchestral writing threatens to get the best of the purely musical argument: yet it is still difficult not to be moved by the sense of a struggling protagonist, condemned and tortured. The 48-minute Symphony which completes the triptych sets itself the task of moving from images of suffering and death to those of rebirth and transcendent affirmation. Its structure, with two preliminary movements lasting around 22 minutes and a grand finale running for 26, leads you to wonder whether the last movement on its own might not have performed the formal and expressive task required. Or you could argue that all three movements are needed to provide an adequate balance to *The World's Ransoming* and the Cello Concerto together. Any early verdict on a work as substantial and wide-ranging as this is bound to be provisional. The performances and recordings are exemplary.

The Berserking[a]. Sowetan Spring[b]. Britannia[b]. Sinfonietta[b].
[a]**Peter Donohoe** *pf*
Royal Scottish National Orchestra / [a]Markus Stenz, [b]James MacMillan.
RCA Victor Red Seal 09026 68328-2 (77 minutes: DDD). Recorded 1995.　　　　Ⓕ

Today's New Music scene is said to be pluralistic: everything is permitted; style is no longer a moral issue. But that supposedly 'pluralistic' scene is still full of people pursuing narrowly exclusive paths. Few composers have been brave enough to attempt a synthesis – Robin Holloway is one noble exception, and James MacMillan is another. Sometimes MacMillan's style-contrasts do take on a moral/political dimension, as in *Britannia*, in which Celtic modality and folk-elements and a moment of radiant protest are submitted to crude onslaughts from drunken versions of *Knees up Mother Brown*, *God save the Queen* and a yobbishly strutting version of the first theme from Elgar's *Cockaigne*, complete with off-beat duck-calls. The militaristic violence at the heart of *Sinfonietta* derives in part from an Ulster Loyalist song, *The Sash*.

MacMillan is a Catholic who can sympathize with the American Indian victims of Catholicism, a Scot who can make an entire piano concerto – *The Berserking* – out of the notion of 'the Scots' seeming facility for shooting themselves in the foot'. His folksiness is not without irony, even when it can seem to offer a haven of peace after a great deal of 'misdirected' energy. Charles Ives is clearly one of MacMillan's synthesizer-heroes. In fact there are moments in *Britannia* that actually sound like Ives. That's one of the reasons why, for all his devout intentions, MacMillan never degenerates into the invention-starved mood-manipulation of the so-called Holy Minimalists. MacMillan is at his least absorbing when he is at his most apparently single-minded, as in the hocketting-dominated *Sowetan Spring* – an impressive technical exercise but perhaps focused a little too narrowly. It is strikingly well performed though, as are all the other works on this disc, and beautifully recorded too.

The Confession of Isobel Gowdie. Tryst.
BBC Scottish Symphony Orchestra / Jerzy Maksymiuk.
Koch Schwann 310502 (54 minutes: DDD). *Gramophone* Award Winner 1993.　　　　Ⓕ

This time the publicity doesn't exaggerate. The première of *The Confession of Isobel Gowdie* at the 1990 Proms was a 'spectacular triumph' – nothing less – and this with an audience drawn largely (one presumes) by Beethoven's Fourth Symphony and Sibelius's Violin Concerto. But success can fade with alarming rapidity. What matters now is that several years later, away from the uplift of that extraordinary reception, *The Confession of Isobel Gowdie* tells its story as stirringly as ever. If MacMillan's programme (the martyrdom of a Scottish Catholic 'witch') seems overpictorial, no problem; the progression from rapt modal string threnody (complete with keening *glissandos*) through mounting violence to the re-emergence and transformation of the modal lament is as easy to follow as the 'narrative' of a Mahler symphony – and the after-effect isn't all that dissimilar. Others may be bothered by undisguised echoes of other composers: Copland, Messiaen, Stravinsky, Ives, the famous single-note *crescendo* from Berg's *Wozzeck* … but the fact that they are undisguised is part of their strength – that and the way they are so obviously drawn into the argument. Of course the quality of the performance matters, and Maksymiuk and his orchestra give the kind of penetrating performance which (usually) only comes from long involvement. *Tryst* also emerges well: the forces may be smaller, but the head-on confrontation of violence with calmer, more humane sounds again generates a compelling musical drama, and the ending, though less spectacular than Isobel Gowdie's final one-tone immolation, works both as an imaginative conclusion and a challenge to go back and dig deeper. Away with caution! Give this a try.

Leevi Madetoja

The Ostrobothnians[a].
Jorma Hynninen *bar* Jussi Harri; **Ritva-Liisa Korhonen** *sop* Liisa; **Raimo Sirkiä** *ten* Antti Hanka;
Monica Groop *mez* Maija; **Ritva Auvinen** *sop* Kaisa; **Pertti Mäkelä** *ten* Salttu;
Aki Alamikkotervo *ten* Kaapo; **Antti Suhonen** *bass* Sheriff;
Esa Ruuttunen *bar* Karjanmaa's Köysti; **Jaakko Hietikko** *bass* Erkki Harri;
La Stelle di Domani; Finnish Radio Chamber Choir.
The Ostrobothnians – Suite, Op. 52[b].
Finnish Radio Symphony Orchestra / Jukka-Pekka Saraste.
Finlandia 3984-21440-2 (two discs: 142 minutes: DDD). Notes, text and translation included.
Recorded live in [a]1997, [b]1993.   Ⓜ

Madetoja belongs to the generation born in the shadow of Sibelius, whose pupil he briefly was.
The Ostrobothnians, based on a folk play by Artturi Järviluoma, was originally intended for another
Sibelius pupil, Toivo Kuula, who was killed during the Finnish civil war. Madetoja's opera, which
draws on folk material from his native Ostrobothnia, dates from 1923 and can lay claim to being
the Finnish national opera. The play struck particularly sympathetic resonances in Finland when it
was first performed in 1914 since it is set against the background of an alien oppression of a
peasant community. The hero, Jussi (Jorma Hynninen), befriends a prisoner on bail for a stabbing,
and defies the tyrannical sheriff. When the prisoner escapes, Jussi is accused of helping him and the
opera culminates in his death and that of his tormentor. It had already notched up over 200
performances by the 1960s and has been staged elsewhere in Scandinavia. If the thematic substance
is folk-derived, the scoring and the dramatic development are well managed. Madetoja knew his
craft, and the opera works well. Hynninen's voice has lost none of its vocal presence or tonal bloom
though it was naturally fresher in his youth, while Monica Groop's Maija and Ritva-Liisa
Korhonen are both excellent. Saraste brings a firm grip to the musical and dramatic flow.
The Ostrobothnians is not a long work, and its three acts run for only a fraction over two hours.
The fill-up is a recording of the short Suite of some 16 minutes that Madetoja made in 1928.

Albéric Magnard

Symphonies – No. 1 in C minor, Op. 4. No. 2 in E major, Op. 6.
BBC Scottish Symphony Orchestra / Jean-Yves Ossonce.
Hyperion CDA67030 (67 minutes: DDD). Recorded 1997.   Ⓕ

Symphonies – No. 3 in B flat minor, Op. 11. No. 4 in C sharp minor, Op. 21.
BBC Scottish Symphony Orchestra / Jean-Yves Ossonce.
Hyperion CDA67040 (73 minutes: DDD). Recorded 1997.   Ⓕ

The name of Albéric Magnard began to impinge on the record public only 30 years ago, and there
have been recordings of three of his symphonies, the opera *Guercoeur*, and a five-disc set of his
chamber music and songs; but he seems doomed to be a composer whose music (highly praised by
several contemporaries) survives only via the gramophone: his impact on the concert life of this
country has been virtually nil, and he has not been much better served in his native France. Not
that he would have cared overmuch: during his life (brought to an abrupt end at the start of the
First World War by German invaders who set fire to his country house) he made little attempt to
get his music performed, being paranoically sensitive to any suspicion of nepotistic influence, as his
father was a powerful newspaper proprietor. By all accounts he was a withdrawn and austere
person, and perhaps in keeping with that image his music is not for the casual listener who looks for
facile attractiveness, but in a somewhat Teutonic way is rewarding for the serious-minded in its
skilfully crafted and thoughtfully lyrical character.

The First Symphony (1890) shows the unmistakable influence of Wagner in the *religioso* slow
movement. Despite the adoption of the cyclic principle championed by his teacher Vincent d'Indy,
under whose watchful eye the work was written and who must have smiled approvingly at his pupil's
fluent contrapuntal technique, Magnard's proliferation of ideas threatens structural continuity,
especially in the first movement. In contrast to that movement's initial brooding atmosphere, the
Second Symphony begins more sunnily and spiritedly (but with a spacious second-subject
paragraph), and the following *Scherzo* (which replaced an earlier fugue) is a bucolic 'Danses' tinged
with introspection. The emotional core of the symphony is the luxuriant *Chant varié*, and the work
ends in an almost light-hearted mood. The Third Symphony's striking organum-like opening leads
to an *Allegro* by turns vigorous and contemplative. Next comes a *Scherzo* headed 'Danses' (as in the
previous symphony), a mocking soufflé with a wistful central section – an altogether captivating
movement that is anything but austere. The movingly tense slow movement's long lines are

subverted by menacing outbursts that build to a stormy climax before subsiding; and there is a finale which combines exuberance and lyricism with a return to the symphony's very first theme. This is certainly the work to recommend to newcomers to Magnard. Several years elapsed before his last symphony in 1913, and by then his overall mood had darkened. The turbulent passion that characterizes the first movement, presented in dramatically colourful orchestration, is also mirrored in the finale: between them come a highly individual *Scherzo* with strange oriental-type passages and a lengthy, anguished slow movement. The BBC Scottish Symphony Orchestra is on splendid form throughout and has been recorded in exemplary fashion.

Gustav Mahler

Austrian 1860-1911

Symphonies – No. 1 in D major; No. 2 in C minor, 'Resurrection'; No. 3 in D minor; No. 4 in G major; No. 5 in C sharp minor; No. 6 in A minor; No. 7 in E minor; No. 8 in E flat major, 'Symphony of a Thousand'; No. 9 in D major; No. 10 in F sharp minor.

Symphonies – No. 1[a]; No. 2[b] (with **Cheryl Studer** *sop* **Waltraud Meier** *mez* **Arnold Schoenberg Choir**); No. 3[b] (**Jessye Norman** *sop* **Vienna Boys' Choir; Vienna State Opera Chorus**);
No. 4[b] (**Frederica von Stade** *mez*); No. 5[a] (**E**); Nos. 6[c] and 7[c];
No. 8[a] (**Studer, Sylvia McNair, Andrea Rost** *sops* **Anne Sofie von Otter** *mez*
Rosemarie Lang *contr* **Peter Seiffert** *ten* **Bryn Terfel** *bass-bar* **Jan-Hendrik Rootering** *bass*
Tölz Boys' Choir; Berlin Radio Chorus; Prague Philharmonic Chorus);
Nos. 9[b] and 10[b] – Adagio.
[a]**Berlin Philharmonic Orchestra**; [b]**Vienna Philharmonic Orchestra**;
[c]**Chicago Symphony Orchestra / Claudio Abbado.**
DG 447 023-2GX12 (12 discs: 718 minutes: ADD/DDD). Texts and translations included.
Recorded 1977-94. Ⓜ **RR**

The current pre-eminence of Gustav Mahler in the concert hall and on disc is not something that could have been anticipated – other than by the composer himself. Hard now to believe that his revival had to wait until the centenary celebrations of his birth in 1960. And yet by 1980 he was more widely esteemed than his longer-lived contemporaries Sibelius and Strauss and could suddenly be seen to tower over twentieth-century music much as Beethoven must have done in a previous age. (Not that he hadn't been there all along: the music of Berg, Shostakovich, Britten and even Copland bears witness to this, disparately but resonantly Mahlerian.) By this time too, a new generation of conductors had come to the fore, further transforming our perceptions of the composer. Claudio Abbado is arguably the most distinguished of this group and, while his interpretations will not satisfy every listener on every occasion, they make an excellent choice for the library shelves, when the price is reasonably competitive and the performances so emblematic (and arguably central to our understanding) of Mahler's place in contemporary musical life.

Of the alternatives, Haitink's package has the fewest expressive distortions while Bernstein's is of course the most ceaselessly emotive of them all; neither has Abbado's particular combination of qualities. It is probably no accident that Donald Mitchell's notes for this set are focused on the nature of Mahler's 'modernity'. For it is that ironic, inquisitive, preternaturally aware young composer who haunts this conductor's performances. Not for Abbado the heavy, saturated textures of nineteenth-century romanticism, nor the chilly rigidity of some of his own 'modernist' peers. Instead an unaffected warmth and elegance of sound allows everything to come through naturally – in so far as the different venues and DG's somewhat variable technology will permit – even in the most searingly intense of climaxes. Increasingly these days, Abbado is presenting Mahler as a fluent classicist, less concerned to characterize the surface battle of conflicting emotions than to elucidate the underlying symphonic structure. The lack of Solti's brand of forthright theatricality can bring a feeling of disappointment. But even where he underplays the drama of the moment, sufficient sense of urgency is sustained by a combination of well-judged tempos, marvellously graduated dynamics and precisely balanced, ceaselessly changing textures. The propulsion comes from within. For those still put off by Mahler's supposed vulgarity the unhurried classicism of these readings may well be the most convincing demonstration of the composer's absolute integrity.

It was in November 1907 that Mahler famously told Sibelius that 'the symphony must be like the world. It must embrace everything.' And perhaps it is only today that we see this as a strength rather than a weakness in his music. He wrote music that is 'about' its own past while at the same time probing into all our futures, music that is so all-embracing and communicates with such directness that we can make it 'mean' whatever we want it to, confident that we alone have really understood the code. Abbado lacks Bernstein's desire to explore these limitless possibilities every time he mounts the podium, but some will count that a blessing. These are committed and authoritative performances.

New York Philharmonic – The Mahler Broadcasts 1948-82.
^a**New York Philharmonic Orchestra,** ^b**Philharmonic Symphony Orchestra of New York /**
^c**Sir John Barbirolli,** ^d**Pierre Boulez,** ^e**Rafael Kubelík,** ^f**Zubin Mehta,** ^g**Dimitri Mitropoulos,**
^h**Sir Georg Solti,** ⁱ**William Steinberg,** ^j**Leopold Stokowski,** ^k**Klaus Tennstedt,** ^l**Bruno Walter.**
New York Philharmonic mono/^mstereo NYP9801/12 (12 discs: 903 minutes: ADD). Also contains
interviews and reminiscences about Mahler. Available at $225 (plus postage and packing) at
selected Tower Records stores or by mail order; in North America call (toll free) 1-800-557-8268;
worldwide 1-317-781-1861; e-mail www.newyorkphilharmonic.org.   Ⓕ ⊞
Symphonies – No. 1 (recorded live in 1959)^{ac}; No. 2 (**Kathleen Battle** *sop* **Maureen Forrester**
contr **Westminster Choir;** rec. 1982)^{afm}; No. 3 (**Yvonne Minton** *mez* **Camerata Singers; Little
Church around the Corner Boys' Choir; Trinity Church Boys' Choir; Brooklyn Boys' Choir**
rec. 1976)^{adm}; No. 4 (**Irmgard Seefried** *sop* rec. 1962)^{ah}; No. 5 (rec. 1980)^{akm}; No. 6
(rec. 1955)^{ag}; No. 7 (rec. 1981)^{ae}; No. 8 (**Frances Yeend, Uta Graf, Camilla Williams** *sops*
Martha Lipton, Louise Bernhardt *contrs* **Eugene Conley** *ten* **Carlos Alexander** *bar*
George London *bass-bar* **Schola Cantorum; Public School No. 12 Boys' Choir, Manhattan;**
rec. 1950)^{bj}; No. 9 (rec. 1962)^{ac}; No. 10 – Adagio; Purgatorio (rec. 1960 and 1958)^{ag}. Lieder eines
fahrenden Gesellen (**Dietrich Fischer-Dieskau** *bar* rec. 1964)^{ai}. Das Lied von der Erde
(**Kathleen Ferrier** *contr* **Set Svanholm** *ten* rec. 1948)^{bl}.

Not your average collection of Mahler symphonies, but one which, with pride, charts in words and
music, the impact of the composer's final two years (1909-11) in and on New York and the
important part the city's orchestra subsequently played in spreading the Mahler message. One might
argue that Walter and Mitropoulos would have pioneered and propagated Mahler performance in
New York even if the composer had never set foot in the place. But if you have the Mahler
connection, and the tradition, then why not make it work for you? That is what the orchestra has
done here, and the result, though highly priced, has the potential for being equally highly prized by
Mahler historians and dedicated collectors alike (English speaking ones, as there are no translations
of the many valuable features in the booklets' 500-odd pages). One of the booklets contains a list of
all the NYPO's Mahler performances since 1904, pin-pointing the broadcasts where tapes 'are
known to exist', and it is from these tapes that this compilation was chosen.

In making the choices, consideration was given to the New York players' own views and memories
of the concerts or conductors (printed in the booklet); and to featuring symphonies from
conductors who never took them into the studio (Barbirolli in the First, Mitropoulos in the Sixth
and Tenth, Stokowski in the Eighth). Bernstein is conspicuous by his absence, but it would seem
that rights are not currently available for the release of his Mahler broadcast tapes. We hear,
though, from the man whose Mahler was Bernstein's model; and Mitropoulos's 1960 Sixth
Symphony must have been a hard act for Bernstein to follow. Follow it Bernstein did, with an
equally powerful but more personal New York Sixth (from 1967, now on Sony Classical), yet
Mitropoulos delivers the symphony's integrity and unpalatable truths with a grim and arguably
more compelling single-mindedness. Apart from the slow movement (placed second, and gloriously
played), there is little relief from the symphony's burdened, battering march to tragedy. Latterly
interpreters have also been more protean in the Eighth's expansive Faust fantasy, and it would be
idle to pretend that other conductors don't make more than Stokowski of the contrasts explicitly
indicated in Mahler's score (angels that dance as well as sing, 'freed from earthly stress'). Stokowski
in 1950 opted for an unusually moderate range of tempos (starting with a swift *Andante*), and it is
impossible to say whether he was playing safe, attempting to dignify the folksy inspiration, or
bringing us something of the manner in which Mahler himself conducted the work (Stokowski was
present at the Eighth's Munich world première in 1910). Whatever the case, along the way there are
as many attractions (especially the string playing) as there are inevitable insecurities, and it is worth
hearing and pondering, not least for the First Part of the symphony, which bears the unmistakable
stamp of greatness (of conception, execution and occasion), and the sound is a marvel for its years.

The earliest recording here is a vital, controlled and incisive 1948 *Das Lied von der Erde* from
Walter, with Kathleen Ferrier making her American début. Set Svanholm tends to press ahead of
the beat, but it is a rare pleasure to hear the tenor songs as resolutely conquered and characterized.
As for Ferrier's contribution, there is little to choose between this and her famous 1952 Decca
Vienna account made with a more relaxed Walter. The later recording perhaps presents the richer
portrait of a unique vocal phenomenon, and a cathartic release of emotion in the final pages not
matched in New York (where the manner is closer to the score's indication of something a little
more serene and understated). Aptly enough for this enterprise, applause has been retained at the
end of the works, even if, in the case of *Das Lied*, one wishes that the audience had waited a few
seconds longer. But audience noise during the music can be frustrating. Time may well be standing
still at the start of Barbirolli's 1959 First Symphony, but the audience is still finding its way to the
seats, and letting loose coughs often enough for some of them to blot out Mahler's birdcalls.
Matters improve, possibly because, as one of the concert's critical notices informs us, only part of

the audience stayed to the end. And the part that did was witness to some engaging features, such as the pronounced, and for the time, deeply unfashionable string *portamentos* (even Stokowski, in his Eighth, opts for discreet slides), and a *Scherzo* with big boots and rustic charm laid on by the barrow-load. The *Scherzo* of Barbirolli's 1962 New York Ninth Symphony is of a consistently coarser cut than his 1964 Berlin studio recording for EMI, and arguably benefits from it, though there is little evidence for the booklet's general assessment of the Berlin Ninth as 'rather disengaged from the work's churning emotions'. And the brightly analytical (and stereo) Berlin recording does allow clearer perception of the details of – future archival revelations apart – Barbirolli's finest taped Mahler symphony interpretation. Solti's Fourth Symphony (also 1962), as we know from his two Decca studio recordings, was unexpectedly graceful and genial, with a long-breathed slow movement, and admirable discipline and refinement, even if that refinement streamlines the work's bolder colours and sardonic edge.

All the New York recordings enjoy good balances; those already mentioned are all in very decent, if occasionally pale, mono sound. The stereo tapings aren't ideally flattering to New York's violins, but benefit from a wider dynamic range (especially the Boulez Third Symphony). For a live recording, the deployment of the various on- and off-stage forces in Mehta's 1982 Second is a major achievement. This was a special occasion for all involved (the orchestra's 10,000th concert), and although Mehta's is neither a particularly lofty nor radical view of the work, the excitement in the hall (as one musician explains in the booklet, 'the players turning each other on') has transferred to disc admirably. The pleasures of Boulez's 1976 performance of the Third Symphony include a typical (and often very sensuous) cultivation of inner workings, concern for outer structure, very precisely graded dynamics, and a strikingly individual rubato (the opening of the finale's hymn, a mesmerizing example). Rarely has the sudden tumult and its immediate aftermath at the end of the third movement – proclamatory brass receding over shimmering strings – cast such a spell. Never mind the horns' tremors in their hushed upper reaches here: as this performance progresses, you gradually become aware of a real time context and continuity almost impossible to create in the studio. Tennstedt had the ability, at the moment of performance, to persuade listeners that the music could and should sound no other way, and his 1980 New York Fifth Symphony runs the full gamut of 'no tomorrow' intensity, intervention, riotous colour and perfectly formed details.

In contrast, the years between Kubelík's Bavarian Radio Seventh (recorded for DG in 1970) and this 1981 New York account appear to have prompted a radical rethink. Or maybe Kubelík is responding to the extra heft of the New York orchestra and ephemeral concert conditions to push out the boundaries. Still recognizable, if moderated, are the sharp features and deliberately soured tone lending menace to both the second and third movements, and an *Andante amoroso* cajoled into a diversion of wonderfully graceful, fresh-voiced charm. But the much broader manner maximizes the far-flung sonorities, in the first movement, at the expense of line and general decorum. You may react differently, particularly if you agree with criticisms of Kubelík's Munich Mahler as lightweight. We mentioned pride at the beginning of this review, and from the general level of playing in this set, it is entirely justified. Naturally there are fluffs, early entries and an occasional rubato prompting untidiness, but the vast majority demonstrates a level of professionalism and innate ability to produce the right sort of sound at the right time that have made and maintained the orchestra as one of the world's ideal Mahler instruments. As to the two-hour-long sequence of audio interviews by William Malloch, 'I Remember Mahler' (New York players' first-hand experiences under Mahler, recorded in the early 1960s), these undoubtedly benefit from editing (which is how they have been presented in the past, on LP as well as CD), but their complete presentation here corresponds with the comprehensive nature of the project, and allows a few more anecdotes currency as cherishable Mahler memorabilia. So, a Mahler marathon with a difference.

Symphonies – Nos. 1 and 2 (**Elly Ameling** *sop* **Aafje Heynis** *contr* **Netherlands Radio Chorus**); No. 3 (**Maureen Forrester** *contr* **St Willibrord Church Boys' Choir; Netherlands Radio Chorus**); No. 4 (**Ameling**); Nos. 5-8 (**Ileana Cotrubas, Heather Harper, Hanneke van Bork** *sops* **Birgit Finnila** *mez* **Marianne Dieleman** *contr* **William Cochran** *ten* **Hermann Prey** *bar* **Hans Sotin** *bass* **St Willibrord and Pius X Children's Choir; Collegium Musicum Amstelodamense; Amsterdam Toonkunst Choir; Amsterdam Stem des Volks Choir**); No. 10 – Adagio.**Concertgebouw Orchestra / Bernard Haitink.**
Philips Bernard Haitink Symphony Edition 442 050-2PB10 (ten discs: 692 minutes: ADD). Recorded 1962-71. Ⓜ

If space is at a premium, this set is undeniably attractive, though the multilingual illustrated booklet dispenses with texts and translations and several symphonies are awkwardly spread between discs. For a generation of record buyers it was these sane, lucid, sometimes (as it now seems) insufficiently demonstrative Concertgebouw readings that represented a way into music previously considered unacceptable in polite society. Haitink's phrasing has an appealing natural simplicity, his rhythmic almost-squareness providing welcome reassurance. The preoccupation with conventional symphonic verities of form and structure does not preclude striking beauty of sound and the recordings have come up well in the remastering. There is some residual hiss. Haitink's early No. 1 (1962), his first taping of a Mahler symphony, is usually reckoned the least satisfactory of his career. Not that it is without interest for the Concertgebouw's reedy woodwinds and vibrato-laden trumpets lend specific character and charm to what is otherwise a comparatively featureless reading. True, the third movement doesn't quite work: Haitink's attempts at 'Jewishness' are so self-conscious that the results sound rhythmically suspect, not quite together rather than convincingly ethnic. The real problem is the boxed-in sound, uncharacteristically rough-and-ready with none of the cool tonal lustre which characterized subsequent LPs from this source.

The Fourth receives a similarly straightforward account with a wonderfully hushed *Poco adagio* and few if any of the aggressive mannerisms which have marred more recent versions. The restraint can border on inflexibility at times. The first movement lacks a certain element of fantasy with everything so very accurate and together, and, while Elly Ameling makes a lovely sound in the finale, the orchestra's animal caricatures are not really vulgar enough, the sense of wonder and awe in the face of heaven rather muted at the close. Though inevitably lacking the gut-wrenching theatricality and hallucinatory colour of Bernstein, the Seventh has none of the staidness and rigidity that occasionally prompts doubts about Haitink's Mahlerian credentials. Now accommodated on a single CD, it emerges as a high point of the series, second only to the celebrated Ninth. The opening is deceptively cool and brooding; thereafter the interpretation is unexpectedly driven and intense, even if Mahler's fantastical sonorities are left to fend for themselves rather than being thrust into the foreground. Only those who feel the nth degree of nightmarish 'exaggeration' to be vital to the expression of the whole need have any doubts. The finale is effectively held together but it should perhaps sound more hollow than this.

To sum up: if you must have the Mahler symphonies under a single conductor, Haitink could arguably be the man to go for. His objectivity will not spoil you for alternative readings. Nevertheless you would not want to miss out on Bernstein, unrelenting in his desire to communicate the essentials of these scores, taking his cue from Mahler's remark that 'the symphony must be like the world. It must be all-embracing'. Haitink is more circumspect, the music's vaunting ambition knowingly undersold.

Symphony No. 1. Lieder eines fahrenden Gesellen.
Dietrich Fischer-Dieskau *bar*
Bavarian Radio Symphony Orchestra / Rafael Kubelík.
DG The Originals 449 735-2GOR (67 minutes: ADD). Text and translation included.
Recorded 1967.   Ⓜ🆁🆁

Rafael Kubelík is essentially a poetic conductor and he gets more poetry out of this symphony than almost any other conductor who has recorded it. Although he takes the repeat of the first movement's short exposition, it is strange that he should ignore the single repeat sign in the *Ländler* when he seems so at ease with the music. Notwithstanding a fondness for generally brisk tempos in Mahler, Kubelík is never afraid of rubato here, above all in his very personally inflected account of the slow movement. This remains a delight. The finale now seems sonically a little thin, with the trumpets made to sound rather hard-pressed and the final climax failing to open out as it can in more modern recordings. The orchestral contribution is very good even if absolute precision isn't guaranteed. Dietrich Fischer-Dieskau's second recording of the *Lieder eines fahrenden Gesellen* has worn rather less well, the spontaneous ardour of his earlier performance (with Furtwängler and the Philharmonia – now reissued on EMI) here tending to stiffen into melodrama and mannerism. There is of course much beautiful singing and he is most attentively accompanied, but the third song, 'Ich hab' ein glühend Messer', is implausibly overwrought, bordering on self-parody. By contrast, Kubelík's unpretentious, Bohemian approach to the symphony remains perfectly valid. A corrective to the grander visions of those who conduct the music with the benefit of hindsight and the advantages of digital technology? Perhaps.

Mahler Symphony No. 1.
Berg (orch. Verbey) Piano Sonata, Op. 1.
Royal Concertgebouw Orchestra / Riccardo Chailly.
Decca 448 813-2DH (70 minutes: DDD). Recorded 1995.   Ⓔ🅱

Chailly gives us a straightforward symphonic overview in which the more overtly programmatic elements are never allowed to threaten the work's structural integrity. Lest it be thought that this implies 'worthy but dull', two things give this performance a very special appeal: the quality of the orchestral playing and the scrupulous attention paid to phrasing and dynamics. The first movement is particularly fresh. How often do we get a genuine *ppp* from the horns before the *cantabile* melody of the cellos and the active part of the development. No doubt the two middle movements will be too emotionally reticent for some: that second movement hardly evokes a peasants' merrymaking, while the third is purged of rusticity, its more bizarre and hysterical elements reduced to a series of incidental if novel orchestral effects. And yet, where a lesser orchestra might have sounded plain, the Royal Concertgebouw imbues the music with real character. The ending goes very well, the horns correctly prominent, the all-too-common percussive thwack on the final crotchet conscientiously eschewed. Chailly's enterprising coupling is much more convincing than you might suppose and much more relevant than another *Blumine*. The recording quality is excellent.

Symphony No. 1.
Chicago Symphony Orchestra / Pierre Boulez.
DG 459 610-2GH (53 minutes: DDD). Recorded 1998.   Ⓕ

Pierre Boulez's Mahler will always be controversial, but here he turns in a fresh and finely detailed account of No. 1 with little to alarm even those temperamentally opposed to his 'objective' approach. It helps that Boulez has been conducting in Chicago for over 30 years, and these players certainly know the idiom. Thanks to DG's analytical recording and Boulez's own close focus, the massive Chicago sonority is less oppressive than usual: woodwinds are bright and characterful and even the obstreperous Chicago brass acquires greater civility, keeping something in reserve for the big moments. Boulez's introduction sets the tone – not as hushed as some yet beautifully articulate, clean and firm. The second movement is faster than the norm, the Ländler very vigorous and lively, the Trio presenting less contrast than usual. Boulez is preoccupied with achieving finely detailed textures at the expense of Hungarian-Jewish swing and there could be more intense nostalgia in the lyric central episode which here seems redolent of the salon. While the finale erupts with exemplary (controlled) attack, Boulez takes care to clarify textures, giving us the inner lines often overlooked. And so Boulez's admirers will not hesitate. For Boulez, the emotional impact of such music may be less important than its texture, orchestration and musical architecture, but, for the wider emotional palate, one can always turn to other interpretations. Boulez has other priorities and in this work there is room for many versions.

Symphony No. 1.
Concertgebouw Orchestra / Leonard Bernstein.
DG 427 303-2GH (56 minutes: DDD). Recorded live in 1987.   Ⓕ

Bernstein's basic view of the First Symphony underwent very little change over the years. How acutely he hears Mahler's early-morning silence. The rising sixth for two oboes in bar 15 is like a deep intake of breath from this rapt observer; the richly harmonized horns some bars later are truly *espressivo*, their dreamy reverie broken only by the sudden *ff* pizzicatos (like a startled animal) which Bernstein points up so vividly a bar later. You will love, too, the way in which the chiming harp really tells as we move into the uneasy middle section (pity about the thump in the orchestra at this point): the chilling entry of tuba and bass drum at fig. 13 casts an appropriately long and ominous shadow across the proceedings. All this is most beautifully and subtly chronicled by the Concertgebouw players. How warmly and generously their strings phrase the wayfarer's music: it takes a great Mahler orchestra and a great Mahler conductor to imply so much suppleness and freedom within the bar without actually labouring the rubato. Their exhilaration in the coda (the euphoric explosion of brass fanfares is hair-raising) is second to none, and again it is the way in which the phrasing spontaneously sings that proves so uplifting. Needless to say, Bernstein gilds the proverbial lily somewhat in the Trio: 'Viennese' isn't the word, and he obviously believes (and why not?) that Mahler simply felt it unnecessary to mark in all the *portamento* – the opening violin phrases being one case in point. There has never been an account of the finale like this one. Masterly control and abandon (such as could only happen in a live performance) go hand in hand: the ferocious onslaught of the opening pages, the touch of rhetoric in the brass declamations of bars 6 and 19, the intense energy in the strings. And then, in repose, the lovingly attended second subject where Bernstein's light and shade in phrasing and dynamics is uniquely affecting. And so on to the tumultuous conclusion. Impressively recorded, this is an almost impossible act to follow.

Symphony No. 2.
Arleen Auger *sop* **Dame Janet Baker** *mez*
City of Birmingham Symphony Chorus and Orchestra / Sir Simon Rattle.
EMI CDS7 47962-8 (two discs: 86 minutes: DDD). Text and translation included. Recorded 1986.
Gramophone Award Winner 1988.   Ⓕ 🆁🆁

Where Simon Rattle's interpretation is concerned, we must go into the realm of a giant Mahlerian like Klemperer. For we are dealing here with conducting akin to genius, with insights and instincts that cannot be measured with any old yardstick. Rattle's sense of drama, of apocalyptic events, is so strong that at the final chords one is awed. None of this could have been achieved, of course, without the CBSO, which here emerges as an orchestra of world class. With such supple and rich string-playing, such expressive woodwind and infallibly accurate and mellow-toned brass, could anyone, coming upon this recording unawares, be blamed for identifying these players as belonging to Vienna, Berlin or Chicago? Attention to dynamics is meticulous throughout and contributes immeasurably to the splendour of the performance. A double *pianissimo* is really that, so when triple *forte* comes along its impact is tremendous. Some of the outstanding features of the performance can be pinpointed: the haunting beauty of the *portamento* horn-playing and the strings' sensitive and perfectly graded *glissandos* at fig. 23; the magical entry of flute and harps just after fig. 3 in the second movement (and, incidentally, the two harps really sound like two throughout, which is rarer than one might think); and the frightening eruption of the two *fortissimo* drum notes just after fig. 51 in the same movement. Then, in the finale, there are the superb woodwind trills, the sense of mounting terror at fig. 8. Dame Janet Baker is at her most tender in 'Urlicht', with Arleen Auger as the soul of purity in the finale. The CBSO Chorus is magnificent, indeed the whole finale, its off-stage brass and echoes beautifully balanced, is an acoustic triumph. This in a spiritual class of its own, a Mahlerian testament. The recording is superb.

Symphony No. 2.
Cheryl Studer *sop* **Waltraud Meier** *mez*
Arnold Schoenberg Choir; Vienna Philharmonic Orchestra / Claudio Abbado.
DG 439 953-2GH2 (two discs: 87 minutes: DDD). Recorded live in 1992. ⓕ 🅂

A live performance should have a headstart in tapping the vital component of spiritual uplift. Abbado presents the score directly with the maximum clarity and precision. In this he is assisted by playing of astounding accuracy and beauty of tone, captured in a recording of (impractically?) wide dynamic range and exquisite detail. Abbado's funeral march is relatively contained, the quiet passages very atmospheric. The deft, restrained manner works well enough in the inner movements, especially the *Andante moderato*. He launches into the third movement *Scherzo* with the audience restive (elsewhere they are pleasingly inaudible); there follows charm but perhaps insufficient sense of threat. The 'Urlicht' is again on the cool side, though Waltraud Meier, beautifully controlling her *legato* while conscientiously projecting to a real public in a large hall, is suddenly impassioned at 'Ich bin von Gott'. The massive finale, conceived here on the very grandest scale, goes well but not quite well enough: the choir is backwardly balanced and, more seriously, there are some agogic touches which impede the natural flow. However, as a document of a great occasion, this set stands up very well indeed.

Symphony No. 3.
Norma Procter *contr* **Wandsworth School Boys' Choir; Ambrosian Singers;**
London Symphony Orchestra / Jascha Horenstein.
Unicorn-Kanchana Souvenir UKCD2006/7 (two discs: 97 minutes: ADD).
Text and translation included. Recorded 1970. Ⓜ 🆁🆁

Every now and again, along comes a Mahler *performance* that no serious collector can afford to be without. Horenstein's interpretation of the Third Symphony is an outstanding example and its reissue on CD at mid-price is a major addition to the Mahler discography. No other conductor has surpassed Horenstein in his total grasp of every facet of the enormous score. Even though the LSO strings of the day were not as powerful as they later became, they play with suppleness and a really tense sound, especially appropriate in the kaleidoscopic first movement, where changes of tempo and mood reflect the ever-changing face of nature. Horenstein gives the posthorn solo to a flügelhorn, a successful experiment. His light touch in the middle movements is admirable, and Norma Procter is a steady soloist in 'O Mensch! Gib acht!', with the Wandsworth School Boys' Choir bimm-bamming as if they were all Austrian-born! Then comes the *Adagio* finale, its intensity and ecstasy sustained by Horenstein without dragging. The recording is not as rich as more recent ones, but it is still a classic.

Symphony No. 3. Four Rückert Lieder. Seven Lieder und Gesänge aus der Jugendzeit.
Martha Lipton *mez* **Dietrich Fischer-Dieskau** *bar*
women's chorus of the **Schola Cantorum; Boys' Choir of the Transfiguration;**
New York Philharmonic Orchestra / Leonard Bernstein *pf*
Sony Classical SM2K47576 (two discs: 142 minutes: ADD). Recorded 1962. Ⓜ

Few who experienced Bernstein's passionate advocacy of Mahler's musical cause in the 1960s were left untouched by it. These recordings date from those years – years when Bernstein's concert and recordings did so much to put Mahler back centre-stage – and the flame of inspiration still burns brightly about them almost 40 years later. The CBS recordings were clearly manipulated, but the sound – at best, big and open but trenchant and analytically clear – suited Mahler's sound world particularly well. Bernstein's account of the Third Symphony is as compelling an experience and as desirable a general recommendation now as it was when it first appeared. The New Yorkers are on scintillating form under the conductor they have most obviously revered in the post-war period. This is a classic account, by any standards. The two-disc set has over 140 minutes of music on it, thanks to the inclusion of recordings by Fischer-Dieskau and Bernstein of 11 Mahler songs. Bernstein himself is a subtle and self-effacing pianist. Fischer-Dieskau scales the musical heights in several of the *Rückert* Lieder but is prone to exaggeration in the less surely written *Jugendzeit* Lieder.

Symphony No. 4[a]. Lieder eines fahrenden Gesellen[b].
[a]**Judith Raskin** *sop* [b]**Frederica von Stade** *mez*
[a]**Cleveland Orchestra / George Szell;** [b]**London Philharmonic Orchestra / Sir Andrew Davis.**
Sony Classical Essential Classics SBK46535 (75 minutes: ADD/DDD). Recorded 1966.　　Ⓑ 🎵🎵

Collectors who waited for years in anticipation of the reappearance on CD of Szell's famous Cleveland Fourth Symphony will not be disappointed. Sony Classical has come through with a pristine digital remastering of the open and exceptionally well-balanced Columbia original. Some hardening of tone under pressure was always a problem, even on LP, but on the whole you would never credit that this was a 1960s recording. As to the performance, the assurance and precision of its execution is something quite remarkable – an orchestra in the very peak of condition: ensemble absolutely unanimous, rubato finely turned to a man, not a blemish in earshot. There is no better tribute to Szell's achievements in Cleveland. Some people have found it dispassionate and calculated in effect and would willingly sacrifice some of the precision for a greater sense of spontaneity at the moment of performance (Szell was always at his best in the concert hall). That's a very subjective reaction, of course, and the cool, pellucid beauty of Szell's Cleveland strings in the slow movement is beyond dispute. The *Lieder eines fahrenden Gesellen* are strong and characterful readings which will give much pleasure. They sound fresh and alert, with tone colouring beautifully controlled.

Symphony No. 4.
Kathleen Battle *sop* **Vienna Philharmonic Orchestra / Lorin Maazel.**
Sony Classical SMK39072 (61 minues: DDD). Recorded 1983.　　Ⓜ

Kathleen Battle sings the symphony's rapt coda in a consciously intimate manner which might roughly be dubbed the 'Listen with Mother' style. By that, no offence is intended. Maazel's version is throughout a very inward-looking one, and in saying that we merely point to the fact that it is a very, very Viennese performance; in Vienna, Mahler's Vienna or Maazel's introspection is an unavoidable condition of being. What's more, only in Vienna will you hear string and, in its special way, wind playing such as is provided here for Maazel in the long-drawn slow movement – it is simply 22-and-a-half minutes of unadulterated pleasure. Maazel has always conducted the symphony's first movement in a relaxed, springy, Bruno Walter-ish way. Away from the score, the ear that is innocent of Mahler's many abstruse changes of tempo may think them rather artificial; but the playing of the VPO is such that one listens, hypnotized. It is difficult not to be tempted by the general ease, introspection and near-morbid nostalgia of the Maazel. Shocking, no doubt: but an indulgence which is very Viennese, very *fin de siècle*. The sound, as you would expect of a recording made in Vienna's Musikvereinsaal, is very satisfying.

Symphony No. 4.
Helmut Wittek *treb* **Concertgebouw Orchestra / Leonard Bernstein.**
DG 423 607-2GH (57 minutes: DDD). Text and translation included. Recorded live in 1987.　　Ⓕ

Occasionally a conductor casts shrewdly a voice able to re-create 'without parody', Mahler's instruction, the feel of this fresh-faced, fresh-voiced, Catholic country boy who is so excited by the prospect in heaven of St Luke slaying whole oxen. Bernstein here uses a remarkably assured chorister from the famous Tölzer Boys' Choir, Helmut Wittek. He is a fearless vocalist with a generally clean top register and a bottom B that puts most of his soprano rivals out of court. He rather yodels the second bar of his solo and skimps the fermata at fig. 14 where he is allowed by an indulgent great-uncle Lenny to toboggan his way spectacularly down to that bottom B. Elsewhere, showing a healthy boyish disregard for pernickety shadings of tone and rhythm, he concentrates on giving a fresh, extrovert, musically confident account of the Wunderhorn verses helped by good diction and some nice word-painting. 'Who have you cast for the soprano solo?' asked Mahler in 1904. 'She must be capable of singing with a naive, childlike expression, and with particularly good diction!' Wittek has both, and the engineers, possibly fearing some lack of presence in his boyish tones, have recorded him fairly prominently where sopranos often have to put up with balances that give them little more than solo instrumental status. As a result, the text is communicated with unusual clarity on this recording. Throughout the finale Bernstein's tempos are uniformly sensible, nearer to Mahler's own, if transcripts of the 1905 Welte Piano Roll are to be trusted, than the rather slower, creamily beautiful Maazel version with Kathleen Battle on CBS. Of course, no orchestra plays Mahler's Fourth better than the Concertgebouw. For simple cogency and grainy clarity of utterance it has no equal, and yet, unlike the Vienna Philharmonic, it doesn't impose its reading on the conductor. This is recognizably Bernstein's own newly-refined but intensely vivid reading. The performance of the slow movement is a special joy, not least because it is touching and profound without being unduly slow. So while you mull over the various alternatives, let us commend to you this original, ungimmicky, musically searching performance as a worthy addendum to any Mahler collection.

Symphony No. 4.
Angela Maria Blasi *sop* **Bavarian Radio Symphony Orchestra / Sir Colin Davis.**
RCA Red Seal 09026 62521-2 (61 minutes: DDD). Text and translation included.
Recorded 1993. Ⓕ

Sir Colin Davis's Fourth is enormously enjoyable. Maybe his Mahler is too restless, too blatantly 'conducted' for some tastes, but that is at least symptomatic of a desire to communicate a personal vision of, and affection for, Mahler's score. Both playing and recording are of exceptional standard, even if the lack of ironic edge to the sound lends the music-making a somewhat old-fashioned air. Davis's *Scherzo* is warm and characterful in a rather cumbersome sort of way, but his slow movement is a marvel – elevated in feeling and blessedly free of the intrusive inflexions which mar an otherwise refreshing account of the opening movement. After this, the finale disappoints just a little. The 'operatic' soloist does not really point her words with sufficient poignancy – nor does she seem willing or able to sing quietly in her upper register – and Sir Colin again insists on playing up the composer's expressive hesitations, adding one or two of his own. This may not be wholly idiomatic Mahler and yet it has abundant humanity and an extraordinary lack of artifice. The sympathetic acoustic of the Herkulessaal, well caught, is a great asset.

Symphony No. 4.
Amanda Roocroft *sop* **City of Birmingham Symphony Orchestra / Sir Simon Rattle.**
EMI CDC5 56563-2 (59 minutes: DDD). Recorded 1997. ⒻⓈ

Rattle springs two big surprises in the first four bars. The first tempo might initially strike you as *over*cautious, but check Mahler's score, and note the words: *Bedächtig – Nicht eilen* ('Cautious; prudent – don't hurry'). In keeping with the accepted view among seasoned Mahlerians that the *poco ritard* in the third bar does not apply to the sleigh bells, Rattle then effects a fleeting moment of disarray as the bells jangle roughshod over this elegant turn into the first theme. A gauche, childlike moment. But then comes the real surprise. The tempo for this charming theme-with-airs (marked *gemächlich* – 'leisurely') is faster, not slower, than the opening tempo. Leisurely, yes, but eager too. The adventure playground of Mahler's youth is up and running. The benefits of this become plainer as the movement unfolds. The second subject sounds completely new (the CBSO cellos manage to persuade us that they've only just discovered it). The first horn is youth's magic horn, the woodwinds beckon raucously. And all the while those startling swings of mood and manner just happen – no rhyme, no reason; just a child's fancy. But beware the bogeyman fiddler. His dance of death – all the sharper, all the more sour (remember he's tuned up a tone) for being so flatly dispatched – comes as a timely reminder that childhood fears are no less real for being the stuff of fairy-tales. Rattle contrasts this beautifully with the rubicund Trio. The transfiguration at its heart, swathed in woozy *portamento*, is simply gorgeous. So, too, the opening of the slow movement, the cellos' legato so fine as to suggest little or no contact with the strings. Rattle's reading is perhaps the most inquisitive (and thus the most intriguing) of recommendable versions.

Symphony No. 4[a]. Lieder eines fahrenden Gesellen[b]. Lieder aus Des Knaben Wunderhorn[c] – Wer hat dies Liedlein erdacht?; Das irdische Leben.
[c]**Elly Ameling,** [a]**Joan Carlyle** *sops* [b]**Anna Reynolds** *mez*
[a]**London Symphony Orchestra;** [bc]**English Chamber Orchestra / Benjamin Britten.**
BBC Music Legends Britten the Performer [a]mono/stereo BBCB8004-2 (75 minutes: ADD).
Item marked [a] recorded live in 1961, [b]1969, [c]1972. ⓂⒽ

This will whet the appetite of even the non-specialist collector! The Fourth had a special place in Britten's affections. Howard Ferguson took him to a Henry Wood Prom performance in 1930 and he heard it subsequently under no less a Mahlerian than Willem Mengelberg. Britten himself did not record nearly enough of other people's music, and the present collection gives us an invaluable opportunity to hear him in repertoire that profoundly influenced his own approach to composition. After a conventionally languorous treatment of the opening bars, Britten darts ahead – bright-eyed and confident throughout a spring-like exposition. The players are momentarily taken aback, but we are soon on firmer ground. This is the eager, lean-sounding LSO familiar from Decca recordings of the period, and, with Britten's help, it is exceptionally alert to dynamic shadings. The brisk, overtly neo-classical manner is very effective in this movement. Britten is well aware of the disquiet at its heart even as he eschews the usual expressive lumps and bumps in the interests of formal cogency. Aptly pungent, the second movement is again chamber-like and transparent, the third as deeply felt as any on disc. Only the boisterous and youthful characterization of the finale is a bit too much of a good thing, banishing the sublime and bringing us dangerously close to caricature. The soloist is not ideal (too operatic) and she anticipates the cue for her last entry. Warmly recommended all the same. The couplings are both apt and generous.

Symphony No. 5.
New Philharmonia Orchestra / Sir John Barbirolli.
EMI CDM5 66910-2 (74 minutes: ADD). Recorded 1969.   Ⓜ 🆁🆁

Sir John Barbirolli's Fifth occupies a special place in everybody's affections: a performance so big in spirit and warm of heart as to silence any rational discussion of its shortcomings. Some readers may have problems with one or two of his sturdier tempos. He doesn't make life easy for his orchestra in the treacherous second movement, while the exultant finale, though suitably bracing, arguably needs more of a spring in its heels. But against all this, one must weigh a unity and strength of purpose, an entirely idiomatic response to instrumental colour and texture (the dark, craggy hues of the first two movements are especially striking); and most important of all that very special Barbirollian radiance, humanity – call it what you will. One point of interest for collectors – on the original LP, among minor orchestral mishaps in the *Scherzo*, were four bars of missing horn obbligato (at nine bars before fig. 20). Not any more! The original solo horn player, Nicholas Busch, has returned to the scene of this momentary aberration (Watford Town Hall) and the absent bars have been ingeniously reinstated. There's even a timely grunt from Sir John, as if in approval. Something of a classic, then; EMI's remastering is splendid.

Symphony No. 5.
Royal Philharmonic Orchestra / Daniele Gatti.
Conifer Classics 75605 51318-2 (70 minutes: DDD). Recorded 1997.   Ⓕ 🅴

Don't let the very opening put you off. Daniele Gatti's Mahler is an expertly prepared eruption of youthful enthusiasm, a display of heart-on-sleeve lyricism. He takes his cue from Mahler's injunction that the upbeat triplets of the trumpet theme should be played somewhat hurriedly, in the manner of military fanfares, and throughout the movement he is wont to place the material in inverted commas. In the subsequent movements, no one is likely to confuse Gatti's flexible rubato with mere mannerism. The wide dynamic range is impressive but subtlety of inflexion is the conductor's trump card. So while the second movement is an almost frantic and at times formidably loud *tour de force*, the famous *Adagietto* is uncommonly slow and sensitive. For the most part, too, Gatti coaxes a properly middle-European sound out of his wind and brass, and, if the RPO's strings cannot yet match those of Vienna, Berlin or Amsterdam, their sound is surprisingly full and rich. Indeed, the musicians sound so grandly confident that the few lapses seem worse than they are. The finale is again thrillingly extrovert, quite without heaviness. In short, this is something of a triumph for all concerned. The production team makes the very best of London's Henry Wood Hall. Above all, Gatti deserves high praise for what must be counted the freshest, most natural-sounding Fifth we have had for a long time.

Symphony No. 5.
Vienna Philharmonic Orchestra / Leonard Bernstein.
DG 423 608-2GH (75 minutes: DDD). Recorded live in 1987.   Ⓕ

Bernstein's tempo for the Funeral march in the first movement of the Fifth Symphony became slower in the 23 years that separated his New York CBS recording from this one, made during a performance in Frankfurt. The strings only passage at fig. 15 in the first movement is exquisitely played, so is the long horn solo in the *Scherzo*. And there is one marvellously exciting moment – the right gleam of trumpet tone at one bar before fig. 29 in the second movement. Best of all is Bernstein himself, here at his exciting best, giving demonic edge to the music where it is appropriate and building the symphony inexorably to its final triumph. Thanks to a very clear and well-balanced recording, every subtlety of scoring, especially some of the lower strings' counterpoint, comes through as the conductor intended. One is made aware of the daring novelty of much of the orchestration, of how advanced it must have sounded in the early years of this century. Here we get the structure, the sound and the emotion. The *Adagietto* is not dragged out, and the scrupulous attention to Mahler's dynamics allows the silken sound of the Vienna strings to be heard to captivating advantage, with the harp well recorded too. Bernstein is strongest in Mahler when the work itself is one of the more optimistic symphonies with less temptation for him to add a few degrees more of *Angst*.

Symphony No. 5.
Berlin Philharmonic Orchestra / Claudio Abbado.
DG 437 789-2GH (69 minutes: DDD). Recorded live in 1993.   Ⓕ

The *Adagietto* is suddenly, almost imperceptibly, there. It is the hallmark of any great performance of the symphony, and Abbado is in amongst the very select few as these magical bars materialize. It might even be the most beautiful, the most subtly inflected account of the movement we have yet heard on disc. How spontaneously the restless heart leaps with Mahler's central diversion; the breathless *pianopianissimo* to a barely grazed *glissando* towards the close is out of this world. So too the huge central *Scherzo*, another of those testing movements separating natural Mahlerians from the would-bes. The key here is patience – respect for space, silence, atmosphere. And the charm. Not even Bernstein quite matches Abbado's relish of the finale's airborne fantasy (how commonly this movement is driven to distraction): it's that delicate balance between tip-toeing sweetness and light and inherently rugged, foot-stomping good humour. Abbado takes an appreciably more dispassionate view of the first movement than Bernstein (doesn't everybody?). Abbado steps back from the tragedy, his funeral march determined to keep up appearances, maintain dignity, the voice (so to speak) cracking only under the stress of Mahler's accentuation. There's a suitably rash development and a splendidly morbid military wind band sound when the march returns centre-stage. Bernstein is at his most wilfully exciting in the second movement. And fine though Abbado is, no one peaks at the climax – the shining trumpet-led premonition of the finale's chorale – quite like Bernstein. Both are special performances (nothing less could challenge the supremacy of Bernstein), both conductors and both orchestras right inside the spirit and sound of this score.

Symphony No. 6. Kindertotenlieder.
Thomas Hampson *bar* **Vienna Philharmonic Orchestra / Leonard Bernstein.**
DG 427 697-2GH2 (two discs: 115 minutes: DDD). Recorded live in 1988.   Ⓕ 🇷🇷

Mahler's tragic Sixth Symphony digs more profoundly into the nature of man and Fate than any of his earlier works, closing in desolation, a beat on the bass drum, a coffin lid closing. Bernstein's reading was at a concert, with all the electricity of such an occasion, and the VPO responds to the conductor's dark vision of Mahler's score with tremendous bravura. Fortunately, the achingly tender slow movement brings some relief, but with the enormous finale lasting over 30 minutes we must witness a resumption of a battle to the death. The coupling is a logical one, for the *Kindertotenlieder* takes up the theme of death yet again. But it is in a totally different, quieter way: these beautiful songs express a parent's grief over the loss of a child, and although some prefer a woman's voice, the sensitive Thomas Hampson makes a good case here for a male singer. The recording of both works is so good that one would not know it was made 'live', particularly as the applause is omitted.

Symphonies Nos. 6 and 7.
London Philharmonic Orchestra / Klaus Tennstedt.
EMI CDS5 55294-2 (three discs: 180 minutes: DDD). Recorded live in 1991 and 1993.   Ⓕ

In spite of the difficulties, Klaus Tennstedt always thrived on the tensions of live performance. Here the conductor is at his most single-minded in music that always brought out the best in him. Not that the results will be to all tastes. This is not all-embracing, world-view Mahler. The sight-lines are too limited for that, the outlook sometimes constrictingly bleak. Despite Tennstedt's inspirational approach there is a lack of tonal variety and the London Philharmonic can sound penny plain for all the dour strength of the brass. This is partly because the conductor is indifferent to the finer points of stylization. You won't find Bernstein's flexibility and emotional range: Tennstedt's rubato, similarly extreme, has a coarser grain and is intended neither to console nor to play up Mahler's sticky Viennese lyricism. What Tennstedt brings to these scores is an aura of integrity and a fierce intensity of expression finally unencumbered by the technical flaws that have sometimes detracted from his achievement. In both works, EMI has obtained good results from the tapes given the acoustic attributes of the venue. The Sixth is the more impressive of the two readings, executed with splenetic zeal at broader tempos than Tennstedt at one time favoured in this music. The Seventh sounds a little less confident. The main body of the movement has the grittily determined demeanour of the Sixth, its second section most obviously emotive, dripping with rubato. In music so reliant on colour and texture there isn't really enough gradation of dynamic: the more sparsely orchestrated passages sound insufficiently hushed and the sluggish alpine reveries offer no refuge from anxious monochrome. The rest of the performance is not uninteresting – the central *Scherzo* incisive, the second *Nachtmusik* carefully prepared and notable for the dusky veiled tone of the strings, the vigorous finale solid rather than crisp. And yet, in attempting to push home every nuance, Tennstedt could in the end be destroying what it is he is trying to create, rocking the boat so much that forward momentum is lost. If you take the Seventh to be an inherently contradictory search for an unrealized ideal of expression, you might find Tennstedt's disruptive manner just the ticket – he never seems quite sure which way to turn. Go elsewhere if you want the music to make more conventional sense. What we have here are two expertly captured performances by a Mahlerian with a singular vision – ungainly and uncomfortable perhaps, but unforgettable.

Symphonies Nos. 6[a] and 8[b].
[b]**Erna Spoorenberg**, [b]**Dame Gwyneth Jones**, [b]**Gwenyth Annear** *sops* [b]**Anna Reynolds** *mez* [b]**Norma Procter** *contr* [b]**John Mitchinson** *ten* [b]**Vladimir Ruzdjak** *bar* [b]**Sir Donald McIntyre** *bass-bar* [b]**Leeds Festival Chorus**; [b]**London Symphony Chorus**; [b]**Orpington Junior Singers**; [b]**Highgate School Choir**; [b]**Finchley Children's Music Group**; [a]**New York Philharmonic Orchestra**; [b]**London Symphony Chorus and Orchestra / Leonard Bernstein.**
Sony Classical Bernstein Royal Edition SM3K47581 (three discs: 157 minutes: ADD). Recorded 1966-67.   Ⓜ

Mahler's Sixth has been the combined object of more lavish praise and contemptuous condemnation than any of the others. It does seem at times the greatest of them all, in its severe formal control of an almost uncontrollable content over such a large span. On the one hand, the work stands as Mahler's most torrential outpouring of naked human feeling, reaching an almost unbearable culmination in the finale's half-hour all-or-nothing battle between hope and despair; yet at the same time it represents his most sustained feat of structural concentration. Or at least it does in a great interpretation. From a recording point of view, this is superlative. As regards the interpretation, it is, as always with this conductor, totally committed and intensely emotional. The slow movement and the finale are unquestionably superb but it is harder to come to terms with the first two movements. The matter of personal reaction features large here, since everything really hinges on the question of the tempo of these two movements, and this is, after all, a matter of individual taste. Both movements are weighty affairs and with Bernstein they are full of neurotic ferocity. The essential character of this material seems to be dogged and sullen, rising to ferocity here and there, certainly, and yet somehow nobly tragic at the same time. Bernstein's quick march tempo cannot accommodate all these feelings, and we are left with ferocity only. However, as stated above, the rest of the interpretation is beyond criticism. The idyllic *Andante moderato* is taken very slowly, and Bernstein's sensitivity to every slight change of atmosphere, spontaneous here, without exaggeration – reveals it as the wonderfully far-ranging movement is really is. As for the vast finale, this is as thrilling a Mahler performance as ever committed to disc. The sheer length of the movement, and the consequent necessity of preserving coherence, justifies a fairly lively march tempo, and here Bernstein does keep it sufficiently steady to accommodate the broadly flowing *alla breve* sections; he builds up the movement into one great moving sweep of sound, in which every contrasting mood still gets its full treatment.

Symphony No. 7.
City of Birmingham Symphony Orchestra / Sir Simon Rattle.
EMI CDC7 54344-2 (77 minutes: DDD). Recorded live in 1991.   ⒻⓇⓇ

You may wonder about the choice of venue – The Maltings, Snape: a great sounding hall – one of the most natural and focused in the world – but for Mahler? Well, there are times here where the hefty tuttis of the outer movements sound fit to burst at the seams. The tonal quality is first-class, the immediacy is to some extent exciting; one can see right into the phantasmagorical scoring of the inner movements – a clear, gently ambient sound serving both intimacy and atmosphere. Last things first. The finale is for once a sensation. From the quasi-baroque splendour of the opening procession right through to a coda which truly flings wide its glorious excess (outreaching trumpets, horns and celestial cowbells), the adrenalin really pumps. Rattle pulls off a mad kind of coherence, a wholeheartedly vulgar apotheosis of Viennese dance with no apologies made for Mahler's seemingly irrational changes of gear and direction. Even the most unruly transitions (and this movement is almost entirely transitional) are met head-on with ferocious energy (the only way), episodes falling over each other in the jostling for centre-stage. The characterization is acute, the colours wonderfully garish (just listen to the squally clarinet trills at 2'48" – hair-raising). Mahler was not one to mince his notes, and neither is Rattle.

Not even Bernstein is as uncompromising in the *Scherzo*. The nightmare comes quickly into focus: the shrieking *glissando* on two clarinets at 00'28" is at once surreal, a flash of grinning skull behind the face. Rapier violin *sforzandos* claw the texture, an emaciated string bass slithers from behind a bellowing tuba, the contra-bassoon grunts and snorts, the strings really relish their grotesque waltz. The dynamic extremes are vicious. Rattle is unique in making it sound thus. On either side of these grisly goings on, the two *Nachtmusiks* could hardly be more beguiling. Poetic sonorities abound. Only the first movement slightly disappoints. Structurally, sonically, it is impressive – organic and elemental. The CBSO violins really are right inside that second subject and as harps draw back the veil on Mahler's central idyll, they could hardly sing more sweetly. But whilst Rattle pulls off the somewhat corny recapitulation with aplomb, there isn't the almost euphoric release that one experiences with Bernstein. But trombones proudly take command in the coda and the first trumpet's fearless ascent to his high-stopped *f* into Tempo 1 brings a genuine tingle of excitement. Few orchestras play the score this well; few conductors have explored it so exhaustively. Against these considerations, any reservations count for little.

Symphony No. 7.
New York Philharmonic Orchestra / Leonard Bernstein.
DG 419 211-2GH2 (two discs: 80 minutes). Recorded live in 1985.　　　　　Ⓕ

Bernstein's version of the Seventh is recorded here in the way he preferred – an amalgam of two or more public performances, though not a sound comes from the audience. The Seventh has always suited Bernstein's volatile way with Mahler. There is a case to be made that it is the most adventurous and progressive of the symphonies, that in it, certainly in the first movement, Mahler came nearest to crossing the sound-barrier into atonalism and that he drew back in the extrovert, Meistersinger-ish Rondo-finale and even further back in No. 8. So it answers well to a conductor who takes it to the limits, revels in its daring risks, and somehow holds it all together. This Bernstein triumphantly does. Such quintessential Mahlerian passages as the soft string chords followed by the violin solo preceding fig. 33 in the first movement, are Bernstein at his most persuasive and the playing is sumptuous. The flickering terrors of the third movement have only been so potently conveyed on record by Abbado, though for a single most exuberant and disarming performance of the Rondo the Bernstein is out on its own. The sound is alarmingly vivid – spare a thought for your neighbours if you play the finale at full blast.

Symphony No. 7.
New York Philharmonic Orchestra / Leonard Bernstein.
Sony Classical Bernstein Century Edition SMK60564 (80 minutes: ADD). Recorded 1965.　　Ⓜ🅷

We are often assured that great conductors of an earlier generation interpreted Mahler from within the Austrian tradition, encoding a sense of nostalgia, decay and incipient tragedy as distinct from the in-your-face calamities and neuroses proposed by Leonard Bernstein. Well, this is one Bernstein recording that should convince all but the most determined sceptics. It deserves a place in anyone's collection now that it has been transferred to a single disc at mid-price. The white-hot communicative power is most obvious in the finale which has never sounded more convincing than it does here; the only mildly questionable aspect of the reading is the second *Nachtmusik*, too languid for some. The transfer is satisfactory, albeit dimmer than one might have hoped, distinctly unspectacular. It sounds historic, but historic in more ways than one.

Symphony No. 8.
Heather Harper, Lucia Popp, Arleen Auger *sops* **Yvonne Minton** *mez* **Helen Watts** *contr*
René Kollo *ten* **John Shirley-Quirk** *bar* **Martti Talvela** *bass*
Vienna Boys' Choir; Vienna State Opera Chorus; Vienna Singverein;
Chicago Symphony Orchestra / Sir Georg Solti.
Decca 460 972-2DM (80 minutes: ADD). Text and translation included. Recorded 1971.　　Ⓜ🆁🆁

Of the so-called classic accounts of the Eighth Symphony, it is Solti's which most conscientiously sets out to convey an impression of large forces in a big performance space, this despite the obvious resort to compression and other forms of gerrymandering. Whatever the inconsistencies of Decca's multi-miking and overdubbing, the overall effect remains powerful even today. The remastering has not eradicated all trace of distortion at the very end, despite some cautious clipping of levels and, given the impressive flood of choral tone at the start of the 'Veni creator spiritus', it still seems a shame that the soloists and the Chicago brass are quite so prominent in its closing stages. As for the performance itself, Solti's extrovert way with Part 1 works tremendously without quite erasing memories of Bernstein's ecstatic fervour. In Part 2, it may be the patient Wagnerian mysticism of Tennstedt that sticks in the mind. Less inclined to delay, Solti makes the material sound more operatic. And yet for its combination of gut-wrenching theatricality and great solo singing, Solti's version makes a plausible first choice – now more than ever. Also, it has been squeezed onto a single CD, albeit at premium price.

Symphony No. 8.
Elizabeth Connell, Edith Wiens, Dame Felicity Lott *sops* **Trudeliese Schmidt,**
Nadine Denize *contrs* **Richard Versalle** *ten* **Jorma Hynninen** *bar* **Hans Sotin** *bass*
Tiffin Boys' School Choir; London Philharmonic Choir and Orchestra / Klaus Tennstedt.
EMI CDS7 47625-8 (two discs: 82 minutes: DDD). Notes, text and translation included.
Recorded 1986. *Gramophone* Award Winner 1987. Ⓕ Ⓢ

Mahler's extravagantly monumental Eighth Symphony, often known as the *Symphony of a Thousand*, is the work that raises doubts in even his most devoted admirers. Its epic dimensions, staggering vision and sheer profligacy of forces required make it a 'difficult work'. Given a great live performance it will sway even the hardest of hearts; given a performance like Tennstedt's, reproduced with all the advantages of CD, home-listeners, too, can be mightily impressed (and so, given the forces involved, will most of the neighbourhood!) – the sheer volume of sound at the climax is quite overwhelming. The work seeks to parallel the Christian's faith in the power of the Holy Spirit with the redeeming power of love for mankind and Tennstedt's performance leaves no doubt that he believes totally in Mahler's creation. It has a rapt, almost intimate, quality that makes his reading all the more moving. The soloists are excellent and the choruses sing with conviction.

Symphony No. 8.
Joyce Barker, Beryl Hatt, Agnes Giebel *sops* **Kerstin Meyer** *mez* **Helen Watts** *contr*
Kenneth Neate *ten* **Alfred Orda** *bar* **Arnold Van Mill** *bass*
BBC Chorus; BBC Choral Society; Goldsmith's Choral Union; Hampstead Choral Society;
Emanuel School Boys' Choir; Orpington Junior Singers;
London Symphony Orchestra / Jascha Horenstein.
BBC Legends/IMG Artists BBCL4001-7 (two discs: 101 minutes: ADD). Recorded live in 1959.
Includes an interview with Jascha Horenstein by Alan Blyth. Ⓜ Ⓗ

This is the first official release of Jascha Horenstein's celebrated Royal Albert Hall concert of March 20th, 1959. It was a curtain-raiser for the centenary cycle mounted by the BBC at the behest of Robert Simpson. The work had been given before in the UK under Sir Henry Wood and Sir Adrian Boult, but it was the present performance that began the indigenous Mahler boom, transfixing not only the nearly 6,000 enthusiasts who packed the hall but a wider listenership beyond. When Leonard Bernstein came to conduct and record the work in London a few years later, the groundwork had already been laid. Not that Horenstein was a Mahlerian of the modern age. A conductor steeped in the German tradition, he made his début in the 1920s with the Vienna Symphony Orchestra in a programme that included Mahler's First Symphony. He brings to his readings of the composer a weight and certainty that can initially disappoint those accustomed to a more febrile, thrustful approach. In other words, don't be put off by the apparently lukewarm opening, the English choral society coloration of the choirs and the dodgy contribution of the second soprano. The performance quickly finds its feet and acquires its own metaphysical brand of tension. Part 2 is if anything even finer. The orchestral preamble is superbly wrought.

There are some incidental problems – how could there not be in a live account of wholly unfamiliar repertoire? – but these are scarcely worth mentioning when the cumulative power of the final build-up is so immense and the recording expands so impressively, encompassing an authentic blaze of choral sonority. For once the Royal Albert Hall really comes into its own, and, all in all, the transfer is better than one dared hope. The coughers are sometimes intrusive, maddeningly so at the start of Part 2, yet there are aspects of Horenstein's performance that no studio-made version can quite rival. This was his finest hour and happily the two-CD set includes a vintage interview to put the achievement in context; there are also authoritative booklet-notes by Bernard Keeffe.

Symphony No. 9.
Berlin Philharmonic Orchestra / Herbert von Karajan.
DG Karajan Gold 439 024-2GHS2 (two discs: 85 minutes: DDD). Recorded live in 1982.
Gramophone Award Winner 1984. Ⓕ ⓇⓇ

Symphony No. 9. Kindertotenlieder. Five Rückert-Lieder.
Christa Ludwig *mez* **Berlin Philharmonic Orchestra / Herbert von Karajan.**
DG Double 453 040-2GTA2 (two discs: 132 minutes: ADD). Recorded 1979-80.
Gramophone Award Winner 1981. Ⓜ

Mahler's Ninth is a death-haunted work, but is filled, as Bruno Walter remarked, 'with a sanctified feeling of departure'. Rarely has this symphony been shaped with such understanding and played with such selfless virtuosity as it was by Herbert von Karajan and the BPO. Choice between the 1982 Karajan classic and the analogue studio recording is by no means easy. Both versions won *Gramophone* Awards in their day, but, whereas the low-profile, mid-price reissue of the analogue LP has Christa Ludwig's magisterial *Kindertotenlieder* and *Rückert-Lieder*, the live account preserves the look and price bracket of the original package. There is no extra music. The performance remains a remarkable one, with a commitment to lucidity of sound and certainty of line. There is nothing dispassionate about the way the Berlin Philharmonic tears into the *Rondo-Burleske*, the agogic touches of the analogue version ironed out without loss of intensity. True, Karajan does not seek to emulate the passionate immediacy of a Barbirolli or a Bernstein, but in his broadly conceived, gloriously played *Adagio* the sepulchral hush is for once as memorable as the eruptive climax. The finesse of the playing is of course unmatched.

For this Karajan Gold reissue, the tapes have been picked over in order to open up the sound and do something about the early-digital edginess of the strings. There is still some occlusion at climactic points; and if those strings now seem more 'plasticky' than fierce, it is impossible to say whether the conductor would have approved. Karajan came late to Mahler and yet, until the release of his (rather more fiercely recorded) 1982 concert relay, he seemed content to regard his earlier studio performance as perhaps his finest achievement on disc. The attraction is greatly enhanced by Christa Ludwig's carefully considered Mahler performances of the mid-1970s. The voice may not be as fresh as it was when she recorded the songs in the late 1950s, but there are few readings of comparable nobility. Ludwig articulates the text with unrivalled clarity and 'In diesem Wetter' at least is positively operatic. How much of the grand scale should be attributed to Karajan? It is difficult to say; the voice *is* sometimes strained by the tempos. Despite the absence of texts, this collection is not to be missed.

Mahler Symphony No. 9.
R. Strauss Metamorphosen, AV142.
Vienna Philharmonic Orchestra / Sir Simon Rattle.
EMI CDS5 56580-2 (two discs: 108 minutes: DDD). Recorded live in 1993 and 1997.   Ⓟ🅴

This may not be a Mahler Ninth for all seasons and all moods, but how thrilling it is to hear the score projected at white heat! Even if Sir Simon Rattle is less frankly emotive than a Barbirolli or a Bernstein, his is still a performance that goes for broke – fidgety, raw and intense. Listeners exclusively committed to the eloquent lucidity of Karajan should perhaps give it a wide berth. This is at various times the loudest, softest, fastest and slowest Mahler Ninth on disc. There are passages where the nuancing is *echt*-Viennese (with some pronounced string *portamentos*, as towards the very end of the work), others where the music is driven forward harshly and with surprising rigidity. There are big rhetorical effects which threaten to reduce a glorious symphonic canvas to a series of neurotic episodes, others where the power and commitment of the playing take the breath away. Test the waters – if you can – with the first movement. This is overwhelming, edge-of-the-seat stuff, yet ultimately just a little monochrome. Despite the impulsive, agitated approach, the mood of brutal obstinacy is oppressively sustained; there is rather less in the way of nobility and repose. In music that responds equally to the tragic subjectivity of a Bernstein and the elevated sense of eternal calm evoked by Karajan, Rattle continues to press home the attack, conveying rather an unquenched commitment to life. Nor does he seek the kind of linear clarity delivered by Bruno Walter, whose remastered stereo recording is much more revealing than its previous LP incarnations. If in the final analysis, the vehemence of execution is not always allied to the generosity of spirit you find in the great performances of the past, is that any more than a recognition that we live in different times? There is little space to discuss the Strauss, except that there is a sense in which it tells the same story, abandoning the familiar berth of Karajan-inspired smoothness for altogether choppier seas. Rattle's music-making lives in the here and now and the immediacy of the performance – passionate but dry-eyed – is gripping in its own way.

Symphony No. 9.
Philharmonia Orchestra / Benjamin Zander.
Telarc 3CD80527 (three discs: 87 minutes: DDD). Recorded live in 1996.   Ⓜ
Includes bonus disc of talk by Zander, 'On Performing and Listening to Mahler's Symphony No. 9'.

Nothing could be less appropriate to Mahler's last complete symphony than the plush, homogenized sound aspired to by some modern orchestras. Take a look at any page of the score of Mahler's Ninth and you'll see that Mahler seems to have gone to extraordinary lengths to emphasize the individuality of the players – widely contrasting colours, dynamics, expression. But you don't have to look at the score – or even listen to Zander's lovingly detailed recorded talk (included on a separate disc – 'The ideal orchestra for the work would be one composed entirely of great individualists, each with the courage to play what he is given, regardless of what the others are doing.'). Just listen to the opening couple of minutes of this recording. Zander has managed to communicate his idea so completely to the Philharmonia that instead of one sound, we hear countless vivid expressive details – all adding up to one organic, multi-dimensional statement. The most remarkable thing about this performance is the emotional intensity and impetus, though Zander manages to get his message across without stretching tempos or underlining climaxes in red. And few recordings convey such a sense of this huge, diverse symphony as a single statement. And the end is remarkably moving; you will find yourself holding your breath through the long silences. No wonder the Barbican audience responds in silence – a full 47 seconds before the applause begins! A great Mahler Nine? If that's the final critical verdict, don't be a bit surprised.

Mahler Symphony No. 9.
K.A. Hartmann Symphony No. 2, 'Adagio'.
Cleveland Orchestra / Christoph von Dohnányi.
Decca 458 902-2DH2 (two discs: 100 minutes: DDD). Recorded 1997 and 1994.   Ⓕ

Christoph von Dohnányi's reputation for brisk, objectified Mahler is not borne out by this unexpectedly long-breathed and evidently long-pondered reading. In the first movement Dohnányi gives himself plenty of space to articulate the structure and clarify detail, presenting the main ideas with the lyricism (and some of the glacial calm) of Herbert von Karajan's famous recordings. The second movement is more characterful than you might expect, its Ländler theme trippingly light at the outset, the waltz more heftily Teutonic. The conductor's relatively straight approach suits the *Rondo-Burleske* and the more lyrical middle section has greater emotive power than other interpreters have allowed. The *Adagio* receives a fine, mainstream performance that really sings. The Hartmann coupling is both unexpected and welcome; it sat in Decca's vaults since 1994. The performance displays all Dohnányi's lucidity and high seriousness, although Hartmann's folk-like material would be more compelling for some extra give and take in the phrasing. Quibbling apart, Dohnányi deserves credit for such adventurous programming and many readers will be intrigued to come across a neglected figure of the post-Mahlerian generation who wears his musical influences with perverse pride – you can detect Reger, Berg, Hindemith, Stravinsky (*The Rite*) and the Bartók of *Bluebeard's Castle*.

Symphony No. 9.
Berlin Philharmonic Orchestra / Sir John Barbirolli.
EMI Studio CDM7 63115-2 (78 minutes: ADD). Recorded 1964.   Ⓜ

This remastered transfer to CD eloquently supports the views of those who regard it as one of the classic interpretations of this symphony, worthy to be ranked with Walter's and Karajan's. There is an almost imperceptible tape hiss to remind us of the recording's age; otherwise the late Kinloch Anderson's sensitive production wears very well. The rapport between Sir John and the Berliners is obvious in the warmth, flexibility and richness of the playing, with the principal horn in particular playing with moving expressiveness. Barbirolli's shaping of the great first movement, like a broad arch, has all the intensity that one so much admired in his conducting and also a sense of architectural structure for which he did not always receive full credit. The savagery of the *Rondo Burleske* is a feature of this performance with Mahler's scoring sounding years ahead of its time. Barbirolli takes fewer than 23 minutes over the *Adagio*-finale, with the result that the melodic pulse never falters. The string playing here is wonderfully heartfelt.

Symphony No. 9.
Vienna Philharmonic Orchestra / Bruno Walter.
Dutton Laboratories Essential Archive mono CDEA5005 (70 minutes: ADD).
Recorded live in 1938. *Gramophone* Award Winner 1989.   Ⓑ Ⓗ

Of course, there is no such thing as a 'definitive' performance but this is as near as one can get to it. Bruno Walter conducted the first performance of the Ninth Symphony in 1912 (it is dedicated to him) as well as this, its first commercial recording. It bestrode no fewer than ten 78rpm discs and consumed many fibre needles! Although later performances (including Walter's) have offered more polished orchestral playing and more vivid recording, none brings one closer to its world of feeling or takes one more deeply into its spirit. For all its blemishes, it has a unique authority and atmosphere. Its fires are white-hot and there is a blazing intensity that has never been surpassed on the gramophone. There is a demonic passion to the *Rondo-Burlesque* (the orchestra plays as if its corporate life is at stake) and the final *Adagio* has a poignancy that once heard is not easily forgotten. Even younger readers unencumbered by nostalgia will recognize the authenticity of feeling here, and everyone who cares about Mahler is urged to listen to it. Although this has appeared in various manifestations, the superiority in every respect of the present transfer is in no doubt. The image is better defined and has both body and presence.

Symphony No. 10 (ed. Cooke).
Bournemouth Symphony Orchestra / Sir Simon Rattle.
EMI CDC7 54406-2 (76 minutes: DDD). Recorded 1980.   Ⓕ

Rattle's superb interpretation of Cooke's performing version of the Tenth Symphony sweeps the board. His achievement is in a special class, empowering the music with such emotional clout that you forget the scholarly debates. There are in fact several adjustments to Schirmer's published score which Rattle explained in the splendid booklet which accompanied the original LP issue, but which is not included with the CD reissue. One example of his innovatory approach is his merging of the drum stroke which ends the fourth movement with the one which triggers the fifth; furthermore the opening pages of the finale are truly awesome here. Tempos are unfailingly appropriate and the orchestra is second to none. With excellent sound this is altogether an essential purchase.

Das Lied von der Erde.
Dame Janet Baker *mez* **James King** *ten*
Concertgebouw Orchestra / Bernard Haitink.
Philips Silver Line 432 279-2PSL (66 minutes: ADD). Recorded 1975. This is also available on a Philips Duo, coupled with Symphony No. 9: 462 299 2PM2 (two discs: 146 minutes: DDD). Ⓜ 🅁🅁

The honours for first capturing the Baker interpretation of the three great songs which in time-span at least make up three-quarters of *Das Lied von der Erde* went to Philips, with Bernard Haitink adding substantially to his already formidable achievement as a Mahlerian. Though there are elements in the reading – and even the conductor's approach – that for some Mahlerians remain controversial, here is above all a version which in total dedication to Mahler encompasses the widest possible expressive range. Interpretatively, it is remarkable how Haitink draws out the fullest range of expressiveness, while keeping a broadly steady tempo, starting with a gloriously bold and thrusting account of the opening bars. He draws out the middle refrain of 'Dunkel ist das Leben' languorously, and the results are very beautiful indeed, managing at the same time to keep the symphonic structure behind the stanzas sharply in focus. Baker's expressiveness is so rich on every level, in musical imagination and in breadth of tone colour. There are moments when far more than usual one relates these songs from *Das Lied* with the songs of *Des Knaben Wunderhorn* or the *Lieder eines Fahrenden Gesellen*. The grey autumn mists of the second song prompt Baker to an inner, almost murmured half-tone on the difficult opening phrases, and the singer's own identity of mood with nature is total, no ordinary weariness this. Her warmth of tone in 'Von der Schönheit' is open and honest, exactly to match the picture of maidens picking flowers. The climax of the song is strong and precise, never frantic in its *accelerando*, while the final stanza brings a smile to the voice and a new element of sensuousness. Most remarkable of all is the reading of the long final song, 'Der Abschied', where again Baker starts on a whispered half-tone. The great final climax on 'Die liebe Erde' finds Baker and Haitink stretching the *pianissimo* markings almost to extremes. Unfortunately, James King does not quite match the imagination of his accompanists. He tries hard to bring out word meaning in detail, but his range of tone colour is limited. In all three of his songs one wants a more beautiful, more lyric range of tone to set against the fine ring of heroic tone, and for that matter to match Haitink. Even so it is a strong, satisfying rendering of the three songs, which are the more sharply contrasted with the meditative contralto songs. But with ravishingly beautiful recording quality – wonderfully analytical but richly co-ordinated too – and the most compellingly individual reading of the contralto songs ever put on record, matched by Haitink's deeply felt conducting, this disc will remain the universal first choice for this much-recorded work.

Das Lied von der Erde.
Agnes Baltsa *mez* **Klaus König** *ten*
London Philharmonic Orchestra / Klaus Tennstedt.
EMI CDC7 54603-2 (67 minutes: DDD). Text and translation included. Recorded 1982-84.   Ⓕ

This is among the most compelling performances of this oft-recorded work in recent times. That makes it all the more incomprehensible that it languished unissued for some nine years in EMI's vaults before its release, apparently because Tennstedt would not approve its release. If he was dissatisfied with the superlative playing and often inspired singing here, he must have been imagining some ideal rendering in heaven. The contribution of the LPO is, in every respect assured, sensitive and life-enhancing. Inspired by Tennstedt's instinctive feeling for both the structure and texture of the work, it plays with alternating intensity and delicacy throughout. Take the passage in the first song before 'Das Firmament blaut ewig' and you'll hear the rich eloquence of the string playing, the acuity of the wind and the incisiveness of the brass, all caught to perfection in the excellent recording. The tempo is slower than on any other version, but Tennstedt is quite able to sustain the song at his chosen pace, indeed it gives it an added weight and significance. Otherwise his speeds tend to the orthodox. In the fourth song, conductor and players catch perfectly the swaying, caressing music of the beautiful girls and their tresses (track 4), then the tumult at the appearance of the lads, here matching Walter's accentuation of this music (on Decca). The third and fifth songs are done with an exhilarating lift making the sombre, eternal thoughts of the finale that much more of a contrast. Tennstedt is blessed with one of the best tenor soloists on disc. König has the heroic tone and steadiness so many others lack. He isn't as poetic and imaginative as the irreplaceable Patzak (Decca), or as youthfully exuberent as Wunderlich (Klemperer/EMI), but he sings with refreshing ease and an innate feeling for the text, especially in the fifth song where he and Tennstedt precisely catch the hectic mood of the drunkard's fatalism. Baltsa doesn't have the language so idiomatically on her tongue, but in the early 1980s she could sing with a grave beauty and restrained vibrancy that is its own justification, and her weighting of tone and notes in the final song is finely wrought more withdrawn and contained than the more open-hearted Ludwig for Klemperer. Others may still prefer the particular responses to words shown by Ludwig (Klemperer) or Ferrier (Walter) and nothing will ever quite replace the peculiarly taut and authoritative accents of the Walter disc, though this one comes close to the same degree of tension and dedication. The recording is well balanced, spacious and immediate.

Das Lied von der Erde (trans. Schoenberg and Riehn).
Monica Groop *mez* **Jorma Silvasti** *ten*
Lahti Chamber Ensemble / Osmo Vänskä.
BIS CD681 (61 minutes: DDD). Texts and translations included. Recorded 1994. Ⓕ

Osmo Vänskä's reading is nothing short of superb in every respect. A recording of demonstration quality, it lets us hear every strand of the translucent scoring; its range and focus are quite remarkable and the balance ideal. All this displays Vänskä's dedicated interpretation and the finely chiselled playing of his ensemble to the greatest advantage, each individual executing his or her part with the utmost refinement and sensibility. Vänskä takes a brisk view of tempo, and the work, especially the final movement, is all the more cohesive and forward-moving as a result, avoiding any hint of sentimentality; nor can one imagine the third movement sounding more effervescent or the fourth more heady. Silvasti has the ideal tenor for this version of the work: it has a silvery sheen yet with a touch of metal in it. As long as you don't mind the occasional use of a fast vibrato, Silvasti is sure to please because he has the words and the music at his command, projecting everything with great aplomb. Groop, better known than her tenor colleague, further enhances her growing reputation with an impassioned performance of the alto's songs. She rises magnificently to all the challenges of the 'Abschied', declaiming with extraordinary Baker-like urgency.

Das Lied von der Erde.
Christa Ludwig *mez* **Fritz Wunderlich** *ten*
Philharmonia Orchestra, New Philharmonia Orchestra / Otto Klemperer.
EMI CDM5 66892-2 (64 minutes: ADD). Recorded 1964-66. Ⓜ

In a famous BBC TV interview Klemperer declared that he was the objective one, Walter the romantic, and he knew what he was talking about. Klemperer lays this music before you, even lays bare its soul by his simple method of steady tempos (too slow in the third song) and absolute textural clarity – where else are the wind parts in the finale so searing because they are so clearly exposed? – but he doesn't quite demand your emotional capitulation as does Walter. Ludwig does that. In the tenor song songs, Wunderlich cannot match Patzak, simply because of the older singer's way with the text; 'fest steh'n' in the opening song, 'Mir ist als wie im Traum', the line plaintive and the tone poignant, are simply unsurpassable. By any other yardstick, Wunderlich is a prized paragon, musical and vocally free. So truthful and natural is the sound on the revived EMI that it easily beats the mono Decca. With voice and orchestra in perfect relationship and everything sharply defined, the old methods of the 1960s have nothing to fear here from today's competition. These two old recordings will never be thrust aside; the Walter for its authority and intensity, the feeling of being present on an historic occasion, the Klemperer for its insistent strength and beautiful singing, even more evident on CD. Both should be in any self-respecting collection.

Das Lied von der Erde.
Kathleen Ferrier *contr* **Julius Patzak** *ten*
Vienna Philharmonic Orchestra / Bruno Walter.
Decca mono 414 194-2DH (ADD). Recorded 1952. ⓂⒽ

'A finer performance than this would not be a song of earth', wrote the *Record Guide* (Collins, 1955) of Decca's legendary performance. The authors also added, 'and the recording is excellent', a view which LP collectors might not have subsequently endorsed but which this altogether superb, historically important transfer to CD in some measure approves. High tessitura string and vocal contributions are occasionally somewhat shrill and lacking in body when set alongside modern recordings but, astonishingly, one might be in the hall with the VPO and these remarkable artists. If what we hear on this transfer from the master tapes in the fifth song is significantly different from what Bruno Walter heard as tenor, solo violin and flute raptly commune, it would be surprising. Equally astounding is the way the transferred recording conveys the sheer weight and body of the Vienna Philharmonic's tone. How easily can we now appreciate the passion, drive, and guile of Walter's conducting, with its subtle colourings and many barely perceptible rubatos. The opening song is especially thrilling, with Patzak quite persuasively 'there' in the musical picture. The post-war VPO winds, the oboe especially, may strike some as curiously nasal. Yet it is the very complexity and idiosyncrasy of the orchestral timbres which help give this reading its special interest. No one has conducted or played the elusive third movement better than this; the pace is ideal, and Patzak, though no longer in his prime, outpoints every rival except possibly Wunderlich on the Klemperer recording. And beyond this there is Ferrier, an artist born to sing this music and singing it here at a time so close to her own death as to make this a real, truly harrowing song of farewell.

Das Lied von der Erde[a]. Lieder eines fahrenden Gesellen[b]. Kindertotenlieder[b]. Rückert-Lieder[c]. Lieder aus Des Knaben Wunderhorn – Wer hat dies Liedlein erdacht?[d]; Des Antonius von Padua Fischpredigt[e]; Wo die schönen Trompeten blasen[d]; Revelge[e]; Der Tambourg'sell[e].
[d]**Lucia Popp** sop [bc]**Dame Janet Baker** mez [a]**Murray Dickie** ten [a]**Dietrich Fischer-Dieskau,** [e]**Bernd Weikl** bars
[a]**Philharmonia Orchestra / Paul Kletzki;** [b]**Hallé Orchestra,**
[c]**New Philharmonia Orchestra / Sir John Barbirolli;**
[de]**London Philharmonic Orchestra / Klaus Tennstedt.**
EMI Rouge et Noir CZS7 62707-2 (two discs: 155 minutes: ADD/DDD). Ⓜ Ⓗ ℞℞

This fascinating, if perverse, mid-price compilation is a typical product of EMI's Rouge et Noir series. That is to say it offers excellent value to those untroubled by peculiar couplings, poorly translated notes and non-existent song texts. It is surprising to find Dame Janet Baker's mid-1960s Mahler in this context. Older readers will recall that these 'classic' performances received some less than enthusiastic notices in the early days, with commentators querying the prevailing intimacy of mood. Twenty years ago, this was assumed to be primarily male (i.e. Fischer-Dieskau) territory. Could it be that Dame Janet's surpassingly beautiful renderings are not that highly prized in France even now? Thanks in no small part to Barbirolli's ultra-sensitive accompaniments, they seem as treasurable as any Mahler on disc and make a tremendous and unexpected bargain here, providing you warm to the idea of *Das Lied* with Fischer-Dieskau in the female (i.e. Dame Janet?) role! That great baritone is in reasonably fresh voice for Paul Kletzki but even so, his generally mellifluous projection is already disfigured by the odd patch of histrionic barking. No doubt Fischer-Dieskau's many admirers will not want to be without this transfer and you do not miss the compassionate warmth of the female touch until the very closing moments, not quite evocative enough here.

The Scottish tenor, Murray Dickie, sings well too; the voice is not large and there are inevitable moments of strain. The conductor, Paul Kletzki, largely forgotten these days, enjoyed a close rapport with the Philharmonia Orchestra in this period and he secures some distinguished playing; the odd mishap reminds us that *Das Lied* was not over-familiar in 1959. His view is refreshingly brisk rather than unacceptably brusque. The sound is good, as with so many of their productions from the late 1950s. The voices are placed well forward and yet the orchestra has great presence with the venue imparting a pleasant bloom. Tennstedt's charmless *Wunderhorn* songs were not well received on their first appearance but even so, you should find something to enjoy in this selection of five, once you get past Weikl's preposterous, melodramatic 'Revelge'. Popp is moving in 'Wo die schönen Trompeten blasen'. The Tennstedt tracks were recorded digitally – the note doesn't give many clues about this or anything else – and the sound is rather brash. A mixed bag then, but well worth investigation.

Lieder aus Des Knaben Wunderhorn.
Jard van Nes contr **John Bröcheler** bass
Arnhem Philharmonic Orchestra / Roberto Benzi.
Ottavo OTRC79238 (55 minutes: DDD). Texts included. Recorded 1992. Ⓕ

Jard van Nes is a natural for Mahler, both from the vocal and interpretative point of view. Particularly admirable is the fresh, spontaneous way in which she approaches her contributions, free from both the long shadow of past performance or awe before such familiar songs. She catches ideally the folk-like charm of 'Rheinlegendchen' and 'Wer hat dies Liedlein erdacht?'. She is also appropriately earthy in 'Das irdische Leben', then marvellously tender as the distant lover in 'Des Schildwache Nachtlied'. Her unadorned mastery of word and tone cannot be praised too highly – listen to the *keck* delivery of 'Verlor'ne Müh': just right – and she crowns her performance with her grave utterance in 'Urlicht'. Bröcheler is among the best, characterizing 'Lob des hohen Verstandes' with enthusiastic vivacity and revelling in St Antony's sermon. Benzi and his orchestra never make the mistake of some more noted performers of over-egging the pudding. Although the detail is all clearly projected and keenly played, in a perfectly balanced recording, the music is kept on the move.

Das klagende Lied (complete version including 'Waldmärchen').
Susan Dunn *sop* **Markus Baur** *boy alto* **Brigitte Fassbaender** *mez* **Werner Hollweg** *ten*
Andreas Schmidt *bar*
Städtischer Musikverein Düsseldorf; Berlin Radio Symphony Orchestra / Riccardo Chailly.
Decca 425 719-2DH (64 minutes: DDD). Text and translation included. Recorded 1989. Ⓕ

Even the musically acute listener would be unlikely to realize that *Das klagende Lied* is the work of a teenager. Mahler's first significant work is as self-assured as anything he was to write in later life. Indeed enthusiastic Mahlerians will recognize here passages which crop up in other works, most notably the Second Symphony. Those same enthusiastic Mahlerians might not recognize much of this recording, however, since only two movements of *Klagende Lied* are usually performed: the 30-minute first movement is considered too rambling. But no one could possibly arrive at that conclusion from this tautly directed, electrifying performance, and it contains some wonderfully imaginative music, including some delightful forest murmurs, which it seems tragic to miss out. For this movement alone this CD is a must for any Mahler fan, but more than that this is a spectacular recording of a one-in-a-million performance. The soloists, choir and orchestra achieve near perfection under Chailly's inspired direction, and the decision to substitute for the marvellous Brigitte Fassbaender a boy alto (Markus Baur) to represent the disembodied voice of the dead brother is a stroke of pure genius. His weird, unnatural voice provides a moment of sheer spine-tingling drama.

Kindertotenlieder[a]. Rückert-Lieder[b]. Lieder eines fahrenden Gesellen[a].
Dame Janet Baker *mez*
[a]**Hallé Orchestra,** [b]**New Philharmonia Orchestra / Sir John Barbirolli.**
EMI CDM5 66981-2 (65 minutes: ADD). Texts and translations included. Ⓕ **RR**

The songs of the *Lieder eines fahrenden Gesellen* ('Songs of a Wayfarer') are directly quoted from Mahler's First Symphony and the same fresh, springtime atmosphere is shared by both works. The orchestration has great textural clarity and lightness of touch. The *Kindertotenlieder*, more chromatically expressive than the earlier work, tap into a darker, more psychologically complex vein in Mahler's spiritual and emotional make-up. The *Rückert-Lieder* are not a song-cycle as such but gather in their romantic awareness and response to the beauties of the poetry a unity and shape that acts to bind them. Together, Baker and Barbirolli reach a transcendental awareness of Mahler's inner musings. Barbirolli draws from the Hallé playing of great delicacy and precision and establishes a clear case for having this CD in your collection.

Kindertotenlieder. Rückert-Lieder. Lieder eines fahrenden Gesellen. Lieder aus Des Knaben Wunderhorn – Das irdische Leben; Des Antonius von Padua Fischpredigt; Urlicht.
Brigitte Fassbaender *mez*
Deutsches Symphony Orchestra, Berlin / Riccardo Chailly.
Decca 425 790-2DH (71 minutes: DDD). Texts and translations included. Recorded 1988-89. Ⓕ

Fassbaender's emotionally charged way of singing is ideally matched to Mahler yet she is just as able to smile and sing gently, wittily. It is in the dramatic declamation, however, that the true flavour of her singing is caught. Throughout the *Fahrenden Gesellen* it is the immediacy, fearlessness of attack and her particular intensity, that makes these readings so arresting. The swiftish speeds throughout ensure that sentimentality is kept at bay; so does Chailly's and the orchestra's biting precision and light touch. Similar characteristics inform a deeply eloquent interpretation of *Kindertotenlieder*. Right from the start the world-weary tone and verbal illumination in the first song catch at the heart and suggest palpably the sense of personal responsibility for the children's deaths on the part of the protagonist. Baker/Barbirolli, with the singer in lovely voice, must be a 'safer' recommendation than the more daring Fassbaender, but the latter is an inviting proposition – and a searing experience.

Mahler Lieder und Gesänge – No. 1, Frühlingsmorgen; No. 2, Erinnerung; No. 3, Hans und Grethe; No. 7, Ich ging mit Lust durch einen grünen Wald; No. 11, Ablösung im Sommer; No. 12, Scheiden und Meiden. Rückert-Lieder – Ich atmet' einem linden Duft; Liebst du um Schönheit; Blicke mir nicht in die Lieder; Ich bin der Welt abhanden gekommen.
Marx Hat Dich die Liebe berhürt. Maienblüten. Und gestern hat er mir Rosen gebracht. Venetianisches Wiegenlied. Wofür.
R. Strauss Acht Lieder aus Letzte Blätter, Op. 10 – No. 3, Die Nacht; No. 8, Allerseelen. Sechs Lieder aus Lotusblättern, Op. 19 – No. 4, Wie sollten wir geheim sie halten; No. 6, Mein Herz ist stumm. Vier Lieder, Op. 27 – No. 1, Ruhe, meine Seele; No. 4, Morgen. Nachtgang, Op. 29 No. 3. Meinem Kinde, Op. 37 No. 3. Begegnung, AV72.
Katarina Karnéus *mez* **Roger Vignoles** *pf*
EMI Debut CDZ5 73168-2 (64 minutes: DDD). Recorded 1998.   ⑧Ⓔ

This is an outright winner, one of the most satisfying CDs of Lieder on the market. Karnéus's absolutely natural voice has an ideal warmth of tone and she connects completely with the text. Karnéus begins with a group that confirms her as an ideal interpreter of Strauss Lieder. She is impressive when deep feelings are invoked by the composer, as in 'Ruhe, meine Seele' and 'Morgen', and both these pieces are all the better for being without the slow tempos and excess of sentiment commonly imposed on them today. The sincere simplicity evinced here is so much more relevant and moving, especially when the phrasing and the German is, as everywhere on the issue, so exemplary, the movement between notes, using gentle *portamento*, so admirable. In the Mahler, there's ebullience and good humour, even a smile in the voice, in 'Ich ging mit Lust' and 'Hans und Grethe', a rich vein of heartfelt, inner feeling so appropriate to 'Liebst du um Schönheit' and 'Ich bin der Welt'. Though in the latter song one misses the orchestral clothing usually encountered, Vignoles consoles us for its absence with his subtle, soft-grained, finely judged playing. Again the rich, even tone and response to the texts add an extra dimension to one's pleasure, particularly in the touching *Venetian Lullaby* which closes a profoundly satisfying programme. The recording is well balanced. The only drawback is that to get texts and translations you are directed to EMI's web site, but don't let that stop anyone acquiring this recital, a real 'must buy' for Lieder lovers.

Marin Marais   French 1656-1728

Alcyone – Suites.
Le Concert des Nations / Jordi Savall.
Auvidis Astrée E8525 (53 minutes: DDD). Recorded 1993.   Ⓕℙ

As one of the greatest exponents of the solo viol tradition perfected by Marais, Savall focuses his insights upon this music and interprets the scoring as Marais might have done. He experiments with all the chamber-music combinations of the day and, typically, hazards some of his own, particularly in the Chaconne. Occasionally, Savall uses winds and sometimes miscalculates his effects, as in the 'Bourrée pour les Bergers et Bergères'. His command of Maraisian ornamentation is, however, everywhere evident and indeed very welcome because of the constant melodic echoes of the solo repertoire in the opera score. With chamber music come more transparent textures, revealing the harmonic and textural richness of the post-Lullian style; cross-rhythms, syncopations and sequences have more impact. By contrast, the opera performances can often sound sluggish and four-square. Savall also includes music that was left out of the opera recording, including the delicately syncopated 'Air pour les Faunes et les Driades' from the Prologue, the exquisitely scored Sarabande, with its beautifully shaded cadences, and the Gigue from Act 1 as well as the 'Sarabande pour les Prêtresses de Junon' from Act 2. In the Prologue and the March and Air 'pour les Matelots' in Act 3, Savall orchestrates passages that were once vocal solos to maintain the proportions of the movements.

Pièces en trio.
Ricercar Consort / Philippe Pierlot *va da gamba*
Ricercar 206482 (two discs: 139 minutes: DDD). Recorded 1998.   Ⓕℙ

Marais's trios are beautifully crafted miniatures, which require the same care and stylistic sensitivity as pieces from his virtuoso solo repertory. They are harmonically much more sophisticated than Lully's, his contemporary, and have more in common with the language of Couperin's early 'sonades' (also dating from the 1690s). Marais's trios seem to have been intended as *musique de chambre*, specially crafted to delight; the allusions to theatre music is in part suggested by his instruction that his pieces would also sound well when played by two *dessus de viole*. The *dessus de viole* makes a much more delicate, soothing sound than the brighter, livelier violin and was better suited to intimate occasions. The two-disc set by the Ricercar Consort explores all these combinations and more, occasionally adding a guitar to the continuo, here mixing a wind instrument with a string instrument, there 'orchestrating' some of the preludes, minuets and large concluding movements.

Pièces de viole, Première livre.
Ricercar Consort / Philippe Pierlot *va da gamba*
Ricercar RIC205842 (three discs: 223 minutes: DDD). Recorded 1995. Ⓜ️Ⓟ

This is music of exquisite refinement, dream-like and reserved, with just those qualities of interpretation from Philippe Pierlot and the Ricercar Consort. Some of the livelier pieces might have been treated more robustly; here, little disturbs the placid surface, but it is ravishing playing for all that. There are nine suites in all, and two occasional pieces (not to be taken in at one sitting, preferably, but savoured individually). This three-CD set (for the price of two) offers excellent value.

Pièces de viole, Livre 2 – Part 1: Ballet en rondeau; Couplets de folies; Prélude; Cloches ou carillon. Part 2: Prélude lentement; Chaconne en rondeau; Tombeau pour M de Ste Colombe; Prélude; Allemande; Courante; Pavan selon de goût des anciens compositeurs de luth; Gavotte; Rondeau en vaudeville; Gigue; Chaconne; Fantaisie.
Markku Luolajan-Mikkola, Varpu Haavisto *vas da gamba*
Eero Palviainen *lte* **Elina Mustonen** *hpd*
BIS CD909 (73 minutes: DDD). Recorded 1997. Ⓕ

The most substantial pieces here are the set of variations of *La folia*, and the *Tombeau pour M de Ste Colombe* in memory of Marais's mentor. His idiom embodies a paradox that is peculiarly French, in that it demands a very high technical standard, yet its proper expression requires the utmost restraint – there is a parallel here with much of Debussy's piano music. The young Finnish viol-player, Markku Luolajan-Mikkola, is a founder-member of Phantasm. Here he holds his own (or, rather, centre-stage) with elegance and reserve, although in the slower pieces one might have wished for more rhythmic flexibility. The continuo section consists of another viol-player, and a theorbo or harpsichord (though in the variations on *La folia*, the two are combined). This works well for the most part, though the high partials of the harpsichord tend to drown the viols: the lute is far less obtrusive. The problem of balance also intrudes when the soloist is in the lower range, though whether this is due to the sound-recording or to the position of the players relative to each other is a moot point. But as an introduction to Marais's art this is hard to fault – try his Pavan 'in the style of the bygone lute composers': a real treat.

Pièces de viole, Quatrième Livre – Marche tartate; Sarabande; La tartarine; Les fêtes champêtres; Gigue la fleselle; Rondeau le bijou; Le tourbillon; L'uniforme; Allemande pour le sujet; Gigue pour la basse; Allemande l'asmatique; Muzette; Caprice ou Sonate; Le labyrinthe; Allemande la bizare; La minaudiere; Allemande la singuliere; L'arabesque; Allemande la superbe; La reveuse; Marche; Gigue; Le badinage; Deux Allemandes.
Christophe Coin, Vittorio Ghielmi *bass viols*
Christophe Rousset *hpd* **Pascal Monteilhet** *theorbo/gtr*
L'Oiseau-Lyre 458 144-2OH (78 minutes: DDD). Recorded 1996. ⒻⒺ

In order to bring the subtleties of music intended to be perceived as in a *goût étranger* to life, a performer must first master the traditional French baroque style. Christophe Coin has done that, both technically and musically, to a degree matched by no other viol player of today. This recording encompasses an astonishing range of moods and effects: he sings ('Fêtes champêtres'), he swaggers ('La fleselle'), he soars ('Caprice'). He revels in the resonance of Marais's exquisite chordal writing ('Sarabande' and 'Muzette') and takes time when it suits the music – always just the right amount (too much would sap the music, too little would betray a lack of *sensibilité* and too frequent would render his performances clichéd). He can be rhetorical ('Fêtes champêtres') but is equally at home with the saucy 'Tartarine'. He is a virtuoso of the first rank (amply in evidence in the 'Tourbillon' and the marathon 'Labyrinthe'), paying attention to the smallest detail – the syncopations of the allemandes ('L'asmatique' and 'La singuliere'), the echoes in the majestic 'Marche tartate' and the graceful 'Arabesque'. He conjures visions in the Rameau-esque 'Minaudiere' and the 'Allemande la superbe'. Central to French viol playing is mastery of the melancholy; so much of the repertory is in minor keys and within the range of the human voice. For performers it is the most revealing of all musical 'affects' and Coin has the character and conviction never to allow it to degenerate into self-indulgence. In his hands such pieces as the rondeaux popularized in the film, *Tous les matins du monde* ('L'arabesque', 'Le reveuse' and 'Le badinage'), and 'Le bijou' are elegant and poetic. With a fine team of accompanists, Christophe Rousset (always moulding his playing to Coin's bow strokes, notably in the 'Allemande la bizare'), Vittorio Ghielmi (whose shuddering low notes in the 'Rondeau le bijou' are especially effective) and Pascal Monteilhet (whose guitar playing contributes so much to the 'Sarabande'), Coin provides entertainment listeners will want to revisit again and again, and sets new standards for viol players today.

Czeslaw Marek

Polish Hymn. Rural Scenes, Op. 30. Death Melody, Op. 23. Greeting. Village Songs, Op. 34. Rückblick, Op. 5.
Elzbieta Szmytka sop **Philharmonia Chorus and Orchestra / Gary Brain.**
Koch Schwann 364412 (59 minutes: DDD). Texts and translations included. Recorded1996.   Ⓕ 🅴

Marek is a truly revelatory composer new to almost everyone, who wrote music of considerable variety and appeal combining late romantic lushness of sound – very much of the time – with a classicality of spirit that was remarkably *forward*-looking. Alongside unsurprising reminiscences of Pfitzner or Richard Strauss in the final piece – but the earliest to be composed – *Rückblick* (1915), there is also a Brahmsian nobility of feeling. More remarkable still is the prize-winning four-part male-voice motet *Death Melody* (1924), with its haunting tenor solo. *Greeting* was written in the same week but is much more than a mere affirmative makeweight. The major items, however, are the two song-cycles, *Rural Scenes* (1929) and *Village Songs* (1934). The titles may be suggestive of Bartók but Marek's idiom was rooted more in the concert hall than the earth of his native Galicia. The best of the songs, such as 'The Shepherd' in *Rural Scenes* or 'Girl's Dream' in *Village Songs*, sustain comparison with Canteloube in Auvergne mode, and both cycles deserve to be much more widely known. The Philharmonia Chorus sings marvellously (Polish speakers might quibble about diction here or there), and the orchestra plays beautifully in the two cycles. Brain's shaping of the music throughout is pretty much ideal, and the rapport between him, the orchestra and the radiant soloist, Elzbieta Szmytka, is clearly audible. A terrific disc.

Luca Marenzio

Madrigali a 4vv ... libro primo.
Concerto Italiano (Rossana Bertini sop Claudio Cavina counterten Giuseppe Maletto ten Sergio Foresti bass Mara Galassi hp Andrea Damiani lte) / **Rinaldo Alessandrini.**
Opus 111 OPS30-117 (62 minutes: DDD). Texts and translations included. Recorded 1994.   Ⓕ

What Concerto Italiano reveals to us is that four-part writing in this expressive and varied milieu makes a virtue out of its limitations: Marenzio capitalizes on exposed dialogues between voices and textural brittleness. Classicism (in the broadest musical sense synonymous with four-part writing long before Bach chorales or Haydn quartets) is what Alessandrini is seeking to impart in this clear juxtaposition of fluent canzonets with intimate rhetoric. The music is so subtly shaded, both by Marenzio and the singers, that unless you are a reincarnated madrigalist this should be experienced in small doses. There is just the same commitment and concentration to the extensive detail in the music. Just observe how much care has gone into *Chi vol udire i miei sospiri in rime* with its beautifully paced *crescendo* on the word 'sospiri' (sighs), the almost imperceptible sketching of the pulse and other wonderful liberties with rhythmic inflexion. So much of this innate understanding is of course expressed through the singers' native tongue (what life those watery vowels bring to Petrarch's later-to-be-famous *Zefiro torna*) and a warm changeable Mediterranean breeze which unselfconsciously manipulates the temperature. None of this would count for much were the ensemble not highly refined in purely abstract terms and this is perhaps the best yet in that respect. Only rarely does the soprano's rich and penetrating tone cause one to worry and when it does this is usually because of a slight tendency to flatness. A small concern in a very fine release.

José Marín

Mi señora Mariantaños. Que se lleva las almas. Aquella sierra nevada. Sin duda piensa menguilla. No piense menguilla ya. Sepan todos que muero. No sé yo cómo es. Al son de los arroyuelos. Le verdad de Perogrullo. Ojos pues me desdeñais. Si quieres dar Marica en lo cierto. Tortolilla sino es por amor. Montes del Tajo escuchad. Niño como en trus mudanças.
Montserrat Figueras sops **Rolf Lislevand** gtrs **Arianna Savall** double hp
Pedro Estevan perc **Adela Gonzalez-Campa** castanets
Alia Vox AV9802 (67 minutes: DDD). Texts and translations included. Recorded 1997.   Ⓕ

José Marín was a guitarist and singer who, despite spending years dodging a term in the galleys for multiple murder, maintained a high popularity in late seventeenth-century Spain as a composer of secular songs, or *tonos humanos*. Concerned almost exclusively with love, sex and longing, these jewels of the songwriter's art are by turns teasing and tortured, playful and poignant, expressing the manifold shades of love with almost bewildering subtlety. Like all the best popular songs, however, they are enjoyable for their sheer melodic charm and rhythmic vitality, even if one does not know precisely what the words are about. There are no early-music obstacles here, just the timeless beauty of the human voice and sensitive accompaniment. Figueras sings with lightness, clarity and, above all, communicativeness, while the various instrumental combinations of guitar, harp and gloriously Spanish-sounding percussion (including bells, castanets, clapping and stamping) help her to make the music really dance. Lislevand's sensitive and alert guitar playing is particularly captivating, and with the modern feel of these songs being enhanced on occasion by his use of a *battente*, or steel-strung guitar. Rarely has Spanish baroque music sounded quite so Spanish as here; the extended vocalizations in *Sepan todos que muero* we assume to have been added by the performers, but they are as evocative and welcome as a warming southern wind. If Marín himself was able to perform these songs with the charm of these musicians it is no wonder that he kept his freedom.

Frank Martin
Swiss 1890-1974

Concerto for Seven Wind Instruments, Timpani, Percussion and Strings[a]. Etudes for String Orchestra[a]. Petite Symphonie concertante[b]. Passacaglia for String Orchestra[c]. Violin Concerto[b]. In terra pax[a].
Ursula Buckel *sop* **Marga Höffgen** *contr* **Ernst Haefliger** *ten* **Pierre Mollet** *bar*
Jakob Stämpfli *bass* **Wolfgang Schneiderhan** *vn* **Pierre Jamet** *hp*
Germaine Vaucher-Clerc *hpd* **Doris Rossiaud** *pf*
Lausanne Choral Union; [c]**Stuttgart Chamber Orchestra / Karl Münchinger;**
[ab]**Suisse Romande Orchestra / Ernest Ansermet.**
Double Decca [bc]mono/[a]stereo 448 264-2DF2 (two discs: 147 minutes: ADD).
Recorded 1951-63.
Ⓜ Ⓗ

This invaluable issue restores not only the pioneering recording of Martin's masterpiece, the *Petite Symphonie concertante* for harp, harpsichord, piano and double string orchestra, but also that of the Violin Concerto. They have great authority and a sense of atmosphere that is very special. The Violin Concerto is an inspired and noble piece, and Schneiderhan's mono recording makes its first appearance since the mid-1950s. In reviewing the original Vox LP the reviewer spoke of the work's 'clarity, restraint and dignity'. Anyone who responds to the Prokofiev D major Concerto or the Bartók and Walton will feel at home here. The *Concerto for seven wind instruments* and the *Etudes* for string orchestra were recorded in the early 1960s and the sound is very fresh. *In terra pax* is a strong work but is here showing its age. Well worth acquiring for the sake of the Violin Concerto.

Der Sturm – Overture; Mein Ariel, hast du, der Luft nur ist; Ein feierliches Lied; Hin sind meine Zauberei'n. Maria-Triptychon. Sechs Monologe aus Jedermann.
Linda Russell *sop* **David Wilson-Johnson** *bar* **Duncan Riddell** *vn*
London Philharmonic Orchestra / Matthias Bamert.
Chandos CHAN9411 (68 minutes: DDD). Recorded 1994.
Ⓕ Ⓔ

The *Maria-Triptychon* was written in the late 1960s in response to a request from Wolfgang Schneiderhan for a work for violin, soprano and orchestra that he could perform with his wife, Irmgard Seefried. Although their recording under the composer himself emanating from a Swiss Radio tape is authoritative, it does not match this Chandos recording in sheer beauty of sound. Linda Russell sings the solo part with great sympathy and intelligence, and Duncan Riddell assumes the mantle of Schneiderhan with no mean success. The transparency of texture that the Chandos team achieves shows this visionary score in the most favourable light. It makes a stronger impression than in any earlier performance, thanks to the dedication of the LPO and its conductor. Bamert distils a strong atmosphere and sense of mystery in all these scores. David Wilson-Johnson is on impressive form in the *Jedermann* Monologues (one of the great song-cycles of the century). His is as perceptive and moving an account as any – and he is no less impressive in the magical *Der Sturm*.

Martin Mass for Double Choir. Passacaille.
Pizzetti Messa di requiem. De profundis.
Westminster Cathedral Choir / James O'Donnell *org*
Hyperion CDA67017 (71 minutes: DDD). Texts and translations included. Recorded 1997.
Gramophone Award Winner 1998.
Ⓕ ⓇⓇ

These are magnificent performances. Written in 1922, the *Agnus Dei* being added four years later, the Mass is one of Martin's most sublime compositions. Surprisingly it gains enormously from using boys' rather than female voices and although one might think women naturally score over boys in terms of understanding and maturity, it is a measure of James O'Donnell's achievement with Westminster Cathedral Choir that the gain in purity and beauty is at no time at the expense of depth and fervour. This is an altogether moving and eloquent performance, often quite thrilling and always satisfying. This disc brings us a fine performance by O'Donnell of the *Passacaille* and the Pizzetti *Messa di Requiem*, also composed in 1922. The received wisdom is that it is in his *a cappella* music that Pizzetti is at his finest and in his 1951 monograph Guido Gatti spoke of his setting as 'the most serene and lyrical of all ... from Mozart's to Gabriel Fauré's'. Serene and lyrical it most certainly is, and it will come as a revelation to those encountering it for the first time. There is a fervour and a conviction about the Westminster performances of both the Requiem and the 1937 *De profundis*. The luminous tone this choir produces in both these inspired and masterly works will ring in your ears long after you have finished playing this splendidly recorded disc.

Mass for Double Choir. Fünf Gesänge des Ariel. Ode à la musique.
Cantate pour le 1er août. Quatre Chansons. Trois Chansons.
Simon Birchall *bar*
The Sixteen / Harry Christophers.
Collins Classics 1467-2 (67 minutes: DDD). Texts and translations included. Recorded 1995. Ⓕ Ⓔ

This is life-enhancing music. After playing the *Mass for Double Choir* one's spirits are lifted. This performance of the Mass has great eloquence and commitment. The *Fünf Gesänge des Ariel* is the set of songs, inspired by Shakespeare's *The Tempest*, which immediately precedes the opera of the same name. The last of the five settings 'Where the bee sucks' is highly virtuosic and imaginative – and is beautifully sung – but then so are they all. The *Cantate pour le 1er août* for chorus and organ comes from the war years. It has the calm dignity that marks all Martin's work and there are many characteristic touches, but generally speaking it is less profoundly individual than his other music from the war years. The 1944 *Chansons*, settings of Roland Stähli and Henri Duvain, are slight but pleasing and they are nicely sung. The same must be said of the delightful 1931 *Chansons* for female voices, to words by Ronsard and others, which are sung with great elegance and charm. The *Ode à la musique* was the last of these pieces to be composed and comes from 1961; it is an inventive and exhilarating setting of a verse by Machaut. All of these works are performed with evident commitment and are expertly recorded.

Requiem.
Elisabeth Speiser *sop* **Ria Bollen** *contr* **Eric Tappy** *ten* **Peter Lagger** *bass*
Lausanne Women's Chorus; Union Chorale; Ars Laeta Vocal Ensemble;
Suisse Romande Orchestra / Frank Martin.
Jecklin Disco JD631-2 (47 minutes: ADD). Text and translation included.
Recorded live in 1973. Ⓕ

Astonishingly, this beautiful score still remains grievously neglected – it deserves to be heard as often as the Fauré Requiem. The work comes from Martin's last years, and was inspired, he tells us, by three cathedrals – St Mark's in Venice, the Montreale in Palermo and the Greek temples of Paestum near Naples. It is a work of vision and devotion of spirit, and casts a strong spell. It is one of those pieces that leaves you with a feeling of enormous tranquillity. The musical language is familiar enough, for there are the same subtle shifts of colour and harmony that you will find in Martin's *Petite Symphonie concertante*. However, there is a dramatic power (*Dies irae*) and a serenity (*In Paradisum*) that are quite new. The short *In Paradisum* is inspired and has a luminous quality and radiance that are quite otherworldly. Martin certainly put all his consummate musical skills into this score with organ and orchestra of equal importance. The 83-year-old composer conducts a completely dedicated and authoritative performance: it might well be improved upon in one or two places in terms of ensemble or security, but the spirit is there. The Swiss Radio recording is eminently truthful and well balanced, and offers a natural enough acoustic. The audience are reasonably unobtrusive.

Bohuslav Martinů

Bohemian 1890-1959

Piano Concertos – No. 2; No. 3; No. 4, 'Incantation'.
Rudolf Firkušný *pf*
Czech Philharmonic Orchestra / Libor Pešek.
RCA Red Seal 09026 61934-2 (67 minutes: DDD). Recorded 1993. Ⓕ Ⓔ

These performances not only have special authority but are in a class of their own. Although the piano concertos are not of comparable importance to the Martinů symphonies, they are not of negligible interest. The disc bears the title 'Tribute to Rudolf Firkušný' and the jewel-case reminds us that he gave the first performance of all three concertos. The Fourth, *Incantation*, is undoubtedly the finest of them all, highly imaginative in its exotic sound world, with what sound like wild Aztec bird calls and war cries, and full of luminous and subtle sonorities. Firkušný's account is a revelation to those who have heard only the Páleníček, Leichner or Havliková recordings. There is the right sense of pace – and space: phrases have time to breathe and make their point. The Czech PO under Libor Pešek gives Firkušný dedicated and sympathetic support. The recording is very good and allows one to hear more orchestral detail than ever before. In Firkušný's hands the Second Concerto has a real sense of warmth and delight. The Third, too, emerges in superlatively fresh and vivid colours. What is also astonishing is that at no time does Firkušný's playing betray his years: he was 81 when these performances were given! He was an aristocrat among pianists and this is a worthy memorial to him.

Symphonies Nos. 1 and 2.
Bamberg Symphony Orchestra / Neeme Järvi.
BIS CD362 (61 minutes: DDD).   Ⓕ

Symphonies Nos. 3 and 4.
Bamberg Symphony Orchestra / Neeme Järvi.
BIS CD363 (63 minutes: DDD).   Ⓕ Ⓢ

Symphonies Nos. 5 and 6.
Bamberg Symphony Orchestra / Neeme Järvi.
BIS CD402 (59 minutes: DDD). Recorded 1988.   Ⓕ

Despite his travels throughout his formative years as a composer, Martinů remained a quintessentially Czech composer and his music is imbued with the melodic shapes and rhythms of the folk-music of his native homeland. The six symphonies were written during Martinů's years in America and in all of them he uses a large orchestra with distinctive groupings of instruments which give them a very personal and unmistakable timbre. The rhythmic verve of his highly syncopated fast movements is very infectious, indeed unforgettable, and his slow movements are often deeply expressive, most potently, perhaps, in that of the Third Symphony which is imbued with the tragedy of war. The Bamberg orchestra plays marvellously and with great verve for Järvi, whose excellently judged tempos help propel the music forward most effectively. His understanding of the basic thrust of Martinů's structures is very impressive and he projects the music with great clarity. The BIS recordings are beautifully clear, with plenty of ambience surrounding the orchestra, a fine sense of scale and effortless handling of the wide dynamic range Martinů calls for. Enthusiastically recommended.

Symphony No. 4. Memorial to Lidice. Field Mass[a].
[a]**Ivan Kusnjer** *bar* **Czech Philharmonic** [a]**Chorus and Orchestra / Jirí Bĕlohlávek.**
Chandos CHAN9138 (65 minutes: DDD). Text and translation included.   Ⓕ

It is doubtful whether the luscious, intricately-scored pages of the big-hearted Fourth Symphony have ever sounded more opulent. Make no mistake, this is, for the most part, glorious playing, intoxicating in its richness (what strings!) and sure-footed poise. Bĕlohlávek has an unexpectedly playful, almost balletic way with the *Scherzo* – the spirit of the dance definitely reigns supreme here; the trio section, too, has a most appealing delicacy and engaging sense of innocence. Reservations? Well, greater bite and tighter focus to Chandos's reverberant sound picture would have been better. More crucially, though, there is some lack of intensity and temperament: you just don't sense the anguish behind the engulfing climax of the slow movement, whilst the finale could certainly do with more unbuttoned exuberance and head-spinning exhilaration. Järvi has the more winning rhythmic flair, though in terms of orchestral polish he honestly can't hold a candle to Bĕlohlávek's super-refined ensemble. In other words, we still await a truly convincing modern recorded account of this wonderful symphony. Bĕlohlávek's account of the *Field* Mass, on the other hand, is an undoubted success. It is wonderfully fervent, boasting a noble-toned, impassioned contribution from the baritone, Ivan Kusnjer, and disciplined, sonorous work from the men of the Czech Philharmonic Chorus. Chandos's recording captures it all to perfection: blend and focus impeccably combined. The moving *Memorial to Lidice* completes this ideally-chosen triptych. Bearing a dedication 'To the Memory of the Innocent Victims of Lidice', Martinů's score was written in response to the notorious mass-destruction of that village by the Nazis in June 1942. One of the composer's most deeply-felt creations, this is an eight-minute orchestral essay of slumbering power, incorporating at its climax a spine-chilling quotation from Beethoven's Fifth. It, too, receives sensitive advocacy here.

Trio for Flute, Violin and Piano. Promenades. Flute Sonata. Five Madrigal Stanzas. Scherzo. Madrigal Sonata.
Alain Marion *fl* **Angèle Dubeau** *vn* **Marc-André Hamelin** *pf/hpd*
Analekta fleurs de lys FL2 3031 (71 minutes: DDD). Recorded 1993.   Ⓜ️**E**

This is a most enjoyable disc. The performances are fresh and exhilarating, vital and intelligent; the recording natural and alive, and the music unfailingly delightful and inventive. The Trio for flute, violin and piano and the *Promenades* were written in Paris just before the war; the Flute Sonata comes from 1945 and the *Madrigal Stanzas* and *Madrigal Sonata* are wartime pieces written in 1942 and 1943 – at about the time of the First Symphony. They are both sunny and full of life, betraying none of the turbulence of the times. These artists give consistent pleasure and delight; the cheeky *Scherzo* of 1929 has rarely been played with quite so much character.

Piano Quartet. Quartet for Oboe, Violin, Cello and Piano. Viola Sonata. String Quintet.
Joel Marangella *ob* **Isabelle van Keulen, Charmian Gadd, Solomia Soroka** *vns*
Rainer Moog, Theodore Kuchar *vas* **Young-Chang Cho, Alexander Ivashkin** *vcs*
Daniel Adni, Kathryn Selby *pfs*
Naxos 8 553916 (73 minutes: DDD). Recorded 1994.   Ⓢ

The Quartet for oboe, violin, cello and piano is a highly attractive piece in the busy yet unfussy neo-classical style that Martinů made so much his own. Its opening theme is quite captivating, but all three movements have charm. The other music is hardly less delightful. The Viola Sonata is an eloquent work from the mid-1950s, composed three years after the *Rhapsody-Concerto* for the same instrument and orchestra. These were vintage years in Martinů's creativity. The String Quintet is the earliest work, dating from his Paris years, and shows the influence of Roussel. Although the first movement is perhaps not top-drawer Martinů, the slow movement is most imaginative. The performances are often touched with distinction and are never less than eminently serviceable. Daniel Adni could perhaps be a little more supple in the Piano Quartet of 1942 though in general he plays with spirit. There is plenty of air round the players and the recording is lifelike and well balanced.

The epic of Gilgamesh.
Eva Depoltová *sop* **Stefan Margita** *ten* **Ivan Kusnjer** *bar* **Ludek Vele** *bass* **Milan Karpíšek** *spkr*
Slovak Philharmonic Choir and Orchestra / Zdeněk Košler.
Marco Polo 8 223316 (56 minutes: DDD). Translation included. Recorded 1989.   Ⓕ

This is one of Martinů's greatest works, completed in 1955, a month or so before the three *Frescoes of Piero della Francesca*. It tells how Gilgamesh, King of Uruk, hears about the warrior Enkidu, a primitive, at home among the works of nature with only animals as friends. He sends him a courtesan to whom he loses his innocence; the King then befriends him but they quarrel and fight before their friendship is really cemented. The second and third parts of the oratorio centre on the themes of death and immortality; the second tells of Enkidu's death and Gilgamesh's grief, his plea to the gods to restore Enkidu and his search for immortality, and the third records his failure to learn its secrets. It is almost impossible to hear the chilling episode of the last words of Enkidu's ghost ('Yes, I saw') with its subtly changing vocal colours without a feeling of awe. With its evocation of a mysterious and remote past, its use of spoken narrative and its distinctive sound world, it is inevitable that it should be compared with Honegger's *Le roi David*. But *Gilgamesh* is far stronger and its invention far more sustained and powerful. The performance is in Czech as, of course, is the narration, which should not limit the dissemination of this disc, for the music deals with universal themes and is Martinů at his most profound and inspired. There are no weaknesses in the cast (the Gilgamesh of Ivan Kusnjer is very impressive indeed), and the chorus and orchestra respond very well to Zdeněk Košler's direction. The recording maintains a generally natural balance between the soloists, narrator, chorus and orchestra, and the somewhat resonant acoustic is used to good advantage.

Giuseppe Martucci   Italian 1856-1909

Piano Concerto No. 2 in B flat minor, Op. 66. La canzone dei ricordi.
Mirella Freni *sop* **Carlo Bruno** *pf*
Orchestra Filarmonica della Scala / Riccardo Muti.
Sony Classical SK64582 (72 minutes: DDD). Text and translation included. Recorded 1995.   Ⓕ**E**

Martucci Orchestral

Both the Piano Concerto and *La canzone dei ricordi* ('The song of memories') date from Martucci's full maturity; they show, however, quite distinct sides of his talent. The concerto is huge, boldly romantic and intensely Brahmsian, but also much more assured and original than most concertos to which such a description might be applied. The first movement, for example, is laid out with great confidence in an ingenious expansion of sonata form, yet with enough variety of incident and splendidly virtuoso pianism to earn every second of its 23 minutes. The slow movement has abundant romantic melody (at times almost recalling – or rather predicting – Rachmaninov) and achieves noble eloquence before its tranquil conclusion. The finale is an entertainingly and resourcefully ingenious sonata rondo with especially brilliant piano writing. Bruno is in fiery and eloquent command of it. *La canzone dei ricordi* is no less opulent but more intimate and much more Italian: a song-cycle of poignant regret for lost love, in a language that owes as much to Martucci's Italian forebears and contemporaries in its vocal writing as it does to Wagner in its harmony. And yet it is also individual, not least in its subtle use of recurring motives and of string textures of great richness. It is a most appealing and effective piece, and Freni seizes all its opportunities for ample lyricism and impassioned gesture with gratitude. The recording is warmly sympathetic.

Martucci Nocturne, Op. 70 No. 1. La canzone dei ricordi.
Respighi Il tramonto.
Brigitte Balleys *mez* **Lausanne Chamber Orchestra / Jésus López-Cobos.**
Claves CD50-9807 (51 minutes: DDD). Recorded 1997.   Ⓜ

Martucci, once director of conservatoires in both Bologna and Naples, and conductor of the first performance in Italy of *Tristan*, is a curious case of a composer totally unfamiliar to the UK's concert life but surprisingly well represented on disc. His warmly nostalgic and tender *Nocturne* would make a worthy alternative to the Mahler *Adagietto* or Barber's overplayed *Adagio*; and the seven poems of his elegiac cycle, *La canzone dei ricordi* are haunting examples of a refined Italian lyricism a world away from his contemporary, Puccini. The setting of Shelley's *Il tramonto* by Martucci's pupil Respighi is suitably poignant but more lush in texture. The admirable Brigitte Balleys sings with her accustomed artistry, but from time to time her voice 'catches' the mike: the playing of the Lausanne Chamber Orchestra is seductively affectionate.

Pietro Mascagni   Italian 1863-1945

Cavalleria rusticana.
Renata Scotta *sop* Santuzza; **Plácido Domingo** *ten* Turiddu; **Pablo Elvira** *bar* Alfio;
Isola Jones *mez* Lola; **Jean Kraft** *mez* Lucia;
Ambrosian Opera Chorus; National Philharmonic Orchestra / James Levine.
RCA Red Seal 74321 39500-2 (71 minutes: ADD). Notes, text and translation included.
Recorded 1978.   Ⓕ 🅁🅁

This was a strong contender in an overcrowded field when it was first released. You would be hard put to find a more positive or a more intelligent Turiddu or Santuzza than Domingo or Scotto. Scotto manages to steer a precise course between being too ladylike or too melodramatic. She suggests all the remorse and sorrow of Santuzza's situation without self-pity. Her appeals to Turiddu to reform could hardly be more sincere and heartfelt, her throbbing delivery to Alfio, 'Turiddi mi tolse l'honore', expresses all her desperation when forced to betray her erstwhile lover, and her curse on Turiddu, 'A te la mala pasqua', while not resorting to the lowdown vigour of some of her rivals, is filled with venom. Domingo proved how committed he was to his role when the part was first given to him at Covent Garden in the mid-1970s. He gives an almost Caruso-like bite and attack to Turiddu's defiance and (later) remorse, and finds a more appropriate timbre than Bergonzi (for Karajan on DG, reviewed under Leoncavallo). He also delivers the Brindisi with an appropriately carefree manner, oblivious of the challenge awaiting him. Pablo Elvira's Alfio is no more than adequate, and the other American support is indifferent. Levine's direction, as positive as Karajan's, is yet quite different. He goes much faster, and time and again catches the passion if not always the delicacy of Mascagni's score. He is well supported by the superb National Philharmonic Orchestra. With a bright and forward recording, this reading that is wholly arresting.

Cavalleria rusticana (sung in English).
Nelly Miricioiu *sop* Santuzza; **Dennis O'Neill** *ten* Turiddu; **Phillip Joll** *bar* Alfio;
Diana Montague *mez* Lola; **Elizabeth Bainbridge** *mez* Lucia;
Geoffrey Mitchell Choir; London Philharmonic Orchestra / David Parry.
Chandos Opera in English CHAN3004 (79 minutes: DDD). Notes and text included.
Recorded 1997.   Ⓕ

One of the most magical beginnings in opera is beautifully played here, and at this early stage one is not getting restive over the slow speeds. Dennis O'Neill sings his *siciliana* like a lover, with touches of an imaginative tenderness that are rare if not unique in this music. His voice distances effectively, and very effective too is the mingling of the church bells with the singing of the off-stage chorus. Santuzza, Nelly Miricioiu, must have been born in another village, but that doesn't matter; her voice has some raw patches but that also troubles less than it might as she brings such concentrated feeling to the part. On the other hand, when the Alfio arrives one can't go on saying it doesn't matter: it does. We want a vibrant Italianate voice if possible, and a firm one at least. Elizabeth Bainbridge is a vivid Mamma Lucia, but Diana Montague, immensely welcome as a singer, has quite the wrong voice-character for Lola, who should be either the local Carmen or a shallow, pert flirt. Still, for those collecting Chandos's Opera in English series this is certainly not one to miss. The drama keeps its hold, the grand old melodies surge, the score reveals more of its inspired detail, and the English language (in Edmund Tracey's translation) does itself credit.

Jules **Massenet**   French 1842-1912

Don Quichotte[a]. Scènes alsaciennes[b].
Nicolai Ghiaurov *bass* Don Quichotte; **Régine Crespin** *sop* Dulcinée;
Gabriel Bacquier *bar* Sancho Panza; **Michèle Command** *sop* Pedro;
Annick Duterte *sop* Garcias; **Peyo Garazzi** *ten* Rodriguez; **Jean-Marie Fremeau** *ten* Juan;
[a]**Suisse Romande Chorus and Orchestra / Kazimierz Kord;**
[b]**National Philharmonic Orchestra / Richard Bonynge.**
Decca 430 636-2DM2 (two discs: 133 minutes: ADD). Notes, text and translation included.
Recorded 1978.   Ⓜ

This heroic comedy was Massenet's last big success (in 1910, when he was 68). People who think of him as only a salon composer should listen to the start of Act 1, set in a Spanish town square at fiesta time; the opening music bursts out of the loudspeakers like that of Verdi's *Otello*, although here the mood is joyous, with tremendous rhythmic verve and gusto. In fact, this opera is closer to Verdi's *Falstaff*, with the same admixture of gentler serious moments amidst the comic bustle and intrigue, and of course, here again the central character is a comic yet lovable figure. The recording, made by a British team in Geneva in 1978, still sounds well although orchestral detail could be clearer. As for the performance by mainly Swiss forces under Kazimierz Kord, and with a Bulgarian bass in the title role (written for Chaliapin), one can only praise it for its idiomatic realization of a 'Spanish' opera by a gifted French composer for the theatre. Though Régine Crespin may be too mature vocally for Dulcinée, the object of the elderly Don Quixote's adoration, she sings splendidly and few will find this a serious weakness. Nicolai Ghiaurov rightly makes Quixote himself a real person, touching and dignified as well as comic, and Gabriel Bacquier gives a rounded portrayal of his servant Sancho Panza, so that Quixote's death scene in the company of his old friend is particularly strong. The lively and tuneful *Scènes alsaciennes* with Bonynge make a fine fill-up.

Hérodiade.
Nadine Denize *mez* Hérodiade; **Cheryl Studer** *sop* Salomé; **Ben Heppner** *ten* Jean;
Thomas Hampson *bar* Hérode; **José van Dam** *bass-bar* Phanuel; **Marcel Vanaud** *bar* Vitellius;
Jean-Philippe Courtis *bass* High Priest; **Martine Olmeda** *mez* Young Babylonian;
Jean-Paul Fouchécourt *ten* Voice in the Temple;
Toulouse Capitole Chorus and Orchestra / Michel Plasson.
EMI CDS7 55378-2 (three discs: 166 minutes: DDD). Notes, text and translation included.
Recorded 1994.   Ⓕ Ⓔ

Written in 1880, *Hérodiade* is typical of the early grand operas with which Massenet courted popularity. It offers five magnificent roles to singers who have the wherewithal to make the most of them, with some glorious show-pieces which are – as always with Massenet – gratefully written for the voice. It is impossible to say whether Massenet consciously took Verdi's *Aida* as a model, but we do know that he put in his request for tickets to see the first performance at the Palais Garnier while he was orchestrating *Hérodiade*. The similarities are inevitable, as both operas are descendants of Meyerbeer. There are copious ballets, mystic off-stage chanting, grand choral finales and exotic settings of Eastern promise. Michel Plasson conducts the opera uncut and has the advantage of a good studio recording. He is not one for taking an objective view of the music and there are times when he rushes frenetically ahead, as if he is as possessed by the lurid goings-on in the drama as the characters on stage. The sense of atmosphere is palpable. In Plasson's hands the heavy chords at the opening of Act 3 resound with a potent mysticism that presages Klingsor's castle (Massenet knew his Wagner too). In fact, we are at the dwelling of Phanuel the sorcerer, a less threatening proposition. José van Dam is marvellous in this big solo, leaning on the opening words of 'Dors, ô cité perverse' with a sinister gleam in his voice that sends shivers down one's back. Silvery pure in tone, Studer's Salomé throws herself into the drama with lustful abandon and Heppner phrases the music with remarkable breadth and seems to have heroic top notes to spare.

Manon.
Ileana Cotrubas sop Manon; **Alfredo Kraus** ten Des Grieux; **Gino Quilico** bar Lescaut;
José van Dam bass-bar Comte des Grieux; **Jean-Marie Frémeau** bar De Brétigny;
Charles Burles ten Guillot; **Ghyslaine Raphanel** sop Poussette;
Colette Alliot-Lugaz sop Javotte; **Martine Mahé** mez Rosette; **Jacques Loreau** bar Innkeeper;
Toulouse Capitole Chorus and Orchestra / Michel Plasson.
EMI CDS7 49610-2 (three discs: 154 minutes: DDD). Notes, text and translation included.
Recorded 1982. Ⓡ

Plasson's version of Massenet's most popular opera would be hard to improve upon. The performance is a genuine piece of company-work, particularly welcome as the company is French and can call upon such gifted singers as Colette Alliot-Lugaz and Charles Burles to take principal supporting roles. Excellent are the brother and father, frequently underestimated as both singing and acting parts but here played with distinction of voice and style by Gino Quilico and José van Dam. It is with the two leading roles that some qualifications have to be introduced among the general praise. Manon and Des Grieux, whatever their sins, have youth on their side, which is something Ileana Cotrubas and Alfredo Kraus in 1982 could not quite claim. Kraus is still marvellously clear in tone, firm in production and resonant throughout his extensive range, but he has developed a way of allowing the emotion (as in 'Ah, fuyez, douce image') to take too external a form of expression and occasionally the music requires a somewhat richer timbre. Cotrubas is usually fine until a high note approaches, affecting the ease and steadiness – and sometimes the charm – of her singing. Even so, both give deeply felt, extressively nuanced performances, presenting genuine characers and not stereotypes. Plasson conducts a performance that is both vigorous and delicate, and production and recorded sound are excellent.

Werther.
José Carreras ten Werther; **Frederica von Stade** mez Charlotte; **Thomas Allen** bar Albert;
Isobel Buchanan sop Sophie; **Robert Lloyd** bass Bailli; **Malcolm King** bass Bailli's friend;
Paul Crook ten Bailli's friend; **Linda Humphries** sop Kätchen; **Donaldson Ball** bar Brühlmann;
Royal Opera House Orchestra, Covent Garden; Children's Choir / Sir Colin Davis.
Philips 416 654-2PH2 (two discs: 131 minutes: AAD/ADD). Notes, text and translation included.
Recorded 1980. *Gramophone* Award Winner 1981. Ⓡ 🇷🇷

The ebb and flow of word and music, the warm, tremulous life of the string playing, and the pacing of each *tableau vivant* is handled so superbly by Sir Colin Davis that there is not a single moment of *longueur*. The Royal Opera House orchestra plays at its very best: the solo detail and the velocity of its every response to Massenet's flickering orchestral palette operates as if with heightened awareness under the scrutiny of the laser beam. The casting polarizes this Werther and this Charlotte. José Carreras is very much a Werther of action rather than of dream, of impetuous self-destruction rather than of brooding lyricism. The real *élan* he brings to lines like 'Rêve! Rêve! Extase! Bonheur!' is more impressive than the conjuring of 'l'air d'un paradis', where the voice can be over-driven at the top. So far as style, line and inflection are concerned, Frederica von Stade's performance can hardly be faulted. Her voice is the very incarnation of Charlotte's essential simplicity of character; but there are times when one could wish for a darker *tinta* to find the shadows in the role, and to bring a greater sense of the undercurrent of emotional conflict as it grows towards the last two acts. Thomas Allen finds unusual breadth in this Albert, noting the slightest giveaway flutter in the line: when he sings 'j'en ai tant au fond du coeur' one does actually begin to believe there may be depths there of which one is too often kept ignorant. Isobel Buchanan's is a small-scale, straightforward Sophie, a real 'oiseau d'aurore'.

Werther.
Jerry Hadley ten Werther; **Anne Sofie von Otter** mez Charlotte; **Gérard Théruel** bar Albert;
Dawn Upshaw sop Sophie; **Jean-Marie Frémeau** bar Magistrate; **Gilles Ragon** ten Schmidt,
Brühlmann; **Frédéric Caton** bass Johann; **Geneviève Marchand** sop Kätchen;
Chorus and Orchestra of the Opéra National de Lyon / Kent Nagano.
Erato 0630-17790-2 (two discs: 121 minutes: DDD). Notes, text and translation included.
Recorded 1995. Ⓡ

The opening scene of this recording promises very well; the orchestra certainly knows how to play Massenet, and Nagano avoids the extremes of quasi-*verismo* style that can mar this essay in masochistic, unrequited passion. Jerry Hadley suggests convincingly the impulsive, romantic young poet. As Charlotte, Anne Sofie von Otter has just the right balance between sounding young (she's meant to be 20) but emotionally mature. She and von Stade (Davis) are among the finest interpreters of the role. Dawn Upshaw makes a very positive, flirty Sophie and Gérard Théruel a good Albert. There is a grandeur about the Davis recording which the Erato version doesn't quite attain. However, von Otter and Hadley sound every bit as dramatic, but in a more intimate, neurotic way.

Werther.
Georges Thill ten Werther; **Ninon Vallin** mez Charlotte; **Marcel Roque** bar Albert; **Germaine Féraldy** sop Sophie; **Armand Narçon** bass Bailli; **Henri Niel** ten Schmidt; **Louis Guenot** bass Johann;
Cantoria Children's Choir; Chorus and Orchestra of the Opéra-Comique, Paris / Elie Cohen.
EMI Références mono CHS7 63195-2 (two discs: 121 minutes: ADD). Notes, text and translation included. Recorded 1931. Ⓜ Ⓗ

If you want to hear just how thoroughly prepared, technically secure, idiomatic and deeply felt French singing could be between the wars, you need only listen to this wonderful performance, here brought to new life on this excellent EMI transfer. The reading shows the benefits of singers sticking to their own language and singing repertory they knew through and through. Vallin develops her portrayal unerringly. The placing of her tone, the way she moves naturally with the music and the consistently warm and steady tone – these are things to treasure. Thill's tone is just as glorious and true as his partner's, his enunciation of the text pleasing and unaffected. Each of Werther's many solos receive a near-ideal reading, with the voice at once plangent and virile. Perhaps what one marvels at more than anything is the way both singers scrupulously follow Massenet's copious markings of feeling and dynamics. The singers surrounding this sovereign pair are no less pleasing. Roque provides a mellow baritone and just the right amount of concern as the solid Albert. Narçon starts off the opera splendidly as a jovial Bailli. Féraldy is pert and lively as Sophie, with the light, airy soprano the role calls for but so seldom gets. Elie Cohen's conducting has elegance, balance and passion – but passion that never becomes overheated as it does in some modern interpretations. Tempos are all perfectly judged and Cohen avoids heavy-handed lingering that doesn't allow Massenet to speak for himself. All in all, a classic set. The sound is adequate.

William Mathias
British 1934-1992

Ave Rex, Op. 45[a]. Elegy for a Prince, Op. 59[b]. This Worlde's Joie, Op. 67[c].
[c]**Janet Price** sop [c]**Kenneth Bowen** ten [b]**Sir Geraint Evans** bar [c]**Michael Rippon** bass
[a]Welsh National Opera Chorus; [c]Bach Choir; [c]St George's Chapel Choir, Windsor Castle;
[ab]London Symphony Orchestra / David Atherton;
[c]New Philharmonia Orchestra / Sir David Willcocks.
Lyrita SRCD324 (79 minutes: ADD). Texts included. Recorded 1973. Ⓕ

These three works were written between 1969 and 1974, and have a good deal in common yet enough separate identity for them to comprise a varied programme, the *Elegy for a Prince* forming a relatively tough and tangy item to be sandwiched in between the choral collections. Of these, *Ave Rex* is a set of carols, 'Sir Christmas' being now by far the best known, and *This Worlde's Joie* a cantata in four movements, nearly 50 minutes long, employing a boys' choir as well as the usual forces of soloists, mixed choir and orchestra. This, of course, makes us think of Britten, and indeed it is difficult not to think of him, and to a lesser extent Tippett, throughout the disc. *This Worlde's Joie* moves delightfully from one good setting to another, always contriving to unify the structure and work effectively towards climax and contrast. The Prince of the *Elegy* is Llywelyn ap Gruffudd, killed by English soldiers in 1282: a stern mood prevails, the orchestral writing harder and more austere than the composer's usual style, though it yields to some tender expression in the last section. Sir Geraint Evans sings with authority and dark coloration. The soloists in the cantata are excellent. All is conducted with vigour and care for detail, and the recordings are admirably clean.

Matteo da Perugia
Italian died before 1418

Helas Avril. Agnus Dei/Ave sancta mundi salus. Puisque la mort. Gloria: Spiritus et alme. Helas que feray. Gloria. Già da rete d'amor. Trover ne puis. Lurea martirii/Conlaudanda est.
Huelgas Ensemble / Paul Van Nevel.
Sony Classical Vivarte SK62928 (61 minutes: DDD). Texts and translations included. Recorded 1996. Ⓕ

Matteo da Perugia Choral and song

Matteo da Perugia is one of the oddly neglected composers of the years around 1400. Though evidently Italian, he wrote largely in the French manner, even when setting Italian texts; so neither national tradition adopts him today. His known output of over 30 pieces is extraordinarily varied in style and inspiration: he seems to have tried everything, often with stunning success. Paul Van Nevel's collection of nine pieces does ample justice to the variety of his output: French songs, Mass movements, motets and an Italian song; from the most chromatic and angular to the most harmonious; from the energetic to the gentle. He is occasionally headstrong in his choice of scoring, from the use of a female chorus in *Helas Avril* to transposing the middle stanza (only) of *Puisque la mort* up a fourth. But everything is done to serve the music, and everything is with an eye to revealing the wayward beauty of this fascinating composer. He helps you to hear inside the music. The sound is good and clear; the singers are excellent; and Van Nevel contributes a characteristically challenging booklet-note that explains his approach.

Siegfried Matthus

German 1934

Matthus String Quartet, 'The Maiden and Death'.
Schubert String Quartet No. 14 in D minor, D810, 'Death and the Maiden'.
Petersen Quartet (Conrad Muck, Gernot Süssmuth *vns* Friedemann Weigle *va* Hans-Jakob Eschenburg *vc*).
Capriccio 10 744 (67 minutes: DDD). Recorded 1997. Ⓕ

Siegfried Matthus, a pupil of Hans Eisler, rose to prominence in the former East Germany as a composer of operas and orchestral music. This quartet was given its première by the Petersen Quartet in 1997. The fearsome yet seductive figure of Death in the Claudius poem set by Schubert is updated; here Death offers himself as a drug. Matthus fashions an absorbing musical drama, with vivid, memorable images (the quartet is quite wonderfully played). The way he portrays the disintegration of personality in the hallucinatory middle movement is particularly convincing. After this, the dirge-like final section is less riveting – the mood is appropriately bleak and empty, but the funeral-march rhythms give an impression of convention and formality. The Schubert, too, is finely played. The Petersen Quartet, taking fewer liberties with the tempos than many other groups, gives an irresistible rhythmic drive to the *Scherzo* and finale. It's meticulous, too, in observing all Schubert's many *pianissimos*. Where these denote sinister, chilling music its whispered playing is brilliantly successful; where the mood is lyrical it's difficult not to feel the style should be more expressive. The recorded sound is excellent.

Judith.
Eva-Maria Bundschuh *sop* Judith; **Werner Haseleu** *bass* Holofernes; **Christiane Röhr** *contr* Mirza; **Hans-Otto Rogge** *ten* Ephraim; **Manfred Hopp** *ten* Daniel; **Hans-Martin Nau** *bass* Osias; **Vladimir Bauer** *bar* Ammon; **Alfred Wroblewski** *bass* Oberpriester; **Klement Slowioczek** *bass* Hosea; **George Jonescu** *bar* Achior; **Horst-Dieter Kaschel** *bass* Hauptmann; **Wolfgang Hellmich** *bar* Kämmerer; **Joachim Vogt** *ten* Bote; **Peter Seufert** *ten* Gesandter aus Edom; **Helmut Völker** *bass* Gesandter aus Moab; **Berlin Radio Men's Chorus;** **Choral Soloists and Orchestra of the Komische Oper, Berlin / Rolf Reuter.**
Berlin Classics 0093392BC (two discs: 118 minutes: DDD). Notes and German text included. Recorded 1986. Ⓕ

The reason for this opera's success is immediately apparent, as is Matthus's gripping ability to evoke a stage picture. The plot is based on the Apocrypha and on Friedrich Hebbel's dramatization of the story, further modified by Matthus himself. In the opera Holofernes is no mere brutish conqueror, but a more complex character, wearied by easy victories, over women as well as nations. Judith, a widow but still a virgin, welcomes the task of slaying her people's conqueror because it will give some point to her life. You've guessed: they each recognize something in each other (and in this version of the story Holofernes knows perfectly well that Judith means to kill him) and she is no longer a virgin when she kills him in his sleep. As the people praise her and their God, her rejected suitor Ephraim (who had seen her with Holofernes) denounces her as 'the whore of Israel' and strips her naked. In a stunning *coup de théâtre* the chorus then marches into the auditorium to sing a powerful but despairing passacaglia while, on stage, all the characters of the drama present a nightmarish dumb-show of Judith's destruction.

And the music? Very powerful. The word-setting is frequently jagged, the orchestra harshly violent, but brief melodic motifs are often repeated obsessively, with pounding rhythms owing something to the later Carl Orff: this is not a difficult score. In the First Act there is much impressive writing for double choir and the larger than life-size characters of Judith and Holofernes are sketched in rhetorical monologues (and a duet) after which the singers in question would probably regard

Elektra or Wotan as a pleasantly relaxing evening off. Act 2 is quieter, focused on the encounter between the two protagonists; after the killing Judith sings as though in a trance, accompanied by a glittering 'continuo' of harp, piano, cymbals and tuned percussion. Like the rest of the opera it is melodrama, but with a kick like a horse. Even if Matthus's score were less striking than it is, this recording would be notable for the fearless vocalism and the electrifying eloquence of Bundschuh's performance in the title-role: she is quite riveting. Haseleu's bass is vehement, effective, a bit rough (Holofernes's music would show up the worn patches in anyone's voice). The lesser roles are all well taken, the choral singing is splendid and the orchestral colours metallically, acidly brilliant. The recording pulls as few punches as Matthus's score. There is only a German libretto, alas.

Nicholas Maw

British 1935

Ghost Dances. La Vita Nuova. Roman Canticle.
Carmen Pelton sop **William Sharp** bar **Twentieth Century Consort / Christopher Kendall.**
ASV CDDCA999 (65 minutes: DDD). Texts and translations included. Recorded 1995.   Ⓕ

Maw's originality may not be the kind that leaps up and yells in your face; but original he certainly is. He can draw on influences as diverse as Britten and Richard Strauss in *La Vita Nuova*, blend elements of Schoenberg's *Pierrot* and Stravinsky's *Petrushka* with the sounds of Latin American and African folk instruments in *Ghost Dances*, and still come up with something that feels like nobody else. The sound of the soprano's sultry tonal phrases in *La Vita Nuova* is a long way from the eerie tone of the African Kalimba at the end of *Ghost Dances* – beautifully described by Malcolm MacDonald in his notes as 'like a phantom piano played with a bony finger'. And yet in context they are obviously the same composer: a romantic with a fertile imagination and a superb technical palate, who clearly delights in enticing and surprising the ear. The performances are of outstanding warmth and finesse. The sound world of *La Vita Nuova* emerges with such richness and depth that it's hard to believe that only ten instruments are playing and Carmen Pelton has a strong sense of the way the vocal lines soar and dip over long periods. William Sharp is eloquent and quite distinct throughout the short *Roman Canticle*. And everything in *Ghost Dances* seems as clear as it should be, with no loss of atmosphere – an excellent recording. It adds up to a perfect introduction to a composer who offers genuine, long-term rewards, not instant, transient gratification.

Sir Peter Maxwell Davies

British 1934

Corpus Christi, with Cat and Mouse. House of Winter. Sea Runes. Lullabye for Lucy.
Apple-Basket: Apple-Blossom. One star, at last. A Hoy Calendar. Westerlings.
BBC Singers / Simon Joly.
Collins Classics 1463-2 (71 minutes: DDD). Texts and translation included. Recorded 1995.   Ⓕ

You might think unaccompanied voices would cramp Maxwell Davies's style. Far from it: the range of colour and texture here is remarkable, all the more so since, with a single exception, all these pieces sound challenging but grateful to sing. The exception is *Westerlings*, which calls for a chorus of virtuosos. Like all this music, save *Corpus Christi*, it uses poems by the late George Mackay Brown, in this case a narrative of the Norse settlement of Orkney, interspersed with magical wordless 'seascapes' and concluding with a setting of the Lord's Prayer in the Orkney dialect of Old Norse: a solemn thanksgiving for a safe landfall. It is closely related to the sea music of Maxwell Davies's symphonies, but the texts and a brilliantly resourceful use of vocal effect and vocal 'scoring' (the illusion of flutes, strings, even an organ, is consummate) make it both dramatic and pictorially evocative. *House of Winter* portrays both the frozen stillness and the violent storms of an Orkney winter, but with poetry and luminous colour rather than onomatopoeia; like its companion piece, *Sea Runes*, its lines are kind to voices. Some of the smaller works here – the very pure melody over rocking 'lullays' of *Lullabye for Lucy*, *A Hoy Calendar* – would not tax a good amateur choir, though some pages of *Corpus Christi* most certainly would. The choral singing, as one would expect of this ensemble and this conductor, is superfine; the recording is both clean and pleasingly spacious.

The Doctor of Myddfai.
Paul Whelan bar Doctor; **Lisa Tyrrell** sop Child; **Gwynne Howell** bass Ruler;
Elizabeth Vaughan mez First Official; **Ann Howard** contr Second Official;
Nan Christie sop Third Official; **Deborah Parry-Edwards** sop Secretary;
Welsh National Opera Chorus and Orchestra / Richard Armstrong.
Collins Classics 7046-2 (two discs: 95 minutes: DDD). Notes and text included.
Recorded live in 1996.   Ⓕ

Maxwell Davies Opera

For Davies's seasoned admirers, *The Doctor of Myddfai* (1996) proves to be a characteristically probing addition to the canon, with much more than mere recycling of familiar gestures and structures. Doctors of Myddfai are legendary figures with magical powers of healing, and the opera concerns one particular Doctor and his difficult relationship with the ruler of an unnamed state. As told by David Pountney's libretto, the story is an uneasy mixture of Celtic mythologizing and Kafkaesque surrealism, in which the purely personal confrontation between the principal characters, Ruler and Doctor, is more fully developed than the social context of disease and environmental damage within which the action supposedly takes place. The tale would carry more conviction if this context were more fully represented. The libretto is also very wordy in places, and the music marks time during some of the long narrations. Where it is most successful is in conveying a sense of compassion for those who suffer, rulers and ruled alike, and it manages to suggest dimensions of feeling well beyond those which the events of the opera actually portray. The performance is a strong one, and all three principals are convincing, confident with the taxing musical idiom. Gwynne Howell is a tower of strength, and Paul Whelan, despite occasional distortions of the English text, ably conveys the Doctor's unearthly and obsessive spirit. Lisa Tyrrell sings persuasively as the Child, and the many small parts are well taken by various WNO stalwarts. Under Richard Armstrong's galvanizing direction the performance builds well to its dance-like apotheosis, and the sound is always clear, if a bit cramped, with stage noise evident but unobtrusive.

Billy Mayerl
British 1902-1959

Mayerl Crystal Clear. Orange Blossom. Piano Exaggerations. Pastorale Exotique. Wistaria. Canaries' Serenade. Shy Ballerina. Puppets Suite, Op. 77. Piano Transcriptions – Body and Soul; Deep Henderson; Tormented; Sing, you sinners; Cheer up; Have you forgotten?; The object of my affection; Is it true what they say about Dixie?; I need you; Love was born; I'm at your service.
Parkin Mayerl Shots, Sets 1 and 2. A Tribute to Billy Mayerl.
Eric Parkin *pf*
Priory PRCD544 (80 minutes: DDD). Recorded 1995.   Ⓕ

Nobody since the master himself has come anywhere near Parkin's easy technical mastery and fastidious musicianship in this delightful music. Some pianists hit the more demanding pieces quite hard: Parkin, like Mayerl, knows better and his playing is consistently light and subtle. This has always been his approach, allied to a faultless sense of pace and rhythm. However, Mayerl, apart from perfecting the piano novelty, also contributed to the English pastoral tradition, which Parkin knows equally well. *Shy Ballerina* is charmingly done with rubato which would be quite out of place in Mayerl's rhythmic numbers. The three-movement *Puppets Suite* is a *tour de force*. As a bonus on this generous 80-minute CD Parkin puts in two sets of his own pieces called *Mayerl Shots*. He explains that, as a result of practising lots of Mayerl, further ideas surfaced spontaneously in a similar idiom. These are all fluent tributes and there are even quotations for the specialists. The piano sound is sharp and clear. Essential listening.

Mayerl Scallywag. Jasmine. Oriental. Minuet for Pamela. Fascinating Ditty. Funny Peculiar. Chopsticks. Carminetta. Mignonette. Penny Whistle. Piano Transcriptions – Me and my girl; Blue velvet; Sittin' on the edge of my chair; The pompous gremlin; My heaven in the pines; Alabamy bound; Stardust; Please handle with care; Two lovely people; Two hearts on a tree; You're the reason why. Studies in Syncopation, Op. 55 – Nos. 7, 10, 14, 15 and 18.
Parkin Mayerl Shots, Set 3.
Eric Parkin *pf*
Priory PRCD565 (76 minutes: DDD). Recorded 1995.   Ⓕ

This release, 'Scallywag', has its own discoveries, notably the *Studies in Syncopation*, which parallel Bartók's *Mikrokosmos* in this field. There are three books of six pieces each, dating from 1930-31, and Parkin plays five of them, proving that they are not just exercises but real music. There are gems in the transcriptions – Carmichael's *Stardust*, Mayerl's own 'You're the reason why' from his 1934 show *Sporting Love*, and a forgotten but lovely tune by Peter York called *Two hearts on a tree*. The Spanish *Carminetta* is Mayerl's equivalent of Joplin's *Solace*. And there is real comedy – totally appreciated and effectively realized by Parkin – in *Chopsticks* and *Penny Whistle*. In addition Parkin gives us his own response to Mayerl in a similar idiom – a third set of his *Mayerl Shots*. The recording is adequate although there is occasionally some background noise.

Piano Transcriptions, Volume 3 – There's a small hotel; The mood that I'm in; So rare; I'm always in the mood for you; Turkey in the straw; For only you; Thanks for the memory; The Highland Swing; I got love; Amoresque; There's rain in my eyes; Patty cake, patty cake, baker man; Blame

it on my last affair; I have eyes; Like a cat with a mouse; Phil the Fluter's Ball; Fools rush in; Peg o' my heart; All the things you are; The Musical Earwig; Transatlantic Lullaby; Tell me I'm forgiven; Japanese Juggler; Poor little rich girl.
Eric Parkin *pf*
Priory PRCD468 (63 minutes: DDD). Recorded 1993. ⒡ ▣

This is pure 1930s music. This is not Mayerl as the lightning-fingered whizz-kid of the 1920s, although many of the transcriptions are tricky enough: it's the style he taught through the Billy Mayerl School of Music, a success story here and abroad until the war. These transcriptions – popular songs of the period arranged in Mayerl's inimitable English accent – are a wonderful encapsulation of an era and they transcend it – as long as they are played like this. The demands on the performer are similar to studying the style of the period at any time. Classically trained pianists have to work hard to play Joplin, Gershwin and Mayerl. But Mayerl belongs to them, as long as their left hand is strong enough, because this is basically a notated tradition rather than an improvised one. Parkin understands it all – the effortless lilt, the light touch, not too much pedal, nothing overdone, everything speaking for itself.

Nikolay Medtner
Russian 1880-1951

Piano Concerto No. 1 in C minor, Op. 33. Piano Quintet in C major, Op. posth.
Dmitri Alexeev *pf*
New Budapest Quartet (András Kiss, Ferenc Balogh *vns* Laszlo Barsony *va* Karoly Botvay *vc*);
BBC Symphony Orchestra / Alexander Lazarev.
Hyperion CDA66744 (59 minutes: DDD). Recorded 1994. ⒡

For Dmitri Alexeev the First Concerto is Medtner's masterpiece, an argument he sustains in a performance of superb eloquence and discretion. Even the sort of gestures later vulgarized and traduced by Tinseltown are given with an aristocratic quality, a feel for a love of musical intricacy that takes on an almost symbolic force and potency, but also for Medtner's dislike of display. Time and again Alexeev makes you pause to reconsider Medtner's quality, and his reserve brings its own distinctive reward. The early *Abbandonamente ma non troppo* has a haunting improvisatory inwardness and later, as the storm clouds gather ominously at 11'55", his playing generates all the necessary electricity. How thankful one is, too, for Alexeev's advocacy of the Piano Quintet where, together with his fully committed colleagues, the New Budapest Quartet, he recreates music of the strangest, most unworldly exultance and introspection. Instructions such as *poco tranquillo (sereno)* and *Quasi Hymn* take us far away from the turbulence of the First Concerto (composed in the shadow of the First World War) and the finale's conclusion is wonderfully uplifting. The recordings are judiciously balanced in both works, and the BBC Symphony Orchestra under Lazarev are fully sympathetic.

Piano Concertos – No. 2 in C minor, Op. 50; No. 3 in E minor, Op. 60.
Nikolai Demidenko *pf*
BBC Scottish Symphony Orchestra / Jerzy Maksymiuk.
Hyperion CDA66580 (74 minutes: DDD). Recorded 1991. *Gramophone* Award Winner 1992.⒡ ▣▣

This splendid disc is given a fine recording, good orchestral playing from a Scottish orchestra under a Polish conductor and, above all, truly coruscating and poetic playing from the brilliant young Russian pianist Nikolai Demidenko. Medtner was a contemporary and friend of Rachmaninov; he settled in Britain in the 1930s, and like Rachmaninov he was an excellent pianist. But while the other composer became immensely popular, Medtner languished in obscurity, regarded as an inferior imitation of Rachmaninov who wrote gushing music that was strong on gestures but weak on substance. The fact is that he can be diffuse (not to say long-winded) and grandiose, and memorable tunes are in short supply, so that his music needs to be played well to come off. When it is, there is much to enjoy, as here in Demidenko's hypnotically fiery and articulate accounts.

Piano Concertos Nos. 2 and 3. Arabesque in A minor, Op. 7 No. 2. Fairy Tale in F minor, Op. 26 No. 3.
Nikolay Medtner *pf*
Philharmonia Orchestra / Issay Dobrowen.
Testament mono SBT1027 (77 minutes: ADD). Recorded 1947. ⒡ ▣

The strong Russian flavour of the ornate writing is evident, as is the composer's masterly understanding of the piano. Listening to the composer himself in the Second's first *molto cantabile a tempo, ma expressivo* or the Third's *dolce cantabile* is to be made doubly aware of his haunting and bittersweet lyricism. The streaming figuration in the Second Concerto's *Romanza* is spun off with deceptive ease, a reminder that while Medtner despised obvious pyrotechnics he was a superb pianist. Two exquisitely played encores are included (the ambiguous poetry of the A minor *Arabesque* could be by no other composer), and the 1947 recordings have been superbly remastered.

Violin Sonatas – No. 1 in B minor, Op. 21; No. 2 in G major, Op. 44.
Lydia Mordkovitch *vn* **Geoffrey Tozer** *pf*
Chandos CHAN9293 (60 minutes: DDD). Recorded 1993.   Ⓕ

Mordkovitch's readings emphasize a lyrical and relaxed approach, and this is particularly so in the lyrical first movement of the short, attractive First Sonata – a little too relaxed perhaps in the outer sections of the lilting second movement 'Danza'. Elsewhere (for instance the *Allegro appassionato* and Finale-Rondo of the Second Sonata), Mordkovitch has an intuitive grasp of structure, allowing the music to unfold with a high degree of ease and direction. These artists are persuasive interpreters of these works and can be strongly recommended to the first-time explorer. The recorded sound is warm and well balanced.

Medtner Violin Sonata No. 3 in E minor, Op. 57, 'Epica'.
Ravel Violin Sonata.
Vadim Repin *vn* **Boris Berezovsky** *pf*
Erato 0630-15110-2 (61 minutes: DDD). Recorded 1996.   Ⓕ

Of Medtner's three sonatas this is perhaps the most intricately worked and, at over 40 minutes, certainly the most substantial. At times it seems almost too long for its own good and for that reason it needs a very persuasive and masterly performance in order to project its strengths. Fortunately this one is about as persuasive as you can get – Repin is lyrical and passionate and has plenty of fiery temperament for this music, and he is ideally complemented by Berezovsky's equally splendid playing. Much is made of the sonata's lyrical and melodic abundance (the *Scherzo* is delivered with great panache) and Repin's choice of tempo for all movements is expertly judged. In the Ravel, Repin and Berezovsky are perhaps even more impressive. As a vehicle for Repin's talent it shows what a marvellous colourist he is, what exceptional subtlety and nuance he brings to the music and, in the 'Blues' movement especially, the sheer *frisson* he is capable of generating. One cannot understate the superb ensemble playing either, with Berezovsky perfectly attuned to every twist and turn of Repin's playing. The recorded sound is very realistic and naturally balanced.

Eight Mood Pictures, Op. 1. Three Improvisations, Op. 2. Three Novelles, Op. 17. Improvisation, Op. 31 No. 1. Etude 'of medium difficulty'. Three Hymns in Praise of Toil, Op. 49.
Geoffrey Tozer *pf*
Chandos CHAN9498 (70 minutes: DDD). Recorded 1995.   Ⓕ

Dithyramb in E flat major, Op. 10 No. 2. Fairy Tale in F minor, 'Ophelia's song', Op. 14 No. 1. Sonatas, Op. 25 – No. 1 in C minor, 'Sonata-Skazka'; No. 2 in E minor, 'The Night Wind'. Sonate-Idylle in G, Op. 56.
Geoffrey Tozer *pf*
Chandos CHAN9618 (72 minutes: DDD). Recorded 1995.   Ⓕ

Medtner's piano music contains glories and riches indeed – an unending sense of intricacy from Russia's most subtle and recondite composer. Even when Medtner reminds you of his debt to others (to, say, Brahms and Schumann) he remains inimitably himself, ranging effortlessly from lyric to epic and essaying everything in between. Take the 'Prologue', from Op. 1, composed when Medtner was 18 and prefaced by some lines from Lermontov telling of a soul carried to earth by an angel. Such serenity and other-worldly preoccupation are expressed in music of rippling complexity, soaring to declamatory heights before resuming its former pensiveness and quiet ecstasy. In total contrast *The Night Wind* Sonata, dedicated to and greatly admired by Rachmaninov, is among the most daunting of all sonatas; of heroic length and ambition. Then there are the *Three Hymns in Praise of Toil*, transcending their seeming workaday proletariat title, their radiant outpouring coloured by a typically Slavic anxiety and unease. 'Nixe' (a water sprite – Op. 2 No. 1), on the other hand, reminds us of Szymanowski in its exoticism, most notably in a magical and shimmering final retreat. The *Improvisation*, Op. 31 No. 1 is another of Medtner's finest, most imaginative offerings, and if the *Dithyramb* exults in Brahmsian fullness, its final pages, which seem to engulf the entire keyboard, are of a vehemence and force peculiar to Medtner. Playing throughout with an enviable strength, grace and subtlety and with an unfailingly beautiful sonority, Geoffrey Tozer is more than equal to every occasion. Hearing him, for example, in the Sonata, Op. 25 No. 2 or in the slow movement from the *Sonata-Skazka* (complete with a melody he describes in his excellent notes as 'one of the loveliest Medtner ever wrote'), you will be made more than aware of his warmth and affection as well as his imperturbable fluency and skill. Played with such conviction all this music acquires a haunting idiosyncrasy which repays constant attention, even when, as Tozer engagingly puts it, 'the themes in Medtner's perorations are like guests leaving a party, standing in the doorway with hats and coats on, saying goodbye, but each unwilling to be the first to leave'. The recordings are of the highest quality.

Sonata in F minor, Op. 5. Two Fairy Tales, Op. 8. Sonata Triad, Op. 11. Sonata in G minor, Op. 22. Sonatas, Op. 25 – No. 1 in C minor, 'Sonata-Skazka'; No. 2 in E minor, 'The Night Wind'. Sonata-Ballade in F sharp major, Op. 27. Sonata in A minor, Op. 30. Forgotten Melodies – Set I, Op. 38; Set II, Op. 39. Sonata romantica in B flat minor, Op. 53 No. 1. Sonata minacciosa in F minor, Op. 53 No. 2. Sonate-Idylle in G major, Op. 56.
Marc-André Hamelin *pf*
Hyperion CDA67221/4 (four discs: 279 minutes: DDD). Recorded 1998.　　　　　　　Ⓜ

With this classic recording of the 14 piano sonatas, Medtner's star soared into the ascendant. Superlatively played and presented, it effects a radical and triumphant transition from years of indifference to heady acclaim. True, Medtner was celebrated by Rachmaninov as 'the greatest composer of our time' and championed by pianists such as Moiseiwitsch, Horowitz and Gilels, yet his music fell largely on deaf ears. Such irony and enigma lie in the music itself, in its distinctive character, colour and fragrance. Listeners were understandably suspicious of music that yields up its secrets so unreadily, almost as if Medtner wished it to remain in a private rather than public domain. Moments of a ravishing, heart-stopping allure, and heroics on the grandest of scales are apt to occur within an indigestible, prolix and recondite context. On paper (and it is virtually impossible to appreciate or consider Medtner without a score) everything is comprehensible, yet the results are never quite what you expect. Much of the writing, too, is formidably complex, with rhythmic intricacies deriving from Brahms and whimsicalities from Schumann supporting a recognizably Slavic yet wholly personal idiom.

Such writing positively demands a transcendental technique and a burning poetic commitment, a magical amalgam achieved with delicacy, drama and finesse by Marc-André Hamelin. Interspersing the sonatas with groups of miniatures containing some of Medtner's most felicitous ideas, he plays with an authority suggesting that such music is truly his language. Wherever you turn you will find a stylistic consistency and aplomb that make you realize that mastery of Medtner's difficulties requires a reflex and elegance beyond mere physical preparation, a capacity to absorb, away from the keyboard, a plethora of ideas, and resolve them into an unfaltering lucidity. Hamelin achieves an unfaltering sense of continuity, a balance of sense and sensibility in music that threatens to become submerged in its own passion. Readers uncertain of Medtner's elusive art should try the *Forgotten Melodies* (and most of all 'Alla reminiscenza'), the *Sonata Triad* and, by contrast, the simple Elysium conjured in the first movement of the *Sonate-Idylle*. Such heaven-sent performances will set you journeying far and wide, their eloquence and calibre accentuated by Hyperion's sound, by clarity, warmth and refinement.

The Angel, Op. 1a. Winter Evening, Op. 13 No. 1. Songs, Op. 28 – No. 2, I cannot hear that bird; No. 3, Butterfly; No. 4, In the Churchyard; No. 5, Spring Calm. The Rose, Op. 29 No. 6. I loved thee well, Op. 32 No. 4. Night, Op. 36 No. 5. Sleepless, Op. 37 No. 1. Songs, Op. 52 – No. 2, The Raven; No. 3, Elegy; No. 5, Spanish Romance; No. 6, Serenade. Noon, Op. 59 No. 1. Eight Songs, Op. 24.
Ludmilla Andrew *sop* **Geoffrey Tozer** *pf*
Chandos CHAN9327 (60 minutes: DDD). Texts and translations included. Recorded 1993.　　　Ⓕ

Musical Opinion, reviewing the newly published Op. 52 in 1931, concluded that, 'very accomplished musician' as he undoubtedly was, Medtner could hardly be considered 'a born song writer': 'These restless, feverish compositions with their incessant chromaticism and modulations are essentially unvocal, though they are dramatic and rhapsodical enough.' It says something for the achievement of Ludmilla Andrew that the 'unvocal' character of Medtner's writing is hardly evident at all, though, to be fair, the first three songs from Op. 52 are perhaps the very ones in which the voice is most hard-pressed and in which it is even possible to feel that they might do very well as piano solos. In the 'Serenade' (No. 6 in the set), the piano part *is* an accompaniment, and the singer brings to it a charm and delicacy worthy of its dedicatee, Nina Koshetz. Geoffrey Tozer is an excellent accompanist. His playing of 'Winter Evening', with its evocative rustling start, is superb; but always, along with the sheer virtuosity, there is a responsive feeling for mood and coloration. There are songs in which the piano takes over. Yet in many the interest is evenly distributed, and these are among the most delightful in the repertoire.

Felix Mendelssohn

German 1809-1847

Piano Concertos – No. 1 in G minor, Op. 25; No. 2 in D minor, Op. 40. Capriccio brillant in
B minor, Op. 22. Rondo brillant in E flat major, Op. 29. Serenade and Allegro giocoso, Op. 43.
Stephen Hough pf
City of Birmingham Symphony Orchestra / Lawrence Foster.
Hyperion CDA66969 (75 minutes: DDD). Recorded 1997. Ⓕ 🆁🆁

With Stephen Hough's Mendelssohn we enter a new dimension. The soft, stylish arpeggios that
open the first work here, the *Capriccio brillant*, announce immediately that something special is on
the way. But this is just a preparation for the First Concerto. Here again, 'stylish' is the word. One
can sense the background – especially the operatic background against which these works were
composed (Weber is very much present). The first solo doesn't simply storm away, *fortissimo*; one
hears distinct emotional characteristics: the imperious, thundering octaves, the agitated semiquavers,
the pleading appoggiaturas. The revelation is the First Concerto's slow movement: not a trace of
stale sentimentality here, rather elegance balanced by depth of feeling. Some of the praise must go
to the CBSO and Lawrence Foster; after all it's the CBSO violas and cellos that lead the singing in
that slow movement. Foster and the orchestra are also effective in the opening of the Second
Concerto – too often dismissed as the less inspired sequel to No. 1. The first bars are hushed,
sombre, a little below the main tempo, so that it's left to Hough to energize the argument and set
the pace – all very effective.

Piano Concerto in A minor. Concerto for Violin, Piano and Strings in D minor.
Rainer Kussmaul vn **Andreas Staier** fp
Concerto Köln.
Teldec Das Alte Werk 0630-13152-2 (72 minutes: DDD). Recorded 1996. Ⓕ 🅿

These two boyhood works of Mendelssohn, dating from his early teens, make an excellent coupling,
providing generous measure too, when the brilliant boy was here writing more expansively than he
did in his later, mature concertos. Given that these works were first heard in the Sunday salons at
the Mendelssohns' home, it is logical that they should be recorded here not just on period
instruments but with a small band of strings, in places one instrument per part. What is less
welcome is that the strings of Concerto Köln adopt what might be regarded as an unreconstructed
view of period string-playing, so that the orchestral tuttis are rather trying, not least in slow
movements, even on an ear well adjusted to period performance. The soloists, both outstanding,
provide a total contrast, and there the violinist, Rainer Kussmaul, is if anything even more
impressive than Andreas Staier, for many years the harpsichordist of Concerto Köln and here the
director as well as soloist. Throughout the Double Concerto Kussmaul plays with rare freshness
and purity, allowing himself just a measure of vibrato, and if Staier takes second place, that is not
just a question of balance between the violin and an 1825 fortepiano by Johann Fritz of Vienna,
but of the young composer's piano writing, regularly built on passagework, often in arpeggios,
rather than straight melodic statements. No doubt that had something to do with the pianos of the
day, with their limited sustaining power. That applies to the piano writing in the Piano Concerto
too, and it is striking that though each work is astonishing from a composer so young, the Double
Concerto, written just a year later, reveals a clear development. The material is not nearly as
memorable in either work as it is in such a masterpiece as the Octet of two years later, yet in every
movement, not least the finales of both works, the composer is clearly identifiable as Mendelssohn.

Double Piano Concertos – E major; A flat major.
Benjamin Frith, Hugh Tinney pfs
RTE Sinfonietta / Prionnsías O'Duinn.
Naxos 8 553416 (74 minutes: DDD). Recorded 1995. Ⓢ

Mendelssohn was 14 when he completed his first two-piano Concerto in E major, and still only 15
when he followed it with a considerably longer (rather too long) and more ambitious second in
A flat. Both concertos were first heard at the family's Sunday morning music parties, with the
composer's much-loved, slightly older sister, Fanny, at the second piano. As her talents were akin to
his own, the two solo parts are indistinguishable in their challenges. And it is to the great credit of
Benjamin Frith and Hugh Tinney that without a score at hand, you would be hard-pressed to guess
who was playing what. You will be as impressed by their attunement of phrasing in lyrical contexts
as by their synchronization in all the brilliant semiquaver passagework in which both works abound.
Their uninhibited enjoyment of the imitative audacities of the later work's finale is a real *tour de
force*. Under Prionnsías O'Duinn the RTE Sinfonietta plays with sufficient relish to allow you to
forget that the recording is perhaps just a little too close. In short, a not-to-be-missed opportunity
to explore the precocious young Mendelssohn at super-bargain price.

Violin Concertos – E minor, Op. 64; D minor.

Violin Concerto in E minor. Symphony No. 4 in A major, Op. 90, 'Italian'. The Hebrides Overture, Op. 26, 'Fingal's Cave'.
Pinchas Zukerman *vn*
New York Philharmonic Orchestra / Leonard Bernstein.
Sony Classical The Royal Edition SMK47592 (73 minutes: ADD). Recorded 1958-69.　Ⓜ🆁🆁

Pinchas Zukerman's 1969 recording of the Violin Concerto is among his first sessions, and remains deeply satisfying and competitive to this day. Phrasing, tone-projection and technical brilliance all contribute to a reading of considerable charm and musicality, and Bernstein's accompaniment is patient and accommodating. But while the Concerto sits happily (and excels) among later arrivals, the symphony finds itself up against a whole host of preferable versions. Bernstein's *Italian* dates back to 1958 and starts out in a mood of uncompromising urgency; it's a robust affair and never short on affection, but decidedly non-*con moto*, both in the *Andante* and the following *Moderato*. The energetic outer movements are best, and the first has the benefit of its important repeat. *The Hebrides* is beefy and busy, with full-blown, weighty textures and bags of energy. The recording sound throughout is very immediate, occasionally rather dry and just occasionally muddled.

Mendelssohn Violin Concerto in E minor.
Bruch Violin Concerto No. 1 in G minor, Op. 26.
Schubert Rondo in A major, D438.
Nigel Kennedy *vn*
English Chamber Orchestra / Jeffrey Tate.
EMI CDC7 49663-2 (71 minutes: DDD). Recorded 1987.　Ⓕ

These are exceptionally strong and positive performances, vividly recorded. When it comes to the two main works, Kennedy readily holds his own against all comers. His view of the Mendelssohn has a positive, masculine quality established at the very start. He may at first seem a little fierce, but fantasy goes with firm control, and the transition into the second subject on a descending arpeggio (marked *tranquillo*) is radiantly beautiful, the more affecting by contrast with the power of what has gone before. Kennedy is unerring helped by Jeffrey Tate's consistently refreshing and sympathetic support. Though it is the English Chamber Orchestra accompanying, there is no diminution of scale whatever. With full and well-balanced sound, the piece even seems bigger, more symphonic than usual. In the slow movement Kennedy completely avoids sentimentality in his simple, songful view, and with Tate a devoted Mendelssohnian, the finale sparkles winningly with no feeling of rush. The coda is always a big test in this work, and Kennedy's and Tate's reading is among the most powerful and exciting on record, thrust home superbly.

The Bruch brings another warm and positive performance, consistently sympathetic, with the orchestra once more adding to the power. Kennedy is more than a match for rival versions, again bringing a masculine strength which goes with a richly expressive yet totally unsentimental view of Bruch's exuberant lyricism as in the central slow movement. The *Rondo* in A major, D438, dating from 1816, was originally written for solo violin accompanied by string quartet. Performed as here with string orchestra, it in effect becomes another *Concertstück*, following a regular Schubertian form, a substantial *Andante* introduction leading to an *Allegro*, lasting here in all some 16 minutes. The 19-year-old was simply enjoying himself with a flow of ideas that may not be very memorable but which in the hands of performers like this are sweetly entertaining.

Violin Concertos – E minor; D minor.
Kyoko Takezawa *vn*
Bamberg Symphony Orchestra / Claus Peter Flor.
RCA Red Seal 09026 62512-2 (53 minutes: DDD). Recorded 1994.　Ⓕ

Kyoko Takezawa and Claus Peter Flor offer performances which consistently reflect the joy of the performers in the music. Many other performances are faster in all but one of the six movements, but Takezawa uses that additional elbow-room to give the music an extra sense of fantasy, often of fun, entirely apt for this composer. In the central Andante of the E minor Takezawa, at her relatively slow speed, is just as fresh and unsentimental as the competition. Rather than power and weight, Takezawa in the outer movements finds a muscular resilience which in context is just as compelling. In the D minor Concerto such qualities are if anything even more striking, and one keeps registering moments of delight, whether in the Mozartian lightness of the first movement, full of fantasy, the Schubertian lyricism of the second, raptly done, with its musing little cadenzas for the soloist, or the Hungarian point of the finale.

String Symphonies – No. 1 in C major; No. 2 in D major; No. 3 in E minor; No. 4 in C minor; No. 5 in B flat major; No. 6 in E flat major; No. 7 in D minor; No. 8 in D major; No. 9 in C major; No. 10 in B minor; No. 11 in F major; No. 12 in G minor; No. 13 in C minor, 'Sinfoniesatz'.

String Symphonies Nos. 1-13.
Hanover Band / Roy Goodman.
RCA Red Seal 09026 68069-2 (three discs: 225 minutes: DDD). Recorded 1992-93. Ⓕ

Mendelssohn's extraordinary precocity is nowhere more comprehensively shown than in the 13 early string symphonies. The inventiveness is dazzling, as with (to take only two examples) the chorale idea in the Minuet of the Sixth Symphony or the brilliant contrapuntal writing in the Eighth Symphony, in which the more immediate inspiration was Mozart, and in particular the *Jupiter* Symphony. Roy Goodman makes use of the version with wind instruments for this symphony, which Mendelssohn made within three days of having written the original, and accepts Mendelssohn's astonishingly fast tempo markings. He brings them off brilliantly, even the helter-skelter bass pizzicatos in the Trio of the Minuet. He also shows, with the use of period string techniques, how quick Mendelssohn's ear was for novel sonorities. An affection for the still underprivileged viola may have come from Mozart, but Mendelssohn would also have heard these sounds pioneered by Weber. There are beautiful string sonorities even in the very earliest works, especially in the often darkly-hued slow movements; and the finales have all the pace and wit of the more mature Mendelssohn (that is to say, when he was in his teens). Goodman judges tempo well, which is to say he has a shrewd sense of weight as well as of pace. He also directs from the keyboard, which it is certain Mendelssohn himself would have done, and he permits himself the occasional contribution: both in theory and in practice, this is entirely in style. This set is intelligently assembled, scrupulously prepared, lucidly recorded and played with freshness and wit.

String Symphonies Nos. 1, 6, 7 and 12.
Nieuw Sinfonietta Amsterdam / Lev Markiz.
BIS CD683 (70 minutes: DDD). Recorded 1994. Ⓕ

Amazing stuff, brilliantly performed. The first of the symphonies fair bursts from the staves, with a chuckling finale that would surely have delighted Rossini. And although the Sixth Symphony's finale harbours hints of miracles to come, Mendelssohn's mature personality is more comprehensively anticipated in the Seventh. Again, the finale suggests the ebullient, life-affirming manner of the orchestral symphonies, albeit sobered by a spot of fugally formal writing later on. The Twelfth Symphony opens with a Handelian sense of ceremony, goes on to incorporate a characteristically tender *Andante* and ends with a finale that, to quote Stig Jacobsson's enthusiastic notes, 'dies away to *pizzicato* and a subsequent *accelerando* which recalls Rossini'. This is truly delightful music, the playing both sensitive and exciting, while BIS's sound is impressively full-bodied.

String Symphonies Nos. 2, 3, 5, 11 and 13.
Concerto Köln.
Teldec 0630-13138-2 (73 minutes: DDD). Recorded 1996. ⒻⓅ

The players have an excellent sense of spontaneity, and of the chamber music element which is part of the style of these works. They listen acutely, and respond sensitively to Mendelssohn's vivid sense of string colour, especially to his love of viola tone (as at the start of No. 11). They also have a just sense of tempo, and never appeal to sensation by playing the fastest movement as fast as they can: cases in point, where a little less than a flat out speed makes far more musical sense, are the *Allegro di molto* that opens No. 3 and the *Presto* concluding No. 5. There are plenty of choices for cycles of these highly enjoyable pieces, with really very little to choose between performances by expert string players of music that does not make very subtle interpretative demands, but these ones are top class.

Symphonies – No. 1 in C minor, Op. 11; No. 2 in B flat major, Op. 52, 'Hymn of Praise'; No. 3 in A minor, Op. 56, 'Scottish'; No. 4 in A major, Op. 90, 'Italian'; No. 5 in D major, Op. 107, 'Reformation'. Overtures – Die Hochzeit des Camacho, Op. 10; A Midsummer Night's Dream Op. 21; The Hebrides, Op. 26, 'Fingal's Cave'; Meeresstille und glückliche Fahrt, Op. 27; The Fair Melusina, Op. 32; Athalie, Op. 74; Ruy Blas, Op. 95.

Symphonies Nos. 1, 2[a] and 3-5. Overtures – The Hebrides; A Midsummer Night's Dream; The Fair Melusina. Octet in E flat major, Op. 20 – Scherzo.
[a]**Elizabeth Connell,** [a]**Karita Mattila** *sops* [a]**Hans-Peter Blochwitz** *ten*
London Symphony Orchestra / Claudio Abbado.
DG 415 353-2GH4 (four discs: 245 minutes: DDD). Recorded 1984-85. Ⓕ🆁🆁

Claudio Abbado gives us a comprehensive collection of Mendelssohn's mature symphonies plus three overtures and the orchestral arrangement (in shortened form) of the *Scherzo* from his String Octet, which at the first British performance in 1829 of the Symphony No. 1 Mendelssohn substituted for the Minuet third movement. If you have a programming facility on your player, you can quite easily insert that *Scherzo* instead of the Minuet, and the idea of having it as an appendix to the symphony, though not new, is a good one. The wide-ranging sound comes out most strikingly in Symphony No. 2. Abbado conveys a keen sense of joy with a wide expressive range. The yearning 6/8 movement is haunting at Abbado's quite slow speed, and though this speed for the *Andante religioso* brings obvious dangers of sweetness and sentimentality, he manages to avoid them completely with his warm but unmannered phrasing. Again, in the choral finale Abbado's speeds tend to be relaxed and the sense of joyful release is all the keener, when in response to the tenor's calls of 'Hüter, ist die Nacht bald hin?' ('Watchman, will the night soon pass?') the soprano gives her radiant call of 'Die Nacht ist vergangen ('The night has departed'). Elizabeth Connell is the more tenderly affecting by being placed at the point slightly at a distance, and then the chorus comes in with even more impact to signal the arrival of day. Earlier Connell and the second soprano, Karita Mattila, are nicely matched in the duet with chorus, 'Ich harrete des Herrn' ('I waited on the Lord'). Though their voices by natural timbre are not so silvery or pure as one ideally wants, the recording helps to give them a sweetness just as apt for the music. Hans-Peter Blochwitz's tenor may be on the light side for the key tenor part, but the tonal beauty and natural feeling for words and phrasing are a delight. So too is the singing of the London Symphony Chorus, particularly beautiful in the chorale, 'Nun danket alle Gott'. Abbado's expansiveness and the luminous choral sound makes for a rich result.

It is that avoidance of Victorian blandness which is striking in Abbado's accounts of Nos. 1 and 5. In No. 1 he is tough and biting in the C minor first movement, slower and simpler in the second, returning to a tough, dark manner for the Minuet and finale. This is a performance which has one marvelling that Mendelssohn could have ever have countenanced the idea of the Octet *Scherzo* as substitute, a piece so different in mood. The first movement of the *Reformation* finds Abbado biting and dramatic, and crisper and again quicker in the second movement *Allegro vivace*. In both the *Scottish* and *Italian* Symphonies Abbado's earlier versions clearly come into contention (these were recorded in 1968 and were long a staple of the Decca catalogue), but where in the *Scottish* the differences of interpretation are relatively unimportant – mainly a question of the slow movement being a little slower and heavier this time – those in the *Italian* are more striking. Here the outer movements are fractionally faster than before, but that difference brings just a hint of breathlessness in the playing of the LSO, where before it was so sparking. By contrast the noticeably faster speed for the second movement *Andante* this time sounds fresher, and the marginally faster speed for the third movement is preferable. As for the overtures, they too bring fresh and attractive performances, very fast and fleet in the fairy music of *A Midsummer Night's Dream* and with the contrast between first and second subjects of *The Hebrides* underlined.

Symphonies Nos. 1 and 5.
Deutsches Symphony Orchestra, Berlin / Vladimir Ashkenazy.
Decca 444 428-2DH (60 minutes: DDD). Recorded 1994.   Ⓕ

Ashkenazy conducts the former Radio Symphony Orchestra in fresh, finely moulded readings of Symphonies Nos. 1 and 5. He allows himself a spacious approach, phrasing affectionately in slow movements marked by consistently gentle *pianissimos*, not just a question of recording balance. So the second movement *Andante* of No. 1 is tender and the slow introduction of the *Reformation* Symphony has plenty of mystery. The *pianissimo* statements of the Dresden Amen introduction to the first movement have you catching your breath, as will the warmth of the initial statement of the *Ein' feste Burg* in the finale, on unaccompanied flute. By contrast Ashkenazy's *allegros* are often faster than other readings, with the Minuet of No. 1 becoming almost a scherzo, as does the second movement of the *Reformation*. There are moments in the first movements of both symphonies, where he comes near to sounding too hectic, but he compensates with springing rhythms. What is slightly disappointing is the relative thinness of the string sound, not as sweet as it could be, but this is only a minor reservation.

Symphony No. 2.
Soile Isokoski *sop* **Mechthild Bach** *sop* **Frieder Lang** *ten*
Cologne Chorus Musicus; Das Neue Orchester / Christoph Spering.
Opus 111 OPS30-98 (65 minutes: DDD). Text and translation included. Recorded 1993.   Ⓕ Ⓟ

The *Hymn of Praise* stands under the shade of Beethoven's *Choral* Symphony, with its considerable length and choral and solo contributions, but it does not reach similar heights of sublimity. What it does possess is an unassuming lyricism, vitality and elegance throughout that is highly attractive.

Christoph Spering is relaxed in his choice of tempos. In no way, however, does he let the music drag or become sentimental. With clean, crisp textures this is a most refreshing performance, full of incidental beauties. In the main *Allegro* of the first movement as well as in the opening section of the big choral cantata-finale, Spering's speeds are fast but refreshing. The rest is different, not just slower in its speeds, but often more affectionate. The duet for the two soprano soloists, 'Ich harrete des Herrn' ('I waited on the Lord'), is especially beautiful, with Soile Isokoski and Mechthild Bach both angelically sweet yet nicely contrasted. The tenor soloist too, Frieder Lang, is exceptionally sweet-toned. The chorus, as recorded in a warm acoustic, are not always ideally clear in inner definition, but the freshness of their singing matches that of the whole performance. Anyone attracted by the advance of period performance into nineteenth-century repertory should certainly investigate this issue.

Symphonies Nos. 3 and 4.
London Symphony Orchestra / Claudio Abbado.
DG 3-D Classics 427 810-2GDC (71 minutes: DDD). Recorded 1984.   ⑧ **RR**

Claudio Abbado's coupling of the *Scottish* and *Italian* Symphonies makes a pretty clear first choice for those wanting these works paired together (the full set is reviewed above). The sound is fresh within a pleasing ambience and the performances show this conductor at his very finest. *Allegros* are exhilarating, yet never sound rushed, and the flowing *Adagio* of the *Scottish* is matched by the admirably paced *Andante* in the *Italian*, with the mood of the 'Pilgrim's March' nicely captured. The *Scherzo* of the *Scottish* is a joy in its infectious gaiety, and the recording here clarifies textures that can often sound muddled, especially at the exuberant horn arpeggios. Both first-movement exposition repeats are included.

Symphonies Nos. 3 and 4.
San Francisco Symphony Orchestra / Herbert Blomstedt.
Decca 433 811-2DH (67 minutes: DDD). Recorded 1989 and 1991.   ⑤

Blomstedt's *Scottish* impresses most by dint of its joyous vigour (outer movements go with a will), rhythmic bounce (perky winds and razor-sharp strings in the *Scherzo*) and unaffected eloquence (as in his affectionately flowing yet never short-winded third movement *Adagio*). This *Italian*, too, is first-rate. Under Blomstedt the opening *Allegro vivace* positively fizzes along, aided by some quite beautifully sprung string playing, whilst the *Saltarello* finale is articulated with real panache. The middle movements are perhaps marginally less memorable, though again the stylish orchestral response yields much pleasure. Although the symphonies were actually set down some 17 months apart, Decca's admirably consistent sound picture possesses the exemplary clarity and sheen we have now come to expect from this particular source. No one can go far wrong with this disc.

Symphonies Nos. 3 and 4.
Leipzig Gewandhaus Orchestra / Kurt Masur.
Teldec Digital Experience 4509-92148-2 (67 minutes: DDD). Recorded 1987.   Ⓜ

If it were not for the characteristically reverberant Leipzig recording, which obscures rather a lot of inner detail in tuttis and does not always allow violin articulation to be heard clearly – as in the *Saltarello* finale of the *Italian* – this would count as near ideal a version of both works as we are likely to get. Masur chooses his speeds judiciously to bring out the freshness of inspiration, avoiding any hint of sentimentality in slow movements, taken at flowing speeds, while never making *allegros* sound fierce or breathless. The bloom on the Leipzig sound is beautifully captured in the lightly scored passages, but then the moment the texture grows thicker, the reverberant acoustic makes for much cloudier results. In the rippling *Scherzo* of the *Scottish*, the notoriously difficult passage where the horns take up the main theme is very murky, but for obvious reasons it can never be ideally clear. Some of the woodwind solos are also rather recessed, though the flute at the start of the finale of the *Italian* is beautifully light and delicate, and the plangent oboe in its prominent solo in the finale of the *Scottish* is given natural balance with no obscuring. Whatever the reservations over the sound, those who in the past have enjoyed Leipzig recordings as engineered by the East Germans need hardly worry. Masur's timing in the outer movements of both symphonies is ideal. His most controversial speeds are those for the inner movements, invariably on the fast side but flowing so easily that they lose nothing in warmth or tenderness. A definite library acqusition.

Symphonies Nos. 3 and 4. Overture – The Hebrides.
Ulster Orchestra / Dimitry Sitkovetsky.
Classic fM 75605 57013-2 (77 minutes: DDD). Recorded 1997.   Ⓜ

Violinist-turned-conductor, Dimitry Sitkovetsky, here draws from the orchestra superb performances of both symphonies as well as the overture, helped by the outstandingly full and rich recording, made in the Ulster Hall. In a way that challenges and generally outshines many rival discs, Sitkovetsky consistently conveys the feeling of live performances caught on the wing. With speeds beautifully chosen and with rhythms crisp and well sprung, his readings are full of light and shade, warmly dramatic, demonstrating an expressive freedom – notably in pressing ahead – which always sounds natural, never self-conscious. With refined playing from every section, at once tense and polished, textures are exceptionally clear and transparent, so that inner details are brought out that are often obscured. In that, the full and immediate recording adds to the impact and vivid sense of presence. The strings in particular produce some magical *pianissimos*, reflecting Sitkovetsky's own mastery as an instrumentalist, yet the stormy passages in the first movement of the *Scottish* also have a physical impact that brings out the inspiration from nature to an exceptional degree. Similarly in the *Hebrides* Overture, after a restrained opening, the atmospheric beauty of the writing comes out vividly. A very generous and apt coupling.

Symphony No. 3. Overture – The Hebrides; A Midsummer Night's Dream. Incidental music, Op. 61: Scherzo; Nocturne; Wedding March.
London Symphony Orchestra / Peter Maag.
Decca The Classic Sound 443 578-2DCS (76 minutes: ADD). Recorded 1957-60.　Ⓜ🄷

The Hebrides and the *Scottish* Symphony offer 'Classic' Decca engineering at its best: airy 1960 Kingsway Hall sound with a real sense of perspective drawing the ear in (woodwind set behind strings but without loss of clarity), pin-point instrumental positioning yet no impression of instruments sealed off from each other, and, for the pre-Dolby period, a remarkable dynamic range, accomplished with low hiss levels and no audible overloading. There is, perhaps, a slight thinness of tone in the middle register, a characteristic that is far more pronounced in the 1957 *Midsummer Night's Dream* excerpts, but the high-key clarity and fizzing presence readily compensate. Maag's intelligent balancing of the orchestra and gauging of the work's proportions and rhetoric do not preclude imaginative handling of their illustrative poetry; in other words, he is a superb Mendelssohnian stylist. Personal rhythmic and dynamic inflexions abound (no doubt eyebrows will rise at such things as his sudden broad delivery of the Mechanicals' clowning in the *Midsummer Night's Dream* Overture). Singing lines are all beautifully wrought, especially that of the symphony's *Adagio* (rather more leisurely than we are used to nowadays), and its 'martial' sections benefit from discreetly balanced timpani. In *The Hebrides*, the balance and range of the sound allow all those swells (superbly observed) to register in proper proportion – here is both delicate impressionism and all the stormy drive and drama that you could want, putting many more recent rivals in the shade. At the heart of this disc's success is, of course, the playing of the revitalized LSO, responding to some challenging tempos with mainly knife-edge precision of ensemble and superb attack – truly vintage LSO champagne.

Overtures – Die Hochzeit des Camacho; A Midsummer Night's Dream; Meeresstille und glückliche Fahrt; Ruy Blas; Athalie; The Hebrides.
Bamberg Symphony Orchestra / Claus Peter Flor.
RCA Red Seal RD87905 (59 minutes: DDD). Recorded 1987-88.　Ⓕ

Die Hochzeit des Camacho ('The Marriage of Camacho') Overture was written in 1825, two years before the masterly evocation of *A Midsummer Night's Dream*, with its gossamer fairies, robust mortals and pervading romanticism, and already demonstrates the teenage composer's enormous musical facility and organizational skills, together with the high quality of his invention. *Meeresstille und glückliche Fahrt* ('Calm sea and prosperous voyage' of 1828) anticipates *The Hebrides* of a year later, and celebrates an ocean voyage on a sailing ship. *Ruy Blas* is a jolly, slightly melodramatic, but agreeably tuneful piece and *Athalie* is also attractive in its melodic ideas. *Fingal's Cave* with its beauty and dramatic portrayal of Scottish seascapes matches the Shakespearian overture in its melodic inspiration (the opening phrase is hauntingly unforgettable) and shows comparable skill in its vivid orchestration. Flor directs wonderfully sympathetic and spontaneous performances, with the Bamberg Symphony Orchestra playing gloriously. There is abundant energy and radiant lyrical beauty in the playing and each piece is unerringly paced and shaped. The glowing recording gives a wonderful bloom to the orchestral textures without preventing a realistic definition.

Overture and Incidental Music to A Midsummer Night's Dream, Opps. 21 and 61.

A Midsummer Night's Dream.
Edith Wiens *sop* **Sarah Walker** *mez*
London Philharmonic Choir and Orchestra / Andrew Litton.
Classics for Pleasure CD-CFP4593 (50 minutes: DDD). Recorded 1987.　Ⓑ🆁🆁

This fine complete version of *A Midsummer Night's Dream* incidental music is a genuine bargain. Andrew Litton not only includes the linking melodramas but makes them seem an essential part of the structure. They are not separately banded, because they prepare for what is to come by echoing what has passed, as in the finale where a grand reprise of the 'Wedding March' and *diminuendo* lead naturally to the brief mentions of the fairy music from the Overture, before the delightful closing chorus, sung with an engaging lyrical felicity. How like Sullivan are the solo vocal lines here! Similarly, fragments of the *Scherzo* (which is played with the lightest touch – nicely articulated but not insubstantial) are used to anticipate the 'Fairies March'. The Overture is most attractively done, the violins light and dainty and the wide dynamic range making the strongest contrast with the full orchestral tuttis. The engineers have, by clever microphone placing and excellent balance, tamed the reverberation of Walthamstow Assembly Hall so that there is bloom on the sound, yet everything projects naturally and clearly. The woodwind detail is a delight and with excellent soloists the vocal numbers have plenty of character and are in the right scale – too much reverberation and the choruses can sound too heavy. The other orchestral movements are well characterized; the 'Nocturne', with a fine horn solo, is spaciously romantic and the 'Intermezzo', taken fast, has the right *appassionato* feeling without being melodramatic. This recording has everything going for it: freshness of approach, spontaneity of feeling and very good sound indeed.

A Midsummer Night's Dream. Symphony No. 4.
Kenneth Branagh *spkr* **Sylvia McNair** *sop* **Angelika Kirchschlager** *mez*
Women of the Ernst-Senff Chorus; Berlin Philharmonic Orchestra / Claudio Abbado.
Sony Classical SK62826 (78 minutes: DDD). Text included. Recorded live in 1995. Ⓟ Ⓔ

It makes an attractive package having Mendelssohn's *A Midsummer Night's Dream* music, dramatically presented (with Kenneth Branagh taking every role from Titania to Puck), very generously coupled with Mendelssohn's most popular symphony. Sony has managed to squeeze in 50 minutes of the *Midsummer Night's Dream* music, which means only a few minor omissions. Some may resist Branagh's style – burring his 'r's for a Mummerset Puck, coming near to an Olivier imitation in Oberon's final speech – but in his versatility he is very persuasive. Having speech over music in melodrama certainly makes sense of the more fragmentary passages of the score. Abbado's performances are a delight, fresh and transparent in the fairy music, with generally fast speeds made exhilarating, never breathless. The chorus is atmospherically balanced, with the two excellent soloists, Sylvia McNair and Angelika Kirchschlager, set more forwardly. The recording, made in the Philharmonie in Berlin, is rather more vivid, a degree less recessed than in the symphony, where the orchestra is placed at a slight distance, an effect one gets used to. In the *Italian* Symphony Abbado's reading has changed little since his earlier LSO version, though here and there, as in the third movement, the phrasing is this time a little more moulded. By any reckoning he remains one of the most persuasive interpreters of this delectable work.

Octet in E flat major, Op. 20. String Quintet No. 2 in B flat major, Op. 87.
Academy of St Martin in the Fields Chamber Ensemble.
Philips 420 400-2PH (63 minutes: ADD). Recorded 1978. Ⓕ

The glorious Octet is a work of unforced lyricism and a seemingly endless stream of melody. The Academy Chamber Ensemble, of fine soloists in their own right, admirably illustrates the benefits of working regularly as an ensemble for they play with uncommon sympathy. The string quintet is a work of greater fervour and passion than the Octet, but it is characterized by the same melodiousness and unfettered lyricism with plenty of opportunities for virtuoso playing, which are well taken. The recordings give a pleasant and warm sheen to the string colour of the ensemble.

String Quintets – No. 1 in A major, Op. 18[a]; No. 2 in B flat major, Op. 87[b].
Raphael Ensemble (Anthony Marwood, Catherine Manson *vns* Timothy Boulton,
Louise Williams *vas* [a]Andrea Hess, [b]Michael Stirling *vcs*).
Hyperion CDA66993 (58 minutes: DDD). Recorded 1997. Ⓕ

These two quintets – both of them masterpieces – emanate from opposite ends of Mendelssohn's career, Op. 18 being very much of a piece with the Overture to *A Midsummer Night's Dream*, Op. 87, presenting more in the way of ardent lyricism. The Raphael Ensemble's smoothly mellifluous performances and ecstatic involvement is tellingly exemplified in the first movement of Op. 18, where converging string lines set up some gloriously full textures, whereas the *Scherzo*'s contrapuntal scurryings inspire quiet-voiced virtuosity. Both performances convey the shimmer and bustle of Mendelssohn's string writing without forcing the issue and score full marks for imagination, tonal integration and musicality. The recordings are well-nigh ideal. This disc provides a rich yield of musical pleasure.

String Quartets – E flat major (1823); No. 1 in E flat major, Op. 12; No. 2 in A minor, Op. 13; No. 3 in D major, Op. 44 No. 1; No. 4 in E minor, Op. 44 No. 2; No. 5 in E flat major, Op. 44 No. 3; No. 6 in F minor, Op. 80. Andante, Scherzo, Capriccio and Fugue, Op. 81 Nos. 1-2.
Melos Quartet (Wilhelm Melcher, Gerhard Voss *vns* Hermann Voss *va* Peter Buck *vc*).
DG 415 883-2GCM3 (three discs: 199 minutes: ADD). Recorded 1976-81.   Ⓜ 🆁🆁

The familiar and misleading cliché of Mendelssohn as the cheerful chappie of early romanticism vanishes at the sound of the F minor Quartet, Op. 80. Here is the intensity, anguish and anger that everyone thought Mendelssohn incapable of. His beloved sister Fanny died in May 1847 (his own death was merely months away), and the ensuing summer saw him leave Berlin for Switzerland, where he began to 'write music very industriously'. And what remarkable music it is. Right from the opening *Allegro assai* one senses trouble afoot, an unfamiliar restlessness mixed in with the more familiar busyness. Furthermore the second movement is surely the most fervent and punishing that Mendelssohn ever wrote – wild, insistent and unmistakably tragic in tone. This gradual intensification and darkening that occurs throughout Mendelssohn's quartet cycle makes it a most revealing guide to his creative development. But much of the earlier music is profoundly 'Mendelssohnian' in the accepted sense of that term: fresh, dynamic, light-textured, beautifully crafted and full of amiable melodic invention. The very early E flat Quartet, Op. posth (composed when Mendelssohn was only 14), although fashioned very much in the style of Haydn and Mozart, points towards imminent developments – a song-like A minor Quartet, already taking its lead from late Beethoven in the same key, the E flat, Op. 12, with its delightful Canzonetta (once popular as a separate 'encore') and the eventful Op. 44 set, three of Mendelssohn's most concentrated full-scale works. And DG also adds the four separate pieces, Op. 81, thus treating us to the entire Mendelssohn string quartet canon. The Melos Quartet comes up trumps with a really superb set of performances – technically immaculate, transparent in tone and full of enthusiasm. The recordings have presence and clarity.

String Quartets Nos. 1 and 2.
Quatuor Mosaïques (Erich Höbarth, Andrea Bischof *vns* Anita Mitterer *va* Christophe Coin *vc*).
Auvidis Astrée E8622 (57 minutes: DDD). Recorded 1997.   Ⓕ 🅿

Saturated in Beethoven, youthfully experimental – these are still two of the finest string quartets written in the nineteenth century. Op. 13 (actually the first to be composed) is especially original: a turbulent, passionate work framed by a prelude and postlude based on a song – a product of an early love affair. There is nothing superficial about these performances. One senses deep, unforced absorption right from the start of both works. The sound of the gut strings (brightly recorded), and the relatively sparing vibrato, might create problems for one or two listeners; but the expressive manner is not significantly different from most conventional modern performances. There is no suggestion of cultivating 'period style' for its own sake, and no hurried tempos in slow movements – the music always has time to breathe. Both performances are refreshing and stimulating, particularly enjoyable in the 'Intermezzo' movements Mendelssohn provides in place of the scherzo or the more classical minuet.

Piano Trios – No. 1 in D minor, Op. 49; No. 2 in C minor, Op. 66.
Vienna Piano Trio (Wolfgang Redik *vn* Marcus Trefny *vc* Stefan Mendl *pf*).
Nimbus NI5553 (55 minutes: DDD). Recorded 1997.   Ⓕ

In Stefan Mendl the Vienna Piano Trio has an exceptionally brilliant pianist. Perhaps the spotlight ought not to be quite so much on the keyboard in the first of these two works, in D minor, but his fingerwork is delectably light and frothy. The composer himself, as an effortless prestidigitator, is of course much to blame in giving it so unrelentingly breathless a stream of notes. In the intervening six years before the C minor Trio, Mendelssohn learnt a lot – no doubt never forgetting his friend Hiller's comment that some of the patterned, arpeggio-type figuration in the earlier work was 'old-fashioned'. You need only compare the elfin *Scherzos* of both to appreciate the infinitely subtler scoring of the latter. Subject-matter is likewise more affirmatively contrasted throughout, notably in the chorale-inspired triumphs of the finale. A more forwardly projected, richer cello song would have helped, but general balance in Nimbus's resonant concert hall is better here than in the D minor. And the enthusiastic freshness and vitality of this young team is a constant stimulus (note their daringly fast tempo risked in both *Scherzos*). In sum, plenty to enjoy here.

Cello Sonatas – No. 1 in B flat major, Op. 45; No. 2 in D major, Op. 58. Variations concertantes, Op. 17. Assai tranquillo. Song without words, Op. 109.
Steven Isserlis *vc* **Melvyn Tan** *fp*
RCA Red Seal 09026 62553-2 (62 minutes: DDD). Recorded 1994.   Ⓕ 🅿 🅴

Isserlis and Tan offer idiomatic, well-turned performances full of freshness and vigour. Try the First Sonata in B flat major (which Mendelssohn wrote for his brother, Paul, in 1838), where the second movement's dual function as scherzo and slow movement is convincingly characterized, and the music's passionate outbursts sound arrestingly potent. Isserlis's and Tan's fine blend of subtlety and panache affectingly conveys the nostalgic mood of the *Variations concertantes*, and culminates powerfully in the work's conclusion. In the D major Second Sonata, Isserlis's and Tan's spontaneity and energy in the outer movements, skilfully controlled variety of timbre and touch in the *Scherzo*, and dramatic opposition of chorale (piano) and recitative (cello) in the third movement sound immensely compelling. In the *Assai tranquillo*, as in the charming *Song without words*, Op. 109, sympathetic tonal balance between cello and fortepiano in the softly lit recording poignantly brings out the music's sentiment. Isserlis and Tan effectively draw out the work's inconclusive ending to create a telling analogy of the eternal nature of friendship. Excellent balance and crisp, restrained recording helps vividly to evoke this music's romantic atmosphere.

Piano Sonata in E major, Op. 6. Variations sérieuses in D minor, Op. 54. Three Preludes, Op. 104*a*. Three Studies, Op. 104*b*. Kinderstücke, Op. 72, 'Christmas Pieces'. Gondellied in A major. Scherzo in B minor.
Benjamin Frith *pf*
Naxos 8 550940 (65 minutes: DDD). Recorded 1994-95. Ⓢ

The multiplicity of notes in Mendelssohn's piano music sometimes lays him open to the charge of 'note-spinning'. So what higher praise for Frith than to say that thanks to his fluency, tact and fancy, not a single work in this second volume seems to outstay its welcome. The unchallengeable masterpiece, of course, is the *Variations sérieuses*, so enthusiastically taken up by Clara Schumann, and still a repertory work today. Frith characterizes each variation with telling contrasts of tempo and touch without sacrificing the continuity and unity of the whole. Equally importantly, never for a moment does he allow us to forget the *sérieuses* of the title. No less impressive is his sensitively varied palette in the early E major Sonata (unmistakable homage to Beethoven's Op. 101) so often helped by subtle pedalling. But surely the recitative of the *Adagio* at times needs just a little more intensity and underlying urgency. Of the miniatures the six *Kinderstücke* ('Christmas Pieces' – written for the children of a friend) emerge with an unforced charm. As music they lack the romance of Schumann's ventures into a child's world, just as the *Three Studies* do of Chopin's magical revelations in this sphere. However, Frith's fingers never let him down. In the first B flat Study he even seems to acquire a third hand to sustain its middle melody. For sheer seductive grace, the independent *Gondellied* haunts the memory most of all. With pleasantly natural sound, too, this disc is quite a bargain.

Lieder – Op. 8: No. 4, Erntelied; No. 8, And'res Maienlied. Op. 9: No. 6, Scheidend. Op. 19*a*: No. 1, Frühlingslied; No. 2, Das erste Veilchen; No. 3, Winterlied; No. 4, Neue Liebe; No. 5, Gruss; No. 6, Reiselied. Op. 34: No. 1, Minnelied; No. 2, Auf Flügeln des Gesanges; No. 3, Frühlingslied; No. 6, Reiselied. Op. 47: No. 1, Minnelied; No. 2, Morgengrüss; No. 3, Frühlingslied; No. 4, Volkslied; No. 6, Bei der Wiege. Op. 57: No. 1, Altdeutsches Lied; No. 2, Hirtenlied; No. 4, O Jugend; No. 5, Venetianisches Gondellied; No. 6, Wanderlied. Op. 71: No. 1, Tröstung; No. 3, An die Entfernte; No. 4, Schilflied; No. 5, Auf der Wanderschaft; No. 6, Nachtlied. Op. 84: No. 1, Da lieg' ich unter den Bäumen; No. 3, Jagdlied. Op. 86: No. 1, Es lauschte das Laub; No. 4, Allnächtlich im Traume; No. 5, Der Mond. Op. 99: No. 1, Erster Verlust; No. 5, Wenn sich zwei Herzen Scheiden. Op. posth.: Das Waldschloss; Pagenlied; Der Blumenkranz; Warnung vor dem Rhein; Schlafloser Augen Leuchte.
Dietrich Fischer-Dieskau *bar* **Wolfgang Sawallisch** *pf*
EMI CMS7 64827-2 (two discs: 95 minutes: ADD). Texts included. Recorded 1970. Ⓜ

Mendelssohn's Lieder offer a challenge all their own, and Fischer-Dieskau takes it up with characteristic alacrity. As the majority of these songs are primarily accompanied melody, with little inherent teasing out or biting on the words, the singer is presented with a comparatively empty stage for his recreative imagination to design and pace. There are passing moments (in the Op. 47 *Morgengrüss*, for example) when the simplicity and ingenuousness of Mendelssohn's settings seems to frustrate Fischer-Dieskau. These moments, though, are rare. His voice, here in its prime, can draw on an extraordinarily wide palette of colour within the legato of the most timeworn strophic song. Both Fischer-Dieskau and Sawallisch, whose light-filled piano playing shows his real sympathy and understanding for this composer, know just when to move into the salon with Mendelssohn. The four Lenau settings and the little drama of mortality offered in *Das erste Veilchen* are re-created with a perfectly-scaled sense of fleeting ardour and melancholy. Best of all, perhaps, are those little vignettes of the dark mythology of the German folk-soul, those diabolic night rides into the forest which find Mendelssohn at his witchy best, and Fischer-Dieskau at his most virtuosic.

Lieder – Op. 8: No. 8, And'res Maienlied. No. 10, Romanze. Op. 9: No. 1, Frage; No. 5, Im Herbst; No. 7, Sehnsucht; No. 8, Frühlingsglaube; No. 9, Ferne; No. 10, Verlust; No. 12, Die Nonne. Op. 19a: No. 3, Winterlied; No. 4, Neue Liebe. Op. 34: No. 2, Auf Flügeln des Gesanges; No. 3, Frühlingslied; No. 4, Suleika; No. 5, Sonntagslied. Op. 47: No. 3, Frühlingslied; No. 5, Der Blumenstrauss; No. 6, Bei der Wiege. Op. 57 No. 3, Suleika. Op. 71: No. 2, Frühlingslied; No. 6, Nachtlied. Op. 86: No. 3, Die Liebende schreibt; No. 5, Der Mond. Op. 99: No. 1, Erster Verlust; No. 5, Wenn sich zwei Herzen Scheiden; No. 6, Es weiss und rät es doch keiner. Pagenlied, Op. posth.
Barbara Bonney sop **Geoffrey Parsons** pf
Teldec 2292-44946-2 (60 minutes: DDD). Texts and translations included. Recorded 1991. Ⓕ

The charm of these songs lies in their simple style and almost endless stream of delightful melody. Unlike other Lieder composers Mendelssohn avoided blatant word-painting or vivid characterizations and certainly the most satisfying songs here tend to be settings of texts which do not on the surface of it offer much scope for musical expression. But while this disc may not give us the very best of Mendelssohn, or indeed the finest examples of nineteenth-century Lied, the singing of Barbara Bonney makes this a CD not to be missed. Here is a rare example of a singer caught on record at the very height of her technical and artistic powers, able to exercise seemingly effortless vocal control in portraying the subtle colours and understated moods of each songs. The partnership with that ever-sensitive accompanist Geoffrey Parsons is inspired. Listen to how Bonney seems to float ethereally above the rippling piano figures in that most famous of all Mendelssohn songs, *Auf Flügeln des Gesanges* ('On wings of song') – a performance which can surely never have been bettered on record.

Lieder – Op. 8: No. 7, Maienlied; No. 8, And'res Maienlied. Op. 9: No. 1, Frage; No. 2, Geständnis; No. 8, Frühlingsglaube. Op 19a: No. 4, Neue Liebe; No. 5, Gruss. Op. 34: No. 2, Auf Flügeln des Gesanges; No. 3, Frühlingslied; No. 4, Suleika. Op. 47: No. 1, Minnelied; No. 4, Volkslied. Op. 57: No. 3, Suleika; No. 6, Wanderlied. Op. 71: No. 4, Schilflied; No. 6, Nachtlied. Op. 86: No. 3, Die Liebende schreibt; No. 5, Der Mond. Op. 99: No. 1, Erster Verlust; No. 6, Es weiss und rät es doch keiner. Op. posth.: Mädchens Klage; Das Waldschloss. Romances (Byron) – There be None of Beauty's Daughters; Sun of the Sleepless.
Dame Margaret Price sop **Graham Johnson** pf
Hyperion CDA66666 (59 minutes: DDD). Texts and translations included. Recorded 1993. Ⓕ 🅴

This recital wholly dispels any lingering doubts there may be about Mendelssohn as a composer of Lieder. He surpassed even Schubert and Brahms in his understanding of Heine's *Die Liebende schreibt*. At the heart of the recital are the settings of Goethe. Besides *Die Liebende schreibt* the pair include the poignant *Erster Verlust* and the two Suleika settings, neither quite a match for Schubert's inspired versions but valid in their own right, particularly when sung with Price's uninhibited, Lehmannesque ardour. Another facet of the performances, a free-ranging *Schwung*, can be heard in *Frühlingslied* and the familiar *Neue Liebe*. The real discoveries here are the two Byron settings uncovered by Johnson. Mendelssohn understood and knew how to set English and the accentuations here are wholly idiomatic. The recording has great presence. Both singer and pianist are in the room with us, anxious and able to please.

Die erste Walpurgisnacht, Op. 60. Songs without Words (orch. Matthus) – Andante con moto, Op. 19 No. 1; Allegro di molto, Op. 30 No. 2; Adagio, Op. 53 No. 4; Andante grazioso, Op. 62 No. 6. Lieder (orch. Matthus) – Op. 34: No. 2, Auf Flügeln des Gesanges; No. 6, Reiselied. Op. 19a: No. 4, Neue Liebe; No. 5, Gruss. And'res Maienlied, Op. 8 No. 8. Pagenlied, Op. posth. Schilflied, Op. 71 No. 4. Der Mond, Op. 86 No. 5.
Jadwiga Rappé contr **Deon van der Walt** ten **Anton Scharinger** bar **Matthias Hölle** bass
Bamberg Symphony Chorus and Orchestra / Claus Peter Flor.
RCA Red Seal 09026 62513-2 (61 minutes: DDD). Texts and translations included. Recorded 1994. Ⓕ

The idea of pagans outwitting their Christian oppressors inspired Mendelssohn to pen some of his most mischievous musical invention: Berlioz was extremely impressed and the rumpus that erupts when Druid guards 'come with prods and pitchforks' (track 8) matches the sailors' choruses from *The Flying Dutchman* for visceral excitement. The lighter Mendelssohn has doughty men tiptoe through a woodland retreat to a Puckish *Scherzo* while the closing 'hymn to faith' recalls the Second Symphony and *Elijah*. Claus Peter Flor directs a performance notable above all for its delicacy, its warmth of texture, its excellent solo singing and the energetic drive of the big choruses. The Overture in particular shows Flor's skill at creating a three-dimensional sound stage, shaping and blending, allowing due prominence to salient musical lines without spoiling the overall balance. The fill-ups are eight delightful Lieder interspersed with four of the *Songs without Words*, piquantly scored by Siegfried Matthus with especially imaginative use of harp and high percussion. 'Spring Song' becomes an oboe solo; 'May Breezes' is shared among solo strings and harp; No. 20 is passed to the solo horn (alluding unmistakably to *A Midsummer Night's Dream*); 'On Wings of Song' incorporates fluid harp writing, and 'Traveller's Song' restlessly shimmering strings (to fit the autumn wind). Deon van der Walt is the pleasingly mellifluous soloist and Flor is as considerate, authoritative and imaginative as he is in the main work. All in all, a super disc, beautifully engineered.

Elijah (sung in English).
Renée Fleming, Libby Crabtree *sops* **Patricia Bardon, Sara Fulgoni** *mezzos*
Matthew Munro *treb* **John Mark Ainsley, John Bowen** *tens* **Neal Davies** *bar*
Bryn Terfel *bass-bar* **Geoffrey Moses** *bass*
Edinburgh Festival Chorus; Orchestra of the Age of Enlightenment / Paul Daniel.
Decca 455 688-2DH2 (two discs: 131 minutes: DDD). Text included. Recorded 1996. Ⓕ 🅿 🄴 🆁🆁

Paul Daniel and Bryn Terfel ensure that this is one of the most dramatic performances of the oratorio on disc. The young conductor, with the advantage of a period instrument orchestra and an excellent one at that, has looked anew at the score and as a consequence reveals much of the rhythmic and dynamic detail not always present in other performances, at least those available on CD in English. His accomplishment in terms of pacing and of balance is also praiseworthy, and he earns further marks for using the trio, quartet and double quartet of soloists Mendelssohn asks for in specific pieces, so as to vary the texture of the music. Terfel simply gives the most exciting and vivid account of the prophet's part yet heard. His range, in terms of vocal register and dynamics, is huge; his expression, mighty and immediate, befits a man of Elijah's temperament. As the score demands, anguish, anger and sympathy are there in full measure, displayed in exceptional definition of words, and when this Elijah calls on the Lord for the saving rain, the Almighty could hardly resist such a commanding utterance. Yet there is always the inwardness part of the role demands, not least in 'It is enough': you sense a man at the end of his tether. As far as the other soloists are concerned, for the concerted numbers Daniel has chosen voices that nicely match each other in timbre. The chorus is alert and unanimous in both attack and well thought-through phrasing, but its actual sound is often a little soft-centred, partly because all-important consonants are ignored. In every respect the orchestral playing is exemplary.

Elijah (sung in German).
Helen Donath, Kerstin Klein *sops* **Jard van Nes** *contr* **Donald George** *ten* **Alistair Miles** *bass*
Leipzig Radio Chorus; Israel Philharmonic Orchestra / Kurt Masur.
Teldec 9031-73131-2 (two discs: 110 minutes: DDD). Text and translation included.
Recorded live in 1992. *Gramophone* Award Winner 1993. Ⓕ 🆂

This is a tremendous performance on almost every count. Never before on disc had the work been treated with such an accent on vivid drama: the Old Testament text and its setting sounds as if it had been created on the spot, all Victorian plush and sentiment disposed of. Nor had any previous recording anything like the immediacy, both choral and orchestral, as this one. The choral singing is fiery, yet disciplined. They sound wholly confident in tone, articulation and accent, responsive to all the roles they have to play, obedient to Mendelssohn's dynamic markings, and totally committed to the discipline imposed on them by Masur's incisive beat. The pace of his reading can be judged by the fact that it takes some 110 minutes over the score as compared with the customary, say, 125. No doubt the live recording has something to do with the sense of electricity in the performance. Chorus and conductor seem to have struck up an ideal rapport with the Israel Philharmonic, on home ground here in every sense. It plays with verve allied to a technical skill capable of keeping up with Masur's exigent demands. In consequence, sections (especially in Part 2) that can seem weak or uninspired in other hands here have a dynamic, driving force that carries all before it. Masur also gains credit for choosing soloists rather than the choir as demanded by Mendelssohn for the trios, quartets and double quartets.

Most of the solo singing is worthy of what surrounds it. With a voice of the right weight and timbre for the part, Alistair Miles sings an honest, strongly limned Elijah. He, more than the other soloists, would sometimes like a little more time than Masur permits him to phrase with more meaning, especially in 'Es ist genug' (even so he fines his tone away sympathetically at its moving close): by and large he stands up well to current competition, both in voice and delivery. Helen Donath is rightly urgent as the grieving widow, though one or two high notes discolour, and mostly belies her years. There is an excellent boy-like soprano as the Youth. Jard van Nes is even better, making a fiery Queen and singing her solos gravely but without sentimentality. The blot on the escutcheon is the wiry tenor and tight vibrato of Donald George, whose voice doesn't record well.

Elijah (sung in German).
Christine Schäfer *sop* **Cornelia Kallisch** *contr* **Michael Schade** *ten* **Wolfgang Schöne** *bass-bar*
Stuttgart Gächinger Kantorei; Stuttgart Bach Collegium / Helmuth Rilling.
Hänssler Classic 98 928 (two discs: 128 minutes: DDD). Text and translation included.
Recorded 1994.　　　　　　　　　　　　　　　　　　　　　　　　　　　　　　Ⓕ🄴

Rilling brings out arrestingly the drama of the piece, turning it into a well-varied, exciting quasi-opera, a far from traditional view of the oratorio. The vicissitudes of the prophet's eventful life, his reaction to events, the challenge to Baal, the encounter with Jezebel, have never sounded so electrifying. For that we have to thank Rilling's disciplined chorus biting in diction, precise and convincing in attack. Yet they can also provide the most sensitive, ethereal tone, as in Nos. 28 and 29, trio and chorus, 'Siehe, der Hüter Israels'. In general, every strand of the complex writing for chorus is made clear yet the overall effect is one of spontaneous combustion. The orchestral playing is no less arresting. Furthermore as Elijah Schöne unerringly or authoritatively captures his many moods. Here is the courageous man of action as he confronts Baal's followers and ironically taunts them, the sense of fiery conviction in 'Ist's nichts des Herrn Wort', of doubt in 'Es ist genug', and finally the wonderful Bachian serenity in 'Ja, es sollen wohl Berge weichen', all evoked in the most positive and imaginative delivery of the text. The voice itself, a firm, expressive bass-baritone, is ideal for the role, one on which the singer has obviously lavished much time and consideration – to excellent effect. The same can be said for Schäfer, who brings a Silja-like conviction to all her work, nowhere more so than in 'Höre Israel'. Anyone hearing her declaim 'Weiche nicht' would never be afraid again. The voice itself is interesting, gleaming yet not without warmth in the tone. Kallisch is almost as convincing in the mezzo solos and gives us a wonderfully malign portrayal of Jezebel. Schade is a fresh-voiced, communicative Obadiah, and he's another who is vivid with his words, especially so in the juniper tree recitative. The recording, however, is slightly too reverberant, but on this occasion the added space around the voices doesn't preclude immediacy of impact.

Paulus, Op. 36.
Juliane Banse *sop* **Ingeborg Danz** *mez* **Michael Schade** *ten* **Andreas Schmidt** *bar*
Stuttgart Gächinger Kantorei; Prague Chamber Choir;
Czech Philharmonic Orchestra / Helmuth Rilling.
Hänssler Classic 98 926 (two discs: 131 minutes: DDD). Text and translation included.
Recorded 1994.　　　　　　　　　　　　　　　　　　　　　　　　　　　　　　　　Ⓕ

Rilling gives dramatic life to a work that can all too easily ramble episodically. His own Stuttgart choir, such a revered group, and the Czech forces partnering them make certain that their conviction comes across to us boldly. Each section is firmly integrated into the whole and offers great clarity. Schmidt is excellent with his steady, warm voice and he is completely inside the role. His singing of 'Gott sei gnädig' is both firmly phrased and movingly interpreted. Young Juliane Banse sings her recitatives and solos, especially 'Jerusalem', with notable beauty of tone. The youthful German-Canadian tenor Michael Schade is an artist of the utmost refinement and intelligence. If you already have the Kurt Masur version on Philips (now deleted) you need not feel you have second-best but if you're a newcomer to the work Schmidt will probably win you over to Rilling.

Aarre Merikanto　　　　　　　　　　　　　　　　　　　　　　Finnish 1893-1958

Piano Concertos Nos. 2 and 3. Two Studies. Two Pieces.
Matti Raekallio *pf*
Tampere Philharmonic Orchestra / Tuomas Ollila.
Ondine ODE915-2 (55 minutes: DDD). Recorded 1997.　　　　　　　　　　　　　　Ⓕ

While it is undeniably true that the principal legacy of Aarre Merikanto lies in his most pioneering music, dating roughly from the period 1918-31, his later, more accessible, style yielded works with much to offer. The Second and Third Piano Concertos (from 1937-8 and 1955 respectively; No. 1 was written prior to the First World War) are typical of his later output – contrapuntally inventive and impressionistic in scoring. Both have an engaging Prokofievan brio in the brisk outer movements and a Rachmaninovesque romanticism in the lyrical central *adagios*. Yet Merikanto never entirely forsook his adventurous harmonic writing, and especially in the Second the net result – allied to considerable formal lassitude – is suggestive of (of all people) Villa-Lobos. Granted it is with a Nordic not a Brazilian accent, but think here of works such as *Momoprecoce* and *Bachiana* No. 3 as much as the piano concertos; those who know both will appreciate the similarity. Matti Raekallio is a pianist of considerable technical ability and musical sensibility. He has the measure of both concertos, and the Second in particular could well become popular as an alternative to Prokofiev's Third or the *Paganini* Rhapsody. The purely orchestral *Two Studies* and *Two Pieces* (1941), though much slighter affairs, are by no means insignificant trifles. Tuomas Ollila secures more than competent performances from the Tampere orchestra, matched by excellent sound. A real delight.

Lemminkäinen, Op. 10. Pan, Op. 28. Four Compositions. Andante religioso. Scherzo.
Tampere Philharmonic Orchestra / Tuomas Ollila.
Ondine ODE905-2 (54 minutes: DDD). Recorded 1997.   Ⓕ

Aarre Merikanto's career divided broadly into three phases, those of apprentice, radical and conservative, and there are works from each present on this valuable issue. Critical hindsight accords (quite rightly) that the brief radical phase, roughly corresponding to the 1920s, was the most valuable, though at the time Merikanto's modernistic approach – and that of his like-minded contemporaries, Ernest Pingoud and Väinö Raito – was derided. Only one piece here represents this period, the highly accomplished tone-poem, *Pan* (1924), a wonderful, evocative, yet robust score, possessed of a very Nordic brand of impressionism. *Lemminkäinen* (1916), by contrast to *Pan*, seems immature, and rather parochial. A Sibelian shadow lies heavily across its quarter-hour duration, yet without a trace of the older composer's own *Lemminkäinen* tone-poems. There is little of the latter's emotional and psychological depth – or musical range – but instead a prevailing rollicking good humour broken occasionally by quieter, more serious moments. The remaining works all date from the early stages of Merikanto's post-modern period, when he reverted to a simpler, more accessible idiom. The *Four Compositions* (1932), which barely exceed *Pan* in length, nevertheless make a very effective and satisfying set, and whereas the *Andante religioso* (1933) seems like a piece out of context, the *Scherzo* (1937) is entirely convincing on its own. The performances are sympathetic and well recorded.

Olivier Messiaen   French 1908-1992

Un sourire[b]. Et exspecto resurrectionem mortuorum[b]. Oiseaux exotiques[a]. La ville d'en-haut[b]. Un Vitrail et des oiseaux[b].
Yvonne Loriod *pf* [a]**Bavarian Radio Symphony Orchestra,**
[b]**Berlin Radio Symphony Orchestra / Karl Anton Rickenbacher.**
Koch Schwann 311232 (70 minutes: DDD). Item marked [a] recorded 1985, [b]1993.   Ⓕ

In *Oiseaux exotiques* Messiaen creates a bower-bird's nest of extravagant, endearingly ramshackle ornateness. *Et exspecto resurrectionem mortuorum*, on the other hand, is one of his grandest and simplest structures, with its litany-like repetitions and responses. Placed between these, the three shorter pieces can be seen both as a useful way of programming works that fit awkwardly in concerts or as a series of further illustrations of Messiaen's use of what one might call 'strophic form'. *Un Vitrail et des oiseaux* ('A stained-glass window and birds'), for example, splits a typical chorale-like theme into four strophes, follows each with a varied 'antistrophe' of birdsong, and each of those with a progressively embellished cadenza, ending with a coda and a solemn restatement of all four strophes of the chorale. It is disarmingly simple and yet audibly related to the cumulative nobility of *Et exspecto*. That tiny but lovely homage to Mozart, *Un sourire*, is a miniature example of the same process; so is *La ville d'en-haut*, which can now be heard as a sort of sketch for Messiaen's last vision of eternity, *Eclairs sur L'au-delà*. These five disparate pieces make a satisfying and illuminating programme. *Oiseaux exotiques* (a cheerful racket of a piece) is rather drily recorded; there's more space around the other pieces in the collection. All are very well played, with proper regard to Messiaen's all-important silences and near-silences as well as his precisely judged juxtapositions.

Chronochromie. La ville d'en-haut. Et exspecto resurrectionem mortuorum.
Cleveland Orchestra / Pierre Boulez.
DG 445 827-2GH (58 minutes: DDD). Recorded 1993.   Ⓕ

Boulez has spoken of his pleasure at performing Messiaen with an orchestra relatively unfamiliar with his music. It sounds as though the Cleveland Orchestra must have enjoyed it too. You would expect them to, perhaps, in such a passage as that in the fourth movement of *Et exspecto*, where the two superimposed plainchant melodies return together with the noble 'theme of the depths' – it has great splendour, as does the chorale melody of the finale, rising at the end to a satisfyingly palpable *fffff*. And in this performance of *Chronochromie* you can hear why Messiaen said that certain pages of it were 'a double homage to Berlioz and Pierre Schaeffer [the French pioneer of electronic music]'. Absolute rhythmic precision and the clarity of colour that comes from meticulous balance are among the other pleasures of these performances. They make a most satisfying coupling, too. The recordings are excellent: clean but not clinical and ample in dynamic range.

Turangalîla-symphonie. Quatuor pour la fin du temps.
Saschko Gawriloff vn **Siegfried Palm** vc **Hans Deinzer** cl **Aloys Kontarsky, Peter Donohoe** pfs
Tristan Murail ondes martenot
City of Birmingham Symphony Orchestra / Sir Simon Rattle.
EMI CDS7 47463-8 (two discs: 130 minutes: DDD/ADD). ⒡

No longer a rarity in the concert hall, Messiaen's epic hymn to life and love has been lucky on record too. Messiaen's luxuriant scoring presents a challenge for the engineers as much as the players and the EMI team comes through with flying colours. Tristan Murail's ondes martenot is carefully balanced – evocative and velvety, neither reduced to inaudibility nor overmiked to produce an ear-rending screech. Peter Donohoe's piano obbligato is similarly integrated into the orchestral tapestry yet provides just the right kind of decorative intervention. Rattle is at his best in the work's more robust moments like the jazzy fifth movement and the many rhythmic passages which recall Stravinsky's *Le Sacre*. But those unfamiliar with Messiaen's extraordinary score should perhaps start with the central slow movement, the beautiful *Jardin du sommeil d'amour*, exquisitely done by the Birmingham team. This *Turangalîla* spills on to a second CD, which leaves room for a distinguished *Quatuor pour la fin du temps*. The music-making here lacks the youthful spontaneity of the main work, but is notable for an unusually slow and sustained performance of the solo-cello movement.

Eclairs sur l'Au-Delà.
Orchestra of the Opéra-Bastille, Paris / Myung-Whun Chung.
DG 439 929-2GH (66 minutes: DDD). ⒡

Eclairs sur L'Au-Delà ('Illuminations of the Beyond') was Olivier Messiaen's last major work. It is almost a summary, musical and spiritual, of the preoccupations of his preceding 60 years but shows him delightedly discovering not only new birds but also entrancingly new sounds: he has not made such startling use before of the contrabass clarinet (in the huge and complex eighth movement, which culminates in a Great Messiaen Tune of sonorous nobility), nor employed (to evoke the Lyrebird) such vertiginous leaps between sections of the orchestra. In one way, then, it is a series of nostalgic revisits. In the fourth movement, for example, there's a sort of two-minute summary of the extremely dense counterpoint of *Chronochromie*; the sixth recalls the 'Dance of fury for the seven trumpets' in the *Quartet for the end of time*. But there's also a touching sense of Messiaen in his eighties preparing to contemplate the beyond. In the ninth of the 11 movements he writes his last birdsong piece, no fewer that 25 birds impersonated simultaneously by 18 woodwind instruments: the image is of Christ as the Tree of Life, the birds are the souls of the blessed, and of course they are all singing at once. He then considers 'The path to the invisible', and if we were expecting a rapt meditation we do not know Messiaen: it is a clamorous and insistent piece, one of his great angular toccatas, expressing the very difficulty of keeping to that path. And finally, most movingly, one of his almost motionless, beginningless and endless string chorales, 'Christ, Light of Paradise'. Chung has a fine orchestra, and the immaculate recording made in the Opéra-Bastille itself sounds impressively spacious.

Six Petites Esquisses d'Oiseaux. Cantéyodjayâ. Quatre Etudes de rythme. Pièce pour le Tombeau de Paul Dukas.
Gloria Cheng pf
Koch International Classics 37267-2 (49 minutes: DDD). Recorded 1993. ⒡

Gloria Cheng is technically fearless and meticulously attentive to complex rhythms, she can sustain a bold melodic line splendidly, and her playing has powerful attack. She is just what the exhilarating but exhausting *Cantéyodjayâ* needs, and she gives it a performance of great *élan* and exciting drama. Similar qualities are needed, of course, in the outer sections of the *Quatre Etudes*, which have all the ferocity that Messiaen asks for. If there is any criticism it is that she tends to mark up Messiaen's quieter dynamics. Thus the famous 'Mode de valeurs et d'intensités', which has a 'mode' of seven degrees of intensity, from *ppp* to *fff*, seems to lack a couple of degrees at the bottom end. However, rarely does one hear this piece sound quite so coherent, and Cheng's concentration in the austere 'Neumes rythmiques' is remarkable. There is admirable precision in the *Petites Esquisses*, but again a slight lack of dynamic range at the quieter end of the spectrum means that each bird does not quite, as Messiaen insists, 'have its own aesthetic'. The recital ends with an impressively austere account of Messiaen's elegy for his teacher.

Huit préludes. Etudes de rythme – No. 1, Ile de feu I; No. 4, Ile de feu II. Vingt regards sur l'Enfant-Jésus – No. 4, Regard de la Vierge; No. 10, Regard de l'esprit de joie; No. 15, Le baiser de l'Enfant-Jésus.
Angela Hewitt *pf*
Hyperion CDA67054 (76 minutes: DDD). Recorded 1998.   Ⓕ

Angela Hewitt has few equals in Messiaen. The very early *Préludes* (Messiaen was still studying with Dukas when he wrote them) might not seem the ideal repertory in which to demonstrate this, but Hewitt plays them throughout with such exquisitely controlled colour, such clarity and such eager love for the music that, if one had ever dared think of them as not wholly characteristic one immediately changes one's mind. Indeed they are full, certainly in this performance, of luminous, shot and shaded colours that are typical of the mature Messiaen, and in the final virtuoso number Hewitt seems even to have discovered an early draft for a theme in the *Turangalîla* Symphony. Her melodic lines are strong, her sonorities rich (but her loud playing is never noisy, never forced) and she has that crucial quality needed of a Messiaen pianist: patience. Patience to let a chord register and fade, patience never to pre-empt a climax. In the two *Ile de feu* pieces she demonstrates that she can produce hard-edged sonorities as well as subtle ones. And all her gifts as a Messiaen pianist are evident in 'Le baiser de l'Enfant-Jésus': the tempo is patient (not slow, but unhurried), the contemplation rapt, the embellishments delicately precise, with a magical change of colour as the sunlit *hortus conclusus* at the centre of the movement is reached. The recording is finely sensitive to the exceptional beauty of Hewitt's sound.

Vingt regards sur l'Enfant-Jésus.
Joanna MacGregor *pf*
Collins Classics 7033-2 (two discs: 128 minutes: DDD). Recorded 1995.   Ⓕ

Joanna MacGregor is a pianist who combines fearless technique with great intelligence and imagination. When these qualities are matched by stunningly beautiful piano sound, we have a distinguished account of the *Vingt regards sur l'Enfant-Jésus*. MacGregor knows very well that some of these pieces require exquisitely vivid colour while others need a narrower chromatic range but one of absolute clarity (the crystalline glistening of the first variation in No. 15, 'La baiser de l'Enfant-Jésus', the cycle's 'slow movement'). But she has few problems with the sheer strength needed elsewhere and only a couple of times do you get a slight impression that either she or the piano had reached its limits (at the height of No. 6, the tumultuous 'Par Lui tout a été fait') or that a little more dynamic variation would have aided her brilliant colour contrasts (in the second development section of No. 10, 'Regard de l'esprit de joie'). Elsewhere, not least in the huge finale, her playing has commanding power and grandeur. Her precision, too, is admirable. Above all, perhaps, she communicates a real love for the sound world of this cycle, which is just as often sensuous and pianistic as it is mystical. We are not short of good recordings of the *Vingt regards*, but MacGregor's is probably the most sheerly beautiful of them all. It was made in the concert hall at Snape on an extremely fine Steinway, but the central achievement here is her perception of Messiaen's prodigal invention of sonorities.

La nativité du Seigneur. Le banquet céleste.
Jennifer Bate *org*
Unicorn-Kanchana DKPCD9005 (62 minutes: DDD). Played on the organ of Beauvais Cathedral. Ⓕ

La nativité du Seigneur comprises nine meditations on themes associated with the birth of the Lord. Messiaen's unique use of registration gives these pieces an extraordinarily wide range of colour and emotional potency and in Jennifer Bate's hands (and feet) it finds one of its most persuasive and capable advocates. Bate was much admired by the composer and is so far the only organist to have recorded his complete works for the instrument. *Le banquet céleste* was Messiaen's first published work for the organ and is a magical, very slow-moving meditation on a verse from St John's Gospel (VI, 56). The very faithful recording captures both the organ and the large acoustic of Beauvais Cathedral to marvellous effect.

Livre du Saint Sacrement.
Jennifer Bate *org*
Unicorn-Kanchana DKPCD9067/8 (two discs: 129 minutes: DDD). Played on the organ of L'Eglise de la Sainte-Trinité, Paris.   ⒻⓈ

The crowning achievement of Messiaen's unique cycle of music for the organ, the *Livre du Saint Sacrement* is also his largest work for the instrument. It is an intensely personal score based on the cornerstone of his faith, the Blessed Sacrament, and spans a wide range of emotions from hushed, private communion to the truly apocalyptic. Jennifer Bate gave the British première of the work in 1986, following which Messiaen invited her to record it using his own organ at the Trinity Church in Paris. The recording is a model of clarity and it is hard to imagine the complex and often very subtle textures of this music being better conveyed. This is a magnificent achievement.

L'Ascension. Apparition de l'église éternelle. Diptyque. Messe de la Pentecôte.
Thomas Trotter *org*
Decca 436 400-2DH (75 minutes: DDD). Recorded on the organ of the Eglise-Collégiale
Saint-Pierre de Douai, France in 1991. Ⓕ🄴

Trotter proves to be in the top rank of Messiaen interpreters. Both the vision and language of *Messe de la Pentecôte* are remote and too often performers fight shy of such musical intensity by concentrating on dazzling registration or displays of technical bravado. Not so Trotter whose sensitivity and self-control are never in doubt. There's nothing remotely silly or contrived about the birdsong element here – it seems a natural and musical expression of joy and peace: which is what we all know Messiaen intended but which so rarely works in performance. The choice of instrument is inspired. Its warm colours glow like sunlight seen through a stained glass window down the length of a dark, incense laden nave. Perhaps the action noise can be a little distracting at first but this is quickly forgotten in these intense and deeply-moving performances.

Poèmes pour Mi. Réveil des oiseaux. Sept Haïkaï.
Françoise Pollet *sop* **Pierre-Laurent Aimard, Joela Jones** *pfs*
Cleveland Orchestra / Pierre Boulez.
DG 453 478-2GH (72 minutes: DDD). Texts and translations included. Recorded 1990s. Ⓕ

All the performances here are excellent, virtuoso indeed, and the recordings are first-class. *Poèmes pour Mi* represent Messiaen at his most lyrically passionate and sensuous, the *Réveil des oiseaux* his 'bird style' at its most intransigent, while the *Sept Haïkaï* stand both for Messiaen's love-affair with Asia and his attempts to convey vivid colour in music. In Françoise Pollet the *Poèmes* get as close as any reading has to Messiaen's specification of a *grand soprano dramatique* as the ideal solo voice. She can sustain a long arch of melody splendidly and, assisted by Boulez's firm control, generates great rhythmic excitement in the fourth and ninth songs of the set. This latter quality gives exhilaration to *Réveil des oiseaux*, as the tangle of exuberant melodies grows ever more complex; Aimard is glitteringly precise here. But it is the *Sept Haïkaï* that are most crucial to Messiaen's later development, with their pairs of movements reflecting each other, their searing saturated colours, their use of juxtaposed 'refrains' and their central homage to the sound of a Japanese orchestra. Boulez has expressed reservations about some of his great teacher's theories, but evidently has few if any about the fantastic sound world imagined by his astonishingly precise ear.

Giacomo Meyerbeer　　　　　　　　　　　German 1791-1864

Dinorah.
Deborah Cook *sop* Dinorah; **Christian du Plessis** *bar* Hoël; **Alexander Oliver** *ten* Corentin;
Della Jones *mez* Goatherd; **Marilyn Hill Smith** *sop* Goatgirl; **Roderick Earle** *bass* Huntsman;
Ian Caley *ten* Reaper;
Geoffrey Mitchell Choir; Philharmonia Orchestra / James Judd.
Opera Rara ORC005 (three discs: 151 minutes: ADD). Notes, text and translation included.
Recorded 1979. Ⓕ

Dinorah is hampered by an awkward plot (involving, for one thing, almost as much retrospective narration as *The Ring*), but the music has a genuine lyric charm. More than that, its strands are skilfully interwoven, with a delightful ending. Deborah Cook is fluent and likeable in the title-role; Christian du Plessis competent in his (the grief-stricken ending of his aria having fine effect); and Alexander Oliver, an excellent comedian, brings a happy touch to the simple but not entirely witless Corentin. Della Jones does admirably in her supporting role, and the Geoffrey Mitchell Choir sings as well as ever. The playing of the Philharmonic Orchestra is of a quality that makes appreciation of Meyerbeer's scoring no problem at all, and James Judd conducts without too much of the rigidity of some modern maestros. As always in Opera Rara's record productions, the presentation is exemplary, and recorded sound, if afflicted in this outdoor opera with distinctly indoor resonance, is clear and well balanced. Meyerbeer and his librettists planned originally a short opera in three scenes; if they had had their way it might have been a masterpiece.

Nikolay Miaskovsky

Miaskovsky Cello Concerto in C minor, Op. 66.
Prokofiev Symphony-Concerto for Cello and Orchestra in E minor, Op. 125
(also includes alternative finale).
Truls Mørk *vc*
City of Birmingham Symphony Orchestra / Paavo Järvi.
Virgin Classics VC5 45282-2 (72 minutes: DDD).   Ⓕ

Whichever way you view it – as attractive repertoire, as dynamic sound, or as distinctive
interpretation – this CD is a sure-fire winner. Neither work yields its strongest virtues without
encouragement: the Prokofiev responds best to focused solo phrasing and firm handling from the
rostrum, while Miaskovsky's concerto can too easily sound discursive. Here, however, musical
impact takes effect right from Prokofiev's introductory bars: Paavo Järvi and his players cut a
commanding profile and the recording conveys a startlingly realistic sound stage, especially from the
lower strings. Truls Mørk might be tagged a 'communicative introvert': his tone is firm and even, his
phrasing refined and his poetic musicianship especially suits the Miaskovsky concerto, with its
subtle asides and winding musical lines. Again, Järvi comes up trumps with a sympathetic
accompaniment and the recording is spectacularly good.

Sinfonietta No. 1 in B minor, Op. 32 No. 2. Theme and Variations. Two Pieces,
Op. 46 No. 1. Napeve.
St Petersburg Chamber Ensemble / Roland Melia.
ASV CDDCA928 (56 minutes: DDD). Recorded 1994.   Ⓕ

The dignity and solid craftsmanship of Nikolay Miaskovsky make him a likeable figure; and the
circumstances in which he maintained those values make him rather more than likeable. The
Variations are consistently attractive, as are the shorter works, despite disconcerting reminiscences
of the *Skye Boat Song* in the first of the Op. 46 Pieces. That's not to say that the music 'holds' you
in the way that Stravinsky, Martinů, Honegger or Tippett do. And, as so often with Miaskovsky,
there are slack moments where ideas seem to be coming back for no better reason than to fill out a
pre-allocated space. The fact remains that if you have got the Miaskovsky bug, or if you want the
fullest possible picture of middle-of-the-road Soviet music, you will find confident, full-bodied
performances here which are the equal of any.

Symphony No. 6 in E flat minor, Op. 23, 'Revolutionary'.
Yurlov Russian Choir; USSR Symphony Orchestra / Kyrill Kondrashin.
Russian Disc mono RDCD15008 (65 minutes: ADD). Recorded 1959.

This is not a flawless performance and the sound is on the thinnish side. But then no other
recording of this work has anything approaching the fire, the expressive ebb and flow, or the sheer
dramatic sweep of Kondrashin. When it first appeared in the early 1920s Miaskovsky's Sixth was
hailed as the first Soviet symphony – not the first composed on Soviet soil, but the first to embody
the cataclysmic experiences, the conflicts and aspirations of Revolution. Of course that begs all
sorts of questions. For instance, does the finale's turn from heroic optimism to funereal tragedy
represent solidarity with past martyrdom or present betrayal of ideals? And what, apart from the
emblematic tunes in that finale, distinguishes the essential message of this music from, say,
Rachmaninov's Second or Glière's Third, to mention two comparable pre-revolutionary Russian
symphonies? Not that it is really necessary to agonize over such things. This is a musically self-
sufficient symphonic drama of aspiration, yearning, frustration and wistfulness, all held in a tense
state of becoming by a squared-off but masterly Wagnerian chromaticism and lit up from time to
time by moments of immensely touching poetic inwardness.

Darius Milhaud

Harp Concerto, Op. 323. Le boeuf sur le toit, Op. 58. La création du monde, Op. 81.
Frédérique Cambreling *hp*
Lyon Opéra Orchestra / Kent Nagano.
Erato MusiFrance 2292-45820-2 (59 minutes: DDD). Recorded 1992.   Ⓕ

Here is music to delight, with performances to match. Milhaud's ballet *Le boeuf sur le toit* was
written for Jean Cocteau in 1919 and is set in an American bar during the Prohibition period
(forbidding the manufacture and sale of alcohol) that was then just beginning. Kent Nagano shows

more Gallic taste and sophistication, and the playing is above all musicianly, while the more uproarious moments come over all the more effectively for this very reason. The playing by the accomplished Lyon orchestra is excellent, not least the wind players who have plenty to do. Written four years later, *La création du monde* was one of the first works by a European composer to take its inspiration from African folklore and the raw black jazz that Milhaud heard in New Orleans. This ballet on the creation myth ends with a mating dance and the whole work is powerfully and darkly sensual. Nagano and his French orchestra bring out all the character of this music and take the jazz fugue in Scene 1 more urgently than usual, to excellent effect. The Harp Concerto dates from 1953, three decades further on into Milhaud's career, and inevitably it has a brighter character, though here, too, there is some jazz influence, though of a far gentler kind. Cambreling is a fine player – an ideal interpreter of this uneven but nearly always fascinating composer.

Symphony No. 3, Op. 271, 'Te Deum'. Les cloches – Symphonic Suite, Op. 259. Saudades do Brasil, Op. 67 – Botafogo; Leme; Tijuca; Laranjeiras.
Russian State Symphony Cappella / Gennadi Rozhdestvensky.
Olympia OCD452 (61 minutes: DDD). Recorded live in 1993.   Ⓕ

Written in 1946, the ballet *Les cloches* was well received at its première in Chicago but was a disaster when performed in New York by an ill-prepared Ballets Russes de Monte-Carlo: Milhaud was obliged to substitute a simpler finale for subsequent performances, but restored the original for the Symphonic Suite now recorded. The work, about a young bride and her groom, begins joyously and melodiously, but at the 'Bronze bells' section the atmosphere becomes heavy with menace, and the hysterical final bacchanale depicts the King of the Ghouls spiriting the bridegroom away. The resonance of the hall in which this live recording was made creates a slightly thick sound, though detail is mostly clear. Rozhdestvensky adopts slower speeds for the 'Silver' and 'Golden' sections than the composer indicates and makes heavy cuts in the finale. The Third Symphony (the only one of Milhaud's first ten not hitherto recorded) was commissioned by French radio to celebrate the ending of the Second World War. Starting with a vigorous, tough movement that could be interpreted as symbolizing wartime struggles, it passes to a meditative, prayerfully intense slow movement (in which a wordless chorus is imaginatively used): a jubilant *Pastorale* suggests the coming of peace, which is finally hailed in a choral *Te Deum*. Again there are marked divergences from Milhaud's printed timings, but the performance is persuasive and exudes great confidence and the two middle movements, at least, represent Milhaud at his best.

Saudades do Brasil, Op. 67 – Leme; Ipanema (arr. Lévy). Suite for Violin, Viola and Piano, Op. 157b. Quatre Visages, Op. 238. Sonatine for Violin and Viola, Op. 226. Sonatas for Viola and Piano – No. 1, Op. 240; No. 2, Op. 244. Sonatine for Viola and Cello, Op. 378.
Paul Cortese *va* **Michel Wagemans** *pf* with **Joaquín Palomares** *vn* **Frank Schaffer** *vc*
ASV CDDCA1039 (78 minutes: DDD). Recorded 1997.   Ⓕ

Paul Cortese here brings his rich, warm tone and flawless, rock-steady technique to Milhaud's viola music. Of the seven works presented here, four were written in the 1940s while Milhaud was teaching at Mills College in the USA. Exceptions are the two arrangements from the early *Saudades do Brasil*; the Suite (which includes a jaunty Provençal-flavoured overture, a lyrical 'Divertissement' and an engagingly cheery finale); and the much later sinewy and prickly *Sonatine* for violin and cello (played here with great finesse), which contains an unexpectedly emotional slow movement. Of the four other works, the violin and viola *Sonatine* is easy-flowing small-talk, unmemorable save for the energetic final fugue; *Quatre Visages*, however, reveals Milhaud's sly wit in its entertaining characterizations of four women – a sunnily contented Californian, a chatterbox from Wisconsin, an earnest creature from Brussels and a vivacious Parisienne. The First Viola Sonata is one of Milhaud's most endearing works. It has Milhaud indulging to the full his penchant for canonic writing. The Second Sonata is less overtly bracing, and its central *Modéré* is charged with expressive drama, while the finale is a rough-and-tumble which tempts Michel Wagemans, alert as he is, into being much too loud for his partner – as indeed he sometimes is elsewhere, notably in the early Suite. But, all in all, this disc does Milhaud proud.

Le boeuf sur le toit, Op. 58a (arr. cpsr). Scaramouche, Op. 165b. La libertadora, Op. 236a. Les songes, Op. 237. Le bal martiniquais, Op. 249. Carnaval à la nouvelle-orléans, Op. 275. Kentuckiana, Op. 287.
Stephen Coombs, Artur Pizarro *pfs*
Hyperion CDA67014 (62 minutes: DDD). Recorded 1997.   Ⓕ

Milhaud was an inveterate traveller, and he absorbed influences from many national styles, illustrated by titles such as *Kentuckiana*, *Le bal martiniquais* and 'Brazileira' (from *Scaramouche*).

The music exudes infectious dance impulses, languid geniality, knockabout humour and sheer *joie de vivre*. It may inhabit a limited expressive sphere, but providing you don't expect introspection or searching profundity you won't be disappointed. There is enjoyment at every turn, whether in the foot-tapping 'Brazileira', the Satie-esque simplicity of the 'Valse' from *Les songes*, or the breezy music-hall atmosphere of *Le boeuf sur le toit*, with its forays into polytonality and its wonderfully imaginative piano writing. The performances are exemplary. Stephen Coombs and Artur Pizarro both enjoy the byways of the piano repertory, and, even if Pizarro is the more starry soloist, they are well matched as a duo. Coombs's top part is suitably bright and sharply lit, and is offset by Pizarro's more subtle colouring. They clearly revel in the protracted playfulness of *Le boeuf sur le toit* (the only work here for piano duet, incidentally, although there is if anything a greater wealth of inner detail than in the two-piano works), where their feeling for Hispanic exoticism is matched by their brilliant virtuosity. The recorded sound is excellent, as are Robert Matthew-Walker's accompanying notes.

Ernest Moeran British 1894-1950

String Quartets – No. 1 in A minor; No. 2 in E flat major. String Trio in G major.
Maggini Quartet (Laurence Jackson, David Angel *vns* Martin Outram *va* Michal Kaznowski *vc*). Naxos 8 554079 (59 minutes: DDD). Recorded 1995. ⑤🅴

The A minor Quartet dates from 1921 when Moeran was a pupil of John Ireland at the Royal College of Music. It is an enormously fluent, folk-song-inspired creation, full of Ravelian poise; indeed the last movement of the three (an exhilarating rondo) owes much to the finale of the French master's F major Quartet. Not surprisingly, Moeran himself always retained his affection for this piece, and the Maggini Quartets accords it wonderfully assured, flexible advocacy. Discovered among Moeran's papers by his widow after his death in 1950, the E flat Quartet appears to be another comparatively early effort. It is cast in just two movements, the second of which is an ambitious linked slow movement and finale, full of ambition and tender fantasy, and containing some truly magical inspiration along the way. Perhaps this movement's intrepid thematic and emotional diversity engendered sufficient niggling doubts in Moeran's mind for him to suppress the whole work. Certainly, in a performance as convinced and convincing as the one here, its melodic fecundity and unpretentious, 'out of doors' charm will endear it to many. That leaves the masterly String Trio of 1931, which, in its impeccable craft, rhythmic pungency (the opening *Allegretto giovale* boasts a time-signature of 7/8), gentle sense of purpose and unerring concentration (above all in the deeply felt slow movement), represents one of Moeran's finest achievements. The members of the Maggini Quartet reveal a relish for Moeran's exquisitely judged part-writing and give an admirably polished, affectionate rendering. Sound and balance are excellent throughout this enterprising, hugely enjoyable collection.

Moeran Songs of Springtime. Phyllida and Corydon.
Warlock A Cornish Carol. I saw a fair maiden. Benedicamus Domino. The full heart. The rich cavalcade. Corpus Christi. All the flowers of the Spring. As dew in Aprylle. Bethlehem Down. A Cornish Christmas Carol.
Finzi Singers / Paul Spicer.
Chandos CHAN9182 (76 minutes: DDD). Texts included. Recorded 1992. ⑤🅴

The Peter Warlock we all know and love from the evergreen *Capriol Suite* and the boisterous songs seems a world away from the introverted and intense artist of these unaccompanied choral carols. Perhaps Warlock's real genius was an ability to create profound expression in short musical structures, but even the more outgoing pieces – the joyful *Benedicamus Domino* and the Cornish Christmas Carol with its gentle hint at 'The First Nowell' – have an artistic integrity which raises them high above the level of the syrup of modern day carol settings. Given performances as openly sincere and sensitive as these few could remain unmoved. In the two Moeran madrigal suites there is an indefinable Englishness – the result of a deep awareness of tradition and love of the countryside. The Finzi Singers' warm-toned, richly expressive voices capture the very essence of this uniquely lovely music.

Federico Mompou Spanish 1893-1987

Música callada.
Herbert Henck *pf*
ECM New Series 445 699-2 (63 minutes: DDD). Recorded 1993. ⑤🅴

Listening to this disc is rather like entering a retreat. There is a rapt, contemplative atmosphere around these 28 miniatures (only two run for as long as three minutes) written between 1959 and 1967 as an attempt to express St John of the Cross's mystic ideal of 'the music of silence'. Practically all slow-moving, using repetition as a structural device but avoiding keyboard virtuosity, and rarely rising even to a *forte*, they seem to acknowledge descent from Erik Satie via the impressionists, though harmonically much freer and sometimes harsher – even, occasionally, stepping inside the area of atonality. No. 3 has a childlike innocence in its folkloric theme: Mompou's fascination with bell-sounds finds echoes in Nos. 5, 17 and 22. Overall there is a sense of tranquil self-communion which, paradoxically, exerts a strange spell on the listener. Herbert Henck, a specialist in twentieth-century music, plays this collection with a tender sensitivity and an ideally suited luminosity of tone, and he is finely recorded. An exceptional and haunting issue, whose sounds seem to hang in the air, as it were.

Cançons i danses – Nos. 1, 3, 5, 7, 8 and 9. Preludes – Nos. 1, 5, 6, 7, 9 and 10. Cants màgics. Charmes. Variations. Dialogues. Paisajes.
Stephen Hough *pf*
Hyperion CDA66963 (77 minutes: DDD). Recorded 1996.
Gramophone Award Winner 1998.   Ⓕ🅂🄴

The music of Federico Mompou may appear at first to consist of little more than charming, delicately scented but dilettantish salon near-improvisations with marked overtones of Erik Satie; but it is significant that his earliest works (in the 1920s) are imbued with a sense of mystery and wonder. Later he was to progress from an ingenuous lyricism (in the *Songs and dances*) to a profounder contemplation and mysticism, to greater harmonic and keyboard complexity (*Dialogues*) and finally, in the 1946-60 *Paisajes* ('Landscapes'), to a more experimental, less tonal idiom. In the hands of an imaginative pianist like Stephen Hough this other-worldly quality becomes revelatory. Hough's command of tonal nuance throughout is ultra-sensitive, he catches Mompou's wistful moods to perfection, and on the rare occasions when the music lashes out, as in *Prelude* No. 7, he is scintillating. In the more familiar *Songs and dances* he is tender in the (mostly melancholy) songs and exhilaratingly crisp rhythmically in the dances. He treats the 'Testament d'Amelia' in No. 8 with a good deal of flexibility, and because Mompou declared (and demonstrated in his own recordings) that 'it's all so free', he takes the fullest advantage of the marking *senza rigore* in No. 5, which reflects Mompou's lifelong fascination with bell-sounds.

Jean-Joseph de Mondonville   French 1711-1772

Six Sonates en symphonies, Op. 3.
Les Musiciens du Louvre / Marc Minkowski.
Archiv Produktion 457 600-2AH (58 minutes: DDD).   Ⓕ🄿🄴

These pieces show Mondonville on ground closest to his heart, and indeed in a position to offer something unique. He was a violinist first and foremost, and his most important legacy is his Op. 3 set of six sonatas for violin and obbligato keyboard of 1734 – among the first of their kind – of which these *Sonates en symphonies* are orchestrations, made by the composer himself and performed with great success in Paris 15 years later. To put it simply, they are pure enjoyment from beginning to end, breathing as they do that spirit of almost pure hedonism which characterizes the most beguiling of mid-eighteenth-century French art. All the symphonies are in three movements, the outer ones being brisk and animated with much busy passagework surviving the transition from solo violin music very effectively, and the middle ones tuneful miniatures evoking the hushed atmosphere of a balmy night scene from a French baroque opera. Marc Minkowski's own dramatic skills help him to create a magical atmosphere in these, while his customary galvanizing energy lends irrepressible and boisterous life to the quick movements. The orchestra plays superbly, and all in all, these are utterly delightful recordings.

Grands motets – Dominus regnavit; In exitu Israel; De profundis.
Sophie Daneman, Maryseult Wieczorek *sops* **Paul Agnew, François Piolino** *tens*
Maarten Koningsberger *bar* **François Bazola** *bass*
Les Arts Florissants / William Christie.
Erato 0630-17791-2 (72 minutes: DDD). Texts and translations included. Recorded 1996.   Ⓕ🄿🄴

Mondonville's *grands motets* were enormously popular for many years at the Concert Spirituel in Paris (of which he was a director for a time). They follow the pattern laid down by Lalande and continued by Rameau, but with more independent instrumental parts and incorporating Italian influences (e.g. *da capo* arias) and operatic elements. These three on psalm texts are deeply impressive. *Dominus regnavit* (1734) was perhaps the earliest of Mondonville's *grands motets* and, besides its polyphonic opening chorus, is notable for two verses entirely for high-register voices and instruments, an operatic *tempête*, and a stunning complex 'Gloria patri'. *De profundis* (1748), written for the funeral of a Chapel Royal colleague, is by its nature sombre, and ends not with the usual 'Gloria patri' but with 'Requiem aeternam' and a fugue. The initial chorus was praised to the sky by contemporaries as 'sublime': other highlights are a baritone aria over a free chaconne bass, and a chorus illustrating 'morning' and 'night' by high and low voices respectively. There is even more illustrative music in the 1755 *In exitu Israel*: what amounts to a dramatic scena, with agitated strings and rushing voices for the 'fleeing sea', dotted figures for the mountains 'skipping like rams', and tremolos and vocal melismas for the 'trembling earth'. The present performances are vivid, with very good soloists, an alertly responsive chorus and a neat orchestra.

Philippus de Monte
Dutch 1521-1603

Missa Si ambulavero. Miserere mei Domine. Peccavi super numerum. Super flumina Babylonis. Domine quid multiplicati sunt. Spes humani generis. Domine Jesu Christe. Angelus Domini descendit de Caelo. Hodie dilectissimi, omnium sanctorum.
New College Choir, Oxford / Edward Higginbottom.
Collins Classics 1527-2 (65 minutes: DDD). Texts and translations included. Recorded 1998. Ⓕ

Philippus de Monte was one of the most prolific composers of his time and held one of the most prestigious posts, that of Kapellmeister at the Imperial court. The insert-note to this anthology remarks that stylistically Monte falls 'between the cool technical assurance of Palestrina and the high drama of Lassus'. When a composer's music is described solely in terms of other people's you know that his critical profile is not what it might be. Yet it is not easy to assess his work more precisely: a superb technician, with an impressive cosmopolitanism and an admirably wide range of genres, Monte offers qualities shared by many composers from this period. Even though the individual character of the works on this disc is not as clearly defined as it might be with Lassus or Palestrina, each yields pleasure and interest. Only occasionally do the composer's rhythmic touches seem to stretch the sense of ensemble uncomfortably (as in the first part of *Domine Jesu Christe* or the 'Hosanna' of the Mass). The distinctive sound of New College's trebles captures the imagination, in an acoustic that lends the recording real character and an admirable clarity of texture.

Claudio Monteverdi
Italian 1567-1643

Il combattimento di Tancredi e Clorinda. Il ballo delle ingrate.
Concerto Italiano / Rinaldo Alessandrini *hpd*
Opus 111 OPS30-196 (58 minutes: DDD). Texts and translations included. Recorded 1998. ⒻⓅ

The graphic realism and dramatic subtlety of both these expanded madrigals are given the most incandescent and powerful readings imaginable here. Concerto Italiano has won many plaudits for its delectable linguistic colouring of the earlier Mantuan madrigal books. *Combattimento*, this *sui generis* dramatic masterpiece from 1624, demonstrates Alessandrini's impeccable instincts for theatrical timing and the *stile concitato*, or agitated style, where extrovert representation of two fighting crusaders has the listener enraptured, not only by the celebrated violence of the figuration, but the poignant foreboding of the Christian knight's discovery that the Saracen warrior whom he has killed is the maiden he loves, in disguise. Stylistically provocative, it is the evocative restraint of Concerto Italiano's expressive world which shuns the self-conscious over-enactment that temporarily stalls even the most established readings. That said, the pace is hot throughout with words spat out by the Testo, or narrator, Roberto Abbondanza. His tenor is dark and often a touch hard-grained but he is remarkable in his dynamic range, contemplative dolour and grounded physicality. He is surrounded by a deeply affecting commentary of well-judged vibrating strings, bright fifths and rhythmic vitality. There are other notable recordings of this great *scena* but the pathos and purity of sentiment of Alessandrini's version have no rival, however, and the post-baptism, reconciliation scene at the end is given an ethereal fragility by Clorinda, the beguiling Elisa Franzetti. The other work here, *Il ballo delle ingrate*, was written in 1608 for Monteverdi's patron Duke but the composer revised the original commission and published it as part of the *Madrigali guerrieri e amorosi* 30 years later. Again, the characterization is penetrating, the recitative style unforced and the string players revel, sometimes a touch scrappily, in the potent undercurrents of women's fate should they resist love. An irresistible release.

Vespro della Beata Virgine (ed. Parrott/Keyte).
Taverner Consort; Taverner Choir; Taverner Players / Andrew Parrott.
Virgin Classics Veritas VMD5 61347-2 (two discs: 106 minutes: DDD). Recorded 1984. Ⓜ🅿🆁🆁

The technical and interpretative problems of the Monteverdi *Vespers* of 1610 are legion. Should the entire volume be performed as an entity, or just the psalms, or perhaps a mixture of psalms and motets? Since the vocal lines in the original publication are heavily ornamented, does this preclude the addition of further embellishment after the manner of contemporary instruction books? Which portions should be sung chorally (and how large should such a 'choir' be?), and which by the soloists? How should the continuo be realized? Many of these difficulties stem from the ambiguities of the original publication of the *Vespers* which remains the source from which all modern performing editions must be made. Others are caused by uncertainties surrounding seventeenth-century liturgical practice. In both these areas this recording offers new ideas. Firstly the liturgy. The central controversy raised by the *Vespers* concerns five non-liturgical compositions inserted among the Marian psalms, hymn and 'Magnificat': 'Nigra sum', 'Pulchra es', 'Duo Seraphim', 'Audi coelum' and the 'Sonata sopra Sancta Maria'. These, the sacred *concerti* described on the title-page as 'suitable for the chapels or private chambers of princes', do not conform textually to any known Marian office but occur in Monteverdi's collection in positions normally occupied by psalm antiphons. These apparent contradictions have led some editors to suggest that they should not be performed as part of the *Vespers*. More convincing is the view, followed here, that the *concerti* are substitutes for the antiphons missing from Monteverdi's collections. And this view is taken even further by seeing them as antiphon-repeats and inserting plainchant for the missing first strain. This is done for three of the psalms; for the remaining two, contemporary instrumental sonatas by Giovanni Paolo Cima are performed. One effect is to make this version feel more unified, more monumental.

Both physically and emotionally the *concerti* are presented here as the focal points of the *Vespers*, the jewels in the crown. Certainly they are the occasion for some of the most spectacular singing on this recording. The essential ingredient here is the performance of Nigel Rogers, surely the most accomplished and convincing singer of the early seventeenth-century Italian virtuoso repertory to be found anywhere. He gives persuasive and seemingly effortless performances in three of the *concerti* in his highly characteristic mellifluous, dramatic yet perfectly controlled manner. In two cases, 'Audi coelum' and 'Duo Seraphim', he is well matched with Andrew King and Joseph Cornwell. By comparison 'Pulchra es', sung by Tessa Bonner and Emma Kirkby, seems rather understated, certainly too much so for this deliberately and deliciously ambiguous text. One important feature of Andrew Parrott's interpretation is its fundamental conception, historically accurate, of the *Vespers* as chamber work rather than a 'choral' one. Thus only one instrument is used per part, the harpsichord is employed very sparingly, and the basic continuo group is restricted to organ and chitarrone. Following the same principle, one voice per part is taken as the norm. The result is a clarity of texture, evident from the opening bars, which allows correct tempos to be used without stifling the often intricate rhythmic features of the writing. 'Nisi Dominus', for example, is taken at a lively speed but does not end up sounding rushed as so often happens. 'Lauda Jerusalem' proceeds at a jaunty pace without loss of detail, and 'Laetatus sum' sounds stately without being leaden-footed. That these effects can be achieved is largely due to decisions about the size and balance of forces.

Finally, mention should be made of another fundamental choice which represents something of a novelty. Both 'Lauda Jerusalem' and the 'Magnificat' are transposed down a fourth here, as indeed they should be according to the convention relating to the clef combinations in which they were originally notated. This brings all the vocal parts into the tessitura of the rest of the work, and also restores the instruments to their normal ranges. Whether or not the result is less 'exciting' than the version we are used to hearing has only partly to do with questions of musicality. For the rest, in this respect as in others, one of the lasting virtues of this well-balanced, unobtrusive recording is that it allows us to hear the *Vespers* sounding something along the lines that Monteverdi intended.

Monteverdi Vespro della Beata Vergine.
Sophie Marin-Degor, Maryseult Wieczorek *sops* **Artur Stefanowicz,**
Fabián Schofrin *countertens* **Paul Agnew, Joseph Cornwell, François Piolino** *tens*
Thierry Félix, Clive Bayley *basses*
Les Sacqueboutiers de Toulouse; Les Arts Florissants / William Christie *hpd/org*
Cima Concerti ecclesiastici – Sonata per il violino, cornetto e violone;
Sonata per il violino e violone.
Members of Les Arts Florissants.
Erato 3984-23139-2 (two discs: 100 minutes: DDD). Text and translation included.
Recorded 1997. Ⓕ

This is in some ways an oddly old-fashioned approach to the 1610 *Vespers*. With a substantial choir and sometimes highly varying orchestration, William Christie creates a warm and glowing sound. Part of his emphasis is on texture and flow, so Monteverdi's often sharp dissonances tend to have a soft edge; and there are some occasionally irrelevant pitches buried in the polyphonic web. He faces the challenge of putting the 'Lauda Jerusalem' and the 'Magnificat' at a pitch-standard a fourth lower than the rest (which he has at a modern concert pitch). And that is where the rich orchestration pays its dividends; the resulting almost impossibly low bass-lines, particularly in the 'Et misericordia' section of the 'Magnificat', sound clear and lucid with their instrumental doubling. He also benefits from the splendid low range of the tenors he uses: they manage to make the 'Gloria Patri' section a true climax to the work, and in particular they give the 'Duo Seraphim' perhaps the most convincing performance available anywhere because they are so beautifully matched. Christie prefaces each of the psalms with a chant introit; and he follows the order of the print except in putting 'Duo Seraphim' before the 'Sonata sopra Sancta Maria'. To fill the gap where Monteverdi put 'Duo Seraphim' he introduces a sonata by Cima, superbly played by a team led by the violinist, François Fernandez; and another excellently performed sonata by Cima separates the 'Lauda Jerusalem' from 'Duo Seraphim'. There is a warmth and generosity here that are undeniably attractive; the movements mentioned go better than anything else available; and everything is done at the level of skill and musicality that we have come to expect from Christie and Les Arts Florissants.

Vespro della Beata Virgine – Domine ad adiuvandum; Dixit Dominus; Laudate pueri; Laetatus sum; Nisi Dominus; Lauda Jerusalem (with plainchant antiphons). Magnificat II.
Motets – O quam pulchra es. Domine, ne in furore. Ego flos campi. Adoramus te, Christe. Laudate Dominum omnes gentes. Ego dormio, et cor meum vigilat. Christe, adoramus te. Cantate Domino.
Concerto Italiano / Rinaldo Alessandrini.
Opus 111 OPS30-150 (75 minutes: DDD). Texts and translations included.
Recorded 1996. Ⓕ ℙ 🄴

Rinaldo Alessandrini and the Concerto Italiano have acquired a formidable reputation, above all for their records of Monteverdi madrigals. The kind of knowledge and detailed understanding of the subtleties of both meaning and pronunciation of the Italian language which only a native speaker can possess, and an impressive command of seventeenth-century vocal styles and techniques are two of the important elements that characterize their distinctive approach. Allied to a profound sense of drama and a lively musicality, these skills have been expertly shaped by Alessandrini to produce some of the finest recordings ever made of this repertory. This makes their foray into Monteverdi's church music all the more intriguing. The first half of the disc is made up of a complete vespers setting assembled from individual pieces published throughout the composer's career. Sung by one voice to a part and richly underpinned by a varied continuo group including theorbos, double harp and contrabass, there is a clarity and intimacy about the result. Details that often disappear in performances with larger forces here speak clearly (the performance of 'Dixit Dominus' from the *Vespers* of 1610 is notable in this respect). The recording is completed by a series of motets including three for solo voice; here it is almost invidious to express preferences, but it is difficult to resist praise for Rossana Bertini's breathtakingly audacious performance of *Laudate Dominum*, invigorated by a good deal of ornamentation executed with great flair and *élan*. This record brims with revelations and surprises – no serious Monteverdian can afford to be without it.

Il primo libro de madrigali. Settimo libro de madrigali – Tempro la cetra; Tirsi e Clori.
The Consort of Musicke / Anthony Rooley.
Virgin Classics Veritas VC5 45143-2 (57 minutes: DDD). Texts and translations included.
Recorded 1991. Ⓕ

Monteverdi's *Primo libro* of 1587 presents a detailed map of his absorption of contemporary madrigalian styles, and above all of his command of the lighter repertories that had become so popular in Italy during the 1580s. At the same time, there is a bittersweet quality about these pieces, for all that they are so episodically structured. This presages the later books when Monteverdi had moved to the Gonzaga court at Mantua, and had become acquainted with the more adventurous music then being written by composers both there and at Ferrara, inspired by the poetry of Guarini and Tasso. This is the first recording to treat the book in its entirety. Here The Consort of Musicke is on fine form, turning in sensitively wrought and carefully considered accounts, with perfect ensemble and tuning, and the textual details sensitively registered. The disc is rounded off with a number of pieces from the *Settimo libro*, clearly more dramatic in conception and effect, which provide an instructive and dramatic contrast with the madrigals from the first book. The continuo grouping here provides a sturdy and richly textured accompaniment to the soloists, and both instrumentalists and vocalists apply discreet and appropriate ornamentation with style.

Il secondo libro de madrigali.
Concerto Italiano / Rinaldo Alessandrini.
Opus 111 OPS30-111 (58 minutes: DDD). Texts and translations included. Recorded 1994. Ⓕ 🅿 🅴

Captivation begins with the very opening of the first piece on the disc, *Non si levav'anchor l'alba novella*, whose gently growing sense of the awakening dawn is itself a delicately drawn metaphor for transition from the urgent desire of the lovers' final embrace after a night of lovemaking to the gentle pain of their parting. The exquisite bittersweet pathos of the scene, whose every nuance and ambiguity is superbly caught in Alessandrini's vision of Monteverdi's music, sets both the standard and the tone for much of what follows in a number of important ways. First, with the exception of *S'andasse amor a caccia* and *Non giacinto o narcisi*, there are no examples here of the lighter *canzonetta*, such a prominent feature of the musical picture in Italy during the 1580s and a strong presence in the composer's own *Primo libro* of 1587. Secondly, and crucially, almost half the contents of the *Secondo libro* of three years later are settings of poetry by Torquato Tasso, whose *Gerusalemme liberata* was the most significant and influential epic to have been written in Italy since Ariosto's *Orlando furioso*, first published in the early decades of the century. Packed with strong images and bright colours, Tasso's verse was much drawn upon by many composers, including Monteverdi who continued to set it throughout his career. In Rinaldo Alessandrini and the Concerto Italiano, the intimate fusion of words and music which the composer embarks upon in this Second Book, and which was to remain a lifelong preoccupation, is delineated with charm, skill and profound understanding.

Il quarto libro de madrigali.
Concerto Italiano / Rinaldo Alessandrini.
Opus 111 OPS30-81 (62 minutes: DDD). Texts and translations included. Recorded 1993.
Gramophone Award Winner 1994.　　　　　　　　　　　　　　Ⓕ 🅿 🅴 🆁🆁

Monteverdi's Fourth Book of Madrigals, first published in 1603, is a wide-ranging collection of pieces written during the previous ten years. Originally written for performance before a select audience by an ensemble of professional virtuoso singers, these madrigals, many of which are set to the sensuous, emotional and epigrammatic verses of Guarini and Tasso, demonstrate Monteverdi's seemingly inexhaustible ability to unite words and music in expressively effective ways. A complete and profound understanding of textual nuance is, then, central to any successful performance and here the Concerto Italiano begins with an obvious and considerable advantage over any group of non-Italians. Some of the finest madrigals in the Fourth Book are those involving direct speech, which allowed Monteverdi to make full use of the court virtuosi, famed for their abilities to combine clear declamation with dramatic gestures and subtle shadings of dynamics and speed. In general the Concerto Italiano has taken the combined messages of music and history to heart; these are performances infused with a flexible approach to tempo and strong projection of text geared to a determination to allow each detail of the words to speak with due force. The singing style itself is muscular without losing its ability to move into a gentler mood, the vocal balance good, the overall sound rich in its lower registers and bright and clear in the upper ones. At its best this record is simply without equal.

Il quinto libro de madrigali.
Concerto Italiano / Rinaldo Alessandrini.
Opus 111 OPS30-166 (65 minutes: DDD). Texts and translations included.
Recorded 1996.　　　　　　　　　　　　　　　　　　　　　　Ⓕ 🅿 🅴

There is a modernity about Monteverdi's poetic choices in the Fifth Book which is in turn reflected in an adventurous harmonic and gestural language which pushes the madrigalian vocabulary of Giaches de Wert and Luca Marenzio to new boundaries. As always with Monteverdi, his main preoccupation here is with an intimate bonding of words and music in a way which goes beyond the illustrative and pictorial manoeuvres of traditional madrigalian styles. This aesthetic priority is one which Rinaldo Alessandrini and the Concerto Italiano have done so much to understand and reveal. Enthusiasts for the Concerto's highly dramatic, yet sensitive and subtle approach, the rich fruit of a winning combination of a true understanding of the textual complexities of Guarini's verse allied to a high order of technical control, will not be disappointed by this disc. The opening diptych, 'Cruda Amarilli/O Mirtillo', sets the tone and style for much of what follows; the pace is stately, the passion being generated by extraordinary dissonances, delineated here with a lingering attention that is truly spine-chilling while still retaining its erotic undertow. Here and elsewhere on this recording, the exactness of the voicing, the gentle underscoring of rhythm and meaning, the authentic sound of the Italian language and the sheer musicality of the final result are united in performances of great expressive power and integrity.

Il ottavo libro de madrigali – Sinfonia; Altri canti d'amor; Non havea Febo ancora, 'Lamento della ninfa'; Vago augelletto; Perchè t'en fuggi, O Fillide?; Altri canti di Marte; Ogni amante è guerrier; Hor ch'el ciel e la terra; Gira il nemico insidioso Amore; Dolcissimo uscignolo; Ardo, ardo, avvampo, mi struggo.
Concerto Italiano / Rinaldo Alessandrini.
Opus 111 OPS30-187 (75 minutes: DDD). Texts and translations included. Recorded 1997.
Gramophone Award Winner 1998. ⓕⓟ

Monteverdi's Eighth Book of Madrigals, issued with the eye-catching title of *Madrigali guerrieri et amorosi* ('Madrigals of Love and War'), was published in 1638. Taking their cue from the prominent position allocated to his cherished *genere concitato* in both the preface and contents of the collection, Rinaldo Alessandrini has made an unusual selection of pieces in which this kind of writing, which in practice involves much rapid chordal repetition, triadic formulas and scale passages to imitate the sounds of war, is prominent. It is a brave choice. The rhetorical gestures of the *genere concitato* are few, simple, obvious and rapidly pall when over-used. Nor are they confined to the *madrigali guerrieri* alone, since the agitation caused by the pains of love can also call them up. The real interpretative difficulty is to invest these moments with sufficient drama and character that they emerge from their somewhat textbook status and come to life. The Concerto Italiano's dramatic readings of these texts involve the deployment of all the familiar devices of severe contrast, occasional changes of pace, subtle underscorings at cadences and the highlighting of dissonant moments. The star performance of the disc is 'Hor ch'el ciel e la terra' which begins with a magically poetic evocation, through exquisitely voiced repeated chords, of the stillness of the night before settling into a depiction of the lover's pain, achieved here through sharp stabbing motions of almost mannerist exaggeration. The Concerto's account of the second part ('Cosi soil d'una chiara fonte viva') is remarkable, not least for its inspired isolation of vocal lines of great lyrical power passed between the voices; the result is a revelation.

Chamber Duets – Chiome d'oro, bel tesoro; Io son pur vezzosetta pastorella; Non è di gentil core; Non è mai le stelle; O come sei gentile, caro augellino; Ohimè, dovè il mio ben?; O viva fiamma; S'el vostro cor, madonna; Soave libertate; Tornate, o cari baci; Vorrei baciarti, O Filli; Book 8: Mentre vaga Angioletta ogn'anima; O sia tranquill'il mare; Book 9: Bel pastor dal cui bel guardo. Scherzi musicali – Zefiro torna. Non vedrò mai le stelle.
Complesso Barocco / Alan Curtis *hpd/org*
Virgin Classics Veritas VC5 45293-2 (68 minutes: DDD). Texts and translations included.
Recorded 1996. ⓕⓟ

Monteverdi's Chamber Duets are of a consistently high quality and include some of his most popular pieces (such as *Zefiro torna*, or the ravishing *Chiome d'oro*). The opening track wonderfully sets the tone, and showcases another of the recording's distinctive features, a particularly full continuo group. As one expects of Complesso Barocco, the standard of interpretation throughout is very high, although some of the more extended pieces seem to lose the thread of the argument, and the male soloists seem almost breathless at the tail-end of certain *passaggi*. The native singers' ease with the language is an essential asset: *Bel pastor*, one of the few duets for unequal voices, is particularly telling in this regard. Moving beyond interpretation, this project brings to the fore Monteverdi's astonishing resourcefulness and diversity of expression: what generous, essential music this is!

L'incoronazione di Poppea.
Helen Donath *sop* Poppea; **Elisabeth Söderström** *sop* Nerone; **Cathy Berberian** *mez* Ottavia;
Paul Esswood *counterten* Ottone; **Giancarlo Luccardi** *bass* Seneca;
Rotraud Hansmann *sop* Virtue, Drusilla; **Jane Gartner** *sop* Fortune, Pallas, Darmigella;
Maria Minetto *contr* Nurse; **Carlo Gaifa** *ten* Arnalta; **Philip Langridge** *ten* Lucano;
Enrico Fissore *bass-bar* Lictor, Mercury; **anonymous** *treb* Love; **Margaret Baker** *sop* Valletto;
Vienna Concentus Musicus / Nikolaus Harnoncourt.
Teldec 2292-42547-2 (four discs: 215 minutes: ADD). Notes, text and translation included.
Recorded 1973-74. ⓕⓟ ⓇⓇ

L'incoronazione di Poppea has always had its staunch admirers, many claiming it to be Monteverdi's greatest masterpiece, even the finest opera of the seventeenth century. However, what's left of the opera amounts to little more than a vocal score, and even then with some scenes missing, others evidently added by hands other than Monteverdi's own. To turn the sketchy, inadequate sources into something that Monteverdi might have recognized as his work requires not only considerable effort but also more than a little self-confidence. Harnoncourt's production is still the best recording of it ever made. With its strong, sensitive cast and excellent pacing, this is a performance that shows the work's true potential, even if the realization is calculated to raise a few eyebrows – and more so today than when it was first released. There are reservations about the use of loud wind instruments, above all in vocal contexts, and about the heavy ornamentation that their players use. Even the scoring of the string orchestra is heavy-handed on occasion. These effects are, of course, entirely of Harnoncourt's own making, since there's nothing in the sources to indicate even the size and nature of the orchestra, let alone its deployment. Also, his decision to associate certain timbres with specific situations could be seen as regrettable. Trumpets for the gods is acceptable enough, but there's nothing subtle about the pair of oboes that surfaces to accompany the comic characters. What saves this performance, however, is the fine cast of singers. There's not a single weak link. It was an imaginative move to cast Elisabeth Söderström as Nerone (originally a high castrato role), and one can forgive her palpable femininity on the grounds that she finds so much to convey in her playing of the part. Equally sure of her role as Ottavia is Cathy Berberian. Even the lesser characters are played superbly well – Jane Gartner as Fortune/Darmigella/Pallas, for example, or Philip Langridge as Lucano. It's as though every member of the cast recognizes the latent power of this marvellous music; and that's what makes this recording such an enduring one.

L'incoronazione di Poppea.
Sylvia McNair sop Poppea; **Dana Hanchard** sop Nerone; **Anne Sofie von Otter** mez Ottavia, Fortune, Venus; **Michael Chance** counterten Ottone; **Francesco Ellero d'Artegna** bass Seneca; **Catherine Bott** sop Drusilla, Virtue, Pallas, Athene; **Roberto Balcone** counterten Nurse; **Bernarda Fink** contr Arnalta; **Mark Tucker** ten Lucano, First Soldier; **Julian Clarkson** bass Lictor, Mercury; **Marinella Pennicchi** sop Love; **Constanze Backes** sop Valleto; **Nigel Robson** ten Liberto, Second Soldier; **English Baroque Soloists / Sir John Eliot Gardiner.**
Archiv Produktion 447 088-2AH3 (three discs: 191 minutes: DDD). Notes, text and translation included. Recorded live in 1993. Ⓕ Ⓟ

The central question was always about how much needs to be added to the surviving notes in order to make *Poppea* viable on stage. Gardiner and his advisers believe that nothing needs adding and that the 'orchestra' indeed played only when explicitly notated in the score but that it was a very small group. To some ears this will have a fairly ascetic effect but it is firmly in line with current scholarly thinking about the opera. To compensate for that asceticism Gardiner has a rich group of continuo players and they play with wonderful flexibility. And Gardiner's spacious reading of the score bursts with the variety of pace that one might expect from a seasoned conductor of early opera. Sylvia McNair is a gloriously sensuous Poppea: from her sleepy first words to the final duet she is always a thoroughly devious character, with her breathy, come-hither tones. Complementing this is Dana Hanchard's angry-brat Nerone, less even in voice than one might hope, but dramatically powerful. Whether they quite challenge Helen Donath and Elisabeth Söderström for Harnoncourt must remain a matter of opinion, but they certainly offer a viable alternative. The strongest performances here, though, come from Michael Chance and Anne Sofie von Otter as Ottone and Ottavia, both of them offering superbly rounded portrayals. Again they face severe challenges from Harnoncourt's unforgettable Paul Esswood and Cathy Berberian, but here the challenge is more equal, being on roughly the same grounds. Francesco Ellero d'Artegna is perhaps the most vocally skilled Seneca to date, with a resonant low C, though Michael Schopper for René Jacobs comes closer to the character of the oddball philosopher with clear political views for which he is happy to die. Catherine Bott is a wonderfully lively Drusilla; and the remainder of the cast are, as one might expect from Gardiner, consistently strong. The fact that this was recorded at a public concert is noticeable only from occasional superfluous noises.

L'Orfeo.
Laurence Dale ten Orfeo; **Efrat Ben-Nun** sop Euridice, Music; **Jennifer Larmore** mez Messenger; **Andreas Scholl** counterten Hope; **Paul Gérimon** bass Charon; **Bernarda Fink** contr Proserpina; **Harry Peeters** bass Pluto; **Nicolas Rivenq** bar Apollo; **Concerto Vocale / René Jacobs.**
Harmonia Mundi HMC90 1553/4 (two discs: 120 minutes: DDD). Notes, text and translation included. Recorded 1995. Ⓕ Ⓟ ⓇⓇ

It is clear right from the start, with the almost aggressive snarling brass and thudding drums of the opening Toccata, that René Jacobs's reading of *L'Orfeo* is a full-blooded one. The tone is set almost immediately by Efrat Ben-Nun, whose approach to the two roles that she sings is refreshingly direct and dramatic; her lines are sensitively shaped and phrased, and only the improvised embellishments to the part of Music, at times quite elaborate, could possibly cause any controversy. Among the other soloists Bernarda Fink delivers a convincingly urgent account of Proserpina's appeal at the opening of the Fourth Act, while Harry Peeters's Pluto presents his measured responses with an attractively lyrical authority. Charon's strangely angular lines, with their air of menace appropriate to one who spends time in contact with the Underworld, are expertly managed by Paul Gérimon, who shows himself to be a true Monteverdi bass. René Jacobs's approach to the thorny question of orchestration is robust. The score is notoriously difficult to interpret in this respect, often contradictory in its indications and in the end any solution can only be judged against some notion of what Monteverdi's sound world might have been. Jacobs's version was originally given at the Salzburg Festival in 1993, and his instrumental resources, based around three continuo instruments spatially separated, are more a reflection of the acoustical properties of a modern pit rather than those of the sort of room in the Ducal Palace in which *L'Orfeo* was first performed. There is nothing necessarily wrong with that, and it has to be said that the result is successful, discriminating and only rarely over-elaborate. In Laurence Dale in the title-role, Jacobs has found a powerful protagonist, a singer capable of negotiating convincingly the sudden changes of emotional state that characterize the part at some of its most critical moments. More to the point, 'Possente spirto' is something of a *tour de force*, conveying the central conception of the power of song with true rhetorical understanding. This is a version of *L'Orfeo* to be reckoned with.

Il Ritorno d'Ulisse in Patria.
Christoph Prégardien *ten* Ulisse; **Bernarda Fink** *contr* Penelope;
Christina Högmann *sop* Telemaco, Siren; **Martyn Hill** *ten* Eumete; **Jocelyne Taillon** *mez* Ericlea;
Dominique Visse *countertenor* Pisandro, Human Fragility; **Mark Tucker** *ten* Anfinomo;
David Thomas *bass* Antinoo; **Guy de Mey** *ten* Iro; **Faridah Subrata** *mez* Melanto;
Jörg Dürmüller *ten* Eurimaco; **Lorraine Hunt** *sop* Minerva, Fortune;
Michael Schopper *bass* Nettuno, Time; **Olivier Lallouette** *bass* Giove;
Claron McFadden *sop* Giunone; **Martina Bovet** *sop* Siren, Love;
Concerto Vocale / René Jacobs.
Harmonia Mundi HMC90 1427/9 (three discs: 179 minutes: DDD). Notes, text and translation included. Recorded 1992. ⓕⓅ

The only surviving manuscript score of this major musical drama, preserved in Vienna, presents an incomplete version of three acts. For this recording, René Jacobs has, within the spirit of seventeeth-century music-making, added more music by Monteverdi and others to expand the work to a satisfying five-act structure suggested by some surviving librettos. He has also considerably expanded the scoring, very much enlivening the instrumental palette that Monteverdi would have had available to him for his original production in Vienna in 1641, and the result is powerful and effective. The extensive cast, led by Christoph Prégardien in the title role, is excellently chosen, not only for vocal quality but also for a convincing awareness of Monteverdi's idiom. Without that, the performance could have seemed tame, and that is nowhere better exemplified than in Act 1, Scene 7 where Ulysses awakes, wondering where he is and what is to happen to him. Prégardien here manages to convey as much depth of feeling as a Pagliaccio yet stays clearly within the bounds of Monteverdi's expressive style. The result is a *tour de force*, one of the many within this production. The adept instrumental contribution certainly helps to maintain variety throughout the work, and an accompaniment suited to the sentiments expressed by the vocalists is always possible with these resources. Ultimately, this production is very much one for our time. It is a practical solution to the problems of performing music of another age, and one that turns out to be inspired, moving and totally compelling.

Cristóbal de Morales

Spanish *c*1500-1553

Morales Mass for the feast of St Isidore of Seville. Missa 'Mille regretz'. Emendemus in melius.
Guerrero O Doctor optime.
Instrumental and organ works by Cabézon, Rogier, Guerrero, Gombert and Santa María.
Gabrieli Consort and Players / Paul McCreesh.
Archiv Produktion 449 143-2AH (76 minutes: DDD). Texts and translations included. Recorded 1995. ⓕⒺ

To begin at the beginning, the instrumental *canciones* by Guerrero and Rogier which open the disc are played with delightful sensitivity: one can understand why instrumentalists were so prized in Spanish cathedrals at this time if they played like this. Morales's Mass itself, performed by an all-male consort, is sung splendidly. There is a real feeling for the work's direction (not easily discerned in music so seamlessly polyphonic as Morales) which, in combination with the seductively rich sonority of the choir, make it a performance of genuine stature. The only reservations concern the stodgy singing of the 'Hosanna' which would surely benefit from a lighter, more rhythmic approach. The plainchant is for the feast of St Isidore of Seville, taken from unspecified sixteenth- and seventeenth-century sources by Robert Snow. It is sung accompanied by a dulcian, as indeed is the polyphony, common Spanish practice of the time. Instruments and choir come together only in

Guerrero's motet, *O Doctor optime*, sung at the Offertory, which is an object lesson in how to achieve blend and balance. Another *canción* by Rogier acts as a recessional, and the disc closes with a short piece by Tomás de Santa María followed by a magnificent performance of Morales's motet *Emendemus in melius*.

Moritz Moszkowski German 1854-1925

Fantaisie Impromptu, Op. 6. Trois Etudes de Concert, Op. 24. Trois Morceaux, Op. 42.
Trois Morceaux, Op. 73. Grande Valse de Concert, Op. 88. Isoldens Tod – Concert Paraphrase after Wagner.
Seta Tanyel *pf*
Collins Classics 1473-2 (65 minutes: DDD). Recorded 1996. Ⓕ🄴

Although Moszkowski could be limited and facile he wrote superbly for the piano, decking out one charming melody after another with the most grateful and scintillating virtuosity. The items presented here span most of Moszkowski's creative career and the full range of his artistry, from the gentle innocence of his salon music (the *Morceaux* of Opp. 42 and 73) to the extrovert virtuosity of the *Etudes de Concert* and the wonderfully pianistic transcription of the final scene from Wagner's *Tristan und Isolde*. Tanyel's playing is gracious, affectionate and polished. The technical demands (often considerable) are surmounted with nonchalant ease and fluency. She tends to eschew idiosyncrasy, but reveals a naturally refined stylishness. The most impressive piece offered here is the paraphrase of Wagner's *Isoldens Tod*, which is in many ways superior to Liszt's famous transcription, and is among Moszkowski's finest piano writing. Tanyel's colourful account is beautifully moulded, giving a sense of inevitability to the ever-intensifying chromaticism. This is a set all enthusiasts of super-virtuosity should investigate. The recording is impeccable.

Fantaisie, 'Hommage à Schumann', Op. 5. Barcarolle, Op. 27 No. 1. Scherzo-Valse, Op. 40.
Etude in G minor, Op. 67 No. 2. Six Morceaux, Op. 83. Trois Morceaux, Op. 86. Trois Morceaux, Op. 87.
Seta Tanyel *pf*
Collins Classics 1519-2 (62 minutes: DDD). Recorded 1998. Ⓕ

Today we take a more genial view of Moszkowski than his contemporaries who dismissed him as a salon composer, and only a puritan could resist 'Sur l'eau' from Op. 87, with its open-hearted embrace of picturesque escapism, its refusal of all *Angst*. The *Barcarolle*, too, is a real discovery, its alternating languor and passion recalling Fauré's early romantic idealism, its final filigree an affectionate tribute to Chopin. 'Complainte' (Op. 87 No. 1) suggests only the gentlest notion of querulousness, yet as one idea streams from another you can't help but marvel at Moszkowski's skill, his endless capacity for conversational elegance and brio. Seta Tanyel's performances are of the most engaging insouciance and dexterity. Other specialists in this repertoire (they include Eileen Joyce, Stephen Hough, Shura Cherkassky and Ilana Vered) may play with a more sharply honed or focused virtuosity but time and again Tanyel's ease and civility make even the slenderest glycerine and rose-water offering delectable. Collins's recordings are exemplary.

Wolfgang Amadeus Mozart Austrian 1756-1791

Clarinet Concerto in A major, K622.

Clarinet Concerto. Clarinet Quintet in A major, K581.
Thea King *basset cl*
[b]**Gabrieli String Quartet** (Kenneth Sillito, Brendan O'Reilly *vns* Ian Jewel *va* Keith Harvey *vc*);
[a]**English Chamber Orchestra / Jeffrey Tate.**
Hyperion CDA66199 (64 minutes: DDD). Ⓕ🆁🆁

The two works on this disc are representative of Mozart's clarinet writing at its most inspired; however, the instrument for which they were written differed in several respects from the modern clarinet, the most important being its extended bass range. Modern editions of both the Clarinet Concerto and the Quintet have adjusted the solo part to suit today's clarinets, but Thea King reverts as far as possible to the original texts, and her playing is both sensitive and intelligent. Jeffrey Tate and the ECO accompany with subtlety and discretion in the concerto, and the Gabrieli Quartet achieves a fine sense of rapport with King in the Quintet. Both recordings are clear and naturally balanced, with just enough distance between soloist and listener.

Clarinet Concerto. Oboe Concerto in C major, K314.
Jack Brymer *cl* **Neil Black** *ob*
Academy of St Martin in the Fields / Sir Neville Marriner.
Philips 416 483-2PH (50 minutes: ADD). Recorded 1973.   Ⓕ

For all the classic status of Jack Brymer's recordings with Beecham (available on EMI with various couplings), we would not now choose them in preference to this Marriner version. His recording here is of the highest distinction, coupled with Neil Black's delightful performance of the Oboe Concerto. They are fine performances, even great ones; with Marriner, Brymer seems to have rethought his approach to a work he must have known almost too well. He has shed none of his elegance, none of that incomparable grace of phrase and creaminess of tone, but there is a greater touch of wistfulness, a hint of tragedy, which lends the music fuller substance. Even in the finale, there is the suggestion that the liveliness is the more precious for an awareness of a darker element. It is the finest of all the recordings displaying Brymer's art at its greatest in one of the greatest works ever written for the instrument. No collector could be disappointed by such a pairing.

Mozart Clarinet Concerto[a].
Spohr Clarinet Concerto No. 1 in C minor, Op. 26.
Weber Clarinet Concerto No. 2 in E flat major, J118.
Ernst Ottensamer *cl/[a]basset cl*
Vienna Philharmonic Orchestra / Sir Colin Davis.
Philips 438 868-2PH (72 minutes: DDD). Recorded 1992.   Ⓕ

Ernst Ottensamer is a virtuoso with a real sense of style, that is to say a musician with an instinct for the difference between the contained romanticism of Mozart's concerto and the overt but differing romanticism of Spohr and Weber. His tone is rich and warm, with a beautiful depth in the lower registers of the basset clarinet in the Mozart, but also a brilliance that has a bit of a wicked glint to it in Weber's finale compared to the dancing ease of Mozart's. Mozart's *Adagio* is beautifully judged in tempo, a song with a seamless line, while Weber's *Romanza* is taken quite differently, like a wordless operatic aria. Spohr's short *Adagio,* a touchingly simple, direct piece, is charmingly delivered, and elsewhere Ottensamer listens with a careful ear to the woodwind and other lines which in this work intermingle so subtly: he is an old Philharmoniker who shows a proper attention to his colleagues. He is given close, sympathetic support by orchestra and conductor. One of Davis's particular qualities is his ear for the telling simplicities in Mozart, so that here a plain arpeggio springs to life with the clarinet's melody, or a set of repeated notes has a sense of direction towards a cadence. How musically the 'accompaniment' is done. The VPO responds with complete understanding, and the recording engineers have missed nothing.

Flute Concertos – No. 1 in G major, K313/K285c; No. 2 in C major, K314/K285d.
Andante in C major, K315/K285e. Flute and Harp Concerto in D major, K299/K297c.

Flute Concerto No. 1. Andante. Flute and Harp Concerto.
Susan Palma *fl* **Nancy Allen** *hp*
Orpheus Chamber Orchestra.
DG 427 677-2GH (58 minutes: DDD). Recorded 1988.   Ⓕ **RR**

Mozart's G major Flute Concerto is a charming work, one by no means without depth. This is an admirable performance by Susan Palma, a remarkably gifted player who is also a member of the Orpheus Chamber Orchestra, a conductorless ensemble of 24 musicians, who play with skill and unanimity (the quality of their phrasing is remarkable) so that all is alert, lithe and yet sensitive. Palma's tone is liquid and bright, with fine tonal nuances, and her cadenzas are no less well imagined. The Concerto for flute and harp was written for the flute-playing Count de Guines to play with his harpist daughter, and combines these two beautiful instruments to fine effect. Again the soloists are highly skilled and, beyond that, their playing is nicely matched, tonally and stylistically. Indeed Palma is as delightful as in the other work and the spacious *Andante* in C major that separates the two concertos, while Nancy Allen makes an exquisite sound and also articulates more clearly than many other harpists. The attractive cadenzas are by Palma and Bernard Rose. The balance between the soloists and the orchestra is natural and the recording from New York's State University has a very pleasing sound.

Flute Concertos Nos. 1 and 2. Andante. Flute and Harp Concerto.
Konrad Hünteler *fl* **Helga Storck** *hp*
Orchestra of the Eighteenth Century / Frans Brüggen.
Philips 442 148-2PH (78 minutes: DDD). Recorded 1990s.   Ⓕ **P**

Konrad Hünteler and Frans Brüggen shape the elegant lines of the G major Concerto with appropriate finesse, enhanced by an exceptionally attractive blend between Hünteler's c1720 Denner flute and the orchestra's pleasingly fine-grained sound. Hünteler's soft flute sound (atmospherically evoking the human voice) and the orchestra's distinctive period instruments bring added dramatic intensity to this music. Likewise, Hünteler and the orchestra capture the direct charm of the C major *Andante*. The C major concerto is Mozart's arrangement for flute of his Oboe Concerto. For this recording, the eighteenth-century flute parts have been compared with those for oboe for a more 'authentic' text, and the resulting exquisitely balanced account makes a wholly convincing masterpiece for the flute. Hünteler and Storck, aided by the orchestra's subtle playing, highlight vividly the flute and harp concerto's perfect match of technical and instrumental resources.

Flute Concertos Nos. 1 and 2. Flute and Harp Concerto. Andante. Rondo in D major, K373 (arr. Galway). Divertimento in D major, K344 – Menuetto (arr. Galway). Serenade No. 13 in G major, K525, 'Eine kleine Nachtmusik'.
Marisa Robles *hp*
Chamber Orchestra of Europe / James Galway *fl*
RCA Red Seal RD87861 (two discs: 109 minutes: DDD). Recorded 1984-85.   Ⓕ

The first work here is the 'Second' Flute Concerto, a 1778 reworking in D major of an Oboe Concerto in C major, K271*k*. Galway draws faithful playing from the musicians of the Chamber Orchestra of Europe so that Mozart's music comes across positively, and the flute is well balanced with the orchestra of two oboes, two horns and strings. The soloist is vivid tonally but could offer more variety of sound, and he and his orchestra are at times strenuous, so that one looks for more poise, subtlety and interpretative range. Furthermore, what are presumably Galway's own cadenzas are fluent and alert but not entirely convincing stylistically. The cadenza to the first movement of the Flute and Harp Concerto seems discursive too. The recording is reverberant, with dynamics on the loud side and a boomy bass, as if the double-basses in particular have been artificially boosted – this is especially noticeable in such passages as the start of the *Adagio ma non troppo* of the G major Concerto. The Concerto for flute and harp is sensuously beautiful and ingenious too. It receives a thoughtful performance from Galway and Marisa Robles, and overall this is an attractive account. One can see that restricting this issue to original works including Mozart's own flute version of the C major Oboe Concerto would still have taken it beyond the length of one CD. As it is, filling two CDs has necessitated incorporating two transcriptions and also the *Eine kleine Nachtmusik* in which, of course, the flute has no place at all but which needs no recommendation as music. As for the transcriptions, Mozart's *Rondo*, K373, was originally for violin and orchestra, but flautists have adopted it in a transposition to D major and it goes well in this form; this arrangement is by James Galway himself, as is that of the Minuet from the *Divertimento* for two horns and strings, K334 – a famous tune that well suits the flute.

Horn Concertos – No. 1 in D major, K412; No. 2 in E flat major, K417; No. 3 in E flat major, K447; No. 4 in E flat major, K495.

Horn Concertos Nos. 1-4. Piano Quintet in E flat major, K452.
Dennis Brain *hn*
Philharmonia Orchestra / Herbert von Karajan.
EMI mono CDM5 66898-2 (55 minutes: ADD). Recorded 1953.   Ⓕ Ⓗ ⓇⓇ

Dennis Brain was the finest Mozartian soloist of his generation. Again and again Karajan matches the graceful line of his solo phrasing (the *Romance* of No. 3 is just one ravishing example), while in the *Allegros* the crisply articulated, often witty comments from the Philharmonia violins are a joy. The glorious tone and the richly lyrical phrasing of every note from Brain himself is life-enhancing in its radiant warmth. The *Rondos* are not just spirited, buoyant, infectious and smiling, although they are all of these things, but they have the kind of natural flow that Beecham gave to Mozart. There is also much dynamic subtlety – Brain doesn't just repeat the main theme the same as the first time, but alters its level and colour. His legacy to the next generation of horn players (and those that have followed on afterwards) was to show them that the horn – a notoriously difficult instrument – could be tamed absolutely and that it could yield a lyrical line and a range of colour to match any other solo instrument. He was tragically killed, in his prime, in a car accident while travelling home overnight from the Edinburgh Festival – his driving was as legendary as his playing. He left us this supreme Mozartian testament which may be approached by others but rarely, if ever, quite equalled, for his was uniquely inspirational music-making, with a quality something like innocence to make it the more endearing. It is a pity to be unable to be equally enthusiastic about the recorded sound. The mono master is, rightly, not given spurious stereo treatment, but the remastering – although the horn timbre, with full Kingsway Hall resonance, is unimpaired – has dried out the strings: added clarity is no fair exchange for loss of amplitude and bloom. But this remains a classic recording.

Horn Concertos Nos. 1-4. Rondos – D major, K514; E flat major, K371, 'Concert Rondo'.
Anthony Halstead *hn*
Academy of Ancient Music / Christopher Hogwood.
L'Oiseau-Lyre 443 216-2OH (60 minutes: DDD). Recorded 1993.   Ⓕ Ⓟ

A particular charm of Halstead's recording lies in cool, understated performances, which are in the best traditions of British horn playing and in the variety in his approach to the different concertos: the broader phrasing and longer lines he brings to the more consciously expansive and symphonic K495, for example, the chamber musical playing in K447 (easily the finest of the concertos), and the gentle lyricism in K417. Everywhere, however, he excels with his shapely moulding of the music and his natural, musical way of rounding off phrases. Playing a period horn, valveless, of course, he 'makes' the notes that are not natural harmonics by deft movements of his hand in the bell. Sometimes this technique can lead to the chromatic notes differing sharply in quality from the open ones, but Halstead seems to have more control over tone quality than most natural horn players: the stopped notes sometimes slip in unobtrusively, but where he wants to use colour to stress them or pick them out, he does so very effectively, with the occasional touch of brassiness or muffling. Clearly his special skill allows him extra options. For the D major Concerto, the last of the four (the correct chronological order is K417, K495, K447, K412), we are given here both the Süssmayr version of the finale (the familiar one, written during the Easter after Mozart's death and including a Lamentation plainsong) and a very capable filling-out of Mozart's incomplete autograph version by John Humphries, who also supplies the skilful completion of the skeletal K371 *Rondo*. With the Academy of Ancient Music under Christopher Hogwood on lively form, with well pointed ritornellos and attentive accompaniments, this is a thoroughly enjoyable and musicianly account of these endearing works.

Horn Concertos Nos. 1-4. Horn Quintet in E flat major, K407/K386c.
David Pyatt *hn*
Kenneth Sillito *vn* **Robert Smissen, Stephen Tees** *vas* **Stephen Orton** *vc*
Academy of St Martin in the Fields / Sir Neville Marriner.
Erato 0630-17074-2 (70 minutes: DDD). Recorded 1996.   Ⓜ Ⓔ

David Pyatt, **Gramophone**'s Young Artist of the Year in 1996, provides performances in which calm authority and high imagination fuse; and this disc is ideally placed in the catalogue to comlement the nobility and urbanity of Dennis Brain. Although there can be no direct comparison with Anthony Halstead, Pyatt's is very much in that mode of supple, understated and often witty playing, accompanied by truly discriminating orchestral forces. Soloist and orchestra create a constantly shifting and lively pattern of dynamic relationships. Pyatt makes the music's song and meditation very much his own. Compared with the dark, dream-like *cantabile* of Brain, he offers in the Second Concerto an *Andante* of cultivated conversation and, in the Third, a *Romanza* of barely moving breath and light. His finales trip the light fantastic. The Second Concerto's springing rhythms reveal wonderfully clear high notes; the Third is nimble and debonair without being quite as patrician as Brain's; and the Fourth creates real mischief in its effervescent articulation. The cadenzas by Terry Wooding (to the first movements of the Third and Fourth Concertos) epitomize Pyatt's performances as a whole: longer and more daringly imaginative than those of Brain, while remaining sensitively scaled and fancifully idiomatic. The concertos are imaginatively and unusually coupled with a fine performance of the Horn Quintet in E flat, with members of the ASMF.

Horn Concertos Nos. 1-4; E major, KAnh98a/K494a. Rondos for Horn and Orchestra – D major, K514 (cptd. Süssmayr); E flat major, K371. Fragment for Horn and Orchestra in E flat major, K370b (both reconstr. Humphries).
Bournemouth Sinfonietta / Michael Thompson *hn*
Naxos 8 553592 (76 minutes: DDD). Recorded 1995.   Ⓢ

This is not just an excellent bargain version of the horn concertos, superbly played and recorded, but a most valuable example of Mozartian scholarship on disc. Michael Thompson, himself directing the Bournemouth Sinfonietta with point and flair, plays the four regular concertos in revised texts prepared by John Humphries, as well as offering reconstructions by Humphries of two movements, designed as the outer movements, an *Allegro*, K370b and a *Rondo*, K371, for an earlier horn concerto written soon after Mozart arrived in Vienna. The other *Rondo*, K514, completed by Süssmayr, is the version generally used in modern performances of the second movement of the so-called Horn Concerto No. 1, K412. This was in fact the last to be composed, and is less demanding technically for the soloist, both in the key chosen and in the range required. Fascinatingly, the *Rondo* played here as the second movement finale of K412 is Humphries's reconstruction from sources recently discovered, much more imaginative than the Süssmayr version. It is a revelation too in the most popular of the concertos, No. 4, to have extra passages, again adding Mozartian inventiveness. For example, the tutti in the first movement before the development section is here extended in a charming few extra bars. The most frustrating, if equally illuminating item is the E major Fragment dating from 1785-86, which consists of a magnificent orchestral tutti, longer than usual, leading into only a few bars of horn solo. Thompson, for ten years the Philharmonia's first horn, is not only technically brilliant, but plays with delectable lightness and point, bringing out the wit in finales, as well as the tenderness in slow movements. As conductor and director, he also draws sparkling and refined playing from the Bournemouth Sinfonietta, very well recorded in clear, atmospheric sound. An outstanding issue for both specialist and newcomer alike.

Oboe Concerto in C major, K314/K271*k*.

Oboe Concerto. Flute Concerto No. 1. Clarinet Concerto.
Nicholas Daniel *ob* **Kate Hill** *fl* **Joy Farrall** *basset cl*
Britten Sinfonia / Nicholas Cleobury.
Classic fM 75605 57001-2 (73 minutes: DDD). Recorded 1997.   Ⓜ **RR**

This collection of Mozart's finest solo woodwind concertos is a winner. All the soloists are distinguished British orchestral players, each having a distinct personality in his or her own right. Joy Farrall's clarinet style combines an easy freedom with warm classical directness. Her performance of the Clarinet Concerto is totally seductive, with Nicholas Cleobury's gracefully phrased opening ritornello setting the scene for the lightly pointed solo entry. Her delicacy of feeling and velvety, luminous timbre immediately cajole the ear, as does the subtlety of her wistful dynamic nuancing. Her fluid line is heard at its most ravishing in the *Adagio*, richly echoed by the strings of the Britten Sinfonia; and the delicacy of the reprise is particularly magical. It is followed by a delicious, bubbling finale with lilting secondary material. Nicholas Daniel is hardly less appealing in the more petite Oboe Concerto and his reedy sweetness of timbre never cloys. He, too, is at his finest in the slow movement, while in the infectious closing *Rondo* finale he provides a neatly succinct cadenza. The Flute Concerto is equally delectable, especially the tender *Adagio* which Cleobury moves forward at exactly the right measured pace and which Kate Hill carols so touchingly. The neatly pointed Minuet finale is captivating. Recorded sound is excellent and well balanced.

Mozart Oboe Concerto.
R. Strauss Oboe Concerto in D major.
Douglas Boyd *ob*
Chamber Orchestra of Europe / Paavo Berglund.
ASV CDCOE808 (44 minutes: DDD).   Ⓕ

This coupling links two of the most delightful oboe concertos ever written. Mozart's sprightly and buoyant work invests the instrument with a chirpy, bird-like fleetness encouraging the interplay of lively rhythm and elegant poise. Boyd's reading of this evergreen work captures its freshness and spontaneity beautifully. If the Mozart portrays the sprightly side of the instrument's make-up the Strauss illustrates its languorous ease and tonal voluptuousness. Again Boyd allows himself the freedom and breadth he needs for his glowing interpretation; he handles the arching melodies of the opening movement and the witty *staccato* of the last with equal skill. Nicely recorded.

Piano Concertos – No. 1 in F major, K37; **No. 2** in B flat major, K39; **No. 3** in D major, K40; **No. 4** in G major, K41; **No. 5** in D major, K175; **No. 6** in B flat major, K238; **No. 8** in C major, K246; **No. 9** in E flat major, K271, 'Jeunehomme'; **No. 11** in F major, K413/K387*a*; **No. 12** in A major, K414/K385*p*; **No. 13** in C major, K415/K387*b*; **No. 14** in E flat major, K449; **No. 15** in B flat major, K450; **No. 16** in D major, K451; **No. 17** in G major, K453; **No. 18** in B flat major, K456; **No. 19** in F major, K459; **No. 20** in D minor, K466; **No. 21** in C major, K467; **No. 22** in E flat major, K482; **No. 23** in A major, K488; **No. 24** in C minor, K491; **No. 25** in C major, K503; **No. 26** in D major, K537, 'Coronation'; **No. 27** in B flat major, K595.

Piano Concertos Nos. 1-27.
English Chamber Orchestra / Murray Perahia *pf*
Sony Classical SX12K46441 (12 discs: 608 minutes: ADD/DDD). Recorded 1975-84.   Ⓜ **RR**

Mozart concertos from the keyboard remain unbeatable. There is a rightness, an effortlessness, about doing the concertos this way which makes for heightened enjoyment. Not that it is the only way; and yet so many of them seem to gain in vividness when the interplay of pianist and orchestra is realized by musicians listening to each other in the manner of chamber music. Provided the musicians are of the finest quality, of course. We now just take for granted that, corporately and individually, the members of the English Chamber Orchestra will match the sensibility of the soloist. They are on top form here, as is Perahia, and the finesse of detail is breathtaking. Just occasionally Perahia communicates an 'applied' quality – a refinement which makes some of his statements sound a little too good to be true, even brittle. But this is to be pernickety. The line of his playing, appropriately vocal in style, is exquisitely moulded; and the only reservations one can have are that a hushed, 'withdrawn' tone of voice, which he is little too ready to use, can bring an air of self-consciousness to phrases where ordinary, radiant daylight would have been even more illuminating; and that here and there a robuster treatment of brilliant passages would have been in place. However, the set is entirely successful on its own terms – whether or not you want to make comparisons with other favourite recordings. Indeed, we now know that records of Mozart piano concertos don't come any better played than here.

Piano Concertos Nos. 1-27. Rondo in D major, K382.
English Chamber Orchestra / Daniel Barenboim *pf*
EMI CZS7 62825-2 (ten discs: 661 minutes: ADD). Recorded 1967-74.   Ⓜ

Mozart's piano concertos explore a number of expressive worlds ranging from buoyant youthful elegance – though there are surprises and formal innovations even in the Salzburg works, like the Minuet section that invades the finale of K271 – to the *Sturm und Drang* of the first movements in K466 and K491, the introspection of the slow movements of K467 and K488 (the latter in F sharp minor, a choice of key the composer made only this once) and the ineffable poise of K595, the last concerto of all. In their performance it is necessary for a soloist and conductor to be at one interpretatively, or better still to be one and the same person, which is what happens here, just as it would have done in Mozart's own time. Daniel Barenboim uses cadenzas of his own along with Mozart's, and others by Beethoven arranged by Edwin Fischer (No. 20 in D minor) and Wanda Landowska (in the *Coronation* Concerto, No. 26). (Barenboim's own may take Mozart rather far in the direction of romanticism.) He gives a legitimate sense of breadth to Mozart's thought that will appeal especially to collectors who have come to these concertos through Beethoven's. At times he can be self-indulgent, sometimes seeming to be unconsciously telling us how exquisitely he can turn a phrase, rather than allowing Mozart to speak for himself (or perhaps more accurately, to seem to do so); but we hasten to say that we feel this only here and there and that not all listeners will agree.

The best way to find out whether you do is to listen to this soloist's shaping of a melody in a slow movement, such as the poignant *Adagio* of No. 23 in A major; undeniably beautiful as this playing is with its ultra-delicate dynamic shading, it could be thought anachronistically romantic in spirit and even narcissistic. Alternatively, but for similar reasons, hear Barenboim in the *Larghetto* of No. 27, with its rather mannered half-tones and hesitations. Again, the performances of the dramatic D minor and C minor Concertos on the eighth CD in this set, which incidentally are the only ones of the series to have a minor key, will tell you if Barenboim's approach to these works that were admired by Beethoven is too overtly Beethovenian, with their *Sturm und Drang* excessively explosive and the Romance in the D minor a heavy-weight affair, not least where the orchestra is concerned. But it is still Murray Perahia, like Barenboim, directing the excellent ECO, who seems to be closest of all to that radiantly self-revealing and self-giving, and yet still elusive, genius which Mozart demonstrated in this wonderful series of concertos.

Piano Concertos Nos. 9 and 12.
Robert Levin *fp*
Academy of Ancient Music / Christopher Hogwood.
L'Oiseau-Lyre 443 328-2OH (56 minutes: DDD). Recorded 1993.   ⒻⓅ

Robert Levin plays with crisp tone, precise articulation and spruce rhythms. His pianism is athletic, alert and very neatly pointed. He makes much of the quicksilver changes of mood in the music, emphasizing them by rhythmic means rather than stressing continuity of line. In the slow movement of K271 he shows a keen sensitivity to the ebb and flow of tension in the music; he has, and he conveys, a strong sense of the direction each phrase is taking, its destiny implicit from its beginning. The articulation in the finale is delightfully clear. The cadenzas are improvised, and (in the best sense) sound it. Levin's accompanying note argues that using new cadenzas preserves the spirit of spontaneity, and there is indeed a sense of something fresh and exciting about the performances. In K414, too, there is the same emphasis on characterizing the music strongly, even at the cost of rhythmic flow from time to time. In the slow movement he draws a beautifully clear line, with his very precise fingerwork; in the finale too the detail is carefully placed. Again, the cadenzas here follow Mozart's design but are his own. Levin's instrument is bright-toned and exceptionally even in quality, and he stands out sharply from the orchestra. The support offered by Christopher Hogwood and the AAM is lively and rhythmically alert, with some nicely shaped detail and a proper touch of swagger to the tuttis. Altogether a very impressive and enjoyable disc, with a happy air of adventure.

Piano Concertos Nos. 9 and 17.
Concerto Köln / Andreas Staier *fp*
Teldec Das Alte Werk 4509-98412-2 (61 minutes: DDD). Recorded 1995.   Ⓕ🅿Ⓔ

Andreas Staier, speaking of the use of period instruments in this outstanding recording of Mozart's
G major Concerto, K453, declares the piece has 'more of the farmyard about it' that way – and he's
absolutely right. From the braying and bellowing of the mid-phrase *crescendos*, the snuffling and
snorting of the bassoons and the hee-hawing of the alternating loud and soft chords, Staier appears
throughout it all the delighted child with a favourite picturebook. Conductorless, the string playing
in the outer movements of both this and the E flat Concerto is buoyant with daring. The impetus
and excitement of both dialogue and modulations in the slow movement of K453 is thrilling – and
so is the dialogue within the orchestral writing itself in the finale. In K271 the music-making has a
bracing immediacy as the almost percussive string playing cuts into the fortepiano's rhetoric, so
imaginatively developed in Staier's fingers.

Piano Concertos Nos. 9 and 21.
English Chamber Orchestra / Murray Perahia *pf*
Sony Classical SK34562 (59 minutes: DDD).   Ⓕ🆁🆁

Perahia's fine Mozart playing is a feature of the musical scene that has been with us for decades, as
this issue reminds us. There is a delightful freshness and crispness as well as the kind of authority
that convinces us that this is the only way to perform the music – that is, until another masterly
account comes along. Perahia's choice of tempos is a case in point, yet he seems natural rather
than merely predictable and one recalls how even fine musicians can often go astray on this matter
which Wagner and Stravinsky alike regarded as crucial. Are there any reservations? Well, perhaps
the CD sound is just that little bit close and bright, but with music-making of this quality that
does not seem to matter. The grave *Andantino* of No. 9 (which Einstein called Mozart's 'Eroica',
perhaps in part because of its key) is given weight without exaggeration. In No. 21, Perahia does
not give the first movement the *maestoso* element which is suggested in some editions: instead
there is a delightful flexibility and Leporello-like charm. However, one may possibly feel that the
G minor passage before the second subject and the E minor one in the development are too soft
and yielding, charming though they are in themselves. Perahia's own cadenza is effective and in
keeping with his chosen approach. In the famous *Andante* also, Perahia plays with great feeling
and poise.

Piano Concertos Nos. 9 and 25.
Richard Goode *pf*
Orpheus Chamber Orchestra.
Nonesuch 7559-79454-2 (63 minutes: DDD). Recorded 1997.   Ⓕ

There is something specially attractive about Richard Goode's collaborations with the Orpheus
Chamber Orchestra. They are occasional and the recordings are made when the musicians feel the
time is right, presumably after a series of public concerts. The opening of No. 25 sounds
tremendous, with a leathery thwack to the kettledrums and the orchestra suitably weighty. Although
the acoustic is a bit dry, there is a satisfying depth to the sonority, and the balance and placing of
the instruments – with the wind as soloists and chorus, and in relation to the piano as well as to the
rest of the orchestra – is absolutely perfect. All the colours are vivid. In contrast to many players of
the modern instrument, Richard Goode does not pull his punches and makes this first movement a
most glorious procession, imposing but never ponderous. His tempo has a propulsive energy and an
underlying fitness that makes possible some relaxation of it in the broader paragraphs of the solo
part. Wonderful slow movement too, flowing admirably, and it's a tricky one to get right. This
concerto has rarely been recorded so successfully, but the Ninth has been done better.

Many of the virtues enjoyed by No. 25 apply here also. It needs a different rhetoric, of course, and
Goode supplies it, but he waxes and wanes and there's something a shade impersonal about him.
Not cool exactly but diffident, as if reluctant to project himself as a personable soloist. The
reservations concern the first movement principally, where it's as if he were saying: 'I do not need to
attract your attention, this beautiful thing Mozart has made we are going to lay out before you'.
One would have preferred him to make us experience it more acutely. However, this is a Mozart
concerto record to give exceptional pleasure. It aims high and wherever you sample it there is no
gap between intention and achievement. And what teamwork! How do these people do it without a
conductor? Is it a workers' co-op? Technical precision in ensemble-playing can be brought about
readily enough, given rehearsal, but the musical focus sustained here is not something often
encountered outside chamber music.

Piano Concertos Nos. 11, 12 and 14.
English Chamber Orchestra / Murray Perahia *pf*
Sony Classical SK42243 (70 minutes: ADD/DDD).   Ⓕ

Piano Concertos Nos. 20 and 27.
English Chamber Orchestra / Murray Perahia *pf*
Sony Classical SK42241 (63 minutes: ADD/DDD).   Ⓕ

These discs happily epitomize some of the best qualities of the complete Perahia/ECO set. Always intelligent, always sensitive to both the overt and less obvious nuances of this music, Perahia is firstly a true pianist, never forcing the instrument beyond its limits in order to express the ideas, always maintaining a well-projected singing touch. The superb ECO reflects his integrity and empathy without having to follow slavishly every detail of his articulation or phrasing. K414 and K413 are charming and typically novel for their time, but do not break new ground in quite the way that K449 does. Here, Mozart's success in the theatre may have suggested a more dramatic presentation and working of ideas for this instrumental genre. K595 is a work pervaded by a serenity of acceptance that underlies its wistfulness. Mozart had less than a year to live, and the mounting depression of his life had already worn him down, yet there is still a sort of quiet joy in this music. The vast range of styles, emotions, and forms that these few works encompass are evocatively celebrated in these performances, and admirably captured in civilized recordings.

Piano Concertos Nos. 11 and 13. Rondo, K386.
Robert Levin *fp*
Academy of Ancient Music / Christopher Hogwood.
L'Oiseau-Lyre 444 571-2OH (57 minutes: DDD). Recorded 1994.   Ⓕ▣

The first impression, at the beginning of the F major Concerto, is of a performance very much in chamber-music style: a neat, compact body of strings, playing attentively in crisp and springy rhythms, with the faint clang of the fortepiano continuo in the background adding sharpness and definition. Robert Levin performs this concerto, one of the less familiar among Mozart's, most beautifully and unassumingly. He draws very precise articulation and sweet tone from the instrument; there is a delightful sense of the brilliance arising naturally and spontaneously rather than as self-conscious virtuosity. Although chamber musical in approach, the performance has its moments of drama too, with hints of the opera house in its characterization and its surprises. Mozart wrote cadenzas for these concertos, but Levin, true to the practice of the time, improvises his own. The music of K415 is thematically less interesting than the other two in the set and possibly the ideas cannot quite support the larger canvas on which Mozart was evidently trying to work. Some of the bravura material seems just a shade empty. Still, this is a very sympathetic reading, with a really splendid improvised cadenza, and again there is some lovely melodic shaping in the slow movement. Mozart used material from his original slow movement draft within the finale, and these sections are handled here with considerable drama. Levin, of course, adds a certain amount of decoration to the lines throughout both concertos, especially in repeated material, and does so with impeccable taste and style and at exactly the points where it seems to be needed. The lone *Rondo*, K386, a charming piece, completes this distinguished disc.

Piano Concertos Nos. 11-13 (arr. cpsr).
Patrick Dechorgnat *pf*
Henschel Quartet (Christoph Henschel, Markus Henschel *vns* Monika Henschel *va*
Mathias D. Beyer *vc*).
EMI Debut CDZ5 72525-2 (79 minutes: DDD). Recorded 1995.   Ⓑ

Writing of these three concertos in 1782, Mozart made an impressive claim: 'They strike a happy medium, neither unnecessarily complex nor overly simple; colourful, pleasant to the ear – but not without substance. At certain moments only the *cognoscenti* will derive any enjoyment from them, but there is something to please the less discriminating too, even if they don't know why.' Heard here in Mozart's own arrangement for piano and string quartet (made for greater accessibility) they make a crystalline, tirelessly inventive trio played with much spirit, articulacy and affection. A faint suspicion that in the opening *Allegro* of K414 (always among Mozart's most economical but endearing works) provided you are clear and tasteful the rest will automatically follow is erased in a most affecting sense of interplay in the *Larghetto* from K413, a grave sense of serenity in the *Andante* from K414 and embellishments that are elegant and discreet throughout. Dechorgnat also achieves a special sense of romantic delicacy in the second subject from the opening movement of K415 and time and again relishes the opportunity for improvisatory freedom and magic in the cadenzas. He is superbly partnered by the Henschel Quartet, and balance and sound are exemplary.

Piano Concertos Nos. 12 and 19.
London Mozart Players / Howard Shelley *pf*
Chandos CHAN9256 (52 minutes: DDD). Recorded 1993.   Ⓕ

These are clear and stylish readings. The playing of both Shelley and the London Mozart Players is
assured, relaxed and unfailingly enjoyable, allowing the music to unfold very naturally. Shelley
demonstrates his fine judgement of tempo, and textures are also well served; the recording gives
quite a bold sound to his modern piano, but its overall immediacy and warmth are not excessive
and the balance is just right. Phrasing is another area deserving praise: Shelley and his expert team
manage to shape the music gracefully without falling into the slightly mannered delivery which can
affect other artists in this repertory. Finally, cadenzas have the right balance of freedom and
formality. Perhaps the two 'slow' movements here – the quotes are because that of K414 is an
Andante and K459's is an *Allegretto* – are richer in style than will suit some tastes: they do not
sound authentic in period-performance terms, but then this is another kind of performance and
perfectly convincing. The recordings are of the high quality we have come to expect from the
Chandos team.

Piano Concertos Nos. 15 and 16.
English Chamber Orchestra / Murray Perahia *pf*
Sony Classical SK37824 (50 minutes: DDD). *Gramophone* Award Winner 1984.   Ⓕ

This is an interpretation of the highest calibre: Perahia's delicious shaping of even the longest and
most elaborate phrases, his unfailingly clear and arresting articulation, and his delicacy and
refinement of tone are without parallel. Perahia's attention is, moreover, by no means restricted to
the solo parts: even the tiniest details of the orchestral writing are subtly characterized, and the
piano and orchestra take on the character of a dialogue – sometimes poignant, often witty or
sparklingly humorous. The two works are admirably contrasted: the Fifteenth is on the whole light
and high-spirited, while the first movement of the Sixteenth is almost Beethovenian in its grandeur
and purposefulness, and both concertos have typically beautiful slow movements. Recordings are
superb: an overly attentive microphone could have done irreparable damage to Perahia's *legato*, but
here the distance is expertly judged and the soloist/orchestra balance is exemplary.

Piano Concertos Nos. 15 and 26.
Robert Levin *fp*
Academy of Ancient Music / Christopher Hogwood.
L'Oiseau-Lyre 455 814-2OH (62 minutes: DDD). Recorded 1997.   Ⓕ Ⓟ Ⓢ Ⓔ

This disc is particularly interesting for several reasons. Firstly, the fortepiano employed (unsigned)
belonged to Mozart himself. Secondly, an earlier version of K450's *Andante* – whose existence is not
even mentioned by Köchel, Einstein, Hutchings or *Grove* – with significant differences in the shape
of the theme, is included besides the usual one. Thirdly, Robert Levin – by playing along in tuttis,
improvising cadenzas, lead-ins and liberal embellishments, providing new left-hand parts for K537
and adopting some of Mozart's original, more difficult readings in K450 – has boldly opted for
performances with an element of spontaneity and non-familiarity such as Mozart's own audiences
would have experienced. The results are delightfully fresh and vital. The wind are excellent, the
finale of K450 is splendidly light-footed; but in K537 Hogwood might have heeded Richard
Strauss's advice not to look encouragingly at the trumpets, who in the first movement are somewhat
overenthusiastic. The biggest surprise comes in the slow movement of K537, where Levin often
offers a free, but stylish paraphrase of the solo part. There is an A just below middle C on this
fortepiano that gives off a curious tinkle whenever it is struck, and in the initial *Allegro* of K537
this can be a bit obtrusive; but it's not enough to put you off a thoroughly illuminating
performance.

Piano Concertos Nos. 17[a] and 21.
Maria João Pires *pf*
Chamber Orchestra of Europe / Claudio Abbado.
DG 439 941-2GH (58 minutes: DDD). Item marked [a] recorded live in 1993.   Ⓕ Ⓔ ⓇⓇ

It is clear from the opening of the G major Concerto that Claudio Abbado and the Chamber
Orchestra of Europe were on good form at this concert in Italy. It springs along, yet unhastily, and
the orchestral sound, while full-bodied, has none of the heaviness that detracts from good
Mozartian style. Playing what sounds like a modern piano of unusual tonal crispness, Maria João
Pires also satisfies, with shapely phrasing and lovely sonorities, and this whole first movement

proceeds with both a keen sense of purpose and unmannered grace, the exchanges of the development section being delightfully done. The cadenza here is Mozart's own and, of course, a model of what cadenzas in his concertos should be but often are not, in other words suiting the music and not overlong. After these unalloyed pleasures, the touching *Andante* is no less satisfying, elegantly sculptured and with marvellous woodwind playing. The playful, variation-form finale is again perfectly judged, and indeed the performance of the whole concerto offers truly outstanding Mozart playing, among the best on disc and unquestionably in the Perahia class. The recording is worthy of it: beautifully balanced and clear for one taken live while also being refreshingly free of audience noise and applause. The C major Concerto is also excellent, the first movement strong yet not pompous, with all concerned thankfully never forgetting that this is Mozart and not Beethoven. The famous 'Elvira Madigan' slow movement is not at all romanticized but admirably poised, and the finale springs along.

Piano Concertos Nos. 17 and 20.
Robert Levin *fp*
Academy of Ancient Music / Christopher Hogwood.
L'Oiseau-Lyre 455 607-2OH (61 minutes: DDD). Recorded 1996. Ⓕ🄿

The performance of the D minor Concerto is a major achievement, one of those recordings that has about it a sense of occasion, a feeling that the artists are creating the music afresh. Well, so they are, to a rather greater extent than usual: Robert Levin improvises the cadenzas and quite a lot else besides. The first-movement cadenza here is a particular triumph. Hogwood and Levin take quite a measured tempo for this movement, and it works very well, giving Levin just the space he needs to shape the music pointedly and with meaning. Here and there he does vary the text more than one might expect. Of course, that is well within his rights, historically speaking, and he never transgresses the boundaries of good taste but at times one might feel there is a little too much ornamentation. In the *Romance*, there are one or two moments where the elaboration of the main theme seems restless, though others, for example the final statement, with a witty touch anticipating Mozart's own variation in the orchestra, are entirely persuasive.

In the lighter G major Concerto Levin is truly on sparkling form, playing the outer movements gracefully and wittily – the finale is especially fine, with the basic speed maintained, to brilliant effect. There is some attractive varying of repeats, which is surely what the music asks for. There is elaboration here too, occasional in the first movement, more generous in the *Andante*. The central issue, however, is that these are very fine performances, with much sensitive and delicate playing from Levin, with admirable support from Hogwood and the AAM musicians; and the balance between piano and orchestra seems particularly happily managed with the glittering fortepiano sound coming clearly through the textures but so translucent as to allow the woodwind details to be heard very sharply too.

Piano Concertos Nos. 18 and 19.
Robert Levin *fp*
Academy of Ancient Music / Christopher Hogwood.
L'Oiseau-Lyre 452 051-2OH (59 minutes: DDD). Recorded 1995. Ⓕ🄿

These are thoughtful and strongly characterized performances which make much of the individuality of the works. K456 is taken at rather steady tempos, with soft and sustained textures and gentle colours, and Levin plays it with rare tenderness and delicacy – there are many sensitive touches of timing in the first movement and less of self-conscious brilliance or assertiveness than the music might permit. This rather inward view is very compelling, and it harmonizes happily with the view he and Hogwood take of the slow movement, a G minor set of variations, which on modern instruments is apt to sound decoratively pathetic but not deeply felt, which it certainly does here. There is a good deal of intensity, and of darker colouring: partly the result of the superior blend of sound resulting from the use of the fortepiano. And some of the solo woodwind playing is of a very high order. Then the finale is taken at quite a measured tempo, not at all as a jolly hunting piece, giving Levin opportunities (which he eagerly takes) to shape and shade individual phrases effectively. Levin improvises the cadenzas, although sets by Mozart survive for both concertos: his argument that a cadenza should have an element of the unexpected is a strong one. The F major, K459 is a lighter work, in a sense; its airy orchestral textures are quite unlike those of the other concertos, especially K456. This is a lively, almost jaunty performance, but in no way superficial; there are countless delectable touches in Levin's playing as well as lightness and elegance, and the effect is very appealing. Similarly, the slow movement, here an *Allegretto*, is quite relaxed, and there is some lovely woodwind playing, counterpointing gracefully with the piano, all exquisitely audible in this aurally translucent recording; at the end you are left under no illusions about the seriousness and stature of the music.

Piano Concertos Nos. 18 and 20.
Richard Goode *pf*
Orpheus Chamber Orchestra.
Nonesuch 7559-79439-2 (58 minutes: DDD). Recorded 1996. Ⓕ ⓈⒺⓇⓇ

With a first-rate balance and quality of sound, here is a Mozart concerto record to transcend considerations of style and stance. The excellence of Richard Goode's playing is not surprising, but the quality of his collaboration with the Orpheus Chamber Orchestra is special: and the beautiful thing about Mozart performance of this calibre is that the two seem inseparable. Of course the freshness and placing of the detail are to be savoured, but it is the long view which holds and persuades. In the D minor Concerto's first movement the brilliant piano writing is so thrilling here because it's projected as being essential to the expression, not just a decoration of it. Goode is particularly impressive in the way he handles the three successive solo statements at the start of the development without slackening pace. They are subtly different in feeling, one from the other, and although he's not the first player to have noticed this, it's characteristic of his distinction to have kept the detail and the overview in balance. He plays his own cadenza in the finale, in place of Beethoven's. He has some good ideas about dynamics in this last movement, and the lightening of mood at the turn to the major key towards the end has rarely sounded such an inspiration – on Mozart's part, of course. The B flat Concerto, K456, is equally enjoyable. The outer movements are brisk and light on their feet, even balletic, but all the colours – and the shadows which pass over the face of the music – are there, just as one wants. Paciness makes for vivacity but never brittleness. At the end, you feel you have had glorious entertainment, and a discourse that has touched on the deepest things. You may well be slightly puzzled as to how Goode achieves so much while appearing to do so little – perhaps it's a question of being so focused, of keeping his eye on the ball! In this the orchestra matches him, as it also matches his spontaneity and relish for the task.

Piano Concerto No. 20. Symphony No. 38 in D major, K504, 'Prague'. Serenade No. 13 in G major, K525, 'Eine kleine Nachtmusik'. Three German Dances, K605.
Vienna Philharmonic Orchestra / Bruno Walter *pf*
Pearl mono GEMMCD9940 (72 minutes: AAD). Recorded 1936-37. ⓂⒽ

Bruno Walter was an accomplished pianist, and his solo work in Mozart's D minor Concerto is full of personality. The first movement cadenza by Reinecke is boring, but otherwise there's much to enjoy in this romantic and subjective interpretation. The VPO plays beautifully both here and in the other Mozart works. The *Prague* Symphony has lots of muscle as well as grace and elegance. If a romantic approach to *Eine kleine Nachtmusik* is sought by the listener then Walter's affectionate interpretations will surely give great pleasure, and the little *German Dances* are charmingly played. Pearl has used commercial pressings for the issue, and a certain amount of surface noise is present. Colin Attwell has reproduced the original sound quality very faithfully and straightforwardly, and his transfers are much kinder to the ears than most others from this period.

Piano Concertos Nos. 22 and 23.
Robert Levin *fp*
Academy of Ancient Music / Christopher Hogwood.
L'Oiseau-Lyre 452 052-2OH (59 minutes: DDD). Recorded 1995. Ⓕ Ⓟ

This is a delectable disc of the two works from 1785-86, the two in which clarinets replace the traditional oboes (the only remaining one with clarinets, K491, needs both). The glitter of the fortepiano – a fine instrument by Christopher Clarke after Anton Walter, whose instruments Mozart used – against the softened, oboe-less orchestral texture is just one of the special delights here. Another is Levin's natural and spontaneous playing – if one can say that about a piece he could undoubtedly have played backwards for years – in the A major work, the first movement especially, where his timing and phrasing sound truly improvisatory, as if he is thinking the music afresh. Which indeed he is; and his touches of ornamentation – listen for example to the main secondary theme in the recapitulation – are witty, inventive and wholly Mozartian. He plays his own cadenza here rather than the Mozart one that everybody else uses, taking that however as his starting-point and moving off in new directions and sampling a different selection of themes. Mozart would have loved it. I'm not entirely certain whether the composer would have enjoyed, quite so much, some of the elaboration of the line in the *Adagio*, tasteful though it undoubtedly is. The finale is full of excitement and high spirits.

Christopher Hogwood directs the E flat Concerto with a fine feeling for its more symphonic character; and Levin too, in his management of the extended solos, is very successful in conveying its breadth with his refined control over the tension while at the same time both brilliant and playful. He gives a deeply felt account of the C minor *Andante* which is enhanced by the admirable AAM wind ensemble playing (and especially the duet for the flute and bassoon) – no one should imagine that the use of period instruments makes it in any way more difficult to realize the darkness of this movement. The finale goes with a splendid swing and of course Levin embellishes the *Andante cantabile* interlude very effectively. The balance favours the orchestra, and the wind instruments in particular, by comparison with recordings that use a modern piano; the piano sound is much more integrated into the texture. But this represents the music as Mozart imagined it and as his own audiences heard it, including the gentle, harmonious clunk of the continuo accompaniment in the tuttis.

Piano Concertos Nos. 23 and 24.
Mitsuko Uchida *pf*
English Chamber Orchestra / Jeffrey Tate.
Philips Solo 442 648-2PM (58 minutes: DDD). Recorded 1987-88.   Ⓜ 𝐑𝐑

These performances from the late 1980s have impressive authority. The balance of sound is a distinctive feature of the recording. How beautifully Mitsuko Uchida plays, and with what freshness and sensibility. Throughout the intimate No. 23, the ease with which she releases and projects the expression is a delight. One wants to hear magic communicated in this music and it is there. After the slow movements, the daylight and brio she brings to the finale is lovely, as if to test the reality of the sublime visions which have gone before. This is some of the best playing of Mozart in recent years. It is an all-round achievement that will not quickly be surpassed and no doubt it will occupy a place in the catalogue as one of the best Mozart concerto recordings of our day. Hers is a thoughtful approach to the great C minor Concerto (No. 24). She eschews the overtly *Sturm und Drang* style that is somewhat fashionable for the first movement. Perhaps her interpretation is helped too by the balancing of the 'percussive' piano rather far back in a way that reveals good orchestral detail while obscuring nothing contributed by the keyboard. But when she plays her own cadenza the piano appears to come forward; the cadenza itself is fairly convincing at first but then goes on too long, wandering stylistically into Beethovenian territory with dreamy recitative and, later, a thumping chord deep in the bass. A poised account of the *Larghetto* and a powerful but well-nuanced finale complete this attractive performance. When you listen to the colour and distinction Jeffrey Tate brings to these works you feel surer still of that. In concertos it is the pianist who must make the running, of course, but it is not many in Mozart who get a collaborator of such calibre.

Piano Concertos Nos. 23 and 24.
Sir Clifford Curzon *pf*
London Symphony Orchestra / István Kertész.
Decca The Classic Sound 452 888-2DCS (57 minutes: ADD). Recorded 1968.   Ⓜ 𝐑𝐑

In a list of all-time best recordings of Mozart piano concertos these should have a place. The balances of piano with orchestra are just right, and the sound has come up freshly on CD, with air as well as clarity and a nicely truthful character. In the No. 24 the wind is not as forward as recordings favour these days, but from the LSO as distinguished soloists and as a wind chorus their contributions tell. Kertész gives Curzon nicely judged support: it sets him off, in a frame, even if it does appear a mite neutral at times and strangely limp in the presentation of the variation theme at the start of the finale of the C minor Concerto. These days, some people might consider the interpretations dated, or unreconstructed. Curzon doesn't decorate the bare, leaping intervals at the close of the slow movement of K488, and he's restrained too in the C minor. But the performances seem to be beyond fashion. The slow movements are especially fine. In the *Larghetto* of No. 24, unfolding at an ideal tempo, Curzon gives the impression of walking while he speaks to us. The gravity of the F sharp minor *Adagio* of No. 23 is a different thing; but there, again, he is unaffected and completely unsentimental, direct in manner even while projecting the deepest feeling. He reminds us that the best interpreters do not impose but find a way of letting the music speak through them.

Piano Concertos Nos. 24 and 25.
András Schiff *pf*
Salzburg Mozarteum Camerata Academica / Sándor Végh.
Decca 425 791-2DH (63 minutes: DDD). Recorded 1988.   Ⓕ 𝐑𝐑

The names of András Schiff and Sándor Végh are distinguished ones in this repertory. The characteristics of these performances are immediately recognizable, though like many good things hard to define. Among them is a generally positive delivery allied to a certain sweetness; listen, for example, to the slow movement of No. 24 and the finale of the No. 25, whose quality owes much to the presence of players like the flautist Aurèle Nicolet. Then there is the pianist's articulation, sometimes *quasi-staccato* in quick passagework but clear and unfailingly expressive even in rapid fingerwork. The conductor and soloist are adroit in their management of transitions, whether of mood, pace, texture or dynamics, and in any combination, and their tempos are also generally well chosen. (Although it is doubtful whether the middle movement of No. 25 is at what Mozart meant by *Andante*, 'a walking pace', it is done with disarming grace.) The recording in the Salzburg Mozarteum is a good one. Finally, these artists are able to balance the component parts of a movement, and of a whole concerto, skilfully, so that, for example, finales seem to flow naturally from slow movements, just as those movements do from opening ones. Schiff and Végh know how to bring out the joy in this music without sacrificing delicacy, a delicacy without the prettification that we occasionally hear from other pianists. In fact, Schiff brings such tonal finesse that it is hard to remember he is playing a big modern Bösendorfer. Performances such as his make a good argument for the viability of modern instruments here as an alternative to period ones.

Piano Concerto No. 26. Rondos – D major, K382; A major, K386.
English Chamber Orchestra / Murray Perahia *pf*
Sony Classical SK39224 (DDD). Ⓕ **RR**

This is certainly one of the most distinguished of Murray Perahia's Mozart concerto recordings. The D major Concerto, No. 26, is not, perhaps, a work of such individuality as the 12 concertos which preceded it, or the only one which succeeded it (No. 27), yet it used to be one of the most popular, probably because it has a convenient nickname (*Coronation*), stemming from the fact that Mozart performed it on October 15th, 1790, at the festivities accompanying the coronation of the Emperor Leopold II in Frankfurt am Main. Now, curiously enough, it is not played all that often and of the available recordings, Perahia leads the field: dignified yet never aloof in the first movement, eloquent in the central *Larghetto* (which he decorates tastefully), and marvellously agile and dexterous in the florid concluding *Rondo*. He plays his own characteristically stylish cadenza in the first movement (Mozart's own has not survived, but for many years the one he wrote for an earlier concerto in the same key, K451, was wrongly associated with the *Coronation* Concerto). As a coupling Perahia gives us the two concert *Rondos*: K382 in D, a Viennese alternative finale for the Salzburg D major Concerto, K175; and K386 in A, presumably the original, rejected finale of K414. The A major *Rondo* has had an eventful history, having been cut into pieces in the nineteenth century for use as greeting cards (!), and patched together subsequently by numerous editors, including Alfred Einstein, Paul Badura-Skoda, Sir Charles Mackerras, and Erik Smith. The version performed here has a different ending which was discovered by Peter Tyson. It was completed by Paul Badura-Skoda and this is its first recording. The performances are sheer delight and, as in the concerto, the ECO plays, quite literally, con amore – a spirit evidently shared by the Sony recording team.

Piano Concerto No. 27. Concerto for Two Pianos and Orchestra in E flat major, K365/K316a.
Emil Gilels, Elena Gilels *pfs*
Vienna Philharmonic Orchestra / Karl Böhm.
DG Galleria 419 059-2GGA (59 minutes: ADD). Ⓜ **RR**

This is the most beautiful of Mozart playing, his last piano concerto given here by Emil Gilels with total clarity. This is a classic performance, memorably accompanied by the VPO and Böhm. Suffice it to say that Gilels sees everything and exaggerates nothing, that the performance has an Olympian authority and serenity, and that the *Larghetto* is one of the glories of the gramophone. He is joined by his daughter Elena in the Double Piano Concerto in E flat, and their physical relationship is mirrored in the quality, and the mutual understanding of the playing: both works receive marvellous interpretations. We *think* Emil plays first, Elena second, but could be quite wrong. The VPO under Karl Böhm is at its best; and so is the quality of recording, with a good stereo separation of the two solo parts, highly desirable in this work.

Violin Concertos – No. 1 in B flat major, K207; No. 2 in D major, K211; No. 3 in G major, K216; No. 4 in D major, K218; No. 5 in A major, K219; D major, K271a/K271*i*. Sinfonia concertante in E flat major, K364/K320*d*.

Violin Concertos – No. 1[a]; No. 2 [b]; No. 3[c]; No. 4[a]; No. 5[c]. Adagio in E major, K261[d]. Rondo in C major, K373[d]. Sinfonia concertante[e].
Arthur Grumiaux *vn* [e]**Arrigo Pelliccia** *va*
[abce]**London Symphony Orchestra / Sir Colin Davis;**
[d]**New Philharmonia Orchestra / Raymond Leppard.**
Philips Duo 438 323-2PM2 (two discs: 153 minutes: ADD). Recorded 1961-64. Ⓜ **RR**

These performances of the five standard violin concertos, the *Sinfonia concertante* and a couple of other pieces were much admired when they came out on LP, and they continue to earn praise for their crispness, lightness and eloquence. Grumiaux was also fortunate in his partner in the *Sinfonia concertante*, for Pelliccia is also an expert Mozartian and they give a performance of this beautiful piece that is expressive but still avoids self-indulgent romanticism. In the solo concertos, too, Grumiaux plays cadenzas that suit the music in length and style. Both Sir Colin Davis and Raymond Leppard are sympathetic partners in this repertory, and since the playing of the two London orchestras is no less satisfying, this issue scores all round artistically. The 1960s recordings do not sound their age, and indeed are pleasing save for a little tape hiss and, it must be said, an excess of bass that hardly suits the style of this translucent music. However, that is a small price to pay when so much else is admirable, and Grumiaux's fine tonal palette is well caught.

Violin Concertos Nos. 1-5[b]. Rondos[b] – B flat major, K269/K261a; C major, K373.
Concertone in C major, K190/K186e[abce]. Adagio in E major, K261[b]. Sinfonia concertante[dh].
Double Concerto in D major, KAnh56/K315f[gh].
Sinfonia concertante in A major, KAnh104/K320e[dfh].
[a]**Richard Morgan** *ob* [b]**Henryk Szeryng**, [c]**Gérard Poulet** *vns* [d]**Nobuko Imai** *va*
[e]**Norman Jones**, [f]**Stephen Orton** *vcs* [g]**Howard Shelley** *pf*
[b]**New Philharmonia / Sir Alexander Gibson;**
[h]**Academy of St Martin in the Fields / Iona Brown** *vn*
Philips Mozart Edition 422 508-2PME4 (four discs: 265 minutes: ADD/DDD).
Recorded 1966-70.   Ⓜ

Mozart's violin concertos agreeably reflect their creator's love and understanding of an instrument which he himself played more than capably. The concertos have much in common with Mozart's cassations, divertimentos and serenades, which also highlight the solo violin and have other concerto-like elements in them. But their lightweight means of expression in no way diminishes their long-term appeal, for Mozart filled them to the brim with wonderful ideas. Henryk Szeryng has a relaxed way with these works and the orchestral contribution from the New Philharmonia under Sir Alexander Gibson is alert yet sensitive. Szeryng's tone is unfailingly beautiful with a sweetness that is greatly appealing. His evident affection for these works makes for pleasing listening and the vivid and witty 'Turkish' episode in the finale of No. 5 has great spirit. This disc also includes the 'doubtful' but agreeable solo Concerto in D major, K271a, together with a rather laid-back account of the *Sinfonia concertante* with Iona Brown and Nobuko Imai as the soloists (beautifully matched and well blended). In addition we have the reconstructions of the incomplete projected Concerto for piano and violin and the single-movement *Sinfonia concertante* in A major for string trio and orchestra. The recordings are satisfying.

Violin Concertos Nos. 1, 2 and 5.
Orchestra of the Age of Enlightenment / Monica Huggett *vn*
Virgin Classics Veritas VC5 45010-2 (77 minutes: DDD). Recorded 1991.   Ⓕ Ⓟ

These fresh, appealing performances stand up well in an awesomely crowded field. With her gut-strung Amati, Monica Huggett does not, of course, rival modern-instrument virtuosos but these concertos gain much from her sweet, slender tone, her light, buoyant articulation and her beautiful control of colour in *piano* dynamics. The passagework in the opening movements of the first two concertos can often seem tedious in high-powered traditional performances; but the lighter period bow and Huggett's deft touches of timing and shading invariably lend wit and point to Mozart's sequences of triplets and semiquavers. The finales of both these concertos are delightfully lithe and airy, while the closing minuet of No. 5 is unusually delicate – though there is plenty of gusto in the A minor 'Turkish' episode. In the three slow movements other performances may be more overtly expressive, freer with rubato; but Huggett's purity and poise, her subtle graduations of vibrato and her gentle eloquence of phrase are very persuasive. These performances have a keen feeling for the music's dance rhythms and a sure sense of style in cadenzas and ornamentation. The orchestral contribution is crisp, transparent and nicely detailed. Clear, naturally balanced sound.

Mozart Violin Concerto No. 3.
Brahms Violin Concerto in D major, Op. 77[a].
Frank Peter Zimmermann *vn*
Berlin Philharmonic Orchestra / Wolfgang Sawallisch.
EMI CDC5 55426-2 (60 minutes: DDD). Item marked [a] recorded live in 1995.   Ⓕ

With the string complement of the Berlin Philharmonic reduced, and Sawallisch at his most sparkling, the Mozart is a delight throughout, with a quicksilver lightness in the outer movements very different from the big bow-wow approach that virtuoso violinists used to adopt. More than in the Brahms Zimmermann finds a vein of fantasy, and in the central *Adagio* he plays with a repose and concentration markedly greater than in his live account of the Brahms slow movement. Curiously, it is not until the finale of the Brahms, where Zimmermann seems to acquire an extra degree of daring, that the advantages of live recording come home at all clearly. Till then, his performance seems just a little too well mannered, with his silvery tone pointing a lack of bravura, however brilliant the playing is technically. Yet in the finale not only does the performance take wing, but Zimmermann becomes more individual, less plain in his manners, as in the little commas of expression he inserts each time in the main Hungarian dance theme.

Violin Concertos Nos. 3-5.
Camerata Academica Salzburg / Augustin Dumay *vn*
DG 457 645-2GH (75 minutes: DDD). Recorded 1996. ⒡

Taking a break from chamber music-making, Augustin Dumay makes his début as soloist and conductor in these vivid and immediate recordings from the Salzburg Mozarteum. The dual role is very much what sets these performances apart. High-fibre, robustly articulated orchestral playing acts as frame and foil for the imaginative *richesse* of Dumay's own free and airy spirit; and the excitement of the players' close mutual engagement gives a real sense of Mozart's youthful energy bursting out of its Salzburg prison walls. Dumay's choice of tempos makes each slow movement appear to breathe the air of another planet: in the G major work, the pizzicato pulse becomes the plucking of a distant lyre, as the bow scarcely seems to shift on the string in a finely suspended song. In the D major, the soloist is *primus inter pares* in a fine weave of wind and strings. And in the A major, whose piercingly true, birdlike first-movement song deliciously anticipates Joachim's larkrise of a cadenza, there is a fluency and sense of wonderment which makes other interpretations seem earthbound by contrast. Dumay can be earthy enough when the occasion demands: in the finales of the D major and A major Concertos, his little moments of rubato make a shapely leg point and stretch forward in a series of high-stepping open-air dances.

Overtures – Le nozze di Figaro; Il re pastore; Die Entführung aus dem Serail; Die Zauberflöte; Idomeneo; Der Schauspieldirektor; Bastien und Bastienne; La clemenza di Tito; Lucio Silla; Così fan tutte; La finta giardiniera; Mitridate, Re di Ponto; Don Giovanni.
Sinfonia Varsovia / Yehudi Menuhin.
Classic fM The Full Works 75605 57032-2 (63 minutes: DDD). Recorded 1998. Ⓜ

This is a highly recommendable issue, offering fresh and alert performances, vividly recorded. Not only that, the choice of overtures is markedly more generous than on any rival disc, including as it does the early pieces, *Il re pastore*, *Bastien und Bastienne* and *Mitridate*. The Overture to *Bastien und Bastienne* may be little more than a flourish, lasting just over a minute and a half, but its opening strikingly anticipates the first theme of the *Eroica*. Like the Overture to *Lucio Silla*, the most inspired of Mozart's teenage operas, the one for *Mitridate* is like a symphony in three movements, just as delightful only even more compact, lasting in all only five and a half minutes. Menuhin's fresh, alert manner at relatively brisk speeds, is most refreshing. And what above all makes this disc compelling is the overall sense of live communication, of players responding in fresh enjoyment. The excellent sound is full and clear with ample bloom.

Serenades – **No. 3** in D major, K185/167a; **No. 4** in D major, K203/K189b; **No. 5** in D major, K204/K231a; **No. 6** in D major, K239, 'Serenata notturna'; **No. 7** in D major, K250/K248b, 'Haffner'; **No. 9** in D major, K320, 'Posthorn'; **No. 10** in B flat for 13 wind instruments, K361/K370a, 'Gran Partita'; **No. 11** in E flat major, K375; **No. 12** in C minor, K388/K384a; **No. 13** in G major, K525, 'Eine kleine Nachtmusik'.

Serenades – Nos. 3 and 4 (with **Iona Brown** *vn*); No. 5 (**Kenneth Sillito** *vn*); Nos. 6 and 7 (**Iona Brown** *vn*); Nos. 9 and 13. Marches – D major, K62; D major, K189/167b; D major, K215/K213b; D major, K237/K189c; D major, K249; D major, K335/K320a No. 1; D major, K335/K320a No. 2. Cassations – G major, K63 (**Kenneth Sillito** *vn*); B flat major, K99/K63a; D major, K100/K62a. Divertimento in D major, K131. Notturno in D major, K286/K269a. Galimathias musicum, K32 (**John Constable** *hpd* **Ambrosian Singers**).
Academy of St Martin in the Fields / Sir Neville Marriner.
Philips Mozart Edition 422 503-2PME7 (seven discs: 404 minutes: DDD). Recorded 1981-89. Ⓜ **RR**

The prospective collector must face the fact that although at medium price this set represents a substantial outlay, it is a pretty good investment for a lifetime's listening pleasure. With Sir Neville Marriner and the Academy of St Martin in the Fields we are in sure and sensitive Mozartian hands, and these performances, by and large, penetrate easily to the heart of the music in all its moods and colours. The recordings are good, too, with crisp sound that nevertheless has a bloom of resonance on it, and there is a natural balance between the orchestral forces, which include a harpsichord. In fact this issue offers Philips engineering at its best. Alongside masterpieces such as the big *Posthorn* and *Haffner* Serenades and the incomparably graceful *Eine kleine Nachtmusik* there is something of a ragbag of music here, and seven CDs make for a lot of listening. But there are few disappointments with the way this music is played. The *Galimathias musicum* is an extraordinary little mixture of themes, with 17 sections in all making up a cheerful 'quodlibet' medley of popular tunes, including a bagpipe-like one in the Lydian mode (in this case G major with C sharps), which the composer seems to have penned in 1766 at the age of ten; here also the Ambrosian Singers and a solo harpsichordist make a useful and idiomatic contribution.

Good nature goes together with inventiveness and compositional brilliance in the best of Mozart's entertainment music, and we can only sit back and admire the wealth of ideas that are laid out before us, including instrumental ones – for example, the *Divertimento*, K131 has four horns, as its last *Adagio* reminds us. Nevertheless, for anyone planning consecutive listening there are seemingly unending stretches of D major – every work on the fourth, sixth and seventh discs is in this key, and most of the fifth as well. The *Eine kleine Nachtmusik* on the fifth is the exception, being in G major, and is nicely played though the orchestra seems on the big side and in its second-movement Romance the bass-line is over-weighty. In the *Haffner* Serenade, Iona Brown is a stylish violin soloist, while the small contribution of the posthorn player Michael Laird in the work named after his instrument (listen for him in the second Minuet) is attractive too, as is that of the other wind players.

Serenade Nos. 3[a]. March, K189/K167*b*. Five Contredanses, K609.
Notturno in D major, K286/K269*a*.
[a]**Arvid Engegard** *vn*
Salzburg Mozarteum Camerata Academica / Sándor Végh.
Capriccio 10 302 (66 minutes: DDD). Recorded 1988-89.   Ⓕ

The main work here is the big *Serenade*, K185, commissioned by the Antretter family of Salzburg and first performed in August 1773 to celebrate the end of the university year. Like other works of its kind it incorporates a miniature two-movement violin concerto within a loose symphonic framework: an *Andante* designed to display the instrument's powers of cantilena, and a brisk *contredanse* with plenty of opportunities for ear-catching virtuosity. There is also a violin solo in the glum D minor trio of the second minuet. But perhaps the finest movements are the sensuous A major *Andante grazioso*, with its *concertante* writing for flutes and horns, and the rollicking 6/8 finale, preceded by an unexpectedly searching *Adagio* introduction. The performance by Végh and his hand-picked Salzburg players is affectionate, rhythmically alive and beautifully detailed, with an imaginative, subtly coloured solo violin contribution from Arvid Engegard. The tempo and specific character of each movement is shrewdly judged: the two minuets, for example, are vividly differentiated, the first properly swaggering, with a nice lilt in the trio, the second spruce and quick-witted. Only in the finale is Végh arguably too leisurely, though here too the style and rhythmic lift of the playing are infectious. Végh follows the serenade with deft, colourful readings of five contredanses from Mozart's last year and a beguiling performance of the *Notturno* for four orchestras, exquisitely imagined open-air music, with its multiple echoes fading into the summer night. All in all a delectable disc, offering a varied concert of Mozart's lighter music performed with exceptional flair and finesse. The recording, too, is outstandingly vivid, with the spatial effects in the *Notturno* beautifully managed.

Serenades Nos. 6, 12 and 13.
Orpheus Chamber Orchestra.
DG Galleria 439 524-2GGA (54 minutes: DDD). Recorded 1985.   Ⓜ **RR**

The *Serenata notturna* (No. 6) can easily seem bland but here is attractively vivacious and alert. The use of light and shade is a constant source of pleasure, the playing itself is extremely fine, and it is altogether a splendid account. *Serenade* No. 12 is a big piece, being in four movements, and it is played so stylishly and with so much refinement and variety that one never becomes satiated with wind tone, as can happen with more ordinary performances. Of course one wonders at the composer's choice of a minor key for the C minor Serenade (No. 12), a work described in Anthony Burton's booklet note as 'dramatic and sombre' which is thus hardly conventional serenade material, but the writer provides no explanation since there is none that fits the facts. But whatever the mystery of its nature, this is a splendid piece, with a tense first movement and a mirror canon (using inversion) for oboes and bassoons in its Minuet that has been described as suggesting 'the image of two swans reflected in still water'. The finale is a terse set of variations, and indeed it is only the *Andante* (in E flat major) of this Serenade that offers real warmth. Since the recording in a

New York location is as successful as the playing, this is the most recommendable version available of this work. There are many worthy recorded performances of Mozart's most famous *Serenade*, the one that is now universally called *Eine kleine Nachtmusik* (No. 13), but this one by the string section of the Orpheus Chamber Orchestra has qualities of refinement and alertness, even enthusiasm, that make it rather special. These players clearly enjoy the music, but bring to it a delightful precision as well as the necessary *joie de vivre* and spontaneity, and each of the four movements is beautifully shaped and characterized, so that this very familiar music comes up as fresh as anyone could wish for.

Serenades Nos. 6 and 13. Divertimento in D major, K136. Adagio and Fugue in C minor, K546.
Ferenc Liszt Chamber Orchestra / János Rolla.
Hungaroton HCD12471 (50 minutes: ADD/DDD).   Ⓕ

The *Eine kleine Nachtmusik Serenade* is a favourite which will never be in any danger of oblivion. The Hungarian Ferenc Liszt Chamber Orchestra plays splendidly with an exceptionally alert style, but with a slightly heavier sound, a slightly solider style, than the Orpheus Chamber Orchestra. Nevertheless, this is to point to minor differences in the two perfectly sensible approaches, not to suggest that either of the performances is in any way materially superior to the other. Another common factor of the two discs is their inclusion, along with the *Nachtmusik*, of *Serenade* No. 6. The Divertimento here offers a degree of instrumental contrast, adding a few wind players to the basic orchestra of strings. Perhaps rather more of the built-in different sounds of these two groups could have been made in the present recording; but the *Serenade* remains an enchanting one. The Divertimento, also in D, lacks corresponding colour, but is nevertheless, quite a strong work; and the C minor *Adagio and Fugue* (an arrangement by Mozart himself from a piano duo) offers a very noticeably strong *Adagio*, and a fugue in which Mozart makes one of his few explorations – a successful one – of an earlier contrapuntal idiom.

Serenades Nos. 10[a] and 11[b]. Adagio in F major, K410/K484d.
[a]**Academy of St Martin in the Fields / Sir Neville Marriner;** [b]**Holliger Wind Ensemble.**
Philips Complete Mozart Edition 446 227-2PM (76 minutes: DDD). Recorded 1984.   Ⓜ 🆁🆁

'A great wind piece of a very special kind': that is how Mozart's Serenade No. 10 for 13 instruments was described on its première in March 1784, and with no exaggeration. It has had many excellent recordings in the past, and this one is certainly among the very finest. It is a matter of taste rather than any kind of chauvinism that leads us to prefer English wind players to any others in the world: the compromise they invariably find between a smooth, well-blended sound and individuality of tone and expression seems to be extremely satisfying. The present disc happily exemplifies it. The ensemble sound, which digital recording doubtless captures the more vividly, has a remarkable warmth and richness yet remains clearly defined, with the result that much inner detail comes through. Sir Neville Marriner's interpretation is characteristically both spirited and graceful. The main *Allegro* of the first movement is quickish yet there seems to be plenty of time for shaping the music; the rhythms are well sprung, the textures lucid. The first trio, for pairs of clarinets and basset-horns is particularly light and happy, and the Ländler-ish lilt of the second one of the second Minuet is nicely caught. It is a pity that in the *Romanze*, again lovingly played and with some finely athletic work from the bassoons in the central section, an evident slip of Mozart's pen is taken seriously and a bar omitted just before the coda. There is much that is exquisite in the variations, above all in the fifth with its wonderful soft textures and the deeply poetic oboe solo above them, played here with great beauty and intensity. The finale is high-spirited, and very neatly played.

Heinz Holliger leads his group of wind players in an exceptionally crisp and light-textured reading of the supreme Eleventh Serenade, marked as you would expect by some winningly imaginative oboe solos. Characterizing the lightness of texture is the unusually reedy, thin-sounding clarinet tone, which will not please everyone. Except for the modern pitch it might almost be from period instruments. The Holliger group can sound too metrical, however crisp in pinpoint precision the ensemble is but in the slow movement the melodic lines soar persuasively. The *Adagio* in F major, K410 is a much shorter, light work, but equally appealing in its Mozartian charm and here receives yet another persuasive performance.

Serenade No. 10.
Berlin Philharmonic Orchestra Wind Ensemble / Zubin Mehta.
Sony Classical SK58950 (50 minutes: DDD). Recorded 1993.   Ⓕ

The 13 players here are of the highest quality and Mehta is a sympathetic conductor. Everything unfolds impressively, and there is a sense of joy in the music-making, the playing natural, easy without slickness, and expressive (sometimes even passionate), without mannerism. To experience the blend of weight and grace that the music and performance offer, listen to the first Minuet, the second of the five movements. The tempo is just right and the shaping of phrases (not least in the delicately scored first trio and the bouncy second one) elegant. Altogether, this is playing of distinction. As for the sound of the *Adagio* which follows, the music which awed Salieri in Shaffer's play *Amadeus*, this is no less poised. Indeed, here is an excellent performance that is complemented by a clear and atmospheric recording made in the Berlin Philharmonie.

Serenade No. 11. Harmoniemusik on 'Die Zauberflöte' (arr. Stumpf).
Nachtmusique (Alf Hörberg *cl/basset hn* Danny Bond, Donna Agrell *bns*
Claude Maury, Teunis Van der Zwart *hns*) / **Eric Hoeprich** *cl/basset hn*
Glossa GCD920601 (65 minutes: DDD). Recorded 1996. Ⓔ Ⓟ

This recording of K375 uses the relatively rare original version, without oboes. In some ways it makes better sense – the later one with oboes never quite justifies their presence. This performance is thoughtful, euphonious (the chording purer than is usual with period instruments) and very musicianly. The opening movement is taken rather deliberately, the central *Adagio* rather more quickly than usual and flowing very gracefully. Eric Hoeprich, who directs from the first clarinet, has a beautifully full and round tone and provides many happy details of expressive timing. In both Minuets (the lighter second taken in lively fashion) the tempo is slightly relaxed for the Trio, to good effect, both at the Trio itself and at the *da capo*. There is some very neat and spirited playing in the finale; the clarinets in particular are tested and show themselves duly agile. If some of the emphatic chords in the opening movement are a little too loudly played, leading to some coarsening of tone, this is nevertheless one of the best available versions of the work, certainly in its sextet form. The *Zauberflöte* wind arrangements are less familiar than those of the Da Ponte operas and particularly enjoyable; more than once the transcription virtually reproduces the original scoring. They follow the same formulae as the others, offering shortened versions of the overture and 13 favourite numbers. The arrangements are mainly by J.C. Stumpf though two pieces are done in other versions, for smaller ensemble, to create variety.

Mozart Serenade No. 13. Adagio and Fugue in C minor, K546.
Anonymous (arr. L. Mozart) Cassation in G major, 'Toy Symphony'.
Pachelbel Canon and Gigue.
Academy of St Martin in the Fields / Sir Neville Marriner.
Philips 416 386-2PH (52 minutes: DDD). Ⓕ

Sir Neville Marriner here collects a miscellaneous group of popular classical and baroque pieces in characteristically polished and elegant performances. The only roughness – and that deliberate – is in the extra toy percussion of Leopold Mozart's *Cassation* with its long-misattributed *Toy Symphony*. The anonymous extra soloists enjoy themselves as amateurs might, not least on a wind machine, but what is very hard to take is the grotesquely mismatched cuckoo-whistle, an instrument which should readily be tunable for pitch. *Eine kleine Nachtmusik* brings a performance plainly designed to caress the ear of traditional listeners wearied with period performance. The second movement Romanze is even more honeyed than usual on muted strings. The oddity of the Pachelbel item is that the celebrated Canon – taken unsentimentally if sweetly at a flowing speed – is given a reprise after the fugue. Warm, well-balanced recording.

Divertimentos – B flat major, K287/K271*h*; D major, K205/K167*a*.
Salzburg Mozarteum Camerata Academica / Sándor Végh.
Capriccio 10 271 (59 minutes: DDD). Recorded 1988. Ⓕ

Mozart's Divertimento, K287 is a six-movement work cast on quite a large scale, and is scored for two violins, viola, two horns and bass, a combination which presents some difficulties of balance. One solution is to use a full orchestral string section, but this can bring its own problems, for Mozart demands playing of virtuoso standard in this score, and anything less than this is ruthlessly exposed. Sandor Végh's smallish string band is of high quality, and has a pleasantly rounded tone quality. The engineers have managed to contrive a satisfactory balance which sounds not at all unnatural, and the sound quality itself is very good. Végh directs an attractive, neatly-pointed performance of the work, one which steers a middle course between objective classicism and expressive warmth. The Divertimento, K205, has five movements, but none of them lasts longer than five minutes, and the work is much shorter and more modest than K287. Scoring in this case is for violin, viola, two horns, bassoon and double bass, to provide another difficult but well resolved problem for the engineers. Végh directs another characterful, delightful performance, to round off a very desirable disc.

Ein musikalischer Spass, K522. Contredanses – C major, K587, 'Der Sieg vom Helden Koburg'; D major, K534, 'Das Donnerwetter'; C major, K535, 'La Bataille'; G major, K610, 'Les filles malicieuses'; E flat major, K607/K605a, 'Il trionfo delle donne'. Gallimathias musicum, K32. German Dances – K567; K605; C major, K611, 'Die Leyerer'. March in D major, K335 No. 1.
Orpheus Chamber Orchestra.
DG 429 783-2GH (69 minutes: DDD). Recorded 1989.   Ⓕ

The celebrated *Musikalischer Spass* ('Musical Joke') which begins the disc is never so crudely funny that it wears thin, but make no mistake, the jokes are there in just about every passage, whether they are parodying third-rate music or wobbly playing, and oddly enough sound still more amusing when the performance is as stylishly flexible as this one by the conductorless Orpheus Chamber Orchestra. One of the tunes here (that of the finale on track four) is that of the BBC's *Horse of the Year* programme – and what a good tune it is, even at the umpteenth repetition as the hapless composer finds himself unable to stop. The rest of this programme is no less delightful and includes miniature pieces supposedly describing a thunderstorm, a battle, a hurdy-gurdy man and a sleigh-ride (with piccolo and sleigh-bells). There is also a *Gallimathias musicum*, a ballet suite of dainty little dances averaging less than a minute in length, which Mozart is supposed to have written at the age of ten. Whatever the case this CD, subtitled 'A Little Light Music', provides proof of his genius, though differently from his acknowledged masterpieces. The recording is as refined as anyone could wish yet has plenty of impact.

Symphonies – No. 1 in E flat major, K16; **No. 2** in B flat major, K17 (attrib. L. Mozart); **No. 4** in D major, K19; **No. 5** in B flat major, K22; **No. 6** in F major, K43; **No. 7** in D major, K45; **No. 7a** in G major, K45a/KAnh221, 'Alte Lambach'; **No. 8** in D major, K48; **No. 9** in C major, K73; **No. 10** in G major, K74; **No. 11** in D major, K84/K73q; **No. 12** in G major, K110/K75b; **No. 13** in F major, K112; **No. 14** in A major, K114; **No. 15** in G major, K124; **No. 16** in C major, K128; **No. 17** in G major, K129; **No. 18** in F major, K130; **No. 19** in E flat major, K132; **No. 20** in D major, K133; **No. 21** in A major, K134; **No. 22** in C major, K162; **No. 23** in D major, K181/K162b; **No. 24** in B flat major, K182/K173dA; **No. 25** in G minor, K183/K173dB; **No. 26** in E flat major, K184/K161a; **No. 27** in G major, K199/K161b; **No. 28** in C major, K200/K189k; **No. 29** in A major, K201/K186a; **No. 30** in D major, K202/K186b; **No. 31** in D major, K297/K300a, 'Paris'; **No. 32** in G major, K318; **No. 33** in B flat major, K319; **No. 34** in C major, K338; **No. 35** in D major, K385, 'Haffner'; **No. 36** in C major, K425, 'Linz'; **No. 38** in D major, K504, 'Prague'; **No. 39** in E flat major, K543; **No. 40** in G minor, K550; **No. 41** in C major, K551, 'Jupiter'; **No. 42** in F major, K75; **No. 43** in F major, K76/K42a; **No. 44** in D major, K81/K73l; **No. 45** in D major, K95/K73n; **No. 46** in C major, K96/K111b; **No. 47** in D major, K97/K73m; **No. 55** in B flat major, K45b; F major, KAnh223/K19a; B flat major, K74g/KAnh216/C11.03.

Symphonies Nos. 1-36; Nos. 38-47; (No. 7a) in G major, 'Alte Lambach', K45a/KAnh221; G major, 'Neue Lambach'.
Berlin Philharmonic Orchestra / Karl Böhm.
DG 453 231-2GX10 (ten discs: 749 minutes: ADD). Recorded 1959-68.   Ⓑ Ⓗ

Böhm's vintage Mozart recordings with the Berlin Philharmonic were in fact just as much a pioneering project as Antál Dorati's Haydn symphonic cycle, completed five years later. This was the first attempt on commercial disc to record the whole Mozart symphony cycle, at a time when virtually none of the works before the little known G minor, No. 25, were at all familiar even to specialists. What the performances tell us, warm and genial, with bold contrasts of dynamic and well-sprung rhythms, is that for the players as well as the conductor this was a voyage of discovery, and their enthusiasm never wanes. On matters of scholarship these performances may have been supplanted by a whole series of recordings since, but as a welcoming way to investigate Mozart early and late they certainly hold their place, with not a hint of routine in the playing. As with Dorati in Haydn, minuets are slow and often heavy by today's standards, but it is interesting to find some of the minuets in the early symphonies taken more briskly, almost as fast *ländlers*. In finales Böhm rarely adopts an extreme speed, but always the springing of rhythm, and the clarity of articulation has the ear magnetized, even with a speed slower than we have grown used to.

When this set was first issued on CD, it involved 12 discs, and it is welcome to have these transfers squeezed on to ten discs instead, particularly when the sound is fuller and more forward, with good body and presence. There is some inconsistency in the recording quality, but not enough to worry about, and even the earliest reading – of the *Haffner*, made in 1959 – is satisfyingly full-bodied, when one or two of the later ones are rather thinner. All the earlier symphonies were recorded in intensive sessions in 1968, and the present bargain box, unlike the previous one, has such information included, as well as essays on Böhm as Mozartian by Peter Cosse and Mozart as symphonist by Heinz Becker. Cosse's memory of Böhm on television drawing a parallel between the slow movement of the Symphony No. 1 and part of the unfinished Requiem is quite delightful. Not surprisingly, Böhm is inconsistent over such matters as exposition repeats. In the *Prague*, for example, though there is no repeat in the first movement, the exposition repeat is observed in the *Presto* finale, a question, one imagines, of Böhm wanting to balance two exceptionally long earlier movements. Then in No. 40 he does observe the first movement repeat, but not in No. 39 or the *Jupiter*, and it is probable that with the *Jupiter* the reason is that DG wanted the symphony to fit comfortably on an LP side. Whatever the reason, it means that the last three symphonies have been squeezed on to a single disc of 79 minutes, and only one of the other discs has a timing of less than 70 minutes, and most are over 75. An excellent bargain, and not just for the historical specialist, but for all Mozartians.

Symphonies Nos. 1, 2, 4 and 5.
Abel (formerly attrib. Mozart) Symphony, Op. 7 No. 3.
Northern Chamber Orchestra / Nicholas Ward.
Naxos 8 550871 (59 minutes: DDD). Recorded 1994.   Ⓢ

Symphonies Nos. 6-10.
Northern Chamber Orchestra / Nicholas Ward.
Naxos 8 550872 (56 minutes: DDD). Recorded 1993.   Ⓢ

These two discs of Mozart's first ten symphonies offer a unique view of the composer's earliest years of apprenticeship as a symphonist. Ward and his orchestra demonstrate a sensitive response to the wealth of stylistic influences apparent in these works. Purists may question the inclusion of two of the symphonies, Nos. 2 and 3, since neither work is actually by Mozart. The former is attributed to the composer's father, Leopold, while the latter is Mozart's orchestration of C.F. Abel's E flat Symphony, Op. 7 No. 3. However, when they are played with such engaging style and elegance as here, these two works add a further important dimension to Mozart's early symphonic output. Where J.C. Bach's influence is most powerful (Symphonies Nos. 1, 4, 5 and 6), the NCO presents the music's contrasting thematic characters with fine clarity, balancing the music's beautifully transparent textures with appropriate lightness of touch. The inclusion of trumpets and drums in the next three symphonies (Nos. 7, 8 and 9) announces the young composer's growing brilliance and stature. In these pieces, the NCO moves into a suitably higher gear, revealing Mozart's new and potent originality, with powerfully dramatic tuttis and expressively sung *andantes*. Mozart made his first trip to Italy in 1770, and the symphony he wrote in Milan that year (No. 10) shows his enthusiastic incorporation of Italian stylistic models. Here the NCO's deliciously spacious orchestral playing demonstrates Mozart's ravishing originality, with dramatic opposition of gesture and instrumentation in the exuberant *allegros* and a beguilingly graceful slow movement that winningly displays a keen awareness of the composer's innovative touches. These are indeed splendid performances, admirably complemented by vivid recordings (made in the spacious acoustic of the Concert Hall, New Broadcasting House, Manchester).

Symphonies Nos. 15-18.
Northern Chamber Orchestra / Nicholas Ward.
Naxos 8 550874 (58 minutes: DDD). Recorded 1994.   Ⓢ

After Mozart returned from his first extended tour of Italy in 1771, he embarked on a number of symphonic projects that show his astonishing assimilation and transformation of the Italian overture, with crisp, transparent orchestration and suppleness of expression. The influence of Sammartini and J.C. Bach – whose music could be heard at concerts in Salzburg during 1772 when these pieces were written – is especially apparent in the bold thematic gestures and civilized discourse between wind and strings. Nicholas Ward and the NCO bring their customary style and eloquence to this music in performances that evocatively portray its blend of formal unity, radiant vitality and occasionally – as in the rhythmically imaginative finale of the C major Symphony – rustic charm. Opening *allegros* are suitably vivacious, *andantes* are graceful and poignant and the vigorous finales bristle with energy. The first movement of the C major Symphony offers a more potent dramatic formula, with subtly poetic triplets and tense tremolos; however, the highlight of the programme is the F major Symphony (No. 18), which Saint-Foix described as 'the first of [Mozart's] great symphonies'. Here, Ward's and the NCO's dramatically compelling account, beautifully presented in a natural, spacious recording, brilliantly highlights the music's operatic qualities.

Symphonies Nos. 16-30.
The English Concert / Trevor Pinnock.
Archiv Produktion 439 915-2AH4 (four discs: 264 minutes: DDD). Recorded 1993-94.   Ⓔ Ⓟ

This set includes all the symphonies Mozart wrote between the spring of 1772 and the end of 1774, his most prolific period of symphony composition. What is exciting about this set is the sweetness of the period-instrument sound (not at all the same as the sweetness of a modern chamber orchestra) and the suppleness and flexibility The English Concert brings to the music. They play, much of the time, as if it were chamber music, particularly in second subjects – the lyrical passages, that is, where they shape the phrases with a warmth and refinement you hardly expect in orchestral music. Timing is quietly witty, yet not at all contrived or artificial: it is the sort of expressive refinement that depends on listening to one another, not on the presence of a conductor. There is large-scale playing too. The opening of the brilliant D major work, K133 has a splendid swing, with its prominent trumpets, and a real sense of a big, symphonic piece. K184 is duly fiery and its accents are neatly judged. The two final symphonies are both very impressively done: an eloquent rather than a fiery account (though something of that too) of the opening movement of K201, with a particularly euphonious and shapely *Andante*, and the finales of both are done with exceptional vitality and the rhythmic resilience that is characteristic of these performances. In short, quite outstanding performances, unfailingly musical, wholly natural and unaffected, often warmly expressive in the slow music and always falling very happily on the ear, with no trace of the harshness that some people think is inevitable with period instruments. They are excellently recorded, with the properly prominent wind balance helping to characterize the sound world of each work.

Symphonies Nos. 21-24 and 26.
Northern Chamber Orchestra / Nicholas Ward.
Naxos 8 550876 (53 minutes: DDD). Recorded 1993.   Ⓢ

This is an opportunity to enjoy Mozart's inexhaustibly imaginative assimilation and transformation of Italian operatic models. To begin, Ward's sensitively balanced orchestral textures reveal Mozart's fragrant orchestration with great clarity in the A major Symphony. Sample the second movement's deftly handled interplay of strings, woodwind and horns, and buoyantly stately Menuetto that culminates effectively in the finale's restless drive. The complete musical satisfaction provided by the four Italian-overture symphonies that comprise the remainder of the programme is due both to the fullness and vigour of the orchestration itself, and to the NCO's lively performances. The opening *allegros* and cheerfully effervescent finales bubble with infectious vitality, while the slow movements provide the opportunity for more intimate instrumental ensembles. Most impressive, however, is the E flat major work, which originated as the overture to the play *Lanassa*. Here, Ward and the NCO compellingly portray the dramatic violence of the opening *Presto*, the profound despair of its minor-key *Andante* and the exuberant rhythms of its finale. The recording is atmospheric.

Symphonies Nos. 25 and 31; D major, K320. Maurerische Trauermusik in C minor, K477/K479a.
Berlin Philharmonic Orchestra / Claudio Abbado.
Sony Classical SK48385 (75 minutes: DDD). Recorded 1992.   Ⓕ

These are exhilarating accounts of Mozart using modern instruments in performances which marry sweetness and purity to crisp rhythms and dramatic bite. The symphony in D major, K320, is the one which Mozart adapted from that same *Posthorn Serenade*, selecting just the first, fifth and seventh movements. It is astonishing that though the three-movement symphony is so much briefer than the seven-movement Serenade, it seems much bolder and more powerful in its arguments. This version of the *Paris* Symphony has the alternative, earlier slow movement as a supplement, as well as the later one in its usual place. No. 29 is presented as a large-scale structure, with both halves of the outer movements repeated. Anyone wanting performances on modern instruments is unlikely to find the approach too massive for Mozart, for although the string band is substantial, the purity and clarity of the playing aerates textures. Woodwind doubling is always clearly audible, as with the bassoons in the second movement of No. 29. Abbado's underlining of light and shade regularly makes for delectable moments, for example in the woodwind trio for the Minuet where the descending scales are made to sound like laughter. The recording also captures very tellingly the intensely serious, lugubrious timbres of the *Maurerische Trauermusik* ('Masonic Funeral Music' of 1785, composed a year after he became a Mason), made dark with extra weight of wind set against a string section without cellos.

Symphonies Nos. 25, 28 and 29.
Prague Chamber Orchestra / Sir Charles Mackerras.
Telarc CD80165 (78 minutes: DDD).   Ⓕ

Here are three symphonies from Mozart's late teens, written in his native Salzburg, in crisply articulated performances. The first of them is a *Sturm und Drang* piece in G minor, a key that the composer reserved for moods of agitation. Mackerras takes the orchestra through the big opening *Allegro con brio* of No. 25 with drive and passion, although it is unlikely that Mozart would have expected a Salzburg orchestra in the 1770s to play as fast as this skilful body of Czech players. The gentle *Andante* comes therefore as a relief, though here too Mackerras keeps a firm rhythmic grasp on the music, and indeed a taut metrical aspect is a feature of all three symphonies as played here, so that minuets dance briskly and purposefully and finales bustle. However, the sunlit warmth of the beautiful A major Symphony, No. 29, comes through and the bracing view of the other two symphonies is a legitimate one, though giving little or nothing in the direction of expressive lingering, much less towards sentimental indulgence. The Prague Chamber Orchestra is an expert ensemble, not overlarge for this style of music, and the recording is admirably clear although a little reverberant.

Symphonies Nos. 28, 29 and 35.
Berlin Philharmonic Orchestra / Claudio Abbado.
Sony Classical SK48063 (74 minutes: DDD). Recorded 1990-91.   Ⓕ**RR**

These are 'big band' versions of Mozart symphonies. Nos. 28 and 29 were recorded live in the Philharmonie, the *Haffner* done in the empty concert hall. The Berlin sound is big and weighty, with horns whooping out richly; the result is not just big-scaled but elegant. Abbado is never a mannered Mozartian, but his phrasing and pointing of rhythm is delicately affectionate. The result, while being warm and elegant, also conveys an element of fun, with tempos never allowed to drag. Slow movements are kept flowing, and finales are hectically fast, but played with such verve and diamond-bright articulation that there is no feeling of breathlessness. Abbado is generous with repeats, though he does not attempt the latter-day 'authentic' habit of including repeats in the *da capos* of minuets. With the score of the *Haffner* sparing of repeats, No. 29 is by far the longest of the three symphonies here, the young Mozart spreading his wings. The Sony engineers have coped splendidly with the acoustic problems of the Philharmonie to give a full and forward sound, not always ideally clear on detail in tuttis but with good presence.

Symphonies Nos. 29, 31-36 and 38-41.
English Baroque Soloists / Sir John Eliot Gardiner.
Philips 442 604-2PH5 (five discs: 309 minutes: DDD). Recorded 1984-89.   Ⓜ**P**

Gardiner took his pilgrimage through the late Mozart symphonies more or less in chronological order over a span of six years. The first disc contains appealing performances of Nos. 29 and 33, the former particularly lyrical and shapely, with an eloquent account of the *Andante*, the latter distinguished for its refinement of line and the properly spirited opening movement. Then comes the *Paris*, No. 31, a piece designed to show off a virtuoso orchestra, which it duly does in this alert and shapely reading, coupled with No. 34, another large-scale piece, in which Gardiner again provides a specially graceful slow movement. In the *Haffner*, *Linz* and *Prague* Symphonies Gardiner is possibly more concerned with classical grandeur than with strong characterization of the ideas. The G minor is the outstanding achievement of the set: the first movement performed with great drive and spaciousness, the second shapely and intense in expression, the finale done with immense vitality, the strings' arpeggios leaping vividly through the texture. The *Jupiter* is almost equally splendid, if slightly flawed by some *piano* effects in the first movement tuttis (this happens too in No. 39) where they do not belong, but the crowning glory, the finale, contains many thrilling things. This is probably the version to choose, under any conductor, of these symphonies on period instruments – indeed perhaps on any instruments.

Symphonies Nos. 29, 33 and 40.
Orpheus Chamber Orchestra.
DG 453 425-2GH (73 minutes: DDD). Recorded 1995.   Ⓕ

The reading of the great G minor symphony here is impressively strong and positive and defies the idea that a corporate interpretation necessarily lacks individuality. The first movement is genuinely *Molto allegro*, very fast indeed but full of detail and not at all breathless sounding, with full, immediate sound heightening the sharp dynamic contrasts. The third and fourth movements bring fast speeds too and crisp attack, while the *Andante*, on the slow side for a latter-day performance, is yet similarly dramatic in its contrasts. It is a powerful, compelling account, and equally recommendable is the Orpheus's reading of No. 33, again with exhilaratingly fast speeds for the outer movements, and with the slow movement relatively expansive and smoother than the others. Though the very opening of No. 29 brings playing a little less tautly compelling, the same qualities quickly emerge in a reading at once fresh and highly polished. And again the immediate, full-bodied sound adds to the impact, with braying horn vividly caught, not least in the exuberant, superbly articulated account of the finale. The Orpheus omits second-time repeats, but until conductors such as Mackerras observed them, few would have expected them anyway in a modern-instrument performance.

Symphony No. 33. Serenade No. 9.
Academy of St Martin in the Fields / Iona Brown.
Hänssler Classic CD98 129 (59 minutes: DDD). Recorded 1997. Ⓕ

Symphony No. 35. Serenade No. 7.
Academy of St Martin in the Fields / Iona Brown *vn*
Hänssler Classic CD98 173 (72 minutes: DDD). Recorded 1997. Ⓕ

Each disc brings together a middle-period symphony and a contemporaneous Serenade. The sound recording has a sharpness of focus and sense of presence more often associated with the finest analogue recordings of the 1960s and 1970s. It is surprising to find that the venue was Henry Wood Hall, for this sounds rather more intimate than most recordings made there, with plenty of bloom but no excessive reverberation. This is Mozart sound, using modern instruments but with some concern for the crisper manners encouraged by period performance, that in its freshness and beauty makes one want to go on listening. The finale of the Symphony No. 33, for example, brings a hectic speed which does not sound at all breathless, with featherlight triplets, and similarly in the finale of the *Posthorn* Serenade with which it is coupled. Exceptionally in that Serenade Iona Brown opts for a more relaxed speed and more moulded style in the lovely minor-key *Andantino* of the fifth movement. The posthorn in the Trio of the second Minuet is this time much more brazen and more forwardly balanced than before. The coupling of the *Haffner* Symphony and *Haffner* Serenade is specially apt. In the Symphony Brown follows the autograph in omitting an exposition repeat. Iona Brown herself is the virtuoso soloist in the Serenade, lighter than ever in the *moto perpetuo* scurryings of the fourth-movement Rondo. For those who continue to resist period performances in this repertory these are very refreshing discs.

Symphonies Nos. 35, 36 and 38-41.
Berlin Philharmonic Orchestra / Karl Böhm.
DG The Originals 447 416-2GOR2 (two discs: 146 minutes: ADD). Recorded 1959-66. Ⓜ Ⓗ ⷵⷵ

These performances come from the first ever complete set of the Mozart symphonies (reviewed above), and they still represent 'big orchestra' Mozart at its most congenial. The contrast between Böhm's sparkling Mozart, both elegant and vigorous, and the much smoother view taken by Karajan on his countless recordings with the same orchestra, works almost entirely in Böhm's favour here. Interpretatively, these are performances very much of their time, with exposition repeats the exception (as in the first movement of No. 40) and with minuets taken at what now seem lumbering speeds. Yet slow movements flow easily, and finales bounce along infectiously. Consistently they convey the happy ease of Böhm in Mozart, even if the recording is beefy by today's standards, not as transparent as one now expects in this repertory, whether on modern or period instruments. There is some inconsistency between the different recordings, all made in the Jesus-Christus Kirche in Berlin. The best sound comes from the sessions in 1966 for the *Linz* and No. 39 – satisfyingly full with no edginess on violins – and the least good from 1959 for the *Prague*, where high violins sound rather fizzy. Yet the very precision of the CD transfers encourages one to highlight such points. In practice most collectors will find the sound more than acceptable enough in all six symphonies to convey the warmth of Böhm in Mozart without distraction.

Symphonies Nos. 36 and 38.
Prague Chamber Orchestra / Sir Charles Mackerras.
Telarc CD80148 (66 minutes: DDD). Ⓕ ⷵⷵ

Mozart wrote his *Linz* Symphony in great haste (five days to be precise), but needless to say there is little evidence of haste in the music itself, except perhaps that the first movement has all the exuberance of a composer writing on the wing of inspiration. The slow movement with its siciliano rhythm certainly has no lack of serenity, although it has drama too. The *Prague* Symphony was written only three years later, yet Mozart's symphonic style had matured and the work is altogether more ambitious and substantial. A glorious spaciousness surrounds Sir Charles's performances. The recording venue is reverberant, yet there is no loss of detail, and the fullness of the sound helps to add weight to climaxes without going beyond the bounds of volume that Mozart might have expected. Sir Charles captures the joy and high spirits that these symphonies embody without in any way undermining their greatness. This vivacity is emphasized by the East European sound of the

Prague Chamber Orchestra, with the out-of-doors timbre of its winds which provides a pleasing contrast both with those of the standard British and Germanic orchestras and specialist, authentic ensembles. Mackerras does, however, adopt some aspects of the modern approach to Mozart performance: he includes harpsichord continuo, his minuets are taken trippingly, one-to-a-bar, and he prefers bowing that is crisper, more detached, and pointed. Phrasing and articulation are taken with a natural grace and without overemphasis, dynamics being graded to provide drama at the right moments. The very rightness of the result is recommendation enough.

Symphonies Nos. 38 and 39.
English Baroque Soloists / Sir John Eliot Gardiner.
Philips 426 283-2PH (66 minutes: DDD). Recorded 1988.   ⓕ P

The spirited yet attentive playing here is, one would think, close in sound to what Mozart might have expected. By Gardiner's standards the performance itself is possibly a little austere. The slow introduction to the *Prague* Symphony, for example, is rather cool and straightforward, with little sense of mystery, the accents strongly marked, and a nervy, edge-of-the-seat atmosphere; when the main *Allegro* begins the strings are hushed, the woodwind response loud, firm and clear – this follows Mozart's dynamic markings, but perhaps overplays them. There is not much change of feeling for the smooth secondary theme. The counterpoint in the development is delivered clearly and sturdily, and indeed with fire. The *Andante* is less naturally lyrical, less warmly shaped, than you might expect. The tempo for the finale is happily chosen and the performance is alive and spirited, its rhythms nicely sprung. In No. 39 the main theme of the *Allegro* is not quite comfortably delivered, and the *Andante*, though marked *con moto*, is decidedly on the slow side and wanting in natural flow. These are, however, impressive performances, and well recorded, with plenty of textural detail coming through. The wind is rather forward at times, especially in No. 38; sometimes they cover the main line of the music (though one might well argue that we have until this recording misconceived what the main line really is).

Symphonies Nos. 38 and 39.
The English Concert / Trevor Pinnock.
Archiv Produktion 449 142-2AH (63 minutes: DDD). Recorded 1993-94.   ⓕ

The *Prague* has a sombre opening, catching the sense of mystery in that remarkable slow introduction, which leads to a bright and spirited account of the main *Allegro*, its structure nicely articulated. The *Andante*, also attentively shaped, has its proper hints of darkness, as well as pastoral grace; and Pinnock offers a reading of the finale with plenty of weight as well as vivacity. The special character of the work as a whole is well captured. The same goes for the great E flat Symphony: what is especially appealing is the sturdiness and the fire of the tuttis in the first movement and the way Pinnock and his orchestra convey the anger, almost despair, in those astonishing tuttis in the *Andante*. There is plenty of lyricism too; but this is not simply a gentle and lyrical symphony, as some conductors would have it – here even the Minuet is done with urgency and intensity.

Symphonies Nos. 40 and 41.
The English Concert / Trevor Pinnock.
Archiv Produktion 447 048-2AH (73 minutes: DDD). Recorded 1994.   ⓕ P RR

The *Jupiter* receives a truly outstanding performance. No. 40 is a perfectly satisfactory but in no way extraordinary performance, though the first movement is for once taken at a true *Molto allegro* while the finale manages to be both poised and full of fire. The *Jupiter*, though, is magnificent. The first movement is duly weighty, but energetically paced and its critical junctures timed with a keen sense of their role within the shape of the whole. In the *Andante* Pinnock draws some extraordinarily beautiful, almost sensuous sound from The English Concert and the lines are moulded with real tenderness. This, above all, is the quality that distinguishes Pinnock's recordings from all the others, this natural and musical sound, deriving from the way the players are intently listening to one another; it is fitting that it reaches its high point in the *Jupiter*. He takes the Minuet at a lively pace and with a fine spring to the rhythm. As for the finale: well, it is decidedly quick, and one has the impression of a performance in which the orchestra is pressed to an extent that its ensemble playing is under stress, though it does of course hold together. It is a very bold, outspoken reading, which leaves one gasping afresh at the music's originality; and the prominence of the woodwind and especially the brass gives different perspectives from usual. It may not be to everyone's taste, but it certainly raises the blood pressure, and the spirits too. The actual sound of the orchestra is very vivid and clean, with sweet, warm and firm string tone, with the wind well forward. It's an exceptionally musical sound.

Symphonies Nos. 40 and 41.
Sinfonia Varsovia / Yehudi Menuhin.
Virgin Classics CUV5 61133-2 (58 minutes: DDD). Recorded 1989.   Ⓜ **RR**

Menuhin, with his brilliant group of Polish players, can be warmly and widely recommended.
Whatever the competition, this combination, recorded in exceptionally vivid, immediate sound, will
have you eager to hear much more. The Sinfonia Varsovia, of which Menuhin was Principal
Conductor, was founded in 1984, largely in his honour, with many members drawn from the Polish
Chamber Orchestra. What is clear is that under the direction of a great string soloist they produce
playing of a precision, clarity and bite which is consistently refreshing. Compared with even the
finest rivals, the articulation of the Varsovia strings has exceptional crispness and definition. That is
partly the result of the recording balance which, set close in what sounds like a smallish hall, has a
vivid sense of presence, revealing inner detail naturally and realistically. What makes these rather
tough, clean-cut readings so attractive is the sense of live music-making, the rhythmic energy, the
natural expressiveness which has nothing of routine or self-consciousness in it. With the close
balance the dynamic range is inevitably reduced at the lower end. All these qualities bring the
performance much closer to what the authenticists have taught us to listen for.

Some may be surprised that Menuhin as a Mozartian here is very much a classicist, generally
preferring speeds on the fast side, rarely indulging in romantic tricks. His speeds for all four
movements of No. 40 are on the fast side. Interestingly for the final *Presto* Menuhin chooses a
relatively relaxed, unrushed speed, but it allows phenomenal articulation, as it does equivalently in
the dashing semiquavers of the finale of No. 39, again not rushed off its feet. Menuhin in No. 39
puts in a note of his own to explain one textual oddity. The *Ländler* rhythms of the Trio, what he
calls the 'hurdy-gurdy' effect, come to a sudden halt at the end, and there is a gaping pause before
the reprise of the Minuet. Menuhin suggests that Mozart's intention is clear at that point in his
manuscript. Menuhin makes it sound the more truncated by refusing to allow any *rallentando* at the
end of the Trio: that is part of its charm. Generally he cannot be faulted on the observance of
repeats, but it is in that same symphony, No. 39, that exceptionally he omits the exposition repeat in
the first movement. Otherwise the only major omissions of repeats are in the *Jupiter*. There, as is
usual, he observes the exposition repeats in the first movement and finale, but not the repeat in the
slow movement or the second half of the finale. Whatever the merits of rival versions, and they are
many, Menuhin's Mozart has a clear claim to a first choice. For those who resist period instruments,
there is much to be said for recommending these positive and immediate readings.

Clarinet Quintet in A major, K581. String Quartet No. 18 in A major, K464.
Janet Hilton *cl*
The Lindsays (Peter Cropper, Ronald Birks *vns* Robin Ireland *va* Bernard Gregor-Smith *vc*).
ASV CDDCA1042 (74 minutes: DDD). Recorded 1998.   Ⓕ **E**

The Lindsays' interpretation of K464 is entirely persuasive, barring a few minor quibbles – the first
movement, though flexible and elegant, is perhaps slightly lacking in urgency and dynamic contrast,
the finale, on the other hand, has all the drama and onward thrust one could wish for, but
occasionally begins to lose its rhythmic poise. The Lindsays play the quartet complete with all its
repeats. If you prefer to have modern instruments in this quartet, go for this recording. The Clarinet
Quintet is given with the finesse and care for phrasing and articulation that characterizes all
Lindsay Mozart issues. It's good for Mozart to sound suave, and Janet Hilton presents the melody
of the *Larghetto* (track 2) with lovely soft articulation, yet the music is more rhetorical and
passionate than she allows, and the hint of vibrato only serves further to soften the expression.
There are, however, fine features in this performance – the exciting, perfectly controlled first-
movement development, a lively, beautifully shaped Minuet, a really melancholic viola in the finale
and a splendidly robust concluding *Allegro*. The recording is clear, intimate, but not dry.

Piano Quintet in E flat major, K452. Clarinet Trio in E flat major, K498, 'Kegelstatt'. Adagio and
Rondo in C minor, K617. Adagio in C major, K356/K617a. Piano Quartets – No. 1 in G minor,
K478; No. 2 in E flat major, K493. Piano Trios – B flat major, K254; D minor, K442 (cptd. Stadler
and Marguerre); No. 1 in G major, K496; No. 3 in B flat major, K502; No. 4 in E major, K542;
No. 5 in C major, K548; No. 6 in G major, K564.
Patrick Ireland, Karl Schouten, Bruno Giuranna *vas* **Jean Decroos** *vc* **Aurèle Nicolet** *fl*
Heinz Holliger *ob* **Eduard Brunner, Jack Brymer** *cls* **Hermann Baumann** *hn*
Klaus Thunemann *bn* **Bruno Hoffmann** *glass harmonica* **Beaux Arts Trio** (Isidore Cohen *vn*
Bernard Greenhouse *vc* Menahem Pressler *pf*); **Alfred Brendel, Stephen Kovacevich** *pfs*
Philips Mozart Edition 422 514-2PME5 (five discs: 274 minutes: ADD/DDD).
Gramophone Award Winner 1991.   Ⓜ

These recordings come from different locations and dates, ranging from 1969 to 1987. Four discs out of the five offer the two piano quartets and seven piano trios, played by the Beaux Arts Trio who are joined in the quartets by the viola player Bruno Giuranna; these are clearly the centrepiece of the issue and the playing of this fine ensemble is strongly characterful yet thoughtful. These are alert, direct and yet refined performances and earn only praise, although the recording in Philips's favoured Swiss location of La-Chaux-de-Fonds could have placed a little more distance between the players and the listener (we also hear the odd intake of breath). But otherwise this clear sound suits the music, and Menahem Pressler's piano tone is well captured. The D minor Trio which ends the series is not wholly authentic, being mainly Maximilian Stadler's compilation from existing material found by Mozart's widow Constanze after his death.

Before we come to the piano quartets and piano trios, the first disc also has important works in fine performances in which Alfred Brendel and Heinz Holliger are just two of the artists involved (the Quintet for piano and wind was among the composer's favourite works). The first disc also offers two pieces featuring the ravishing sound of the glass harmonica (musical glasses), which is played by its leading exponent, Bruno Hoffmann, and the solo *Adagio* in C major is quite ethereally beautiful, if rather closely recorded. This unique instrument is usefully described and illustrated in the booklet.

String Quintets – No. 1 in B flat major, K174; No. 2 in C minor, K406/K516b; No. 3 in C major, K515; No. 4 in G minor, K516; No. 5 in D major, K593; No. 6 in E flat major, K614.
Arthur Grumiaux, Arpad Gérecz vns **Georges Janzer, Max Lesueur** vas **Eva Czako** vc
Philips Mozart Edition 422 511-2PME3 (three discs: 170 minutes: ADD). Recorded 1973.
Gramophone Award Winner 1991. Ⓜ

Of the six works which comprise Mozart's complete *oeuvre* for string quintet, that in B flat major, K174, is an early composition, written at the age of 17. It is a well-made, enjoyable work, but not a great deal more than that. The C minor work, K406, is an arrangement by Mozart of his Serenade for six wind instruments, K398. It is difficult not to feel that the original is more effective, since the music seems to sit a little uncomfortably on string instruments. But the remaining four works, written in the last four years of Mozart's life, are a different matter. The last string quintets from Mozart's pen were extraordinary works, and the addition of the second viola seems to have encouraged him to still greater heights. It has been suggested that Mozart wrote K515 and K516 to show King Friedrich Wilhelm II of Prussia that he was a better composer of string quintets than Boccherini, whom the King had retained as chamber music composer to his court. There was no response, so he offered these two quintets for sale with the K406 arrangement to make up the usual set of three. K593 and K614 were written in the last year of his life. Refinement is perhaps the word that first comes to mind in discussing these performances, which are affectionate yet controlled by a cool, intelligent sensitivity. The recordings have been well transferred, the quality is warm and expansive and Grumiaux's tone, in particular, is a delight to the ear but all the playing is stylish.

String Quintet No. 3. String Quartet No. 16 in E flat major, K428.
Louise Williams va **The Lindsays** (Peter Cropper, Ronald Birks vn Robin Ireland va Bernard Gregor-Smith vc).
ASV CDDCA992 (67 minutes: DDD). Recorded 1995. Ⓕ

Here's a really fine performance of the great C major Quintet. The Lindsays take the first movement at a true *Allegro*, so that it bowls along in top gear, the details vivid and sharply etched. Much of this grandest and most spacious movement in Mozart's chamber output is marked to be played softly: in the Lindsays' hands the wonderful counterpoint in the development section can be heard with exceptional clarity as the tension builds up, but not the dynamic. The *Andante* sounds the more touching for never being overplayed, and it's a special pleasure to hear how the most florid passages for first violin and first viola fit effortlessly into the rhythmic scheme. In the finale, Peter Cropper introduces some beautifully played *portamentos* in the main theme, and the whole movement sounds delightfully witty and happy. The E flat Quartet, K428 is cool and stylish, which suits this enigmatic work rather well. The Lindsays' way of using Mozart's marks of expression and articulation to make the music speak feels absolutely right, especially in their delicate, refined *Andante*, and it's good to hear the quartet played with all its repeats. The recording has a nice intimate quality.

Flute Quartet No. 1 in D major, K285. Oboe Quartet in F major, K370/K368b. Clarinet Quintet.
Jaime Martin fl **Jonathan Kelly** ob **Nicholas Carpenter** cl **Brindisi Quartet** (Jacqueline Shave, Patrick Kiernan vns Katie Wilkinson Krososhunin va Anthony Pleeth vc).
EMI Debut CDZ5 69702-2 (64 minutes: DDD). Recorded 1996. Ⓕ

Do you like your Mozart refined and graceful? Or robust and spontaneously expressive? A combination of both would be perfect, you may think, but in practice it's not always easy to achieve. The Brindisi Quartet and its three colleagues play with exceptional finesse, and excellent balance and blend, well captured by the recording. These are predominantly light-toned performances, with the phrases shaped convincingly and with unfailing elegance. Their approach seems just about ideal in the Flute Quartet, where the joyful, vivacious atmosphere of the outer movements is enhanced by thoughtful attention to detail. Jaime Martin's sensitive, sensuous flute-playing in the *Adagio* provides a delightful contrast. There are many good things in the other two pieces, too. Jonathan Kelly's virtuosity in the Oboe Quartet's finale is really exciting, as is the brilliant, superbly balanced development section in the Clarinet Quintet's first movement. But there are places where you might long for something less cool and detached. The recording of the Oboe Quartet by Nicholas Daniel and members of the The Lindsays (reviewed further on with the String Quartet No. 17 and the Horn Quintet) manage to combine stylishness with strong expression.

Piano Quartets – No. 1 in G minor, K478; No. 2 in E flat major, K493.
Isaac Stern *vn* **Jaime Laredo** *va* **Yo-Yo Ma** *vc* **Emanuel Ax** *pf*
Sony Classical SK66841 (56 minutes: DDD). Recorded 1994.　　　　　　　　Ⓕ

There is no shortage of good recordings of this favourite coupling of two Mozart masterpieces, and this grouping of star names offers performances of comparable imagination and insight. In the E flat Quartet, K493, it is not just Isaac Stern and Yo-Yo Ma whose solo entries have one sitting up, but also Jaime Laredo in the rare moments when Mozart gives a solo opportunity to his own instrument, the viola. Speeds are beautifully chosen, and in both works the performances consistently convey a sense of happy spontaneity. Emanuel Ax shows what a natural, individual Mozartian he is. The G minor work is in many ways parallel to the great piano concertos of the period, with the piano regularly set against the strings in ensemble, and Ax readily establishes the sort of primacy plainly required, even in such company as this. He is a shade robust at the start of the central *Andante* but in fast music as in slow his gift of pointing rhythms and moulding phrases is consistently persuasive and imaginative. The recording, made in the Manhattan Center, New York, is a degree drier than in many of the current rival versions, but there is ample bloom on the sound, fitting very well in a domestic listening room.

String Quartets – No. 1 in G major, K80/K73f; **No. 2** in D major, K155/K134a; **No. 3** in G major, K156/K134b; **No. 4** in C major, K157; **No. 5** in F major, K158; **No. 6** in B flat major, K159; **No. 7** in E flat major, K160/K159a; **No. 8** in F major, K168; **No. 9** in A major, K169; **No. 10** in C major, K170; **No. 11** in E flat major, K171; **No. 12** in B flat major, K172; **No. 13** in D minor, K173; **No. 14** in G major, K387; **No. 15** in D minor, K421/K417b; **No. 16** in E flat major, K428/K421b; **No. 17** in B flat major, K458, 'Hunt'; **No. 18** in A major, K464; **No. 19** in C major, K465, 'Dissonance'; **No. 20** in D major, K499, 'Hoffmeister'; **No. 21** in D major, K575; **No. 22** in B flat major, K589; **No. 23** in F major, K590.

String Quartets Nos. 1-23.
Quartetto Italiano (Paolo Borciani, Elisa Pegreffi *vns* Piero Farulli *va* Franco Rossi *vc*).
Philips Mozart Edition 422 512-2PME8 (eight discs: 474 minutes: ADD). Recorded 1966-73.
Gramophone Award Winner 1991.　　　　　　　　Ⓜ

These are classic performances which have won praise ever since they began to appear back in 1967. Admittedly, a little allowance has to be made for the sound. For example, it is a touch heavy and close in the 1966 recording of the D minor Quartet that is one of the wonderful set of six that Mozart dedicated to Haydn. In a way, this accords to some extent with the playing of the Quartetto Italiano, which is at times rather earnest – and in the first movement of this work, rather deliberate in its pace. But these are really the only criticisms of a generally splendid issue, and the innate seriousness of these fine Italian artists is almost always a plus feature: indeed, they bring an overall intelligence, refinement and, above all, range of interpretative values to this often superb and always attractive music. As for quality of ensemble, they are impeccable. This is undeniably still the best general survey of Mozart's string quartets available, and at mid-price the eight discs represent a safe investment that should yield many years of pleasure.

String Quartets No. 14-19.
Chilingirian Quartet (Levon Chilingirian, Mark Butler *vns* Nicholas Logie *va* Philip de Groote *vc*).
CRD3362: Nos. 14 and 15 (59 minutes: ADD). CRD3363: Nos. 16 and 17 (56 minutes: ADD). CRD3364: Nos. 18 and 19 (68 minutes: ADD). Recorded 1979.　　　　　　　　Ⓕ

For reticent, confidential performances that reach deeply into this wonderful music we suggest you try the Chilingirian Quartet's versions of the 'Haydn' Quartets, first issued on LP in 1980. They effectively move you from a public to a private domain of music-making. The Chilingirian may be slightly less adroit technically than some of their competitors, the Alban Berg Quartet particularly, especially as regards intonation (Levon Chilingirian is sometimes a bit wayward in this respect); nor does it aspire to the Alban Berg's tonal opulence and power, but its performances of these six inexhaustible works represent some of the most searching, naturally expressive Mozart playing on disc today. Its tendency, in contra-distinction to the Alban Berg, is towards understatement. Tempos are frequently a little slower than average, dynamic contrasts vivid without exaggeration (*fortes* are never harsh or explosive), phrasing is alive and imaginative, yet with no attempt to beautify the moment. In *Allegros*, notably the first movements of Nos. 17 and 19, and the finale of No. 16, the Chilingirian may appear over-leisurely, slightly lacking in bite and brio; but its uncommonly thoughtful, intimate approach consistently reveals depths and shadows in this music that elude more obviously dynamic performances. Rarely, if ever, will you hear No. 18 played with such grace, such gentle, reflective intensity; more than ever its Minuet, spare and absorbed, seems to look forward through Beethoven's Op. 18 No. 5 to the corresponding movement in the late A minor Quartet, Op. 132. And profound reflective tenderness is a quality the Chilingirian consistently brings to the slow movements: listen to its hushed, veiled tone at the start of the *Andante* of No. 19, for instance, or the subtly judged ebb and flow of tension in the astonishing chromatic *Andante* of No. 16, not, perhaps, *con moto*, as Mozart asks, but haunting in its subdued disquiet. The Chilingirian receives an ideally truthful, rounded recording that reveals with ideal clarity its exceptional care for inner detail. Few other current versions of the 'Haydn' Quartets offer richer rewards.

String Quartets Nos. 15-17 and 20.
Franz Schubert Quartet (Florian Zwiauer, Helge Rosenkranz *vns* Hartmut Pascher *va* Vincent Stadlmair *vc*).
Nimbus NI5455/6 (two discs: 115 minutes: DDD). Recorded 1994.   Ⓕ

Mozart's profound debt to Haydn in the six string quartets he dedicated to the composer (of which the Franz Schubert Quartet here plays K421 and K428) is most evident in their innovative approach to texture. Moreover, the true equality between the four parts – demonstrating a critical relationship between instrumentation and musical substance – has inspired startlingly different interpretative approaches. The Chilingirian Quartet's elegantly refined, charmingly understated accounts convincingly present the music in an intimate, private context. By contrast, like the Alban Berg Quartet, the Franz Schubert Quartet offers more dramatic readings, whose wider dynamic range projects the music in a more public manner. Nimbus's impressively truthful recording reveals the music's varied textures with pellucid clarity in the opening *allegros*, and relatively fast *andantes* imbue the performers' lush ensemble with appropriately increased animation. The minuets are more passionate than those of the Chilingirian, and the finales are likewise bold and dramatic, with the variation finale of the D minor work, in particular, confirming a satisfying sense of overall unity. Despite their striking contrasts, though, the Franz Schubert Quartet does not quite achieve the extremes of the Alban Berg, whose powerfully arresting 1979 recording of the *Hunt* Quartet (K458) still sounds exceptionally fresh. The Franz Schubert Quartet's comparatively relaxed approach to the first movement, for example, fails to match the Berg's exhilarating evocation of the chase. Nevertheless, for those who find the latter too highly charged, the Franz Schubert Quartet here offers an alternative whose beautiful textural clarity and vivid thematic detail many will find irresistible. To the *Hoffmeister* Quartet, the Franz Schubert Quartet brings delicacy and finesse, most notably in their dynamic control and contrapuntal clarity. Try them in the first movement's development section, their lucid counterpoint in the second movement's introspective trio (in the tonic minor), their heartfelt expression in the *Adagio*, and their enthralling, symphonic conception of the finale. These distinguished accounts deserve an assured place among the very best.

String Quartets Nos. 17 and 19.
Alban Berg Quartet (Günther Pichler, Gerhard Schulz *vns* Hatto Beyerle *va* Valentin Erben *vc*).
Teldec 2292-43037-2 (57 minutes: DDD).   Ⓕ **ⓇⓇ**

In String Quartet No. 17 Mozart saw the Trio section and the main Minuet section as a unity, and in the Berg performance, they quite obviously belong to each other – the players hold the tempo steady all through the movement. Dynamic contrasts can be extreme and you may find them close to being excessive, but they certainly make for excitement, and some of the effects can be enthralling; you will rarely hear the *calando* at the end of the exposition of No. 17, the falling away from *piano* to *pianissimo*, so sensitively managed. The *Dissonance* Quartet (No. 19) is played with unusual subtlety. You know you are in for a striking performance from the very first bars of the 'dissonance' slow introduction. The slow movement is particularly impressive here; in some other performances the little four-note figure that keeps being tossed from one instrument to another sometimes seems to outstay its welcome. By adopting quite a slow tempo, the Alban Berg manages to give this little phrase an unexpected dignity. The players bring unusual skill and musicianship to both of these quartets and they have a particularly neat way with *staccato* passages.

String Quartet No. 17. Oboe Quartet in F major, K370/K368*b*. Horn Quintet in E flat major, K407/K386*c*.
Nicholas Daniel *ob* **Stephen Bell** *hn* **The Lindsays** (Peter Cropper *vn* Ronald Birks *vn/va* Robin Ireland *va* Bernard Gregor-Smith *vc*).
ASV CDDCA968 (68 minutes: DDD). Recorded 1995. ⓕ

The Lindsays really make the *Hunt* Quartet sparkle. One could describe their approach as middle-of-the-road; they're as meticulous as many period-instrument groups about details of phrasing, and avoid excessive accents and vibrato, yet their sound is modern, and the care over detail doesn't preclude a very spontaneous approach in which the music's feeling is compellingly communicated. In the Oboe Quartet Nicholas Daniel matches the string players' care over articulation and detailed expression, and plays with exceptional technical polish and brilliance. His gleaming tone is capable of great expressive range. The Horn Quintet is perhaps not quite such an individual or remarkable work as the two quartets. And you may find yourself longing for the extra character and beauty that a fine performance with the natural horn would have had. Yet this is a highly recommendable reading, too. The recording is very lifelike, with clear spacing of the instruments.

String Quartets Nos. 21 and 23.
Quatuor Mosaïques (Erich Höbarth, Andrea Bischof *vns* Anita Mitterer *va* Christophe Coin *vc*).
Auvidis Astrée E8659 (60 minutes: DDD). Recorded 1998. ⓕⓅ

The Mosaïques here turn to Mozart's last quartets; the sheer refinement of its playing – its silk-sewn ensemble and its uncanny ability to sense out the living pulse and pace of a work – comes into its own in the *sotto voce* movements of No. 21. A single ascending or descending scale can take on a rare beauty. And when these characteristic scales return to seal the first movement in a tiny coda, they are enlivened by the little touches of rubato which breathe air into this performance. That same touch of rubato awakens the spirit of dance in the Menuetto, lifting the heel and pointing the toe. It is details like these which reanimate this music and give the edge of character to the Mosaïques' playing, over and above their rivals in this repertoire. In No. 21, the mercurial playing of the Mosaïques, with the light, close harmony and subtly shaded inner voices, which is such a hallmark of this group, combines with a perfectly judged pace for the 6/8 *Allegretto*. And again the Mosaïques takes little moments to catch its breath, so that the hurtling round-dance of a finale leaves us a little less dizzy than it does in the hands of most other groups.

Piano Trios – No. 1 in G major, K496; No. 3 in B flat major, K502. Divertimento in B flat major, K254.
Augustin Dumay *vn* **Jian Wang** *vc* **Maria João Pires** *pf*
DG 449 208-2GH (73 minutes: DDD). Includes bonus CD featuring short works by Brahms, Franck, Grieg, Mozart and Ravel. Recorded 1995. ⓕⒺ

This disc of early Mozart trios is radiant with the discriminating, fanciful and exuberant music-making which characterizes this rare trio of friends. A *crescendo* of joy shooting up through the opening scalic and arpeggio figures of K496 is answered by finely tapered violin playing and a cello which draws the ear to its contributions long before the true dialogue of the *Andante*. This ensemble finds a truly lilting 6/8 (rather than the illusion of a sturdier 3/4) for the second movement, and the finale is full of a sense of wonder, in its platinum-tipped violin and the drawing back into finely nuanced tones of grey for the sombre fifth variation. For K502, Pires picks up on the sense of forward impetus inherent in the rhythm of the opening theme and in the slow movment her phrasing makes its melody more shapely above the unsurpassed beauty of sustained tone in violin and cello. A delicious performance of the little *Divertimento*, K254 reveals the ancestry of these two trios; and there is yet another bonus in a 48-minute disc of extracts from the six recordings of Mozart, Brahms, Franck, Ravel and Grieg made over six years by the incomparable duo of Pires and Dumay.

Violin Sonatas – No. 1 in C major, K6; No. 2 in D major, K7; No. 3 in B flat major, K8; No. 4 in G major, K9; No. 5 in B flat major, K10; No. 6 in G major, K11; No. 7 in A major, K12; No. 8 in F major, K13; No. 9 in C major, K14; No. 10 in B flat major, K15; No. 11 in E flat major, K26; No. 12 in G major, K27; No. 13 in C major, K28; No. 14 in D major, K29; No. 15 in F major, K30; No. 16 in B flat major, K31.
Gérard Poulet *vn* **Blandine Verlet** *hpd*
Philips Duo 438 803-2PM2 (two discs: 135 minutes: ADD). Recorded 1975. ⓜⓅ

The early keyboard and violin sonatas include the boy composer's first works to appear in print: K6-9 were composed during his five-month Paris stay of 1763-64; K10-15 followed in 1765, when the Mozarts resided in London's Belgravia for over a year. The Sonatas, K26-31 appeared a month or two later when the family moved to The Hague. The precociously lively invention is consistently ear-catching, especially in the spunky violin part in the *allegros* and the often graceful lyrical writing. Even if the keyboard dominates the musical partnership, the violinist is always contributing attractive comments. The performances here are very well played, being vital and fresh, and very spontaneous sounding; moreover, they are well balanced and naturally recorded. There is much to intrigue here and many of these miniature works are extremely rewarding in their simplicity and direct melodic appeal.

Piano Sonatas – No. 1 in C major, K279/K189*d*; **No. 2** in F major, K280/K189*e*; **No. 3** in B flat major, K281/K189*f*; **No. 4** in E flat major, K282/K189*g*; **No. 5** in G major, K283/K189*h*; **No. 6** in D major, K284/K205*b*; **No. 7** in C major, K309/K284*b*; **No. 8** in A minor, K310/K300*d*; **No. 9** in D major, K311/K284*c*; **No. 10** in C major, K330/K300*h*; **No. 11** in A major, K331/K300*i*; **No. 12** in F major, K332/K300*k*; **No. 13** in B flat major, K333/K315*c*; **No. 14** in C minor, K457; **No. 15** in F major, K533/K494; **No. 16** in C major, K545; **No. 17** in B flat major, K570; **No. 18** in D major, K576.

Piano Sonatas Nos. 1-18. Fantasia in C minor, K475.
Christoph Eschenbach *pf*
DG 419 445-2GX5 (five discs: 339 minutes: ADD). Recorded 1967-70.   Ⓜ 🆁🆁

Born in 1940, Christoph Eschenbach established himself during the 1960s and made these recordings not long after: they show him as an accomplished Mozartian and fully deserved their reissue. This having been said, Eschenbach's playing of the sonatas here is characterized by a pleasingly straightforward musicianship. For all their occasional easy *galanterie*, they deserve to be more frequently recorded, although many good recordings do exist: the most obviously recommendable rival to this is that of Mitsuko Uchida. Still, Eschenbach offers good value. His firm yet flexible way with quick outer movements is very likeable, and his delicate but purposeful handling of slow ones; here and there (as in the outer movements of No. 10) his phrasing is a little clipped and Prussian-sounding, but not so often as to be a problem, and his nimble yet sensitive fingerwork is always pleasing – try the finales of Nos. 1 and 5 for early examples – while minuets dance in the right stately way. His gracefully songful accounts of movements where some other pianists find less charm are delightful, such as the finale of No. 7 and the first movement of No. 12. The C minor *Fantasia* Sonata is strongly done, but the powerful Eighth Sonata needs more punch and so does the 'Turkish Rondo' in No. 11. The recordings have come up remarkably well in this digital remastering and need no apology, with crisp yet warm piano tone. Be warned, though, that the accompanying insert-notes are useless and pretentious.

Piano Sonatas Nos. 1-18. Fantasia, K475.
Mitsuko Uchida *pf*
Philips Mozart Edition 422 517-2PME5 (five discs: 325 minutes: DDD).
Gramophone Award Winner 1989 and 1991.   Ⓜ

By common consent, Mitsuko Uchida is among the leading Mozart pianists of today, and her recorded series of the piano sonatas won critical acclaim as it appeared and finally *Gramophone* Awards in 1989 and 1991. Here are all the sonatas, plus the *Fantasia* in C minor, K475, which is in some ways a companion piece to the sonata in the same key, K457. This is unfailingly clean, crisp and elegant playing, that avoids anything like a romanticized view of the early sonatas such as the delightfully fresh G major, K283. On the other hand, Uchida responds with the necessary passion to the forceful, not to say *Angst*-ridden, A minor Sonata, K310. Indeed, her complete series is a remarkably fine achievement, comparable with her account of the piano concertos. The recordings were produced by Erik Smith in the Henry Wood Hall in London and offer excellent piano sound; thus an unqualified recommendation is in order for what must be one of the most valuable volumes in Philips's Complete Mozart Edition. Do not be put off by critics who suggest that these sonatas are less interesting than some other Mozart compositions, for they are fine pieces written for an instrument that he himself played and loved.

Piano Sonatas Nos. 1-3.
Ronald Brautigam *fp*
BIS CD835 (58 minutes: DDD). Recorded 1996.   Ⓕ 🅿

Ronald Brautigam brings uncommon energy and excitement to these sonatas, playing them with a freshness and sense of novelty that few manage to produce for music familiar to most pianists from their schoolroom days. One might find the first movement of K279 a little breathless, perhaps wanting in elegance; Brautigam doesn't always bother to round off a phrase gracefully. But the *Andante* is beautifully played, with much delicacy of timing, just the right vein of sentiment and a fine command of the textures available on the fortepiano. He is indeed masterly in all the slow movements here. In the beautiful F minor middle movement of K280 his understanding of the expressive nature of Mozart's harmony is particularly telling, and in the recapitulation especially he produces an almost Chopinesque poetry with the soft-textured left hand against a right-hand melody: let no one say this isn't Mozartian, for if you can do it as tastefully as this, on the instrument Mozart used, you may be sure Mozart would have done something like it. Mozart might have made the repeats (all of which are observed) a little more elaborate; Brautigam ornaments very little but he does play the music slightly differently second time round in details of timing and shading. There are few recordings of these sonatas on the fortepiano, and these are extremely musical and imaginative performances.

Piano Sonatas Nos. 5, 6 and 10.
Maria João Pires *pf*
DG 437 791-2GH (73 minutes: DDD). Recorded 1990.   Ⓕ

Maria João Pires presents these sonatas with clear yet lightly pedalled textures and an overall directness that still allows room for tonal and rhythmic flexibility – which, generally speaking, is not overdone. Largely, her playing seems to let the music speak for itself, although of course just offering the notes is not enough and what we here appreciate is the art that conceals art. However, one might question the occasional detail: for example, less than a minute into the G major Sonata, Pires's longish trill on the D preceding the second subject is questionable, which gives us a bar with four beats in it instead of three. The *Andante* of the same work begins with repeated Cs that seem too emphatically *staccato*, and its central section is a little overdramatized. The dance movement called *Rondeau en Polonaise* in K284 is on the slow side, though it still holds together, and the variation-form finale varies considerably in pace. Pires consistently observes repeats, including the second halves of movements (thus we get virtually every note of K283 twice), as is indicated. These are clear, commendable performances, and the kind of grace that Pires brings to this music, in which other pianists can sound a touch severe, is most appealing. The recording is pleasing and faithful.

Piano Sonatas Nos. 15 and 16. Fantasia, K475 (all arr. Grieg).
Sviatoslav Richter, Elisabeth Leonskaja *pfs*
Teldec 4509-90825-2 (62 minutes: DDD). Recorded 1993.   Ⓕ

When Grieg added an accompaniment for a second piano to Mozart's keyboard sonatas, he did it primarily with teaching in mind. It was apparently common practice in the 1880s for teachers to accompany their pupils on a second piano. But the resulting compositions soon found their way into the concert hall where, according to Grieg, 'the whole thing sounded surprisingly good'. And so it does today. In trying to 'impart to several of Mozart's sonatas a tonal effect appealing to our modern ears' Grieg left a telling little document or two on just what those late nineteenth-century Norwegian ears expected. If the C major 'Sonata facile' seems to sit even more sedately in the drawing-room, then it soon becomes clear that the light glinting through its windows is not a million miles away from that bouncing off the fjord waters which lap around Troldhaugen. The C minor *Fantasia* becomes a dark salon melodrama (shades of *Bergljot*) which moves from conversation with not a little chromatic prevarication to the hanging of whimsical icicles of figuration around the major-key section. Gently exuberant harmonies cross-weave their way through the sparse trio-sonata-like textures of the opening F major before a trotting bass makes a high-stepping mountain horse of the rondo-finale. These are Mozart-Kugeln with a *bonne bouche* or two of the finest Gravadlax on the side. And if these fond tributes are good enough for Elisabeth Leonskaja and Sviatoslav Richter, who could resist tasting them?

Piano Variations[a] – G major, K24; D major, K25; C major, K179/K189a; G major, K180/K173c; C major, K264/K315d; C major, K265/K300e; F major, K352/K374 (with **Koopman**); E flat major, K353K/300f; E flat major, K354/K299a; F major, K398/K416e; G major, K455; A major, K460/K454a (**Koopman**); B flat major, K500; D major, K573; F major, K613. Minuets[c] – F major, K1d; G major/C major, K1/K1e/K1f; F major, K2; F major, K4; F major, K5; D major, K94/K73h; D major, K355/K576b (**Uchida**). Fantasia in D minor, K397/K385g[b]. Rondos[b] – D major, K485; A minor, K511. Adagio in B minor, K540[b]. Gigue in G major, K574[b]. Klavierstück in F major, K33B[c]. Capriccio in C major, K395/K300g[c]. March No. 1 in C major, K408/K383e[c]. Prelude and Fugue in C major, K394/K383a[c]. Allegros[c] – C major, K1b; F major, K1c; B flat major, K3; C major, K5a; G minor, K312/K590d; B flat major, K400/K372a (cpted Stadler). Suite in C major,

K399/K385/ᶜ. Kleine Trauermarsch in C minor, K453aᶜ. Andante in C major, K1aᶜ. Fugue in G minor, K401/K375eᶜ (with **Tini Mathot** *hpd*)
ᵃ**Ingrid Haebler,** ᵇ**Mitsuko Uchida** *pfs* ᶜ**Ton Koopman** *hpd*
Philips Mozart Edition 422 518-2PME5 (five discs: 274 minutes: ADD/DDD).
Gramophone Award Winner 1991.　　　　　　　　　　　　　　　　　　　Ⓜ Ⓟ

These five mid-price discs offer music of fine and often superb quality in a convenient format. Of the three artists here, two are generally fine and satisfying, though the third is more controversial. Ingrid Haebler was recorded back in 1975, but the piano sound is good and little tape background remains, and her performances of the variation sets, which take up the first three discs, are delicate without cuteness, effortlessly encompassing the music's wide range of moods. Mitsuko Uchida, on the fourth disc, performs individual pieces including the two rondos and the beautiful *Adagio* in B minor (the only piece Mozart wrote in this key) in a highly refined manner, a touch over-sophisticated perhaps but still beautiful and expressive and taking full, unashamed advantage of the sound of a modern grand. By contrast, Ton Koopman's disc of minuets and other miscellaneous things is played on a harpsichord at a semitone below modern concert pitch and offers a recording of such immediacy that some listeners will regard it as too bright. Koopman puts gusto into everything he does, but not always to good effect. However, even if grace is in short supply in his performances, they undeniably offer ample personality, and such reservations as one may have about his playing should not affect the desirability of the set as a whole.

Suite in the style of Handel in C major, K399 – Overture. Adagio and Allegro in F minor, K594 (ed. Trotter). Londoner Notenskizzenbuch, KAnh109b – Allegro in F major, K15a; Andante in E major, K15o; Andante in B flat major, K15q. Andante in B flat major, K15ii. Adagio in B minor, K540. Allegro in G major, K72a. Fugue in G minor, K401/K375e. Gigue in G major, K574. Prelude and Fugue in C major, K394/K383a. Andantino in E flat major, K236. Andante für eine Walze in eine kleine Orgel in F major, K616. Adagio in C major, K356/K617a. Fantasia für eine Uhr, K608 (ed. Trotter).
Thomas Trotter *org*
Decca London 443 451-2LH (66 minutes: DDD). Recorded on the organ of the Nederlandse Hervormde Kerk, Farmsum, The Netherlands in 1993.　　　　　　　　　　　　　Ⓕ

It takes much scratching around in the dirt to find enough Mozart organ music to fill a CD. Mozart left so little organ music for posterity; he was such a fluent improviser that he never really needed to write anything down. What we have here, apart from pieces for other instruments which probably wouldn't get much of an airing if they weren't played on the organ (K594 and K608, originally for mechanical clock, are, ironically, generally considered to be the greatest organ works between Bach and Mendelssohn), are fragments and miniatures, tantalizing crumbs from the table of a genius, which in the hands of most players would seem little more than worthwhile curiosities. Thomas Trotter is an openly communicative player and while his discography to date centres around the extensive romantic repertoire, he proves himself here to be equally compelling in both classical repertoire and in short musical structures. Helped by a ravishing instrument which he handles with admirable fluency (although the action noise is horribly obtrusive), Trotter's Mozart truly comes to life. The big pieces (including a breathtakingly virtuosic account of K608) sit comfortably alongside the miniatures and the whole disc presents a thoroughly rewarding musical experience.

Concert Arias – Ah! se in ciel, benigne stelle, K538; Vorrei spiegarvi, oh Dio!, K418; No, no che non sei capace, K419; Se tutti i mali miei, K83/K73p; Popoli di Tessaglia! ... Io non chiedo, eterni Dei, K316/K300b; Mia speranza adorata ... Ah, non sai qual pena sia, K416; Alcandro, lo confesso ... Non so d'onde viene, K294; Ma che vi fece, o stelle ... Sperai vicino il lido, K368.
Natalie Dessay *sop*
Orchestra of the Opéra de Lyon / Theodor Guschlbauer.
EMI CDC5 55386-2 (64 minutes: DDD). Texts and translations included. Recorded 1994.　　Ⓕ

Natalie Dessay's range extends upward far into the leger lines yet without incurring breathiness of a pallid coloration in the lower notes. She has a sylph's grace and lightness, and yet the timbre or character of her voice is thoroughly human. The profusion of scales and more intricate passagework common in some degree to all these pieces finds in her an unostentatious virtuoso, mind and breath giving well-regulated support, and a sensitive feeling for phrase and line making good musical sense throughout. Where vehemence and a dramatic quality of voice are in demand, as in the opening of *Popoli di Tessaglia*, we can find some reassurance in their absence because at least the young singer does not try to force an effect. In less strenuous attack, as in *No, no che non sei capace*, she conveys the energy of a determined spirit yet still has some way to develop as an expressive artist. The more sorrowful and tender phrases of *Se tutti i mali miei*, for example, evoke only a mild response in her. Occasionally, too, Dessay's purity forfeits normal resonance and for what seems to be an involuntary note or two the voice flutes with a kind of disembodied hollowness. An instance occurs just before the second part of *Vorrei spiegarvi*, yet this is such a lovely performance, so graceful in its leisurely interplay of voice and instruments, that grumbling really is out of order. Orchestra, conductor and recorded sound all make their contributions.

Missae breves – G major, K49/K47*d*[a]; D minor, K65/K61*a*[b]; D major, K194/K186*h*[a]; C major, K220/K196*b*[b], 'Spatzenmesse'.
[a]**Christine Schäfer,** [b]**Angela Maria Blasi** *sops* [a]**Ingeborg Danz,** [b]**Elisabeth von Magnus** *mezzos* [a]**Kurt Azesberger,** [b]**Uwe Heilmann** *tens* [a]**Oliver Widmer** *bar* [b]**Franz-Josef Selig** *bass*
Arnold Schoenberg Choir; Vienna Concentus Musicus / Nikolaus Harnoncourt.
Teldec Das Alte Werk 3984-21818-2 (69 minutes: DDD). Texts and translations included.
Recorded 1994.　　　　Ⓔ **P**

These youthful Masses, composed between 1768 and 1775, are among Mozart's most concise – K65, in particular, is a *Missa brevis* with a vengeance. Brevity was, of course, *de rigueur* in the Salzburg liturgy and we can hardly blame Mozart for rattling unceremoniously through the long texts of the *Gloria* and *Credo*. With minimal scope for musical development, much of the writing in the two earlier works, especially, is frankly perfunctory – the 12-year-old composer dutifully going through the motions. As so often in late-eighteenth-century Masses, the central mystery of the 'Et incarnatus est – Crucifixus' prompts a more individual musical response; and the *Benedictus* of K65 is a touching little duet for soprano and alto soloists based, surprisingly, on a descending chromatic motif, a traditional trope of lamentation. For all the conventional bustle of their faster movements, the two later Masses are more varied in their textures (though, *pace* the booklet-note, elaborate counterpoint is still at a premium) and more memorable in their ideas. Both the settings of the *Benedictus* have the grace and airiness of eighteenth-century Austrian churches. But the high point in each work is the *Agnus Dei*, especially that of K194, with its harmonic poignancy and dramatic alternations of solo and chorus. Just occasionally Nikolaus Harnoncourt's direction can sound over-insistent – in, say, the *Kyrie* of K49, with its almost aggressive *marcato* articulation. But for the most part he chooses apt, mobile tempos, keeps the rhythms buoyant and characterizes vividly without betraying the music's essential blitheness and innocence of spirit. The playing of the Concentus Musicus is typically polished and responsive and the Arnold Schoenberg Choir, with little to tax them here, do all that is asked of them. Both individually and in consort the soloists make the most of their limited opportunities, with delectable tone and phrasing from the two sopranos, Christine Schäfer and Angela Maria Blasi. The recorded balance is excellent, catching all of Harnoncourt's sharply etched orchestral detail while giving ample presence to the choir.

Mass in C major, K257, 'Credo'. Litaniae de venerabili altaris sacramento, K243.
Angela Maria Blasi *sop* **Elisabeth von Magnus** *contr* **Deon van der Walt** *ten*
Alistair Miles *bass*
Arnold Schoenberg Choir; Vienna Concentus Musicus / Nikolaus Harnoncourt.
Teldec Das Alte Werk 9031-72304-2 (61 minutes: DDD). Notes, texts and translations included.
Recorded 1991.　　　　Ⓔ **P**

The *Litaniae de venerabili altaris sacramento* of 1775 has powerful claims to be reckoned the finest of Mozart's church works before the C minor Mass and Requiem; but it has never quite had the recognition it deserves. Or the performance: until now, that is. It is clearly a deeply felt work, from the grave, warm opening of the 'Kyrie', through the imposing 'Verbum caro factum' and the graceful 'Hostia' that succeeds it, the 'Tremendum' with its almost Verdian menace and the appealing 'Dulcissum convivium' (a soprano aria with soft textures supplied by flutes and bassoons), the highly original 'Viaticum' and the resourcefully and lengthily developed 'Pignus' to the 'Agnus', a beautiful soprano aria with solo writing for flute, oboe and cello. The performance here under Nikolaus Harnoncourt rightly sees no need to apologize for the stylistic diversity of the work. The issue is made still more attractive by the inclusion of a Mass setting of the same year, one of Mozart's most inventive and original in its textures and its treatment of words. Altogether a very attractive record.

Mass in C major, K317, 'Coronation'.

Coronation Mass. Vesperae solennes de confessore in C major, K339. Epistle Sonata in C major, K278/K271*e*.
Emma Kirkby *sop* **Catherine Robbin** *mez* **John Mark Ainsley** *ten* **Michael George** *bass*
Winchester Cathedral Choir; Winchester Quiristers;
Academy of Ancient Music / Christopher Hogwood with **Alastair Ross** *org*
L'Oiseau-Lyre 436 585-2OH (54 minutes: DDD). Texts and translations included.
Recorded 1990.　　　　Ⓔ **P** **RR**

647

It is difficult to think of many recordings of Mozart's church music that so happily captures its character – the particular mixture of confidence, jubilation and contemplation – as Hogwood's. His unfussy direction, his broad phrasing, his lively but generally unhurried tempos and his happy details of timing serve splendidly in the *Coronation* Mass, the finest of Mozart's completed mass settings; the solemnity of the *Kyrie*, the fine swing of the *Gloria* and the energy of the *Credo*, with due pause for its rapt moment at the 'Et incarnatus', all these come over with due effect. Arguably the 'Osanna' is rather quick, but its jubilation is splendid. And the sweetness of the *Benedictus* is ravishing. Not more so, however, than the *Agnus*, for there, at a decidedly slow tempo, Hogwood allows Emma Kirkby to make the most of this very sensuous music, which she duly most beautifully does. The soloists are altogether an excellent team, with two refined voices in the middle and Michael George a firm and sturdy bass. The inclusion of the K278 Epistle Sonata is a happy notion. The *Vesperae solennes de confessore* is a setting of the five vesper psalms and the *Magnificat*, made in 1780, a year after the Mass, for some church feast in Salzburg. With admirable singing from the choir, a fresh-voiced group whose boys have a fine bright ring, and a spacious recording with exceptionally good stereo separation that properly conveys the ecclesiastical ambience, this is a disc to treasure.

Masses – C minor, K427/K417a, 'Great'; D minor, K62, 'Requiem'.

Masses – Coronation[a]; C minor[b]; Requiem[c].
Helen Donath, [b]**Heather Harper** *sops* [a]**Gillian Knight,** [c]**Yvonne Minton** *mezzos*
Ryland Davies *ten* [ab]**Stafford Dean,** [c]**Gerd Nienstedt** *basses* [ac]
John Alldis Choir; London Symphony [b]**Chorus and** [ab]**Orchestra,**
[c]**BBC Symphony Orchestra / Sir Colin Davis.**
Philips Duo 438 800-2PM2 (two discs: 135 minutes: ADD). Recorded [ab]1971, [c]1967.   Ⓜ

These seem rather old-fashioned performances nowadays, but they are vigorous and full of conviction and many readers will find them wholly sympathetic. The *Coronation* Mass has a splendidly imposing start, and the two long movements, the *Gloria* and *Credo*, are done with plenty of spirit at rather rapid tempos: the effect is brilliant and affirmative, though with these rather large forces it does seem a shade driven. The 'Osanna' is also decidedly speedy. There is some really lovely, heartfelt solo singing from Helen Donath, especially in the *Agnus Dei*. The soloists are recorded unnaturally forward, giving the impression of their being very close with a big choir in the distance. The orchestral balance doesn't seem quite right, either, with the trombones in particular too prominent at times. Davis's reading of the C minor Mass is very much more weighty; his interpretations certainly accentuate the difference between these two works, only three or four years apart. The sombre, intense opening can readily be justified, but the heavy 'Domine Deus' and the very slow 'Et incarnatus', beautifully sung though it is, again by Donath, do seem exaggerated, and even if the 'Quoniam' is quickish it seems somewhat ponderously *legato*. There is certainly a feeling for the grandeur of the work and also its drama (listen for example to the *Sanctus*), and the sturdy, forthright 'Benedictus' is very effective too.

Donath excels again in the 'Laudamus te' (her semiquaver runs neat and crystalline) and her duetting with Heather Harper in the 'Laudamus te' is very enjoyable, although the voices do not really match well: there are of course arguments either way, for blend or contrast, in music with such close interplay. The performance of the Requiem is also available on a single CD and it is one that has been much, and justly, recommended. It is certainly a rather operatic reading, with much drama and passion and eloquence, and it is very musical and compelling, though some may feel that the variations in tempo and the general consciousness of effect are not what they want in an ecclesiastical work. Again, there is sure and strong choral singing, and Donath shines once more as the soprano, with Ryland Davies in his best voice in the tenor music. These are not, then, the versions of these works that one would necessarily choose first of all, but they are musical and persuasive and, at a moderate price, well worth considering.

C minor Mass (ed. Maunder).
Arleen Auger, Lynne Dawson *sops* **John Mark Ainsley** *ten* **David Thomas** *bass*
Winchester Cathedral Choir; Winchester Quiristers;
Academy of Ancient Music / Christopher Hogwood.
L'Oiseau-Lyre Florilegium 425 528-2OH (51 minutes: DDD). Text and translation included.
Recorded 1988.   Ⓜ 🅿 🆁🆁

Mozart left unfinished the work that ought to have been the choral masterpiece of his early Viennese years but there is enough of it to make up nearly an hour's music – music that is sometimes sombre, sometimes florid, sometimes jubilant. Christopher Hogwood avoids any charge of emotional detachment in his steady and powerful opening *Kyrie*, monumental in feeling, dark in tone; and he brings ample energy to the big, bustling choruses of the *Gloria* – and its long closing fugue is finely sustained. The clarity and ring of the boys' voices serve him well in these numbers. There is a strong solo team, headed by the late Arleen Auger in radiant, glowing voice and, as usual, singing with refined taste; Lynne Dawson joins her in the duets, John Mark Ainsley too in the trio. But this is essentially a 'soprano mass' – Mozart wrote it, after all, with the voice of his new wife (and perhaps thoughts of the much superior one of her sister Aloysia) in his mind – and Auger, her voice happily stealing in for the first time in the lovely 'Christe', excels in the florid and expressive music of the 'Et incarnatus' (where Richard Maunder has supplied fuller string parts than usual, perhaps fuller than Mozart would have done had he finished the work). Hogwood directs with his usual spirit and clarity.

C minor[a]. Masonic Funeral Music, K477.
[a]**Christiane Oelze** sop [a]**Jennifer Larmore** mez [a]**Scot Weir** ten [a]**Peter Kooy** bass
Collegium Vocale; La Chapelle Royale Choir;
Champs Elysées Orchestra / Philippe Herreweghe.
Harmonia Mundi HMC90 1393 (60 minutes: DDD). Texts and translations included.
Recorded 1991.   Ⓕ**P**

Herreweghe's reading of the Mass also uses period instruments, with a slightly larger choir than Hogwood's. It is, however, a more traditional kind of performance, very slow and deliberate at the opening, with an impressive choral build-up; if the choral *crescendo* was unknown or at best rare in Mozart's time, Herreweghe makes a strong case for its being justified or even implied by the music. The 'Christe' is highly expressive, too, indeed passionate. He offers a very powerful 'Gratias', with strong rhythms and well-marked contrasts, a slower and more *staccato* 'qui tollis', and a 'Cum sancto spiritu' fugue more consciously shaped – it is a long movement and benefits from an expressed awareness of its architecture. You will relish the prominent brass in the 'Jesu Christe' and the incisive choral singing in the 'Hosanna'. The solo quartet in the *Benedictus*, carefully and musically shaped, blended particularly effectively, and Christiane Oelze does well in all the first soprano's music, clear, expressive and controlled in the 'Et incarnatus'. The second soprano (as it ought to be) is rather heavily contralto-like for the 'Laudamus te'. The 'Domine Deus' depends rather critically on a good match (or appropriate contrast) of the two upper voices and when they differ in style as much as they do here something is forfeit. This affects the 'Quoniam' trio too. Still, this is an impressive performance, and on the whole one that makes more of the work than most. The fill-up is the *Masonic Funeral Music*, an impassioned account: so impassioned, perhaps, in its sense of protest against death as seemingly to contradict Mozart's famous quotation, in his last letter to his father, about death as man's best friend. The plainsong, incidentally, is sung here by the choir.

C minor (ed. Eder).
Arleen Auger, Barbara Bonney sops **Hans Peter Blochwitz** ten **Robert Holl** bass
Berlin Radio Chorus; Berlin Philharmonic Orchestra / Claudio Abbado.
Sony Classical SK46671 (53 minutes: DDD). Text and translation included. Recorded 1990.   Ⓕ

'Comfortable' is not a fashionable word to use by way of praise; 'disturbing' is. However, Abbado's is comfortable. No doubt part of the warmth is due to another unfashionable feature, the use of a large orchestra not playing on period instruments. That it plays magnificently and that the choir is a particularly fine one will have something to do with it too. Perhaps the balance of the recording overweights the orchestral bass, and a little less reverberance might not come amiss in the hall acoustic, but these are matters of degree, not disqualifying objections. Rather similarly, when it comes to the style of the performance, one might prefer a more jolly, a-hunting-we-will-go bounce for the rhythms of the *Credo*, but again this is a matter of degree for Abbado is not lacking in vitality or colour. Of course if you take the view that the 'Qui tollis' should be like sitting on spikes you will find Abbado too well cushioned and will prefer an alternative version. But there is no feeling of superficiality or blandness in Abbado, and the double choir is well recorded to carry weight and to enforce the pictorial effect of the music. In tempo, too, he judges well. Abbado's singers are well forward and very distinct. Abbado brings a vigorous touch to the *Kyrie* without impairing the profundity. The other great strength here is the excellence of the two sopranos. With the happy emulation of the seraphim they place their high As and B flats, their semiquaver runs and long held notes in the 'Domine Deus'. Auger has warmth, Bonney brightness, and she sings the 'Et incarnatus est' with blissfully assured control. There have been many lovely accounts of this work on disc, few better than here.

Requiem Mass (cptd. Süssmayr).
Sylvia McNair sop **Carolyn Watkinson** contr **Francisco Araiza** ten **Robert Lloyd** bass
Chorus and Academy of St Martin in the Fields / Sir Neville Marriner.
Philips 432 087-2PH (50 minutes: DDD). Text and translation included. Recorded 1990.   Ⓕ**RR**

Mozart's Requiem may not be wholly Mozart's, as we all know: but performers certainly show no reservations in the power or the conviction they bring to its music, whoever it may be by. This one under Sir Neville Marriner is among the noblest and most powerful of them all; an unusually thoughtful and careful reading. The first thing that strikes you is the passionate nature of the choral singing, right from the start: the Academy chorus sings the beginning almost as if it were a personal protest against death, and the chromaticisms and dissonances of the 'Requiem aeternam' make their due effect. And the 'Kyrie', taken at a vigorous pace, has great energy. The dynamics in the 'Dies irae' are strongly made, almost exaggerated (the shape of the violin phrases does perhaps invite that); there is a finely solemn 'Rex tremendae majestatis', with sharply dotted rhythms, a slow 'Lacrimosa' with finely detailed shaping, a lively 'Domine Jesu' and an 'Agnus Dei' so grandly sombre that it unmistakably emerges as the expressive climax of the whole work.

There is superlative solo singing, too – Robert Lloyd in dark and noble voice in the 'Tuba mirum', Sylvia McNair as moving as always with her beautiful sound and refinement of nuance, in that number, in the 'Benedictus' and in the 'Lux aeterna'. The inner voices too are satisfactory though Francisco Araiza's expressive taste is possibly not quite in line with that of the others. Possibly the slowish tempos do not work quite so well for the solo ensemble numbers as they do for the choruses: the 'Recordare' seems just a shade static, however refined the shaping of the music, and perhaps so too does the 'Benedictus'. The version used is billed as Süssmayr's, but that isn't quite the whole truth: for example, his trombone parts are sometimes omitted (as in part of the 'Tuba mirum' and the 'Benedictus') and there is a basset horn chromaticism omitted in the 'Agnus' – though that may be simply a mistake. Marriner's Requiem is a powerful and distinctive interpretation: a consistent, considered view of the work, faithfully and carefully carried through.

Requiem Mass. Ave verum corpus in D major, K618.
Anna Maria Panzarella sop **Nathalie Stutzmann** contr **Christoph Prégardien** ten
Nathan Berg bass
Les Arts Florissants / William Christie.
Erato 0630-10697-2 (54 minutes: DDD). Texts and translations included. Recorded 1994.　ⒻⓅ

Les Arts Florissants provides a substantial, dramatic reading: the tempo for the 'Requiem aeternam' is slow, but malleable, and Christie is ready to make the most of the changes in orchestral colour or choral texture and indeed to dramatize the music to the utmost. Clearly he has little truck with any notion that this is an austere piece: he sees it as operatic, almost romantic – and the result is very compelling. There are surprising things: 'Quantus tremor', in a very weighty account of the 'Dies irae', for example, is hushed rather than terrifying; the 'Recordare' is slow to the point of stickiness; there are rather mannered *crescendos* in the *Sanctus*; and often cadences are drawn out, for example in the 'Hostias'. The powerful choruses of the Sequence are imposingly done, and the grave 'Lacrimosa' wonderfully catches the special significance not only of the music itself but also of the fact that this is the moment where Mozart's last autograph trails off. The choral singing is sharply etched and generally distinguished: the choir gives a vigorous yet finely dovetailed *Kyrie* fugue and the 'Quam olim Abrahae' is splendidly sturdy. Although the solo singing is not uniformly outstanding the soprano's melting tone is sometimes very appealing, and Prégardien is an excellent stylist; the *Benedictus* is particularly impressive, very shapely and refined. In short, this is a reading full of character and imaginative ideas, very much a conscious modern interpretation of the work and very finely executed. The disc is completed by perhaps the only piece which can reasonably follow the Requiem, the *Ave verum corpus*, in a slow, hushed, rather romantic reading that is undeniably moving.

Requiem Mass. Kyrie in D minor, K341/K368a.
Sibylla Rubens sop **Annette Markert** contr **Ian Bostridge** ten **Hanno Müller-Brachmann** bar
La Chapelle Royale; Collegium Vocale;
Orchestra of the Champs-Elysées, Paris / Philippe Herreweghe.
Harmonia Mundi HMC90 1620 (54 minutes: DDD). Texts and translations included.
Recorded live in 1996.　ⒻⓅ

This is a direct, unaffected recording of the familiar Süssmayr version of the Requiem, marked by its vigorous choral singing and its strong rhythmic underpinning. Philippe Herreweghe is not afraid of slowish tempos, more traditional ones than those favoured by most period-instrument practitioners. His conducting provides its own justification. The opening 'Requiem aeternam' moves with deliberation and a firm, steady tread; so too in a different way does the 'Dies irae', but with no lack of energy. The momentum of the 'Rex tremendae majestatis' is quite out of the ordinary; in the 'Confutatis' Herreweghe makes the most of the contrast between the sharp rhythms of the men's voices and the female angelic choir, softening it, however, by easing the tempo from one to the other. The 'Lacrimosa' is unusually impassioned. There is a finely energetic 'Quam olim Abrahae' fugue, in which the Chapelle Royale and Collegium Vocale sing cleanly and vigorously, as indeed they also do in the *Kyrie* fugue. These are of course female sopranos and altos, but steady and concentrated in tone; perhaps here and there the choral sound seems a shade pallid, lacking the brilliance of the best English choirs. The clarity of the recording is a delight in the big contrapuntal choruses. The solo quartet too comes across with unusual definition, for example in the 'Recordare' (where there is some passionate singing from them, coupled with pleasantly reedy basset-horn tone) and in the *Benedictus*, which is done with an agreeable flow. Individually, the soloists do some pleasing things, especially perhaps the soprano and the tenor; all do well in the 'Tuba mirum'. While not perhaps the most arresting Requiem in the catalogue, this is certainly a very accomplished version, especially for Herreweghe's direction, with its firmness and resilience and its clear sense of shape and direction. The coupling of the fine D minor *Kyrie*, now widely taken to be a relatively late work (in spite of its K number), in a shapely reading, is a happy choice.

Requiem Mass. Symphony No. 25.
Lisa della Casa *sop* **Ira Malaniuk** *contr* **Anton Dermota** *ten* **Cesare Siepi** *bass*
Vienna State Opera Concert Choir; Vienna Philharmonic Orchestra / Bruno Walter.
Orfeo D'Or mono C430961B (76 minutes: ADD). Recorded live in 1956.　　　　Ⓕ Ⓗ

Listening to this is a moving experience. Though he may not have known it at the time, this was Walter's farewell to a festival with which he had been closely associated over 30 years: he conducted there from 1925 to 1937 after which he was forced to withdraw because of Austria's Anschluss with Nazi Germany. He returned again in 1946 and off and on, mostly conducting Mahler, until this final meeting with his beloved Mozart. Yet there is nothing in the least sentimental, or indeed inappropriately romantic, about these contributions from a conductor on the verge of his eightieth birthday. As a contemporary critic (Karl Schumann) put it, the little G minor Symphony is given as an 'eerie vision of night and suffering' with consolation coming only in the *Andante*. Of the other work Schumann commented: 'Bruno Walter understands the Requiem logically as Catholic church music, as a musical interpretation of the liturgy' and thus banishes thoughts about a 'swansong elegy'. The performance is taut, closely worked, never broad or indulgent. Listen to the counterpoint of 'Quam olim Abrahae' and you will hear the sharp rhythms that characterize the whole. Even so, Walter's beloved Vienna Philharmonic is allowed to display its warm, ethereal string tone as circumstances allow. Four of the leading soloists of the day contribute positively. Siepi inhabits the bass-line as to the manner born, and on the top of the quartet, della Casa provides tones fit for the contemplation of heavenly matters. In-between Malaniuk's soothing mezzo and Dermota's plaintive tenor are heard to advantage. The one drawback of the performance is the unsteady tone of the Vienna Opera chorus's sopranos, encountered on so many recordings of the period. But as a whole, the choral singing is as dedicated as the rest. The recording is in well-focused mono. This was undoubtedly the best of Walter's Requiems and so worth an hour or so of anyone's time.

Così dunque tradisci, K432. Alcandro, lo confesso, K512. Mentre ti lascio, K513. Per questa bella mano, K612. Rivolgete a lui lo sguardo, K584. Die Zauberflöte – Der Vogelfänger bin ich ja; In diesen heil'gen Hallen; Ein Mädchen oder Weibchen. Le nozze di Figaro – Hai già vinta la causa! ... Vedrò mentr'io sospiro. Don Giovanni – Madamina, il catalogo è questo; Deh! vieni alla finestra.
Thomas Quasthoff *bar*
Württemberg Chamber Orchestra / Jörg Faerber.
RCA Victor Red Seal 09026 61428-2 (56 minutes: DDD). Texts and translations included.
Recorded 1996.　　　　Ⓕ

With a voice hovering usefully between bass and baritone, and a rich, vibrant tone, the greatly talented Quasthoff reminds one of Ramey at his most convincing but with more colouring in his tone. In what is a taxing recital devoted to concert and opera arias, there is virtually nothing to criticize. Quasthoff has the versatility and imagination to move easily between roles in the same opera; thus after the Sarastro aria, he shows himself a wholly delightful Papageno, singing with a ready smile in his tone and a nice variety between verses of the bird-catcher's two songs. Then a suave, seductive Serenade from his Giovanni is followed by an appropriately oily 'Madamina' from his Leporello. In *Figaro* he undertakes only the Count and changes coats again, as it were, to exhibit anger and command. From *Così fan tutte* he chooses Guglielmo's discarded aria, 'Rivolgete', which can sound too long, but not when sung with such relish as here. It's particularly rewarding to have modern recordings of the four concert arias unaccountably neglected by basses, especially when sung with such warm tone, firm line and pointed diction. Quasthoff couldn't have better partners than the experienced, seemingly ageless Faerber and his orchestra, prompt in rhythm and well balanced with the voice.

Così fan tutte – Ah, scostati! ... Smanie implacabili. Le nozze di Figaro – Non so più cosa son. Idomeneo – Non ho colpa; Il padre adorato; March of the priests. Mitridate, rè di Ponto – Venga pur, minacci; Già dagli occhi. Don Giovanni – Vedrai, carino; In quali eccessi ... Mi tradì quell'alma ingrata. Lucio Silla – Il tenero momento. La clemenza di Tito – Marcia; Deh per questo istante; Non più di fiori. Io ti lascio, o cara, addio, KAnh245/K621a.
Vesselina Kasarova *mez*
Staatskapelle Dresden / Sir Colin Davis.
RCA Victor Red Seal 09026 68661-2 (74 minutes: DDD). Texts and translations included.
Recorded 1996.   Ⓕ 🇪

Being the questing, individual spirit Kasarova is, she can be controversial as she breaks new ground in interpretation. She does nothing by halves, so some of these performances could divide lovers of Mozart singing. However, most of the arias in this vivid recital are thrilling in all the right kinds of ways. Defiant Dorabella, despondent Elvira and confused Vitellia are all unerringly portrayed, but it is in the great castrato roles that Kasarova excels most of all. Both sides of Farnace's character in *Mitridate* are explored in his arias, the first fiercely proud, the single word 'barbaro' saying it all. Then in the second we hear the gently palpitating voice of repentance, 'son pentito'. In Cecilio's aria from *Lucio Silla*, another aspect of Kasarova's singing brings a smile of pleasure – the wonderful variety she brings to her runs. The aria, *Io ti lascio* displays her grave beauty of tone, enhanced by the slightest of vibrations, revealing a singer of high intelligence with the means to fulfil her earnest intents. Who better to partner such an elevated singer than Sir Colin? He provides the know-how of a loving Mozartian, prompt in every phrase, and singer and conductor are seconded by playing of idiomatic firmness from the orchestra. Everything is admirably recorded.

Così fan tutte – In uomini, in soldati; Temerari! … Come scoglio; Ei parte … Per pietà, ben mio. Le nozze di Figaro – E Susanna non vien! … Dove sono; Giunse alfin il momento … Al desio (K577a). Don Giovanni – Batti, batti, o bel Masetto; In quali eccessi … Mi tradì quell' alma ingrata. Davidde penitente, K469 – Lunghi le cure ingrate. Exsultate, jubilate, K165/K158a.
Cecilia Bartoli *mez*
Vienna Chamber Orchestra / György Fischer.
Decca 443 452-2DH (61 minutes: DDD). Texts and translations included. Recorded 1993.   Ⓕ

There are relatively few Italian mezzos, or sopranos for that matter, who sing a lot of Mozart and Bartoli's very Italian characteristics are immediately identifiable: brilliance of execution, vitality of words, sharpness of mind. She tears into the recitative before Donna Elvira's 'Mi tradì' with a blistering fury that leaves most interpreters of the role standing and has no problems with the *fioriture* of the aria itself. Her Fiordiligi has the bite for 'Come scoglio', but comparisons with a variety of lyric sopranos show up a want of depth to the tone, both here and in 'Per pietà'. Her Countess delivers her lines with appropriately aristocratic weight, though one senses her natural temperament being suppressed with difficulty. However much she tries to disguise herself, the real Bartoli is likely to pop her head out. There are unlikely to be any complaints about her effervescent Despina or Zerlina, both portrayals for which she has stage experience. In the concert hall she is also a spirited interpreter of *Exsultate, jubilate*. From the opening line Bartoli makes other singers seem bland by comparison, getting the Latin words to tingle with a sense of elation that only an Italian-speaker would dare. The orchestral sound might be more firmly focused (the sound picture in 'Batti, batti' has the solo cello close, while the wind struggle to be heard from some deep recess) but Fischer accompanies his soloist with energy and tact.

Le nozze di Figaro – Giunse alfin il momento … Deh, vieni; Giunse alfin il momento … Al desio di chi t'adora, K577a. Don Giovanni – In quali eccessi … Mi tradì. Die Entführung aus dem Serail – Ach, ich liebte. Il rè pastore – L'amerò, sarò costante[a]. Die Zauberflöte – Ach, ich fühl's. La finta giardiniera – Geme la tortorella; Crudel, Oh Dio! fermate; Ah, dal pianto, dal singhiozzo. Zaïde – Ruhe sanft, mein holdes Leben. Il sogno di Scipione – Lieve son al par del vento. Nehmt meinen Dank, ihr holden Gönner, K383.
Renée Fleming *sop* [a]**Krista Bennion Feeney** *vn*
Orchestra of St Luke's / Sir Charles Mackerras.
Decca 452 602-2DH (60 minutes: DDD). Recorded 1995.   Ⓕ 🇪

Renée Fleming's exceptionally beautiful voice has a depth to it which first reminds you of de los Angeles in her prime and then, in the context of *Le nozze di Figaro*, of the mistress rather than the maid. It also points up the slight oddity that as regards tessitura (or the 'lie' of the voice) the two roles differ very little, while the voice-characters are nevertheless quite distinct. It suggests also good reasoning on the part of Fleming, who is quoted in an article on the disc as saying 'I wanted to do this high-lying Mozart before it's too late.' She does indeed mingle 'high-lying Mozart' with the medium. In several items she faces the heights and takes them with zest and success. The Germanic use of head-voice in 'Ach, ich liebte' (*Die Entführung*), for instance, is forsworn in favour of a full-bodied voice in the upper notes. In La Fortuna's aria from *Il sogno di Scipione* not only are the C major scales similarly brave and full, but the cadenza is topped with a *staccato* E and G, both *in alt*. But this is the record of more than a singer. Mackerras and the St Luke's Orchestra contribute greatly towards its distinction. The playing of the big scene for Sandrina in *La finta gardiniera*, for instance, is something very special. In the *Zauberflöte* and *Zaïde* arias a fast tempo is chosen, with a loss of the more luxurious loveliness and a gain in eighteenth-century refinement. In everything, orchestral parts as well as the voice, the sound is suited to the sense, and both give plentiful delight.

Le nozze di Figaro – Non so più cosa son; Porgi, amor. Don Giovanni – Batti, batti; In quali eccessi … Mi tradì. Così fan tutte – Temerari … Come scoglio; Ei parte … Per pietà, ben mio. La clemenza di Tito – Deh per questo istante; Ecco il punto … Non più di fiori vaghe catene. Oh, temerario Arbace! … Per quel paterno amplesso, K79/K79*d*. Ch'io mi scordi di te … Non temer, amato bene, K505*a*.
Véronique Gens *sop*
Orchestra of the Age of Enlightenment / Ivor Bolton with **Melvyn Tan** *fp*
Virgin Classics Veritas VC5 45319-2 (59 minutes: DDD). Texts and translations included. Recorded 1998. Ⓕ🅴

Véronique Gens is one of the most engaging and stylish Mozart sopranos around, as this sampler of her art confirms. Her early training has made her a particularly happy collaborator with the Orchestra of the Age of Enlightenment. Under the exacting baton of Ivor Bolton, they show sharp and eager teeth to match her own highly-strung recitative in 'In quali eccessi'. And this Donna Anna demonstrates more than one-dimensional *Angst* as the orchestra's wind soloists breathe in sympathy with every moment of *palpitando* in Gens's own supple phrasing. There's a similar focus on the emotional potential of breath in a 'Non so più' whose fierce frustration flies out of eloquent consonants. Steady control of breath and tone bring a moving poise to 'Non più di fiori', where Vitellia's horrified introspection finds empathy in Lesley Schatzberger's basset-horn obbligato. And as Sesto, Gens moulds the moist clay of some of Mozart's most beautiful melodic contours in 'Deh, per questo istante'. Two concert arias circle in the orbit of that earlier great *opera seria*, *Idomeneo*: Idamante's 'Non temer', in which Gens sighs poignantly with the dying fall of Melvyn Tan's sweetly articulated fortepiano; and the youthful Arbace aria 'Per quel paterno amplesso', to whose lilting farewell Gens brings eloquent breadth. There's her Countess and Zerlina to enjoy as well and, particularly, the two exquisitely sculpted and sparingly but powerfully ornamented arias from *Così*.

Die Entführung aus dem Serail – Martern aller Arten. Die Zauberflöte – Ach, ich fühl's. Vorrei spiegarvi, oh Dio, K418. No, che non sei capace, K419. Ah, se in ciel, benigne stelle, K538. Il rè pastore – L'amerò, sarò costante. Voi avete un cor fedele, K217. Chi sà, chi sà, qual sia, K582. Le nozze di Figaro – Deh vieni, non tardar. Der Schauspieldirektor – Bester Jüngling. Nehmt meinen Dank, ihr holden Gönner, K383. Schon lacht der holde Frühling, K580.
Sumi Jo *sop*
English Chamber Orchestra / Kenneth Montgomery.
Erato 0630-14637-2 (65 minutes: DDD). Texts and translations included. Recorded 1995. Ⓕ

Sumi Jo's disc naturally begs comparison with Renée Fleming's (reviewed above). Both singers give delightful performances, and if a contrast claims attention it lies rather more in the instrumental work and perhaps that of the conductors. In 'Ach, ich fühl's' (*Die Zauberflöte*) Mackerras, conducting for Fleming, takes an unusually fast tempo, while Kenneth Montgomery, still quick compared with what became the norm, avoids the suspicion of didacticism. Interestingly, it is Sumi Jo who forfeits elegance in the difficult high run on 'Herzen', while Fleming, at the faster speed, uses her technique to more secure advantage. In *Nehmt meinen Dank* comparison focuses more exclusively upon the singers, for here Fleming is distinctly the more expressive: warmer ('bleibt immer dar'), more responsive ('so feurig, als mein Herz ihn sprich'). Delights abound. Sumi Jo has the apt Susanna voice, and her 'Deh vieni' is delicious. In *Vorrei spiegarvi* the delicate charm is winningly captured, with a beautifully judged interplay between voice and instruments. 'Martern aller Arten' has its scales and broad intervals clearly articulated, with plenty of spirit and never a harsh note. Throughout the recital this lovely singer shows herself a worthy exponent of the tradition handed on from Mozart's own time.

Margaret Price sings Mozart
Mozart La clemenza di Tito – Parto, parto (**Thea King** *cl*)[a]. Le nozze di Figaro – Voi che sapete[a]; E Susanna non vien! … Dove sono[a]; Giunse alfin il momento … Deh vieni, non tardar[a]. Die Entführung aus dem Serail – Martern aller Arten[a]. Il rè pastore – L'amerò, sarò costante[a]

Mozart Concert and Opera arias

(Jose-Luis Garcia vn)[a]. Don Giovanni – In quali eccessi ... Mi tradì quell' alma ingrata[a]; Crudele! Ah no mio bene ... Non mi dir[a]. Idomeneo – Parto, e l'unico ... Idol mio, se ritroso[b]. Concert arias – Vado, ma dove? oh Dei!, K583[b]; Vorrei spiegarvi, oh Dio, K418[b]; Ch'io me scordi di te ... Non temer, amato bene, K490 (**Dennis Simons** vn)[b]; Al desio, K577[b]; Bella mia fiamma ... Resta, oh cara, K528[b]. Ch'io mi scordi di te ... Non temer, amato bene, K505[b]; Nehmt meinen Dank, ihr holden Gönner, K383[b]. Eine kleine deutsche Kantate, K619[c].
Mussorgsky The Nursery[c]. **Liszt** Sonetti di Petrarca, S270[c].
Dame Margaret Price sop [a]**English Chamber Orchestra;**
[b]**London Philharmonic Orchestra / James Lockhart** [c]pf
RCA Victor Gold Seal 09026 61635-2 (two discs: 151 minutes: ADD). Texts and translations included. Recorded [a]1973, [b]1975, [c]1970.　Ⓜ

Margaret Price's early recordings announced to the world a unique singer: nobody could mistake that purity of tone or the way she has of moving from note to note, as though each is a separate gem in a row of pearls. Although complete recordings followed of some of the Mozart operas, the disc of individual arias holds its own. 'Idol mio' from *Idomeneo* has never been more ravishing; the Countess's 'Dove sono' is an example of the purest classical poise, despite some plummy Italian vowels. A touch of breathiness intrudes in fast passages where the voice is asked to move around, but even mentioning it seems unfair, when there is so much beauty on all sides. At this stage of her career Margaret Price was not the kind of artist to inject drama into Mozart's more formal concert arias, but that disc also contains some favourite tracks. Her *Nehmt meinen Dank* lights upon an unexpectedly sweet tone and *Vorrei spiegarvi* seems even more spectacular today than it did at the time, given that the young Mozartian soprano has subsequently gone on to sing Aida. The fillers are taken from Price's 'Wigmore Hall' song recital. There is no room for the Italian songs, but we do get her fearless singing of Liszt's Petrarch Sonnets, accompanied in a drily unromantic fashion by James Lockhart. The verdict is clear-cut: not to be missed.

Ah, lo previdi ... Ah, t'invola, K272. A questo seno ... Or che il cielo, K374. Alma grande e nobil core, K578. Grabmusik, K42a/K35a – Betracht dies Herz und frage mich. Vado, ma dove? oh Dei!, K583. Bella mia fiamma ... Resta, o cara, K528. Misera! dove son ... Ah! non son io, K369.
Gundula Janowitz sop
Vienna Symphony Orchestra / Wilfried Boettcher.
DG The Originals 449 723-2GOR (61 minutes: ADD). Texts and translations included. Recorded 1966.　Ⓜ

An 'original' is exactly what this disc is, as it reproduces Janowitz's first solo recital record, issued in 1967. Listening back, we can marvel not just at the purity of tone and silken vocal line, but also a refinement of style that marks out a fully formed artist. The highlights include a delicate *Vado, ma dove?* and a performance of *Bella mia fiamma* which lights up the music with the subtlest of colours from within. Some of the recitatives might have been more dramatic, but Wilfried Boettcher and the Vienna Symphony Orchestra provide alert accompaniment. There is also a bonus: the original LP did not have room for the ravishing G minor lament 'Betracht dies Herz' from the *Grabmusik*, K42, and that is now issued for the first time here, a minor treasure in its own right.

Mozart Exsultate, jubilate, K165/K158a. Zaïde – Ruhe sanft, meine holdes Leben. Nehmt meinen Dank, ihr holden Gönner, K383. Mia speranza adorata ... Ah non sai qual pena sia, K416. Vorrei spiegarvi, oh Dio, K418. Ch'io mi scordi di te … Non temer, amato bene, K505[a].
R. Strauss Morgen, Op. 27 No. 4. Liebeshymnus, Op. 32 No. 3. Der Rosenband, Op. 36 No. 1. Wiegenlied, Op. 41 No. 1. Das Bächlein, AV118.
Christine Schäfer sop [a]**Maria João Pires** pf
Berlin Philharmonic Orchestra / Claudio Abbado.
DG 457 582-2GH (65 minutes: DDD). Texts and translations included. Recorded 1997.　Ⓕ🅔

Schäfer must now be rated in the royal line of Schwarzkopf, Seefried, Ameling, Popp and most recently Bonney as an interpreter of Mozart and Strauss. Yet, she is, like those renowned singers, very much her own person with her own distinctive voice and style. Her almost vibrato-less, at times slightly acerbic tone won't be to all tastes but her unadorned, clear and imaginative singing of all the Mozart arias demands and holds attention. In *Nehmt meinen Dank*, the single word 'Geduld' carries a wealth of meaning; the whole of K416 – Mozart at his most pained and searching – has an intense feeling of farewell as Schäfer delivers it and again a single word, 'addio' at the end of the recitative, is drenched in sadness. In *Non temer, amato bene*, with Pires providing an ideal counterpoint to the singer, Schäfer etches into the mind the full import of the emotions being expressed, without a hint of sentimentality. *Ruhe sanft* disarms criticism, so touchingly, simply, is it sung, with the little cadenza before the reprise deftly touched in. The more extrovert pieces, *Exsultate, jubilate* and *Vorrei, spiegarvi* are, appropriately enough, sung more objectively. Abbado and the Berlin Philharmonic support Schäfer in the most refined fashion possible, all the instrumental detail finely honed. They are just as ingratiating in Strauss. Most recent interpreters have had richer, warmer voices than Schäfer's. She is a throwback to, say, Elisabeth Schumann, who sang *Wiegenlied* with just the same kind of artless, silvery beauty, combined with a pure, keen line – a real winner. But so is each of these beautifully composed and sung pieces, the texts fully understood so that the words are ideally melded with their settings: note especially the extra tranche of intensity at the climax of *Liebeshymnus* and the ideal delineation of the elegiac *Morgen*'s reflective mood, the tempo for once not too slow. Indeed it's in this last song, that one hears, as well as anywhere, the soprano's special gift of plaintive eloquence. The recording could not be better balanced.

Le nozze di Figaro – Non so più; Voi che sapete; Giunse alfin il momento ... Deh vieni. Così fan tutte – E'amore un ladroncello. Don Giovanni – Vedrai, carino. La clemenza di Tito – Parto, parto; Deh, per questo; Ecco il punto, o Vitellia ... Non piu di fiori. Concert Arias – Chi sa, chi sa, qual sia, K582; Alma grande e nobil core, K578; Ch'io mi scordi di te?, K505.
Cecilia Bartoli *mez* **András Schiff** *pf* **Peter Schmidtl** *basset cl/basset hn*
Vienna Chamber Orchestra / György Fischer.
Decca 430 513-2DH (58 minutes: DDD). Texts and translations included. Recorded 1989-90.   Ⓕ

Mozart wrote some of his most appealing music for the mezzo-soprano voice with the roles of Cherubino and Susanna in *Le nozze di Figaro*, Dorabella in *Così fan tutte* and Zerlina in *Don Giovanni* each boasting at least one memorable aria. Alongside these this disc includes a handful of concert arias including *Ch'io mi scordi di te?* which was written for the farewell performance of the great mezzo Nancy Storace with Mozart himself playing the concertante piano role. Here with as innate an interpreter of Mozart's piano writing as András Schiff and a voice so remarkably self-assured as Cecilia Bartoli's the electricity of that first, historic performance seems almost to be recreated. And, here as elsewhere, György Fischer directs the splendid Vienna Chamber Orchestra with disarming sensitivity while the recording is wonderfully warm and vibrant. Cecilia Bartoli boasts a voice of quite extraordinary charm and unassuming virtuosity: her vocal characterizations would be the envy of the finest actresses and her intuitive singing is in itself a sheer delight. But she also brings to these arias a conviction and understanding of the subtleties of the language which only a native Italian could. Listen to the subtle nuances of 'Voi che sapete', the depth of understanding behind Dorabella's seemingly frivolous 'E'amore un ladroncello'; these are not mere performances, but interpretations which penetrate to the very soul of the music. No Mozart lover should be without this CD.

La clemenza di Tito.
Uwe Heilmann *ten* Tito; **Della Jones** *mez* Vitellia; **Cecilia Bartoli** *mez* Sesto;
Diana Montague *mez* Annio; **Barbara Bonney** *sop* Servillia; **Gilles Cachemaille** *bar* Publio;
Academy of Ancient Music Chorus; Academy of Ancient Music / Christopher Hogwood.
L'Oiseau-Lyre 444 131-2OHO2 (two discs: 137 minutes: DDD).Notes, text and translation included. Recorded 1993.   ⒻⓅⒺ

The appeal of *La clemenza di Tito*, if less immediate and less obvious than that of the other operas of Mozart's maturity, is still very powerful and very individual. Hogwood has assembled a quite remarkable cast, with certainly two, perhaps three, outstanding interpretations. First among them must be Cecilia Bartoli, who rightly establishes Sextus as the central character, the one whose actions and whose feelings are the focal point of the drama. The opening number is the duet 'Come ti piace, imponi', where the firm and pure sound of Bartoli's voice, in contrast with the contained hysteria of Vitellia's, at once defines the opera's basis. It is clear from her singing that she reads Sextus, for all his weakness in giving way to Vitellia, as a man of integrity, one of the noblest Romans of them all. Then there is Della Jones's remarkable Vitellia. There are lots of interesting and emotionally suggestive touches in her singing, which is very committed and very passionate, if not perhaps immaculately tidy – but then, tidiness is no part of Vitellia's persona. Her rich bottom register is magnificent and the top Bs have no fears for her. Uwe Heilmann's Titus is marked by much subtle and finely shaped singing and a keen awareness of how phrasing conveys sense. Occasionally the tone is inclined to be nasal, but that does not interfere with a very sympathetic and often moving reading. Hogwood's keen awareness of what, expressively speaking, is going on in the music, and his refusal to be tied to a rigid rhythmic pulse in order to make it manifest, is one of the strengths of this recording. The recitatives are sung with a great deal of life and awareness of meaning, not simply gabbled through at maximum speed. These, of course, are not Mozart's own work and are usually heavily cut. While some may feel that the inclusion of every note, as in the present version, is an advantage to the opera, others may not unreasonably take the opposite view. At any rate, the discs' tracking is arranged so that a new track begins for each aria, which enables listeners to make their own cuts without difficulty.

La clemenza di Tito.
Gösta Winbergh *ten* Tito; **Carol Vaness** *sop* Vitellia; **Delores Ziegler** *mez* Sesto;
Martha Senn *mez* Anno; **Christine Barbaux** *sop* Servilia; **László Polgár** *bass* Publio;
Vienna State Opera Chorus; Vienna Philharmonic Orchestra / Riccardo Muti.
EMI CDS5 55489-2 (two discs: 136 minutes: ADD). Notes, texts and translation included.
Recorded live in 1988.   ⓕ 🅴

Riccardo Muti, oblivious to or at least putting aside attempts at period practice, interprets the work
unashamedly as a grand, incisive near-tragedy. Nor is he averse to the players of the Vienna
Philharmonic drawing the most sensuous sounds from the score, yet he never indulges Mozart,
favouring swiftish, though flexible tempos and sharp rhythms. Muti is also notable for catching the
tinta, the individual colour, of this work. Listen to the trio of contrasted feeling, 'Quello di Tito', in
Act 2 and you'll divine the calibre of this reading, or a little earlier to the way Muti persuades the
chorus into the most mellifluous sounds in 'Ah, grazie si rendamo'. Muti's approach is admirably
seconded by the generous voices taking the three central roles: Vaness is in her element as Vitellia,
alternately amorous, vindictive, scheming and forgiving. Her account is boldly and confidently sung
throughout a longish evening. As Sextus, Ziegler is fully the equal of her/his loved one,
encompassing both her arias with richly contoured tone and courageously delivered coloratura, all
tending to convey Sesto's torture of the mind. The only drawback is a certain similarity in the two
singers' refulgent tone. At the centre of the emotional chasm stands Winbergh's commanding,
concerned Tito, perhaps the most heroically sung on any version yet sufficiently flexible for his
arias' runs (given a few unwanted aspirates). If the other singers aren't quite in the same category,
they are all well in the vocal and dramatic picture. It is good to hear the true sound of a theatre
acoustic on this live recording. Of course, on the other hand you have to cope with applause at the
end of many numbers and one intrusion, happily only in dry recitative, of an audible aeroplane. So,
a formidable addition to the work's discography, totally engrossing on its own terms and
recommendable as a contender to any newcomer to the piece on disc.

Così fan tutte.
Dame Elisabeth Schwarzkopf *sop* Fiordiligi; **Christa Ludwig** *mez* Dorabella;
Hanny Steffek *sop* Despina; **Alfredo Kraus** *ten* Ferrando; **Giuseppe Taddei** *bar* Guglielmo;
Walter Berry *bass* Don Alfonso;
Philharmonia Chorus and Orchestra / Karl Böhm.
EMI CMS7 69330-2 (three discs: 165 minutes: ADD). Notes, text and translation included.
Recorded 1962.   Ⓜ 🆁🆁

Così fan tutte is the most balanced and probing of all Mozart's operas, formally faultless, musically
inspired from start to finish, emotionally a matter of endless fascination and, in the second act,
profoundly moving. It has been very lucky on disc, and besides this delightful set there have been
several other memorable recordings. However, Böhm's cast could hardly be bettered, even in one's
dreams. The two sisters are gloriously sung – Schwarzkopf and Ludwig bring their immeasurable
talents as Lieder singers to this sparkling score and overlay them with a rare comic touch. Add to
that the stylish singing of Alfredo Kraus and Giuseppe Taddei and the central quartet is
unimpeachable. Walter Berry's Don Alfonso is characterful and Hanny Steffek is quite superb as
Despina. The pacing of this endlessly intriguing work is immaculate. The emotional control of the
characterization is masterly and Böhm's totally idiomatic response to the music is arguably without
peer. However, two modern recordings, using period instruments, do offer stimulating alternative
views.

Così fan tutte.
Amanda Roocroft *sop* Fiordiligi; **Rosa Mannion** *sop* Dorabella; **Eirian James** *mez* Despina;
Rainer Trost *ten* Ferrando; **Rodney Gilfry** *bar* Guglielmo; **Carlos Feller** *bass* Don Alfonso;
Monteverdi Choir; English Baroque Soloists / Sir John Eliot Gardiner.
Archiv Produktion 437 829-2AH3 (three discs: 134 minutes: DDD). Recorded live in 1992.   ⓕ 🅿

Gardiner's is a *Così* with a heart, and a heart in the right place. It comes from a stage performance
given in the Teatro Comunale at Ferrara – the city from which, of course, the sisters in the story
hail – in 1992. The vitality and the communicativeness of the recitative is one result of recording a
live performance; it is flexible, conversational and lively, as it ought to be, and the Italian
pronunciation is remarkably good considering there isn't a single Italian in the cast. Amanda
Roocroft makes a capable Fiordiligi, with a big, spacious 'Come scoglio', and shows real depth of
feeling in what is a very beautiful account of 'Per pietà'; her tone is bright and forward. Rosa
Mannion, as Dorabella, acts effectively with her voice in 'Smanie implacabili' and is full of life in
her Act 2 aria. The Guglielmo, Rodney Gilfry, is quite outstanding for his light, warm and flexible

baritone, gently seductive in Act 1, showing real brilliance and precision of articulation in 'Donne mie'. Eirian James's Despina is another delight, spirited, sexy and rich-toned, and full of charm without any of the silliness some Despinas show. Period instruments notwithstanding, this is a fairly traditional performance. Gardiner often uses quite generous rubato to highlight the shape of a phrase, and he is alert, as always, to how the orchestral writing can underline the sense.

Così fan tutte.
Soile Isokoski sop Fiordiligi; **Monica Groop** mez Dorabella; **Nancy Argenta** sop Despina; **Markus Schäfer** ten Ferrando; **Per Vollestad** bar Guglielmo; **Huub Claessens** bass Don Alfonso; **La Petite Bande and Chorus / Sigiswald Kuijken.**
Accent ACC9296/98 (three discs: 181 minutes: DDD). Notes, text and translation included. Recorded live in 1992.   Ⓔ Ⓟ

Kuijken's live recording is lighter in mood than Gardiner's. Nearly all the tempos are quicker and there is more sense of spontaneity. Mozart very rarely wrote dynamic or accentuation marks into his singers' parts; the singers were expected to learn their music from a repetiteur (or Mozart himself) and take their cues from what they heard in performance. Gardiner has his singers follow, meticulously, the orchestral dynamics; Kuijken leaves them, more or less, to sing with what they hear. This is a symptomatic difference: one performance is highly wrought, the other freer and more natural. The sisters in the Kuijken version are excellently done by Soile Isokoski, even in voice and with an attractive ring, and Monica Groop, again a pleasing and even voice intelligently and musically used. Their duets are both very appealing, with a happy sense in 'Prenderò quel brunettino' that they might be getting up to a little mischief. The Alfonso here, Huub Claessens, more baritone than bass, is particularly successful in the recitative, which here again is done with much care for its meaning. A pleasing and lively Così, it would be a good recording with which to get to know the opera, whereas the Gardiner is a connoisseur's performance, subtle and sophisticated, and communicating important things about the opera.

Don Giovanni.
Eberhard Waechter bar Don Giovanni; **Dame Joan Sutherland** sop Donna Anna; **Dame Elisabeth Schwarzkopf** sop Donna Elvira; **Graziella Sciutti** sop Zerlina; **Luigi Alva** ten Don Ottavio; **Giuseppe Taddei** bar Leporello; **Piero Cappuccilli** bar Masetto; **Gottlob Frick** bass Commendatore; **Philharmonia Chorus and Orchestra / Carlo Maria Giulini.**
EMI CDS5 56232-2 (three discs: 162 minutes: ADD). Notes, text and translation included. Recorded 1959.   Ⓔ Ⓗ ⓇⓇ

Although this set is over 40 years old, none of its successors is as skilled in capturing the piece's drama so unerringly. It has always been most recommendable and Giulini captures all the work's most dramatic characteristics, faithfully supported by the superb Philharmonia forces of that time. At this stage of Giulini's career, he was a direct, lithe conductor, alert to every turn in the story and he projects the nervous tension of the piece ideally while never forcing the pace, as can so easily happen. Then he had one of the most apt casts ever assembled for the piece. Waechter's Giovanni combines the demonic with the seductive in just the right proportions, Taddei is a high-profile Leporello, who relishes the text and sings with lots of 'face'. Elvira was always one of Schwarzkopf's most successful roles: here she delivers the role with tremendous intensity. Sutherland's Anna isn't quite so full of character but is magnificently sung. Alva is a graceful Ottavio. Sciutti's charming Zerlina, Cappuccilli's strong and Italianate Masetto and Frick's granite Commendatore are all very much in the picture. The recording still sounds well.

Don Giovanni.
Rodney Gilfry bar Don Giovanni; **Luba Orgonasova** sop Donna Anna; **Charlotte Margiono** sop Donna Elvira; **Eirian James** mez Zerlina; **Christoph Prégardien** ten Don Ottavio; **Ildebrando d'Arcangelo** bass Leporello; **Julian Clarkson** bass Masetto; **Andrea Silvestrelli** bass Commendatore; **Monteverdi Choir; English Baroque Soloists / Sir John Eliot Gardiner.**
Archiv Produktion 445 870-2AH3 (three discs: 176 minutes: DDD). Notes, text and translation included. Recorded 1994.   Ⓔ Ⓟ

John Eliot Gardiner's set has a great deal to commend it. The recitative is sung with exemplary care over pacing so that it sounds as it should, like heightened and vivid conversation, often to electrifying effect. As an adjunct, ensembles, particularly the Act 1 quartet, are also treated conversationally, as if one were overhearing four people giving their opinions on a situation in the street. The orchestra, perfectly balanced with the singers in a very immediate acoustic, supports them, as it were 'sings' with them. That contrasts with, and complements, Gardiner's expected ability to empathize with the demonic aspects of the score, as in Giovanni's drinking song and the final moments of Act 1, which fairly bristle with rhythmic energy without becoming rushed. The arrival of the statue at Giovanni's dinner-table is tremendous, the period trombones and timpani achieving an appropriately brusque, fearsome attack. Throughout this scene, Gardiner's penchant for sharp accents is wholly appropriate; elsewhere he is sometimes too insistent. As a whole, tempos not only seem right on their own account but also, all-importantly, carry conviction in relation to each other. Where so many conductors today rush 'Mi tradì', Gardiner prefers a more meditative approach, allowing his soft-grained Elvira to make the most of the aria's expressive possibilities.

As in his other Mozart opera recordings, Gardiner benefits from working with singers whom he knows well. Gilfry's Giovanni is lithe, ebullient, keen to exert his sexual prowess; an obvious charmer, at times surprisingly tender yet with the iron will only just below the surface. Suave and appealing, delivered in a real baritone timbre, his Giovanni is as accomplished as any on disc. Ildebrando d'Arcangelo was the discovery of these performances: this young bass is a lively foil to his master and on his own a real showman, as 'Madamina' indicates, a number all the better for a brisk speed. Orgonasova once more reveals herself a paragon as regards steady tone and deft technique – no need here to slow down for the coloratura at the end of 'Non mi dir' – and she brings to her recounting of the attempted seduction a real feeling of immediacy. In 'Or sai chi l'onore' she manages just the right kind of supple urgency. As Anna, Margiono sometimes sounds a shade stretched technically, but consoles us with the luminous, inward quality of her voice and her reading of the role, something innate that cannot be learnt. Nobody in their right senses is ever going to suggest that there is one, ideal version of *Don Giovanni*; the work has far too many facets for that, but for sheer theatrical *élan* complemented by the live recording, Gardiner is among the best, particularly when one also takes into account a recording that is wonderfully truthful and lifelike.

Don Giovanni.
Bo Skovhus *bar* Don Giovanni; **Christine Brewer** *sop* Donna Anna;
Dame Felicity Lott *sop* Donna Elvira; **Nuccia Focile** *sop* Zerlina; **Jerry Hadley** *ten* Don Ottavio;
Alessandro Corbelli *bar* Leporello; **Umberto Chiummo** *bass* Masetto, Commendatore;
Scottish Chamber Chorus and Orchestra / Sir Charles Mackerras.
Telarc CD80420 (three discs: 183 minutes: DDD). Notes, text and translation included.
Recorded 1995. Ⓕ 🇪

This set has no astonishing or brilliant individual interpretations here, but the whole is full of life and energy and freshness. The Scottish Chamber Orchestra is not a period-instrument group, but Mackerras, as he explains in his thoughtful note in the accompanying booklet (and as we hear), uses valveless horns and trumpets and something close to period timpani – hence the alarming sound of the opening chords. He also calls for sharper attack and quicker decay from the string players and a very forward wind balance. Tempos are often but by no means always on the fast side. But he also allows his singers plenty of time to phrase their music expressively, for example in the Giovanni-Zerlina scene in the first finale, in the trio at the beginning of Act 2 (some wonderfully sensual orchestral colours here), in Giovanni's serenade, in the great sextet (very powerfully done) and in the cemetery scene, which has a proper sense of the hieratic and yet a knife-edge tension too. In sum, it is a highly theatrical interpretation, one that constantly has you on the edge of your seat.

Umberto Chiummo makes a good, incisive Masetto and (perhaps with a little help) a truly formidable Commendatore in the final scenes. Nuccia Focile provides a beguiling Zerlina, with a sweet upper range and more than a touch of sensuousness and charm. Alessandro Corbelli, the Leporello, is a lively, lowish baritone who uses the sound of the words to advantage and can phrase with just the right hint of elegance. His voice is very close, arguably too close, in general sound to that of the Giovanni, Bo Skovhus, yet the master-servant relationship is conveyed convincingly. Skovhus's sharp vitality (listen to 'Metà di voi'), his virile Champagne Aria and his deeply sensual *portamentos* in the Serenade stress those aspects of Giovanni's character that underlie the plot. Jerry Hadley offers an Ottavio of some intensity, not the smoothest or most graceful, but stronger in expression than most and Dame Felicity is in full, creamy voice in a role she has often sung with distinction. On the question of versions, Mackerras gives the Prague original first (with 'Dalla sua pace' inserted in Act 1), so if you play the second disc through to the end, you should then skip the first ten tracks of the third disc to continue; or, if you want the Vienna version, you should skip the last six of the second and pick up at the beginning of the third, where you will hear the rare (and rather silly, though musically agreeable) Zerlina-Leporello duet and Elvira's scene (but not 'Il mio tesoro'). This is an excellent solution for listeners who can be bothered to press a couple of buttons. Lazy ones will hear some of the music twice over. All round, an immensely enjoyable version of *Don Giovanni*.

Die Entführung aus dem Serail[a]. Exsultate, jubilate, K165/K158a[b].
Maria Stader *sop* Constanze (Beate Guttmann); **Rita Streich** *sop* Blonde;
Ernst Haefliger *ten* Belmonte (Sebastian Fischer); **Martin Vantin** *ten* Pedrillo (Wolfgang Spier);
Josef Greindl *bass* Osmin; **Walter Franck** *spkr* Bassa Selim;
[a]**Berlin RIAS Chamber Choir and Orchestra,**
[b]**Berlin Radio Symphony Orchestra / Ferenc Fricsay.**
DG Dokumente [a]mono/[b]stereo 445 412-2GDO2 (two discs: 125 minutes: ADD). Notes, texts
and translations included. Recorded 1954. Ⓜ Ⓗ

Fricsay was an advocate of crisp, zestful, pared-down Mozart *avant la lettre*. This was the first in
his distinguished series of Mozart opera recordings, throughout which he used Berlin Radio forces
and singers familiar with his work. They prove formidable advocates. The orchestra, recorded in
resonant, honest mono, plays superbly throughout for their conductor. Stader was a particular
favourite with Fricsay. If not the most refulgent of sopranos, she had both the consistency of voice
and thoroughness of technique to cope with almost all the demands of Constanze's music.
Although one ideally wants a more dramatic singer in the part, her feeling for the shape of a
Mozart phrase is always admirable. She is suitably partnered by the fluent, lyrical Haefliger, who
also sang Belmonte at Glyndebourne in the 1950s. Although his voice hasn't quite the bite and
positive characteristics of other Belmontes, it is used with consummate style. Rita Streich is the
ideal Blonde, singing with pure tone and spirited attack: she has the individuality of voice, the hint
of vibrato most attractive, to please the most fastidious listener. Vantin is a more than adequate
Pedrillo, who sings his Serenade in an appropriate *mezza voce*. Greindl brings a fully fledged bass to
bear on Osmin's music and fills it with a nice combination of vicious sadism leavened by comedy.
Although his singing is occasionally marred by intrusive aspirates, he is among the most enjoyable
Osmins on disc. Happily he and Streich are allowed to speak their own dialogue so that their Act 2
encounter goes particularly well. As was a dubious custom with DG at the time, the other singers
are doubled by speaking voices that hardly match their own. Those who have come to appreciate
Fricsay's many attributes as a conductor will not be disappointed by this reissue, and will gain as a
generous bonus Stader's delightful account of *Exsultate, jubilate*. In absolute terms those without
Die Entführung in their collection should hear this one.

Die Entführung aus dem Serail.
Ingrid Habermann *sop* Constanze; **Donna Ellen** *sop* Blonde; **Piotr Bezcala** *ten* Belmonte;
Oliver Ringelhahn *ten* Pedrillo; **Franz Kalchmair** *bass* Osmin; **Harald Pfeiffer** *spkr* Bassa Selim;
Linz Landestheater Choir; Linz Bruckner Orchestra / Martin Sieghart.
Arte Nova Classics 74321 49701-2 (two discs: 115 minutes: DDD). Notes, text and translation
included. Recorded live in 1996-97. Ⓢ

This is a real bargain, just about as enjoyable as any performance given by more prominent artists
on better-known labels. Recorded live, it is not surprising to find such a natural sense of ensemble
among the principals or such a well-integrated account of the score from Sieghart, who is also
aware of the latest research on this score in terms of orchestration and small embellishments. His
reading is a shade strict and unsmiling, but it has the virtue of keeping the drama on the move in a
work that can outstay its welcome in more self-indulgent performances, and the playing of the small
band is exemplary. Dialogue is included but kept to the minimum essential to clarify the action.
Ingrid Habermann has the dramatic coloratura, the technique and all the notes to encompass the
fearful demands of Constanze's role and shows the dramatic resolution it requires. The Polish tenor
Piotr Bezcala has also been judiciously cast for his part: his voice is firm and sappy, and he discloses
an ability to make his four taxing arias sound relatively simple. One or two unwanted lachrymose
moments apart, he is a model of Mozartian style. The Canadian soprano, Donna Ellen, is a
mettlesome Blonde, happy in the dizzy heights reached in her first aria. Her Pedrillo is a lively
singer but one prone to questionable pitch, particularly in his Serenade. Best of all is the native
Austrian, Franz Kalchmair as an Osmin with a rotund, pleasing bass, as happy at the bottom as at
the top of his range and he is obviously a formidable actor. The Bassa Selim's role has been severely
curtailed; what remains of it is spoken with the appropriate blend of menace and authority by
Harald Pfeiffer. The recording is reasonably good.

Idomeneo, re di Creta.
Anthony Rolfe Johnson *ten* Idomeneo; **Anne Sofie von Otter** *mez* Idamante;
Sylvia McNair *sop* Ilia; **Hillevi Martinpelto** *sop* Elettra; **Nigel Robson** *ten* Arbace;
Glenn Winslade *ten* High Priest; **Cornelius Hauptmann** *bass* Oracle;
Monteverdi Choir; English Baroque Soloists / Sir John Eliot Gardiner.
Archiv Produktion 431 674-2AH3 (three discs: 211 minutes: DDD). Notes, text and translation
included. Recorded 1990. *Gramophone* Award Winner 1991. Ⓕ Ⓟ ⓇⓇ

This is unquestionably the most vital and authentic account of *Idomeneo* to date on disc. We have here what was given at the work's first performance in Munich plus, in appendices, what Mozart wanted, or was forced, to cut before that première and the alternative versions of certain passages, so that various combinations of the piece can be programmed by the listener. Gardiner's direct, dramatic conducting catches ideally the agony of Idomeneo's terrible predicament – forced to sacrifice his son because of an unwise row. This torment of the soul is also entirely conveyed by Anthony Rolfe Johnson in the title role to which Anne Sofie von Otter's moving Idamante is an apt foil. Sylvia McNair is a diaphanous, pure-voiced Ilia, Hillevi Martinpelto a properly fiery, sharp-edged Elettra. With dedicated support from his own choir and orchestra, who obviously benefited from a long period of preparation, Gardiner matches the stature of this noble *opera seria*. The recording catches the excitement which all who heard the live performances will recall.

Idomeneo, re di Creta.
Plácido Domingo *ten* Idomeneo; **Cecilia Bartoli** *mez* Idamante; **Heidi Grant Murphy** *sop* Ilia; **Carol Vaness** *sop* Elettra; **Thomas Hampson** *bar* Arbace; **Frank Lopardo** *ten* High Priest; **Bryn Terfel** *bass-bar* Oracle;
Chorus and Orchestra of the Metropolitan Opera, New York / James Levine.
DG 447 737-2GH3 (three discs: 176 minutes: DDD). Notes, text and translation included.
Recorded in 1994. Ⓕ **E**

After Gardiner's lithe, slimline *Idomeneo*, Levine brings us back to a 'traditional' reading, with a big orchestra and a cast starry enough to make the Golden Horseshoe thoroughly happy. There can be little question that this must be the most recommendable recording for those not wanting a period-instrument 'authentic' version. First, however, a word of explanation is needed, in view of the great divergences among current recordings of the opera, to clarify what this consists of. It is more or less the Munich first performance version: we get both arias for Arbace (particularly welcome in view of Thomas Hampson's fine singing), Idamante's acceptance of death 'No, la morte' and Elettra's final venomous 'D'Oreste, d'Aiace', but not Idomeneo's 'Torna la pace' and only the shorter version of his 'Fuor del mar' (with a changed ending). Recitatives are given almost complete, and though words are most expressively coloured throughout, this results in many recitatives almost turning into *ariosos*. Appoggiaturas are applied, if not very consistently, but only one artist, Heidi Grant Murphy, ventures to ornament an aria, in the reprise section of 'Se il padre perdei'. Murphy's Ilia is a gentle, youthful, sweet-voiced *ingénue*; her *fioriture* in 'Zeffiretti' are sung with delicious purity and clarity. Bartoli as Idamante is utterly convincing and deeply involved in every nuance of the character's emotions, and her 'No, la morte' is memorable. Carol Vaness may be forgiven for a rather screamy 'D'Oreste, d'Aiace' but her earlier 'Tutto nel cor' shows the right bitterness and fury, and she persuasively softens her tone when Elettra feels that fate seems to be favouring her. As Idomeneo, Plácido Domingo gives a reading of the nobility and intelligence we might expect from him, one which makes him an outstanding interpreter of the role. Aided by a well-judged production that successfully conveys the various perspectives in the opera, Levine presides over a coherently planned performance satisfying both from the dramatic and the lyrical viewpoints.

Mitridate, re di Ponto.
Giuseppe Sabbatini *ten* Mitridate; **Natalie Dessay** *sop* Aspasia; **Cecilia Bartoli** *mez* Sifare; **Brian Asawa** *counterten* Farnace; **Sandrine Piau** *sop* Ismene; **Juan Diego Flórez** *ten* Marzio; **Hélène Le Corre** *sop* Arbate;
Les Talens Lyriques / Christophe Rousset.
Decca Ⓕ 460 772-2DHO3 (three discs: 179 minutes: DDD). Notes, text and translation included.
Recorded 1998. Ⓕ **P**

Mozart was not quite 15 when he composed *Mitridate*, as the first carnival opera for the Milan opera house, the one that was shortly to become La Scala. Operas of that period were, of course, composed specifically for the cast that created them: Mozart more than once referred to fitting an aria to the voice as a tailor fitted a suit to the figure. And some of the original cast of *Mitridate* thought their arias ill-fitting: Mozart was required to rewrite several of them (one of them five times over, it seems, before the tenor was satisfied – though the sublime result justifies it). Many of the arias are expansive pieces, with a semi-*da capo*, and make heavy demands on the singers' agility and compass. This set has a starry cast. The *primo uomo* role, Sifare, was written for an unusually high-lying castrato voice. Here it is sung, with great character, by Cecilia Bartoli. Perhaps the finest of her four arias is the slow one in Act 2 with horn obbligato, 'Lungi da te, mio bene', which is sung here with real depth of feeling, shapeliness of line and richness of tone. But her caressing of the phrases in the slow part of her second Act 1 aria, and her exact and clearly articulated semiquaver *fioriture* in the fast part, are a delight too, as they are in her opening number, a virtuoso piece which she dispatches imperiously. The only reservation is that the part does lie very high for her: the top B flats sound strained, and indeed the quality from G upwards is slightly impaired. Still, it is a marvellous performance and she brings to the music a real sense of drama and care for the words and their meaning, in the recitative as well as the arias. There is nothing but praise, too, for Natalie Dessay in the prima donna role of Aspasia, beloved of Sifare, lusted after by his brother Farnace, betrothed to their father Mitridate (that more or less summarizes the basis of the plot). Full, creamy tone, brilliantly thrown-off rapid music, a firmly sustained line (try 'Pallid'ombre', in Act 3, taken very slowly), a keen sense of drama, high notes struck loud and clear and bang in the middle: one could ask for nothing more. Her duet with Bartoli, the single concerted number, at the end of Act 2, is a joy: they seem to have all the time in the world for sensitive phrasing and refined detail.

Then Brian Asawa, in the castrato role of Farnace, offers some very fine countertenor singing, with a full, almost throaty tone, not at all in the usual countertenor manner, and extraordinarily even across a wide range. In his final aria (where Farnace repents his misdeeds) there is a powerfully sustained line in what is the longest and possibly the most deeply felt piece in the opera. Sandrine Piau sings tenderly and gracefully in Ismene's rather lighter role. Giuseppe Sabbatini copes well in the role of Mitridate but does not always manage so happily either in the lyrical music or the expressions of anger (of which there are several). He is inclined to sing too loudly or too softly: there is no comfortable mean. His first aria, 'Se di lauri', the most beautiful piece in the score (this is the one at which Mozart had five shots), is too forceful and grandiose where softness and warmth are wanted, and the *pianissimo* recapitulation is not persuasive. Still, this is accurate, technically accomplished and perfectly tuned singing. In the angry arias he is apt to rant; the effect is fiery enough but the sound is not very musical. In the two small roles, Hélène Le Corre sings very pleasantly in Arbate's aria and Juan Diego Flórez shows a substantial, slightly nasal voice in Marzio's. Christophe Rousset directs his period instrument band with vigour and conviction.

Le nozze di Figaro.
Sesto Bruscantini bar Figaro; **Graziella Sciutti** sop Susanna; **Franco Calabrese** bass Count Almaviva; **Sena Jurinac** sop Countess Almaviva; **Risë Stevens** mez Cherubino; **Monica Sinclair** contr Marcellina; **Ian Wallace** bass Bartolo; **Hugues Cuénod** ten Don Basilio; **Daniel McCoshan** ten Don Curzio; **Gwyn Griffiths** bar Antonio; **Jeanette Sinclair** sop Barbarina; **Glyndebourne Festival Chorus and Orchestra / Vittorio Gui.**
Classics for Pleasure CD-CFPD4724 (two discs: 158 minutes: ADD). Recorded 1955. Ⓑ Ⓗ ℞℞

This comes from what might be termed the second generation of Glyndebourne performances, those dominated by Vittorio Gui, whose approach to Mozart was more volatile, more Italianate, possibly a little less warm than that of his equally individual predecessor, Fritz Busch. This is immediately evident in the Overture, which tells us very definitely that we are to hear a tale of intrigue and emotional turmoil, da Ponte as prominent as Mozart. To achieve his purpose, Gui imported a cast that included three Italians. Bruscantini is a mercurial, light-voiced, mobile Figaro, Calabrese a dark-browed Almaviva, very much a dominant personality in his household (he is also, for the most part, strong and vibrant in tone and excellent in Mozartian diction). Graziella Sciutti, who was to be Glyndebourne's Susanna only in 1958, was brought in for the recording, and a lively, if a little thin-voiced Susanna she proves. Wonderful to hear all three pronouncing their own tongue so pointedly. For all that, the most compelling reason for obtaining this set is the Countess of the irreplaceable Sena Jurinac, a noble, aristocratic assumption sung in the warmest, most palpitating tones – a lovable singer at the height of her powers. A drawback is Risë Stevens's tired-sounding and unidiomatic Cherubino, but even she fits well enough into the ensemble. Among the casting of smaller roles, Hugues Cuénod's idiosyncratic, utterly delightful Basilio (he has his Fourth Act aria) and Ian Wallace's splendid Bartolo are definite assets. So is Raymond Leppard's harpsichord support in the recitatives.

This was one of EMI's earliest stereo efforts, and the placings are well managed, with the sense of intimacy you get in the theatre at Glyndebourne and which so often eludes modern recordings but it has to be said that the orchestral sound now seems a little confined and lacking in bloom. But then – regardless of the countless excellent modern recordings available – listen again to Jurinac's touching 'Dove sono' (sustained at a slow speed) and Gui's very theatrical way with the score and you will know that you will always need to have this set. Gui's matching of tempos is laudable and he draws playing from the RPO, then doubling as the Glyndebourne orchestra, that is at once disciplined and full of character. And it is an exceptional bargain. For about £10·00 you get some 158 minutes of music. So, the impecunious newcomer should hurry to catch this set.

Le nozze di Figaro.
Bryn Terfel bass-bar Figaro; **Alison Hagley** sop Susanna; **Rodney Gilfry** bar Count Almaviva; **Hillevi Martinpelto** sop Countess Almaviva; **Pamela Helen Stephen** mez Cherubino; **Susan McCulloch** sop Marcellina; **Carlos Feller** bass Bartolo; **Francis Egerton** ten Don Basilio,

Don Curzio; **Julian Clarkson** bass Antonio; **Constanze Backes** sop Barbarina;
Monteverdi Choir; English Baroque Soloists / Sir John Eliot Gardiner.
Archiv Produktion 439 871-2AH3 (three discs: 179 minutes: DDD). Notes, text and translation
included. Recorded live in 1993. Ⓕ Ⓟ

The catalogue of *Figaro* recordings is a long one, and the cast lists are full of famous names. In this
version only one principal had more than a half-dozen recordings behind him, and some had none
at all. It is a commentary on the astuteness of the casting and on the capacity of a strong conductor
to make the whole so much more than the sum of its parts that this version can stand comparison
with any, not only for its grasp of the drama but also for the quality of its singing. It is, of course, a
period-instrument recording, more evidently so than many under Gardiner. The string tone is pared
down and makes quite modest use of vibrato, the woodwind is soft-toned (but happily prominent).
The voices are generally lighter and fresher-sounding than those on most recordings of the opera
and the balance permits more than usual to be heard of Mozart's instrumental commentary on the
action and the characters. The recitative is done with quite exceptional life and feeling for its
meaning and dramatic import, with a real sense, during much of it, of lively and urgent
conversation, especially in the first half of the work. Bryn Terfel and Alison Hagley make an
outstanding Figaro and Susanna. Terfel is quite a deep bass-baritone with enough darkness in his
voice to sound pretty menacing in 'Se vuol ballare' as well as bitter in 'Aprite un po' quegli occhi'; it
is an alert, mettlesome performance – and he also brings off a superlative 'Non più andrai', done
with tremendous spirit to its rhythms and richly and pointedly coloured. Hagley offers a reading of
spirit and allure. The interplay between her and the woodwind in 'Venite inginocchiatevi' is a
delight, and her cool but heartfelt 'Deh vieni' is very beautiful. Once or twice her intonation seems
marginally under stress but that is the price one pays for singing with so little vibrato, and it's worth
it. Hillevi Martinpelto's unaffected, youthful-sounding Countess is enjoyable; both arias are quite
lightly done, with a very lovely, warm, natural sound in 'Dove sono' especially. Some may prefer a
more polished, sophisticated reading, of the traditional kind, but this is closer to what Mozart
would have wanted and expected.

Rodney Gilfry provides a Count with plenty of fire and authority, firmly focused in tone; the
outburst at the *Allegro assai* in 'Vedrò mentr'io sospiro' is formidable. Pamela Helen Stephen's
Cherubino sounds charmingly youthful and impetuous; 'Voi che sapete' is taken a good deal
quicker than usual, and with a touch of comedy, and benefits from it. There is no want of dramatic
life in Gardiner's direction. His tempos are marginally quicker than most, and the orchestra often
speaks eloquently of the drama. Gardiner adopts the Moberly/Raeburn order of events in Act 3.
This involves placing 'Dove sono' before, instead of after, the sextet and in the last Act he places
Susanna's aria before, instead of after, Figaro's.

Le nozze di Figaro.
Cesare Siepi bass Figaro; **Hilde Gueden** sop Susanna; **Alfred Poell** bar Count Almaviva;
Lisa della Casa sop Countess Almaviva; **Suzanne Danco** sop Cherubino;
Hilde Rössl-Majdan contr Marcellina; **Fernando Corena** bass Bartolo;
Murray Dickie ten Don Basilio; **Hugo Meyer-Welfing** ten Don Curzio;
Harald Pröglhöf bass Antonio; **Anny Felbermayer** sop Barbarina;
Vienna State Opera Chorus; Vienna Philharmonic Orchestra / Erich Kleiber.
Decca Grand Opera Series 417 315-2DM3 (three discs: 172 minutes: ADD). Recorded 1955. Ⓜ Ⓗ

Erich Kleiber's *Figaro* is a classic of the classics of the gramophone: beautifully played by the
Vienna Philharmonic, conducted with poise and vitality and a real sense of the drama unfolding
through the music. It's very much a Viennese performance, not perhaps as graceful or as
effervescent as some but warm, sensuous and alive to the interplay of character. At the centre is
Hilde Gueden, whose Susanna has echoes of Viennese operetta singing although she remains a true
Mozartian stylist – her 'Deh vieni' is impeccably graceful and perfectly timed. Lisa della Casa's
Countess may not be one of the most dramatic but the voice is full yet focused, and 'Dove sono' is
a delight in particular. Suzanne Danco's Cherubino is not exactly impassioned, and is really as
much girlish as boyish, but it is still neat and musical singing. The balance among the men is
affected by the casting of Figaro with a weightier singer than the Count. But Alfred Poell's Count
makes up in natural authority and aristocratic manner what he lacks in sheer power, and he shows
himself capable, too, of truly sensual singing in the Act 3 duet with Susanna.

There are excellent performances, too, from Corena's verbally athletic Bartolo and Dickie's alert,
ironic Basilio. However, the true star is Erich Kleiber. The beginning of the opera sets your
spine a-tingling with theatrical expectation. Act 1 goes at pretty smart tempos, but all through
he insists on full musical value. There is no rushing in the confrontations at the end of Act 2 – all
is measured and properly argued through. And everything is truly sung: the singers are never
allowed, even had they wanted to, to skimp on the music to convey the drama, and they have

rather to use the music to convey it. With Kleiber and the VPO behind them, they do so utterly convincingly. The sound is satisfactory, for a set of this vintage – no lover of this opera should be without it.

Zaïde.
Lynne Dawson sop Zaïde; **Hans-Peter Blochwitz** ten Gomatz; **Olaf Bär** bar Allazim;
Herbert Lippert ten Sultan Soliman; **Christopher Purves** bass Osmin;
Academy of Ancient Music / Paul Goodwin.
Harmonia Mundi HMU90 7205 (75 minutes: DDD). Notes, text and translation included.
Recorded 1997. Ⓕ Ⓟ

Mozart began composing the work known as *Zaïde* in 1779-80, but left it unfinished, ostensibly because no performance was in prospect, but perhaps also because, very soon after he broke off, he came to see that this rather static kind of musical drama was not the sort of piece he wanted to write. Moreover, the character relationships are difficult to deal with: the libretto and the music (as far as it goes) imply a powerful attraction at the beginning of the opera between Zaïde and Gomatz, but ultimately, in the final scene, which Mozart never reached, they turn out to be brother and sister: very touching, and well attuned to the sensibilities of the time, but cramping to the composer. Nevertheless, the music of *Zaïde* is full of fine things, often foreshadowing not only the similar *Entführung* but also *Idomeneo*. This recording captures its beauties and its depth of feeling beautifully. This is partly because of the sympathetic conducting of Paul Goodwin, who paces it with excellent judgement, bringing to it just the right degree of flexibility, and achieves orchestral textures that are both clear and warm – much more so than usual from period-instrument groups. The melodramas, tellingly shaped, perfectly catch the tone of passion. The AAM plays at its best for him (notably, and understandably, the principal oboist).

It is hard to imagine a better cast. Lynne Dawson sings the title-role with a frail beauty that is very appealing. Hans-Peter Blochwitz's shapely lines and full, eloquent tone make Gomatz's arias a delight, too; and Herbert Lippert, the second tenor, as the Sultan (in love, or lust, with Zaïde), is almost his match in evenness and lyrical quality. It is also a luxury to have Olaf Bär as Allazim: the music is sung with a refinement of tone and ease of articulation that you don't imagine it has often had before. Christopher Purves sings Osmin cleanly without perhaps quite fully realizing the comedy. In sum, this far excels any previous recording.

Die Zauberflöte.
Ruth Ziesak sop Pamina; **Sumi Jo** sop Queen of Night; **Uwe Heilmann** ten Tamino;
Michael Kraus bar Papageno; **Kurt Moll** bass Sarastro; **Andreas Schmidt** bar Speaker;
Heinz Zednik ten Monostatos; **Lotte Leitner** sop Papagena; **Adrianne Pieczonka** sop
Annette Kuettenbaum, Jard van Nes mezzos First, Second and Third Ladies;
Max Emanuel Cencic, Michael Rausch, Markus Leitner trebs First, Second and Third Boys;
Wolfgang Schmidt ten **Hans Franzen** bass Two Armed Men; **Clemens Bieber** ten
Hans Joachim Porcher bar Two Priests;
Vienna Boys' Choir; Vienna State Opera Concert Choir;
Vienna Philharmonic Orchestra / Sir Georg Solti.
Decca 433 210-2DH2 (two discs: 152 minutes: DDD). Notes, text and translation included.
Recorded 1990. Ⓕ ℞℞

Sir Georg Solti's relationship with *Die Zauberflöte* is long and illustrious. When, in 1937, he was musical assistant to Toscanini in Salzburg, it was Solti's fingers which conjured the sound from Papageno's glockenspiel. In Salzburg in 1990, Solti turned from rostrum to celesta and duetted with Papageno once again. This recording is a fitting celebration of Solti's own long Mozartian journey. Solti's 1969 recording, also for Decca and available as a three-disc reissue, was praised for its feeling for excitement, where a very slight excess of solemnity or relaxation can be deadly. It is exactly that quality which epitomizes this newer recording: if anything, tempos are even more finely judged, more intuitively moulded to the shape of the score's harmonic dramas and emotional breathing. Solti's tempos and pacing are in fact the inspiration of this *Flute*. Marginally faster than in 1969, the Overture now springs rather than stings on its way. Sarastro's crew are a merry, totally unpompous lot: there is no more joyful entry than for this Sarastro, truly *mit Freuden* in the finale of Act 1. Solti also pays tribute to the *Flute* as fairy-tale. Largely by pacing, he never allows Schikaneder's little motto couplets (Ladies, Boys, Speaker) to become ponderous moralistic asides: each one bounces into its natural place in the dramatic scheme of things. Solti gives time and space enough, though, for melodically or harmonically self-isolating lines such as Tamino's response to the Speaker, 'Der Lieb' und Tugend Eigentum'; for the vibrancy of the inner string parts for Isis and Osiris and the Armed Men; to Pamina's cry of 'Die Wahrheit!'. This cry is one of the most moving on disc.

Ruth Ziesak's fresh, highly intelligent performance here restores to Pamina that fusion of innocence and strength, vulnerability and courage which the character and her music demand. With Solti's tempo, and sprung orchestral chords pulsing like a heartbeat, her first pure phrase of 'Bei Männern' catches the breath with delight; her genuflecting cry of pain to Sarastro pierces the heart; her 'Ach, ich fühl's' is shaped by deep desperation, not mere melancholy. The casting of Tamino epitomizes a major difference between the two Solti versions. Uwe Heilmann, raw, penetrating and a little Schreier-like of timbre, is a livelier dramatic presence than Stuart Burrows (1969), if not as aristocratic and well-groomed a voice. The 1969 version is singerly: this newer recording primarily dramatic.

By the same token, Hermann Prey's Papageno (1969) is easier to listen to than that of Michael Kraus, who tends to bounce clean off the end of a phrase, and whose chattering quality can be sometimes less purely musical but often more plausible than Prey. This Queen of Night is not merely an Olympia with a crown. Sumi Jo was truly in her ascendant here. A truly rhythmic brightness and glow of melodic phrasing suffuses her singing, and this is considerable relief from the muscular gymnastics of other interpreters on record. Her lunar beauty seems to take its strength, as it surely must, from Sarastro himself. Kurt Moll, appropriately, sings on an entirely other vocal plane: the depth of his voice is fully equal to the breadth of his music. In his musical temple there are indeed many mansions. His slaves and his Monostatos (Heinz Zednik) are ably aided and abetted by the natural, well-paced dialogue, often whispering and wondering, sometimes crackling with tension; never over-directed. Effects, too, both meteorological and avian, surpass those on previous recordings. To sum up, then, Solti's earlier recording bears up well musically, but is eclipsed dramatically by the live presence and meticulous recording balance of this newer version.

Die Zauberflöte.
Rosa Mannion sop Pamina; **Natalie Dessay** sop Queen of Night;
Hans-Peter Blochwitz ten Tamino; **Anton Scharinger** bass Papageno;
Reinhard Hagen bass Sarastro; **Willard White** bass Speaker; **Steven Cole** ten Monostatos;
Linda Kitchen sop Papagena; **Anna Maria Panzarella** sop **Doris Lamprecht** mez
Delphine Haidan contr First, Second and Third Ladies;
Damien Colin, Patrick Olivier Croset, Stéphane Dutournier trebs First, Second and Third Boys;
Christopher Josey ten First Armed Man, First Priest;
Laurent Naouri bass Second Armed Man, Second Priest;
Les Arts Florissants / William Christie.
Erato 0630-12705-2 (two discs: 150 minutes: DDD). Notes, text and translation included.
Recorded 1995.   ⓕⓟ

With a background primarily in the French baroque, William Christie comes to *Die Zauberflöte* from an angle quite unlike anyone else's; yet this is as idiomatic and as deeply Mozartian a reading of the work as any. Interviewed in the booklet-note, Christie says wise things about the work and ways of performing it, and in particular remarks on the unforced singing that is one of his objectives, much more manageable with the gentler sound of period instruments. All of this is borne out by the performance itself, which falls more sweetly and lovingly on the ear than any other. All this gives Christie opportunities to shape the work subtly and sensitively, with finer levels of nuance than are available to most modern performances. Mozartians will relish it, and it will prompt fresh thought about the work.

His tempos, for example, often set tradition aside. Many are quickish, but not all: 'Der Hölle Rache' is distinctly slower than usual, deliberate rather than fiery; so in particular is the union of Pamina and Tamino in the second finale, which gives it a *gravitas* that establishes it as the true emotional climax of the work. Yet overall the performance is quick and light-textured – and often quite dramatic. These light and soft textures and graceful phrasing are what above all characterize this recording. Some may find Christie less responsive than many more traditional interpreters to the music's quicksilver changes in mood, yet this is a part of his essentially broad and gentle view of *Die Zauberflöte*. His cast has few famous names. There is of course Hans-Peter Blochwitz, probably the finest Tamino around these days. As Pamina, Rosa Mannion has much charm and a hint of girlish vivacity but blossoms into maturity and indeed passion in 'Ach, ich fühl's' – the final phrases, as the wind instruments fall away and leave her alone and desolate, are very moving. Natalie Dessay's Queen of Night is forthright, clean and well tuned, with ample weight and tonal glitter. The orchestral playing from Les Arts Florissants is as polished as always, and the translucent sound is a joy on the ear. Christie offers a very satisfying, acutely musical view of the work.

Die Zauberflöte.
Tiana Lemnitz sop Pamina; **Erna Berger** sop Queen of Night; **Helge Roswaenge** ten Tamino;
Gerhard Hüsch bar Papageno; **Wilhelm Strienz** bass Sarasto; **Walter Grossmann** bass

Speaker, Second Armed Man; **Heinrich Tessmer** *ten* Monostatos, First Armed Man;
Irma Beilke *sop* Papagena, First Boy; **Hilde Scheppan** *sop* First Lady;
Elfriede Marherr-Wagner *sop* Second Lady; **Rut Berglund** *contr* Third Lady, Third Boy;
Carla Spletter *sop* Second Boy; **Ernest Fabbry** *ten* Priest;
Favres Solisten Vereinigung; Berlin Philharmonic Orchestra / Sir Thomas Beecham.
EMI Références mono CHS7 61034-2 (two discs: 130 minutes: ADD). Notes, texts and translation
included. Also available on Pearl mono GEMMCDS9371. Recorded 1937-38.   Ⓜ Ⓗ

Beecham's feeling for both the grandeur and the delicacy, and the evident command he has of his
forces, ensure attentiveness and delight at every turn. Every appearance of Gerhard Hüsch is a joy:
we have had good Papagenos since this, the first of all complete recordings of *Die Zauberflöte*, but
he surely remains the best. Tiana Lemnitz sings with such surpassing beauty for so much of the
time that the occasional scoop is forgiven. Erna Berger's Queen of Night is firm and technically
accomplished, and there are splendid performances by the Three Ladies. The Tamino is not well
cast: Roswaenge lacks finesse though he is a positive enough character. Wilhelm Strienz is literally
out of his depth, producing nasty, unresonant low notes and generally sounding more like a Hans
Sachs than a Sarastro. Walter Grossmann is a woolly Speaker, and Heinrich Tessmer, perfect as
Monostatos, is no use as First Armed Man. The absence of dialogue, as the anonymous writer of
EMI's admirable sleeve-note says, 'turns music-drama into a sort of song-cycle'. Altogether a set to
pick one's way through, essential though it is to have it at hand. And this also applies to the Pearl,
warily recommending it over its rival with the caution that there is surface-sound (however reduced)
and, alas, no text and translation. The Pearl transfer provides the greater enjoyment, although it is
true that EMI has all but eliminated the surface-sound; true also that the EMI transfer has greater
sharpness of sibilants and 't's with all that that may imply about frequency range.

Santiago de Murcia   Spanish 17th-18th century

Fandango. Zarambegues o Muecas. La Jotta. Gaitas. Cumbees. Jácaras por la E. Marizápalos.
Gallardas. Tarantelas. Preludio Grabe. La Cadena. Una Giga de Corelli. Passacalles por la E.
Marionas por la B. Payssanos. Folías Ytalianas. Las Penas. Allegros I and II. Otros canarios.
Canarios.
Paul O'Dette, Pat O'Brien, Stephen Player *baroque gtrs*
Andrew Lawrence-King *hp/psaltery* **Pedro Estevan** *perc*
Harmonia Mundi HMU90 7212 (78 minutes: DDD). Recorded 1997.   Ⓕ

This disc is titled '¡Jácaras!'. 'A group of scamps and high-spirited people who walk around at night
making a racket and singing in the streets.' No, not English holiday-makers, but a Spanish
dictionary's description of the so-called *jaques*, whose lifestyle is depicted in the style of music
known as the *jácaras*. The music on this disc, for all its own high spirits, is not drawn directly from
the repertoire of these 'underworld ruffians' (as *Grove* calls them), but instead from two manuscript
collections of guitar music by Santiago de Murcia, guitarist to a succession of royals and aristocrats
in Spain, Naples and Mexico during the first half of the eighteenth century. As one might expect
then, there is music here of a courtly and cultured sort (including adaptations of violin music by
Corelli, all of which Paul O'Dette plays with customary grace and languid lyrical ease). But what
listeners will undoubtedly find more striking are the boisterous and highly rhythmic dances,
characterized by the sort of hard-driven guitar-strumming which those English holiday-makers may
well be more used to hearing. A glance at the titles above should suffice to give an impression of
their exotic range, and played here by assorted ensembles of guitars, harp and percussion, they are
utterly irresistible in their infectious rhythms and often surprisingly modern-sounding harmonies
and textures. Clearly Murcia's employers enjoyed letting their hair down from time to time; indeed,
anyone who could remain still while listening to this music must have feet of stone.

Modest Mussorgsky   Russian 1839-1881

Pictures at an Exhibition (orch. Ravel). A Night on the Bare Mountain (arr. Rimsky-Korsakov).

Mussorgsky Pictures at an Exhibition.
Stravinsky The Rite of Spring.
Philadelphia Orchestra / Riccardo Muti.
EMI Studio Plus CDM7 64516-2 (64 minutes: ADD). Recorded 1978.   Ⓜ ℝℝ

Pictures at an Exhibition was the first commercial recording to do full justice to the sheer range and
depth of sonority that the remarkable Philadelphia Orchestra could command. The recording venue

was the Metropolitan Church of Philadelphia and the generous acoustic of the hall enabled this great orchestra to be heard to best advantage. And what orchestral playing it offers us. The lower strings in 'Samuel Goldenberg and Schmuyle' have an extraordinary richness, body and presence, and 'Baba Yaga' has an unsurpassed virtuosity and attack. The glorious body of tone, the richly glowing colours, the sheer homogeneity of the strings and perfection of the ensemble is a consistent source of pleasure. Muti's reading is second to none and the orchestral playing is altogether breathtaking. There are many other fine recordings of this work but they do not possess quite that homogeneity of tone and the extraordinary sheen that is and has been the hallmark of the Philadelphians for many decades. The recording is amazingly lifelike and truthful.

Muti directs a performance of *The Rite of Spring* which is aggressively brutal but yet presents its violence not in coldly clinical terms but with red-blooded conviction. He favours a tempo a degree faster than usual, but no faster than the composer himself recommends and certainly not breathlessly fast. The great compulsion of the whole performance lies in his ability to draw playing from his orchestra which is not just precise and brilliant, but passionately committed. Wildness and barbarity are so clearly part of the mixture to a degree not matched by most other recordings, so it is not surprising that Muti's interpretation has continued to remain among the front-runners. The recording is gloriously full and dramatic with wide dynamic range and fine separation. The brass and percussion are caught with special vividness helped by one of the most impressive bass responses heard in this work.

Mussorgsky Pictures at an Exhibition. A Night on the Bare Mountain.
Ravel Valses nobles et sentimentales.
New York Philharmonic Orchestra / Giuseppe Sinopoli.
DG 429 785-2GH (67 minutes: DDD). Recorded 1989.   Ⓕ

Sinopoli's recording of *Pictures at an Exhibition* has great panache and is full of subtle detail and sharply characterized performances. Of course none of this would be possible without the marvellous virtuosity of the NYPO, whose brass section plays with a wonderful larger-than-life sonority and whose woodwind section produces playing of considerable delicacy and finesse, as for example in 'Tuileries' and the 'Ballet of the Unhatched Chicks'. Sinopoli clearly revels in the drama of this work and this is nowhere more noticeable than in his sinister readings of 'Catacombs' and 'Baba-Yaga'. *A Night on the Bare Mountain* is no less impressive, where again the flair and virtuosity of the orchestra have an almost overwhelming impact. Less successful are Ravel's *Valses nobles et sentimentales* which are perhaps too idiosyncratic for an individual recommendation despite some superb performances and moments of great beauty. The sound is very well balanced and engineered.

Mussorgsky Pictures at an Exhibition.
Respighi The Pines of Rome. The Fountains of Rome.
Chicago Symphony Orchestra / Fritz Reiner.
RCA Victor Gold Seal 09026 61401-2 (70 minutes: ADD). Recorded 1957-59.   Ⓜ Ⓗ

This 1957 *Pictures at an Exhibition* was, alongside Karajan's famous Philharmonia version for EMI (currently out of the catalogue), one of the first two outstanding stereo recordings of this piece. Both records showed the startling instrumental virtuosity which each great orchestra could command. Reiner's performance is full of character, and marvellously played, especially by the famous Chicago brass, although the full string sonority is equally impressive (in 'Goldenberg and Schmuyle', for instance), and besides the spectacle, there are tender moments like the hauntingly nostalgic picture of 'The old castle'. The climax of the closing 'Great Gate of Kiev' is superbly built to produce a very grand final statement, but note also the venom of the attack in the fierce scalic flourish at 1'28" (track 15). The extraordinary thing about this reissue is that the channels are reversed. It is almost unbelievable that this was not noticed. With excellent notes, however, this is an indispensable reissue. (This recording is, incidentally, also included in a compilation disc which is reviewed in the Collections section.)

Reiner's legendary performances of Respighi's *Pines* and *Fountains of Rome* were recorded in Orchestra Hall, Chicago, in 1959. This recording still has the power to astonish, both by the sheer quality of the orchestral playing and the richly translucent sound and incredibly subtle detail. The ecstatic moment when the strings swell out in 'The Pine of the Janiculum' (track 18 – first at 1'53", then even more rapturously at 3'37"), is unforgettable and the portrait of the Villa Medici fountain at sunset has a similar element of rapture, with the bell gently tolling at the end. The wonderful internal balances in the music's quieter passages are a credit to conductor and engineers alike, and of course also to the unique hall acoustics. The playing of the Chicago orchestra is quite glorious and the many touches from the percussion department add to the uniquely atmospheric quality of these remarkable recordings. The big splashes of sound, like the turning on of the Triton Fountain, or great Neptune processional, associated with the Trevi at midday, so spacious in Reiner's hands, are splendidly brought off. But it is the gentle moments that one remembers most, utterly alluring in their soft focus, almost decadent in their glowing seduction of colour.

A Night on the Bare Mountain. Pictures at an Exhibition. Boris Godunov – Symphonic synthesis. Khovanshchina – Act 4 Entr'acte (all arr. Stokowski).
BBC Philharmonic Orchestra / Matthias Bamert.
Chandos CHAN9445 (69 minutes: DDD). Recorded 1995.　　　　　　　　　　　　　　Ⓕ

Oliver Daniel (Stokowski's biographer) wrote extensively about doubts expressed by various musicians that Stokowski's orchestral transcriptions were entirely his own work, explaining that Lucien Cailliet (a clarinet player in the Philadelphia Orchestra) did a good deal of the physical work of score-writing. Yet Cailliet himself stated that the conductor and he discussed each piece in detail first, and it is known that Stokowski was always amending the instrumentation in the course of performances. In any case, Cailliet's association with the conductor ended in 1938 and while he might have contributed to the skilfully tailored 24-minute *Boris Godunov* synthesis, the *Pictures at an Exhibition* was all Stokowski's own and *Night on Bald Mountain* (the correct title, and nearer the original Russian meaning) was scored for Disney in 1940. Anyone who has seen *Fantasia* finds the imagery in this last piece unforgettable and the powerfully plangent orchestration (especially the use of percussive effects) is in many respects nearer to Mussorgsky's *St John's Night on the Bare Mountain* than the Rimsky version. It sounds really superb here, as indeed does the *Pictures*. The sombre power of the operatic synthesis, with its Kremlin bells and chanting monks and the haunted portrait of Boris himself, emerges with distinction. The Entr'acte from *Khovanshchina* is even finer, one of Stokowski's most effective transcriptions, rich in sonority and played very movingly under Matthias Bamert.

The vividness of Stokowski's *Pictures* is immensely likeable too, particularly the way in which the orchestration is varied – the unison horns sing out splendidly near the climax of 'Bydlo', while to feature a cor anglais for the main theme in 'The old castle' is quite as telling as Ravel's saxophone, perhaps more so. Stokowski uses the violins rather more than Ravel, as instanced by the opening 'Promenade'. The one moment when Ravel's scoring is truly inspired is the interchange between Goldenburg and Schmuyle; Stokowski has the woodwind echo the solo trumpet and the effect, mockingly piquant though it is, becomes less bleatingly obsequious than Ravel's version. Not surprisingly, the 'Catacombes' sequence makes a sumptuously weighty impact and 'Baba-jaga' is searingly grotesque and bizarrely full of imaginative orchestral comments. Two numbers are omitted: 'Tuileries' and 'Limoges', as Stokowski considered them 'too French' and 'not Mussorgskian'. 'The Great Gate of Kiev', scored for massive forces, including bells and organ, makes a huge final apotheosis – how Stokowski must have revelled in its grand climax.

Pictures at an Exhibition. A Night on the Bare Mountain. Khovanshchina – Prelude (Dawn on the Moscow River).
Atlanta Symphony Orchestra / Yoel Levi.
Telarc CD80296 (50 minutes: DDD). Recorded 1991.　　　　　　　　　　　　　　Ⓕ

When this was released, Telarc established a position for it as sonically the most spectacular set of *Pictures* among the many in the current catalogue. And it is a very fine performance too. The programme opens with *A Night on the Bare Mountain* – the brass sound is special, with great richness and natural bite with no exaggeration. The performance is well paced and exciting. Perhaps Levi's evil spirits are not as satanic as some, but they certainly make an impact and the contrasting melancholy of the closing section is very touching, with the tolling bell nicely balanced and the clarinet solo poignantly taking over from the gently elegiac strings. The characterization of *Pictures at an Exhibition* is no less successful, although it is an essentially mellower view than, for example, Sinopoli's highly praised DG version with the NYPO. Levi's is a performance where throughout the conductor makes the most of the colour, and brilliant orchestral effects of Ravel's inspired score, revealing much that often goes unheard – the grotesquerie of 'Gnomus' is not accentuated, but one greatly enjoys the attack of the lower strings which are very tangible indeed; a doleful bassoon introduces 'The Old Castle' and the saxophone solo has a satin-like finish on the timbre to produce an elegant melancholy; the woodwind in 'Tuileries' is gentle in its virtuosity. Levi holds back a little for the delicate string entry and the whole piece has a captivating lightness of touch. 'Baba-Yaga' makes a grand entrance, her music much less plangent than with Sinopoli, but again with the orchestral sounds tickling the ear. The reprise is dramatic and weighty and we are led naturally into the great finale, very grandiloquent. The final climax is unerringly built and at the very close the brass and strings produce an electrifying richness and weight of sound, to bring a *frisson* of excitement, with the tam-tam resounding clearly. Then there is silence, and out of it steals the exquisite opening of the *Khovanschchina* Prelude, with its poetic evocation of dawn over the Kremlin. Levi goes for atmosphere above all else and does not make too much of the climax, but the coda with its fragile woodwind halos is most delicately managed. This disc is a first choice if state-of-the-art recording is your prime consideration.

Mussorgsky Pictures at an Exhibition.
Tchaikovsky Piano Sonata in G major, Op. 37.
Sviatoslav Richter *pf*
Melodiya mono 74321 29469-2 (61 minutes: ADD). Recorded 1956-58.　　　Ⓜ Ⓗ

The blend of German and Russian backgrounds must have something to do with the unique power of Richter at his best. Certainly that comes across in the tempering of rhetoric with structural insight which elevates the Tchaikovsky Sonata beyond any other performance of this unwieldy piece; again Richter's sweeping panache and volcanic sense of flow make for a colossal Mussorgsky *Pictures* (Moscow, 1958), far better recorded than the famous, though currently unavailable, live Sofia account. Richter's interpretations in these years had an elemental power and unselfconscious abandon that was refined and tempered in later life. The mono sound is acceptable.

Complete Songs.
Boris Christoff *bass* **Alexandre Labinsky, Gerald Moore** *pfs*
French Radio National Orchestra / Georges Tzipine.
EMI Références mono CHS7 63025-2 (three discs: 191 minutes: ADD). Notes, texts and translations included. Recorded 1951-56.　　　Ⓜ Ⓗ

This set is undoubtedly one of the all-time glories of the gramophone and should be in any worthwhile song collection. This is unquestionably Boris Christoff's most important legacy. Even on the first disc, in the earlier and slightly less remarkable songs, Mussorgsky offers a range of personalities and emotions as then unknown in Russian song. There are the war-like King Saul, the sad figure of Wilhelm Meister in the *Song of the Old Man* (what we know as 'An die Türen'), the desolate landscape of *The Wind Howls*, the folk-hero, Calistratus. Then we hear a wide variety of styles from the recitative-like *Cast-off Woman* to the gentle lyricism of *Night*. In this last song Christoff produces that magical *mezza voce* of his to suggest the intimacy of the loved one portrayed within. But, by then – the eleventh song – he has already given us an amazing palette of sound colours, everything from the utterly ferocious to the gentlest whisper. With the second disc, we come to many of the better-known songs but few of them have ever been better interpreted than here. In *Hopak*, the bass has a rollicking time of it, relishing every word. In *Savishna*, a wonderfully vivid song, he subtly portrays the idiot. He catches the bitter satire of *The Classicist* and the humour of *The Seminarist*, where the Latin recitation is gleefully projected.

The rather weak *Puppet Show* is almost saved here by Christoff's identity with its twists of irony. Then he can change style again to produce a hypnotically sweet tone for *Evening Song*, a tender lyric built on only five notes. But the centrepiece of this disc is, of course, the *Nursery* cycle, where Christoff manages to adapt his big tone to a convincing impersonation of a small boy. He finds yet other voices for the Nurse and for the Mother. This is a *tour de force*. Similarly rewarding are his performances of the *Sunless* and *Songs and Dances of Death* cycles. He catches all the bleak gloom of the first, the histrionic force of the second, where his variety of timbre is once more astonishing, but in the *Songs and Dances* he uses a corrupt orchestration. After these two cycles, Mussorgsky's inspiration seemed to falter, though *On the Dnieper*, a lyrical piece of surpassing beauty, and the ever-popular *Song of the flea*, which ends the set, are remarkable achievements in their way and are here excellently interpreted. Labinsky and Moore are vivid and imaginative partners.

Songs and Dances of Death. The Nursery. The Peep-show. Forgotten. The Seminarist. Darling Savishna. The he-goat: A worldly story. Mephistopheles' song of the flea.
Sergei Leiferkus *bar* **Semion Skigin** *pf*
Conifer Classics CDCF229 (66 minutes: DDD). Texts and translations included. Recorded 1993.　　　Ⓕ Ⓔ

Few have interpreted Mussorgsky with the kind of confidence, understanding and sheer vocal bravura that Leiferkus shows here. He has all the necessary *gravitas*, vocal presence and tonal nuance. Leiferkus has recorded *Songs and Dances of Death* before with orchestra but the version with piano is to be preferred because their very intimacy in this form makes the pieces that much more frightening. At present there is no version with piano in the catalogue to rival Leiferkus's for intensity of expression or breadth of characterization. Here Death in all its terrifying guises as so arrestingly depicted by the composer, comes starkly into your home, courtesy of the singer, his vivid partner and an ideal recording. The accomplishment in *The Nursery* cycle is, if possible, even more astonishing as the baritone completely changes the character of his tone for impersonating the child. Usually assigned to a soprano, it has been attempted in the past on disc, and successfully so, by Christoff. Leiferkus at once emulates his great predecessor's achievement yet manages to give these delightful songs his own, very definite profile. More delights follow. The satire of *The Peepshow* is brilliantly realized. In the rest of the songs Mussorgsky's gift for strongly flavoured story-telling and figure-painting is conveyed in abundance through Leiferkus's ebullient delivery, closing with a rollicking but never overdone *Song of the flea*.

Epitaph. The Sphinx. Not like thunder, trouble struck. Softly the spirit flew up to heaven. Pride. Is spinning man's work?. The Vision. It scatters and breaks. On the Dnieper. Eremushka's lullaby. The Feast. The Classicist. From my tears. Sunless.
Sergei Leiferkus *bar* **Semion Skigin** *pf*
Conifer Classics 75605 51248-2 (59 minutes: DDD). Texts and translations included.
Recorded 1995. Ⓕ **E**

Leiferkus so much *enjoys* singing. That's evident from first to last on this, the second instalment of his absolutely riveting account of Mussorgsky's songs. His success is based on his amazing variety of tone colour and textual inflexion. The singer who is so embittered, so biting in a big, baritonal manner for projecting the harshness in *Not like thunder* dissolves into the warm, all-enveloping, bass-like interpreter of *Softly the spirit flew up to heaven*, one of the composer's most melodically inspired songs. Then in the next song, another voice, another character is met as Leiferkus catches to perfection the heroic irony of *Pride*. In *The Vision*, and again in the Schumannesque *From my tears*, we hear a lyrically vibrant baritone, dispensing an appropriately erotic charge so strongly contrasting with the deliberately light, almost mincing tone employed to convey the sharp satire of *The Classicist*. The grand passion of that Cossack lament, *On the Dnieper*, and the extrovert good cheer of *The feast* are further triumphs – and all that is before we reach his reading of the *Sunless* cycle, where Leiferkus sounds suitably world-weary as he plumbs the depths of this profoundly depressing work. In everything his confident and pointed delivery of the text is exemplary yet verbal histrionics never get in the way of good singing. With Skigin once again a wonderfully responsive partner and a fine recording, we recommend this disc unreservedly and urge you to acquire it.

Songs[a] – Where are thou, little star? Night. Gopak. The Nettle mountain. You drunken sot! The Orphan. The Magpie. Child's song. The Ragamuffin. Evening Song. Gathering mushrooms. The Wanderer. The garden by the Don. Hebrew song. Meines Herzens Sehnsucht. Ich wollt' meine Schmerzen ergössen. *Piano Pieces*[b] – Méditation. On the southern shore of the Crimea. Au village. Intermezzo in modo classico. Une larme. Gopak. Impromptu passionne.
Sergei Leiferkus *bar* [a]**Semion Skigin**, [b]**Vovka Ashkenazy** *pfs*
Conifer Classics 75605 51274-2 (74 minutes: DDD). Texts and translations included.
Recorded 1996. Ⓕ

Leiferkus enjoys himself immensely with Mussorgsky's songs; and this is infectious. The range of colour he displays would be self-indulgent, were it not for the fact that the nature of many of them demands a dramatic identification. Moreover, the artist who can lull the senses with such beautiful warmth of tone in *Night* or *Evening song* or *The Wanderer* has not only the right but really the duty to throw it to one side for the bawling of the energetically faithless wife in *Gopak* (with wonderfully exuberant playing by the ever-admirable Semion Skigin), or the termagant's screeching tirade of 'Akh, ti' at the homecoming drunkard. There is a sharper edge and a lightening of tone for *The Magpie*, and a very cleverly judged irony in the sweetness as in *Gathering mushrooms* it dawns on the listener that the crop being picked is poisoned, and destined for use in the near future. The taunting of the old woman in *The Ragamuffin*, one of Mussorgsky's most brilliant *tours de force*, is a real piece of virtuosity. With the towering exception of *Pictures at an Exhibition*, Mussorgsky's piano music is of little account, consisting of either salon musings like *Une larme* and *Méditation* or genre pieces with some Russian melodic colouring. The most interesting is the *Intermezzo in modo classico*, inspired by a peasant scene and demonstrating that he was only really inspired by words or imagery. Vovka Ashkenazy plays them gracefully and lightly. This is a splendid disc.

Scherzo in B flat major. Intermezzo 'in modo classico'. Khovanshchina – Dance of the Persian Slave Girls; Intermezzo; Golitsyn's journey. Boris Godunov – Introduction and Polonaise (all orch. Rimsky-Korsakov). Sorochinsky Fair – Overture; Gopak (both orch. Liadov); Parassia's Song. Sunless (orch. Svetlanov).
Natalia Gerasimova *sop*
Russian State Symphony Orchestra / Evgeni Svetlanov.
RCA Victor Red Seal 09026 68406-2 (71 minutes: DDD). Recorded 1994. Ⓕ

Mussorgsky by name, but not necessarily by nature. Virtually everything on this musically varied CD has been orchestrated by another hand. Svetlanov's performances are unforced and malleable, while the recordings have considerable impact: the double-basses at the start of *Khovanshchina*'s Entr'acte are virtually tangible. The 'Dance of the Persian Slave Girls' is very much 'pre-*Polovtsi*' and Liadov's felicitous orchestrations of music from *Sorochinsky Fair* are appealing. The performances are nicely judged and Natalia Gerasimova – a stylish, brittle-voiced soprano with a pronounced Slavic vibrato – gives a winning account of Parassia's schizoid 'Dumka'. However, the disc's highlight is Svetlanov's sensitive orchestration of the *Sunless* cycle. Here Gerasimova tames her exuberance for an appropriately inward performance, and the recording keeps her in perfect aural perspective with the orchestra. The first and fourth songs are scored for strings, the second for woodwind, the third for brass and woodwind, whereas the fifth makes economical use of larger forces (including percussion) and the sixth – 'On the river' – recalls the world of Rachmaninov's *The isle of the dead*. Svetlanov's mastery of mood and texture suggests active parallels with the superb Mussorgsky orchestrations of Shostakovich and Markevitch. The recordings are excellent.

St John's Night on the Bare Mountain. Pictures at an Exhibition (orch. Ravel). The destruction of Sennacherib[a]. Salammbô – Chorus of priestesses[a]. Oedipus in Athens – Chorus of people in the temple[a]. Joshua[b].
[b]**Elena Zaremba** *mez*
[a]**Prague Philharmonic Chorus; Berlin Philharmonic Orchestra / Claudio Abbado.**
DG 445 238-2GH (65 minutes: DDD). Texts and translations included. Recorded live in 1993. Ⓕ

St John's Night on the Bare Mountain is the original version of *A Night on the Bare Mountain*. Abbado obviously relishes the odd grotesque spurts of colour from the woodwind, and the Mussorgskian ruggedness. The composer's structural clumsiness is not shirked and the lack of the smooth continuity found in the Rimsky arrangement does not impede the sense of forward momentum; indeed at the close the Russian dance element is emphasized, rather than the sinister pictorialism. (Of course the luscious slow ending is not here at all – that was added by Rimsky.) The choral pieces are gloriously sung and again Abbado brings out their Russian colour, especially in the glowing yet sinuous 'Chorus of priestesses'. *Joshua* is made to seem a minor masterpiece with its lusty opening (hints of Borodin's Polovtsians) and its touching central solo ('The Amorite women weep'). This is most eloquently sung by Elena Zaremba and the theme is then movingly taken up first by the women of the chorus and then the men, before the exultant music returns. The performance of *Pictures at an Exhibition*, like the choral items, gains from the spacious ambience and sumptuous overall textures. It is very dramatic in its contrasts and very beautifully played.

St John's Night on the Bare Mountain. Scherzo in B flat major. Intermezzo 'in modo classico' in B minor. Khovanshchina – Prelude, Act 1, 'Dawn over the Moscow River'; Mysterious powers; In the Streltsy quarter all are sleeping; Dance of the Persian Slave Girls; The departure of Prince Golizyn. Mlada – Festive March.
Marianna Tarasova *mez* **Anatoly Kotcherga** *bass*
Berlin Radio Chorus; Südtiroler Kinderchor;
Berlin Philharmonic Orchestra / Claudio Abbado.
Sony Classical SK62034 (60 minutes: DDD). Texts and translations included.
Recorded 1995-96. Ⓕ

No work of Mussorgsky's has a more tangled history than *St John's Night on the Bare Mountain*. To cut a long story short, in 1867 Mussorgsky wrote the orchestral *Bare Mountain*, but, dismayed by Balakirev's withering comments, shelved it. Then, to the opera-ballet *Mlada*, commissioned in collaboration with Rimsky-Korsakov, Cui and Borodin, he contributed a scene, based on the orchestral piece and now lost, sometimes known as 'The Sabbath of the Black Goat'. This he adapted for the never-to-be-finished opera, *Sorochintsy Fair*, for chorus and orchestra, as 'The Young Peasant's Dream'. Despite the title given it on the record (as above), it is this operatic vocal and choral scene which is here recorded. Based on it, Rimsky-Korsakov made the orchestral transcription which has been so widely performed and recorded. There is more to it than that; but all that need be added here is that there have been various versions of the opera: Cui (1917) and Tcherepnin (1923) took a hand, but the best known performing score is by Shebalin (1931). Abbado gives the piece a formidable charge of energy here, strong, potent and dynamic. It is a powerful piece, especially in the original operatic scene rather than in the more appealing Rimsky-Korsakov orchestral guise which we know so well. He also gives a gentle, evocative performance of the *Khovanshchina* Prelude depicting dawn over the River Moscow, and accompanies his singers well in the two scenes from the opera, with Kotcherga a gloomy Shaklovity and Tarasova powerfully conjuring up the spirits of darkness in one of Mussorgsky's greatest arias. There is also a lively performance of the dance, and a vivid one of the *Intermezzo*, a lively response by Mussorgsky to a scene he witnessed of some peasants blundering through the snow.

Boris Godunov (first version).
Nikolai Putilin *bar* Boris Godunov; **Viktor Lutsiuk** *ten* Grigory; **Nikolai Okhotnikov** *bass* Pimen;
Fyodor Kuznetsov *bass* Varlaam; **Konstantin Pluzhnikov** *ten* Shuisky;
Nikolai Gassiev *ten* Missail; **Zlata Bulycheva** *mez* Fyodor; **Olga Trifonova** *sop* Xenia;
Yevgenia Gorokhovskaya *mez* Nurse; **Liubov Sokolova** *mez* Hostess;
Evgeny Akimov *ten* Simpleton; **Vassily Gerello** *bar* Shchelkalov; **Grigory Karassev** *bass* Nikitich;
Evgeny Nikitin *bass* Mityukha; **Yuri Schikalov** *ten* Krushchov.

Boris Godunov (second version).
Vladimir Vaneyev *bass* Boris Godunov; **Vladimir Galusin** *ten* Grigory;
Olga Borodina *mez* Marina; **Nikolai Okhotnikov** *bass* Pimen; **Fyodor Kuznetsov** *bass* Varlaam;
Konstantin Pluzhnikov *ten* Shuisky; **Nikolai Gassiev** *ten* Missail; **Evgeny Nikitin** *bass* Rangoni,
Mityukha; **Zlata Bulycheva** *mez* Fyodor; **Olga Trifonova** *sop* Xenia;
Yevgenia Gorokhovskaya *mez* Nurse; **Liubov Sokolova** *mez* Hostess;
Evgeny Akimov *ten* Simpleton; **Vassily Gerello** *bar* Shchelkalov;
Grigory Karassev *bass* Nikitich; **Yuri Schikalov** *ten* Krushchov;
Andrei Karabanov *bar* Lavitsky; **Yuri Laptev** *ten* Chernikovsky;
Chorus and Orchestra of the Kirov Opera / Valery Gergiev.
Philips 462 230-2PH5 (five discs: 306 minutes: DDD). Notes, texts and translations included.
Recorded 1997.   Ⓜ

What we have here is, literally, two operas for the price of one. That is to say, the two discs
containing Mussorgsky's first *Boris Godunov* and the three containing his second are available at
five discs for the normal cost of three. And what we are dealing with is, in a real sense, two operas.
First, a brief resumé of the facts. In 1868-69 Mussorgsky composed seven scenes: outside the
Novedevichy Monastery, Coronation outside the Kremlin, Pimen's Cell, the Inn, the Tsar's rooms in the
Kremlin, outside St Basil's Cathedral, Boris's Death in the Kremlin. When these were rejected by the
Imperial Theatres in 1872, he made various revisions. To meet objections about the lack of female roles,
he added the two scenes with the Polish princess Marina Mniszek; he also substituted the final Kromy
Forest scene for the St Basil's scene (causing a problem by duplicating the episode with the *yurodivy*, or
holy fool). He made a large number of adjustments, some minor, some more significant (such as
dropping Pimen's narration of the murder of the young Tsarevich), and one huge, the complete
rewriting of the original fifth scene, in the Kremlin, sometimes known as the Terem scene (*terem* is an
obsolete word for a room in a tower). This was the work he resubmitted, and which was first performed
in St Petersburg in 1874. Rimsky-Korsakov's famous version (which does much more than
reorchestrate) was first heard in 1896, and for many years superseded its predecessors.

However, it has increasingly been recognized that *Boris* II is not a revision of *Boris* I but a different
work, both as regards the view of the central character and his place in the historical narrative, and
also as regards the rethought musical technique and sometimes change of idiom which this has
brought about. So the present set makes a real contribution to our understanding and enjoyment of
Russia's greatest opera. It follows that there have to be two singers of the central role. Putilin (*Boris* I)
is in general more capacious in tone, more brooding and lofty, in the Terem scene more embittered and
harsh, willing to act with the voice. Vaneyev is a more immediate and human Boris, tender with his son
Fyodor (a touching, engaging performance from Zlata Bulycheva) both in the Terem and at the end,
not always as dominating as this Tsar should be but sympathetic, allowing his voice to blanch as death
approaches, and especially responsive to the melodic essence of Mussorgsky's speech-delivered lines.
This enables him to be rather freer with the actual note values. It does not necessarily matter:
Mussorgsky changed his mind over various details, and the important thing is to use his notes to create
character rather than be too literal with what the different versions propose. Pimen, strongly sung with
a hint of the youthful passions he claims to have abjured, is sung by Nikolai Okhotnikov more or less
identically in both performances.

The only character, apart from Boris, to be accorded two singers is Grigory, the False Dmitri. Viktor
Lutsiuk (*Boris* I) is strenuous, obsessed, vital; Vladimir Galusin (*Boris* II) can sound more frenzied, and
has the opportunity with the addition of the Polish acts to give a convincing portrayal of a weak man
assuming strength but being undermined by the wiles of a determined woman. Here, she is none other
than Olga Borodina, moodily toying with her polonaise rhythms and then in full sensuous call.
Yevgenia Gorokhovskaya is a jolly old Nurse in the *Boris* II Terem scene. The rest of the cast do not
really change their interpretations from one *Boris* to another, and indeed scarcely need to do so: it is
not really upon that which the differences depend. Liubov Sokolova sings a fruity Hostess, welcoming
in Fyodor Kuznetsov a Varlaam who can really sing his Kazan song rather than merely bawling it.
Konstantin Pluzhnikov makes Shuisky move from the rather sinister force confronting Boris in the
Terem to a more oily complacency in the Death scene: many Shuiskys make less of the part. Evgeny
Nikitin is a creepy, fanatical Rangoni, Vassily Gerello a Shchelkalov of hypocritical elegance, Evgeny
Akimov a sad-toned Simpleton. Gergiev directs strong, incisive performances, accompanying

sympathetically and controlling the marvellous crowd scenes well. However, it is a pity that he allows fierce whistles completely to drown the speeding violins opening the Kromy Forest scene (the music can be heard only when it returns), and he has not been given sufficient clarity of recording with the chorus. The words are often obscure, even with the boyars in the Death scene, and far too much is lost in the crowd exchanges. This is regrettable for a work that, in either incarnation, draws so much on realistic detail of articulation. Nevertheless, these five discs form a completely fascinating set, one which no admirer of this extraordinary creative achievement can afford to ignore.

Boris Godunov.
Anatoly Kotcherga bass Boris; **Sergei Larin** ten Grigory; **Marjana Lipovšek** mez Marina;
Samuel Ramey bass Pimen; **Gleb Nikolsky** bass Varlaam; **Philip Langridge** ten Shuisky;
Helmut Wildhaber ten Missail; **Sergei Leiferkus** bar Rangoni; **Liliana Nichiteanu** mez Feodor;
Valentina Valente sop Xenia; **Yevgenia Gorokhovskaya** mez Nurse;
Eléna Zaremba mez Hostess; **Alexander Fedin** ten Simpleton;
Albert Shagidullin bar Shchelkolov; **Wojciech Drabowicz** ten Mitukha, Krushchov;
Slovak Philharmonic Chorus; Berlin Radio Chorus; Tölz Boys' Choir;
Berlin Philharmonic Orchestra / Claudio Abbado.
Sony Classical S3K58977 (three discs: 200 minutes: DDD). Notes, text and translation included.
Recorded 1993. Ⓕ

Few conductors have been more diligent than Abbado in seeking the truth about this vast canvas. He chooses the definitive 1872-74 version, adding scenes, including the complete one in Pimen's cell and the St Basil's scene from 1869. His is a taut, tense reading, grand, virtuosic, at times hard-driven, favouring extremes of speed and dynamics. The orchestra is very much in the foreground, sounding more emphatic than would ever be the case in the opera house. Kotcherga has a superb voice, firmly produced throughout an extensive register. His is a Boris avoiding conventional melodrama and concerned to show the loving father. The ambitious lovers are well represented. Indeed, Larin is quite the best Grigory yet on disc, sounding at once youthful, heroic and ardent, and quite free of tenor mannerisms. Lipovšek characterizes Marina forcefully: we are well aware of the scheming Princess's powers of wheeler-dealing and of erotic persuasion. The recording is of demonstration standard: most potent in the way it captures the incisive and pointed singing of the combined choruses in their various guises. Here all is vividly brought before us by conductor and producer in the wide panorama predicated by Mussorgsky's all-enveloping vision.

Boris Godunov (arr. Rimsky-Korsakov).
Ivan Petrov bass Boris Godunov; **Vladimir Ivanovsky** ten Grigory; **Irina Arkhipova** mez Marina;
Mark Reshetin bass Pimen; **Alexey Geleva** bass Varlaam; **Georgy Shulpin** ten Shuisky;
Nikolay Zakharov ten Missail; **Yevgeny Kibkalo** bass Rangoni;
Valentina Klepatskaya mez Feodor; **Tamara Sorokina** sop Xenia;
Yevgeniya Verbitskaya mez Nurse; **Veronika Borisenko** mez Innkeeper;
Anton Grigoryev bass Simpleton, Nikitich; **Alexey Ivanov** bar Shchelkalov;
Vladimir Valaitis bar Lavitsky; **Yury Galkin** bass Chernikovsky;
Leonid Ktitorov bass Mityukha; **Anatoly Mishutin** ten Krushchov, Boyar;
Chorus and Orchestra of the Bolshoi Theatre, Moscow / Alexander Melik-Pashayev.
Melodiya 74321 29349-2 (three discs: 175 minutes: ADD). Notes, text and translation included.
Recorded 1962. Ⓜ

This is certainly the most authentic-sounding version of the Rimsky arrangement so far recorded. Under Melik-Pashayev's conducting, which combines discipline, an innate understanding of the score's rhythmic and melodic requirements and sheer experience in directing the work, it flows onwards in a steady stream of musical and dramatic consistency. Nowhere else will you hear such a cast of singers, steeped in the best tradition of performing the work at the Bolshoi, and at the same time so apt for their given roles. Petrov isn't at all in the Chaliapin or Christoff (Dobrowen) mould of performing the work: his performance is entirely free of melodrama and is sung with all the vocal verities observed in a rounded, warm bass. In his more modest way, Petrov invests his role with just as much feeling and drama as his more histrionic rivals – his is a richly rewarding portrayal on all counts. Even better is the Marina of the young Arkhipova. In her case, one can assert with certainty that she has no peer, let alone a better on any other set. The proud carriage of her voice and the finely nuanced character of her loud and soft singing are just what one wants from the ambitious Polish Princess. Her Grigory, Ivanovsky, isn't vocally quite in her class – the voice sounds strained under pressure – but, like everyone else in the cast, he is very much inside his role and declaims it with real passion. In the Polish act Kibkalo makes an ideally insinuating Rangoni. Reshetin is perfectly cast as grave old Pimen; he is another bass whose tone is well supported and easily produced. Shulpin has one of those sharp-edged tenors that many British ears abhor, but it seems to be absolutely the right voice for that crepuscular, two-faced boyar. Grigoryev is a plangent, touching Simpleton. Most of the supporting cast is in the same mould, peculiarly Russian, and therefore idiomatic in timbre. Some may baulk at the backward recording of the orchestra. The excellent singing of the chorus is vividly caught. The stereo spread is a trifle too marked. If you enjoy Rimsky's admittedly inauthentic scoring, you should seriously consider this well-remastered Melodiya set.

Boris Godunov (arr. Rimsky-Korsakov).
Boris Christoff *bass* Boris, Pimen, Varlaam; **Nicolai Gedda** *ten* Grigory;
Eugenia Zareska *mez* Marina, Feodor; **André Bielecki** *ten* Shuisky, Missail, Krushchov;
Kim Borg *bass* Rangoni, Shchelkalov; **Ludmila Lebedeva** *sop* Xenia;
Lydia Romanova *mez* Nurse, Hostess; **Wassili Pasternak** *ten* Simpleton;
Raymond Bonte *ten* Lavitsky; **Eugène Bousquet** *bass* Chernikovsky;
Choeurs Russes de Paris; French Radio National Orchestra / Issay Dobrowen.
EMI Références mono CHS5 65192-2 (three discs: 178 minutes: ADD). Recorded 1952. Ⓜ Ⓗ

Dobrowen's lean, vivid, acutely shaped direction, benefiting from taut rhythms and fastish tempos, is as vital as that on any version since. Its other main attribute is, of course, Christoff's first complete reading on disc of the tortured Tsar, whose role he sings with an enviable combination of firm tone, vital diction and concentrated histrionics, never overstepping the mark. His assumption of two other parts has always been frowned on, but he so subtly varies his tone – softer, greyer for Pimen, rotundly rollicking for Varlaam – that the tripling only worries in the final scene when Pimen comes face to face with the dying ruler. The contrast of his finely shaded Pimen with Ramey's one-dimensional singing on the Abbado version is most marked. If that were not enough, there is the beauty and ardour of the young Gedda as Grigory to please the ear and Zareska's seductive, vocally appealing Marina. She also sings a likeable Feodor. Kim Borg doubles successfully as Shchelkalov and an oily Rangoni. The choral singing is good. We have heard much better on disc since, but few orchestras, in the West at least, have sounded so Russian as these French players but then few have had the benefit of being tutored by Dobrowen. The digital transfers bring out the excellence of the original engineering.

Khovanshchina.
Aage Haugland *bass* Ivan Khovansky; **Vladimir Atlantov** *ten* Andrey Khovansky;
Vladimir Popov *ten* Golitsin; **Anatolij Kotscherga** *bar* Shaklovity;
Paata Burchuladze *bass* Dosifey; **Marjana Lipovšek** *contr* Marfa;
Brigitte Poschner-Klebel *sop* Susanna; **Heinz Zednik** *ten* Scribe;
Joanna Borowska *sop* Emma; **Wilfried Gahmlich** *ten* Kouzka;
Vienna Boys' Choir; Slovak Philharmonic Choir;
Vienna State Opera Chorus and Orchestra / Claudio Abbado.
DG 429 758-2GH3 (three discs: 171 minutes: DDD). Notes, text and translation included.
Recorded live in 1989. Ⓕ

The booklet-essay suggests that Mussorgsky's music constantly poses a question to his Russian compatriots: 'What are the causes of our country's continuing calamities, and why does the state crush all that is good?'. Anyone who follows today's news from Russia and then experiences this opera will understand what is meant, and while we observe with sympathy we seem no nearer than the citizens of that great, tormented country to finding solutions for its endemic problems. However, Mussorgsky was not the least of those Russian musicians who found lasting beauty in her history and he expressed it in a powerfully dramatic idiom that drew on folk-music and had both epic qualities and deep humanity as well as an occasional gentleness. There is also an element here of Russian church music, since *Khovanshchina* has a political and religious theme and is set in the 1680s at the time of Peter the Great's accession. Since the work was unfinished when Mussorgsky died, performances always involve conjectural work, and the version here – which works convincingly – is mostly that of Shostakovich with the choral ending that Stravinsky devised using Mussorgsky's music. The cast in this live recording is not one of star opera singers, but they are fully immersed in the drama and the music, as is the chorus and the orchestra under Claudio Abbado, and the result is deeply atmospheric. The booklet has the Russian text and a translation.

Conlon Nancarrow
Mexican 1912-1997

Nancarrow Three Canons for Ursula. Studies for Player Piano Nos. 3c, 6 and 11.
Bach The Art of Fugue, BWV1080.
Joanna MacGregor *pf*
Collins Classics 7043-2 (two discs: 108 minutes: DDD). Recorded 1995. Ⓕ

In her witty and incisive notes, MacGregor compels us to hear a vital relationship between eighteenth- and twentieth-century composers who see fugue and canon as the highest musical good, a 'sounding mathematics' which 'achieves a depth and simplicity and at times a luminous serenity' and the performances testify to her sense of Bach's richness and intellectual grace. Immaculate, lucid and sensitive she reveals *The Art of Fugue* as an incomparable act of meditation. MacGregor has recorded Bach and Nancarrow before but here the juxtaposition is the thing. Using multi-track techniques she emulates and excels Nancarrow's original player piano capacity for intricacy. Very short quaver-durations in Study No. 11 end in a fantastic virtuoso uproar and remind one of a related complexity in 'Canon B', the second of the *Three Canons for Ursula*. The difficulties are immense but in Joanna MacGregor such music has a superlative champion. All her performances in their power and eloquence positively beg you to share her sense of discovery and exhilaration. This is an indispensable issue for all musicians who relish a supreme play of the mind and imagination. The recordings are magnificent.

Carl Nielsen

Danish 1865-1931

Flute Concerto, FS119[a]; Clarinet Concerto, FS129[b]. Maskarade[a] – Overture; Magdalone's dance scene; Prelude, Act 2; Dance of the cockerels.
Holger Gilbert-Jespersen *fl* **Ib Erikson** *cl*
Danish State Radio Symphony Orchestra / [a]**Thomas Jensen**, [b]**Mogens Wöldike**.
Dutton Laboratories mono CDLXT2505 (62 minutes: ADD). Recorded 1954.   Ⓜ Ⓗ

In the early 1920s Nielsen heard the Copenhagen Wind Quintet rehearsing some works by Mozart and was moved to compose his enchanting Wind Quintet. He subsequently planned to write each of its members a concerto but only lived long enough to compose the two recorded here – the Flute Concerto of 1926 and the Clarinet Concerto of two years later. The soloist at the former's première was Holger Gilbert-Jespersen and it was he who made its first recording over a quarter of a century later. Gilbert-Jespersen was by all accounts an artist of refined taste and strong Gallic sympathies, and much of the piece was inspired by his temperament. The burlesque gestures of the trombone at the end are a joke which Nielsen made at his expense. Unless it is discreetly handled, the affectionate little jest can itself sound crude; but here all is perfection, particularly in such a superb CD transfer as this. Aage Oxenvad, who was the original dedicatee of the Clarinet Concerto, was to have recorded it but died shortly before the sessions were due to take place. At the time, Ib Erikson was Principal Clarinet of the fine Danish State Radio Symphony Orchestra. This version conveys better than so many more modern ones the unearthly quality of the Concerto, its rarefied and bracing air. These performances carry a special authority and cannot be too strongly recommended.

Nielsen Violin Concerto, FS61[a].
Sibelius Violin Concerto in D minor, Op. 47[b].
Cho-Liang Lin *vn*
[a]**Swedish Radio Symphony Orchestra**, [b]**Philharmonia Orchestra** / **Esa-Pekka Salonen**.
Sony Classical SK44548 (69 minutes: DDD). Recorded 1987-88. *Gramophone* Award Winner 1989.   Ⓕ

At the time this was the best recording of the Sibelius Concerto to have appeared for more than a decade and probably the best ever of the Nielsen. Cho-Liang Lin brings an apparently effortless virtuosity to both concertos. He produces a wonderfully clean and silvery sonority and there is no lack of aristocratic finesse. Only half-a-dozen years separate the two concertos, yet they breathe a totally different air. Lin's perfect intonation and tonal purity excite admiration and throughout them both there is a strong sense of line from beginning to end. Esa-Pekka Salonen gets excellent playing from the Philharmonia Orchestra in the Sibelius and almost equally good results from the Swedish Radio Symphony Orchestra. This is one of the classic concerto recordings of the century.

Violin Concerto. Flute Concerto. Clarinet Concerto.
Toke Lund Christiansen *fl* **Niels Thomsen** *cl* **Kim Sjøgren** *vn*
Danish National Radio Symphony Orchestra / **Michael Schønwandt**.
Chandos CHAN8894 (80 minutes: DDD). Recorded 1990.   Ⓕ

Kim Sjøgren may not command the purity of tone of Cho-Liang Lin but he has the inestimable advantage of totally idiomatic orchestral support: Michael Schønwandt has an instinctive feeling for this music – and this shows throughout the whole disc. The perspective between soloist and orchestra is well judged (Sjøgren is never larger than life) and so is the internal balance. In the Flute Concerto, which veers from Gallic wit to moments of great poetic feeling, Toke Lund Christiansen is an excellent soloist. He has no want of brilliance or authority and his performance also has plenty of character. Niels Thomsen's account of the Clarinet Concerto is one of the very finest now before the public. If there is any music from another planet, this is it! There is no attempt to beautify the score nor to overstate it: every dynamic nuance and expressive marking is observed by both the soloist and conductor. Thomsen plays as if his very being is at stake and Michael Schønwandt secures playing of great imaginative intensity from the Danish Radio Orchestra.

Symphonies – No. 1 in G minor, FS16; No. 2, FS29, 'The Four Temperaments'; No. 3, FS60, 'Sinfonia espansiva'; No. 4, FS76, 'The inextinguishable'; No. 5, FS97; No. 6, FS116, 'Sinfonia semplice'.

Symphonies Nos. 1 and 6.
San Francisco Symphony Orchestra / Herbert Blomstedt.
Decca 425 607-2DH (67 minutes: DDD). Recorded 1989. ⓕ 🆁🆁

Nielsen always nurtured a special affection for his First Symphony – and rightly so, for its language is natural and unaffected. It has great spontaneity of feeling and a Dvořákian warmth and freshness. Blomstedt's recording is vital, beautifully shaped and generally faithful to both the spirit and the letter of the score. The recording is very fine: the sound has plenty of room to expand, there is a very good relationship between the various sections of the orchestra and a realistic perspective. Blomstedt gives a powerful account of the Sixth, too, with plenty of intensity and an appreciation of its extraordinary vision. It is by far the most challenging of the cycle and inhabits a very different world from early Nielsen. The intervening years had seen the cataclysmic events of the First World War and Nielsen himself was suffering increasingly from ill health. Blomstedt and the fine San Fransisco orchestra convey the powerful nervous tension of the first movement and the depth of the third, the *Proposta seria*. A splendid issue.

Symphony No. 1. Flute Concerto. Rhapsody Overture: An imaginary trip to the Faroe Islands, FS123.
Patrick Gallois *fl*
Gothenburg Symphony Orchestra / Myung-Whun Chung.
BIS CD454 (63 minutes: DDD). Recorded 1989.

This recording of the First Symphony is hardly less fine than Blomstedt's. Tempos are generally well judged and there is a good feeling for the overall architecture of the piece. It gets off to a splendid start and Chung shapes the second group affectionately. He pulls back further later on, interpreting the *molto tranquillo* as an agogic rather than a character marking. However, he does not put a foot wrong in the slow movement, which has a splendid sense of line, and phrasing which is attentive but never overemphatic. In the *Scherzo* he does pull back fractionally for the wind on their second appearance though not the first time round. The finale is exhilaratingly played. Throughout the work Chung knows how to build up to a climax and keep detail in the right perspective. As always, the Gothenburg orchestra plays with enthusiasm and spirit, as if it has always lived with this music and yet, paradoxically, is discovering it for the first time. The Rhapsody Overture, *An imaginary trip to the Faroe Islands*, begins most imaginatively but inspiration undoubtedly flags. The performance of the Flute Concerto is rather special. It is most strongly characterized by Patrick Gallois who plays with effortless virtuosity and an expressive eloquence that is never over- or under-stated. His purity of line in the first movement is quite striking and he has the measure of the poignant coda. His dynamic range is wide, the tone free from excessive vibrato and his approach fresh.

Symphonies Nos. 2 and 3.
Nancy Wait Fromm *sop* **Kevin McMillan** *bar*
San Francisco Symphony Orchestra / Herbert Blomstedt.
Decca 430 280-2DH (67 minutes: DDD). Recorded 1989.
Gramophone Award Winner 1991. ⓕ 🆁🆁

This disc couples two of Nielsen's most genial symphonies, both of which come from the earliest part of the century, in performances of the very first order. The Second (1902), inspired by the portrayal of *The Four Temperaments* (Choleric, Phlegmatic, Melancholic, Sanguine) that he had seen in a country inn, has splendid concentration and fire and, as always, from the right pace stems the right character. Moreover the orchestra sounds inspired, for there is a genuine excitement about its playing. Indeed Blomstedt's accounts are by far the most satisfying available. The Third, *Espansiva*, is even more personal in utterance than *The Four Temperaments*, for during the intervening years Nielsen had come much further along the road of self-discovery. His melodic lines are bolder, the musical paragraphs longer and his handling of form more assured. It is a glorious and richly inventive score whose pastoral slow movement includes a part for two wordless voices.

Blomstedt gives us an affirmative, powerful reading and in the slow movement, the soprano produces the required ethereal effect. The Decca sound is very detailed and full-bodied, and in the best traditions of the company. Blomstedt's *Espansiva* has greater depth than most rival accounts; the actual sound has that glowing radiance that characterizes Nielsen, and the tempo, the underlying current on which this music is borne, is expertly judged – and nowhere better than in the finale. Blomstedt is an experienced guide in this repertoire and this shows, while his orchestra plays with refreshing enthusiasm.

Symphony No. 2. Aladdin – Suite, FS89.
Gothenburg Symphony Orchestra / Myung-Whun Chung.
BIS CD247 (56 minutes: DDD). Recorded 1983. Ⓕ

Myung-Whun Chung has a real feeling for this repertoire and his account of the Second Symphony is very fine. Nielsen himself had a strong association with the Gothenburg Symphony Orchestra, and the present orchestra is an enthusiastic and responsive body. Tempos are excellently judged, there is a splendid sense of forward movement and completely idiomatic feeling. The recording is impressive too, with the excellent acoustic of the Gothenburg Hall being used to great advantage. Until this release the *Aladdin* music had been out of the catalogue for some time so it was doubly welcome. It certainly receives a beguiling and spirited performance under Chung. The strings produce excellent quality in 'Aladdin's Dream' and the playing is alert and sensitive throughout. All in all, a very distinguished set.

Symphonies Nos. 2 and 3.
National Symphony Orchestra of Ireland / Adrian Leaper.
Naxos 8 550825 (68 minutes: DDD). Recorded 1994. Ⓢ

The vital current on which every phrase must be borne in Nielsen needs to flow at higher voltage. This is music which needs to be played at white heat. Well, there is no lack of electricity in Leaper's reading of the Second. He sets a cracking pace for the first movement, the choleric temperament, and hardly puts a foot wrong in its three companions. His tempos in the *Sinfonia espansiva* are well judged and sensible throughout all four movements. The finale, where many conductors get it wrong, seems to be just right. These are more than just serviceable performances: they are very good indeed and the Irish orchestra sounds well rehearsed and inside the idiom. You can pay more and do worse although some collectors will be inclined to think the additional polish one gets from Blomstedt or Myung-Whun Chung is worth the extra outlay. These latter performances continue to grow in stature, and it is no mean compliment to the Naxos versions to say that they give them a very good run for their money. Naxos does not identify the singers in the slow movement of the *Espansiva*. No one investing in this issue and then going on to either of the Blomstedt accounts is going to feel that they have been let down. The recording team secures a very decent balance: well laid-back wind and brass, with good front-to-back perspective and transparency of texture.

Symphonies Nos. 3[a] and 5.
[a]**Ruth Guldbaek** *sop* [a]**Niels Møller** *ten*
[a]**Royal Danish Orchestra; New York Philharmonic Orchestra / Leonard Bernstein.**
Sony Classical The Royal Edition SMK47598 (71 minutes: ADD). Recorded 1962-65. Ⓜ

These particular performances are extremely fine, the finest Fifth ever on record in the opinion of many – it is an essential library supplement. To some tastes it is an overdriven performance and an aggressively balanced recording; to most Nielsen lovers it has charisma and a sense of discovery without ever violating the spirit of the music (Nielsen, it should be remembered, was happy to let great conductors follow their instincts in his music – including Furtwängler in this very work). Overall, this disc shows Bernstein at something close to his greatest. Under his direction the accompaniments revel in the music, and the understanding between orchestra and both soloists is excellent. In No. 5 there is the magnificent playing of the NYPO, with the best side-drum and clarinet solos on record, ensuring that the menace with which Nielsen's humanity has to wrestle is fully embodied. The sense of anticipation Bernstein generates is not the least factor which makes this performance so thrilling – plus the way expectation shades into depression, desperation or exaltation. The Third Symphony is scarcely less fine. The finale is more subtly grasped by Blomstedt, but no one who cares about Nielsen should miss Bernstein in the remaining movements.

Symphonies Nos. 3 and 5.
Catherine Bott *sop* **Stephen Roberts** *bar* **Royal Scottish Orchestra / Bryden Thomson.**
Chandos CHAN9067 (71 minutes: DDD). Recorded 1991. Ⓕ

Bryden Thomson and the Royal Scottish Orchestra give fresh and direct readings of the *Espansiva* and the Fifth which are eminently satisfying. At no point are we aware of the conductor interposing himself between composer and listener, and one can sense an evident enthusiasm on the part of the players. This is Nielsen plain and unadorned without any frills. Thomson has a very good feeling for Nielsen's tempos and his account of the finale feels just right. All in all, a splendidly sane performance with good singing from the fine soloists in the slow movement. The Fifth Symphony is another unaffected and straightforward performance that has a great deal going for it – not least the beautiful clarinet playing in the coda, and the thoroughly committed second movement. One is, perhaps, more aware of the beat in the first movement than in Blomstedt's Decca account and it rarely seems to float or sound disembodied as it does with him. However, Thomson gets very spirited playing from all departments of the orchestra and the recordings are very good and present, even if the sound lacks the transparency Decca achieves for Blomstedt. These are eminently enjoyable, ardent performances that can hold their head high amongst any competition.

Symphonies Nos. 4 and 5.
San Francisco Symphony Orchestra / Herbert Blomstedt.
Decca 421 524-2DH (72 minutes: DDD). Recorded 1987.   Ⓔ **RR**

These are two of Nielsen's most popular and deeply characteristic symphonies. Blomstedt's are splendid performances. The Fourth Symphony occupied Nielsen between 1914 and early 1916 and reveals a level of violence new to his art. The landscape is harsher; the melodic lines soar in a more anguished and intense fashion (in the case of the remarkable slow movement, 'like the eagle riding on the wind', to use the composer's own graphic simile). Blomstedt's opening has splendid fire and he is not frightened of letting things rip. The finale with its exhilarating dialogue between the two timpanists comes off splendidly. The Fifth Symphony of 1922 is impressive, too: it starts perfectly and has just the right glacial atmosphere. The climax and the desolate clarinet peroration into which it dissolves are well handled. The recording balance could not be improved upon: the woodwind are well recessed (though clarinet keys are audible at times), there is an almost ideal relationship between the various sections of the orchestra and a thoroughly realistic overall perspective. Blomstedt has a good rapport with his players who sound in excellent shape and respond instinctively to these scores.

Symphonies Nos. 4 and 5.
Finnish Radio Symphony Orchestra / Jukka-Pekka Saraste.
Finlandia 3984-21439-2 (72 minutes: DDD). Recorded 1997.   Ⓕ

This is an impressive account of the Fourth Symphony which can hold its own among the very best available. The Finnish RSO brings a feeling of urgent intensity to the slow movement and Saraste is carefully attentive to matters of dynamics and phrasing. He builds up the musical argument powerfully to a strong and convincing climax. Nor can the Fifth be faulted: it is also powerfully conceived with a strong command both of detail and the overall architecture of the piece. The opening moves but is atmospheric, with careful attention to dynamic nuance and texture. The *tranquillo* section (two bars before fig. 24: track 5) is most sensitively handled: it is both poetic and mysterious. The engineers cope admirably with the dryish acoustic of the Helsinki Culture Hall: they produce exemplary clarity and it is only at the ends of movements or in the general pause that precedes the final *Allegro* of No. 4 where one becomes aware of this. Among modern recordings, this Finlandia issue deserves to be recommended alongside Blomstedt's San Francisco coupling. Some may even prefer it.

Symphonies Nos. 4 and 6.
Royal Scottish National Orchestra / Bryden Thomson.
Chandos CHAN9047 (70 minutes: DDD). Recorded 1991.   Ⓕ

Bryden Thomson's accounts of the Fourth and Sixth call to mind the ardent intensity of the pioneering Danish recordings (no longer available) by Launy Gróndahl and Thomas Jensen, such are their fire. The orchestra plays with total commitment and the underlying violence of No. 4 makes a powerful impact, both at the opening and in the finale. But his Sixth is arguably the very finest version of the work on disc, notwithstanding the cultured and splendidly recorded account by Herbert Blomstedt. Thomson strikes exactly the right tempo for the first movement and the problematic 'Humoreske' has never made better sense. He takes it at a steadier pace than most rival conductors, so that its questioning spirit registers. The third movement, the 'Proposta seria', is both eloquent and searching. Even in a strongly competitive field this splendidly recorded Chandos account brings one closer to this extraordinary work than any other.

Aladdin – Suite, FS89. Maskarade – Overture; Prelude, Act 2; The Cockerels' Dance. Rhapsody Overture: An imaginary trip to the Faroe Islands, FS123. Helios Overture, FS32. Saga-Drøm, FS46. Pan and Syrinx, FS87.
Gothenburg Symphony Orchestra / Neemi Järvi.
DG 447 757-2GH (72 minutes: DDD). Recorded 1995.   Ⓕ

Järvi gets totally committed playing from his fine orchestra; its members convey the feeling that they all believe in every note they utter. *Aladdin* is given with great spirit and spontaneity. The recording, made by the same team and in the same venue as the orchestra's earlier recording of the work, under Myung-Whun Chung, is excellent, though the 1983 BIS account has marginally greater depth and transparency. In only one instance does Järvi get it wrong and that is in the *Helios Overture*, which is too fast for its sunrise to cast its spell! Thoughts turn to Jupiter where the sun rises every ten hours. Everything else here calls for straightforward applause.

Nielsen Wind Quintet, FS100.
Fernström Wind Quintet, Op. 59.
Kvandal Wind Quintet, Op. 34. Three Sacred Folktunes, Op. 23*b*.
Oslo Wind Quintet (Tom Ottar Andreasson *fl* Lars Peter Berg *ob* Arild Stav *cl*
Hans Peter Aasen *bn* Jan Olav Marthinsen *hn*).
Naxos 8 553050 (70 minutes: DDD). Recorded 1993.   Ⓢ

This is a thoroughly entertaining CD, combining three very different and unfamiliar works with what is probably the finest wind quintet ever penned. The major item here, of course, is the Nielsen: a glorious work which achieves the rare combination of seriousness of expression as well as being utterly relaxed in tone. The Oslo ensemble is a little slower than usual, but its measured tempos are most convincing; indeed, in the finale they highlight musical connections with Nielsen's Fifth and Sixth Symphonies in ways rarely heard elsewhere. The Swede John Axel Fernström was undeniably a minor composer. If his music does not possess many visionary qualities it is certainly well crafted and his 1943 Quintet is an engaging and worthwhile concert opener. Johan Kvandal from Norway is a weightier proposition and better-known outside of his native country than is Fernström. Kvandal's Quintet, Op. 34 (1971), was written for the Oslo ensemble (apparently for a couple of cases of wine!) and is serious and high-minded in tone, contrasting effectively with both the Fernström and Kvandal's own *Sacred Folktunes* of 1963. In the Quintet's fast second movement Kvandal adopts a rather Shostakovichian manner, even alluding to the Soviet master's Twelfth Symphony, though to what purpose (if deliberate at all) is unexplained. The idiomatic playing is reproduced in a slightly flat recording (made in the studios of Norwegian Radio), although the Naxos sound has great immediacy.

String Quartets – No. 1 in G minor, FS4; No. 2 in F minor, FS11; No. 3 in E flat major, FS23; No. 4 in F major, FS36. Movements for String Quartet, FS3*c*.
Danish Quartet (Tim Frederiksen, Arne Balk-Møller *vns* Claus Myrup *va* H. Brendstrup *vc*).
Kontrapunkt 32150/1 (two discs: 138 minutes: DDD). Recorded 1992.   Ⓕ

Nielsen composed two quartets and a string quintet during his student years. There was a gap of eight years between the F minor Quartet and the Third, in E flat, Op. 14 (FS23) during which Nielsen had written his First Symphony, and another eight before the F major, Op. 44 (FS36) saw the light of day. By this time he had written his opera, *Saul and David* and the best part of *Maskarade* as well as the Second Symphony. The Danish Quartet is very sensitive to dynamic nuance and phrases imaginatively. Of course, the F major Quartet goes deeper than the Third. There is a grace, an effortless fluency and a marvellous control of pace. Ideas come and go just when you feel they should; yet its learning and mastery is worn lightly. Though the earlier quartets are not such perfect works of art, they are nevertheless always endearing. The Danish Quartet is completely inside this music and is totally persuasive. In spite of the closely balanced recording this set gives real pleasure and can be recommended with enthusiasm.

Five Pieces, FS10. Humoresque Bagatelles, FS22. Chaconne, FS79. Suite, FS91. Three Pieces, FS131.
Leif Ove Andsnes *pf*
Virgin Classics VC5 45129-2 (54 minutes: DDD). Recorded 1995.   Ⓕ 🅴

This music on this disc is quite wonderful and deserves the widest dissemination. Although the *Suite* (*Suite luciferique*) was dedicated to Schnabel, the great pianist never played it in public. On record the finest advocate of the piano music was Arne Skjold Rasmussen, whose three-LP set appeared fleetingly in this country in a Vox box during the 1960s. Without the slightest disrespect to him, it now has to be said that this music has at last found its true interpreter in the Norwegian Leif Ove Andsnes. He has the measure both of the fresh and charming early pieces, FS10 and 22, and the later more searching, other-worldly *Suite* and the *Three Pieces*. The *luciferique* of the former alludes, incidentally, to the messenger of light, not the prince of darkness, and Nielsen subsequently withdrew the title. This is music of great substance and a deep and powerful originality. Andsnes has such a natural feeling for it that you will probably never find yourself questioning his interpretative judgements. He brings wit and subtlety to pieces like the 'Spinning Top' and 'Jumping Jack' from FS10, and there is always a splendid rhythmic grip, tonal sensitivity and variety of keyboard colour. He communicates real conviction to the listener, a feeling that this is the only way this music can sound. There is an impressive eloquence and nobility here, and the recorded sound is in every respect exemplary. It is 'present', natural and lifelike. Because this music is unfamiliar, collectors may be cautious or slow in exploring it. To judge from his BBC Proms performance in 1995, Andsnes has quite a following and it is to be hoped that he will lead his admirers on to this music which he has here served so well.

Aladdin.
Mette Ejsing *contr* **Guido Paevatalu** *bar* **Danish National Radio Chamber Choir; Danish National Radio Symphony Orchestra / Gennadi Rozhdestvensky.**
Chandos CHAN9135 (79 minutes: DDD). Text and translation included. Recorded 1992.　　Ⓕ🅴

Nielsen's music to Adam Oehlenschläger's *Aladdin* comes from 1917-18, and was commissioned for a particularly lavish production of the play at the Royal Theatre in Copenhagen. More than half the music consists of orchestral interludes to accompany processions and dances, most of which come in the Third Act. Many are delightful and endearing, and once heard difficult to get out of one's head. Robert Simpson summed the work up in his Nielsen monograph: 'The market-square in Isfahan where four orchestras play in four different tempos suggesting marvellously the clashing colours, movements and sounds of an eastern market-place is undoubtedly the most striking and original part of the music. Some of it is not very interesting (the rather commonplace Blackamoors' Dance, for instance) but most is intensely perceptive and colourful.' It is full of characteristic Nielsenesque touches, and although it is not the composer at his very best, it offers many irresistible delights. Performance and recording are superb.

Springtime in Funen, Op. 42. Aladdin – Suite, FS89.
Inga Nielsen *sop* **Kim von Binzer** *ten* **Jørgen Klint** *bass* **St Klemens School Children's Choir; University Choir 'Little Muko'; Odense Symphony Orchestra / Tamás Vetö.**
Unicorn-Kanchana DKPCD9054. Notes, text and translation included. Recorded 1985.　　Ⓕ

If you have ever wondered why Nielsen's music inspires such devotion among his followers, this recording offers perhaps an even better explanation than the high-powered issues of his symphonies. *Springtime in Funen* was a commission from the Association of Danish Choral Societies and the *Aladdin* suite is taken from incidental music for Oehlenschläger's play; they were composed in the aftermath of the Fifth and Fourth Symphonies respectively. Yet neither needs any apologies on account of its origins as 'occasional music' and neither is overshadowed by those symphonic masterpieces. Rather, the symphonies seem to have cleared the air and allowed the gentler, more relaxed side of Nielsen's character to emerge with a special purity. The Nielsen-lover will only need to know that these are marvellous performances, excellently recorded. The Hungarian-born Tamás Vetö has that crucial instinct for natural pacing which so often eludes non-Danish conductors in Nielsen; the Odense orchestra produces a full-blooded and thoroughly idiomatic sound, with a characteristically Danish raw quality at times which one accepts as part of the spontaneity and relish of the playing. In *Springtime in Funen* Inga Nielsen is outstanding, and though the tenor and bass are marginally less characterful, they too sing with much feeling. The tenderness of the tenor's strophic song sums up the unobtrusive genius of the work – it is a discovery as simple and miraculous as the sun on your face on a spring morning. Both adult and children's choruses are superb. If only there was a singable English translation (and perhaps if the very end were not quite so abrupt), *Springtime in Funen* would surely be a huge success in this country. Likewise the *Aladdin* suite, given the right kind of advocacy, might well enjoy something like the popularity of *Peer Gynt*. Every one of its seven movements is a winner, catchy and memorable, and the range of mood is just as wide. This disc is simply a joy from start to finish, and if you think we are exaggerating, all we can say is – try it.

Maskarade.
Aage Haugland *bass* Jeronimus; **Susanne Resmark** *contr* Magdelone;
Gert Henning Jensen *ten* Leander; **Bo Skovhus** *bar* Henrik; **Michael Kristensen** *ten* Arv;

Kurt Ravn *bar* Leonard; **Henriette Bonde-Hansen** *sop* Leonora;
Marianne Rørholm *contr* Pernille; **Johan Reuter** *bar* Night Watchman, Master of the
Masquerade; **Christian Christiansen** *bass* Tutor;
Danish National Radio Choir and Symphony Orchestra / Ulf Schirmer.
Decca 460 227-2DHO2 (two discs: 145 minutes: DDD). Notes, text and translation included.
Recorded 1996. Ⓕ **E**

If you can keep a straight face through the master/servant antics of the club-addicts Leander and
Henrik, if you can stay uncharmed by the ageing, repressed Magdelone when she shows she can still
cut a caper, if you can stop your foot tapping in the Act 3 Maskarade itself, and if you can remain
unmoved by the gentle pathos of the demasking scene, then you're made of very stern stuff indeed.
It is, not surprisingly, thoroughly idiomatic. Since the first production in 1906 *Maskarade* has been
Denmark's national opera, and all the principals here have the music in their blood. Gert Henning
Jensen may be a rather tremulous Leander, but he sounds appropriately youthful, and the love duets
with his well-matched Leonora, Henriette Bonde-Hansen, are wonderfully touching (strong echoes
of Brahms's *Liebeslieder* waltzes here). Bo Skovhus is in superb voice as the Figaro-esque Henrik,
though an even sharper sense of fun in the characterization would not have come amiss; Michael
Kristensen's blockhead Arv is also a paler impersonation than it should be. Aage Haugland is in
magnificent voice and almost steals the show in Act 1 as the crusty old Jeronimus; the vulnerable
but lovable Magdelone of Susanne Resmark instantly brings a lump to the throat. Ulf Schirmer
conducts with excellently judged tempos and an obvious deep affection for the idiom. Above all he
has a grasp of the underlying momentum of each act, what Nielsen would have called the 'current'.

This recording uses a score prepared by the government-sponsored Carl Nielsen Edition, which
restores traditionally cut or displaced passages and corrects a host of textual and musical details.
The resulting play of contrasts and effective large-scale pacing, especially in the supposedly
problematic Second and Third Acts, entirely vindicates this full-length version. Having said all that,
Schirmer does miss a trick or two. The Overture could do with a bit more lilt and swagger (the
Danish strings could be more full-bodied here); the end of Act 2, where a preview of the
Maskarade is heard as if through half-open doors, is too loud; synchronization is initially dodgy in
Act 3, as though the chorus can't quite believe the swift tempo; and the choral interpolations in the
Tutor's strophic song sound a little contrived. So collectors wedded to the lovable Unicorn-
Kanchana Frandsen set (sadly somewhat dimmed in its CD transfer) will find reasons for returning
to it; and the richest comedy of all in Act 1 is to be found in the 1954 Grøndahl set on Danacord
(whose heavy cuts rule it out as a top recommendation, however). The balance sheet comes out
strongly in favour of this Decca set, even before taking into account the excellent recording quality
and high quality of booklet presentation. This is a life-enhancing comic opera, comparable in many
ways to Britten's *A Midsummer Night's Dream*, and it's wonderful to hear it done full justice.

Luigi Nono
Italian 1924-1990

Nono Il canto sospeso.
Mahler Kindertotenlieder. Rückert-Lieder – Ich bin der Welt abhanden gekommen.
Susanne Lothar, Bruno Ganz *spkrs* **Barbara Bonney** *sop* **Susanne Otto** *mez*
Marjana Lipovšek *contr* **Marek Torzewski** *ten*
Berlin Radio Chorus; Berlin Philharmonic Orchestra / Claudio Abbado.
Sony Classical SK53360 (70 minutes: DDD). Recorded live in 1992. Ⓕ

More talked about than performed, at least in the UK, Nono's '20th-century classic' is a key work
of the European avant-garde, one in which serial processes and Communist ideology are brought
together in a dramatically compelling memorial to the victims of Fascism. Cynics might contend
that the advantage of such harrowing subject matter lies in its dialectical correctness – even Soviet
composers were able to incorporate moments of extreme dissonance so long as these could be said
to depict the horrors of Nazism – but this is to disregard the obvious emotional commitment which
suffuses Nono's often intractable idiom. Under Abbado, the playing is as tight and stylish as might
be expected from these forces: choral singing is unprecedentedly secure and Barbara Bonney is
especially radiant. Less welcome for repeated listening are the interpolated readings, by Bruno Ganz
and Susanne Lothar, of the letters from which Nono builds his cantata, the last dispatches of
members of the Resistance condemned to death. There are delivered coolly and unsensationally, not
in Italian, and can be programmed out according to taste. It is a powerful idea to juxtapose the two
main works. Nono's texts include many painful messages from children to parents – they too might
have been subtitled *Kindertotenlieder* – and Mahler's familiar *Rückert* verses are lent a new
resonance from the very first. Marjana Lipovšek, born and trained in what was once Yugoslavia,
sings well, with long, resonant and well-balanced phrases, yet her dark, solemn manner does not
efface memories of such female exponents as Ferrier, Ludwig and Baker. There is not quite enough

wistful tenderness, at least until the last song, where the *frisson* of a live performance comes across strongly in the consolatory calm of the closing stages. This is, as it should be, marvellously hushed, heart-rending stuff. The 20-bit technology does not entirely offset the drawbacks of live recording in the Philharmonie, but the results are perfectly acceptable here.

Per Nørgård
Danish 1932

Symphony No. 3. Piano Concerto.
Per Salo *pf* **Danish National Radio Choir and Symphony Orchestra / Leif Segerstam.**
Chandos New Direction CHAN9491 (73 minutes: DDD). Text and translation included.
Recorded 1996. Ⓕ

Chandos has provided typically opulent sound for this rich, variegated score of Symphony No. 3 (1972-5), and in the depth and presence of the recording one finds a wealth of detail that could otherwise be missed. Although in the first movement some sonorities could be projected more prominently, in the half-hour-long second movement the disc comes into its own, both sonically and as a performance. Segerstam's experience as a Mahler conductor enables him to weld the disparate elements most convincingly, though one feels bound to say that the music is never really symphonic. Nørgård's Piano Concerto is more recent, having been completed in 1996. Readers who know his viola and cello concertos *Between* and *Remembering Child* will find that this concerto approaches the genre from a quite different tack. Gone is the traditionally confrontational nature of the form: here the keyboard is first amongst equals, an ally of the orchestra whose concern it is to fuse and reconcile the opposing tempos. In fact, two entirely new ones emerge, but along the way Nørgård traverses some extraordinary terrain, as for instance in the weird cadenza in the piano's lowest register just over half-way through. Per Salo is undaunted by the technical difficulties, giving us a fascinating disc.

Ib Nørholm
Danish 1931

Symphonies – No. 4, Op. 76, 'De-creation'; No. 5, Op. 80, 'The Elements'.
Nina Pavlovski *sop* **Stefan Dahlberg** *ten* **Per Høyer** *bar* **Ib Nørholm** *narr*
Danish National Radio Choir; Odense Symphony Orchestra / Eduard Serov.
Kontrapunkt 32212 (74 minutes: DDD). Recorded 1995. Ⓕ

Like Per Nørgård, Ib Nørholm was a pupil of Vagn Holmboe and is currently Professor of Composition in Copenhagen. His early music was in a lyrical Nordic style very much in the tradition of Nielsen and Holmboe. But unlike his master, Nørholm has been keenly responsive to the European avant-garde and has, perhaps, embraced 'the new internationalism' too eagerly. The very titles of some of his works betray their self-consciousness: the Sixth Symphony is called 'Moralities, or There may be many miles to the nearest spider'. Nørholm possesses a sophisticated aural imagination and a fine ear for texture. Both symphonies offer us moments of considerable beauty and many others that are not. Basically the Fourth Symphony is deficient in thematic vitality and although there is a great deal of activity, there is little real musical movement. The Fifth Symphony is the more interesting of the two pieces. The opening of its third movement, *Poco fluente*, is quite beautiful but there is, arguably, too much neo-expressionistic hysteria and too little sense of momentum. The performances are dedicated and the recording copes admirably with the complex textures and reproduces them with lucidity.

Mikhail Nosyrev
USSR 1924-1981

Symphonies Nos. 3 and 4.
St Petersburg Academic Symphony Orchestra / Vladimir Verbitzky.
Olympia OCD653 (72 minutes: DDD). Recorded 1997. Ⓕ

In 1943 a 19-year-old violinist in Leningrad's Musical Comedy Theatre was arrested, accused of counter-revolutionary activity and sentenced to death by firing squad. The sentence was commuted to ten years' imprisonment, and having served his term, Mikhail Nosyrev returned to his profession, first as conductor then as composer. Shostakovich assisted in his induction into the Soviet Composers' Union in 1967. All this is according to Per Skans's fascinating booklet-essay, and a sad, though to Sovietologists all too familiar tale it is. Yet to go on to refer to Nosyrev's music as a 'time-bomb' is to raise expectations too high. To be sure, Nosyrev's penchant for grotesque juxtaposition makes for some memorable and vivid moments, but the lack of firm discipline and the general crudity of structure mean that the full potential of such moments is never realized. The two symphonies recorded here were composed shortly before Nosyrev's premature death. No. 3 begins with snarling bass clarinet, bassoons and tam-tam, rather like someone sitting on the bass end of a wheezy reed organ. A lamenting low flute line begins a succession of intense tableaux, each one set in stark relief from its surroundings. A central *Presto* with sudden, scary intrusions, like a ride in a ghost train, precipitates a passionate but curiously unmotivated climax, after which a return of the flute melody has a certain wan poignancy. Cartoon grotesquerie and rapid juxtapositions again dominate the second movement, while the finale is in pure Shostakovich oom-pah music-hall style, with a lamenting central section also indebted to the master. Tinkling triangles lead off the Fourth Symphony, whose 23-minute first movement alternates sonoristic and expressionistic sections in a way which rather touchingly fails to get going. The 13-minute second movement starts again as if to emulate a Shostakovich finale but develops its own individual line in gruesomeness. Of all the possible coded messages in Soviet music this movement's SOS patterns (from around 5'00") constitute one of the most intriguing. Performances are vivid and authoritative and recording quality is clean. All in all, this is a release of considerably more than average interest.

Vítezslav Novák
Bohemian 1870-1949

Piano Quintet in A minor, Op. 12. 13 Slovak Folksongs. Songs of a Winter Night, Op. 30.
Magdalena Kožená *mez* **Radoslav Kvapil** *pf*
Kocian Quartet (Pavel Hůla, Jan Odstrčil *vns* Zbynek Padourek *va* Václav Bernášek *vc*).
ASV CDDCA998 (67 minutes: DDD). Texts and translations included. Recorded 1996.   Ⓕ

Novák's A minor Piano Quintet of 1896 was composed in the wake of his first fruitful study of the folk-song traditions of both Moravia and Slovakia. It is an accomplished creation, comprising a finely sustained *Allegro molto moderato*, an effective central theme and variations (based on a fifteenth-century Czech love-song) and a joyous, swaggering finale. Seven years later, Novák produced his piano suite, *Songs of a Winter Night*. Its four movements make a charming set, ranging in mood from the wistful intimacy of the opening 'Song of a moonlight night' to the gleeful merry-making of the last in the series ('Song of a carnival night'). Even during the ecstatic pealing that marks the climax of the memorable 'Song of a Christmas night', Novák's piano writing always remains wonderfully pellucid, a factor that also adds to the listener's enjoyment of his six volumes of Slovak songs, 13 of which are heard here. Gems include the plaintive *Sedla mucha* ('A fly sat on a cornflower') with its bewitching piano traceries, the harmonically searching *Svic, mila, mas komu* ('Light the lamp, my love') and the haunting, tragic tale of *Chodzila Mariska* ('Mariska's walking along the bank'). Radoslav Kvapil and the Kocian Quartet form a thoroughly convincing alliance in the early Piano Quintet. The excellent Kvapil also shines in the solo suite (though the balance is slightly too close for comfort), and in the song sequence he provides tenderly idiomatic support to the characterful mezzo, Magdalena Kožená.

Michael Nyman
British 1944

The Piano Concerto. MGV (Musique à Grande Vitesse).
Kathryn Stott *pf*
Royal Liverpool Philharmonic Orchestra; Michael Nyman Band; orchestra / Michael Nyman.
Argo 443 382-2ZH (59 minutes: DDD). Recorded 1994.   Ⓕ

Considering the international success of Jane Campion's film *The Piano*, it seems quite logical that Nyman should adapt his celebrated score into a concert piece. Though performed uninterrupted, the 32-minute concerto is divided into four clear-cut sections. The Scottish folk-songs on which much of the score is based imbue the piece with a yearning, heartfelt quality not usually associated with this composer. Indeed, the whole concerto, as so convincingly advocated by Kathryn Stott and the RLPO, throbs with an unbridled romantic fervency (the second movement and the end of the third almost Rózsa-like in their ardour) that may come as something of a shock to hardened Nymanites or those who appreciate the less grandiose scoring for the film. More recognizably Nymanesque is *MGV*, a sort of *Pacific 231* for the 1990s, composed for the inauguration of the TGV North-European line in France. Here the composer's abstract style is eminently suited to describing a non-stop, imaginary railway journey through five regions between Paris and Lille; his repeated phrases and chugging, insistently propulsive rhythms create an effect that is totally spellbinding, with the strings adding an especially effective sense of speed and visual sweep. A rewarding disc that will appeal to Nyman fans old and new.

The Draughtsman's Contract – An Eye for Optical Theory; Queen of the Night. And do they do –
Songs 1, 2 and 4. The Piano – Here to There. Carrington – Outside Looking In; The Infinite
Complexities of Christmas. La traversée de Paris – Le Palais Royal; De l'Hôtel de la Ville à la
Concorde. Plotting for the Shopkeeper (all arr. Brady/Gregory and Roach).
London Saxophonic.
Tring International TRING007 (66 minutes: DDD). Recorded 1997.   Ⓜ🄴

Anybody interested in Michael Nyman's music should hear this disc. With the title 'An Eye for a
Difference' it consists of arrangements of many of Nyman's strongest pieces for London
Saxophonic, an ensemble made up of 10 saxophones, piano and electric bass. It is a measure of the
seriousness of this project that the production and all the arrangements have been carried out by
musicians who have had direct experience of playing in the Michael Nyman Band; and that Martin
Elliott and Andrew Findon, the bass guitarist and bass saxophone players who for so long have
been the 'bass powerhouse' of the Nyman sound, are also taking part. As David Roach points out
in his booklet-note, the Michael Nyman Band original scorings may create a more sharply
differentiated sound through the interplay of strings, saxes and brass, but the London Saxophonic
arrangements blend to a point that you do indeed, as Roach suggests, get the impression of 'one
giant instrument, sometimes clamorous, sometimes sweet but balanced in a way no other ensemble
could achieve'. If anything, the use of one basic tone colour makes Michael Nyman's music even
more punchy than usual and even less polite through the absence of a string section.

The London Saxophonic versions sound at times more complex than the originals, with musical
figures that were originally kept distinct in tone colour now rubbing up against each other in a way
that is very exciting. The dark, elemental quality of this recording makes you appreciate afresh not
only the sheer verve of Nyman's invention, but his extraordinary, effortless mastery of harmonic
progression. The production values of this disc similarly maximize performance energy, even if it
sometimes comes at the expense of absolutely perfect ensemble, the odd hard-sounding edit and
some slightly questionable artificial reverberation – although the latter could simply be the electric
wind instrument lurking. Nevertheless, this funky, rough-and-ready approach feels fully in keeping
with the spirit of the music and of this recording. This could well prove to be your favourite disc of
Michael Nyman's music. Play this disc at sufficiently high volume and make up your own mind.

String Quartet No. 4. Three Quartets.
Camilli Quartet (Elisabeth Perry, Rachel Browne *vns* Prunella Pacey *va* Melissa Phelps *vc*)
Michael Nyman Band / Michael Nyman.
EMI CDC5 56574-2 (56 minutes: DDD). Recorded 1997.   Ⓕ

Those who admire and enjoy Nyman's first three string quartets (available on Argo), will find much
to enjoy in this, his Fourth. The Quartet derives from a piece called *Yamamoto perpetuo* which was
especially composed for Yohji Yamamoto's autumn fashion show in Paris, and also makes use of
material from Nyman's score to Christopher Hampton's film *Carrington*, and a Scottish melody that
was noted down for *The Piano* but in the event wasn't used. The Camilli Quartet gives an
invigorating and sensitive performance. *Three Quartets* dates from 1994 and is so named because it
is scored for a string quartet, saxophone quartet and brass quartet. It's an interesting textural mix,
allowing the opportunity to explore and develop nicely contrasting passages in Nyman's typically
kaleidoscopic, frenetic manner, and is superbly performed here by the Michael Nyman Band. Good
recorded sound.

Fernando Obradors   Spanish 1897-1945

Obradors El poema de la Jungla.
Rodó Symphony No. 2.
Gran Canaria Philharmonic Orchestra / Adrian Leaper.
ASV CDDCA1043 (65 minutes: DDD). Recorded 1998.   Ⓕ🄴

The Spanish Gran Canaria Philharmonic is here paying tribute to two of its past conductors, both
virtually unknown as composers. In *El poema de la Jungla* Obradors was inspired by Rudyard
Kipling's classic. Written in 1938 and winning a Government of Catalonia prize, it was perhaps
intended to serve as a ballet, but no projected scenario is known, and it exists as a symphonic suite
in three movements, with an idyllic but rather diffuse Nocturne in its centre. Simple in outline, with
well-defined themes, and transparent in texture, it is imaginatively scored: the most striking
movement, as well as by far the longest, is the finale, which builds from an initial mysterious poetry
to increasingly energetic and often brilliant action, though with occasional broader, more tranquil

episodes. The Second Symphony by Gabriel Rodó, a distinguished cellist and successful conservatoire director, dates from 1957: its composition was reputedly stimulated by the news of the death of Sibelius. It is certainly an extremely serious-minded work – even the fast movements are shot through with disquiet and anxiety – and very well written. Rodó is really something of a find, and Adrian Leaper is to be thanked for bringing him to our notice. Playing and recording alike are of a very high order.

Johannes Ockeghem Flanders *c*1410-1497

Missa prolationum.
The Clerks' Group / Edward Wickham.
ASV Gaudeamus CDGAU143 (65 minutes: DDD). Recorded 1995.   Ⓕ🅴
Obrecht (attrib.) Humilium decus. **Busnois** Gaude coelestis Domina. In hydraulis.
Pullois Flos de spina. **Josquin Desprez** Illibata Dei Virgo nutrix.

This recording focuses on one of the most astonishing compositional feats of the second half of the fifteenth century: Ockeghem's *Missa prolationum.* The successive movements of the Ordinary of the Mass are based on double canons that progress from the unison to the octave, while at the same time the composer also exploits the inherent ambiguity of the mensural system (hence the work's title) of the later Middle Ages so that the rhythmic relationships between the voices are constantly being transformed. The astonishing thing is how effortlessly Ockeghem weaves his complex polyphonic web, and this is reinforced here by the unfettered, direct way in which The Clerks' Group approaches the music. Although there are only eight singers in the group (so a maximum of two voices to a part), they bring a very satisfactory mix of the vocal agility one might expect from a small ensemble and the ability to sing through the long-breathed lines favoured by Ockeghem, without ever sounding strained or thin. The overall sound is immediate, crystal clear and closely recorded, but it never lacks for richness or blend – much credit to the ASV production team, too, in this respect. Although at first sight the five motets on the disc seem only loosely related to each other and to the Mass (the works date variously from the 1460s through to the 1490s), there are potentially illuminating links: several of the composers appear to pay homage, whether directly or indirectly, to one another's pieces and in general they all opt for quite self-consciously complex structures yet create a musical idiom that is lucid and full of emotional responses to the texts (mostly Marian) they chose to set. This is the Franco-Netherlandish school at its best.

Ockeghem Missa 'l'homme armé'. Ave Maria. Alma redemptoris mater.
Josquin Desprez Memor esto verbi tui.
Plainchant Alma redemptoris mater. Immittet angelus Domini.
Anonymous L'homme armé.
Oxford Camerata / Jeremy Summerly.
Naxos 8 554297 (57 minutes: DDD). Texts and translations included.   Ⓢ

The centrepiece of this recording is Ockeghem's *L'homme armé* Mass. It may be one of Ockeghem's earliest Masses, dating perhaps from the early 1450s. It is also one of his most curious. For the most part it lies in a relatively high register, belying the composer's usual predilection for low bass ranges; but every now and again the basses descend in spectacular fashion. In the third *Agnus*, they hold down the tune in very long notes, with the other voices seeming to float above them. Seldom before in the history of music can the articulation of time have been so clear a feature of a piece's design: it seems almost to have been suspended altogether. It is an extraordinary moment, and extraordinarily difficult to pull off in performance, but here the singers seem to have got it right. Elsewhere, Summerly's approach is nicely varied, but on the whole more meditative than emphatic; one might say that the performance grows in stature with each movement, as though keeping pace with the cycle's ambition. In its details the reading is not without the odd glitch, but taken as a whole it is a fine achievement. The accompanying motets work very well but it is a shame that the choir's richness of sound is not quite matched by the acoustic. They deserve a more inspiring venue. But the overall impression is resoundingly positive: those new to Ockeghem should find this super-budget disc too good an opportunity to pass up.

Missa 'Mi-Mi'. Intemerata Dei mater.
Cappella Pratensis / Rebecca Stewart *sop*
Ricercar RIC206402 (56 minutes: DDD). Texts and translations included. Recorded 1997-98.   Ⓕ

This recording of the *Mi-Mi* Mass offers a refreshingly different approach. Rebecca Stewart has thought a great deal about the work and proposes a mystical, symbolic interpretation of its modal structure. Mystical, too, is Cappella Pratensis's performance under her direction: tempos are drawn-out and the singing is characterized by expressive swells on long notes that sound very different from the much straighter delivery adopted by English groups. If the tempos seem almost too extreme in the longer-texted movements (some listeners may find the word 'almost' a bit rich: the *Credo* lasts nearly 12 minutes), in the melismatic movements especially the purposeful shaping of lines makes for deeply involving listening. The ensemble is recognizably Flemish in tone, but sings at a consistently low dynamic: the effect is not so much muted as inward, which gives the women's voices an intriguing graininess. There are some bizarre decisions regarding sharpened notes, particularly those on final chords, most audibly in the *Kyrie* and in an otherwise solid rendition of *Intemerata Dei mater*. It might be easy to point out occasional roughnesses of intonation and delivery, but for those who worry that a certain depressing uniformity is taking hold of this repertory, Stewart's approach is not so much a breath of fresh air as a much-needed hit of oxygen. Don't pass it by. This recording is utterly compelling.

Missa 'De plus en plus'. Presque transi. Prenez sur moi vostre exemple. O rosa bella o dolce anima mia. Aultre Venus estés. Petite camusette. Tant fuz gentement. Mort tu as navré.
Orlando Consort (Robert Harre-Jones *counterten* Charles Daniels, Angus Smith *tens* Donald Greig *bar*).
Archiv Produktion 453 419-2AH (73 minutes: DDD). Texts and translations included. Recorded 1996. Ⓕ

This is a superb recording of Ockeghem's Mass, *De plus en plus*, by the Orlando Consort. The Orlandos' mixed programme of sacred and secular music offers a good, rounded picture of Ockeghem's art. In the Mass, the Orlandos are obvious first choice for those who prefer a soloistic approach, or for whom anything other than countertenors on top lines smacks of heresy. They are experienced singers with logical phrasing and breathing in solo passages, great interpretative acuteness, and a quality of ensemble that is of itself expressive. The Orlandos seem to achieve more with less: that is part of the magic of hearing Ockeghem sung this way. The accompanying songs certainly makes the case for Ockeghem's versatility as a song composer, a point emphasized by the differences of scoring to which they are especially sensitive. If this recording demonstrates anything, it is that the sacred and the secular are very different worlds. If the Orlandos seem to have trouble shifting gears between the two they are certainly not alone, either in England or abroad.

Ockeghem Requiem. Fors seulement. Missa 'Fors seulement'.
Brumel Du tout plongiet/Fors seulement.
La Rue Fors seulement.
The Clerks' Group / Edward Wickham.
ASV Gaudeamus CDGAU168 (71 minutes: DDD). Texts and translations included. Recorded 1996.
Gramophone Award Winner 1997. Ⓕ Ⓔ

Top billing goes to the Requiem, Ockeghem's most widely recorded work and perhaps his most enigmatic piece, stylistically very wide-ranging and diverse. Aesthetic judgement is hard to pass, since it may well be incomplete; but the surviving movements contain some of his most arresting inspirations. This is the first version of any quality to feature sopranos on the top lines. Incidentally, no recording of the Requiem is uniformly excellent; on the other hand, the words of the Mass for the dead conjure up many associations, and The Clerks deserve praise for the verve and imagination with which they respond to the work's interpretative challenges. The fillers are the works built on Ockeghem's song *Fors seulement* (which includes Antoine Brumel's *Du tout plongiet*). It is difficult to decide which to praise more highly: the pieces themselves, which are incomparable, or the singing, which represents The Clerks' finest achievement to date. *Fors seulement* inspired a flowering of astonishing pieces scored for very low voices (initiated, it appears, by the composer himself): in both the Mass and in *Du tout plongiet*, the basses descend to written low Cs. In addition, these pieces are exceptionally richly scored (the Mass and the La Rue song are five-voice works), creating polyphony as dense and as dark as a strong Trappist ale. The Clerks achieve almost miraculous linear definition here, without losing an iota of the music's sensuous appeal: quite a feat, given the low pitch and awesome contrapuntal complexity involved. This is a major achievement.

Jacques Offenbach   German/French 1819-1880

Offenbach (arr. M. Rosenthal) Gaîté parisienne.
Rossini (arr./orch. Respighi) La boutique fantasque.
Boston Pops Orchestra / Arthur Fiedler.
RCA Victor Living Stereo 09026 61847-2 (64 minutes: ADD). Recorded 1954-56. Ⓜ Ⓗ

Arthur Fiedler and the Boston Pops, for so long the guardians of traditional concert-hall light music in America, never made a better stereo recording than the amazing early (1954) complete Offenbach/Rosenthal *Gaîté parisienne* ballet score. It scintillates with effervescence and vitality, has just the right degree of brash vulgarity, yet the richly embracing acoustics of Symphony Hall ensure that the entry of the great 'Barcarolle' has warmth as well as allure. This transfer makes the very most of the outstanding mastertape. The coupling comprises some 27 minutes from the hardly less delectable Rossini/Respighi *La boutique fantasque* also brightly and atmospherically played and again given first-class sound from two years later. A real collector's item, not to be missed by anyone who cares about the history of stereo reproduction and also for the sheer *joie de vivre* of the music.

Les contes d'Hoffmann.
Raoul Jobin *ten* Hoffmann; **Renée Doria** *sop* Olympia; **Vina Bovy** *sop* Giulietta;
Géori Boué *sop* Antonia; **Fanély Revoil** *mez* Nicklausse; **Louis Musy** *bar* Lindorf;
André Pernet *bass* Coppélius; **Charles Soix** *bass* Dapertutto; **Roger Bourdin** *bar* Dr Miracle;
René Lapelletrie *ten* Spalanzani; **Camille Maurane** *bar* Hermann;
Chorus and Orchestra of the Opéra-Comique, Paris / André Cluytens.
EMI mono CMS5 65260-2 (two discs: 130 minutes: ADD). Notes and text included.
Recorded 1948. Ⓜ H RR

In the 1930s in Paris, Raoul Jobin and José Luccioni were the two great opera matinée-idols. Jobin was a French Canadian, made his début in 1930 and was soon singing at both the Opéra, as Faust, Lohengrin and Raoul in *Les Huguenots*, and at the Opéra-Comique, where he was a favourite Hoffmann and Don José. This recording may perhaps find him just a little late in his career. His years at the Metropolitan (throughout the German occupation) obviously took their toll, when he sang roles that were too heavy for him in such a huge theatre. However, the splendour of this set is the authenticity of the vocal style and the diction of such stalwarts of the Opéra-Comique ensemble as Louis Musy, Roger Bourdin, Fanély Revoil (better known as an operetta singer) and, luxurious casting, Camille Maurane in the small part of Hermann.

The three heroines are well inside their roles, but are afflicted with a little strain in the higher-lying passages. Renée Doria sang all these parts later in her career – when this recording was made she was just at the outset, having made her début in Paris in 1944. Her Olympia is strong on the *staccato* notes but a bit fragile in the long phrases – this doll broke quite easily, one imagines. In the same act, André Pernet, a great figure from pre-war Paris is a superb Coppélius. In the Venice act, Vina Bovy is dramatically convincing as Giulietta, but hasn't much vocal sheen left (she made her début in 1919). Géori Boué, the Antonia, is one of the great figures from French post-war opera, but one feels that Giulietta would have been her role ideally. As for Jobin, despite some strain, he makes a convincing poet. Although there is such strong competition on CD where *Hoffmann* is concerned, this historic version is essential listening for a sense of style if the work absorbs you.

Les contes d'Hoffmann.
Plácido Domingo *ten* Hoffmann; **Dame Joan Sutherland** *sop* Olympia, Giulietta, Antonia, Stella;
Gabriel Bacquier *bar* Lindorf, Coppélius, Dapertutto, Dr Miracle;
Huguette Tourangeau *mez* La Muse, Nicklausse; **Jacques Charon** *ten* Spalanzani;
Hugues Cuénod *ten* Andrès, Cochenille, Pitichinaccio, Frantz; **André Neury** *bar* Schlemil;
Paul Plishka *bass* Crespel; **Margarita Lilowa** *mez* Voice of Antonia's Mother;
Roland Jacques *bar* Luther;
Lausanne Pro Arte Chorus; Du Brassus Chorus;
Suisse Romande Chorus and Orchestra / Richard Bonynge.
Decca 417 363-2DH2 (two discs: 143 minutes: ADD). Notes, text and translation included.
Recorded 1968. Ⓕ

This is a wonderfully refreshing set, made the more sparkling in the CD transfer, which enhances the sense of presence and immediacy in the often-complicated action. The story emerges crystal-clear, even the black ending to the Giulietta scene in Venice, which in Bonynge's text restores the original idea of the heroine dying from a draught of poison, while the dwarf, Pitichinaccio shrieks in delight. One also has to applaud his rather more controversial decision to put the Giulietta scene in the middle and leave the dramatically weighty Antonia scene till last. That also makes the role of Stella the more significant, giving extra point to the decision to have the same singer take all four heroine roles. With Dame Joan available it was a natural decision, and though in spoken dialogue she is less comfortable in the Giulietta scene than the rest, the contrasting portraits in each scene are all very convincing, with the voice brilliant in the doll scene, warmly sensuous in the Giulietta scene and powerfully dramatic as well as tender in the Antonia scene. Gabriel Bacquier gives sharply intense performances, firm and dark vocally, in the four villain roles, Hugues Cuénod contributes delightful vignettes in the four *comprimario* tenor roles, while Domingo establishes at the very start the distinctive bite in his portrait of Hoffmann; a powerful and a perceptive interpretation. The recording is vivid, with first-class playing from the Suisse Romande Orchestra.

Orphée aux enfers (ed. Minkowski/Pelly).
Yann Beuron *ten* Orphée; **Natalie Dessay** *sop* Eurydice; **Jean-Paul Fouchécourt** *ten* Aristée-Pluton; **Laurent Naouri** *bar* Jupiter; **Lydie Pruvot** *sop* Juno; **Ewa Podles** *mez* Public Opinion; **Steven Cole** *ten* John Styx; **Véronique Gens** *sop* Vénus; **Patricia Petibon** *sop* Cupid; **Jennifer Smith** *sop* Diane; **Etienne Lescroart** *ten* Mercury; **Virginie Pochon** *sop* Minerva; **Grenoble Chamber Orchestra;**
Chorus and Orchestra of the Opéra National de Lyon / Marc Minkowski.
EMI CDS5 56725-2 (two discs: 110 minutes: DDD). Notes, text and translation included. Ⓟ🄴
Recorded 1997.

Orphée aux enfers may be Offenbach's best-known operetta, but it has had limited attention on disc. The lightly scored original 1858 version was in two acts and four scenes. The spectacular 1874 version had lots of extra songs and ballet numbers. Since this latter demands huge forces, it is scarcely viable on stage today. The usual solution in the theatre is thus to add selected numbers from the 1874 version to the 1858 text, and this is what was done for the performances at Geneva, Lyons and Grenoble that formed the basis of this recording. Home listeners may prefer to make their own selections of numbers, and musicologically questionable decisions such as the rescoring of 1874 pieces for 1858 orchestral resources become more exposed. What matters most, though, is the quality of performance, and the pleasures of this one are formidable. Above all, Natalie Dessay's exchanges in the First Act with her despised violinist husband (the admirable Yann Beuron) are superbly done. So is her sighing over Jean-Paul Fouchécourt's Aristeus, whose two big solos show equal elegance. Later come Laurent Naouri's formidable Jupiter and cameos such as Etienne Lescroart's agile performance of Mercury's song and Patricia Petibon's deliciously winning account of Cupid's 'Couplets des baisers' (both interpolations from the 1874 version). Ensemble numbers are extremely well done and throughout, Marc Minkowski provides thoughtful and lively direction.

What causes doubt is the tendency towards overstatement, from the opening monologue of Eva Podles's Public Opinion, where almost every word seems to be given exaggerated emphasis, through Aristeus's crude falsetto in his opening solo, to a curiously mechanical version of John Styx's 'Quand j'étais roi de Béotie' and some gratuitous vocal gymnastics in the 'Hymne à Bacchus'. Ultimately, however, those doubts are banished by the positive virtues. Whereas those who want virtually every note Offenbach composed for *Orphée aux enfers* must stick with the 1978 Plasson/EMI recording (reissued on CD some years ago), Minkowski's version offers a more faithful impression of Offenbach's original compact creation, with selected 1874 additions as a bonus. It is a consistently imaginative performance, altogether livelier than its predecessor, and at its best a superbly musical version of Offenbach's sparkling creation.

Carl Orff German 1895-1982

Carmina Burana.
Gundula Janowitz *sop* **Gerhard Stolze** *ten* **Dietrich Fischer-Dieskau** *bar*
Schönberg Boys' Choir;
Chorus and Orchestra of the Deutsche Oper, Berlin / Eugen Jochum.
DG The Originals 447 437-2GOR (56 minutes: ADD). Text and translation included.
Recorded 1967. Ⓜ🆁🆁

Since its original release, Jochum's performance has consistently been a prime recommendation for this much-recorded piece. Listening to it again in the superbly remastered sound, one can easily hear why. He pays great attention to detail – particularly with regard to tempo and articulation – yet the performance as a whole has a tremendous cogent sweep and the choruses have terrific power. The more reflective sections are not neglected, however, and movements such as 'Stetit Puella', with Janowitz sounding alluring and fey, have surely never been more sensitively handled. Stolze is ideal as the roasted swan and Fischer-Dieskau encompasses the very varied requirements of the baritone's music with ease. This distinguished performance, authorized by the composer and here sounding better than ever, retains its place at the head of the queue.

Carmina Burana.
Beverly Hoch *sop* **Stanford Olsen** *ten* **Mark Oswald** *bar*
F.A.C.E. Treble Choir; Montreal Symphony Chorus and Orchestra / Charles Dutoit.
Decca 455 290-2DH (59 minutes: DDD). Texts and translations included. Recorded 1996. Ⓔ

Dutoit's is the most satisfying and sheerly enjoyable modern performance of *Carmina Burana* to have appeared for some time. He is scrupulous in his attention to the many markings to be found in the score and ensures that details of articulation and orchestration are clearly audible, without obtruding from the overall texture. His tempos, almost without exception, feel just right, and Dutoit has conveyed his evident enthusiasm for the music to his performers, who respond accordingly. Stanford Olsen's roasted swan song is appropriately weird – helped by Orff's strange accompaniment being superbly pointed, whilst Beverly Hoch compensates for some thinness of tone with expressive phrasing, including a sensuous *portamento* in her 'In trutina' solo. Apart from his first number, which is somewhat ponderous, Mark Oswald delivers the baritone's music with an equal measure of sensitivity and gusto. The choral singing is exceptionally fine. The recording, clear and full-bodied, makes this release the most recommendable of digital versions.

Orff Carmina Burana.
Holst The Planets.
Penelope Walmsley-Clark *sop* John Graham-Hall *ten* Donald Maxwell *bar*
Southend Boys' Choir; London Symphony Chorus and Orchestra / Richard Hickox.
Carlton Classics LSO Doubles 30368 01107 (two discs: 114 minutes: DDD). Recorded 1987.   Ⓑ

One of the best all-rounders of this Carlton series is the unexpected Hickox coupling of *Carmina Burana* with Holst's *The Planets*. The former is especially successful and indeed is among the best of all the available bargain versions, partly because the excellent LSO Chorus is joined by the Southend Boys' Choir, whose knowing sexual joy in 'Oh, oh, oh, I am bursting out all over' gives the 'Cours d'amour' sequence an exhilarating lift. Penelope Walmsley Clarke, too, is rapturously seductive as the 'Girl in the red dress'. Hickox directs the proceedings with precision and enthusiasm and the digital sound has fine presence. *The Planets* is also pretty impressive, opening with a snarling account of 'Mars', followed by a translucently peaceful 'Venus'. 'Jupiter' and 'Uranus' rather lack ripeness, if not vitality, but the withdrawn atmosphere of 'Saturn' is very compelling, as is the closing hush of 'Neptune'. The recording is vivid rather than rich, but has a spectacular range. This pairing is surely worth any collector's outlay.

Trionfi – Carmina Burana[a]; Catulli Carmina[b]; Trionfo di Afrodite[c].
[a]**Barbara Hendricks**, [bc]**Dagmar Schellenberger**, [c]**Lisa Larson**, [c]**Eva Maria Nobauer** *sops*
[c]**Barbara Reiter** *contr* [a]**Michael Chance** *counterten* [bc]**Lothar Odinius**, [c]**Robert Swensen** *tens*
[c]**Klaus Kuttler**, [a]**Jeffrey Black** *bars* [c]**Alfred Reiter** *bass*
[a]**St Albans Abbey Choir**; [a]**London Philharmonic Choir**; [bc]**Linz Mozart Choir**;
[a]**London Philharmonic Orchestra**; [bc]**Munich Radio Orchestra** / Franz Welser-Möst.
EMI CDS5 55519-2 (two discs: 137 minutes: DDD). Texts and translations included.   Ⓕ
Recorded 1989.

Catulli Carmina and *Trionfo di Afrodite* are under-represented in the current catalogue, unlike *Carmina Burana*, and it is here given a lithe and vigorous reading with spectacular playing from the LPO and fine singing from the choruses. Barbara Hendricks's vibrato may not be to all tastes and Jeffrey Black is too genial, lacking the requisite *slancio* quality his part demands, whilst Michael Chance's beautiful tone is not what was intended by the composer since a tenor singing in his highest register is specified. Nevertheless, this performance is more than the sum of its parts and Welser-Möst's attention to detail is evidence of his careful and considered approach. In the central section of *Catulli Carmina*, the unaccompanied settings of Catullus are well realized with secure intonation and variety of expression and the prologue, with its insistent ostinatos for four pianos and percussion, is quite electrifying. *Trionfo di Afrodite* receives a thrilling and compelling performance and the final, orgiastic shouts of the chorus greeting the appearance of the goddess, make it the climax of the whole triptych. As bride and bridegroom, Dagmar Schellenberger and Lothar Odinius rise to the challenges of their parts with their wide-ranging and melismatic melodic lines. The other soloists and chorus sing with conviction and enthusiasm, supported by colourful and confident orchestral playing. Just occasionally, Welser-Möst presses ahead when Orff directs otherwise, but he draws out the dramatic qualities inherent in these works which were conceived for the theatre and despite blemishes, this set is now the preferred version of *Trionfo*.

Johann Pachelbel

German 1653-1706

Musicalische Ergötzung.
Les Cyclopes (Manfred Kraemer, Laura Johnson *vns* Nina Diehl *vc* Bibiane Lapointe *hpd*
Thierry Maeder *org*).
Pierre Verany PV794111 (53 minutes: DDD). Recorded 1994.   Ⓔ Ⓟ

This recording is a sobering reminder that the likes of Pachelbel and Muffat from the German-speaking world are on the same level and sometimes even better than, for example, the likes of Biber. Indeed, it is most likely that Biber published his partitas for *scordatura* violins, *Harmonia artificioso–ariosa*, as a direct consequence of this very set, which Pachelbel sent to the press in 1691. One can quite believe it, judging by the way Biber articulates and circumnavigates the contours of the sarabande as Pachelbel does equally well in the third *Partie*. But there is more to it than that: it is the freedom of the polyphonic textures and coloration achieved through the special *scordatura* tuning of the violins (an elaborate system to facilitate double- and triple-stopping and diversify the tonal properties of the instrument) which both composers share. The relatively restricted structure of the dance, the chaconne and the suite as a whole gives the spirit of free invention and variation a context in which Pachelbel would seem to have set a trend for his Moravian colleague to contemplate.

Pachelbel's *scordatura* music is arguably more instantly appealing than Biber's more arcane examples, though less intricate and rhetorically concentrated. Pachelbel was, after all, a more cosmopolitan figure by the very nature of his geographical situation, a world of less maverick virtuosity than Biber's though one which exhibits a greater range of up-to-date sonata techniques from Italy and mature dance movements from France. As with Muffat, and so many other Germans, the marriage is fortuitous and, as the sonata *allegro* of the third *Partie* shows, the rigours of indigenous counterpoint blend effortlessly into the merry hybrid. In all the six suites – each one for two violins and basso continuo – Les Cyclopes is admirably forthright, yet capable, too, of portraying with a rich palette an intensity of feeling and immediacy which few baroque chamber ensembles achieve so effortlessly. The character of the dances is clearly and often humorously communicated and the passagework is always executed with precision and a sleight of hand, even if the tuning is occasionally a touch wayward. These committed performances can be safely recommended to those searching for attractive and finely wrought music of the pre-Bach period.

Giovanni Pacini
Italian 1796-1867

Maria, Regina d'Inghilterra.
Nelly Miricioiu *sop* Mary Tudor; **Bruce Ford** *ten* Riccardo Fenimoore;
José Fardilha *bass* Ernesto Malcolm; **Mary Plazas** *sop* Clotilde Talbot;
Alastair Miles *bass* Gualtiero Churchill; **Susan Bickley** *mez* Page; **Benjamin Bland** *bass* Raoul;
Geoffrey Mitchell Choir; Philharmonia Orchestra / David Parry.
Opera Rara ORC15 (three discs: 172 minutes: DDD). Notes, text and translation included.
Recorded 1995-96.   Ⓕ

Pacini wrote happily within the formal conventions of Italian opera in his time. Opening chorus, aria and cabaletta, duet likewise in two 'movements', big ensemble as finale of the middle act, 'brilliant' solo for prima donna just before the final curtain. The form (like sonata form or sonnet) is a good one, perhaps the best for opera to be itself in, rather than a play set to music; and for the most part Pacini exploits the form admirably. The plot is adapted from the play by Victor Hugo, and tells of Mary I's love for a scheming courtier, an Italian in Hugo, the Scotsman Fenimoore in Pacini. This Fenimoore, being the tenor, is loved by two ladies and is deceiving both. The other woman, Clotilde, is protected and loved by the baritone Ernesto, who of course finds out about Fenimoore, to accomplish the downfall of whom he puts himself at the disposal of Fenimoore's enemy, the Lord Chancellor (bass). A great point about such a set-up is the scope it provides for duets, and these are both plentiful and good. There are choruses of merrymakers, soldiers and Londoners out for blood. The ensemble, an excellent example of its kind, comes at the point when Fenimoore is cornered and feelings run high.

So do the voices. We are lucky to have Bruce Ford. At a *fortissimo* he may sound underpowered, and he does not play imaginatively with *mezza voce* effects, but he much more than copes: in florid passages he moves swiftly and gracefully, he appears to be comfortable with the tessitura, and in the Prison scene, which provided Ivanov with his greatest success, he sings with feeling and a sense of style. The women have suitably contrasting voices, Mary Plazas's fresh and high, Nelly Miricioiu's older in tone, more dramatic in timbre. Both are expressive singers, and though Miricioiu too habitually resorts to the imperious glottal emphasis associated with Callas and Caballé, she brings conviction to all she does. The baritone, José Fardilha, has a touch of the flicker-vibrato that can give distinctive character, and Alastair Miles confers nobility of utterance upon the vindictive Chancellor. The cast, in fact, is worthy of the opera, which in this recording has probably its most important performance since the première of 1843. There is fine work from the Geoffrey Mitchell Choir and the Philharmonia under David Parry. Recorded sound is clear and well balanced, and the production handles the drama well. You are likely to play it straight through from start to finish, chafing at any interruption; and that says something for both the music and the drama.

Ignacy Paderewski

Polish 1860-1941

Symphony in B minor, Op. 24, 'Polonia'.
BBC Scottish Symphony Orchestra / Jerzy Maksymiuk.
Hyperion CDA67056 (74 minutes: DDD). Recorded 1998. ⒡

Best-known as a legendary concert pianist and appointed first Prime Minister of Poland in 1919, Ignacy Jan Paderewski also found time to compose. In 1903 he embarked on his vast *Polonia* Symphony, which cost him some five years of labour and was to be his final major creation. First heard privately in Lausanne on Boxing Day, 1908, the symphony received its public première in Boston some eight weeks later under Max Fiedler and was soon taken up by both Hans Richter and André Messager. In its unashamedly epic countenance and theatrical sense of rhetoric, *Polonia* most closely resembles the two symphonies of Liszt as well as Tchaikovsky's *Manfred*, though it perhaps lacks the distinctive thematic profile of those masterworks. That said, the mighty opening movement (some half-an-hour in duration) is an impressive achievement, its stately introductory material sowing the seeds for much of what is to follow as well as acting as a most effective foil to the rousingly patriotic, defiant *Allegro vivace* proper. At first, the central *Andante con moto* meanders along moodily in an introspective, Rachmaninovian manner, but, about half-way through, the skies darken further and the music acquires a distinctly troubled, sombre flavour that cannot be dispelled (the bleak coda offers no consolation). The finale's truculent battle-cries (which manage to incorporate a cleverly disguised motif based on the first two bars of the Polish national anthem) are temporarily assuaged by two tranquil episodes. The BBC Scottish SO and its longstanding Polish chief Jerzy Maksymiuk mastermind a performance of eloquence and dashing commitment (only in the closing minutes does any hint of raggedness creep into the violins' bustling – and, by the sound of it, none-too-rewarding – passagework). The recording, too, is pretty resplendent, and collectors with a sweet tooth for precisely this sort of heady, late-romantic 'spectacular' shouldn't hesitate for a moment.

Nicolò Paganini

Italian 1782-1840

Violin Concertos – No. 1 in E flat major, Op. 6; No. 2 in B minor, Op. 7, 'La campanella'.

Violin Concertos Nos. 1 and 2.
Salvatore Accardo *vn*
London Philharmonic Orchestra / Charles Dutoit.
DG 415 378-2GH (69 minutes: ADD). Recorded 1975. ⒡

Paganini's violin music was at one time thought quite inaccessible to lesser mortals among the violin-playing fraternity, but as standards of technique have improved master technicians are now able to do justice to such works as these concertos. Salvatore Accardo is certainly among them, and we can judge his skill as early as the opening violin solo of the First Concerto. This is typical of the style, with its authoritative and rhetorical gestures and use of the whole instrumental compass, but so is the second theme which in its refinement and songlike nature demands (and here receives) another kind of virtuosity expressed through a command of tone, texture and articulation. Dutoit and the London Philharmonic Orchestra have a mainly subordinate role, certainly when the soloist is playing, but they fulfil it well and follow Accardo through the kind of rhythmic flexibilities which are accepted performing style in this music and which for all we know were used by the virtuoso performer-composer himself. The recording is faithful and does justice to the all-important soloist.

Violin Concertos Nos. 1 and 2.
Ilya Kaler *vn*
Polish National Radio Symphony Orchestra / Stephen Gunzenhauser.
Naxos 8 550649 (67 minutes: DDD). Recorded 1992. Ⓢ

Ilya Kaler is a Russian virtuoso (born in Moscow in 1963), a pupil of Leonid Kogan. He is a first-rate fiddler and an excellent musician. Paganini's once fiendish pyrotechnics hold no terrors for him, not even the whistling harmonics, and how nicely he can turn an Italianate lyrical phrase, as in the secondary theme of the first movement of the First Concerto. Then he can set off with panache into a flying *staccato*, bouncing his bow neatly on the strings when articulating the delicious *spiccato* finales of both works. Stephen Gunzenhauser launches into the opening movements with plenty of energy and aplomb and is a sympathetic accompanist throughout – he is never heavy in orchestral writing that can easily sound vapid or stodgy. How nicely the violins shape the lyrical ritornello introducing the first movement of the Second, and there is some sensitive horn playing in the *Adagio*. Kaler's intonation is above suspicion and he is naturally balanced: there is none of the scratchiness that can ruin one's pleasure in Paganinian pyrotechnics. With excellent notes, this is a superior product at super-bargain price. The recordings were made in the Concert Hall of Polish Radio in Katowice. It has an ideal ambience for this music: nicely warm, not clouded. Great value on all counts.

Paganini Violin Concerto No. 1.
Saint-Saëns Havanaise in E major, Op. 83. Introduction and Rondo capriccioso in A minor, Op. 28.
Sarah Chang vn
Philadelphia Orchestra / Wolfgang Sawallisch.
EMI CDC5 55026-2 (55 minutes: DDD). Recorded 1993-94. (F)

Paganini would surely have been utterly astonished at Sarah Chang's version of his No. 1. She made her début with the piece in the Avery Fisher Hall at the age of eight(!), but had reached more advanced years (12) when she recorded it in Philadelphia for EMI. The performance is dazzling, particularly the finale where her light rhythmic touch and deliciously pert sliding 'harmonized harmonics' are a wonder of technical assurance. Note too, in the first movement, the relaxed ease of the decorated bouncing bow passages and the gently tender reprise of the second subject. The slow movement is not overtly romantic, but the freshness is never in doubt. One does not expect her to sound maturely sophisticated like Perlman and she slightly understates the sultry atmosphere of the Saint-Saëns *Havanaise* to pleasing effect, yet manages the coda with spruce flexibility of phrase and the most subtle graduations of timbre. The *Introduction and Rondo capriccioso* has plenty of dash and she catches the Spanish sunlight in the *Introduction* without an overtly sensuous response. She is not flattered by the recording: balanced close. Sawallisch directs with plenty of verve and he supports his soloist admirably.

Centone di sonate Nos. 7-12.
Moshe Hammer vn **Norbert Kraft** gtr
Naxos 8 553142 (72 minutes: DDD). Recorded 1994. (S)

The *Centone di sonate* (a 'hotchpotch of sonatas') consists of 18 'sonatas' which are really salon works with a variety of movements – none of them in sonata form. Whether Paganini, who wrote them sometime after 1828, intended these pieces for public performance or merely for the use of the then abundant amateur musicians is not known. As usual in his works of this genre, it is the violin which hogs the limelight while the guitar remains a humble bag-carrier. The guitar parts are indeed so simple that they would have been within the reach of any amateur who was capable of keeping his end up with another musician; Segovia considered them beneath his dignity and refused many invitations to play them with famous partners! Nothing is harder than to be 'simple': Mozart managed it whilst at the same time being deceptively complex; Paganini did it at a far less sublime level, with sentimental, cheerful and pert tunes. Truth to tell, they are not the kind of works which impel one to listen to them at one sitting except for the most devoted *aficionado* of Paganini's violinistic voice or of hearing the guitar in an unremittingly subservient though genuinely complementary role. These splendid performances on modern instruments make no claim to 'authentic' status, but they are no less appealing for that. They squeeze every last drop from the music with (inauthentically) full sound, and a Siamese-twin tightness of ensemble that was probably rare amongst those who played these works in Paganini's own time. In the end, these works have a charm that is hard for any but the most straitlaced to resist. It is unlikely that the *Centone* will ever be better played and/or recorded.

Six Sonatas for Guitar and Violin, Op. 3. Sonata concertata in A major, Op. 61. 60 Variations on 'Barucabà', Op. 14. Cantabile in D major, Op. 17.
Scott St John vn **Simon Wynberg** gtr
Naxos 8 550690 (54 minutes: DDD). Recorded 1993. (S)

Six Sonatas for Guitar and Violin, Op. 2. Cantabile e Valtz, Op. 19. Variazioni di bravura on Caprice No. 24. Duetto amoroso. Sonata per le gran viola e chitarra.
Scott St John vn **Simon Wynberg** gtr
Naxos 8 550759 (59 minutes: DDD). Recorded 1993. (S)

Several of the violin/guitar duos testify to Paganini's amorous inclinations: the sections of the *Duetto amoroso* spell out the course of an affair, from beginning to separation, and may have been aimed (unsuccessfully, one imagines) at the Princess Elisa Baciocchi in Lucca. His conservative harmonic vocabulary springs few surprises and his melodies sometimes verge on banality, but by dint of sheer charm and technical ingenuity he somehow gets away with it; only the po-faced could resist an admiring smile at his effrontery. Collectively, these works present the full range of Paganini's technical armoury – the left-hand pizzicatos, high harmonics, double-stopping, 'sneaky' chromatic runs and the rest, and Scott St John betrays no difficulty in dealing with every googly that comes his way. More than that, in the daunting *Sonata per le gran viola e chitarra* (celebrating Paganini's acquisition of a Stradivarius instrument) cocks a snook at every viola joke that ever was. The guitar's role in the action varies from purely supportive subservience to more equal (though at a lower acrobatic level) partnership, as in the *Sonata concertata* and from time to time in the Op. 3 Sonatas. Wynberg proves as well matched a partner as St John could have wished for. Violinists, guitarists and lovers of winsomeness for its own sake should revel in these very well recorded discs and will find much information in the booklet.

---

24 Caprices, Op. 1.
Itzhak Perlman *vn*
EMI CDC7 47171-2 (72 minutes: ADD).   Ⓕ

This electrifying music with its dare-devil virtuosity has long remained the pinnacle of violin technique, and the *Caprices* encapsulate the essence of the composer's style. For a long time it was considered virtually unthinkable that a violinist should be able to play the complete set; even in recent years only a handful have produced truly successful results. Itzhak Perlman has one strength in this music that is all-important, other than a sovereign technique – he is incapable of playing with an ugly tone. He has such variety in his bowing that the timbre of the instrument is never monotonous. The notes of the music are dispatched with a forthright confidence and fearless abandon that are ideal. The frequent double-stopping passages hold no fear for him. Listen to the fire of No. 5 in A minor and the way in which Perlman copes with the extremely difficult turns in No. 14 in E flat; this is a master at work. The set rounds off with the famous A minor Caprice, which inspired Liszt, Brahms and Rachmaninov, amongst others, to adapt it in various guises for the piano.

---

24 Caprices.
Leonidas Kavacos *vn*
Dynamic CDS66 (77 minutes: DDD). Recorded 1989-90.   Ⓕ

The Greek Leonidas Kavacos, who won first prize at the 1988 Paganini Competition in Genoa, as well as taking the 1991 *Gramophone* Concerto Award for the Sibelius Violin Concerto, is given a recorded sound that favours the lower strings of the violin, so much so that the sonority resembles a viola. He takes a truly intelligent view of the musical potential of Paganini's frequently tortuous-sounding Caprices. He also has a pretty formidable playing equipment and manages to capture the mysterious and obsessive side of the music. The acoustic is spacious and thus one can take an objective and balanced view of the music. He does not treat the *Caprices* as if they were merely *études*, but follows the composer's tempo markings with fidelity, notably in the Sixth Caprice. Kavacos manages to save up his best playing for last: the final, and best-known, Caprice is quite superb, with a real sense of fantasy.

---

24 Caprices.
Michael Rabin *vn*
EMI CDM7 64560-2 (69 minutes: ADD). Recorded 1958.   Ⓜ Ⓗ

The almost legendary American, Michael Rabin, who died tragically early in 1972 at the age of 35 after slipping on a parquet floor, was ultimately a stupendous technician not greatly concerned with stylistic considerations. He is so close to the microphone that one hears every detail with razor-sharp clarity. This closeness has the undesirable effect of ironing-out virtually all the dynamic shadings of his bowing, so that the playing has an unnatural evenness. The tone is nearly always astringent. The Eighth Caprice, in E flat, is excruciating on an aural level. In terms of technical finesse and sheer dexterity, however, Rabin is an utterly brilliant player, and in the immense number of passages where double-stopping raises its ugly head, his control of pitch is stunning. In the final Caprice, Rabin is notable for his wonderful singing quality in the highest register, where his controlled use of vibrato reigns supreme.

Giovanni Palestrina   Italian *c*1525/6-1594

Palestrina Missa Benedicta es. Missa Nigra sum. Missa Papae Marcelli. Missa brevis. Missa Nasce la gioia mia. Missa Assumpta est Maria. Missa Sicut lilium inter spinas.

Nigra sum. Assumpta est Maria. Sicut lilium inter spinas.
Anonymous Benedicta es. Assumpta est Maria in caelum. **Josquin Desprez** Benedicta es,
celorum regina. **Lheritier** Nigra sum. **Primavera** Nasce la gioia mia.
The Tallis Scholars / Peter Phillips.
Gimell 454 890-2PM4 (four discs: 249 minutes: ADD/DDD). Recorded 1980-89.
Gramophone Award Winner 1991. Ⓜ Ⓢ

From the 100-plus Masses that he could have recorded, Peter Phillips has chosen so shrewdly that
the selection here offered appears as comprehensive a cross-section of Palestrina's achievement as
you could possibly wish in the space of four hours. The variety of texture and audible technique
among these Mass settings is quite remarkable. Among the seven Masses collected here, a profound
development takes place between the massive sonority of the *Missa Benedicta es*, audibly both
Palestrina's homage to, and his measuring of himself against, his great predecessor Josquin Desprez
(Josquin's motet and its plainchant base are included, to make the point crystal-clear), and the
division of the voices in the *Missa Assumpta est Maria* into two dissimilar, antiphonal choirs,
projecting and dramatizing the text with urgent force as well as beauty. The music is most
beautifully but not too beautifully sung. Balance, intonation, chording and clarity of texture are all
immaculate, but the performances respond to the changes of emotional temperature between the
Masses also; they are expressively sung, in the best sense of that word. The recordings, in ample but
not obscuring acoustics, are very fine.

Ave Maria. Alma Redemptoris mater a IV. Veni sponsa Christi. Surge, propera amica mea. Quae est
ista. Magnificat IV toni. Hodie beata virgo. Ave regina coelorum a IV. Magnificat VII toni. Ave Maria
a V. Ave maris stella.
Camerata Nova / Luigi Taglioni.
Stradivarius STR33375 (59 minutes: DDD). Texts and translations included. Recorded 1996. Ⓕ

This is the new Italian sound of renaissance church music: a gentle vibrato, but a wonderfully loose
and relaxed sound with a kind of breathy production. In the normal four-voice Palestrina texture
both the two top voices are taken by women; but the sopranos are extremely light in their sound so
they never dominate the texture, and the altos are of that wonderful variety that one usually only
hears from Italians, with a firm and infinitely attractive chest register that goes confidently down to
a low F. If the texture here is quite unlike what we are used to hearing from the best British
ensembles, that is partly because there is an emphasis on line rather than on sonority. It's a sound of
tremendous restraint, as though none of the singers is attempting to project a 'voice'. If one can say
with confidence that this was not the sound Palestrina was expecting (any more than he was
expecting the sound of The Tallis Scholars and their like), one can say with equal confidence that
the Camerata Nova brings across the spirit and the polyphonic vitality of his music with
astonishing power. Considerable credit must go to Luigi Taglioni for producing such a gentle and
controlled ensemble. The music is also nicely chosen: a group of Marian motets, two Magnificat
settings and a Marian hymn to form a neatly contrasted programme, with several pieces gloriously
sung by four solo women's voices. If you thought that Palestrina was a composer of seamless and
immaculate textures with just a touch too much surface gloss for comfort, this may be a record to
help you to hear one of the world's most influential composers in a different light.

Palestrina Surge, illuminare Jerusalem. Missa Papae Marcelli. Stabat mater. Alma Redemptoris
mater. Magnificat Primi Toni. Nunc dimittis.
Allegri Miserere mei.
The Tallis Scholars / Peter Phillips.
Gimell 454 994-2PH (73 minutes: DDD). Texts and translations included. Recorded live in 1994. Ⓕ

The sense of a memorable occasion is quite tangible here. The largely Italian audience, assembled in
Palestrina's own great Basilica of Santa Maria Maggiore to mark the 400th anniversary of his
death, is clearly impressed by The Tallis Scholars' virtuosity. The *Missa Papae Marcelli* is in fact a
good four minutes faster than in their previous recording, made in 1980. No doubt they know the
piece even better now, and no doubt Phillips has changed his view of it. But it really seems as
though the building and its acoustic both had an effect, firstly in encouraging the singers really to
sing out (the *Sanctus* has an extraordinary full-throated fervour), but perhaps also the knowledge
that this was the very spot where Palestrina worked with his choir prompted an even greater
awareness of the music's eloquence. The Allegri *Miserere* doesn't really belong in this collection, of
course; it was written for another building entirely (the Sistine Chapel) decades after Palestrina's
death. It may have been included because Peter Phillips, alongside his scholarship and his gifts as a
choir-trainer, has a feeling for drama and the spatial effects of this music could not be rendered
nearly so spectacularly in the Sistine. It is stunning, with Deborah Roberts in the florid solo
soprano part floating high Cs and roulades up into the vast space with luminous clarity. The

Palestrina pieces have their own drama, and they are shrewdly programmed. It was a good choice to begin the disc with the almost rollicking jubilation of *Surge, illuminare*, wise to follow the showy *Miserere* with Palestrina at his most sublime in the *Stabat mater*. To follow that with the hymn-like, homophonic *Alma Redemptoris mater*, and that with the joyous *Magnificat* (for two choirs, but sounding like at least six, of quite different colours) is programme-building of a very high order. To add the eight-part *Nunc dimittis* as an encore, with its wonderful arching lines and a firework-display of counterpoint at the end, has a touch of genius to it. The recorded sound is splendid, the acoustic always perceptible but the singers never lost in it.

Masses – Viri Galilaei; O Rex gloriae. Motets – Viri Galilaei; O Rex gloriae.
Westminster Cathedral Choir / James O'Donnell.
Hyperion CDA66316 (68 minutes: DDD). Texts and translations included. Recorded 1988.　　Ⓕ

This is music in which Westminster Cathedral Choir excels: its response to the richly reverberant acoustic is warm and generous; it performs with the ease and freedom of kinship – a far cry from the studied perfection of many other choirs. Each motet is heard before its reworking as a Mass. The six-part scoring of *Viri Galilaei* (two trebles, alto, two tenors and bass) invites a variety of combinations and textures, culminating in the joyful cascading Alleluias at the end of Part I and the jubilant ascending series in Part II. In the Mass the mood changes from triumph to quiet pleading – a change partly due to revised scoring: the two alto parts beneath the single treble produce a more subdued sound. The Choir clearly relishes this exploration of the deeper sonorities: in the *Creed* one entire section is entrusted to the four lowest voices. The four-part motet *O Rex gloriae* is lithe and fast-moving. The corresponding Mass, largely syllabic in style, gives the Choir the chance to demonstrate its superb command of phrasing and accentuation: the Latin comes over with intelligibility and subtlety. Listen, also, to the wonderful solo boys' trio in the 'Crucifixus', and for the carefully crafted canons in the *Benedictus* and the *Agnus Dei*.

Victimae Paschali. Magnificat. Nunc dimittis. Dum complerentur. Ad Dominum cum tribularer. Ad te levavi. Stabat mater. Alma Redemptoris mater. Recordare. Veni sancte spiritus.
New College Choir, Oxford / Edward Higginbottom.
Collins Classics 1509-2 (56 minutes: DDD). Texts and translations included. Recorded 1997.　　Ⓕ

Palestrina's motets do not enjoy the sort of coverage garnered by his Masses. They often appear alongside a Mass, but rarely are they allowed to stand on their own, as here. For Palestrina enthusiasts, that is reason enough to investigate this disc. But there are other attractions, not least the very distinctive sound of the Choir of New College, Oxford. The boys' full and reedy tone makes them sound slightly older than one was used to (on previous recordings by them). This greater experience would account for their admirable sureness in the matter of phrasing (an added and welcome bonus in recordings of this kind). The altogether more robust timbre in evidence here is most apposite, reflecting a move away from the angelicism of performances of Palestrina's music (hinted at in Noel O'Regan's notes). The difference in sound is welcome enough in itself, but here it serves a fresh perception of the music. The recordings took place in the chapel of New College and the slightly dry acoustic underlines the aesthetic preference for precision of expression as opposed to an impressionistic wash of sound. If the voices' staggered breathing is occasionally audible (and the odd insecurity of attack exposed), the gain in distinctiveness is ample compensation.

Sir Andrzej Panufnik　　　　　　　　　　　　Polish/British 1914-1991

Sinfonia concertante. Concerto for Timpani, Percussion and Strings. Harmony.
Karen Jones *fl* **Rachel Masters** *hp* **Richard Benjafield** *perc* **Graham Cole** *timp*
London Musici / Mark Stephenson.
Conifer Classics CDCF217 (55 minutes: DDD). Recorded 1993.　　Ⓕ

All of the works recorded here, as with most of Andrzej's Panufnik's later music, are quite rigorously built from spare basic resources (*Harmony* and the *Sinfonia concertante* from two three-note cells, the *Concertino* from a single motif of four notes). They ought to sound 'same-y', and in a sense they do, in that all three have a certain serenity at their core, with frequent recourse to quietness, and all three are harmonically transparent. That is Panufnik's idiom, and one wouldn't complain of two Mozart symphonies that they both sound Mozartian. But all three pieces are also 'about' the unification of dissimilarity. The basic material of the *Sinfonia concertante* is put to lyrical, meditative, tranquil use in the first of its main movements but is shown in the second to be just as capable of generating abrupt discontinuity, swift movement and vigorous rhythm; the brief concluding 'Postscriptum' reflects on how very simple the raw material for such contrast can be.

The 'method' is tested more severely in the five-movement *Concertino*, which was written as a test-piece, and, since the two soloists are percussionists, as something of a display vehicle as well. *Harmony* takes the unifying of dualities a step further: here we have two instrumental groups (wind octet and a small string ensemble without double-basses) that engage in serene dialogue until they eventually merge and the music intensifies through angular stress to passionate but austere tenderness. It is a memorable image, surely not coincidentally dedicated to Panufnik's wife on the occasion of their silver wedding; it is subtitled 'Poem', and is indeed poetic, but the poetry and severity of the technique are inseparable. All three works are beautifully played and very cleanly recorded.

Sir Hubert Parry British 1848-1918

Shulbrede Tunes. Theme and 19 Variations in D minor. Hands across the Centuries.
Peter Jacobs pf
Priory PRCD451 (73 minutes: DDD). Recorded 1992.   Ⓕ

This likeable anthology usefully expands our appreciation of a figure best known for his choral and symphonic offerings. The three works gathered here span some 38 years. Nearly three decades separate the publication dates of the *Theme and 19 Variations* and Parry's next piano work, the charming ten-movement suite of 1914 entitled *Shulbrede Tunes*. The twelfth-century Shulbrede Priory in Sussex was the home of Parry's elder daughter, Dorothea, her husband, Arthur Ponsonby, and their two children, Elizabeth and Matthew. Each family member, as well as the house and grounds, is lovingly evoked by Parry in this winsome, nicely contrasted series of character pieces. Indeed, Dorothea (or 'Dolly', as she is named here) is represented by two portraits, the second of which comprises the emotional core of the series. Parry's seven-movement suite from 1916, *Hands across the Centuries*, instantly recalls his earlier *Lady Radnor's Suite* (and the *English Suite* to come) in its easy tunefulness and reliance on baroque dance forms. Peter Jacobs's playing here betokens total commitment and idiomatic warmth. The engineering, too, is eminently truthful (if just a touch hissy).

Parry English Lyrics: Set 2 – O mistress mine; Take, O take those lips away; No longer mourn for me; Blow, blow, thou winter wind; When icicles hang by the wall. Set 4 – Thine eyes still shine for me; When lovers meet again; When we two parted; Weep you no more; There be none of beauty's daughters; Bright star. Set 5 – A Welsh lullaby. Set 6 – When comes my Gwen; And yet I love her till I die; Love is a bable. Set 7 – On a time the amorous Silvy. Set 8 – Marian; Looking backward. Set 9 – There. Set 10 – From a city window.
Vaughan Williams Songs of Travel. Linden Lea.
Robert Tear ten **Philip Ledger** pf
Belart 461 493-2 (77 minutes: ADD). Recorded c1979.   Ⓑ

This selection of Parry's songs is very welcome in these fine and intelligent performances by Robert Tear and Philip Ledger. Parry does not always measure up to his texts (in the sonnets of Keats and Shakespeare especially), and is best when renouncing his teatime-Brahms style in favour of a more personal and imaginative idiom, as in 'When icicles hang by the wall' and 'From a city window'. Vaughan Williams's great song-cycle, *Songs of Travel*, has a freshness partly deriving from the comparative rarity of hearing it in higher keys for the tenor voice. Both artists give the impression of having studied the songs as it were 'from scratch'. Tear's phrasing is a delight, showing exceptional sensitivity to the words, and Ledger's playing, with very sparing use of pedal, is scrupulously clean and careful over detail. The recorded sound is fine. No texts are included but it hardly matters: the diction is so clear you are unlikely to miss a word.

I was glad when they said unto me. Evening Service in D major, 'Great'. Songs of Farewell. Hear my words, ye people. Jerusalem.
Timothy Woodford, Richard Murray-Bruce trebs **Andrew Wickens,**
Colin Cartwright countertens **David Lowe, Martin Pickering** tens **Bruce Russell,**
Paul Rickard bars **John Heighway** bass **Roger Judd** org
Choir of St George's Chapel, Windsor / Christopher Robinson.
Hyperion CDA66273 (58 minutes: DDD). Texts included. Recorded 1987.   Ⓕ

The more of Parry's music one comes to know, the more apparent it becomes that the 'received opinion' of him is askew. Take the 1882 settings of the *Magnificat* and *Nunc dimittis*, for instance. These, amazingly, were not published until 1982. This recording – another example of Hyperion's courageous policy – shows how un-Victorian in the accepted sense they are. In other words, they are bold, unconventional and unsanctimonious – like quite a lot of Victorian church music, one may add. Perhaps the big anthem, *Hear my words* (1894) shows more signs of conventionality, but it has an attractive part for solo soprano (treble here) and ends with the hymn 'O praise ye the Lord'. The St George's Chapel Choir, conducted by Christopher Robinson, sings these works with more ease than it can muster for the famous and magnificent Coronation anthem *I was glad*, ceremonial music that not even Elgar surpassed. A sense of strain among the trebles is always evident. Although a wholly adult choir in the *Songs of Farewell* might be preferable, these are assured and often beautiful performances – excellent diction – of these extraordinarily affecting motets. English music does not possess much that is more perfect in the matching of words and music than the settings of 'There is an old belief' and 'Lord, let me know mine end', invidious as it is to select only two for mention. A stirring *Jerusalem* completes this enterprising recording, which brings the sound of a great building into our homes with absolute fidelity.

Arvo Pärt Estonian 1935

Fratres (seven versions). Festina Lente. Cantus in Memory of Benjamin Britten. Summa.
Peter Manning *vn* **France Springuel** *vc* **Mireille Gleizes** *pf* **I Fiamminghi.**
Telarc CD80387 (79 minutes: DDD). Recorded 1994. ⓕ

Telarc's *Fratres-Fest* proves beyond doubt that good basic material can be reworked almost *ad infinitum* – if the manner of its arrangement is sufficiently colourful. This sequence is particularly imaginative in that it alternates two varied pairs of *Fratres* with atmospheric original string pieces, then separates the last two versions with the sombre pealing of *Festina Lente*. The first *Fratres* opens to a low bass drone and chaste, ethereal strings: the suggested image is of a slow oncoming processional – mourners, perhaps, or members of some ancient religious sect – with drum and xylophone gradually intensifying until the percussive element is so loud that it resembles Copland's *Fanfare for the Common Man*. One envisages aged protagonists who have been treading the same ground since time immemorial, whereas the frantically propelled, arpeggiated opening to the version for violin, strings and percussion leaves a quite different impression. Still, even here the music does eventually calm and Peter Manning provides an expressive solo commentary. All six arrangements share a common 'approach-and-retreat' formula, with ideas that arrive from – and subsequently retreat to – some distant horizon. Next comes the gentle cascading of Pärt's *Cantus in Memory of Benjamin Britten*, with its weeping sequences and lone, tolling bell. The eight-cello *Fratres* uses eerie harmonics (as does the cello and piano version that ends the programme), whereas *Fratres* for wind octet and percussion is cold, baleful, notably Slavonic-sounding and occasionally reminiscent of Stravinsky. The alternation of *Summa* (for strings) and the quartet version of *Fratres* works nicely, the former more animated than anything else on the disc; the latter, more intimate. The performances are consistently sympathetic, and the recordings are excellent.

Pärt Annum per annum. Pari intervalli. Mein Weg hat Gipfel und Wellentäler. Trivium I-III.
Cage Souvenir.
Scelsi In nomine lucis[a].
Christoph Maria Moosmann *org*
New Albion NA074CD (64 minutes: DDD). Recorded on the organ in St Martin's Cathedral, Rottenburg in 1994; [a]recorded at Collegiate Church of St Hippolyte, Poligny, France in 1992. ⓕ

The pieces by Pärt constitute his complete organ output to date. *Pari intervalli*, originally written for woodwind as a memorial tribute, and *Trivium I-III* are the earliest, dating from 1976 when Pärt broke a three-year composing silence. Then came *Annum per annum* (1980) where five movements representing sections of the Mass are framed by one long sustained chord of D – loud going down to soft in the prelude, and the opposite in the postlude. The latest piece, *Mein Weg* (1989), is closely based on a poem about the spiritual journey through life. Most of the Pärt works have a veritable fixation on D, which comes up resplendently in the loud second piece of *Trivium* which, like the first one, is on a pedal. This is the organ music of spiritual minimalism, restrained but powerful if you are on the right wavelength. The Cage and Scelsi are first recordings. Cage's *Souvenir* (1984), commissioned by the American Guild of Organists, at times sounds like an improvisation on a recurrent theme suggesting plainsong. But, being Cage, the piece contains irreverent squawks and eruptions of clusters to put things into perspective. The interaction between textures is – for Cage – unusually structured and satisfying. *In nomine lucis* (1974) by the eccentric Italian Giacinto Scelsi, who died in 1988, is in memory of his younger colleague Franco Evangelisti. This is a most unusual, atmospheric piece, where Moosmann uses assistants to operate the organ's mechanical stops very precisely to obtain microtones. *In nomine lucis* seems to be Scelsi's only organ work and there is nothing quite like it. The organ at Rottenburg, although modern, sounds exactly right for the neo-medievalism of Pärt's timeless message, and the recording is outstanding.

Berliner Messe. The Beatitudes. Annum per Annum. Magnificat. Seven Magnificat Antiphons.
De profundis.
Polyphony / Stephen Layton with **Andrew Lucas** org
Hyperion CDA66960 (74 minutes: DDD). Texts and translations included. Recorded 1997.   Ⓕ

Pärt's music is about equilibrium and balance – balance between consonance and dissonance, between converging voices and, in the context of a CD such as this, between the individual works programmed. Stephen Layton has chosen well, starting with the variegated *Berliner Messe* and closing with the starkly ritualistic *De profundis*, a memorable and ultimately dramatic setting of Psalm 130 for male voices, organ, bass drum and tam-tam, dedicated to Gottfried von Einem. The Mass features two of Pärt's most powerful individual movements, a gently rocking 'Veni Sancte Spiritus' and a *Credo* which, as Meurig Bowen's unusually perceptive notes remind us, is in essence a major-key transformation of the better-known – and more frequently recorded – *Summa*. Everything here chimes to Pärt's tintinnabulation style, even the brief but fetching organ suite *Annum per Annum*, where the opening movement thunders an alarm then tapers to a gradual *diminuendo*, while the closing coda shoulders an equally well-calculated *crescendo*. The five movements in between are mostly quiet, whereas *The Beatitudes* flies back to its opening tonality on 'a flurry of quintuplet broken chords'. It is also the one place that witnesses a momentary – and minor – blemish on the vocal line, but otherwise Layton directs a fine sequence of warmly blended performances. If you are new to Pärt's music, then this disc would provide an excellent starting-point. We would suggest playing the individually shaded *Seven Magnificat Antiphons* first, then tackling the *Berliner Messe*, followed, perhaps, by the *Magnificat*. Polyphony employs what one might roughly term an 'early music' singing style, being remarkably even in tone, largely free of vibrato and alive to phrasal inflexions. As to rival discs, none is significantly better performed; but as each Pärt programme is, in a sense, a concept in itself, we would recommend listening as widely as possible. We would also suggest experimenting with playing sequences: by so doing you will maximize the subtle differences between individual pieces.

Te Deum. Silouans Song, 'My soul yearns after the Lord … . Magnificat. Berliner Messe.
Estonian Philharmonic Chamber Choir; Tallinn Chamber Orchestra / Tõnu Kaljuste.
ECM New Series 439 162-2 (66 minutes: DDD). Texts and translations included. Recorded
1993.   Ⓕ Ⓔ

Pärt's *Te Deum* sets the standard liturgical text to a wide range of nuances, shades and dynamics; brief string interludes provide heart-rending wordless commentaries, and the work's closing pages provide a serenely moving affirmation of holiness. Although relatively static in its musical narrative, Pärt's *Te Deum* is both mesmerizing and enriching. *Silouans Song* (1991), an eloquent study for strings, is as reliant on silence as on sonority. It is again austere and chant-like, although its dramatic interpolations approximate a sort of sacral protest. The brief *Magnificat* for *a cappella* choir (1989) positively showers multi-coloured resonances. However, the *Te Deum's* closest rival – in terms of substance and appeal – is surely the 25-minute *Berliner Messe* (1990-92). Here again Pärt employs the simplest means to achieve the most magical ends: 'Veni Sancte Spiritus' weaves a luminous thread of melodic activity either side of a constant, mid-voice drone, while the weighted phrases of the *Sanctus* take breath among seraphic string chords. And how wonderful the gradual darkening of the closing *Agnus Dei*, where tenors initially answer sopranos and an almost imperceptible mellowing softens the work's final moments. Beautiful sounds, these – gripping yet remote, communicative yet deeply personal in their contemplative aura, while the all-round standard of presentation – performance, engineering, documentation – serves Pärt as devotedly as Pärt serves the Divine Image.

Statuit et Dominus. Missa Sillabica. Beatus Petronius. Seven Magnificat Antiphons. De profundis.
Memento mori. Cantate Domino. Solfeggio.
Estonian Philharmonic Chamber Choir / Tõnu Kaljuste
with **Christopher Bowers-Broadbent** org
Virgin Classics VC5 45276-2 (61 minutes: DDD). Texts and translations included.
Recorded 1995-96.   Ⓕ Ⓔ

Pärt's demands on the organ as an accompaniment to voices are neither particularly complex nor technically demanding but do require exceptional sensitivity from the player. It is largely through skilful use of registration that Bowers-Broadbent displays his profound understanding of the music. He balances his role admirably, keeping a discreet distance from the singers for the most part and measuring the long drawn-out *crescendo* of *De profundis* to perfection. However, this is, of course, a disc devoted to Pärt's choral music and it is the choir, rather than the organist, who are the real heroes. The Estonian Philharmonic Choir doesn't sound as if it's studied the music long and hard, but these performances feel as if they come from the heart; there is a tangible sense of spiritual empathy. Listen to the magical, ethereal quality of the singing in the divine *Gloria* from the *Missa Sillabica* which Tõnu Kaljuste draws from his singers. And in the magical *Magnificat Antiphons* the Estonian choir reveal an even greater depth of feeling. The recording is gloriously atmospheric.

Anthony Payne
British 1936

Symphonies of Wind and Rain. The Song Streams in the Firmament. Evening Land.
Paraphrases and Cadenzas. A Day in the Life of a Mayfly.
Jane Manning *sop* **Dov Goldberg** *cl* **Owen Gordon** *va* **Dominic Saunders** *pf*
Jane's Minstrels / Roger Montgomery.
NMC NMCD056 (78 minutes: DDD). Text included. Recorded 1996.   Ⓕ

Like most British composers who emerged during the 1960s, Payne was acutely aware of disparities between local and continental, conservative and radical predispositions. The earliest work here, *Paraphrases and Cadenzas* for clarinet, viola and piano (1969, rev. 1979) has clear points of contact with post-Schoenbergian expressionism, and there is engaging interplay between the rhythmic and harmonic bite which derives from that source, and the expansiveness and warmth of expression that flourish nearer home. The most recent work, *Symphonies of Wind and Rain* for wind sextet, string quintet and percussion (1991), has less in the way of overt intensity and concentration – this combination of wind and rain never blows up a storm, and the music tends more to the reflective than the assertive – but its ideas are attractive and its design well shaped, avoiding those still-familiar English vices of flabby harmony and ill-defined form. *Evening Land*, a cycle for voice and piano setting Auden's translations of Per Lagerkvist (1981), is no less effective as a cumulative structure, even if one questions Payne's decision to alternate speech and song quite so determinedly in the early stages. But there are no reservations about the two other purely instrumental works included here. *A Day in the Life of a Mayfly* (1981) easily transcends the merely whimsical with its vivid ideas and brilliantly resourceful instrumentation, while *The Song Streams in the Firmament* (1986) confirms the special strengths of Payne's distinctive personal synthesis of the hard-edged and the lyrical. Performances are uniformly first-class, and recordings likewise, save for a slightly over-resonant piano sound.

Krzysztof Penderecki
Polish 1933

St Luke Passion (Passio et mors Domini nostri Jesu Christi secundam Lucam).
Sigune von Osten *sop* **Stephen Roberts** *bar* **Kurt Rydl** *bass* **Edward Lubaszenko** *narr*
Cracow Boys' Choir; Warsaw National Philharmonic Chorus;
Polish Radio National Symphony Orchestra / Krzysztof Penderecki.
Argo 430 328-2ZH (76 minutes: DDD). Text and translation included. Recorded 1989.   Ⓕ

The first performance in Münster Cathedral in 1966 of Penderecki's *Passio et mors Domini nostri Jesu Christi secundum Lucam* brought overnight fame and world recognition to the then 33-year-old composer, and succeeded, where many others had failed, in bringing the methods and language of the avant-garde to a much wider and respective audience. Part of its immediate success must surely lie in his skilful fusion of past musical techniques (renaissance-like polyphony, Gregorian melismata and Venetian *cori spezzati*) with the colouristic avant-garde devices that he had been developing in the years preceding its composition. Mind you, it was not without its detractors. Some critics, for the very reasons stated above, accused Penderecki of 'courting the masses' and of 'pure sensation-seeking', not to mention the fact that here was a young composer who had the audacity to court comparison with the sublime creations of Bach. Time, however, has proved some justification for the initial enthusiasm as the many hundreds (yes, hundreds!) of performances since its première testify – no mean feat for a contemporary work of these proportions. It unfailingly creates an impressive impact on the listener with its dramatic energy and waves of tension, even if some of its language does sound a little dated. The performance, under the guiding hand of the composer, is all one could wish for with splendid performances from orchestra, chorus and soloists alike, while the recording, made in the Cathedral of Christ the King, Katowice, has a beautifully spacious and resonant sound that gives the work a somewhat timeless quality.

St Luke Passion – Stabat mater; Miserere; In pulverem mortis. Magnificat – Sicut locutus est.
Agnus Dei. Song of Cherubim. Veni creator. Benedicamus Domino. Benedictus.
Tapiola Chamber Choir / Juha Kuivanen.
Finlandia 4509-98999-2 (52 minutes: DDD). Texts and translations included. Recorded 1993.   Ⓕ Ⓢ

There is a neat correspondence in the way the earliest and most recent pieces included here – *Stabat mater* (1962) and *Benedictus* (1992) – both move to resolutions on simple major triads. The difference is in the extent to which the triads in the later work govern the musical fabric throughout. In the 1960s such common chords had to be fought for, and could even seem tacked on rather arbitrarily. In general, however, it is another kind of consistency that makes this disc musically worthwhile. Although all the works tend to be reflective and devotional in character, the contrapuntal medium of the unaccompanied chorus inspires the composer to an economical intensity all too often absent from his later instrumental works. Indeed, it is as part of that intensity that elements of his early, much more dissonant style, so powerfully represented in the three extracts from the *St Luke Passion* and the fragment from the *Magnificat*, re-emerge within the more traditional harmonic world of the later pieces – especially the *Veni creator*. Yet it should also be said that Penderecki's austere response to this celebratory text seems more than a little strange. Of the later works *Song of Cherubim* is the most powerful, ending as it does with remarkably rapt 'Alleluias'. A note tells us that the composer regards the *Benedictus* as a draft to be reworked at a later stage. These performances are on the whole models of pure-toned clarity. The recordings are full of atmosphere but well balanced and not excessively resonant.

Anaklasis[a]. Threnody for the victims of Hiroshima. Fonogrammi. De natura sonoris I. Capriccio. Canticum canticorum Salomonis. De natura sonoris II. Dream of Jacob.
Wanda Wilkomirska *vn* **Cracow Philharmonic Chorus; Polish National Radio Symphony Orchestra; [a]London Symphony Orchestra / Krzysztof Penderecki.**
EMI Matrix CDM5 65077-2 (75 minutes: ADD). Recorded 1972-75. Ⓜ

Works such as the *Threnody for the victims of Hiroshima* delve deep within the recesses of collective memory, often triggering disturbing images. Even that master musical psychologist Alban Berg could hardly have approximated the *Threnody*'s chamber of horror – the blinding light of its opening bars, the aural swerve as trees bend and houses shatter, the jittery aftermath as fall-out spreads its poisonous message, and the myriad gestures and effects that amount to a terrifying experience. No other twentieth-century instrumental work quite equals the *Threnody* for graphic impact and no other composer has provided the victims of Hiroshima and Nagasaki with such a dramatic or telling memorial. What of the rest? Penderecki's invariable preference for slow motion, dense tonal clusters, roaring sonorities (*De natura sonoris II* rises to a deafening primeval groan), wailing vocalizations and sundry instrumental effects (tapping and screeching), not to mention a virtual absence of melody and definable rhythm, make for a pretty draining listening session. One wonders whether the musical metaphors that Penderecki used during this phase of his career are actually capable of expressing anything brighter than *Angst*, terror, fear, disorientation and – very occasionally – black humour. Yet it is a fascinating sound world for all that, and the *Threnody* is surely its most profound justification. The recordings report all with merciless clarity.

Giovanni Pergolesi   Italian 1710-1736

Stabat mater. Salve regina in C minor.
Emma Kirkby *sop* **James Bowman** *counterten*
Academy of Ancient Music / Christopher Hogwood.
L'Oiseau-Lyre Florilegium 425 692-2OH (52 minutes: DDD). Texts and translations included. Recorded 1988. ⒻⓅ

Pergolesi's *Stabat mater*, written in the last few months of his brief life, enjoyed a huge popularity throughout the eighteenth century. But modern performances often misrepresent its nature, either through over-romanticizing it or by transforming it into a choral work. None of these are qualities overlooked in this affecting performance, for Emma Kirkby and James Bowman are well versed in the stylistic conventions of baroque and early classical music – and their voices afford a pleasing partnership. Both revel in Pergolesi's sensuous vocal writing, phrasing the music effectively and executing the ornaments with an easy grace. Singers and instrumentalists alike attach importance to sonority, discovering a wealth of beguiling effects in Pergolesi's part writing. In the *Salve regina* in C minor Emma Kirkby gives a compelling performance, pure in tone, expressive and poignant, and she is sympathetically supported by the string ensemble. The recording is pleasantly resonant.

Pergolesi Stabat mater.
A. Scarlatti Stabat mater.
Gemma Bertagnolli *sop* **Sara Mingardo** *contr*
Concerto Italiano / Rinaldo Alessandrini *org*
Opus 111 OPS30-160 (70 minutes: DDD). Text and translation included. Recorded 1998. ⒻⒺ

One thing which commends this recording of Pergolesi's *Stabat mater* above others seems to lie in the imaginative and stylistically assured direction of Rinaldo Alessandrini. He lays emphasis on the relationship between words and music, and he has come up with some ideas which probe deeper than many, in his aim to bring the piece to life with expressive fervour. And it was an inspired move to pair the work with another, earlier *Stabat mater* by Alessandro Scarlatti. Both settings were commissioned by the same Neapolitan brotherhood, Pergolesi's to replace the other which the brethren reckoned a little old-fashioned. It isn't really, for though it does not breathe the theatrical atmosphere of Pergolesi's iridescent music, it is far from being archaic and overall, perhaps, makes a stronger appeal to the contemplative spirit. Both settings are similarly scored for soprano and alto soloists with strings and continuo. Gemma Bertagnolli's secure technique – which allows her on occasion to indulge in virtuosic vocal athletics – and her clear, forceful delivery, are immediately appealing. It is Sara Mingardo, though, who makes the stronger impression with her slightly more disciplined approach and her fervent declamation. Both singers make much of the vivid word-painting – present in each of the settings – but wholeheartedly revelling in the melodic allure of the Pergolesi.

Livietta e Tracollo[a]. La serva padrona[b].
[a]**Nancy Argenta** *sop* Livietta; [a]**Werner van Mechelen** *bass* Tracollo;
[b]**Patricia Biccire** *sop* Serpina; [b]**Donato di Stefano** *bass* Uberto;
La Petite Bande / Sigiswald Kuijken *vn*
Accent ACC96123D (80 minutes: DDD). Notes and texts included. Recorded live in 1996. Ⓕ P

La serva padrona, most famous of *intermezzi*, is given here with a rare but comparable companion-piece. *Livietta e Tracollo* is also for two characters, light soprano and *buffo* bass, with two sections, originally to be played in the intervals of the evening's *opera seria*. Rather more complicated and improbable than *La serva padrona*, it tells of a girl disguised as a French peasant (male) seeking vengeance on a robber who in turn appears disguised as a pregnant Pole. She succeeds in the first half, while in the second the man, now disguised as an astrologer, has more luck and they agree to get married. Musically it is not so very inferior to the *Serva*. Both have more wit in the music than in the libretto, with deft parodies of *opera seria* and a popular appeal in the repeated phrases of their arias, catchy without being coarse. The performance here is a lively one with Nancy Argenta as a resourceful and not too pertly soubrettish Livietta. Kuijken's Petite Bande plays with a distinctively 'period' tone; the speeds are sprightly and the rhythms light-footed. In both works, the women are better than the men, who (on this showing) lack the comic touch. Patricia Biccire sings attractively, especially in her 'sincere' aria, 'A Serpina penserate', and she paces her recitatives artfully. A lower baroque pitch is used and the final number is the short duet, 'Per te io ho nel core', as in the original score.

Pérotin

French c1160-c1225

Pérotin Viderunt omnes. Alleluia, Posui Adiutorium. Dum sigillum summi Patris. Alleluia, Nativitas. Beata viscera. Sederunt principes.
Anonymous Veni creator spiritus. O Maria virginei. Isias cecinit.
Hilliard Ensemble (David James *counterten* John Potter, Rogers Covey-Crump, Mark Padmore, Charles Daniels *tens* Gordon Jones *bar*) **/ Paul Hillier** *bar*
ECM New Series 837 751-2 (68 minutes: DDD). Texts included. Ⓕ

This is a superb and original recording. It gives musical individuality to a group of works that have hitherto tended to sound much the same. Moreover, as a special attraction for those wanting to see artistic individuality in early composers, it includes all but one of the identifiable works of Pérotin. Inevitably his two grand four-voice organa take up much of the record. At nearly 12 minutes each they may have been the most ambitious polyphonic works composed up to the end of the twelfth century. The Hilliard Ensemble adopts a wonderfully suave and supple approach to both *Viderunt* and *Sederunt*, softening the pervasive rhythms that can make them a shade oppressive and showing a clear view of the entire architecture of each piece. They surge irrepressibly from one section to another, creating a musical momentum that belies the admirably slow speeds they generally adopt. They also beautifully underline the musical differences between the two works, producing a sound which seems a credible reflection of what one might have heard at Notre Dame in the late twelfth century. What is particularly exciting here is the way in which the musicians grasp at the individual dynamic of each work: the enormous open spaces they create to project the text of the magical *O Maria virginei*; the breakneck virtuosity in their swirling performance of *Dum sigillum*, the ever so gently modulated rhythms in the strophic *Veni creator*; the harder edge in their tone for *Alleluia Nativitas*; and so on. With a splendidly judged note by Paul Hillier, this is a recording of the highest distinction.

Allan Pettersson

Symphonies Nos. 5 and 16.
John-Edward Kelly *sax* **Saarbrücken Radio Symphony Orchestra / Alun Francis.**
CPO CPO999 284-2 (65 minutes: DDD). Recorded 1995.

The orchestral playing is full of commitment, the account of the 40-minute Fifth (1960-62) sounding tremendously vivid; Francis has the edge over rival versions where it counts, in his overall view of this magnificent work. Yet the coupling – the last symphony the Swede managed to complete – is better still. No. 16 was written in 1979 for the American saxophonist Frederik Hemke. Here Kelly, who has made some minor modifications to the solo part for reasons explained in the booklet (the ailing composer appears to have been uncertain of the instrument's range), glides through the hair-raising virtuosity with breathtaking ease. This is the kind of advocacy Pettersson, who never heard the work, can only have dreamed of. An excellent disc.

Symphonies Nos. 7 and 11.
Norrköping Symphony Orchestra / Leif Segerstam.
BIS CD580 (70 minutes: DDD). Recorded 1992.
Ⓕ

Most of Pettersson's major works are constructed as large, unified movements (although he was an accomplished miniaturist) and Nos. 7 and 11, respectively 46 and 24 minutes in length, are no exceptions. The former in some ways is unrepresentative of the composer; the obsessiveness of mood and hectoring tone are present, especially in the *Angst*-ridden first and third spans, but the range of expression is much wider than in most of his other works. Composed in 1967-68, it has a unique atmosphere, both haunting and haunted, which will stay with you for a long time. His melodic genius is confirmed in the long and heartfelt central threnody, as well as by the beautiful quiet coda, truly music to 'soften the crying of a child'; its delivery by the Norrköping players has just the right amount of detachment. Segerstam's tempos permit the work to breathe and resonate not unlike Mahler. The Eleventh Symphony (1974) is less combative in tone, although it has its moments, and is not on the same elevated plane as the Seventh. The recording quality is first-rate, allowing both the devastating power and delicate fine detail of these scores to emerge equally well.

Hans Pfitzner

Pfitzner Palestrina – Preludes, Acts 1, 2 and 3. Das Herz – Liebesmelodie. Das Käthchen von Heilbronn, Op. 17 – Overture.
R. Strauss Guntram – Overture. Capriccio – Prelude. Feuersnot – Liebesszene.
Orchestra of the Deutsche Oper, Berlin / Christian Thielemann.
DG 449 571-2GH (75 minutes: DDD). Recorded 1995.
Ⓕ🄴

Christian Thielemann shows a marked fondness for broad tempos: even more obviously he loves big gestures and sumptuously rich sound. You can hear both tendencies in Pfitzner's *Käthchen von Heilbronn* Overture. On the face of it this is a problematic piece: very long (16 minutes) and with especially leisured transitions between its sections. After the big, bold, martial music of the opening you might expect a conductor to be a little nervous of the fact that Pfitzner allows a particularly lengthy transition to ensue before he even begins to prepare for his 'second subject', in fact the superbly romantic melody that represents Käthchen herself. Quite admirably, Thielemann does not hurry nor does he overstate the Käthchen theme: full, impassioned eloquence is reserved for its grandiose return. Although he allows the overture's big moments ample space to expand, there is no sense of mere waiting between them: he shows great care and sensitivity in Pfitzner's quieter pages. He obviously loves this music, and that is still more obvious in the *Palestrina* preludes, where the luminously pure textures of the first Prelude receive no less scrupulous attention than the nobly baying brass in the second or the velvety denseness of string sonority in some pages of the last. Thielemann's Strauss is no less effective. He finds a genuine Straussian line and ardour even in the not yet wholly mature *Guntram* Overture, builds a huge climax from the exquisite string sounds that begin the *Feuersnot* love scene and only falters just a little in the *Capriccio* Sextet; here he allows his solo strings to play just a little too forcefully. A distinguished début marked by ravishing orchestral playing. The recording is richly ample: you can almost reach out and stroke it.

Palestrina.
Nicolai Gedda *ten* Palestrina; **Dietrich Fischer-Dieskau** *bar* Borromeo;
Gerd Nienstedt *bass* Master of Ceremonies; **Karl Ridderbusch** *bass* Christoph Madrusch, Pope Pius IV; **Bernd Weikl** *bar* Morone; **Herbert Steinbach** *ten* Novagerio; **Helen Donath** *sop* Ighino;

Brigitte Fassbaender *mez* Silla; **Renate Freyer** *contr* Lukrezia; **Victor von Halem** *bass* Cardinal of Lorraine; **John van Kesteren** *ten* Abdisu; **Peter Meven** *bass* Anton Brus; **Hermann Prey** *bar* Count Luna; **Friedrich Lenz** *ten* Bishop of Budoja; **Adalbert Kraus** *ten* Theophilus; **Franz Mazura** *bass* Avosmediano; **Tölz Boys' Choir; Bavarian Radio Chorus and Symphony Orchestra / Rafael Kubelík.**
DG 20th Century Classics 427 417-2GC3 (three discs: 206 minutes: ADD). Notes, text and translation included. Recorded 1970s. (M)

Rafael Kubelík's magnificent, sumptuously cast DG recording of *Palestrina* is an almost impossible act to follow, indeed it's hard to imagine such an extravagance of vocal riches being encountered in a German opera recording nowadays: Brigitte Fassbaender ardently impulsive in the brief role of Palestrina's pupil Silla, Helen Donath pure-voiced and touching as his son Ighino, and an absolute constellation of superb basses and baritones, often doubling quite small parts: Karl Ridderbusch, Bernd Weikl, Hermann Prey, Franz Mazura, with at their head Dietrich Fischer-Dieskau as a surely unsurpassable Borromeo: dangerously powerful, intensely concerned and in magnificent voice. And those are just the 'secondary' roles! Pfitzner's text is one of the finest librettos ever written, and Gedda's singing gives the impression that the beauty of the words and their portrayal of Palestrina's dignity and suffering are more important to him than concern for his own voice. Kubelík's urgent conducting has a visionary quality, with a marvellous ear for the radiance of this wonderful score.

Astor Piazzolla
Argentinian 1921-1992

Piazzolla Libertango (arr. Calandrelli). Tango Suite (arr. S. Assad) – Andante; Allegro. Le Grand Tango (arr. Calandrelli). Sur – Regreso al amor. Fugata. Mumuki. Tres minutos con la realidad. Milonga del ángel. Histoire du Tango – Café 1930 (all arr. Calandrelli).
Calandrelli Tango Remembrances.
Yo-Yo Ma *vc* **Antonio Agri** *vn* **Nestor Marconi, Astor Piazzolla** *bandoneón* **Horacio Malvicino, Odair Assad, Sérgio Assad, Oscar Castro-Neves** *gtrs* **Edwin Barker, Héctor Console** *db* **Kathryn Stott, Gerardo Gandini, Leonardo Marconi, Frank Corliss** *pfs*
Sony Classical SK63122 (64 minutes: DDD). Recorded 1987-97. (F)

Yo-Yo Ma is the latest international artist to surrender to the spell of the Argentinian dance: he can also be heard on the soundtrack of the film, *The Tango Lesson*. Here, surrounded by a brilliant group of experts in the genre, he presents with wholehearted commitment a well-varied programme of Piazzolla pieces. They range from the melancholy or sultry to the energetic or fiery. Among the latter, *Fugata* is ingenious, *Mumuki* richly eloquent, and *Tres minutos con la realidad* nervily edgy: in this last, Kathryn Stott understandably earned the admiration of her Argentinian colleagues. She also shines with Yo-Yo Ma in an exciting performance of *Le Grand Tango*: his playing in the *Milonga del ángel* is outstandingly beautiful. Special mention must also be made of some spectacular virtuosity by the Assad brothers in the *Tango Suite*. The characteristic bandoneón is featured with the cellist in *Café 1930*; and by technological trickery Yo-Yo Ma partners Piazzolla himself (recorded in 1987) in a confection called *Tango Remembrances*. Those who are already fans of this genre will be in no need of encouragement to procure this disc.

María de Buenos Aires (arr. Desyatnikov).
Julia Zenko, Jairo *vocs* **Horacio Ferrer** *narr*
Buenos Aires Coral Lírico; Kremerata Musica / Gidon Kremer *vn*
Teldec 3984-20632-2 (two discs: 94 minutes: DDD). Notes, text and translation included. Recorded 1997-98. (F) (E)

María de Buenos Aires is victim, lover, heroine and *femme fatale*, a powerful illusion given substance and pathos by the approachable surrealism of the opera's librettist, Horacio Ferrer. Piazzolla's music harbours a Weill-like sense of foreboding; minor-key heartache invades almost everywhere, even when the dancing starts, the air thickens and the drink starts to flow. If you want to sample prior to purchasing, then try disc 1, track 4, 'I am María', potentially the set's hit number; the saucy 'Fugue and Mystery' (track 6 – an 'instrumental' where María walks the city streets), the aromatic 'Waltz-poem' (track 7) or the gorgeous, rambling bandoneón solo that opens the next track but which soon gives way to a rhythmically ferocious but heavily sentimental 'Accusation Toccata'. María is a textile-worker whose spirit is conjured from an asphalt-covered grave for various fresh encounters – not least with a gaggle of psychoanalysts who, in real life (Argentina around 1960) helped cope with a national neurosis caused by severe economic problems. Piazzolla's madcap 'Aria of the Analysts' (disc 2, track 4) recalls Bernstein's 'Gee, Officer Krupky' from *West Side Story*, but elsewhere the musical style has that air of ineffable sadness, melancholy and 'tragedy bravely borne' that is so typical of Piazzolla's music in general. Then again, *María de*

Buenos Aires is a 'Tango Operita' and this remarkable performance keeps the dance element very much to the fore. Leonid Desyatnikov's arrangement takes heed of various recorded predecessors (the most famous being a two-LP release that was issued not long after the piece was completed), but centres mainly on 'the graphically stark style of the Astor Quartet, a style that struck me [Desyatnikov] as the most natural one to adopt in a modern re-working of the music'. This latest set is fresher in tone, texturally more inventive and more tellingly astringent than any rival. Julia Zenko is a sensually alluring singer and Jairo recalls the passionate, jazz-inflected delivery of that great tango past-master, Carlos Gardel. And then there's Kremer himself, agile, personable, tonally changeable, a template in sound for the tragic but elusive main protagonist, 'María tango, slum María, María night, María fatal, María of love'. Through him, you learn to love her.

Walter Piston
American 1894-1976

The Incredible Flutist – Suite. Fantasy for English Horn, Harp and Strings. Suite for Orchestra. Concerto for String Quartet, Wind Instruments and Percussion. Psalm and Prayer of David.
Scott Goff *fl* **Glen Danielson** *hn* **Theresa Elder Wunrow** *hp*
Juilliard Quartet (Robert Mann, Joel Smirnoff *vns* Samuel Rhodes *va* Joel Krosnick *vc*);
Seattle Symphony Chorale and Orchestra / Gerard Schwarz.
Delos DE3126 (68 minutes: DDD). Recorded 1991-92. Ⓕ

Gerard Schwarz's flutist fixes you with his limpid tone. However, it will always be known as the score with the Tango. Schwarz goes with the flow, the sway of the melody, but it can never linger long enough. The *Fantasy* enters darkened Elysian fields – Piston's lyricism sits well with this distinctive voice of sorrow and regret. We can trace their kinship right back to the composer's first published work – the orchestral *Suite* of 1929. At its heart is a long and intense pastorale: the cor anglais is there at the inception. Framing it, motoric syncopations carry us first to a kind of drive-by the blues with bar-room piano and Grappelli violin. The finale is essentially a fugal work-out: high-tech Hindemith. Piston's very last work, the *Concerto*, is ten eventful minutes where the imperative is once again pitted against the contemplative. The mixing of timbres is masterly, a fleck of woodwind or a brush of tambourine or antique cymbal speaking volumes. But at the centre of gravity is the Juilliard Quartet, moving in mysterious ways, leading on to a closing viola solo – another dark voice posing both unanswered question and valediction. In fact, the last words uttered here are those of the *Psalm and Prayer of David* – a rare vocal setting for Piston, and as such, refreshingly open, unhackneyed, unhieratical. Performance and recording are superb.

Ephrem Podgaits
USSR 1949

Podgaits Missa Veris.
Bortnyansky Liturgy.
Vesna Children's Choir, Moscow / Alexander Ponomarev.
Opus 111 OPS30-224 (68 minutes: DDD). Texts and translations included. Recorded 1997. Ⓕ

The music of Ephrem Podgaits may be new to you, but on the evidence of his *Missa Veris* ('Spring Mass') he has something to say and is not afraid to say it. The work, which on the testimony of the choir members here was an immediate and lasting success, is often disconcertingly reminiscent of Britten (*Psalm 150*, *Missa brevis*, *St Nicholas* ...), and at times recalls Fauré (though always filtered through the curiously British sound of the Vesna Children's Choir, Moscow). None the less it is written with great assurance and *élan*. The most consistently striking and original movement is the haunting *Credo*, a winding chromatic chant, though there is also an immediately engaging playfulness in the 'Benedictus' and the final 'Alleluia', for example, which must have won not only the hearts of the Vesna Choir but of its audiences. Bortnyansky's three-voice *Liturgy* sets seven sections from the Divine Liturgy of St John Chrysostom in a fresh, appealing manner (and with an unbelievably rapid *Credo*) and deserves to be heard more often. The Vesna Choir, sprightly, beautifully in tune and full toned, does it more than justice. In all, a delightful disc.

Manuel Ponce
Mexican 1882-1948

Piano Concerto[a]. Violin Concerto[b]. Concierto del sur[c].
[b]**Henryk Szeryng** *vn* [c]**Alfonso Moreno** *gtr* [a]**Jorge Federico Osorio** *pf*
[b]**Royal Philharmonic Orchestra,** [ac]**State of Mexico Symphony Orchestra / Enrique Bátiz.**
ASV CDDCA952 (78 minutes: DDD). Recorded [ac]1994 and [b]1984. Ⓕ

Manuel Ponce has been called the 'father of Mexican musical nationalism'; but in his Piano Concerto (his first sizeable work) there is little, if any, trace of local colour. This is a showy, conventional late-romantic work of the barnstorming variety, and despite a great deal of bravura piano writing – Ponce himself was the soloist in its first performance in 1912 – its sound and fury do not amount to much musically. Osorio (who made an agreeable record of Ponce's solo piano music for ASV) is suitably exhibitionist: the orchestral sound is a bit shrill. By 1941, the year of the *Concierto del sur*, Ponce's style had changed and matured, he having meanwhile studied in Paris with Dukas; and this is one of the best guitar concertos in the repertory; its Mexican character is evident in the festive finale. Moreno's performance is strong in urgency and intensity though it could have had a greater sense of poetry in the *Andante*. Ponce's only other concerto, that for violin two years later, is his best-known thanks to the championship of Szeryng, its dedicatee, and through the inclusion in its melancholy second movement of references to his famous song *Estrellita* (whose rights he had unwittingly surrendered to an astute publisher). Szeryng plays the virtuoso solo part – which includes a lengthy cadenza, as does the guitar concerto – brilliantly, but in the acoustic of the Mexican hall used for this mid-1980s recording the tuttis are somewhat thick and rowdy.

Amilcare Ponchielli

Italian 1834-1886

La Gioconda.
Maria Callas *sop* La Gioconda; **Fiorenza Cossotto** *mez* Laura Adorno;
Pier Miranda Ferraro *ten* Enzo Grimaldo; **Piero Cappuccilli** *bar* Barnaba;
Ivo Vinco *bass* Alvise Badoero; **Irene Companeez** *contr* La Cieca;
Leonardo Monreale *bass* Zuane; **Carlo Forte** *bass* A Singer, Pilot; **Renato Ercolani** *ten* Isepo,
First Distant Voice; **Aldo Biffi** *bass* Second Distant Voice; **Bonaldo Giaiotti** *bass* Barnabotto;
Chorus and Orchestra of La Scala, Milan / Antonio Votto.
EMI mono CDS5 56291-2 (three discs: 167 minutes: DDD). Notes, text and translation included.
Recorded 1959. Ⓜ Ⓗ

Ponchielli's old warhorse has had a bad press in recent times, which seems strange in view of its melodic profusion, his unerring adumbration of Gioconda's unhappy predicament and of the sensual relationship between Enzo and Laura. But it does need large-scale and involved singing – just what it receives here on this now historic set. Nobody could fail to be caught up in its conviction. Callas was in good and fearless voice when it was made, with the role's emotions perhaps enhanced by the traumas of her own life at the time. Here her strengths in declaiming recitative, her moulding of line, her response to the text are all at their most arresting. Indeed she turns what can be a maudlin act into true tragedy. Ferraro's stentorian ebullience is most welcome. Cossotto is a vital, seductive Laura. Cappuccilli gives the odious spy and lecher Barnaba a threatening, sinister profile, whilst Vinco is a suitably implacable Alvise. Votto did nothing better than this set, bringing out the subtlety of the Verdi-inspired scoring and the charm of the 'Dance of the Hours' ballet. The recording sounds excellent for its age.

Francis Poulenc

French 1899-1963

Concerto for Organ, Strings and Timpani in G minor.

Organ Concerto. Suite française, d'après Claude Gervaise. Concert champêtre.
Elisabeth Chojnacka *hpd* **Philippe Lefebvre** *org*
Lille Symphony Orchestra / Jean-Claude Casadesus.
Naxos 8 554241 (59 minutes: DDD). Recorded 1997. Ⓢ Ⓔ ⓇⓇ

Elisabeth Chojnacka gets off to a head start against most others who have recorded the *Concert champêtre* by using the right kind of instrument: she understands that it is much sillier to play newish music on a period instrument than old music on a modern one. The effective proportions secured here between her deft playing and the orchestra also owe much to Jean-Claude Casadesus's nice sense of judgement and to the work of an excellent recording team. It was particularly perverse of Poulenc to ask a harpsichord to contend with large brass and percussion sections and then, a decade later, employ only strings and timpani in his concerto for the intrinsically far more powerful organ; and that perversity is underlined here by using the massive organ of Notre Dame, Paris (whose imposing specification is supplied for the satisfaction of organ buffs) – though once again the recording technicians have skilfully succeeded in producing a string sonority that does not suffer beside the organ's awesome thunders. You can't help wondering whether Poulenc really had such a giant sound in mind, but it's undeniably thrilling; and the quieter moments are captured with commendable clarity and calm. From the interpretative point of view, it's quite a performance.

The wind and percussion of the Lille orchestra get a chance to demonstrate their quality in accomplished playing of the spry dances of the *Suite française*. An eminently recommendable disc.

Organ Concerto. Piano Concerto[a]. Double Piano Concerto in D minor.
[a]**Pascal Rogé, Sylviane Deferne** pfs **Peter Hurford** org
Philharmonia Orchestra / Charles Dutoit.
Decca 436 546-2DH (60 minutes: DDD). Recorded 1992. Ⓕ

The Piano Concerto has the right blend of melodic and textural richness, wit and warmth in the hands of performers who understand the music well enough to bring out all its felicitous detail without exaggeration. The mood of its expansive first movement is more tender than usual here, with its incisive wit and spiky Stravinskian instrumentation being correspondingly less in evidence. But the music can take this approach, and the climaxes are not underplayed, while the ecstatically chorale-like music towards the end of the movement is done to perfection. In the gentle *Andante con moto*, Rogé and Dutoit are in their element, but here again the powerful passages also make their impact, while the romp of a finale has the right *joie de vivre*. The Double Piano Concerto comes over with great vivacity, with Deferne and Rogé (playing second piano) skilfully unanimous and crisply recorded. The Organ Concerto, recorded in St Alban's Cathedral, is also successful; Peter Hurford's mastery in Bach serves him well in its more darkly baroque aspects, but he is equally idiomatic in the uninhibitedly bouncy passages.

Poulenc Les biches – suite. Les animaux modèles. Matelote provençale. Pastourelle. Valse. Les mariés de la Tour Eiffel – Discours du Général; La baigneuse de Trouville. Aubade[a].
Satie (orch. Poulenc) Fête donnée par les Chevaliers Normands en l'honneur d'une jeune demoiselle. Prélude du Nazaréen No. 1. Gnossienne No. 3.
[a]**Pascal Rogé** pf **French National Orchestra / Charles Dutoit.**
Decca 452 937-2DH (79 minutes: DDD). Recorded 1996. Ⓕ

The majority of the works here date from the first half of Poulenc's life, up to the age of 30. The disc's three main pillars all owe their origin to the world of ballet, *Les biches* (written at the age of 20 for Diaghilev) being the work that, with its *joie de vivre*, first put him in the public eye. Aided by the clearest sound ever produced from the Salle Wagram, Dutoit gives a vivid performance of this Bright Young Things score, less slinky than others in the 'Adagietto' but light-footed in the 'Rag-Mazurka' and spikily brash in the outer movements. There was more maturity of feeling by the time *Aubade*, for a private ballet with choreography by Nijinska, was composed six years later: with its mood veering between harshly dramatic, gently melancholy and madcap-gay and its stylistic inconsistency, it has never been as popular as his other works (also depending more on a knowledge of the scenario), and recordings have often been dogged by problems of balance. The present performance gets this right, however, and without much question this is the most satisfactory version currently available. But for sheer lyrical beauty there is little in Poulenc to match the luscious outer movements of the splendid score for Lifar's 1940 *Animaux modèles*. The orchestral imagination in its 'Two roosters' movement is to be found again in Poulenc's arrangement of two of his mentor Satie's starkly hieratic Rosicrucian pieces – a clear case of making a silk purse out of a sow's ear (the exotically chromatic *Gnossienne* is more intrinsically interesting musically). Rounding off an exceptionally well-filled and desirable disc is a handful of Poulenc miniatures, ranging from the vulgarity of his early *Valse* via the farcical *Mariés de la Tour Eiffel* pieces to the rumbustiously jolly *Matelote provençale*.

Sinfonietta. Concert champêtre. Pièce brève sur le nom d'Albert Roussel. Bucolique. Fanfare. Deux Marches et un Intermède. Suite française.
Pascal Rogé hpd
French National Orchestra / Charles Dutoit.
Decca 452 665-2DH (78 minutes: DDD). Recorded 1994. Ⓕ

The *Concert champêtre* is a difficult work to bring off, and Poulenc himself is largely to blame: owing to his unfamiliarity with the then little-known harpsichord he seriously miscalculated the balance, employing far too large an orchestra, and his many hesitations and delays in completing the work make themselves manifest in the bitty structure, with abrupt and inconsequential changes of pace in the outer movements that few performances manage to make convincing. On record the concerto has usually suffered from too puny a harpsichord sound, and even here the instrument could with advantage have been more closely recorded to make its full effect. Poulenc was equally dilatory in finishing the *Sinfonietta*. Though the work is considerably more substantial than its title suggests, it does not outstay its welcome, at least in this engaging reading, which Dutoit shapes with vitality and sensitive phrasing, though even he cannot make the finale sound other than a patchwork. This is a vigorous and alert interpretation. The pleasurably neat and characterful performances of the *Suite française* for wind, percussion and harpsichord, based on themes by the sixteenth-century Claude Gervaise of the three-movement *musique de table* for a banquet at the 1937 Exposition Universelle, and of the tributes for the sixtieth birthday of Roussel and the seventy-fifth of his friend Marguerite Long add to the disc's attractions.

Poulenc Sextet for Piano and Wind Quintet.
Milhaud La création du monde.
Saint-Saëns Septet in E flat major, Op. 65.
Elizabeth Mann *fl* **Stephen Taylor** *ob* **David Shifrin** *cl* **Dennis Godburn** *bn* **Richard Todd** *hn*
Thomas Stevens *tpt* **Ani Kavafian, Julie Rosenfeld** *vns* **Toby Hoffman** *va* **Carter Brey** *vc*
Jack Kulowitsch *db* **André Previn** *pf*
RCA Victor Red Seal 09026 68181-2 (50 minutes: DDD). Recorded 1993.   Ⓕ

Predictably, one feels that Previn is the moving spirit behind these performances of three vivid French pieces for biggish chamber ensembles, and that it is especially his *joie de vivre* that informs Poulenc's sextet, where his charming solo at 2'13" in the first movement is just the first of many delights that help us to forget that its construction is not of the tightest. His colleagues also deserve every credit, and this crisply recorded account of the work is admirable, sparkling without glare. This version of Milhaud's ballet score, *La création du monde*, is a five-movement suite for piano plus string quartet that the composer made at his publisher's request. This is hard on its primitive elements, and indeed is no substitute for the original, but the performers offer all the vigour and sexiness that they can and it comes across well enough. After the uninhibited Poulenc and Milhaud, the programming of Saint-Saëns makes one fear a let-down in musical temperature, but the composer of the *Carnival of the Animals* had five years before already penned a jolly, witty and busy score in his Septet of 1881, whose scoring includes a trumpet and double-bass. This is another sparkling performance and rounds off an excellent, enterprising disc.

Capriccio[a]. Sonata for Two Pianos[a]. Elégie[a]. Sonata for Piano Duet[a]. L'embarquement pour Cythère[a]. Violin Sonata. Elégie.
Chantal Juillet *vn* **André Cazalet** *hn* **Pascal Rogé,** [a]**Jean-Philippe Collard** *pfs*
Decca 443-968-2DH (70 minutes: DDD). Recorded 1989-94.   Ⓕ

Few records could be more haunting or thought-provoking than this. For the lasting and predominant impression is of how Poulenc's music is so frequently clouded by a sense of elegy, by an uneasy if richly fruitful truce between levity and despair. The presence of two *Elégies*, and by implication, a third, is therefore hardly insignificant. Yet how typical of Poulenc, given so sombre a setting, to ring the changes with infinite elegance and poetry. The *Elégie* for horn and piano, composed in memory of Dennis Brain's tragic death in 1957, sounds the darkest note, the *Elégie* for two pianos, on the other hand, is intended to evoke the aroma of cognac and Gauloises, while the Violin and Piano Sonata's central 'Intermezzo' and 'Presto tragico' luxuriantly and tersely recall the death of Federico Garcia Lorca, murdered by Franco's minions in 1936 for his combined liberalism and homosexuality. Elsewhere the light shines through. *L'embarquement pour Cythère* is classic Poulenc, mischievously linking Watteau's painting of idealized love and the comforting world of seaside chips, accordions and cheap perfume (both Watteau and Poulenc were frequent holiday visitors to Nogent-sur-Marne). Here is witty and dazzling relief indeed. Both performances and recording are superb. Pascal Rogé, who has the lion's share of the proceedings, could hardly sound more authentically Gallic, more stylishly aware of the composer's tears and laughter. Jean-Philippe Collard, Chantal Juillet and André Cazalet are distinguished partners.

Les soirées de Nazelles. Deux Novelettes – No. 1 in C major; No. 2 in B flat minor. Novelette 'sur un thème de M de Falla'. Pastourelle (arr. pf). Trois mouvements perpétuels. Valse.
15 Improvisations – No. 1 in B minor; No. 2 in A flat major; No. 3 in B minor; No. 6 in B flat major; No. 7 in C major; No. 8 in A minor; No. 12 in E flat major, 'Hommage à Schubert'; No. 13 in A minor; No. 15 in C minor, 'Hommage à Edith Piaf'. Trois Pièces.
Pascal Rogé *pf*
Decca 417 438-2DH (67 minutes: DDD). Recorded 1986. *Gramophone* Award Winner 1988.   Ⓕ Ⓢ

Humoresque. Nocturnes. Suite in C major. Thème varié. 15 Improvisations – No. 4 in A flat major; No. 5 in A minor; No. 9 in D major; No. 10 in F major, 'Eloge des gammes'; No. 11 in G minor; No. 14 in D flat major. Two Intermezzos. Intermezzo in A flat major. Villageoises. Presto in B flat major.
Pascal Rogé *pf*
Decca 425 862-2DH (63 minutes: DDD). Recorded 1989.   Ⓕ

These beautifully recorded and generously filled discs offer a rich diversity of Poulenc's output. On the first disc, the masterly *Soirées de Nazelles* were improvised during the early 1930s at a country house in Nazelles as a memento of convivial evenings spent together with friends. It paints a series of charming portraits – elegant, witty and refined. The *Trois mouvements perpétuels* are, like so many of the works represented here, lighthearted and brief, improvisatory in flavour and executed with a rippling vitality. The *Improvisations* constantly offer up echoes of the piano concertos with their infectious rhythmic drive – the 'Hommage à Schubert' is a tartly classical miniature in three-time played with just the right amount of nonchalant ease by Pascal Rogé. The 'Hommage à Edith Piaf' is a lyrical and touching tribute – obviously deeply felt. The *Humoresque* which opens the second recital is open-air and open-hearted in style, yet songlike too in its melodic richness. The simplicity of this music is deceptive, as is that of the warmly caressing C major Nocturne that follows, for both pieces need subtle phrasing, rubato and the kind of textures only obtainable through the most refined use of the sustaining pedal. Rogé has these skills, and he is also fortunate in having an excellent piano at his disposal as well as a location (the Salle Wagram in Paris) that gives the sound the right amount of reverberation. There are many delights in this music and the way it is played here: to mention just one, listen to the masterly way that the composer and pianist together gradually bring around the flowing freshness of the C major Nocturne towards the deeply poignant feeling of the close. They should especially delight, and to some extent reassure, anyone who deplores the absence of charm and sheer romantic feeling in much of our century's music.

Un soir de neige. Chansons françaises. Sept chansons. Chanson à boire. Petites voix. Figure humaine.
New London Chamber Choir / James Wood.
Hyperion CDA66798 (67 minutes: DDD). Texts and translations included. Recorded 1995.　　Ⓕ

Poulenc's unaccompanied secular choral works, which demand virtuoso choirs, evidently hold no terrors for James Wood and his choir. The major work here is the wartime *Figure humaine*, whose finale, 'Liberté', became an inspiration to the Resistance movement. The choir at once impresses by the vividness with which it treats words and by its intelligent verbal phrasing (though some vowels, especially nasal ones, are not entirely native-sounding): it commands a wide dynamic range, thrilling at climaxes, with perceptive tonal nuances; and the chording of the difficult chromaticisms is commendably assured. The most characteristic movement of the cantata, 'Toi ma patiente', is beautifully shaped, and the final cadence of 'En chantant' is perfectly 'placed', thanks to the bright-voiced sopranos. The accelerating passion in 'Liberté' is scarifying, and the final cry (complete with a blood-curdling top E) is overwhelming. The other wartime work, *Un soir de neige*, is finely moulded throughout, with a movingly deep appreciation of its mood of melancholy contemplation. These all illustrate Poulenc's serious side. In the earlier *Sept chansons* there is a mixture of moods, which are well caught, though the nimble 'Marie' could have been better defined. There is energy and obvious enjoyment in the performance of the eight folk-song arrangements, especially 'Les tisserands', but also quiet pathos in 'La belle se sied au pied de la tour'.

Le bestiaire ou Cortège d'Orphée. Cocardes. Trois poèmes de Louise Lalanne. A sa guitare. Tel jour, telle nuit. Miroirs brûlants – Tu vois le feu du soir. Banalités. Métamorphoses. Voyage. Le souris. La dame de Monte-Carlo.
Dame Felicity Lott *sop* **Graham Johnson** *pf*
Forlane UCD16730 (64 minutes: DDD). Texts and translations included. Recorded 1994.　　Ⓕ

This programme of *mélodies* is perfectly chosen and balanced. Juxtaposing song cycles and single numbers from the whole of Poulenc's career, putting them in chronological order, it highlights the extreme modernity of Poulenc's choice of poetry with his universal appeal as a songwriter. *Le Bestiaire* from 1918, to Apollinaire's verses, is his earliest substantial group and it is remarkable how vivid and strong the Poulenc sound already was, when he was just 19. Of the three early Cocteau settings, *Cocardes*, Poulenc said he wanted 'the smell of French fries, the accordion, Piver perfume' – once one has that in mind, both pianist and singer do splendidly, with lines such as 'Lionoléum en trompe-l'oeil. Merci. Cinéma, nouvelle muse'. *Tel jour, telle nuit* was, of course, one of the great cycles composed for Pierre Bernac but the brighter colours of Lott's voice make it more romantic than, for instance, Souzay's interpretation. Graham Johnson as accompanist is the worthy successor to Dalton Baldwin and the composer himself as the perfect interpreter of these *mélodies*.

Le bal masqué. Le bestiaire. Rapsodie nègre. Cocardes. Trois mouvements perpétuels. Le gendarme incompris. Quatre poèmes de Max Jacob.
Dominique Visse *counterten* **François Le Roux** *bar* **Lambert Wilson** *narr* **Pascal Rogé** *pf* **soloists of the French National Orchestra / Charles Dutoit.**
Decca 452 666-2DH (76 minutes: DDD). Texts and translations included. Recorded 1995.　　Ⓕ

This is a disc that fans of the early *gamin* Poulenc will fall on with cries of joy. The biggest surprise is probably the four poems by Max Jacob, here recorded for the first time: it was thought that Poulenc had discarded them, but a few years ago Milhaud's widow found the manuscript among the papers of her husband, who had conducted the first performance. The surprise is not this reappearance but Poulenc's musical language: while the second and fourth poems are set in his familiar frolicsome madcap style, the other two, largely atonal, reveal that in 1921 he had been toying with Schoenbergian ideas. The other near novelty (its first modern recording) is the 'playlet interspersed with songs' *Le gendarme incompris*, a farce about a marquise cross-dressed as a priest who is arrested by a periphrastic gendarme and brought before an easily corruptible police chief. The whole piece is wildly hilarious (quite apart from the literary joke of cocking a snook at Mallarmé and Verlaine).

On rather more familiar ground Le Roux, as usual, shines with his subtle sense of style – Poulenc insisted that even his most frivolous pieces should be treated *au grand sérieux* – and his exemplary enunciation. Pascal Rogé sparkles in the 'Intermède' of the impudent *Bal masqué* (as does a solo violinist in its 'Bagatelle'), performed with zest by all, and equally gambols in the 'Ronde' of that *blague*, Poulenc's first work to be publicly performed, the *Rapsodie nègre* (here presented in its original 1917 version). On the other hand, the popular *Mouvements perpétuels* are given in a later instrumentation, possibly by another hand than Poulenc's own. Le Roux's versatility is again demonstrated in the circus/fairground atmosphere of the *Cocardes* and the epigrammatic *Bestiaire*. The excellent soloists from the French National Orchestra are recorded with great clarity; and James Harding, braving Jacob's and Cocteau's minefield of puns, Joycean wordplay and surrealist juxtapositions, provides spirited translations.

Tel jour, telle nuit[b]. Cocardes[b]. Une chanson de porcelaine[b]. Calligrammes[b]. Le bestiaire ou Cortège d'Orphée[b] – La colombe; Le serpent; La puce. Le travail du peintre[b]. A sa guitare[b]. Cinq poèmes de Ronsard[b]. Deux poèmes[b]. Vive Nadia[b]. Nuage[c]. Dans le jardin d'Annac. Rosemonde[c]. Chansons villageoises[c]. Dernier poème[c]. Mais mourir[c]. Le disparu[c]. Hymne[c]. Quatre poèmes[c]. La fraîcheur et le feu[c]. Cinq poèmes[b]. Parisiana[c]. Huit chansons polonaises[a]. Paul et Virginie[b]. Trois chansons[b]. Pierrot[b]. Epitaphe[b]. Mazurka[b].
[a]**Urszula Kryger** *mez* [b]**François Le Roux**, [c]**Gilles Cachemaille** *bar* **Pascal Rogé** *pf*
Decca 460 326-2DH2 (two discs: 139 minutes: DDD). Also available as part of a four-disc, mid-price set of the complete *mélodies* (460 599-2DM4). Texts and translations included. Recorded 1998.
Ⓕ

During the final years of his life, Poulenc described his own personality, 'What has often been praised as my charming modesty is fundamentally nothing more than an inferiority complex.' This sometimes seems to be reflected in his music, especially in the way that the little bursts of melody which are so haunting often burn themselves out before one can catch hold of them. It was Poulenc's own opinion that his music could be divided between those pieces that evoked his childhood beside the Marne, the works that were inspired by the countryside of the Touraine and third, the Parisian-inspired pieces. With the poets Eluard, Cocteau and Apollinaire prominent, it's natural that Poulenc's *mélodies* are mostly Paris-bound affairs. In this two-disc set the lion's share of the singing goes to François Le Roux. With Gilles Cachemaille and Urszula Kryger joining in on the second disc, this completes Decca's project to record all of Poulenc's songs. Le Roux does these three Cocteau settings with wonderful timing and diction here. He occasionally sounds taxed by the high-lying phrases Poulenc composed for Pierre Bernac in *Tel jour, telle nuit* and *Calligrammes*. He is one of the few singers of today who really knows how to employ head-tones without sounding false but *A sa guitare*, composed for Yvonne Printemps, really is soprano territory. He's absolutely superb in the three extra songs for *Le bestiaire*, only recently published (taking the snake, the dove and the flea as their subjects).

The second disc begins with Cachemaille singing one of Poulenc's latest and most beautiful songs, *Nuage*, to a poem by Laurence de Beylié. This is followed by two other songs from the 1930s and 1950s, both to Apollinaire poems, *Dans le jardin d'Anna* and *Rosemonde*. These make a neat group, as do the two contrasting poems by Robert Desnos, *Dernier poème* and *Le disparu* with an Eluard setting, *Mais mourir* in between – evocations of the occupation, of the poet's friend and then his own transportation to the death camps. Cachemaille's voice is more sensual than Le Roux's but he doesn't have such a range of expression at his command. Cachemaille sings the *Chansons villageoises* with plenty of firm tone – Poulenc asked for a Verdi baritone of the Iago type for these. They really benefit from being heard with orchestra, but Pascal Rogé certainly plays them with splendid verve. His contribution to the arrangements of Polish folk-songs – Poulenc's homage to Chopin – is also crucial. *La fraîcheur et le feu*, seven songs composed from one long Eluard poem, is a big challenge and Cachemaille doesn't altogether avoid a sense of strain. In general both Cachemaille and Le Roux are somewhat more at home in the lighter songs. The more you listen to Poulenc's *mélodies*, the more fascinating they become.

Gloria[a]. Stabat mater[a]. Litanies à la vierge noire[b].
[a]**Françoise Pollet** *sop*
[a]**French Radio Choir;**
[b]**Maîtrise de Radio France; French National Orchestra / Charles Dutoit.**
Decca 448 139-2DH (62 minutes: DDD). Texts and translations included. Recorded 1994. Ⓕ🅁🅁

Dutoit, with his sensitivity, vitality and insight, outdoes his recorded rivals in two of these works. The finest performance here is undoubtedly of the *Litanies*, whose orchestral introduction immediately impresses by its wonderfully hushed sense of reverence. Dutoit respects the composer's desire for the work to be performed with simplicity: this is an intimate, not an exteriorized, plea (occasioned by the death in a horrible accident of Poulenc's friend Ferroud, a composer now largely forgotten), and the refrain 'Ayez pitié de nous' is uttered with true intensity by a chorus of unmistakably French timbre. There is thoughtful phrasing too in the *Gloria*, again and again marked by Dutoit's vision and care over detail. He accents the deliberately-paced initial movement strongly, is light-footed in the Stravinskian 'Laudamus te', is not too slow and avoids sentimentality in 'Domine Deus Agnus Dei', and gives grandeur to the start of the final movement. Françoise Pollet, warm and sweet-voiced in the repeated 'Qui tollis peccata mundi', is radiant in the final Amens. The *Stabat mater* presents difficulties of balance which here are satisfactorily solved (the basses' first entry is, for once, not too obscure, and the orchestra does not overwhelm everyone in the fury of 'Quis est homo'). And again Dutoit is illuminating in the vigour of 'Cujus animam' and the well-judged restraint of 'Quae moerabat' (which in Yan Pascal Tortelier's reading sounds inappropriately cheerful). But in this work the chorus, though good in the unaccompanied sections of 'O quam tristis', too often sings on the underside of notes. Ah well, it was perhaps too much to hope that all three works would reach the same level of excellence.

Gloria. Stabat mater.
Janice Watson *sop*
BBC Singers; BBC Philharmonic Orchestra / Yan Pascal Tortelier.
Chandos CHAN9341 (56 minutes: DDD). Texts and translations included. Recorded 1994. Ⓕ

We are immediately struck, at the start of the *Gloria*, by the radiantly warm but clean orchestral sonority: only later does an uneasy suspicion arise that, apparently seduced by the sound, the recording engineers may be favouring it at the expense of the chorus, especially at orchestral *fortes*. But it is committed and thoroughly secure choral singing, perhaps most easily appreciated in some of the unaccompanied passages – tender in the almost mystic 'O quam tristis' and firm-toned at 'Fac ut ardeat' (both in the *Stabat mater*); it gives real attack at 'Quis est homo' (just holding its own against the orchestra); the sopranos can produce a bright, ringing tone; and only the very first line of the *Stabat mater*, lying low in the basses, needed to be a bit stronger (as in most performances). Janice Watson is a sweet-voiced soloist with very pure intonation; but she could with advantage have strengthened her consonants throughout. Tortelier gives intensely felt readings of both works – the murmurous ending of the *Stabat mater* and the thrilling *fortissimo* chords at 'Quoniam' in the *Gloria* spring to mind – and fortunately he keeps the vocal 'Domine Deus' entry moving at the same pace as at its introduction. He takes the Stravinskian 'Laudamus te' fast and lightly; the only questionable speed is of 'Quae moerebat', which sounds too cheerful for the words ('mourning and lamenting'). Taken all in all, these are performances of undoubted quality.

Mass in G major. Quatre motets pour le temps de Noël. Quatre petites prières de Saint François d'Assise. Quatre motets pour un temps de pénitence. Laudes de Saint Antoine de Padoue. Salve regina. Ave verum corpus. Exultate Deo.
Trinity College Choir, Cambridge / Richard Marlow.
Conifer Classics CDCF151 (70 minutes: DDD). Texts and translations included. Ⓕ

The lusciously chromatic harmony of the Mass in G major can easily cloy but the bright, radiant textures of the singing of the Trinity College Choir avoids this entirely. Readers unfamiliar with this work will be surprised how potent it is. The *Ave verum corpus* for high high voices is quite exquisite and in the St Francis *Prières* Marlow is assured and musically aware. The choir does, however, produce occasional curious French pronunciation, with some very odd mute 'e's. An interesting personal sidelight on these graceful and expressive pieces for male voices is revealed by the dedication to Frère Jérome of Champfleury 'in memory of his grandfather, my uncle Camille Poulenc'. The interpretation of the penitential motets is very dramatic and the short motet *Salve regina* is graceful and serene. Caution needs to be taken not to listen to too many of these works – virtually entirely homophonic, and nearly all characterized by Poulenc's special brand of tartly sweet harmonies – one after the other. The performances, with fine balance, expressive dynamic shadings, pure intonation, intelligent phrasing and excellent enunciation, are very impressive. Marlow, of course, is operating on home ground, in the almost ideal acoustics of Trinity College Chapel in Cambridge. The accompanying notes are interesting and informative.

Mass in G major. Quatre motets pour un temps de pénitence. Quatre motets pour le temps de Noël. Exultate Deo. Salve regina.
Berlin RIAS Chamber Choir / Marcus Creed.
Harmonia Mundi HMC90 1588 (52 minutes: DDD). Texts and translations included. Recorded 1995. (F)

There has never been a more beautiful performance of the *Salve regina*. And elsewhere this virtuoso choir displays, beyond impeccably pure intonation and chording (chorus-masters everywhere will note with envy the sopranos' clean, dead-sure attacks on high notes), a sensitivity to verbal meaning, dynamics and vocal colour that argues not only skilful direction but a complete ease and absorption into the music's often chromatic nature by all the singers. They bring a bright-eyed tone to the *Exultate Deo*, awe to 'O magnum mysterium' (in the Christmas motets), and a striking diversity of timbre to 'Tristis est anima mea' (in the penitential motets); in the Mass they interpret to perfection the *doucement joyeux* indication of the *Sanctus*. They appear to have been recorded in some large church, but without any problems of resonance and the words are extremely clear throughout: a first-class disc.

Dialogues des Carmélites.
Catherine Dubosc *sop* Blanche de la Force; **Rachel Yakar** *sop* Madame Lidoine;
Rita Gorr *mez* Madame de Croissy; **Brigitte Fournier** *sop* Soeur Constance;
Martine Dupuy *mez* Mère Marie; **José van Dam** *bass-bar* Marquis de la Force;
Jean-Luc Viala *ten* Chevalier de la Force; **Michel Sénéchal** *ten* L'Aumônier;
François Le Roux *bar* Le Geôlier;
Lyon Opéra Chorus and Orchestra / Kent Nagano.
Virgin Classics VCD7 59227-2 (two discs: 152 minutes: DDD). Notes, text and translation included. *Gramophone* Award Winner 1993. (F)

Poulenc's *chef d'oeuvre* is one of the few operas written since *Wozzeck* that has survived in the repertory – and deservedly so. It is written from, and goes to, the heart, not in any extrovert or openly histrionic way but by virtue of its ability to explore the world of a troubled band of Carmelite nuns at the height of the terrors caused by the French Revolution, and do so in an utterly individual manner. Poulenc unerringly enters into their psyches as they face their fatal destiny. Nagano responds keenly to the sombre, elevated mood and intensity of Poulenc's writing and unfailingly delineates the characters of the principals as they face their everyday martyrdom. The magisterial authority of Martine Dupuy's Mère Marie, the agony of Rita Gorr's Old Prioress, the inner torment of Catherine Dubosc's Sister Blanche, the restraint of Rachel Yakar's Madame Lidoine, the eager charm of Brigitte Fournier's Sister Constance are only the leading players in a distribution that is admirable in almost every respect. The score is for once given complete. The recording is atmospheric and suggests stage action without exaggeration.

Les mamelles de Tirésias.
Barbara Bonney *sop* Thérèse; **Jean-Philippe Lafont** *bar* Director;
Jean-Paul Fouchécourt *ten* Husband; **Wolfgang Holzmair** *bar* Policeman;
Gordon Gietz *ten* Journalist; **Graham Clark** *ten* Lacouf;
Akemi Sakamoto *mez* Marchande de journaux; **Mark Oswald** *bar* Presto;
Anthony Dean Griffey *ten* Son;
Tokyo Opera Singers; Saito Kinen Orchestra / Seiji Ozawa.

Le bal masqué.
Wolfgang Holzmair *bar*
members of the **Saito Kinen Orchestra / Seiji Ozawa.**
Philips 456 504-2PH (72 minutes: DDD). Notes, texts and translations included. Recorded 1996. (F)**E**

Les mamelles de Tirésias is Poulenc's *Così fan tutte*. On the surface it can seem merely an absurd romp. Poulenc, though, has used Apollinaire's *sur-réaliste* drama – in 1917 it was the play that gave the word to the language – as a starting-point for a work that is full of emotion – regrets, nostalgia and longing, then finally at the end the rebirth of hope. Poulenc worked on and off on the piece in the early 1940s, but finished it in a great burst of creative energy after the end of the Second World War. During the German occupation of France, Poulenc mostly being away from Paris, like the characters in the play stranded in a mythical Zanzibar, he amused himself with details about the city and its *arrondissements* – the score is full of little musical references that match Apollinaire's untranslatable puns. This recording is the first since the classic André Cluytens version, which included several members of the original cast, including Poulenc's favourite soprano, Denise Duval; after she created the part of Thérèse, Poulenc described her as 'stunning Paris with her beauty, her acting talent and her voice'. It's a hard act to follow, but Barbara Bonney succeeds in creating a vivid character without imitating Duval.

Seiji Ozawa has always had a special feeling for French opera of this period. The biggest advantage of this recording is the clarity of the orchestral sound – in the 1953 version the voices are so prominent that one loses all the beautiful detail in those heart-catching Poulenc juxtapositions, as the composer put it, 'in the midst of the worst buffoonery a phrase can effect a change in the lyric tone'. The vocal coach, Pierre Valet, deserves a medal for the way he has succeeded in getting the Tokyo Opera Singers to articulate the French. As Presto and Lacouf, Mark Oswald and Graham Clark get to sing the wonderful duet about their gambling debts, 'Monsieur Presto, je n'ai rien gagné'. Wolfgang Holzmair is luxury casting as the Gendarme, and in the crucial role of Thérèse's husband, Jean-Paul Fouchécourt is splendidly clear, whether looking after the babies or discussing Picasso's art. Those who already know this opera will delight in this performance, and if you have not yet become acquainted with the taste of the banana leaf and the strawberry together – the symbol Apollinaire offers his lovers at the end – you have a treat in store. *Les mamelles* is such a jewel on its own, but *Le bal masqué* makes a good fill-up.

Dialogues des Carmélites[a].
Denise Duval *sop* Blanche de La Force; **Régine Crespin** *sop* Madame Lidoine;
Denise Scharley *mez* Madame de Croissy; **Liliane Berton** *sop* Soeur Constance;
Rita Gorr *mez* Mère Marie; **Xavier Depraz** *bass* Marquis de La Force; **Paul Finel** *ten* Chevalier de La Force; **Janine Fourrier** *sop* Mère Jeanne; **Gisèle Desmoutiers** *sop* Soeur Mathilde;
Louis Rialland *ten* L'Aumônier; **René Bianco** *bar* Le Geôlier; **Jacques Mars** *bar* L'Officier;
Raphael Romagnoni *ten* First Commissaire; **Charles Paul** *bar* Second Commissaire;
Michel Forel *ten* Thierry;**Max Conti** *bar* Javelinot;
Chorus and Orchestra of the Opera, Paris / Pierre Dervaux.

Le gendarme incompris[b].
Nicolas Rivenq *bar* Monsieur Médor; **Jean-Paul Fouchécourt** *ten* Marquise de Montonson;
Jean-Christoph Benoit *bar* Pénultième;
Soloists Ensemble of the Garde Républicaine / François Boulanger.

Les mamelles de Tirésias[c].
Duval *sop* Thérèse, Fortune-teller; **Marguérite Legouhy** *mez* Marchande de journaux,
Grosse Dame; **Jean Giraudeau** *ten* Husband; [c]**Emile Rousseau** *bar* Policeman;
Robert Jeantet *bar* Director; **Julien Thirache** *bar* Presto; **Frédéric Leprin** *ten* Lacouf;
Serge Rallier *ten* Journalist; **Jacques Hivert** *sngr* Son; **Gabriel Jullia** *sngr* Monsieur barbu;
Chorus and Orchestra of the Opéra-Comique / André Cluytens.

Les chemins de l'amour[d].
Yvonne Printemps *sop* orchestra / Marcel Cariven.

Fanfare[e].
Toulouse Capitole Orchestra / Stéphane Cardon.

L'histoire de Babar[f].
Sir Peter Ustinov *narr* **Paris Conservatoire Orchestra / Georges Prêtre.**

La dame de Monte Carlo[g].
Mady Mesplé *sop* **Monte Carlo Philharmonic Orchestra / Prêtre.**

La voix humaine[h].
Duval *sop* La Femme; **Orchestra of the Opéra-Comique, Paris / Prêtre.**

Le bal masqué[i].
Benoit *bar* **Maryse Charpentier** *pf* **Soloists of the Paris Conservatoire Orchestra / Prêtre.**

L'invitation au château[j].
David Grimal *vn* **Romain Guyot** *cl* **Emmanuel Strosser** *pf*

Sécheresses[k].
French Radio Choir; French New Philharmonic Orchestra / Prêtre.

Figure humaine[l]. Un soir de neige[m].
The Sixteen / Harry Christophers.
EMI Poulenc Edition [acd]mono/stereo CMS5 66843-2 (five discs: 380 minutes: [acdfhi]ADD/DDD) .
Texts included. Recorded [a]1958, [b]1998, [c]1953, [d]1941, [e]1998, [f]1965, [g]1985, [h]1959, [i]1965,
[j]1998, [lm]1989.   Ⓜ

Poulenc's stage works might seem to be divided between those that hark back to his youth as a
member of Les Six, and the more pessimistic mood that overtook him after the Second World War.
It doesn't really work like that, however, since it was after composing *Dialogues des Carmélites* that
he returned to the work of Jean Cocteau to produce two contrasting monologues – *La voix humaine*
and *La dame de Monte Carlo* in which the frivolous and the tragic are mixed with exquisite irony. It
must have been quite a long-term investment when *Les mamelles de Tirésias* was recorded in 1953.
This classic version under André Cluytens can never be surpassed as a souvenir of the earliest
performances of what is still Poulenc's most successful opera, but the orchestral detail is much more
vivid on the modern Ozawa set. Denise Duval was Poulenc's favourite soprano and although her
voice has that slightly astringent quality in the upper reaches so typical of French female singers,
her performances are so complete, musically and dramatically, that they ought to be studied by any
aspiring soprano who wants to sing in French.

Cocteau wanted Poulenc to compose *La voix humaine* for Callas but he would only consider Duval.
It's a very difficult role to act and sing and again, although many famous divas have tackled it –
Olivero, Scotto, Norman and Söderström among them – Duval's 'Elle' is sublime. Public and critics
have always been somewhat divided by *Dialogues de Carmélites*. The *Gramophone* Award-winning
Nagano version boasts as strong a cast as you could imagine for the time, but again, Duval,
Crespin, Berton and the others have an intensity that it's difficult to imagine ever being equalled.
EMI has provided texts but no translations. Monsieur Poulenc would not have been amused. He
insisted that *Carmélites* should be performed in translation outside France. The other items that
make up the set include Poulenc's humorous and really beautiful incidental music for Anouilh's play
L'invitation au château. As in so many other instances this finds Poulenc using little quotations and
self-quotations. The fourth number 'Mouvement de valse hésitation' is a delicate variation on the
Berger-De Féraudy waltz *Amoureuse* and elsewhere there is a hint of his 15th *Improvisation*.
Similarly in *Le bal masqué*, there is a little five-note phrase which is a pre-echo of the husband's
demand 'Donnez-moi du lard' in *Mamelles*. At the end of the fourth CD we do get to hear
Mme Fresnay, the delectable Yvonne Printemps, in her waltz-song from Anouilh's *Léocadia*,
'Les chemins de l'amour'. It was Poulenc himself who called her singing 'literally divine'.

La dame de Monte Carlo, composed as a concert number for Denise Duval, is beautifully sung by
Mady Mesplé. It's a bit like an opera-composer's take on the 'Let's face the music and dance' scene
from the Astaire-Rogers movie *Follow the Fleet*, the gambler facing ruin outside the casino. The
secular cantatas that end the last CD, two of them newly recorded by The Sixteen, provide yet more
scope for contrasting Poulenc's shifts of mood between the cabaret and the chapel. Poulenc himself
wrote: 'The vocal style of the *Stabat* or that of *Dialogues des Carmélites* is in fact as far removed
from the song as the string quartet is from the string orchestra.'

Michael Praetorius   German 1571-1621

Lutheran Christmas Mass.
Roskilde Cathedral Boys' Choir and Congregation;
Gabrieli Consort; Gabrieli Players / Paul McCreesh.
Archiv Produktion 439 250-2AH (79 minutes: DDD). Text and translation included.
Recorded 1993.   Ⓕ Ⓟ

The aesthetic of contrast, so central to early baroque spectacle (sacred or profane), is inspired here
by the traditional part played by the congregation in Lutheran worship. Praetorius's music for the
figuraliter (the vocal/instrumental choirs) is greatly influenced by fashionable Venetian techniques.
But what is striking is the way the old *alternatim* practices of the Protestant church blend so
naturally with the intricate textures and scorings of a colourful Italian-style canvas, ranging from
intimate dialogues to full grandiloquent sonority. What is more, the centrality of the chorale is
never compromised. Despite all these ingredients, it is McCreesh's research and imagination that
make this service such a powerful testament to the faith expressed by Lutherans of Praetorius's
generation, and indeed by subsequent generations to which Bach was so indebted. The service
follows, to all intents and purposes, the Mass of the Roman rite (sung with distinction by the
Gabrieli Consort though the sopranos seem a little unsure in the *Kyrie*) interspersed with a versatile
array of motets, hymns, prayers, intoned readings, a superbly conceived and suitably mysterious
Pavan by Schein for the approach to Communion and several rhetorically positioned organ

preludes. For a congregation, the Gabrieli Consort and players are joined by the boys of Roskilde Cathedral, Denmark and a some local amateur choirs. The effect is remarkable for its fervour in the hymns; now one can see why *Von Himmel hoch da komm ich her* inspired so many settings in the seventeenth century. Other familiar tunes include *Quem pastores*, *Wie schön leuchtet der Morgenstern* in a shimmering prelude by Scheidt followed by a delicately nuanced motet on the same tune. *In dulci jubilo* is treated to a flamboyant setting by Praetorius featuring six trumpets. The spacious acoustic of the cathedral exhibits McCreesh's acute timbral sense; definition is not ideally sharp but this is a small price to pay for a natural perspective which embraces the sense of community worship essential for this project.

Zbigniew Preisner
Polish 20th century

Requiem For My Friend.
Elzbieta Towarnicka *sop*
Varsov Chamber Choir; Sinfonia Varsovia / Jacek Kaspszyk.
Erato 3984-24146-2 (74 minutes: DDD). Text and translation included. Recorded 1998.　Ⓕ

As the success of his film scores shows, Zbigniew Preisner knows exactly how to compose effective and immediately impressive music with an acute sense of timing. *Requiem For My Friend*, his first work written specifically for concert performance, also shows this ability, but placed in a new context. Scored for five voices, organ, string quintet and percussion, the first part, 'Requiem', employs words from the Latin *Missa pro defunctis*, and one feels that the ghosts of chant and the polyphonic tradition are often not far away (particularly in the opening 'Officium' and the *Kyrie*). A good deal of other music is suggested during the course of the work: one occasionally thinks of the Górecki of the Third Symphony or *O Domina nostra*, or Pärt, and also other composers of film music such as Vangelis or Jerry Goldsmith. This said, however, the work has its own sense of direction and cohesion and the relatively limited resources are put to very effective use: the only section that does not work is the *Agnus Dei*, which relies too heavily on sentiment and whose Wurlitzerish combination of organ and strings is very saccharine. The most effective movement is the unaccompanied 'Lux aeterna', simple and folk-like, but there are memorable things particularly in the 'Lacrimosa', which attains a real dramatic power with its repetitive melodic tag, and the 'Offertory', whose character is defined by the subtle use of recitative-like vocal writing.

The second part of the work, 'Life', for much larger forces and also in nine movements, is generally less successful in that it has less sense of unity and relies not so much on distinctive musical material as on the kind of symphonic film music gestures which work excellently in context but which fail to sustain interest or to cohere as a concert work (try the Orff-Jerry Goldsmith sounds of 'Veni et vidi' for an example of this). There are nevertheless some fine things, such as the saxophone writing (and playing) in 'The beginning', or the hushed, valedictory 'Prayer'. This is music which wears its heart on its sleeve, and as a personal memorial to a friend (the film director, Krzysztof Kieslowski) that is entirely appropriate.

André Previn
German/American 1929

A Streetcar Named Desire.
Renée Fleming *sop* Blanche DuBois; **Rodney Gilfry** *bar* Stanley Kowalski;
Elizabeth Futral *sop* Stella Kowalski; **Anthony Dean Griffey** *ten* Harold Mitchell;
Judith Forst *mez* Eunice Hubbell; **Matthew Lord** *ten* Steve Hubbell;
Jeffrey Lentz *ten* Young Collector; **Josepha Gayer** *mez* Flower Woman;
San Francisco Opera Orchestra / André Previn.
DG 20/21 459 366-2GX3 (three discs: 163 minutes: DDD). Notes and text included.
Recorded live in 1998.　Ⓜ

Tennessee Williams always resisted the operatic stage. Requests to turn *Streetcar* into an opera (and there were, not surprisingly, a good many) were always denied. His plays – and *Streetcar* in particular – were quite operatic enough without being sung. The music of Williams's poetry was always implicit. And yet … In 1964, as a gesture to composer Lee Hoiby, who underscored his ill-fated *Slapstick Tragedy*, Williams gave Hoiby the option to adapt any of his plays (including *Streetcar*) as an opera. Hoiby chose *Summer and Smoke*. But the door was finally open. André Previn came to it only in 1998. The offer, from Lotfi Mansouri of the San Francisco Opera, was nothing if not timely. After almost half-a-century of writing dramatic music for the movies, for the stage, to say nothing of his recent developments as a songsmith, opera was impatient for his touch. But *Streetcar*? It's perfect and yet not. The greater part of Previn's success has to do with his respect for, and understanding of, the music of Williams's text. Librettist Philip Littell has done an excellent job of adapting it, condensing it, mindful of how opera, by its very nature, seeks to elaborate and intensify the nodal points of any drama. In *Streetcar* those are easy enough to identify, but the real challenge (and accomplishment) here has been to preserve the play's narrative strength whilst losing more than an hour of its duration. You don't feel as if you've lost anything. All your favourite lines are just where you last left them.

Or seem to be. Previn's word-setting is now well practised and very skilled. His acute awareness of Williams's speech rhythms means that you hear every word (I don't recall too many intrusive sung vowels). The jokes all land (you can hear the audience testify to that). The poetry takes wing. The tone of the play rings true. Previn's *Streetcar* begins with the ominous lowing of a tuba and a sleazy, twice-sounded, trumpet-laden chord slurred through too much heat and booze. There is no jazz in Previn's score – just the allusion to it, the smell of it, the flavour of it. The sound world is late, late, romantic. Berg crossed with Barber and suffused with Britten (if you must have specific antecedents). The threat of violence restlessly, spikily, agitates just below the surface. Previn's score is rich in atmospherics. But richer yet is the way it takes Williams's lead in aspiring to a heady, ready lyricism where the play and players dare to dream of enchantment, tenderness, hope. This, of course, is especially true of Blanche whose vain belief that 'soft people have got to shimmer and glow' is reflected in music almost as sweet as it is extinct. Previn is sparing with this music, but when it comes, it floats, untouched and unsullied by the grubbiness, the brutality, of the real world below. And just as Blanche retreats more and more into her imagined world, so Previn's music for her grows more fragrant, more voluptuous, transporting her and us to higher and flightier regions. 'I want magic' is everything – and more – that she craves.

Renée Fleming must have been such an inspiration for Previn. She is currently at the peak of her powers. Indeed, you cannot imagine another singer of this stature who sounds and looks, in operatic terms, as one might imagine Blanche to sound and look. But then, you've only got to glance at the production photographs in the booklet to see just how carefully, and effectively, the opera has been cast. Fleming may have been a given for Blanche, but Rodney Gilfry's Stanley (big on baritonal bluster as well as biceps), Elizabeth Futral's Stella, and Anthony Dean Griffey's Mitch (whose idealism – not least the one brief, shining moment in Act 2 where he is able to articulate something of his belief in love – is so touching) are each outstanding. All in all, then, a considerable piece of work. Not everything sits quite as you would like it to sit, not everything comes off the page with quite the force you may have envisaged (Blanche's rape music, for instance, is very much Previn in B-movie mode). The play, of course, remains something else altogether. A masterpiece. But Previn and Littell and their cast have gone further than you would have thought possible towards effecting a theatrically viable transition from page to musical stage. It is probably a score that will knit together in the mind, though at first the ideas may seem too fragmented. Opera-goers have their own streetcar, which they board fearfully yet hopefully whenever a new opera comes along; it sounds at that moment very much as though they have stopped at a setting-down point they might actually recognize as Desire.

Sergey Prokofiev Russian/USSR 1891-1953

Prokofiev Symphony-Concerto (Sinfonia concertante) for Cello and Orchestra in E minor, Op. 125.
Tchaikovsky Variations on a Rococo Theme for Cello and Orchestra, Op. 33. Andante cantabile for Cello and Strings.
Yo-Yo Ma *vc*
Pittsburgh Symphony Orchestra / Lorin Maazel.
Sony Classical SK48382 (68 minutes: DDD). Recorded 1991.   Ⓕ

The *Symphony-Concerto* – a reworking of Prokofiev's earlier Cello Concerto – states that 'the title was prompted by the enhanced role of the orchestra which sounds at par in the ensemble with the solo cello'. This revision, like that of the Fourth Symphony, has its detractors; those who feel Prokofiev's second (even third) thoughts were not necessarily an improvement. However, you are likely to come away from this performance less aware of patchwork and padding and more excited about what this music is capable of expressing. Take the last half of the finale: the theme rings out slowly and majestically on full brass, then, in an instant, confidence withers at the icy *sul ponticello* from orchestral cellos, and we are transported to the nursery accompanied by a funereal tread from timpani and basses. The solo cello rises from this to fix on the home key with a fast and furious ostinato while the brass intones an outline of the theme – menacing, like the *Dies Irae*. At the end we are left with the cello hanging on to his *ostinato* for grim life and a final peremptory chord from the orchestra. When this work was substantially recast, for Prokofiev in his final years, times were pretty grim.

It's tempting to say that Ma and Maazel emphasize the lyrical and elegiac elements at the expense of the dramatic and sardonic ones, but their reading is not that easily pigeon-holed. In the second movement there is a marvellous wit, fantasy and playfulness from Ma, and refined tone of great beauty for the *cantabile* at 3'13", without a doubt one of Prokofiev's loveliest melodies. Was there restricted session time for the *Rococo* Variations? The woodwind seem too loud for their *piano* markings in the fifth bar, and at 1'53" the oboist thinks there's no repeat of the second half of the theme. The slower woodwind refrain isn't too convincing, which prior to the second variation, draws attention to the fact that Ma and Maazel race off here 50 per cent faster (the marking is *tempo della thema*). Despite all of this, Ma lends his playing a blend of aristocratic finesse, caprice and elevated lyricism. The *Andante cantabile* is slow, almost a lullaby and quite hypnotic – even the silences soothe. As to the recording, quite apart from the truthful perspectives which allow the listener to perceive details of orchestration normally obscured, the soundstage has openness and coherence.

Piano Concertos – No. 1 in D flat major, Op. 10; No. 2 in G minor, Op. 16; No. 3 in C major, Op. 26; No. 4 in B flat major, Op. 53 (left-hand); No. 5 in G major, Op. 55.

Piano Concertos Nos. 1-5.
Vladimir Ashkenazy *pf*
London Symphony Orchestra / André Previn.
Decca 452 588-2DF2 (two discs: 126 minutes: ADD). Recorded 1974-75.　　　Ⓜ 🆁🆁

While it's true that the Prokofiev piano concertos are an uneven body of work, there's enough imaginative fire and pianistic brilliance to hold the attention even in the weakest of them; the best, by common consent Nos. 1, 3 and 4, have stood the test of time very well. As indeed have these Decca recordings. The set first appeared in 1975, but the sound is fresher than many contemporary digital issues, and Ashkenazy has rarely played better. Other pianists have matched his brilliance and energy in, say, the Third Concerto, but very few have kept up such a sure balance of fire and poetry. The astonishingly inflated bravura of the Second Concerto's opening movement is kept shapely and purposeful and even the out-of-tune piano doesn't spoil the effect too much. And the youthful First has the insouciance and zest its 22-year-old composer plainly intended. Newcomers to the concertos should start with No. 3: so many facets of Prokofiev's genius (including that wonderfully piquant lyricism) are here, and Ashkenazy shows how they all take their place as part of a kind of fantastic story. But there are rewards everywhere, and the effort involved in finding them is small. Why hesitate?

Piano Concertos Nos. 1-5.
Vladimir Krainev *pf*
Frankfurt Radio Symphony Orchestra / Dmitri Kitaienko.
Teldec 9031-73257-2 (two discs: 123 minutes: DDD). Recorded 1991.　　　Ⓕ

Far too little heard of in the West, Vladimir Krainev reminds us, if anyone needed reminding, how sheerly exciting these concertos can be in the hands of a virtuoso on top form. Here are the dash and flamboyance, the spacious and rhythmic grasp, the balletic poise and acrobatic daredevilry which announce a born Prokofiev player. Only in the Third Concerto, far and away the most popular of the five, does Krainev succumb to the temptations of smash-and-grab overstatement – perhaps he has played the piece too often, or maybe he was conscious of the plethora of fine rival recordings. In this case the first movement pushes forward in a crude, attention-grabbing manner, the second is laboured in places, and the finale is again rather roughly handled. Not that pussy-footing is what Prokofiev needs, but here the impression is of a foreground-only portrait of the music. The finest performances are of the First, Fourth and Fifth Concertos, all of which have a splendid cut and thrust. Krainev revels in their extravagance and physicality, and he is backed up by beautifully prepared, sensitive orchestral playing. The massive Second Concerto is also fine, though here the recorded balance tends to swallow up important woodwind solo lines in a generalized warmth of ambience (elsewhere, for the most part, this warmth is a definite advantage). This set can hold its own against most of the competition.

Piano Concertos Nos. 1 and 3[a].
Evgeni Kissin *pf*
Berlin Philharmonic Orchestra / Claudio Abbado.
DG 439 898-2GH (42 minutes: DDD). Item marked [a] recorded live in 1993.　　　Ⓕ

Kissin always seems to have time to acknowledge the implications of Prokofiev's harmony, to allow the left hand to converse with the right (always naturally, never tricksily), and to gauge the relationship of his part to the orchestra. He is also scrupulous with dynamics. At the first entry in the C major Concerto he manages, as few pianists do, the *piano* contrast after the first three notes without losing soloistic presence. And he resists the temptation to shout out *forte* passages, so that Prokofiev's *fortissimos* stand in proper relief, as do his carefully placed accents (hear the opening theme of the same concerto's finale). Perhaps none of that strikes you as exceptional, but it is so in Prokofiev, where the sheer athletic demands are extreme and refinement seems like too much to ask. With a technique like his and an orchestra as responsive as the Berlin Philharmonic there are just a few places in the C major Concerto, such as the final pages, where Kissin might have allowed himself to be a bit more carried away. But there is no shortage of exhilaration in the youthful D flat Concerto, which is a model blend of attack, wit, poetry and drive. In fact there is little discernible difference between this studio recording and the live C major, either in accuracy or in excitement. It would be wrong to say that Kissin surpasses Ashkenazy (reviewed above). Bronfman on Sony Classical is virtually a match for him and offers the Fifth Concerto in addition. But DG's recording is clearer than the 20-year-old Decca set, and Abbado and the Berliners are far superior to Mehta and the Israel Philharmonic. Full price for 42 minutes of music may seem a bit steep; but what Kissin and Abbado have to offer is certainly in the luxury class.

Piano Concertos Nos. 1, 3 and 5.
Yefim Bronfman *pf*
Israel Philharmonic Orchestra / Zubin Mehta.
Sony Classical SK52483 (66 minutes: DDD). Recorded 1992.   Ⓕ

The opening of the First Concerto rather sits back on its haunches in this performance, and for all the subtle virtues of Bronfman's playing there is little of the blood-on-the-keys fanatical edge that would make you sit up and take notice. But that is not the abiding impression of this issue. For one thing the subtleties are so persuasive, the articulation so clean and the entire approach so considered and idiomatic that Bronfman starts to convince on his own terms. The finale of the Third Concerto will win you over completely; from its rabbits-out-of-the-hat opening to its tintinnabulating conclusion it is simply bursting with life and colour. And Mehta and the orchestra, hitherto rather passive-sounding, are sparked into action – hear the trombones at the clinching of C major in the final pages. The Fifth Concerto is also a triumph. Bronfman's way with the lolloping second movement is as enthralling as Ashkenazy's more garish extremes, and although Previn and the LSO constantly outdo their Israel counterparts for pointed characterization, this recording will have you revelling in every note of the music. Overall, then, this is an excellent mainstream version of these concertos. Superbly recorded, with a top-quality piano, and properly balanced with the soloist well to the fore, it surpasses virtually all the contenders in this exact repertoire.

Prokofiev Piano Concertos Nos. 1 and 3.
Bartók Piano Concerto No. 3, Sz119.
Martha Argerich *pf*
Montreal Symphony Orchestra / Charles Dutoit.
EMI CDC5 56654-2 (70 minutes: DDD). Recorded 1998.   Ⓕ🅴

Martha Argerich's return to the studios in two concertos she has not previously recorded is an uplifting moment. As always with this most mercurial of virtuosos, her playing is generated very much by the mood of the moment, and those who heard her in Prokofiev's First Concerto with Riccardo Muti at London's Royal Festival Hall some years ago – a firestorm of a performance – may well be surprised at her relative geniality with Dutoit. Her entire reading is less hard-driven, her opening arguably more authentically *brioso* than ferocious, her overall view a refreshingly fanciful view of Prokofiev's youthful iconoclasm. The central *Andante assai* is inflected with an improvisatory freedom she would probably not have risked earlier in her career and in the *Allegro scherzando* she trips the light fantastic, reserving a suitably tigerish attack for the final octave bravura display. Again, while her performance of the Third Concerto is less fleet or nimble-fingered than in her early legendary disc for DG with Abbado (reviewed below); it is more delectably alive to passing caprice. Part-writing and expressive detail interest her more than in the past and there is certainly no lack of virtuoso *frisson* in the first movement's concluding quasi-fugal *più mosso* chase. Once more Argerich is unusually sensitive in the central *Andantino*, to the fourth variation's plunge into Slavic melancholy and introspection. Personal and vivacious throughout, she always allows the composer his own voice.

This is true to an even greater extent in Bartók's Third Concerto where her rich experience in chamber music makes her often *primus inter pares*, a virtuoso who listens to her partners with the greatest care. In the *Adagio religioso* she achieves a poise that has sometimes eluded her in the past and her finale is specially characterful, her stealthy start to the concluding *Presto* allowing the final pages their full glory. Dutoit and the Montreal Symphony achieve a fine unity throughout, a sense of like-minded musicians at work. The recordings are clear and naturally balanced and only those in search of metallic thrills and rushes of blood to the head will feel disappointed.

Piano Concertos Nos. 2 and 4. Overture on Hebrew Themes in C minor, Op. 34.
Yefim Bronfman *pf* **Giora Feidman** *cl*
Juilliard Quartet (Robert Mann, Joel Smirnoff *vns* Samuel Rhodes *va* Joel Krosnick *vc*);
Israel Philharmonic Orchestra / Zubin Mehta.
Sony Classical SK58966 (65 minutes: DDD). Recorded 1993-94. Ⓕ 🄴

Bronfman's technical facility makes light of the Second Concerto's massive first movement cadenza,
and when the Israeli brass breaks through at 9'45" – all brawn and thunder – the effect is quite
overwhelming. The *Scherzo* is neat and mechanized, the *Intermezzo*'s initial 'fee-fi-fo-fum' brisk but
grimly intimidating, while the long, dizzyingly eventful finale is effectively held in check. As to the
Fourth (left-hand) Concerto, this is, perhaps, the work's finest recording to date. The first movement
has an appropriately cool demeanour, with nimble pianism and precise orchestral support. Then
there is the *Andante*, one of Prokofiev's most introspective narratives, here given with just the right
balance of mobility and restraint. The *Moderato*, too, has great charisma, its quick-fire mood
changes (from menace to laughter, and back again) inspiring from these players a combination of
energy, poise and finesse. It is a beautifully recorded, trim, dapper and above all stylish account of
Prokofiev's most underrated concerto. As if that were not enough, Sony throws in an extraordinary
rendition of the tangy *Overture on Hebrew Themes*, where the Juilliard Quartet mimics and
humours Giora Feidman's saucy, Klezmer-style clarinet playing, an authentic flashback to old-time
Yiddish theatre or street song: caustic, lovable and primary-coloured in the manner of Chagall. It
makes a wonderful encore.

Piano Concerto No. 3[a]. Violin Concerto No. 1 in D major, Op. 19[b]. Lieutenant Kijé – Suite,
Op. 60[c].
[a]**Martha Argerich** *pf* [b]**Shlomo Mintz** *vn*
[a]**Berlin Philharmonic Orchestra;**
[bc]**Chicago Symphony Orchestra / Claudio Abbado.**
DG Classikon 439 413-2GCL (69 minutes: ADD). Recorded [a]1967, [b]1983, [c]1977. Ⓑ 🆁🆁

There have been others to match the bustle and brilliance of Argerich's Prokofiev, her coloristic
range, her drive, her flashiness, her straining at the leash; but none who has so satisfyingly
combined all those qualities, who has given us such a rocket-launched recapitulation in the first
movement, such circus-routine vividness in the following variations, or such monstrous, hyperbolic
fairy-tale imagery in the finale, and all done with the most engaging reckless abandon. Claudio
Abbado has a highly-developed feeling for Prokofiev's sound world. Rarely has the fairy-tale
atmosphere of the First Violin Concerto been more keenly evoked. He distills a sense of wonder
and enchantment that is quite special. Textures are delicately coloured, dynamic nuances
scrupulously observed and there are feather-light string sonorities. Shlomo Mintz phrases with
imagination and individuality; you need only hear the way he shapes the first bars for that to
register. He plays with great polish and beauty of tone. Occasionally he colours a phrase by playing
on the flat side of the note though his intonation is fine throughout. Abbado's otherwise excellent
Lieutenant Kijé is marred by strange lapses of concentration from the Chicago Symphony Orchestra
– split horn notes, a misread in the 'Troïka' (which is probably the movement you would most often
want to play for friends) and some dicey solos besides. But mostly it's fine. The slightly grubby
double-bass and saxophone solos in the 'Romance' are most characterful. The engineers produce a
beautifully refined and homogeneous balance and it is very impressive indeed. There is plenty of
space round the instruments and the sound is truthful.

Prokofiev Piano Concerto No. 5[a].
Rachmaninov Piano Concerto No. 2 in C minor, Op. 18[b].
Sviatoslav Richter *pf*
Warsaw Philharmonic Orchestra / [a]**Witold Rowicki,** [b]**Stanislaw Wislocki.**
DG 415 119-2GH (58 minutes: ADD). Recorded 1959. Ⓕ 🄷

Prokofiev was to find no more dedicated an advocate for his keyboard works than Richter. So how
good that this artist's now legendary account of the Fifth Piano Concerto has been granted a new
lease of life on CD. Although it has never enjoyed the popularity of Prokofiev's Nos. 1 and 3, here,
however, attention is riveted from first note to last. Richter delights in the music's rhythmic vitality
and bite, its melodic and harmonic unpredictability. Both piano and orchestra are so clearly and
vividly reproduced that it is difficult to believe that the recording is 35 years old. Though betraying
its age slightly more, notably in the sound of the keyboard itself, Rachmaninov's No. 2 is no less
gripping. Not all of Richter's tempos conform to the score's suggested metronome markings, but his
intensity is rivalled only by his breathtaking virtuosity. Never could the work's opening theme
sound more laden, more deeply and darkly Russian.

Violin Concertos – No. 1 in D major, Op. 19; No. 2 in G minor, Op. 63.

Violin Concertos Nos. 1 and 2. Solo Violin Sonata in D major, Op. 115.
Gil Shaham *vn*
London Symphony Orchestra / André Previn.
DG 447 758-2GH (60 minutes: DDD). Recorded 1995.   ⓕ E RR

Rarely, if ever, have there been performances where soloist, orchestra and conductor connect with such unerring intuition, where the music is treated so naturally. Previn ushers in the First Concerto's crystalline opening with gentle intensity, raising the curtain for Gil Shaham's warmly tended first entry. Both make great play with the march theme that follows. The effect is like spicy gossip shared between friends while the *Scherzo* is equally rich in dialogue. Shaham's tone is at its most expressive at the beginning of the third movement, and at its most delicate just prior to the last big climax. This natural exegesis extends to the darker Second Concerto, even where Shaham or Previn linger about a particular phrase. The recording, too, is extremely impressive, with well defined string lines and a fine body of winds, brass and percussion (the all-important bass drum especially). Note how, beyond the raucous happenings of the second movement's central episode, the violins waft back with the principal theme (at 6'56"). Similar felicities occur regularly throughout both concertos, while the Second's finale – a riotous, slightly tongue-in-cheek *danse macabre* – is here sensibly paced and very well articulated. If all that weren't enough, Shaham treats us to a substantial encore in the lively Solo Sonata that Prokofiev intended to be performed in unison by a group of young players.

Violin Concertos Nos. 1 and 2.
Itzhak Perlman *vn*
BBC Symphony Orchestra / Gennedy Rozhdestvensky.
EMI CDC7 47025-2. (49 minutes: DDD/ADD)   ⓕ

The catalogue contains enough recommendable rival versions of these technically demanding, astringent, yet warmly romantic concertos to suit all tastes (including Shaham, Mintz, Vengerov – in a *Gramophone* Award-winning performance, reviewed under Shostakovich – as well as Perlman). The mastery of Perlman's technique and feeling for these two works makes this a strong recommendation indeed. The soloist is too far forward in the musical balance; yet one soon accepts this degree of prominence and indeed very little of the fine orchestral detail is lost as a result. And so the choice may well come down to Perlman's authority against the imagination and individuality of other interpreters. He is splendidly accompanied by Rozhdestvensky and the BBC Symphony Orchestra.

Cinderella, Op. 87. Summer Night – Suite, Op. 123.
Russian National Orchestra / Mikhail Pletnev.
DG 445 830-2GH2 (two discs: 138 minutes: DDD).   ⓕ E RR

This is an outstanding release. If Pletnev launches *Summer Night* somewhat brusquely, what follows is beyond reproach. Most striking of all is the radical clarity of texture which makes Prokofiev's modest suite seem at once unprecedentedly modern and that much more shrewdly realized in terms of colour. The score was extrapolated from the opera *The Duenna* (or *Betrothal in a Monastery*) in 1950 and its neglect, as Pletnev shows, is unaccountable. It is curious that a ballet as familiar as *Cinderella* should be so seldom heard in its entirety. Like *Romeo and Juliet*, *Cinderella* gives an impression of immense assurance, belying the obvious hazards of cultural production under Stalin. It is strong without being daring, colourful without being extravagant, and once again exhibits an emotional involvement often hidden in the past. This sounds reassuringly Tchaikovskian and yet there is also something pale and elusive in its make-up, perhaps designed to reflect the character of its main protagonist. The motif of Cinderella repressed, first heard at the very start of the ballet, is given a heavy tread, the orchestra dragging its metaphorical feet to intensify the pensive mood. As for the second motto theme, anticipating her eventual happiness with her dream prince, it is not so much broad and impassioned as achingly beautiful. Nor is the conducting without humour. The sisters' 'dancing lesson' has never been more vividly evoked, their unruly behaviour and slow learning curve precisely delineated in the truculent attack of the two solo violins. 'The Prince's first galop' (thrice he rushes off impetuously in search of his beloved) is as light as a feather, executed with matchless finesse by the Russian strings. The sound is good, the orchestral playing superb.

Cinderella[a]. Symphony No. 1[b].
London Symphony Orchestra / André Previn.
EMI Forte CZS5 68604-2 (two discs: 127 minutes: [a]DDD/[b]ADD). Synopsis included.
Recorded [a]1983, [b]1977.   Ⓜ

Previn's admirable *Cinderella* appeared originally on LP in 1983 but was never transferred to CD in its entirety, EMI opting for a single-disc 'highlights' compilation instead. It has come up quite beautifully in this transfer, the Abbey Road production (Grubb/Parker) possessing a most appealing warmth and lustre. Previn's imaginative, highly sympathetic direction combines both warm-hearted affection as well as a most seductive theatrical flair (the whole of Act 2 is particularly memorable in this regard). Throughout, the LSO responds with considerable dash and character: just occasionally, the strings are wanting in the last ounce of finesse and absolute technical security, but the woodwind contribution is especially felicitous. Comparing it with the immaculately honed but comparatively chilly Pletnev set, many readers may well prefer this competitively priced reissue. Unfortunately, the 'bonus' item – an enthusiastic, but distractingly scrappy *Classical* Symphony is far from ideal. No matter, a bargain all the same.

Peter and the Wolf, Op. 67.

Prokofiev Peter and the Wolf[a].
Bizet Jeux d'enfants.
Saint-Saëns Le carnaval des animaux.
[a]**Sir John Gielgud** *narr*
Royal Philharmonic Orchestra / Andrea Licata.
Tring International Royal Philharmonic Collection TRP046 (69 minutes: DDD).
Recorded 1994. Ⓢ**RR**

This *Peter and the Wolf* is very enjoyable indeed and more than worth its modest price. The famous voice is noticeably more mature, but the manner is just as charmingly avuncular and Gielgud participates in the narrative with steadily increasing excitement. The moment when the wolf catches and swallows his prey is wonderfully involving (and the oboe soloist here portrays a poignantly unlucky little duck). The following sequence, when the bird does his stuff from the branch of the tree is equally delightful – nice flute playing – Gielgud obviously enjoys the resourcefulness of all the characters (except the duck and the wolf) and even has his own spontaneous little vocal grin at the thought that 'the wolf's jumping only made the rope round his tail tighter'. The final procession is suitably grand and the moral of the tale could hardly be better pointed. At the very end Gielgud's glee in discovering that the duck is still alive inside the wolf is palpable, and this will surely appeal to young children. Every word of the narration communicates a great actor's joy in the English language, and Gielgud's vocal inflexions and changes of colour are a continual delight to the ear. So to the orchestral performance, which has a concert-hall ambience. The joining up is not always completely smooth (as when the hunters come out of the woods), but overall the continuity is well managed, and the orchestral playing has a nicely light touch.

The *Carnival of the Animals*, with a pair of excellent pianists, Vivian Troon and Roderick Elms (who make fun of themselves with clumsy wrong notes in their self-portrait), is a vividly straightforward and lively account, with individual instruments close-miked, altering the balance between numbers: the double-bass solo brings him well forward; 'The Swan', however, is unusually melancholy, as if he has just lost his mate. Bizet's *Jeux d'enfants* makes a good encore, again well played and recorded.

Prokofiev Peter and the Wolf.
Debussy La boîte à joujoux.
Patrick Stewart *narr* **Orchestra of Opéra de Lyon / Kent Nagano.**
Erato 4509-97418-2 (61 minutes: DDD). Text included. Recorded 1993. Ⓕ

Choosing the 'right' *Peter and the Wolf* is particularly difficult in that the versions that most please young children tend to drive parents mad, while the more urbane productions can challenge a child's concentration span. *Star Trek* veteran Patrick Stewart manages to straddle the borders with a narration that is both involving and restrained, an intimate yet lively reading, beautifully integrated into the orchestral score – which is itself superbly played by the Orchestra of Opéra de Lyon. Kent Nagano's roster of insights is far too substantial to itemize individually, so suffice to say that anyone in search of a stylishly tailored, tastefully phrased account is unlikely to complain. The recording, too, is exceptionally well balanced, albeit in the slightly cavernous acoustic of the Opéra de Lyon; whereas the location chosen for *La boîte à joujoux* – Lyon's Auditorium Maurice Ravel – is near ideal. This, too, is a performance of rare refinement and poise – a keenly inflected, tender and texturally luminous reading, with graphic characterization and phrasing that suggests lightning reflexes all round. However, as each of the four movements is positively crammed with dramatic incident, anyone interested in following the storyline will need some sort of synopsis. Regrettably, all Erato gives us is the bare text for *Peter and the Wolf*, plus essential recording details. Kent Nagano's conducting is superb, the recordings are generally excellent, Patrick Stewart tells a mean tale – it's just a shame that Erato's presentation is inadequate.

Romeo and Juliet, Op. 64.

Romeo and Juliet.
Cleveland Orchestra / Lorin Maazel.
Decca Double 452 970-2DF2 (two discs: 141 minutes: ADD). Synopsis included.
Recorded 1973.   ⓜ **RR**

It was George Szell who made the Cleveland Orchestra into a highly responsive virtuoso body, and
when he died in 1970 he was in due course succeeded by Lorin Maazel, himself a renowned
orchestral trainer. Here is Maazel's first Cleveland recording of Prokofiev's masterpiece, *Romeo and
Juliet*, notable for a quite outstanding quality of orchestral playing. The strings in particular have a
remarkable depth of tone, though they play with great delicacy when it is needed; but then the
orchestra as a whole plays with extraordinary virtuosity, tonal weight and exactness of ensemble. If
the woodwind have a somewhat piquant blend this suits the music, which throughout is admirably
served by Maazel's highly rhythmic, dramatic conducting. This vibrant complete recording, reissued
yet again on CD, has the added advantage of being at mid-price. There is a useful synopsis
contained in the notes, where the story of the ballet is explained cue by cue. If the orchestral
playing is a notable feature, then so is the high-quality recording, which is well balanced and wide in
range. It suffers little in comparison with the best of today and is indeed a tribute to the excellent
standards which Decca engineers achieved in the early 1970s. There are many other fine versions in
the catalogue but none surpasses this for passionate feeling, extraordinary orchestral virtuosity and
colour. The Cleveland never made a finer recording than this.

Romeo and Juliet.
London Symphony Orchestra / André Previn.
EMI Forte CZS5 68607-2 (two discs: 149 minutes: ADD). Notes included. Recorded 1973.   ⓜ

It is good to have André Previn's set of *Romeo and Juliet* restored to circulation at such a
reasonable price. The EMI recording (masterminded by Christopher Parker) still sounds pretty
sumptuous and the legendary Kingsway bloom remains mercifully intact on CD. Compared with
Maazel's dazzlingly assured Clevelanders, Previn's hard-working LSO can sound just a touch
cautious and technically fallible. Yet Previn's affectionate, wittily pointed reading has its place too:
many will rightly respond to its sense of easy spontaneity, tender restraint and unaffected honesty.
It is, in sum, a more relaxed, less relentlessly high-powered affair than his distinguished transatlantic
rivals, but no less compelling for that.

Romeo and Juliet.
Kirov Theatre Orchestra / Valery Gergiev.
Philips 432 166-2PH2 (two discs: 144 minutes: DDD). Recorded 1990.   Ⓕ

This great ballet score has been very lucky on records. Both Previn's EMI set and the Decca Maazel
recording, are very distinguished and make a powerful impression on the listener. This Russian
recording could not be more different. It was made in the Kirov Theatre in Leningrad and has the
fullness and amplitude characteristic of the finest western recordings, not surprising, as the
recording team was from Philips. The orchestral playing, too, is superb by any international
standard and has none of the sharp edges or raucousness we used to associate with Soviet
fortissimos. Indeed, if there were a criticism of the playing it would be to suggest it is at times
almost over-cultivated. The Introduction has a striking grace and flexibility, a sophistication of light
and shade that some listeners might not expect. The action of the opening street scene and the
sequence of events which follows is delineated with much delicacy of effect, crisp clear rhythms,
great energy when called for, in the 'Morning dance', for instance and the most stylish instrumental
response from all departments of the orchestra.

Perhaps it is all a shade mellow (Maazel showed how pungent Prokofiev's scoring could sound) and
the mood of the 'Balcony scene' is pure romanticism, relaxed and without sexual ardour: the strings
float ethereally, there is a beautifully played violin solo, and at the climax one is quite carried away.
The great climax of 'Juliet's funeral' (track 20) generates richly intense string playing and
resoundingly powerful brass. But there is no sense of utter despair. So this is a performance to enjoy
for the lyric feeling of Prokofiev's score and for the marvellous orchestral playing, but the starkness
of the tragedy is more heartrendingly conveyed elsewhere.

Romeo and Juliet – Suites Nos. 1-3: excerpts. Chout, Op. 21 – ballet suite.
London Symphony Orchestra / Claudio Abbado.
Decca Ovation 425 027-2DM (54 minutes: ADD). Recorded 1966.   ⓜ

It was an excellent idea to couple nine items from the familiar *Romeo and Juliet* ballet score with a similar sequence from the unjustly neglected *Chout* – the blackly comic tale of a village trickster, the Buffoon of the alternative title. *Romeo and Juliet* is more popular than ever these days, but Abbado's mid-1960s selection – less predictable than most – retains its freshness and appeal; only his sluggish *Dance of the girls with lilies* lacks something in charm. The sound is pretty good, the brass very immediate. While *Chout* has that rather sadistic plot – and the audiences of 1921 had ultra-modern cubist sets, costumes and choreography to object to – its neglect seems unaccountable today, given the quality of the music. Here, Prokofiev was clearly inspired by Stravinsky's *Petrushka*. Even if there remains some loosely-written connective tissue, there is also a fund of melodic invention that could only have come from the younger man. The orchestration glitters throughout, sharp-edged and totally distinctive. Decca's analogue recording remains impressive.

Prokofiev Romeo and Juliet – Suites Nos. 1 and 2[a].
Mussorgsky A Night on the Bare Mountain[b].
[a]Minneapolis Symphony Orchestra / Stanislav Skrowaczewski;
[b]London Symphony Orchestra / Antal Dorati.
Mercury Living Presence 432 004-2MM (67 minutes: ADD). Recorded 1960-62.　　　Ⓜ

Skrowaczewski's version of the *Romeo and Juliet* ballet suites is one of the very best things he has recorded. The LP made an extremely strong impression when it first appeared here in 1965, after Dorati had brought the Minneapolis orchestra to a high peak of achievement. The playing is often electrifying in its precision and delicacy – witness the very opening filigree on the high violins in the 'Folk Dance' of Suite No. 1 or the delectably precise articulation of the portrayal of Mercutio which follows. Skrowaczewski's subtlety of rubato, both in the latter (track 2) and the wonderfully delicate 'Madrigal' which follows (when Romeo first approaches Juliet), is equally memorable for the wistful character of the orchestral playing. The 'Balcony scene' with its gently soaring string line is ravishingly done, and then in the 'Death of Tybalt' there is a frenzied burst of sheer bravura from the violins, with exhilaratingly sharp articulation that makes the nape of the neck tingle. 'Juliet as a young girl' in Suite No. 2 brings playing which combines a gossamer touch with unpretentious virtuosity of the highest order, while at the closing climax of 'Romeo at Juliet's grave' the music's pungent agony and sense of apotheosis is powerfully expressed (the bite of the violin line well matched by the turbulent horns and mordant brass). The acoustics of Edison High School in Minneapolis and the refined clarity of the recording seem ideal for Prokofiev's scoring. There are many fine modern selections of these Suites but none which captures its unique atmosphere and character more tellingly. Dorati's (1960) *A Night on the Bare Mountain* (rather more sumptuously recorded, in Watford Town Hall) makes a good filler. It is a dramatic performance, not always conventional in pacing, with a particularly poignant closing section – again, Mercury engineering at its most impressive, with the resonant sonorities never clouding the detail.

Symphonies – No. 1 in D major, Op. 25, 'Classical'; No. 2 in D minor, Op. 40; No. 3 in C minor, Op. 44; No. 4 in C major, Op. 47 (original 1930 version); No. 4 in C major, Op. 112 (revised 1947 version); No. 5 in B flat major, Op. 100; No. 6 in E flat minor, Op. 111; No. 7 in C sharp minor, Op. 131.

Symphonies Nos. 1-7.
Royal Scottish National Orchestra / Neeme Järvi.
Chandos CHAN8931/4 (four discs: 260 minutes: DDD). *Gramophone* Award Winner 1985.　Ⓕ🆁🆁

Prokofiev was not a natural symphonist. Albeit successful in emulating Haydn in the *Classical* Symphony, the Sixth Symphony is his only undisputed integrated symphonic structure (and an epic-tragic utterance as intense as any by Shostakovich). It has been suggested that his symphonies all have a sense of some unstaged scenario, and the Third and Fourth (and to a lesser extent, the Seventh) Symphonies actually rework material from his music for the stage. The Fourth (in both versions) in particular fails to convince as a symphony owing to the profusion and individuality of its often strikingly beautiful thematic ideas – it's a real patchwork quilt of a piece. Enter Neeme Järvi, nothing if not a man of the theatre, to give maximum dramatic intensity and character to all Prokofiev's ideas, whether they add up symphonically or not; capable of overawing his Scottish forces into playing of aerial lightness and easeful lyricism in the *Classical* Symphony, and pulling no punches where Prokofiev's inspiration (as in the Second and Third Symphonies) is at its most strident, violent and hysterical. Make no mistake, though, these are also readings of real stature: where there is symphonic 'line', Järvi unerringly finds it. Drawbacks? Some may feel the need for a deeper pile of string sound, particularly in the Fifth Symphony; and these typically spacious Chandos productions do not always ensure adequate projection for the woodwind, but more often than not one cannot fail to be impressed by the coherence and co-ordination, both musically and technically, of some of this century's most fabulous and fraught orchestral essays. As a cycle, this is unlikely to be challenged for some time.

Symphony No. 1. Peter and the Wolf[a]. March in B flat minor, Op. 99. Overture on Hebrew Themes, Op. 34bis[b].
[a]**Sting** narr [b]**Stefan Vladar** pf
Chamber Orchestra of Europe / Claudio Abbado.
DG 429 396-2GH (50 minutes: DDD). Recorded 1986-90.   Ⓕ 🔲🔲

Abbado's elegant and graceful reading of the *Classical* Symphony is one of the finest in the catalogue, and is particularly notable for its beautifully shaped phrasing, clarity of inner detail and crisp articulation. He seems to make all the right choices at all the right tempos. His first movement, the right side of measured, is dapper in the best sense and marked by keen detailing in the fugal development: note the clinching flourish in the timpani line – an exciting touch. Everywhere is elegance and rhythmic grace. Abbado's strings tread air through the *Larghetto*, the finale is indeed *molto vivace* with quicksilver articulation from the COE woodwinds, chortling and darting in and around the bar-lines. Abbado and the multi-talented Sting offer a lively and beautifully crafted account of Prokofiev's ever popular *Peter and the Wolf*. Any fears that the original freshness of Prokofiev's creation may be lost in favour of a less formal approach are soon dispelled – Sting is an effective and intelligent storyteller capable of capturing the imagination of adults and children alike, and there is never a feeling of contrivance or mere gimmickry. The orchestral playing is a real delight too; sharply characterized and performed with great affection. The *Overture on Hebrew Themes* is more commonly heard in its drier, more acerbic version for clarinet, piano and string quartet, but makes a welcome and refreshing appearance on this disc in Prokofiev's own arrangement for small orchestra. The spry *March* in B flat is a wartime novelty which seems to scent victory: it's a little like *Kijé*'s Wedding march with a twist from a certain *Three Oranges* – this version of it will do very nicely.

Symphonies Nos. 1 and 5.
Berlin Philharmonic Orchestra / Herbert von Karajan.
DG Galleria 437 253-2GGA (71 minutes: ADD).   Ⓜ 🔲🔲

The playing throughout the First Symphony is beautifully cultured and there is wonderful lightness and delicacy. The first movement could sparkle more and the same could be said of the finale, yet the slow movement is very beautiful indeed. The sound has marvellous clarity and definition as well as exemplary range. Even more than 30 years after its first release, Karajan's Fifth Symphony still remains incomparable. The playing has wonderful tonal sophistication and Karajan judges tempos to perfection so that the proportions seem quite perfect. The recording, too, is extremely well balanced and has excellent ambience, and this reissue strikes you as smoother and more refined than both the original LP and any previous reissue. No other available version of this symphony begins to match this in distinction and stature. Even at full price this would still sweep the board and at its mid-price level it is a clear first choice.

Symphonies Nos. 1 and 5.
Los Angeles Philharmonic Orchestra / André Previn.
Philips Solo 442 399-2PM (57 minutes: DDD). Recorded 1987.   Ⓜ

This is an almost unqualified success, one of the finest records Previn made. Prokofiev strikes a particularly sympathetic chord in this conductor; indeed, he has as strong a natural affinity with him as he has with Walton and Shostakovich, though neither his Sixth nor Seventh came off as successfully. Since these were recorded, there have been several versions of this coupling and turning to the mid-price field Karajan in the Fifth is the most perfectly proportioned and sumptuous account, though artistically it still takes second place to the Koussevitzky. All the same, Karajan is not recorded with the same clarity and presence as the Previn version. This can still take its place high among the very best.

Symphonies Nos. 1 and 5. Romeo and Juliet – Suite No. 2. Chout, Op. 21 – Danse finale.
Boston Symphony Orchestra / Serge Koussevitzky.
RCA Victor Gold Seal mono 09026 61657-2 (73 minutes: ADD). Recorded 1945-47.   Ⓜ Ⓗ

Although there have been many fine and some thrilling performances of Prokofiev's Fifth Symphony since it first appeared on record, this is one of the best. Of course, there are many more modern and better recorded versions that can be recommended but (to put an unwelcome scenario) were the bomb about to drop, and one had only time to play one version of the Fifth, for many people it would be this one. Not even the Berlin Philharmonic under Karajan can match the strings of the Boston Symphony in sheer power and eloquence under Koussevitzky. They possess a lyrical intensity matched by few others. Above the stave they sing with unerring purity of intonation: the sound is marvellously clean and their tone can only be called luminous. The wind and brass are of comparable excellence. This account dates from 1946, yet the musicians sound as if they have known this music all their lives. The *Classical* is both vivacious and enchanting. Superb performances, in a class of their own, which produce even better results now than they did on vinyl.

Symphonies Nos. 1 and 7. The Love for Three Oranges – Suite, Op. 33*a*.
Philharmonia Orchestra / Nicolai Malko.
Classics for Pleasure CD-CFP4523. Recorded 1955. ⑧ 🄷

A good record is always a good record and this one is a very good one indeed. Considering the date of the recording, its quality is astonishing. The balance is excellent and the actual sound seems hardly dated. It is bright and vivid without being artificial and the natural resonance of the hall never clouds detail. The playing of the Philhamonia at its peak is marvellous: try the deliciously elegant string line in the *Larghetto* of the *Classical* Symphony, or the chortling humour of both strings and wind in the finale of the Seventh. What attractive works these are in Malko's hands, with delicacy and a warm but not cloying romanticism and with everything part of the overall picture. The suite from *The Love for Three Oranges* is no less tellingly characterized, the 'March' crisply buoyant, the romantic interlude touchingly lyrical. Highly recommended on all counts.

Symphony No. 5. Scythian Suite, Op. 20.
City of Birmingham Symphony Orchestra / Sir Simon Rattle.
EMI CDC7 54577-2 (64 minutes: DDD). Recorded 1992. ⑤

Here is a Prokofiev Fifth as vibrant, intelligent and meticulously prepared as you'd expect from this partnership. In the mighty opening movement, there's real mystery about those fairy-tale slumberings at the start of the development, and how naturally Rattle quickens the pulse during the pages which follow, the sense of expectancy and adventure palpably conveyed. Enter the coda, and Rattle's expertly-graduated dynamics ensure a riveting succession of spectacular climaxes. Here, too, EMI's impressive recording opens out magnificently. Rattle's scherzo is a marvellously quick-witted conception, the slow movement etched with genuine tenderness and bustling good humour reigns supreme in the admirably spirited finale. The coupling is a stunning *Scythian Suite*, combining foundation-threatening pagan spectacle and heart-stopping beauty in ideal equilibrium. Brilliant!

String Quartets – No. 1 in B minor, Op. 50; No. 2 in F major, Op. 92.
American Quartet (Mitchell Stern, Laurie Carney *vns* Daniel Avshalomov *va* David Geber *vc*).
Olympia OCD340 (50 minutes: ADD). Recorded 1982. Ⓜ

Prokofiev's wider popularity has never extended to his chamber music. Of his two quartets, the Second is by far the better known and comes from the war years when Prokofiev was evacuated to the Caucasus, where he made a study of the musical folklore of Kabarda – indeed, it is sometimes known as the 'Kabardinian' Quartet. Although the material is folk-derived, it is completely absorbed into Prokofiev's own melodic bloodstream and doesn't sound in the least bit 'folksy'. The second movement quotes a Kabardinian love song of great lyrical beauty, and at one point in the slow movement, the accompaniment imitates a Caucasian stringed instrument, the kamancha. It is a work of real quality which has the astringent flavouring and poetic flair that characterizes Prokofiev at his best. Although the First Quartet, written at the behest of the Library of Congress in 1930, is not so immediately appealing it, too, is a work of substance which grows on the listener. Prokofiev's friend and colleague, Nikolay Miaskovsky, who composed 13 string quartets and more than twice as many symphonies, particularly admired the last movement, and encouraged Prokofiev to score it for full strings. The American Quartet communicates conviction and belief in this music: theirs is a persuasive account, sensitive and yet full-blooded, and they are very well recorded.

Violin Sonatas – No. 1 in F minor, Op. 80; No. 2 in D major, Op. 94*a*. Five Melodies, Op. 35*b*.
Vadim Repin *vn* **Boris Berezovsky** *pf*
Erato 0630-10698-2 (63 minutes: DDD). Recorded 1995. Ⓕ 🄴

A clear first choice in this repertoire and heartening confirmation of the young Vadim Repin's considerable violinistic skills. Tension sets in right from the First Sonata's opening bars: the tone is bright, sweet, tremulous and warmly expressive, while the music's sombre mood is precisely gauged. Repin phrases with considerable sensitivity and his attack in the work's faster episodes – the *Allegro brusco*'s outer sections and most of the finale – has a Heifetzian 'edge'. Nervous energy is also much in evidence, while the *Andante* – one of Prokofiev's most haunting creations – has a wistfully distracted air that Boris Berezovsky matches with some notably perceptive piano playing. The *Allegrissimo* finale, too, is arresting: deftly fingered, percussively insistent and with a truly heartfelt projection of the work's tender closing phrase. One of Repin's leading qualities is his obvious interpretative sincerity; nowhere does one sense the suave affectation that afflicts some of his contemporaries, a fact that registers with particular force in the Second Sonata's opening *Moderato*. Here lesser artists often sound either matter-of-fact or uninterested, and even superior ones opt for relative coolness. Repin and Berezovsky, on the other hand, are both tender and relaxed; phrasal 'crossfire' and keen inflexion keep sparks flying in the *Scherzo*, the *Allegretto leggiero e scherzando* is appropriately limpid, and although the finale could have swaggered rather more freely, there are magical moments to spare. Both players achieve an impressive range of colour throughout and the five delightful *Melodies* make for a welcome sequence of encores. Very well recorded.

Prokofiev Violin Sonata No. 2.
K. Khachaturian Violin Sonata, Op. 1.
Szymanowski Violin Sonata in D minor, Op. 9.
David Oistrakh *vn* **Vladimir Yampolsky** *pf*
Testament mono SBT1113 (65 minutes: ADD). Recorded 1955. Ⓕ ◨

David Oistrakh's playing is, at its best, a calming force in an agitated world – intelligent, considered (just occasionally overcalculated), invariably poised, big-toned and confident. You know what to expect and are rarely disappointed, and these excellent refurbishments of key Oistrakh performances from the 1950s lend a characteristic narrative quality to a wide variety of repertoire. Best perhaps is the Prokofiev sonata, which Oistrakh himself instigated in reaction to hearing the flute-and-piano original. The playing is quietly confidential in the first and third movements, pert in the *Scherzo* and exuberant in the closing *Allegro con brio*. Oistrakh's phrasing is incisive without sounding aggressive (most notes retain their full measure of tone, even at speed), while his handling of rhythm is both supple and muscular. Szymanowski's post-romantic Op. 9 is lusciously full-toned and expertly negotiated by Yampolsky, while the reading of Karen Khachaturian's Op. 1 – a pleasant piece reminiscent of Kabalevsky, the lighter Shostakovich and, very occasionally, Gershwin – is another masterly performance, especially in the delightful *Andante*. All in all, this is a superb disc, expertly annotated and very well presented. The Prokofiev Second Sonata is as near 'definitive' as anyone has a right to expect, while the rest is typical of a violinist whose aristocratic playing and artistic diplomacy were – and remain – an inspiration to us all.

Piano Sonatas – No. 1 in F minor, Op. 1; No. 2 in D minor, Op. 14; No. 3 in A minor, Op. 28; No. 4 in C minor, Op. 29; No. 5 in C major, Opp. 38/135; No. 6 in A major, Op. 82; No. 7 in B flat major, Op. 83; No. 8 in B flat major, Op. 84; No. 9 in C major, Op. 103; No. 10 in E minor, Op. 137.

Piano Sonatas Nos. 1, 4 and 6.
Yefim Bronfman *pf*
Sony Classical SK52484 (52 minutes: DDD). Recorded 1991. Ⓕ ◳

These are performances which are highly considered, thoroughly idiomatic, possessed of exceptionally clean fingerwork and articulation and rich in subtleties and expressive nuance. Bronfman opens the disc with a particularly impressive and bold-hearted account of the Sixth Sonata; one of those interpretations that seizes and holds the listener's attention from the first to last bar. There's a real sense of dramatic narration about this performance, as opposed to the sometimes overtly (and exclusively) virtuosic readings of some pianists. That's not to deny the virtuosic elements of Bronfman's performance, of which there are plenty, though more impressive is the deceptive ease and finesse with which he traverses some of Prokofiev's excessive demands. In the Fourth Sonata every mood change is superbly caught, and Bronfman's lyricism and delicacy in the tender, probing central section of the slow movement is particularly memorable. The short, youthful First Sonata, always a difficult work to bring off successfully, is played with great verve and panache. Good recorded sound.

Piano Sonatas Nos. 2 and 7. The Love for Three Oranges, Op. 33*ter* – March. Ten Pieces from Cinderella, Op. 97 – No. 10, Waltz. Six Pieces from Cinderella, Op. 102 – No. 4, Amoroso. Three Pieces, Op. 96 – No. 1, War and Peace – Waltz, Op.96 No. 1.
Barry Douglas *pf*
RCA Victor Red Seal RD60779 (56 minutes: DDD). Recorded 1991. Ⓕ

There has often been a tendency with Prokofiev's piano music for pianists to overplay the percussive, steely qualities of the piano writing at the expense of the lyrical aspects. Barry Douglas, however, attains the perfect blend – muscular and athletic where power and agility are called for, but ever alert to the lyricism which lies beneath the surface. The Second Sonata is a prime example. Douglas has the full measure of this youthful, energetic masterpiece, and one feels that he has fully assimilated this piece before committing it to disc. The first movement with its restless oscillation between expressive melody and ruminative figuration is thoughtfully fashioned, and the knockabout scherzo and fleet-footed energetic finale are delivered with much vigour and flair. The Seventh Sonata (the central work of Prokofiev's 'War Trilogy') is impressive too, with Douglas fully in command of its bristling difficulties. As for the rest of the disc, Douglas offers some of the less frequently heard piano transcriptions, of which the delirious 'love' Waltz from *Cinderella* and the March from *The Love for Three Oranges* crave particular attention. The recording is beautifully engineered and balanced.

Piano Sonatas Nos. 2, 3, 5 and 9.
Yefim Bronfman *pf*
Sony Classical SK53273 (66 minutes: DDD). Recorded 1995.   Ⓕ

Yefim Bronfman is most impressive here. As before, his readings are considered, idiomatic and technically immaculate and refreshingly free of the idiosyncrasies that so many of his rivals bring to these sonatas. Nowhere is this more evident than in his beautifully crafted account of the Ninth Sonata, the opening movement of which is certainly one of the most exquisitely simple and poetic readings currently in the catalogue. His account of the Fifth Sonata is an excellent example of his faithfulness to Prokofiev's written note and his uncluttered, direct and often powerful approach. Every change in mood is superbly crafted and judged (especially in the single-movement Third Sonata) and in the youthful, rumbustious Second Sonata Bronfman's pristine fingerwork comes very much into its own. There are, of course, a number of rival recordings available in this repertoire; however, Bronfman can safely compete with the finest on offer. Good recorded sound.

Prokofiev Piano Sonata No. 8. Visions fugitives, Op. 22 – Nos. 3, 6 and 9.
Debussy Estampes. Préludes, Book 1 – Voiles; Le vent dans la plaine; Les collines d'Anacapri.
Scriabin Piano Sonata No. 5 in F sharp major, Op. 53.
Sviatoslav Richter *pf*
DG Dokumente 423 573-2GDO (67 minutes: ADD). Recorded 1963.   Ⓜ

Richter has long been acclaimed as one of the most dedicated champions of Prokofiev's keyboard music, with the Eighth Sonata always particularly close to his heart. It would certainly be hard to imagine a more profoundly and intensely experienced performance than this, or one of greater keyboard mastery. After the yearning introspection of the temperamental opening movement and the *Andante*'s evocation of a more gracious past, the rhythmic tension and sheer might of sonority he conjures in the finale make it easy to understand why the composer's biographer, I.V. Nestyev, suspected some underlying programme culminating in 'heroic troops resolutely marching ahead, ready to crush anything in their path'. In the uniquely Prokofievian fantasy of the three brief *Visions fugitives* he is wholly bewitching. As for the Fifth Sonata of Scriabin, his impetuous start at once reveals his understanding of its manic extremities of mood. For just these Russian performances alone, this excellently refurbished disc can be hailed as a collector's piece. And as a bonus there is Debussy too, with infinite subtleties of tonal shading to heighten atmospheric evocation.

Ten Pieces from Romeo and Juliet, Op. 75. War and Peace – Waltz, Op. 96 No. 1. The Love for Three Oranges, Op. 33b – March; Scherzo. Six Pieces from Cinderella, Op. 102.
Vladimir Ashkenazy *pf*
Decca 452 062-2DH (60 minutes: DDD). Recorded 1993-94.   Ⓕ

In the *Ten Pieces from Romeo and Juliet* it is gratifying to find this indefatigable artist complementing fierceness with finesse, his sometimes chaffing mastery with much delicacy of expression. His 'Folk Dance' is bright and ceremonious with pungently accented *sf* chording. 'Juliet' is as headstrong as she is introspective, while 'Mercutio' brandishes his rapier wit in gloriously assured and articulate style. The sinister undertow of 'Masques' erupts into open belligerence in 'Montagues and Capulets' but, overall, there is a true sense of how a world of overheated emotions is resolved in the most engaging mix of exuberance and *gravitas*. In *Cinderella*, 'Quarrel' suggests a debate as mock-acrimonious as any in the House of Commons and the enchanting 'Amoroso' ends the suite in a manner alternatively forceful and ethereal. Readily recommendable alternatives of this repertoire are few and far between and Decca's superbly successful sound enriches the effect of Ashkenazy's unfailingly expert performances.

Alexander Nevsky, Op. 78. Scythian Suite, Op. 20.
Linda Finnie *sop*
Scottish National Chorus and Orchestra / Neeme Järvi.
Chandos CHAN8584 (60 minutes: DDD). Text and translation included. Ⓕ 🆁🆁

At the chill opening of Järvi's fine version of *Alexander Nevsky* one can really feel the bitter wind of the Russian winter. The acoustics of the Caird Hall in Dundee where these Chandos recordings were made adds an extra atmospheric dimension to this splendidly recorded performance. The choral entry has an affecting poised melancholy, yet their geniality in the call to 'Arise ye Russian people' has a ring of peasantry. The 'Battle on the Ice' is the enormously spectacular climax, with the bizarre dissonance of the orchestral *scherzando* effects given tremendous pungency capped by the exhilarating shouts of fervour from the singers. Linda Finnie's contribution is most eloquent too and Järvi's apotheosis very moving. The *fortissimo* force of Chandos's recording is especially telling. As a coupling, Järvi chooses the ballet *Ala and Lolly*, originally written for Diaghilev which, when rejected by him, became the *Scythian Suite*. Its aggressive motoric rhythms are as powerful as anything Prokofiev wrote (indeed, their primitive force has an element of almost brutal ugliness to which you may not wholly respond) but the lyrical music is top-quality Prokofiev. 'It remains one of his most richly imaginative, harmonically sophisticated and wonderfully atmospheric scores', suggests Robert Layton in the notes. Certainly Järvi has its measure and so do the Chandos engineers, but it's not music for a small flat.

Ivan the Terrible, Op. 116.
Liubov Sokolova *mez* **Nikolai Putilin** *bar*
Chorus of the Kirov Opera; Rotterdam Philharmonic Orchestra / Valery Gergiev.
Philips 456 645-2PH (65 minutes: DDD). Text and translation included. Recorded 1996. Ⓕ

This studio account of *Ivan* ranks with the best of Gergiev's opera recordings. Of course, recommending just one version for the collection is not easy when the work, rather like the film itself, does not exist in a definitive form. Part 1 of Eisenstein's masterpiece was released in 1946 to worldwide acclaim, although Stravinsky for one did not care for its mix of iconography and melodrama. Prokofiev's health was so poor that he recommended that Gavriil Popov take over as composer for Part 2. Later he was able to resume work on the project – only to find it withheld from distribution. Soviet officials found its portrayal of Ivan's psychological decline too negative and, no doubt, too close to home. Which is not to say that Prokofiev intended to encode any criticism of Stalin in the notes. The film was released in the USSR in 1958 by which time plans to complete the trilogy had been abandoned, its prime movers long dead. Prokofiev thought highly enough of the score to reuse sections of it, but he left no guidelines for presenting it in the concert hall. Reshaping the music to fit a chronological narrative, Abram Stasevich fabricated an overlong oratorio. Gergiev's version is based on Stasevich; only here the music is left to fend for itself without the interpolated Russian texts. The Russian choir and some notably forward timpani help Gergiev build the right atmosphere. The wide vibrato of his young mezzo is nothing if not authentic and there will be no complaints about the robust singing of Nikolai Putilin. James Agee acclaimed the film as 'A visual opera, with all of opera's proper disregard of prose-level reality' but if you want the music divorced from the images, Gergiev's account is among the most sheerly dramatic.

Betrothal in a Monastery.
Nikolai Gassiev *ten* Don Jerome; **Alexander Gergalov** *bar* Ferdinand;
Anna Netrebko *sop* Louisa; **Larissa Diadkova** *contr* Duenna; **Evgeny Akimov** *ten* Antonio;
Marianna Tarassova *mez* Clara; **Sergei Alexashkin** *bass* Mendoza;
Yuri Shkliar *bass* Don Carlos;
Kirov Opera Chorus and Orchestra / Valery Gergiev.
Philips 462 107-2PH3 (three discs: 153 minutes: DDD). Notes, text and translation included.
Recorded live in 1997. Ⓕ

Betrothal in a Monastery.
Alexei Maslennikov *ten* Don Jerome; **Vladimir Redkin** *bar* Ferdinand;
Lyudmilla Sergienko *sop* Louisa; **Galina Borisova** *mez* Duenna; **Arkady Mishenkin** *ten* Antonio;
Marina Shutova *mez* Clara; **Mikhail Krutikov** *bass* Mendoza;
Vladislav Verestnikov *bass* Don Carlos;
Bolshoi Theatre Chorus and Orchestra / Alexander Lazarev.
Melodiya 74321 60318-2 (two discs: 154 minutes: DDD). Notes included. Recorded 1990. Ⓜ

Prokofiev's genial *Betrothal in a Monastery* may not be his most consistently inspired score, but it is immensely likeable, so it's very welcome to have two first-rate recordings to fill what was a gap in the catalogue. Collectors following the Philips Kirov series will probably look forward to adding another handsome-looking light-blue box set to their shelves. But three full-price discs? With almost identical timings the Bolshoi performance fits comfortably on to two, and at mid-price the Melodiya issue works out (presumably) at roughly half the cost. Furthermore, Lazarev and his cast and orchestra are not a whit inferior to Gergiev and Co., and the two conductors have very similar approaches to pacing and characterization. If anything the slightly saltier Bolshoi style is more appropriate than the smoother Kirov, and Melodiya's richer, more resonant studio recording is in many ways preferable to Philips's dry-throated theatre acoustic.

And yet, go for the Melodiya set and you have to do without the libretto. Who these days is prepared to forgo the text, especially given that the score, itself by no means easily obtainable, has the words in Russian only? Melodiya does admittedly supply a detailed synopsis (as does Philips, of course), and if you want to keep abreast of the three couples who finally plight their troths after a double elopement and a variety of disguises and mistaken identities, it's the synopsis rather than the text that you need. But for closer acquaintance, you need the words. Though there's precious little to choose between the two casts, generally speaking the male roles are slightly more successful at the Bolshoi (in particular Alexei Maslennikov's Don Jerome is superior to the initially rather hoarse Nikolai Gassiev), while the female ones are better at the Kirov (this goes especially for Anna Netrebko's mellifluous Louisa). Both Duennas are appropriately fruity. The Moscow chorus savours its chance to cavort as drunken monks in Act 4 even more than do its St Petersburg counterparts. So faced with an either/or choice you may find yourself having to go for the Philips set for the sake of having the text and translation, but will probably find it hard not to resent the unnecessary expense of the extra disc.

The Fiery Angel.
Galina Gorchakova *sop* Renata; **Sergei Leiferkus** *bar* Ruprecht; **Vladimir Galusin** *ten* Agrippa;
Konstantin Pluzhnikov *ten* Mephistopheles; **Sergei Alexashkin** *bass* Faust;
Vladimir Ognovanko *bass* Inquisitor; **Evgeni Boitsov** *ten* Jakob Glock;
Valery Lebed *bass* Doctor; **Yuri Laptev** *ten* Mathias; **Mikhail Kit** *bar* Servant;
Evgenia Perlasova *mez* Landlady; **Larissa Diadkova** *mez* Fortune teller;
Olga Markova-Mikhalenko *contr* Mother Superior; **Yevgeny Fedotov** *bass* Innkeeper;
Mikhail Chernozhukov *bass* First Neighbour; **Andrei Karabanov** *bar* Second Neighbour;
Gennadi Bezzubenkov *bass* Third Neighbour; **Tatiana Kravtsova** *sop* First Nun;
Tatiana Filimoniva *sop* Second Nun;
Chorus and Orchestra of the Kirov Opera / Valery Gergiev.
Philips 446 078-2PH2 (two discs: 119 minutes: DDD). Notes, text and translation included.
Recorded live in 1993. *Gramophone* Award Winner 1996. Ⓕ🅴

The opera is no blameless masterpiece – Prokofiev's indulgence in lurid sensationalism sometimes gets the better of his artistic judgement. But that sounds a pretty po-faced judgement in the face of the overwhelming power which so much of this score exudes. This Maryinsky performance comes live from what is clearly a highly-charged occasion in one of the world's great opera houses. That brings with it the disadvantage of a constrained opera-pit acoustic, which makes some of Prokofiev's over-the-top scoring seem pretty congested. But the immediacy and clarity of the sound, plus the orchestra's rhythmic grasp, ensures that the effect is still properly blood-curdling. If Leiferkus's distinctive rich baritone at first sounds a touch microphoney, the ear can soon adjust to that too, and Gorchakova brings intense beauty as well as intensity to Renata's hysterics, taking us right inside the psychological drama. The supporting roles are filled with distinction and this makes a huge difference to the sustaining of dramatic tension, the *crescendo* which Prokofiev aimed to build through his five acts. Considering the extent of the stage goings-on there is remarkably little audience distraction on the recording.

The Love for Three Oranges (sung in French).
Gabriel Bacquier *bar* King of Clubs; **Jean-Luc Viala** *ten* Prince; **Hélène Perraguin** *mez* Princess Clarissa; **Vincent Le Texier** *bass-bar* Leandro; **Georges Gautier** *ten* Truffaldino;
Didier Henry *bar* Pantaloon, Farfarello, Master of Ceremonies; **Gregory Reinhart** *bass* Tchelio;
Michèle Lagrange *sop* Fata Morgana; **Consuelo Caroli** *mez* Linetta;
Brigitte Fournier *sop* Nicoletta; **Catherine Dubosc** *sop* Ninetta; **Jules Bastin** *bass* Cook;
Béatrice Uria Monzon *mez* Smeraldina;
Chorus and Orchestra of Lyon Opéra / Kent Nagano.
Virgin Classics VCD7 59566-2 (two discs: 102 minutes: DDD). Notes, text and translation included. *Gramophone* Award Winner 1990. Ⓕ

This is a wonderfully zany story about a prince whose hypochondriac melancholy is lifted only at the sight of a malevolent witch tumbling over, in revenge for which she casts on him a love-spell for three oranges: in the ensuing complications he encounters an ogre's gigantic cook who goes all gooey at the sight of a pretty ribbon, princesses inside two of the oranges die of oppressive desert heat, and the third is saved only by the intervention of various groups of 'spectators' who argue with each other on the stage. The music's brittle vivacity matches that of the plot, and though there are no set-pieces for the singers and there is practically no thematic development – the famous orchestral March and Scherzo are the only passages that reappear – the effervescent score is most engaging. The performance is full of zest, with lively orchestral playing and a cast that contains several outstanding members and not a single weak one; and the recording is extremely good. Those desirous of so doing can delve into the work's symbolism and identify the objects of its satire – principally Stanislavsky's naturalistic Moscow Arts Theatre: others can simply accept this as a thoroughly enjoyable romp.

War and Peace.
Lajos Miller *bar* Prince Andrei Bolkonsky; **Galina Vishnevskaya** *sop* Natasha Rostova;
Katherine Ciesinski *mez* Sonya; **Maria Paunova** *mez* Maria Akhrosimova;
Dimiter Petkov *bass* Count Ilya Rostov; **Wieslaw Ochman** *ten* Count Pytor Bezukhov;
Stefania Toczyska *mez* Helena Bezukhova; **Nicolai Gedda** *ten* Anatol Kuragin;
Vladimir de Kanel *bass-bar* Dolokhov; **Mira Zakai** *contr* Princess Maria Bolkonskya;
Malcolm Smith *bass* Colonel Vasska Denisov; **Nicola Ghiuselev** *bass* Marshal Mikhail Kutuzov;
Eduard Tumagian *bar* Napoleon Bonaparte;
Radio France Chorus; French National Orchestra / Mstislav Rostropovich.
Erato Libretto 2292-45331-2 (four discs: 247 minutes: DDD). Notes, text and translation included. Recorded 1986. Ⓜ

Over four hours long, 72 characters, 13 scene changes: is it any wonder that Prokofiev's *War and Peace*, adapted from Tolstoy's famously epic novel, has had few performances and even fewer forays into the recording studio? At the front of the booklet Rostropovich recalls how, as Prokofiev lay dying, he reiterated one wish, that Rostropovich should make this opera known to the world. It comes as no surprise, then, to find a deeply committed performance from both soloists (only 45 of them due to some adroit doubling), chorus and orchestra. Prokofiev adapted the novel into seven 'peace' and six 'war' tableaux, thus sustaining drama through contrast throughout its Wagnerian length. With few exceptions the multinational cast sings in good Russian and among them Lajos Miller is particularly affecting as Prince Andrei, pleasingly ardent in his opening moonlit aria. The central female role of Natasha is taken by Galina Vishnevskaya. She sang the role in the 1959 première and inevitably no longer sounds like an innocent 16 year old. Unfortunately, problems are compounded by a hardness in her tone and a lack of attention to detail in some of the quieter sections – particularly in her exchanges with Helena where the asides sound like part of the normal conversation. Stefania Toczyska as the treacherous Helena makes a great impression, as does Katherine Ciesinski as Natasha's confidante, Sonya. Of the men, Nicolai Gedda as Prince Anatol sings with character and great style and Eduard Tumagian is a suitably heroic and steadfast Napoleon. An added attraction of the recording are the sound effects, particularly in the war scenes, convincing but never overly obtrusive. Good translations are provided in three languages, crowning a laudable achievement.

Francesco Provenzale
Italian 1624-1704

Provenzale Cantemus, psallamus. O Jesu mea spes. Audite caeli. Angelicae mentes.
Avitrano Sonate a Quattro, Op. 3 – No. 2 in D major, 'L'Aragona'; No. 10 in C major, 'La Maddaloni'.
Marchitelli Sonata II.
Roberta Invernizzi, Emanuela Galli *sops* Giuseppe de Vittorio *ten*
Cappella de' Turchini / Antonio Florio *vc*
Opus 111 OPS30-211 (62 minutes: DDD). Texts and translations included. Recorded 1998. Ⓕ

Antonio Florio and Cappella de' Turchini's ambitious survey of the finest baroque Neapolitan music turns to the well-nigh accepted father of the so-called Neapolitan School, Francesco Provenzale. Whilst scholars have argued that much of what is deemed 'Neapolitan' is really just 'Italian', this series has proved that such a view demonstrates a limited knowledge of both the sources and the sheer range of musical idioms and 'dialects' which became established in the second half of the seventeenth century. Provenzale's three motets for two sopranos, published in 1689 (*Audite caeli* is for soprano and tenor) are hardly masterpieces but they are still good. The bold challenges to the singer's techniques are often thrilling, but the flavour is less one of operatic transplantation than an indigenous sacred virtuosity which Provenzale jealously guarded; both the extensive *O Jesu mea spes* and *Angelicae mentes* see both Roberta Invernizzi and Emanuela Galli put through their paces, but they both sail through with well-matched timbres and nonchalant Mediterranean breeziness; only occasionally does their instinct for spontaneous moulding lead to questionable intonation, of the sort which cannot be argued away in the name of increased expression. For the most part, the easy, imitative dialogue of Provenzale's motets are revitalized by textually alert and finely projected singing. Of the instrumental interludes, Marchitelli's Sonata II for three violins is a winner.

Giacomo Puccini Italian 1858-1924

Opera Arias: La rondine – Chi il bel sogno di Doretta. La bohème – Sì, mi chiamano Mimì; Donde lieta uscì. Gianni Schicchi – O mio babbino caro. Manon Lescaut – In quelle trine morbide; Sola, perduta, abbandonata. Suor Angelica – Senza mamma, O bimbo. Tosca – Vissi d'arte. Madama Butterfly – Un bel dì vedremo; Che tua madre; Tu, tu, piccolo iddio.
Turandot – Signore, ascolta!; In questa reggia; Tu, che di gel sei cinta.
Julia Varady *sop*
Berlin Radio Symphony Orchestra / Marcello Viotti.
Orfeo C323941A (52 minutes: DDD). Recorded 1993. Ⓕ

A lovely and somewhat surprising record by the most fascinating and patrician lyric soprano of the present age: 'surprising' because, though Varady is associated closely enough with Verdi, the Puccini connection is less readily made, 'lovely' because the voice is still so pure, the style so musical and (above all) the response so intelligent, immediate and full-hearted. She adjusts wonderfully well to the Italian idiom, lightening the vowels, freeing the upper range, allowing more *portamento* than she would probably do in other music, yet employing in its use the finest technical skill and artistic judgement. Her singing of Magda's song in *La rondine* opens the record and introduces a singer who sounds (give or take a little) half her actual age: Varady's début dates back to 1962. In Mimì's narrative she sings with so fine a perception of the character – the hesitancies, the joy in 'mi piaccion quelle cose' – that Schwarzkopf's exquisite recording comes to mind, just as, from time to time, and especially in the *Madama Butterfly* excerpts, the finely concentrated, tragic restraint of Meta Seinemeyer is recalled. It is good to hear, too, how sensitively Varady differentiates between characters, Manon Lescaut having that essential degree of additional sophistication in tone and manner. What runs as a thread through all of these characterizations is a feeling for their dignity. Mimì does not simper. Sister Angelica does not sob. Lauretta has resolution in her pleading. Butterfly, Liù and Tosca are what they should be: women whose pathos lies not in their weakness but in a passionate, single-minded fidelity. That leaves Turandot which is a mistake. That is, she is outside the singer's scope and should remain so: it is not merely a matter of vocal thrust, weight and stamina, but also of voice-character, although the performance of her aria has clear merits (the imperiousness of 'Mai nessun m'avrà' for instance). Welcome would have been printed texts, though it is true the excerpts are all pretty well known. None of that should deter purchase; this is singing to treasure.

Opera Arias: Turandot – Non piangere, Liù!; Nessun dorma!. Gianni Schicchi – Avete torto! Firenze è come un albero fiorito. Il Tabarro – Hai ben ragione; Io voglio la tua bocca ... Folle di gelosia!. La rondine – Parigi! è la citta dei desideri ... Forse, come la rondine; Dimmi che vuoi seguirmi. La fanciulla del West – Una parola sola! ... Or son sei mesi; Risparmiate lo scherno ... Ch'ella mi creda libero. Madama Butterfly – Dipende dal grado di cottura ... Amore o grillo; Addio, fiorito asil. Tosca – Recondita armonia; E lucevan le stelle. La bohème – Che gelida manina. Manon Lescaut – Tra voi, belle; Donna non vidi mai; Ah! Manon, mi tradisce; Ah! non v'avvicinate!; Manon ... senti, amor mio ... Vedi, son io che piango. Edgar – Orgia, chimera dall'occhio vitreo. Le villi – Ecco la casa ... Torna ai felici dì.
José Cura *ten*
Philharmonia Orchestra / Plácido Domingo.
Erato 0630-18838-2 (71 minutes: DDD). Texts and translations included. Recorded 1997. Ⓕ

For those of us who can feast on a good tenor voice as if there were no tomorrow, this is (to put it crudely) the goods. First, however, a peculiarity of this programme is that it goes backwards. It starts with *Turandot* and recedes along a strict chronological line to *Le villi*. That of itself is an attractive idea, but it means that the terminus is a long and somewhat inconclusive excerpt, while the starting-point is 'Nessun dorma!'. We all know what that means these days, and it looks suspiciously like making a bid for the market if not for the kingdom. A dark, rather throaty, big and uncharming voice reiterates the famous command. As it takes the high As we realize that this is special, rising easily and thrillingly out of the baritonal middle register; Cura holds his high B ('vincerò') for the maximum length compatible with holding on to the succeeding A for even longer. But he is a man with surprises in store. 'Non piangere, Liù!' begins quietly and is thoughtfully phrased. Similarly he shows his unpredictability in the *Tosca* arias: 'Recondita armonia' is stolid, almost routine, but then 'E lucevan le stelle' becomes the real expression of a man facing the prospect of imminent execution, and writing a poem. Throughout, Cura displays a thrilling voice with an individual timbre. His 'face' wears too much of a scowl and he does not give the impression of thinking about the person he is nominally addressing, but this is a solo recital and perhaps it would be different in a complete opera. He is accompanied here with uncommon sympathy by a conductor who has a good deal more experience of singing than has the singer himself.

La bohème.
Victoria de los Angeles *sop* Mimì; **Jussi Björling** *ten* Rodolfo; **Lucine Amara** *sop* Musetta;
Robert Merrill *bar* Marcello; **John Reardon** *bar* Schaunard; **Giorgio Tozzi** *bass* Colline;
Fernando Corena *bass* Benoit, Alcindoro; **William Nahr** *ten* Parpignol;
Thomas Powell *bar* Customs Official; **George del Monte** *bar* Sergeant;
Columbus Boychoir; RCA Victor Chorus and Orchestra / Sir Thomas Beecham.
EMI mono CDS5 56236-2 (two discs: 108 minutes: ADD). Notes, text and translation included.
Recorded 1956. Ⓕ H RR

The disadvantages of this famous Beecham *Bohème* are obvious. It is a mono recording and is restricted in dynamic range. The sheer sense of space that is needed if the complex crowd scene of Act 2 is to emerge with the maximum impact is inevitably lacking; the climaxes here and elsewhere are somewhat constricted; no less important, it is sometimes harder to focus on the subtleties of Puccini's orchestration. It was also made in a great hurry, and this shows in a number of patches of slightly insecure ensemble, even a couple of wrong entries. But there is no other important respect in which it does not stand at least half a head (often head and shoulders) above its more recent rivals, admirable in many respects though many of them are. Nobody has ever been so predestinately right for the role of Mimì than Victoria de los Angeles: right both in vocal quality and in sheer involvement with every word and every musical phrase that Mimì utters. Beyond a certain point (usually a certain dynamic level) most sopranos stop being Mimì and simply produce the same sound that they would if they were singing Aida or Tosca. De los Angeles rarely does this; even under pressure (and Beecham's unhurried tempos do put her under pressure at times, as does the fact that a full-throated Italianate high C was never her strongest suit), the very difficulties themselves are used as an expressive and interpretative resource. Hers is the most moving and involving Mimì ever recorded. And Björling's is unquestionably the most musical Rodolfo. He has the reputation of having been a bit of a dry stick, dramatically (on stage he looked like the other Bohemians' elderly, portly uncle), but on record he is the one exponent of the role to be credible both as a lover and as a poet. His voice is fine silver rather than brass, it can caress as well as weep, and his love for Mimì is more often confided than it is bellowed for all Paris to hear.

This, indeed, is one of the most conspicuous differences between Beecham's account and most others: its simple belief that when Puccini wrote *pp* he meant it. Beecham (whose spell over his entire cast – in which there is no weak link – extends as far as teaching his Schaunard, John Reardon, an irresistibly funny, cut-glass English accent for the parrot-fancying milord) makes one realize what an intimate opera this is, how much of it is quiet, how many of its exchanges are *sotto voce*, and he thus enables his singers to use the full range of their voices and to employ subtleties of colour, phrasing and diction that are simply not available to a voice at full stretch (and in the process he largely cancels out the disadvantage of his recording's restricted dynamic range). It is the same with his handling of the orchestra: one would expect Beecham to seem understated, but again and again one turns back to his reading and discovers nothing missing – he has achieved as much or more with less. This is as complete a distillation of Puccini's drama as you are likely to hear.

La bohème.
Mirella Freni *sop* Mimì; **Luciano Pavarotti** *ten* Rodolfo; **Elizabeth Harwood** *sop* Musetta;
Rolando Panerai *bar* Marcello; **Gianni Maffeo** *bar* Schaunard; **Nicolai Ghiaurov** *bass* Colline;
Michel Sénéchal *bass* Benoit, Alcindoro; **Gernot Pietsch** *ten* Parpignol;
Schoenberg Boys' Choir; Berlin German Opera Chorus;
Berlin Philharmonic Orchestra / Herbert von Karajan.
Decca 421 049-2DH2 (two discs: 110 minutes: ADD). Notes, text and translation included.
Recorded 1972. Ⓕ

Pavarotti's Rodolfo is perhaps the best thing he has ever done: not only the finest recorded account of the role since Björling's on the Beecham set, but adding the honeyed Italianate warmth that even Björling lacked. He cannot quite match Björling's poetic refinement, no doubt, and he is less willing to sing really quietly, but Pavarotti's honest sincerity counts for a great deal: his pride as he declares his vocation as a poet, the desperate feigning of his 'Mimì è una civetta' are points that most tenors miss or treat as mere opportunities for a big sing. His latter-day image may sometimes tend to hide it, but this recording is a reminder that Pavarotti is an artist of intelligence and delicacy as well as splendour of voice. His Mimì, Freni, sings most beautifully and sensitively. Panerai is a strong and vividly acted Marcello. Harwood is an interesting Musetta: her tiny narration, in Act 4, of her meeting with the stricken Mimì is a gripping moment, and there is no shadow of doubt that her waltz-song in Act 2 is a passionate (and irresistible) avowal to Marcello. Karajan is a great Puccini conductor who can linger over the beauties of the orchestration without ever losing his grip on the drama or relaxing his support of the singers. There are not many operas of which a better case can be made for having more than one account in one's collection. For a modern *La bohème* to supplement the Beecham this Karajan set must go to the top of the list.

La bohème (sung in English).
Cynthia Haymon *sop* Mimì; **Dennis O'Neill** *ten* Rodolfo; **Marie McLaughlin** *sop* Musetta;
Alan Opie *bar* Marcello; **William Dazeley** *bar* Schaunard; **Alastair Miles** *bass* Colline;
Andrew Shore *bar* Benoit, Alcindoro; **Mark Milhofer** *ten* Parpignol;
Simon Preece *bar* Customs Official; **Paul Parfitt** *bass-bar* Sergeant;
Peter Kay Children's Choir; Geoffrey Mitchell Choir; Philharmonia Orchestra / David Parry.
Chandos Opera in English CHAN3008 (two discs: 111 minutes: DDD). Notes and text included.
Recorded 1997. Ⓕ Ⓔ

The text (Grist and Pinkerton amended by David Parry) is a very acceptable rendering of a libretto which was, after all, first known in England … in English. However well sung, that first performance, at Manchester in 1897, is unlikely to have offered orchestral playing as fine as the Philharmonia's in this recording, and David Parry's well-considered control of tempo is another strong factor at work in making this a special recording of the opera irrespective of language. The singers have that first requisite of a good *Bohème* cast: they work as a team. Cynthia Haymon is a gentle Mimì, perfectly lovely in the middle register of her voice, just a little worn on top. Dennis O'Neill provides a rare pleasure in this music, singing softly at the right moments (in the Quartet, for example); he also produces such a very good top C in his aria that he has no need to give us another at the end of the Act instead of obliging with the composer's harmonies. Marie McLaughlin's Musetta is not quite the sparkler one had in mind, but the fellow Bohemians are capital, in voice as in spirits. The ensemble in Act 2 is first-rate, the contribution of the Peter Kay Children's Choir even better than that. The recording is superb.

La Fanciulla del West.
Carol Neblett *sop* Minnie; **Plácido Domingo** *ten* Dick Johnson; **Sherrill Milnes** *bar* Jack Rance;
Francis Egerton *ten* Nick; **Robert Lloyd** *bass* Ashby; **Gwynne Howell** *bass* Jake Wallace;
Paul Hudson *bass* Billy Jackrabbit; **Anne Wilkens** *sop* Wowkle;
Chorus and Orchestra of the Royal Opera House, Covent Garden / Zubin Mehta.
DG 419 640-2GH2 (two discs: 130 minutes: ADD). Notes, text and translation included.
Recorded 1977. *Gramophone* Award Winner 1978. Ⓕ

This opera depicts the triangular relationship between Minnie, the saloon owner and 'mother' to the entire town of gold miners, Jack Rance, the sheriff and Dick Johnson (alias Ramerrez), a bandit leader. The music is highly developed in Puccini's seamless lyrical style, the arias for the main characters emerge from the texture and return to it effortlessly. The vocal colours are strongly polarized with the cast being all male except for one travesti role and Minnie herself. The score bristles with robust melody as well as delicate scoring, betraying a masterly hand at work. Carol Neblett is a strong Minnie, vocally distinctive and well characterized, whilst Plácido Domingo and Sherrill Milnes make a good pair of suitors for the spunky little lady. Zubin Mehta conducts with real sympathy for the idiom and the orchestra responds well.

Madama Butterfly.
Renata Scotto *sop* Madama Butterfly; **Carlo Bergonzi** *ten* Pinkerton;
Rolando Panerai *bar* Sharpless; **Anna di Stasio** *mez* Suzuki; **Piero De Palma** *ten* Goro;
Giuseppe Morresi *ten* Prince Yamadori; **Silvana Padoan** *mez* Kate Pinkerton;
Paolo Montarsolo *bass* The Bonze; **Mario Rinaudo** *bass* Commissioner;
Rome Opera House Chorus and Orchestra / Sir John Barbirolli.
HMV Classics HMVD5 72886-2 (two discs: 142 minutes: ADD). Notes, text and translation included. Recorded 1966. Ⓑ ⓇⓇ

This is Barbirolli's *Butterfly*; despite Scotto's expressiveness and Bergonzi's elegance it is the conductor's contribution that gives this set its durability and its hold on the affections. The Rome Opera Orchestra is not the equal of the Vienna Philharmonic for Karajan. But it is an Italian orchestra and it evidently recognized a compatriot and a seasoned fellow Puccinian in the London-born Giovanni Battista Barbirolli: he played in rehearsals at Covent Garden directed by the composer and had made his conducting début there in this opera. The rapport between conductor and orchestra and their mutual affection for Puccini are evident throughout, and they make this the most Italianate of all readings. It is hugely enjoyable, not just in the big emotional outpourings (like the Act 2 interlude, where Barbirolli's passionate gasps and groans spur the orchestra to great eloquence) but in many tiny moments where you can almost see the conductor and his players lovingly and absorbedly concentrating on subtleties of phrasing and texture. There is a lot of good singing, too. Scotto's voice will not always take the pressure she puts on it, but her portrayal is a touching and finely detailed one. The ever stylish Bergonzi sings with immaculate phrasing and perfect taste, Panerai is an outstanding Sharpless (beautifully sung, the embodiment of anxious, pitying concern) and di Stasio's Suzuki is attractively light-voiced and young-sounding. The recording, however, is a bit narrow in perspective, rather close (really quiet singing and playing rarely register as such) and some of the voices are edged or slightly tarnished in loud passages. Barbirolli's set is perhaps for those who find the meticulously refined detail of Karajan studied (also ravishing and stunningly recorded); those, in short, for whom Latin warmth and impulsive open-heartedness are indispensable in this opera. They will find those qualities here, with singing to match, and will not mind the occasional patch of stridency.

Madama Butterfly.
Mirella Freni *sop* Madama Butterfly; **Luciano Pavarotti** *ten* Pinkerton;
Robert Kerns *bar* Sharpless; **Christa Ludwig** *mez* Suzuki; **Michel Sénéchal** *ten* Goro;
Giorgio Stendoro *bar* Prince Yamadori; **Elke Schary** *mez* Kate Pinkerton;
Marius Rintzler *bass* The Bonze; **Hans Helm** *bass* Commissioner;
Vienna State Opera Chorus; Vienna Philharmonic Orchestra / Herbert von Karajan.
Decca 417 577-2DH3 (three discs: 145 minutes: ADD). Notes, text and translation included.
Recorded 1974.   Ⓕ

In every way except one the transfer of Karajan's radiant Vienna recording for Decca could hardly provide a firmer recommendation. The reservation is one of price – this Karajan is on three discs, not two, at full price. However it does allow each act to be self-contained on a single disc, and for such a performance as this no extravagance is too much. Movingly dramatic as Renata Scotto is on the Barbirolli set, Mirella Freni is even more compelling. The voice is fresher, firmer and more girlish, with more light and shade at such points as 'Un bel dì', and there is an element of vulnerability that intensifies the communication. In that, one imagines Karajan played a big part, just as he must have done in presenting Luciano Pavarotti – not quite the super-star he is today but already with a will of his own in the recording studio – as a Pinkerton of exceptional subtlety, not just a roistering cad but in his way an endearing figure in the First Act. Significantly CD brings out the delicacy of the vocal balances in Act 1 with the voices deliberately distanced for much of the time, making such passages as 'Vienna la sera' and 'Bimba dagli occhi' the more magical in their delicacy. Karajan, both in that duet and later in the Flower duet of Act 2, draws ravishing playing from the Vienna Philharmonic strings, getting them to imitate the *portamento* of the singers in what is also an *echt-Viennes* manner, ravishing to the ear. Christa Ludwig is by far the richest and most compelling of Suzukis.

Madama Butterfly.
Miriam Gauci *sop* Madama Butterfly; **Yordi Ramiro** *ten* Pinkerton; **Georg Tichy** *bar* Sharpless;
Nelly Boschkowá *mez* Suzuki; **Josef Abel** *ten* Goro; **Robert Szücs** *bar* Prince Yamadori;
Alzbeta Michalková *mez* Kate Pinkerton; **Jozef Spaček** *bass* The Bonze;
Vladimir Kubovčik *bass* Commissioner, Registrar;
Slovak Philharmonic Chorus; Bratislava Radio Symphony Orchestra / Alexander Rahbari.
Naxos 8 660015/6 (two discs: 141 minutes: DDD). Notes and text included. Recorded 1991.   Ⓢ

Though this would never be a first-choice *Butterfly*, it might serve quite happily as a *Butterfly* first-choice. That is, coming upon the opera fresh, never having heard it before, one could well find it a good introduction. It is consistently musical, avoids cheapness or exaggerated sentiment, and, while presenting worthily the enchanting and infinitely poignant score, it leaves plenty to be discovered with a widening knowledge of other and greater performances. An attractive feature is the youthfulness of the Butterfly and Pinkerton. The Pinkerton, a Mexican lyric tenor, Yordi Ramiro, gives as likeable, sincere a version of the character as any. And this is not a falsification of the part, at the very heart of which is the painful truth that likeable people may do very unlikeable things. It is a good voice: limited, but well defined and with a youthful freshness in its tone. The Butterfly is also young-sounding: Miriam Gauci, born in Malta. She sings uncompromisingly as a light lyric soprano, with an especially lovely quality in the upper range. The lightness itself brings limitations in this colossal role, and they are compounded by the immaturity of her acting-portrayal: she does many of 'the right things' but it is rare to find in her the flash of expressiveness that illuminates a character from within. A newcomer to the opera is not likely to be troubled by this, but will on the contrary be delighted by the quality of the voice and touched by the general appeal of the character. Alexander Rahbari conducts a performance that captures both the opera's charm and seriousness, not, however, its intensity.

Manon Lescaut.
Mirella Freni *sop* Manon Lescaut; **Luciano Pavarotti** *ten* Des Grieux; **Dwayne Croft** *bar* Lescaut;
Giuseppe Taddei *bar* Geronte; **Ramon Vargas** *ten* Edmondo; **Cecilia Bartoli** *mez* Singer;
Federico Davia *bass* Innkeeper, Captain; **Anthony Laciura** *ten* Dancing Master;
Paul Groves *ten* Lamplighter; **James Courtney** *bass* Sergeant;
Chorus and Orchestra of the Metropolitan Opera / James Levine.
Decca 440 200-2DHO2 (two discs: 120 minutes: DDD). Notes, text and translation included.
Recorded 1992. ⒻⓇⓇ

With Luciano Pavarotti as a powerful Des Grieux, James Levine conducts a comparably big-boned performance of *Manon Lescaut*, bringing out the red-blooded drama of Puccini's first big success, while not ignoring its warmth and tender poetry in exceptionally full, vivid sound with the voices well in front of the orchestra. In the title-role Freni's performance culminates in an account of the big Act 4 aria, more involving and passionate than any of the others on rival versions, with the voice showing no signs of wear, and with her sudden change of face at the words 'terra di pace' ('a land of peace') bringing a magical lightening of tone. That aria makes a thrilling climax, when too often this act can seem a letdown. In this as in so much else, Levine conveys the tensions and atmosphere of a stage performance in a way that owes much to his experience at the Metropolitan. More completely than other versions, it avoids the feeling of a studio performance. Reactions to Pavarotti as Des Grieux will differ widely. The closeness of balance means that in volume his singing rarely drops below *mezzo forte*, but there is little harm in having so passionate a portrait of Des Grieux as Pavarotti's. Needless to say, the hero's big emotional climaxes in each of the first three acts come over at full force. The rest of the cast is strong too, with Dwayne Croft a magnificent Lescaut who, as well as singing with rich, firm tone, brings out the character's wry humour. Many collectors will count this a clear first choice among current versions. For the sheer power of Puccinian drama, vividly conveyed, it will be hard to beat.

Manon Lescaut.
Maria Callas *sop* Manon Lescaut; **Giuseppe di Stefano** *ten* Des Grieux;
Giulio Fioravanti *bar* Lescaut; **Franco Calabrese** *bass* Geronte; **Dino Formichini** *ten* Edmondo;
Fiorenza Cossotto *mez* Singer; **Carlo Forti** *bass* Innkeeper; **Vito Tatone** *ten* Dancing master;
Giuseppe Morresi *bass* Sergeant; **Franco Ricciardi** *ten* Lamplighter;
Franco Ventrigilia *bass* Captain;
Chorus and Orchestra of La Scala, Milan / Tullio Serafin.
EMI CDS5 56301-2 (two discs: 120 minutes: ADD). Notes, text and translation included.
Recorded 1957. ⒻⒽ

This performance is unique, with Act 4 for once a culmination in Callas's supreme account of the death scene. She may present a rather formidable portrait of a young girl in Act 1, but here the final act with its long duet and the big aria, 'Sola, perduta, abbandonata', is far more than an epilogue to the rest, rather a culmination, with Callas at her very peak. Di Stefano, too, is on superb form and Serafin's pacing of the score is masterly. Di Stefano wipes the floor with most of his rivals past and present: in Act 4 he has a concerned tenderness for Manon that others can only sketch, his debonair charm in 'Tra voi belle' is incomparable and (rarest of virtues among tenors) he never sings past the limits of his voice. Fioravanti as Lescaut and Calabrese as Geronte sing well if not very characterfully. However, digital CD remastering in this instance loses out. A break has to be made in Act 2 – in a fairly innocuous place before the duet 'Tu, tu, amore tu'. The first two acts make up a total timing only a few seconds over the 75-minute limit, but evidently it was enough to prevent them going on to a single CD. That said, the CD brings the same advantages in refining the original boxy sound without glamorizing it in false stereo, plus the usual advantages of absence of background and ease of finding places. For an account of *Manon Lescaut* which comes fully to terms with the opera's huge contrasts of colour and mood you will also have to have a modern recording, for with all its improvements the sound here necessarily remains very dry.

La rondine. Le Villi – Prelude; L'Abbandono; La Tregenda;
Ecco la casa … Torna ai felice di. Morire!.
Angela Gheorghiu *sop* Magda; **Roberto Alagna** *ten* Ruggero; **Inva Mula-Tchako** *sop* Lisetta;
William Matteuzzi *ten* Prunier; **Alberto Rinaldi** *bar* Rambaldo; **Patricia Biccire** *sop* Yvette;

Puccini Opera

Patrizia Ciofi *sop* Bianca; **Monica Bacelli** *mez* Suzy; **Riccardo Simonetti** *bar* Périchaud;
Toby Spence *ten* Gobin; **Enrico Fissore** *bar* Crébillon;
London Voices; London Symphony Orchestra / Antonio Pappano *pf*
EMI CDS5 56338-2 (two discs: 131 minutes: DDD). Texts and translations included.
Recorded 1996. *Gramophone* Award Winner 1997.   Ⓕ🅔

It could not be more welcome when a recording transforms a work, as this one does, setting it on a new plane. *La rondine* ('The Swallow'), Puccini's ill-timed attempt to emulate Lehár in the world of operetta, completed during the First World War, has long been counted his most serious failure, 'a bird with half-broken wings' as Mosco Carner called it. Puccini's cunning has never been in doubt either, for he and his librettists cleverly interweave elements not just of *La traviata* but of *The Merry Widow* and *Die Fledermaus*, not to mention earlier Puccini operas. His melodic style may for the most part be simpler than before, but one striking theme follows another with a profusion that any other composer might envy. What Pappano reveals far more than before is the subtlety with which Puccini interweaves his themes and motifs, with conversational passages made spontaneous-sounding in their flexibility. Above all, Pappano consistently brings out the poetry, drawing on emotions far deeper than are suggested by this operetta-like subject, thanks also to Gheorghiu's superb performance, translating her mastery as Violetta to this comparable character. Magda's first big solo, 'Che il bel sogno di Doretta' (neatly forecast by the poet, Prunier, in the preceding section) finds Gheorghiu at her most ravishing, tenderly expressive in her soaring phrases, opening out only at the final climax. From first to last, often with a throb in the voice, her vocal acting convinces you that Magda's are genuine, deep emotions, painful at the end, intensified by the ravishing beauty of her voice.

As Ruggero, the hero, Alagna has a far less complex role, winningly characterizing the ardent young student. What will specially delight Puccinians in this set is that he is given an entrance aria about Paris, 'Parigi e un citta', which transforms his otherwise minimal contribution to Act 1. The partnership of Gheorghiu and Alagna highlights the way that Puccini in the melodic lines for each of his central characters makes Ruggero's more forthright, Magda's more complex. Among much else, the role of the poet, Prunier, is transformed thanks to the clear-toned William Matteuzzi in what is normally a *comprimario* role. Not only is his relationship with Magda beautifully drawn, his improbable affair with the skittish maid, Lisetta, is made totally convincing too, mirroring Magda's affair. For the fill-ups, the excerpts from *Le Villi*, warm and dramatic, make one wish that Pappano could go on to record that first of Puccini's operas, with Alagna giving a ringing account of Roberto's aria, as he does of the song, *Morire!* – with Pappano at the piano. Originally an album-piece written for a wartime charity, Puccini used it, transposed up a semitone, with different words, as the entrance aria for Ruggero. Altogether a set to treasure for bringing out the full genius of a tenderly moving work too long discounted.

Il trittico.

Il tabarro.
Carlo Guelfi *bar* Michele; **Maria Guleghina** *sop* Giorgetta; **Neil Shicoff** *ten* Luigi;
Riccardo Cassinelli *ten* Tinca; **Enrico Fissore** *bass* Talpa; **Elena Zilio** *mez* Frugola;
Barry Banks *ten* Ballad-seller; **Angela Gheorghiu** *sop* Lover; **Roberto Alagna** *ten* Lover;
London Voices; London Symphony Orchestra / Antonio Pappano.

Suor Angelica.
Cristina Gallardo-Domâs *sop* Suor Angelica; **Bernadette Manca di Nissa** *contr* Princess;
Felicity Palmer *mez* Abbess; **Elena Zilio** *mez* Monitoress;
Sara Fulgoni *mez* Mistress of the Novices; **Dorothea Röschmann** *sop* Sister Genovieffa;
Judith Rees *sop* Sister Osmina; **Rachele Stanisci** *sop* Sister Dolcina;
Francesca Pedaci *sop* Nursing Sister; **Anna Maria Panzarella** *sop* First Almoner Sister;
First Lay Sister; **Susan Mackenzie-Park** *sop* Second Almoner Sister;
Deborah Miles-Johnson *contr* Second Lay Sister; **Rosalind Waters** *sop* Novice;
London Voices; Tiffin Boys' School Choir; Philharmonia Orchestra / Antonio Pappano.

Gianni Schicchi.
José van Dam *bass-bar* Gianni Schicchi; **Angela Gheorghiu** *sop* Lauretta;
Roberto Alagna *ten* Rinuccio; **Felicity Palmer** *mez* Zita; **Paolo Barbacini** *ten* Gherardo;
Patrizia Ciofi *sop* Nella; **James Savage-Hanford** *treb* Gherardino;
Carlos Chausson *bass* Betto di Signa; **Luigi Roni** *bass* Simone; **Roberto Scaltriti** *bar* Marco;
Elena Zilio *mez* La Ciesca; **Enrico Fissore** *bass* Spinelloccio; **Simon Preece** *bar* Pinellino;
Noel Mann *bass* Guccio;
London Symphony Orchestra / Antonio Pappano.
EMI CDS5 56587-2 (three discs: 162 minutes: DDD). Notes, texts and translations included.
Recorded 1997.   Ⓕ🅔 🆁🆁

734

No previous recordings bring quite such warmth or beauty or so powerful a drawing of the contrasts between each of the three one-acters in Puccini's triptych as these. It is Pappano above all, with his gift for pacing Puccini subtly, who draws the set together. In each opera he heightens emotions fearlessly to produce unerringly at key moments the authentic gulp-in-throat, whether for the cuckolded bargemaster, Michele, for Sister Angelica in her agonized suicide and heavenly absolution, or for the resolution of young love at the end of *Gianni Schicchi*. It will no doubt disappoint some that the starry couple of Angela Gheorghiu and Roberto Alagna do not take centre-stage, but quite apart from their radiant singing as Lauretta and Rinuccio in *Gianni Schicchi* – not least in that happy ending, most tenderly done – they make a tiny cameo appearance in *Il tabarro* as the off-stage departing lovers, a heady 45 seconds. It is the sort of luxury touch that Walter Legge would have relished. No doubt Gheorghiu would have been just as persuasive as Giorgetta in *Il tabarro* and as Sister Angelica, but having different sopranos in each opera sharpens the contrasts between them. Maria Guleghina makes a warm, vibrant Giorgetta, and the touch of acid at the top of the voice adds character, pointing to the frustration of the bargemaster's wife.

Even more remarkable is the singing of the young Chilean soprano, Cristina Gallardo-Domâs as Sister Angelica. Hers is a younger, more vulnerable Angelica than usual. Her vocal subtlety and commanding technique go with a fully mature portrayal of the nun's agony, her defiance of the implacable Princess as well as her grief over her dead son. As with Gheorghiu, the dynamic shading brings *pianissimos* of breathtaking delicacy. The Princess is powerfully sung by Bernadette Manca di Nissa, her tone firm and even throughout. Felicity Palmer, with her tangy mezzo tone, is well contrasted as the Abbess, and she is just as characterful as the crabby Zita in *Gianni Schicchi*. The casting in *Suor Angelica* is as near flawless as could be, with Elena Zilio and Dorothea Röschmann outstanding in smaller roles. Zilio is the only singer who appears in all three operas, just as effective as Frugola in *Il tabarro*, though there her full, clear voice is not always distinguishable from Guleghina as Giorgetta. Among the men Carlo Guelfi makes a superb Michele, incisive, dark and virile. He brings out not just the anger but the poignancy of the bargemaster's emotions, as in the duet with Giorgetta, when they lament what might have been. Neil Shicoff makes a fine Luigi, the nerviness in his tenor tone aptly bringing out a hysterical quality in the character. The male *comprimarios* are vocally more variable, if always characterful, as they are too in *Gianni Schicchi*.

As Schicchi himself José van Dam is in fine voice. This, after all, is a role with little sustained lyricism, and there is none of the dryness noted in one or two of the veteran singer's more recent recordings. The clean focus of van Dam's voice perfectly conveys the sardonic side of Schicchi, and the top Gs he has to negotiate are wonderfully strong and steady. Maybe the full voice he uses for the name 'Gianni Schicchi', when in impersonation of old Buoso he is dictating the new will, makes too obvious a contrast with the quavering old man imitation, but it is what Puccini asked for. Also worthy of praise is the comfortingly sumptuous and atmospheric sound, very wide in its dynamic range. Off-stage effects are magical, and always thanks to Pappano and fine playing from both the LSO and Philharmonia, the beauty and originality of the carefully textured instrumentation can be appreciated with new vividness. Thanks to Pappano and his well-chosen team, this is a set to renew one's appreciation of operas that represent Puccini still at his peak. He may have had doubts over the length of his triptych, but on disc in performances such as these they are utterly magnetic.

Il tabarro[a].
Tito Gobbi *bar* Michele; **Margaret Mas** *sop* Giorgetta; **Giacinto Prandelli** *ten* Luigi;
Piero De Palma *ten* Tinca; **Plinio Clabassi** *bass* Talpa; **Miriam Pirazzini** *mez* Frugola.

Suor Angelica[b].
Victoria de los Angeles *sop* Suor Angelica; **Fedora Barbieri** *mez* Princess;
Mina Doro *mez* Abbess, Mistress of the Novices; **Corinna Vozza** *mez* Monitoress;
Lidia Marimpietri *sop* Sister Genovieffa, First Almoner Sister; **Santa Chissari** *sop* Sister Osmina,
Second Almoner Sister, Novice; **Anna Marcangeli** *sop* Sister Dolcina;
Teresa Cantarini *mez* Nursing Sister; **Silvia Bertona** *sop* First Lay Sister;
Maria Huder *mez* Second Lay Sister.

Gianni Schicchi[c].
Tito Gobbi *bar* Gianni Schicchi; **Victoria de los Angeles** *sop* Lauretta;
Carlo del Monte *ten* Rinuccio; **Anna Maria Canali** *mez* Zita; **Adelio Zagonara** *ten* Gherardo;
Lidia Marimpietri *sop* Nella; **Claudio Cornoldi** *ten* Gherardino; **Saturno Meletti** *bass*
Betto di Signa; **Paolo Montarsolo** *bass* Simone; **Fernando Valentini** *bar* Marco;
Giuliana Raymondi *sop* La Ciesca;
Rome Opera Chorus;
Rome Opera Orchestra / [a]Vincenzo Bellezza, [b]Tullio Serafin, [c]Gabriele Santini.
EMI mono/[c]stereo CMS7 64165-2 (three discs: 161 minutes: ADD). Texts and
translations included. Recorded [a]1955, [b]1957, [c]1958. Ⓜ Ⓗ

Unless you insist on the most up-to-date recorded sound, or on buying the individual operas of Puccini's trilogy separately, this is the classic *Trittico*. Gobbi's blackly authoritative but pitiful Michele in *Il tabarro* and his genially authoritative Schicchi (the two outer panels of the triptych *do* match, in an odd sort of way) have seldom been equalled, let alone surpassed. De los Angeles's Angelica is more purely and movingly sung than any other on record, and her Lauretta in *Gianni Schicchi* is enchanting. Could it be said, even so, that *Il tabarro* is the weak link in this trilogy? It is a three-hander, surely, and neither the soprano nor the tenor are quite in Gobbi's league. Mas is a bit plummy and mezzoish, true, but the slight implication this gives that Giorgetta's liaison with the young stevedore Luigi is her last chance at escape from a hateful life and a marriage that has soured adds an extra twinge of pain to a plot in which all three principals are victims. And in this context Prandelli's slightly strenuous rawness of tone characterizes Luigi rather well. In *Gianni Schicchi*, Carlo del Monte as Rinuccio also looks like under-casting but in fact he's one of the few tenors who've recorded the part who sounds convincingly young, and his ardent praise of Florence and the 'new men' who are reinvigorating the city is proudly sung. Here, too, Gobbi is surrounded by a constellation of pungent character actors, and de los Angeles in *Suor Angelica* is teamed with a charmingly girlish, impulsive Genovieffa and with Fedora Barbieri's rigidly implacable Princess (is there another parallel here, with the stiff-necked Zita, 'La Vecchia', in *Gianni Schicchi*?). With generally very stylish conducting throughout (only Belezza in *Il tabarro* is a touch staid, and he omits nearly all of Puccini's off-stage sound effects) only the rather elderly recordings might be seen as a drawback. EMI boldly labels the whole set 'stereo', but both *Il tabarro* and *Suor Angelica* sound like minimally 'processed' mono: a touch congested in fuller pasages, a hint of fizzy brightness here and there but nothing that's not abundantly worth putting up with for such performances as these.

Tosca.
Montserrat Caballé *sop* Tosca; **José Carreras** *ten* Cavaradossi; **Ingvar Wixell** *bar* Scarpia;
Samuel Ramey *bass* Angelotti; **Piero De Palma** *ten* Spoletta;
Domenico Trimarchi *bar* Sacristan; **William Elvin** *bar* Sciarrone, Gaoler;
Ann Murray *mez* Shepherd Boy;
Chorus and Orchestra of the Royal Opera House, Covent Garden / Sir Colin Davis.
Philips Duo 438 359-2PM2 (two discs: 118 minutes: ADD). Recorded 1976. Ⓜ **RR**

Caballé's Tosca is one of the most ravishingly sung on record, with scarcely a less than beautiful note from one end of the role to the other, save where an occasional phrase lies a touch low for her. She doesn't quite have the 'prima donna' (in quotes, mind) temperament for the part (the coquettish malice of 'but make her eyes black!', as Tosca forgives Cavaradossi for using a blonde stranger as model for his altarpiece of the Magdalen, is not in Caballé's armoury; either that or she knows that her voice would sound arch attempting it), but her portrayal is much more than a display of lovely sounds. She is precise with words, takes minute care over phrasing, and although some may not care for her characteristic scoops at the outset of 'Vissi d'arte', she knows to a split second where dead-centre precise pitching becomes crucial. Carreras's Cavaradossi is one of his best recorded performances: the voice untarnished, the line ample, and if he's tempted at times to over-sing (he quite drowns the Sacristan's interjections in 'Recondita armonia') one forgives the fault for the sake of his poetic ardour (a very good 'E lucevan le stelle'). Wixell is the fly in the ointment: a capable actor and an intelligent artist, but his gritty timbre lacks centre and thus the necessary dangerous suavity. Davis's direction is considerably flexible but dramatic and finely detailed; the secondary singers (Murray a convincingly boy-like Shepherd, Trimarchi an uncaricatured Sacristan, Ramey an aristocratic Angelotti) are all very good indeed. The recording, despite some rather unconvincing sound effects, still sounds very well, with space around the voices and a natural balance between them and the orchestra. It's pity that Philips, in its otherwise praiseworthy decision to pack two CDs into a jewel-case no thicker than those normally holding just one, should have saved space by omitting the libretto.

Tosca.
Leontyne Price *sop* Tosca; **Giuseppe di Stefano** *ten* Cavaradossi;
Giuseppe Taddei *bar* Scarpia; **Carlo Cava** *bass* Angelotti; **Piero De Palma** *ten* Spoletta;
Fernando Corena *bass* Sacristan; **Leonardo Monreale** *bass* Sciarrone;
Alfredo Mariotti *bass* Gaoler; **Herbert Weiss** *treb* Shepherd Boy;
Vienna State Opera Chorus; Vienna Philharmonic Orchestra / Herbert von Karajan.
Decca 452 620-2DF2 (two discs: 114 minutes: ADD). Text and translation included.
Recorded 1962. Ⓑ

Karajan's classic version of *Tosca* was originally issued on the RCA label, but produced by John Culshaw of Decca at a vintage period. The first surprise is to find the sound satisfying in almost every way, with a firm sense of presence and with each voice and each section of the orchestra cleanly focused within the stereo spectrum. That is a spectacular tribute to Decca engineering of the time, and to the detailed production of Culshaw. What is less surprising is the superiority of this version as an interpretation. He was always a master Puccinian, and this set was a prime example of that mastery. A typical instance comes at the end of Act 1, where Scarpia's *Te Deum* is taken daringly slowly, even more so than in Berlin, and conveys a quiver of menace that no other version begins to match. An extra nicety is the way that in the instrumental introduction to Cavaradossi's first aria, 'Recondita armonia', he treats it as the musical equivalent of a painter mixing his colours, the very point Puccini no doubt had in mind. Karajan, though individual, and regularly challenging his singers (as he does with Taddei in the slow speed for the *Te Deum*) is most solicitous in following the voices. It is fascinating to note what expressive freedom he allows his tenor, di Stefano, and he makes Leontyne Price relax, giving a superb assumption of the role, big and rich of tone, intense of expression; the voice is the more beautiful for not being recorded too closely.

Tosca.
Maria Callas *sop* Tosca; **Giuseppe di Stefano** *ten* Cavaradossi; **Tito Gobbi** *bar* Scarpia;
Franco Calabrese *bass* Angelotti; **Angelo Mercuriali** *ten* Spoletta;
Melchiorre Luise *bass* Sacristan; **Dario Caselli** *bass* Sciarrone, Gaoler;
Alvaro Cordova *treb* Shepherd Boy;
Chorus and Orchestra of La Scala, Milan / Victor de Sabata.
EMI mono CDS5 56304-2 (two discs: 108 minutes: ADD). Notes, text and translation included.
Recorded 1953. Ⓕ Ⓗ

The producer Walter Legge used to quite often question the necessity of stereo. Now more strikingly than ever in this remastering of one of the great classic performances of the gramophone, one of his own masterpieces as a creative recording producer, it is easy to see what he meant. With off-stage effects, for example – so important in Puccini – precisely placed, there is a sense of presence normally reserved for two-channel reproduction. In the long duet between Tosca and Cavaradossi in Act 3 you can even detect a difference of placing between the two singers, Callas set at a slight distance, though whether or not to offset a microphone problem with so biting a voice one can only guess. The immediacy is astonishing, and the great moment of the execution with trombones rasping and the fusillade reproduced at a true *fortissimo* has never been represented on record with greater impact. What is especially delightful is that where on most previous CD transfers of mono originals the results have emphasized the single-channel flatness, often with sound lacking in body, this is full and weighty. The slightly jangling brightness on some percussion instruments gives some hint of the age of the recording, but with mono of this vintage it is amazing what bloom there is even on the violins, and when it comes to the voices, there one simply forgets the years, and drinks in the glory of one of the really great recorded opera performances as never before. The contrasts of timbre are beautifully brought out – amazingly wide with Gobbi as with Callas and with di Stefano producing his most honeyed tones. Wonderful as Gobbi's and di Stefano's performances are, and superbly dramatic as de Sabata's conducting is, it is the unique Callas in the title-role that provides the greatest marvel, and here more than ever one registers the facial changes implied in each phrase, with occasional hints of a chuckle (usually ironic) apparent.

Tosca (sung in English).
Jane Eaglen *sop* Tosca; **Dennis O'Neill** *ten* Cavaradossi; **Gregory Yurisich** *bar* Scarpia;
Peter Rose *bass* Angelotti; **John Daszak** *ten* Spoletta; **Andrew Shore** *bass* Sacristan;
Christopher Booth-Jones *bass* Sciarrone; **Ashley Holland** *bass* Gaoler;
Charbel Michael *mez* Shepherd Boy;
Peter Kay Children's Choir; Geoffrey Mitchell Choir; Philharmonia Orchestra / David Parry.
Chandos Opera in English CHAN3000 (two discs: 118 minutes: DDD). Notes and text included.
Recorded 1995. Ⓕ

This is an issue to delight far more than devotees of opera in English, a gripping account of Puccini's red-blooded drama. Above all, it offers the first major recording to demonstrate the powers of Jane Eaglen at full stretch in one of the most formidable, vocally satisfying portrayals of the role of Tosca in years. David Parry here demonstrates his full understanding of Puccini and the bite and energy in the playing of the Philharmonia, not to mention the expressive warmth in the love music, will have you riveted as though hearing the music for the first time. The opulent Chandos sound, cleanly focused with plenty of atmosphere and presence, adds to the impact, whether in the power of the big tuttis or in the subtlety of whispered string *pianissimos*. Off-stage effects are nicely evocative, though the sequence of bell-sounds at the start of Act 3 is so clear it suggests an orchestra rather than a Roman landscape. Otherwise, the slightly forward balance of voices against orchestra is very well judged for a set in which the audibility of words is paramount. The translation is Edmund Tracey's as used by ENO at the Coliseum and generally very good because unobtrusive, even if you get occasional awkwardnesses. Eaglen is well matched by

Dennis O'Neill as Cavaradossi, aptly Italianate in every register, and betraying only a slight unevenness occasionally, not a wobble, on high notes under pressure. Gregory Yurisich makes a powerful Scarpia, younger-sounding than most, and therefore a more plausible lover. The others are well cast too, notably Peter Rose as an outstanding, fresh-voiced Angelotti.

Turandot.
Dame Joan Sutherland *sop* Princess Turandot; **Luciano Pavarotti** *ten* Calaf;
Montserrat Caballé *sop* Liù; **Tom Krause** *bar* Ping; **Pier Francesco Poli** *ten* Pang,
Prince of Persia; **Piero De Palma** *ten* Pong; **Nicolai Ghiaurov** *bass* Timur;
Sir Peter Pears *ten* Emperor Altoum; **Sabin Markov** *bar* Mandarin;
Wandsworth School Boys' Choir; John Alldis Choir;
London Philharmonic Orchestra / Zubin Mehta.
Decca 414 274-2DH2 (two discs: 117 minutes: ADD). Notes, text and translation included.
Recorded 1972. Ⓕ 🆁🆁

Turandot is a psychologically complex work fusing appalling sadism with self-sacrificing devotion. The icy Princess of China has agreed to marry any man of royal blood who can solve three riddles she has posed. If he fails his head will roll. Calaf, the son of the exiled Tartar king Timur, answers all the questions easily and when Turandot hesitates to accept him, magnanimously offers her a riddle in return – 'What is his name?'. Liù, Calaf's faithful slave-girl, is tortured but rather than reveal his identity kills herself. Turandot finally capitulates, announcing that his name is Love. Dame Joan Sutherland's assumption of the title role is statuesque, combining regal poise with a more human warmth, whilst Montserrat Caballé is a touchingly sympathetic Liù, skilfully steering the character away from any hint of the mawkish. Pavarotti's Calaf is a heroic figure in splendid voice and the chorus is handled with great power, baying for blood at one minute, enraptured with Liù's nobility at the next. Mehta conducts with great passion and a natural feel for Puccini's wonderfully tempestuous drama. Well recorded.

Turandot.
Maria Callas *sop* Princess Turandot; **Eugenio Fernandi** *ten* Calaf;
Dame Elisabeth Schwarzkopf *sop* Liù; **Mario Borriello** *bar* Ping; **Renato Ercolani** *ten* Pang;
Piero De Palma *ten* Pong; **Nicola Zaccaria** *bass* Timur; **Giuseppe Nessi** *ten* Emperor Altoum;
Giulio Mauri *bass* Mandarin;**Chorus and Orchestra of La Scala, Milan / Tullio Serafin.**
EMI mono CDS5 56307-2 (two discs: 118 minutes: ADD). Notes, text and translation included.
Recorded 1957. Ⓜ 🅷

To have Callas, the most flashing-eyed of all sopranos as Turandot, is – on record at least – the most natural piece of casting. Other sopranos may be comparably icy in their command, but Callas with her totally distinctive tonal range was able to give the fullest possible characterization. With her, Turandot was not just an implacable man-hater but a highly provocative female. One quickly reads something of Callas's own underlying vulnerability into such a portrait, its tensions, the element of brittleness. With her the character seems so much more believably complex than with others. It was sad that, except at the very beginning of her career, she felt unable to sing the role in the opera house, but this recording is far more valuable than any memory of the past, one of the most thrillingly magnetic of all her recorded performances, the more so when Schwarzkopf as Liù provides a comparably characterful and distinctive portrait, far more than a Puccinian 'little woman', sweet and wilting. Even more than usual one regrets that the confrontation between princess and slave is so brief. Next to such supreme singers it was perhaps cruel of Walter Legge to choose so relatively uncharacterful a tenor as Eugenio Fernandi as Calaf, but at least his timbre is pleasingly distinctive. What fully matches the singing of Callas and Schwarzkopf in its positive character is the conducting of Serafin, sometimes surprisingly free, but in its pacing invariably capturing rare colour, atmosphere and mood as well as dramatic point. The Ping, Pang and Pong episode of Act 2 has rarely sparkled so naturally, the work of a conductor who has known and loved the music in the theatre over a long career. The conducting is so vivid that the limitations of the mono sound hardly seem to matter. As the very opening will reveal, the CD transfer makes it satisfyingly full-bodied. Though with its rich, atmospheric stereo the Mehta set remains the best general recommendation, it is thrilling to have this historic document so vividly restored.

Henry Purcell

British 1659-1695

Complete Ayres for the Theatre – The History of Dioclesian, or The Prophetess, Z627[b].
King Arthur, Z628[b]. The Fairy Queen, Z629[b]. The Indian Queen, Z630[b]. The Married Beau, Z603[a].
The Old Bachelor, Z607[b]. Amphitryon, Z572[a]. The Double Dealer, Z592[a]. Distressed Innocence,

Z577ᵃ. The Gordian Knot Unty'd, Z597ᵃ. Abdelazer, Z570ᵃ. Bonduca, Z574ᵃ. The Virtuous Wife, Z611ᵃ. Sonata While the Sun Rises in 'The Indian Queen'ᵇ. Overture in G minorᵃ. Sir Anthony Love, Z588 – Overtureᵃ. Timon of Athens, Z632ᵃ. The Indian Queen, Z630 – Symphonyᵇ.
ᵃThe Parley of Instruments; ᵇThe Parley of Instruments Baroque Orchestra / Roy Goodman.
Hyperion CDA67001/3 (three discs: 209 minutes: DDD). Recorded 1994.　　　Ⓕ🅴

All these works were published within 18 months of Purcell's death. The 13 suites of choice movements from plays and semi-operas, entitled *A Collection of Ayres, compos'd for the Theatre, and upon other occasions*, may well have been the editing work of Purcell's brother, Daniel. Whoever it was had a rare combination of musical integrity and commercial flair: the pieces lifted from Purcell's interpolations to plays are often reordered and arranged with a deftness and charm which conveys the spirit of the theatre as well as heightening the loss and poignancy of Purcell's passing. How moving the Rondeau Minuet from *The Gordian Knot Unty'd* must have seemed to those who knew and loved Purcell. As a major retrospective of Purcell's life in the theatre, the *Ayres for the Theatre* mainly comprise instrumental dances from their original sources, though there are several movements readapted from sung airs, such as 'Fairest isle' from *King Arthur* and 'If love's a sweet passion' from *The Fairy Queen*. The tunes are wonderful and varied, the inner part-writing skilful and the rhythmic imagination knows no bounds. Even so, this is not music where more than a suite at a time can be recommended for ultimate satisfaction: stop while you still want more. And more you will most certainly want with Roy Goodman's alert and distinctive direction. If a few of the movements sound a touch mundane and lack dynamism as one follows on from another, the positive side is that the performances are never forced and rarely mannered. For the semi-opera 'suites', Goodman employs a full orchestra. What The Parley of Instruments has in abundance is a cordiality of expression which seems so absolutely right, especially in the slower airs.

Fantasia in F major, Z745, 'Upon one note'. Fantasias – three part, Z732-34; four part, Z735-43. In Nomines – G minor Z746; G minor, Z747, 'Dorian'.
Hespèrion XX (Sophie Watillon, Eunice Brandao, Sergi Casademunt, Wieland Kuijken, Marianne Müller, Philippe Pierlot *viols*) **/ Jordi Savall** *treb viol*
Auvidis Astrée E8536 (54 minutes: DDD). Recorded 1994.　　　Ⓕ🅿

Purcell's music for viols represents the final flowering of the English consort tradition. Viol consorts had been out of fashion for at least 20 years, ousted by the Italian violin sonatas and French ballet music. Purcell's polished essays in this antique form were neither published nor, apparently, widely circulated. Nevertheless, we cherish them today for their sublime expressiveness and craftsmanship. Jordi Savall and his group have achieved a state of abstraction seldom experienced in music. It almost goes without saying that Hespèrion's playing is always extremely beautiful: the music demands it. But any need to be rhetorical, to lean on a dissonance or pronounce a cadence, has been outgrown and discarded. The scale within which these features and more (most notably the rhythmic life of the music) are articulated is so minimal, so subtle and yet ultimately so compelling, that from the first track the listener is transported into a rarefied aural dimension usually reserved for single movements or even phrases. Don't miss it.

Fantasias – three part, Z732-4; four part, Z735-43; five part, 'upon one note', Z745. In Nomines – G minor, Z746; G minor, 'Dorian', Z747.
Joanna Levine, Susanna Pell, Catherine Finnis *viols*
Phantasm (Laurence Dreyfus, Wendy Gillespie, Jonathan Manson, Markku Luolajan-Mikkola *viols*).
Simax PSC1124 (51 minutes: DDD). Recorded 1994. *Gramophone* Award Winner 1997.　　　Ⓕ🅿

Purcell's contrapuntal mastery is dazzling, with the points of imitation in the various sections of each fantasia treated in double or triple counterpoint, inversion, augmentation and all other technical devices – for instance, the initial subjects of fantasias Z739, 742 and 743 at once appear in mirror images of themselves – but the music's deep expressiveness and the dramatic tension created by its chromaticisms and unpredictable harmonies make it clear that he certainly had performance in mind (a matter of some dispute), even if, because of the king's dislike of such intellectual pursuits, only privately by conservative-minded music-lovers. It is this expressiveness which Phantasm emphasizes in this recording, both in their varied dynamics and in their use of vibrato. Speeds here are in general fast and there is great variety of bowing and hence of articulation.

---

12 Sonatas of Three Parts, Z790-801 – No. 1 in G minor; No. 2 in B flat major; No. 3 in D minor; No. 4 in F major; No. 5 in A minor; No. 6 in C minor; No. 7 in E minor; No. 8 in G major; No. 9 in C minor; No. 10 in A minor; No. 11 in F minor; No. 12 in D major.
Pavlo Beznosiuk, Rachel Podger *vns* **Christophe Coin** *bass viol* **Christopher Hogwood** *org*
L'Oiseau-Lyre 444 449-2OH (72 minutes: DDD). Recorded 1994.　　　Ⓕ

If the lyrical refinement and other-worldliness of the *Fantasias* is largely absent, Purcell manipulates the flighty drama of the Italian spirit with a seasoned individuality. For a start he never entirely rejects the Englishness of the *Fantasias*, both in terms of harmonic unpredictability and the contrapuntal texture which forced Roger North to describe the sonatas as 'clog'd with somewhat of an English vein'. Sonata No. 5 is a case in point and one which the performers here relish with an imploring *legato* and doleful accentuation, plentifully endowed with rhetorical detail. Indeed, characterization – and just how far one goes in music whose gestures are mapped out with great clarity – is what makes this such an interesting recording. There is a grandeur and interpretational scope which gives each sonata its own measure of distinction. The violin playing of Pavlo Beznosiuk and Rachel Podger is beautifully matched and coloured, warm-toned in the opening of the Corellian Sixth Sonata but 'just and quick', crisp and precise in the canzona-style *allegros* of Sonatas Nos. 2 and 12. Hogwood performs on a chamber organ throughout (often in tandem – when Purcell decrees it – with Christophe Coin's eloquent if slightly restrained gamba). However, youthful abandon and effervescent personality are what makes this disc such an infectious addition to the catalogue.

A Choice Collection of Lessons – Suites: No. 1 in G major, Z660; No. 2 in G minor, Z661; No. 3 in G major, Z662; No. 4 in A minor, Z663; No. 5 in C major, Z666; No. 6 in D major, Z667; No. 7 in D minor, Z668; No. 8 in F major, Z669; Chaconne in G minor, Z T680. Ground in Gamut in G major, Z645. Ground in C minor, Z D221. Ground in D minor, Z D222. Prelude in G minor. The Second Part of Musick's Hand-maid – A New Ground in E minor, Z T682; Suite in C major, Z665. Sarabande with Division, Z654. Hornpipe in D minor, Z T684, 'Round-O'.
Sophie Yates *hpd*
Chandos Chaconne CHAN0587 (70 minutes: DDD). Recorded 1994. ⒻⓅ

A Choice Collection of Lessons – Suites: Nos. 1-8. The Second Part of Musick's Hand-maid – March in C major, Z647; Minuet in A minor, Z649; A New Scotch Tune in G major, Z655; A New Ground in E minor, Z T682; A New Irish Tune in G major, Z646; Sefauchi's Farewell in D minor, Z656. Ground in Gamut in G major, Z645. Ground in C minor, Z T681. Ground in D minor, Z D222. Air in G major, Z641. Air in D minor, Z675. Hornpipe in D minor, Z T684, 'Round-O'. Hornpipe in E minor, Z T685.
Olivier Baumont *hpd*
Erato 0630-10695-2 (64 minutes: DDD). Recorded 1995. ⒻⓅ

Considering Purcell's long involvement with keyboard instruments, it is curious, and certainly disappointing, that he wrote so little of any substance for them. Not many are likely to echo the late Professor Westrup's claim that the eight three- or four-movement suites are 'worthy predecessors of Bach's'; but they do contain fine individual movements, such as the Almands of Nos. 8 and, particularly, 7. Other than the suites, the harpsichord works consist of brief dance movements, popular tunes, grounds (of which Purcell was a supreme master) and transcriptions from his theatre music. There is a good deal of overlap between these two discs – the suites, three grounds and the *Round-O* Hornpipe which Britten used as the basis for his virtuosic orchestral *tour d'horizon*.

Sophie Yates, playing on a copy of a 1681 Vaudry harpsichord, takes it at Britten's sturdily stately pace; Olivier Baumont, on the 1664 Hatley virginals at Fenton House in London (though employing that collection's 1752 Kirckman harpsichord for the suites) takes it up-tempo as a real hornpipe, to startling effect. Features of Yates's playing, throughout, are its freshness and neatness (especially of ornaments), and she is always stylish – her unmeasured preludes convey a true improvisatory feeling – but overall her readings are more sober than Baumont's and have less sense of fantasy. He shows more boldness, more dash in the energetic Preludes to Suites Nos. 2, 3 and 5, is more springy in all the corants, and almost everywhere adopts faster speeds which tend to give the miniature movements more character. In two of the grounds, particularly the moving E minor 'Here the deities approve', he also makes the melody line stand out better. Baumont extends the Fifth Suite with a skippety Jigg taken from the 1689 volume which was the only one to be printed in Purcell's lifetime, and is daring enough to precede the Seventh Suite (which has no prelude) with a Prelude from a seventeenth-century manuscript now in Oxford which he has transposed for the occasion.

Complete Anthems and Services, Volume 7 – I was glad when they said unto me[b]. I was glad when they said unto me, Z19[a]. O consider my adversity, Z32[b]. Beati omnes qui timent Dominum, Z131. In the black dismal dungeon of despair, Z190. Save me, O God, Z51[b]. Morning and Evening Service in B flat major, Z230 – Te Deum; Jubilate. Thy Way, O God, is Holy, Z60. Funeral Sentences for the death of Queen Mary II[b] – Drum Processional; March and Canzona in C minor, Z860; Man that is born of Woman, Z27; In the midst of Life, Z17[b]; Thou know'st Lord, Z58[b]; Thou know'st Lord, Z58[c].

Mark Kennedy, Eamonn O'Dwyer, James Goodman *trebs* Susan Gritton *sop*
James Bowman, Nigel Short *countertens* Rogers Covey-Crump, Charles Daniels,
Mark Milhofer *tens* Michael George, Robert Evans *basses*
[a]New College Choir, Oxford; [b]The King's Consort Choir; The King's Consort / Robert King.
Hyperion CDA66677 (70 minutes: DDD). Recorded 1993.

This recording is made up predominantly of anthems, devotional songs and a morning service
(a functional, though not perfunctory, setting of the *Te Deum* and *Jubilate*) most of which disclose
the range and quality of the composer's sacred *oeuvre* near its best. Of the two settings of *I was
glad*, the first was, until not long ago, thought to be the work of John Blow. This full anthem more
than whets our appetite with its agreeable tonal and melodic twists; when the *Gloria* arrives, we are
assured that this is vintage Purcell by the sensitive pacing as much as an exquisite contrapuntal
denouement. The earlier setting is more poignant. Opening with a string symphony in the spirit of a
Locke consort, the music blossoms into a deliciously Elysian melodic fabric. Good sense is made of
the overall shape and the soloists are, as ever, excellent. *Beati omnes* is a positive gem; this may well
have been written for the composer's wedding. Of the small-scale pieces, *In the black dismal dungeon*
is the real masterpiece and it is delivered astutely by the secure and musicianly voice of Susan
Gritton. Finally to the funeral pieces. Here we have an ominous procession from the Guild of
Ancient Fifes and Drums and the first appearance of four 'flatt' trumpets – as opposed to two plus
two sackbuts; the effect of this subtle timbral change makes extraordinary sense of the music,
engendering a new grandeur and uncompromising clarity as would have befitted such an occasion.
The vocal performances are earthy and impassioned.

Music for the Funeral of Queen Mary – March and Canzona in C minor, Z860. Funeral Sentences
for the death of Queen Mary II. The Bell Anthem, Z49, 'Rejoice in the Lord alway'. Remember not,
Lord, our offences, Z50. Give sentence with me, O Lord, Z12. Jehova, quam multi sunt hostes
mei, Z135. O, I'm sick of life, Z140. My beloved spake, Z28. Hear my prayer, O Lord, Z15. O God,
thou art my God, Z35. Voluntaries[a] – No. 1 in C major, Z717; No. 4 in G major, Z720.
Winchester Cathedral Choir; Hilary Brooks *vc* **Baroque Brass of London;**
The Brandenburg Consort / David Hill [a]*org* with **David Dunnett** *org*
Argo 436 833-2ZH (66 minutes: DDD). Texts included. Recorded 1992.

David Hill is a master of long-breathed melody and sustained intensity and he brings to Purcell's
anthems a breadth of vision inspired by the time-span of earlier genres. Indeed, it is the range of
anthems skilfully chosen from amongst Purcell's finest church music which distinguishes this disc as
much as the funeral pieces. *Jehova, quam multi sunt hostes mei* is particularly effective, exemplifying
not only Hill's astute pacing but also his vigorous sense of the dramatic declamatory style which
Purcell must have gleaned from continental sources. The open-throated treble sound is equally
appropriate and characterizes the vocal colouring of almost all the works. The soloists for the verse
anthems are drawn both from the ranks of the choir and a pool of professional soloists. Between
them they shape the music with spirit and eloquence as can be relished in the abundant fruits of
My beloved spake. The strings of The Brandenburg Consort balance the buoyant vocal style here
with sparkling rhythmic exchanges. Winchester benefits from that fragility and loneliness which a
solo treble can give to 'In the midst of life', especially in a gothic acoustic. The Baroque Brass of
London captures the doleful strains with finesse and makes wonderful musical sense of the
Canzona.

Odes for St Cecilia's Day – 1692, Hail, bright Cecilia, Z328;
1683, Welcome to all the pleasures, Z339.

Hail, bright Cecilia. My beloved spake, Z28. O sing unto the Lord, Z44.
Gabrieli Consort and Players / Paul McCreesh.
Archiv Produktion 445 882-2AH (70 minutes: DDD). Texts included. Recorded 1994.

Paul McCreesh's performance of the 1692 Ode for St Cecilia's Day is exceptionally receptive to the
brilliance of the score. The trumpets are bold and brassy (only occasionally overblown) and the
ensemble as a whole moves effortlessly from discretion and intimacy to the imposing timbral
homogeneity of McCreesh's most extrovert Venetian exploits. His tempos – especially in the grand
opening instrumental sinfonia – are irrepressible and invigorating; there is a danger that this
eight-section introduction can seem too much of a good thing, if not briskly negotiated. The solo
singing is almost uniformly outstanding: Peter Harvey is the busiest of the basses and he delivers
his splendid music, including 'Wondrous machine!', with authority and variety of colour. Charles
Daniels must, by now, have sung almost everything by Purcell but there is no sign of flagging:
''Tis Nature's voice' has a magical sense of unfolding as the music's captivating charms are
gradually exposed. His duet with Mark le Brocq, 'In vain the am'rous flute' has its moments,
though the intonation of the recorders is languorous to say the least. Susan Hemington Jones

sounds bright and alert though she seems just a touch unsettled and she is guilty of the occasional rather ugly 'early-musicy' swell, though to pick out a couple of bars there should certainly not detract attention from some notable singing in the verse anthem, *O sing unto the Lord*, especially in an extraordinarily moving close where the Gabrieli Consort's warmth of tone is exquisitely caught. *My beloved spake* is the other filler: a wonderful work and again very well performed.

Hail, bright Cecilia; Welcome to all the pleasures.
Susan Hamilton, Siri Thornhill *sops* **Robin Blaze, Martin van der Zeijst** *countertens*
Mark Padmore *ten* **Jonathan Arnold, Peter Harvey, Jonathan Brown** *basses*
Collegium Vocale / Philippe Herreweghe.
Harmonia Mundi HMC90 1643 (73 minutes: DDD). Texts included. Recorded 1997.   Ⓕ

The two famous St Cecilian Odes reflect a remarkable polarity in the composer's creative priorities: the shorter of the two, *Welcome to all the pleasures*, is a supreme amalgamation of Fishburn's words and Purcell's music, bursting with contained subtlety and enchantment. There is also a unique sense of conveying something novel, in this case an inaugural tribute on November 22nd, 1683, to the patron saint of music, henceforth annually celebrating 'this divine Science'. *Hail, bright Cecilia* from 1692 is three times longer and explores all the startling orchestral sounds which changed English music towards something approaching a Handelian palette. It is also truly *fin de siècle* (some might say Newtonian) in ambition and the imagery is as breathtakingly splendid now as it was when the Victorians first revered it for its boldness and scale. Such qualities clearly animate Herreweghe and he shapes this music with rapture and precision. The whole is infectiously fresh and never rushed. If not as brilliant or as full as McCreesh, Herreweghe is rather more sensitive to the nuances which irradiate from Purcell's colouring of words. He largely uses English voices. 'Hark! hark! each tree' boasts the versatile and effortless alto of Robin Blaze who, with the assured Peter Harvey, achieves a delightfully naturalistic lilt. This version certainly rivals McCreesh (for whom Peter Harvey also sings 'Wondrous machine' splendidly) for elevated characterization. One blip here is the piping soprano in 'Thou tun'st this world' (Susan Hamilton) where the voice seems technically and expressively limited. For beauty of sound, then, Herreweghe is your man. For dramatic immediacy and excitement, look no further than McCreesh.

Welcome to all the pleasures. Funeral Sentences for the death of Queen Mary. Birthday Ode, Z323, 'Come ye sons of art away'. March and Canzona in C minor, Z860. Funeral Music for the death of Queen Mary.
Emily Van Evera *sop* **Timothy Wilson** *counterten* **John Mark Ainsley, Charles Daniels** *tens*
David Thomas *bass* **Taverner Consort, Choir and Players / Andrew Parrott.**
Virgin Classics Veritas VC5 45159-2 (55 minutes: DDD). Recorded 1998.   Ⓕ

Whilst McCreesh makes the score sparkle with his energetic view of tempos, Andrew Parrott parades his smooth and integrated forces with less instant theatricality. Instead we have a typically homogeneous and unfolding scenario which complements McCreesh's more effervescent and lush reading. The reappearance of Parrott's recordings of Purcell's earlier Cecilian ode, *Welcome to all the pleasures* and the time-honoured and particularly accessible *Come ye sons of art away* is also received with open arms. Some may distrust the low pitch (A=392) but the high tenor of Charles Daniels and the satisfying registral blend of Timothy Wilson and John Mark Ainsley in 'Sound the trumpet' are more than adequate recompense and the former's mellifluous rendering of 'Here the deities approve' is a real gem to be savoured.

She loves, and she confesses, Z413. Amintas, to my grief I see, Z356. Corinna is divinely fair, Z365. Amintor, heedless of his flocks, Z357. He himself courts his own ruin, Z372. No, to what purpose, Z468. Sylvia, 'tis true you're fair, Z512. Lovely Albina's come ashore, Z394. Spite of the godhead, pow'rful love, Z417. If music be the food of love, Z379/3. Phyllis, I can ne'er forgive it, Z408. Bacchus is a pow'r divine, Z360. Bess of Bedlam, Z370, 'From silent shades'. Let formal lovers still pursue, Z391. I came, I saw, and was undone, Z375. Who can behold Florella's charms?, Z441. Cupid, the slyest rogue alive, Z367. If prayers and tears, Z380. In Chloris all soft charms agree, Z384. Let us, kind Lesbia, give away, Z466. Love is now become a trade, Z393. Ask me to love no more, Z358. O Solitude! my sweetest choice, Z406. Olinda in the shades unseen, Z404. Pious Celinda goes to prayers, Z410. When Strephon found his passion vain, Z435. The fatal hour comes on apace, Z421. Sawney is a bonny lad, Z412. Young Thirsis' fate, ye hills and groves, deplore, Z473.
Barbara Bonney, Susan Gritton *sops* **James Bowman** *counterten* **Rogers Covey-Crump,**
Charles Daniels *tens* **Michael George** *bass* **Mark Caudle, Susanna Pell** *vas da gamba*
David Miller *lte/theorbo* / **Robert King** *org/hpd*
Hyperion CDA66730 (76 minutes: DDD). Texts included. Recorded 1993-94.   ⒻⓅ

This third and last volume of Purcell's non-theatrical secular songs consummates a most rewarding survey of 87 songs with more of the same: a vocal palette of six singers who are by now so steeped in the nuances of Purcell's strains that even the slightest offering sparkles with something memorable. The treasure is shared between Barbara Bonney and Susan Gritton who complement each other superbly. Gritton, becoming more refined in characterization and tonal colour by the day, is allotted the free-style and dramatic pieces whilst to Bonney's fluid and sensual melisma is designated the more strophic or *cantabile* settings. *Lovely Albina's come ashore*, at one time thought to be 'the last song that Mr. Henry Purcell sett before he Dy'd', is at any rate one of the composer's most mature creations, tantalizingly hinting at a new, tautly designed and classically balanced type of song. This work, *If music be the food of love* (the best of the three versions) and *I came, I saw* are striking examples of how exceptionally Bonney negotiates Purcell's skipping and curling contours and makes these songs sound even finer creations than we previously thought. *From silent shades* ('Bess of Bedlam') is Purcell's quintessential mad-song and Gritton has the measure of it all the way; packed full of incident, imagery and musical detail, her narration is clear and finely judged, reporting the tale with irony and change of colour, thereby never resorting to the more usual overexaggeration which tends to lessen the impact of Bess's condition. The CD is beautifully and thoroughly documented.

Odes and Welcome Songs, Volumes 6-8.
Gillian Fisher, Mary Seers, Susan Hamilton, Tessa Bonner sops **James Bowman, Nigel Short, Michael Chance** countertens **Mark Padmore, Andrew Tusa, Rogers Covey-Crump, Charles Daniels, John Mark Ainsley** tens **Michael George, Robert Evans** basses **New College Choir, Oxford; The King's Consort / Robert King.**

Love's goddess sure was blind, Z331. Raise, raise the voice, Z334. Laudate Ceciliam, Z329. From those serene and rapturous joys, Z326.
Hyperion CDA66494 (68 minutes: DDD).Texts included. Recorded 1991. ⒻⓅ

Of old, when heroes thought it base, Z333. Swifter, Isis, swifter flow, Z336. What, what shall be done on behalf of the man?, Z341.
Hyperion CDA66587 (66 minutes: DDD).Texts included. Recorded 1991. ⒻⓅ

Come ye sons of art, away, Z323. Welcome, viceregent of the mighty king, Z340. Why, why are all the Muses mute?, Z343.
Hyperion CDA66598 (68 minutes: DDD).Texts included. Recorded 1991. ⒻⓅ

These three CDs represent the final instalments in Hyperion's complete recording of Purcell's Odes and Welcome Songs. Purcell composed a number of these celebratory works between 1680 and 1695, and 24 survive. They were written for a considerable range of events: most of them for royal birthdays, of King James II and Queen Mary, but also for a royal wedding, educational celebrations, and the 'Yorkshire Feast' of 1689. This cornucopia of wonderful music has largely been ignored, and Hyperion's edition is to be warmly welcomed, not only for bringing to the catalogue such magnificent music, but also for the extremely sympathetic and musical performances by the The King's Consort under the direction of Robert King. Of all the works on these discs, probably the most well known is *Come ye sons of art, away* written for Queen Mary in 1694 (Volume 8). This joyous work contains some of Purcell's most ebullient music, typified by the duet for two countertenors, 'Sound the trumpet'. Like all of the works in the set this is surrounded by a well contrasted group of solos and duets for individual voices, instrumental interludes, and the occasional chorus. Less famous, but equally full of Restoration pomp and ceremony is the Yorkshire Feast song (Volume 7). Like many of the odes, the text for this is second-rate, ostensibly telling the story of York from the Roman occupation to the seventeenth century. However, this is merely the pretext for a splendidly varied set of vocal and instrumental items, the climax of which might be more fitting for a coronation than for a dinner of Yorkshire worthies!

Volume 6 contains four of the least well known if no less rich and varied odes, two of which are dedicated to the patron saint of music, St Cecilia. While composed for slightly smaller forces than the more ceremonial odes, these contain music which is equally jaunty and exhilarating. Throughout all three volumes the most striking fact is Purcell's extraordinary inventiveness, and his incredible facility at word setting: even the most lame texts come alive in his hands, and the variety of expression throughout is astonishing. Robert King's direction is always sensitive to both the broad span and individual nuances of Purcell's kaleidoscopic writing for voice and instruments. The King's Consort plays with great understanding throughout and has clearly wholly absorbed the often elusive style of this music, in which many influences, most notably those from France, are combined. The vocal soloists are uniformly excellent, but special mention must be made of the ravishing soprano Gillian Fisher, and the versatile countertenor James Bowman. Hyperion's recordings throughout are without fault, achieving both excellent internal balance and appropriate atmosphere and perspective.

O Solitude! my sweetest choice, Z406. Not all my torments can your pity move, Z400. Stript of their green our groves appear, Z444. The Blessed Virgin's Expostulation – Tell me, some pitying Angel, Z196. If music be the food of love, Z379/1. The fatal hour comes on apace, Z421. The Queen's Epicedium, 'Incassum, Lesbia, rogas', Z383. Cupid, the slyest rogue alive, Z367. Bess of Bedlam, 'From silent shades', Z370. An Evening Hymn on a Ground – Now that the sun hath veiled his light, Z193. O Solitude! my sweetest choice, Z406. Tyrannic Love – Ah! how sweet it is to love. The Fairy Queen – Hark! the echoing air. Pausanias – Sweeter than roses. The Tempest – Dear pretty youth. The Comical History of Don Quixote – From rosy bow'rs. Sophonisba – Beneath the poplar's shadow. The Indian Queen – I attempt from love's sickness. The History of Dioclesian – Let us dance, let us sing. King Arthur – Fairest isle.
Nancy Argenta sop **Nigel North** lte/gtr **Richard Boothby** va da gamba **Paul Nicholson** hpd/org
Virgin Classics Veritas VC7 59324-2 (74 minutes: DDD).Texts included. Recorded 1992.   ℗Ⓔ

Here we can delight in one of the best recordings of Purcell's songs (mainly taken from *Orpheus Britannicus*) to have emerged in recent times and arguably the most literary-sensitive accounts since Alfred Deller. Nancy Argenta proves that declamatory and strophic songs (and many sub-genres in between) can be negotiated in the same recital with supreme technical finesse, profound understanding of the texts and the type of inventive nuances which enhance the implied conceits of an extraordinary range of songs. Moreover, she has the technical and temperamental control to explore the expressive gamut, from impish and deliberately impersonal no-nonsense texts (such as 'Stript of their green', where the singer's rolling spontaneity is just what is called for) to the impulsive gestures and psychological tensions in 'Tell me, some pitying Angel' and 'From rosy bow'rs'. The former is an especially fine portrayal with its sustained organ continuo commentating alongside sundry plucks (always astutely gauged by Nigel North, Richard Boothby and Paul Nicholson) whilst Argenta delivers the Virgin's touching and anxious expostulation with a rare understanding and empathy. Sheer technical bravura, however, is what performances of these songs too frequently lack and the quality of pitching (notoriously awkward leaps abound) and tuning sets this disc in a class of its own; only very occasionally does shrillness or a rather lifeless vibrato detract from an otherwise exquisite release – one which should sit on the shelves of all those who need convincing that Purcell's solo vocal music of this ilk is anything but a glorious testament to the human voice.

Dioclesian, Acts 1-4.
Catherine Pierard sop **James Bowman** counterten **John Mark Ainsley, Mark Padmore** tens
Michael George bass
Collegium Musicum 90 Chorus; Collegium Musicum 90 / Richard Hickox.
Chandos Chaconne CHAN0568 (54 minutes: DDD). Text included. Recorded 1994.   ℗

It was *Dioclesian*, the least known of the four semi-opera masterpieces of Purcell, for which the composer initially earned a reputation for writing stage music. The 'opera' was by all accounts a roaring success, though music played a less important part in the stage works of the 1690s than it did in the masque-related works of the previous decades – ironically just at the time when England could at last boast a dramatic master who could stand tall amongst the 'greats' of France and Italy. If the paucity of tableaux means a less atmospheric scenic context, such as we experience in *The Fairy Queen* or *King Arthur*, there is still much fine music which deserves to be highly regarded. Hickox is evidently committed to this score: the instrumental movements are all disciplined and yet display the buoyancy and variety of expression of one who senses the freshness of Purcell's first foray into the theatre. His soloists are authoritative Purcellians and they never disappoint and he manages to sustain the tension and climate he sets from the start.

Dido and Aeneas.
Catherine Bott sop Dido; **John Mark Ainsley** ten Aeneas; **Emma Kirkby** sop Belinda;
David Thomas bass Sorceress; **Elizabeth Priday** sop First Witch;
Sara Stowe sop Second Witch; **Julianne Baird** sop Second Woman;
Daniel Lochmann treb First Sailor; **Michael Chance** counterten Spirit;
Academy of Ancient Music Chorus and Orchestra / Christopher Hogwood.
L'Oiseau-Lyre 436 992-2OHO (52 minutes: DDD). Notes and text included.
Recorded 1992.   ℗RR

Emma Kirkby (whose Dido, for Parrott on Chandos, remains one of the finest on record) sings Belinda for Hogwood; David Thomas (whose Aeneas, on the same recording, was outstanding) sings the Sorceress; Michael Chance takes the tiny part of the Spirit, thereby putting its moment into centre stage as the gloriously conceived turning-point of the story. A few innovations, too. Following the arguments that the Sorceress could be a man, Hogwood's choice of Thomas has offered us perhaps the most eloquent version on disc so far. Thomas gives full value to the words and the music. Less convincing is the use of a boy for the sailor's song; despite direct and spirited singing, its text is quite inappropriate for a boy. Much more successful is the use of the Drottningholm wind-machines to interpret the various stage-instructions and give the entire performance a real sense of verisimilitude. Catherine Bott is a fine Dido, even-voiced across the range and powerfully expressive if occasionally a touch free with the rhythms. John Mark Ainsley easily stands as the finest Aeneas since David Thomas. This is a very difficult role to handle dramatically, because its moods change so fast; and Ainsley handles all this with heartbreaking ease. This is a classic interpretation. So too is Hogwood's reading of the score, with his faultless sense of the right speed and the right rhythm as well as his ability to see the moment when everything must be interrupted to give space to the drama.

Dido and Aeneas.
Véronique Gens *sop* Dido; **Nathan Berg** *bass-bar* Aeneas; **Sophie Marin-Degor** *sop* Belinda; **Claire Brua** *sop* Sorceress; **Sophie Daneman** *sop* Second Woman, First Witch; **Gaëlle Mechaly** *sop* Second Witch; **Jean-Paul Fouchécourt** *ten* Spirit, Sailor; **Les Arts Florissants / William Christie.**
Erato 4509-98477-2 (52 minutes: DDD). Notes and text included. Recorded 1994. Ⓕ Ⓟ

William Christie's reading of *Dido* is very much in terms of the reputed French influence on Purcell. Overdotting, reverse dotting and *inégalité* are used throughout; the lines are often heavily embellished in the manner of Lully. This is a perfectly justifiable approach to the music, since there is little direct evidence to say exactly how much the French style dominated in England. This version – with single strings, an excellent small choir and a slightly obtrusive harpsichord – stands well alongside what is otherwise available: if you prefer *Dido* in the French manner this is the record you will want; if not, you will probably still want it as a very different view of a major work. Apart from a few moments' inattention in Belinda's 'Haste, haste to town', you would hardly notice that most of the cast are Francophone, except in that Nathan Berg's imposing bass-baritone finds it slightly easier to exploit the colour and the meaning of Aeneas's words. Véronique Gens is a lucid and sensible Dido, partnered by a sprightly Belinda from Sophie Marin-Degor and a good Second Woman from Sophie Daneman. Claire Brua's Sorceress is a splendidly insinuating conception, with a slithering melodic style that neatly characterizes her evil. Perhaps the main musical distinction of this version is the way Christie presents the final paragraphs. Up to this point he has taken generally quick speeds, and he runs the final confrontation of Dido and Aeneas at a headlong tempo, which works very well. Then he comes almost to a standstill at the moment when Aeneas leaves the stage, choosing an unusually slow speed for the chorus 'Great minds against themselves conspire'. This makes way for a dangerously slow Lament, which is heart-stopping, and the final chorus, which is not.

The Fairy Queen.
Gillian Fisher, Lorna Anderson *sops* **Ann Murray** *mez* **Michael Chance** *counterten* **John Mark Ainsley, Ian Partridge** *tens* **Richard Suart, Michael George** *basses* **The Sixteen Choir and Orchestra / Harry Christophers.**
Collins Classics 7013-2 (two discs: 133 minutes: DDD). Text included. Recorded 1990. Ⓕ Ⓟ

Of Purcell's four semi-operas in which extended musical set pieces or masques are mixed with substantial dialogue, it is *The Fairy Queen* that stands the best chance of catching the public's imagination, not only because of its superb music but also on account of its foundation in such a well-loved part of England's literary heritage as *A Midsummer Night's Dream*. Much has been made of the liberties taken by Purcell's anonymous librettist for this work, but no one who has heard the music could deny that the composer conjures just as truthfully as Shakespeare the pains and pleasures of love, the interludes of low comedy, and the magical atmosphere of the fairy wood. Harry Christophers has assembled a strong cast. With singers like Gillian Fisher, Michael Chance, John Mark Ainsley and Ian Partridge aboard, things are unlikely to go far astray, while the contribution of the always excellent Sixteen Choir means, too, that this is a performance without any serious weakness. The orchestra, it's true, could sound more committed at times, while Ann Murray seems a little out of place in this particular company; but in general there is a refreshing lightness, an authentic Englishness, to this recording that serves the music well. Perhaps the highlight is the gentle Second Act Masque which lulls Titania to sleep, but also highly enjoyable are the comic scenes, such as the one in which a drunken poet suffers an uncomfortable encounter with some fairies. This is not a recording which has everything – it lacks sheer splendour for one thing – but it is among the best.

The Indian Queen.
Emma Kirkby, Catherine Bott *sops* **John Mark Ainsley** *ten* **Gerald Finley** *bar*
David Thomas *bass* **Tommy Williams** *sngr*
Chorus and Orchestra of the Academy of Ancient Music / Christopher Hogwood.
Also includes additional Act by Daniel Purcell.
L'Oiseau-Lyre 444 339-2OHO (73 minutes: DDD). Notes and text included.
Recorded 1994.   Ⓕ P RR

Christopher Hogwood makes us realize that for all the constraints, this score is not inherently
small-scale and that it warrants all the subtlety of colour that can be achieved using 12 soloists and
a decent sized choir and orchestra. Needless to say, Hogwood conveys a consistent, logical and
meticulous understanding of the score. The orchestral playing is crisp and transparent, the
Academy of Ancient Music's articulation allowing the integrity of the inner parts to be heard to the
full without compromising blend. Amongst a distinguished line-up of singers, John Mark Ainsley
gets the lion's share and is perhaps marginally more effective as the Indian Boy than as Fame, but
such gloriously mellifluous and controlled singing can only enhance the reputation of this work.
Emma Kirkby is in fine fettle and she executes the justly celebrated song 'I attempt from love's
sickness' with her usual communicative panache. Then comes the pleasurably contrasted voice of
Catherine Bott: 'They tell us that your mighty powers' could not be in better hands. David Thomas
as Envy, with his two followers in the Act 2 masque, highlights this brilliant scene as the work of a
true connoisseur of the theatre. Mature Purcell is most strongly felt in the deftly ironic invocation
by the conjurer, Ismeron, whose 'Ye twice ten thousand deities' is delivered authoritatively by
Gerald Finley, though the lulling to sleep, before the God of Dream's gloomy non-prediction, is
strangely unconvincing. Taken as a whole, the quality of music shines very brightly in Hogwood's
reading. It is perhaps a touch calculated in places. The inclusion of Daniel Purcell's Act 5 masque is
interesting but not much more than that.

The Indian Queen.
Tessa Bonner, Catherine Bott *sops* **Rogers Covey-Crump** *ten* **Peter Harvey** *bass*
Purcell Simfony Voices; Purcell Simfony / Catherine Mackintosh *vn*
Linn Records CKD035 (60 minutes: DDD). Recorded 1994.   Ⓕ

If *The Indian Queen* is less ambitious than the other three 'operas' there is the sure touch here of
the composer at his most mature and adept (as his last great work for the theatre, there is a strong
possibility that Purcell may never have lived to hear it). The Prologue, in which he had the rare
opportunity to set an extended dialogue, is beautifully balanced, the humour in Act 2 delicate and
inimitably charming, and the music in Act 3 – when Zempoalla's ill-fated love is prophesied by
Ismeron the magician in 'Ye twice ten thousand deities' – ranks alongside the finest moments in
Purcell's output and was praised by Dr Burney nearly 100 years later. The small-scale character of
the work, compared to its siblings, is taken a stage further by the Purcell Simfony, which employs a
minute chamber-size group of four strings, doubling oboe and recorder, single trumpet and drums.
The soloists sing with airy restraint but each responds to these Hilliardesque proportions with a
rhythmic buoyancy and direct intimacy which projects a finely gauged overall conception of the
work. If the expressive power of the music is at times rather glazed, there is a sure atmosphere
which is captured by a delightful perspective on the recorded sound, ensuring that the light
puff-pastry of 'I come to sing great Zempoalla's story' and 'I attempt from love's sickness' is both
warm and yet never imposing. The ensemble is not always first-rate but there is nothing too
worrisome and the instrumental numbers are elegantly shaped. Tessa Bonner gets the lion's share of
the solo soprano numbers, ahead of the more colourful Catherine Bott, though the former's
comparatively brittle sound has a crystalline quality which suits director Catherine Mackintosh's
consistent, if austere strategy. To sum up, this release is consistently touching, one which in a
paradoxical way gets under the skin despite the recessed emotional climate it conveys.

King Arthur.
Véronique Gens, Claron McFadden, Sandrine Piau, Susannah Waters *sops* **Mark Padmore,
Iain Paton** *tens* **Jonathan Best, Petteri Salomaa, François Bazola-Minori** *basses*
Les Arts Florissants Chorus and Orchestra / William Christie.
Erato 4509-98535-2 (two discs: 90 minutes: DDD). Notes and text included. Recorded 1995.
Gramophone Award Winner 1995.   Ⓕ P E

If the co-operation with John Dryden led to a unity of vision in terms of music's expressive role in
the overall drama, Purcell was limited to a historical patriotic fantasy with little room for the magic
and pathos of, say, the superior *Fairy Queen*. Yet in the context of a stage presentation, Purcell's
music shines through strongly. On disc though, with just the music, not even the dramatic powers of

William Christie can restore its place in the overall scheme. But never mind, this is a score with some magnificent creations and Christie is evidently enchanted by it. The choral singing is richly textured, sensual and long-breathed, yet always alert to a nuance which can irradiate a passage at a stroke, as Christie does in the bittersweet close of 'Honour prizing' – easily the best moment in Act 1. The instrumental movements are finely moulded so that sinewy counterpoint and rhythmic profile are always strongly relayed. The songs, too, have been acutely prepared and are keenly characterized without resorting to excess. All the basses deliver their fine music with aplomb. If there is one drawback to extracting the musical numbers from the 'opera' when they have so clearly been delivered within a theatrical context, it is that the highly contextual characterizations lend themselves less well to the musical continuity of a CD. But *King Arthur* without the play is dramatically a nonsense so why try to pretend? Christie does not but makes the strongest case for this music to date.

Richard Pygott

British c1485-1549

Pygott Missa Veni sancte spiritus.
Mason O rex gloriose.
Choir of Christ Church Cathedral, Oxford / Stephen Darlington.
Nimbus NI5578 (52 minutes: DDD). Recorded 1993-94.   Ⓕ

Nick Sandon has done a meticulous piece of reconstruction to produce a performing edition of Richard Pygott's five-part *Missa Veni sancte spiritus* from the incomplete set of Peterhouse partbooks. Replacement of the missing tenor would in itself have been fairly straightforward: it simply repeats the first 11 pitches of the plainchant antiphon for the Vespers psalmody of the Saturday before Pentecost. The listener will have no difficulty in picking out the statements of the *cantus firmus* as they occur. The task of reconstruction was more arduous for those sections requiring a freely composed tenor. But Sandon has managed to overcome this difficulty, and his achievement has resulted in the resurrection of a long-forgotten work and made possible this splendid recording from Dorchester Abbey. The bright, resonant acoustic produces a warm response from the singers. The restoration of John Mason's *O rex gloriose* presented a more complex problem, since the treble part was missing as well as the tenor. But once the tenor was identified, it strode through, providing a firm basis on which to reconstruct the treble. The Sarum Passiontide chant *O rex gloriose* is a strange hybrid – a troped antiphon in the shape of a responsory, with verses, repeats and all, to be sung with the Compline canticle *Nunc dimittis*. This painstaking reconstruction enables us to hear something very near the original: we owe Christ Church Choir and Nick Sandon a vote of thanks.

Roger Quilter

British 1877-1953

Shakespeare Songs, Op. 23 – No. 3, It was a lover and his lass; No. 4, Take, o take those lips away. O mistress mine, Op. 6 No. 2. How shall I your true love know?, Op. 30 No. 3. Orpheus with his lute, Op. 32 No. 1. Hark! Hark! the lark!. The Arnold Book of Old Songs – Ye banks and braes; Charlie is my darling; Ca' the yowes to the knowes. I arise from dreams of thee, Op. 29. Songs, Op. 25 – No. 3, An old carol; No. 5, Music, when soft voices die. Songs, Op. 3 – No. 1, Love's philosophy; No. 2, Now sleeps the crimson petal. Spring is at the door, Op. 18 No. 4. Passing dreams, Op. 10 No. 2. Three Pastoral Songs, Op. 22. Go, lovely rose, Op. 24 No. 3. Songs, Op. 14 – No. 1, Autumn evening; No. 3, A last year's rose. Amaryllis at the fountain, Op. 15 No. 2. I dare not ask a kiss, Op. 28 No. 3. To Julia, Op. 8. Rosmé – Love calls through the summer night.
Lisa Milne sop **Anthony Rolfe Johnson** ten **Graham Johnson** pf
Duke Quartet (Louisa Fuller, Rick Koster vns John Metcalfe va Ivan McCready vc).
Collins Classics 1512-2 (70 minutes: DDD). Texts included. Recorded 1997.   Ⓕ

Quilter, in his small output, and output of small things, was almost always, utterly and unmistakably, himself. 'Almost always': two items in this programme prompt that. One is the very last, a duet with a waltz-refrain, dated 1940. He hadn't quite the courage to carry on and make a really big thing of it, adding the bold banality that might have ensured success. The other is the setting of Shelley's *Indian Serenade* ('I arise from dreams of thee'). The longest of the songs and the most elaborate, it is also the furthest from the drawing-room and nearest to art-song; and it is the least characteristic. The delicacy and restrained passion of Quilter's characteristic writing finds a sensitive exponent in Graham Johnson. Both singers bring an affectionate touch. Lisa Milne is delightful in the Ophelia song, *How shall I your true love know?* and in the spirited *Charlie is my darling*. Anthony Rolfe Johnson is most gratefully heard in the quieter songs such as *An old carol* ('I

747

sing of a maiden'). It is interesting to hear the Herrick cycle, *To Julia*, in the arrangement Quilter made for accompaniment by piano quintet. Also moving and fascinating to hear again the song in which he really did extend – and remain – himself: his arrangement of *Ca' the yowes to the knowes*.

Sergey Rachmaninov   USSR/American 1873-1943

Piano Concertos – No. 1 in F sharp minor, Op. 1; No. 2 in C minor, Op. 18; No. 3 in D minor, Op. 30; No. 4 in G minor, Op. 40. Rhapsody on a Theme of Paganini, Op. 43.

Piano Concertos Nos. 1-4. Paganini Rhapsody.
Earl Wild *pf*
Royal Philharmonic Orchestra / Jascha Horenstein.
Chandos CHAN8521/2 (two discs: 134 minutes: ADD). Recorded 1965.   Ⓟ **RR**

Such is the luxuriance of sound revealed in these remasterings, it is difficult to believe the recording date; and such is the quality of the piano playing that it is easy to understand why Chandos should have wanted to go to such trouble. There are not so many Rachmaninov pianists who dare to throw caution to the wind to the extent that Earl Wild does in the outer movements of the First Concerto, fewer still who can keep their technical poise in the process. The improvisatory feel to the lyricism of the slow movement is no less remarkable. Wild's panache is every bit as seductive in No. 4, and the *Paganini Rhapsody* is a rare example of a performance faster than the composer's own – devilishly driven in the early variations and with tension maintained through the following slower ones so that the famous eighteenth can register as a release from a suffocating grip, rather than an overblown, out-of-context exercise in grandiosity. Because of his lightness and touch Wild's tempos never seem excessive. Undoubtedly he shifts the balance from languishing pathos and overwhelming grandeur towards straightforward exuberance; but that may be no bad thing for refreshing our view of the composer. It keeps us in touch with an earlier tradition, at the same time feeling supremely youthful in its energy and sounding fully up to date thanks to Chandos's outstanding refurbishment of the sound. The RPO appears to be revelling in the whole affair, in a way one would not have immediately associated with Horenstein. To pick on the very few weaknesses, the very relaxed clarinet tone in the slow movement of Concerto No. 2 rather misses the character, and elsewhere in this work the balance engineers rather crudely stick a microphone under the cello section's nostrils. But then the solo playing in this concerto is generally a little disappointing too, as though Wild had actually played the piece rather too often. A miss-hit in bar 6 is an ominous sign, and the thoughtless disregard for soft dynamics is as disturbing as the comparative glibness of most of the lyrical themes. In No. 3 there are the hateful cuts to contend with, and one senses that the performance has been rather thoughtlessly modelled on the composer's own, idiosyncrasies and all. None the less, for the sake of the outstanding performances of Nos. 1 and 4 and the *Rhapsody*, and for the unique combination of old-style bravura and modern sound, this issue earns a strong recommendation.

The Complete Recordings.
Piano Concertos – Nos. 1[b], 2[a], 3[b] and 4[b]. Paganini Rhapsody[a]. The isle of the dead, Op. 29[c]. Vocalise, Op. 34 No. 14[c]. Symphony No. 3 in A minor, Op. 44[c]. Daisies. Nine Etudes tableaux, Op. 33 – No. 2 in C major; No. 7 in E flat major. Etude tableau in A minor, Op. 39 No. 6. Lilacs (two versions, recorded in 1923 and 1942). Six Moments musicaux, Op. 16 – Allegretto. Sérénade in B flat minor, Op. 3 No. 5. Humoresque in G major, Op. 10 No. 5. Oriental Sketch in B flat major. Polka de W.R. (three versions, recorded in 1919, 1921 and 1928). Preludes – C sharp minor, Op. 3 No. 2 (three versions, recorded in 1919, 1921 and 1928); G minor, Op. 23 No. 5; G flat major, Op. 23 No. 10; E major, Op. 32 No. 3; G major, Op. 32 No. 5; F minor, Op. 32 No. 6; G sharp minor, Op. 32 No. 12. **Beethoven** Violin Sonata No. 8 in G major, Op. 30 No. 3. 32 Variations on an original theme in C minor, WoO80. **Schubert** Violin Sonata in A major (Duo), D574. **Grieg** Violin Sonata No. 3 in C minor, Op. 45. **Schumann** Carnaval, Op. 9. **Chopin** Piano Sonata No. 2 in B flat minor, Op. 35. Also includes solo piano works by other composers.
Fritz Kreisler *vn* **Sergey Rachmaninov** *pf* **Philadelphia Orchestra /** [a]**Leopold Stokowski,** [b]**Eugene Ormandy,** [c]**Sergey Rachmaninov.**
RCA Victor Gold Seal mono 09026 61265-2 (ten discs: 640 minutes: ADD). Recorded 1919-42.
Gramophone Award Winner 1993.   Ⓜ **H**

Here, on RCA's superbly remastered ten-disc set, is awe-inspiring and scintillating confirmation of Rachmaninov's greatness; as composer, pianist, chamber musician and conductor. Controversy over his stature as a composer may live on in the dustier corners of academia, but today once confident assertions that his music would never last, that it lacked the regenerative force of true tragedy or that it was, in essence, little more than a precursor of Hollywood, have been triumphantly erased.

Works such as the Second Symphony, the Third Piano Concerto and the Second Piano Sonata are played without the once acceptable and debilitating cuts so sadly sanctioned by the composer, and innovative as well as traditional elements in Rachmaninov's writing are celebrated. What is indisputable, however, is Rachmaninov's quality as a pianist. Alternatively teasing and granitic in other composer's music (his way with Schumann's *Carnaval* and Chopin's Second Sonata, to name but two, will always incite argument) his performances of his own works are, quite simply, inimitable, imbued with a brio and aristocracy entirely his own. The most immediately appealing include all four concertos and the Paganini *Rhapsody*, Handel's *Harmonious Blacksmith* Variations (pure pianistic sorcery) and Rachmaninov's own second *Moment musical* and *Mélodie*, Op. 3 No. 2; the former of a mind-bending virtuosity, the latter aglow with the *cantabile* and rubato of another, far-off age. But everything is absorbing, nothing without interest. These recordings blazen out Rachmaninov's stature both as creator and re-creator in every golden bar.

Piano Concertos Nos. 1-4.
Vladimir Ashkenazy *pf*
London Symphony Orchestra / André Previn.
Double Decca 444 839-2DF2 (two discs: 135 minutes: ADD). Recorded 1970-72.　　Ⓜ

Despite the recording dates, the sound and balance are superb and there is nothing to cloud or impede one's sense of Ashkenazy's greatness in all these works. From him every page declares Rachmaninov's nationality, his indelibly Russian nature. What nobility of feeling and what dark regions of the imagination he relishes and explores in page after page of the Third Concerto. Significantly his opening is a very moderate *Allegro ma non tanto*, later allowing him an expansiveness and imaginative scope hard to find in other more 'driven' or hectic performances. His rubato is as natural as it is distinctive and his way of easing from one idea to another shows him at his most intimately and romantically responsive. There are no cuts, and his choice of the bigger of the two cadenzas is entirely apt, given the breadth of his conception. Even the skittering figurations and volleys of repeated notes just before the close of the central *Intermezzo* cannot tempt Ashkenazy into display and he is quicker than any other pianist to find a touch of wistfulness beneath Rachmaninov's occasional outer playfulness (the *scherzando* episode in the finale). Such imaginative fervour and delicacy are just as central to Ashkenazy's other performances. His steep unmarked *decrescendo* at the close of the First Concerto's opening rhetorical gesture is symptomatic of his romantic bias, his love of the music's interior glow. And despite his prodigious command in, say, the final pages of both the First and Fourth Concertos, there is never a hint of bombast or a more superficial brand of fire-and-brimstone virtuosity.

Previn works hand in glove with his soloist. Clearly, this is no one-night partnership but the product of the greatest musical sympathy, of a mutual skill and affection. The opening of the Third Concerto's *Intermezzo* (where the orchestra momentarily steps into the limelight) could hardly be given with a more idiomatic, brooding melancholy, a perfect introduction for all that is to follow. If you want playing which captures Rachmaninov's always elusive, opalescent centre then Ashkenazy is hard to beat. (The Second Concerto, our first choice in this work, is available on a single disc and is reviewed below.)

Piano Concertos Nos. 1 and 4. Paganini Rhapsody.
Zoltán Kocsis *pf*
San Francisco Symphony Orchestra / Edo de Waart.
Philips Solo 446 582-2PM (72 minutes: DDD). Recorded 1982.　　Ⓜ

Piano Concertos Nos. 2 and 3. Vocalise (arr. Kocsis).
Zoltán Kocsis *pf*
San Francisco Symphony Orchestra / Edo de Waart.
Philips Solo 446 199-2PM (75 minutes: DDD). Recorded 1978-84.　　Ⓜ

Few if any readings of the piano concertos and the *Paganini* Rhapsody spark or scintillate with such daredevilry, are of such unapologetic virtuoso voltage, as these. True, Kocsis can sometimes be more voluble than poised, breezing through the Third Concerto's haunting opening theme at the fastest flowing tempo and – for lovers of the ever-romantic Variation No. 18 from the *Paganini* Rhapsody, in particular – sometimes sacrificing heart's-ease for high-octane bravura. Again, you may question his near *allegretto* spin through the Second Concerto's central *Adagio*, eagerly glimpsing so many dazzling athletic opportunities ahead. Even so, try him in the Third Concerto's cadenza (the slimmer and better of the two) and you will hear it topped and tailed with a ferocious and almost palpable aplomb. Listen to him snapping off phrase ends in the intricate reel of the *Paganini* Rhapsody's Variation No. 15 or flashing fire in the *Allegro leggiero* from the First Concerto's finale and you may well wonder when you last encountered such fearless brilliance, pace and relish. Even those attuned to the darker, more introspective Rachmaninov of Ashkenazy will surely pause to wonder. Edo de Waart and the San Francisco Symphony Orchestra are no match for the LSO for Previn; yet, overall, this is the most propulsive and exciting set of the complete concertos. Kocsis's whirlwind tempos even allow him time for an encore – his own ardent elaboration of the *Vocalise*, a performance sufficiently ecstatic to set even the least susceptible heart a-flutter.

Piano Concerto No. 1[a]. Paganini Rhapsody[b].
Vladimir Ashkenazy *pf*
[a]**Concertgebouw Orchestra**; [b]**Philharmonia Orchestra / Bernard Haitink.**
Decca 417 613-2DH (52 minutes: DDD).   Ⓕ

Showpiece that it is, with its lush romantic harmonies and contrasting vigorous panache, the First Concerto has much to commend it in purely musical terms and although its debts are clear enough (most notably perhaps to Rimsky-Korsakov), it stands on its own two feet as far as invention, overall design and musical construction are concerned. The *Paganini* Rhapsody is one of the composer's finest works and arguably the most purely inventive set of variations to be based on Paganini's catchy tune ever written. The wealth of musical invention it suggested to Rachmaninov is truly bewildering and his control over what can in lesser hands become a rather laboured formal scheme is masterly indeed. Ashkenazy gives superb performances of both works and the Concertgebouw and the Philharmonia are in every way the perfect foils under Bernard Haitink's sympathetic direction. There is weight, delicacy, colour, energy and repose in equal measure here and it is all conveyed by a full-bodied and detailed recording.

Piano Concerto No. 2. Paganini Rhapsody.
Vladimir Ashkenazy *pf*
London Symphony Orchestra / André Previn.
Decca Ovation 417 702-2DM (58 minutes: ADD). Recorded 1970-72.   Ⓜ 🅁🅁

What emerges most obviously here is the keen poetic individuality of Ashkenazy as a Rachmaninov interpreter. The composer himself is far rougher with his music than Ashkenazy ever is. Those who like Rachmaninov concertos to sound forceful above all will no doubt have reservations, but rarely has this work sounded so magically poetic. That is not just Ashkenazy's doing – his rubato is consistently natural – but the work of Previn and his players. The delicacy of the LSO playing, in the feathery lightness of so many string passages, in Previn's mastery at keeping expressive players in precise ensemble together, is a constant delight. Indeed, if one compares this version with Ashkenazy's earlier one with Kondrashin and the Moscow Philharmonic (also available on a mid-price Decca CD), the main differences lie not with the soloist so much as with the accompaniment, this time altogether more refined and where necessary richer. Previn lets the music do more work on its own. The pointing of phrase, rhythm and dynamic is generally subtle and the bravura passages for orchestra are sharply defined and dramatic. Orchestral detail emerges more clearly than on other recordings, but thanks to finely balanced orchestral recording (no exaggeration of big violin tone) there are no gimmicks. The flute and clarinet *staccatos* for example after fig. 39 in the finale are clear but unexaggerated, where too often engineers are tempted to bring those instruments unnaturally forward. The playing of both Ashkenazy and the LSO continually conveys the impression not of a warhorse but of a completely new work; even such a favourite passage as the return of the slow-movement main theme just before fig. 26 is pure and completely unhackneyed. But the performance which clinches the success of this delightful venture is that of the *Paganini Rhapsody*, magical from beginning to end in its concentrated sense of continuity, with the varying moods over the 24 variations leading inevitably from one to another. No great splurge of emotion on the great eighteenth variation, but a ripe sense of fulfilment, utterly tasteful. Although the final surprising quiet cadence could be pointed with more wit, the rest has so much delicacy that it is a marginal reservation. At the recording sessions Ashkenazy and Previn simply did two complete performances, and decided that no 'patching' was needed. The finished recording confirms that.

Rachmaninov Piano Concerto No..3[a].
Tchaikovsky Piano Concerto No. 1 in B flat minor, Op. 23[b].
Martha Argerich *pf*
[a]**Berlin Radio Symphony Orchestra / Riccardo Chailly;**
[b]**Bavarian Radio Symphony Orchestra / Kyrill Kondrashin.**
Philips 446 673-2PH (73 minutes: DDD). Recorded live in [a]1982 and [b]1980.   Ⓕ Ⓔ 🅁🅁

To describe both performances as 'live' is to deal in understatement, for rarely in her entire and extraordinary career has Argerich sounded more exhaustingly restless and quixotic, her mind and fingers flashing with reflexes merely dreamt of by other less phenomenally endowed pianists. Yet her Rachmaninov is full of surprises, her opening *Allegro* almost convivial until she meets directions such as *più vivo* or *veloce*, where the tigress in her shows her claws and the music is made to seethe and boil at a white-hot temperature. The cadenza (the finer and more transparent of the two) rises to the sort of climax that will make all pianists' hearts beat faster and her first entry in the 'Intermezzo' interrupts the orchestra's musing with the impatience of a hurricane. But throughout these pages it is almost as if she is searching for music that will allow her virtuosity its fullest scope. In the finale she finds it, accelerating out of the second movement with a sky-rocketing propulsion. Here the music races like wildfire, with a truly death-defying turn of speed at 7'21" and an explosive energy throughout that must have left audience, conductor and orchestra feeling as if hit by some seismic shock-wave. The Tchaikovsky, too, finds Argerich at her most inflammatory. Those of a nervous disposition or, more precisely, those who like their Tchaikovsky to be more magisterial and composed will, of course, look elsewhere but who would miss volleys of octave spun off like single notes, or a second movement central *Prestissimo* dispatched at a scarcely credible tempo? A performance, then, for those who like life in the fast lane, though it has to be said that such incandescence is hardly flaunted, more a 'spontaneous overflow of powerful feelings' of emotion recollected not so much in tranquillity as in a cloud of fire and fury. The recordings, given the tricky circumstances, are remarkably successful.

Rachmaninov Piano Concerto No. 3.
Tchaikovsky Piano Concerto No. 1 in B flat minor, Op. 23.
Vladimir Horowitz *pf*
New York Philharmonic Symphony Orchestra / Sir John Barbirolli.
APR mono APR5519 (66 minutes: ADD). Recorded live in 1940-41. ⓅⒽ

This is the Rachmaninov Third to end all Rachmaninov Thirds, a performance of such super-human pianistic aplomb, pace and virtuosity that it makes all comparisons, save with Horowitz himself, a study in irrelevance. It was Horowitz's 1930 recording with Albert Coates that made Artur Rubinstein pale with envy; goodness knows how he would have reacted had he heard Horowitz and Barbirolli! Taken from a 1941 New York broadcast (with apologies from the producer for snaps, crackles, pops and the like) Horowitz's tumultuous, near-apocalyptic brilliance includes all his unique and tirelessly debated attributes; his swooning rubato, thundering bass and splintering treble, his explosive attack, his super-erotic inflexions and turns of phrase. Try the skittering *scherzando* variation just before the close of the central *Intermezzo* and note how the pianist's velocity eclipses even his legendary recording with Fritz Reiner. This ultimate wizard of the keyboard is in expansive mood in the Tchaikovsky. There are ample rewards, too, for those who rejoice in Horowitz at his most clamorous, for the thunder and lightning of this 'Tornado from the Steppes'. The performance ends in what can only be described as a scream of octaves and an outburst by an audience driven near to hysteria. Barbirolli and the New York Philharmonic Symphony Orchestra are equal to just about every twist and turn of their volatile soloist's argument and so these performances (and most notably the finale of the Rachmaninov) are, quite simply, beyond price.

Rachmaninov Piano Concerto No. 4.
Ravel Piano Concerto in G major.
Arturo Benedetti Michelangeli *pf*
Philharmonia Orchestra / Ettore Gracis.
EMI CDC7 49326-2 (47 minutes: ADD). Recorded 1957. ⓅⒽ

In crude and subjective terms Michelangeli makes the spine tingle in a way no others can approach. How does he do it? Of course this is the secret every pianist would love to know, and which no writer can ever pin down. But it is possible to give some general indications. It is not a question of technique, at least not directly, because Ashkenazy, for example (on Decca) can match their most virtuosic feats; indirectly, yes, it is relevant, in that there are dimensions in Michelangeli's pianism which allow musical conceptions to materialize which might not dawn on others. It is not a question of structure, in the narrow sense of the awareness of overall proportions, judicious shaping of paragraphs, continuity of thought; but the way structure is projected and the way it is transmuted into emotional drama; of course these things are critical. In one way or another most of the recordings in this section respond vividly to the excitement of Rachmaninov's dramatic climaxes; but with Michelangeli these climaxes seem to burst through the music of their own volition, as though an irresistible force of nature has been released. It is this crowning of a structure by release, rather than by extra pressure, which gives the performance a sense of exaltation and which more than anything else sets it on a different level. It enables him to be freer in many details (some of which may not be universally approved) and yet seem more inevitable as a whole. The impact of all this would be negligible without a sympathetically attuned conductor and orchestra. Fortunately that is exactly what Michelangeli has. Michelangeli's Ravel is open to criticism, partly because many listeners feel uncomfortable with his persistent left-before-right mannerism in the slow movement and with his unwarranted textual tinkerings (like changing the last note). But there is no doubt that he is as finely attuned to this aloof idiom as to its temperamental opposite in the Rachmaninov. And although the recording cannot entirely belie its vintage, it does justice to one of the finest concerto records ever made.

Symphonies – No. 1 in D minor, Op. 13; No. 2 in E minor, Op. 27; No. 3 in A minor, Op. 44. Symphonic Dances, Op. 45.

Symphonies Nos. 1-3. Symphonic Dances, Op. 45. The isle of the dead, Op. 29. Vocalise (arr. cpsr). Aleko – Intermezzo; Gipsy Girls' Dance.
London Symphony Orchestra / André Previn.
EMI CMS7 64530-2 (three discs: 227 minutes: ADD). Recorded 1974-76.   Ⓑ

Rachmaninov's three symphonies reflect three very different phases in his creative development: the first (1895) is a stormy synthesis of contemporary trends in Russian symphonic music, the Second (1906-07), an epic study in Tchaikovskian opulence, and the third (1935-36) a seemingly unstoppable stream of original ideas and impressions. The Second was the first to gain wide acceptance, and with good reason. It shares both the key and general mood of Tchaikovsky's Fifth. Cast in E minor, its initial gloom ultimately turns to triumph, and the symphony includes enough glorious melodies to keep Hollywood happy for decades. The First Symphony had a difficult birth, largely through the incompetent musical midwifery of Alexander Glazunov whose conducting of the work's première apparently left much to be desired. It is, however, an immensely promising piece and although undeniably the product of its times, prophetic not only of the mature Rachmaninov, but of other Northern voices, including – occasionally – the mature Sibelius. Both the Third Symphony and its near-contemporary, the *Symphonic Dances* find Rachmaninov indulging a fruitful stream of musical consciousness, recalling motives and ideas from earlier compositions, yet allowing gusts of fresh air to enliven and rejuvenate his style. Both works have yet to receive their full due in the concert hall, although the strongly evocative *Isle of the dead* is more securely embedded in the repertoire. What with these and a trio of warming shorter pieces, André Previn's mid-1970s LSO package makes for an excellent bargain. The performances are entirely sympathetic, avoiding familiar interpretative extremes such as slickness, bombast and emotional indulgence. Previn shows particular understanding of the Third Symphony, the *Symphonic Dances* and *The isle of the dead,* works that represent Rachmaninov at his most innovative and assured. The Second Symphony is played without cuts (not invariably the case, even today) and the recordings are generous in tone and revealing of detail, especially among the woodwinds.

Symphonies Nos. 1-3.
Concertgebouw Orchestra / Vladimir Ashkenazy.
Double Decca 448 116-2DF2 (two discs: 140 minutes: DDD). Recorded 1980-82.   Ⓜ

Ashkenazy has made few more distinguished discs as conductor than his Rachmaninov symphony recordings of the early 1980s. They are to that decade what Ormandy's were to the 1960s or Previn's to the 1970s and their appearance in this two-disc format has the obvious attraction of economy. The downside of the repackaging is that you have to put up with a change of disc half-way through the Second Symphony and lose the shorter orchestral works included in the Previn set. Previn is the most natural but not always the most electrifying of Rachmaninov interpreters and many will find Ashkenazy preferable, particularly in No. 1. Although some of Ashkenazy's speeds seem unnaturally pressed – he fairly tips us into the first movement reprise having declined to cap the climax with unvalidated bells – the excitement is infectious. Previn's LSO is not at its best in the *Larghetto* (placed third), but in the corresponding movement of the Second Symphony the boot is on the other foot. Not that Ashkenazy isn't convincing too – so long as you can forget the Previn. Ashkenazy's volatile approach is at its most extreme in the Third, the mood much less autumnal than it usually is (and perhaps should be), with the fruity Concertgebouw brass unconstrained. Such an unashamedly episodic rendering of the score has its drawbacks, but the virtuosic energy and romantic gush are hard to resist. Throughout the cycle, the players are unfailingly alert and the recordings sound very well indeed.

Symphony No. 2. The Rock, Op. 7.
Russian National Orchestra / Mikhail Pletnev.
DG 439 888-2GH (64 minutes: DDD). Recorded 1993.   ⒻⓈⒺⓇⓇ

Mikhail Pletnev's achievement is to make us hear the music afresh: a performance characterized by relatively discreet emotionalism, strong forward momentum and a fanatical preoccupation with clarity of articulation. When there is no Slavic wobble, it scarcely matters that his winds display an individuality which once or twice fails to transcend mere rawness – so much the better in this music! The strings, forceful and husky (with separated violin desks) are beyond reproach. The most remarkable playing comes in the finale. The lyrical effusions are superbly characterized without undermining the sense of inexorability, the climaxes not just powerful but affecting too. The closing pages bring a rush of adrenalin of the kind rarely experienced live, let alone in the studio. This is great music-making, the rubato always there when required, the long phrases immaculately tailored yet always sounding spontaneous. DG's unexpected coupling is *The Rock*, an early, rather bitty piece which is however very deftly scored and intriguingly Scriabinesque in places. In Pletnev's hands, the central climax is surprisingly powerful, with just a hint of the buzz-saw in the brass playing. The fabulous delicacy elsewhere is alone worth the price of admission.

Symphony No. 3. Symphonic Dances.
St Petersburg Philharmonic Orchestra / Mariss Jansons.
EMI CDC7 54877-2 (72 minutes: DDD). Recorded 1992. Ⓕ 🅴 🆁🆁

This is one of the more distinguished Rachmaninov issues of recent years. While no Rachmaninov Third unfolds as inexorably as Previn's (reviewed above), it is refreshing to hear the opening 'motto' theme played perfectly in tune by an orchestra on even more dazzling form than the LSO, and Jansons unearths such exquisite details of sonority and texture that criticism is all but silenced. There have been more haunting, more fundamentally pessimistic accounts, but none with such an ear for Rachmaninov's sometimes risky orchestral effects. The *Symphonic Dances* are even more impressive. The insinuating waltz movement is irresistible, very free with idiomatic-sounding rubato, while the dynamic outer portions of the finale are superbly articulated, dazzling in the closing stages. EMI's close-miking of instrumental lines may inhibit the sort of tonal blend implied by Rachmaninov's scoring, but the distinctive heft and huskiness of Mravinsky's string section is not betrayed. In its lush, extrovert way, this disc is unbeatable.

Symphony No. 3. Morceaux de fantaisie, Op. 3 – No. 3, Mélodie in E major; No. 4, Polichinelle in F sharp minor (both orch. anon.).
National Symphony Orchestra of Ireland / Alexander Anissimov.
Naxos 8 550808 (52 minutes: DDD). Recorded 1996. Ⓢ

Can Anissimov hope to compete in a field that includes Ashkenazy's high-octane digital accounts in sundry bargain formats, not least a Double Decca two-pack offering all three symphonies? Perhaps surprisingly the answer turns out to be yes, for the conductor produces a highly distinctive performance of the Third, inspiring his orchestra to playing of considerable warmth and flair. Sound quality is excellent too. String tone is crucially important with this composer, and here again any worries prove unfounded. Not for Anissimov the 'neurotic' Russian-ness of Ashkenazy's Rachmaninov. Like Jansons, he disregards the first-movement exposition repeat, but he makes the orchestral voices speak with an altogether gentler tone. There are shattering climaxes when the music calls for them, and the symphony ends in rousing style; elsewhere the sophisticated languor and careful phrasing recall André Previn's famous recording. Although some will be disappointed with the generally slow tempos (relaxed even further for those succulent second subjects), there is an unusual wholeness of musical vision and pacing which never sacrifices the needs of the larger structure to the lure of momentary thrills. The couplings are somewhat mysterious as no arranger is cited. Despite the short measure, this is thoroughly recommendable at the price.

Rachmaninov Symphonic Dances.
Janáček Taras Bulba.
North German Radio Symphony Orchestra / Sir John Eliot Gardiner.
DG 445 838-2GH (56 minutes: DDD). Recorded live in 1993. Ⓕ

Rachmaninov's *Symphonic Dances* are played with great sharpness here, emphasizing the extraordinary originality of his last completed work and serving as a reminder that the original title was *Fantastic Dances*: this might be more suitable for a performance that, though not lacking in lyrical grace, sets some familiar characteristics in a novel, strange and even somewhat disquieting context. The waltz of the central movement (once to have been called 'Twilight') has a rhythmic fluency that suggests not so much elegance as a faintly uncertain atmosphere; and there are shadows lying across the urgency of the finale. A fascinating score, intelligently and imaginatively read. *Taras Bulba* is also very well played. Here, the problems include unusual instrumental balance but, still more, getting the relationships between the many tempo changes into the right perspective. Gardiner is sensitive to these, without always following the instructions in the score to the letter. For the most part, his reading justifies this, though in the first movement, 'The Death of Andri', the move into the *Allegro vivo* is not done *accelerando* but abruptly, three bars early, which seems to go against the nature of the melodic phrases. But this is a small point, and for the rest the performance is admirably detailed and well judged; and in both works the orchestral playing is full of virtuosity and clarity.

Symphonic Dances. The bells, Op. 35.
Elizaveta Shumskaya *sop* **Mikhail Dovenman** *ten* **Alexei Bolshakov** *bar*
Russian Republican Chamber Choir; Moscow Philharmonic Orchestra / Kyrill Kondrashin.
Melodiya 74321 32046-2 (69 minutes: ADD). Recorded 1964. ⓜ

The *Symphonic Dances* receive a terrific, no-holds-barred performance. As you might expect, Kondrashin ignores the curious *Non allegro* tempo direction for the first movement and, unlike so many conductors, he is unfazed by Rachmaninov's unexpected reprise of the Orthodox chant, *Blagosloven esi, Gospodi*, towards the end of the last. Ploughing on with no loss of tension he finds additional adrenalin for the final bars. The concluding gong stroke, not taken literally as a dotted crotchet, is allowed to resonate a while. The transfers are not particularly distinguished. The picture is inclined to break up at climaxes, something odd has happened to the dynamic range and the tone is raw. Nevertheless, collectors will want this disc. Neither work was at all familiar in the 1960s – fashionable opinion having all but silenced *The bells* in the UK – so Kondrashin's LPs were an important step towards the rehabilitation of a major composer. The performance of the choral work may strike some listeners as unsophisticated – neither instrumentalists nor singers (certainly not the solo soprano) are as tonally ingratiating as we expect today – but the music-making is hugely exciting in the classic Kondrashin manner. It is sung in Russian, of course, and it is extraordinary how this, together with the very Russian solo voices, turns it into a completely Russian work. Even if the soprano and baritone have a pretty wide vibrato and even sometimes tend to scoop, their singing is extremely exciting. The chorus is excellent. In both works, Kondrashin offers maximum impact, minimum fuss.

Trios élégiaques – G minor; D minor, Op. 9.
Copenhagen Trio (Søren Elbaek *vn* Troels Svane Hermansen *vc* Morten Mogensen *pf*).
Kontrapunkt 32187 (65 minutes: DDD). Recorded 1994. ⓕ

The shade of Tchaikovsky haunts both these works. In the first, there are turns of phrase from his Trio, and much of the style and the textural approach to the problems derive from his example – not always a very good one, when it came to dealing with a virtuoso piano part against the weaker sound of the strings. Rachmaninov is ingenious, and handles his material expertly in a long, shapely movement. Tchaikovsky is more consciously the exemplar of the second Trio. Deeply impressed by the younger composer's *The Rock*, he had agreed to conduct the first performance in January 1894, a rare gesture of appreciation. On Tchaikovsky's death in October, the shocked Rachmaninov wrote his Trio 'in memory of a great artist', just as Tchaikovsky had once written a Trio in memory of another great artist, Nikolay Rubinstein. And here, too, there is a substantial variation movement, on a theme from *The Rock*. It is lyrically varied, not with conscious allusions after the manner of Tchaikovsky's elegy but with a sense of indebtedness that is unmistakable. Rachmaninov initially intended to have the opening statement of the theme played on the harmonium; he later revised the work, removing this appalling idea, and it is the second version which is recorded here, and well recorded in a fine performance that does full justice to a lengthy but affecting piece.

Variations on a Theme of Chopin, Op. 22. Variations on a Theme of Corelli, Op. 42. Mélodie in E major, Op. 3 No. 3. Piano Sonatas – No. 1 in D minor, Op. 28; No. 2 in B flat minor, Op. 36 (orig. version); No. 2 in B flat minor, Op. 36 (rev. version). Ten Preludes, Op. 23. 13 Preludes, Op. 32. Prelude in D minor. Prelude in F major. Morceaux de fantaisie, Op. 3. Morceau de fantaisie in G minor. Song without words in D minor. Pièce in D minor. Fughetta in F major. Moments musicaux, Op. 16. Fragments in A flat major. Oriental Sketch in B flat major. Three Nocturnes – No. 1 in F sharp minor; No. 2 in F major; No. 3 in C minor. Quatre Pièces – Romance in F sharp minor; Prélude in E flat minor; Mélodie in E major; Gavotte in D major. 17 Etudes-tableaux, Opp. 33 and 39. Transcriptions – **Rimsky-Korsakov** The Tale of Tsar Saltan – The Flight of the Bumble-bee. **Kreisler** Liebesleid. Liebesfreud. **Bizet** L'Arlésienne Suite No. 1 – Menuet. **Schubert** Die schöne Müllerin, D957 – Wohin? **Mussorgsky** Sorochinsky Fair – Gopak. **Bach** Solo Violin Partita No. 3 in E major, BWV1006 – Preludio, Gavotte, Gigue. **Rachmaninov** Daisies, Op. 38 No. 3. Lilacs, Op. 21 No. 5. Vocalise, Op. 34 No. 14 (arr. Kocsis). **Mendelssohn** A Midsummer Night's Dream, Op. 61 – Scherzo. **Behr** Lachtäubchen, Op. 303 (pubd. as Polka de VR). **Tchaikovsky** Cradle Song, Op. 16 No. 1.
Howard Shelley *pf*
Hyperion CDS44041/8 (eight discs: 449 minutes: DDD). Recorded 1978-91. ⓜ

This Hyperion set is a significant testament to Howard Shelley's artistry. Pianistically impeccable, he understands what Rachmaninov was about. The original piano works span some 45 years of the composer's life. The earliest pieces here, the *Nocturnes*, strangely owe allegiance neither to Field nor Chopin, but are very much in the mid-to-late nineteenth-century Russian salon style. The Third, in C minor, has nothing whatever to do with its title. Nicely written too, but still uncharacteristic, are four pieces from 1888, which amply demonstrate that from his early teens the composer had something individual to say. The *Mélodie* in E major (not to be confused with that from Op. 3) is memorable for its hypnotic use of piano tone. Hyperion's recording quality can be heard at its very best here; there is real bloom and colour. Written shortly after his First Piano Concerto in the early 1890s, the *Morceaux de fantaisie*, Op. 3 bring us to familiar Rachmaninov. The ubiquitous Prelude in C sharp minor is the second number but Shelley tries to do too much with it; he is more effective in the *Sérénade* with its Spanish overtones. In the E flat minor *Moment musical*, Op. 16 one feels that he is able to master Rachmaninov's swirling accompaniments idiomatically. In Variation No. 15 of the seldom-heard *Variations on a Theme of Chopin* (the theme is the Prelude in C minor from Op. 28) Shelley succeeds in bringing the notes to life, getting his fingers around the fleet *scherzando* writing.

The first set of Preludes is, of course, mainstream repertoire and, as such, easier to assess. In the warmly expressive D major Prelude he lends the piece a strong Brahmsian feel and it emerges as very well focused, especially since the voices are so subtly separated. He manages to transform the C minor into a restless mood picture. The First Sonata is conventionally dismissed as being unwieldy but Shelley gives it a symphonic stature and allows it to be seen in conjunction more with the composer's orchestral writing. Within a couple of years Rachmaninov was at the height of his powers and shortly after the Third Concerto he wrote the Op. 32 Preludes. Shelley conjures up an exquisite moonlit scene for the G major, but he is not as impressive in the B minor. However, with him it is always the music that dictates the course of the interpretation. In the two sets of *Etudes-tableaux* he excels as he does too in the Second Sonata. He draws together the disparate elements of the finale with terrific mastery and shows himself the equal of the 'Horowitz clones' in matters of technique. In the *Corelli* Variations he is not quite in tune with the scope of the work but is outstanding in the transcriptions, if a little straight-faced. The recorded sound is never less than serviceable and is sometimes excellent.

Rachmaninov Piano Sonata No. 1.
Scriabin Piano Sonatas – No. 1 in F minor, Op. 6; No. 4 in F sharp, Op. 30.
Sergio Fiorentino *pf*
APR APR5556 (72 minutes: DDD). Recorded 1995.　　　　　Ⓜ

Sergio Fiorentino's reading of Scriabin's Fourth Piano Sonata is more intense and focused than most recent recordings. The delineation between melody and accompaniment in the opening movement is brilliantly accomplished and the winged *Prestissimo volando* which follows is exhilarating and superbly controlled. The First Sonata is no less impressive. His reading has youthful impetuosity in the first movement coupled with a powerful, tragic undertone in the second and fourth, and there is an imperious authority in his interpretation. Rachmaninov's First Piano Sonata has immense authority too, especially in the opening movement which is given a forceful, yet finely controlled, reading. Fiorentino strides through its formidable demands with consummate ease, and in the *Lento* there is much to be admired in his *cantabile* and beautiful phrasing. A very rewarding disc from a pianist of tremendous stature. Recorded sound is good.

Piano Sonata No. 2 (original version). Preludes – Op. 23: No. 1 in F sharp minor; No. 7 in C minor; Op. 32: No. 2 in B flat minor; No. 6 in F minor; No. 9 in A major; No. 10 in B minor.
Etudes-tableaux – Op. 39: No. 2 in B minor; No. 7 in C minor; F minor, Op. 33 No. 1.
Morceaux de fantaisie, Op. 3 – No. 3 in E major, 'Mélodie'; No. 5 in B flat minor, 'Sérénade'.
Zoltán Kocsis *pf*
Philips 446 220-2PH (61 minutes: DDD). Recorded 1994.　　　　ⓅⒺ🆁🆁

This richly exploratory recital – far removed from a popular or commercial programme – contradicts at every turn stale, still prevailing notions concerning Rachmaninov. For not only is the Second Sonata played in its original 1913 version rather than the stitched-together 1931 revision, but the shorter items include many of the composer's finest works. The seventh rather than the first C minor *Etude-tableau*, Op. 39, for example, is an elegy of the most startling modernity with its *lamentoso* outcries, its memory of the Russian liturgy and its massive central carillon. How refreshing, too, to open with the Brahmsian syncopation and expressive richness of the A major Prelude, Op. 32 No. 9 and to mix mood and key to such kaleidoscopic and dazzling effect. Throughout, Kocsis's performances are as bold and stimulating as his choice of works, gloriously free-spirited and of an immense pianistic brio and command. Indeed his performance of the

Second Sonata is as fulminating and rhapsodic as any on record. Action-packed in an exhausting and enthralling way, his reading never sounds arch or contrived. Kocsis possesses a stupendous technique, stepping out in dazzling style in the ultra-Russian *Etude-tableau*, Op. 33 No. 1 and clarifying the Siberian whirlwind of the F minor Prelude, Op. 32 No. 6 with a breathtaking clarity and focus. Kocsis's accompanying essay is no less stimulating and astringent than his playing (he is unsparing over the 1931 revision of the Sonata) and he has been magnificently recorded.

---

24 Preludes, Opp. 23 and 32. Prelude in D minor. Morceaux de fantaisie, Op. 3. Lilacs. Daisies. Mélodie in E major. Oriental Sketch in B flat major. Moments musicaux, Op. 16.
Dmitri Alexeev *pf*
Virgin Classics VCD7 59289-2 (two discs: 138 minutes: DDD). Recorded 1987-89. Ⓕ

Alexeev's all-Russian mastery has seldom been heard to such advantage and his technical force and authority throughout are unarguable. True, he hardly wears his heart on his sleeve in the quixotic Minuet of Op. 23 No. 3, is less than poetically yielding in the Chopinesque tracery of Op. 23 No. 4. He does, however, capture the Slavonic malaise of No. 1 with rare insight and his punishing weight and rhetoric in Op. 23 Nos. 2 or 7 will make even the most sanguine listener's pulse beat faster. He unleashes the central build-up of Op. 32 No. 7 with the impact of a Siberian whirlwind and time and again his icy, determinedly unsentimental approach gives added strength and focus to the composer's brilliant fury. Alexeev is more convincing in the more vertiginous numbers from the *Moments musicaux*, in Nos. 2, 4 and 6 rather than in the opening rhythmic play of No. 1 where he sounds altogether too literal and austere. Yet you only have to hear his way of making even *Polichinelle*'s well-worn phrases come up as fresh as paint or his trenchancy in *Oriental Sketch* to realize that you are in the presence of a master pianist. The recordings are of demonstration quality and the accompanying essay mirrors the rare toughness and integrity of these performances; the essential nobility of Rachmaninov's genius.

Etudes-tableaux: Op. 33ᵃ – No. 5 in D minor; No. 6 in E flat minor; No. 9 in C sharp minor; Op. 39 – No. 1 in C minor; No. 2 in A minor; No. 3 in F sharp minor; No. 4 in B minor; No. 7 in C minor; No. 9 in D major. Preludes: Op. 23 – No. 1 in F sharp minor; No. 2 in B flat major; No. 4 in D major; No. 5 in G minor; No. 7 in C minor; No. 8 in A flat major; Op. 32 – No. 1 in C major; No. 2 in B flat minor; No. 6 in F minor; No. 7 in F major; No. 9 in A major; No. 10 in B minor; No.12 in G sharp minor.
Sviatoslav Richter *pf*
Olympia OCD337 (74 minutes: DDD/ADD). Items marked ᵃ recorded 1983, others 1971. Ⓕ

As in previous volumes in this valuable series, sound quality is on the dry side. But Richter's is the sort of playing which positively benefits from close analytical scrutiny, and serious collectors of piano recordings should need no further encouragement. Recorded in 1971 and 1983 they show a Richter in transition. Still in evidence is the prime-of-life virtuoso who burst on to the Western scene in the 1960s; but increasingly taking over is the uncompromising, ascetic philosopher-pianist of the 1980s. Metaphysics in Rachmaninov? Certainly. And not just the apparently superhuman fingerwork in the E flat minor *Etude-tableau* or the first C minor of Op. 39. What comes across is something beyond expression. It is an overriding fatalism, a sense of the immense sadness of Russia, broken only by moments of heroic resistance. The Preludes are more resonantly recorded, with a rather disappointing tubby bass. If you can live with that there is a quite unique Rachmaninov to be heard here – a brave, noble spirit, expressed in writing of an unquenchable fervour and orchestral solidity.

Etudes-tableaux, Opp. 33 and 39.
John Lill *pf*
Nimbus NI5439 (64 minutes: DDD). Recorded 1995. Ⓕ

The *Etudes-tableaux* are known to be musical evocations of various pictorial or perhaps narrative ideas, though quite rightly Rachmaninov did not let on where the stimuli came from; there is certainly no sign that John Lill is much preoccupied with such matters. He is a powerful keyboard technician, which is the first necessity in approaching these virtuoso studies, and this puts him in a strong position for dealing with the bold assertiveness of some of them, for instance the first piece of all. He also has a very vivid sense of tempo (balancing speed and texture sympathetically), and equally a sense for the slight lifting of pressure as well as slowing up, or the reverse, which is the essence of true romantic rubato. Where he can seem less responsive than some of his colleagues is with the more delicate pieces, whose fantasy he perhaps underrates. But if he also loses something in introspection, he can command admiration with his magisterial delivery. In sum, a very strong set of performances of some fascinating music.

Etudes-tableaux: Op. 33 – No. 2 in C major; No. 8 in G minor; Op. 39 – No. 3 in F sharp minor; No. 4 in B minor; No. 5 in E flat minor. Preludes: Op. 23 – No. 1 in F sharp minor; No. 3 in D minor; No. 5 in G minor; No. 7 in C minor; No. 10 in G flat major; Op. 32 – No. 6 in F minor; No. 8 in A minor; No. 10 in B minor; No. 12 in G sharp minor. Five Morceaux de fantaisie, Op. 3.
Nikolai Demidenko pf
Hyperion CDA66713 (70 minutes: DDD). Recorded 1994.   Ⓕ

Nikolai Demidenko's performances couple immense pianistic tact and skill, though the rushes of adrenalin, when they come (the searing central climax of the Op. 3 'Elégie' or the A minor Prelude, Op. 32 where a tiny motif is tempest-tossed seemingly in all directions at the same time) are almost palpable. The C major *Etude-tableau*, Op. 23 No. 2 rises and falls with supreme naturalness and impetus and the absence of all lushness or luxuriance in the G minor *Etude-tableau*, Op. 32 No. 8 is a pointed reminder of Rachmaninov's serious, religious inspiration. Demidenko creates a magnificent carillon of Moscow bells in the great B minor Prelude and his E flat minor *Etude-tableau*, Op. 39 is arrestingly sombre and dry-eyed, its conclusion articulated with a rare sense of ebbing drama, of all passion spent. If you prefer Rachmaninov's emotional storms viewed acutely but from a distance then Demidenko is your man. The recordings faithfully mirror this pianist's very distinctive sound world.

Rachmaninov The bells.
Prokofiev Alexander Nevsky, Op. 78.
Sheila Armstrong sop **Anna Reynolds** mez **Robert Tear** ten **John Shirley-Quirk** bar
London Symphony Chorus and Orchestra / André Previn.
EMI Studio CDM7 63114-2 (78 minutes: ADD). Recorded 1975 and 1971.   Ⓜ

This is an ideal coupling with first-rate soloists in both works. Sheila Armstrong is especially fine in *The bells* and Anna Reynolds provides genuine Slavonic intensity in her contribution to the Prokofiev. The chorals singing too, if without the special vocal timbre and enunciation of a Russian group, has undoubted fervour, while in the famous 'The Battle on the Ice' sequence in *Alexander Nevsky*, the orchestral playing has thrilling pungency and bite. The orginal analogue recordings, made in London's Kingsway Hall, were exceptionally well balanced and on LP the combination of ambient effect and sharpness of detail was ideally judged. Undoubtedly the remastering increases the clarity and projection of the sound with, perhaps, a slight loss of warmth and atmosphere. However, the overall effect is certainly vividly spectacular and compulsively dramatic. This disc is a very real bargain for the performances are both very fine indeed.

Vespers, Op. 37.
Olga Borodina mez **Vladimir Mostowoy** ten
St Petersburg Chamber Choir / Nikolai Korniev.
Philips 442 344-2PH (56 minutes: DDD). Texts and translations included. Recorded 1993.   Ⓕ

The St Petersburg Chamber Choir sing the *Vespers*, or *All-Night Vigil*, dramatically. Korniev follows the composer's markings carefully, but he is evidently concerned to give a concert performance of vivid immediacy, and there are places where this departs from the reflective or celebratory nature of music that is so strongly grounded in Orthodox tradition. This is most marked with Olga Borodina, who is not the first fine singer to bring too operatic a note to her solo in 'Blagoslovi, dushe moya' ('Bless the Lord, O my soul'); Vladimir Mostowoy is more discreet in 'Blagosloven esi' ('Blessed art Thou'). The choir itself is excellent, with particularly fine sopranos who can chant high above the others in beautifully pitched thirds; while there is, as ever in Russian church choirs, a splendid bass section that can underpin the textures with effortlessly rich low Cs, and find no difficulty with the famous descending scale down to a sonorous bottom B flat at the end of 'Nyne otpushchayeshi' (the *Nunc dimittis*). The recording is not always as clear as it could be with the textures and especially the words. A strength of the issue, which distinguishes it from almost all others available, is the booklet, which includes not only the full text in transliteration (with English, German and French translations), but also excellent essays.

12 Songs, Op. 21. 15 Songs, Op. 26. Were you hiccoughing?. Night.
Joan Rodgers sop **Maria Popescu** mez **Alexandre Naoumenko** ten **Sergei Leiferkus** bar
Howard Shelley pf
Chandos CHAN9451 (72 minutes: DDD). Texts and translations included. Recorded 1994-95.   Ⓕ

Two figures in particular haunt this second volume of Chandos's survey of Rachmaninov's songs – Feodor Chaliapin and Rachmaninov himself. They had become friends in the years when they worked together in an opera company and when Rachmaninov was concentrating on developing his piano virtuosity. As a result the Op. 21 songs are dominated by an almost operatic declamatory manner coupled with formidably difficult accompaniments. Leiferkus rises splendidly to the occasion, above all in 'Fate' (Op. 21 No. 1), and so throughout the songs does Howard Shelley. He is unbowed by the technical problems and he understands the novel proportions of songs in which the piano's participation has an unprecedented role. He also enjoys himself in the roisterous exchanges with Leiferkus in what is really Rachmaninov's only lighthearted song, *Were you hiccoughing?* The songs for the other voices are less powerful, in general more lyrical and intimate. Alexandre Naoumenko only has five songs, and they are not, on the whole, among the more striking examples, but he responds elegantly to 'The fountain' (Op. 26 No. 11). Maria Popescu gives a beautiful account of one of the most deservedly popular of them all, 'To the children' (Op. 26 No. 7), and of the remarkable Merezhkovsky setting, 'Christ is risen' (Op. 26 No. 6), no outburst of Orthodox jubilation but a grieving for the sorry state of the world into which a reborn Christ would now come. Joan Rodgers is enchanting in 'The Lilacs' (Op. 21 No. 5) and moving in the song acknowledging that love is slipping away, 'Again I am alone' (Op. 26 No. 9). She has complete mastery of the style, and nothing here is finer than her arching phrase ending 'How peaceful' (Op. 21 No. 7) – 'da ty, mechta moya' (and you, my dream) – with Shelley gently articulating Rachmaninov's reflective piano postlude from the world of Schumann.

Letter to K. S. Stanislavsky. 14 Songs, Op. 34. From the Gospel of St John. Six Songs, Op. 38. A prayer. All wish to sing.
Joan Rodgers *sop* **Maria Popescu** *mez* **Alexandre Naoumenko** *ten* **Sergei Leiferkus** *bar* **Howard Shelley** *pf*
Chandos CHAN9477 (68 minutes: DDD). Texts and translations included. Recorded 1994-95. Ⓕ

This set opens with a powerful dramatic outpouring. It is in fact a formal letter of apology, for unavoidable absence from a gathering, which Rachmaninov sent for Chaliapin to sing to Stanislavsky; and one of the most touchingly elegant phrases is simply the date on the letter, October 14th, 1908. Perhaps he was showing a rare touch of irony in using his full lyrical powers in such a context; but at any rate, the piece nicely prefaces the two collections of his last phase of song-writing, before he left Russia for exile. Some of his greatest songs are here, coloured in their invention by the four great singers whose hovering presence makes the disposition of this recital between four similar voices a highly successful idea. The Chaliapin songs go to Sergei Leiferkus, occasionally a little overshadowed by this mighty example (as in 'The raising of Lazarus', Op. 34 No. 6) but much more often his own man, responding to the subtly dramatic, sometimes even laconic melodic lines with great sympathy for how they interact with the words, as with the strange Afanasy Fet poem 'The peasant' (Op. 34 No. 11). Alexandre Naoumenko inherits the mantle of Leonid Sobinov, and though he sometimes resorts to a near-falsetto for soft high notes, he appears to have listened to that fine tenor's elegance of line and no less subtle feeling for poetry. Pushkin's 'The muse' (Op. 34 No. 1) is most tenderly sung, and there is a sensitive response to line with 'I remember this day'. Maria Popescu has only two songs, 'It cannot be' and 'Music' (Op. 34 Nos. 7 and 8), but she has a light tone and bright manner. Joan Rodgers is exquisite in the most rapturous and inward of the songs (the great Felia Litvinne was the original here). Of the Op. 38 set, Rachmaninov was particularly fond of 'The rat-catcher' (No. 4), and especially of 'Daisies' (No. 3), which she sings charmingly, but it is hard to understand why he did not add 'Sleep'. He might have done had he heard Rodgers's rapt performance with Howard Shelley, the music delicately balanced in the exact way he must have intended between voice and piano as if between sleep and waking.

Aleko.
Sergei Leiferkus *bar* Aleko; **Maria Gulegina** *sop* Zemfira; **Anatoly Kocherga** *bass* Old Gipsy; **Ilya Levinsky** *ten* Young Gipsy; **Anne Sofie von Otter** *mez* Old Gipsy Woman.

The Miserly Knight.
Anatoly Kocherga *bass* Servant; **Sergei Aleksashkin** *bass* Baron; **Sergei Larin** *ten* Albert; **Ian Caley** *ten* Jew; **Vladimir Chernov** *bar* Duke.

Francesca da Rimini.
Sergei Leiferkus *bar* Lanciotto Malatesta; **Maria Gulegina** *sop* Francesca; **Ilya Levinsky** *ten* Dante; **Sergei Aleksashkin** *bass* Virgil; **Sergei Larin** *ten* Paolo;
Gothenburg Opera Chorus and Orchestra / Neeme Järvi.
DG 453 452-2GH3 (three discs: 174 minutes: DDD). Notes, texts and translations included. Recorded 1996. Ⓕ

Rachmaninov's three one-act operas that survive give evidence of real dramatic talent. Who else has written so accomplished a graduation exercise as *Aleko*? Tchaikovsky was dazzled, no doubt also flattered, by some suggestions of imitation. It is a number opera, based on Pushkin's dramatic poem *The Gipsies*, warning that the urban sophisticate cannot recapture pristine wildness, and has at its centre a superb soliloquy of lost love. Leiferkus takes a lyrical approach; this is a beautiful, tragic performance, ironically set against Ilya Levinsky's carelessly superficial charm as the Young Gipsy. Zemfira is sung with fierce spirit by Maria Gulegina, especially in her cruel 'Old husband' song, and at the end with a lingering caress that seems to be for neither man but for Death itself. The other operas are different matters, both tinged with Bayreuth experiences that Rachmaninov had absorbed more thoroughly than is sometimes allowed. *The Miserly Knight* is one of the 'little tragedies' in which Pushkin presents a moral issue but does not offer a solution. Here, it is the contrast between the old knight, claiming that his devotion to gold has taken him beyond passion into a realm of serenity, and his son, who merely needs the ready. The long central soliloquy, perhaps Rachmaninov's finest piece of dramatic writing, is superbly delivered by Sergei Aleksashkin, with the wide range of his eloquence drawing sympathy to the miser. Sergei Larin portrays his son Albert as a selfish extrovert; and Ian Caley does what he can to make the Jewish moneylender more human than an unpleasant caricature.

Francesca da Rimini requires Rachmaninov to triumph over an inept libretto by Modest Tchaikovsky. This he does to a remarkable degree, using Modest's inability to produce a text for the chorus of the damned to good advantage with wordless wails, and filling out the sketchy love duet with some 50 bars of a sensuous orchestral kiss. However, he should have rejected the banal placing of the final line, about the lovers reading no more that day, in favour of its breathtaking place in Dante, when their poring over Lancelot and Guinevere reveals their own love to them. Ilya Levinsky brings a more intensely lyrical line and manner to this than in *Aleko*, and Maria Gulegina ranges from docility before Lanciotto (Leiferkus again a jealous husband) to rapture in the love duet. Neeme Järvi leads all three operas, as the orchestra should do for much of the time, and the beautiful playing he draws from the Gothenburg orchestra helps to make these three records a set extolling Rachmaninov's operatic talent. It is an excellent 'trilogy', excellently presented.

Jean-Philippe Rameau French 1683-1764

Ouvertures – Les fêtes de Polymnie; Les indes galantes; Zäis; Castor et Pollux; Naïs; Platée; Les fêtes d'Hébé; Zoroastre; Dardanus; Les paladins; Hippolyte et Aricie; Le temple de la gloire; Pygmalion; Les surprises de l'Amour; Les fêtes de l'Hymen et de l'Amour; Acante et Céphise.
Les Talens Lyriques / Christophe Rousset.
L'Oiseau-Lyre 455 293-2OH (70 minutes: DDD). Recorded 1996.
Gramophone Award Winner 1998. Ⓕ🅿🅴

Rameau was an orchestrator of rare and individual genius and his operas, ballets and smaller entertainments are generously provided with some of the most original and alluring dance music to emerge from the eighteenth century. Roughly speaking, the music on this disc was written between 1733, the date of Rameau's first opera *Hippolyte et Aricie*, and 1761, when he produced his *comédie-lyrique*, *Les Paladins*. Lovers of Rameau's music will be thoroughly familiar with most of the music played on the disc but will be delighted to find some rarities, too. The most remarkable of these is the overture to the *pastorale-héroïque*, *Acante et Céphise*. It was commissioned to celebrate the birth of the Duke of Burgundy in 1751. Adulatory prologues were out of fashion by the 1750s but instead Rameau attempted something entirely new – a portrayal in music of the good wishes of the nation, and the public rejoicing at the news of the Prince's birth. Rameau experimented with programmatic elements and vivid tone-painting elsewhere in his overtures, notably in those of *Platée* (1745), and *Zaïs* (1748). The overture to *Acante et Céphise* is different again, with its inclusion of specific 'occasional' references. Its three sections are marked 'Voeux de la Nation', 'Feu d'Artifice' (whose bass-line is punctuated by cannon-fire – thunderously captured in the recording) and 'Fanfare'. Les Talens Lyriques responds admirably to this music, relishing every bar of it in performances which are refined in ensemble and articulate in speech. Rousset has proved himself a fine exponent of this hugely rewarding repertoire.

Suites – Les fêtes d'Hébé; Acante et Céphise.
Orchestra of the Eighteenth Century / Frans Brüggen.
Glossa GCD921103 (67 minutes: DDD). Recorded live in 1996-97. Ⓕ🅿

Frans Brüggen's affection for Rameau's orchestral music is confirmed by the many previous issues of dances from his operas. Those are on the Philips label but, for this programme of suites from Rameau's *opéra-ballet*, *Les fêtes d'Hébé* and the *pastorale-héroïque*, *Acante et Céphise*, Brüggen has defected to the Spanish label, Glossa. In respect both of presentation and sound, this recently established label has, as they say, done him proud, for this is certainly the most satisfying issue so far in Brüggen's occasional series. While the music of *Les fêtes d'Hébé*, one of Rameau's most successful operas, is comparatively well known, that of *Acante et Céphise* is not. It is an unjustly neglected piece, making Brüggen's suite of the overture and 15 dances all the more welcome. The Orchestra of the Eighteenth Century responds atmospherically if not always unanimously to Brüggen's sensitive direction. He is a wonderfully rhythmic musician whose imagination is clearly and understandably fired by some of the most innovative and evocative orchestration to have emerged from the first half of the eighteenth century. *Acante et Céphise* was one of the earliest pieces in which Rameau introduced clarinets and these are at once heard to great effect in the brilliant overture, whose horn writing sometimes foreshadows Gluck. It is a splendid *pièce d'occasion* which many readers will find sufficient enticement to explore further. In summary, this is a captivating programme, marred only occasionally by restrictions imposed by live recordings.

Premier livre de pièces de clavecin. Pièces de clavecin en concerts. Nouvelles suites de pièces de clavecin. Les petits marteaux de M. Rameau. La Dauphine.
Christophe Rousset *hpds*
L'Oiseau-Lyre 425 886-2OH2 (two discs: 129 minutes: DDD). Recorded 1989.
Gramophone Award Winner 1992. Ⓕ Ⓟ

This recording of Rameau's solo harpsichord music outdistances most of the competition. Rousset does not include everything that Rameau wrote for the instrument but he does play all the music contained in the principal collections of 1706, 1724 and *c*1728 as well as *La Dauphine*. Rousset's phrasing is graceful and clearly articulated, the inflexions gently spoken and the rhythmic pulse all that one might wish for. Tempos are, for the most part, well judged and the playing admirably attentive to detail and delightfully animated. Only occasionally does Rousset perhaps just miss the mark with speeds that are uncomfortably brisk and lacking that choreographic poise which is such a vital ingredient in French baroque music. But at his strongest he is irresistible and this is how we find him in 'Les niais de Sologne' and its variations, the reflective 'L'entretien des Muses', the animated 'Les cyclopes', 'La poule', 'L'enharmonique' and the dazzling A minor Gavotte and variations. In these and in many other of the pieces, too, Rousset's impeccable taste and seemingly effortless virtuosity provide the listener with constant and intense delight. The quality of the recording is ideal as are the two instruments which Rousset has chosen to play.

Deus noster refugium. In convertendo. Quam dilecta.
Sophie Daneman, Noémi Rime *sops* **Paul Agnew** *ten* **Nicolas Rivenq** *bar*
Nicolas Cavallier *bass* **Les Arts Florissants / William Christie.**
Erato 4509-96967-2 (70 minutes: DDD). Texts and translations included. Recorded 1994.
Gramophone Award Winner 1995. Ⓕ Ⓟ

All three motets date from relatively early in Rameau's career, before he had really made a name for himself, yet all show to a certain extent some of the characteristics that 20 years or so later would so thrillingly illuminate his operas. *Deus noster refugium*, for instance, features impressive depictions of nature in turmoil that would not sound out of place in *Hippolyte et Aricie*, and all three begin with long, expressive solos not unlike the opening of an act from a *tragédie-lyrique*. *Quam dilecta* does sound a little more 'churchy' than the others, with its impressive, rather Handelian double fugue, but *In convertendo* – a work which Rameau heavily revised well into his operatic Indian summer in 1751 – absolutely reeks of the theatre. Drop anyone familiar with the composer's operas into the middle of this piece, and surely only its Latin text would give away that this is church music. It comes as no surprise to find Christie going to town on this dramatic element. The slightly dry acoustic of the Radio France studio is a help, as are the forceful, penetrating qualities of the solo and choral singers. But it is Christie's command of gesture, pacing and contrast which really gives these performances such an invigorating character.

Castor et Pollux.
Howard Crook *ten* Castor; **Jérôme Corréas** *bass* Pollux; **Agnès Mellon** *sop* Télaïre;
Véronique Gens *sop* Phebe; **René Schirrer** *bar* Mars, Jupiter; **Sandrine Piau** *sop* Venus,
Happy Spirit, Planet; **Mark Padmore** *ten* Love, High Priest; **Claire Brua** *sop* Minerve;
Sophie Daneman *sop* Follower of Hebe, Celestial Pleasure; **Adrian Brand** *ten* First Athlete;
Jean-Claude Sarragosse *bass* Second Athlete;
Les Arts Florissants / William Christie.
Harmonia Mundi HMC90 1435/7 (three discs: 173 minutes: DDD). Notes, text and translation included. Recorded 1992. Ⓕ Ⓟ

Castor et Pollux was Rameau's second *tragédie en musique*. Its first performance took place in October 1737 but the opera was greeted with only moderate enthusiasm. It was only with the composer's thoroughly revised version of 1754 that the opera enjoyed the popularity that it unquestionably deserved. The revision tautened a drama which had never been weak but it dispensed with a very beautiful Prologue. Christie and Les Arts Florissants perform Rameau's first version complete with its Prologue. The librettist, Pierre-Joseph Bernard, was one of the ablest writers with whom Rameau collaborated and his text for *Castor et Pollux* has been regarded by some as the best in the history of eighteenth-century French opera. Bernard focuses on the fraternal love of the 'heavenly twins' and specifically on the generosity with which Pollux renounces his immortality so that Castor may be restored to life. Christie's production was staged at Aix-en-Provence in the summer of 1991 and recorded by Harmonia Mundi a year later. This performance realizes the element of tragedy, above all in the First Act, and Christie's singers sound very much at home with French declamation. A very beautiful score, affectionately and perceptively interpreted that will afford deep and lasting pleasure.

Les fêtes d'Hébé.
Sophie Daneman *sop* Hébé, Une Naïde, Eglé; **Gaëlle Méchaly** *sop* L'amour;
Paul Agnew *ten* Momus, Le ruisseau, Lycurgue; **Sarah Connolly** *mez* Sapho, Iphise;
Jean-Paul Fouchécourt *ten* Thélème, L'oracle, Mercure; **Luc Coadou** *bass* Alcée;
Laurent Slaars *bar* Hymas; **Matthieu Lécroart** *bar* Le fleuve; **Maryseult Wieczorek** *mez*
Une Lacédémonienne, Une bergère; **Thierry Félix** *bar* Tirtée, Eurilas;
Les Arts Florissants / William Christie.
Erato 3984-21064-2 (two discs: 148 minutes: DDD). Notes, text and translation included.
Recorded 1997. *Gramophone* Award Winner 1998. Ⓕ **E**

Rameau produced one of his most engaging scores for *Les fêtes d'Hébé*. The entertainment comprises a prologue and three *entrées*. All is prefaced with a captivating two-movement Overture whose playful second section has much more in common with a Neapolitan *sinfonia* than a traditional opera overture in the French mould. The dances belong to one of the composer's fruitiest vintages and Christie has capitalized upon this with a sizeable band which includes, where appropriate, a section of musettes, pipes and drums. The singers are carefully chosen for their contrasting vocal timbres and the line-up, by and large, is strong. The leading roles in each of the opera's four sections are fairly evenly distributed between Sophie Daneman, Sarah Connolly, Jean-Paul Fouchécourt, Paul Agnew and Thierry Félix. The first three of this group are consistently engaging; their feeling for theatre, and their intuitive ability to seek out those aspects of Rameau's vocal writing which enliven it, seldom fail, and they bring considerable charm to their performances. Agnew, too, is on strong form though in the lower end of his vocal tessitura, required for the role of Momus in the Prologue, he sounds less secure than in his more accustomed *haute-contre* range. That can be heard to wonderful effect elsewhere and, above all, in a duet for a Stream and a Naiad (first *Entrée*) in which he is joined by Daneman. This beguiling little love-song is proclaimed with innocent fervour and tenderness. Félix has a rounded warmth and resonance and his occasional weakness of poorly focused tone has here been largely overcome. *Les fêtes d'Hébé* contains a wealth of inventive, instrumentally colourful and evocative dances. Small wonder that audiences loved it so much in the 1720s: with music of such vital originality, how could it be otherwise? Christie and Les Arts Florissants have possibly never been on crisper, more disciplined form than here, revelling in Rameau's beguiling pastoral images, tender and high-spirited in turn. A ravishing entertainment, from start to finish.

Hippolyte et Aricie.
Mark Padmore *ten* Hippolyte; **Anne-Maria Panzarella** *sop* Aricie; **Lorraine Hunt** *sop* Phèdre;
Laurent Naouri *bass* Thésée; **Eirian James** *mez* Diane; **Gaëlle Mechaly** *sop* L'Amour, Female
Sailor; **Nathan Berg** *bass* Jupiter, Pluton, Neptune; **Katalin Károlyi** *mez* Oenone; **Yann Beuron** *ten*
Arcas Mercure; **François Piolino** *ten* Tisiphone; **Christopher Josey** *ten* Fate I; **Matthieu Lécroart**
bar Fate II; **Bertrand Bontoux** *bass* Fate III; **Mireille Delunsch** *sop* High Priestess;
Patricia Petibon *sop* Priestess, Shepherdess; **Les Arts Florissants / William Christie.**
Erato 0630-15517-2 (three discs: 182 minutes: DDD). Notes, text and translation included.
Recorded 1996. *Gramophone* Award Winner 1997. Ⓕ **P**

William Christie adheres throughout to the 1733 original (Rameau revised the start of Act 2 in 1757), in so doing opening up some passages previously omitted. He uses an orchestra with a good string weight and it plays with security both of ensemble and intonation, and with splendidly crisp rhythms. Despite the opera's title, the main protagonists are Theseus and his queen Phaedra, whose guilty passion for his son Hippolytus precipitates the tragedy. Phaedra is strongly cast with a passionate Lorraine Hunt who is particularly impressive in the superb aria, 'Cruelle mère des amours', which begins Act 3. Throughout the opera, indeed, one is also struck alike by the profusion of invention, the unobtrusive contrapuntal skill, the charm and colour of the instrumentation and the freedom allotted to the orchestra. The work's final scene, for example, set in a woodland, is filled with a truly enchanting atmosphere, ending, after the customary chaconne, with 'Rossignols amoureux' (delightfully sung by Patricia Petibon). Anna-Maria Panzarella makes an appealingly youthful Aricia (to whom Rameau allocates surprisingly little on her own), and Mark Padmore is easily the best Hippolytus on record, making the most of his despairing Act 4 aria, 'Ah, faut-il, en ce jour, perdre tout ce que j'aime?'. Pains have been taken with the whole cast over the expressive delivery of words and over neatness of ornamentation; and production values such as the proper perspective for the entry of the crowd rejoicing at Theseus's return have been well considered. All told, this is one of William Christie's best achievements, an obvious labour of love for a masterpiece which, he confesses, has entranced him for 30 years.

Les Indes galantes – Prologue.
Claron McFadden *sop* Hébé; **Jérôme Corréas** *bar* Bellone; **Isabelle Poulenard** *sop* L'Amour.

Le Turc généreux.
Nicolas Rivenq *bass* Osman; **Miriam Ruggieri** *sop* Emilie; **Howard Crook** *ten* Valère.

Les Incas du Pérou.
Bernard Deletré *bass* Huascar; **Isabelle Poulenard** Phanie; **Jean-Paul Fouchécourt** *ten* Carlos.

Les fleurs.
Fouchécourt Tacmas; **Corréas** Ali; **Sandrine Piau** *sop* Zaïre; **Noémi Rime** *sop* Fatime.

Les sauvages.
Rivenq Adario; **Crook** Damon; **Deletré** Don Alvar; **McFadden** Zima;
Les Arts Florissants / William Christie.
Harmonia Mundi HMC90 1367/9 (three discs: 203 minutes: DDD). Notes, text and translation included.   Ⓕ Ⓟ

Les Indes galantes was Rameau's first *opéra-ballet*. He completed it in 1735 when it was performed at the Académie Royale in Paris. *Opéra-ballet* usually consisted of a prologue and anything between three and five *entrées* or acts. There was no continuously developing plot but instead various sections might be linked by a general theme, often hinted at in the title. Such is the case with *Les Indes galantes* whose linking theme derives from a contemporary taste for the exotic and the unknown. Following a prologue come four *entrées*, 'Le Turc généreux', 'Les Incas du Pérou', 'Les fleurs' and 'Les sauvages'. William Christie and Les Arts Florissants give a characteristically warm-blooded performance of one of Rameau's most approachable and endearing stage works. Christie's control of diverse forces – his orchestra consists of some 46 players – his dramatic pacing of the music, his recognition of Rameau's uniquely distinctive instrumental palette and his feeling for gesture and rhythm contribute towards making this a lively and satisfying performance. The choir is alert and well disciplined and the orchestra a worthy partner in respect of clear textures and technical finesse; this can be readily appreciated in the splendid, spaciously laid out and tautly constructed orchestral Chaconne which concludes the work. The booklet contains full texts in French, English and German and the music is recorded in a sympathetic acoustic.

Karol Rathaus   Polish 1895-1954

Symphony No. 1, Op. 5. Der letzte Pierrot.
Deutsches Symphony Orchestra, Berlin / Israel Yinon.
Decca Entartete Musik 455 315-2DH (77 minutes: DDD). Recorded 1996.   Ⓕ

Karol Rathaus was one of those indirect victims of Nazism that Decca's Entartete Musik series has been so indispensable in rediscovering. He was briefly very successful in pre-war Germany (an opera was premièred by Bruno Walter; Furtwängler and Horenstein also took him up). Seeing the way the wind was blowing he left Germany the year before Hitler came to power, wrote film music and a ballet in Paris and London but found few openings and fewer performances in America, where he eventually settled. The First Symphony (there are two others) was roundly abused at its première in 1926; this recording is its first performance since then, and the composer – not yet 60 – went to his early grave believing the score to be lost. It is a prodigiously inventive work, 40 minutes long though in only two movements, in a frowning, sinewy post-romantic style that might remind you just a little of the symphonies of Honegger or of the more austere pages of Martinů. The thematic language, though, is much closer to the Viennese tradition and its roots in Mahler, Reger and (Rathaus's teacher) Schreker are clearly perceptible. But it has an individual emotional vein, often grim, sombre or shadowed, rising at times to a bitter eloquence that is very striking; orchestrally, too, it is highly accomplished. According to an accompanying note Rathaus was frightened by the reaction to the work and by the anti-Semitism of some of his critics; it is hard not to hear some such prejudice in dismissals of the symphony as 'atonal'. It is no such thing, and although many of its melodies are angular and some of its dissonances harsh, it is by no means especially innovative for its period.

Even so, Rathaus apparently changed his style soon afterwards. Not radically, if his ballet *The last Pierrot* is anything to go by. Its melodies are sometimes smoother; no doubt association with dance added an element of grace to his manner, but the music is evidently by the same composer as the symphony. Jazz elements are introduced (and adroitly used to convey real menace at one point) and there is a violent forcefulness that aptly reflects the plot – this is a Pierrot in modern times, seeking his Columbine among factories and dance halls. It is effective and was for a while very popular. But it is the Symphony that whets one's appetite for more of this impressively gifted composer's music, especially in such eloquent performances as these. The Symphony is a tough piece to bring off – it had to wait five years for its première, because conductors were scared of it – but Israel Yinon has its full measure.

Einojuhani Rautavaara

Finnish 1928

Cantus arcticus, Op. 61 (Concerto for Birds and Orchestra) with taped birdsong. Piano Concerto No. 1, Op. 45[a]. Symphony No. 3, Op. 20.
[a]**Laura Mikkola** pf
Royal Scottish National Orchestra / Hannu Lintu.
Naxos 8 554147 (74 minutes: DDD). Recorded 1997. Ⓢ

No other new music stands to benefit more from extensive exposure, not so much because of its quality (which is beyond question), as because of an almost tangible connection with nature, than that by Rautavaara. One constantly senses the joy of a man alone with the elements: awe-struck, contented and inspired. Bird-song comes from all directions, quite literally in the case of the 'Concerto for birds and orchestra' or *Cantus arcticus*, that sets taped bird-song against a rustic though often peaceful orchestral backdrop. The piece ends with the reassuring cacophony of 'Swans Migrating', excellently recorded here. The young Finnish conductor, Hannu Lintu, directs a fine performance, though the flutes at the beginning of 'The Bog' (*Cantus*'s first movement) are rather overaccentuated. The bird-song tape blends well with the music and is very atmospheric. The First Piano Concerto and Third Symphony (out of seven) receive good performances, most notably the Brucknerian Symphony, an impressive and often dramatic work that begins and ends in the key of D minor. Rautavaara's orchestration incorporates four Wagner tubas, though some of the finest material is also the quietest. The slow movement is sullen but haunting, the *Scherzo* occasionally suggestive of Nielsen or Martinů and the finale brings the parallels with Bruckner fully within earshot. The First Piano Concerto has a brilliance and immediacy that should please both orchestral adventurers and piano *aficionados*. The solo writing employs clusters and much filigree fingerwork, but it is the noble, chorale-like second movement that leaves the strongest impression. Laura Mikkola gives a good performance. Naxos provides a full sound picture and viewed overall, this is an excellent CD, concisely annotated by the composer.

Flute Concerto, Op. 63, 'Dances with the Winds'[a]. Anadyomene. On the Last Frontier[b].
[a]**Patrick Gallois** fl
[b]**Finnish Philharmonic Choir; Helsinki Philharmonic Orchestra / Leif Segerstam.**
Ondine ODE921-2 (59 minutes: DDD). Recorded 1998. Ⓕ🅔

Anadyomene (1968) suggests a Turner canvas re-cast in sound. It opens restlessly among undulating pastels, the tone darkens further, there are brief comments from flute and bass clarinet, the brass prompts a swelling climax, then the mood gradually becomes more animated before we are ferried back from whence we came. It is 'a homage to Aphrodite, born of the sea foam, the goddess of love', and a very appealing one at that. The colourful Flute Concerto *Dances with the Winds* is a more extrovert piece with Nielsen as a fairly certain forebear. It shares its material between ordinary flute, bass flute, alto flute and piccolo. The action-packed opening movement withstands some fairly aggressive interjections from the brass, the brief second movement recalls the shrill sound world of fifes and drums; the elegiac *Andante moderato* offers plenty of jam for the alto flute, and the finale's striking mood-swings have just a hint of Bernsteinian exuberance about them. Rautavaara's prompt for *On the Last Frontier* (1997) was an early encounter with *The Narrative of Arthur Gordon Pym* by Edgar Allan Poe. He calls it 'a seafaring yarn in the typical boys' reading mould' and responds accordingly with a 24-minute slice of descriptive musical reportage, not of Poe's exact 'narrative', but of an imagined *Last Frontier* based on ideas from the story's closing section. It is an eventful, majestic, slow-burning tone-poem, nourished further by some distinctive instrumental solos and with telling use of a full-blown chorus. No texts are provided, and yet the aura of unexplored maritime depths and a sense of mystery associated with them carry their own wordless narrative. All three works are expertly performed and exceptionally well recorded.

Symphony No. 7, 'Angel of Light'. Annunciations.
Kari Jussila org **Helsinki Philharmonic Orchestra / Leif Segerstam.**
Ondine ODE869-2 (65 minutes: DDD). Recorded 1995. ⓕⓈⒺ

The Seventh Symphony's opening *Tranquillo* evokes a calm though powerful atmosphere, with many Sibelian points of reference – most especially in recognizable echoes of the *Largo* fourth movement from Sibelius's Fourth Symphony, whereas the closing *Pesante-cantabile* is more in line with the symphonic world of Alan Hovhaness. The Angel idea originates in a series that already includes a number of other works (*Angels and Visitations* and *Angel of Dusk*, for instance), the reference being (as the composer himself explains) to 'an archetype, one of mankind's oldest traditions and perennial companions'. This Jungian axis is reflected in monolithic chords, ethereal harmonic computations (invariably broad and high-reaching) and an unselfconscious mode of musical development. Readers schooled in the more contemplative works of Górecki, Pärt and Tavener will likely respond to this spatially generous essay, though Rautavaara's language is more a celebration of nature and her works than of any specific religious ritual. Comparisons with the *Annunciations* (for organ, brass quintet, wind orchestra and percussion) find the earlier work far harsher in tone, much more demanding technically (it calls for a formidable organ virtuoso) and more radical in its musical language. Here the style ranges from the primeval drone that opens the work through canon, 'bird forest' activity (a recurring strategy in Rautavaara's music) and the novel effect of having the 'notes of a dense chord weirdly circulating in the room' when the organ motor is switched off. Kari Jussila rises to the various challenges set for him with what sounds like genuine enthusiasm (his fast fingerwork is amazing) while Leif Segerstam and the Helsinki Philharmonic fully exploit the tonal drama of both works. The recordings are warm and spacious.

String Quartets Nos. 1 and 2. String Quintet, 'Unknown Heavens'.
Jan-Erik Gustafsson vc **Jean Sibelius Quartet**
(Yoshiko Arai-Kimanen, Jukka Pohjola vns Matti Hirvikangas va Seppo Kimanen vc).
Ondine ODE909-2 (62 minutes: DDD). Recorded 1997. ⓕ

Here we encounter not one Rautavaara, but three: the fledgling student captivated by folklore; the dodecaphonic zealot stretching the expressive potential of 'the system'; and lastly, the triumphant melodist basking in his own unique brand of harmonic complexity. The stylistic leap from Rautavaara's Second Quartet to his Quintet, or *Unknown Heavens* is more a matter of tone than temperament. All three works are ceaselessly active, the First (1952) being perhaps the leanest (certainly the shortest), and the last (1997) the richest in texture. *Unknown Heavens* takes its name from an earlier work for male chorus, which Rautavaara actually quotes, initially in the second bar of the first movement ('when the second violin answers the question opposed by the first,' as Rautavaara himself writes), many times thereafter, and then significantly revised ('in inverted intervals') at the start of the fourth movement. The third begins as a cello duet, sure justification of why – and how – five players are employed where the Kuhmo Music Festival originally commissioned a piece for four. 'The work seemed to acquire a will of its own,' writes Rautavaara and indeed, the Quintet bears witness to a warming stream of consciousness. The equally well-performed string quartets are stylistically rather more challenging. The First Quartet plays for just over 11 minutes and inhabits a mildly rustic world roughly akin to Kodály. Best here is the *Andante*'s haunting coda, whereas the 1958 Second Quartet is at its most inventive for the faster second and fourth movements. The current Rautavaara is more relaxed, more contemplative, more wise and softer-grained than his former self. He seems happier reflecting nature than organizing abstract patterns: you sense that the Quintet is authentically self-expressive, whereas the quartets speak interestingly about nothing in particular. The recordings are full-bodied and well balanced.

Vigilia.
Pia Freund sop **Lilli Paasikivi** mez **Topi Lehtipuu** ten **Petteri Salomaa** bar **Jyrki Korhonen** bass
Finnish Radio Chamber Choir / Tino Nuoranne.
Ondine ODE910-2 (64 minutes: DDD). Text and translation included. Recorded 1997. ⓕⒺ

Although grounded in the faith of the Finnish Orthodox Church, *Vigilia* somehow manages to excavate a spiritual path beyond the confines of denominational dogma. Rautavaara's delicious blend of ancient and modern modes is pointedly exemplified in the 'First Katisma', where soprano and contralto, then tenor and baritone, proclaim 'Blessed is the man that walketh not in the counsel of the ungodly'. There, the harmonic drift is decidedly 'post-renaissance', whereas the 'Alleluias' that follow update to 'post-romantic' and the subsequent assurance that 'the Lord knoweth the way of the righteous' brings us on line with the wistful, nature-loving Rautavaara of the Seventh Symphony and *Cantus arcticus*. The *a cappella Vigilia* was a joint commission from the Helsinki Festival and the Finnish Orthodox Church; the original Evening and Morning Services date from 1971 and 1972, respectively, with this concert version following on later. Possible influences include Bartók, Stravinsky and Messiaen, though early music is a more palpable prompt and Rautavaara himself is always the leading voice. Rautavaara's employment, or rather absorption, of ancient modes runs roughly parallel with Steve Reich's in works such as *Tehillim* and *Proverb*, though by contrast with Reich, harmonic colouring takes its lead from poetic imagery rather than from the sounds of specific words. *Vigilia* uses variation technique to impressive effect; it is a refreshingly open-hearted piece, one that – whether sombre or celebratory, traditional or innovative – grants ritual narrative a vibrant voice and should earn its composer wide-scale recognition. The performance is beautifully sung and the recording bold and realistic.

Maurice Ravel

French 1875-1937

Piano Concerto in G major[ab]. Piano Concerto for the Left Hand[ac]. Valses nobles et sentimentales (orch. cpsr)[b].
[a]Krystian Zimerman *pf*
[b]Cleveland Orchestra, [c]London Symphony Orchestra / Pierre Boulez.
DG 449 213-2GH (56 minutes: DDD). Recorded 1994.　　　　　　　Ⓕ**E** **RR**

Zimerman's pianism is self-recommending. His trills in the first movement of the G major Concerto are to die for, his passagework in the finale crystal-clear, never hectic, always stylish. For their part Boulez and the Clevelanders are immaculate and responsive; they relish Ravel's neon-lit artificiality and moments of deliberate gaudiness. That goes equally for the *Valses nobles*, which have just about every nuance you would want to be there, and none that you wouldn't. The recording is generous with ambience, to the point where some orchestral entries after big climaxes are blurred. Otherwise detail is razor-sharp and one of the biggest selling-points of the disc. Zimerman's humming may be a slight distraction for some listeners, especially in the Left-Hand Concerto, where you may not be always convinced that the LSO knew quite what it was supposed to do with the long notes of the main theme, and where there is a slight lack of tension in exchanges between piano and orchestra. There again, had the G major Concerto not been so wonderful those points might not have registered at all, for this certainly is playing of no mean distinction. In the Left-Hand Concerto, Zimerman's phenomenal pianism sets its own agenda and brings its own rich rewards.

Piano Concerto in G major. Piano Concerto for the Left Hand. Menuet antique. Une barque sur l'océan. Fanfare pour 'L'éventail de Jeanne'.
Pascal Rogé *pf*
Montreal Symphony Orchestra / Charles Dutoit.
Decca 410 230-2DH (57 minutes: DDD). Recorded 1982.　　　　　　　Ⓕ

Ma mère l'oye. Pavane pour une infante défunte. Le tombeau de Couperin. Valses nobles et sentimentales.
Montreal Symphony Orchestra / Charles Dutoit.
Decca 410 254-2DH (67 minutes: DDD). Recorded 1983. *Gramophone* Award Winner 1985.　Ⓕ**RR**

It is, of course, possible to build a satisfying Ravel library from different sources, but that would bring unavoidable duplication of repertoire. Yet collections like this are rarely consistent in quality. This is that rare case: not one of these recordings is seriously outclassed, either interpretatively or sonically. Dutoit and his Montreal orchestra are superb stylists; Ravel was just as much of a musical magpie as Stravinsky, with few historical, contemporary, or popular styles remaining exempt from a sophisticated Ravelian transformation (in some works they rub shoulders, for example, the *Valses nobles et sentimentales*). Dutoit ensures that the styles register, but without labouring the point – the result is always pure Ravel. There is also a consistent elegance, both of execution and expression, though Dutoit has a cunning (or sixth sense) in knowing when to let the players off the leash, and by how much (the G major Piano Concerto abounds in examples). A balletic stance goes hand in hand with rare departures from Ravel's suggestions of pace; for example, the virtuosity of his orchestra allows him to take the mercurial 'Prélude' to *Le tombeau de Couperin* at Ravel's marking, without loss of composure. One radical departure from the score is his slow tempo for the strings' melody as we enter the 'Jardin féerique' in *Ma mère l'oye*, but even the most fastidious Ravelian will surely succumb to the rapt beauty of the result. Ravel, the time traveller, from the childhood, fairy-tale world of *Ma mère l'oye* to *Le tombeau de Couperin*'s homage to the French baroque, also benefits from an acoustic setting where space can add an extra dimension, a depth for, say, the horn fanfares at the 'once upon a time' start of *Ma mère l'oye* or the last post resonances that the trumpet imparts in the Trio of *Le tombeau*'s Minuet. St Eustache in Montreal has just such an acoustic, where the perspective laid out by the different planes draws you in and envelops you. Unlike so many recordings made in churches these days, there's no blurring of detail, or ungainly weight in *fortissimos*; and microphone placement gives a discreet presence to all that glitters.

Le tombeau de Couperin. Pavane pour une infante défunte. Ma mère l'oye. Une barque sur l'océan. Alborada del gracioso.
Orchestra of the Opéra National de Lyon / Kent Nagano.
Erato 0630-14331-2 (69 minutes: DDD). Recorded 1994.   Ⓕ🅔

The fairytale wonders and crystalline textures of *Ma mère l'oye* rarely fail to bring out the best in performers and sound engineers. And Nagano joins the score's other master magicians of the past decade, namely, Dutoit, Rattle and Boulez. But no consideration would be complete without putting into the frame Monteux's 1964 recording (reviewed in the Collections section) – it takes but a few seconds to hear 'through' a moderate degree of tape hiss to a group of crack musicians gathered around the revered *maître* and producing sublime chamber music, with the most finely gauged seeking out and savouring of expressive colour, character and period *charme*. Nagano enjoys perhaps the most present and tactile recorded sound of all available versions (a distinctively 'hairy' contrabassoon in 'Beauty and the Beast'), with a fine bloom, if not quite the depth of the Dutoit or Boulez, or the comprehensive focus for detail of the Rattle. Interpretatively, Nagano shares most with Rattle, preferring a wide variety of tempo; not as slow as him in Beauty's 'Pavane', though one might complain that 'Tom Thumb' suggests more movement than Nagano's tempo allows (he turns it into a dreamy woodland interlude). 'Pagodaland', by contrast, is more lively than usual, with the opening piccolo solo nicely inflected.

Both the Boulez and Nagano discs offer *Une barque sur l'océan*, and Nagano's account is one of the most most gripping ever heard. It is a piece whose transcription tends to find more apology than advocacy among Ravel commentators, and is a less frequent inclusion among Ravel anthologies on disc. A pity, as its alternating gentle sunlit sway (and what enchantment lies in the dappled detailing) and the huge waves of sound that arise from it are a gift to conductors who fancy themselves as Poseidon for eight minutes. The 'Prelude' of *Le tombeau de Couperin* is reminiscent of water music (an enchanted babbling brook?). Here Nagano eschews Dutoit's gentle rapids (and the score's challengingly fast metronome mark), facilitating more precise articulation and lovely colouring (wonderfully liquid woodwinds, so well caught by the recording). And in the 'Forlane', precise accentuation and articulation give the main theme a real lift. Questions of balance in *Le tombeau* between baroque manners and romantic warmth tend to find different answers from different interpreters, and different expectations from listeners. And some may feel that Nagano's 'expressive' haltings in the central sections of the 'Forlane' and 'Rigaudon' are more affectation than affection. Still, it would be wrong to end with a complaint. This is a distinguished Ravel collection.

Boléro. Ma mère l'oye. Rapsodie espagnole. Une barque sur l'océan. Alborada del gracioso.
Berlin Philharmonic Orchestra / Pierre Boulez.
DG 439 859-2GH (76 minutes: DDD). Recorded 1993.   Ⓕ 🆁🆁

You would hardly recognize Boulez's Ravel here from its previous chilly, chiselled self. Those early 1970s collaborations with the Cleveland and New York orchestras on Sony Classical are superseded on all grounds, not least on account of their close, contrived balances. But most striking of all is the clear superiority of the Berlin Philharmonic Orchestra's playing; something that says more about Boulez's development as a podium technician than any relative deficiency in either of the American orchestras. If Boulez's earlier manner might have been likened to that of an investigative pathologist at a post-mortem, his 1990s role could be described as a layer on of hands (with the occasional hint of the micro-surgeon; no bad thing in Ravel). In *Ma mère l'oye*, he is among the master magicians: subtleties of nuance and timing (previously in short supply) now abound; here is playing of a wholly different order of grace and beauty, not the kind that lingers in passages in danger of becoming too exquisite to bear, nor the kind that parades the score's exoticism. A sense of drama and proportion are held in perfect equilibrium, with a moderate range of tempos for the set pieces, but slower tempos than before for the scene-setting 'Prélude' and linking interludes in order to realize their atmosphere and sheer sorcery. In the Spanish items, some may find the Berlin woodwinds too cultured in tone and artful in phrasing for their various improvisatory solos: it is rare (and initially unsettling) to hear the first few minutes' solos in *Boléro* quite as strongly contoured as this (they are, too, predictably *legato*; do these players ever draw breath?). You may find yourself craving a hint of abandon from the brass, particularly in the 'Féria' from the *Rapsodie*; and here and in the *Alborada*, as before, tempos remain slower than average (the

'Habanera' is utterly hypnotic), strikingly so in the 'Féria' which now, quite aptly, sounds as much like Chabrier as Ravel: festive as opposed to driven and explosive. The sound is both present and resonant in the right degrees. Boulez's Ravel was always provocative; it is now evocative.

Fanfare pour 'L'éventail de Jeanne'. Shéhérazade. Alborada del gracioso. Miroirs – La vallée des cloches (arr. Grainger). Ma mère l'oye. La valse.
Maria Ewing mez **City of Birmingham Symphony Orchestra / Sir Simon Rattle.**
EMI CDC7 54204-2 (75 minutes: DDD). Text and translation included. Recorded 1989.   Ⓕ

In the past there have been instances of Rattle's intensive preparation for setting down a much loved masterpiece precluding spontaneity in the end result. Not here. Along with the customary refinement and revelation of texture, there is a sense of Rattle gauging the very individual fantasy worlds of this varied programme with uncanny precision: an aptly childlike wonder for *Ma mère l'oye*'s fairy tale illustrations; the decadence and decay that drive *La valse* to its inevitable doom; and the sensual allure of the Orient in *Shéhérazade* providing a vibrant backdrop for soprano Maria Ewing's intimate confessions. The three shorter items that make up this indispensable (and generously filled) disc are equally successful, all recorded with stunning realism.

Rapsodie espagnole. Menuet antique. Ma mère l'oye. La valse.
Boston Symphony Orchestra / Bernard Haitink.
Philips 454 452-2PH (63 minutes: DDD). Recorded 1995.   Ⓕ

Alborada del gracioso. Le tombeau de Couperin. Valses nobles et sentimentales. Boléro.
Boston Symphony Orchestra / Bernard Haitink.
Philips 456 569-2PH (63 minutes: DDD). Recorded 1996.   Ⓕ

Haitink returns here, with the wisdom of experience, to Ravel pieces he recorded two-and-a-half decades ago (Haitink's 1970s Amsterdam Concertgebouw Ravel is still available, rather more of it than is offered here, at half the asking price, on a Philips Duo). Are there good reasons for preferring Haitink's newer recordings to the old? The answer has to be 'yes'. Haitink's regular Philips producer and balance engineer, Volker Straus, reproduces this in, by today's standards, quite a close balance, but one that captures enough of Boston Symphony Hall's very open acoustic. That said, there isn't quite the spatial dimension and ambient warmth of Haitink's previous Concertgebouw recordings (where one has to tolerate a degree of analogue tape hiss). Also, some listeners may be alarmed by the vivid presence for both Boston's principal flute – generously phrased playing requiring 'generous' intakes of breath – and the very high incidence of platform noise (sample track 10 of *Ma mère l'oye* from 4'32"). As to Haitink's own contribution, the differences are small, but taken as a whole, justify the venture. Here or there you will find a rubato more easefully achieved, or a passage pointed or shaded with more imagination or emotion (the accentuation of the woodwind at the start of the 'Danse de rouet' from *Ma mère l'oye* and the rapt string playing at the start of its 'Le jardin féerique'); and here or there, a marginally faster or slower tempo, mainly to the music's benefit. The newer *La valse* avoids most of the stretchings and slowings, except the marked ones, of the old, its sights more firmly set on the final climax. And the tempo is more successfully maintained in *Boléro* – definitely 'a class act' with a veiled, silky blend of muted trumpet and flute tone from 4'13" and wonderfully suave but streetwise solos from the saxophones and trombone.

In short, other interpreters might live a little more dangerously, might sometimes 'hear' the music in more interesting ways, might evoke more period charm. But for a modern collection, these discs deserve to be taken very seriously. Haitink's new-look Ravel is central. And it is Ravel of great conviction and composure.

Daphnis et Chloé. Rapsodie espagnole. Pavane pour une infante défunte.
Chorus of the Royal Opera House, Covent Garden;
London Symphony Orchestra / Pierre Monteux.
Decca The Classic Sound 448 603-2DCS (74 minutes: ADD). Recorded 1959-61.   Ⓜ H RR

Diaghilev's ballet *Daphnis et Chloé*, based on a pastoral romance by the ancient Greek poet Longus, was first produced in June 1912, with Nijinsky and Karsavina in the title roles and choreography by Mikhail Fokine. Pierre Monteux conducted the first performance, and 47 years later he recorded his peerless interpretation for Decca. Though the Second Suite from the ballet is familiar to concert-goers and makes an effective piece in its own right, the full score, with wordless chorus, conveys still greater atmosphere and magic. No work of more sheer sensual beauty exists in the entire orchestral repertoire, and Monteux was its perfect interpreter. He conducts with a wonderful sense of clarity and balance: every important detail tells, and there is refinement of expression, yet inner strength too. The LSO plays with superlative poetry and skill, and the chorus is magnificent in its tonal blend and colour. The *Rapsodie espagnole* and *Pavane* are also given ideal performances, and the recordings show off Decca's exceedingly high standards during the late 1950s and early 1960s.

Daphnis et Chloé. La valse.
Berlin Radio Chorus; Berlin Philharmonic Orchestra / Pierre Boulez.
DG 447 057-2GH (71minutes: DDD). Recorded 1993-94.   Ⓕ Ⓢ Ⓔ

Increasingly, for considering modern recordings of *Daphnis*, it seems you must banish memories of 1959 Monteux; put behind you the most playful, mobile, texturally diaphanous, rhythmically supple account of the score ever recorded; one that is uniquely informed by history and selfless conductorial wisdom. For some, Monteux's view may remain a rather moderate one – certainly in terms of basic tempo and basic dynamic range; and Ravel's score suggests tempos and dynamics which modern performances, and especially recordings, have more faithfully reproduced (not necessarily to its advantage). Boulez has, of course, acquired a vast wealth of experience of conductorial wisdom (not least in subtle accommodations of pace and general phrasing) since his first New York recording of *Daphnis*. And here he has the Berlin Philharmonic Orchestra – on top form – to sustain and shape melody within some of his strikingly slow tempos (such as the opening, and Part 3's famous 'Daybreak'), and who remain 'composed' in his daringly fast ones (the 'Dance of the young girls around Daphnis' and the 'Danse guerrière' – one of the most exciting on disc). Just occasionally, you feel that there are parts of the work that interest him less than others (Chloé's 'Danse suppliante', and the 'amours' of the 'Pantomime'). But anyone who doubts Boulez's ability to achieve, first, a sense of ecstasy should hear this 'Daybreak'; secondly, a refined radiance (rather than ripe refulgence), should try the first embrace (track 5, 2'49"; at this point, this is also one of the very few recordings where you can hear the chorus); or, thirdly, to characterize properly the supernatural, listen to the 'flickering' accents he gives the string *tremolo* chords in the 'Nocturne'.

The chorus work, not least in the so-called 'Interlude', is outstanding; the harmonic boldness of this passage was just as startling in New York, but the Berlin chorus, unlike the New York one, is here properly set back. Vowel sounds are varied; the dynamics are just as powerfully graded and the passage builds superbly to the 'Danse guerrière', with off-stage brass perfectly placed and timed. In general, DG's recording – a sumptuous Jesus-Christus Kirche production – strikes exactly the right compromise between clarity and spaciousness, much as Decca's did for Dutoit. With the added lure of an expansive and often massively powerful *La valse* (spectacular timpani), this is now the most recommendable modern *Daphnis* available.

Daphnis et Chloé.
New England Conservatory Choir; Boston Symphony Orchestra / Charles Munch.
RCA Victor Living Stereo 09026 61846-2 (54 minutes: ADD). Recorded 1955.   Ⓜ Ⓗ

This landmark *Daphnis*, made in stereo, sounds quite astonishing in this transfer. Robert Layton, writing in *Gramophone*, and comparing Monteux with Munch 'succumbed more readily to the heady intoxication, the dazzling richness of colour and virtuosity' of the Munch. Both Monteux and Munch understood the dangers of extremes and excessive lingering in this score; of sentiment turning into syrup and Ravel's 'Choreographic Symphony' (his own term) falling apart. It should be noted that, though their recordings balance Ravel's complex score more skilfully and imaginatively than most modern contenders, the score's huge range of dynamics could not be fully realized by the technology of the time.

String Quartet in F major[a]. Violin Sonata in G major[b]. Piano Trio in A minor[c].
[a]**Quartetto Italiano** (Paolo Borciani, Elisa Pegreffi *vns* Piero Farulli *va* Franco Rossi *vc*);
[b]**Arthur Grumiaux** *vn* [b]**István Hajdu** *pf*
[c]**Beaux Arts Trio** (Daniel Guilet *vn* Bernard Greenhouse *vc* Menahem Pressler *pf*).
Philips Solo 454 134-2PM (ADD).). Recorded [a]1968, [bc]1965.   Ⓜ ⦿⦿

The playing by the Quartetto Italiano in the String Quartet is superb. The first movement is very languorous and though there is not quite enough contrast in the *Scherzo* between the loud pizzicato at the start and the soft bowed music a few seconds later – it sounds more like *mf* than Ravel's *pp* and *ppp* – the movement goes well and the slow music in the middle is most sensitively managed. In the slow movement, the main tune on the viola (it comes 14 bars from the start) is covered by the second violin, and this happens later on as well whenever the tune recurs. Yet here again most of the movement is beautifully played. The balance of the recorded sound is splendid. (Incidentally, this same recording is also reviewed with the Debussy String Quartet – see the review under

Debussy). The Beaux Arts Trio is very much at home in Ravel. The account of the Trio is a fine one, sensitively paced and perceptive of the music's volatile ebb and flow, of its refined textures. The recording has the wide dynamic range this work needs and there is a good stereo balance between the three instruments, at least in the first three movements. The sombre dignity of the *Passacaille* is particularly moving, but one never tires of any part of this score. It is still one of the best performances of this work in the catalogue. Grumiaux is very communicative in the Violin Sonata, maintaining a beautifully long line in the first movement, although here he could have sometimes employed a little more of a sense of fantasy. Both he and Hajdu make a convincing job of this work's central Blues section. A most recommendable reissue.

Violin Sonatas – 1897; 1927. Tzigane. Pièce en forme de Habanera. Berceuse sur le nom de Gabriel Fauré. Sonata for Violin and Cello. Kaddisch (trans. Garban).
Chantal Juillet *vn* **Truls Mørk** *vc* **Pascal Rogé** *pf/pf luthéal*
Decca 448 612-2DH (78 minutes: DDD). Recorded 1995. *Gramophone* Award Winner 1997.　　Ⓕ

The piano luthéal, used at the Paris première of *Tzigane*, is an instrument modified to sound like a cimbalom. Its timbre isn't quite the same, but Pascal Rogé produces a wonderful range of sparkling metallic sounds, lending an exciting and exotic atmosphere to the performance. The violin playing in *Tzigane* is special too – Chantal Juillet's gipsy style is absolutely convincing, the opening solo passage delivered with brilliantly characterized rhythms and a fine sense of timing. If *Tzigane* is the most striking item on the disc, the other performances aren't far behind. The short pieces are especially enjoyable – the velvety tone Juillet produces for *Kaddisch*, the elegant variations of tone (from both players) in the *Pièce en forme de Habanera*, and the delicate textures and gentle phrasing of the *Berceuse*. In the two Violin Sonatas with piano the playing is fastidious and very well balanced. Rogé never dominates – in the loudest passages he produces a clear sound, with resonance carefully controlled. In the 'big' passages of the 1927 Sonata there's no attempt to rival the barnstorming excitement or the romantic warmth and urgency of some of the many other recommendable versions. Juillet's and Rogé's playing is cooler, but always expressive, with imaginative and beautiful variations of tone colour. Juillet and Mørk match each other excellently in the Sonata for Violin and Cello. Again, there's a wide range of sonorities, including some suitably grotesque sounds in the second movement, and infectious rhythmic *élan* in the finale. The recording is clear and bright.

Ravel Violin Sonatas – 1897; 1927.
Debussy Violin Sonata.
Pierné Violin Sonata, Op. 36.
Gérard Poulet *vn* **Noël Lee** *pf*
Arion ARN68228 (65 minutes: DDD). Recorded 1993.　　ⒻⒺ

The special significance of this performance of Debussy's Sonata – his last work – is that it was written for the violinist's father Gaston Poulet, who gave the première in 1917 with the composer at the piano; a second performance by the same artists in the same year was Debussy's last public appearance. Gérard Poulet is very impressive in this beautiful, mercurial and ultimately melancholy piece – which, he says, his father taught him 'in every detail'. This performance, therefore, is probably as close as we can get to the authentic preservation of the composer's intentions. His tone is warm yet delicate, and the lilt and fantasy of the sonata emerge strikingly, with an idiomatic flexibility of tempo and dynamics. The recording, too, is a good one, with just the right amount of atmosphere, although the piano could have been placed a bit more forwardly, not least because Lee is such a fine artist: Nadia Boulanger called him 'one of the finest musicians I have ever met'. Ravel's Violin Sonata of 1927 also gets a strong performance. Rightly, the playing style is quite different here, and the edgy lyricism of the first movement is perfectly caught, as is the bittersweet quality of the Blues and the barely suppressed hysteria of the *Perpetuum mobile*. As for Ravel's one-movement Sonata of 1897, which remained unplayed until 1975, this performance brings out its naïve charm, though it reveals little of the composer we know. Pierné's Sonata (1900) is a welcome addition to the current catalogue, passionate and brilliant and in every way rewarding. Altogether, an outstanding disc.

Gaspard de la nuit. Valses nobles et sentimentales. Jeux d'eau. Miroirs. Sonatine. Le tombeau de Couperin. Prélude. Menuet sur le nom de Haydn. A la manière de Borodine. Menuet antique. Pavane pour une infante défunte. A la manière de Chabrier. Ma mère l'oye[a].
Pascal Rogé, [a]**Denise-Françoise Rogé** *pfs*
Double Decca 440 836-2DF2 (two discs: 142 minutes: ADD). Recorded 1973-1994.　　Ⓜ

Everything is expressed with a classic restraint, elegance and economy, an ideal absence of artifice or idiosyncrasy. Rogé, exemplifying the finest French pianism, knows precisely where to allow asperity to relax into lyricism and vice versa, and time and again he finds that elusive, cool centre at the heart of Ravel's teeming and luxuriant vision. True, those used to more Lisztian but less authentic Ravel may occasionally find Rogé diffident or *laissez-faire*. But lovers of subtlety will invariably see him as illuminating and enchanting. How often do you hear *Ma mère l'oye* given without a trace of brittleness or archness, or find *Jeux d'eau* presented with such stylish ease and tonal radiance? Rogé may lack something of Thibaudet's menace and high-flying virtuosity in 'Scarbo' (also on Decca) but how memorably he re-creates Ravel's nocturnal mystery. Even if one misses a touch of cruelty behind Ondine's entreaty, few pianists can have evoked her watery realm with greater transparency. Arguably one of the finest Ravel recordings available.

Shéhérazade[bl]. Vocalise en forme de habanera[dj]. Chants populaires[abdef]. Sur l'herbe[ej]. Histoires naturelles[ej]. Cinq mélodies populaires grécques[bj]. Tripatos[bj]. Ballade de la reine morte d'aimer[bj]. Manteau de fleurs[bj]. Rêves[bj]. Don Quichotte à Dulcinée[fj]. Ronsard à son âme[fj]. Sainte[fj]. Les grands vents venus d'outre-mer[fj]. Un grand sommeil noir[fj]. Deux mélodies hébraïques[fj]. Trois poèmes de Stéphane Mallarmé[al]. Noël des jouets[al]. Deux épigrammes de Clément Marot[al]. Chansons madécasses[cgh]. Chanson du rouet[cj]. Si morne[cj].
[a]**Dame Felicity Lott**, [b]**Mady Mesplé**, [c]**Jessye Norman** *sops* [d]**Teresa Berganza** *mez*
[e]**Gabriel Bacquier** *bar* [f]**José van Dam** *bass*
[g]**Michel Debost** *fl* [h]**Renaud Fontanarosa** *vc* [j]**Dalton Baldwin** *pf*
[k]**Toulouse Capitole Orchestra**, [l]**Orchestre de Paris Chamber Ensemble / Michel Plasson.**
EMI Rouge et Noir CZS5 69299-2 (two discs: 136 minutes: DDD). French texts included. Ⓜ
Recorded *c*1982.

Despite the enormous popularity of Ravel's music, many of his songs remain comparatively little known and seldom recorded. This collection was the last in the series of editions of French song that Dalton Baldwin recorded for EMI. The first CD opens with Berganza's performance of *Shéhérazade*. Very accomplished, beautifully accompanied by Plasson and the Toulouse orchestra, it makes an interesting contrast to some of the versions done by sopranos. Berganza follows it with a splendid rendition of the *Vocalise en forme de habanera*, and the 'Chanson espagnole' from the *Chants populaires*. These last are divided among four singers – Gabriel Bacquier sings the 'Chanson française', José van Dam the Italian and Hebrew songs, while Dame Felicity Lott sings the least known, the Scottish (words by Burns). Bacquier and van Dam really steal the show on this set. This is the most enjoyable performance ever recorded of *Histoires naturelles*. The smile in Bacquier's voice, his exquisite diction and timing make this the highlight of the first CD. Mady Mesplé's performance of the five Greek songs are splendid, and the four songs that follow – *Tripatos* (another Greek-inspired setting), *Ballade de la reine morte d'aimer*, *Manteau de fleurs* and *Rêves* – are all rarities. The second CD has van Dam's celebrated performance of the three *Don Quichotte* songs. His version with piano is very characterful. Norman contributes the *Chansons madécasses*; she has so often included this cycle in her recital programmes that it is now closely associated with her voice and personality. Dame Felicity Lott's group includes the *Mallarmé* songs, the early *Clémont Marot* songs (very good) and the charming *Noël des jouets*, and then the 'Chanson écossaise' – the fifth popular song, reconstructed by Arbie Orenstein in the 1970s. This set is well worth acquiring for the sake of near completeness (it doesn't include *Fascination*, the slow waltz-song Ravel composed for Paulette Darty, much recorded in the days when it was attributed to the publisher Marchetti) and above all for the contributions from Gabriel Bacquier and José van Dam and, of course, Dalton Baldwin himself, sensitive, eloquent as always.

Alan Rawsthorne
British 1905-1971

Violin Concertos – No. 1; No. 2. Cortèges – fantasy overture.
Rebecca Hirsch *vn*
BBC Scottish Symphony Orchestra / Lionel Friend.
Naxos 8 554240 (64 minutes: DDD). Recorded 1996. Ⓢ

Rawsthorne enthusiasts should waste no time in snapping up this disc, containing as it does music-making of perceptive dedication and impressive polish. He completed his First Violin Concerto in 1947, dedicating the score to Walton (listen for the tongue-in-cheek quotation from *Belshazzar's Feast* just before the end). Cast in just two movements, it is a lyrically affecting creation that weaves quite a spell, especially in a performance as dignified and consistently purposeful as the present one. However, the revelation comes with the Second Concerto of 1956. Rebecca Hirsch and Lionel Friend locate a deceptive urgency and symphonic thrust in the opening *Allegretto* that genuinely compel. If anything, the succeeding *Poco lento* wears an even more anguished, nervy demeanour, the music's questing mood very well conveyed. By contrast, the finale (a theme and variations) proceeds in serene, almost carefree fashion, its witty coda forming a delightfully unbuttoned conclusion to a genuinely striking, much-underrated work. As a curtain-raiser, Naxos gives us the fantasy overture, *Cortèges*. Commissioned by the BBC and premièred at the 1945 Proms by the LSO under Basil Cameron, it is an approachable, well-wrought essay, pitting an eloquent *Adagio* processional ('wistfully expressive rather than tragic in tone', as annotator Sebastian Forbes astutely observes) against an irrepressible *Allegro molto vivace* tarantella (echoes here of Rawsthorne's own exuberant *Street Corner* Overture from the previous year). The composer develops his material with customary skill, and Friend draws a committed and alert response from the BBC Scottish SO (which seems to enjoy the experience hugely). Boasting a spacious, bright and admirably balanced sound picture (no attempt to spotlight the soloist), here is an enormously rewarding issue as well as a bargain of the first order.

Paul Reade

British 1943-1997

Far from the Madding Crowd.
Royal Ballet Sinfonia / Paul Murphy.
Black Box BBM1006 (75 minutes: DDD). Recorded 1997.   Ⓕ

Paul Reade's *Far from the Madding Crowd* is a successor to his other ballets, already available on CD. His *Hobson's Choice* was a big hit for Sadler's Wells Royal Ballet in 1989, and his *Cinderella* has also received extended CD coverage (both on ASV). The present Hardy setting is gently evocative of its rural setting, and is immediately accessible, with opulent orchestral effects, intensely romantic, consistently lyrical and richly tuneful. It even uses folk melodies, played by an on-stage 'folk-fiddler', that are taken from collections at Dorchester's county museum in Hardy's own hand. The documentation here is detailed, though this is a ballet that can stand on its own feet and should appeal readily enough to all lovers of light music. The sadness is that it proved Reade's last ballet score, since shortly after it opened he was diagnosed as suffering from lymphoma, from which he died in June 1997. It makes for undemanding but attractive listening.

Jean-Féry Rebel

French 1661-1747

Recueil de douze Sonates – La Flore; La Junon; La Venus; Le Tombeau de Monsieur de Lully; La Pallas; L'Immortelle; L'Apollon.
Ensemble Rebel (Jörg-Michael Schwarz, Karen-Marie Marmer *vns*
Gail Ann Schroeder *va da gamba* Pieter Dirksen *hpd/org*).
Deutsche Harmonia Mundi 05472 77382-2 (62 minutes: DDD). Recorded 1994-96.   ⒻⓅ

Lully's gifted pupil, Jean-Féry Rebel is chiefly remembered nowadays for *Les élémens*, his entertaining *symphonie de danse*, with its strikingly original representation of 'Chaos'. His collection of seven trios and five solos, though harmonically less bold than parts of *Les élémens*, are nevertheless innovative. Rebel's trios compare favourably with those of his contemporary, François Couperin. They are full of interest, revealing many extended passages of effective part-writing for the violins. Five of the trios have an evocative subtitle, inspired by the gods and goddesses of classical mythology, while a sixth, 'L'Immortelle', seems to embrace the entire concept. The last of the trios, though, strikes a more personal note inasmuch as it is a musical-poetic tribute, or *tombeau* to Lully. The piece, by far the most often played in modern times, introduces a deep note of pathos. These are stylish performances, full of spirit yet receptive to subtler, underlying expressive currents. Few readers will be disappointed either by the music or by the recorded sound, which is sympathetic and intimate.

Violin Sonatas – No. 1 in A major; No. 3 in A minor; No. 4 in E minor; No. 5 in D major; No. 6 in B minor; No. 7 in G minor; No. 8 in D minor; No. 9 in F major.
Andrew Manze *vn* **Jaap ter Linden** *va da gamba* **Richard Egarr** *hpd*
Harmonia Mundi HMU90 7221 (78 minutes: DDD). Recorded 1998.   ⒻⓅⒺ

This is Andrew Manze's first-ever foray into the French baroque repertory with eight of Rebel's 12 seldom-heard violin sonatas of 1713. Manze, never short of genius or fire in the Italian and Austrian repertory, here relaxes his sound, making gentle and subtle use of tempo and dynamics and only occasionally breaking out into impassioned lyricism. But that does not mean to say that he has simply plugged into the fashionable French baroque sound with its easy grace and polite twiddles; one can easily imagine these sonatas being played in just such a pretty manner, but Manze has instead looked deep into the music and extracted from it a great variety of expression, including in many places an unexpected darkness, a brooding restraint immediately apparent in the *Grave* movements with which some of these sonatas open, but seldom far away even in the apparently carefree musettes, rondeaux or allemandes. It brings to the music an unexpected emotional edge, even a touch of menace. It would be a mean spirit who could not admire the intelligence and imagination which is so lovingly brought to this neglected music. Combined with the sympathetic contributions of Richard Egarr and Jaap ter Linden, this is baroque chamber music-making of the highest order.

Max Reger
German 1873-1916

Eine Lustspielouvertüre, Op. 120. Symphonic Rhapsody, Op. 147. Suite in A minor, Op. 103a. Scherzino in C major.
Marie Luise Neunecker hn **Walter Forchert** vn
Bamberg Symphony Orchestra / Horst Stein.
Koch Schwann 31498-2 (60 minutes: DDD). Recorded 1994.   Ⓕ

The American violinist Florizel von Reuter concocted the so-called *Symphonic Rhapsody* for violin and orchestra from a mere 130 bars of Max Reger's manuscript. Reger had been preparing an *Andante and Rondo capriccioso* for violin and small orchestra at the time of his death, and von Reuter courted wide-scale controversy by working a modicum of material into a 25-minute epic that does not even approximate the form that Reger himself had in mind. Reger left precious few clues as to how he might have proceeded. Von Reuter's continuous structure falls into four distinct sections, with a perky little fugue at 16'22" and a fairly elaborate cadenza at 19'11". Fans of the expansive Violin Concerto (a work that even Reger himself had some misgivings about) will delight in this lyrical hybrid, a genuine meeting of like-minds though its principal composer would no doubt have produced something finer still. Walter Forchert gives an excellent performance, much as he does of the delightful A minor Suite, most of which was orchestrated from a violin-and-piano original by Adalbert Baranski. Here the tone is unashamedly Bachian, with a droning Trio to the 'Gavotte' and a most beautiful 'Aria' – the only movement that Reger himself refashioned – that takes its cue from Bach's Third Orchestral Suite. Horst Stein's programme opens and closes with winning examples of Reger in extrovert mode: the once-popular *Lustspiel* Overture, cast in sonata form and full of contrapuntal mischief, and the brief but fetching *Scherzino* in C major for horn and orchestra, composed in Weiden for the local music society. Stein's advocacy is all that one could wish for; the orchestral playing is quietly characterful and the recordings are exceptionally faithful.

Suite im alten Stil, Op. 93. Serenade in G major, Op. 95.
Bamberg Symphony Orchestra / Horst Stein.
Koch Schwann 315662 (66 minutes: DDD). Recorded 1993.   Ⓕ▣

There are few orchestral works composed during the last 100 years that have been more unfairly neglected than Reger's delightful Serenade, Op. 95. And what a beauty it is! The opening theme is unalloyed delight, while the first movement's expansive workings are eventful, affectionately discursive and formally well crafted. The second subject is one of Reger's loveliest melodies and the harp chimes that signal the melting return of the opening idea spell genuine magic. The contrapuntal finale is full of fun and the work ends – in thematic terms – from whence it began, in a mood of pastoral reverie. As to the orchestra, Reger employs winds, brass and timpani framed by two separate string groups, one playing with mutes (the one placed on the right-hand side of the stage), the other without, so that antiphonal interplay between them is underlined. Lovers of mainstream romantic repertory cannot fail to respond and Stein's performance is, viewed overall, the most polished we have had so far. The *Suite in the Olden Style* started life as a duo for violin and piano but the orchestral version dates from the very end of Reger's tragically short career. The rumbustious first movement opens in the manner of Bach's Third *Brandenburg Concerto*; the *Largo* hints at Bruckner and the fugal finale is built on a puckish theme that seems to wind on into infinity. Here, then, is an excellent CD to counter all those unfounded rumours about Reger's 'dry, dull, academic' composing style. If you love Bach, Brahms, Bruckner or Dvořák – then you have the potential to love at least Reger's Serenade virtually as much.

Four Symphonic Poems after Arnold Böcklin, Op. 128. Variations and Fugue on a Theme of J.A. Hiller, Op. 100.
Royal Concertgebouw Orchestra / Neeme Järvi.
Chandos CHAN8794 (67 minutes: DDD). Recorded 1989.   Ⓕ

Mention of Reger's name in 'informed' circles is likely to produce a conditioned reflex: 'Fugue!'. In his day he was the central figure of the 'Back to Bach' movement, but he was also a romantic who relished all the expressive potential of the enormous post-Wagnerian orchestra. Chandos, not surprisingly, exploits the open spaces of the Amsterdam Concertgebouw, forsaking some healthy transparency for an extra spatial dimension; a more sumptuous glow. With Järvi's instinct for pacing in late romantic music, and his great orchestra's evident delight in the copious riches of the discovery, for the *Hiller* Variations, this disc is very tempting. Anyone who warms to Vaughan Williams's *Tallis Fantasia* will immediately respond to the 'Hermit playing the violin', the first of the four *Böcklin* tone-poems; Debussy's 'Jeux de vagues' from *La mer* was obviously in Reger's mind for the second poem 'At play in the waves'; and the 'Isle of the dead' is Reger's no less doom- and gloom-laden response to the painting that so captured Rachmaninov's imagination. The final painting, 'Bacchanal', was described as a Munich beer festival in Roman costume – an entirely fitting description for Reger's setting of it!

Variations and Fugue on a Theme of Beethoven, Op. 86. Eine Ballettsuite in D major, Op. 130. Four Symphonic Poems after Arnold Böcklin, Op. 128.
Norrköping Symphony Orchestra / Leif Segerstam.
BIS CD601 (72 minutes: DDD). Recorded 1993.   Ⓕ

This disc is well programmed to show off the contrasting sides of orchestral Reger: firstly, the familiar champion of absolute music and the German tradition in the Variations; secondly, in *Eine Ballettsuite*, the unlikely purveyor of a relatively lightly scored *divertissement* of six dance or character portraits 'for musical epicures'; and finally, in the *Böcklin* Poems, one who succumbed to the lure of programme music and 'impressionist' colour and timbre. In both the first and third *Böcklin* Poems Segerstam is closer to Reger's metronome markings than the faster, more freewheeling Järvi. Segerstam is also, throughout the Poems, more acutely responsive to the extremes – and the minutest gradations in between – of both pace and dynamics. For the first and third poems (and parts of the second) this means that you are now aware just how much of this music dwells in the regions of *pianissimo* and beyond, and also how fine an impressionist Reger was. In the Poems, Järvi, it has to be said, has the advantage of a great orchestra, rather than a very good one, and a more accommodating acoustic. BIS gives Segerstam another of its textbook recordings, that is to say: an ears only, halfway back in an average size, modern concert-hall experience (levels are lower for the *Böcklin* Poems).

Piano Trios – B minor, Op. 2; E minor, Op. 102.
Gunter Teuffel *va* **Parnassus Trio** (Wolfgang Schröder *vn* Michael Gross *vc* Chia Chou *pf*).
Dabringhaus und Grimm MDG303 0751-2 (67 minutes: DDD).   Ⓕ

It was very wise to programme the masterly E minor Trio before its B minor predecessor. Unsuspecting listeners who jump straight in at Op. 2 will discover a pleasing if discursive piece, forged in the shadow of Brahms, with an opening *Allegro appassionato* which, although half the length of its disc-companion's first movement, actually seems twice as long. The *Scherzo* is frumpish, the closing *Adagio con variazioni* sombre and somewhat long-winded. And yet the use of viola in place of a cello has its attractions, and there are numerous telling glimpses of the mature Reger. The E minor Trio is something else again, a rugged masterpiece, with a finely structured opening *Allegro moderato, ma con passione* (the three stages of its argument are divided equally within a 15-minute framework), a mysterious *Allegretto* that opens in the manner of later Brahms then suddenly lets in the sunlight, and a noble, hymn-like *Largo* that recalls 'The Hermit with the Violin' from the *Böcklin* Portraits. Reger's Second Trio is full of audacious modulations and striking dramatic gestures; it *is* long (something in excess of 40 minutes), but never outstays its welcome. No one could reasonably ask for more than the Parnassus Trio offers, either in terms of drama or of interpretative subtlety. If you love Brahms and fancy diving in among a plethora of stimulating musical complexities, invest without delay. And if you love melody, then there's plenty of that, too.

Six Morceaux, Op. 24. Silhouetten, Op. 53. Blätter und Blüten, Op. 58.
Jean Martin *pf*
Naxos 8 550932 (79 minutes: DDD). Recorded 1994.   Ⓢ

A valuable treat for all inquisitive piano buffs and dedicated Regerians, even if some of the music is of variable quality. Least impressive, perhaps, are the *Six Morceaux*, Op. 24 (1898) – all of them fairly derivative, especially of Chopin (No. 2), Schubert (No. 4) and Brahms (No. 5). Whether they quite repay their taxing demands is open to some doubt, whereas the *Silhouetten* Op. 53 (1900) and *Blätter und Blüten* Op. 58 (1900-02) are quite another matter. Both sets are rich in playful modulations and lyrical ideas. Op. 53's opening 'Äusserst lebhaft' anticipates the mischievous Reger of the *Hiller* Variations; the Ninth recalls the Grieg of the *Lyric Pieces*, the Tenth, Reger's own *Ballettsuite* (of some 13 years later), and the Twelfth, Brahms's late *Intermezzos*. All could enrich any programme of late-romantic piano music, while the more aphoristic (and technically simpler) *Blätter und Blüten* are lighter in tone, their high-points being (at least on first acquaintance) a charming 'Frühlingslied' and a thoughtful pair of 'Romanzen', the second of which recalls Smetana's piano music at its finest. Seventy-nine minutes constitute a fair chunk out of anyone's leisure timetable but, with the present context, 44 of them (that is, Op. 53 and 58) could be very happily spent listening. And certainly Jean Martin plays well and is realistically recorded.

Six Preludes and Fugues, Op. 131a. Preludes and Fugues, Op. 117 – No. 1 in B minor; No. 2 in G minor; No. 3 in E minor; No. 5 in G major; No. 6 in D minor; No. 7 in A minor; No. 8 in E minor.
Mateja Marinkovič *vn*
ASV CDDCA876 (two discs: 82 minutes: DDD). Recorded 1993. ⓜ

Reger's knowledge of, and feeling for, the violin were all-embracing, and although his winding melodic lines can sometimes prove maddeningly discursive, there is much beauty in the writing – the A minor Prelude, or the E minor Prelude, Op. 131a providing particularly good sampling points. Bach is of course an overwhelming presence: quite apart from direct quotations there is the all-pervasive influence of the unaccompanied Sonatas and Partitas, especially with regard to Reger's fugues, which invariably start with a hint of Bachian *déjà-vu* before modulating way beyond the baroque's customary orbit. All 13 works here are surprisingly varied in theme and tone, although even the most enthusiastic listener is advised not to take in more than a few at a time. The prize-winning violinist Mateja Marinkovič is professor at both the Royal Academy of Music and the Guildhall School of Music, and his warm-centred, tonally true performances serve Reger handsomely. A major addition to the solo violin repertory on CD, and a must for all Regerians.

Drei geistliche Gesänge, Op. 110. Drei Gesänge, Op. 39.
Danish National Radio Choir / Stefan Parkman.
Chandos CHAN9298 (56 minutes: DDD). Texts and translations included. Recorded 1993-94. Ⓕ

Visions of myriad notes covering the page would frighten most choirs away, but these singers are made of sterner stuff. For them complex contrapuntal structures, devious chromatic harmonies and textures so thick you need a forage knife to get through them, hold no terrors. Rather they not only weave their way through Reger's characteristically tangled scores without a moment's doubt, but illuminate the paths so clearly one hardly notices the dense musical undergrowth all around. Parkman has a clear-sighted view of what is wanted and, aided by singers whose pure, perfectly blended tone is in itself a joy to hear, he follows his vision unfalteringly: everything falls neatly into place making real musical sense. The hefty Op. 110 Motets (ostensibly in five, but often diverging into as many as nine independent parts) can, and usually do, sound oppressively heavy, but here offer some of the most sublimely beautiful moments yet captured on CD. A triumph of skill over adversity.

Jacob Regnart

Dutch *c*1530/45-1599

Mariale.
Weser-Renaissance Bremen / Manfred Cordes *tbn/org*
CPO CPO999 507-2 (72 minutes: DDD). Texts and translations included. Recorded 1996. Ⓕ

Jacob Regnart held the post of vice-chapel master of the Imperial Court at Prague until his death in 1599. Lassus thought enough of his younger contemporary to recommend him for the post of chapel master to the Elector of Saxony (though both Lassus and Regnart himself declined the position). His best-regarded compositions are the *Mariale* of 1588, written during his service at Innsbruck under Archduke Ferdinand of Tyrol, brother of the Emperors Rudolph II and Matthias II. The list of titles shows it to be a conspectus of the most famous Marian texts. Fifteen of its 23 pieces are recorded here. They are strongly reminiscent of de Monte's music (unsurprisingly, since he was Regnart's superior at Prague). They offer a great variety of vocal scorings, and reflect several approaches and traditions (the *Stabat mater* refers obliquely to Josquin's setting in a few places, much as Lassus's does; and the *Regina caeli* quotes the plainsong episodically). In short, this is admirably well-made and accomplished music, making its point discreetly and inviting repeated listening. The same applies to the music-making of the Weser-Renaissance Bremen. Each motet is given a different scoring, and the mix between voices, high instruments (cornetts and trombones) and continuo is consistently sensitive. Both the singers and instrumentalists are secure enough as ensembles in their own right to go it alone; conversely, some motets include only one voice, which gives each soloist a chance to impress. Like the music itself the general approach is understated, but this has the effect of drawing listeners in rather than distancing them. Hopefully, the composer's relative obscurity will not prevent a very fine disc from getting the exposure it deserves. Specialists, collectors or the open-minded shouldn't hesitate.

Steve Reich

American 1936

Music for 18 Musicians.
Anonymous Ensemble / Steve Reich pf
ECM New Series 821 417-2 (57 minutes: ADD). Recorded 1978.   Ⓕ

Steve Reich's first recording of *Music for 18 Musicians* was a landmark release in the history of new music on record and confirmed what a towering masterpiece it is. The recording was actually produced by Rudolf Werner for DG, following the release of a three-LP set of *Drumming, Six Pianos* and *Music for Mallet Instruments, Voice and Organ*. Legend has it that Roland Kommerell, at that time head of German PolyGram, foresaw the commercial potential of Reich's piece but realized that DG was not the best vehicle to market the recording. Kommerell therefore offered the recording instead to Manfred Eicher of ECM, a company which had hitherto only released jazz and rock. The ECM release sold well over 100,000 copies, around ten times higher than might be expected of a new music disc. This episode changed the nature of ECM and signalled a new approach to marketing new music that has since been taken up by other companies. The 1978 recording still sounds beguilingly fresh. When Steve Reich and Musicians came to re-record *Music for 18 Musicians* for Nonesuch's ten-CD box set in 1996, their performance was amazingly 11 minutes longer than the ECM version. Normally, you would expect such a big difference to come from a slower tempo, but in fact the underlying pulse of both recordings is virtually identical. This is because of the unusual structure of *Music for 18 Musicians*, where the gradual fading-in and fading-out of different elements are not given a fixed number of repetitions but are played simply as long as it takes for this process to happen. In the 1996 version, these fade-ins and fade-outs are more finely graded and require more repetitions than in the 1978 version.

Proverb. Nagoya marimbas. City life.
Bob Becker, James Preiss *marimbas* **Theatre of Voices** (Andrea Fullington, Sonja Rasmussen, Allison Zelles *sops* Alan Bennett, Paul Elliott *tens*);
Steve Reich Ensemble / Paul Hillier; Bradley Lubman.
Nonesuch 7559-79430-2 (42 minutes: DDD). Recorded 1996.   Ⓕ Ⓔ

The Wittgenstein quotation ('How small a thought it takes to fill a whole life') serves as the basis of *Proverb* for three sopranos, two tenors, vibraphones and two electric organs, a composition that was premièred as a partial work 'in progress' at a 1995 Prom. The complete piece (it plays for some 14 minutes) holds together very well. Three sopranos 'sing the original melody of the text in canons that gradually augment, or get longer', whereas Perotin's influence can be heard in the tenor parts. Reich's skill at inverting, augmenting and generally transforming his material has rarely sounded with such immediacy. After a virtuosic, pleasantly up-beat *Nagoya marimbas* lasting four-and-a-half minutes comes *City life*, probably Reich's best piece since *Different Trains*. The sound-frame includes air brakes, pile drivers, car alarms, boat horns and police sirens, all of which are loaded into a pair of sampling keyboards and played alongside the instrumental parts (two each of flutes, oboes, clarinets and pianos, plus string quartet and bass).

The first movement opens with what sounds like a distant relation of Stravinsky's *Symphonies of Wind Instruments* then kicks into action on the back of a Manhattan street vendor shouting 'Check it out'. The second and fourth movements witness gradual acceleration – the second to a pile driver, the fourth to a heartbeat – and the third has the two sampling keyboards engaging in top-speed crossfire based on speech samples. The last and most dissonant movement utilizes material taped when the World Trade Centre was bombed in 1993. *City life* is a tightly crafted montage, formed like an arch (A-B-C-B-A), lean, clever, catchy and consistently gripping. In fact the whole disc (all 42 minutes of it) should thrill dyed-in-the-wool Reichians and preach convincingly to the as-yet unconverted. The sound is excellent.

Ottorino Respighi

Italian 1879-1936

Piano Concerto in A minor. Toccata. Fantasia slava.
Konstantin Scherbakov pf
Slovak Radio Symphony Orchestra / Howard Griffiths.
Naxos 8 553207 (51 minutes: DDD). Recorded 1994.   Ⓢ

Respighi Orchestral

All these pieces are otherwise available in decent performances, but at this price how could anyone with the slightest weakness for Respighi hesitate? Scherbakov and Griffiths do a good deal more than dutifully go through the motions, the soloist in particular playing with delicacy and affection, grateful for the (quite frequent) opportunities to demonstrate how well he would play Liszt or Rachmaninov, but in the *Toccata* he is interested as well in Respighi's more characteristic modal vein; as a Russian, he demonstrates that this too, like so much in Respighi, was influenced by the time he spent in Russia. Russian soloist, English conductor and Slovak orchestra all enjoy the moment in the *Fantasia slava* where Respighi presents a morsel of Smetana in the evident belief that it's a Russian folk-dance, but the Concerto and the *Fantasia*, both very early Respighi, are not patronized in the slightest. The central slow section of the Concerto, indeed, achieves something like nobility, and although there is a risk of the pianism in this work seeming overblown and rhetorical, Scherbakov's fondness for Respighi's more fleet-footed manner doesn't let this happen often. The *Toccata* is not so much an exercise in the neo-baroque, often though its dotted and florid figures promise it, more of an essay on how far one can be neo-baroque without giving up a post-Lisztian keyboard style and comfortable orchestral upholstery. But in a slow and florid central section, a rather melancholy aria that passes from the soloist to the oboe, to the strings and back again, there is a real quality of Bachian utterance translated not unrecognizably into a late romantic language (you may be momentarily reminded of Gerald Finzi). Scherbakov sounds touched by it, and obviously wants us to like it. Indeed these are likeable performances of music that needs that sort of help, but repays it. The recordings are more than serviceable, but each work is given only a single track.

Respighi Concerto gregoriano. Poema autunnale.
Saint-Saëns Violin Concerto No. 3 in B minor, Op. 61.
Pierre Amoyal *vn*
French National Orchestra / Charles Dutoit.
Decca 443 324-2DH (69 minutes: DDD). Recorded 1993.   Ⓕ

This is big, bold, romantic violin playing, just what both concertos need. The Respighi especially, perhaps: he had recently discovered Gregorian chant and modality, and the *Concerto gregoriano* was the first big work to exploit these. But Respighi was a violinist long before he discovered plainchant, and the noun of the work's title is at least as important as its adjective. Moreover in numerous of his compositions he shows himself well acquainted with Saint-Saëns, who also knew about chant and the modes, as the 'third subject' of his Third Concerto's finale demonstrates. The two concertos make a good coupling, in short, and an excellent demonstration that the manner appropriate to Saint-Saëns's work, conceived for a great virtuoso (Sarasate), pays dividends in the Respighi as well. The *Concerto gregoriano*'s problem is that its first two movements are both rhapsodic and relatively slow. However, in a performance as sumptuous as this, one finds strength and drama in what can seem dulcet meandering; and when the finale arrives and is given suitable vigour we seem to be hearing another of Respighi's Roman pictures, a jubilant and richly coloured one. The Saint-Saëns is just as good: Amoyal's tone is sweetly seductive in *legato* playing, opening out admirably to the more flamboyant gestures, never becoming hectic in the virtuoso passages. That 'third subject' in the finale is not played ethereally, as some violinists take it: Amoyal knows very well that its function is to return triumphantly in the brass (Saint-Saëns might well have subtitled it, as Respighi did his finale, 'Alleluia') and he plays it firmly and brightly. Both Amoyal and Dutoit seem to be enjoying Respighi's richly coloured, warmly elegiac *Poema autunnale*, discovering maybe that a work dutifully chosen as an appropriate filler is perhaps the best music here. The recording manages both to place Amoyal in a flatteringly forward perspective and to allow a satisfying fullness to orchestral tuttis.

Roman Trilogy – Pines of Rome; Fountains of Rome; Roman Festivals.

Roman Trilogy.
Orchestra dell'Accademia di Santa Cecilia / Daniele Gatti.
Conifer Classics 75605 51292-2 (66 minutes: DDD). Recorded 1996.   Ⓕ 🔲🔲

This was Daniele Gatti's début as an orchestral conductor and it is an auspicious one. Although Respighi's trilogy might not seem ideal repertory for the purpose, nor perhaps the Santa Cecilia the ideal orchestra, both orchestra and repertoire have in fact been rather shrewdly chosen. The recording documents the results of a five-year, obviously happy, relationship with the orchestra and it plays quite beautifully for him in music that they must know backwards – it gave the first performances of *Pines* and *Fountains* and the European première of *Festivals*. The reputation of these works as orchestral showpieces means that there are quite precise expectations of every performance, and Gatti fulfils these expectations admirably. But there are many signs that he has his own ideas about this music, and they are convincing as well as refreshing. 'The fountain of Valle Giulia at dawn', for example, is slower than usual, making for an attractively gentle pastoral. The breathless hush at the end of 'The Medici fountain at sunset' is very beautiful, too, and in the pitfall-ridden 'Pines of the Janiculum' pretty well everything is right: the appearance of the recorded nightingale magically timed and placed, against a softly warm string background (but with ardent solo playing), the rubato and phrasing finely judged, the piano and clarinet poetically evoking moonlight. At the other end of the dynamic spectrum there is a huge and satisfying *crescendo* to conclude 'Epiphany' (No. 4 of *Festivals*) and a magnificent blare of extra brass at the end of 'Pines of the Appian Way'. The recording is also first-class: realistically spacious and atmospheric, with a huge dynamic range.

Roman Trilogy.
Pittsburgh Symphony Orchestra / Lorin Maazel.
Sony Classical SK66843 (64 minutes: DDD). Recorded 1994-96.   Ⓕ

In ripely committed performances like Maazel's, there are few works to match Respighi's trilogy in showing off the glories of a modern orchestra in full cry. Maazel's is an exceptionally fine recording. The orchestral sound is perfectly natural and perfectly believable; the acoustic is both perceptible and credible; Respighi's textures are satisfyingly rich but always comprehensible; instruments are in the right perspective, and when a solo line is prominent there is no sense that it has been artificially spotlit or moved forward. Once you've got over the pleasurable relief of hearing such a sound again, you notice of course what a splendid orchestra this is: in *Pines* alone, what wonderfully velvety strings to evoke the shadows of the pines near a catacomb, what sensitive woodwind soloists as companions to the nightingale (poetically distant but beautifully clear) on the moonlit Janiculum! And then you enjoy not only the fine control of Maazel's big *crescendos* in the second and fourth movements, but the fact that you don't have to fiddle with the volume controls to appreciate both the quiet and the loud ends of those *crescendos*. Sony's booklet, artfully, is in monochrome; the sound is not only in full colour but in three-dimensional relief.

Roman Trilogy.
Royal Philharmonic Orchestra / Enrique Bátiz.
Naxos 8 550539 (61 minutes: DDD). Recorded 1991.   Ⓢ

This Naxos disc is an extraordinary bargain. It has such excitement and verve that one can accept an extra degree of brazen extroversion, indeed revel in it. In *Roman Festivals* the opening 'Circuses' is immensely spectacular, its character very much in the unfettered gladiatorial tradition of the Coliseum: the trumpets and drums are quite thrilling. The gossamer opening of 'The Jubilee' leads to the most dramatic climax. In the 'October Festival' the strings play their Latin soliloquy very exotically for Bátiz. The closing section brings a gentle mandolin serenade; with Marriner it is almost too distanced and hazy, as if in a dream, certainly effective enough. The great clamour of the Epiphany celebrations which follow unleashes a riotous *mêlée* from the RPO, which sounds as if it is enjoying itself hugely, and the obvious affinity with the final fairground scene of Petrushka is the more striking when the strings have that bit more bite. The *Pines* and *Fountains* are also very fine. When the unison horns signal the turning on of the Triton Fountain, and the cascade splashes through the orchestra, the RPO unleashes a real flood. Yet the lovely, radiant gentle evocation of the central movements of *The Pines*, and the sensuous Italian light of the sunset at the Villa Medici, are most sensitively realized by the RPO, and at the very beginning of the finale, 'The Pines of the Appian Way', the ever present sound, with its growling bass clarinet, gives a sinister implication of the advancing Roman might. This disc would be recommendable at full price; in the super-bargain area it is unbeatable.

Church Windows. Brazilian Impressions. Roman Festivals.
Cincinnati Symphony Orchestra / Jesús López-Cobos.
Telarc CD80356 (71 minutes: DDD). Recorded 1993.   Ⓕ🅴

One could easily argue that neither *Church Windows* nor *Brazilian Impressions* is quite as successful as the 'essential' Respighi of *Pines, Fountains* and *Festivals* (and that *Festivals* is the weakest of the Roman trilogy anyway). The only answer to that, López-Cobos seems to suggest, is to take the music perfectly seriously and pay scrupulous attention not just to its potential for sonorous spectacle but to its wealth of beautifully crafted detail. The gong at the end of the second movement of *Church Windows* is magnificently resonant, as is the organ in the finale, and the work is given an extra inch or two of stature by sensitive handling of those moments that need but don't always get delicacy. He pays such care to character and detail in 'Butantan', that creepy depiction of a snake-farm in *Brazilian Impressions*, that you can not only recapture the real, crawling horror that Respighi experienced there, but discover in the music also a queer sort of Debussian grace as well. And as for *Roman Festivals*, well, what's wrong with 20-odd minutes of wide-screen spectacular once in a while? But if every colour is precisely rendered, the quiet passages as affectionately turned as they are here, what skill there is to be found in it, what a gift for immaculately precise instrumental detail. With that sort of handling all three pieces sound quite worthy of sharing shelf space with *Pines* and *Fountains*. The recording is spectacular.

Gli uccelli. Antiche danze ed arie per liuto – Suites Nos. 1 and 3. Trittico botticelliano.
Orpheus Chamber Orchestra.
DG 437 533-2GH (69 minutes: DDD). Recorded 1991.   Ⓕ

This is astonishing playing. To do without a conductor when performing Respighi might seem an easier task than in an authentic masterpiece, but these suites require so much care over details of phrasing, colour, balance and articulation that not a few skilled conductors have failed to distil their freshness and charm unalloyed. But there are no conducted performances that excel these in their immaculate care over texture, delicacy of nuance and precision of tuning. Nor do they lack character, by any means: the orchestra's method of rehearsal, democracy tempered by the authority of a leader elected for each work, seems to have ensured a pretty well ideal balance between unanimity and soloistic individuality. If you add an infectious sense of enjoyment (the not quite respectable enjoyment of Respighi's hand-colouring of his monochrome originals) and solo playing of great refinement, it's hard to imagine better readings than these. Excellent recording.

Cinque canti all'antica. Sei liriche. Deità silvane. Ballata alla luna. Stornello. Stornellatrice. Contrasto. Tanto bella. Invito alla danza. L'ultima ebbrezza. Notturno. Luce.
Leonardo de Lisi *ten* **Reinild Mees** *pf*
Channel Classics CCS9396 (60 minutes: DDD). Texts and translations included. Recorded 1996.Ⓕ

Leonardo de Lisi is a lyric tenor of real quality with a Lieder singer's subtlety, taste and responsiveness to words. In fact by the colour of the voice you might not take him to be an Italian and his French diction is almost impeccable in the two settings by Respighi (among the *Sei liriche*) of French texts, the quite magical 'Le repos en Egypte' and the striking 'Noël ancien'. If you have not so far thought of Respighi as a song composer you are in for a surprise. Sopranos quite often programme his charming *Stornellatrice* as an encore but it has equals and indeed superiors here. *Tanto bella*, for example: ample grateful melody over a lilting accompaniment, with a haunting middle section. The *Canti all'antica* are fresh and very simple, sometimes rather like a Monteverdian *arioso*. But with the *Sei liriche* of 1912 we reach audible French influence as well as French texts and by 1917 and *Deità silvane* Respighi's smooth lines have become flexible and his idiomatic keyboard writing is now filled with vivid imagery. Reinild Mees is obviously as fond of *Deità silvane* as de Lisi is. Both are excellently recorded, the voice a little close but not disturbingly so.

Deità silvane[a]. Nebbie[b]. Aretusa[b]. La sensitiva[b].
[a]**Ingrid Attrot** *sop* [b]**Linda Finnie** *mez*
BBC Philharmonic Orchestra / Richard Hickox.
Chandos CHAN9453 (60 minutes: DDD). Texts and translations included. Recorded 1995.   Ⓕ

In some of Respighi's comparatively neglected pieces, his accustomed richness and subtlety of orchestral colour go with a certain lack of melodic individuality. Once or twice in *Deità silvane* ('Woodland gods'), for example, one wishes that the poems' classical imagery would lead him towards an evocation or even a direct quotation from Italian music's 'classical' past of the kind that so often renders his better-known music so memorable. In *La sensitiva* ('The sensitive plant'), however, his care for the imagery and especially the prosody of Shelley's poem (in Italian translation) was so responsive that really striking melodic invention was the result. The orchestral colour of the piece is exquisite, the succession of ideas (the sensitive plant is image both of unhappy lover and spurned artist) a good deal more than merely picturesque. In a performance as expressive as this it seems one of Respighi's best works, and a good deal more sophisticated than he is generally given credit for. *Aretusa* is fine, too, with bigger dramatic gestures, even richer colour and some magnificent sea music. The much better-known *Nebbie* ('Mists'; though seldom heard in its rich orchestral dress) is another example of Respighi finding a genuinely sustained melodic line in response to a text which obviously meant a great deal to him. Everything here is played with a real care for Respighi's line as well as his sumptuous but never muddy colours. The recording is first-class.

Aretusa. Il tramonto. Lauda per la natività del Signore. Trittico botticelliano.
Patricia Rozario *sop* **Dame Janet Baker, Louise Winter** *mezzos* **Lynton Atkinson** *ten*
Richard Hickox Singers; City of London Sinfonia / Richard Hickox.
Collins Classics 1349-2 (72 minutes: DDD). Texts and translations included. Recorded 1991.   Ⓕ

Aretusa and *Il tramonto* are set to translations of poems by Shelley: colourful works with a wide range of expression, stimulating just that kind of boldness and generosity of utterance in which Dame Janet is expert. She is in fine voice here, and at the end of *Il tramonto* ('The tomb of the dead self') her tone is stern, strong and dark, intensely personal. Even so, coming to the disc initially for these tone-poems for solo voice and orchestra, one may eventually be most glad of the purchase for its introduction to the choral *Lauda per la natività del Signore.* This is a most lovely work. It has solo parts for Mary, the Angel and a shepherd (all well taken), but the great joy lies in the choral and orchestral writing, rich and imaginative, showing evident delight in the medievalism. The better-known *Trittico botticelliano* is very enjoyable too, and all are fine in performance and recorded sound.

Julius Reubke German 1834-1858

Reubke Piano Sonata in B flat minor.
Schumann Kreisleriana, Op. 16.
Till Fellner *pf*
Erato 0630-12710-2 (63 minutes: DDD). Recorded 1996.   Ⓕ

Reubke's B flat minor Piano Sonata was completed just before his untimely death at 24 and here Till Fellner's performance has outstanding imaginative sympathy and pianistic command. The prime inspirational source for his expansive, thematically metamorphosed and interlinked three-movement work was undoubtedly Liszt's B minor Sonata, not only in form but in so much of its general style of keyboard expression and its emotional questings and conflicts. Not a note played here sounds second-hand. One is lost in admiration at the concentrated intensity Fellner brings to arresting challenges, soul-searching recitative, spiritual repose and majestic grandeur. For the triumphant home-coming he draws a near organ-like fullness and depth of sonority from his instrument.

'A positively wild love is in some of the movements, and your life and mine, and the way you look.' So Schumann wrote to Clara about *Kreisleriana*, dashed off in a mere four days during their enforced separation. Here there is not quite the same immediacy or urgency of response as in the Reubke Sonata. Perhaps Fellner is more closely attuned to the visionary Eusebius than the impulsive Florestan. The two dreams of Clara (Nos. 4 and 6) are questionably slow here. That said, it is a deeply thoughtful, poetic performance, carried out with exemplary keyboard refinement and tonal beauty.

Silvestre Revueltas Mexican 1899-1940

La coronela. Itinerarios. Colorines[a].
Santa Barbara Symphony Orchestra, [a]English Chamber Orchestra / Gisèle Ben-Dor.
Koch International Classics 37421-2 (50 minutes: DDD). Recorded 1997.   Ⓕ

With this recording, the enterprising and charismatic Uruguayan conductor Gisèle Ben-Dor usefully extends the already considerable representation in the catalogue of Silvestre Revueltas, whose irregular lifestyle led to his death at the age of 40 after a mere decade of creativity as a composer. His *Colorines*, stridently exotic in instrumentation and rhythmically pungent, shows influences from native folk music (particularly in a less frantic section) and, conspicuously, from *The Rite of Spring*; the work's weakness lies in its stylistic inconsistency, but it is brilliantly performed by the ECO and equally brilliantly recorded. More substantial and less eagerly striving for effect, but just as virtuosically scored, and often very moving (especially in the section for solo soprano saxophone), is *Itinerarios*, an extended threnody for the Spain which had just become engulfed in a bitter civil war. *La coronela*, a ballet first performed two years later, in 1940, is something of a confection. Not only did Revueltas die before completing it (it was finished by Blas Galindo and orchestrated by Candelario Huízar), but all their performance material was then lost, and the score had, as far as possible, to be reconstructed by the conductor of the première; but the final movement is in fact a compilation from two of Revueltas's earlier film scores. The scenario, developed from a series of skeleton figure engravings illustrated in the booklet, deals with the overthrow by the peasant class of the decadent bourgeoisie. The opposing factions are delineated, not without touches of satiric humour, in a generally less radical idiom – the 'For the fallen' episode reveals an unexpectedly diatonic lyricism – though the composer makes it abundantly clear that his ardent sympathies lie with the revolutionaries. As with many ballets, however, a detailed knowledge of the scenario is necessary to make sense of the course of the music, however vividly it is presented here.

Nicolay Rimsky-Korsakov

Russian 1844-1908

Scheherazade, Op. 35. Capriccio espagnol, Op. 34. Russian Easter Festival Overture, Op. 36.

Scheherazade[a]. Capriccio espagnol[b]. Russian Easter Festival Overture[c].
Herman Krebbers *vn* [ac]**Concertgebouw Orchestra /** [a]**Kyrill Kondrashin;**
[b]**London Symphony Orchestra /** [bc]**Igor Markevitch.**
Philips Solo 442 643-2PM (74 minutes: ADD). Recorded [a]1980, [b]1963, [c]1965. Ⓜ️ 🆁🆁

Kondrashin's performance of *Scheherazade* is one of the very finest made of Russian music in the
Concertgebouw; it has glamour and brilliance, and the resonance brings a wonderful feeling of
spaciousness in the first movement and adds a thrill to the spectacle of the finale. Kondrashin has
the full measure of this colourful score, while the finale builds up to a feeling of excitement which
leads to a riveting climax at 'The Shipwreck'. Of course, any performance of this masterpiece
stands or falls by the portrayal of Scheherazade herself by the solo violin, and here the
Concertgebouw's leader, Herman Krebbers dominates the action from the gentle, beguiling opening
to his exquisite closing solo, suggesting that all is well at last between the Sultan and his bewitching
Sultana. A brilliant performance of Rimsky's *Capriccio espagnole* follows, very well played by the
LSO under Igor Markevitch; indeed, the 1963 recording sounds far more lustrous than it did on LP.
It is upstaged, however, by Markevitch's performance of the composer's *Russian Easter Festival
Overture*, made two years later, when again the aura of the Concertgebouw ambience adds a glow
to more remarkable playing from this great orchestra. Altogether a superb disc, and generously full.

Scheherazade. Capriccio espagnol.
London Symphony Orchestra / Sir Charles Mackerras.
Telarc CD80208 (60 minutes: DDD). Recorded 1990. Ⓕ

Sir Charles Mackerras throws himself into this music with expressive abandon, but allies it to
control so that every effect is realized and the London Symphony Orchestra plays these familiar
works as if it was discovering them afresh. Together they produce performances that are both vivid
and thoughtful, while the solo violin in *Scheherazade* is seductively and elegantly played by Kees
Hulsmann, not least at the wonderfully peaceful end to the whole work. The finale featuring a
storm and shipwreck is superbly done, the wind and brass bringing one to the edge of one's seat.
This sensuous and thrilling work needs spectacular yet detailed sound, and that is what it gets here,
the 1990 recording in Walthamstow Town Hall being highly successful and giving us a CD that
many collectors will choose to use as a demonstration disc to impress their friends. The
performance and recording of the *Capriccio espagnol* is no less of a success.

Scheherazade. Capriccio espagnol.
London Philharmonic Orchestra / Mariss Jansons.
EMI CDC5 55227-2 (62 minutes: DDD). Recorded 1994. Ⓕ

This has got to be one of EMI's finest recordings, not as analytically transparent as some but vivid
and immediate with a thrillingly wide dynamic range. As to Jansons's interpretation of the main
work, he follows up the big bold, brassy opening with a surprisingly restrained account of the main
theme as it develops, keeping power in reserve, building up more slowly than usual. What then is
consistently striking in all four movements is Jansons's pointing of rhythm, lilting, bouncy and
affectionate in a way that distinguishes this from most other versions. This is a *Scheherazade* that
dances winningly, less earnest than usual, often suggesting a smile on the face. That is very welcome
in a work that, for all its exotic colour and memorable themes, needs persuasive handling if it is not
to seem like a lot of introductions leading to introductions, and codas leading to codas, with little
meat in the middle. Jansons's control of structure leads to a masterly sense of resolution at the great
climax towards the end of the finale, as the main theme returns *fortissimo*. Nowhere does this seem
like a virtuoso exercise, brilliant as the playing of the LPO is, not least that of the warmly
expressive violin soloist, Joakim Svenheden. Rather, emotionally involved, Jansons finds a rare
exuberance in Rimsky-Korsakov's stream of ideas and colours, leading compellingly from one to
another. The *Capriccio espagnol* brings a similar combination of expressive warmth and
exuberance. In the brilliant 'Alborada' at the beginning of the *Capriccio* Jansons's speed is less
hectic than some, and with springy rhythms it is made to sound relaxed, jolly rather than fierce. Not
that in either work is there any shortage of biting excitement.

Scheherazade. Russian Easter Festival Overture.
Vienna Philharmonic Orchestra / Seiji Ozawa.
Philips 438 941-2PH (58 minutes: DDD). Recorded live in 1993. Ⓕ

Scheherazade is a work which brings the very best out of Seiji Ozawa, a colourist who likes to mould the music and make it dance. Instead of his own Boston Symphony, here he conducts the even richer-toned Vienna Philharmonic, with strings all the more sensuous in a live recording. It was made during a concert in the orchestra's home, the Musikvereinsaal in Vienna, and the tensions of a live performance consistently add compulsion to a work which can seem disconcertingly episodic. The violin solo of the leader, Rainer Honeck, from the start gives one a sense of firm purpose in the unfolding of these musical fairy-tales. Except in the love-scene of the third movement, 'The Young Prince and Princess', Ozawa's speeds tend to be on the slow side, but he readily sustains them, building up the climaxes with satisfying weight and concentration. The performance surprisingly tends to fall short in the dance-rhythms of the second movement, the 'Kalender Prince', with the oboe and bassoon solos sounding self-conscious and rather jerky. But the Viennese strings are also at their most sumptuous. The recording, forward balanced, is satisfyingly warm and full. Not everyone will relish the inclusion of applause at the end of the fourth movement. The welcome fill-up, though recorded in the same venue during a studio session, has similar characteristics.

Scheherazade. The Tale of Tsar Saltan, Op. 57 – Tsar's farewell and departure; Tsarina in a barrel at sea; The three wonders.
Philharmonia Orchestra / Enrique Bátiz.
Naxos 8 550726 (61 minutes: DDD). Recorded 1992. Ⓢ

Bátiz proves an impulsive, purposeful interpreter. In the second movement, his performance is more lilting Ozawa's, with rubato more persuasive, helped by superb Philharmonia wind-playing. The fanfares which interrupt in echelon (track 2) are brisk rather than weighty, confirming a more volatile approach than Ozawa's. In the third movement the Philharmonia strings may not be quite as rich as the Viennese, but with the excellent, well-balanced recording revealing more inner detail the result is more refined, with a delectably lilting clarinet entry on the *grazioso* dance-rhythm (track 3). David Nolan's violin solos are more individually rhapsodic, if not always as immaculate tonally as the Viennese. In short, this budget issue is at least as compelling and just as exciting as its full-priced rival, and rather better recorded, standing comparison with the best of previous versions. The fill-up can be warmly recommended too, three movements from the five which Rimsky included in the orchestral suite of musical pictures from *Tsar Saltan*, starting with the delectable march entitled the 'Tsar's farewell and departure'. The other movements are 'Tsarina in a barrel at sea' and 'The three wonders', with the over-played 'Flight of the Bumble-Bee' hardly missed.

Symphonies – No. 1 in E minor, Op. 1; No. 2 (Symphonic Suite), Op. 9, 'Antar'; No. 3 in C major, Op. 32. Russian Easter Festival Overture. Capriccio espagnol.
Gothenburg Symphony Orchestra / Neeme Järvi.
DG 423 604-2GH2 (two discs: 125 minutes: DDD). Ⓕ

No one is going to claim Rimsky's First and Third Symphonies to be neglected masterpieces. He came to refer to his First (partly written whilst the young naval officer was on duty!) as a 'disgraceful composition', and along with the other two symphonies, it was subjected to extensive revision by the later learned master of musical technique. The beautifully lyrical second theme reminds us that Rimsky was reared in the country and had the early advantage of a good soaking in folk-song. Though the debt to Glinka is obvious, to our ears classical concerns seem uppermost throughout, and the music is free from anything that could be called exoticism. Not so the Second. Rimsky was a member of the 'Mighty Five', a group of composers (including Mussorgsky, Balakirev and Borodin) sworn to the nationalist cause, professing horror at anything tinged with German academicism and ever searching for subjects on which they could lavish a preference for orchestral colour above form. Rimsky's *Antar* combined these ideals, and more. Our hero of the title is allocated a Berliozian *idée fixe*, an oriental location (the desert of Sham) and the joys of vengeance, power and love from the grateful fairy Gul-Nazar as a gift for saving her from a winged monster.

It is, in every way, an antecedent of *Sheherazade* and, after hearing Järvi's rich and eloquently descriptive account, one wonders why it has never attained anything like the same popularity. His Third Symphony reverts to a more academic manner. In 1871 he was invited to join the theory and composition faculty at the St Petersburg Conservatory and, in Tchaikovsky's words, 'from contempt of schooling he had turned all at once to the cult of musical technique'. Despite a paucity of truly memorable ideas, it is a symphony to admire for its construction and light-as-air orchestration. The set is completed with urgent, vibrant accounts of the *Capriccio espagnol* and the *Russian Easter Festival Overture*, quite the most colourful and exciting versions on disc, and they confirm that the less familiar symphonies could not be in better hands. DG's engineers resist the temptation to glamorize the music and offer a lucid and spacious panorama of sound.

Symphony No. 3. Sadko, Op. 5. Mlada – Procession of the Nobles. The Maid of Pskov –
Overture. The Tale of Tsar Saltan – The three wonders. The Tsar's Bride – Overture.
Russian State Symphony Orchestra / Evgeni Svetlanov.
RCA Victor Red Seal 09026 62684-2 (76 minutes: DDD). Recorded 1993.　　　　　Ⓕ

Borodin and Tchaikovsky were both hostile to Rimsky-Korsakov's Third Symphony when they
heard it in its first version, but not as critical as the composer himself. What we have here is its third
and final revision, purged of the excesses of technique that, he wrote in his memoirs, made it all too
dry. In this version, which has had several recordings, it is enjoyable less as the solemn exercise to
which Borodin objected than as a piece of vivid orchestral writing with some attractive ideas
guiding it. It therefore fits easily into a programme of Korsakov orchestral show-pieces, of which
the most substantial is the musical picture *Sadko*. Svetlanov is an old hand with this music, and he
draws properly colourful performances from the orchestra, clearly and brightly recorded. Serious
collectors of Rimsky-Korsakov's symphonies will no doubt have acquired the fine set by Neeme
Järvi with the Gothenburg Symphony Orchestra on DG (reviewed above). For what might be called
a Rimsky-Korsakov taster, even if not of his best music, the present disc is very acceptable.

Sadko.
Vladimir Galusin *ten* Sadko; **Valentina Tsidipova** *sop* Volkhova;
Sergei Alexashkin *bass* Okean-More; **Marianna Tarassova** *mez* Lyubava Buslayevna;
Larissa Diadkova *contr* Nezhata; **Bulat Minjelkiev** *bass* Viking Merchant;
Gegam Grigorian *ten* Indian Merchant; **Alexander Gergalov** *bar* Venetian Merchant;
Vladimir Ognovenko *bass* Duda; **Nikolai Gassiev** *ten* Sopel; **Nikolai Putilin** *bar* Apparition;
Yevgeny Boitsov *ten* Foma Nazarich; **Gennadi Bezzubenkov** *bass* Luka Zinovich;
Kirov Opera Orchestra / Valery Gergiev.
Philips 442 138-2PH3 (three discs: 173 minutes: DDD). Notes, text and translation included.
Recorded live in 1993.　　　　　Ⓕ

Rimsky-Korsakov's operas are not so well represented in the catalogue that one can afford to give
anything but a welcome to this complete version from the Maryinsky company, for all its
drawbacks. *Sadko* is a panoramic work, packed with numbers, rather less packed with event or with
character. The various characters delivering themselves of a song or a ballad or an address are
reasonably well contrasted, partly because of Rimsky-Korsakov's skills in drawing on different
Russian influences and in differentiating between a simple tonal language for the real world and a
more chromatic idiom for the seductive realm of the Sea King (Okean-More) and his daughter
Volkhova. It needs a numerous and strong cast who can make the most of its opportunities. Sadko
himself is sung by Vladimir Galusin pretty steadily at full volume. He settles down a little as the
opera proceeds, and by Act 3 is finding a somewhat more pacific manner. Valentina Tsidipova
returns his advances, and makes her own, with a good feeling for line, if one can overcome
resistance to the steady vibrato. The Sea King is strongly sung by Sergei Alexashkin, truculent at
first but warming his tone somewhat as he comes to accept Sadko. But it is a pity that the best-
known number from the opera, the song of the Indian Merchant, should be sung as half-heartedly
as it is by Gegam Grigorian. Valery Gergiev leads his forces well, and draws some vigorous,
colourful singing from the choruses in their various manifestations. There is, however, a good deal
of noise occasioned by the many stage comings and goings, with clumpings and hoarse whisperings
as well as tunings-up and applause. The recording has difficulty in catching all the singers equally in
their various peregrinations across the stage, but for the most part this is a fair representation of a
score that is nothing if not colourful.

Joaquin Rodrigo　　　　　　　　　　　　　　　　　Spanish 1901-1999

Concierto de Aranjuez[a]. Three Piezas españolas[b]. Invocacíon y danza[c].
Fantasía para un gentilhombre[d].
Julian Bream *gtr*
[a]**Chamber Orchestra of Europe;**
[d]**RCA Victor Chamber Orchestra / **[a]**Sir John Eliot Gardiner;** [d]**Leo Brouwer.**
RCA Victor Julian Bream Edition 09026 61611-2 (69 minutes: DDD).
Recorded [abc]1982-83, [d]1987.　　　　　Ⓜ **RR**

In the early 1980s Bream had entered a phase in which both his musical and technical powers
were at their height, which he too recognized and celebrated in this remarkable album. With it he
confirmed that he is Segovia's truest and best successor, though in no sense his imitator, and
established a benchmark in the history of the guitar on record. Everything he touched turns to

music and is here recorded with the utmost reality. If anyone is wondering why he should here have taken his third bite at Aranjuez's cherry, it was in order to 'go digital' but in the event this proved a subsidiary *raison-d'être*. At the time the Chamber Orchestra of Europe was no casual band assembled for a session but a newly-formed orchestra of young players from several countries, greeting the concerto as a fresh experience and playing it with splendid precision and vitality. John Eliot Gardiner's conducting is unfailingly idiomatic. Who catalyzed whom is hard to say but Bream certainly responded with the *Aranjuez* of his life, clean as a whistle, eloquently phrased and passionate; nothing is lost in the recording and the guitar is 'prestidigitalized' into unfailing audibility. *Aranjuez*s come and go but this one must remain as the touchstone for a very long time, reaffirming the thoroughbred character of a warhorse that so often sounds tired through overworking. The concerto may be very familiar territory but the other items are not. Prior to this recording only Eric Hill on Saga Records had previously resisted the temptation to sever the 'Fandango' from the other two *Piezas españolas*; Bream too reassembles the triptych by restoring the exciting 'Zapateado' and the un-Rodrigo-like 'Passacaglia'. This triptych is a strongly atmospheric work whose difficulty has helped to keep it out of the concert halls until relatively recently. Bream's interpretation of *Invocación y danza* is equally masterly – one cannot imagine who else could have made it.

Leo Brouwer is a man of so many musical parts that the loss of one of them, his role as a virtuoso guitarist, has passed almost unnoticed; here he plays one of the others – that of conductor. What better than to provide the ammunition for others to fire, and to direct the campaign yourself? *Fantasía para un gentilhombre* has its own merits and demerits, with Bream stressing the musical rather than the virtuosic elements, adopting somewhat slower tempos than other interpreters in most of the movements – that of the final 'Canarios' is more in keeping with the character of the dance itself. Brouwer's splendid control of the orchestra reflects his experience of both sides of the concerto 'fence'. This disc is a 'must.

Concierto de Aranjuez[ac]. Fantasía para un gentilhombre[ac]. Cançoneta[bc]. Invocacíon y danza[a]. Tres Pequeñas piezas[a].
[a]Pepe Romero *gtr* **[b]Augustín Léo Ara** *vn*
[c]Academy of St Martin in the Fields / Sir Neville Marriner.
Philips 438 016-2PH (64 minutes: DDD). Recorded 1992.   Ⓕ

What we have here is simply one of the best: Pepe Romero, a close friend of Rodrigo, has the technique to do whatever he pleases, though his capacity for high speed does not tempt him to display it for its own sake. There is elegance and a certain nobility in his interpretations, though he lacks the warmth of Bream, for instance, and the 'flamenco steeliness' of his *rasgueados* does perhaps stand in uncomfortable contrast with the rest. The ASMF must by now know these scores by heart but, perhaps stimulated by the presence of a soloist who is so completely in command of his material, its immaculate support bears no trace of staleness. The *Cançoneta* (1923) is one of Rodrigo's earliest works, a small (just under three minutes) island of peaceful romantic dreams in a sea of guitar music, sweetly played by Ara (Rodrigo's son-in-law) and ignored in the annotation. There is no better recording of the *Invocacíon y danza*, and only one other (also by Romero) of the *Tres Pequeñas piezas*, in the last of which the steely *rasgueados* are entirely in character. If you are not already liberally provided with recordings of the two main items you may rightly be tempted by this outstanding recording.

Concierto de Aranjuez. Fantasía para un gentilhombre. Un tiempo fue Itálica famosa. Zarabanda lejana. Adela. Villancicos – Pastorcito Santo; Coplillas de Belén. Coplas del pastor enamorado.
Manuel Barrueco *gtr*
Philharmonia Orchestra / Plácido Domingo *ten*
EMI CDC5 56175-2 (67 minutes: DDD). Texts and translation included. Recorded 1995-97.   Ⓕ

Concierto de Aranjuez. Fantasía para un gentilhombre. Concierto para una fiesta.
David Russell *gtr*
Naples Philharmonic Orchestra (Florida) / Erich Kunzel.
Telarc CD80459 (72 minutes: DDD). Recorded 1997.   Ⓕ

Both these discs are amongst the best recordings of the *Concierto de Aranjuez* and *Fantasia para un gentilhombre*. Barrueco and Russell are members of the guitar's top-drawer élite – giving performances of crystalline clarity – and they are both excellently supported by their orchestras. In both these recordings the guitar is foregrounded to the extent that it achieves greater dominance than it ever does in the concert hall. One might regard this as a distortion, but as it more faithfully represents what was/is in the composer's inner ear it should be enjoyed in its own right. Neither do these comments apply only to the guitar and orchestra works of Rodrigo. If you already have top-rated versions of either or both of these pieces you may rest content with them, but if you decide (for whatever reason) to add one of these new recordings to your collection then your choice may depend on the other items they contain. In Russell's case it is the *Concierto para una fiesta*. The thought 'where have I heard this before?' may cross your mind – in relation to both musical elements and the mode of orchestration. But you may find these familiar echoes lovably welcome. Barrueco adds two solos, neither one yet dulled by overfamiliarity. The *Zarabanda lejana* is given with the utmost expressivity, and *Un tiempo fue Itálica famosa* is delivered with panache; rapid passages in Rodrigo's guitar works are almost invariably scales, appropriately testifying to the influence of flamenco. Barrueco has one more trump card to play – his partnership with Plácido Domingo in four songs, selected from those for which Rodrigo himself has made adaptations for the guitar of the original piano accompaniments (the texts are given in four languages). Both are longstanding devotees of Rodrigo's music, and it shows. Domingo also conducts the orchestra, an exercise in which both parties demonstrate their happy meeting of minds.

Cipriano de Rore
Italian 1515/16-1565

Rore Missa Praeter rerum seriem. Motets – Infelix ego; Parce mihi; Ave regina; Descendi in hortum meum.
Josquin Desprez Praeter rerum seriem.
The Tallis Scholars / Peter Phillips.
Gimell 454 929-2PH (72 minutes: DDD). Texts and translations included.
Gramophone Award Winner 1994.   Ⓕ

This record begins with a magisterially concentrated and evocative account of one of Josquin's most inspired and tightly-constructed motets, the six-voice *Praeter rerum seriem*. This in turn is the starting-point for Rore's Mass – which takes as its cue Josquin's antiphonal approach – wherein the song on which the Mass is based is passed from the upper to the lower voices in succession. Rore, whose piece is in one sense an act of homage to Josquin was, if briefly, Josquin's successor at the d'Este court at Ferrara. It is in this context that Rore's work is an act of homage in a second sense, since to Josquin's already rich texture Rore adds an additional soprano part, while the first alto voice carries throughout a *cantus firmus* to the text 'Hercules secundus dux Ferrarie quartus vivit et vivet'. Around this structural scaffolding the remaining voices weave an endlessly inventive sequence of carefully-worked motives reminiscent of Josquin's original. This performance is characterized by great sensitivity to textual inflexion and to the many moments of exquisite bonding of words and music. Nevertheless, in the end it is Peter Phillips's ability to control the overall architecture of the music, as well as its detail, that provides the basis for a reading of such conviction; his direction, combined with The Tallis Scholars's strongly-focused singing and well-balanced ensemble, results in a gripping performance of rare beauty, intelligence and power. No less fine is the group of four motets that completes the recording, and which reveals Rore as one of the greatest and last exponents of the Franco-Flemish tradition.

Ned Rorem
American 1923

Piano Concerto for the Left Hand[a]. Eleven Studies for Eleven Players[b].
Kathy Lord *ob* **Gregory Raden** *cl* **Elizabeth Ostling** *fl* **Katerina Englichova** *hp* **Jack Sutte** *tpt*
Anthony Lafargue, Ryan Leveille *perc* **Steven Copes** *vn* **Choong-Jin Chang** *va*
Jeffrey Lastrapes *vc* [a]**Gary Graffman,** [b]**Reiko Uchida** *pfs* / [b]**Rossen Milanov;**
[a]**Curtis Institute Student Orchestra / André Previn.**
New World 80445-2 (62 minutes: DDD). Recorded 1993.   Ⓕ

In an appealingly candid booklet-essay, Ned Rorem describes his Left-Hand Concerto (his fourth for piano so far) as an 'entertainment' – an entirely apt epithet, as it turns out, but one even more well suited to the earlier companion work on this valuable New World offering, namely the austerely titled *Eleven Studies for Eleven Players*. Dating from 1959-60, this charming suite is full of sparkling invention, nostalgic and witty by turns, and everywhere Rorem's scoring displays a very Gallic refinement. The Left-Hand Concerto of 1991 is another multi-movement work, eight in all, spread across three varying sections. Again, Rorem's inspiration impresses by dint of its appealing lyrical fervour and colourful, assured instrumentation, nowhere more so than in the strikingly beautiful 'Hymn' and 'Duet' which together form the emotional core of the concerto. The *Eleven Studies* receive a thoroughly sensitive, polished rendering from New World's *ad hoc* ensemble. In the concerto, Gary Graffman is a committed exponent (though his chosen instrument is not in the best of health) and André Previn draws an enthusiastic orchestral response from the students of the Curtis Institute.

Johann Rosenmüller

Vespro della beata Vergine.
Canticum; Cantus Cölln; Concerto Palatino / Konrad Junghänel.
Harmonia Mundi HMC90 1611/2 (two discs: 131 minutes: DDD). Texts and translations included.
Recorded 1996. ⓕ 🄴

The Marian cycle of devotions set by Johann Rosenmüller continues Cantus Cölln's important mission of illuminating Germany's finest seventeenth-century offerings, and this is a magnificent vindication of their efforts. His style is something of a godsend to Cantus Cölln, and vice versa. As a fluent and brilliant colourist of the most grandiloquent styles, he also never forsakes Teutonic contrapuntal discipline; the combination, at its best, produces a meticulously voiced control of texture and tautness of conception. These are attributes long admired in the performances of this eminent vocal ensemble also, and they are heard with concentrated fervour in five Psalms and a Magnificat, interspersed with plainsong, motets (with texts expertly reworked to fit the Vespers) and two fine instrumental sonatas. Whilst 'Dixit Dominus', in terms of scale (it is over 600 bars long), is a memorable compendium of glistening scoring, rhythmic vitality, snappy declamation and textual characterization, often of a masterly kind, there are other works – less structurally ambitious – where the totality of Rosenmüller's invention flatters rather more. 'Laudate pueri' evolves mesmerizingly, capped by a thrilling extended 'Sicut erat' (so too in the C minor Magnificat, whose opening chords resemble an early romantic opera overture). Cantus Cölln gives a virtuoso performance of this work – 'He raiseth the poor out of the dust' is punctuated wonderfully by the instrumental commentary – and also 'Laetatus sum', where the singers' invigorating dialogue distracts the listener from D major overkill, a small Achilles' heel in Rosenmüller's dazzling armoury. 'Laude Jerusalem' is in the same vein, yet with a rolling sarabande momentum and an unusual *obbligato* combination of trumpet and cornetto. Cantus Cölln and Concerto Palatino demonstrate how a relatively small consort can sound majestic through extreme care in all matters of ensemble and intonation. A fine achievement.

Gioachino Rossini

Overtures – Tancredi; L'italiana in Algeri; L'inganno felice; La scala di seta; Il barbiere di Siviglia; Il Signor Bruschino; La cambiale di matrimonio; Il turco in Italia. Introduction, Theme and Variations in E flat (attrib.).
Charles Neidich cl **Orpheus Chamber Orchestra.**
DG Masters 445 569-2GMA (66 minutes: DDD). Recorded 1984. Ⓜ 🆁🆁

This is one of the finest of all collections of Rossini overtures to have been recorded in recent decades. The superbly stylish playing apart, one of the reasons for the disc's success is the fact of its working within shrewdly appointed boundaries of chronology and style. All the overtures are early, dating from the years in which Rossini put his own indelible mark on the operatic overture (or 'musical visiting card' as Gino Roncaglia so elegantly expressed it). They also date from the time, pre-Naples, when Rossini was writing for smallish orchestras; no danger here of us being ricocheted from early Rossini to late by some grand maestro and his souped-up symphony orchestra. It is also nice to hear overtures that do not normally get a look-in in such anthologies. One can imagine a few collectors being disturbed by the dryness of the recording and the fierce brilliance of the playing. But that, too, is part of the disc's allure; its ability to conjure afresh the aggressive radicalism of the young Rossini. It is doubtful whether the clarinet piece (attributed to Rossini, and certainly using music by him) adds greatly to the disc's value. Inevitably, the Orpheus players have the whole thing fizzing as appetizingly as a glass of sharply chilled champagne.

Overtures – Armida; Il barbiere di Siviglia; Bianca e Falliero; Demetrio e Polibio; La gazza ladra; Guillaume Tell; L'inganno felice; Matilde di Shabran; Semiramide; Il Signor Bruschino.
Orchestra of La Scala, Milan / Riccardo Chailly.
Decca 448 218-2DH (75 minutes: DDD). Recorded 1995. ⓕ 🄴

This collection is a truly memorable day out at the Rossini fair. Musically everything is top notch. Chailly's conducting is characteristically full-blooded, but stylish and witty too. Milan's La Scala orchestra responds to his masterly direction with playing of tremendous colour, verve and corporate virtuosity. And Decca's engineers have achieved a sound whose mixture of warmth, brilliance and immediacy ensures that all the overtures, big and small, come up in a razor-sharp focus. For the most part, the collection juxtaposes the familiar with the rather less familiar. Nor are the less familiar pieces of lesser interest. The overture to *Armida*, with its solemn drum-beats and vertiginous warbling horns, is a case in point. And it was a very clever move indeed to include the overture to *Bianca e Falliero* which is itself a kind of guided tour of the later Neapolitan operas, containing as it does themes for *La donna del lago*, *Ricciardo e Zoraide* and *Ermione*. This is one of those discs when everything goes right. It offers an hour-and-a-quarter of untrammelled pleasure.

Overtures – Guillaume Tell; La scala di seta; Il Signor Bruschino; Il barbiere di Siviglia; La gazza ladra; La Cenerentola.
Chicago Symphony Orchestra / Fritz Reiner.
RCA Victor Gold Seal GD60387 (47 minutes: ADD). Recorded 1958.   Ⓜ 🄷

This is one of the most famous of all collections featuring this sparkling repertoire. By the time of this recording, Fritz Reiner had built the Chicago Symphony into one of the world's greatest ensembles, and their swaggering yet supremely flexible virtuosity is heard to superb effect on this survey. Not that these accounts are in any sense overdriven or that Rossini's music is used merely as an excuse for high-powered orchestral display; far from it: Reiner's direction possesses elegance, genial high-spirits and (at times) an almost Beechamesque wit – sample, say, the pointed woodwind dialogue in the scintillating reading of *La Cenerentola* to hear this. In fact, the only regret one could possibly have about this simply marvellous music-making is that, with a total duration of just under 47 minutes there isn't more of it! Despite some (inevitable) residual hiss, the RCA transfer engineers have worked wonders with these elderly tapes, producing a far more full-blooded, transparent sound picture than one would have thought possible. At mid-price, this is unmissable. Buy it!

Rossini Sonate a quattro – No. 1 in G major; No. 2 in A major; No. 3 in C major; No. 4 in B flat major; No. 5 in E flat major; No. 6 in D major.
Bellini Oboe Concerto in E flat major.
Cherubini Horn Sonata in F major.
Donizetti String Quartet in D major (1828).
Roger Lord *ob* **Barry Tuckwell** *hn*
Academy of St Martin in the Fields / Sir Neville Marriner.
Double Decca 443 838-2DF2 (two discs: 112 minutes: ADD). Recorded 1964-68.   Ⓜ

Rossini's six string sonatas are usually heard performed by a string orchestra, although they were in fact composed for a quartet of two violins, cello and double bass. The sonatas, which display amazing musical dexterity and assurance, may date from as early as 1804. The world of eighteenth-century opera is never far away, with the first violin frequently taking the role of soprano soloist, particularly in the slow movements. Written for Rossini's friend Agostino Triosso, who was a keen double bass player, the sonata's bass parts are full of wit and suavity. There are other thoroughly recommendable modern digital versions, yet there is something very special about Marriner's Academy set, made for Argo in the late 1960s. The playing has an elegance and finesse, a sparkle and touch of humour that catches the full character and charm of these miraculous examples of the precocity of the 12-year-old composer. The Double Decca format here is ideal because of the substantial bonuses. Donizetti's String Quartet sounds elegant in its string-orchestra version, Bellini's Oboe Concerto is played stylishly by Roger Lord and Cherubini's mini-concerto for horn and strings is dispatched with aplomb by by Barry Tuckwell. Highly recommendable.

Petite messe solennelle.
Helen Field *sop* **Anne-Marie Owens** *mez* **Edmund Barham** *ten* **John Tomlinson** *bass*
David Nettle, Richard Markham *pfs* **Peter King** *harm*
City of Birmingham Symphony Orchestra Chorus / Simon Halsey.
Conifer Classics CDCF184 (78 minutes: DDD). Text and translation included.
Recorded 1989.   Ⓕ Ⓢ 🆁🆁

Of Rossini's later works, none has won such affection from the general listening public as the *Petite messe solennelle*. He called it 'the final sin of my old age' and, as with the other of his *péchés de vieillesse*, he declined to have it published. Editions issued in 1869, the year after his death, failed to retain his original scoring and contained numerous inaccuracies, yet these have been the basis of most subsequent recordings of the work. The Conifer disc presents the Mass in a revelatory Oxford University Press edition by Nancy Fleming, using two pianos in addition to a fine French harmonium. That alone would mark it out for prime consideration, even if the reading were only passable, but here we have the bonus of dedicated, heartfelt performances from all involved. Above all, the scale of the work is finely captured – it was intended for chamber performance and both writing and scoring reflect the intimacy of Rossini's ideas. Much praise must go to Simon Halsey for so clearly establishing the parameters for this performance, and to the recording engineers for making it all seem so convincing. The whole issue establishes a benchmark for assessing recordings of this work.

Petite messe solennelle.
Daniella Dessì *sop* **Gloria Scalchi** *mez* **Giuseppe Sabbatini** *ten* **Michele Pertusi** *bass*
Chorus and Orchestra of the Teatro Comunale, Bologna / Riccardo Chailly.
Decca 444 134-2DX2 (two discs: 82 minutes: DDD). Text and translation included.
Recorded 1993. Ⓜ E

A proper representative of the orchestrated version has been long overdue. Chailly's performance is a glorious heart-warming affair. Not that you are likely to be convinced right away. To ears accustomed to the *Kyrie* in its original form, the texturing here is pure suet. Nor does the sound of the largish and here rather distantly placed choir seem especially well focused in the *Christe eleison*. Gradually, though, the ear adjusts, the musicians warm to their task, the performance gets into its stride. The Bologna Chorus sings the *Gloria* and *Credo* with passion, clarity and love. The tenor is adequate, the bass superb, the two girls absolutely fabulous. (The *Qui tollis* is sung with near-shameless allure.) If the *Crucifixus* can never be as painful as it is in the sparer original version, this is amply offset by the sheer beauty of Daniella Dessì's singing and by the hair-raising force of the 'Et resurrexit' (superbly recorded) as Chailly and his choir realize it. By the end, after Gloria Scalchi's deeply affecting account of the *Agnus Dei*, you begin to wonder whether the orchestral version wasn't more than a match for the original. It isn't, but it is an indication of the cumulative eloquence of this utterly inspired performance that it comes to seem so.

Stabat mater.
Luba Orgonasova *sop* **Cecilia Bartoli** *mez* **Raúl Giménez** *ten* **Roberto Scandiuzzi** *bass*
Vienna State Opera Concert Choir; Vienna Philharmonic Orchestra / Myung-Whun Chung.
DG 449 178-2GH (59 minutes: DDD). Text and translation included. Recorded 1995. Ⓟ E RR

Chung's conducting of the *Stabat mater* is somewhat Karajanesque: extremely beautiful orchestral playing; a choir which sings expressively but who yields something in focus and clarity of sound to the best rival English choirs; a strong dramatic sense with some unusual tempos that lead to the performance occasionally seeming mannered; and much fine solo singing, the singers encouraged to sing with great inwardness, with a special kind of *quiet* beauty. Raúl Giménez is encouraged by Chung to husband his rescources and sing with honeyed charm; for Cecilia Bartoli 'Fac ut portem' is a dramatic oration, for Bartoli and Chung it is a private meditation. The soloists are as fine as any on record and the text is nursed with special care by both soloists, choir, and conductor. The integration of singers, orchestra and acoustic is well managed in the secular sounding Golden Hall of the Vienna Musikverein. There are things – the rather too jaunty 'Sancta mater', the rather too protracted 'Quando corpus morietur' – that seem irksome on a first hearing, let alone on repetition. However, this recording can be regarded as first among equals among what is currently a distinguished field.

Stabat mater. Petite messe solennelle.
Lucia Popp, Catherine Malfitano *sops* **Brigitte Fassbaender, Agnes Baltsa** *mezzos*
Nicolai Gedda, Robert Gambill *tens* **Dimitri Kavrakos, Gwynne Howell** *basses*
Katia and **Marielle Labèque** *pfs* **David Briggs** *harm*
Choir of King's College, Cambridge / Stephen Cleobury;
Chorus and Orchestra of the Maggio Musicale, Florence / Riccardo Muti.
EMI Forte CZS5 68658-2 (two discs: 147 minutes: DDD). Recorded 1981-84. Ⓜ

Florence recording of the *Stabat mater* first appeared on CD in 1987; he paints the work in glowing colours and directs it grandly (not to say grandiloquently) and with much passion. The spaces of the Palazzo Vecchio are aglow with sound; the way the chorus is set relatively far back, diffusing the sonorities, is particularly appealing. This may not make for absolutely clear detailing of each and every note but it creates a wonderful atmosphere. At the time the recording was made, tenors were falling like flies and Muti had to accept last-minute substitutions, neither of which was ideal. Robert Gambill is adequate, but he is not in the Gwynne Howell class. The King's, Cambridge recording of the *Petite messe solennelle* has long been one of the most successful versions of this rare and wonderful but not especially lucky work on record. Rossini would have blenched at the thought of his *Messe* being sung by boys' voices ('sour and out of tune') but not these boys' voices. The King's boys sing sublimely, and how Rossini would have loved the Labèque sisters. Again, alas, there are some problems with the soloists. Gedda is past his best and Kavrakos is a rather unwieldy Rossini singer. Lucia Popp is fine, and so is Brigitte Fassbaender. The two works would normally spread across three CDs. To have them on two CDs, and at mid-price, is a great boon. Neither performance is perfect, but what performances of these works are? Cleobury's refinement and Muti's passion are well matched and contrasted in this sensible and economical coupling.

Rossini Otello – Che ascolto? ... Ah come mai non senti pietà. Guillaume Tell – Ne m'abandonne pas ... Asile héréditaire. Stabat mater – Cujus animam gementem. L'italiana in Algeri – Languir per una bella; Ah, come il cor di giubilo. Le siège de Corinthe – Avançons, oui ces murs ... Grand Dieu faut-il qu'un peuple qui t'adore.

Donizetti La favorite – Un ange, une femme inconnue; Je ne méritais pas ... Qui ta voix m'inspire; La maîtresse du roi? ... Ange si pur. Messa da Requiem – Ingemisco. Gabriella di Vergy – Si compia il sacrificio ... Io l'amai.

Justin Lavender *ten*
Bournemouth Symphony Orchestra / Howard Williams.
IMP Classics 30367 0010-2 (73 minutes: DDD). Recorded 1994.   Ⓢ

Rodrigo's long and incredibly difficult aria from Rossini's *Otello* announces Lavender's ability both to spin a secure *legato* and negotiate divisions with facility. But it is the second item that places him in the forefront of Rossini singing today. Every note of Arnold's strenuous outpouring is hit dead centre; up to the high C near the aria's close, the runs are cleanly delivered, the tone is clear and unfettered. Lavender's kind of tenor with its keen, pointed head voice may well be very much the sound Rossini had in mind for that part – and for Néocles in *Siège*, whose Act 3 scena is interpreted with the involvement possible only to an artist who has already sung the part on stage. In both these pieces Lavender's French is idiomatic. *La favorite* is at last being restored to the original language and Lavender demonstrates how much smoother Fernand's arias sound in French. Note also his long breath and his feeling for the shape of a Donizettian phrase. His Italian is no less excellent than his French. Perhaps there isn't enough light and shade in Lindoro's pieces from *L'italiana* but Raoul's romantic outpouring from *Gabriella* goes well. One piece in Latin from each composer finds Lavender full of the right conviction, the top D flat in 'Cuius animam' taken fearlessly. Howard Williams is the ideal partner, breathing life into every bar of the orchestration, especially notable in the Rossini pieces. The only reservations concern the recording – too much air around the voice – and the insert-notes which are inadequate. Let neither prevent you hearing a notable and fascinating début recital.

Zelmira – Riedi al soglio. Le nozze di Teti e di Peleo – Ah, non potrian reistere. Maometto II – Ah! che invan su questo ciglio; Giusto ciel, in tal periglio. La donna del lago – Tanti affetti in tal momento. Elisabetta, Regina d'Inghilterra – Quant' è grato all'alma mia; Fellon, la penna avrai. Semiramide – Serenai vaghirai ... Bel raggio lusinghier.

Cecilia Bartoli *mez*
Chorus and Orchestra of the Teatro La Fenice, Venice / Ion Marin.
Decca 436 075-2DH (59 minutes: DDD). Texts and translations included. Recorded 1991.   Ⓕ

This sparkling disc brings together a collection of arias composed by Rossini for one of the great prima donnas of the nineteenth century, who was also his wife, Isabella Colbran. It is tempting to wonder whether even she had a voice to match that of Cecilia Bartoli, one of the most luscious, most exciting voices in opera. All those dazzling chromatic runs, leaps, cadenzas and cascading coloraturas are handled with consummate ease. Throughout, Bartoli sounds as if she's enjoying the music; there is always an engaging smile in the voice, although she is properly imperious in the extracts from *Elisabetta* and disarmingly simple in the prayerful 'Giusto ciel, in tal periglio' ('Righteous heaven in such danger') from *Maometto II*. The orchestral and choral forces bring a delightful intimacy to the proceedings, with some cheeky woodwind solos and fruity brass passages. The recording, produced at the Teatro La Fenice by Decca veteran Christopher Raeburn, favours the voices but gives it just enough distance to accommodate high Cs and astounding A flats at the bottom of the range. The orchestral perspective is changeable but satisfactory. For Rossini and Bartoli fans, this disc is a must.

Il barbiere di Siviglia.
Roberto Servile *bar* Figaro; **Sonia Ganassi** *mez* Rosina; **Ramon Vargas** *ten* Count Almaviva;
Angelo Romero *bar* Bartolo; **Franco de Grandis** *bass* Don Basilio;
Ingrid Kertesi *sop* Berta; **Kázmér Sarkany** *bass* Fiorello;
Hungarian Radio Chorus; Failoni Chamber Orchestra, Budapest / Will Humburg.
Naxos 8 660027/9 (three discs: 158 minutes: DDD). Notes and text included.
Recorded 1992.   Ⓢ Ⓔ ⓇⓇ

Not everyone will approve, but there are ways in which this super-budget recording of *Il barbiere di Siviglia* puts to shame just about every other version of the opera there has yet been. Those it may not please are specialist vocal collectors for whom *Il barbiere* is primarily a repository of vocal test pieces, a kind of musical Badminton. If, on the other hand, you regard *Il barbiere* (Rossini, ex-Beaumarchais) as a gloriously subversive music drama – vibrant, scurrilous, unstoppably vital –

then this set is guaranteed to give a great deal of pleasure. 'Performance' is the key word here. Humburg is described in the Naxos booklet as 'Conductor and Recitative Director'; and for once the recitatives really are part of the larger drama. The result is a meticulously produced, often very funny, brilliantly integrated performance that you will almost certainly find yourself listening to as a stage play – rather than an opera with eminently missable (often arbitrarily abbreviated) recitatives. With a virtually all-Italian cast, the results are a revelation. The erotic allure of the duet 'Dunque io son' is striking, arising as it does here out of the brilliantly played teasing of Rosina by Figaro about her new admirer. Similarly, Don Basilio's Calumny aria, superbly sung by Franco de Grandis, a black-browed bass from Turin who was singing for Karajan, Muti and Abbado while still in his twenties. This takes on added character and colour from the massive sense of panic created by de Grandis and the admirable Dr Bartolo of Angelo Romero when Basilio comes in with news of Almaviva's arrival in town.

The Overture is done with evident relish, the playing of the Failoni Chamber Orchestra (a group from within the Hungarian State Opera Orchestra) nothing if not articulate. Aided by a clear, forward recording, a *sine qua non* with musical comedy, the cast communicates the Rossini/ Sterbini text – solo arias, ensembles, recitatives – with tremendous relish. They are never hustled by Humburg, nor are they spared: the *stretta* of the Act 1 finale is a model of hypertension and clarity. It would have been nice to have an English version of the libretto, but you can't have everything at rock-bottom prices and Naxos does provide an excellent track-by-track synopsis. Super-Scrooges might complain that 158 minutes of music could have been shoe-horned on to two CDs, but three CDs is a fair deal for a complete *Il barbiere*, and the layout is first-rate. This *Il barbiere* jumps to the top of the pile in a single leap. As operatic pole-vaulters, this puts Naxos in the Olympic class.

Il barbiere di Siviglia.
Thomas Allen *bar* Figaro; **Agnes Baltsa** *mez* Rosina; **Francisco Araiza** *ten* Count Almaviva; **Domenico Trimarchi** *bar* Dr Bartolo; **Robert Lloyd** *bass* Don Basilio; **Matthew Best** *bass* Fiorello; **Sally Burgess** *mez* Berta; **John Noble** *bar* Official; **Ambrosian Opera Chorus; Academy of St Martin in the Fields / Sir Neville Marriner.**
Philips 446 448-2PH2 (two discs: 147 minutes: ADD). Notes, text and translation included.
Recorded 1982. Ⓕ

This was the most stylish and engaging account of *Il barbiere* to have appeared on record since the famous de los Angeles/Bruscantini set recorded by EMI with Glyndebourne forces in 1962. Here, making a rare but welcome appearance in an opera recording, is the stylish Academy of St Martin in the Fields. It is as pointed and sure-footed an account of the score as you could hope to hear, a reading which entirely belies the fact that this was Neville Marriner's operatic début on record. Quite how the producer, in duets, ensembles and recitatives, created so live a sense of theatre in so essentially unconvivial a place as Watford Town Hall, north west of London, must for ever remain a mystery; there is here a real and rare sense of the delighted interplay of character: a tribute, in the first place, to the degree to which Thomas Allen, Francisco Araiza, Domenico Trimarchi, Agnes Baltsa, Robert Lloyd and their fellows are inside their roles musically and dramatically. There is no vulgar horseplay in the recording; but equally there is nothing slavish or literal about the way in which Rossini's, and Beaumarchais's comic felicities have been realized. The text is Zedda, more or less. Robert Lloyd takes the Calumny aria in C (D is the 'authentic' key), rightly so, for his is a magnificent bass voice. It's a grand characterization, very much in the Chaliapin style. Thomas Allen's Figaro and Francisco Araiza's Count bring out the opera's virility, its peculiarly masculine strength. (Agnes Baltsa is by turns cunning, charming, and passionate; but this is a man's world, one feels, full of an ardour and energy which she complements but never initiates.) Allen has a vivid sense of character and a brilliant technique. He also has a ripe sense of comedy.

Araiza is similarly compelling. Technically he is first-rate. His divisions are unusually bright and clean (though rapid triplets tend to go unshaded), the top (including some flashy cadences) true, shaped in a way which is both musically vivid and dramatically right, rounding out Araiza's portrait of an aristocrat distinguished by his ability to dominate and dispel mere domestic imbroglio. Equally, Araiza can be confiding, and funny. His whining music-master is a delight, right down to an unscripted attempt at a reprise of 'Pace e gioia' at the end of the scene, cut off by a petulant 'Basta!' from the excellent Bartolo, Domenico Trimarchi. Baltsa's Rosina, too, is infected by the set's general liveliness: witness the delighted gurgle of joy which escapes from her at the news of the Count's intentions. Recitatives, edited down here and there, are very alert, theatrically pointed; and Nicholas Kraemer's accompaniments on a sweet-sounding fortepiano are an added pleasure. Philips preferred a dryish, intimate acoustic; the small-theatre atmosphere this confers is very likeable, the more so as it allows Marriner the opportunity to conduct with a tautness and vigour which a boomier, more open acoustic would disallow. With excellent choral work in the all important ensembles, and with a delightful Berta from Sally Burgess, this is undoubtedly one of the very best *Barbers* the gramophone has given us.

Il barbiere di Siviglia.
Sesto Bruscantini *bar* Figaro; **Victoria de los Angeles** *sop* Rosina;
Luigi Alva *ten* Count Almaviva; **Ian Wallace** *bass* Dr Bartolo; **Carlo Cava** *bass* Don Basilio;
Duncan Robertson *ten* Fiorello; **Laura Sarti** *mez* Berta;
Glyndebourne Festival Chorus; Royal Philharmonic Orchestra / Vittorio Gui.
EMI Rossini Edition CMS7 64162-2 (two discs: 141 minutes: ADD). Notes, text and translation
included. Recorded 1962. Ⓜ

Perhaps it is a shade misleading to refer to this classic EMI recording as a 'Glyndebourne' set. It
has all the ingredients of a Glyndebourne production: notably the cast, the orchestra and chorus,
and that doyen of Rossini conductors, Vittorio Gui. But as far as can be ascertained, there was no
actual stage production of *Il barbiere* in 1962. Nor was the recording, for all its dryness and sharp-
edged immediacy, actually made in Glyndebourne. It is a well-honed, conservatively staged
stereophonic studio recording made by EMI in its Abbey Road Studio No. 1 at the conclusion of
the 1962 Glyndebourne season. Gui's performance is so astutely paced that whilst the music bubbles
and boils every word is crystal-clear. This is a wonderfully declaimed reading of the score, but also
a beautifully timed one. Gui's steady tempos also allow the music to show its underlying toughness.
He also secures characterful playing from the RPO, from the wind players in particular. Back in
1962, the RPO (still very much Beecham's creation) was the resident Glyndebourne orchestra.
Where Victoria de los Angeles is so memorable is in the beauty of her singing and the originality of
the reading. There has never been a Rosina who manages to be both as guileful and as charming as
de los Angeles. Team her up with the incomparable Sesto Bruscantini and, in something like the
nodal Act 1 duet, 'Dunque io son', you have musical and dramatic perfection. Gui's Dr Bartolo, Ian
Wallace, is a fine old character actor, given plenty of space by Gui, allowing his portrait of
Dr Bartolo to emerge as a classic compromise between the letter and the spirit of the part.

La Cenerentola.
Teresa Berganza *mez* Angelina; **Luigi Alva** *ten* Don Ramiro; **Renato Capecchi** *bar* Dandini;
Paolo Montarsolo *bar* Don Magnifico; **Margherita Guglielmi** *sop* Clorinda;
Laura Zannini *contr* Tisbe; **Ugo Trama** *bass* Alidoro;
Scottish Opera Chorus; London Symphony Orchestra / Claudio Abbado.
DG 423 861-2GH2 (two discs: 144 minutes: ADD). Notes, text and translation included.
Recorded 1971. Ⓕ 🆁🆁

Rossini's Cinderella is a fairy-tale without a fairy, but no less bewitching for the absence of a magic
wand. In fact the replacement of the winged godmother with the philanthropic Alidoro, a close
friend and adviser of our prince, Don Ramiro, plus the lack of any glass slippers and the presence
of a particularly unsympathetic father character, makes the whole story more plausible.
La Cenerentola, Angelina, is more spunky than the average pantomime Cinders, not too meek to
complain about her treatment or to beg to be allowed to go to the ball. She herself gives Don
Ramiro one of her pair of bracelets, charging him to find the owner of the matching ornament and
thus taking in hand the control of her own destiny. Along the way, Don Ramiro and his valet
Dandini change places, leading to plenty of satisfyingly operatic confusion and difficult situations.
This recording, when originally transferred to CD, was spread across three discs, but it has now
been comfortably fitted into two. It gives a sparkling rendition of the score with a lovely light touch
and well-judged tempos from Abbado and the London Symphony Orchestra and virtuoso vocal
requirements are fully met by the cast. The chief delight is Teresa Berganza's Angelina, gloriously
creamy in tone and as warm as she is precise. The supporting cast is full of character, with Luigi
Alva a princely Don Ramiro, Margherita Guglielmi and Laura Zannini an affected and fussy pair
of sisters, and Renato Capecchi as Dandini, gleeful and mischievous as he takes on being prince for
a day. The recording sounds more than usually well for its age.

Le comte Ory.
Juan Oncina *ten* Comte Ory; **Sari Barabas** *sop* Comtesse Adèle;
Cora Canne-Meijer *mez* Isolier; **Michel Roux** *bar* Raimbaud; **Ian Wallace** *bass* La Gouverneur;
Jeannette Sinclair *sop* Alice; **Monica Sinclair** *contr* Ragonde; **Dermot Troy** *ten* Chevalier;
Glyndebourne Festival Chorus and Orchestra / Vittorio Gui.
EMI Rossini Edition mono CMS7 64180-2 (two discs: 113 minutes: ADD). Notes, text and
translation included. Recorded 1956. Ⓜ 🅗

This now legendary production of *Le comte Ory*, finest of all French-language comic operas, was
one of Glyndebourne's principal glories in the 1950s. It was seen there over 30 times between 1954
and 1958; it also visited Paris (coals to Newcastle) and the Edinburgh Festival. Like Jane Austen's
Emma it could be said to be faultless despite its faults. There are cuts. The French is not consistently

good. The singing is variable, yet the Glyndebourne recording has several trump cards to play. Juan Oncina as the philandering Comte Ory has a matchless presence and charm. He is occasionally taxed by the tessitura of the role; but his diction is superb, and, with Gui in attendance, there is a flawless ease of emission where Rossini's melodies are at their most beguiling. Oncina and Gui do the supremely Rossinian thing of cultivating elegance of line and sweetness of sound above all else. Gui is also flawless in his pacing of the score, never regimenting the music. This recording is one of the last masterpieces of the mono era. Don't be put off by slightly rusty sound in the Overture. As soon as the voices come into play it is clear how astutely the recording has been staged for the gramophone by Gui and the engineers. It is occasionally quite remarkable in terms of clarity and guileful pointing of dramatic perspectives. And in Rossini's big ensembles that is a huge plus. Put on track 19 of the first disc, the Act 1 finale, and see if you don't agree. As far as many collectors are concerned, at moments like this God and Rossini are in their respective heavens and everything is right with the world.

Guglielmo Tell (in Italian).
Sherrill Milnes bar Guglielmo Tell; **Luciano Pavarotti** ten Arnoldo; **Mirella Freni** sop Matilde;
Della Jones mez Jemmy; **Elizabeth Connell** mez Edwige; **Ferrucio Mazzoli** bass Gessler;
Nicolai Ghiaurov bass Gualtiero; **John Tomlinson** bass Melchthal;
Cesar Antonio Suarez ten Un pescatore; **Piero De Palma** ten Rodolfo;
Richard Van Allan bass Leutoldo;
Ambrosian Opera Chorus; National Philharmonic Orchestra / Riccardo Chailly.
Decca 417 154-2DH4 (four discs: 235 minutes: ADD). Notes, text and translation included.
Recorded 1980.   Ⓕ

If ever there was a case for armchair opera – and on CD at that – it is Rossini's *Guglielmo Tell*. The very limitations which have made it, so far, a non-repertory work, give space for the imagination to redress the balance: the short, Rousseau-esque scenes of life by Lake Lucerne, the distant entrances and exits of shepherds and huntsmen, the leisurely but perfectly balanced side-vignettes of fisherman, hunter, child. Thanks to the clarity and liveliness of the recording itself and, above all, the shrewd casting, this set creates a vivid *charivari* of fathers, sons, lovers and patriots, all played out against some of Rossini's most delicately painted pastoral cameos. Riccardo Chailly keeps up the undercurrent of tension between private love and public loyalty, as well as working hard the rustic jollity of the score. Tell himself could hardly have a better advocate than Sherrill Milnes, who succeeds in portraying the moral rectitude of a man who casts himself in the role of his brother's keeper, while managing to glow with true ardour and integrity in the cause for which he is fighting. Arnoldo and Matilde, too, are cleverly cast. Pavarotti contains the coarse, direct impulsiveness of Arnoldo's shepherd stock with the tenderness of love, in his characteristic charcoal *cantabile* and, indeed, the numbness of his remorse. Freni, singing opposite him as the forbidden Princess Matilde, phrases with aristocratic poise, folding into every fragment of embryonic *bel canto* the fragile ardour of a young girl's love. The vocal chemistry between them in their Act 2 declaration of love is a lively incarnation of their respective roles. A similarly interesting patterning of vocal timbres is produced by the casting of Elizabeth Connell as Edwige, Tell's wife, and of Della Jones as Jemmy, their son. Their last-act Trio with Matilde is matched by the contrasting colours of the basses of Ghiaurov, Tomlinson and Van Allan: their roles may be small, but their characters are vividly stamped on what is an excellent ensemble performance.

L'inganno felice.
Annick Massis sop Isabella; **Raúl Giménez** ten Bertrando; **Rodney Gilfry** bar Batone;
Pietro Spagnoli bass Tarabotto; **Lorenzo Regazzo** bar Ormondo;
Le Concert des Tuileries / Marc Minkowski.
Erato 0630-17579-2 (78 minutes: DDD). Notes, text and translation included.
Recorded live in 1996.   Ⓕ

This is a fine and tremendously enjoyable recording of an exquisite early Rossini one-acter that in the first flush of Rossini's national and international success in the years 1812-24 was, without question, one of his most popular operas. The plot resembles that of a late Shakespearian comedy. Set in a seaside mining community, it is concerned with the discovery and rehabilitation of Isabella, Duke Bertrando's wronged and, so he thinks, long-dead wife. It is a work that is comic and serious, witty and sentimental; and there, perhaps, lies the rub. Rossini, especially early Rossini, is meant to be all teeth and smiles, yet *L'inganno felice* is not quite like that. The very *mise-en-scène* is odd: 'seaside' and 'mining' being, in such a context, strangely contradictory concepts. This is a splendid performance, using a chamber ensemble of about 30 players. It is a live performance, recorded with pleasing immediacy, that begins bullishly but settles to intimacy when the drama requires. The score is full of vocal pitfalls, not least for the tenor and for the baritone Batone. But Giménez and Gilfry cope more than adequately, with enough in reserve to produce moments of genuine ease and beauty. Annick Massis is a charming Isabella, good in her first aria, ravishing in her second. The final scene of *L'inganno felice*, its finest sequence, is set at night amid the mining galleys and is beautifully performed here, looking forward in some respects to the wonderful Act 2 Nocturne of *Le comte Ory*; they are, indeed, works of similar pedigree, albeit an age apart.

L'italiana in Algeri.
Jennifer Larmore *mez* Isabella; **Raúl Giménez** *ten* Lindoro; **Alessandro Corbelli** *bar* Taddeo;
John del Carlo *bass* Mustafà; **Darina Takova** *sop* Elvira; **Laura Polverelli** *mez* Zulma;
Carlos Chausson *bass-bar* Haly;
Geneva Grand Theatre Chorus; Lausanne Chamber Orchestra / Jésus López-Cobos.
Teldec 0630-17130-2 (two discs: 147 minutes: DDD). Notes, text and translation included.
Recorded 1997. ⒻⒺ🆁🆁

This recording is hard to fault on any count. López-Cobos revels in all aspects of this dotty comedy, timing everything to perfection, enthusing his accomplished orchestra and cast to enjoy their collective self. First there's a magic moment as Isabella and Lindoro espy each other for the first time, and comment on the joy of reunion; then the main section gets under way to a perfectly sprung rhythm from the conductor, with all the passage's detail made manifest; finally the *stretta* is released with the kind of vitality that sets the feet tapping. Larmore obviously thoroughly enjoys the role and conveys that enjoyment in singing that matches warm, smiling tone to bravura execution of her *fioriture*. She is a mettlesome Isabella, who knows how to tease, then defy her would-be lover, Mustafà, and charm her real amour, Lindoro, her 'Per lui che adoro' sung with an immaculate line and sensuous tone, its repetition deftly embellished. Finally 'Pensa alla patria' evinces a touch of true *élan*. Lindoro is taken by that paragon among Rossini tenors, Raúl Giménez, who presents his credentials in 'Languir per una bella', honeyed tone succeeded by fleet runs. He is no less successful in his more heroic Cavatina in Act 2. Corbelli, another master-Rossinian, is witty as the put-upon Taddeo, his textual facility a marvel. The American bass-baritone, John del Carlo, is a characterful Mustafà, managing to suggest, as Rossini surely intended, a paradox of lovesick tyrant and ludicrous posturing without ever overstepping the mark into farce, and rolling Italian and his rotund roulades off his tongue with idiomatic assurance. Chausson is well in the picture as Haly. And the recording is up to Teldec's impeccably high standard.

L'italiana in Algeri.
Marilyn Horne *mez* Isabella; **Ernesto Palacio** *ten* Lindoro;
Domenico Trimarchi *bar* Taddeo; **Samuel Ramey** *bass* Mustafà; **Kathleen Battle** *sop* Elvira;
Clara Foti *mez* Zulma; **Nicola Zaccaria** *bass* Haly;
Prague Philharmonic Chorus; I Solisti Veneti / Claudio Scimone.
Erato Libretto 2292-45404-2 (two discs: 140 minutes: ADD). Notes and text included.
Recorded 1980. Ⓜ

Written within the space of a month during the spring of 1813, and with help from another anonymous hand, Rossini's *L'italiana in Algeri* was an early success, and one which went on to receive many performances during the nineteenth century, with an increasingly corrupt text. A complete reconstruction was undertaken by Azio Corghi and published in 1981; this recording uses this edition which corresponds most closely to what was actually performed in Venice in 1813. *L'italiana* is one of Rossini's wittiest operas, featuring as did a number of his most successful works a bewitching central character, in this case Isabella, who makes fun of her various suitors, with the opera ending with a happy escape with her beloved, Lindoro, a typical *tenorino* role. This fine recording on Erato has plenty of vocal polish. Scimone's biggest asset is Marilyn Horne as Isabella: possibly the finest Rossini singer of her generation and a veteran in this particular role, she sings Rossini's demanding music with great virtuosity and polish. Her liquid tone and artful phrasing ensure that she is a continuous pleasure to listen to. She is strongly supported by the rest of the cast: Kathleen Battle is a beguiling Elvira, Domenico Trimarchi a most humorous Taddeo, and Samuel Ramey a sonorous Bey of Algiers – Isabella's opponent and pursuer. Ernesto Palacio's Lindoro, however, has patches of white tone and is correct rather than inspiring. Scimone's conducting is guaranteed to give considerable pleasure.

Semiramide.
Dame Joan Sutherland *sop* Semiramide; **Marilyn Horne** *mez* Arsace;
Joseph Rouleau *bass* Assur; **John Serge** *ten* Idreno; **Patricia Clark** *sop* Azema;
Spiro Malas *bass* Oroe; **Michael Langdon** *bass* Ghost of Nino; **Leslie Fryson** *ten* Mitrane;
Ambrosian Opera Chorus; London Symphony Orchestra / Richard Bonynge.
Decca 425 481-2DM3 (three discs: 168 minutes: ADD). Notes, text and translation included.
Recorded 1966. Ⓜ

Wagner thought it represented all that was bad about Italian opera and Kobbe's *Complete Opera Book* proclaimed that it had had its day – but then added what looked like second thoughts, saying that 'were a soprano and contralto to appear in conjunction in the firmament the opera might be successfully revived'. That was exactly what happened in the 1960s, when both Sutherland and Horne were in superlative voice and, with Richard Bonynge, were taking a prominent part in the reintroduction of so many nineteenth-century operas which the world thought it had outgrown. This recording brought a good deal of enlightenment in its time. For one thing, here was vocal music of such 'impossible' difficulty being sung with brilliance by the two principal women and with considerable skill by the men, less well known as they were. Then it brought to many listeners the discovery that, so far from being a mere show-piece, the opera contained ensembles that possessed quite compelling dramatic intensity. People who had heard of the duet 'Giorno d'orroré' were surprised to find it remarkably unshowy and even expressive of the ambiguous feelings of mother and son in their extraordinary predicament. It will probably be a long time before this recording is superseded, admirably vivid as it is in sound, finely conducted and magnificently sung.

Il Signor Bruschino.
Samuel Ramey *bass* Gaudenzio; **Claudio Desderi** *bar* Bruschino padre;
Kathleen Battle *sop* Sofia; **Frank Lopardo** *ten* Florville; **Michele Pertusi** *bass* Filiberto;
Jennifer Larmore *mez* Marianna; **Octavio Arévalo** *ten* Bruschino figlio, Commissario;
English Chamber Orchestra / Ion Marin.
DG 435 865-2GH (76 minutes: DDD). Notes, text and translation included. Recorded 1991. Ⓕ

Witty and sentimental but also at times hair-raisingly cruel, *Il Signor Bruschino* is the last, and arguably the best, of the one-acters Rossini wrote for the tiny Teatro San Moisè in Venice between 1810 and January 1813. These early *farse* can get by on tolerably good singing. What they absolutely can't do without is first-rate conducting – and, on record, clear, sharply defined orchestral sound. Choosing between the conducting of DG's Ion Marin and Claves's Marcello Viotti isn't all that difficult. Marin is far more vital; and what a cast there is on DG – a cast so expert and experienced they can't fail to bring the score wonderfully to life. Central to the whole enterprise is the Bruschino of Desderi, a superbly rounded portrait of a man who, despite the sweltering heat and the machinations of everyone around him, finally gives as good as he gets. Ramey's portrait of Gaudenzio is masterly, acted with relish and richly sung. Battle gives a ravishing account of Sofia's aria 'Ah!, donate il caro sposo' with its cor anglais colourings. This *Bruschino* is probably the one to have. Whatever reservations one may occasionally have about the conducting and the focus of the recording, it is difficult to imagine a better-cast account.

Tancredi.
Ewa Podles *contr* Tancredi; **Sumi Jo** *sop* Amenaide; **Stanford Olsen** *ten* Argirio;
Pietro Spagnoli *bar* Orbazzano; **Anna Maria di Micco** *sop* Isaura; **Lucretia Lendi** *mez* Roggiero;
Capella Brugensis; Collegium Instrumentale Brugense / Alberto Zedda.
Naxos 8 660037/8 (two discs: 147 minutes: DDD). Notes and Italian text included. Ⓢ Ⓔ
Recorded 1994.

Tancredi is a seminal work in the Rossini canon, a work which mingles a new-found reach in the musical architecture with vocal and instrumental writing of rare wonderment and beauty. Philip Gossett's new Critical Edition of the score is the one used here, albeit somewhat pragmatically, by Alberto Zedda. The singing is splendid throughout, with a cast that is unusually starry. Podles has sung the role of Tancredi (to acclaim) at La Scala, Milan; the Amenaide, Sumi Jo, is a touch cool at first, too much the pert coloratura but this is not an impression that persists. Hers is a performance of wonderful vocal control and flowering sensibility. Podles, a smoky-voiced Pole, likes to go her own way at times. In recitatives, rests are ignored and emphases freely redistributed. In arias, it is not unusual to find the pulse beating faster or slower as the musical temperature rises or falls. In the event, though, she and Sumi Jo work well together, and they sound marvellous. Podles also manages, chameleon-like, to adjust to the purer, more obviously stylish Rossini manner of a singer who is very unlike herself, the American tenor Stanford Olsen. His portrait of the conscience-stricken father Argirio matches singing of grace and impetus with great fineness of dramatic sensibility. As a result, something like the scene of the signing of his daughter's death-warrant emerges here as the remarkable thing it is. Zedda is lucky to have at his disposal another of those wonderfully stylish chamber orchestras and chamber choirs that Naxos seem able to conjure at will. The aqueously lovely preface to Tancredi's first entrance is a fairly representative example of the players' ear for Rossini's delicately-limned tone-painting. And the recording itself is beautifully scaled. As usual with Naxos, you get a multilingual synopsis plus an original-language libretto without translation; but in the case of an opera like *Tancredi*, where it is very much a case of 'Prima la musica', this is not a great disincentive to buy. All in all, then, this is a fine set; the first-ever studio recording of *Tancredi*, and a palpable hit.

Il turco in Italia.
Michele Pertusi *bass* Selim; **Cecilia Bartoli** *mez* Fiorilla; **Alessandro Corbelli** *bar* Don Geronio;
Ramón Vargas *ten* Don Narciso; **Laura Polverelli** *mez* Zaida; **Francesco Piccoli** *ten* Albazar;
Roberto de Candia *bar* Prosdocimo;
Chorus and Orchestra of La Scala, Milan / Riccardo Chailly.
Decca 458 924-2DHO2 (two discs: 142 minutes: DDD). Notes, text and translation included.
Recorded 1997. *Gramophone* Award Winner 1998.   Ⓕ

Add a star mezzo of Cecilia Bartoli's stature to a conductor of Riccardo Chailly's sympathies and *Il
turco in Italia* was asking to be recorded. Chailly, of course, has recorded the work before – for CBS
back in 1981 – but in the years since, he has matured as a Rossini conductor and the Scala orchestra
has this music under its collective fingers; indeed there is an energy and vitality to this playing that
is wholly infectious. For Chailly's earlier recording, Montserrat Caballé was a very underpowered
Fiorilla; Bartoli is full of fire and mettle (her 'Sqallido veste bruna' is sensational). Michele Pertusi
is a fine Selim and his performance seems to breathe stage experience – it is a characterization that
is as vocally fine as it is theatrically adept. Alessandro Corbelli, reinforcing his credentials as a
Rossini singer of flair and panache, is a strongly characterized Geronio. This is a recording that
smacks of the theatre, and unlike so many so-called comic operas, has lost nothing in its transfer to
disc. Under Chailly's baton it fizzes and crackles like few other sets – recitatives are dispatched with
the assurance of native Italian speakers and with a genuine feeling for the meaning of the text.
Decca's recording is beautifully judged and the set makes a fine modern alternative to the now
classic (but cut) 1954 recording under Gavazzeni, with Maria Callas incomparable as Fiorilla.

Il viaggio a Reims.
Sylvia McNair *sop* Corinna; **Cheryl Studer** *sop* Madama Cortese; **Luciana Serra** *sop* Contessa
di Folleville; **Lucia Valentini Terrani** *mez* Marchesa Melibea; **Raúl Giménez** *ten* Cavalier Belfiore;
William Matteuzzi *ten* Conte di Libenskof; **Samuel Ramey** *bass* Lord Sidney;
Ruggero Raimondi *bass* Don Profondo; **Enzo Dara** *bar* Barone di Trombonok;
Giorgio Surian *bar* Don Prudenzio; **Lucio Gallo** *bar* Don Alvaro;
Berlin Radio Chorus; Berlin Philharmonic Orchestra / Claudio Abbado.
Sony Classical S2K53336 (two discs: 135 minutes: DDD). Notes, text and translation included.
Recorded live in 1992.   Ⓕ

The rediscovery of Rossini's dazzling, sophisticated coronation entertainment *Il viaggio a Reims* was
one of the musical highlights of the 1980s; and it was Abbado's DG recording that brought the
work to the public at large (it was voted *Gramophone*'s Record of the Year in 1986). No one who
already has the DG recording need feel compelled to go out and buy the Sony. After all, the music
is the same, and so are no fewer than six of the 11 principal singers. Of the singers who are
repeating their roles, both Ramey and Dara now surpass their already superb earlier performances.
Dara has transformed the aria in which Baron Trombonok catalogues national foibles. What was
previously more or less a straight recitation is now a miracle of subversive inflexion, with Abbado
and the Berlin players adding wonderful new colours that seem to lie dormant in the earlier
recording. When it comes to the singers, the Sony set has its weaknesses. Not Gallo. His
Don Alvaro is less cumbersome than Nucci's on DG. Nor perhaps Serra as the fashion-crazed
young French widow. But for Count Libenskof DG's Francisco Araiza is far more in command of
the role than William Matteuzzi. On balance, though, collectors will be better off with the Sony,
and it is better recorded.

Nino Rota   Italian 1911-1979

Symphonies – No. 1 in G major; No. 2 in F major, 'Tarantina – Anni di pellegrinaggio'.
Norrköping Symphony Orchestra / Ole Kristian Ruud.
BIS CD970 (63 minutes: DDD). Recorded 1998.   Ⓕ

It is fascinating to encounter these early works by Nino Rota, written when he was in his twenties,
after a period of study in the USA. Rota's early career was as a church musician, something to
which he returned late in life, after decades composing for the screen and the theatre. The influences
to be detected in the First Symphony (1935-39) include Sibelius and Stravinsky but perhaps more
significantly Copland and Hindemith. It is clearly a youthful work, a bit long-winded, but showing
Rota's already firm grasp of complicated and sophisticated orchestration. The last, fourth,
movement especially seems to have a maturity that points towards future greatness. The Second
Symphony, which he began while still at work on the First, in 1937, is even more Coplandesque.
What would this have sounded like to an audience in the 1930s (it wasn't performed until 1970)? In

one way it would have seemed conservative in the extreme, showing no tendency towards atonality or any influence of jazz. The score carries a subtitle, 'Tarantina – Anni di pellegrinaggio', referring to the period Rota spent in the extreme south of Italy, teaching in Taranto. It could be dismissed as 'light music' and the style wouldn't have offended the most sensitive ears, yet each movement is full of beautiful instrumental detail and constructed in a pleasing way. Rota had yet to find his unmistakable voice, one infused with irony and humour, which would make him the perfect match for Federico Fellini. Devotees of his film music may find these symphonies on the bland side, but anyone who enjoys, for instance, the contemporary style of Alwyn or Coates in England, will find these works worthwhile. The orchestra under Ole Kristian Ruud plays both symphonies with a good sense of period manner, never overdoing the lush sound. Recommended for the adventurous.

Piano Concertos – E minor; C major.
Massimo Palumbo *pf*
I Virtuosi Italiani / Marco Boni.
Chandos CHAN9681 (64 minutes: DDD). Recorded 1998.   Ⓕ

Both of these works are unashamedly romantic and nostalgic in style. The E minor Piano Concerto was composed in 1960 – at the same time as Rota's music for Fellini's film *La Dolce Vita*. As if in answer to the latter's extreme cynicism, the concerto seems to be a questioning exploration of the remaining possibilities in a modern, romantic form. It is doubtful if anyone would immediately associate it with the 1960s. The opening *Allegro-tranquillo* movement begins with a dreamlike theme on the piano which is then taken up by the orchestra and developed as a sort of conversation – the orchestra insisting on a heroic, almost martial sound, while the piano and woodwind reiterate the original soft mood. The first movement is over 16 minutes (the main failing of the piece is its length): away from the rule of the film-editor's stop-watch Rota felt free to indulge himself. The same four-note figure that runs through the opening is taken up in the second movement, a quiet, slow section with a haunting intensity. The finale continues the awake-in-a-dream contrasts. Rota composed four piano concertos, but the date of that in C major seems to be in doubt. It is earlier than 1960, and is a sparer, jauntier work, more redolent in mood of the 1920s. It, too, presents a dialogue between the quest-like piano part and the orchestra asserting a darker mood. Both concertos are played by Massimo Palumbo with brilliant technique, the recorded sound is excellent and I Virtuosi Italiani under Marco Boni provides excellent support.

Film Music – The Godfather. Il gattopardo. Prova d'orchestra. La dolce vita. Otto e mezzo. Rocco e i suoi fratelli.
La Scala Philharmonic Orchestra / Riccardo Muti.
Sony Classical SK63359 (71 minutes: DDD). Recorded 1979.   Ⓕ

The influences on Nino Rota's music for *The Godfather* aren't hard to identify – Stravinsky, Ravel, Puccini. It's an ironic commentary on the sordid story to back it with surging neo-romantic symphonic music. Coppola's two-part epic of Italian immigrants in the USA and the drift into mob rule was probably the biggest assignment of Rota's long career. The score made a huge contribution to the film's success – so much so that after his death the studio returned to his music for *Godfather III*. Its mixture of Neapolitan folk-song spattered with jazzy honky-tonk makes for a pleasant opening to this second CD of Rota's music by Riccardo Muti and the Scala Philharmonic. Rota's career was inextricably bound up with those of the two most influential Italian film-makers of the 1950s and 1960s – Fellini and Visconti. Fellini's two big successes of the early 1960s, *La dolce vita* and *Otto e mezzo* are represented by brief extracts – the open-air circus-parade finale of the latter score still has a mysterious, exuberant feel. The sources Rota drew on for this are similar to those in *The Godfather* but his use of them is surer and more original. The last collaboration with Fellini was the comedy about a rehearsal – *Prova d'orchestra*. Time is not being kind to a lot of Fellini's work which now seems self-indulgent, but conversely Visconti's films have a massive grandeur that is overwhelming. Muti's first volume of Rota had the ballroom sequence; here there is a brief suite of themes from the film. *Rocco e i suoi fratelli* caused a scandal in Italy in 1960 with its depiction of organized crime and corruption and it led to Visconti's rift with La Scala because of government interference. He would surely have smiled to think, nearly 40 years later, of the orchestra playing Rota's score for the film.

Albert Roussel   French 1869-1937

Bacchus et Ariane, Op. 43. Le festin de l'araignée, Op. 17.
BBC Philharmonic Orchestra / Yan Pascal Tortelier.
Chandos CHAN9494 (68 minutes: DDD). Recorded 1995.   ⒻⒺ

As compared to his contemporary Dukas, Roussel has been somewhat sidelined as a 'connoisseur's composer'. That presumably means that he did not write fat, lush tunes that could be exploited in television commercials, but produced works of vigorous ideas and more subtle quality. Record companies used to fight shy of his music – the Third and Fourth Symphonies have indeed maintained a foothold, but with the ballet *Bacchus et Ariane*, which is closely linked with the Third, we have mostly been given only its second half. Here are alert, rhythmically vital performances of Roussel's two most famous ballets, which even at the most exuberantly excited moments (like the 'Bacchanale' in *Bacchus*) preserve a truly Gallic lucidity, and which Tortelier marks by a captivating lightness of touch; and when it comes to quiet passages one could not ask for greater tenderness than in the beautiful end of Act 1 of *Bacchus* (shame on those conductors who neglect this for the more extrovert Act 2), when Bacchus puts Ariadne to sleep. *Le festin de l'araignée*, written 18 years earlier, is in a quite different style. Where *Bacchus*'s trenchant idiom at times makes one think of Stravinsky's *Apollon Musagète*, *Le festin* (which had the misfortune to be overshadowed by *The Rite of Spring*, produced only eight weeks later) is atmospheric and more impressionistic (in the same vein as Roussel's First Symphony). It is a score full of delicate invention, whose one weakness is that for its full appreciation a knowledge of its detailed programme is needed – and that is provided here in the booklet. The BBC Philharmonic play it beautifully. If this is 'connoisseur's music', then be happy to be called a connoisseur: you will find it delectable.

Roussel Symphony No. 3 in G minor, Op. 42.
Franck Symphony in D minor.
French National Orchestra / Leonard Bernstein.
DG Masters 445 512-2GMA (69 minutes: DDD). Recorded live in 1981.   Ⓜ

This 1981 Roussel Third is recognizably via Bernstein, and is more kaleidoscopic and meaningful than you are likely to have heard it, unless you possess his first New York account. The *Rite of Spring*-cum-*Age of Steel* stamping rhythms of the first movement are now a little slower, the effect possibly a little relaxed until you arrive at the central climax (astonishing 'whooping' horns and crashing metal) and the coda (now superbly emphatic with ringing trumpets and lots more crashing metal). The slow movement's songful yearning is, as it was before, slow, sublime and intensely searching in the manner of its counterpart in Mahler's Sixth, though the contrasting *più mosso* is not now fast enough and has its limp moments. That said, the general control is superior, particularly at and around the movement's now awesome final climax. Bernstein's New Yorkers were uninhibitedly rowdy and brash in the finale; the finale's moments of brashness are now offset by rather more sophistication (at, again, a slower tempo). The recording, which has a less than ideally focused bass drum, is both spacious and present, with an appropriate touch of astringency on top. Bernstein's Franck is atmospheric, big on rhetoric, extreme in its range of tempo and dynamics and typically intense. On the grand return in the finale of the slow movement's theme, Bernstein broadens massively. Vulgar? Well, perhaps, depending on your viewpoint. His control is again superb, with the orchestra's winds mellifluous in tone.

Impromptu, Op. 21. Deux Poèmes de Ronsard, Op. 26. Joueurs de flûte, Op. 27.
Violin Sonata No. 2 in A major. Segovia, Op. 29. Sérénade, Op. 30. Duo. Vocalises – Aria No. 2.
Irene Maessen *sop* **Paul Verhey** *fl* **Hans Roerade** *ob* **Jos de Lange** *bn*
Jean-Jacques Kantorow *vn* **Erika Waardenburg** *hp* **Jan Goudswaard** *gtr*
Quirijn van Regteren Altena *db* **Jet Röling** *pf* **Schoenberg Quartet** (Janneke van der Meer,
Wim de Jong *vns* Henk Guittart *va* Viola de Hoog *vc*).
Olympia OCD459 (65 minutes: DDD). Recorded 1994.   Ⓕ

While Roussel's orchestral music has won a following in this country, his chamber music still, for the most part, enjoys only cult status here. This excellent volume covers the period from 1919 to 1928, when Roussel, firmly rejecting the impressionism of his contemporary Ravel, had adopted what is often (though loosely) referred to as neo-classical style. Try as one may, it is difficult to avoid the use of the adjective 'astringent' commonly applied to his music; but along with its clean-cut clarity (like that of a good dry wine) and a rhythmic alertness often manifested in unusual time-signatures and changeable tempos goes a dry humour – as in the comic *Duo* for bassoon and double-bass, the fourth piece of the *Joueurs de flûte* (in the vein of Debussy's *Prélude*, 'General Lavine, eccentric') or the angular finale (mostly in 10/8) of the Second Violin Sonata. What is in short supply, however, except in the Aria played here on the oboe, is lyricism: Roussel can be seductive (the charmingly sung Ronsard songs, with their elaborate flute arabesques) or exotic ('Krishna', the third of the 'flute players'), he can even indulge in pastiche, as in the guitar *Segovia*, but – even if this sounds like heresy – his themes remain obstinately unmemorable and he lacks purely melodic invention. Throughout the disc the performances merit the highest praise but special mention must be made of Erika Waardenburg's beautiful playing, with superfine tonal gradations, of the *Impromptu* for harp.

Miklós Rózsa

Rózsa Cello Concerto, Op. 32.
Schurmann The Gardens of Exile.
Peter Rejto *vc*
Pecs Hungarian Symphony Orchestra / Howard Williams.
Silva Classics SILKD6011 (60 minutes: DDD). Recorded 1995.   Ⓕ

Rózsa's Cello Concerto (1969) is substantial, concentrated and accomplished. What is immediately striking is not so much the beguilingly tangy harmonic resource and rhythmic flair of his inspiration (the composer's native Hungarian roots shine through in every bar) as the effortless technical assurance and irresistible colour of it all (Rózsa's expert scoring is a real treat throughout). The eventful, beautifully proportioned first movement is rich in strong ideas, persuasively worked out, and features a cadenza which combines eloquence and riveting virtuosity. By contrast, the central *Lento con grand espressione* is songful and tinged with anguish, whereas the *Allegro vivo* finale, save for a brief, shadowy slower episode, positively swaggers with spiky energy and (again) terrific rhythmic *élan*. Like Rózsa, Gerard Schurmann has gained a reputation as a composer of both film and 'serious' music. Scored for cello obbligato and orchestra, *The Gardens of Exile* (1991) bears a dedication to Sir Michael Tippett. In an introductory note the composer explains: 'The condition of exile referred to in the title of this piece is internal, while the metaphorical gardens in which to dwell contain cultivated memories of the past, back to childhood. Superimposed on this idea were my recollections of a vast expanse of semi-wild tropical gardens in Java. Elegantly structured and the product of a sophisticated aural imagination (the orchestration is exotic, luscious even), Schurmann's music has something of the craft and angular lyricism of his teacher, Alan Rawsthorne. In fact *The Gardens of Exile* is a most beguiling score. Rejto is a commanding, highly articulate soloist and his contribution has both discipline and tonal lustre to commend it. The accompaniment is watchful and dedicated and although balance is well judged, the overall sound could have done with more bloom. A most enjoyable pairing.

Piano Concerto, Op. 31. Cello Concerto, Op. 32.
Brinton Smith *vc* **Evelyn Chen** *pf* **New Zealand Symphony Orchestra / James Sedares.**
Koch International Classics 37402-2 (62 minutes: DDD). Recorded 1997.   Ⓕ

Brinton Smith (a prize-winning pupil of Zara Nelsova at the Juilliard School) is the eloquent, impassioned soloist in the Cello Concerto and he receives accomplished support from Sedares and the New Zealand SO. What a pity, then, that the uncomfortably cavernous, slightly synthetic sound picture doesn't really do full justice to their sterling efforts. For anyone coming to this splendid work for the first time, we would therefore recommend the Rejto/Williams version ahead of this admittedly altogether more commanding newcomer. Enthusiasts, on the other hand, will be delighted to learn that the two performances on this disc complement each other beautifully: the sheer bravura of Smith's reading is infectious, whereas Rejto is a degree more reticent. The Piano Concerto (1966) is big-boned, virtuosic in the extreme and full of the most engaging local colour; it is cast in traditional three-movement form, the finale being an especially eventful creation. What's more, Rózsa's unerring sense of proportion ensures that the work never threatens to outstay its welcome. Evelyn Chen is a dazzlingly secure, sympathetic exponent, and she builds a fine rapport with Sedares and the NZSO. Happily, the resonant acoustic is noticeably better controlled here, and the balance is excellent.

Variations on a Hungarian Peasant Song, Op. 4. North Hungarian Peasant Songs and Dances, Op. 5. Duo, Op. 7. Solo Violin Sonata, Op. 40.
Isabella Lippi *vn* **John Novacek** *pf*
Koch International Classics 37256-2 (62 minutes: DDD). Recorded 1994.   Ⓕ

In his autobiography, *A Double Life* (Midas Books: 1982) Rózsa proudly declares that 'the music of Hungary is stamped indelibly ... on virtually every bar I have ever put on paper', and nowhere are the fervent, rustic rhythms of the composer's beloved homeland more vividly assimilated than in his music for solo violin. This is especially true of Opp. 4 and 5, two early successes from 1929, both of which blaze with potent memories of the Magyar peasant music that Rózsa felt was all around him, and which he would jot down 'in a kind of delirium' during his youth on the family estate. Op. 7 was written two years later and marked the end of his term as a student in Leipzig. Though evoking once again the gipsy fiddlers of his boyhood, the themes here are actually Rózsa's own and reveal some of the surging romanticism that would later characterize his film scores. Following his memorable career in Hollywood, Rózsa made a satisfying return to 'pure' music with the Solo Violin Sonata of 1986. Dedicated to his friend Manuel Compinsky, this passionate, energetic piece pays another loving tribute to the mother country that provided Rózsa with a 'living source of inspiration'. Isabella Lippi is a highly expressive soloist. She tackles the many fiendishly animated passages with great panache but also displays a keen understanding of the music's pastoral colouring and darkly romantic fervour. Sympathetic support from her accompanist and clear, warm sound.

Edmund Rubbra
British 1901-1986

Violin Concerto, Op. 103. Viola Concerto, Op. 75.
Tasmin Little *vn* **Rivka Golani** *va*
Royal Philharmonic Orchestra / Vernon Handley.
Conifer Classics CDCF225 (54 minutes: DDD). Recorded 1994. Ⓕ

The Viola Concerto, a première recording, is a work of striking euphony and depth. There are none of the piquant dissonances of, say, the Bartók or Walton concertos; the Rubbra concentrates on linear development; the satisfaction this concerto gives resides primarily in the subtlety with which its lines evolve and grow. The pensive, rhapsodic opening puts one immediately under its spell. The most poetic of the three movements is the finale, subtitled *Collana musicale* or 'musical necklace', nine linked sections, each of them self-contained and offering thoughts on the theme rather than conventional variations. Rivka Golani gives a fine account of the solo part, her playing committed and intelligent even though her tone could at times do with greater opulence. The Violin Concerto, too, is a three-movement piece, though here it is the middle movement, *Poema,* that is the emotional centre of gravity; it has both depth and serenity. The invention unfolds seamlessly and organically, each idea growing out of and developing from the preceding one. Tasmin Little's playing is thoughtful and eloquent and her virtuosity conveys a sense of effortless ease. Moreover, in Vernon Handley she is supported by a conductor who both knows what this music is about, and has its measure.

Symphonies – No. 3, Op. 49; No. 7 in C major, Op. 88.
BBC National Orchestra of Wales / Richard Hickox.
Chandos CHAN9634 (71 minutes: DDD). Recorded 1997. ⒻＢ

For some years the Third Symphony was a repertory piece, at least on BBC programmes, but it fell completely out of favour in the late 1950s. Commentators have noticed a certain Sibelian cut to its opening idea (with woodwind in thirds) but everything else strikes you as being completely personal. There is a whiff of Elgarian fantasy in the fourth variation of the finale. It has been called the most genial and relaxed of Rubbra's symphonies but there is a pastoral feel to many of the ideas, bucolic even, in the same way that there is about the Brahms Second Symphony. Brahms springs to mind in the masterly variations and fugue of the finale, for not long before, Rubbra had orchestrated the Brahms *Handel* Variations. Richard Hickox and his fine players give a very persuasive and totally convincing account of the symphony. Anyone coming to the Seventh for the first time, particularly in this performance, will surely not fail to sense the elevated – indeed exalted – quality of its musical thought. Its opening paragraphs are among the most beautiful Rubbra ever penned and it is evident throughout that this is music that speaks of deep and serious things. This performance speaks with great directness and power. The horn playing in the opening is eloquent and the orchestral playing throughout is of a uniformly high standard. To sum up, these are magnificent and impressive accounts and the recording is truthful and splendidly balanced.

Symphonies – No. 4, Op. 53; No. 10, Op. 145, 'Sinfonia da camera'; No. 11, Op. 153.
BBC National Orchestra of Wales / Richard Hickox.
Chandos CHAN9401 (58 minutes: DDD). Recorded 1993-94. Ⓕ

Rubbra's music lacks the kind of surface allure that captivates the ear at first acquaintance. Nor does he possess the dramatic power of Vaughan Williams or his immediate contemporary Walton, but he does have a sense of organic continuity that is both highly developed and immediately evident to the listener. Wilfrid Mellers put it in a nutshell when he said of the symphonies, there is 'nothing abstruse about their tonality and harmony, which is basically diatonic', but they are difficult because 'the continuity of their melodic and polyphonic growth is logical and unremitting. The orchestration shows scarcely any concern for the possibilities of colour, nothing on which the senses can linger and the nerves relax. Second subjects are hardly ever contrasting ideas but rather evolutions from or transfigurations of the old.' The opening of the Fourth Symphony is one of the most beautiful things not just in Rubbra but in the English music of our time. These pages are free from any kind of artifice, and their serenity and quietude remain with the listener for a long time. The Fourth (1940-42) was a wartime work, though no one would ever guess so. The Tenth and

Eleventh Symphonies are late works from 1974 and 1979 respectively. Both symphonies are highly concentrated one-movement affairs which unfold with the seeming inevitability and naturalness so characteristic of the composer. To sum up, this is music made to last. Richard Hickox has the measure of its breadth and serenity, and secures a sense of total commitment and dedication from his excellent players. The Chandos recording is in the best traditions of the house.

Symphony No. 9, 'Sinfonia sacra', Op. 140. The Morning Watch, Op. 55.
Lynne Dawson sop **Della Jones** mez **Stephen Roberts** bar
BBC National Chorus and Orchestra of Wales / Richard Hickox.
Chandos CHAN9441 (57 minutes: DDD). Texts included. Recorded 1993.   Ⓕ🅔

The Ninth is Rubbra's most visionary utterance and its stature has so far gone unrecognized (this is its only recording). After its first performance in Liverpool in 1973 it remained on the shelf, apart from a BBC broadcast in the early 1980s, which Richard Hickox also conducted. Its subtitle, *Sinfonia sacra*, gives a good idea of its character. It tells the story of the Resurrection very much as do the Bach Passions. There are three soloists: the contralto narrates from the New Testament while the soprano takes the part of Mary Magdalen and the baritone that of Jesus. Other parts – those of disciples and angels – are taken by the chorus which also functions outside the action, in four settings of meditative Latin texts from the Roman liturgy or in Lutheran chorales to which Rubbra has put verses by Bernard de Nevers. The symphonic dimension is reinforced by the opening motive, which pretty well dominates the work or, as the composer puts it, casts its shadow over everything. Its argument unfolds with a seeming inevitability and naturalness that is the hallmark of a great symphony. Its depth and beauty call to mind only the most exalted of comparisons and it should be heard as often as *Gerontius* or the *War Requiem*. This is music of an inspired breadth and serenity and everyone connected with this magnificent performance conveys a sense of profound conviction. *The Morning Watch* is one of Rubbra's most eloquent choral pieces. It dates from 1946, and so comes roughly half-way between the Fourth and Fifth Symphonies. A setting of the seventeenth-century metaphysical poet, Henry Vaughan, it too is music of substance and its long and moving orchestral introduction is of the highest order of inspiration. Richard Hickox and his fine team of singers and players deserve thanks and congratulations, as indeed does Chandos for giving it such excellent sound.

Rubbra A Hymn to the Virgin, Op. 13[ab]. Rosa mundi, Op. 2[ab]. Fukagawa[b]. Pezzo ostinato, Op. 102[b]. Songs, Op. 4 – The Mystery[a]; Jesukin[ab]. Orpheus with his Lute, Op. 8[ab]. Transformations, Op. 141[b]. The Jade Mountain, Op. 116[ab]. Improvisation, Op. 124[c]. Discourse, Op. 127[bc].
L. Berkeley Nocturne[b].
Howells Prelude[b].
[a]**Tracey Chadwell** sop [b]**Danielle Perrett** hp [c]**Tim Gill** vc
ASV CDDCA1036 (67 minutes: DDD). Texts included. Recorded 1995.   Ⓕ

All but ten minutes of this CD is devoted to Rubbra and several works here are in fact first recordings, including the impressive *Transformations* for harp, Op. 141, and the early miniatures that open the disc, the *Hymn to the Virgin* and *Rosa mundi*. Both reflect the world of Holst and Scott. Many of the pieces also reflect the strong attraction Rubbra felt for the Orient, from the early *Fukagawa* arrangement (1929), to *The Jade Mountain* (1962), as well as the inspiring harp pieces: the *Pezzo ostinato* and the *Transformations*, the most extended (and perhaps the most exalted) piece on the disc. Both derive inspiration from the Indian *raga*. Danielle Perrett plays with finesse and sensitivity and her free, imaginative handling of the *Pezzo ostinato* is admirable. She brings authority to the *Improvisation*, Op. 124 (1964). Tracey Chadwell proves an intelligent interpreter of the songs, although (and this is a minor reservation) she appears more backwardly balanced and there is just a shade too much echo round her voice. Generally speaking, however, the recording is first-rate. The overall character of this music is meditative and readers should select a few pieces at a time: the repertoire – in particular the big harp pieces – benefits from and rewards the listener's rapt concentration. Both the Lennox Berkeley *Nocturne* and the Howells *Prelude* are attractive pieces. This is a mandatory acquisition for Rubbra *aficionados*.

Anton Rubinstein   Russian 1829-1894

Rubinstein Piano Concerto No. 4 in D minor, Op. 70[a].
Shura Cherkassky pf
[a]**Royal Philharmonic Orchestra / Vladimir Ashkenazy.**
Decca 448 063-2DH (76 minutes: [a]DDD/[b]ADD). Recorded [a]1994, [b]1974.   Ⓕ

Encores[b]: **Rubinstein** Melody in F major, Op. 3 No. 1. **J. Strauss II/Godowsky** Wein, Weib und Gesang. **Godowsky** Waltz-poem No. 4 (for left hand). Triakontameron – Alt Wien. **Saint-Saëns/Godowsky** Le carnaval des animaux – No. 13, The swan. **Schubert/Godowsky** Moment musical in F minor, D780 No. 3. **Tchaikovsky** Nocturne in C sharp minor, Op. 19 No. 4. **Glazunov** Valse in D major, Op. 42 No. 3. **Chaminade** Autrefois, Op. 87 No. 4. **Moszkowski** Caprice espagnole, Op. 37.

What other pianist possessed so succulent or teasing a sense of sophistication? Every glistening strand of Godowsky's *Wein, Weib und Gesang*, his polyphonic, poly-rhythmic maze, is highlighted with uncanny virtuoso resource, and even Sir Clifford Curzon – that incomparable Schubertian – might have smiled rather than frowned over Cherkassky's Schubert-Godowsky, an arrangement he abhorred. Glazunov's *Valse* in D is spun off with a delicate, vertiginous brilliance entirely Cherkassky's own and Chaminade's *Autrefois* is a charming pastiche. Then there is Rubinstein's Fourth Concerto, another work for long at the centre of Cherkassky's affections. That august publication, *The Record Guide* (Collins: 1951) may have offered a sniping estimate ('the swelling introduction promises great things, but what emerges is perhaps only a rather large mouse') but played with Cherkassky's musical commitment even the most outwardly conventional gestures take wing. A passing sense of frailty is instantly erased by Cherkassky's tip-toe delicacy in the whirlwind finale, by a shot-silk tonal finesse in the central *Andante*, and by a capacity to take all the time in the world to make his points, whether piquantly or expressively. Ashkenazy's partnership with his quicksilver soloist could hardly be more sympathetic and the recordings capture Cherkassky's tonal bloom and colour to perfection.

Poul Ruders

Danish 1949

Violin Concerto No. 1[a]. Etude and Ricercare. The Bells[b]. The Christmas Gospel[c].
Lucy Shelton *sop* **Rolf Schulte** *vn*
[b]**Speculum Musicae / David Starobin** *gtr* [a]**Riverside Symphony Orchestra / George Rothman;** [c]**Malmö Symphony Orchestra / Ola Rudner.**
Bridge BCD9057 (62 minutes: DDD). Texts included. Recorded 1994-95.   Ⓕ **E**

Ruders's First Violin Concerto (from 1981) begins as routine minimalist auto-hypnosis. But it develops some wonderfully inventive ways of disrupting and reassembling itself. Admittedly the last movement, with its chaconne based on Vivaldi and Schubert, tiptoes on the border of sensationalism. Otherwise the work could join Schnittke's Fourth as one of the few contemporary violin concertos with a strong claim to standard-repertoire status. Rolf Schulte gives an intense account of the solo part; the Riverside orchestra is tight in discipline, the recording close. All these factors help to make the overall musical impression extremely vivid. Less persuasive is Ruders's vocal writing in *The Bells* (the same Edgar Allen Poe texts as set by Rachmaninov), and there is something not quite convincing about the instrumental setting too – perhaps too uniform an intensity, too much frantic heterophony. Oliver Knussen has done this sort of thing rather more successfully. *The Christmas Gospel*, tossed off in two weeks for a mixed animation and live-action film, is darkly impressive – necessarily simple and direct, but still rewarding, even when divorced from the visual images. Superb performances and recordings throughout.

Four Dances in One Movement. Dramaphonia. Corpus cum figuris.
Erik Kaltoft *pf*
Aarhus Sinfonietta / Søren Kinch Hansen.
BIS CD720 (70 minutes: DDD). Recorded 1995-96.   Ⓕ

The name *Corpus cum figuris* ('body with figurations') comes from Thomas Mann's novel about a fictional German composer, *Dr Faustus*. There's no programmatic significance, says Poul Ruders; it was the title itself that set his imagination working. At times the piece does sound like a grotesque, terrifying break-dance, full of jagged, joint-dismembering syncopations. But something of Mann's apocalyptic conception seems to have got into Ruders's music too – the smell of sulphur, the sense of prevailing desolation. It comes over well in this moody but very precise performance. So too does *Dramaphonia*, a one-movement piano concerto with an 'orchestra' of 11 instruments. This is more sombre still than *Corpus cum figuris*, the pace prevailingly slow and brooding. But Ruders knows how to hold the attention, even when very little seems to be happening. *Four Dances in One Movement* makes an excellent contrast. Now we're nearer to the 'lighter' Ruders – the composer who could win over a Last Night of the Proms audience with his brilliant and entertaining *Concerto in Pieces*. The darkness of the other two works isn't entirely absent from *Four Dances*, but the sweetly parodistic waltz tune of the second dance is delicious. Perhaps the performance could be a little more satirically stylish. The recording is lucidity itself.

John Rutter

Requiem[a]. Hymn to the Creator of Light. God be in my head. A Gaelic Blessing. Psalmfest – No. 5, Cantate Domino. Open thou mine eyes[b]. A Prayer of St Patrick. A Choral Fanfare. Birthday Madrigals – No. 2, Draw on, sweet night; No. 4, My true love hath my heart. The Lord bless you and keep you.
[a]Rosa Mannion, [b]Libby Crabtree *sops*
Polyphony; Bournemouth Sinfonietta / Stephen Layton.
Hyperion CDA66947 (69 minutes: DDD). Texts and translations included. Recorded 1997.   Ⓕ🄴

Here is music finely crafted, written with love for the art and an especial care for choral sound. It is melodious without being commonplace, harmonically rich without being sticky, modern in the graceful way of a child who grows up responsive to newness but not wanting to kick his elders in the teeth. He gives us, in large measure, the heart's desire: we listen saying 'Ah yes!' and with a half-foreseen satisfaction 'Yes, of course! Lovely!' But he's on too familiar terms with our heart's desires, doesn't extend them, or surprise us into realizing that they were deeper and subtler than we thought. This is by way of cautiously savouring a remembered taste, which could readily be indulged without perceived need for an interval: one item leads to another and before we know it the pleasurable hour is over. The Requiem itself lasts for 36 minutes; the other pieces vary from under two minutes to just over six. Most are unaccompanied and show the choir of 25 voices as another of those expert groups of assured and gifted professionals that are among the principal adornments of modern musical life. Their capacity as a virtuoso choir is tested in the *Cantate Domino* and *Choral Fanfare*, but Rutter writes for real singers (not just singer-musicians) and their tone is unfailingly beautiful. Rosa Mannion and Libby Crabtree are excellent soloists.

Rutter Five Traditional Songs.
Vaughan Williams Five English Folksongs.
Traditional (arr. Rutter) I know where I'm going. Down by the sally gardens. The bold grenadier. The keel row. The cuckoo. She's like the swallow. Willow song. The willow tree. The miller of Dee. O can ye sew cushions? Afton water. The sprig of thyme. She moved through the fair (arr. Runswick). The lark in the clear air (arr. Carter).
Cambridge Singers; City of London Sinfonia / John Rutter.
Collegium COLCD120 (66 minutes: DDD). Texts included. Recorded 1992.   Ⓕ

Pleasure in singing is almost the *raison d'être* of this disc. John Rutter not only provides those of us over 30 with a healthy dollop of nostalgia, but gives these songs a whole new lease of life in some characteristically scrumptious arrangements. He is not attempting to follow in the footsteps of the great folk-song arrangers (he pays tribute to this tradition by including Vaughan Williams's *Five English Folksongs*). His arrangements belong more to the light music tradition; what Messrs Binge, Coates and Tomlinson achieved with orchestral colours Rutter finds primarily through vocal ones – and it's significant that the very finest arrangements here (including a ravishing 'Golden Slumbers') are unaccompanied. He is supported throughout by an outstanding group of singers.

Harald Saeverud

Saeverud Peer Gynt, Op. 28 – Suites Nos. 1 and 2.
Grieg Peer Gynt Suites Nos. 1 and 2, Opp. 46 and 55.
Anne-Margrethe Eikaas *sop*
Norwegian Radio Orchestra / Ari Rasilainen.
Finlandia 0630-17675-2 (74 minutes: DDD). Recorded 1996.   Ⓕ

To juxtapose the *Peer Gynt* music of Grieg and Saeverud on record is such an obvious idea that it is astonishing that no one has thought of it before. It was inevitable that there should be a reaction against the pictorialism and romanticism of Grieg's *Peer Gynt*, particularly after the upheaval of the Second World War and the Nazi occupation of Norway, and when Saeverud was approached by Hans Jacob Nilsen to compose his incidental music, it was for a realistic production shorn of sentiment and glamour. Saeverud's score for the play has no vestige of romanticism, not a trace of gentility, and its musical language is robust and uncouth. It is full of character, whether it is in 'Peerludium', the portrayal of the cocky Peer himself, the wild and lascivious 'Anitra' (nothing demure about her) or the splendidly earthy 'Devil's Five-hop' and the equally brilliant 'Dovretroll jog'. The Norwegian Radio Orchestra is a highly accomplished body with great refinement of colour and tone, and Ari Rasilainen draws splendid, well-characterized playing from them. The familiar Grieg suites are hardly less fine. The recording is refined, most realistic in perspective and ideally balanced.

Camille Saint-Saëns
French 1835-1921

Cello Concerto No. 1 in A minor, Op. 33.

Cello Concerto No. 1. Le carnaval des animaux – The swan[a]. Romance in F major, Op. 36[b]. Romance in D major, Op. 51[b]. Cello Sonata No. 1 in C minor, Op. 32[b]. Chant saphique in D major, Op. 91[b]. Gavotte in G minor, Op. posth.[b]. Allegro appassionato in B minor, Op. 43[b]. Prière, Op. 158[c].
Steven Isserlis vc [a]**Dudley Moore,** [b]**Pascal Devoyon** pfs [c]**Francis Grier** org
London Symphony Orchestra / Michael Tilson Thomas.
RCA Victor Red Seal 09026 61678-2 (67 minutes: DDD). Recorded 1992.   Ⓕ

'Concerto!' was a Channel Four TV series that showed participating soloists in rehearsal, in conversation with Dudley Moore and Michael Tilson Thomas and, ultimately, in performance, which resulted in several recordings, of which this is one. This disc is recommendable not so much for Steven Isserlis's Cello Concerto – smooth and intelligent as that is – as for the additional fill-ups. *The swan* has Moore and Tilson Thomas as joint accompanists, elegantly executed, but the items with Pascal Devoyon are especially valuable, the First Cello Sonata full of elegantly tailored drama, the two *Romances*, *Chant saphique* and *Gavotte* palpable charmers, tastefully played; and the headstrong, thematically memorable *Allegro appassionato*, one of the finest shorter pieces in the cellist's repertory. The disc is enhanced by the opportunity of hearing the rather affecting but relatively unfamiliar *Prière*, composed for André Hekking just two years before Saint-Saëns's death.

Cello Concertos – No. 1; No. 2 in D minor, Op. 119. Suite, Op. 16 (arr. vc/orch). Allegro appassionato in B minor, Op. 43. Le carnaval des animaux – The swan.
Maria Kliegel vc
Bournemouth Sinfonietta / Jean-François Monnard.
Naxos 8 553039 (62 minutes: DDD). Recorded 1995.   Ⓢ

This issue neatly plugs two gaps in the catalogue. The cello and orchestra version of the Op. 16 Suite (originally with piano) is extremely effective, with the composer's own colourful and transparent instrumentation. The 'Romance' sounds particularly fine with its expressive, original harmonies, and prominent woodwind, and Maria Kliegel and the Bournemouth players are thoroughly in tune with the spirit of the music. The Second Cello Concerto of 1902, the last of Saint-Saëns's ten concertos, lacks the highly memorable melodies of the popular First Concerto, but it has other qualities – a *fin de siècle* richness of harmony in the slower music, and a two-movement form that's both original and cogent. It's also very virtuosic, and Maria Kliegel performs with impressive panache and precision. A most welcome addition to the catalogue, then, especially in such a persuasive performance – and at a super-bargain price. The First Concerto, too, is well played, but on its own wouldn't be the first recommendation (János Starker's performance on a Mercury disc – see the review under Lalo – is our first choice). The performance here seems a little disconnected, with some beautiful sections, like the second theme in the finale, next to others that are 'milked' for immediate effect.

Cello Concerto No. 1[a]. Suite, Op. 16 (arr. cpsr)[a]. Cello Sonata No. 1[b]. Romance, Op. 36[a]. Allegro appassionato[a]. Le carnaval des animaux – The swan[a].
Mischa Maisky vc [b]**Daria Hovora** pf
[a]**Orpheus Chamber Orchestra.**
DG 457 599-2GH (70 minutes: DDD). Recorded 1997.   Ⓕ

Mischa Maisky's rich, velvety tone and brilliant technique give all the works here an arresting, memorable quality. The recordings, too, are full and resonant and, in the concerto, the Orpheus players sound as passionately involved as the soloist; the tuttis lose all feeling of formality. (By comparison, the LSO for Isserlis lacks intensity.) You will be swept along by Maisky's performance until the third movement, where he takes the main theme very slowly, more *Andante* than *Allegro moderato*, then speeds up substantially for the virtuoso passages. Isserlis shows how much more satisfying a performance can be without these extreme tempo variations. For the Suite, though, Maisky is preferable over the Naxos recording with Maria Kliegel, attractive and stylish though it is. Playing and recording are more vivid, with the *Molto adagio tempo* of the 'Romance' beautifully sustained. Maisky's warmth and verve carry him through the *Allegro appassionato* and the Op. 36 *Romance* in fine style, but 'The swan' is very disappointing – hold-ups (often big ones) on nearly every bar-line destroy the serenity. Though the Maisky and Isserlis discs contain several of the same pieces, there's a very different emphasis – Isserlis mostly with piano, Maisky with orchestra, so they only come into direct competition for the concerto and the sonata. The performances of the latter are very different, Maisky and Hovora bringing out the music's dark passion, Isserlis and Devoyon stressing classical refinement. The Isserlis/Devoyon *Andante* is definitely preferable– the different elements come together more persuasively – but for the outer movements it's more difficult to say; you really need to hear both.

Piano Concerto No. 2 in G minor, Op. 22.

Piano Concertos – No. 1 in D major, Op. 17[a]; No. 2[b]; No. 3 in E flat major, Op. 29[c]; No. 4 in C minor, Op. 44[a]; No. 5 in F major, Op. 103, 'Egyptian'[b].
Pascal Rogé *pf*
[a]**Philharmonia Orchestra;** [b]**Royal Philharmonic Orchestra;**
[c]**London Philharmonic Orchestra / Charles Dutoit.**
Double Decca 443 865-2DF2 (two discs: 140 minutes: ADD). Recorded 1978-79. Ⓜ **RR**

Saint-Saëns's First Concerto was written when the composer was 23 years old, and it is a sunny, youthful, happy work conventionally cast in the traditional three-movement form. A decade later he wrote the Second Concerto in a period of only three weeks. This concerto begins in a mood of high seriousness rather in the style of a Bach organ prelude; then this stern mood gives way to a jolly fleet-footed *Scherzo* and a *presto* finale: it is an uneven work, though the most popular of the five concertos and this is its most recommendable version. The Third Concerto is perhaps the least interesting work, whilst the Fourth is the best of the five. It is in effect a one-movement work cast in three ingeniously crafted sections. Saint-Saëns wrote his last, the *Egyptian*, in 1896 to mark his 50 years as a concert artist. Mirroring the sights and sounds of a country he loved, this is another brilliant work. Pascal Rogé has a very secure, exuberant sense of rhythm, which is vital in these works, as is his immaculate, pearly technique. Dutoit is a particularly sensitive accompanist and persuades all three orchestras to play with that lean brilliance which the concertos demand. The recordings are true and well balanced.

Saint-Saëns Piano Concerto No. 2.
Rachmaninov Piano Concerto No. 3 in D minor, Op. 30.
Shostakovich Prelude and Fugue in D major, Op. 87 No. 5.
Emil Gilels *pf*
Paris Conservatoire Orchestra / André Cluytens.
Testament mono SBT1029 (65 minutes: ADD). Recorded 1954-56. Ⓔ **H**

Gilels was a true king of pianists and these Paris and New York based recordings can only strengthen and confirm his legendary status. Here, once more, is that superlative musicianship, that magisterial technique and, above all, that unforgettable sonority; rich and sumptuous at every level. What breadth and distinction he brings to the first movement of the Saint-Saëns, from his fulmination in the central octave uproar to his uncanny stillness in the final pages. High jinks are reserved for the second and third movements, the former tossed off with a teasing lightness, the latter's whirling measures with infinite brio. An approximate swipe at the *Scherzo's* flashing double-note flourish, a false entry and a wrong turning five minutes into the finale offer amusing evidence of Gilels's high-wire act; this performance was, after all, recorded before today's obsession with a gleaming and artificial perfection. No performance of this concerto is more 'live', and it is small wonder that Claudio Arrau included it among his desert island favourites. Gilels's Rachmaninov is altogether more temperate yet, once more, this is among the few truly great performances of this work. His tempo is cool and rapid, and maintained with scintillating ease through even the most formidable intricacy. The cadenza – the finer and more transparent of the two – billows and recedes in superbly musical style and the climax is of awe-inspiring grandeur and the central *scherzando* in the finale is as luminous as it is vivacious. The finale's *meno mosso* variation is excluded (a beautiful passage that Gilels would doubtless have reinstated in our more enlightened times) and, it has to be said, Cluytens's partnership is distant and run of the mill. But the recordings hardly show their age in such admirably smooth transfers. Gilels's 'encore', Shostakovich's piquant Prelude and Fugue No. 5 shines like a brilliant shaft of light after the Rachmaninov. The performance is perfection, entirely justifying Artur Rubinstein's comment after hearing him play in Russia: 'If that boy comes to the West, I shall have to shut up shop'.

Saint-Saëns Violin Concerto No. 3 in B minor, Op. 61.
Wieniawski Violin Concerto No. 2 in D minor, Op. 22.
Julian Rachlin *vn*
Israel Philharmonic Orchestra / Zubin Mehta.
Sony Classical SK48373 (52 minutes: DDD). Recorded 1991. Ⓕ

Saint-Saëns's expansive Third Violin Concerto has the rare distinction of providing a showcase for virtuosos without compromising purely musical values. In terms of thematic material and orchestration, it has all the gracefulness and restraint of a classical concerto (as well it might, given its composer's admiration for Beethoven), but, additionally, it manages to find space for passion (first movement) and tenderness (second), as well as encourage a highly musical brand of technical display (third). Written for Sarasate in the early 1880s, the Concerto has long attracted the attention of leading players, yet has still to achieve the popularity of Saint-Saëns's more celebrated shorter works for violin and orchestra, his *Havanaise* and *Introduction and Rondo capriccioso*. Tchaikovsky was much taken with Henryk Wieniawski's Second Concerto (1862), a less ambitious piece than the Saint-Saëns but one that, over the years, has proved more popular. A great violinist himself, Wieniawski knew how to challenge his interpreters with devilishly difficult passagework and gorgeous melodies (such as we encounter at the heart of this D minor Concerto), and it is a pleasure to encounter a young player who so fully understands its idiom. Lithuanian-born Julian Rachlin has a smooth, velvety tone and a lightning left hand; his playing has something of the cultured refinement of the late Nathan Milstein, yet it has its own personality and on this particular CD enjoys the added advantage of superb accompaniments, beautifully recorded. Incidentally, in the Wieniawski, the orchestral tutti passages are played complete.

Danse macabre in G minor, Op. 40. Phaéton in C major, Op. 39. Le rouet d'Omphale in A major, Op. 31. La Jeunesse d'Hercule in E flat major, Op. 50. Marche héroïque in E flat major, Op. 34. Introduction and Rondo capriccioso in A minor, Op. 28[a]. Havanaise in E major, Op. 83[a].
[a]**Kyung-Wha Chung** *vn*
[a]**Royal Philharmonic Orchestra; Philharmonia Orchestra / Charles Dutoit.**
Decca 425 021-2DM (66 minutes: ADD).   Ⓜ

It's enough to make you weep – at the age of three, Saint-Saëns wrote his first tune, analysed Mozart's *Don Giovanni* from the full score when he was five, and at ten claimed he could play all of Beethoven's 32 piano sonatas from memory. There is some consolation in the fact that, according to a contemporary, physically 'he strangely resembled a parrot', and perhaps even his early brilliance was a curse rather than a blessing, as he regressed from being a bold innovator to becoming a dusty reactionary. In his thirties (in the 1870s) he was at the forefront of the Lisztian avant-garde. To Liszt's invention, the 'symphonic poem' (Saint-Saëns was the first Frenchman to attempt the genre, with César Franck hard on his heels), he brought a typically French concision, elegance and grace. Charles Dutoit has few peers in this kind of music; here is playing of dramatic flair and classical refinement that exactly matches Saint-Saëns intention and invention. Decca's sound has depth, brilliance and richness.

Symphony No. 3 in C minor, Op. 78, 'Organ'.

Symphonies – A major; F major, 'Urbs Roma'; No. 1 in E flat major, Op. 2; No. 2 in A minor, Op. 55; No. 3.
Bernard Gavoty *org*
French Radio National Orchestra / Jean Martinon.
EMI CZS5 69683-2 (two discs: 156 minutes: ADD). Recorded 1972-75.   Ⓜ

Saint-Saëns's four early symphonies have rather tended to be eclipsed by the popularity of his much later *Organ* Symphony. It's easy to see why the latter, with its rich invention, its colour and its immediate melodic appeal has managed to cast an enduring spell over its audiences, but there is much to be enjoyed in the earlier symphonies too. The A major dates from 1850 when Saint-Saëns was just 15 years old and is a particularly attractive and charming work despite its debt to Mendelssohn and Mozart. The Symphony in F major of 1856 was the winning entry in a competition organized by the Societé Sainte-Cécile of Bordeaux but was immediately suppressed by the composer after its second performance. The pressures of writing for a competition no doubt contribute to its more mannered style but it nevertheless contains some impressive moments, not least the enjoyable set of variations that form the final movement. The Symphony No. 1 proper was in fact written three years before the *Urbs Roma* and shares the same youthful freshness of the A major, only here the influences are closer to Schumann and Berlioz. The Second Symphony reveals the fully mature voice of Saint-Saëns and in recent years has achieved a certain amount of popularity which is almost certainly due in part to this particularly fine recording. Inevitably we arrive at the *Organ* Symphony, and if you don't already have a recording then you could do a lot worse than this marvellously colourful and flamboyant performance. Indeed, the performances throughout this generous set are persuasive and exemplary. A real bargain, well worth investigating.

Symphony No. 3[a]. Samson et Dalila – Bacchanale[b]. Le déluge – Prélude[b]. Danse macabre[b].
[a]**Gaston Litaize** *org*
[a]**Chicago Symphony Orchestra,** [b]**Orchestre de Paris / Daniel Barenboim.**
DG Galleria 415 847-2GGA (56 minutes: ADD). Recorded 1976.   Ⓜ ℞℞

Daniel Barenboim's recording of the Third Symphony has dominated the catalogue ever since it first appeared on LP. There is not a rival version to match it in its warmth and power. If anyone for whatever reason has been holding back from buying a recording of this massively enjoyable symphony, then they should wait no longer. This is one of the most exciting, physically involving recordings ever made of this work. Barenboim secures not only fine ensemble from his Chicago players but conveys supremely well the mounting excitement of a live performance, without ever falling into hysteria. The organ part has been superimposed on to the Chicago tape. It has Gaston Litaize at the organ of Chartres Cathedral, and though there may be objections in principle, the result is more sharply defined than on most rival recordings. The reissue is generous in offering an exhilarating 'Bacchanale' from *Samson et Dalila*, a sparkling *Danse macabre* in which Luben Yordanoff plays his violin solo beautifully, if not especially diabolically, and the rather engaging and not too sentimental Prélude from *Le déluge*. The remastering has brought a brighter overall sound picture, with the bass response drier, and a very slight loss of bloom on the upper strings. At the famous organ entry in the finale the ear notices that the top is harder, but the spectacle remains and retains its thrill; the *Scherzo* gains from the enhanced inner clarity. When it was first reviewed in 1976 it was predicted that it would be a demonstration record for years to come, and so it has proved.

Symphony No. 3[a]. Le carnaval des animaux[b].
Peter Hurford *org* **Pascal Rogé, Christina Ortiz** *pfs*
[a]**Montreal Symphony Orchestra;** [b]**London Sinfonietta / Charles Dutoit.**
Decca Ovation 430 720-2DM (58 minutes: DDD). Recorded 1980-82. Ⓜ

In 1886 Saint-Saëns poured his considerable experience as an unequalled virtuoso of the organ, piano and practitioner of Lisztian unifying techniques into his *Organ* Symphony; it instantly put the French Symphony on the map, and provided a model for Franck and many others. With its capacity for grand spectacle (aside from the organ and a large orchestra, its scoring includes two pianos) it has suffered inflationary tendencies from both conductors and recording engineers. Dutoit's (and Decca's) achievement is the restoration of its energy and vitality. The private and affectionate portraits in the 'zoological fantasy', *The carnival of the animals*, benefit from more intimate though no less spectacular sound, and a direct approach that avoids obvious clowning.

Saint-Saëns Symphony No. 3.
Debussy La mer.
Ibert Escales.
Berj Zamkochian *org*
Boston Symphony Orchestra / Charles Munch.
RCA Living Stereo 09026 61500-2 (73 minutes: ADD). Recorded 1956-59. Ⓜ Ⓗ

Charles Munch made his famous recording of this Symphony in Symphony Hall, Boston. To get round the problems of the hall resonance the RCA engineers moved many of the seats from the body of the hall so that the orchestra could spread out, while the organ (situated behind the stage) was miked separately. The result was a wonderfully rich, sumptuous sound which at the same time achieved internal clarity – one notices that in the *Scherzo* and the filigree passages for piano in the introduction to the finale. However, it is the spectacular moments that one remembrs: the rich bonding of organ and strings in the *Poco adagio* and the full-blooded organ entry from Berj Zamkochian in the finale. Munch's superb reading moves forward with a powerful lyrical impulse in a single sweep from the first note to the last. To make this issue even more enticing Munch's 1956 versions of Debussy's *La mer* and Ibert's *Escales* ('Port of call') have been included. There is some marvellous playing in both, especially from the lustrous Boston violins. Here, however, the original recordings were more closely balanced and the effect is less rich, the dynamic range less wide. The adrenalin runs high in both performances and the picturesque imagery of *Escales* is vividly conveyed.

Le carnaval des animaux.

Saint-Saëns Le carnaval des animaux.
Poulenc Double Piano Concerto in D minor.
Güher Perkinel, Süher Pekinel *pfs*
French Radio Philharmonic Orchestra / Marek Janowski.
Teldec 4509-97445-2 (38 minutes: DDD). Recorded 1990. Ⓜ ⓇⓇ

Güher and Süher Pekinel, highly talented twins of mixed Turkish-Spanish parentage, playing together on a single piano, set off vivaciously into the Introduction of *Le carnaval des animaux*, tripping along with irresistible charm and gaiety. Throughout, there is such an engaging lightness of touch underneath the surface sparkle that they readily dominate the performance. Yet the balance is well managed, and the partnership with Janowski and the French orchestra works quite admirably, so that time and again the ear is delighted, whether by the squawking hens and cockerels, the gentle, unhurried Offenbachian tortoises, the elephantine sylph, obviously parading on points (the double-bass solo so neatly focused by Gérard Soufflard), the galumphing kangaroos, the fragile, watery aquarium and the dainty fluttering within the aviary. The 'Pianists', for once, are deftly purposeful and sure of themselves; then the fossils forget any macabre associations and dance past with perky insouciance. Perhaps the finest orchestral solo of all is 'The swan' (Eric Levionnais), who swims by with natural grace and simple dignity (and without coming too close). A lovely performance. The finale is as spirited as the opening and it is doubtful if there is a finer account of the Saint-Saëns, nor one more beautifully recorded, with every detail crystal-clear within a most pleasing ambience.

Not surprisingly this personable and perceptive duo then turn to the scintillating wit of Poulenc's Concerto for two pianos. They perform this work equally persuasively, and with plenty of dash and dazzle. Yet the secondary theme of the first movement is given a special haunting nostalgia, half-way between Satie and Ravel, and the delicious Mozartian pastiche of the *Larghetto* is equally relished. How nicely they make the melody sing, while the orchestral backing has the appropriate veiled sensuality and the docile coda is exquisite. Then the finale erupts with bouncing pianistic articulation and rather more strident comments from the orchestra, but again there is an exotic lyrical secondary tune that blossoms nicely before the brief closing burst of pianistic fireworks. The only drawback is the short playing time: 38 minutes; but it may be counted fair value at mid-price.

Saint-Saëns Le carnaval des animaux.
Ravel Ma mère l'oye.
Joseph Villa, Patricia Prattis Jennings *pfs*
Pittsburgh Symphony Orchestra / André Previn.
Philips 400 016-2PH (49 minutes: DDD).   Ⓕ

With the transfer to CD of the Ravel work, the mellowness of the original LP, atmospheric but finely transparent, is further enhanced. The same qualities are a great asset in *Le carnaval des animaux*, notably so in the beautifully transparent account of 'Aquarium' and in the finely judged, not-too-close balance of the solo cello in 'The swan', played with exquisite tenderness by Anne Martindale Williams. The piano tone is extremely faithful too, bright but never aggressive, with the piano chords rightly kept as a pulsing background against the string melody (Offenbach-based) of 'Tortoises', and though the double-basses sound rather distant in 'The elephant', the sepulchral quality in their timbre is very realistic. The full ensemble used in the opening and closing movements is not so transparent, but that is mostly a question of instrumentation. There has rarely, if ever, been a more exuberant account of the final procession of the animals. This is one of the finest versions of this work. The one reservation is a purely technical one. There is no banding except between the two works, which means that if you simply want to play 'The swan' – as many will with such a performance as this – you have to use the fast-forward button.

Saint-Saëns String Quartets – No. 1 in E minor, Op. 112; No. 2 in G major, Op. 153.
Fauré String Quartet in E minor, Op. 121.
Miami Quartet (Ivan Chan, Cathy Meng Robinson *vns* Chauncey Patterson *va* Keith Robinson *vc*).
Conifer Classics 75605 51291-2 (75 minutes: DDD). Recorded 1997.   ⒻⒺ

Saint-Saëns was 64 when he wrote the First Quartet, a closely argued, intense piece, and didn't follow it up for another 20 years; the Second Quartet is not dissimilar in style to those far more popular fruits of his old age, the three woodwind and piano sonatas. Though neither quartet has the melodic memorability of his best-known music, the neglect is hard to understand – there's an effortless mastery of string textures, inventive and original use of counterpoints, and a delightfully fresh approach to form, with continual surprises enlivening the overall unity. The Miami Quartet is a brilliant ensemble. Exceptionally well balanced, there's an uncomplicated, unexaggerated *élan* to their playing, which seems just right for this music, in which intellectual playfulness is an important ingredient. The contrapuntal fun and games of No. 2's finale has a stunning light-fingered virtuosity, yet the more serious moments are just as effective – the sweet serenity of the opening of No. 1's *Adagio*, for instance. The Miami are highly recommended, even without taking into account their beautiful performance of the Fauré; the subtle harmonic and emotional shifts of this unique piece are captured in the most convincing way, with wonderfully affecting changes of tone colour. All round it's an outstanding disc. The Conifer recording is admirably realistic; its clarity highlights the exceptional precision of the playing.

Piano Trios – No. 1 in F major, Op. 18; No. 2 in E minor, Op. 92.
Joachim Trio (Rebecca Hirsch *vn* Caroline Dearnley *vc* John Lenehan *pf*).
Naxos 8 550935 (65 minutes: DDD). Recorded 1993.   ⓈⒺ

1863 and 1892 are the dates of these trios, of which No. 1 was written by a composer not yet 30 but already a confident master of his craft. Bland his voice may be, but it is intelligent and agreeable: a French Brahms without genius, one dares suggest, although Mendelssohn also comes to mind. At the same time, there are passages unlike either of these composers, such as the bare and angular main theme of the A minor slow movement in No. 1, though Grieg might have written it. Such music needs sympathetic, unfussy interpretation and the skilful and sensitive Joachim Trio gives it just that; as for the First Trio as a whole, the work is charming (try the fleet *Scherzo* for a sample) and the booklet-essay rightly notes the 'delicate brilliance' of the piano writing by a composer who was also an expert player. The E minor Trio, a more dramatic five-movement piece is played here with fine judgement and thus warmly expressive without sentimentality or mannerism. The recording is excellent.

Chanson (Nouvelle chanson sur un vieil air). Guitare. Rêverie. L'attente. Le chant de ceux qui s'en vont sur la mer. Le pas d'armes du Roi Jean. La coccinelle. A quoi bon entendre. Si vous n'avez rien à me dire. Dans ton coeur. Danse macabre. Mélodies persanes, Op. 26 – La brise; Sabre en main; Au cimetière; Tournoiement. Marquise, vous souvenez-vous?. La Cigale et la Fourmi. Chanson à boire du vieux temps. Nocturne. Violons dans le soir. Guitares et mandolines. Une flûte invisible. Suzette et Suzon. Aimons-nous. Temps nouveau. Le vent dans la plaine. Grasselette et Maigrelette.
François Le Roux *bar* **Krysia Osostowicz** *vn* **Philippa Davies** *fl* **Graham Johnson** *pf*
Hyperion CDA66856 (78 minutes: DDD). Texts and translations included. Recorded 1996. Ⓕ

This is the most resounding blow yet to be struck for the *mélodies* of Saint-Saëns. François Le Roux with his incisive diction and ability to characterize each song, is a real champion for the man, once so successful, who became, as Graham Johnson puts it in the booklet, 'a footnote' rather than a chapter in the history of French music. Many of the poems that Saint-Saëns set were used by other composers, for instance *Dans ton coeur*, which became Duparc's *Chanson triste*, by 'Jean Lahor' (Henri Cazalis). Graham Johnson playfully suggests what a fortune Saint-Saëns might have made if he had survived long enough to write for the movies a bit more. The first song of the *Mélodies persanes*, 'La brise', is full of eastern promise, the second, 'Sabre en main' a rollicking bit of toy-soldier galloping away, but just as one is beginning to think that Johnson is shooting himself in the foot by being so ironic about the music they're performing comes the hauntingly beautiful fifth song, 'Au cimetière', with its quietly rippling accompaniment and the languorous poem about the lovers sitting on a marble tomb and picking the flowers. Le Roux sings this with controlled, quiet intensity. Johnson makes the point that it is of little importance from which part of the composer's life the songs come, he embodies that totally French nineteenth-century style, sometimes anticipating Hahn and Massenet, sometimes harking back to Boieldieu. If a setting of La Fontaine's fable about the cicada and the ant is pure salon charm, then the final 'Grasselette et Maigrelette' Ronsard *chanson*, composed when Saint-Saëns was 85 in 1920, is a vivacious *café-concert*-style evocation of old Paris.

Samson et Dalila.
Plácido Domingo *ten* Samson; **Waltraud Meier** *mez* Dalila; **Alain Fondary** *bar* Priest;
Jean-Philippe Courtis *bass* Abimelech; **Samuel Ramey** *bass* Old Hebrew;
Christian Papis *ten* Messenger; **Daniel Galvez-Vallejo** *ten* First Philistine;
François Harismendy *bass* Second Philistine;
Chorus and Orchestra of the Bastille Opera, Paris / Myung-Whun Chung.
EMI CDS7 54470-2 (two discs: 124 minutes: DDD). Notes, text and translation included.
Recorded 1991. Ⓕ 🆁🆁

Without doubt this is the most subtly and expertly conducted performance of this work to appear on CD, excellent as others have been in this respect, and also the best played and sung. Chung's achievement is to have welded the elements of pagan ruthlessness, erotic stimulation and Wagnerian harmony that comprise Saint-Saëns's masterpiece into a convincing whole. His success is based on the essentials of a firm sense of rhythm and timing allied to a realization of the sensuousness and delicacy of the scoring. Whether in the lamenting of the Hebrews, the forceful music written for the High Priest, the heroics of Samson, the sensual outpourings of Dalila, or the empty rejoicing of the Bacchanale, he and his orchestra strike to the heart of the matter – and that orchestra plays with Gallic finesse, augmented by a dedicated discipline, not always a feature of French playing. The choral singing, though too distantly recorded, is no less alert and refined, with a full range of dynamic contrast. Meier's Dalila is a fascinating portrayal of this equivocal anti-heroine, seductive, wheedling, exerting her female wiles with the twin objects of sexual dominance and political command. All her sense of purpose comes out in her early greeting to the High Priest, 'Salut à mon père'; then she's meditative and expectant as Dalila ponders on her power at 'Se pourrait-il'. The set numbers are all sung with the vocal ease and long phrase of a singer at the zenith of her powers.

She makes more of the text than Domingo who sings in his now familiar, all-purpose style, admirable in itself, somewhat missing the particular accents brought to this music by the great French tenors of the past. They exist no more and one must salute the sterling and often eloquent tones of Domingo. You may occasionally be conscious that he sounds in a different acoustic from the other singers.

Fondary is superb as the High Priest, firm and rich in tone, commanding and vengeful in delivery: the most compelling interpreter of the part on disc, *tout court*. Ramey is luxury casting as the Old Hebrew, but as this is a part once sung by Pinza, Ramey probably felt he wasn't slumming it. After an unsteady start, he sings the small but important role with breadth and dignity. As Abimelech, Courtis makes much of little. Apart from the two reservations already made, the recording is admirable, with a wide and spacious sound, and the soloists forward, but well integrated into the whole. The Bastille would seem a successful venue for opera recording. This must now be the outright recommendation for this work, one that will give constant and rewarding pleasure.

Samson et Dalila.
Carlo Cossutta *ten* Samson; **Marjana Lipovšek** *mez* Dalila; **Alain Fondary** *bar* Priest;
Yves Bisson *bar* Abimelech; **Harald Stamm** *bass* Old Hebrew;
Constantin Zaharia *ten* Messenger; **Jérôme Engramer** *ten* First Philistine;
Ionel Pantea *bass* Second Philistine;
Sofia Chamber Choir; Bregenz Festival Chorus; Vienna Volksoper Chorus;
Vienna Symphony Orchestra / Sylvain Cambreling.
Koch Schwann 317742 (two discs: 127 minutes: DDD). Notes, text and translation included.
Recorded live in 1988.   Ⓕ

Cambreling draws as much sensuousness and delicacy from the score as any, and also attends to its pagan element with suitable brio. Though like some of his predecessors, he is inclined to linger unduly against the composer's express wishes, as in the marginally too slow tempo for 'Mon coeur s'ouvre à ta voix', he uses the gained time to underline the refinement of the scoring, helped by some lovely playing from his orchestra, which is in true theatrical balance with the singers. Although by rights the polyglot cast should tell against the set, the French is in fact as idiomatic as any. While Lipovšek sometimes, like Meier for Chung, indulges in dramatic gestures strictly outside the realm of style appropriate to the piece, she sings for the most part with a luscious tone and is as pleasing to listen to as Meier and instils the whole role, by vocal means alone, with a sense of Dalila's dangerous powers of seduction. Working in a live performance she has an advantage over all her rivals in creating theatrical intensity. She is matched in that by Cossutta. The then 56-year-old tenor has just the kind of *élan* in his attack that sometimes eludes Domingo (Chung). Some may find the vibrato that is part and parcel of Cossutta's timbre disturbing. Once that is taken on board, Cossutta's is as vigorous, pliable and musically attentive a Samson as any. Fondary was Chung's High Priest, and here he repeats his formidable assumption. The smaller roles are adequately taken and the choral singing is excellent. Stage noises are minimally distracting even during the dances; applause is confined to ends of acts. As a whole the recording has more presence than the backwardly recorded Chung set which is undoubtedly the safer recommendation, Cambreling is the more exciting, both because it is taken live and because of the special *frisson* the two principals give to their music. Do hear one or other version of this superbly integrated score.

Aulis Sallinen   Finnish 1935

Variations for Orchestra, Op. 8. Violin Concerto, Op. 18. Some aspects of Peltoniemi Hintrik's funeral march, Op. 19. The nocturnal dances of Don Juanquixote, Op. 58.
Eeva Koskinen *vn* **Torleif Thedéen** *vc*
Tapiola Sinfonietta / Osmo Vänskä.
BIS CD560 (63 minutes: DDD). Recorded 1992.   Ⓕ

Sallinen's operas and symphonies have stolen the limelight in recent years at the expense of other works fully worthy of attention as this well-played and well-recorded disc proves. Whereas the Variations (1963) are somewhat anonymous if deftly written, the Violin Concerto (1968) is an altogether maturer work, unusually sombre for so bright a solo instrument. The Third String Quartet (1969) is subtitled *Some aspects of Peltoniemi Hintrik's funeral march*. This arrangement for string orchestra dates from 1981. *The nocturnal dances of Don Juanquixote* is an extended fantasia for cello and strings, the title being the only parody of Strauss (although a solo violin enters late as Sancho Panza-leporello!). Sallinen is fond of playing games and all is never as it seems: one can almost hear the collective thud of critics' jaws falling open at this Arnold-like spoof, yet there are darker moments too: bravo to Sallinen and BIS for this intriguing issue.

Songs of Life and Death, Op. 69. The Iron Age – Suite, Op. 55*b*ª.
Margit Papunen *sop* **Jorma Hynninen** *bar* **Opera Festival Chorus;** ª**East Helsinki Music
Institute Choir; Helsinki Philharmonic Orchestra / Okko Kamu.**
Ondine ODE844-2 (75 minutes: DDD). Texts and translations included. Recorded 1995. Ⓕ

Listening to these two works by Aulis Sallinen is a bit like looking at two different photographs of
the composer: the face is undeniably the same but not the perspective. *Songs of Life and Death*
(1993-94) arose, rather by mischance, from a failed effort to compose a Requiem on verses by Lassi
Nummi. Although title and outward form suggest Mahlerian associations, the conservative musical
language rather brings Verdi to mind, and in a very real sense this cycle is a twentieth-century
equivalent of the latter's Requiem: both are symphonic in construction and operatic in idiom,
composed from spiritual rather than religious standpoints, and make use of secular elements. There
are differences, of course, not least in scale and conception. And while Sallinen's songs are also very
much songs of *life*, death is not here perceived as a grim or tragic end, and this imparts to the whole
a peculiarly late twentieth-century aspect. Here at last is the choral-and-orchestral masterpiece
Sibelius should have written, Finnish to the core yet international in appeal. It is one of the very
finest compositions Sallinen has yet produced. Where in the *Songs of Life and Death* voices are the
principal element, in the *Iron Age* Suite (1978-82) the focus is rather on the orchestra, the chorus
being an important but more colouristic extra. The suite originated in music written for a series of
prize-winning Finnish TV documentaries and in it the more familiar Sallinen of the symphonies
and early operas is on display. Both works receive terrific performances from Sallinen's longstanding
champion, Okko Kamu, and his forces.

Dino Saluzzi
20th century

Kultrum – Cruz del Sur. Salón de tango. Milonga de los morenos. … y solos – bajo una luna
amarilla – discuten sobre el pasado. Miserere. El apriete. … y se encaminó hacia el destierro.
Recitativo final.
Dino Saluzzi *bandoneon*
Rosamunde Quartet (Andreas Reiner, Simon Fordham *vns* Helmut Nicolai *va* Anja Lechner *vc*).
ECM New Series 457 854-2 (60 minutes: DDD). Recorded 1998. ⒻⒺ

Too often, recordings that attempt to cross-breed musical forms are contrived by record companies
who think there's a fast buck to be made if they can turn opera into dance music, or early music
into rock, or rock into classical music. However, there have always been a few whose genuinely
multifaceted history allows a natural growing-together of elements from several musical sources.
ECM has been releasing records like this for years, without feeling the need to market them as
'crossover'. Arriving at a critical stance for such music is another matter. For example, this
particular recording is perhaps a prime example of a music that arises naturally from its mixture of
influences – here the South American tango and folk traditions and the European string quartet –
but the only way to describe it adequately would be to dismantle the critical traditions of each form
and reassemble an entirely new model from the relevant components, much as the music itself does.
Clearly that is impossible here, so we can only offer a few rather facile-sounding pointers. Saluzzi's
eminently listenable but uncompromised compositions draw on his own diverse background in
tango, chamber music and avant-garde jazz; the result is evocative of all of these. Excitement,
poignancy, virtuosity and sheer emotional strength permeate these eight pieces. Comparisons with
Bartók, Ives, Piazzolla, Weill and Skempton come to mind at a considerable push, but the
uniqueness of this disc is paramount. Buy it!

Giuseppe Sammartini
Italian 1695-1750

Giovanni Battista Sammartini
Italian 1700-1775

G. Sammartini Recorder Concerto in F major. Concerti grossi – No. 6 in E minor; No. 8 in
G minor.
G.B. Sammartini Symphonies – G major; D major. String Quintet in E major.
Conrad Steinmann *rec*
Ensemble 415 / Chiara Banchini *vn*
Harmonia Mundi Musique d'abord HMA190 1245 (63 minutes: DDD). Recorded 1986. ⒷⓅ

Giuseppe Sammartini, the elder brother and virtuoso oboist, here contributes a recorder concerto
and two concerti grossi sandwiched between two symphonies and a quintet for strings by the more

progressive Giovanni Battista. The differences in style – one emanating from London and bearing the stamp of the conservative English taste, the other from Milan and one of the instigators of an important new genre – are unmistakable. Giuseppe's restless E minor 'Spiritoso' from the Sixth Concerto Grosso, the G minor *French Overture* and graceful minuets belong to a different musical world from that of G.B.'s brash symphonies. Under the capable and lively direction of Chiara Banchini, Ensemble 415 presents these works at their best: lightly textured with brisk tempos, articulated with unusual precision (which the resonant church acoustic only slightly blunts) and sympathetically read; for though the quality of the music varies – the Symphony in G major is especially appealing, that in D major embarrassingly thin with its empty Vivaldian *arpeggios* – the performance never falters. Giuseppe's recorder concerto, rescued from a manuscript in Sweden, is nicely played by Conrad Steinmann. Banchini's solo in the *Largo* of GB's late String Quintet is most affecting, showing herself to be equally at home on the platform and in the front desk.

Erik Satie French 1866-1925

Parade. Trois Gymnopédies – Nos. 1 and 3 (orch. Debussy); No. 2 (orch. Corp). Mercure. Three Gnossiennes (orch. Corp). Rêlache.
New London Orchestra / Ronald Corp.
Hyperion CDA66365 (66 minutes: DDD). Recorded 1989. Ⓕ

In 1918, the year after Diaghilev's Russian Ballet staged Satie's *Parade* in Paris, Poulenc wrote that 'to me, Satie's *Parade* is to Paris what *Petrushka* is to St Petersburg'. Satie was thenceforth adopted as the spiritual father of 'Les Six', whose ideal was the marriage of serious music with jazz, vaudeville, and the circus. Those who only know Satie from his early *Gymnopédies* and *Gnossiennes* – take heed: *Parade* shuffles along its apparently aimless, deadpan and wicked way with interjections from typewriters, lottery wheels, pistols and sirens. What does it all mean? Ronald Corp could be accused of retaining a slightly stiff upper lip, but there may well be a seriousness of purpose behind Satie's balletic miniatures. Certainly, there is little here of the uproarious debunking of some of 'Les Six'. His orchestrations of the *Gnossiennes* and the remaining *Gymnopédie* are idiomatic, and his performances of all six have the requisite cool beauty. Hyperion's sound is spacious and natural.

The Essential Erik Satie
Trois Gymnopédies. Le piège de Méduse. Croquis et agaceries d'un gros bonhomme en bois. Poudre d'or. Chapitres tournés en tous sens. Trois préludes du fils des étoiles. Le Piccadilly. Préludes en tapisserie. Véritables préludes flasques. Je te veux. Sonatine bureaucratique. Pièces froides. Sports et divertissements. Vexations.
Peter Dickinson pf
Conifer Classics CDCF183 (77 minutes: DDD). Ⓜ ᴿᴿ

We are not short of recordings of Satie's piano music, but this generously filled disc is recommended, not merely because it seems to be closer than most to conveying the character of this elusive but fascinating musician, whom his friend Darius Milhaud called 'poor Satie', but also because it's a little different in presentation from a straightforward recital. For a start, the booklet-notes are also by Peter Dickinson, who is a composer as well as a scholar; they are enlightened and sensitive as well as informative, and preceded by a self-portrait drawing of the composer which is touching and skilful (he sent it to Cocteau in 1917). Peter Dickinson says that he has aimed here 'to represent the best of Satie's unique personality in mystical, comic and popular veins' and a note at the end of the booklet tells us too that he has 'sought to present The Essential Erik Satie, both by his selection of the works and by stripping away any inessential indulgencies of interpretation'.

The proof of these precepts lies in the playing, we may say – and very nice it is too. The title of Satie's most popular work is hardly ever understood save by scholars, but one suspects that the three *Gymnopédies* which evoke the choral dances of naked boys in ancient Sparta reflect his sexual taste; if they do, their deep innate delicacy and sadness (one is marked *douloureux* and another *triste*) must win sympathy. Dickinson plays them with a quiet grave beauty, though ideally the recording here and elsewhere could have allowed a more remote *pianissimo*. After this comes a series of further pleasures: the pianist is a little straight-faced in the humorous pieces such as those of *Le piège de Méduse*, but this is arguably the right approach – we should not forget that Satie's mother was Scottish and this characteristic humour is what the Scots call pawky or even dour. It's a wry twinkle that Dickinson gives us, rather than a belly-laugh, but make no mistake, the humour's all there. And he can instantly create a mood for pieces which are sometimes very brief, such as the 21 that make up *Sports et divertissements* and the final 'Quadrille' of *Le piège* which lasts a mere 20 seconds – not a very striking 20 seconds musically, however. Satie was a melodist too – listen to the café-concert waltzes called *Poudre d'or* and *Je te veux*, not very individual if you like, but how agreeable when played like this, with just the right degree of Gallic schmaltz! The Rosicrucian music of *Le fils des étoiles* is both deeply serious and original in language; orchestrated, it could pass as being by the Debussy of two decades later. This Satie disc will convince you of just how much worthwhile piano music came from the pen of this composer. A good recording adds to one's pleasure; with a certain softness to the piano sound, it was made in The Maltings, Snape.

Six Gnossiennes. Ogives. Petite ouverture à danser. Sarabandes. Trois Gymnopédies.
Reinbert de Leeuw *pf*
Philips 446 672-2PH (67 minutes: DDD). Recorded 1992.   ⒡

Tender, solemn, droll, silly and occasionally plain boring, Satie's piano music has certainly proved its appeal for performers and record collectors, judging from the number of recitals devoted to it. But this one is out of the ordinary, for unlike the majority of artists, who offer a mixed bag of pieces, Reinbert de Leeuw has chosen music that is entirely solemn and even hieratic in utterance. He begins with the archaically beautiful *Gnossiennes*, taking the first of them unusually slowly but with compelling concentration. The composer's devotees will be thrilled, though you have to surrender completely to get the message of this repetitive, proto-minimalist music. The four *Ogives* derive their name from church architecture and their unbarred, diatonically simple music has clear affinities with plainchant although unlike chant it is richly harmonized. Monotonous it may be, but that is part of its charm, if that term can apply to such a contemplative style. The very brief *Petite ouverture à danser* is a mere meandering sketch in lazy waltz-time, but all Satie is sacred to the converted and the writer of the booklet-essay accords it four lines, finding in it (as translated here) 'a suggestion of indifference, vacillating between a melancholy melody and indecisive harmony'. (Not exactly Beethoven, one might say.) The two pensively sad triptychs of *Sarabandes* and *Gymnopédies* – here very slow yet tonally most refined – complete this finely played and recorded disc, which offers nothing whatsoever of the bouncier *café-concert* Satie.

Sports et divertissements. Enfantillages pittoresques. Valse-ballet. Fantaisie-valse. Le piège de Méduse. Petite musique de clown triste. Première pensée Rose + Croix. Le fils des étoiles – La vocation; L'initiation. Carnet d'esquisses et de croquis. Petit prélude de 'La Mort de Monsieur Mouche'. Gambades. Caresse. Trois Peccadilles importunes. La diva de l'Empire. Les pantins dansent. Danse de travers. Petite ouverture à danser. Rêverie du pauvre.
Pascal Rogé *pf*
Decca 455 370-2DH (61 minutes: DDD). Recorded 1996.   ⒡

This unusual collection displays a broader diversity of style and expression than we expect from Satie. It contains the rarely heard *Sports et divertissements*, comprising 20 snap-shots, none lasting more than a minute or so, each evoking a sport or recreational activity. This is surely one of Satie's finest works, and it ought to be better known. Also recorded are early pieces, including the *Valse-ballet* and *Fantaisie-valse*, published in 1885. Much of this music displays a childlike innocence and simplicity, but here we also find wit, pastiche and evocation. Pascal Rogé has already consolidated his reputation as a performer of French repertoire. His responses are generally cool and reserved; this undoubtedly suits the ethereal timelessness of much of Satie's output, but occasionally one wishes, if only for contrast in the context of the disc as a whole, that Rogé would let himself go a bit more (the 'Esquisses et Sketch montmartrois' from the *Carnet d'esquisses et de croquis*, for example). That said, his playing is wholly idiomatic and vividly captures the spirit of Satie's idiosyncratic imagination. This collection of miniatures (the disc has 60 tracks) allows for selective listening, although each work, especially the *Sports et divertissements*, should be heard in full. Recorded with a wonderfully natural, if very close, piano sound, this is one of the most enjoyable and varied Satie recitals on disc.

Trois Gymnopédies. Six Gnossiennes. Cinq Nocturnes. Trois Embryons desséchés.
Trois avant-dernières pensées. Valse-ballet. Fantaisie-valse. Je te veux.
Ronan O'Hora *pf*
Tring International TRP069 (61 minutes: DDD). Recorded 1995.   Ⓢ

Ronan O'Hora is a sensitive pianist in this repertoire, where there are now many recorded contenders and a fair range of interpretative styles. The sad tenderness of the *Gymnopédies* comes across, although he is brisker than some artists with the meltingly beautiful flow of Nos. 1 and 3. If O'Hora is justifiably concerned to eschew an inappropriately romantic approach, this is not at the expense of the occasional discreet rubato (as towards the end of No. 2) without which the music would lack humanity. Not all this music has the gravity of this triptych, or the *Gnossiennes*.

Elsewhere Satie gives us his characteristic caperings and banalities, and O'Hora responds neatly and wittily, doing the best he can with the silly repetitive endings of at least two pieces. Indeed, his programme is well played and planned. As suggested, there are many rival Satie pianists on disc but there is so much of Satie's piano music now available that you can purchase several discs without duplicating repertory, save perhaps for the ubiquitous *Gymnopédies*. O'Hora's disc offers a pleasingly intimate, atmospheric recording.

Emil von Sauer

German 1862-1942

Sauer Piano Concerto No. 1 in E minor.
Scharwenka Piano Concerto No. 4 in F minor, Op. 82.
Stephen Hough *pf*
City of Birmingham Symphony Orchestra / Lawrence Foster.
Hyperion CDA66790 (70 minutes: DDD). Recorded 1994. *Gramophone* Award Winner 1996. Ⓕ Ⓔ

In Scharwenka's Fourth Piano Concerto grand, Lisztian ambitions are fulfilled and embellished in writing of the most ferocious intricacy and the tarantella finale throws everything at the pianist, seemingly simultaneously. It is therefore hardly surprising that after early triumphs the Fourth Concerto fell into neglect. At its second performance, given in 1910 with Scharwenka as soloist and Mahler as conductor, it was described as being of a 'truly Dionysian and bewildering brilliancy', a phrase that, lifted into our own times, encapsulates Stephen Hough's astonishing performance. Then there is Sauer's First Concerto, its key a warm, over-the-shoulder memory of Chopin's E minor Concerto, yet with a style and content to make even the least susceptible listeners' heads nod and feet tap. The *Cavatina* is as luscious and enchanting as the finale is teasingly brief and light-hearted. Throughout, haunting melodies are embroidered with the finest pianistic tracery and, once again, the performance is bewitching. In the *Cavatina* Hough's caressing, fine-spun tone and long-breathed phrasing are a model for singers as well as pianists, and in the finale there is a lightly deployed virtuosity that epitomizes his aristocratic style. Naturally, the spotlight falls unashamedly on the soloist in such music, but the orchestra has no small part in the proceedings, and Lawrence Foster and the City of Birmingham Symphony Orchestra are superbly resilient and enthusiastic, with strings that sing their hearts out, notably in the third movement of the Sauer. These are both première recordings, and the sound and balance are exemplary.

Alessandro Scarlatti

Italian 1660-1725

Già lusingato appieno da Zeffiri. Arianna. Poi che riseppe Orfeo. Bella madre de'fiori.
Christine Brandes *sop* **Arcadian Academy** (Elizabeth Blumenstock, Lisa Weiss *vns*
Mary Springfels *va da gamba* David Tyler *archlte/theorbo* Nicholas McGegan *hpd*).
Conifer Classics 75605 51293-2 (72 minutes: DDD). Texts and translations included.
Recorded 1996. Ⓕ Ⓟ Ⓔ

Alessandro Scarlatti wrote some 700 cantatas: so it's four down, around 690-odd to go. Not that there'll be any complaint if they are all as delectable as this. Scarlatti's range of invention is as wide as his technical diversity, which even in this one genre – and he also wrote about 60 operas – is astonishing. Introductory sinfonias can be, as here, in one, two or three movements or absent altogether (*Orfeo*); arias can be in *da capo* form (his favourite) or *devisen* ('motto') or strophic, with midway and final ritornellos, as in *Bella madre de'fiori*, or without, accompanied only by continuo (as throughout in *Orfeo*) or with imitative or independent violin lines; recitatives are either accompanied or *secco*, but always expressive, often dramatic. Possessed of an Emma Kirkby-like light and pure-toned voice, Christine Brandes invests all her words with meaning, colouring her tone and dynamics in accordance with the mood, and able to convey fury as well as heartache. Technically, too, she is ideally suited to this repertoire: she is at ease with florid writing, demonstrates a finely controlled *messa di voce* at the words 'Al trono' in *Già lusingato* and elsewhere, and is stylish in ornamenting repeat sections. The vitality, freshness and character brought by the Arcadian Academy to its playing earns this disc an enthusiastic recommendation.

Il rosignolo (first version). Perchè tacete, regolati concenti?. Infirmata, vulnerata. Ombre tacite e sole. Il genio di Mitilde mente non vè. O pace del mio cor.
David Daniels *counterten*
Arcadian Academy / Nicholas McGegan.
Conifer Classics 75605 51325-2 (74 minutes: DDD). Texts and translations included.
Recorded 1998. Ⓕ

The American countertenor, David Daniels has a fine, firmly produced voice, even throughout its range; both his intonation and his enunciation are impeccable; he is exact in his handling of florid passages; and his ornamentations (seemingly spontaneous) are very stylish. If there is one reservation, it is that for too much of the time (except in *Infirmata, vulnerata*) he sings at one constant level of dynamics – though he produces an arresting *messa di voce* on the first word of *Ombre tacite*. It is possible that the recording contributes to this: it is certainly responsible for the harpsichord sounding much weaker in some cantatas than in others. By far the most substantial work here is the earliest, *Perchè tacete*, probably dating from the mid-1690s. It is the only one with a Venetian opera-type overture (three movements, the outer ones with Corellian suspensions, enclosing an intermittent *fugato*), and the numerous movements include four arias, three of which are of two strophes.

At the other extreme is *Il rosignolo*, scored only for continuo and consisting of just two *da capo* arias joined by a recitative: the nightingale's song, it emerges, is a lament for love. Love is also the subject of *O pace del mio cor* (the lover vainly seeking peace of mind) and the 1716 *Ombre tacite* (the most fully scored of the present works), the despairing lament of a deceived lover. In the recitatives of both of these, Scarlatti underlines emotive words with extraordinary harmonic progressions. A contrast to all of these is provided by *Il genio di Mitilde* (for continuo alone), where the flightiness and capricious moods of the loved ones are reflected in an ultra-busy, athletic cello part. The one remaining work is something of an enigma: though in Latin and printed as a 'sacred concerto', the words could be interpreted as referring either to divine love or to human (which is presumably why McGegan includes it here). The style is certainly plainer than in the others except for the vigorous ending: there are chromatic harmonies in the first aria, and a later aria is unusual in being constructed on a seven-bar ground bass. The disc as a whole demonstrates Scarlatti's range of styles and the diversity of his scoring, even within a single work.

Cain, overo il primo omicidio.
Graciela Oddone, Dorothea Röschmann *sops* **Bernarda Fink** *contr* **Richard Croft** *ten*
Antonio Abete *bass*
Academy for Ancient Music, Berlin / René Jacobs *counterten*
Harmonia Mundi HMC90 1649/50 (two discs: 138 minutes: DDD). Text and translation included.
Recorded 1997.   Ⓕ

This is a remarkable work, startling from the very outset (where the vigorous overture is preceded by a solo violin), and this performance is stunning. To be precise, the work was classified at the time not as an oratorio but as a *trattenimento sacro* ('sacred entertainment'), which suggests that its first performance, in 1707 in Venice (to which Scarlatti, normally based in Rome, had for once been lured by commissions for two operas), took place in a private palace rather than a church. But Scarlatti brought to the work, besides his seemingly inexhaustible invention, all the dramatic instinct that had made him famous as a composer of operas (of which he had already written about 40). Anyone charged with extracting a 'highlights' selection from this would find themselves in a quandary, since almost every number could be considered a highlight. How could he omit, for example, the brilliant opening aria (with violin interpolations) for Adam, two remorseful arias, with affecting chromaticisms, for Eve, two contrasting D minor arias in succession for the brothers out in the fields, one feeling Nature sinister, the other peaceful, the jealous Cain floridly swearing vengeance at being slighted or movingly bidding farewell to his parents, Lucifer (with excited violins) tempting Cain, Adam and Eve grieving over the absence of their sons, Abel in Heaven sending consolation, and so on and so on? René Jacobs has assembled an absolutely outstanding cast whose technical accomplishment, dramatic commitment and stylish ornamentation could scarcely be bettered. The instrumental playing, too, is first-class.

A. Scarlatti Humanità e Lucifero.
Corelli Trio Sonatas – B flat major, Op. 3 No. 3; C major, Op. 4 No. 1.
Rossana Bertini *sop* **Massimo Crispi** *ten*
Europa Galante / Fabio Biondi *vn*
Opus 111 OPS30-129 (61 minutes: DDD). Text and translation included. Recorded 1990s.   ⒻⓅ

Alessandro Scarlatti's oratorio, *Humanità e Lucifero*, here receives its first recording. It dates from 1704 when it was first performed at the Collegio Nazareno in Rome on the Feast of the Blessed Virgin Mary. The text is written in the Italian vernacular, more widely understood than Latin. It takes the form of a dispute between Humanity – who celebrates the birth of the Virgin – and Lucifer, who struggles with her for supremacy. Eventually, Lucifer recognizes that in Humanity he has more than met his match and he returns to Lake Avernus and the nether regions 'neither prince nor king'. The imagery evoked by the unidentified librettist is charmingly naive and sometimes colourful, both aspects of which are characteristically capitalized upon by Scarlatti. This is a vibrant score of instant melodic and harmonic appeal, very well sung by Rossana Bertini (Humanity) and marginally less so by Massimo Crispi (Lucifer). Bertini has a particularly bright vocal timbre which suits her role admirably. Her intonation is deadly accurate and her performance radiates light throughout. Crispi is more variable in the success with which he negotiates some of Scarlatti's exacting passagework. The voice is less refined in tone quality than Bertini's and, while this is appropriate to his Stygian role, there is a tendency towards bluster which adversely affects tonal focus. The music itself holds the attention throughout and, as so often with Scarlatti, there are moments of outstanding beauty, enhanced by delicate scoring perhaps for solo violin, cello or sopranino recorder. In contrast with these delicate touches are passages of resonant scoring for solo trumpet. The insertion of two trio sonatas by Scarlatti's contemporary, Corelli, from Opp. 3 and 4 are also very affecting in context. They are sensitively played by Biondi and his instrumentalists who bring a rare sense of poetry to the slow movements. In summary, this is a rewarding issue and one which readers so far unacquainted with Scarlatti's vocal music are likely to find a very enjoyable introduction. Recorded sound is excellent and full texts with translations are included.

Domenico Scarlatti ·   Italian 1685-1757

Missa Breve, 'La Stella'. Te Deum in C major. Stabat mater in C minor. Iste Confessor.
The Sixteen / Harry Christophers with **Ian Watson** *org* **Siobhan Armstrong** *hp*
Robin Jeffrey, Elizabeth Kenny *theorbos*
Collins Classics 1504-2 (60 minutes: DDD). Texts and translations included. Recorded 1997.   Ⓕ

Domenico Scarlatti's church music is often unfairly underrated because we cannot dismiss from our minds the harmonic and rhythmic exuberance that characterize his keyboard sonatas; it dates from earlier, mostly from his time in Rome, before he flowered in the heady atmosphere of Spain, where he was to spend most of his life. Judged on their merits and without reference to Domenico's mature Spanish output, a couple of these works, at least, are by no means without depth and tension, as The Sixteen makes abundantly clear in these committed and technically splendidly assured performances. The Mass is stylistically mixed, as if Domenico was still feeling his way into an idiom in which he could feel at home; nevertheless, it is quite impressive. But after the smooth, richly chordal *Kyrie* and an unexpectedly restrained *Gloria* the bold harmonies at 'Et incarnatus est' in the *Credo* pull one up with a jerk. A surprise of another kind is the omission of the *Benedictus* in favour of 'Cibavit eos Dominus'; then the *Agnus Dei* refers back to the *Sanctus*. Admittedly *Iste Confessor* is no more than a simple melodious hymn in five verses alternating between solo soprano and chorus, and the *Te Deum*, very diatonic until the final 'Non confundar', is little more than a generalized elation. The *Stabat mater*, however, is on a far more distinguished level; Harry Christophers's admirable singers invest it with a compelling passion and intensity. The appropriately ecclesiastical acoustic of the recording venue has been cleanly captured.

Keyboard Sonatas – Kk1; Kk3; Kk8; Kk9; Kk11; Kk17; Kk24; Kk25; B minor, Kk27; Kk29; Kk87; Kk96; Kk113; Kk141; Kk146; Kk173; Kk213; Kk214; Kk247; Kk259; Kk268; Kk283; Kk284; Kk380; Kk386; Kk387; Kk404; Kk443; Kk519; Kk520; Kk523.
Mikhail Pletnev *pf*
Virgin Classics VCD5 45123-2 (two discs: 140 minutes: DDD). Recorded 1994.
Gramophone Award Winner 1996.   Ⓕ Ⓔ ⓇⓇ

Every so often a major pianist reclaims Scarlatti for the piano with an outstanding recording and this is certainly such an occasion. As Ralph Kirkpatrick put it, Scarlatti's harpsichord, while supremely itself, is continually menacing a transformation into something else. True, the relation of the music to harpsichord sound could hardly be closer – you can't argue on that point! – and of course it wouldn't have been composed the way it is for a different instrument. Scarlatti is marvellous at suggesting imaginary orchestrations and stimulating our own imagination. He makes us aware of the different vantage points as the music passes before us, of the different tones of voice and rhetorical inflexions – as various in these sonatas as the events in them are unpredictable. There are dances and fiestas and processions here, serenades and laments, and evocations of everything from the rudest folk music to courtly entertainments and churchly polyphony; and as the kaleidoscope turns you marvel at the composer who could embrace such diversity and shape it and put it all on to the keyboard. No wonder Chopin found Scarlatti a kindred spirit.

This is strongly individual playing, be warned. Pletnev's free-ranging poetic licence may not be to your taste, and admittedly it does beg a few questions. Not that his spectacular virtuosity is likely to be controversial: this really is *hors de catégorie* and enormously enjoyable. And the evocations of the harpsichord are often very witty – only a fool would play Scarlatti on the piano as if the harpsichord had never existed. But Pletnev doesn't shrink from using the full resources of the piano, sustaining pedal included, and if you baulk at the prospect of that as the means to an end he will probably not be for you. The sustaining pedal is indeed dangerous in music which is almost wholly to do with lines, not washes of colour; its effect is to make us see Scarlatti as if through Mendelssohn's eyes. Yet moments of such falsification are rare. As often as not when Pletnev appears to be on the verge of stepping outside Scarlatti's world, or reinventing a little bit of it, it's because of some shaft of insight vouchsafed to his extraordinary musical mind that is well worth having. Characterization is everything, and though he can be a mite coy in the reflective sonatas he generally goes straight to the heart of the matter. The vigorous, full tone in the quick numbers is a joy to have, and most admirable of all is the way he makes sound immediately command character. That is something only the best artists are able to do. There are no doubts about the recorded sound: this is one of the best piano recordings available.

Keyboard Sonatas – C major (manuscript – Yale University); G major; D major; C major (all three ed. Henle); G major (ed. Sociedad Española de Musicología, Madrid); D minor; A major; G major (all ed. Unión Musical Española, Madrid); A major (ed. Musica Antiqua, Lisbon); A major; E major (both MS – Biblioteca de Catalunya, Barcelona); A major (MS – British Library, London); A major (MS – Real Conservatorio de Música, Madrid). Fandango in D minor.
Mayako Soné *hpd*
Erato 4509-94806-2 (51 minutes: DDD). Recorded 1993.　　　　　　　　　　ⒻⓅ

It's a bit silly of Erato to label this disc 'Unpublished sonatas' when the publishers of eight of the present 14 are actually listed: if they meant 'recently discovered sonatas', why not say so? Apart from this, however, a certain scepticism is called for by the claim that these are by Scarlatti. A few may well be by him; the majority, to differing extents, are of doubtful authenticity. The most convincing 'possibles' are the robustly exuberant Yale C major and three sonatas (two of them longer than usual) found in Valladolid and published by UME in Madrid. The *Fandango* has been worked up by the player here from a sketch (an impression of Scarlatti's improvisation?) in a private collection in Tenerife: shorter than the famous example attributed to Soler but closely resembling it in style. It is played with tremendous gusto – like everything else on this disc – on a Blanchet copy by Mayako Soné, a young harpsichordist who is making quite a name for herself. Her experience as a continuo player has doubtless been a contributory factor in her splendidly strong rhythmic sense; and her crisp articulation is a pleasure to hear. Regardless of the authenticity or otherwise of these pieces, this is a very attractive disc.

Keyboard Sonatas – Kk69; Kk113; Kk114; Kk115; Kk116; Kk208; Kk209; Kk215; Kk216; Kk246; Kk247; Kk394; Kk395; Kk414; Kk415; Kk426; Kk427; Kk513.
Andreas Staier *hpd*
Teldec Das Alte Werk 0630-12601-2 (74 minutes: DDD). Recorded 1995.　　　　ⒻⓅ

Staier is adept at capturing the mercurial changes of mood and still surprising harmonic quirks of Scarlatti's unpredictable genius, and even when we disagree with his readings they always hold the interest. In particular, he manages to convey the spirit of Scarlatti's spur-of-the-moment inventive powers, not merely by adding spontaneous extra ornaments or inserting buckshee pauses-for-thought, but by his very flexible pace – which may take some getting used to. Kk427, which is marked 'as fast as possible', has never been played faster than here, but Kk114 – one of two sonatas including the direction *Tremulo* to indicate a continuous trill – sounds rushed, and Kk208 is preternaturally slow, drawing attention to a left-hand-before-right mannerism that also affects the pensive Kk69. Staier makes big variations within Kk394 and Kk395, for example, and starts the second half of the bright Kk414 at a new tempo. Yet he only does it to tease, and he can, when he wants to, maintain an admirably direct forward impulse, as in the C sharp minor Sonata, Kk246, his wonderfully springy Kk209, or in Kk113, with its exhilarating cross-hand leaps. Scarlatti styles exemplified here range from the Neapolitan three-section Pastorale, Kk513 to the savage Spanish scrunches of Kk215, and from continuity – even isorhythm in Kk415 – to constant stop-and-start tactics, as in Kk426 (which, together with its companion Kk427, calls for an instrument with a top G, which this Keith Hill copy of a mid-eighteenth-century German harpsichord evidently has).

Keyboard Sonatas – Kk213; Kk214; Kk318; Kk319; Kk347; Kk348; Kk356; Kk357; Kk380; Kk381; Kk454; Kk455; Kk478; Kk479; Kk524; Kk525; Kk526; Kk527.
Ralph Kirkpatrick *hpd*
DG Classikon 439 438-2GCL (52 minutes: ADD). Recorded 1970.　　　　　　Ⓜ Ⓟ

An infectious zest characterizes these attractive performances of Scarlatti sonatas, most of them among the less well known. And Scarlatti's own zest is manifest in their wonderfully imaginative diversity: unmistakable, for example, is the sheer glee with which he constantly plunges from one end of the keyboard to the other in Kk356 and K357 (to write which he resorted to the use of four staves), indulges in bold modulations (Kk526 and K319), and writes a couple of sonatas in the then *ultima Thule* key of F sharp major. Kirkpatrick's presentation accords with the theory that the sonatas were intended to be paired; and the insert-note, informative as to the background but silent about the works selected, rightly disagrees with the absurd theory that the 500-plus sonatas were all written in the composer's last few years. The bright-toned instrument employed here (and vividly recorded) was by Rainer Schütze of Heidelberg. An exhilarating disc.

Franz Xaver Scharwenka
Polish 1850-1924

Piano Concertos – No. 2 in C minor, Op. 56; No. 3 in C sharp minor, Op. 80.
Seta Tanyel *pf*
Hanover Radio Philharmonic Orchestra / Tadeusz Strugała.
Collins Classics 1485-2 (79 minutes: DDD). Recorded 1996. (F)

Scharwenka would surely have been heartened by Seta Tanyel's admirable campaign on his behalf. Here, she continues with the Second and Third Piano Concertos, once again surmounting every ferocious obstacle with an ease that allows her an unblemished freedom to concentrate on the composer's musical character. Those with a taste for full-blown rhetoric in an ultra-nineteenth-century style and for some notably beguiling slow movements (the *Adagio* from the Third is hard to resist) will, of course, hardly need persuading, but other more sceptical listeners will surely be convinced when the performances temper an enviable fluency and expertise with discretion. True, Tanyel's playing does not always scintillate with the most concentrated virtuoso aplomb, yet in the Third Concerto's massive cadenza she is as impressive in octave thunder as in filigree delicacy. Tadeusz Strugala's partnership is suitably enthusiastic and the recordings, as always from this source, are exemplary.

Four Polish Dances, Op. 47. Menuet, Op. 65 No. 1. Scherzo, Op. 65 No. 2. Six Waltzes, Op. 28. Variations on a Theme by C. H., Op. 57. Drei Klavierstücke, Op. 86. Erzählungen am Klavier (Legends), Op. 5.
Seta Tanyel *pf*
Collins Classics 1474-2 (72 minutes: DDD). Recorded 1995. (F)

Chopin's spirit may hover over the *Polish Dances* (all four are *mazurkas*), Brahms over the *Waltzes* and Schumann over large sections of Opp. 5, 57 and 86, with terms such as *langsam-innig* or *langsam und zart* telling their own affectionate tale. Yet by the time Scharwenka reached his *Drei Klavierstücke*, Op. 86 he felt increasingly free of the past; able to venture into a greater harmonic subtlety, modulatory ease and cunning. The 'Nocturne' is more impressionistic than Chopinesque and, after the sprightly 'Serenade', 'Marchen' blossoms into considerable expressive richness. The *Variations on a Theme by C. H.*, too, increase in interest and although Vars. 9 and 11 are haunted by Schumann's *Faschingsschwank aus Wien* and *Davidsbundler-tänze* respectively, they transform their bias into music of a special distinction and freshness. So, far from scraping the barrel there is much here to surprise and enliven. Tanyel's performances are beyond reproach. Strong, sensitive and stylish, she is warmly sympathetic. The recordings are excellent.

Samuel Scheidt
German 1587-1654

Ludi Musici – Alamande a 4; Canzon ad imitationem Bergamas angl a 5; Canzon super Cantionem Gallicam a 5; Canzon super O Nachbar Roland a 5; Five Courants a 4; Courant dolorosa a 4; Two Galliards a 4; Galliard a 5; Galliard battaglia a 5; Three Paduanas a 4.
Hespèrion XX / Jordi Savall *viol*
Auvidis Fontalis ES8559 (62 minutes: DDD). Recorded 1995. (F)(P)

Scheidt's *Ludi Musici* reflects the fusion of English and German traditions in the emergent world of instrumental music in early seventeenth-century Germany and is a mouth-watering diverse and inventive mixture of dance, canzona and variation. These are works which brim over with character and nonchalantly brilliant craftsmanship. Scheidt has that rare knack, for the 1620s and 1630s, of sustaining an instrumental piece for more than two minutes without bombarding us with a new idea every ten bars; the longer pieces such as the Paduanas and the brilliant Canzon a 5 *ad imitationem Bergamas angl*, with its thrilling close, convey admirable long-term direction amid a concentrated love of ephemeral effect. This is a cocktail which Hespèrion XX relishes. The Pavans are, as you would expect from Jordi Savall, eventful. There are moments when an indulgence from Savall's treble viol stifles the potential for a more reflective allusion, but the overriding effect is of a performer striving to find a meaningful discourse, not content just to 'let the music play itself'; the colour and shape he brings to line and texture is often beguiling (disarmingly poignant in the stillness of the final Paduana), at times too much of a good thing but always engaging.

Johann Hermann Schein German 1586-1630

Israelis Brünnlein.
Ensemble Vocal Européen / Philippe Herreweghe.
Harmonia Mundi HMC90 1574 (79 minutes: DDD). Texts and translations included.
Recorded 1995.   Ⓕ

Anyone who hears this sympathetic account of *Israelis Brünnlein* ('The Fountains of Israel' –
26 sacred madrigals in five and six parts with a *basso seguente*) from Ensemble Vocal Européen will undoubtedly be convinced that this is one of the great pillars of German baroque music. It is fascinating not only as a demonstration of how the best German music incorporates foreign styles within indigenous techniques but also for Schein's discovery of his own unique expressive horizons, in ways which cannot directly be attributed to either Mantua or Leipzig. As in the *Lagrime di San Pietro* of Lassus (a composer whose poised contrapuntal craft is transmuted with profound respect by Schein), secular idioms successfully serve the sacred vision. Herreweghe, whose cool and collected reading of the Lassus masterpiece (see review under Lassus; refer to the Index) is vocally peerless, finds fresh priorities here. The exposed solo context draws out a greater sense of quasi-spontaneous attention, particularly in upbeat examples like 'Freue dich des Weibes' and the concentrated brilliance of 'Ist nicht Ephraim?'. Emotional intensity is, however, inclined to sound overmeasured in works like 'Die mit Tränen säen' and 'Was betrübst', where dramatic urgency is required above the restrained shapeliness and refinement that is Herreweghe's hallmark. There are some fine singers here (underpinned by the splendid Peter Kooy), even if the tenor tuning is not always beyond reproach; as an almost comprehensive – five pieces are left out – volume of 80-odd minutes, this further assures Schein's reputation as a master of exquisite characterization.

Johann Heinrich Schmelzer Austrian c1620/23-1680

Schmelzer Sonatae unarum fidium – Nos. 1-6. Sonata for Violin and Continuo in A minor, 'Il cucù'.
Biber (arr. A. Schmelzer) Sonata for Violin and Continuo, 'Victori der Christen'.
Romanesca (Andrew Manze *vn* Nigel North *theorbo* John Toll *hpd/org*).
Harmonia Mundi HMU90 7143 (67 minutes: DDD). Also includes a free sampler disc of Biber
violin sonatas. Recorded 1995.   ⒻⓅ

Performances of works from the indigenous Austrian seventeenth-century 'school' have made a significant impact on the *status quo* of mainstream baroque instrumental music of late. This is not to say that the more formalized Italian traditions, that dominated in Vienna until Schmelzer's gradual and unspectacular rise to Kappelmeister of the imperial court in 1679, have been in any way shown up; rather that the distinctive rhetorical flavour of *Mittel Europa* has both broadened our horizons and encouraged players and listeners to think more flexibly about the unique language of composers such as Biber and Schmelzer. These are men who have left a remarkable amount to the imagination: and yet, a step of faith, technical brilliance and a commitment to find the dramatic and emotional heart of these solo works reaps untold rewards. Whilst Biber has enjoyed the most marked renaissance of those in the employ of the imperial court, Schmelzer is the spiritual father of this colourful native expression.

Coming to these recordings (the first to include all six of Schmelzer's pioneering *Sonatae unarum fidium*, or 'Sonatas for one violin' of 1644) from Biber's extravagant and incomparably theatrical sonatas, one is immediately struck by common stylistic threads but also by Schmelzer's studied lyricism, a searing and disarming feel for melodic progression (heard in the close of the *Cucù* Sonata) and the sense of a man who, when he is not following his tail with ostinato basses, has thoroughly mastered the canzona-sonata mentality and takes full advantage of its freedom. All Biberian features certainly, but as Andrew Manze both explains in his note and demonstrates in his playing, there is less overall ostentation here; whilst the extraordinary Sonata No. 4 latterly contains gloriously extended and potent outbursts, it is the patient arching direction of Schmelzer's melodic frame which draws one into his web. Manze and his accomplished continuo players (the contribution of the theorbo is both exquisite and distinctive) are wonderful exponents in this mesmerizing baroque byway.

Franz Schmidt

Symphony No. 4 in C major. Variations on a Hussar's Song.
London Philharmonic Orchestra / Franz Welser-Möst.
EMI CDC5 55518-2 (72 minutes: DDD). Recorded 1994. *Gramophone* Award Winner 1996.   Ⓕ🄴

Writing in *The Symphony* (ed. Robert Simpson, Penguin Books: 1967) the late Harold Truscott made out a strong case for Franz Schmidt. He robustly dismissed the notion that his music does not travel. 'It "travels" very well, when allowed to do so, and I will go so far as to say that anyone who claims a love and understanding of Beethoven, Brahms or Sibelius, should have no difficulty with Schmidt. There could,' he went on, 'scarcely be a more positive work than No. 4, whose confidence is complete and without bombast' and it is obvious that Schmidt's mastery of the art of symphonic thinking and of the orchestra is everywhere in evidence. The symphony is in one unbroken span whose material derives from the haunting opening 21-bar theme on solo trumpet – in itself an idea of remarkable originality. Unlike Reger, whose influence can at times be clearly heard, Schmidt was a late developer and far from prolific. Indeed apart from the four symphonies, there is only one other orchestral work, the *Variations on a Hussar's Song* recorded here. For those who have never encountered his music, it is perhaps best if loosely described as rich in palette, in much the same way as Elgar, chromatic in its harmonic language yet never cloying, and above all it has an innate nobility, an elegiac dignity of utterance and a sense of vision. Not without reason did Truscott call Schmidt the 'only real successor to Bruckner – in so far as there is one at all'. Welser-Möst shows great feeling for and sympathy with this music and carries his fine players with him. Theirs is playing of eloquence and dedication, and the recording has truthful and well-detailed sound.

Das Buch mit sieben Siegeln.
Christiane Oelze *sop* **Cornelia Kallisch** *contr* **Stig Andersen, Lothar Odinius** *tens*
René Pape, Alfred Reiter *basses* **Friedemann Winklhofer** *org*
Bavarian Radio Chorus and Symphony Orchestra / Franz Welser-Möst.
EMI CDS5 56660-2 (two discs: 107 minutes: DDD).
Text and translation included. Recorded live in 1997.   Ⓕ🄴

Franz Welser-Möst shows complete sympathy with Schmidt's world and sensibility in what many admirers consider Schmidt's masterpiece, *Das Buch mit sieben Siegeln* ('The Book with Seven Seals'). Schmidt turned to the last book of the New Testament, the Revelation of St John the Divine, for his text. Nobility shines through almost every bar of the score – mind you, one can say this of almost everything Schmidt wrote. The recording offers fine sound, and a performance of great commitment and grandeur. Schmidt portrays John as a young man and apparently wished to have a Heldentenor rather than a lyric tenor sing the role, and this is observed here. The singing throughout is of impressive quality from all concerned – and in particular Stig Andersen – and the sensitive orchestral response leaves no doubt of all the artists' belief in this visionary and often inspired work. On almost every count this Bavarian performance does justice to Schmidt's masterpiece. The technical balance of the recording has been most expertly and musically done.

Das Buch mit sieben Siegeln.
Hilde Gueden *sop* **Ira Malaniuk** *contr* **Anton Dermota, Fritz Wunderlich** *tens*
Walter Berry *bass-bar*
Vienna Singverein; Vienna Philharmonic Orchestra / Dimitri Mitropoulos.
Sony Classical Festspieldokumente mono SM2K68442 (two discs: 111 minutes: ADD).
Text included. Recorded live in 1959.   Ⓜ🄷

As a composer himself and a man of deep religious conviction Mitropoulos responded to Schmidt's oratorio; such haunting passages as the duet for two survivors of the pestilence and death spread by the horsemen of the Apocalypse, or the tremendous earthquake chorus that follows the breaking of the seventh seal have a powerful sense of drama which is emphasized by Mitropoulos's precise care for contrapuntal and instrumental detail. Yes, in this live performance there are a few untidinesses but the impact and the devout urgency of the reading are not in the least diminished by them. In the hugely taxing central role of St John, Dermota is deeply impressive. Although the part is often given to a dramatic tenor it responds to a lyric voice that is capable at times of ringing fullness. Dermota matches Mitropoulos's urgency, and clearly means every word of the role. At one point, where a descending vocal line illustrates the text's reference to the four beasts and the elders falling down before the Lamb, it is obvious that the bottom note of the phrase is not within his range. Instead, quietly and reverently, he speaks it, and the expressive effect of this is characteristic of his whole performance. The other soloists, Gueden and Berry especially, are distinguished, and both chorus and orchestra audibly respond to Mitropoulos's conviction. The mono recording is a little constricted at times, with patches of acid string tone, but it improves and gains impact as it proceeds.

Florent Schmitt

La tragédie de Salomé.
Marie-Paule Fayt *sop*
Rhineland-Pfalz State Philharmonic Orchestra / Patrick Davin.
Marco Polo 8 223448 (59 minutes: DDD). Recorded 1991. ⓕ

This is a real rarity. We have had recordings of the large-orchestra suite from *La tragédie de Salomé* before but here, apparently for the first time, is the complete ballet which runs to twice the length of the suite and calls for only a chamber orchestra (the theatre couldn't accommodate more). Schmitt's virtuosity in drawing rich sonorities and a voluptuous, barbaric atmosphere from it is astonishing. Unlike the treatments of the biblical story by Strauss or Massenet, in the scenario here there is no question of Salome being in love with John the Baptist. Schmitt composed a well-structured score of exotic and sensual colour that includes broad lyrical episodes as well as vividly orgiastic sections. Compared to the suite for full orchestra, these lose nothing in impact or impressiveness by the smaller forces employed – indeed, the music gains in clarity and pungency thereby. It is not surprising that Stravinsky, to whom the work was dedicated, described it as 'one of the greatest masterpieces of modern music'. The performance, and the recording, are deserving of the highest commendation.

Alfred Schnittke

Concerto grosso No. 1[a]. Quasi una sonata[b]. Moz-Art à la Haydn[c].
Tatiana Grindenko *vn* **Yuri Smirnov** *hpd/prep pf/pf*
Chamber Orchestra of Europe / [a]**Heinrich Schiff,** [bc]**Gidon Kremer** [a]*vn*
DG 439 452-2GCL (62 minutes: DDD). Recorded live in 1988. Ⓜ

For a single representative of Alfred Schnittke's work you could choose nothing better than the first *Concerto grosso* of 1977. Here are the psychedelic mélanges of baroque and modern, the drastic juxtapositions of pseudo-Vivaldi with pseudo-Berg, producing an effect at once aurally exciting and spiritually disturbing. The piece has had many recordings, but never with the panache of Kremer and friends and never with the vivid immediacy of this live DG recording (in fact the solo violins are rather too closely miked for comfort, but that's only a tiny drawback). *Quasi una sonata* was originally composed in 1968 for violin and piano and it was something of a breakthrough piece for Schnittke as he emerged from what he called 'the puberty rites of serialism', letting his imagination run riot for the first time. No one could call it a disciplined piece, but if that worries you, you should leave Schnittke alone anyway. The transcription for solo violin and string orchestra is an ingenious one and Kremer again supplies all the requisite agonized intensity. *Moz-Art à la Haydn* is a very slight piece of work, and it really depends on visual theatricality to make its effect. Still, it complements the other two pieces, and this disc makes an excellent introduction to this composer.

Schnittke Concerto grosso No. 6[a]. Violin Sonata.
Weill Concerto for Violin and Wind Orchestra, Op. 12.
Takemitsu Nostalgia.
Daniel Hope *vn* [a]**Simon Mulligan** *pf/hpd*
English Symphony Orchestra / William Boughton.
Nimbus NI5582 (73 minutes: DDD). Recorded 1998. ⓕ

Full marks to Nimbus for variety. The danger is that three such different composers, combined in a way you would never expect in a concert, will cancel each other out. Fortunately, the performances are strong enough – even when heard in close succession – to justify the enterprise, and the recordings are no less successful in the way they capture the intimacy of tone characteristic of all four compositions. With the earlier of the Schnittke works, the Sonata, a textual point of some interest emerges. Usually, the harpsichord functions as the violinist's *alter ego* throughout, but Hope, with Schnittke's agreement, has the keyboardist move from harpsichord to piano from the final stages of the second movement onwards. The change is certainly justified in the finale, and adds an extra dimension to a commendably unexaggerated account of this turbulent score. There is room for a degree of detachment in the fraught *Concerto grosso* No. 6 and this the Nimbus team provides. The early Weill Violin Concerto can easily sprawl, and sound too earnest for its own good. Here there is an appropriate fluency, and excessive gravity is avoided. Daniel Hope is able to project the required authority, especially in the cadenza, and although some listeners might prefer a more forward placement for the soloist, the excellent qualities of Hope's playing are no less appealing. As for Takemitsu's song of farewell for the film-maker Andrei Tarkovsky, the music is a model of how to balance emotional restraint and expressive warmth, and the performance does it justice.

Violin Concertos[a] – No. 2; No. 3. Stille Nacht. Gratulations rondo.
Gidon Kremer *vn*
[a]**Chamber Orchestra of Europe / Christoph Eschenbach** *pf*
Teldec 4509-94540-2 (61 minutes: DDD). Recorded 1994.   Ⓕ

Schnittke's Second Violin Concerto opens with the kind of jagged, convulsive, Webern-crossed-with-Shostakovich cadenza that is a trademark of his string writing. The structure is based on Christ's life, death and resurrection, and the double-bass is a Judas figure, an anti-soloist (shades of Liszt's Faust/Mephistopheles perhaps). That may or may not affect one's reactions to the music. Do Berg's Violin Concerto and Chamber Concerto, for instance, stand by their hidden programmes or by the notes composed as a result of them? And the Third Concerto is certainly not a piece to be trifled with. Its unusual scoring for 13 winds and four strings is partly modelled on Berg's Chamber Concerto, and at one stage the composer was toying with another Biblical subtitle, *The Song of Songs*. But the musical invention seems more self-sufficient, more concentrated and more finished than that of the Second Concerto. The violin's trills convey the alarm of a whole psychic world tottering, and all three movements have their nerve-endings exposed. The Mahlerian chorale of the finale carries bittersweetness to the *n*th degree. Throughout the disc Kremer's personality is a compelling presence, and the Chamber Orchestra of Europe is terrific in its support. Eschenbach's contribution is perhaps less overt but certainly no less vital, and in the two contrasted miniatures (in many ways the outstanding compositions in the programme) his discretion is the ideal foil for his charismatic partner. Recording quality is of the very finest.

Schnittke String Quartet No. 3. Piano Quintet.
Mahler/Schnittke Piano Quartet.
Borodin Quartet (Mikhail Kopelman, Andrei Abramenkov *vns* Dmitri Shebalin *va*
Valentin Berlinsky *vc*); **Ludmilla Berlinsky** *pf*
Virgin Classics VC7 59040-2 (66 minutes: DDD). Recorded 1990.   Ⓕ

Schnittke's chamber music does not have the high public profile of some of his symphonies and concertos, but in many ways it is more fastidiously composed and it certainly makes for equally rewarding listening at home. The Piano Quintet is the outstanding feature of this disc. Predominantly slow and mournful (it is dedicated to the memory of the composer's mother) and with a haunting waltz on the notes of the BACH monogram, it is here played with compelling intensity, especially by the pianist Ludmilla Berlinsky, daughter of the Borodin Quartet's cellist. The Piano Quartet is a conflation of the 16-year-old Mahler's first movement with his incomplete second movement in Schnittke's own paraphrase – another haunting experience, beautifully played and recorded. Less satisfying as a performance, because slightly glossed over, is the Third Quartet; but this is perhaps the finest and undoubtedly the most often performed of Schnittke's chamber works, and as a whole the disc can be warmly recommended to those looking for a representative sample of Schnittke rather than a comprehensive library.

String Trio. Violin Sonatas – No. 1; No. 2, 'Quasi una sonata'.
Mateja Marinković *vn* **Paul Silverthorne** *va* **Timothy Hugh** *vc* **Linn Hendry** *pf*
ASV CDDCA868 (65 minutes: DDD).   Ⓕ

This performance is extremely satisfying. It is atmospherically recorded, and convincingly reinforces the Trio's claims to be considered one of Schnittke's major works. The music is surely to be preferred in this original version, rather than as the 'Trio Sonata' of Yuri Bashmet's orchestral arrangement. Dating from 1985, and written in response to a commission from the Alban Berg Society of Vienna, the Trio is notable for the extent to which its reminiscences and re-creations are far less contrived and self-indulgent than is often the case with this composer. They are not merely backward-looking, nostalgic gestures, but suggest a blueprint for a new, romantically tinged post-modernism. Whether or not you go along with this analysis, it is difficult to deny that the Trio puts the pair of early violin sonatas into the shade. They are not negligible pieces, even so, and these performances have much to commend them. Mateja Marinković and Linn Hendry make a first-rate duo: even the most piano-bashing bits of the Second Sonata are not deprived of all musical sense, and the urgent interplay between the instruments is authentically intense.

Suite in the Old Style. Moz-Art à la Haydn. Praeludium in memoriam Dmitri Shostakovich. A Paganini. Stille Musik. Stille Nacht. Madrigal in Memoriam Oleg Kagan. Gratulations rondo.
Mateja Marinković, Thomas Bowes *vns* **Timothy Hugh** *vc* **Linn Hendry** *pf*
ASV CDDCA877 (68 minutes: DDD). Recorded 1993.   Ⓕ

At first glance, this disc presents a rather scrappy impression. It contains no large-scale pieces, and the largest work – the early *Suite in the Old Style* – is for the most part an uneventful exercise in dutiful imitation. It is what the *Suite* only hints at that the other works realize more fully. In the *Gratulations rondo* Schnittke again wears the mask of conformity to an old, easygoing classicism. When the mask begins to slip, we wonder what to think. Is this a serious lesson about the potential banality of classicism's familiar formulas? Are the distortions of those formulas expressive of affection or hostility? These issues come most fully into focus in *Stille Nacht*, as Gruber's sweet little tune, with its obediently basic harmony, is subjected to quiet but ruthlessly dissonant deconstruction. 'Silent Night' acquires the connotations of Rachel Carson's *Silent Spring*, suggesting an environmental disaster rather than a cosy spirituality. Schnittke's ability to create memorable musical laments is well displayed here, in the Shostakovich and Kagan memorial pieces, in *Stille Musik* and even in *A Paganini*, which traces an absorbing contest between an apparent distaste for virtuosity and a celebration of it. The impact of these compositions is the greater for their relative concentration – not an invariable virtue in Schnittke – and Mateja Marinković is a player of admirable technical refinement. The recording is first-class, and the disc can serve as an ideal introduction to Schnittke for listeners who may have doubts about his larger-scale works. 'Scrappy' it is not.

---

12 Penitential Psalms.
Swedish Radio Choir / Tõnu Kaljuste.
ECM New Series 453 513-2 (53 minutes: DDD). Text and translation included. Recorded 1996. Ⓕ

Schnittke's 12 *Penitential Psalms* (1988) are not biblical: Nos. 1-11 use sixteenth-century Russian texts and No. 12 is a wordless meditation which encapsulates the spirit and style of what precedes it. Though at times dark and despairing in tone, this is in no sense liturgical music. It is too expansive, and reaches towards the ecstatic too consistently, to qualify as ascetic or austere. Indeed, the warmly euphonious chorale-like textures with which several of the movements end are sumptuous enough for one to imagine a soulful saxophone weaving its way through them. As this suggests, the recording is extremely, and not inappropriately, resonant, and the performance is polished to a fault, the individual lines superbly controlled and the textures balanced with a fine feeling for their weight and diversity. Although some listeners may find this issue just a little too refined for its own good, it realizes the work's expressive world with imposing and irresistible authenticity. In these works, Schnittke seems to be doing penance for the extravagant indulgences of works such as *Stille Nacht* and the Viola Concerto, abandoning modernism in general and expressionism in particular. The music nevertheless retains strong links with the images of lament and spiritual aspiration, and there is nothing in the least artificial or contrived about its emotional aura. It is difficult to imagine a more convincing or better recorded account of it than this one.

Othmar Schoeck

Swiss 1886-1957

Elegie, Op. 36.
Andreas Schmidt *bar*
Musikkollegium Winterthur / Werner Andreas Albert.
CPO CPO999 472-2 (58 minutes: DDD). Text and translation included. Recorded 1997. Ⓕ

This is a wonderful disc. The *Elegie* was the first of Othmar Schoeck's song-cycles and among his most haunting. Its emotional origins are to be found in the turbulent affair he had with the pianist Mary de Senger, whose course Dr Chris Walton charts in his authoritative notes. They first met when de Senger auditioned for him in 1918 and their relationship survived various quarrels, depressions and reconciliations until 1923. The previous year Schoeck had begun composing a series of songs that in time came to form the present cycle. It can be said to portray 'the narrative of a dying love' and though the impulse was primarily autobiographical, his relationship with de Senger was not to disintegrate finally until after its completion and first performance. He began in the summer of 1922 by setting Eichendorff's poem, *Der Einsielder* – whose title he subsequently changed to *Der Einsame* ('The lonely one') – which he placed at the very end of the cycle.

The cycle comprises two dozen settings for baritone and chamber orchestra of poems by Lenau and Eichendorff. Right from the first notes the listener is drawn into Schoeck's world and remains under his spell for the remaining hour. What imaginative miniatures these are, powerful in atmosphere, full of inventive resource and sensitive colouring. Take, for example, the third song, 'Stille Sicherheit' ('Quiet certainty'), which takes one-and-a-half minutes but is so concentrated in feeling and heady in atmosphere that it conveys as much as a miniature tone-poem. The same may be said of No. 11, 'Vesper', with its evocative tolling bells and powerful scents – and practically any of the later songs in this cycle. Not only is Schoeck's harmonic and orchestral palette subtle, but the vocal line is beautifully drawn and, it goes without saying, given the distinction of this artist, beautifully sung. This is one of the outstanding song-cycles of its period, very naturally recorded: its beauties resonate in the mind long after you have played it.

Penthesilea.
Helga Dernesch *sop* Penthesilea; **Jane Marsh** *sop* Prothoe; **Mechtild Gessendorf** *sop* Meroe;
Marjana Lipovšek *mez* High Priestess; **Gabriele Sima** *sop* Priestess;
Theo Adam *bass-bar* Achilles; **Horst Hiestermann** *ten* Diomede; **Peter Weber** *bass* Herold;
Austrian Radio Chorus and Symphony Orchestra / Gerd Albrecht.
Orfeo C364941B (80 minutes: ADD). Notes and text included. Recorded live in 1982. Ⓕ Ⓔ

Schoeck's one-act opera, *Penthesilea* is an astonishing and masterly score. It seems barely credible that a work so gripping in its dramatic intensity, and so powerful in atmosphere, should be so little known. It has the listener on the edge of the seat throughout its 80 short minutes and, like any great opera, it continues to cast a spell long after the music has ended. In the *Grove Dictionary of Opera*, Ronald Crichton wrote that 'at its most intense, the language of *Penthesilea* surpasses in ferocity Strauss's *Elektra*, a work with which it invites comparison'. In so far as it is a one-act work, set in the Ancient World, highly concentrated in feeling and with strongly delineated characters, it is difficult not to think of Strauss's masterpiece. Yet its sound world is quite distinctive. Though he is a lesser figure, Schoeck similarly renders the familiar language of Straussian opera entirely his own. The vocabulary is not dissimilar yet the world is different. We are immediately plunged into a vivid and completely individual world, packed with dramatic incident: off-stage war cries and exciting, dissonant trumpet calls. There is an almost symphonic handling of pace, but the sonorities are unusual: for example, there is a strong wind section, some ten clarinets at various pitches, while there are only a handful of violins; much use is made of two pianos in a way that at times almost anticipates Britten. This performance emanates from the 1982 Salzburg Festival; Helga Dernesch in the title-role commands the appropriate range of emotions as Penthesilea and the remainder of the cast, including the Achilles of Theo Adam, rise to the occasion. The important choral role and the orchestral playing under Gerd Albrecht are eminently committed and the recording is good without being state-of-the-art. There is a useful essay and libretto, though in German, not English or French.

Arnold Schoenberg
Austro/Hungarian 1874-1951

Verklärte Nacht, Op. 4.

Verklärte Nacht. Pelleas und Melisande, Op. 5.
Berlin Philharmonic Orchestra / Herbert von Karajan.
DG The Originals 457 721-2GOR (74 minutes: ADD). Recorded 1973-74. Ⓜ ℞℞

This is a very distinguished coupling, superbly played by the Berlin Philharmonic Orchestra – a truly 'legendary' reissue, quite unsurpassed on record. Karajan never approached contemporary music with the innate radicalism and inside knowledge of a composer-conductor like Boulez; yet he cannot be accused of distorting reality by casting a pall of late-romantic opulence and languor over these works. He is understandably most at home in the expansive and often openly tragic atmosphere of Schoenberg's early tone-poems *Verklärte Nacht* and *Pelleas und Melisande*. The richly blended playing of the BPO provides the ideal medium for Karajan's seamless projection of structure and expression. He remains especially sensitive to the music's lyricism, to the connections that to his ears override the contrasts. Although *Verklärte Nacht* has certainly been heard in performances less redolent of nineteenth-century tradition, as well as less calculated in terms of recorded acoustic, this remains a powerfully dramatic reading. One man's view, then: but, given the man, a notably fascinating one.

Verklärte Nacht. Five Orchestral Pieces, Op. 16. Three Piano Pieces, Op. 11. Six Piano Pieces, Op. 19. Piano Piece, Op. 11 No. 2 (arr. Busoni).
Chicago Symphony Orchestra / Daniel Barenboim *pf*
Teldec 4509-98256-2 (77 minutes: DDD). Recorded 1995. Ⓕ

Barenboim's version begins with the evident belief that Schoenberg's initial marking of *Sehr langsam* is not an invitation to linger lovingly over every last semiquaver. The expressive trajectory of the whole is magnificently natural and persuasive, as one might expect from the experienced Wagnerian that Barenboim has become. Only at the very end does he risk too weighty an articulation and too broad a tempo, a tendency confirming that his reading is stronger in passion than it is in tenderness. The recorded sound is also spacious in the extreme. Barenboim's superbly played account is a superior example of the kind of 'wide screen' approach to Schoenberg's early masterwork favoured by conductors like Karajan and Sinopoli. The appeal of this disc is greatly enhanced by the other items. There is a marvellously vivid performance of the Op. 16 *Pieces* which, for clarity of texture and depth of expression, counts – along with Robert Craft's – as one of the most convincing of current versions. And we also hear Barenboim as pianist in the Op. 11 and Op. 19 *Pieces*. There are minor idiosyncracies in Op. 19 – for example, a rather brisk tempo for No. 6 – but Op. 11 is excellent. As a bonus Barenboim also plays Busoni's 'amplification' (perhaps 'dilution' is a better term) of Op. 11 No. 2. This is one of the more pointless attempts by one talent to render another, very different talent more 'comprehensible', but it provides a distinctive and far from insignificant footnote to a Schoenberg disc of unusual substance and distinction.

Schoenberg Verklärte Nacht.
Schubert (arr. Mahler) String Quartet No. 14 in D minor, D810, 'Death and the Maiden'.
Norwegian Chamber Orchestra / Iona Brown.
Chandos CHAN9616 (69 minutes: DDD). Recorded 1994.   Ⓕ

Given the wrong sort of performance, *Verklärte Nacht* can drag on interminably – but not here. Iona Brown's reading with the Norwegian Chamber Orchestra lends every instrumental exchange the immediacy of live theatre: her lovers are voluble, unstinting and spontaneously communicative. There is colour in every bar: Schoenberg's ceaseless shifts in tone and tempo seem freshly credible, and the sum effect is extraordinarily compelling. The up-front recording further compounds a sense of urgency; only the closing pages seem a trifle uncomfortable with such close scrutiny. Rivals, however, are plentiful. Among older alternatives, Karajan and the Berlin Philharmonic are the most tonally alluring; but Brown runs it close, and her young Norwegian players are with her virtually every bar of the way. No digital rival is quite as good. The Schubert-Mahler also offers further confirmation of a genuine artistic alliance. Mahler's bolstered textures work least well in the second movement (where dramatic gesture plays a subsidiary role), something that even Brown's advocacy doesn't quite compensate for; but the rest is shot through with genuine passion and vitality. A memorable disc.

Variations for Orchestra, Op. 31. Pelleas und Melisande.
Chicago Symphony Orchestra / Pierre Boulez.
Erato 2292-45827-2 (62 minutes: DDD). Recorded 1991.   Ⓕ

The two faces of Schoenberg could scarcely be more starkly juxtaposed than they are on this superbly performed and magnificently recorded disc – Boulez and the CSO at their formidable best. *Pelleas und Melisande* can be taken not only as Schoenberg's 'answer' to Debussy's opera (also based on Maeterlinck's play) but as his challenge to Richard Strauss's supremacy as a composer of symphonic poems. It is indeed an intensely symphonic score in Schoenberg's early, late-romantic vein, with an elaborate single-movement structure and a subtle network of thematic cross-references. Yet none of this is an end in itself, and the music is as gripping and immediate a representation of a tragic love story as anything in the German romantic tradition. To move from this to the abstraction of the 12-note Variations, Op. 31 may threaten extreme anticlimax. Yet from the delicate introduction of the work's shapely theme to the turbulent good humour of the extended finale Schoenberg proves that his new compositional method did not drain his musical language of expressive vitality. The elaborate counterpoint may not make for easy listening, but the combination of exuberance and emotion is irresistible – at least in a performance like this.

Chamber Symphony No. 1, Op. 9[a]. Erwartung[b]. Variations for Orchestra, Op. 31[c].
Phyllis Bryn-Julson *sop* [a]**Birmingham Contemporary Music Group;**
[bc]**City of Birmingham Symphony Orchestra / Sir Simon Rattle.**
EMI CDC5 55212-2 (75 minutes: DDD). Text and translation included. Recorded 1993.   Ⓜ Ⓔ
Gramophone Award Winner 1995.

This well-filled disc offers an unusually comprehensive survey of the essential Schoenberg – the irascible late-romantic of the *Chamber Symphony* (1906), the radical expressionist of *Erwartung* (1909) and, in the *Variations* (1928), the synthesizer of expressionist moods with techniques that set up neo-classical associations. Rattle's account of the *Chamber Symphony* may well surpass that of the Orpheus Chamber Orchestra (reviewed below) in the demonstration quality of the sound, which has remarkable depth and realism. Rattle ensures a superbly well characterized and integrated performance, which only veers towards over-emphasis at the very end. There is also ample refinement where that is called for, and this quality is no less abundant in *Erwartung*. Here the almost impressionistic sheen of the orchestral sound fits well with Phyllis Bryn-Julson's generally restrained approach to the vocal line. When it comes to the *Variations for Orchestra*, Rattle and the CBSO are supreme. This recording may well be the first to convey the full, astonishing range of the work's textures, from the most delicate chamber music to dense tuttis, without a hint of artificiality. But it is the interpretation which counts for most. Rattle brings all these textures to rhythmic and expressive life, avoiding the lumpiness and stridency which occasionally afflict other conductors. He has evidently taken enormous care to follow Schoenberg's detailed markings, yet the result has a sovereign spontaneity. Despite strong competition from Boulez this performance is a triumph.

Chamber Symphonies – No. 1; No. 2, Op. 38. Verklärte Nacht.
Orpheus Chamber Orchestra.
DG 429 233-2GH (69 minutes: DDD). Recorded 1989.   Ⓕ

In the late twentieth century there's increasing evidence that the early twentieth century's most radical music is becoming so easy to perform that it may at last be losing its terrors for listeners as well as players. This can only be welcomed, provided that performances do not become bland and mechanical, and the conductorless Orpheus Chamber Orchestra triumphantly demonstrates how to combine fluency with intensity. If you like your Schoenberg effortful – to feel that the players are conquering almost insuperable odds – these recordings may not be for you. But if you like spontaneity of expression that is never an end in itself, and communicates Schoenberg's powerfully coherent forms and textures as well as his abundant emotionalism, you should not hesitate. The DG disc is the first to place Schoenberg's two Chamber Symphonies alongside *Verklärte Nacht*. The First Chamber Symphony shows Schoenberg transforming himself from late-romantic into expressionist, while in the Second the recent American immigrant, in the 1930s, looks back to his romantic roots and forges a new, almost classical style. With superb sound, this is a landmark in recordings of twentieth-century music.

String Quartets – No. 1, Op. 7; No. 2 in F sharp minor, Op. 10; No. 3, Op. 30; No. 4, Op. 37.
Dawn Upshaw *sop* **Arditti Quartet** (Irvine Arditti, David Alberman *vns* Garth Knox *va* Rohan de Saram *vc*).
Auvidis Montaigne MO782024 (two discs: 139 minutes: DDD). Recorded 1993.   Ⓕ

These recordings were made in London, in collaboration with the BBC, and the sound is consistently spacious, with a natural clarity and an even balance; the details of Schoenberg's complex counterpoint, as evident in No. 1 as in No. 4, can be heard with a minimum of stress and strain. Although one occasionally gets the impression that the Arditti is relatively cool in its response to this often fervent music, the overall mood they create is far from anti-romantic, and they call on a remarkably wide range of dynamics and tone colours. Even if every nuance in Schoenberg's markings is not followed, this is warmly expressive playing. Dawn Upshaw's contribution to the Second Quartet also helps to heighten the sense of drama although she misses some of that mysterious, ecstatic quality which makes this music so haunting. It is in the Third and Fourth Quartets that the superior sound quality of the Auvidis Montaigne issue pays the greatest dividends. Textural clarity is vital here, and although even the Arditti struggles to sustain the necessary lightness in the long second movement of No. 4, their wider dynamic range brings you consistently close to the toughly argued, emotionally expansive essence of this music. Yet the performance of No. 3 is the finest achievement of the set: clarity of form and emotional conviction combine to create an absorbing account of a modern masterwork. It sets the seal on a most distinguished enterprise.

Schoenberg String Quartet in D major. String Trio, Op. 45ª.
Zemlinsky Two Movements for String Quintet. Two Movements for String Quartet.
Andrea Wennberg *va* **Corda Quartet** (ªOlga Nodel, Christiane Plath *vns* ªFrauke Tometten-Molino *va* ªEdith Salzmann *vc*).
Stradivarius STR33438 (79 minutes: DDD). Recorded 1996.   Ⓕ

While it is no longer necessary to introduce Zemlinsky as Schoenberg's brother-in-law and musical mentor, rather than as a composer in his own right, it is still interesting to hear programmes which compare and contrast their compositional developments. This well-performed disc confirms that, although after a similar start the two grew ever further apart, Zemlinsky's later music was much more than the unadventurous outpouring of a lesser talent. Written in the mid-1890s, Zemlinsky's Two Movements for string quintet are accomplished and personable studies whose obvious echoes of various late-romantic masters enhance rather than diminish their appeal. Much the same can be said (though the influences are slightly different) of Schoenberg's D major Quartet of 1897, even more impressive as a student piece in avoiding any hint of that diffuseness in which Zemlinsky occasionally indulged. By 1929, the date of the Two Movements for string quartet, Zemlinsky was still a late-romantic, though with an intensity suggesting familiarity with Berg's more recent pieces, like the *Lyric Suite* (dedicated to Zemlinsky). At that time, Schoenberg was already well on the road that would lead to the fragmented, atonal expressionism of the String Trio, exceptional though that work is in its impatience with the kind of links to classical and romantic traditions that Schoenberg usually admitted. The Corda Quartet conveys the full emotional range of these works.

Schoenberg Verklärte Nacht, Op. 4 (orig. version).
Schubert String Quintet in C major, D956.
Alvin Dinkin *va* **Kurt Reher** *vc*
Hollywood Quartet (Felix Slatkin, Paul Shure *vns* Paul Robyn *va* Eleanor Aller *vc*).
Testament mono SBT1031(73 minutes: ADD). Recorded 1950-51.
Gramophone Award Winner 1994. ⒻⒽ

This was the first ever recording of *Verklärte Nacht* in its original sextet form and it remains unsurpassed. When it was first reviewed in *Gramophone*, Lionel Salter wrote of it as being 'beautifully played with the most careful attention to details of dynamics and phrasing, with unfailing finesse, with consistently sympathetic tone, and, most important, with a firm sense of the basic structure'. The Schubert too fully deserves its classic status. The tranquillity of the slow movement has never been conveyed with greater nobility or more perfect control. The Hollywood Quartet made music for the sheer love of it and as a relaxation from their duties in the film-studio orchestras, for which they were conspicuously overqualified. They have incomparable ensemble and blend; and their impeccable technical address and consummate tonal refinement silence criticism. The transfers could not be better.

Five Orchestral Pieces, Op. 16. A Survivor from Warsaw, Op. 46. Begleitmusik zu einer Lichtspielszene, Op. 34. Herzgewächse, Op. 20. Serenade, Op. 24ᵃ.
Eileen Hulse *sop* **Stephen Varcoe** *bar* **Simon Callow** *narr* **London Voices;**
ᵃ**Twentieth Century Classics Ensemble; London Symphony Orchestra / Robert Craft.**
Koch International Classics 37263-2 (69 minutes: DDD). Recorded 1994. Ⓕ

This is an absorbing issue, not least for the sheer variety of works that it contains. The two largest compositions, Op. 16 and Op. 24, define the disc's range. The *Five Orchestral Pieces*, in which expressionism can be heard emerging from the chrysalis of late romanticism, are played with supreme finesse by the LSO, and Robert Craft probes the richly diverse textures with exemplary concentration and precision. The downside is some loss of immediacy, a general feeling of caution. There are also slight reservations about the balance in *A Survivor from Warsaw*, where Simon Callow is, one imagines, placed behind the orchestra, depriving this harrowing work of its visceral impact. Since Callow's style can veer in a flash from the conversational to the melodramatic, a closer focus would have been preferable. *Herzgewächse* and *Begleitmusik zu einer Lichtspielszene* are both well performed, the latter with a recessed perspective, similar to that in Op. 16, which ensures an extremely well-blended texture without loss of detail. Nevertheless, there is no doubt that the finest performance here is that of the *Serenade*, Op. 24, where the sound (recorded in New York, not in London) is cleaner, and the characterization is superb from beginning to end. Stephen Varcoe is a rather breathy singer in the dauntingly angular and wide-ranging 'Sonnet', but the performance as a whole makes a convincing case for the work's high level of musical thought and purely technical mastery.

Cabaret Songs – No. 1, Galathea; No. 2, Gigerlette; No. 3, Der genügsame Liebhaber. Drüben geht die Sonne scheiden. Vier Lieder, Op. 2. Die Aufgeregten, Op. 3 No. 2. Lieder, Op. 6 – No. 1, Traumleben; No. 4, Verlassen; No. 8, Der Wanderer. Gedenken. Jane Grey, Op. 12 No. 1. Zwei Lieder, Op. 14. Folksong arrangements – Der Mai tritt ein mit Freuden; Es gingen zwei Gespielen gut; Mein Herz ist mir gemenget; Mein Herz in steten Treuen.
Mitsuko Shirai *mez* **Hartmut Höll** *pf*
Capriccio 10 514 (63 minutes: DDD). Texts and translations included. Recorded 1993. Ⓕ

Mitsuko Shirai has pretty well the ideal voice for these songs. It's not large, but her subtle control of dynamics enables her to encompass surprisingly big gestures. Her intimacy and deft way with words bring great rewards, too. Most of these songs are early Schoenberg, still within hailing distance of Brahms or Wolf (who would not have been ashamed of the long, lyrical line of 'Traumleben', with its overt quotation from Wagner's *Tristan*). Even in Op. 14, where atonality is in sight, close motivic working and, in 'In diesen Wintertagen', a graceful vocal line, retain a close kinship to the nineteenth-century Lied, and Shirai's easy negotiation of awkward intervals prevents them from ever sounding ungrateful. The strangest pieces here, but oddly attractive, are Schoenberg's folk-song arrangements (who would ever have thought he had much time for such things?). Much later than any of the original songs in this collection, in their close and sometimes busy counterpoint they are a touching homage to Brahms (who loved, collected and arranged such songs himself) and even to Bach: they are 'chorale preludes' in all but name. Shirai, very properly, sings them beautifully but plainly. Her husband is an ideally responsive partner; the recording is satisfactory, if a bit too close.

Friede auf Erden, Op. 13. Kol nidre, Op. 39. Drei Volkslieder, Op. 49. Zwei Kanons – Wenn der schwer Gedrückte klagt; O dass der Sinnen doch so viele sind!. Drei Volkslieder (1929) – Es gingen zwei Gespielen gut; Herzlieblich Lieb, durch Scheiden; Schein uns, du liebe Sonne. Vier Stücke, Op. 27. Drei Satiren, Op. 28. Sechs Stücke, Op. 35. Dreimal tausen Jahre, Op. 50. De profundis (Psalm 130), Op. 50*b*. Modern Psalm (Der erste Psalm), Op. 50*c*. A Survivor from Warsaw, Op. 46.
John Shirley-Quirk, Günter Reich *narrs*
BBC Singers; BBC Chorus and Symphony Orchestra; London Sinfonietta / Pierre Boulez.
Sony Classical SM2K44571 (two discs; 105 minutes: DDD/ADD). Texts and translations included. Recorded 1976-86.

Ⓜ

Pierre Boulez's recordings of Schoenberg have been appearing at irregular intervals over many years. This two-disc compilation of choral works includes performances recorded on three separate occasions in 1982, 1984 and 1986, as well as transferring the 1976 recording of *A Survivor from Warsaw*, originally coupled on LP with three purely orchestral works. There is no lack of interpretative consistency in what we hear, however. By 1976 Boulez was a seasoned Wagner conductor, and while it may be simplistic to ascribe the weightiness and spaciousness of these Schoenberg performances to his experiences at Bayreuth, the generally recessed sound-perspective strongly suggests a desire to turn the BBC's Maida Vale studios into a much larger and more resonant hall. This distancing is especially evident in John Shirley-Quirk's declamation of the text of *Kol nidre*, one of Schoenberg's later and more substantial sacred compositions. Once you adjust to the balance, the performance itself has an appropriately fervent atmosphere, as do the accounts of the other works involving narrator, chorus and orchestra, the unfinished *Modern Psalm* and *A Survivor from Warsaw*. Both are characteristically intense and exultant, the *Psalm* with some particularly telling orchestral interjections, *A Survivor from Warsaw* with its climactic choral hymn (sung in Hebrew, though the booklet fails to provide transliterations of the Hebrew text both for this and for Psalm 130). Günter Reich's memorably dramatic (but not melodramatic) narration in *A Survivor from Warsaw* benefits from his relatively forward placing.

Most of the music on the discs is for chamber choir, usually unaccompanied. Boulez's expressiveness tends to be fairly generalized, creating and sustaining an overall mood rather than responding to every nuance of the text. The BBC Singers are technically excellent, but the recording magnifies the collective vibrato, the tonal fruitiness which can blur textural definition, especially in the close-knit part-writing of the six pieces for male choir, Op. 35. Where the late-romantic sheen Boulez casts over Schoenberg's harmony works best is in such beautifully turned exercises in nostalgia as the German folk-song arrangements, especially the ravishingly beautiful 'Schein uns, du liebe Sonne'. Fortunately the singers find the necessary incisiveness for the Op. 27 and Op. 28 collections, even if a drier acoustic might have helped to clarify the convoluted lines of the problematic Op. 27 No. 4, 'Der Wunsch der Liebhabers'. It is a pity that Sony Classical didn't take a little more care with the booklet but that doesn't detract from a firm recommendation.

Gurrelieder.
Susan Dunn *sop* **Brigitte Fassbaender** *mez* **Siegfried Jerusalem, Peter Haage** *tens*
Hermann Becht *bass* **Hans Hotter** *narr*
St Hedwig's Cathedral Choir, Berlin; Dusseldorf Musikverin Chorus;
Berlin Radio Symphony Orchestra / Riccardo Chailly.
Decca 430 321-2DH2 (two discs: 101 minutes: DDD). Text and translation included. Recorded 1985.

Ⓕ Ⓢ ⓇⓇ

'Every morning after sunrise, King Waldemar would have a realization of the renewing power of nature, and would feel the love of Tove within the outward beauty of Nature's colour and form' (thus said Leopold Stokowski, who made the first-ever recording of *Gurrelieder*). This vast cantata, a direct descendant of Wagnerian music-drama, was for the turn-of-the-century musical scene in general, more the ultimate gorgeous sunset. Schoenberg started work on it in 1899, the same year as his *Verklärte Nacht*, but delayed its completion for over a decade, by which time some of his more innovatory masterpieces were already behind him. Schoenberg's forces are, to put it mildly, extravagant. As well as the six soloists and two choruses, the orchestra sports such luxuries as four piccolos, ten horns and a percussion battery that includes iron chains; and so complex are some of the textures that, to achieve a satisfactory balance, a near miracle is required of conductor and recording engineers. Decca has never been mean with miracles where large-scale forces are concerned and this set is no exception. Chailly gives us a superbly theatrical presentation of the score. The casting of the soloists is near ideal. Susan Dunn's Tove has youth, freshness and purity on her side. So exquisitely does she float her lines that you readily sympathize with King Waldemar's rage at her demise. Siegfried Jerusalem has the occasional rough moment but few previous Waldemars on disc have possessed his heroic ringing tones and range of expression. And Decca makes sure that its trump card, the inimitable Hans Hotter as the speaker in 'The wild hunt of the summer wind', is so tangibly projected that we miss not one single vowel or consonant of his increasing animation and excitement at that final approaching sunrise.

Gurrelieder.
Deborah Voigt sop **Jennifer Larmore** mez **Thomas Moser, Kenneth Riegel** tens
Bernd Weikl bar **Klaus Maria Brandauer** spkr Dresden State Opera Chorus;
Leipzig Radio Chorus; Prague Men's Chorus; Staatskapelle Dresden / **Giuseppe Sinopoli.**
Teldec 4509-98424-2 (two discs: 113 minutes: DDD). Texts and translations included.
Recorded live in 1995. (F)

Sinopoli's account is more luxurious, he is more likely than Chailly to let his orchestra rip (the Staatskapelle Dresden letting rip is an awesome sound) and he is more generous with ample rubato. These qualities, together with Teldec's sumptuous live recording (if an audience were present they must have been bound and gagged: not a single intrusive sound) count for a great deal in this piece, and for their sake you might be prepared to put up with one or two less than ideal soloists. Deborah Voigt's voice is bright, vibrant, fearless in *ff* and in the upper register, but needing hard work to fine it down to really expressive, quiet singing. But when she does work hard she is impressive. So is Thomas Moser, sometimes a stalwartly baritonal Waldemar, once or twice a little unsteady, but with ringing, heroic top notes. Larmore is even brighter than Voigt, with a penetrating fast vibrato: strongly dramatic, but not as gravely moving as the best Waldtaube ever, Chailly's Brigitte Fassbaender. No actor in the Speaker's role, not even one as distinguished as Brandauer, will ever surpass Chailly's Hans Hotter, much richer of voice and rising to a splendidly full-throated (and *sung*!) final word, but Brandauer has wit and character on his side. The choral singing in the later scenes is opulent. Sinopoli takes 12 minutes longer over the piece than Chailly. Yes, his speeds are generally slower, and the long sequence of love-songs in Part 1 occasionally loses urgency as a result, but a good deal of the difference of timing is accounted for by flexible rubato, which will strike anti-Sinopolists as fussy but others as voluptuous.

Pierrot lunaire, Op. 21. Herzgewächse, Op. 20. Ode to Napoleon, Op. 41.
Christine Schäfer sop **David Pittman-Jennings** narr
Ensemble InterContemporain / **Pierre Boulez.**
DG 457 630-2GH (53 minutes: DDD). Texts and translations included. Recorded 1997. (F)

Pierre Boulez's third recording of *Pierrot lunaire* is his first to use the Ensemble InterContemporain. The result is an intense yet intimate reading, recorded (doubtless to the conductor's specifications) in a way that is positively anti-resonant, and which veers, like the music itself, between harshness and reticence. Boulez's second recording (for Sony Classical), with Yvonne Minton, has long been notorious as the 'sung' *Pierrot*, flouting the composer's specific instructions about recitation. This time Christine Schäfer is more speech-orientated, the few fully sung notes perfectly pitched, and although slidings-away from sustained sounds are on the whole avoided, the effect is superbly dramatic in the work's more expressionistic movements. There are only a very few places (like the end of No. 11) where the voice is too softly projected in relation to the instruments, and only one movement (No. 18) which seems a little short of the necessary sense of menace. Overall, nevertheless, the work's existence in a strange world half-way between cabaret and concert hall is admirably caught. Boulez's first recording of the *Ode to Napoleon* was with David Wilson-Johnson and the Ensemble InterContemporain (also Sony Classical), and this one is a more than adequate replacement. David Pittman-Jennings has a heavy voice, but he skilfully inflects the sketchily notated dynamics of the vocal part, and the instrumental backing is appropriately forceful and well nuanced. The sound may be clinically dry, but when the performance itself has such expressive immediacy, this is scarcely a serious drawback. The disc is completed by the brief, exotic Maeterlinck setting from 1911, whose hugely demanding vocal line deters all but the hardiest. Christine Schäfer copes, while the accompaniment for celesta, harmonium and harp weaves its usual spell. A memorable disc, and a clear front-runner among current versions for all three works.

Moses und Aron.
David Pittman-Jennings narr Moses; **Chris Merritt** ten Aron; **László Polgár** bass Priest;
Gabriele Fontana sop Young Girl, First Naked Woman; **Yvonne Naef** mez Invalid Woman;
John Graham Hall ten Young Man, Naked Youth; **Per Lindskog** ten Youth;

Henk de Vries *bar* Young Man; **Siegfried Lorenz** *bar* Another Young Man;
Chorus of the Netherlands Opera; Royal Concertgebouw Orchestra / Pierre Boulez.
DG 449 174-2GH2 (two discs: 106 minutes: DDD). Notes, text and translation included.
Recorded 1995. Ⓟ Ⓢ

Moses und Aron is respected rather than loved, with the reputation of being a tough assignment for
all concerned. One of the essays in the booklet accompanying this recording calls it a didactic
opera. Pierre Boulez, however, is a conductor in whom didacticism is close to a passion, and he is
obviously passionate about this opera (this is his second recording of the piece). We take it for
granted that in any work to which he feels close, every detail will be both accurate and audible. But
for Schoenberg *Moses und Aron* was a warning as well as a homily, and as much a confession of
faith as either. Boulez, often himself a Moses preaching against anti-modern backsliding, is at one
with Schoenberg here. Some such reason, surely, has led to this being not only a performance of
immaculate clarity, but of intense and eloquent beauty and powerful drama too. The recording was
made during a run of stage performances, but in the Concertgebouw in Amsterdam, not in the
theatre. In the beautiful acoustic of their own hall, the orchestra plays with ample richness as well
as precision, and the at times complex textures benefit enormously from a perceptible space around
them. The choral singing matches the orchestral playing in quality: beautiful in tone, eloquently
urgent, vividly precise in the difficult spoken passages. The soloists are all admirable, with no weak
links. Merritt in particular seems to have all that the hugely taxing role of Aron demands: a fine
control of long line, intelligently expressive use of words, where necessary the dangerous
demagogue's glamour. Pittman-Jennings is a properly prophetic Moses, grand of voice. But the set
is Boulez's achievement above all: he is as good at dramatic excitement (the transformations of
Moses's staff) as at soberly or poignantly expressive melody (the memorably beautiful closing
scene), and the long, orgiastic worship of the Golden Calf has all that one hopes for from it: power,
menace, hysteria, the grotesque, but also a queerly impressive sensuous lyricism which is
disturbingly alluring. This is one of Boulez's finest achievements, a compelling argument for *Moses
und Aron* as an anything but coldly didactic opera.

Franz Schreker Austrian 1878-1934

Die Gezeichneten.
Heinz Kruse *ten* Alviano Salvago; **Elizabeth Connell** *sop* Carlotta;
Monte Pederson *bar* Count Vitelozzo Tamare; **Alfred Muff** *bass* Duke Adorno/Capitaneo
di Giustizia; **Lászlo Polgar** *bass* Lodovico Nardi, Podesta; **Christiane Berggold** *mez* Martuccia;
Martin Petzold *ten* Pietro; **Robert Wörle** *ten* Guidobald Usodimare;
Endrik Wottrich *ten* Menaldo Negroni; **Oliver Widmer** *bar* Michelotto Cibo;
Matthias Goerne *bass-bar* Gonsalvo Fieschi; **Kristin Sigmundsson** *bass* Julian Pinelli;
Petteri Salomaa *bass* Paolo Calvi; **Marita Posselt** *sop* Ginevra Scotti;
Reinhard Ginzel *ten* First Senator; **Jörg Gottschick** *bass* Second Senator;
Friedrich Molsberger *bass* Third Senator; **Herbert Lippert** *ten* A youth;
Berlin Radio Chorus; Deutsches Symphony Orchestra, Berlin / Lothar Zagrosek.
Decca Entartete Musik 444 442-2DHO3 (three discs: 171 minutes: DDD). Notes, text and
translation included. Recorded 1993-94. Ⓟ Ⓔ

The mingling in *Die Gezeichneten* of post-*Salome* opulence (Strauss with rich admixtures of
Scriabin, Szymanowski, Korngold and Puccini) with post-*Salome* gaminess of subject matter is
indeed strong stuff. Carlotta, a beautiful but gravely ill painter knows that her health would never
withstand physical love. She is loved, he believes hopelessly, by the monstrously ugly nobleman
Alviano; she is desired by the licentious Count Tamare. Drawn by the beauty of Alviano's soul she
at first declares her love for him, but then deserts him for Tamare. On learning that she gave herself
to Tamare voluntarily, knowing the fatal consequences, Alviano first kills his rival, then goes mad.
Schreker's sheer resourcefulness is breathtaking. Each character seems to have not merely an
identifying theme but a whole sound world. Scenes of extreme complexity are handled with total
assurance. The score is melodious, fabulously multi-coloured and has great cumulative power. One
reservation was hinted at by Alban Berg's reaction to the libretto: he found it superb but 'a bit
kitschy'. It is, and this quality is intensified in the music by a curious impassivity, as though
Schreker were observing his characters from outside. Carlotta's 'conversion' from spiritual to
physical love is not accompanied by much change in her alluringly mysterious music; her
characterization is fantastically detailed but has no depth. She, Alviano and Tamare are ideas, not
people. It is an opera in which richness of detail, complexity of texture and sheer glamour replace
humanity. The end is 'effective' but not tragic. Nevertheless, as a document of its time (1918) and as
a score of unprecedented richness it abundantly deserves recording. Zagrosek's reading is superb,
his cast almost without flaw. Connell has all Carlotta's glamour, together with a purity of tone and
a subtle response to words and phrasing that come close to giving her a soul. Kruse is less

imaginative, one or two of Alviano's high notes give him trouble, but he sings strongly and lyrically; Pederson makes a grippingly formidable, physical opponent. The precision and detail of the subsidiary characters are praiseworthy throughout; even very small roles have been cast from strength. The recording is remarkably fine, spacious and sumptuous, with not a single detail out of focus.

Franz Schubert Austrian 1797-1828

Overtures – Der Teufel als Hydraulicus; Der Spiegelritter; Des Teufels Lustschloss; Der vierjährige Posten; Claudine von Villa Bella; Die Freunde von Salamanka; Die Zwillingsbrüder; Alfonso und Estrella; Die Verschworenen; Fierrabras.
Haydn Sinfonietta, Vienna / Manfred Huss.
Koch Schwann 311212 (68 minutes: DDD). Recorded 1997.   Ⓟ Ⓟ

The works here cover a span of some dozen years, ranging from the jaunty, bustling *Der Teufel als Hydraulicus* and the more ambitious *Der Spiegelritter*, both composed around the time of Schubert's fifteenth birthday, to the overtures to his richest and grandest stage works, *Alfonso und Estrella* (1821) and *Fierrabras* (1823). The teenage overtures, while giving few hints of Schubert's melodic genius, are full of striking dramatic gestures. There are intermittent echoes of Mozart and affinities between two effervescent operetta overtures of 1815, *Der vierjährige Posten* and *Claudine von Villa Bella*, and the contemporary Second Symphony. The boldest and most colourful of these early overtures is that to Schubert's first completed opera, *Des Teufels Lustschloss*, a grisly Gothic horror tale whose hero undergoes blood-curdling ordeals worthy of Indiana Jones. Schubert evidently relished the opportunity for orchestral grotesquerie, whether in the eerie chorale for horns and trombones in the development or the screeching, cackling coda, with its piercing woodwind and high trumpets. Of the later overtures, those to the one-act *Singspiels*, *Die Zwillingsbrüder* and *Die Verschworenen*, are delightfully conspiratorial, with a nod to Mozart's *Figaro* in the former and a strong dash of Rossini in the latter. *Alfonso und Estrella* and *Fierrabras* are altogether more imposing affairs. Each opens with a brooding, atmospherically scored slow introduction, while the main *Allegro* of *Alfonso* has a tremendous cumulative rhythmic force that points ahead to the *Great* C major Symphony. With his Viennese-based orchestra Manfred Huss does ample justice to Schubert's exhilarating invention. Tempos are lively, rhythms strong and propulsive and textures sharply etched, with Huss making the most of the composer's theatrical contrasts. The recording has admirable clarity and impact.

Symphonies – No. 1 in D major, D82; No. 2 in B flat major, D125; No. 3 in D major, D200; No. 4 in C minor, D417, 'Tragic'; No. 5 in B flat major, D485; No. 6 in C major, D589; No. 8 in B minor, D759, 'Unfinished'; No. 9 in C major, D944, 'Great'.

Symphonies Nos. 1-6, 8 and 9. Grand Duo in C major, D812 (orch. J. Joachim).
Rosamunde, D644 – Overture, 'Die Zauberharfe'.
Chamber Orchestra of Europe / Claudio Abbado.
DG 423 651-2GH5 (five discs: 320 minutes: DDD). Recorded 1986-87.
Gramophone Award Winner 1989.   Ⓕ

Even from a conductor who had actively encouraged the Chamber Orchestra of Europe from the start, it is a remarkable tribute that Claudio Abbado chose this superb band of young musicians, founded by former members of the European Community Youth Orchestra, for this major Schubert project. A more obvious choice would have been the Vienna Philharmonic, or for that matter either of the other great orchestras with which he had been closely associated, the Chicago Symphony or the London Symphony Orchestra. But Abbado's confidence in his young players was repaid with compound interest. For all their fine qualities, his previous recordings of the central Viennese classics have never been remarkable for their warmth. With the COE in Schubert it is different. These are performances, recorded in three different venues, mainly in the Konzerthaus in Vienna, but also at Watford Town Hall, which have an authentic Schubertian glow. Anyone worried that a band with the words 'Chamber Orchestra' in the title might sound too puny for the later symphonies, need have no worries at all. The playing here is as satisfyingly powerful as it is polished, Abbado bringing an extra imaginative dimension without losing anything in freshness. Added to that, he uses specially edited texts for the six symphonies not included in the Neue Schubert-Ausgabe, with important and at times striking results. As Abbado says in a note, it was surprising, when so much scholarship had gone into reconstructing unfinished works, that 'symphonies which existed complete in autograph had not yet been edited from the original version'. He asked Stefano Mollo, a member of the orchestra, to do research on the original source material in Vienna, a task of detective work and collation that took him two years, and the results are included here.

So the middle section of the first subject in the Great C major Symphony has a semiquaver figure in the oboe melody quite different from what we have become used to, and four bars which Brahms cut from the *Scherzo* when he was editing the old Schubert-Ausgabe have been restored. Conversely the additional bars that Brahms added to the Fourth and Sixth Symphonies have been omitted. Abbado admits: 'There was some soul-searching on my part about the desirability of reversing some of Brahms's quite sensitive editorial decisions: the four bars he cut in the *Scherzo* of the Great C major, for example, are not Schubert's strongest'. No, not the strongest, one has to admit, but very striking none the less in their brassiness. On any count Schubertians will find refreshment here not just in the performances but in the texts too, and though any idea that the *Grand Duo* for piano duet was the missing 'Symphony No. 7' has long been exploded, it is good to have that as a supplement to the authentic cycle in the arrangement made – at Brahms's suggestion – by Joseph Joachim. In principle the lovely slow movement of the *Tragic* Symphony may be too romantic as Abbado presents it, but with yearningly tender oboe playing (a mark of the whole set, from, we assume, Douglas Boyd the regular principal), it is the most winning account of all on record. The only place where Abbado's subtle pointing dangerously draws attention to itself is in the *Unfinished* Symphony. There in the first movement, the second subject has Abbado starting each phrase with a slight agogic hesitation, very beautiful and very refined, but not really so effective as the simpler, folk-like treatment favoured by others. Yet his slowing for the ominous opening of the development section in that movement adds superbly to the tremendous power of the climax as it builds up, a totally justified freedom of expression, the mark of a master interpreter.

In the Great C major, too, the hand of a master, the touches of individuality, the moments of freedom, give Abbado's reading an extra weight lacking in other interpretations. Much is owed to the crispness of the COE ensemble, not least in the enunciation of dotted rhythms or – in the finale – the scurrying triplets, where this is as clean in texture as a performance on period instruments. Though in conventional style Abbado allows a momentary easing into the second subject of the first movement of that symphony, and draws out the cello melody after the big climax of the slow movement, his choice of basic speeds makes those modifications seem naturally expressive and not at all self-indulgent. Abbado's extra items are generous too, not just the *Rosamunde* Overture but the Joachim arrangement of the *Grand Duo*, not likely to be confused with an original Schubert symphony but bringing illumination to a work which in the very forces involved – piano duet – gets unjustly neglected. With its fresh look at the texts, with its refined and imaginative performances, sunnily expressive, powerful and intense, this Abbado set has to be the first recommendation, guaranteed to bring joy and illumination.

Symphonies Nos. 1-6, 8 and 9.
Royal Concertgebouw Orchestra / Nikolaus Harnoncourt.
Teldec 4509-91184-2 (four discs: 284 minutes: DDD). Recorded live in 1992.　　　ⓟⒺ

Harnoncourt, like Abbado on DG, has researched Schubert's own manuscripts, and corrected many unauthentic amendments that found their way into the printed editions of the symphonies, such as the eight bars later added to the Fourth Symphony's first movement exposition; but the differences between Harnoncourt's interpretative Schubert and Abbado's are startling. The Ninth's finale, unlike Abbado's, a whirling, spinning *vivace* – is borne aloft on astonishingly precise articulation of its rhythms and accents, and a springy delivery of the triplets. Characteristics, of course, one has come to expect from a Harnoncourt performance. Still, what a joy to hear this *Allegro*, and those of most of the earlier symphonies, seized with such bright and light-toned enthusiasm. Here is urgent, virile and vehement playing, never over-forceful, over-emphatic or burdened with excessive weight. What came as a surprise was the consistent drawing out of these scores' potential for sadness and restlessness. Harnoncourt does not set apart the first six symphonies as merely diverting, unlike Abbado (out-and-out charm is seldom part of Harnoncourt's Schubertian vocabulary): their bittersweet ambiguities and apparent affectations of anxiety here acquire a greater significance, and the cycle, as a whole, a greater continuity.

Up to a point, the darker, more serious Schubert that emerges here, derives from the type of sound Harnoncourt fashions from his orchestra; not least, the lean string tone and incisive brass. And maybe, up to a point, from the corrections: Harnoncourt refers to the manuscripts as often being 'harsher and more abrupt in tone [than the printed editions], juxtaposing extreme dynamic contrasts', though you can't help feeling that contrasts in general have been given a helping hand. Trios are mostly much slower than the urgent minuets/scherzos that frame them (with pauses in between the two). And Schubert's less vigorous moments are very noticeable as such, and are inflected with varying degrees of melancholy – it is uncanny how the string playing, in particular, often suggests a feeling of isolation (along with the sparing vibrato is an equally sparing use of that enlivening facility: *staccato*). The *Unfinished* Symphony's first movement is a stark, harrowing experience (yet it remains a well-tempered musical one: gestures are never exaggerated); the opening is as cold as the grave itself; the second subject knows its song is short-lived. In both movements, the elucidation and balance of texture can only be described as masterly: just listen to the trombones casting shadows in both codas. This, then, is as seriously pondered, coherent and penetrating a view of the complete cycle as we have had. Whether or not you feel Harnoncourt focuses too much on Schubert's darker side, you have to marvel at his ability to realize his vision. The recorded sound offers that inimitable Concertgebouw blend of the utmost clarity and wide open spaces.

Symphonies Nos. 1-6, 8 and 9.
Staatskapelle Dresden / Sir Colin Davis.
RCA Victor Red Seal 09026 62673-2 (four discs: 269 minutes: DDD). Recorded 1994. Ⓕ

Back in 1981, Davis was the first to give us a Ninth with 'all' the repeats, as he does here. Since 1981, we've had Ninths that have also given us the repeats in the *da capo* of the *Scherzo* (which Davis didn't then, and doesn't now). But, with repeat-extended recordings of the Ninth, there is a fine line between being borne along by it, and, to be frank, becoming bored by it. Drive and energy play their part, but there are many other influencing factors – contrasts of tempo and dynamics, consistently spirited and incisive accentuation and articulation, and weight of orchestral sound, to which you might feel Davis has not quite enough of the first two, and maybe a touch too much of the third. Perhaps the jury needs further deliberation on the Davis Ninth; sample it extensively and you will continue to be impressed by the general magnificence of playing (trombones are never blatant), and by the beauty and airy articulacy of the sound (bass-lines are particularly well defined). The cumulative effect of Davis's maintained tempos is heard to greater advantage in his *Unfinished*, among the finest of recent recordings, as are the Abbado and Harnoncourt. In Davis's first movement, there is none of their hastening for the dramatic and energetic moments and the benefit is heard in the coda's 'incomparable song of sorrow' (Einstein). There must be no doubt that Davis's achievement in the first six symphonies will have collectors cherishing this set. The delights are far too numerous to mention, and if reservations in the Ninth Symphony have caused alarm, not one of them applies here. His instincts never desert him: for the general pacing and weighting of the music (slow introductions with an old-world patience, but no false grandeur); for knowing when to charm with a small slowing; and for knowing when to leave well alone (the serene and steady progress of the Fifth's *Andante*) and when to intervene (the gradual increase of tempo in the Sixth's finale). And where Abbado is scrupulous about dynamics, Davis is more selective; the Fourth's *Andante* is properly sublime and shapely, and the wind-down from the agitated second idea, with all those dying falls, has never been more affectingly done.

The First Symphony's first movement immediately announces a satisfyingly rich and varied spectrum of tone colour allied to a lightness of touch, and then a beautifully sung second subject, the whole informed with a blithe Mozartian grace. What more could one ask for? Well, perhaps for the small adjustments in balance and dynamics that Davis makes in the movement's coda that speak volumes about the kind of preparation (study or experience; probably both) that has obviously gone into the majority of these realizations. And then there is the orchestra itself, retaining a few features of its former self. The horns have lost the old Eastern European vibrato, but it is still a warm sound; one, in the balance here, always clearly in the picture. The clarinets remain an acquired taste; their characteristic 'hoot' is very likeable (a joy in the yodelling which opens the *Allegro con brio* of the Third Symphony's first movement); their tone always individual enough to remain a distinct feature of the woodwind choir, indeed of tuttis in general. String tone is not full-bodied in the Berlin manner, but sweet, the playing always possessed of grace of movement (and when called on, power), their famed articulation rarely deserting them. Much is made of the spacious Lukaskirche acoustic; there are only a few places where it prevents an ideally focused image (the same could be said of the Harnoncourt Concertgebouw set) and one can't imagine many collectors forgoing the bloom for something more clinical. It must be said, though, that Abbado's cycle set new standards of textural clarity which are unlikely ever to be equalled on either modern or period instruments.

Symphonies Nos. 3, 5 and 6.
Royal Philharmonic Orchestra / Sir Thomas Beecham.
EMI Studio CDM7 69750-2 (78 minutes: ADD). Recorded 1955-59. Ⓜ Ⓗ ⓇⓇ

Beecham was well into his seventies when he made these recordings with the Royal Philharmonic, the orchestra he had founded in 1946. His lightness of touch, his delight in the beauty of the sound he was summoning, the directness of his approach to melody, and his general high spirits will all dominate our memory of these performances. But listening again, we may be reminded that Beecham could equally well dig deep into the darker moments of these works. Schubert's elation was rarely untroubled and the joy is often compounded by its contrast with pathos – Beecham had that balance off to a tee. It should be noted that he does not take all the marked repeats and he doctored some passages he considered over-repetitive. However, these recordings may also serve as a reminder of the wonderful heights of musicianship that his players achieved, as in the trio of the Third Symphony's Minuet, where a simple waltz-like duet between oboe and bassoon attains greatness by the shapeliness, ease and poignancy of its execution. Despite some signs of age, these recordings still preserve the brilliance of their readings and the tonal quality of this orchestra. Altogether, a disc to lift the heaviest of spirits.

Symphonies Nos. 3 and 4. Overture in D major, D590, 'In the Italian style'.
Stockholm Sinfonietta / Neeme Järvi.
BIS CD453 (62 minutes: DDD).   (F)

The Overture is a delight, even if the Stockholm woodwinds lack that last ounce of agility for their perky Rossinian imitations. About the Abbado DG set of the symphonies (Nos. 3 and 4 are available separately but without the Overture), we have extolled the wonderfully spontaneous sounding playing. But alongside Järvi, Abbado can sound positively calculating. As remarked about Järvi's set reviewed below (Symphonies Nos. 5 and 6), it is the 'freshness' of Järvi's approach that is so infectious, and that quality is here in abundance as well. The Stockholm Sinfonietta, though, lacks the corporate virtuosity of the Chamber Orchestra of Europe; in the finale of the Third Symphony both conductors set similarly brisk speeds, but the Swedes simply don't have the muscle to leap for joy like their COE counterparts, and in the finale of the Fourth you miss the clean articulation of those accompanying quavers on the strings that run through most of this movement and give it so much of its excitement and tension. Neither is the engineering free of fault. The recording location is the same as for Nos. 5 and 6 (the Stockholm Concert Hall), but you sense that the microphones have been moved back. The overall balance is uncannily natural, but a little more mellow than before. Timpani and brass are vivid (wonderful horns!), but in the tuttis and faster passages there ought to be a clearer profile of the strings. The Third Symphony is less afflicted than the Fourth, perhaps because it is more lucidly scored. So, Järvi for warmth, grace and the occasional impression of a rushed job, Abbado for drama rhythmic stability and sound of striking clarity.

Schubert Symphony No. 3.
Schumann Symphony No. 3 in E flat major, Op. 97, 'Rhenish'.
North German Radio Symphony Orchestra / Günter Wand.
RCA Red Seal 09026 61876-2 (56 minutes: DDD). Recorded live 1991-92.   (F)

If Harnoncourt's Schubert is a nervous athlete hurrying among ghostly forerunners of a darker age, Wand's is a healthy bearer of the central classical tradition – plain-speaking, keen-eared and perennially youthful. Comparing the two in the Third Symphony's opening *Adagio maestoso* tells all, Harnoncourt thoughtfully attenuated and pensive, Wand more obviously Teutonic, though never stodgy or overbearing. Under Wand's direction, the *Allegro con brio*'s little clarinet melody has a delightful sing-song quality, although main arguments later on (played with exposition repeat intact) are fairly sturdy and well 'grounded'. Contrasts are even more marked in the Minuet and *Presto*, where Harnoncourt's punch and panic (listen to his machine-gun horns near the start of the *Presto*) inhabit a different world to Wand's Beethovenian brio. The *Rhenish* is forthright and unfussy, the opening *Lebhaft* swift, almost breathless in its impetuosity, the *Scherzo*, a rumbustious tavern song with brazen horns to close. The third movement is perhaps just a little sedate – we continue to stand by the incomparably poetic Kubelík here (our top choice in this work) – but the 'Cologne Cathedral' *Feierlich* and closing *Lebhaft* set up an admirable contrast between nobility and festive cheer. The orchestra follows Wand every note of the way and the live recordings have warmth and immediacy. Altogether a splendid affirmation of the then 80-year-old Günter Wand's undiminished interpretative skills.

Symphonies Nos. 4 and 8.
Bavarian Radio Symphony Orchestra / Carlo Maria Giulini.
Sony Classical SK66833 (64 minutes: DDD). Recorded live in 1993 and 1995.   (F)

Giulini's Eighth is noble and beautiful, but his way with the Fourth needs a warning. On the face of it, the Fourth's first movement *Vivace* marking and the leisurely chugging motion on offer here don't have much to do with each other. One could argue that by beating in four (the *Allegro* is in common time), Giulini is actually giving us a *vivace*. Yet one could just as easily retort that such an approach may occasion a lively conductor's baton, but not much else. Still, if the stormy vehemence and athletics (incisive accentuation and drive) of many another recording are not your cup of tea, you may well respond to Giulini's patient, mannerly and beautifully turned approach. You certainly will to the Fourth's finale: hardly 'in-a-spin' in the modern manner, but decently propelled and opening out finally into a moment of genuine splendour. Such things as the *decrescendoes/crescscendoes* in the brass parts, and a suddenly reflective moment in the development are no more radical (and no less relevant) than some of Harnoncourt's 'adjustments'. And there is gentle humour here too: the horns with the 'pah' of the 'oompah' in the second subject's recapitulation (all horn parts are clear in this typically open, naturally informative Herkukssaal recording). As ever, Giulini knows how to make Schubert sing, and if, in the *Unfinished*, he lingers in the first movement second subject's only brief moment of relative radiance (bars 94-103, and in the repeat), he does so without inflating it. What a pity it was that the Munich audience only allowed one second before bursting in on Schubert's 'music of the spheres'.

Symphonies Nos 5 and 6. Overture in D major in the Italian style, D591.
Stockholm Sinfonietta / Neeme Järvi.
BIS CD387 (72 minutes: DDD).   Ⓕ

A quality that this Järvi disc abounds in is freshness. As so often with Järvi, one notices an unusual degree of light and shade, while the phrasing always sounds spontaneous. He makes the music breathe, and the textures always sound deliciously airy without an accompanying loss of tonal weight in louder passages; a bright, well-focused BIS recording helps. In the Trio of the Sixth Symphony *Scherzo*, his balance of *forte*-piano accents, and *legato* continuation, is convincing but he does tend to come down on each accent so decisively that one hardly has time to recover before the next one – the intervening woodwind phrases leave little impression. Nevertheless, this is a recommendable coupling, with the Overture, D591, a generous filler.

Symphonies Nos. 5 and 8.
Concertgebouw Orchestra / Leonard Bernstein.
DG 427 645-2GH (57 minutes: DDD). Recorded live in 1987.   Ⓕ

Bernstein is surprisingly brisk in the first movement of the *Unfinished*, making it much more clearly a sonata-form *Allegro*, with the semiquavers of the main theme given an almost Mendelssohnian quality in their lightness. Perhaps even more surprisingly he refuses to linger over the haunting melody of the second subject, keeping it very fresh, hardly at all moulding it in the way that Abbado does, for example, with the Chamber Orchestra of Europe. In the slow movement Bernstein opts for a rather heavily moulded treatment at an unusually slow tempo – almost a reversion to the romantic manne. However, with the *fortissimo* interjections all the weightier at Bernstein's speed, it remains a strong and convincing reading. The sound in both No. 5 and the *Unfinished* is comparably full and atmospheric to that for the *Great* C major (reviewed below). In the Fifth Symphony some may similarly have reservations over Bernstein's relatively slow tempo for the second movement *Andante con moto*, which again is fairly heavily moulded. Yet the refinement of the playing and the detailed imagination puts it in a league of its own. In all three fast movements of No. 5, not least the finale, he adopts a dashing speed; light as well as brisk. Whatever detailed reservations there may be, Bernstein is consistently at his most magnetic, justifying even more than usual his latter-day technique of having live recordings edited together and tidied up afterwards.

Symphonies Nos. 8 and 9.
Berlin Philharmonic Orchestra / Günter Wand.
RCA Victor Red Seal 09026 68314-2 (two discs: 85 minutes: DDD). Recorded live in 1995. Ⓜ 🆁🆁

The advantages of these Berlin readings over Wand's 1991 Hamburg Musikhalle/North German RSO recordings (also live) are, often, as you might expect: greater facility (in, say, the infamous string triplets in the Ninth's last movement), generally richer string sonority (a proper 'heft' for those stamping C major chords also in the Ninth's finale), sweeter, more vibrant and more focused woodwind (wonderful solos in the Eighth's second movement second subject), a generally wider (though far from excessive) range of dynamics in the Eighth, more expansive phrasing, and accents more consistently placed (and recorded sound with marginally greater presence). The ground-plans remain the same, in other words, the basic tempo and its modification (and what ingenious and effective plans they are, and how marvellous it has been to re-encounter Wand's sublimely wrought rubato; as does the conductor's views on repeats (taken in the Eighth's first movement, but not in the Ninth's outer movements). It is pointless to speculate whether the small details that *have* changed (for example, the now truly *pianissimo* second subject of the Eighth's first movement) are due to Wand's further four years' thoughts on the works, or changes brought about by the Berlin orchestra's own musical collective, or just 'another time, another place'. Maybe a bit of all three. If you already own the Hamburg recordings, there is no need to rush out to buy this set (and, of course, you will also be the proud owner of the finest Schumann Fourth of the last two decades – the Hamburg Schubert Eighth's coupling). If you don't, this set is an obvious choice. Wand's Schubert is informed by a very special devotion, wisdom and insight, and a very individual spirit of adventure.

Symphony No. 9.
Concertgebouw Orchestra / Leonard Bernstein.
DG 427 646-2GH (50 minutes: DDD). Recorded live in 1987. Ⓕ

In the *Great* Symphony, with its built-in reputation for 'heavenly length', Bernstein opts in all four movements for relatively fast speeds. It is not until the main *Allegro* of the first movement that Bernstein really shows his hand. The slow introduction, warmly moulded, flows at a normal enough speed, but then he launches into an exhilaratingly brisk and rhythmic account of the first movement, refusing even a momentary *tenuto* for the entry of the second subject, let alone a slowing. He draws from the Concertgebouw the most delicate playing in the recapitulation, and keeps up the momentum in the coda past the first return of the theme of the introduction, making up for that with the biggest possible rallentando at the end for the final statement. He is markedly fast in the *Andante con moto* of the second movement, making the main theme light and jaunty. He makes no *accelerando* in the big *ostinato crescendo*, and shows his cunning in the following cello theme, slowing the tempo in the traditional way but with far less than usual of a feeling of gear-change at the end, when the main tempo is resumed. The *Scherzo* is tough rather than charming at Bernstein's brisk speed, but well sprung, and the urgency of the finale goes with satisfying weight and fine articulation of triplets by the Concertgebouw strings. The rasp of horns and trombones is beautifully caught, adding to the exhilaration of this live performance. In his urgency Bernstein omits exposition repeats in the outer movements, as well as the second repeat in the *Scherzo*.

Symphony No. 9.
Vienna Philharmonic Orchestra / Sir Georg Solti.
Decca 430 747-2DM (55 minutes: DDD). Recorded 1982. Ⓜ

Solti's Ninth is likely to bowl you over when you first hear it – you somehow don't expect him to be such a mellow and smiling Schubertian, and of course the VPO playing has great vitality too. As a performance it is quite glorious and can hold its own with any of its rivals, and in terms of recorded sound it is amazing (one of Decca's very best, and in the demonstration class, still). In its LP format, it was notable for its wide-ranging dynamics, its warmth and real 'presence'. The sound is, indeed, full-bodied and well-defined. Yet the CD remaster is undoubtedly superior: the instruments seem positively tangible. Initially, you may wonder whether the higher transfer level of the CD is responsible for the greater sense of immediacy but adjusting the controls still leaves the CD sounding firmer, more 'present' and richer. Altogether a most impressive disc and though one might quibble about the balance (one is placed very forward in the concert hall), there is no doubt that this is a winner among the many recordings of this heavenly symphony.

Symphony No. 9. Gesang der Geister über den Wassern, D714.
Monteverdi Choir; Vienna Philharmonic Orchestra / Sir John Eliot Gardiner.
DG 457 648-2GH (64 minutes: DDD). Text and translation included. Recorded live in 1997. Ⓕ

An outstanding example of the programmer's art. From the close of the choral song's watery passage of the soul, the common key of C allows the symphony's opening horn call then to ease us magically on to firmer ground for its own world of more confident journeying. Schubert might almost have intended it! An outstanding *performance* of the song, too; heard in the supremely evocative version for male voice and lower strings. These days, it is more difficult for new versions of the symphony to be 'outstanding'. Outstanding versions have fallen into two categories. Old masters, like Giulini and Wand, revisiting a score barnacled by traditional speedings and slowings, and bringing their own lifetimes' gained insights and affection to it (barnacles and all); and those who have thrown late-nineteenth- and twentieth-century traditions and instruments out of the window and started afresh, such as Norrington and Mackerras.

Gardiner, despite the generally lively tempos and light touch, is happy to embrace most of the barnacles. Obviously, you won't find Gardiner making cuts and halving the tempo for the finale's famous unison stamping Cs (which, in any case, is less of a barnacle than a massive holing below the water-line); but neither is there any incidence of Norrington's 'historical' phrasing vocabulary. Whether all this is how Gardiner feels the symphony should sound, or is born out of respect for a Viennese tradition, is hard to say. Whatever the case, in general, they play magnificently for him; the Vienna strings – with all the violins on the left – their familiar sweet-toned selves (showing little inhibition in their use of vibrato); and the special colours of their woodwinds' voices are always heard where they should be (memorably rustic, rueful oboes in the second movement, and a joyous 'singing out' of the entire section in the *Scherzo*'s Trio). As for the recorded sound, DG manages a satisfying compromise between spaciousness and presence. Of an audience there is not a hint.

Symphony No. 10 in D major, D936*a* (realized Newbould).
Symphonic fragments – D major, D615; D major, D708*a* (orch. Newbould).
Scottish Chamber Orchestra / Sir Charles Mackerras.
Hyperion CDA67000 (54 minutes: DDD). Recorded 1997. Ⓕ

Someone will have to find another name for Schubert's *Unfinished* Symphony (the B minor) before too long. In fact there are six unfinished Schubert symphonies: there are two whole movement expositions for D615, torsos of three movements and a nearly complete *Scherzo* for D708*a*, and enough sketch material for Brian Newbould to attempt a complete conjectural reconstruction of D936*a*, the symphony Schubert began writing in the last weeks of his life. Inevitably some will ask, why bother? Well, apart from the increase in the sense of wonder at Schubert's sheer productivity, there is some wonderful music here, especially the slow movement of D936*a*, desolate and warmly consoling by turns. As a whole, D936*a* suggests that, even at this late stage, Schubert was still thinking in terms of new developments. The concluding third movement, contrapuntally fusing elements of scherzo and finale, is like nothing else in Schubert – or in any other composer of the classical period. Of course, Newbould has had to do some guessing here, but the results are on the whole strikingly authoritative. The performances carry plenty of conviction and the recordings are atmospheric while allowing one to hear all significant detail. Altogether this is a fascinating disc – and not just for musicologists.

Octet in F major, D803.
Academy of St Martin in the Fields Chamber Ensemble (Kenneth Sillito, Malcolm Latchem *vns* Stephen Shingles *va* Denis Vigay *vc* Raymund Koster *chbr bass* Andrew Marriner *cl* Timothy Brown *hn* Graham Sheen *bn*).
Chandos CHAN8585 (60 minutes: DDD). Recorded 1987. Ⓕ 🆁🆁

This recording offers wonderful sound, not just in the quality itself, which is superlative, but in the impression of an unartificial balance – for though the strings are quite clearly in the picture, they don't seem to be given quite such a helping hand as in most other recordings. A thoughtful, measured first-movement introduction sets the tone for the performance. A good, moderate basic tempo is chosen for the movement's main *allegro* section, but within that framework there is some flexibility of phrase and pulse, so that the music breathes naturally and spontaneously. There is indeed something of a relaxed, intimate Viennese flavour in the music-making which is immensely enjoyable, though some listeners might well prefer a stronger, more outgoing approach. In the *Adagio* Andrew Marriner floats his clarinet solo exquisitely, and the whole movement is most sensitively realized: each phrase seems to be pregnant with meaning. In the third movement *Allegro vivace* the players find an attractive, dancing rhythm, and the variations which follow are deliciously inflected. After a Minuet shaped with a good deal of subtlety and affection the performance is well rounded off with a strong, purposeful finale.

Octet. Minuet and Finale in F major, D72.
Vienna Octet; Vienna Wind Soloists.
Decca Eclipse 448 715-2DEC (72 minutes: DDD). Recorded 1990. Ⓑ

Over the years Decca has made a speciality of recording the Schubert Octet in Vienna, and this budget-priced reissue by the Vienna Octet, captured within the glowing acoustics of the Mozartsaal of the Vienna Konzerthaus, and ideally balanced by Christopher Raeburn, is most winning. The enticing warmth of the opening *Adagio* catches the listener's attention at once, and the central movements – the *Scherzo* bustling with vitality and the deliciously played *Andante con variazioni* – are unforgettable. Then comes the lovingly Schubertian *Menuetto*, and after an arresting *tremolando* introduction, the joyfully bucolic finale rounds things off in sparkling fashion. At its price, this Vienna version is now in a class of its own. As a bonus we are offered the *Minuet and Finale*, D72, two engaging miniatures from the composer's youth, nicely elegant in the hands of the Vienna Wind Soloists. The demonstration-standard recording makes this a bargain not to be passed by.

Piano Quintet in A major, D667, 'Trout'.

Piano Quintet[a]. Quartet in G major, D96[b].
[b]**Wolfgang Schulz** *fl* [a]**Gerhard Hetzel** *vn* **Wolfram Christ** *va* **Georg Faust** *vc*
[a]**Alois Posch** *db* [b]**Göran Söllscher** *gtr* [a]**James Levine** *pf*
DG 431 783-2GH (65 minutes: DDD). Recorded 1990. Ⓕ 🅴🆁🆁

Schubert composed the *Trout* Quintet in his early twenties for a group of amateur musicians in the town of Steyr in Upper Austria, which lies upon the River Enns which was then noted for its fine fishing and keen fishermen. The Quintet was certainly tailored for special circumstances, but like all great occasional music it stands as strongly as ever today, with its freshly bubbling invention and sunny melodiousness. The *Trout* Quintet's widespread popularity is due partly to its cheerful radiance and warmth, reflective of Schubert's happy experiences in the summer of 1819, and partly to the spirit of friendship and camaraderie which it seems to embody. In the present version by James Levine and members of the Vienna Philharmonic, the unity of ensemble and common sense of purpose are most compelling. Both acoustically and musically, their performance has an affecting intimacy. Particularly noticeable are the warmth of Faust's cello playing within the texture and the heavenly phrasing of the Vienna Philharmonic's leader, Gerhard Hetzel, who was tragically killed in a walking accident in 1993. The piano is attractively balanced as a member of the ensemble, rather than as a soloist, which makes the variation fourth movement unusually appealing. Like most of their rivals, this group does not repeat the exposition in the finale. A rarity has been included which ensures that any Schubertian will want this issue in their collection. The so-called Guitar Quartet, D96, is an arrangement of a trio by Wenzel Matiegka which Schubert made in 1814. It is a charming work, presumably intended for domestic use, whose grace and elegance are highly infectious in this delightful performance.

Piano Quintet[a]. String Trios – B flat major, D581; B flat major, D111*a*.
Members of the **Leipzig Quartet** (Andreas Seidel *vn* Ivo Bauer *va* Matthias Moosdorf *vc*);
[a]**Christian Zacharias** *pf* [a]**Christian Ockert** *db*
Dabringhaus und Grimm MDG307 0625-2 (66 minutes: DDD). Recorded 1998.　　　　　Ⓕ

This *Trout* must surely be one of the very best versions of this much-recorded work – the sound is wonderfully natural, and so is the performance. You get the impression that here was an occasion when everything 'clicked', giving the playing a friendly, relaxed feeling that's just right for this carefree piece. Zacharias has the knack of making even the simplest phrase sound expressive, and the strings, without any exaggeration, produce the most beautiful tonal shadings. All five players, too, have an impressive sense of line; the phrasing and points of emphasis are balanced so that Schubert's expansive designs are projected compellingly. If the *Trout* shows a typically Schubertian spaciousness, his one completed String Trio is unusually compact. Another distinguished feature is the florid, Spohr-like elegance of much of the violin writing – Andreas Seidel is splendidly stylish and confident. Indeed, this is another very fine performance, emphasizing the predominating gentle lyricism, but with plenty of vigour and panache when required. The String Trio fragment, less than two minutes, continues the same, 'let's hear everything' approach; it's a sketch for what subsequently became the comparatively familiar B flat Quartet, D112.

Schubert Piano Quintet.
Mozart Piano Quartet in G minor, K478.
Thomas Zehetmair *vn* **Tabea Zimmermann** *va* **Richard Duven** *vc* [a]**Peter Riegelbauer** *db*
Alfred Brendel *pf*
Philips 446 001-2PH (75 minutes: DDD). Recorded 1994.　　　　　Ⓕ

Brendel is of course the lynchpin here and, as ever, balances heart and mind with innate good taste. Time and again you find yourself overhearing detail that might otherwise have passed for nothing: every modulation tells (needless to say, this *Andante* probes deeper than most); every phrase of dialogue has been polished, pondered and carefully considered. And yet it *is* a dialogue, with the loose-limbed Thomas Zehetmair leading his supremely accomplished colleagues through Schubert's delightful five-tier structure. The *Scherzo* and *Allegro giusto* frolic within the bounds of propriety (some will favour an extra shot of animal vigour), whereas the first, second and fourth movements are rich in subtle – as opposed to fussy – observations. The recording, too, is exceedingly warm, with only the occasional want of inner detail to bar unqualified enthusiasm. As ever, Philips achieves a well-rounded, almost tangible piano tone. Mozart's G minor Quartet makes for an unexpected, though instructive, coupling, treading as it does on the *Trout*'s playful tail. Here again there is much to learn and enjoy, especially in terms of phrasal dovetailing and elegant articulation (Brendel's opening flourish is a model of Mozartian phrase-shaping). Still, you may sometimes crave rather more in the way of *Sturm und Drang* – a fiercer, more muscular attack, most especially in the first movement. Yet there will be times when the conceptual unity and executive refinement of this performance – its articulate musicality – will more than fit the bill. Both works include their respective first movement repeats.

Piano Quintet. Adagio and Rondo concertante in F major, D487.
Jenö Jandó *pf* **Kodály Quartet** (Attila Falvay, Tamás Szabo *vns* Gábor Fias *va* János Devich *vc*);
IstvánTóth *db*
Naxos 8 550658 (53 minutes: DDD).　　　　　Ⓢ

This disc is further proof of Naxos's impressive ability to produce outstanding recordings at an astonishingly low price. Jenö Jandó's recording of the *Trout* Quintet, in a version which is based on the first edition of 1829, is buoyant and vigorous. The string support from members of the Kodály Quartet and István Tóth, despite some rough edges, is generally sonorous and appropriate. Balance is good, with the piano agreeably highlighted. The result is a performance which is a most desirable acquisition. Although Schubert wrote no concertos, he did write a *concertante* work for piano and strings which is also included here. Notwithstanding limitations of thematic invention, the *Adagio and Rondo* makes an attractive coupling. Jandó's sheer enthusiasm for this music provides a compelling alternative to other full-price accounts.

Piano Quintet[a]. String Quartet No. 14 in D minor, D810, 'Death and the Maiden'[b].
Sir Clifford Curzon *pf* [a]members of the **Vienna Octet** (Willi Boskovsky *vn* Gunther Breitenbach *va* Nikolaus Hübner *vc* Johann Krump *db*); [b]**Vienna Philharmonic Quartet** (Willi Boskovsky, Otto Strasser *vns* Rudolf Streng *va* Robert Scheiwein *vc*).
Decca 417 459-2DM (71 minutes: ADD). Item marked [a] recorded 1957, [b]1963. Ⓜ Ⓗ

Willi Boskovsky's gentle and cultured mind is very much responsible for the success of these performances of Schubert's two best-known chamber works. In the delectable *Trout* Quintet there is real unanimity of vision between the players, as well as an immaculate attention to the details of the scoring. Clifford Curzon's part in the performance is memorable especially for his quiet playing – the atmosphere is magical in such moments. Everywhere there is a great awareness of the delicacy and refinement of Schubert's inventiveness. The *Death and the Maiden* Quartet is no less successful. Schubert's strikingly powerful harmonies, together with a sustained feeling of intensity, all go to heighten the urgency of the first movement. Despite this, string textures are generally kept light and feathery. In the *Andante* all is subtly understated and although a mood of tragedy is always lurking in the background, never is it thrown at the listener. Boskovsky's understanding of the music is very acute and the performance cannot fail to satisfy even the most demanding. These are two vintage recordings and in the quartet the quality of sound is quite remarkable.

String Quintet in C major, D956.

String Quintet.
Douglas Cummings *vc* **The Lindsays** (Peter Cropper, Ronald Birks *vns* Roger Bigley *va* Bernard Gregor-Smith *vc*).
ASV CDDCA537 (DDD). Recorded 1985. Ⓕ ⓇⓇ

Schubert's sublime C major Quintet is eminently well served on disc. With this version one is immediately struck by its naturalness. You are left with the impression that you are eavesdropping on music-making in the intimacy of a private home. Although there is plenty of vigour and power, there is nothing of the glamourized and beautified sonority that some great quartets give us. (The two cellos, incidentally, are both by the same maker, Francesco Rugeri of Cremona.) They observe the first-movement exposition repeat, and the effortlessness of their approach does not preclude intellectual strength. The first movement surely refutes the notion that Schubert possessed an incomplete grasp of sonata form, an idea prompted by the alleged discursiveness of some of the sonatas. This is surely an amazing achievement even by the exalted standards of his day, and The Lindsays do it justice, as indeed they do the ethereal *Adagio*. Here they effectively convey the sense of it appearing motionless, suspended as it were, between reality and dream, yet at the same time never allowing it to become static. The quartet sound is not so full-bodied or richly burnished as that produced by many rivals, lacking quite the splendour or richness given to the best sound-recordings, but they have what can only be called a compelling wisdom. Their reading must be placed at the top of the list and for many readers will be an obvious first choice.

Schubert String Quintet.
Boccherini String Quintet in E major, G275.
Isaac Stern, Cho-Liang Lin *vns* **Jaime Laredo** *va* **Yo-Yo Ma, Sharon Robinson** *vcs*
Sony Classical SK53983 (76 minutes: DDD). Recorded 1993. Ⓕ

A glamorous line-up of soloists is, of course, far from a guaranteed recipe for success in chamber music, especially in a work as democratic as the Schubert Quintet. But at the 1952 Prades Festival, Stern, Casals and colleagues achieved the miraculous in their now legendary recording, reissued by Sony with Casals's hitherto unpublished 1953 Schubert Fifth Symphony (reviewed below). Over 40 years on, Stern teamed up with an equally starry first cellist, Yo-Yo Ma, and three distinguished colleagues in a reading that often recalls the Prades performance in style and spirit. The quality of the string playing is predictably fabulous, the communion between the five players close and intent, and the music-making marries keen intellectual and structural command with a generosity and spontaneity of impulse. The manner in which the players realize all the disturbing power of Schubert's muscular, rebarbative counterpoint is wholly admirable. Like Stern, Casals *et al* in 1952, the players bring to the *Scherzo* tigerish attack and demonic drive, suggesting an edge of desperation to the rollicking dance; the Trio, by contrast, is uncommonly slow and searching, evoking the haunted world of the *Heine* songs composed a few months earlier. The finale, too, has a desperate, almost manic energy. With the successive quickenings of the pace in the coda, here sounding absolutely inevitable, the gaiety becomes increasingly hysterical, even nightmarish; and the massive accent on the final D flat makes the close even more ominously ambivalent than usual.

The one real reservation about this powerful and disquieting performance is the lack of true *pianissimo* quality, partly, though one suspects not wholly, a consequence of close microphone placing. This, of course, affects the slow movement above all. On the other hand, the players go for broke in the central F minor catastrophe, Stern and Ma singing their great despairing melody with an abandon that rivals (and a purity of intonation that surpasses) Stern and Casals in the 1952 recording. So while the outer sections of the *Adagio* lack the last degree of inwardness and spirituality, this is an intensely compelling reading of the Quintet that realizes to the full the unease and terror that shadow the music. It certainly ranks among the finest available. The disc's attractions are enhanced by the inclusion of all marked repeats and by the presence of the Boccherini E major Quintet, the one with the world's most famous minuet. The other three movements prove no less delightful, with their characteristic mixture of sensuality and leisurely grace enlivened in the finale by touches of exotic Spanish colour; Stern and his colleagues give a highly appealing performance, full of subtle touches of timing and colour and savouring alike Boccherini's delicate detail and his often luscious textures.

String Quintet.
Borodin Quartet (Mikhail Kopelman, Andrei Abramenkov *vns* Dmitri Shebalin *va*
Valentin Berlinsky *vc*); **Mikhail Milman** *vc*
Teldec 4509-94564-2 (52 minutes: DDD). Recorded 1994.   Ⓕ

Decades of experience has taught the Borodin Quartet that there is more to late Schubert than resignation and dream. In each movement, it is harmonic instability, suddenness of dynamic contrast, harshness of rhythm and texture which are emphasized – and all caught faithfully in the outstanding engineering and production. Comparison in the case of this work, and this performance, really is odious. But surely there are few other accounts with a longer, more intense inner *crescendo* at the very core of those opening chords, or a more starkly rhythmic cut-off? The fierceness of those ever-tautening sequences and imitations at the start do away with any need for over-sweetness in the second, lyrical subject: it simply becomes set into gentle, natural relief. The great slow movement convinces entirely in its pulse-rate and pacing, with great dignity drawn from the full, sustained dotted note values in the violin parts. The *presto* of the *Scherzo* is restrained by a certain heavy-heeled ballast, so that the velocity of every note counts, and this most sober of Trios is given a frame of fitting substance. Few quartets capture so movingly the anxious tremor in the heart of the finale, as it lunges savagely between major and minor. But then few quartets have learned to look so far away from themselves and so deep into the very centre of the music.

String Quintet. Symphony No. 5.
Isaac Stern, Alexander Schneider *vns* **Milton Katims** *va* **Paul Tortelier** *vc*
Prades Festival Orchestra / Pablo Casals *vc*
Sony Classical Casals Edition mono SMK58992 (76 minutes: ADD). Recorded 1952-53.   Ⓜ Ⓗ

This should have an in-built fail-safe against hasty consumption, in that their interpretative ingredients are so rich, varied and unpredictable that to experience it all at once is to invite mental and emotional exhaustion. Casals is, of course, the lynchpin. A charismatic presence, he embraces everything with the passion of a devoted horticulturist tending his most precious flowers, and that his love extended beyond the realms of music to mankind itself surely enriched his art even further. The most celebrated Prades recording ever is still the Stern/Casals/Tortelier reading of the C major Quintet, a masterful traversal graced with elastic tempos, songful phrasing, appropriate rhetorical emphases (especially in the first and second movements) and fabulous string playing. The coupling here is a 'first release' of Schubert's Fifth Symphony, recorded in 1953 – a warm, keenly inflected performance, jaunty in the outer movements and with an adoring, broadly paced *Adagio*. One presumes that it has been held from previous view only because of a few minor executant mishaps. It is certainly well worth hearing. The transfer of the Quintet reveals itself as marginally warmer but occasionally less well-focused than previous incarnations. Still, the original was no sonic blockbuster to start with but this shouldn't deter you from hearing this disc.

String Quartets – No. 10 in E flat major, D87; No. 12 in C minor, D703, 'Quartettsatz'; No. 13 in A minor, D804; No. 14 in D minor, D810, 'Death and the Maiden'; No. 15 in G major, D887.

String Quartets Nos. 10 and 13. Quartettsatz in C minor, D703.
Artis Quartet (Peter Schuhmayer, Johannes Meissl *vns* Herbert Kefer *va* Othmar Muller *vc*).
Sony Classical SK66720 (66 minutes: DDD). Recorded 1994.   Ⓕ

The Artis Quartet has all the right Viennese qualifications to play Schubert – its playing is graceful and stylish, with genuine warmth of tone and expression. In the A minor Quartet it takes its cue from Schubert's many expression marks – making the accents and *crescendos* sound absolutely spontaneous; pointers to the underlying emotion. It helps that it plays the many soft passages so delicately; by contrast the more intense, dramatic moments come over strongly without any hint of overplaying, using imaginative variations of tone colour to point the different shades of feeling. The flowing *Andante* is a delight, and the restrained lilt of the Minuet, maintaining the melancholic mood, is equally successful. Only in the finale are some of the rhythms not ideally poised, but even here there's much to admire. The early E flat Quartet is played beautifully too; in the finale the leader's elegant *portamentos*, and the rhythmic fizz of the opening, remind us that the young Schubert was writing in the era of both Spohr and Rossini. The C minor *Quartettsatz* is less pleasing. Though in essence it's another fine and brilliant performance, the frequent hold-ups for accents start to sound rather contrived.

String Quartets Nos. 10 and 13.
Quatuor Mosaïques (Erich Höbarth, Andrea Bischof *vns* Anita Mitterer *va* Christophe Coin *vc*).
Auvidis Astrée E8580 (68 minutes: DDD). Recorded 1995.   Ⓕ Ⓟ Ⓔ

This recording of the A minor Quartet was the first ever on period instruments. With unusually broad tempos, the Mosaïques consistently stresses the music's pathos, loneliness and fatalism. The Hungarian-flavoured finale is normally seen as a stoically cheerful reaction to the pain that has gone before. But here it steals in as if in a dream from the spectral close of the Minuet, the opening melody delicately floated, its off-beat accents barely flicked; where the Alban Berg brings a faintly military strut to the C sharp minor melody (2'11"), the Mosaïques, suppressing any hint of swagger in the dotted rhythms, distils a doleful balletic grace. In the *Andante* of the *Rosamunde* the Mosaïques, while slower than its rivals, never loses sight of the *gehende Bewegung*, the walking motion that underlies so many of Schubert's *andantes*. It matches its rivals in its tender, sentient phrasing, subtly flexing the pulse in response to harmonic movement. The Minuet, with its glassy, vibratoless *pianissimos*, is more eerily remote, less human in its desolation, than from the Alban Berg. For the coupling the Mosaïques offers the early E flat Quartet, written when Schubert was just 16. Not even this affectionate, considered advocacy can do much for the dull, harmonically stagnant opening movement. But the players relish the raw energy of the *Scherzo*, with its braying donkey evocations, and bring a delicious demure wit to the Rossinian second theme of the finale (0'58"). And, as in the absorbing, moving reading of the A minor Quartet, the delicacy of nuance and clarity of texture, easier to obtain from the sparer-toned period instruments, is often revelatory. The recording is clean, vivid and immediate. In sum, an outstanding disc in every way.

String Quartets Nos. 10[b] and 14[a].
Alban Berg Quartet (Günther Pichler, Gerhard Schulz *vns* Thomas Kakuska *va* Valentin Erben *vc*).
EMI CDC5 56470-2 (57 minutes: DDD). Item marked [a] recorded live in 1994, [b]1997.   Ⓕ

String Quartets Nos. 12 and 15.
Alban Berg Quartet (Günther Pichler, Gerhard Schulz *vns* Thomas Kakuska *va* Valentin Erben *vc*).
EMI CDC5 56471-2 (60 minutes: DDD). Recorded live in 1997.   Ⓕ

The Alban Berg Quartet's policy of making recordings at concert performances certainly produces impressive results: interpretations that avoid any feeling of routine or of being overcareful. What impresses above all is the flexibility and sensitivity of these performances. In the first movement of D887 the Alban Berg, by subtly drawing our attention to the precise emotional colour of all Schubert's magical harmonic shifts, finds a touching, intimate quality within the grand design. And it's certainly an advantage for any group performing this quartet to be able to produce such a magnificent *tremolando* – whether it's the forest murmurs of the first movement or the Gothic shuddering of the *Andante*'s middle section. The G major Quartet is the outstanding performance on these discs, but *Death and the Maiden* isn't far behind, particularly the *con fuoco Scherzo* and finale. There are a few places, where Schubert is straightforwardly tuneful (in D703 and in the outer movements of D87, especially) where one wishes Günther Pichler would play in a simpler, more direct manner. The Busch Quartet's 1930s recordings of D810 and D887 are smoother, less emphatic than that of modern groups, and this enables it to convey the emotional nuances, particularly of the D minor Quartet, in a more inward and profound way. And the two quartets are available (with some repeats missing) on a single CD. But it's a measure of the Alban Berg Quartet's exceptional quality to realize that it is in the same league, with the same sense of players totally absorbed in the music. And of course the recorded sound is immeasurably more vivid and lifelike.

String Quartets Nos. 12[a], 13[b], 14[a] and 15[b].
Quartetto Italiano (Paolo Borciani, Elisa Pegreffi *vns* Piero Farulli *va* Franco Rossi *vc*).
Philips Duo 446 163-2PM2 (two discs: 142 minutes: ADD). Recorded [a]1965, [b]1976-77. Ⓜ 🆁🆁

The Italians' playing has freshness, affection, firm control and above all authority to a degree that no relative newcomer can match. It is notable not only for the highest standards of ensemble, intonation and blend, but also for its imaginative insights; these attributes readily apply to the music-making on this Duo reissue, particularly in the slow movements. Indeed, the players' progress through the wonderful set of variations in the *Andante con moto*, which reveals the *Death and the Maiden* Quartet's association with the famous Schubert song of that name, has unforgettable intensity (it is a grand conception packed with memorable detail – the evocation of terror in the early stages of the first movement coda has never been bettered). The comparable *Andante* of No. 13, with its lovely *Rosamunde* theme – which is approached here in a relaxed, leisurely manner – is held together with a similar (almost imperceptible) sureness of touch. Incidentally, when this work was originally issued, the first-movement exposition repeat was cut in order to get the quartet complete on to a single LP side. Here it has been restored. Finest of all is the great No. 15, a work of epic scale. In this performance the first movement alone runs to nearly 23 minutes, and the players' masterly grip over the many incidents that make up the *Allegro molto moderato* is effortless. For an encore we are given No. 12, a piece on a smaller scale, but here presented with a comparable hushed intensity of feeling. This, like No. 14, was recorded in 1965 and the textures are rather leaner than on the others, with a fractional edge on *fortissimos*. Nevertheless, the ear soon adjusts when the playing is as remarkable as this. The other recordings have more body, and a fine presence. The CD transfers throughout are a great tribute to the Philips engineering team.

String Quartets Nos. 14 and 15.
Busch Quartet (Adolph Busch, Gösta Andreasson *vns* Karl Doktor *va* Hermann Busch *vc*).
EMI Références mono CDH7 69795-2 (73 minutes: ADD). Recorded 1936-38. Ⓜ 🄷

Death and the Maiden is the best served of Schubert's quartets on CD. The Busch Quartet's account is now well over 60 years old but it still brings us closer to the heart of this work than any other. The slow movement, in particular, has an unmatched and marvellous eloquence. The same must also be said of the G major Quartet, a performance of surpassing beauty which reveals more of the depth and humanity of the score than any subsequent recording. Such are these performances that the music is quick to engross your thoughts to the exclusion of any consideration of the age of the recordings. The present recording is, on the whole, good: exceptionally so in the quieter passages.

Piano Trios – B flat major, D28 (Sonata in one movement); No. 1 in B flat major, D898; No. 2 in E flat major, D929. Notturno in E flat major, D897. String Trios – B flat major, D471; B flat major, D581.
Beaux Arts Trio (Menahem Pressler *pf* Daniel Guilet *vn* Bernard Greenhouse *vc*);
Grumiaux Trio (Arthur Grumiaux *vn* Georges Janzer *va* Eva Czako *vc*).
Philips Duo 438 700-2PM2 (two discs: 127 minutes: ADD). Recorded 1966-69. Ⓜ

These performances are polished, yet the many solo contributions from each of the players emerge with a strong personality. The Beaux Arts cellist brings lovely phrasing and a true simplicity of line, so right for Schubert – memorably in the lovely slow movement melody of the Trio No. 2 in E flat. In addition to the great piano trios (B flat, D898 and E flat, D929) the set includes the extremely personable, very early Sonata in B flat, D28, where the lyrical line already has the unmistakable character of its young composer. Also included is the *Notturno*, D897, a raptly emotive short piece played here with a remarkable depth of feeling that recalls the gentle intensity of the glorious slow movement of the String Quintet. The recording is naturally balanced, although a little dry in the treble. Of the two rarer string trios, also early works, the four-movement Trio D581 is totally infectious, with that quality of innocence that makes Schubert's music stand apart. Given such persuasive advocacy, and vivid recording, both pieces cannot fail to give the listener great pleasure.

Piano Trios Nos. 1 and 2. Sonata in A minor, D821, 'Arpeggione'. Notturno in E flat major, D897.
Yuuko Shiokawa *vn* **Miklos Perényi** *vc* **András Schiff** *pf*
Teldec 0630-13151-2 (two discs: 127 minutes: DDD). Recorded 1995. Ⓕ

This set begins with an outstanding performance of the *Arpeggione* Sonata. The recording is clear and spacious, and the outer movements have an effortless sense of momentum that is not too inflexible to allow for some expressive rubato and pointing of the phrases. There's no hint in Perényi's playing that this is a difficult work for the cello, and he produces a most beautiful, warm, serene tone for the *Adagio*. Schiff's special feeling for Schubert is apparent even in the most subsidiary details of the piano part and particularly in the more dominating roles of the trios and the *Notturno*. These three well-matched players find exactly the right tone and feeling. In the first *Allegro* of the B flat Trio the superior recording helps them to convey the music's grandeur and the following *Andante* is played with a flowing, evocative style. Shiokawa's clear-toned, elegant violin playing is a great asset here. In the *Notturno*, too, a flowing tempo doesn't spoil the tranquillity of the opening melody, but allows the contrasting episode to emerge triumphantly. In the monumental E flat Trio Schiff, Shiokawa and Perényi seem sometimes a little polite and decorous but their interpretation is certainly not lacking in vitality or variety. The finale in this performance lasts nearly 20 minutes: the players have gone back to the original version of the movement – Schubert made cuts when preparing the trio for publication. If you're an admirer of Schubert's 'heavenly length' you'll hear it as the true culmination of one of his greatest instrumental works.

Overture in F major, D675. Eight Variations on a theme from Hérold's 'Marie', D908. Rondo in D major, D608. Marches héroïques, D602. Fantasie in F minor, D940. Variations in B flat major, D603/D968a. Divertissement à la hongroise, D818. Six Polonaises, D824.
Yaara Tal, Andreas Groethuysen *pf duet*
Sony Classical S2K58955 (two discs: 137 minutes: DDD). Recorded 1993. Ⓕ

Tal and Groethuysen explain that they have used a Fazioli Model 308 piano and thank their recording team for its 'exceptional abilities'. Indeed, an impressive sound comes from this big instrument, which the artists consider necessary to re-create the 'symphonic ambitions' and 'extremes' of the music, although it is unlike anything Schubert could have heard, and they play with a fine tonal and dynamic range which allows intimacy as well as power. The treble is bright yet not glaring, as we hear in the closing page of the *Overture*. The recording is fairly reverberant but produces a satisfying aural picture. The performances are strong and compelling, with plenty of momentum, yet flexible. The *Rondo* has a winning *galanterie*, and the players know that *Allegretto* marking here applies to style as well as tempo. The F minor *Fantasie* is Schubert's best-known keyboard duet and, of course, inhabits a more private world in which despair features strongly. Tal and Groethuysen's basic tempo is a genuine *Allegro molto moderato*, and they know how to make transitions from one mood to the next, as when approaching the doom-laden F sharp minor section at 4'55". Furthermore, they rightly bring out the 'smiles through tears' aspect of the more lyrical music, do not hurry the *Scherzo* (which is consequently all the stronger) and shape the fugue finely. Very impressive. The sound is very clear and firm.

Divertissements – à la hongroise, D818; sur des motifs originaux français, D823.
Andreas Staier, Alexei Lubimov *fp duet*
Teldec 0630-17113-2 (66 minutes: DDD). Recorded 1997. Ⓕ**P**

Schubert's *Divertissement à la hongroise*, his most flamboyant essay in the Hungarian vernacular style, has always overshadowed the *Divertissement* on French themes. Yet the less favoured work is in some ways the more compelling. Its profoundly un-divertimento-like first movement has a haunting, quintessentially Schubertian second theme and one of the composer's most turbulent and tonally audacious developments. The *Andantino*, a set of variations on a glum little theme that sounds more plausibly French than anything else in the work, is transfigured by its ravishing final variation in the major; and the finale is a sprawling, colourful rondo, built on a theme that equivocates between G major and E minor. Using a fine copy by Christopher Clarke of an 1826 Graf instrument, Staier and Lubimov give performances which, in poetry, *élan* and sheer relish have never been surpassed. One immediate advantage of a fortepiano in this music is the way it clarifies the textures, especially in the bass regions, which can too easily sound murky on a modern grand. Then there is the unique array of colours available through the use of no fewer than five pedals – the harp-like sonorities of the *una corda* pedal, for instance, or the 'bassoon' pedal, with its buzzing lower strings. The instrument's *coup de grâce* is its so-called Turkish pedal, attached to bass drum, bells and cymbals, which the players unleash at strategic points with swashbuckling effect. If you're a sceptic about period performance, then these hugely enjoyable performances should convert you.

Allegro in A minor, D947, 'Lebensstürme'. Four Polonaises, D599. Variations in E minor on a French song, D624. Divertissement, D823. Grandes marches, D819. Rondo in A major, D951.
Yaara Tal, Andreas Groethuysen *pf duet*
Sony Classical S2K66256 (two discs: 153 minutes: DDD). Recorded 1994. Ⓕ

The first discs in the Schubert series from Tal and Groethuysen are reviewed above. This pair of discs features the same Fazioli Model 308 grand piano, its big modern sound clearly unauthentic but surprisingly effective in conveying what the artists call the 'symphonic' aspects of the music. The recording is splendidly clear yet atmospheric, with a fine dynamic range. As for the playing, it is wonderfully controlled, affectionate while subtly poised and textured, with flexible tone and tempo – a model of Schubert duet style. Tal and Groethuysen are winningly persuasive with great responsiveness and refinement. The little-known 'Lebensstürme' *Allegro* that opens the first disc is a vivid and intense piece in Schubert's tragic key of A minor that is not unworthy of comparison with the *Fantasie* and was composed a month after that masterpiece of the composer's final year. The *Four Polonaises* of 1818 are more ordinary, but still delightful when played as elegantly as this, and the same may be said of the E minor *Variations on a French song* – a work from the same year that the young Schubert dedicated to Beethoven. The later *Divertissement* ('sur des motifs originaux français'), a three-movement suite in all but name, is in the same key of E minor but more striking: its central variation-form *Andantino* is among the best and most personal music that Schubert wrote, with subtleties of every kind that Tal and Groethuysen respond to consistently. All this music is on the first disc. The second offers the same mixed bag: medium to highest quality in the music but outstanding playing. Thus the six *Grandes marches* are frankly conventional despite their occasional Hungarian flavour; they also last far too long, occupying well over an hour in all and with No. 5 alone lasting nearly 20 minutes – though the latter, funereal and in the unusual key of F flat minor, is rather special and was later transcribed for orchestra by Liszt. However, the very late *Rondo* in A is rich in invention and emotionally deep.

Sonata for Piano Duet in C major, D812, 'Grand Duo'. Eight Variations in A flat major, D813.
Trois marches militaires, D733.
Daniel Barenboim, Radu Lupu *pf duet*
Teldec 0630-17146-2 (77 minutes: DDD). Recorded 1993.   Ⓕ🅴

One might expect this combination of artists playing Schubert to produce winning results, and so it does. Rarely will you hear duet playing of such refined elegance and multicoloured animation. Here, the playing is vivid and glamorous; the dynamic and colouristic range of Barenboim's and Lupu's performances suggests a public environment. After the spirited brio of the familiar *Marches militaires*, the remainder of the disc contains music of greater seriousness and architectural breadth. The Variations in A flat are beautifully played, with subtle and discerning pianism. The largest work on this disc is the C major Sonata: here it runs to 43 minutes, longer than any of Schubert's solo sonatas. It can reasonably be classed alongside Schubert's two other late masterpieces in C, the *Great* Symphony and the String Quintet. The *Grand Duo* is symphonic in scope and expression, although the writing is innately pianistic. The fine detail of Barenboim's and Lupu's account, their diversity of colour and attack and their voicing of melodic and inner lines, suggests an image of suitably orchestral depth and variety. Furthermore, the surface gloss of these performances is underpinned by the most crystalline lucidity and poetry. The recording is excellent.

Violin Sonatas – D major, D384; A minor, D385; G minor, D408.
Angèle Dubeau *vn* **Anton Kuerti** *pf*
Analekta fleurs de lys FL2 3042 (55 minutes: DDD). Recorded 1990.   Ⓜ

These performances are really impressive. Angèle Dubeau and Anton Kuerti are at one in maintaining the intimate tone of these works; they manage to make each detail expressive, yet keeping to a natural, unforced utterance. It helps, in such memorably tuneful music, that they both know exactly how to present a singing, *legato* melodic line. Even when playing very quietly, Dubeau keeps some tension in the way the notes are joined together; this art, which many modern string-players seem to have forgotten, enables her to convey effortlessly the feeling behind the notes – the sweet melancholy of the minor episode in D384's *Andante*, for instance. The lively music, such as the finales of D384 and D408, is played with splendid verve, and they're aware, too, of the more dramatic moments. The major drawback of this issue is the recording quality. By comparison, for instance, with DG's vivid, beautifully balanced recording of Kremer and Maisenberg, this sounds dim and distant and the violin, especially, lacks presence. Recording quality aside, however, Dubeau and Kuerti give by far the more winning, affecting interpretation.

Violin Sonatas – D384; D385; D408.
Gidon Kremer *vn* **Oleg Maisenberg** *pf*
DG 437 092-2GH (62 minutes: DDD). Recorded 1991.   Ⓕ

The front cover of the booklet here refers to these works as sonatinas, while the notes and back cover have sonatas. In fact they have been called both and, as the notes explain, the diminutive designation was bestowed on them by their publisher. The writer makes a case for the grander title, and indeed they are hardly slight, with the A minor and G minor lasting over 20 minutes and only the popular D major having something of the miniature about it. Furthermore, the minor mode of D385 and D408 (which here precede the D major) adds to one's feeling that these are not lightweight pieces. Clearly this is also the view of Gidon Kremer and Oleg Maisenberg, who invest the first movement of the A minor work with a lilting melancholy, taking it slowly even for *Allegro moderato* and often lingering over expressive details longer than might be thought desirable; however, this is better than applying pressure to the music and they mostly maintain momentum. Yet in their playing as a whole you feel that they aim to give these works a depth and drama that they do not altogether bear. Indeed, it is a touch mannered, and whether you find it excessively so must be a matter of taste. The same is true of this violinist's characteristic tone: it has a certain thinness along with vibrant sweetness, although it is undoubtedly touching. This said, the two artists are very well attuned, and Maisenberg is an admirable pianist. The recording is well balanced and very natural.

Violin Sonata in A major (Duo), D574. Rondo brillant in B minor, D895. Fantasy in C major, D934.
Gidon Kremer *vn* **Valery Afanassiev** *pf*
DG 431 654-2GH (67 minutes: DDD). Recorded 1990. ⒡

Few recitals can offer the listener such unalloyed pleasure as this gloriously played and generously conceived recording from Kremer and Valery Afanassiev. Rarer yet by far, though, are releases capable of generating the kind of communicative ambience more normally revealed by the intimacy of live music-making. The very opening bars of Afanassiev's piano introduction at the start of the *Duo* in A major, D574, with its restrained yet expectant dignity of utterance would mesmerize the heart of the sternest critic, whilst Kremer exhibits charm, wit, understatement and sheer delight in this work. The B minor Rondo and the magnificent Fantasy in C major were written a decade after the *Duo* and were both intended to display the talents of the composer's friend, the Czech violinist, Josef Slavic, who had settled in Vienna during 1826. Neither work found favour at the time, and quite possibly the dark premonitions of the Rondo, whose emotional sympathies recalled those of the *Unfinished* Symphony, were unsuited to Viennese popular tastes. However, although Kremer's approach avoids mere rhetoric here, this superb recording is surely crowned by a magisterial performance of the *Fantasy*. It combines bravura, elegance and a deep affinity with the Schubertian genre, captured with splendid realism by a recording which is technically beyond criticism.

Schubert Sonata in A minor, D821, 'Arpeggione'.
Schumann Märchenbilder, Op. 113. Adagio and Allegro in A flat major, Op. 70.
Bruch Kol nidrei, Op. 47.
Enescu Konzertstück.
Yuri Bashmet *va* **Mikhail Muntian** *pf*
RCA Red Seal RD60112 (73 minutes: DDD). Recorded 1989. ⒡

Thanks should go to Yuri Bashmet with his glorious tone, and his closely attuned pianist, Mikhail Muntian, for enriching the CD catalogue with Georges Enescu's rarely heard *Konzertstück*, written in Paris in the composer's impressionable early twenties, and played here with intuitive understanding of its fantasy and lyrical rapture. Like that work, the four miniatures of Schumann's *Märchenbilder* of 1851 were also inspired by the viola itself, whereas Schumann's *Adagio and Allegro*, Bruch's *Kol nidrei* (based on one of the oldest and best-known synagogue melodies) and Schubert's charming A minor Sonata were originally written for valve-horn, cello and the now obsolete arpeggione respectively. But with his wide range of colour and his 'speaking' phrasing Bashmet makes them all entirely his own, only causing the occasional raised eyebrow with slower tempos for slow numbers (such as Schumann's lullaby-like Op. 113 No. 4 and the *Adagio* of Schubert's Sonata) than could be enjoyed from players without his own fine-spun, intimately nuanced line. Strongly recommended.

Andante in C major, D29. Minuet in A minor, D277a. Minuet in A major, D334. 13 Variations in A minor on a theme by Anselm Hüttenbrenner, D576. Andante in A major, D604. Fantasy in C major, D605a, 'Grazer Fantasie'. Three Impromptus, D946.
James Lisney *pf*
Olympia OCD479 (65 minutes: DDD). Recorded 1995. ⒡

James Lisney's unusual Schubert recital offers an illuminating programme of lesser-known works, demonstrating the composer's exploitation of tonal colour and keyboard sonority. After a sensitive performance of the enchanting C major *Andante*, D29, Lisney plays a group of pieces that exploit the expressive potential of A major/minor tonality. Two minuets establish the emotional contrast between these tonal colours: the A minor one is bold and defiant, with a tranquil F major trio, while the carefree, amiable A major work is balanced by a poignantly lyrical trio in E major. The *Variations on a theme by Anselm Hüttenbrenner* demonstrates a more complex and dramatic A major/minor dichotomy, which Lisney here presents beautifully with subtle control of the theme's different transformations and telling modal shifts. In addition, Lisney offers a thoroughly absorbing, searching account of the brooding, introspective A major *Andante* and a poetically romantic, finely conceived performance of the *Grazer Fantasie*. To conclude, carefully observed interpretations of the three *Impromptus*, D946, whilst perhaps lacking the spontaneity of Brendel's reissued versions (on a two-disc set), nevertheless confirm Lisney as a thoughtful and perceptive Schubertian. This fascinating concert, which benefits from satisfyingly faithful recorded sound, should attract a wide audience.

Schubert Fantasy in C major, D760, 'Wandererfantasie'.
Schumann Fantasie in C major, Op. 17.
Maurizio Pollini pf
DG The Originals 447 451-2GOR (52 minutes: ADD). Recorded 1973.   Ⓜ

The cover shows Caspar David Friedrich's familiar *The Wanderer above the Sea of Fog*. Pollini, on the other hand, is a wanderer in a transparent ether or crystalline light and both of these legendary performances, recorded in 1973 and beautifully remastered, are of a transcendental vision and integrity. In the Schubert his magisterial, resolutely un-virtuoso approach allows everything its time and place. Listen to his flawlessly graded triple *piano* approach to the central *Adagio*, to his rock-steady octaves at 5'23" (where Schubert's merciless demand is so often the cause of confusion) or to the way the decorations in the *Adagio* are spun off with such rare finesse, and you may well wonder when you have heard playing of such an unadorned, unalloyed glory. Pollini's Schumann is no less memorable. Doubting Thomases on the alert for alternating touches of imperiousness and sobriety will be disappointed, for, again, Pollini's poise is unfaltering. The opening *Moderato* is *sempre energico*, indeed, its central *Etwas langsamer* is so sensitively and precisely gauged that all possible criticism is silenced. The coda of the central march (that *locus classicus* of the wrong note) is immaculate and in what someone once called the finale's 'shifting sunset vapour' Pollini takes us gently but firmly to the shores of Elysium. Here is a record that should grace every musician's shelf.

Impromptus – D899; D935. Drei Klavierstücke, D946. Allegretto in C minor, D915.
Maria João Pires pf
DG 457 550-2GH2 (two discs: 108 minutes: DDD). Recorded 1997.   Ⓕ

This is something very special indeed. Maria João Pires's two-disc set of Schubert's *Impromptus*, significantly dedicated to Sviatoslav Richter, contains a booklet in which standard notes are replaced by carefully chosen extracts from Pires's own reading: reflections on time, space and wilderness from Yves Simon's *Le voyageur magnifique*; meditations on Schubert as Wanderer; and thoughts from a neuroscientist on the 'physiology' of great music. Like so many prefaces, these words are best read afterwards, when certain fragments, different for each listener, may well close-focus in the mind elements still resonating in the ear. Pires's characteristic impassioned absorption in all she plays – that concentration which makes the listener appear to be eavesdropping on secrets shared between friends – could hardly find a truer soul mate than in the sensibility of Schubert. Each *Impromptu* has a rare sense of integrity and entirety, born of acute observation and long-pondered responses.

Pires's instinct for tempo and pacing brings a sense of constant restraint, a true *molto moderato* to the *Allegro* of the C minor work from D899, created by a fusion of right-hand *tenuto* here with momentary left-hand rubato there. Then there is the clarity of contour within the most subtly graded undertones of the G flat major of D899 which re-creates it as a seemingly endless song. Or an *Andante* just slow, just nonchalant enough for the *Rosamunde* theme of the D935 B flat major to give each variation space and breath enough to sing out its own sharply defined character. The *Allegretto*, D915 acts as a *Pause* between the two discs, a resting place, as it were, for reflection and inner assessment on this long journey. Its end – which could as well be its beginning – is in the *Drei Klavierstücke*, D946 of 1828. The first draws back from the fiery impetuousness within the *Allegro assai*'s tautly controlled rhythms, to an inner world with its own time scale; the second, more transpired than played, has an almost unbearable poignancy of simplicity. The paradox of these totally unselfregarding performances is how unmistakably they speak and sing out Pires and her unique musicianship. To draw comparisons here would be not so much odious as to miss the point.

Drei Klavierstücke, D946. 12 Waltzes, D969. Six Moments musicaux, D780.
Peter Katin fp
Athene ATHCD7 (74 minutes: DDD). Recorded 1995.   ⒻⓅ

One of the most attractive features of Katin's Schubert disc is its comfortable intimacy, conjuring images of the composer's own domestic music-making. The Clementi square piano sounds wholly appropriate in the *Waltzes*, highlighting Schubert's magical blend of Viennese gaiety and warmer harmonic shades. In the *Drei Klavierstücke*, Katin further underlines his relaxed approach with some beautifully atmospheric effects and the inclusion of all repeats. Witness the timeless quality in the slower sections of the first piece; the menacing tremolos of the C minor music and the ethereal upper register of the A flat minor music in the second piece, and the subtly coloured textures and boldly projected voice-leading in the third one.

Piano Sonatas – No. 1 in E major, D157; **No. 2** in C major, D279; **No. 3** in E major, D459; **No. 4** in A minor, D537; **No. 5** in A flat major, D557; **No. 6** in E minor, D566; **No. 7** in E flat major, D568; **No. 8** in F sharp minor, D571; **No. 9** in B major, D575; **No. 11** in C major, D613; **No. 12** in F minor, D625; **No. 13** in A major, D664; **No. 14** in A minor, D784; **No. 15** in C major, D840, 'Relique'; **No. 16** in A minor, D845; **No. 17** in D major, D850; **No. 18** in G major, D894; **No. 19** in C minor, D958; **No. 20** in A major, D959; **No. 21** in B flat major, D960.

Piano Sonatas Nos. 1-21.
András Schiff *pf*
Decca 448 390-2DM7 (seven discs: 498 minutes: DDD). Recorded 1992-93.　　Ⓜ

András Schiff's Schubert sonatas, of course, come into direct competition with the masterly set from Wilhelm Kempff, which is very special indeed (these were recorded in the mid- to late 1960s and are available on a seven-disc DG set). Kempff's unsurpassed performance of the last great B flat Sonata (No. 21), for instance, is ravishingly beautiful, full of the insights of his long experience. But throughout his series Schiff's freshness of approach is spring-like in its appeal, and his response to these 19 works (he includes the fragments of the Eighth Sonata, which Kempff omits) – which he describes as 'among the most sublime contributions written for the piano' – is no less individual and certainly not short of poetic feeling or a sense of the music's overall design. Anyone who wants modern recordings of these great sonatas should be well content with Schiff's survey, even though the catalogue also includes many individual performances of great distinction. The excellent recordings were made in the Brahms-Saal of the Vienna Musikverein. Schiff's sonatas, incidentally, are all available separately and many of these individual sets are reviewed below.

Piano Sonatas Nos. 1, 3 and 13.
András Schiff *pf*
Decca 440 311-2DH (71 minutes: DDD). Recorded 1992-93.　　Ⓕ

This seventh volume in Schiff's Schubert sonata cycle spotlights the young composer, starting with the E major work (D157) which, at the age of 18, he chose as his official No. 1. Schiff plays it with a delectable, springlike freshness and tonal charm – banishing every vestige of the 'impersonality' the insert-note writer warns us to expect in the opening *Allegro ma non troppo*. His delicate keyboard 'orchestration' is no less a delight in the slow movement, with its plaintive reminders of Mozart's Barbarina and her lost pin. It is easy to understand why the E major Sonata (D459) of the following year first appeared in print, posthumously, as *Fünf Klavierstücke*. Each of the five movements inhabits a world of its own. And each is as unpredictable in sequence of ideas and modulation as in actual keyboard texture. Schiff himself revels in the music's romantic pre-echoes, not least in the demonstrative finale unusually headed *Allegro patetico*. The disc is completed by the A major Sonata of 1819, the last of Schubert's youthful essays in the genre before a four-year break, but the first of these early works to find a regular place in the repertory. Its gracious, lyrical charm is caught by Schiff in a reading of winning simplicity. No detail is overlooked (there are endless subtleties to enjoy just from his left hand) but never does his point-making intrude. Even in the spirited final *Allegro* his relaxed approach suggests not a hard-working concert pianist but a Schubert playing at home for the delectation of his friends.

Piano Sonatas Nos. 2, 12 and 21.
András Schiff *pf*
Decca 440 310-2DH (78 minutes: DDD). Recorded 1992.　　Ⓕ

In his own contribution to the insert-notes, Schiff writes, '[Schubert's] music is most sensitive to tonal quality, especially in soft and softest dynamics. He's also a quintessentially Viennese composer, and for this reason a Bösendorfer Imperial has been chosen.' The C major Sonata, D279, eloquently reinforces Schiff's argument. Despite its strong Beethovenian flavour, most notably in the first two movements, Schiff is undemonstrative with the music's overt virtuosity, preferring to allow his sensitive *cantabile*, attractively enhanced by the Bösendorfer's delicate edge, to express Schubert's radiant lyricism. Schubert left the first movement of the F minor Sonata, D625, incomplete and Schiff poignantly breaks off where the composer did. His graceful, elegant playing charmingly conveys the music's Biedermeier character in the second movement, and he shows a profound sympathy for Schubert's musical and expressive language through effective opposition of the finale's dramatic forces in a performance that matches Richter's affectionately attentive account. In the B flat major Sonata, D960, Schiff's inclusion of the exposition repeat emphasizes the music's discontinuities for a potent expression of the underlying unease, first apparent in the bass trills. Subtle shifts of key and colour are powerfully effective in both the slow movement and the finale, and deft control in the *Scherzo* yields much revelatory detail – further evidence of the appropriateness of the Bösendorfer sound.

Piano Sonatas Nos. 3, 5 and 18.
Martino Tirimo *pf*
EMI Eminence CD-EMX2278 (78 minutes: DDD). Recorded 1995. Ⓜ

Piano Sonatas – No. 2 with Allegretto, D346 (cptd. Tirimo); No. 17.
Menuetto (Allegro) in A minor, D277a.
Martino Tirimo *pf*
EMI Eminence CD-EMX2279 (70 minutes: DDD). Recorded 1995. Ⓜ

Martino Tirimo's interpretation of the A flat Sonata is particularly interesting. After the opening *Allegro*, his leisurely pace in the slow movement accentuates the boldness of his reading, which he further reinforces by repeating the second part of the finale instead of the first as Schiff does. Tirimo's performance of the C major Sonata (including the *Allegretto* as finale) is also arresting. Schubert-scholar Walter Rehberg first suggested (in 1928) the fragmentary *Allegretto* as a possible fourth movement, and Tirimo's completion of it convincingly reveals its mirroring of the first movement's thematic gestures. Tirimo's slow tempo in the *Andante* creates a wistful quality that is less striking than with Schiff; but, since Schiff makes no attempt to complete the sonata, this can easily be understood as an appropriate difference in structural emphasis. The inclusion of the earlier version of the Minuet (D277a) is valuable for those wishing to make comparisons. Schubert possessed a fantastic ability to create hybrid forms and his sonatas often exhibit a remarkably fluid, through-composed quality.

The E major Sonata was originally published in 1843 as *Fünf Klavierstücke*. Nevertheless, Tirimo highlights the structural coherence in this work's five movements with sensitivity and idiomatic elegance. The opening *Allegro* flows naturally into the graceful first *Scherzo* (here marked *Andante*). Tirimo's heartfelt emotion in the *Adagio* gives moment for pause before the second *Scherzo*'s opposition of light, graceful dance and dark-hued atmosphere (in the trio). He concludes with a winning account of the finale's delightful interplay of operatic and balletic characters. The first movement of the G major Sonata was entitled *Fantasie* in the first printed edition, and the Bösendorfer piano's unique tonal palette enhances Schiff's presentation of its melodic threads to magical effect. Tirimo gives an eloquent reading of this work's broad, introspective moods; yet there are slight reservations in the *Scherzo*, where Schiff plays with a good deal more gusto, and, in the finale, where Tirimo's faster speed encourages a plainer presentation of the music's contrasts. Also Tirimo's weighty playing in the *Scherzo* of the D major Sonata lacks Schiff's persuasive style. Ultimately, though, Tirimo's blend of thoughtful scholarship, technical precision and fresh spontaneity remains compelling.

Piano Sonatas Nos. 4 and 20.
Malcolm Bilson *fp*
Hungaroton HCD31587 (59 minutes: DDD). Recorded 1995. ⒸⓅ

Bilson's is not the first disc to highlight the close affinity between Schubert's A minor Piano Sonata, composed in March 1817, and the great A major Sonata from the composer's final year. In a recording of the same two works, Schiff – aided by the modern Bösendorfer piano's capacity for sustained serene tone – perceptively reveals the A minor Sonata's voice-leading threads in a compelling blend of romantic, dance-like grace and lyrical warmth. With judicious use of the moderator pedal, Bilson here effectively exploits the 1815 Lagrassa fortepiano's robust tone in a reading which, though less dramatic than Schiff's, atmospherically opposes different tonal regions. Schubert miraculously transformed the duple-metre theme of the A minor Sonata's slow movement into the flowing lines of the A major Sonata's rondo finale. Schiff's concentration on detail throughout this later work could be seen to be impeding the music's natural impetus. However, the spaciousness of his account does successfully convey the music's broad landscape. Bilson's blend of spontaneity and distinctive contrasts of tonal colour in all movements winningly conveys both the music's potently dramatic use of motivic material and its large-scale psychological spans.

Piano Sonatas Nos. 4 and 15.
Ralf Gothóni *pf*
Ondine ODE797-2 (56 minutes: DDD). Recorded 1991. Ⓕ

When Schubert's C major Piano Sonata, D840 was first published in 1861, it was given the title *Relique* in the mistaken belief that it was the composer's last work. In fact, it was composed in April 1825, around the same time as Schubert began work on the *Great* C major Symphony. Usually, only the first two completed movements are played, but like Richter (reviewed further on), Gothóni also includes the fragmentary third and fourth ones. Gothóni's is a thoughtful performance that shows a sympathetic response to Schubert's harmonic language and the various tonal colours associated with it. Richter's characteristically profound concentration creates an exceptionally broad landscape – notably in the first movement – but Gothóni's account, though less challenging intellectually, offers a comparable technical and expressive range and he gives a vivid and powerful performance of the work's dramatic extremes. The reverberant recording adds emphasis to the music's volcanic outbursts.

Piano Sonatas Nos. 5, 9 and 18.
András Schiff *pf*
Decca 440 307-2DH (76 minutes: DDD). Recorded 1992. Ⓕ

Schubert's piano music from András Schiff always lifts the spirits, and this time quite a bit higher than most comparable available versions. Typically, he chooses his favourite Bösendorfer Imperial with its Viennese accent and writes in an introduction to the notes of its Schubertian sensitivity to tone-quality, particularly in the softest dynamics. Schiff cites the opening of the G major Sonata, D894 as an example and, indeed, this movement, which the composer originally called a Fantasy, has a gentle luminosity about it. Schiff's approach to the vast first movement more closely resembles Lupu's (reviewed further on) in its meditative, long-sighted qualities; but Schiff again triumphs, in coaxing both a wider and a more finely controlled tone palette out of his instrument. Schiff's greatest achievement here, though, is his organic view of the inner and outer worlds of this sonata. As in the song, 'Der Lindenbaum' (from *Winterreise*), images of both tender dream and harsh reality seem to shape the piece. Schiff makes them seem simply different sides of the same persona. One flows into and out of another, with the dark concentration of rhythm in the eye of the storm. In the last movement, Schiff outdoes Lupu in the dance of constantly shifting weights and measures, lights and half-lights which dapple the rondo's returns. Schiff seems to play through the childlike ears and eyes of Schubert himself. This outstanding performance of D894 is nicely balanced by a deliciously understated D557, the most classically conceived of all Schubert's sonatas, and by the more adventurous D575. Here, Schiff continues to exploit the qualifying *ma non troppo* of the opening *Allegro* to create a sense of a plethora of ideas and energies being held back within an unquiet serenity. If the slow movement is a little over-deliberate, the finale again seems to be constantly surprising itself with the new ideas which sing out as if they had only just been imagined.

Piano Sonatas Nos. 7 and 19.
András Schiff *pf*
Decca 440 308-2DH (61 minutes: DDD). Recorded 1992. Ⓕ

Those who like their C minor Sonata bulging with Byronic sentiment or exploding with theatrical sparks will no doubt find Schiff's unshowy approach intolerably ascetic though the absorption, the inner penetration of his playing here is worth the loss of a few histrionic thrills. His understanding is revealed in tiny, delicate touches – the way the C minor's first movement eases gently into the second subject, or the nicely timed silences in the Menuetto, with the *Allegro* finale arising after another short but pregnant pause. At the same time there's a profound grasp of the Schubertian pulse: the tension between subtle rubato and what Theodor Adorno called the 'somnambulistic' forward tread. It's beautifully judged, whether in minute details (the slight holding back in the running quavers near the start of the E flat Sonata is a perfect example) or in the longer term – the way D568's Minuet resumes the first movement's basic pulse. Schiff is emphatically not one of those pianists that wants to show you at every stage what a fabulously rich palette he possesses, but the sound he coaxes from his Bösendorfer is hauntingly lovely, and the Decca recording captures it, and the Vienna Musikverein Brahms-Saal's intimate warmth, superbly.

Piano Sonatas Nos. 9, 12 and 13. Moment musical in C major, D780 No. 1.
Sviatoslav Richter *pf*
BBC Legends BBCL4010-2 (78 minutes: ADD). Recorded live in 1979. Ⓜ

Richter's Schubert is simply in a class of its own. No pianist did more to overturn the traditional view of the composer as a blithe, unreflecting child of nature. And in this Festival Hall recital three sonatas from 1817-19 unfold with a grandeur of conception, a spirituality and a stoical timelessness that were unique to Richter. The first two movements of the A major Sonata are, on the face of it, implausibly slow: but with his mesmeric, self-communing intensity Richter convinces you for the duration of the performance that no other way is admissable. Phrases, paragraphs are shaped with calm inevitability, underpinned by the sublime, luminous simplicity of Richter's *cantabile*; and no pianist is more sensitive to Schubert's magical harmonic strokes or understands more surely their place in the larger scheme. As Richter conceives them, the first two movements of the A major foreshadow the rapt, philosophical contemplation of the late G major and B flat Sonatas; and even the finale, projected with Richter's characteristic mastery and subtlety of rhythm, has something rarefied in its playfulness. Richter is equally lofty and far-sighted in the two lesser-known sonatas. The BBC recording, while perhaps a shade bass-light, is warm, and does ample justice to Richter's vast dynamic and tonal palette. A bronchial March audience can intrude at the start of tracks, especially in finales. But no matter. All but those terminally resistant to Richter's uniquely introspective, long-spanned view of the composer should acquire as a matter of urgency these visionary performances by one of the greatest Schubertians of the century.

Piano Sonatas No. 9, 15 and 18.
Sviatoslav Richter *pf*
Philips 438 483-2PH2 (two discs: 117 minutes: ADD). Recorded live in 1979.   Ⓕ

Facts first. The G major Sonata, D894 takes up an entire CD, in comparison with the average 16 or 17 minutes. Richter's first movement is no less than 26'51" long. Then the C major, D840 appears not *unvollendet* at all, but with its little unfinished Menuetto and Rondo taking their own eye- and ear-opening place. Behind these facts lie the concepts which set these performances apart. The heavenly length of the first movement of D894 is created out of Richter's relationship with time itself. The more one listens to his late Schubert, the more one realizes that movement and momentum are not conceived as linear. Rather they are cyclical, very much in the spirit of the final song of *Winterreise* in which the Leiermann's turning melody could be eternal. No wonder that it is to Richter that singers like Peter Schreier turn when working out the when and the how of their Schubert. The opening *Molto moderato* is read as extremely slow: the ear begins by being on tenterhooks for what might come next – then shocked by the sudden, harsh brightening of tone as the first temporary modulation is prepared. As the movement progresses, the opening motif becomes like a mantra in an extended meditation in which the listener must go through the same discipline of private pacing as the performer. At a practical level, Richter's tempo allows the mood of *Molto moderato e cantabile* to be unbroken by busy-ness even as the theme metamorphoses into quaver figuration. The *Andante*, when at last it arrives, moves with a contrastingly lithe, blithe ease, more songlike, more forceful at its centre. The simplicity and clarity of movement created by Richter's fingers in the bright dance of weight and measure which is the final *Allegretto* (and which makes for an archaic, hymn-like *Andante* in D575) is Schubert's sweetness and light. His dark side, in both these sonatas, is explored uncompromisingly by Richter in modulations of key and dynamics abrupt enough to hurt. Richter's complete incomplete Sonata, D840 is another extraordinary journey. Another endless *Moderato* (22 minutes) is this time relentless in the bare, unbeautiful resonance of its repeated figures which, all the more miraculously, become song accompaniment. It is followed by a strange, minimalist Menuetto and an almost surreal sense of bleakness as the pirouetting Rondo melts into thin air.

Piano Sonatas Nos. 11, 14 and 21.
Stephen Hough *pf*
Hyperion CDA67027 (76 minutes: DDD). Recorded 1998.   Ⓕ

Stephen Hough's moving performance of Sonata No. 21 is marked throughout by refined, discerning pianism and an uncommonly subtle ear for texture. In all four movements, even the *Scherzo* and finale, he seeks out the music's inwardness and fragility, its ethereal, self-communing remoteness. The opening *Molto moderato*, unfolding in vast, calm spans, has a hypnotic inevitability; there are countless felicities of timing and colour, but always a vital sense of forward motion. Hough adopts a dangerously slow tempo in the *Andante* but sustains it through the breadth and concentration of his line, the subtlety of his tonal palette (listen, for instance to his infinitely tender, infinitely poignant colouring) and his pointing of rhythmic detail. His rarefied grace and delicacy, his gentle probing of the music's vulnerability and loneliness, are of a piece with his conception of the sonata as a whole. As usual, Hyperion does not stint over playing time, offering another complete sonata in addition to the two-movement fragment, No. 11. No. 14, perhaps Schubert's most depressive instrumental work, is magnificently done. Hough distils an immense weight of suffering from the pervasive two-note motif that dominates the first movement like some massive, Wagnerian pendulum; but, typically, the lyrical music is limpidly coloured and poignantly inflected, with an unusually precise observation of Schubert's accents. The *Andante* is flowing and long-arched, with some ravishing soft playing and he a brings a superb rhythmic impulse to the eerily scudding counterpoint of the main subject and a piercing tenderness to the contrasting F major theme (0'51"). The fragmentary C major Sonata, one of numerous Schubert torsos from the years 1817-22, is no great shakes: two pleasant but uneventful movements, both incomplete. It's unsurprising that Schubert lost interest in mid-flight. But Schubertians will be happy to have the fragment as a bonus to Hough's individual and searching readings of the two great sonatas, which take their place alongside the most recommendable in the catalogue. The pleasure is enhanced by the exemplary clarity, warmth and truthfulness of the recording.

Piano Sonatas Nos. 14 and 17.
Alfred Brendel *pf*
Philips 422 063-2PH (63 minutes: DDD). Recorded 1987.   Ⓕ

There is an extraordinary amount of highly experimental writing in Schubert's piano sonatas. The essence of their structure is the contrasting of big heroic ideas with tender and inner thoughts; the first impresses the listener, the second woos him. The two works on this CD are in some ways on a varying scale. The D major lasts for 40 minutes, the A minor for around 23. However, it is the latter that contains the most symphonically inspired writing – it sounds as if it could easily be transposed for orchestra. Alfred Brendel presents the composer not so much as the master of Lieder-writing, but more as a man thinking in large forms. Although there are wonderful quiet moments when intimate asides are conveyed with an imaginative sensitivity one remembers more the urgency and the power behind the notes. The A minor, with its frequently recurring themes, is almost obsessive in character whilst the big D major Sonata is rather lighter in mood, especially in the outer movements. The recorded sound is very faithful to the pianist's tone, whilst generally avoiding that insistent quality that can mar his loudest playing.

Piano Sonatas Nos. 15 and 18.
Mitsuko Uchida *pf*
Philips 454 453-2PH (70 minutes: DDD). Recorded 1996.   Ⓕ

Schubert's G major Sonata, D894, is the ultimate *Frühlingstraum*. Pervading the entire work is that oscillation between light-filled dream and stark waking reality. These may be juxtaposed in dramatic motivic contrast, but they are, quintessentially, twin sides of a single consciousness; and it is Mitsuko Uchida's supreme achievement to understand and re-create precisely this quality. She creates a true opening *molto moderato* of profound stillness and long distances. Chords really resonate and breathe out, yet her quick intakes of breath as the second subject steps into dance are tempered with the more flexible, whimsical intimacy of a Schiff. Uchida's gentleness of touch is ballasted by a firmly delineated bass and a weight of rhythmic articulation. She finds an easy, instinctive pace for the *Andante*, creating compacted shocks in the ringing chords of its minor-key episodes. These chords announce a Menuetto in which the Trio slinks in as the merest spectre of a Ländler, and leads to a finale in which Uchida creates a dance of the spirit within a deep inner stillness. The *Relique* Sonata, D840, one of Schubert's great and tantalizingly unfinished works, sounds entire, fully achieved in Uchida's hands. She shares with Schiff a leisured playing-out of the first movement. And her *Andante* is no less intimate in its *bel canto* of minute nuance and inflexion, starker and bleaker still than Schiff's masterpiece.

Piano Sonata No. 16. Impromptus, D946.
Alfred Brendel *pf*
Philips 422 075-2PH (61 minutes: DDD).   Ⓕ

Piano Sonatas Nos. 16 and 18.
Radu Lupu *pf*
Decca 417 640-2DH (74 minutes: ADD).   Ⓕ

Though love of the music alone, as pianists know, is not enough to master these pieces, it is essential, and in this big A minor Sonata Brendel presents us with a drama that is no less tense for being predominantly expressed in terms of shapely melody. There is a flexibility in this playing that reminds us of the pianist's own comment that in such music 'we feel not masters but victims of the situation': he allows us plenty of time to savour detail without ever losing sight of the overall shape of the music, and the long first movement and finale carry us compellingly forwards, as does the *Scherzo* with its urgent energy, while the *Andante* second movement, too, has the right kind of spaciousness. In the *Impromptus* which date from the composer's last months, Brendel is no less responsive or imaginative. Richly sonorous digital recording in a German location complements the distinction of the playing on this fine disc. Radu Lupu also understands Schubert's style as do few others and the way in which he is able to project this essentially private world is outstanding. His tone is unfailingly clear, and this adds substantially to the lucidity of the readings. The simplicity of the opening themes of the A minor Sonata is a marvel of eloquence and when it is reset in the development section of the first movement one is amazed to hear Lupu transforming it into something far more urgent and full of pathos. The G major Sonata again fires Lupu's imagination and in the Minuet third movement he uses a considerable amount of rubato for the dance; its solid rhythmic pulse is an ideal foil to offset the extraordinary transitions of the finale that follows. The recorded sound is excellent.

Piano Sonata No. 16. Impromptus, D946.
Andreas Staier *fp*
Teldec Das Alte Werk 0630-11084-2 (62 minutes: DDD). Recorded 1995. Ⓕ🅿

Once again, it is Andreas Staier's imagination and insight as a musician, rather than Staier-as-fortepianist, which comes to the fore in this rich recital. In the Sonata, for instance, Staier sets up a wide gulf between the two poles of Schubert's musical material – the sustained and lyrical, and the percussive and propulsive – in metaphysical terms, if you like, between the inner and outer, the contemplative and active life of this movement. Then he starts to paint with the pedal: there is a choice of four on this 1825 Viennese Johann Fritz fortepiano, and his changing use of them as the hands wander through the development creates a wide landscape for the journey, reminiscent of some of the piano writing in *Winterreise*. Here, and in the even more far-reaching expressive palette of the E flat major *Impromptu*, Staier really does realize the truth of his own statement that this – unlike the multi-purpose modern concert grand – is truly a 'specifically Romantic instrument'. In the slow movement's variations, the shifting balance between the hands are uniquely tailored to the resonating scale of the instrument, to uniquely revelatory effect. None of this could happen, of course, without Staier's own exceptionally sensitive imagination. At the start of the E flat minor *Impromptu* he creates a wide area of open space for the *Andante*, with the little, high, cadenza-like scalic figure appearing, as a sudden and wonderful bright light, as time is momentarily suspended.

Piano Sonata No. 19. Impromptus, D899. Deutsche Tänze, D783.
Imogen Cooper *pf*
Ottavo OTRC78923 (70 minutes: DDD). Recorded 1989. Ⓕ

This is in fact the last of Imogen Cooper's six-disc cycle of the piano music of Schubert's last six years, a cycle launched in 1988 hard on the heels of similar cycles given on the concert platform in both London and Amsterdam. Like its predecessors, it confirms her as a Schubert player of exceptional style and finesse. Intuitively perceptive phrasing and a willingness to let the music sing within a wholly Schubertian sound world are prime virtues. And though (like her erstwhile mentor, Alfred Brendel) she is no slave to the metronome when contrasting first and second subjects in sonata expositions, she still makes the music her own without the self-consciously mannered kind of interpretation heard from one or two more recent rivals in this strongly competitive field. Her urgent yet poised performance of the late C minor Sonata certainly confirms her admission (in a 1988 *Gramophone* interview) that the comparatively clinical atmosphere of an audience-less recording venue worries her not at all. In London's Henry Wood Hall her Yamaha is as clearly and truthfully reproduced (save for a slight suspicion of pedal-haze in the sonata's demonically driven finale) as most else in the series. The *Impromptus* reveal an acutely sensitive response to Schubert's dynamic subtleties and surprises of key, while the 16 *German Dances* tell their own simple Viennese tale.

Piano Sonatas Nos. 19 and 21.
Sviatoslav Richter *pf*
Olympia OCD335 (78 minutes: ADD). Recorded 1972. Ⓕ

As any follower of Richter's Schubert knows, you have to allow his sense of time to take over. Resist it and you will draw a blank. Submit to it and you will pass through an unsuspected doorway into an inner world of timeless inevitability. The C minor first movement is all fierce concentration and bleakness, the second all intense inner singing, the third deceptive simplicity with silences weighted as if hovering over the music's own demise, and the finale has a hellish drive to it – an utterly compelling experience. Monumental as ever, the first movement of the B flat Sonata is immensely slow, the tempo chosen not with the opening theme in mind but with a view to the G flat trill and the following silence, reminders of the chasm beneath. Don't expect any consolation from the slow movement or Grecian lightness from the *Scherzo*; all is directed towards the controlled desperation of the finale. Any duffer (to paraphrase Goethe) can make this sonata touching; but with Richter it becomes (to risk malicious misunderstanding) appalling. It bores into the soul.

Piano Sonatas Nos. 19-21.
Andreas Staier *fp*
Teldec Das Alte Werk 0630-13143-2 (two discs: 119 minutes: DDD). Recorded 1996.　　　Ⓕ🅿

The harpsichord has all but replaced the concert grand in baroque keyboard music. But resistance to the fortepiano is still strong; that clattery tone, the lack of sustaining power in high registers – it just doesn't sing like a modern piano. However, there are many instances where the sound of the 1825 Johann Fritz piano, and especially Andreas Staier's handling of it, are simply revelatory. Staier uses the fortepiano's moderator pedals and the *una corda* pedal, which shifts the hammers so that they strike only one string each, to great effect. Staier's use of these tools never seem excessive or misplaced, and it's hard to believe that Schubert wouldn't have made similar use of them. It isn't only in the special effects department that the fortepiano scores. In the middle of the slow movement of D959 there's a remarkable, violent cadenza-like passage which is rarely effective on modern concert pianos. On the fortepiano you can strain and pound for all you're worth, and yet the *scale* of the sound feels absolutely right. The later recitative-like contrast of the *ffz* chords and short, pleading *piano* phrases at the climax of the second movement of D959 works wonderfully here. Similarly, Staier can play the *fzp* and *ffzp* accents in the trio section of D960's *Scherzo* with due emphasis without destroying the music's prevailing lightweight character. But it is Staier's handling of the instrument, not the instrument itself, that makes these recordings so exceptional. In matters of tempo, phrasing and so on, his approach is thoroughly modern; in fact his performances would probably translate very effectively to a modern piano without any – or much – sense of incongruity. This is a most impressive fortepiano recording. And that goes for the sound quality too. A strong recommendation for anyone who isn't terminally prejudiced.

Piano Sonata No. 20. Moments musicaux, D780.
Stephen Kovacevich *pf*
EMI CDC5 55219-2 (66 minutes: DDD). Recorded 1994.　　　Ⓕ

Here is Schubert playing as compulsive and single-minded as any on record. Formidably serious and concentrated this is not for lovers of 'lilac time' or of softly focused, lyrical options. Indeed, it is often as if the Grim Reaper himself had cut a swathe through Schubert, forbidding at a glance even a touch of solace, let alone *Gemütlichkeit*. Yet the force and authenticity of such an outwardly controversial view is made unarguable and few pianists have penetrated more deeply to the dark, restlessly beating heart beneath Schubert's outwardly genial surface. The ferocity of Kovacevich's *fortissimo* chording in the development section of the sonata's first movement is wholly typical of his refusal of all polite circumspection, and rarely can the *Andantino*, with its central elemental uproar, have sounded more spare or disconsolate. Even the *Scherzo* becomes both a memory of Beethoven's fierce whimsy and a presage of Chopin's irony, and more than touch of unease erases much chance of a conventionally meandering or leisurely view of the finale. For Kovacevich, then, this is surely Schubert's sonata equivalent of *Winterreise*; a savage journey into oblivion. Many will look for light relief in the *Moments musicaux*, but once again Kovacevich refuses all obvious sentiment or enticement. His tone remains lean and acidulous, and he possesses a rare ability to drain his sonority of all colour substance, accentuating the hectic flush of No. 5 and achieving an extreme sense of desolation in No. 6. This record, then, is for those who concede that Schubert could be 'full of sorrow/And leaden eyed despair', a composer who had more than his share of life's vicissitudes. Competition from other great Schubertians (Schnabel, Brendel, Pollini, Lupu and Imogen Cooper, to name but five!) is intense, yet Kovacevich's Schubert surely inhabits a world of its own and is in a sense beyond compare; an extraordinary achievement. The recordings are spectacularly bold.

Piano Sonata No. 21. Allegretto in C minor, D915. 12 Ländler, D790.
Stephen Kovacevich *pf*
EMI CDC5 55359-2 (58 minutes: DDD). Recorded 1994.　　　Ⓕ🅴🆁🆁

Kovacevich creates his own ambience with such force and fidelity that he achieves an ultimate musical illusion: a definitive and unarguable statement indelibly and disturbingly true to Schubert's always ambiguous genius. Of course, those wedded to a less savage sense of experience, to a lightness and civility that are part of Schubert's appeal, will look elsewhere. For even in his selection of encores, Kovacevich retreats at every opportunity into a crepuscular, near hallucinatory world, his sense of elegy all pervasive. In the sonata's first-movement repeat (the nine bars despised by Brendel but, clearly, relished by Kovacevich) the distant thunder of the opening erupts in a violent upheaval. The outwardly innocent quaver flourish at 4'03" flashes with sudden anger, a startling gesture, yet one wholly in keeping with a work where desperation so easily surfaces through autumnal sadness and resignation. The *Andante*, too, is a marvel of the most concentrated musical thinking, there are some swingeing *sforzandos* in the finale to remind us, once more, of underlying menace and even the *Scherzo*'s brightly tripping outer sections are shadowed by an unusually dark-hued way with the central trio. Throughout, the effort of interpretation is immense and so although you will doubtless return to other deeply cherished recordings you will probably find a special place for Kovacevich. No more darkly questing performance exists. The recordings faithfully capture Kovacevich's awe-inspiring dynamic range, from the merest whisper to an elemental uproar.

Piano Sonata No. 21. Drei Klavierstücke, D946.
Mitsuko Uchida *pf*
Philips 456 572-2PH (71 minutes: DDD). Recorded 1997.   Ⓕ

Mitsuko Uchida's concentration and inwardness are of a rare order in her absorbed, deeply poetic reading of the B flat Sonata. No pianist makes you so aware how much of the first two movements is marked *pp* or even *ppp*; and none conjures such subtlety of colour in the softest dynamics: listen, for instance, to her playing of the three unearthly C sharp minor chords that usher in the first-movement development, or her timing and colouring of the breathtaking sideslip from C sharp minor to C major in the *Andante*. Other pianists may find a stronger undercurrent of foreboding or desperation in these two movements – though Uchida builds the development of the initial *Molto moderato* superbly to its dramatic climax. But none probes more hauntingly the music's mysterious contemplative ecstasy or creates such a sense of inspired improvisation. And her limpid *cantabile* sonorities are always ravishing on the ear. Uchida is equally attuned to the less rarefied world of the *Scherzo* and finale, the former a glistening, mercurial dance, *con delicatezza* indeed, the latter graceful and quixotic, with a hint of emotional ambiguity even in its ostensibly cheerful main theme and a tigerish ferocity in its sudden Beethovenian eruptions. The coupling is generous: the three *Klavierstücke*, D946, composed, like the sonata, in Schubert's final year, 1828, and assembled by Brahms for publication. She brings a wonderfully impassioned sweep, with razor-sharp rhythms, to the opening of the E flat minor, No. 1, and mesmerically floats its slow B major episode. She also restores the beguiling barcarolle-like episode in A flat that Schubert excised from his autograph manuscript. The recording finely captures Uchida's subtle, pellucid sound world. In sum, a revealing disc from a Schubertian of rare insight and spirituality.

Masses – No. 1 in F major, D105; No. 2 in G major, D167; No. 3 in B flat major, D324; No. 4 in C major, D452; No. 5 in A flat major, D678; No. 6 in E flat major, D950. Stabat mater, D383.

Masses – No. 1; No. 2; No. 3; No. 4; No. 5; No. 6. Stabat mater. Also contains six other short works.
Lucia Popp, Helen Donath, Maria Venuti *sops* **Brigitte Fassbaender** *mez*
Adolf Dallapozza, Peter Schreier, Francisco Araiza, Josef Protschka *tens*
Dietrich Fischer-Dieskau *bar*
Bavarian Radio Chorus; Bavarian Radio Symphony Orchestra / Wolfgang Sawallisch.
EMI Sawallisch Edition CMS7 64778-2 (four discs: 297 minutes: ADD/DDD).
Texts and translations included. Recorded 1980s.   Ⓜ

Schubert's sacred choral works seem very much the poor relation in an output comprising so many indisputable masterpieces of vocal, piano, chamber and orchestral music. Yet he also wrote prolifically in this genre. This set includes six of his Masses, including the majestic one in B flat major (No. 3), and the intense *Stabat mater*, not to mention a host of smaller pieces and fragments. Quantity doesn't necessarily imply quality, even where Schubert is concerned. The rather meagre representation this music has always received in the catalogue would seem to suggest that much of what is included in these discs is of little more than academic interest. Certainly not even Schubert's greatest advocates would describe everything he wrote for the Church as a masterpiece; his use of counterpoint, most notably in the Sixth Mass, is often dismissed as rudimentary. But there can never be any doubting the sincerity of Schubert's intentions and given sensitive, well-conceived performances, his unquenchable gift for melodic invention and ability to write instantly attractive music overrides any technical shortcomings. Such are Sawallisch's performances. His clear sense of direction, his natural feel for the line and his unpretentious approach never fail to reveal the inherent beauty in almost everything Schubert wrote. The Bavarian Radio Chorus, with its rich, vibrant tone, won't be to everyone's liking, but it shows a consistent level of technical accomplishment, following Sawallisch's naturally shaped lines and beautifully moulded hairpin dynamics with a wholly natural flow. Similarly, with such accomplished Schubertians as Lucia Popp and Fischer-Dieskau one can expect some memorable performances. The highlight of these discs is the deliciously delicate trio between Popp, Adolf Dallapozza and Dietrich Fischer-Dieskau, supported by some extraordinarily elegant orchestral playing, in the *Benedictus* of the Second Mass: if you had to take just one recording of Schubert to a desert island, this would be a strong contender. Sawallisch's is an impressive achievement for maintaining so consistent an approach and producing performances of exemplary musicianship, even in works of less than uniform quality themselves. The recordings are first-rate, with the older analogue transfers coming up unusually well.

Mass No. 5. Deutsche Messe, D872.
Stefan Preyer *treb* **Thomas Weinhappel** *counterten* **Jörg Hering** *ten* **Harry van der Kamp** *bass*
Arno Hartmann *org*
Vienna Boys' Choir; Chorus Viennensis;
Orchestra of the Age of Enlightenment / Bruno Weil.
Sony Classical Vivarte SK53984 (60 minutes: DDD). Texts and translations included.
Recorded 1993.   Ⓕ 🄿

In the *Deutsche Messe* Bruno Weil makes no attempt to impose interpretative individuality on music designed purely for liturgical use: he is content merely to oversee neat ensemble and balance. The orchestra, consisting mainly of wind instruments, doubles the chorus parts and while its role might seem largely superfluous it does provide a comfortable cushion on which the choir can relax while making its way effortlessly through such unchallenging music. It's a different story with the sparkling A flat major Mass, but again Bruno Weil's understated direction results in an immensely satisfying performance. There is a youthful vigour and infectious enthusiasm here. Of course, much of that comes from the superb singing of the Vienna Boys' Choir. Their exuberant 'Hosanna's in the *Sanctus* and *Benedictus* are more unashamedly joyful than such music has a right to be. The two boy soloists sing with a musical maturity way beyond their years. That is not to belittle the splendid contribution from the adult voices nor the exquisite playing of the Orchestra of the Age of Enlightenment. Weil achieves the perfect tonal blend: nothing disturbs the open-hearted honesty of this genuinely sincere performance.

Mass No. 6. Tantum ergo, D962. Offertorium, D963.
Helen Donath, Lucia Popp *sops* **Brigitte Fassbaender** *mez*
Francisco Araiza, Peter Schreier *tens* **Dietrich Fischer-Dieskau** *bar*
Bavarian Radio Chorus and Symphony Orchestra / Wolfgang Sawallisch.
EMI Studio CDM7 69223-2 (71 minutes: DDD). Recorded 1980.   Ⓜ 🆁🆁

This reissue sounds every bit as fine as the original LP issue, and the CD transfer does it full justice. On almost all points Sawallisch's performance scores over the current rivals. What tends to be missing elsewhere is the attention to detail as well as to long phrasing that Sawallisch brings. You hear it in the opening oboe and clarinet phrases of the *Kyrie* – every one of Schubert's off-beat accents tells – and it brings far sharper feature- and colour-contrast to the long fugal sections without disrupting the flow. One of the triumphs of the Sawallisch version is its vindication of Schubert's contrapuntal writing – frequently sneered at in the past by reviewers. Even the famous 'solecism' in the *Agnus Dei* carries dramatic conviction. Sawallisch is dramatic, expressive, flowingly lyrical (the solo *Benedictus* is quite lovely) and utterly in command of movements – and of the work as a whole – as single, long-breathed structures. It's interesting that while his timings suggest tempos consistently slower than others, his performance has greater sense of pace, of movement to a definite goal. The *Dona nobis* has an urgency that fits closely with conventional ideas of late Schubert, and the contrasting *Agnus Dei* sections have an enormous amount of stark power. Sawallisch's fillers are both very enjoyable, especially the ardent *Offertorium*.

Mass No. 6.
Benjamin Schmidinger *treb* **Albin Lenzer** *counterten* **Jörg Hering** *ten* **Kurt Azesberger** *ten*
Harry van der Kamp *bass*
Vienna Boys' Choir; Chorus Viennensis;
Orchestra of the Age of Enlightenment / Bruno Weil.
Sony Classical Vivarte SK66255 (48 minutes: DDD). Text and translation included.
Recorded 1994.   Ⓕ 🄿

The most striking thing about this disc is the recording balance. It is as if there's a microphone behind every music-stand. The effect is of a group of disparate musicians more than a conglomerate whole but, with individual playing as good as this, it does provide a real listening treat, although it won't be to everyone's taste. To even fewer tastes will be the unequivocal bias towards orchestral playing. After all, what is a Schubert Mass if not primarily a choral work? There is some lovely singing here, not least from the quintet of soloists; yet all the voices are relegated to play second fiddle to the orchestra. Of all his Masses the E flat work (Schubert's last) is the least concerned with expressing a belief or in presenting fundamental Christian texts (although it wasn't the only Mass from which he unilaterally omitted unpalatable sections of the *Credo*) and its intricate orchestral textures and delightful instrumental writing are worthy of the closest inspection. Bruno Weil has already proved himself to be a deeply sympathetic Schubertian with a clear sense of what works, and what on first hearing comes as something of a shock is shown on repeated listening to make perfectly good musical sense. This view of Schubert may be from an unusual angle, but it is an infinitely rewarding approach to this unutterably beautiful music.

Psalm 23, D706. Im Gegenwärtigen Vergangenes, D710. Gesang der Geister über den Wassern, D714. Gondelfahrer, D809. Coronach, D836. Nachthelle, D892. Grab und Mond, D893. Nachtgesang im Walde, D913. Ständchen, D920. Die Nacht, D983c. Gott im Ungewitter, D985.
Birgit Remmert *contr* **Werner Güra** *ten* **Philip Mayers** *pf*
Scharoun Ensemble; RIAS Chamber Choir, Berlin / Marcus Creed.
Harmonia Mundi HMC90 1669 (59 minutes: DDD). Texts and translations included.
Recorded 1998. Ⓕ

Most of the part-songs here evoke some aspect of night, whether benevolent, romantic, transfigured or sinister. Between them they give a fair conspectus of Schubert's achievement in the part-song genre, ranging from the mellifluous, Biedermeier *Die Nacht*, forerunner of many a Victorian glee, and the gently sensuous *Gondelfahrer* to the eerie, harmonically visionary *Grab und Mond* and the brooding *Gesang der Geister über den Wassern*. Other highlights here include the alfresco *Nachtgesang*, with its quartet of echoing horns, *Ständchen*, a delicious nocturnal serenade, the austere, bardic Scott setting *Coronach* and the serenely luminous *Nachthelle*. The RIAS Chamber Choir confirms its credentials as one of Europe's finest, most virtuosic ensembles. It sings with rounded, homogeneous tone, wellnigh perfect intonation (crucial in this repertoire) and an excitingly wide dynamic range. Characterization tends to be very vivid, whether in the ecstatic central climax in *Nachthelle*, sharp contrasts in *Gesang der Geister über den Wassern* or the great sense of awe – and palpable feeling for Schubert's strange modulations – in *Grab und Mond*. Birgit Remmert, the alto soloist in *Ständchen* (sung, incidentally, in the version with women's voices), sings well enough but with insufficient lightness and sense of fun. But Werner Güra negotiates what one of Schubert's friends called 'the damnably high' tenor solo in *Nachthelle* gracefully and with no sense of strain. Philip Mayers is a serviceable rather than specially imaginative pianist, though the delicate, silvery treble of the early nineteenth-century instrument is enchantingly heard in *Psalm 23* and the shimmering high repeated notes of *Nachthelle*; and the other instrumentalists make their mark – splendid rotund horns in *Nachtgesang im Walde*, sombrely intense strings in *Gesang der Geister*. The recorded sound is clear and warm, with a well-judged vocal-instrumental balance.

Psalm 23. Gott in der Natur, D757. Gesang der Geister über den Wassern – D538; D714. Nachtgesang im Walde, D913. Gondelfahrer. Psalm 92, D953. Nachthelle. Der Tanz, D826. Mondenschein, D875. Ständchen, D920. Die Geselligkeit, D609. Mailied, D202. Lützows wilde Jagd, D205. Sehnsucht, D636.
BBC Singers / Jane Glover; members of the **City of London Sinfonia; Susan Tomes** *pf*
Collins Classics 1499-2 (74 minutes: DDD). Texts and translations included. Recorded 1996. Ⓕ

Of all the hundreds of settings of Psalm 23 ('The Lord is my shepherd') surely none exudes such calm and inner peace as Schubert's. And few recordings have ever yielded such sublime beauty from this setting as does this dreamily shaped, exquisitely moulded account from the BBC Singers under the wonderfully relaxed hand of Jane Glover. It sets the scene for a disc of exceptional beauty and charm. The BBC Singers have been criticized for sounding like a collection of 28 solo voices. There's certainly more than a grain of truth in that, but in this repertoire that's exactly what's needed. These are part-songs rather than choral pieces, with each part demanding both the musical and technical skill of a full-fledged soloist. That individual voices are discernible only enhances the sense of intimacy, but where a solo voice is projected above the others, as in the enchanting setting of *Ständchen* where an effectively fresh-voiced Jacqueline Fox is given the most exquisite support from the male voices (and the ever-sensitive Susan Tomes, whose piano playing throughout is an absolute treasure), Jane Glover has no problems achieving the ideal balance. These performances capture perfectly the essential spirit of the music. Enhanced by a top-notch recording this is a truly exceptional disc.

Stabat mater. Magnificat in C major, D486. Offertorium in B flat major, D963.
Sheila Armstrong *sop* **Hanna Schaer** *mez* **Alejandro Ramirez** *ten* **Philippe Huttenlocher** *bar*
Lausanne Vocal Ensemble; Lausanne Chamber Orchestra / Michel Corboz.
Erato 4509 96961-2 (59 minutes: ADD). Recorded 1979. Ⓜ

Schubert's strikingly fresh setting of the *Stabat mater* (in a German translation) was written in the composer's nineteenth year, yet it displays clear anticipations of his later music, especially in the terzetto (No. 11) for soprano, tenor, baritone and chorus and the striking chorus 'Wer wird Zähren sanften Mitleids' (No. 5) with its superb horn writing. There is a beautiful tenor aria with oboe obbligato, in which Alejandro Ramirez is very stylish, while the bass aria 'Sohn des Vaters' is dark and strong. Here Philippe Huttenlocher may not be quite sombre enough, yet his contribution is still most enjoyable. The singing of the Lausanne Vocal Ensemble, with the Lausanne CO under Corboz, combines clarity of focus with a firm sonority, and Schubert's lively, if somewhat uncharacteristic, fugues certainly have plenty of vigour. The two shorter Schubert pieces that make up the rest of the disc, the Magnificat (again with a fine contribution from Ramirez) and the Offertorium, are also given strong performances from Corboz. The recording, although not crystal clear, has transferred vividly.

Complete Secular Choral Works.
Elisabeth Flechl, Ruth Ziesak *sops* **Martina Steffl, Angelika Kirchschlager** *mezzos*
Birgit Remmert *contr* **Franz Leitner, Thomas Künne, Christoph Prégardien,**
Herbert Lippert *tens* **Oliver Widmer** *bar* **Karl Heinz Lehner, Hiroyuki Ijichi, Edgard Loibl,**
Robert Holl *basses* **Barbara Moser, András Schiff, Andreas Staier, Werner Schröckmayr** *pfs*
Arnold Schoenberg Choir; Vienna Concert-Verein / Erwin Ortner.
Teldec 4509-94546-2 (seven discs: 480 minutes: DDD). Texts and translations included.
Recorded 1995-96.   Ⓕ

The scheme of presentation here is both sensible and imaginative. Each of the discs has a subject-heading and each has its share of the treasures. The first, 'Transience', opens with the setting of Goethe's *Gesang der Geister über den Wassern* for men's voices and string quartet (without violins), probably the supreme masterpiece of the whole collection. The fascinating contrapuntal treatment of Schiller's *Dreifach ist der Schritt der Zeit* in its male-voice setting, and the gentle melancholy of Scott's *Coronach* are also memorable. The love-songs on the second disc begin and end with the *Ständchen*, 'Zögernd leise', its second version, with male-voice chorus, being so much the more attractive in these performances. Under the heading of 'Eternity' (third disc) comes much that has perhaps a questionable place in a secular anthology: good to have, nevertheless, the anthem known to British choristers as *Where Thou reignest* as *Schiksalslenker, blicke nieder*. The fourth disc has 'Heroism' as its theme, with *Mirjams Siegesgesang* as its lengthiest work. 'Nature' (fifth disc) produces several masterpieces, including Kleist's *Gott in der Natur* and the magical *Nachthelle*. The sixth, devoted to 'Celebration', has some longer occasional pieces, none so delightful as the brief cantata written for his father's birthday in 1813, with guitar accompaniment. The last disc, 'Circle of Friends', begins, beguilingly, with *Der Tanz* and ends with *Zur guten Nacht*. Ortner's soloists do well, but it is in the choral singing that the great merit of these performances lies. The Arnold Schoenberg Choir is a fine body of musicians and here they show a virtually unflawed beauty and opulence of tone. The pianists, headed by András Schiff, are excellent.

Lieder, Volumes 1-3.
DG 437 214-2GX21 (21 discs: 1463 minutes: ADD). Volumes also available separately,
as detailed below. Recorded 1966-72.   Ⓑ

234 Lieder, written between 1811 and 1817.
Dietrich Fischer-Dieskau *bar* **Gerald Moore** *pf*
DG 437 215-2GX9 (nine discs: 404 minutes: ADD). Recorded 1966-68.   Ⓑ

171 Lieder, written between 1817 and 1828.
Dietrich Fischer-Dieskau *bar* **Gerald Moore** *pf*
DG 437 225-2GX9 (nine discs: 395 minutes: ADD). Recorded 1969.   Ⓑ

Die schöne Müllerin, D795. Winterreise, D911. Schwanengesang, D957.
Dietrich Fischer-Dieskau *bar* **Gerald Moore** *pf*
DG 437 235-2GX3 (three discs: 184 minutes: ADD). Recorded 1971-72.   Ⓑ

Twenty-one discs at under £100 bringing together two of this century's greatest Lieder interpreters – it sounds like a recipe for success, as indeed it is, fulfilling the highest expectations. The recordings were made when Dietrich Fischer-Dieskau was at his peak and Gerald Moore could draw on a lifetime's experience and love of this repertoire. Though the set makes no claims to completeness (in the way that Graham Johnson's ongoing Schubert series on Hyperion does), most of the songs for male voice are included here. The use of a single singer and pianist gives the set a unity that allows the listener to gasp anew at the composer's wide-ranging inspiration and imagination. Fischer-Dieskau brings a unique understanding, an elegant line and a diction that renders the text clear without resort to the written texts. If occasionally he imparts an unnecessary weightiness to the lighter songs, this quibble is as nothing when his historic achievement is taken as a whole. And though he made many recordings of the song cycles these are perhaps the finest, with Moore the ideal partner. Try for example, the bleakness of 'Ihr Bild' from *Schwanengesang* or the hallucinatory happiness of 'Der Lindenbaum' from *Winterreise*. The songs themselves are basically in chronological order (but with the three song cycles collected together in the final box). It is unfortunate there is no index – trying to find individual songs can be frustrating. It should also be added that the translations are distinctly quirky in places; better to use Richard Wigmore's excellent book *Schubert: The Complete Song Texts* (Gollancz: 1988) if you have a copy to hand. This is undoubtedly one of the greatest bargains in the *Guide*. Buy, without fear of disappointment.

Lieder[a] – Gretchen am Spinnrade, D118. Was bedeutet die Bewegung?, D720. Ach, um deine feuchten Schwingen, D717. Schwestergruss, D762. Schlummerlied, D527. An die untergehende Sonne, D457. Heiss' mich nicht reden, D877 No. 2. So lasst mich scheinen, D877 No. 3. Nur wer die Sehnsucht kennt, D877 No. 4. Kennst du das Land, D321. Berthas Lied in der Nacht, D653. Epistel an Herrn Josef Spaun, D749. Raste, Krieger, D837. Jäger, ruhe von der Jagd, D838. Ave Maria, D837. Hin und wieder, D239. Lieber schwärmt, D239 No. 6. An die Nachtigall, D497. Schlafe, schlafe, D498. Delphine, D857. Wiegenlied, D867. Die Männer sind méchant, D886 No. 3. Iphigenia, D573. Das Mädchen, D652. Die junge Nonne, D828. Am Grabe Anselmos, D504. Abendstern, D806. Die Götter Greichenlands, D677. Gondelfahrer, D808. Auflösung, D807. Lieder[b] – Die Forelle, D550. Rastlose Liebe, D138. Auf dem Wasser zu singen, D774. Der Tod und das Mädchen, D531. An die Musik, D547. Frühlingsglaube, D686. Der Musensohn, D764. An Sylvia, D891. Litanei, D343. Heidenröslein, D257. Nacht und Träume, D827. Du bist die Ruh', D776.
Dame Janet Baker mez [a]**Gerald Moore,** [b]**Geoffrey Parsons** pf
EMI Forte CZS5 69389-2 (two discs: 155 minutes: ADD). Recorded 1870-80. Ⓜ

When the major part of this issue, the first 25 songs, appeared in 1971 under the title 'A Schubert Evening', the reviewer gave it a glowing review in **Gramophone**. EMI provided a lavish booklet with annotations on each song, texts and translations, and illustrations of the artists and of Schubert. Virtually nothing of that remains. The briefest summary of the notes, no pictures (just fancy and irrelevant artwork), no words. In a spectacular piece of mis-marketing, EMI seems to be setting out to frighten away those at whom this mid-price issue is aimed – among them many newcomers to Lieder. That is a great shame as this set has some of the most glorious Schubert singing you can imagine. 'A Schubert Evening' was in part instigated as a complementary issue to Fischer-Dieskau's contemporaneous recording of all Schubert's songs suited to a male interpreter. Dame Janet chose those he had abjured, ones specifically written for a female protagonist. She fulfils almost every aspect of her riveting selection in terms of vibrant tone, immaculate line, control of dynamics, insights into the poems' meaning and lively storytelling, where that's called for. EMI, in its documentation, seems to have overlooked the fact that five of the songs, Nos. 7-11 on the second CD, come from an earlier recital. They are in fact five of the songs that Baker often sang at recitals from the start of her career and to which she was particularly attached; *Am Grabe Anselmos* and *Gondelfahrer*, two superb pieces, are perhaps the most telling of a wonderful group. The remainder of the recordings from a 1980 recital with Parsons, showing no deterioration in the mezzo's singing, offer several of the composer's most popular pieces, all sung *con amore*. Even with such inadequate packaging, this is an issue to treasure.

An den Mond, D193. Wandrers Nachtlied I, D224. Der Fischer, D225. Erster Verlust, D226. Heidenröslein, D257. Erlkönig, D328. Litanei auf das Fest Allerseelen, D343. Seligkeit, D433. Ganymed, D544. An die Musik, D547. Die Forelle, D550. Frühlingsglaube, D686. Im Haine, D738. Der Musensohn, D764. Wandrers Nachtlied II, D768. Der Zwerg, D771. Auf dem Wasser zu singen, D774. Du bist die Ruh, D776. Nacht und Träume, D827. Fischerweise, D881. Im Frühling, D882. An Silvia, D891.
Ian Bostridge ten **Julius Drake** pf
EMI CDC5 56347-2 (69 minutes: DDD). Texts and translations included. Recorded 1996. ⒻE

Bostridge's growing band of devoted admirers are sure to be satisfied by this selection from Schubert's most popular songs. They will once more wonder at his famed engagement with the text in hand and his innate ability both to sing each piece in an entirely natural manner and at the same time to search out its inner meaning, everything achieved without a vocal or technical mishap within hearing. His gift for finding the right manner for each song is exemplified in the contrast between the easy simplicity he brings to such apparently artless pieces as *Fischerweise*, *Frühlingsglaube* and the less familiar *Im Haine* (this a wondrous performance of a song that is the very epitome of Schubert the melodist) and the depth of feeling found in *Erster Verlust* (a properly intense reading), *Nacht und Traüme*, *Wandrers Nachtlied* I and II, *Du bist die Ruh* (so elevated in tone and style) and *Litanei*. Bostridge also characterizes spine-chillingly the intense, immediate drama of *Erlkönig* and *Der Zwerg*, though here some may prefer the weight of a baritone. In the latter piece Drake is particularly successful at bringing out the originality of the piano part, and in a much simpler song, *An Sylvia*, he gives to the accompaniment a specific lift and lilt that usually goes unheard. *An die Musik* might have benefited from a slightly simpler treatment and the piano in *Fischerweise* is a touch heavy, but the faults are marginal, and in these songs, as in everything else, the ear responds eagerly to the tenor's fresh, silvery tone and his ever-eager response to words. The recording and notes are faultless.

Der Musensohn, D764*b*. Schwanengesang, D957 – Liebesbotschaft; Abschied; Die Stadt; Die Taubenpost. Der Schiffer, D536. Die Forelle, D550*e*. An eine Quelle, D530. Auf der Bruck, D853. Das Rosenband, D280. Rastlose Liebe, D138. Winterreise, D911 – Der Lindenbaum. Auf dem Wasser zu singen, D774. Im Freien, D880. Im Abendrot, D799. Wandrers Nachtlied II, D768. Im Frühling, D882. An den Mond, D296. Auf dem Strom, D943.
Hans-Peter Blochwitz *ten* **Marie-Luise Neunecker** *hn* **Rudolf Jansen** *pf*
Philips 438 932-2PH (64 minutes: DDD). Texts and translations included. Recorded 1992.   Ⓕ

This choice of songs gives a true and rewarding conspectus of Schubert's genius as a writer of Lieder. Here is Schubert's world, its emotions and mysteries, encapsulated in miniature. On the other hand, even if you are a collector well versed in Schubert, and perhaps investing in the Hyperion Edition, and/or with Fischer-Dieskau by your side, you could still profit by the purchase of this one-off CD, simply because Blochwitz's voice is exactly right for this repertoire: a silvery, easily produced tenor, owned by an artist who sings German as a natural speaker and as an unaffected musician. Every piece makes its point yet with the kind of innate art that conceals art. As he has the ever-perceptive and musically faultless Jansen, so pellucid in his playing, as his partner, this is a delight from start to finish; and that finish, a fitting climax to an intelligently planned programme, is the grandly romantic *Auf dem Strom*, beautifully balanced and clearly recorded, completing one's pleasure in this CD.

Im Frühling, D882. Die Blumensprache, D519. Die gefangenen Sänger, D712. Der Schmetterling, D633. An den Mond, D259. An den Mond, D296. Die Gebüsche, D646. Der Fluss, D693. Der Knabe, D692. Nacht und Träume, D827. Im Abendrot, D799. Glaube, Hoffnung und Liebe, D955. Vom Mitleiden Mariä, D632. Beim Winde, D669. Des Mädchens Klage, D6. Blanka, D631. Das Mädchen, D652. Die Rose, D745. Die junge Nonne, D828. Nähe des Geliebten, D162.
Christine Schäfer *sop* **Irwin Gage** *pf*
Orfeo C450971A (79 minutes: DDD). Texts and translations included. Recorded 1997.   Ⓕ

What makes Schäfer such a special artist is the candid, plaintive, natural quality of her tone and her simplicity of phrasing. These are combined with clear, unaffected diction, and a sense of vulnerability in the timbre, to evoke the pure spirit of each song. Some, used to more vibrant, luscious voices, may find Schäfer's tone too narrow or they may be troubled by moments when she is deliberately on the flat side of a note but they are part of her vocal personality and perhaps nearer to what was heard in Schubert's day. Her attributes as a Schubertian, already disclosed in her contributions to the Hyperion Edition, are confirmed by her discerning choice of songs in this generously filled programme. Whether the pieces are grave or cheerful, Schäfer finds the right expression. The simplicity at the start of *An den Mond* (D296) is succeeded by heightened intensity at just the appropriate moment, in the fifth stanza. In that underrated Schlegel setting, *Der Fluss*, she adds special urgency to the last line. In better-known songs, such as *Nacht und Träume* and *Im Abendrot*, which succeed one another here, the soprano refreshes the familiar through a new draught of feeling, simple yet inward, and that is the epithet that comes most readily to mind in those two melancholic songs, *Das Mädchen* and *Die Rose*, the one about an unloved girl, the other about a flower speaking of its mortality. To end she catches the perfect Schubert/Goethe accord of *Nähe des Geliebten*, where 'Ich denke dein' and 'Ich bin bei dir' are affirmations of a deep love. Irwin Gage partners his singer with many touches of subtle, finely shaded phrasing. Add a surely balanced recording and Lieder lovers are in for a generous treat.

Ave Maria, D839. Ganymed, D544. Kennst du das Land, D321. Heiss mich nicht reden, D877 No. 2. So lasst mich scheinen, D877 No. 3. Nur wer die Sehnsucht kennt, D877 No. 4. Liebhaber in allen Gestalten, D558. Heidenröslein, D257. Nahe des Geliebten, D162. Die Forelle, D550. Auf dem Wasser zu singen, D774. Im Abendrot, D799. Ständchen, D889. Du bist die Ruh, D776. Gretchen am Spinnrade, D118. Gretchens Bitte, D564. Der Hirt auf dem Felsen, D965.
Barbara Bonney *sop* **Sharon Kam** *cl* **Geoffrey Parsons** *pf*
Teldec 4509-90873-2 (73 minutes: DDD). Texts and translations included. Recorded 1994.   Ⓕ

Bonney's programme is most carefully planned. She begins with a substantial selection of Goethe settings, going to the heart of the matter in all the Mignon songs, singing *Ganymed* with exemplary *legato* and breath control. Then she makes a well-varied selection from many of the better-known pieces. She crosses paths with Blochwitz only in *Die Forelle* and *Auf dem Wasser zu singen*. Both take the same time over each, but it is worth noting that Jansen, for Blochwitz, finds more variety and lift in the barcarolle-like accompaniment of the latter song than does Parsons. Vocally speaking, both versions are enjoyable in their natural accomplishments. Bonney's line and breath are again remarkable in *Du bist die Ruh*, which also demonstrates, as do all the other offerings, the purity of her tone – more North American clear-aired than Viennese creamy – yet that is never allowed to exclude depth of feeling. Indeed when she returns to the Goethe settings with *Gretchen am Spinnrade* she shows particular eloquence in the way that, at a deliberate pace, she builds the song unerringly to its climaxes and also catches the inwardness of Gretchen's state of mind. The recording is faultless.

Heidenröslein, D257. Wonne der Wehmut, D260. Der Jüngling an der Quelle, D300. Erntelied, D434. Im Walde, D708. Geheimes, D719. Suleika I, D720. Dass sie hier gewesen, D775. Viola, D786. Im Abendrot, D799. Abendstern, D806. Ave Maria, D839. Totengräbers Heimweh, D842. Bei dir allein, D866 No. 2. Der Wanderer an den Mond, D870. Im Frühling, D882. An Silvia, D891. Ständchen, D920.
Anne Sofie von Otter *mez* **Bengt Forsberg** *pf* with **Swedish Radio Chorus.**
DG 453 481-2GH (69 minutes: DDD). Texts and translations included. Recorded 1996. Ⓕ

Anne Sofie von Otter waited with some trepidation to make her first Schubert disc, conscious of the high degree of both literary awareness and musical commitment necessary for such an undertaking. In songs such as *An Silvia* and *Geheimes* the wide-eyed wonder of her own discovery incarnates that of the songs' own subjects. Tiny moments of gentle emphasis, and a little spring on each note of its rising sequences adds to the wondering incredulity of *An Silvia*'s questionings; and von Otter's vocal heritage of the baroque and of Mozart have, of course, schooled her voice to articulate perfectly the tapering phrases and shy note-pairs that convey the glancing secrets of *Geheimes*. The recital grows gradually darker, moving, by way of *Ständchen*, D920, to the twilight of *Im Abendrot*. Here, long, firmly-grounded vowels are backlit by the afterglow of Forsberg's piano line before some deep, passionate digging into the *Angst* of *Totengräbers Heimweh*, and a wonderfully breathless, intimately urgent imprecation of an *Ave Maria*.

Schiller Lieder – Die Bürgschaft, D246; Hoffnung, D637; Hektors Abschied, D312; An Emma, D113; Des Mädchens Klage, D191; Gruppe aus dem Tartarus, D583; Der Pilgrim, D794; Der Alpenjäger, D588; Leichenfantasie, D7; Die Götter Griechenlands, D677; Sehnsucht, D636.
Christoph Prégardien *ten* **Andreas Staier** *fp*
Deutsche Harmonia Mundi 05472 77296-2 (74 minutes: DDD). Texts and translations included. Recorded 1993. Ⓕ Ⓟ Ⓔ

In *Die Götter Griechenlands*, Prégardien encompasses all the most compelling aspects of such notable tenor interpreters of Lieder as Patzak, Pears and Schreier. The plangent timbre is perfect for this elegiac lament, the *legato* ideal, the phraseology touching. Because this is perhaps Schubert's most telling setting of Schiller, to whose poetry the disc is devoted, it heads the many reasons for buying it. The performance of a quite different song, the ballad *Die Bürgschaft*, is another, as here Prégardien brings to bear quite different attributes – a darker tone, a powerful sense of the song's drama and an innate feeling for the pulse of this long but ultimately rewarding piece. Over and above that, the singer makes every word tell. The same is true of the jejune but entertaining *Leichenfantasie*. All the other songs, even the more intractable ones, are interpreted with the high intelligence and sense of style one would expect. Staier is both an alert and persuasive player, but once or twice, such as in *Der Pilgrim*, one longs for the softer timbre of a modern instrument instead of a fortepiano. Recording is first-rate.

Lieder, Volume 23 – Der Tod Oscars, D375. Das Grab, D377ᵃ. Der Entfernten, D350. Pflügerlied, D392. Abschied von der Harfe, D406. Der Jüngling an der Quelle, D300. Abendlied, D382. Stimme der Liebe, D412. Romanze, D144. Geist der Liebe, D414. Klage, D415. Julius an Theone, D419. Der Leidende, D432. Der Leidende (second version), D432b. Die frühe Liebe, D430. Die Knabenzeit, D400. Edone, D445. Die Liebes-götter, D446. An Chloen, D363. Freude der Kinderjahre, D455. Wer sich der Einsamkeit ergibt, D478. Wer nie sein Brot mit Tränen ass, D480. An die Türen, D479. Der Hirt, D490. Am ersten Maimorgen, D344. Bei dem Grabe meines Vaters, D496. Mailied, D503. Zufriedenheit, D362. Skolie, D507.
Christoph Prégardien *ten* ᵃ**London Schubert Chorale; Graham Johnson** *pf*
Hyperion CDJ33023 (78 minutes: DDD). Texts and translations included. Recorded 1994. Ⓕ

When the Hyperion Schubert Edition is completed, this latest wondrous offering will rank among its most precious jewels. Prégardien is a prince among tenor interpreters of Lieder at present, on a par with Blochwitz in instinctive, natural and inevitably phrased readings. Johnson, besides, of course, finding exactly the right performers for these songs, surpasses even his own high standard of playing in this series. Then there is Schubert himself, the Schubert of 1816 by and large, who was, Johnson tentatively suggests in his notes, going through a phase of 'bringing himself under control'. That means, largely but far from entirely, writing gently lyrical strophic songs, most of them of ineffable beauty and simplicity, starkly contrasting with the Harfenspieler settings from *Wilhelm Meister*, two of which were written in 1816, the other in 1822. In such an outright masterpiece as *Der Jüngling an der Quelle*, Prégardien and Johnson confirm the latter's view that this piece 'makes time stand still'. They emphasize, in *Stimme der Liebe*, how Schubert uses shifting harmonies to indicate romantic obsession. They show in the two similar but subtly different versions of *Der Leidende* ('The suffering one') what Johnson calls 'two sides of the same coin', with the tenor's plangent, tender singing, line and text held in perfect balance, an unalloyed delight. The two Hölty songs that follow, *Die frühe Liebe* and *Die Knabenzeit*, evince a wonderful affinity with thoughts of childhood on the part of poet and composer, again ideally captured here. So is the 'chaste and wistful' mood of Klopstock's *Edone*. These are just a few of many discoveries on this generously timed disc. Ideally balanced recording.

Lieder, Volume 24 – Schäfers Klagelied, D121. An Mignon, D161. Geistes-Gruss, D142 (two versions). Rastlose Liebe, D138. Der Gott und die Bajadere, D254. Tischlied, D234. Der Schatzgräber, D256. Der Rattenfänger, D255. Bundeslied, D258. Erlkönig, D328. Jägers Abendlied, D215. Jägers Abendlied, D368. Wer nie sein Brot mit Tränen ass, D480 (two versions). Nur wer die Sehnsucht kennt, D359. So lasst mich scheinen, D469a and D469b (two fragments). Nur wer die Sehnsucht kennt, D481. Nur wer die Sehnsucht kennt, D656. An Schwager Kronos, D369. Hoffnung, D295. Mahomets Gesang, D549 (cptd. R. Van Hoorickx). Ganymed, D544. Der Goldschmiedsgesell, D560. Gesang der Geister über den Wassern, D484 (cptd. R. Van Hoorickx). Gesang der Geister über den Wassern, D705 (cptd. E. Asti).
Christine Schäfer sop **John Mark Ainsley** ten **Simon Keenlyside** bar
Michael George bass **Graham Johnson** pf
London Schubert Chorale / Stephen Layton.
Hyperion CDJ33024 (79 minutes: DDD). Texts and translations included. Recorded 1993-94. Ⓕ

Renewed praise first of all for Graham Johnson. This volume is as cogent an example as any of his method, a masterly exposition, in written words and musical performance, of the crucial relationship between Goethe and Schubert upon which Johnson throws a good deal of new light. As ever here the familiar happily rubs shoulders with the unfamiliar. Not all is notable Schubert, but the lesser songs, among them one or two hearty occasional pieces, merely serve to place in perspective the greater ones. The CD begins with one of the latter, *Schäfers Klagelied*, in a finely honed, dramatic performance by Ainsley, who is heard later on the disc always to advantage. Good as Christine Schäfer is in the first version of *An Mignon*, she is better in the sadly neglected *Der Gott und die Bajadere*, as Johnson avers. This is the only song in the genre about prostitution, and a haunting one too, even though, throughout its appreciable length, it relies on just one melody, and Schäfer precisely catches its haunting atmosphere. But the climax of her contribution comes in *Ganymed* – with Johnson providing exactly the right rhythmic lilt at the piano, her voice conveys all the elation of poem and music. Schäfer is the child in a three-voice rendering of *Erlkönig*, a manner of performing the piece that has the composer's blessing. Johnson has surely never surpassed his account here of the hair-raisingly difficult piano part. Then he is just as accomplished with Keenlyside in a thrilling account of another masterpiece engendered by response to Goethe's genius, *An Schwager Kronos*. George, who perhaps has the least ingratiating songs to perform, sings with feeling and style but sometimes an excess of vibrato. This is an invaluable addition to this series.

Lieder, Volume 26 – Der Einsame, D800. Des Sängers Habe, D832. Lied der Delphine, D857 No. 1. Lied des Florio, D857 No. 2. Mondenschein, D875. Nur wer die Sehnsucht kennt, D877 No. 1. Heiss mich nicht reden, D877 No. 2. So lasst mich scheinen, D877 No. 3. Nur wer die Sehnsucht kennt, D877 No. 4. Totengräberweise, D869. Das Echo, D990C. An Silvia, D891. Horch, horch! die Lerch', D889. Trinklied, D888. Wiegenlied, D867. Widerspruch, D865. Der Wanderer an den Mond, D870. Grab und Mond, D893. Nachthelle, D892. Abschied von der Erde, D829.
Christine Schäfer sop **John Mark Ainsley** ten **Richard Jackson** bar
London Schubert Chorale; Graham Johnson pf
Hyperion CDJ33026 (76 minutes: DDD). Texts and translations included. Recorded 1995. Ⓕ🄴

As another wondrous addition to this unique venture, it is hard to know where to begin in its praise. It has several centres of excellence, the first being Schäfer's beseeching, urgent account of the

Mignon settings from Goethe's *Wilhelm Meister* that make plain her pre-eminence today among sopranos in Lieder. Next comes Ainsley's winningly fresh account of *An Silvia*. You may be surprised at how wholly new-minted Ainsley's ardent tones and Johnson's elating piano manage to make of such a hackneyed song. Schäfer and Johnson do the same service for *Horch, horch! die Lerch'*. Then comes the extraordinary discovery of this volume. As a rule, Johnson has excluded unaccompanied vocal pieces from his project; happily, he has made an exception in the case of the astonishingly original Seidl setting *Grab und Mond*, which touches on eternal matters, or rather the permanence of death, a message starkly expressed in typically daring harmony. The London Schubert Chorale gives it a spellbinding interpretation and also contributes positively to a performance of another Seidl setting, the better-known *Nachthelle*, where the high-lying tenor lead provides no problems for Ainsley. There have to be reservations over the work of Richard Jackson. No amount of creative intelligence can mask the fact that his dried-out tone is inadequate to the demands of *Der Einsame*, the unjustly neglected *Totengräberweise* and *Der Wanderer an den Mond*, which call for a richer palette of sound. Throughout, Johnson's playing and, of course, his admirable notes are their customary sources of pleasure and enlightenment. The recording is well-nigh faultless.

Lieder, Volume 27 – Lob der Tränen, D711. Lebensmelodien, D395. Sprache der Liebe, D410. Wiedersehn, D855. Sonett I, D628. Sonett II, D629. Sonett III, D630. Abendröte, D690. Die Berge, D634. Die Vögel, D691. Der Fluss, D693. Der Knabe, D692. Die Rose, D745. Der Schmetterling, D633. Der Wanderer, D649. Das Mädchen, D652. Die Sterne, D684. Die Gebüsche, D646. Blanka, D631. Der Schiffer, D694. Fülle der Liebe, D854. Im Walde, D708.
Matthias Goerne *bar* **Christine Schäfer** *sop* **Graham Johnson** *pf*
Hyperion CDJ33027 (78 minutes: DDD). Texts and translations included. Recorded 1995-96. Ⓕ

Goerne's brief is Schubert's settings of the brothers Schlegel, whose volatile character and life are amply and fascinatingly described in Johnson's introduction to the booklet. As ever in this series, there are songs that we should curse ourselves for neglecting for so long. Among the few settings of August von Schlegel is the interesting *Lebensmelodien*, where the Swan and the Eagle engage in a colloquy – the one all tranquil, the other all disturbed – and are observed by doves on whom Schubert lavishes his most beautiful music. In the formal *Wiedersehn*, as Johnson avers, Schubert imitates the style of a Handelian aria. The second of three Petrarch translations prefigures, arrestingly, the mood of *Winterreise*. When we come to brother Friedrich and the quasi-cycle *Abendröte* we are in an even more exalted world where *Der Fluss*, another of Schubert's miraculous water songs, *Der Knabe*, above all *Die Rose*, where the fading of the rose is a metaphor for lost virginity (this, movingly done by Schäfer), and *Der Wanderer* show just how willingly Schubert responded to Schlegel's imagery. About Goerne's singing as such, ably assisted by Johnson's playing, there need be no reservations, particularly in the visionary *Die Sterne*, but as the CD progresses his interpretations begin to seem a shade soporific; one wonders if he has lived long enough with these songs to penetrate to their heart. His easily produced, slightly vibrant and mellifluous baritone and sense of Schubertian style make him, by and large, a rewarding interpreter. The recording is superb.

Lieder, Volume 32 – An die Sonne, D439. Beitrag zur fünfzigjährigen Jubelfeier des Herrn von Salieri, D407. Das war ich, D174a/D450a. Didone Abbandonata, D510a (both cptd. Hoorickx). Der Entfernten, D331. Entzückung, D413. Der Geistertanz, D494. Gott der Weltschöpfer, D986. Gott im Ungewitter, D985. Grablied auf einen Soldaten, D454. Das Grosse Halleluja, D442. Des Mädchens Klage, D389. Licht und Liebe, D352. Naturgenuss, D422. Ritter Toggenburg, D397. Schlachtgesang, D443. Die verfehlte Stunde, D409. Der Wanderer, D489. Zufriedenheit, D501. Zum Punsche, D492.
Lynne Dawson, Patricia Rozario, Christine Schäfer *sops* **Ann Murray,**
Catherine Wyn-Rogers *mezzos* **Paul Agnew, John Mark Ainsley, Philip Langridge,**
Jamie MacDougall, Daniel Norman, Christoph Prégardien, Michael Schade,
Toby Spence *tens* **Simon Keenlyside, Maarten Koningsberger, Stephan Loges,**
Christopher Maltman, Stephen Varcoe *bars* **Neal Davies, Michael George** *basses*
Graham Johnson *pf*
London Schubert Chorale / Stephen Layton.
Hyperion CDJ33032 (78 minutes: DDD). Notes, texts and translations included. Ⓕ

Like the previous Schubertiads in the Hyperion Edition, this disc mixes solo songs and partsongs, the familiar and the unfamiliar. In fact, the only really famous number here is *Der Wanderer*, that archetypal expression of romantic alienation whose popularity in Schubert's lifetime was eclipsed only by that of *Erlkönig*. Some of the partsongs – *Zum Punsche*, *Naturgenuss* and the tub-thumping *Schlachtgesang* – cultivate a vein of Biedermeier heartiness that wears a bit thin today. Nor will Schubert's consciously archaic tribute to his teacher Salieri have you itching for the repeat button – though, like several other numbers, it shows the 19-year-old composer rivalling Mozart in his gift for musical mimicry. In compensation, though, are partsongs like the sensual *Der Entfernten*, with its delicious languid chromaticisms (relished here by the London Schubert Chorale), and the colourful setting of *Gott im Ungewitter*. The slight but charming setting of *Das war ich* is appealingly done by the light-voiced Daniel Norman, and Ann Murray brings her usual charisma and dramatic conviction to the pathetic Italian scena *Didone Abbandonata*. Christine Schäfer is equally charismatic in the unjustly neglected *Die verfehlte Stunde* (recorded here for the first time), catching perfectly the song's mingled yearning and ecstasy and negotiating the mercilessly high tessitura with ease. Other happy discoveries include Schubert's virtually unknown third setting of *Des Mädchens Klage*, with its soaring lines, a melancholy tale of courtly love, sung by Christoph Prégardien with as much drama and variety as the music allows, and the surging *Entzückung* ('music for an infant Lohengrin,' as Graham Johnson puts it), for which Toby Spence has both the flexibility and the necessary touch of metal in the tone. Doubts were fleetingly raised by Lynne Dawson's slight tremulousness in *Des Mädchens Klage*, and by Christopher Maltman's prominent vibrato at *forte* and above in an otherwise involving performance of *Der Wanderer*. But, these cavils apart, no complaints about the singing or Graham Johnson's vivid accompaniments.

Lieder – Gruppe aus dem Tartarus, D583. Litanei auf das Fest Allerseelen, D343. Die Forelle, D550. An die Leier, D737. Lachen und Weinen, D777. Schwanengesang, D957 – Ständchen; Das Fischermädchen; Die Taubenpost. Meerestille, D216. Der Wanderer, D489 (formerly D493). Erlkönig, D328. Der Tod und das Mädchen, D531. Heidenröslein, D257. Wandrers Nachtlied II, D768. An die Musik, D547. Auf der Bruck, D853. Schäfers Klagelied, D121. An Silvia, D891. Du bist die Ruh', D776. An die Laute, D905. Rastlose Liebe, D138. Ganymed, D544. Der Musensohn, D764.
Bryn Terfel *bass-bar* **Malcolm Martineau** *pf*
DG 445 294-2GH (69 minutes: DDD). Texts and translations included. Recorded 1994.
Gramophone Award Winner 1995.

Terfel's gift, now well known, is a generous, individual voice, a natural feeling for German and an inborn ability to go to the heart of what he attempts. His singing here is grand in scale – listen to any of the dramatic songs and the point is made – but like Hotter, whom he so often resembles, he is able to reduce his large voice to the needs of a sustained, quiet line, as in *Meerestille*. When the two come together as in *Der Wanderer*, the effect can be truly electrifying, even more so, perhaps, in *Erlkönig* where the four participants are superbly contrasted. Yet this is a voice that can also smile, as in *An die Laute* and 'Die Taubenpost' or express wonder, as in *Ganymed*, a most exhilarating interpretation, or again explode in sheer anger as in the very first song, the strenuous *Gruppe aus dem Tartarus*. Terfel is not afraid to employ rubato and vibrato to make his points and above all to take us right into his interpretations rather than leave us admiring them, as it were, from afar. Throughout, Martineau's at once vigorous and subtle playing is an apt support: his accompaniment in *Erlkönig* is arrestingly clear and precise.

Heidenröslein, D257. Die Forelle, D550. An die Nachtigall, D497. Im Frühling, D882. Die junge Nonne, D828. Nacht und Träume, D827. Auf dem Wasser zu singen, D774. Ave Maria, D839. Frühlingsglaube, D686. Gretchen am Spinnrade, D118. Du bist die Ruh, D776. Der Tod und das Mädchen, D531. Viola, D786. Die Männer sind méchant, D866 No. 3.
Renée Fleming *sop* **Christoph Eschenbach** *pf*
Decca 455 294-2DH (66 minutes: DDD). Texts and translations included. Recorded 1996.

When yet another recital of Schubert Lieder appears, composed in the main of well-known songs, one looks for some special attributes to set it off from what has gone before in such profusion. Renée Fleming frequently supplies just those touches of individual response and high art which the ear is seeking. Like Dame Margaret Price she brings considerable stage experience to bear on her readings in terms of dramatic immediacy. That is particularly true of *Die junge Nonne* and *Gretchen am Spinnrade*, both of which carry the charge of emotions made manifest at the moment of recording. There is almost as much to enjoy and appreciate in the more reflective, inward pieces. *Im Frühling*, in both voice and piano, catches very precisely the sense of longing evoked by the spring, with Eschenbach pointing up the poignancy of alternating major-minor. In *An die Nachtigall*, Fleming's tone is poised, finely controlled, even more so in the more difficult *Du bist die Ruh*, where she shades the end of the final two couplets with a ravishing *piano*. *Nacht und Träume*, still harder to sustain, is as time-stopping as it should be. In the sadly neglected flower-ballad *Viola* the pair suggest a true partnership of thought and execution. At least three other songs, *Auf dem Wasser zu singen*, *Ave Maria* and *Frühlingsglaube* seem marginally too slow. Here, and sometimes elsewhere, a shade more rhythmic verve, a greater attention to consonants, would improve on what is already a formidable array of virtues, and Eschenbach's habit of indulging in *ritenutos* sometimes becomes a distraction. These small points apart, this is a Liederabend to savour and it has been faultlessly recorded.

Lieder[a] – Im Abendrot, D799. Die Sterne, D939. Nacht und Träume, D827. Der liebliche Stern, D861. Der Vollmond strahlt, D797 No. 3*b*. Der Einsame, D800. Schlaflied, D527. An Silvia, D891. Das Mädchen, D652. Minnelied, D429. Die Liebe hat gelogen, D751. Du liebst mich nicht, D756. An die Laute, D905. Der Blumenbrief, D622. Die Männer sind méchant, D866.No. 3. Seligkeit, D433. Nachtviolen, D752. Du bist die Ruh, D776. Das Lied im Grünen, D917. Der Schmetterling, D633. An die Nachtigall, D497. An die Nachtigall, D196. Der Wachtelschlag, D742. Im Freien, D880. Die Vögel, D691. Fischerweise, D881. Die Gebüsche, D646. Im Haine, D738. Kennst du das Land, D321. Nur wer die Sehnsucht kennt, D877 No. 4. Heiss mich nicht reden, D877 No. 2. So lasst mich scheinen, D877 No. 3. Die Liebende schreibt, D673. Nähe des Geliebten, D162. Heidenröslein, D257. Liebhaber in allen Gestalten, D558. Die junge Nonne, D828. Der König in Thule, D367. Gretchen am Spinnrade, D118. Gretchens Bitte, D564. Szene aus Goethes Faust, D126 (with Meinard Kraak *ten, chorus* and *org*). Suleika I, D720. Suleika II, D717. Raste Krieger!, D837. Jäger, ruhe von der Jagd, D838. Ave Maria, D839. An die Musik, D547. Schwestergrüss, D762. Sei mir gegrüsst, D741. Die Blumensprache, D519. An den Mond, D296. Abendbilder, D650. Frühlingssehnsucht, D957 No. 3. Erster Verlust, D226. Nachthymne, D687. Die Sterne, D684. Der Knabe, D692. Wiegenlied, D498. Berthas Lied in der Nacht, D653.
Lieder[b] – Ganymed, D544. Die Götter Griechenlands, D677. Der Musensohn, D764. Fülle der Liebe, D854. Sprache der Liebe, D410. Schwanengesang, D744. An den Tod, D518. Die Forelle, D550. Am Bach im Frühling, D361. Auf dem Wasser zu singen, D774. Der Schiffer, D694. An die Entfernte, D765. Sehnsucht, D516. An die untergehende Sonne, D457. Abendröte, D690.
Elly Ameling *sop* [a]**Dalton Baldwin,** [b]**Rudolf Jansen** *pf*
Philips The Early Years 438 528-2PM4 (four discs: 260 minutes: ADD/DDD). Texts included.
Recorded 1972-84.　　　　　　　　　　　　　　　　　　　　　　　　　　　　　　　Ⓜ

The first *Im Abendrot* (the Lappe setting) introduces the smiling Ameling of 1973, her voice basking in the images of golden shafts of light, and rapt in an easeful *legato*. In the shorter vowels and pulsing pianistic light of *Die Sterne*, she still finds serenity, just as in *Der Einsame* the poet's solitude is sensed at the heart of a tingling, sentient world. The expressive subtlety of these performances comes from an unique fusion of response between Ameling and Baldwin during this period. In the second disc, their creative empathy is turned to Schubert's settings of Goethe. Ameling focuses on the vulnerability and childlike eagerness of Mignon, missing, perhaps, the nervous feverishness which lies just below the surface of these songs, and which Wolf was to exploit to the full. After one of the most perfectly-scaled performances of *Heidenröslein* on disc, Ameling and Baldwin turn to Goethe's Gretchen and Suleika, and to Scott's Ellen. Gretchen's searing vision at the spinning-wheel is answered by the rarely heard *Szene aus Goethes Faust* in which Ameling finds herself in the company of an anonymous and very spooky *Böser Geist*, as well as a ghostly choir who seem piped in from another planet. Seven years later, Ameling turns to a still stranger spirit world. The third disc, recorded in 1982, includes the lunar beauty of Schubert's Bruchmann setting, *Schwestergrüss*, articulated by a voice bleached of any colour. It is almost impossible to detect any sense of ageing in the voice here. Characterized by songs which search out the most elusive of soul moods, this third recital reveals Ameling's soprano at its most finely nuanced, in songs such as *Abendbilder* and the Novalis *Nachthymne*. In the final disc, at the age of 50, Ameling took on the challenge of some of Schubert's most visionary songs: facing Schiller's Greek gods, Goethe's *Ganymed*, Schlegel's *Der Schiffer* and moving through Mayrhofer's longing to Schlegel's final sunset. These songs stretch the voice and the mind to its very limits, yet Ameling's artistry seems to grow with the music itself. The set includes full texts but no translations. In the end, though, Ameling's singing renders them all but redundant.

Songs to poems by Goethe.
Am Flusse, D160. Trost in Tränen, D120. Schäfers Klagelied, D121. Meeres Stille, D216. Heidenröslein, D257. Jägers Abendlied, D368. Sehnsucht, D123. Die Liebe, D210. Rastlose Liebe, D138. Nähe des Geliebten, D162. Der Fischer, D225. Erster Verlust, D226. Der König in Thule, D367. Wer sich der Einsamkeit ergibt, D478. An die Türen, D479. Wer nie sein Brot mit Tränen ass, D480. An Schwager Kronos, D369. An Mignon, D161. Ganymed, D544. An die Entfernte, D765. Versunken, D715. An den Mond, D259. Der Musensohn, D764. Auf dem See, D543. Geistes-Gruss, D142.
Christoph Prégardien *ten* **Andreas Staier** *fp*
Deutsche Harmonia Mundi 05472 77342-2 (70 minutes: DDD). Texts and translations included.
Recorded 1994.　　　　　　　　　　　　　　　　　　　　　　　　　　　　　　　Ⓕ Ⓟ

Prégardien proves himself just as adept at such a light piece as *Heidenröslein* as in the still, solemn thoughts of *Meeres Stille*, or the forceful challenge of *An Schwager Kronos*; the eager striving of *Ganymed*, or the spring-like joy of *Der Musensohn*, adapting his flexible tone to the varying requirements of each. The reading of the *Harfenspieler Lieder* forms the centrepiece of the recital, the singer catching the melancholy and mystery so unerringly suggested by the composer himself.

The books speak unkindly of *Sehnsucht*, but Prégardien, a superb Bach interpreter, brings out the connection with the older composer in the recitative of this cantata-like song. Staier again seems the ideal partner for this singer. His luminous playing of his fortepiano, notably in such a piece as *An den Mond*, exactly matches the ethereal beauty of the tenor's performance. Once or twice we may wish for the more substantial tones of a Fischer-Dieskau or a Schreier with their attendant 'modern' pianists, but the older interpreters' gifts are, in a sense, complementary to and different from the younger artists. The natural, well-balanced recording allows us to hear all the subtleties to be found in these performances, which pay homage, in their verbal detailing, as much to poet as to composer.

Lieder on Record, Volumes 1 and 2.
Various artists.
EMI mono CHS5 66150-2/154-2 (two sets of three discs each: 205 and 202 minutes: ADD). Ⓜ Ⓗ
Texts and translations included. Recorded 1898-1952.
Sopranos – **Pauline Cramer, Ursula van Diemen, Elise Elizza, Kirsten Flagstad, Marta Fuchs, Dusolina Giannini, Ria Ginster, Frieda Hempel, Lilli Lehmann, Lotte Lehmann, Frida Leider, Minnie Nast, Flora Nielsen, Aaltje Noordewier-Reddingius, Margaret Ritchie, Lotte Schöne, Elisabeth Schumann, Dame Elisabeth Schwarzkopf, Irmgard Seefried, Meta Seinemeyer, Susan Strong.**
Mezzo-sopranos – **Therese Behr-Schnabel, Julia Culp, Elena Gerhardt, Marie Götze, Susan Metcalfe-Casals, Edyth Walker.**
Contraltos – **Edith Clegg, Ottilie Metzger, Maria Olszewska, Sigrid Onegin.**
Tenors – **Friedrich Brodersen, Karl Erb, Heinrich Hensel, John McCormack, Franz Naval, Julius Patzak, Sir Peter Pears, Aksel Schiøtz, Leo Slezak, Richard Tauber, Georges Thill, Gustav Walter.**
Baritones – **David Bispham, Leopold Demuth, Hans Duhan, Dietrich Fischer-Dieskau, Sir George Henschel, Gerhard Hüsch, Herbert Janssen, Charles Panzéra, Bernhard Sonnerstedt, Harold Williams.**
Bass-baritones – **Harry Plunkett Greene, Hans Hotter, Friedrich Schorr.**
Basses – **Feodor Chaliapin, Wilhelm Hesch, Alexander Kipnis, Paul Knüpfer, Endré Koréh, Lev Sibiriakov, Vanni-Marcoux, Ernst Wachter.**

Much has happened to the interpretation of Lieder since 1952 and quite a bit since 1982 when this issue first appeared on LP. Yet there is still much to be learnt from listening to these 93 songs interpreted by 64 singers in a total of 129 performances. Styles have changed radically since the early decades of the century. Nowadays we insist on accuracy over every aspect of interpretation; in these older performances the text and its meaning takes precedence over almost everything else: nearly all these singers are keen to tell an urgent message and never mind if that involves excessive rubato, *ritardandos*, playing about with note values. Practically every singer is an individualist, the voice and style immediately recognizable. Today the manner is more uniform, the personal, eccentric approach often frowned upon. The transfers are almost identical with those made by Keith Hardwick for the LP set, very many taken off vinyl, giving you the singers in very present form, no scratch intervening. The oldest discs – many rarities – are intractable: 1990s technology might has not improved on what we encounter here. These are fascinating and rewarding issues that no lover of Schubert and/or Lieder should be without.

Die schöne Müllerin, D795. Schwanengesang, D957. Winterreise, D911.

Die schöne Müllerin, with a reading of six poems not set by Schubert.
Ian Bostridge *ten* **Dietrich Fischer-Dieskau** *narr* **Graham Johnson** *pf*
Hyperion CDJ33025 (73 minutes: DDD). Text and translation included. Recorded 1994-95.
Gramophone Award Winner 1996. Ⓕ ℞℞

The 20 songs of *Die schöne Müllerin* portray a Wordsworthian world of heightened emotion in the pantheistic riverside setting of the miller. The poet, Wilhelm Müller, tells of solitary longings, jealousies, fears and hopes as the river rushes by, driving the mill-wheel and refreshing the natural world. Bostridge and Johnson go to the heart of the matter, the young tenor in his aching tones and naturally affecting interpretation, the pianist in his perceptive, wholly apposite playing – and, of course, in his extensive notes. The sum of their joint efforts is a deeply satisfying experience. Bostridge has the right timbre for the protagonist and a straightforward approach, with an instinctive rightness of phrasing. His peculiarly beseeching voice enshrines the vulnerability, tender feeling and obsessive love of the youthful miller, projecting in turn the young lover's thwarted passions, self-delusions and, finally, inner tragedy. Nowhere does he stretch beyond the bounds of the possible, everything expressed in eager then doleful tones. Johnson suggests that 'Ungeduld' mustn't be 'masterful and insistent' or the youth would have won the girl, so that even in this superficially buoyant song the sense of a sensitive, sad, introverted youth is maintained. The daydreaming strophic songs have the smiling, innocent, intimate sound that suits them to perfection, the angry ones the touch of stronger metal that Bostridge can now add to his silver, the tragic ones, before the neutral 'Baches Wiegenlied', an inner intensity that rends the heart as it should. An occasional moment of faulty German accenting matters not at all when the sense of every word is perceived. As a bonus we have here a recitation of the Prologue and Epilogue and of the Müller poems not set by Schubert: Fischer-Dieskau graces it with his speaking voice. The ideal Hyperion recording catches everything in very present terms, as it does Johnson's own adumbration in his playing of what he writes in his notes. In all musical matters, everything Johnson writes only enhances one's enjoyment, if that is the right word, of a soul-searching interpretation.

Die schöne Müllerin.
Håkan Hagegård bar **Emanuel Ax** pf
RCA Red Seal 09026 61705-2 (61 minutes: DDD). Texts and translations included.
Recorded 1987. Ⓕ

Die schöne Müllerin.
Wolfgang Holzmair bar **Jörg Demus** pf
Preiser 93337 (68 minutes: ADD). Recorded 1984. Ⓕ

Simply as a voice Hagegård's is perhaps superior to any other singers reviewed here. It is, paradoxically, a light yet heroic sound, typically Swedish in timbre, flexible throughout its range and – relevant to the work in hand – tenor-like in tone. Its owner uses it with marked attention to vocal verities, never disturbing a sure *legato*, placing his words firmly and naturally on it. The eager youth of the early songs is unerringly enacted, perhaps without quite the sense of vulnerability suggested by Holzmair and other tenor interpreters, although by the same token he suggests an appropriately open-air, fresh youth. When sorrow, jealousy and eventually heartbreak enter the lad's life, Hagegård projects these with as much conviction yet without a hint of exaggeration or sentimentality. He, and the sensitive but never obtrusive Ax, allow Schubert to speak for himself in sensible, moderate speeds and discreet phrasing: in the context of frequent repetitions, this has undoubted advantages. Holzmair and Demus do much the same. It would be hard to choose among these three versions if you wanted a straightforward reading, but the sheerly beautiful sound of Hagegård's voice places him marginally in front. Fischer-Dieskau peers deeper into the songs and the youth's psychology – but Hagegård and his partner probably come closer to a truly Schubertian ideal. The recording is ideally balanced.

Die schöne Müllerin.
Dietrich Fischer-Dieskau bar **Gerald Moore** pf
EMI CDC7 47173-2 (59 minutes: ADD). Text and translation included. Recorded 1961 Ⓕ

This reissue is the best of Fischer-Dieskau's three recordings of this work, made at the height of his – and Moore's – powers. Fischer-Dieskau's interpretation is simply more idiomatic and more natural. He and Moore are here more spontaneous than in 1951 (for EMI), less affected than in 1972 (reissued on a DG CD in 1985). The conglomeration of Fischer-Dieskau's subtleties and insights are almost overwhelming but here they are mostly subsumed in the immediacy of a highly individual, always alerting performance. But the difference between conscious interpretation and interior restraint can be felt if you compare Fischer-Dieskau and Patzak in the phrase 'sie mir gab' in 'Trockne Blumen'. Moore throughout offers a discerning and musically valid characterization of the participating stream: nothing is overplayed yet all is made manifest. So the intending purchaser is embarrassed with riches in a work that almost always brings the best out of its interpreters. Whichever other interpretation you opt for, you will certainly want Fischer-Dieskau for complete command and understanding of this glorious work.

Die schöne Müllerin.
Julius Patzak ten **Michael Raucheisen** pf
Preiser mono 93128 (61 minutes: AAD). Recorded 1943. Ⓕ Ⓗ

'Der Mensch hat so eine Stimme' ('The man has a tone of voice') says Rocco of Florestan, and it's always a phrase that seems particularly apt for the voice of the great Viennese tenor, Julius Patzak, who was, of course, an unsurpassed Florestan himself. The same plangent utterance that was so affecting in his portrayal of Beethoven's suffering hero informs his famous interpretation of Schubert's cycle about the lovelorn miller-hand. Indeed, his account of 'Die liebe Farbe' is so subjectively intense as to be hardly bearable, and the whole reading, with its poignant diction and lambent tone, places it quite in a class of its own. None reaches to the heart of the matter with quite Patzak's unerring skill. The range of his tone colour and methods of expression are evident not only in 'Die liebe Farbe' but also in the two great songs that succeed it. In 'Die liebe Farbe', such phrases as 'grüne Rasen' and 'hat's jagen so gern' carry an enormous weight of grief as does the piercing enunciation of 'tote liebe' in 'Trockne Blumen'. The end of this song is taken very fast, as if in a fever of unjustified hope. But in earlier, happier moments, Patzak is no less eloquent – try the third verse of 'Des Müllers Blumen' or the whole of 'Morgengruss', where he creates the illusion of actually talking to the girl, or hear the intimate articulation in 'Der Neugierige' while, by contrast, the words tumble out abruptly in the fierce hatred of 'Der Jäger' and the following song. This is an interpretation that is *hors concours*, and not perhaps an interpretation one would wish to hear every day – it is simply too despairing. It is immensely detailed (though never at the expense of *legato*) and subjective, free and spontaneous seeming, never calculated and sophisticated. Raucheisen is at times revelatory at the piano, at times wayward. The recording, though very immediate, has the occasional distortion, and the piano is backward. But the greatness of the reading overrides any drawbacks, although listening to it does require a degree of faith.

Schwanengesang. Herbst, D945. Der Wanderer an den Mond, D870. Am Fenster, D878. Bei dir allein, D866 No. 2.
Peter Schreier *ten* **András Schiff** *pf*
Decca 425 612-2DH (63 minutes: DDD). Texts and translations included. Recorded 1989.
Gramophone Award Winner 1990.

Though *Schwanengesang* is not a song-cycle but a collection of Schubert's last (or 'swan') songs by their first publisher, it is generally felt to form a satisfying sequence, with a unity of style if not of theme or mood. This is certainly not weakened by the addition on the Decca disc of the four last songs which were originally omitted, all of them settings of poems by Johann Seidl. Seidl is one of the three poets whose work Schubert used in these frequently sombre songs and it is strange to think that all concerned in their creation were young men, none of the poets being older than Schubert. The listener can scarcely be unaware of a shadow or sometimes an almost unearthly radiance over even the happiest (such as 'Die Taubenpost', the last of all) and that is particularly true when the performers themselves have such sensitive awareness as here. Peter Schreier is responsive to every shade of meaning in music and text; graceful and charming in 'Das Fischermädchen', flawlessly lyrical in 'Am Meer', he will sometimes risk an almost frightening raw-boned cry as in the anguish of 'Der Atlas' and 'Der Doppelgänger'. András Schiff's playing is a miracle of combined strength and delicacy, specific insight and general rightness.

Schwanengesang. Sehnsucht, D879. Der Wanderer an den Mond, D870. Wiegenlied, D867. Am Fenster, D878. Herbst, D945.
Brigitte Fassbaender *mez* **Aribert Reimann** *pf*
DG 429 766-2GH (68 minutes: DDD). Texts and translations included. Recorded 1989-91.
Gramophone Award Winner 1992.

Fassbaender and Reimann offer something equally compelling but rather different in their account of *Schwanengesang*. Fassbaender's interpretation, idiosyncratic in every respect, pierces to the heart of the bleak songs with performances as daring and challenging as the playing of her partner. More than anyone, these two artists catch the fleeting moods of these mini-dramas, and their searing originality of concept. Even the lighter songs have a special individuality of utterance. This is a starkly immediate interpretation that leaves the listener shattered. The extra Seidl settings, rarely performed, are all worth hearing. Both of these notable partnerships are superb in their own ways.

Winterreise.
Peter Schreier *ten* **András Schiff** *pf*
Decca 436 122-2DH (72 minutes: DDD). Text and translation included. Recorded 1991.

Winterreise can lay claim to be the greatest song cycle ever written. It chronicles the sad, numbing journey of a forsaken lover, recalling past happiness, anguishing over his present plight, commenting on how the snow-clad scenery reflects or enhances his mood. Schreier himself, in his note in the booklet accompanying this recording, refers to the unique density and spiritual concentration of the songs; that, and their hallucinatory nature, inform this riveting performance from start to finish, nowhere more so than in 'Wasserflut' and 'Einsamkeit'. The latter is a paradigm of the whole searing, almost unbearable experience. If you can tolerate it you will be engaged and surely moved by the whole. In this song, Schreier leans into the words and notes of 'Ach, das die Luft so ruhig!' suggesting the cry of a desperate, tormented soul – as does the emphatic enunciation of the single word 'Bergstroms' earlier, in 'Irricht'. Also arresting is the curiously daring way Schreier asks the question at the end of 'Die Post', as if it were a spontaneous afterthought. These make the moments of calm and repose all the more eerie. The sad delicacy of

Schiff's playing at the start of 'Frühlingstraum' sets the scene of the imagined May to perfection, and the flowing lift of his left hand in 'Täuschung' is as deceptively friendly as the light described by the singer. 'Das Wirtshaus' is all false resignation: voice and piano tell us of the man's tired emptiness. Anger and defiance are registered in raw, chilling tone and phraseology. Then, in the pair's revelatory way, they draw attention anew to the originality of concept of 'Letzte Hoffnung'. The final songs taken simply, speak beautifully of acceptance. The recording is warm yet clear.

Winterreise.
Bernd Weikl *bar* **Helmut Deutsch** *pf*
Nightingale Classics NC070960-2 (70 minutes: DDD). Text and translation included.
Recorded 1993.   Ⓕ

For those who prefer a baritone, Weikl seriously challenges the hegemony, among lower-voiced singers, of the many available versions. Indeed it is the absolute vocal security and evenness of Weikl's actual singing that so impresses even before one considers his view of the work. Nowhere is there any sign of strain, over-emphasis, faltering in pitch, or failure of nerve in executing a phrase with a long breath, and as the singer has such a strong voice one feels throughout that there is always something held in reserve. As a reading the Weikl unerringly keeps that balance between detachment and subjectivity. Tempos are in every case perfectly judged – and here Deutsch's well-observed and well-balanced playing makes a significant contribution – a wonderful frozen feeling in 'Auf dem Flusse', for instance. Weikl displays many gradations of tone to enhance his thought-through reading – 'Gefrorne Tränen' is a good example – but he uses vocal emphases more sparingly, reserving his most pointed verbal accents for such things as 'Gras' in 'Erstarrung', 'Hähne' in 'Frühlingstraum' and 'Hunde' in 'Im Dorfe', but even these never upset the verities of line and firm tone, and the sheer beauty of the singing, as in 'Der Lindenbaum', is balm to the ear. For those who find Fischer-Dieskau's more agonized, psychological readings too much to bear, or find his style too interventionist, Weikl is the obvious choice. A superb recording.

Winterreise.
Dietrich Fischer-Dieskau *bar* **Jörg Demus** *pf*
DG The Originals 447 421-2GOR (71 minutes: ADD). Text and translation included.
Recorded 1965.   Ⓜ

On the verge of his fifth decade, the singer was in his absolute prime – and it shows. Indeed listening to his interpretation is like coming home to base after many interesting encounters away from the familiar. Indeed, it is possibly the finest of all in terms of beauty of tone and ease of technique – and how beautiful, how smooth and velvety was the baritone's voice at that time. That this is the most interior, unadorned and undemonstrative of Fischer-Dieskau's readings perhaps arises from the fact that Demus, a discerning musician and sure accompanist, is the most reflective of all the singer's many partners in the cycle. Demus never strikes out on his own, is always there unobtrusively and subtly supportive, with the right colour and phrasing, literally in hand. Given an intimate, slightly dry recording, finely remastered, the whole effect is of a pair communing with each other and stating the sad, distraught message of Schubert's bleak work in terms of a personal message to the listener in the home. A deeply rewarding performance. Certainly if you want Fischer-Dieskau in the cycle you need look no further.

Winterreise.
Christoph Prégardien *ten* **Andreas Staier** *fp*
Teldec Das Alte Werk 0630-18824-2 (74 minutes: DDD). Texts and translations included.
Recorded 1996.   Ⓕ 🅿

Prégardien and Staier have something new and important to offer. From the very first song, we are in the presence of a sensitive, inward man in fear of his fate. Something is actually happening to this sufferer's soul at the second 'des ganzen Winters Eis'; indeed the whole final verse of the second song expresses the youth's anguish. Just as memorable are the stab of pain in the repeated final line 'Da ist meiner Liebstens Haus' at the end of 'Wasserflut', the introverted misery of the ice-carving of the loved one's name in 'Auf dem Flusse' and the almost mesmeric feeling in the final verse as the torrent rages in the protagonist's heart. This is what the singing of this cycle is about: the exposing of raw nerves. Staier is just as revelatory. Using his fortepiano to maximum effect, he finds so many fresh perceptions in his part, as in the precise weighting at the start of 'Einsamkeit' and, as important, ones that accord perfectly with those of his regular partner. Here you have the sense of performers who have lived together with the cycle and conceived a unified, thought-through vision. Listen to the way the pair mesh together to searing effect at the end of 'Irrlicht', or how they make use of the pregnant pause to increase the work's drama as at the start of 'Rast', in which Prégardien displays an unexpected range of dynamics. The ineffable sadness of 'Frühlingstraum' (the text ideally articulated, the close quite properly trance-like), the raw blast of winter in 'Der stürmische Morgen', the tense weariness of 'Der Wegweiser', the weary half-voice of 'Das Wirtshaus' – these and so much else contribute to the impression of a truly great performance. The recording is very finely balanced.

Die Verschworenen, oder Der häusliche Krieg.
Soile Isokoski *sop* Countess Ludmilla; **Peter Lika** *bass* Count Heribert von Lüdenstein;
Rodrigo Orrego *ten* Astolf von Reisenberg; **Andreas Fischer** *ten* Garold von Nummen;
Christian Dahm *bass* Friedrich von Trausdorf; **Thomas Pfützner** *bass* Knight;
Mechthild Georg *mez* Udolin; **Anke Hoffmann** *sop* Isella; **Lisa Larsson** *sop* Helene;
Susanne Behnes *sop* Luitgarde; **Marion Steingötter** *sop* Camilla; **Iris Kupke** *sop* Woman;
Chorus Musicus; Das Neue Orchester / Christoph Spering.
Opus 111 OPS30-167 (64 minutes: DDD). Notes, text and translation included.
Recorded 1996.   ©℗

Ignaz Castelli's neatly wrought text, loosely based on Aristophanes' *Lysistrata*, prompted, early in 1823, Schubert's most dramatically viable stage-work, a one-act *Singspiel*. Aristophanes' story of aggrieved womenfolk withholding their favours until their husbands abandoned their warmongering is transposed here to Vienna during the Crusades and softened with a liberal injection of Biedermeier sentiment. Schubert's parodistic martial music for the macho warriors can occasionally grow wearisome, especially in the finale. Otherwise, though, he scarcely puts a foot wrong. His dramatic pacing is sure and lively, his invention witty, touching and colourful, with its intermittent echoes of Mozart. The opera's gem is Helene's bittersweet F minor *Romanze*, with its sinuous clarinet obbligato (beautifully played here) and haunting modulation to the major in the very last bars. With his polished orchestra and fresh-toned chorus Christoph Spering gives a sympathetic, shrewdly paced account of the score, allowing the lyrical numbers plenty of breathing space and revealing a light, pointed touch in the comic ensembles. Of the singers, Peter Lika's Count has plenty of 'face', though his bass can become coarse under pressure. Rodrigo Orrego, as the knight Astolf, displays an agreeable, soft-grained tenor; and all four principal female roles are well taken, with Lisa Larsson showing a bright, pure tone and a shapely sense of phrase as Helene, and Soile Isokoski bringing real distinction to the role of the Countess, her warm, vibrant soprano, with its hint of mezzo richness and depth, more than once reminiscent of Schwarzkopf. The recording is vivid and well balanced, giving ample presence to the voices while allowing Schubert's felicitous scoring its due.

Ervin Schulhoff   Bohemian 1894-1942

Symphonies Nos. 3 and 5.
Prague Radio Symphony Orchestra / Vladimír Válek.
Supraphon 11 2161-2 (53 minutes: DDD). Recorded 1994.   Ⓕ

Posthumous premières of these works in the 1950s aroused little interest, but Schulhoff has acquired quite a following in recent years and this latest addition to his discography should not be overlooked. As always in music where there is no performance tradition to speak of, the range of interpretative possibilities is wide. On this showing, Vladimír Válek is the most deft and neo-classical of Schulhoff conductors, offering well-prepared, notably fluent accounts of both pieces; his aim seems to be to reconcile their blatant Communistic idiom with the lighter, Roaring Twenties manner of the composer's previous creative period. In Israel Yinon's recording of the Third Symphony, you sense that the music is not just being given room to breathe; it can only be considered in the light of the composer's death in a Nazi concentration camp. Accordingly, Yinon adopts a much weightier tempo in the first movement, its ostinato unrelenting, its drums militantly thwacked. Albrecht's idea of *moderato* is yet more funereal, suggesting that it is the Czech conductor who is out of line. Nevertheless, Válek's account is arguably the most persuasive of the three, executed with commendable crispness. In the Fifth Symphony, risking some loss of *gravitas*, Válek is again nothing if not urgent. The music makes better sense in his hands and any lack of clarity in the orchestral textures would seem to derive from deficiencies in the writing. Even the lack of a clinching melodic idea is made to appear less important. This is a valuable disc, well annotated.

Sextet. String Quartet in G major, Op. 25. Duo[a]. Solo Violin Sonata[b].
Rainer Johannes Kimstedt *va* **Michael Sanderling** *vc* **Petersen Quartet**
([b]Conrad Muck, [a]Gernot Sussmuth *vns* Friedemann Weigle *va* [a]Hans-Jakob Eschenburg *vc*).
Capriccio 10 539 (77 minutes: DDD). Recorded 1994.   Ⓕ

As Schulhoff enthusiasts will have come to expect, the works represented are not at all uniform in style. The early quartet is prematurely neo-classical. It was conceived in 1918 when the composer was still serving in the Austrian Army. The German group certainly gives it their all. Taut and tough, they seem intent on radicalizing the discourse whether through a heightened response to its finer points or a profound understanding of the Beethovenian models that lurk beneath the surface invention. As a result, the Quartet emerges as a witty, substantial piece. The string Sextet was completed six years later but sounds quite different, its Schoenbergian first movement well integrated with the more eclectic idiom of the rest. Whatever the outward manner, Schulhoff's rhythmic phraseology is metrically conceived. Even if you already know the Sextet the Petersen makes a plausible first choice. The aggressive communication of their playing is emphasized by the bright, not quite top-heavy sound balance. The Janáček-Bartók-Ravel axis of the *Duo* is equally well served. The Sonata for solo violin (1927) is at least as interesting as similar works by Hindemith, less emotionally wrenching than the Bartók. That work was composed a couple of years after Schulhoff's premature death. A thoroughly distinguished issue by an ensemble seemingly incapable of giving a dull performance.

Schulhoff String Quartet No. 1.
Hindemith String Quartet No. 3, Op. 22.
Weill String Quartet.
Brandis Quartet (Thomas Brandis, Peter Brem *vns* Wilfried Strehle *va* Wolfgang Boettcher *vc*).
Nimbus NI5410 (60 minutes: DDD). Recorded 1992.   Ⓕ

All three works bear witness to a culture that, in terms of tempo and sensation, was in the process of excited transformation. The period covered is 1923-24, the time of rocketing German inflation, the establishment of the USSR, Rilke's *Duino Elegies* as well as major Kafka (who died in 1924), Mann, Musil, Cocteau and Bréton (his Surrealist manifesto). This music is full of it all. Hindemith's bold Third Quartet – one of the composer's most arresting and accessible pieces – launches its explorations within a relatively formal framework, certainly in comparison with Schulhoff and Weill. Rich invention is tempered by a sense of outward propriety. Weill's Quartet opens with considerable expressive warmth, although it soon busies itself with a whole range of interesting ideas (the finale is particularly rich in incident), with a hoot of a *Scherzo* that suddenly swerves to a Reger-like March, then waltzes gently forth in a manner that suggests Shostakovich before embarking on further discursive episodes and scurrying off to a cheeky *diminuendo*. Granted, one feels that Weill is in search of something he never quite finds, but the very act of searching makes for an absorbing adventure.

Even more compelling, however, is Schulhoff's dazzling First Quartet, the last piece in the programme and a highly dramatic musical mystery tour. Urgency rules right from the opening bars, while Schulhoff's tonal palette is both wide-ranging and ingeniously employed: pizzicato, *col legno*, *sul ponticello*, harmonics (wonderfully effective in the finale), dense harmonic computations and a rhythmic vitality that recalls Bartók at full cry (most especially in the third movement). The work's pale, equivocal coda recalls the parallel quartet mysteries of Schulhoff's fellow Holocaust victims Krása and Haas, while the work as a whole is far more than the sum of its restless and endlessly fascinating parts. A fine programme, lustrously recorded.

Robert Schumann   German 1810-1856

Cello Concerto in A minor, Op. 129.

Schumann Cello Concerto. Adagio and Allegro in A flat major, Op. 70. Fantasiestücke, Op. 73. Fünf Stücke im Volkston, Op. 102. Mass in C minor, Op. 147 – Offertorium.
Bargiel Adagio in G major, Op. 38.
Steven Isserlis *vc* Dame Felicity Lott *sop* David King *org*
Deutsche Kammerphilharmonie / Christoph Eschenbach *pf*
RCA Red Seal 09026 68800-2 (75 minutes: DDD). Recorded 1996.   Ⓕ ⓅⓈⒺⓇⓇ

Only two of the works in this forwardly recorded anthology – the *Fünf Stücke im Volkston* of 1840 and the Cello Concerto of a year later – were originally inspired by the cello. But in closely attuned, super-sensitive partnership with Eschenbach as both conductor and pianist, Steven Isserlis somehow persuades us that no instrument better revealed 'the beloved dreamer whom we know as Schumann', as Tovey once put it. Helped by unhurried tempos and a lovely-voiced *c*1745 Guadagnini cello, Isserlis draws out the rich, nostalgic poetry of the concerto's first two movements with the eloquence of speech. And with his buoyancy of heart and bow he silences all criticism of the finale – even its low-lying cadenza (this he subsequently plays again with the composer's surely less effective flourish for the soloist in the closing bars). The five engaging *Volkston* pieces with piano are vividly characterized and contrasted in mood. And the Op. 73 and Op. 70 miniatures lose nothing through transfer from clarinet and horn respectively to one of the composer's two optional alternatives. The *Adagio and Allegro* for horn surely gains in expressive intimacy and vitality when bowed rather than blown. The *Offertorium* (with its telling accompanying cello thread) is sung by Felicity Lott with heart-easing beauty. The inclusion of a hitherto unrecorded, noble *Adagio* by Clara Schumann's gifted half-brother, Woldemar Bargiel, also helps to make this disc something of a collector's piece.

Cello Concerto[a]. Adagio and Allegro in A flat major, Op. 70[b]. Fantasiestücke, Op. 73[b]. Funf Stücke im Volkston, Op. 102[b].
Heinrich Schiff *vc*
Gerhard Oppitz *pf* **Berlin Philharmonic Orchestra / Bernard Haitink.**
Philips 422 414-2PH (60 minutes: DDD). Item marked [a] recorded 1988, [b]arr. Grützmacher, recorded 1991. Ⓕ 🇪

Schumann's Cello Concerto is a fairly dark, troubled work, and sometimes cellists are tempted to adopt a somewhat overwrought approach when playing it. In fact, it responds best to a more balanced approach, as exemplified in the performance by Heinrich Schiff. His playing is very eloquent, and quite strong, but there is also a feeling of dignity and refinement in his response to the music. Everything is perfectly in scale, and the work's essential nobility is allowed to emerge in a most moving fashion. Schiff's technique is faultless, and his tonal quality is very beautiful. Haitink and the BPO seem totally in sympathy with the soloist, and the recording is warm and well detailed. The three items with piano accompaniment comprise a series of short pieces which are for the most part sunnier in outlook than the Concerto, and they make an effective contrast to the larger-scale work. Again Schiff's playing is expressive, but his phrasing is full of subtlety and poetry, and Oppitz is a highly responsive partner.

Cello Concerto[a]. Piano Trio No. 1 in D minor, Op. 63[b]. Funf Stücke im Volkston, Op. 102[c].
Pablo Casals *vc* [b]**Alexander Schneider** *vn* [b]**Mieczyslaw Horszowski**, [c]**Leopold Mannes** *pfs* [a]**Prades Festival Orchestra / Eugene Ormandy.**
Sony Classical Casals Edition mono SMK58993 (74 minutes: ADD). Recorded 1952-53. Ⓜ 🇭

This disc provides a prime sampling of the Casals manner at its most inspired. His 1953 recording of Schumann's Cello Concerto is a startlingly demonstrative affair with heavily thrashed accents, savage entries and a general proneness to exaggeration that makes a meal out of Schumann's already heightened psycho-musical pathology. And yet Casals's unique brand of poetry is always heart-rending: try from 11'25" into the first movement and follow through to the next, and you'll hear palpable premonitions of the Elgar Concerto as well as some exquisite cello playing. Prior to an enjoyable (but, again, rather bullishly projected) set of *Stücke im Volkston*, we are offered an extremely fine reading of Schumann's sombre D minor Trio – this is undoubtedly a near-contender for 'best ever' status of this work.

Piano Concerto in A minor, Op. 54.

Piano Concerto[a]. Introduction and Allegro appassionato in D minor (Concertstück), Op. 92[a]. Violin Concerto in D minor, Op. posth[b]. Cello Concerto[c]. Konzertstück in F major, Op. 86[d].
Daniel Barenboim *pf* **Gidon Kremer** *vn* **Paul Tortelier** *vc* **Gerd Seifert, Norbert Hauptmann, Christopher Kohler, Manfred Klier** *hns*
[a]**London Philharmonic Orchestra / Dietrich Fischer-Dieskau;**
[b]**Philharmonia Orchestra / Riccardo Muti;**
[c]**Royal Philharmonic Orchestra / Yan Pascal Tortelier;**
[d]**Berlin Phiharmonic Orchestra / Klaus Tennstedt.**
EMI Rouge et Noir CZS7 67521-2 (two discs: 121 minutes: ADD).
Items marked [a] recorded 1974, [b]1982, [cd]1978 Ⓜ

If ever a performance of Schumann's Piano Concerto stressed the principle of dialogue between soloist and conductor, then this is it. True, the Philharmonia's string ensemble isn't as water-tight under Fischer-Dieskau as it might have been under some other conductors; and poetry is invested at the premium of relatively low-level drama. Orchestral textures are absolutely right for Schumann – warm yet transparent, full-bodied yet never stodgy – and poetry is a major priority. Add Barenboim's compatible vision and keyboard finesse, and you indeed have a memorable reading. Despite the extensive competition, Stephen Kovacevich's memorable recording with Sir Colin Davis remains the top recommendation for this work (reviewed under Grieg). The more discursive *Introduction and Allegro appassionato* has plenty of interest, but remembering that this isn't exactly top-drawer Schumann, the performance could be more arresting. Conversely, the *Konzertstücke* has as much forthrightness as it could possibly take, certainly in terms of engineering: the four magnificent horns ring out with Olympian force, keenly supported by an animated BPO. The Cello Concerto is more smoothly recorded, but although Tortelier *père* had the measure of this fragile masterpiece's troubled spirit, his son was, at least at this stage in his career, less comprehensively perceptive. As for the Violin Concerto, one finds oneself frequently moved by Kremer's solo playing – his handling of the slow movement has a tonal richness – but less than happy with Muti's indulgent accompaniment. The repetitions in this work are frequently misunderstood as symptoms of creative decline rather than as the trenchant rhetorical devices that they in fact are, and Muti gives the impression of being unconvinced by them. Nevertheless, Kremer and Muti are, within the useful context of this competitively-priced set, certainly up to the task of communicating what is still a scandalously underrated work. They also have the benefit of good engineering.

Schumann Piano Concerto.
R. Strauss Burleske in D minor, AV85.
Hélène Grimaud *pf*
Deutsches Symphony Orchestra, Berlin / David Zinman.
Erato 0630-11727-2 (52 minutes: DDD). Recorded 1995.   Ⓕ

Such is Grimaud's immediacy of response to every change of mood in the opening *Allegro affettuoso* of Schumann's concerto that some listeners may think it a little too excitable – at the expense of maturer composure and poise. But never in this movement, nor in a finale of unflagging vitality and *joie de vivre*, is there any hint of mere keyboard display. You could certainly never hope to hear the first movement's nostalgic main theme played with a more eloquent simplicity. Piano and orchestra are in exceptionally close accord throughout, and not least in the intimate conversational exchanges of the *Andantino grazioso*. Written when Strauss was a mere 22, the *Burleske* cries out for youthful virtuosity, volatility, caprice and charm – which we're given here with effortless fluency by all concerned. In what could vaguely be described as lyrical 'second subject' territory (from the start of track 5, *tranquillo*) who could fail to enjoy those amazing pre-echoes of irresistibly seductive, smiling (*con amore*) things-to-come a quarter of a century later in *Der Rosenkavalier*? The Erato sound is clear-cut rather than lusciously cushioned, but never hard-edged: it falls agreeably on the ear.

Piano Concerto. Introduction and Allegro appassionato in G major, Op. 92.
Introduction and Allegro in D minor, Op. 134.
Murray Perahia *pf*
Berlin Philharmonic Orchestra / Claudio Abbado.
Sony Classical SK64577 (57 minutes: DDD). Recorded 1994.   Ⓕ

With a considerable number of versions already available, the Piano Concerto needs no special pleading. From Perahia and Abbado it comes across with refreshing eagerness, as if Schumann could scarcely pause for breath in an uprush of inspiration. But unflagging strength of direction by no means excludes the personal. The first movement, in particular, brings intimately revealing nuances of phrasing from Perahia, with a finely shaped, richly expressive cadenza before a delectably light-fingered, effervescent coda. Free of coy cosseting the *Andante* has a natural, gracious flow. However, a more expansive melodic glow in the middle section would not have gone amiss, not least when the violins soar into the upper reaches (a masterstroke of orchestration) near its end. Piquantly crunched acciaccaturas at the start inject the finale with inexhaustible rhythmic buoyancy. Recorded in Berlin's Philharmonie, the sound quality is vibrantly full and forward. Perahia adds Schumann's two later works for piano and orchestra as couplings, of which the sorely neglected last in D minor was part of his birthday present for Clara barely six months before his breakdown. Though less immediately ear-catching than the Mendelssohnian G major work (where Perahia's exhilarating homecoming silences often heard accusations of protraction), Schumann's farewell to the genre – as played here – is striking as by far the more intense and laden of the two, with eventual major-key victory won after deeper internal struggle.

Schumann Piano Concerto[a].
Prokofiev Piano Concerto No. 3 in C major, Op. 26[b].
Van Cliburn *pf*
Chicago Symphony Orchestra / [a]Fritz Reiner, [b]Walter Hendl.
RCA Living Stereo 09026 62691-2 (61 minutes: ADD). Recorded 1960.   Ⓜ

The outright winner of the first Tchaikovsky Competition, Van Cliburn's playing left an indelible mark and an enduring legend. Returning to these two wholly characteristic performances is to be forcibly reminded of his cardinal and unique qualities. Here, captured in RCA's magnificent remastering, is that sumptuously rich and burnished tone, that generous elasticity of phrase and rhythm, that open-hearted rhetorical splendour. Tempos, as so often with Cliburn, are expansive, allowing him an imperial breadth and majesty. Listen to the fullness and clarity he finds in Schumann's first movement *passionato* elaboration, or the way he sweeps all before him in the finale's exultant conclusion. On the other hand Cliburn's romantic generosity would probably have angered Prokofiev, whose austere performance of his own Third Concerto was bleak and angular. Yet even he would surely have marvelled at the way every note is made audible in his scintillating score. Given such superb assurance the final variation in the second movement sounds more than ever like two different forms of motion proceeding simultaneously and, all in all, both performances provide awe-inspiring evidence of Cliburn's once towering genius. In these too often lean times, when emotional aridity is often applauded highly, such magnificence is doubly rewarding.

Symphonies – No. 1 in B flat major, Op. 38, 'Spring'; No. 2 in C major, Op. 61; No. 3 in E flat major, Op. 97, 'Rhenish'; No. 4 in D minor, Op. 120.

Symphonies Nos. 1-4. Overture, Scherzo and Finale, Op. 52.
Staatskapelle Dresden / Wolfgang Sawallisch.
EMI Sawallisch Edition CMS7 64815-2 (two discs: 148 minutes: ADD). Recorded 1972.　Ⓜ 🆁🆁

Schumann's symphonies come in for a lot of criticism because of his supposed cloudy textures and unsubtle scoring, but in the hands of a conductor who is both skilful and sympathetic they are most engaging works. Sawallisch's recordings, brightly transferred, provide us with a much admired set. His style, fresh and unforced, is not as high powered as some other conductors but it is sensible, alert and very pleasing. He achieves great lightness in the First and Fourth Symphonies – there's always a sense of classical poise and control but never at the expense of the overall architecture of the pieces. The Second and Third Symphonies, larger and more far-reaching in their scope, again benefit from Sawallisch's approach. The playing of the Staatskapelle Dresden is superlative in every department, with a lovely veiled string sound and a real sense of ensemble. These are real bargains and with the *Overture, Scherzo and Finale* thrown in for good measure, definitely not to be missed.

Symphonies Nos. 1 and 2.
Bavarian Radio Symphony Orchestra / Rafael Kubelík.
Sony Classical Essential Classics SBK48269 (74 minutes: ADD). Recorded 1978-79.　Ⓑ 🆁🆁

Symphonies Nos. 3 and 4. Manfred, Op. 115 – Overture.
Bavarian Radio Symphony Orchestra / Rafael Kubelík.
Sony Classical Essential Classics SBK48270 (76 minutes: ADD). Recorded 1978-79.　Ⓑ 🆁🆁

It is difficult to understand why Kubelík's wonderful cycle failed to make an impact when it was first issued. His sensitivity to detail, his refusal to bully Schumann's vulnerable structures and his ability to penetrate occasional thickets of orchestration, make these especially memorable. Just listen to the cheeky bassoon backing clarinet, 1'44" into the *Spring* Symphony's fourth movement, the limpid phrasing of the *Rhenish* Symphony's *Nicht schnell* third movement, or the to-ing and fro-ing between first and second violins (usefully separated, as virtually always with Kubelík) in the last movement of the Second. Only the first movement of the Fourth seems a little heavy-handed, but then the poetry of the *Romanze* and the exuberance of the finale more than make amends. First movement repeats are observed and the playing throughout is rich in felicitous turns of phrase. The sound, though, is a minor stumbling block: violins are thin (one of the few disadvantages of having them separated is that their massed tone becomes mildly diluted), brass a little fuzzy and the whole production less focused than Sawallisch's set. But Kubelík's insights are too varied and meaningful to miss, and there is much pleasure to be derived from them. What with a stirring *Manfred* Overture added for good measure, they also constitute exceptional value for money.

Symphonies Nos. 1-3; No. 4 (1841 and 1851 versions); G minor, WoO29, 'Zwickauer'. Overture, Scherzo and Finale, Op. 52. Konzertstück in F major, Op. 86.
Roger Montgomery, Gavin Edwards, Susan Dent, Robert Maskell *hns*
Orchestre Révolutionnaire et Romantique / Sir John Eliot Gardiner.
Archiv Produktion 457 591-2AH3 (three discs: 202 minutes: DDD). Recorded 1996.　Ⓕ 🅿🅴

The first point to note is how much more comprehensive this is than previous cycles, even the outstanding RCA set of period performances from Roy Goodman and the Hanover Band. That offers the *Overture, Scherzo and Finale* in addition to the four numbered symphonies, but No. 4 comes in the rare first version of 1841. Gardiner offers both versions, 1841 and 1851, and his performances of them are very well geared to bringing out the contrasts. Still more fascinating is the inclusion of both the early, incomplete Symphony in G minor, and the *Konzertstück* of 1849 for four horns, with the ORR soloists breathtaking in their virtuosity in the outer movements, using horns with rotary valves crooked in F. Otherwise, except in three specified movements, natural horns are used, braying clearly through orchestration which always used to be condemned as too thick. In his note, Gardiner fairly points out the merits of the 1841 version in transparency and other qualities, suggesting, as others have, that the doublings in the later version make it safer and more commonplace. Paradoxically in performance, Gardiner is if anything even more electrifying in the later, more thickly upholstered version, as ever clarifying textures and building up to a thrilling conclusion. Even the *Zwickauer* Symphony of 1832 emerges as very distinctive of Schumann. It is, incidentally, a merit of the layout of this set on three well-filled discs that the eight works appear in chronological order.

The contrasts between Gardiner and Goodman in their approach to the numbered works are not as marked as expected, often as much a question of scale and recording quality as of interpretative differences, with Goodman's orchestra more intimate, and with the RCA sound a degree less brightly analytical. Both prefer fast speeds, with Goodman a shade more relaxed and Gardiner more incisive, pressing ahead harder, with syncopations – so important in Schumann – more sharply dramatic. One advantage that Gardiner has in his slightly bigger scale is that he brings out more light and shade, offering a wider dynamic range. Hence the solemn fourth movement of the *Rhenish* Symphony inspired by Cologne Cathedral – as with Goodman taken at a flowing speed – builds up more gradually in a bigger, far longer *crescendo*, in the end the more powerful for being held back at the start. Though the Goodman set still holds its place, Gardiner offers a conspectus of Schumann as symphonist that is all the richer and more illuminating for the inclusion of the extra rarities.

Symphonies Nos. 1-4. Manfred, Op. 115 – Overture.
Cleveland Orchestra / George Szell.
Sony Classical Masterworks Heritage MH2K62349 (two discs: 135 minutes: ADD). Recorded 1958-60.

This famous set gives us the heart of George Szell, his feeling for style, for line and for Schumann's warming but fragile symphonic structures. Szell loved the Schumann symphonies (his eloquent booklet annotation makes that abundantly clear), but readers should be warned that he attempts to correct – and here we quote the Szell himself – 'minor lapses [in orchestration] due to inexperience' with 'remedies' that range from 'subtle adjustments of dynamic marks to the radical surgery of re-orchestrating whole stretches'. More often than not, the musical results serve Schumann handsomely. Szell sometimes takes *crescendo* to imply *accelerando*, but his insistence on watertight exchanges invariably facilitates a snug fit between various instrumental choirs, the strings especially. Markings such as *Animato* (in the First Symphony's *Allegro molto vivace*) or *piano dolce* (in the same movement) are scrupulously observed, and so are most of Schumann's metronome markings. Playing standards are uncommonly high, but the close-set recordings occasionally undermine Szell's painstaking efforts to clarify Schumann's orchestration, the *Rhenish* being the worst offender (paradoxically, it is also from the most recent session).

The *Rhenish* again yields high musical dividends, with sensitively shaped central movements, but were we to single out just one track on the whole set, it would have to be the Second Symphony's *Adagio espressivo*, a performance of such warmth, nobility and elasticity (the latter not a quality normally associated with Szell) that it is tempting to grant it the accolade of 'best ever'. The *Manfred* Overture is given a wildly spontaneous performance (Szell's rostrum footwork is dramatically audible), with extreme tempos and some brilliant playing. Sometimes you may feel that Szell was being overprotective towards the music and that the same interpretations played live might have thrown caution to the wind. Still, Szell should certainly be granted equal status with his bargain stablemates Kubelík and Sawallisch. Both are perhaps marginally more spontaneous in the First and Third Symphonies, but Szell's loving exegeses underline details in the music that you won't have heard on many other recordings. Transfers and presentation are superb.

Symphony No. 2. Konzertstück in F major, Op. 86. Manfred, Op. 115 – Overture.
Philharmonia Orchestra / Christian Thielemann.
DG 453 482-2GH (76 minutes: DDD). Recorded 1996.

This programme is brilliantly designed for continuous listening. Thielemann is his own man, making no stylistic concessions to 'historically informed' performance. The disc begins with the *Manfred* Overture: its opening three chords are very smoothly delivered (they are usually incisive and strong), but they are justified by the spacious gravity and dignity of what follows. You may find this *Manfred* too ready to yield to introspective slower motion (a feature of the performance of the

Second Symphony). Then *Manfred*'s interior world is blown away by 'something quite curious' as Schumann described his *Konzertstück* for four horns and orchestra. Replace 'curious' with 'dazzling', even 'reckless', and you might gain a better idea of the piece. Here is playing of great brilliance and bravado.

We've not had a performance of the Second Symphony as satisfying since Karajan's and Sawallisch's from the early 1970s. On first hearing, one occasionally feels that Thielemann had lost his sense of proportion, principally in the *Scherzo*, whose much slower Trios can sound self-conscious. But, more often than not, a few bars further on, and the nature of the expression released by that slower tempo makes clear the reason for its choice. And in the Symphony's outer *Allegros* Thielemann always ensures enough urgent propulsion and springing energy to make workable his many slowings. Never do you feel the tension sagging as a result of a slowing; on the contrary, the contrasts invariably intensify the drama. The Symphony's *Adagio* (over 12 minutes of it; ten minutes is the average) is the disc's principal glory: a wondrously sustained and shaped *cantabile*, with the essential bass-line well defined. It might be thought a risky business recording Schumann in a church, but the microphones are close and this ample sound offers a convincing focus and proportion.

Schumann Symphony No. 4.
Schubert Symphony No. 8 in B minor, D759, 'Unfinished'.
North German Radio Symphony Orchestra / Günter Wand.
RCA Red Seal RD60826 (57 minutes: DDD). Recorded live in 1991. Ⓕ 🆁🆁

Wand's Schumann Fourth has impressive cumulative power; something the composer obviously intended with all four movements linked and sharing common themes. Wand's purposeful manner does not preclude many individual touches early in the work (the *Romanze* is darkly coloured and beautifully phrased), but as Schumann's thematic unity in continuity becomes more established, so Wand tightens his grip: the finale's introductory 'darkness to dawn', for example, is here no interpolated episode, but an amassing of energies already in the air. The sound is full, deep and natural. Wand's is a traditionally unhurried unfolding of Schubert's *Unfinished*, and one which does not exploit its troubled lyrical expanses, bar by bar, for the utmost drama. Perceptible deviations from his well maintained pulse give heightened expressiveness to crucial moments in the 'symphonic' drama, such as the fearful start of the first movement's development section, and the second movement's haunting central transition. But the quality here that is most easy to recognize, and just as impossible to analyse, is its spirituality. The live origins may help to explain this, as they do a few trifling imprecisions in the playing.

Schumann Symphony No. 4.
Schubert Symphony No. 4 in C minor, D417, 'Tragic'.
Mendelssohn Die schöne Melusine, Op. 32.
Berlin Philharmonic Orchestra / Nikolaus Harnoncourt.
Teldec 4509-94543-2 (77 minutes: DDD). Recorded live in 1995. Ⓕ

'I think of it as one of the greatest symphonic poems' Harnoncourt has said of *Die schöne Melusine*. A bold claim, but here indeed is a bold and beauteous performance. Beauty first, 'the beauty of calm waters' as Tovey described the opening: upwardly curling mother-of-pearl Berlin winds and strings. Then boldness: and here the strongly rhythmic second theme is subjected to such a dramatic *animato* that its definition may strike you as initially blurred (a momentary impression though, and the Overture as a whole benefits from Harnoncourt's tempo contrasts).

The Berliners' musical collective would appear to have had a profound (and positive) effect on Harnoncourt in the Schubert. Compare the slow movement with his Concertgebouw recording (part of a cycle: see the review under Schubert; refer to the Index to Reviews): there, the *Andante*'s relatively detached period manners are here (at a slower tempo, though still an *Andante*) transformed into a very real beauty and eloquence of phrase and expression. Very startling, if you don't know Harnoncourt's Amsterdam recording, is the removal of eight bars (from the printed editions) in the first movement's exposition, and Harnoncourt's fateful ('Tragic'?) half-tempo delivery of the finale's closing unison C chords. Dramatic delaying tactics – whether tiny hesitations, or huge fermatas – have always been a feature of Harnoncourt's conducting. Together with his insistent accentuation, sudden contrasts of dynamics, texture and tempo (for example, *Scherzo*/Trio tempos), you may feel that this Schumann Fourth (the familiar revision) sets out to contradict the symphony's apparent continuity, certainly compared to a performance like Wand's on RCA. But then, this is a performance that can catch fire spectacularly in a way that few others do, especially in the symphony's closing stages. The Berliners' playing is magnificent, and the sound is both present and spacious.

Piano Quintet in E flat major, Op. 44. Andante and Variations, Op. 46. Piano Quartet in
E flat major, Op. 47. Fantasiestücke, Op. 73. Adagio and Allegro in A flat major, Op. 70.
Märchenbilder, Op. 113. Violin Sonata No. 2 in D minor, Op. 121[a].
Marie-Luise Neunecker hn [a]**Dora Schwarzberg, Lucy Hall** vns **Nobuko Imai** va
Natalia Gutman, Mischa Maisky vcs [a]**Martha Argerich, Alexandre Rabinovitch** pf
EMI CDS5 55484-2 (two discs: 146 minutes: DDD). Recorded live in 1994.   Ⓕ

After 'one memorable day of rehearsal', as the introductory note puts it, Martha Argerich and a
group of friends recorded this generously long programme at a public concert in Holland 'with the
enthusiasm and intimate inspiration of a house-party'. The rarity is the *Andante and Variations*,
Op. 46, here brought up with all the spontaneous freshness of new discovery in a performance as
enjoyable for its self-generating continuity as its diversity. Argerich and her fellow pianist,
Rabinovitch divide keyboard responsibilities in the remainder of the programme. Her own major
triumph comes in the Quintet (with truly inspirational help from Maisky's cello). Every note tingles
with life and colour in an arrestingly imaginative reading of exemplary textural transparency. In
none of the more familiar works in the concert is that little extra stimulus of live as opposed to
studio recording combined with more finesse and finish than here. In the Quartet Rabinovitch is a
little less successful in concealing Schumann's inclination to entrust too much to his own
instrument, with some aggressive accentuation *en route*. The finale is breathlessly, albeit excitably,
fast. Rabinovitch is joined by Marie-Luise Neunecker in a hearty performance on the second disc of
the *Adagio and Allegro* for horn and piano. In the smaller pieces Argerich reaffirms herself as an
artist of 'temperament', much given to the impulse of the moment. In place of clarinet, the Op. 73
Fantasiestücke are played here with cello (Natalia Gutman), one of Schumann's two sanctioned
alternatives despite its low-lying voice. However, in the *Märchenbilder* she partners the prescribed
viola (Nobuko Imai). The recording itself is pleasingly natural. And there is heartening audience
applause, judiciously unprotracted, as a further reminder that we are at a live performance.

Piano Trios – No. 1 in D minor, Op. 63; No. 2 in F, Op. 80.
Florestan Trio (Anthony Marwood vn Richard Lester vc Susan Tomes pf).
Hyperion CDA67063 (57 minutes: DDD). Recorded 1998.   Ⓕ Ⓔ

For those who have always thought of Schumann's First Piano Trio as his finest chamber work
after the Piano Quintet, the Florestan Trio may encourage you to think again about the Second
Trio – a wonderful piece, full of poetic ideas. The artists make vigorous work of the first movement's
urgent thematic interrelations but the real surprise is the third movement, a lilting barcarolle awash
with significant counterpoint, although the heart of the Trio is surely its slow second movement –
deeply personal music. The differences in the trios are more marked than their similarities. The
Second Trio is mellow, loving and conversational, but the First is troubled, tense, even tragic – save,
perhaps, for its unexpectedly Mendelssohnian finale. The Florestan Trio realizes the music's myriad
perspectives, coaxing its arguments rather than confusing them. Marwood employs some subtle
portamento and varies his use of vibrato, whereas Susan Tomes never forces her tone. Real
teamwork, equally in evidence for the gently cantering *Scherzo* and the fine, elegiac slow movement.

Piano Trios – No. 2; No. 3 in G minor, Op. 110.
Fontenay Trio (Michael Mücke vn Niklas Schmidt vc Wolf Harden pf).
Teldec 4509-90864-2 (54 minutes: DDD). Recorded 1993.   Ⓕ

This Fontenay coupling of the Second and Third Trios has plenty to commend it in youthful verve
and vividness of characterization, particularly welcome in No. 3 in G minor, where excessive
repetition of initially arresting ideas can so easily sound merely patterned. Bigger tests come in the
more personally motivated F major work, composed exactly ten years after Schumann's clandestine
engagement to his beloved Clara, with the opening phrase of his 1840 love-song *Intermezzo* ('In the
depths of my heart I keep a radiant image of you') as the secret underlying clue. Its introduction by
the violin in the course of the first movement's development, though heartfelt, is just a little too
backward. Also worrying is the almost aggressive accentuation of the pianist (a player certainly
never backward in coming forward) in this movement's launching theme. All three artists respond
warmly to the slow movement's *Mit innigem Ausdruck*, and they honour the third movement's
slowish metronome marking rather than transforming it into a scherzo. Their relish of its quaint
coda is particularly arresting. The recording is bright albeit a bit hard.

Violin Sonatas – No. 1 in A minor, Op. 105; No. 2 in D minor, Op. 121.
Gidon Kremer vn **Martha Argerich** pf
DG 419 235-2GH (49 minutes: DDD).   Ⓕ ⓇⓇ

Schumann's two violin sonatas are late works, dating from 1851, and both were written quickly, apparently in four and six days respectively. This rapidity of composition is nowhere evident except perhaps in the vigour and enthusiasm of the music. Argerich and Kremer, both mercurial and emotionally charged performers, subtly balance the ardent Florestan and dreamily melancholic Eusebius elements of Schumann's creativity. This is even more striking in the Second Sonata, a greater work than its twin, thematically vigorous with a richness and scope that make it at once a striking as well as ideally structured work. Kremer and Argerich have established a close and exciting duo partnership and this fine recording shows what like minds can achieve in music so profoundly expressive as this.

Violin Sonatas Nos. 1 and 2; No. 3 in A minor – Intermezzo.
Ilya Kaler vn **Boris Slutsky** pf
Naxos 8 550870 (51 minutes: DDD). Recorded 1993.   Ⓢ

These performances, powerfully recorded in Indiana by these two young Russian artists, are most enjoyable. The passion of their playing is perhaps not wholly Germanic, but every artist legitimately brings something of himself to the music he performs, and nothing here takes us out of touch with Schumann's world. Indeed, there is an impressive intensity to this playing, although refinement and tenderness are rightly also present. Kaler and Slutsky mould these melodies well; it's a matter of timing as well as tone and dynamics, as the *Allegretto* of the A minor Sonata shows. The same movement also demonstrates how they follow Schumann naturally through his characteristically rapid changes of mood, while the finale that follows has power and purpose. The single movement from the composite 'FAE Sonata' dedicated to Joseph Joachim, in which Schumann collaborated with the young Brahms and Albert Dietrich, makes a useful bonus in a disc which would otherwise last under 50 minutes. The Naxos disc at super-bargain price represents fine value.

Fantasiestücke, Op. 12ᵃ – No. 1, Des Abends; No. 2, Aufschwung; No. 3, Warum?; No. 5, In der Nacht; No. 7, Traumes Wirren; No. 8, Ende von Lied. Etudes symphoniques, Opp. 13 and posthᵇ. Faschingsschwank aus Wien, Op. 26ᶜ.
Sviatoslav Richter pf
Revelation RV10012 (77 minutes: ADD). Items marked ᵃ recorded live in 1970, ᵇ1972, ᶜ1976.   Ⓜ

Here are 77 minutes of delight from Russia's recently unearthed Aladdin's Cave beginning with Schumann's Op. 12 *Fantasiestücke*, recorded in May 1970. The *Etudes symphoniques* followed in January 1972. In what is perhaps the most pianistically rather than autobiographically inspired of all the major works of Schumann's twenties, Richter reminds us in no uncertain terms of his sleight of hand. The five supplementary variations (Op. posth.) he wisely inserts as a self-contained group of exquisite youthful dreams before returning to reality in the *con gran bravura* storms of No. 6. Finally, *Faschingsschwank aus Wien*, recorded in October 1976. It is difficult to recall a more plaintive account of the 'Romanze' from anyone, achieved by simplicity within a questionably slow tempo. For the most part it is the work's teasing charm that he conveys with fingers of gossamer lightness and fleetness. Gallic rather than German Schumann, perhaps, but irresistible. Good tonal reproduction.

Fantasie in C major, Op. 17. Faschingsschwank aus Wien, Op. 26. Papillons, Op. 2.
Sviatoslav Richter pf
EMI Studio CDM7 64625-2 (67 minutes: ADD/DDD). Recorded 1961-62.   Ⓜ 🅗 🆁🆁

There can surely be no doubt as to Richter's current status as elder statesman of the piano world. And collectors now have a bewildering array of his recent, mainly live performances and reissues to choose from. Richter's Schumann is unequalled. The *Fantasia* is arguably Schumann's keyboard masterpiece. And Richter plays it better than other pianists. Nobody can phrase as beautifully as he can, or produce those marvellously soft accompaniments beneath quietly singing tunes or toss off the middle movement with such speed and brilliance. There is astonishing poetry in his playing. It almost amounts to a rediscovery of the work. And the same could be said of *Faschingsschwank aus Wien* and *Papillons*. (The way he plays the main theme of the latter should make you buy this disc if nothing else does – he seems to add stature to the work.) His assets in all of these works are, first, an unusually musical sense of phrasing. Secondly, he can reduce an accompaniment to a mere murmur without any loss of evenness so that a tune above it can sing even when it is soft. Thirdly, he uses a great deal of rubato, but always with impeccable taste; his rubato in slow passages has a mesmeric quality only partly due to the fact that he usually plays such passages much slower than other pianists. Fourthly, he has faultless technique. His superiority is apparent throughout. The recording is magnificent for its date. These are classic performances which no serious devotee of piano music should be without.

Schumann Fantasie. March in G minor, Op. 76 No. 2. Concert Studies on Caprices by Paganini, Op. 10 – No. 4 in C minor; No. 5 in B minor; No. 6 in E minor. Novellette in F major, Op. 21 No. 1. Blumenstück in D flat major, Op. 19. Vier Nachtstücke, Op. 23.
Brahms Piano Sonatas – No. 1 in C major, Op. 1; No. 2 in F sharp minor, Op. 2. Variations on a Theme by Paganini, Op. 35. Capriccio in C major, Op. 76 No. 8. Intermezzo in E minor, Op. 116 No. 5. Ballade in G minor, Op. 118 No. 3. Rhapsody in E flat major, Op. 119 No. 4.
Sviatoslav Richter *pf*
Philips 438 477-2PH3 (three discs: 184 minutes: DDD).   Ⓕ

Variable reproduction, coupled with this highly-strung artist's own unpredictability, inevitably results in ups and downs. But for the one-and-a-half discs of Schumann alone, this album can be cherished as a collector's piece. There is surely no one more finely attuned to Schumann's secret inner world. The miniatures give particular pleasure and how keenly he responds to that element of 'strangeness blended with the beautiful' (as romanticism was once defined) in the four *Nachtstücke* written with a supernatural premonition of his brother's death. All technical challenges are dissolved into the purest poetry in the three all-too-rarely heard *Concert Studies on Caprices by Paganini* and in the major work, the great Op. 17 *Fantasie*, his own emotional warmth is fortunately matched by some of the ripest sonority that we're given in this album. It's a performance which obviously comes from the deepest places of his heart.

There are memorable things too in the two early Brahms sonatas, not least the strain of nostalgic lyricism so beautifully drawn from the first movement of No. 1 in C major. The two sets of *Paganini* Variations in their turn bring bewitchingly light and delicate prestidigitation and seductively sung melody. But in burlier bravura, and notably in both excitable homecomings, there are some gaucheries and inaccuracies that would certainly not have got through in a studio recording. Of the miniatures, the intimate, elusive E minor *Intermezzo* is exquisitely phrased and shaded.

Fantasiestücke, Op. 12[a] – No. 1, Des Abends; No. 2, Aufschwung; No. 3, Warum?; No. 5, In der Nacht; No. 7, Traumes Wirren; No. 8, Ende von Lied. Humoreske in B flat major, Op. 20[a]. Novelletten, Op. 21[b] – No. 1 in F major; No. 2 in D major; No. 8 in F sharp minor.
Sviatoslav Richter *pf*
Melodiya mono 74321 29464-2 (71 minutes: ADD). Items marked [a] recorded 1956, [b]1960.   Ⓜ Ⓗ

The booklet contains an anecdote about Arthur Rubinstein hearing Richter for the first time, 'It really wasn't anything out of the ordinary. Then at some point I noticed my eyes growing moist: tears began rolling down my cheeks ...'. What produces such a reaction cannot be put into words, but it probably has to do with Richter's uncanny ability to convey a sense of inevitability. In Schumann, for instance, Richter takes characterization and virtuosity in his stride and aims at the emotional truth beyond. Impetuosity and fantasy are there, but at the structural level rather than in the detail. The simplicity of his *Humoreske* gets to the heart of the matter as unerringly as the *élan* of his *Fantasiestücke* and the tensed steel of his *Novelettes*. Decent mono sound.

Humoreske in B flat major, Op. 20. Kinderszenen, Op. 15. Kreisleriana, Op. 16.
Radu Lupu *pf*
Decca 440 496-2DH (75 minutes: DDD). Recorded 1993.   Ⓕ Ⓔ

As piano playing this disc has an aristocratic distinction reminiscent of Lipatti. As music-making it is underpinned by a totally unselfconscious kind of intuition, making you feel you are discovering the truth of the matter for the first time. It is difficult to recall a more revealing performance of Schumann's *Humoreske*. Lupu captures all the unpredictability of its swift-changing moods while at the same time imparting a sense of inevitability to the sequence as a whole. Florestan's caprice is as piquant as Eusebius's tenderness is melting. Yet there is an underlying unity in the diversity from Lupu, enhanced by most beautifully timed and shaded 'links'. Goodness knows how long this work has been in his repertory. But here it emerges with the keen edge of new love. Next, *Kinderszenen*: simplicity is its keynote. To begin with (as notably in the opening 'Von fremden Ländern und Menschen') you wonder if, in rejection of sentimentality, he might not be allowing himself enough time for wide-eyed wonderment. But you are soon won over by his limpid tonal palette and the sheer purity of his phrasing. Each piece tells its own magical little tale without the slightest trace of special pleading. Such pristine grace will never pall, however often heard. *Kreisleriana* in its turn offers rich contrasts of desperation, dedication and Hoffmannesque drollery. And except, perhaps, in the impetuous No. 7 (taken dangerously fast), it brings further reminders that we are in the presence of a master pianist – amongst so much else able to rejoice in this work's endless dialogues between left hand and right with his opulent bass and gleaming treble. Reproduction is totally faithful throughout.

Piano Sonata No. 1 in F sharp minor, Op. 11. Fantasie in C major, Op. 17.
Maurizio Pollini *pf*
DG 423 134-2GH (63 minutes: ADD). (F)

These works grew from Schumann's love and longing for his future wife Clara. Pollini's performances are superb, not least because they are so truthful to the letter of the score. By eschewing all unspecified rubato in the *Fantasie*, he reminds us that the young Schumann never wrote a more finely proportioned large-scale work; this feeling for structure, coupled with exceptional emotional intensity, confirms it as one of the greatest love-poems ever written for the piano. His richly characterized account of the Sonata is refreshingly unmannered. Certainly the familiar charges of protracted patterning in the faster flanking movements are at once dispelled by his rhythmic *élan*, his crystalline texture and his ear for colour. The CD transfer is most successful.

Piano Sonata No. 1. Fantasie in C major, Op. 17.
Leif Ove Andsnes *pf*
EMI CDC5 56414-2 (64 minutes: DDD). Recorded 1996. (F) **E**

Leif Ove Andsnes never lets us forget that Schumann was a mere 25 when writing his First Piano Sonata. His recording, with its youthful lightness of heart, is most refreshing. With fastish tempo and delectably light, scintillating fingerwork he dances through the first movement's sometimes all-too-persistent fandango rhythm, and though adopting an unspecified slower tempo for the smoother second subject maintains an unbroken continuity of flow from first note to last. The Aria sings with a spring-like wonderment and grace. And even if the tongue-in-cheek pomposity at the start of the 'Intermezzo' section is not fully relished, his lightness and clarity of texture and his rhythmic buoyancy win the day in the *Scherzo*, and yet again in the finale, which in heavier hands can so easily sound protracted. The *Fantasie* comes across with arrestingly impulsive immediacy. Andsnes's extreme contrasts of urgency and poetic musing in the first movement might be thought over-episodic, but the requested fantasy and passion are all there. The central movement is brilliantly excitable and his acute response to every passing innuendo makes the finale a truly moving human confession – albeit in a different world from Pollini's trance-like, superhuman inner calm. Apart from brief loss of refinement in the *Fantasie*'s moments of heightened fervour, the tone-quality of the recording matches the distinction of the playing.

Etudes symphoniques, Op. 13 (1852 version). Arabeske in C major, Op. 18. Davidsbündlertänze, Op. 6. Blumenstück in D flat major, Op. 19.
András Schiff *pf*
Teldec 4509-99176-2 (76 minutes: DDD). Recorded 1995. (F)

Schumann was a great re-thinker, in Schiff's opinion not always for the better in later life – hence his choice of Schumann's original (1837) conception of the *Davidsbündlertänze* rather than its more usually heard 1851 revision. Except for a touch of mischief (subsequently removed) at the end of No. 9, textual differences are slight. But Schiff prefers the fewer repeat markings in the first edition, so that ideas never lose their freshness. More importantly, the exceptional immediacy and vividness of his characterization reminds us that initially Schumann signed nearly all of these 18 'bridal thoughts' with an F (the impetuous Florestan) or an E (the introspective, visionary Eusebius) – or sometimes both – as well as including literary inscriptions (and one or two more colourful expression marks) as a clue to the mood of the moment. Schiff laughs and teases, storms and yearns, as if the hopes and dreams of the youthful Robert, forbidden all contact with his distant beloved, were wholly his own – there and then. The impatient Florestan fares particularly well. For the much metamorphosed *Etudes symphoniques* Schiff chooses the generally used late version of 1852 with its admirably tautened finale. Here, his bold, firmly contoured approach reaffirms it as the most magisterially 'classical' work the young Schumann ever wrote. Schiff emphasizes its continuity and unity as a whole. Even the five so-called supplementary variations emerge as more purposeful, less ruminative, than often heard. These Schiff wisely offers as a completely independent group at the end. The recital is completed by the *Arabeske* and *Blumenstück*, again played with a very strong sense of direction, even if Schiff is not yet Richter's equal in disguising the repetitiveness of the latter. Nothing but praise for the naturalness of the reproduction.

Etudes symphoniques, Op. 13. Carnaval, Op. 9. Kreisleriana, Op. 16. Papillons, Op. 2. Kinderszenen, Op. 15. Davidsbündlertänze, Op. 6. Fantasiestücke, Op. 12 – No. 1, Des Abends. Waldszenen, Op. 82 – No. 7, Vogel als Prophet.
Alfred Cortot *pf*
Music & Arts mono CD-858 (two discs: 131 minutes: ADD). Recorded 1928-48. (F) **H**

It is good to have this Music & Arts sharply focused issue of Cortot's evergreen, ever-fresh performances on a well-presented two-CD set. These recordings have been reissued many times before. How many artists, today, one wonders, could hope to garner such tribute? So here, again, is that magically floated *cantabile* tugging at the heart-strings in 'Des Abends' (how one longs for the rest of the cycle) yet maintained with the flawless line and impetus of a great singer. In the *Davidsbündlertänze*, one of Cortot's most poetically potent if battle-scarred recordings, his confusion in Florestan's *schneller* in No. 3 or in the vaulting leaps of No. 12 is, perhaps, not quite what the composer had in mind in his instruction, *Mit Humor*. Yet who can resist his *dolce cantando* in No. 14, the gem of his Schumann, alive with a rich polyphonic pianistic tradition that Alfred Brendel so sadly claims has virtually vanished from the music scene. In *Kinderszenen* the 'poet' of the epilogue is at once Schumann and Cortot, creator and re-creator, and in the *Etudes symphoniques* the gold-dust scattering of the posthumous studies throughout the main work is done with such passion and inwardness that only a Beckmesser could possibly object. Playing like this seems light years away from today's style or standard. But *pace* Cortot, his idiosyncrasy, his pell-mell virtuosity and poetic ecstasy may strike a foreign and even alien note in our more puritan times yet, as Yvonne Lefebure so eloquently put it, 'even his wrong notes were those of a god'.

Theme and Variations on the name 'Abegg', Op. 1. Fantasie in C major, Op. 17. Faschingsschwank aus Wien, Op. 26.
Vladimir Ashkenazy *pf*
Decca 443 322-2DH (58 minutes: DDD). Recorded 1991.   Ⓕ

The *Fantasie* in C is the centrepiece of this issue. Ashkenazy plays with a strong and consistently sustained sense of direction, as if trying to emphasize the continuity and coherence of the argument no less than the music's passion. It is an urgently committed, full-bodied performance and needless to say his command of the keyboard is superb, not least in the central march with its recklessly fast coda. It could well have been in response to Clara's plea for something less searching, something more brilliant and easily understood by the general public, that Schumann came up with the *Faschingsschwank aus Wien*. Ashkenazy gives a spirited enough performance to justify his resort to a considerably swifter tempo than prescribed for the three fast movements. The Decca recording is pleasingly warm and true.

Allegro in B minor, Op. 8. Novelletten, Op. 21. Drei Fantasiestücke, Op. 111. Gesänge der Frühe, Op. 133.
Ronald Brautigam *pf*
Olympia OCD436 (79 minutes: DDD). Recorded 1993.   Ⓕ

The note reminds us that even the eight *Novelletten* chosen as the centrepiece here are not often heard in sequence as a set. Brautigam prefaces them with the early (1831-32) B minor *Allegro* originally intended as the first movement of a sonata. They are followed by the last two suites Schumann ever wrote for the piano – the *Gesänge der Frühe* only a year before his final breakdown. Most enjoyable is Brautigam's vitality – vitality of imagination no less than of fingers. You are immediately gripped by his plunge into the Op. 8 *Allegro*, with its arresting octave 'motto'. His mercurial fancy and ear for hidden melodic strands in the ensuing stream certainly makes nonsense of hasty dismissal of this work as mere old-style virtuoso note-spinning. Moreover, such is his unflagging impulse in the eight *Novelletten* that never for a moment are you tempted to accuse Schumann of over-repetitively patterned figuration. Potently characterized and contrasted as are the three *Fantasiestücke*, Op. 111 of 1851, Brautigam leaves you in no doubt as to their unity as a set – as he does again, still more subtly and movingly, in the more elusive spiritual world of the five *Gesänge der Frühe*. The bright, clear tonal reproduction is acceptable enough.

Davidsbündlertänze, Op. 6. Fantasiestücke, Op. 12.
Benjamin Frith *pf*
Naxos 8 550493 (63 minutes: DDD). Recorded 1991.   Ⓢ

The young prize-winning British pianist Benjamin Frith indulges the *Davidsbündlertänze*'s caprice, highlighting the contrasts between fast and slower pieces, and summoning his excellent technique for some exciting pianism. But then contrast lies at the very heart of Schumann's inspiration. Frith favours impulse over refinement, and isn't afraid to throw caution to the winds, if the mood dictates. His *Fantasiestücke*, too, are forthright and outspoken, although 'Des Abends', 'Warum' and 'Ende vom Lied' each contain plenty of poetry. Naxos's recording is excellent. Certainly recommended, not only for the budget-conscious collector, but for those who enjoy youthful pianistic exuberance.

Drei Gedichte, Op. 30. Sechs Gedichte, Op. 36. Fünf Lieder, Op. 40. Romanzen und Balladen,
Opp. 45, 49 and 53. Belsazar, Op. 57. Der Handschuh, Op. 87.
Olaf Bär bar **Helmut Deutsch** pf
EMI CDC5 56199-2 (72 minutes: DDD). Texts and translations included. Recorded 1996. Ⓕ

'Die beiden Grenadiere' apart, Schumann's ballads crop up too rarely in recital and on disc. All the
more welcome, then, are Olaf Bär's bold and perceptive readings of some of the finest of them. In
Op. 45 he graphically realizes the *grand guignol* of 'Der Schatzgräber' ('The treasure-seeker'), with
Helmut Deutsch relishing the onomatopoeic keyboard part. Equally compelling is the neglected
chivalric ballad, *Der Handschuh* ('The glove'): making vivid use, as ever, of his consonants, Bär slyly
mocks the pomposity of the royal retinue in the opening recitative, savours Schumann's lion and
tiger imitations (gleefully abetted by Deutsch) and catches to perfection the simpering, wheedling
Lady Kunigunde. Scarcely better known than these ballads are the three Geibel settings, Op. 30,
and the six songs, Op. 36 to homely, faded verses by Robert Reinick. Bär is virile and incisive in the
alfresco cheerfulness of 'Der Knabe mit dem Wunderhorn' and the macho bravado of 'Der
Hidalgo', with its swaggering bolero rhythms.

Bär's freshness and unsentimental tenderness are very well suited to the relatively modest songs
of Op. 36. And he and Deutsch respond sharply to the character sketches of Op. 40, from the
shy delicacy of 'Märzveilchen' ('March violets') through the sinister, twilit 'Muttertraum' to the
aching intensity of 'Der Soldat' and the desperation behind the wedding merriment in 'Der
Spielmann'. These days Bär's softer singing can sometimes be a shade breathy and unfocused,
with high notes not quite integrated into the line; nor is his *legato* always seamless. Random
comparison with Dietrich Fischer-Dieskau also finds the older baritone predictably wider in
his emotional and coloristic range, freer and more fluid in his phrasing and often more subtle
in his individual insights. But the more open, direct Bär is invariably a sympathetic singer and an
involving and, in the ballads, vividly dramatic interpreter. He and the ever-attentive Deutsch
certainly make a persuasive case for these less favoured products of Schumann's great song
year of 1840.

Frauenliebe und -leben, Op. 42. Gesänge, Op. 31 – No. 1, Die Löwenbraut; No. 2,
Die Kartenlegerin. Gedichte, Op. 35 – No. 1, Lust der Sturmnacht; No. 8, Stille Liebe. Rose, Meer
und Sonne, Op. 37 No. 9. Fünf Lieder, Op. 40. Der Schatzgräber, Op. 45 No. 1. Volksliedchen,
Op. 51 No. 2. Die Soldatenbraut, Op. 64 No. 1. Lieder-Album für die Jugend, Op. 79 – No. 5,
Vom Schlaraffenland; No. 22, Des Sennen Abscheid; No. 26, Schneeglöcken. Mein schöner
Stern!, Op. 101 No. 4. Abendlied, Op. 107 No. 6. Die Meerfee, Op. 125 No. 1. Dein Angesicht,
Op. 127 No. 2.
Anne Sofie von Otter mez **Bengt Forsberg** pf
DG 445 881-2GH (79 minutes: DDD). Texts and translations included. Recorded 1993. Ⓕ Ⓔ

This is one of those records where the promise of something exceptional in the first phrases is
fully borne out by all that follows. The *Frauenliebe* cycle is sung by a character, as vividly defined
as any Fiordiligi, Senta or Mimì in opera. Von Otter is one of those rare artists who can adapt
the voice and yet be true to its natural identity. In these songs of Schumann (not only in the
Frauenliebe) she seems, unselfconsciously, to find a new voice-personality for each and still to
confine herself to what lies naturally within her scope, forcing nothing and falsifying nothing.
The woman of the 'life and love' starts out as a girl. 'Seit ich ihn gesehen' has a shy, private
rapture which then grows bold for 'Er, der Herrlichste von allen', frank in its enthusiasm,
buoyant in the spirit of its rhythm, radiant as the voice rises to its highest notes. 'Ich kann's nicht
fassen, nicht glauben' is fully outgoing, an expression of utter commitment, and the smile is
always in the voice. The engagement-ring induces maturity, the girl now a woman. The wedding-
day preparations, confiding of motherhood, dandling the baby, and then the emptiness of life
at the husband's death: all are caught as in reality and in character. It is a completely absorbed
and absorbing performance.

The generous selection of songs which follows works its spell partly by contrasts. The pastoral
sweetness of 'Des Sennen Abschied' gives way to a grim, predatory ferocity of utterance in 'Der
Schatzgräber', and the big Brahmsy sweep of 'Lust der Sturmnacht' throws into relief the wistfully
tender mood of 'Dein Angesicht'. In these and in all else von Otter lights upon the right tone, and
the right shades of that tone. The programme is well planned, too, rounded off with 'Rose, Meer
und Sonne', sketching the melodies of *Frauenliebe und -leben* with which the recital began.
Occasionally the piano is recorded too heavily or too prominently for the voice. But generally the
sympathy and unanimity of singer and pianist are all that could be desired – as is the recital *in toto*.
No comparisons: it doesn't matter how much of Schumann you already have on the shelves, this
will still be a prized addition.

Liederkreis, Op. 24. Dichterliebe, Op. 48. Belsatzar, Op. 57. Abends am Strand, Op. 45 No. 3.
Die beiden Grenadiere, Op. 49 No. 1. Lieder und Gesänge, Op. 127 – No. 2, Dein Angesicht;
No. 3, Es leuchtet meine Liebe. Vier Gesänge, Op. 142 – No. 2, Lehn deine Wang; No. 4,
Mein Wagen rollet langsam.
Ian Bostridge ten **Julius Drake** pf
EMI CDC5 56575-2 (69 minutes: DDD). Texts and translations included. Recorded 1997.
Gramophone Award Winner 1998.　　　　　　　　　　　　　　　　　　　　　　Ⓕ E RR

Bostridge makes one think anew about the music in hand, interpreting all these songs as much
through the mind of the poet as that of the composer and, being youthful himself, getting inside the
head of the vulnerable poet in his many moods. That, quite apart from his obvious gifts as a singer
and musician, is what raises Bostridge above most of his contemporaries who so often fail to live
the words they are singing. Every one of the magnificent Op. 24 songs has some moment of
illumination, whether it's the terror conveyed so immediately – and immediacy of reaction is of the
essence all-round here – in 'Schöne Wiege', the breathtaking beauty and sorrow of 'Anfang wollt
ich' or the breadth and intensity of 'Mit Myrten und Rosen'. In between the two cycles comes a
group of the 1840 Leipzig settings that adumbrates every aspect of Bostridge's – and his equally
perceptive partner's – attributes. The vivid word-painting in *Belsatzar* brings the Old Testament
scene arrestingly before us. The inward fantasy of *Abends am Strand* is keenly evoked with an
appropriately raw touch on the word 'Schrein' ('howl'). Then there's the unexpected heroic touch
the tenor brings to *Die beiden Grenadiere*, where Drake's imaginative contribution helps to paint the
patriotic picture. Perhaps best of all is the unjustly neglected *Es leuchtet meine Liebe*, a melodrama
here perfectly enacted by both performers. *Mein Wagen rollet langsam* forms a perfect introduction,
in its lyrical freedom, to *Dichterliebe*, an interpretation to rank with the best available in terms of
the sheer beauty of the singing and acute response to its sustained inspiration. Listen to the wonder
brought to the discovery of the flowers and angels in 'Im Rhein', the contained anger of 'Ich grolle
nicht', the sense of bereavement in 'Hör ist das Liedchen' and you will judge this is an
interpretation of profundity and emotional identification, the whole cycle crowned by the sensitivity
of Drake's playing of the summarizing postlude. To complete one's pleasure EMI has provided an
exemplary and forward recording balance.

Schumann Dichterliebe, Op. 48.
Mendelssohn Lieder, Op. 19a – No. 4, Neue Liebe; No. 5, Gruss. Lieder, Op. 34 – No. 2, Auf
Flügeln des Gesanges; No. 6, Reiselied. Morgengruss, Op. 47 No. 2. Allnächtlich im Träume,
Op. 86 No. 4.
Schubert Schwanengesang, D957 – Der Atlas; Ihr Bild; Das Fischermädchen; Die Stadt;
Am Meer; Der Doppelgänger.
Christoph Prégardien ten **Andreas Staier** fp
Deutsche Harmonia Mundi 05472 77319-2 (57 minutes: DDD). Texts and translations included.
Recorded 1993.　　　　　　　　　　　　　　　　　　　　　　　　　　　　　　　　Ⓕ P

In their deeply poignant reading of *Dichterliebe,* these artists expose the wounded pain of the
protagonist, and the participation of a fortepiano gives the performance an intimacy that a grand
piano cannot match. The simple beauty of the singing in the early songs is rightly countermanded
by the darker, more dramatic tone and manner in 'Im Rhein' and 'Ich grolle nicht', with the top A
on 'Herzen' piercing to the heart. These in turn give way to the plaintive sorrow of 'Und wüssten's
die Blumen', the *Innigkeit* of 'Hör ich das Liedchen', the delicately etched line and feeling of 'Am
leuchtenden Sommermorgen', and the numbed emptiness, of 'Ich hab im Traum geweinet'. The
draining of all passion is summed up in the repeated final line of the penultimate song, 'Zerfliesst
wie alte Schaum', with the fortepiano's afterthought so translucently played by Staier, whose
postlude to the whole cycle, restrained and understated though it is, speaks volumes of the sadness
experienced throughout. The truthfulness of the interpretation is seconded by the tenor's command
of line and phrase, the player's close rapport with his partner. This intelligently planned programme
then offers more Heine in the shape of settings by Mendelssohn and Schubert. The less demanding
Mendelssohn group allows an emotional respite between the soulful Schumann and the searing
Schubert. From *Schwanengesang,* that extraordinary pair of anguished songs, 'Ihr Bild' and 'Die
Stadt', are given their full measure of grief, with a gentle, rather fast 'Das Fischermädchen' in
between. Prégardien's silver-voiced sorrowing and communing in 'Am Meer' is just right, the verbal
accents present but never overdone. And so on to that Everest of a song, 'Der Doppelgänger',
a stark, nerve-tingling interpretation that is a fitting climax to a superb recital, faultlessly recorded.

Liederkreis, Op. 24. Dichterliebe, Op. 48.
Matthias Goerne bar **Vladimir Ashkenazy** pf
Decca 458 265-2DH (50 minutes: DDD). Texts and translations included. Recorded 1997.　Ⓕ E

Matthias Goerne is with little doubt the most probing male Lieder singer to emerge from Germany in recent years, an artist of extraordinary magnetism both in his live performances and on disc. With his dark, velvet timbre, intense *legato* line and searching response to the fluctuating shades of Heine's bittersweet verses, Goerne gives mesmeric readings of both *Dichterliebe* and the Op. 24 *Liederkreis*. Partly because of the colour of his voice, partly because of some unusually broad tempos, both cycles emerge as more sombre and haunted than in the comparably fine recordings by Wolfgang Holzmair and Ian Bostridge. The fourth song of the *Liederkreis*, 'Lieb Liebchen', seems suffused with genuine death-weariness – barely a hint here of wryness or irony. In the following 'Schöne Wiege meiner Leiden', Goerne captures the feverishness of Heine's original which Schumann's lulling, nostalgic melody tends to mitigate; later in the song the lover's tottering reason and death-longing are chillingly realized. In the first two songs of *Dichterliebe* Goerne underlines the sense of sorrow and regret with which Schumann shadows Heine's limpid love lyrics. And this sets the tone for a brooding, intensely inward reading, flaring into self-lacerating bitterness in 'Ich grolle nicht' and 'Das ist ein Flöten und Geigen', hardening into an iron stoicism in the closing song, before the overwhelming sense of longing and loss in the last line. Throughout, Ashkenazy is a positive, sympathetic partner, though here and there his sharply etched playing can be overassertive. If some may understandably prefer a higher, lighter voice in these cycles, Goerne is the equal of both Holzmair and Bostridge in interpretative insight and tonal beauty, and ventures a more daring range of expression than either.

Liederkreis, Op. 24. Myrthen, Op. 25 – No. 7, Die Lotosblume; No. 21, Was will die einsame Träne?; No. 24, Du bist wie eine Blume. Romanzen und Balladen – Op. 45: No. 3, Abends am Strand; Op. 49: No. 1, Die beiden Grenadiere; No. 2, Die feindlichen Brüder; Op. 53: No. 3, Der arme Peter; Op. 64: No. 3, Tragödie. Belsatzar, Op. 57. Lieder und Gesänge, Op. 127 – No. 2, Dein Angesicht; No. 3, Es leuchtet meine Liebe. Gesänge, Op. 142 – No. 2, Lehn deine Wang; No. 4, Mein Wagen rollet langsam.
Stephan Genz bar **Christoph Genz** ten **Claar ter Horst** pf
Claves CD50-9708 (59 minutes: DDD). Texts and translations included. Recorded 1996-97.　　Ⓕ

This is a recital of promise and fulfilment. Stephan Genz's voice and style are as wide-ranging as his mode of expression. He lives every moment of Op. 24, entering into all aspects of Schumann's settings and Heine's originals yet never overstepping the mark in his verbal painting. The other Heine settings receive no less than their due. The sensuous and plaintive qualities in Genz's tone are well suited to the three Heine poems in *Myrthen*. In contrast he rises to the histrionic challenges of *Die beiden Grenadiere, Belsatzar* and the rarely encountered *Die feindlichen Brüder*, performances that are felt as immediately as if at the moment of composition. In *Abends am Strand* the voice follows to the full the song's romantic import. In the third song of Op. 64, *Tragödie*, the baritone is joined by his talented tenor brother: their voices naturally blend well. Finally, Genz is inspired by that amazingly original song, *Mein Wagen rollet langsam*, to give of his absolute best. Here, as throughout, Claar ter Horst matches the perceptions of her partner, and both are caught in an amenable acoustic.

Liederkreis, Op. 39. Frauenliebe und -leben, Op. 42.
Soile Isokoski sop **Marita Viitasalo** pf
Finlandia 0630-10924-2 (49 minutes: DDD). Texts and translations included. Recorded 1993-95.Ⓕ

This interpretation from this young Finnish soprano can stand comparison with the best. In her wonderfully straightforward and musical performance, she marries a sincere spontaneity with a warming sense of line and phrase, a style well learnt yet put to her own, positive purpose. Before you is the rapturous bride-to-be in all her moods, then the young woman struck almost dumb by unexpected grief. Nothing in her portrayal is forced or in the least contrived yet everything, felt from the heart, goes to it. And the voice itself? Well, reminders of Flagstad's richness, Ameling's naturalness and Price's precision are here to be heard and enjoyed. She is just as imaginative in Op. 39 as in Op. 42, giving a very central, unaffected account of the *Liederkreis* encompassing all its varied moods and one that makes its points unobtrusively and, as with Op. 42, with the emphasis on long-breathed phrasing and rock-steady tone. The partnership with Viitasalo is obviously a fruitful one. The two artists think and 'breathe' alike though in Op. 42 he is just occasionally too prominent, at least as recorded.

Complete Lieder, Volume 1. Das verlassene Mägdlein, Op. 64 No. 2. Melancholie, Op. 74 No. 6. Aufträge, Op. 77 No. 5. Op. 79 – No. 7a, Zigeunerliedchen I; No. 7b, Zigeunerliedchen II; No. 23, Er ist's!. Die Blume der Ergebung, Op. 83 No. 2. Röslein, Röslein!, Op. 89 No. 6. Sechs Gedichte und Requiem, Op. 90. Op. 96 – No. 1, Nachtlied; No. 3 Ihre Stimme. Lieder und Gesänge aus Wilhelm Meister, Op. 98a – No. 1, Kennst du das Land?; No. 3, Nur wer die Sehnsucht kennt;

No. 5, Heiss' mich nicht reden; No. 7, Singet nicht in Trauertönen; No. 9, So lasst mich scheinen. Sechs Gesänge, Op. 107. Warnung, Op. 119 No. 2. Die Meerfee, Op. 125 No. 1. Sängers Trost, Op. 127 No. 1. Mädchen-Schwermut, Op. 142 No. 3.
Christine Schäfer sop **Graham Johnson** pf
Hyperion CDJ33101 (75 minutes: DDD). Texts and translations included. Recorded 1995.
Gramophone Award Winner 1997.   Ⓕ

This disc launches Hyperion's Schumann Lieder project as auspiciously as Dame Janet Baker's recital opened their Complete Schubert Edition. As ever, Graham Johnson shows an unerring gift for matching singer and song. These are almost all late pieces, written between 1849 and 1852 under the shadow of depression and sickness; and their intense chromaticism can all too easily seem tortuous. However, imaginatively supported by Johnson, Christine Schäfer illuminates each of these songs with her pure, lucent timbre, her grace and breadth of phrase and her unselfconscious feeling for verbal meaning and nuance. The voice is an expressive, flexible lyric-coloratura; she can spin a scrupulously even *legato*, integrates the high notes of, say, 'Er ist's' perfectly within the melodic line, and has the breath control to sustain the long phrases of 'Requiem' with apparent ease. Aided by Johnson's lucid textures and uncommonly subtle feel for rubato and harmonic direction, Schäfer avoids any hint of mawkishness in songs like 'Meine Rose', Op. 90 No. 2, 'Mädchen-Schwermut' and 'Abendlied'. Several songs here have been overshadowed or totally eclipsed by the settings by Schubert, Wolf or Brahms, and Schäfer and Johnson do much to rehabilitate them.

Schäfer brings an exquisite wondering stillness to the Goethe 'Nachtlied', more disturbed and earthbound than Schubert's sublime setting, but here, at least, scarcely less poignant. She also has the dramatic flair to bring off the difficult Mignon songs, especially the volatile, quasi-operatic 'Heiss' mich nicht reden' and 'Kennst du das Land', where the final verse, evoking Mignon's terrifying passage across the Alps, builds to a climax of desperate, almost demented yearning. At the other end of the emotional spectrum, Schäfer brings a guileful, knowing touch to the first of the *Zigeunerliedchen*; the Mendelssohnian 'Die Meerfee' glistens and glances and 'Aufträge' has a winning eagerness and charm, with a delicious sense of flirtation between voice and keyboard. In sum, a delectable, often revelatory recital. The recording is natural and well balanced, while Graham Johnson's typically searching commentaries complement the performances perfectly.

Complete Lieder, Volume 2. Drei Gedichte, Op. 30. Die Löwenbraut, Op. 31 No. 1. 12 Gedichte, Op. 35. Lieder und Gesänge aus Wilhelm Meister, Op. 98a – No. 2, Ballade des Harfners; No. 4, Wer nie sein Brot mit Tränen ass; No. 6, Wer sich der Einsamkeit ergibt; No. 8, An die Türen will ich schleichen. Vier Husarenlieder, Op. 117.
Simon Keenlyside bar **Graham Johnson** pf
Hyperion CDJ33102 (70 minutes: DDD). Texts and translations included. Recorded 1997.   Ⓕ ▣

In his notes Graham Johnson says that what we have always lacked is a convincing way of performing late Schumann songs, often spare in texture and elusive in style. Well, he and Keenlyside seem to have found one here in their wholly admirable versions of the very different Opp. 98a and 117. The Op. 98a settings of the Harper's outpourings from *Wilhelm Meister* have always stood in the shade of those by Schubert and Wolf. This pair show incontrovertibly that there's much to be said for Schumann's versions, capturing the essence of the old man's sad musings, as set by the composer in a typically free and imaginative way, alert to every nuance in the texts. The extroverted Lenau *Husarenlieder* could hardly be more different. Keenlyside identifies in turn with the bravado of the first, the cynicism of the second, and the eerie, death-dominated mood of the fourth. The third, as Johnson avers, is a bit of a dud. Then it's back to the miracle year of 1840 for three seldom-heard Geibel *Knabenhorn* settings, Op. 30. The pair enter into the open-hearted mood called for by these songs, most of all in the irresistible 'Der Hidalgo'. Keenlyside is just as forthright in the ballad *Die Löwenbraut* and in those of Op. 35, the well-known Kerner settings, which display Schumann's Florestan side, and he brings impressive control to the Eusebius ones, not least the all-enveloping 'Stille Tränen'. The interpretation of this quasi-cycle is convincing and unerringly paced. The recording and Johnson's persuasive playing are, as usual, of the highest standard.

Manfred – Incidental Music, Op. 115 (arr. Beecham).
Gertrud Holt sop **Claire Duchesneau** mez **Glyndwr Davies, Ian Billington** tens **Niven Miller** bar **Laidman Browne, Jill Balcon, Raf de la Torre, David Enders** spkrs
BBC Chorus; Royal Philharmonic Orchestra / Sir Thomas Beecham.
Sir Thomas Beecham Trust mono BEECHAM4 (78 minutes: ADD). Recorded 1954-56.   Ⓜ Ⓗ

Schumann was haunted by Byron's autobiographically-inspired dramatic poem, *Manfred*, from a very early age. When eventually writing his incidental music for it (15 numbers and an overture) in 1848-49 he confessed to never having devoted himself to any composition before 'with such lavish love and power'. No one in this country has ever done more for it than Sir Thomas Beecham, who even staged it at the Theatre Royal, Drury Lane, London, way back in 1918, some 36 years before reviving it for the BBC and at the Festival Hall in performances leading to this now legendary recording. Score-followers will at once note Beecham's appropriation and scoring of two of the composer's roughly contemporaneous keyboard miniatures as additional background music for the guilt-wracked, soliloquizing Manfred. But their choice and placing is so apt that even Schumann himself might have been grateful. By present-day standards Laidman Browne might be thought a shade too overtly emotional in the title-role. But speakers (including a splendidly awesome Witch of the Alps and rustic chamois-hunter), like singers, orchestra and the magnetic Sir Thomas himself, are all at one in vividness of atmospheric evocation. Splendid remastering also plays its part in making this medium-priced disc a collector's piece.

Das Paradies und die Peri, Op. 50ª. Overture, Scherzo and Finale, Op. 52.
Julie Faulkner, Heidi Grant Murphy sops **Florence Quivar, Elisabeth Wilke** contrs
Keith Lewis, Robert Swensen tens **Robert Hale** bass-bar
Dresden State Opera Chorus; Staatskapelle Dresden / Giuseppe Sinopoli.
DG 445 875-2GH2 (two discs: 112 minutes: DDD). Text and translation included.　　　Ⓕ
Item marked ª recorded live in 1994.

How gratified Schumann would be at today's great new interest in his larger-scale choral works, not least the first, *Das Paradies und die Peri*, of which he was justifiably so proud. It was Armin Jordan and his Swiss forces who first introduced it to the British CD catalogue, a *Gramophone* Record Award-winning Erato issue, sadly now deleted. However, Schumann lovers still have several versions from which to choose, all of them, in different ways, sufficiently characterful to win the work new friends. This one, a full-bodied, forwardly reproduced recording in Dresden's Semperoper, has the throb of a live event – plus one or two minor imperfections of ensemble and of balance that might have prompted re-takes in a studio. Julie Faulkner is a pleasing Peri, touching in this fallen angel's pathos, and in triumph soaring effortlessly over choir and orchestra. There is very much to enjoy from the mellifluous Keith Lewis, a tellingly expressive yet never over-operatic tenor narrator. And the lyrical warmth of Robert Hale as the penitent sinner (and the baritone soloist in 'Jetzt sank des Abends goldner Schein') removes all danger of the unctuous or lugubrious in Part 3. Florence Quivar's compassionate Angel is slightly marred by obtrusive vibrato. All supporting soloists are good. The Dresden choir responds well to heartier challenges – as also to the hushed holiness of 'O heilge Tränen' near the end. Sinopoli and his orchestra are rarely the equal of Jordan and the Suisse Romande Orchestra in subtlety of shading and phrasing. But response is generously open-hearted. The second disc includes an infrequently heard extra – here, Schumann's Op. 52, which, because of the lack of a slow movement, he declined to call a symphony. Perhaps more could have been done to disguise the *Scherzo*'s repetitive patterning. But the outer movements are full of spirit.

Der Rose Pilgerfahrt, Op. 112.
Inga Nielsen, Helle Hinz sops **Annemarie Møller, Elizabeth Halling** mezzos
Deon van der Walt ten **Guido Päevatalu** bar **Christian Christiansen** bass
Danish National Radio Choir and Symphony Orchestra / Gustav Kuhn.
Chandos CHAN9350 (62 minutes: DDD). Text included. Recorded 1993.　　　Ⓕ

Amidst today's great upsurgence of interest in Schumann's later choral undertakings, the work's long neglect is no doubt due to its all-too-naive tale of a rose who, after an eagerly sought transformation into a maiden to experience human love, chooses to sacrifice herself for her baby. Schumann's own ready response to Moritz Horn's poem can best be explained by its underlying moral message together with a strain of German rusticity then equally close to the composer's heart. Having said that, how grateful Schumann lovers should be to Chandos for at last introducing the work to the English catalogue in so sympathetic yet discreet a performance from this predominantly Danish cast. All credit to the conductor, Gustav Kuhn, for revealing so much fancy in fairyland, so much brio in peasant merriment, and so much charm in more tender lyricism without ever making heavy weather of this essentially *gemütlich* little score. No praise can be too high for the Danish National Radio Choir: such immediacy of response leaves you in no doubt as to their professional status. Nor do the soloists or orchestra disappoint. Tonal reproduction is agreeably natural.

Der Rose Pilgerfahrt. Nachtlied, Op. 108.
Camilla Nylund, Anke Hoffmann, Simone Kermes sops **Claudia Schubert** contr
Rainer Trost ten **Jochen Kupfer, Andreas Schmidt** bars **Chorus Musicus;**
Das Neue Orchester / Christoph Spering.
Opus 111 OPS30-190 (69 minutes: DDD). Text and translation included. Recorded 1996.　　ⒻⓅ

This charming little choral work is best described as a musical fairy-tale for the young at heart. Spering's version has the special interest of using chamber-like forces, with 'period' wind and brass, to reveal new subtleties of balance and colour in this composer's often unjustly criticized orchestration. The pleasing solo voices are tellingly contrasted and the lyrical eloquence of the narrator, Rainer Trost, deserves special mention; likewise the supersensitive response, whether as elves, peasants or angels, of the chorus. The overriding reason for recommending this disc rather than the Chandos set (above) is its inclusion of the rarely heard *Nachtlied*. Inspired by a Hebbel poem, Schumann conveys the onset of night and the wonder of the nocturnal sky in a magnificent arch of arrestingly scored sound, before subsiding into sleep that 'comes softly as a nurse towards a child'. Lasting barely nine minutes, it surely ranks among Schumann's masterpieces – or so this finely shaped and deeply felt, mellow-toned performance persuades you.

Szenen aus Goethes Faust.
Karita Mattila, Barbara Bonney, Brigitte Poschner-Klebel, Susan Graham *sops*
Iris Vermillion *mez* **Endrik Wottrich, Hans-Peter Blochwitz** *tens* **Bryn Terfel** *bass-bar*
Jan-Hendrik Rootering, Harry Peeters *basses*
Tölz Boys' Choir; Swedish Radio Chorus; Berlin Philharmonic Orchestra / Claudio Abbado.
Sony Classical S2K66308 (two discs: 115 minutes: DDD). Notes, text and translation included.
Recorded live in 1994.   Ⓕ

No one before Schumann had ever attempted to set Goethe's mystical closing scene, which he finished in time for the Goethe centenary in 1849. What eventually emerged as his own Parts 1 and 2 (in turn portraits of Gretchen and the by now repentant Faust) followed later, after his move from a Mendelssohn-dominated Leipzig to a Wagner-ruled Dresden, hence the striking difference in style. Nothing Schumann ever wrote is more dramatic than Faust's blinding and death in the course of Part 2. The Berlin Philharmonic is very forwardly recorded – occasionally perhaps a little too much so for certain voices. But never in the case of Bryn Terfel in the title-role. Any advance fears that he might disappoint were immediately banished not only by the generosity and flow of his warm, round tone but also the total commitment and conviction of his characterization. Moreover as Dr Marianus in Part 3 he offers some wonderfully sustained *mezza* and *sotto voce*. Karita Mattila's Gretchen is always sympathetically pure-toned, clean-lined and assured. At times, as positioned, the other male soloists seem a little outweighed by the orchestra. No praise can be too high for the Four Grey Sisters (so tellingly contrasted in vocal colour) led by Barbara Bonney: their midnight encounter with Faust and his eventual blinding is brilliantly done. And there is splendidly characterful choral singing throughout from both adult and youthful choirs. In the more operatically conceived Parts 1 and 2 and the visionary Part 3, Abbado himself takes the music to heart and what he draws from his orchestra makes nonsense of the charge that Schumann was an inept scorer. This is worth every penny of its full-price.

Genoveva.
Ruth Ziesak *sop* Genoveva; **Deon van der Walt** *ten* Golo; **Rodney Gilfry** *bar* Hidulfus;
Oliver Widmer *bar* Siegfried; **Marjana Lipovšek** *mez* Margaretha; **Thomas Quasthoff** *bar* Drago;
Hiroyuki Ijichi *bass* Balthasar; **Josef Krenmair** *bar* Caspar;
Arnold Schoenberg Choir; Chamber Orchestra of Europe / Nikolaus Harnoncourt.
Teldec 0630-13144-2 (two discs: 129 minutes: DDD). Notes, text and translation included.
Recorded live in 1996.   Ⓕ

For most listeners, Schumann's only opera is still a relatively unknown quantity but lovers of Schumann will celebrate a work that is at once intimate, thought-provoking and gloriously melodious. The libretto (by Schumann himself, after Tieck and Hebbel) deals with secret passion and suspected adultery, while the music mirrors emotional turmoil with great subtlety, and sometimes with astonishing imagination. Copious foretastes are provided in the familiar overture, and thereafter, discoveries abound. Sample, for example, the jagged counter-motif that shudders as Genoveva's husband Siegfried entreats Golo (his own *alter ego*) to guard his wife while he is away at war (disc 1, track 5, at 1'58"); or the off-stage forces representing drunken servants at 2'22" into track 9; or the almost Expressionist writing at 4'00" into track 10 where Golo responds – with seething hatred – to Genoveva's vengeance. You might also try track 2 on disc 2, at 3'37", where Golo brings Siegfried news of Genoveva's supposed adultery, music that is both pained and equivocal. The entreaties of Drago's ghost aren't too far removed from Siegmund's 'Nothung!' in Act 1 of *Die Walküre* (track 4, at 6'10"), and Genoveva's singing from 'a desolate, rocky place' (track 5, first minute or so), sounds fairly prophetic of Isolde (who was as yet unborn, so to speak). Harnoncourt suspects that Genoveva was a 'counterblast' to Wagner, and although Wagner apparently thought the opera 'bizarre', there remains a vague suspicion of sneaking regard, even a smidgen of influence. Teldec's balancing is mostly judicious and the musical direction suggestive of burning conviction. The worthy though relatively conventional Gerd Albrecht (in Orfeo's mellow

1992 recording) only serves to underline the leaner, more inflected and more urgently voiced profile of Harnoncourt's interpretation. As to the two sets of singers, most preferences rest with the latter's line-up. Stage effects are well handled and the sum effect is of a top-drawer Schumann set within an unexpected structural context.

Heinrich Schütz

German 1585-1672

Symphoniae sacrae, SWV341-67.
Emma Kirkby, Suzie Le Blanc sops **James Bowman** counterten **Nigel Rogers,
Charles Daniels** tens **Stephen Varcoe, Richard Wistreich** basses
Jeremy West, Nicholas Perry cornets **Purcell Quartet** (Catherine Mackintosh,
Catherine Weiss vns Richard Boothby va da gamba Robert Woolley hpd).
Chandos Chaconne CHAN0566/7 (two discs: 139 minutes: DDD). Text and translation included.
Recorded 1993-94.   ⓕ🅿🅴

These discs are in various ways revelatory. Schütz's collection is difficult to get through in one sitting, but each item in the collection is a jewel, albeit not ostentatiously displayed. This is church music on a small scale in terms of physical resources, but of enormous invention and beauty. Sometimes the Purcell Quartet do not push the music along quite enough. In general, however, the instrumentalists respond with enthusiasm and great understanding of the style of these rather recondite works. It takes considerable sensitivity to bring out the rich textures of *Meine Seele erhebt den Herren* or *Der Herr ist meine Stärke* without enjoying such moments at the expense of the vocal soloist. The relatively well-known bass solo *Herr, nun lässest du deinen Diener* is another example of a perfect match between voice and instruments. Emma Kirkby brings all her customary charm and precision to her two solo arias. Both tenors are in their element, if sometimes a little understated, and Stephen Varcoe and Richard Wistreich really understand and communicate the glowing black and gold colours of Schütz's writing for the bass voice. Schütz's debt to Monteverdi is very much evident in *Der Herr ist mein Licht* and even more so in *Es steh Gott auf*, but Schütz's natural reluctance to 'deck out my work with foreign plumage' means that his own voice as a composer is always in evidence. This reconciliation of Italian *stile concertato* with Schütz's northern reticence is one of the challenges in performing his music, and one to which this recording rises magnificently.

Freue dich des Weibes deiner Jugend, SWV453. Liebster, sagt in süssem Schmerzen, SWV441. Nachdem ich lag in meinem öder Bette, SWV451. Glück zu dem Helikon, SWV96. Haus und Güter erbat man von Eltern, SWV21. Tugend ist der beste Freund, SWV442. Teutoniam dudum belli atra pericla, SWV338. Wie wenn der Adler, SWV434. Siehe, wie fein und lieblich ists, SWV48. Vier Hirtinnen, gleich jung, gleich schön, SWVAnh1. Lässt Salomon sein Bette nicht umgeben, SWV452. Die Erde trinkt für sich, SWV438. Wohl dem, der ein Tugendsam Weib hat, SWV20. Itzt blicken durch des Himmels Saal, SWV460. Syncharma musicum, SWV49.
Weser-Renaissance Bremen / Manfred Cordes.
CPO CPO999 518-2 (71 minutes: DDD). Texts and translations included. Recorded 1997.   ⓕ

Here is a discovery of several unrecorded byways of Schütz's miscellaneous secular *oeuvre*. Of course, the seventeenth century being what it is, secular and sacred are deliberately dovetailed into a cultural pea soup: these works are embedded in the literary morality of the age and are not entirely profane. There is a pleasing lightness of touch from the soloists (especially the soprano) and the instrumental consort does not attempt, as is so mistakenly regarded these days as the ideal, to ape the vocal lines at every turn in a wash of homogeneity; there are many distinctive virtuosic commentaries, as in *Tugend ist der beste Freund*, which Cordes (enhanced by the excellent recorded sound) allows to breathe naturally. Noble intensity and harmonious accord are the order of the day in the splendidly uplifting concerto *Teutoniam dudum*, which through its extraordinary structural clarity immediately delights the listener with a celebration of the cessation of hostilities after the miserable Thirty Years War. Most impressive, though, is the sympathetic and gentle treatment of the words from Weser-Renaissance, beautifully complemented by the soft articulation of the winds, especially in *Siehe, wie fein* and the domestic charm of *Wohl dem, der ein Tugendsam*. This is chamber music-making from the heart, tempered convincingly by the intellect and affectionately delivered.

Geistliche Chormusik, SWV369-97 – Herr, auf dich traue ich, SWV377; Die mit Tränen säen, SWV378 ; So fahr ich hin zu Jesu Christ, SWV379 ; O lieber Herre Gott, SWV381; Ich bin eine refende Stimme, SWV383; Die Himmel erzählen dei Ehre Gottes, SWV386; Herzlich lieb hab ich dich, o Herr, SWV387; Das ist je gewisslich wahr, SWV388; Unser Wandel ist im Himmel, SWV390; Selig sind die Toten, SWV391; Was mein Gott will, das gescheh allzeit, SWV392. Kleiner

geistlichen Concerten, Erster Theil, SWV282-305 – Eile mich, Gott, zu erretten, SWV282; O süsser, o freundlicher, SWV285; Schaffe in mir, Gott, ein reines Herz, SWV291. Kleiner geistlichen Concerten, Anderer Theil, SWV306-37 – Ich liege und schlafe, SWV310; Wann unsre Augen schlafen ein, SWV316.
Agnes Mellon sop **Mark Padmore** ten **Peter Kooy** bass
Collegium Vocale / Philippe Herreweghe.
Harmonia Mundi HMC90 1534 (61 minutes: DDD). Texts and translations included.
Recorded 1994.   Ⓕ 🅟

This anthology shows both sides of Schütz's output: the solid *prima prattica* training which is evident in his fine handling of counterpoint, and the Monteverdian lessons learned and shown off in the *Kleiner geistlichen Concerten*. Common to both styles is an impressive economy of means, so that with very limited resources Schütz obtains an extraordinary variety of colour and responds with immediacy to each text. To all this Collegium Vocale brings a brilliance of colour and a splendid choral blend (particularly evident in *Herr, auf dich* and *Die mit Tränen*) and a vivid response to Schütz's often difficult tempo changes. The speech-propelled writing in such motets as *O lieber Herre Gott* or *Die Himmel erzählen* is far from easy to bring across convincingly, but both are rendered here with impressive conviction and power. The *Concerte* are rather disappointing after such magnificent concerted choral singing, their highly baroque word-setting seeming superficial, but they are superbly sung, and it is especially good to hear Peter Kooy shown to such advantage.

Ich hab mein Sach Gott heimgestellt, SWV305. Ich will dem Herren loben allezeit, SWV306. Was hast du verwirket, SWV307. O Jesu, nomen dulce, SWV308. O misericordissime Jesu, SWV309. Ich leige und schlafe, SWV310. Habe deine Lust an dem Herren, SWV311. Herr, ich hoffe darauf, SWV312. Bone Jesu, verbum Patris, SWV313. Verbum caro factum est, SWV314. Hodie Christus natus est, SWV315. Wann unsre Augen schlafen ein, SWV316. Meister, wir haben die ganze Nacht gearbeitet, SWV317. Die Furcht des Herren, SWV318. Ich beuge meine Knie, SWV319. Ich bin jung gewesen, SWV320. Herr, wann ich nur dich habe, SWV321. Rorate coeli desuper, SWV322. Joseph, du Sohn David, SWV323. Ich bin die Auferstehung, SWV324.
Tölz Boys' Choir / Gerhard Schmidt-Gaden with **Roman Summereder** org
Capriccio 10 388 (77 minutes: DDD). Texts and translations included. Recorded 1989-90.   Ⓕ 🅟

Getting music published evidently encountered economic difficulties during the Thirty Years' War, for Heinrich Schütz had to issue his *Kleiner geistlichen Concerten* ('Little Sacred Concertos') – short motets for vocal soloists and continuo – in two parts in, respectively, 1636 and 1639. The voices of the soloists here are typically very individual and characterful, and all are remarkably adroit and stylish, so the personal witness that is so pronounced in the text is particularly well portrayed. These are performers well used to the subtleties of baroque word-setting and they highlight all the ingenuity that Schütz lavished on these seemingly simple parts. There is an evident delight in the way the composer deployed his limited resources, constantly ringing the changes on traditional formulas to produce a richness of ideas that it took a Bach or Handel to emulate. The rather close recording allows all these intricacies to emerge undiminished and although the resonance of the acoustic seems restrained, this is no bad thing for repertoire that, despite its title, has the feel of chamber music.

Psalmen Davids sampt etlichen Moteten und Concerten, SWV22-47.
Cantus Cölln (Elisabeth Scholl, Annette Labusch sops Elisabeth Popien mez Stratton Bull counterten Gerd Türk, Wilfried Jochens, Jörn Lindemann tens Stephan Schreckenberger, Stephan MacLeod basses)
Concerto Palatino / Konrad Junghänel.
Harmonia Mundi HMC90 1652/3 (two discs: 143 minutes: DDD). Texts and translations included.
Recorded 1997.   Ⓕ

Here is something to get excited about. Nearly 32 years have passed since the only complete recording (on DG, long unavailable), under Hanns-Martin Schneidt, of this, Schütz's first monumental publication of sacred music. Whether anything can be worth waiting for that long is a moot point, but Cantus Cölln and Concerto Palatino give us an interpretation that is unlikely to be surpassed. With eight singers and no fewer than two dozen instrumentalists, the scale is little short of symphonic. For sheer splendour, who can top *Danket dem Herren* (SWV45) or the next piece in the collection, *Zion spricht*? It is easy enough to single out the most opulent pieces, but as Peter Wollny remarks in his admirable booklet-notes, the whole point of the *Psalmen Davids* is its variety in the treatment of a medium whose potential for cliché is very great. The musicians respond to Schütz's demands with verve and perception and the sort of confidence that would carry any music aloft in triumph. The sound-recording does them full justice. You will almost certainly listen, enthralled, to the entire collection – nearly two-and-a-half hours – in one sitting. Aside from a slip or two in proof-reading, the notes and texts are instructive and well presented.

Alexander Scriabin

Scriabin Piano Concerto in F sharp minor, Op. 20.
Tchaikovsky Piano Concerto No. 1 in B flat minor, Op. 23.
Nikolai Demidenko *pf*
BBC Symphony Orchestra / Alexander Lazarev.
Hyperion CDA66680 (65 minutes: DDD). Recorded 1993. Ⓕ

The chief attraction here is the unusual coupling which pairs two sharply opposed examples of
Russian romanticism, and although the reasons for the neglect of Scriabin's Piano Concerto are not
hard to fathom (its lyrical and decorative flights are essentially inward-looking), its haunting,
bittersweet beauty, particularly in the central *Andante*, is hard to resist. Demidenko's own
comments, quoted in the accompanying booklet, are scarcely less intense and individual than his
performance: 'in the ambience, phrasing and cadence of his music we meet with a world almost
without skin, a world of nerve-ends where the slightest contact can bring pain.' His playing soars
quickly to meet the music's early passion head on, and in the first *più mosso scherzando* he
accelerates to produce a brilliant lightening of mood. His flashing *fortes* in the *Andante*'s second
variation are as volatile as his *pianissimos* are starry and refined in the finale's period reminiscence,
and although he might seem more tight-lipped, less expansive than Ashkenazy on Decca, he is
arguably more dramatic and characterful. Demidenko's Tchaikovsky, too, finds him ferreting out
and sifting through every texture, forever aiming at optimum clarity. While this is hardly among the
greatest Tchaikovsky Firsts on record, it is often gripping and mesmeric. The orchestra responds
admirably to its mercurial soloist and certainly comes alight at key moments in both concertos. The
recorded balance is not always ideal and the piano sound is sometimes uncomfortably taut.

Piano Concerto[a]. Prometheus, Op. 60, 'Le poème du feu'[b]. Le poème de l'extase, Op. 54[c].
Vladimir Ashkenazy *pf*
Ambrosian Singers; [ab]**London Philharmonic Orchestra;** [c]**Cleveland Orchestra / Lorin Maazel.**
Decca 417 252-2DH (66 minutes: ADD). Recorded [ab]1971, [c]1978. Ⓕ

This CD gives us the essential Scriabin. The Piano Concerto has great pianistic refinement and
melodic grace as well as a restraint not encountered in his later music. With *Le poème de l'extase*
and *Prometheus* we are in the world of art nouveau and Scriabin in the grip of the mysticism (and
megalomania) that consumed his later years. They are both single-movement symphonies for a huge
orchestra: *Prometheus* ('The Poem of Fire') calls for quadruple wind, eight horns, five trumpets,
strings, organ and chorus as well as an important part for solo piano in which Ashkenazy shines.
The sensuous, luminous textures are beautifully conveyed in these performances by the LPO and
the Decca engineers produce a most natural perspective and transparency of detail, as well as an
appropriately overheated sound in the sensuous world of *Le poème de l'extase*.

Symphonies – No. 1 in E major, Op. 26[a]; No. 2 in C minor, Op. 29; No. 3 in C minor, Op. 43,
'Divin poème'. Le poème de l'extase, Op. 54[b]. Prometheus, Op. 60, 'Le poème du feu'[c].
[a]**Stefania Toczyska** *mez* [a]**Michael Myers** *ten* [c]**Dmitri Alexeev** *pf* [b]**Frank Kaderabek** *tpt*
[a]**Westminster Choir;** [c]**Philadelphia Choral Arts Society;**
Philadelphia Orchestra / Riccardo Muti.
EMI CDS7 54251-2 (three discs: 188 minutes: DDD). Text and translation included.
Recorded 1985-90. Ⓕ RR

There can be few more thrilling sounds on disc (and no more compelling reason for a totally
sound-proofed listening room) than the climax to Muti's *Poème de l'extase*. The clamour of bells
here (both literal and imitative) reveals an essentially Russian heart at the core of this score's most
cosmopolitan of Russian composers, and the *maestoso* proclamation of the theme of self assertion
has the raised Philadelphia horns in crucially sharp focus. As in the corresponding climax in
Prometheus (at 18'21"), this 'éclat sublime' is filled out with a floor-shaking contribution from the
organ. Like the organ, the wordless chorus at this point in *Prometheus* registers more as a device for
enriching and exalting the texture, rather than as a striking new presence. Muti's *Prometheus* is,
arguably, the most complete realization of the mind-boggling demands of this score ever to have
been recorded. The inert opening ('Original chaos' – lovely *pp* bass drum!) and mysterious
awakening have rarely sounded so atmospheric. Alexeev's first entry is not as strong willed as some,
but he seems to be saving a more imperious attack for the same point in the recapitulation. Muti
builds the work superbly: the imposing clash of states in the development (and the changes of
tempo) charted with mighty assurance (beware of the *ff* dissonance at fig. 21, 10'23"!). And
thereafter *Prometheus* is airborne, with Alexeev both agile and articulate in the 'Dance of Life'
(16'44"). Throughout the cycle, the tonal allure of the Philadelphia Orchestra is fully in evidence.
Only in the Third Symphony, *Divin poème*, do Muti and the EMI team seem to be on less than their

indomitable form. Compared with some versions, the tempo relationships in the first movement don't fully convince. However, it is unlikely that this cycle will be seriously challenged for many a year. Taken as a whole it immeasurably enhances Scriabin's stature as a symphonist and offers the kind of playing and recording which, as recently as a couple of decades ago, Scriabin enthusiasts could only have imagined in their dreams.

Scriabin Prometheus.
Stravinsky The Firebird.
Alexander Toradze pf
Kirov Opera Chorus and Orchestra / Valery Gergiev.
Philips 446 715-2PH (72 minutes: DDD). Recorded 1997.　　　　　Ⓕ**E**

Stravinsky and the short-lived Scriabin were almost contemporaries; of these two exactly contemporary works (1909-10), *Prometheus*, as Oliver Knussen has put it, is 'so much more than a period piece; pregnant with possibilities for the future', whereas *The Firebird*, aside from its 'Infernal Dance', rarely does anything more startling than pick up from where Rimsky-Korsakov left off – indeed, in certain sections, it shows that Stravinsky also knew his Scriabin rather well (for example, the Firebird's 'Dance of Supplication'). Gergiev's *Firebird* is certainly a startling performance. All manner of things contribute to the impression of distinction, among them the fact that this is that rare thing on record, an all-Russian complete *Firebird*. The music-making seems alive with a special presence: the orchestra is fairly close, though there is a real sense of the hall, never more so than when a heart-stopping crack is let loose from the drums on Kashchey's appearance. But the primary presence here (obvious enough, but it needs saying) is of a man of the theatre, maybe too audibly (for some) breathing life into the proceedings, moving from one section of the ballet to the next with the transitional mastery of a Furtwängler, and taking risks with tempo (do hear the end of the 'Infernal Dance'). The darkness to light of the ballet's last few minutes is nothing less than mesmeric. *Prometheus* is equally compelling. Toradze's solo contribution is slightly less the centre of the piece's universe than Argerich in the sensational Abbado recording, in terms of both imaginative daring and recorded scale, though it never lacks character. The only reservation about the Abbado concerned the relatively fined down impression of Scriabin's huge orchestra. Yet with the more imposing-sounding Russian team you really know about it. Gergiev's is also a much broader view of the piece (some four minutes longer), but it never sounds overly languid, indeed it enables him and Toradze, unlike Argerich and Abbado, to achieve a dizzying *accelerando prestissimo* in the final bars that is faster than anything that has preceded it.

Etude in C sharp minor, Op. 2 No. 1. 12 Etudes, Op. 8. Etudes, Op. 42. Etude in E flat major, Op. 49 No. 1. Etude, Op. 56 No. 4. Three Etudes, Op. 65.
Piers Lane pf
Hyperion CDA66607 (56 minutes: DDD). Recorded 1992.　　　　　Ⓕ**S**

Although Scriabin's *études* do not fall into two neatly packaged sets in the same way as Chopin's celebrated contributions, there is nevertheless a strong feeling of continuity and development running throughout the 26 examples produced between the years 1887 and 1912. This is admirably demonstrated in this excellent issue from Hyperion, which, far from being an indigestible anthology proves to be an intriguing and pleasurable hour's worth of listening charting Scriabin's progression from late-romantic adolescence to harmonically advanced mystical poet. Indeed, although these studies can be counted as amongst the most digitally taxing and hazardous of their kind, Scriabin also saw them as important sketches and studies for his larger works, and as experiments in his gradually evolving harmonic language and mystical vision. Piers Lane attains the perfect balance between virtuoso display and poetic interpretation. Expressive detail and subtle nuance are finely brought out, and he is more than receptive to Scriabin's sometimes highly idiosyncratic sound world; rarely, for instance, has the famous 'Mosquito' *Etude* (Op. 42 No. 3) been captured with such delicate fragility as here, and in No. 1 of the three fiendishly difficult *Etudes,* Op. 65 the tremulous, ghostly flutterings are tellingly delivered with a gossamer-light touch and an appropriate sense of eerie mystery. The clear, spacious recording is exemplary.

Scriabin Etudes – C sharp minor, Op. 2 No. 1; Op. 8: No. 5 in E major; No. 11 in B flat minor; Op. 42: No. 2 in F sharp minor; No. 3 in F sharp major; No. 4 in F sharp major; No. 5 in C sharp minor; No. 6 in D flat major; No. 8 in E flat major; Trois Etudes, Op. 65. Piano Sonata No. 6 in G major, Op. 62.
Miaskovsky Piano Sonata No. 3 in C minor, Op. 19.
Prokofiev Piano Sonata No. 7 in B flat major, Op. 83.
Sviatoslav Richter pf
Melodiya mono 74321 29470-2 (68 minutes: ADD). Recorded 1952-58.　　　　　Ⓜ**H**

Richter's interpretations in the 1950s had an elemental power and unselfconscious abandon that was refined and tempered in later life; the problem is the unreliable 1950s Soviet recording quality, compounded, presumably, by some decay in the master-tapes over the years, and not entirely redeemed by the NoNoise remastering technique. Nevertheless, here is an other-worldly Scriabin, cataclysmic and elevated, culminating in a vaporous, explosive, ultimately clamorous account of the Sixth Sonata. The Miaskovsky – formulaic Scriabin with an academic safety net – is probably better heard on other versions; from the amount of background noise on Melodiya you might think a *babushka* with her vacuum cleaner was competing for attention. Finally comes a muscular and emotionally searing Prokofiev Seventh which presents the only serious alternative to Pollini.

Piano Sonatas – No. 1 in F minor, Op. 6; No. 2 in G sharp minor, Op. 19, 'Sonata-fantasy'; No. 3 in F sharp minor, Op. 23; No. 4 in F sharp, Op. 30; No. 5 in F sharp major, Op. 53; No. 6 in G major, Op. 62; No. 7 in F sharp major, Op. 64, 'White Mass'; No. 8 in A major, Op. 66; No. 9 in F major, Op. 68, 'Black Mass'; No. 10 in C major, Op. 70.

Piano Sonatas Nos. 1-10. Fantasie in B minor, Op. 28. Sonata-fantaisie in G sharp minor.
Marc-André Hamelin *pf*
Hyperion CDA67131/2 (two discs: 146 minutes: DDD). Recorded 1989-90.   Ⓕ

Scriabin was an ambitious composer. A romantic alchemist, he saw his music as a transmuting agent. Through its influence pain would become happiness and hate become love, culminating in a phoenix-like rebirth of the universe. With Shakespearian agility he would change the world's dross into 'something rich and strange'. Not surprisingly, given Scriabin's early prowess as a pianist, the ten sonatas resonate with exoticism, ranging through the First Sonata's cries of despair (complete with magnificent Russian funeral march), to the Second Sonata's Baltic Sea inspiration, the Third Sonata's 'states of being', the 'flight to a distant star' (No. 4) and 'the emergence of mysterious forces' (No. 5). Nos. 7 and 9 are *White* and *Black Mass* Sonatas respectively, and the final sonatas blaze with trills symbolizing an extra-terrestrial joy and incandescence. Even less surprisingly such music makes ferocious demands on the pianist's physical stamina and imaginative resource. However, Marc-André Hamelin, a cool customer, takes everything in his stride. Blessed with rapier reflexes he nonchalantly resolves even the most outlandish difficulties. He launches the First Sonata's opening outcry like some gleaming trajectory and, throughout, his whistle-stop virtuosity is seemingly infallible. You might, however, miss a greater sense of the music's Slavonic intensity, its colour and character; a finer awareness, for example, of the delirious poetry at the heart of the Second Sonata's whirling finale. Hamelin's sonority is most elegantly and precisely gauged but time and again his fluency (admittedly breathtaking) erases too much of the work's originality and regenerative force. However, he shows a greater sense of freedom in the Fifth Sonata, and in the opalescent fantasy of the later sonatas, he responds with more evocative skill to subjective terms, as well as to moments where Scriabin's brooding introspection is lit by sudden flashes of summer lightning. Hyperion's recordings are a little tight and airless in the bass and middle register, but their two-disc set is beautifully presented and includes a superb essay on Scriabin.

Scriabin Piano Sonatas Nos. 2 and 9. Etudes – F sharp minor, Op. 8 No. 2; B major, Op. 8 No. 4; E major, Op. 8 No. 5; F sharp major, Op. 42 No. 3; F sharp major, Op. 42 No. 4; F minor, Op. 42 No. 7. Four Pieces, Op. 51. Vers la flamme, Op. 72.
Prokofiev Visions fugitives, Op. 22.
Nikolai Demidenko *pf*
Conifer CDCF204 (73 minutes: DDD).   Ⓕ 🆁🆁

This is special – very special. Demidenko clearly has an extraordinary affinity and affection for the music of Scriabin and this is nowhere more apparent than in his remarkably beautiful performance of the Second Piano Sonata. The first movement (surely one of the most gorgeous movements Scriabin ever wrote) lives and breathes in the hands of this virtuoso artist. His tone gradation and dynamic nuances are perfectly judged, and the ebb and flow and surging climaxes of what Scriabin called 'a vision of the sea remembered' are superbly crafted. The tender lyrical second subject is brought unerringly to life in Demidenko's exquisitely tender and spine-tingling performance. His breathtaking account of the second movement, an exhilarating *Presto* in 3/4 time, is a subtle blend of precision and poetry, and one constantly marvels at his delicate and expressive pedalling. The six *Etudes* and the *Four Pieces*, Op. 51 that follow confirm just how consummate a Scriabin interpreter Demidenko is; each miniature being beautifully crafted and jewelled to perfection.

The Ninth Sonata is given a spacious though tightly controlled and cogent performance. Perhaps Demidenko doesn't quite achieve as great a satanic thrill as some performances but here there is subtlety and wider nuance coupled with an impressive overall conception of the work. The remaining Scriabin item, *Vers la flamme* is a single emotional *crescendo* without pause from the first note to the last. Indeed, it is an extraordinarily intense and elevating experience that places immense demands on the pianist's resources during its relatively short duration. Demidenko plays it with a burning inner intensity that is hard to resist. With barely time to recover from the all-consuming flames of the Scriabin we are confronted with a performance of Prokofiev's *Visions fugitives* that can only be described as magical and compelling. Demidenko's performance stands in a class of its own. Each fleeting vision is irridescent with inspiration, and for sheer sonority, colour and tonal variation quite simply the finest on disc. The recording, made at The Maltings, Snape is immaculate and faultless. A remarkable début recording.

Piano Sonatas Nos. 3-5. 12 Etudes, Op. 8.
Yuki Matsuzawa pf
Pianissimo PP10394 (72 minutes: DDD). Recorded 1993. Ⓕ🄴

Yuki Matsuzawa has an unassailably secure technical mastery, dealing with apparent ease and panache with the formidable virtuosity required by, for example, the Ninth, Tenth and Twelfth Studies of Op. 8 – and it is rare to find a pianist observing indications so absolutely exactly yet so seemingly naturally. As the first *Etude* reveals, she possesses that almost teasing lightness that Pasternak (who knew Scriabin) tells us was typical of his playing; and in lyrical passages such as the dreamy poetic *Andante* of the Third Sonata her tone is ravishingly beautiful. She is meticulous about detail and has a sensitive feeling for phrase and structure and a proper appreciation of the expressive implications of key shifts (e.g. in Op. 8 No. 8). She brings off the self-questioning of the Third Sonata, lingering over its initial subject, and the neurosis of the Fourth, with its passing echoes of *Tristan*, the chromatic *appoggiaturas* which give the first movement's harmonies a special character, and a truly fleeting *volando* in its second movement (which contains that direction in an Italian that never was, *giobilosco*). In the Fifth Sonata, written when Scriabin was making so great a change in his idiom, she is convincingly deft, if taking the *languido* sections very freely. This is a brilliant recording début.

Scriabin 24 Preludes, Op. 11.
Shostakovich 24 Preludes, Op. 34.
Artur Pizarro pf
Collins Classics 1496-2 (68 minutes: DDD). Recorded 1997. Ⓕ🄴

In Scriabin's 24 Preludes, Op. 11, Artur Pizarro once again confirms his glittering array of first prizes in performances of rare pianistic refinement, arguing the composer's volatility, his sudden calms and squalls, with unfaltering conviction. Nothing is hectic or rushed, everything sings and flows with a natural ease and impetus. The majority of Scriabin's aphorisms, with their affectionate memories of Chopin, are romantically self-communing and in this enraptured dreamworld Pizarro could hardly show a more consistent poise or subtlety. His rubato (in No. 4) is telling but never affected or excessive, his pedalling both lavish and acute (in No. 11, with its insinuating lilt and sultry undertow). In No. 16 his way of pushing each sinister phrase forward suggests the music's darkness, its emerging and receding violence, and, throughout, his flexibility and warmth are almost tangible. Pizarro's easy and immaculate technique, too, make light of Shostakovich's more quirky Op. 34 Preludes. Here, he is equally at home in the vaudeville pranks of No. 6, or the stillness of No. 17, the *Presto tarantella* whirl of No. 9 or the dark ceremonial of No. 14. Collins's sound beautifully captures Pizarro's unfailing tonal bloom.

Peter Sculthorpe
Australian 1929

Piano Concerto. Little Nourlangie. Music for Japan. The song of Tailitnama.
Kirsti Harms mez **Mark Atkins** didjeridu **Tamara Anna Cislowska** pf **David Drury** org
Sydney Symphony Orchestra / Edo de Waart.
ABC Classics 8 770030 (53 minutes: DDD). Text included. Recorded 1996. Ⓕ

Little Nourlangie dates from 1990. It takes its name from a small outcrop of rocks in Australia's Kakadu National Park on which can be found the Aboriginal Blue Paintings, depicting fish, boats and ancestral figures and which inspired the composer. *Little Nourlangie* is a characteristically striking creation, scored with much imaginative flair. It shares its diatonic main theme with that of Sculthorpe's 1989 guitar concerto, *Nourlangie*, and comprises four-and-a-half minutes of 'straightforward, joyful music' (to quote the composer). By contrast, *Music for Japan* exhibits a much more uncompromising demeanour. It was written in response to the Expo '70 exhibition in Osaka and according to annotator Graeme Skinner, is at once 'his most abstract and modernist orchestral score'. The work's title should be carefully heeded: the piece remains very much 'about'

Australia, an impression doubly confirmed by the incorporation of a tape featuring a didjeridu played by Mark Atkins. Sculthorpe has long been preoccupied with the music from other countries situated in and around the Pacific – and Japanese music in particular, elements of which he has incorporated into other works such as the present Piano Concerto of 1983. Sculthorpe's Piano Concerto is an imposing creation, less indigenous-sounding and 'pictorial' than many of his other compositions, including *The song of Tailitnama* (1974). Conceived for high voice, six cellos and percussion, this haunting piece was in fact written for a TV documentary. Edo de Waart presides over a set of performances that exhibit great commitment and exemplary finish. The recording and presentation are excellent too.

Déodat de Séverac
French 1873-1921

Ritournelle. Renouveau. Chevrier. Paysages tristes. Musette. Les hiboux. Ne dérangez pas le monde. Le ciel est, par-dessus le toit. Le roi a fait battre tambour. Un rêve. Les cors. Temps de neige. Pour le jour des rois. Chanson pour le petit cheval. L'infidèle. Philis. Chanson de la nuit durable. Le cotillon couleur de rose. La chanson de Blaisine. L'éveil de Pâques. Ba be bi bo bu!. Chanson de Jacques. Offrande. Ma poupée chérie[a]. Chant de Noël[a]. Aubade. A l'aube dans la montagne.
François Le Roux *bar* **Graham Johnson** *pf* with [a]**Patricia Rozario** *sop*
Hyperion CDA66983 (79 minutes: DDD). Texts and translations included. Recorded 1997.   Ⓕ

On his periodic detours down the byways of French song Graham Johnson has produced some very worthwhile discoveries, of which this latest disc devoted to the neglected Déodat de Séverac is certainly one. It would not be easy, or very helpful, to try to sum up Séverac's style in a single phrase. Perhaps because he preferred the provinces to metropolitan Paris, Séverac may have felt under less pressure to stand out from the crowd. From the songs selected here we can trace a wide range of influences with Debussy as his closest musical relative and Duparc, Chabrier and even Canteloube as his second musical cousins. There is not a dull moment: impressionist tone-painting, eighteenth-century pastiche, folk-song arrangements all find a place here. The songs that best reveal Séverac's stature are those composed under the influence of *Pelléas et Mélisande*, such as *Un rêve* and the lofty *A l'aube dans la montagne*, which display a sensitivity for word-setting worthy of Debussy. François Le Roux knows his way around this style of music. Although the recording shows a marked decline in the freshness and focus of his voice, there is no baritone better placed to be our guide to Séverac's varied song output. Le Roux is just as engaging in the light-hearted folk-songs as in the masterly setting of Baudelaire's mournful *Les hiboux* with its owls' calls echoing in the accompanist's right hand. Where Fauré or Debussy composed rival settings, it would be too much to say they had met their match, but Séverac has attractions of his own. The tuneful lullaby *Ma poupée chérie* would make a nice addition to any recital programme and, a few blushes notwithstanding, so would the wickedly naughty ditty *Offrande*. This is another of Johnson's spot-on discoveries, with Patricia Rozario making an appealing guest appearance in two songs.

Rodion Shchedrin
USSR 1932

Symphony No. 2 (25 Preludes for Orchestra). Concerto for Orchestra No. 3, 'Old Russian Circus Music'.
BBC Philharmonic Orchestra / Vassily Sinaisky.
Chandos CHAN9552 (80 minutes: DDD). Recorded 1996.   Ⓕ

After a long period of suffering from relative obscurity, the music of Rodion Shchedrin is making new friends in the West and this recording of the Second Symphony is especially welcome. A key work of Russian-Soviet music, premièred in 1965, it is a rare example of officially sanctioned experimentalism, reminding us that the composer occupied a paradoxical position as licensed modernist of the *ancien régime*. There have been attempts to reposition him politically in recent years but this should not be allowed to obscure the extraordinary dexterity of his music. While many of his earlier works clatter away amiably enough, consciously eschewing the profound, the Second Symphony is made of sterner stuff. It consists of 25 preludes that fall into five broad 'movements', the frequent recourse to radical musical languages presumably validated by the theme – Peace and War, Life and Death. Some sections draw upon the symphonic rhetoric of Shostakovich and Prokofiev, albeit without the tonal moorings, so don't expect that old diatonic tunefulness. There are earnest emotings and there are novelties – like the fantasy on the sound of an orchestra tuning up and the very 1960s deployment of House of Horror harpsichord. It is at the very least a fascinating document from an enormously skilful operator. While some of the high-lying string passages are taxing and sound it, the playing is remarkably good. The sound is clear and rich.

John Sheppard

British c1515-1559/60

Aeterne Rex altissime. Dum transisset Sabbatum II. Hostis Hérodes impie. In manus tuas III.
Te Deum laudamus. Mass 'The Western Wynde'. The Second Service: Magnificat; Nunc dimittis.
The Sixteen / Harry Christophers.
Hyperion CDA66603 (63 minutes: DDD). Texts and translations included. Recorded 1992.   Ⓕ

This disc centres round one of Sheppard's best-known four-part Masses, *The Western Wynde*. Though largely syllabic in style, in accordance with liturgical prescriptions at a time when taste in church music was turning towards ever greater emphasis on the text, this Mass still has moments that recapture the earlier visionary style in all its wonder. The section 'Et incarnatus est', coming after an amazing cadence at 'descendit de coelis' in the *Credo*, is a case in point. 'Pleni sunt coeli' is another, and also the opening of the *Benedictus*, where the melody unfolds unhurriedly over the delicate counterpoint of the mean and the bass. In such passages as these The Sixteen is in its element, each singer relating to his or her colleagues with the intimacy and mutual understanding of performers of chamber music. The supporting programme includes *alternatim* hymn settings, responsories and a *Te Deum*. In all of these the chant is sung with excellent phrasing and a smooth *legato*, avoiding completely those intrusive 'aitches' one hears so often. Some subtle repercussions in the intonation to *Dum transisset Sabbatum* are particularly pleasing. In all five pieces, though, the tempo of the chant sections bore little relationship to the polyphony – the least far removed being that of the hymn *Aeterne Rex altissime*, where the individual chant notes had roughly the duration of a half-beat of the polyphony. The English *Magnificat and Nunc dimittis* reveal Sheppard fully conforming to the later syllabic style in a rich and joyful texture. Here, and in the Latin *Te Deum* The Sixteen display to the full their glowing vocal qualities. This is wonderful singing, with a sense of freedom and flow that is almost overpowering.

The Lord's Prayer. The Second Service – Magnificat; Nunc dimittis. Gaude, gaude, gaude Maria. Filie Ierusalem. Reges Tharsis et insulae. Spiritus sanctus procedens. Laudem dicite Deo nostro. Hec dies. Impetum fecerunt unanimes. Libera nos, salva nos.
Choir of Christ Church Cathedral, Oxford / Stephen Darlington.
Nimbus NI5480 (67 minutes: DDD). Texts and translations included. Recorded 1995.   Ⓕ

This enjoyable recording opens with two works in English which were probably written within days of John Sheppard's early death, as Roger Bowers's introductory essay explains. The hypothesis is an intriguing one, for *The Lord's Prayer* and the Second Service largely lack the wayward dissonances that play an integral (and controversial) part in this composer's style. Whether the difference is due to the switch to the vernacular is a moot point, for the Latin Responds that make up most of the disc show off the older style more conspicuously. The most impressive of these is undoubtedly the elaborate *Gaude, gaude, gaude Maria*, but the piece that most clearly enunciates its composer's idiosyncrasies has to be the concluding *Libera nos* (Sheppard wrote two identically scored settings of this text, but neither the programme details nor Bowers's essay makes clear which one is performed here). Sheppard's special predilection for high voices makes the participation of boy trebles here particularly appropriate. In such traditional choral establishments, unanimity of ensemble is crucial given the number of boys involved. From that standpoint this choir is difficult to fault, although towards the end of the recital a certain tiredness is just perceptible. If anything, the sound is a shade top-heavy at times (as in *Filie Ierusalem*), but a couple of the Responds dispense with trebles altogether, providing a welcome contrast.

Dmitry Shostakovich

Russian/USSR 1906-1975

Cello Concertos – No. 1 in E flat major, Op. 107; No. 2 in G major, Op. 126.

Cello Concertos Nos. 1 and 2.
Mischa Maisky *vc*
London Symphony Orchestra / Michael Tilson Thomas.
DG 445 821-2GH (65 minutes: DDD). Recorded 1993.   Ⓕ Ⓔ RR

The Second Cello Concerto is one of the major concertos of the post-war period – as potent a representative of the composer's later style as the last three symphonies, be it through irony (second movement), poetry (first and third) or anger (beginning of the third). Few cellists have tended the *piano espressivo* of the *Largo*'s opening bars as lovingly as Mischa Maisky does, while the rapt quality of his soft playing and the expressive eloquence of his double-stopping wring the most from Shostakovich's extended soliloquy. Michael Tilson Thomas points and articulates with his usual skill. Only the opening of that movement (with its furious whoop horns) seems marginally underprojected, although the main climax later on is both immensely powerful and extraordinarily clear. The First Concerto harbours fewer mysteries than the Second and yet remains a pivotal work. Maisky phrases beautifully, while Tilson Thomas and the LSO again come up trumps, even though 1'33" into the finale the dramatic switch to 6/8 sounds less spontaneous than it does under, say, Maxim Shostakovich. In other respects, however, this is a forceful and fairly outgoing interpretation, beautifully recorded and a suitable coupling for the disc's star act – the finest available studio recording of the Second Concerto. In fact, this CD is now the prime recommendation for the two concertos coupled together.

Cello Concertos Nos. 1 and 2.
Heinrich Schiff vc
Bavarian Radio Symphony Orchestra / Maxim Shostakovich.
Philips 412 526-2PH (61 minutes: DDD).   Ⓕ

In the First Concerto, Heinrich Schiff's excellent version with the Bavarian Radio Symphony Orchestra under Shostakovich *fils* can hold its own against all opposition. The first movement is taut and well held together and the second is beautifully shaped, the passion and poignancy of the climax being particularly well conveyed. Schiff makes one listen to every nuance and wait upon every rest. The Second Concerto comes between the Thirteenth and Fourteenth Symphonies, neither of which endeared Shostakovich to the Soviet Establishment. The concerto did not meet with the enthusiastic acclaim that had greeted No. 1 and has not established itself in the repertory to anywhere near the same extent as its predecessor, perhaps because it offers fewer overt opportunities for display. It is a work of eloquence and beauty, inward in feeling and spare in its textures. The opening *Largo* could hardly be in stronger contrast to the corresponding movement of No. 1. It is intimate and withdrawn in feeling, and on first encounter appears closer to the ruminative *Nocturne* of the Violin Concerto No. 1. It seems rhapsodic and fugitive, and it takes time before one realizes how purposeful is the soloist's course through the shadowy landscape. Yet the sonorities have the asperity so characteristic of Shostakovich. It is a haunting piece, lyrical in feeling, and gently discursive, sadly whimsical at times and tinged with a smiling melancholy that hides deeper troubles. The balance is generally excellent: the soloist is perhaps marginally forward, but the result is still very natural yet very clear and there is quite outstanding definition and realism. Recommended with enthusiasm.

Piano Concertos – C minor for Piano, Trumpet and Strings, Op 35;
No. 2 in F major, Op. 102.

Piano Concertos Nos. 1 and 2. The Unforgettable Year 1919, Op. 89 – The assault on beautiful Gorky.
Dmitri Alexeev pf **Philip Jones** tpt
English Chamber Orchestra / Jerzy Maksymiuk.
Classics for Pleasure CD-CFP4547 (48 minutes: DDD).   Ⓑ **RR**

Shostakovich's piano concertos were written under very different circumstances, yet together they contain some of the composer's most cheerful and enlivening music. The First, with its wealth of perky, memorable tunes, has the addition of a brilliantly-conceived solo trumpet part (delightfully done here by Philip Jones) that also contributes to the work's characteristic stamp. The Second Concerto was written not long after Shostakovich had released a number of the intense works he had concealed during the depths of the Stalin era. It came as a sharp contrast, reflecting as it did the optimism and sense of freedom that followed the death of the Russian dictator. The beauty of the slow movement is ideally balanced by the vigour of the first, and the madcap high spirits of the last. The poignant movement for piano and orchestra from the Suite from the 1951 film *The Unforgettable Year 1919*, 'The assault on beautiful Gorky', provides an excellent addition to this disc of perceptive and zestful performances by Alexeev. He is most capably supported by the ECO under Maksymiuk, and the engineers have done them proud with a recording of great clarity and finesse. A joyous issue.

Piano Concertos. Three Fantastic Dances, Op. 5. 24 Preludes and Fugues, Op. 87 – No. 1 in C major; No. 4 in E minor; No. 5 in D major; No. 23 in F major; No. 24 in D minor.
Dmitri Shostakovich pf **Ludovic Vaillant** tpt
French Radio National Orchestra / André Cluytens.
EMI Composers in Person mono CDC7 54606-2 (76 minutes: ADD). Recorded 1958-59.   Ⓕ **H**

Before devoting himself entirely to composition Shostakovich pursued a successful parallel career as a concert pianist, playing mostly romantic repertoire. These recordings were made at a time when he still played his own works in public, and they show him to have been a highly skilled player. His performances of both concertos are quite brilliant, and have a particularly vivacious, outgoing quality. In the First Concerto Ludovic Vaillant plays the trumpet part with character and great virtuosity, and the orchestral playing under Cluytens matches that of the composer in its joyous high spirits. The three little *Fantastic Dances* are wittily brought to life. A different, far more serious and academic world is evoked by Shostakovich in his Preludes and Fugues. Here the composer shapes his own long contrapuntal lines with great skill, and these are very compelling, highly concentrated performances. The mono recordings are all very acceptable, save that of the last Prelude and Fugue, where a certain rustiness creeps into the sound. All these items have historical importance, but they also offer many rewards to the listener who is primarily interested in the music.

Violin Concertos – No. 1 in A minor, Op. 99; No. 2 in C sharp minor, Op. 129.

Violin Concertos Nos. 1 and 2.
Lydia Mordkovitch *vn*
Scottish National Orchestra / Neeme Järvi
Chandos CHAN8820 (69 minutes: DDD). Recorded 1989.
Gramophone Award Winner 1990.   ⓅRR

This coupling completely explodes the idea of the Second Violin Concerto being a disappointment after the dramatic originality of No. 1. Certainly No. 2, completed in 1967, a year after the very comparable Cello Concerto No. 2, has never won the allegiance of violin virtuosos as the earlier work has done, but here Lydia Mordkovitch confirms what has become increasingly clear, that the spareness of late Shostakovich marks no diminution of his creative spark, maybe even the opposite. In that she is greatly helped by the equal commitment of Neeme Järvi in drawing such purposeful, warmly expressive playing from the Scottish National Orchestra. With such spare textures the first two movements can be difficult to hold together, but here from the start, where Mordkovitch plays the lyrical first theme in a hushed, beautifully withdrawn way, the concentration is consistent. The première recording of the work from David Oistrakh (on Chant du Monde but currently out of the catalogue), dedicatee of No. 2 as of No. 1, has remained unchallenged for a generation, and Mordkovitch does not always quite match her mentor in the commanding incisiveness of the playing in bravura passages. But there is no lack of power in her reading, and in any case much the more vital element in this work is the dark reflectiveness of the lyrical themes of the first two movements.

It is not just that Mordkovitch has the benefit of far fuller recording and a less close recording balance, but that her playing has an even wider range of colouring and dynamic than Oistrakh's. She conveys more of the mystery of the work and is perfectly matched by the orchestra. As in the First Concerto the principal horn has a vital role, here crowning each of the first two movements with a solo of ecstatic beauty in the coda. The Russian player on the Chant du Monde version is first-rate, no Slavonic whiner, but the SNO principal is far richer still, with his expressiveness enhanced by the wider dynamic and tonal range of the recording. The range of the recording helps too in the finale, where the *Allegro* has a satisfyingly barbaric bite, while the *scherzando* element is delectably pointed, as it is in the first movement too. In the First Concerto Mordkovitch is hardly less impressive. As in Concerto No. 2 one of her strengths lies in the meditative intensity which she brings to the darkly lyrical writing of the first and third movements. Here, too, she has never sounded quite so full and warm of tone on record before. In the brilliant second and fourth movements she may not play with quite the demonic bravura of Oistrakh, but as in No. 2 there is no lack of power or thrust, and in place of demonry she gives rustic jollity to the dance rhythms, faithfully reflecting the title of the finale, *Burlesque*. She is helped by recorded sound far fuller than Oistrakh's. This is a superb disc.

Shostakovich Violin Concerto No. 1.
Prokofiev Violin Concerto No. 1 in D major, Op. 19.
Maxim Vengerov *vn*
London Symphony Orchestra / Mstislav Rostropovich.
Teldec 4509-92256-2 (62 minutes: DDD). Recorded 1994. Includes bonus sampler disc.
Gramophone Award Winner 1995.   ⓅE

There is an astonishing emotional maturity in Vengerov's Shostakovich. He uses Heifetz's bow but it is to David Oistrakh that he is often compared. His vibrato is wider, his manners less consistently refined, and yet the comparison is well founded. Oistrakh made three commercial recordings of the Shostakovich and one can guess that Vengerov has been listening to those earlier Oistrakh renditions as there is nothing radically novel about his interpretation. It is possible that some will find Vengerov's impassioned climaxes a shade forced by comparison. Yet he achieves a nobility and poise worlds away from the superficial accomplishment of most modern rivals. He can fine down his tone to the barest whisper; nor is he afraid to make a scorching, ugly sound. While his sometimes slashing quality of articulation is particularly appropriate to the faster movements, the brooding, silver-grey 'Nocturne' comes off superbly too, though it seems perverse that the engineers mute the low tam-tam strokes. Rostropovich has the lower strings dig into the third movement's passacaglia theme with his usual enthusiasm. Indeed the orchestral playing is very nearly beyond reproach.

Vengerov and Rostropovich take an unashamedly epic view of the Prokofiev concerto and it works well. Closely observed digital recording uncovers a wealth of detail, most of it welcome, with the conductor's erstwhile clumsy tendency barely noticeable. Towards the end of the first movement, the approach to the reprise of the opening melody on solo flute with harp, muted strings and lightly running tracery from the soloist is very deliberately taken, and the long-breathed finale builds to a passionate, proto-Soviet climax. The central *Scherzo* is predictably breathtaking in its virtuosity. Need one go on? If you're looking for a recording of the Shostakovich, Vengerov's coupling may be less logical than Lydia Mordkovitch's (see above) but do not be deterred from investigating this extraordinary disc. However committed you are to alternative interpretations, these demand to be heard.

Shostakovich Violin Concerto No. 1.
Prokofiev Violin Concerto No. 2 in G minor, Op. 63.
Vadim Repin *vn*
Hallé Orchestra / Kent Nagano.
Erato 0630-10696-2 (59 minutes: DDD). Recorded 1995. Ⓕ

Vadim Repin's interpretation of the Shostakovich comes across as less quintessentially Russian than Maxim Vengerov's in its avoidance of rhetorical overkill. Without in any way underplaying the bravura passages (the *Scherzo* is taken at an incredible speed), he stresses rather the chamber-like intimacy of Shostakovich's score. Rather surprising, perhaps, is the flowing tempo for the slow third movement, but, thanks also to Nagano and the Hallé, we do actually hear the music as a passacaglia. With Vengerov and Rostropovich intent on heightening strong emotions rather than clarifying textures, the LSO's contribution is comparatively impenetrable on Teldec. In the 'Nocturne' the tam-tam, inaudible in Abbey Road, is perfectly caught in Manchester. Given Repin's dazzling achievement in the Shostakovich concerto, his Prokofiev is a shade disappointing. The violin is less sweetly caught and Repin sometimes makes the kind of uningratiating noises which imply some impatience with the straightforward *Romeo and Juliet*-style lyricism of the work. The finale sounds spontaneous but the lovely slow movement could do with more space to indulge its sweetly singing lines. However, if the coupling appeals, Repin represents a clear first choice – and anyone who cares about the Shostakovich will want to hear this disc.

Shostakovich Violin Concerto No. 1.
Tchaikovsky Violin Concerto in D major, Op. 35.
Midori *vn*
Berlin Philharmonic Orchestra / Claudio Abbado.
Sony Classical SK68338 (73 minutes: DDD). Recorded live in 1997. Ⓕ

It makes an original and attractive coupling having the Tchaikovsky concerto together with this twentieth-century Russian masterpiece. The implication is that Shostakovich in this darkly introspective work is less a modernist than a successor to the romantic Tchaikovsky, and Midori's readings, recorded live, do bring out the likenesses quite as much as the obvious contrasts. With the solo instrument naturally balanced, the most striking point about both performances is the way that Midori, never lacking in virtuoso bravura, makes an even more distinctive impression in the many passages where she plays in a hushed, intimate half-tone. At the beginning of the *Moderato* first movement of the Shostakovich her tone is so withdrawn that one has to listen hard to detect precisely when she starts playing. In the passacaglia third movement she conveys an ethereal poignancy in her *pianissimo* playing. Even in the Tchaikovsky the degree to which Midori brings out a meditative quality in passages normally treated merely as sweet and songful is striking, a point established at the very start in her first ruminative solo.

As these are live recordings, it is not surprising that in both works Midori is often rhythmically free, always sounding spontaneous, though the central *Canzonetta* of the Tchaikovsky, at a markedly slow tempo, does run the risk of sounding a little sticky, with marked agogic hesitations. Even so the hushed intensity is most compelling, sparkling and volatile in the flourishes at the beginning of the finale of the Tchaikovsky. She adopts the tiny traditional cuts in the finale, arguably the preferable course. In both works Abbado is a powerful and sympathetic, yet discreet accompanist, with tuttis designed to support the soloist, rarely drawing attention to himself. In the finale of the

Shostakovich it is striking how even before Midori enters Abbado finds an element of jollity in a movement which more often is treated as thrustful and demonic. Not that there is ever any lack of weight in the Berlin Philharmonic's playing, with a recording that is both warm and well detailed.

Shostakovich Violin Concerto No. 2.
Prokofiev Violin Concerto No. 2 in G minor, Op. 63.
Maxim Vengerov *vn*
London Symphony Orchestra / Mstislav Rostropovich.
Teldec 0630-13150-2 (62 minutes: DDD). Recorded 1996. Ⓕ

This is an exceptionally fine peformance of the Shostakovich, the desperate bleakness perfectly realized. There has been no finer account since that of the dedicatee, David Oistrakh (Chant du Monde). With Rostropovich rather than Kondrashin on the podium, tempos are comparatively deliberate in the first two movements, but there is no lack of intensity in the solo playing and rather more in the way of light and shade. In the stratospheric writing of the *Adagio*, Vengerov is technically superb, while the all-pervading atmosphere of desolation has never been more potently conveyed. The finale is more extrovert than some will like, the fireworks irresistible, and yet you do not lose the disquieting sense of a composer at the end of his tether, seemingly contemptuous of his own material. The Prokofiev is rather less successful, however. The balance there is partly to blame – the orchestra a remote presence, the soloist rather too closely scrutinized – but also there is a lack of intimacy in the interpretation itself. Vengerov self-consciously scales down his tone for the first movement's exquisite second subject, but the second movement, very slow and grand, is plagued by Rostropovich's over-insistent nuancing. Even if the finale has its impressive passages, there isn't quite enough light-hearted Spanishry in a piece written not to Soviet order but for Robert Soëtans to play in Madrid. Vengerov's sometimes 'overwrought' manner fits this music like a glove.

The Counterplan, Op. 33 – Presto; Andante (with Alexander Kerr, vn); The Song of the Counterplan. Alone, Op. 26 – March; Galop; Barrel Organ; March; Altai; In Kuzmina's hut; School children; Storm Scene. The Tale of the Silly Little Mouse, Op. 56 (arr. Cornall). Hamlet, Op. 116 – Introduction; Palace Music; Ball at the Castle; Ball; In the Garden; Military Music; Scene of the Poisoning. The Great Citizen, Op. 55 – Funeral March. Sofia Perovskaya, Op. 132 – Waltz. Pirogov, Op. 76a (arr. Atovmian) – Scherzo; Finale. The Gadfly, Op. 97 – Romance (Kerr).
Royal Concertgebouw Orchestra / Riccardo Chailly.
Decca 460 792-2DH (78 minutes: DDD). Recorded 1998. Ⓕ Ⓔ

Only ardent film buffs and die-hard Shostakovich completists will cavil at this selection of Riccardo Chailly's rather offbeat collection, cutting across as it does several more serious-minded projects. He gives us some genuine novelties too. 'The Song of the Counterplan' (track 3) was transmogrified into an MGM production number in the 1940s for the film *Thousands Cheer*. Producer Andrew Cornall's new (non-vocal) suite from the *Tom and Jerry*-like *Tale of the Silly Little Mouse* was sanctioned by the composer's estate and makes its début here. The 'Funeral March' from *The Great Citizen* turns up again in the Eleventh Symphony (track 22). And the much later 'Waltz' from *Sofia Perovskaya* is also unfamiliar. Less committed listeners should perhaps sample track 11 for Shostakovich's take on the spooky weirdness of the theremin, and track 25 for the ubiquitous 'Romance' from *The Gadfly*. There may be no great music here – some of the darker numbers from *Hamlet* come closest with their echoes of *Stepan Razin* and the Thirteenth Symphony – but with music-making of this quality it scarcely matters. For once you probably won't miss the raw primary colours and fish-glue pungency of an older interpretative tradition. Chailly has rarely sounded so unbuttoned in the studio and the selection is generous, if random. Only the final chord of the 'Finale' from *Pirogov* is a bit of a puzzle. Given the top-notch Decca production values on display, what sounds here like a drop-out or similar technical fault could be either the conductor executing a tricksy hairpin *diminuendo* or Shostakovich perpetrating a Mahler 7-type joke. Warmly recommended in any event.

Moscow-Cheryomushki, Op. 105 – concert suite (ed. Cornall). The Bolt – ballet suite, Op. 27a (1934 version). The Gadfly, Op. 97 – Overture; The Cliff; Youth; Box on the Ear; Barrel Organ; Contredanse; Galop; At the Market Place; The Rout; The Passage of Montanelli; Finale; The Austrians; Gemma's Room.
Philadelphia Orchestra / Riccardo Chailly.
Decca 452 597-2DH (73 minutes: DDD). Recorded 1995. Ⓕ Ⓔ

Although entitled 'The Dance Album', interestingly only one of the items on this disc (*The Bolt*) is actually derived from music conceived specifically for dance. However, what the disc reveals is that Shostakovich's fondness for dance forms frequently found expression in his other theatrical/film projects. The world première recording of a suite of four episodes from the 1959 operetta *Moscow-Cheryomushki* will be of particular interest to Shostakovich devotees. Despite the somewhat mundane plot, the score produces some surprisingly attractive and entertaining numbers, most notably perhaps the invigorating 'A spin through Moscow' and the 'Waltz'. For the suite from the ballet *The Bolt* Chailly brings us the less frequently heard 1934 version in which the composer dropped two of the eight numbers and changed some of the titles in order to deflect from the story-line of the ballet. Lots of parody and plenty of Shostakovich with his tongue planted firmly in his cheek is what we get, and if this aspect of the composer's output appeals then you will certainly enjoy Chailly's and his players' spirited and colourfully buoyant performances of this energetic score. Less familiar light is also shed on the music from the film *The Gadfly* which is heard here in a version which brings together 13 of the score's episodes and preserves Shostakovich's original orchestration, as opposed to the suite prepared and re-orchestrated by Levin Atovmyan. All the performances on the disc are superbly delivered and the recorded sound is excellent.

The Golden Age.
Royal Stockholm Philharmonic Orchestra / Gennadi Rozhdestvensky.
Chandos CHAN9251/2 (two discs: 134 minutes: DDD). Recorded 1993.　　　　Ⓕ

The Golden Age (1930) is an industrial exhibition organized in a capitalist country, at which a group of Soviet sportsmen have been invited to compete. The general idea of Shostakovich's characterization is to differentiate between goodies and baddies by assigning them respectively healthy-folk and decadent-bourgeois idioms. But then the trouble was, he couldn't stop himself enjoying being decadent. Not all of the 37 movements stand up independently of the stage-action. But the finales and the whole of Act 3 are top-notch stuff, at times surprisingly threatening in tone and symphonic in continuity; and there are several movements which could undoubtedly be promoted alongside the four in the familiar concert suite (the Tap Dance of Act 2 is especially appealing, for instance). Those who know their Shostakovich will be constantly intrigued by foretastes of *Lady Macbeth*, the Fourth Symphony and the *Hamlet* music, and by the appearance of Shostakovich's 'Tea for Two' arrangement as an Interlude in Act 2. This first complete recording is a major coup for Chandos. Admittedly not even their flattering engineering can disguise a certain lack of confidence and idiomatic flair on the part of the Royal Stockholm Philharmonic Orchestra. But let that not deter anyone with the least interest in Shostakovich, or ballet music, or Soviet music, or indeed Soviet culture as a whole, from investigating this weird and intermittently wonderful score.

Symphonies – No. 1 in F minor, Op. 10; **No. 2** in B major, Op. 14, 'To October'; **No. 3** in E flat major, Op. 20, 'The first of May'; **No. 4** in C minor, Op. 43; **No. 5** in D minor, Op. 47; **No. 6** in B minor, Op. 54; **No. 7** in C major, Op. 60, 'Leningrad'; **No. 8** in C minor, Op. 65; **No. 9** in E flat major, Op. 70; **No. 10** in E minor, Op. 93; **No. 11** in G minor, Op. 103, 'The year 1905'; **No. 12** in D minor, Op. 112, 'The year 1917'; **No. 13** in B flat minor, Op. 113, 'Babiy Yar'; **No. 14**, Op. 135; **No. 15** in A major, Op. 141.

Symphonies Nos. 1 and 3[a].
London Philharmonic [a]Choir and Orchestra / Bernard Haitink.
Decca London 425 063-2DM (65 minutes: ADD/DDD). Texts and translations included.
Recorded 1980-81. The cycle is also available as an 11-disc set: Ⓑ 444 430-2LC11.　　Ⓜ 𝗥𝗥

Symphonies Nos. 2[a] and 10.
London Philharmonic [a]Choir and Orchestra / Bernard Haitink.
Decca London 425 064-2DM (76 minutes: ADD/DDD). Texts and translations included.
Recorded 1981.　　Ⓜ 𝗥𝗥

Symphony No. 4.
London Philharmonic Orchestra / Bernard Haitink.
Decca London 425 065-2DM (68 minutes: ADD/DDD). Texts and translations included.
Recorded 1979.　　Ⓜ 𝗥𝗥

Symphony Nos. 5[a] and 9[b].
[a]Concertgebouw Orchestra; [b]London Philharmonic Orchestra / Bernard Haitink.
Decca London 425 066-2DM (76 minutes: ADD/DDD). Texts and translations included.
Recorded 1981. *Gramophone* Award Winner 1982-83.　　Ⓜ 𝗥𝗥

Symphony Nos. 6 and 12.
Concertgebouw Orchestra / Bernard Haitink.
Decca London 425 067-2DM (74 minutes: ADD/DDD). Texts and translations included.
Recorded 1983.　　Ⓜ Ⓢ 𝗥𝗥

Symphony No. 7.
London Philharmonic Orchestra / Bernard Haitink.
Decca London 425 068-2DM (79 minutes: ADD/DDD). Texts and translations included.
Recorded 1979. Ⓜ RR

Symphony No. 8.
Concertgebouw Orchestra / Bernard Haitink.
Decca London 425 071-2DM (62 minutes: ADD/DDD). Texts and translations included.
Recorded 1982. Ⓜ

Symphony No. 11.
Concertgebouw Orchestra / Bernard Haitink.
Decca London 425 072-2DM (61 minutes: ADD/DDD). Texts and translations included.
Recorded 1983. Ⓜ S RR

Symphony No. 13.
Marius Rintzler *bass* **Concertgebouw Choir and Orchestra / Bernard Haitink.**
Decca London 425 073-2DM (64 minutes: ADD/DDD). Texts and translations included.
Recorded 1982. Ⓜ RR

Symphony No. 14. Six Marina Tsvetaeva Poems, Op. 143.
Julia Varady *sop* **Ortrun Wenkel** *contr* **Dietrich Fischer-Dieskau** *bar*
Concertgebouw Orchestra / Bernard Haitink.
Decca London 425 074-2DM (72 minutes: ADD/DDD). Texts and translations included.
Recorded 1980. Ⓜ RR

Symphony No. 15[a]. From Jewish Folk Poetry, Op. 79[b].
Elisabeth Söderström *sop* **Ortrun Wenkel** *contr* **Ryszard Karczykowski** *ten*
[a]**London Philharmonic Orchestra;** [b]**Concertgebouw Orchestra / Bernard Haitink.**
Decca London 425 069-2DM (73 minutes: ADD/DDD). Texts and translations included.
Recorded 1978. Ⓜ RR

This, the first complete Western cycle of the symphonies, conducted by Bernard Haitink, returns to the catalogue at mid price, Decca having jettisoned a few minor works and decoupled several major ones. It is hard to argue with this presentation when it includes modern annotations and full recording data. Concerned for tradition, and with the need to challenge it, the young Shostakovich could be classical and modern, polemical and prankish by turns. Haitink, not entirely po-faced, turns in a thoroughly decent account of the First Symphony, missing just a little of the element of pastiche. The recoupling with the Third does strike sparks, the language of the later music variously foreshadowed in divergent contexts. In the Fourth Symphony, Haitink offers no stupendous revelations, content to bring out the dignity of the writing in a piece where we have come to expect something more sensational, less perfectly controlled. Even the hurtling *moto perpetuo fugato* passage for strings, which triggers the main climax of the first movement, seems just a little studied. His outer movements are helpfully split, by additional cues – but his literalness and sobriety fall short of the ideal, as, marginally, does the playing.

Haitink's Fifth, deeply considered and almost indecently well upholstered, is not easy to assess. Originally greeted with extreme reverence in these pages – its release followed hard on the heels of the publication of *Testimony* which surely influenced the critical response – it is an earnest attempt to make structural sense of the music's grand symphonic aspirations. It is only because the orchestral playing is generally so immaculate that one registers the curious glitch 2'13" into the *Largo*. That movement is generally less affecting than it can be, yet the preceding *Allegretto* is triumphantly brought off as a heavy-footed Mahlerian ländler. Then again, the first movement's long-limbed second subject chugs along reluctantly, dourly unphrased, with none of the easeful balm to be found in other interpretations. Haitink's Fifth is now generously paired with his solid, untrivial but scarcely earth-shattering Ninth. His Sixth and Twelfth are characterized by playing of predictable *gravitas* and tonal splendour. This Twelfth could be seen as the 'best' modern version.

The *Leningrad* is another matter. It has rightly been praised for its symphonic integrity and splendid sound. Haitink's stoical view of the Eighth is highly impressive, though not very varied in mood. Curiously, the finale is mis-cued. Kurt Sanderling's reading (Berlin Classics) is also highly impressive. The Tenth has always seemed less dependent on a conductor steeped in the Russian tradition, and the only drawback of Haitink's well-played, well-recorded account is his unsubtle, over-confident tone in the enigmatic third movement *Allegretto*. There is real demonic abandon in the *Scherzo*. Karajan's Tenth (DG) is very desirable but he offers no makeweight. Haitink offers a carefully prepared account of No. 2, where the choral contribution has the odd awkward moment but the overall effect is very arresting. His Eleventh too has such weight and precision that his customary detachment is mostly less noticeable than his phenomenal control. Haitink's Thirteenth boasts another of Decca's huge, reverberant recordings, of such 'cinematic' brilliance and range that it threatens to dwarf the music-making. The chorus and orchestra are on terrific form and the soloist, Marius Rintzler, would seem to be at one with Haitink's brooding approach (this is reviewed in much greater depth on page 903). As one of the first of Shostakovich's late scores to be taken seriously in the West, it is odd that the Fourteenth should have been so poorly represented in the CD catalogue. Haitink's polyglot reading does not really represent a viable solution – too much vital and specific tone colour is lost along with the original note-values. To make matters worse, Fischer-Dieskau is in hectoring mode and both soloists' proximity to the microphones makes for uncomfortable listening, though the orchestral contribution is excellent. Barshai (Russian Disc) can lay claim to *absolute* authenticity. It is a fascinating document, as he and Vishnevskaya rage against the dying of the light in every song, slicing seconds (sometimes minutes) off the timings of the Western account. Generally speaking the sound is close and crude, by no means intolerable but sufficiently prone to distortion to inhibit a general recommendation. In its way, however, this disc is indispensable.

Haitink's Fifteenth has always been highly regarded, despite some less than needle-sharp contributions from the percussion where it matters most. At medium price, and with a rather high-level transfer of its coupling (whose historical significance is ably outlined in the insert-note), this merits a place at or near the top of anyone's list. To sum up: Haitink's set, superbly engineered, is nothing if not reliable. For those who prize technical finesse over raw passion, Haitink remains a plausible first choice. These are endlessly fascinating, endlessly equivocal works.

Symphonies Nos. 1 and 6.
Scottish National Orchestra / Neeme Järvi.
Chandos CHAN8411 (64 minutes: DDD). Recorded 1984-85.   Ⓕ

The First Symphony, the 19-year-old composer's graduation piece from the then Leningrad Conservatory in 1925, may be indebted to Stravinsky, Prokofiev, Tchaikovsky and even Scriabin. But it rarely sounds like anything other than pure Shostakovich. The sophisticated mask of its first movement is drawn aside for a slow movement of Slav melancholy and foreboding, and the finale brilliantly stage-manages a way out. The Sixth (1939) takes the familiar Shostakovichian extremes of explosive activity and uneasy contemplation (that the composer reconciles in the finale of the First) and separates them into individual movements. Two swift movements (a mercurial but menacing *Scherzo*, and a real knees-up of a finale) follow on from an opening *Largo* whose slow lyrical declamations eventually all but freeze into immobility. Järvi has a will (and Chandos, the engineering) to explore the extremes of pace, mood and dynamics of both symphonies; his account of the First Symphony convinces precisely because those extremes intensify as the work progresses. Some may crave a fuller, firmer string sound, but the passionate intensity of the playing (in all departments) is never in doubt.

Symphonies Nos. 2 and 3.
London Voices; London Symphony Orchestra / Mstislav Rostropovich.
Teldec 4509-90853-2 (48 minutes: DDD). Recorded 1993.   Ⓕ

Rostropovich's disc is cut at a low level, which will make the dark opening pages of the Second Symphony implausibly opaque unless you reset the controls. The string playing then emerges as impressively polished, the wind aptly angular and spiky, more characterful than their rivals as the music gains pace. Only the LSO's leader seems a trifle thin of tone (as recorded). Under Rostropovich, uniquely among recent exponents of the score, the factory whistle is not doubled by brass. Thereafter the churchy acoustic ensures that his London Voices sounds at least as numerous as rival recordings; and the men at least are more comfortable with the idiom. The climax is both fervent and unusually secure of pitch. Rostropovich's account of the Third is an outstanding achievement. Relishing the opportunities for display, the LSO finds its best form – crisper of ensemble than in previous outings with this inspirational, if not always ideally lucid, conductor – and the recorded sound is surely the best in Teldec's cycle. The opening clarinet theme is exquisitely done and, amid the corybantic tumult of Revolution, the lyrical moments are empowered here with rare emotional clout. Already we hear the authentic voice of the composer Rostropovich knew as friend and mentor, the disillusioned chronicler of Soviet reality.

Shostakovich Symphony No. 4.
Britten Russian Funeral.
City of Birmingham Symphony Orchestra / Sir Simon Rattle.
EMI CDC5 55476-2 (68 minutes: DDD). Recorded 1994.   Ⓕ

This could just be the most important Western recording of the Fourth since the long-deleted Ormandy and Previn versions. Naturally, it complements rather than replaces Kondrashin's reading (Chant du Monde), taped shortly after the work's belated unveiling in December 1961: papery strings and lurid brass cannot disguise that conductor's unique authority even when Shostakovich's colouristic effects are muted by rudimentary Soviet sound engineering. In his recording, Rattle's approach is more obviously calculated, supremely brilliant but just a little cold. A certain firmness and self-confidence is obvious from the first. The restrained Hindemithian episode is relatively square, the first climax superbly built. The second group unfolds seamlessly with the glorious *espressivo* of the strings not much threatened by the not very mysterious intrusions of harp and bass clarinet. Tension builds again, some way into the development, with the lacerating (Kondrashin-like) intensity of the strings' *moto perpetuo fugato* passage.

Six miraculously terraced discords herald the two-faced recapitulation. Kondrashin and Järvi (Chandos) find more emotional inevitability in Shostakovich's destabilizing tactics hereabouts. Rattle doesn't quite locate a compensating irony, although his closing bars are convincingly icy, with nicely audible gong. Even in Rattle's experienced hands, the finale is not all plain sailing. The initial quasi-Mahlerian march is underpinned by disappointingly fuzzy timpani strokes which lose the point of their own lopsidedness. But then the section's mock-solemn climax is simply tremendous (and tremendously loud). The incisive *Allegro* is launched with (deliberate?) abruptness at an unbelievably fast tempo and, even if the music doesn't always make sense at this pace, the results are breathtaking. The denouement is approached with real flair. A superbly characterized trombone solo, hushed expectant strings and the most ambiguous of all Shostakovich perorations is unleashed with devastating force. The coda is mightily impressive too. After this, the Britten encore risks seeming beside the point; this really is emotional play-acting. In sum, neither Kondrashin's nor Järvi's more direct emotional involvement are easily passed over. On the other hand, Rattle does give us a thrilling example of what a relatively objective, thoroughly 'modern' approach has to offer today. With its huge dynamic range and uncompromising, analytical style, EMI's recording pulls no punches, and the awesome precision of the CBSO's playing makes for an unforgettable experience.

Symphony No. 5. Ballet Suite No. 5, Op. 27a.
Scottish National Orchestra / Neeme Järvi.
Chandos CHAN8650 (76 minutes: DDD). Recorded 1988.   Ⓕ

There are more Shostakovich Fifths than you can shake a stick at in the CD catalogue at present, and several of them are very good. Järvi's makes perhaps the safest recommendation of them all: it has a generous coupling (which cannot be said of many of its rivals), it has no drawbacks (save, for some tastes, a slight touch of heart-on-sleeve in the slow movement) and a number of distinct advantages. A profound seriousness, for one thing, and an absolute sureness about the nature of the finale, which many conductors feel the need to exaggerate, either as brassy optimism or as bitter irony. Järvi takes it perfectly straight, denying neither option, and the progression from slow movement (the overtness of its emotion finely justified) to finale seems more natural, less of a jolt than usual. The SNO cannot rival the sheer massiveness of sound of some of the continental orchestras who have recorded this work, but while listening one hardly notices the lack, so urgent and polished is the playing. A very natural and wide-ranging recording, too, and the lengthy Suite (eight movements from Shostakovich's early ballet *The Bolt*, forming an exuberantly entertaining essay on the various modes that his sense of humour could take) makes much more than a mere fill-up.

Symphonies Nos. 7 and 10.
Chicago Symphony Orchestra / Leonard Bernstein.
DG 427 632-2GH2 (two discs: 120 minutes: DDD). Recorded live in 1988.   Ⓕ

The *Leningrad* Symphony was composed in haste as the Nazis sieged and bombarded the city (in 1941). It caused an immediate sensation, but posterity has been less enthusiastic. What business has the first movement's unrelated long central 'invasion' episode doing in a symphonic movement? Is the material of the finale really distinctive enough for its protracted treatment? Michael Oliver, in his original *Gramophone* review, wrote that in this performance 'the symphony sounds most convincingly like a symphony, and one needing no programme to justify it'. Added to which the work's epic and cinematic manner has surely never been more powerfully realized. These are live recordings, with occasional noise from the audience (and the conductor), but the Chicago Orchestra has rarely sounded more polished or committed under any conditions. The strings are superb in the First Symphony, full and weightily present, and Bernstein's manner in this symphony is comparably bold and theatrical of gesture. A word of caution: set your volume control carefully for the *Leningrad* Symphony's start; it is scored for six of both trumpets and trombones and no other recording has reproduced them so clearly, and to such devastating effect.

Symphony No. 8.
London Symphony Orchestra / André Previn.
EMI Matrix CDM5 65521-2 (61 minutes: ADD). Recorded 1973.　　Ⓜ🆁🆁

The Eighth Symphony, written in 1943, two years after the *Leningrad*, offers a wiser, more bitterly disillusioned Shostakovich. The heroic peroration of the Seventh's finale is here replaced by numbed whimsy and eventual uneasy calm. André Previn has since re-recorded the symphony but this youthful account serves to remind us that the music is the product of a young man's imagination. The remake has greater breadth in every sense and, note for note, the orchestral playing is often finer. However, many will prefer the urgency of this earlier version. At that time, Previn seemed content to add a patina of mid-Atlantic gloss, and a good deal of subtlety, to the raw expressivity of the earlier Soviet recordings; he had not yet adopted the self-consciously epic manner thought appropriate today. There are few who know how to bring off the symphony as a gloomy and spiritless *in memoriam*, but the lithe freshness of the Previn is a compelling alternative. EMI's transfer is punchy and focused.

Symphonies Nos. 9 and 15.
Moscow Philharmonic Orchestra / Kyrill Kondrashin.
Melodiya 74321 19846-2 (54 minutes: ADD). Recorded 1965 and 1974.　　Ⓜ

After Mravinsky's politically motivated refusal to undertake the première of the Thirteenth in 1962, Shostakovich found a stalwart interpreter in Kyrill Kondrashin. Shostakovich recordings don't come any more authentic than this. Objectively speaking, the playing of the Moscow Philharmonic is not uniformly distinguished. Kondrashin can be startlingly brisk, the panache and brilliance hardening into mannerism. The transfers are no more than serviceable and the badly translated accompanying notes are untrustworthy at best. That said, here is unbeatable music-making, and these are arguably among Kondrashin's greatest recordings. The classic Ninth (from 1965) is conveniently paired with a superbly vivid Fifteenth (from 1974), generally hard-driven *à la* Mravinsky but far more convincingly poised. The first movement goes at a frightening lick, deserting the toy shop for the asylum, the slow movement lacks only the very last ounce of desolation and the finale, always intelligently conceived, is suitably emotive at the close. The sound has immediacy and just enough depth. Though of earlier vintage, the Ninth enjoys a more generous acoustic, the tape a little prone to distortion at moments of stress (which for Kondrashin come more often than usual). Both interpretations have a tonal weight and sarcastic intent which cannot fail to shock the uninitiated. To sum up: he finds in these scores an unrivalled degree of dramatic tension, bringing to the surface raw emotions that more smoothly executed Western accounts play down. We may be impressed by the diligent literalness and sobriety of Haitink, but to what extent should we worry if he illuminates aspects of the music the composer himself thought unimportant? It isn't simply a matter of 'authentic' orchestral timbre. Kondrashin's versions document a very special kind of insight.

Shostakovich Symphony No. 10.
Mussorgsky (orch. Shostakovich) Songs and Dances of Death.
Robert Lloyd *bass*
Philadelphia Orchestra / Mariss Jansons.
EMI CDC5 55232-2 (72 minutes: DDD). Recorded 1994.　　Ⓕ

Stalin died on March 5th, 1953, the same day as Prokofiev. In the summer of that year Shostakovich produced a symphony which can be taken as his own return to life after the dark night of dictatorship – the last two movements included, for the first time in his output, his personal DSCH signature (the notes D, E flat, C, B natural, in the German spelling). In the West the Tenth Symphony is now widely regarded as the finest of the cycle of 15, not just for its sheer depth of personal feeling, but because it finds the purest and subtlest musical representation of that feeling. Perhaps this is why it is less dependent than some of Shostakovich's major works on a conductor steeped in the Russian idiom. Anyone expecting a welter of hairpin *diminuendos* and expressive nudges will be disappointed by Jansons's Shostakovich – solid, sturdy and rhythmically taut rather than overly individualistic for the most part. Jansons's first movement is basically brisk, with thrustful strings and conscientiously Soviet-style woodwind. It is a cogent enough view and yet the sense of underlying desolation is lacking, despite the conductor's vocal exhortations. The *Scherzo* is brilliantly articulated – even if the relatively leisurely pace robs the music of its potential to intimidate. The 'difficult' third movement is more convincing, though again unusually confident in tone. It would be churlish not to single out the superb horn playing. The main body of the finale (the introduction is separately tracked by the way) is launched with precise rhythmic clarity rather than irrepressible enthusiasm. In short, this is an excellent, sometimes dazzling choice among modern versions but it may strike seasoned listeners as slightly sterile, at once tightly controlled and spiritually disengaged. There is more passion in the coupling. Robert Lloyd is curiously under-represented on CD in the Russian repertoire that suits him so well. His admirers are bound to want this performance, which is very impressive as sheer singing. Throughout the disc, the close focus of the recording exposes a few instances of less than perfect synchronization but with playing so spectacularly accomplished, if not recognizably Philadelphian, this must be counted an outstanding achievement in its way.

Symphony No. 11.
Leningrad Philharmonic Orchestra / Evgeny Mravinsky.
Praga PR254 018 (61 minutes: ADD). Recorded live in 1967.   Ⓕ

Despite the rawness and occasional congestion of the sound this is a performance of extraordinary vehemence. There is an element in the work, of course, that is very close to agitprop; there are pages in the terrifying *Scherzo* and in the finale that are not so much composed in primary colours as splashed on to a wall in broad strokes of dripping red and black. Many recent performances have refined this element with sheer orchestral virtuosity, but that is not Mravinsky's way: his brass players yell at the tops of their voices, his percussion threatens to overwhelm the rest of the orchestra, his violins come within an ace of breaking their strings with the sheer scorch of their bows' impact. It is valuable too for the unique sound of a Soviet orchestra during the Soviet period playing a profoundly Soviet work: you really do get the impression that every member of the orchestra knows and has complex reactions to all those quoted revolutionary or pre-revolutionary songs. The work is about a revolt against intolerable oppression. Such a revolt, suppressed like that in Leningrad in 1905, took place in Prague not long after this performance. It has such eloquence that you can almost persuade yourself that it played a part in that.

Symphony No. 11.
St Petersburg Philharmonic Orchestra / Vladimir Ashkenazy.
Decca 448 179-2DH (55 minutes: DDD). Recorded 1994.   Ⓕ

There are many felicitous touches here, rather less in the way of *gravitas*. For once, the motto theme is clearly audible from the start, just as, at the very end of the piece, the alternating major and minor thirds ring out cleanly against the orchestral clamour. Detail emerges vividly throughout, with the recording team favouring relatively close balances to convey the orchestra's distinctive sonority. The trumpets blaze through with the old fervour at key points in the second movement; the strings retain their characteristic huskiness even if they sound thinner than they used to. And yet to adopt generally brisk tempos without Mravinsky's insistent ferocity of address is to risk taming the beast. If the work is to be associated with big, universalized ideas of requiem and redemption – a (Brittenish?) search for eternal rest in the face of violence and death – it will require careful handling. Ashkenazy is a discreet interpreter in the best sense but, given his avoidance of the *self-consciously* profound, you may feel that Shostakovich's rhetoric is not always empowered with sufficient clout to banish the doubts. To sum up: this is a fresh, unaffected reading.

Symphony No. 12ᵃ. The Execution of Stepan Razin, Op. 119.
Siegfried Vogel bass
Leipzig Radio Chorus and Symphony Orchestra / Herbert Kegel
ᵃ**Leipzig Gewandhaus Orchestra / Ogan Durjan**.
Philips Collector Series 434 172-2PM (74 minutes: ADD). Recorded 1967.   Ⓜ

Since no one has yet seen fit to restore the classic Kondrashin Melodiya recording (from the late 1960s) of *The Execution of Stepan Razin*, the reappearance of this full-blooded account from Leipzig is most welcome. True, Siegfried Vogel is somewhat limited in his range of colour, but he and the chorus make a good stab at idiomatic Russian while Herbert Kegel manages to secure a high level of intensity from the orchestra, whether in passages of glacial stillness or of hyperactivity. Together they capture the denunciatory tone of the conclusion, so typical of Shostakovich's music at this time (two years on from the Symphony No. 13). The absence from the booklet of Evtushenko's text or even a translation is a serious drawback, but the performance itself is a class above its only current rival on Koch International. The Twelfth Symphony receives almost as good a performance, marred only by imperfect tuning in solo woodwind and brass lines – the brooding second movement is particularly badly affected. Ogan Durjan's interpretation does not touch hysterical extremes in the Mravinsky manner (on a mid-price Erato disc without a coupling), but it is finely paced and ultimately rather stirring. Good value for money overall, but what a shame about the absence of texts.

Symphony No. 13.
Anatoly Kocherga *bass*
National Male Choir of Estonia; Gothenburg Symphony Orchestra / Neeme Järvi.
DG 449 187-2GH (58 minutes: DDD). Text and translation included. Recorded 1995.　　　Ⓕ

This is the most entertaining modern recording of what is usually counted a forbidding work. You may even feel that the conductor's flexible tempos and extrovert manner represent a distraction from the real issues. That would be unfair, although the changes of pace in *Babiy Yar* are undeniably abrupt and deprive the closing bars of their usual solidity and impact. The Estonian choir sound very confident and the bullish effect is enhanced by willing if not always refined playing from an orchestra that lacks great weight of string tone. The big, spacious recording helps of course but Anatoly Kocherga is the crucial player, not a deep bass perhaps but an authentic Boris with a range of expressive nuance and a ready responsiveness to text that some will find overstated. In the paradoxical finale, Yevtushenko's joke at the expense of the compliant Soviet writer Alexei Tolstoy is unusually well pointed, and the final pages are intensely poignant even if they no longer feel like the inevitable outcome of a symphonic journey as undertaken by Haitink. Järvi may lack his *gravitas* but his alternative could well appeal to those put off by the perceived severity of the piece. Transliterated Russian text and translations are provided.

Symphony No. 13.
Marius Rintzler *bass*
Concertgebouw Orchestra Choir (male voices); **Concertgebouw Orchestra / Bernard Haitink.**
Decca 425 073-2DM (64 minutes: DDD). Notes, texts and translations included.
Recorded 1984.　　　Ⓜ🆁🆁

With one single reservation Haitink's account of *Babiy Yar* is superb. The reservation is that Marius Rintzler, although he has all the necessary blackness and gravity and is in amply sonorous voice, responds to the anger and the irony and the flaming denunciations of Yevtushenko's text with scarcely a trace of the histrionic fervour they cry out for: he is more like a sympathetic but detached observer than an impassioned orator, and he shows little relish for the sound of Russian words. The excellent chorus, though, is very expressive and it makes up for a lot, and so does the powerful and sustained drama of Haitink's direction. He has solved the difficult problems of pacing a symphony with three slow movements (one is so gripped throughout that one is scarcely aware that there are such problems) and the atmosphere of each movement is vividly evoked, with a particular care for the subtleties of Shostakovich's orchestration. The orchestral sound, indeed, is magnificent: one can readily believe that the huge forces called for in the score were actually provided, but this does not necessitate any unnatural focusing on (say) the celeste in order that it shall register. The perspective is very natural throughout, and there is an excellent sense of the performance taking place in a believable space.

Symphony No. 13.
Vitaly Gromadsky *bass* **USSR State Academic Choir; Yurlov Russian Choir;**
Moscow Philharmonic Orchestra / Kyrill Kondrashin.
Russian Disc RDCD11191 (57 minutes: AAD). Text and translation included.
Recorded live in 1962.　　　Ⓕ

This will be a self-recommending issue for many readers. Rival, Western accounts, like those of Järvi and Haitink, make a different sort of impact. More concerned with the symphonic than the dramatic, they bring a touch more subtlety to the ironic equivocations of 'A Career' but are less successful in putting across the straightforward, 'dissident' anger of previous movements. Like early Western commentators they remain at one remove from the emotional life of the piece. Shostakovich confounds expectations not merely by selecting these vivid, dissenting verses (imagine Copland setting Bob Dylan *c*1963) but by presenting them in an idiom of Mussorgskian simplicity, unimpeachably 'correct' from the official Soviet point of view. It is no accident that the composer follows the Twelfth's revolutionary *Dawn of Humanity* with a consecutive opus focusing on the enduring legacy of Stalinism. On Russian Disc's rediscovered (stereo) tape, the finer points are forgotten as every syllable of text is projected with maximum force.

For anyone unconvinced by Haitink's monolithic conception – for all his technical assurance, he can seem to be missing the point – this disc is the one to have, whatever its exact provenance. The choral singing is outstanding and, in place of Marius Rintzler's impassive manner (and occasional habit of sliding up to the note), we have Vitaly Gromadsky, risking more than critical disfavour by taking on this controversial new work, supremely committed (if not without moments of uncertain pitch), gloriously, unmistakably Russian. He does miss a vital cue in the desolate third movement, 'In the store', here taken at an easy, flowing pace. As for the sound quality, it is vivid enough, by no means impossibly crude, although the vocal image can 'bleed' across the sound stage and there are some worrying drop-outs five minutes into 'Babi Yar'. Even if the booklet's claim that we are eavesdropping on the première is not supported by the recording details on the insert-note, this is an indispensable piece of musical history.

Symphony No. 14. Two Pieces for String Quartet (arr. Sikorski).
Margareta Haverinen *sop* **Petteri Salomaa** *bass*
Tapiola Sinfonietta / Joseph Swensen.
Ondine ODE845-2 (59 minutes: DDD). Text and translation included. Recorded 1994-95.   Ⓕ

The multilingual version of the Fourteenth Symphony was sanctioned by the composer but it remains something of a rarity on disc; some vital and specific tone colour is lost along with the original note values, and the 'three lilies' adorn the grave of 'The Suicide' more elegantly in the Russian. Bernard Haitink may not agree. He elected to use the multilingual text in his 1980 recording and now Joseph Swensen presents this compelling alternative. We tend to take sonic excellence for granted these days but this is a true state-of-the-art recording with the soloists more naturally placed than in the rival Decca issue and an orchestral sound combining great clarity with just enough hall resonance. The performance has character too, if lacking the pervasive chill of the earliest Soviet accounts. The conductor secures excellent results from the Tapiola Sinfonietta. It is a lean and super-efficient group, yet without the loss of character this can sometimes imply.

Of the soloists, the bass-baritone Petteri Salomaa is particularly impressive: his is a voice of rare tonal beauty, a Billy Budd rather than a Boris. His pronunciation is a little odd at times – something more noticeable in a version which has the singers feigning familiarity with four languages – but you may not see this as a problem. Tempos are perceptibly more 'extreme' than Haitink's, with the opening 'De profundis' dangerously slow in the modern manner and a strikingly well-characterized instrumental contribution to 'A la Santé' ('In the Santé Prison'). The fillers, larger than life, brilliantly dispatched and curiously inappropriate, are based on original quartet pieces which only came to light in the mid-1980s. The first shares material with *Lady Macbeth of Mtsensk*; the second appears as the polka from *The Age of Gold*! This is nevertheless a more rewarding, more probingly conducted disc than most of the current Shostakovich crop.

Shostakovich (arr. Derevianko) Symphony No. 15.
Schnittke Praeludium in memoriam Dmitri Shostakovich.
Gidon Kremer *vn* **Clemens Hagen** *vc* **Vadim Sakharov** *pf/celesta*
Michael Gärtner, Edgar Guggeis, Peter Sadlo *perc*
DG 449 966-2GH (47 minutes: DDD). Recorded 1995.   Ⓕ

While the last of Shostakovich's symphonies has chamber-like qualities, it is also acutely imagined in terms of orchestral sonority, so much so that you may be somewhat taken aback by this version. Viktor Derevianko's arrangement of the Fifteenth is by no means unsympathetic – it would appear to have had the blessing of the composer – but it cannot have been easy to find aural equivalents for the densely scored climaxes of the slow movement and finale. Certainly these passages no longer stand out from the rest as they do in the original work. Nor do the snatches of Wagner which open that finale have anything like their original emotive force: there's no getting away from the fact that quotations from *The Ring* sound incongruous on piano. On the other hand, Derevianko's skeleton exposes the nub of the argument in a way that may prove instructive for those who prize Shostakovich above all as a manipulator of symphonic form. And what a relief to encounter a properly articulated percussion pattern at the close. There are some implausibly tinny moments along the way, but much of the music-making is spellbinding, and one is struck again and again by the players' unerring sensitivity. The Schnittke makeweight is equally well served; it is one of his more effective lamentations, concise as well as deeply felt. Notwithstanding the short measure, this package is recommended to adventurous spirits.

String Quartets – No. 1 in C major, Op. 49; **No. 2** in A major, Op. 68; **No. 3** in F major, Op. 73; **No. 4** in D major, Op. 83; **No. 5** in B flat major, Op. 92; **No. 6** in G major, Op. 101; **No. 7** in F sharp minor, Op. 108; **No. 8** in C minor, Op. 110; **No. 9** in E flat major, Op. 117; **No. 10** in A flat major, Op. 118; **No. 11** in F minor, Op. 122; **No. 12** in D flat major, Op. 133; **No. 13** in B flat minor, Op 138; **No. 14** in F sharp minor, Op. 142; **No. 15** in E flat minor, Op. 144.

String Quartets Nos. 1-15.
Fitzwilliam Quartet (Christopher Rowland, Jonathan Sparey *vns* Alan George *va* Ioan Davies *vc*).
Decca 455 776-2LC6 (six discs: 377 minutes: ADD). Recorded 1975-77.
Gramophone Award Winner 1977.   Ⓑ ⓇⓇ

If Shostakovich's cycle of 15 symphonies can be said to represent a musical thread passing through the whole of the composer's public life, then it can be argued that his cycle of 15 string quartets represents the private persona of the man behind the mask, from the beginning of his personal anguish in the late 1930s, until his death in 1975. At the time of his First Quartet, composed in 1938, he was already an experienced and respected composer with five symphonies to his credit as well as much music for stage and film. Thenceforth his symphonic music inscrutably presented the emotions – albeit largely ironically – that the State expected from its leading composer, while the quartets provided an outlet for the emotions within and for his personal responses to the events taking place in the world around him. If the music is rich in irony, then the language that the composer uses is quite straightforward, with a defined tonality, simple melodies, uncluttered rhythms and clear textures. There is only one possible composer, so recognizably individual is the voice.

The Fitzwilliam Quartet originally recorded its cycle in the mid-1970s, shortly after a concentrated period of study with the composer. Despite being recorded in analogue, the sound quality is still remarkably good. The group has a remarkable understanding of the idiom and of the music's underlying motivation. In the First Quartet it captures the uneasy mood (reminiscent of the contemporary Fifth Symphony) behind the seemingly placid surface. In the Fourth Quartet, it gives the Jewish idioms – a metaphor for the oppressed artist and never far away in Shostakovich's music – a more deliberate, and thus more natural-sounding, tempo. Probably the best known of the quartets is No. 8, composed in Dresden in 1960 and dedicated to the victims of Fascism and of the War, and in view of the constant use of the DSCH motif and the quotations from several of his own pieces, there can be little doubt that Shostakovich considered himself among their number. It's a grim, often macabre, work and once again the Fitzwilliam captures the loneliness of the composer. So often, his solo melodies, set against a stark and sombre accompaniment, sound like a voice crying in the wilderness. The quartets are well worth getting to know and the performances by the Fitzwilliam Quartet, despite their age, still seem to reach the heart of the composer's intentions.

String Quartets Nos. 1, 3 and 4. Two Pieces for String Quartet (1931).
Shostakovich Quartet (Andrei Shishlov, Sergei Pishchugin *vns* Alexander Galkovsky *va* Alexander Korchagin *vc*).
Olympia OCD531 (77 minutes: ADD). Recorded 1978-85.   Ⓕ

String Quartets Nos. 2, 5 and 7.
Shostakovich Quartet
Olympia OCD532 (78 minutes: ADD). Recorded 1978-85.   Ⓕ

String Quartets Nos. 6, 8 and 9.
Shostakovich Quartet
Olympia OCD533 (74 minutes: ADD). Recorded 1978-85.   Ⓕ

String Quartets Nos. 10, 11 and 15.
Shostakovich Quartet
Olympia OCD534 (78 minutes: ADD). Recorded 1978-85.   Ⓕ

String Quartets Nos. 12-14.
Shostakovich Quartet
Olympia OCD535 (73 minutes: ADD). Recorded 1978-85.   Ⓕ

Any attempt to rank these players in relation to their more widely acclaimed opposite numbers in the Borodin Quartet seems pointless at this level of dedication; both teams have lived through this most extraordinary of twentieth-century quartet-cycles many times. If any general observation about the two can be made, it is that the Borodin finds more corporate subtleties and passing shades in some of the earlier quartets, while the individual members of the Shostakovich Quartet make even stronger, more vibrant soloists. In the context of Shostakovich's many, very vocal solos and recitatives, it hardly seems invidious to single out the first violinist, Andrei Shishlov – dark, powerful and flawless of intonation throughout. Listen to his sleight-of-hand freedom in the unaccompanied melody of No. 6's finale: the Borodin's Mikhail Kopelman doesn't begin to touch imagination like that. These players also teach us to hold in equal awe the more classically contained quartets – No. 6 and the outer movements of No. 10 have a special grace – and all the slow movements are impressively unfolded with a steady fluency (notable in the passacaglias). As for the last rites of No. 15, not even the Borodin finds such implicit human warmth in the still *fugato* of the Elegy. In tandem with the impassioned solos of the later movements, it's an impressive summing-up of this team's best intentions. Balances in the earlier recordings are less than kind to second fiddle and cellist and are uncomfortably boxy. You'll also have to adjust the volume-level for consecutive listening. If you seek only a single-disc token of the achievement, Vol. 4 (featuring Quartets Nos. 10, 11 and 15) is the one to have.

String Quartets Nos. 1 and 15.
Borodin Quartet (Mikhail Kopelman, Andrei Abramenkov *vns* Dmitri Shebalin *va*
Valentin Berlinsky *vc*).
Teldec 4509-98417-2 (53 minutes: DDD). Recorded 1995.　　　　　　　　　　　　　　Ⓕ

The point of coupling Shostakovich's first and last string quartets is obvious, and the contrast
between what the composer himself called his 'Springtime Quartet' and the unprecedented sequence
of six slow movements written months before his death could not be more poignant. The
performances take full account of this contrast, not only in sheer amplitude of gesture (the
single-note *crescendos* in the second movement of the Fifteenth Quartet are scorching) but also in
command of scale: the desolation of the Fifteenth's opening movement, as long as all four of the
First put together, is unrelieved, but it is never for one moment monotonous. There are big gestures
even in the First Quartet, but these players have the tonal range to encompass an almost naïve
sweetness in its second movement as well. The recordings are very fine.

String Quartets Nos. 4, 11 and 14.
Hagen Quartet (Lukas Hagen, Rainer Schmidt *vns* Veronika Hagen *va* Clemens Hagen *vc*).
DG 445 864-2GH (71 minutes: DDD). Recorded 1993-94.　　　　　　　　　　　　　　Ⓕ

The Hagen has chosen a fascinating journey to the unusual at-one-with-the-world radiance that
ends the Fourteenth. Already in this interpretation of the Fourth we hear those voices from beyond
the grave that trouble the later quartets. The introspective shading of the *Andantino*'s earlier stages,
climax included, sounds as if the mutes are already on. And when in fact the players do take them
up – for the rest of the movement and the whole of the ensuing *Allegretto* – the sound becomes
even more refined; note how first violin Lukas Hagen sings out his solo at fig. 29 (track 2, 3'31")
with a frail, unearthly beauty which sounds as if it emanates from a viola d'amore. Corporate work
is faultlessly and subtly in sympathy with the essence of the piece; the only individual weakness
occurs when Shostakovich asks the cellist to come to the fore in the finale's build-up of tension –
Clemens Hagen's tone doesn't really make itself felt here – though the collective *fortissimo* cry from
the heart shortly afterwards makes amends with even more intensity than some of the Hagen's
senior counterparts (including the Shostakovich Quartet on Olympia) have previously found there.

Clemens does rather lack the presence to take the lead in Quartet No. 14, dedicated to the cellist of
the Beethoven Quartet, and emphasizing his role accordingly; the sound can be lovely, but right at
the start he has the misfortune to be echoed by his more characterful brother. Still, the F sharp
major ending is as implicitly moving as it can be, and joint string power in crises comes very close
to the genuine Russian article. Indeed, in the fifth-movement *Humoresque* of the Eleventh the
limelighted second violin – Rainer Schmidt, the quartet's febrile and ever-impressive outside
influence – brings so much forceful tone to the swelling of his two repeated notes that it sounds for
all the world as if two violins are playing in unison, not just the one. Again, the joint approach to
chants and combats, not to mention Lukas's extraordinary handling of the *glissandos* in the second
movement, bring an urgently vocal quality to the work.

Shostakovich String Quartet No. 8.
Schnittke String Quartet No. 2.
Tchaikovsky String Quartet No. 1 in D major, Op. 11.
Duke Quartet (Louisa Fuller, Rick Koster *vns* John Metcalfe *va* Ivan McCready *vc*).
Collins Classics 1450-2 (70 minutes: DDD). Recorded 1995.　　　　　　　　　　　　Ⓕ

Shostakovich has 15 string quartet masterpieces to choose from, none of which is either 'early' or
musically insubstantial; but because the Eighth has historical-political connotations it tends to be
the most often recorded; the others tend to get ignored, at least outside of recorded or live cycles.
The Duke Quartet goes for the jugular, especially in the three *Largos*: the second in particular yields
a handsome body of tone while the sudden ray of light at 3'44" has real pathos. The only minor
reservation concerns the *Allegretto*, which sounds just a mite too cheerful for the ghostly, cynical
statement that it is. Placing Schnittke's Second Quartet directly after Shostakovich's Eighth was a
stroke of genius, especially as its opening harmonies seem to echo the D-S-C-H motif that closes
the earlier work. Schnittke's piece incorporates a frenzied *Agitato* (with wild arpeggios to the fore),
a prayer-like *Mesto* and an intense *Moderato* finale that retreats among ethereal harmonics. It is a
very powerful piece; the programme ends with Tchaikovsky's classically proportioned First Quartet.
Here the Duke Quartet's phrasing is somewhat fussy, especially in the first movement, and there are
also some uncomfortable tempo relations. Still, the last two movements are sprightly enough, the
recordings are good and the whole adds up to a programme that is certainly worth hearing –
especially for the sake of the Shostakovich and the Schnittke.

Piano Quintet in G minor, Op. 57[a]. Piano Trio No. 2 in E minor, Op. 67.
Elisabeth Leonskaja *pf* **Borodin Quartet** (Mikhail Kopelman, [a]Andrei Abramenkov *vns* [a]Dmitri Shebalin *va* Valentin Berlinsky *vc*).
Teldec 4509-98414-2 (63 minutes: DDD). Recorded 1995. Ⓕ RR

The Piano Quintet is almost symphonic in its proportions, lasting some 35 minutes, and has been popular with audiences ever since its first performance in 1940. Much of its popularity stems from Shostakovich's highly memorable material, particularly in the boisterous and genial *Scherzo* and finale movements. Because of the presence of a piano and of the powerful emotions expressed in them, the Quintet and Trio are commonly given very big performances indeed. Those on this recording are by no means small, but they are chamber music, and that seems to be the view of the pianist as well as the string players. The finale of the Piano Trio actually gains in power from this, the greatest weight of tone being reserved for the true climax, and half the intensity of the Quintet, in this reading, comes from a remarkably wide and masterfully controlled range of sonority and dynamic: note how very gradually the fugal second movement acquires warmth and how the poignant 'Intermezzo' gains pathos from the delicate clashes of the piano line. Leonskaja is a superb partner in both works. The recordings are very fine, with the balance just right in both works.

Shostakovich Piano Trios – No. 1 in C minor, Op. 8; No. 2 in E minor, Op. 67.
Schnittke Trio.
Vienna Piano Trio (Wolfgang Redik *vn* Marcus Trefny Stefan Mendl *pf*).
Nimbus NI5572 (69 minutes: DDD). Recorded 1998. Ⓕ

Shostakovich's adolescent First Trio's ramshackle structure seems to matter less than its surprisingly Gallic-sounding, passionately late-romantic invention. The Vienna Piano Trio offers a rich-toned and meticulously prepared account. The tricky cello opening to the Second Trio is wonderfully ethereal here, and the even more tricky accumulating tempo over the entire movement is steady and logical, though this and the main tempo for the *Scherzo* are both more reined in than in the composer's own account (once available on Supraphon). The passacaglia and finale are properly intense and none the worse for being kept within the bounds of euphony, though the ideal performance, yet to be realized on CD, would be one which drained bitterer dregs of sorrow and took excitement closer to the point of hyperventilation. Schnittke's Trio is more than an interesting makeweight. The String Trio original dates from 1985, the fateful year of the composer's first stroke and a period when he seemed to have a direct line to a kind of other-worldly inspiration (far more so than in later years when he claimed that more or less explicitly). True, the two longish movements occasionally seem at a loss, and at such times the gaucheness curiously echoes that of the teenage Shostakovich. Overall though this is one of Schnittke's most economical and restrained scores, and one of his finest. At every turn the Vienna Piano Trio is sensitive to the character and flow of this haunting music. A fine disc, then – imaginative programming, accomplished performances, and rich, well-balanced recording.

Cello Sonata. Piano Quintet in G minor, Op. 57.
Mstislav Rostropovich *vc* **Dmitri Shostakovich** *pf*
Beethoven Quartet (Dmitry Tsyganov, Vasily Shirinsky *vns* Vadim Borisovsky *va* Sergey Shirinsky *vc*).
Revelation mono RV70005 (55 minutes: ADD). Recorded 1957 and1950. Ⓜ H

Shostakovich's piano playing is all that you might expect it to be, brilliant in the Cello Sonata and intense in the Quintet – virtues that mirror the two works' leading musical qualities. Both recordings have been reissued before, though the present transfer of the Quintet was dubbed from acetate rather than direct from tape. In other respects, the sound is more than respectable. Performance-wise, the sonata parades some notably accomplished cello playing, warm and full-bodied in the first movement and hugely energetic in the finale. The darker Piano Quintet is more impressive still, with the sweetest string tone imaginable at the start of the fugue (Dmitry Tsyganov's lead violin is extremely distinctive) and plenty of drive elsewhere. It is, above all, a supremely authoritative reading, drily though clearly recorded, a significant release, both musically and historically.

---

24 Preludes and Fugues, Op. 87 – No. 1 in C major; **No. 2** in A minor; **No. 3** in G major; **No. 4** in E minor; **No. 5** in D major; **No. 6** in B minor; **No. 7** in A major; **No. 8** in F sharp minor; **No. 9** in E major; **No. 10** in C sharp minor; **No. 11** in B major; **No. 12** in G sharp minor; **No. 13** in F sharp major; **No. 14** in E flat minor; **No. 15** in D flat major; **No. 16** in B flat minor; **No. 17** in A flat major; **No. 18** in F minor; **No. 19** in E flat major; **No. 20** in C minor; **No. 21** in B flat major; **No. 22** in G minor; **No. 23** in F major; **No. 24** in D minor.

Shostakovich Preludes and Fugues Nos. 4, 12, 14, 15, 17 and 23.
Scriabin Poème-nocturne, Op. 61. Two Danses, Op. 73. Vers la flamme, Op. 72. Fantasie in B minor, Op. 28.
Prokofiev Piano Sonatas – No. 4 in C minor, Op. 29; No. 6 in A major, Op. 82. Pieces, Op. 12 – Legend. Visions fugitives, Op. 22 – Allegretto; Animato; Molto giocoso; Con eleganza; Commodo; Allegretto tranquillo; Con vivacita; Feroce; Inquieto; Con una dolce lentezza. Pieces, Op. 32 – Danse; Waltz. Three Pieces from Cinderella, Op. 95 – Gavotte. Ten Pieces from Cinderella, Op. 97 – Autumn fairy; Oriental dance. Six Pieces from Cinderella, Op. 102 – Grand waltz; Quarrel.
Sviatoslav Richter pf
Philips 438 627-2PH2 (two discs: 152 minutes: DDD).   Ⓕ **RR**

Richter's greatest triumphs are in the Shostakovich Preludes and Fugues. From the glacial spaces of the E flat Prelude to the benediction of the F major, each is placed in its own world, each projected as a long, steady accumulation of musical thought. No recorded performances, not even the composer's own, are as compelling. This two-disc set is a mixture of live and studio recordings. At times the piano tone lacks lustre (particularly in the Prokofiev Sixth Sonata, one of the studio recordings), but overall the quality is fine. Which is to say that while this may not be exactly a voluptuous sonic experience at least there are no barriers between the listener and Richter's elevated music-making. The compilation begins with four of the most vaporous and highly charged of Scriabin's late pieces. Disdaining their invitations to lurid nuance and indulgent phrasing, Richter brings to them an intensity and concentration which dispel any thoughts of decadence. In its place are purity and idealism, and the apparent restriction of tone colour conceals a myriad of precisely chiselled lines and weighted chords. So without making any obvious show of it he manages to release the inner power of the music – the menace in the galloping triplets of 'Flammes sombres' (second of the two *Danses*, Op. 73), the fierce ecstasy of *Vers la flamme*, for instance.

Less successful, however, is the earlier *Fantasie*, which runs out of steam rather seriously in the culminating stages. But this is virtually the only sign of any decline in Richter's virtuoso powers. If any work puts those powers to the test it is Prokofiev's Sixth Sonata, and here the finale goes at a tremendous lick, as irresistible as a river in full spate. Both middle movements are also fast-flowing streams, but again it is structural inevitability rather than surface excitement which makes the pulse race, the more so for the fact that the opening *Allegro* is deliberately held back – obstinately insistent in rhythm and dry in tone. As the Sonata's first performer back in his student days Richter speaks with obvious authority in this work. And over the years he has made the smaller-scale Fourth Sonata very much his own property too, investing every moment of it with meaning. In the shorter Prokofiev pieces it is good to hear him in more mellow mood. The Op. 12 *Legend* is dreamy and seductive, the *Visions fugitives* full of fantasy and grace, and he clearly loves every tiniest corner of the *Cinderella* pieces, the more secretive the better.

Preludes and Fugues Nos. 1-24.
Tatyana Nikolaieva pf
Melodiya 74321 19849-2 (three discs: 168 minutes: DDD). Recorded 1987.   Ⓕ

Tatyana Nikolaieva was in at the birth of Shostakovich's Preludes and Fugues, and she made them one of the cornerstones of her repertoire. But you don't need to know those facts in order to sense the authority and insight of her interpretations. She gives the three-hour cycle a wonderful over-arching sense of unity, of an unbroken voyage of exploration. That may not have been the composer's intention (he actually spoke out specifically against such a view of the work), but there are plenty of indications in the structure and character of his music to justify Nikolaieva's approach. Her recordings of the complete Preludes and Fugues are undoubtedly the finest monuments to a much lamented artist. It is truly sad that her playing was not fully appreciated in the West until so late in her career. Not that her performances are seriously flawed; and if the acoustic is a fraction too close and dry, better this than an over-resonant sound. It gives space for the music to breathe rather than suffocating it with unwanted stage-mist; and it enables many more of Nikolaieva's nuances to register.

Preludes and Fugues Nos. 1-24.
Vladimir Ashkenazy pf
Decca 466 066-2DH2 (two discs: 142 minutes: DDD). Recorded 1995.   Ⓕ **E**

Here is a Shostakovich Preludes and Fugues cycle to be reckoned with. Admittedly, it starts none too promisingly with, by the highest standards, a rhythmically stiff, tonally lumpy C major Prelude and some overpedalling in the fugue. The neo-baroque figuration of the A minor Prelude and its spiky Fugue, on the other hand, presents his true credentials. On form and well prepared, as here,

Ashkenazy remains a formidably fluent pianist, and the clarity and energy he brings to the faster, denser pieces is surpassed only by Richter (Philips). The sound itself is quite 'pingy', with a generous ambience behind it. That serves to heighten the impact of the more demonstrative pieces, but makes it difficult for Ashkenazy to sustain the atmosphere of the more meditative ones. Or maybe he simply doesn't feel the music that way. In the final D minor Fugue (No. 24), where you can almost hear Shostakovich's Tenth Symphony being born, Ashkenazy fails to build the texture as mightily as the early stages lead you to expect. Nikolaieva surpasses him here, and in general she reveals both subtler and grander perspectives, especially in her tauter, more drily recorded 1987 Melodiya set. Even so the balance-sheet for Ashkenazy comes out comfortably in the black. For consistency of pianism, straightforward integrity of interpretation and high quality of recording, his set can be warmly recommended.

From Jewish Folk Poetry, Op. 79. The New Babylon – suite (arr. Rozhdestvensky).
Tatyana Sharova sop **Ludmila Kuznetsova** mez **Alexei Martynov** ten
Russian State Symphony Orchestra / Valéry Polyansky.
Chandos CHAN9600 (70 minutes: DDD). Text and translation included. Recorded 1995-96. Ⓕ

This recording of Shostakovich's song-cycle *From Jewish Folk Poetry* is first-rate. For a start Polyansky's three vocal soloists are uncommonly well chosen: the light, youthful, slightly vulnerable soprano, the rich, world-weary mezzo and the ardent but unheroic tenor are ideally suited to the texts Shostakovich cunningly chose to convey his solidarity with mass suffering. Polyansky sets spacious tempos which allow every nuance of that suffering to register, and his orchestra is responsive and idiomatic in colouring. The recording, by Russian engineers, feels almost too good to be true in its excessive warmth; otherwise this version is easily preferable to the rival Rozhdestvensky on RCA. Polyansky's choice of the first of Shostakovich's 35 or so film scores makes for a more than welcome coupling. Polyansky offers an admirably idiomatic version of the Suite. He is especially adept at choosing timbres to reflect mood and situation. Even if you don't know the story-line the music was designed to accompany, this performance is so vividly characterized it can hardly fail to engage you.

Six Romances on Japanese Poems, Op. 21. Six Poems of Marina Tsvetayeva, Op. 143.
Suite on Verses of Michelangelo, Op. 145.
Elena Zaremba contr **Ilya Levinsky** ten **Sergei Leiferkus** bar
Gothenburg Symphony Orchestra / Neeme Järvi.
DG 447 085-2GH (71 minutes: DDD). Texts and translations included. Recorded 1994. Ⓕ

Leiferkus has recorded nothing finer than this rightly daunting interpretation of the *Suite on Verses of Michelangelo*, Shostakovich's greatest, most monolithic song-cycle – equal first if you include the Fourteenth Symphony. One should never underestimate Leiferkus's sheer vocal beauty of line and sheen in the superb declamatory settings of 'Dante' and its companion-piece hymn to the exiled poet (parallels with Solzhenitsyn were inescapable in 1974); nor is there that lack of a deeper understanding elsewhere in the cycle sometimes sensed in previous recordings by Leiferkus. As for the orchestral playing, the shadowy chords underpinning the earlier songs and punctuating the wonderful exchange of verses between Strozzi and Michelangelo on the sculptor's sleep in 'Night' are carefully projected with all the infinite atmosphere one has come to expect from Järvi's rapport with his supremely resonant Gothenburg strings. The similar mood of the near-contemporary Tsvetayeva settings, no less profound in their reflection on creativity and the State, make a perfect coupling for the *Michelangelo* Suite. Zaremba is another great Russian voice – very impressive indeed, like Leiferkus, in majestic declamation, but more distractingly loud (and her up-front role in the recording doesn't help) when she should be withdrawn. That is also true of the tenor, Ilya Levinsky in the *Romances on Japanese Poems*. A dark sidelight on *Lady Macbeth of the Mtsensk District*, the plangent aspect of the sequence is best served when Levinsky plays respectively the rejected and the unrequited lovers of the fourth and the fifth songs. Investigate the first two cycles to check the vocal progress of two fine young Russian singers; but don't miss Leiferkus's *Michelangelo* Suite.

The Nose.
Edvard Akimov bar Kovalyov; **Valery Belykh** bass Ivan Yakolevich;
Nina Sasulova sop Praskovya Osipovna; **Boris Tarkhov** ten District Inspector;
Boris Druzhinin ten Ivan; **Aleksandr Lomonosov** ten Nose; **Igor Paramonov** bass Footman;
Valery Solovyanov bass Clerk; **Lyudmila Sokolenko** sop Bread-roll seller;
Ashot Sarkisov sop Doctor; **Alexander Braim** ten Yaryzhkin; **Lyudmila Sapegina** mez Alexandra Grigoryevna Podtochina; **Lyudmila Ukolova** sop Daughter;
Moscow Chamber Theatre Chorus and Orchestra / Gennadi Rozhdestvensky.

Shostakovich Opera

The Gamblers.
Vladimir Rybasenko bass Alexei; **Vladimir Tarkhov** ten Ikharyov;
Valery Belykh bass Gavryushka; **Nicolai Kurpe** ten Krugel; **Ashot Sarkisov** bass Shvokhnyev;
Yaroslav Radivonik bar Utyeshitelny;
Leningrad Philharmonic Orchestra / Gennadi Rozhdestvensky.
Melodiya 74321 60319-2 (two discs: 150 minutes: DDD). Recorded 1974 and 1978.   Ⓜ

With upwards of 70 solo roles and a repertoire of grotesqueries apparently designed to put *Wozzeck* in the shade, *The Nose* was always calculated to be provocative. No wonder its first production in 1930 was reviewed (not unsympathetically) as The Hand-bomb of an Anarchist; and no wonder it soon fell foul of the increasingly vicious dumbing-down of the Soviet arts, not to be heard again in Russia until 1974 when Boris Prokovsky and Gennadi Rozhdestvensky mounted it at the Moscow Chamber Theatre. That production was immortalized in this classic recording, whose belated appearance on CD ought to be cause for unqualified celebration. So it would be if artistic grounds were all. Goodness knows how much rehearsal it took to master the manic complexities of the score, but the sheer clarity and confidence in characterization achieved is little short of miraculous. Edvard Akimov scores a personal triumph as the physiognomically challenged Kovalyov, and Rozhdestvensky is on the ball throughout. Even the recording quality has by and large stood the test of time. This was the biggest remaining gap in the Shostakovich CD discography, and we'll be lucky to have anything to rival it in the foreseeable future. More's the pity then that we get no libretto or translation. Without one or other of these it's hard to see how you can ever get more than a surface impression of the piece. Even the otherwise helpful synopsis is silent about the insertion of a couple of minutes of text from the original story near the end, which Shostakovich only agreed to at the time of the 1974 production and which isn't given in the (Russian-only) Complete Edition score. Shostakovich's other Gogol opera, the unfinished *The Gamblers*, also receives a wonderful performance, full-blooded and idiomatic. It makes a generous and appropriate filler.

Jean Sibelius   Finnish 1865-1957

Violin Concerto in D minor, Op. 47.

Sibelius Violin Concerto.
Tchaikovsky Violin Concerto in D major, Op. 35.
Kyung-Wha Chung vn
London Symphony Orchestra / André Previn.
Decca The Classic Sound 425 080-2DCS (66 minutes: ADD). Recorded 1970.   Ⓜ 𝐑𝐑

If the vital test for a recording is that a performance should establish itself as a genuine one, not a mere studio run-through, Chung's remains a disc where both works leap out at you for their concentration and vitality, not just through the soloist's weight and gravity, expressed as though spontaneously, but through the playing of the LSO under Previn at a vintage period. The great melodies of the first two movements of the Sibelius are given an inner heartfelt intensity rarely matched, and with the finale skirting danger with thrilling abandon. Chung's later Montreal version of the Tchaikovsky (also Decca) is rather fuller-toned with the tiny statutory cuts restored in the finale. Yet the very hint of vulnerability amid daring, a key element in Chung's magnetic, volatile personality, here adds an extra sense of spontaneity. This remains breathtaking playing, and the central slow movement, made to flow without a hint of sentimentality, has an extra poignancy. The Kingsway Hall sound, full and sharply focused, gives a sense of presence to match or outshine today's digital recordings.

Violin Concerto. Serenade in G minor, Op. 69 No. 2. En saga, Op. 9.
Julian Rachlin vn
Pittsburgh Symphony Orchestra / Lorin Maazel.
Sony Classical SK53272 (60 minutes: DDD). Recorded 1992.   Ⓟ 🅴

Julian Rachlin was only 18 when he made this recording and here he is in one of the most challenging of concertos, whose difficulties he takes easily in his stride. He has consistent beauty of tonal colour, a pure silvery tone with intonation to match, and possesses the aristocratic quality this music calls for. He is technically flawless – stunning in fact – and his eloquence is unfailingly persuasive: for example, the beautifully articulate way in which he echoes the questioning phrase in the slow movement (track 2, 2'34"). The tiny mannerisms in which he indulges would not inhibit a placing alongside such classics as Oistrakh (Melodiya) and Perlman (EMI). Certainly his artistry and sensitivity place him securely among the finest players of today. The G minor *Serenade* is quintessential Sibelius. It has a poignant, wistful melancholy all its own, and there are few pieces which more keenly evoke the magic of the white nights of the Scandinavian summer. Rachlin, coming as he does from the Baltic, though he left Lithuania when he was six, would understand all that. Lorin Maazel's *En saga* is a straight, often very fast, but thoroughly atmospheric account of the score. The recording is splendidly balanced. Outstanding.

Finlandia, Op. 26. Karelia Suite, Op. 11. Tapiola, Op. 112. En saga.
Philharmonia Orchestra / Vladimir Ashkenazy.
Decca Ovation 417 762-2DM (63 minutes: DDD). Recorded 1980-85.   Ⓜ

More than 30 years separate *En saga* and *Tapiola*, yet both works are quintessential Sibelius. The latter is often praised for the way Sibelius avoided 'exotic' instruments, preferring instead to draw new and inhuman sounds from the more standard ones; and the former is, in many ways, just as striking in the way Sibelius's orchestration evokes wind, strange lights, vast expanses and solitude. Both works suggest some dream-like journey: *En saga* non-specific though derived from Nordic legend; *Tapiola* more of an airborne nightmare in, above and around the mighty giants of the Northern forests inhabited by the Green Man of the Kalevala, the forest god Tapio (the final amen of slow, bright major chords brings a blessed release!). Ashkenazy's judgement of long term pacing is very acute; the silences and shadows are as potent here as the wildest hurricane. And Decca's sound allows you to visualize both the wood and the trees: every detail of Sibelius's sound world is caught with uncanny presence, yet the overall orchestral image is coherent and natural. In addition, his *Finlandia* boasts some of the most vibrant and powerful brass sounds on disc.

Six Humoresques, Opp. 87 and 89. Two Serenades, Op. 69. Two Pieces, Op. 77.
Overture in E major. Ballet scene.
Dong-Suk Kang *vn*
Gothenburg Symphony Orchestra / Neeme Järvi.
BIS CD472 (62 minutes: DDD). Recorded 1989.   Ⓕ

The music for violin and orchestra here is marvellously rewarding and gloriously played. The six *Humoresques*, Opp. 87 and 89 come from the same period as the Fifth Symphony, at a time when Sibelius was toying with the idea of a second violin concerto, and some of the material of the *Humoresques* was possibly conceived with a concerto in mind. Sibelius wrote that these radiant pieces convey something of 'the anguish of existence, fitfully lit up by the sun', and behind their outward elegance and charm, there is an all-pervasive sadness. This is even more intense in the *Serenades*, which are glorious pieces and quintessential Sibelius. Dong-Suk Kang is an outstanding player. His impeccable technique and natural musical instinct serve this repertoire well and he seems to have established an excellent rapport with Järvi and the Gothenburg orchestra. The two fill-ups are juvenilia and are only intermittently characteristic. The Overture is very much in his *Karelia* idiom, though they are of undoubted interest to all Sibelians. The recording up to BIS's usual high quality.

Karelia Suite. Incidental music – King Christian II; Pelleas and Melisande (all original versions).
Anna-Lisa Jakobsson *mez* **Raimo Laukka** *bar*
Lahti Symphony Orchestra / Osmo Vänskä.
BIS CD918 (78 minutes: DDD). Texts and translations included. Recorded 1997-98.   Ⓕ

Sibelius supplied four numbers for the February 1898 Helsinki première of Adolf Paul's historical drama *King Christian II* – the 'Minuet', 'The Fool's Song', 'Elegy' and 'Musette' – and these eventually took their place in the five-movement concert suite alongside the 'Nocturne', 'Serenade' and 'Ballade' which the composer completed the same summer. The street music of the 'Musette' is simply delightful in its original garb without added strings, and in both the 'Serenade' and 'Ballade' Vänskä uncovers strong thematic and stylistic links with the almost exactly contemporaneous First Symphony. The defiant quality these fine artists bring to 'The Fool's Song' (eloquently delivered by Raimo Laukka) is also very likeable. Music-making of refreshing perception and meticulous sensitivity similarly illuminates this first complete recording of Sibelius's original incidental music for a 1905 production of Maeterlinck's symbolist play (the venue was again Helsinki's Swedish Theatre). There are ten numbers in all.

The performance of the *Karelia Suite* in its original scoring (which acts as a splendid curtain-raiser here) has been compiled from Vänskä's complete recording of the original *Karelia* music. Both outer movements have a real sense of pageantry about them (Vänskä directs with exhilaratingly clean-limbed swagger), though there are certain reservations about his occasional predilection for exaggerated and affected *pianopianissimos*. Thus, at around 3'30" in the central 'Ballade' (track 2), the dynamic level drops almost below the threshold of audibility and has you rushing to boost the volume control (Vänskä repeats this trick twice in the *King Christian II* 'Elegy', and towards the end of the final number in *Pelléas*). For optimum results, therefore, playback needs to be higher than many listeners may think reasonable. That said, the engineering is quite spectacularly truthful throughout and there is no doubt that this is an unusually absorbing collection.

Kullervo, Op. 7.

Kullervo.
Marianne Rørholm *contr* **Jorma Hynninen** *bar*
Helsinki University Chorus; Los Angeles Philharmonic Orchestra / Esa-Pekka Salonen.
Sony Classical SK52563 (70 minutes: DDD). Text and translation included. Recorded 1992.   Ⓕ

Sibelius's *Kullervo* was the symphonic poem-cum-symphony with which he made his breakthrough in Finland in 1892. Common to all recordings, including Salonen's, is the magisterial presence of Jorma Hynninen. Salonen keeps a firm grip on the proceedings and maintains a real sense of momentum throughout. Moreover, temptations to dwell on beauty of incident or to indulge in expressive emphasis are resisted, and this extraordinary piece is all the more telling as a result. The drama of the central scena is vividly realized and both Marianne Rørholm and Jorma Hynninen are impressive – as indeed are the male voices of the Finnish chorus. An impressive performance, and the orchestral playing and recording are absolutely first-class.

Kullervo.
Eeva-Liisa Saarinen *mez* **Jorma Hynninen** *bar*
Estonian State Academic Male Choir; Helsinki University Male Choir;
Helsinki Philharmonic Orchestra / Paavo Berglund.
EMI Matrix CDM5 65080-2 (72 minutes: DDD). Text and translation included. Recorded 1985.   Ⓜ

This will be an obvious choice for many collectors. When comparing the present performance with Berglund's pioneering 1971 account (once available on an HMV LP), there is much greater lyrical intensity in the shaping of phrases and altogether greater fantasy in the treatment of detail – almost every point is better made in this new account which is fresher and comes more from the heart than its predecessor. Although there was greater warmth in the 1971 analogue recording, there is no mistaking the clarity and presence of this excellent Matrix issue. This issue also benefits from the presence of Jorma Hynninen. The dramatic intensity of the central scena is also impressively conveyed by Berglund's soprano, Eeva-Liisa Saarinen. Berglund's fourth movement is preferable; Salonen is just a bit headlong here. This present issue is recommendable on all counts, both artistically and in terms of sound, and at mid price is excellent value.

Legends, Op. 22, 'Lemminkäinen Suite'. Tapiola.
Helsinki Philharmonic Orchestra / Leif Segerstam.
Ondine ODE852-2 (70 minutes: DDD). Recorded 1995.   Ⓕ

The four *Legends* first began to surface in Sibelius's mind in 1893, at the same time as he was working on his *Kalevala* opera, *The Building of the Boat*, the prelude to which became 'The swan of Tuonela'. (It is not the only thing from the opera that found its way into the *Legends*. The lovely A minor idea for muted strings in the middle section of 'Lemminkäinen in Tuonela' is also among the sketches, where Sibelius scribbled over it the words, 'the Maiden of Death'. In the opera she would have rowed Väinämöinen across the river to Tuonela. In the tone-poem she symbolizes the very opposite, the loving mother whose ministrations return Lemminkäinen to life.) In 1954 Sibelius reversed the order of the inner movements so that 'The swan' preceded 'Lemminkäinen in Tuonela'. Perversely Segerstam disregards the composer's wishes and places them in the old order. To be fair, there is a case for this order in that you otherwise have two highly dramatic pieces ('Lemminkäinen in Tuonela' and 'Lemminkäinen's Homeward Journey') placed alongside each other, and in any event we can readily forgive him this liberty since most CD players are programmable. Segerstam gets very good results from the Helsinki orchestra which responds with a keen enthusiasm that is inspiriting. The performance is free from excessive mannerisms and his account of *Tapiola* is very impressive. He tellingly evokes the chilling terrors and the awesome majesty of the Nordic forest.

Luonnotar, Op. 70. Karelia Suite. Andante festivo. The Oceanides, Op. 73. King Christian II, Op. 27 – Suite. Finlandia.
Soile Isokoski *sop*
Gothenburg Symphony Orchestra / Neeme Järvi.
DG 447 760-2GH (72 minutes: DDD). Text and translation included. Recorded 1992-95.   Ⓕ

This CD offers the *Karelia* and *King Christian II* suites, both from the 1890s, together with outstanding accounts of two of the strangest and most haunting masterpieces of Sibelius's maturity, *Luonnotar* and *The Oceanides*. Of special interest is *Luonnotar*, which tells of the creation of the world as related in Finnish mythology and was written for the legendary Aino Ackté. Not surprisingly, perhaps, it places cruel demands on the soloist both in terms of tessitura and dynamics. Soile Isokoski is magnificent and possesses an impressive accuracy both in intonation and dynamics above the stave. Järvi gets an excellent response from his fine Gothenburg players and tellingly conveys the atmosphere and mystery of this extraordinary score. The excellent note speaks of it as 'unlike anything else in the entire repertoire' – which indeed it is! What a wonderfully evocative score *The Oceanides* is, and what an atmospheric, and indeed magical account, we have here. The performances of the *Karelia* and *King Christian II* suites are not quite in this class but they are enjoyable, and the recording is quite exemplary.

Pelleas and Melisande – Incidental Music, Op. 46. Swanwhite, Op. 54 – The Harp; The Maiden with the Roses; The Prince Alone; Swanwhite and the Prince; Song of Praise. King Christian II – Incidental Music, Op. 27.
Sauli Tiilikainen *bar*
Iceland Symphony Orchestra / Petri Sakari.
Chandos CHAN9158 (79 minutes: DDD). Text and translation included. Recorded 1992.   Ⓕ **E**

These performances are natural and unaffected and radiate immense care and pleasure in music-making. The *King Christian II* music includes 'The Fool's Song', complete with soloist, and very good he is too, and a short 'Minuet'. Petri Sakari's performance is totally unaffected and full of enthusiasm; the players sound as if they are enjoying this score and communicate their pleasure. Phrasing is attentive, musical through and through but never fussy. The *Pelleas and Melisande* is a version many collectors would want to have. It is imaginative, totally musical, strong on atmosphere and observant of dynamic subtleties. There may be readers who might find some of the tempos on the slow side; they are unhurried, but in context they feel right. Unfortunately there is only room for five movements from the *Swanwhite* music. All are beautifully played; every detail is allowed to take its time and the phrasing, though attentive, is free of the slightest taint of narcissism. Let 'Swanwhite and the Prince' serve as an example of how well thought out and natural in feeling the phrasing is! Added to this, the Chandos recording is beautifully transparent, warm and well detailed.

The Tempest – Incidental Music, Op. 109ᵃ. Scènes historiques: Op. 25 – No. 3, Festivo; Op. 66ᵃ. Karelia Suite – No. 1, Intermezzo; No. 3, Alla marciaᵇ. Finlandiaᶜ.
ᵃ**Royal Philharmonic Orchestra;** ᵇ**BBC Symphony Orchestra;**
ᶜ**London Philharmonic Orchestra / Sir Thomas Beecham.**
EMI Beecham Edition mono CDM7 63397-2 (73 minutes: ADD). Recorded 1938-55.   Ⓜ **H** **RR**

Symphonies – No. 4 in A minor, Op. 63ᵃ; No. 6 in D minor, Op. 104ᵇ. The Tempest – Incidental Music, Op. 109: Preludeᵃ. Legends, Op. 22 – Lemminkäinen's returnᵃ. The bard, Op. 64ᵃ.
ᵃ**London Philharmonic Orchestra;** ᵇ**Royal Philharmonic Orchestra / Sir Thomas Beecham.**
EMI Beecham Edition mono CDM7 64027-2 (79 minutes: ADD). Recorded 1937-47.   Ⓜ **H**

One of the special things about Beecham's Sibelius was its sheer sonority: there was a fresh, vernal sheen on the strings quite different from the opulence of Koussevitzky or Karajan but with all their flexibility and plasticity of phrasing, and a magic that is easier to discern than define. Suffice it to say that his feeling for atmosphere in Sibelius was always matched by a strong grip on the architecture. His 1956 recording of the two suites from *The Tempest* enjoys legendary status and is pure magic. The 1952 performances of four of the *Scènes historiques* have that similar ring of authenticity that transcend any sonic limitations. Beecham's stark account of the Fourth Symphony carries special authority since it was done after a long correspondence with the composer; and the 1947 RPO performance of the Sixth enjoyed Sibelius's imprimatur. The Prelude to *The Tempest* is as chillingly realistic as *Lemminkäinen's return* is exciting.

The Wood Nymph, Op. 15. The Wood Nymph (melodrama). A lonely ski-trail. Swanwhite, Op. 54 – incidental music (original version).
Lasse Pöysti *narr*
Lahti Symphony Orchestra / Osmo Vänskä.
BIS CD815 (62 minutes: DDD). Recorded 1996.   Ⓕ **S**

Although most Sibelians will know of the tone-poem, *The Wood-Nymph*, they will not have heard it, as the score has remained in Helsinki University Library. It opens very much in *Karelia* mode, and as one might expect, inhabits much the same world as the Lemminkäinen *Legends*. Though it is less developed than the 1892 *En saga*, let alone the *Legends* in their definitive form, it still bears the characteristic Sibelian hallmarks. The present disc gives us an opportunity to put it alongside the melodrama of the same name, scored for speaker, horn, strings and piano. This is a setting of the mainland-Swedish poet, Viktor Rydberg, best known in the Sibelius context for *Autumn Evening* ('Höstkväll'). The tone-poem which was given a month after the première of the melodrama follows much the same basic layout, though the chamber music-like texture offers numerous felicities. Not content with these interesting novelties, the CD also gives us two other works new to the catalogue, another short melodrama, *A lonely ski-trail* to words by Bertel Gripenberg, which in its piano form dates from 1925 and which Sibelius scored for harp and strings as late as 1948, a short, slight and atmospheric piece; and above all, the complete incidental music to Strindberg's *Swanwhite*. The score runs to some 30 minutes and is full of that special light and sense of space characteristic of *Pelleas and Melisande*. The playing of the Lahti orchestra under Osmo Vänskä is excellent and the recording, too, is very fine: spacious, well detailed and refined. Obviously a self-recommending issue which no Sibelian should miss.

Symphonies – No. 1 in E minor, Op. 39; No. 2 in D major, Op. 43; No. 3 in C major, Op. 52; No. 4 in A minor, Op. 63; No. 5 in E flat major, Op. 82; No. 6 in D minor, Op. 104; No. 7 in C major, Op. 105.

Symphonies Nos. 1-7. The Oceanides. Kuolema – Scene with cranes. Nightride and Sunrise[a].
City of Birmingham Symphony Orchestra, [a]Philharmonia Orchestra / Sir Simon Rattle.
EMI CMS7 64118-2 (four discs: 267 minutes: DDD). Ⓜ🆁🆁

Simon Rattle's reissued Sibelius cycle is now accommodated on four mid- (as opposed to five full-) price CDs, losing among the fill-ups only Kennedy's well-played account of the concerto. The first movement of Symphony No. 1 is impressive and its epic quality is splendidly conveyed. You may be less taken with the slow movement: the rather mannered closing bars, not particularly acceptable in the concert hall, are distinctly worrying on disc. The measured tempo of the *Scherzo* is also a problem: it is slower than the metronome marking and the movement lacks fire. However, *The Oceanides* is the finest on disc. In the Second Symphony, Rattle's first movement is again on the slow side and the Trio section of the *Scherzo* is pulled about. The Fourth and Seventh find him at his finest and the magnificent EMI recording is very richly detailed and well defined. The Fourth distils a powerful atmosphere in its opening pages; one is completely transported to its dark landscape with its seemingly limitless horizons. Only Beecham has surpassed Rattle in the slow movement. Rattle's version of the Sixth is still among the best around, with tremendous grip and concentration. In both the Third and the Fifth he is equally impressive, though his handling of the celebrated transition in the first movement of the Fifth in his Philharmonia version is preferable (reviewed below). However, the inducement of *The Oceanides*, *Nightride and Sunrise* and an evocative account of the 'Scene with cranes' from *Kuolema* tips the scales in Rattle's favour.

Symphonies Nos. 1 and 7. Karelia Overture, Op. 10.
London Symphony Orchestra / Anthony Collins.
Beulah mono 1PD8 (62 minutes: ADD). Recorded 1952-55. Ⓕ🅷

Symphonies Nos. 2 and 6.
London Symphony Orchestra / Anthony Collins.
Beulah mono 2PD8 (69 minutes: ADD). Recorded 1953-55. Ⓕ🅷

Symphony No. 3. Pohjola's Daughter, Op. 49. Pelleas and Melisande – No. 2, Melisande; No. 6, Pastorale; No. 7, At the spinning wheel; No. 8, Intermezzo; No. 9, Death of Melisande. Nightride and Sunrise.
London Symphony Orchestra / Anthony Collins.
Beulah mono 3PD8 (68 minutes: ADD). Recorded 1954-55. Ⓕ🅷

The name Anthony Collins (1893-1963) probably doesn't mean a great deal to the majority of younger readers, but for quite a few serious Sibelius *aficionados* his 1950s Decca recordings hold cult status. In these transfers the original recordings are revealed for the fine achievements they were: beautifully balanced, clear and vivid, allowing us to hear these performances in intimate detail – which is how they deserve to be heard. Collins is a first-rate musical landscape-painter. He doesn't just give us the bold sweeping brush-strokes, important as they are; he shows how the landscapes team with minute life. Rustling string textures aren't blandly homogenized – tiny details catch the ear, and then vanish again. Woodwind bird calls or horn calls can be acutely expressive – some passages remind one of Sibelius's comments about quasi-human voices in the nature sounds around his forest-home. But exaggeration is alien to the Collins approach. Nothing is forced, almost everything is fresh and vital, and it isn't only in the symphonies that the Collins touch is refreshing.

Pohjola's Daughter comes to life as effectively as the symphonies, and the third disc contains a real rarity, an entirely satisfactory *Nightride and Sunrise*.

Symphonies Nos. 1-7.
Philharmonia Orchestra / Vladimir Ashkenazy.
Decca Double 455 402-2DF2 and 455 405-2DF2 (two two-disc sets: 144 and 150 minutes: ADD/DDD). Recorded 1980-96. Ⓜ

Of all the cycles of Sibelius's symphonies recorded during recent years this is one of the most consistently successful. Ashkenazy so well understands the thought processes that lie behind Sibelius's symphonic composition just as he is aware, and makes us aware, of the development between the Second and Third Symphonies. His attention to tempo is particularly acute and invariably he strikes just the right balance between romantic languor and urgency. The Philharmonia plays for all it's worth and possesses a fine body of sound. The recordings are remarkably consistent in quality and effectively complement the composer's original sound world.

Symphony No. 1. Karelia Suite. Finlandia.
Oslo Philharmonic Orchestra / Mariss Jansons.
EMI CDC7 54273-2 (62 minutes: DDD). Recorded 1990. Ⓕ

Jansons's account of the First Symphony is thrilling. It has excitement and brilliance without exaggerations. Tempos throughout are just right, the phrasing breathes naturally and the sonority is excellently focused. Jansons never presses on too quickly but allows each phrase, each musical sentence to register so that the listener feels borne along on a natural currrent. Moreover, excitement is not whipped up but arises naturally from the music's forward momentum. The Oslo Philharmonic is a highly responsive orchestra of no mean virtuosity and it plays with a splendid intensity and fire not only in the symphony but also the *Karelia Suite* and *Finlandia* which sound very fresh. All the artistic decisions in this reading seem to be right and the orchestral playing further enhances the high renown this ensemble now enjoys. Very good recording too.

Symphonies Nos. 1 and 4.
London Symphony Orchestra / Sir Colin Davis.
RCA Red Seal 09026 68183-2 (78 minutes: DDD). Recorded 1994.
Gramophone Award Winner 1997. Ⓕ

Sir Colin Davis takes us completely inside the Fourth Symphony – we become part of it and feel we inhabit it. It is arguably the finest and most powerful reading of the work to have emerged since the days of Karajan. It was always one of the triumphs of his Boston survey on Philips. Along with the 1937 Beecham and the 1966 Berlin Philharmonic Karajan sets the Colin Davis was one of the most inward and searching readings committed to disc. We are not long – indeed barely a few bars – into the first movement before we realize that we are in a totally different world from most other interpretations. There is a far greater sense of breadth but it is in terms of imaginative insight that Davis scores. What is there to say of his First save that it, too, has an excitement, a sense of immediacy and authenticity of feeling that is equally convincing. This is Sibelius conducting of real stature and the LSO responds with total commitment. RCA provides a first-rate recording.

Symphonies Nos. 1 and 7.
San Francisco Symphony Orchestra / Herbert Blomstedt.
Decca 444 541-2DH (62 minutes: DDD). Recorded 1993-94. Ⓕ

This performance of the Seventh is magisterial and majestic Sibelius without a trace of interpretative egotism. It is built up with real feeling for balance and proportion and as a whole, the reading is powerful and marvellously controlled, with no want of dignity or nobility. The First Symphony is among the best to have appeared in recent years. We have not been short of good versions in recent years – Ashkenazy and the Philharmonia, Jansons and the Oslo Philharmonic and Bernstein and the Vienna Philharmonic to name only three. Blomstedt admits no concessions to the gallery; we are given this symphony with plenty of fire and no lack of virtuosity on the part of the orchestra. Here we get Sibelius straight and unadorned. The sound is well balanced.

Symphonies Nos. 2 and 6.
London Symphony Orchestra / Sir Colin Davis.
RCA Victor Red Seal 09026 68218-2 (73 minutes: DDD). Recorded 1994. Ⓕ 🆁🆁

The eloquent polyphony, purity of utterance and harmony of spirit give the Sixth Symphony a special place in the canon. Sibelius's mastery enables him to move with a freedom so complete that the musical events are dictated by their own inner necessity. And in Davis's hands this music unfolds with a freedom and naturalness that are totally convincing. As Sibelius said of the Fourth Symphony, this is music 'with nothing of the circus about it', and in this reading there is no playing to the gallery. There is no playing to the gallery either in Sir Colin's account of the Second Symphony. He views the work as a whole and does not invest detail with undue expressive vehemence at its expense, but strikes just the right balance between the nationalist-romantic inheritance on the one side and the classical power of Sibelius's thinking on the other. The first movement has dignity and breadth, and as with Karajan (EMI), the pacing of climaxes is magisterial. The recording has splendid presence and space.

Symphony No. 2. Pohjola's Daughter, Op. 49. Legends – No. 2, The Swan of Tuonela; No. 4, Lemminkäinen's return. Finlandia.
NBC Symphony Orchestra / Arturo Toscanini.
Naxos Historical mono 8 110810 (76 minutes: ADD). Recorded live in 1940.　　　　Ⓢ🅷

As the symphony's finale builds to its apotheosis, you'll have to contend with trumpets that sound as if they more usually play at wedding parties for *The Godfather*. This is presumably how Toscanini liked his trumpets (and woodwinds and strings) to sound when singing, just as he liked them to deliver more forceful, rhythmical figures with a vengeance – the 'vengeance' perhaps a result of close microphones and/or little evidence of a hall acoustic. All of which means that if your notions of Nordic nobility in the symphony are gathered across the decades from recordings by Kajanus, Collins, Koussevitzky and Karajan, you should probably give Toscanini a wide berth. If you did, however, you would be depriving yourself of perhaps the most dramatically intense and physically exciting performances of the symphony and *Pohjola's Daughter* ever recorded. The present Naxos accounts of the symphony and *Pohjola's Daughter* are already available (at twice the price) in RCA's Toscanini Edition. The only audible difference lies in the more 'filtered' (and arguably smoother) sound of the Naxos transfer. The same could be said of *Pohjola's Daughter*, but here Naxos has used a different source, with a noisier surface, though less flutter. By way of shorter items, the Naxos release offers, as does RCA's, 'The Swan of Tuonela' and *Finlandia*, but the RCA performances are later ones with cleaner, clearer and more boldly projected sound. Which leaves Naxos's extra carrot (apart from the price) – a 'Lemminkäinen's return' electric with energy.

Symphonies Nos. 3 and 5.
London Symphony Orchestra / Sir Colin Davis.
RCA Red Seal 09026 61963-2 (61 minutes: DDD). Recorded 1992.　　　　Ⓕ

Some 20 years have passed since Davis's last Sibelius cycle, with the Boston Symphony Orchestra for Philips. Generally speaking Sir Colin's version of the Third has greater breadth and sense of scale than his previous account or any other. His first movement has a majestic stride and great power; and he has the measure of the slow movement's pantheistic musings. The Fifth is more tautly held together than before; the first movement moves forward and onwards with a powerful feeling of inevitability and purpose. The transition in the first movement to the *Scherzo* section is masterly. Listening to this disc, one wonders anew at the sheer originality of this piece, and that is, of course, the touchstone of a great performance. Sir Colin Davis understands Sibelius as do few others and senses the vital currents that flow through these symphonies, and the LSO know this and respond with playing of distinction. The recording is in every way first-class, vivid in detail and truthful in perspective.

Symphonies[a] Nos. 3 and 5. March of the Finnish Jaeger Battalion, Op. 91 No. 1[b].
[a]**London Symphony Orchestra;** [b]**Helsinki Philharmonic Orchestra / Robert Kajanus.**
Koch Historic mono 37133-2 (62 minutes: ADD). Recorded 1928-1933.　　　　Ⓜ🅷

Finlandia has already reissued all Kajanus's London recordings on a three-disc set. That edition contains transfers made by Anthony Griffith for World Records, issued in the 1970s, and they still sound very good indeed. Griffith had the advantage of working from original masters: Koch's Mark Obert-Thorn has been obliged to use commercial pressings and while he has obtained good sound, there is inevitably more background noise and an unevenness in the quality which is not present in Finlandia's transfers. However, Koch has scored an important point by including Kajanus's only Sibelius recording with his own Helsinki orchestra. The piece itself is perhaps the composer's weakest, but the performance has great historical importance, for it is played by an orchestra with which Sibelius had close links, and under a conductor who was his chosen interpreter. We can hear clearly just why Sibelius admired Kajanus so much in the two symphonies here. At the age of 76 he was still able to generate a good deal of tension and energy in the LSO's playing, yet there is a particular sense of balanced, logical music-making, a seemingly natural authority in the phrasing and an apparent inevitability in the way he unfolds the composer's symphonic argument. Everything seems perfectly in place, and the music speaks to us in a very direct and compelling fashion.

Symphonies Nos. 4 and 7. Kuolema – Valse triste.
Berlin Philharmonic Orchestra / Herbert von Karajan.
DG Galleria 439 527-2GGA (66 minutes: ADD). Recorded 1965-67.   Ⓜ

Karajan recorded the Fourth Symphony three times, once in the 1950s with the Philharmonia and twice with the Berlin Philharmonic. The work obviously meant a great deal to him. He insisted on its inclusion in his very first concert on his appointment at the Berlin Philharmonic in the early 1960s at a time when Sibelius's cause had few champions in Germany, so keen was he to stake its claim as one of the great symphonies of the day. Karajan's account has withstood the test of time as one of the most searching, profound and concentrated performances of this masterpiece, and its reappearance at mid price was very welcome. The Seventh is finer than his earlier Philharmonia version but does not enjoy quite the same classic status. Karajan's *Valse triste* is wonderfully seductive. Indispensable!

Sibelius Symphony No. 5[a].
Nielsen Symphony No. 4, FS76, 'The inextinguishable'[b]. Pan and Syrinx FS87[b].
[a]**Philharmonia Orchestra,** [b]**City of Birmingham Symphony Orchestra / Sir Simon Rattle.**
EMI CDM7 64737-2 (78 minutes: DDD). Recorded 1981-84.   Ⓜ 🆁🆁

Simon Rattle's 1982 recording of the Sibelius Fifth is a remarkable achievement for a young man; it was (and remains) one of the very best in the catalogue. He handles the transition between the first movement and the *Scherzo* section in masterly fashion – more convincingly than in his later CBSO performance (reviewed above), good though that is. It received (and more to the point, deserved) numerous accolades at the time and it is a pleasure to have it reissued here at mid-price. EMI has found room, too, for Rattle's version of *Pan and Syrinx*, again one of the most poetic interpretations of this little masterpiece ever committed to disc. Rattle's account of Nielsen's Fourth is perceptive and well shaped, though it lacks something of the fire and abandon recalled from a broadcast he made with the Philharmonia Orchestra in the late 1970s. Strongly recommended.

Symphonies – No. 5 (original 1915 version). En saga (original 1892 version).
Lahti Symphony Orchestra / Osmo Vänskä.
BIS CD800 (58 minutes: DDD). Recorded 1995. *Gramophone* Award Winner 1996.   Ⓟ 🆂🅴

Every so often a CD appears which, by means of some interpretative insight, changes our view of a piece of music. This disc changes our whole perspective in a wholly different sense, for it gives us a glimpse of two familiar masterpieces in the making. Sibelius struggled with the Fifth Symphony for almost seven years from about 1912 until it reached its definitive form in 1919. Although the finished score of the first version does not survive, the orchestral material does, and thus it was not difficult to reconstruct the score. The 1915 score is now available to the public at large in dedicated performance. To study how the two scores differ is to learn something important about the creative process and it is this mystery that makes this disc imperative listening – and not just for Sibelians. The four-movement 1915 score has a more complex harmonic language than the final score and so it provides a missing link, as it were, between the Fourth Symphony and the definitive Fifth. The opening horn motive has yet to emerge, and the finale's coda has yet to acquire its original hammer-blow chords. And in between you will find that the various themes, some distinctly recognizable, others taking off in totally unexpected directions and charting unknown regions. Something of the cosmic feel of this music emerges in a letter Sibelius wrote in 1914, 'God opens the door for a moment and his orchestra was playing the Fifth Symphony'. Of course, Sibelius knew what he was doing, and in the 1919 version, he managed to keep the door open for rather longer! The version of *En saga* with which we are familiar does not come between the *Kullervo* Symphony and the *Karelia* music but from 1901 between the First and Second Symphonies and was made for Busoni. The original offers fascinating material for comparison: there is a brief glimpse of Bruckner, whose work he had encountered in Vienna a year or two earlier, and the orchestral writing, though not always as polished as in the later version, still has flair. All praise to the Lahti orchestra and their fine conductor, and the excellent and natural balance.

Symphony No. 7. Rakastava, Op. 14. En saga. Kullervo.
Hillevi Martinpelto sop **Karl-Magnus Fredriksson** bar
London Symphony Chorus and Orchestra / Sir Colin Davis.
RCA Red Seal 09026 68312-2 (two discs: 138 minutes: DDD). Text and translation included.
Recorded 1994-96.   Ⓕ

Those who recall Sir Colin Davis's performance with the LSO of *Kullervo* at London's Barbican
Centre in 1992 (subsequently televised) will not have forgotten its epic sweep and magisterial
control. On record, Sir Colin's account brings us not only Sibelius's first essay in the form but also
his last. The set also includes two other works conceived in the 1890s, *En saga* and *Rakastava*. The
latter is one of Sibelius's most affecting pieces. It is affectingly played, too. In Davis's hands the
Seventh Symphony is by turns powerful, epic and serene, its climaxes expertly placed. But to turn to
Kullervo: what works in the concert hall may not make the same impression when heard in the
intimacy of the home. The LSO plays with refinement and spirit, and the London Symphony
Chorus is responsive. The first movement is slower than than the Barbican performance yet after a
few bars it seems exactly right. It is spacious and broad which underlines the Brucknerian feeling to
the piece. The slow movement, 'Kullervo's Youth', is splendidly characterized, as is the central
'Kullervo and his Sister' movement. Both singers acquit themselves well. The remaining two
movements are paced with unerring judgement. It is puzzling that Sibelius should have entertained
such strong doubts about *Kullervo* as to discourage performances during his lifetime. Sir Colin's
excellently recorded performance reveals *Kullervo* as the great work it is.

Five Pieces, Op. 81. Novelette, Op. 102. Five Danses champêtres, Op. 106. Four Pieces,
Op. 115. Three Pieces, Op. 116.
Nils-Erik Sparf vn **Bengt Forsberg** pf
BIS CD625 (57 minutes: DDD). Recorded 1993.   Ⓕ

No one listening to this music would doubt that Sibelius had a special feeling for the violin.
Whether he is composing lighter music such as the captivating 'Rondino' from the Op. 81 set or the
more substantial later pieces, such as the first of the *Danses champêtres*, which comes close to the
world of *The Tempest*. Neither the Op. 115 nor the Op. 116 set contains great music but they are
much finer than they have been given credit for. Both 'On the heath' and the 'Ballade', Nos. 1 and 2
of Op. 115, have an innocence that calls to mind the wonderful *Humoresques* for violin and orchestra.
In particular 'The Bells', Op. 115 No. 4 is a rather cryptic miniature and the 'Scène de danse' of
Op. 116, with its striking tonal juxtapositions, is a kind of Finnish equivalent of the Bartók
Romanian Dances. Nils-Erik Sparf and Bengt Forsberg are dedicated and sensitive exponents who
make the most of the opportunities this repertoire provides. The piano tone sounds a little thick at
the bottom end of the spectrum, and the violin is by no means the dominant partner in the aural
picture. This reservation is a small one and the performances are enthusiastically recommended.

King Christian II, Op. 27 – Fool's Song of the Spider. Five Christmas Songs, Op. 1. Eight Songs,
Op. 57. Hymn to Thaïs. Six Songs, Op. 72 – No. 3, The kiss; No. 4, The echo nymph; No. 5,
Der Wanderer und der Bach; No. 6, A hundred ways. Six Songs, Op. 86. The small girls.
Monica Groop mez **Love Derwinger** pf
BIS CD657 (66 minutes: DDD). Texts and translations included. Recorded 1994.   Ⓕ

Monica Groop, following her success in the Cardiff Singer of the World Competition, has built up
a busy career. Communication is her strength, and unevenness of line a relative weakness. Sibelius's
songs are a rich and still undervalued part of the song repertoire. Still only four or five are really
well known, and none of those is included here. Not all are of very special quality: the title is
probably the best thing about the 'Fool's Song of the Spider' (from *King Christian II*), and the
Hymn to Thaïs gains interest through being Sibelius's only song in English rather than through
intrinsic merit. Yet there are many delights here, including the closing waltz-song, *The small girls*.
The acoustic is perhaps somewhat too reverberant but has plenty of presence.

Songs, Volume 3. Seven Songs, Op. 13. Six Songs, Op. 50. Six Songs, Op. 90. The Wood
Nymph. Belshazzar's Feast – The Jewish Girl's Song. Resemblance. A Song. Serenade.
The Thought[a].
Anne Sofie von Otter, **[a]Monica Groop** mezzos **Bengt Forsberg** pf
BIS CD757 (67 minutes: DDD). Texts and translations included. Recorded 1994-95.   ⒻⒺ

The vast majority of Sibelius's songs are in Swedish, the language with which he grew up as a child,
and here they are given by a distinguished native Swedish partnership. The *Seven Songs*, Op. 13, are

all Runeberg settings and come from the composer's early years (1891-2). Best known, perhaps, are 'Spring is flying' and 'The dream', but there are others, such as 'The young hunter', that are no less delightful and characterful. The other Runeberg settings here, the *Six Songs*, Op. 90, come towards the end of Sibelius's career as a song composer (1917-18). 'The north', as in all the nature poetry of Runeberg, touches a very special vein of inspiration. Along with 'Die stille Nacht', Op. 50 No. 5, which is equally affectingly given by these two artists – it is among his finest songs. Interest naturally focuses on the rarities. *The Wood Nymph*, not to be confused with the melodrama or the tone-poem, is recorded here for the first time. As well as *A Song*, there are two other early Runeberg settings, the 1888 *Serenade* and *Resemblance*, both of them also première recordings. 'The Jewish Girl's Song' will be familiar from the incidental music to *Belshazzar's Feast*, and is affecting in this form – particularly sung as it is here. Given the artistry and insight of this splendid partnership, and the interest and beauty of the repertoire, this is a self-recommending issue.

Arioso, Op. 3. Seven Songs, Op. 17. Row, row duck. Six Songs, Op. 36. Five Songs, Op. 37. Pelleas and Melisande, Op. 46 – The three blind sisters. Six Songs, Op. 88. Narcissus.
Anne Sofie von Otter *mez* **Bengt Forsberg** *pf*
BIS CD457 (57 minutes: DDD). Texts and translations included. Recorded 1989. Ⓕ

In all, Sibelius composed about 100 songs, mostly to Swedish texts but his achievement in this field has, naturally enough, been overshadowed by the symphonies. Most music lovers know only a handful like 'Black roses', Op. 36 No. 1, and 'The Tryst' and the most popular are not always the best. Sibelius's output for the voice has much greater range, diversity and depth than many people suppose. For collectors used to hearing them sung by a baritone, the idea of a soprano will seem strange but a lot of them were written for the soprano Ida Ekman. Anne Sofie von Otter not only makes a beautiful sound and has a feeling for line, but also brings many interpretative insights to this repertoire. The very first song from the Op. 17 set is a marvellous Runeberg setting, 'Since then I have questioned no further' and it was this that Ida Ekman sang for Brahms. Von Otter captures its mood perfectly and has the measure of its companions too. Her account of 'Black roses' is particularly thrilling and she is very persuasive in the weaker Op. 88 set. She sings throughout with great feeling for character and her account of 'Astray', Op. 17 No. 6, has great lightness of touch and charm. The Opp. 36 and 37 sets are among the finest lyrical collections in the whole of Sibelius's song output, and they completely engage this artist's sensibilities. These are performances of elegance and finesse; Bengt Forsberg proves an expert and stylish partner and both artists are well recorded.

Incidental Music – Everyman, Op. 83; Belshazzar's Feast, Op. 51. The Countess's Portrait, Op. posth.
Lilli Paasikivi *mez* **Petri Lehto** *ten* **Sauli Tiilikainen** *bar* **Pauli Pietiläinen** *org*
Leena Saarenpää *pf*
Lahti Chamber Choir; Lahti Symphony Orchestra / Osmo Vänskä.
BIS CD735 (65 minutes: DDD). Texts and translations included. Recorded 1995. Ⓕ

These are all first recordings and interest centres on the score Sibelius wrote for Hofmannsthal's morality play, *Jedermann* ('Everyman') in 1916. The final score comprises 16 numbers and runs to some 40 minutes. Some of the music is fragmentary and hardly makes sense out of context, though most of it is atmospheric and all of it is characteristic. The sustained *Largo* section for muted, divided strings (track 11), is among the most searching music Sibelius ever wrote for theatre and, artistically, is fit to keep company with *The Tempest* music. Overall the material does not lend itself to being turned into a suite in the same way as *Belshazzar's Feast* but this recording rescues from obscurity some strangely haunting and at times really inspired music – the last 25 minutes are very powerful. By all accounts Hjalmar Procopé's *Belshazzar's Feast* was a feeble play and when it first appeared, one newspaper cartoon showed the playwright being borne aloft in the composer's arms. There seems little doubt that his name would not be alive were it not for Sibelius's music. The latter certainly makes an expert job of creating an effective and (in the case of the 'Notturno') a moving concert suite. The present issue gives us an additional six minutes or so of unfamiliar music; there are 11 numbers in all, though familiar passages from the suite are broken up. *The Countess's Portrait* (1906) is a wistful, pensive and charming piece for strings, which was only published two years ago. Obviously this is a self-recommending issue of exceptional interest.

Incidental Music – Karelia; Kuolema. Valse triste, Op. 44 No. 1 (1904 versions).
Heikki Laitinen, Taito Hoffren *sngrs* **Kirsi Tiihonen** *sop* **Raimo Laukka** *bar*
Lahti Symphony Orchestra / Osmo Vänskä.
BIS CD915 (76 minutes: DDD). Texts and translations included. Recorded 1997. ⒻⓈ

Sibelius Choral and song

This is a disc which will be of great interest to Sibelians. The original score of the *Karelia* music was discovered in the conductor Kajanus's library after his death in 1933 and his widow returned it to Sibelius three years later. The music extended to eight tableaux which portrayed various episodes in Karelian history. In the 1940s Sibelius destroyed the score, about which he had had second thoughts since its première in 1893, sparing only the overture, the movements familiar from the suite and the first number, 'A Karelian Home – News of War'. Fortunately for posterity, a set of orchestral parts came to light, albeit incomplete, and were put into shape by Kalevi Kuoso. It was these that the composer Kalevi Aho used in preparing the edition on which this recording is based. In all there are some 40 minutes of music, over half of which is new. Those familiar with the 'Ballade' from the Op. 11 Suite will no doubt be slightly disconcerted to hear the familiar cor anglais melody taken by a baritone and will find the piece too long in its original form. The opening of the fifth tableau, 'Pontus de la Gardie at the gates of Käkisalmi [Kexholm Castle] in 1580', is highly effective and leads into the famous 'Alla marcia'. It is fascinating to hear what the piece is like, and what Sibelius was prepared to lose. Listening to this reaffirms and illumines both the sureness of his artistic judgement and the vitality of his creative imagination. Sibelius's incidental music to *Kuolema*, the play by his brother-in-law, Arvid Järnefelt, dates from 1903. The most familiar music from it is the *Valse triste*, which Sibelius revised the following year, adding flute, clarinet, horns and timpani and making it altogether more sophisticated harmonically and melodically. Osmo Vänskä and his Lahti players prove reliable and responsive guides in this atmospheric music and it is hard to imagine their performances being improved on. Wide-ranging and expertly balanced recorded sound.

The Tempest – Incidental Music, Op. 109.
Kirsi Tiihonen *sop* **Lilli Paasikivi** *mez* **Anssi Hirvonen, Paavo Kerola** *tens* **Heikki Keinonen** *bar* **Lahti Opera Chorus and Symphony Orchestra / Osmo Vänskä.**
BIS CD581 (68 minutes: DDD). Text and translation included. Recorded 1992.   Ⓕ **S**

A first recording of the full score! Sibelius's music for *The Tempest,* his last and greatest work in its genre, was the result of a commission for a particularly lavish production at the Royal Theatre, Copenhagen in 1926. The score is far more extensive than the two suites and consists of 34 musical numbers for soloists, mixed choir, harmonium and large orchestra. Readers will be brought up with a start by the music for the 'Berceuse', the second item, which uses a harmonium rather than the strings with which we are familiar from the two suites and although it is still more magical in the familiar orchestral suite, the original has an other-worldly quality all its own. The music is played in the order in which it was used in the 1927 production of the play and there are ample and excellent explanatory notes. The 'Chorus of the Winds' is also different but no less magical in effect. Of course, taken out of the theatrical context, not everything comes off – but even if the invention is not consistent in quality, at its best it is quite wonderful. The singers and chorus all rise to the occasion and Osmo Vänskä succeeds in casting a powerful spell in the 'Intermezzo', which opens Act 4. The recording is marvellously atmospheric though it needs to be played at a higher than usual level setting as it is a little recessed. For Sibelians this is a self-recommending issue.

Partsongs, Op. 18[a] – No. 1, The Broken Voice; No. 3, The Boat Journey of Väinämöinen; No. 4, Fire on the Island; No. 6, The Song of my Heart. Busy as a Thrush[a]. Play, Beautiful Girl[a]. Rakastava, Op. 14[a]. The Thrush's Toiling[a]. Festive March[a]. Cantata for the Helsinki University Ceremonies of 1897, Op. 23[a]. To Thérèse Hahl[a]. Nostalgia[c]. Not with Grief[a]. Wonderful Gifts[c]. March of the Finnish Jaeger Battalion, Op. 91 No. 1. Three Runeberg Songs[a]. Awaken![a]. Choir of the Winds. Ballad[a]. The Son's Bride. Men from Plain and Sea, Op. 65a[a]. Dreams[a]. Christmas Song[a]. Give Me No Splendour, Op. 1 No. 4[a]. Bell Melody of Berghaill Church, Op. 65b[a]. Three Introductory Antiphons, Op. 107b. Ode, Op. 113 No. 11[a]. Carminalia[bc]. Primary School Children's March[c]. In the Morning Mist[c]. Hail, O Princess[a]. The Landscape Breathes, Op. 30[a]. Three American School Songs. The Way to School[a]. School Song[a]. March of the Labourers[a]. The World Song, Op. 91b. Song of the Athenians, Op. 31 No. 3[bc]. To the Fatherland[a]. Song for the People of Uusimaa[a]. Finlandia[a].
[a]**Tapiola Chamber Choir;** [b]**Friends of Sibelius / Hannu Norjanen;**
[c]**Tapiola Choir / Kari Ala-Pöllänen** with **Ilmo Ranta** *pf* **Johanna Torikka** *org/harm*
Finlandia 0630-19054-2 (two discs: 147 minutes: DDD). Texts and translations included. Recorded 1996-97.   Ⓕ

This survey of Sibelius's complete choral songs is important – and irresistible – not only for its consistently fine performances, but for the historical context it provides for a deeper understanding of both Sibelius and his later contemporaries. The two-disc set begins where – in the mythology of Finnish oral tradition – all music began: with the life-giving song of Väinämöinen from the *Kalevala's* compilation of folk poetry; the verse which tuned Sibelius's ear to the musicality of the Finnish language (at a time when he and his social class still spoke Swedish) also inspired his first distinctive song settings. Here, excellent production most sensitively captures the division and shifting of the finely blended voices of the Tapiola Chamber Choir, as solo and ensemble voices trace the asymmetrical metres and modal cadences of works such as 'The Boat Journey' from Op. 18 and 'The Lover'. References to the *Kalevala* return in the group of songs for ceremonies and festivities in which solo exhortations are pitted against shifting choral harmonies, as images of journey, hope and freedom are expressed in the supple melodies of ten songs for a university degree ceremony from 1897 (Op. 23). A fervent and optimistic tribute to Finland's great national romantic painter Albert Edelfelt sets works by Sibelius's beloved Swedish-language poet, Rüneberg: and his 'Autumn Evening' could be an aural re-creation of one of the painter's own canvases. Sibelius's music pierces dark, close harmonies with high lines of anguish, presaging the imaginative virtuosity of later masterpieces such as 'Men from Plain and Sea' and 'Dreams' with their sense of the wandering and yearning of the human spirit. The second disc follows three simple Christmas carols with the composer's sacred and liturgical pieces. Among these early prentice works, the bells of Helsinki's great Kallio Church ring out: the peal which Sibelius wrote for the fine 1912 Nordic Jugendstil building still rings out twice a day, and here we are treated to the words as well. The songs for children range from distinctly uninspired English-language commissions for American schools, to a tiny and perfect setting of 'The Landscape Breathes', in which the girls' voices slowly and chromatically thaw from their unison freeze. Finland's and Sibelius's unique species of unjingoistic patriotism returns at the end with gently yet distinctively harmonized hymns to specific regions of the motherland and, finally and inevitably, with the great *Finlandia* hymn.

Valentin Silvestrov
USSR/Ukrainian 1937

Symphony No. 5. Postludium.
Alexei Lubimov *pf*
Deutsches Symphony Orchestra, Berlin / David Robertson.
Sony Classical SK66825 (65 minutes: DDD). Recorded 1995. Ⓟ 🄴

Silvestrov's Fifth is one of the best-kept secrets of the ex-Soviet symphonic repertoire. It was composed in 1980-82, and its 1988 Melodiya recording, never widely available in the West, became something of a cult hit with his fellow-Ukrainians and with Russian musicians and students. Like the *Postludium* with which it is coupled here, it is quite deliberately nostalgic – a symphony composed, as it were, after the death of the genre and consisting only of poignant memories. In musical terms those memories are of the melodic and accompanimental figures characteristic of nineteenth-century song; so the structure consists of quietly ecstatic extended melodies spaced by even more ecstatic efflorescences of piano-accompaniment-derived textures. Throughout the symphony's unbroken, slow-moving 47-minute span, Silvestrov's precise ear for harmony, his extreme sensitivity to orchestral texture, and his subtlety of large-scale control, are remarkable. Just as importantly, his visions of timeless beauty are set in the context of 'here-and-now' emotional pain (if you are sampling before buying, be sure to hear past the first three minutes where that context is set up). The way these contrasting phases foreshadow, overlap and echo one another has the feeling of genuine symphonic mastery. Find yourself a quiet hour and let this masterpiece cast its magic spell.

Robert Simpson
British 1921-1997

Canzona[a]. Media morte in vita sumus[b]. Tempi[c]. Eppur si muove[d].
[d]**Iain Quinn** *org* [ab]**Corydon Brass Ensemble;** [bc]**Corydon Singers / Matthew Best.**
Hyperion CDA67016 (68 minutes: DDD). Texts included. Recorded 1997. Ⓕ

Simpson would never have claimed that choral music was his *métier*. Yet for lovers of his music there is something especially revealing about the two pieces recorded here. In *Media morte in vita sumus* ('In the midst of death we are in life') he deliberately reverses the scriptural motto in order to articulate his personal 'anti-pessimist' creed. The musical setting for chorus, brass and timpani is appropriately austere, and Simpson's own words are translated into Latin for the sake of universality. *Tempi* for *a cappella* chorus is a *jeu d'esprit*, the text consisting entirely of Italian tempo and character markings. The Corydon Singers offers superbly confident performances, as does the Corydon Brass Ensemble which also shines in the comparatively well-known *Canzona*. It's impossible to avoid comparisons with Nielsen when it comes to the 31-minute *Eppur si muove* ('But it does move') for organ. This 12-minute *ricercare* followed by a 19-minute passacaglia sets its jaw squarely against conventional organ-loft grandiosity. Its intellectual monumentality is clearly in the *Commotio* mould, though it's only fair to say it's considerably tougher going than Nielsen's late masterpiece. Iain Quinn joins the long line of dedicated performers who have made Hyperion's Simpson series such a consistent triumph. The recording quality leaves nothing to be desired.

String Quartet No. 13. String Quintet No. 2. Clarinet Quintet.
Thea King *cl* **Christopher van Kampen** *vc* **Delmé Quartet** (Galina Solodchin, John Trusler *vns*
John Underwood *va* Jonathan Williams *vc*).
Hyperion CDA66905 (64 minutes: DDD). Recorded 1997.   Ⓕ

This invigorating and thought-provoking disc forms another welcome instalment in Hyperion's
invaluable Simpson cycle. In the Clarinet Quintet of 1968 the wind partner is treated as an equal of
the strings, which makes the linear and contrapuntal inventiveness all the more remarkable and
absorbing, though for some it may make the music seem no more than monochrome. Like late
Beethoven, Simpson seems to begin by charting a realm just out of emotional reach yet somehow
crucial to one's psychic well-being. The mental energy gained then spills over into actual fast music,
even into an engaging jigginess. The Quintet feels as though it could go on much longer than its
actual 31 minutes without the inventive resources drying up. The rarefied conclusion is all the more
moving for its steadiness of gaze. The Thirteenth Quartet (1989) retains many familiar Simpson
hallmarks. It opens with a sinewy, deceptively triadic theme which soon gives way to spidery,
triplety counterpoint. It is all very ascetic and self-denying and the second and fourth movements
go into an interior, attenuated world in which it is difficult to feel entirely at home. The even more
recent String Quintet No. 2 keeps its cards just as close to its chest. Again the design alternates
austere, lyrical music with a knotty *Allegro*, initially short-lived but gradually expanding, while the
slower sections remain more or less constant in duration. The impression is less of conflict and
resolution than of a stand-off between the two tempo-types, eyeing one another in mutual
suspicion; the conclusion is bleak-Sibelian. The Delmé is a longstanding Simpson advocate and it
seems to have the ideal sound for him – crystalline, alert and focused, as though beyond obvious
human expressiveness in a realm of higher wisdom. The same goes for their admirable partners,
Thea King and Christopher van Kampen. This may be one of the less immediately accessible
Simpson programmes, but it is still richly rewarding.

Nikos Skalkottas   Greek 1904-1949

Violin Concerto, AK22ª. Largo Sinfonico, AK4a. Greek Dances, AK11 – Epirotikos; Kretikos;
Tsamikos; Thessalikos; Mariori mou-Mariori mou; Arkadikos; Kleftikos (arr. cpsr).
ªGeorgios Demertzis *vn*
Malmö Symphony Orchestra / Nikos Christodoulou.
BIS CD904 (78 minutes: DDD). Recorded 1997.   Ⓕ

From Nikos Skalkottas's earliest works, a personal idiom was evident, combining European
modernism with the rhythmic dynamism of Greek traditional music, and characterized by a tensile
strength and translucency of sound. Like Bartók, Skalkottas wrote 'popular' music without
compromise. The *Greek Dances* are ideal encore pieces, not least in these suave arrangements for
strings. The Violin Concerto of 1937 is among his major works, with a solo part that is demanding
yet integral to the symphonic nature of the score – something that Georgios Demertzis's vital
account readily conveys. The close of the *Andante* has true lyrical repose, before the finale provides
fireworks as well as clinching the musical design. The *Largo Sinfonico*, completed in 1944, embodies
some of Skalkottas's most personal music; its 26-minute span is a seamless fusion of variation and
sonata forms, as satisfying formally as emotionally. Nikos Christodoulou's notes speak of a private
musical universe, yet the plangency of the cello theme and the remorseless tread of the central
climaxes betray an unease surely inseparable from the time of composition. The final bars, with the
thematic material recast as a series of unearthly chords, feel as much a stoic acceptance of reality as
they are a 'harmony of the spheres'. With the Malmö orchestra fully attuned to the idiom,
Christodoulou's powerfully shaped reading makes for a compelling experience.

Bedřich Smetana   Bohemian 1824-1884

Má vlast.
Czech Philharmonic Orchestra / Rafael Kubelík.
Supraphon 11 1208-2 (78 minutes: DDD). Recorded live in 1990.   Ⓕ 🆁🆁

Smetana's great cycle of six tone-poems, *Má vlast*, celebrates the countryside and legendary heroes
and heroines of Bohemia. It is a work of immense national significance encapsulating many of the
ideals and hopes of that country. What a triumphant occasion it was when Rafael Kubelík returned
to his native Czechoslovakia and to his old orchestra after an absence of 42 years and conducted
Má vlast at the 1990 Prague Spring Festival. Supraphon's disc captures that live performance – not

perfectly, since the sound is efficient rather than opulent – but well enough to show off what is arguably the finest performance on record since Talich's early LP set. You would never imagine that Kubelík had emerged from five years of retirement and a recent serious illness, such is the power and eloquence of his conducting. Typically he takes a lyrical rather than a dramatic view of the cycle, and if there is strength enough in more heroic sections there is also a refreshing lack of bombast. Kubelík's intimate knowledge of the score (this is his fifth recording of it) shows time and time again in the most subtle touches. Even the weakest parts of the work are most artfully brought to life, and seem of much greater stature than is usually the case. 'Vltava' flows beautifully, with the most imaginative flecks of detail, and in 'From Bohemia's Woods and Fields' there are vivid visions of wide, open spaces. The orchestra, no doubt inspired by the occasion, rewards its former director with superlative playing.

Má vlast.
Concertgebouw Orchestra / Antál Dorati.
Philips Solo 442 641-2PM (79 minutes: DDD). Recorded 1987. ⓜ

The Concertgebouw Orchestra, vividly directed by Antál Dorati, gives a strongly characterized performance of this epic cycle. The romantic opening of 'Vyšehrad' benefits from the glowing hall ambience, while 'Vltava' builds impressively from the gentle trickling streams to the river's powerful course through the St John's rapids – and how beautifully the Concertgebouw strings sing the main theme. 'Šárka', for all its bloodthirsty scenario, never descends into melodrama, 'From Bohemia's woods and fields' is gloriously diverse, and the darkly sombre opening of 'Tábor' contrasts with the hammered forcefulness of 'Blaník', which never becomes bombastic because of the crisply pointed orchestral articulation, while the performance is enhanced by the lovely playing in its enchanting pastoral interlude. Dorati's imaginative grip on this last, wayward 15-minute piece holds the listener throughout all its episodes to the grandiloquent final peroration. The recording is out of Philips's top-drawer.

Má vlast.
Czech Philharmonic Orchestra / Václav Talich.
Supraphon mono 11 1896-2 (74 minutes: AAD). Recorded 1954. ⓕ **Ⓗ**

Try listening from just before six minutes into 'From Bohemia's Woods and Fields' and you reach the very heart of this great performance. The CPO brass lunges towards the main melody with unconstrained eagerness, their impact much aided by smiling *glissandos*. And as Talich and his players climb aboard Smetana's homespun melody, everything assumes a sunny glow: it's almost as if the entire work thus far had prepared for that one magical moment. But there are of course countless additional splendours: the luminous mobility of 'Vltava', the grimness of 'Šárka' (so different here to the excitable Kubelík), the sense of foreboding in 'Tábor' and the chest-swelling patriotism of 'Blaník'. The strings retain more than a hint of the *portamentos* that were such a distinctive feature of Talich's 1929 recording, but the woodwinds are notably superior and the basically excellent sound releases more of the music's dynamism than was easily audible on 78s. The transfer makes a warmer case for the original tapes than did the old LPs, and generally serves Talich well – except in one maddening respect. A couple of bars have dropped from 'Tábor', thus utterly ruining the contour of a major climax. The offending cut was not present on the original recording. If you can write off the missing bars as 'historical wear and tear', then expect a *Má vlast* that's way above average, an inspired affirmation of national pride by a wonderful people who had only recently escaped one form of tyranny, and would subsequently fall prey to another.

Smetana Piano Trio in G minor, B104.
Tchaikovsky Piano Trio in A minor, Op. 50.
Golub Kaplan Carr Trio (Mark Kaplan *vn* Colin Carr *vc* David Golub *pf*).
Arabesque Z6661 (75 minutes: DDD). Recorded 1994. ⓕ

The Tchaikovsky Trio is well represented on CD as opposed to less than a dozen recordings of the Smetana. The Tchaikovsky is more often than not coupled with Arensky and the Smetana with Dvořák or Suk. No other version offers the current works together. The Golub Kaplan Carr Trio gives exemplary, well-shaped accounts of both works, which grip the listener with their musicality and unforced, natural eloquence. The Tchaikovsky Trio is performed complete, without any of the cuts that the composer sanctioned and played without the slightest overstatement. All three are fine players but when one sees the discography of some cellists (no disrespect intended to any of them), it is puzzling that Colin Carr has not enjoyed greater exposure as a soloist. The recording has great presence and though it may be a bit too forward for some tastes it is still well balanced. In any event, both performances are thoroughly enjoyable.

Má vlast – Vltava. The bartered bride – Overture; Polka; Furiant; Dance of the Comedians.
The Kiss – Overture. Libuše – Prelude. The two widows – Overture.
Cleveland Orchestra Chorus; Cleveland Orchestra / Christoph von Dohnányi.
Decca 444 867-2DH (57 minutes: DDD). Text and translation included. Recorded 1993-94.　　Ⓕ

Pride of place must go to the magnificent Overture to *Libuše*, a work that was completed in 1872
but not actually premièred until 1881, two years before Dvořák composed his *Hussite* Overture
along vaguely similar lines. The opening brass-and-timpani fanfare anticipates Janáček's *Sinfonietta*,
although ensuing incident is more reminiscent of Smetana's own *Má vlast* and, especially, Wagner.
Dohnányi effects ideal pacing and tapers a beautifully graded *diminuendo* away from the bold
opening, but the strings are occasionally less than precise. *The two widows* opens somewhat in the
manner of late Verdi though the overall flavour is unmistakable. Then there is the delightful 'Polka'
and the lively Overture to *The Kiss*, both prime-cut samplings of Smetana's mature style. *The
bartered bride* suite is very nicely done, although don't expect Dohnányi's 'Dance of the Comedians'
to match Szell's Cleveland recording of 30 years earlier for precision, especially among the strings.
In the 'Polka', vivid stereophony lends considerable presence to the chorus, which makes a very
bold entrance: You may feel you have been gatecrashed by a crowd of unannounced guests! 'Vltava'
is equally effective, what with its stylishly phrased opening, sensitive transitions (especially into the
'Peasant's Wedding' episode) and powerful current later on. The sound is resonant and full-bodied.

The bartered bride.
Gabriela Beňačková *sop* Mařenka; **Peter Dvorský** *ten* Jeník; **Miroslav Kopp** *ten* Vašek;
Richard Novák *bass* Kecal; **Jindřich Jindrák** *bar* Krušina; **Marie Mrázová** *contr* Háta;
Jaroslav Horáček *bass* Mícha; **Marie Veselá** *sop* Ludmila; **Jana Jonášová** *sop* Esmeralda;
Alfréd Hampel *ten* Circus master; **Karel Hanuš** *bass* Indian;
Czech Philharmonic Chorus and Orchestra / Zdeněk Košler.
Supraphon 10 3511-2 (three discs: 137 minutes: DDD). Notes, text and translation included.
Recorded 1980-81.　　Ⓕ

There is something special about a Czech performance of *The bartered bride* and this one is no
exception. The hint of melancholy which runs through the work is wonderfully evoked, as well as its
marvellous gaiety. Zdeněk Košler has the rhythm and lilt of the music in his bones, like any Czech
conductor worth his salt. The Czech Philharmonic has long had one of the finest of all woodwind
sections, and especially in this music they play with a sense of their instruments' folk background,
with phrasing that springs from deep in Czech folk-music. This sets the musical scene for some
moving performances. The warm, lyrical quality of Gabriela Beňačková's voice can lighten easily to
encompass her character's tenderness in the first duet, 'Věrné milování', or 'Faithful love', the
considerable show of spirit she makes when Jeník appears to have gone off the rails. Her Act 1
lament is most beautifully song. Peter Dvorský as Jeník plays lightly with the score, as he should, or
the character's maintaining of the deception can come to seem merely cruel. Even old Kecal comes
to new life, not as the conventional village bumbler, but as a human character in his own right as
Richard Novák portrays him – quite put out, the old boy is, to find his plans gone astray. In fact, all
of the soloists are excellent. The chorus enjoys itself hugely, never more so than in the Beer chorus.
Altogether a delightful, touching and warming performance.

Libuše.
Gabriela Beňačková *sop* Libuše; **Václav Zítek** *ten* Přemysl; **Antonín Svorc** *bass* Chrudoš;
Leo Marian Vodička *ten* Stáhlav; **Karel Průša** *bass* Lubtor; **René Tuček** *bar* Radovan;
Eva Děpoltová *sop* Krasava; **Věra Soukupová** *mez* Radmila;
Prague National Theatre Chorus and Orchestra / Zdeněk Košler.
Supraphon 11 1276-2 (three discs: 166 minutes: DDD). Notes, text and translation included.
Recorded live in 1983.　　Ⓕ

Libuše is a patriotic pageant, static and celebratory, with such plot as there is concerning the
mythical founder of Prague, Libuše, and her marriage to the peasant Přemysl, founder of the first
Czech dynasty. Václav Zítek makes a fine, heroic Přemysl; but the triumphant performance comes,
as it must, from Gabriela Beňačková. The opera concludes with a series of tableaux in which Libuše
prophesies the future kings and heroes who will assure the stability and greatness of the nation. At
the end of a long performance her voice is undimmed in its ringing splendour; and earlier, as near
the very start, the beauty of her tone and line seeks out all the warmth, character and humanity
which she proves to be latent in Smetana's spacious but seemingly plain vocal writing. *Libuše* is
scarcely Smetana's greatest opera, as he liked to claim, but especially in so splendid a performance
from Beňačková, and under the grave but impassioned direction of Zdeněk Košler, it makes
compelling listening. The live recording includes some applause, but little other distraction.

Dame Ethel Smyth

String Quintet in E major, Op. 1. String Quartet in E minor.
Joachim Griesheimer *vc* **Mannheim Quartet** (Andreas Krecher, Claudia Hohorst *vns*
Niklas Schwarz *va* Armin Fromm *vc*).
CPO CPO999 352-2 (68 minutes: DDD). Recorded 1994.   Ⓕ

The Mannheim Quartet, reinforced in the early String Quintet by the cellist Joachim Griesheimer,
gives superb performances of keenly inventive works which belie the old idea that Smyth was
influenced above all in her chamber music by Brahms. As is pointed out in the note (poorly
translated from the German), the delightfully fresh first movement of the Quintet, written in 1881
when Smyth was in her mid-twenties, keeps reminding one of Dvořák, notably the *American*
Quartet and the *New World* Symphony. Yet those two works were written after this, not before, and
one wonders just what the influence was. In the five-movement scheme the outer movements are by
far the most substantial, with the three middle movements as contrasting interludes, a delicate
Andantino, a jolly *Scherzo* and a raptly lyrical *Adagio* which in a tantalizingly brief three-and-a-half
minutes has the composer taking on the role of visionary, with a nod in the direction of the
Cavatina from Beethoven's B flat Quartet, Op. 130. Delightful and refreshing as the Quintet is, it is
the Quartet, begun in 1902 but not completed till ten years later, which demonstrates the composer's
originality most clearly. It was bold of her, instead of starting with an *Allegro*, to have an easily
lilting *Allegretto lirico* as a sonata-form first movement. It is the more remarkable when you realize
that this predominantly gentle and sweet inspiration dates from the years when Smyth was most
active in the Suffragette cause, finally getting ending up in prison. The second movement is a jaunty
scherzo with a hint of English folk music in the themes, and the lively finale, starting with a *fugato*,
also has an English flavour. The beautiful, extended slow movement, like the brief *Adagio* of the
Quintet, is peacefully lyrical, again belying the composer's often violent personality. These are
outstanding performances, well recorded.

Antonio Soler

Soler Keyboard Sonatas – No. 36 in C minor; No. 72 in F minor; No. 88 in D flat major;
No. 119 in B flat major. Fandango.
D. Scarlatti Keyboard Sonatas – Kk7; Kk84; Kk185; Kk187; Kk193; Kk208; Kk491; Kk492.
Virginia Black *hpd*
Cala United CACD88005 (58 minutes: DDD).   ⒻⓅ

This highly recommendable disc is particularly exhilarating, even among a multitude of Scarlatti
recordings. Thought has been given to the order of the sonatas selected, so as to provide a smooth
key-sequence as well as contrasts of mood and pace. Black starts off in fine style with the sturdy
Kk491 Sonata, complete with trumpet tuckets: she shows that it is perfectly possible to maintain
strict time without any danger of sounding mechanical. On the other hand, her slight flexibility for
expressive purposes in Kk208 is judged to a nicety. There is joyousness in Kk492, with its quasi-
guitar thrummings and rushing scales, and noisy high spirits in Kk187; the exuberant vivacity of
Kk7 really needed to be seen – not to check that there was no cheating in the perversely lengthy
cross-handed sections (for who could not trust Virginia Black), but to enjoy the left-hand leaps, as
we do the sixths and thirds of Kk84. The chosen sonatas by Scarlatti's disciple Soler are equally
pleasurable. The chattering repeated notes of No. 88 and the right-hand leaps of tenths in No. 119
are entirely in the tradition of his mentor: the modulations in the second half of No. 36 and
No. 119 point to Soler's special interest in that subject. (By an unfortunate misreading, this latter is
billed as *Allegro arioso* instead of *Allegro airoso*, which is a very different thing.) A disappointment
in the disc is the amazing and spectacular *Fandango* (which may or may not be by Soler, but is
remarkable whoever wrote it): not only does Virginia Black make numerous cuts in this, but her
small inflexions of pace undermine the relentlessly cumulative drive of the dance rhythm. No details
are given of the harpsichord employed, but it is a fine instrument with a magnificently rich tone.

Fernando Sor

Fantaisies – No. 12, Op. 58; No. 13, Op. 59, 'Fantaisie élégiaque'. Studies, Op. 60.
Nicholas Goluses *gtr*
Naxos 8 553342 (65 minutes: DDD). Recorded 1994.   Ⓢ

Sor's guitar works is an *oeuvre* that is perhaps the most consistent in quality, and most manageable
in quantity of any major guitar composer of the period. Whilst Sor was born and died later than

Beethoven his language was closer to that of Mozart, barely on the edge of romanticism. He was a polished and elegant composer, whose works have more quiet emotional content and expressiveness than those of any of his contemporaries, and though he often calls for technical virtuosity he doesn't lean too heavily on it. The *Fantaisie*, Op. 58 is not one of Sor's more riveting works. Goluses plays it in a somewhat matter-of-fact way. The *Fantaisie élégiaque*, arguably Sor's finest single work, elicits a very different response, a deeply sensitive and dignified reading in which the moments of silent grief are given the breathing-space and time they call for. Sor devoted five opus numbers to his 97 studies, of which Op. 60 was the last. Each has a clear technical and/or musical purpose and even the simplest is lovingly crafted music – which is how Goluses treats it, with lots of care lavished on it. It should be remembered that the guitar of Sor's time differed from today's in construction, stringing and sound, and that Sor played without using the right-hand nails. Goluses uses a modern instrument and plays with nails, which inevitably leads to differences in sound and, to some extent, interpretation. Given and accepting the differences, Goluses sets a benchmark for present-day guitarists.

Grand Sonatas – C major, Op. 22; C major, Op. 25. Divertissement, Op. 23.
Eight Short Pieces, Op. 24.
Adam Holzman *gtr*
Naxos 8 553340 (75 minutes: DDD). Recorded 1994. ⑤

The major works in Holzman's programme are the two sonatas, each with four movements. Of these Op. 25 is by far the finer – and the best work of its kind from the period; the last movement is a Minuet, a final lightening of the atmosphere that was not then uncommon. The *Divertissement*, Op. 23 contains ten pieces – *Valses*, *Allegrettos*, *Andantes*, a *Minuetto* and an *Allemande*. With a few exceptions they are, like the studies, more likely to be of interest to guitarists than to the general listener. Holzman plays very well, with a softer sound than Goluses (see above), and in a tighter acoustic. At slower tempos he exercises a pleasing degree of rubato and commendable dynamic shading; one wishes he had done likewise in the quicker ones, which incline to the metronomic. These are two discs that should, both in their own right and at super-budget price, be irresistible to guitarists.

Introduction and Variations on 'Que ne suis-je la fougère!', Op. 26. Introduction and Variations on 'Gentil Housard', Op. 27. Introduction and Variations on 'Malbroug', Op. 28. 12 Studies, Op. 29. Fantaisie et Variations brillantes, Op. 30.
Jeffrey McFadden *gtr*
Naxos 8 553451 (62 minutes: DDD). Recorded 1995. ⑤

This contribution to Naxos's integral archive of Sor's guitar music consists neatly of the last works he published with Meissonnier, before transferring to the more prestigious house of Pacini. Sets of variations, whether *per se* or framed in the *Fantaisie*, Op. 30, abound. The *12 Studies*, Op. 29 are described as 'Book 2', those of Op. 6 being 'Book 1', and are here given as Nos. 13-24, as they were in the original edition of 1827. Jeffrey McFadden, a Canadian, is a squeaky-clean and very musical player, with the clear and three-dimensional tone for which his fingers are admirably suited. No composer for the guitar of the time wrote studies that were more truly expressive than those of Sor; McFadden plays them, and everything else here, with humanity and respect. This outstanding disc would be cheap at twice the price.

Bent Sørensen

Danish 1958

Minnewater. Sirenengesang. Shadowland. The Deserted Churchyards. Clairobscur.
Esbjerg Ensemble / Jules Van Hessen.
Da Capo 8 224075 (63 minutes: DDD). Recorded 1997. ⑤

The titles of these five pieces composed between 1987 and 1994 point to the shamelessly allusive, evocative and entirely distinctive character of Sørensen's work. He is a composer of the twilight zones, fascinated by the natural processes of change and decay, and creating his own fluid soundscapes characteristic from complex patternings of microtones, *glissandos* and floating rhythms. The tautologically titled *Minnewater* plays for 12 minutes, with the tensions built and released by shifting levels of dynamic and rhythmic recession: the opening trilling vibration of microtones, like the surface of water grazed by a light wind, becomes criss-crossed by the sounds of distant bells and the flight formations of woodwind. *The Deserted Churchyards* (whose only programme-note is a monochrome photo of an overgrown heathland with a rune stone) offers bells aplenty; but there is silence, too, and a stark toccata of percussive wind and piano figures.

Sirenengesang is the newest work here and it offers an overview of Sørensen's repertoire of resources. The wonder of this piece, and of Sørensen's writing in general, is the acute understanding he brings to his writing for each instrument. Here the voices of the Esbjerg Ensemble merge mesmerically in the most subtle interplay of timbres and figuration whose movement in space is most beautifully captured in this Danish recording.

Louis Spohr

German 1784-1859

Violin Concertos – No. 1 in A major, Op. 1; No. 14 in A minor, Op. 110, 'Sonst und Jetzt'; No. 15 in E minor, Op. 128.
Ulf Hoelscher *vn*
Berlin Radio Symphony Orchestra / Christian Fröhlich.
CPO CPO999 403-2 (66 minutes: DDD). Recorded 1995. Ⓕ

Hoelscher has the elegance and almost vocal quality with which Spohr's violin writing is associated, but he can also master the virtuosity which is needed for the oddest work here, entitled *Sonst und Jetzt*, or 'Then and Now'. There is something of an in-joke for violinists here. Irritated by the playing of the Norwegian virtuoso, Ole Bull, whom Schumann regarded as the equal of Paganini, Spohr wrote this piece contrasting the lyrical qualities of the violin (in an expansive re-creation of the Minuet) with a hectic *Tarantella* embodying all he disliked in the showy 'modern' style. The idea falls flat as a piece of music criticism, simply because Spohr produces rather a good *Tarantella* and integrates it ingeniously and not contentiously with his more lyrical music. Hoelscher could have made the point by playing the two kinds of music in more extreme fashion; but, if it is true that nothing is colder than the ashes of dead controversies, the more musical course is to play the work as he does, warmly and without *parti-pris*. The Concerto No. 15 is a rather more weary piece, in which Spohr goes through the motions expertly but without his full creative attention. Op. 1 is a juvenile work (he was 18), obviously close to his beloved Mozart in spirit but also heavily influenced by Kreutzer, Rode and especially Viotti. The best movement is the delightful *Siciliano*, which Spohr embellishes lovingly.

Nonet in F major, Op. 31. Octet in E major, Op. 32. Waltz in A major, Op. 89, 'Erinnerung an Marienbad'.
Academy of St Martin in the Fields Chamber Ensemble.
Philips 438 017-2PH (74 minutes: DDD). Recorded 1992. Ⓕ

Spohr's two most popular chamber works go well together, here in performances that emphasize their lyrical, reflective, even sometimes wistful manner. The Academy suggests greater depths than most interpreters, sometimes at the expense of the music's gaiety in the faster movements. The finale of the Octet can sound livelier than on this disc, and perhaps should, though there is at least consistency with all that has gone before; and the 'Harmonious Blacksmith' depicted in the variation movement is a more melancholy fellow than Handel surely intended. But the playing is thoughtful and well judged, not only in matters of living ensemble (something more than merely timing) but in exploring and bringing to life the music through a flexible and sensitive application of its form. So the first movements of both works come off well as sonata structures as powerful and supple as Spohr must have intended, which will doubtless give these performances lasting satisfaction. The sound is well balanced, with a proper attention to the rich middle registers. As a *bonne bouche*, there is the waltz which he wrote in salon manner for the typical spa ensemble of the day.

Piano Trios – No. 3 in A minor, Op. 124; No. 4 in B flat major, Op. 133.
Borodin Trio (Rostislav Dubinsky *vn* Laszlo Varga *vc* Luba Edlina *pf*).
Chandos CHAN9372 (66 minutes: DDD). Recorded 1994. Ⓕ

Spohr's late piano trios are virtuoso works, in every sense. They are ingeniously composed and are difficult to balance with true effect; above all they demand great technical dexterity, and the dexterity to allow many extremely difficult passages to play a secondary or supporting role. In particular No. 3 in A minor places demands on the players who need virtuosity of the kind which the Borodin Trio are well able to provide. Their skills need no recommendation by now; here, they also have a subtlety and quickness of response that come from a proper sympathy with Spohr's idiom. They rise to the occasion with, for instance, the racing piano fingerwork in the Variations of No. 3; they also respond with the flexibility of tempo the music needs for its full expressive effect. Moreover, in places where Spohr seems to have lost concentration for a moment or two – his capacity to meander down beguiling but distracting chromatic paths, his habit of striking a cliché chord like a dramatic attitude, his gear-changing modulations – the Borodin hold faith and make the music come off effectively. The A minor Trio is the more worthwhile piece, and deserves all this interpretative concentration; but the rather less well invented work in B flat, apparently here receiving a first recording, is worth having for some pleasant and recreational music. The recording team cannot always have had an easy task with balance; it all works excellently.

Sir John Stainer

British 1840-1901

The Crucifixion.
Martyn Hill *ten* **Michael George** *bass*
BBC Singers; Leith Hill Festival Singers / Brian Kay with **Margaret Phillips** *org*
Chandos CHAN9551 (71 minutes: DDD). Text included. Recorded 1997.   Ⓕ

It is easy to dismiss Stainer's *Crucifixion* as the epitome of English musical disfunctionality in the nineteenth century. Yet, over 100 years after its première at Marylebone Parish Church in 1887, this work still has a following. Despite moments of questionable taste Stainer's formula strikes a chord for a surprisingly broad audience. In its favour, it unfolds with a seamless ease, never jolting the listener with gratuitous theatricality or the type of rhetorical intensity which the English find mildly embarrassing. Emotional engagement here is about an unintrusive sobriety, affected by a glowing sentimental identification with the Saviour's plight – all very Victorian but clearly a strong residue of such a temperament still remains. One has to admire Stainer for writing a challenging work of sensible length which, without an orchestra, is achievable and satisfying for a capable parish choir: Stainer's *Crucifixion* is a celebration of amateurism, that cherished English virtue. Brian Kay has worked a great deal with committed amateurs, in this case the Leith Hill Festival Singers, the festival of which he is director. There is indeed an underlying freshness of expression here, of singers with eyes and ears on stalks and a real sense of purpose to the performance. They are fortified by the excellent BBC Singers. Margaret Phillips's imaginative and genial registrations, not to mention her skilful accompaniment, provide notable support to the excellent contributions of Martyn Hill and Michael George. An unselfregarding and genuine performance.

Carl Stamitz

German 1745-1801

Symphonies – F major, Op. 24 No. 3; Op. 13 – No. 4 in G major; No. 5 in C major;
D major, 'La chasse'.
London Mozart Players / Matthias Bamert.
Chandos CHAN9358 (62 minutes: DDD). Recorded 1994.   Ⓕ

Besides showing Stamitz's flair for melody and effective use of contrast, the London Mozart Players are responsive to the touches of genuine originality in these pieces. Try the first movement of the C major Symphony, Op. 13 No. 5, where the slow introduction ingeniously returns as a coda, or the textural variety in the G major Symphony, Op. 13 No. 4, where flutes replace oboes in the outer movements, while the second movement, in which the LMP elegantly conveys the music's spaciousness, is scored for strings and continuo alone. Bamert's firm, sympathetic direction is also evident in the F major Symphony, Op. 24 No. 3, where the second and third movements are particularly effective for the subtlety with which the LMP defuses the slow movement's dramatic intensity, with delightfully buoyant playing in the work's radiantly cheerful finale. *La chasse* is the highlight of the disc. The declamatory character of the slow introduction gives way to operatic brilliance in the subsequent *Allegro*, and the slow movement's graceful stateliness culminates in a vividly descriptive portrayal of the hunt in the finale. The stylish performances make a strong case for this repertoire.

Sir Charles Villiers Stanford

Irish/British 1852-1924

Stanford Symphony No. 3 in F minor, Op. 28, 'Irish'.
Elgar Scenes from the Bavarian Highlands, Op. 27.
Bournemouth Symphony Chorus; Bournemouth Sinfonietta / Norman Del Mar.
EMI British Composers CDM5 65129-2 (70 minutes: ADD). Text included. Recorded 1981-82.   Ⓜ

A valuable addition to the catalogue on its initial appearance, Norman Del Mar's characteristically enterprising 1982 recording of Stanford's *Irish* Symphony re-emerges in splendidly vital fashion on this beautifully presented release. Compared with Vernon Handley and the excellent Ulster

Orchestra on Chandos, Del Mar is perhaps just a touch lacking in charm and it is undoubtedly the former who more effectively minimizes the element of dutiful convention which occasionally afflicts both outer movements (Handley is nearly three minutes quicker in the opening *Allegro moderato*, yet there is no feeling of undue haste). However, Del Mar draws the threads together most satisfyingly for the symphony's ample peroration, and his Bournemouth band responds with commendable vigour throughout. Preceding the Stanford here is a rare outing for the orchestral version of Elgar's *Scenes from the Bavarian Highlands*. This six-movement choral suite shows Elgar at his most carefree and joyous, qualities savoured to the full in Del Mar's exuberant performance. A thoroughly enjoyable reissue.

Requiem, Op. 63[a]. The Veiled Prophet of Khorassan[b]: Overture; Ballet music – No. 1; No. 2; There's a bower of roses.
Frances Lucey, Virginia Kerr *sops* **Colette McGahon** *mez* **Peter Kerr** *ten*
Nigel Leeson-Williams *bass*
RTE Philharmonic Choir;
National Symphony Orchestra of Ireland / [a]Adrian Leaper, [b]Colman Pearce.
Marco Polo 8 223580/1 (two discs: 104 minutes: DDD). Texts and translations included.
Recorded 1994.   Ⓕ

It is most moving to hear this Requiem and to reflect that for the best part of a century a work so rich in feeling and craftsmanship has lain largely silent and unregarded. The opening *Requiem aeternam* ought of itself, one would think, to have ensured at least the occasional revival: a warm, lyrical composition, firmly structured and with something unmistakably personal about it, rather as with Dvořák. The *Kyrie* seems to express affection, though 'For what?' one wonders – perhaps for the sheer beauty of sound. The 'Gradual' allows interest to slip, recaptured by the 'Sequence', plentiful in ideas and rising to a generous climax in the 'Lacrimosa'. The 'Offertorium' brings a touch of nineteenth-century Grand Manner, tightening up later with a robust, fugal 'Quam olim Abrahae'. The *Sanctus* ends vigorously with its 'Pleni sunt caeli', and a sweet, well-sustained orchestral passage (perhaps with Beethoven in mind) leads into the 'Benedictus'. A Funeral March introduces the *Agnus Dei*, and the whole work, not all that much shorter than the Verdi Requiem, ends with a spacious, steadily developed 'Lux aeterna'. Soloists and chorus are used with relish for the capabilities of the human voice, and in listening one thinks quite as much of opera as of oratorio. As a fill-up on the second disc we are given further rarities, the Overture and other excerpts from *The Veiled Prophet of Khorassan*, the first of Stanford's operas. The Overture, more Brahms than Mendelssohn and with a genial suggestion of the Irish jig, is a thoroughly likeable piece, so once more we are left feeling that here is still another area of Stanford's output that might reward attention. The performances are able and enthusiastic. Recorded sound might be sharper, but at least it falls more kindly on the ears than do many of more vaunted origin. In any case, we are deeply in Marco Polo's debt for this revival.

Stabat mater, Op. 96. Te Deum, Op. 10 No. 1. Six Bible Songs, Op. 113.
Ingrid Attrot *sop* **Pamela Helen Stephen** *mez* **Nigel Robson** *ten* **Stephen Varcoe** *bar*
Ian Watson *org*
Leeds Philharmonic Chorus; BBC Philharmonic Orchestra / Richard Hickox.
Chandos CHAN9548 (74 minutes: DDD). Texts and translations included. Recorded 1995.   Ⓕ

Writing of his old teacher in 1952, Vaughan Williams foretold that his time would come round again: 'With the next generation the inevitable reaction will set in and Stanford will come into his own.' It has taken more than a generation, but at last it does begin to look as though he was right. This recording of a 'symphonic cantata', the *Stabat mater*, strong in ideas, deeply felt and structurally assured, will certainly strengthen the steadily growing appreciation of his worth. The Prelude, impressive as it is, is almost *too* soundly constructed, and the first choral movement, rich in its Verdi-like foreground of soloists, signs off with a slightly self-conscious repetition of the opening words by the soprano. Stanford is never abashed by the prospect of melodic commitment, and the orchestral Intermezzo comes out boldly with what promises to be a good, old-fashioned Grand Tune; but then he seems to remember where he is, and the piece ends with murky explorations that seem not quite to find what they may be seeking. The work itself ends, as Lewis Foreman suggests in his useful notes, in Eternity: 'we seem to reach the crest of a hill only to find the path stretching onward and upward to another.' The performance carries conviction, with Hickox exercising that natural rightness of his so that in a work such as this, without predecessors on record, a listener will feel that this is how it should 'go'. Fine orchestral playing and choral singing give pleasure throughout. The solo quartet is led by Ingrid Attrot's colourful but none too evenly produced soprano, and in the *Bible Songs* Stephen Varcoe sings sensitively to the judiciously registered organ accompaniment of Ian Watson. The most tuneful of *Te Deum*s follows, blithe and buoyant in its orchestrated version.

Morning and Evening Services in B flat major, Op. 10ᵃ. Evening Services – A major, Op. 12ᵃ;
F major, Op. 36ᵃ; E flat majorᵇ. Two Anthems, Op. 37ᵇ. Three Motets, Op. 38. Pater noster.
The Lord is my Shepherdᵃ.
Winchester Cathedral Choir / David Hill with ᵃ**Stephen Farr**, ᵇ**Christopher Monks** *org*
Hyperion CDA66964 (78 minutes: DDD). Texts included. Recorded 1997.   Ⓕ

Delius, in an extremity of wonder and dismay, is said to have remarked that Parry would have set
the whole 'something' Bible to music if he had had the 'something' time. Stanford similarly must
have been suspected of a purpose, under similar conditions, to set the Evening canticles in every key
in the *Well-tempered Clavier*. A major, B flat major, C major, F major and G major are familiar to
us already; here Hyperion comes up with E flat major; and this is but Vol. 1. The *Magnificat and
Nunc dimittis* in E flat major dates back to 1873 and, according to the valuable notes by Dr Jeremy
Dibble, is not with any certainty known even to have been performed. Perhaps this is because both
settings are almost indecently tuneful. The 23-year-old Irishman comes out with an apocalyptic
'scattered the proud', a broadly melodious 'to be a light' and 'Gloria's as catchy as a comic opera.
In these clap-happy days it might enjoy a new lease of life, except of course that it is far too good.
As for the B flat major settings written six years later, these (both Morning and Evening services)
have long owed their popularity to a melodic gift that is almost Schubertian and a correspondingly
deft mastery of construction.

The A major and F major settings also lie within the scope of this first volume, leaving G major
(with the treble solo) and C major (best of all) for another day. Winchester Cathedral Choir is
surely one of the best in the UK. Under David Hill, the trebles have acquired something of the
bright, distinctive tone of the Westminster Cathedral boys. The men are excellent, and all of
them sound as though they are singing for the joy of it. Several of these works involve more
than the customary four parts, and the eight-part *Pater noster*, recorded for the first time, has
splendid richness, with the choir forming massive columns or pillars of sound in the powerful
climax. Stanford's writing for the organ, endowing the accompaniment with an independent
life, is also a delight and at times we might wish that the fine playing of both organists had
been brought into sharper focus. The choir we hear with rare clarity, and to do so is an unmixed
pleasure.

Evening Service in G major, Op. 81. Morning Service in C major, Op. 115.
Six Bible Songs and Hymns, Op. 113.
Winchester Cathedral Choir / David Hill *org* with **Stephen Farr, Christopher Monks** *orgs*
Hyperion CDA66965 (67 minutes: DDD). Texts included. Recorded 1997.   Ⓕ

Stanford's *Bible Songs* are occasionally introduced into programmes one or two at a time, but it is
rare to have all six. Four of the songs take their text from the Psalms, the others from Isaiah and
Ecclesiasticus, but each has a generic title: 'A Song of Freedom', 'A Song of Wisdom' and so forth.
They are written for baritone with organ accompaniment and here we hear what is a rarity indeed,
namely the alternation of songs and hymns as Stanford intended. The songs were published in 1909,
the hymns a year later, but they are designed to slot in so that the cycle takes the form of a cantata.
This bare description gives no idea of the enriched effect. The hymns are mostly well known (*Let us
with a gladsome mind* is the first), and there is always a strong emotional effect to be gained from
such a process. Stanford had no formulated design, as upon an audience, but if he had he could
hardly have achieved it with a surer touch. The great revelation of this disc is afforded by the
performance of the songs and hymns as an entity. Only four of the six songs fall to William
Kendall, who sings them well though the tessitura is occasionally a little low for him. The baritone
Plunket Greene was the dedicatee and first performer, but one of the songs (No. 4) had a separate
dedication to the soprano Agnes Nicholls. It was presumably with this in mind that 'A Song for
Peace' is allocated to the choir's fine treble soloist, Kenan Burrows. The corresponding allocation
of 'A Song of Wisdom', however, seems not entirely an *act* of wisdom: the visionary text and
broad, powerful setting call for a different kind of timbre. The choral singing is excellent, as
are the organists. In particular, it is good to find the changes of tempo in the *Te Deum* so
effectively carried through. And that *Te Deum* – indeed, the whole of the C major Service – is
surely the masterpiece.

Evening Service in C major, Op. 115. Ye Choirs of New Jerusalem, Op. 123. Gloria in B flat major,
Op. 128. St Patrick's Breastplate. Motets, Op. 135 – No. 2, Eternal Father; No. 3, Glorious and
Powerful God. For lo, I raise up, Op. 145. Magnificat in B flat major, Op. 164. Lighten our
darkness. How beauteous are their feet.
Winchester Cathedral Choir / David Hill with **Stephen Farr, Christopher Monks** *orgs*
Hyperion CDA66974 (64 minutes: DDD). Texts included. Recorded 1997.   Ⓕ

This disc includes some of Stanford's best work, starting with the Evening Service in
C. At Winchester they take a broad view of this, bringing out a meditative grandeur rather than the
more pressing enthusiasm in favour elsewhere. In general, the tempo is brisk, matched with verbal
and rhythmic life in abundance. *For lo, I raise up* is particularly exciting. Written in 1914, this
marvellous setting of Habakkuk's vision of a war-torn world that is eventually to 'be filled with the
knowledge of the glory of the Lord' needs a choir that can forget it is 'in church'. The narrative
must be eager-eyed, crisp on the words, intense in drive and attack like Toscanini conducting The
Ride of the Valkyries; and that is just about how it is here. In the eight-part *Magnificat* the speed is
risky, and may indeed be a little too headlong at the expense of clarity; but again it is rhythmically
exhilarating. The anthem *Lighten our darkness* is recorded here for the first time (Stanford wrote it
in 1918 for St George's, Windsor, but the manuscript got lost, and having been found in 1935 was
neglected till the present day). The prayer is lovingly treated, and the performance is worthy of the
honour bestowed.

Wilhelm Stenhammar Swedish 1871-1927

Piano Concerto No. 1 in B flat minor, Op. 1. Symphony No. 3 in C major – fragment.
Mats Widlund *pf*
Stockholm Philharmonic Orchestra / Gennadi Rozhdestvensky.
Chandos CHAN9074 (51 minutes: DDD). Recorded 1992.   Ⓕ

Piano Concerto No. 2 in D minor, Op. 23ᵃ. Serenade in F major, Op. 31ᵇ.
Florez och Blanzeflor, Op. 3ᵇ.
Ingvár Wixell *bar* **Janos Solyom** *pf*
ᵃ**Munich Philharmonic Orchestra;** ᵇ**Swedish Radio Symphony Orchestra / Stig Westerberg.**
EMI Matrix CDM5 65081-2 (73 minutes: ADD). Text and translation included.
Recorded 1970-74.   Ⓜ

The First Piano Concerto comes from 1893, when Stenhammar was 22, and such was its success
during the 1890s that he was invited to play it with the Berlin Philharmonic under Richard Strauss.
In time, however, he grew tired of it and became careless as to its fate. Both the autograph and the
orchestral parts were destroyed when Breslau was bombed during the Second World War. But
recently a copy probably made for the American première came to light in the Library of Congress.
Chandos also offers a short fragment from the Symphony No. 3 in C major, on which Stenhammar
embarked in 1918-19. At not much under 50 minutes it is perhaps overlong, but still has much
charm, and Widlund and Rozhdestvensky make a most persuasive case for it. The recording has
great depth and warmth and the strings of the Stockholm orchestra have great richness of sonority.
The *Serenade* is arguably Stenhammar's masterpiece. In its Overture the writing is vibrant and
luminous, full of subtly changing textures and colours, and like the finale is of symphonic
proportions. Apparently Stenhammar toyed at one stage with the idea of adding the word *selvaggio*
or 'wild' to the title of the *Scherzo*, the mercurial centrepiece of the whole work, which is played
with captivating spirit here. Stig Westerberg's recording comes up very fresh indeed. The playing
throughout is ardent, sensitive and vital. This issue offers two additional pieces, most notably János
Solyom's brilliant account of the Second Piano Concerto with the Munich Philharmonic, sounding
as if it were recorded yesterday. It is strongly indebted to Saint-Saëns, and the *Scherzo* has a
Mendelssohnian effervescence and delicacy. The early and endearing if Wagnerian *Florez och
Blanzeflor,* finely sung by Ingvár Wixell, is the admirable makeweight.

Symphony No. 2 in G minor, Op. 34. Excelsior!, Op. 13. Two Songs, Op. 4 (orch. cpsr).
Reverenza.
Anne Sofie von Otter *mez*
Royal Stockholm Philharmonic Orchestra / Paavo Järvi.
Virgin Classics VC5 45244-2 (76 minutes: DDD). Text and translation included.
Recorded 1996.   ⒻⒺ

This account of the G minor Symphony has a lot going for it. Paavo Järvi is eminently
straightforward and sensitive, the architecture of the piece is well shaped and detail attentively
handled. He hardly puts a foot wrong and obviously has great feeling for the piece. It is a
distinguished performance – and what a wonderful score! The fill-ups are generous: the *Reverenza*
movement which Stenhammar included in the original version of the *Serenade* for orchestra but
subsequently excised, comes off well. The two Op. 4 Songs – 'The girl came from meeting her lover'
is a subtle and refined song and its companion, 'The girl on Midsummer's Eve', is even lovelier –
have never been recorded before in their orchestral form. Von Otter is on home ground and in
radiant voice. The exhilarating *Excelsior!* overture, which comes from the mid-1890s, is the standard

coupling, and is given here with great panache and spirit. The only caveat is the recording which though perfectly acceptable, is not in the top flight. There is insufficient transparency in climaxes and the sound is two-dimensional with little front-to-back depth. *Reverenza* fares much better and so do the songs. In any event these performances score strongly on artistic grounds and will give pleasure and delight.

Bernard Stevens

British 1916-1983

Stevens Fantasia on 'Giles Farnaby's Dreame'. Piano Sonata in one movement, Op. 25. Aria.
Howells Gadabout. Three Pieces, Op. 14. Sonatina.
Jeremy Filsell *pf*
Guild GMCD7119 (70 minutes: DDD).   Ⓕ

This is an effective, but slightly odd coupling of composers, since all the Howells is available from Margaret Fingerhut and the best of his keyboard music is probably for the organ, with the notable exception of the outstanding clavichord works, all of which John McCabe has recorded on the piano. The earliest Howells here lacks his mature fingerprints, but the late *Sonatina* (1971) is pared down but recognizable, especially in the slow movement. Filsell approaches everything sympathetically, but 'Procession' from Op. 14 is not sufficiently rhythmically regular to reflect its subject. The Stevens works, headed by the Sonata (1954), are not otherwise represented in the catalogue. The single movement is in the rhetorical tradition of the British piano sonata, in a rather grey, mainstream dialect less personal than Rawsthorne but not far from some of Hoddinott's or Mathias's works. The slow central section (based on the two-chord alternation from the finale of Vaughan Williams's Symphony No. 6) starting at 6'30" is pleasantly lyrical, then it meanders until overtaken by a kind of jig (11'32") to finish. The *Aria* from the early 1960s is delightful – is this the core of Stevens, who was said to be always smiling? The *Farnaby* Variations are resourceful, a considered exploration of the virginal piece bridging the gap between the centuries, ending rather surprisingly with a diatonic fugue. All this is convincingly played, in a slightly metallic piano sound.

Alessandro Stradella

Italian 1644-1682

Ah! troppo è ver. Si apra al riso ogni labro. Sonata di viole.
Lavinia Bertotti, Emanuela Galli, Barbara Zanichelli *sops* **Roberto Balconi** *counterten*
Maurizio Sciuto *ten* **Carlo Lepore** *bass*
Orchestra Barocca della Civica Scuola di Musica di Milano / Enrico Gatti.
Arcana A79 (67 minutes: DDD). Texts included. Recorded 1997.   Ⓕ

Ferma, ferma il corso. Frena o filli il fiero orgoglio. Fuor della Stigia sponda. Non avea il sole ancora. Si salvi chi può. Sinfonias – No. 12; No. 22.
Christine Brandes *sop* **Paul O'Dette** *lte* **Ingrid Matthews** *vn* **Mary Springfels** *va da gamba*
Barbara Weiss *hpd/org*
Harmonia Mundi HMU90 7192 (69 minutes: DDD). Recorded 1997.   ⒻⓅ

These two releases represent different aspects of Stradella's work. The Arcana issue features two Christmas cantatas, *Si apra al riso* for three mixed solo voices, two violins and continuo, and the larger *Ah! troppo è ver* for mixed solo voices, with a concertino of violin, cello and continuo, and ripieno strings supplying the concerto grosso. The disc also contains a Sonata consisting of concertino and ripieno elements, a *concerto grosso*, in fact, of which form Stradella was a pioneer. The other disc contains five chamber cantatas for solo voice – here, a soprano – and continuo, whose sequence is interrupted by two interesting and lively instrumental *Sinfonias*. The movements of the first are strikingly varied, while the second is a set of variations on a moderately extended 'ground'. Enrico Gatti and his almost all-Italian ensemble of singers and instrumentalists enliven this music, his imagination responding unfailingly to Stradella's often individual, at times, quirky style, and his feeling for texture and declamation most impressive. These and other qualities may be sensed at once in the splendid, larger-than-life account of *Ah! troppo è ver*. Some may find the acoustic a shade over-reverberant but the ear quickly grows accustomed. The performances certainly have rough patches, vocally and instrumentally, but they convey with fervour the spirit and occasional atmosphere of the music. The chamber cantatas disc is technically accomplished, maintaining a level of finesse and attention to detail not always present in the other. Christine Brandes has a lightly coloured, ingenuous voice, just a little pinched in her uppermost register and strained to its limits in the ferociously demanding cantata *Ferma, ferma il corso*. Her diction is clear and her inflexions pay close attention to the meaning and mood of the texts. As in the Christmas cantatas, so too in these more intimate pieces Stradella often surprises us with melodies that strike off in unexpected directions, sometimes requiring virtuosity from the singer and a fine sensibility from the continuo support. Both are present in these performances of pieces, few, if any, of which have been previously recorded. Stradella's cantatas will handsomely reward ears that savour expressive subtlety.

San Giovanni Battista.
Catherine Bott, Christine Batty sops **Gérard Lesne** counterten
Richard Edgar-Wilson ten **Philippe Huttenlocher** bar
Les Musiciens du Louvre / Marc Minkowski.
Erato 2292-45739-2 (61 minutes: DDD). Notes, text and translation included.
Recorded live in 1991. *Gramophone* Award Winner 1993. ⓕⓅ

Stradella's amorous adventures, which eventually led to his murder in Genoa at the age of 37, subsequently gave rise to a novel, an opera by Flotow, a poem, a play and a song text. Though an outstanding oratorio composer he was considered in his own lifetime foremost as a composer for the theatre, and his great gifts in this direction enabled him to treat the New Testament story of the imprisonment and murder of John the Baptist with considerable dramatic force. *San Giovanni Battista* was first performed in Rome in 1657. The librettist, a Sicilian priest, Girardo Ansaldi, dispensed with a *testo* or narrator, concerning himself more directly with the exchanges between Herod and John the Baptist. Stradella portrays this relationship with great subtlety as he does equally that between Herod, his wife Herodias and their daughter Salome. The work is in two parts. Events in Part 1 are presented in three stages. After a *Sinfonia* follows a pastoral scene in which John bids farewell to the countryside as he prepares to travel to Herod's court. In the second stage the scene moves to the court where the king's birthday festivities are in full swing. Stage three is marked by the arrival of John who interrupts the proceedings with a command that Herod give up his brother's wife. Herod is enraged and orders John to be thrown into prison. Part 2 contains the well-known events leading to the beheading of John and concludes with a masterly duet in which the contrasting emotions of foreboding and joy are expressed by Herod and Salome, respectively.

Marc Minkowski has assembled a strong team of soloists with Gérard Lesne in the title-role. Additionally there are three brief sections allotted to a chorus fulfilling various functions in the first part of the oratorio. Minkowski paces the music well, making the most of Stradella's admirably effective contrasts of texture and mood. Lesne's portrayal of John the Baptist is affecting and his warm tone and subdued vocal colour suits the music in Part 2 especially well. Herodias and Salome both come over well though neither singer succeeds in concealing the difficulties presented by Stradella's wide tessitura. Catherine Bott gives a virtuoso performance of her aria 'Sù, coronatemi' underlining both the callousness and the streak of cruelty which characterize the role. Huttenlocher's Herod is splendid. Sometimes you may find his voice ill-focused but here he conveys with equal conviction the king's vacuous authority on the one hand, and his tortured soul on the other. In conclusion, this animated and imaginative approach to a masterly score does the work justice. Minkowski realizes the inherent richness of invention and the sheer beauty of the music with insight, affection and, a lively awareness of its dramatic intent. The recording is excellent and full texts in translation are provided in the booklet.

Eduard Strauss
Austrian 1835-1916

Johann Strauss I
Austrian 1804-1849

Josef Strauss
Austrian 1827-1870

Johann Strauss II
Austrian 1825-1899

Ein Straussfest II
E. Strauss Ohne Aufenthalt, Op. 112. **Josef Strauss** Plappermäulchen, Op. 245. Sphären-Klänge, Op. 235. Jockey, Op. 278. **J. Strauss I** Chinese Galop, Op. 20. **J. Strauss II** Ägyptischer Marsch, Op. 335ª. Künstler-Quadrille, Op. 71. Kaiser-Walzer, Op. 437. Freikugeln, Op. 326. Jubelfest-Marsch, Op. 396. Tritsch-Tratsch-Polka, Op. 214. Geisselhiebe, Op. 60. Klipp Klapp, Op. 466. Wein, Weib und Gesang, Op. 333. Perpetuum mobile, Op. 257.
Cincinnati Pops Chorale and Orchestra / Erich Kunzel.
Telarc CD80314 (68 minutes: DDD). Recorded 1991-92. ⓕ

This collection deliberately sets out to adorn popular Strauss pieces with sound effects to outdo anything one hears at a Vienna New Year Concert. It starts with a performance of Eduard Strauss's

Ohne Aufenthalt that is accompanied throughout by steam railway effects, has bullets flying mercilessly in the *Freikugeln* Polka, and includes neighing nags and swishing whips in the *Jockey* Polka. The fun is increased by the inclusion of the *Künstler-Quadrille*, a sort of 1850s 'Hooked on Classics' number that begins with Mendelssohn's 'Wedding March' and continues through the likes of Mozart's Symphony No. 40 and Chopin's 'Funeral March' Sonata to Beethoven's *Ruins of Athens* and *Kreutzer* Sonata. If the Viennese lilt is just a shade lacking in the waltzes, the playing is nevertheless excellent and lively throughout. The Strausses themselves would have approved.

New Year's Day Concert, 1998
Hellmesberger I Kleiner Anzeiger. **E. Strauss** Bahn frei!, Op. 45. **J. Strauss I** Marianka-Polka, Op. 173. Radetzky Marsch, Op. 228. **J. Strauss II** Annen-Polka, Op. 117ᵃ. Nachfalter, Op. 157. Tritsch-Tratsch-Polka, Op. 214ᵃ. Wiener Bonbons, Op. 307. An der schönen, blauen Donau, Op. 314. Nur fort!, Op. 383. Rosen aus dem Süden, Op. 388. Nordseebilder, Op. 390. Wo uns're Fahne weht, Op. 473. Prinz Methusalem – Overture. **Josef Strauss** Die Schwebende, Op. 110. Jocus Polka, Op. 216. In der Heimat!, Op. 231. Plappermäulchen, Op. 245. Neue Melodien-Quadrille, Op. 254.
ᵃVienna Boys' Choir; Vienna Philharmonic Orchestra / Zubin Mehta.
RCA Red Seal 09026 63144-2 (two discs: 91 minutes: DDD). Recorded live in 1998.   Ⓜ

The Vienna Philharmonic on this recording is still the orchestra that seems to have the edge over all others in allying technical perfection to capturing the sparkle and lilt of the music. As with recent custom, this release contains the main concert on the first CD, with the encores on a short second disc. Applause is retained to create the live atmosphere. As ever, the concert mixes traditional items with others that are less well known. Alongside favourites such as *An der schönen, blauen Donau* and *Rosen aus dem Süden*, the *Plappermäulchen* and *Bahn frei!* polkas and the *Radetzky Marsch*, eight pieces are new to the concerts. Not that all their music will necessarily be unfamiliar. The overture to *Prinz Methusalem*, for instance, contains a theme that Marischka and Korngold filched for their adaptation of *Eine Nacht in Venedig*, while Josef Strauss's *Neue Melodien-Quadrille* provides opportunities to spot quotations from operas by Donizetti and Verdi. Very much in the unjustly neglected category are Johann Strauss II's elegant waltzes, *Nachfalter* and the picturesque *Nordseebilder*, while the younger Josef Hellmesberger's *Kleiner Anzeiger* galop means that he is represented in these concerts for the second year running. As a further novelty there is the appearance of the Vienna Boys' Choir to give variety to a couple of familiar polkas. This disc is fully up to the standard of its predecessors in choice of items, performance and recording quality.

New Year's Day Concert, 1999
J. Strauss I Furioso-Galopp, Op. 114. Radetzky March, Op. 228. Walzer à la Paganini, Op. 11ᵃ (arr. Rot).
J. Strauss II Scherz-Polka, Op. 72 (arr. Rot)ᵃ. Sinngedichte, Op. 1. G'schichten aus dem Wienerwald, Op. 325. Tritsch-Tratsch-Polka, Op. 214. Donauweibchen, Op. 427. Hopser-Polka, Op. 28. Künstlerleben, Op. 316. Banditen-Galopp, Op. 378. Unter Donner und Blitz, Op. 324. Perpetuum mobile, Op. 257. An der schönen, blauen Donau, Op. 314.
Vienna Philharmonic Orchestra / Lorin Maazel ᵃ*vn*
RCA Red Seal 74321 61687-2 (77 minutes: DDD). Recorded live in 1999.   Ⓕ

This is the tenth time that Lorin Maazel has conducted the New Year's Concert in Vienna, more often than anyone since Willi Boskovsky. What is always endearing is that Maazel, unlike any maestro since that former concert-master, boldly takes up his solo violin, entering into the fun in a way that lightens his once-severe image. He sets the right atmosphere with his two *concertante* items, the *Scherz-Polka* of Johann Strauss II and the *Walzer à la Paganini* of Strauss I, both arranged for him by Michael Rot, and what does it matter if most of the violin section of the Vienna Philharmonic could play them just as well? The distinctive point about the 1999 concert is that it marked the centenary of the death of the younger Johann and the 150th of his father. Aptly the programme starts with the very first of his hundreds of opuses, the 'Epigram Waltz', *Sinngedichte*, precisely setting out the pattern he always favoured in waltzes, just as winningly lyrical as the many later favourites. Some New Year's Concerts take you by storm with their bite and energy. This one makes its points above all by charming. The seductive languor of the introduction to *G'schichten aus dem Wienerwald* ('Tales from the Vienna Woods'), with its haunting zither solo, sets the pattern, followed by such rarities as the late *Donauweibchen Waltz* ('Little Woman of the Danube') on themes from the operetta, *Simplicius*, and the *Hopser-Polka*, insinuating rather than thrusting. The uproarious *Banditen-Galopp*, with its police-whistles and gunshots, then raises the temperature, and the well-known sequence of favourites at the end sparkles as brightly as ever, even if the audience's clapping in the inevitable encore, the *Radetzky March*, is no better disciplined than usual. As ever, a winning disc.

J. Strauss II Complete Works, Volume 34.
Russischer Marsch, Op. 426. Slaven-Potpourri, Op. 39. Fünf Paragraphe, Op. 105.
La favorite, Op. 217. Nikolai-Quadrille, Op. 65. Abschied von St Petersburg, Op. 210.
Der Kobold, Op. 226. Im russischen Dorfe, Op. 355 (orch. Schönherr). Dolci pianti
(with Jozef Sikora vc). Niko-Polka, Op. 228.
[a]**Bratislava Radio Symphony Orchestra / Michael Dittrich;**
Marco Polo 8 223234 (69 minutes: DDD). Recorded 1991.   (F)

J. Strauss II Complete Works, Volume 35.
Zivio!, Op. 456 (orch. Fischer). Architecten-Ball-Tänze, Op. 36. Jäger, Op. 229. Accelerationen,
Op. 234. Der Liebesbrunnen, Op. 10 (orch. Kulling). Die Zeitlose, Op. 302. Königslieder, Op. 334.
Im Sturmschritt, Op. 348. Der Blitz, Op. 59 (orch. Babinski). Heut' ist heut', Op. 471
(orch. Babinski). Die Wahrsagerin, Op. 420.
Košice State Philharmonic Orchestra / Johannes Wildner.
Marco Polo 8 223235 (74 minutes: DDD). Recorded 1991.   (F)

J. Strauss II Complete Works, Volume 36.
Matador-Marsch, Op. 406 (orch. Fischer). Kreuzfidel, Op. 301. D'Woaldbuama (Die Waldbuben),
Op. 66 (orch. Babinski). Process, Op. 294. Elfen-Quadrille, Op. 16 (orch. Kulling). Mephistos
Höllenrufe, Op. 101. Bitte schön!, Op. 372. Die Extravaganten, Op. 205. Fledermaus-Quadrille,
Op. 363. Der Klügere gibt nach, Op. 401. Neu-Wien, Op. 342. Diplomaten-Polka, Op. 448.
Košice State Philharmonic Orchestra / Alfred Walter.
Marco Polo 8 223236 (68 minutes: DDD). Recorded 1989-91.   (F)

Volume 34 offers a distinct Russian flavour. The most obviously familiar item is the opening
Russischer Marsch while the waltz *Abschied von St Petersburg* will also be familiar to some. It's a
fine swinging waltz, with an attractive cello solo in the introduction. *Dolci pianti*, one of three
romances surviving from Strauss's Russian visits, provides further material for a cello soloist, while
the piquant *Niko-Polka* offers as good an example as any of the delights to be found among the
unfamiliar works of the Waltz King. Not the least attraction of Vol. 34 is the conductor Michael
Dittrich and his alert, *echt-Wienerisch* performances here. On Vol. 35 Johannes Wildner's
conducting shows up to much better effect than has often been the case. Marches have always been
his strong point, and the collection thus gets off to a good start with *Zivio!* from the operetta
Jabuka. There are other attractive pieces on offer, too, from the perpetual favourite *Accelerationen,*
through the delicate polka-mazurka *Die Zeitlose* to the magisterial *Königslieder* (a waltz from
Strauss's most successful period) and the polka-mazurka *Die Wahrsagerin* on melodies from *The
Gipsy Baron.*

Volume 36 offers perhaps the most attractive music of the three volumes. Again the performance of
the haunting waltz *Mephistos Höllenrufe* may not erase memories of some previous versions, but
such pieces as the *Neu-Wien* waltz and the excellently played *Fledermaus-Quadrille* are among the
composer's most agreeable creations. Perhaps the most pleasant surprise of all comes from the waltz
Die Extravaganten which, with its endearing themes and richly inventive harmonic and orchestral
touches, shows above all the merits of Marco Polo's voyage of Straussian rediscovery.

J. Strauss II Complete Works, Vol. 43.
Reitermarsch, Op. 428. Walzer-Bouquet No. 1. Postillon d'amour, Op. 317. Simplicius-Quadrille,
Op. 429. Wilde Rosen, Op. 42 (arr. Babinski/Kulling). Die Tauben von San Marco, Op. 414.
Auf dem Tanzboden, Op. 454 (arr. Pollack). Des Teufels Antheil (arr. Pollack). Trifolien (comp. with
Josef and Eduard Strauss). Herrjemineh, Op. 464.
Slovak State Philharmonic Orchestra, Košice / Christian Pollack.
Marco Polo 8 223243 (58 minutes: DDD). Recorded 1992.   (F)

Maskenfest-Quadrille, Op. 92. Aschenbrödel-Walzer. Von der Börse, Op. 337. Monstre-Quadrille
(with Josef Strauss). Autograph Waltzes (arr. Cohen). Auf freiem Fusse, Op. 345. Schützen-
Quadrille (with Josef and Eduard Strauss). Altdeutscher Walzer (arr. Pollack). Nur nicht mucken,
Op. 472 (arr. Peak). Hinter den Coulissen (comp. with Josef Strauss).
Slovak State Philharmonic Orchestra, Košice / Christian Pollack.
Marco Polo 8 223244 (56 minutes: DDD). Recorded 1992.   (F)

Fest-Marsch, Op. 452. Zigeunerbaron-Quadrille, Op. 422. Ischler Walzer. Ritter Pasman – ballet
music. Pasman-Quadrille (arr. Pollack). Eva-Walzer. Potpourri-Quadrille. Der Carneval in Rom –
ballet music (arr. Schönherr).
Slovak State Philharmonic Orchestra, Košice / Alfred Walter.
Marco Polo 8 223245 (59 minutes: DDD). Recorded 1993.   (F)

This Marco Polo series delves increasingly into the more remote corners of the Waltz King's output. Vols. 43 and 44 include as many as four collaborations between Johann and his two brothers, of which the *Trifolien* waltz and *Schützen-Quadrille* most engagingly permit a comparison of all three brothers' strengths. Both volumes also include a waltz from the composer's 1876 visit to the USA. The *Walzer-Bouquet* No. 1 (originally the *Manhattan Waltzes*) is a convincingly authentic Strauss arrangement of themes from his earlier waltzes, but it is difficult to feel as sure of the worth or authenticity of the *Autograph Waltzes*, which may merely comprise themes thrown off by Strauss and worked up by an eager US publisher. The other particular curiosities of these two volumes are *Auf dem Tanzboden*, a musical evocation of a painting, and the *Altdeutscher Walzer*, which is really no more than an *entr'acte* from the operetta, *Simplicius*. The attractive early waltz *Wilde Rosen* receives a compelling performance from Christian Pollack, without the somewhat heavy beat he imparts to the *Walzer-Bouquet*. Generally Pollack seems better in the polkas and quadrilles, which he gives genuine 'lift' and sparkle, as here in several delightful polkas and the *Maskenfest-Quadrille*, which contains themes familiar to anyone who knows *Graduation Ball*.

By contrast, Vol. 45 is relatively free of the polkas and polka-mazurkas that tend to sound somewhat leaden in the hands of Alfred Walter. Over half this CD is devoted to items from Strauss's only opera *Ritter Pasman* – not just the ballet music (played in a fuller version than on some occasions), but also the *Pasman-Quadrille* and *Eva-Walzer* arranged by other hands from the score. The posthumous *Ischler Walzer* proves a piece of genuine charm, and the *Potpourri-Quadrille* compiled by Strauss for his visit to London in 1867 provides fun value with its quotations from earlier Strauss quadrilles interspersed with a selection of Scottish airs. The inclusion of the *Carneval in Rom* ballet music in a modern arrangement seems unfortunate in a collection such as this with an accent on authenticity. As a whole, though, this proves one of the best of Walter's volumes, and all three CDs rank among the more interesting and enjoyable in this adventurous series.

J. Strauss I Radetzky March, Op. 228.
J. Strauss II Die Fledermaus – Overture. Perpetuum mobile, Op. 257. Accelerationen-Waltz, Op. 234. Unter Donner und Blitz-Polka, Op. 324. Morgenblätter-Waltz, Op. 279. Persischer Marsch, Op. 289. Explosionen-Polka, Op. 43. Wiener Blut-Waltz, Op. 354. Ägyptischer Marsch, Op. 335. Künstlerleben-Waltz, Op. 316. Tritsch-Tratsch-Polka, Op. 214.
J. Strauss II/Josef Strauss Pizzicato Polka.
Vienna Philharmonic Orchestra / Willi Boskovsky *vn*
Decca Ovation 417 747-2DM (65 minutes: ADD). Recorded 1958-73.   Ⓜ Ⓗ

There have been no finer recordings of Johann Strauss than those by Boskovsky and the Vienna Philharmonic. The velvety sheen and elegance of the orchestra's sound, combined with the unique lilt that comes so naturally to Viennese players, produced magical results. For this compilation Decca has sensibly mixed seven of the most famous waltzes and polkas from those sessions with other popular Strauss compositions in various rhythms, from the celebrated *Die Fledermaus* Overture, through popular polkas and novelty pieces (for *Perpetuum mobile* Boskovsky himself can be heard explaining that it has no ending) to the ever-popular *Radetzky March*. The recorded sound is not up to the most modern digital standards, but reprocessing has produced a remarkably homogeneous sound for recordings originating over a 15-year period.

J. Strauss I (arr. Weinmann) Wiener Gemüths, Op. 116. Beliebte Annen, Op. 137. Eisele und Beisele Sprünge, Op. 202. **J. Strauss II** Schatz, Op. 418 (arr. Webern). Wein, Weib und Gesang, Op. 333 (arr. Berg). Kaiser-Walzer, Op. 437 (arr. Schoenberg). **Lanner** (arr. Weinmann) Marien-Walzer, Op. 143. Steyrische-Tänze, Op. 165. Die Werber, Op. 103.
Wolfgang Schulz *fl* **Ernst Ottensamer** *cl* **Alois Posch** *db* **Heinz Medjimorec** *pf*
Alfred Mitterhofer *harm*
Alban Berg Quartet (Günter Pichler, Gerhard Schulz *vns* Thomas Kakuska *va* Valentin Erben *vc*).
EMI CDC7 54881-2 (62 minutes: DDD). Recorded 1992.   Ⓕ

In the Alexander Weinmann arrangements of Lanner and the elder Johann Strauss, one is able to appreciate to the full the clear lyrical lines of works whose full orchestration is very much built upon the foundation of the string quartet. Likewise, in the large-scale waltzes of the younger Strauss one cannot but admire the skill and affection with which Webern, Berg and Schoenberg used the limited resources available to their Society for Private Musical Performances. Indeed, if string quartet, piano, flute and clarinet inevitably struggle to capture the full splendour of the march introduction to the *Kaiser-Walzer*, the imaginative way in which Schoenberg finds a chamber ensemble substitute for Strauss's full orchestral sound is perhaps the most impressive aspect of the various arrangements here. On its own terms, the collection is extremely impressive. The Alban Berg Quartet has made a fine selection of some of the most melodic works from over half a century of prodigious invention, and it plays them with affection and relish. From Lanner's tender *Marien-*

Walzer, through to Strauss Junior's most magisterial waltz, the clarity and refinement of the playing is tempered with a sense of lightheartedness and fun. If you fancy a Viennese dance collection with a different slant, don't hesitate to go for this admirable release.

Die Fledermaus.
Julia Varady *sop* Rosalinde; **Lucia Popp** *sop* Adele; **Hermann Pre**y *ten* Eisenstein;
René Kollo *ten* Alfred; **Bernd Weikl** *bar* Doctor Falke; **Ivan Rebroff** *bass/mez* Prince Orlofsky;
Benno Kusche *bar* Frank; **Ferry Gruber** *ten* Blind; **Evi List** *sop* Ida;
Franz Muzeneder *bass* Frosch;
Bavarian State Opera Chorus and Orchestra / Carlos Kleiber.
DG 415 646-2GH2 (two discs: 107 minutes: ADD). Notes, text and translation included.
Recorded 1975.   Ⓕ RR

Twenty-five years after its original release there is still no recording of *Die Fledermaus* that, for many collectors, matches this one for the compelling freshness of its conductor's interpretation – the attention to every nuance of the score and the ability to bring out some new detail, all allied to extreme precision of vocal and instrumental ensemble. The ladies, too, as so often seems to be the case in recordings of *Die Fledermaus*, are quite superlatively good, with ideally characterized and projected singing. If the men are generally less outstandingly good, one can have no more than minor quibbles with the Eisenstein of Hermann Prey or the Alfred of René Kollo. But it is less easy to accept Ivan Rebroff singing the role of Orlofsky falsetto. Some collectors find that his contribution quite ruins the whole set, but most will find it tolerable enough for the glories to be found elsewhere on the recording. DG remastered the set to make it sound as though it were recorded only yesterday; but it continues to provoke puzzlement by the break between discs, which occurs during the Act 2 finale. If a split into such uneven lengths is to be made, why not have it between Acts 1 and 2? Enough of minor quibbles – this set is a 'must buy'.

Die Fledermaus.
Dame Elisabeth Schwarzkopf *sop* Rosalinde; **Rita Streich** *sop* Adele;
Nicolai Gedda *ten* Eisenstein; **Helmut Krebs** *ten* Alfred; **Erich Kunz** *bar* Doctor Falke;
Rudolf Christ *ten* Prince Orlofsky; **Karl Dönch** *bar* Frank; **Erich Majkut** *ten* Blind;
Luise Martini *sop* Ida; **Franz Böheim** *bar* Frosch;
Philharmonia Chorus and Orchestra / Herbert von Karajan.
EMI Great Recordings of the Century CDM5 67074-2 (two discs: 110 minutes: ADD).
Recorded 1955.   Ⓜ H

This 1955 recording can readily be recommended to anyone less concerned with modernity of sound than with enjoying a well-proven, classic interpretation of Strauss's operetta masterpiece. Herbert von Karajan, whose preference for slow tempos and beauty of sound above all else was then still in the future, here directs with affection and *élan*. Amongst the principals Elisabeth Schwarzkopf leads the cast majestically and ravishingly. Notably in the *Csárdás*, her firm lower notes swell gloriously into a marvellously rich and individual register. As her maid, Adele, Rita Streich is an agile-voiced, utterly charming foil, launching her 'Laughing Song' with deliciously credible indignation. Nicolai Gedda also enters into the fun with supreme effect. Throughout he sings with youthful ardour and freshness, but he also has a high old time impersonating the stammering Blind in the Act 3 trio. Erich Kunz's rich, characterful baritone is also heard here to good effect as Doctor Falke, the character who arranges the 'bat's revenge' which forms the story of *Die Fledermaus*. Unconventionally, the young Prince is played by a tenor rather than the mezzo-soprano for whom the role was written. Purists may object, but the result is dramatically convincing, and musically could hardly be bettered when the singer is the sweet-toned Rudolf Christ. Altogether this set can still rival any later one in theatrical effectiveness, and EMI has done a good job in refurbishing it, with the disc-break sensibly placed between Acts 1 and 2.

Die Fledermaus (sung in English).
Rosemarie Arthars *sop* Rosalinde; **Adey Grummet** *sop* Adele; **David Fieldsend** *ten* Eisenstein;
Khosrow Mahsoori *ten* Alfred; **Gordon Sandison** *bar* Doctor Falke;
Deborah Hawksley *mez* Prince Orlofsky; **Lynton Black** *bar* Frank; **Howard Ludlow** *ten* Blind;
Wendy Schoemann *sop* Ida; **Paul Barnhill** *spkr* Frosch;
D'Oyly Carte Opera Chorus and Orchestra / John Owen Edwards.
Sony Classical S2K64573 (two discs: 111 minutes: DDD). Notes and texts included.
Recorded 1995.   Ⓕ

Recordings of *Die Fledermaus* in English were common enough during the early days of LP. Since then the work has tended to be regarded as the province of international star opera casts, which makes the D'Oyle Carte release all the more welcome. Comparisons with those international, German-language versions are scarcely appropriate, though on any terms the present recording is a resounding success. It presents the score, extremely well played and sung (in Alistair Beaton's new translation), in a form that enables English-speaking listeners to keep unusually well apace of a notoriously complex plot. The tone of the performance is admirably set by the overture, in which symphonic pretensions are set aside in favour of a light and leisurely journey through the engaging material. John Owen Edwards never forces the tempo but allows the melodies to unfold naturally, and eases gently into the big waltz tunes. Musical standards remain uniformly high throughout the performance, which omits any ballet music but restores the two brief passages in Act 2 (in the opening chorus and the *Csárdás*) that are usually cut. Without ever being sent up, the work once more becomes part of the international popular musical theatre tradition rather than part of an overblown operatic form. The cast is almost universally strong, with David Fieldsend (Eisenstein), Adey Grummet (Adele) and Gordon Sandison (Falke) each admirable in his or her way and Rosemarie Arthars a particular joy as she switches effortlessly between a testing singing part and dialogue that contributes so much to making this *Fledermaus* an integral experience.

Der Zigeunerbaron.
Pamela Coburn *sop* Saffi; **Herbert Lippert** *ten* Barinkay; **Wolfgang Holzmair** *bar* Homonay;
Rudolf Schasching *ten* Zsupán; **Christiane Oelze** *sop* Arsena; **Júlia Hamari** *mez* Czipra;
Elisabeth von Magnus *contr* Mirabella; **Jürgen Flimm** *bar* Carnero;
Robert Florianschutz *bass* Pali; **Hans-Jürgen Lazar** *ten* Ottokar;
Arnold Schoenberg Choir; Vienna Symphony Orchestra / Nikolaus Harnoncourt.
Teldec 4509-94555-2 (two discs: 150 minutes: DDD). Notes, text and translation included.
Recorded live in 1994.   Ⓕ

This set comes with a sticker proclaiming the inclusion of 40 minutes of unpublished music. Well, 14 perhaps – certainly no more than 15. False claims aside, though, this proves an uncommonly interesting and enjoyable release. The extra music comes because Nikolaus Harnoncourt and Johann Strauss specialist Norbert Linke have sought to restore *Der Zigeunerbaron* to the form it had before Strauss made various cuts. The real merits of the set lie elsewhere. Not least, Harnoncourt has stripped away generations of Viennese schmaltz and performing tradition. This is the very first recording to include every number of the published score, and for once the music is sung at its original pitch, without the usual downward transpositions for Zsupán and Homonay. Most particularly Harnoncourt has completely rethought the style of the performance.

Der Zigeunerbaron is a long work, described as 'Komische Oper' rather than 'Operette', and much of its music is unusually solid for Strauss. Harnoncourt gives the major numbers full weight, phrasing them beautifully, drawing refined singing from the soloists, among whom Herbert Lippert and Pamela Coburn combine beautifully in the duet 'Wer uns getraut?', and Christiane Oelze is a delectably sweet Arsena. The necessary light relief comes not only from Zsupán (Rudolf Schasching in fine voice) but from usually omitted subsidiary numbers. Elisabeth von Magnus sings Mirabella's 'Just sind es vierundzwanzig Jahre' with exhilarating comic zest, and joins with Jürgen Flimm (more actor than singer) to make the trio 'Nur keusch und rein' an irresistible delight. The recording comes from a live concert performance, with some audience laughter and coughs but with applause suppressed. This deserves to win new admirers both for Harnoncourt and for Strauss's masterly score.

Richard Strauss   German 1864-1949

Horn Concertos Nos. 1 and 2. Duett-Concertino, AV147. Serenade, Op. 7.
David Pyatt *hn* **Joy Farrall** *cl* **Julie Andrews** *bn*
Britten Sinfonia / Nicholas Cleobury.
EMI Eminence CD-EMX2238 (66 minutes: DDD). Recorded 1994.
Gramophone Award Winner 1996.   Ⓜ 🆁🆁

David Pyatt won the BBC's 'Young Musician of the Year' Competition back in 1988. Since then the fledgling has well and truly flown. This is sensationally good horn playing. Primarily, there's his noble *legato*: the heart of the matter, a beautiful sound, full, even and unclouded. He is sparing with the brassy timbres, holding them in reserve for dramatic effect, for such times as the instrument's well-rounded jocularity must take on a brazen, huntsmen-like air, or rise to shining heroics – like the challenging motto theme of the First Concerto. His shaping of the big phrases rolls off the page with ease and authority, but equally, so much of his personality is conveyed in the rhythmic articulation: a dashing, Jack-be-nimble mischievousness (even a touch of impudence?) in Strauss's athletic *allegros*. Most of all, though – and this is rare – he loves to play quietly, really quietly. He is a master of those dreamy, far-away departures – twilit forest-murmurings: mysterious, unreal. The recording helps in this, too, with a beautifully integrated balance. The sound of the early *Serenade*, Op. 7, is particularly fine with ripe, euphonious tuttis and room enough for individual personalities (and the Britten Sinfonia boasts several) to open up. And that is the most remarkable aspect of the piece, the utterly natural way it blends and contrasts across the whole spectrum of wind voices. Two of them take centre-stage in the delightful *Duett-Concertino*. Joy Farrall's clarinet and Julie Andrews's bassoon are like Octavian and the Baron Ochs in this gentle but spirited opus. A spendid disc, then, sympathetically directed by Nicholas Cleobury.

Horn Concertos Nos. 1 and 2. Oboe Concerto, AV144. Duet Concertino. Burleske in D minor, AV85. Parergon, Op. 73. Panathenäenzug: Symphonic Study in the form of a Passacaglia, Op. 74. Till Eulenspiegels lustige Streiche, Op. 28. Don Juan, Op. 20. Ein Heldenleben, Op. 40.
Peter Damm hn **Manfred Clement** ob **Manfred Weise** cl **Wolfgang Liebscher** bn
Malcolm Frager, Peter Rösel pfs
Dresden Staatskapelle / Rudolf Kempe.
EMI CMS7 64342-2 (three discs: 224 minutes: ADD). Recorded 1970-75. Ⓜ

Violin Concerto in D minor, Op. 8. Symphonia domestica, Op. 53. Also sprach Zarathustra, Op. 30. Tod und Verklärung, Op. 24. Der Rosenkavalier – Waltzes. Salome – Dance of the Seven Veils. Le bourgeois gentilhomme – Suite, Op. 60. Schlagobers – Waltz. Josephslegende – Suite.
Ulf Hoelscher vn
Dresden Staatskapelle / Rudolf Kempe.
EMI CMS7 64346-2 (three discs: 222 minutes: ADD). Recorded 1970-75. Ⓜ

Metamorphosen for 23 Solo Strings, AV142. Eine Alpensinfonie, Op. 64. Aus Italien, Op. 16. Macbeth, Op. 23. Don Quixote, Op. 35. Dance Suite on Keyboard Pieces by François Couperin, AV107.
Paul Tortelier vc **Max Rostal** va
Dresden Staatskapelle / Rudolf Kempe.
EMI CMS7 64350-2 (three discs: 208 minutes: ADD). Recorded 1970-75. Ⓜ

'From the store of glorious memories of my artistic career, the tones of this master orchestra ever evoke feelings of deepest gratitude and admiration' (thus spoke Richard Strauss when greeting the Dresden orchestra in 1948 on its 400th Anniversary). You get the feeling that this orchestra is justifiably proud of its tones, and its Straussian associations; it takes only a few minutes of the wind concertos disc (the first CD in Volume 1), with the principals as soloists, to be aware of those tones, and to detect a special radiance that probably derives from that pride. Kempe, it seems, was the man to draw it out, and give it purpose; after his *Till Eulenspiegel*, for example, virtually all others either affect character, or are characterless. Some may find Kempe an occasionally circumspect Straussian, one who preferred decorum to decibels in the protracted cacophony that concludes the *Symphonia domestica*, and who ensures that the famous '2001' opening to *Also sprach Zarathustra* isn't so awesome that the rest of the piece is an anti-climax. It is difficult, though, to think of many other Straussians with the imagination and understanding to bring these scores to life from within. To catalogue Kempe's Straussian credentials would take up more space than is available; suffice it to say that, like Fritz Reiner, clarity of texture and a natural flexibility of pacing were prerequisites for the characterful animation and interaction of orchestral soloists or instrumental groups, but never at the expense of the long-term direction of the music. His technique, too, ensured the kind of feats of ensemble and precision that you might have expected from the Chicago Symphony Orchestra under Reiner, but Kempe's orchestra, of course, retains its warmer and cherishably Old World tones.

There are many self-evidently great Strauss performances here. A lithe, demon-driven *Don Juan*; perhaps the most vital and communicative *Don Quixote* ever recorded (greatly ennobled by Tortelier's presence); and *Ein Heldenleben* whose hero is drawn with humanity, even vulnerability and self-doubt (the reaction to the critics is unbearably sad; the scene with the hero's wife, properly reactive), and the ideal choice for those who find the work's egotism unpalatable. EMI has mixed the familiar with the unfamiliar in each box, and dedicated Straussians will find the by-ways explored with comparable commitment and skill. The recordings, made between 1970 and 1975 (the year before Kempe's premature death), vary in perspective from an ideally distanced, natural layout (*Till* and *Aus Italien*), to the closer and slightly 'contained' (*Eine Alpensinfonie* and *Ein Heldenleben*), and the vividly present (*Le bourgeois gentilhomme* and *Metamorphosen*). Clear, light-toned timpani with very little bass resonance further enhance Kempe's precise rhythmic control (even though they sound like tom-toms at the start of *Also sprach Zarathustra*), and soloists are invariably up-front, but rarely at the expense of orchestral detail. The recordings benefit from the warm acoustics of the Lukaskirche in Dresden.

Also sprach Zarathustra. Ein Heldenleben.
Chicago Symphony Orchestra / Fritz Reiner.
RCA Living Stereo 09026 61494-2 (76 minutes: ADD). Recorded 1954. Ⓜ ⒣ RR

It is astonishing to reflect that this recording of *Also sprach Zarathustra* was made on March 8th, 1954, in stereo when Toscanini was still (just) recording in low-fi in New York's Carnegie Hall. The sound may be tonally fierce by current standards (less so than many oft-praised Mercury reissues) but the balance is fully acceptable, with the first and second violins set close to the listener (and the microphones) on either side of the podium, and the basses hard left. Reiner's *Also sprach* is intense and extrovert. In his second year with the Chicago Symphony Orchestra, the conductor was already getting a thrilling response from the strings, although woodwind intonation could be a problem. Confident and well played as it is, the spectacular opening sunrise inevitably lacks the impact of modern recordings. What we have instead is a measure of raw passion and forward thrust unequalled on disc. In reflective passages, conductor and/or engineers display some reluctance to achieve a real *pianissimo*, but as the tempo builds Reiner invariably creates great excitement and the orchestral playing is marvellous. Reiner's reading of *Ein Heldenleben* has humanity as well as virtuosity – the touching closing section is memorable.

Don Juan[a]. Till Eulenspiegels lustige Streiche[a]. Ein Heldenleben[b].
[a]**Cleveland Orchestra / George Szell;** [b]**Philadelphia Orchestra / Eugene Ormandy.**
Sony Classical Essential Classics SBK48272 (75 minutes: ADD). Recorded 1957-60. Ⓑ ⒣ RR

Ormandy's hero is a transatlantic with a fat cigar in his mouth, and that he's out to impress is obvious from the start. He employs glamorous representatives, too: slick brass and percussion, smartly ordered winds and a plush, generous army of strings. Yet, he is not without soul, as his 'Works of Piece' and 'Retirement from the World and the Fulfilment of his Life' ably illustrate. In fact, his having been fulfilled earlier on in the score only goes to underline his profound change of heart. And with Ansel Brusilow an eloquent solo commentator, and truthful if rather opaque sound, his 'Indian summer' is most eloquently reported. Turn then to Szell, and the contrast is quite startling. Szell used to play his own piano-solo arrangement of *Till Eulenspiegel* to Strauss, and his recording of the work reveals the depth of his perception. No hint of brashness here, just wit, myriad detail and astonishing orchestral virtuosity. There can't be many better *Don Juan*s on CD. The transfers from fair-to-middling originals are absolutely first-rate.

Don Juan. Eine Alpensinfonie.
San Francisco Symphony Orchestra / Herbert Blomstedt.
Decca 421 815-2DH (70 minutes: DDD). Recorded 1988. Ⓕ

The *Alpine Symphony* is the last of Richard Strauss's great tone-poems and is in many ways the most spectacular. The score is an evocation of the changing moods of an alpine landscape and the huge orchestral apparatus of over 150 players encompasses quadruple wind, 20 horns, organ, wind machine, cowbells, thunder machine, two harps and enhanced string forces. Its pictorialism may be all too graphic but what virtuosity and inspiration Strauss commands. Herbert Blomstedt's reading penetrates beyond the pictorialism into the work's deeper elements. It emerges as a gigantic hymn to nature on a Mahlerian scale. Tempos are slower, but these are justified by the noble expansiveness of the final pages, towards which the whole performance moves with impressive inevitability. The San Francisco Symphony's playing is magnificent, with subtle use of vibrato by the strings and superb performances, individual and corporate, by the wind sections. The *Don Juan* performance is fine too. The recording is excellent, the big climaxes really thrilling and the whole well balanced.

R. Strauss Don Juan[a]. Ein Heldenleben[b].
Wagenaar Cyrano de Bergerac, Op. 23[a].
[a]**Concertgebouw Orchestra;**
[b]**New York Philharmonic Symphony Orchestra / Willem Mengelberg.**
Pearl mono GEM0008 (71 minutes: ADD). Recorded 1928-42. Ⓜ ⒣

Mengelberg's changes to *Ein Heldenleben* were designed to emphasize the score's brilliance. So the opening triplets are bowed separately rather than slurred and *Luftpausen* are inserted to articulate the phrasing. Later in the work, Mengelberg's famous *portamentos* are worked on and the melodic lines put together gradually to perfect intonation and ensemble. Illicit emendations are clearly audible in this 72-year-old recording. You might expect such interventionist conducting to sound artificial or calculated, as it almost invariably does in the forays made by present-day period orchestras into early twentieth-century repertoire, but nothing could be further from the truth.

Whatever Mengelberg's methods, there is nothing artificial about this glorious, ardent account of Strauss's score. The hero can seldom have sounded more ebullient, whether in love or war. The critics' mixture of incomprehension and petty spite is realized to perfection, and those string *portamentos* (sounding utterly natural) are well to the fore as the hero retreats from worldly concerns. The secret of all this has to lie in Mengelberg's familiarity with the score, although it may help that the American orchestra's style of playing was markedly more 'modern' than that of Mengelberg's Concertgebouw. As Pearl's excellent documentation states, by the time this recording was made Mengelberg had 'nearly three decades' worth of *Heldenlebens* under his belt'. Only hours after these sessions were completed, the orchestra gave the first performance of *An American in Paris*. In Mark Obert-Thorn's transfer, the recording seems little short of miraculous given its age; apart from the restricted dynamic range, it sounds better than many made 20 years later, combining deep, solid bass with astonishing clarity – including, alas, perfect reproduction of the subway trains passing underneath Carnegie Hall! So what if there is a whiff of contrivance about the 1938 Concertgebouw performance of *Don Juan*. The main work remains indispensable for anyone remotely interested in Strauss or in the history of recording. Perhaps, as the booklet says, this is the definitive *Heldenleben*. The bonus item, Wagenaar's *Cyrano de Bergerac* Overture, makes little odds; it is *Don Juan* crossed with *Die Meistersinger* and here we have the real thing.

Don Quixote. Don Juan.
Milton Preves *va* **Antonio Janigro** *vc*
Chicago Symphony Orchestra / Fritz Reiner.
RCA Living Stereo 09026 68170-2 (59 minutes: ADD). Recorded 1954-59. Ⓜ Ⓗ ⓇⓇ

Fritz Reiner's posthumous reputation is such that an enthusiastic recommendation for this well-packed reissue is probably superfluous. But even now there is a sense in which the disc brings together two sides of Reiner's music-making. The *Don Juan*, recorded as early as December 1954, is one of the most exciting of all time, racing panther-like from the opening gestures, lush and self-consciously *espressivo* in the sweeping string theme. The hushed playing is as exquisite as contemporary technology would permit (the opening is disfigured by noticeable wow). And yet one can see why earlier commentators were reluctant to endorse it without reservation. It is a self-consciously brilliant reading and just a shade heartless. No such reservations surround the *Don Quixote*, made in April 1959 during Antonio Janigro's American début, and recorded with astonishing fidelity using a different orchestral set-up (without divided violins). As so often in this revelatory series, the transfers have been carefully handled, drying out the sound just enough to maximize inner detail but retaining all the distinctive bloom of the venue. This is disciplined yet red-blooded music-making of a kind in short supply these days.

Don Quixote. Lieder – Morgen, Op. 27 No. 4; Der Rosenband, Op. 36 No. 1; Wiegenlied, Op. 41 No. 1; Freundliche Vision, Op. 48 No. 1; Waldseligkeit, Op. 49 No. 1; Die heiligen drei Könige, Op. 56 No. 6.
Dame Felicity Lott *sop* **André Vauquet** *va* **François Guye** *vc*
Suisse Romande Orchestra / Armin Jordan.
Mediaphon MED72 165 (69 minutes: DDD). Recorded 1996. Ⓕ

Above all, this disc is notable for taking advantage of the superlative acoustic of the Victoria Hall in Geneva, home of the Suisse Romande Orchestra, thus giving us the most impressively recorded *Don Quixote* yet, in sound terms. The detail of the brilliant scoring is clearly delineated while at the same time the whole picture is one of amazing warmth and resplendence. The spread of sound and its wonderful luminosity are things to marvel at and, of course, they are ideal for this inspired score. Happily Jordan and his orchestra offer a performance worthy of the place and the production – no aspect of the score missed. François Guye brings out all Quixote's endearing and aggravating qualities without a hint of exaggeration, his tone always full and poised. His viola partner makes a suitable companion, and the individual soloists from the orchestra also distinguish themselves. The songs are more than a makeweight. Lott, the leading Straussian soprano of the day, knows just how to make the most of six of the composer's best-loved songs with ethereal, fine-grained tone and line. As with the tone-poem, Jordan presents the music without any excess of sentiment. What a pity, then, that texts and translations aren't provided, the only blot on a disc that will give much pleasure and satisfaction.

R. Strauss Feuersnot – Love scene. Salome – Dance of the Seven Veils. Die Frau ohne Schatten – Symphonic Fantasy.
Weber Overtures – Der Freischütz; Oberon.
Staatskapelle Dresden / Giuseppe Sinopoli.
DG 449 216-2GH (57 minutes: DDD). Recorded 1995. Ⓕ

In his complete recording of *Salome* for DG, made in Berlin (reviewed further on), Sinopoli has already shown us how warmly sympathetic he is to Strauss's operatic music. With his Dresden orchestra the results are if anything even more sensuous, with ravishing string tone perfectly married to Sinopoli's moulded and flexible style. The Love scene from Strauss's very first opera, *Feuersnot*, is drawn from the closing pages of the work, a delectable lollipop that ought to be much better known, in places looking forward to the later Strauss of *Der Rosenkavalier*. Salome's Dance is given a luscious performance with no holding back, and with each section of a piece that can seem bitty leading magnetically to the next. Much the longest piece on the disc is the Symphonic Fantasy from *Die Frau ohne Schatten*. Again Sinopoli's concentration and the gorgeous playing of the orchestra, sumptuously recorded, give cohesion to an obviously sectional piece. Inevitably, it is second best to the opera, with the symbolism eliminated, but thanks to Strauss's cunning it makes a welcome item for those with a sweet tooth. The link with the two popular Weber overtures is a tenuous one, presumably a reference to the association of each composer with Dresden. In Weber some may resist Sinopoli's moulded, warmly expressive style in the slow introductions, but with such superb playing, it would take a curmudgeon not to be seduced.

Serenade, Op. 7. Suite in B flat major, Op. 4. Sonatina No. 2 in E flat major, AV143, 'Fröhliche Werkstatt'.
Wind soloists of the **Chamber Orchestra of Europe / Heinz Holliger.**
Philips 438 933-2PH (74 minutes: DDD). Recorded 1993.　　　　Ⓕ

With the second of the composer's late *Sonatinas* (also known as the Symphony for Wind Instruments) the COE wind players have made sure that outer-movement lines have plenty of muscle, that the bigger harmonies bloom without ever sounding overblown and that the whole adds up to a rainbow of generous invention, effects and colours such as one would hardly have thought possible even given Strauss's extraordinary knowledge of the medium. With a sophisticated, easy-going team like the Netherlands Wind Ensemble, the Indian summer burble has an instant charm that palls rather quickly; but while not even the COE team can quite stop the mind from wandering in the very prolix finale, there is a dynamic and tonal rigour about the first movement which rivets attention. The line of easy invention between the teenage Strauss's first characteristically happy inspirations in the *Serenade* and the octogenarian's refuge in his 'happy workshop' is broken by the more uneven qualities of the Op. 4 *Suite*. The COE players do it the credit of taking it seriously, making the most of the characteristic swing from an assumed pale cast of thought into the character of a prototype *Till Eulenspiegel*. Again, the full chordings – closely but deliciously captured by the excellent recording – are a constant delight, and one assumes Holliger's shaping hand in the flexible vocalizing of the many *bel canto* lines. A winner.

Strauss Symphonia domestica.
Wagner Tristan und Isolde – Prelude and Liebestod (arr. Humperdinck).
Lohengrin – Preludes, Acts 1 and 3.
Berlin Philharmonic Orchestra / Herbert von Karajan.
EMI Karajan Edition CDM5 66107-2 (76 minutes: ADD). Recorded 1973.　　Ⓜ🆁🆁

Symphonia domestica remains something of a black sheep in Strauss's mature output. Lacking a compelling narrative thrust, it tends to come apart at the seams in an unsympathetic performance, exposing its composer as a vapid musical rambler – but not so here. Patiently we awaited the restoration of much of Karajan's recordings and here at last is his opulent 1970s Strauss, not always ideally urgent but ever suave and sophisticated. The remastering has retained the wide range of the originals, focusing detail better in a big, sometimes cavernous, acoustic space even if that fabulous Berlin string tone is not always so well served. The most important of Karajan's Strauss performances is the *Symphonia domestica*. The conductor recorded it only the once and, as is often the case in his overstuffed discography, the one-offs are rarely also-rans. The playing is not absolutely impeccable – the trumpet intonation was criticized in the original review – but only those implacably opposed to Karajan's brand of manipulated orchestral sonority need hesitate. Rudolf Kempe (reviewed above) is less insistently luxurious, as befits some of Strauss's more exquisitely tender and beguiling invention. EMI's generous supplement of Wagnerian bleeding chunks is derived from a couple of generally well-received LPs from the same period. The charge of over-refinement is not entirely avoided in *Lohengrin* excerpts but the blood courses more strongly in the excerpts from *Tristan*, though again some will feel that the sensuous moulding of sound takes undue precedence over substantive communication.

Symphonia domestica. Tod und Verklärung.
Bavarian Radio Symphony Orchestra / Lorin Maazel.
RCA Red Seal 09026 68221-2 (74 minutes: DDD). Recorded 1995.　　　　Ⓕ

Despite the comments above, *Symphonia domestica* contains some exquisitely tender and beguiling invention, something of which Lorin Maazel must be acutely conscious as this is his second digital recording. The conductor's quest for technical perfection can sometimes produce an alienating effect but only those who demand Karajan's saturated sonorities in this repertoire will be dissatisfied with the chamber-like results achieved here. Maazel keeps a sophisticated yet altogether less ostentatious grip on the proceedings, concerned to let individual lines register without strain. This *Tod und Verklärung* is his fourth on disc and, again, with the rhetoric pared down, the awkward corners seem to disappear. These are refreshing, thoughtful, superbly prepared performances which will inevitably strike some listeners as understated. The orchestral playing is remarkably fine, the recordings faithful and true, with just a hint of artificiality in the placing of instrumental solos: the sound of the solo violin in Tod's evocation of childhood is not ideally pure. In the *Symphonia domestica*, Maazel's approach is subtler, belying the glitzy packaging favoured by RCA.

Symphonies – D minor, AV69[a]; F minor, Op. 12[b].
[a]**Bavarian Radio Symphony Orchestra,**
[b]**Berlin Radio Symphony Orchestra / Karl Anton Rickenbacher.**
Koch Schwann 365322 (74 minutes: DDD). Recorded 1996-97.   Ⓕ

The D minor Symphony is of purely specialist interest, the work of a well-schooled 16-year-old rather than a Mendelssohnian prodigy. No less a conductor than Hermann Levi conducted its first performance, but Strauss was soon anxious to suppress it altogether and would no doubt have been horrified to read of its resuscitation today. The beautiful acoustic of the Herkulessaal flatters the orchestra and its not inappropriately 'provincial' horns. The more familiar work in F minor was admired by several distinguished contemporaries. Brahms nevertheless thought it no more than 'quite pretty'. The piece gets under way with a descending scale that seems to anticipate the *Alpensinfonie*, but the dutiful academicism of what follows gives little foretaste of the mature Strauss. While the inner movements have greater individuality, *Don Juan* is worlds away. Rickenbacher's performance is commendably fresh and alert.

Till Eulenspiegels lustige streiche[a]. Also sprach Zarathustra[a]. Don Juan[a]. Ein Heldenleben[b]. Eine Alpensinfonie[c]
[a]**Chicago Symphony Orchestra,** [b]**Vienna Philharmonic Orchestra,**
[c]**Bavarian Radio Symphony Orchestra / Sir Georg Solti.**
Decca Double 440 618-2DF2 (two discs: 152 minutes: ADD). Recorded 1970s.   Ⓜ 🔲🔲

This set is remarkable value. The formidable power of Sir Georg Solti's personality dominates all these brilliantly played performances. The intensity is never in doubt; one cannot but be continually gripped by this kind of music-making, for the great Hungarian conductor is never daunted by the recording studio. *Eine Alpensinfonie*, with the Bavarian Radio Symphony Orchestra, has the most glorious tone (especially the brass). Such is the amplitude of the sound – and the warm commitment of the playing – that it counteracts the conductor's tendency to press forward, almost as if he is driven by some remorseless spirit. *Till Eulenspiegel, Also sprach Zarathustra, Ein Heldenleben* and *Don Juan* were recorded at the peak of Solti's reign as Music Director of the Chicago Symphony in the early and mid-1970s. The playing is magnificently opulent, even Germanic in feeling, and the bravura is tremendously assured. *Till Eulenspiegel* brings a particularly vivid start with the sound most clearly placed in its natural setting and atmosphere. Solti's version is excellent on very count. It is impossible to resist the sweep and intoxicating power of this great orchestra unleashed, yet at the same time held by the conductor in an absolutely firm grip. Even if other performances of Strauss's music have more subtlety of feeling, Solti's admirers will count this anthology a great bargain. The CD transfers of these brilliant Decca analogue recordings of 1975 are certainly impressive.

Tod und Verklärung. Metamorphosen.
Berlin Philharmonic Orchestra / Herbert von Karajan.
DG 410 892-2GH (52 minutes: DDD). Recorded 1982.
Gramophone Award Winner 1982-83.   Ⓕ 🔲🔲

These are a clear first-choice in both works. Karajan's *Metamorphosen* has almost unbearable intensity and great emotional urgency – it is a very gripping and involving account. The sound is marginally more forward and cleaner than is ideal, though the rich ambience is very appealing. *Tod und Verklärung* is not so spectacularly recorded as some more modern versions but it is a greater performance that just about any other, and finer than any of Karajan's earlier versions. Indeed, it is quite electrifying, with superb playing from all departments and a life-and-death intensity to the climaxes. It is more vividly recorded than his most recent previous version and the performance is tauter (25'23" against 27'00" in 1974) and more powerful. In both works, it would be difficult to improve on these performances by the greatest Richard Strauss conductor of his day and the glorious BPO, and the quality of the recording gives no cause for reproach.

R. Strauss Gesänge, Op. 33 – No. 3, Hymnus; No. 4, Pilgers Morgenlied. Gesänge, Op. 51. Grössere Gesänge, Op. 44 – No. 1, Notturno.
Mahler (orch. Berio) Lieder und Gesänge – No. 1, Frühlingsmorgen; No. 3, Hans und Grethe; No. 6, Um schlimme Kinder artig zu machen; No. 7, Ich ging mit Lust durch einen grünen Wald; No. 10, Zu Strassburg auf der Schanz; No. 13, Nicht wiedersehen!
Andreas Schmidt *bar*
Berlin Radio Symphony Orchestra / Cord Garben.
RCA Red Seal 09026 61184-2 (62 minutes: DDD). Texts and translations included.
Recorded 1992.   Ⓕ

The real discovery here is Strauss's 15-minute-long, wholly neglected 'Notturno', a narrative accompanied by an orchestra to a poem by Richard Dehmel. It tells of the vision of a dream of Death in the shape of a much-loved friend who appears in bright moonshine, in the depths of the night, playing a beseeching air on his violin. As Norman Del Mar says in Vol. 3 of his biography of the composer (London: 1972): 'The title *Notturno* is Dehmel's own and the long poem is one of great emotional intensity.' So is Strauss's extraordinary hypnotic and original setting. The mood of the piece is hallucinatory and tormented, uncannily recalling that of Tristan's desperate outbursts in Act 3. Schmidt interprets it with a notable feeling for its haunting, eerie quality, in a recording of presence. Almost as neglected are the two songs that comprise Strauss's Op. 51. 'Das Thal', is the most ambitious, describing someone who wants to get away from it all. Its sustained lyricism and atmospheric scoring are Strauss at his most compelling. Berio's orchestrations of some of Mahler's early settings don't sound entirely Mahlerian, but Schmidt sings them beautifully.

Deutsche Motette, Op. 62[a]. Gesänge, Op. 34. An den Baum Daphne (epilogue to 'Daphne'), AV137[b]. Die Göttin im Putzzimmer, AV120.
[a]**Tina Kiberg,** [b]**Marianne Lund** *sops* [b]**Christian Lisdorf** *treb* [a]**Randi Stene** *contr*
[a]**Gert Henning-Jensen** *ten* [a]**Ulrik Cold** *bass*
[b]**Copenhagen Boys' Choir; Danish National Radio Choir / Stefan Parkman.**
Chandos CHAN9223 (57 minutes: DDD). Texts and translations included. Recorded 1993.   Ⓕ

Under Stefan Parkman the Danish National Radio Choir has established a reputation second to none. Parkman handles his singers as if they were a fully fledged symphony orchestra; which is not at all inappropriate in this programme by the supreme master of orchestral colour. From the heart of the 16 chorus parts of the *Deutsche Motette* a further seven are projected by solo voices emerging imperceptibly from the midst of a dense, luxuriant texture. The depth of colour and range of emotions are every bit as extensive in these works as in the great orchestral tone-poems; indeed few orchestral tone-poems evoke dusk and sunset so vividly as 'Der Abend', the first of the 1897 *Zwei Gesänge*. There is a wonderfully luminous soundscape here; a combination of superb compositional skill, sensitive musical direction, superlative choral singing and a warm, full-bodied recording.

Lieder – Op. 10: No. 2, Nichts; No. 9, Allerseelen; Winternacht, Op. 15 No. 2; Ständchen, Op. 17 No. 2; All' mein Gedanken, Op. 21 No. 1; Op. 22: No. 3, Efeu; No. 4, Wasserrose; Op. 27: No. 2, Cäcilie; No. 3, Heimliche Aufforderung; Op. 29: No. 1, Traum durch die Dämmerung; No. 3, Nachtgang; Op. 32: No. 2, Sehnsucht; No. 3, Liebeshymnus; Der Rosenband, Op. 36 No. 1; Op. 37: No. 3, Meinem Kinde; No. 4, Mein Auge; No. 5, Herr Lenz; No. 6, Hochzeitlich Lied; Befreit, Op. 39 No. 4; Op. 49: No. 1, Waldseligkeit; No. 6, Junggesellenschwur; Weihnachtsgefühl, AV94.
Simon Keenlyside *bar* **Malcolm Martineau** *pf*
EMI Eminence CD-EMX2250 (64 minutes: DDD). Texts and translations included.
Recorded 1995.   Ⓜ

Simon Keenlyside understands and respects both Strauss's sentiment and his sentimentality for what it is. With steady, thoughtfully considered word-placing, he relieves *Allerseelen* of its sicklier scents and keeps its movement light and fresh, bringing the song to a strong, firmly syllabic climax. This skill in estimating the expressive potential of verbal weight and measure also strengthens the contours of his *Sehnsucht*; and in *Ständchen* keeps the vocal focus clear and bright in the more fleet, high notes. Keenlyside exploits the heroic character of his baritone in the bold rhetorical questions of *Nichts*, and in *Liebeshymnus* where the voice rings out with fearless resilience in its top register. This sense of heroic address and acclamation tends to replace, for Keenlyside, the more tremulous, passionate response some singers find in songs such as the *Hochzeitlich Lied* and *Heimliche*

Aufforderung: the lip seldom trembles here, the voice yields little to Strauss's harmonic sidesteps and melodic melismas. Whether you miss that, or find it a relief, will be purely a matter of taste. With Martineau delighting equally in the complexity and simplicity of the piano writing displayed in these love-songs, the recital should certainly take a significant place in any Strauss collection.

Four Last Songs, AV150 (Op. posth.).

R. Strauss Four Last Songs.
Wagner Wesendonk Lieder. Tristan und Isolde – Prelude and Liebestod.
Cheryl Studer *sop*
Dresden Staatskapelle / Giuseppe Sinopoli.
DG 439 865-2GH (61 minutes: DDD). Notes, texts and translations included. Ⓕ **E**

In the Strauss, Cheryl Studer's voice, lyrical yet with dramatic overtones, seems near-ideal for Strauss and for this work in particular, quite apart from the sheer beauty and technical accomplishment of her singing. In the first two songs there is the necessary ecstasy and longing in her singing as Strauss reviews, elegiacally, his musical credo. For example, one could cite the loving treatment in 'September' of the phrases beginning 'Langsam tut er', the singer's tone poised, the shading of the line perfectly natural. It is the seamless *legato* and lovely voice that again make 'Beim Schlafengehen' so rewarding while, in the final song, Studer is suitably hushed and reflective. Sinopoli and the Staatskapelle Dresden provide ideal support for their singer with the playing in all these works as lyrically expressive as the singing above it, all tempos ideally judged. Similar praise can be given to the reading of the *Wesendonk Lieder*. Here, once again, one notes Studer's amazing combination of vocal mastery and interpretative insight. Every dynamic and expressive mark is scrupulously followed (listen to the *piano* at 'Luft' and 'Duft' in the second song) in the pursuit of seamless phrasing and a due attention to the text. The richness of her singing, the thorough mastery of German diction and phraseology, make this another special performance. Sinopoli's reading of the Prelude to *Tristan* is flowing, intense and spontaneous and the playing is predictably superb, all adding to the disc's worth. The recordings are for the most part happily spacious and well focused.

Four Last Songs[a]. Capriccio – Morgen mittag um elf! ... Kein andres[b]. Tod und Verklärung[c].
[ab]**Gundula Janowitz** *sop*
[a]**Berlin Philharmonic Orchestra / Herbert von Karajan;**
[b]**Bavarian Radio Symphony Orchestra, **[c]**Staatskapelle Dresden / Karl Böhm.**
DG Classikon 439 467-2GCL (65 minutes: ADD). Recorded 1971-72. Ⓜ

Here is a feast of glorious Strauss at bargain price, though the performances are anything but bargain in quality. In spite of strong challenges from far and wide, the singing of them by Gundula Janowitz has, arguably, still not been surpassed for Straussian opulence and tenderness – we emphasize 'arguably', for people feel passionately about interpretations of this work! – and Karajan conducts a near-ideal account of the orchestral score. Janowitz, in glorious voice, sings the *Four Last Songs* flowingly. The recording is more hazy than on the other two exemplary performances. The fashion of the moment to denigrate Böhm is incomprehensible when you encounter readings as splendid as his two contributions here, in which he again proves himself an ideal Straussian. The live account of *Tod und Verklärung* caught at the 1972 Salzburg Festival but not released until 1988 (in memoriam) builds naturally to its various incandescent climaxes and the music is never allowed to drag or descend, as it can in lesser hands, into sentimentality. The playing of the Dresden orchestra is lithe and warm. The final scene of *Capriccio* comes from the complete set recorded in Munich in 1971. Once more Böhm judges tempos and texture to a nicety, the music always moving forward in perfect balance to its end.

Four Last Songs[a]. Arabella – Er ist der Richtige nicht[b]; Der Richtige so hab ich stets zu mir gesagt[c]; Das war sehr gut, Mandryka[b]. Ariadne auf Naxos – Es gibt ein Reich[b]. Capriccio – Closing scene[c].
Lisa della Casa, Hilde Gueden *sops* **Alfred Poell** *bar* **Paul Schoeffler** *bass-bar*
Franz Bierbach *bass*
Vienna Philharmonic Orchestra / **[a]Karl Böhm, **[b]**Rudolf Moralt, **[c]**Heinrich Hollreiser.**
Decca Historic mono 425 959-2DM (67 minutes: ADD). Texts and translations included. Ⓜ **H**
Recorded 1953-54.

Four Last Songs, AV 150[a]. Capriccio – Morgen mittag um Elf[a]. Arabella[b] – Ich danke, Fräulein ... Aber der Richtige; Mein Elemer; Sie wollen mich heiraten; Das war sehr gut.
Dame Elisabeth Schwarzkopf, Anny Felbermeyer *sops* **Josef Metternich** *bar*
Philharmonia Orchestra / **[a]Otto Ackermann, **[b]**Lovro von Matačic.**
EMI Références mono CDH7 61001-2 (68 minutes: ADD). Recorded 1953-54. Ⓜ **H**

R. Strauss Choral and song

Strauss's *Four Last Songs* are a perfect summation of the composer's lifelong love-affair with the soprano voice deriving from the fact that he married a soprano, Pauline Ahna. They are also an appropriate and deeply moving farewell to his career as a composer and to the whole romantic tradition and they have inspired many glorious performances. In recent times there has been a tendency to linger unnecessarily over what are already eloquent enough pieces. Lisa della Casa, in her naturally and lovingly sung performance under Karl Böhm (the first-ever studio recording of the pieces back in 1953) makes no such mistake. In this incarnation this is a wonderful offering at medium price backed by other invaluable Strauss interpretations from the Swiss diva. Her particular gift is to sing the pieces in a natural, unforced manner with gloriously unfettered tone. Her and Böhm's tempos tend to be faster than those employed by most of her successors.

The *Four Last Songs* are sung with equal beauty by Elisabeth Schwarzkopf. She sings 'Im Abendrot' even more beautifully than della Casa, and with an even more serene feeling of the coming of Death. Her interpretation is extraordinarily moving. The songs gain a great deal also, by being sung in the published order. It is good to have these outstanding performances on CD, especially as they also allow us to hear Schwarzkopf in two Strauss operatic roles she never sang on stage. The voice is at its best and there are moments of rare insight, such as the lovely *pp* 'Du kennst mich wieder' in 'Frühling'. Also the Philharmonia of 1953 was something special, and the excellent balance of the recording brings out Straussian subtleties galore. The *Capriccio* finale was recorded before Schwarzkopf made the complete recording. It is a more forceful, less lovable performance. The *Arabella* excerpts, on the other hand, exacerbate regret that she didn't record the whole opera. She brings just the right mixture of hauteur and impulsiveness to the enigmatic heroine.

R. Strauss Ariadne auf Naxos – Ein schönes war; Es gibt ein Reich. Arabella – Mein Elemer!.
Wagner Die Walküre – Der Männer Sippe; Du bist der Lenz. Lohengrin – Einsam in trüben Tagen. Tannhäuser – Dich teure Halle; Allmächt'ge Jungfrau. Der fliegende Holländer – Joho hoe! ... Traft ihr das Schiff. Tristan und Isolde – Mild und leise.
Elisabeth Meyer-Topsøe *sop*
Copenhagen Philharmonic Orchestra / Hans Norbert Bihlmaier.
Kontrapunkt 32249 (60 minutes: DDD). Texts included. Recorded 1996. Ⓕ

There are few, if any, sopranos today who can sing this repertory more securely than Meyer-Topsøe. A pupil of Nilsson, she sings with her teacher's ringing confidence, tone and technique solid and unblemished. It is heartening to hear once more a Scandinavian interpreter of Wagner with such a thrilling sound, one for whom the challenge of Senta, Elsa, Elisabeth and Isolde are as nothing. All that said, there is as yet room in some items for more dramatic involvement. One might expect more sense of obsession in Senta's Ballad, more intensity of longing in Elsa's Dream, more interior ecstasy in 'Du bist der Lenz'. Studio restrictions and/or a somewhat careful conductor may not be a help in that respect. An exception to this stricture is the Liebestod where Meyer-Topsøe sounds a Nilsson-like touch of transfiguration. Her Straussian credentials are impeccable and are amply confirmed here in her Ariadne and Arabella. Here's evidence, most of all in a gloriously outgoing 'Es gibt ein Reich', of identification with a given role. Her Arabella is hardly less engrossing as she ponders on her 'Fremde Mann', the soprano's even, youthful timbre exactly right for the eager yet thoughtful girl. Bihlmaier seems happier in Strauss than in Wagner. The recording rightly has the singer centre-stage, the exciting voice caught in a natural acoustic. The fact that the accompanying notes contain German texts only, without translations, shouldn't prevent connoisseurs from acquiring this disc.

Der Rosenkavalier – Wie du warst! Wie du bist; Da geht er hin ... Ach, du bist wieder da! ... Die Zeit, die ist ein sonderbar Ding; Mir ist die Ehre; Mein Gott, es war nicht mehr ... Heut oder morgen ... Marie Theres'... Hab' mir's gelobt ... Ist ein Traum.
Régine Crespin, Elisabeth Söderström, Hilde Gueden *sops* **Heinz Holecek** *bar*
Vienna State Opera Concert Choir; Vienna Philharmonic Orchestra / Silvio Varviso.
Decca 452 730-2DC (62 minutes: ADD). Recorded 1964. Ⓑ

This, one of the most desirable discs in the whole recorded history of the opera, has led a Cinderella existence since it first appeared 33 years ago. Now invited to the ball, it ought to be accorded status as a princess. Crespin, quite heart-rending as the Marschallin, is in pristine voice. She fills her music with silvery, sensuous tone and at the same time judges every note, every phrase to perfection, whether in the monologue, or the final scenes of Acts 1 and 3. These extracts benefit from having, as Strauss intended, a soprano Octavian – and what a soprano! Söderström's vibrant, impassioned singing is just what the role calls for. Together she and Crespin make the close of Act 1 a thing to savour. Then in the Silver Rose Presentation she is joined by Gueden still able in her late-forties to float Sophie's high-lying phrases as to the manner born, while in the last act Gueden finds just the right sense of embarrassment in the presence of the Marschallin. It is a thousand pities the opera was not recorded complete, not least because Varviso, as at those Covent Garden performances, is in his absolute element, elegant and ardent, finding an idiomatic Straussian ebb and flow with the VPO on rapturous form, all recorded with Decca's 1960s skill. Christopher Raeburn provides the notes, filling in the plot as best he can in the absence of texts and translations. This is a must for all Straussians.

R. Strauss Salome – Ach, du wolltest mich nicht deinen Mund küssen lassen. Guntram – Fass'ich sie bang. Ariadne auf Naxos – Es gibt ein Reich. Arabella – Mein Elemer!. Die ägyptische Helena – Zweite Brautnacht!.
Mozart Lucio Silla – Ah, corri, vola ... Quest'improvviso tremito. Don Giovanni – Or sai chi l'onore; Crudele! Ah no, mio bene ... Non mi dir. Idomeneo – Idol mio, se ritroso; Oh smania! oh furie! ... D'Oreste, d'Aiace.
Jane Eaglen *sop*
Israel Philharmonic Orchestra / Zubin Mehta.
Sony Classical SK60042 (65 minutes: DDD). Texts and translation included. Recorded 1997. Ⓕ

The partnership of Eaglen and the Israel Philharmonic under Zubin Mehta is at its strongest in the Richard Strauss tracks of this Mozart and Strauss compilation. The orchestra's superbly balanced wind soloists create dark shadows for *Guntram*'s Freihild, as she reflects within them, at first perplexed and then, in unflaggingly focused voice, thankful for her love for the Minnesinger – and for the glory of her top B. If Ariadne's distraction is captured rather less convincingly, then the sustained rapture of *Die ägyptische Helena*'s 'Zweite Brautnacht!' draws the full effulgence from Eaglen's golden soprano in what seems to be one breathless sentence. The five Mozart arias here remind us just what a formidable Mozartian Eaglen is; and one only wishes that Mehta were her equal in this respect – one longs for a livelier orchestral presence. Eaglen's own skills at pacing and charging with emotion Elektra's passages of accompanied recitative make for real momentum, lit by a bright platinum gleam in the voice in 'Oh smania! ... D'Oreste, d'Aiace'; and her instinctive phrasing gives eloquent voice to Elektra's more demure moments in 'Idol mio'.

Die ägyptische Helena – excerpts[a].
Viorica Ursuleac, Margit Bokor *sops* **Franz Völker, Helge Roswaenge** *tens* **Alfred Jerger** *bar*
Die Frau ohne Schatten – excerpts[b].
Hilde Konetzni, Emmy Loose, Else Schulz *sops* **Else Boettcher** *mez* **Melanie Frutschnigg, Elisabeth Höngen** *contrs* **Torsten Ralf, Wenko Wenkoff, William Wernigk, Josef Herrmann, Alfred Poell, Tomislav Neralic** *bars* **Herbert Alsen, Georg Monthy, Marjan Rus, Roland Neumann** *basses*
Daphne – excerpts[c].
Maria Reining *sops* **Anton Dermota, Alf Rauch** *tens*
Vienna State Opera Chorus and Orchestra / [a]**Clemens Krauss,** [b]**Karl Böhm,** [c]**Rudolf Moralt.**
Koch Schwann mono 314552 (two discs: 145 minutes: ADD). Item marked [a] recorded live in 1933, [b]1943, [c]1942. Ⓜ Ⓗ

This enshrines valuable extracts from the original Viennese performances of *Helena* and *Daphne*, and some 90 minutes from what proves to be one of the most convincing readings ever of *Die Frau ohne Schatten*. The *Helena* provides the final proof that the somewhat maligned Ursuleac was, in the 1930s, a Strauss soprano *par excellence* and, supported by her husband Krauss's inspiriting direction, she fills the famous solo 'Zweite Brautnacht' and other equally taxing passages with refulgent tone and soaring phraseology. For 1933 the sound is remarkable, and has the minimum amount of distortion. When *Die Frau* is sung and conducted as here at a 1943 revival, it does indeed sound like Strauss's outright masterpiece as many experts on the composer declare it to be. Böhm recognizes the virtues of sheerly beautiful sound (amply provided by his cast and the Vienna Philharmonic), textural clarity of a chamber-music kind and keeping the score on the move. Excellent as have been her successors as the Empress, Konetzni just about surpasses them all for the steadiness of her tone, her firm *legato* and her involvement. The first Daphne at the State Opera was Maria Reining. In her long opening solo, she is inclined to spoil her lovely singing by sliding into notes from below, but she reaches her glorious best in her duet with Apollo and from then on goes from strength to strength, making light of the extraordinary demands Strauss places on his soprano. Both Moralt and Böhm are ardent advocates of this vital but flawed score. Any Straussian must have this issue. Others who wish to find out just how to sing and conduct the composer's operas authentically may well like to sample it too.

Arabella.
Julia Varady *sop* Arabella; **Helen Donath** *sop* Zdenka; **Dietrich Fischer-Dieskau** *bar* Mandryka; **Walter Berry** *bass* Waldner; **Helga Schmidt** *mez* Adelaide; **Elfriede Höbarth** *sop* Fiakermilli;

Adolf Dallapozza *ten* Matteo; **Hermann Winkler** *ten* Elemer; **Klaus-Jürgen Küper** *bar* Dominik;
Hermann Becht *bar* Lamoral; **Doris Soffel** *mez* Fortune Teller; **Arno Lemberg** *spkr* Welko;
Bavarian State Opera Chorus; Bavarian State Orchestra / Wolfgang Sawallisch.
Orfeo C169882H (two discs: 144 minutes: DDD). Notes, text and translation included.   ⓕ

Complete except for a brief cut in Matteo's part in Act 3, Sawallisch's 1981 Orfeo recording of
Arabella has been easily fitted on to two CDs. Sawallisch is the most experienced conductor of
Strauss's operas alive today and at his best in this one, his tempos just right, his appreciation of its
flavour (sometimes sentimental, at others gently ironic and detached) unequalled. Helen Donath's
delightful Zdenka is a perfect foil for Varady's Arabella. Varady's singing of the title-role is
characterful and intelligent. One should be left with ambivalent feelings about this heroine; is she
lovable or a chilling opportunist? Or both? And while Fischer-Dieskau's singing of Mandryka has
not the total security of his earlier DG recording of the role with Keilberth, he remains the best
Mandryka heard since the war.

Ariadne auf Naxos.
Dame Elisabeth Schwarzkopf *sop* Ariadne; **Irmgard Seefried** *sop* Composer;
Rita Streich *sop* Zerbinetta; **Rudolf Schock** *ten* Bacchus; **Karl Dönch** *bar* Music-Master;
Hermann Prey *bar* Harlequin; **Fritz Ollendorff** *bass* Truffaldino; **Helmut Krebs** *ten* Brighella;
Gerhard Unger *ten* Scaramuccio; **Lisa Otto** *sop* Naiad; **Grace Hoffman** *mez* Dryad;
Anny Felbermayer *sop* Echo; **Hugues Cuénod** *ten* Dancing Master;
Alfred Neugebauer *spkr* Major-Domo;
Philharmonia Orchestra / Herbert von Karajan.
EMI Great Recordings of the Century mono CMS5 67077-2 (two discs: 128 minutes: ADD/mono).
Recorded 1954.   ⓕ Ⓗ ℞℞

Karajan's *Ariadne* is perfectly cast, magnificently performed, and very well recorded. The scoring,
for a small orchestra, demands virtuoso playing from what, in effect, is a group of soloists: and the
members of the Philharmonia Orchestra rise brilliantly to the occasion. There is a warmth and
beauty of tone, a sweep of phrase, that gives lively promise of the wonderful playing we hear
throughout the opera. Karajan's genius has never been more apparent than in his treatment of the
Bacchus-Ariadne scene, in which he makes the score glow with a Dionysiac ardour and in which, at
the tremendous climax when Bacchus enters and is greeted by Ariadne as the herald of Death, he
gets an ample volume of tone from his players. Every character is vividly brought to life – Karl
Dönch's harassed music master is offset by the cynical dancing master of Hugues Cuénod, and
Alfred Neugebauer, in his speaking role, conveys with a superbly calm pomposity his contempt for
both sets of artists. The way he enunciates his words is superb. The other small parts, all sung by
experienced artists, are wholly in the picture. Rita Streich sings the lyrical phrases of Zerbinetta
beautifully. Technical difficulties do not appear to exist for her and all she does is musical. Irmgard
Seefried, as the Composer, has less beauty of tone but more variety. The ineffably lovely trio for the
Naiad, Dryad and Echo is exquisitely sung by Lisa Otto, Grace Hoffman and Anny Felbermayer,
paralleled by the equally beautiful singing of the other trios. They are simply ravishing and, like all
the concerted music, have a perfect ensemble. The *commedia dell'arte* characters are all very good,
especially Hermann Prey: and their ensembles between themselves and with Zerbinetta are a great
delight. After an awkward start, Elisabeth Schwarzkopf, as Ariadne, brings the dark tone that is
needed, to Ariadne's sorrows, and gives us much lovely singing thereafter, and also all the rapture
called for at the end of her great address to the herald of Death and in her greeting to Bacchus.
Rudolf Schock sings the latter with heroic tone and sufficient nuance to make one believe in the
youthful god. The general impression is of a truly magnificent performance and recording in which
all concerned have, under Karajan's superb direction, been inspired to give of their best.

Ariadne auf Naxos.
Gundula Janowitz *sop* Ariadne; **Teresa Zylis-Gara** *sop* Composer;
Sylvia Geszty *sop* Zerbinetta; **James King** *ten* Bacchus; **Theo Adam** *bass-bar* Music Master;
Hermann Prey *bar* Harlequin; **Siegfried Vogel** *bass* Truffaldino;
Hans Joachim Rotzsch *ten* Brighella; **Peter Schreier** *ten* Scaramuccio, Dancing Master;
Erika Wustmann *sop* Naiad; **Annelies Burmeister** *mez* Dryad; **Adele Stolte** *sop* Echo;
Erich-Alexander Winds *spkr* Major-Domo;
Staatskapelle Dresden / Rudolf Kempe.
EMI Opera CMS7 64159-2 (two discs: 118 minutes: ADD). Notes, text and translation included.
Recorded 1968.   Ⓜ

At mid-price this classic set cannot be recommended too highly. Nobody knew more about how to
pace Strauss's operas than Kempe and he was at his best when working with the Staatskapelle
Dresden, a group of players who have Strauss in their veins. This reading brings out all the

sentiment and high spirits of this delightful work, and the results are beautifully recorded. Janowitz's golden tones were ideal for the title-role, which she sings with poise and inner feeling, though she makes little of the text. Zylis-Gara is a suitably impetuous Composer in the engaging Prologue where 'he' meets and has a gently erotic encounter with the charming but flighty Zerbinetta, a role here taken with brilliant accomplishment by Sylvia Geszty, who made it her own in the 1960s. James King is a forthright though none too flexible Bacchus. The smaller parts are also well taken.

Elektra.
Birgit Nilsson *sop* Elektra; **Regina Resnik** *mez* Klytemnestra; **Marie Collier** *sop* Chrysothemis;
Gerhard Stolze *ten* Aegisthus; **Tom Krause** *bar* Orestes; **Pauline Tinsley** *sop* Overseer;
Helen Watts *contr* **Maureen Lehane, Yvonne Minton** *mezzos* **Jane Cook,**
Felicia Weathers *sops* First, Second, Third, Fourth and Fifth Maidservants;
Tugomir Franc *bass* Tutor;
Vienna Philharmonic Orchestra / Sir Georg Solti.
Decca 417 345-2DH2 (two discs: 108 minutes: ADD). Notes, text and translation included.
Recorded 1966-67.

Elektra is the most consistently inspired of all Strauss's operas and derives from Greek mythology, with the ghost of Agamemnon, so unerringly delineated in the opening bars, hovering over the whole work. The invention and the intensity of mood are sustained throughout the opera's one-act length, and the characterization is both subtle and pointed. It is a work peculiarly well suited to Solti's gifts and he has done nothing better in his long career in the studios. He successfully maintains the nervous tension throughout the unbroken drama and conveys all the power and tension in Strauss's enormously complex score which is, for once, given complete. The recording captures the excellent singers and the Vienna Philharmonic in a warm, spacious acoustic marred only by some questionable electronic effects. Notwithstanding the latter, this is undoubtedly one of the greatest performances on record and sounds even more terrifyingly realistic on this magnificent transfer.

Elektra.
Inge Borkh *sop* Elektra; **Jean Madeira** *mez* Klytemnestra; **Lisa della Casa** *sop* Chrysothemis;
Max Lorenz *ten* Aegisthus; **Kurt Böhme** *bass* Orestes; **Alois Pernerstorfer** *bass-bar* Tutor;
Anny Felbermayer *sop* Confidante; **Karol Loraine** *mez* Trainbearer; **Erich Majkut** *ten* Young
Servant; **György Littasy** *bass* Old Servant; **Audrey Gerber** *sop* Overseer; **Kerstin Meyer,**
Sonja Draksler, Sieglinde Wagner, Marilyn Horne *mezzos* **Lisa Otto** *sop* First, Second, Third,
Fourth and Fifth Maidservants;
Vienna State Opera Chorus; Vienna Philharmonic Orchestra / Dimitri Mitropoulos.
Orfeo mono C456972I (two discs: 107 minutes: ADD). Recorded live in 1957.

This is an enthralling performance that every Straussian will want to experience. Mitropoulos made a speciality of the score, his most important contribution to opera interpretation. Souvenirs exist of his performances at the Metropolitan in 1949 with Varnay in the title-part and at the Maggio Musicale in Florence the following year with Ann Konetzni, but his Salzburg reading is the one to have. Those present were apparently bowled over by the occasion. No other conductor, not even Böhm or Solti in the studio quite matches the *frisson* of this literally overwhelming performance. And Mitropoulos is working with Inge Borkh, who confirms that she is indeed the most comprehensively equipped soprano for the title-role (even more so than Nilsson), vocally secure – high C apart – and emotionally capable of fulfilling every demand of the strenuous part. In the great scene with Orestes that lies at the heart of the piece she first expresses ineffably the sorrow at his supposed death, the 'tausendmal' and 'nie wiederkommt' passage done with such a searing sense of loss; then comes the great release of recognition – sung with immense warmth – followed by yet another, almost silvery voice as Elektra recalls her lost beauty. It is a passage of singing to return to again and again for its many insights. Borkh is hardly less impressive in her psychologically tense tussle with her mother, in her wheedling flattery of her sister when she wants Chrysothemis's co-operation in killing Klytemnestra, or in the charm offensive to fool Aegisthus where her command of textual detail is so sure.

Chrysothemis finds in della Casa an unusual interpreter, wonderfully ecstatic and pure of voice if not as emotionally involving as some and, it is said, dramatically overparted. Madeira is a formidable Klytemnestra, her nightmarish thoughts expressed in a firm voice, accurately deployed. Naturally, caught on stage, she is even more involved than in the studio. Böhme, a real bass, presents an implacable, angry Orestes, not as subtle or as sympathetic as Krause for Solti. Lorenz's fading *Heldentenor* is ideal to express Aegisthus's fatuity. The maids have never, surely, been cast with such secure voices, Kerstin Meyer positive in her few important phrases, and Horne tucked away as Fourth Maid. Inevitably, cuts are made as is almost always the case in the theatre where, otherwise, Elektra might be left voiceless by the end. If you want the complete score, the famous Solti set will do very nicely. If you want Borkh, you must choose between the Böhm in stereo, still excellent, at mid-price on DG, or this unique experience, also at mid-price. Dedicated Straussians might like it as an addition to one of the stereo versions. The more recent recordings are really not competitive.

Die Frau ohne Schatten.
Julia Varady sop Empress; **Plácido Domingo** ten Emperor; **Hildegard Behrens** sop Dyer's Wife;
José van Dam bar Barak the Dyer; **Reinhild Runkel** contr Nurse;
Albert Dohmen bar Spirit-Messenger; **Sumi Jo** sop Voice of the Falcon;
Robert Gambill ten Apparition of a Young Man; **Elzbieta Ardam** mez Voice from above;
Eva Lind sop Guardian of the Threshold; **Gottfried Hornik** bar One-eyed Brother;
Hans Franzen bass One-armed Brother; **Wilfried Gahmlich** ten Hunchback Brother;
Vienna Boys' Choir; Vienna State Opera Chorus;
Vienna Philharmonic Orchestra / Sir Georg Solti.
Decca 436 243-2DHO3 (three discs: 195 minutes: DDD). Notes, text and translation included.
Recorded 1989-91. *Gramophone* Award Winner 1992.   Ⓕ

This was the most ambitious project on which Strauss and his librettist Hugo von Hofmannsthal collaborated. It is both fairy tale and allegory with a score that is Wagnerian in its scale and breadth. This Solti version presents the score absolutely complete in an opulent recording that encompasses every detail of the work's multi-faceted orchestration. Nothing escapes his keen eye and ear or that of the Decca engineers. The cast boasts splendid exponents of the two soprano roles. Behrens's vocal acting suggests complete identification with the unsatisfied plight of the Dyer's Wife and her singing has a depth of character to compensate for some tonal wear. Varady gives an intense, poignant account of the Empress's taxing music. The others, though never less than adequate, leave something to be desired. Domingo sings the Emperor with customary vigour and strength but evinces little sense of the music's idiom. José van Dam is likewise a vocally impeccable Barak but never penetrates the Dyer's soul. Runkel is a mean, malign Nurse as she should be, though she could be a little more interesting in this part. It benefits from glorious, dedicated playing by the VPO.

Friedenstag.
Bernd Weikl bar Commandant; **Sabine Hass** sop Maria; **Jaakko Ryhänen** bass Sergeant;
Jan Vacik ten Rifleman; **Jan-Hendrik Rootering** bass Corporal; **Alfred Kuhn** bass Musketeer;
Gerhard Auer bar Bugler; **Eduardo Villa** ten A Piedmontese; **Florian Cerny** bar Officer;
Thomas Woodman bar Front-line Officer; **Kurt Moll** bass Holsteiner;
Robert Schunk ten Burgomaster; **Karl Helm** bass Prelate;
Cornelia Wulkopf mez Woman of the People;
Bavarian State Opera Chorus and Orchestra / Wolfgang Sawallisch.
EMI CDC5 56850-2 (77 minutes: DDD). Notes, text and translation included.
Recorded live in 1988.   Ⓕ 🆁🆁

In 1988, the Munich Festival presented every one of the operas of its native son, Richard Strauss. The concert performance of *Friedenstag* was scheduled to be issued on CD the following year. In fact it took 11 years for the recording to be released, at least in the UK. The work has always been frowned on, even in the most exalted circles of Strauss *aficionados*, but it is difficult not to be moved by the passion and sincerity of the relationship between the seemingly strict, militaristic Commandant and his wife Maria, starved of love and affection as her husband devotes all his energies to prosecution of his part in the Thirty Years War. Admittedly much of the first part of the 80-minute, one-act work is less than inspired but once the tortured, uptight Commandant takes centre-stage, the composer's inspiration takes off. This splendidly committed performance offers excellent advocacy for the opera. Sawallisch, then in charge of the Bavarian State Opera, was and is the most authoritative among today's Strauss conductors. His reading here and the playing of his orchestra are convincing and technically assured. The role of the Commandant was written for Hans Hotter and he sings it superbly on the Koch Schwann/Krauss set reviewed below, but Weikl is almost in his noble predecessor's class. At the peak of his career in 1988 he pours out strong, untiring tone and conveys all the man's inner agony evinced in his relationship with his troops and with his wife. As Maria, Sabine Hass, who died while still in her forties, could have no better memorial than this assumption, her impassioned, rich-toned voice soaring to the heights as she seeks to rekindle her husband's interest in her. The role seems to draw the best from its interpreters – Viorica Ursuleac gives a blinding performance on the alternative set. That has, on the whole, the better support, but of course this more recent version is far better recorded and will satisfy anyone wanting to add the piece – a snip on one CD – to their collection.

Friedenstag[a].
Hans Hotter *bass-bar* Commandant; **Viorica Ursuleac** *sop* Maria; **Herbert Alsen** *bass* Sergeant;
Josef Witt *ten* Rifleman; **Hermann Wiedemann** *bass* Corporal; **Carl Bissuti** *bass* Musketeer;
Nikolaus Zec *bass* Bugler; **Anton Dermota** *ten* A Piedmontese; **Hermann Gallos** *ten* Officer;
Georg Monthy *bass* Front-line Officer; **Karl Kamann** *bass* Holsteiner;
Willy Franter *ten* Burgomaster; **Viktor Madin** *bar* Prelate;
Mela Bugarinovic *mez* Woman of the People.

Arabella – excerpts[b]. Ariadne auf Naxos – excerpts[c].
[b]**Margit Bokor**, [bc]**Adele Kern**, [c]**Dora Komarek**, [c]**Anny Konetzni**,
[c]**Elisabeth Rutgers**, [c]**Else Schulz**, [b]**Viorica Ursuleac** *sops* [c]**Elena Nikolaidi**,
[b]**Gertrud Rünger** *mezzos* [c]**Friedrich Jelinek**, [c]**Alexander Pichler**, [c]**Richard Sallaba**,
[c]**Set Svanholm**, [c]**William Wernigk** *tens* [c]**Hermann Baier**, [c]**Alfred Poell** *bars*
[bc]**Alfred Jerger** *bass-bar* [b]**Richard Mayr**, [c]**Alfred Vogel** *basses* [c]**Alfred Muzzarelli** *spkr*
Vienna State Opera [ab]**Chorus and Orchestra** / [ab]**Clemens Krauss**, [c]**Rudolf Moralt.**
Koch Schwann mono 314652 (two discs: 143 minutes: ADD). Item marked [a] recorded live in
1939, [b]live in 1933, [c]1941. Ⓜ Ⓗ

This issue offers us a complete performance of Strauss's underrated and under-recorded *Friedenstag*
given by its creators in 1939, shortly after its première in Munich. Here Krauss, Ursuleac and
Hotter prove incontrovertibly that the work has a strength and validity not often accorded it by
even the most dedicated of Straussians. You marvel at the immense conviction and energy Krauss
brings to it. Then, his wife Ursuleac gives the performance of her life as Maria. She is fearless and
tireless in tackling the high As, B flats and Bs in which the role abounds, singing with vibrant tone
and in a possessed manner fitting an overwrought woman starved of the love of her husband (the
Commandant) who has poured all his energies into war. Finally, she provides the necessary ecstasy
when she wins him back and sees the war come to an end. As ever, Strauss glories in his writing for
a *lirico-spinto*, and Ursuleac glories with him. The 30-year-old Hotter, in towering voice, gives to the
Commandant's part the right sense of a man dedicated to his role of defending his Kaiser's cause
and honour at whatever cost to his men or to his personal life. A team of Viennese stalwarts of the
day fills the smaller roles satisfactorily, with the young Dermota notable as the Piedmontese youth
musing on his beloved Italy and its girls. The music is so different from most of what Strauss was
writing at the time. Instead of harking back to romanticism, as in *Arabella* and *Daphne*, he
composes here in a tougher style more in keeping with his own time, bringing into play
Hindemithian, even Bergian ideas. The final paean to peace recalls the Mahler of the symphonies'
choral sections. Mind you, the piece – as many have commented – is more dramatic oratorio than
opera. The recorded sound, taken in this case off a broadcast, is good by the standard of these sets,
but by no means anything special. However, the voices don't distort and much of the orchestral
detail can be gleaned. *Friedenstag* is flanked by excerpts from two other works by Strauss. Those
from a 1933 *Arabella*, also a Viennese 'first', featuring the original singers of the two main roles, are
not so desirable since Ursuleac and Jerger recorded the most important passages commercially (for
Decca-Polydor in 1933). Nevertheless, it is good to hear Krauss conducting with such *élan*.

Der Rosenkavalier.
Dame Elisabeth Schwarzkopf *sop* Die Feldmarschallin; **Christa Ludwig** *mez* Octavian;
Otto Edelmann *bass* Baron Ochs; **Teresa Stich-Randall** *sop* Sophie;
Eberhard Waechter *bar* Faninal; **Nicolai Gedda** *ten* Italian Tenor; **Kerstin Meyer** *contr* Annina;
Paul Kuen *ten* Valzacchi; **Ljuba Welitsch** *sop* Duenna; **Anny Felbermayer** *sop* Milliner;
Harald Pröglhöf *bar* Notary; **Franz Bierbach** *bass* Police Commissioner;
Erich Majkut *ten* Feldmarschallin's Major-domo; **Gerhard Unger** *ten* Faninal's Major-domo,
Animal Seller; **Karl Friedrich** *ten* Landlord;
Loughton High School for Girls and Bancroft's School Choirs;
Philharmonia Chorus and Orchestra / Herbert von Karajan.
EMI CDS5 56242-2 (three discs: 191 minutes: ADD). Notes, text and translation included.
Recorded 1956. *Gramophone* Award Winner 1988. Ⓟ Ⓗ
Also available on EMI mono CDS5 56113-2 (three discs: 182 minutes: ADD). Ⓟ Ⓗ

Der Rosenkavalier concerns the transferring of love of the young headstrong aristocrat Octavian
from the older Marschallin (with whom he is having an affair) to the young Sophie, a girl of
nouveau riche origins who is of his generation. The portrayal of the different levels of passion is
masterly and the Marschallin's resigned surrender of her ardent young lover gives opera one of its
most cherishable scenes. The comic side of the plot concerns the vulgar machinations of the rustic
Baron Ochs and his attempts to seduce the disguised Octavian (girl playing boy playing girl!). The
musical richness of the score is almost indescribable with stream after stream of endless melody,
and the final trio which brings the three soprano roles together is the crowning glory of a

masterpiece of our century. This magnificent 1956 recording, conducted with genius by Karajan and with a cast such as dreams are made of, has a status unparalleled and is unlikely to be challenged for many a year. The Philharmonia plays like angels and Elisabeth Schwarzkopf as the Marschallin gives one of her greatest performances. The recording, lovingly remastered, is outstanding. In 1956 stereo recording was new to the commercial recording world and, unwilling to gamble everything on the new medium, producer Water Legge arranged for the sessions to be captured in both mono and stereo, using separate microphone layouts and separate balance engineers. The mono recording has never before been issued on CD. One is, in fact, immediately struck by the mono recording's warmer, closer balance: Schwarzkopf, for example, a significantly more rounded, fuller and essentially dominant presence, never in danger of being overwhelmed by the orchestra. The detail and transparency of the overall canvas on the stereo recording is more naturally convincing but the mono will make a special appeal to those who prefer intimate access to these great singers. The dilemma is that each recording is impressive in its way and yet so very different. Students of the voice will almost certainly favour the mono release; devotees of the opera itself may well prefer the stereo.

Der Rosenkavalier.
Maria Reining sop Die Feldmarschallin; **Sena Jurinac** sop Octavian;
Ludwig Weber bass Baron Ochs; **Hilde Gueden** sop Sophie; **Alfred Poell** bar Faninal;
Anton Dermota ten Italian Tenor; **Hilde Rössl-Majdan** mez Annina; **Peter Klein** ten Valzacchi;
Judith Hellweg sop Leitmetzerin; **Berta Seidl** sop Milliner; **Walter Berry** bass Police
Commissioner; **Harald Pröglhöf** bass Feldmarschallin's Major-domo;
August Jaresch ten Faninal's Major-domo; **Erich Majkut** ten Animal Seller, Landlord;
Franz Bierbach bass Notary;
Vienna State Opera Chorus; Vienna Philharmonic Orchestra / Erich Kleiber.
Decca Historic mono 425 950-2DM3 (three discs: 197 minutes: ADD). Notes, text and translation
included. Recorded 1954.   Ⓜ 🔲🔲

Decca has done wonders in cleaning the sound on this reissued classic recording. It seems warmer and more spacious than in any of its LP guises. The bloom on the playing of the Vienna Philharmonic is grateful to the ear and the voices stand ideally in relation to the instruments. That is doubly heartening given the fact that Kleiber's interpretation still stands above that of any of his successors. His innate and deep understanding of the score and his instinctive feeling for this area of the Viennese idiom remains unsurpassed; so does his convincing treatment of the score's weaker pages (it is here given complete). Above all, Kleiber never makes the mistake of lingering too long over the work's purple passage, nor does he overheat its more active ones: the key to his reading is a combination of lightness, line and incandescence – try the opening of Act 2. Once you have his reading under your skin you can proceed to more self-indulgent and/or brilliant performances. The vocal glory of the set remains Sena Jurinac's Octavian. Here in more refulgent voice perhaps than anywhere else on disc, she gives the performance of one's dreams. How gleaming yet how warm is her voice, how naturally impetuous and intense her colloquies with her elders. Jurinac carefully denotes Octavian's growing fascination with Sophie. Then, as the maudlin Mariandl of Act 3, she changes her tone subtly, never exaggerating. Finally, her voice soars gloriously in the trio and duet that crown the work. It is a definitive interpretation, and will surely remain so.

Maria Reining's Marschallin has been badly underrated. Her approach is natural, stylish and very moving in its simplicity – and its obedience to the score. Not a trace of self-consciousness or arch phrasing spoils the patent honesty of her portrayal. The voice itself sounds a little tremulous at the start, and it never quite gains the warmth other Marschallins achieve, but the unmannered yet absolutely idiomatic enunciation of the text is compensation enough, and her partnership with Jurinac's Octavian is often memorable. Hilde Gueden's singing may be a shade sophisticated for Sophie (and she shouldn't show dislike for Ochs before she has met him), but the accuracy and firm focus of her singing count for much. Ludwig Weber's Ochs is a ripe, assured assumption sung with total command of the text and in an authentic Viennese accent. Among the smaller parts, one notes Dermota's lyrical Italian Tenor, Alfred Poell's fussily excited Faninal, Peter Klein's properly nasty Valzacchi and Walter Berry's imposing Police Commissioner. All are versed in that essential, command of Strauss's *parlando* style, so that Hofmannsthal's racy, keenly fashioned libretto is given wit and point. Although admiration for Karajan remains undiminished – and, of course, it benefits from stereo placing as compared with the mono here – but Kleiber is the performance to take to your desert island. Its renaissance, lovingly prepared by Decca, is more than welcome.

Salome.
Cheryl Studer sop Salome; **Bryn Terfel** bar Jokanaan; **Horst Hiestermann** ten Herod;
Leonie Rysanek sop Herodias; **Clemens Bieber** ten Narraboth; **Marianne Rørholm** contr Page;
Friedrich Molsberger bass First Nazarene; **Ralf Lukas** bass Second Nazarene;

William Murray *bass* First Soldier; **Bengt Rundgren** *bass* Second Soldier;
Klaus Lang *bar* Cappadocian;
Orchestra of the Deutsche Oper, Berlin / Giuseppe Sinopoli.
DG 431 810-2GH2 (two discs: 102 minutes: DDD). Notes, text and translation included.
Recorded 1990. Ⓕ 🆁🆁

Strauss's setting of a German translation of Oscar Wilde's play is original and erotically explicit. It
caused a sensation in its day and even now stimulates controversy. Sinopoli's recording is a
magnificent achievement, mainly because of Cheryl Studer's representation of the spoilt Princess
who demands and eventually gets the head of Jokanaan (John the Baptist) on a platter as a reward
for her striptease ('Dance of the Seven Veils'). Studer, her voice fresh, vibrant and sensuous,
conveys exactly Salome's growing fascination, infatuation and eventual obsession with Jokanaan,
ending in the arresting necrophilia of the final scene. She expresses Salome's wheedling, spoilt
nature, strong will and ecstasy in tones apt for every aspect of the strenuous role. She is supported
to the hilt by Sinopoli's incandescent conducting and by Bryn Terfel's convincing Jokanaan,
unflaggingly delivered, by Hiestermann's neurotic Herod, who makes a suitably fevered, unhinged
sound as the near-crazed Herod, and Rysanek's wilful Herodias. The playing is excellent and the
recording has breadth and warmth. This is eminently recommendable. For a newcomer to the work,
Studer's superb portrayal may just tip the balance in favour of Sinopoli, though Sir Georg Solti's
famous version is in a class of its own, with a gloriously sung Salome and the ravishingly beautiful
playing of the Vienna Philharmonic.

Salome.
Birgit Nilsson *sop* Salome; **Eberhard Waechter** *bar* Jokanaan; **Gerhard Stolze** *ten* Herod;
Grace Hoffman *mez* Herodias; **Waldemar Kmentt** *ten* Narraboth; **Josephine Veasey** *mez* Page;
Tom Krause *bar* First Nazarene; **Nigel Douglas** *ten* Second Nazarene;
Zenon Koznowski *bass* First Soldier; **Heinz Holecek** *bass* Second Soldier;
Theodore Kirschbichler *bass* Cappadocian;
Vienna Philharmonic Orchestra / Sir Georg Solti.
Decca 414 414-2DH2 (two discs: 99 minutes: ADD). Notes, text and translation included.
Recorded 1961. Ⓕ

Sir Georg Solti's *Salome* was one of Decca's notable Sonic-stage successes and still beats most of its
operatic competitiors in terms of sound alone. There is a real sense here of a theatrical
performance, as directed by John Culshaw, with an imaginative use of movement. Of course, the
vivid, nervous energy of Strauss has always been Solti's territory and this is an overwhelming
account of Strauss's sensual piece, sometimes a little too hard-hitting for its or our good: there are
places where the tension might be relaxed just a shade, but throughout, the VPO answers Solti's
extreme demands with its most aristocratic playing. With only a single break, the sense of mounting
fever is felt all the more. Nilsson's account of the title-role remains another towering monument to
her tireless singing. Here, more even than as Brünnhilde, one notices just how she could fine away
her tone to a sweet and fully supported *pianissimo*, and her whole interpretation wants nothing of
the erotic suggestiveness of sopranos more familiar with the role on stage. Stolze's Herod is properly
wheedling, worried and, in the final resort, crazed, but there are times, particularly towards the end
of his contribution, when exaggeration takes over from characterization. Other interpretations show
how effects can be created without distortion of the vocal line. Waechter is an aggressive rather
than a visionary Jokanaan. Grace Hoffman is a suitably gloating Herodias. Much better than any
of these, Nilsson apart, is Kmentt's wonderfully ardent Narraboth. Hardly any of the rivals since
1961 has managed a true challenge to this outstanding set.

Salome.
Inga Nielsen *sop* Salome; **Robert Hale** *bass-bar* Jokanaan; **Reiner Goldberg** *ten* Herod;
Anja Silja *sop* Herodias; **Deon van der Walt** *ten* Narraboth; **Marianne Rørholm** *contr* Page;
Bent Norup *bar* First Nazarene; **Morten Frank Larsen** *bar* Second Nazarene;
Per Høyer *bar* First Soldier; **Stephen Milling** *bass* Second Soldier;
Anders Jokobsson *bass* Cappadocian; **Henriette Bonde Hansen** *sop* Slave;
Danish National Radio Symphony Orchestra / Michael Schønwandt.
Chandos CHAN9611 (two discs: 99 minutes: DDD). Notes, text and translation included.
Recorded 1998. Ⓕ

You may wonder if there is any place for another *Salome*, given the already well-stocked field. But
Inga Nielsen, who proves a Salome of quite exceptional talent, even inspiration, answers that
question. Better than any of her predecessors she creates a princess who sounds credibly teenaged
with surely just the pearl-like yet needle-sharp tone Strauss intended. Nobody has so convincingly
conveyed the impression of a spoilt, petulant innocent with the will and determination to get her

way – and then exploited her manipulative character to frightening effect as, sexually awakened, Salome becomes obsessed with the body of Jokanaan. In a performance that is vocally stunning from Salome's first entrance, Nielsen fashions her reading with supreme intelligence in her response to words and notes. Throughout she sings keenly, even maliciously off the text. While still having nothing but praise for Studer's beautifully sung portrayal on the Sinopoli set – her tone is more refulgent, less narrow than Nielsen's but she is not so much inside the role – or for Nilsson's vocally overwhelming portrayal for Solti, Nielsen simply seems a Salome by nature, made for the part.

Happily Nielsen's riveting interpretation receives suitable support. Schønwandt yields to none of his illustrious predecessors in impressing on us the still-extraordinary originality, fascination and tense horror of Strauss's score, carrying us unerringly into what Michael Kennedy in his excellent notes calls 'the strange, sultry, moonlit world where "something terrible" is about to happen'. From start to finish, including an electrifying account of the Dance, his is a fiercely direct, highly charged yet never vulgar reading. Hale, who has partnered Nielsen in this work at the Brussels Opera, is a noble-sounding, resolute Jokanaan of long experience. Although he doesn't attempt the larger-than-life, tremendous performance of Terfel for Sinopoli, nor is his tone as steady, his reading is surely more of a piece with the opera as a whole. Goldberg is just right as the degraded, superstitious, lecherous Herod, vocally astute and characterful. Silja is a well-routined, sometimes over-the-top Herodias. The smaller roles are particularly well sung by mainly Danish singers. Chandos provides a recording of extraordinary range and breadth, yet one that makes sure that the singers take stage front. Anyone who already has the highly regarded Sinopoli version will probably not feel the need to invest in this set, but newcomers are urged to hear it, as it must now be a recommendation alongside the DG. Nielsen is really unmissable.

Igor Stravinsky
Russian/French/American 1882-1971

The reviews which follow comprise part of 'The Complete Edition' (Sony Classical S22K46290 22 CDs: ADD Ⓜ). The items reviewed here were subsequently issued as separate sets.

The Complete Edition, Volume 1.
The Firebird[a]. Scherzo à la russe[a]. Scherzo fantastique[b]. Fireworks[a]. Petrushka[a].
The Rite of Spring[a]. Renard[c]. L'histoire du soldat – Suite[c]. Les noces[d].
Mildred Allen sop **Regina Sarfaty** mez **Loren Driscoll, George Shirley** tens
William Murphy bar **Richard Oliver, Donald Gramm** basses **Toni Koves** cimbalom
Samuel Barber, Aaron Copland, Lukas Foss, Roger Sessions pfs
[d]**American Concert Choir;** [d]**Columbia Percussion Ensemble;** [a]**Columbia Symphony Orchestra;** [b]**CBC Symphony Orchestra;** [c]**Columbia Chamber Ensemble / Igor Stravinsky.**
Sony Classical SM3K46291 (three discs: 194 minutes: ADD). Recorded 1959-63.   Ⓜ Ⓗ

Inspiration for this collection of mainly stage music came from Stravinsky's native folk-song, folk-dance, folk-tale and folk ritual; and the set contains virtually all the music from Stravinsky's 'Russian' period, including the three great ballets. It is fascinating to chart his development from the 1908 *Scherzo fantastique* with its orchestral colours scintillating in the best Rimsky-Korsakovian manner, to the wholly original language of *Les noces* with its almost exclusively metrical patterns and monochrome scoring (soloists, chorus, pianos and percussion) begun only six years later. The links are there: witness the Rimskian bumble-bee that flies through the *Scherzo* to find its winged counterpart two years on in *The Firebird*; and the primitive rhythmic force of Kastchei's 'Infernal dance' in *The Firebird* finding its fullest expression, another three years later, in *The Rite of Spring*; and so on. Each work is a logical, if time-lapse progression from the previous one. The set concludes with the 15-minute long animal rites of the farmyard opera-cum-burlesque *Renard* (1916); and *L'histoire du soldat* (1918), a morality play designed for a small touring theatre company (the Suite included here omits the speaking roles); both, like *Les noces*, leaving behind the lavish orchestra of *The Rite* for small and unusual instrumental and vocal combinations.

To have the composer at the helm, and a consistent approach to the way the music is recorded, ensures that those links are clearly established. And the orchestra that takes the lion's share of the task, the Columbia Symphony, was assembled by CBS to include many of the finest players in America. It is possible to criticize the recordings (made between 1959 and 1963) for close balances and spotlighting, but many modern contenders, more distantly recorded, will more often than not deprive you of adequate articulation of the music's linear and rhythmic ingenuity. The dynamic range and contours of *The Rite of Spring* do seem momentarily reduced and disturbed by the techniques, otherwise all these recordings reproduce with good tone, range, openness and presence. As to Stravinsky the conductor, only *Les noces* finds him at less than his usual rhythmically incisive self. This *Petrushka* is more representative: it pulsates with inner life and vitality – incidentally, Stravinsky uses his leaner, clearer 1947 revision, not the original 1911 score as the booklet claims.

The Complete Edition, Volume 2.
Apollo[a]. Agon[b]. Jeu de cartes[c]. Scènes de ballet[d]. Bluebird – Pas de deux[a]. Le baiser de la fée[a].
Pulcinella[a]. Orpheus[e].
Irene Jordan *sop* **George Shirley** *ten* **Donald Gramm** *bass*
[a]**Columbia Symphony Orchestra;** [b]**Los Angeles Festival Symphony Orchestra;** [c]**Cleveland
Orchestra;** [d]**CBC Symphony Orchestra;** [e]**Chicago Symphony Orchestra / Igor Stravinsky.**
Sony Classical SM3K46292 (three discs: 210 minutes: ADD). Recorded 1963-65.　　Ⓜ

Volume 2 comprises ballets written between 1919 and 1957. *Pulcinella* was based on music
originally thought to have been written by Pergolesi, but now known to be the work of various
eighteenth-century composers. In 1919 Stravinsky had not long embraced neo-classical style, but
here was a brilliant example of old wine in new bottles, with the melodies sounding as if they come
from the pen of Stravinsky himself. The composer conducts a lively, sharply-accented account of
the score. 1928 saw the production of two Stravinsky ballets. *Apollo*, a mainly quiet, contemplative
score, written for string orchestra, has many passages of great beauty. Stravinsky the conductor
does not linger over these, but allows the work's cool classical elegance to speak for itself. In
Le baiser de la fée Stravinsky used themes by Tchaikovsky as the basis for his score. Once again, the
music seems quite transformed, and the result is a most captivating work. Stravinsky's watchful,
affectionate performance is perfectly proportioned. His arrangement of the 'Pas de deux' from
Tchaikovsky's *Sleeping Beauty* is no more than a reduction for small pit orchestra, however, and a
mere curiosity. In *Jeu de cartes*, which dates from 1936, Stravinsky used music by Rossini and
others, but here the references are only fleeting, and merely enhance the humour of this robust,
outgoing score. His performance brings out all the work's vigour and personality very effectively,
but here and there rhythms become slightly unstuck, and a slightly hectic quality manifests itself.

Scènes de ballet was written in 1944, and possesses a slightly terse quality in the main, though there
are some more lyrical passages. Stravinsky does nothing to soften the work's edges in his
performance, and it emerges as a strong, highly impressive piece. *Orpheus* was completed in 1947,
and shows Stravinsky's neo-classical style at its most highly developed. Much of the music is quiet,
after the manner of *Apollo*, but then the orchestra suddenly erupts into a passage of quite savage
violence. Stravinsky conducts this passage with amazing energy for a man in his eighties, and
elsewhere his performance has characteristic clarity and a very direct means of expression typical of
a composer performance. Finally *Agon*, written in 1957, attracts the listener with its colourful
opening fanfares, and then pursues an increasingly complex serial path in such a brilliant and highly
rhythmical fashion that one is hardly aware that the technique is being used. This work, brilliantly
conducted by Stravinsky, is an ideal introduction to his late style, and to the serial technique itself.
Remastering has been carried out with the greatest skill, and all the recordings in this set sound
very well indeed for their age.

The Complete Edition, Volume 4.
Symphonies – No. 1 in E flat major[a]. Stravinsky in rehearsal. Stravinsky in his own words.
Symphony in Three Movements[b]. Symphony in C[c]. Symphony of Psalms[d].
Toronto Festival Singers; [ad]**Columbia Symphony Orchestra;**
[b]**Columbia Symphony Orchestra;** [c]**CBC Symphony Orchestra / Igor Stravinsky.**
Sony Classical SM2K46294 (two discs: 143 minutes: ADD). Recorded 1961-66.　　Ⓜ

The word 'symphony' appears in the title of each work on these two discs, but this term covers
some very diverse material. Stravinsky was in his mid-twenties when he wrote his Symphony in
E flat, and the score is very much in the style of his teacher Rimsky-Korsakov. It has genuine colour
and flair, however, and the octogenarian conductor brings paternalistic affection and a good deal of
vigour to his performance. The *Symphony in C* dates from 1940, when Stravinsky was in his neo-
classical phase. The work has many beautiful pages, as well as much pungent wit. In this
performance Stravinsky drives the music much harder than he did in his 1952 mono recording with
the Cleveland Orchestra, and although there are some exciting moments the music does tend to lose
its elements of grace and charm. The performance of the *Symphony in Three Movements* is also
characterized by the use of fastish tempos. But this violent work, written in 1945, and inspired by
events in World War Two, responds more readily to a strongly driven interpretation. Stravinsky
wrote his *Symphony of Psalms* in 1930, and this composition reflects his deep religious convictions
in varied settings from the Book of Psalms. His use of a chorus is interestingly combined with an
orchestra which lacks upper strings. Stravinsky conducts a fervent, serious, beautifully balanced
performance. All the 1960s recordings in this set sound very well in their CD transfers. In some
quarters the elderly Stravinsky has been wrongly portrayed as a frail, inadequate figure who only
took over performances when works had been thoroughly rehearsed for him. Nothing could prove
more clearly that this was not true than the rehearsal excerpts in this set, which show a vigorous,
alert octogenarian very much in control of proceedings, and rehearsing passages in some detail.

Stravinsky Violin Concerto in D major[a].
Lutosławski Partita for Violin, Orchestra and Obbligato Solo Piano (1985)[b]. Chain 2 (1984)[b].
Anne-Sophie Mutter *vn* **Phillip Moll** *pf*
[a]**Philharmonia Orchestra / Paul Sacher;** [b]**BBC Symphony Orchestra / Witold Lutosławski.**
DG 423 696-2GH (56 minutes: DDD). Ⓕ 🇷🇷

This disc contains some spellbinding violin playing in a splendidly lifelike recording, and it's a
bonus that the music, while unquestionably 'modern', needs no special pleading: its appeal is
instantaneous and long-lasting. Mutter demonstrates that she can equal the best in a modern classic
– the Stravinsky Concerto – and also act as an ideal, committed advocate for newer works not
previously recorded. The Stravinsky is one of his liveliest neo-classical pieces, though to employ that
label is, as usual, to underline its rough-and-ready relevance to a style that uses Bach as a
springboard for an entirely individual and unambiguously modern idiom. Nor is it all
'sewing-machine' rhythms and pungently orchestrated dissonances. There is lyricism, charm, and
above all humour: and no change of mood is too fleeting to escape the razor-sharp responses of
this soloist and her alert accompanists, authoritatively guided by the veteran Paul Sacher.
Lutosławski's music has strongly individual qualities that have made him perhaps one of the most
approachable of all contemporary composers. This enthralling collaboration between senior
composer and youthful virtuoso is not to be missed.

Apollon musagète (1947 version). The Firebird – Suite. Scherzo fantastique, Op. 3.
Royal Concertgebouw Orchestra / Riccardo Chailly.
Decca 458 142-2DH (71 minutes: DDD). Recorded 1994-95. Ⓕ Ⓢ Ⓔ 🇷🇷

The fact that Stravinsky's revision dispensed with 'half the woodwind, two of the three harps,
glockenspiel and celesta from the original scoring' (to quote the excellent insert-note) hardly
constitutes the bleaching process that a less colour-sensitive performance might have allowed. Part
of the effect is due to a remarkably fine recording where clarity and tonal bloom are complementary,
but Chailly must take the credit for laying *all* Stravinsky's cards on the table rather than holding this
or that detail to his chest. Everything tells, much as it does in the *Scherzo fantastique* – whether the
euphonious winds and brass at 3'52", the motorized repeated notes later on (at 8'31") or the
ornamental swirlings that, in stylistic terms, dance us all the way from Rimsky's Arabian Nights to
the unmistakably Russian world of *The Firebird. Apollon musagète* is of course something else again
and Chailly takes the lyrical line, pointing without punching and allowing his excellent strings their
head. The coda is jaunty, the 'Apothéose' suitably mysterious and 'Variation d'Apollon' features fine
solo work from the orchestra's leader, Jaap van Zweden. Viable alternatives include leaner, more
ascetic readings but Chailly balances gracefulness with tonal substance and the sound is glorious.

Apollon musagète. Pulcinella – suite. Capriccio.
John Ogdon *pf*
Academy of St Martin in the Fields / Sir Neville Marriner.
Decca The Classic Sound 443 577-2DCS (70 minutes: ADD). Recorded 1967-70. Ⓜ

The Academy's 1968 coupling of the *Pulcinella* suite and *Apollon* was their first foray into
twentieth-century repertoire on disc and it now returns with *Capriccio* a substantial bonus. The
transfers are excellent. In *Pulcinella*, the unprecedented crispness of the Academy's ensemble may
no longer inspire particular awe – we are accustomed to squeaky-clean Stravinsky nowadays – so it
is the elegant, characterful solos and clear, warm (not quite plummy) Kingsway Hall ambience that
places this account in a special category. *Apollon* sounds superb too, that final 'Apotheosis' as
blissful as ever, although, as its final chord dies, the improved clarity in the bass alerts us to the
presence of an unwelcome intruder – the London Underground. *Capriccio*, not perhaps one of
Stravinsky's more inspiring works, is well served by John Ogdon, less so by the over-resonant
acoustic of The Maltings, Snape, which sometimes obscures instrumental detail. Notwithstanding
these reservations, this is an outstanding collection.

Le baiser de la fée. Faun and Shepherdess, Op. 2. Ode.
Lucy Shelton *sop*
Cleveland Orchestra / Oliver Knussen.
DG 449 205-2GH (64 minutes: DDD). Text and translation included. Recorded 1995-96. Ⓕ Ⓔ

Oliver Knussen offers us the best-played, best-recorded and most sensitively interpreted account of
Le baiser de la fée that we have had so far on CD, with meticulous attention to Stravinsky's dynamic
markings and delicate instrumental pointing. Stravinsky's subtle Tchaikovsky orchestrations (the

musical 'grid' of *Le baiser*) inspire a reading that exhibits delicate sensibilities and quick reflexes, and Knussen's fill-ups respond equally well to those same qualities. The mildly erotic *Faun and Shepherdess* is seductively played, with soprano Lucy Shelton sounding agile and vocally appealing. The tripartite *Ode* is a quietly eventful memorial for Natalie Koussevitzky. Even Stravinsky's own 1965 Columbia Symphony Orchestra recording, although full of lovely things and obviously of great historical interest, is outclassed by DG's superior recording.

Le baiser de la fée[a]. Symphony in C[b]. Pulcinella[c]. L'histoire du soldat – Suite[d]. Octet[e].
[c]**Mary Simmons** *mez* [c]**Glenn Schnittke** *ten* [c]**Philip MacGregor** *bass*
[abc]**Cleveland Orchestra,** [de]**Chamber Ensemble / Igor Stravinsky.**
Sony Classical Masterworks Heritage mono MH2K63325 (two discs: 155 minutes: ADD).
Recorded 1952-55.   Ⓜ Ⓗ

This two-CD set calls itself 'The Mono Years 1952-55' to distinguish the recordings from those Stravinsky made in the following decade, of the same repertoire – in stereo – gathered together by Sony Classical for its 22-disc Stravinsky Edition and subsequent reissues. The four orchestral works here benefit from a refinement of tone and elegance of manner not equalled by the Columbia and CBC Symphony Orchestras in the stereo remakes. To be fair, the more closely miked strings and woodwinds of the stereo recordings, though undeniably vivid, and occasionally better at profiling leading thematic lines, could be unkind to string tone. And given the effortlessness with which many orchestras nowadays handle the difficulties of a Stravinsky score, it must be said that not everything in these Cleveland sessions speaks with the poetry of precision. Here or there in Cleveland, you will find slightly faster or slower tempos, some of the slower ones allowing more expressive shaping of song (*The Fairy's Kiss*) or clearer exposition of intricate ingenuity (the first movement of the Symphony in C). There is a graceless (even grotesque) plod for the fiancée's short solo variation in *The Fairy's Kiss* 'Pas de deux' (track 6), but the more flowing tempo for the ballet's haunting final 'Berceuse' is a definite plus; as are the chamber items (*The Soldier's Tale* and the Octet), recorded with the cream of New York's players, and sounding like Stravinsky's happiest studio sessions. Quite apart from the expertise of the playing, the pleasure these musicians took in two of Stravinsky's wittiest scores is communicated so vividly that one completely forgets the source is mono.

Stravinsky Circus Polka. Ode. Scherzo à la Russe. Scènes de ballet. Concertino. Agon. Greeting Prelude 'Happy Birthday to you'. Canon on a Russian popular tune. Variations 'Aldous Huxley in memoriam'.
Stafford Smith/Key (arr. Stravinsky) The star-spangled banner.
London Symphony Orchestra / Michael Tilson Thomas.
RCA Red Seal 09026 68865-2 (76 minutes: DDD). Recorded 1996.   Ⓕ

This CD has been absorbingly programmed to chart the progress from Stravinsky's early years in America, awkwardly coming to terms with a new language, a new and rather harsh economic climate and a musical public that welcomed him warmly enough but was at the same time welcoming scores of other refugee musicians. Acutely conscious of money and the absence of it, he attempted in vain to obtain film music commissions from Hollywood and tried to write pop songs and to make money in the relatively prosperous world of jazz. But the *Scherzo à la Russe*, originally for jazz band (played here in its orchestral version), sounds like a rejected movement from *Petrushka*. Rather more shrewdly he wrote the *Scènes de ballet* for a Broadway revue, and was rewarded with a respectable run of performances. The *Concertino*, written for string quartet long before Stravinsky's arrival in America, arranged there for a chamber orchestra of 12 instruments, is a neat demonstration of how much of his late style was already present in his earlier work. The proto-serial *Agon* and the super-serial *Variations* both represent Stravinsky's relief and sheer exuberance, not so much at finding serialism as at realizing that he had been writing quasi-serially all his life and that he could exploit its techniques while still remaining himself. What makes this a hugely entertaining as well as an instructive survey is the infectious zest of the performances. The enjoyable racket of the *Circus Polka*, the gorgeous trumpet tune in *Scènes de ballet*, the sheer delight in inventing entrancing new sonorities that is central to *Agon*, the more arcane but none the less obvious pleasure in the *Aldous Huxley* Variations of constructing perfect, crystalline mechanisms – all these are conveyed with exemplary precision. The recordings are brilliant.

The Firebird. The Rite of Spring. Perséphone.
Stephanie Cosserat *narr* **Stuart Neill** *ten*
Ragazzi, The Peninsula Boys Chorus; San Francisco Girl's Chorus;
San Francisco Symphony Chorus and Orchestra / Michael Tilson Thomas.
RCA Red Seal (special price) 09026 68898-2 (three discs: 119 minutes: DDD). Text and translation included. Recorded live in 1996-98.   Ⓔ

On the face of it, an odd compilation. Why issue one of Stravinsky's least-known ballets in harness with two of his most popular? The answer lies partly in *Perséphone*'s revisiting, 20 years on, of the theme of *The Rite* (earth and rebirth) with Homer's Greece replacing pagan Russia in a neo-classical piece described by Elliott Carter as 'a humanist *Rite of Spring*'. Rather more difficult to explain is the presence of *The Firebird* (the complete 1910 score plus a piano), but a performance as good as this is its own justification. And if three discs – avoiding a mid-ballet disc change – appears extravagant, RCA obligingly prices them as two. We have no idea how much post-concert 'patching' there was after the two live recordings (*The Firebird* and *The Rite*), but the playing is superbly 'finished'. Possibly, the ballet's ending was better on that particular night than any of the others; certainly, Tilson Thomas's timing and shading of the last minutes' darkness-to-light is spellbinding, the management of the *crescendo* on the final chord, even more so. Perfumes are distinctly French, with the *Firebird*'s 'supplication' as seductive as any on disc. The general exuberance of the playing in *The Rite* might also be thought French, though the virtuoso delivery and flamboyance are recognizably American. It isn't a *Rite* that investigates the score's radicalism; rather it is one to send you home from the concert hall exhilarated by the experience.

You would be lucky to catch *Perséphone* in the concert hall. Rather baffling given the quality of a piece which shares with *Oedipus Rex* an inspired blend of distancing and direct appeal, and with *Apollo* and *Orpheus*, an archaic beauty and limpidity. The singers rise to that challenge (and others) with superb choral work. Stravinsky called *Perséphone* a 'melodrama', referring to the spoken title-role. And as Persephone *is* Spring, RCA has cast an aptly youthful-sounding actress in the part, very good at eagerness, passion and compassion. It may be that the voice is too young for *gravitas*; it may equally be that, as recorded (she doesn't sound on-stage with the musicians, and if she was, then her microphone was too close) there was no need to project in the same way, and stage projection might have helped create an element of *gravitas*. It is a small point, and her relative immediacy is always appealing. In all other respects, RCA's balance is beyond criticism.

Petrushka (1947 version). Symphony in Three Movements.
Peter Donohoe *pf*
City of Birmingham Symphony Orchestra / Sir Simon Rattle.
EMI CDC7 49053-2 (57 minutes: DDD). Recorded 1986.   Ⓕ **RR**

Stravinsky's second great ballet score, *Petrshka*, has been well served on disc from the earliest days of LP. He recorded it himself (rather indifferently), but there is in any event a good case for preferring the brilliance and clarity of digital sound in this of all works. Simon Rattle's performance is most notable for its fresh look at details of scoring and balance, with pianist Peter Donohoe making a strong impression. The results are robust and persuasive, though one sometimes has the impression that the characters are being left to fend for themselves. The atmospheric sound with its generous middle and bass is certainly very natural. The symphony too is eminently recommendable, sounding more high-spirited than it sometimes has, with Rattle particularly relishing the jazzy bits.

Petrushka (1947 version). Pulcinella.
Anna Caterina Antonacci *sop* **Pietro Ballo** *ten* **William Shimell** *bar*
Royal Concertgebouw Orchestra / Riccardo Chailly.
Decca 443 774-2DH (73 minutes: DDD). Text and translation included. Recorded 1993.   Ⓕ **E**

In *Petrushka* Chailly has his players characterize even the smallest detail. Note the tongue-in-cheek lead-in to the 'Russian Dance' and the carefree 'squeeze-box' character of the dance itself (with dynamic crossfire between wind and brass and some excellent piano playing). 'Petrushka' (second tableau) is played *con amore*, with much humanity and not entirely without malice: perhaps the anger and frustration aren't as blatant as they might be; but the pain and humiliation certainly are. It's a performance that breathes, that sings and neither rushes its fences nor loses sight of the score's very specific rhythmic profile. As for the recording, given top-ranking engineers – who could rightly expect anything less than exceptional? The coupling, too, is equally colourful: a pert, sweet-centred *Pulcinella*, with an expressive *concertino* in the 'Ouverture', winsome phrasing elsewhere and extremely brilliant accounts of the two *Allegro assais* (tracks 23 and 35). Here there is an incisiveness, attack and buoyancy to the rhythms. The singing is vividly characterized and, again, the recording is spectacular, with a trombone 'Vivo' that should serve the same 'demonstration' function as Ansermet's and Marriner's did in the days of LP.

Pulcinella. Renard. Two Suites. Rag-Time.
Jennifer Larmore *mez* **John Aler, Frank Kelly** *tens* **Jan Opalach, John Cheek** *basses*
Saint Paul Chamber Orchestra / Hugh Wolff.
Teldec 4509-94548-2 (73 minutes: DDD). Texts and translations included. Recorded 1994.   Ⓕ

Hugh Wolff's *Pulcinella* is a witty, incisive alternative. Just try the *Vivo* with its frolicking trombone and wilting double-bass solo and note how stylishly they phrase their closing duet. His singers are generally above par, Jennifer Larmore especially. Wolff offers for couplings the best *Rag-Time* for 11 instruments on disc – gently swinging and without a hint of self-consciousness – plus keenly focused accounts of the two Suites for small orchestra and an exceedingly enjoyable *Renard*. Here the singing is again excellent and there's a novelty in that Wolff has tweaked the published translation and in so doing has effected a more natural flow to the comedy. Again, there is a plethora of detail – subtle underlinings, useful clarifications and felicitous turns of phrase – and the recording is excellent.

The Rite of Spring (two versions).
Philharmonia Orchestra / Igor Markevitch.
Testament mono/stereo SBT1076 (67 minutes: ADD). Mono version recorded 1951, stereo 1959.

Markevitch's 1959 stereo *Rite* is in a league of its own. This is a model of how to balance the score (and of how to create the illusion of a wide dynamic range within more restricted parameters). Markevitch would have been totally familiar with every note of the piece (in 1949, he sent Stravinsky a list of mistakes he had noticed in the recently revised edition), and by 1959 he clearly knew what it needed in performance, including how to keep its shock-value alive. There are 'improprieties' here, such as the slowing for the 'Evocation of the Ancestors' (making the most of those timpani volleys), but nothing serious. As it happens, Markevitch's 'Introduction' to Part 2 is unusually fast but he is able to take in the following small marked variations of tempo, providing valuable contrasts. And in any case, the playing is so alive, alert and reactive, whatever the dynamic levels: listen to the incisive clarinets' entry in the 'Mystic Circles' and the *frisson* it imparts to the following *pianissimo tremolando* from the strings (track 4 after 4'06"). We could fill the rest of the page with similar highlights, and other features unique to the performance, but that would be to spoil the fun of discovery (or rediscovery – and what a transfer – of what an original!). This is a great *Rite* for lots of reasons, not the least of which is the sessions were obviously electric. As a fascinating bonus, Testament also offers a 1951 mono recording of a great *Rite* in the making. The differences are not radical, but enough to justify the idea.

The Rite of Spring. Apollon musagète.
City of Birmingham Symphony Orchestra / Sir Simon Rattle.
EMI CDC7 49636-2 (65 minutes: DDD).

Recordings of *The Rite of Spring* are legion, but it is rare to find Stravinsky's most explosive ballet score coupled with *Apollon musagète*, his most serene. The result is a lesson in creative versatility, confirming that Stravinsky could be equally convincing as expressionist and neo-classicist. Yet talk of lessons might suggest that sheer enjoyment is of lesser importance, and it is perfectly possible to relish this disc simply for that personal blend of the authoritative and the enlivening that Simon Rattle's CBSO recordings for EMI so consistently achieve. Rattle never rushes things, and the apparent deliberation of *The Rite*'s concluding 'Sacrificial Dance' may initially surprise, but in this context it proves an entirely appropriate, absolutely convincing conclusion. Rattle sees the work as a whole, without striving for a spurious symphonic integration, and there is never for a moment any hint of a routine reading of what is by now a classic of the modern orchestral repertoire. The account of *Apollon* has comparable depth, with elegance transformed into eloquence and the CBSO strings confirming that they have nothing to fear from comparison with the best in Europe or America. The recordings are faithful to the intensity and expressiveness of Rattle's Stravinsky, interpretations fit to set beside those of the composer himself.

The Rite of Spring. Pulcinella[a].
[a]**Olga Borodina** *mez* [a]**John Mark Ainsley** *ten* [a]**Ildebrando d'Arcangelo** *bass*
Berlin Philharmonic Orchestra / Bernard Haitink.
Philips 446 698-2PH (71 minutes: DDD). Text and translation included.

The booklet's interior artwork – a jagged cubist pattern of white print on a black background and vice-versa – will strike you either as inventive or deeply irritating, but its contrasts are mirrored in the success and failure of the two performances. Despite occasional instances of affectionate pointing, and finely done solos from the tenor and bass, conditions for this *Pulcinella* – among them, a possible unfamiliarity with the notes – do not lend themselves to buoyancy, fun and quick wittedness, and a wonderfully effervescent score is rendered, for the most part, four-square and flat. But how different is this *Rite*; and if the opening bassoon solo – a very melancholy air, beautifully eased into – hints at a performance more ear-caressing than earth-cracking, what emerges is as comprehensive a realization of the many elements of this score as any on record. The light-toned recording combines vividly present and analytical clarity with a mostly audible sense of space; its sophistication only slipping in those moments where the parts don't relate to the whole. Opinions will differ about whether those 'moments' are few or many, but the balance allows a very high yield of the score's intricacies and radicalism, and provides a clear window on the wonderful expressive variety of the playing. But what of Haitink's parameters? As it happens, they are mainly Stravinsky's, with tempos that keep the work on its feet, an avoidance of inflexions alien to the score, and an appreciation of how much more radical *The Rite* can sound if not turned into a percussion concerto. When all is said and done, you have to ask yourself with any performance of *The Rite*, are you left shaken by it? You will be by this one.

The Rite of Spring. Canticum sacrum[a]. Requiem canticles. Choral Variations on 'Vom Himmel hoch'.
Irène Friedli *mez* **Frieder Lang** *ten* **Michel Brodard** *bar*
[a]**Lausanne Pro Arte Choir; Suisse Romande Chamber Choir and Orchestra / Neeme Järvi.**
Chandos CHAN9408 (75 minutes: DDD). Texts and translations included. Recorded 1994. Ⓕ

Järvi's is a weighty account of *The Rite* and it packs a massive punch. He does not opt for showily fast tempos (save towards the end of the 'Sacrificial Dance', where a combination of high speed and rather heavy sonority garbles a little of the detail) and at times – in the 'Mystical Circle', for instance – he leans on the accents, diminishing the springiness of the rhythm. Elsewhere, though, the articulation tingles appropriately, and the orchestral sound is often beautiful, often cleanly detailed. One would not, even so, put it among the top half-dozen current recordings of *The Rite of Spring* were it not for the quite splendid couplings, where the very qualities that are a slight disadvantage in *The Rite* give urgency and eloquence to a couple of scores that are still regarded as among Stravinsky's most difficult. Both soloists are good, especially the elegantly lyrical tenor, and the chorus sings with wonderfully jubilant confidence. A slight tendency to overmark dynamics, noticeable in *The Rite*, is evident at the beginning of the *Requiem canticles*, where Stravinsky firmly instructs that the strings are not to play loudly and Järvi just as firmly begs to differ. But he has obviously been moved by the fervour of the piece, and he demonstrates that a sonorous, full-voiced account can be just as effective as the more usual reading of the score as a quiet chamber ritual. After that there is no doubting how much fun Stravinsky had in so industriously outdoing Bach's contrapuntal ingenuity in the *Choral Variations*. Järvi obviously loves all those extra twiddly bits too, and is more successful than any other conductor at demonstrating what a Christmassy work it is. Decent recordings throughout, little lacking in resonance in the *Canticum sacrum* (its pauses very precisely tailored to the reverberation time of St Mark's in Venice, after all) and the organ-blower motor of the Victoria Hall in Geneva sounds as though it needs servicing. Otherwise a highly recommendable coupling, especially to those who love *The Rite*.

Two Suites. Four Etudes, Op. 7[a]. Four Norwegian Moods. Concerto for Two Solo Pianos. Ode. Rag-time. Piano-rag music[a]. Renard.
Thom Baker, Drew Martin *tens* **David Evitts, Wilbur Pauley** *basses*
[a]**Mark Wait, Tom Schultz** *pfs*
St Luke's Orchestra / Robert Craft.
MusicMasters 67110-2 (76 minutes: DDD). Text and translation included. Recorded 1991-93. Ⓕ

This is Stravinsky on a relatively small scale – slick, light-textured and free-flowing, purged of expressive exaggeration but by no means slavishly literal. Indeed, the opening number of the Suite No. 1 is surprisingly romantic in feeling. More predictably, subsequent items find the musicians trying to achieve the appropriate spikiness in what can seem a rather resonant performance space. The short orchestral pieces are interleaved with an unpredictable assortment of keyboard works, the piano tone generally a little shallow though perfectly acceptable. Craft's restraint points up the unchanging aspects of Stravinsky's musical language. The effective English-text version of *Renard* uses a variant of Stravinsky's own translation but on its own, more intimate, fairy-tale terms Craft's performance is an undoubted success. The *Ode* will come as a delightful discovery to many. Its second movement (very convincingly done here) is drawn from music originally composed for the hunting scene in the Hollywood film of *Jane Eyre* (starring Orson Welles); its third achieves real profundity in a three-minute span.

Rag-time. Octet. Three Pieces. L'histoire du soldat – Suite. Pastorale. Concertino. Septet. Epitaphium.
Lorna McGhee *fl* **Dmitri Ashkenazy** *cl* **Alan Brind** *vn* **Cristina Bianchi** *hp*
European Soloists Ensemble / Vladimir Ashkenazy *pf*
Decca 448 177-2DH (59 minutes: DDD). Recorded 1994. Ⓕ

This is probably Ashkenazy's finest Stravinsky CD. The catchy but immensely clever Septet scores a double bulls-eye by employing formal ingenuity (the closing Gigue features four separate fugues on four versions of an eight-note row) without 'losing' the untutored listener. Written for violin, viola, cello, clarinet, horn, bassoon and piano, it is followed by the disc's closing selection, a 1'29" *Epitaphium* that offers brief confirmation of the older Stravinsky's serial leanings. The journey started with *Rag-time*, composed in 1918 and peppered with the metallic twang of a cimbalom. Ashkenazy's performance of this is very well played, as is the Octet, with its scampering variations and gentle, bossa-nova style final bars (did Stravinsky ever write anything more charming than this?). Again, the performance is confident and unfussy, while Dmitri Ashkenazy blows plenty of spirit into the *Three Pieces* for solo clarinet (the third especially) and Ashkenazy *père* joins him – together with violinist Alan Brind – for a no-nonsense account of a trio arrangement of *The Soldier's Tale* Suite. Here Brind favours light bowing and bland characterization, whereas the elegant *Pastorale* and lively *Concertino* are, by turns, colourful and punchy. Decca's recordings are uniformly good throughout; so is the standard of playing, and although one might maintain other preferences in this or that individual piece, the programme is both stimulating and entertaining.

Piano-rag music. Circus Polka. Sonata. Serenade in A major. Tango. Four Studies, Op. 7. Scherzo. Sonata in F sharp minor.
Victor Sangiorgio pf
Collins Classics 1374-2 (71 minutes: DDD). Recorded 1991.   Ⓕ

Victor Sangiorgio launches his Stravinsky programme with a superbly colourful account of the *Piano-rag music*. He commands an excellent variety of attack and resonance, and this combines with his natural rhythmic *élan* and his fine ear for textural voicing to make the *Circus Polka* and the *Tango* especially effective. The *Studies* go well too, especially the Chaplinified Scriabin of No. 4. The short 1902 *Scherzo* is the only seriously flawed performance, marred as it is by a tendency towards spasmodic over-punctuation. But at least Sangiorgio pays this slight piece, and the anything-but-slight F sharp minor Sonata, the compliment of meticulous preparation. Third-hand Tchaikovsky the Sonata may be, but there is still something irresistible about the Russian gung-ho of its finale. The recording is very immediate in its impact, possessing both warmth and clarity.

Pastorale. Deux poèmes de Paul Verlaine. Two poems of Konstantin Bal'mont. Three Japanese lyrics. Three little songs, 'Recollections of my childhood'. Pribaoutki. Cat's Cradle Songs. Four Songs. Mavra – Chanson de Paracha. Three Songs from William Shakespeare. In memoriam Dylan Thomas. Elegy for J.F.K. Two Sacred Songs (after Wolf).
Phyllis Bryn-Julson sop **Ann Murray** mez **Robert Tear** ten **John Shirley-Quirk** bar
Ensemble InterContemporain / Pierre Boulez.
DG 20th Century Classics 431 751-2GC (58 minutes: ADD). Texts and translations included.
Recorded 1980.   Ⓜ

It may be true that this disc lacks the focus of a single major work, but it is also much more than a random compilation of unrelated miniatures. Principally, it offers an aurally fascinating contrast between two groups of pieces: Stravinsky's relatively early Russian settings, as he worked through his own brand of nationalism, reaching from the salon style of *Pastorale* to the folk-like vigour of a work like *Pribaoutki*; then the late serial compositions, written in America, which prove that the rhythmic vitality and melodic distinctiveness of the early works survived undimmed into his final years. Stravinsky may have regarded texts as collections of sounds whose natural rhythms had no role to play in their musical setting, but the essential meaning still comes through unerringly, whether it is that of the plaintive Paracha's song from the opera *Mavra* or the sombre *Elegy for J.F.K.* (to an Auden text). The disc is rounded off by the very late Wolf arrangements, and whilst one might quibble here and there about Boulez's choice of tempo, or the balance of voice and instruments, the disc as a whole is immensely satisfying.

L'histoire du soldat – Suite. La Marseillaise. Valse pour les enfants. Sketches for a Sonata. Pribaoutki. Cats' Cradle Songs. Monumentum pro Gesualdo di Venosa ad CD annum. Mass. The dove descending breaks. Canticum sacrum ad honorem Sancti Marci nominis.
Catherine Ciesinski mez **Jon Humphries** ten **David Evitts** bar **Rolf Schulte** vn **Mark Wait** pf
The Gregg Smith Singers; Orchestra of St Luke's / Robert Craft.
MusicMasters 67152-2 (78 minutes: DDD). Recorded 1992-94.   Ⓕ

Craft's 'hands-on' relationship with this music tells at virtually every juncture. *Canticum sacrum*, for example, sounds so much more confident than it does under the composer's own direction. Compare the two versions of the second movement ('Euntes in mundum') and Craft's extra urgency and superior blending immediately hold one's attention. Taken overall, the newer recording is notably faster than its predecessor, whereas the performance of the *Mass* seems to acknowledge Stravinsky's early music influences, especially in terms of a singing style which, in Stravinsky's own recording sounds – at least next to Craft – strangely unidiomatic. Craft was responsible for introducing Stravinsky to the work of Carlo Gesualdo, and the *Momentum pro Gesualdo di Venosa ad CD annum* – a wonderfully supple recomposition of three five-part madrigals for woodwinds, brass and strings – is in fact dedicated to him. Again, the playing is cleanly accomplished, while the *L'histoire du soldat* Suite is the only performance that rivals Stravinsky's third recording (included in Sony's 22-disc retrospective). Craft has taken great pains over the percussion parts, which are placed here as per the original score. The remaining items on this generously filled collection include a sensitive account of the *a cappella* anthem, *The dove descending*, the lively *Pribaoutki* (the first of which was particularly admired by Prokofiev), the *Cats' Cradle Songs* (admired by Webern) and three comparative rarities: the première on record of two gnomic piano pieces based on orchestral sketches (total timing: 44 seconds), a 50-second *Valse pour les enfants* and a highly palatable solo violin arrangement of *La Marseillaise* (composed on New Year's Day 1919, seven weeks after the Armistice), again presented for the first time on disc and extremely well played by Rolf Schulte. It would make a splendid recital 'encore'. An excellent disc, then. Craft balances scholarship and enthusiasm with perceptive musicianship.

Les noces[a]. Mass[b].
Anny Mory *sop* **Patricia Parker** *mez* **John Mitchinson** *ten* **Paul Hudson** *bass*
English Bach Festival Chorus; Trinity Boys' Choir; Martha Argerich, Krystian Zimerman, Cyprien Katsaris, Homero Francesch *pfs* [a]
English Bach Festival Percussion Ensemble;
[b]members of the **English Bach Festival Orchestra / Leonard Bernstein.**
DG 20th Century Classics 423 251-2GC (44 minutes: ADD). Texts and translations included.　　Ⓜ

Stravinsky Les noces.
Traditional Russian Village Wedding Songs Play, Skomoroshek. River. Trumpet. Cosmas and Demian. The drinker. Green forest. God bless, Jesus. My white peas. Steambath. Berry. Black beaver. In the house. Bunny with short legs. The bed. Birch tree.
Pokrovsky Ensemble / Dmitri Pokrovsky.
Nonesuch 7559-79335-2 (54 minutes: DDD). English texts included.　　ⒻⒺ

Many readers will probably look askance at the timing here – could DG really not have done anything with the spare 30 minutes' capacity? However, never mind the width, feel the quality – these are top-drawer Bernstein performances, excellently recorded. *Les noces* sports an impressive array of pianists; but that need not be a decisive factor, since rhythmic precision and good balance are far more at a premium than individual flair or power – fortunately these individuals are equally fine ensemble players. It is even more important that the choir should be meticulously prepared (which they are), that the vocal soloists should be precise and full-blooded (which they are) and that the conductor should impart a sense of the profundity of the whole conception (which Bernstein emphatically does). The Mass is an ideal coupling for *Les noces*, not just because of the shared importance of the chorus, but because it, too, displays a fundamental ritual experience, in this case the sacrament of worship rather than marriage, with archetypal clarity. Bernstein's reading has all the calm devotion of the composer's own, even if the soloists are rather variable. A highly recommendable reissue. For the Nonesuch recording Dmitri Pokrovsky and the singers in his ensemble travelled to southern and western Russia in search of melodies and texts related to *Les noces*; and they found rich pickings. True, the melodic similarities are not as tangible as the folk sources for *Petrushka* but the 15 songs, here recorded with immense flair and enjoyment to a variety of instrumental accompaniments, will be a revelation to non-specialists and specialists alike. Be prepared for some fairly acerbic sounds. Authentic Russian folk polyphony is an extraordinarily modern-sounding experience, as is authentic open-throated singing. The value of the disc is multiplied by the fact that the singers have carried over the style and expressive content of the folk-songs into their performance of *Les noces* itself, bringing it to life in a way that must surely be unprecedented and uniquely illuminating. Not only that, but Pokrovsky had the inspired idea of recreating the instrumental parts on an Apple Macintosh computer, thus continuing Stravinsky's search for the ideal mechanical realization.

Stravinsky The Flood. Abraham and Isaac. Variations 'Aldous Huxley in memoriam'. Requiem canticles.
Wuorinen A Reliquary for Igor Stravinsky.
Susan Bickley *sop* **Peter Hall** *ten/spkr* **David Wilson-Johnson** *bar* **Stephen Richardson** *bass*
Michael Berkeley, Bernard Jacobson, Lucy Shelton *spkrs*
New London Chamber Choir; London Sinfonietta / Oliver Knussen.
DG 447 068-2GH (70 minutes: DDD). Texts and translations included. Recorded 1994.　　Ⓕ

There is a confidence and spontaneity about the music-making on this disc that signal something special. Under Oliver Knussen's authoritative direction the performances leap from the speakers with a vividness that is the ideal complement to the music's rhythmic litheness and intensity of colour. Not all the Stravinsky works represent the composer at his best. *The Flood* (a 'musical play' for television) has marvellous episodes, not least the 'flood' music itself, but other passages, like the melodrama in which God gives Noah his instructions, are less inspired. All four works make strong impressions in these recordings, however, and the *Huxley* Variations and *Requiem canticles* are the crowning glory, with an excellent balance between sharpness of detail and shapely, expressive phrasing. In *The Flood* Michael Berkeley's narration is rather too matter of fact alongside Bernard Jacobson's more actorish Noah, and in the *Requiem canticles'* 'Tuba mirum' David Wilson-Johnson is not ideally focused in tone, but these are very minor cavils. In *Abraham and Isaac* Wilson-Johnson is exemplary in projecting the lyricism as well as the drama of one of Stravinsky's most complex pieces of vocal writing. Charles Wuorinen's *Reliquary* refers to material which Stravinsky was working on at the time of his death, but the last thing Wuorinen was aiming at was pious imitation of the master. There's an exuberant elaboration here that is almost Schoenbergian, at least until the understated coda, and this strong piece fully earns its place on the disc. All the recordings are crisply focused, the sound very immediate.

Symphony of Psalms. Oedipus Rex.
Ivo Zídek *ten* Oedipus; **Věra Soukupová** *mez* Jocasta; **Karel Berman** *bass* Créon;
Eduard Haken *bass* Tiresias; **Antonin Zlesák** *ten* Shepherd; **Zdeněk Kroupa** *bar* Messenger;
Jean Desailly *narr*
Czech Philharmonic Chorus and Orchestra / Karel Ančerl.
Supraphon Historical 11 1947-2 (73 minutes: AAD). Recorded 1964-66. ⒻⒽ🆁🆁

Oedipus Rex is one of Stravinsky's most compelling theatre pieces, a powerful drama that re-enacts the full force of a glorious highspot in ancient culture. The text is by Jean Cocteau, who once said, pertaining to his work on *Oedipus,* that 'any serious work, be it of poetry or music, of theatre or of film, demands a ceremonial, lengthy calculation, an architecture in which the slightest mistake would unbalance the pyramid' (quoted from *Diary of an Unknown,* pub. Paragon House). The fusion of words and music in *Oedipus,* indeed its very 'architecture' is masterly and arrests the attention consistently, from the animated severity of the opening narration, through the cunningly calculated tension of its musical argument, to the tragic restraint of its closing pages. Karel Ančerl was one of Stravinsky's most committed exponents. This particular recording of *Oedipus Rex* was taped in the Dvořák Hall of the House of Artists, Prague, and earned itself at least three major gramophone awards. Ančerl traces and intensifies salient points in the tragedy yet maintains a precise, sensitive touch; his vocal collaborators include the noble Karel Berman (Créon) who, like Ančerl himself, suffered considerably during the Nazi occupation of Czechoslovakia; then there's a fine Jocasta in Věra Soukupová and the convincing but occasionally unsteady Ivo Zídek singing the part of Oedipus. Both here and in the *Symphony of Psalms* – one of the most serenely perceptive performances of the work ever recorded – the Czech Philharmonic Chorus excels, while Supraphon's 1960s engineering (not, alas, the DDD suggested on the box) has an appealing brightness.

The Rake's Progress.
Jerry Hadley *ten* Tom Rakewell; **Dawn Upshaw** *sop* Anne; **Samuel Ramey** *bass* Nick Shadow;
Grace Bumbry *mez* Baba the Turk; **Steven Cole** *ten* Sellem; **Anne Collins** *contr* Mother Goose;
Robert Lloyd *bass* Trulove; **Roderick Earle** *bass* Keeper;
Chorus and Orchestra of Opéra de Lyon / Kent Nagano.
Erato 0630-12715-2 (two discs: 138 minutes: DDD). Recorded 1995.　　　Ⓕ

Any number of the world's opera houses would have given their eye teeth for the privilege of presenting the première of Stravinsky's only true opera, but he, intensely money-conscious though he was (and he had worked on the piece for three years without a commission fee), insisted on La Fenice in Venice. Because he was fond of the city, of course, but also because *The Rake's Progress* is a chamber opera. And this is a chamber performance of it, with a fairly small orchestra, much singing of almost *parlando* quality and crystal-clear words. It is also intimate, with a strong sense of the stage, of characters reacting to each other. With Nagano's on the whole brisk tempos, it gives the impression of a real performance, and a gripping one. Upshaw's is not the purest soprano voice to have attempted the role of Anne, and there have been more spectacular high Cs than hers, but she is movingly vulnerable, totally believable. So is Hadley, acting at times almost too vividly for the music's line: as he occasionally demonstrates he has a wonderfully beautiful head voice. He is not, therefore, quite the touchingly likeable 'shuttle-headed lad' that Alexander Young portrayed so unforgettably in the composer's own recording, but no other Tom Rakewell surpasses him. Ramey's is a bigger voice than most of the others here – firm and superbly produced. Collins and Lloyd are both first-class as Mother Goose and Trulove, Cole an unusually light-voiced, confidingly conspiratorial Sellem. If any, Bumbry is the disappointment of the cast, somewhat over-loud and baritonal almost throughout, but the French chorus sings nimbly and in admirable English. Stravinsky's own recording is still to be cherished, but of modern recordings of *The Rake's Progress* this is by some way the most enjoyable.

Josef Suk
Bohemian 1874-1935

Asrael, Op. 27.
Bavarian Radio Symphony Orchestra / Rafael Kubelík.
Panton 81 1101-2 (64 minutes: ADD). Recorded 1981.   Ⓕ

To use large scale symphonic form for the purging of deep personal grief carries the danger that the result will seriously lack discipline. In 1904-05 Suk's world was shattered by two visits from Asrael (the Angel of Death in Muslim mythology): he lost his father-in-law (and revered teacher) Dvořák, and his beloved wife, Otylka. Forgivably, Suk does perhaps linger a little too long in the fourth movement's gentle, mainly lyrical portrait of Otylka, but elsewhere the progress is as satisfying psychologically as it is symphonically. Much of the music has a concentrated dream-like quality; at the extremes, spectral nightmare visions merge with compensatory surges of lyrical ardour. Set Kubelík's reading alongside any of the other modern versions and one is immediately aware of a wholly compelling imaginative intensity and interpretative flair that betoken a true poet of the rostrum. Kubelík's control throughout is awesome and he conjures up playing of enormous expressive subtlety from his fine Munich orchestra. No other recorded performance – not even Václav Talich's legendary 1952 Supraphon account – succeeds in conveying the intensely personal nature of this music with such devastating emotional candour. Technically, too, one need have no qualms about this Panton disc – the Bavarian Radio engineers secure most truthful results.

Epilogue, Op. 37. A Fairy Tale, Op. 16.
Luba Orgonasova *sop* **Iván Kusnjer** *bar* **Peter Mikuláš** *bass*
Royal Liverpool Philharmonic Choir and Orchestra / Libor Pešek.
Virgin Classics VC5 45245-2 (70 minutes: DDD). Text and translation included. Recorded 1997.   Ⓕ

Scored for soprano, baritone, bass, large and small mixed choruses and orchestra, and running for 40 minutes without a break, *Epilogue* was described by its creator as 'the last part of a cycle, the spirit of which manifested itself for the first time in *Asrael*: it goes through the whole of human life, into reflection on death and the dread of it, before the appearance of the song of earthly love – all this leading up to the exhilarating song of liberated mankind.' Pešek's massed forces bring genuine enthusiasm, vigour and dedication to Suk's extraordinarily ambitious, subtly clothed creation, the music's kaleidoscopic range of colour and mood conveyed with commendable sensitivity and unerring perception. Pešek's ever-involving conception is extremely satisfying in its clear-headed rigour and cumulative thrust. The lucidly balanced, spectacularly full and wide-ranging engineering handles those positively seismic tuttis in the last section with some aplomb. John Tyrell's notes carry the requisite authority but there are, however, some irritating discrepancies in the booklet presentation.

Pešek's account of *A Fairy Tale* (into which we are plunged after a gap of a mere four seconds) faces formidable competition from his own 1981 recording with the Czech PO (available on Supraphon). In the gorgeous opening tableau the excellent violin soloist (surprisingly uncredited, though it is in fact RLPO Principal Malcolm Stewart) plays with a poignant restraint and unaffected purity that is extremely moving. Again, Pešek directs with considerable imagination and flair (the arresting start of the last movement certainly generates a heady sense of spectacle here). If that earlier account continues to have the edge in terms of tangy local colour and dramatic cutting edge, Suk's radiant score is imbued with an extra human warmth and wistful intimacy on Merseyside that provide ample compensation. A most welcome issue.

Ripening, Op. 34. Praga, Op. 26.
Royal Liverpool Philharmonic Choir and Orchestra / Libor Pešek.
Virgin Classics VC7 59318-2 (67 minutes: DDD). Recorded 1992.   Ⓕ Ⓔ

Completed in 1917, *Ripening* shows Suk at the height of his powers. This vast yet tightly organized tone-poem shares many of the autobiographical concerns of its large-scale orchestral predecessors (*Asrael* and *A Summer Tale*). Throughout, Suk handles his outsize forces with a truly Straussian confidence and virtuosity, nowhere more strikingly than in the extended Fugue which attains a climax of truly devastating proportions; the profound serenity of the ensuing coda (where a wordless female chorus is used to magical effect) could not have been harder won. The coupling, *Praga*, is an affectionate, enjoyably grandiloquent portrait-in-sound of that fair city dating from 1904. Pešek and the RLPO are accomplished and communicative. The engineering, too, is first-class.

Chamber works, Volumes 1-3.
Supraphon 11 1874-2 (three discs, aas: 208 minutes: ADD/DDD). Recorded 1966-92.
Ⓜ

String Quartets – No. 1 in B flat major, Op. 11[a]; No. 2, Op. 31[b]. Tempo di menuetto[b]. Meditation on an old Czech hymn, Op. 35a[b]. Quartet movement in B flat major[a].
Suk Quartet ([a]Antonín Novák, [b]Ivan Straus, Vojtěch Jouza *vns* Karel Rehák *va* Jan Stros *vc*).
Supraphon 11 1531-2 (71 minutes: ADD/DDD). Recorded 1966-92.
Ⓜ

Piano Trio in C minor, Op. 2. Elégie, Op. 23. Piano Quartet in A minor, Op. 1. Piano Quintet in G minor, Op. 8.
Josef Suk *vn* **Jan Talich** *va* **Michaela Fukačová** *vc* **Pavel Stěpán** *pf*
Suk Trio (Josef Suk *vn* Josef Chuchro *vc* Josef Hála, Jan Panenka *pfs*);
Suk Quartet (Antonín Novák, Vojtěch Jouza *vns* Karel Rehák *va* Jan Stros *vc*).
Supraphon 11 1532-2 (74 minutes: ADD/DDD). Recorded 1966-92.
Ⓜ

Mélodie. Minuet. Balada in D minor. Four Pieces, Op. 17. Ballade in D minor, Op. 3 No. 1. Serenade in A major, Op. 3 No. 2. Bagatelle, 'Carrying a bouquet'. Barcarolle in B flat major. Balada in D minor. Elégie, Op. 23. Sousedská.
Jiří Válek *fl* **Josef Suk, Jitka Nováková, Ludmila Vybíralová, Miroslav Kosina, Jaroslav Krištůfek, Zdeněk Mann** *vns* **Marek Jerie, František Host, Ivo Laniar** *vcs* **Tomáš Josífko** *db* **Renata Kodadová** *hp* **Josef Hála** *pf/harm* **Jan Panenka, Iván Klánský** *pfs* **Josef Fousek, Libor Kubánek** *perc* **Suk Quartet.**
Supraphon 11 1533-2 (63 minutes: ADD/DDD). Recorded 1966-92.
Ⓜ

A treasure-trove of heartfelt music performed with refinement and flair. Volume 1 concentrates on Suk's string quartet output (Suk himself was the second violinist in the great Czech Quartet for 40 years). If the First Quartet (1896) doesn't quite show the same freshness or entrancing melodic vein of the String Serenade of four years earlier, it remains a delightfully unassuming creation with the genial presence of Suk's teacher Dvořák looming large over the proceedings. It is followed by a rare hearing for the alternative finale Suk composed some 19 years later in 1915. By this time, of course, the composer had already found his own strongly personal voice. Both the resourceful Second Quartet of 1911 (an ambitious one-movement essay of nearly 28 minutes' duration and considerable emotional variety) and the deeply-felt *Meditation on an old Czech Hymn* (1914) are works of some substance well worth exploring, and these passionate accounts enjoy excellent sound. The remaining two volumes perhaps contain more to interest Suk *aficionados* than newcomers, though the adorable *Four Pieces* for violin and piano, Op. 17, have always remained great favourites.

Volume 2 features youthful offerings: the Piano Trio, the Piano Quartet, the likeable, if rather garrulous, Piano Quintet of 1893 and the touching *Elégie* for piano, violin and cello from 1902, written to celebrate the anniversary of the death of the poet and dramatist, Julius Zeyer. Apart from the *Four Pieces* already mentioned, the third and final volume also contains, amongst much else, the *Elégie* in its original guise for violin, cello, string quartet, harmonium and harp, no fewer than three different *Ballades* in D minor conceived for various instrumental combinations during Suk's days at the Conservatory, the 'Barcarolle' slow movement of a very early String Quartet from 1888, as well as the composer's last completed piece from 1935, the engaging *Sousedská* for five violins, double-bass, cymbals and triangle. Recording dates range from 1966 to 1992 (most of the material is designated as AAD), but the quality is consistently praiseworthy and the volumes are available either separately or gathered together within an attractive slipcase.

Six Pieces, Op. 7. Spring, Op. 22a. Summer moods, Op. 22b. About Mother, Op. 28.
Radoslav Kvapil *pf*
Unicorn-Kanchana DKPCD9159 (74 minutes: DDD). Recorded 1994.
Ⓕ

Suk wrote some 60-odd short piano pieces, many of them collected into groups sharing an experience; about a third of them are here, in four collections. Three of these, the Six Pieces (Op. 7), and the connected *Spring* and *Summer moods* (Op. 22), antedate the dreadful double blow that befell him in 1904 and 1905; the sequence *About Mother* belongs to 1907, and is more backward-looking and reflective, marked by sorrow but not with the darkness that was shadowing his large-scale orchestral works in these years. The latter are pieces written for his son, touching domestic vignettes that avoid sentimentality, and are marked by foreboding in the last of them, when the irregularity of the rhythms reflects the frail beat of his wife's heart. The pieces make an excellent anthology of Suk's music, and Kvapil has their manner ideally. He can touch off a mood of gentleness or wit or, more rarely, something almost wry in its oblique, private feeling. Some of the pieces are very simple, and would buckle under playing of greater intensity; some need a little intelligent help in holding them together, or in making the most of Suk's handling of a single idea permeating the invention; Kvapil is unerringly sensitive to their mood.

Sir Arthur Sullivan British 1842-1900

Sullivan Cello Concerto in D major (reconstr. Mackerras and Mackie)[a]. Symphony in E major, 'Irish'[b]. Overture di ballo[b].
Elgar Romance, Op. 62 (arr. vc)[a].
[a]Julian Lloyd Webber *vc*
[a]London Symphony Orchestra / Sir Charles Mackerras;
[b]Royal Liverpool Philharmonic Orchestra / Sir Charles Groves.
EMI British Composers CDM7 64726-2 (71 minutes: ADD/DDD). Items marked [a]recorded 1986; [b]1968. Ⓜ

Sir Charles Groves's sturdy yet affectionate reading of Arthur Sullivan's wholly charming *Irish* Symphony was always one of the best of his EMI offerings with the RLPO, and the 1968 recording remains vivid. In the sparkling *Overture di ballo*, again, Groves conducts with plenty of character. There are also first-rate performances of Sullivan's undemanding Cello Concerto from 1866 (in a fine reconstruction by Sir Charles Mackerras – the manuscript was destroyed in Chappell's fire of 1964) as well as Elgar's wistful little *Romance* (originally for bassoon). This is a thoroughly attractive mid-price reissue.

Overtures – Cox and Box; The Sorcerer; HMS Pinafore; The Pirates of Penzance; Patience; Iolanthe; Princess Ida; The Mikado; Ruddigore (arr. Toye); The Yeomen of the Guard; The Gondoliers; The Grand Duke.
Royal Ballet Sinfonia / Andrew Penny.
Naxos 8 554165 (70 minutes: DDD). Recorded 1997. Ⓢ

The first thing that sets this apart from other collections of Sullivan overtures is that – for the first time – it covers the entire Gilbert and Sullivan output. The only works that are missing are *Thespis*, *Trial by Jury* and *Utopia Limited*, none of which had overtures as such. The sensible addition of the overture to *Cox and Box* means that all the Sullivan comic operas likely to be of interest to the general collector are here. An even more intelligent feature is that they are presented in chronological order, so that one can chart the progression of Sullivan's comic opera style from the very French-sounding ending of *Cox and Box* and the equally French-sounding opening of *The Sorcerer* through to more distinctively Sullivanesque sounds of the later pieces. Of course, none of this would count for much if the performances were not up to scratch. Happily they are models of their kind. Andrew Penny has an agreeably light touch, alternatively reflective and sparkling, and gets graceful phrasing from the Royal Ballet Sinfonia – ideal performers of light music. Nobody wanting a collection of Sullivan's comic opera overtures should need to look elsewhere.

Victoria and Merrie England.
RTE Sinfonietta / Andrew Penny.
Marco Polo 8 223677 (78 minutes: DDD). Recorded 1993. Ⓕ

Five years before Edward German's comic opera *Merrie England*, this Sullivan ballet score was staged at the Alhambra Theatre as part of the celebrations of Queen Victoria's Diamond Jubilee. The original full score appears not to have survived. However, a complete piano reduction was published, along with an orchestral suite, and in addition Sullivan reused earlier material such as his *Imperial March* and music from his early ballet *L'île enchantée*. From all these sources Roderick Spencer has made this very convincing re-creation of the full score. And very worthwhile it proves too. As the notes explain, British ballet in those days was not classical ballet as we know it today but mime-drama. Spectacle was what it was all about, and Sullivan rose to the occasion admirably. There are some most attractive passages – not only in the recycled material but also, for instance, the Solo Variation for the May Queen and perhaps above all the Waltz of Wood Nymphs, which would well repay taking over into the light music repertory. In addition Sullivan skilfully weaves in various patriotic British melodies as well as traditional dances such as a morris dance and a sailors' hornpipe. Such pastiche is the sort of thing that Sullivan did particularly well, and Andrew Penny

and the RTE Sinfonietta do the whole score proud. This is as rewarding as any of the CDs of
Sullivan without Gilbert that Marco Polo have issued.

The Gondoliers. Overture di ballo (1870 version).
Richard Suart bar Duke of Plaza-Toro; **Philip Creasey** ten Luiz; **John Rath** bass Don Alhambra;
David Fieldsend ten Marco; **Alan Oke** bar Giuseppe; **Tim Morgan** bar Antonio;
David Cavendish ten Francesco; **Toby Barrett** bass Giorgio; **Jill Pert** contr Duchess of
Plaza-Toro; **Elizabeth Woollett** sop Casilda; **Lesley Echo Ross** sop Gianetta;
Regina Hanley mez Tessa; **Yvonne Patrick** sop Fiametta; **Pamela Baxter** mez Vittoria;
Elizabeth Elliott sop Giulia; **Claire Kelly** contr Inez;
D'Oyly Carte Opera Chorus and Orchestra / John Pryce-Jones.
TER CDTER2 1187 (two discs: 109 minutes: DDD). Recorded 1991.   Ⓕ

This is one of a series of recordings by the new D'Oyly Carte Opera Company that offers a vastly
better quality of sound than any of its ageing competitors. Orchestral detail is the most immediate
beneficiary, and the overture serves to demonstrate John Pryce-Jones's lively tempos and lightness of
touch. Outstanding among the singers are perhaps John Rath, who gives Don Alhambra's 'I stole
the prince' and 'There lived a king' real presence, and Jill Pert, a formidable Duchess of Plaza-Toro.
Richard Suart not only provides the leading comedy roles with exceptionally clear articulation and
musicality, but also adds considerable character to his portrayals; his 'I am a courtier grave and
serious' is a sure winner. David Fieldsend and Alan Oke provide attractive portrayals of the two
gondoliers, and Lesley Echo Ross and Regina Hanley are also most agreeable. Seasoned listeners
may note numerous changes of detail as a result of the purging of the performance material of
changes made to the parts around the time of the 1920s Savoy Theatre revivals. There is no
dialogue, but added value is provided by Sullivan's sunniest comic opera score being accompanied
by the sparkling *Overture di ballo*, played in its original version with some traditional cuts opened up.

HMS Pinafore.
Richard Suart bass Sir Joseph Porter; **Felicity Palmer** mez Little Buttercup;
Rebecca Evans sop Josephine; **Thomas Allen** bar Captain Corcoran;
Michael Schade ten Ralph Rackstraw; **Donald Adams** bass Dick Deadeye;
Valerie Seymour sop Hebe; **Richard Van Allan** bass Bill Bobstay;
John King, Philip Lloyd-Evans bars Bob Becket;
Welsh National Opera Chorus and Orchestra / Sir Charles Mackerras.
Telarc CD80374 (74 minutes: DDD). Notes and text included. Recorded 1994.   ⒻⒺ

As always, Mackerras keeps the livelier numbers moving along comfortably without ever a hint of
rushing, whilst giving full weight to the tender moments and, above all, caressing all the details of
Sullivan's delicious orchestration. Right from the overture, with its beautifully shaped *Andante*
section, this is music-making to perfection. Of the singers, Felicity Palmer's Buttercup truly oozes
plumpness and pleasure, while Thomas Allen's Captain does not just the crew of the *Pinafore*, but
all of us, proud. If Rebecca Evans's Josephine is a shade lacking in colour, Mackerras has found in
Michael Schade's Ralph Rackstraw a most elegant addition to his G&S team. As for Richard
Suart's Sir Joseph Porter, this is surely as stylish a demonstration of patter singing as one can find
anywhere on disc, while Donald Adams's Dick Deadeye is no worse for his 40-odd years singing the
role. Add orchestral playing of refinement, choral work whose perfection extends from the formal
numbers to the varied inflexions of 'What nevers?', plus a recording that brings out the instrumental
detail to perfection, and one has a *Pinafore* that is unadulterated delight from first note to last.

The Mikado.
John Holmes bass The Mikado; **John Wakefield** ten Nanki-Poo; **Clive Revill** bar Ko-Ko;
Denis Dowling bar Pooh-Bah; **John Heddle Nash** bar Pish-Tush;
Marion Studholme sop Yum-Yum; **Patricia Kern** mez Pitti-Sing; **Dorothy Nash** sop Peep-Bo;
Jean Allister mez Katisha.
Iolanthe – excerpts.
Elizabeth Harwood, Elizabeth Robson, Cynthia Morey sops **Heather Begg,**
Patricia Kern mezzos **Stanley Bevan** ten **Eric Shilling, Denis Dowling, Julian Moyle** bars
Leon Greene bass
Sadler's Wells Opera Chorus and Orchestra / Alexander Faris.
Classics for Pleasure CD-CFPD4730 (two discs: 135 minutes: ADD). Recorded 1962.   Ⓑ

At the core of these performances are some of the finest British singers of 30 years ago, all of
whom were chosen not just for their singing but for their sense of the theatricality and humour of
Gilbert and Sullivan. Just listen, for instance, to how John Heddle Nash gives full expression to

every word of Pish-Tush's 'Our great Mikado'. Here, too, is Marion Studholme's delicious Yum-Yum and Elizabeth Harwood's joyous Phyllis. If one singles out Clive Revill for special mention, it is because his Ko-Ko is uniquely well judged and imaginative, combining superb comic timing, verbal clarity and vocal dexterity. His 'little list' is hilarious, and one can almost feel one's hand gripped at the words 'shake hands with you *like that*'. At the helm in both works is Alexander Faris who knew supremely well how to capture the lightness and sparkle of operetta. The new Overture put together for *The Mikado* by Stephen Dodgson may come as a surprise, but it is apt and cleverly done. The sound is inevitably dated when compared to more recent recordings, but it scarcely mars the enjoyment.

The Pirates of Penzance.
Eric Roberts *bar* Major-General Stanley; **Malcolm Rivers** *bar* Pirate King;
Gareth Jones *bar* Samuel; **Philip Creasy** *ten* Frederic;
Simon Masterton-Smith *bass* Sargeant of Police; **Marilyn Hill Smith** *sop* Mabel;
Patricia Cameron *sop* Edith; **Pauline Birchall** *mez* Kate; **Susan Gorton** *contr* Ruth;
D'Oyly Carte Opera Chorus and Orchestra / John Pryce-Jones.
TER CDTER2 1177 (two discs: 85 minutes: DDD). Recorded 1990.   Ⓕ

The revival of the D'Oyly Carte Opera Company produced the first digital recordings of complete Gilbert and Sullivan scores, and this TER set is a very happy example. Philip Creasy is an engaging and vocally secure Frederic, and Marilyn Hill Smith trips through 'Poor wandering one' with a delectable display of vocal ability and agility. The couple's interplay with the chorus in 'How beautifully blue the sky' is quite enchanting, and their exchanges in 'Stay, Frederic, stay' splendidly convincing. Eric Roberts makes the Major-General a thoroughly engaging personality, and the dotty exchanges between Simon Masterson-Smith's Sargeant of Police and his police force are sheer joy. Even such details as the girls' screams at the appearance of the pirates in Act 1 have a rare effectiveness. John Pryce-Jones keeps the score dancing along. Those who want the dialogue as well as the music must look elsewhere, but this version is certainly to be recommended.

The Yeomen of the Guard.
Peter Savidge *bar* Sir Richard Cholmondeley; **Neill Archer** *ten* Colonel Fairfax;
Donald Adams *bass* Sergeant Meryll; **Peter Hoare** *ten* Leonard; **Richard Suart** *bar* Jack Point;
Donald Maxwell *bar* Shadbolt; **Alwyn Mellor** *sop* Elsie; **Pamela Helen Stephen** *mez* Phoebe;
Felicity Palmer *mez* Dame Carruthers; **Clare O'Neill** *sop* Kate; **Ralph Mason** *ten* First Yeoman;
Peter Lloyd Evans *bar* Second Yeoman.

Trial by Jury.
Rebecca Evans *sop* Plaintiff; **Barry Banks** *ten* Defendant; **Richard Suart** *bar* Judge;
Peter Savidge *bar* Counsel; **Donald Adams** *bass* Usher; **Gareth Rhys-Davies** *bar* Foreman;
Welsh National Opera Chorus and Orchestra / Sir Charles Mackerras.
Telarc CD80404 (two discs: 121 minutes: DDD). Recorded 1995. Notes and texts included.   Ⓕ

Between them, *The Yeomen of the Guard* and *Trial by Jury* contain all that is best in Sullivan's music for the theatre. In the former there is some of his more serious and ambitious writing, in the latter some of his most consistently light-hearted and engaging. All of this is brought out in Telarc's series of recordings with Welsh National Opera. As always, Sir Charles Mackerras paces the music impeccably, and he has assured contributions from such stalwarts as Donald Adams, Felicity Palmer and Richard Suart. The last-named may be a shade light-voiced compared with some of the more comic performers of Jack Point and the Learned Judge; but in *The Yeomen* it is surely his performance that stands out. His handling of the dialogue after 'Here's a man of jollity' is masterly, and his 'Oh, a private buffoon' is as winning as any, with impeccable clarity of diction and a perfectly judged French accent for 'jests ... imported from France'. Neill Archer and Alwyn Mellor are admirable as Fairfax and Elsie; but Pamela Helen Stephen could have displayed more of the minx in Phoebe Meryll's personality, while in *Trial by Jury* Barry Banks has too small a voice to convince as the Defendant. Recommended, especially if you want both works on the same set.

Franz von Suppé   Austrian 1819-1895

Overtures – Leichte Kavallerie; Tricoche und Cacolet; Boccaccio. Afrikareise – Titania Waltz.
Fatinitza. Humorous variations on the popular song, 'What comes there from on high?'
Die Heimkehr von der Hochzeit. Herzenseintracht – polka. Franz Schubert. Triumph Overture.
Slovak State Philharmonic Orchestra, Košice / Alfred Walter.
Marco Polo 8 223683 (62 minutes: DDD). Recorded 1994.   Ⓕ

This volume of Marco Polo's Suppé series offers another fascinating insight into the wider output of a composer unjustly typecast through the brilliance of his rousing overtures. Here the familiar *Leichte Kavallerie* and *Fatinitza* overtures serve to demonstrate the thoroughly reliable conducting and playing of Alfred Walter and the Košice orchestra, without quite offering a challenge to the most rousing interpretations available elsewhere. What are of interest are the rarities. Of the unfamiliar overtures, that to *Tricoche und Cacolet*, a Viennese adaptation of a Meilhac and Halévy play, is perceptibly in the French style of Offenbach, with some attractive themes and a marvellous passage for bassoon, while the *Triumph Overture* has a typically exciting ending. The overture to *Die Heimkehr von der Hochzeit* is perhaps less striking, while that to *Franz Schubert* (a one-act operetta portraying the composer on stage) is mainly notable for its use of Schubertian themes – *Der Erlkönig, Der Wanderer*, the German Dance No. 7 (also used later in *Lilac Time*), *Der Schäfer und der Reiter* and *Die Taubenpost*. Among the other pieces, the *Afrikareise* waltz finds Suppé very much in Straussian territory, while *Herzenseintracht* proves that he could also produce a polka with the best. Perhaps the most intriguing item is Suppé's set of humorous variations on the *Fuchslied*, a popular Viennese student song which we would recognize as *A-hunting we will go*. It all provides further enjoyable proof that Suppé's entertaining writing extended way beyond his overtures.

Requiem in D minor.
Aleksandra Baranska sop **Katarzyna Suska** contr **Jerzy Knetig** ten **Andrzej Hiolski** bass
Cracow Philharmonic Chorus and Orchestra / Roland Bader.
Koch Schwann 312482 (71 minutes: DDD). Text and translation included. Recorded 1989. Ⓕ

Suppé composed his Requiem in 1855 in memory of Franz Pokorny, the theatre manager to whom he owed much of his early conducting and compositional experience. After a few performances it lay forgotten. Then in 1988 it was performed at the Montpellier Festival and although recorded in 1989 we have had to wait some time for its appearance. The demands of a large-scale religious work held no terrors for Suppé, a thoroughly trained and proficient musician. The work is powerfully and imaginatively written, with much of the operatic flavour of Verdi's Requiem of 19 years later. The chorus has the major vocal contribution, with the bulk of the solo opportunities going to the two lower voices. Anyone wishing to sample the riches of the work should try the hauntingly beautiful 'Hostias', with its eerie brass and woodwind and stirring bass solo, or the 'Agnus Dei', with its plaintive funeral march developing into a typically expansive Suppé theme. This Koch release offers a spacious reading, notably in the 'Dies irae' and the 'Rex tremendae'. This is an impressive and moving work that has much more to offer than mere curiosity value.

Giles Swayne
British 1946

Cry.
BBC Singers / John Poole.
NMC NMCD016 (76 minutes: DAD). Recorded 1984. Ⓕ

The 'cry' is that of a composer who, by the late 1970s, was utterly disenchanted with the stuffy and self-regarding world of contemporary art music. His desire was for a new balance, especially between vernacular and cultivated traditions, and the result is a synthesis, a new world of basically euphonious modal harmony that reflects the impact of musical regions well beyond the borders of Europe – Africa, in particular. Twenty years on we might be inclined to pigeon-hole Swayne as a Tavener-like minimalist and *Cry* undoubtedly represents a kind of musical 'Back to Basics'. Its seven movements parallel the seven days of creation, but there's no biblical text telling the story, simply a tapestry of vocal sounds that aim for a pure, pre-verbal intensity of experience. Swayne's willingness to open up his vocal sound world to electronic transformation creates parallels with Stockhausen and Berio, to name the most obvious, and it is easy to see how *Cry* might disappoint listeners to whom the poetic, intellectual content of vocal works by those avant-garde masters is crucial. Given its extreme dependence on atmosphere, *Cry* has a relatively narrow expressive range. Hearing it remains an absorbing experience, nevertheless, and this is due in large part to the remarkably sustained intensity of this performance by 28 members of the BBC Singers. The insert-note recounts the headaches that confronted NMC in their remastering of the original recording, but what matters to the listener is that the result preserves a raw sonic immediacy that fits Swayne's urgent idealism like a glove.

Magnificat. Nunc dimittis. Missa brevissima. Three Shakespeare Songs. The Tiger. Veni creator II. O magnum mysterium. Ophelia Drowning. Missa Tiburtina.
BBC Singers / Stephen Cleobury with Philippa Davies fl **David Goode** org
Collins Classics 1531-2 (77 minutes: DDD). Texts and translations included. Recorded 1998. Ⓕ

Giles Swayne shares with his British near-contemporaries, Colin Matthews and Diana Burrell, an ability to write music of very direct expressive character, and this is superbly conveyed in these stunningly assured performances of his smaller choral works. Every one of these pieces, ranging in date from 1969 to 1996 but mainly written during the 1980s, is attractive and distinctive. Swayne might at times flirt with minimalism, and make frequent recourse to rhythmic patterns reflecting his interest in African music, but the result is never routine or mechanical. Echoes of Britten's *Rejoice in the Lamb* and *Missa brevis* indicate another important source for Swayne's style, and his music is at its best when lively, joyous – or angry. The *Magnificat* and *Nunc dimittis*, *Veni creator II*, and *The Tiger* (using Blake's famous poem) all display these qualities. *Ophelia Drowning* is less interesting, suggesting that Swayne finds restraint more difficult, and some effects, like the evocation of Tallis-like spaciousness in the *Missa Tiburtina*, are a little too artlessly deployed for their own good. All the same, the way this Mass's final movement, 'Dona nobis pacem', seems to move from confidence to doubt is highly affecting, and none the worse for being obvious and uncomplicated. All the texts set by Swayne here are familiar, and his ability to come up with so many new ideas and effects is remarkable. The excellent recordings match totally convincing performances.

Jan Pieterszoon Sweelinck

Dutch 1562-1621

Toccata in C major. Ballo del granduca. Ricercar. Malle Sijmen. Mein junges Leben hat ein End'. Aeolian Echo Fantasia. Onder een linde groen. Toccata in A minor I. Erbarm dich mein, o Herre Gott. Poolsche dans.
James David Christie org
Naxos 8 550904 (64 minutes: DDD). Played on the C.B. Fisk Organ, Houghton Chapel, Wellesley College, USA. Recorded 1993. Ⓢ

James David Christie presents what is, in effect, a most satisfactory re-creation of one of Sweelinck's organ recitals, given daily between 1580 and 1621, for the burghers of Amsterdam. One hopes they were properly appreciative of the most consistently witty and generous-spirited keyboard music before the era of Buxtehude, Couperin and Bach. While Christie may not possess the lyricism of a Leonhardt, the humane warmth of a Piet Kee, or the mercurial whimsy of a Koopman, he is, in his own right, a bold, stylish, unhasty player, clearly thoroughly versed in early performance practice, with an incisive technique disclosing musical intelligence and common sense. He is particularly successful in the five major variation sets here, relishing the variety of decorative motifs but still conveying an impression of structural coherence and unity. Just occasionally his articulation might have worked better in a somewhat larger acoustic: at times a more obviously singing touch might have suggested greater tenderness in quieter moments and more ample majesty in louder ones. However, with appealing registrations, an almost ideal choice of programme, good notes and undistractingly natural recording, this disc merits general recommendation.

Ab Oriente. Angelus ad pastores ait. Beati omnes. Beati pauperes. Cantate Domino. De profundis. Diligam te Domine. Domine Deus meus. Ecce nunc benedicite. Ecce prandium. Ecce virgo concipet. Euge serve bone. Gaudate omnes. Gaude et Laetare. Hodie beata Virgo Mariae. Hodie Christus natus est. In illo tempore. In te Domine speravi. Iusti autem. Laudate Dominum. Magnificat. Non omnis. O Domine Jesu Christe. O quam beata lancea. O sacrum convivium. Paraclectus autem. Petite et accipietis. Qui vult venire post me. Regina coeli. Tanto tempore. Te Deum laudamus. Timor Domini. Ubi duo vel tres. Venite, exultemus Domino. Vide homo. Videte manus meas. Viri Galilaei.
Clare College Choir, Cambridge / Timothy Brown
with **James Grossmith, Andrew Henderson** org
Etcetera KTC2025 (two discs: 141 minutes: DDD). Notes, texts and translations included. Recorded 1998. Ⓕ

Lurking suspicion that Jan Pieterszoon Sweelinck is a true doyen of sacred vocal music is emphatically confirmed in an important and invigorating world première recording of the complete 1619 *Cantiones Sacrae*. This collection of 37 motets in five-voices demonstrates, above all, the quality of his aesthetic, one in which textual representation and pure contrapuntal pleasure converge with effortless mastery; you only have to hear the first minute of the first track, a quasi-introit, 'Gaudete', of infectious energy, to dance to its affirmative and buoyant rhythms and bask in the clarity of the harmonic conception. *Cantiones Sacrae* projects a distinctive containment, both in scale and emotional judgement, which should appeal to choirs of all shapes and sizes – and listeners too; drawing close parallels with William Byrd can be a hazardous exercise, though there is some common territory, borne out by biography, that Sweelinck survived as a Catholic in a Protestant working environment. By turning to the Roman vulgate in later years for his texts, as he does here, Sweelinck mirrors Byrd's own practice in the *Gradualia*, if far less methodically. As these pieces would not, therefore, have adorned the liturgy, their use was most likely limited to domestic situations and to the Collegium Musicum in Amsterdam, an institute founded especially to promote Sweelinck's compositions. These performances by the young, effervescent voices of Clare College Choir, Cambridge are impressive. Timothy Brown expertly circumnavigates his disciplined larger forces of about 26 voices around an *oeuvre* which is at once both introspective and ecstatic. The smaller-scale consort is perhaps a little less polished, the tuning of the sopranos has a tendency to 'dip' intermittently, and there is an occasional 'piping kettle' quality to the timbre. Generally, too, the lack of colorific range and resonance belies the youthful membership of the choir; this can be telling in some of the slower music where prettiness tends to prevail above projection of sentiment. These are small gripes in a project which stands out for a pioneering place in the catalogue and its fine advocacy of Sweelinck's seemingly unlimited resource.

Karol Szymanowski Polish 1882-1937

Violin Concertos – No. 1, Op. 35; No. 2, Op. 61. Three Paganini Caprices, Op. 40.
Romance in D, Op. 23.
Thomas Zehetmair *vn* **Silke Avenhaus** *pf*
City of Birmingham Symphony Orchestra / Sir Simon Rattle.
EMI CDC5 55607-2 (65 minutes: DDD). Recorded 1996. *Gramophone* Award Winner 1997. Ⓕ 🆁🆁

They make an admirable coupling, the two Szymanowski violin concertos, but a demanding one for the soloist. They are both so beautiful that it must be tempting to embellish both with a similarly glowing tone. They inhabit quite different worlds (they were written 16 years apart) and Zehetmair shows how well they respond to quite different approaches. In the First, after a rapt solo entry, he uses for the most part a lovely but delicate tone, expanding to athletic incisiveness but not often to lushness. It fits very well with Rattle's handling of the orchestra: occasionally full and rich but mostly a sequence of exquisitely balanced chamber ensembles. Generous but finely controlled rubato from both soloist and conductor allows the concerto's improvisatory fantasy to flower; and the quiet close even has a touch of wit to it. Zehetmair's sound is immediately less ethereal, more robust, for the opening melody of the Second Concerto. This is the sort of tone, you suspect, that he would use in Bartók's Second Concerto, and it points up a vein of indeed Bartókian strength to this work's longer and firmer lines. Rattle, too, seeks out bolder and more dense colours. It is characteristic that even the more musing lyrical pages here are given a warmer colour than superficially similar moments in the First Concerto.

The *Paganini Caprices* were equipped by Szymanowski not with deferential accompaniments but with independent and quite freely composed piano parts. They change Paganini, even where the violin part is unmodified (most of the time but not quite all), into a late romantic virtuoso, with a hint of Lisztian poetry alongside the expertly pointed-up fireworks of the Twenty-Fourth *Caprice*; even here Zehetmair is a listening violinist, not one to upstage his excellent pianist. The *Romance*, the warmest and most luscious piece here, is beautifully done but with a touch of restraint to prevent it cloying. A first-class coupling, and a recording that makes the most of the superb acoustic of Symphony Hall in Birmingham.

Harnasie, Op. 46ᵃ. Symphony No. 4, Op. 60, 'Symphonie concertante'ᵇ. Mazurkas, Op. 50 –
No. 1 in C major; No. 2 in A major. Theme and Variations in B flat minor, Op. 3.
Andrzej Bachleda *ten* **Wiesław Kwasny** *vn* **Felicja Blumental** *pf*
ᵃ**Cracow Radio Chorus and Symphony Orchestra / Antoni Wit;**
ᵇ**Polish National Radio Symphony Orchestra / Jerzy Semkow.**
EMI Matrix CDM5 65307-2 (75 minutes: ADD). Recorded 1974-79.   Ⓜ

With the exception of the early and accomplishedly Brahmsian *Theme and Variations*, this is all late Szymanowski, Szymanowski giving up just a little of the colour and opulence of his middle period to respond with delight to the fresh and invigorating rawness of the folk music of the Tatra region. He responds most obviously, of course, in the folk ballet *Harnasie*, with its frequent imitations of raucous folk fiddling and the fervour of choral folk-song and its heartfelt evocations of Poland's mountain country. But surely the wonderfully poised opening theme of the *Symphonie concertante* owes something to this influence too (a theme so beautiful that Szymanowski cannot resist returning to it as the true destination of all the previous beauties of his slow movement)? The last movement might almost be a supplement to *Harnasie*, but the use throughout of wind and string solos sounds very much like a 'refinement' of the peasant fiddle and trumpet in the ballet. Since the performances are very good indeed, and the recordings clean and decent, the coupling is a very recommendable one. All the more so since Western pianists still seem reluctant to programme the *Symphonie concertante*, and *Harnasie*, which calls for tenor and violin soloists and a chorus as well as orchestra, is unlikely ever to prove popular in the concert hall. Both are full of delights. The *Theme and Variations* and the two *Mazurkas* are well played; the latter will undoubtedly whet your appetite for the more intimate and subtle aspects of 'late Szymanowski', and will send you off hunting for the other 18 *Mazurkas*.

Métopes, Op. 29. 12 Etudes, Op. 33. Masques, Op. 34. Mazurkas, Op. 50 – No. 7, Poco vivace; No. 13, Moderato; No. 15, Allegretto dolce. Two Mazurkas, Op. 62.
Mikhail Rudy *pf*
EMI CDC5 55390-2 (72 minutes: DDD). Recorded 1994.   (F)

'Big' and 'strong' are words that spring to mind quite often during these readings; not perhaps the first adjectives one would choose to describe Szymanowski, yet they seem highly appropriate here. What do the *Métopes* have in common? They are portraits of women (the Sirens, Calypso, Nausicaa), all of whom at least threaten to be too strong for Odysseus. 'Isle of the Sirens' is a big piece, for all its florid voluptuousness; there is firm strength as well as impressionist colour to the portrait of Calypso; Szymanowski's Nausicaa is an exotic enchantress as well as a seductive one. The *Masques*, of course, respond still more to strong and purposeful virtuosity, and Rudy brings richness of colour as well as bold pianism to 'Shéhérazade', while in 'Tantris le bouffon' he somehow suggests the humiliation of Tristan, in this version of the legend forced to disguise himself as a jester to gain access to Isolde; there is even something of frustration or of desperation beneath the ardour of his 'Sérénade de Don Juan'. After all this, the *Mazurkas* come as a surely deliberate shock: a distilled, pared-down music after all that richness and colour and, in the late *Mazurka*, Op. 62 No. 1, an outpouring of the purest lyricism. All in all, enormously enjoyable, not least the ample acoustic which matches the scale of the performances so well. If you want to convert someone to Szymanowski's piano music, start here.

---

20 Mazurkas, Op. 50. Two Mazurkas, Op. 62.
Pawel Kamasa *pf*
Koch Schwann 310662 (57 minutes: AAD). Recorded 1992.   (F)(S)

Kamasa himself adds a note to the accompanying booklet explaining why it was decided not to record these performances digitally. One can only report that the piano tone as reproduced here is very beautiful, very subtle of colour, indeed very responsive to Kamasa's poetic handling of this music. Another note, by the late Witold Lutosławski, praises his 'tremendous understanding' of Szymanowski's harmonies and his 'precise and purposeful' use of the pedal. Indeed he is a pianist of such exceptional gifts that this disc is recommended even to listeners who are not especially interested in Szymanowski. But they will surely soon become so under the influence of playing such as this, in which keyboard colour is so exquisitely clear, in which quite dense chords are never opaque. In them one can hear Szymanowski's excitement at discovering in the supposedly 'crude' folk music of the Tatra Mountains not only a harmonic asperity and a rhythmic boldness that excited him but a nobility of utterance that gives these brief pieces a quite disproportionate stature. They are indeed, as Kamasa says with a rueful apology for such seeming overstatement, 'symphonic', and his performances also have the urgency and fantasy to reveal what big pieces they are, despite their brevity.

Stabat mater, Op. 53. Litany to the Virgin Mary, Op. 59. Symphony No. 3, Op. 27, 'The song of the night'.
Elzbieta Szmytka *sop* **Florence Quivar** *contr* **Jon Garrison** *ten* **John Connell** *bass*
City of Birmingham Symphony Orchestra and Chorus / Sir Simon Rattle.
EMI CDC5 55121-2 (56 minutes: DDD). Texts and translations included. Recorded 1994.
Gramophone Award Winner 1995.   (F)(E)

The first impression here is that Rattle is relatively new to Szymanowski. There's a huge enthusiasm here, a missionary quality that bespeaks the recent convert. On the other hand the care over matters of balance, the knowledge of just those points where Szymanowski's complexity needs very careful handling if it's not simply to blur into opacity, suggest a conductor who has been there before and knows the dangers. You get the feeling that a conscious decision was made to delay recording this music until the circumstances were right. The CBSO Chorus sounds thoroughly at home not only in the music but in the language too. The clincher on the decision to go ahead with this recording might well have been Rattle's realization that in Elzbieta Szmytka he had a soprano who might have been born to sing Szymanowski's pure, floated and very high-lying soprano lines (in the *Stabat mater* and the *Litany*; in the symphony he uses a tenor, which was Szymanowski's own first choice). The result is very fine indeed: one of the most beautiful Szymanowski recordings ever made. And yet 'beautiful Szymanowski' isn't all that hard if the orchestra's good enough and the conductor capable. Rattle's insistence that all of the music be heard, its bones and sinews as well as its flesh, its urgency and passion as well as its deliquescent loveliness, makes for uncommonly gripping Szymanowski as well. He reminds one of how much more there is to the Third Symphony than voluptuous yearning: solemnity, for one thing, and a fierce ardour that can indeed knock you sideways. The choice of soloists for the *Stabat mater* is interesting: alongside Szmytka's radiant purity are Quivar's throaty vibrancy and Connell's weighty darkness. Not a matching trio, but the contrast is appealing; it adds to the rich differentiation of sonority that Rattle draws from his chorus and orchestra. Garrison in the symphony is a touch hard and strenuous, less enraptured than one or two of the Polish tenors (and sopranos) who've recorded it, but he's a musicianly and likeable singer. The recording is outstanding: lucid, rich and spacious, with tremendous and perfectly focused climaxes.

Germaine Tailleferre
French 1892-1983

Intermezzo. Larghetto. Jeux de plein air. Toccata. Suite Burlesque. Two Waltzes. Fandango. La nouvelle Cythère. Image. Sonata for two pianos.
Mark Clinton, Nicole Narboni *pfs*
Elan ELAN82278 (64 minutes: DDD). Recorded 1996.   Ⓕ Ⓔ

Milhaud was responsible for introducing the young Germaine Tailleferre, who had been brilliantly carrying off prize after prize at the Conservatoire, to Satie, who on hearing her *Jeux de plein air* in 1917 declared her his 'musical daughter' and brought her into contact with other young musicians who later were to be dubbed 'Les Six'. His enthusiasm was understandable, for the two traditional games depicted (the second being 'Hunt the slipper') had drawn from her witty, light-hearted music (though with infinitely greater invention and technique than he had ever shown). *Gaminerie* also dominates the Poulenc-like *Toccata*, a perky piece played here with deliciously pointed *staccato*. At this time Tailleferre was also experimenting with polytonality, as can be heard in the initially meditative *Image*. Her background of Satie and Ravel (a friend of hers), however, emerges in the *Two Waltzes* of 1925, the first utterly charming but harmonically spiced, the second sprucely brilliant. All the pieces on this disc are unpretentious, concise and very brief: even the 1974 so-called Sonata, bubbling with Gallic gaiety, lasts a mere six minutes, and the *Suite Burlesque*, wonderfully frisky for an 87-year-old, consists of fragmentary chippings.

The sparkling *Intermezzo* and the *Larghetto* are taken from her quite considerable film music; but her theatrical sense is best illustrated by the only work here of any length – *La nouvelle Cythère*, written in 1929 for Diaghilev's Ballets Russes but never performed because of his death. It is an attractive work, full of freshness, vitality and variety, and if only it were orchestrated would surely be welcomed by some ballet company today. No fewer than seven of the present ten works (six of which are still unpublished) here make their first appearance on disc. The Clinton-Narboni duo is absolutely first-rate, with an immensely engaging spirit, delicacy, variety of touch and subtle shadings, and the recording matches it in quality. An irresistibly joyous disc.

Toru Takemitsu
Japanese 1930-1996

Day Signal. From Heaven. Quotation of Dream[a]. How Slow the Wind. Twill by Twilight. Archipelago S. Dream/Window. Night Signal.
[a]**Paul Crossley,** [a]**Peter Serkin** *pfs*
London Sinfonietta / Oliver Knussen.
DG 20/21 453 495-2GH (71 minutes: DDD). Recorded 1996.   Ⓕ

'Dream', 'Slow', 'Twilight': these are the kind of words that give the key to Takemitsu's later style, and all the works on this disc were written between 1985 and 1993. The Debussy connection is easy to hear but, simply because of that, Takemitsu's own personal blend of the flowing and the disjunctive, against a harmonic background consistently more dense than Debussy's, stands out as one of the most significant late twentieth-century responses to an early twentieth-century master. Second-hand impressionism it is not. Oliver Knussen's performances are models of balance and clarity, with the music's purely colouristic qualities not excessively indulged. Also crucial here is the excellent quality of the DG recording, extremely well-designed for the way most of these pieces alternate so subtly between soloistic writing and fuller yet no less richly imagined textures. *Dream/Window* sets the tone for the kind of restrained yet eloquent ceremonies that can also be heard in the tribute to Feldman, *Twill by Twilight* and the two beautifully constructed works, *How Slow the Wind*, and *Quotation of Dream*. It is tempting to say that this is the best single CD of Takemitsu's music so far issued.

To the Edge of Dream. Folios – I, II and III. Toward the Sea III. Here, There and Everywhere.
What a Friend. Amours Perdues. Summertime. Vers, l'Arc-en-ciel, Palma.
John Williams *gtr* **Sebastian Bell** *alto fl* **Gareth Hulse** *ob d'amore*
London Sinfonietta / Esa-Pekka Salonen.
Sony Classical SK46720 (60 minutes: DDD).   Ⓕ

Toru Takemitsu is an original, refined composer and something of a latter-day impressionist, as
titles like *To the Edge of Dream* suggest. It may therefore come as a surprise to find him arranging
songs by Lennon and McCartney, Gershwin and others, for solo guitar. Yet these prove to have
attractive touches of the subtlety found in Takemitsu's own compositions, and they also provide
useful contrast to the more substantial works on this beguiling disc. *Folios*, the earliest composition
included, already reveal Takemitsu's musical catholicity in its reference to a Bach chorale. *Toward
the Sea* and *Vers, l'Arc-en-ciel, Palma* are both more expansive mood pieces, the former (for guitar
and alto flute) almost too reticent and hesitant beside the richer textures of the latter, which is
enhanced by the additional solo role given to the oboe d'amore as well as its beautifully laid out
orchestral accompaniment. *To the Edge of Dream* is in effect a guitar concerto, with a wider range
of mood and an even more developed role for the orchestra than *Vers, l'Arc-en-ciel, Palma*. It
provides a particularly satisfying focus for a sensitively performed and well recorded disc. Even if
we hear rather more of the guitar relative to the orchestra than we would in the concert hall, this is
not unreasonably artificial.

Thomas Tallis
British *c*1505-1585

Beati immaculati. Puer natus est nobis. Mass Puer natus est nobis. Viderunt omnes.
Dies sanctificatus. Celeste organum. Viderunt omnes. Suscipe quaeso Dominus.
Gaude gloriosa Dei mater.
Chapelle du Roi / Alistair Dixon.
Signum Records SIGCD003 (65 minutes: DDD). Texts and translations included.
Recorded 1997.   Ⓕ

The illuminating insert-notes by Nick Sandon place Mary's short reign within the bewilderingly
stormy context of the sixteenth century with a calm understanding that enables the listener to see
how this Latin music came to be written. Incidentally, the first piece was originally an English
setting of *Beatus vir*. Sandon says it falls naturally into place with its Latin text. But the verses
given in the booklet don't exactly correspond to what is being sung, which raises an unnecessary
question mark. Sandon's edition of the Proper Salisbury chants for the Third Mass of Christmas
are performed between the polyphonic items. Meticulously researched, they serve as a foil to the
sumptuous settings of the Ordinary. If only they had been sung with more solemnity and gusto,
omitting those irritating little bursts of volume on the high notes! All these chants, including the
sequence, would have sounded more authentic at a slower tempo with the occasional semi-metrical
dactyl: as it is, they comes across rather as a poor relation beside the magnificence of Tallis's seven-
part polyphony. The polyphonic singing is exemplary, the clarity of the individual parts and the
rhythmic interplay well under control. The singers enter into the spirit of the liturgical texts, in
particular in the third section of the *Agnus Dei*, with its manifold pleading repetitions of 'Dona
nobis pacem'. In the final motet, *Gaude gloriosa*, which presents major difficulties because of its
structure and length, their interpretation at times almost touches the visionary.

Lamentations of Jeremiah. Motets – Absterge Domine; Derelinquat impius; Mihi autem nimis;
O sacrum convivium; In jejunio et fletu; O salutaris hostia; In manus tuas; O nata lux de lumine.
Salve intemerata virgo.
The Tallis Scholars / Peter Phillips.
Gimell 454 925-2PH (68 minutes: DDD). Texts and translations included.   Ⓕ

This, the third volume of the survey by The Tallis Scholars of the music of the Tudor composer,
Thomas Tallis, contains the well-known *Lamentations*, eight motets, and the extended motet *Salve
intemerata virgo*. The *Lamentations* and motets are typical of the style of late Renaissance English
composers. The overall mood is one of considerable austerity and their simplicity is indicative of
the probability of their having been written for the private use of loyal Catholics rather than for
formal ritual. *Salve intemerata virgo,* on the other hand, looks back to the glories of the late
fifteenth century. In particular Tallis's use of the phrygian mode gives the work as a whole a strong
sense of the medieval. Despite this disparity of styles the Tallis Scholars acquit themselves, as
always, with great distinction. In the *Lamentations* and motets they achieve an appropriate sense of
intimacy, while in *Salve intermerata virgo* they rise fully to the challenges of one of the more

extended and demanding examples of Tudor choral composition. In addition the formidable challenges which this latter work sets for the conductor, such as the sense of pace, variation of dynamics, and overall architecture of the work, are all extremely well handled by Peter Phillips. The recording is very fine.

Lamentations of Jeremiah[a]. Absterge Domine[b]. In jejunio et fletu[a]. If ye love me[a]. O sacrum convivium[b]. Audivi vocem de caelo[a]. Derelinquat impius[a]. Salvator mundi, salva nos I[a]. Solfa-ing Song a 5[b]. In Nomine a 4 No. 1[b]. Benedictus[a]. Fond youth is a bubble[b]. Psalm Tunes for Archbishop Parker's Psalter[a] – No. 3, Why fum'th in sight; No. 8, Tallis's Canon. Like as the doleful dove[b]. When shall my sorrowful sighing slake[b]. Te lucis ante terminum I[a].
[a]**Theatre of Voices / Paul Hillier;** [b]**The King's Noyse / David Douglass.**
Harmonia Mundi HMU90 7154 (71 minutes: DDD). Recorded 1995.   Ⓕ

This is imaginative programme planning – atmospheric renaissance music performed by choral and instrumental forces in amiable juxtaposition rather than combination. The 16-strong Theatre of Voices, who are based at the University of California at Davis, sing throughout with a dark-browed *gravitas* and warmth of feeling that are thoroughly appropriate and give considerable pleasure. The secular music plus (surprisingly perhaps, but interestingly) *Absterge Domine* and *O sacrum convivium* are done by The King's Noyse, an expert renaissance violin consort, though they realize the sombre harmonic undertow so characteristic of Tallis less successfully than the singers. It ends with the tranquil evening office hymn, *Te lucis ante terminum* (complete with its alternating plainchant). Unlike most English groups in this repertoire, the Theatre of Voices do not use falsettists (authenticity may be on their side). Compared with The Tallis Scholars, the high-lying tenor parts here – often assigned by other groups to male altos – are perhaps not always impeccably blended, and the female voices sometimes have a slight flatward colouring. But, in compensation, this American group certainly taps a rich vein of pathos in this affecting music while remaining stylistically convincing, and Tallis's two most famous psalm-tunes are done with much relish. A distinctive, and on the whole, commendable issue, warmly recorded, and with a sumptuously produced CD booklet.

Spem in alium. Salvator mundi (I, II). Sancte Deus, sancte fortis. Gaude gloriosa Dei mater. Miserere nostri. Loquebantur variis linguis.
The Tallis Scholars / Peter Phillips.
Gimell 454 906-2PH (43 minutes: DDD). Recorded 1984.   Ⓕ 🆁🆁

For the 1985 quatercentenary of Tallis's death, Peter Phillips and The Tallis Scholars produced this version of *Spem in alium*; in many respects it is clearly the most successful ever recorded. Not only is the choir superb and the interpretation an intelligent one; this is also the only recording in which the eight choir choirs seem genuinely to sing from different positions in the stereo spread, a technical achievement that leads to some thrilling antiphonal exchanges. Above all, Phillips's reading is a confident and assertive one. The effect is more that of a plea than a prayer, and the overall shaping is most characterful. Inevitably there are problems of balance, both at the top of the texture (several of the trebles are given rather too much prominence) and in the middle, where in full sections the music of the inner voices sometimes blends too readily into rich chords rather than emerging as a complex web of counterpoint. But these are relatively small complaints to be made against what is frankly an outstanding achievement. This is a *Spem in alium* to be cherished. Phillips has paired *Spem in alium* with another of Tallis's largest and most celebrated works, *Gaude gloriosa Dei mater*. Here the texture is absolutely crystal, with verse sections sung by solo voices, and again the music has been paced with great care. It is certainly highly accomplished; and the same must be said of the readings of the five shorter pieces that complete the disc. What a fitting tribute to Tallis in his centenary year. No one who cares for Tudor choral music should be without it.

Tan Dun   Chinese/America 1957

Symphony 1997.
Yo-Yo Ma *vc*
Imperial Bells Ensemble of China; Yip's Children's Choir;
Hong Kong Philharmonic Orchestra / Tan Dun.
Sony Classical SK63368 (72 minutes: DDD). Text and translation included. Recorded 1997.   Ⓕ

Writing history into music is nothing new. The reunification of Hong Kong with China has inspired numerous commissions of one sort or another, Dun's *Symphony 1997* being among them. However, few will have utilized musical instruments that date back 2,400 years. The bianzhong is a family of tuned bells that, collectively, spans a five-octave range. They were discovered in an ancient tomb that as excavated as recently as 1978 and Dun's symphony gives them pride of place. In 'Heaven' (the symphony's first main episode), the bianzhong's grandeur 'rises from the earth's grave', though their presence is scarcely less imposing elsewhere. *Symphony 1997* opens and closes with a simple, touching 'Song of Peace'. It is cast in three sections ('Heaven', 'Earth' and 'Mankind'), the solo cello taking the role of commentator through wordless song. 'Water' (track 8) is a sub-division of 'Earth' and includes a demonstrative solo cadenza reminiscent of the finale from Kodály's Op. 8 Solo Sonata, whereas the following track has the orchestra slowly re-enter like some huge, sonorous community. Needless to say, Yo-Yo Ma's playing has great panache and intensity. 'Earth' represents Dun at his most characteristically inventive, but elsewhere dominant influences include Chinese popular music, various European late-romantics, Hindemith, Stravinsky and Varèse. There are also reminiscences of Beethoven (a quotation from 'Ode to Joy') and Puccini (an old love-song used in *Turandot*). *Symphony 1997* is a highly theatrical, lavishly scored montage, frequently rhythmic, richly atmospheric and with merging styles that reflect both China and the neighbour that has once again become family.

Marco Polo.
Thomas Young *ten* Polo; **Alexandra Montano** *mez* Marco; **Dong-Jian Gong** *bass* Kublai Khan; **Susan Botti** *sop* Water; **Shi-Zheng Chen** *sngr* Rustichello, Li Po; **Nina Warren** *sop* Sheherazada, Mahler, Queen; **Stephen Bryant** *bar* Dante, Shakespeare;
Cappella Amsterdam; Netherlands Radio Chamber Orchestra / Tan Dun.
Sony Classical S2K62912 (two discs: 100 minutes: DDD). Notes and text included.
Recorded live in 1996. Ⓕ

Mobility and re-creation are key concepts in Tan Dun's 'opera within an opera', although readers expecting gravy-train minimalism will be disappointed. Tan uses rhythm in the old-fashioned way, at key dramatic moments or in support of internal and external action. The 're-creative' element concerns opera directors and their potential responses 'to different elements of these tales [concerning Marco Polo] in creating the dramatic world of the opera'. The 'plot', which has been skilfully rendered verbal by Paul Griffiths (although words in this context have a strongly allusive function), concerns three journeys, one physical, the other two spiritual and musical, respectively. The components of the name 'Marco'/'Polo' are initially polarized to represent 'Marco the traveller' and 'Polo the memory' (their words are similarly divided), although the two do eventually join forces for a duet. Musically, *Marco Polo* is based on the interconnection of two very separate currents – Eastern operatic and instrumental traditions ('Opera 1'), and Western opera traditions with a blend of Eastern and Western instruments ('Opera 2'). The forceful opening (a recurring idea) is shared among Chinese percussion, whereas much of the string writing that follows curves in the style of Chinese popular music. The 'physical' aspect of the journey calls on medieval, Middle Eastern, Indian, Tibetan, Mongolian and Chinese influences. Mahler counts among the 'Western' components (Shakespeare and Dante are two others), quite literally on track 14 of the second disc where 'Der Trunkene im Frühling' from *Das Lied von der Erde* makes a cameo appearance. Tan Dun's instrumentalists and vocal team give virtuoso performances, but special mention should be made of Susan Botti and Thomas Young, although the most astonishing vocal contribution of all comes from Shi-Zheng Chen, whose range and agility are remarkable. *Marco Polo*'s instrumentation includes a substantial battery of percussion, various national instruments (pipa, sitar, Tibetan bells and so on), 'optional' old instruments, plus woodwind, brass and strings. Documentation is intriguing, albeit occasionally cryptic, and the recording is excellent.

Alexander Taneyev
Russian 1850-1918

String Quartets – No. 1 in G major, Op. 25; No. 2 in C major, Op. 28; No. 3 in A major, Op. 30.
Talan Quartet (Vladimir Talanov, Alexander Talanov *vns* Olga Bulakova *va* Alexei Steblov *vc*).
Olympia OCD543 (68 minutes: DDD). Recorded 1994. Ⓜ

Alexander Taneyev was yet another of the amateurs who contributed so much to Russian music, scribbling away secretly under his desk at the Imperial Chancellery, and even managing to write a couple of operas as well as orchestral and chamber music. In his three string quartets, at any rate, he reveals a fluent charm that owes most to the Russian lyrical tradition upheld by his namesake, among many others, and glorified by Tchaikovsky, but also taking account of the long Viennese inheritance. His qualities show best in a melodic charm and an ability to produce music in various manners well suited to the medium; he was also professional enough to write a decent fugue. If he does not really sustain the forms of the movements well, and can occasionally seem to get a bit caught up in processes that do not have sufficient musical motivation, there are some lively *Scherzos* and some lyrical meditations in the *Larghetto* movements of, in particular, Nos. 2 and 3. Collectors of Russian music will no doubt want to add these rarities to their shelves, and may find themselves taking them down to play for relaxation quite often; they will also find sympathetic and well-turned performances from the Talan Quartet.

Giuseppe Tartini
Italian 1692-1770

Violin Concertos – C major, D12; D minor, D45; E major, D51; B flat major, D117.
Gordan Nikolitch *vn*
Auvergne Orchestra / Arie van Beek.
Olympia OCD476 (59 minutes: DDD). Recorded 1996.

Tartini's violin concertos come and go in a wide variety of performing styles; Nikolitch and the Auvergne Orchestra are not practitioners of period instruments but they are at one in their approach to the music, disciplined in matters of expression, mainly clean and lively in their ensemble and appreciative of qualities which make Tartini's concertos the distinctive and rewarding pieces that they undoubtedly are. The expressive focal point of many of the concertos is the slow middle movement. There are some lyrical examples in this programme including, in the case of the C major Concerto (D12), not one slow movement, but two. This was a distinctive Tartini hallmark, the provision of alternative slow movements providing a poetic motto mainly drawn from Metastasio and Tasso, to establish the basic mood of the piece in question. Both of the slow movements of the C major work contain mottoes from Metastasio's *Demofoonte*, while the single slow movement of the E major Concerto (D51) has an unidentified one concerning a turtle-dove. There is plenty that is rewarding in this programme. Nikolitch is an athletic player who, nevertheless, turns his back on any opportunity for vacuous showmanship. This conjunction of soloist and orchestra under the direction of Arie van Beek is an effective one. A slight acidity of tone in the ripieno section of the E major Concerto is not sufficient to dampen one's spirits.

Violin Concertos – D major, D15; G major, D78; B flat major, D123; G major, D80; A minor, D115.
Gordan Nikolitch *vn*
Auvergne Orchestra / Arie van Beek.
Olympia OCD475 (76 minutes: DDD). Recorded 1996.

The Auvergne Orchestra is not a period instrument ensemble but it demonstrates a lively and playful rapport with late baroque music. The performances are full of vitality and caprice. Nikolitch is a sensitive player who is constantly aware of the underlying poetry in Tartini's music, above all in slow movements. In these Tartini sometimes appended poetic mottoes, often in secret code, mainly drawn from Tasso and Metastasio. These established the mood of the movement in question and, more and more, became the focal point of the work. Sometimes, too, Tartini would provide a concerto with an alternative slow movement, one of which he might regard as definitive. One such instance is included in this programme (in the G major Concerto, D80) where, happily, Nikolitch gives us both slow movements. The dance-like character of many of the outer movements is an attractive feature of Tartini's concertos. Bright and clear recorded sound.

Violin Sonatas – G minor, 'Devil's Trill', B:g5; A minor, B:a3. Variations on a Gavotte by Corelli, B:F11 – excerpts. Pastorale in A major, B:A16 (all arr. Manze).
Andrew Manze *vn*
Harmonia Mundi HMU90 7213 (69 minutes: DDD). Recorded 1997.

The romantic connotations of Tartini's Violin Sonata in G minor, the *Devil's Trill*, deriving from the composer's own account of an appearance by the devil in a dream, have contributed towards making it one of the great *morceaux favoris* of the nineteenth and twentieth centuries. It is, furthermore, just about the only remaining piece of baroque music where a piano accompaniment can still be countenanced without uniformly raised eyebrows. Some traditions do, indeed, die hard. But, of course, Tartini never intended anything of the kind; in fact, he probably never envisaged a keyboard continuo part at all, since none of his surviving autographs contains a figured bass for keyboard realization. They do, however, mostly include unfigured bass parts though, as Tartini himself remarked, he provided them, often as an afterthought, and more for reasons of convention than any other. Andrew Manze sees this as a justification for playing all the pieces in his programme without bass accompaniment. On the whole the experiment works well, since the expressive content and structural *puissance* of the music lies foremost in Tartini's melodic line. There are moments, however, where harmonic support from the bass is required, and at such times, above all in the *Devil's Trill* Sonata, Manze has had to introduce chords in the violin part to compensate for the absence of a cello. Manze's athletic technique, his musical sensibility and perhaps, too, his engaging sense of fun, ensure fascination and entertainment in equal measure. The 'diabolical' finale of the G minor Sonata has rhythmic poise, expressive delicacy and commendable virtuosity, and few admirers of this challenging piece will feel seriously compromised by the absence of a string bass. None will regret the passing of the piano in this context. A stimulating release, beautifully recorded, and rich in fantasy.

John Tavener

British 1944-

... Depart in Peace. My Gaze Is Ever Upon You. Tears of the Angels.
Patricia Rozario sop **Matthew Rooke** tambura
BT Scottish Ensemble / **Clio Gould** vn
Linn Records CKD085 (59 minutes: DDD). Recorded 1998. Ⓕ🄴

The most immediately striking work on this disc is the meditative, extremely beautiful ... *Depart in Peace*, for soprano, violin, tambura and strings. Dedicated to the memory of Tavener's father, it is a setting of the *Nunc dimittis*, interspersed with Alliuatic antiphons. The work follows a hypnotic sequence of repeating segments – an ecstatic string sequence with soprano (the first Alliuatic antiphon); the Song of Simeon (soprano, solo violin, tambura and cellos); an exquisitely beautiful, hymn-like sequence (the second Alliuatic antiphon) and finally an ecstatic Middle-Eastern sounding chant (the third Alliuatic antiphon). As the work progresses the antiphons lengthen on each repetition – the effect, over 25 minutes, is spellbinding and stunning. Tavener describes *My Gaze Is Ever Upon You* as 'a series of sixteen gazes, moments and ecstatic breaths, written in Trinitarian guise' for solo violin, with taped violin and string bass drone. Although less obviously immediate to the ear than ... *Depart in Peace*, it nevertheless weaves a magical spell over the listener, as does *Tears of the Angels* for solo violin and strings, which Tavener asks, at the head of the score, to be played 'at the extreme breaking point of tenderness'. All is performed with great authority, conviction and beauty, and Patricia Rozario's singing in … *Depart in Peace* is extraordinarily fine. A beautiful disc.

Akathist of Thanksgiving.
James Bowman, Timothy Wilson countertens **Martin Baker** org
Westminster Abbey Choir; BBC Singers; BBC Symphony Orchestra / **Martin Neary.**
Arc of Light SK64446 (78 minutes: DDD). Text and translation included. Recorded live in 1994. Ⓕ

With the success of the ecstatic *Protecting Veil*, it has perhaps been easy to forget just how rigorous and austere Tavener's music was only a few years previously. In 1986, his music had reached an extreme of 'inner silence'. *Eis Thanaton* was the work which broke through the barrier, moving painfully from darkness to light, but nevertheless the blaze of light of pieces such as the *Akathist* was hardly to be predicted. An *akathistos* is a long hymn used in the Orthodox rite, prescribed liturgically in the modern Russian use to be sung at Matins on the Saturday in the fifth week of Great Lent. The prototype *akathist* (others were written later) is addressed to the Mother of God and was written during the seventh century. The text Tavener sets is not liturgical, but was written strictly according to liturgical structure by Archpriest Gregory Petrov in a Siberian prison camp shortly before his death in the 1940s. The poetry is remarkable, for the quality and variety of its life-affirming imagery as much as for the fact that it was written at all in circumstances of such adversity. The danger in setting such poetry of course is that the music will be correspondingly diverse and lack structure. To an extent Tavener has avoided this by founding each section on a pedal note which furnishes the mode, though to claim this as a Byzantine procedure is extremely misleading since no Byzantine composer would ever use all eight tones of the *oktoechos* in a single work. The undeniable musical richness of each of the sections is therefore contained within each modal 'frame', but somehow this does not generate a real harmonic structure for the work.

Having said that, the score is a catalogue of riches. The dark-hued, quasi Bulgarian male-voice sections, the sparkling countertenor duets, the variety of the scoring and the deeply moving recurring 'Amin', and the unexpected quiet climax in the ninth *kontakion* sung by a solo countertenor, are all things of extraordinary power. They are very well sung indeed on this live recording (though the tenors have trouble maintaining control when in the higher registers and the basses are perhaps not quite convincingly Russian-sounding enough); in particular the trebles are beyond reproach, and the duets sung by Bowman and Wilson are wonderfully sensitive.

Akhmatova Requiem[a]. Six Russian Folksongs[b].
Phyllis Bryn-Julson, Elise Ross sops **John Shirley-Quirk** bar
[b]**Nash Ensemble;** [a]**BBC Symphony Orchestra** / **Gennadi Rozhdestvensky.**
BBC Radio Classics 15656 9197-2 (69 minutes: ADD). Text of Requiem included. Item marked [a] recorded live in 1981, [b]1979. Ⓑ

The *Akhmatova Requiem* is one of John Tavener's darkest, most austere large-scale works and is a setting of a cycle of poems by the Russian poet Anna Akhmatova written as a testimony to the horrors of the Stalinist regime. 'I have tried to convey the grim, numbing cold of the poetry' says Tavener, and it has to be said that the unremitting bleakness and sombre hues of this piece succeed in every respect. The *Requiem* is amongst Tavener's finest and important compositions. At times the bleak sound world of Shostakovich is brought to mind, but there are unmistakably Tavenerisms too – whooping horn figurations, tolling bells, long, sustained string passages and the largely intoned, declamatory and uncompromising vocal writing. The recording on this disc was taken from its Prom performance in 1981 and is an incredibly intense, exceptionally fine rendition under the baton of Gennadi Rozhdestvensky. The *Six Russian Folksongs* make a very attractive, lightweight companion to the *Akhmatova Requiem* and are effectively delivered here by the soprano Elise Ross and the Nash Ensemble. The settings, which include the famous 'Kalinka', are colourfully embellished with the sound of the domra – a Russian folk instrument similar in sound to the balalaika.

Eternity's Sunrise[a]. Funeral Canticle[b]. Petra: A Ritual Dream[c]. Sappho: Lyrical Fragments[d]. Song of the Angel[e].
[ade]**Patricia Rozario**, [d]**Julia Gooding** *sops* [bc]**George Mosley** *bar* [e]**Andrew Manze** *vn*
Academy of Ancient Music [bc]**Chorus and Orchestra / Paul Goodwin.**
Harmonia Mundi HMU90 7231 (65 minutes: DDD). Notes, texts and translations included. Recorded 1998. (F)

Once upon a time we dreamt of breaking down musical barriers, but nowadays we can happily recount how many have been broken. This particular venture reconciles genres and generations on various fronts – between father and son, religious denominations, old and new musical modes, poetry and liturgy, and old instruments newly employed. The title-piece, *Eternity's Sunrise*, was born in the wake of loss. Tavener's late father was its prompting inspiration, and Diana, Princess of Wales its dedicatee. The tonal structure is simple: earth is represented by the solo soprano, angels by hand bells and heaven by a modest instrumental ensemble. It is a deceptively simple work, and rendered especially appealing in this context by Harmonia Mundi's vivid recording. Tavener devotees will love it. The brief and warmly harmonized *Song of the Angel* for soprano and solo violin is set at a further distance but works well. *Petra: A Ritual Dream* calls on the Greek poet Giorgios Seferis to help reinvent the transcendent (represented, in terms of music, by violin harmonics). George Mosley intones the text, backed by a small chorus. Some of Tavener's word setting is fairly dramatic, and there is a folkloric slant to selected melodic lines. Tavener's *Sappho: Lyrical Fragments* (1981), the earliest work on the programme, is set for two sopranos with brief instrumental interludes between sections. Mysterious yet gripping, the *Fragments* owe something to Stravinsky (of, say, *Apollo*) whereas the last and longest piece on the disc – the *Funeral Canticle* for Tavener's father – cradles its texts between disparate styles, from plainchant to a reassuring variation on the Bach-style chorale. Could this be the son holding the father's hand, or vice versa? Whatever the unconscious subtext, *Funeral Canticle* is probably the most durable piece here.

Innocence. The Lamb. The Tiger. The Annunciation. Hymn to the Mother of God. Hymn for the Dormition of the Mother of God. Little Requiem for Father Malachy Lynch. Song for Athene.
Patricia Rozario *sop* **Leigh Nixon** *ten* **Graham Titus** *bass* **Alice Neary** *vc*
Charles Fullbrook *bells* **Martin Baker** *org*
Westminster Abbey Choir; English Chamber Orchestra / Martin Neary.
Sony Classical SK66613 (64 minutes: DDD). Texts included. Recorded 1994-95. (F)

This is recommended as a single disc to convince anyone of the mastery of John Tavener. As well as the superb new work, *Innocence*, specially written for Westminster Abbey – encapsulating in 25 minutes what many of his more expansive pieces have told us – we have a rich and rewarding selection of other shorter choral pieces. They include not just the established favourites like the two intense Blake settings, *The Lamb* and *The Tiger*, and the two hymns for the Mother of God – here more openly passionate than in previous recordings – but the bald and direct *Little Requiem for Father Malachy Lynch*, the sharply terraced *Annunciation* and the *Song for Athene* of two years ago, all among Tavener's most beautiful and touching inspirations. The theme of *Innocents* is Innocent Victims, which prompted Tavener to compose a ritual built on texts from varied sources, Christian, Jewish, Islamic and Hindu. This involves a range of elements, set physically apart from each other. So the main choir, soprano (representing Holy Wisdom) and cello are at the centre, with the baritone soloist on one side intoning prayers for mercy in the language of the Orthodox church, and with the tenor soloist entering behind with Islamic prayers, and far away the pure sounds of a boys' choir. The result is both moving and atmospheric, with the climax introducing one element after another in rich *crescendo*, to provide a resolution very comparable to Britten's in the *War Requiem*. Neary draws intensely committed singing from his choir, with the principal soloists, Patricia Rozario and Graham Titus, both excellent, as well as the tenor, Leigh Nixon, with Alice

Neary an expressive cellist. All the performances have a warmth of expressiveness which defies any idea of ecclesiastical detachment. The discs of shorter Tavener works from both The Sixteen (Collins, 6/94) and St George's Chapel Choir (Hyperion) offer excellent performances of the four shortest and best-known works, but they seem relatively cool next to Neary's, whose reading of the *Hymn to the Mother of God* is overwhelmingly powerful within its three-minute span. The recording vividly captures Westminster Abbey's acoustic with extreme dynamics used impressively to convey space and distance.

Svyati. Eternal Memory. Akhmatova Songs. The Hidden Treasure. Chant.
Patricia Rozario *sop* **Daniel Phillips, Krista Bennion Feeney** *vns*
Todd Phillips *va* **Steven Isserlis** *vc*
Kiev Chamber Choir / Mykola Gobdych; Moscow Virtuosi / Vladimir Spivakov.
RCA Victor Red Seal 09026 68761-2 (70 minutes: DDD). Text included. Recorded 1995.　　Ⓕ Ⓔ

'O Holy One', or 'Svyatiy', to quote its correct transliteration) sets a religious text as a backdrop to Isserlis's warm, soaring solo oration. *Eternal Memory* recalls the 1992 **Gramophone** Award-winning *The Protecting Veil*, albeit with its own very individual structure: it opens with a paradisiacal passage in the style of Byzantine chant (think of the *1812* Overture's first few minutes), then turns restless for a middle section that suggests Biber's 'Drunken Revellers' (in *Battalia*) gate-crashing a Shostakovich string quartet. The revellers eventually hobble off, the Byzantine mood returns and 'Paradise persists'. And if proof were needed that not all Tavener sounds the same, then the six stark but startling *Akhmatova Songs* would surely provide it. All are utterly unalike, varying in style from the wailing declamations of 'Dante', through the more comforting tones of 'Pushkin and Lermontov' to the concise mini-drama of 'The Muse'. Soprano Patricia Rozario is a vivid vocal actress who commands an astonishingly wide range. *The Hidden Treasure* Quartet is, in a sense, a cello solo with string trio accompaniment. The work follows a sort of bridge from the Paradise 'from which we have fallen' to the 'Paradise which Christ promised to the repentant thief'. The CD ends with palindromic *Chant* for unaccompanied cello, a four-minute encore from the eloquent soloist who more-or-less predominates throughout 70 arresting minutes. One hesitates to offer a blanket recommendation in an area where critical reaction is frequently polarized, but do at least try the *Akhmatova Songs*, music that could profitably sit alongside similarly compelling song-cycles by Mussorgsky and Shostakovich. RCA's sound quality is excellent throughout.

John Taverner

British *c*1490-1545

Hodie nobis caelorum Rex. Mater Christi sanctissima. Magnificat sexti toni. Nesciens mater. Quemadmodum a 6. Missa Mater Christi sanctissima. In nomine a 4.
Fretwork (Wendy Gillespie, Richard Campbell *treble viols* Susanna Pell, Julia Hodgson, Richard Boothby *bass viols* William Hunt *great bass viol*);
The Sixteen / Harry Christophers.
Hyperion CDA66639 (65 minutes: DDD). Texts and translations included. Recorded 1992.　　Ⓕ Ⓟ

The Sixteen offer an impressive account of the composer's five-part *Missa Mater Christi sanctissima*, based on his votive anthem of the same name. It is a lively and vigorous work, beautifully crafted, and this performance amply matches that craftsmanship. Harry Christophers attempts no liturgical reconstruction, concentrating instead upon sheer musical quality. Three female sopranos replace the boy trebles. The music is all pitched up a tone, which has the effect of adding brilliance to every climax. He demonstrates the surprisingly good acoustic of St Jude's in Hampstead – an acoustic of space and definition, ideal for the interweaving of the strands of early Tudor polyphony; indeed, clarity and a sense of space are hallmarks of the recording. The supporting programme of the Christmas responsory, *Hodie*, the votive anthem *Mater Christi* and a four-part *Magnificat* is completed – unexpectedly, but most delightfully – by two pieces for viols.

Missa Gloria tibi Trinitas. Kyrie, 'Leroy'. Dum transisset Sabbatum I. Mass a 4, 'Western Wynde'.
The Tallis Scholars / Peter Phillips.
Gimell 454 995-2PH (79 minutes: DDD). Texts and translations included. Recorded 1984-93.　　Ⓕ

This disc shows a striking panorama of The Tallis Scholars over the past ten years. Most of this comes from a CD of 1986. But by adding their more recent recording of the *Western Wynde* Mass they have created an anthology containing some of Taverner's most remarkable music: the two most famous Masses alongside two of his loveliest smaller works. For the *Western Wynde* Mass The Tallis Scholars present themselves at their most mandarin: everything beautifully in place, gentle, soothing, immaculate. The marvellous range of inventive lines that Taverner weaves around this

trite little melody is given full scope to blossom and grow. Nothing is hurried or allowed to stand
out too much. This is in striking contrast to their much earlier approach to the Mass *Gloria tibi
Trinitas*: here Peter Phillips takes the music very much by the scruff of the neck, changing pace and
textures to articulate the massively complex six-voice textures. This is a tremendously exciting
performance because it so often throws caution to the winds. In other words, some listeners may
find the *Western Wynde* a touch bland and *Gloria tibi Trinitas* a touch rough, but it makes for an
exciting disc. And nobody could possibly resist the still beauty they give to the *Leroy Kyrie*.

Missa Sancti Wilhelmi. Motets – O Wilhelme, pastor bone; Dum transisset Sabbatum;
Ex eius tumba.
The Sixteen / Harry Christophers.
Hyperion CDA66427 (52 minutes: DDD). Texts and translations included. Recorded 1990.   Ⓕ

The *Missa Sancti Wilhelmi* is not one of Taverner's best known works, but there is no reason why
this should be the case. Though it does not have the sometimes rather wild melodic beauty of the
six-voice Masses, it is nevertheless an impressive work in a more modern imitative style, in keeping
with its model *O Wilhelme, pastor bone*. The Sixteen perform with their customary clarity and
precision, and convey enthusiasm even in the somewhat syllabic *Gloria* and *Credo* movements of the
Mass, something which is not always easy to do. While both the 'Wilhelm' works and *Dum
transisset Sabbatum* are among Taverner's later works, there is no doubt at all that *Ex eius tumba* is
one of the earliest. It is firmly late medieval in style, and the intricate tracery of its construction, so
well captured here by The Sixteen, makes a thought-provoking contrast to the pieces in a more
'continental' imitative style. At 15 minutes this is a substantial composition, and one can only be
surprised that it is so little-known: perhaps the large amount of chant which forms an integral part
of the work has discouraged performers. *Dum transisset Sabbatum* is, however, the high point of the
disc, and if The Sixteen do not quite attain the ecstatic heights achieved in the recording by The
Tallis Scholars (reviewed above), neither do they fail to rise to Taverner's inspiration.

Pyotr Ill'yich Tchaikovsky   Russian 1840-1893

Piano Concertos – No. 1 in B flat minor; No. 2 in G major, Op. 44;
No. 3 in E flat major, Op. 75.

Piano Concerto No. 1ª. The Nutcracker – Suite, Op. 71a (arr. Economou)ᵇ.
Martha Argerich, ᵇNicolas Economou *pfs*
ªBerlin Philharmonic Orchestra / Claudio Abbado.
DG 449 816-2GH (53 minutes: DDD). Item marked ª recorded live in 1994.   Ⓕ Ⓔ 𝗥𝗥

Tchaikovsky's First Concerto has already appeared twice on disc from Martha Argerich in
complementary performances: live and helter-skelter on Philips with Kondrashin (reviewed under
Rachmaninov; refer to the Index), studio and magisterial with Dutoit on DG. Now, finely recorded,
here is a third, live recording with the Berlin Philharmonic and Claudio Abbado surpassing even
those earlier and legendary performances. Argerich has never sounded on better terms with the
piano, more virtuoso yet engagingly human. Lyrical and insinuating, to a degree her performance
seems to be made of the tumultuous elements themselves, of fire and ice, rain and sunshine. The
Russians may claim this concerto for themselves, but even they will surely listen in disbelief, awed
and – dare one say it – a trifle piqued. Listen to Argerich's *Allegro con spirito*, as the concerto gets
under way, where her darting *crescendos* and *diminuendos* make the triplet rhythm speak with the
rarest vitality and caprice. Her nervous reaching out towards further pianistic frays in the
heart-easing second subject is pure Argerich and so are the octave storms in both the first and third
movements that will have everyone, particularly her partners, tightening their seat belts. The
cadenza is spun off with a hypnotic brilliance, the central *Prestissimo* from the *Andantino* becomes a
true 'scherzo of fireflies', and the finale seems to dance off the page; a far cry from more emphatic
Ukranian point-making and brutality. For encores DG have reissued Argerich's 1983 performance
of *The Nutcracker* where she is partnered by Nicolas Economou in his own arrangement, a marvel
of scintillating pianistic prowess, imagination and finesse.

Violin Concerto in D major, Op. 35.

Piano Concertosª Nos. 1-3. Violin Concertoᵇ.
Kyung-Wha Chung *vn* **Victoria Postnikova** *pf*
ªVienna Symphony Orchestra / Gennadi Rozhdestvensky;
ᵇMontreal Symphony Orchestra / Charles Dutoit.
Double Decca 448 107-2DF2 (two discs: 142 minutes: DDD). Recorded 1981-82.   Ⓜ

Our top recommendation in this work is Kyung-Wha Chung's 1970 version on Decca with André Previn – see the review under Sibelius. If your main priorities in Tchaikovsky concertos are visceral excitement, barnstorming virtuosity and nifty tempos, then Chung's later version is probably not the set for you. Tempos here are generally broad, and although there is no lack of pianistic thunder – Victoria Postnikova commands a handsome tone – the interpretative accent falls securely beneath the music's surface. The First Concerto is revealing in the sense that dialogue between soloist and orchestra is particularly sensitive; listen, for example, to the delicately voiced woodwinds at 6'38" (in the first movement), to Postnikova's subsequent response and, most especially, to the pianist's free yet nimble handling of the second movement's treacherous *valse-prestissimo* (4'05"). As Tchaikovsky Firsts go, this is among the most searching, the most personal and certainly the most individual available, though one can already hear a loud opposition: '*too* slow, *too* mannered, *too* indulgent, *too* soft-grained, orchestrally'.

Again, in the Second and Third Concertos Postnikova plumbs the depths. Her handling of Tchaikovsky's epic cadenzas is second to none – starting at 1'55" into the Second Concerto's first movement, then (most notably) between 13'26" and 19'13", where the solo writing is so massive in scale that you temporarily forget the mute presence of an orchestra. Rozhdestvensky views Tchaikovsky's orchestral architecture with a fine sense of perspective. This is *real* interpretation and presents a powerful case for a much maligned work (torso though it is). True, there is still room for critical controversy (the Second Concerto's first movement is hardly *Allegro brillante*), but Postnikova and Rozhdestvensky have so much to say about the music. Decca also offers a poised and elegantly phrased account of the Tchaikovsky Violin Concerto, where a rather edgy-sounding Kyung-Wha Chung is offered blandly 'regular' support by the Montreal Symphony Orchestra under Dutoit. Not a world-beater by any means, but a sensible makeweight, very well recorded. As indeed is the rest of the set, although the Vienna Symphony strings will strike some as rather thin in tone. An altogether riveting reissue and a genuine bargain as well.

Tchaikovsky Violin Concerto.
Brahms (arr. Joachim) Hungarian Dances – No. 1 in G minor; No. 2 in D minor; No. 4 in B minor; No. 7 in A major.
Sarah Chang *vn* **Jonathan Feldman** *pf*
London Symphony Orchestra / Sir Colin Davis.
EMI CDC7 54753-2 (49 minutes: DDD). Recorded 1992-93. Ⓕ

The range of dynamic truthfulness conveyed in Sarah Chang's performance, helped by a clear, full, naturally-balanced recording, brings not just momentary delight in individual phrases but cumulative gain, in this reading which so strongly hangs together. Not only does Chang play with exceptionally pure tone, avoiding heavy coloration, but her individual artistry does not demand the wayward pulling-about often found in this work. In that she is enormously helped by the fresh, bright and dramatic accompaniment provided by the LSO under Sir Colin Davis. In the outer movements Chang conveys wit along with the power and poetry, and the intonation is immaculate. Brahms's *Hungarian Dances* are delectable, marked by the sort of naughty pointing of phrase and rhythm that tickles one's musical funny-bone just as the playing of Kreisler always did. Here is a young artist who really does live up to the claims of the publicists. (See also the review in the Collections section – 'Sir Georg Solti – A Celebration' which includes Maxim Vengerov's stunning live performance of the Violin Concerto, with the London Philharmonic Orchestra under Mstislav Rostropovich.)

Tchaikovsky 1812 Overture, Op. 49[a]. Capriccio italien, Op. 45[b].
Beethoven Wellingtons Sieg, Op. 91, 'Die Schlacht bei Vittoria'[c].
[a]**University of Minnesota Brass Band;** [ab]**Minneapolis Symphony Orchestra;**
[c]**London Symphony Orchestra / Antál Dorati.**
Mercury Living Presence 434 360-2MM (66 minutes: ADD). Also includes commentary by Deems Taylor on the making of the recordings. Recorded 1955-60. Ⓜ Ⓗ ⓇⓇ

Both battle pieces incorporate cannon fire recorded at West Point, with *Wellington's Victory* adding antiphonal muskets and *1812*, the University of Minnesota Brass Band and the bells of the Laura Spelman Rockefeller carillon. In a recorded commentary on the *1812* sessions, Deems Taylor explains how, prior to 'battle', roads were blocked and an ambulance crew put on standby. The actual weapons used were chosen both for their historical authenticity (period instruments of destruction) and their sonic impact, the latter proving formidable even today. In fact, the crackle and thunder of *Wellington's Victory* could easily carry a DDD endorsement; perhaps we should, for the occasion, invent a legend of Daring, Deafening and potentially Deadly. Dorati's conducting is brisk, incisive and appropriately dramatic. *1812* in particular (Dorati's second Minneapolis recording of the piece for Mercury) suggests a rare spontaneity, with a fiery account of the main 'conflict' and a tub-thumping peroration where bells, band, guns and orchestra conspire to produce one of the most riotous key-clashes in gramophone history. *Capriccio italien* was recorded some three years earlier (1955, would you believe) and sounds virtually as impressive. Again, the approach is crisp and balletic, whereas the 1960 LSO Beethoven recording triumphs by dint of its energy and orchestral discipline. As 'fun' CDs go, this must surely be one of the best – provided you can divorce Mercury's aural militia from the terrifying spectre of real conflict (such as we see almost daily via the media). Wilma Cozart Fine has masterminded an astonishingly effective refurbishment while the documentation – both written and recorded – is extremely comprehensive.

1812 Overture. Romeo and Juliet – Fantasy Overture. Marche slave, Op. 31. Francesca da Rimini, Op. 32.
Royal Liverpool Philharmonic Orchestra / Sian Edwards.
EMI Eminence CD-EMX2152 (66 minutes: DDD).   Ⓜ

It is an extraordinary achievement that the young British conductor, Sian Edwards, should have made her recording début with a Tchaikovsky programme of such distinction. She immediately achieves a splendid artistic partnership with the Royal Liverpool Philharmonic Orchestra, whose playing is so full of vitality, and whether in *1812* with its vigour and flair, its cluster of lyrical folk melodies, and a spectacular finale with thundering canon, or in *Marche slave*, resplendently patriotic, in a uniquely Russian way, together they bring the music tingling to life in every bar. *Romeo and Juliet*, on the other hand, needs a finely judged balance between the ardour and moonlight of the love music, the vibrant conflict of the battle, and the tragedy of the final denouement, which is uncannily well managed. Most intractable interpretatively is *Francesca da Rimini*, with its spectacularly horrifying picture of Dante's inferno which the composer uses to frame the central sequence depicting the lovers, Francesca and Paolo, and the doom-laden atmosphere which surrounds their intense mutual passion. Edwards's grip on this powerfully evocative sequence of events is unerringly sure, and she takes the orchestra through the narrative as only an instinctive Tchaikovskian could. The work opens with an unforgettable sense of nemesis and ends with a truly thrilling picture of the whirlwinds of Hell, into which the lovers are cast, still in their final passionate embrace. All in all this is one of the best Tchaikovsky discs in the mid-price catalogue. The recording is excellent.

Francesca da Rimini, Op. 32. Hamlet – Fantasy Overture, Op. 67.
New York Stadium Orchestra / Leopold Stokowski.
dell'Arte CDDA9006 (43 minutes: ADD). Recorded 1958.   Ⓕ 🄷

A good record is always a good record, and this comment applies even more to a great record. Stokowski's inspired performance of *Hamlet* is far, far superior to any other recorded version. *Francesca* is nearly as fine and generates enormous tension at the sequence just before the lovers are discovered where their passion is encompassed in polyphonic string textures of the greatest intensity. Then, after the dramatic moment of their death, they are consigned to the whirlwinds of Dante's Inferno, which rage frenziedly until the riveting final climax, where the gong is not allowed to drown the nemesis of bold orchestral dissonances at the last few bars. Stokowski's reading is equally memorable for the beguiling wind solos in the romantic middle section – depicting the idyll of the lovers – shaped with characteristic magic. *Hamlet* is sensational. It is also even better recorded than *Francesca* and the sonority of the lower strings is particularly telling at the electrifying opening, while at the big climax the weight of the trombones and tuba is splendidly caught. But perhaps the most spectacular moment is the forboding march-like sequence, dominated by the side-drum, which is sinisterly dramatic each time it appears: this device anticipates Shostakovich at the climax of the first movement of the Fifth Symphony and the emotional character of the playing is very Russian in its fervour. The desolation of mood of the coda is intensely moving, with a power of melancholy to equal that at the close of the *Pathétique* Symphony.

Hamlet does not have a love theme to match *Romeo and Juliet*, but its equivalent possesses a unique colour when it appears in the woodwind. Ophelia's melody on the oboe is utterly poignant and when it returns there is a rustling in the strings which subtly creates a sense of uneasiness. If you are wondering about the identity of the New York Stadium Orchestra, Bert Whyte, the brilliant engineer of this recording, and also one of the founders of the Everest label, has affirmed that it is the New York Philharmonic under a pseudonym. This was the pre-Bernstein era and the ensemble isn't always immaculate, but the tremendous commitment of the playing more than compensates. It is not clear whether Bryan Crimp's remastered version (which dell'Arte issued on a 12-inch 45rpm disc) is used for the CD, but certainly the sound is cleaner than originally, if perhaps a little drier. During the closing years of his life Stokowski said, 'When I get to Heaven I shall shake Tchaikovsky by the hand and thank him for all the wonderful music he has given us'.

Manfred Symphony, Op. 58. The Tempest, Op. 18.
Russian National Orchestra / Mikhail Pletnev.
DG 439 891-2GH (76 minutes: DDD). Recorded 1993.　　　　　　　　　Ⓕ **E**

There are no cheap thrills in Pletnev's *Manfred*. Percussion and brass are very carefully modulated, their brilliance and power reserved quite noticeably for what Pletnev sees as the few crucial climactic passages in the outer movements. Timpani in particular provide support rather than make a show – it is the lower strings that course through Manfred's outburst in the second movement (from 5'50"), not the almost standard spurious timpani swells. It is the strong, dark woodwind, not the more usual stuttering horns, that you initially hear in the first movement's concluding *Andante con duolo* (from 13'09"). The deep satisfaction to be had from this account comes from the superlative strings, and from Pletnev's pacing which, more often than any of the listed additional recommendations takes notice of Tchaikovsky's tempo indications, most obviously in the properly flowing third movement's pastoral, and in the successful bonding of the finale's episodic structure (the magniloquent Muti's Achilles' heel). More eccentric is Pletnev's drop in tempo for those rising unison scales on strings at the start of the bacchanale (from 0'18"), but it is less troubling than Toscanini's and particularly Jansons's speeding up for those hammering chords before Astarte returns; and, mercifully, there are none of the cuts made by Toscanini. *The Tempest*, a generous coupling, brings much the same priorities and equal rewards – no more need be said, except to observe that the horns receive a better deal from the balance than in the symphony. As to the recording generally, timpani is probably less focused than Pletnev would have wanted; in all other respects, the sound does full justice to the riches of his orchestra and the seriousness of his intent.

The Nutcracker, Op. 71.

The Nutcracker[a]. Queen of Spades – Duet of Daphnis and Chloë[b].
[b]**Cathryn Pope** *sop* [b]**Sarah Walker** *mez*
[a]**Tiffin Boys' School Choir; London Symphony Orchestra / Sir Charles Mackerras.**
Telarc CD80137 (two discs: 88 minutes). Recorded 1986.　　　　　　　Ⓕ **RR**

This is Tchaikovsky's most rewarding ballet score, and for those readers who like a fairly clear decision in such matters, this must be first choice, if only just. Indeed, it is the marvellous sound of the Telarc CDs that clinches the matter. The recording engineer is the illustrious Jack Renner who masterminded all the early digital Cleveland CDs. Here he has the advantage of the acoustics of Watford Town Hall and his microphone placing is very perceptive. The set has the subtle extra resonance of a concert hall, which adds a little glamour to the violins and a glowing extra warmth to the middle and lower range. Yet there is no blurring and no 'empty-hall' feeling – the reverberation sounds just right. Now to the performance. Mackerras is renowned for the vitality of his conducting and he takes the 'Miniature Overture' quite fast. But the playing is deliciously neat and the sweetness of the recorded violin timbre adds a little mellowness. Throughout the party scene Mackerras presses, yet he is never inflexible and has a fine flair for detail. From scene 5 onwards the action becomes quite riveting; the recording opens up its spectacularly wide dynamic range, and we have a taste of what is to come when 'The magic spell begins', the Christmas tree grows to a great orchestral climax and we are made aware of how Tchaikovsky adds to the depth and sonority with his writing for the tuba (this is especially striking again in the gloriously sumptuous sound for the climax of the great Act 2 *pas de deux*). Mackerras creates an *1812*-like excitement in 'The Battle between the Nutcracker and the Mouse King' and Jack Renner interpolates some real canon and gunshots to add to the sense of spectacle. But it is done judiciously and good-humouredly, for this is a battle and the effect stays in perspective. ('Caution!' says a note on the sleeve and even notes the location of the two canon shots in case 'damage could result to speakers or other components'. But, frankly, that is hardly likely.)

One of the key moments in the ballet is Tchaikovsky's thrilling climbing melody when Clara and Prince travel through the pine forest to the Prince's fairy kingdom, and Mackerras gives this a glorious serenity helped by the glowing sound and the fine LSO playing. The LSO is on top form in the 'Divertissement' that forms the main part of Act 2. Mackerras's approach is sparkling rather than elegant. Yet in the choral 'Waltz of the Snowflakes' Mackerras's spry lightness is very pleasurable, the chorus timbre is warm and the *accelerando* at the end is convincing. The gorgeously expansive recording is most impressive when Tchaikovsky lets himself go, and no other nineteenth-century composer could score a romantic orchestral climax better than he. As an appendix we are offered the 'Duet of Daphnis and Chloë,' a charming vignette from *The Queen of Spades*. It is nicely sung and the recording is distanced. The Telarc notes are splendid, a model of their kind, with a long discussion on the ballet, plus a detailed synopsis and then more information about the artists involved.

The Nutcracker.
Kirov Opera Chorus and Orchestra / Valery Gergiev.
Philips 462 114-2PH (81 minutes: DDD). Recorded 1998.   Ⓕ

This is *The Nutcracker* as a short ride in a fast machine. You may find that your most positive
responses to this *Nutcracker* will come after a higher than usual intake of caffeine. Obviously, a fair
measure of Tchaikovsky's score is meant to be continuous, but the Kirov's animated action never
lets up for a moment. It may have something to do with squeezing it on to a single disc (no pauses
for breath, even between the First and Second Acts); and under the circumstances, it is not
surprising that Gergiev doesn't want to relax the momentum with the usual repeat of the leisurely
'Grandfather Dance'. But this is probably how he conducts *The Nutcracker* at the Kirov (the
recording was, in fact, made in Baden-Baden), and the elegance with which he moves from loud or
fast sections of the score to quieter or slower ones – for example, the Arabian dance starting with a
diminuendo – speak of ease gained from experience.

What we don't have here is a *Nutcracker* to enhance the ambience of a room lit by Christmas tree
lights and a log fire. What we do have, however, is a realization that makes it clear why Stravinsky so
loved the Tchaikovsky ballets. If there is an ostinato working away in the accompaniment, Gergiev
gives it prominence and energy (the swift tempos help, of course). And credit for the very high yield
of unusual features of this most inventively scored of all Tchaikovsky's ballets should probably be
evenly divided between Gergiev, the specific timbres of the orchestra and the very immediate sound.
When not caught up in the colourful exuberance of it all, one may stop to notice that the image
lacks depth, the violins are a little thin in upper regions, and the brass occasionally play-out with
the familiar Russian welly, wobble and weather (moderate amounts). Equally, the ear may be briefly
diverted by minor imprecisions and the odd extraneous noise. But has there ever been a *Nutcracker*
so captured apparently 'on the wing', or, for that matter, so exciting?

The Nutcracker. The Sleeping Beauty – Aurora's Wedding.
Montreal Symphony Orchestra / Charles Dutoit.
Decca 440 477-2DH2 (two discs: 135 minutes: DDD). Recorded 1992.   Ⓕ

Many of the favourite characteristic dances seem freshly minted, notably the 'Dance of the
Sugar-plum Fairy', with its deliciously liquid celesta, and the perky 'Chinese Dance'. The 'Waltz of
the Snowflakes' (Act 1) with the children's chorus also has great charm. The transparency of the
recorded sound, which helps to make all this possible, is immediately noticeable in the delightful
gossamer string textures of the 'Miniature Overture'. But the big Act 2 *Adagio*, too, is exceptionally
satisfying, its histrionics conveyed with passionate flair, yet without hysterical rhetoric at the
excitingly grand climax. The recording is extremely vivid: bright but without glare, and the balance
between detail, weight and hall resonance seems exactly right. 'Aurora's Wedding' is the very much
truncated version of *The Sleeping Beauty* which Diaghilev adopted in repertory after his
extravagant London production of the complete ballet in 1921 nearly bankrupted him. The music,
after introducing both Carabosse and the Lilac Fairy, passes on to the christening, includes the
hunting scene in Act 2, where the Prince has a vision of his sleeping princess, then moves on to the
happy ending and the dances which form the highlight of the last act.

Serenade in C major, Op. 48. Souvenir de Florence, Op. 70.
Vienna Chamber Orchestra / Philippe Entremont.
Naxos 8 550404 (65 minutes: DDD). Recorded 1990.   Ⓢ

This is one of the many CDs now on the market that dispel the myth once and for all that only full-
price recordings contain really outstanding performances. The Naxos label is just about as 'bargain'
as you can get, and here they have given us superlative performances of two of Tchaikovsky's most
endearing works. The Serenade in C contains a wealth of memorable and haunting music,
beautifully and inventively scored and guaranteed to bring immense pleasure and delight to those
dipping their toes in to the world of classical music for the first time. Philippe Entremont and the
Vienna Chamber Orchestra give a marvellously polished and finely poised performance full of
warmth, affection and high spirits, and the famous second movement Waltz in particular is played
with much elegance and grace. The *Souvenir de Florence*, originally written for string sextet,
makes a welcome appearance here in Tchaikovsky's own arrangement for string orchestra. This
is a delightfully sunny performance, full of suavity, exuberance and romantic dash, but always
alert to the many subtleties of Tchaikovsky's skilful and intricate part-writing. The *Adagio
cantabile* is particularly notable for some extremely fine and poetic solo playing from the violin
and cello principals of the VPO. The beautifully spacious recording does ample justice to the
performances.

The Sleeping Beauty, Op. 66.

The Sleeping Beauty.
Czecho-Slovak State Philharmonic Orchestra / Andrew Mongrelia.
Naxos 8 550490/92 (three discs: 174 minutes: DDD). Recorded 1991. ⓢ

Andrew Mongrelia is clearly a ballet conductor to his fingertips. His account of *The Sleeping Beauty* is not only dramatic, when called for, but graceful and full of that affectionate warmth and detail which readily conjure up the stage imagery. Moreover, the House of Arts in Košice seems to have just the right acoustics for this work. If the sound is too brilliant the louder passages of Tchaikovsky's score can easily hector the ear; if the effect is too mellow, the result can become bland. Neither happens here – the ear is seduced throughout and Mongrelia leads the listener on from number to number with an easy spontaneity. The woodwind playing is delightful (try track 9 with its 'singing canaries' – so like Delibes in its scoring). At the end of Act 1 the Lilac Fairy's tune is given a spacious, *frisson*-creating apotheosis. The alert Introduction to Acts 2 and 3 bring crisp brass and busy strings on the one hand, arresting hunting horns on the other, and what sparkling zest there is in the strings for the following 'Blind-man's buff' sequence, while the famous Act 2 Waltz has splendid rhythmic lift. Act 3 is, of course, essentially a great extended *Divertissement*, with Tchaikovsky's imagination working at full stretch through some two dozen characterful dance numbers of every conceivable balletic flavour, are all played here with fine style. Quite irrespective of price, this vies with Gergiev as a first choice among current recordings of the score and you get about two-and-a-half hours of music for about the cost of one full-price CD. The value is even more remarkable when the excellent notes clearly relate the ballet's action to each of the 65 separate cues.

The Sleeping Beauty.
Kirov Theatre Orchestra / Valery Gergiev.
Philips 434 922-2PH3 (three discs: 164 minutes: DDD). Recorded 1992. Ⓕ

Many authorities regard this as Tchaikovsky's finest ballet score and, indeed, one of the greatest ballet scores of all time. It contains many wonderful things: the Waltz from Act One includes some wonderfully arching phrasing that soars with tremendous passion, while the 'Panorama' of Act 2 is one of the composer's finest melodic ideas. The 'Pas de six' of Act 1 and the contrasted Fairy dances of Act 3 bring the same almost Mozartian grace (combined with Tchaikovsky's own very special feeling for orchestral colour) that he displays in the *Nutcracker* characteristic dances, which turn simple ballet vignettes into great art. Valery Gergiev, the conductor of the Kirov Theatre Orchestra of St Petersburg is at home in this score. He secures splendidly alive and sympathetic playing from his orchestra and the Philips recording is full and sumptuous, with a rich theatrical atmosphere. Tchaikovsky's big climaxes expand properly, the strings are full and natural and the woodwind colours glow.

Suite No. 2, Op. 53. The Tempest.
Detroit Symphony Orchestra / Neeme Järvi.
Chandos CHAN9454 (64 minutes: DDD). Recorded 1994-95. Ⓕ

Tchaikovsky's elusive blend of instrumental precision and free-flowing thematic fantasy in the Second Suite meets its match in the Detroit/Järvi partnership: the conductor's imagination works alongside the lean, clean Detroit sound with interesting results. The strings are not always the ideal: the lush chordings and central fugal energy of the opening movement, 'Jeu de sons', cry out for a richer, Russian tone. But the semiquaver patter is beautifully done, the lower lines clear and personable. Keen articulation and driving force go hand-in-glove as Järvi prepares for the entry of the four accordions in the virile 'Rondo-Burlesque', sweeping on to the folk-song of the central section with characteristic aplomb. And yes, the accordions are here: 'the engagement of these instruments is not indispensible ... but the composer believes that their sonority is apt to increase the effectiveness', it says in the score. It is in the Schumannesque phrases and the subtly shifting moods of the most poetic movement, 'Rêves d'enfant', that Järvi really comes into his own; the short-lived, other-worldly radiance at the heart of the movement seems more than ever like a preliminary study for the transformation scenes of *The Nutcracker*, just as the woodwind choruses throughout the work look forward to that and *Sleeping Beauty*.

The magical haze surrounding Prospero's island in *The Tempest* doesn't quite come off; here it's Pletnev (reviewed on page 984) who surprises us with the true magician's touch, but then his Russian horns, and later his trumpeter, cast their incantations more impressively. Järvi is no more successful than any other conductor in stitching together Tchaikovsky's strong impressions of the play, though a little more forward movement in the love-music might have helped.

Swan Lake, Op. 20.

Swan Lake.
Montreal Symphony Orchestra / Charles Dutoit.
Decca 436 212-2DH2 (two discs: 154 minutes: DDD). Recorded 1991.　　Ⓕ 🆁🆁

No one wrote more beautiful and danceable ballet music than Tchaikovsky, and this account of *Swan Lake* is a delight throughout. This is not only because of the quality of the music, which is here played including additions the composer made after the première, but also thanks to the richly idiomatic playing of Charles Dutoit and his Montreal orchestra in the superb and celebrated location of St Eustache's Church in that city. Maybe some conductors have made the music even more earthily Russian, but it is worth remembering that the Russian ballet tradition in Tchaikovsky's time was chiefly French and that the most influential early production of this ballet, in 1895, was choreographed by the Frenchman Marius Petipa. Indeed, the symbiosis of French and Russian elements in this music (and story) is one of its great strengths, the refinement of the one being superbly allied to the vigour of the other, notably in such music as the 'Russian Dance' with its expressive violin solo. This is a profoundly romantic reading of the score, and the great set pieces such as the Waltz in Act 1 and the marvellous scene of the swans on a moonlit lake that opens Act 2 are wonderfully evocative; yet they do not for that reason overshadow the other music, which supports and strengthens them as gentler hills and valleys might surround and enhance magnificent, awe-inspiring peaks, the one being indispensable to the other. You do not have to be a ballet *aficionado* to fall under the spell of this wonderful music, which here receives a performance that combines romantic passion with an aristocratic refinement and is glowingly recorded.

Swan Lake.
Philadelphia Orchestra / Wolfgang Sawallisch.
EMI CDS5 55277-2 (two discs: 159 minutes: DDD). Recorded 1993-94.　　Ⓕ

Full marks to EMI for capacity-filled discs with the minimum necessary missing (two short double bar line repeats in Act 3's early stages). Forest, lake, moonlight and melancholy; these are the scenes that find Sawallisch in his element. The superb solo oboe is free to float his sad song in the swan scene (end of Act 1 and beginning and end of Act 2; how marvellous to hear the slurred *staccato* so well taken); the tempo is broad, the perspective deep, and Sawallisch's control of dynamics and his fluid pace (different in all three scenes) is masterly. Also impressive is the ballet's storm-tossed finale, less elemental at the start than Dutoit, but the moment these strings ride that storm, you know you are in Philadelphia. At this point, Sawallisch loosens the reins on his elsewhere tightly controlled brass (Dutoit's use of the brass is more judiciously opportunist). In general, Sawallisch uses a narrow range of tempos: Tchaikovsky's slower dances, such as the 'Intrada' to the Act 1 'Pas de trois', can initially seem surprisingly brisk, and the difference between the *Andante* and the *Allegro* in the second part of the succeeding 'Pas de deux' is small. Arguably, this moderation of speed brings an appreciable continuity to the musical scheme of things, and is a welcome corrective to the short-term, maximum contrast approach. The symphonic aspirations of the ballet can be overstressed, and it is significant that Sawallisch is at his most convincing in the most obviously 'symphonic' section of the score—the whole of Act 4. Significant, too, is Sawallisch's complete avoidance of the familiar theatrical tricks of the trade, such as rhetorical slowings at the ends of numbers. EMI's sound, apart from an occasional hollow 'ring' to tuttis, is full, spacious and well balanced. Woodwind are more consistently featured than on the Dutoit set, and percussion is well controlled. The tracking is generous; the documentation, wide ranging; and the presentation, classy. All in all, a deeply considered, seriously intentioned *Swan Lake*; one to stir the mind, if not the limbs.

Symphonies – No. 1 in G minor, 'Winter Daydreams', Op. 13; No. 2 in C minor, Op. 17, 'Little Russian'; No. 3 in D major, Op. 29, 'Polish'; No. 4 in F minor, Op. 36; No. 5 in E minor, Op. 64; No. 6 in B minor, Op. 74, 'Pathétique'.

Symphonies Nos. 1-6.
Berlin Philharmonic Orchestra / Herbert von Karajan.
DG Symphony Edition 429 675-2GSE4 (four discs: 264 minutes: ADD). Recorded 1975-79.　Ⓜ 🆁🆁

Those who are looking for an outstanding bargain, one of the most enticing we can think of, need go no further than this Karajan set. All six numbered symphonies are squeezed on to only four CDs, selling at mid-price. The minor snag is that Nos. 2 and 5 are broken between discs, but even there one is no worse off than with an ordinary LP. Karajan's discography reveals no fewer than seven versions of the *Pathétique*, six each of Nos. 4 and 5, but the ones here, dating from 1975 and 1976, are in almost every way, both for sound and as interpretations, the finest he has done, certainly far preferable to his more recent DG series made with the Vienna Philharmonic.

Symphonies Nos. 1, 2 and 3, dating from 1979 are Karajan's only recordings of those earlier works, but ones which saw him at his very finest, combining high polish with freshness and lyrical spontaneity. There are points where he is clearly preferable even to Jansons (a Karajan devotee incidentally who counts the maestro as his most cherished mentor), as in the superb building of the final climax on the horn theme in the slow movement of No. 1. Many will also prefer Karajan's faster speed in the first movement of No. 2, where for once Jansons takes an unusually measured, if finely pointed, view. Though in the opening of No. 4 with Karajan, the digital transfer makes the brassy motto theme a little too fierce, generally these are among the best of his 1970s recordings from Berlin, fuller and more detailed than the digital sound on his Vienna versions of Nos. 4-6.

Symphonies Nos. 1-6. Manfred Symphony, Op. 58. Romeo and Juliet – Fantasy Overture. Capriccio italien, Op. 45. 1812 Overture, Op. 49. Marche slave, Op. 31. Francesca da Rimini, Op. 32. The Storm, Op. 76.
Concertgebouw Orchestra / Bernard Haitink.
Philips Bernard Haitink Symphony Edition 442 061-2PB6 (six discs: 423 minutes: ADD). Recorded 1961-79. Ⓜ

It is clear that Haitink is more at home with symphonic substance than the shorter colourful showpieces. This set documents his development as a conductor (and a Tchaikovskian) – the shorter pieces being recorded between 1961 and 1972, the symphonies between 1974 and 1979. The exception is the student Tchaikovsky's overture, *The Storm*, recorded with the symphonies, and the performance of which is so masterful, colourful and exciting, that you might think it a more mature work (though exactly *whose* 'more mature' work it might be isn't always easy to say). As eighty per cent of the contents of this package comprise the symphonies, let us briefly deal with the rest. You might wonder if Haitink had ever heard an Italian singing an Italian song as anything less capricious or Italian would be hard to imagine. There are moments in the feud music of *Romeo and Juliet* that suggest Haitink's resolve, and his communication of that resolve, was not what it was shortly to become. From eight years later, we have the brilliantly realized (and recorded) letter of the score in *Francesca*, the *1812* Overture and *Marche slave*. On to the symphonies: as a symphonic cycle, it remains temperate, considered and patient, living mostly at a fair distance from the edge, with rarely a hint of exaggeration or overemphasis – sterling qualities indeed. Haitink's grand and dignified manner is immensely stirring and satisfying. Throughout the symphonies, tempos and dynamics are chosen to guarantee impeccable articulation, beauty of tone production, flawless instrumental balances and a typical awareness of the important climactic moment. These recordings of the symphonies have all been available on CD before, with the exception of *Manfred* which was long overdue for reissue. Its pastoral and orgy (third and fourth movements) encapsulate what is both most frustrting and most formidable in Haitink's Tchaikovsky. Philips's Concertgebouw engineering broke new ground with the symphonies. The tuttis here reproduce with a clarity and epic splendour that have rarely, if ever, been bettered.

Symphony No. 1.
Oslo Philharmonic Orchestra / Mariss Jansons.
Chandos CHAN8402 (44 minutes: DDD). Ⓕ

Symphony No. 2. Capriccio italien, Op. 45.
Oslo Philharmonic Orchestra / Mariss Jansons.
Chandos CHAN8460 (48 minutes: DDD). Recorded 1985. Ⓕ

The composer himself gave the work the title *Winter Daydreams*, and also gave descriptive titles to the first two movements. The opening *Allegro tranquillo* he subtitled 'Dreams of a winter journey', while the *Adagio* bears the inscription 'Land of desolation, land of mists'. A *Scherzo* and finale round off a conventional four-movement symphonic structure. In the slow movement Jansons inspires a performance of expressive warmth and tenderness, while the *Scherzo* is managed with great delicacy and sensitivity. Both the opening movement and the finale are invested with vigour and passion, and everywhere the orchestral playing is marvellously confident and disciplined. The recording has not only impact and immediacy but also warmth and refinement. Jansons also has the full measure of Tchaikovsky's Second Symphony. It is a direct performance – the first movement allegro is relatively steady, but never sounds too slow, because of crisp rhythmic pointing – and the second movement goes for charm and felicity of colour. The finale is properly exuberant, with the secondary theme full of character, and there is a fine surge of adrenalin at the end. The *Capriccio italien,* a holiday piece in which the composer set out to be entertaining, is also played with great flair and the hint of vulgarity in the Neapolitan tune is not shirked. Again the closing pages produce a sudden spurt of excitement which is particularly satisfying. The recording here is just short of Chandos's finest – the massed violins could be sweeter on top, but the hall resonance is right for this music and there is a proper feeling of spectacle.

Symphonies Nos. 4-6.
Leningrad Philharmonic Orchestra / Evgeny Mravinsky.
DG 419 745-2GH2 (two discs: 129 minutes: ADD). Recorded 1960. Ⓕ

These recordings are classics of the gramophone, landmarks not just of Tchaikovsky interpretation, but of recorded orchestral performances in general. The Leningrad Philharmonic plays like a wild stallion, only just held in check by the willpower of its master. Every smallest movement is placed with fierce pride; at any moment it may break into such a frenzied gallop that you hardly know whether to feel exhilarated or terrified. The whipping up of excitement towards the fateful outbursts in Symphony No. 4 is astonishing – not just for the discipline of the *stringendos* themselves, but for the pull of psychological forces within them. Symphony No. 5 is also mercilessly driven and pre-echoes of Shostakovichian hysteria are particularly strong in the coda's knife-edge of triumph and despair. No less powerfully evoked is the stricken tragedy of the *Pathétique*. Rarely, if ever, can the prodigious rhythmical inventiveness of these scores have been so brilliantly demonstrated. The fanatical discipline is not something one would want to see casually emulated – few orchestras would stand for it in any case – but it is applied in a way which sees far into the soul of the music and never violates its spirit. Strictly speaking there is no real comparison with Mariss Jansons's Chandos issues, despite the fact that Jansons had for long been Mravinsky's assistant in Leningrad. His approach is warmer, less detailed, more classical, and in its way very satisfying. Not surprisingly there are deeper perspectives in the Chandos recordings, but DG's refurbishing has been most successful, enhancing the immediacy of sound so appropriate to the lacerating intensity of the interpretations.

Symphony No. 4.
Oslo Philharmonic Orchestra / Mariss Jansons.
Chandos CHAN8361 (42 minutes: DDD). Ⓕ Ⓢ

A high emotional charge runs through Jansons's performance of the Fourth, yet this rarely seems to be an end in itself. There is always a balancing concern for the superb craftsmanship of Tchaikovsky's writing; the shapeliness of the phrasing; the superb orchestration, scintillating and subtle by turns; and most of all Tchaikovsky's marvellous sense of dramatic pace. Rarely has the first movement possessed such a strong sense of tragic inevitability, or the return of the 'fate' theme in the finale sounded so logical, so necessary. The playing of the Oslo Philharmonic Orchestra is first rate: there are some gorgeous woodwind solos and the brass manage to achieve a truly Tchaikovskian intensity. Recordings are excellent: at once spacious and clearly focused, with a wide though by no means implausible dynamic range.

Symphonies Nos. 4-6. Romeo and Juliet – Fantasy Overture.
Serenade in C major, Op. 48 – Waltz.
Concertgebouw Orchestra / Willem Mengelberg.
Music and Arts mono CD809(two discs: 149 minutes: AAD). Recorded 1928-37. Ⓕ Ⓗ

Those readers who treat Tchaikovsky's written scores as sacrosanct will likely baulk at these provocative re-creations; but, be warned, those who risk sampling Mengelberg's realization of the music's emotional core could quite easily be mesmerized into forgetting the very existence of a printed source. So forget his dynamic adjustments, his re-harmonizing a crucial chord at the end of the Fifth Symphony, or the dazzling array of tempos that he inflicts on the Fourth's finale. That was his way, his manner of communication; yet the end products are nothing short of spellbinding, even on those occasions when we are prompted to shake our heads at the sheer nerve of it all. Mengelberg's charting of the Fourth Symphony's first movement is a masterpiece of interpretative rhetoric: the central development is angrily impatient, the final build-up a terrifying tread towards some unimaginable catastrophe. The *Andantino* is played with a degree of rubato that would tax even an accomplished soloist, while the *Romeo and Juliet* Fantasy Overture, the *1812* Overture and the first two movements of the Fifth Symphony rage, riot or relax as the spirit dictates. Under Mengelberg's inspired baton, the Fifth's first movement in particular is like a tightly-coiled spring that snaps loose whenever the temperature rises, and the equally charismatic *Pathétique* climaxes with a desperately weeping *Adagio lamentoso*. The Music and Arts transfers are remarkably quiet and detailed but the Fifth Symphony is split between two CDs.

Symphony No. 5.
Oslo Philharmonic Orchestra / Mariss Jansons.
Chandos CHAN8351 (43 minutes: DDD). Recorded 1984. Ⓕ ⦗RR⦘

With speeds which are fast but never breathless and with the most vivid recording imaginable, this is as exciting an account as we have had of this symphony. In no way does this performance suggest anything but a metropolitan orchestra, and Jansons keeps reminding one of his background in Leningrad in the great years of Mravinsky and the Philharmonic. Nowhere does the link with Mravinsky emerge more clearly than in the finale, where he adopts a tempo very nearly as hectic as Mravinsky's on his classic DG recording. In the first movement he resists any temptation to linger, prefering to press the music on, and the result sounds totally idiomatic. In the slow movement Jansons again prefers a steady tempo, but treats the second theme with delicate rubato and builds the climaxes steadily, not rushing his fences, building the final one even bigger than the first. In the finale it is striking that he follows Tchaikovsky's notated slowings rather than allowing extra *rallentandos* – the bravura of the performance finds its natural culmination. The Oslo string ensemble is fresh and bright and superbly disciplined, while the wind soloists are generally excellent with an attractively furry-toned but not at all wobbly or whiny horn solo in the slow movement. The Chandos sound lives up to its reputation, very specific and well focused despite a warm reverberation, real-sounding and three-dimensional with more clarity in tuttis than the rivals provide. This was the first issue in Jansons's Tchaikovsky cycle and could hardly have been more promising.

Symphony No. 5.
Vienna Philharmonic Orchestra / Valery Gergiev.
Philips 462 905-2PH (46 minutes: DDD). Recorded live in 1998.   Ⓕ🅔

This is the genuine article – live and alive – an unpatched one-off performance bursting at the seams with passion, presence, theatre and vitality. But make no mistake, this is *not* lofty Tchaikovsky. We can't tell you whether Gergiev's very physical bursts of tone and tempo manoeuvres, particularly in the first two movements, are what you will want to hear in a recorded performance of this symphony. That is for you to decide. Reactions may differ from one hearing to the next, always admiring such things as the dramatic effectiveness of the strong bass pedal link between the end of the finale's opening *Andante* and the start of its ensuing *Allegro vivace*, but occasionally being left uneasy by some of the tempo contrasts (the radical slowing for the first-movement recapitulation's bassoon solo almost suggesting that Rumpole of the Bailey had inadvertently wandered on to the scene). 'Love at first sight', as Gergiev's collaboration with the orchestra has been described, translates here into body-and-soul compliance with the conductor's expressive intentions. And for its own part the orchestra does what it does best: strings lacing the lyricism with their famed vibrato-rich playing, and bouncing the outer sections of the third movement *Waltz* as only they know how to do. The slight compression of the Austrian Radio recording for Gergiev is not troublesome; on the contrary, it enables a higher than usual transfer level, and thus greater immediacy for the feel and the features of what was clearly an 'event'.

Tchaikovsky Symphony No. 5.
Mussorgsky Songs and Dances of Death.
Anatoly Kotscherga *bass*
Berlin Philharmonic Orchestra / Claudio Abbado.
Sony Classical SK66276 (65 minutes: DDD). Text and translation included.
Recorded live in 1994.   Ⓕ

Sony's booklet tells us that Shostakovich's orchestration was used for the Mussorgsky songs; 'Shostakovich ed. Abbado' would be more accurate, though you will need a score to pick up most of Abbado's changes, mainly small additions and alterations to the string parts. These alterations tie in with an approach to all four songs that finds soloist and conductor generally avoiding the Grand Guignol tactics and timing that Hvorostovsky and Gergiev so obviously relish. Kotscherga has the richer, darker bass voice that seems ideal for these songs, and which he varies to great effect: ashen-voiced and gravelly for the opening of 'Lullaby', turning to a silken whisper for its haunting refrain; and he judiciously coarsens tone and manner to mimic and menace the doomed drunkard in 'Trepak'. When Kotscherga 'opens up', the power and pitching are thrilling, not least in the 'Ty maja!' ('You are mine!') at the end of 'Serenade'. With Abbado's alterations giving the strings a little more to do, and the Berlin strings at their expressive finest, their contribution to the success of the Mussorgsky songs is considerable.

And so it is in the Tchaikovsky. Though they never appear to dominate the scene, as has often been the case in DG's Berlin recordings, such moments as their full-toned, impassioned song at the climax of the symphony's slow movement, and *feroce* and *marcatissimo* playing in the finale's main *Allegro*, duly astonish. This is Abbado's third recording of Tchaikovsky's Fifth and, as before, he allows himself a fair measure of freedom in pacing (considerably more than Jansons). On balance,

Abbado finds more shadow in the score than the breezy Jansons, especially in the symphony's opening minutes and the finale is one of the most exciting on disc, with superb brass. The orchestra are present, but the Philharmonie's ambience adds just enough warmth and space to the proceedings. Those who prefer the more obviously spacious setting that Chandos gave to Jansons may find it a little dry.

Symphony No. 6. Marche slave, Op. 31. The Seasons, Op. 37b. Six morceaux composés sur un seul thème, Op. 21. The Sleeping Beauty (arr. Pletnev) – excerpts.
Russian National Orchestra / Mikhail Pletnev pf
Virgin Classics VBD5 61636-2 (two discs: 138 minutes: DDD).   Ⓜ 🆁🆁

There's no denying that Russian orchestras bring a special intensity to Tchaikovsky, and this Symphony in particular. But, in the past, we have had to contend with lethal, vibrato-laden brass, and variable Soviet engineering. Not any more. Pianist Mikhail Pletnev formed this orchestra in 1990 from the front ranks of the major Soviet orchestras, and the result here has all the makings of a classic. The brass still retain their penetrating power, and an extraordinary richness and solemnity before the Symphony's coda; the woodwind (soft, veiled flute tone, dark-hued bassoons) make a very melancholy choir; and the strings possess not only the agility to cope with Pletnev's aptly death-defying speed for the third movement march, but beauty of tone for Tchaikovsky's yearning cantabiles, and their lower voices add thunderous black density to the first movement's development's shattering intrusion. Pletnev exerts the same control over his players as he does over his fingers, to superb effect. The dynamic range is huge and is comfortably reproduced here with clarity, natural perspectives, a sense of instruments playing in a believable acoustic space, and a necessarily higher volume setting than usual. *Marche slave*'s final blaze of triumph, under the circumstances, seems apt.

Pletnev finds colours and depths in *The Seasons* that few others have found even intermittently. Schumann is revealed as a major influence, not only on the outward features of the style, but on the whole expressive mood and manner. The opening of 'May' is straight from the contemplative Schumann – his Eusebius persona – while the mercurial *staccato-legato* exchanges near the start of 'January' are intrusions from the lighter Florestan. That alternation of civilized soulfulness and delicious, faintly wicked humour recurs again and again in this performance. Even the melancholy song of 'October' has its tiny touches of Pletnevian naughtiness, but how beautifully the tune itself sings. And as a display of pianism the whole set is outstanding, all the more so because Pletnev's brilliance isn't purely egoistic. Even when he does something unmarked – like attaching the hunting fanfares of 'September' to the final unison of 'August' – he's so persuasive that you could believe that this is somehow inherent, if not actually explicit, in the material. The six *Morceaux*, Op. 21, emerge here as fascinating, richly enjoyable works. This is all exceptional playing, and the recording – bright in the treble, but also warm in tone – is ideally attuned to all its moods and colours.

Symphony No. 6. Piano Concerto No. 1 in B flat minor, Op. 23.
Vladimir Horowitz pf
NBC Symphony Orchestra / Arturo Toscanini.
Naxos Historical mono 8 110807 (71 minutes: ADD). Recorded live in 1941.   Ⓢ 🄷

Every home should probably have one. After all, Horowitz, that ultimate wizard of the keyboard, was preserved for posterity in the concerto on five different occasions. This performance from Carnegie Hall was taped the month before Horowitz and his father-in-law Toscanini made their better-known studio recording for RCA. Both performances marshal an old war-horse into a thoroughbred racer (past the finishing-post, mane flying in the wind, minutes before most of the competition), and the differences between them owe as much to the sound as the performances themselves. RCA's bursts more vibrantly into the living-room, but the orchestral bass booms, throwing into unfortunate relief a comparatively narrow-range, shallow piano sound with an unhelpful 'ring' in the instrument's middle register. In the end, despite its dazzle, the impression the performance leaves is one of antics, aggression and impatience. The live performance has a less uniform presence and body, but there is a parity of sound between orchestra and piano, and a less confused picture of Horowitz's playing, which allows you to register a greater variety of touch, colour, maybe even timing. Toscanini's *Pathétique* always was 'the real thing', in the sense of expression being honestly and directly communicated. But here, there is no mistaking Toscanini pushing out the boundaries in, say, a more brilliant scherzo/March; and a broader finale where the extra playing-out in the finale's second theme contrasts very effectively with the quiet sobbing from high cellos with the same theme just before the end. The latter might seem a cliché, but it convinces in the context of a reading that holds all the elements of this symphony – its passion, its pathos, its pity and its grace – in perfect poise.

Variations on a Rococo Theme, Op. 33. Nocturne No. 4, Op. 19. (arr. Tchaikovsky).
Pezzo capriccioso, Op. 62. When Jesus Christ was but a child No. 5, Op. 54. Was I not a little
blade of grass? No. 7, Op. 47. (both orch. Tchaikovsky) Andante cantabile, Op. 11.
(arr. Tchaikovsky).
Raphael Wallfisch vc
English Chamber Orchestra / Geoffrey Simon.
Chandos CHAN8347 (48 minutes: DDD). Recorded 1984.　　　　　　　　　　Ⓕ 🆁🆁

This account of the *Rococo* Variations is the one to have: it presents Tchaikovsky's variations as he
wrote them, in the order that he devised and including the *allegretto moderato con anima* that the
work's first interpreter, 'loathsome Fitzenhagen', so high-handedly jettisoned. (See also the review
under Dvořák on page 331 where Mstislav Rostropovich uses the published score rather than the
original version.) The first advantage is as great as the second: how necessary the brief cadenza and
the *andante* that it introduces now seem, as an up-beat to the central sequence of quick variations
(Fitzenhagen moved both cadenza and *andante* to the end). And the other, shorter cadenza now
makes a satisfying transition from that sequence to the balancing *andante sostenuto*, from which the
long-suppressed eighth variation (not a major musical discovery in itself) is an obvious build-up to
the coda – why, the piece has a form, after all! Raphael Wallfisch's fine performance keeps the
qualifying adjective 'rococo' in mind – it is not indulgently over-romantic, in short – but it has
warmth and beauty of tone in abundance. The shorter pieces are well worth having: the baritone
voice of the cello suits the *Andante cantabile* and the Tatyana-like melody of the *Nocturne*
surprisingly aptly. The sound is quite first-class: cello tone is rendered with great realism, and the
smallish orchestra appears in a very natural perspective.

String Quartets – No. 1 in D major, Op. 11; No. 2 in F major, Op. 22; No. 3 in E flat minor, Op. 30.
Quartet Movement in B flat major. Souvenir de Florence, Op. 70.
Yuri Yurov va **Mikhail Milman** vc **Borodin Quartet** (Mikhail Kopelman, Andrei Abramenkov vns
Dmitri Shebalin va Valentin Berlinsky vc).
Teldec 4509-90422-2 (two discs: 151 minutes: DDD). Recorded 1993.
Gramophone Award Winner 1994.　　　　　　　　　　　　　　　　　　　　　　　Ⓕ

Who could fail to recognize the highly characteristic urgency and thematic strength of the F major
Quartet's first movement development section, or miss premonitions of later masterpieces in the
Third Quartet's *Andante funèbre*. None of these works is 'late' (the last of them pre-dates the
Fourth Symphony by a couple of years), yet their rigorous arguments and sweeping melodies
anticipate the orchestral masterpieces of Tchaikovsky's full maturity. So why the neglect – that is, of
all but the First Quartet? The most likely reason is our habitual expectation of orchestral colour in
Tchaikovsky, a situation that doesn't really affect our appreciation of the early, almost Schubertian
D major Quartet (the one with the *Andante cantabile* that moved Tolstoy to tears). The Second and
Third Quartets are noticeably more symphonic and particularly rich in the kinds of harmonic
clashes and sequences that Tchaikovsky normally dressed for the orchestral arena. Even minor
details, like the quick-fire exchanges near the beginning of No. 3's *Allegretto*, instantly suggest
'woodwinds' (you can almost hear oboes, flutes and clarinets jostle in play), while both finales could
quite easily have been transposed among the pages of the early symphonies. But if these and other
parallels are to register with any conviction, then performers need to locate them, and that's a
challenge the Borodins meet with the ease of seasoned Tchaikovskians. They are natural and
spontaneous, most noticeably in the first movement of the exuberant *Souvenir de Florence* sextet,
and in that wonderful passage from the Second Quartet's first movement where the lead violin calms
from agitated virtuosity to a magical recapitulation of the principal theme – an unforgettable
moment, superbly paced in this Teldec reading. We also get a bonus in the shape of a 15-minute
B flat Quartet movement – an appealing torso imbued with the spirit of Russian folk-song – which
is accommodated partially at the expense of the First Quartet's last movement repeat .

Tchaikovsky Capriccio italien. Swan Lake (arr. Debussy). The Sleeping Beauty
(arr. Rachmaninov). Marche slave (arr. Batalini).
Scriabin Fantasy in A minor.
Katia Labèque, Marielle Labèque pfs
Philips 442 778-2PH (56 minutes: DDD). Recorded 1994.　　　　　　　　　　　　　　Ⓕ

This is a fascinating and, for the most part, brilliantly played collection. The 20-year-old Debussy's
arrangement of three dances from *Swan Lake* opens with a glittering flourish, and then presents the
music in totally pianistic terms: the 'Danse russe' is most engaging and the 'Danse napolitaine'
invites and receives scintillating brilliance at its close. Rachmaninov was just 18 when he arranged
the suite from *Sleeping Beauty* and Tchaikovsky was greatly displeased with the result. 'It was a

mistake to entrust this work to a *boy*', said he angrily to Ziloti, who had arranged the commission. The latter hastily re-edited Rachmaninov's work. But Rachmaninov deplored his failure and probably had a hand in revising the final version, which is certainly pianistically effective. The Labèques obviously enjoy the drama of the 'Introduction', attacking it with relish and then putting in a splendid pianistic 'bang' at the climax of 'La fée des lilas'. The surprise here is that they entirely miss the rhythmic point (and all the magic) of the famous 'Panorama', playing it too fast, and failing to notice that it should float gently above the (almost syncopated) bass, which here rocks prosaically. They are at home in the 'Waltz', however, which is played with fine sparkle, and they make the most of Rachmaninov's extra decorations, though they are inclined to rush their fences a little here and there.

Alexandra Batalini's transcription of the *Marche slave* ends the recital grandiloquently – the orchestral detail is all there, particularly the effulgent twiddly bits in the treble, and it is made to sound so commandingly pianistic that one does not miss the orchestra (and that's saying a good deal with a composer like Tchaikovsky). The coda is quite splendid and this performance, with its thrilling fireworks at the end, would deservedly bring the house down at a live recital, which is just what it sounds like, with a very real and immediate piano recording. It is a pity the recital was programmed to open with Tchaikovsky's own four-handed piano transcription of the *Capriccio italien*, for the composer (although he admired his own efforts) showed no real skill at re-thinking a spectacular orchestral show-piece for the piano. It opens with the famous bugle call played by one hand(!), and as 'the rest of the brass joins in', the extended fanfare is little short of tedious. Fortunately when the Labèque sisters get to the echo theme they are able to invest it with their own effervescence, even if they are a bit impetuous, and the 'Tarantella' finale certainly tests their virtuosity, just as the composer intended. The Scriabin *Fantasy* follows, opening nocturnally and later becoming harmonically more complex.

Morceaux – Op. 10; Op. 19 – No. 1, Rêverie du soir, No. 5, Capriccioso; Op. 40 – No. 2, Chanson triste, No. 8, Valse; Op. 51 – No. 1, Valse de salon, No. 3, Menuetto scherzoso, No. 5, Romance; Op. 72 – No. 5, Méditation, No. 12, L'espiègle, No. 15, Un poco di Chopin. Romance in F minor, Op. 5. Valse-scherzo in A major, Op. 7. The Seasons, Op. 37*b* – No. 1, January; No. 5, May; No. 6, June; No. 11, November.
Sviatoslav Richter *pf*
Olympia OCD334 (80 minutes: DDD/ADD). Recorded 1983.   Ⓕ

Richter elevates Tchaikovsky's miniatures far beyond the salon. No interpretative frills, just trenchant fingerwork and perfectly sculpted sound, so that slight unbendings become immensely touching. The effect is to convey not so much the surface melancholy of these pieces as their underlying strength of character. A curious sense of permanence comes through, as though the music is being contemplated rather than felt. Not for imitation, perhaps (and who could imitate such perfect harmonic and structural weighting?), but this is breathtaking, inspiring artistry, and it sets its own terms. Sound quality is on the dry side. But Richter's is the sort of playing which positively benefits from close analytical scrutiny, and serious collectors of piano recordings should need no further encouragement.

Liturgy of St John Chrysostom, Op. 41. Nine Sacred Pieces. An angel crying.
Corydon Singers / Matthew Best.
Hyperion CDA66948 (75 minutes: DDD). Texts and translations included. Recorded 1997.   Ⓕ

Tchaikovsky's liturgical settings have never quite caught the popular imagination which has followed Rachmaninov's (his All-Night Vigil, at any rate). They are generally more inward, less concerned with the drama that marks Orthodox celebration than with the reflective centre which is another aspect. Rachmaninov can invite worship with a blaze of delight, setting 'Pridite'; Tchaikovsky approaches the mystery more quietly. Yet there is a range of emotion which emerges vividly in this admirable record of the Liturgy together with a group of the minor liturgical settings which he made at various times in his life. His ear for timbre never fails him. It is at its most appealing, perhaps, in the lovely 'Da ispravitsya' for female trio and answering choir, beautifully sung here; he can also respond to the Orthodox tradition of rapid vocalization, as in the Liturgy's Creed and in the final 'Blagosloven grady' (in the West, the Benedictus). Anyone who still supposes that irregular, rapidly shifting rhythms were invented by Stravinsky should give an ear to his Russian sources, in folk poetry and music but also in the music of the Church. Matthew Best's Corydon Singers are by now old hands at Orthodox music, and they present these beautiful settings with a keen ear for their texture and their 'orchestration'. The recording was made in an (unnamed) ecclesiastical acoustic of suitable resonance, and sounds well. Transliterated texts and translations are provided in a booklet that includes an outstandingly good essay on the tradition and the music by Ivan Moody.

My genius, my angel, my friend. Take my heart away. Songs, Op. 6 – No. 1, Do not believe, my friend; No. 2, Not a word, o my friend; No. 5, Why?; No. 6, None but the lonely heart. Cradle song, Op. 16 No. 1. Reconciliation, Op. 25 No. 1. The fearful minute, Op. 28 No. 6. It was in the early spring, Op. 38 No. 2. Songs, Op. 60 – No. 6, Frenzied nights; No. 7, Gipsy's song; No. 12, The mild stars shone for us. Songs, Op. 63 – No. 4, The first meeting; No. 5, The fires in the rooms were already out. Serenade, Op. 65 No. 1. Songs, Op. 73 – No. 2, Night; No. 4, The sun has set; No. 6, Again, as before, alone.
Olga Borodina *mez* **Larissa Gergieva** *pf*
Philips 442 013-2PH (60 minutes: DDD). Translations included. Recorded 1993.　　　　ⒻⒺ

Olga Borodina is among the most considered of Tchaikovsky interpreters on disc. In the 'Cradle song', one of Tchaikovsky's most haunting pieces, Joan Rodgers sounds carefree as she rocks her baby to sleep, where Borodina is heavier, sensing dark threats all around. Larissa Gergieva adds to the unsettling atmosphere of that song by stressing the chromatic tensions in the accompaniment. In general, it might have been better to have had a pianist less amenable to slow speeds than Gergieva, but Borodina has such a range of colour and expression in her voice that she can fill the time profitably. One marvels at the beauty of the singing and admires its sustained intensity. In 'Night' a darkness descends over the voice from the opening lines, but in 'Again, as before, alone' she tries something even more daring, draining all the life and vibrancy from her tone in a way that is quite unforgettable. One would hardly dare play the final track often. There is also a free CD, 'Presenting Olga Borodina' in three excerpts from existing Philips opera sets. In fact, there is no need to persuade us that Borodina is a star: this recital demands that she be accepted on her own terms.

Songs, Op. 6 – No. 1, Do not believe, my friend; No. 2, Not a word, o my friend; No. 4, A tear trembles; No. 5, Why?; No. 6, None but the lonely heart. Reconciliation, Op. 25 No. 1. No response, or word, or greeting, Op. 28 No. 5. Songs, Op. 38 – No. 1, Don Juan's Serenade; No. 2, It was in the early spring; No. 3, At the ball; No. 5, The love of a dead man. Songs, Op. 47 – No. 3, Dusk fell on the earth; No. 4, Sleep, poor friend; No. 5, I bless you, forests. Songs, Op. 57 – No. 2, On the golden cornfields; No. 5, Death. Frenzied nights, Op. 60 No. 6. I should like in a single word. My genius, my angel, my friend.
Sergei Leiferkus *bar* **Semion Skigin** *pf*
Conifer Classics 75605-51266-2 (62 minutes: DDD). Texts and translations included.　　　　Ⓕ

This first volume in Leiferkus's collection of Tchaikovsky's songs with Semion Skigin contains a good number of favourites. He has the innate sympathy for the melodic lines to refresh even so well known, and often abused, a song as the one usually called in this country *None but the lonely heart*. This is beautifully sung, with a tinge of mournfulness in the tone and a long, carefully crafted shading of the melody. He can also turn to a hearty, even ruthless tone for the vehemence of *Don Juan's Serenade*, a fine partnership with Skigin as the piano hurtles forward mercilessly under the rollicking of the tune. Two songs of oblique love are among the best in the whole recital. *My genius, my angel, my friend* is tenderly phrased, as if all leading towards the long, held note that closes the song, on the cherished words 'moy drug' – 'my friend'. There is also gentleness, and that sense of love never wholly grasped which haunted Tchaikovsky so bitterly, in *At the ball* – one of his most moving songs – as the singer cannot bear to let the vision glimpsed across the crowded dance floor vanish altogether. Leiferkus seems in a few of the songs to be placed a little far back for the best effect, but in general the balance is carefully arranged so as to keep voice and piano in proper focus with each other. Certainly this is necessary in songs where melodic lines can blend so skilfully. Here is a recital of the quality one would expect from so fine an artist.

Songs, Op. 6 – No. 1, Do not believe, my friend; No. 2, Not a word, o my friend; No. 4, A tear trembles; No. 5, Why?; No. 6, None but the lonely heart. Cradle Song, Op. 16 No. 1.
Op. 38 – No. 2, It was in the early Spring; No. 3, At the ball. Reconciliation, Op. 25 No. 1.
Op. 47 – No. 1, If only I had known; No. 5, I bless you, forests; No. 6, Does the day reign?;
No. 7, Was I not a little blade of grass?. Do not ask, Op. 57 No. 3. Op. 60 – No. 4,
The Nightingale; No. 7, Gipsy's Song; No. 11, Exploit. I opened the window, Op. 63 No. 2.
Op. 73 – No. 2, Night; No. 6, Again, as before, alone. To forget so soon. I should like in a single word.
Lina Mkrtchyan *contr* **Evgeny Talisman** *pf*
Opus 111 OPS30-219 (74 minutes: DDD). Texts and translations included. Recorded 1998.　　　　Ⓕ

Deep purple velvet is the best way to describe this Armenian contralto's voice. The timbre is rich, the quality unflawed. No less remarkable is the lady's art, strikingly personal and in tune with Tchaikovsky's inward-looking mind and feeling for inner drama. With ample resources of volume, she nevertheless chooses to sing quietly for much of the time in these essentially private utterances, so that when the full voice is used it is as though the powerful emotions are breaking through and will brook no further restraint. And yet they are, quite speedily, brought again under the control of a mind preoccupied with its own thoughts and addressing at most an imagined presence, and never a concert-audience. In *Not a word, o my friend* Mkrtchyan is mindful that this is a song (partly) about silence: the 'droog' in question is as though at her side and she murmurs her confidences. In *It was in the early Spring* she sings all first three-and-a-half verses in a unified tone of musing reminiscence till exclamations in the lyric prompt a *crescendo*, and then a light caress of rhythm and melody restores the gentle affection. The pianist, Evgeny Talisman, is less than ideally clear, whether in recorded sound or in his playing; yet this seems to provide added insight, more sense of the piano's function in so many of these songs.

Op. 16 – No. 3, Accept just once; No. 4, O sing that song; No. 5, Thy radiant image; No. 6, In dark Hell. Op. 25 – No. 2, As o'er the burning ashes; No. 3, Mignon's song; No. 5, I never spoke to her; No. 6, As they reiterated, 'Fool!'. Op. 27 – No. 2, Look, yonder cloud; No. 5, Was it the mother who bore me?; No. 6, My spoilt darling. Op. 38 – No. 4, Oh, if only you could for one moment; No. 6, Pimpinella. Softly the spirit flew up to heaven, Op. 47 No. 2. Op. 57 – No. 3, Do not ask; No. 4, Sleep; No. 6, Only thou alone. Op. 60 – No. 8, Forgive; No. 11, Exploit. Blue Eyes of Spring. Mezza notte. We have not far to walk.
Nina Rautio sop **Sergei Leiferkus** bar **Semion Skigin** pf
Conifer Classics 75605 51269-2 (66 minutes: DDD). Texts and translations included.
Recorded 1997. Ⓕ

Only a third of the songs in this volume (part of Conifer's complete Tchaikovsky song series) are sung by Leiferkus, but they include some of the finest, and the finest performances. There is a superb irony in his singing of *As they reiterated, 'Fool!'*, as he curls his voice around the phrases and hardens his tone into a snarl for the reproach to the drunkard; yet the cavernous pain in one of Tchaikovsky's strangest songs, *In dark Hell*, matches without any emotional distancing the poem's grim mood. With *Exploit* he controls the growth of tone towards the climax superbly, then dropping to a hushed, exhausted quality for the quiet final verse. This is singing of Russian song at its finest, intense yet personal, eloquent but never straying into the operatic. Nina Rautio is not so sure-footed. At her best, she can respond with grace and a fresh sense of colour, as with the pretty *Pimpinella*. In *Sleep* she pays close attention to the words, which hold the key (as so often with Tchaikovsky) to phrasing that can be elusive. But when less at ease with a song, she can take refuge in operatic declamation of a kind that loses the idiom, as with *Softly the spirit*, or snatch at the phrasing, as with *Thy radiant image*. The setting of Mignon's *Kennst du das Land* (in Tyutchev's translation) is more successfully handled, not least because of the beautiful playing of Semion Skigin. He has the idiom of these songs in his veins, and the skill to match his singers and respond to the best in them. There is no finer Russian song pianist performing today.

Why did I dream of you?, Op. 28 No. 3. 16 Children's Songs, Op. 54. 12 Songs, Op. 60 – No. 1, Last night; No. 2, I'll tell you nothing; No. 3, O, if only you knew; No. 5, Simple words; No. 10, Behind the window in the shadow.
Ilya Levinsky ten **Semion Skigin** pf
Conifer Classics 75605 51268-2 (65 minutes: DDD). Texts and translations included.
Recorded 1995. Ⓕ

Ilya Levinsky's disc chiefly consists of the *16 Children's Songs*, the best of them delightful pieces in Tchaikovsky's most direct and well-crafted vein. They do, of course, need a comparable craft from the singer, and Levinsky very intelligently takes the words that touched Tchaikovsky as his own starting point. Though his tenor is light, poised and graceful – his singing of 'Why did I dream of you?' suggests that he must be a good Lensky – it is not a voice of naturally great range, but he uses it so expressively and eloquently that each of his interpretations has real meaning. 'Christ had a garden' (from Op. 54), rubbed almost smooth by countless soupy arrangements and soupier performances, is here sung with an attention that entirely refreshes it. Levinsky can also make a good comic turn out of 'The Cuckoo' from the same set, as the wretched bird ends up by insisting interminably on the merits of its song. He is wittily accompanied here by Semion Skigin, whose perception and skill is a hallmark of this generally excellent series. A word, too, for David Brown's helpful notes and for excellent translations of the texts (printed in transliteration).

The Snow Maiden.
Irina Mishura-Lekhtman mez **Vladimir Grishko** ten
Michigan University Musical Society Choral Union;
Detroit Symphony Orchestra / Neeme Järvi.
Chandos CHAN9324 (79 minutes: ADD). Text and translation included. Recorded 1994. Ⓕ

Tchaikovsky Opera

Tchaikovsky wrote his incidental music for Ostrovsky's *Snow Maiden* in 1873, and though he accepted it was not the best of which he was capable, he retained an affection for it and was upset when Rimsky-Korsakov came along with his full-length opera on the subject. The tale of love frustrated had its appeal for Tchaikovsky, even though he was not to make as much as Rimsky was of the failed marriage between Man and Nature. But though he did not normally interest himself much in descriptions of the natural world, there are charming numbers that any lover of Tchaikovsky's music will surely be delighted to encounter. A strong sense of a Russian folk celebration, and of the interaction of the natural and supernatural worlds, also comes through, especially in the earlier part of the work. There is a delightful dance and chorus for the birds, and a powerful monologue for Winter; Vladimir Grishko, placed further back, sounds more magical. Natalia Erassova (also for Chistiakov) gets round the rapid enunciation of Lel's second song without much difficulty, but does not quite bring the character to life; Irina Mishura-Lekhtman has a brighter sparkle. Chistiakov's Shrove Tuesday procession goes at a much steadier pace than Järvi's, and is thus the more celebratory and ritual where the other is a straightforward piece of merriment. Both performances have much to recommend them, and it is not by a great deal that Järvi's is preferable. The balance is further tilted by CdM providing only an English (and French) translation of the text unmatched to a Russian text or transliteration; Chandos provide transliteration and English translation.

Iolanta – Who can compare with my Mathilde. Iolanta and Vaudémont duet. Oprichnik – Natalya's arioso. Mazeppa – The old man's gone, how my heart beats – Sleep my baby, my pretty. The Maid of Orleans – Farewell, Forests. The Queen of Spades – Stay, I beg of you!. I love you beyond all measure. Undina – Undina's song. The Voyevoda – Bastryukov's aria. Vakula the Smith – Oskana's aria. Eugene Onegin – Let me perish, but first let me summon (Letter Scene). The Enchantress – Kuma's arioso.
Inessa Galante, Marina Shaguch *sops* **Alexander Fedin** *ten* **Sergei Leiferkus** *bar*
Royal Opera House Orchestra, Covent Garden / Neeme Järvi.
Royal Opera House Records 75605 55022-2 (79 minutes: DDD). Recorded 1997.   Ⓕ

There can scarcely be a more beautiful or subtler account of the Letter Scene from *Eugene Onegin* than that given here by Inessa Galante. She makes us believe that these are the inner thoughts of an obsessed young girl as she moulds her phrases with a sense of spontaneous feeling: you can almost see Tatyana writing in her boudoir. The voice itself shows that it has blossomed into a warm, vibrant, evenly produced instrument and its owner uses it with unfailing musicality, aided by Järvi's sympathetic support. This is the glorious centrepiece of 'The Tchaikovsky Experience', with excerpts from all his operas. Galante possibly even more moving as vulnerable Iolanta learning of her blindness from her admirer Vaudémont in the composer's last opera. This, one of the most touching duets in Tchaikovsky, perhaps in all opera, is compellingly sung here by Galante and the tenor Alexander Fedin. Marina Shaguch deserves almost as much praise. Her voice isn't as easily produced as Galante's but is more dramatic in character. She has some of the rarer material to interpret, such as the haunting solo from *Undina* and as poor, demented Maria at the end of *Mazeppa*, singing a lullaby to her sweetheart dying in her arms. Sergei Leiferkus sings with his customary conviction in Robert's soliloquy from *Iolanta*. Though his account of Yeletsky's solo from *The Queen of Spades* isn't as ingratiating as some, it is delivered with compensating intelligence. Järvi conducts all the music with command of idiom, drawing refined playing from the ROH Orchestra. Unfortunately texts and translations aren't included but you can write off for them. None the less this is an important disc, well recorded, and generously filled.

Tchaikovsky Eugene Onegin – Let me perish, but first let me summon. The Queen of Spades – What am I crying for, what is it?. The Enchantress – Where are you, beloved? ... Hurry to my side. Oprichnik – I heard voices and footsteps.
Verdi La forza del destino – Son giunta! ... Madre, pietosa Vergine; Pace, pace, mio Dio. Otello – Mia madre aveva ... Piangea cantando ... Ave Maria. Aida – Qui Radames verra? ... O patria mia. Il trovatore – Tacea la notte placida ... Di tale amor.
Galina Gorchakova *sop*
Chorus and Orchestra of the Kirov Opera / Valery Gergiev.
Philips 446 405-2PH (60 minutes: DDD). Texts and translations included. Recorded 1995.   Ⓕ Ⓔ

Gorchakova promises to be one of the vocal giants of her generation. This recital programme marks her first steps into the Italian repertoire on disc. For a star of the Kirov, Verdi's St Petersburg opera – *La forza del destino* – makes an apt choice. Arriving at the monastery gate, her Leonora immediately announces herself as a Verdi soprano of tragic stature, shaping 'Madre, pietosa Vergine' with the dark colouring of a troubled soul. The Willow Song from *Otello* is predictably doom-laden, for Gorchakova is no simple, creamy, lyrical Desdemona. The Aida is less successful and sounds as if it is not yet fully in her voice. It might have been better to offer 'Ritorna vincitor', as she seems uncomfortable with long, slow phrases around the top of the stave. The top C is very loud and the conclusion, broken off sharply in full voice, is not what Verdi asks for. After that, the *Trovatore* goes much better: the aria has splendid vocal depth and the cabaletta (one verse only) is surprisingly nimble, especially at Gergiev's brilliant pace. Elsewhere his conducting of the Verdi could do with more pace. As an interpreter of Tchaikovsky, Gorchakova has already won her laurels on the stage. Despite the size and dark colour of the voice, her soprano is still youthful enough for her to play a plausible Tatyana and the Letter Scene will be one of the major reasons for acquiring this disc. The heart of the scene is sung with the kind of *pianissimo* that one would use to carry to the back of the theatre, rather than an inward *pianissimo* intended for the microphone. The *Queen of Spades* aria (Lisa's short solo from Act 1, not her main aria) is so full of beautiful, soaring tone that one resents being cut off just at the point where Herman enters for their duet. The brief aria from *The Enchantress* includes an exciting high B. Elsewhere there is one worrying sign to be mentioned. That is a tendency to go flat when the music is soft and slow (both the *Otello* and the *Aida* suffer from passages of sinking pitch) and one has to hope that difficulties like this are not allowed to defeat her. Gorchakova is no highly polished automaton as a singer, as we know from a couple of problematical live appearances. Her artistry is about letting this voice out of its cage and harnessing its formidable energy. The Philips recording team has done well to capture it so truthfully in the studio. A vocal beast like this is not easily tamed.

Eugene Onegin.
Dmitri Hvorostovsky *bar* Eugene Onegin; **Nuccia Focile** *sop* Tatyana;
Neil Shicoff *ten* Lensky; **Olga Borodina** *mez* Olga; **Alexander Anisimov** *bass* Prince Gremin;
Sarah Walker *mez* Larina; **Irina Arkhipova** *mez* Filipievna; **Francis Egerton** *ten* Triquet;
Hervé Hennequin *bass-bar* Captain; **Sergei Zadvorny** *bass* Zaretsky;
St Petersburg Chamber Choir; Orchestre de Paris / Semyon Bychkov.
Philips 438 235-2PH2 (two discs: 141 minutes: DDD). Notes, text and translation included.
Recorded 1992.

Entirely at the service of Tchaikovsky's marvellous invention, Semyon Bychkov illuminates every detail of the composer's wondrous scoring with pointed delicacy and draws playing of the utmost acuity and beauty from his own Paris orchestra – enhanced by the clear, open recording – and the St Petersburg Choir are superbly disciplined and alert with their words. Focile offers keen-edged yet warm tone and total immersion in Tatyana's character. Aware throughout of the part's dynamic demands, she phrases with complete confidence, eagerly catching the girl's dreamy vulnerability and heightened imagination in the Letter scene, which has that sense of awakened love so essential to it. Hvorostovsky is in his element. His singing has at once the warmth, elegance and refinement Tchaikovsky demands from his anti-hero. Together he, Focile and Bychkov make the finale the tragic climax it should be; indeed the reading of this passage is almost unbearably moving. Shicoff has refined and expanded his Lensky since he recorded it for Levine and Anisimov is a model Gremin, singing his aria with generous tone and phrasing while not making a meal of it. Olga Borodina is a perfect Olga, spirited, a touch sensual, wholly idiomatic with the text – as, of course, is the revered veteran Russian mezzo Arkhipova as Filipyevna, an inspired piece of casting.

Eugene Onegin.
Evgeny Belov *bar* Eugene Onegin; **Galina Vishnevskaya** *sop* Tatyana;
Sergei Lemeshev *ten* Lensky; **Larissa Adyeva** *mez* Olga; **Ivan Petrov** *bass* Prince Gremin;
Valentina Petrova *sop* Larina; **Evgenya Verbitskaya** *mez* Filipyevna; **Andrei Sokolov** *ten* Triquet;
Igor Mikhailov *bass* Zaretsky; **Georgi Pankov** *bass* Captain;
Bolshoi Theatre Chorus and Orchestra / Boris Khaikin.
Melodiya mono 74321 17090-2 (two discs: 140 minutes: ADD). Recorded 1955.

The classic Khaikin version, generally accepted as the most convincing and knowledgeable performance the work has yet received, wears its 45 years lightly: indeed, the recording of the voices and even the orchestra, albeit in mono, has a great deal to teach producers today in terms of a natural sound. The reading's virtues are, above all, Khaikin's unforced, unexaggerated, wholly integrated direction, with players and singers who know the score from the inside giving an entirely idiomatic reading (if you can forgive the watery horns). From the very first scene you feel the impetus of the performance and are drawn into its truly Russian ambience. Khaikin brings into perfect balance the dramatic and yearning aspects of the score in a lyrical, delicate reading. With his incisive but sympathetic beat, he clearly characterizes those many passages of intimate feeling without which any account of the piece crucially fails. The young Vishnevskaya is a near-ideal Tatyana, having exactly the right voice for the part and totally convincing us that she *is* Tatyana. She is incomparable. What a genuine, unsophisticated outpouring of passion the Letter scene becomes as she interprets it, and how superbly she sings it! Few tenors before or since Lemeshev have offered precisely the right tone and character for Lensky. From his first entry we hear a plaintive timbre and easy way with the language that proclaim a true poet. Belov's Onegin, though not quite in that class, is a resolute member of a real ensemble and rises to the challenge of the final scenes. All that disappoints is the presentation: numerous spelling mistakes and no libretto.

Iolanta.
Galina Gorchakova sop Iolanta; **Gegam Grigorian** ten Vaudémont;
Dmitri Hvorostovsky bar Robert; **Sergei Alexashkin** bass King René;
Nikolai Putilin bar Ibn-Hakia; **Larissa Diadkova** mez Martha; **Nikolai Gassiev** ten Alméric;
Tatiana Kravtsova sop Brigitta; **Olga Korzhenskaya** mez Laura;
Gennadi Bezzubenkov bar Bertrand;
Chorus and Orchestra of the Kirov Opera, St Petersburg / Valery Gergiev.
Philips 442 796-2PH2 (two discs: 96 minutes: DDD). Notes, text and translation included.
Recorded 1994.   Ⓕ

Iolanta, the touching little princess, blind and virginal, into whose darkness and isolation there eventually shines the 'bright angel' of Duke Robert, is delightfully sung by Galina Gorchakova. There is a freshness and sense of vulnerability here, especially in the opening scenes with Martha in the garden as she sings wistfully of something that appears to be lacking in her life: the *Arioso* is done charmingly and without sentimentality. Gegam Grigorian sometimes sounds pinched and under strain, even in the Romance. He is also overshadowed by Dmitri Hvorostovsky who is here at his best: warm and with a somewhat dusky tone, responding with great sensitivity to the often elusive melodic lines which Tchaikovsky writes in this, his last opera. The King, Provence's 'bon roi René', is benignly if a little throatily sung by Sergei Alexashkin, and he has at hand a sturdy-voiced Ibn-Hakia in Nikolai Putilin. Valery Gergiev conducts a sensitive performance, responding constructively to the unusual scoring (much disliked by the possibly jealous Rimsky-Korsakov), and not overplaying the more demonstrative elements in a score that gains most through some understatement. The booklet very sensibly prints in parallel columns a transliteration of the Russian, then English, German and French; the text in the original Cyrillic is printed separately at the end.

Mazeppa.
Nikolai Putilin bar Mazeppa; **Irina Loskutova** sop Maria; **Sergei Alexashkin** bass Kochubey;
Larissa Dyadkova mez Lyubov; **Viktor Lutsiuk** ten Andrei; **Viacheslav Luhanin** bass Orlik;
Vladimir Zhivopistsev ten Iskra; **Nikolai Gassiev** ten Drunken Cossack;
Kirov Opera Chorus and Orchestra / Valery Gergiev.
Philips 462 206-2PH3 (three discs: 170 minutes: DDD). Notes, text and translation included.
Recorded live in 1996.   Ⓕ 🆁🆁

This Kirov recording is taken live from performances at the Maryinsky Theatre, and it's extremely telling at all the crucial moments, without emerging as consistently superior to Järvi on DG. Nikolai Putilin's Mazeppa has a heavier voice than his DG counterpart, and he shows more strain (Tchaikovsky takes his baritone to a high A flat at one point). But his dramatic range is greater and he is more believable both as ruthless tyrant and love-struck old man. So honours are fairly even here. Similarly Irina Loskutova's Maria cannot compete with DG's Galina Gorchakova for beauty of tone and purity of line, and in anything above a *mezzo piano* her voice spreads quite alarmingly. Yet it is Loskutova who is the more moving at the opera's quiet conclusion. It's the same story but in reverse with the two Kochubeys. For Philips Sergei Alexashkin is heftier of voice in Act 1, but it's DG's Anatoly Kocherga, initially rather dry and underpowered, who grows in dramatic stature in the Prison and Execution scenes, darkening the timbre and timing his delivery to perfection, where Alexashkin can only add stagey sobs and routine barks of defiance.

The balance-sheet is fairly even with the smaller roles too. Larissa Dyadkova repeats her moving portrayal of the agonized mother; Viktor Lutsiuk's Andrei sounds at first no better than a cardboard-cut-out ardent lover but largely redeems himself in Act 3; Nikolai Gassiev hams up the Drunken Cossack in a way that was probably more effective on stage than it is on CD. Scientific measurement would probably show little difference between the Kirov Orchestra's instinctive *sostenuto* and the plausible copy of it manufactured by the Gothenburgers, or between the full-throated Russian of a native chorus and the Stockholm Royal Opera's more than passable imitation. However, the extra sense of dramatic immediacy here is unmistakable. Järvi was swift in the 'Gopak', stomach-churning in the Prison and Execution scenes, and vivid in the 'Battle of Poltava'; Gergiev is even more so. Incidentally, Gergiev departs from the score in the Battle, bolstering it with a forceful return of the famous *Slava!* folk-song and omitting Tchaikovsky's transition to the following scene. The booklet makes no mention of it, merely reprinting the DG essays and synopsis (cutting the musical example in the German essay). But that at least means that whichever version you choose you get the considerable benefit of Richard Taruskin's erudition.

The orchestra-pit sound is dryish, with little or no bloom on the strings and indifferently balanced woodwind. The *frisson* of curtain going up, audience presence, applause between scenes, and movement of voices on stage, offers some compensation, and you soon adapt. But the results of editing together more than one live performance are not entirely satisfactory. There are some bumpy edits on held vocal notes and voices sometimes jump to different positions on stage (if you think you're likely to be put off, try to hear the first disc, track 3, at 0'27' and 1'34'). Musically both sets are distinguished, but if forced to choose we would take the Gergiev, for an extra sense of the drama being lived out. However, owners of the DG discs will enjoy better sound quality and marginally more consistent singing.

Mazeppa.
Sergei Leiferkus *bar* Mazeppa; **Galina Gorchakova** *sop* Maria;
Anatoly Kotscherga *bass* Kochubey; **Larissa Dyadkova** *mez* Lyubov; **Sergei Larin** *ten* Andrei;
Monte Pederson *bar* Orlik; **Richard Margison** *ten* Iskra; **Heinz Zednik** *ten* Drunken Cossack;
Stockholm Royal Opera Chorus; Gothenburg Symphony Orchestra / Neeme Järvi.
DG 439 906-2GH3 (three discs: 166 minutes: DDD). Notes, text and translation included.
Recorded 1993. Ⓕ

It was *Eugene Onegin* that turned Tchaikovsky into Russia's best-loved composer, not the more calculated recipes for success of *The Maid of Orleans*, *Mazeppa* or *Charodeyka* ('The Enchantress'). *Onegin* works for us today because it is sincerely felt from start to finish; but the fascination of those lesser-known operas lies in the way they move in and out of scenes and predicaments which clearly touched the composer. Of the three, *Mazeppa* has the greatest share of first-rate music, extending our appreciation of Tchaikovsky's blacker side as he attempts to reflect the cruelty inflicted by the anti-hero. Gorchakova's response to Mazeppa's patriotic scheme in Act 2 gives us a fairer picture of the Gorchakova phenomenon than ill-focused earlier stages of this semi-interpretation: shining strength above the stave goes some way towards redeeming the placidity of the whole. It takes Larissa Dyadkova's far more committed cut and thrust in the electrifying scene between Maria and her mother to spur Gorchakova to a more consistent sense of occasion. Anatoly Kotscherga would clearly like to deliver more than his limited vocal resources permit him as the outraged father seethes in Act 1 but he rises to his supreme challenge as Tchaikovsky plumbs the depths for Kochubey's prison monologue: here, indeed, are the range of tone colour and introspection missing from Gorchakova's mad scenes.

Leiferkus has less to deal with as the headstrong tyrant; even so, he strikes firmly at the heart of darkness, and there could be no more free- and easy-sounding delivery of the wonderful aria that Tchaikovsky gave his baritone at a late stage in the compositional process. In the cases of both the victim's darkest hour and this, the conqueror's most sensitive one, Järvi reinforces the orchestra's role as an equal partner in characterization – driving home the lower-instrument gloom and terror of Kochubey's circumstances, underlining the light and lovely, woodwind-dominated scoring of 'O, Maria!' as Mazeppa muses Gremin-like on the sincerity of his late-flowering love. As a whole the set is a faithful testament to *Mazeppa*'s power to move and appal.

The Queen of Spades.
Gegam Grigorian *ten* Herman; **Maria Gulegina** *sop* Lisa; **Irina Arkhipova** *mez* Countess;
Nikolai Putilin *bar* Count Tomsky; **Vladimir Chernov** *bar* Prince Yeletsky;
Olga Borodina *mez* Pauline; **Vladimir Solodovnikov** *ten* Chekalinsky;
Sergei Alexashkin *bass* Surin; **Evgeni Boitsov** *ten* Chaplitsky; **Nikolai Gassiev** *ten* Major-domo;
Gennadi Bezzubenkov *bass* Narumov; **Ludmila Filatova** *mez* Governess;
Tatiana Filimonova *sop* Masha;
Kirov Theatre Chorus and Orchestra / Valery Gergiev.
Philips 438 141-2PH3 (three discs: 166 minutes: DDD). Notes, text and translation included.
Recorded 1992. Ⓕ

There are major problems with all the current sets of *The Queen of Spades*, but Valery Gergiev, one of the outstanding Tchaikovskians of the day, here coaxes from a thoroughly Western-sounding Kirov Theatre Orchestra what is surely the most refined account of the score yet recorded, and one that is never lacking energy or full-blooded attack. His is not so much a compromise approach as one which stresses fatalism and underlying sadness. The recording was made in the Kirov Theatre itself, and there is admittedly some constriction to the orchestral sound picture; but for many the atmosphere of a real stage-venue will be a plus, and the all-important balance between voices and orchestra is just right. If the spine still fails to tingle as often as it should, that is mainly a reflection of the respectable but unexciting singing, though it would be folly to expect greater thrills from any of the three rival sets, and in many ways Gergiev's conducting elevates his above them all.

Alexander Tcherepnin

Piano Concertos – No. 1, Op. 12; No. 4, Op. 78, 'Fantaisie'; No. 5, Op. 96.
Murray McLachlan *pf*
Chetham's Symphony Orchestra / Julian Clayton.
Olympia OCD440 (71 minutes: DDD). Recorded 1995.   Ⓕ

The Tcherepnin piano concertos are in their various ways cast in the same exuberant, heartfelt romantic manner. However, there is considerable variety within this general approach. The First, written in Paris in 1920, takes not the slightest interest in what was beginning to occupy French musicians and most other Parisian expatriates at the beginning of that exciting decade: it looks east, to a Georgia which Tcherepnin had known before exile, and north to an influence from, of all composers, Sibelius. The result is inventive but, predictably, less original than the later concertos. The Fourth, written in 1947, looks further east to China, a country which Tcherepnin had toured in the 1930s and where he met his future wife. It is more a set of three tone-poems, lightly accommodating Chinese musical gestures into the familiar romantic language, than a symphonic concerto. The Fifth belongs to 1963, and is a much more enigmatic work, and also by some way the most original of the entire set of six. Murray McLachlan is a fine advocate of this music, which is technically demanding and, in the Fifth Concerto, also demanding of a subtle understanding if the most is to be made of its laconic gestures and rather greyer lyricism. The Chetham's Symphony Orchestra reaffirms its ability to cope with technically testing scores and, guided by Julian Clayton, to make musical sense of them with the command of more experienced musicians.

Narcisse et Echo, Op. 40.
The Hague Chamber Choir; The Hague Residentie Orchestra / Gennadi Rozhdestvensky.
Chandos CHAN9670 (53 minutes: DDD). Recorded 1998.   Ⓕ

Nikolay Tcherepnin's *Narcisse et Echo* was one of the first of Diaghilev's Paris ballets, produced in 1911 and hence anticipating Ravel's *Daphnis et Chloé* by a year. Tcherepnin's ear is actually a match for Ravel's in orchestral subtlety, and his skill in scoring for his very large orchestra decorates the ballet with some ravishing sounds. The work was reproached at the time for being static, which it could hardly help being when Narcissus spends the last quarter of an hour gazing adoringly at his reflection in a pool. Not even Nijinsky could do much with that, it seems, even though Tcherepnin's most sensuous music was twining itself lovingly around him. There is also a dance for Narcissus with the hapless Echo, and some set pieces for a group of Boeotians. Neither of these generates much musical exhilaration, nor, despite a flurry of rhythmic complexity, does the arrival of a troop of depressingly sober Bacchantes. Tcherepnin gives them all lovely sounds, but there is nothing of Ravel's intoxicating energy, let alone his exquisite melodic invention. The comparison between these two adjacent ballets invoking a Greek pastoral idyll is inevitably to Tcherepnin's disadvantage. But simply as aural sensation it is captivating, especially when played as beautifully as it is here.

Georg Philipp Telemann

Concerto for Three Horns, Violin and Orchestra in D major. Overture-Suites – C major, TWV55:C5, 'La Bouffonne'; F major, TWV55:F11, 'Alster Echo'. Concerto in G major, 'Grillen-Symphonie'.
Anthony Halstead, Christian Rutherford, Raul Diaz *hns*
Collegium Musicum 90 / Simon Standage *vn*
Chandos Chaconne CHAN0547 (70 minutes: DDD). Recorded 1993.   Ⓕ🅿

This release shows Telemann at his most irrepressibly good-humoured and imaginative. There's a concerto for three rattling horns and a solo violin (a splendid sound, with the horns recorded at what seems like the ideal distance), and an elegant suite for strings which sounds like Handel, Bach and a few French composers all thrown in together. More striking, though, is the most substantial piece on the disc, the *Alster Echo* Overture-Suite, a nine-movement work for strings, oboes and horns full of tricks and surprises occasioned by a whole host of representative titles. Thus 'Hamburg Carillons' brings us horns imitating bells, 'Concerto of Frogs and Crows' has some mischievously scrunchy wrong notes, and in 'Alster Echo' there's a complex network of echoes between oboes and horns. But the show-stealer by a long way on this disc is the *Grillen-Symphonie* ('Cricket Symphony'), which Telemann jokingly noted on the manuscript as being 'in the Italian, English, Scottish and Polish styles'. What he meant by that is hardly the point; this is a work for the gloriously silly scoring of piccolo, alto chalumeau, oboe, violins, viola, and two double-basses, a somewhat Stravinskian combination that you're unlikely to encounter every day. But it's not just the instrumentation that's irresistibly odd. There is a slow movement with curious, melancholy woodwind interventions a little reminiscent of *Harold in Italy*, and a finale which is quite a hoot.

Concerto for Two Oboes, Three Trumpets, Timpani and Strings. Overture-Suite in G minor, TWV55:g4. Musique de table – Overture-Suite in D major, TWV55:D1.
Paul Goodwin, Lorraine Wood *obs* **Mark Bennett, Michael Harrison, Nicholas Thompson** *tpts*
The English Concert / Trevor Pinnock.
Archiv Produktion 439 893-2AH (59 minutes: DDD). Recorded 1993. Ⓕ🅿

This extensive D major concerto is well represented in the catalogue. The flawless G minor Suite is a little-known gem displaying Telemann's brilliant and variegated ideas of blending and offsetting three *concertante* oboes with strings. After the exquisitely balanced overture the picturesque dances are executed with refined characterization, most notably in the robustly Ramellian, 'Les Irresoluts'. If the inclusion of the Produktion II suite (from Musique de table) is perhaps a missed opportunity for more *objets inconnus*, it is certainly not a waste of air time. Pinnock's approach is about right in its bold gestures, with the forward placing of the trumpet and oboe making for a persuasive dialogue, even if Mark Bennett's gleaming tone tends to predominate. Bennett's virtuoso 'natural' trumpet playing is demanded again in a performance of one or two extant concertos Telemann wrote for three trumpets. He and his colleagues are meticulously matched here in a thrilling performance which simply has to be heard by those who relish baroque music at its grandest and most rhetorical.

Concertos – A minor for Violin; E minor for Flute and Violin (with Rachel Brown *fl*); G major for Four Unaccompanied Violins; A major for Four Violins (Micaela Comberti, Miles Golding, Andrew Manze *vns*); E major for Violin. Overture-Suite in G minor, 'La Changeante'.
Collegium Musicum 90 / Simon Standage *vn*
Chandos CHAN0519 (63 minutes: DDD). Recorded 1990-91. Ⓕ🅿

Concertos – G major for Violin; D major for Two Flutes, Violin and Cello (Brown, Siu Peasgood *fls* Jane Coe *vc*); F sharp minor for Violin; G major for Two Violins (Comberti). Overture-Suite in B flat major, 'Ouverture burlesque'.
Collegium Musicum 90 / Simon Standage *vn*
Chandos CHAN0512 (64 minutes: DDD). Recorded 1990-91. Ⓕ🅿

It is difficult to mention Telemann without referring to the prolific and eclectic nature of his output, reflected in his very numerous concertos, and in these recordings the two works that are *not* concertos – *La Changeante* and *Ouverture burlesque*, both of which evoke the spirit of the *commedia dell'arte*. What changes in *La Changeante* is not only the moods of the movements but also their keys; only the first and last of the eight are in the home key of G minor, the others are in a variety of different ones, a most unusual feature at that time. The overture-suites are predominantly French in style but the concertos represent Telemann's highly individual variant of Venetian models. Whilst Vivaldi's concertos are predominantly in three movements (quick-slow-quick), Telemann's are usually in four or five, with no set pattern of pace, and they take both *da chiesa* and *da camera* forms. Telemann's muse seems rarely to have slept, likewise his acute sense of instrumental colour. When Playford wrote of 'Sprightly and cheerful musick' he was referring to that of the cittern; had he lived a little longer he might have felt the same about that of Telemann, not least if he had heard it played so expertly by Collegium Musicum 90, who are brought into your home by most faithful recorded sound.

Overture-Suite in A minor[a]. Concerto in E minor for Recorder and Flute[b]. Viola Concerto No. 1 in G major[c]. Overture des Nations anciens et modernes for Strings and Continuo, TWV55[b].
Franz Verster *fl* **Paul Doctor** *va*
[a]**South-West German Chamber Orchestra / Friedrich Tilegant;**
[b]**Amsterdam Chamber Orchestra / André Rieu;** [c]**Concerto Amsterdam / Frans Brüggen** *rec*
Teldec Das Alte Werk 9031-77620-2 (69 minutes: ADD). Recorded 1967-68. Ⓜ🅿

Four performances of the highest calibre, marvellously recorded in the 1960s and now sounding as fresh as the day they were made. Two of them feature the distinguished recorder player Frans Brüggen (who is now more often heard on disc as a conductor). He is at his inimitable finest, and this is very fine indeed, in the masterly Suite in A minor for recorder and strings (every bit as fine a work as the Bach B minor Suite for the same instrumentation) and the E minor Concerto for recorder, transverse flute and strings with its attractive interplay of solo texture. Here he is joined by Franz Verster. Brüggen then moves to the conductor's podium to direct the Concerto Amsterdam, joined by a superb viola player, Paul Doctor, in the justly famous G major Viola Concerto. The *Overture des Nations anciens et modernes* is another suite (comprising nine movements), full of the composer's most felicitious invention. The music is played with great character and the CD transfer is exemplary.

Overture-Suite in C major, TWV55:C3, 'Hamburger Ebb und Fluth'. Overture-Suite in D major. Concerto in A minor for Two Recorders, Two Oboes and Strings. Concerto in E minor for Recorder, Flute and Strings.
Dominique Gauthier *fl* **Philippe Foulon** *va da gamba*
Orchestre Musica Antiqua / Christian Mendoze *rec*
Pierre Verany PV796022 (68 minutes: DDD). Recorded 1995. Ⓕ Ⓟ

An attractive programme of suites and concertos. Musica Antiqua was founded some 15 years ago but its representation on disc, at least in the UK, has been infrequent. As we might expect, these musicians bring a markedly French atmosphere to Telemann's Suites. And why not? Telemann was drawn to French *ouvertures* and their appended suites of dances at an early age and his love of them never deserted him. In the Suite in C major, variously subtitled *Wassermusik* and *Hamburger Ebb und Fluth*, indigenous French gestures especially can be felt in rhythmic *inégalités* and in the ornamented resolution of several final cadences. This Suite is colourfully scored for pairs of recorders and oboes with bassoon and strings and it is the woodwind department of the Ensemble which gives the performance its lustre. That is not to imply any serious shortcoming in the string playing but rather that the recording balance favours the wind instruments. None of the four works, in fact, is well served by the acoustic, which is hollow in sound and reverberant in a way that only intermittently captures the character of the instruments; and the solo and *concertino* players are placed too close to the microphone. Whatever the shortcomings of the recording itself, however – and anyway this is purely a matter of personal preference – the spirited and mainly stylish playing of these musicians is hardly open to question. In the D major Suite the solo viola da gamba, to which Telemann gives pride of place throughout, is expressively played by Philippe Foulon. He is a gambist who proves his eloquence above all in the fine Sarabande of the work. The two concertos are for solo woodwind and strings. The A minor work is scored for pairs of recorders, oboes and violins with basso continuo, while that in E minor, the best-known piece in the programme, features an unusual partnership of recorder and flute, the old and the new, so to speak. The A minor Concerto is the slighter of the two and is the one work here which Telemann enthusiasts may not have in their library. It is an engaging piece with lively dialogue among the three instrumental groups; but it lacks the colourful invention of the E minor Concerto, with its tender slow movements and wild, swirling Polish dance finale. What the performances lack in finesse is generously compensated for in sheer interpretative *esprit*.

Overture-Suite in G major, 'La changeante'. Overture des Nations anciens et modernes. Suite in D major.
Northern Chamber Orchestra / Nicholas Ward.
Naxos 8 553791 (58 minutes: DDD). Recorded 1996. Ⓢ

These are three particularly attractive orchestral suites from an almost daunting legacy of some 130 such pieces from Telemann's pen. Ward directs the modern-instrument band from his position as first violin, securing tidy ensemble and maintaining buoyant rhythms. The least performed of the Suites is *La changeante*, framed by the key of G minor. Ward brings plenty of charm and some graceful gesture to the dances, yet too often underplays their character. Better this, by far, than those occasionally encountered mannerisms which exaggerate the importance of Telemann's sometimes elusive subtitles; but some of this playing may strike you as just a little too serious. The *Overture des Nations anciens et modernes*, like *La changeante*, is scored for strings and continuo. This is a delicious piece, full of witty contrasts, and prefaced by one of Telemann's most supple French overtures. The performance fails either to convey fully its nobility or to capitalize upon the radiance of Telemann's affable harmonies; but the playing is anything but lifeless, and repeats are scrupulously observed. While these two Suites probably date from Telemann's early years in Hamburg or even, in the case of *Les Nations*, slightly earlier, the remaining Suite in D major belongs to the very last years of his life. Scored for woodwind, two horns and strings it possesses some of the hallmarks of early classicism, demonstrating not only the octogenarian Telemann's fluency with a newly emerging idiom but also a certain flair for it. As before, the playing is rhythmic and sympathetic. In summary, an attractive release which does not, however, realize the music's full potential to entertain. But the playing is so good that it deserves inclusion in this guide.

Overture-Suites – G minor, TWV55:g4; A minor, TWV55:a2; C major, TWV55:C6; D major, TWV55:D15; D minor, TWV55:d3; F minor, TWV55:f1.
Vienna Concentus Musicus / Nikolaus Harnoncourt.
Teldec Das Alte Werk 4509-93772-2 (two discs: 148 minutes: ADD). Recorded 1978. Ⓜ Ⓟ

Harnoncourt is nowhere more at home than in the aesthetic world of this music. The Overtures of the ravishing G minor Suite and the bolder C major work show him to be a master of noble gesture and purposeful articulation. There is a robust, biting energy about Harnoncourt which is infectious; often, as in the Bourée *en trompette* of the C major work, one imagines that the exaggerated contrasts and deliberate accentuations would appear mannered if executed by anyone other than Harnoncourt. Throughout, he conjures up subtle rhythmic deviations, each paragraph flexibly shaped but still controlled and naturally breathed. If pliancy of this kind is an answer to making sense of baroque phrasing, then texture speaks volumes too: Telemann's oboe writing in particular, and its place within a string body is exceptionally skilled; his scoring of three oboes is especially effective and the oboists play with irresistible *esprit*. The D major Suite is full of instances where their performances brim with personality, contributing greatly to that fruity and ever so musty nose which characterizes Concentus Musicus on vintage form. The recorded sound is full of presence. With Harnoncourt one can imagine few exponents better suited to this colourful repertoire. This release is full of many unique delights and it contains three works not otherwise available in the catalogue.

Overture-Suites – G major, TWV55:G4, 'Des Nations anciens et modernes'; B flat major, 'Völker-Overture'. Concerto for Two Chalumeaux and Strings in D minor. Sonata for Two Chalumeaux and Continuo in F major. Viola Concerto in G major.
Colin Lawson, Michael Harris *chalumeaux*
Collegium Musicum 90 / Simon Standage *vn/va*
Chandos Chaconne CHAN0593 (77 minutes: DDD). Recorded 1995. Ⓕ🅿Ⓔ

The seemingly endless supply of Telemann's orchestral music shows no sign of palling in this release from Collegium Musicum 90, which mixes two colourful overture-suites with works for that mellow forerunner of the clarinet, the chalumeau, and the Concerto for viola which is famous mainly for being, well, a concerto for viola. The last three works are somewhat conventional, it must be admitted, but all show how readily the adaptable Telemann was able to find distinctive and attractive qualities in individual instruments, however unusual; the concerto for two chalumeaux, especially, has a calming summer-night feel to it. All are expertly played by their respective soloists. Undoubtedly of more interest, though, are the two suites, both of which feature a sequence of movements depicting the peoples of different European nations. Telemann's allusions are sometimes a little obscure – it's not easy to work out what makes one movement Swedish and another Swiss – but the results are certainly fun; try 'Les turcs', or the brief but extraordinary 'Les moscovites', with its three-note bell ostinato not unlike Bizet's *L'Arlésienne*. The performances are clean, neatly characterized and brightly recorded, from an orchestra that is really beginning to settle into a character of its own these days.

Essercizii Musici.
Cologne Camerata.
Deutsche Harmonia Mundi 05472 77361-2 (four discs: 236 minutes: DDD). Recorded 1994-95. Ⓕ🅿

Essercizii Musici consists of 12 trios, ten sonatas for melody instrument with basso continuo and two suites for solo harpsichord. The contents are satisfying on two levels since not only do they furnish the listener with unflagging entertainment but they also provide the performer with music written with unusual sympathy for the instruments in question. Telemann could turn his hand to almost anything and, it would seem, at the drop of a hat, did so. Here we have music both of intrinsically high calibre and of a cast which effortlessly explores the most alluring vocal range of each instrument. It is music which, in short, fulfils one of the composer's fervently declared aims, to give each instrument what suits it best, thus pleasing both player and audience. The members of Cologne Camerata, individually and corporately, enliven the music with stylistic and instrumental fluency. Telemann's distinctive expressive inflexions are not difficult to translate in performance yet their very ingenuousness, simplicity and lack of contrivance too often results in their being glossed over. These musicians revel in the melancholy suspensions, playful gymnastics and convivial instrumental dialogue with which these solos and trios abound. Certainly not all the pieces are of equal depth, but in trios such as that in C minor (No. 1), A major (No. 4), B flat (No. 8) and E flat (No. 12), Telemann reveals an extraordinary *puissance*, making a contribution to mid-eighteenth century chamber music that is both significant and inspired. In short, this is an important and delightful issue which will appeal to all lovers of eighteenth-century music. Fine recorded sound.

Sonates Corellisantes – No. 1 in F major, TWV42:F2. Paris Quartets, 'Nouveaux quatuors en Six Suites' – No. 6 in E minor, TWV43:e4. Essercizii Musici – Trio No. 8 in B flat major, TWV42:B4. Quartets – A minor, TWV43:a3; G minor, TWV43:g4.
Florilegium Ensemble.
Channel Classics CCS5093 (53 minutes: DDD). Recorded 1992. Ⓕ🅿

The rarity here is the *Sonata Corellisante* for two violins and continuo in which Telemann pays tribute to Corelli. The remaining works are the sixth and perhaps finest of the 1738 *Nouveaux Quatuors* or *Paris Quartets* as they have become known, a little *Quartet* (or *Quadro*) in G minor, a B flat Trio from the *Essercizii Musici* collection (*c*1739) and a fine Concerto da camera (Quartet) in A minor, very much along the lines of Vivaldi's pieces of the same kind in which each instrument other than the continuo has an obbligato role. The finest work here is the *Paris Quartet* which consists of a Prelude, a sequence of dance-orientated movements and an elegiac Chaconne that lingers long in the memory. The performance is full of vitality and probes beneath the music's superficialities. There is, throughout the programme, an intensity and a youthful spontaneity about this playing which has considerable appeal.

Kleine Cammer-Music – Partita No. 2 in G major, TWV41:G2. Essercizii Musici – Solo No. 5 in B flat major, TWV41:B6; Solo No. 11 in E minor, TWV41:e6; Trio No. 12 in E flat major, TWV42:Es3. Der getreue Music-Meister – Sonata in A minor, TWV41:a3. Der Harmonische Gottesdienst – No. 26, Am Sonntage Jubilate in C minor, TWV1:356[a]; No. 31, Am ersten Pfingstfeiertage in G major, TWV1:1732[a].
Paul Goodwin *ob* **Nigel North** *lte/theorbo* **Susan Sheppard,** [a]**Lynden Cranham** *vcs*
John Toll *hpd*
Harmonia Mundi HMU90 7152 (65 minutes: DDD). Recorded 1995.   Ⓕ ℗ Ⓔ

Paul Goodwin is surely one of the finest baroque oboists of the moment, so when he turns his mind to such a master of agreeable and skilfully composed chamber music as Telemann, it must be worth our while listening in. Every piece has its own character and charms: here is a seven-movement Partita from the *Kleine Cammer-Music* of 1716, then a couple of Solos and a quirky Trio involving an obbligato harpsichord from the *Essercizii Musici* of 1739, while a Lesson from the giant 1720s part-work, *Der getreue Music-Meister*, sits alongside movements with oboe obbligato from the slightly earlier sacred cantata collection *Der harmonische Gottesdienst*. The variety of form and nomenclature is more than matched on this disc by that of accompaniments which, as so many of the best continuo teams do these days, make an indispensable creative contribution to the success of the performance as a whole. With the boisterous and inspired Romanesca pair of Nigel North and John Toll on board this is no surprise. A cello also takes the original vocal line in the cantata movements, though the identity of the player (Susan Sheppard) is not made clear in the booklet. As for Goodwin himself, his playing is bold and bright with solid, versatile technique and fluid phrasing, and his interpretations are detailed and intelligent while losing nothing in spontaneity. The recorded sound for all instruments is perhaps rather aggressive over the space of an hour's listening, but then these are performances which by their very refusal to be timid demand full attention.

Trio Sonatas – F major, TWV42:F10; G minor, TWV42:g7. Quartets – C major, TWV43:C2; B minor, TWV43:b3; G major, TWV43:G12.
Limoges Baroque Ensemble (Maria-Tecla Andreotti *fl* Sergio Azzolini *bn*
Gilles Colliard *vn* Vittorio Ghielmi *va da gamba* Bruno Cocset *vc/violone*
Willem Jansen *hpd*) / **Christophe Coin** *va da gamba*
Auvidis Astrée E8632 (56 minutes: DDD). Recorded 1997.   Ⓕ ℗ Ⓔ

This discerningly assembled programme of chamber music with viola da gamba shows off the composer in some of his finest and most varied colours. Each and every one of the pieces here is of sustained musical interest and expressive charm. Christophe Coin, who plays viola da gamba and directs the ensemble, is certainly one of the most interesting minds at work in this period, and his performances are full of rhythmic energy, expressive fervour and technical expertise. Coin has made a point of highlighting Telemann's sensibility towards colour and texture, a feature that becomes strikingly apparent in the Quartet in B minor. It is scored for flute, viola da gamba, bassoon and continuo and, like its companion, in C major, conforms with an Italian *concerto a quattro*. The two slow movements of the B minor work are enormously expressive, the one tinged with melancholy, the other more conventionally lyrical. More startling than either of these, though, is the exotic finale with its central European folk-dance rhythmic inflexions, so beloved by the composer. The remaining pieces are all delightful, especially, perhaps, the Quartet in G major, scored for flute, two violas da gamba and harpsichord. Why is the companion piece always ignored? It is on a comparable inspirational level. This is a first-rate release and certainly one of the most invigorating discs of Telemann's chamber music available. The recorded sound is outstanding.

---

12 Fantaisies for Violin without Continuo, TWV40:14-25. Der Getreue Music-Meister – 'Gulliver' Suite in D, TWV40:108.
Andrew Manze, Caroline Balding *vns*
Harmonia Mundi HMU90 7137 (78 minutes: DDD). Recorded 1994.   Ⓕ ℗

Andrew Manze brings a very definite and distinctive angle to the 12 *Fantaisies*. We have learnt to take virtuosity for granted with Manze – his remarkable feats allow the most prejudiced to forget that he is playing a baroque fiddle. But without such an instrument he could barely create such a biting astringency in the more self-effacing and tortured moments (*Fantaisie* No. 6) or a cultivated assurance and definition in articulation to the recognizably regular sections, such as *Fantaisie* No. 10, where Telemann is working in established forms – particularly in the latter works in the set where dance forms predominate. If characterization is the key, Manze is arguably the most persuasive of all his rivals. He grows through phrases in the Gigue of the Fourth *Fantaisie* in a fashion which gives the work a peculiarly stoical strength, purrs through the contrapuntally conceived *Fantaisies* (Nos. 1-6 in particular) with nonchalant disdain for their often extreme technical demands and leaves sighs and pauses hanging with supreme eloquence. With sheer lucidity, breadth of imagination and colour, he most acutely captures the sense of a famous public figure ensconced in a private world against the backdrop of a musical world in a state of flux. To add spice to an already outstanding release, we have the short and delightful *Gulliver* Suite for two violins where Manze is joined by Caroline Balding – trust Telemann to be up-to-the-mark only a year or two after *Gulliver's Travels* was published!

---

12 Sonate metodiche.
Barthold Kuijken *fl* **Wieland Kuijken** *va da gamba* **Robert Kohnen** *hpd*
Accent ACC94104/5D (two discs: 140 minutes: DDD). Recorded 1994. ⓟ🅿

No, the title is hardly an incentive to part with one's pocket-money. But with Telemann we should know better than to be taken in by such packaging details. These are, in fact, 12 skilfully written and entertaining sonatas, published in two sets of six and issued in 1728 and 1732. Telemann seems, right from the start, to have had two instruments in mind: flute or violin, and though Barthold Kuijken has elected to play all of them on a baroque flute, he does so with such technical mastery that there is little cause for regret. He savours the many playful ideas contained in the faster movements and realizes a touching sense of melancholy in several of the slow ones. Among the most impressive of the sonatas is that in B minor which Kuijken plays with sensitivity and technical panache. The interpretation is on a sufficiently elevated level to warrant unqualified praise. The recorded sound is first-rate.

Hamburger Admiralitätsmusik, TWV24:1. Overture-Suite in C major, TWV55:C3,
'Hamburger Ebb und Fluth'.
Mieke van der Sluis *sop* **Graham Pushee** *counterten* **Rufus Müller** *ten* **Klaus Mertens,**
David Thomas, Michael Schopper *basses* **Alsfeld Vocal Ensemble;**
Bremen Baroque Orchestra / Wolfgang Helbich.
CPO CPO999 373-2 (two discs: 119 minutes: DDD). Text and translation included.
Recorded live in 1995. ⓟ🅿

The orchestral suite *Hamburger Ebb und Fluth* has been recorded many times and is one of the most engaging examples from Telemann's pen of a form at which he excelled. The Bremen Baroque Orchestra gives a lively and elegantly shaped performance of the work, introducing to its French overture a degree of *gravitas* appropriate to the occasion. Following the orchestral suite comes the *Admiralitätsmusik* serenade itself whose own introductory French overture's opening gestures call to mind the overture to Handel's *Music for the Royal Fireworks* written a quarter of a century later. Richey's poem is a paean to Hamburg, its institutions, its government and, not least, its prosperity. Each of the soloists assumes a role. Hamburg (Harmonia) is assigned to the soprano, judicial wisdom (Themis) to a countertenor, prosperity (Mercurius) to a tenor, the Elbe (Albis), North Sea (Neptunus) and republican liberty (Mars) to three basses. Recitatives and arias for these dramatis personae make up the greater part of Richey's text, lightly seasoned with occasional choruses for nymphs, tritons and the like. While it is more than likely that the audience in whose honour the serenade was written responded more readily to the topical and topographical allusions in Richey's text than to Telemann's music, quite the reverse applies today. Richey's platitudinous, at times flatulent sentiments are not likely to fire the imagination of late twentieth-century landlubbers. The solo team is a strong one, but the Alsfeld Vocal Ensemble does not always match them in tonal precision. The string playing is clean but would have better served the music if it had been more rhythmically incisive. In summary, this is a fascinating issue. Clear sound from a live recording.

Der Herr ist König, TWV8:6. Die Donner-Ode, TWV6:3.
Ann Monoyios, Barbara Schlick *sops* **Axel Köhler** *counterten* **Wilfried Jochens** *ten*
Harry van der Kamp, Hans-Georg Wimmer, Stephan Schreckenberger *basses*
Rheinische Kantorei; Das Kleine Konzert / Hermann Max.
Capriccio 10 556 (65 minutes: DDD). Texts and translations included. Recorded 1990-92. ⓟ

The *Donner-Ode* was one of Telemann's biggest public successes during his lifetime and is a striking piece in its own right, a vivid reaction to the Lisbon earthquake of 1755. The shock caused to the international community by this dreadful event (in which some 60,000 people were killed) was enormous, and in Hamburg a special day of penitence was the occasion for this 'Thunder Ode', though it does perhaps suggest a rather smug satisfaction that such a disaster didn't befall northern Germany. 'The voice of God makes the proud mountains collapse', the text proclaims, 'Give thanks to Him in His temple!'. The music, too, both in its mood and in that extraordinarily up-to-date style of Telemann's later years, frequently conjures the benign, entertainingly song-like pictorial mood of a Haydn Mass or oratorio. Entertaining is the word, though, especially in this energetic performance under Hermann Max. He is fleet-footed and buoyantly athletic, benefiting from what is becoming his customary excellent team of German soloists. For the coupling Max chooses another German work, the cheerful cantata *Der Herr ist König*, written much earlier in the composer's life and rather more Bach-like in character and form (though it is worth pointing out that since it survives partly in Bach's hand, we ought perhaps to conclude that Telemann was the one wielding the influence here). As in the *Ode*, choir, soloists and orchestra are bright, tight-knit and well recorded, making this release as a whole an enjoyable one.

Die Hirten an der Krippe zu Bethlehem, TWV1:797. Siehe, ich verkündige Euch, TWV1:1334. Der Herr hat offenbaret, TWV1:262.
Constanze Backes *sop* **Mechthild Georg** *contr* **Andreas Post** *ten* **Klaus Mertens** *bass*
Michaelstein Chamber Choir; Telemann Chamber Orchestra / Ludger Rémy.
CPO CPO999 419-2 (65 minutes: DDD). Texts and translations included. Recorded 1996. Ⓕ Ⓟ

The tenderly expressive and ingenuous character of German Protestant Christmas music of the baroque seldom fails to exert its magic. Though the greatest achievements in this tradition greatly diminished after Bach, there were exceptions. One of them is Telemann's intimate and characteristically imaginative oratorio *Die Hirten an der Krippe zu Bethlehem* ('The Shepherds at the Crib in Bethlehem'). The text is by the Berlin poet, Ramler and though Ramler's taste for classical forms sometimes makes his work stiff and austere, nothing could be further removed from this than his intimate account and celebration of Christ's birth. Certainly, it touched a chord in Telemann who responded with music of expressive warmth and irresistible charm. This is not at all the world of Bach's *Christmas Oratorio*, indeed it is only approximately a sixth of the length of Bach's masterpiece. Telemann's concept is one rather of noble simplicity, a sought-after goal in post-Bach church music which, in this respect, at least, provided a perfect foil to Ramler's text. Every reader will recognize the melody of the opening number as belonging to the Latin carol *In dulci jubilo*. Telemann's harmonization of the sixteenth-century tune, straightforward but with an occasional harmonic piquancy, sets the scene concisely and intimately. Thereafter, follows one delight after another. Of outstanding beauty are the 'Shepherd's Song' and the bass aria, 'Hirten aus den goldnen Zeiten'. This is an extremely pleasurable, well-filled, disc with a pervasive charm. The remaining two items are both Christmas cantatas, of 1761 and 1762 respectively and contain music of enormous appeal. Performances are excellent, with outstanding singing by Klaus Mertens and Mechthild Georg. Both choir and orchestra rise to the occasion under the sensitive and stylish direction of Ludger Rémy. Three hitherto unrecorded pieces in performances of such vitality make this comfortably a very strong issue.

Lobet den Herrn, alle seine Heerscharen, TWV1:061. Wer nur den lieben Gott lässt walten, TWV1:593. Der Tod ist verschlungen in den Sieg, TWV1:320.
Dorothee Fries *sop* **Mechthild Georg** *contr* **Andreas Post** *ten* **Albert Pöhl** *bass*
Friedemann Immer Trumpet Consort (Friedemann Immer, Klaus Osterloh, Ute Hübner *tpts*
Stefan Gawlik *timp*)
Bach Collegium Vocale, Siegen; Hanover Hofkapelle / Ulrich Stötzel.
Hänssler Classic CD98 179 (56 minutes: DDD). Texts and translations included. Recorded 1997. Ⓕ

While Telemann's concertos, suites, instrumental chamber music and oratorios have been well explored by performers, his large-scale cantatas, comparatively speaking, have not. Part of the problem is that there is a truly daunting number of them – many, many more for instance than those of his contemporary, Bach. And, it need hardly be said, the quality is variable. But few are utterly devoid of inspiration and the three pieces contained in this programme rise well beyond that category. Until now they have remained very possibly unperformed, but certainly unrecorded. These are not domestic pieces of the kind which characterize his well-known Hamburg anthology, *Der harmonische Gottesdienst*, but generously, sometimes colourfully orchestrated works with choruses, recitatives, arias and chorales. The format, in short, is Bach-like, though with nothing remotely comparable to the great opening choral fantasies of which Bach was the unchallenged master. Indeed, Telemann usually treats his hymn melodies simply, this very approach lending them a distinctive, ingenuous charm.

The three cantatas offer the listener strong contrasts of colour and of mood. The New Year piece, *Lobet den Herrn* has glittering trumpet parts with timpani and Telemann's deployment of them is deft and effective. The Neumeister setting, on the other hand, with an orchestra confined to strings and woodwind, is quietly spoken and more reflective. Performances are stylish and the director, Ulrich Stötzel, has a lively feeling for Telemann's frequent use of dance rhythms. The soloists are expressive – notably, perhaps, Mechthild Georg, who offers a lyrical account of her aria with oboe in the Easter cantata, *Der Tod ist verschlungen in den Sieg*. In short, this is a release which should interest and delight all readers with a taste for the music of this imaginative, astonishingly prolific and seemingly indefatigable composer, whose fecundity too often prompts generalizations that are as unwelcome as they are unjustified.

Orpheus.
Roman Trekel *bar* Orpheus; **Ruth Ziesak** *sop* Eurydice; **Dorothea Röschmann** *sop* Orasia; **Werner Güra** *ten* Eurimedes; **Maria Cristina Kiehr** *sop* Ismene; **Hanno Müller-Brachmann** *bar* Pluto; **Isabelle Poulenard** *sop* Cephisa, Priestess; **Axel Köhler** *counterten* Ascalax; **RIAS Chamber Choir, Berlin; Academy for Ancient Music, Berlin / René Jacobs.**
Harmonia Mundi HMC90 1618/9 (two discs: 159 minutes: DDD). Notes, text and translation included. Recorded 1996.   Ⓕ Ⓔ

This is the first performance on disc of an opera that was recognized as being the product of Telemann's pen only some 20 years ago. The original libretto was by a Frenchman, Michel du Boullay. Telemann himself seems to have adapted the text to suit Hamburg taste but though the libretto has survived virtually complete, a small part of the score is lost. For the edition used here, Peter Huth – who has also contributed a useful essay – Jakob Peters-Messer and René Jacobs, have filled the lacunae with music from other Telemann sources. Telemann's *Orpheus* has an additional dimension to the standard version of the legend in the person of Orasia, widowed Queen of Thrace. She occupies a key position in the drama first as murderess of Eurydice of whose love for Orpheus she is jealous, then of Orpheus himself, since he, understandably, rejects her advances. The plot develops effectively, contributing greatly to the dramatic coherence and overall satisfaction provided by text and music alike. In common with a great many operas for the Hamburg stage, *Orpheus* contains arias sung in languages other than the German vernacular. Italian was the usual alternative, but here there are airs in French, too, and Telemann, on these occasions, lends emphasis to the 'mixed style' aesthetic, in which he was an ardent believer, by retaining the distinctive stylistic character of each country. But the German arias are often both the most interesting and the most varied, since it is the Lied and the *arioso*, as developed in the Passion-Oratorio settings, that provide those additional ingredients which vitalize, refresh and give distinction to his music.

The cast is first-rate. Dorothea Röschmann projects a passionate and temperamental Orasia for whom Telemann has provided several strongly characterized arias. Orpheus is sung by Roman Trekel, Eurydice by Ruth Ziesak. Telemann adorns both roles with an affecting blend of lyricism and pathos. Eurydice's part in the drama is, perforce, relatively small but her music is often alluring and nowhere more so, perhaps, than when she welcomes the shades, who gather to prevent an opportunity for the lovers to look upon one another during the rescue scene. There are some forward-looking harmonies here which foreshadow later developments in opera. Orpheus's music is, appropriately, captivating more often than not; and it is strikingly varied in character. The other major beneficiary of Telemann's musical largesse is Orpheus's friend, Eurimedes, a tenor role expressively sung by Werner Güra. Pluto, a bass-baritone role sung with resonance and authority by Hanno Müller-Brachmann, appears in Act 1 only; but he has some splendid music'. The remaining roles are small but, of these, Ismene, one of Orasia's ladies-in-waiting, deserves mention for the aria, 'Bitter und süss sind Rachgier und Liebe'. This double-edged piece is ravishingly sung by Maria Cristina Kiehr. And another, for Pluto's servant Ascalax, contains moments of vivid word-painting fluently if, perhaps, tamely handled by Axel Köhler. In choosing a soprano of the calibre of Isabelle Poulenard to sing the minor role of Cephisa, a nymph, Jacobs showed shrewd judgement, since Telemann wrote a virtuoso aria for her which Poulenard sings with brilliance and technical skill. Cephisa also shares some delightful music with a chorus of nymphs. There are several fine choruses, lightly and articulately sung by the RIAS Chamber Choir and a handful of invigorating instrumental numbers. Jacobs and his musicians deserve congratulations, and so does Harmonia Mundi for the first-rate recording. This is an important and hugely enjoyable release.

Johannes Tinctoris   Flanders *c*1435–?1511

Missa L'homme armé. Missa sine nomine No. 1.
The Clerks' Group / Edward Wickham.
Cyprès CYP3608 (69 minutes: DDD). Recorded 1997.   Ⓕ

Johannes Tinctoris is remembered as perhaps the most influential theorist of the fifteenth century. What is not so well known is that he was no mean composer himself and The Clerks' Group reveals here how fine a composer he was. In the four-voice *L'homme armé* cycle he sets out to make his mark on a growing tradition of settings of that famous tune. His florid, at times fierce, prolixity fairly takes the breath away and The Clerks respond in kind with a raw, almost raucous performance that is very exciting to listen to. The top line is shared by a countertenor and a female alto. Although some may find the result at times just a bit rough, the energetic approach adopted here is certainly impressive. There are thrills of a slightly different nature in the *Missa sine nomine* No. 1, and it is remarkable that the low register can be sustained over half an hour's music. But the effort betrays itself in a slight loss of poise and shaping of lines, and an occasional suggestion of blandness about the ensemble's sound. As in the *L'homme armé* Mass, The Clerks' cast is slightly different from their usual sound, and one or two voices obtrude uncomfortably on occasion. The microphones, placed very close to the singers, emphasize these jagged edges. Yet the lyricism of the three-voice Mass provides effective contrast with the *L'homme armé* Mass, and suggests a variety of compositional approaches that marks Tinctoris as a composer of true inspiration.

Sir Michael Tippett
British 1905-1998

Concerto for Double String Orchestra. Fantasia concertante on a Theme of Corelli.
The Midsummer Marriage – Ritual Dances.
BBC Symphony Chorus and Orchestra / Sir Andrew Davis.
Teldec British Line 4509-94542-2 (64 minutes: DDD). Text and translation included. Recorded 1993. Ⓕ

Sir Andrew Davis's formidable Tippettian credentials shine through in every bar of this outstanding anthology. Aided by realistic, firmly focused sound, the *Concerto for Double String Orchestra* sounds glorious here. What's more, Davis directs a performance of enormous humanity, intelligence and dedication – even Sir Neville Marriner's excellent EMI remake now seems a little matter-of-fact by comparison. In the slow movement Davis secures a rapt response from his BBC strings (the exquisite closing bars are drawn with ineffable tenderness), while the finale bounds along with irrepressible vigour and fine rhythmic panache. Davis's *Fantasia concertante* is an even more remarkable achievement. This is another inspirational display: sensitive and fervent, yet marvellously lucid and concentrated too. Once again, the BBC strings are on radiant form, and the lyrical intensity of their playing during the central climax has to be heard to be believed. Davis's identification with this sublime music is total. Much the same applies, for that matter, to the committed and incisive account of the 'Ritual Dances' from *The Midsummer Marriage*, a veritable *tour de force* to which the BBC Symphony Chorus contributes thrillingly in the final dance.

Divertimento on Sellinger's Round. Little Music for Strings. The Heart's Assurance (orch. Bowen). Concerto for Double String Orchestra.
John Mark Ainsley *ten*
City of London Sinfonia / Richard Hickox.
Chandos CHAN9409 (71 minutes: DDD). Text included. Recorded 1995. Ⓕ

Chandos has here secured the first recording of the orchestral version of Tippett's major song-cycle, *The Heart's Assurance*. The *Concerto for Double String Orchestra* is Tippett's first masterwork, and it's marvellous to have a recording that does justice to all those antiphonal textural subtleties. One might wish for a touch more brio in the first movement, and a richer, stronger tone in places: for example, the slow movement's sublime outer sections. But this is still a very satisfying performance, not least because the finale comes across with such a winning blend of vitality and eloquence. Meirion Bowen's orchestration of *The Heart's Assurance* had Tippett's approval, and it is undoubtedly a resourceful piece of work. What makes the effect so different from the voice and piano original is that the all-important doublings of voice and instrument seem so much more prominent when the instrument in question can sustain the sound for as long as the voice itself. For this reason the original may be preferable, and in addition, despite John Mark Ainsley's excellent contribution to this recording, the final song doesn't build to its overwhelming climax as inexorably as it should. However, this is a valuable Tippett disc, and the recording is satisfyingly rich in detail.

The Rose Lake[a]. The Vision of St Augustine[b].
John Shirley-Quirk *bar*
London Symphony Chorus and Orchestra / [a]Sir Colin Davis, [b]Sir Michael Tippett.
Conifer Classics 75605 51304-2 (68 minutes: [b]ADD/[a]DDD). Text and translation included. Recorded [a]1997, [b]1971. Ⓕ Ⓢ

Although Tippett let it be known that *The Rose Lake* would be his last orchestral work, it does not sound valedictory. It is based on the profound impression made on him, during a holiday in Senegal, of a small lake which at midday was transformed from whitish green to translucent pink. Tippett imagines the lake singing and frames the five verses of its song with glittering ostinatos and bright toccatas, with much tuned percussion including three octaves of the rototoms of which he made such effective use in *Byzantium*. It is a simple, rondo-like structure but a satisfying one, with the lake first awakening (calm, woodland horns), its song then echoing from the sky (woodwind and string counterpoint) and reaching 'full song' (a long, eloquent string line underpinned by drums) at the centre. The latter half of the work is not a literal mirror-image of the first, but a series of poetic and ingenious 'doubles' of what went before, ending with magical horn calls recalling those in *The Midsummer Marriage*, a quiet rattle of xylophone and rototoms and, as a surprising coda, an abrupt sequence of *staccato* wind chords. It is a lovely and a moving piece, brimming with characteristically Tippettian melody. Almost as important, it is of just the right length to couple with the composer's own recording of one of his greatest but also one of his least often performed masterpieces. *The Vision of St Augustine* is hideously difficult to perform, but the choral singing here is quite heroic, and John Shirley-Quirk's account of the taxing solo part is nothing short of superb. It is truly visionary and profoundly moving. Sir Colin Davis's account of *The Rose Lake* is as urgently communicative as Tippett's own of the cantata, and the older recording is by no means put in the shade by the newer: both are excellent. This, in short, is an essential coupling for all admirers of Tippett's music.

Symphony No. 1. Piano Concerto.
Howard Shelley *pf*
Bournemouth Symphony Orchestra / Richard Hickox.
Chandos CHAN9333 (72 minutes: DDD). Recorded 1994.   Ⓕ**S**

The riot of proliferating counterpoint that is Tippett's Symphony No. 1 presents enough problems of orchestral balance to give recording teams (not to mention conductors) nightmares. Chandos has managed highly creditable degrees of containment and clarity, without loss of realism, and the impact, when the last movement finally settles on to its long-prepared harmonic goal, is powerful and convincing. As with other Hickox performances in this Tippett series, doubts as to whether initial impetus is sufficient to keep the complex structures on course prove groundless. This is a fine account, well balanced between lively rhythmic articulation and broad melodic sweep. The performance of the Piano Concerto is no less notable for the inexorable way in which its mighty design unfolds. There may be too much decorum, too little passion, in certain episodes, yet Howard Shelley makes persuasive sense of the *con bravura* marking in the finale, and his shaping of the first movement's long, dreamingly decorative lines is as alert and sensitive as his control of the second movement's more dynamic discourse. This is a truly symphonic concerto, with a wealth of invention, remarkable textural ingenuity and a particularly imaginative use of the orchestra to complement the bright colours of the solo instrument. The recording is faultless.

Symphony No. 2. New Year – Suite.
Bournemouth Symphony Orchestra / Richard Hickox.
Chandos CHAN9299 (65 minutes: DDD). Recorded 1994.   Ⓕ**B**

The balance Hickox achieves between attention to detail and large-scale symphonic sweep is exemplary, and especially impressive in the tricky finale, where he conveys the essential ambiguity of an ending which strives to recapture the optimistic *élan* of the work's opening without ever quite managing it. The Chandos recording, too, gives us much more of the symphony's contrapuntal detail. The first recording of music from Tippett's latest opera *New Year*, premièred in 1989, is thoroughly welcome. The music of this suite may seem over-emphatic to anyone who hasn't experienced the opera in the theatre, and the recording relishes the booming electric guitars and wailing saxophones, as well as the taped spaceship effects. Yet there are many imaginative moments, like the use of the 'paradise garden' sarabande borrowed from *The Mask of Time*, and the exotic arrangement of *Auld Lang Syne* near the end. This is Tippett firing on all cylinders, with a performance and recording to match.

Praeludium. Symphony No. 3.
Faye Robinson *sop*
Bournemouth Symphony Orchestra / Richard Hickox.
Chandos CHAN9276 (64 minutes: DDD). Text included. Recorded 1993.   Ⓕ

The Third Symphony, first heard in 1972, is one of Tippett's most complex and highly charged attempts to create a convincing structure from the collision between strongly contrasted musical characteristics. The work evolves from a purely orchestral drama – fast first movement, slow second movement, both large-scale, followed by a shorter *Scherzo* – to a less extended but also tripartite sequence of blues settings, the whole capped by a huge, climactic coda in which the soprano voice finally yields the last word to the orchestra. The first two movements (Part 1, as Tippett calls it) remain a considerable technical challenge, especially to the strings, but this performance manages to sustain an appropriate level of tension without sounding merely effortful, and without skimping on the opportunities for eloquence of phrasing. It could well be that Tippett has over-indulged the percussion in the slow movement, but this vivid and well-balanced Chandos recording lets us hear ample detail without exaggerating the bright colours and hyper-resonant textures. The later stages have the advantage of a superbly characterful singer in Faye Robinson. She has the power, the edge, and also the radiance, to make Tippett's progression from idiosyncratic blues to Beethoven-quoting peroration utterly convincing. The work ends, famously, on a question-mark, dismissing the unrestrained affirmation of Beethoven's *Choral* finale in favour of the unresolved opposition of loud brass and soft strings. Will that 'new compassionate power/To heal, to love' which the text 'senses' actually be achieved? Nearly thirty years on, the jury is still out on Tippett's great humanist challenge. Meanwhile, there can be no questioning the achievement of this performance and recording, coupled strikingly with the highly characteristic *Praeludium* for brass, bells and percussion of 1962.

String Quartets – No. 1[a]; No. 2 in F major[a]; No. 3[a]; No. 4[b]; No. 5[c].
The Lindsays (Peter Cropper, Ronald Birks *vns* [a]Roger Bigley, [bc]Robin Ireland *vas* Bernard Gregor-Smith *vc*).
ASV CDDCS231 (two discs: 123 minutes: ADD/DDD). Recorded 1975-92.   Ⓕ

Tippett coached the The Lindsays for these recordings of his first three quartets, and the other two were written for it. In a note written for the quartet's twenty-fifth anniversary in 1992 he said that in these recordings they were 'concerned to establish good precedents in matters of style, so that succeeding generations of interpreters start at an advantage'. In fact one of the most enjoyable things about these readings is that they are so very characteristic of the The Lindsays. Of course a number of the qualities that one might call 'characteristic' are uncommonly well suited to Tippett's earlier quartets: big tone, sheer vigour of attack and an infectious enjoyment of his lithe sprung rhythms. These performances are indeed excellent precedents for later interpreters. They do establish a style – big-scaled, urgently communicative – that is presumably 'authentic' and yet they challenge listeners as well as other performers to imagine how else they might be done. They also affirm the aching absence of a quartet between the Third and the Fourth (Tippett intended to write one in the late 1940s or early 1950s but got side-tracked by *The Midsummer Marriage* and did not write another for over 20 years) and make one wonder what the rejected two movements of the First Quartet might be like. It is wonderful, though, to hear the five as a sequence in such authoritative readings. The recordings sound very well, but have been transferred at an exceptionally high level.

Tippett String Quartet No. 5.
The Lindsays (Peter Cropper, Ronald Birks *vns* Robin Ireland *va* Bernard Gregor-Smith *vc*).
ASV CDDCA879 (76 minutes: DDD). Recorded 1992.   Ⓕ
Brown Fanfare to welcome Sir Michael Tippett. **Purcell** Fantasias – F major, Z737; E minor, Z741; G major, Z742. **Morris** Canzoni Ricertati – No. 1, Risoluto; No. 6, Lento sostenuto.
C. Wood String Quartet in A minor.

This curious mixture of a programme is a precise re-creation of the concert at which Tippett's Fifth String Quartet had its first performance. Music by two of his teachers and one of his great inspirers is preceded by a greeting prelude that quotes both Purcell and Tippett himself. Tippett's Quartet is quite typical of him, both in its exquisitely singing lyricism and in the fact that it is by no means a mere looking back towards his earlier lyrical phases. Here intensification of expression is often achieved by distillation, towards such a simplicity of utterance that at crucial moments the music thins sometimes to one, often to no more than two, of the quartet's voices. R.O. Morris's *Canzoni Ricertati* subject faintly folk-like melodies to ingenious fugal and canonic treatment. In Charles Wood's quartet, the ingenious interplay of short motives in his *Scherzo* is something that might have caught the young Tippett's ear, and his finale dresses up the Irish folk-song *The lark in the clear air* in its best Sunday clothes. The Purcell *Fantasias* point up Tippett's Purcell-ancestry rather touchingly as does Christopher Brown's miniature *Fanfare*. The Lindsays' beautiful performances are cleanly but not clinically recorded.

Piano Sonatas Nos. 1-3.
Nicholas Unwin *pf*
Chandos CHAN9468 (55 minutes: DDD). Recorded 1995.   Ⓕ

These are very big performances indeed, giving a clear and infectious impression of how satisfying these sonatas must be when you have a technique as commanding as Nicholas Unwin's. The tireless toccata vein in Tippett's piano writing, the abrupt grandeur of some of his juxtapositions, what one might call the 'Beethoven-plus' element (angular dotted figures not far from the *Grosse Fuge*, a buoyant humour closely related to the late *Bagatelles*) – all these are finely conveyed. Possibly missing is the blithely springy lightness of touch that some other pianists have found, especially in the First Sonata. Unwin is capable of light, transparent textures, and of fluid lyricism, so he provides pretty well 90 per cent or more of what these sonatas require. No one has supplied more, though it might have been a different 90 per cent. Which is to say that these are works that can take a variety of interpretations and gain from them. The recordings match the performances well, with a commandingly big piano sound, but there is no lack of more sober colour.

The Windhover. The Source. Magnificat and Nunc dimittis, 'Collegium Sancti Johannis Cantabrigiense'. Lullaby. Four Songs from the British Isles. Dance, Clarion Air. A Child of Our Time – Five Negro Spirituals. Plebs angelica. The Weeping Babe.
Finzi Singers / Paul Spicer with **Andrew Lumsden** *org*
Chandos CHAN9265 (55 minutes: DDD). Texts included. Recorded 1994.   Ⓕ

The Finzi Singers are eloquent in the Spirituals, and polished in the *British Songs* (especially the beguiling 'Early One Morning'). However, it is especially good to have the works which represent early sightings of Tippett's later, less lusciously lyrical style – the *Lullaby* (with countertenor, reminding us that it was written for the Deller Consort) and the *Magnificat* and *Nunc dimittis*: here not only are the intonation and phrasing of the tricky lines supremely confident, but the accompanying organ is recorded with exemplary naturalness. The vocal sound throughout is generally no less successful. There may be almost too full and rich a texture for the linear intricacies of *Plebs angelica* and *The Weeping Babe* to make their maximum effect, but there is no lack of exuberance in *Dance, Clarion Air* and the other secular pieces.

Tippett Music. Songs for Ariel. Songs for Achilles. Boyhood's End. The Heart's Assurance.
Purcell If music be the food of love, Z379/2. The Fairy Queen – Thrice happy lovers. The Fatal hour comes on apace, Z421. Bess of Bedlam, Z370. Pausanias – Sweeter than roses.
Martyn Hill *ten* **Craig Ogden** *gtr* **Andrew Ball** *pf*
Hyperion CDA66749 (70 minutes: DDD). Texts included. Recorded 1994.   Ⓕ🅔

The two longest works – the cantata *Boyhood's End* and song-cycle *The Heart's Assurance* – challenge the musicianship and sensitivity of singer and pianist alike. *Boyhood's End* (1943), a setting of prose that is never prosaic, shows the ecstasy of *Midsummer Marriage* to be already within the system, and the profusion of notes has to be mastered so that the dance shall seem as delicate and natural as graceful improvisation. In *The Heart's Assurance* (1951) the spirit is similar though the technical accomplishment of all concerned, composer and performers, is heightened. For the singer, in addition to fearsome difficulties of pitch and rhythm, there is likely to be some problem of tessitura, particularly in the third of the songs, 'Compassion'. For the pianist, concentration has to be divided between the virtuosic writing of his own part and responsiveness to the singer, his notes, words and expression. Martyn Hill and Andrew Ball are wonderfully at one in all this, and the balancing of voice and piano has been finely achieved. The *Songs for Achilles*, with guitar, also convey a sense of ardent improvisation, and the voice rings out freely. The *Songs for Ariel* here work their natural magic. Tippett's affinities with Purcell are felt at one time or another in most of these compositions, starting indeed with the opening of the programme, the setting of Shelley's *Sleep*. It is good also to have the Purcell 'realizations' included. The recording was issued to mark the composer's ninetieth birthday, a most touching and eloquent tribute.

A Child of Our Time. The Weeping Babe[a].
[a]**April Cantelo, Elsie Morison** *sops* **Pamela Bowden** *contr*
Richard Lewis *ten* **Richard Standen** *bass*
[a]**John Alldis Choir;**
Royal Liverpool Philharmonic Choir and Orchestra / Sir John Pritchard, [a]**Sir Colin Davis.**
Belart 461 123-2 (69 minutes: ADD). Recorded 1957.   Ⓢ🄷🆁🆁

A Child of our Time, first performed in 1941, is a twentieth-century Passion Music in which the protagonist is not divine, but human. The form is that of a Passion, with a narrator, with choruses and arias sometimes narrative, sometimes reflective, sometimes in commentary. Instead of chorales, there are Negro spirituals. In theory, this may seem a rather startling and perhaps inappropriate idea: but when we hear the music, we find that the introduction of the spirituals is natural, fitting and deeply moving. The work is not even; but at least two-thirds of it is inspired and original, in the sort of way that Berlioz's *Infant Christ* is. Tippett's counterpoint and his peculiar, unconventional scoring sound the overtones of human experience: the deep communicativeness of his compassionate and visionary music is not something that can be put into words; it must be experienced. And in many ways, we can experience it even more profoundly in this very fine performance than in the concert hall: we hear the voices – of the Boy, of his Mother, of the oppressed multitudes. Without distraction, we are put directly in touch with the music. The performance is, almost without qualification, a superb one. Richard Lewis and Richard Standen are both excellent. Elsie Morison sings with feeling and understanding, but her actual timbre is a little more bright, almost boyish, than one would ideally like to hear in music which calls for the sort of soprano that Joan Cross had. Pamela Bowden, too, has a rather odd timbre, strangely like a falsetto-tenor or countertenor around F on the treble stave. The words of the Liverpool Choir are not distinct, but their singing is otherwise very fine. Sir John Pritchard's reading of the score is masterly and extremely sensitive. *The Weeping Babe* is a wartime piece, written in 1944 to especially written words of Dame Edith Sitwell; a beautifully wrought piece, thoroughly diatonic in idiom and simple in feeling. The recording is extremely vivid and lifelike.

A Child of Our Time.
Faye Robinson *sop* **Sarah Walker** *mez* **Jon Garrison** *ten* **John Cheek** *bass*
City of Birmingham Symphony Chorus and Orchestra / Sir Michael Tippett.
Collins Classics 1339-2 (69 minutes: DDD). Text included. Recorded 1992.   Ⓕ

Sir Michael Tippett made this recording in his eighty-seventh year, some 50 years after completing this, his first wholly characteristic large-scale work. We may well come to regret that he recorded so few of his compositions when he was younger – and *A Child of Our Time* in particular, since youthful impetuosity is so essential to its character. There are places where a firmer hand and a more forceful rhythm might have been more appropriate. Yet the performance as a whole has a touching gravity and an honest expressiveness that make the final vision of 'an abiding hope' unusually telling. Pritchard's recording was distinguished particularly by the contributions of the soprano and tenor soloists; this release, made in Symphony Hall Birmingham, excels in the work's vivid orchestral and choral textures. The soloists might have been given a more forward position, but their contributions are generally good, despite Faye Robinson's occasionally excessive vibrato, and John Cheek's rather lachrymose way with his recitatives. Tippett's preference for deliberate tempos is most obvious in the Spiritual 'Nobody knows the trouble I see', which has less 'swing' than in other performances. At first, Part One seems to hang fire, and the orchestral accompaniment to the first soprano solo 'How can I cherish my man in such days?' is overweighted. But the tension gradually builds, with 'Go down, Moses' splendidly broad and sonorous, and the later stages achieve the right balance between the dramatic and contemplative dimensions proper to an oratorio. At a time when national aspirations are once again a cause of instability in the world, Tippett's message has renewed relevance, and his music, and his interpretation of it, retains its special power to move.

The Mask of Time.
Faye Robinson *sop* **Sarah Walker** *mez* **Robert Tear** *ten* **John Cheek** *bass*
BBC Symphony Chorus and Orchestra; BBC Singers / Sir Andrew Davis.
EMI British Composers CMS7 64711-2 (two discs: 91 minutes: DDD). Notes and text included.
Recorded live in 1986. *Gramophone* Award Winner 1987.   Ⓜ

The problems which *The Mask of Time* presents to a recording producer are formidable: complex and closely-set ensembles in which both chorus and soloists must be audible, an all-too-coagulable electric organ, blindingly brilliant high brass, an exuberant use of percussion (of which the bashing of brake-drums with a couple of coke-hammers is only the most conspicuous example: it sounds like a gargantuan xylophone) – all these are juxtaposed with chamber textures of luminous beauty and delicacy that could very easily be distorted by any attempt to compensate for their relative lack of decibels. It is difficult to imagine the problems being better solved than they are by this outstandingly successful recording: the rendering of voices is splendidly direct and natural, any discreet help that the final section may have needed to clarify the soloists' contributions is unobtrusive, the alluring strangeness of Tippett's orchestral palette is engrossingly conveyed without ever robbing the chorus of satisfying impact. The recorded sound, in short, has the measure of the work's stature. That stature is implicit from the very beginning (a memorable choral image of the creation of sound), but it first becomes fully evident in the fourth movement ('The ice-cap moves South-North'), a huge choral double *Scherzo* of marvellously sustained invention. This combines impressive technical resource with the sort of naivety that can reach areas that sophistication cannot: the first part of the movement, an exhilarating evocation of man the hunter, concludes with an onomatopoeic percussion interlude (to describe a stampede of buffalo); the second, in which mankind learns agriculture and religion, unaffectedly quotes both Handel and Beethoven within its first few bars and ends with the dawning of a magnificent sun (choir and brass so vivid that you shield your eyes). Balancing this in the second half of the piece is another scherzo, also double, but this time a fearsome one. Shelley's vision of human life as a triumphant but terrifying juggernaut is set as a Berliozian *Lacrimosa*, careering along over a lumbering ostinato, drums and brass adding elements of *Tuba mirum* and *Dies irae*. Shelley's death at sea is then described in a scudding, headlong storm-piece of reeling impetus, but both sections of the movement salvage images of permanence from the wreckage: a choral shout of 'Life!' and a calm contemplation of the poet's immortality.

Such contradictions are at the very heart of *The Mask of Time*: the 'paradise garden' scene that lies between the two scherzos mingles radiantly Purcellian evocations of Milton and a sort of blues-madrigal with some of Tippett's most engagingly daft dialogue. Soaring towers (the ululatory 'endless singing' of the finale, the movingly plangent *Akhmatova* setting in the eighth movement) are set alongside cunningly crafted lapidary work (the three chorale preludes and three alchemical invocations that make up the seventh), and for such moments as these you will be more than willing to pay the price of a few botched details: Tippett has never been a composer of flawless masterpieces. He needed this towering structure in order to support the sheer size of the images he was creating; they contain some of his most masterly music and provided abundant evidence that his imaginative grasp was still expanding. Who could complain that some elements of the structure are a bit rickety? The performance is a marvellous one, distinguished especially by choral singing of breathtaking assurance and by the fervour and grip of Andrew Davis's direction; the soloists are all better than good and the orchestral playing is virtuoso. A performance worthy of the music, indeed: high praise.

The Knot Garden[a].
Raimund Herincx *bass* Faber; **Yvonne Minton** *mez* Thea; **Jill Gomez** *sop* Flora;
Dame Josephine Barstow *sop* Denise; **Thomas Carey** *bar* Mel; **Robert Tear** *ten* Dov;
Thomas Hemsley *bar* Mangus;
Orchestra of the Royal Opera House, Covent Garden / Sir Colin Davis.

A Child of Our Time[b].
Jessye Norman *sop* **Dame Janet Baker** *mez* **Richard Cassilly** *ten* **John Shirley-Quirk** *bar*
BBC Singers; BBC Choral Society; BBC Symphony Orchestra / Sir Colin Davis.
Philips 446 331-2PH2 (two discs: 145 minutes: ADD). Notes and texts included. Item marked [a]
recorded 1993, [b]1975. Ⓕ

The Knot Garden is a classic of its period and a central work in its composer's output. Some of the more enthusiastic reviews after its first performance were rather perplexed by its structure: it is a short opera, but its three acts are divided into 23 scenes, often brief and abruptly juxtaposed. However, the form of the piece now seems to be admirably clear, musically strong and ideally appropriate to the subject. It is not so much a narrative as an examination of a set of relationships. The First Act introduces six of the seven characters, briefly demonstrates their problems and then introduces a catalyst in the person of Denise, the freedom-fighter disfigured by torture. She sings an updated version of an ancient operatic form – the virtuoso display aria, here brilliantly put to new purposes – which in turn prompts an ensemble-finale in the again updated form of a blues with a fast boogie-woogie middle section. As an opera about relationships it needs particularly sensitive handling by the singers, and the cast (that of the first performance) is outstanding. Tear gives his character ('a homosexual in pink socks!', sneered one reviewer) real charm and pathos as well as singing his uncommonly difficult lines with great flair. Barstow is even finer: an electric presence with a visionary intensity to her aria of remembered anguish. Minton and Herincx are both excellent, Gomez touchingly vulnerable, while Hemsley's immaculate diction and gentlemanly tones are perfect for Mangus, the psychiatrist Prospero who 'puts them all to rights'. Davis is as eloquently urgent in the opera as in the oratorio, *A Child of Our Time*, which, in a generally fine, rather opera-scaled reading, makes an ideal coupling: two complementary aspects of Tippett the maker of healing images.

Loris Tjeknavorian   Iranian 1937

Tjeknavorian Piano Concerto, Op. 4.
Babadzhanian Heroic Ballade. Nocturne.
Armen Babakhanian *pf*
Armenian Philharmonic Orchestra / Loris Tjeknavorian.
ASV CDDCA984 (58 minutes: DDD). Recorded 1996. Ⓕ

Tjeknavorian Orchestral

Tjeknavorian's concerto may have too many notes, but it is endearingly like a pastiche of a Khachaturian concerto, with added dissonances. It opens in this vein, but almost immediately there is a strenuous orchestral tutti, with the piano splashing about wildly in a kind of accompanied toccata. This is not a style with which the more conservative Khachaturian would have been comfortable, until suddenly a rather touching, sinuous Armenian melody arrives, which he would certainly have acknowledged. The pianist gently and thoughtfully soliloquizes on this attractive lyrical idea until he receives some romantic support from the orchestra. A repeated *pianissimo* solo ostinato (played with remarkable concentration by Babakhanian) then gradually gathers pace and leads to the reprise and a pianistic climax of glittering, even thundering bravura before the orchestra riotously returns. The *Andante* then brings a yearning horn solo and the piano ruminates until the orchestra joins him to build a dissonantly lyrical climax. The soloist gives a brilliant performance, with stunning bravura where needed, yet he is quite melting in the lyrical passages. With the composer at the helm of the obviously well-rehearsed Armenian Orchestra it is difficult to think that the work could receive more compelling advocacy and the recording is extremely vivid.

Babadzhanian won a USSR State Prize for his *Heroic Ballade*, and it opens in the orchestra as if it were going to produce a title-theme for a David Lean movie. But the piano enters gently with a sub-Rachmaninovian melody, with Armenian touches. The Rachmaninov influences remain strong, but the composer's eclectic style does not mean that he is not inventive: there are plenty of reflective poetic opportunities for the soloist. The work overall is distinctly enjoyable. The *Nocturne* is not just crossover music – it has already crossed over, for it begins with a gentle rhythm backing, which continues throughout. The piano enters and soon the full strings take up the melody and expand it: cheap music, but as Noel Coward observed, there is nothing more potent. Again, the playing is splendidly enthusiastic (and stylish) and the sound excellent.

Haukur Tómasson
Icelandic 1960

Gudrún's Fourth Song.
Berit Maeland *sop* Gudrún; **Merete Sveistrup** *sop* Kostbera, First Norn;
Ulla Kudsk Jensen *mez* Glaumvör, Second Norn; **Isabel Piganiol** *mez* Brynhildur;
Rudi Sisseck *bass-bar* Atli; **Sverrir Gudjónsson** *counterten* Knéfröour, Third Norn;
Thórunn Kristjánsdóttir *sop* Erpur; **Herdís A. Jónasdóttir** *contr* Eitill;
Fóstbraedur Male Choir; Ensemble Caput / Christian Eggen.
BIS CD908 (60 minutes: DDD). Notes, text and translation included. Recorded 1997. Ⓕ

In truth, this disc presents just the music for the opera *Gudrún's Fourth Song* (1994-96), since in performance its 12 numbers are linked by spoken, unset narratives, omitted here. This imitates the fragmentary quality of the Icelandic Eddas from which the text derives, and is echoed in the title – there being three traditional lays associated with Gudrún, the opera is therefore the fourth. Gudrún is promised by her brothers, Gunnar and Högni, to the hero Sigurd. This last-named has previously killed a treasure-hoarding dragon and awakened a princess surrounded by fire with whom he has fallen in love; having then betrayed her (by marrying her off to Gunnar) he has been slain in revenge. Sound familiar? Well this is the same legend as in *Siegfried* and *Götterdämmerung*, bereft of its divine aspect and presented from the viewpoint of Gudrún (Wagner's Gutrune). Gunnar and Högni equate to Gunther and Hagen, Sigurd to Siegfried (yes, the dragon is Fafnir), while the Valkyrie Brynhildur is not Wotan's daughter but Attila the Hun's sister. Attila (here called Atli) duly marries Gudrún. His vengeance on Gunnar and Högni, and Gudrún's Medea-like response, extend the story beyond Wagner in true Icelandic fashion. The music, however, bears no echo of *The Ring*. This is a chamber opera, delicate in texture (there are some lovely instrumental and vocal solos) however much the individual lines are forged of steel. The magical score has an inner radiance, particularly during Gudrún's solos (tracks 1, 5 and 12), that is more redolent of Judith Weir than Wagner. Captured beautifully on this recording, this performance sounds perfect.

Thomas Tomkins
British 1572-1656

Prelude. Fancy. Three In Nomines. Voluntary. Pavan and Galliard of Three Parts. Fancy (arr. cpsr). Toy, 'Made at Poole Court'. Pavan. Robin Hood. Two Pavans. Ground.
Bernhard Klapprott *hpd/virg*
Dabringhaus und Grimm MDG607 0704-2 (72 minutes: DDD). Recorded 1995. ⒻⓅ

Tomkins is perhaps best known as a later representative of the school of English madrigalists, and one of Byrd's most talented pupils; yet he composed in all the genres available to him, and left a substantial quantity of keyboard music. Indeed, he was a keen student of the works of other virginalists and, like Byrd, extended his activity in this area to the very last years of his life. Tomkins is at his best when unfettered by pre-ordained conceits, and while he cannot match his great mentor's grasp of form or his knack for writing instantly memorable tunes, the best pieces here are not without charm (the little *Toy*, for example). Bernhard Klapprott plays mostly on a harpsichord, and more rarely on a much softer virginal, which seems the more effective of the two instruments for conveying the music's unaffected delicacy. He strives to find the right expression for each piece; rubato is applied differently from one work to the next according to each piece's character, rather than exclusively by genre. Tempos could have been equally varied: they are uniformly on the slow side, even where greater agility would at least be warranted (as in the Galliard). The choice of instrument may have something to do with this: the virginal's softer sound encourages more rapid runs, whereas the harpsichord's seems to do the opposite. Still, a pleasing disc: Klapprott's advocacy of Tomkins reminds us how much of this first golden age of the keyboard remains unexplored.

Third Service. O Lord, let me know mine end. O that the salvation were given. Know you not. In Nomine (1648). In Nomine (1652). Voluntaries – G major; C major; A minor.
New College Choir, Oxford / Edward Higginbottom with **David Burchell** *org*
CRD CRD3467 (62 minutes: DDD). Texts included. Recorded 1990. Ⓕ Ⓔ

This is a well-balanced programme of sacred music by Thomas Tomkins. The four movements of the Third, or Great Service, together with the three anthems are spaced out with five organ pieces – two *In Nomines* and three voluntaries – chosen and arranged in such a way that the resulting key sequence has a satisfying natural flow. After an unassuming intonation, the truly royal *Te Deum* of the Great Service takes off with great verve and vigour, the rich ten-part texture of the full sections contrasting well with the lighter scoring of the verses. This energy and these contrasts are characteristic of the performances as a whole. There is some delightful solo singing in the verse anthems, in particular the alto solo in *O Lord, let me know mine end.* The two solo trebles are kept busy: they have a rather distinctive but complementary tone-quality, which makes up for a slight imbalance in volume. In general, however, the balance is good and the ensemble excellent. The trebles are a confident group with good articulation; they soar up to their top B flats with ease.

Michael Torke

Overnight Mail. Telephone Book. July. Flint. Change of Address.
Anton Lukoszevieze *vc* **Mark Thistlewood** *db* **Philip Bush** *pf*
Apollo Saxophone Quartet (Tim Redpath, Rob Buckland, Andrew Scott, Will Gregory *saxes*);
Present Music (Marie Sander *fl* Bill Helmer *cl* Eric Segnitz *vn* Paul Gmeinder *vc*);
Michael Torke Band / Michael Torke *pf* **Orkest de Volharding / Jurjen Hempel.**
Argo 455 684-2ZH (67 minutes: DDD). Recorded 1996-97. Ⓕ Ⓔ

At his best, Torke manages to capture a feeling of glowing euphony and an effortless quality that is rare in new music today. If the highlights of this disc are *Telephone Book* and *July*, a great deal of credit is due to the performances which are superb. It is hard to imagine a more expressive and beautifully timed rendition of *July* than the one given by the Apollo Saxophone Quartet, whose approach manages to combine considerable refinement of tonal blending with the spontaneity almost of a live performance. The first movement of *Telephone Book* is none other than *The Yellow Pages*, which Torke has recorded before for Argo. The two versions are remarkably similar in approach but this recording with Present Music is funkier, fuller in sound and shows greater insight into the work's structure. The two movements, 'The Blue Pages' and 'The White Pages', which feature the same technique of 'static transposition', are also well characterized and sustained. However, the CD as a whole lacks contrast and prospective listeners might be advised not to hear it all the way through but to concentrate on individual works. 'Priority', the first movement of *Overnight Mail*, is particularly impressive, and both *Flint* and *Change of Address* have many striking ideas. This recording confirms Torke as one of the foremost compositional talents in America today.

Veljo Tormis

Estonian Calendar Songs – Martinmas Songs; St Catherine's Day Songs; Shrovetide Songs; Swing Songs; St John's Day Songs for Midsummer's Eve; Three Estonian Game Songs.
Estonian Philharmonic Chamber Choir / Tõnu Kaljuste.
Virgin Classics VC5 45185-2 (52 minutes: DDD). Texts and translations included.
Recorded 1995. Ⓕ Ⓔ

Works by Veljo Tormis, particularly those for voices, seem altogether more natural than the better-known output of Pärt which can strike you as artificial by comparison. The present collection of songs, inspired by the rituals of the Estonian folk calendar, resonates in the mind long after actual listening has ceased. Tormis has a predilection for cycles and sets – indeed sets of cycles; these 32 songs (all composed 1966-67) are grouped into six sets, ranging from simple triptychs (the *Shrovetide* and *Game Songs* – the games all relating to Christmas) to fully fledged cycles for Martinmas (nine songs) and St John's Day (seven). The *Martinmas Songs*, like most of their companions here but unlike the *Forgotten Peoples* cycle, are tiny – none exceeds 100 seconds and six last under a minute. The *St John's Day Songs*, however, are a different matter: bigger-boned if mostly brief ('Fire Spell', with its insistent declamations, is electric), although the final 'St John's Song', at over five-and-a-half minutes, is more a small cantata or motet than a 'mere' song. The Estonian choir under its Chief Conductor, Tõnu Kaljuste, does itself and the music proud in beautifully sung renditions.

Charles Tournemire
French 1870-1939

Symphonies – No. 5 in F minor, Op. 47; No. 8 in G minor, Op. 51, 'Le triomphe de la mort'.
Liège Philharmonic Orchestra / Pierre Bartholomée.
Auvidis Valois V4793 (69 minutes: DDD). Recorded 1997.   Ⓕ

The Liège Philharmonic may not be a world-class orchestra, but it plays with wholehearted commitment and sensitive dynamics, and is directed by a conductor who is clearly in sympathy with the Franckian school, so that these performances offer a very satisfactory presentation of this deeply felt, passionate music. Tournemire (one of Franck's successors at Ste Clotilde) could best be described as a romantic mystic: unlike some other enormously prolific composers, his ideas have quality and his treatment of them is both original and extremely effective. Those wishing to sample his style are recommended to start with the beatific *Pastorale* of the Fifth Symphony, a work written in 1913-14 and inspired by Alpine scenery which produced in him a poetic mood of exaltation.

The Eighth Symphony of a decade later, which employs a gigantic orchestra in virtuoso and varied fashion and is somewhat bolder in harmonic idiom, is subtitled *Triumph over death* and was written on the death of the composer's dearly loved wife (to whom the Fifth had been dedicated). Both works are most unorthodox in form. The Fifth consists of a first movement in which a chorale appears three times, each time followed by an *Allegro* section: the second movement is the tender *Pastorale* that then leads into a joyous finale headed 'Towards the light'. The Eighth is still more unusual in that a single theme ingeniously runs throughout its two movements, the first a sorrowing *Lento* that is followed by a luminous more light-hearted section. The second continues for a while in similar vein but with more brilliant scoring, gives way to an intimate meditation and ends in a transport of radiance. A remarkably individual and gripping work that demands to be heard.

Tournemire Suite Evocatrice, Op. 74.
Vierne Symphony No. 3, Op. 28.
Widor Symphonie Gothique, Op. 70.
Jeremy Filsell *org*
Herald HAVPCD145 (71 minutes: DDD). Recorded in 1991 on the Harrison and Harrison organ
of Ely Cathedral.   Ⓕ

Compared with, say, the symphonies of Tchaikovsky or Sibelius the organ symphonies of Widor and his pupil Vierne are not particularly long. But in terms of organ music they are among the longest single works in the repertory. Within their five-movement form the composers set out to exploit the full expressive range of the organ and it was no coincidence that the organ symphony developed in turn of the century France. The great French organ builder Aristide Cavaillé-Coll was then producing instruments capable of hitherto undreamt-of colour and expression. Both Widor (at St Sulpice) and Vierne (at Notre Dame) had at their disposal the finest instruments in Paris and they indulged themselves fully in their symphonies. The subtitle of Widor's Ninth (*Gothic*) says it all. The structure is vast, intricately detailed, and almost forbidding in its grandness. Vierne's Third also presents an awesome spectacle, full of complex music and technically demanding writing, while Tournemire's neo-classical Suite provides a moment almost of light relief in such heavyweight company. Jeremy Filsell is an outstanding virtuoso player with a gift for musical communication and, in the Ely Cathedral organ, an instrument which produces the range of the great French instruments, but within an altogether clearer acoustic. These are performances and recordings of exceptional quality.

Joaquín Turina

Danzas fantásticas, Op. 22. La procesión del Rocio, Op. 9. Sinfonía sevillana, Op. 23. Ritmos, Op. 43.
Bamberg Symphony Orchestra / Antonio de Almeida.
RCA Red Seal RD60895 (63 minutes: DDD).   Ⓕ

Turina was a magnificent orchestrator and although he was – as Antonio de Almeida points out in his useful booklet annotations – a 'quintessential Sevillian', he was also acutely aware of musical trends beyond his own locality. His style approximates the youthful opulence of early Debussy (whose sensuous *Printemps* frequently comes to mind), yet the piquant instrumentation that graces, say, 'Exaltación' from the *Danzas fantásticas*, or the whole of *La procesión del Rocio* is refreshingly individual – beautifully aired and crafted, with the sum of its gleaming parts amounting to an appealing tonal blend. Were it not for the give-away nature of specifically Spanish melodies, Dvořák (of the *Slavonic Dances*) would as likely come to mind as Falla – particularly in the *Danzas*. *La procesión* (1912) predates the other pieces on the disc, while *Ritmos* was composed as late as 1928. It was premièred by Casals, but here more than anywhere else on the disc, one is reminded of Almeida's great mentor, Sir Thomas Beecham. Just listen to the way he points *Ritmos*'s atmospheric 'Danza lenta', or sample the excitement he generates in the 'Danza exótica' from the same work; then turn back to 'Fiesta en San Juan de Aznalfarache' from *Sinfonía sevillana* – awash with colour from the first bar to the last – and witness how the Bamberg players exploit Turina's varied tonal palette. As for the recording (a co-production between BMG Classics and Bavarian Radio), it's truly demonstration-worthy; a fair sampling point is the 'Valse trágico' from *Ritmos*, which features a spectacular mushrooming tam-tam. Turina's use of winds, brass and percussion, in particular, is as judicious as it is impressive, and he never overcrowds his orchestral climaxes. Unalloyed delight.

Turina Piano Trios – No. 1, Op. 35; No. 2, Op. 76. Círculo, Op. 91.
Granados Piano Trio, Op. 50.
Beaux Arts Trio (Ida Kavafian *vn* Peter Wiley *vc* Menahem Pressler *pf*).
Philips 446 684-2PH (73 minutes: DDD). Recorded 1995.   Ⓕ

The youthful Granados Trio (the first performance was given in 1895), which occupies a third of the disc, is a pleasantly lyrical, if rather inconsequential and bland (except in the excitable finale) work whose only obvious Hispanicism is an isolated phrase at the end of the Trio to the elfin *Scherzetto*. Turina's works for trio, written over a quarter of a century later, are altogether more skilful, more subtle and rewarding, and considerably more nationalistic (though coloured by impressionist influences) – conspicuously in the First Trio's harmonically evocative theme followed by five variations in regional dance styles, including a *muñeira*, a *zortzico* and a *soleares*. The swaying rhythms in its finale too – which in the best Schola Cantorum tradition recapitulates earlier material – and of the more restrained Second Trio's initial movement and its sparkling second-movement *zortzico*, are idealized-Spanish in style. Turina's talent for romantically picturesque music is demonstrated in his *Círculo*, which depicts sunrise, midday and sunset, a programme that allows him again to utilize the cyclic form he had learnt from Vincent d'Indy. The accomplished performances can, despite a rather often over-hefty piano, be recommended to all interested in this seldom heard area of Spanish music.

Mark-Anthony Turnage

Blood on the Floor.
Martin Robertson *sax/bass cl* **John Scofield** *elec gtr* **Peter Erskine** *drum kit*
Ensemble Modern / Peter Rundel.
Argo 455 292-2ZH (69 minutes: DDD). Recorded live in 1996.   Ⓕ

Blood on the Floor is an impressive demonstration of the composer's ability to straddle the worlds of jazz, rock and art music without descending to the modish doodling of his crossover peers. The overall title comes from a painting by Francis Bacon, while the music ranges widely in its references and allusions. Understandably, the disc's packaging plays upon the theme of urban alienation and, of course, *Blood on the Floor* has its harrowing aspects. A younger brother of the composer died as a consequence of drug addiction and several of its nine movements could scarcely be more explicitly titled. At the same time, the punchy, amplified, vernacular element should not disguise the fact that this is also an elegantly crafted suite, ingeniously laid out for the 30-odd musicians of Ensemble Modern plus a solo trio of electric guitar, drum kit and saxophone. The participation of John Scofield puts flesh on the bones of Turnage's longstanding idiomatic involvement with Miles Davis, and the 'classical' influences include the usual culprits – Stravinsky, Britten and, conceptually at least, Hans Werner Henze. Somehow, the contradictions don't jar as you'd expect. Operating in an age in which the acquisition of a unified and personal voice is no longer considered top priority, Turnage's eclecticism does not lead to the usual anonymity. His bluesy, shell-shocked lyricism is very much his own. The abrasive opening movement spews out key thematic material in a series of angry, violent climaxes, and yet this is not the dominant mood. 'Junior Addict', inspired by a poem by Langston Hughes, is powerfully melodic with its bleak soprano saxophone solo weaving through woodwinds above a subterranean bass. Get this far and you should be hooked. Elsewhere the symphonic Turnage is in the ascendant, seeming to aim for the clinching quasi-Mahlerian expression of hope tempered by fatalism, dispelling the fears. The recording is edited together from live performances given in a variety of venues and the immediate style of miking, pop-influenced track-listings and (trilingual) annotations will not be to everyone's taste. That said, the playing is undeniably superb and, for the moment, this feels like a major release whether it represents the last gasp of the Third Stream or a radical new beginning.

Erkki-Sven Tüür
Estonia 1959

Architectonics VI. Passion. Illusion. Crystallisatio. Requiem.
Estonian Philharmonic Chamber Choir; Tallinn Chamber Orchestra / Tõnu Kaljuste.
ECM New Series 449 459-2 (64 minutes: DDD). Text and translation included.
Recorded 1994-95.   Ⓕ

Architectonics VI sounds like one of those titles that are too good to resist, and it is to the credit of Erkki-Sven Tüür that he admits as much in the brief interview in the booklet to this beguiling disc (the sumptuous annotation in English is translated in reduced form in German and French). Tüür's piece – written in 1992 – isn't architectonic in construction (well, any more than the music of a hundred other composers), but it is well put together and effective on its own terms. *Passion* and *Illusion*, both for string orchestra and composed in 1993, are closer in spirit to the prevailing 'New Simplicity' of current East Baltic composition. *Passion*, indeed, is occasionally reminiscent of Tüür's better-known compatriot, Arvo Pärt, although the brief *Illusion* has a curiously English feel to it. The title track, *Crystallisatio* (1995), is scored for three flutes, bells, string orchestra and live electronics and is somewhat more demanding in scope. It is here that Tüür's synthesis of minimalism with serial techniques is heard most eloquently; not wholly achieved, perhaps, but fascinating in application. By far the biggest piece is the Requiem (1992-93; in memory of the conductor Peeter Lilje). It is a deeply felt, half-hour-long setting of the mass for the dead, and is of markedly different character to the other pieces here. This is a handsomely produced, thought-provoking release. Anyone wanting to hear up-to-the-minute new music that will not sear the ears off his or her head should try it.

Viktor Ullmann
Austro/Hungarian 1898-1944

Ullman Die Weise von Liebe und Tod des Cornets Christoph Rilke. Variationen und Doppelfuge über ein Thema von Arnold Schoenberg, Op. 3a.
Schoenberg Sechs Klavierstücke, Op. 19. Ode to Napoleon, Op. 41.
Gert Westphal, Roland Hermann *spkrs* **Tim Vogler, Frank Reinecke** *vns* **Stefan Fehlandt** *va*
Michael Sanderling *vc* **Michael Allan, Günther Herzfeld, Frank-Immo Zichner** *pf*
Edition Abseits EDA008-2 (65 minutes: DDD). Texts and translations included. Recorded 1994.   Ⓕ

Coupling Ullmann and Schoenberg makes sense. Even in the desperate conditions of the concentration camp Theresienstadt, where his Rilke setting was composed, Ullmann followed a more recognizably German compositional path than his fellow internees. His teacher's work was the yardstick against which he would have gauged his own development. Listening to the *Variations* in conjunction with *Die Weise von Liebe und Tod des Cornets Christoph Rilke* one is aware of a simplification of technique and expression not solely attributable to the practical constraints of Ullmann's last years. But then he was never a slavish Schoenbergian: the *Variations* begin with an artfully academic inversion of the theme, extend its possibilities in a language that owes more to Berg and take a quasi-Hindemithian line in the rhetorical counterpoint of the fugue. Herzfeld gives what seems to be an accurate, often bravura performance, whereas his Schoenberg Op. 19 pieces (the source of Ullmann's theme) lack a certain tension, the sound itself rather too soft-grained. Competition in this repertoire is fierce.

Ullmann's setting of 12 extracts from Rilke's novella is a quirky but compelling assertion of self against insurmountable odds. The problem of integrating speech and music into a unified whole is not so much solved as avoided, in favour of a series of vignettes depicting stages in the protagonist's journey towards a mythical future. Simple leitmotivic fragments provide overall coherence, although the text's evocative qualities are inevitably cramped by the two-dimensional effect of the medium: Ullmann did not live to complete an orchestral version. When performed with this degree of conviction, *Die Weise von Liebe und Tod des Cornets Christoph Rilke* is more than a historical curiosity, even if Ullmann cannot match the ironic force that Schoenberg draws from Lord Byron's withering 'tribute'. The present performance of the *Ode to Napoleon* lacks the flexibility and *élan* one expects to hear in the English language original but Hermann makes a solid case for Schoenberg's own (unpublished) German translation. The players capture the intricacy, if not always the immediacy, of the instrumental commentary – the recording is spacious but could be better focused. An uneven disc then, but definitely one of the more interesting Ullmann offerings to date.

Galina Ustvol'skaya   USSR 1919

Concerto for Piano, Strings and Timpani[a]. Octet[b]. Piano Sonata No. 3[b]. Grand Duet[c].
A. Kosoyan, Kh. Chinakov obs **A. Stang, A. Liskovich, A. Dukor, F. Soakov** vns
Oleg Stolpner vc **V. Znamensky** timp **Pavel Serebryakov, M. Karandashova,**
Oleg Malov pfs **Chamber Orchestra of the Leningrad State Philharmonic Society.**
Melodiya 74321 49956-2 (75 minutes: ADD). Recorded [a]1970, [b]1975, [c]1985.   Ⓜ

Here's an excellent CD for anyone wanting to sample the music of Galina Ustvol'skaya. The repertoire offers only a restricted chronological survey (up to 1959), but the performances have the fanatical intensity which is a *sine qua non* for her peculiar mode of agonized communication. The Concerto for piano, strings and timpani shows the roots of her style in Prokofiev and Shostakovich – in 1946 Ustvol'skaya was still in Shostakovich's Leningrad composition class. Pavel Serebryakov gives the instrument an appropriately hard time, knocking it out of tune fairly early in the proceedings, but something of the *frisson* of playing previously banned music (the première was not until 1969) certainly comes across. By 1950 Ustvol'skaya was writing the kind of stripped-bare textures which Shostakovich recognized as an influence on him. The Octet (for two oboes, four violins, timpani and piano!) is a case in point, and it climaxes in percussive blows of a quite fearsome insistence. Oleg Malov, the one performer closest to Ustvol'skaya over the years, delves deep into the ascetic mysteries of the Third Piano Sonata. Malov and Oleg Stolpner show what a massively impressive piece the *Grand Duet* can be in the right hands. Once again the piano's treble register doesn't survive more than a couple of minutes before becoming seriously detuned, though otherwise the recording quality is fine. Rival performances pale by comparison. In sum, here is a chance to hear all the music on this disc as it should be heard.

Moishei Vainberg   Polish 1919-1996

Chamber Symphonies – No. 1, Op. 145; No. 4, Op. 153[a].
[a]**Bengt Sandström** cl
Umeå Symphony Orchestra / Thord Svedlund.
Olympia OCD651 (62 minutes: DDD). Recorded 1998.   Ⓕ

The prolific Vainberg's chamber symphonies are sometimes no more 'chamber' than his other symphonies: rather engagingly, he confessed that he had got into a muddle and felt the numbers were getting too high. These are both appealing works. No. 1 owes much to Prokofiev, especially to the *Classical* Symphony in the two outer movements. Here, the appealing melodiousness comes close to being actual quotations, or perhaps gestures of homage. The two middle movements are plainer, but fresh and likeable in Vainberg's most fluent manner. The Fourth *Chamber Symphony* is altogether odder. The piece is described as being for string orchestra and clarinet, but it is difficult to sense where Vainberg is writing a string serenade and where a kind of clarinet concerto. In two of the linked movements, the clarinet plays a leading role, with a strong entry on to the stage and some vigorous soloistic work that gives it domination over the strings. There is also a prominent cadenza for a solo cello in the work's third section. It is difficult to feel that the experiment is a success, but Vainberg's skill and the sympathetic nature of his music-making hold the interest. The performances are lively and responsive, the recording fresh and, especially in No. 4, intelligently geared to what seem to be Vainberg's curious intentions.

String Quartets – No. 1, Op. 2/141; No. 10, Op. 85; No. 17, Op. 146.
Gothenburg Quartet (Ingrid Sjönnemo, Elin Anderberg vns Mia Wassenius va
Anders Robertson vc).
Olympia OCD628 (61 minutes: DDD). Recorded 1997.   Ⓕ

Vainberg Chamber

Vainberg's First Quartet was his first essay in the form, when he was 18 and seemingly impressed by both Berg and Schoenberg. The vicissitudes of his life (if one can use so light a term to cover his and his family's sufferings at the hands of both Nazi and Communist anti-Semitism) caused the work to be lost; and in 1985 he wrote it down again from memory. He is said to have been possessed of a phenomenal memory but it is difficult to suppose that some element of revision or recomposition all those years later was not involved. At any rate, the outcome is an odd work, well written and individual in character. However, it lacks the distinctive nature of either the Tenth Quartet of 1964 or still more the Seventeenth of 1987. It is a very interestingly written work, inserting a slow movement in the course of a sonata movement rather in the manner of the so-called *Phantasy* once suggested to English composers by W.W. Cobbett and successfully achieved by, especially, Frank Bridge. Vainberg can have known nothing of this, but he reaches a comparable solution to a formal problem, and does so with real invention and structural good judgement. The Gothenburg Quartet plays these three pieces with liveliness and perception, and anyone curious about this remarkable sequence of works would find a good sampler here.

---

24 Preludes, Op. 100. Solo Cello Sonata No. 1, Op. 72.
Yosif Feigelson *vc*
Olympia OCD594 (57 minutes: DDD). Recorded 1996.   Ⓜ

Vainberg composed the cycle of 24 Preludes for Rostropovich, but, for reasons which are not disclosed by Per Skans in his otherwise admirably informative insert-notes, the two men fell out, and the work, written in 1968, was not performed until 1996 by the present artist. It is a remarkably impressive and entertaining piece. The longest of the Preludes lasts only just over three minutes; most of the others last under two. The tonal design – a climb 12 degrees up the chromatic scale from C, followed by a similar descent – gives the music coherence, but what holds the forefront of the listener's attention is a virtuoso variety of invention, some of it witty, some of it grave and with baroque overtones, some of it allusive, with references to colleagues including Vainberg's friend and advocate Shostakovich (whose DSCH motif from his Cello Concerto marks No. 21). It is a pity that Rostropovich did not take the work up, as his reputation could have done much to make the music known and to have helped Vainberg when he needed all the help he could get. But the performances of the cycle, and of the rather less remarkable Solo Cello Sonata, are outstanding, and collectors who acquire this disc are more than likely to find themselves wondering why he is not better known.

Edgar Varèse   French/American 1883-1965

Ionisation[a]. Amériques[a]. Arcana[a]. Density 21.5. Offrandes[b]. Octandre[b]. Intégrales[b].
Rachel Yakar *sop* **Lawrence Beauregard** *fl*
[a]**New York Philharmonic Orchestra;**
[b]**Ensemble InterContemporain / Pierre Boulez.**
Sony Classical SMK45844 (77 minutes: ADD/DDD). Texts and translations included.   Ⓜ

Varèse was a pioneer, a quester and above all a liberator. Music for him was a form of twentieth-century alchemy – the transmutation of the ordinary into the extraordinary, an alchemical wedding of intellectual thought with intuitive imagination. It was the writings of the fourteenth-century cosmologist and alchemist Paracelsus that formed the inspiration behind his orchestral work *Arcana*, a vast canvas of sound built entirely out of one melodic motive. Echoes of Stravinsky and others are discernible, but the totality of *Arcana* is pure Varèse. The same is true of *Amériques*, a title that Varèse emphasized was not to be taken as 'purely geographical but as symbolic of discoveries – new worlds on earth, in the sky or in the minds of men'. Here romanticism and modernism seem to coexist side by side, where allusions from works such as *La mer* and *The Firebird* seem like memories carried into his brave new world. The remaining items consist of smaller chamber works which display Varèse's most radical, though equally rewarding, styles. Boulez and his players give committed, virtuosic performances of these challenging and intriguing works. Well worth exploring.

Tuning Up. Amériques. Poème électronique. Arcana. Nocturnal. Un grand sommeil noir (orig. version/orch. Beaumont). Offrandes. Hyperprism. Octandre. Intégrales. Ecuatorial. Ionisation. Densité 21.5. Déserts. Dance for Burgess.
Sarah Leonard, Mireille Delunsch *sops* **Kevin Deas** *bass* **Jacques Zoon** *fl*
François Kerdoncuff *pf* **Edgard Varèse** *electronics*
Prague Philharmonic Choir; ASKO Ensemble;
Royal Concertgebouw Orchestra / Riccardo Chailly.
Decca 460 208-2DH2 (two discs: 151 minutes: DDD). Texts and translations included.
Recorded 1992-98.   ⒫ 🄴

This set is announced as 'The Complete Works' of Edgard Varèse, with Chailly setting new standards for an overall collection. 'Complete' requires clarification. Excluded are the electronic interlude, *La procession du Vergès*, from the 1955 film *Around and About Joan Miró* (is this still extant?) and the 1947 *Etude* Varèse wrote as preparation for his unrealized *Espace* project – material from which, according to Chou Wen-Chung, found its way into later works. Successively Varèse's pupil, amanuensis and executor, Professor Chou would appear ideally placed to advise on a project of this nature. Yet it does seem surprising to omit the *Etude*, completed, performed and apparently extant, while including *Tuning Up*, which Varèse never realized as such, and *Dance for Burgess*, which does not exist in a definitive score. That said, the former is an ingenious skit on the orchestral machine, while the latter is an unlikely take on the Broadway dance number: the light they shed on Varèse's preoccupations in the late 1940s makes their inclusion worth while. Works such as *Octandre* and *Intégrales* require scrupulous attention to balance if they are to sound more than crudely aggressive: Chailly secures this without sacrificing physical impact – witness the explosive *Hyperprism*. He brings out some exquisite harmonic subtleties in *Offrandes*, Sarah Leonard projecting the texts' surreal imagery with admirable poise. The fugitive opening bars of *Ionisation* sound slightly muted in the recorded ambience, though not the cascading tuned percussion towards the close.

The instrumentational problems of *Ecuatorial* are at last vindicated, allowing Varèse's inspired combination of brass and electronic keyboards to register with awesome power. Chailly opts for the solo bass, but a unison chorus would have heightened the dramatic impact still further. *Amériques*, the true intersection of romanticism and modernism, is performed in the original 1921 version, with its even more extravagant orchestral demands and bizarre reminiscences of *The Rite of Spring* and Schoenberg's *Five Orchestral Pieces*, understandably replaced in the revision. *Arcana* was recorded back in 1992, Chailly probing beyond the work's vast dynamic contours far more deeply than any other rival on disc. No one but Varèse has drawn such sustained eloquence from an ensemble of wind and percussion, or invested such emotional power in the primitive electronic medium of the early 1950s. *Déserts* juxtaposes them in a score which marks the culmination of his search for new means of expression. The opening now seems a poignant evocation of humanity in the atomic age, the ending is resigned but not bitter. The tape interludes in Chailly's performance have a startling clarity, as does the *Poème électronique*, Varèse's untypical but exhilarating contribution to the 1958 Brussels World Fair. The unfinished *Nocturnal*, with its vocal stylizations and belated return of string timbre, demonstrates a continuing vitality that only time could extinguish. Varèse has had a significant impact on post-war musical culture, with figures as diverse as Stockhausen, Charlie Parker and Frank Zappa acknowledging his influence. Chailly's recordings demonstrate, in unequivocal terms, why this music will continue to provoke and inspire future generations.

Ralph Vaughan Williams
British 1872-1958

Symphonies – No. 1, 'A Sea Symphony'; No. 2, 'A London Symphony'; No. 3, 'A Pastoral Symphony'; No. 4 in F minor; No. 5 in D major; No. 6 in E minor; No. 7, 'Sinfonia antartica'; No. 8 in D minor; No. 9 in E minor.

Symphonies – No. 1[a]; No. 2; No. 3[b]; Nos. 4-6; No. 7[c]; Nos. 8-9. Flos campi. Serenade to Music.
[a]Joan Rodgers, [b]Alison Barlow, [c]Alison Hargan *sops* William Shimell *bar*
Christopher Balmer *va*
Liverpool Philharmonic Choir; Royal Liverpool Philharmonic Orchestra / Vernon Handley.
EMI Eminence CDBOX-VW1 (six discs: 396 minutes: DDD). No. 2 **E**; Nos. 2 and 8 **S**.   Ⓜ**RR**

Symphonies Nos. 6 and 9.
Royal Liverpool Philharmonic Orchestra / Vernon Handley.
EMI Eminence CD-EMX2230 (67 minutes: DDD). Recorded 1994.   Ⓜ**E**

Handley's performances can withstand comparison with the very best. The first to appear was the Fifth Symphony. Rightly acclaimed on its initial release, this remains a gloriously rapt, yet formidably lucid realization. The coupling, a supremely dedicated rendering of the exquisite *Flos campi*, is just as distinguished. Handley's masterly pacing is a compelling feature of both the *Sea Symphony* and *Sinfonia antartica*, but, whilst it is difficult to fault either performance on artistic grounds, here more than elsewhere one notes the limitations of the slightly cramped acoustic of Liverpool's Philharmonic Hall. There are no technical shortcomings about the illuminatingly intense Third or the Fourth, with its unbridled ferocity and orchestral virtuosity. The Second and Eighth bring outstandingly perceptive, marvellously communicative music-making, with both scores emerging as fresh as the day they were conceived. Handley's interpretation of the Sixth Symphony is a model of cogency and long-term control. Don't be deceived by the element of slight reserve in the opening movement. It soon transpires that Handley already has his eyes firmly set on the work's terrifying apex, namely the baleful climax of the succeeding *Moderato*. Handley's *Scherzo* teems with busy detail, its feverish contrapuntal workings laid out before us with maximum clarity and force. So many performances have come to grief in the extraordinary finale; Handley's is a triumphant exception. In this desolate, inconsolable landscape (with not an *espressivo* marking in sight), Handley, achieves a truly awesome hush and concentration. And what of the Ninth, VW's other 'E minor'? Few interpreters on disc have probed much beneath the surface of this elusive, craggy masterpiece. Handley captures the music's mordant wit, whilst allowing the listener to revel afresh in the astonishing vitality and startlingly original sonorities of VW's ever-imaginative inspiration. The overriding impression left is one of supreme sensitivity and utter dedication to the cause. In the visionary finale, whose monumental, block-like structure gradually takes shape before our eyes like Stonehenge itself, Handley's conception just has the edge over his rivals in terms of elemental power and effortless inevitability. The recordings are admirably natural.

Symphony No. 1.
Dame Felicity Lott *sop* **Jonathan Summers** *bar*
Cantilena; London Philharmonic Choir and Orchestra / Bernard Haitink.
EMI CDC7 49911-2 (71 minutes: DDD). Text included. Recorded 1989. Ⓕ

A firm hand on the tiller is needed to steer a safe course through this, Vaughan Williams's first and most formally diffuse symphony, completed in 1909. Haitink is clearly an ideal choice of helmsman and he is helped by a remarkably lucid recording that resolves details that would rarely be revealed in live performance. What might be more unexpected here is the obvious affinity he shows for this music: whilst never transgressing the bounds of Vaughan Williams's characteristically English idiom, he manages to place the work in the European mainstream, revealing a whole range of resonances, from Bruckner and Mahler to the Impressionists. Not all the glory should go to the conductor, of course. Both soloists are particularly fine, the vulnerability behind the spine-tingling power of Felicity Lott's voice providing excellent contrast to the staunch solidity of Jonathan Summers. The LPO Chorus, aided by Cantilena, is on top form and the whole enterprise is underpinned by the LPO's total commitment and expertise.

Symphony No. 1.
Dame Isobel Baillie *sop* **John Cameron** *bar*
London Philharmonic Choir and Orchestra / Sir Adrian Boult.
Belart mono 450 144-2 (68 minutes: ADD). Recorded 1952. Ⓢ Ⓗ

'Classic recording of Symphony No. 1' proclaims the sleeve of this super-budget Belart CD. That assessment is, of course, absolutely spot-on. Fine as is Boult's own 1968 stereo remake (available on an EMI reissue), this Decca performance undoubtedly surpasses it in terms of sheer fervour and concentration: no one before or since has held the finale together with quite such effortless mastery. Vaughan Williams himself lent his supervision to the sessions, and the mono sound remains remarkably full-blooded, if inevitably rather lacking in range. No Vaughan Williams enthusiast can afford to overlook the present reissue: if you missed out on it first time round on Decca's sadly defunct British Collection series, you've no excuse now. The singular lack of texts is, however, an irritating oversight.

Symphonies Nos. 3 and 4.
Amanda Roocroft *sop*
London Philharmonic Orchestra / Bernard Haitink.
EMI CDC5 56564-2 (72 minutes: DDD). Recorded 1996. Ⓕ

These are thought-provoking interpretations of great dedication and intelligence. If Haitink's deeply felt conception of *A Pastoral Symphony* is the most daringly broad we've yet had on disc, its concentration and abundant character grip from first measure to last. Aided by orchestral playing of the highest quality, the opening movement unfolds with a luminous serenity, its climaxes unerringly 'placed', yet Haitink is also acutely aware of the ominous stirrings just beneath the surface. Most distinctive of all is the *Moderato pesante* third movement which, as Haitink views it, is a monumentally sombre, even intimidating affair. This is an interpretation of compelling individuality and tragic intensity which all Vaughan Williams *aficionados* should investigate forthwith. The same holds true for the Fourth. Again, Haitink presides over a performance of immense integrity and perceptive long-term rigour. Speeds here are less controversial. By not driving the first movement too hard, Haitink ensures that we can savour the full expressive eloquence of the strings' *appassionato sostenuto* secondary idea. What's more, the *Scherzo* possesses fine rhythmic point, and the transition into the finale generates a tremendous expectancy. In this last movement Haitink keeps a firm hand on the tiller and steadfastly refuses to whip up any artificial excitement, but its rugged symphonic strength must surely command enormous respect.

Symphonies Nos. 4[a] and 5[b].
[a]**BBC Symphony Orchestra / Ralph Vaughan Williams;** [b]**Hallé Orchestra / Sir John Barbirolli.**
Dutton Laboratories mono CDAX8011 (66 minutes: ADD). Item marked [a] recorded 1937; [b]1944.　　　　Ⓜ️🅷

No performance on record of Vaughan Williams's Fourth Symphony has ever quite matched this very first one, recorded under the composer's baton in October 1937. As Michael Kennedy says in his highly illuminating note for the Dutton Laboratories reissue, it is 'taken at a daredevil pace', and more importantly has a bite and energy beyond any rival. If early listeners to this violent work were shocked by the composer's new boldness, here his conducting demonstrates the passionate emotion behind the piece – paradoxically the most conventional of his symphonies in structure, as it is the most radical in idiom. The remastered sound is so vivid and immediate, so full of presence, that in places one almost has the illusion of stereo before its time. Sir John Barbirolli's première recording of the Fifth Symphony, made in February 1944 eight months after the first performance, is hardly less remarkable. This, too, has never quite been matched since for the stirring passion of the great climaxes in the first and third movements, with Barbirolli in each carefully grading the intensity between exposition and recapitulation. It is also a revelation to find him taking the triple-time of the Passacaglia finale much faster than latter-day rivals, relating it far more closely than usual to the great example of the finale of Brahms's Fourth Symphony, making it no pastoral amble but a searing argument. Here again hiss – very high on the original wartime 78s – has been virtually eliminated, but that has left the high violins sounding rather papery. Even so, there is no lack of weight or bite in the big climaxes, with brass and wind atmospherically caught. An outstanding issue for all lovers of this composer's music, not just those who specialize in historic recordings.

Symphony No. 5[a]. Valiant-for-truth[b]. The Pilgrim Pavement[c]. Psalm 23 (arr. Churchill)[b]. Hymn-tune Prelude on 'Song 13' by Orlando Gibbons (arr. Glatz)[a]. Prelude and Fugue in C minor[a].
[c]**Ian Watson** *org* [bc]**Richard Hickox Singers;**
[a]**London Symphony Orchestra / Richard Hickox.**
Chandos CHAN9666 (71 minutes: DDD). Texts included. Recorded 1997.　　　　Ⓕ

This is an exceptionally powerful yet deeply moving account of the Fifth. Aided by glowing, wide-ranging engineering, Hickox's is an urgently communicative reading. The first and third movements in particular emerge with an effortless architectural splendour and rapt authority, the climaxes built and resolved with mastery. The *Scherzo* is as good a place as any to sample the lustrous refinement of the LSO's response (its golden-toned cello section consistently catches the ear throughout). Hickox ensures that the symphony's concluding bars positively glow with gentle ecstasy: here is a Fifth that can surely hold its own in the most exalted company. Material from *The Pilgrim's Progress* made its way into the Fifth Symphony and two of the five enterprising couplings here provide further links with John Bunyan's timeless allegory: the 1940 motet for mixed voices with organ, *Valiant-for-truth* and John Churchill's 1953 arrangement for soprano and mixed chorus of Psalm 23 (originally sung by The Voice of a Bird in Act 4 of *The Pilgrim's Progress*). The latter receives its finely prepared recorded début on this occasion, as do both *The Pilgrim Pavement* (a 1934 processional for soprano, chorus and organ written for New York City's Cathedral of St John the Divine) and Helen Glatz's string-orchestra arrangement of the solo-piano *Hymn-tune Prelude on 'Song 13'* by Gibbons. Which just leaves the Prelude and Fugue, originally written for organ in 1921, but heard here in a sumptuous orchestration. A stimulating Vaughan Williams compilation.

Symphony No. 6. Fantasia on a Theme by Thomas Tallis. The Lark Ascending.
Tasmin Little *vn*
BBC Symphony Orchestra / Sir Andrew Davis.
Teldec British Line 9031-73127-2 (62 minutes: DDD). Recorded 1990.　　　　Ⓕ🆂

Sir Andrew Davis clearly thought long and hard before committing this enigmatic and tragic symphony to disc, and the result is one of the most spontaneous and electrifying accounts of the Sixth Symphony available. The urgency and vigour of the first and third movements is astonishing, leaving one with the impression that the work might have been recorded in one take. His treatment of the second subject's reprise in the closing pages of the first movement is more underplayed and remote than the beautifully sheened approach of some recordings, but is arguably more nostalgic for being so. The feverish, nightmare world of the *Scherzo* is a real *tour de force* in the hands of an inspired BBC Symphony Orchestra, and the desolate wasteland of the eerie final movement has rarely achieved such quiescence and nadir as here. Davis's searchingly intense *Tallis Fantasia* is finely poised with a beautifully spacious acoustic. The disc concludes on a quietly elevated note with Tasmin Little's serene and gently introspective reading of *The Lark Ascending*. The recording is excellent.

Symphony No. 6. In the Fen Country. On Wenlock Edge.
Ian Bostridge *ten*
London Philharmonic Orchestra / Bernard Haitink.
EMI CDC5 56762-2 (69 minutes: DDD). Text and translation included. Recorded 1998.   Ⓕ Ⓔ

This is a noble, rewarding and profoundly musical account of the Sixth. Drawing some magnificently clean and sonorous playing from the LPO (and aided by a ripe and wide-ranging recording), Haitink steers a characteristically purposeful course through the first movement, alighting on precisely the right tempo for the second subject's final ecstatic metamorphosis. Right from the outset, one notes how the supreme articulation of the orchestral playing helps to make so much sense of the composer's trenchant counterpoint. However, it's in the succeeding *Moderato* that Haitink really pulls ahead of most of his rivals, his eloquent conception displaying a riveting long-term rigour. No complaints, either, about the implacable mystery and tingling concentration of Haitink's epilogue. Altogether a distinguished Sixth, and one which deserves to rank alongside the finest currently available. It's also difficult to imagine a more refined, sympathetic rendering of *In the Fen Country* than Haitink's. It unfolds with melting beauty and tender grace. A cherishable display indeed, and the delights continue with *On Wenlock Edge*. Ian Bostridge sings with moving ardour and intelligence (his 'Is my team ploughing?' is an especially compulsive interpretation), whilst Haitink's support is a model of scrupulous sensitivity and delicate nuance. All in all, a release to savour.

Symphony No. 7.
Sheila Armstrong *sop*
London Philharmonic Choir and Orchestra / Bernard Haitink.
EMI CDC7 47516-2 (42 minutes: DDD). Recorded 1984.   Ⓕ

Scored for wordless soprano solo and chorus plus a large orchestra, this Seventh Symphony was based on the composer's music for the film *Scott of the Antarctic*. It comprises five movements; the Prelude, which conveys mankind's struggle in overcoming hostile natural forces; a *Scherzo*, which depicts the whales and penguins in their natural habitat; 'Landscape', which portrays vast frozen wastes; Intermezzo, a reflection of the actions and thoughts of two members of the party; and 'Epilogue', describing the final tragic assault on the South Pole. Bernard Haitink's conducting is highly imaginative, very concentrated and very committed, and the LPO responds to him with some wonderfully atmospheric playing, full of personality and colour. Armstrong's eerie disembodied soprano voice and the remote chorus heighten the atmosphere, so that the score emerges as a powerful, coherent essay in symphonic form. The recording is magnificently sonorous and spacious.

Symphony No. 9. Piano Concerto in C major.
Howard Shelley *pf*
London Symphony Orchestra / Bryden Thomson.
Chandos CHAN8941 (57 minutes: DDD). Recorded 1990.   Ⓕ Ⓢ

Alongside the scorching account of the apocalyptic Fourth Symphony, this clear-headed, perceptive traversal of the enigmatic Ninth has fair claims to be regarded as the best thing in Bryden Thomson's underrated VW cycle for Chandos. Thomson's urgent conception of the opening *Moderato maestoso* in particular has a sweep and momentum one might not have previously associated with this movement, yet the gain in terms of sheer concentration and symphonic stature is irrefutable. Granted, some may find the outer sections of the succeeding *Andante sostenuto* just a little too lacking in evocative magic, but there's no gainsaying the effectiveness of gallumphing woodwind in the oafish *Scherzo*; certainly, the LSO's saxophone trio seems to be enjoying its day out hugely. In the finale, too, Thomson's approach is more boldly assertive than usual – not the way one would always want to hear this music, perhaps, but a thoroughly valid and convincing performance all the same. The coupling, Howard Shelley's distinguished remake of the same composer's craggily elusive Piano Concerto, is both imaginative and desirable. All in all, a highly recommendable disc: the LSO is in fine fettle throughout, whilst the glowing sound is close to ideal.

Vaughan Williams Job – A masque for dancing[a]. The Wasps – Overture[a].
Arnold Four Scottish Dances, Op. 59[b].
London Philharmonic Orchestra / [a]Sir Adrian Boult, [b]Sir Malcolm Arnold.
Everest EVC9006 (57 minutes: ADD). Recorded 1958.   Ⓕ Ⓗ

This is the third of Sir Adrian Boult's four recordings of *Job*, a work he conducted with peerless authority for over 40 years (he was, of course, the score's dedicatee). The performance is one of enormous dedication and considerable insight, achieving a rare serenity in Scene 3 ('Minuet of the Sons of Job and their Wives'), Scene 5 ('Dance of the Three Messengers') and, above all, in the Epilogue, which is more movingly realized than ever before or since. However, the chosen venue of London's Royal Albert Hall evidently brought problems for the Everest recording team: it's an odd sound, tightly miked and rather lacking in body, with brass balance closer than is ideal. Nor was the London Philharmonic in the healthiest of shape at the time: string tone can be unreliable and intonation occasionally suspect. Boult also directs a cherishable, delectably pointed rendering of *The Wasps* Overture, whose glorious central melody really does seem to unfold with all the time in the world here. Finally, Sir Malcolm Arnold conducts his own, irresistibly tuneful *Scottish Dances*. The sound in both these items is impressively vivid for its late-1950s vintage. A very welcome reissue.

Dona nobis pacem. Sancta civitas[a].
Yvonne Kenny *sop* **Philip Langridge** *ten* **Bryn Terfel** *bass-bar*
[a]**St Paul's Cathedral Choir; London Symphony Chorus and Orchestra / Richard Hickox.**
EMI British Composers CDC7 54788-2 (63 minutes: DDD). Texts included. Recorded 1992.　ⒻⓈ

This is a generous and inspiring coupling of two of Vaughan Williams's most important choral utterances. Hickox coaxes magnificent sounds from the LSO throughout: in *Dona nobis pacem*, for example, the sense of orchestral spectacle during 'Beat! Beat! drums!' is riveting in its physical impact. As ever, the contribution of the London Symphony Chorus combines full-throated discipline and sensitivity to nuance, and Hickox's trio of soloists is all excellent, with Bryn Terfel outstandingly eloquent. *Sancta civitas* is a work whose multi-layered scoring places great demands on both conductor and production team alike: suffice it to report, it is difficult to see Hickox's inspirational account of this still-underrated score (with its striking pre-echoes of *Job* and the Fourth Symphony) being surpassed for years to come. EMI's clean, wide-ranging sound is admirable.

Vaughan Williams Mass in G minor. Te Deum in G major.
Howells Requiem. Take him, earth, for cherishing.
Mary Seers *sop* **Michael Chance** *counterten* **Philip Salmon** *ten* **Jonathan Best** *bass*
Corydon Singers / Matthew Best with **Thomas Trotter** *org*
Hyperion CDA66076 (60 minutes: ADD). Texts included.　　　　　　　　　Ⓕ

Vaughan Williams's unaccompanied Mass in G minor manages to combine the common manner of Elizabethan liturgical music with those elements of his own folk-music heritage that make his music so distinctive, and in so doing arrives at something quite individual and new. The work falls into five movements and its mood is one of heartfelt, if restrained, rejoicing. Howells's Requiem dates from 1936, a year after the death of his only son. The work was not released in his lifetime but was reconstructed and published in 1980 from his manuscripts. It is a most hauntingly beautiful work of an obviously intensely personal nature. *Take him, earth, for cherishing* was composed to commemorate the assassination of J.F. Kennedy. The text is an English translation by Helen Waddell of Prudentius's fourth-century poem, *Hymnus circa Exsequias Defuncti*. Again it demonstrates the great strength of Howells's choral writing, with a clear outline and aptly affecting yet unimposing harmonic twists. The Corydon Singers give marvellous performances and the sound is very fine.

A Cotswold Romance. Death of Tintagiles.
Rosa Mannion *sop* **Thomas Randle** *ten* **Matthew Brook** *bar*
London Philharmonic Choir; London Symphony Orchestra / Richard Hickox.
Chandos CHAN9646 (54 minutes: DDD). Text included. Recorded 1997.　　　　　Ⓕ

A Cotswold Romance is a gift from Vaughan Williams, delivered through the good offices of his experienced arranger, Maurice Jacobson, to those who hold the music of *Hugh the Drover* in deep affection but who, under torture, would probably have to admit that the opera itself is less than perfect. *Hugh*, first produced in 1924, enjoyed sufficient immediate success for a set of records to be produced with the original cast. It then had to wait till 1979 for a complete recording on LP (reissued on EMI), and till 1994 for a new one on CD. The adaptation as a dramatic cantata came out in 1951, reducing the two-act opera to ten numbers and rescoring some of the music so as to allow a (still) larger part for the chorus. Possibly, just possibly, Jacobson was a little too much in love with the score himself to exercise an objective judgement in his enrichments (for that is what they are). The addition of wordless choruses as accompaniment, and the appropriation of some of the solo music by the chorus, are features one might hold in some suspicion. However, it is delightful, not least when the chorus sings the first part of Hugh's song of the road and re-enters with delicious harmonies at 'All the scented night'. Thomas Randle, who has the voice of a man of the road and a lover, is admirably cast. Rosa Mannion, with a slight hint of turning tremulous under pressure, is otherwise an ideal Mary, and the chorus, upon whom much depends, is excellent. Hickox conducts with brio and with due feeling for the romance. *Death of Tintagiles* (14'46" to the *Cotswold Romance*'s 39'30") comprises incidental music written for a play by Maeterlinck, performed without much success in 1913. In his interesting notes, Stephen Connock associates it with *Riders to the Sea* and the *Sinfonia antartica*; and it is true that there are sternly impressive moments, of menace and darkness. It hardly seems viable as an orchestral suite, but is good to have on this disc, partly for reference, partly for contrast, and, to this rather limited extent, in that it is austerely and intermittently impressive in its own right.

On Wenlock Edge. Five Mystical Songs. Four Hymns – No. 1, Lord, come away; No. 3, Come Love, come Lord. Three Poems by Walt Whitman – No. 1, Nocturne; No. 3, Joy, shipmate, Joy!. Four Poems by Fredegond Shove – The water mill. Four Last Songs – No. 2, Tired. The House of Life – No. 2, Silent Noon. The Splendour falls. It was a lover and his lass. Dirge for Fidele. Two English Folksongs.
Anthony Rolfe Johnson *ten* **Simon Keenlyside** *bar* **Graham Johnson** *pf*
Duke Quartet (Louisa Fuller, Rick Koster *vns* John Metcalfe *va* Ivan McCready *vc*).
Collins Classics 1488-2 (78 minutes: DDD). Texts included. Recorded 1996. Ⓕ

This makes an auspicious start to an ambitious series from Collins Classics devoted to English song. At its heart lies Keenlyside's sincere, unobtrusive account of the *Five Mystical Songs* in its version for voice and piano, one wholly in accord with these lovely Herbert settings. His warm, firm tone, smooth line and refined way with words combine to create an unforgettable impression. Keenlyside is no less impressive in the individual songs assigned to him, notably the late song 'Tired', one of four poems the elderly composer wrote to texts by his wife, Ursula, in 1956, and in the two Whitman settings, the hypnotic 'Nocturne' and the exuberant 'Joy, Shipmate, Joy!', which Keenlyside delivers with appropriate brio. He brings his wry sense of humour to 'The Lawyer', one of two folk-song settings with violin dating from 1925. The other, 'Searching for Lambs' is one of Rolfe Johnson's sensitive contributions. The latter also delivers a typically sympathetic, subtly phrased, musing account of the famous 'Silent Noon' from *The House of Life* cycle. Then he draws a wide range of emotion and colour from the familiar *On Wenlock Edge*. Once or twice these Housman settings reveal his tone under stress, as at the end of 'Heron Hill'; till then that moving song receives an inward, deeply felt reading. The cycle is suitably supported by the intense, characterful playing of the Duke Quartet and Graham Johnson. Johnson's contribution to the rest of a well-filled CD is as thoughtful as one would expect. The disc begins and ends with two little-known and pleasing Shakespeare duets where the singers' voices blend nicely. Splendid recording.

Vaughan Williams On Wenlock Edge[a]. Songs of Travel[a].
Butterworth Love blows as the wind blows[b].
Elgar Pleading, Op. 48 No. 1[b]. Song Cycle, Op. 59[b]. Two Songs, Op. 60[b].
Robert Tear *ten* **Thomas Allen** *bar*
City of Birmingham Symphony Orchestra / [a]Sir Simon Rattle, [b]Vernon Handley.
EMI British Composers CDM7 64731-2 (69 minutes: DDD/ADD). Texts included.
Recorded 1979-83. Ⓕ

Neither of Vaughan Williams's song cycles was originally written with orchestral accompaniment. *On Wenlock Edge* was scored for accompaniment of piano and string quartet, while the *Songs of Travel* were written with piano. Both lose a little when sung with orchestra but the gain seems to considerably outweigh any loss, especially when three such superb artists are involved. Tear's singing is notable for some wonderfully long phrases (as also is Allen's in the other cycle) together with the other Tear qualities, of clarity of words and such matters. The CBSO plays especially well for Rattle – all in all, superb performances that do real justice to Vaughan Williams's imagination, his care for words and his orchestration. The Tear/Handley Elgar and Butterworth items are rarities and were all première recordings. Throughout, Tear sings with his customary sensitivity and the CBSO under Handley gives irreproachably alert imaginative support. The recording is vivid and well balanced.

Serenade to Music. Flos campi. Five mystical songs[a]. Fantasia on Christmas carols[a].
Elizabeth Connell, Linda Kitchen, Anne Dawson, Amanda Roocroft *sops*
Sarah Walker, Jean Rigby, Diana Montague *mezzos* **Catherine Wyn-Rogers** *contr*
John Mark Ainsley, Martyn Hill, Arthur Davies, Maldwyn Davies *tens* [a]**Thomas Allen,**
Alan Opie *bars* **Gwynne Howell, John Connell** *basses* **Nobuko Imai** *va*
Corydon Singers; English Chamber Orchestra / Matthew Best.
Hyperion CDA66420 (68 minutes: DDD). Texts included. Recorded 1990. Ⓕ

In 1938 Sir Henry Wood celebrated his 50 years as a professional conductor with a concert. Vaughan Williams composed a work for the occasion, the *Serenade to Music*, in which he set words by Shakespeare from Act 5 of *The Merchant of Venice*. Sixteen star vocalists of the age were gathered together for the performance and Vaughan Williams customized the vocal parts to show off the best qualities of the singers. The work turned out to be one of the composer's most sybaritic creations, turning each of its subsequent performances into a special event. Hyperion has gathered stars of our own age for this outstanding issue and Best has perceptively managed to give each their head whilst melding them into a cohesive ensemble. A mellow, spacious recording has allowed the work to emerge on disc with a veracity never achieved before. The coupled vocal pieces are given to equal effect and the disc is completed by Nobuko Imai's tautly poignant account of *Flos campi*, in which the disturbing tension between solo viola and wordless chorus heighten the work's crypticism.

Five Tudor Portraits. Five Variants of 'Dives and Lazarus'.
Jean Rigby *mez* **John Shirley-Quirk** *bar*
London Symphony Chorus and Orchestra / Richard Hickox.
Chandos CHAN9593 (55 minutes: DDD). Text included. Recorded 1997. Ⓕ

First heard at the 1936 Norwich Festival, Vaughan Williams's *Five Tudor Portraits* find the composer at his most dazzlingly inventive, the resourceful and witty writing fitting Skelton's words like a glove. Moreover, an irresistible humanity illuminates the most ambitious of the settings, 'Jane Scroop (Her Lament for Philip Sparrow)', which contains music as compassionate as Vaughan Williams ever conceived. It is a life-enhancing creation and well deserving of this first-rate recording. Aided by disciplined, ever-willing orchestral support, the London Symphony Chorus launches itself in lusty fashion into the ale-soaked narrative of 'The Tunning of Elinor Rumming', though the resonant acoustic rather precludes ideal clarity of diction. Hickox is exuberant in this sparkling tableau, while Jean Rigby's characterful contribution should raise a smile. John Shirley-Quirk's is a touching presence in 'My Pretty Bess', and the mordant, black humour of 'Epitaph of John Jayberd of Diss' is effectively captured. Jane Scroop's lament in the fourth (and surely best) movement finds these fine artists at their most perceptive. How ravishingly Hickox moulds his strings in the hushed passage following 'It was proper and prest!' where the music movingly anticipates the poignancy of the closing section. Listen out, too, for the wealth of exquisitely observed woodwind detail in the enchanting funeral processional. The concluding 'Jolly Rutterkin' goes with a swing, though Shirley-Quirk is a mite unsteady at the top of his range. The coupling is a heart-warming *Dives and Lazarus*, with the LSO strings producing their most lustrous tone.

The Pilgrim's Progress.
Gerald Finley *bar* Pilgrim; **Peter Coleman-Wright** *bar* John Bunyan;
Jeremy White *bass* Evangelist, Envy, Third Shepherd; **Donaldson Bell** *bar* Pontius Pilate;
Gidon Saks *bass* Apollyon, Lord Hate-Good, Mistrust; **Richard Coxon** *ten* Pliable, Mister By-Ends; **Francis Egerton** *ten* Timorous, Usher; **Roderick Williams** *bar* Obstinate, Watchful, First Shepherd; **Adrian Thompson** *ten* Lord Lechery, Celestial Messenger;
Rebecca Evans *sop* Madam Wanton, Shining One; **Pamela Helen Stephen** *mez* Madam Bubble, Shining One, Heavenly Being II; **Anne-Marie Owens** *mez* Madam By-Ends, Pickthank;
Christopher Keyte *bass* Simon Magus; **John Kerr** *bass* Judas Iscariot;
Susan Gritton *sop* Malice, Bird, Shining One, Heavenly Being I; **Neil Gillespie** *ten* Worldly Glory;
Jonathan Fisher *bar* Demas; **Mark Padmore** *ten* Interpreter, Superstition, Second Shepherd;
Robert Hayward *bar* Herald; **Mica Penniman** *sop* Woodcutter's Boy;
Chorus and Orchestra of the Royal Opera House, Covent Garden / Richard Hickox.
Chandos CHAN9625 (two discs: 130 minutes: DDD). Notes and text included.
Recorded 1997. Ⓕ🆁🆁

The Royal Northern College of Music mounted a highly successful production in 1992, serving for a new generation to bring the kind of understanding and enjoyment fostered by the famous performances at Cambridge 40 years earlier. It was the recollection of those that made Christopher Bishop (producer of the Boult recording) say that 'perhaps the future of *Pilgrim* lies not in the opera house but with amateurs, and VW would be the last composer to be dismayed at that'. There is nothing amateur*ish* about the RNCM (available on the company's own label), where of course the students are in a sense already professional; but the performance, especially in the Vanity Fair scene and other concerted passages, comes through with the energy and well-rehearsed precision of the best amateur productions. Otherwise it is a matter of choice between Hickox's excellent version and the classic Boult. Both have more forward recorded sound than the RNCM, and are inevitably stronger in soloists, voice for voice. Voice for voice, Boult does better than Hickox, though with an exception that is crucial. John Noble was a fine Pilgrim on the earlier recording, but Gerald Finley brings not only a voice that is as good and well suited but also a dramatic quality that is more colourful and intense. But Boult's cast is very strong, with several of the short parts, such as the

Herald (Terence Sharpe) better sung than as here (Robert Hayward). In the Valley of Humiliation the voice of Apollyon comes as an amplified sound from off-stage, but on record the trick is to catch an overpowering terror, and this they manage better on EMI, partly by virtue of having Robert Lloyd to strike it, and also by the producer's decision to bring it (and the menacing wordless chorus) closer. Nor, in the comparison, is there any sense of a confrontation of 'bright young feller' and 'grand old fuddy-duddy'. Boult does not *sound* like an old man, any more than Hickox sounds like a youngster. The Boult recording, finely remastered, is a strong survivor. Hickox has a bigger canvas for the recorded sound, and achieves a clearer texture. The newer version also has Gerald Finley, and is a fine performance anyway.

The Pilgrim's Progress.
John Noble bar Pilgrim; **Raimund Herincx** bass John Bunyan, Lord Hate-Good;
John Carol Case bar Evangelist; **Wynford Evans** ten Pliable; **Christopher Keyte** bass Obstinate,
Judas Escariot, Pontius Pilate; **Geoffrey Shaw** bass Mistrust, Demas;
Bernard Dickerson ten Timorous, Usher; **Sheila Armstrong** sop Shining One 1;
Marie Hayward Segal sop Shining One 2, Madam Wanton; **Gloria Jennings** mez Shining One 3,
Madam By-Ends; **Ian Partridge** ten Interpreter, Superstition; **John Shirley-Quirk** bar Watchful;
Terence Sharpe bar Herald; **Robert Lloyd** bass Apollyon; **Norma Burrowes** sop Branchbearer,
Malice; **Alfreda Hodgson** contr Cupbearer, Pickthank; **Joseph Ward** bar Lord Lechery;
Richard Angas bass Simon Magus, Envy; **John Elwes** ten Worldly Glory;
Delia Wallis mez Madam Bubble; **Wendy Eathorne** sop Woodcutter's Boy;
Gerald English ten Mister By-Ends;
London Philharmonic Choir and Orchestra / Sir Adrian Boult.
EMI British Composers CMS7 64212-2 (two discs: 153 mintues: ADD). Notes and texts included.
Recorded 1970-71. Ⓜ

When this glowing performance of one of Vaughan Williams's most raptly beautiful works first appeared in 1972 as a centenary offering to the composer, it was hoped that the record would lead to more stage performances on both sides of the Atlantic. That hope, alas, was not fulfilled. That Vaughan Williams drew from a whole series of Bunyan inspirations over 30 years has made for meatiness of material and little or no inconsistency of style. 'They won't like it,' predicted the composer after the first performance at Covent Garden. 'They don't want an opera with no heroine and no love duets – and I don't care. It's what I meant, and there it is.' Though he described the work as a 'morality', he was aggressively concerned that it should be treated as an opera, not as an oratorio. One can see what he meant. He wanted the work's strength and cohesion brought out, not just its piety, but in truth precious little is lost from not having it staged, and the format of recording might well be counted as ideal, allowing the listener to picture his own staging.

Sir Adrian's portrait, marvellously characterful, stands as one of the very finest of his many records of Vaughan Williams's music, beautifully paced and textured with the fascinating references to the symphonies – not just No. 5 which took material from the previously written Act 1 but (at least by implication) Nos. 3, 4 and 7 as well, not to mention the *Serenade to Music*. In every way Vaughan Williams's Bunyan inspirations permeated his music, and this opera stands as their centre-point. John Noble, who as a very young singer scored a great success in the 1954 Cambridge production, may not have the richest or most characterful baritone, but his dedication and understanding make for compelling results. Outstanding among the others are such singers as Sheila Armstrong, Ian Partridge, Norma Burrowes and John Shirley-Quirk. The chorus – subject of rather tough treatment from Boult (this set has the bonus of Boult's sharp-tongued rehearsals: to the chorus: 'You talk … you talk like market-women') sings with fervour, and the sound – using the always helpful London Kingsway Hall – remains first-rate.

Riders to the Sea[a].
Norma Burrowes sop Nora; **Dame Margaret Price** sop Cathleen; **Helen Watts** contr Maurya;
Benjamin Luxon bar Bartley; **Pauline Stevens** mez Woman;
Ambrosian Singers; Orchestra Nova of London / Meredith Davies.

Epithalamion[b].
Stephen Roberts bar Jonathan Snowden fl Howard Shelley pf
Bach Choir; London Philharmonic Orchestra / Sir David Willcocks.

Merciless Beauty[b].
Philip Langridge ten
members of the **Endellion Quartet** (Andrew Watkinson, James Clark vns David Waterman vc);
EMI British Composers CDM7 64730-2 (75 minutes: ADD/DDD). Texts included.
Recorded [a]1970 and [b]1986. Ⓜ

Vaughan Williams completed his masterly setting of J.M. Synge's one-act drama, *Riders to the Sea*, in 1932. Although it has enjoyed the occasional revival, it remains one of the least-known and most under-appreciated of Vaughan Williams's major works. Indeed, with scoring that is both economical and intensely evocative, it can be a gripping experience, especially when presented as sympathetically as here. The cast is a uniformly strong one, and Meredith Davies inspires everyone to give of their very best. The 1970 sound has come up superbly, creating a rather more vivid impression, in fact, than its modern partners from 1986. These are also both considerable rarities. *Epithalamion* is a large-scale cantata from 1957 based on Edmund Spenser's love-poem of the same name: musically, it draws extensively on material used in VW's 1938 masque, *The Bridal Day*, and its emotional centrepiece, 'The Lover's Song', boasts a viola solo of exquisite beauty. Finally, there is *Merciless Beauty*, three pithy Chaucer settings for tenor and string trio dating from 1921. Performances are all one could wish.

Francesco Veracini

Italian 1690-1768

Sonate accademiche, Op. 2 – No. 7 in D minor; No. 8 in E minor; No. 9 in A major; No. 12 in D minor. Capriccio sesto con due soggetti in G minor.
Fabio Biondi *vn* **Maurizio Naddeo** *vc* **Rinaldo Alessandrini** *hpd* **Pascal Monteilhet** *theorbo*
Opus 111 OPS30-138 (61 minutes: DDD). Recorded 1995.　　　　　　　　　　Ⓕ🅿

Despite the continuing rediscovery of so much of the Italian baroque, Veracini's music remains comparatively unknown both in the concert hall and on record. This neglect is as unjustified as the traditional unfavourable comparison of his music with that of Vivaldi. He was a performer whose curious style was already noticed during his lifetime by the English writer Charles Burney, who once said that by travelling and playing all over Europe Veracini had formed a 'style of playing peculiar to himself'. The same might be said of his composing, which far from being simply an assimilation of contemporary modes, speaks with a sharply individual voice that constantly surprises with its freshness and originality. This almost kaleidoscopic shifting of moods and manners is fully evident in the *Sonate accademiche*, a collection of pieces published in 1744, but the fruits of a lifetime's experience playing in Dresden, London and Venice. As such they are shot through with virtuoso passagework, double-stopping and other technical features characteristic of Veracini's performances. These are here negotiated by Fabio Biondi with an easy brilliance that nevertheless does not sacrifice poetry for mere outward display. His approach is vigorous, with plenty of tone when required, and attractively alive. The overall sound is sharp and clean. Both he and the other performers use either period instruments or modern copies, and Rinaldo Alessandrini's informed and committed direction, and support, brings out all the delicacy of Veracini's rich and varied textures.

Giuseppe Verdi

Italian 1813-1901

Overtures and Preludes – Oberto; Un giorno di regno; Nabucco; Ernani; Giovanna d'Arco; Alzira; Attila; I masnadieri; Macbeth; Il corsaro; La battaglia di Legnano; Luisa Miller; Rigoletto; La traviata; I vespri Siciliani; Un ballo in maschera; La forza del destino; Aida.
Berlin Philharmonic Orchestra / Herbert von Karajan.
DG 453 058-2GTA2 (two discs: 113 minutes: ADD). Recorded 1975.　　　　　　Ⓜ

Karajan was one of the most adaptable and sensitive of dramatic conductors. His repertoire in the theatre is extraordinarily wide being at home equally in Verdi, Wagner, Richard Strauss and Puccini. In this celebrated 1975 collection of all of Verdi's overtures, he gives us some fine insights into the composer's skill as an orchestrator, dramatist and poet. Though Karajan had only recorded *Aida* complete his dramatic instincts bring some fine performances of the lesser known preludes. The earliest, *Nabucco* from 1842 (the collection is arranged chronologically), already shows a mastercraftsman at work, with a slow introduction promising much. *La traviata* shows a quite different skill – the delicate creation of a sensitive poet working in filigree. The final four preludes are great works fully worthy of this individual presentation. Even the lesser known preludes are enhanced by Karajan's dramatic instincts. Good recordings, though less than outstanding.

Overtures and Preludes – Oberto; Nabucco; Giovanna d'Arco; Alzira; La battaglia di Legnano. Attila; I masnadieri; Il corsaro; Un giorno di regno; Ernani; I due Foscari; Macbeth; Ballet Music – Macbeth.
BBC Philharmonic Orchestra / Sir Edward Downes.
Chandos CHAN9510 (76 minutes: DDD). Recorded 1996.　　　　　　　　　Ⓕ

Verdi Orchestral

These performances from an experienced British operatic stalwart have dignity (witness the brass in *Nabucco*), panache, and splendidly colourful orchestral playing, including real string virtuosity, using the widest range of dynamic. The *crescendo* at the opening of *Giovanna d'Arco* is most compelling. Some of the shorter preludes are full of atmosphere. The brief *Macbeth* Prelude is particularly potent and the ballet music is both dramatic and rumbustious while *I masnadieri* closes with a swooning cello solo. *La battaglia di Legnano* which ends the programme has plenty of full-blooded brass at the opening and close. The recording is spectacular.

Messa da Requiem[a]. Quattro pezzi sacri[b].
[a]**Luba Orgonasova**, [b]**Donna Brown** *sops* **Anne Sofie von Otter** *mez* **Luca Canonici** *ten*
Alastair Miles *bass*
Monteverdi Choir; Orchestre Révolutionnaire et Romantique / Sir John Eliot Gardiner.
Philips 442 142-2PH2 (two discs: 120 minutes: DDD). Notes, texts and translations included.
Recorded 1992.   Ⓕ ℙ Ⓔ ℝℝ

Gardiner's Verdi Requiem is in a class of its own. His are readings that combine a positive view and interpretative integrity from start to finish, something possible only in the context of the superb professionalism of the (augmented) Monteverdi Choir, which sings with burnished, steady tone throughout and suggests, rightly, a corporate act of worship. Its contribution is beyond praise – and Verdi would surely have marvelled at that. He might also have been surprised and delighted to hear the soloists' contribution sung with such precision by such a finely integrated quartet, who perform the important unaccompanied passages with special grace and sensitivity. Instead of hearing the usual jostle of vibratos, here the four voices are firm and true. Individually they are also distinguished. Pride of place must go to Orgonasova who gives the performance of her life. The exactly placed high B in the 'Quid sum miser' section of the *Dies irae*, the perfect blending with von Otter at 'Dominum', the whole of the *Andante* section of the 'Libera me', sung with ethereal tone and a long breath, make the heart stop in amazement. In 'Oro supplex' Gardiner follows Verdi's tempo marking. More often he follows tradition, with slower speeds than those suggested, and he allows more licence than the score, or conductors like Toscanini. But as his liberties all seem so convincing in the context of the whole, who should complain? In the *Pezzi sacri*, Gardiner gives the most thrilling account yet to appear. The recording, made in Westminster Cathedral, has a huge range which may cause problems in confined spaces. You are liable to be overwhelmed by the *Dies irae*.

Messa da Requiem. Quattro pezzi sacri.
Elena Filipova *sop* **Gloria Scalchi** *mez* **César Hernández** *ten* **Carlo Colombara** *bass*
Hungarian State Opera Choir and Orchestra / Pier Giorgio Morandi.
Naxos 8 550944/5 (two discs: 126 minutes: DDD). Texts and translations included.
Recorded 1996.   Ⓢ Ⓔ

Morandi brings to his interpretation a youthful, Italian energy and generosity of expression. Given a judicious choice of young soloists, all up to their exigent tasks, an excellent chorus (a shattering *Dies irae*, an alert, not too drilled *Sanctus*, a disciplined 'Libera me' fugue) and a well-fashioned recording, this set makes a compelling case for recommendation as an alternative to Gardiner's period-performance set. Try track 7, the 'Rex tremendae', where you can hear how Morandi builds a movement unerringly to an appropriately tremendous climax. The soloists show how involved they are in the work, form a good ensemble and individually exhibit the intelligence to sing quietly as needed. Elena Filipova and Scalchi combine into a rich-toned duo in 'Liber scriptus', spoilt a little by moments of indeterminate pitch from the soprano (later the two contrast well in the *Agnus Dei*). Hernández, with his warm, baritonal, Spanish-style tenor, sings a sensitive 'Ingemisco' (a touch of insecurity at the start excepted), succeeded by Colombara's truly magisterial conjuring of the flames of hell at 'Confutatis maledictis'. Filipova's floated entry at 'huic ergo' in the succeeding trio and the sheer intensity of the whole 'Lacrymosa' bring the *Dies irae* to a fitting close. The rest of the performance is on an equivalent level of achievement, Morandi always judging speeds to a nicety. The fill-up to this large-scale reading is a fine performance of the *Quattro pezzi sacri*.

Opera choruses: Nabucco – Gli arredi festivi giù cadano infranti; Va, pensiero, sull'ali dorate.
I Lombardi – Gerusalem!; O Signore, dal tetto natio. Macbeth – Tre volte miagola; Patria oppressa.
I masnadieri – Le rube, gli stupri. Rigoletto – Zitti zitti. Il trovatore – Vedi! le fosche notturne spoglie;
Squilli, echeggi la tromba guerriera. La traviata – Noi siamo zingarelle ... Di Madride nio siam
mattadori (with **Marsha Waxman** *mez* **David Huneryager, Richard Cohn** *basses*). Un ballo in
maschera – Posa in pace. Don Carlos – Spuntato ecco il dí. Aida – Gloria all'Egitto. Otello – Fuoco
di gioia. Requiem – Sanctus.
Chicago Symphony Chorus and Orchestra / Sir Georg Solti.
Decca 430 226-2DH (70 minutes: DDD). Texts and translations included. Recorded 1989.   Ⓕ

Verdi's choruses occupy a special place in his operas. They are invariably red-blooded and usually make a simple dramatic statement with great impact. The arresting 'Chorus of the Hebrew Slaves' ('Va, pensiero') from *Nabucco* is probably the best-known and most popular chorus in the entire operatic repertoire, immediately tugging at the heart-strings with its gentle opening cantilena, soon swelling out to a great climax. Solti shows just how to shape the noble melodic line which soars with firm control, yet retaining the urgency and electricity in every bar. He is equally good in 'Gli arredi festivi', from the same opera, not only in the bold opening statement, shared between singers and the resplendent sonority of the Chicago brass, but also later when the mood lightens, and women's voices are heard floating over seductive harp roulades. The dramatic contrasts at the opening of 'Gerusalem!' from *I Lombardi* are equally powerfully projected, and the brass again makes a riveting effect in 'Patria oppressa' from *Macbeth*. But, of course, not all Verdi choruses offer blood and thunder: the volatile 'Fire chorus' from *Otello* flickers with an almost visual fantasy, while the wicked robbers in *I masnadieri* celebrate their excesses (plunder, rape, arson and murder) gleefully, and with such rhythmic jauntiness that one cannot quite take them seriously. The 'Gipsies' chorus' from *La traviata* has a nice touch of elegance, and the scherzo-like 'Sanctus', from the *Requiem*, which ends the concert, is full of joy. But it is the impact of the dramatic moments which is most memorable, not least the big triumphal scene from *Aida*, complete with the ballet music, to provide a diverse interlude in the middle. The recording is in the demonstration class.

Opera Arias: Nabucco – Ben io t'avenni ... Anch'io dischiuso un giorno. Il trovatore – Tacea la notte placida ... Di tale amor; Timor di me? ... D'amor sull'ali rosee. La traviata – E strano! ... Ah, fors'è lui ... Follie! Sempre libera[a]; Teneste la promessa ... Addio del passato. Un ballo in maschera – Ecco l'orrido campo ... Ma dall'arido stelo divulsa ... Morro, ma prima in grazia.
La forza del destino – Pace, pace, mio Dio.
Julia Varady sop [a]**Lothar Odinius** ten
Bavarian State Orchestra / Dietrich Fischer-Dieskau.
Orfeo C186951 (51 minutes: DDD). Recorded 1995. Ⓕ

Varady endows these arias we have heard hundreds of times, and of which we all have our favourite memories and recordings, with renewed life through an art which is fully responsive, highly fastidious, lovely in the quality of its sound and individual in its timbre and inflexion. The beauty of tone is evident first of all in its well-preserved purity (and Varady, born in 1941, is of an age when normally allowances have to be made). Here is not a full-bodied, rich Ponselle-like voice, but she makes wonderfully effective use of her resources, which include a surprisingly strong lower register and an upward range that (as we hear) easily encompasses the high D flat and has an E flat available. She is dramatic in style yet also thoroughly accomplished in her scales, trills and other *fioriture*. Her first *Trovatore* aria, for instance, includes the cabaletta with its full complement of technical brilliances. The musical instinct seems almost infallible – a 'wrong' *portamento* or rubato always irritates and here everything seems right. A remarkable sensitivity is at work throughout. The orchestra is conducted by Fischer-Dieskau, Varady's husband, and here too is a fine example of a positive, non-routine collaboration, the pacing and shading of the orchestral parts so frequently having something specific to offer (for example, in the letter passage from *La traviata*). The recording is well balanced.

Luisa Miller – Oh! fede negar potessi ... Quando le sere al placido. I Lombardi alla prima crociata – La mia letizia infondere. Aida – Se quel guerrier ... Celeste Aida. Ernani – Mercè, dilette amici ... Come rugiada al cespite ... O tu che l'alma adora (with **London Voices**). Un ballo in maschera – Forse la soglia ... Ma se m'è forza perderti. Otello – Dio! mi potevi; Niun mi tema (with **Andrew Busher** ten **James Bobby** bar **Richard Fallas, Noel Mann** basses). La forza del destino – Prelude, Act 3; La vita è inferno ... O, tu che in seno. Macbeth – O figli, o figli miei! ... Ah, la paterna mano. Jérusalem – L'émir auprès de lui ... Je veux encore entendre. Il trovatore – Ah! si, ben mio ... Di quella pira (with **Angela Gheorghiu** sop **London Voices**).
Roberto Alagna ten
Berlin Philharmonic Orchestra / Claudio Abbado.
EMI CDC5 56567-2 (64 minutes: DDD). Texts and translations included. Recorded 1997. Ⓕ 🅴

Alagna here shows, in the most demanding programme imaginable, that there is little if anything wrong with his technique and a great deal right with his sense of Verdian style. Indeed, he takes the score as his bible. That is evident, for instance, in his treatment of Otello. In the great Act 3 Monologue, besides thinking himself into the Moor's deep well of despondency at this juncture of the tragedy, evinced in a slightly juddering tone, he sings the opening passage as written, staying on the A flat and E flat, not going for unwanted melodrama. Then the cantilena is sung with the appropriate touch of pained nobility. In the Death scene he finds the right pent-up voice for 'Come sei pallida' and the repeated 'Desdemona', then sings 'Or morendo' with a *pp* on the high G, as Verdi enjoins. So much else in the recital is just as thoughtfully interpreted. He solves the problem of the high B flat at the end of 'Celeste Aida' by starting it *mezzo-forte* and shading it away affectingly in a well-executed *diminuendo*, having sung the whole aria in a suitably poetic manner. Alagna is the brigand to the life in Ernani's introductory aria. Riccardo's (or if you like Gustaf's) Act 3 aria is charged with emotion, the tone properly plaintive and darkened for the middle section. Then there's perhaps the most taxing aria for tenor in all Verdi: Alvaro's 'O, tu che in seno' from *Forza*. Following the most eloquent playing by the Berlin Philharmonic's clarinet in the long introduction, Alagna catches the Inca's sense of longing in the recitative and then rises to the challenge of the aria's relentless tessitura with fine-grained, almost heroic tone. Nor does he shirk the high Cs in 'Di quella pira'. The rarity here is the item from *Jérusalem*, sung in Alagna's other tongue. The Berlin Philharmonic's contribution, under Abbado's distinguished direction, is as accomplished as you might expect. The recording allows us to hear the full bloom of Alagna's voice, but occasionally the sound of the voice appears to stray or float around the sound spectrum, a disconcerting effect, but that's not enough of a distraction to prevent a strong recommendation.

Aida.
Montserrat Caballé *sop* Aida; **Plácido Domingo** *ten* Radames;
Fiorenza Cossotto *mez* Amneris; **Piero Cappuccilli** *bar* Amonasro;
Nicolai Ghiaurov *bass* Ramphis; **Luigi Roni** *bass* King of Egypt;
Esther Casas *sop* Priestess; **Nicola Martinucci** *ten* Messenger;
Chorus of the Royal Opera House, Covent Garden; New Philharmonia Orchestra; Trumpeters of the Royal Military School of Music, Kneller Hall / Riccardo Muti.
EMI CDS5 56246-2 (three discs: 148 minutes: ADD). Notes, text and translation included. Recorded 1974. Ⓕ 🆁🆁

Caballé for Muti gives what is generally considered her most successful Verdi performance on record, full of those vocal subtleties and beauties that inform her best singing, at its finest perhaps in the lovely floated passages, but no less effective when it comes to the power needed to fill Verdi's phrases generously. Moreover, the characterization, perhaps inspired by Muti, fulfils almost every aspect of the role's demands. In contrast to Caballé's delicacy and plangency, there is Cossotto's imperious, fiercely sung Amneris, just as electrifying when she is at the end of her tether in Act 4 as when she is baiting Aida in Act 2. Domingo sings an upright, musical Radames, Cappuccilli is a forthright, unsubtle Amonasro, Ghiaurov a properly merciless Ramphis. Muti gives an impassioned, subjective account of the score, sometimes indulging in sudden *accelerandos* and *crescendos* that are unwarranted by the score. The balance between this set and Claudio Abbado on DG is a fine one. Ricciarelli (Abbado), though not vocally anywhere near so reliable as Caballé, is still an Aida to be reckoned with because she understands the emotions of the part so well. But Domingo on the Abbado set offers the most heroic Radames on any available set, and one fashioned in long breaths and refined phrasing. Abbado himself is inclined to take a more measured view of the score than Muti and he is just as able as Muti to create the right atmosphere for a scene, by his attention to Verdi's illustrative detail. With Muti digitally remastered, the differences in recorded quality are even more marked. The EMI sound is bigger in scale, more reverberant and spacious, but in the indoor scenes, as it were, the Abbado often seems the more natural. Both choruses and orchestras are well caught, and distinguish themselves with splendidly vital contributions. By a hair's breadth Muti is preferable.

Aida.
Maria Callas *sop* Aida; **Richard Tucker** *ten* Radames; **Fedora Barbieri** *mez* Amneris;
Tito Gobbi *bar* Amonasro; **Giuseppe Modesti** *bass* Ramphis; **Nicola Zaccaria** *bass* King of Egypt; **Elvira Galassi** *sop* Priestess; **Franco Ricciardi** *ten* Messenger;
Chorus and Orchestra of La Scala, Milan / Tullio Serafin.
EMI Callas Edition mono CDS5 56316-2 (two discs: 144 minutes: ADD). Notes, text and translation included. Recorded 1955. Ⓕ 🅷

Aida, the daughter of the Ethiopian king, is a prisoner at the Egyptian court where she falls in love with Radames, an Egyptian captain of the guard; Amneris, the Egyptian princess, also loves him. The tensions between these characters are rivetingly portrayed and explored and the gradual build-up to Aida's and Radames's union in death is paced with the sureness of a master composer. Callas's Aida is an assumption of total understanding and conviction; the growth from a slave-girl torn between love for her homeland and Radames, to a woman whose feelings transcend life itself represents one of the greatest operatic undertakings ever committed to disc. Alongside her is Fedora Barbieri, an Amneris palpable in her agonized mixture of love and jealousy – proud yet human. Tucker's Radames is powerful and Gobbi's Amonasro quite superb – a portrayal of comparable understanding to stand alongside Callas's Aida. Tullio Serafin is quite simply ideal and though the recording cannot compete with modern versions (it was never, in fact, a model of clarity), nowhere can it dim the brilliance of the creations conjured up by this classic cast.

Un ballo in maschera.
Katia Ricciarelli *sop* Amelia; **Plácido Domingo** *ten* Riccardo; **Renato Bruson** *bar* Renato;
Edita Gruberová *sop* Oscar; **Elena Obraztsova** *mez* Ulrica; **Ruggero Raimondi** *bass* Sam;
Giovanni Foiani *bass* Tom; **Luigi De Corato** *bar* Silvano; **Antonio Savastano** *bar* Judge;
Gianfranco Manganotti *ten* Servant;
Chorus and Orchestra of La Scala, Milan / Claudio Abbado.
DG 453 148-2GTA2 (two discs: 127 minutes: ADD). Notes included. Recorded 1981. Ⓜ **RR**

This recording is a wholly satisfying and unified performance of *Un ballo in maschera*, largely
because Abbado and his La Scala forces give us a total sense of a theatrical experience and because
Abbado's conducting is so stable and of a piece. Listening to his direction, you will be struck by his
attention to detail and his sensible tempos. Though not quite so exciting as Votto's, it seems to make
better sense as a whole. Ricciarelli is always inside the part of Amelia, giving us the very epitome of
the girl torn between love and duty. Domingo doesn't have, never has had, the 'ping' of a Pavarotti,
but his Riccardo is as involved and as involving a performance as that of his Amelia; together with
Abbado, they give an eloquent account of the love duet. Bruson, in fine voice, is hardly less
expressive. The sound could be a little more open and clear but it's quite acceptable.

Un ballo in maschera.
Giuseppi di Stefano *ten* Riccardo; **Tito Gobbi** *bar* Renato; **Maria Callas** *sop* Amelia;
Fedora Barbieri *mez* Ulrica; **Eugenia Ratti** *sop* Oscar; **Ezio Giordano** *bass* Silvano;
Silvio Maionica *bass* Samuel; **Nicola Zaccaria** *bass* Tom; **Renato Ercolani** *bar* Judge;
Chorus and Orchestra of La Scala, Milan / Antonino Votto.
EMI Callas Edition mono CDS5 56320-2 (two discs: 130 minutes: ADD). Notes, text and
translation included. Recorded in 1956 Ⓕ **H**

Ballo manages to encompass a vein of lighthearted frivolity (represented by the page, Oscar) within
the confines of a serious drama of love, infidelity, noble and ignoble sentiments. None of the more
recent recordings has quite caught the opera's true spirit so truly as this one under Votto's unerring
direction. Callas has not been surpassed in delineating Amelia's conflict of feelings and loyalties,
nor has di Stefano been equalled in the sheer ardour of his singing as Riccardo. Add to that no less
a singer than Tito Gobbi as Renato, at first eloquent in his friendship to his ruler, then implacable
in his revenge when he thinks Riccardo has stolen his wife. Fedora Barbieri is full of character as
the soothsayer Ulrica, Eugenia Ratti a sparky Oscar. It is an unbeatable line-up.

Don Carlos.
Plácido Domingo *ten* Don Carlos; **Montserrat Caballé** *sop* Elisabetta; **Shirley Verrett** *mez* Eboli;
Sherrill Milnes *bar* Rodrigo; **Ruggero Raimondi** *bass* Philip II;
Giovanni Foiani *bass* Grand Inquisitor; **Delia Wallis** *mez* Thibault;
Ryland Davies *ten* Count of Lerma; **Simon Estes** *bass* Monk; **John Noble** *bar* Herald;
Ambrosian Opera Chorus;
Royal Opera House Orchestra, Covent Garden / Carlo Maria Giulini.
EMI CDS7 47701-8 (three discs: 208 minutes: ADD). Notes, text and translation included.
Recorded 1970. Ⓕ **RR**

In no other Verdi opera, except perhaps *Aida*, are public and private matters so closely
intermingled, so searchingly described as in this large-scale, panoramic work, in which the political
intrigues and troubles of Philip II's Spain are counterpointed with his personal agony and the lives
and loves of those at his court. This vast canvas inspired Verdi to compose one of his most varied
and glorious scores. Giulini, more than any other conductor, searches out the inner soul of the piece
and his cast is admirable. The young Plácido Domingo makes a vivid and exciting Carlos, whilst
Montserrat Caballé spins glorious tone and phrases in encompassing Elisabeth's difficult music.
Shirley Verrett is a vital, suitably tense Eboli, Sherrill Milnes an upright, warm Rodrigo and
Ruggero Raimondi a sombre Philip. The Covent Garden forces sing and play with fervour.

Don Carlo.
Roberto Alagna *ten* Don Carlo; **Karita Mattila** *sop* Elisabeth; **Waltraud Meier** *mez* Eboli;
Thomas Hampson *bar* Rodrigue; **José van Dam** *bass-bar* Philippe II;
Eric Halfvarson *bass* Grand Inquisitor; **Csaba Airizer** *bass* Monk; **Anat Efraty** *sop* Thibault;
Scot Weir *ten* Comte de Lerme, Herald; **Donna Brown** *sop* Voice from Heaven;
Chorus of the Théâtre du Châtelet; Orchestre de Paris / Antonio Pappano.
EMI CDS5 56152-2 (three discs: 206 minutes: DDD). Notes, text and translation included.
Recorded live in 1996. Ⓕ **RR**

This is an eloquent and inspiriting performance of Verdi's singular music-drama depicting private tragedy within public conflict, and a recording of the French version. Text-wise, Pappano excludes the opening scene for the chorus at Fontainebleau, cut by the composer before the first night; he includes the important dress-changing scene at the start of Act 3 (which explains Carlos's ardour towards the 'wrong' woman), a snippet of the Elisabeth-Eboli duet in Act 4, and the whole of the Carlos/Philippe duet after Posa's death (the theme of which was reused in the Requiem). Pappano also chooses some of the alternative settings, notably in the Posa-Philippe duet in Act 2 and the farewell encounter of Elisabeth and Carlos in Act 5, amendments that Verdi made for the neglected 1872 Naples revision. Neither seems an improvement. Pappano's is a subtly shaped, superbly paced and vital interpretation from start to finish. He is as able to encompass the delicacies of the Veil Song and the succeeding exchanges as he is to purvey the grand, tragic passion of Elisabeth and Carlos in Act 2, the intricacies and changes of feeling in the colloquy between Rodrigue and Philippe, the terrible menace of the Grand Inquisitor. The Orchestre de Paris supports him with playing of dedication and sensitivity. Giulini's noble conducting of the Italian version (reviewed above) comes to mind when listening to Pappano and his players. Praise cannot be higher.

By and large he has singers who can sustain his vision. Mattila sings a lovely Elisabeth. Her soft-grained yet strong tone and exquisite phrasing in all her solos and duets is balm to the ear. By Mattila's side Alagna offers an equally involving Carlos. presenting a more vulnerable picture of the unbalanced infante. His is a fully rounded portrayal that will please his many admirers, the difficult tessitura seldom troubling him and his French, of course, is impeccable. As Rodrigue, Marquis de Posa, Hampson also has idiomatic French. His mellifluous baritone well suits this French version and he provides many moments of vocal beauty. Arguably, the death needs a more imposing voice but the added decibels can easily be borne to appreciate Hampson's intelligence. Van Dam nicely balances the exterior authority and interior agony of Philippe, everywhere in command of line, language, phrase. The recording catches the *frisson* of the theatrical experience. The positioning of the singers on stage never causes problems; everything is clear and in its place, and the balance with the pit sounds natural. This is a landmark in the *Don Carlos* discography.

Ernani.
Plácido Domingo *ten* Ernani; **Mirella Freni** *sop* Elvira; **Renato Bruson** *bar* Don Carlos;
Nicolai Ghiaurov *bass* Don Ruy, Gomez de Silva; **Jolanda Michieli** *sop* Giovanna;
Gianfranco Manganotti *ten* Don Riccardo; **Alfredo Giacomotti** *bass* Iago;
Chorus and Orchestra of La Scala, Milan / Riccardo Muti.
EMI CDS7 47083-8 (three discs: 128 minutes: DDD). Notes, text and translation included.
Recorded live in 1982.   Ⓕ

Renato Bruson's Don Carlo is an assumption that is as gripping dramatically as it is vocally. In his portrayal more than anywhere, the musical tension of *Ernani* becomes manifest and everywhere Bruson offers superb Verdi singing. Domingo's Ernani is hardly less impressive and he benefits from being caught live on stage. His opening aria and cabaletta are full of delicate touches and obedience to the dynamic marks. In the last act, his recitative, 'Tutto ora tace d'intorno' has great pathos, and his contributions to the final trio an overwhelming eloquence. Here, too, Freni achieves most, the etching in of 'Il riso del tuo volto fa ch'io veda', a brief utterance of happiness, most affecting, and her desperate appeals to Silva for mercy sung with brio. In her opening aria and cabaletta, the famous 'Ernani, Ernani', too much is asked of a voice not really meant by nature for this kind of heavy duty, but none can quite match the sorrow and heartbreak of Elvira's predicament that Freni manages in the theatre. Ghiaurov, rusty as his voice had become, creates a great impression of dignity and implacable strength, and many of those qualities are carried over into his singing. 'Infelice' is delivered with mature nobility, 'Ah, io l'amo' is intensely moving. Ghiaurov is denied Silva's probably spurious cabaletta. Otherwise the work is given complete. Muti conducts the score in exemplary manner. He has learnt when to allow his singers licence to phrase with meaning and when to press on. The La Scala chorus gives us the genuine sound of Italian voices in full flight, sounding much more inside their various assumptions than their rivals. The audience is occasionally in evidence as are the on-stage effects, but the atmosphere of being in an opera house and taking part, as it were, in a real occasion has all the advantages over the aseptic feeling of a studio.

Falstaff.
Tito Gobbi *bar* Falstaff; **Rolando Panerai** *bar* Ford;
Dame Elisabeth Schwarzkopf *sop* Alice Ford; **Anna Moffo** *sop* Nannetta;
Luigi Alva *ten* Fenton; **Fedora Barbieri** *mez* Mistress Quickly; **Nan Merriman** *mez* Meg Page;
Tomaso Spataro *ten* Dr Caius; **Renato Ercolani** *ten* Bardolph; **Nicola Zaccaria** *bass* Pistol;
Philharmonia Chorus and Orchestra / Herbert von Karajan.
EMI Great Recordings of the Century CMS5 67083-2 (two discs: 120 minutes: ADD). Notes, text and translation included. Recorded 1956.   Ⓜ Ⓗ ⓇⓇ

This *Falstaff* still stands (with Toscanini) peerless in the catalogue. At its centre stands Tito Gobbi, and his is a presence large enough to encompass both the lord and the jester, the sensuous and the sensual, and the deep seriousness as well as the deep absurdity of his vision. Few Falstaffs have such a measure of the simplicity of his first monosyllables in the bustle around him; few find the poise as well as the confusion within his music. Karajan's recording is incomparable in its quartet of merry wives. Schwarzkopf's Alice radiates both the 'gioia nell'aria' and the 'gioia nel'cor' of Verdi's writing, Fedora Barbieri's redoubtable Mistress Quickly, with her stentorian cries of 'Povera donna!', puts other readings in the shade; Anna Moffo's Nannetta, perfectly matched in timbre and agility with Luigi Alva's Fenton, is a constant delight. It is, above all, their corporate presence which works at such a distinctively higher level. Rolando Panerai is a magnificent Ford; his 'E sogno? o realtà?' is a high point of the performance. This 1956 recording has been discreetly and skilfully doctored, but a little background hiss does remain. But one doesn't actually end up hearing it. This great recording is a-flutter with pungent solo detail, realizing, with Nannetta, that the world is 'tutto deliro, sospiro e riso'. The episodes of the opera, its exits and entrances, its subjects and counter-subjects, pass with the unique sensibility of Verdi's final great exuberant fugue of life.

Falstaff.
Domenico Trimarchi *bar* Falstaff; **Roberto Servile** *bar* Ford;
Julia Faulkner *sop* Alice Ford; **Dilbèr** *sop* Nannetta; **Maurizio Comencini** *ten* Fenton;
Anna Maria di Micco *sop* Mistress Quickly; **Anna Bonitatibus** *mez* Meg Page;
Enrico Facini *ten* Doctor Caius; **Alessandro Cosentino** *ten* Bardolph;
Franco de Grandis *bass* Pistol;
Chorus and Orchestra of Hungarian State Opera / Will Humburg.
Naxos 8660050/1 (two discs: 120 minutes: DDD). Notes and synopsis included.
Recorded 1996. ⑤ 🄴

This set from Naxos does a good job in challenging the best in the field. Humburg, responsible for the well-liked *Barbiere* from the same stable, strikes just the right balance between the high spirits and the delicacy in Verdi's last and most miraculous score, and secures a sympathetic response from his singers and players. He has sensibly chosen a predominantly Italian cast for a work that depends, more than any other in Verdi, on pinpoint enunciation of the text, Boito's delightful refashioning of Shakespeare. Nobody is better at this than Trimarchi, a veteran of many stage performances and recordings of the comic roles in Italian opera, and a Falstaff of wit and resource. He, like the rest, adopts the conversational, intimate style needed, nowhere more so than in the interview with 'Fontana' where, in the *sotto voce* Verdi wants, he tells how Ford is about to be cuckolded. It is just one point in a reading full of ripe understanding, the characterization nicely held between comedy and autumn melancholy. Another advantage is that his voice lies, as the role requires, ideally poised between baritone and bass. It is true that his vibrato has loosened and when he places pressure on his tone it becomes unsteady – but that is true of a number of other interpreters on CD and hardly detracts from a lovable portrait all-round.

Servile, Humburg's expert Figaro, proves a formidable Ford, quick to anger, truly anguished in his monologue of jealousy, always secure in voice, adept with his words. Around their men are gathered a lively group of merry wives, most notably the lightly scheming, even-voiced, soul-of-the-party Alice of Julia Faulkner, whose Italian is so idiomatic you'd hardly know she wasn't native-born, and the vocally smiling, irrepressible Quickly of di Micco, who sensibly avoids the exaggerations often imposed on the part but follows Verdi's markings to the letter. The Meg is more than adequate. Although the Nannetta and Fenton sing well, they miss the ethereal beauty and steadiness of tone to be found elsewhere, but they, like the Caius, Bardolph and Pistol, enter into the spirit of a well-produced set that employs just enough devices to suggest a stage performance. The sound is sensibly balanced, although once or twice the voices seemed disconcertingly either closer or further away from the microphones. However, this is a *Falstaff* to savour and one that surely bears repetition.

Falstaff.
Giuseppe Valdengo *bar* Falstaff; **Frank Guarrera** *bar* Ford; **Herva Nelli** *sop* Alice Ford;
Teresa Stich-Randall *sop* Nannetta; **Antonio Madasi** *ten* Fenton;
Cloe Elmo *contr* Mistress Quickly; **Nan Merriman** *mez* Meg Page;
Gabor Carelli *ten* Dr Caius; **John Carmen Rossi** *ten* Bardolph; **Norman Scott** *bass* Pistol;
Robert Shaw Chorale; NBC Symphony Orchestra / Arturo Toscanini.
RCA Gold Seal mono GD60251 (two discs: 117 minutes: ADD). Notes, text and translation included. Recorded 1950. Ⓜ 🄷

This *Falstaff* remains, as it always has been, one of the half a dozen greatest opera sets ever recorded. It is a miracle in every respect. How Toscanini loved Verdi and how he strained every sinew to fulfil this amazing score's variety in line, feeling and colour. Whether it is the clarity and discipline of the ensembles, the extraordinary care taken over orchestral detail or the alert control of dynamics, Toscanini is supreme, yet nothing is done for effect's sake; everything seems natural, inevitable, unforced, as though the score was being created anew before us with chamber-music finesse – and the atmosphere of a live performance adds to the feeling of immediacy. Nobody dares, or seems to want to interrupt the magic being laid before them. Toscanini in his old age is matching the subtlety and vitality of the composer's own Indian summer – or one might say spring, so delicate and effervescent does the scoring sound. If, vocally, the main glory is the wonderful sense of ensemble gained through hours of hard rehearsals, individual contributions are almost all rewarding. Indeed, Valdengo's Falstaff, under Toscanini's tutelage, has not been surpassed on disc even by Gobbi. Flexibility, charm, exactness, refinement inform his beautifully and wisely sung portrayal. He is no less pointed and subtle in his encounter with Frank Guarrera's imposing Ford. Another great joy of the set is the women's ensemble, their contribution the very epitome of smiling chatter. The Alice, Meg and Nanetta (Stich-Randall – none better), all sound, as they were, fresh and youthful. Herva Nelli is a lively and delightful Alice and Cloe Elmo's Quickly is as rich and ripe of voice and diction as any on disc, though a trifle coarse at times. The Fenton is sweet and Italianate in tone, but not as stylish as others. The smaller roles are all very much part of the team. This set should be a source of revelation to a new generation of collectors who may have a wrong-headed view of what Toscanini was about. The remastering gives it clearer, more immediate sound than ever heard before from the originals.

La forza del destino (1869 version).
Martina Arroyo *sop* Leonora; **Carlo Bergonzi** *ten* Don Alvaro; **Piero Cappuccilli** *bar* Don Carlos;
Ruggero Raimondo *bass* Padre Guardiano; **Biancamaria Casoni** *mez* Preziosilla;
Sir Geraint Evans *bar* Melitone; **Antonio Zerbini** *bass* Marchese;
Florindo Andreolli *ten* Trabuco; **Mila Cova** *mez* Curra; **Virgilio Carbonari** *ten* Mayor;
Derek Hammond-Stroud *bar* Surgeon;
Ambrosian Opera Chorus; Royal Philharmonic Orchestra / Lamberto Gardelli.
EMI Opera CMS7 64646-2 (three discs: 168 minutes: ADD). Notes, text and translation included.
Recorded 1969.

This wonderfully multifarious opera demands an array of principal singers who need to be skilled in an unusually wide range of vocal and dramatic skills. It is a 'chase' opera in which Carlos pursues Alvaro and Leonora through two countries, through cloister and convent, through scenes popular and martial, all treated on the most expansive scale. It is dominated by its series of magnificent duets that are composed so that the music marches with the development of situation and character. Gardelli's reissue is an excellent mid-price buy. It features Bergonzi, that prince among Verdi tenors, as an exemplary and appealing Alvaro, and Piero Cappuccilli – like Bergonzi at the peak of his powers when this set was made – as a full-blooded and Italianate Carlos. In the three all-important duets, their voices blend ideally. Leonora was the most successful of Arroyo's recorded roles, and she sings here with a feeling and urgency appropriate to Leonora's desperate situation. Casoni's vital Preziosilla, Raimondi's grave but over-lugubrious Padre Guardiano and Sir Geraint's keenly characterized Melitone complete a well-chosen cast. Over all presides Gardelli, a Verdi conductor with an instinctive feeling for the ebb and flow of his music, always attending to the needs of the music, never calling attention to himself.

La forza del destino (1862 version).
Galina Gorchakova *sop* Leonora; **Gegam Grigorian** *ten* Don Alvaro;
Nikolai Putilin *bar* Don Carlos; **Mikhail Kit** *bass* Padre Guardiano;
Olga Borodina *mez* Preziosilla; **Georgy Zastavny** *bar* Melitone;
Askar Abdrazakov *bass* Marchese; **Nikolai Gassiev** *ten* Trabuco; **Lia Shevtzova** *mez* Curra;
Gennadi Bezzubenkov *bass* Mayor; **Yuri Laptev** *ten* Surgeon;
Kirov Theatre Chorus and Orchestra / Valery Gergiev.
Philips 446 951-2PH3 (three discs: 158 minutes: DDD). Notes, text and translation included.
Recorded 1995.

It is appropriate that the first recording of the first version of *Forza* should come from St Petersburg, where the work had its première in 1862. However, whilst the première was predominantly an Italian affair, Gergiev's set is given entirely by Russian artists. By and large, they fare splendidly, four of the five principals enjoying the weight of voice and command of the appropriate style to make their roles tell. Gorchakova evinces the weight of voice, also the broad sweep of tone and line, that her solos demand. Added to that there is a feeling for dramatic situation. 'Pace, pace', for instance is suitably filled with foreboding, the lustrous, dark timbre recalling that of Ponselle – and there can be no higher praise. Just once or twice, at the top, the voice becomes a shade strident and ideally one wants more pointed articulation of the text – how familiar is that complaint today in opera singers' performances! – but it is an interpretation of formidable achievement. Grigorian is an exciting Alvaro; no other tenor today, and few in the past, could fulfil the exacting demands of the part as easily as he does: the confident *spinto* thrust in the voice is just right. He effortlessly rises to the generosity of phrase the role calls for and fills the many elegiac phrases with the feeling of melancholy they need. Only Bergonzi for Gardelli surpasses him by virtue of more idiomatic Italian and a finer line, but the superiority is slight and Bergonzi doesn't have to contend with the added music of 1862. Grigorian finds a worthy adversary in Putilin's Carlos. Putilin need fear no comparisons even with the admirable Cappuccilli for Gardelli. Although, like his predecessors and coevals in the role, he is shy of following Verdi's dynamic markings, in other respects his refulgent baritone is just the instrument for Carlos and he breathes the right fire in his implacable hatred of his imagined enemy Alvaro. Borodina easily encompasses the high-lying (for a mezzo) demands of Preziosilla and sounds the right seductive and martial notes for her role. The one disappointment is the singing of the veteran Kit, who sounds grey and woolly, with no real centre to his tone. As the humorous element in Verdi's mix, Zastavny seems at first a shade faceless but as his part progresses, one begins to admire the fact that it is being sung truly, not guyed, which makes his sermon seem a proper successor to the monologues of Rigoletto and Macbeth, albeit in a comic vein. The minor parts are well done. Excellent recording.

La forza del destino.
Stella Roman *sop* Leonora; **Frederick Jagel** *ten* Don Alvaro; **Lawrence Tibbett** *bar* Don Carlos;
Ezio Pinza *bass* Padre Guardiano; **Irra Petina** *mez* Preziosilla;
Salvatore Baccaloni *bass* Melitone; **Louis d'Angelo** *bar* Marquese; **Thelma Votipka** *mez* Curra;
Alessio de Paolis *ten* Trabuco; **Lorenzo Alvary** *bass* Mayor; **John Gurney** *bass* Surgeon;
Metropolitan Opera Chorus and Orchestra, New York / Bruno Walter.
Naxos Historical mono 8 110038/40 (three discs: 168 minutes: AAD). Recorded live in 1943. Ⓢ 🅷

There has never been quite so electrifying a *Forza* as Walter's vital, brilliantly executed reading, which encapsulates the essence of the forthcoming drama. It confirms what few may know today, that Walter was a superb interpreter of Verdi, renowned in pre-war days as an advocate of the composer on the Continent. Yet this was the first time he had conducted *Forza*, so his lithe, finely honed reading is all the more remarkable. The other revelation is the Leonora of Stella Roman, a greatly underrated soprano brought to the Met in 1941, who yields few points to such notable interpreters of the part as Ponselle, Milanov and Tebaldi. They apart, you would go far to hear a Leonora so well equipped for the role, and so committed to it, one who uses her warm, generous voice to unerring effect in projecting the woman's dire predicament. Padre Guardiano appears in the guise of Pinza, none better, and sounding, one uncertain high E apart, secure, concerned and authoritative. Indeed their duet, one of the most telling in all Verdi, is among this performance's pleasures. Jagel as Don Alvaro passes easily the test of the taxing aria of sad recollection at the start of Act 3. Tibbett as Don Carlos compels attention at every entry with his distinctive timbre and faultless style, but truth to tell the glorious tone had dulled since his great days in the 1930s and at times he sounds stretched by the part. Both his arias suffer cuts. Carlos's second (of three) duets with Alvaro is also excised as was then the custom, and *strettas* throughout are foreshortened. Baccaloni enjoys himself hugely as Melitone and obviously relishes his encounters with his superior, the Padre Guardiano, the two Italians revelling in the text. Petina is a lively but lightweight Preziosilla. The sound is a bit crackly and restricted but good enough to enjoy an absorbing account of the score. It is strange that Naxos did not see fit to exclude the Spanish introductions to the broadcast. This vivid version has much to commend it at the price.

I Lombardi alla prima crociata.
June Anderson *sop* Giselda; **Luciano Pavarotti** *ten* Oronte; **Samuel Ramey** *bass* Pagano;
Richard Leech *ten* Arvino; **Ildebrando d'Arcangelo** *bass* Pirro; **Yanni Yannissis** *bass* Acciano;
Jane Shaulis *mez* Sofia; **Anthony Dean Griffey** *ten* Prior; **Patricia Racette** *mez* Viclinda;
Chorus and Orchestra of the Metropolitan Opera, New York / James Levine.
Decca 455 287-2DHO2 (two discs: 129 minutes: DDD). Notes, text and translation included.
Recorded 1996. Ⓕ

Pavarotti appeared in the Metropolitan Opera production of *I Lombardi* in 1993 and this recording is the delayed result, following after a gap of three years. Little, if anything, seems to have been lost in the interim. He is in good voice and sings Oronte's aria with a fine sense of *legato*, binding the decorative turns of the cabaletta beautifully into the vocal line and throwing in a respectable top C to show us he still can. *I Lombardi* is a viscerally exciting opera. The first complete recording, conducted by Lamberto Gardelli (Philips), set a good benchmark in 1972, but that need not deter us from welcoming this lively newcomer. The Metropolitan Opera Orchestra plays with splendid precision and, as Turks and Crusaders, women of the harem and virgins, the Met Chorus has a high old time on both sides of *I Lombardi*'s war-zone. Levine himself has improved beyond recognition as a Verdian; this studio recording is well paced and has a good sense of theatre. Everything is swift and crisp on the surface. The best role goes to the soprano Giselda, specially tailored for the delicate skills of Erminia Frezzolini. Among the current crop of Verdi sopranos, June Anderson is probably as plausible a modern Frezzolini as any. There is some lovely, pure-toned singing in her big scene at the end of the Second Act and her coloratura is shining bright, both in this cabaletta and later in 'In fondo all'alma'. Samuel Ramey makes a relatively lightweight Pagano, who alone decorates his second verses. In the second tenor role Richard Leech holds his own, though his voice does not take well to the microphone. Ildebrando d'Arcangelo proudly represents the younger generation of Italian singers in the small role of Pirro and Patricia Racette sings brightly as Viclinda. Gardelli's crusading first recording has a rough Italianate vigour that lovers of early Verdi will enjoy, but Levine and his forces more than hold their ground with pace and brilliance, and a bright, modern recording with on balance a better cast and the voices well forward.

Luisa Miller.
Montserrat Caballé sop Luisa; **Luciano Pavarotti** ten Rodolfo; **Sherrill Milnes** bar Miller;
Bonaldo Gaiotti bass Count Walter; **Anna Reynolds** mez Federica;
Richard Van Allan bass Wurm; **Annette Céline** mez Laura; **Fernando Pavarotti** ten Peasant;
London Opera Chorus; National Philharmonic Orchestra / Peter Maag.
Decca 417 420-2DH2 (two discs: 144 minutes: ADD). Notes, text and translation included.
Recorded 1970s   Ⓕ

This transitional work shows Verdi enhancing his skills and refining his musical style. The plot, based on a Schiller drama, involves the tragedy and death of Luisa and her beloved Rodolfo brought about by the evil Wurm, apt predecessor of Verdi's Iago. The title-role could not find a more appealing interpreter than Caballé, who spins a fine line and is highly responsive to Luisa's sad situation. She is partnered by Pavarotti at the height of his powers as Rodolfo. He excels in 'Quando le sere al polacido', the work's most famous aria. As Luisa's equivocal father, Miller, Milnes gives one of his best performances on disc and Van Allan is a properly snarling Wurm. Maag, an underrated conductor, directs a strong, well-proportioned performance. He gives the impression of being in love with this opera and he goes right to the heart of the score, finding its seriousness as well as its fire. The last act is specially fine, containing what are regarded as among the gramophone classics, the two duets of Luisa, first with her father, then with Rodolfo. The production is unobtrusively effective in creation of atmosphere and is spaciously recorded.

Macbeth.
Piero Cappuccilli bar Macbeth; **Shirley Verrett** mez Lady Macbeth;
Nicolai Ghiaurov bass Banquo; **Plácido Domingo** ten Macduff;
Antonio Savastano ten Malcolm; **Carlo Zardo** bass Doctor;
Giovanni Foiani bass Servant; **Sergio Fontana** bass Herald;
Alfredo Mariotti bass Assassin; **Stefania Malagú** mez Lady-in-waiting;
Chorus and Orchestra of La Scala, Milan / Claudio Abbado.
DG The Originals 449 732-2GOR2 (two discs: 154 minutes: ADD). Notes, text and translation
included. Recorded 1976.   Ⓜ **RR**

Verdi's lifelong admiration for Shakespeare resulted in only two operas based on his plays. *Macbeth*, the first, originally written in 1847, was extensively revised in 1865. Without losing the direct force of the original, Verdi added greater depth to his first ideas. Once derided as being un-Shakespearian, it is now recognized as a masterpiece for its psychological penetration as much as for its subtle melodic inspiration. Abbado captures perfectly the atmosphere of dark deeds and personal ambition leading to tragedy, projected by Verdi, and his reading holds the opera's disparate elements in the score under firm control, catching its interior tensions. He is well supported by his Scala forces. Shirley Verrett may not be ideally incisive or Italianate in accent as Lady Macbeth, but she peers into the character's soul most convincingly. As ever, truly inspired by Abbado, Cappuccilli is a suitably haunted and introverted Macbeth who sings a secure and unwavering *legato*. Domingo's upright Macduff and Ghiaurov's doom-laden Banquo are both admirable in their respective roles.

Otello.
Plácido Domingo ten Otello; **Cheryl Studer** sop Desdemona; **Sergei Leiferkus** bar Iago;
Ramon Vargas ten Cassio; **Michael Schade** ten Roderigo; **Denyce Graves** mez Emilia;
Ildebrando d'Arcangelo bass Lodovico; **Giacomo Prestia** bass Montano;
Philippe Duminy bass Herald; **Hauts-de-Seine Maîtrise;**
Chorus and Orchestra of the Opéra-Bastille, Paris / Myung-Whun Chung.
DG 439 805-2GH2 (two discs: 132 minutes: DDD). Notes, text and translation included.
Recorded 1993.   Ⓕ Ⓢ Ⓔ **RR**

Just as *Othello* is a difficult play to bring off in the theatre, so *Otello* is a difficult opera to bring off out of it. For some years now, Domingo has been, on stage, the greatest Otello of our age. On record, though, he has had less success. Leiferkus and Domingo have worked closely together in the theatre; and it shows in scene after scene – nowhere more so than in the crucial sequence in Act 2 where Otello so rapidly ingests Iago's lethal poison. By bringing into the recording studio the feel and experience of a stage performance – meticulous study subtly modified by the improvised charge of the moment – both singers help defy the jinx that so often afflicts *Otello* on record. The skill of Leiferkus's performance is rooted in voice and technique: clear diction, a disciplined rhythmic sense and a mastery of all ornament down to the most mordant of mordents. Above all, he is always *there* (usually stage right in this recording), steely-voiced, rabbiting on obsessively. We even hear his crucial interventions in the great Act 3 *concertato*. Domingo is in superb voice; the sound seems golden as never before. Yet at the same time, it is a voice that is being more astutely deployed. To take that cruellest of all challenges to a studio-bound Otello, the great Act 3 soliloquy 'Dio! mi potevi', Domingo's performance is now simpler, more inward, more intense. It helps, perhaps, that his voice has darkened, winning back some of its russet baritonal colourings.

Chung's conducting is almost disarmingly vital. Verdi's scoring is more Gallic than Germanic. The score sounds very brilliant in the hands of the excellent Opéra-Bastille orchestra, and, in Act 4, very beautiful. Maybe Chung is wary of the emotional depths and, occasionally, the rhythmic infrastructure is muddled and unclear. And yet, the freshness is all gain. He is already a master of the big ensemble, and the line of an act. Tension rarely slackens. Where it does the mixing and matching of takes is probably to blame. Studer's is a carefully drawn portrait of a chaste and sober-suited lady. Perhaps Verdi had a sweeter-voiced singer in mind for this paragon of 'goodness, resignation, and self-sacrifice' (Verdi's words, not Shakespeare's). Studer's oboe tones keep us at a certain distance, yet you will look in vain for a better Desdemona. What's more, Studer is a singer who can single-mindedly focus the drama afresh, as she does more than once in Act 3. DG's recording is clear and unfussy and satisfyingly varied; Studer, in particular, is much helped by the beautifully open acoustic the engineers provide for the closing act. This is undoubtedly the best *Otello* on record since the early 1960s. It also happens to be the first time on disc that a great Otello at the height of his powers has been successfully caught in the context of a recording that can itself be generally considered worthy of the event, musically and technically.

Otello.
Ramon Vinay *ten* Otello; **Herva Nelli** *sop* Desdemona; **Giuseppe Valdengo** *bar* Iago;
Virginio Assandri *ten* Cassio; **Leslie Chabay** *ten* Roderigo; **Nan Merriman** *mez* Emilia;
Nicola Moscona *bass* Lodovico; **Arthur Newman** *bass* Montano;
NBC Chorus and Symphony Orchestra / Arturo Toscanini.
RCA Gold Seal mono GD60302 (two discs: 125 minutes: ADD). Recorded 1947.   Ⓜ Ⓗ

One of the century's legendary achievements on record confirms its reputation on this well-managed reissue. Here Toscanini's blazing intensity, his full comprehension of every facet of the score are evident throughout. The attack and dedication of chorus and orchestra are apparent throughout; so is the discipline and textural clarity on all sides. The sound remains dry but somehow this very close, confined quality accords with the work's own claustrophobic quality – if only Otello had gone out into the open air and thought about the reality of the evidence before him, he might not have been so easily caught up in Iago's web of deceit. Valdengo's Iago continues to put others in the shade. His light, almost elegant and seemingly cheerful tone, his mordant, sinister delivery of the *Credo*, his insinuating and perfectly accurate delivery of the imagined Dream all tell of his willingness to follow Toscanini's guidance, for he never sang so well for anyone else. This is a faultless performance. So, in terms of interpretation, is Vinay's Otello – the tormented, fearsomely commanding Moor to the life. Nelli's sincerity of purpose, her accuracy and her true tone compensate for a slightly pallid reading of Desdemona's thoughts and feelings. The smaller roles are all worthily taken. Any incidental drawback should not prevent anyone hearing this overwhelming interpretation. Toscanini identifies so sympathetically with the human condition, as did Verdi himself – and it is from Verdi, at whose feet he sat, that Toscanini learnt his trade.

Otello.
Giuseppe Giacomini *ten* Otello; **Dame Margaret Price** *sop* Desdemona;
Matteo Manuguerra *bar* Iago; **Dino di Domenico** *ten* Cassio; **Alain Gabriel** *ten* Roderigo;
Martine Mahé *mez* Emilia; **Luigi Roni** *bass* Lodovico; **Vincent le Texier** *bass-bar* Montano;
Anton Kúrňava *bass* Herald;
Slovak Philharmonic Chorus; Les Petits Chanteurs de Bordeaux;
Orchestre National de Bordeaux Aquitaine / Alain Lombard.
Forlane 216774 (two discs: 128 minutes: DDD). Notes, text and translation included.
Recorded live in 1991.   Ⓕ

On the evidence of this *Otello*, and much else, Giacomini is more viscerally exciting than any of the famous Three. Certainly no tenor in this role since Del Monaco in his prime had the elemental, almost frightening power evinced by Giacomini's reading, but his talents go well beyond the possession of a real *tenore robusto*. His dark, louring tone and agonized delivery of the text exactly match the passion and jealousy of the Moor, alternately achingly sorrowful as he imagines his wife's infidelities, and fierily tormented as he rants and raves at her supposed wrongdoing. There is much to study in this searing interpretation, which is on a par with Vinay's for Toscanini and sung in the same dark-grained, tormented fashion. Giacomini's overwhelming portrayal is worthily supported. Dame Margaret Price provides rounded, cleanly produced tone, even if there are a few signs of wear, and her interpretation – in response to a real occasion – is emotionally compelling. In the Act 3 duet, she brings to the passage beginning 'Mi guarda!' and the line 'E son io l'innocente' the depth of Desdemona's heart-stricken soul as she tries to defend herself against Otello's accusations, and her Act 4 scene is shaped and executed with the expected sense of impending doom.

Matteo Manuguerra, an experienced and sympathetic Verdian, was already in his mid-sixties when this performance took place and there are times when his voice has to be husbanded, but he shows much intelligence in portraying the subtlety of Iago's evil. The smaller roles are decently if not exceptionally cast. Alain Lombard keeps the performance consistently on the boil. He handles the public scenes, most notably the Act 3 ensemble (given uncut), with the urgency and large scale they call for. His chorus and orchestra, while not quite in the highest class, perform with keen awareness of the score's pithy quality. This set may not entirely challenge the hegemony of the 1947 Toscanini and Serafin sets, but it is histrionically exciting, largely because of the live ambience (the audience is remarkably quiet, clapping only at the end of acts) and there is a straightforward honesty about it that has eluded more glamorous recordings. Stage noise is seldom in evidence. The recording is at times over-resonant, but catches the excitement of the occasion. With Giacomini giving such an authentically vivid account of the title-role, most Verdians will want to own this set.

Rigoletto.
Tito Gobbi *bar* Rigoletto; **Maria Callas** *sop* Gilda; **Giuseppe di Stefano** *ten* Duke;
Nicola Zaccaria *bass* Sparafucile; **Adriana Lazzarini** *mez* Maddalena;
Plinio Clabassi *bass* Monterone; **Giuse Gerbino** *mez* Giovanna;
Renato Ercolani *ten* Borsa; **William Dickie** *bar* Marullo;
Elvira Galassi *sop* Countess Ceprano; **Carlo Forti** *bar* Count Ceprano;
Chorus and Orchestra of La Scala, Milan / Tullio Serafin.
EMI mono CDS5 56327-2 (two discs: 118 minutes: ADD). Notes, text and translation included.
Recorded 1955. (P)(H)(RR)

That one recording should continue to hold sway over many other attractive comers after 45 years is simply a tribute to Callas, Gobbi, Serafin and Walter Legge. Whatever the merits of its successors, and they are many, no *Rigoletto* has surpassed Gobbi in tonal variety, line, projection of character and understanding of what Rigoletto is about; no Gilda has come anywhere near Callas in meaningful phrasing – listen to 'Caro nome' or 'Tutte le feste' on any other set if you are disbelieving – nor achieved such a careful differentiation of timbre before and after her seduction; no conductor matches Serafin in judging tempo and instrumental detail on a nicety; nor benefited from a chorus and orchestra bred in the tradition of La Scala; no producer has equalled Legge in recording voices rather than the space round them. And di Stefano? Well, he may not be so stylish a Duke as some others, but the 'face' he gives his singing, and the sheer physical presence he conveys, not to mention his forward diction, are also unique in this opera. Nothing in this world is perfect, and so there are some small drawbacks here. Serafin sadly makes small cuts in the first Gilda/Rigoletto duet and omits entirely the Duke's cabaletta as used to be practice in the theatre. Gobbi could be said not to have quite the weight of voice ideally called for by a Verdi baritone role. Finally, the recording, although immeasurably improved from previous issues of the set, still has one or two places of distortion obviously present on the original tape. In every other way, this remains the classic performance on record, and one that should be on every Verdi collector's shelf.

Rigoletto.
Renato Bruson *bar* Rigoletto; **Andrea Rost** *sop* Gilda; **Roberto Alagna** *ten* Duke;
Dimitri Kavrakos *bass* Sparafucile; **Mariana Pentcheva** *contr* Maddalena;
Giorgio Giuseppini *bass* Monterone; **Antonella Trevisan** *mez* Giovanna;
Ernesto Gavazzi *ten* Borsa; **Silvestro Sammaritano** *bass* Marullo;
Nicoletta Zanini *mez* Countess Ceprano; **Antonio de Gobbi** *bass* Count Ceprano;
Marilena Laurenza *sop* Page; **Ernesto Panariello** *bass* Usher;
Chorus and Orchestra of La Scala, Milan / Riccardo Muti.
Sony Classical S2K66314 (two discs: 121 minutes: DDD). Notes, text and translation included.
Recorded live in 1994. (F)

You immediately feel that added *frisson* of a 'real' occasion in this live recording and that continues throughout a well-prepared and well-integrated performance, applause restricted to ends of acts, virtually no audience noise. As for Muti's interpretation, it is rewardingly vital, rhythmically speaking. Every moment is acutely and alertly sprung with speeds tending to be on the brisk side. It is a pleasure to hear how Muti observes the importance Verdi gives to oboe, clarinet and bassoon, how profitably he makes all his singers observe to the letter what Verdi wrote. Ah, Roberto Alagna! Many will want this set for his participation alone. Listen to the Duke's aria and cabaletta at the start of Act 3 and you will hear this young tenor's tone perfectly suited and his phrasing immaculately turned. Both in 'La donna è mobile' and the opening of the Quartet one might like a shade more variation in dynamics and tonal colour, but then Alagna has the sappy, brilliant voice and, above all, the *slancio* the part demands, and his singing reflects the Duke's wilful, libidinous nature. His is a most attractive contribution to the set. At the end of the Duke-Gilda duet, Muti demands and gets the full cadenza written into the score. It is finely turned by Alagna, and by Rost, who offers an altogether lovely performance, ideal in almost every respect. With just the right weight of voice for the role, all her singing is full-toned and precisely articulated, and the tone itself is vibrant and tangy. Rost hasn't the specifically Italian sound but she is an accomplished technician, and dies heart-rendingly.

The years have been kind to Bruson's voice (he was 58 when this recording was made), but it has to be said that, especially in the first half of the opera, the vibrato is now disturbing when the tone comes under pressure. Perhaps because he is afraid he cannot sustain a line at a lower dynamic level, he seems unwilling to sing at less than *mezzo-forte*. His remains a considered, eloquent interpretation through which courses a father's concern and anguish. Only Gobbi for Serafin provides a range of colour and shades of meaning beyond all his rivals. Kavrakos is a suitably sturdy, dour Sparafucile. After a blowzy start Pentcheva proves a seductive-sounding Maddalena. Alagna's superbly vital Duke and Rost's greatly appealing Gilda may well sway you in favour of this set. However, as engineered here – the action seems somewhat distanced, as though you are sitting in the balcony rather than the stalls – you need a very high volume setting to get a satisfactory level from the singers; then the orchestra sounds too loud. Of course the Serafin will remain unrivalled for many, but its aged sound and the disfiguring cuts must be a serious drawback to anyone coming afresh to the work's discography.

Simon Boccanegra.
Piero Cappuccilli *bar* Simon Boccanegra; **Mirella Freni** *sop* Amelia; **José Carreras** *ten* Gabriele; **Nicolai Ghiaurov** *bass* Fiesco; **José van Dam** *bass-bar* Paolo; **Giovanni Foiani** *bass* Pietro; **Antonio Savastano** *ten* Captain; **Maria Fausta Gallamini** *sop* Maid; **Chorus and Orchestra of La Scala, Milan / Claudio Abbado.**
DG The Originals 449 752-2GOR2 (two discs: 136 minutes: ADD). Notes, text and translation included. Recorded 1977. ⓜ

This famous recording has become a gramophone classic, a performance in the studio after a series of performances at La Scala in the Strehler staging. The close, slightly claustrophobic recording exactly mirrors the mood of nefarious activities and intrigues following Boccanegra's rise to be Doge of Genoa, he and his lovely daughter victims of the dark deeds round them. In his plebeian being, clement exercise of authority and warm, fatherly love, Simon Boccanegra is made for Cappuccilli who, under Abbado's tutelage, sings it not only *con amore* but with exemplary, delicately tinted tone and unbelievably long-breathed phrasing. As his daughter Amelia, Freni was just entering her quasi-*spinto* phase, and expands her lyric voice easily into the greater demands of this more dramatic role. Similarly heavier duties had not yet tarnished the youthful ardour and sap in the tone of the 30-year-old Carreras. As implacable Fiesco, Ghiaurov exudes vengeful command and van Dam evil machinations as the villain Paolo. Over all presides Abbado in what remains one of his greatest recordings, alert to every facet of the wondrous score, timing every scene, in an opera tricky to pace, to near-perfection, and in sum bringing theatrical drama into the home. This set should now be an essential adornment to any reputable collection of Verdi.

Stiffelio.
José Carreras *ten* Stiffelio; **Sylvia Sass** *sop* Lina; **Matteo Manuguerra** *bar* Stankar; **Wladimiro Ganzarolli** *bass* Jorg; **Ezio di Cesare** *ten* Raffaele; **Maria Venuti** *mez* Dorotea; **Thomas Moser** *ten* Federico;
Austrian Radio Chorus and Symphony Orchestra / Lamberto Gardelli.
Philips 422 432-2PM2 (two discs: 109 minutes: ADD). Notes, text and translation included. Recorded 1979. ⓜ

Stiffelio's rediscovery in the late 1960s enabled this reassessment, fully discussed in Julian Budden's introduction to the set. The drama has greater unity. Stiffelio himself is almost a dry run for Otello, a man of generous instincts who is forced into a ruinous situation. As a whole the score is, as Budden suggests, the most unjustly neglected of Verdi's operas. Had it not been suppressed by the censors, and then unsatisfactorily revised, it would surely have a regular part in the repertory as the story and its handling are far superior to what preceded them in the Verdi canon. The title-role is a gift for an accomplished tenor: Carreras catches the moral fervour and uncertainties of the part with his open-hearted, spontaneous performance. As Lina, who is torn between steadfastness and vulnerability, Sylvia Sass also offers a rewarding performance, alternating delicacy with fiery strength, though technically she isn't always as secure as one might ideally wish. Manuguerra is appropriately venomous as Stankar but his voice hasn't any particular distinction, tending to sound nasal, nor has his reading much individuality, but he is never less than adequate. Gardelli here adds another vital performance to his long series of Verdi readings. But any reservations pale before the importance of the work in hand to all Verdians, and enough is achieved to prove its worth. Besides, it is an essential purchase for Carreras enthusiasts.

La traviata.
Ileana Cotrubas sop Violetta; **Plácido Domingo** ten Alfredo; **Sherrill Milnes** bar Germont; **Stefania Malagù** mez Flora; **Helena Jungwirth** sop Annina; **Walter Gullino** ten Gastone; **Bruno Grella** bar Baron; **Alfredo Giacomotti** bass Marquis; **Giovanni Foiani** bass Doctor; **Walter Gullino** ten Giuseppe;
Bavarian State Opera Chorus and Orchestra / Carlos Kleiber.
DG 415 132-2GH2 (two discs: 106 minutes: ADD). Notes, text and translation included. Recorded 1977. Ⓕ 🆁🆁

This performance is so compelling dramatically, and as a recording much more natural than most of its rivals, that it really should be a newcomer's first choice. The interpretation of Violetta by Ileana Cotrubas, superbly partnered by Kleiber's conducting, makes it an imperative. Cotrubas's peculiarly plaintive, vibrating timbre and highly individual nuances seem to be perfectly fitted to the part. To those she adds more of a sense of involvement and spontaneity than any other on disc. In Act 2, if she does not have you close to tears, you must have a hard heart indeed. At 'Più non esiste', this Violetta leaves no doubt that all previous experience has been erased from her mind in Alfredo's arms. Then, the very precise articulation and observance of note values, so typical of the set as a whole, at 'non sapete' emphasizes the sudden realization that all she now lives for is to be taken from her, just as at 'Così alla misera' she feels the blow has fallen as she communes to herself, the tears held back on the accentuated word 'implacabil'. At 'Amami, Alfredo' the whole bottled-up sense of mortality and lost happiness breaks forth uncontrollably. This is a superb interpretation.

That first scene of Act 2 is the clue to any great reading of the role of Violetta. It is not undermined by the rest of Cotrubas's performance. 'Sempre libera', at Kleiber's fast pace, is nervously exciting as it should be, with firm attack from the singer. The exchanges with Annina and the Doctor in Act 3 could not be more touching, the dots over the semiquavers at 'ogni speranza è morta!' properly observed and proving the dramatic effect Verdi intended for them. Kleiber gives the score a Toscanini-like sense of dramatic purpose and impending doom. You can hear that in the final *allegro* section of the Violetta/Germont duet, with note values, double dots and the like, firmly observed. Much earlier in the score Kleiber and his excellent Munich players give the dance music *chez* Violetta a chilling emptiness. Domingo gives Alfredo one of his most winning performances, singing with sensitivity and grace – note the real *pianissimo* at the end of the first-act duet with Violetta – and altogether following her and their conductor away from routine. His outburst at Flora's party has an Otello-like sense of wrong and jealousy. Kleiber's volatile, incisive direction, sometimes in questionable tempos, has worn perhaps a little less well than the rest. But then you hear Cotrubas's heart-rending 'Amami, Alfredo' and inevitably lean towards this set. You won't be disappointed, and will certainly enjoy the theatrical-like sound and you will be unable to avoid getting caught up in the drama.

La traviata.
Tiziana Fabricini sop Violetta; **Roberto Alagna** ten Alfredo; **Paolo Coni** bar Germont; **Nicoletta Curiel** mez Flora; **Antonella Trevisan** mez Annina; **Enrico Cossutta** ten Gastone; **Orazio Mori** bass Baron; **Enzo Capuano** bass Marquis; **Francesco Musinu** bass Doctor; **Ernesto Gavazzi** ten Giuseppe; **Ernesto Panariello** bass Servant; **Silvestro Sammaritano** bass Messenger;
Chorus and Orchestra of La Scala, Milan / Riccardo Muti.
Sony Classical S2K52486 (two discs: 136 minutes: DDD). Notes, text and translation included. Recorded live in 1992. Ⓕ Ⓔ

An exciting and eloquent reading on all sides, this version must now be rated with the established frontrunners – but, as with some of those, most notably any of Callas's versions, it is not for the fainthearted, or for those who like their Violettas to have full, equally, produced voices. Fabriccini is evidently not an Act 1 Violetta. But even without assured coloratura and with problems at the *passagio*, she is one who is going to hold our attention and move us. In the Second Act so much bespeaks not only complete identification with Violetta's predicament but also vocal acumen of an exceptional kind, often based on the seemingly lost art of *portamento*. Because this is a live performance we are conscious that the singer's acting is part of the secret of the reading's success, that and the obvious youth of a soprano who is not yet a preening prima donna. The final tragedy is still better, very much modelled on Callas. The voice, more settled now than anywhere in the performance manages her role with long-breathed phrasing and pathetic accents, the result of a true understanding of Verdian style yet never self-conscious in its effect – this is undoubtedly great singing *and* interpretation. The death is deeply moving. Alagna, in the role that brought him to attention, is just the Alfredo for this Violetta; youthfully ardent, with keen-edged tone, finely attuned to the *legato* essential in Verdi. The recording is taken from four performances, given at La Scala, and is a theatrical view full of electricity, vitally executed by the forces of La Scala, as vital as any in the recorded history of the work. Don't miss it.

La traviata.
Angela Gheorghiu *sop* Violetta; **Frank Lopardo** *ten* Alfredo; **Leo Nucci** *bar* Germont;
Leah-Marian Jones *mez* Flora; **Gillian Knight** *mez* Annina; **Robin Leggate** *ten* Gaston;
Richard Van Allan *bass* Baron; **Roderick Earle** *bass* Marquis; **Mark Beesley** *bar* Doctor;
Neil Griffiths *ten* Giuseppe; **Bryan Secombe** *bass* Messenger; **Rodney Gibson** *ten* Servant;
Chorus and Orchestra of the Royal Opera House, Covent Garden / Sir Georg Solti.
Decca 448 119-2DHO2 (two discs: 127 minutes: DDD). Notes, text and translation included.
Recorded live in 1994. Ⓕ

For Angela Gheorghiu, Violetta was the right role at the right time. The whole drama is there in her voice, every expression in the eyes and beat of the heart reflected in the way she shapes and colours Verdi's vocal lines. Her quiet singing is particularly lovely, affording subtle variations of tenderness and inner anxiety. When she does choose to make a point with force, as in her sudden warmth of feeling towards Giorgio Germont at 'Qual figlia m'abbracciate' or her chilling cry of 'Morro!', accompanied by a loud thump on the table, her ideas always hit home. A few moments of vocal weakness are accentuated by the microphone, mainly a tendency to go sharp and some hardness at the top of the voice that was not troublesome in the theatre. Otherwise, she is the most complete and moving Violetta we have had since her compatriot, Ileana Cotrubas. These live performances were remarkably the first time that Sir Georg Solti, at the age of 82, had conducted a staged *La traviata* and he wanted two young singers who were coming fresh to the opera, as he was himself. What was so spellbinding in the theatre was the touching intimacy they brought to their scenes together. Instead of the duets for Violetta and Alfredo turning into standard Italian operatic bawling, they became lovers' whispers, each phrase floating like a kiss from one set of lips to the other. The effect comes across here in the cadenzas, where Gheorghiu and Frank Lopardo really seem to be listening to each other. Elsewhere, one is more aware than in the theatre that Lopardo's light tenor is far from being an idiomatic Italian voice. His idiosyncratic tone quality and un-Italian vowels can be problematical, as is some ungainly lifting up into notes.

Leo Nucci, Decca's resident Verdi baritone at the time, makes a standard Giorgio Germont, not more, and apart from Leah-Marian Jones's energetic Flora, the smaller roles do not say a great deal for the Royal Opera's depth of casting, with its selection of gruff bass voices and prim Anglo-Saxon accents. Solti insisted that the opera be performed complete (more unusual in the theatre than it is on disc). But there is nothing studied about his conducting: the performance is fresh and alive from the first note to the last, the result of a lifetime's experience of how to pace a drama in the opera house. With the increasing number of live opera sets, a recommendation for *La traviata* is likely to be based on whether one is prepared to accept noises-off or not. Decca's recording is well balanced and vivid, dancing feet and banging doors included. Among the live sets, Giulini and Callas at La Scala in 1955 must be *hors concours*, an unforgettable performance of the greatest inspiration, but in rather awful sound. Muti's more recent La Scala set, in which he has to wrestle with Tiziana Fabbricini's wayward talents as Violetta, is the nearest comparison.

Il trovatore.
Maria Callas *sop* Leonora; **Giuseppe di Stefano** *ten* Manrico;
Rolando Panerai *bar* Count di Luna; **Fedora Barbieri** *mez* Azucena;
Nicola Zaccaria *bass* Ferrando; **Luisa Villa** *mez* Ines; **Renato Ercolani** *ten* Ruiz, Messenger;
Giulio Mauri *bass* Old Gipsy;
Chorus and Orchestra of La Scala, Milan / Herbert von Karajan.
EMI CDS5 56333-2 (two discs: 129 minutes: ADD). Notes, text and translation included.
Recorded 1956. Ⓕ Ⓗ ℞℞

Callas and Karajan took the world by the ears in the 1950s with this *Il trovatore*. Leonora was one of Callas's finest stage roles and this recording is wonderfully intense, with a dark concentrated loveliness of sound in the principal arias that puts one in mind of Muzio or Ponselle at their best. Walter Legge always managed to team Callas with the right conductor for the work in question. Often it was Serafin, but Karajan in *Il trovatore* is utterly compelling. This opera, like Beethoven's Seventh Symphony and Stravinsky's *The Rite of Spring*, is one of music's great essays in sustained rhythmic intensity; dramatically it deals powerfully in human archetypes. All this is realized by the young Karajan with that almost insolent mastery of score and orchestra which made him such a phenomenon at this period of his career. There are some cuts, but, equally, some welcome inclusions (such as the second verse of 'Di quella pira', sung by di Stefano with his own unique kind of *slancio*). Although the EMI sound is very good, one or two climaxes suggest that in the heat of the moment, the engineer, Robert Beckett, let the needle run into the red and you might care to play the set in mono to restore that peculiar clarity and homogeneity of sound which are the mark of Legge's finest productions of the mono era. But whatever you do don't miss this set.

Il trovatore.
Plácido Domingo *ten* Manrico; **Leontyne Price** *sop* Leonora; **Sherrill Milnes** *bar* Count di Luna;
Fiorenza Cossotto *mez* Azucena; **Bonaldo Giaiotti** *bass* Ferrando;
Elizabeth Bainbridge *mez* Ines; **Ryland Davies** *ten* Ruiz; **Stanley Riley** *bass* Old Gipsy;
Neilson Taylor *bar* Messenger;
Ambrosian Opera Chorus; New Philharmonia Orchestra / Zubin Mehta.
RCA Red Seal 74321 39504-2 (two discs: 137 minutes: ADD). Notes, text and translation
included. Recorded 1969. Ⓜ 𝐑𝐑

There are details here which fully justify its inclusion and will be enough to tempt any collector's palette. The Leonora of Leontyne Price is the high point of the Mehta recording: her velvety, sensuous articulation of what is certainly an 'immenso, eterno amor' is entirely distinctive and dramatically astute. The New Philharmonia is a no less ardent protagonist. Mehta's pacing may be uneven, his accompanying breathless, but he draws robust playing in bold primary colours to which the recording gives vivid presence. The acoustic serves Manrico less well: he seems to be singing in the bath when we first overhear him. This, though, is a younger, simpler Domingo than the one we encounter elsewhere, and there are passages of wonderfully sustained intensity. Cossotto's Azucena is disappointing. All the vocal tricks and techniques are there, but it is very much a concert performance in which she, and therefore we, are never entirely engaged.

Il trovatore.
Plácido Domingo *ten* Manrico; **Aprile Millo** *sop* Leonora; **Vladimir Chernov** *bar* Conte di Luna;
Dolora Zajick *mez* Azucena; **James Morris** *bass* Ferrando; **Sondra Kelly** *contr* Ines;
Anthony Laciura *ten* Ruiz; **Glenn Bater** *bass* Old Gipsy; **Tim Willson** *ten* Messenger;
New York Metropolitan Opera Chorus and Orchestra / James Levine.
Sony Classical S2K48070 (two discs: 129 minutes: DDD). Notes, text and translation included.
Recorded 1991. Ⓕ

This is the most recommendable among modern versions of *Trovatore*, with a reading all-round that finely balances the lyrical and melodramatic elements in the score. Once Leonora appears, the reading takes on true Verdian style. This is a reading to please the ear and move the heart. Immediately this Leonora is confronted with Conte di Luna, we hear the firm, vibrant, implacable tones of Chernov. His voice is in its absolute prime and he sings everything with the confident panache that suggests as much. Our upright hero is Domingo, aged a little since his earlier recordings of Manrico for Mehta and Giulini (listed overleaf). The artistry and management of the voice are as rewarding as of old and Domingo reserves his best for the last and greatest scene when both his sovereign phrasing – 'Riposa, o madre' sung in a single breath – and his involvement take on the aura of active participation. Manrico's feelings of love for his mother, momentary contempt for Leonora and eventual tragic pathos are firmly targeted: we hear once more the noble tenor we know and can listen to in sappier voice for Giulini. As Azucena, Zajick gives an effective and strong-willed performance, wanting only the last ounce of character: she is also at her best in the final act. The Met chorus is no more than adequate on this occasion, but as ever the house's orchestra plays with the virtuosity it reserves for its Musical Director. Levine's reading is well timed, properly earthy yet refined in the many delicate touches Verdi evinces in arias and duets. Luciano Pavarotti's predominantly lyrical tenor (for Mehta on Decca) is not ideal for Manrico but he sings it with such unfailing musicality and sense of line that Pavarotti enthusiasts need not hesitate to acquire this version, confident that their hero's portrayal is set in suitable surroundings. However, the whole reading is not as well integrated as the Levine, and by a hair's breadth that is probably the better sung. Mehta's earlier, much-lauded recording for RCA remains very much in the frame.

Sándor Veress

Hommage à Paul Klee. Concerto for Piano, Strings and Percussion. Six Csárdás.
András Schiff, Dénes Várjon pfs
Budapest Festival Orchestra / Heinz Holliger.
Teldec 0630-19992-2 (63 minutes: DDD). Recorded 1997.   Ⓕ

So, who exactly was Sándor Veress? He assisted László Lajtha at the Budapest Ethnological
Museum, worked with Bartók in the folk music department of the Hungarian Academy of
Sciences, emigrated to the West and received various prizes towards the end of his life. Initial
impressions are misleading: a comfortably *crescendoing* string chord followed by simple keyboard
chiming, a bit like a fragment from a soap-opera soundtrack. But then the fun really starts: the two
pianos combine or converge, the ray of string tone finds some pizzicatos for company, and the
chiming starts to sound like a page out of Lou Harrison. The first of the 'Fantasies for two pianos
and string orchestra' that comprise Veress's 1951 *Hommage à Paul Klee* strikes a tone that could as
well have been achieved by, say, Rautavaara, Hovhaness or indeed Harrison. The second piece, 'Fire
Wind', blows in like a hurricane, shivering or snapping to *col legno* strings and pizzicatos; the third
is an 'Old Sound' that superficially resembles the slow movement of Rodrigo's much-loved
Concierto de Aranjuez, then there's the dry weaving of 'Below and Above', the guitar-like
strumming of 'Stone Collection', the textural richness of 'Green on Green' and a lively 'Little Blue
Devil' to close. András Schiff and Dénes Várjon leave no phrase open to question, and the
Budapest Festival strings under Heinz Holliger play brilliantly – and lusciously – throughout.

Veress evidently enjoyed concocting sweet-toned first subjects: the Concerto for piano, strings and
percussion (1952) again opens with disarming lightness and simplicity. The first two movements are
in ternary form, while in the third, 'the scurrying writing is controlled by a twelve-note row' (as the
excellent notes remind us). Bartók is a strong influence, especially in the first movement's driving
rhythms and the atmospheric music of the central *Andante* (very reminiscent of Bartók's Second
Piano Concerto). The string writing is highly distinctive, though the percussion part tends
occasionally to be of the crash-bang-wallop variety (witness the finale's opening). Schiff's
performance is naturally sympathetic, while his droll accounts of the six pre-war *Csárdás* –
contrapuntal miniatures that possess something of Copland's boldness and candour – round off a
rare and unexpected musical treat. The recordings are excellent.

Tomás Luis de Victoria

Laetatus sum. Missa Laetatus sum. Veni Creator Spiritus. Vadam et circuibo civitatem. Vidi
speciosam. Ad caenam Agni providi. Magnificat sexti toni.
The Sixteen / Harry Christophers.
Collins Classics 1521-2 (69 minutes: DDD). Texts and translations included. Recorded 1997.   Ⓕ

This volume of The Sixteen's Victoria series explores yet another facet of this composer's works: his
polychoral music. He composed his 12-voice setting of the psalm *Laetatus sum*, while he was still in
Rome and it was included in his printed collection of 1573, making it the earliest triple-choir music
to be published, and showing him to be at the forefront of the latest trends in sacred music in Italy.
His 1600 collection of polychoral pieces, printed in Spain after his return there, including this
parody Mass of the earlier psalm-setting as well as the triple-choir *Magnificat* also recorded here,
made an important contribution to the development of the idiom in the Iberian peninsula. This CD
is, then, all the more welcome for exploring this underperformed repertory and with all the polished
assurance we would expect of The Sixteen; it also serves as an important reminder that Victoria did
not only write in the sombre, austere manner so closely associated with him through his much
better-known music for Holy Week and the Requiem.

On this disc, and following the latest thinking, the three choirs combine voices and instruments in
different manners: Choir I is all-vocal (SSAB); in Choir II the voices (SATB) are accompanied by
organ and bass dulcian; and Choir III has voices (SATB) doubled by cornett and sackbuts. The
overall sonority, especially in the tuttis, is impressively rich and expansive, and Collins Classics
achieves a good balance and just the right amount of textural clarity in the resonant acoustic of
St Jude's, Hampstead. Harry Christophers's unhurried and appropriately spacious interpretation of
both Mass and motet captures well the sense of serene but joyful affirmation at the heart of the
psalm text. The two hymns, *Veni Creator Spiritus* and *Ad caenam Agni providi*, are performed with
the correct chant in alternate verses, and the pair of six-voice motets flow smoothly, but
expressively, with secure shaping of the vocal lines and sensitivity to the balancing of the
contrapuntal texture. This is a beautifully prepared and rewarding recording that deepens our
appreciation of one of the greatest masters of the renaissance.

Missa O quam gloriosum. Missa Ave maris stella. Motet – O quam gloriosum.
Westminster Cathedral Choir / David Hill.
Hyperion CDA66114 (57 minutes: DDD). *Gramophone* Award Winner 1985.   Ⓕ

This is likely to become one of your most cherished discs. It is notable for its spacious depth of sound, volatile unpredictability of interpretation, and above all the soaring *sostenuto* of the boy trebles, with their forward and slightly nasal tone quality. With their magnificently controlled *legato* lines, the Westminster boys treat Victoria's music as though it were some vast plainchant, with a passion that excites and uplifts. The choir is recorded in the exceptionally resonant Westminster Cathedral, at a distance and with great atmosphere. *Ave maris stella* is not one of Victoria's familiar Masses, quite simply because no music publisher has made it available to choirs in a good, cheap edition. To have it rescued from obscurity is laudable in itself, but to have it sung with such poise and sensitivity is an unexpected double treat. Unlike *O quam gloriosum*, this is a work that thrills with echoes of Victoria's Spanish upbringing, of Morales and his predecessors, even of Josquin Desprez, whose own *Ave maris stella* Mass was brought to the cathedrals of the Iberian peninsula earlier in the century. The plainchant melody, familiar to all of us through Monteverdi's setting in the 1610 Vespers, completely dominates Victoria's music, for it is placed most often in huge treble lines that wheel high above the general texture. Magnificent as the early parts of the work are, nothing quite matches the final five-part *Agnus Dei*, sung here with admirable support and breadth and exquisitely shaped by David Hill. This can be recommended without any reservation.

Officium defunctorum (1605).
Gabrieli Consort / Paul McCreesh.
Archiv Produktion 447 095-2AH (60 minutes: DDD). Text and translation included.
Recorded 1994.   Ⓕ🅔

This is a remarkable recording. In some ways it is like a rediscovery, for here is an approach not too far from Pro Cantione Antiqua at their best and yet that group never recorded the work. The Gabrieli Consort adds chant to the Requiem Mass itself, thus creating more of a context for Victoria's magisterial work. We have therefore the Epistle and preceding prayer, the Tract, Sequence, Gospel, Preface, Lord's Prayer and Postcommunion in addition to the polyphony; this also means, for example, that the *Kyrie* is sung nine-fold with alternating chant instead of simply three-fold only in polyphony. One may presume that the chant was taken from a suitable Spanish source by Luis Lozano Virumbrales, an expert in this field and author of the insert-notes together with Paul McCreesh. The performance itself is stately and imposing, with a tremendous homogeneity of sound: the use of an all-male choir, together with the added chant, lends it a tangibly monastic feel, though it would have been a fortunate monastery indeed that had falsettists of this quality. About the performance of the chant there are two points of interest: firstly, that it is doubled, like the polyphony, by a bajón, common Spanish practice at this period, and secondly, that McCreesh is not afraid to have the falsettists singing the chant too. The pace of the polyphony often seems to be unhurried, but it never feels slow, and Westminster Cathedral Choir is of course faced with the hugely reverberant acoustics of its home building. From the beginning the singing is involving and incarnate, but the real magic comes nearer the end: from the *Agnus Dei* onwards one feels that the Gabrieli Consort has really got the measure of the music and is allowing it to speak through them. The final great responsory, the 'Libera me' is performed with heart stopping power and conviction. McCreesh's approach shows how the Mass would have fitted into and complemented the liturgical framework without ever losing its own internal power and drama (for that of course is what it was intended for). A revelatory disc.

Officium Hebdomadae Sanctae – Lamentations of Jeremiah. Vexilla Regis. Pange lingua gloriosi.
The Sixteen / Harry Christophers.
Collins Classics 1518-2 (76 minutes: DDD). Texts and translations included. Recorded 1997.   Ⓕ🅔

This is what recording should be about: a project with a vision in which thoughtfully planned programming is allied to excellent performances and recorded sound to flesh out our knowledge of a repertory while at the same time giving great pleasure to the listener. Pleasure may seem an odd word to use in the context of a recording of *Lamentations* and hymns for Holy Week as there is absolutely no sense in which Victoria's music is anything other than emotionally harrowing, especially when sung with the appropriately fierce intensity brought to it by The Sixteen under the direction of Harry Christophers. Vocal scoring, balancing of chords and the sense of tension and release generated by carefully prepared suspensions become crucial components in these spare textures, and all are comprehended superbly well in this recording. The essentially homophonic idiom also inspires much more shaping of phrase and use of dynamic contrasts than is commonly encountered today in performances of sacred polyphony of a more contrapuntal kind. It is noticeable that in the two hymns inserted between the *Lamentations*, the greater contrapuntal complexity and comparatively florid melodic writing of the polyphonic verses results in less shaping, the overlapping movement of the voices having a continuous swell that tends to diffuse such arresting effects. The last two verses of the Passiontide hymn *Vexilla Regis* are, however, no less dramatic than the *Lamentations*: the sixth verse ('O crux ave, spes unica'), which would usually have been sung with the singers kneeling before the Crucifix, is strikingly sustained, while the last verse ('Te summa Deus Trinitas') has a triumphal quality that almost exuberantly communicates the central message of the Passion of Christ. The insert-notes are exemplary. Rush out and buy this beautiful and moving recording.

Veni Sancte Spiritus. Dum complerentur. Missa Dum complerentur. Popule meus. Vexilla Regis. Veni Creator Spiritus. Pange lingua gloriosi. Lauda Sion.
Westminster Cathedral Choir / James O'Donnell with **Joseph Cullen** *org*
Hyperion CDA66886 (70 minutes: DDD). Texts and translations included. Recorded 1996.   Ⓕ

Westminster Cathedral Choir here makes a special contribution to the music of Tomás Luis de Victoria. The *Missa Dum complerentur*, for Pentecost, is based on Victoria's own motet; he adds an extra voice in the parody Mass setting and draws much on the opening material of the motet as well as its distinctive 'Alleluia' sections which ring out like a peal of bells – especially in this excellent performance. Indeed, the motet is finely conceived, with Victoria characteristically responding to the imagery of the text with changes of texture and pacing within the essentially contrapuntal idiom: a true master. The choir, with its full-bodied sound and well-sustained vocal lines, has, over long years of tradition in singing this particular part of the repertory, achieved an almost intuitive feel for the flow of the music, which is perhaps as near as we'll ever get today to the authentic situation of professional church singers in Rome or the Spanish cathedrals in the sixteenth century. What we'll never know is whether the sonority – in particular the timbre of the boys' voices – resembles anything Victoria might have heard, that distinctive focus and intensity of tone well illustrated by the two Holy Week settings on the disc: the homophonic *Popule meus* and the hymn *Vexilla Regis*. This, and the two Pentecost hymns, are performed *in alternatim* with alternate verses in plainchant and polyphony. This is a superb and compelling disc that adds to our knowledge and appreciation of Victoria's art.

Louis Vierne
French 1870-1937

Symphonies – No. 2, Op. 20; No. 3, Op. 28.
Colin Walsh *org*
Priory PRCD446 (72 minutes: DDD). Played on the organ of Lincoln Cathedral. Recorded 1992. Ⓕ

Here is something out of the ordinary. It's not just that Colin Walsh is an impassioned advocate of the French romantic school or that he possesses a technique which all but takes one's breath away. Neither is it the ravishing Lincoln instrument, glorious though it sounds here in one of Priory's most vivid recordings. It's the way Walsh brings the music itself into such sharp focus. Vierne's creation takes centre stage, unobscured either by a player's virtuosity or an organ's enticing allure: the latter something of a rare feat since organ buffs seem to prefer to listen to the instrument rather than what's being played on it. Walsh manages the instrument deftly enough – after all, he knows it as intimately as anyone – so we never really notice his subtle and skilful registrations, giving all the more impact to those great climactic moments. So often a Vierne symphony can sound like a well-ordered sequence of individual pieces, but here the essential interdependence of the movements is most powerfully demonstrated. The composer's marvellous sense of structure and ingenious architectural designs are shown for the great musical gifts they are.

Henry Vieuxtemps
Belgian 1820-1881

Violin Concertos – No. 2 in F sharp minor, Op. 19; No. 3 in A major, Op. 25.
Misha Keylin *vn*
Janáček Philharmonic Orchestra / Dennis Burkh.
Naxos 8 554114 (57 minutes: DDD). Recorded 1995.   Ⓢ

By good fortune Naxos has chosen a splendid player to introduce us to Nos. 2 and 3. The Russian artist, Misha Keylin, emigrated to the USA at the age of nine and by 15 was already a soloist at Carnegie Hall. His timbre is rich, with a duskily subtle control of colour, his technique impeccable, and there is the kind of Slavonic flair that can bring these lightweight but masterly concertos fully to life. As the opening ritornello of the Second Concerto immediately demonstrates, Burkh's accompaniments with the leonine Janáček Philharmonic are extremely vivid and supportive, polished too. In the *Andante* Keylin phrases the melody most enticingly, in a heartfelt but never cloying manner and the finale is just as graceful, with the histrionics ever tasteful. The Third Concerto opens with a throbbing, spirited tutti; the solo entry, with its rhythmic snap, is arresting and has an exciting, Paganini-like progress and a dainty secondary theme. The *Adagio* is a darkly eloquent cantilena and the finale, marked *con delicatezza*, the soloist launches into a scintillating rondo, with attractive contrasting episodes. In short one cannot conceive that these two thoroughly diverting concertos could be given a more auspicious CD début. The Naxos recording is first-rate. A genuine bargain.

Heitor Villa-Lobos
Brazilian 1887-1959

Bachianas Brasileiras – Nos. 4, 5, 7 and 9. Chôros No. 10, 'Rasga o coração'.
Renée Fleming *sop*
BBC Singers; New World Symphony / Michael Tilson Thomas.
RCA Red Seal 09026 68538-2 (78 minutes: DDD). Recorded 1996.   Ⓟ **RR**

In his booklet-note, the commentator here calls *Chôros* No. 10 the masterpiece of that quintessentially Brazilian series. It is certainly the most ambitious, with very large orchestral and choral forces in a complex mélange of urban street song (a popular *schottisch* by Medeiros), chattering native Indian chants and bird-song twitterings, of mysterious jungle atmosphere, compulsive ostinato rhythms and virtuoso orchestral effects. The present performance is excellent. The couplings here are illuminating, consisting as they do of more Villa-Lobos – four of his highly individual tributes to Bach's influence. By far the best known of the *Bachianas Brasileiras* is, of course, No. 5, whose Aria demonstrates the composer's ability to spin a haunting long-flowing melody. Renée Fleming is the sweet-toned soloist with the cello section of this accomplished orchestra of young graduates from American conservatoires: warmly lyrical as she is, however, and brilliantly exact in the dartings of the Dansa, her words are not very distinct even in the slow-moving Aria. By his deeply expressive shaping of No. 4's Preludio Tilson Thomas avoids any satiety with its extreme monothematicism, and in the second movement secures coherent continuity despite the (rather loud) insistent interventions of the araponga bird's repeated note. He produces a beautifully poetic tranquillity in the brief Prelude of No. 9 and complete lucidity and rhythmic buoyancy in its Fugue. If that is the most Bachian of the series, the much more substantial No. 7 also has its moments of homage: its first movement has a fine breadth, and its finale is an impressive and serious-minded large-scale fugue that begins quietly and culminates in a grandiose blaze of sound; but the busy Toccata is characteristically and challengingly Brazilian, and the first part of its Giga (before it goes all Hollywood) is delightfully fresh in this invigorating performance.

Bachianas Brasileiras Nos. 2, 4 and 8.
Cincinnati Symphony Orchestra / Jesús López-Cobos.
Telarc CD80393 (70 minutes: DDD). Recorded 1995.   Ⓟ **E**

If any parallels existed between Bach and Brazilian idioms, they were largely in Villa-Lobos's mind – even the Fugue in No. 8 of these *Bachianas Brasileiras* is totally un-Bach-like; so anyone coming fresh to these exotically coloured, rather sprawling works should not be misled by false expectations. But fascinating, indeed haunting, in a highly individual way, they are. In view of the composer's sublime indifference to instrumental practicalities (as, for instance, the feasible length of a trombone *glissando*), his carelessness over detail in his scores, his Micawber-like trust that problems of balance he had created would be sorted out in performance, the chaotic state of the printed scores and orchestral parts of his music (littered as they are with wrong notes and questionable points), and numerous misreadings in past performances, the only half-way reliable yardstick for conductors or critics is the composer's own recordings, made in the 1950s and now preserved in a six-CD box on EMI. Compared to them, the present issue shows a number of differences. Chief of these is the warmer, more generalized sound, with less emphasis on clarity of detail. This works reasonably well in the Preludio of No. 8, where concentration on the melodic line and the adoption of a slower tempo aid the movement's lyricism (likewise the more sentimental approach to the Aria of No. 2); the Aria of No. 8 is unquestionably more poetic and the Dansa of No. 4 lighter; but in the most famous movement, the hilarious and ingenious 'Little train of the Caipira' of No. 2, the rasps near the start and the clatter of wheels on the track (evoked by the fiendishly difficult piano part) are far too subdued in favour of the 'big tune'. López-Cobos deals persuasively with knotty questions of balance such as in the middle section of No. 3's Toccata, and brings to the fore the bell-like araponga bird's cry in No. 4's Coral, but makes less of that movement's jungle screeches. He makes clear the thematic link between the sections of No. 4's Aria, and seeks to overcome the repetitious pattern of its Preludio by taking a faster speed rather than by the wealth of tonal nuance the composer himself introduced. Perhaps such detailed comparisons are superfluous: enjoy, enjoy!

Chôros No. 11.
Ralf Gothóni *pf*
Finnish Radio Symphony Orchestra / Sakari Oramo.
Ondine ODE916-2 (62 minutes: DDD). Recorded 1998. ⒡

Villa-Lobos wrote five piano concertos as well as other works for piano and orchestra with less *concertante* titles, such as *Momoprecoce* and the third of the *Bachianas Brasileiras*: in fact *Chôros* No. 11 is the largest-scale of them all, though despite its ferociously demanding solo part it has been described rather as a 'mammoth concerto grosso'. If that term conjures up for you an image of a neat neo-classical work, forget it: this is Villa-Lobos in his usual excitably coloured, hyper-exuberant style, writing in a grandiose loose form that – since few of its vast proliferation of themes are developed – defies analysis but whose overall effect is strangely riveting. Every so often lyrical passages occur among the manic busyness, and the linked second movement, profligately overscored as it is, is really romantic, with three related but not identical melodic ideas (and a big cadenza). The finale, which begins with a *fugato*, is thematically more integrated than the rest (for a time, at least) and consequently could be considered the most successful movement. The sound is vivid, Ralf Gothóni contributes prodigious feats of virtuosity and the Finnish orchestra shows total commitment to this extraordinary work.

Gênesis. Erosño (Origem do rio Amazonas). Amazonas. Dawn in a tropical forest.
Czecho-Slovak Radio Symphony Orchestra, Bratislava / Roberto Duarte.
Marco Polo 8 223357 (62 minutes: DDD). Recorded 1990. ⒡

Do not be deterred by the thought of an Eastern European orchestra playing unfamiliar Villa-Lobos. The Czecho-Slovak Radio Orchestra is clearly a very skilled and flexible body, and the conductor Roberto Duarte, a Brazilian authority on Villa-Lobos, has instilled South American colour and rhythmic vitality into his players quite brilliantly. The best of the four works is probably the earliest, *Amazonas*, which was written in 1917. Here, at the age of 30, Villa-Lobos's imagination was extraordinarily fertile, and this early evocation of Brazilian folklore, with its use of unusual instruments and strange orchestral timbres, is remarkably advanced for its date. The short tone poem *Dawn in a tropical forest* is a late work dating from 1953, and this has a more lyrical, more classical style. The remaining two works also come from the last phase in Villa-Lobos's career, and have similar themes. *Gênesis*, written in 1954, is a large-scale symphonic poem and ballet which depicts its enormous subject with all the extravagant colour and use of complex rhythms which were the composer's trademark. *Erosño*, or *The origin of the Amazon*, composed in 1950, is another ambitiously complex work. All four items are captured in faithful, wide-ranging sound.

Bachianas Brasileiras – No. 2: Toccata; No. 4; No. 5. Miniaturas – No. 2, A Viola. Modinhas e Cançōes, Series I – No. 3, Cantilena. Momoprecoce. Chôros No. 10, 'Rasga o coração'.
Victoria de los Angeles *sop* **Frederick Fuller** *bar* **Magda Tagliaferro** *pf*
Chorale des Jeunesses Musicales de France;
French Radio National Orchestra / Heitor Villa-Lobos *pf*
EMI Composers in Person mono CDC5 55224-2 (78 minutes: ADD). Recorded 1948-57. ⒡ Ⓗ

No one disc could fully illustrate the extent of Villa-Lobos's bewilderingly vast and unruly output's stylistic diversity; but this one makes a very good attempt. For those encountering him for the first time the simplest approach is via his purely lyrical side – the two songs so sympathetically sung by Frederick Fuller, *A Viola* with its gently insistent rumba rhythm and *Cantilena* wending its way above an unchanging pedal-note before repeating the melody wordlessly. The same wordless treatment is adopted in the haunting first movement of the *Bachianas Brasileiras* No. 5 for soprano and eight cellos (which has become Villa-Lobos's best-known piece, thanks partly to commercial exploitation): the radiance of Victoria de los Angeles's voice more than compensates for the less than tidy ensemble in places that the composer achieves as conductor. Moving to the non-vocal works, nobody could fail to enjoy the Toccata from the Second *Bachianas Brasileiras*, a brilliantly vivid sound picture of a little country train determinedly and happily chuffing along – as inventive as Honegger's earlier *Pacific 231* but more fun: the final exhausted long emission of steam cannot but make you laugh. The orchestral virtuosity which that piece demands reappears in the complex rhythms of the finale of *Bachianas Brasileiras* No. 4, whose much more straightforward first three movements, however, provide some clue to the composer's avowed preoccupation with Bach. Villa-Lobos's lifelong interest in children is illustrated by the noisily high-spirited fantasy

Momoprecoce (derived from the piano suite *Children's carnival*): its dedicatee, Magda Tagliaferro, brings to it all the requisite energy and boisterousness. The newcomer to Villa-Lobos, having weathered its strikingly individual scoring and sometimes strident dissonances, can now advance to the exotic atmosphere of the heartfelt cry for 'Brazilian heart and Brazilian earth' of the *Chôros* No. 10, which brings into play a chorus chanting against a hail of *staccato* syllables: the overall effect is totally unique and immensely exciting. The quality of transfer is bright and clear.

Missa São Sebastião. Bendita sabedoria. Praesepe (Ansy Boothroyd *mez*).
Cor dulce, cor amabile. Panis angelicus. Sub tuum praesidium. Ave Maria (a 5).
Ave Maria (a 6). Pater noster. Magnificat-alleluia (Elizabeth McCormack *mez*).
Corydon Singers and Orchestra / Matthew Best.
Hyperion CDA66638 (77 minutes: DDD). Texts and translations included. Recorded 1992-93   Ⓕ

Any listener not informed in advance and asked to identify the composer of all these religious works except the Mass (the earliest here) would be most unlikely to think of Villa-Lobos. That larger-than-life exotic, that extravagantly experimental and boisterous figure, the composer of such chastely restrained music, the sweetly gentle *Cor dulce*, the mellifluous imitative counterpoint of the first of the *Bendita sabedoria* (six brief choral pieces on biblical texts), the controlled fervour of the *Pater noster*? Even the impressive and grandiose *Magnificat-alleluia* (written in 1958 at the request of Pope Pius XII to celebrate Lourdes Year) gives no hint of its country of origin. The one clue here might be that, of the two *Ave Marias*, the (earlier) five-part setting is in Portuguese. It is only the Mass that reveals all. Amid its austere style and purely diatonic, contrapuntal idiom the *Sanctus* suddenly seems to come from a different background: then one remembers that Sebastian is the patron saint of Rio de Janeiro; and looking into the score one finds that the liturgical heading of each movement is followed by a local one, the final *Agnus Dei* bearing the subtitle 'Sebastian, protector of Brazil'. This programme, all of unaccompanied music except for the *Magnificat-alleluia*, should not be listened to as a continuity if some feeling of sameness is to be avoided: the Corydon Singers are most efficient in all they do, but the outstanding performance is of the Mass.

Antonio Vivaldi   Italian 1678-1741

Bassoon Concertos – C major, RV472; D minor, RV482; E minor, RV484; F major, RV491;
G major, RV494; G minor, RV495; A minor, RV499.
Klaus Thunemann *bn*
I Musici.
Philips 446 066-2PH (57 minutes: DDD). Recorded 1994.   Ⓕ

Vivaldi's distinctive individuality is in full flower in the rich invention which characterizes the tuttis of the fast movements of his bassoon concertos; and in the slow movements, as so often elsewhere, he proves himself a poet with the most delicate of sensibilities. In all of them, he seems to have been inspired by the colour and range of the instrument itself, exploring almost every possibility available to him in the bassoon of his day and, like Rameau in France, writing especially rewardingly for it in the tenor register. Thunemann, of course, plays an instrument of present-day manufacture, in keeping with the modern string instruments of I Musici; but he makes a very beautiful sound indeed, capitalizing on the inherent virtues of up-to-date technology. To all but the most committed Vivaldians only one of the seven concertos here may seem at all familiar. That is the atmospheric Concerto in E minor (RV484) with its undulating first movement tuttis inspired, one might suspect, by Venetian waters. Thunemann instils life into every bar of his interpretation, performing dazzling feats of athleticism apparently with the utmost of ease, while at the same time giving thought to ornamentation. Not a note is either out of tune or misplaced and, in slow movements, many of which possess beguiling lyrical charm, Thunemann reveals himself as a musician of great sensitivity. The *Largo* of the first concerto on the disc (RV491) is a striking example. Readers familiar with Vivaldi's sacred vocal music will recognize its derivation in part from a passage to be found both in his *Magnificat* (RV610) and his *Kyrie* (RV587). In the present context Vivaldi imbues an already arresting harmonic pattern with a drowsy, almost dreamlike fantasy in which the bassoon writing, treated here with an affecting improvisatory freedom, ranges widely with some striking intervals against sustained, softly modulating strings. It's a brief moment of magic.

Bassoon Concertos – C major, RV474; F major, RV489; A minor, RV498.
Chamber Concertos – F major, RV571; G minor, RV576; G minor, RV577.
Danny Bond *bn*
Academy of Ancient Music / Christopher Hogwood.
L'Oiseau-Lyre 436 867-2OH (58 minutes: DDD). Recorded 1992.   ⒻⓅ

One of the mysteries surrounding Vivaldi's 37 complete bassoon concertos is that they are so difficult; recordings tended to prove the point – they *are* tough nuts. But here Danny Bond surmounts every obstacle with rounded tone, secure intonation, every note clearly played, with musicality to match that of his colleagues – and on a period bassoon to boot. The other three works are *concerti grossi* ('*con molti strumenti*') of which RV571 is the most virtuosic. The Concertos, RV576 and 577 were, as their large wind band proclaims, written for the ample resources of the Dresden orchestra. All the soloists are on superb form, the ensemble is spirited and beautifully balanced – as is the recording thereof. A wholly delightful disc.

Cello Concertos – C major, RV400; C minor, RV401; D minor, RV405; G major, RV415ᵃ; G minor, RV417; A minor, RV419; B flat major, RV423.
Roel Dieltiens *vc/ᵃvc piccolo* **Ensemble Explorations** (Christine Busch, Natsumi Wakamatsu *vns* Frans Vos *va* Richte van der Meer *vc* Anthony Woodrow *db* Attilio Cremonesi *hpd/org* Mike Fentross *lte/gtr*).
Harmonia Mundi HMC90 1655 (68 minutes: DDD). Recorded 1997.　　　　　　　　Ⓕ🅿

Though himself a violinist, Vivaldi nevertheless proved, in 27 cello concertos and nine cello sonatas, that he was able to write just as expressively for other instruments. One of the loveliest of the cello concertos is RV401. Roel Dieltiens knows how best to project and enliven the late baroque syntax. Phrases are elegantly shaped, effectively punctuated and delivered with inflective charm. Intimate, conversational, sometimes animated, sometimes affectionate – a wide variety of moods touches the listener. Vivaldi's music is seldom lacking in expressive subtlety and the sheer simplicity of so many of the ideas is often the secret of its affective allure. All is played with panache and the music is underpinned by a continuo richly endowed with variety of colour and texture. Apart from the C minor Concerto, Dieltiens has skilfully chosen pieces which are infrequently performed, playing the last in the programme, RV415, on a violoncello piccolo. It's an attractive piece, much favoured by cellists but, alas, unlikely to be the product of Vivaldi's pen. A rewarding issue.

Cello Concertos – C minor, RV402; D minor, RV406; G major, RV414.
Sonatas – A minor, RV44; E flat major, RV39; G minor, RV42.
Christophe Coin *vc*
Academy of Ancient Music / Christopher Hogwood *hpd*
L'Oiseau-Lyre 433 052-2OH (67 minutes: DDD). Recorded 1990.　　　　　　　　Ⓕ🅿

Christophe Coin's feeling for dance rhythms, his clear articulation and musical phrasing and his sharp ear for detail bring the concertos and sonatas alive in an infectious way. He is both firmly and imaginatively supported in the sonatas by a fine continuo group, and in the concertos by the strings of the Academy of Ancient Music. In the sonatas Christopher Hogwood varies the colour of the accompaniments by moving between harpsichord and organ while cello and baroque guitar add further variety and support. In the concertos, fast movements are characterized by vigorous, idiomatic passagework for the solo instrument punctuated by pulsating Vivaldian rhythms in the tuttis. In the slow movements, richly endowed with lyricism, the expressive intensity of the music is, on occasion, almost startling, revealing Vivaldi as a composer capable of far greater affective gestures than he is often given credit for. This music never fails to move the spirit.

Cello Concerto in A minor, RV422. Violin Concerto in D minor, Op. 4 No. 8. String Concertos – C major, RV117; E minor, RV134; G major, RV151, 'Alla rustica'. Amor, hai vinto, RV683. Cessate, omai cessate, RV684.
Sara Mingardo *mez* Francesca Vicari *vn* **Luigi Piovano** *vc*
Concerto Italiano / Rinaldo Alessandrini *hpd*
Opus 111 OPS30-181 (60 minutes: DDD). Texts and translations included.
Recorded 1996.　　　　　　　　Ⓕ🅿🅴

This thoughtfully and attractively devised programme by Rinaldo Alessandrini and Concerto Italiano breaks up a sequence of five well contrasted concertos with two of Vivaldi's chamber cantatas. The two vocal pieces are both for alto with divided violins, viola and continuo; and their subject matter, dealt with in the customary pattern of two alternating recitatives and arias, concerns the efficacy of Cupid's arrows on those incredibly susceptible denizens of Arcadia. Sara Mingardo enlivens this music at every turn. Her voice is warm in tone, evenly projected and, in a pastoral setting where the cruel pangs of love are felt in almost every bar, appropriately anguished. The chamber cantatas are still among Vivaldi's better kept secrets and there is much that satisfies heart and mind alike. Of the five concertos three are *concerti a quattro*, or strings without soloist; in the solo concertos cellist Luigi Piovano and violinist Francesca Vicari, who also leads Concerto Italiano, are fluently stylish and technically assured. Like Alessandrini and his ensemble, they bring plenty of graceful gesture and effective articulation to the music. A most satisfying recital of Vivaldi's music, both on account of interpretation and for the window it opens on to the composer's widely ranging expressive vocabulary.

Chamber Concertos – D major, RV93; D major, RV94; F major, RV98, 'La tempesta di mare'; G minor, RV104, 'La notte'; G minor, RV107; A minor, RV108; F major, RV442. Trio Sonata in D minor, RV63.
Il Giardino Armonico.
Teldec 4509-91852-2 (67 minutes: DDD). Recorded 1990-92.   Ⓕ Ⓟ

There are baroque groups that are frankly dull and there are others on whom stylistic felicity sits naturally and gracefully. Il Giardino Armonico, an 11-strong group of young Italians, is one of the best. Italy, the birthplace of the baroque, has been curiously slow in coming forward with a specialized unit such as this, but the wait has been worthwhile; Il Giardino Armonico is as Italian as the music itself – brightly coloured, individualistic, confident, stylish, arrestingly decorated, bubbling with enthusiasm and ... add your own adjectives. The only un-Italian thing about them is their collective unanimity! Set these performances against any others in the catalogue and, with no detriment to the others, the differences are likely to deal you a blow to the solar plexus. Any sneaking fear that such unbridled *élan* leads to a uniformly vigorous approach is unfounded; equally 'Italian' is their wide dynamic range, dramatically exploited in RV104 and RV63, and all calls for serenity are answered. The recording is as bright and clear as the music.

Concertos for Two Violins and Strings – C major, RV505; D major, RV511; A minor, RV523 (with Micaela Comberti *vn*). Concerto for Two Cellos and Strings in G minor, RV531 (Jane Coe, David Watkin *vcs*). Concerto for Two Oboes and Strings in D minor, RV535 (Anthony Robson, Catherine Latham *obs*). Concerto for Two Violins, Oboe and Strings in C major, RV554.
Collegium Musicum 90 / Simon Standage *vn*
Chandos Chaconne CHAN0528 (65 minutes: DDD). Recorded 1991.   Ⓕ Ⓟ

It was natural, with so many talented young ladies available at the Pietà, that Vivaldi should have written a large number of concertos with two or more soloists. More than two dozen are for two violins; RV505 and 511 are both mature works, the former leaning towards *galant* style and the latter 'unified' by elements that are common to its outer movements. RV554, originally a triple concerto for violin, oboe and organ, was rewritten by Vivaldi for oboe and two violins, in which latter form it is given in this recording. The Concerto for two oboes, RV535, is 'Corellian' in its four-movement *da chiesa* form and in its 'conversations' between the soloists and the *ripieno* strings – a Vivaldian rarity. If Vivaldi wrote a more eloquently pathetic melody than that of the *Largo* of the Double Cello Concerto, RV531, it is hard to bring it to mind. Collegium Musicum 90 fields a modest string band, which adds leanness of sound to its other virtues of stylishness and crispness of ensemble. Excellent oboe soloists contribute to the allure of this recording.

Concertos – G major, RV151, 'Alla rustica'; B flat major for Violin and Oboe, RV548; G major for Two Violins, RV516; A minor for Oboe, RV461; G major for Two Mandolins, RV532; C major, RV558.
The English Concert / Trevor Pinnock.
Archiv Produktion 415 674-2AH (53 minutes: DDD).   Ⓕ Ⓟ

The *Concerto con molti stromenti*, RV558, calls for a plethora of exotic instruments and Vivaldi's inventiveness, everywhere apparent, seems to know no bounds. The vigorous melodies have splendid verve whilst the slow movements are no less exciting. The concertos which employ plucked instruments, are particularly entrancing to the ear – here is virtuosity indeed, with Pinnock sensibly opting for an organ continuo to emphasize the difference between the plucked strings and the bowed. The Double Mandolin Concerto, RV532, is beautifully played with a real build-up of tension in the tuttis. The English Concert is affectionate and rhythmically precise and the recording is good, with the gentler sounding instruments well brought out of the fuller textures.

Concerto for Four Violins and Strings in D minor, RV549. Cello Concertos – G major, RV413; A minor, RV418. Concerto for Violin, Cello and Strings in B flat major, RV547[a]. Concerto for Two Violins, Two Cellos and Strings in G major, RV575[b]. String Concertos – C major, RV117; E minor, RV134; F minor, RV143; A major, RV159.
[b]**Stephen Marvin, Chantal Rémillard, Cynthia Roberts** *vns*
[ab]**Anner Bylsma,** [b]**Christina Mahler** *vcs*
Tafelmusik / Jeanne Lamon [ab]*vn*
Sony Classical Vivarte SK48044 (66 minutes: DDD). Recorded 1990.   Ⓕ Ⓟ

This is a first-rate recording of concertos for various combinations of strings. Though Vivaldi himself was a violinist he wrote for almost every other instrument of his day with informed skill. One of those to benefit was the cello, which features as a solo instrument to a greater or lesser extent in five of the concertos in this programme. The soloist is the Dutch virtuoso Anner Bylsma whose animated playing generates a feeling of excitement and spontaneity by no means easily captured on disc. If he has a fault then it is that he is too often attracted by breakneck tempos and it is that which detracts from the opening movement of the G major Concerto (RV413). Apart from that one minor criticism the disc is one to be treasured not only for the excellence of the playing but also for the judicious choice of repertory. The Concerto in G major for two violins, two cellos and strings (RV575) is a beautifully crafted work with notably expressive writing for the solo instruments. The four concertos for ripieno strings, in which Vivaldi foreshadows the early classical symphonists, provide a rewarding contrast with the remaining programme and are played here with accomplishment and affection.

Double Concerto for Two Oboes and Strings in D minor, RV535. Concertos for Multiple Instruments – A major, RV552, 'per eco in lontano'; D major, RV562; F major, RV568; F major, RV569; G minor, RV577, 'per l'orchestra di Dresda'.
Philharmonia Baroque Orchestra / Nicholas McGegan.
Reference Recordings RRCD77 (72 minutes: DDD). Recorded 1996. Ⓕ🅟

Here is Vivaldi-playing with a commendably light, athletic touch. It is so easy to make a meal out of his orchestral tuttis yet these performances inspire the music with expressive delicacy and rhythmic vitality. The programme is a colourful one of concertos for a variety of instruments, wind and strings, in various combinations. Apart from occasional instances of predictable passagework, present above all in some of the wind writing, this music is engaging on many different levels. Slow movements such as the wonderfully free violin fantasy of RV562 reveal the exhilarating flights of fancy of which Vivaldi was capable, while the profusion of alluring inflexions present in fast and slow movements alike, makes strong appeal to the senses. Vivaldi was no stranger to the art of parody and, in the opening movement of RV568, we find him introducing sensuous, sighing quaver motifs present in the finale of the *Concerto a due Cori per la Santissima Assenzione di Maria Vergine* (RV535). This kind of approach to Vivaldi's music greatly enlivens and refreshes its innate character. The disc is superbly recorded, allowing us to revel in every sonorous detail of solo and continuo playing alike.

Double and Triple Concertos – Two Cellos and Strings in G minor, RV531; Violin, Cello and Strings in F major, RV544, 'Il Proteo ò sia il mondo rovescio'; Three Violins and Strings in F major, RV551; Two Violins and Strings in A major, RV552, 'per eco in lontano'; Violin, Two Cellos and Strings in C major, RV561; Two Violins, Two Cellos and Strings in D major, RV564.
Christophe Coin *vc*
Il Giardino Armonico / Giovanni Antonini.
Teldec Das Alte Werk 4509-94552-2 (64 minutes: DDD). Recorded 1994.
Gramophone Award Winner 1996. Ⓕ🅔

This is a strong programme which almost unfailingly presents the Venetian composer in his most colourful clothing. Though Vivaldi often wrote imaginatively for pairs of wind instruments his musical ideas were of necessity confined by their technical limitations. With violins and cellos, on the other hand, he was better able to extend his creative faculties, which resulted in music of more sustained interest. This is certainly true of the two concertos which he wrote for two violins, two cellos and strings, one of them (RV564) included here. Making an even rarer appearance on disc is a Concerto in F major for violin and cello (RV544), the least well known of three such works from Vivaldi's pen. Two versions of this concerto exist, the other (RV572) containing additional parts for pairs of flutes and oboes. Both carry the engaging title *Il Proteo ò sia il mondo al rovescio*. Infrequently performed, too, is a C major piece for violin, two cellos and strings (RV561), though the characteristically Vivaldian ritornello of the opening movement may recall other contexts in the minds of listeners. The three remaining works are fairly mainstream Vivaldi: the G minor Concerto for two cellos (RV531), the F major Concerto for three violins (RV551) and the A major Concerto for two violins, one of them functioning as an echo, the *violine per eco in lontano* (RV552). From this, readers will infer a pleasing variety of texture and, within the limits of a purely string programme, colour. Il Giardino Armonico has thought carefully about the latter, ringing the changes in the keyboard continuo between organ and harpsichord, and introducing a theorbo, too. But what makes this disc a real winner is the exhilarating character of the playing, both solo and ripieno. Playing of vitality and lyricism brings Vivaldi's music to life in a thrilling manner. Indeed, the integrity and musicianly character of these performances is in no small measure heightened by the presence of Christophe Coin. Fine music, fine playing and a fine recording. An outstanding issue.

12 Concertos, Op. 3, 'L'estro armonico'.
Academy of Ancient Music / Christopher Hogwood.
L'Oiseau-Lyre Florilegium 414 554-2OH2 (two discs: 96 minutes: DDD). ⓂⓅ

This set of Concertos is arranged as a display of variety, and ordered in a kaleidoscopic way that would maintain interest were it to be played in its entirety. These works are often played with an inflated body of *ripieno* (orchestral) strings, but in this recording they are played as Vivaldi intended them; only four violins are used. The contrast does not come from antiphony or weight of numbers but is provided through the *tutti* versus episodic passages. One could not assemble a more distinguished 'cast' than that of the AAM in this recording, showing clearly just why this music is best played on period instruments, by specialists in baroque style, who are not afraid to add a little embellishment here and there. Performances and recording are splendid. This is required listening.

L'estro armonico.
Europa Galante / Fabio Biondi *vn*
Virgin Classics Veritas VMD5 45315-2 (two discs: 100 minutes: DDD). Recorded 1997-98 ⒻⓅⒺ

No other set of Vivaldi's concertos contains the sheer variety on display in *L'estro armonico*. The catalogue has seldom been without a decent recording of these ceaselessly fascinating concertos, though none begins to approach this version in respect of fantasy and exuberance. Fabio Biondi and his Italian ensemble, Europa Galante, bring something entirely fresh and vital to oft-performed repertoire, illuminating well-trodden paths with affective articulation and eloquently voiced inflexions. Not all of their extravagant, Mediterranean gestures, perhaps, will find favour with readers; indeed, some of Biondi's own embellishments can be a little inapposite. Tempos are well chosen, by and large, and ensemble is clear-textured and evenly balanced. The continuo group, which includes harpsichord, organ, archlute and baroque guitar, makes an important contribution to the overall success. This music is wonderful stuff, rejuvenating and immensely satisfying.

Six Flute Concertos, Op. 10.
Patrick Gallois *fl*
Orpheus Chamber Orchestra.
DG 437 839-2GH (49 minutes: DDD). Recorded 1992. ⒻⒺ

Patrick Gallois is a player of agility and sensitivity, an intelligent artist who can make his metal flute speak with all the subtlety of varied articulation and tone colour that some of us had come to assume was only possible on the wooden baroque instrument. These are deliciously light performances, in the best sense of the word; plenty of air allowed in, sparing and thoughtful use of vibrato, and above all an infectious bounce to the music-making in general. Gallois's sunny approach is matched by the excellent string players of the Orpheus Chamber Orchestra, whose stunning unanimity of ensemble, crispness of attack and sheer concentration-level once again make it hard to believe that they operate without a conductor. And both soloist and orchestra are equally responsive, too, to the uniquely tranquil beauties of the Vivaldian slow movement.

Oboe Concertos – C major, RV447[a]; F major, RV457[b]; A minor, RV461[b]; A minor, RV463[a]; D minor, RV535. Concerto for Two Clarinets, Two Oboes and Strings in C major, RV559.
[a]**Frank de Bruine,** [b]**Stephen Hammer** *obs* **Eric Hoeprich, Antony Pay** *cls*
Academy of Ancient Music / Christopher Hogwood.
L'Oiseau-Lyre 433 674-2OH (60 minutes: DDD). Recorded 1991. ⒻⓅ

This delightful miscellany of concertos by Vivaldi for one and two oboes – in a single instance, here, they are joined by a pair of clarinets – confirms Stephen Hammer as one of the very finest baroque oboe players around. He and Christopher Hogwood have achieved a happy partnership which realizes on the one hand the exuberant vitality of Vivaldi's rhythms, and on the other the rich seam of fantasy running through so much of his music. Few if any of Vivaldi's 18 or so surviving solo concertos for the instrument are disappointing. Stephen Hammer and Frank de Bruine have picked four of the best constructed and most alluring of them, taking two concertos each. They join forces in the D minor Concerto for two oboes, and are further joined by Eric Hoeprich and Antony Pay for one of Vivaldi's two concertos for two oboes and two clarinets. The latter piece is effectively written with the focus on the contrasting sonorities of the single and double reed families. Hammer negotiates the solo writing with consummate skill, athletic, precise in tuning and articulation and tasteful in his ornamentation and the remainder comes over with comparable panache. Both oboists unfailingly bring out the poetry in the music with sensibility and restraint. Fine recorded sound.

Oboe Concertos – C major, RV447; C major, RV450; D major, RV453; A minor, RV461;
A minor, RV463. Concerto for Violin and Oboe in B flat major, RV548.
Douglas Boyd *ob* **Marieke Blankestijn** *vn*
Chamber Orchestra of Europe.
DG 435 873-2GH (59 minutes: DDD). Recorded 1991. Ⓕ

Vivaldi wrote 17 solo oboe concertos, three for two oboes and another for oboe and violin. In this
virtuoso programme the oboist, Douglas Boyd, has chosen five of the solo oboe concertos together
with the more modestly conceived but no less captivating Concerto in
B flat for oboe and violin. The oboe concertos have been selected discerningly, not only for their
musical interest but also, it would seem, with an eye to their rarity value on the concert platform.
Boyd, playing a modern oboe, gives fluent, sensitively shaped performances and is supported in a
lively manner by the strings of the Chamber Orchestra of Europe. Boyd is expressive in slow
movements – they almost invariably possess considerable lyrical appeal – and athletic in faster ones;
and he needs to be, for Vivaldi seldom showed mercy on his soloists. From among the many
beautiful movements here the *Larghetto* of the Concerto in A minor (RV461) stands out and may
be ranked among Vivaldi's happiest creations for the oboe. Fine recorded sound.

Sinfonia for Strings in G major, RV149. Concertos for Violin and Strings, Op. 8 – No. 5 in
E flat major, RV253, 'La tempesta di mare'; No. 6 in C major, RV108, 'Il piacere'. Double Concerto
for Viola d'amore, Lute and Strings in D minor, RV540. Concertos for Multiple Instruments –
A major, RV552, 'per eco in lontano'; C major, RV558.
Academy of Ancient Music / Andrew Manze *vn*
Harmonia Mundi HMU90 7230 (65 minutes: DDD). Recorded 1996. ⒻⓅ

In one respect or another all the pieces here are vintage Vivaldi and, taken together, they offer a fair
conspectus of his expressive range, his feeling for instrumental colour and his originality. Three of
the four works performed have become firm favourites among twentieth-century audiences: the
Concertos for viola d'amore and lute (RV540), for violin, echo violins and strings (RV552) and
con molti istromenti (RV558). The fourth item, a wonderfully spirited *Sinfonia* (RV149), Vivaldi
wrote as an introduction to a serenata, now lost, by another composer. The performances are
splendid. Manze has a pleasing awareness of the inherent poesy and fantasy in Vivaldi's music and
has the technique to make the most of it. *La tempesta di mare* is particularly enjoyable and the
tenderly expressive Concerto for viola d'amore and lute – the gently swung rhythm of the sublime
Largo is as pleasing as Manze's ornamented repeats. The orchestra is generally on good form,
responsive to Vivaldi and Manze alike. These aspects can be savoured above all in the C major
Concerto with its treble recorders, tenor chalumeaux, mandolins, theorbos, violins, cello and string
tutti. Vivaldi was clearly intent on showing off the diverse, multicoloured musical talents of his
pupils in this rhythmically infectious piece. This is a delightful programme, executed with refinement.

String Concertos – C major, RV117; C minor, RV118; D major, RV123; D minor, RV128;
F major, RV136; F minor, RV143; G major, RV146; A major, RV159; A major, RV160;
B flat major, RV163, 'Conca'.
I Musici.
Philips 438 876-2PH (55 minutes: DDD). Recorded 1992. Ⓕ

Here is a generous and varied selection from among the concertos which Vivaldi wrote for strings
without soloist. He composed over 40 such pieces of which ten are included here. Anyone who
still thinks that one Vivaldi concerto sounds much the same as another should listen to these
vital, often forward-looking pieces. They are full of striking contrasts and ideas which point
strongly in the direction of the early symphony and the tautly constructed fugues at the conclusion
of the Concerto in D major (RV123) and the beginning of the Concerto in F minor (RV143) are but
two reminders of how effective a contrapuntist Vivaldi could be if he so wished. I Musici gives a
lively view of these engaging concertos with tidy ensemble and good intonation and should
disappoint only those who don't enjoy listening to baroque repertory played on modern
instruments.

String Concertos – D minor, RV129, 'Concerto madrigalesco'; E flat major, RV130,
'Sonata al santo sepolcro'; C minor, RV202; G minor, RV517; B flat major, RV547;
C minor, RV761. Sinfonia in B minor, RV169, 'Sinfonia al santo sepolcro'.
Adrian Chamorro *vn* **Maurizio Naddeo** *vc*
L'Europa Galante / Fabio Biondi *vn*
Opus 111 OPS30-9004 (52 minutes: DDD). Recorded 1990. ⒻⓅ

This invigorating programme contains well-known and less well-known concertos by Vivaldi. The performances sparkle with life and possess an irresistible spontaneity. The Concertos for one and two violins (RV761 and RV202) are comparative rarities and are played with agility and insight by the soloist director Fabio Biondi and his alert and responsive ensemble. Biondi himself is capable of light and articulate bowing and has a natural feeling for graceful turns of phrase. Vivaldi's virtuoso writing occasionally finds chinks in his armour but with enlightened music-making of this order it matters little. Everywhere Vivaldi's infectious rhythms are tautly controlled and the music interpreted with character and conviction. Perhaps the highlight of the disc is the Concerto in B flat for violin and cello. Outer movements are crisply articulated and played with almost startling energy while the poignant lyricism of the *Andante* is touchingly captured. A refreshing and illuminating disc; the recorded sound is clear and ideally resonant.

Viola d'amore Concertos – D major, RV392; D minor, RV393; D minor, RV394; D minor, RV395; A major, RV396; A minor, RV397.
Orchestra of the Age of Enlightenment / Catherine Mackintosh *va d'amore*
Hyperion CDA66795 (67 minutes: DDD). Recorded 1995. ⒻⓅ

John Evelyn (1620-1706) was beguiled and surprised by the sound of the viola d'amore, but he should hardly have been so by the fact that it was on that occasion 'played ... by a *German*'; that was the nationality of most of the composers who wrote for it – Bach, Biber, Telemann and Mattheson. The instrument was distinguished by its wide compass, its use of sympathetic strings (not bowed but allowed to resonate), and the fact that it lent itself to playing 'the lyra way' (as with the bass viola da gamba), facilitating the use of multiple stopping and contrapuntal textures. Vivaldi was obviously no less attracted by it; six concertos are a lot for such an unusual instrument, and it is fair to say that they represent some of the most beguiling music he wrote. Mackintosh, on top form, acts her role with the utmost virtuosity, lovely tone, unimpeachable intonation, and fine style – with some elegant embroidery. The OAE is admirable, making this splendidly engineered recording one to treasure.

Dresden Concertos – D major, RV213; D major, RV219; D major, RV224; D minor, RV240; E flat major, RV260; A major, RV344; B minor, RV388.
Cristiano Rossi *vn*
Accademia I Filarmonici / Alberto Martini.
Naxos 8 554310 (67 minutes: DDD). Recorded 1998. Ⓢ

The Dresden link was forged by Vivaldi's friend and one-time pupil, Johann Georg Pisendel. Pisendel visited Venice in 1716 when he appears to have struck up a warm friendship with Vivaldi, who dedicated several sonatas and concertos to him. The seven violin concertos on this disc have survived in manuscripts preserved in the Dresden Sächsische Landesbibliothek. Much of this music will be entirely new to most collectors. By and large these are pieces which do not wear their hearts on their sleeves. There are few extravagant flourishes and perhaps less than we might expect in the way of extrovert gesture. But there is no lack of brilliance in the solo violin writing – Pisendel's reputation as a virtuoso was hardly less than Vivaldi's – and, as ever, the music contains a profusion of effective rhythmic ideas. The solo violin parts are entrusted to Cristiano Rossi who often, though not always, discovers the fantasy in Vivaldi's solo writing. The bowing is graceful and relaxed even if intonation is occasionally awry. The A major Concerto, RV344 affords a good instance of soloist and orchestra at their most persuasive. But the lyrically expressive violin melody against a dotted rhythm continuo of the *Largo* of RV224 is unquestionably the most alluring. The more you hear this music, the more you are likely to be captivated by it. The recorded sound seems a little boxy and confined, but textures come through clearly all the same.

Violin Concertos – D major, RV223; D major, RV229; D minor, RV248; F major, RV267; A major, RV343; A major, RV349.
Israel Chamber Orchestra / Shlomo Mintz *vn*
MusicMasters 67120-2 (59 minutes: DDD). Ⓕ

Shlomo Mintz has hit on the charming idea of assembling six concertos which Vivaldi intended expressly at one time or another for his gifted pupil, Anna Maria at the Pietà in Venice. If the music is anything to go by then Signora Anna Maria must have been prodigiously talented; much of the music here is of a markedly virtuoso character and of enormous appeal, melodic and rhythmic. Mintz himself does considerable justice to the works, effortlessly surmounting the technical difficulties posed by Vivaldi's writing. Equally admirable is his spirited approach and the wholehearted enthusiasm with which he throws himself into the playful invention, often strikingly varied, of the outer movements. The only reservation, a small one, lies in the recorded sound which has a slight hollowness, especially noticeable in slow movements and in passages where the solo violin is accompanied solely by cello and keyboard continuo. A captivating issue.

Violin Concertos, Op. 8, 'Il cimento dell'armonia e dell'inventione' – Nos. 1-4, 'The Four Seasons'; No. 5 in E flat major, RV253, 'La tempesta di mare'; No. 6 in C major, RV180, 'Il piacere'; No. 7 in D minor, RV242; No. 9 in D minor, RV236; No. 10 in B flat major, RV362, 'La caccia'; No. 11 in D major, RV210; No. 12 in C major (two versions, RV178 and RV449).

Violin Concertos, Op. 8 – Nos. 1-4, 8 and 9.
Enrico Onofri vn **Paolo Grazzi** ob
Il Giardino Armonico / Giovanni Antonini.
Teldec 4509-96158-2 (61 minutes: DDD). Recorded 1993. 　　　　Ⓕ🅿

Il Giardino Armonico doesn't do anything extraordinary; it is more a matter of its demonstration of what can be achieved with small forces – 5.1.2.1 plus soloist and continuo. Here, small is flexible and it highlights the differences in colour achieved by varying the continuo – bassoon, cello, organ, harpsichord and theorbo, unobscured by the *ripieno*, all have their moments. Numbers of 'chamber' dimensions also favour unanimity of attack and changes of dynamics and pace, all vividly accomplished by IGA. The dog barks harshly in 'Spring' but without disturbing the shepherd's peaceful dreams, and the chill of 'Autumn' in the *Adagio molto* is conveyed by the ethereal strings with the harpsichord firmly relegated to a supporting role. Onofri is as good a soloist as may be met in a long march, pitch-perfect, incisive but not 'edgy', and effortlessly alert to every nuance. All the foregoing good things are also to be found in the other two concertos from Op. 8, together with Grazzi's liquid-toned and agile oboe playing in that in D minor, attractively supported in the *Largo* by theorbo and bassoon. A tasty addition to any collection.

Violin Concertos, Op. 8[a] – Nos. 1-5. Oboe Concerto in A minor, RV461[b].
Bassoon Concerto in D minor, RV481[c].
[b]**Robin Williams** ob [c]**Ursula Leveaux** bn [a]**Anthony Marwood** vn
Scottish Chamber Orchestra / Nicholas McGegan.
Classic fM The Full Works 75605 57045-2 (67 minutes: DDD). Recorded 1998. 　　　Ⓜ

The aim of Classic fM's The Full Works series is to make classical music more accessible. Although modern instruments and pitch are used in these recordings, should any listener be persuaded to take the further step of trying and liking fully 'authentic' recordings, that would be the icing on very well-baked and tasty cakes. Anthony Marwood gets just about everything stylistically right, and shows an instinctive flair for embellishment in *The Four Seasons*. These performances (and that of the comparably programmatic *La tempesta di mare*), with sprucely pointed and sensitively controlled support, succeed in the difficult task of making these concertos sound fresh. Likewise, there is nothing but praise for Robin Williams's oboe playing (with some passages of remarkable 'snake's-tongued' articulation) and Ursula Leveaux's concealment of the difficulty of meeting Vivaldi's often near-outrageous demands on bassoon players, past and present. Both put their skills at the service of pure music-making. Authentic or not, all these beautifully balanced performances are some of the most enjoyable available.

Violin Concertos, Op. 8 – Nos. 1-4. Oboe Concertos, Op. 7 – No. 1 in B flat major, RV465; No. 5 in F major, RV285a.
Andrew Manze vn **Marcel Ponseele** ob
Amsterdam Baroque Orchestra / Ton Koopman.
Erato 4509-94811-2 (56 minutes: DDD). Recorded 1993-94. 　　　Ⓕ🅿

This is a splending set, valid for a lifetime of pleasure. Little differences in attention to detail soon begin to show, first at 0'17" of the first movement of 'Spring', where the chords that are usually hit hard are here given a happy little squeeze. Amsterdam Baroque (consisting here of 13 instrumentalists) plays with the unanimity of one mind and body, with extreme changes of volume that never sound theatrically contrived, as concerned with the fate of every note as with the shaping of each phrase. Manze's bow breathes vocal life into his strings; in the slow movements many notes whisper their way into being, and his *fortissimo* whiplashes have rasp-free edges. There are many delightful little personal touches – his slurred resolution of the sighing appoggiatura at 2'50" in the third movement of 'Spring', and the way he nudges his way up the ladder of trills in the first movement of 'Autumn' are just two. The remaining works come from Op. 7, in the first of which (RV465) the oboe is the designated soloist; its transcribed role in No. 5 (RV285a) accords with baroque practice. Both are charming works with a high level of inspiration, played with no less affection than the *Seasons*.

Violin Concertos, Op. 8 – Nos. 1-6.
Mariana Sirbu *vn*
I Musici.
Philips 446 699-2PH (60 minutes: DDD). Recorded 1995.   Ⓕ

Mariana Sirbu here joins the company of the many artists who have recorded *The Four Seasons*. Sirbu is no less incisive than any of the others and, particularly in the slow movements which she plays with little added adornment, her lines are fine and imaginatively nuanced. I Musici remains crisp and responsive, and a novel touch is its addition of a lute to the continuo; it is from time to time audible, providing the little fill-ins usually the prerogative of the harpsichord, as for example in the final *Presto* of 'Summer' and the *Adagio molto* of 'Autumn', though in the latter its economical comments perhaps lack the icy edge of the harpsichord. The two other concertos from Op. 8 (*La tempesta di mare* and *Il piacere*) are no less compellingly played. This may be counted among the very best middle-of-the-road versions of *The Four Seasons*, strongly recommended to first-time buyers. The well-balanced recording has brightness and life.

Violin Concertos, Op. 8 – Nos. 5-7, 9-11 and 12 (two versions).
Enrico Onofri *vn* **Paolo Grazzi** *ob*
Il Giardino Armonico / Antonini.
Teldec Das Alte Werk 4509-94566-2 (74 minutes: DDD). Recorded 1994-95.   ⒻⓅ

In the completion disc of Il Giardino Armonico's Op. 8, as two of the concertos exist in alternative forms, with oboe *vice* violin (RV236 = 454, RV178 = 449), they are given in both versions – with negligible differences in tempo. The virtues of Il Giardino Armonico are, if anything, even more vividly apparent in this recording. Onofri is once again spellbinding in his imaginative use of a varied continuo, here highlighted in the *Adagio* of RV362 (*La caccia*) played only by violin and theorbo. One complaint: if there is logic behind the order in which the concertos are presented, it is not apparent. The first volume has six concertos (61 minutes), Vol. 2 has eight (74 minutes), whereas to place Nos. 1-6 and RV454 on one disc, and Nos. 7-12 and RV449 on the other would have created no apparent problem. One would, however, need a far more compelling reason not to make a beeline for the nearest record store in search of these magical and finely recorded discs.

Cello Sonatas – E flat major, RV39; E minor, RV40; G minor, RV42; A minor, RV44; B flat major, RV45; B flat major, RV46.
Pieter Wispelwey *vc*
Florilegium Ensemble (Elizabeth Kenny, William Carter *ltes/theorboes/gtrs*
Daniel Yeadon *vc* Neal Peres da Costa *hpd/org*).
Channel Classics CCS6294 (66 minutes: DDD). Recorded 1994.   ⒻⓅ

Vivaldi wrote with great imagination for the cello, and the sonatas, like the concertos, are plentifully endowed with affecting melodies – the third movement of the E minor Sonata is a superb example – and virtuoso gestures. It would seem, on the strength of these pieces, that Vivaldi possessed a rare sensibility to the expressive *cantabile* possibilities in writing for the cello. Certainly, few baroque composers other than Bach and perhaps Geminiani realized the instrument's solo potential better than he. Wispelwey is a sensitive player who draws a warm if at times under-assertive sound from his instrument. Fast movements are clearly articulated, slow ones lyrically played with some feeling for the poetry of the music. The performances are thoughtful and enlightened, with a continuo group that includes organ, harpsichord, cello, archlutes, theorboes and guitars in a variety of combinations. The recorded sound is fine.

Trio Sonatas for Two Violins and Continuo, Op. 1 – No. 7 in E flat, RV65; No. 8 in D minor, RV64; No. 9 in A flat, RV75; No. 10 in B flat, RV78; No. 11 in B minor, RV79; No. 12 in D minor, RV63, 'Variations on La Follia'.
L'Arte dell'Arco / Christopher Hogwood *hpd/org*
Deutsche Harmonia Mundi 05472 77350-2 (54 minutes: DDD). Recorded 1997.   ⒻⓅ

The stronger works of Vivaldi's Op. 1 are concentrated within the second half of the set, recorded here. Among them is the best known of the Trios from the collection, the 20 variations on the theme of Spanish origin, *La Follia*. The instruments are tuned fractionally higher than today's concert pitch, rather than the lower A=415, around which most current period-instrument groups prefer to hover. Recent research points to a Venetian tradition of a higher, therefore brighter, pitch in the seventeenth and eighteenth centuries. Another feature of the recording lies in the instruments themselves, which belong to the collection of the Ospedale della Pietà with which Vivaldi was associated, on and off, throughout his working life. The performances are extremely appealing: great consideration is given to instrumental sonority and interplay, and careful thought has gone into the punctuation and phrasing of the music. In this way the listener is at once engaged both in the gesture and oratory of these beautifully crafted pieces. Vivaldi's layout of movements, in all but the last sonata of the set, loosely conforms with that of a typical *sonata da camera* and, within his chosen schemes, he injects all the expressive contrasts and rhythmic vitality which characterize his concertos. L'Arte dell'Arco sensibly, and to some effect, rings the changes of colour and texture in the basso continuo; cello, theorbo, harpsichord and chamber organ are all called upon but, in one of the sonatas, the two violins are supported by cello, without either keyboard or plucked string. With Hogwood's exemplary playing and tasteful judgement, the pleasure in this disc is complete.

---

12 Violin Sonatas, 'Manchester Sonatas' – No. 1 in C major, RV3; No. 2 in D minor, RV12; No. 3 in G minor, RV757; No. 4 in D major, RV755; No. 5 in B flat major, RV759; No. 6 in A major, RV758; No. 7 in C minor, RV6; No. 8 in G major, RV22; No. 9 in E minor, RV17a; No. 10 in B minor, RV760; No. 11 in E flat major; RV756; No. 12 in C major, RV754.
La Romanesca (Andrew Manze *vn* Nigel North *lte/theorbo/gtr* John Toll *hpd*).
Harmonia Mundi HMU90 7089/90 (two discs: 145 minutes: DDD). Recorded 1992.　　ⒻⒿⒺ

Vivaldi is so well known for his concertos that we are apt to overlook his admittedly much smaller output of sonatas. This set of 12 for violin and continuo was discovered in Manchester's Central Music Library during the 1970s though five of them exist in versions which have been known for much longer. It is probable that all of them date from the early- to mid-1720s when Vivaldi assembled them to present to Cardinal Ottoboni on the occasion of his visit to Venice, the city of his birth, in 1726. The violinist Andrew Manze has an appealing rapport with this music and is expressive in his shaping of phrases. He reveals sensibility towards Vivaldi's pleasing melodic contours. Indeed, this is a quality in which these sonatas abound, not only in the varied Preludes with which each Sonata begins but also in the brisker, sometimes very brisk allemandes and correntes. He ornaments the music with an effective blend of fantasy and good taste and he dispenses with bowed continuo instruments, preferring the lighter textures provided by harpsichord, archlute, theorbo or guitar. This is music of great beauty and vitality which will delight most if not all lovers of the late baroque; and it is sympathetically interpreted and warmly recorded.

Confitebor tibi Domine, RV596[a]. Deus tuorum militum, RV612[b]. Stabat mater in F minor, RV621[c]. In turbato mare, RV627[d]. O qui coeli terraeque serenitas, RV631[d]. Non in pratis aut in hortis, RV641[e].
[d]**Susan Gritton** *sop* [abe]**Jean Rigby** *mez* [c]**Robin Blaze** *counterten*
[ab]**Charles Daniels** *ten* [a]**Neal Davies** *bass*
The King's Consort / Robert King.
Hyperion CDA66799 (78 minutes: DDD). Texts and translations included. Recorded 1998.　　ⒻⒿ

This release in Robert King's complete cycle of Vivaldi's church music mainly features works unconnected with the Ospedale della Pietà including a motet written in Rome and the famous *Stabat mater* composed for a church in Brescia. All are for solo voice or voices and orchestra, and for the most part they carry the typical Vivaldi trademarks: boisterous energy alongside a tender if angular lyricism; a vivid and excitable responsiveness to verbal imagery; and what the insert-notes describe as 'a shocking radicalism: a willingness to strip music down to its core and reconstitute it from these simplest elements.' The best works on this disc are the first three. *In turbato mare* is a rip-roaring 'simile' motet which makes use of the old operatic device of comparing a troubled soul to a storm-tossed ship finding peace in port. The noble *Non in pratis aut in hortis* is an *introduzione*, a short motet designed to precede a performance of a lost *Miserere*; since it ends on a half-close, it is followed here (with musical if not liturgical logic) by the *Stabat mater*. All are excellently sung; few recordings exist of the first two, but it is hard to imagine the ebulliently virtuosic Susan Gritton and the movingly firm-voiced Jean Rigby being significantly bettered. By contrast, the *Stabat mater* is well-trodden territory, but the warmly mellifluous Robin Blaze easily matches his rivals on disc. The King's Consort is a little raw in the string department, but in general it shows bright and lively form and is well served by an acoustic perfectly suited to the occasion. Under King's direction, too, they capture splendidly the spirit of this uncomplicated but atmospheric music.

Dixit Dominus in D major, RV595[ab]. Domine ad adiuvandum me, RV593[a].
Credidi propter quod, RV605. Beatus vir in B flat major, RV598[ab]. Beatus vir in C major, RV597[abc].
[a]**Susan Gritton,** [b]**Catrin Wyn-Davies** *sops* [b]**Catherine Denley** *mez* [c]**Charles Daniels** *ten*
[c]**Neal Davies** *bar* [c]**Michael George** *bass*
Choir of The King's Consort; The King's Consort / Robert King.
Hyperion CDA66789 (70 minutes: DDD). Texts and translations included. Recorded 1997.　　ⒻⒿ

Vivaldi Choral and song

Here are two of Vivaldi's most extended and impressive psalm settings. These are the single-choir *Dixit Dominus*, RV595 (Psalm 110), and double-choir *Beatus vir*, RV597 (Psalm 112). Vivaldi set both psalms more than once and King's programme also includes the single movement *Beatus vir*, RV598, as well as the response, *Domine ad adiuvandum me*, RV593, and the conservatively styled Vesper psalm, *Credidi propter quod*, RV605. One aspect of this music which ought to strike listeners is its sheer variety. Not just variety in colour but also of expressive nuance achieved, as so often by Vivaldi, by gently beguiling inflexions, and by a simple directness of communication. Both of the generously proportioned psalm settings on this disc provide ample evidence of his originality in the sphere of sacred vocal music. The King's Consort Choir, some 20 voices in all, makes a lively and warm-textured contribution; the solo line-up is also quite strong; with Susan Gritton and Catrin Wyn-Davies providing an evenly matched, lightly articulated partnership in their two duets. Neal Davies and Michael George are splendidly robust in their vigorous 'Potens in terra' duet from *Beatus vir* (RV597). Catherine Denley gives an appropriately strongly inflected account of 'Judicabit in nationibus', but is intimate and tender in her beautiful 'De torrente in via bibet' (from *Dixit*). The remaining soloist, Charles Daniels, delivers the virtuoso 'Peccator videbit' (*Beatus vir*, RV597) with articulate lightness and comfortable agility. Though consisting of only three movements and of short duration, the G major *Domine ad adiuvandum me*, is easily on a level with the larger-scale pieces. Its expressive warmth is irresistible, its textual illustration effective and its structure taut, coherent and satisfying. A rewarding issue, well documented and spaciously recorded.

Domine ad adiuvandum me, RV593. Beatus vir, RV597. Stabat mater, RV621.
Magnificat, RV610a.
Ex Cathedra Chamber Choir and Baroque Orchestra / Jeffrey Skidmore.
ASV Gaudeamus CDGAU137 (70 minutes: DDD). Texts and translations included.
Recorded 1991.   Ⓕ Ⓟ

This is an interesting and mainly successful attempt to place a handful of Vivaldi's sacred pieces in a liturgical context. The most well-known work here is the *Stabat mater* for alto voice and strings, but the others deserve to be heard more often than they are. Ex Cathedra Chamber Choir is a well-disciplined, youthful sounding ensemble whose contribution to the recording is first-rate. And it is from the choir that solo voices emerge as required, giving the performances a homogeneity of sound and intent. The instrumentalists, too, make a strong contribution and together with the voices project interpretations which are full of vitality. There are, of course, rival versions on disc of all the music sung here but, on the strength of the thoughtful way it has been presented by the director of Ex Cathedra, Geoffrey Skidmore, this is perhaps the most affecting of them. Few will be disappointed, for example, by the gently inflected, poignant account of the *Stabat mater* by the countertenor Nigel Short. Hardly a detail has been overlooked, even to the extent of allowing the listener to hear a distant bell during the opening Versicle. In short, only the painfully and unnecessarily small typeface of the accompanying texts fails to please.

Gloria in D major, RV589. Magnificat in G minor, RV611. Concerto for Strings in D minor, RV243.
Concerto for Oboe, Trumpet and Strings in D major, RV563.
Deborah York, Patrizia Biccire *sops* **Sara Mingardo** *contr* **Andrea Mioh** *ob*
Gabriele Cassone *tpt*
Akademia; Concerto Italiano / Rinaldo Alessandrini.
Opus 111 OPS30 195 (60 minutes: DDD). Texts and translations included. Recorded 1997.   Ⓕ Ⓔ

Once you recover from the shock of hearing the opening chorus of Vivaldi's *Gloria* sung at what initially strikes you as a breakneck tempo, you will quickly begin to enter into the vital spirit of Rinaldo Alessandrini's performance. In fact it is not only this introductory movement that is thought-provoking but also the carefully considered tempos of several other sections of the work, some of them much slower than we have become used to. Alessandrini lays far greater emphasis than many of his rivals on the meaning of the Latin text. The two supplicatory sections, 'Domine Deus, Rex caelestis' and 'Domini Deus, Agnus Dei', are both sensitively handled with affective dynamic shading; in the first of them Alessandrini avails himself of Vivaldi's option for a violin solo rather than the more customarily heard oboe. The piece is lyrically sung by Deborah York with a beautifully sustained and imaginatively ornamented violin accompaniment played by Francesca Vicari. The soloist in the second of these movements, Sara Mingardo, also makes a favourable impression. The other sacred vocal work in this release is the latest of several adaptations Vivaldi made of a *Magnificat* which he had originally written for the Pietà. One of the principal differences between this version and the earlier ones lies in five effectively contrasted arias for named singers among the *figlie di coro* of the Pietà. In this performance the solos are distributed among three rather than five artists, but it hardly matters since each is sung with distinctive character and accomplished technique. Two concertos of contrasting aspect and instrumentation complete this very attractive programme. Both have been recorded previously, though, in the case of RV563 (sometimes encountered under the catalogue number RV781), not quite in the way it is performed here, with a natural trumpet and oboe as playful protagonists in the outer movements. In the slow movement the trumpet is tacet, the oboe assuming a solo role with scalewise passages of a somewhat vacuous character. Never mind, this is a rewarding issue above all, perhaps, for the expressive performance of the *Magnificat*.

In furore gustissimae irae, RV626. Longe mala, umbrae, terrores, RV629. Clarae stellae, scintillate, RV625. Canta in prato, ride in monte, RV623. Filiae mestae Jerusalem, RV638.
Nulla in mundo pax, RV630.
Deborah York *sop* **Catherine Denley** *mez* **James Bowman** *counterten*
The King's Consort / Robert King.
Hyperion CDA66779 (69 minutes: DDD). Texts and translations included. Recorded 1996. Ⓕ ⒫

This volume in Robert King's exploration of Vivaldi's sacred music offers five of his motets for solo voice and strings, together with RV623, one of the *Introduzioni* he composed to precede his liturgical choral pieces. As ever with Vivaldi, they are utterly beguiling pieces of music, impossible to dislike and easy to be beguiled by. Their Latin texts – which usually allow for two arias separated by a recitative and followed by an 'Alleluia' – are about as profound as the sonnets which accompany *The Four Seasons*, but they inspire in Vivaldi just the same kind of charmingly uncomplicated reaction. Nightingales, scenes of general Arcadian bliss, the storms of God's wrath and the touching sorrow of the mournful daughters of Jerusalem before the Cross – all bring forth what you might be tempted to call stock responses were it not for the fact that the music is always so instantly recognizable as being by Vivaldi. Vivaldi's singers must have been good to judge from these pieces, which show a brand of virtuosity more at home in the instrumental concerto than the aria. James Bowman and Catherine Denley are both on good form (the latter having a particularly taxing number to sing), but the star of the disc is Deborah York, yet another of the many outstanding young sopranos to have arrived on the scene in recent years. Her *In furore iustissimae irae* is a *tour de force* of vocal power and agility with a teasing little top C at the end of the first aria; while the deceptive beauties of *Nulla in mundo pax sincera* are artfully conjured by sly little *portamentos*. The string accompaniments throughout are buoyant but beefy, aided by an excellent recorded sound, and the tempos seem well judged.

Magnificat in G minor, RV610a[a]. Lauda Jerusalem in E minor, RV609[b]. Kyrie in G minor, RV587[c].
Credo in E minor, RV591[d]. Dixit Dominus in D major, RV594[e].
[abe]**Susan Gritton,** [abe]**Lisa Milne** *sops* [ae]**Catherine Denley** *mez* [ae]**Lynton Atkinson** *ten*
[e]**David Wilson-Johnson** *bar*
The King's Consort Choristers and Choir; The King's Consort / Robert King.
Hyperion CDA66769 (63 minutes: DDD). Texts and translations included. Recorded 1994. Ⓕ ⒫ Ⓔ

King's 'super-group' featuring choristers drawn from seven English cathedral and collegiate choirs sounds better than ever – technically reliable, with a good, full sound – and are a credit to King's vision in bringing them together. This volume has five typically uplifting works, three of which – *Lauda Jerusalem, Dixit Dominus* and the G minor *Kyrie* – offer the opulent sound of double choir and orchestra. *Dixit Dominus* is the most substantial, a colourful 23-minute sequence of varied solos and choruses, with trumpets, oboes and two organs all chipping in, most notably in an awe-inspiring depiction of the Day of Judgement. The other two are perhaps less striking, though *Lauda Jerusalem* is certainly charming in its two-soprano interchanges. Highlights of the single-chorus works include another exquisite soprano duet and a fiery 'Fecit potentiam' in the *Magnificat*, and an extraordinary 'Crucifixus' in the *Credo* which departs from the pain-wracked norm by seemingly depicting with lugubrious slow tread Christ's walk to Calvary. King manages very well in capturing the essence of Vivaldi's bold, sometimes disarmingly straightforward style. These tidy performances are driven with just the right amount of springy energy – neither too much nor too little – and are well recorded in the warm resonance of St Jude's Church, Hampstead in London.

Salve regina in C minor, RV616. Introduzione al Miserere, RV641. Introduzione al Gloria, RV637.
Salve regina in G minor, RV618. Concerto for Violin and Strings in C major, RV581
('per la Santissima Assenzione di Maria Vergine').
Gérard Lesne *counterten* **Fabio Biondi** *vn*
Il Seminario Musicale.
Virgin Classics Veritas VC7 59232-2 (77 minutes: DDD). Texts and translations included.
Recorded 1991. Ⓕ ⒫

The principal works here are two settings of the Marian antiphon *Salve regina*, but the French countertenor Gérard Lesne follows this with an extended *Introduzione* to a *Miserere*, one of two by

Vivaldi, and an *Introduzione* to a *Gloria*; and by way of making up a programme, he divides the four vocal pieces into two groups inserting a Violin Concerto between them. The main bias of this music is contemplative, often deeply so, as is the case with the darkly expressive, sorrowful introduction to the *Miserere non in pratis*. Lesne approaches the music with style. Indeed, a stronger advocate for these affecting compositions is hard to imagine since he is technically almost faultless. Then there is the Concerto in C major (*in due cori*), a splendid example of Vivaldi's skill in this medium, admirably played by the violinist Fabio Biondi with Lesne's own group Il Seminario Musicale. Vivaldi enthusiasts will require no further proof of this disc's merit, but readers in general should also find much to enjoy here, both in the singing and playing. The recorded sound is pleasantly resonant, serving the best interests of Lesne's voice and of the instruments too. A fine release.

Stabat mater, RV621. Cessate, omai cessate, RV684. Filiae mestae Jerusalem, RV638. String Concertos – C major, RV114; E flat major, RV130, 'Sonata al Santo Sepolcro'.
Andreas Scholl *counterten*
Ensemble 415 / Chiara Banchini *vn*
Harmonia Mundi HMC90 1571 (52 minutes: DDD). Texts and translations included.
Recorded 1995. ***Gramophone*** Award Winner 1996.　　　　　　　　　　Ⓕ**S**E

Here is a very attractively prepared menu whose main course is the *Stabat mater* for countertenor and strings. Hors-d'oeuvres and side-dishes consist of a ripieno concerto (RV114), a chamber cantata for countertenor and strings (RV684), a string sonata in E flat (RV130) and an introductory motet to a lost *Miserere* (RV638). Taken together, the pieces demonstrate something of Vivaldi's diverse style as a composer. The two instrumental works offer the strongest contrasts, the Concerto suggestive, above all in its opening movement, of an opera sinfonia, the Sonata redolent with poignant suspensions and darkly sonorous in its first movement, but yielding to a tautly constructed fugue in the second. The chamber cantata, if closely related to the two sacred vocal items on the disc in respect of tonal colour, differs from them in character. Conforming with the standard Italian cantata pattern at the time of two pairs of alternating recitative and *da capo* aria Vivaldi enlivens his pastoral idyll with two particularly affecting arias, the first with a palpitating pizzicato violin, the second a virtuoso vocal *tour de force* illustrating the plight of the forsaken lover. Andreas Scholl brings the whole thing off superbly with only a moment's faulty intonation at the close of the first aria. Unlike settings of the *Stabat mater* by Pergolesi and others, Vivaldi used only the first ten of the 20 stanzas of the poem. His deeply expressive setting of the poem will be familiar to many readers but few will have heard such an affecting performance as Scholl achieves here. The lyrical prayer of human yearning for faith contained in the 'Fac ut ardeat' movement is tenderly sung and here, as throughout the programme, sympathetically supported by Ensemble 415 under Chiara Banchini's experienced direction.

Juditha Triumphans, RV644.
Maria Cristina Kiehr *sop* **Ann Murray, Susan Bickley, Sarah Connolly, Jean Rigby** *mezzos*
The King's Consort Choir; The King's Consort / Robert King.
Hyperion CDA67281/2 (two discs: 148 minutes: DDD). Text and translation included.
Recorded 1997.　　　　　　　　　　　　　　　　　　　　　　　　　　　　Ⓕ

All the solo roles in Vivaldi's only surviving oratorio, *Juditha Triumphans*, were written for the female voices of the Ospedale della Pietà in Venice, where Vivaldi was, at the time, acting choirmaster. The work, with its Latin libretto by Giacomo Cassetti, dates from 1716. In his introduction, Michael Talbot surmises that the oratorio would have been introduced by a sinfonia. That seems likely, but none has survived, so two movements from one of Vivaldi's colourfully scored concertos *con molto stromenti* (RV555) serve as a preface to Robert King's recording. The cast, with Ann Murray in the title-role, is a strong one, and the wonderfully diverse instrumental obbligatos are a constant delight; yet the sum of the parts does not always add up to an entirely rewarding whole. The powerful drama is understated, overall, but this is the most stylish if not always the most dramatically satisfying of the versions to have appeared on disc. Certainly, Maria Cristina Kiehr turns in a performance of constant pleasure as Holofernes's servant Vagaus and Sarah Connolly's fuller-textured voice, with its warmth of timbre, conveys a sympathetic picture of Abra, Judith's servant. There is more passion to the story of Judith and Holofernes and Vivaldi's setting of it than we are allowed to hear in this performance but that said, King's reading, more than any other, allows us to revel in the sheer beauty and kaleidoscopic brilliance of Vivaldi's score. His singers and players have served him well.

Opera Arias and Sinfonias: Griselda – Sinfonia; Ombre vane, ingiusti orrori; Agitata da due venti.
Tito Manlio – Non ti lusinghi la crudeltade. Ottone in Villa – Sinfonia; Gelosia, tu già rendi l'alma

mia; L'ombre, l'aure, e ancora il rio[a]. L'Atenaide – Ferma, Teodosio. Bajazet – Sinfonia. L'Incoronazione di Dario – Non mi lusinga vana speranza. Catone in Utica – Se mai senti spirarti sul volto; Se in campo armato.
Emma Kirkby, [a]**Liliana Mazzarri** *sops*
The Brandenburg Consort / Roy Goodman.
Hyperion CDA66745 (75 minutes: DDD). Texts and translations included. Recorded 1994.   Ⓕ🅟

This release of arias and sinfonias from Vivaldi's operas gives us a *bonne bouche* of what lies in store for artists and record companies inclined to explore this still somewhat overlooked aspect of Vivaldi's output. The programme is also an entertaining one in its own right and it is far from being a mere highlights disc. The arias have been chosen with discernment, thoughtfully grouped and effectively interspersed with three of Vivaldi's opera *sinfonias*. The formula proves so successful that it even occurs to you that this was maybe the happiest solution to reviving at least the more problematic of Vivaldi's operas. Emma Kirkby's voice is still maturing, filling out, and she is able to achieve an ever increasing variety of colour. Her 'Ombre vane, ingiusti orrori', a ravishing piece from *Griselda* (1735), is beautifully and effortlessly controlled, delicately shaded and rhythmically vital; and her feeling for apposite embellishment comes across with pleasing spontaneity and stylistic assurance. The voice is supported and highlighted by the sympathetic partnership of The Brandenburg Consort conducted by Roy Goodman. This disc will delight Vivaldi enthusiasts. Excellent recorded sound.

Ottone in Villa.
Monica Groop *mez* Ottone; **Nancy Argenta** *sop* Caio Silio; **Susan Gritton** *sop* Cleonilla;
Sophie Daneman *sop* Tullia; **Mark Padmore** *ten* Decio;
Collegium Musicum 90 / Richard Hickox.
Chandos Chaconne CHAN0614 (two discs: 145 minutes: DDD). Notes, text and translation included. Recorded 1997.   Ⓕ🅟

Vivaldi claimed to have written over 90 stage works, but he may have been exaggerating. What is undeniable is that, much as we may marvel at the profusion of his concertos, which certainly brought him fame, he was most successful in his day as an opera composer. This, his very first opera, premièred in Vicenza in 1713, was an instant hit, and Vivaldi himself thought well enough of it to employ the music of one aria no fewer than five more times. The work was produced very simply, without special scenery or effects, and with modest forces – only five singers (one a castrato) and a small orchestra of strings, a pair of very economically used oboes doubling recorders, and continuo. The story is a relatively uncomplicated one by the standards of baroque opera, of amatory pretences and misunderstandings: it has been admirably summarized by Eric Cross (who has edited the work) as a 'light-weight, amoral entertainment in which the flirtatious Cleonilla consistently has the upper hand, and gullible Emperor Ottone (a far from heroic figure) never discovers the truth about the way he has been deceived'. The score proceeds in a succession of *secco* recitatives (with just a very occasional *accompagnato*) and *da capo* arias – which the present cast ornament very stylishly.

There are no duets or ensembles except for a perfunctory final chorus in which the characters merely sing in unison; but there is an abundance of tuneful arias, and when Vivaldi can be bothered to write proper accompaniments to them – he often merely has violins doubling the voice, plus a bass-line – he can provide interesting imitative counterpoint. Several arias employ only the upper strings without cello and bass except in ritornellos. The small Vicenza theatre could not afford star singers, so only limited opportunities were provided for vocal virtuosity; but the present cast makes the most of its opportunities, both in display and in meditative mood. It is not always easy to tell the three sopranos apart, but Susan Gritton well suggests the scheming minx Cleonilla; Nancy Argenta with her bright voice has the castrato role that includes several fine arias, and displays a *messa di voce* in an echo aria; and Sophie Daneman, in a breeches role, produces a wide range of colour. Monica Groop slightly undercharacterizes Ottone except when roused to dismiss Rome's anxiety at his dalliance. It is quite a relief to hear one male voice, and Mark Padmore is excellent. Richard Hickox keeps a firm rhythmic hand on everything and delivers quite the best and neatest Vivaldi operatic recording yet.

Tito Manlio.
Giancarlo Luccardi *bass* Tito Manlio; **Norma Lerer** *mez* Decio; **Margaret Marshall** *sop* Lucio;
Júlia Hamari *mez* Servilia; **Rose Wagemann** *mez* Manlio; **Birgit Finnilä** *mez* Vitellia;
Domenico Trimarchi *bar* Lindo; **Claes Hakon Ahnsjö** *ten* Geminio;
Berlin Radio Chorus; Berlin Chamber Orchestra / Vittorio Negri.
Philips 446 332-2PM4 (four discs: 238 minutes: ADD). Notes, text and translation included. Recorded 1977.   Ⓜ

Vivaldi Opera

Tito Manlio was produced for the Mantuan Carnival season in 1719 and, if we are to believe a note by Vivaldi himself at the head of the score, was written in the space of five days. This recording of the work was first issued on LP in 1978. *Tito Manlio* certainly ranks among one of the most successful of the Vivaldi operas so far commercially recorded. The libretto, by Matteo Noris, whom Vivaldi set on more than one occasion, centres round a dispute between the Romans and the Latins which has arisen because the Roman Senate, headed by Titus Manlius, has denied the Latins a consul of Latin birth. The Latins declare war on Rome but, since until now the opposing camps have been on friendly terms, Titus forbids his son Manlius to engage the enemy in single combat. Manlius disobeys him and is sentenced to death by his father. These events, together with drama provided by lovers separated by war, sustain the opera successfully by and large, through three substantial acts. All this takes place in about BC340, by the way.

Vivaldi's melodic invention is alluring and, if the libretto is no masterpiece, at least it provides a wealth of opportunities for evocative image painting. The role of Lucio is stylishly sung by Margaret Marshall. Titus's daughter Vitellia, sung by Birgit Finnilä, is also allotted some engaging music. Then there is Titus's music, sung by Giancarlo Luccardi; he had a reputation as a stern consul and Vivaldi underlines this side of his character with some robust arias. Manlius, Titus's son, sung by Rose Wagemann, also has some strong arias – not surprisingly since his predicament seems hopeless on all fronts. In short, this is an opera which both in content and performance, albeit dated in some respects, goes some way towards rehabilitating Vivaldi in the minds of readers who, over the years, have encountered more than their fair share of indifferent recordings. The cast is mainly a strong one, with the Berlin Chamber Orchestra (using modern instruments) providing solid support. If the overture to the work has survived it can no longer be identified. Negri, instead, has chosen three movements from three different concertos (RV562, 579 and 141). The solution is both apt in context and extremely effective. A welcome and stimulating reissue.

Kevin Volans

South African 1949

This is How it is[a]. Walking Song. Leaping Dance[a]. Concerto for Piano and Wind Instruments[bc]. Untitled (In memoriam G.H.V.)[ad].
[c]**Peter Donohoe,** [d]**Kevin Volans** *pfs*
Netherlands Wind Ensemble / [a]**Wim Steinmann,** [b]**Daniel Harding.**
Chandos New Direction CHAN9563 (59 minutes: DDD). Recorded 1995-96.   Ⓕ

Often Volans will end a piece with new material in such a way that the listener is left hanging (as at the end of *Leaping Dance* and *Untitled*), waiting for a sense of closure that never comes; the vernacular African elements on this disc are presented almost raw, giving them a poignancy peculiar to Volans's music. At his best he can create a sound that is arrestingly beautiful and sustain interest in the way it is developed for the whole of the piece. For this reason *Walking Song*, *Leaping Dance* and *Untitled* are the pieces to listen to first, for they communicate their ideas with a rare combination of directness and sophistication. But it is surprising that *This is How it is* was placed at the start of the CD as it seems by far the weakest piece and, although the Concerto has many striking textures, it is doubtful whether it sustains them effectively throughout. Despite Peter Donohoe's remarkably sensitive performance, the Concerto's frequent references to the slow wind chords from Stravinsky's *Symphony of Wind Instruments* inevitably lead to a loss of musical tension. However, there is much to entrance the listener here, played with commitment and textural sensitivity by the Netherlands Wind Ensemble. Anyone who has fallen under the spell of *White Man Sleeps* should definitely consider buying this disc.

Jan Voříšek

Bohemian 1791-1825

12 Rhapsodies, Op. 1. Le désir, Op. 3. Le plaisir, Op. 4.
Artur Pizarro *pf*
Collins Classics 1477-2 (75 minutes: DDD). Recorded 1996.   Ⓕ Ⓔ

Voříšek's output was small: having already recorded the better known piano works (also on Collins Classics), Artur Pizarro here virtually completes the solo piano music with the youthful *Rhapsodies* and two other early works. Commended by Beethoven, the 12 *Rhapsodies* are all similar in form (a basic ternary ABA), expression (fast and often virtuosic outer sections with a contrasting lyrical middle section), and style (strong rhythmic elements including frequent accents and syncopation, diminished chords, and rapid modulation). Pizarro's performances are exceptional in every respect: the spiritual bravura of his *perpetuum mobile* playing is matched by his complete control, crystalline clarity and rhythmic incisiveness. The articulation of the *Third Rhapsody* (similar in texture and profile to the second movement of the *Fantasia*), the softer focus of the delicate Sixth *Rhapsody*, and the rhythmic momentum of the Eleventh (a daring precursor to Alkan's fearsome 'Comme le vent' from *Etudes dan les tons mineurs*) are by turns enchanting and astonishing. The remaining two works are played with equal stylishness, although ultimately they are not quite so involving. The recordings are suitably bright – a wonderful disc.

Richard Wagner

German 1813-1883

Lohengrin – Prelude. Tannhäuser – Overture. Siegfried Idyll. Götterdämmerung – Siegfried's Rhine Journey; Siegfried's Funeral March.
Lucerne Festival Orchestra; Vienna Philharmonic Orchestra / Wilhelm Furtwängler.
Testament mono SBT1141 (61 minutes: ADD). Recorded late 1940s.   Ⓕ 🅷

This is, as they say, something else. The *Lohengrin* Act 1 Prelude opens the disc of studio recordings, the only item of five – all Walter Legge produced – with the Lucerne Festival Orchestra. The way the Swiss brass *crescendos* on the upbeat to the climactic delivery of the hymn must rate as among the most elating of all Furtwängler moments. Why this and the *Tannhäuser* Overture have never been issued before remains a mystery, as probably do *all* the reasons why, in the latter piece, the Vienna Philharmonic sounds on fire for Furtwängler and on duty for, say, Knappertsbusch in 1953 (once available on a Decca LP). Siegfried's Rhine Journey evolves in one seamless sweep, barring the split-second but disconcerting rhythmic hiatus at the moment of take-off (4'51"). And mercifully Furtwängler doesn't tag on the trite concert ending (as did Reiner and Toscanini), giving a chance to wonder at the uniquely resonant low brass sounds of the VPO. Then on to the Funeral March, every dark sound fully charting the depths, every phrase carrying special import, and, as in the *Siegfried Idyll*, the occasional passage reminding us of standards of tuning of the day. The latter account, Furtwängler's only recording of the piece, engages rather than diverts and charms, with Vienna string playing typically sweet and rapturous, and 'Siegfried, Hope of the World' tensely built to an almost delirious climax. Depth, presence and a very naturally achieved clarity characterize all these recordings, and 78 sources only occasionally make their presence felt.

Der Ring des Nibelungen – spoken introduction with 193 musical examples.
Deryck Cooke *narr* **various singers;**
Vienna Philharmonic Orchestra / Sir Georg Solti.
Decca The Classic Sound 443 581-2DCS2 (two discs: 141 minutes: ADD). Booklet of musical illustrations included. Recorded 1967.   Ⓜ

Deryck Cooke died, prematurely, in 1976 before he completed his comprehensive study on *The Ring*. Fortunately, in 1967, Decca had had the foresight to invite him to record this introduction to the cycle. In this he developed at length his ideas on its leitmotifs using 193 examples, most of them taken from the Solti recording, and a few made specifically to illustrate a point Cooke was making. Wagner, as he avers, described the motifs as 'melodic moments of feeling', not signposts or tags. He also adds that their psychological significance and development are of the essence in comprehending *The Ring*, and divides them into four groups – character, objects, events and emotions – which he then proceeds to describe, in simple, pungent language, how they are deployed throughout the work. His straightforward, unfussy method and delivery, so typical of a man quite without egotistical pretension, enhances one's understanding and, more important, enjoyment of this mighty work. It is an essential adjunct to anybody's recording of the cycle.

Tannhäuser – Overture and Venusberg Music. Die Meistersinger von Nürnberg – Prelude, Act 3. Tristan und Isolde – Prelude and Liebestod.
Berlin Philharmonic Orchestra / Herbert von Karajan.
DG Karajan Gold 439 022-2GHS (50 minutes: DDD). Recorded 1984.   Ⓕ

What is so special about Karajan's digital recordings that they are reissued at full price and, ungenerously in this case, with only their original programme? The answer might be another question: when, in modern times, have you heard from Berlin (or anywhere else) such long-drawn, ripe, intense, characterful, perfectly formed and supremely controlled Wagner playing? Not from some other sources with the *Tannhäuser* Overture, whose Pilgrims are less solemn and grand and whose revellers produce less of Karajan's joyous *éclat*. Moving on a few minutes, and the passage where Karajan's Venus succeeds in quelling the riot finds Karajan effecting a spellbinding sudden *diminuendo* (from 4'41", track 2), leaving us with the enchanted eddying of the orchestra. It must surely qualify as one of Karajan's 'greatest moments', had not the seemingly unstoppable tidal wave that preceded it already done so. The true keeper of Berlin's 'Wagner on record' latterly has been

Daniel Barenboim. His *Tristan* Prelude (taken from the complete set, reviewed below), is more conventionally paced (i.e. faster) than Karajan's, with the phrasing just as steeply raked, and the balance and control, in some respects, even more accomplished. But the breadth of Karajan's conception is matched by his concentration (it never feels too slow), the playing is achingly intense, the whole superbly built, and the reserves of tone he is able to draw on for the climax seem limitless.

Tristan und Isolde – Love Music (arr. Stokowski). Die Walküre – Ride of the Valkyries; Wotan's Farewell and Magic Fire Music. Götterdämmerung – Siegfried's Death and Funeral March (both arr. Gerhardt). Siegfried Idyll.
National Philharmonic Orchestra / Charles Gerhardt.
Chesky CD161 (78 minutes: DDD). Recorded 1985-95. Ⓕ

Charles Gerhardt opens with Stokowski's unashamedly indulgent synthesis of the themes from *Tristan und Isolde*, with the vocal parts seamlessly welded into the orchestration, beginning at the Introduction to Act 2, including the Love Music from the same act and the Liebestod. Gerhardt moves naturally from yearning and languishing to real passion, following Stokowski in using divided strings, employing 16 first violins, ten second violins, 12 violas and 12 double-basses. The off-stage six-part hunting-horn episode (at 1'35") sounds glorious with the expansion to ten horns weighted with a bass trombone, Wotan's infinitely touching Farewell to his daughter, Brünnhilde, in *Die Walküre*, and the following truly magical Fire Music. Even without the voices the tremendously committed string playing is very moving indeed, and the recording is superb. The *Siegfried Idyll* is also beautifully played and makes a flowing, gentle interlude. Gerhardt lets the tension slip a little in the middle but gathers the themes together magnetically in the involving closing section. He then begins Siegfried's Death and Funeral March earlier than Stokowski, at the moment when Hagen kills Siegfried. The result is very direct and powerful with fine brass playing. The Valkyries then ride, or rather gallop in at breakneck speed to finish the concert exuberantly. The recordings were made in Walthamstow (*Tristan*, 1985), All Saint's, Petersham (*Die Walküre*, 1994 – the best sound of all), Air Studios (*Siegfried Idyll*, 1995), (*Götterdämmerung*, St John's, Smith Square, 1990), and the Valkyries bring another clear, bright studio offering (1995). This is a record for hi-fi buffs, and on really discerning equipment it is fascinating to compare the way the five different engineers have coped with the widely varying ambience effects, with their microphone placing.

Die Walküre – Ride of the Valkyries; Wotan's Farewell and Magic Fire Music. Siegfried – Forest murmurs. Götterdämmerung – Siegfried's Rhine Journey; Siegfried's funeral march and Immolation scene. Siegfried Idyll.
Staatskapelle Dresden / Donald Runnicles.
Teldec 0630-17109-2 (74 minutes: DDD). Recorded live in 1996. Ⓕ

These excerpts are taken not from opera performances, but from an orchestral concert in the Dresden Staatsoper – and what a magnificently expansive acoustic it has! At the opening of the programme the Valkyries ride in with tremendous weight and purpose; and if when following on, the tearingly poignant scene of 'Wotan's Farewell' begins rather in mid-stream, from then onwards one has the sense of a firm and continuing narrative line. Runnicles paces with the experience of the opera house and creates the most natural ebb and flow of tempo, conveying at first great tenderness, and then on through Wotan's very human grief to the passion of Loge's Fire music (glorious string playing throughout). The Forest murmurs acts as a central interlude, Wagner's tone-painting delightfully evoked, with flashes of urgency anticipating Siegfried's coming quest. In the great Immolation scene so powerful is that final conflagration of brass, with its overriding lyrical string apotheosis, that one is almost aware of the heat of the flames. Throughout, Runnicles generates maximum tension, and one never has the sense that these are just excerpts, purple patches; instead one is carried satisfyingly onwards to the gods' final nemesis and the destruction of Valhalla. The glorious *Siegfried Idyll* acts as a touchingly romantic epilogue. Again the orchestra plays very beautifully indeed. Overall this is one of the finest and most moving single-disc summations of what Wagner's orchestral writing is all about, and in the *Ring* the orchestra tells us everything that is happening on stage.

Tannhäuser – Dich teure Halle. Die Walküre – Der Männer Sippe. Der fliegende Holländer – Joho hoe! Traft ihr das Schiff. Götterdämmerung – Höre mit Sinn; Starke Scheite. Lohengrin – Einsam in trüben Tagen. Parsifal – Grausamer! Fühlst du im Herzen. Tristan und Isolde – Wie lachend sie.
Waltraud Meier *mez*
Bavarian Radio Symphony Orchestra / Lorin Maazel.
RCA Red Seal 09026 68766-2 (72 minutes: DDD). Texts and translations included.
Recorded 1996-97. ⒻⒺ

This is without question the most thrilling Wagner disc to appear in years. Bleeding chunks have had a bad press, but when they are performed like this, with utter conviction, verbal acuity and vocal control, producing results at once inspiriting and deeply moving, criticism is silenced. Meier and Maazel have reached, instinctively or not, an ideal rapport: together they create a unanimity of outlook based on urgency in conveying the sense of each passage, so that each heroine comes before us newly minted, at speeds in every case faster than what has become the custom today. In Senta's Ballad, Meier and Maazel bring before us, so immediately, the distraught, possessed woman of Wagner's imagining. Then we hear an Elsa totally convinced of her saviour's arrival, as Meier, with her ever vivid word-painting, mentions 'Ein golden Horn', a more positive girl than usual. Waltraute's Narration, benefiting from Maazel's forward-moving tempo and Meier's deeply felt utterance, coheres into a symbol of Wagner's late mastery. Kundry is portrayed as truly trying to win back Parsifal. Isolde's irony is felt in every bar of her Narration and Curse: it's the ability to imprint the smallest phrase on the mind that so distinguishes all these readings and makes them special. You hear that again in Sieglinde's compelling description of Wotan's appearance, even more in Brünnhilde's Immolation. Meier is reaching towards the pinnacle of Wagner singing represented by this latter role; here are the strength of will and the pathos called for by the great finale. The Bavarian Radio Symphony sounds truly committed to Maazel, who faithfully follows the ebb and flow of Meier's singing, and the recording, sympathetic to the voice, offers worthy support.

Tannhäuser – Overture. Siegfried Idyll. Tristan und Isolde – Prelude and Liebestod.
Jessye Norman *sop*
Vienna Philharmonic Orchestra / Herbert von Karajan.
DG 423 613-2GH (54 minutes: DDD). Text and translation included. Recorded live in 1987.   Ⓕ

For the Wagner specialist who has a complete *Tannhäuser* and *Tristan* on the shelves, this disc involves some duplication. Even so, it is not hard to make room for such performances as are heard here. For the non-specialist, the programme provides a good opportunity for a meeting halfway, the common ground between Master and general music-lover being the *Siegfried Idyll*. This offers 20 minutes of delight in the play of musical ideas, structured and yet impulsive, within a sustained mood of gentle affection. The orchestration is something of a miracle, and it can rarely have been heard to better advantage than in this recording, where the ever-changing textures are so clearly displayed and where from every section of the orchestra the sound is of such great loveliness. It comes as a welcome contrast to the *Tannhäuser* Overture, with its big tunes and *fortissimos*, the whole orchestra surging in a frank simulation of physical passion. A further contrast is to follow in the *Tristan* Prelude, where again Karajan and his players are at their best in their feeling for texture and their control of pulse. Jessye Norman, singing the Liebestod with tenderness and vibrant opulence of tone, brings the recital to an end. There is scarcely a single reminder that it was recorded live.

Wesendonk Lieder. Tristan und Isolde – Prelude, Act 1; Mild und leise. Götterdämmerung – Dawn and Siegfried's Rhine Journey; Starke Scheite.
Julia Varady *sop*
Deutsches Symphony Orchestra, Berlin / Dietrich Fischer-Dieskau.
Orfeo C467981A (71 minutes: DDD). Texts and translations included. Recorded 1997.   Ⓕ 🅑

This is a truly riveting recital of Wagner from Varady (magnificent singing) and Fischer-Dieskau. There have been few such warmly and intelligently sung versions of the Immolation. Maybe on stage Brünnhilde might have been beyond Varady; here there's not a sign of strain as she rides the orchestra, sympathetically supported by her husband. But what makes it stand out from performances by possibly better-endowed sopranos is her deep understanding of the text: again and again, nowhere more so than at 'Ruhe, ruhe, du Gott', where Varady's vibrating lower register is so effective, you feel the tingle factor coming to the fore. Earlier, the passage starting 'Wie Sonne lauter' benefits from the lyrical sound and faultless line Varady exhibits; then in the more heroic final sections, this Brünnhilde is like a woman transfigured. And transfiguration is, of course, a feature of Varady's concentrated, urgent Liebestod, her complete absorption with the text as much as with the music an object-lesson in great Wagner singing. Her reading of the *Wesendonk Lieder* is no less remarkable, no less enthralling. Nothing here of the slow, wallowing approach often favoured today. The feeling of the words is one of very present emotions. Try the final section of 'Stehe still!' starting 'Die Lippe verstummt' or the emphasis on the single word 'Smaragd' in 'Im Treibhaus' or the whole of a most beautifully etched 'Träume'. She is surely helped here by Fischer-Dieskau's refusal to indulge the music. On his own the *Tristan* Prelude and the *Götterdämmerung* Dawn and Rhine Journey are keenly shaped. The players of his Berlin orchestra cover themselves in glory. The recording is exemplary. A 'must' for admirers of this astonishing artist and for Wagnerians.

Der fliegende Holländer.
Theo Adam *bar* Holländer; **Anja Silja** *sop* Senta; **Martti Talvela** *bass* Daland;
Ernst Kozub *ten* Erik; **Annelies Burmeister** *mez* Mary; **Gerhard Unger** *ten* Steuermann;
BBC Chorus; New Philharmonia Orchestra / Otto Klemperer.
EMI CDS5 55179-2 (three discs: 152 minutes: ADD). Notes, text and translation included.
Recorded 1968. Ⓕ **RR**

Klemperer's magisterial interpretation of this work was unavailable in any form for far too long so that its reissue was most welcome. As ever, Klemperer by and large justifies some moderate tempos by the way in which he sustains line and emphasizes detail. Only once or twice – in the Spinning and Sailors choruses – do you sense a lack of propulsion. Otherwise there is throughout a blazing intensity to the reading that brooks no denial. The storm and sea music in the Overture and thereafter is given stunning power, and the Dutchman's torture and passion is evoked in the orchestra. Indeed, the playing of the New Philharmonia is a bonus throughout. Klemperer catches as convincingly as anyone the elemental feeling of the work – the sense of the sea, basic passions and the interplay of character unerringly adumbrated. There have been few baritones before or since Theo Adam who have sustained the line of the Dutchman so well and so intelligently reached the heart of the matter where the text is concerned. Silja's bright, sometimes piercing timbre isn't to everyone's taste, but hers is a most moving portrayal of trust and loyalty and love unto death, the interpretation of an outstanding singing-actress. Martti Talvela, singing magnificently and suggesting a formidable presence, is a bluff, burly Daland. Ernst Kozub's Erik has its clumsy moments but one admires the shining tone. Gerhard Unger offers an ardent, cleanly articulated Sailor. Annelies Burmeister is a ripe Mary. The BBC Chorus is very much in the picture. The overall sound is a shade on the dry side, but better that than the excessive reverberation on so many opera sets today.

Der fliegende Holländer.
Robert Hale *bass-bar* Holländer; **Hildegard Behrens** *sop* Senta; **Kurt Rydl** *bass* Daland;
Josef Protschka *ten* Erik; **Iris Vermillion** *mez* Mary; **Uwe Heilmann** *ten* Steuermann;
Vienna State Opera Concert Choir;
Vienna Philharmonic Orchestra / Christoph von Dohnányi.
Decca 436 418-2DHO2 (two discs: 145 minutes: DDD). Notes, text and translation included.
Recorded 1991. Ⓕ **E**

Singers, conductor, chorus, orchestra and engineers combine to make Dohnányi's set the most successful modern recording of the work. With the Vienna Philharmonic responding to Dohnányi's precise and energizing beat from start to finish the sea does really seem to course through the score as Wagner intended. Dohnányi emphasizes the raw, even untutored sound of much of the orchestration, giving the wind and brass the prominence they deserve. Taut, springy rhythms abound from the Overture onwards. He opts for the three-act version and the full ending. Hale is an exemplary Dutchman and sings with great depth and understanding. This is evident throughout a masterly traversal of his long monologue, where the required torment in the tone is revealed to the full. Behrens captures Senta's single-minded passion and infatuation, singing the quieter passages with refined sensitivity, the forceful ones with fearless attack; and satisfaction extends to the lesser roles. The chorus is superb as sailors, ghost crew and townspeople, singing with firm tone and exact attack. Nothing here is left unconsidered yet, amazingly, for the most part a real sense of the theatre is achieved throughout. For that we have to thank the Decca team. Balance, depth, perspectives all seem blessedly natural; undoctored and inevitable, so that one is able to take the sound picture for granted.

Lohengrin.
Paul Frey *ten* Lohengrin; **Cheryl Studer** *sop* Elsa; **Gabriele Schnaut** *sop* Ortrud;
Ekkehard Wlaschiha *bar* Telramund; **Manfred Schenk** *bass* King Henry;
Eike Wilm Schulte *bar* Herald;
Bayreuth Festival Chorus and Orchestra / Peter Schneider.
Philips 434 602-2PH4 (four discs: 212 minutes: DDD). Notes, text and translation included.
Recorded 1990. Ⓜ **RR**

Schneider's is a splendidly absorbing performance of *Lohengrin*. This underrated conductor provides a straightforward, no-nonsense reading in the best *Kapellmeister* tradition, avoiding the extremes of tempo interpretation of some more highly-powered conductors. He obtains playing and singing of the highest calibre from the Bayreuth orchestra and chorus, sustains the long and sometimes tedious-seeming paragraphs of Acts 1 and 2 without ever allowing boredom to intervene, and brings extraordinary tension to such forward-looking scenes as Lohengrin's arrival, the

Ortrud-Telramund dialogue and the psychologically intense duet for Elsa and Lohengrin in Act 3. Elsa was one of the roles with which Studer made her name on the international scene; she sings it here once more with refulgent tone, understanding of the text and comprehension of Elsa's dreamy then troubled personality. Particularly affecting is her desperate appeal to Lohengrin at the end of Act 2. Paul Frey is a sensitive, chivalrous Lohengrin, even if his voice hasn't quite the Heldentenor strength of some of his predecessors. Evil is reasonably well represented. Wlaschiha is a vital and nasty Telramund, keenly projecting the character's chip-on-the-shoulder malevolence of the words. Schnaut has an imposing, powerful soprano although more could have been made of the words than she achieves. Schenk is a well-routined King, Schulte a superb Herald. Incidentally, Schneider observes the traditional (Wagner's) cut just before Lohengrin's Farewell, although the passage is printed in full in the booklet. This set is well worth considering in a sparse recommendable field of available versions.

Lohengrin.
James King *ten* Lohengrin; **Gundula Janowitz** *sop* Elsa; **Dame Gwyneth Jones** *sop* Ortrud;
Thomas Stewart *bar* Telramund; **Karl Ridderbusch** *bass* King Henry;
Gerd Nienstedt *bass* Herald;
Bavarian Radio Chorus and Symphony Orchestra / Rafael Kubelík.
DG 449 591-2GX3 (three discs: 222 minutes: ADD). Notes, text and translation included. Ⓜ
Recorded 1971.

The attributes of Kubelík's *Lohengrin* have been underestimated. It will hold your interest from first to last, not least thanks to Kubelík's masterly overview. Not only does he successfully hold together all the disparate strands of the sprawling work, he also imparts to them a sense of inner excitement through his close attention to the small notes and phrases that so often delineate character in this score and through his vital control of the large ensembles. He is helped inestimably by the Bavarian Radio forces – gloriously singing strings, characterful winds, trenchant, involving chorus – of which he was, in 1971, a beloved chief. There's never a dull moment in his vivid, theatrical *Lohengrin*. The recording imparts a suitably spacious atmosphere to the piece but also places the principals up front where they should be except when distancing is required – as at Lohengrin's first appearance and at the moment when Elsa appears on the balcony to address the night breezes. Janowitz's Elsa is one of the set's major assets. Pure in tone, imaginative in phrasing, she catches the ear from her first entry, very much suggesting Elsa's vulnerability. Later she eloquently conveys her deep feelings in the love duet, followed by her voicing of all the doubts that beset her character.

King's Lohengrin is more ordinary; today we would be grateful for such solid, musical and well-judged singing. Few if any Lohengrins can sing the passage starting 'Höchstes Vertraun' (third disc, track 5) with anything like King's true tone and powerful conviction. Though not as detailed or subtle in his colouring of the text as some, Thomas Stewart sings a sturdy Telramund, managing the high tessitura with consummate ease. He is horribly plausible in his complaints against Elsa. This portrayal discloses him as a grossly undervalued singer. Dame Gwyneth Jones's portrayal, taken all-round, is reasonably convincing despite turning a vibrato that might flatteringly be called opulent into something more objectionable. Her Ortrud registers high on the scale of vicious malevolence in the part. The difficulty, as it always has been with this intelligent artist, is that the subtlety evinced in quiet passages is vitiated when the tone comes under pressure – but some Ortruds today are far more guilty in that respect than Jones. As King Henry, Ridderbusch offers a judicious blend of sympathy and authority dispensed in fluent, warm tone. Nienstedt makes the Herald's pronouncements moments to savour. The chorus are nothing short of superb. So, this makes an irresistible bid for recommendation. It is well recorded, sounding wholly resplendent and as cogently conducted as any of its rivals.

Lohengrin.
Peter Seiffert *ten* Lohengrin; **Emily Magee** *sop* Elsa; **Deborah Polaski** *sop* Ortrud;
Falk Struckmann *bar* Telramund; **René Pape** *bass* King Henry; **Roman Trekel** *bar* Herald;
Chorus of the Deutsche Oper, Berlin; Staatskapelle Berlin / Daniel Barenboim.
Teldec 3984-21484-2 (three discs: 211 minutes: DDD). Notes, texts and translations included. Ⓕ
Recorded 1997.

This recording is based on the cast with which Barenboim performed the opera at the Berlin State Opera in 1996, although the tenor taking the title-role is different, and it benefits from that stage experience in terms of dedicated, confident readings on all sides, most of all in the execution of Barenboim's superbly disciplined chorus and orchestra. The chorus, so important in this work, sings with refinement, discipline and enthusiasm in its many roles while all departments of the orchestra play the score to the hilt. Barenboim himself manages to give an overriding unity to a work that can, in lesser hands, sprawl. That's particularly true as regards Act 2, where all the comings-and-goings can test a listener's concentration; not here when the conductor so unerringly weaves the disparate elements into a coherent, forward-moving whole. Barenboim is also to be commended for playing Act 3 complete, restoring not only the theatre cuts often made in recording but also the second verse of Lohengrin's Grail narration, cut by Wagner before the first night. In the opera house it is sensibly omitted because it lengthens the act unduly and gives a flagging tenor too much to do, but it's good to have it included here. The only reservation concerns the famous Prelude to Act 3 which seems too brash and too fast; perhaps Barenboim was trying to say something new about the overfamiliar. All the singers, bar one, are regulars at the Berlin State Opera. The exception is Seiffert as Lohengrin, who in tone, phrasing and sheer lyrical ardour makes a near-ideal white knight. His Elsa is Emily Magee, her tone full and refulgent, her interpretation deeply felt. The one worry is that her voice is so much like that of Polaski that they are hard to tell apart in their long confrontation in Act 2. Polaski makes a splendidly forceful and articulate Ortrud, only very occasionally sounding taxed by heavier passages, most worryingly in her closing imprecations. Struckmann's Telramund isn't as tortured as Fischer-Dieskau's in Kempe's set, but these vital, involving interpretations have their own validity. Pape is a model King Henry, pouring out his concerns in golden tone. Trekel is a strong Herald. The set is enhanced by a perfectly balanced and warm recording.

Die Meistersinger von Nürnberg.
Bernd Weikl bar Hans Sachs; **Ben Heppner** ten Walther; **Cheryl Studer** sop Eva;
Kurt Moll bass Pogner; **Siegfried Lorenz** bar Beckmesser; **Deon van der Walt** ten David;
Cornelia Kallisch contr Magdalene; **Hans-Joachim Ketelsen** bar Kothner;
Michael Schade ten Vogelgesang; **Hans Wilbrink** bar Nachtigall; **Ulrich Ress** ten Zorn;
Hermann Sapell bar Eisslinger; **Roland Wagenführer** ten Moser; **Rainer Büse** bass Ortel;
Guido Götzen bass Schwarz; **Friedmann Kunder** bass Foltz; **René Pape** bass Nightwatchman;
Bavarian State Opera Chorus; Bavarian State Orchestra / Wolfgang Sawallisch.
EMI CDS5 55142-2 (four discs: 257 minutes: DDD). Notes, text and translation included.
Recorded 1993. Ⓕ 🆁🆁

Sawallisch's *Meistersinger* is very much a version for today – profoundly musical, as it was bound to be under him, sung with a consistent beauty of sound, and recorded truthfully and spaciously. Anybody coming to the work for the first time, and wanting a version backed by modern sound, will find it a sensible choice, a performance for the most part measuring up to the score's many demands on its interpreters. Sawallisch obtains singing and playing on the highest level of achievement, observant of detail, rich in texture, sure in pacing and – very important in this score – anxious to move forward where there is any danger of the music seeming over-extended, as in the recital of the tones and the Act 2 episode of Beckmesser's courting. Sawallisch's reading also catches the warmth that pervades the whole opera, yet is also successful in deftly projecting its comedy. It must be said, however, that with Sawallisch the earth doesn't move, the spirit is seldom lifted as it should be. On the other hand, nobody is better than Sawallisch at characterizing the disputes between the Masters in Act 1, or the pointed humour of the Act 2 Sachs/Beckmesser scene, and much else of that nature is unobtrusively right. Where the recording itself is concerned, great care has been taken over the placing of the singers in relation to one another and the correct distancing of the voices where called for. The balance in relation to the orchestra seems just about ideal. In the modern manner the chorus is placed a little too far back. Even so, Sawallisch takes an honoured place in the illustrious company of interpreters. His reading is full of thoughtful *aperçus* and natural flow, and displays a sensible overview of the score. Vocally it will satisfy all but those with the most demanding tastes in, and/or, long experience in Wagnerian interpretation.

Die Meistersinger von Nürnberg.
Otto Edelmann bass Hans Sachs; **Hans Hopf** ten Walther; **Dame Elisabeth Schwarzkopf** sop Eva; **Friedrich Dalberg** bass Pogner; **Erich Kunz** bar Beckmesser; **Gerhard Unger** ten David;
Ira Malaniuk contr Magdalene; **Heinrich Pflanzl** bar Kothner; **Erich Majkut** ten Vogelgesang;
Hans Berg bass Nachtigall; **Josef Janko** ten Zorn; **Krl Mikorey** ten Eisslinger;
Gerhard Stolze ten Moser; **Heinz Tandler** bass Ortel; **Heinz Borst** bass Schwarz;
Arnold van Mill bass Foltz; **Werner Faulhaber** bass Nightwatchman;
Bayreuth Festival Chorus and Orchestra / Herbert von Karajan.
EMI Références mono CHS7 63500-2 (four discs: 267 minutes: ADD). Notes and text included.
Recorded live in 1951. Ⓜ 🅷

In his well-researched note to this reissue, Richard Osborne very properly writes that 'the miracle of Karajan's conducting is that it marries fervour with lucidity in particular measure'. That can be heard most tellingly in the work's most inspired section – the first four scenes of Act 3. The instrumental detail that characterizes and describes Beckmesser's movements as he steals into Sachs's study is delineated with a refined clarity that ideally brings out its humour. Then in the following scene Karajan is inspired to heights of intensity and concentration as Sachs and Eva play out their emotional entanglement culminating in 'O Sachs, mein Freund' and the Quintet. It is here, too, that Schwarzkopf's Eva and Edelmann's Sachs add a further touch of eloquence to their already finely wrought performances. The underrated Edelmann gives the best sung Sachs in any complete recording. He has the prime virtues of perfect firmness, a true *legato* and a strong, full-bodied, unforced, totally likeable tone. You may not find the individuality of phrase here that other, older interpreters give us, but in his varied responses to the masters, Eva, Walther and Beckmesser, he is unfailingly true to Sachs as the poet-cobbler, and his voice proves virtually tireless. One might argue as to whether the youthful Schwarzkopf is quite as lovable and outgoing an Eva as she might be, but in respect of radiant tone, musical phrasing, wit allied to beauty, she hasn't a peer. Nor has Gerhard Unger as David, who sings his role with the fresh tone and eager responses it calls for. With the rest of the singers, a few – but not many – reservations have to be made. This set won't be for those who mind occasional coughs – they're most troublesome in the Third Act Prelude, just when you want silence to admire Karajan's deeply moving interpretation – or who must have stereo and perfect voice/orchestra balance. But for anyone who appreciates a true-to-life, responsive and exceptionally intense experience this is a version to cherish.

Die Meistersinger von Nürnberg.
Thomas Stewart *bar* Hans Sachs; **Sándor Kónya** *ten* Walther; **Gundula Janowitz** *sop* Eva;
Franz Crass *bass* Pogner; **Thomas Hemsley** *bar* Beckmesser; **Gerhard Unger** *ten* David;
Brigitte Fassbaender *mez* Magdalene; **Kieth Engen** *bass* Kothner;
Horst Wilhelm *ten* Vogelgesang; **Richard Kogel** *bass* Nachtigall; **Manfred Schmidt** *ten* Zorn;
Friedrich Lenz *ten* Eisslinger; **Peter Baille** *ten* Moser; **Anton Diakov** *bass* Ortel;
Karl Christian Kohn *bass* Schwartz; **Dieter Slembeck** *bass* Foltz;
Raimund Grumbach *bass* Nightwatchman;
Bavarian Radio Chorus and Symphony Orchestra / Rafael Kubelík.
Calig CAL50971/4 (four discs: 272 minutes: ADD). Recorded 1967.   Ⓕ

There could be no more fitting memorial to Kubelík than the appearance of this, probably the most all-round satisfying *Meistersinger* in the era of stereo. It was recorded in 1967 by Bavarian Radio to mark the work's centenary the following year. Kubelík conducts an unforced, loving interpretation, showing a gratifying grasp of overall structure. As a whole the reading has an unobtrusive cohesion achieved within flexible tempos and dynamics. Everything proceeds at an even, well-judged pace with just the right surge of emotion at the climaxes. All this is conveyed unerringly to his own Bavarian Radio Symphony forces. Stewart's Sachs is certainly his most successful performance on disc. He offers a finely moulded, deeply considered reading that relies on firm, evenly produced, mostly warm tone to create a darkish, philosophical poet-cobbler. Kónya is simply the most winning Walther on any set, superseding Sawallisch's excellent Heppner by virtue of a greater ardour in his delivery. Kónya pours out consistently warm, clear tone, his tenor hovering ideally between the lyric and the heroic. Nor are there many better Evas than the young Janowitz, certainly none with a lovelier voice. Franz Crass, a less pompous Pogner than some, sings his part effortlessly, with noble feeling. Hemsley, though singing his first Beckmesser, evinces a close affinity with the Town Clerk's mean-mindedness, and his German is faultless. Unger is a paragon among Davids, so eager in his responses and finding just the right timbre for the role. His Magdalene, again perfect casting, is the young Fassbaender. With a characterful Kothner in Engen, the requirements for a near-ideal *Meistersinger* ensemble are in place. As the recording doesn't betray its age this would undoubtedly be the first choice among stereo versions.

Parsifal.
Jess Thomas *ten* Parsifal; **George London** *bass-bar* Amfortas; **Hans Hotter** *bass* Gurnemanz;
Irene Dalis *mez* Kundry; **Gustav Neidlinger** *bass* Klingsor; **Martti Talvela** *bass* Titurel;
Niels Möller *ten* First Knight; **Gerd Neinstedt** *bass* Second Knight;
Sona Cervená *mez* Ursula Boese *contr* Gerhard Stolze, Georg Paskuda *tens* Squires;
Gundula Janowitz, Anja Silja, Else-Margrete Gardelli, Dorothea Siebert, Rita Bartos *sops*
Sona Cervená *mez* Flower Maidens;
Bayreuth Festival Chorus and Orchestra / Hans Knappertsbusch.
Philips 416 390-2PH4 (four discs: 250 minutes: ADD). Notes, text and translation included.
Recorded live in 1962.   Ⓕ **RR**

There have been many fine recordings of this great Eastertide opera, but none have so magnificently captured the power, the spiritual grandeur, the human frailty and the almost unbearable beauty of the work as Hans Knappertsbusch. This live recording has a cast that has few equals. Hotter is superb, fleshing out Gurnemanz with a depth of insight that has never been surpassed. London's Amfortas captures the frightening sense of impotence and anguish with painful directness whilst Thomas's Parsifal grows as the performance progresses and is no mean achievement. Dalis may lack that final degree of sensuousness but gives a fine interpretation. Throughout Knappertsbusch exercises a quite unequalled control over the proceedings; it is a fine testament to a great conductor. The Bayreuth acoustic is well reproduced and all in all it is a profound and moving experience.

Parsifal.
Peter Hofmann *ten* Parsifal; **José van Dam** *bass-bar* Amfortas; **Kurt Moll** *bass* Gurnemanz;
Dunja Vejzovic *mez* Kundry; **Siegmund Nimsgern** *bass* Klingsor; **Victor von Halem** *bass* Titurel;
Claes Hakon Ahnsjö *ten* First Knight; **Kurt Rydl** *bass* Second Knight;
Marjon Lambriks, Anne Gjevang *mezzos* **Heiner Hopfner** *ten* **Georg Tichy** *bass* Squires;
Barbara Hendricks, Janet Perry, Inga Nielsen *sops* **Audrey Michael** *mez*
Doris Soffel, Rohângiz Yachmi Caucig *contrs* Flower Maidens;
Hanna Schwarz *mez* Voice from above;
Berlin Deutsch Opera Chorus; Berlin Philharmonic Orchestra / Herbert von Karajan.
DG 413 347-2GH4 (four discs: 256 minutes: ADD). Notes, text and translation included.
Recorded 1979-80. *Gramophone* Award Winner 1981.   Ⓕ

Karajan's *Parsifal* seems to grow in stature as an interpretation on each rehearing; on its CD transfer it appears to have acquired a new depth, in terms of sound, because of the greater range of the recording and the greater presence of both singers and orchestra. As in practically all cases, CD offers a more immediate experience. Karajan's reading, a trifle stodgy in Act 1, grows in intensity and feeling with the work itself, reaching an almost terrifying force in the Prelude to Act 3 which is sustained to the end of the opera. Moll's Gurnemanz is a deeply expressive, softly-moulded performance of notable beauty. Vejzovic, carefully nurtured by Karajan, gives the performance of her life as Kundry. Hofmann's tone isn't at all times so steady as a Parsifal's should be, but he depicts the character's anguish and eventual serenity in his sincere, inward interpretation. Van Dam is a trifle too placid as Amfortas but his singing has admirable power and steadiness. Nimsgern is the epitome of malice as Klingsor. The choral singing hasn't quite the confidence of the superb orchestral playing which has both qualities of Keats's imagining of beauty and truth in abundance.

Das Rheingold.
John Tomlinson *bass* Wotan; **Linda Finnie** *mez* Fricka; **Graham Clark** *ten* Loge;
Helmut Pampuch *ten* Mime; **Günter von Kannen** *bar* Alberich; **Eva Johansson** *sop* Freia;
Kurt Schreibmayer *ten* Froh; **Bodo Brinkmann** *bar* Donner; **Birgitta Svendén** *mez* Erda;
Matthias Hölle *bass* Fasolt; **Philip Kang** *bass* Fafner; **Hilde Leidland** *sop* Woglinde;
Annette Küttenbaum *mez* Wellgunde; **Jane Turner** *mez* Flosshilde;
Bayreuth Festival Orchestra / Daniel Barenboim.
Teldec 4509-91185-2 (two discs: 149 minutes: DDD). Notes, text and translation included.
Recorded live in 1991.   Ⓕ

Die Walküre.
Poul Elming *ten* Siegmund; **Nadine Secunde** *sop* Sieglinde; **Anne Evans** *sop* Brünnhilde;
John Tomlinson *bass* Wotan; **Linda Finnie** *mez* Fricka, Siegrune; **Matthias Hölle** *bass* Hunding;
Eva Johansson *sop* Gerhilde; **Eva-Maria Bundschuh** *sop* Helmwige; **Ruth Floeren** *sop* Ortlinde;
Shirley Close *mez* Waltraute; **Hebe Dijkstra** *mez* Rossweisse; **Birgitta Svendén** *mez* Grimgerde;
Hitomi Katagiri *mez* Schwertleite;
Bayreuth Festival Orchestra / Daniel Barenboim.
Teldec 4509 91186-2 (four discs: 233 minutes: DDD). Notes, text and translation included.
Recorded live in 1992.   Ⓕ

These are enthralling performances. Tomlinson's volatile Wotan is the most potent reading here. He manages to sing every word with insistent meaning and forceful declamation while maintaining a firm *legato*. His German is so idiomatic that he might have been speaking the language his whole life and he brings breadth and distinction of phrase to his solos at the close of both operas. Anne Evans has a single, important advantage over other recent Brunnhildes in that her voice is wholly free from wobble and she never makes an ugly sound. Hers is a light, girlish, honest portrayal, sung with unfailing musicality if not with the ultimate insights. Linda Finnie is an articulate, sharp-edged Fricka, and Graham Clark a sparky, incisive Loge. Nadine Secunde's impassioned Sieglinde is matched by the vital, exciting Siegmund of Poul Elming and Matthias Hölle as both Hunding and Fasolt is another of those black basses of which Germany seems to have an inexhaustible supply. The whole of *Das Rheingold* is magnificently conducted by Barenboim, a more expansive Wagnerian than Böhm. By 1991 he had the full measure of its many facets, brought immense authority and power to building its huge climaxes, yet finds all the lightness of touch for the mercurial and/or diaphanous aspects of this amazing score. He has the inestimable advantage of a Bayreuth orchestra at the peak of its form, surpassing – and this says much – even the Metropolitan orchestra for Levine, and Barenboim's reading is more convincing as a whole than Levine's. Similar qualities inform his interpretation of *Die Walküre*. Barenboim has now learnt how to match the epic stature of Wagner's mature works, how to pace them with an overview of the whole and there is an incandescent, metaphysical feeling of a Furwänglerian kind in his treatment of such passages as Wotan's anger and the Valkyrie ride. Again, the orchestra is superb. It is backed by a recording of startling presence and depth, amply capturing the Bayreuth acoustic.

Rienzi.
René Kollo *ten* Cola Rienzi; **Siv Wennberg** *sop* Irene; **Janis Martin** *sop* Adriano;
Theo Adam *bass* Paolo Orsini; **Nikolaus Hillebrand** *bass* Steffano Colonna;
Siegfried Vogel *bass* Raimondo; **Peter Schreier** *ten* Baroncelli;
Günther Leib *bass* Cecco del Vecchio; **Ingeborg Springer** *sop* Messenger of Peace;
Leipzig Radio Chorus; Dresden State Opera Chorus;
Staatskapelle Dresden / Heinrich Hollreiser.
EMI CMS7 63980-2 (three discs: 225 minutes: ADD). Notes, text and translation included.
Recorded 1974-76. Ⓜ

Rienzi is grand opera with a vengeance. Political imperatives count for more than mere human feelings, and politics means ceremony as well as warfare: marches, ballet music and extended choruses are much in evidence, while even the solo arias often have the rhetorical punch of political harangues. It could all be an enormous bore. Yet the young Wagner, basing his work on Bulwer Lytton's story of the tragic Roman tribune, did manage to move beyond mere tub-thumping into a degree of intensity that – for those with ears to hear – prefigures the mature genius to come. In the end, Rienzi himself is more than just a political animal, and the existential anguish of Tannhäuser, Tristan and even Amfortas glimmers in the distance. It would be idle to pretend that this performance is ideal in every respect, either musically, or as a recording. But its virtues outweigh its weaknesses by a considerable margin. Siv Wennberg was not in best voice at the time, but the other principals, notably René Kollo and Janis Martin, bring commendable stamina and conviction to their demanding roles. Above all the conductor Heinrich Hollreiser prevents the more routine material from sounding merely mechanical, and ensures that the whole work has a truly Wagnerian sweep and fervour.

Der Ring des Nibelungen.
Das Rheingold.
George London *bass-bar* Wotan; **Kirsten Flagstad** *sop* Fricka; **Set Svanholm** *ten* Loge;
Paul Kuen *ten* Mime; **Gustav Neidlinger** *bass* Alberich; **Claire Watson** *sop* Freia;
Waldemar Kmentt *ten* Froh; **Eberhard Waechter** *bar* Donner; **Jean Madeira** *contr* Erda;
Walter Kreppel *bass* Fasolt; **Kurt Böhme** *bass* Fafner; **Oda Balsborg** *sop* Woglinde;
Hetty Plümacher *sop* Wellgunde; **Ira Malaniuk** *mez* Flosshilde.

Die Walküre.
James King *ten* Siegmund; **Régine Crespin** *sop* Sieglinde; **Birgit Nilsson** *sop* Brünnhilde;
Hans Hotter *bass-bar* Wotan; **Christa Ludwig** *mez* Fricka; **Gottlob Frick** *bass* Hunding;
Vera Schlosser *sop* Gerhilde; **Berit Lindholm** *sop* Helmwige; **Helga Dernesch** *sop* Ortlinde;
Brigitte Fassbaender *mez* Waltraute; **Claudia Hellmann** *sop* Rossweisse;
Vera Little *contr* Siegrune; **Marilyn Tyler** *sop* Grimgerde; **Helen Watts** *contr* Schwertleite.

Siegfried.
Wolfgang Windgassen *ten* Siegfried; **Hans Hotter** *bass-bar* Wanderer;
Birgit Nilsson *sop* Brünnhilde; **Gerhard Stolze** *ten* Mime; **Gustav Neidlinger** *bass* Alberich;
Marga Höffgen *contr* Erda; **Kurt Böhme** *bass* Fafner; **Dame Joan Sutherland** *sop* Woodbird.

Götterdämmerung.
Birgit Nilsson *sop* Brünnhilde; **Wolfgang Windgassen** *ten* Siegfried; **Gottlob Frick** *bass* Hagen;
Gustav Neidlinger *bass* Alberich; **Dietrich Fischer-Dieskau** *bar* Gunther;
Claire Watson *sop* Gutrune; **Christa Ludwig** *mez* Waltraute;
Dame Gwyneth Jones *sop* Wellgunde; **Lucia Popp** *sop* Woglinde;
Maureen Guy *mez* Flosshilde; **Helen Watts** *contr* First Norn; **Grace Hoffman** *mez* Second Norn;
Anita Välkki *sop* Third Norn;
Vienna State Opera Chorus; Vienna Philharmonic Orchestra / Sir Georg Solti.
Decca 455 555-2DMO14 (14 discs: 876 minutes: ADD). Notes, texts and translations included.
Recorded 1958-65. *Also available separately.* ⒷⒽℝℝ

Classics of the gramophone have to move with the times, and in its latest manifestation, 40 years from the first LP issue of *Das Rheingold*, the Solti/Decca *Ring*, first issued on CD in 1985, is now available at bargain price. As perspectives on the Solti/Culshaw enterprise lengthen, and critical reactions are kept alert by the regular appearance of new, or newly issued, and very different recordings, it may seem increasingly ironic that of all conductors the ultra-theatrical Solti should have been denied a live performance. There are indeed episodes in this recording that convey more of the mechanics of the studio than of the electricity of the opera house – the opening of *Die Walküre*, Act 2, and the closing scenes of *Siegfried* and *Götterdämmerung*, for example. Yet, in general, dramatic impetus and atmosphere are strongly established and well sustained, sometimes more powerfully than is usually managed in the theatre. As just one example one would instance the superb control with which the intensity of Donner's summoning up of the thunder in *Das Rheingold* is maintained across Froh's greeting to the rainbow bridge (which often falls flat in the theatre) into Wotan's own great salutation. At the majestic climax of this scene the power of feeling conveyed by George London's fine performance counts for more than any 'artificiality' in the way the voice is balanced against the orchestra. Equally memorable in a totally different context is Solti's management of the long transition in *Götterdämmerung* between Hagen's Watch and the appearance of Waltraute. Nothing could be less mannered or unnatural than Solti's grasp of perspective and feeling for the life of each phrase in this music.

Even so, we are not proposing to offer a full-blown revisionist interpretation of Solti's *Ring*, arguing that he always prefers deliberation to impetuosity and that the recording itself has the ideal natural balance. On CD the clarity of instrumental detail is consistently remarkable, and while not all the singers sound as if they are constantly in danger of being overwhelmed (Hagen's Watch is a good example of an appropriately forward vocal balance) there are some vital episodes especially those involving Wolfgang Windgassen and Birgit Nilsson. Awareness of what these artists achieved in other recordings strengthens the suspicion that they may have been giving more than we actually get in this case. Windgassen in particular is not allowed to dominate the sound picture in the way his part demands, and Nilsson can seem all-too relaxed within the comforting cocoon of the orchestral texture. Factors like these, coupled with those distinctive Soltian confrontations between the hard-driven and the hammily protracted, have prevented the Decca cycle from decisively seeing off all its various rivals over the years.

It is nevertheless still open to question whether any studio recording of *The Ring* could reasonably be expected to be more atmospheric, exciting or better performed than this one. The Vienna Philharmonic is not merely prominent, but excellent, and such interpretations as Svanholm's Loge, Neidlinger's Alberich and Frick's Hagen remain immensely impressive. Above all, there is Hans Hotter, whose incomparably authoritative, unfailingly alert and responsive Wotan stands up well when compared to his earlier Bayreuth accounts. Nowhere is he more commanding than in *Siegfried*, Act 1, where one even welcomes Stolze's mannerisms as Mime for the sparks they strike off the great bass-baritone. Earlier in this act the interplay of equally balanced instruments and voices in relatively intimate conversational phrases displays the Culshaw concept at its most convincing. The care taken over the SonicStage production was graphically chronicled by Culshaw in *Ring Resounding* (Secker & Warburg: 1967). He would have been astonished to hear what his successors have achieved in renewing his production through digital remastering. One now realizes how much of the original sound was lost on the old pressings. What we now have is exactly what was achieved and recorded in the Sofiensaal in Vienna in those pioneering days back in 1958. Which brings us to comparisons with the 1980 Janowski/RCA version (reviewed below). The approaches of the two recordings are so different that they almost seem like different experiences. Whereas Culshaw was intent on creating a theatre on record with all the well-known stage effects, the rival version eschews all such manifestations. In general, Janowski presents a much more intimate view of the work, more contained than Solti's. So there can be no doubt that, despite the occasional thumps from Solti, despite somewhat skimpy presentation (the *Götterdämmerung* tracks are not timed), and however many other *Rings* you may have, your collection will needs this one.

Der Ring des Nibelungen.
Das Rheingold.
Theo Adam *bass-bar* Wotan; **Annelies Burmeister** *mez* Fricka; **Wolfgang Windgassen** *ten* Loge; **Erwin Wohlfahrt** *ten* Mime; **Gustav Neidlinger** *bass* Alberich; **Anja Silja** *sop* Freia; **Hermin Esser** *ten* Froh; **Gerd Nienstedt** *bass* Donner; **Vera Soukupova** *mez* Erda; **Martti Talvela** *bass* Fasolt; **Kurt Boehme** *bass* Fafner; **Dorothea Siebert** *sop* Woglinde; **Helga Dernesch** *sop* Wellgunde; **Ruth Hesse** *mez* Flosshilde;
Bayreuth Festival Chorus and Orchestra / Karl Böhm.
Philips 412 475-2PH2 (two discs: 137 minutes: ADD). Notes, text and translation included. Recorded live in 1967. ⓕ

Die Walküre.
James King *ten* Siegmund; **Leonie Rysanek** *sop* Sieglinde; **Birgit Nilsson** *sop* Brünnhilde; **Theo Adam** *bass* Wotan; **Annelies Burmeister** *mez* Fricka, Siegrune; **Gerd Nienstedt** *bass* Hunding; **Danica Mastilovic** *sop* Gerhilde; **Liane Synek** *sop* Helmwige;

Helga Dernesch *sop* Ortlinde; **Gertraud Hopf** *mez* Waltraute; **Sona Cerverá** *mez* Rossweisse;
Elisabeth Schärtel *contr* Grimgerde; **Sieglinde Wagner** *contr* Schwertleite;
Bayreuth Festival Chorus and Orchestra / Karl Böhm.
Philips 412 478-2PH4 (four discs: 210 minutes: ADD). Notes, text and translation included.
Recorded live in 1967. Ⓕ

Siegfried.
Wolfgang Windgassen *ten* Siegfried; **Theo Adam** *bass* Wanderer;
Birgit Nilsson *sop* Brünnhilde; **Erwin Wohlfahrt** *ten* Mime; **Gustav Neidlinger** *bass* Alberich;
Vera Soukupova *mez* Erda; **Kurt Boehme** *bass* Fafner; **Erika Köth** *sop* Woodbird;
Bayreuth Festival Orchestra / Karl Böhm.
Philips 412 483-2PH4 (four discs: 223 minutes: ADD). Notes, text and translation included.
Recorded live in 1967. Ⓕ

Götterdämmerung.
Birgit Nilsson *sop* Brünnhilde; **Wolfgang Windgassen** *ten* Siegfried; **Josef Greindl** *bass* Hagen;
Gustav Neidlinger *bass-bar* Alberich; **Thomas Stewart** *bar* Gunther;
Ludmila Dvořáková *sop* Gutrune; **Martha Mödl** *mez* Waltraute; **Dorothea Siebert** *sop* Woglinde;
Helga Dernesch *sop* Wellgunde; **Sieglinde Wagner** *contr* Flosshilde;
Marga Höffgen *contr* First Norn; **Annelies Burmeister** *mez* Second Norn;
Anja Silja *sop* Third Norn;
Bayreuth Festival Chorus and Orchestra / Karl Böhm.
Philips 412 488-2PH4 (four discs: 249 minutes: ADD). Notes, text and translation included.
Recorded live in 1967. Ⓕ

Wagner's *Der Ring des Nibelungen* is the greatest music-drama ever penned. It deals with the eternal
questions of power, love, personal responsibility and moral behaviour, and has always been open to
numerous interpretations, both dramatic and musical. For every generation, it presents a new
challenge, yet certain musical performances have undoubtedly stood the test of time. One would
recommend the recording made at Bayreuth in 1967 because, above all others, it represents a true
and living account of a huge work as it was performed in the opera house for which it was largely
conceived. Every artist who appears at Bayreuth seems to find an extra dedication in their
comportment there, and on this occasion many of the singers and the conductor surpassed what
they achieved elsewhere. Böhm's reading is notable for its dramatic drive and inner tension. For the
most part he also encompasses the metaphysical aspects of the score as well, and he procures
playing of warmth and depth from the Bayreuth orchestra. Birgit Nilsson heads the cast as an
unsurpassed Brünnhilde, wonderfully vivid in her characterization and enunciation, tireless and
gleaming in voice. Wolfgang Windgassen is equally committed and alert as her Siegfried and Theo
Adam is an experienced, worldly-wise Wotan. No *Ring* recording is perfect or could possibly tell the
whole story but this faithfully recorded version conveys the strength and force of the epic's
meaning.

Der Ring des Nibelungen.
Das Rheingold[a].
Theo Adam *bass-bar* Wotan; **Yvonne Minton** *mez* Fricka; **Peter Schreier** *ten* Loge;
Christian Vogel *ten* Mime; **Siegmund Nimsgern** *bass-bar* Alberich; **Marita Napier** *sop* Freia;
Eberhard Büchner *ten* Froh; **Karl-Heinz Stryczek** *bass* Donner; **Ortrun Wenkel** *contr* Erda;
Roland Bracht *bass* Fasolt; **Matti Salminen** *bass* Fafner; **Lucia Popp** *sop* Woglinde;
Uta Priew *mez* Wellgunde; **Hanna Schwarz** *contr* Flosshild.

Die Walküre[b].
Siegfried Jerusalem *ten* Siegmund; **Jessye Norman** *sop* Sieglinde;
Jeannine Altmeyer *sop* Brünnhilde; **Theo Adam** *bass-bar* Wotan; **Yvonne Minton** *mez* Fricka;
Kurt Moll *bass* Hunding; **Eva-Maria Bundschuh** *sop* Gerhilde; **Ruth Falcon** *sop* Helmwige;
Cheryl Studer *sop* Ortlinde; **Ortrun Wenkel** *contr* Waltraute; **Uta Priew** *mez* Rossweisse;
Christel Borchers *mez* Siegrune; **Kathleen Kuhlmann** *contr* Grimgarde;
Anne Gjevang *contr* Schwertleite.

Siegfried[c].
René Kollo *ten* Siegfried; **Theo Adam** *bass-bar* Wanderer; **Jeannine Altmeyer** *sop* Brünnhilde;
Peter Schreier *ten* Mime; **Siegmund Nimsgern** *bass-bar* Alberich; **Ortrun Wenkel** *contr* Erda;
Norma Sharp *sop* Woodbird.

Götterdämmerung[d].
Jeannine Altmeyer *sop* Brünnhilde; **René Kollo** *ten* Siegfried; **Matti Salminen** *bass* Hagen;
Siegmund Nimsgern *bass-bar* Alberich; **Hans Günter Nöcker** *bar* Gunther;

Norma Sharp sop Gutrune; **Ortrun Wenkel** contr Waltraute; **Uta Priew** mez Wellgunde;
Lucia Popp sop Woglinde; **Anne Gjevang** contr First Norn;
Daphne Evangelotos mez Second Norn; **Ruth Falcon** sop Third Norn.
**Men's Voices of the Leipzig State Opera; Dresden State Opera Chorus; Staatskapelle
Dresden / Marek Janowski.**
RCA Red Seal 74321 45417-2 (14 discs: 839 minutes: DDD).
Notes, texts and translations included. Recorded ᵃ1980, ᵇ1981, ᶜ1982, ᵈ1983.   Ⓑ

Here's a true and desirable bargain. This, the first digitally recorded cycle to appear on CD, has
always had a great deal to commend it, and at budget price it becomes even more attractive. One of
its most telling assets is the actual recording, still the most natural, clear and most sensitively
balanced available. Then it has the Dresden Staatskapelle playing with the utmost beauty from start
to finish and with lean power when that's called for. Voices and players are in an ideal relationship.
Which is not to say that such purple passages as the Magic Fire Music, Ride of the Valkyries,
Rhine Journey and Funeral March want anything in visceral excitement. Janowski conducts a
direct, dramatic interpretation, concerned throughout with forward movement. His clear-sighted
conducting conveys theatrical excitement from start to finish without fuss or attempts at portentous
readings. All this makes it an ideal introduction to the *Ring* for any young collector, who can later
go on to more philosophically inclined interpretations. The casts are by and large excellent. *Das
Rheingold* is dominated by three central performances – Nimsgern's vibrant, articulate Alberich,
Schreier's wonderfully vital, strikingly intelligent and articulate Loge and Adam's experienced
Wotan. But Fricka, Giants and Rhinemaidens are all well cast, and the whole performance grips
one's attention from start to finish as the kaleidoscopic drama unfolds.

Die Walküre introduces us to Norman's involving if not wholly idiomatic Sieglinde and, even
better, the youthful Jerusalem's near-ideal Siegmund, forthright and sincere, not forgetting Moll's
granite Hunding. Adam is so authoritative, so keen with the text, so inside his part that an
occasional unsteadiness can be overlooked. With Altmeyer's Brünnhilde we come to the one
drawback of the set. Though in this and the succeeding operas, we are thankful for such clear,
clean and youthful tone, her reading is unformed and one-dimensional, lacking the essential
insights of a Varnay or Behrens. In the title-role in *Siegfried* Kollo gives one of his most attractive
portrayals on disc, full of thoughtful diction poised on clear-cut tone. Schreier misses nothing in
his interpretation of the dissembling, wily Mime, Adam is at his very best as the wise, old
Wanderer, and the smaller parts are well catered for. In *Götterdämmerung*, Salminen is a
commanding, often subtle Hagen, though inclined to bark in his call, Nöcker a splendid Gunther.
This set is particularly recommended to anyone wanting a reasonably priced introduction to the
cycle. Even at a higher level, it has much going for it in comparison with supposedly more
prestigious recordings.

Der Ring des Nibelungen – abridged.
Sopranos – **Florence Austral, Noel Eadie, Florence Easton, Tilly de Garmo, Nora Gruhn,
Genia Guszalewicz, Frida Leider, Göta Ljüngberg, Elsie Suddaby, Louise Trenton.**
Mezzos – **Evelyn Arden, Lydia Kindermann, Elfriede Marherr-Wagner, Maartje Offers,
Maria Olczewska.**
Contraltos – **Emmi Leisner, Gladys Palmer, Nellie Walker.**
Tenors – **Waldemar Henke, Rudolf Laubenthal, Kennedy McKenna, Lauritz Melchior,
Albert Reiss, Heinrich Tessmer, Walter Widdop.**
Baritones – **Howard Fry, Emil Schipper, Deszö Zádor.**
Bass-baritones – **Rudolf Bockelmann, Friedrich Schorr.**
Basses – **Ivar Andrésen, Frederick Collier, Arthur Fear, Eduard Habich, Emanuel List.**
Orchestras – **Berlin State Opera, London Symphony, Vienna State Opera.**
Conductors – **Karl Alwin, Sir John Barbirolli, Leo Blech, Albert Coates,
Lawrance Collingwood, Robert Heger, Karl Muck.**
Pearl mono GEMMCDS9137 (seven discs: 500 minutes).   ⓂⒽ

Here we have, in its entirety, what one might term the Old Testament of *The Ring* recordings, the
discs made in the late 1920s and early 1930s in London and Berlin. The operas given the major
share are *Die Walküre* and *Siegfried*. The four extracts from *Das Rheingold* are notable only for
Friedrich Schorr's magisterial 'Abendlich strahlt'. *Götterdämmerung* suffers most from being
reduced to brief extracts, although the passages have been well chosen to give a substantial flavour
of the vast work. Coates and the slightly less admirable Blech share the conducting with a few
incursions from Heger, the young Barbirolli and others. The playing, mostly by the LSO of the day
and the Berlin State Opera Orchestra, is remarkable for its sweep, also for its care over detail, much
of which has astonishing clarity considering the dates of the recordings. Coates is particularly
successful in projecting the ardour of the *Walküre* love duet and the forging of the sword in
Siegfried. His speeds are always on the swift side.

Of course, the singing is the most treasurable aspect of the whole enterprise. Encountering Leider again one realizes anew that few, if any, have equalled her combination of vocal security, close-knit line and phrasing, and that matching of feeling with a goddess's natural dignity. Her Brünnhilde is an assumption all aspiring heroic sopranos should closely study (but they don't!). Fledgling Heldentenors would be unwise to listen to Melchior for they might be inclined to suicide. The sheer *élan*, strength and verbal acuity of his singing are, and will surely remain, unique. For these reasons alone he is unsurpassable as Siegfried, a role that ideally suited his remarkable attributes. Schorr's Wotan is just as remarkable. Once again tone, technique and text are in perfect accord as his noble bass-baritone fills every passage grandly, movingly. The sound is vivid throughout these seven (for the price of five), generously filled CDs. The voices are recorded more successfully than in most modern versions of these works, and their relationship with the orchestra is more natural than that favoured in studios today. This is a set no enquiring Wagnerian should be without.

Tannhäuser (Paris version).
Plácido Domingo *ten* Tannhäuser; **Cheryl Studer** *sop* Elisabeth; **Andreas Schmidt** *bar* Wolfram; **Agnes Baltsa** *mez* Venus; **Matti Salminen** *bass* Hermann; **William Pell** *ten* Walther; **Kurt Rydl** *bass* Biterolf; **Clemens Biber** *ten* Heinrich; **Oskar Hillebrandt** *bass* Reinmar; **Barbara Bonney** *sop* Shepherd Boy;
Chorus of the Royal Opera House, Covent Garden;
Philharmonia Orchestra / Giuseppe Sinopoli.
DG 427 625-2GH3 (three discs: 176 minutes: DDD). Notes, text and translation included. Ⓕ

Plácido Domingo's Tannhäuser is a success in almost every respect. He evokes the erotic passion of the Venusberg scene and brings to it just the right touch of nervous energy. This is boldly contrasted with the desperation and bitterness of the Rome Narration after the hero's fruitless visit to the Pope seeking forgiveness: Domingo's description of how Tannhäuser avoided every earthly delight on his pilgrimage is delivered with total conviction. In between he berates the slightly prissy attitude of his fellow knights on the Wartburg with the dangerous conceit of someone who knows a secret delight that they will never enjoy in their measured complacency. His tenor must be the steadiest and most resplendent ever to have tackled the part, although his German is far from idiomatic with several vowel sounds distorted. Baltsa also has some problems with her German, but she has the range and attack, particularly in the upper register, for an awkwardly lying part.

It is obviously Sinopoli's concern throughout to bring out every last ounce of the drama in the piece, both in terms of orchestral detail, which receives very special attention from the Overture, given a big, full-blooded reading, onwards, but also in his awareness in this opera of the longer line, often sustained by the upper strings. The Philharmonia's violins respond with their most eloquent playing. The kind of *frisson* Sinopoli offers is evident in the anticipatory excitement at the start of Act 2 and the iron control he maintains in the big ensemble later in the same act. Cheryl Studer's secure, beautiful voice has no difficulty coping with Sinopoli's deliberate tempos. She takes her part with total conviction, both vocal and interpretative, phrasing with constant intelligence. Andreas Schmidt is a mellifluous, concerned Wolfram, Salminen a rugged, characterful Landgrave and Barbara Bonney an ideally fresh Shepherd Boy. As knights, ladies and pilgrims the Covent Garden Chorus sings with consistent beauty of sound, and has been sensibly balanced with the orchestra. Domingo and Studer make this version a winner, as does the wide range of the fine recording.

Tristan und Isolde.
Ludwig Suthaus *ten* Tristan; **Kirsten Flagstad** *sop* Isolde; **Blanche Thebom** *mez* Brangäne; **Josef Greindl** *bass* King Marke; **Dietrich Fischer-Dieskau** *bar* Kurwenal;
Edgar Evans *ten* Melot; **Rudolf Schock** *ten* Shepherd, Sailor; **Rhoderick Davies** *ten* Helmsman;
Chorus of the Royal Opera House, Covent Garden;
Philharmonia Orchestra / Wilhelm Furtwängler.
EMI mono EMI CDS5 56254-2 (four discs: 236 minutes: ADD). Notes, text and translation included. Recorded 1952. Ⓕ ⓇⓇ Ⓗ

Those of us who had worn out our original HMV pressings of this recording of *Tristan und Isolde* were grateful to EMI for marking the Furtwängler centenary by reissuing this recording on CD. We should now be doubly grateful. It was remastered again in 1997, achieving a marked improvement over its 1985 transfer. At best, the sound is remarkable. At the start of Act 2, for instance, there is an exceptional depth of perspective to the mono sound. Elsewhere, in the big climaxes, the sound does become congested; though it never breaks up or distorts, there is some perceptible hardening of the musical arteries. The digital remastering also makes studio noises more audible: for instance, the brief rumpus at the end of Tristan's first phrase in 'O sink hernieder'. The performance, as is well known by now, is memorable for the reach, beauty and re-creative power of Furtwängler's conducting and Flagstad's authoritative, beautifully pointed account of Isolde's role. Though it lacked opera house experience, the Philharmonia Orchestra, in 1952, was probably the world's finest orchestra. It is difficult to accept the view, sometimes stated, that Flagstad was unsuited at this time to the role of Isolde. It would have been better caught younger; but that said, there were no contemporary Isoldes to better Flagstad's. The young Dietrich Fischer-Dieskau is a superb Kurwenal; there could be tiny reservations about other members of the cast: the hugely impressive but perhaps rather too formal Tristan of Ludwig Suthaus, Josef Greindl's King Marke, and so on. A unique listening experience.

Tristan und Isolde.
Wolfgang Windgassen *ten* Tristan; **Birgit Nilsson** *sop* Isolde; **Christa Ludwig** *mez* Brangäne;
Martti Talvela *bass* King Marke; **Eberhard Waechter** *bar* Kurwenal; **Claude Heater** *ten* Melot;
Erwin Wohlfahrt *ten* Shepherd; **Gerd Nienstedt** *bass* Helmsman; **Peter Schreier** *ten* Sailor;
Bayreuth Festival Chorus and Orchestra / Karl Böhm.
Philips 434 425-2PH3 (three discs: 219 minutes: ADD). Notes, text and translation included.
Recorded live in 1966.   Ⓜ

Tristan und Isolde.
Siegfried Jerusalem *ten* Tristan; **Waltraud Meier** *mez* Isolde; **Marjana Lipovšek** *mez* Brangäne;
Matti Salminen *bass* King Marke; **Falk Struckmann** *bar* Kurwenal; **Johan Botha** *ten* Melot;
Peter Maus *ten* Shepherd; **Roman Trekel** *bar* Helmsman; **Uwe Heilmann** *ten* Sailor;
Berlin State Opera Chorus; Berlin Philharmonic Orchestra / Daniel Barenboim.
Teldec 4509-94568-2 (four discs: 235 minutes: DDD). Notes, text and translation included.
Recorded 1994   Ⓕ

Böhm's recording is a live Bayreuth performance of distinction, for on stage are the most admired Tristan and Isolde of their time, and in the pit the 72-year-old conductor directs a performance which is unflagging in its passion and energy. Böhm has a striking way in the Prelude and *Liebestod* of making the swell of passion seem like the movement of a great sea, sometimes with gentle motion, sometimes with the breaking of the mightiest of waves. Nilsson characterizes strongly and her voice with its marvellous cleaving-power can also soften quite beautifully. Windgassen's heroic performance in the Third Act is in some ways the crown of his achievements on record, even though the voice has dried and aged a little. Christa Ludwig is the ideal Brangäne, Waechter a suitably-forthright Kurwenal, and Talvela an expressive, noble-voiced Marke. Orchestra and chorus are at their finest.

Over several seasons of conducting the work at Bayreuth, Barenboim has by now thoroughly mastered the pacing and shaping of the score as a unified entity. Even more important he has peered into the depths of both its construction and meaning, emerging with answers that satisfy on almost all counts, most tellingly so in the melancholic adumbration of Isolde's thoughts during her narration, in the sadly eloquent counterpoint of bass clarinet, lower strings and cor anglais underpinning King Marke's lament, and in the searingly tense support to Tristan's second hallucination. These are but the most salient moments in a reading that thoughtfully and unerringly reveals the inner parts of this astounding score. The obverse of this caring manner is a certain want of spontaneity, and a tendency to become a shade self-regarding. You occasionally miss the overwhelming force of Furtwängler's metaphysical account or the immediacy and excitement of Böhm's famous live Bayreuth reading but the very mention of those conductors suggests that Barenboim can live in their world and survive the comparisons with his own perfectly valid interpretation. Besides, he has the most gloriously spacious yet well-focused recording so far of this opera and an orchestra not only familiar with his ways but ready to execute them in a disciplined and sensitive manner. The recording also takes account of spatial questions, in particular the placing of the horns offstage at the start of Act 2.

Salminen delivers a classic account of Marke's anguished reproaches to Tristan, his singing at once sonorous, dignified and reaching to the heart, a reading on a par with that of his fellow-countryman Talvela for Böhm. Meier's Isolde is a vitally wrought, verbally alert reading, which catches much of the venom of Act 1, the visceral excitement of Act 2, the lambent utterance of the Liebestod. Nothing she does is unmusical; everything is keenly intelligent, yet possibly her tone is too narrow for the role. Lipovšek's Brangäne tends to slide and swim in an ungainly fashion, sounding at times definitely overparted. Listening to Ludwig (Böhm) only serves to emphasize Lipovšek's deficiencies. Then it is often hard on the newer set to tell Isolde and Brangäne apart, so alike can be their timbre. As with his partner, Jerusalem sings his role with immaculate musicality; indeed he may be the most accurate Tristan on disc where note values are concerned, one also consistently attentive to dynamics and long-breathed phrasing. On the other hand, although he puts a deal of feeling into his interpretation, he hasn't quite the intensity of utterance of either Windgassen (Böhm), or, even more, Suthaus (Furtwängler). His actual timbre is dry and occasionally rasping: in vocal terms alone Suthaus is in a class of his own. Yet, even with reservations about the Isolde and Tristan, this is a version that will undoubtedly hold a high place in any survey of this work, for which one performance can never hope to tell the whole story.

Die Walküre.
Poul Elming ten Siegmund; **Alessandra Marc** sop Sieglinde; **Gabriele Schnaut** mez Brünnhilde; **Robert Hale** bass-bar Wotan; **Anja Silja** sop Fricka; **Alfred Muff** bass Hunding; **Michèle Crider** sop Gerhilde; **Ruth Falcon** sop Helmwige; **Susan Marie Pierson** sop Ortlinde; **Karin Goltz** mez Waltraute; **Susan Shafer** mez Rossweisse; **Katherine Ciesinski** mez Siegrune; **Sandra Walker** mez Grimgerde; **Penelope Walker** mez Schwertleite; **Cleveland Orchestra / Christoph von Dohnányi.**
Decca 440 371-2DHO4 (four discs: 225 minutes: DDD). Notes, text and translation included. Recorded 1992.   Ⓕ

Dohnányi conducts a well-paced, thought-through reading that at once creates dramatic excitement and attends to the longer view. We sense the inner pleasures and anxieties of each character in turn: Siegmund's extended defiance, Sieglinde's ecstasy in Act 1, even more her spiritual desperation in Act 2 and final elevation when she knows she is pregnant, Wotan's misery, fury, love, Brünnhilde's missionary zeal in Act 2, her remorse in Act 3. In brief the conductor persuades singers and players alike to give us the essence of the work. One can hardly ask for more, apart from a level of excellence in execution on both sides. Neither orchestra nor cast disappoints, the players responding with a fiery, expertly played and vital performance. In Act 1 we encounter the warm, dark-grained Sieglinde of Alessandra Marc, whose slightly covered, expressive tone and phrasing recall that of Rysanek in the part. Poul Elming is an almost ideal Siegmund, his tone pleasing with that slightly metallic touch common in Scandinavian singers, especially tenors. His antagonist, Hunding, is sung with astonishing immediacy and biting venom by Alfred Muff, every syllable made to tell.

In Act 2 we meet at once Gabriele Schnaut's very positive Brünnhilde. Bright and forceful in her war cry, she shows suitable concern at her father's distress, and is wise and dignified in her colloquy with Siegmund. In Act 3 her appeal to Wotan 'War es so schmählich?' is lovingly projected with more than a touch of Varnay in her voice, praise enough. Robert Hale's Wotan is a more familiar quantity. With a voice properly poised for the part between baritone and bass, he has no difficulty with either his high or low notes, can sing a true line and is fully conversant with every facet of Wotan's dilemma. He is no less successful in trying to defy Fricka or in thundering against his errant daughter. You may find the ultimate in psychological insight missing, but most of the interior anguish of the part is there, impeccably delivered. As his Fricka, Anja Silja gives a typically intelligent, keenly articulated performance. The recording, including a few unobtrusive sound effects, is large in scale. A grand, satisfying performance on almost every count.

Emile Waldteufel   French 1837-1915

Flots de joie, Op. 145. Château en Espagne, Op. 225. Gaîté, Op. 164. Tout à vous, Op. 142. Bella, Op. 113. Brune ou blonde, Op. 162. Acclamations, Op. 223. La Barcarolle, Op. 178. Béobile.
Slovak State Philharmonic Orchestra, Košice / Alfred Walter.
Marco Polo 8 223684 (66 minutes: DDD). Recorded 1992-95.   Ⓕ

Alfred Walter's Waldteufel series is distinguished by his characteristic professionalism and the Slovak orchestra at Košice plays with warmth and considerable polish. This volume contains entirely unfamiliar repertoire, and much of it deserves to be better known: Gaîté, Brune ou blonde and La Barcarolle all have attractive ideas, the last-named nothing like Offenbach, but with a gently bouncing lilt. There are several striking numbers: Rêverie and the nostalgic Au revoir are aptly named, while Trésor d'amour uses flutes to usher in a tune of graceful delicacy. Coquetterie, too, has a capricious, winningly scored introduction entirely in keeping with its title. The highlight of the disc is Béobile, a pizzicato novelty of such verve that if better known it could be a great favourite. The recording is excellent, with a nice ballroom resonance.

Sir William Walton   British 1902-1983

Cello Concerto. Symphony No. 1 in B minor.
Lynn Harrell vc
City of Birmingham Symphony Orchestra / Sir Simon Rattle.
EMI British Composers CDC7 54572-2 (74 minutes: DDD). Recorded 1990-91.   Ⓕ ⓇⓇ

Walton Orchestral

Simon Rattle's version of Walton's First Symphony is as intelligent and dynamic a traversal as one would expect from this talented figure. Texturally speaking, the inner workings of Walton's score are laid bare as never before, aided by what sounds like a meticulously prepared CBSO. Some may find a touch of contrivance about Rattle's control of dynamics in the scorching first movement, but there's absolutely no gainsaying the underlying tension or cumulative power of the whole. Under Rattle the *Scherzo* darts menacingly (the most convincing account of this music since the classic 1966 Previn account – see below), whilst the slow movement is an unusually nervy, anxious affair. Certainly, the finale is superbly athletic and lithe, though by now one is beginning to register that EMI's sound is, for all its transparency and natural perspective, perhaps a little lightweight for such enormously red-blooded inspiration. Overall, though, Rattle's is a very strong account – indisputably one of the finest we've had in recent years – and his disc's claims are enhanced by the coupling, a wholly admirable performance of the same composer's luxuriant Cello Concerto (though see page 1083 for an alternative coupling). Here Rattle and Lynn Harrell form an inspired partnership, totally dedicated and achieving utter concentration throughout – no mean feat in this of all works which demand so much from both performers and listeners.

Cello Concerto. Symphony No. 1.
Robert Cohen *vc*
Bournemouth Symphony Orchestra / Andrew Litton.
Decca London 443 450-2LH (74 minutes: DDD). Recorded 1993.　　　Ⓕ

Belshazzar's Feast. Henry V. Crown Imperial.
Bryn Terfel *bass-bar*
Waynflete Singers; L'Inviti; Bournemouth Symphony Chorus and Orchestra / Andrew Litton.
Decca London 448 134-2LH (60 minutes: DDD). Text included. Recorded 1995.　　　Ⓕ

More than anyone since Previn, Litton thrillingly conveys the element of wildness in Walton's finest inspirations, notably in the works of the pre-war period. It is partly a question of his treatment of the jazzy syncopations which are such a vital element in Walton. Litton is not alone in treating them with a degree of idiomatic freedom – the composer himself as interpreter set the pattern – but as with Previn, Litton's affinity with the jazz element comes from inside, clearly reflecting his American background. Consistently he makes the music crackle with high voltage electricity, and again he echoes Previn in the way he can screw tension up to the limit and beyond, resolving grinding dissonances on heart-warming concords. That is particularly important in the First Symphony. The Rattle version is superb, but next to Litton's it seems almost too safe, too closely controlled, lacking the extremes of tension, the wildness. Litton even surpasses Previn in the climactic resolution of the finale. With him this movement in no way seems a let-down after the rest, as it easily can – reflecting the composer's problems over completing it. The climactic resolution on an outburst from multiple timpani and percussion is more shattering than ever before on disc, with the Decca recording team achieving wonders in the weight and brilliance of the sound. In general the transfer level is a degree lower than in most rival versions. In the Cello Concerto too the sound is a degree less immediate than in Rattle's version with Lynn Harrell, and that matches a broad contrast of interpretation. Where Harrell remains unrivalled in power and tonal resonance, Robert Cohen for Litton follows a deeper, more hushed, more meditative approach, even when as in the first movement he has a more flowing speed.

In both discs the exceptionally full and vivid recording brings out the opulence as well as the sensuousness of Walton's orchestration, regularly enhancing Litton's expressive warmth as a Waltonian in the great romantic melodies. Not only that, the bitingly dramatic contrasts of brass and percussion have never been more vivid, with the Bournemouth orchestra playing magnificently, not just with brilliance but with passionate commitment. Whereas the first disc was recorded in the helpful acoustic of the Southampton Guildhall, *Belshazzar's Feast* was put into the grander setting of Winchester Cathedral. The problems for the engineers must have been daunting, for the reverberation time is formidably long, yet thanks to brilliant balancing there is ample detail and fine focus in exceptionally incisive choral and orchestral sound. The great benefit is that this emerges as a performance on a bigger scale than its rivals, with the contrasts between full chorus and semi-chorus the more sharply established. The vividly dramatic soloist is Bryn Terfel, spine-chilling in his narration describing the writing on the wall. In *Crown Imperial* a cathedral acoustic does bring some lack of clarity, but it is a stirring performance. Andrew Litton's years as Principal Conductor of the Bournemouth Symphony Orchestra could hardly have had a richer culmination on disc.

Viola Concerto in A minor. Symphony No. 2. Johannesburg Festival Overture.
Lars Anders Tomter *va*
English Northern Philharmonia / Paul Daniel.
Naxos 8 553402 (61 minutes: DDD). Recorded 1995.　　　Ⓢ

This disc opens with one of the wittiest, most exuberant performances of the *Johannesburg Festival Overture*: characteristically Daniel encourages the orchestra's virtuoso wind and brass soloists to point the jazz rhythms idiomatically, making the music sparkle. The Viola Concerto is just as delectably pointed, the whole performance instantly magnetic. Tomter's tone, with its rapid flicker-vibrato, lacks the warmth of Kennedy's (reviewed below), but the vibrato is only obtrusive in that upper-middle register and his intonation is immaculate, his attack consistently clean, to match the crisp ensemble of the orchestra. Although he adopts relatively measured speeds both for the *Scherzo* and the jaunty opening theme of the finale, the rhythmic lift brings out the *scherzando* jollity of the latter all the more.

Daniel's keen observance of dynamic markings is again brought out in the stuttering fanfare theme of the *Scherzo*, with muted trumpets and trombones for once played *pianissimo* as marked. The close of the slow epilogue has never been recorded with such a profound hush as here, subsiding in darkness, and the recording team is to be complimented on getting such beautiful sound, clean with plenty of bloom. Paul Daniel adopts a relatively broad tempo in the Symphony's first movement, which makes less impact than in Andrew Litton's powerful Decca version (reviewed above), and the flowing tempo for the central slow movement makes for a lighter, less passionate result too. The finale, with its brassy first statement of the Passacaglia theme, brings fine dynamic contrasts, but again Litton and others produce a fatter, weightier sound, which on balance is preferable. Yet Daniel's view is a very valid one, to round off most convincingly an invaluable addition to the Walton discography.

Walton Viola Concerto[a].
Bruch Violin and Viola Concerto in E minor, Op. 88[b]. Romance, Op. 85[c]. Kol Nidrei, Op. 47[c].
Yuri Bashmet *va* [b]**Viktor Tretyakov** *vn*
London Symphony Orchestra / **[a]André Previn,** [bc]**Neeme Järvi.**
RCA Red Seal 09026 63292-2 (64 minutes: DDD). Recorded 1994 and 1996.   Ⓕ

Presumably, this outstanding version of the Walton Viola Concerto from Yuri Bashmet, warm and intense, recorded in 1994, was held up for lack of a suitable coupling. Having the three Bruch works may seem odd, but with the passionate Bashmet the mixture works well. After all, both composers are at their most richly lyrical and though in style they are worlds apart, the Bruch Double Concerto and the Walton Concerto date from successive decades, written respectively in 1911 and 1929. In the Walton, Bashmet adopts a very slow speed for the opening *Andante*, but is fast and incisive in the vigorous third subject, and the central *Scherzo* brings a dazzling display of virtuosity. In the finale, Bashmet finds plenty of fun in Walton's *scherzando* writing, but then draws out the epilogue at a very slow speed, beautifully sustained, not just by him but by Previn and the orchestra, the ideal accompanists. The rarely-played Bruch Double Concerto in three compact movements, slow, medium and fast, is better known in the version for clarinet and viola. As performed here by Bashmet with his pure-toned violinist colleague, Viktor Tretyakov, it gains in sensuousness from having the solo instruments closely allied rather than sharply contrasted. It is amazing what a fund of melodic invention Bruch kept into his seventies, not just in this concerto but in the glorious *Romance* for viola and orchestra of 1912. Bashmet again gives a heartfelt performance, as he does of *Kol Nidrei*. With Bashmet at his finest, and the LSO playing beautifully for both conductors, this is a disc to recommend to anyone with a taste for romantic viola music.

Violin Concerto. Viola Concerto.
Kennedy *vn/va*
Royal Philharmonic Orchestra / André Previn.
EMI CDC7 49628-2 (57 minutes: DDD). Recorded 1987.   Ⓕ Ⓢ

These concertos are among the most beautiful written this century. Walton was in his late twenties when he composed the viola work and in it he achieved a depth of emotion, a range of ideas and a technical assurance beyond anything he had so far written. Lacking in the brilliance of the violin, the viola has an inherently contemplative tonal quality and Walton matches this to perfection in his score, complementing it rather than trying to compensate as other composers have done. There is a larger element of virtuosity in the Violin Concerto, but it is never allowed to dominate the musical argument. Kennedy gives wonderfully warm and characterful performances which are likely to stand unchallenged as a coupling for a long time. He produces a beautiful tone quality on both of his instruments, which penetrates to the heart of the aching melancholy of Walton's slow music, and he combines it with an innate, highly developed and spontaneous-sounding sense of rhythmic drive and bounce which propels the quick movements forward with great panache. Previn has long been a persuasive Waltonian and the RPO responds marvellously, with crisp and alert playing throughout. The recordings are very clear and naturally balanced with the solo instrument set in a believable perspective.

Belshazzar's Feast. Overtures – Portsmouth Point; Scapino. Improvisation on an Impromptu of Benjamin Britten.
John Shirley-Quirk *bar*
London Symphony Chorus and Orchestra / André Previn.
EMI CDM7 64723-2 (68 minutes: ADD). Text included. Recorded 1972. Ⓜ 𝐑𝐑

Previn's 1972 version of *Belshazzar's Feast*, recorded at the time of the composer's 70th birthday, is preferable to his 1986 version for ASV. The bite of the choral sound and the closer focus make the result far sharper and more dramatic, even though some of the speeds are more spacious. John Shirley-Quirk as soloist is also preferable to the less firm Benjamin Luxon, having more subtlety and refinement as well as a firmer voice The transfer is outstandingly good with fine bloom and plenty of weight. EMI also provides most generous couplings.

Walton Façade – Suites Nos. 1-3[a]. Siesta[b]. Sinfonia concertante[a]. Portsmouth Point[a].
Arnold Popular Birthday[a].
Eric Parkin *pf*
London Philharmonic Orchestra / [a]**Jan Latham-König,** [b]**Bryden Thomson.**
Chandos CHAN9148 (59 minutes: DDD). Recorded 1990-92. Ⓕ

The *Sinfonia concertante* (1926-27) with its sharply memorable ideas in each movement and characteristically high voltage, has never had the attention it deserves, and that is all the more regrettable when there is such a dearth of attractive British piano concertos. The soloist, Eric Parkin, is perfectly attuned to the idiom, warmly melodic as well as jazzily syncopated. He points rhythms infectiously and shapes melodies persuasively, though the recording sets the piano a little backwardly, no doubt to reflect the idea that this is not a full concerto. Jan Latham-König proves most understanding of the composer's 1920s idiom, giving the witty *Façade* movements just the degree of jazzy freedom they need. The Third Suite, devised and arranged by Christopher Palmer, draws on three apt movements from the *Façade* entertainment, ending riotously with the rag-music of 'Something lies beyond the scene'. That is a first recording, as is Constant Lambert's arrangement of the Overture, *Portsmouth Point. Siesta* is given an aptly cool performance under Thomson, and the *Popular Birthday* is Malcolm Arnold's fragmentary linking of *Happy Birthday to You* with the 'Popular Song' from *Façade*, originally written for Walton's seventieth birthday. The impact of some of the pieces, notably in *Façade,* would have been even sharper, had the warmly atmospheric Chandos recording placed the orchestra a fraction closer.

Overtures – Johannesburg Festival; Portsmouth Point; Scapino. Capriccio burlesco.
The First Shoot (orch. Palmer). Granada Prelude. Prologo e Fantasia. Music for Children.
Galop final (orch. Palmer).
London Philharmonic Orchestra / Bryden Thomson.
Chandos CHAN8968 (70 minutes: DDD).

While enthusiasts for Walton's music may justifiably complain that there is not enough of it, they usually concede that what there is is readily available in good recorded performances. However, thanks to the dedicated and skilful work of Christopher Palmer, still more of it is now coming to light. How many people, one wonders, have ever heard *The First Shoot*, a miniature ballet written for a C.B. Cochran show in 1935, the *Granada Prelude* devised for that television company in the 1960s, or the *Prologo e Fantasia* which was the composer's last work, written for Rostropovich and his National Symphony Orchestra of Washington. Such fresh and welcome goodies as these appear along with familiar material such as the splendidly open-air, nautical overture *Portsmouth Point* that Walton wrote nearly 40 years earlier, at the very start of his career. The Cochran piece, as orchestrated by Palmer, has five little sections that are delightfully jazzy in a way that recalls *Façade* and one's only regret is that there's not more of it. All this music is in the excellent hands of Bryden Thomson and the LPO, and Palmer's booklet essay is a model of stylish, informative writing. The recording is richly toned, which takes some edge off the composer's characteristically sharp scoring.

Spitfire Prelude and Fugue. Sinfonia concertante[a]. Variations on a Theme by Hindemith.
March – The History of the English Speaking Peoples.
[a]**Peter Donohoe** *pf*
English Northern Philharmonia / Paul Daniel.
Naxos 8 553869 (53 minutes: DDD). Recorded 1996.

Naxos opts for the original version of the *Sinfonia concertante* rather than Walton's revision, with piano writing and orchestration slimmed down. Walton himself, before he died, suggested such a return. As soloist Peter Donohoe plays with power and flamboyance, brought home the more when the piano is very forwardly balanced, too much so for a work which does not aim to be a full concerto, leaving the orchestra a little pale behind. Even so, hopefully this account, broad in the first movement, flowing in the central *Andante*, will persuade others to take it up, young man's music built on striking, colourful ideas, used with crisp concision. Paul Daniel is splendid at interpreting the jazzy syncopations with the right degree of freedom, and in the *Spitfire Prelude and Fugue* he adds to the impact by taking the big march tune faster than many, similarly demonstrating that *The History of the English Speaking Peoples* March, buried for too long, is a match for Walton's other ceremonial marches. Best of all is the performance of the *Hindemith* Variations, given here with winning panache. The strings of the English Northern Philharmonia may not be as weighty as in some rival versions, but the articulation is brilliant, and the complex textures are all the more transparent. The fire and energy of the performance has never been surpassed on disc. A very welcome issue.

Walton Symphony No. 1.
Vaughan Williams The Wasps – Overture.
London Symphony Orchestra / André Previn.
RCA Gold Seal GD87830 (52 minutes: ADD). Recorded 1966, 1971.   Ⓜ

André Previn's 1966 version of Walton's First Symphony with the LSO marked a breakthrough in his recording career, instantly establishing him as a major new figure, not least in interpreting British music and Walton above all. As a performance it has still not been surpassed or even matched on record, and this fine transfer issued at mid-price simply confirms this opinion. Even now Previn has rarely made a record as bitingly intense as this. A slight emotional reticence in the slow movement and in the epilogue to the finale with its elegiac trumpet solo add rather than detract from its merits. Also, the flute solo at the start of the slow movement has rarely sounded so chill and bare as here, where other interpreters can seem too overtly emotional, too warm for this melancholy music. *The Wasps* Overture is a most enjoyable makeweight. There is a hint of rasp on the brass tone at times, betraying the age of the recording, but the precision of focus and balance on CD are all the more impressive, with plenty of body in the sound.

Symphony No. 1. Belshazzar's Feast.
Thomas Hampson *bar*
Cleveland Orchestra Chorus;
City of Birmingham Symphony Chorus and Orchestra / Sir Simon Rattle.
EMI CDC5 56592-2 (78 minutes: DDD). Recorded 1990-97.   Ⓕ

This is a winning coupling, with Walton's two searing masterpieces from the 1930s given electrifying performances under Rattle. This recording of the symphony first appeared coupled with the Cello Concerto (reviewed above), but *Belshazzar's Feast* is more recent, recorded with a combination of atmospheric warmth and clarity unmatched in any other version, another tribute to the acoustic of Symphony Hall, Birmingham. Rattle, with players he knows so well, combines expressive freedom with knife-edged precision of ensemble, and it is the same in *Belshazzar's Feast*. It is true that compared with Previn in his vintage version – still sounding wonderfully well, with the transfer of the analogue recording full and forward – the opening sections are not quite so warmly expressive, have less elbow-room rhythmically. Also, with Previn the celebrations after the king's death have more jollity in them, where Rattle, with syncopations made exceptionally sharp and biting, conveys much more a manic intensity entirely in keeping with the subject. Rattle's total timing is over three minutes shorter than those of either Previn or Litton (reviewed above). That, incidentally, has made all the difference in allowing these two works to be fitted on a single CD. Not that there is any feeling of haste in Rattle's reading, just of extra tautness, with incisive playing and singing from both the orchestra and the massive chorus. It was an inspired idea to bring in the Cleveland Orchestra Chorus alongside the Birmingham chorus. Though other versions have ample weight of choral sound, this one consistently scores in the terracing of sound, with dynamic shading wonderfully precise and with the semi-chorus magically distinct. As baritone soloist Thomas Hampson sings immaculately with warm tone and clear focus, and if the description of the writing on the wall is not quite as mysterious as it can be, that again reflects Rattle's tautness and urgency.

Symphony No. 1. Partita.
English Northern Philharmonia / Paul Daniel.
Naxos 8 553180 (64 minutes: DDD). Recorded 1994.   Ⓢ🅔

Daniel demonstrates clearly here his natural affinity with Walton's music. In the sustained paragraphs of the First Symphony he knows unerringly how to build up tension to breaking point, before resolving it, and then building again – a quality vital above all in the first and third movements. He is freer than many in his use of rubato too, again often a question of building and resolving tension, as well as in the degree of elbow-room he allows for jazzy syncopations, always idiomatic. This symphony, with its heavy orchestration, would certainly have benefited from rather drier sound, but well-judged microphone balance allows ample detail through. Only occasionally do you feel a slight lack of body in high violin tone, a tiny reservation. Daniel's reading of the *Partita*, originally written for Szell and the Cleveland Orchestra, brings out above all the work's joyfulness. It may not be quite as crisp in its ensemble as that of the dedicatees, but the degree of wildness, with dissonances underlined, proves a positive advantage in conveying enjoyment. In the slow movement Daniel at a relatively slow speed is markedly more expressive than those brilliant models, again a point which makes the performance more endearing, and if Daniel's speed for the finale is just a little cautious, the precision and rhythmic bounce readily justify his approach. Irrespective of price, this is a version of the much-recorded symphony that competes with the finest ever, and outshines most.

Piano Quartet[a]. Violin Sonata[b]. Five Bagatelles.
Janice Graham *vn* **Paul Silverthorne** *va* **Moray Welsh** *vc* **Tom Kerstens** *gtr*
[a]**Israela Margalit**, [b]**John Alley** *pfs*
EMI Anglo-American Chamber Music CDC5 55404-2 (69 minutes: DDD). Recorded 1994-95.　　Ⓕ

This is a splendid addition to EMI's Anglo-American Chamber Music series, with superb string players from the LSO, and with Israela Margalit making a distinguished contribution. A bonus is an outstanding performance of the *Five Bagatelles* for guitar, originally written for Julian Bream. With Israela Margalit injecting fire, the performance of the Piano Quartet is light and volatile. That impression is enhanced by the EMI recording balance, with open textures, letting the solo work stand out. The EMI team's treatment of the slow movement – light, flowing yet still warm – is apt for the work of a precocious 16-year-old composer, and though the finale is not quite as biting as it could be, there is still vigour, and the players readily respond to the moments of repose, as in the pause before the final coda. Janice Graham is the brilliant, winningly expressive violinist in both works, fanciful and volatile, notably in the first movement of the Sonata. Her performance is outstanding, bringing warmth and purposefulness to what can easily seem one of the more wayward of Walton's major works. The excellent sound is remarkably consistent.

Anon in love. A Song for the Lord Mayor's Table. Façade – Long steel grass; Tango-pasodoble; Popular Song (all arr. Palmer); Daphne; Through Gilded Trellises; Old Sir Faulk. Winds. Tritons. Christopher Columbus – Beatriz's Song. As You Like It – Under the Greenwood Tree.
Dame Felicity Lott *sop* **Martyn Hill** *ten* **Craig Ogden** *gtr* **Graham Johnson** *pf*
Collins Classics 1493-2 (52 minutes: DDD). Texts included. Recorded 1996.　　Ⓕ

Walton was not the most prolific of composers, but he contributed a masterpiece to practically every genre in which he worked. Similarly, while we do not often think of him in association with the song or the song-cycle, his solo cantata, *A Song for the Lord Mayor's Table* is surely something special. So, you might say, is *Anon in love*, the sequence of Elizabethan lyrics originally set (as heard here) for tenor and guitar and premièred at Aldeburgh in 1960. It was rescored for strings, harp and (very sparingly) percussion, and the *Lord Mayor* for full orchestra, which, as Michael Kennedy notes in his introductory essay, Walton really had in mind from the first. The performances match their accompaniments. Dame Felicity Lott might well have characterized the *Lord Mayor* on a larger scale had she been singing with orchestra. In the songs from *Façade*, the difference is most marked in 'Old Sir Faulk', where Lott sounds merely pretty and high-spirited. However 'irksome' Walton found the labour, he wrote very well for the piano; so, at least, it seems when Graham Johnson is the pianist. Even *Façade* sounds pianistic in his hands, and in the second set (arranged by the late Christopher Palmer) the partnership works brilliantly. As a milk-white witness of Spanish night-life, Martyn Hill makes scary magic of 'Long Steel Grass'. The shorter pieces go well too, particularly the 16-year-old's turbulent accentuations in his setting of Swinburne's *Winds*. The recital is a valuable addition to Collins's English Song series.

Belshazzar's Feast[a]. Coronation Te Deum. Gloria[b].
[b]**Ameral Gunson** *contr* [b]**Neil Mackie** *ten* [a]**Gwynne Howell**, [b]**Stephen Roberts** *bars*
Bach Choir; Philharmonia Orchestra / Sir David Willcocks.
Chandos CHAN8760 (62 minutes: DDD). Texts included. Recorded 1989.　　Ⓕ

With Sir David Willcocks in charge of the choir which he has directed since 1960, one need have no fears that the composer's many near-impossible demands of the chorus in all three of these masterpieces will not be met with elegance and poise. There is as well, in *Belshazzar*, a predictably fine balance of the forces to ensure that as much detail as possible is heard from both chorus and orchestra, even when Walton is bombarding us from all corners of the universe with extra brass bands and all manner of clamorous percussion in praise of pagan gods. Such supremely musical concerns bring their own rewards in a work that can often seem vulgar. The revelation here is the sustained degree of dramatic thrust, exhilaration and what Herbert Howells called 'animal joy' in the proceedings. How marvellous, too, to hear the work paced and scaled to avoid the impression of reduced voltage after the big moments. Gwynne Howell is the magnificently steady, firm and dark toned baritone. The *Gloria* and *Coronation Te Deum* are informed with the same concerns: accuracy and professional polish are rarely allowed to hinder these vital contributions to the British choral tradition. The recording's cathedral-like acoustic is as ideal for the *Te Deum*'s ethereal antiphonal effects, as it is for *Belshazzar*'s glorious spectacle; and Chandos matches Willcocks's care for balance, bar by bar.

Walton Façade[a]. Overtures – Portsmouth Point; Scapino[b]. Siesta[b].
Arnold English Dances, Op. 33[b].
Dame Edith Sitwell, Sir Peter Pears *spkrs*
[a]**English Opera Group Ensemble / Anthony Collins;**
[b]**London Philharmonic Orchestra / Sir Adrian Boult.**
Decca London mono 425 661-2LM (74 minutes: DDD). Recorded 1954.   Ⓜ Ⓗ

This is the classic and authoritative reading of the fully approved selection of *Façade* settings. Dame Edith herself reads two-thirds of the numbers, Sir Peter the remaining third. The poetess herself reads them with such *joie de vivre*, such a natural feeling for her own verses and inflexions that nobody could be expected to rival her. Her timing is perfect, her delivery deliciously idiosyncratic, the intonations obviously what she and presumably Walton wanted. Sir Peter isn't far behind her in ability to relish the writing and the instrumental ensemble plays with refinement allied to virtuosity. The 1950s mono recording stands the test of time remarkably well.

The Bear.
Della Jones *mez* Madame Popova; **Alan Opie** *bar* Smirnov; **John Shirley-Quirk** *bar* Luka;
Northern Sinfonia / Richard Hickox.
Chandos CHAN9245 (53 minutes: DDD). Text included. Recorded 1993.   Ⓕ

If Walton's sense of humour was firmly established from the start in *Façade*, his one-acter, *The Bear*, among his later works brings out very clearly how strong that quality remained throughout his life. In this Chekhov tale, Walton times the melodramatic moments marvellously – notably the climactic duel between the mourning widow and her husband's creditor (the bear of the title) and Hickox brings that out most effectively. Walton also deftly heightens the farcical element by introducing dozens of parodies and tongue-in-cheek musical references, starting cheekily with echoes of Britten's *Midsummer Night's Dream*. Hickox brings out the richness of the piece as well as its wit, helped by the opulent Chandos recording which still allows words to be heard clearly. The casting of the three characters is as near ideal as could be. Della Jones is commanding as the affronted widow, consistently relishing the melodrama like a young Edith Evans. Alan Opie as Smirnov, 'the bear' is clean-cut and incisive, powerfully bringing out the irate creditor's changing emotions, while John Shirley-Quirk, still rich and resonant, is very well cast as the old retainer, Luka.

Troilus and Cressida.
Judith Howarth *sop* Cressida; **Arthur Davies** *ten* Troilus; **Clive Bayley** *bass* Calkas;
Nigel Robson *ten* Pandarus; **Alan Opie** *bar* Diomede; **James Thornton** *bar* Antenor;
David Owen-Lewis *bass* Horaste; **Yvonne Howard** *mez* Evadne; **Peter Bodenham** *ten* Priest;
Keith Mills *ten* Soldier; **Bruce Budd** *bass* First Watchman; **Stephen Dowson** *bass* Second
Watchman; **Brian Cookson** *ten* Third Watchman;
Chorus of Opera North; English Northern Philharmonia / Richard Hickox.
Chandos CHAN9370/1 (two discs: 133 minutes: DDD). Notes and text included. Recorded 1995.
Gramophone Award Winner 1995.   Ⓕ

Troilus and Cressida is here powerfully presented as an opera for the central repertory, traditional in its red-blooded treatment of a big classical subject. Few if any operas since Puccini's have such a rich store of instantly memorable tunes as *Troilus and Cressida*. Walton wrote the piece in the wake of the first great operatic success of his rival, Benjamin Britten. What more natural than for Walton, by this time no longer an *enfant terrible* of British music but an Establishment figure, to turn his back on operas devoted like Britten's to offbeat subjects, and to go back to an older operatic tradition using a classical love story, based on Chaucer (not Shakespeare). Though he was much praised for this by early critics in 1954, he was quickly attacked for being old-fashioned. Even in the tautened version of the score he offered for the 1976 Covent Garden revival – with the role of the heroine adapted for the mezzo voice of Dame Janet Baker – the piece was described by one critic as a dodo. Yet as Richard Hickox suggests, fashion after 40 years matters little, and the success of the Opera North production in January 1995 indicated that at last the time had come for a big, warmly romantic, sharply dramatic work to be appreciated on its own terms. This recording was made under studio conditions during the run of the opera in Leeds in the UK. The discs amply confirm what the live performances suggested, that Walton's tautening of the score, coupled with a restoration of the original soprano register for Cressida, has proved entirely successful.

Hickox conducts a performance that is magnetic from beginning to end. The scene is atmospherically set in Act 1 by the chorus, initially off-stage, but then with the incisive Opera North chorus snapping out thrilling cries of 'We are accurs'd!'. The libretto is unashamedly archaic in its use of 'opera-speak' like that, with 'thee's and 'thou's and the occasional 'perchance'. Though the text may put some off, it is plainly apt for a traditional 'well-made opera' on a classical subject. The first soloist one hears is the High Priest, Calkas, Cressida's father, about to defect to the Greeks, and the role is superbly taken by the firm, dark-toned Clive Bayley. Troilus's entry and his declaration of love for Cressida bring Waltonian sensuousness and the first statements of the soaring Cressida theme. Arthur Davies is not afraid of using his head voice for *pianissimos*, so contrasting the more dramatically with the big outbursts and his ringing top notes. This is a young-sounding hero, Italianate of tone. Similarly, Judith Howarth's Cressida is quite girlish and she brings out the vulnerability of the character along with sweetness and warmth. After Calkas has defected to the Greeks, her cry of 'He has deserted us and Troy!' conveys genuine fear, with her will undermined. All told, although some fine music has been cut, the tautened version is far more effective both musically and dramatically, with no *longueurs* at all. The role of Diomede, Cressida's Greek suitor, can seem one-dimensional, but Alan Opie in one of his finest performances on record sharpens the focus, making him a genuine threat, with the element of nobility fully allowed. As Antenor, James Thornton sings strongly, but is less steady than the others, while Yvonne Howard is superb in the mezzo role of Evadne, Cressida's treacherous servant and confidante. Not just the chorus but the orchestra of Opera North, the English Northern Philharmonia, respond with fervour. Naturally and idiomatically they observe the Waltonian rubato and the lifting of jazzily syncopated rhythms which Hickox as a dedicated Waltonian instils, echoing the composer's own example. As for the recorded sound the bloom of the acoustic enhances the score, helped by the wide dynamic range.

Peter Warlock
British 1894-1930

The Wind from the West. To the Memory of a Great Singer. Take, o take those lips away. As ever I saw. The Bayly berith the bell away. There is a lady sweet and kind. Lullaby. Sweet content. Late summer. The Singer. Rest, sweet nymphs. Sleep. A Sad Song. In an arbour green. Autumn Twilight. I held love's head. Thou gav'st me leave to kiss. Yarmouth Fair. Pretty Ring Time. A Prayer to St Anthony of Padua. The Sick Heart. Robin Goodfellow. Jillian of Berry. Fair and True. Ha'nacker Mill. The Night. My Own Country. The First Mercy. The Lover's Maze. Cradle Song. Sigh no more, ladies. Passing by. The Contented Lover. The Fox.
John Mark Ainsley ten **Roger Vignoles** pf
Hyperion CDA66736 (69 minutes: DDD). Texts included. Recorded 1994. Ⓕ Ⓔ

Philip Heseltine, so strangely renamed, did not facilitate either the singing or the playing of his songs. For the voice they have a way of passing awkwardly between registers, and though the high notes are not very high they tend to be uncomfortably placed. The pianist, caught for long in a pool of chromatics, suddenly finds his hands flying in both directions. Yet for the singer with the control of breath and command of voice that John Mark Ainsley so splendidly employs here, and for a pianist with Roger Vignoles's sureness of touch and insight, they must be wonderfully satisfying to perform, for there is such a love of song implicit in them and such a personal voice speaks through them. The programme here is arranged chronologically, from 1911 to 1930. Early and Elizabethan poems are the favourite source, and then the poems of contemporaries such as Belloc, Symons and Bruce Blunt. Even the earliest of the songs, *The Wind from the West*, has the characteristic touch of a lyrical impulse, directly responsive to words, and a fastidious avoidance of strophic or harmonic banality. Often a private unease works within the chromaticism as in the *Cradle Song* ('Be still, my sweet sweeting'), yet nothing could be more wholehearted in gaiety when he is in the mood for it (viz. *In an arbour green, Robin Goodfellow, Jillian of Berry*). Ainsley sings with fine reserves of power as well as softness; he phrases beautifully, and all the nuance that is so essential for these songs (in *Sleep*, for instance) is most sensitively judged. Vignoles is entirely at one with singer and composer. There are excellent notes by Fred Tomlinson, and a fine watercolour by Peter de Wint graces the booklet.

Franz Waxman

Waxman The Song of Terezína[a].
Zeisl Requiem Ebraico[b].
[b]**Deborah Riedel** sop [a]**Della Jones** mez [b]**Michael Kraus** bass-bar
[a]**Berlin Radio Children's Choir;**
Berlin Radio Chorus and Symphony Orchestra / Lawrence Foster.
Decca 460 211-2DH (59 minutes: DDD). Texts and translations included. Recorded 1997. Ⓕ

The booklet accompanying this CD is illustrated by a stark photograph of the crematorium at Terezín in 1945. Of the 15,000 children who were interned there only 100 survived. In 1964 when Franz Waxman was invited to compose a work 'involving children' for the Cincinnati May Festival he decided to set some of the poems that had been found by rescue workers after the liberation of the concentration camp. Some of these are anonymous, but some have the children's names and even ages attached. The texts themselves are very touching, really beautiful, with the sort of direct imagery and use of language that only the young have access to. Waxman has set eight poems, some for choir, some for a mezzo-soprano soloist. Although the music is in his style familiar from many large-scale Hollywood film scores, with strong influences drawn from the post-Schoenberg school, Waxman has matched the clarity of the children's verses with urgent yearning precision. The first song ends with the words 'I'd like to fly up but I don't know how' and each poem in its way carries something of the same message – the desire for release from the nightmare of reality. The message that Waxman has so brilliantly conveyed in these children's voices, 'Do not forget us!', could be taken as the theme for the whole Entartete Musik enterprise which has given us such a wealth of diverse and beautiful music over recent years. Like Waxman, Eric Zeisl had a career in Hollywood, as well as one composing for the concert hall. His setting of the 92nd Psalm, composed in 1944, is more conventional in mood and style, aimed at a wider public, but none the worse for that. Lawrence Foster, who studied with Waxman, conducts the Children's Choir and the Symphony Orchestra of Berlin Radio. There is no answer to the question that one asks each time one confronts the history of the Holocaust, but this music brings a very special sense of release, and that is the greatest possible tribute to the spirit of bravery expressed in the poems written by these children as they faced death and destruction.

Carl Maria von Weber

Clarinet Concertos – No. 1 in F minor, J114. No. 2 in E flat major, J118. Grand duo concertant, J204.
Sharon Kam cl **Itamar Golan** pf
Leipzig Gewandhaus Orchestra / Kurt Masur.
Teldec 0630-15428-2 (64 minutes: DDD). Recorded 1996. Ⓕ 🄴

Teldec provides a good programme in having the two Weber clarinet concertos coupled with a work which is virtually another concerto but with piano accompaniment, the *Grand duo concertant*. Sharon Kam is a young Israeli whom Kurt Masur heard in her home country, immediately inviting her back to Leipzig to play concertos. She was contracted by Teldec in 1994, but this is the first disc entirely devoted to her playing, revealing her as a most imaginative and individual artist, using the widest tonal and dynamic range, and with a very sure technique, with every note cleanly in place. As the opening movement of the First Concerto demonstrates, she has the gift of magicking a phrase, and one mark of her magnetism and flair is the way she can hold tension over an exaggerated pause or *tenuto*. Most remarkable of all is the dark intensity of Kam's account of the slow minor-key *Romanza* of the Second Concerto, with the soloist clearly the one insisting on a very measured tempo, when Masur's preference is always towards flowing *Andantes*. She is similarly impressive in the *Grand duo concertant*, though there the piano tone of Itamar Golan is on the shallow side.

Clarinet Concertos – Nos. 1 and 2. Clarinet Concertino in E flat major, J109.
Clarinet Quintet in
B flat major, J182.
Kari Kriikku cl **New Helsinki Quartet** (Jan Söderblom, Petri Aarnio vns Ilari Angervo va
Jan-Erik Gustafsson vc);
Finnish Radio Symphony Orchestra / Sakari Oramo.
Ondine ODE895-2 (76 minutes: DDD). Recorded 1996. Ⓕ

Kari Kriikku's are brilliant performances of works that more or less reinvented the clarinet as an instrument of brilliance, at any rate in the hands and under the flashing fingers of Weber's friend Heinrich Baermann. The formidable difficulties hold no terrors for Kriikku; indeed, wonderfully fluent as his playing is in, for instance, the fireworks music that ends the Second Concerto and the Quintet, one almost wants there to be more sense of difficulties overcome as witness of the virtuoso as hero. But that would be to quibble, especially when Kriikku has such a wide range of expression and such an intelligent approach to the music. He plays the First Concerto as a slightly tense, witty work, giving the *Adagio* a long-breathed lyricism and the finale humour as well as wit. The only questionable element is his own over-long cadenza to the first movement. The Second Concerto is treated as a more lyrical and dramatic work, with an elegant *polacca* finale, and there is a beautiful length of phrasing in the *Andante*, as there is in the 'Fantasia' movement of the Quintet. Kriikku neatly touches off the mock-sinister intervention in the Quintet's finale, refusing to take it seriously. He is well accompanied throughout.

Piano Sonatas – No. 1 in C major, J138; No. 2 in A flat major, J199. Rondo brillante in E flat major, J252, 'La gaité'. Invitation to the dance, J260.
Hamish Milne *pf*
CRD CRD3485 (76 minutes: DDD). Recorded 1991.   Ⓕ

Weber's piano music, once played by most pianists, has since suffered neglect and even the famous *Invitation to the dance* is now more often heard in its orchestral form. Since he was a renowned pianist as well as a major composer, the neglect seems odd, particularly when other pianist composers such as Chopin and Liszt are at the centre of the concert repertory; but part of the trouble may lie in the difficulty of the music, reflecting his own huge hands and his tendency to write what the booklet-essay calls 'chords unplayable by others'. Hamish Milne makes out a real case for this music, and his playing of the two sonatas is idiomatic and resourceful, even if one cannot banish the feeling that Weber all too readily used the melodic and harmonic formulae of eighteenth-century *galanterie* and simply dressed them up in nineteenth-century salon virtuosity. From this point of view, a comparison with Chopin's mature sonatas or Liszt's magnificent single essay in the form reveals Weber as a lightweight. A hearing of the first movement in the First Sonata will quickly tell you if this is how you may react, while in its *Presto* finale you may praise a Mendelssohnian lightness but also note a pomposity foreign to that composer. Leaving aside the musical quality of these sonatas, this is stylish playing which should win them friends. The *Rondo brillante* and *Invitation to the dance* make no claim to be other than scintillating salon music, and are captivating in Milne's shapely and skilful performances. The recording is truthful and satisfying.

Meine Lieder, meine Sänge, J73. Klage, J63. Der Kleine Fritz an seine jungen Freunde, J74. Was zieht zu deinem Zauberkreise, J86. Ich sah ein Röschen am Wege stehn, J67. Er an Sie, J57. Meine Farben, J62. Liebe-Glühen, J140. Über die Berge mit ungestüm, Op. 25 No. 2. Es stürmt auf der Flur, J161. Minnelied, J160. Reigen, J159. Sind es Schmerzen, J156. Mein Verlangen, J196. Wenn ich ein Vöglein war', J233. Mein Schatzerl is hübsch, J234. Liebesgruss aus der Ferne, J257. Herzchen, mein Schätzchen, J258. Das Veilchen im Thale, J217. Ich denke dein, J48. Horch'!, Leise horch', Geliebte, J56. Elle était simple et gentillete, J292.
Dietrich Fischer-Dieskau *bar* **Hartmut Höll** *pf*
Claves CD50-9118 (52 minutes: DDD). Texts and translations included. Recorded 1991.   Ⓕ

'In my opinion the first and most sacred duty of a song-writer is to observe the maximum of fidelity to the prosody of the text that he is setting.' Weber was writing in defence of a number he composed for an obscure play, but his words can stand as an apologia for his 90-odd songs. His contribution to German song has been underrated, for his ideas were different from those of his contemporaries. Fischer-Dieskau used to resist suggestions that he might take up Weber's songs, and it is good that he has now done so, even late in his career. Always sensitive to words, he now responds with the subtlety of understanding that comes from many years of closeness to German poetry. Only very occasionally is there the powerful emphasis on the single expressive word that sometimes used to mar his interpretations, keeping them too near the surface of the poetry. He can still use individual colour marvellously: the tonal painting of 'blue', 'white' and 'brown' in *Meine Farben* is exquisitely done. But more remarkable, here and in other songs, is the manner in which he follows the novel melodic lines which Weber has contrived out of the poetry.

Ein steter Kampf is a masterly example; so is *Was zieht zu deinem Zauberkreise*, one of the few songs in which Weber enters Schubertian territory; so are *Es stürmt auf der Flur* and *Liebesgruss aus der Ferne*. Not even Fischer-Dieskau can quite bring off the coy *Der Kleine Fritz* by slightly sending it up (the only hope), and there is something a bit hefty about *Reigen*, a very funny wedding song full of 'Heissa, lustig!' and 'Dudel, didel!', though Hartmut Höll does wonders with the clanking accompaniment. Höll varies his tone so much here from the warmth and depth of his touch elsewhere that one wonders if the engineers did not take a small hand: why not? These are charming, touching, witty, colourful verses, often by minor figures of Weber's circle, and they drew from him music that heightens their point. Fischer-Dieskau's intelligent artistry could not more eloquently support the praise for Weber from Wilhelm Müller, poet of *Die schöne Müllerin* and *Winterreise*, as 'master of German song'.

Der Freischütz.
Peter Schreier *ten* Max (Hans Jörn Weber); **Gundula Janowitz** *sop* Agathe (Regina Jeske);
Edith Mathis *sop* Aennchen (Ingrid Hille); **Theo Adam** *bass* Caspar (Gerhard Paul);
Bernd Weikl *bar* Ottokar (Otto Mellies); **Siegfried Vogel** *bass* Cuno (Gerd Biewer);
Franz Crass *bass* Hermit; **Gerhard Paul** (spkr) Samiel; **Günther Leib** *bar* Kilian (Peter Hölzel);
Leipzig Radio Chorus; Staatskapelle Dresden / Carlos Kleiber.
DG 415 432-2GH2 (two discs: 130 minutes: ADD). Notes, text and translation included.
Recorded 1973. Ⓕ

Carlos Kleiber's fine set of *Der Freischütz* earns reissue on CD for a number of reasons. One is the excellence of the actual recorded sound with a score that profits greatly from such attention. Weber's famous attention to details of orchestration is lovingly explored by a conductor who has taken the trouble to go back to the score in manuscript and observe that there are differences between that and most of the published versions. So not only do we hear the eerie sound of low flute thirds and the subtle contrast of unmuted viola with four-part muted violins in Agathe's 'Leise, leise', among much else, with a new freshness and point, but all the diabolical effects in the Wolf's Glen come up with a greater sense of depth, down to the grisliest detail. The beginning of the Overture, and the opening of the Wolf's Glen scene, steal upon us out of a primeval silence, as they should. All this would be of little point were the performance itself not of such interest. There is a good deal to argue about but this is because the performance is so interesting. Whatever one may feel about some of Kleiber's tempos, and one may feel some of them to be unwise in both directions, they spring from a careful, thoughtful and musical mind. The singing cast is excellent, with Gundula Janowitz an outstanding Agathe to a somewhat reflective Max from Peter Schreier, at his best when the hero is brought low by the devilish machinations; Edith Mathis is a pretty Aennchen, Theo Adam a fine, murky Caspar. The dialogue, spoken by actors, is slightly abbreviated and occasionally amended. Kleiber's reading produces much new insight to a magical old score.

Anton Webern Austrian 1883-1945

Webern Passacaglia, Op. 1. Six Pieces, Op. 6. Five Pieces, Op. 10. Variations, Op. 30.
Bach (arr. Webern) Musikalisches Opfer, BWV1079 – Ricercar a 6.
Schoenberg A Survivor from Warsaw, Op. 46.
Gottfried Hornik *narr*
Vienna State Opera Chorus; Vienna Philharmonic Orchestra / Claudio Abbado.
DG 431 774-2GH (50 minutes: DDD). Text and translation included. Recorded 1989-92. Ⓕ

This is a fine reading of the rarely-heard and forcefully dramatic Variations, Op. 30. Abbado and the VPO are predictably responsive to the romantic intensity of the early *Passacaglia*, with nothing routine in their performance, and the sets of expressionist miniatures are even more convincing in their blend of delicacy and power. The fourth piece from Op. 6, the closest Webern ever came to concentrating the essence of a Mahlerian funeral march, and ending with an ear-splitting percussion *crescendo*, is all the more effective for Abbado's refusal to set a self-indulgently slow tempo. Technically, these recordings outshine the competition, though there are other memorable interpreters – Boulez especially in Op. 30. Given the evident rapport between Webern and Abbado it seems odd that the disc doesn't include more of Webern's music – for example, the Symphony, Op. 21. The Bach arrangement is nevertheless an ear-opening exercise in passing baroque counterpoint through a kaleidoscope of expressionist tone colours, and Schoenberg's *A Survivor from Warsaw* retains its special power to move and disturb.

Webern Passacaglia, Op. 1. Five Pieces, Op. 5. Six Pieces, Op. 6. Im Sommerwind.
Bach (orch. Webern) Musikalisches Opfer, BWV1079 – Ricercar a 6.
Schubert (orch. Webern) Deutsche Tänze, D820.
Berlin Philharmonic Orchestra / Pierre Boulez.
DG 447 099-2GH (67 minutes: DDD). Recorded 1993-94. ⒻⓈ

With the exception of the Bach and Schubert arrangements this is all relatively early, pre-serial Webern, yet Boulez devotes as much care and as much affection to the D minor *Passacaglia* and to the undeniably immature but irresistibly luscious *Im Sommerwind* as to the far more characteristic Op. 5 and Op. 6 pieces. Indeed, if the *Passacaglia* is anything to go by, a Brahms symphony cycle from Boulez would be a fascinating prospect, while his reading of the 'idyll for large orchestra' suggests that his Delius might be no less interesting. Boulez does not imply that the mature Webern is present here in embryo; but he does perhaps make us ask how much of that later music is, like this, inspired by nature. To be reminded of Brahms by the *Passacaglia* is no less appropriate. This is a Janus of a piece, looking back not only to Brahms's Fourth Symphony but beyond (the presence of the Bach/Webern *Ricercar* points that up), and at the same time moving onwards from the delicate chamber passages in *Im Sommerwind* towards the 'orchestral chamber music' of Op. 5 and Op. 6. Boulez looks both ways too, with rich orchestral amplitude and expressive phrasing (very broad rubato) but he also notices Webern's already marked liking for transparent textures, quiet subtleties of string colour and the sound of the muted trumpet. And yes: heard in this context the shorter pieces are a logical progression. They are intensely expressive, with a wide range of emotion often within a very few bars; no wonder Boulez prefers the earlier, richer scoring of Op. 6. He obviously loves their Mahler-derived dissolution of the boundary between orchestral and chamber music, and encourages the Berlin Philharmonic to play with great tonal beauty, aware that a recurrent marking in mature Webern is 'tenderly'. Those qualities recur in the Bach and Schubert arrangements; the rubato in the Fourth Schubert Dance and the Viennese charm of the Fifth suggest that a Boulez *Fledermaus*, even, might be a gleam at the back of his mind. The recordings, very properly, are warm as well as clean.

Complete works, Opp. 1-31.
Passacaglia, Op. 1 (**London Symphony Orchestra / Pierre Boulez**). Entflieht auf leichten Kähnen, Op. 2 (**John Alldis Choir / Boulez**). Five Songs from 'Der siebente Ring', Op. 3. Five Songs, Op. 4 (**Heather Harper** *sop* **Charles Rosen** *pf*). Five Movements, Op. 5 (**Juilliard Quartet**). Six Pieces, Op. 6 (**LSO / Boulez**). Four Pieces, Op. 7 (**Isaac Stern** *vn* **Rosen** *pf*). Two Songs, Op. 8 (**Harper** *sop* **chamber ensemble / Boulez**). Six Bagatelles, Op. 9 (**Juilliard Qt**). Five Pieces, Op. 10 (**LSO / Boulez**). Three Little Pieces, Op. 11 (**Gregor Piatigorsky** *vc* **Rosen** *pf*). Four Songs, Op. 12 (**Harper** *sop* **Rosen** *pf*). Four Songs, Op. 13. Six Songs, Op. 14 (**Harper** *sop* **chbr ens / Boulez**). Five Sacred Songs, Op. 15. Five Canons on Latin Texts, Op. 16 (**Halina Lukomska** *sop* **chbr ens / Boulez**). Three Songs, Op. 18 (**Lukomska** *sop* **John Williams** *gtr* **Colin Bradbury** *cl* **/ Boulez**). Two Songs, Op. 19 (**John Alldis Ch, mbrs LSO / Boulez**). String Trio, Op. 20 (**mbrs Juilliard Qt**). Symphony, Op. 21 (**LSO / Boulez**). Quartet, Op. 22 (**Robert Marcellus** *cl* **Abraham Weinstein** *sax* **Daniel Majeske** *vn* **Rosen** *pf* **/ Boulez**). Three Songs from 'Viae inviae', Op. 23 (**Lukomska** *sop* **Rosen** *pf*). Concerto, Op. 24 (**mbrs LSO / Boulez**). Three Songs, Op. 25 (**Lukomska** *sop* **Rosen** *pf*). Das Augenlicht, Op. 26 (**John Alldis Ch; LSO / Boulez**). Piano Variations, Op. 27 (**Rosen** *pf*). String Quartet, Op. 28 (**Juilliard Qt**). Cantata No. 1, Op. 29 (**Lukomska** *sop* **John Alldis Ch; LSO / Boulez**). Variations, Op. 30 (**LSO / Boulez**). Cantata No. 2, Op. 31 (**Lukomska** *sop* **Barry McDaniel** *bar* **John Alldis Ch; LSO / Boulez**). Five Movements, Op. 5 – orchestral version (**LSO / Boulez**).
Bach (orch. Webern) Musikalischen Opfer, BWV1079 – Fuga (Ricercata) No. 2 (**LSO / Boulez**). **Schubert** (orch. Webern) Deutsche Tänze, D820 (**Frankfurt Radio Orchestra / Anton Webern**. Recorded live in 1932).
Various artists.
Sony Classical SM3K45845 (three discs: 223 minutes: ADD). Notes, texts and translations included. Recorded 1967-72. *Gramophone* Award Winner 1978. Ⓜ

Webern is as 'classic' to Pierre Boulez as Mozart or Brahms are to most other conductors, and when he is able to persuade performers to share his view the results can be remarkable – lucid in texture, responsive in expression. Despite his well-nigh exclusive concern with miniature forms, there are many sides to Webern, and although this set is not equally successful in realizing all of them, it leaves the listener in no doubt about the music's sheer variety, as well as its emotional power, whether the piece in question is an ingenious canon-by-inversion or a simple, folk-like *Lied*. From a long list of performers one could single out Heather Harper and the Juilliard Quartet for special commendation; and the smooth confidence of the John Alldis Choir is also notable. The recordings were made over a five-year period and have the typical CBS dryness of that time. Even so, in the finest performances which Boulez himself directs – as indicated in the review above, the *Orchestral Variations*, Op. 30 is perhaps the high point – that remarkable radiance of spirit so special to Webern is vividly conveyed. It is a fascinating bonus to hear Webern himself conducting his Schubert arrangements – music from another world, yet with an economy and emotional poise that Webern in his own way sought to emulate.

Symphony, Op. 21. Das Augenlicht, Op. 26. Cantatas – No. 1, Op. 29; No. 2, Op. 31. Variations, Op. 30. Five Pieces, Op. posth. Drei Lieder.
Christiane Oelze *sop* **Gerald Finley** *bar*
BBC Singers; Berlin Philharmonic Orchestra / Pierre Boulez.
DG 447 765-2GH (59 minutes: DDD). Texts and translations included. Recorded 1994. Ⓕ

Pierre Boulez has been conducting this music for 40 years, and his interpretations have evolved from the youthful Domaine Musical recordings, through the incisive CBS readings of 1967-72 (reviewed above), to this present 'late' style. Boulez encourages the Berlin Philharmonic to play with great tonal beauty, and the recordings are warm as well as clean. Tempos are generally broader than they were 30 years ago, and forms are outlined more expansively. There are moments of high drama – the sudden outburst from the solo horn in the second movement of Op. 21, the representations of thunder and lightning in the first movement of Op. 29 – but these are balanced by an eloquent spaciousness and refinement, as with the glowing canonic lines in the first movement of Op. 21. Only in Boulez's account of the *Variations*, Op. 30 do you feel that the emphasis on lyric inwardness risks an excess of decorum, the raw contrasts of texture and mood so strong in the CBS version sacrificed to an overall blend that deprives Webern of some of his power to shock. That power is explosively present in the *Five Pieces* from 1913, especially in the astonishing No. 3, and also, less aggressively, in the whispered *Sprechgesang* of the *Drei Lieder*. But the other side of Webern, the sheer tenderness of his lyrical imagination, is conveyed here with particular distinction by the solo singing and the beautifully integrated BBC Singers, superbly accurate in the cantatas and *Das Augenlicht*. A distinguished disc.

Drei Gedichte (1899-03). Acht frühe Lieder (1901-04). Fünf Lieder (1906-08). Fünf Lieder aus 'Der siebente Ring', Op. 3. Fünf Lieder, Op. 4. Vier Lieder nach Gedichten von Stefan George (1908-09). Vier Lieder, Op. 12. Drei Lieder aus 'Viae inviae', Op. 23. Drei Lieder, Op. 25.
Christiane Oelze *sop* **Eric Schneider** *pf*
DG 447 103-2GH (76 minutes: DDD). Texts and translations included. Recorded 1994. Ⓕ

Webern's songs are quiet and mostly brief (there are 40 of them here in the space of 76 minutes). They are intimate, ethereal, more concerned with distilling subtle emotional states than with telling stories or painting pictures. Christiane Oelze's voice and musicianship are well suited to them. Her voice is not large, but by careful control of dynamics she can easily encompass those infrequent moments where a big phrase or an ample gesture is required. The sound is pure and bright, her sense of line as admirable as her intonation and her pianist is an artist of great intelligence, refinement and command of colour. The recording balances them very well, not tempted by Oelze's confiding manner to come too close. The first mature songs here are those with opus numbers, the three earlier sets an account of how that maturity was achieved. In the two outer songs of the *Drei Gedichte* we already hear a prediction of Webern's later manner, but the central setting of Richard Dehmel's 'Nachtgebet der Braut' might be by another composer, with its four verses of overheated Wagnerian passion. Real urgency arrives with serialism and the last three sets of songs on this disc. With it arrives also fantasy, wit and a feeling of being at ease with the past; now Webern can make subtle but unmistakable allusions to (among others) Bachian aria and Viennese *Ländler* (this latter hint beautifully picked up by Oelze and Schneider). And by now he is also choosing poems, either very simple or exaltedly religious, that are ideally suited to his distilled, immaculate precision. Webern became a great songwriter with Op. 12, but the path to that achievement is absorbingly charted on this disc.

Kurt Weill

Symphony No. 2. Violin Concerto, Op. 12. Aufstieg und Fall der Stadt Mahagonny – Suite (arr. Brückner-Rüggeberg).
Frank Peter Zimmermann *vn*
Berlin Philharmonic Orchestra / Mariss Jansons.
EMI CDC5 56573-2 (70 minutes: DDD). Recorded 1997. ⒻⒺ

For works that are so seldom performed in the concert hall, Weill's Second Symphony and his Violin Concerto have both notched up a healthy number of recordings. The Second Symphony was composed in the summer of 1933 as a commission from the Princesse de Polignac, when Weill was living in France having fled from the Nazis. It has many textural and melodic affinities with *Der Silbersee*, the last work Weill completed in Germany, and *Die sieben Todsünden*, the first piece he wrote in France. Within the whole picture of Weill's life and works, the Symphony could be seen as a farewell to his youth and to his country of birth. After 1933 he would declare that he had no nationality (until he could say 'I'm an American!' in 1941). The agitated, distressed sound of the opening movement gives way to the second part – with its resigned, marching theme at the start, like the two men at the end of *Silbersee* going forth into the unknown. But towards the end of this second movement, despite its melancholy mood the music seems to look forward with a five-note phrase which anticipates exactly the refrain of Rose's aria from Act 1 of *Street Scene*, with the words 'maybe it will be'. Jansons and the BPO give the symphony its most sumptuous performance and recording to date – one feels like thumbing one's nose at Schoenberg who dismissed Weill completely (as did Webern). In this year of his centenary, Weill's music is becoming more and more established and the two halves of his career merge into one. The Violin Concerto is the earliest of his compositions to have achieved a place in the repertory. Zimmermann makes a splendid soloist in this performance, highlighting the neo-classical characteristics of the piece. The suite of tunes from *Mahagonny* was obviously designed by Wilhelm Brückner-Rüggeberg to match the wit of Weill's own *Dreigroschenoper* suite. It doesn't quite work since the big operatic ensemble and arias sound a bit lost when boiled down to orchestral effects. But for those who shy away from Weill's music-theatre works this CD might be the ideal introduction to his music.

Der Silbersee – Ich bin eine arme Verwandte (Fennimores-Lied); Rom war eine Stadt (Cäsars Tod); Lied des Lotterieagenten. Die Dreigroschenoper – Die Moritat von Mackie Messer; Salomon-Song; Die Ballade von der sexuellen Hörigkeit. Das Berliner Requiem – Zu Potsdam unter den Eichen (arr. Hazell). Nannas-Lied. Aufstieg und Fall der Stadt Mahagonny – Alabama Song; Wie man sich bettet. Je ne t'aime pas. One Touch of Venus – I'm a stranger here myself; Westwind; Speak low.
Ute Lemper *sop*
Berlin Radio Ensemble / John Mauceri.
Decca New Line 425 204-2DNL (50 minutes: DDD). Texts and translations included.   Ⓕ

The songs in this collection are mostly from the major works Weill composed between 1928 and 1933, but also included are one from his years in France and three items from the 1943 Broadway musical *One Touch of Venus*. By comparison with the husky, growling delivery often accorded Weill's songs in the manner of his widow Lotte Lenya, Ute Lemper has a voice of appealing clarity and warmth. What distinguishes her singing, though, is the way in which these attributes of vocal purity are allied to a quite irresistible dramatic intensity. Her 'Song of the Lottery Agent' is an absolute *tour de force*, apt to leave the listener emotionally drained, and her *Je ne t'aime pas* is almost equally overwhelming. Not least in the three numbers from *One Touch of Venus*, sung in perfect English, she displays a commanding musical theatre presence. This is, one feels, how Weill's songs were meant to be heard.

Lost in the Stars.
Gregory Hopkins *ten* Leader; **Arthur Woodley** *bass-bar* Stephen Kumolo;
Reginald Pindell *bar* Absalom, John, Man, Villager; **Cynthia Clarey** *sop* Irina;
Carol Woods *sngr* Linda; **Jamal Howard** *treb* Alex; **Richard Vogt** *spkr* Stationmaster, Judge;
New York Concert Chorale; St Luke's Orchestra / Julius Rudel.
MusicMasters 67100-2 (72 minutes: DDD). Recorded 1992.   Ⓕ

Lost in the Stars is subtitled 'A Musical Tragedy' and was adapted by Maxwell Anderson from Alan Paton's novel *Cry the Beloved Country*. Weill and Anderson's use of a chorus to comment on the action and advance the story makes the play difficult to stage, and Anderson's sentimentalization of the Paton original has made it one of the most dated of Weill's works. Julius Rudel conducted a production of *Lost in the Stars* for the New York City Opera in 1959, and observes in the booklet that he found these recording sessions 'somewhat akin to a religious experience'. This certainly communicates itself, especially in the choral sequence 'Cry the Beloved Country' which frames the death-cell confrontation between father and son. Without much recorded dialogue, the condescending sugariness of the Anderson contribution is reduced and Weill's experimentation with the choruses as well as his usual high quota of great melodies make this one of the finest modern recordings of his work. In the main role of the black preacher, Kumolo, Arthur Woodley sings with fervour and fine diction and the Orchestra of St Luke's manage an accurate 1940s sound; a real achievement. This is a major addition to the catalogue and essential to any collection of Weill's work – or of twentieth-century opera.

Die sieben Todsünden[a]. Symphony No. 2[b].
Teresa Stratas, Nora Kimball *sops* **Frank Kelley, Howard Haskin** *tens*
Herbert Perry, Peter Rose *basses*
Chorus and Orchestra of the Opéra National de Lyon / Kent Nagano.
Erato 0630-17068-2 (65 minutes: DDD). Text and translation included.
Recorded [a]1993; [b]1996.   Ⓕ Ⓔ

Weill and Brecht's *Seven Deadly Sins*, written in haste just after their flight from Hitler's Germany, was their last major collaboration. The question of its interpretation will always be bound up with the memory of Lotte Lenya, who created the role of Anna I. This performance of *Sins* was recorded at the same time that Stratas performed it for Peter Sellars's film of the work (available on video from Decca). There is a certain amount of stage noise in this recording, especially in 'Lust' – the heart of the work. Stratas's singing isn't pretty, but then it's not meant to be; she uses all her declamatory powers, and projects text and music in such a dramatic and heartfelt way that it puts this version immediately in the front rank. Nagano's conducting begins with a very slow introduction, which may sound off-putting to those familiar with the much sprightlier Rattle or Masur versions, which also have soprano soloists. As the performance progresses though, Nagano's control of the drama seems just right – this isn't a concert reading, but a full-scale theatrical event. The recorded sound of the symphony is noticeably better than that of *Sins*. As Weill's only major orchestral work, it has never really caught on, though the orchestral writing is as sophisticated as anything in his operas. With so many versions of *Die sieben Todsünden*, preferences for voice and coupling are important. Fassbaender and von Otter both have a selection of Weill songs and arias, Réaux with Masur has the *Lulu* suite, Ross with Rattle, Stravinsky's *Pulcinella*. For first-time Weill buyers, we are inclined to recommend this version over all the others; Stratas is terrific and the coupling is perfect.

Street Scene.
Kristine Ciesinski *sop* Anna Maurrant; **Richard Van Allan** *bass* Frank Maurrant;
Janis Kelly *sop* Rose Maurrant; **Bonaventura Bottone** *ten* Sam Kaplan;
Terry Jenkins *ten* Abraham Kaplan; **Meriel Dickinson** *mez* Emma Jones;
Angela Hickey *mez* Olga Olsen; **Claire Daniels** *sop* Jennie Hildebrand;
Fiametta Doria *sop* First Nursemaid; **Judith Douglas** *mez* Second Nursemaid;
English National Opera Chorus and Orchestra / Carl Davis.
TER Classics CDTER21185 (two discs: 146 minutes: DDD). Recorded 1989.   Ⓕ

Street Scene is the most ambitious product of Weill's American years. It's something of a *Porgy and Bess* transferred from Catfish Row to the slum tenements of New York. Where *Porgy and Bess* is through-composed with recitatives, though, *Street Scene* offers a mixture of set musical numbers, straight dialogue, and dialogue over musical underscoring. The musical numbers themselves range from operatic arias and ensembles to rousing 1940s dance numbers. It is consistently well sung, particularly where style is concerned. Weill described the work as a 'Broadway opera', and it demands a vernacular rather than a classical operatic singing style. This it duly gets from Kristine Ciesinski as Anna Maurrant, while Janis Kelly's beautifully clear but natural enunciation and her sense of emotional involvement make daughter Rose's 'What good would the moon be?' a performance of real beauty. Praiseworthy too is Richard Van Allan as the murderous husband, his 'Let things be like they always was' creating a suitably sinister effect. Among the subsidiary attractions is the appearance of Catherine Zeta Jones, performing the swinging dance number 'Moon-faced, starry-eyed'.

Leó Weiner

Hungarian 1885-1960

Weiner Serenade, Op. 3.
Bartók Cantata profana, Sz94[a].
Kodály Psalmus Hungaricus, Op. 13[b].
Tamás Daróczy *ten* Alexander Agache *bar*
Hungarian Radio and Television [ab]Chorus and [b]Children's Chorus;
[b]Schola Cantorum Budapestiensis; Budapest Festival Orchestra / Sir Georg Solti.
Decca 458 929-2DH (59 minutes: DDD). Texts and translations included. Recorded 1997.   Ⓕ 🅔

It is apt, if ironic, that these very last recordings of Sir Georg Solti, product of sessions in Budapest 1997, three months before his death, should make up the perfect valedictory disc. Ironically too, these were his very first recordings made in his native Hungary with Hungarian musicians. Solti's plan was to pay tribute to his three great teachers at the Liszt Conservatoire in Budapest, not only in this recording but in a concert of the same three representative works, designed to round off the 1998 Budapest Spring Festival. In the event the concert went ahead as a memorial to Solti with most of the same performers conducted by Iván Fischer.

The rarity here is the Serenade of Leó Weiner, the teacher closest to Solti in his student days, one who both challenged him and drew him out. The amiability of this music, far less individual, less specifically Hungarian than that of Bartók or Kodály, seems to reflect Weiner's character as Solti's mentor. Beautifully written in four cleanly constructed movements, this is a delightful piece full of fresh, crisply conceived ideas, as in the easygoing sonata-form first movement. The warmly responsive woodwind soloists of the Budapest Festival Orchestra come into their own in the interlude of the third movement with its sequence of solos getting faster, in turn for clarinet, bassoon, oboe and flute. Solti could never have conceived a more winning last offering on disc. In his final reconciliation with his native land (which, as he always pointed out, rejected him twice over, both under the Fascists and the Communists) Solti found extra warmth in music he loved, while keeping the biting intensity which was always a hallmark of his conducting. As he explains in the accompanying booklet, Solti came finally to feel that the story of Bartók's *Cantata profana* – about nine sons turned by magic into stags, who finally return home – symbolized his own life-story. The chorus sings superbly, with the Romanian baritone, Alexander Agache, a strong and dark soloist, though the powerful and strenuous tenor, Tamás Daróczy, sings with too wide a vibrato to give much pleasure on disc. His singing is the drawback in the Kodály too, a more serious one when the tenor plays such a central part in this psalm sequence. None the less, what matters is the incandescence of the whole performance. With glowing sound, reflecting the helpful acoustic of the Italian Institute in Budapest, the piece receives here idiomatic singing and playing.

Judith Weir

British 1954

The Art of Touching the Keyboard. I Broke off a Golden Branch. El Rey de Francia. The King of France[a]. Distance and Enchantment[a]. The Bagpiper's String Trio. Ardnamurchan Point[bc].
[a]**Susan Tomes**, [b]**William Howard**, [c]**Petra Casén** *pfs* **Schubert Ensemble of London;
Domus** (Krysia Osostowicz *vn* Timothy Boulton *va* Richard Lester *vc*).
Collins Classics 1453-2 (58 minutes: DDD). Recorded 1995.   Ⓕ

Judith Weir's music is not simplistic, nor does it ape any style from the past, and it is not in the least minimalist, but it has qualities that could appeal to a vastly wider audience than the 'contemporary music public'. Her music is bold, clean and uncluttered, with a strong melodic line and purposeful forward movement. Those qualities are present even when she is paying an overt homage to Schubert, as in the exquisitely lyrical opening of *I Broke off a Golden Branch* (written for the Schubert Ensemble of London, and for the forces of the *Trout* Quintet), all the more so since the other preoccupation of this fine work is to avow a debt: to the beautiful, ancient folk music of the region we used to call Yugoslavia. Anyone who can carry out both of these objectives – and the gesture to Schubert is as delightfully affectionate as the tribute to Croatia is eloquent – and still remain unmistakably herself is evidently a very considerable composer. Strong melody is a feature of all these pieces: long, eventful, often florid melody. Indeed, despite changes of mood, direction, tempo and texture you can hear each piece as a single long melody.

Even *The Art of Touching the Keyboard*, an avowed study of types of keyboard attack, has a surprising unity, a feeling that the whole piece is in a single span. *Ardnamurchan Point*, despite being for two keyboards, is mostly a single line throughout, a sort of journey; as with the tortuous road that suggested the title, you know that there will be a grand view at the end of it. That this sort of line has its roots in folk music is acknowledged in *Distance and Enchantment*, a piano quartet based on two folk melodies about mysterious vanishings (an appendix, in fact, to Weir's opera *The Vanishing Bridegroom*) and in *The Bagpiper's String Trio*. Nearly all these pieces were written for close friends, in most cases the artists on this disc; Weir says that of all her works these (for that very reason?) are the ones she most enjoys listening to. That quality too, of the anticipation of shared pleasure, is clearly audible in the performances.

Silvius Weiss

German 1686-1750

Lute Sonatas, Volume 1 – No. 36 in D minor; No. 42 in A minor; No. 49 in B flat major.
Robert Barto *lte*
Naxos 8 553773 (72 minutes: DDD). Recorded 1996.   ⓈⓅ

Silvius Weiss, the greatest lutenist of his age, was an almost exact contemporary of Bach, his most famous admirer. The style of lute music was dominated by French influence until the end of the seventeenth century, when the instrument's 'centre of gravity' moved to Eastern Europe, where Weiss was born in Breslau (now Wrocław) and spent much of his working life. The ornate *style précieux*, of which harpsichordists had learnt much from lutenists, gave way to a simpler *cantabile* one, a stepping-stone on the road to the *galant*. In many of Weiss's solo lute sonatas and suites the French influence survived in the *non mesuré* elements in the preludes and fantasias, and the appearance of various character pieces. Baroque lute music often sounds like an archbishop delivering a solemn sermon, but Weiss runs the gamut from profoundly solemn allemandes and sarabandes to light-footed *galanteries* and joyously prancing gigues. Everything, not least the harmonic adventurousness, bespeaks a composer who was no less renowned as an extemporizer. Weiss's music abounds in technical difficulty but Robert Barto has no apparent problem in concealing the fact. He is a supple and stylish performer, and this excellently recorded disc contains some of the finest playing of Weiss around.

Samuel Wesley

In exitu Israel. Ave regina caelorum. Magnificat anima mea. 12 Short Pieces with a Voluntary added – A minor; Gavotte in F. Services in F – Te Deum laudamus; Jubilate Deo. Ostende nobis Domine. Ecce panis angelorum. Domine salvam fac regem nostrum. Omnia vanitas (Carmen funebre). Voluntary in D. Tu es sacerdos. Might I in Thy sight appear. O Lord God most Holy. Dixit Dominus.
Gonville and Caius College Choir, Cambridge / Geoffrey Webber org
ASV Gaudeamus CDGAU157 (65 minutes: DDD). Recorded 1995.   Ⓕ

Samuel, the father, has been rather neglected in favour of Samuel Sebastian, the son. This disc opens with the eight-part motet, *In exitu Israel* which is probably his masterpiece. Notoriously difficult to sing without some smudging of the quavers, it also requires firm direction to stop it from 'running away'. Here the cleanness of line is impeccable as is the steadiness of tempo, and the clarity of the performance is both aided and tested by the unreverberant acoustic of Selwyn Chapel. The Gonville and Caius College Choir has a deservedly growing reputation, with voices of good, fresh quality, ears well attuned to each other, and admirable alertness in matters of phrasing and rhythm. The inner parts perhaps need strengthening, especially in relation to the robust bass-line, which one would not wish to hear 'tamed' at the expense of colour and character. The sopranos are as good treble-substitutes as any, and provide some very adequate soloists. Wesley's genius worked largely within the restraints of his period: essentially he was an eighteenth-century composer, his unostentatious style graceful and economical. He had an unfashionable enthusiasm for Bach, which brings a contrapuntal vigour into many of his best pieces. The bravura accompaniment to *Domine salvam fac* reminds us that he was also the leading British organist of his time, and an attractive feature of this recital is its inclusion of organ works that are not always easy to play. Geoffrey Webber gives a tasteful account, playing (for instance) the Gavotte as a dance-movement, and not in the grandiose disguise of its frequent appearances at the end of Cathedral Evensong.

Christoph Weyse

Christmas Cantata No. 3. Easter Cantata No. 1.
Bodil Anderson sop **Dorthe Elsebet Larsen** sop **Kirsten Dolberg** mez
Peter Grønlund ten **Stephen Milling** bass
Tivoli Concert Choir; Tivoli Symphony Orchestra / Michael Schønwandt.
Da Capo 8 224049 (52 minutes: DDD). Recorded 1997.   Ⓕ

Christoph Weyse was a Danish composer of German extraction. From 1789 he was based in Copenhagen, becoming distinguished as a pianist and church organist. He was the court composer from 1819, producing cantatas, songs, symphonies and much more. Among his important works are the innovatory *Allegri di bravura* for piano (1796), the fine if traditional ensembles in his sacred cantatas, and above all the songs, particularly the spiritual ones to texts by Ingemann (1837-38). This is a delightful disc. He may not have been a particularly original composer, but these two cantatas (from 1836 and 1821 respectively) are full of fresh vitality and some glorious melodies. The singers bring to them the conviction that the words are significant poetry, however naive they may appear at first sight. Michael Schønwandt directs flawless performances, captured in vivid sound.

Percy Whitlock

Dignity and Impudence (arr. Riley). Seven Sketches on Verses from the Psalms.
Two Fantasie Chorals. Three Reflections.
Graham Barber org
Priory PRCD525 (72 minutes: DDD).
Recorded on the Willis organ of Hereford Cathedral in 1995.   Ⓕ

Malcolm Riley has arranged *Dignity and Impudence* from the orchestral score Whitlock wrote in 1932, although the composer used to play it on the organ himself. Falling between the swashbuckling public manner of Elgar and Walton, it is well worth having and the orchestral originals belong to the tradition of British light music and should be revived. A landmark is the first complete recording of the *Seven Sketches on Verses from the Psalms*. Surprisingly Whitlock said he didn't care for the third one, 'Plaint', although this piece seems a particularly personal statement where he moves away from his predictable Georgian cathedral idiom, occasionally spiced up with chromatics from Delius or impressionist chords from Debussy, to something closer to Frank Bridge. The slender beauties of the folk-like opening 'Pastorale' are slightly rushed by Barber but he demonstrates a sympathetic command of the idiom, especially high spots such as the tuba rhetoric of the 'Exultemus'. The sonorities on Hereford's Willis, which Whitlock himself tried out, are ideal. In the two *Fantasie Chorals* Whitlock is more ambitious, following the model of Franck's masterpieces but coming closer to Bruckner's improvisatory meandering. The second one manages a strong peroration. At his best Whitlock is a kind of organist's Fauré, modal and subtle, and in Barber's performances he gets the strongest possible advocacy. The recording is sometimes light on bass and there are a few mechanical noises, but it's a resplendent sound.

Sing praise to God who reigns above. Jesu, grant me this I pray. Solemn Te Deum. Three Introits. The Saint whose praise today we sing. Communion Service in G. Glorious in heaven. Magnificat and Nunc dimittis (1924). O gentle presence. Come let us join our cheerful songs. O gladsome light. Magnificat and Nunc dimittis (1930).
Rochester Cathedral Choir / Roger Sayer with **William Whitehead** *org*
Priory PRCD583 (70 minutes: DDD). Texts included. Recorded 1996.   Ⓕ

A pupil of Vaughan Williams, Whitlock wrote a symphony and other full-scale orchestral works, but it is by some short organ pieces, anthems and other liturgical settings that he is remembered: a cheerful style, usually, practical and professional, not wasting his own notes or anybody else's time. A very fair selection is given here, ranging in chronology from a teenage composition (*O gladsome light*) to a hymn anthem (*Come let us join our cheerful songs*) published in the year of his death. His Communion Service of 1928 is typical of his effective, unpretentious workmanship. Unaccompanied anthems, such as *Jesu, grant me this I pray* and *The Saint whose praise today we sing*, are perhaps more personal: exercises in a loved and ancient tradition. One feels too that he *deserves* to be remembered: a shy, frail young man, and courageous as in middle age he faced the prospect of blindness armed with a magnifying glass and a memory he trained to learn the accompaniments of whole oratorios by heart.

Henryk Wieniawski   Polish 1835-1880

Violin Concertos – No. 1 in F sharp minor, Op. 14; No. 2 in D minor, Op. 22. Fantaisie brillante on Themes from Gounod's 'Faust', Op. 20.
Marat Bisengaliev *vn*
Polish National Radio Symphony Orchestra / Antoni Wit.
Naxos 8 553517 (70 minutes: DDD). Recorded 1995.   Ⓢ

By the time Wieniawski wrote his Second Violin Concerto, ten years after the First (which he wrote when in his teens) his finesse as a composer was more developed, and it is the Second, with its haunting melodies, that has remained more consistently in the repertory. Even so, this coupling of the two is apt and welcome on this super-budget Naxos issue. Marat Bisengaliev quickly demonstrates Wieniawski's positive qualities. Though he is not as persuasive an interpreter as some of his rivals in this repertoire, rather less individual and imaginative in his phrasing, and less bold in bravura writing, the security of his technique is formidable, with a wide tonal range. His gentle half-tones in the slow movements of both works are strikingly beautiful, magically caught in this excellent Polish recording. Wit and the Polish National Radio Symphony Orchestra provide most sympathetic support. In the 20-minute *Fantaisie* on themes from *Faust* Wieniawski shuffles the melodies skilfully, with Mephistopheles's Calf of Gold aria providing a brilliant display passage. It makes a charming show-piece, if not one that bears much repetition. An excellent bargain.

Sir David Willcocks   British 1919

Magnificat. Three Sea Shanties. Infant Holy. Can you count the stars?. A Spotless Rose. In paradisum. The Holly and the Ivy. God be in my head. Gift of Life. Regina caeli. Draw near. Sing we now!. O holy Jesus. Blessing.
English Cathedral Singers / Jonathan Willcocks with **Carys Lane** *sop* **Jane Watts** *org*
The Wallace Collection; Royal Academy Brass.
Priory PRCD668 (74 minutes: DDD). Texts included. Recorded 1998.   Ⓕ

This music is melodious, rhythmical, colourful, responsive; above all, it is expert in the understanding of voices, individual and in combination, *a cappella* or with varied types of accompaniment. It is written for use. Recognizing the need church choirs and choral societies have for music which is modern but traditional, liberated but reverent, it conforms happily to such conditions. In mood it can encompass the *Magnificat*'s rejoicing and the sea shanty's plaintive 'Woe is me'. In resources it can seem equally content with parish-church organ or festival choir with brass and percussion. The idiom acknowledges its century (the syncopations of jazz, the sweet nostalgic appeal of the musical) while its roots and perhaps its heart are elsewhere. A John Rutter or even a Stanford (his superb professionalism transported from another age) could conceivably have written this music; a Benjamin Britten or a Kenneth Leighton could not. It deals in gratification: no bad thing in itself, but limiting. The performances exactly match the requirements. The voices are fresh, the players accomplished; and all are well recorded.

Hugo Wolf

Austrian 1860-1903

Wolf Eichendorff Lieder – Der Freund; Der Musikant; Verschwiegene Liebe; Das Ständchen; Der Soldat I; Der Soldat II; Nachtzauber; Der Schreckenberger; Der Glücksritter; Lieber Alles; Heimweh; Der Scholar; Der verzweifelte Liebhaber; Unfall; Liebesglück; Seemanns Abschied; Erwartung; Die Nacht. In der Fremde – I, UP87; II, UP88; VI, UP93. Rückkehr, UP90. Nachruf, UP81.
Korngold Einfache Lieder, Op. 9 – No. 1, Schneeglöckchen; No. 2, Nachtwander; No. 3, Ständchen. Der Kranke, Op. 38 No. 2.
Boje Skovhus *bar* **Helmut Deutsch** *pf*
Sony Classical SK57969 (62 minutes: DDD). Texts and translations included. Recorded 1993. Ⓕ

Lovers of good Lieder singing will surely respond eagerly to Skovhus's bold and velvet-toned singing and welcome a disc of songs which are currently under-represented in the catalogue. Eichendorff and Wolf are here predominantly outside, walking or riding along, and Wolf is free of the cares marking the Mörike settings that went before in his opus. Skovhus is the Musician, Soldier, Sailor, Swashbuckler, Fortune-hunter and Scholar to the life. But he can also encompass a more thoughtful mood, as expressed in pieces such as *Die Nacht*, where his quiet singing is perfection. Deutsch's mastery of Wolf's intricate rhythms and harmonies is never less than masterly, and he is recorded as an equal partner with the singer. Four of Korngold's Eichendorff settings form a neat pendant to the Wolf. Although his version of *Ständchen* is more obviously sentimental than Wolf's, it has its own character. *Schneeglöckchen* is suffused in Debussian harmony (Op. 9 was composed in 1917), and the final song, written 30 years later, is peculiarly Korngoldian in its passing-note harmony and deliberately post-romantic idiom. The interpreters are just as subtle yet unexaggerated in their performing here as in the Wolf.

Goethe Lieder – Harfenspieler I-III; Der Rattenfänger; Coptisches Lied I; Frech und froh I and II: Epiphanias; Genialisch Treiben; Der Schäfer; Blumengruss; Frühling übers Jahr; Anakreons Grab; Phänomen; Ob der Koran von Ewigkeit sei?; Trunken müssen wir alle sein!; So lang man nüchtern ist; Sie haben wegen der Trunkenheit; Hätt' ich irgend wohl Bedenken; Komm, Liebchen, komm!; Wie sollt'ich heiter bleiben; Wenn ich dein gedenke; Ganymed.
Wolfgang Holzmair *bar* **Thomas Palm** *pf*
Collins Classics 1402-2 (55 minutes: DDD). Texts and translations included.
Recorded live in 1988. Ⓕ 🄴

Holzmair is a refreshing and challenging singer. He follows no known school and quite avoids the influence of Fischer-Dieskau. His voice is individual and tangy; his interpretations here, as elsewhere, are apparently spontaneous (the live recording helps) and unmarked by convention. His tone doesn't please everyone; it has a quick vibrato of a kind more frequently encountered in the earlier decades of the century than in the later, and it can harden under pressure. That's part of the price of taking risks: like Wolf he isn't always well behaved – and he's all the more stimulating for his immediacy of manner. Nowhere is that more apparent than in *Ganymed* where the wonder of the poem and its setting is wholly conveyed in this soaring interpretation. At the other end of the emotional scale in the inexhaustible variety of the Goethe settings is the desolation of the *Harfenspieler* ones, in the first of which the line 'Dann bin ich micht allein' carries all the inner torment of the mysterious old man. Nor at the end of the next verse is Holzmair averse to bursting out in operatic-like pain at 'Mich Einsamen die Pein'. The all-important piano parts are in the safe hands of Thomas Palm, a most sensitive player. He is placed a shade too far backward in relation to the voice but this probably reflects what you would have heard in the concert hall. Too much applause is included and the length is short by today's standards on CD. But, as they say, the quality is what matters and here it is high.

Italienisches Liederbuch.
Dawn Upshaw *sop* **Olaf Bär** *bar* **Helmut Deutsch** *pf*
EMI CDC5 55618-2 (78 minutes: DDD). Texts and translations included. Recorded 1996. Ⓕ 🄴

Both these singers approach the songs with such a natural style of interpretation that it is as if they had just discovered the wonders contained within this ever-delightful book and are only too eager to convey them to their audience – absolutely nothing of artifice or over-refinement found on some noted versions. They also convey in their singing a consistency of thought that is matched to perfection by the playing of their superb pianist, Helmut Deutsch. Yet individually the singers' attributes are different: Upshaw's open sincerity is everywhere in evidence, ideally complementing Bär's greater sophistication and urbanity. You can hear their skills wonderfully adumbrated in five successive songs in the middle of the recital. First Upshaw catches all the sadness of 'Mir ward gesagt' to be answered by the soft-grained, warm, impassioned outpouring of Bär in 'Und willst du deinen Liebsten sterben'. Then comes the inward feeling of 'Sterb' ich', so unerringly articulated by Bär, and the revelation of Upshaw's sense of humour in 'Mein Liebster ist so klein'. Finally, Bär's pure sense of *legato* in 'Benedeit dir sel'ge Mutter' keenly contrasts with the right touch of irony in the middle section.

From that you will have noted that the duo doesn't sing this collection in the printed order but one of Bär's own devising that makes eminent sense. Thus, for example, the railing songs are grouped together, the singers vying with each other in projecting scorn and anger. Later Upshaw shows the variety of her skills by catching, quite without exaggeration, the pain of 'Was soll der Zorn' and the cheeky teasing of 'Nein, junger Herr', itself nicely answered by Bär's 'Hoffartig seid Ihr'. So much else needs remarking on but listeners will want to discover for themselves the many pleasures of this rewarding issue. Drawbacks? Upshaw's peculiarly clear, clean tone just occasionally jars the ear and Bär doesn't quite match the range of colour or the many *aperçus* of Fischer-Dieskau's unique art. But this disc is its own best advocate, well supported by a finely achieved recording.

Liederstrauss. Sechs Reinick Lieder. An ***. Traurige Wege. Herbstentschluss. Ernst ist der Frühling. Spätherbstnebel. Wo ich bin, mich ringsum dunkelt. Du bist wie eine Blume. In der Fremde IV. Rückkehr. Lieder aus letzte Blätter – Die Nacht. Eichendorff Lieder – Erwartung. Nachruf.
Nico van der Meel ten **Dido Keuning** pf
Globe GLO5149 (63 minutes: DDD). Texts and translations included. Recorded 1996.　　　　Ⓕ

Wolf's early songs have been unduly neglected. Setting in turn Lenau, Heine, Eichendorff and Reinick, inspiration for so many Lieder composers, Wolf seems to have based his style, at this time, on Schumann and to a lesser extent Brahms. Apart from influences, almost all these songs are a delight in themselves, requiring no need for comparisons, odious or otherwise. Wolf is not yet the wholly original composer of his master-songs written from 1888 onwards, but his unerring ability to distil the core of the poems of the romantic writers he was setting is already there for all to hear; so too are his innate gift for lyrical melody, attractively fashioned piano parts and subtle harmony. These attributes inform almost all these pieces. 'Meine Liebchen, wir sassen beisammen' from the *Liederstrauss* Heine settings, is typical with its rippling accompaniment and well-defined vocal line. Another song from the same group, 'Es blasen die blau'n Husaren' looks forward in its march-like rhythm to later attempts in this manner.

The Eichendorff setting, *In der Fremde*, pre-echoes even more significantly mature Wolf, while the Eichendorff 'Die Nacht' and the haunting *Nachruf* are songs to savour by any yardstick. Even so, it is the six Reinick settings of 1882-83 that bring the greatest rewards, every one a miniature to cherish and, to quote the insert-note, 'revealing a charm and tenderness that shows us the kinder side of Wolf's personality'. Among them 'Nachtgruss' and 'Frühlingsglocken' demand repeated hearing, particularly when sung in the light, plangent tenor of Nico van der Meel. His may be a slightly dry, monochrome voice but after a while the almost vulnerable sound of his tone becomes an asset in these sorts of pieces, to which he also brings high intelligence and a keen ear for verbal nuance. Dido Keuning, perfectly balanced with van der Meel in an excellent recording, completes pleasure in a disc that lovers of Lieder should not overlook.

Mörike Lieder – Der Genesene an die Hoffnung; Ein Stündlein wohl vor Tag; Der Tambour; Nimmersatte Liebe; Fussreise; Verborgenheit; Im Frühling; Auf einer Wanderung; Der Gärtner; In der Frühe; Gebet; Neue Liebe; Wo find'ich Trost?; Frage und Antwort; Lebe wohl; Heimweh; Denk'es, o Seele!; Der Jäger; Storchenbotschaft; Bei einer Trauung; Selbstgeständis; Abschied.
Peter Schreier ten **Karl Engel** pf
Orfeo C142981A (60 minutes: DDD). Texts and translations included. Recorded 1996.　　Ⓕ🅔

Peter Schreier's ever-supple tenor, honed by keen-eyed intelligence and a verbal palate sharp enough to taste and try every last word, makes him a Wolf interpreter of the highest order. In this meticulously shaped programme of 22 of Wolf's eager settings of Mörike, one wonder appears after another. Schreier and his ever-sentient pianist, Karl Engel, move from a gentle awakening of love, which grows in intensity towards the innermost core of songs of doubt and fear, and on through a gallery of wonderfully dry, wry tableaux to the final farewell and the kicking of the critic downstairs. The first song here, *Im Frühling*, epitomizes the equilibrium, security and entirety of performances which have grown from long-pondered consideration. The long, drowsy vowels, and Schreier's sensitivity to the high-register placing of crucial words of longing all fuse into the slow-walking movement of cloud, wing, river, breeze, as language becomes expanded and enriched by tone. Schreier's remarkable steadiness of line in *Verborgenheit* reveals the song's secrets only reluctantly: the fierce intensity of sudden illumination is all the more searing. Grotesquerie and poignancy coexist in *Bei einer Trauung*, and we feel every catch of the voice as Schreier turns weird and whimsical tale-teller in *Storchenbotschaft*.

Mörike Lieder – Im Frühling; Auf eine Christblume I; Lied vom Winde. Goethe Lieder – Philine; Mignon; Der Schäfer; Blumengruss; Frühling übers Jahr; Anakreons Grab; Phänomen; Ganymed. Spanisches Liederbuch – Mühvoll komm' ich und beladen; In dem Schatten meiner Locken; Bedeckt mich mit Blumen; Wer tat deinem Füsslein weh; Wehe der, die mir verstrickte. Italienisches Liederbuch – Nun lass uns Frieden schliessen. Sechs Lieder für eine Frauenstimme – Mausfallen-Sprüchlein. Sechs alte Weisen.
Dame Elisabeth Schwarzkopf *sop* **Gerald Moore** *pf*
EMI Festspieldokumente mono CDH7 64905-2 (71 minutes: ADD). Texts included.
Recorded live in 1958. Ⓕ Ⓗ Ⓔ

'A blissful experience of the purest lied art' reported the *Salzburger Nachrichten* on Schwarzkopf's recital. The recording derives from the Austrian Broadcasting Corporation's archive. It gives a marvellous sense of presence, recalling most vividly what it was that made the memory of Schwarzkopf's song recitals precious. First, the quality of voice, caught here at its purest and most radiant; then the full concentration of a total sensibility, emotion and intellect fused, upon the songs: every one of them lived a special life on each separate occasion. The riches of this recital are beyond the scope of a short review. Every song here deserves a paragraph to itself, and the appreciation of Gerald Moore's work would have a large share in each. The disc, for one who cares for Wolf's songs and the art of their performance, is beyond price.

Hugo Wolf Society Edition
Mörike Lieder – excerpts. Spanisches Liederbuch – excerpts. Italienisches Liederbuch – excerpts. Eichendorff Lieder – excerpts. Goethe Lieder – excerpts. Drei Gedichte von Michelangelo. Gedichte von Scheffel, Mörike, Goethe und Kerner – excerpts. Gedichte von Richard Reinick – excerpt. Lieder für eine Frauenstimme – excerpts. Gedichte nach Heine, Shakespeare und Lord Byron – excerpts.
Marta Fuchs, Ria Ginster, Tiana Lemnitz, Elisabeth Rethberg, Alexandra Trianti *sops*
Elena Gerhardt *mez* **Karl Erb, John McCormack, Helge Roswaenge** *tens*
Herbert Janssen, Gerhard Hüsch *bars* **Friedrich Schorr** *bass-bar*
Alexander Kipnis, Ludwig Weber *basses* with various pianists.
EMI mono CHS5 66640-2 (five discs: 375 minutes: ADD). Texts and translations included.
Recorded 1931-38. Ⓜ Ⓗ

Whatever has since been achieved in Wolf interpretation, the old Hugo Wolf Society recordings hold their place not only as regards the distinction of the readings but as evidence of the pioneering work done by Ernest Newman and Walter Legge in the promulgation of the composer's highly original style. Six volumes were issued on 78rpm discs between 1931 and 1938, but a planned seventh was not released as a set (because of the war intervening) until the LP reissue came out in 1981. Here a further six titles have been unearthed from the EMI archives. The CD box has a suitably distinguished cover and texts and translations have been provided. This is a cornucopia of delights for the Lieder lover. Gerhardt had the whole of the first volume to herself, and launches the project with a typical honesty of approach. Her slightly grand voice and inimitable style may not be to modern tastes but persist and you'll surely respond to the generosity of her singing. The next volumes are dominated by the mellow tones and deeply felt performances of Hüsch, Janssen and Kipnis, to whom Legge assigned exactly the right pieces for their respective styles. All are deeply rewarding, but Hüsch in love-songs from the *Spanish Songbook* and Kipnis in the *Michelangelo* Songs and so much else make particularly memorable contributions. Among the women, the much underrated Greek soprano, Alexandra Trianti brings just the right lightness of touch to some of the teasing, airy pieces from the *Italian Songbook*. Ria Ginster is a fresh, pleasing soprano, but she slightly undercharacterizes her offerings. Not so Elisabeth Rethberg, who encompasses the grander passions of the *Italian Songbook* and is unsurpassed in the sorrowful abasement of 'Mühvoll komm' ich und beladen' from the *Spanish Songbook*. Legge perceptively brought in Schorr for a defiant 'Prometheus' (in Wolf's orchestral version) and McCormack for an elevating 'Ganymed'. In 1937, Roswaenge sings a hair-raising 'Feuerreiter'.

Other singers in the later volumes who bring their special individuality of utterance to bear on specific areas of Wolf's output are Fuchs (touching as Mignon and so eager in the great love-song, 'Geh, Geliebter, geh jetzt!'), the refined, sensitive Erb and the lovely Lemnitz, whose 'In der Frühe, Schlafendes Jesuskind' and 'Wiegenlied im Sommer' are unmissable. Janssen also returned in 1937 for deeply eloquent accounts of some of the most inspired pieces in the *Spanish Songbook*, including a 'Schlafendes Jesuskind' almost as rewarding as Lemnitz's reading. The gem among the previously unpublished items is Kipnis's sensual, intimate 'Verschwiegene Liebe'. Then to round things off Gerhardt is heard again in a newly issued version of a rarely heard, grief-laden song, 'Uber Nacht', on which she lavishes all her love for Wolf. The pianists from Bos to Moore are uniformly excellent, though not always as perceptive as their successors today. It is Wolf and the singers who make this one of the great enterprises of the pre-war gramophone.

Spanisches Liederbuch.
Anne Sofie von Otter *mez* **Olaf Bär** *bar* **Geoffrey Parsons** *pf*
EMI CDS5 55325-2 (two discs: 109 minutes: DDD). Texts and translations included.
Recorded 1992-94.   Ⓕ 🅁🅁

The songs are performed not in the published order but in one devised by Bär for several recitals of the set given by this trio, and now carried over into the recording studio. For the ten religious songs the reordering works well. In any case here the two singers show a deep and rewarding comprehension of the agony and ecstasy of poems and music. Listen, too, to von Otter's sense of smiling wonder in 'Ach, des Knaben Augen' as the holy mother looks into her son's eyes. By contrast in 'Mühvoll komm' ich und beladen' she changes to a searing, soul-searching manner that captures completely the woman's remorse, magnificently so at the climactic 'Nimm mich an'. Bär is as tense and inward in the great 'Herr, was trägt der Boden hier', capturing the voices of penitent and Christ to perfection. Note, too, Parsons's deliberately heavy gait in 'Die du Gott gebarst'. There are problems, however, in the more numerous secular songs.

With von Otter, apart from downward transpositions that make the piano parts sound unduly dark and Parsons consequently a shade heavy-handed, there is little to quarrel with. She teases, flirts, falls in love with the best of them, alert with her words, but never overdoing the archness. Bär, though, is not only up against the perhaps more formidable challenge of Fischer-Dieskau (on DG) but also against his own reordering. He does not have the immense tonal range and emotional charge of the older baritone. 'Herz, verzage nicht geschwind' is broader, more biting in Fischer-Dieskau's reading, for instance, 'Ach im Maien' that much more mellifluous, but you could say that Bär's more contained, but by no means reticent approach has its own, Wolfian justification. But it is entirely Bär's fault that songs Nos. 21 and 24, which should be sung as a group, lose some of their force when separated as here, thoughtfully as Bär sings each in its turn. However, the readings as a whole are worthy of the collection. In the modern manner there is more space around the voices than on the closer-miked DG set, where Fischer-Dieskau is very much a presence in the room with you: you listen to the newer pair in more of a recital ambience. This newer version doesn't replace the old, but those who want another, fresh, valid view of the *Spanisches Liederbuch* or just want to hear von Otter in her element will wish to acquire these two absorbing discs.

Spanisches Liederbuch – Die ihr schwebet um diese Palmen; Ach, des Knaben Augen; Mühvoll komm' ich und beladen; In dem Schatten meiner Locken; Sagt, seid Ihr es, feiner Herr; Mögen alle bösen Zungen; Alle gingen, Herz, zur Ruh; Tief im Herzen trag' ich Pein; Komm, o Tod, von Nacht umgeben; Ob auch finstre Blicke glitten; Bedeckt mich mit Blumen; Sie blasen zum Abmarsch; Wer tat deinem Füsslein weh; Geh' Geliebter, geh' jetz. Mörike Lieder – Das verlassene Mägdlein; Nimmersatte Liebe; Verborgenheit; Im Frühling; Elfenlied; Auf ein altes Bild; Lied vom Winde.
Elly Ameling *sop* **Rudolf Jansen** *pf*
Hyperion CDA66788 (59 minutes: DDD). Texts and translations included. Recorded 1991.   Ⓕ

This is a gratifying distillation of Ameling as a Wolf interpreter, a late flowering of her art in which we are consoled for some loss in the quality and quantity of tone by the insights offered. Indeed, in so many of these readings, her performance represents Wolf singing of the most telling kind. The four central songs tell us all. To 'Ob auch finstre Blicke glitten' she brings a depth of verbal accent and inner expression that places it among Wolf's highest achievements. There follow a properly weary, care-ridden account of 'Alle gingen, Herz, zur Ruh', a languorous evocation of 'Bedeckt mich mit Blumen' and a tragic entry into the abasing world of 'Mühvoll komm' ich und beladen'. The two sacred songs are hardly less impressive. Her choice ends with a reading of 'Geh' Geliebter', in which Ameling sheds the years to give us all the ardent thoughts of the girl reluctant at dawn to leave her lover. If you have hesitated before buying the complete EMI set, you might prefer to try this rewarding and distinguished selection. Ameling shows equal discernment in her choice from the

Mörike settings, catching – as the best Wolf interpreters can do – the specific mood of each. If there is a favourite here it has to be 'Das verlassene Mägdlein', where the dreadful anguish of the abandoned girl, so unerringly caught by Wolf, is expressed in a mood of almost toneless lassitude – just right. As ever, Jansen is an ideal partner for this singer, nowhere more so than when he rightly underplays the rhythm of 'Sie blasen zum Abmarsch'.

Haydn Wood

A May-Day Overture. Soliloquy. Variations on a once popular humorous song. Paris Suite. Roses of Picardy (orchestral version). A Manx Rhapsody. Frescoes – Sea shanties; The Bandstand, Hyde Park. An Evening Song. A Day in Fairyland – Dance of a whimsical elf. London Landmarks – The Horse Guards, Whitehall.
Slovak Radio Symphony Orchestra, Bratislava / Ernest Tomlinson.
Marco Polo British Light Music 8 223605 (73 minutes: DDD). Recorded 1993. Ⓕ

This pleasing collection of music by Haydn Wood features veteran light music conductor Ernest Tomlinson, who coaxes the best out of the Bratislava players. The familiarity of Wood's 'Montmartre' march must have left many longing to hear the rest of the *Paris Suite*, and it is unlikely that anyone could be disappointed with the languorous waltz and dreamy meditation that form its first two movements. Here, too, in Wood's own orchestral version, is that most beautiful of melodies, *Roses of Picardy* and the stirring march 'The Horse Guards, Whitehall', the signature tune of *Down Your Way*. Less familiar items include another stirring march, 'The Bandstand' – a sort of 'Montmartre' without the string of onions – and there are a couple of delightful miniatures in *An Evening Song* and 'Dance of a whimsical elf'. The more ambitious pieces include reminders of Wood's Manx upbringing, and there is a curiosity in the *Variations on a once popular humorous song* (the song in question being *If you want to know the time, ask a policeman*), which has some enigmatic Elgarian touches to it. Wood brought a classical resource to his stirring melodies, and this is a thoroughly worthwhile release.

Hugh Wood

String Quartets – No. 1; No. 2, Op. 13; No. 3, Op. 20; No. 4.
Chilingirian Quartet (Levon Chilingirian, Charles Stewart *vns* Simon Rowland *va* Philip de Groote *vc*).
Conifer Classics 75605-51239-2 (78 minutes: DDD). Recorded 1994. Ⓕ

Wood's style is evident in the First Quartet, where the angular gestures of the introduction propose ideas for future discussion, thus prompting references back to the opening movement, while another strategy gradually reveals ideas that become dominant in the finale. The result is a sketch, as yet somewhat tentative, of a quartet whose four movements are unified, finale-directed rather than first-movement dominated. The Second and Third Quartets, seemingly stepping aside from this path, in fact investigate it further. The Second, in 39 very brief linked sections, some of them mildly aleatoric, gradually builds a powerful sense of forward impetus from an opening in which each brief and violently juxtaposed musical event seems to propose a different direction. The Third has fewer sections and a longer span, but a still greater emotional range, from its chilly opening to the big, confident gestures with which it ends. Here there is no hint of the aleatory nor of disjunct juxtaposition, but a gradual growth of eloquence, of a hard-won long line. It was written after an unproductive period, and towards the end there is a distinctly Beethovenian sense of 'feeling new strength'. The recent Fourth Quartet is a superb demonstration of that strength at full stretch: an expository prelude, a tense *Scherzo* (itself expository also), a noble *Adagio* whose long lines can easily bridge silences and quite sharp angles, and a finale that is most satisfyingly the audible destination of all that preceded it. It is a masterly piece, enhanced by being heard as the culmination of its predecessors. Finely recorded, the Chilingirian Quartet is passionately involved with this music.

James Wood

Two men meet, each presuming the other to be from a distant planet. Phainomena.
Venancio Mbande talking with the trees.
Kuniko Kato *marimba* **Steven Schick** *perc*
New London Chamber Choir; Critical Band / James Wood.
NMC NMCD044 (66 minutes: DDD). Recorded 1993-97. Ⓕ

Wood Orchestral

This disc offers a great opportunity to explore James Wood's challenging but never incoherent compositions. If the mixture of elaborate titles and prominent percussion leads you to suspect a degree of pretentiousness, the quality of thought and the sensitivity to design as well as texture should reassure you that Wood is a real composer, as well as a fine performer, and the recordings could hardly be better. In *Phainomena* a touch of the pretentious can be detected in the way the music diffuses its strengths through over-insistence on ritualistic vocal writing and repetitive instrumental dance-patterns. But the other works are more effective, and vindicate Wood's own personal brand of modernism. The plan of *Two men meet*, to proceed from confrontation to reconciliation, could be simplistically schematic, but the subtlety of the interactions between percussion soloist and orchestra makes this a consistently absorbing and appealing score. In *Venacio Mbande talking with the trees*, the blend of intricate thought and clear, purposeful structure is if anything even more satisfying, with a poetic quality to the writing that lingers in the mind. Fans of Evelyn Glennie ought to try this disc, simply to see how well other percussion specialists match up to her achievements.

Charles Wuorinen
American 1938

Time's Encomium. Piano Sonata No. 1. String Quartet No. 1.
Robert Miller *pf*
Fine Arts Quartet (Leonard Sorkin, Abram Loft *vns* Bernard Zaslav *va* George Sopkin *vc*).
Music & Arts CD932 (75 minutes: ADD). Recorded 1968-71.   Ⓕ

The years 1968-70, when these works were composed, were of particular significance in Wuorinen's development. Then in his early thirties, he had become aware that he was losing patience with New Music's 'directionlessness'. On this evidence he was still quite happy with New Music's inherent complexity of utterance. But in Wuorinen's best compositions persistent density of texture is offset by an expressive exuberance redolent of the laid-back New York culture of the time. The ability of advanced and elaborate composition to project a strong vein of witty inventiveness is best shown here in *Time's Encomium*. The subtitle – 'for synthesised and processed synthesised sound' – makes the piece appear forbidding in the extreme, but Wuorinen evidently relished the technical possibilities of a medium that dispenses with live performers. As with Nancarrow's *Studies* for player piano, there's an element of sending-up the routines of traditional 'live' composition which adds greatly to the fun. Yet this is a substantial musical statement, not to be written off as incidental music for an unmade *Tom and Jerry* cartoon. The other works are more demanding. The Piano Sonata shares some of *Time's Encomium*'s fantasy and volatility: nevertheless, both the Sonata and the String Quartet, with their large-scale, intensely active forms, risk precisely that sense of directionlessness which the composer was seeking to avoid. The Quartet, in particular, seems determined to shun the kind of rhapsodic flow that makes the other works more appealing. Even so, there's no denying the power of the musical mind at work here, and the performances – aided by excellent remastering – will keep you listening.

Iannis Xenakis
Greek/French 1922

A Colone. Nuits. Serment. Knephas. Medea.
New London Chamber Choir; Critical Band / James Wood.
Hyperion CDA66980 (58 minutes: DDD). Texts and translations included. Recorded 1997.   Ⓕ

This enterprising Hyperion release is a great success, showing just how varied – and unintimidating – Xenakis's music can be. The performances are nothing short of phenomenal in their technical assurance and emotional power, and the recording is also something special, giving the singers just the right degree of space and resonance to project the often complex textures with all the necessary precision. The earliest works offer different angles on the composer's ultra-expressionist idiom, with *Nuits* (1967) adopting a very direct way of representing its anguished lament for the martyrs of Greece's struggle for freedom after 1945. *Medea* (also 1967) uses much more text, and its chant-like style has affinities with Stravinsky's *Les noces*, but the overall effect is much harsher, with abrasive yet imaginative instrumental writing. *A Colone* (1977) also has Stravinskian affinities, and the text (Sophocles's description of the delights of Colonus) prompts music which is uninhibitedly exuberant, even dance-like. This warmer, more celebratory side of Xenakis is carried over into *Serment* (1980), a short setting of a text derived from the Hippocratic Oath and not, one suspects, an entirely serious effort, though there is nothing trivial about it either. Finally, the superb *Knephas* ('Darkness') of 1990 begins in an appropriately unsparing manner, but ends with a hymnic apotheosis which recalls Messiaen in its harmonic character and warmth of atmosphere. Here is one of the twentieth century's most important musical voices, and this recording does it full justice.

Eugène Ysaÿe

Solo Violin Sonatas, Op. 27 – No. 1 in G minor; No. 2 in A minor; No. 3 in D minor, 'Ballade'; No. 4 in E minor; No. 5 in G major; No. 6 in E major. Poème élégiaque, Op. 12. Rêve d'enfant, Op. 14.
Philippe Graffin *vn* **Pascal Devoyon** *pf*
Hyperion CDA66940 (78 minutes: DDD). Recorded 1996.   Ⓕ

Philippe Graffin has one major advantage over his rivals: his pure intonation. Even the most demanding of Ysaÿe's flights of virtuosic fancy sound beautiful. Graffin refuses to overplay the music; tone and expression are always natural and unforced. Though he follows Ysaÿe's very detailed instructions more exactly than most violinists, there's also a strong element of fantasy, the music developing in a seemingly unconstrained and spontaneous way, the individual movements sharply characterized. The stunning bowing variations and rubato of the *Presto* finale of the Fourth Sonata, and the playful grace of the *Allegretto poco scherzoso* in the First Sonata are just two examples. You may be bothered by one thing in Graffin's playing – occasional rhythmic weakness. In the First Sonata's finale, the rubato gets out of hand, losing the underlying rhythmic impetus, and the opening *Allemande* of Sonata No. 4 is similarly undermined by his unwillingness to dwell sufficiently on the longer notes. Graffin's *Danse Rustique* in Sonata No. 5, on the other hand, is splendidly poised and bouncy. The beautifully played additional items are a real bonus, as are the thoughtful and illuminating notes by Graffin himself. Graffin, as a 'grand pupil' of Ysaÿe, shows himself well placed to carry on the tradition of Ysaÿe performance, inspired by the great violinist's own recordings. The recording is excellent.

Jan Dismas Zelenka

Capriccios – No. 2 in G major; No. 3 in F major. Concerto a 8 in G major. Hipocondrie a 7 in A major.
Das Neu-Eröffnete Orchestre / Jürgen Sonnentheil.
CPO CPO999 458-2 (61 minutes: DDD). Recorded 1996.   Ⓕ Ⓟ Ⓔ

This disc contains two of Zelenka's five *Capriccios*, a Concerto for eight instruments and the intriguingly titled *Hipocondrie*, which occupies ground somewhere between suite and concerto. Zelenka was skilled in the art of combining instruments of differing colours, ordering them about in a way that makes us wonder if he had a grudge against players. The horn-writing in the *Capriccios* is merciless, with uncommonly high parts often emerging in exposed moments in the texture. Zelenka's melodic facility, rhythmic imagination and instinctive feeling for effective instrumental ranges and colours are sufficient to sustain interest. There is an inventive freshness about his music which contains surprises at almost every turn. Sometimes, however, as in the finale of the Concerto in eight parts, sequential patterns are overworked, giving the movement a somewhat amorphous, unsatisfying shape. Initial rather good ideas, almost always arresting, are less well sustained than, say, Telemann's, even if they are sometimes bolder and more adventurous. Sonnentheil achieves spirited, amiable performances from Das Neu-Eröffnete Orchestre, an able body of period-instrumentalists. The two horns are excellent and, if oboes and strings sound a shade unrefined occasionally, it does little to spoil enjoyment of an entertaining programme.

Trio Sonatas – No. 1 in F major; No. 3 in B flat major; No. 4 in G minor.
Ensemble Zefiro (Paolo Grazzi, Alfredo Bernardini *obs* Alberto Grazzi *bn* Manfred Kraemer *vn* Lorenz Duftschmid *violone* Gian Carlo Rado *theorbo* Rinaldo Alessandrini *hpd/org*).
Auvidis Astrée E8563 (52 minutes: DDD). Recorded 1995.   Ⓕ Ⓟ

Zelenka was one of a gifted group of composers associated with the Dresden court during the first half of the eighteenth century. The court orchestra, one of the best around at that time, boasted a particularly accomplished wind section, and it may have been for some of these players that Zelenka wrote his six trios. The sources have not survived complete in all cases and the realization, for example, of the bass parts in the First and Third Sonatas, both of them included here, must always be conjectural. Ensemble Zefiro has thought carefully about this and has arrived at a solution which is both idiomatic and, it seems, in keeping with the surviving material. The playing is spirited and plentifully endowed with virtuosity. The oboists Paolo Grazzi and Alfredo Bernardini are technically secure and tastefully imaginative in their ornamentation. Bassoonist Alberto Grazzi is also fluent and furthermore a sensitive ensemble player. Keyboard continuo is stylishly provided by Rinaldo Alessandrini, sometimes playing harpsichord, at other times organ; and additional continuo support includes violone and theorbo. Readers so far unacquainted with these sonatas are in for a treat for this is music rich in fantasy, exciting for its virtuosic content, unusually extended in the working out of its ideas, and effectively constructed.

Trio Sonatas – No. 2 in G minor, No. 5 in F major; No. 6 in C minor.
Ensemble Zefiro (Paolo Grazzi, Alfredo Bernardini *obs* Alberto Grazzi *bn* Roberto Sensi *db*
Rolf Lislevand *theorbo* Rinaldo Alessandrini *hpd/org*).
Auvidis Astrée E8511 (52 minutes: DDD). Recorded 1993.　　　　　　　　　　　　　Ⓕ Ⓟ

For sheer *élan* and spirit the baroque instrumental players on this disc take some beating. Zelenka's
six sonatas for two oboes, bassoon and continuo are among the most rewarding and at times most
difficult pieces of baroque chamber music in the oboe repertory. Indeed, pieces demanding such
virtuosity from these instruments were probably without precedent at the time (1715). The writing is
often such as to make us wonder if they were destined for friends or enemies of the composer. Here,
then, is splendidly invigorating playing of music which offers a great deal beyond face value. The
sounds of the solo instruments themselves, together with an effective continuo group of double-
bass, harpsichord/organ and theorbo are admirably captured in the recording.

The Lamentations of Jeremiah.
Michael Chance *counterten* **John Mark Ainsley** *ten* **Michael George** *bass*
Chandos Baroque Players.
Hyperion CDA66426 (73 minutes: DDD). Texts and translations included. Recorded 1990.　　　Ⓕ Ⓟ

Between the incomparable settings by Thomas Tallis and the extremely austere one by Stravinsky
(which he called *Threni*) the 'Lamentations of Jeremiah' have attracted surprisingly few composers.
Perhaps the predominantly sombre tone, without even the dramatic opportunities presented by the
Dies irae in a Requiem, is off-putting. Be that as it may, Zelenka showed remarkable resourcefulness
in his 1722 setting for the electoral chapel at Dresden, where he was *Kapellmeister*. His musical
language is in many ways similar to that of J.S. Bach but there are also daring turns of phrase
which are entirely personal. The six *Lamentations* feature each singer twice; this performance is
intimate, even mystical, slightly spacious in tempo and with a resonant acoustic.

Alexander Zemlinsky　　　　　　　　　　　　　　　　　　　　　　Austrian 1871-1942

String Quartets – No. 1 in A major, Op. 4; No. 4, Op. 25. Two Movements for String Quartet.
Pražák Quartet (Vaclav Remes, Vlastimil Holek *vns* Josef Klusoň *va* Michal Kaňka *vc*).
Praga Digitals PRD250 107 (70 minutes: DDD). Recorded 1997.　　　　　　　　　　　　　Ⓕ

String Quartets – No. 1; No. 2, Op. 15.
Artis Quartet (Peter Schuhmayer, Johannes Meissl *vns* Herbert Kefer *va* Othmar Muller *vc*).
Nimbus NI5563 (65 minutes: DDD). Recorded 1997.　　　　　　　　　　　　　　　　　Ⓕ

Zemlinsky's four quartets have never quite become part of the established chamber music repertory.
That they deserve a place in that repertory is eloquently argued by both these couplings. Nimbus
announces that the Artis Quartet will be recording the Third and Fourth Quartets in due course;
Praga make no such promise about the Pražák completing their survey, but it would be a great pity
if they did not. In the richly post-Brahmsian First Quartet the Artis produces splendidly ample
tone, warm intensity of expression and, in the demurely lilting *Scherzo*, a touch of humour. The
Pražák does not have quite their Austrian colleagues' variety of colour (the Artis plays a
Montagnana, an Andrea Guarneri, a Guadagnini and an Andrea Amati, which helps) and its
slower tempos, though adding a touch of geniality to the first movement, also adds a hint of heavy-
footedness to the *Scherzo*. On the other hand it is readier to play quietly, and reveals more shadow
in the slow movement.

The Artis completes its disc with an account of the Second Quartet which is startlingly successful in
conveying its abrupt, at times violent oscillations of mood and its extraordinary vehemence, while
very properly finding the centre of its emotional world to be a poignant lyricism. The Pražák has
the still harder task of the Fourth Quartet, one of the most demanding pieces for the medium ever
written. If you unworthily suspect that its slowish *Scherzo* in the First Quartet is due to caution, its
account of the Fourth's concluding double fugue convincingly demonstrates its hair-raising
virtuosity. And in the rest of this work its very slightly rougher, brighter sound is a positive
advantage, though in the elaborately florid textures of the penultimate variation movement it shows
that it can also produce sweet tone and a fine line. It will be fascinating to hear what the Artis will
make of this work. Until both quartets complete their cycles you shouldn't part with either of these
discs. If you insist on a recommendation at this stage it would have to be, but only by a whisker, for
the Artis. But the Pražák adds a substantial bonus in the form of a pair of movements from an
abandoned quartet of 1927, the first strangely based on an almost derisive fragment of *Yankee*

Doodle, the second an apparent attempt to fuse a slow movement, at times mysterious, at times intense, with more aggressive music that eventually gives birth to an enigmatic Minuet. Both discs are well recorded, the Nimbus sound being a little warmer than the Praga.

Zemlinsky Sechs Gesänge, Op. 13.
Mahler Lieder eines fahrenden Gesellen. Rückert-Lieder.
Anne Sofie von Otter *mez*
North German Radio Symphony Orchestra / Sir John Eliot Gardiner.
DG 439 928-2GH (56 minutes: DDD). Texts and translations included.
Recorded live in 1993.   Ⓕ Ⓔ

This is another absolute winner for both von Otter and Gardiner. The three works make an ideal programme, the two Mahler pieces forming a sensible frame for the central Zemlinsky. In all three offerings von Otter offers that peculiar gift of hers consisting of utter conviction allied to wonderful musicianship. In terms of tempo, phrasing, balance and sheer interpretative know-how, the pair take no false steps and very many fruitful ones. You will look hard to find a version of *Lieder eines fahrenden Gesellen* filled with such sense of emotions being felt and expressed so immediately. Von Otter and Gardiner make the work live here and now for our time, Gardiner rewardingly alert to every nuance and subtlety in Mahler's orchestral writing, which the clear recording admirably seconds. The Zemlinsky is the real revelation, though, far preferable to the piano version of these shadowy Maeterlinck settings. These songs of sexual liberation and *fin de siècle* decadence, which mirror precisely the world of *Jugendstil* as exemplified in Klimt's paintings – and are equally multi-mirrored, highly coloured and erotic – cry out for instrumental clothing. Gardiner revels in the dream-world orchestration while von Otter perfectly catches their hothouse atmosphere and underlines the texts' meaning without ever indulging in any overemphases. It's almost a relief to come up into the open air of Mahler's Rückert setting, 'Ich atmet' einen linden Duft', where von Otter lightens her timbre, bringing a gentle smile into her tone. In these settings, she once more finds the right 'face' for each song – even expanding grandly into the affirmations at the end of 'Um Mitternacht' – and then ends a compelling disc with just the other-worldly serenity predicated by 'Ich bin der Welt'. There's no need to seek out any other recording of these pieces: this is the one to have.

Ein lyrische Symphonie, Op. 18. Symphonische Gesänge, Op. 20.
Alessandra Marc *sop* **Håkan Hagegård** *bar* **Willard White** *bass*
Royal Concertgebouw Orchestra / Riccardo Chailly.
Decca Entartete Musik 443 569-2DH (65 minutes: DDD). Texts and translations included.
Recorded 1993. *Gramophone* Award Winner 1995.   Ⓕ Ⓔ

With the Concertgebouw, one has no fear that the sheer beauty of Zemlinsky's orchestral textures will be understated, but the urgency and strength beneath the surfaces are evident too, and it's quite an achievement for such an orchestra of Mahler specialists to get Zemlinsky's sound, so like Mahler and yet so very unlike, unerringly right. The soloists are simply superb: Marc is voluptuously caressing, not least in her sensuous use of *portamento*, but very intelligent in her use of words, her understanding of the dramatic gist of her three songs, and her extended lower register gives her both security at the bottom of the range and a beautiful shading of mezzo-ish warmth; Hagegård has nobility and strength as well as tenderness, and the Lieder singer's subtlety that the third and last songs need. Throughout, the orchestral playing is immaculately balanced. Was Willard White chosen for the *Symphonische Gesänge* because they are settings of black American poets? If so, he has the intelligence to realize that there is nothing especially 'ethnic' about them; to realize also, as does Chailly, that although only one opus number separates them from *Ein lyrische Symphonie* they inhabit a different world, harsher and more bitter. They require great vocal splendour but also a certain reserve. White and Chailly succeed admirably.

Posthumous Songs – Sechs Lieder. Zwei Lieder. Zwei Preislieder. Wandl' ich im Wald des Abends. Vier Lieder. Zwei Brettl-Lieder. Drei Lieder. Zwei Balladen. Lieder auf Gedichte von Richard Dehmel – Ansturm; Vorspiel; Auf See. Vier Lieder. Und einmal gehst du.
Ruth Ziesak *sop* **Iris Vermillion** *mez* **Hans-Peter Blochwitz** *ten*
Andreas Schmidt *bar* **Cord Garben** *pf*
Sony Classical SK57960 (70 minutes: DDD). Texts and translations included. Recorded 1993.   Ⓕ

These are the songs Zemlinsky didn't publish; why not? When sung as they are here in chronological order the reason for a while seems obvious: they have little individuality until about a third of the way through the collection. From then on things get much more interesting. The three settings of Richard Dehmel have a concentrated, poignant intensity so impressive that one is tempted to speculate about hidden reasons for Zemlinsky's reticence. 'Jane Grey' (from *Zwei Balladen*), for example, was entered for a competition to which Schoenberg submitted a setting of exactly the same text. Is that why it almost out-Schoenbergs Schoenberg in its tenuous hold on tonality, its curiously gripping bare angularity? But in 'Der verlorene Haufen' (*Zwei Balladen*), also set by Schoenberg for the same competition, Zemlinsky seems to be out-Mahlering Mahler in the fearsome march-toccata that accompanies this grim tale of a front-line regiment contemplating death each morning. The manner of the Dehmel songs is recaptured in a haunting group of settings of Hofmannsthal (*Vier Lieder*); there are also two curious comic ballads (the *Brettl-Lieder*, one quite funny, the other – about a man who eats so much that he bursts – rather disgusting), a most beautiful cradle-song over a dead child ('Über eine Wiege', *Drei Lieder*) and a much later, nobly stoic contemplation of old age (*Und einmal gehst du*) that are in no way inferior to the best of Zemlinsky's published songs. Blochwitz, Schmidt and Garben are splendid, Vermillion matches them admirably and Ziesak, if a little hard and bright at times, can fine her voice down to an effective intimacy. The recordings are excellent.

Zemlinsky Eine florentinische Tragödie.
Iris Vermillion *mez* Bianca; **Heinz Kruse** *ten* Guido Bardi; **Albert Dohmen** *bar* Simone.
A. Mahler (orch. Colin and David Matthews) Die stille Stadt. Laue Sommernacht. Bei dir ist es traut. Licht in der Nacht. Waldeinsamkeit. Erntelied.
Iris Vermillion *mez*
Royal Concertgebouw Orchestra / Riccardo Chailly.
Decca Entartete Musik 455 112-2DH (71 minutes: DDD). Notes, texts and translations included.
Recorded 1996. Ⓕ Ⓔ

Zemlinsky's *Florentine Tragedy* is a disturbing, shocking piece, but to make its fullest impact it also needs to sound ravishingly beautiful. Zemlinsky's sumptuous scoring often demands an orchestra of the Royal Concertgebouw's stature, and in this reading it sounds quite magnificent. But the score also needs a conductor of subtlety and shrewdness to point up the two passages of contrasting serene lyricism, one where Simone's wife Bianca assures Count Bardi of her eternal love and another when husband and wife rediscover their love for each other. Vermillion is very fine at both these points, her mezzo timbre adding warmth to her line. Kruse is admirable too, fining down his ringing tenor in that duet scene, and, as Simone, Dohmen is forceful and dangerous. But Chailly is the real star of the performance, pacing the opera so well that it seems over in no time, drawing richly complex but never muddy textures from his remarkable orchestra. On hearing the Alma Mahler songs one is struck by the benefits of their orchestration. But here again, exquisitely though Vermillion sings these songs, Chailly must take at least half the credit. Each song is taken faster than in most recordings with piano, and every one of them gains from it in impulsive urgency. In both Zemlinsky's opera and Alma Mahler's songs the recording leaves nothing to be desired: the colours are rich but beautifully clean.

Der König Kandaules (cptd. Beaumont).
James O'Neal *ten* König Kandaules; **Monte Pederson** *bar* Gyges; **Nina Warren** *sop* Nyssia;
Klaus Häger *bass* Phedros; **Peter Galliard** *ten* Syphax; **Mariusz Kwiecien** *bar* Nicomedes;
Kurt Gysen *bass* Pharnaces; **Simon Yang** *bass* Philebos; **Ferdinand Seiler** *ten* Sebas;
Guido Jentjens *bar* Archelaos;
Hamburg State Philharmonic Orchestra / Gerd Albrecht.
Capriccio 60 071/2 (two discs: 128 minutes: DDD). Recorded live in 1996. Notes, text and
translation included. Ⓕ

King Candaules, based on a play by André Gide, is Zemlinsky's last opera, written during the Nazis' rise to power and complete in short score when he fled to America in 1938. He showed it to his pupil Artur Bodanzky, then a Principal Conductor at the Met, but Bodanzky seems to have warned him that the libretto would not be acceptable – in one scene Candaules tricks his wife into undressing in front of a fisherman he has recently befriended, then into sleeping with him. Zemlinsky never completed the orchestration of *Der König Kandaules* but left a large number of indications of scoring. Antony Beaumont's orchestration sounds perfectly convincing. When two excerpts from the score were performed and recorded in 1994 it already looked as though a major work by Zemlinsky was about to be revealed. And that indeed is the case: a marvellous and quite characteristic score, but in some ways a dismaying one. All the orchestral richness and the voluptuously singing lines that one expects are there, but wedded to a plot that seems all too accurately to reflect the disorder and disillusion of the times in which it was written. Nyssia, the wife so chaste and beautiful that until now no one but Candaules has seen her unveiled, is portrayed in music of quite sumptuous allure, but her reaction to his betrayal is more Salome-like than tragic: she orders the fisherman Gyges to kill her husband and take his place, in her bed as well as on the throne. Gyges, the poor but honest peasant (and his music has a touch of nobility to it), is a murderer himself: he killed his own wife because, as Candaules would have agreed, she was his property. And Candaules the seeming altruist, whose greatest pleasure is to share his wealth with others, is in fact simply boasting of his good fortune: even his wife's beauty is a sort of torment to him if other men are not jealous of it. And in Zemlinsky's musical portrayal the more his baseness becomes obvious the more glamorous and sympathetic he is. The performance is a fine one, O'Neal lacking only the last touch of heroic vocal stature for Candaules, Warren only a little stretched by the Ariadne-like role of Nyssia, Pederson first class (a moment or two of suspect intonation aside) as Gyges. Albrecht is perfectly at home in this sort of music, the orchestra's admirable richness of tone does not obscure detail, and the recording is atmospheric (stage business audible) but clear. Zemlinsky's reputation has been growing year by year recently. It can only be enhanced by this ravishing, richly complex, disturbing opera.

Bernd Alois Zimmermann

German 1918-1970

Concertos – Oboe and Small Orchestra; Trumpet and Orchestra, 'Nobody knows the trouble I see'; Canto di speranza; Cello and Orchestra, 'en forme de pas de trois'.
Heinz Holliger *ob* **Håkan Hardenberger** *tpt* **Heinrich Schiff** *vc*
South-West German Radio Symphony Orchestra / Michael Gielen.
Philips 434 114-2PH (71 minutes: DDD). Recorded 1989-92.   Ⓕ

The Oboe Concerto (1952) vigorously confronts the central post-war challenge: if you want to embrace the new (serialism) alongside the old (neo-classicism), how do you keep your balance? The answer, for Zimmermann, was 'precariously'. In the Trumpet Concerto (1954) the absorption of a negro spiritual and elements of jazz serve to intensify the trauma of a search for stylistic equilibrium. Yet again the result is an impressive work of art strongly built and progressing inexorably to a bleak conclusion. *Canto di speranza* (1953-57) brings us still closer to the apocalyptic modernism of the opera *Die Soldaten* (begun in 1958) as models – notably Webern – become objects of mockery. The Cello Concerto *en forme de pas de trois*, written after the opera in 1965-66, completes the process of re-creative rejection. It is a haunting fantasy, at once ballet score and concert work, a parody of nineteenth-century terpsichorean conventions which is as bitter in tone as it is beguiling in sound. Philips have assembled three star soloists for this well-recorded disc, and with sterling orchestral support they do the music proud.

Antiphonen. Omnia tempus habent. Présence.
Julie Moffat *sop* **Peter Rundel** *vn* **Tabea Zimmermann** *va* **Michael Stirling** *vc*
Hermann Kretzschmar *pf*
Ensemble Modern / Hans Zender.
RCA Red Seal 09026 61181-2 (56 minutes: DDD). Recorded 1992.   Ⓕ

Omnia tempus habent sets verses from Ecclesiastes for soprano and an instrumental ensemble which, with copious use of flute and vibraphone, echoes then-contemporary Boulez and Berio. Like those masters, Zimmermann could turn a highly fragmented style to strong expressive ends, with an elaborate vocal line that tests Julie Moffat in what is in any case an unflatteringly close recording. The other works fare better. *Antiphonen* is in effect a viola concerto, and, like many such compositions, it involves its gentle protagonist in an Orpheus-like attempt to tame the instrumental furies embodied by snarling brass and menacing percussion. The contest is nothing if not melodramatic, the end an uneasy, exhausted compromise rather than a victory for one side or the other. Zimmermann even includes a variety of texts to be declaimed by the instrumentalists: maddeningly, these are not set out in the booklet and, in any case, the device is of dubious value. Far more effective are the purely instrumental textures of *Présence*, where the need to work with just three instruments seems to have refined Zimmermann's thinking. The result is one of his finest works. *Présence* is a ballet score, and the composer shows great resource in allowing hints of conventionally patterned dance music to infiltrate the spiky, scary idiom of the remainder. Although the drama reflects *Antiphonen*'s alternation of aggressive and submissive moods, the music is absorbing on its own terms, and the piece is performed with great spirit by members of the Ensemble Modern.

Requiem für einen jungen Dichter.
Vlatka Orsanic *sop* **James Johnson** *bar* **Michael Rotschopf, Bernhard Schir** *spkrs*
Christoph Grund *org* **Alexander von Schlippenbach Jazz Band; Cologne Radio Chorus;**
Stuttgart Radio Chorus; Edinburgh Festival Chorus; Bratislava Slovak Chorus;
Bratislava City Chorus; South-West German Radio Symphony Orchestra / Michael Gielen.
Sony Classical SK61995 (64 minutes: DDD). Recorded 1995.   Ⓕ

Zimmermann's *Requiem for a young poet* is a humbling polyphony of twentieth-century misdeeds – riveting, provocative, uncompromising and as essential to our understanding of 1960s 'serious' music as The Beatles are to an informed perception of that decade's pop culture. In fact, the two momentarily converge when Zimmermann quotes The Beatles' song *Hey Jude* (something of a horrific pun, especially given the *Requiem*'s use of the German language and of Hitler's voice in particular). The work opens to a hollow drone, a sort of post-Holocaust *Zarathustra* framing a gallery of voices, three of them, like Zimmermann's own, being suicides: the poets Vladimir Mayakovsky, Konrad Bayer and (via Mayakovsky) Sergei Essenin. The spoken word is crucial throughout; in fact it was Bayer who provided the *Requiem*'s chilling motto: 'What can we hope for? There is nothing that awaits us except death'. Recited extracts from Wittgenstein's 'Philosophical Investigations' (relating specifically to the idea of 'language games') precede the voice of Pope John XXIII, a reading from 'Molly Bloom's Monologue' (Joyce's *Ulysses*), Alexander Dubček addressing the Czech people; then Hitler, Chamberlain, the former Greek Prime Minister Andras Papandreou, readings from Pound, Schwitters, Camus, Sándor Weöres and musical fragments by Wagner (*Tristan*), Milhaud (*La création du monde*) and Messiaen (*L'ascension*) – a tumbling stream of consciousness where thinkers and artists have the definite upper hand. Most texts are spoken in German and although there are no detailed texts or translations provided (a bit of a nuisance, admittedly), one presumes that the point of quotation was more a matter of evoking memory and specific events than pondering the wisdom (either genuine or suspect) of those present. The *Requiem* climaxes to the unsettling sound of massed demonstrations and ends with a forcefully punctuated choral declamation (or affirmation) of the words 'Do ... /na ... /no ... /bis ... /pa ... /cem'! Fans of Zimmermann's opera *Die Soldaten* will have already braced themselves.

'The piece is inscribed to all the catastrophes that the human race has brought down upon itself and addresses those aspects of human behaviour that have opened up the way to such a Day of Wrath or that threaten to do so.' Hiekel's words ring true but barely touch the aural scope and emotional impact of this incredible piece, its sustained tension, telling juxtapositions (voices that echo or mix in various perspectives), the devastating effect of those 'montage-like' chords and the rude (but rare) invasions of humour. No one was better qualified for the interpreter's role than Michael Gielen; he and his soloists, choral forces and orchestra acquit themselves with distinction.

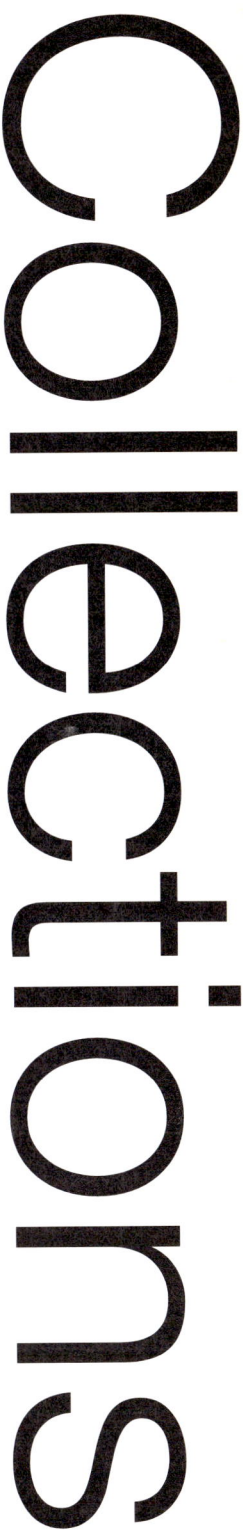

Orchestral

A la carte
Itzhak Perlman *vn*
Abbey Road Ensemble / Lawrence Foster
EMI CDC5 55475-2 (63 minutes: DDD). Recorded 1995.   Ⓕ
Massenet Thaïs – Méditation. **Glazunov** Mazurka-Oberek in D major. Meditation, Op. 32.
Rachmaninov Vocalise, Op. 34 No. 14. **Sarasate** Zigeunerweisen, Op. 20. Introduction and
Tarantella, Op. 43. **Rimsky-Korsakov** (arr. Kreisler) Fantasia on Two Russian Themes, Op. 33.
Tchaikovsky (orch. Glazunov) Scherzo in C minor, Op. 42 No. 2. **Wieniawski** Légende,
Op. 17. Zigeunerweisen. **Kreisler** The Old Refrain. Schön Rosmarin.

A most enjoyable programme. Perlman approximates the 'old school' with something of an actor's
skill: he feels the period, not as a first-hand witness (even at 50, he is far too young for that), but as
a respectful recipient of a great tradition. His 'Méditation' is an elevated 'easy listen', sensitively
accompanied. The Glazunov *Mazurka-Oberek* should be at least as popular as Saint-Saëns's concert
pieces for violin and orchestra, and Perlman does it proud. The initial pages of Rachmaninov's
Vocalise are a little over-sweet (too many well-oiled slides), but its latter half achieves genuine
expressive eloquence. Glazunov's *Meditation* is suitably honeyed and the Kreisler-Rimsky *Fantasia*
(where Goldmark's A minor Concerto hovers around the main theme) is given a truly splendid
performance. Of the rest, the two Kreisler pieces are exceptional, *Schön Rosmarin* especially, while
Lawrence Foster's expert Abbey Road Ensemble provides a discreet but flavoursome orchestral base.

American Light Music Classics
New London Orchestra / Ronald Corp.
Hyperion CDA67067 (73 minutes: DDD). Recorded 1998.   Ⓕ
Sousa (orch. Winter) The Washington Post. **Mills** (orch. Crooke) Whistling Rufus.
Gould American Symphonette No. 3 – Pavanne. **Arndt** (orch. Zamecnik) Nola. **Pryor** The
Whistler and His Dog. **Anderson** The Belle of the Ball. Plink, Plank, Plunk! **Guion** (orch. Schmid)
The Arkansas Traveller. **Bratton** (orch. Saddler) The Teddy Bears' Picnic. **MacDowell**
(orch. Woodhouse) To a Wild Rose, Op. 51 No. 1. **Holzmann** Blaze away. **Friml** (orch. Minot)
Chanson, 'In Love'. **Scott** (orch. Lane) The Toy Trumpet. **Gershwin** (orch. Berkowitz)
Promenade. **Herbert** (orch. Langey) March of the Toys. **Rose** Holiday for Strings. **Nevin**
(orch. Myddleton) Narcissus, Op. 13 No. 4. **Gillis** Symphony No. 5½, 'A Symphony for Fun'.
Rodgers (orch. Walker) Carousel Waltz.

Leroy Anderson, John Philip Sousa and Rudolf Friml are all still household names (well, to many
readers, at any rate) but no matter how well you know the tune, how many can remember the name
of the composer of *The Teddy Bears' Picnic* – composed by John W. Bratton in 1907 decades before
words were set to it – or *Narcissus*, a little masterpiece by Ethelbert Nevin from 1891? The latter
had two English adaptations. In the 1890s it was used as the tune for one of Marie Lloyd's successes
at the Palace in Cambridge Circus, *There they are, the two of them on their own*, and 50 years later
Joyce Grenfell and Norman Wisdom used it for their 'Laughter' record. Anyone who grew up in the
era of the BBC Light Programme will recognize many of the other pieces played on this CD. In his
notes, Andrew Lamb fills us in, for instance, where Frederick Allen Mills is concerned. His
Whistling Rufus sounds familiar, and surely Lehár knew it and took some inspiration from it when
he composed the Cake-Walk in Act 3 of the *Merry Widow*. Mills's best-known work is the song,
Meet me in St Louis, Louis revived 40 years after its composition for the Minelli film. The longest
item on the disc is Don Gillis's Symphony No. 5½ subtitled *A Symphony for Fun*. Originally a
trombonist, Gillis went on to a radio career and became Toscanini's producer. Once the staple of
bandstand and palm court orchestras, these lovely old tunes have a freshness and charm akin to the
best light-hearted literature or illustration from the same period. Easy listening, yes, but produced
with formidable skill. Ronald Corp and the New London Orchestra play the whole sequence with
verve and dedication. Clear, good recording.

American Music
Boston Symphony Orchestra / Serge Koussevitzky.
Pearl mono GEMMCD9492 (79 minutes: AAD). Recorded 1934-40.   Ⓜ Ⓗ
Foote Suite in E minor, Op. 36. **McDonald** San Juan Capistrano.
Copland El salón México. **Harris** Symphonies – No. 1; No. 3.

Music lovers with a romantic hankering for the American desert and the Great Outdoors may well
know Roy Harris's high, wide and handsome Third Symphony already, but the chances of having

heard Serge Koussevitzky's 1939 recording of it are somewhat more remote. If you can accept and enjoy the soundtracks of classic Westerns, then you'll have no trouble with this CD: the playing of the Boston Symphony burns through a veil of surface hiss with the ease and accuracy of a blow-torch, and Koussevitzky's conducting tends to confirm the judgement of many, that this is indeed the greatest American symphony. It's a tremendous experience, and although the work is barely 17 minutes long, it none the less constitutes an epic journey. Koussevitzky was a great musical pioneer, and his recordings of Copland's saucy *El salón México* and Arthur Foote's delightful Suite (easily as appealing as, say, Grieg's *Holberg Suite*) are rightly regarded as classics. Add Harris's First Symphony – a poorer recording, but a fascinating prophecy of greater work to come – and Harl McDonald's colourful essays, and you have the basis of an absorbing concert, one that is likely to give you a great deal of enjoyment.

Les Ballets Russes
London Philharmonic Orchestra, London Symphony Orchestra / Antál Dorati.
Pearl mono GEM0036 (74 minutes: ADD). Recorded 1937. Ⓜ Ⓗ
J. Strauss II (arr. Desormière) Le beau Danube. **d'Erlanger** Les cent baisers.
Chabrier (arr. cpsr, Mottl and Rieti) Cotillon. **Boccherini** (arr. Françaix) Scuola di ballo.

The impact of Diaghilev's Ballets Russes on the artistic and musical world in the West was so widespread that when he died in 1929 it was assumed that his ballet company would go with him. In the 1930s, however, under the joint management of René Blum and Colonel Vassily de Basil, the Ballet Russe de Monte-Carlo emerged with a new generation of stars and soon the dynamic young Antál Dorati as Music Director. Apart from still photographs and stage designs, there is so little to help a modern audience imagine what those glittering seasons were like that this CD has an almost dreamlike quality. When the company danced at Covent Garden, the London Philharmonic was the orchestra in residence, so these performances are authentic – unlike so many concert readings of ballet scores, this is how the music would have sounded in the theatre.

The four ballets represented were all popular items on the programme for several seasons. Although the last to be recorded, in 1939, *Scuola di ballo*, Jean Françaix's arrangement of ten pieces by Boccherini, was one of the first works presented by the company in 1933. It was choreographed by Léonide Massine, based on a play by Goldoni. Massine himself danced the central male role, with two of the most glamorous ballerinas as his partners – Irina Barnonova and Tatiana Riabouchinska. The sound is, as Françaix put it, 'full of Parisian modernisms'. Balanchine's ballet, *Cotillon*, was also one of the earliest post-Diaghilev efforts by the company. Chabrier's music was mostly orchestrated by Vittorio Rieti, and the ballet was designed by Christian Bérard. Unlike Balanchine's later, more abstract work, it had a narrative about guests at a formal dance in a private house, with the theme of 'The hands of fate'. Balanchine himself danced the First Guest at the première, with Tamara Toumanova as the Daughter of the House.

Le beau Danube, with Johann Strauss's music arranged by Roger Desormière, was one of the most enduringly popular of Massine's ballets. The sets were by Vladimir Polunine, based on the drawings of Constantin Guys. Alexandra Danilova had a great success as the Street Dancer, with Massine himself as the Hussar. The finale, with Baronova's solo culminating in 32 *fouettés* and then the rival Hussar and Dandy trying to outdo each other in pirouettes can easily be imagined in Dorati's ecstatic conducting. The rarest piece is Baron Frédéric d'Erlanger's *Les cent baisers*. Dorati conducted the world première at Covent Garden in July 1935 – the choreography was by Bronislava Nijinska with designs by Jean Hugo, and Baronova and Lichine in the main roles. The Hans Andersen tale of the Princess and the Swineherd is a story of romantic disillusion and d'Erlanger's music, although evoking courtly traditions, has a swooning almost Korngold-like mood. The sound of these recordings from the 1930s is very clear and free of distortion. Anyone with a curiosity about the great days of the Ballets Russes is likely to be utterly enthralled by this enchanting disc.

Baroque Trumpet Concertos
Håkan Hardenberger *tpt*
I Musici.
Philips 442 131-2PH
(54 minutes: DDD). Items marked ᵃ transcribed for trumpet. Recorded 1993. Ⓕ
Vivaldi (rev. Malipiero) Concerto for Two Trumpets and Strings in C major, RV537 (with Reinhold Friedrich, tpt). **Corelli** Sonata for Trumpet and Strings in D major. **Albinoni** Concerto in B flat major, Op. 7 No. 3ᵃ. **Torelli** Sonata a 5 con tromba, G7. **A. Marcello** Oboe Concerto in D minorᵃ. **Viviani** Capricci armonici – Sonata prima. **Franceschini** Sonata for Two Trumpets, Strings and Continuo in D major (Friedrich). **Baldassare** Sonata for Cornett, Strings and Continuo in F majorᵃ.

No trumpet player can make a career as a baroque player on a modern instrument without performing music originally written for other instruments; the domestic repertoire is simply not sustainable (it could be argued that the Torelli and Corelli works only sound truly colourful on a natural trumpet and tonally bland even with Hardenberger's modern playing). No complaints with transcriptions *per se*: a good one can leave the original looking to its laurels. Some disappointment must be registered, however, that Hardenberger has not investigated his own fare from the multifarious collections of fine eighteenth-century concertos. Most listeners will enjoy this highly exacting playing and his silky articulation and rhythmic discipline – the Vivaldi is as high-tech and effortless as you will ever hear. I Musici are a curious choice of accompanists. Still sporting their timelessly vigorous and yet unashamedly Mediterranean approach to baroque chamber playing, there is quite a temperamental polarity here, one would suspect, between their style and Hardenberger's Nordic and less overtly emotional playing. The result, however, is not as marked as you might expect, since Hardenberger vocalizes more in this recording than in the past (all slow movements are warmer and less 'worked out' than in previous discs of this nature) and he responds to I Musici's full-blooded playing in a similarly jaunty way. The Marcello D minor Concerto has some especially sweet moments.

Sir Thomas Beecham The RPO Legacy.
Royal Philharmonic Orchestra / Sir Thomas Beecham.
Dutton Laboratories mono CDLX7027 (74 minutes: ADD). Recorded 1946-47. Ⓜ Ⓗ
Berlioz Le corsaire, Op. 21. **Sibelius** Tapiola, Op. 112. **Mussorgsky** Khovanshchina – Dance of the Persian Slaves. **Debussy** Printemps. **Bach** Christmas Oratorio, BWV248 – Sinfonia. **Smetana** The Bartered Bride – Overture; Polka; Dance of the Comedians. **Chabrier** Joyeuse marche.

With astonishingly full mono sound, this first disc in the RPO Legacy series vividly captures the tense excitement of the months following Beecham's founding of the orchestra in 1946. It starts with the recording of the Berlioz *Corsaire* Overture which was the very first from the RPO to be issued. Beecham at hectic speed in the opening flourish challenges his violins to keep up, and the result has an apt element of wildness while offering fine ensemble. *Tapiola*, recorded a few weeks later in November 1946, similarly has a rugged intensity as well as polish, with the terracing of texture and dynamic beautifully brought out even in mono. Finest of all in the collection is the Debussy *Printemps* which Beecham conducted as early as 1913, but which he never recorded again. Though the sessions began on the very day that *Tapiola* was recorded, the contrast of mood is astonishing. Finnish ruggedness and severity give way to sensuousness and beauty in the first of the two sections and to energy and colour in the second. Bach, not a composer generally associated with Beecham, inspires him to a performance which suggests French rather than German music, sweet and elegant, and the Smetana and Chabrier are electrifying, not least the horn trills in the Chabrier. The Dutton transfers have a vivid sense of presence with contrasts of dynamic and texture more clearly established than is common in mono recordings of the 1940s.

Brian Kay's British Light Music Discoveries
Royal Ballet Sinfonia / Gavin Sutherland.
ASV White Line CDWHL2113 (70 minutes: DDD). Recorded 1998. Ⓜ
Alwyn Suite of Scottish Dances. **Arnold** The Roots of Heaven – Overture. **Bennett** Little Suite.
Jacob The Barber of Seville Goes to the Devil. **Johnstone** Tarn Hows. **Langford** Two Worlds.
Langley The Coloured Counties. **Lyon** Joie de vivre. **Parker** The Glass Slipper – Overture.
Sargent Impression of a Windy Day, Op. 9.

Though Brian Kay's name and portrait are used to promote this splendid collection, one suspects the driving force may have been its producer and annotator, Philip Lane, who has done such a lot for British light music on CD. With so much of Malcolm Arnold's music available, it is astonishing that his typically ebullient and tuneful overture *The Roots of Heaven* is here receiving its first recording. The same goes for William Alwyn's attractive set of Scottish dances, which are largely based on traditional tunes. Gordon Jacob's witty take-off of Rossini's best-known overture is the best-known piece here, but all the rest are very well worth getting to know. Richard Rodney Bennett's utterly charming *Little Suite* includes a waltz in best *Murder on the Orient Express* style, and the ebullient overture by David Lyon is a splendid representation of his work. You may never have thought of Sir Malcolm Sargent as a composer, but his contribution proves as rewarding as any, being a most attractive tone-poem with some appropriately breezy melodies. Then there is Clifton Parker's dainty overture to the musical play *The Glass Slipper*, plus three tone-poems by sometime BBC producers – Alan Langford contrasting the old world and the new, and Maurice Johnstone and James Langley elegantly depicting some of England's loveliest countryside. This really is a most enterprising and enjoyable collection, with stylish playing from the Royal Ballet Sinfonia.

Cello Concertos
Pablo Casals *vc*
London Symphony Orchestra / Sir Landon Ronald;
BBC Symphony Orchestra / Sir Adrian Boult.
Biddulph mono LAB144 (79 minutes: ADD). Recorded 1936-46. Ⓜ Ⓗ
Elgar Cello Concerto in E minor, Op. 85. **Boccherini** (arr. Grützmacher) Cello Concerto in
B flat major, G48. **Bruch** Kol Nidrei, Op. 47. **Haydn** (arr. Gevaërt) Cello Concerto No. 2 in
D major, HobVIIb/2 – Allegro moderato; Adagio.

The leonine growl that prefaces Elgar's most introspective orchestral masterpiece is played here with uncompromising defiance, whereas the weary solo ascent that follows can rarely – if ever – have conveyed a deeper sense of disorientation. Casals's handling of the solo line is wistful, sometimes wilful, profoundly personal and ideally accompanied by the ever-attentive Sir Adrian Boult. Just listen to the *Scherzo*'s cheeky banter (track 7, from 1'25"), to the pointing of wind phrases in particular – precise yet unforced and always musically responsive. The most affecting passage of all occurs at around 6'31" into the finale (track 9), at the moment where Elgar seems overwhelmed by feelings almost too painful to bear. No other performance is quite as successful in contrasting the 'brave front' of Elgar's bolder tuttis with the ineffable sadness of his solo writing. Occasional hiccups in the cello line (the odd spot of discoloration) go for nothing and Casals's distant groaning merely serves – like Glenn Gould's humming and Toscanini's singing – to compound an impression of total commitment.

Biddulph's annotation relates how a changing critical climate gradually became sympathetic to Casals's account of the Elgar Concerto (initial reactions were fairly hostile), and how Britain's handling of the Franco situation in Spain deeply offended Casals. Projected sessions never materialized and the Haydn Concerto recording that is here issued for the first time (it was set down the day after the Elgar) remained incomplete. What we do have, however, is very well recorded, typically eloquent and full of interpretative incident, with sundry expressive subtleties and an especially memorable account of the *Adagio*. Of course purists will baulk at Gevaërt's arrangement, just as they will lament Grützmacher's handiwork in a famous – and equally characterful – account of the Boccherini B flat Concerto. *Kol Nidrei*, on the other hand, is given one of the slowest, purest and most deeply felt readings imaginable, perfectly reflecting the pain, resolution and quiet victory that mark the three stages of repentance (Kol Nidrei is the pivotal evening prayer for the Jewish Day of Atonement). Transfers are, again, excellent (Ward Marston was at the control desk), and if you are in search of 'The Essential Casals' – no, 'The Quintessential Casals' – then you need look no further.

Classical Trumpet Concertos
John Wallace *tpt* John Anderson *ob d'amore* Peter Thomas *vn*
Philharmonia Orchestra / Christopher Warren-Green, Simon Wright.
Nimbus NI7016 (75 minutes: DDD). Recorded 1983-88. Ⓕ
Haydn Concerto in E flat major, HobVIIe/1. **Neruda** Concerto in E flat major. **Hummel** Concerto
in E flat major. **F. Weber** Variations in F major. **Fasch** Concerto for Trumpet, Oboe d'amore,
Violin and Strings in E major.

The famous Haydn Concerto sounds bright and forthright with trumpeter and orchestra freshly caught in the spacious Church of All Saints, Tooting. Wallace's technical strength and impish articulation are characterized by crisp tonguing and a strident (if at times fairly uncompromising) trumpet sound in the outer movements. Peace is restored in a beautifully judged slow movement in which Wallace floats rather than imposes. Less refined than some other recordings of this work (track 2 at 3'43" has an extraordinary blemish in the lower register of the strings), there is a natural freshness here which one rarely hears in this old war-horse. The Neruda Concerto, written originally for the corno da caccia, makes an attractive trumpet piece, flawed only by its unbalanced episodic structure. Hummel's Concerto is a persuasive work, by and large, and it is given a bold reading here by Wallace, full of incident, some examples of which trip out of the bell in a fairly conventional manner. Others are decidedly quirky, such as the mock antiquated tuning on the opening trill of the second movement. Rather more effective are the dazzling embellishments which look forward to the salon and the new virtuoso tradition of the nineteenth century which the trumpet inhabited once valves had been invented. Friedrich Dionysius Weber's Variations in F major are typical of this musically slight but entertaining world in which the cornet/trumpet was beginning to thrive. Wallace is utterly at home in this idiom, bringing to the music the swagger and facility upon which its characterization depends. Finally we step back to the Indian summer of the trumpet, the early classical years and the stratospherically high trumpet range demanded by Carl Friedrich Christian Fasch. His Concerto for trumpet, oboe d'amore and violin is an exciting work, brilliantly played.

Favourite Cello Concertos
Julian Lloyd Webber *vc* with various artists.
Philips 462 115-2PM2 (two discs: 155 minutes: DDD). Recorded 1984-98. Ⓜ
J. Lloyd Webber Jackie's Song (**BBC Concert Orchestra / Barry Wordsworth**).
Dvořák Cello Concerto in B minor, B191 (**Czech Philharmonic Orchestra / Václav Neumann**).
Elgar Cello Concerto in E minor, Op. 85 (**Royal Philharmonic Orchestra / Yehudi Menuhin**).
Romance, Op. 62 (**Academy of St Martin in the Fields / Sir Neville Marriner**). Une idylle in
G major, Op. 4 No. 1 (**John Birch** *org*). **Tchaikovsky** Variations on a Rococo Theme in A major,
Op. 33 (**London Symphony Orchestra / Maxim Shostakovich**). **Fauré** Elégie, Op. 24.
Saint-Saëns Cello Concerto No. 1 in A minor, Op. 33. Allegro appassionato in B minor, Op. 43
(**English Chamber Orchestra / Yan Pascal Tortelier**). **Albinoni** (arr. Palmer) Adagio in G minor.
Gounod Ave Maria. **Saint-Saëns** Le carnaval des animaux – Le cygne. **Schumann** (arr. Palmer)
Kinderszenen, Op. 15*d* – Träumerei, Op. 15 No. 7 (**English Chamber Orchestra / Nicholas
Cleobury**). **Bach** (arr. Palmer) Cantata No. 147 – Jesu, joy of man's desiring (**Royal Philharmonic
Orchestra / Nicholas Cleobury**).

A first-class package in every way. As we know from his live performances, Julian Lloyd Webber has
a firm, richly coloured and full-focused tone; moreover it records well. His lyrical warmth projects
tellingly over the entire range and his involvement in the music communicates consistently and
tellingly. He has chosen his accompanists well too. His account of the great Dvořák concerto is full
of passionate feeling, with a tender *Adagio*, and Neumann and the Czech Philharmonic give him
thoroughly persuasive backing, playing with plenty of bite in tuttis, the Slavonic exuberance always
to the fore. His performance of the Elgar concerto has the huge advantage of Lord Menuhin as his
partner, a true Elgarian if ever there was one. It is a performance of real understanding and rare
intensity, which never oversteps the work's emotional boundaries and is imbued with innate
nostalgia: the *Adagio* has a haunting Elysian stillness. The Saint-Saëns is played for the splendid
bravura war-horse that it is, and we are also given a rare chance to hear the original, uncut version
of Tchaikovsky's *Rococo* Variations. Lloyd Webber soon proves that it is superior to the truncated
version used in most other recordings; moreover his spontaneous warmth in Tchaikovsky's long-
drawn lyrical lines, which he makes sound very Russian in character, makes a perfect foil for the
sparkling virtuosity elsewhere. Among the encores the lovely *Träumerei* stands out for its freely
improvisational feeling and Lloyd Webber's own catchy, slight but romantic personal tribute to
Jacqueline du Pré is played as an ardent, tuneful and timely postscript.

Favourite Overtures, Volume 2.
London Philharmonic Orchestra, [a]Berlin Philharmonic Orchestra / Sir Thomas Beecham.
Dutton Laboratories mono CDLX7009 (75 minutes: ADD). Recorded 1933-40. Ⓜ Ⓗ
Mozart Le nozze di Figaro. Don Giovanni. Die Zauberflöte[a]. **Weber** Oberon. Der Freischütz.
Brahms Tragic Overture. **Wagner** A Faust Overture. **Berlioz** Le carnaval romain.
Rossini La scala di seta.

The *Zauberflöte* Overture is taken from Beecham's complete recording of the opera, and he shows a
measured, profound response to Mozart's inspiration. All his characteristic elegance is still there,
but the 43 players of the Berlin Philharmonic are made to play in a concentrated, highly
characterful fashion. He provides a strong, arrestingly dramatic account of the *Don Giovanni*
Overture, yet his *Nozze di Figaro* bubbles over with charm and wit. He finds plenty of drama in the
Wagner, and the Brahms has an appropriate and highly impressive strength and profundity of
feeling. A reading such as this effectively gives the lie to Beecham's reputation in some quarters as a
lightweight interpreter. Perhaps the best performance of all is the overture by his beloved Berlioz,
for energy and excitement are matched by playing of the most affecting delicacy and poetry in the
piece's more reflective passages. All the engineering is outstanding.

French Orchestral Works
[a]French Radio National Orchestra, [b]Royal Philharmonic Orchestra / Sir Thomas Beecham.
EMI Beecham Edition CDM7 63379-2 (68 minutes: ADD). Ⓜ Ⓗ
Bizet Carmen – Suite No. 1[a]. **Fauré** Pavane, Op. 50 [a]. Dolly Suite, Op. 56 (orch. Rabaud)[a].
Debussy Prélude à l'après-midi d'un faune[b]. **Saint-Saëns** Le rouet d'Omphale, Op. 31[b].
Delibes Le roi s'amuse – Ballet Music[b].

Even to those who never heard him in the flesh there is no mistaking Beecham's relish in, and flair
for, the French repertoire. His combination of mischievous high spirits, almost dandyish elegance,
cool outer classicism masking passionate emotion, swagger, refined nuance and delicate charm was
perhaps unique – not matched even by such committed Francophiles as Constant Lambert. *Elan* is
at once in evidence here in the *Carmen* prelude, and subtle dynamic gradations in the entr'actes to

Acts 2 and 4; there is lightness, vivacity and tenderness in Fauré's *Dolly Suite* and a true Gallic reserve in his *Pavane*; and he enters with prim finesse into Delibes's pastiche dances. Debussy's erotic study, on repeated hearings of this performance, becomes the more Grecian and effective for its conscious understatement; and only the Saint-Saëns symphonic poem, for all the RPO's delicacy, seems to hang fire. But four or five bull's-eyes out of six is a pretty good score, and at medium price not to be missed.

German Operetta Overtures
Academy of St Martin in the Fields / Sir Neville Marriner.
Philips 456 576-2PH (67 minutes: DDD). Recorded 1997. Ⓕ E
Heuberger Der Opernball – Overture. **Humperdinck** Hänsel und Gretel – Prelude.
Lortzing Zar und Zimmermann – Overture. **Marschner** Hans Heiling – Overture.
Nicolai Die lustigen Weiber von Windsor – Overture. **Rezniček** Donna Diana – Overture.
J. Strauss II Die Fledermaus – Overture. **Suppé** Dichter und Bauer – Overture.
Weber Euryanthe – Overture.

This collection should more aptly be named 'Opera and Operetta Overtures'. But there is no denying the warmth and colour of all these works, with Marriner and the Academy inspired to produce the most brilliant playing, flawless in ensemble, opulent in tone and ripely recorded. It is a joy to have such war-horses as Suppé's *Poet and Peasant* presented like this, and when Heuberger's operetta, *The Opera Ball*, has spawned such a favourite number as the song, 'Im chambre separée', it is good to find that hit-tune as a waltz in the middle of the Overture, leading on to a riotous final galop. Setting the pattern best of all is Rezniček's *Donna Diana* Overture, a piece guaranteed to raise one's spirits. It is also good to have such a rarity as Marschner's Overture to the high romantic drama, *Hans Heiling*, not so different in tone from the overtures to such comic operas as *Zar und Zimmermann*. In short, a delightful cocktail of a disc.

The Guitarist
John Williams *gtr*
orchestra / William Goodchild.
Sony Classical SK60586 (63 minutes: DDD). Recorded 1998. Ⓕ
Anonymous Lamento di Tristan. Ductia. Saltarello. **Satie** Gnossiennes Nos. 1 and 2.
Gymnopédie No. 3 (all arr. Williams). **Domeniconi** Koyunbaba. **Houghton** Stélé.
Theodorakis Three Epitafios. **J. Williams** Aeolian Suite.

The seemingly polarized but reconcilable elements of protest and a yearning for space and time for contemplation appear to be buried in Williams's psyche. Here they find full expression. Turkish, Greek and Greek-influenced music are the backbone of the programme: Domeniconi's programmatic *Koyunbaba* speaks for itself, as does the music of Theodorakis ('love, loneliness and freedom of expression'), and Satie's is seen as an 'early reaction against 19th-century Romanticism'; Houghton's *Stélé* and Williams's own skilfully wrought *Aeolian Suite*, too, have declared connections with Greek music. Total technical mastery is something that has never been lacking in Williams's performances (barring the occasional slips that all artists make in concert), and to it he here adds a modest but unfailingly tasteful ability as an arranger. *Koyunbaba* is a work that can seem interminable – and in many hands it *does*, but Williams's performance of it is heartfelt, not contrived, and Houghton's *Stélé* reveals the longings that can dwell in the souls of composers who began with jazz, rock and media music. If you have to live with only one recording by Williams it should be this one. It is perhaps the most personal musical statement he has yet made, and it is in every sense immaculately recorded.

Homage to Benny Goodman
Sabine Meyer, Wolfgang Meyer *cls*
Bamberg Symphony Orchestra, Bamberg Symphony Big Band / Ingo Metzmacher.
EMI CDC5 56652-2 (70 minutes: DDD). Recorded 1997. Ⓕ E
Paganini Caprice in A minor, Op. 24 No. 1. **Powell** Clarinade. **Prima** Sing, sing, sing.
B. Goodman Rachel's Dream. **Sauter** Clarinet à la King. **Traditional** Tiger Rag (all arr. Walden).
G. Jenkins Goodbye (arr. Luis). **Arnold** Clarinet Concerto, Op. 115. **Bernstein** Prelude, Fugue
and Riffs. **Copland** Clarinet Concerto. **Stravinsky** Ebony Concerto.

Starting with a dazzling account of Sir Malcolm Arnold's Second Concerto, the one written for Benny Goodman, this is not just a tribute to the great polymath among clarinettists but a most attractive collection of music that is middle-of-the-road in the best sense, echoing the achievement of Goodman himself in crossing barriers. Not everything was composed for him – the Stravinsky for example was written for Woody Herman – but this is music which suited his style, as it does that of Wolfgang Meyer, even more than that of his celebrated sister, Sabine. One notes that only one of the longer works, the *Ebony Concerto*, and one of the shorter ones, the Paganini *Caprice* in jazzed-up form, feature Sabine Meyer, though four of the big band arrangements feature them both in duet. It is not hard to deduce that the brother is the prime mover behind this whole programme, when in his flamboyant way he plays with an extra freedom and panache compared with his sister. Where he revels in the extrovert show of such a movement as the pre-Goodman Rag which closes the Arnold Concerto, Sabine Meyer is more reticent. She gives a slightly understated performance of the *Ebony Concerto*, characteristically subtle in phrasing and tonal shading but not quite sharp enough to bring out the full point of Stravinsky's angular cross-rhythms. It remains a fine performance, crisply accompanied by the Bamberg Symphony Big Band under Metzmacher. Even so, Wolfgang Meyer and the Bambergers play at higher voltage and with sharper attack whether in the Arnold, the Copland or the Bernstein. In the big band arrangements, duetting alongside her brother, Sabine then loses all inhibitions, equally bringing out the fun in these jazz arrangements. And what other orchestra is constituted formally in big band formation, as the Bambergers appear to be here, playing with flair? Though it is a pity that Bartók's *Contrasts* – written for Szigeti as well as Benny Goodman – is not also included, this makes an excellent, generous mixture, not only well played but well recorded too.

Hungarian Connections
[a]Laurence Kaptain *cimb*
Chicago Symphony Orchestra / Sir Georg Solti.
Decca 443 444-2DH (72 minutes: DDD). Recorded live in 1993.　　Ⓟ 🄴
Bartók Hungarian Sketches, Sz97. Romanian folkdances, Sz68. **Kodály** Háry János, Op. 15 – Suite[a]. **Liszt** Two Episodes from Lenau's Faust, S110 – Der Tanz in der Dorfschenke. Hungarian Rhapsody No. 2 in D minor (orch. Döppler). **L. Weiner** Csongor és Tünde, Op. 10*b* – Introduction; Scherzo.

This is a terrific programme. The sequence is imaginative, the material extremely attractive, and the standard of performance high. The *Mephisto Waltz* swirls in heady abandon, with strings as delicate as thistledown, and some snappy work from the Chicago brass. The once-ubiquitous Second *Hungarian Rhapsody* is wittily turned, although Döppler's sundry added counterpoint and rather tame orchestration tend to mute the rustic edge of Liszt's original. The performance, though, has plenty of life and the recording conjures up a realistic sense of aural perspective. Sir Georg's empathy for this idiom is everywhere in evidence, and never more so than in Bartók's *Romanian folkdances*, where lightness of touch and sensitive rubato re-create a crucial feeling of improvisation. The *Hungarian Sketches* are tellingly pointed, with fluid lines in 'Evening in the Village' and 'Melody', a hilarious *ff* trombone/tuba belch in 'A Little Tipsy' and cleanly differentiated percussion in the 'Bear Dance'. Solti's version is now perhaps the current front-runner, and makes for a most entertaining musical diversion. Nice, too, to hear music by the much underrated Leó Weiner, his *Csongor és Tünde* ballet with its subtle reminiscences of Nicolai's *Merry Wives of Windsor* Overture and Liszt's *Dante* Symphony. The busy *Scherzo* is the sort of thing Bartók might have composed had he not outgrown the worlds of Strauss and Dohnányi, while the Introduction is reminiscent of Kodály in pastoral vein. Kodály himself is represented by a genial, often brilliantly played account of the *Háry János* Suite, superbly recorded and with some distinctive solo work.

Les introuvables de Jacqueline Du Pré
Jacqueline du Pré *vc*
[a]Gerald Moore, [b]Ernest Lush, [c]Stephen Kovacevich *pfs*
[d]London Symphony Orchestra / Sir John Barbirolli;
[e]Royal Philharmonic Orchestra / Sir Malcolm Sargent;
[f]New Philharmonia Orchestra, [g]Chicago Symphony Orchestra,
[h]English Chamber Orchestra / Daniel Barenboim [i]*pf*
EMI CZS5 68132-2 (six discs: 857 minutes: ADD).　　Ⓑ
Elgar Cello Concerto in E minor, Op. 85[d]. **Delius** Cello Concerto[e]. **Saint-Saëns** Cello Concerto No. 1 in A minor, Op. 33[f]. **Schumann** Cello Concerto in A minor, Op. 129[f]. **Dvořák** Cello Concerto in B minor, B191[g]. Silent woods, B182[g]. **Haydn** Cello Concertos – No. 1 in C major[h]; No. 2 in D major[d]. **Monn** (arr. Schoenberg) Cello Concerto in G minor[d]. **Chopin** Cello Sonata, Op. 65[i]. **Franck** Violin Sonata in A major[i] (arr. *vc/pf*). **Fauré** Elégie, Op. 24[a]. **Bruch** Kol Nidrei, Op. 47[a]. **Bach** Cello Suites – No. 1 in G major, BWV1007; No. 2 in D minor, BWV1008 (rec. live 1962). **Handel** Oboe Concerto in G minor, HWV287[b] (arr. *vc/pf* Slatter. rec. live 1961). **Beethoven** 12 Variations on Handel's 'See the conqu'ring hero comes', Wo045[i]. Seven Variations in E flat major on Mozart's 'Bei Männern, welche Liebe fühlen', Wo046[i]. 12 Variations in F major on 'Ein Mädchen oder Weibchen', Op. 66[i] (recorded live in 1970). Cello Sonatas[c] – No. 3 in A major, Op. 69; No. 5 in D major, Op. 105 No. 2.

As the title suggests, this fine six-disc retrospective of Jacqueline du Pré's recording career – a mere ten years long – was masterminded by French EMI. Aptly the English commentary by Jeremy Siepmann quotes Sir John Barbirolli's memorable remark in Christopher Nupen's television film, *Jacqueline*: "If you have no excesses in the full bloom of youth, what will there be to pare away on the long road to maturity?" The wonder was that Jacqueline du Pré was mature in her artistry from the start, and it is good that from the period even before the first official EMI sessions the collection includes three BBC recordings: Bach's Cello Suites Nos. 1 and 2 and a Handel sonata arranged from the Oboe Concerto in G minor. Those early BBC recordings are inevitably flawed, but the sheer scale of the artistry is never for a moment in doubt. Of the handful of items recorded by EMI in July 1962 with Gerald Moore accompanying, only Bruch's *Kol Nidrei* is included.

The Delius was du Pré's first concerto recording, and she was not nearly as much at ease as she came to be later. The CD transfers do not minimize any of the flaws in the original recordings, notably the disappointing sound given to her Chicago recording of the Dvořák Concerto. Not only is the orchestral sound both coarse and thin with a high degree of background hiss, the cello is balanced far too close. Even with that balance one registers clearly the wide dynamic range of du Pré's playing, down to a whispered *pianissimo*. It was right to include it and also the cello sonata recordings of Chopin and Franck, the last recordings ever made by du Pré in December 1971. The tone may not have been quite so even as earlier, but the fire and warmth are undiminished. All the concerto recordings are welcome with the tear-laden quality in the slow movement of the Schumann matching that in the Elgar. It is good that the supreme Beethoven sonata recordings she made with Stephen Bishop (later Kovacevich) are included here, both sparkling and darkly intense. From the Beethoven series recorded at the 1970 Edinburgh Festival by the BBC only the three sets of variations are included, artistically fascinating but with sound curiously distanced and uninvolving. A must for anyone who was ever magnetized by du Pré's playing.

Les introuvables de János Starker
János Starker *vc* [a]Gerald Moore *pf*
Philharmonia Orchestra / [b]Carlo Maria Giulini, [c]Walter Susskind.
EMI mono/stereo CZS5 68485-2 (six discs: 398 minutes: ADD). Recorded 1956-59.　Ⓜ Ⓗ
Bach Solo Cello Suites, BWV1007-12. **Kodály** Solo Cello Sonata, Op. 8. **Dohnányi** Konzertstück in D major, Op. 12[c]. **Boccherini** Cello Concerto in B flat major, G482[b]. **Haydn** Cello Concerto No. 2 in D major, HobVIIb/2[b]. **Schumann** Cello Concerto in A minor, Op. 129[b]. **Saint-Saëns** Cello Concerto No. 1 in A minor, Op. 33[b]. **Dvořák** Cello Concerto in B minor, B191[c]. **Fauré** Elégie, Op. 24[c]. **Milhaud** Cello Concerto No. 1, Op. 136[c]. **Prokofiev** Cello Concerto in E minor, Op. 58[c]. Also contains short items [a] by Bach, Chopin, Debussy, Kreisler, Mussorgsky, Paganini, Popper, Saint-Saëns, Schubert, Schumann and Tcherepnin.

János Starker is a supremely accomplished player whose tough, dry, vibrant sound was fuller in youth than in older age but whose every stroke of the bow suggests profound musicality, at once forthright and ardently expressive. In the Bach Cello Suites the approach is 'classical-romantic' rather than 'authentic baroque', with propulsive Preludes, buoyant Bourrées, Gavottes and Gigues, and deeply introspective accounts of the slower movements. He has recorded the Kodály Sonata on other occasions, but it would be difficult to upstage the well-employed virtuosity of this 1957 performance, especially in the raging final *Allegro molto vivace*, a dazzling dance sequence and the nearest Kodály ever came to sounding like Bartók. Of the concerto's, the Dvořák, in particular, features a most touching account of the slow movement, but EMI slip up in its tracking of the individual movements of the Saint-Saëns Concerto (the *Allegretto con moto* actually starts during track 7, and not at the beginning of track 8). The Schumann Concerto is very full-bodied but not especially subtle; Dohnányi's delightful *Konzertstück* receives smiling advocacy, Fauré's *Elégie* weeps inwardly, while both the Milhaud and Prokofiev concertos – the former with its Mahlerian resonances (try the *Grave* second movement for side-glances towards *Das Lied*), the latter, a restless precursor of a musically superior *Symphony-Concerto* – are treated to typically lithe, finely honed playing. Boccherini (with cadenzas by Hutter) and Haydn (where the cellist provides his own cadenzas) both respond to Starkerian tonal tapering, and then there are the encores – wistful, lean and tastefully turned. The transfers are mostly excellent.

Let the Trumpet Sound
Crispian Steele-Perkins *tpt*
Bournemouth Sinfonietta / Richard Studt *vn*
Carlton Classics 30366 0038-2 (76 minutes: DDD). Recorded 1996.　Ⓜ
J. James Trumpet Concerto in D major, 'The Four Seasons'. **Vivaldi** Concerto for Two Trumpets and Strings in C major, RV537. **Stanley** Trumpet Concerto in D major. **J. Clarke** Three Trumpet Ayres. **Handel** Airs from Vauxhall Gardens. **Purcell** Ayres for the Theatre (both arr. Steele-Perkins).

Anyone who has seen Crispian Steele-Perkins in recital will know how persuasively he communicates his art, often fortified by instructive and entertaining verbal interludes. The somewhat clichéd title of this disc belies an unusually satisfying blend of recognizable trumpet music and imaginative arrangements, all made by the soloist. From a technical point of view, there is a degree of hidden virtuosity in that the natural trumpet Steele-Perkins plays is keyed at a higher than normal pitch to accommodate the modern instruments of the Bournemouth Sinfonietta. This hybrid of old and new is, if not unique, certainly rare; the juxtaposition is particularly successful here because the strings are sympathetic (if not always quite as stylish as a period band) to the special tonal nuances of the natural trumpet. Moreover, Steele-Perkins makes the most of the brighter but no less full sound of his 'old' instrument: he wafts with a languid, vocalized elegance in the impressive Concerto by John James and demonstrates the expressive power of articulation and embellishment on such an instrument, especially in his suite of great Handel tunes and the resourceful *Ayres for the Theatre* by Purcell. Recorded in a resonant acoustic, this is a thoroughly entertaining, fresh and invigorating programme. If a touch unrefined in the strings, the eager-sounding ensemble more than makes up for it.

Moura Lympany in recital
Dame Moura Lympany *pf*
[ae]Philharmonia Orchestra / [a]Herbert Menges, [e]Walter Susskind.
Dutton Laboratories mono CDCLP4000 (77 minutes: ADD). Ⓕ Ⓗ
Mozart Piano Concertos[a] – No 12 in A major, K414/K385*p*; No. 21 in C major, K467.
Albéniz (arr. Godowsky) Tango, Op. 165 No. 2[b]. **Chopin** Fantaisie-impromptu in C sharp minor, Op. 66[c]. **Granados** Goyescas – No. 4, Quejas o la maja y el ruiseñor[d]. **Turina** Rapsodia sinfónica, Op. 66[e].

Now that Dame Moura Lympany has ended her performing career, this recorded tribute comes as a special blessing. For long associated with the romantic virtuoso repertoire which she played with an unalloyed polish and graciousness, Dame Moura possessed the most catholic of tastes and her 1955 disc of Mozart's Concertos, K414 and K467, is surely among her finest offerings. Every change of mood, every subtlety of modulation is registered without fuss, narcissism or the sort of self-consciousness so often taken for an authentic style; her performances are of superfine quality and in impeccable taste. There are distinguished contributions from individual members of the Philharmonia and although the orchestra under Herbert Menges occasionally moves with a heavier tread than their soloist, they are none the less satisfyingly robust with no scaling down of drama or gesture. In Turina's picture-postcard charmer there is less heat and dazzle than in some other readings, yet you could say that both here and in Granados's 'Maiden and the Nightingale' there is delicate rather than lurid colouring. The recordings are adequate.

Marches and Overtures à la Française
Detroit Symphony Orchestra / Paul Paray.
Mercury Living Presence 434 332-2MM (66 minutes: ADD). Recorded 1959-60. Ⓜ
Meyerbeer Coronation March[a]. **Gounod** Marche funèbre d'une marionnette[a]. **Saint-Saëns** Suite algérienne in C major, Op. 60 – March militaire française[a]. Marche héroïque in E flat major, Op. 34[a]. **Rouget de Lisle** La marseillaise[a]. **Adam** Si j'étais roi – Overture[b]. **Boieldieu** La dame blanche – Overture[b]. **Offenbach** La belle Hélène – Overture[c]. Orphée aux enfers – Overture[c]. Les contes d'Hoffmann – Prelude[c]. **Rossini** Guillaume Tell – Overture[d].

They don't make collections like this any more! Or so it seems. Yet can musical tastes really have changed so radically from the days when people would patiently turn over a 78rpm record for the second half of Boieldieu's *La dame blanche* Overture? Unlikely, and there must surely be a welcome for such a collection of charmingly melodious, unpretentious and yet well-crafted pieces as on this CD. Paul Paray (1886–1979) was a genuine son of Normandy who in his seventies could still bring out the Gallic warmth, excitement and sparkle of these pieces. The recording sounds just a shade raw with the violins at the top of their range, but generally the warmth and richness of sound make it quite unbelievable that these recordings are now 38-odd years old.

Pierre Monteux Edition
[a]San Francisco Symphony Orchestra; [b]Chicago Symphony Orchestra;
[c]Boston Symphony Orchestra; [d]RCA Victor Symphony Orchestra / Pierre Monteux.
RCA Pierre Monteux Edition mono/stereo 09026 61893-2 (15 discs: 16 hours 55 minutes: ADD). Ⓜ Ⓗ

Beethoven Die Ruinen von Athen – Overture[a] (recorded 1949). Symphonies[a] – No. 4 in B flat major, Op. 60; No. 8 in F major, Op. 93. **Bach** (orch. Respighi) Passacaglia and Fugue in C minor, BWV582[a]. **Berlioz** Symphonie fantastique, Op. 14[a]. Benvenuto Cellini – Overture[a] (rec. 1952).

Les troyens – Prélude, Act 3[a] (rec. 1945). La damnation de Faust, Op. 24 – Hungarian March[a] (rec. 1951). **Brahms** Symphony No. 2 in D major, Op. 73[a] (rec. 1945). Schicksalslied, Op. 54[a] (with **Stanford University Chorus**, rec. 1949). **Mahler** Kindertotenlieder[a] (**Marian Anderson** *contr*). **Chausson** Symphony in B flat major, Op. 20 (rec. 1950). Poème de l'amour et de la mer, Op. 19[d] (**Gladys Swarthout** *mez* rec. 1947). **Chabrier** Le roi malgré lui – Fête polonaise[a] (rec. 1947). **Debussy** Images[a] (rec. 1951). Images oubliées – Sarabande[a] (orch. Ravel, rec. 1946). Nocturnes[c] (**Berkshire Festival Chorus**, rec. 1955). La mer[c] (rec. 1954). **Liszt** Les Préludes, S97[c]. **Scriabin** Le poème de l'extase, Op. 54[c] (rec. 1952). **Saint-Saëns** Havanaise in E major, Op. 83[c] (Leonid Kogan *vn*). **Delibes** Coppélia – Suite[c]. Sylvia – Suite[c] (rec. 1953). **Gounod** Faust – Ballet Music[a] (1947). **Franck** Symphony in D minor[b] (rec. 1961). Pièce héroïque in B minor[a] (orch. O'Connell). **d'Indy** Istar, Op. 42[a] (rec. 1945). Symphonie sur un chant montagnard français in G major, Op. 25a (**Maxim Shapiro** *pf* rec. 1941). Fervaal, Op. 40 – Prélude[a] (rec. 1945). Symphony No. 2 in B flat major, Op. 57[a] (rec. 1942). **Ravel** Daphnis et Chloé – Suite No. I[a] (rec. 1946). Valses nobles et sentimentales[a] (rec. 1946). Alborada del gracioso[a] (rec. 1947). La valse[a]. **Lalo** Le roi d'Ys – Overture[a] (rec. 1942). **Ibert** Escales[a] (rec. 1946). **Rimsky-Korsakov** Scheherazade, Op. 35[a] (rec. 1942). Sadko, Op. 5[a] (rec. 1945). Symphony No. 2, Op. 9, 'Antar'[a] (rec. 1946). **R. Strauss** Ein Heldenleben, Op. 40[a] (rec. 1947). Tod und Verklärung, Op. 24[a] (rec. 1960). **Stravinsky** Petrushka[a] (rec. 1959). The Rite of Spring[a] (rec. 1951). **Tchaikovsky** Symphonies[c] – No. 4 in F minor, Op. 36; No. 5 in E minor, Op. 64; No. 6 in B minor, Op. 74, 'Pathétique'.

'Under-heralded, under-sung, under-appreciated except by those who knew' runs Leon Fleischer's tribute, one of many, in the booklet of this important box-set. Inevitably, as the majority of these RCA recordings were made during Monteux's 17-year tenure in San Francisco, you may wonder how to interpret the claims of colleagues at the time that Monteux had achieved marvels there. Be not anxious: the only San Francisco recording here that reveals the orchestra as seriously less than world-class is the *Tod und Verklärung* which Monteux recorded in 1960 as a guest, eight years after his directorship there had ceased. For the rest, what this playing lacks in ultimate refinement of tone, it more than makes up for with unfailing responsiveness to its conductor's priorities; and as the conductor is Monteux, that means a lot. There is not one single routinely played or badly balanced bar of music, though tolerance may be needed for unexpected gremlins in the machinery (moments of distortion and congestion) in the pre-tape San Francisco recordings (i.e. about a third of the set).

As Monteux was the conductor of the most (in)famous première this century, Stravinsky's *Rite*, and its subsequent champion, you might expect these two restored recordings of the work (he recorded it four times) to shine more brightly than they do. Ensemble is generally tighter in Boston but there are moments of untypical laxity and coarseness. The less heavyweight Paris Conservatoire reading (in stereo) shares much with the 1960 Stravinsky: not as incisive but quite as revealing of the score's no less revolutionary intimate secrets, in other words, for the connoisseur, more rewarding than the endless list of modern recordings that turn the work into a percussion concerto. Throughout the stereo account of *Petrushka*'s Fair scenes, the characterization is earthy without ever being clumsy, and Petrushka himself is pathos in person. Again, if you are looking for the general whipcrack impact of many a modern version, you will be disappointed, though there are numerous instances where Monteux knows and shows how to articulate a difficult figure or a whole passage (for example, the final chase and death of Petrushka) with greater precision than in the average showpiece account. Stravinsky also praised Monteux's 1950 San Francisco Beethoven Eighth. No wonder. Here is the jester in the Age of Elegance; and Monteux has the measure of both.

His airborne 1952 Beethoven Fourth is strong without heaviness or overemphasis; and that, to oversimplify, is the secret of Monteux's success in the Austro-German repertoire; the repertoire he loved more than any other, but which the public, or to be more precise, those that chose what the public should receive, decided was not his forte. All credit to RCA for the courage to release this previously unissued 1947 San Francisco *Heldenleben*; as well as the wisdom to record it in the first place. Monteux recorded Brahms's Second Symphony four times, and the first two were made in San Francisco. The box includes his first (1945) recording and it has all the *joie de vivre* and superb string detailing that you would expect from a Monteux performance, but the extent of which always takes you by surprise. Another surprise is the tensely blazing first movement development. Don't be put off by the constricted sound, or the lack of a proper *sotto voce* at the start of the finale; most Brahms Seconds sound hopelessly retentive after this. His 1945 Berlioz *Symphonie fantastique* is a properly volatile reading: one that lives close to the edge.

The playing in an excitable and sharp-featured Waltz (with superbly managed *rits.*) may perhaps strike you as often too loud, but Monteux will then suddenly surprise you with a brilliantly placed hush. This was a real Monteux speciality – establishing a mean of quiet that was practical for projecting clarity (especially for gramophone listeners) and to allow players to phrase properly, and then to select the right moment to drop from it. Was there ever a more accomplished architect of the climactic paragraph? The accomplishment is that you are rarely aware of the mechanics of the operation. To analyse how he does it would probably take a week-long conductors' symposium, so let us settle for shorthand and call it an inspired mix of planning and spontaneity.

The set contains all Monteux's d'Indy recordings. A good decision; d'Indy needs his champion's recordings returned to circulation as a new generation of French conductors take up the cause. If the record moguls and opera impresarios of the time were unwilling to allow Monteux to indulge his passion for Wagner, he undoubtedly found a ready outlet in d'Indy, Franck and Chausson (and Lalo's *Le roi d'Ys* Overture). His celebrated 1961 Chicago Franck Symphony must be in the collection of anyone who loves the work. Monteux's Delibes and Gounod ballet suites are stylish, but also vital and strong. Typically, tempos here and in his Rimsky-Korsakov, are swift but fluid. There are references in the accompanying booklets to his knack of finding *Le tempo juste*, and time and again a phrase of Christoph von Dohnányi's came to mind: 'when the music is on its feet, it does the right thing'. Music on its feet was, of course, the making of Monteux, but well before the Diaghilev connection, the teenage Monteux had played second violin in the Folies Bergères. Years later Gershwin complimented him on his marvellous rhythmic sense, and Monteux cited his Folies experience as the training for it. This rhythmic sense … the spirit of the dance (call it what you will) permeated everything Monteux conducted, especially his Ravel. The Boston Debussy *La mer* and *Nocturnes* – 1954 and 1955 respectively, the latter in stereo – are among the finest on disc. Suffice it to say that Monteux understood that Debussy knew exactly what he wanted. This *La mer* is an all too rare case of the conductor working *with* the composer, not imagining he knows better. The discs are also available separately.

Pierre Monteux
The Early Years.
[a]Concertgebouw Orchestra; [b]London Symphony Orchestra / Pierre Monteux.
Philips The Early Years 442 544-2PM5 (five discs: 311 minutes: ADD). Recorded 1961-64. Ⓜ
Beethoven Symphony No. 3 in E flat major, Op. 55, 'Eroica'[a]. **Schubert** Symphony No. 8 in B minor, D759, 'Unfinished'[a]. **Tchaikovsky** Swan Lake – excerpts[b]. **Brahms** Symphony No. 2 in D major, Op. 73[b]. Academic Festival Overture, Op. 80[b]. Tragic Overture, Op. 81[b] (recorded 1962). **Ravel** Boléro[b]. La valse[b]. Ma mère l'oye[b]. **Debussy** Images[b]. Le martyre de St Sébastien – symphonic fragments[b].

'The Early Years – Pierre Monteux' it says on the box. The early years are, of course, those of Philips, not Monteux. This mid-price set offers his very last stereo recordings, made between 1962 and 1964, when Monteux was in his late eighties – vintage years to be sure, for the conductor, the LSO and Philips engineering – on five discs for the price of four. The new CDs have been 'digitalized by Bitstream', a process which has fractionally opened out and brightened up the treble. Compared with today's average offerings from London or Amsterdam, hall ambience is minimal (especially in the Brahms symphony), but the balances are flawless, and the benefits of Monteux's separated first and second violin sections are everywhere to be heard. Of Monteux's two *Eroica* recordings, this 1962 Amsterdam account is the one to have: 'textures have a Stravinskyan bite and clarity … the Concertgebouw are producing that fierce, bright, glistening tone which has always been a sure sign that their collective psyche is aflame', wrote *Gramophone*'s Richard Osborne in 1988. The first movement of Monteux's Amsterdam *Unfinished* (with repeat) is unusually fast, relaxing beautifully for the second subject (good, focused tone and phrasing here, not the common *pianissimo* thread). The LSO *Swan Lake* selection (with some numbers pruned, and a couple of concert endings) is well chosen for contrast, and the opening number sets the scene with some rapid string playing of effortless precision and point. Rarely, if ever, do you hear the swan theme (solo oboe) sung with such dignity and melancholy, the syncopations in the Act 1 *Pas de Deux* Waltz handled with such elegance, or the ballet's closing minutes played with such tragic grandeur. On occasions Tchaikovsky sounds like Delibes, but Tchaikovsky would undoubtedly have approved of that. In the last of Monteux's four recordings of the Brahms Second Symphony, subtleties of nuance and timing, and modifications of pacing, reflect a lifetime's love and experience of the work. Typically, it is light-toned and gentle in cast, almost symphonic chamber music.

You would expect a Monteux *Academic Festival Overture* to raise the spirits, and you won't be disappointed. The *Tragic Overture* is articulated more powerfully than the symphony, always on its feet, and with heaven-sent, *pianissimo* muted violins preparing the way for the noble brass transformation of the opening theme. Monteux's LSO strings come into their own for the Debussy and Ravel items. There is a very good case for suggesting that, in the range of expression he was capable of encouraging from his string desks, Monteux (himself originally an orchestral violinist, and then a violist in a string quartet) had no peers. You will hear a great range of vibrato, very prominent, for example, in the gorgeous husky tone for the viola and violin gipsy song solos in the first two movements of 'Ibéria' (it is worth mentioning that Monteux's ancestors were Spanish), or the more exalted moments from *Le martyre*. And if you are unable to succumb totally to the maximum vibrato and extraordinary textures as Monteux leads us through the 'Fairy Garden' at the end of *Ma mère l'oye*, then you are a lost cause.

New World Jazz
Tad Calcara, Jerome Simas *cls*
New World Symphony / Michael Tilson Thomas *pf*
RCA Red Seal 09026 68798-2 (68 minutes: DDD). Recorded 1997.   Ⓕ **Ⓔ**
J. Adams Lollapalooza. **Antheil** A Jazz Symphony. **Bernstein** Prelude, Fugue and Riffs.
Gershwin Rhapsody in Blue. **Hindemith** Ragtime. **Milhaud** La création du monde.
Raksin The Bad and the Beautiful – main theme. **Stravinsky** Ebony Concerto.

The Ultimate Jazz Album, this, imaginatively programmed and impeccably realized by all involved. We kick off with the dazzling world première recording of John Adams's six-and-a-half-minute *Lollapalooza* (1995), whose infectiously rhythmic, post-modern cavortings are relished to the full by Tilson Thomas and his superb young band. This *Rhapsody in Blue* evinces an improvisatory fantasy and edge-of-seat, theatrical fervour to make one appreciate anew the extraordinary boldness, reckless danger even, of Gershwin's ground-breaking inspiration. Bernstein's exhilarating *Prelude, Fugue and Riffs* receives the outing of a lifetime, a gloriously idiomatic, stunningly assured display which, like the wonderfully poised reading of Stravinsky's *Ebony Concerto*, invites and fully withstands comparison with the best rivals. We also get a singularly deft and atmospheric performance of Milhaud's 1923 ballet masterpiece, *La création du monde*, whose striking pre-echoes of Gershwin have never seemed more potent than here. All of which just leaves Hindemith's 'well-tempered' *Ragtime*, a mischievous reworking from 1921 of the C minor Fugue from Book 1 of the *48* (and dispatched on this occasion with a gleeful exuberance), George Antheil's endearingly outrageous *A Jazz Symphony* and David Raksin's gorgeous main title for Vincente Minnelli's *The Bad and the Beautiful* (1952). Thrillingly realistic sound throughout. Not to be missed!

Orchestral works
Cristina Ortiz *pf*
Royal Philharmonic Orchestra / Moshe Atzmon.
Decca 414 348-2DH (58 minutes: DDD). Recorded 1984.   Ⓕ
Rachmaninov Piano Concerto No. 2 in C minor, Op. 18. **Addinsell** Warsaw Concerto.
Litolff Concerto Symphonique No. 4 in D minor, Op. 102 – Scherzo. **Gottschalk** (orch. Hazell)
Grande fantaisie triomphale sur l'hymne national brésilien, RO108.

The C minor Concerto of Rachmaninov symbolizes romanticism at its ripest. Its combination of poetry and sensuous warmth with languorously memorable melodic lines balanced by exhilarating pianistic brilliance happily avoids any suggestion of sentimentality. The simple chordal introduction from the soloist ushers in one of the composer's most luscious tunes, yet the slow movement develops even greater ardour in its melodic contour, and the composer holds back a further haunting expressive idea to bring lyrical contrast to the scintillating finale. The couplings here are most apt. The genuinely inspired pastiche *Warsaw Concerto* by Richard Addinsell has a principal theme worthy to stand alongside those of Rachmaninov and its layout shows satisfying craftsmanship. Ortiz plays this main theme with great affection and she is equally beguiling in the delicious Litolff *Scherzo*. The effect here is of elegance rather than extrovert brilliance: this is reserved for the Gottschalk *Grande fantaisie triomphale*, which is played with a splendid panache that almost covers its inherent vulgarity and certainly emphasizes its ingenuous charm. Throughout the recording balance is realistic and the reverberation adds the most attractive bloom.

Russian Showpieces
Chicago Symphony Orchestra / Fritz Reiner.
RCA Living Stereo 09026 61958-2 (71 minutes: ADD). Recorded 1957-59.   Ⓜ **Ⓗ**
Mussorgsky (orch. Ravel) Pictures at an Exhibition[a]. A Night on the Bare Mountain[a].
Tchaikovsky Suite No. 1, Op. 43 – Marche miniature[b]. Marche slave, Op. 31[b]. **Borodin**
Prince Igor – Polovtsian March[b]. **Kabalevsky** Colas Breugnon – Overture[b]. **Glinka** Ruslan
and Lyudmila – Overture[b].

Reiner's *Pictures at an Exhibition* was one of the glories of the early stereo LP catalogue offering orchestral playing of the highest calibre. The richness of the brass sounds is apparent in the very opening 'Promenade' and 'Bydlo' really does sound like a heavy ox wagon. Reiner pictures the 'Tuileries' lightly but nostalgically and the 'Unhatched chicks' daintily, while the image of 'Samuel Goldenburg' is unctiously conveyed by the full-bodied lower strings, which makes Schmuyle's bleating the more telling in consequence, 'Market Place at Limoges' becomes a lightly articulated orchestral *Scherzo*. The finale is predictably and grandly spacious. After Mussorgsky's sonorous climax dies away, Tchaikovsky's piquant little march sounds like a gnat after an elephant, and makes a charming diversion before the menacing brass growls of *Night on the Bare Mountain* (in Rimsky's version) and the robustly accented Borodin 'Polovtsian March', which takes us back to the world of Slavonic orchestral spectacle. *Marche slave* is slow and sombre, but certainly makes a powerful climax. Then the mood lightens again for the last two items, the *Colas Breugnon*, with its exuberant cross sycopations, matched by the racy *Ruslan and Lyudmila* Overture. One can only marvel at the consistency of the recording, so resplendent in its opulent concert hall ambience.

Sir Georg Solti – A Celebration
Angela Gheorghiu *sop* Anne Sofie von Otter *mez* Maxim Vengerov *vn*
London Philharmonic Orchestra / Zubin Mehta, [a]Mstislav Rostropovich.
Decca 466 000-2DH (77 minutes: DDD). Texts and translations included. Recorded live in 1998. Ⓕ
Beethoven Egmont, Op. 84 – Overture. **Mozart** Mass in C minor, K427/K417a – Laudamus te.
Le nozze di Figaro – Voi che sapete. **Puccini** Gianni Schicchi – O mio babbino caro.
Tchaikovsky Violin Concerto in D major, Op. 35ª. **Verdi** La forza del destino – Pace, pace, mio Dio. **Wagner** Götterdämmerung – Dawn; Siegfried's Rhine Journey; Zurück vom Ring (orchestral finale).

This is a recording of a concert given in October 1998 at the Royal Albert Hall in London, celebrating the life and music of Sir Georg Solti. Seen on television a week afterwards, it was a great occasion, but one which inevitably had a hole in the middle in the absence of the great man himself. That, too, is felt on the disc in the two items without soloists, Beethoven's *Egmont* Overture at the beginning and the *Götterdämmerung* excerpts at the end. It would have been too much to expect Zubin Mehta, for all his fine qualities, to match the high voltage of a Solti performance. Enough to say that after a slightly tepid start the LPO plays beautifully, though again inevitably, a live recording in the Albert Hall cannot live up to the usual Decca brilliance or clarity. What above all makes this a very desirable disc are the contributions of the three soloists. Anne Sofie von Otter's florid singing of 'Laudamus te' is immaculate, with trills and divisions of diamond precision, and with dynamic shading finely controlled. In Cherubino's 'Voi che sapete' she is then as strong and positive as on stage. Angela Gheorghiu is caught splendidly in a thrilling account of Leonora's 'Pace, pace, mio Dio' from Verdi's *Forza*, not just powerful but poignant too, ending with a hair-raising top B flat, which brings the house down. 'O mio babbino caro', on the slow side, is glowingly full-toned. But best of all is the Tchaikovsky Violin Concerto with the two Russians in partnership, Vengerov leading Rostropovich something of a dance on the podium, just as the great cellist has himself done to many an unwary conductor. The virtuosity is spectacular in its dazzling clarity, and the heart's-easing beauty of the central *Canzonetta* is breathtakingly intense: a great performance.

Stokowski Transcriptions
Philadelphia Orchestra / Wolfgang Sawallisch.
EMI CDC5 55592-2 (66 minutes: DDD). Recorded 1995. Ⓕ
Bach Cantatas: No. 208 – Schafe können sicher weiden; No. 140 – Wachet auf!; No. 80 – Ein' feste Burg. Toccata and Fugue in D minor, BWV565. **Boccherini** String Quintet in E major, G275 – Minuet. **Beethoven** Piano Sonata No. 14 in C sharp minor, Op. 27 No. 2, 'Moonlight' – Adagio sostenuto. **Chopin** Prelude in E minor, Op. 28 No. 4. **Franck** Panis angelicus. **Tchaikovsky** String Quartet No. 1 in D major, Op. 11 – Andante cantabile. At the ball, Op. 38 No. 3 (with Marjana Lipovšek *mez*). **Debussy** Suite bergamasque – Clair de lune. Préludes, Book 1 – No. 10, La cathédrale engloutie. **Rachmaninov** Prelude in C sharp minor, Op. 3 No. 2.

Quite apart from reissues of the Stokowski's own recordings, there are several other discs of these highly coloured arrangements. Though Stokowski's own recordings, even those he made in extreme old age, generally have a degree more flair and dramatic bite than any others, the contrasts are not always what you would expect. So it is surprising to find that the BBC Philharmonic strings are more ripely resonant than those of the Philadelphia Orchestra in Franck's *Panis angelicus*, though that is an exception, and possibly Sawallisch simply wanted to minimize the piece's bold vulgarity. One of the items common to these discs is the *Adagio* from Beethoven's *Moonlight* Sonata, and there Sawallisch brings out far more of the mystery of what becomes an evocative, atmospheric piece, making the Bamert disc seem clinical. This collection also gains in glamour from having Marjana Lipovšek as an appropriately Slavonic-sounding soloist in the orchestration of the Tchaikovsky song, *At the ball*. This EMI disc provides a generous programme together with richly rounded recording, well defined in the bass. Yet Bamert's even more generous selection of 15 encore pieces overlaps on only three items, and includes more in which Stokowski has the greatest fun tweaking the ear provocatively, such as Mozart's *Turkish Rondo*: the advice to anyone with a sweet tooth is to get both discs for maximum indulgence.

Arturo Toscanini
Philharmonic Symphony Orchestra of New York / Arturo Toscanini.
Pearl mono GEMMCDS9373 (three discs: 230 minutes: ADD). Ⓕ Ⓗ
Beethoven Symphonies – No. 5 in C minor, Op. 67 (recorded live in 1933); No. 7 in A major,
Op. 92 (rec. 1936). **Brahms** Variations on a Theme by Haydn, Op. 56a, 'St Antoni Chorale'.
Dukas L'apprenti sorcier. **Gluck** Orfeo ed Euridice – Dance of the Blessed Spirits. **Haydn**
Symphony No. 101 in D major, 'Clock'. **Mendelssohn** A Midsummer Night's Dream, Op. 61 –
Scherzo (two versions); Nocturne. **Mozart** Symphony No. 35 in D major, K385, 'Haffner'.
Rossini Semiramide – Overture. L'Italiana in Algeri – Overture. Il barbiere di Siviglia – Overture.
Verdi La traviata – Preludes, Acts 1 and 3. **Wagner** Götterdämmerung – Dawn; Siegfried's Rhine
Journey. Lohengrin – Preludes, Acts 1 and 3. Siegfried Idyll.

Almost every non-vocal classical record collection in the 1930s included some of Toscanini's
recordings with the Philharmonic Symphony Orchestra of New York. They were the classical
orchestral records of their day, and were universally admired. Nearly 60 years on they still make an
enormous impact. In general they have more freedom of spirit than his later recordings with the
NBC SO. All the terrific tension and drive of a Toscanini performance is there, but tempered at this
stage with a rare lyricism and beauty of phrase. Play the *Traviata* Preludes and hear how the New
York strings speak with an extraordinary depth of feeling and richness of tone; Dukas's *Scherzo* is
taken at breakneck speed, but there is still room for the most finely sculpted turns of phrase and
telling changes of pulse – even now, when superlative orchestral playing is commonplace, this
performance seems a miracle of refined, flexible virtuosity, and how extraordinary it must have
seemed 60 years ago. These recordings are part of the conductor's 1929 series for Victor. Three
years earlier he had had a brief flirtation with the Brunswick company, making just the two
Mendelssohn sides.

These comparatively cautious performances do not really add to our knowledge of Toscanini and
they are difficult to find in their original 78rpm form, but Pearl were right to include them as part
of a complete survey of his New York recordings. The 1929 series did nothing to change the great
conductor's aversion to making records, and it was not until 1936 that Victor persuaded him to
record again. In the meantime efforts had been made to record him in live performance, and these
he always rejected. But somehow test pressings of a Beethoven Fifth Symphony from 1933 have
survived and are included here. It is an enormously powerful, direct performance, full of fire and
passion. The plum of the 1936 Victor sessions is surely Beethoven's Seventh Symphony, a
performance of miraculous clarity, expressive force and explosive, titanic rhythm. Many judges feel
that this is the greatest ever recording of the symphony, and once heard it stays in the mind
permanently as the yardstick for other and lesser interpretations. Pearl's transfer engineering isn't
up to its usual high standard. At its best the sound is tonally very good and full-bodied, but there is
evidence of computerized filtering throughout the set in a general coarseness and unevenness of the
sound image, where continual sampling results in rapid changes in the nature of the signal.
However, despite reservations about the sound, here is a treasure trove indeed.

Trumpet Concertos
Håkan Hardenberger *tpt*
Academy of St Martin in the Fields / Sir Neville Marriner.
Philips 420 203-2PH (59 minutes: DDD). Recorded 1986. Ⓕ Ⓡ Ⓡ
Hummel Trumpet Concerto in E flat major. **Hertel** Trumpet Concerto in D major.
J. Stamitz (realized Boustead) Trumpet Concerto in D major. **Haydn** Trumpet Concerto
in E flat major, HobVIIe/1.

This recording made such a remarkable impression when it first appeared in 1987 that it created
overnight a new star in the firmament of trumpeters. The two finest concertos for the trumpet are
undoubtedly those of Haydn and Hummel and Hardenberger plays them here with a combination
of sparkling bravura and stylish elegance that are altogether irresistible. Marriner and his Academy
accompany with characteristic finesse and warmth, with the lilting dotted rhythms of the first
movement of the Hummel, seductively jaunty. The lovely *Andante* of the Haydn is no less beguiling
and both finales display a high spirited exuberance and an easy bravura which make the listener
smile with pleasure. He is no less distinctive in the lesser concerto of Johann Hertel and the other
D major work attributed to Johann Stamitz but probably written by someone with the unlikely
name of J.B. Holzbogen. This takes the soloist up into the stratosphere of his range and provides
him also with some awkward leaps. The Hertel work also taxes the soloist's technique to the
extremities but Hardenberger essays all these difficulties with an enviably easy aplomb and
remains fluently entertaining throughout. The recording gives him the most vivid realism and
presence but it is a pity that the orchestral backcloth is so reverberant; otherwise the sound is
very natural.

Trumpet Concertos
Crispian Steele-Perkins *tpt* [a]Neil Black, [a]James Brown *obs*
English Chamber Orchestra / Anthony Halstead.
Carlton Classics 30366 0066-2 (63 minutes: DDD). Recorded 1986. Ⓜ
Haydn Trumpet Concerto in E flat major, HobVIIe No. 1. **M. Haydn** Trumpet Concerto in C major,
MH60. **Humphries** Trumpet Concerto in D major, Op. 2 No. 12. **Neruda** Trumpet Concerto in
E flat major (ed. Steele-Perkins). **Telemann** Concerto for Two Oboes, Trumpet and Strings No. 1
in D major[a]. **Torelli** Trumpet Concerto No. 2 in D major.

This reissue from 1986 contains a pleasing mixture of the familiar and the rediscovered. Though
frequently recorded, there are surprisingly few versions of the Haydn Trumpet Concerto which one
would be happy to experience on a regular basis but this is certainly one of them. Steele-Perkins's
playing is concerned with shape and decorum, not just demonstrative virtuosity. To this end, he
brings a lively buoyancy to the fast movements with especially well-judged articulation; the little-
known Michael Haydn Concerto (just as stratospheric as the better-known work) is a case in point
with its lyrical vocalizing, disarmingly complemented by a shimmering texture of languid flutes.
Steele-Perkins brings his cultivated sense of line to both this work and the Torelli, though the
Telemann Concerto for trumpet and two oboes – a rather pedestrian piece it has to be said – is
altogether less invigorating. The resonant acoustic is advantageous throughout, particularly in the
Neruda, a work where momentum, in less distinguished company, is inclined to sag. Anthony
Halstead and the ECO provide sensitive and tasteful accompaniments throughout.

Twentieth-Century Flute Concertos
Jennifer Stinton *fl* Geoffrey Browne *cor ang*
Scottish Chamber Orchestra / Steuart Bedford.
Collins Classics 1210-2 (66 minutes: DDD). Ⓕ
Honegger Concerto da camera. **Ibert** Flute Concerto. **Nielsen** Flute Concerto, FS119.
Poulenc (orch. L. Berkeley) Flute Sonata.

Strictly speaking, two of the four works on this disc are not flute concertos at all: the Honegger, like
the Richard Strauss *Duet Concertino*, is a chamber concerto for two equal instruments and the
Poulenc is an orchestral transcription of the Flute Sonata, but let that pass! Here is an intelligently
planned and excellently recorded programme which forms a wonderful showcase for this highly
accomplished soloist. In the Nielsen, Steuart Bedford adopts a rather measured tempo for the first
movement. Jennifer Stinton plays with considerable dash and virtuosity (her first movement
cadenza is very fine indeed – even if it is not quite as breathtaking as Gallois). More perhaps could
have been made of the contrast in mood in the second movement and generally speaking, the
impression conveyed is that the orchestra is less inside the idiom than in the more straightforward
Ibert and Poulenc score. Honegger's own *Concerto da camera* comes from the late 1940s at much the
same time as the Fourth Symphony (*Deliciae basiliensis*), and inhabits much the same landscape.
Indeed, part of the slow movement could come from the Larghetto of the symphony. Stinton and
Geoffrey Browne play with great sympathy for the idiom and their performance will hopefully make
more friends for this civilized and rewarding score. There are good, thoroughly expert performances
of the popular Ibert Concerto and Sir Lennox Berkeley's transcription of the Poulenc. This is an
enjoyable disc and Stinton plays with artistry and charm – and the recording is first-class.

Violin Concertos
Elizabeth Wallfisch *vn*
Brandenburg Orchestra / Roy Goodman.
Hyperion CDA66840 (79 minutes: DDD). Recorded 1995. Ⓕ
Mysliveček Violin Concerto No. 4 in B flat major. **Schubert** Rondo for Violin and Strings in
A major, D438. **Spohr** Violin Concerto No. 8 in A minor, Op. 47, 'in modo di scena cantate'.
Viotti Violin Concerto No. 22 in A minor, G97.

The revival in the popularity of the violin concerto during the latter part of the eighteenth century
is winningly celebrated in this delightful, superbly recorded programme. Mysliveček's Fourth
Concerto sets the tone with music of graceful charm, in which Wallfisch engagingly deploys her
fluent virtuosity to reveal the music's full expressive potential. With sensitive accompaniment from
the Brandenburg Orchestra, she presents a satisfying feeling of orderly balance in the first
movement, poignantly expresses the *Larghetto*'s affecting melodiousness with incisive phrasing, and
negotiates the athletic leaps in the finale with compelling vitality. Wallfisch and the Brandenburg go
on to give a truly enchanting account of Viotti's A minor Violin Concerto (No. 22) that exploits the
valuable insights offered by Ferdinand David's performing edition of the piece. Although Schubert
never wrote a violin concerto, he did leave some impressive *concertante* violin music that attests to

his own early training on the instrument. Finally, Spohr's A minor Concerto (No. 8) gives an intriguing theatrical element to the programme and Wallfisch and his forces vividly evoke the music's striking vocal character.

Works for Violin and Orchestra
Gidon Kremer *vn* [c]Andrei Gavrilov *pf*
[a]Berlin Philharmonic Orchestra / Herbert von Karajan;
[b]Philharmonia Orchestra / Riccardo Muti.
EMI Forte CZS5 69334-2 (two discs: 151 minutes: ADD). Recorded 1976-82. (M)
Brahms Violin Concerto in D major, Op. 77. **Sibelius** Violin Concerto in D minor, Op. 47.
Schumann Violin Concerto in D minor, Op. posth. **Weber** Grand duo concertant, J204.
Hindemith Violin Sonata in E flat major, Op. 11. **Schnittke** Quasi una Sonata.

It would be hard to imagine a finer showcase for Kremer's talent. The Schumann has been a benchmark performance for some years, strong and purposeful in the outer movements, hushed and dedicated in the central slow movement. With Muti a challenging yet sympathetic partner, the Sibelius is also given a remarkable performance, notable not just for Kremer's expressive warmth, but for his inner intensity in the great opening melodies of the first two movements, each played as a hushed meditation, but with the first flowing freely, fanciful and poetic, not too slow for an *Allegro moderato*. The finale is then fast and volatile. This recoupling for the two-disc format is also valuable for offering Kremer's glowing account of the Brahms Concerto, his first collaboration with Karajan, one which plainly inspired them both. The spaciousness of the first movement brings total concentration, to justify Kremer's freedom of expression. The slow movement possesses poise and purity, leading to a beautifully sprung account of the finale, with dance rhythms brought out. The analogue recording is comparably spacious. In the three new items Gavrilov proves a comparably inspired partner, with the Weber so winningly characterized – fiery in the first movement, dedicated in the *Andante* and exuberant in the finale – that one almost forgets the original clarinet version, so satisfying is the transformation. The early Hindemith Sonata can rarely have been played with such warmth and intensity, and the Schnittke work, full of extended, pregnant pauses, is superbly held together by the concentrated interplay of the performers, an astonishing 20-minute tapestry.

Chamber

Amber Waves American Clarinet Music.
Richard Stoltzman *cl* Irma Vallecillo *pf*
RCA Red Seal 09026 62685-2 (66 minutes: DDD). Recorded 1994. (F)
Gershwin (arr. Gach) Three Preludes. **Bernstein** Clarinet Sonata. **McKinley** Clarinet Sonata.
C. Fisher Clarinet Sonatine. **Hyman** Clarinata. **Rowles** The Peacocks.
Traditional (arr. Stoltzman) Amazing Grace.

Richard Stoltzman could be claimed as the James Galway of the clarinet. He has developed the personality of the instrument in new ways, often drawing on jazz effects, in what he regards as an American tradition. And he has a considerable following. He has recorded major pieces like the Corigliano Concerto, but in this collection he's simply relaxing. He starts with an ingenious arrangement of Gershwin's piano pieces, the *Three Preludes*, where the few extra effects in both clarinet and piano are completely idiomatic. Then there's Bernstein's early Sonata, another American classic. W.T. McKinley makes his début in the British catalogue with a rather overblown, four-movement Sonata and so does Clare Fisher with *Sonatine*. There's nothing very individual in either work, but Stoltzman obviously enjoys playing them. The real gems come when he goes deeper into jazz, especially Jimmy Rowles's *The Peacocks*, which was used in the soundtrack of *Round Midnight*. This brings out everything in Stoltzman's unique style – bent notes and microtonal slides in near vocal effects. Magical! Dick Hyman is another jazz pianist and composer. His *Clarinata* is a red-hot encore with a soupy middle section. Finally Stoltzman plays his own arrangement of *Amazing Grace*, and very touching it is too. An attractive collection, well recorded.

Black Angels
Kronos Quartet (David Harrington, John Sherba *vns* Hank Dutt *va* Joan Jeanrenaud *vc*).
Nonesuch 7559-79242-2 (62 minutes: DDD). (F)
Crumb Black Angels. **Tallis** (arr. Kronos Qt) Spem in alium. **Marta** Doom. A sigh. **Ives** (arr. Kronos Qt/Geist) They are there! **Shostakovich** String Quartet No. 8 in C minor, Op. 110.

This is very much the sort of imaginative programming we've come to expect from this talented young American quartet. With an overall theme of war and persecution the disc opens with George Crumb's *Black Angels*, for electric string quartet. This work was inspired by the Vietnam War and bears two inscriptions to that effect – *in tempore belli* (in time of war) and 'Finished on Friday the Thirteenth of March, 1970', and it's described by Crumb as 'a kind of parable on our troubled contemporary world'. The work is divided into three sections which represent the three stages of the voyage of the soul – fall from grace, spiritual annihilation and redemption. As with most of his works he calls on his instrumentalists to perform on a variety of instruments other than their own – here that ranges from gongs, maracas and crystal glasses to vocal sounds such as whistling, chanting and whispering. *Doom. A sigh* is the young Hungarian composer István Marta's disturbing portrait of a Roumanian village as they desperately fight to retain their sense of identity in the face of dictatorship and persecution. Marta's atmospheric blend of electronic sound, string quartet and recorded folk-songs leave one with a powerful and moving impression. At first sight Tallis's *Spem in alium* may seem oddly out of place considering the overall theme of this disc, but as the insert-notes point out the text was probably taken from the story of Judith, in which King Nebuchadnezzar's general Holofernes besieged the Jewish fortress of Bethulia. Kronos's own arrangement of this 40-part motet (involving some multi-tracking) certainly makes a fascinating alternative to the original. A particularly fine account of Shostakovich's Eighth String Quartet (dedicated to the victims of fascism and war) brings this thought-provoking and imaginative recital to a close. Performances throughout are outstanding, and the recording first-class.

Cello Moods
Julian Lloyd Webber *vc* [a]Jayson Kouchak *pf*
[b]Royal Philharmonic Orchestra / James Judd; [c]BBC Concert Orchestra / Barry Wordsworth.
Philips 462 588-2PH (74 minutes: DDD). Ⓕ
Bach Orchestral Suite No. 3 in D major, BWV1068 – Air[b]. **Borodin** String Quartet No. 2 in D major – Notturno[b]. **Caccini** Ave Maria[b]. **Chopin** Nocturne No. 2 in E flat major, Op. 9 No. 2[b]. **Debussy** Rêverie[b]. **Elgar** Chanson de matin, Op. 15 No. 2[b]. Salut d'amour, Op. 12[b]. **Rheinberger** Organ Sonata No. 11 in D minor, Op. 148 – Cantilena (all arr. Cullen)[b]. **Boccherini** Cello Concerto No. 9 in B flat major, G482 – Adagio[b]. **Bruch** Kol Nidrei, Op. 47[b]. **Franck** Panis angelicus[b]. **Glazunov** Mélodie, Op. 20 No. 1[b]. **J. Lloyd Webber** Jackie's Song[c]. **Massenet** Thaïs – Méditation[b]. **Traditional** Sakura Sakura[a].

This collection of Julian Lloyd Webber's recordings is of popular encore pieces (mostly transcriptions). He opens with a tastefully 'vocal' rendering of Franck's *Panis angelicus* and ends with a noble *Cantilena* from Rheinberger; however, the highlight is a movingly warm, yet not over-the-top account of Bruch's *Kol Nidrei*. His own charming little tribute to Jacqueline du Pré, and the Massenet *Méditation* on a cello rather than a violin is very appealing. Other highlights are Caccini's gently touching *Ave Maria*, which is the kind of half-familiar, nostalgic piece one can't put a name to. The Russian melodies are played romantically, but without swooning: the most enjoyable is the least-known, Glazunov's *Mélodie*, Op. 20 No. 1. However the Chopin *Nocturne* in E flat major stands out as an example of an untranscribable piano piece. Lloyd Webber has a firm, richly coloured and full-focused tone which records well. If you enjoy typical lollipops played on the cello with affectionate flair, then neither the warm recording, nor the quantity of music offered, can be faulted.

Cello Song
Julian Lloyd Webber *vc* John Lenehan *pf*
Philips 434 917-2PH (53 minutes: DDD). Recorded 1992. Ⓕ
Villa-Lobos O Canto do capadócio. **Bach** Cantata No. 156, Ich steh mit einem Fuss im Grabe – Sinfonia. **Castelnuovo-Tedesco** Sea murmurs, Op. 24a. **Schumann** Funf Stücke im Volkston, Op. 102 – No. 2, Langsam. **Scriabin** Etudes in B flat minor, Op. 8 No. 11. **Rachmaninov** Romance in F minor. **Grieg** Lyric Pieces, Book 3, Op. 43 – To the Spring. **Delius** Hassan – Serenade. **Elgar** Romance, Op. 62. **Chopin** Cello Sonata in G minor, Op. 65 – Largo. **Brahms** Five Lieder, Op. 105 – Wie Melodien zieht es mir. **Dvořák** Seven Gipsy Melodies, B104 (Op. 55) – Songs my mother taught me. **Debussy** Beau soir. **Messiaen** Quatuor pour la fin du temps – Louange à l'Eternité de Jésus. **Traditional** The Star of the County Down.

As the title of this disc implies, all the pieces contained therein are rather in the same slowish-paced, lyrical vein, but their sequence has been cleverly chosen so that there is still plenty of variety to keep the listener's attention. Some of the items are original cello and piano pieces, others are skilful arrangements, and there is a good mixture of well known and unusual offerings. Elgar's bassoon *Romance* translates particularly well to the cello, as do the Brahms, Debussy and Dvořák songs and only in the arrangement of Grieg's piano piece, *To the Spring* does one feel that a cello is a little out of place. The Messiaen excerpt is the longest and the most profound item, and it exists quite happily as an entity away from the rest of the *Quatuor*. Throughout the programme Julian Lloyd Webber plays with exceptional sensitivity, sympathy and tonal beauty – in fact it would be difficult to find better performances of this kind of repertoire anywhere on records of today or yesterday. John Lenehan gives good support, and Philips have provided a mellow, roomy recording.

Cello World

Steven Isserlis *vc* Dame Felicity Lott *sop* Maggie Cole *hpd*
Thomas Adès, Michael Tilson Thomas, Dudley Moore *pfs*
RCA Red Seal 09026 68928-2 (74 minutes: DDD). Recorded 1997.   Ⓕ
Beethoven Andante con Variazioni, WoO44 No. 2. **Schumann** Violin Sonata No. 3, WoO27 – Intermezzo. **Fauré** Morceau de concours. **Léonard** L'âne et l'ânier, Op. 61 No. 4.
Dvořák Romantic Piece, B150 No. 4. **Seiber** Dance Suite (all arr. Isserlis). **Debussy** Nocturne et Scherzo. **Berlioz** La captive, Op. 12. **Saint-Saëns** Le carnaval des animaux – The Swan.
Villa-Lobos O Canto do Cisne Negro. **Martinů** Duo. **Rachmaninov** Lied. **Scriabin** Romance.
Popper Dance of the Elves, Op. 39. **J. Isserlis** Souvenir Russe. **Tavener** The Child Lived.
Tsintsadze Miniatures – Chonguri. **Vine** Inner World.

As one might expect from so characterful an artist as Steven Isserlis, this is a cello recital with a difference, attractive in a delightfully offbeat way. The last and longest item, *Inner World* by the Australian Carl Vine, for amplified cello with electronic support, could easily become a cult piece. Starting like a cadenza for some romantic cello concerto, it grows ever more elaborate, always tonal and lyrical, with the soloist in duet with himself at times, culminating in a wild, exciting coda. You might regard that as the most controversial item, but for a very wide audience it could be a winner. Otherwise, there are only two regular cello showpieces, Saint-Saëns's 'The Swan' exquisitely done with a final whispered half-tone (in a recording evidently taken from the television series with Michael Tilson Thomas and Dudley Moore) and Popper's *Dance of the Elves*, as flamboyant as you will ever hear it. It may seem gimmicky that the opening item, the Beethoven Variations, transcribed from a Sonatina for mandolin and piano (1796), should here have anachronistic harpsichord accompaniment. Yet as a performance it certainly works, with exhilarating pointing of the final syncopated variation. Most of Isserlis's transcriptions are from violin originals, including the comic Léonard piece, full of ever more exaggerated hee-haws, set against the carter's song in the middle. The Fauré *Morceau de concours* is an exception, transcribed from a flute piece.

In all those items Thomas Adès is an inspired accompanist, specially relishing the witty 1920s parodies in Mátyás Seiber's *Dance Suite*, including one delectable *glissando* near the end. The Cuban cross-rhythms of the jolly pizzicato piece by the Georgian, Sulkhan Tsintsadze, are also wittily pointed by both artists. Other oddities include the jolly little Martinů *Duo* (with Isserlis taking both parts), and the unlikely *Nocturne et Scherzo*, in fact a little waltz, which Debussy wrote in an anonymous style in Russia in 1882. It is good too to have Isserlis's tribute to his grandfather, the pianist Julius Isserlis, in a nostalgic folk-based Russian piece. The two items with Felicity Lott bring extra freshness and beauty, not just the Berlioz song but the Tavener piece with accompaniment for cello alone. With first-rate sound this is going to give great pleasure to Isserlis's many admirers.

A Choice Collection

Palladian Ensemble (Pamela Thorby *rec* Rachel Podger *vn* Susanne Heinrich *va da gamba*
William Carter *gtr/theorbo*).
Linn Records CKD041 (66 minutes: DDD). Recorded 1995.   Ⓕ
Locke Broken Consorts – D major; C major. **Matteis** Setts of Ayres – Book 2: No. 10, Preludio in ostinatione; No. 12, Andamento malincolico; Book 3: No. 7, Preludio-Prestissimo; No. 8, Sarabanda-Adagio; No. 9, Gavotta con divisioni; Book 4: No. 27, Bizzararrie sopra un basso malinconico; No. 28, Aria amorosa-Adagio. **Baltzar** John come kiss me now. **Weldon** Sett of Ayres in D major. **Blow** Ground in G minor. **Butler** Variations on Callino Casturame. **J. Banister** Divisions on a Ground. **Anonymous** Old Simon the King.

The 'choice collection' of 'music of Purcell's London' is of items such as might have been heard at the concerts of then contemporary music held on the premises of Thomas Britton, the 'small coal man', surely one of the most unlikely patrons in the history of music. It is in effect complementary to the Palladian Ensemble's earlier disc ('An Excess of Pleasure', also on Linn Records, CKD010), with another liberal helping of Matteis's various and sometimes agreeably bizarre *Ayres* and two more of Locke's *Broken Consorts*, which we find absorbing rather than confusing – as Charles II did. With this disc John Weldon and Henry Butler are newcomers to the catalogue, the former with what amounts to an irregularly ordered suite, the latter with splendid variations on *Callino Casturame* in which Susanne Heinrich plays most expressively – and proves that chords played on the viola da gamba do not have to sound like teeth being pulled. *Old Simon the King* could not have been heard in Purcell's own time in this anonymous setting from *The division flute* of 1706, but the tune was printed as early as 1652. If you are not already aware of the high quality of the instrumental playing, stylish musicality and imaginative approach of the Palladian Ensemble this disc provides a good opportunity to find out what you have been missing.

Devil's Trill
Yuval Yaron *vn* **Jeremy Denk** *pf*
Naim Audio NAIMCD018 (48 minutes: DDD). Recorded 1996.　　　　　　　　Ⓕ
Gluck Orfeo ed Euridice – Dance of the Blessed Spirits.
Leclair Sonatas for Violin and Continuo – D major, Op. 8 No. 2; C minor, Op. 5 No. 6.
Tartini Sonata for Violin and Continuo in G minor, 'Devil's Trill'. **Vivaldi** (arr. Respighi)
Sonata for Violin and Continuo in D major, Op. 2 No. 11.

This is truly beautiful violin playing, elegant in the opening *Larghetto* of Tartini's *The Devil's Trill* Sonata and with the truest intonation later on. The cadenza, too, is extremely brilliant, though never 'showy'. Both sonatas by the eighteenth-century dancer-turned-composer Jean Leclair find Yaron in fine fettle, with a winsome tone and tastefully controlled vibrato. Respighi's naughty-but-nice reworking of a sonata that Vivaldi dedicated to Frederick IV of Norway and Denmark features some delicious piano harmonies beneath the solo line and you would be hard put to find a more eloquent voicing of the Gluck/Kreisler 'Mélodie'. So who, you may ask, *is* Yuval Yaron? Violin *aficionados* may already have encountered him, but the more general reader might like to know that he won First Prize at the 1975 Sibelius Competition in Helsinki, studied with Gingold and at Heifetz's masterclasses and is currently Professor of Violin at the Indiana University School of Music in Bloomington, where his excellent pianist Jeremy Denk also serves and where Naim's recordings were. The timing is stingy but, as already suggested, Yaron's playing is a joy to behold.

Jacqueline du Pré – Her Early BBC Recordings
Jacqueline du Pré, [f]William Pleeth *vcs* [deg]Ernest Lush, [c]Stephen Kovacevich *pf*
EMI Studio mono CDM7 63165/6-2 (two discs: 112 minutes: ADD). Recorded live 1962-65.　Ⓜ Ⓗ
CDM7 63165-2 **Bach** Solo Cello Suites – No. 1 in G major, BWV1007[a]; No. 2 in D minor, BWV1008[b]. **Britten** Cello Sonata in C major, Op. 65 – Scherzo and March[c]. **Falla** (arr. Maréchal) Suite populaire espagnole[d].
CDM7 63166-2 **Brahms** Cello Sonata No. 2 in F major, Op. 99[e]. **F. Couperin** Nouveaux Concerts – Treizième concert[f]. **Handel** (arr. Slatter) Oboe Concerto in G minor, HWV287[g].

We owe the BBC and EMI a debt of gratitude for making these valuable recordings available on disc. The performances date from her mid- to late-teens, and reveal a maturity and passion that is rare in so young a performer. This, together with her wonderful gift of communication, make these performances very special indeed. The two Bach Cello Suites have a magical, intimate poetry that transfixes the attention from the very first note and her beautifully phrased and lyrical readings more than compensate for any slight imperfections of articulation. Sadly we have only the '*Scherzo*' and 'March' movements from the Britten Cello Sonata, and judging by the quality of these, a complete performance would surely have been a recording to treasure. These are sparkling performances, full of wit and good humour, reflecting the obvious rapport between the two young artists. The recording of Falla's *Suite populaire espagnole* dates from 1961 when du Pré was only 16 but is no less assured or technically accomplished. The performance is full of life and rhythmic vitality, with some very tender and expressive playing, as in the cantabile melodies of the 'Nana' and 'Cancion' movements. The mono recordings are not of the highest quality (the Bach Suites are taken from transcription discs, so there are traces of surface noise and clicks) but this is of little relevance when we are presented with playing as beautiful and captivating as this.

Espana!
Katia and Marielle Labèque *pf*
Philips 438 938-2PH (59 minutes: DDD). Recorded 1993.　　　　　　　　　Ⓕ
Falla La vida breve – Danses espagnoles. El amor brujo – Ritual Fire Dance. **Lecuona** Malagueña. **Albéniz** Suite española, Op. 47 – Sevilla; Cádiz; Aragon; Castilla. Pavana capricho, Op. 12. Iberia – Triana. Navarra. **Infante** Danses andalouses.

The Labèque sisters give us the right Iberian mixture of vigour, brilliance, shadows and languor, and seem to be thoroughly enjoying themselves in music that they know well. There is no more exciting keyboard performance of Falla's 'Ritual Fire Dance'. This is actually a transcription by Mario Bragiotti. Indeed, save for the *Danses Andalouses* by Manuel Infante, every piece here is a transcription and the Labèques themselves have had a hand in that of Lecuona's exquisitely sultry *Malagueña*, which includes quietly plucked strings at the two-minute mark. But no one would know that this music was not originally written for two pianos, for everything is idiomatic. Indeed, the transcription of Albéniz's *Suite española* and *Pavana capricho* is by the composer, while that of his 'Triana' (music that beautifully blends vivacity and delicacy) is by his friend Granados. The recording is intimate yet atmospheric.

Fantaisie for Flute and Harp
Anna Noakes *fl* Gillian Tingay *hp*
ASV White Line CDWHL2101 (76 minutes: DDD). Recorded 1996. Ⓜ
Traditional El diablo suelto. La partida. Spanish Love Song (trans. Galway). Urpila. Bailecito de procesión. **Villa-Lobos** Modinha. Bachianas Brasileiras No. 5. **Fauré** Fantaisie, Op. 79. Après un rêve, Op. 7 No. 1. Sicilienne, Op. 78. Pièce. **L. Boulanger** Nocturne. **Saint-Saëns** Romance, Op. 37. **Ravel** Pavane pour une infante défunte. **Caplet** Rêverie. **Piazzolla** Histoire du Tango.

Here is a lightweight but entertaining collection, which happily juxtaposes French insouciance with Latin American sparkle. The pair of South American folk-songs which opens the programme are real lollipops; then comes some lilting Villa-Lobos; first the sultry rhythmic *Modinha*, nudged with a nice rhythmic subtlety, and then the famous (soprano/cello) *Bachianas Brasileiras* No. 5, which sounds seductive enough on the flute. The disc includes flowing, coolly beautiful Fauré and a gentle, haunting *Nocturne* by Lili Boulanger (meltingly phrased by Anna Noakes), followed by a romantic *morceau* by Saint-Saëns. One of the most enticing later pieces is the chimerical *Rêverie* of André Caplet and the recital ends with a highly individual and immediately arresting suite of four strongly flavoured miniatures by Astor Piazzolla called *Histoire du Tango*, bewitching in their combination of Latin rhythmic inflexions with a smoky Parisian night-club atmosphere. They are presented with much *élan* and sparkle and given added lift by various uninhibited percussive thwacks from both players. Although the harp sounds somewhat recessed, it always provides a glowing web of sound.

Fantasías Mediterráneas Spanish Music for Clarinet and Piano.
Joan Enric Lluna *cl* Jan Gruithuyzen *pf*
Clarinet Classics CC0017 (72 minutes: DDD). Recorded 1997. Ⓕ
J. Menéndez Introducción, Andante y Danza. Contemplación. **Yuste** Estudio melódico.
A. Romero Fantasía, sobre temas de la ópera 'Lucrecia de Borgia' de Donizetti.
Montsalvatge Self-Paráfrasis. **Guinjoan** Fantasía. **C. Cano** Vigilias. **Brotons** Sonata, Op. 64.

According to the artist featured here (the principal clarinet of the Bournemouth Sinfonietta), the clarinet is, after the guitar, one of the most popular instruments in Spain – largely as a result of the numerous wind bands, whose tradition goes back well over a century. Little of the extensive Spanish solo repertoire for the instrument has found its way outside the country, however; and this conspectus of a century-and-a-half of composers for it will be practically virgin territory for all but the best-informed. The three earliest figures represented here were all primarily virtuosos who held posts in leading Spanish orchestras and, in two cases, as teachers at the Madrid Conservatory. The opening *Fantasía* by Antonio Romero is one of those old-fashioned competition or audition test-pieces which makes every kind of terrifying demand on a player – which, however, Lluna sails through effortlessly and with total assurance, also retaining quality in the highest register.

Born half a century and more later, Miguel Yuste and Julián Menéndez both produced music of more intrinsic value, though the latter's *Introducción, Andante y Danza* (the last section of which shows a nice turn of fantasy) again puts the emphasis on technical adroitness, but now with a command of colour: his *Contemplación* is a charming pastoral, and Yuste's *Estudio melódico* has a long-breathed romantic lyricism. After these, Montsalvatge's dissonant grotesqueries in a brief paraphrase of a section of his 1958 Partita come like an invigorating splash of cold water, preparing the ground for the rhythmically vital, freely dodecaphonic *Fantasía* by the now 68-year-old Joan Guinjoan (which puts both players on their mettle) and for two major works on the disc by two much younger composers. César Cano's (b.1960) *Vigilias* utilizes some unorthodox instrumental techniques (not all of which are particularly rewarding musically) and presents formidable difficulties, which Lluna (the work's dedicatee) and his excellent pianist seem to take in their stride; but most impressive of all is the 1986 two-movement Sonata by Salvador Brotons (b.1959, once a pupil of Montsalvatge), an imaginative and mainly lyrical work with a vivacious angular finale – a sonata that richly deserves to be taken into virtuoso players' repertoire.

First and Foremost
Apollo Saxophone Quartet (Tim Redpath, Rob Buckland, Andrew Scott, Jonathan Rebbeck *saxes*); John Harle ᵃ*alto sax*/ᵇ*keybds* ᶜRoy Powell *keybds*
ᵈWill Gregory *bar and bass saxes* ᵉMike Hamnett *perc*
Argo 443 903-2ZH (52 minutes: DDD). Recorded 1993. Ⓕ

Corea (arr. Apollo Saxophone Quartet) Children's Songs – Nos. 2-4, 6, 7, 11, 16 and 18[be].
Nyman Four Songs for Tony. **D. Bedford** Fridiof Kennings[e]. **W. Gregory** Hoe Down[ade].
R. Powell Bow out[c].

All this music was written or arranged (by the composer) for saxophone quartet, and it spans a
variety of idioms from that of classical music to those of jazz, the hoe down, film music and the
Icelandic saga. A saxophone quartet is in effect a 'whole consort', to be listened to (unless you are
certifiably allergic to its sound) like any other – a recorder consort, a brass ensemble, or a string
quartet. In their first recording, the Apollo Quartet proves to be musically sensitive, tight in
ensemble and painless in intonation. Dear old Adolphe, who even proposed the erection of a giant
'muzak machine' overlooking Paris, could never have visualized anything like this. Powell's
comment on *Bow out* perhaps epitomizes the best approach to the programme as a whole: 'neither
'jazz' nor 'classical' ... [it] occupies its own space'. The recording is of high quality in all respects.

French Chamber Music
Rainer Kussmaul, Madeleine Carruzzo *vns* Wolfram Christ *va* Georg Faust *vc* Alois Posch *db*
Margit-Anna Süss *hp* Ensemble Wien-Berlin (Wolfgang Schulz *fl* Hansjörg Schellenberger *ob*
Karl Leister *cl* Milan Turkovič *bn* Günter Högner *hn*).
Sony Classical SK62666 (71 minutes: DDD). Recorded 1996.   Ⓕ Ⓔ
Debussy Sonata for Flute, Viola and Harp. **Françaix** Octet. **Ibert** Trois pièces brèves.
Jolivet Chant de Linos. **Ravel** Introduction and Allegro.

This is a well-assembled programme, played by an expert ensemble and recorded with striking
fidelity. The quality of the individual players can perhaps best be heard in the second of the Ibert
pieces, the Debussy trio and the virtuoso flute threnody by Jolivet (originally a 1944 Conservatoire
test-piece when Jean-Pierre Rampal was the winner), here performed in the later version when he
rescored the piano part. The intensity and greater profundity of the latter two works particularly
suit this group of rich-toned and serious-minded artists, whose ensemble is flawless; they excel in
lyrical passages, such as the tender opening of the Françaix Octet's slow movement, but their
extremely emotional reading of the first part of the Ravel (for which a leisurely pace is taken) is at
variance with the Gallic spirit of understatement and limpidity. This is the only reservation about
these interpretations: the waltz in the third Ibert piece could have been more playful and the *gamin*
example in the finale of the entertaining Françaix Octet (a superbly crafted work) more carefree.

Impressions d'enfance
Gidon Kremer *vn* Oleg Maisenberg *pf*
Teldec 0630-13597-2 (63 minutes: DDD). Recorded 1996.   Ⓕ Ⓔ
Bartók Violin Sonata No. 2, Sz76. **Enescu** Impressions d'enfance, Op. 28.
Schulhoff Violin Sonata No. 2. **Plakidis** Two Grasshopper Dances.

This is a fabulous recital, the sort that suggests wet ink on the page and performances born more of
impulse than of duty. The Enescu sequence is pure delight, from the gipsy-like cadences of the
unaccompanied 'Minstrel' that opens the suite, through the virtual-reality chirruping of 'The bird in
the cage and the cuckoo on the wall', to the ingenious 'linking' miniatures – half a minute apiece or
less – that etch a cricket and 'Wind in the chimney'. *Impressions d'enfance* (1940) ends with an
extraordinarily graphic 'Sunrise'. The idiom straddles late Debussy and mature Bartók, though
Enescu's characteristically Romanian flavouring soon gives the game away. Kremer's performances
are agile, lean and impetuous, with copious slides and numerous flushes of warmth. Furthermore,
he carries the camp-fire element into the Bartók, rhapsodizing rapturously over the final climax and
effecting a magical *diminuendo* towards the sonata's close. Maisenberg commands a multi-shaded
tonal palette and it's a delight to encounter a work that can be – in unsympathetic hands – a
listening trial transformed into a sort of cerebral Hungarian rhapsody. Again, agility is a keyword.
Which leaves Ervín Schulhoff's outspoken Second Violin Sonata, a product of 1927, touched by
Hindemith's influence in the first movement, and by heated emotions in the second. Kremer and
Maisenberg give it showcase treatment and the recording is, as elsewhere, first-rate. The encore is
unaccompanied, a pair of folky, heavily double-stopped *Grasshopper Dances* by Peteris Plakidis.

Industry
Bang on a Can All-Stars (Maya Beiser *vc* Evan Ziporyn *saxes* Mark Stewart *gtrs* Robert Black *db*
Lisa Moore *kbds* Steven Schick *perc*); **Cees van Zeeland, Gerard Bouwhuis** *pfs*
Amy Knowles *congas* Icebreaker (Katherine Pendry, James Poke *panpipes* Richard Craig *sax*
Damian le Gassick *fender rhodes*).
Sony Classical SK66483 (61 minutes: DDD). Recorded 1994.   Ⓕ
Wolfe Lick. **L. Andriessen** Hout. Hoketus. **D. Lang** The Anvil Chorus. **Gordon** Industry.

The All-Stars come across here as a fiercely aggressive group, combining the power and punch of a rock band with the precision and clarity of a chamber ensemble. The individual pieces cover a considerable idiomatic range but share the minimalist fascination with repetitive, gradually evolving structures. Rhythm is constant and vital, melody and harmony either stunted or non-existent. The programme kicks off with Julia Wolfe's *Lick* – sensibly enough as it's the most approachable work on the disc. In a surprisingly affectionate tribute to the rock music of her youth, Wolfe toys with the expectations of the genre with considerable formal cunning; and no one could deny the extraordinary panache of the playing. The Andriessen compositions lack any comparable lightness of touch. This is not to deny that they matter. They articulate in purest form the seminal impulse behind the other music here, remaking the static, consonant sounds of Terry Riley, Steve Reich and the rest into a vehicle of protest – edgy, jarring and *Angst*-ridden. *Hout* and *Hoketus* are as severe in their canonic processes as any of Reich's early phase pieces, and their halting angular ideas evoke the back streets of some dark and impenetrable urban jungle (possibly best left unexplored). Is there another composer who would think of obtaining a monolithic sonority from panpipes and saxophones over acoustic and electric pianos with bass guitars and a conga rhythm? Like it or not, this disc makes an impressively cogent, individualistic statement. The music certainly isn't subtle: it's a bruising assault on the soothing, pseudo-spiritual escapism of the Holy Minimalists on the one hand and the excessive, barely-heard complexities of the Modernist Old Guard on the other. The results are technically outstanding but definitely not for the faint-hearted.

In the Name of Bach
[b]Catherine Bott *sop* [a]Julian Podger, [a]Robert Evans *tens* [a]Michael McCarthy *bass* Florilegium.
Channel Classics CCS9096 (75 minutes: DDD). Notes and texts included. Recorded 1995. Ⓕ
G.C. Bach Siehe, wie fein und lieblich (Geburtstagkantate)[a]. **J.E. Bach** Violin Sonata in F minor.
W.F. Bach Adagio and Fugue in D minor, F65. Duetto for Two Flutes in E minor, F54. **J.E. Bach** Sammlung auserlesener Fabeln I – Die ungleichen Freunde[b]; Die Unzufriedenheit[b]; Der Affe und die Schäferin[b]; Der Hund[b]. **J.C. Bach:** Sonata for Keyboard, Violin and Cello in G major, T313/1 (Op. 2 No. 2). **J.B. Bach:** Overture in D major – Passepieds Nos. 1 and 2; La Joye.

Here is a Bach family anthology featuring three members of the clan whose music seldom finds its way into record catalogues. The earliest representative is Georg Christoph, one of Sebastian Bach's uncles. He was, for a time, town Kantor at Schweinfurt in Franconia where in 1684 he received a visit on his birthday from his two brothers. Georg Christoph was so delighted that, shortly afterwards, he wrote a cantata to record the event, *Siehe, wie fein und lieblich* ('Behold, how good and how pleasant it is for brethren to dwell together in unity'). Tenors Julian Podger and Robert Evans, with bass Michael McCarthy, provide a well-focused and evenly balanced ensemble seemingly to savour the spirit in which the piece was written. Next in the family chronology comes Johann Bernhard Bach, a cousin of J.S.B. Not a great deal of his music survives but among that which does are four orchestral suites which may well have resulted from his exposure to those of Telemann who was already a fluent master of the form. It is a pity that Florilegium saw fit to include only three short dances from the Fourth Suite in D major. The music is well worth performing without omission. The highly gifted but emotionally complex Wilhelm Friedemann is represented by the long-admired, poignant and oft-recorded *Adagio and Fugue* in D minor for two flutes and strings, and by one of his several *Duettos* for two flutes, this one in E minor. Florilegium, corporately and individually, plays the music with heartfelt expression and a sensibility that mirrors the stylistic idiom.

It is the music of J.S. Bach's nephew and pupil, Johann Ernst, which occupies the greater part of the programme. This member of the family seems wholeheartedly to have embraced the early classical idiom, further demonstrating, both in the Violin Sonata in F minor and in the four songs selected from his *Sammlung auserlesener Fabeln*, that he was a composer with a distinctive and affecting musical vocabulary at his disposal. Catherine Bott gives warmly expressive performances, savouring the considerable lyrical content of a little-known area of Bach family industry. The prodigious talent of this dynasty once again reaches a peak in Florilegium's programme with a Quartet in G major by Johann Christian, the 'London Bach'. Musically speaking, the expansive opening movement is especially engaging but the entire work is played with elegance and charm by these artists. In summary, this is varied and enjoyable entertainment, well off the beaten track. Although the absence of any translation from the German of the texts of the four songs is regrettable, it does not prevent a warm recommendation.

Journey to the Amazon
Sharon Isbin *gtr* with [a]Gaudencio Thiago de Mello *perc* [b]Paul Winter *sax*
Teldec 0630-19899-2 (55 minutes: DDD). Recorded 1997. ⒻⒺ
L. Almeida Historia do Luar[a]. **Lauro** Seis por derecho. El marabino. Valses venezolanos – No. 3, Natalia. **Barrios** Waltz, Op. 8 No. 4. Julia Florida. **Thiago de Mello** A Hug for Pixingha.

Chants for the Chief – No. 1, A Chamada dos ventos/Canção Nocturna; No. 2, Uirapurú do Amazonas (both arr. cpsr). Lago de Janaucá. A Hug for Tiberio. Cavaleiro sem Armadura (arr. Wolff). **Montaña** Porro. **Savio** Batucada. **Brouwer** Canción de cuna, 'Berceuse' (arr. Grenet). **Canonico** Aire de Joropo (arr. Lauro/Diaz). **Vianna** Cochichando (arr. Barbosa-Lima).

No one is currently doing more to free the guitar from its rent-a-programme image than Sharon Isbin. She is not South American, nor does the Amazon flow through Cuba, Colombia, Venezuela or Paraguay, but none of this matters in the least. Others before her have hitched rides with specialists in particular areas and sounded like uncomfortable passengers, but Isbin has loved and felt this music for over a quarter of a century and in the company of Thiago de Mello and Paul Winter is entirely at home. One might fear the addition of assorted percussive sounds and 'rain-forest' noises to be intrusive, especially in the familiar items, but they are atmospherically enhancing, handled with great discretion (delightfully in Grenet's arrangement of Brouwer's *Canción de cuna*) and often rhythmically uplifting. Lauro's setting of the traditional *Seis por derecho* has never sounded more full of vitality. The guitar has a wide range of tone colour, which Isbin exploits with skill and taste in traversing the gamut from tenderness to joyously rhythmic energy. The excellent annotation resides in a concertina-form booklet, which is user-friendly in that respect, but whose printing in white on a 'rain-forest' background is not equally so. Recording is beautifully clear and well balanced. Waste no time in getting your hands on this disc.

Kremerata Musica
[a]**Sabine Meyer** cl [b]**Gidon Kremer** vn [c]**Veronika Hagen** va [d]**Clemens Hagen** vc
[e]**Oleg Maisenberg** pf
DG 447 112-2GH (76 minutes: DDD). Recorded 1994.   Ⓕ
Mahler Quartet in A minor[bcde]. **Schoenberg** Piece in D minor[be]. String Trio, Op. 45[bcd].
Phantasy, Op. 47[be]. **Webern** Two Pieces for Cello and Piano[de]. Four Pieces, Op. 7[bc]. Three Little
Pieces, Op. 11[de]. Cello Sonata[de]. **Berg** Four Pieces, Op. 5[ae]. Chamber Concerto –
Adagio (arr. cpsr)[abe].

This is a Second Viennese School disc that revels in extremes: for example, there could hardly be a greater contrast than that between Schoenberg's very early, very anodyne piece for violin and piano (it could easily be mistaken for Schubert at his least poetic) and his last instrumental work, the forceful, economical *Phantasy*. Even so, the playing throughout is so refined and expressive that the later music's eroded but still potent links with the romantic tradition are unmistakable. The result is fascinating, and one of the best releases of its kind for some years. Mahler's honorary membership of the Schoenberg school – as early patron and model – is acknowledged in his own youthful movement for piano quartet, an evocative mixture of Brahmsian and Wagnerian elements that showed the way forward with exemplary clarity. As for Schoenberg's pupils, Webern's rapid progress from languid late romanticism (in the two cello pieces of 1899) to aphoristic expressionism is powerfully displayed, the close positioning of the cello in the Op. 11 Pieces adding to the larger-than-life impression of these performances. Sabine Meyer's clarinet is also closely recorded in the Berg pieces, but music so rich in striking incident can stand such immediacy, as can Berg's arrangement of the *Chamber Concerto*'s slow movement for clarinet, violin and piano. Nevertheless, the finest music-making of all is heard in Schoenberg's Trio, an account in which technical mastery and expressive fantasy combine to brilliant effect.

Kronos Quartet – 25 Years
Kronos Quartet (David Harrington, John Sherba vns Hank Dutt va Joan Jeanrenaud vc).
Nonesuch 7559-79504-2 (ten discs: 653 minutes: ADD/DDD). Recorded 1973-98.   Ⓜ
Adams John's Book of Alleged Dances. **Ali-Zade** Mugam Sayagi. **Benshoof** Traveling Music.
Song of Twenty Shadows. **Crumb** Black Angels. **Feldman** Piano Quintet (**Aki Takahashi** pf).
Glass String Quartets – No. 2, 'Company'; No. 3, 'Mishima'; No. 4, 'Buczak'; No. 5.
Golijov The Dreams and Prayers of Isaac the Blind (with **David Krakauer** cl/bass, cl/basset hn).
Górecki String Quartets – No. 1, Op. 62, 'Already it is Dusk'; No. 2, Op. 64, 'Quasi una fantasia'.
Gubaidulina String Quartet No. 4. **Pärt** Fratres. Psalom (arr. Höfer). Summa. Missa Sillabica
(**Ellen Hargis** sop **Suzanne Elder** contr **Neal Rogers** ten **Paul Hillier** bass). **Phan** Tragedy at the
Opera. **Piazzolla** Five Tango Sensations (**Astor Piazzolla** bandoneón). Four, for Tango.
Reich Different Trains. **Riley** Cadenza on the Night Plain. G Song. Salome Dances for Peace –
Echoes of Primordial Time; Good Medicine Dance. **Schnittke** String Quartets – No. 2; No. 4.
Collected Songs Where Every Verse is Filled with Grief (arr. Kronos). **Sculthorpe** String Quartets
– No. 8; No. 11, 'Jaribu Dreaming'. From Ubirr (**Michael Brosnan, Mark Nolan** didjeridoos).
Volans String Quartet No. 1, 'White Man Sleeps'.

The string quartet is both the most exclusive and the most approachable of small instrumental combinations. On the one hand it has hosted some of the most profound and ethereal repertory in

Western music, while on the other it is peculiarly responsive to popularization. Perhaps having a head-count that approximates the average pop group helps, and there is plenty of scope for projected 'personality'. But there is also something intriguing about a good piece for string quartet, a sense of being a privileged fly on the wall, eavesdropping on conversations that were only really meant to be shared among four – a sort of cerebral or spiritual voyeurism. The Kronos Quartet has always known how to make audio theatre out of chamber music, what with its numerous commissions, imaginative programmes, flexible playing style and an openness to world music that is particularly apparent in this majestic 25th anniversary collection. Kronos knows the meaning of quality, but also has the common touch. Nonesuch offers us a generous helping of reissues, supplemented by around two hours' worth of new material. So *Summa* (which is among the most sensual of Pärt's tintinnabulatory works) and the concise *Missa Sillabica* appear here for the first time. John Adams is represented by the up-tempo delights of *John's Book of Alleged Dances* and Steve Reich by his durable – and partly autobiographical – *Different Trains*. Taxing as this is, it is hard to imagine that Gubaidulina's compelling Fourth Quartet – which also calls for multiple quartets – would have been much easier to realize. But if you put on the first movement of Kevin Volans's *White Man Sleeps* and sample its closing pages, you hear what must surely have been a thematic prompt for *Different Trains* (Volans's piece dates from 1984, Reich's from 1988). The similarity is striking.

George Crumb's terrifying *Black Angels* is a sort of anti-Vietnam War protest in sound that anticipates Schnittke in its juxtaposition of the old (in this case Schubert's *Death and the Maiden* Quartet) and the new. Both Schnittke and Górecki suggest profound inner conflicts laid bare, though the specific manners of their personal expression are highly contrasted: those who are rested by Górecki's ubiquitous Third Symphony (reviewed under Górecki) should brace themselves for his chamber music. Kronos back-packs across city, desert or plain, sighing deeply with Astor Piazzolla (on bandoneón) for his *Five Tango Sensations* and toughening up for his more aggressive *Four, for Tango* (another first release). Turn then to Osvaldo Golijov and you confront the Jewish world of klezmer, with clarinettist David Krakauer spicing up *The Dreams and Prayers of Isaac the Blind*. Franghiz Ali-Zadeh conjures folk motives from Azerbaijan, and Peter Sculthorpe (in *Jabiru Dreaming*, Quartet No. 8, *From Ubirr*) reinvents the music of the Aborigines (offered here for the first time on CD). P.Q. Phan's tragi-comic *Tragedy at the Opera* recalls a Vietnamese singer who died in the line of stage duty (trying to sing a female role) and among the Americans, Ken Benshoof gives us his accessible, mostly upbeat *Traveling Music* (the Kronos's first commission) and the extraordinarily moving elegy *Song of Twenty Shadows* – again a first release. Morton Feldman is represented by his slow-breathing, delicately textured Piano Quartet (with Aki Takahashi), Philip Glass by four surprisingly variegated Quartets (Nos. 2-5) and Terry Riley by excerpts from *Salome Dances for Peace* (the most minimalistic music on the set), the neo-baroque *G Song* (Riley's first piece for Kronos) and the colourful *Cadenza on the Night Plain*. The last two are first releases. Nonesuch's presentation is a minor work of art in itself and the documentation an informed easy read, though there is precious little to indicate what is – or what is not – a first release. You would be hard pressed to find a friendlier, or more attractive *entrée* to the world of new music.

Mnemosyne
Jan Garbarek *saxes*
The Hilliard Ensemble
ECM New Series 465 122-2 (two discs: 105 minutes: DDD). Texts and translations included.
Recorded 1998.   Ⓕ
Anonymous Alleluia nativitatis. Eagle Dance. Fayrfax Africanus. Novus novus. Russian Psalm.
Athenaeus Delphic Paean. **Billings** When Jesus Wept. **Brumel** Agnus Dei. **Dufay** Gloria.
Garbarek Loiterando. Strophe and Counter-Strophe. **Guillaume le Rouge** Se je fayz dueil.
Hildegard of Bingen O ignis Spiritus Paracliti. **Mesomedes** Hymn to the Sun. **Tallis** O Lord,
in Thee is all my trust. **Tormis** Estonian Lullaby. **Traditional** Mascarades. Quechua Song.
Remember me, my dear (all arr. Hilliard Ensemble).

'A sign we are, inexplicable without pain ... .' The words are by the nineteenth-century German poet Friedrich Hölderlin, taken from *Mnemosyne*, one of the cryptic hymns that he wrote before descending into madness. ECM publishes the entire first strophe as a sort of legend, and the reference is telling. 'Mnemosyne' was the mother of the muses, and the word also means 'memory'. For Hölderlin, song was an 'abandoned, flowing nature', a description that fits this album beautifully. Memory, ecstasy, pain, joy, reconciliation: all are, at one time or another, signalled in the present programme. Garbarek spices the English thirteenth-century *Alleluia nativitatis* that opens the second disc with some unexpectedly Eastern-sounding modulations. The *Delphic Paean* that follows dives headlong among some absorbing dissonances, whereas Garbarek's own *Strophe and Counter-Strophe* enjoys a more sophisticated harmonic climate. Add Basque folk-song fragments warmed by the breathy aural contours of Garbarek's saxophone, and you have a characteristic sampling of a sequence that lasts, in total, for one-and-three-quarter hours. Both discs feature twilit Estonian lullabies (placed third on disc 1, and sixth on disc 2). Dufay's *Gloria* (sung *sans* Garbarek) ends on a desolate, protracted Amen, with Fayrfax Africanus marking an exultant point of contrast. Brumel's *Agnus Dei* allows Garbarek to temporarily monopolize the main melody line, but perhaps the most striking collaboration of all is for Hildegard's *O ignis Spiritus* which reaches spine-tingling levels of ecstasy. The second CD includes a Russian Psalm where Garbarek adopts a resonant bass presence, an up-tempo Iroquois and Padleirmiut Eagle dance and, to close, works by William Billings and Mesomedes that complete the musical arch with something close to perfection. It is a difficult disc to categorize. Maybe we should view it as a collaborative original composition which balances ancient and modern, sacred and profane, body and soul.

Neapolitan Chamber Works
Il Giardino Armonico Ensemble / Giovanni Antonini *rec*
Teldec Das Alte Werk 4509-93157-2 (54 minutes: DDD). Recorded 1993.   Ⓕ Ⓟ
Sarri Concerto for Recorder, Two Violins, Viola and Continuo in A minor. **D. Scarlatti** Sonata for Mandolin and Continuo in D minor, Kk90. **Durante** Concerto for two Violins, Viola and Continuo in G minor. **A. Scarlatti** Sonata for Recorder, two Violins and Continuo in A minor. **Mancini** Sonata for Recorder, Two Violins and Continuo in D minor.

The idea of a selection of music that might have been heard in early eighteenth-century Naples is not a new one but, in the area of chamber music, it has not been more vividly brought to life than on this disc. Domenico Scarlatti's Sonata is one of several believed to have been intended for a solo instrument with continuo, and here the soloist is as clean and quick-fingered a mandolinist as you could find, even if you hired a private detective (he is also the violist!) – a beguiling performance indeed. The remaining items lack any other recording, and all are to be welcomed. Sarri was a prolific composer of vocal music and the Concerto was his only instrumental work, with the recorder singing 'arias' that would tax any diva. There is something in each of the others to surprise and delight, such as the subtly tear-shedding chromatics of the opening *Affetuoso* of Durante's Concerto and the *Piano* of Alessandro Scarlatti's Sonata, a recorder/violin duo. Every item is illuminated by sensitivity to expressive nuance and dynamics, and the recording is close to perfection.

Paris French Flute Sonatas.
Emmanuel Pahud *fl* **Eric Le Sage** *pf*
EMI CDC5 56488-2 (66 minutes: DDD). Recorded 1997.   Ⓕ Ⓢ
Dutilleux Sonatine. **Ibert** Jeux. Aria. **Jolivet** Chant de Linos. **Messiaen** Le merle noir.
Milhaud Sonatina for Flute and Piano, Op. 76. **Poulenc** Flute Sonata. **Sancan** Sonatine.

Examinations are usually viewed with aversion and some suspicion, but the Paris Conservatoire's custom of commissioning new works for its final examinations has valuably enriched the repertoire for wind instruments: three of the works on this disc – the *Sonatinas* (of 1943 and 1946 respectively) of the exact contemporaries Dutilleux and Sancan, and Messiaen's *Le merle noir* – owe their origin to these competitive exams. By their nature they lay stress on technical virtuosity, as indeed do nearly all the works here, which though differing widely in idiom share a certain Gallic style recognizable by its 'clarity, refinement and lightness of touch', as the insert-note puts it. These qualities are also characteristic of the playing of the Swiss-born Emmanuel Pahud, Principal Flute of the Berlin Philharmonic, who has a lighter tone than some of his distinguished predecessors. All the items here have been recorded before, however. Excellent partnered by Eric Le Sage, Pahud's brilliant and sensitive performances are outstanding. Exhilaratingly skittish in the brief *scherzando* finale of the Sancan and that of the Poulenc, intense in the Jolivet, mysteriously atmospheric in the first movement of the Dutilleux (a work undervalued by its composer), tender in the Ibert *Aria* and powerfully athletic at the end of the Messiaen, this is a winner of a disc.

Pastoral
Emma Johnson *cl* [b]**Judith Howarth** *sop* [a]**Malcolm Martineau** *pf*
ASV CDDCA891 (74 minutes: DDD).   Ⓕ
Ireland Fantasy-Sonata in E flat major[a]. **Vaughan Williams** Six Studies in English folk song[a]. Three Vocalises for Soprano Voice and Clarinet[b]. **Bax** Clarinet Sonata[a]. **Bliss** Pastoral (posth.)[a]. Two Nursery Rhymes[b]. **Stanford** Clarinet Sonata, Op. 129.

A lovely programme, radiantly performed and most judiciously chosen. Things get under way in fine style with John Ireland's marvellous *Fantasy-Sonata*: beautifully written, passionately argued and encompassing (for Ireland) a wide range of moods; it's certainly a work that shows this underrated figure at the height of his powers. The Clarinet Sonata by Ireland's teacher, Stanford, is one of that composer's most successful works: formally elegant and most idiomatically laid out, it boasts a central *Adagio* (entitled 'Caoine' – an Irish lament) of considerable eloquence. Johnson is a gloriously mellifluous exponent in both Vaughan Williams's *Six Studies* and the Bax Sonata, and in the first movement of the latter she manages to convey a slumbering mystery that is somehow almost orchestral in its imaginative scope. Judith Howarth joins Johnson for the haunting *Three Vocalises* (one of Vaughan Williams's very last utterances from his final year) and makes an equally agile showing in Bliss's delightful *Two Nursery Rhymes* and touching *Pastoral*. A real pleasure, then, from start to finish and Malcolm Martineau proffers superb accompaniments.

Perilous Night

Joanna MacGregor *pf* with [a]Lulu Bates, [b]Keith Turnbull *vocs* [c]Talvin Singh *tablas*
SoundCircus SC003 (two discs: 114 minutes: DDD). Recorded 1998.   Ⓕ
Cage Sonatas and Interludes. The Perilous Night. Bacchanale. **Bates** You Live and Learn[a].
Black Dead Sheep. **Fairclough** Inside Out. **Gribbin** The Broken Piece of the Moon. **Harvey** Homage to Cage, à Chopin (und Ligeti ist auch dabei). **O'Brien** Rasavan. **Pratt** Studies on Cage Nos. 1 and 2. **Singh/MacGregor** Endgame[c]. **Toovey** You May Not (Want) to (be) Hear/Here[b].
Wilson/Zoetrope ALF – The Vegan Gravy Mix.

Joanna MacGregor is aiming at her own audience that crosses categories in a way that bewilders record shops. To emphasize the fact, this two-CD set is in cardboard wrappers which open out, and the whole thing stands up like a slim book, although the title is not clear on the spine. The contents are built around Cage, even to the extent of commissioning new pieces for the same prepared piano as his *Sonatas and Interludes* with the option of added tape. MacGregor, who says she 'fell profoundly in love' with Cage's magic box, delivers a characteristically vivid performance of his first piece for the adapted instrument, the *Bacchanale* from 1940. This is rhythmically energetic and exciting, spooky in the middle. Her treatment of *The Perilous Night* is poetic and sensitive but the *Sonatas and Interludes* are disappointing. As interested readers will doubtless be aware, there is plenty of competition on CD for this Cage classic. MacGregor's rhythmic sense is weak, some rests get cut (as in the Fourth and Eighth Sonatas) and her piano preparations are sometimes less than scintillating. The new pieces make odd bedfellows – and some of them are forced into close proximity. Tracks 9 and 10 run on and so do tracks 12 and 13. The new piece by Jonathan Harvey is provocatively framed by two short fragments by Mary Black called *Dead Sheep*. The Harvey is a witty response to Chopin in a mad prepared-piano context and the best of the other pieces are the longer ones – Deirdre Gribbin's exploitation of Tibetan monks chanting, and Talvin Singh's tablas in *Endgame*. Notes are not provided for all pieces so you never know what's coming – but a must for MacGregor fans.

Portes Ouvertes The Twentieth-Century Cello, Volume 3.

Matt Haimovitz *vc* [a]Philippe Cassard *pf*
DG 457 584-2GH (64 minutes: DDD). Recorded 1996.   Ⓕ
Britten Cello Soanta, Op. 65[a]. Tema-Sacher. **Debussy** Cello Sonata in D minor[a].
Dutilleux Trois Strophes sur le nom de Sacher. **Reger** Suite in A minor, Op. 131c No. 3.
Webern Three Little Pieces, Op. 11[a].

This recital of twentieth-century cello compositions sustains the thesis that extreme contrast, not merely variety, has been the spice of twentieth-century musical life. To juxtapose two works from 1914, Reger's Third Suite and Webern's *Three Little Pieces*, the former expansive and retrospective, the latter aphoristic and reaching nervously into an unknowable future, makes the point with admirable immediacy. The rest of the music here is more mainstream, the Britten Sonata showing that there was as much mileage left in the old classical genres in 1960 as Debussy had found in his Sonata more than 40 years before. With these works, of course, Haimowitz is competing against a long series of distinguished predecessors on disc, and his partnership with Cassard can't match their empathy in the Britten, or – it goes without saying – of Rostropovich and Britten himself in both sonatas. The recording as such is at its best in the unaccompanied works, its closeness and resonance reinforcing the powerful musical profile of Dutilleux's elegant yet forceful *Strophes*, and helping to ensure that Reger does not seriously outstay his welcome. In Webern, Debussy and Britten the piano sound has an abrasive aspect to it, as if the object were to underline the incompatibility of two such different instruments. But the playing is technically first-rate, and should certainly open doors (why the French title?) to anyone exploring this repertory for the first time.

Henry Purcell and his Time

Scaramouche (Andrew Manze, Caroline Balding *vns* Jaap ter Linden *bass viol*
Ulrike Wild *hpd/org* [a]Foskien Kooistra *vn* [b]Konrad Junghänel *theorbo*
Channel Classics CCS4792 (60 minutes: DDD). Recorded 1992.   ⒻⓅ

Locke The Broken Consort – Suites Nos. 3[b] and 4. **W. Lawes** Fantasia-Suite No. 7 in D minor. **Jenkins** Fantasia in three parts. **C. Simpson** Prelude. Divisions on a Ground[b]. **Baltzar** Divisions on 'John Come Kiss me Now'[b]. **Purcell** Pavans – B flat major, Z750; G minor, Z752[a]. Fantasia upon a Ground, Z731[ab].

On this disc of English seventeenth-century chamber music, Scaramouche offers a homogeneous selection of music and instrumental combinations. (The disc advertises itself, by the way, as offering the music of 'Henry Purcell and His Time', a claim whose level of accuracy – Lawes, for one, died over a decade before Purcell was born – is eloquently symbolized by a portrait of an unmistakably Elizabethan lady on the front of the box!) Here the innocent charm of other selections of this nature is largely replaced by the weightier, more sober pronouncements of Lawes, Locke and Purcell, but also by a bold interpretative vigour which makes it just as lively a listen in its own way. Jaap ter Linden's rendition of his Simpson piece is suitably poetic, while Andrew Manze's version of *John Come Kiss me Now* has a Turkey-in-the-Straw ending that will make you chuckle. This may be a less polished and fluent recording than some others maybe, but in the end, moments like these – as well as the fact that there is lastingly rewarding music to be heard here – will make you want to play it again and again.

Recital
David Pyatt *hn* Martin Jones *pf*
Erato 3984-21632-2 (66 minutes: DDD). Recorded 1996. Ⓕ
Beethoven Horn Sonata in F major, Op. 17. **F. Strauss** Nocturno, Op. 7. **Koechlin** Horn Sonata, Op. 70. **Damase** Pavane variée. Berceuse, Op. 19. **Hindemith** Horn Sonata. **Abbott** Alla caccia. **Schumann** Adagio and Allegro in A flat major, Op. 70.

Beethoven's Horn Sonata – in its day successfully premièred by the famous Bohemian virtuoso and composer, Punto – is nevertheless written rather clumsily for the horn (the composer suggested the cello as a viable alternative) and even Dennis Brain had problems with it. David Pyatt – *Gramophone*'s Young Artist of the Year in 1996 – sails off into the work with aplomb and gives it one of the finest performances on or off record. He makes it seem to sit easily on the instrument and provides just the right kind of timbre and buoyant lyrical flow – indeed it sounds like a masterpiece, which it very nearly is. He is helped both by a first-rate partnership with Martin Jones and an excellently balanced recording, which does not let the horn overwhelm the piano. The second piece here is an attractive novelty by Franz Strauss, the father of Richard, and another famous player who advised Wagner on the format of Siegfried's horn call. Koechlin's Sonata, more fluent than Beethoven's, has a rather fine *Andante très tranquille*, and another Frenchman, Jean-Michel Damase, provides two short but memorable occasional pieces. The Hindemith Sonata is wayward: it never seems quite sure where it is progressing harmonically, but Pyatt and Jones are so naturally and spontaneously attuned to the work that it becomes readily assimilable. Allan Abbott's *Alla caccia* is an endearing lollipop while Schumann's *Adagio and Allegro* here emerges flowing almost as easily as if it had been written by Mozart – who knew just what a horn could manage without sounding effortful. Altogether this is a splendid recital, which will give much pleasure to any lover of this intractable but highly rewarding instrument.

Smetana Quartet
[b]Pavel Stěpán *pf*
Smetana Quartet (Jiří Novák, Lubomir Kostecký *vns* Milan Skampa *va* Antonín Kohout *vc*).
Testament SBT1074/5 (two discs, oas: 79 and 77 minutes: ADD). Recorded 1965-66. Ⓕ
SBT1074 **Dvořák** String Quartet No. 12 in F major, B179, 'American'[a]. Piano Quintet in A major, B155[b]. **Janáček** String Quartet No. 1, 'The Kreutzer Sonata'[d].
SBT1075 **Dvořák** Terzetto in C major, B148[c]. String Quartet No. 14 in A flat major, B193[c].
Janáček String Quartet No. 2, 'Intimate Letters'[d].

Listening to these discs tempts one to think that in the 1960s the Smetana was the Berlin Philharmonic of quartets – just as in the 1950s the Hollywoods might have been fancifully called the Philadelphia Orchestra of quartets. Much of the playing here is in a class of its own, only later equalled by the Borodin and Alban Berg Quartets in terms of finesse and ensemble. The Dvořák performances must be numbered among the very best now in the catalogue: their phrasing has none of the artificiality that marks some professional quartets (that is to say that a phrasing once rehearsed becomes, as it were, mechanically reproduced so that while the line rises and falls it doesn't genuinely breathe) and it is an enormous relief to hear genuine *pianissimo* tone and so natural and unforced an ensemble. There are numerous recordings of each of the Janáček Quartets but in terms of tonal finesse, perfection of ensemble and depth of feeling the present issues would be difficult to beat.

A St Petersburg Recital

Olivier Baumont *hpd* with **Myriam Gevers** *vn*
Erato 3984-21665-2 (53 minutes: DDD). Recorded 1996. Ⓟ Ⓟ
Anonymous Seven Variations on 'Katenka was known as the most beautiful girl in the village'.
Bortnyansky Sonatas – F major; B flat major. Concerto di Cembalo in D major.
Gurilyov Preludes – E flat minor; D major; C minor. **Karaülov** 10 Variations on 'You, Little
Orpheus'. **Kozlovsky** Polonaise on a Ukrainian Song. **Manfredini** Sonata in D minor.
Paisiello Preludio e Rondo in E flat majora. Sinfonia, 'Alcide al Bivio'.

Full marks to Olivier Baumont for enterprise! He has here sought out almost completely unknown
harpsichord pieces by Russian and Russia-based composers (the instrument continued to be
popular in Russia into the early nineteenth century) and recorded them on a Shudi/Broadwood of
1770, most appropriately, since it is known that Shudi shipped two of his harpsichords to Russia in
1772 and 1773. At the St Petersburg court, Italian influence was strong: Manfredini and, 20 years
later, Paisiello were both in the service of Catherine the Great; Bortnyansky, a pupil of Galuppi
(who had succeeded Manfredini there), had spent some time in Italy and adopted a purely Italian
style. Of the pieces by these three composers, Manfredini's three-movement Sonata has an
attractively vivacious central *Allegro*, and the single-movement binary sonatas by Bortnyansky
have impressive moments and are technically more showy, though containing rather too many
conventional bass figurations (broken octaves and Alberti basses). Of greater structural, if not
musical, interest is the latter's Concerto which (like Bach's infinitely greater *Italian Concerto*)
suggests an interplay of solo and tutti, which is realized here thanks to the Shudi machine stop.
Oddly to our ears, the violin in Paisiello's *Rondo* merely provides an accompaniment to the
dominating harpsichord: his opera sinfonia is to a work performed at the Hermitage a year
before his *Serva padrona* and two years before his *Barber of Seville*. As far as character is
concerned, however, all this music is put into the shade by the purely Russian pieces. Two of
the present preludes by Gurilyov (published in 1810) are striking, and the three larger works,
all based on native folk-songs, presuppose – particularly the variation sets – a high level of
virtuosity among Russian harpsichordists. This, of course, poses no problem for Baumont,
for whose spirited championship of this rare repertoire we should be most grateful. A
revelatory disc.

The String Quartet in Eighteenth-Century England

Salomon Quartet (Simon Standage, Micaela Comberti *vns* Trevor Jones *va*
Jennifer Ward-Clarke *vc*).
Hyperion CDA66780 (69 minutes: DDD). Recorded 1995. Ⓟ Ⓟ
Abel String Quartet in A major, Op. 8 No. 5. **Shield** String Quartet in C minor, Op. 3 No. 6.
Marsh Quartetto in B flat major in imitation of the Stile of Haydn's Opera Prima.
Webbe Variations in A major on 'Adeste Fideles'. **S. Wesley** String Quartet in E flat major.

For various reasons connected with the patterns of its social life, the string quartet was slow to
become established in England. The work that opens this CD, by the German-born Abel, comes
from the first set of quartets to be published in London (in 1769); it is an amiable piece, graceful
enough, harmonically rather static and texturally unenterprising. The few Englishmen who ventured
into the string quartet genre did rather better. William Shield's work, the sixth of a set published in
1782, begins with a passionate C minor gesture and has some echoes of Haydn both in the
ingenuity of its humour and in its seriousness, though not in his technique nor his sureness of taste;
but the *Adagio* is very remarkable, quite individual in the tone of its expression and reaching an
extraordinarily imaginative climax in each half with a sort of free-flying violin passage, in its way
breathtaking. The finale too is sombre in quite an original way. John Marsh (a lawyer and a
landowner, though music was his passion), wrote his quartet 'in imitation of the Stile of Haydn's
Opera Prima' in the 1780s: it is a very fluent, polished piece, close in manner to Haydn's Op. 1
No. 1, with a spirited 6/8 opening movement, two minuets (the second particularly delightful) with
an appealing *Largo* of charm and warmth, between them, and a witty finale with some lively
invention.

Samuel Webbe, too, used Haydn as his model – the slow movement of the *Emperor* Quartet – for
his variations on *Adeste Fideles*: it is a beautiful, highly ingenious piece, harmonically rich,
exquisitely crafted. But the most unexpected work here is certainly the Samuel Wesley Quartet,
usually supposed to date from the very beginning of the nineteenth century but surely more likely,
as Peter Holman says in his note, to be 20 years later – the energetic, leaping lines, the complex
figuration, the abrupt gestures, the free textures: all this speaks of a later, post-classical era. It is a
substantial and powerful piece, wholly individual in tone. The Salomon brings a good deal of fire to
this piece, and indeed, once past the Abel, it plays this music with splendid conviction, as it amply
merits. This CD is something of a revelation.

Trios for 4
Palladian Ensemble (Pamela Thorby *recs* Rachel Podger *vn* Susanne Heinrich *va da gamba*
William Carter *archlte/gtr*).
Linn Records CKD050 (63 minutes: DDD).   Ⓕ🅿
Handel Trio Sonatas, Op. 2 – No. 1 in B minor; No. 4 in F major. **Telemann** Trio Sonatas –
G minor, TWV42:g9; A minor, TWV42:a4. **Leclair** Ouverture in G major, Op. 13 No. 1.
Quantz Trio Sonata in C major.

The programme has been artfully chosen to demonstrate the diversity of styles current at more or
less the same period of time. The Handel sonatas, the earliest works here though not published until
1730, are fundamentally Italianate; Leclair, despite this overture in the French style, also displays
goûts réunis; Telemann, catholic in his tastes, is happy to include robust folk influences; and Quantz,
less contrapuntal and more *galant* than the others, looks ahead to pre-classical style. The present
performances exude a sense of enjoyment in the verve the artists bring to the second and last
movements of the Handel F major and the delicious lightness of the initial *Allegro* of the Quantz;
and in the Telemann A minor (from the *Essercizii musici*) Pamela Thorby and Rachel Podger
exhibit virtuoso tonguing and bowing (though the finale is too rushed). Equally attractive, however,
is the shaping of *affettuoso* movements, notably the *Grave* of the Telemann G minor. The *Largo* of
Handel's Op. 2 No. 1 can often sound lumbering, but the ensemble's adoption of the *Andante* speed
indicated in the C minor version is much more convincing and effective. The only reservations about
this disc – and they are very slight indeed – concern some of William Carter's contributions: his
accents in the finale of Telemann's G minor Trio are rather too rumbustious, and in the lively first
Allegro of Handel's Op. 2 No. 1 the archlute continuo is too dry.

Variaciones del Fandango español
Andreas Staier *hpd* with ᵃ**Christine Schornsheim** *hpd* ᵃ**Adela Gonzáles Cámpa** *castanets*
Teldec 3984-21468-2 (65 minutes: DDD). Recorded 1998.   Ⓕ
Albero Recercata, Fuga and Sonata – G major; D major. **Boccherini** Guitar Quintet in D major,
G341 – Fandango (arr. Staier/Schornsheim)ᵃ. **Ferrer** Adagio and Andantino in G minor. **Gallés**
Keyboard Sonatas – No. 9 in C minor; No. 16 in F minor; No. 17 in C minor. **López** Variaciones
del Fandango español. **Soler** Fandango.

The heyday of the fandango dance was in the eighteenth century (Mozart introduced a form of it in
Figaro, following Gluck's *Don Juan*). It was danced by a single couple who did not touch but whose
movements were highly erotic; and there were several local varieties of it, including the malagueña,
the granadina, the rondeña and the murciana. Andreas Staier does not, despite the disc's title,
confine himself to the fandango rhythm or to the key of D minor which was so prevalent for it. He
kicks off with stunning virtuosity with Soler's famous piece (if it really *was* by him), with its
exciting build-up and fearsome hand-crossings. After the initial *tiento* (which he pulls about with
violent changes of speed), he tears at a most un-fandango-like breakneck pace into the dance,
whirling breathlessly to the end and employing a free range of registrations on his German-type
instrument. He does not make the mistakes of spoiling the cumulative effect by rubatos and
changes of speed or tacking on a reprise which wrongly ends the work on the tonic instead of the
dominant. He adopts the same fast pace for the very similar but shorter variations on the fandango
by López (which he discovered), who was an organist in the royal chapel in Madrid under
Charles III and IV. It is a distinct relief to find a more authentic speed adopted in a free
arrangement for two harpsichords of a fandango from a Boccherini quintet, which is enlivened by
(obbligato) castanets. Albero's *recercatas* and gigantic fugues are every bit as astonishing in their
chromaticisms and eccentric key-shifts as Bach's *Chromatic Fantasia and Fugue* – in fact, more
outlandish. The *recercatas* resemble the older lute *préludes non-mésurés*; the lively sprawling fugues
(that in D minor a gigue) call forth brilliantly virtuosic playing and splendidly rhythmic stamina;
and each work closes with a binary sonata movement which contains Scarlattian chordal scrunches.
Of the other non-fandango works here, the most interesting is an F minor Sonata by Josep Gallés, a
Catalan whose other sonatas disclose a somewhat disorganized musical mind.

Virtuoso Music for Trumpet
Sergei Nakariakov *tpt* Alexander Markovich *pf*
Teldec 4509-94554-2 (59 minutes: DDD). Items marked ᵃ arr. Markovich, ᵇNakariakov, ᶜDokshitzer.
Recorded 1994.   Ⓕ
Waxman Carmen Fantasiaᵃ. **Arban** Variations on a theme from Bellini's 'Norma'ᵃ. Variations on a
Tyrolean Themeᵃ. **Falla** La vida breve – Danse espagnoleᵇ. **Saint-Saëns** Le carnaval des
animaux – The swanᵇ. **Paganini** Caprice in E flat major, Op. 1 No. 17ᵇ. Moto perpetuo in
C major, Op. 11ᵇ. **Tchaikovsky** Valse-scherzo in C major, Op. 34ᵇ. **Sarasate** Zigeunerweisen,
Op. 20ᶜ. **Fauré** Le réveilᵇ. **W. Brandt** Concert Piece No. 2.

Sergei Nakariakov is an extraordinary talent. It is one thing to be able to play the violin at the age of 17 with the technical aplomb of one's elders but a brass instrument – on a purely physical level – requires a strength and maturity which can be accelerated only so fast. His prowess as a trumpeter lies not only in the sphere of technical wizardry, which he has in super-abundance, but in a security of tone and interpretational vision: the subtle tuning in this selection of mainly-transcribed violin pieces and the gipsyish portamentos are astute and accomplished. The Russian-ness of his playing is fascinating; he has that intensity of tone that Westerners find so hard to emulate without sounding corny or chastened. Nakariakov has a focused but fat, epic sound (though no doubt it will get even more wholesome with age) and a total security and command in all registers. His technique is particularly admirable in the lower reaches where he seems rarely to need the air at his disposal to progress through phrases. Nakariakov's slow playing is fluid, especially in Fauré's *Le réveil*.

Virtuoso Works for Violin and Piano
Maxim Vengerov *vn* Itamar Golan *pf*
Teldec 9031-77351-2 (67 minutes: DDD). Recorded 1993.   Ⓕ
Wieniawski Polonaise No. 1 in D major, Op. 4. Légende, Op. 17. **Paganini** I palpiti, Op. 13.
Kreisler Schön Rosmarin. Tambourin chinois. Caprice viennois. **Bloch** Baal shem – Nigun.
Tchaikovsky Souvenir d'un lieu cher, Op. 42 – No. 2, Scherzo in C minor; No. 3, Mélodie in
E flat major. **Messiaen** Thème et Variations. **Sarasate** Caprice basque, Op. 24.
Bazzini La Ronde des lutins, Op. 25.

Maxim Vengerov is such a masterful musician that everything he touches turns to gold. Firstly, his intonation is impeccable. The purity and steadiness of Paganini's *I palpiti* is such that one never has the impression of his being under any strain. The double-stopping episodes in Wieniawski's *Légende* appear to come as naturally to him as single notes. He captures the mawkish Slavonic melancholy with real intensity. In the Kreisler selection Vengerov is gentle and generous-spirited, charmingly pure in *Schön Rosmarin* and idiomatic for the tongue-in-cheek *Tambourin chinois*. The Bazzini has terrific attack, too, though it might have been more impish. The piece is undeniably inconsequential, but one is left gawping at the phenomenal accuracy and confidence of the left-hand pizzicato section at the end. In conclusion it must be said that rarely if ever does one hear the Tchaikovsky *Mélodie* played with more eloquence or refined tone colour.

Instrumental

Martha Argerich Début Recital.
Martha Argerich *pf*
DG The Originals 447 430-2GOR (71 minutes: ADD). Recorded 1960-71.   Ⓜ 🆁🆁
Chopin Scherzo No. 3 in C sharp minor, Op. 39. Barcarolle in F sharp major, Op. 60.
Brahms Two Rhapsodies, Op. 79. **Prokofiev** Toccata in D minor, Op. 11. **Ravel** Jeux d'eau.
Liszt Hungarian Rhapsody No. 6 in D flat major. Piano Sonata in B minor, S178.

Here, on this richly filled CD, is a positive cornucopia of musical genius. Martha Argerich's 1961 disc remains among the most spectacular of all recorded débuts, an impression reinforced by an outsize addition and encore: her 1972 Liszt Sonata. True, there are occasional reminders of her pianism at its most fraught and capricious (Chopin's *Barcarolle*) as well as tiny scatterings of inaccuracies, yet her playing always blazes with a unique incandescence and character. The Brahms *Rhapsodies* are as glowingly interior as they are fleet. No more mercurial Chopin *Scherzo* exists on record and if its savagery becomes flighty and skittish (with the chorale's decorations sounding like manic bursts of laughter), Argerich's fine-toned fluency will make other, lesser pianists weep with envy. Ravel's *Jeux d'eau* is gloriously indolent and scintillating and the Prokofiev *Toccata* (a supreme example of his early iconoclasm) is spun off in a manner that understandably provoked Horowitz's awe and enthusiasm. Liszt's Sixth *Hungarian Rhapsody* is a marvel of wit and daring and the B minor Sonata is among the most dazzling ever perpetuated on disc. The recordings have worn remarkably well and the transfers have been expertly done.

The Composer-Pianists
Marc-André Hamelin *pf*
Hyperion CDA67050 (68 minutes: DDD). Recorded 1998.   Ⓕ 🅴
Godowsky Toccata in G flat major, Op. 13. **Scriabin** Poème tragique in B flat major, Op. 34.
Deux Poèmes, Op. 71. **Bach/Feinberg** Kommst du nun, Jesu, vom Himmel herunter BWV650.

Haydn/Alkan Symphony No. 94 in G major, 'Surprise' – Andante. **Alkan** Esquisses,
Op. 63 – No. 46, Le premier billet-doux; No. 47, Scherzetto. **Busoni** Fantasia after J. S. Bach.
Rachmaninov Moment musical in E flat minor, Op. 16 No. 2. Etude-tableau in E flat major,
Op. 33 No. 4. **Feinberg** Berceuse, Op. 19a. **Medtner** Improvisation in B flat minor, Op. 31
No. 1. **Sorabji** Pastiche on Hindu Song from Rimsky-Korsakov's 'Sadko'. **Hamelin**
Etudes – No. 9, 'd'après Rossini'; No. 10, 'd'après Chopin'; No. 12 (Prelude and Fugue).

Here is a cunning and potent mix of every conceivable form of pianistic and musical intricacy (it
excludes the merely decorative, salon or ephemeral). Everything is of the most absorbing interest;
everything is impeccably performed. Hamelin's richly inclusive programme ranges from Godowsky's
Toccata, music of the most wicked, labyrinthine complexity, to three of his own projected cycle of
12 *Etudes*, among them a ferociously witty and demanding Prelude and Fugue and a reworking of
Chopin's Op. 10 No. 5, full of black thoughts as well as black notes. Then there is Alkan's sinister
absorption of the *Andante* from Haydn's *Surprise* Symphony (loyal to Haydn, Alkan's teasing
perversity also makes such music peculiarly his own); a *Berceuse* by Samuel Feinberg that prompts
Francis Pott, in his brilliantly illuminating notes, to question what sort of child would be lulled by
such strangeness; some superb Medtner and Scriabin and a cloudy, profoundly expressive *Fantasia
after J. S. Bach* by Busoni. Clearly among the most remarkable pianists of our time, Hamelin makes
light of every technical and musical difficulty, easing his way through Godowsky's intricacy with
yards to spare, registering every sly modulation of Alkan's 'Le premier billet-doux' and generating a
white-hot intensity in Rachmaninov's admirably revised version of his Second *Moment musical*.
Here, Hamelin's maintenance of a 'line' set within a hectically whirling complexity is something to
marvel at. Taut, sinewy and impassioned, this performance is a worthy successor to Rachmaninov's
own legendary disc (see review under Rachmaninov). More generally, every phrase and note of
these performances is coolly appraised within its overall context and the results are audacious and
immaculate as required. Hyperion's sound is superb.

Danish Organ Works
Kevin Bowyer *org*
Nimbus NI5468 (70 minutes: DDD). Recorded on the Marcussen organ of Odense Cathedral,
Denmark in 1995.   Ⓕ
Gade Three Tone Pieces, Op. 22. **Syberg** Prelude, Intermezzo and Fugato.
Nørgård Partita concertante, Op. 23. **Nielsen** Commotio, FS155.

This disc contains four large and little-known works, although with the exception of *Prelude,
Intermezzo and Fugato* by Franz Syberg, all are currently represented in the catalogue. Gade's three
pleasant but unexceptional pieces are decidedly Mendelssohnian, Per Nørgård presents a work
crammed full of diverse stylistic allusions (including a remarkably Shostakovich-like slow
movement which Bowyer clearly relishes), while Nielsen's powerful *Commotio*, undeniably one of
the glories of twentieth-century organ music, rules itself out of most organists' portfolios by being
long and difficult. Bowyer's declared purpose in putting this programme together is to celebrate the
Danish town of Odense – only Gade had no direct connection with the place. Bowyer himself has
spent a considerable part of this decade there – winning the Odense international organ
competition in 1990 and subsequently making most of his recordings there. He hardly needs an
excuse for using the Marcussen in Odense Cathedral, however – it makes a simply lovely sound and
he is clearly very much at ease with it.

Divers styles dans l'Eloquence Pieces from the Bauyn Manuscript, Volume 2.
Jane Chapman *hpd*
Collins Classics 1421-2 (71 minutes: DDD). Recorded 1994.   Ⓕ℗
L. Couperin Suites – A minor; D minor; Prélude in C major. Pavanne in F sharp minor.
Froberger Toccatas in A minor and G major. Suite in A minor. Ricercare in C major.
Frescobaldi Capriccio in G major. Fantasia in E minor. **Anonymous** Four Pavannes.

Here are pieces by three of the undisputed keyboard masters of the early baroque. Louis Couperin
provides the main substance of the programme, in the shape of two large-scale suites, a lengthy
Pavanne in the unusual key of F sharp minor to open the disc, and a solemn *Prélude* to end. One of
the advantages, however, of this type of release over the single-composer (or, for that matter, single-
country) species is that new cross-connections can be illustrated, and it is fortunate the Bauyn
collection contains both a Couperin *Prélude* explicitly 'a l'imitation de Mr Froberger' and the
Froberger *Toccata* which was its model. Chapman includes both, and then takes the opportunity to
give us more of the German composer's attractive and influential music, including a three-
movement suite to go with the *Toccata*. Two pieces by Froberger's teacher Frescobaldi complete the
disc, along with four short *Pavannes* which are anonymous but by no means worthy of disownment.
Chapman's grasp of the French idiom is secure, her application of it once again eloquent and

attractive. If she is a shade more convincing in the dance movements than in the grander *Préludes* and *Toccatas*, then that could well be partly down to her instrument, a 1614 Ruckers from Dartington Hall which has its own beauties, for sure, but which doesn't quite have the resonance and sheer weighty presence of a French model. If that's the only drawback, though, it's not much of one; this is a thoroughly worthwhile and enjoyable release.

Carnegie Hall Highlights
Artur Rubinstein *pf*
RCA Gold Seal 09026 61445-2 (64 minutes: ADD). Recorded live in 1961.   Ⓜ
Debussy Préludes – La cathédrale engloutie; Ondine. Images – Hommage à Rameau;
Poissons d'or. **Szymanowski** Mazurkas, Op. 50 – Nos. 1-4. **Prokofiev** Vision fugitives,
Op. 22 – Nos. 1-3, 9-14 and 16. **Villa-Lobos** Próle do bébé, Book 1.
Schumann Arabeske in C major, Op. 18. **Albéniz** Navarra.

Artur Rubinstein had a unique flair for live musical communication and these concert performances have great spontaneity. In fact, the whole disc might have been billed as 'The Essential Rubinstein', thus providing one of the few occasions where the 'essential' epithet would have been fully justified. And it's certainly all here – the wistful reverie (*Arabeske*), the mastery of rhythm and exotic colours (Szymanowski *Mazurkas*, *Navarra*, *Próle do bébé*), acute sensitivity to miniature forms (*Visions fugitives*), unforced virtuosity employed to musical ends (*Próle*) and a natural inclination towards musical impressionism (Debussy). RCA is more active with its back catalogue than most of its rivals so we can only hope that more Rubinstein is waiting in the wings.

Alfred Cortot
Alfred Cortot *pf*
Biddulph mono LHW014/15 (two discs: 133 minutes: ADD). Recorded 1919-25.   Ⓜ Ⓗ
Piano works by Albéniz, Chopin, Debussy, Fauré, Liszt, Mendelssohn, Ravel, Saint-Saëns,
Scriabin and Weber.

Cortot was, arguably, the most vivacious of all keyboard sophisticates, one whose dazzling mind and fingers flashed with a happy disregard for mere accuracy or musical propriety. Like the heroine of Muriel Spark's novel, *The Prime of Miss Jean Brodie*, Cortot proclaimed that beauty and truth rather than safety always came first. With exemplary completeness Biddulph presents in this invaluable two-disc set Cortot's complete acoustic recordings, admirably transferred by Ward Marston. Cortot's inimitable wit and seduction grace Albéniz's *Triana* as well as *Seguidilla* and *Malagueña*, and two Fauré items offer further enchantment. Elsewhere there is a reminder in Cortot's death-defying spin through Saint-Saëns's *Etude en forme de valse* of a brilliance and rapidity that aroused the awe and envy of Horowitz and, in Scriabin's D sharp minor *Etude*, of a blazing rhetoric and insinuation that suggest total sympathy for the Russian romantic idiom. Alas, there are savage cuts in several pieces (Chopin's Op. 22 *Grande Polonaise*, minus its introductory *Andante Spianato*, is butchered virtually beyond recognition, the price of early recording techniques. This would also explain a pell-mell rush in several other works (try the 1923 Chopin *Berceuse*). Cortot preferred to take risks rather than modify his mood of the moment for the sake of mere expediency.

Alfred Cortot
Alfred Cortot *pf*
Biddulph mono LHW020 (77 minutes: ADD). Recorded 1925-39.   Ⓜ Ⓗ
Piano Works by Albéniz, Bach, Brahms, Chopin, Handel, Liszt, Purcell, Saint-Saëns and Schubert.

Biddulph has unearthed some astonishing gems. Cortot's whirl through Albéniz's *Malagueña* and joyous charge through the *Seguidillas* (a kind of Spanish *Chopsticks*) may be familiar, but what of *Sous la Palmier*? Here Cortot spins a tale beneath the palms that would seduce a saint. As the insert-note so nicely puts it, all these performances have 'an almost tangible Iberian heat', a lilt and insinuation that can make even the redoubtable Alicia de Larrocha sound sober and lacking in *joie de vivre*. Schubert's *12 Ländler*, D681, too, seem to dance off the page, and in the *Arioso* from Bach's F minor Concerto (the pianist's own arrangement) Cortot shows himself an incomparable 'singer' of the keyboard. Even his finest partners in artistry (and they include Dame Maggie Teyte and Gérard Souzay) must have marvelled at that exquisitely floating *pianissimo* and his alternately full and delicate *cantabile*. Then there is Cortot's Purcell selection, all within style but with that instantly recognizable rhythmic spring and vivacity, yet another recording of Saint-Saëns's *Etude en forme de valse* (which made Horowitz pale with envy) and Chopin performances as sprightly and elemental as any on record. The *Berceuse*'s figurations foam and race with a happy disregard for tranquillity yet the playing is as mesmeric as it is iridescent. And although the First *Ballade* and

Second *Impromptu* are periodically invaded by inaccuracies like swarms of locusts, nothing can detract from Cortot's innate elegance, fire and poetry. Ward Marston's transfers are exemplary, beautifully transcending age and crackles to capture performances which make most contemporary piano playing seem as insignificant as chaff in the wind.

Shura Cherkassky Piano Works.
Shura Cherkassky *pf*
ªPhilharmonia Orchestra / Anatole Fistoulari.
Testament mono SBT1033 (62 minutes: ADD). Recorded 1952-58.　　　　Ⓕ**H**
Liszt Piano Concerto No. 1 in E flat major, S124ª. Liebestraum in A flat major, S541 No. 3.
Réminiscences de Don Juan (Mozart), S418. Hungarian Rhapsody No. 13 in A minor, S244.
Faust (Gounod) – Waltz, S407. **Saint-Saëns** Le carnaval des animaux – Le cygne.
Liadov A musical snuffbox, Op. 32.

Here, in excellent transfers of HMV recordings dating from the 1950s, is a vintage Cherkassky recital. Mercurial and hypnotic, his way with Liszt's E flat Concerto reminds us in every nook and cranny that he has always been able to enliven and transform even the most over-familiar score. True, there are moments – such as the start of the *Allegro vivace* – where he is less than ideally poised or balletic (one of those instances where his elfin caprice can seem close to uncertainty and where he leads Fistoulari and the Philharmonia a Puckish dance: now you hear me, now you don't), yet his sparkle and charm are inimitable. Again, in Var. 1 of the *Don Juan* Fantasy he is perhaps more flustered than *elegantamente*, but even when his virtuosity is less than watertight, his playing is infinitely more fascinating and imaginatively varied. Cherkassky can be garrulous or somnolent, his phrasing languorous or choppy, yet in the ecstatic, long-breathed descent just before the coda of the *Liebestraum* No. 3 and in all of the *Hungarian Rhapsody* No. 13 and the *Faust* Waltz, his mastery has seldom sounded more effortless or unalloyed. Finally, two encores of *friandises*: Godowsky's fine-spun elaboration of Saint-Saëns's 'Le cygne'.

Fingerbreaker
Morten Gunnar Larsen *pf*
Decca 460 499-2DH (67 minutes: DDD). Recorded 1998.　　　　Ⓕ
Blake Brittwood Rag. Dictys on Seventh Avenue. **Joplin** The Cascades. The Entertainer.
Scott Joplin's New Rag. Solace. **Lamb** American Beauty Rag. The Ragtime Nightingale.
Sensation. **Jelly Roll Morton** Don't you leave me here. Fingerbreaker. Kansas City Stomp.
Scott Grace and Beauty. Kansas City Rag. The Ragtime Betty. **Smith** Echo of Spring.
Finger Buster. Rippling Waters.

Norwegian pianist Morten Gunnar Larsen's résumé as a specialist in ragtime and early jazz styles mirrors his considerable keyboard artistry in a recital that instructs as much as it delights. Larsen is able to point up the stylistic differences between the six composers here in purely pianistic terms. He revels as much in Jelly Roll Morton's blues roots and hard-edged chord voicings, for instance, as he does the New Orleans legend's brass-band tinged polyrhythms and eloquent melodic invention in *Kansas City Stomp* and *Don't you leave me here*. For all of the title cut's virtuosic ebullience, Larsen is not afraid to roughen up the sonority when needed, yet curiously misinterprets Morton's rhythmic intentions in the second chorus. The pianist is totally in sync, though, with Eubie Blake's extrovert, Tin Pan Alley-influenced brand of ragtime, and serves up the composer's trademark 'backward boogie woogie' effects with gusto. By contrast, Larsen's reserved decorum in the Joplin selections seems rather sober and prim. He sheds his inhibitions, though, in the James Scott and Joseph Lamb triumvirates, and imbues stride master Willie 'The Lion' Smith's decorative flourishes with a wistful, patrician quality: a convincing foil to the composer's own forthright playing style.

French Baroque Harpsichord Works
Sophie Yates *hpd*
Chandos Chaconne CHAN0545 (71 minutes: DDD). Recorded 1993　　　　Ⓕ**P**
D'Anglebert Pièces de Clavecin – Suite in G minor; Tombeau de M. de Chambonnières.
F. Couperin L'Art de toucher le clavecin – Prélude in D minor. Livre de clavecin, Deuxième ordre
– Seconde Courante; Sarabande, 'La Prude'; Les Idées heureuses; La Voluptueuse. **Forqueray**
La Rameau; La Boisson; La Sylva; Jupiter. **Rameau** L'enharmonique. L'Égyptienne. La Dauphine.

Sophie Yates has a real understanding of the French style – so difficult to capture, with its special conventions and elaborate ornamentation. Her phrasing is subtle as well as musical; and she proves herself capable of the flexibility proper to this music without risk to the underlying pulse or to continuity. Her reading of *La Dauphine*, Rameau's last harpsichord piece, is justifiably free and improvisatory, since it is thought to be a transcription of Rameau's extemporization at the wedding of the Dauphin in 1747. She savours Rameau's bold enharmonics, too, shows drive and energy in his *L'Egyptienne*, impressive dignity in Forqueray's tribute to his great contemporary and in a d'Anglebert sarabande, expressiveness in Forqueray's *La Sylva* and a sense of enjoyment in the trenchant drama of the flashing thunderbolts of his *Jupiter*. Yates also has the advantage of admirable recording of a particularly beautiful and rich-sounding instrument (a copy of a Goujon).

French Organ Works

Simon Lindley *org*

Naxos 8 550581 (74 minutes: DDD). Recorded on the organ of Leeds Parish Church in 1991.　Ⓢ
Guilmant Grand Choeur in D major, 'alla Handel'. Cantilene pastorale, Op. 19. **Vierne** 24 Pièces en stile libre, Op. 31 – Epitaphe; Berceuse. Stèle pour un enfant défunt. **M-A. Charpentier** Te Deum, H146 – Prelude. **Langlais** Trois méditations (1962). **Bonnet** Romance sans paroles. **de Maleingreau** Suite mariale. **Boëllmann** Suite gothique, Op. 25. **Widor** Symphony No. 5 in F minor, Op. 42 No. 1 – Toccata.

Two of the most popular organ showpieces are here – Widor's Toccata and the Toccata which comes as the last movement of Boëllmann's *Suite gothique*. In addition there is the majestic *Te Deum* Prelude by Charpentier (familiar to a wide audience as the Eurovision signature tune) and the gentle *Berceuse* which Vierne wrote for his baby daughter. Alongside these evergreens, mainstays of any organ-lover's CD collection, are some more unusual but no less enjoyable pieces: Guilmant's glorious *Grand Choeur 'alla Handel'*, Bonnet's delightful *Romance sans paroles* and Paul de Maleingreau's *Suite mariale*. In short, a real feast of some of the best French organ music. Simon Lindley, organist at the musically-renowned Leeds Parish Church, gives fine, no-nonsense performances which should appeal especially to those exploring this music for the first time. The organ makes a super noise, and the Naxos recording is highly commendable. It may not be an instrument of which the *cognoscenti* of French organ music would immediately approve, but there is enough sensitivity and interpretative insight in Lindley's performances to make this a worthwhile buy for casual listener and specialist alike.

From Stanley to Wesley, Volume 6.

Jennifer Bate *org*

Unicorn-Kanchana DKPCD9106 (65 minutes: DDD). Recorded 1989-90.
Recorded on the organs of Adlington Hall, Cheshire; The Dolmetsch Collection, Haslemere, Surrey; The Chapel of St Michael's Mount, Cornwall; The Iveagh Bequeast, Kenwood, London; Killerton House, Broadclyst, Exeter, Devon and The Chapel of Our Lady and St Everilda, Everingham, Yorkshire in 1989-91.　ⒻⓈ
Boyce Voluntary in D major. **Handel** Fugue in G major. Voluntary in C major.
Heron Voluntary in G major. **Hook** Voluntary in C minor. **Russell** Voluntary in F major.
Stanley Voluntaries – A minor, Op. 6 No. 2; D minor, Op. 7 No. 4; G major, Op. 7 No. 9.
Stubley Voluntary in C major. **S. Wesley** Voluntaries – E flat major, Op. 6 No. 7; B flat major.

Whilst most people would regard Bach and his North German contemporaries as synonymous with all that is best in eighteenth-century organ music there was also a significant school of organist-composers thriving in England. Chief amongst these was John Stanley whose music was greatly admired at the time, in particular by a recent immigrant from Germany, one George Frederic Handel (two fine examples of his own organ music are to be found on this CD). But while the German composers were writing for their great, majestic organs, their English counterparts were faced with something far humbler in scope and more delicate and intimate in character. To hear this music played on such an instrument is to have its true beauty revealed: here it is played not just on one authentic contemporaneous instrument, but the Unicorn-Kanchana team has scoured the length and breadth of England, from Cornwall to Yorkshire, to unearth six classic, and virtually unaltered examples. Jennifer Bate's immense musical and technical powers and her innate, native sense of style, imbues this disc with compelling musical authority which, added to the captivating sound of these six delightful organs, makes it an intriguing historical document – real 'living history', if you like. This CD is the sixth in a series and while each is a valuable addition to the recorded legacy of English music, this one in particular gives the less specialist collector a representative and varied selection of this wonderful, yet woefully overlooked area of our musical heritage.

Grand Piano – The Polish Virtuoso

[a]Josef Hofmann, [b]Ignaz Friedman, [c]Ignaz Jan Paderewski *pf*

Nimbus NI8802 (71 minutes: DDD). From piano rolls released between 1919 and 1932.　ⓂⒽ
Hofmann Impressions for Piano – No. 3, The Sanctuary[a]. Kaleidoscope, Op. 40 No. 4[a].
Moszkowski La jongleuse, Op. 52 No. 4[a]. Etincelles, Op. 36 No. 6[a]. Serenata, Op. 15 No. 1[b].

Guitarre, Op. 45 No. 2ª. Caprice espagnol, Op. 37ª. **Friedman** Viennese Waltzes on Themes from Gärtner – Nos. 1-4ᵇ. Estampes, Op. 22 – Nos. 2 and 4ᵇ. Elle danse, Op. 10 No. 5ᵇ. **Paderewski** Humoresques de concert, Op. 14ᶜ – No. 1, Minuet; No. 3, Caprice; No. 6, Cracovienne fantastique. Miscellanea, Op. 16ᶜ – No. 1, Légende in A flat major; No. 4, Nocturne in B flat major. Mélodie, Op. 8 No. 3ᶜ.

Josef Hofmann pf
Nimbus NI8803 (76 minutes: DDD). From piano rolls released between 1920 and 1927. Ⓜ Ⓗ
Chopin Piano Sonata No. 2 in B flat minor, Op. 35. Nocturnes – D flat major, Op. 27 No. 2; F minor, Op. 55 No. 1. Polonaises – A major, Op. 40 No. 1; A flat major, Op. 53. Scherzos – No. 1 in B minor, Op. 20; No. 3 in C sharp minor, Op. 39. Waltz in A flat major, Op. 42. Berceuse in D flat major, Op. 57.

These performances taken from Duo-Art rolls are played, via a 'robot' created in 1973, on a modern concert Steinway under the supervision of Gerald Stonehill, a world authority on the Duo-Art catalogue. As a result, they sound as vivid and sparkling as if they had been given yesterday – indeed, so vivid is the piano tone that it emphasizes brightness at the expense of warmth. To some extent this may be due to the difference in tone-quality between the instruments on which the recordings were made and that used for the reproduction, but sneaking doubts remain about the matching of the robot's responses, resulting in some lack of really soft passages.

Doubts about realism are lessened by a performance of Chopin's 'funeral march' Sonata by Hofmann (Cherkassky's teacher), revered by contemporaries such as Rachmaninov. Though the dynamic range in the piece is not large (the limitations being at the *ff* end), it sounds a convincingly natural reading. But better still are the A flat *Polonaise*, which boasts a fine crisp *élan*, the B minor *Scherzo*, which employs a very full dynamic range and, like the C sharp minor *Scherzo*, illustrates the real meaning of *Presto con fuoco*, and a delicately pearly A flat *Waltz*. The *Berceuse*, coolly played, slightly suffers from a weakness also found elsewhere in the series – too obtrusive a middle register in relation to the melody above, whether due to the voicing of the piano or to a miscalculation in the adjustment of Duo-Art's two dynamic systems ('accompaniment' and 'theme'). Hofmann is heard again, and at his stunning best, on the disc devoted to three Polish virtuosos. A group of five pieces by his teacher Moszkowski is notable for perfectly controlled *staccato* touch, vital rhythmicality, neat rapid repeated notes and some delectable lightness, while Hofmann's own *Kaleidoscope* shows his breath-taking mercurial virtuosity .

Ignaz Friedman is represented by Moszkowski's once popular *Serenata* and by a handful of his own pieces in which he can display the superb technique for which he was famous. There is undeniably an air of exhibitionism about *Elle danse* and the elaborate fantasias on waltz themes by a singer friend (No. 3 particularly lavishly ornate); but with such coruscating playing who would want to complain? Paderewski did not have the natural facility of the others – he was a late starter – but attracted huge and adoring crowds everywhere and was the most highly paid. There is a sparkle about his lively 'Caprice' in the style of Scarlatti and a quite attractive, if conventional, nationalist feeling in the 'Cracovienne fantastique'. The series is provided with first-class notes and Nimbus is to be applauded for its courageous enterprise.

Great European Organs, Volume 26.
Keith John org
Priory PRCD370 (73 minutes: DDD). Recorded on the organ of Gloucester Cathedral, UK in 1991. Ⓕ Ⓢ
Stanford Fantasia and Toccata in D minor, Op. 57. **Reger** Five Easy Preludes and Fugues, Op. 56 – No. 1 in E major. **Shostakovich** Lady Macbeth of the Mtsensk district – Passacaglia. **Schmidt** Chaconne in C sharp minor. **Ravanello** Theme and Variations in B minor.

On the face of it this CD might look as if its appeal is purely for those with a specialist taste in large-scale post-romantic organ music. Certainly Schmidt's gargantuan *Chaconne* represents a daunting prospect both to player and listener, while Shostakovich's only organ solo begins with the kind of chilling dissonance which would certainly scare off those of a delicate disposition. Similarly neither Stanford nor Reger usually attract a crowd when their organ music played – and who has ever heard of Ravanello? But if ever a recording was made to shatter preconceptions, this is it. For a start the Gloucester organ makes a wondrous sound and Priory's recording is in a class of its own; in terms of sound alone this surely ranks as one of the best ever CDs of organ music. Then Keith John quite literally pulls out all the stops to produce an unparalleled display of virtuosity and musicianship. His technical prowess turns the Schmidt into a thrilling *tour de force* while few could question, after hearing his performances, that the Stanford is one of the best works ever written by a British composer or that Ravanello's music doesn't deserve the neglect it currently suffers. An essential disc.

Great European Organs, Volume 48.
Gerard Brooks *org*
Priory PRCD558 (79 minutes: DDD). Recorded on the Cavaillé-Coll organ in the Abbey Church of
St Ouen, Rouen in 1995. Ⓕ
Commette Scherzo. **Guilmant** Marche funèbre et chant séraphique, Op. 17 No. 3.
Ibert Trois Pièces. **Philip** Toccata and Fugue in A minor. **Dallier** Cinq Invocations.

Here we have a magnificent recording of one of the truly Great European Organs. In Gerard
Brooks, Priory has found a player as eager to reveal the glories and subtleties of one of Cavaillé-
Coll's greatest creations as his own impressive virtuosity. Widor's description of this as a
'Michelangelo of an organ' seems singularly apt in the light of a disc which displays the instrument
so vividly.

A simple reading of the track list might imply that such opulent resources are being squandered on
a collection of oddities drawn from the ample dark recesses of French organ literature. If Guilmant
is the only familiar name (so far as organists are concerned Ibert is an obscure figure – although on
the strength of his *Trois Pièces* alone he could stand as a significant figure in early twentieth-
century French music), the music of the others is as familiar as a new Andrew Lloyd Webber score
– we're sure we've heard it all before but can't quite remember where. Edouard Commette's *Scherzo*
is clearly first cousin to Henri Mulet's famous *Carillon sortie*, Achille Philip's *Toccata* comes from
the same stable as that from Boëllman's *Suite gothique*, while Henri Dallier's *Invocations* inspired by
Latin Marian texts could easily pass for Vierne, especially the glittering final Toccata. But if the
idioms are familiar and the ideas derivative, the musical quality in both intellectual and emotional
terms is undeniable. Simply put, this is a programme of immensely enjoyable music, all of which
bears repeated listening and certainly deserves a place both in the catalogues and on the shelves of
lovers of good organ music.

Great European Organs, Volume 51.
Peter King *org*
Priory PRCD618 (78 minutes: DDD). Recorded on the Klais organ of Bath Abbey in 1997. Ⓕ
Bach Pastorale in F major, BWV590. **G. Böhm** Vater unser im Himmelreich, WK ii 138.
Buxtehude Prelude, Fugue and Chaconne in C major, BuxWV137. **Eben** Homage to Dietrich
Buxtehude. **Guridi** Triptico del Buen Pastor. **Liszt** (trans. Schaab) Orpheus, S98.
Saint-Saëns Fantaisie in D flat major, Op. 101.

This seems rather a peculiar programme with a focus on Buxtehude and the North German
baroque and with a few other disparate pieces thrown in to spice up the menu. Peculiar or not, it
works superbly. The new Bath Abbey instrument is adorable – a complete rejection of the argument
often propounded that, on purely musical terms, an organ built outside the British Isles is
inappropriate for a major English ecclesiastical building – and it makes everything here sound
convincing and impressive. This sumptuous instrument is well served by a beautifully proportioned
recording. For those interested in the music rather than the instrument, Peter King's performances
range from the solid (Buxtehude's *Praeludium* in G minor) to the near-inspired (Bach's *Pastorale*).
Eben's *Homage* is based on material from the two Buxtehude pieces on the disc and uses
Buxtehudian structures and figurations in a typically astute Eben manner. The inclusion of the
Liszt and Saint-Saëns is obviously inspired by King's deep fondness for these pieces – it shows in
every bar of these lovingly nurtured performances – while the Guridi has moments which allow us
to hear the organ's more atmospheric qualities. Not everybody will be immediately attracted to this
disc by the music, but for the sheer pleasure of hearing a truly wonderful, modern instrument, this
release cannot be recommended too highly.

Le Groupe des Six
Marcelo Bratke *pf*
Olympia Explorer OCD487 (62 minutes: DDD). Recorded 1996. Ⓜ
Auric Adieu New York. **Durey** Trois Préludes à la mémoire de Juliette Méérowitch, Op. 26.
Honegger Sept Pièces brèves. **Milhaud** Printemps – Volume 1, Op. 25; Volume 2, Op. 66.
Poulenc Trois Mouvements perpétuels. Trois Pièces. **Tailleferre** Romance.
Les Six Album des Six.

With his clean-cut technique, tonal sensitivity and verve, Marcelo Bratke confirms the very
favourable impression created by his previous discs in this present focus on composers in France
around 1920, the immediate post-First-World-War period of the Bright Young Things. Yet,
contrary to the popular image, few of these pieces by Les Six are nose-thumbingly facetious: the
only real exception, clearly intended to shock the *bourgeois*, is the much too long and rather bad

foxtrot with 'wrong-note' harmonies by Auric, the youngest of the six. The oldest was the now almost completely forgotten Durey; the highly charged first, at least, of his sombre tributes to a friend, and his contribution to a 1920 album, suggest an original mind. Of the three composers born in 1892, the most traditionally diatonic music comes from Tailleferre, with an entirely Fauré-esque *Romance*; Milhaud is represented by a predominantly calm set of pastorals, polytonal in idiom but, except for the first, not altogether free from a charge of note-spinning; and the most interesting is Honegger, who besides a thoughtfully dreamy 'Sarabande' in the collective album contributes seven varied, tersely packed miniatures that experiment in polytonality and atonality. Born in 1899 were Auric and his senior by five weeks, Poulenc, who of course became much the most popular. His familiar *Mouvements perpétuels* are, however, trivia as compared with the *Trois Pièces*, the Scriabinesque harmonies and exotic arabesques of whose 'Pastorale' hint at mysterious depths, and whose improvisatory 'Hymne' furnished several ideas for the later *Concert champêtre*; the brittle final 'Toccata', with its rapid-fire note-repetitions, provides a scintillating vehicle for Bratke's brilliance of articulation. The recording quality matches his excellence.

Guitar Recital
Jason Vieaux *gtr*
Naxos 8 553449 (64 minutes: DDD). Recorded 1995. ⓢ
Barrios Waltzes, Op. 8 – Nos. 3 and 4. Julia Florida – Barcarola. **Bustamente** (arr. Morel)
Misionera. **Pujol** Preludios – Nos. 2, 3 and 5. **Krouse** Variations on a Moldavian Hora.
Merlin Suite del recuerdo. Morel Chôro. Danza Brasileira. Danza in E minor. **Orbón**
Preludio y Danza.

This is the début recording by an artist of great talent. His technical prowess is impressive to say the least, as near flawless as one may get, and his tone is as clear and expressive as his musical thinking. There are now many finger-perfect guitarists on tap but those of Vieaux's natural musicality are rare indeed; everything in the moulding of the phrases comes from within – you just can't *programme* sensitivity of this kind. The main thrust of the music is Latin-American, a nice juxtaposition of the well known (Morel, Barrios, Pujol and Bustamente) with some unfamiliar but substantial (of their kind) pieces by Merlin and Orbón. The apparent 'misfit' is the work by Krouse, far removed from Latin America, but why should music of this quality be excluded, for whatever reason? It is included for the best of reasons, because the performer loves it and is right to do so. The theme is Moldavian and the language of the imaginative and technically punishing variations convincingly matches it. Vieaux plays everything with chameleon-like felicity of style and feeling. Superb recording and excellent notes complete an issue of the greatest distinction.

Myra Hess 1938-42 HMV Recordings.
Dame Myra Hess *pf*
Biddulph mono LHW025 (76 minutes: ADD). Recorded 1938-42. Ⓜ Ⓗ
Schumann Carnaval, Op. 9. **Matthay** Elves, Op. 17. Stray Fancies, Op. 22. **Bach** (arr. Hess)
Cantata No. 147, Herz und Mund und Tat und Leben – Jesu, bleibet meine Freude ('Jesu, joy of man's desiring'). **D. Scarlatti** Keyboard Sonata in G major, Kk14. **Brahms** Piano Pieces, Op. 76
– No. 2, Capriccio in B minor; No. 3, Intermezzo in A flat major. Capriccio in D minor, Op. 116
No. 7. Intermezzo in E flat major, Op. 117 No. 1. Intermezzo in C major, Op. 119 No. 3.
Ferguson Piano Sonata in F minor, Op. 8.

Those who, sadly, retain an image of Dame Myra Hess as either a sober-suited pianist inclined towards severity or a 'graciousness' that excluded the toughest, most durable virtues, are in for a surprise. For here, on this truly glorious record, she ranges effortlessly from sheer wit and style (Schumann's *Carnaval*) to a dancing rhythmic magic (Scarlatti), from a glowing poetic inwardness (all the Brahms, with perhaps Op. 76 No. 3 as the distantly shining star of the set) to a matchless eloquence (Howard Ferguson's tragic masterpiece, his 1938-40 Piano Sonata). Yet all such qualities are seamlessly joined. Nothing is forced and whether you consider her regal tonal resource (tirelessly celebrated by Stephen Kovacevich, her finest pupil), or a naturalness and candour easy to underestimate, everything is achieved with supreme authority; an illusion achieved by only the truest artists. What an object-lesson, then, for today's harassed young pianists, jostling for attention in an increasingly commercial market-place, a reminder of a poetic and speculative artistry beyond price. Finally, David Lennick's transfers are masterly and Wayne Kiley's notes refer movingly to the legendary wartime National Gallery concerts held in London, where Hess's performances created an 'indelible image of hope and vision in adversity'.

Vladimir Horowitz The solo European recordings, 1930-36, Volumes 1 and 2.
Vladimir Horowitz *pf*
APR mono APR5516/7 (two discs, oas: 69 and 71 minutes: ADD). Ⓜ Ⓗ

APR5516: Chopin Etudes – C sharp minor, Op. 10 No. 4; G flat major, 'Black Keys', Op. 10 No. 5; F major, Op. 10 No. 8; F major, Op. 25 No. 3 (recorded 1934). Mazurkas – F minor, Op. 7 No. 3; E minor, Op. 41 No. 2; C sharp minor, Op. 50 No. 3. Scherzo No. 4 in E major, Op. 54. Piano Sonata No. 2 in B flat minor, 'Funeral March', Op. 35 – Grave ... doppio movimento (rec. 1936). **Liszt** Funérailles, S173 No. 7. Piano Sonata in B minor, S178.
APR5517: D. Scarlatti Keyboard Sonatas – B minor, Kk87; G, Kk125. **Haydn** Keyboard Sonata in E flat major, HobXVI/52. **Beethoven** 32 Variations on an Original Theme in C minor, WoO80. **Bach/Busoni** Nun freut euch, lieben Christen gmein, BWV734. **Schumann** Presto passionato in G minor (rec. 1932). Arabeske in C major, Op. 18. Traumes Wirren, Op. 12 No. 7. Toccata in C major, Op. 7. **Debussy** Etude No. 11 'Pour les arpèges composés'. **Poulenc** Pastourelle. Toccata. **Rimsky-Korsakov/Rachmaninov** The tale of Tsar Saltan – Flight of the bumble-bee. **Stravinsky** Petrushka – Russian dance (rec. 1932). **Rachmaninov** Prelude in G minor, Op. 23 No. 5. **Prokofiev** Toccata in D minor, Op. 11 (rec. 1930).

Horowitz's 1930-36 European recordings are beyond price and so it is more than gratifying to have them permanently enshrined on APR rather than fleetingly available elsewhere. This is notably true of Horowitz's legendary, forever spine-tingling 1932 recording of the Liszt Sonata. Here, once more, is that uniquely teasing and heroic sorcery with octaves and passagework that blaze and skitter with a manic force and projection; an open defiance of all known musical and pianistic convention. Horowitz's virtuosity, particularly in his early days, remains a phenomenon, and hearing, for example, the *vivamente* elaboration of the principal theme or the octave uproar preceding the glassy, retrospective coda is to be reminded of qualities above and beyond the explicable. His way with the Chopin *Mazurkas* unites their outer dance elements and interior poetry with a mercurial brilliance and idiosyncrasy and who but Horowitz could use his transcendental pianism to conjure a *commedia dell'arte* vision of such wit and caprice in Debussy's *Etude, Pour les arpèges composés*? Schumann's *Traumes Wirren* is spun off with a delicacy and dancing magic and in the same composer's *Presto passionato* Horowitz's performance hints at the schizophrenic violence and darkness that finally engulfed Schumann. Of the previously unpublished recordings, the first movement from Chopin's Second Sonata is as macabre and tricky as ever, with a steady, oddly menacing tempo. Prokofiev's *Toccata*, on the other hand, is tossed off at a nail-biting speed and not even a small but irritating cut, a wild, approximate flailing at the end and an added chord by way of compensation, can qualify the impact of such wizardry. In Rachmaninov's G minor Prelude, however, Horowitz's volatility gets the better of him. If Horowitz, in common with virtually every other pianist, was not equally convincing in every composer and was even 'a master of distortion' for some, he was a Merlin figure of an indelible, necromantic brio for all others. Bryan Crimp explains the origin of the recordings at admirable length and if they, though expertly transferred, show their age, nothing can lessen the impact of Horowitz's early charisma.

Vladimir Horowitz Piano works.
Vladimir Horowitz pf
RCA Gold Seal mono/ᵃstereo GD60377 (65 minutes: ADD).   Ⓜ Ⓗ
Prokofiev Piano Sonata No. 7 in B flat major, Op. 83 (recorded 1945). Toccata, Op. 11.
Poulenc Presto in B flat major (both rec. 1947).
Barber Piano Sonata in E flat major, Op. 26 (rec. 1950). **Kabalevsky** Piano Sonata No. 3, Op. 46 (rec. 1947). **Fauré** Nocturne No. 13 in B minor, Op. 119ᵃ (rec. 1977).

Even today, when there is a six-deep queue of virtuosos who, laid end to end, would stretch halfway round the world, Vladimir Horowitz's playing is something to make the listener gasp and sit up. He has been called, with justification, 'the greatest pianist alive or dead'. Horowitz was associated with all three of the sonatas on this disc from their very beginnings. Prokofiev wrote his Seventh Sonata in 1942, and Horowitz gave the first American performance less than two years later. He sent a copy of this 1945 recording to the composer, and Prokofiev sent him an autographed copy of the score in return, inscribed 'to the miraculous pianist from the composer'. The performance is indeed superlative, with playing of extraordinary virtuosity, and Horowitz responds with equal flair to the sonata's 'barbaric' and lyrical elements. Kabalevsky's Third Sonata dates from 1946, and Horowitz gave the American première in February 1948, two months after he made this recording. The work is of lesser stature than the Prokofiev, but its three well-contrasted movements make up an effective enough sonata. Again, Horowitz plays brilliantly and very sympathetically throughout the work. The world première of Barber's Piano Sonata was given by Horowitz in 1949. This piece is brilliantly written and technically extremely demanding to play – a perfect vehicle, in fact, for Horowitz the virtuoso. The great pianist brings great flair to the shorter Poulenc and Prokofiev items: the Fauré was recorded at a later stage of his career, and is played in a more deliberate, though perfectly idiomatic fashion. Four of the items have been transferred from 78s in good sound. The Barber and Fauré come from tape sources and sound well – the latter is even in stereo. This is a disc all pianists and piano enthusiasts should have – and it's mid-price too!

Vladimir Horowitz The Last Recording.
Vladimir Horowitz *pf*
Sony Classical SK45818 (58 minutes: DDD). Recorded 1989.   Ⓕ
Haydn Piano Sonata in E flat major, HobXVI/49. **Chopin** Mazurka in C minor, Op. 56 No. 3.
Nocturnes – E flat major, Op. 55 No. 2; B major, Op. 62 No. 1. Fantaisie-impromptu in
C sharp minor, Op. 66. Etudes – A flat major, Op. 25 No. 1; E minor, Op. 25 No. 5. **Liszt** 'Weinen,
Klagen, Sorgen, Zagen', Präludium, S179. **Wagner/Liszt** Paraphrase on Isolde's Liebestod from
'Tristan und Isolde', S447.

More than any other pianist of his generation, Vladimir Horowitz was a legend in his lifetime, not
only for his staggering technique but also for the personality and authority of his playing. Other
pianists such as Rubinstein and Arrau may have been finer all-rounders (there were gaps in his
repertory even in the classical and romantic field), but none has left so many performances
distinguished by a special individuality that is covered, though hardly explained, by the word magic.
As Murray Perahia has written, from the point of view of a pianist over 40 years his junior, 'he was
a man who gave himself completely through his music and who confided his deepest emotions
through his playing'. The performances in this last of his recordings, made in New York in 1989
and with superlative piano sound, are wonderfully crystalline and beautifully articulated, yet there
is warmth, too, in the Haydn sonata that begins his programme and nothing whatever to suggest
that octogenarian fingers were feeling their age or that his fine ear had lost its judgement. The rest
of the disc is devoted to Chopin and Liszt, two great romantic composers with whom he was always
associated, the last piece being Liszt's mighty transcription of Wagner's *Liebestod*, in which the
piano becomes a whole operatic orchestra topped by a soprano voice singing out her love for the
last time. Apparently this was the last music Horowitz ever played, and no more suitable ending can
be imagined for a great pianistic career informed by a consuming love of music that was expressed
in playing of genius. A uniquely valuable record.

The Hungarian Anthology
Peter Frankl *pf*
ASV CDDCA860 (78 minutes: DDD). Recorded 1992.   Ⓕ
Liszt Csárdás macabre, S224. **Dohnányi** Gavotte and Musette. **Kodály** Seven Pieces, Op. 11.
Bartók (trans. cpsr.) Dance Suite, Sz77. **Weiner** Three Hungarian Rural Dances. **Kurtág** Plays
and Games for Piano, Book 3 – excerpts. **Szöllösy** Paesaggio con morti.

An important reminder, this, of how and where Hungarian piano music is progressing. The last
piece of Peter Frankl's programme dates from 1988; the *Paesaggio con morti* by András Szöllösy, an
impressive, 11-minute study in musical shades and textures. Working back from there, and tracing
the general direction of Szöllösy's route, is a relatively simple task. Oddly, Kodály more than Bartók
seems – in this case, at least – the overriding influence: his *Seven Pieces*, Op. 11 have never sounded
more engaging than here, and the largest of them, 'Epitaphe', is surely among the composer's most
dramatic inspirations. With György Kurtág's *Plays and Games for Piano*, credits revert back to
Bartók. Leó Weiner's spicy *Hungarian Rural Dances* include a 'Ronde de Marosszek'; but here
again, it's more Bartók than Kodály who springs to mind. Bartók's own *Dance Suite* is, of course, a
pivotal creation in its use of Eastern European and Arabic modes, and the way they are so expertly
welded on to the work's overall structure. And then to Dohnányi and Liszt, although the former's
pleasant *Gavotte and Musette* seems more a side-long glance at Smetana than an extension of the
bold, bald and audacious world of Liszt's menacing *Czárdás macabre*. Here we can locate the seeds
of Bartók's mature style, sown not merely among the realms of local folklore (although this
disturbing *Csárdás* is profoundly Hungarian in spirit), but deep within the furthest recesses of our
collective musical unconscious. Performances and recording are sympathetic.

Evgeni Kissin in Tokyo
Evgeni Kissin *pf*
Sony Classical SK45931 (73 minutes: DDD). Recorded live in 1987.   Ⓕ
Rachmaninov Lilacs, Op. 21 No. 5. Etudes tableaux, Op. 39 – No. 1 in C minor; No. 5 in
E flat minor. **Prokofiev** Piano Sonata No. 6 in A major, Op. 82. **Liszt** Concert Studies, S144 –
La leggierezza; Waldesrauschen. **Chopin** Nocturne in A flat major, Op. 32 No. 2. Polonaise in
F sharp minor, Op. 44. **Scriabin** Mazurka in E minor, Op. 25 No. 3. Etude in C sharp minor,
Op. 42 No. 5. **Anonymous** (arr. Saegusa) Natu – Wa Kinu. Todai – Mori. Usagi.

One reason for buying this CD is that it contains dazzling piano playing by a 15-year-old Russian
set fair for a career of the highest distinction. A better reason is that the recital contains as full a
revelation of the genius of Prokofiev as any recording ever made in any medium. The Sixth Sonata
is the first of a trilogy which sums up the appalling sufferings of Russia under Stalin in a way only

otherwise found in Shostakovich's 'middle' symphonies. Kissin plays it with all the colour and force of a full orchestra and all the drama and structural integrity of a symphony, plus a kind of daredevilry that even he may find difficult to recapture. As for the rest of the recital only the Rachmaninov pieces are as memorable as the Prokofiev, though everything else is immensely impressive (the Japanese encore-pieces are trivial in the extreme, however). Microphone placing is very close, presumably in order to minimize audience noise; but the playing can take it, indeed it may even be said to benefit from it.

Fritz Kreisler The Complete Victor Recordings.
Fritz Kreisler vn with various artists.
RCA Gold Seal mono 09026 61649-2 (11 discs: 781 minutes: ADD).
Recorded 1910-46. Ⓜ Ⓗ
Works by Albéniz, Bach, Balogh, Bass, Beethoven, Berlin, Bizet, Boccherini, Braga, Brahms, Böhm, Cadman, Chaminade, Chopin, Cottenet, De Curtis, Dawes, Debussy, Dohnányi, Drdla, Dvořák, Earl, Falla, Foster, Friedberg, Friml, Gärtner, Gluck, Godard, Godowsky, Gounod, Grainger, Granados, Grieg, Handel, Haydn, Herbert, Heuberger, Hirsch, Hubbell, Jacobi, Johnson, Korngold, Koschat, Koželuch, Krakauer, Kramer, Kreisler, Lalo, Lehár, Lemare, Leroux, Liliuokalani, Logan, Mascagni, Massenet, Mendelssohn, Meyer-Helmund, Moszkowski, Nevin, Offenbach, Openshaw, Owen, Paderewski, Paganini, Poldini, Rachmaninov, Raff, Rameau, Ravel, Rimsky-Korsakov, Romberg, Schubert, Schütt, Scott, Seitz, Smetana, Spencer, Tchaikovsky, Thomas, Tosti, Townsend, Valdez, White and Winternitz.

If Jascha Heifetz was the firebrand among virtuosos, Bronislaw Huberman the passionate intellectual and Joseph Szigeti the articulate thinker, Fritz Kreisler was the ultimate gentleman – an easygoing, genial and comforting old-world master whose large discography centres mainly on the many sweetmeats associated with his name. This neatly packaged and beautifully transferred collection of 'The Complete Victor Recordings' is in many respects the ultimate tribute: over 200 tracks covering the period 1910-46 and tracing a subtle stylistic curve from the vibrant and quick-wristed performances of the teens to the wistful, elegant and slightly off-colour 1946 recording of Kreisler's Straussian *Viennese Rhapsodic Fantasietta*. However, readers unable to stomach acoustic 78s are duly warned that primitive technology dominates the first six CDs, whereas the rest is made up of generally well-engineered electrical recordings. Still, such was Kreisler's sure projection and richness of tone that, like certain great singers of the period (McCormack being a fair case in point), he triumphed over inadequacies of sound. High points of his early discography include revealing 'one off' recordings of the 'Canzonetta' from Tchaikovsky's Violin Concerto and the *Scherzando* from Lalo's *Symphonie espagnole* (both 'first commercial releases'), Kreisler's own arrangement of Chopin's A minor *Mazurka*, Op. 67 No. 4, a truncated Bach Double Concerto with Efrem Zimbalist and the various items with John McCormack.

Kreisler's electrical RCA recordings are dominated, at least in terms of repertoire, by the oft-reissued sonata performances with Rachmaninov, all of them combining violinistic poise with taut, muscular pianism. As to the rest, there are countless gems and a plethora of duplications: six of the *Thaïs* 'Méditation', five each of *Caprice viennois*, *Liebesleid* and *Liebesfreud*, four of Dvořák's *Humoresque*, etc. – so many subtle varieties of a single basic conception, whether in terms of colour, rubato or phrasing. Some contrasts are fairly marked; one can think in particular of *Mighty Lak' a Rose*, where the electrical recording with pianist Carl Lamson is so much more stylish than Kreisler's acoustical duet with Geraldine Farrar. Then there are the previously unissued 1929 sessions with Lamson and poignant, reflective performances. 'The King of Violinists' (as he was sometimes known) was an undisputed master of musical aperitifs and desserts: taken in moderation, these recordings will give boundless pleasure.

Dinu Lipatti The Last Recital.
Dinu Lipatti pf
EMI Références mono CDH5 65166-2 (73 minutes: ADD). Recorded live in 1950. Ⓜ Ⓗ
Bach Partita in B flat major, BWV825[a]. **Mozart** Piano Sonata No. 8 in A minor, K310/K300d[a].
Schubert Impromptus, D899[a] – No. 2 in E flat major; No. 3 in G flat major.
Chopin Waltzes[b] – Nos. 1 and 3-14.

Apart from the two Schubert *Impromptus*, the programme of Lipatti's last recital consisted of works he had recorded only some ten weeks earlier for EMI, in a Geneva studio, while enjoying a miraculous cortisone-wrought new lease of life. However, when honouring this Besançon Festival engagement on September 16th, 1950, very much against the advice of his doctors, leukaemia had once more gained the upper hand. Less than three months later he was dead, aged only 33. As those of us who have long cherished the original LPs already know, the only evidence of weakness was the omission of the last of the concluding Chopin *Waltzes* (in his own favoured sequence, that in

A flat major, Op. 34 No. 2). For the rest, the recital stands as 'one of the great musical and human statements, a testimony to his [Lipatti's] transcendental powers, an almost frightening assertion of mind over matter' as the sympathetic introductory note puts it in the insert-booklet. One has to marvel at the clarity of articulation and part-playing in the Bach Partita, at once so attentive to craftsmanly cunning yet so arrestingly unpedagogic and alive. For Mozart he finds a wonderfully translucent sound world, rich in subtleties of colouring – not least in the slow movement's laden song. And as in the two Schubert *Impromptus*, the musical message is all the more affecting for its totally selfless simplicity and purity of expression. Even if just one or two of the *Waltzes* might be thought too fast, with over-swift internal tempo changes for contrasting episodes, his gossamer lightness of touch and mercurial imaginative fancy explain why his way with them has now acquired legendary status. The only small regret is that this most excellently remastered medium-price CD deprives us of the endearingly spontaneous extended arpeggio with which Lipatti prefaced the opening Partita, as if in greeting to his instrument, and likewise the improvisatory modulation with which he carried his Besançon listeners from Bach's B flat major to Mozart's A minor.

Mandelion Twentieth Century Organ Works.
Kevin Bowyer *org*
Nimbus NI5580/1 (two discs: 138 minutes: DDD). Recorded on the Marcussen organ, Tonbridge School Chapel, Kent in 1998. Ⓕ
Burrell Arched Forms with Bells. **Ferneyhough** Sieben Sterne. **Gowers** Toccata and Fugue.
Graham Three Pieces. **Iliff** Trio. **Mellers** Opus Alchymicum. **Pärt** Pari intervalli.
Ridout The Seven Last Words. **Tavener** Mandelion.

This is an extraordinary collection, another tribute to Bowyer's prodigious exploratory fervour. It is surprising to find how much such a diverse group of composers has in common in the period following Messiaen's stupendous innovations which redefined the personality of the organ. This is emphasized by the use of a single instrument throughout. But the religious shadow of Messiaen also falls on Tavener in *Mandelion*, an eloquent 1981 piece which has given the title to the whole collection. *Mandelion* is a meditation on icons and the various images of the face of Christ. Not Roman Catholic, of course, but by no means Tavener's spiritual minimalism of more recent times and there is a blazing triadic climax at 16'10" and C major to end with. Nothing like that in the magisterially confident *Seven Stars* which Ferneyhough wrote in 1970. There are passages where the player has to improvise in the style set and no registration is specified. Bowyer takes it all in his capacious stride, as he does the half-hour *Opus Alchymicum* by Mellers where he had a special role in the work's final form. It seems overextended but the final 'Illuminatio' makes a superb toccata on its own. An even older work is probably the best part of the weaker second CD – *The Seven Last Words* by Alan Ridout (1934-96). Written for Alan Wicks in 1967, this is a vivid evocation of the chosen scenario, pertinent and concentrated, where every section has audible coherence. There's a striking elegy for two-part pedal solo. Of the remaining pieces Diana Burrell's *Arched Form with Bells* is genuinely inventive in both textures and continuity and there really are church bells at the end; Pärt's 1976 memorial tribute is placidly minimal; and Patrick Gowers's *Toccata and Fugue*, already available on CD twice without its fugue (Priory and OxRecs), dwarfs its much later partner. There's plenty to explore in this imaginative anthology.

Nocturnal
Julian Bream *gtr*
EMI CDC7 54901-2 (73 minutes: DDD). Recorded 1992. Ⓕ
Martin Quatre Pièces Brèves. **Britten** Nocturnal after John Dowland, Op. 70. **Brouwer** Guitar Sonata. **Takemitsu** All in Twilight. **Lutosławski** (trans. cpsr): 12 Folk Melodies.

No one can truly reach into the depths of Britten's *Nocturnal* until Life has taught them some hard lessons, nor, perhaps, can they perceive the *Innigkeit* of Martin's work. The veteran, Julian Bream, with his technical armoury totally at the service of his emotions, demonstrates the truth of this in performances of moving intensity. Age has not dimmed his enthusiasm for pastures new: Brouwer's strong, and in places wryly humorous, Sonata with its teasing references to the composers to whom its three movements pay tribute, and Takemitsu's introspective *All in Twilight*, were written at his behest and are communicated with wonderful clarity. What the insert-notes aptly describe as the 'simple charm' of Bream's arrangements of Polish folk-melody settings by Lutosławski brings the recital to a lighter conclusion. Bream has rarely played (or been recorded) better than here.

Organ Fireworks, Volume 6.
Christopher Herrick *org*
Hyperion CDA66778 (76 minutes: DDD). Recorded on the Norman and Beard organ in the Town Hall, Wellington, New Zealand in 1995. Ⓕ

Hollins A Trumpet Minuet. **Elgar** Organ Sonata No. 1 in G major, Op. 28. **Cocker** Tuba tune.
Sumsion Introduction and Theme. **Spicer** Kiwi Fireworks – Variations on 'God defend New
Zealand'. **C.S. Lang** Tuba tune. **Lemare** Concertstück in the form of a Polonaise, Op. 80.
Wagner (trans. Lemare, arr. Westbrook and Herrick) Die Meistersinger von Nürnberg – Prelude,
Act 1.

This series turned into something of a world tour for Christopher Herrick and the 'Organ
Fireworks' team, and here they travel to New Zealand. They have come up with one genuine piece
of 'home-grown' music (although C.S. Lang left New Zealand for England almost before he could
tell a nappy from a nazard) and a connection with Edwin Lemare; he played this organ three
months after its completion in 1906. However, the starting-point for this programme is the tradition
of civic organ concerts which was exported from the town halls of Edwardian England to such far-
flung corners of the British Empire as Singapore, South Africa and, of course, New Zealand. The
Wellington Town Hall organ is typical of a large turn-of-the-century English symphonic organ and
while it might seem a little extravagant to go half-way round the world to find one, it is, following
its 1985-86 restoration, rare in being substantially unaltered and in excellent working condition.
Full organ is gloriously meaty, the flue tone beautifully blended and the solo reeds a joy to behold –
a silvery Tromba perfect for Hollins's elegant Minuet; a gusty Tuba ideal for both Cocker and Lang.
As ever Herrick's performances have both musical integrity and great communicative flair: his is a
matchless performance of the Elgar Sonata, in which the composer's strangely awkward use of the
organ, in places treating it almost orchestrally, is immaculately managed.

Organ Fireworks, Volume 7.
Christopher Herrick org
Hyperion CDA66917 (70 minutes: DDD). Recorded on the Klais organ of the Hallgrímskirkja,
Reykjavík in 1996.   Ⓕ
Johnson Trumpet Tune in F major. **Guilmant** Deuxième Offertoire sur des Noëls, Op. 33.
Litaize Variations sur un Noël angevin. **Bonnet** In Memoriam – Titanic, Op. 10 No. 1.
Karg-Elert Improvisation, Op. 81, 'Nearer my God to Thee'. **Reubke** Sonata on the 94th Psalm
in C minor. **Lefébure-Wély** Noël varié. **Pachelbel** Prelude, 'Vom Himmel hoch'. **Edmundson**
Toccata, 'Vom Himmel hoch'.

Iceland: Land of Volcanoes. What an appropriate place for Christopher Herrick to set off this
batch of fireworks. But in keeping with the awesome, almost vengeful spectacle of an Icelandic
volcano in full spate these are not all the cheerful, colourful sparklers of a British Guy Fawkes
Night. Central to the disc is a stunning performance of Julius Reubke's massive Sonata on the 94th
Psalm ('O God, to whom vengeance belongeth'). It must be said straight away that this
performance surpasses any version yet to appear on CD. Herrick throws himself into the work with
almost manic intensity, culminating in a breathtakingly virtuosic account of the fugue. Equally
spectacular is this magnificent Klais; its *chamade* reeds punching into the air with primeval ferocity,
its dark, full-throated chorus reeds seeping over the music like molten lava. And all this captured in
a recording of exceptional clarity and presence. Maintaining the tradition of choosing music to
match the recording's geographical location, Herrick has come up with two pieces (by Bonnet and
Karg-Elert) linked in some respect to the sinking of the *Titanic*. (Of course, it actually sank off
Greenland but, in the scale of things, Iceland isn't *that* far away!) The rest of the programme (with
the exception of a harmless *Trumpet Tune* by David Johnson) has a Christmassy flavour; reflecting,
one supposes, the preponderance of snow in Iceland. There are splendid *Noëls* by Guilmant,
Lefébure-Wély and Litaize, and the disc ends with a sizzling account of Edmundson's *Toccata* on
the chorale *Vom Himmel hoch*. The recording is magnificent.

Philips Great Pianists of the 20th Century

Martha Argerich pf
Philips Great Pianists of the 20th Century 456 700-2PM2 (two discs: 158 minutes: ADD).
Released in association with Steinway & Sons.   Ⓜ
Bach Partita No. 2 in C minor, BWV826. **Liszt** Piano Concerto No. 1 in E flat major, S124 (with
London Symphony Orchestra / Claudio Abbado). **Prokofiev** Piano Concerto No. 3 in C major,
Op. 26 (**Berlin Philharmonic Orchestra / Abbado**). **Rachmaninov** Piano Concerto No. 3 in
D minor, Op. 30 (**Berlin Radio Symphony Orchestra / Riccardo Chailly**). **Ravel** Piano Concerto
in G major (**Berlin Philharmonic Orchestra / Abbado**). Sonatine. Gaspard de la nuit.

Martha Argerich's concerto work, including that represented here, has always been dazzling; but the
piano is an intimate instrument, and full artistic assessment demands sustained, intimate listening.
The only solo repertoire here are just two pieces by Ravel (a luminescent and classical reading of
the *Sonatine* and her mighty *Gaspard de la nuit*) and a Bach Partita. Her overpowering live
Rachmaninov Concerto No. 3 of 1982, recorded with Chailly, remains a peculiarly heart-wrenching

performance, filled with the pianist's mercurial way with tempos, redolent with a tragedy made all the more poignant by her eerie and almost resigned sense of composure. It is exhilarating, yet profoundly sad, with the aura of a valedictory reading which, thankfully, it is not. The sparks with Chailly are extraordinary. Equally thrilling is the Prokofiev Third, with Abbado, a favourite partner and one well represented in this collection. Her Bach Partita in C minor is a funny little afterthought in such weighty and dramatic company. The playing is delightfully unstudied, fluid, natural and, somehow, very un-Argerich. The piece becomes a kind of strange pendant to the rest of the material, but an enticing reminder of the deeply vulnerable, mesmerizingly self-reflective player that Argerich was when she had nothing between her and the audience but a piano. It is achingly exposed music-making, so much so that it becomes almost hard to keep listening. It awakens the old craving to hear her again on the empty stage.

Claudio Arrau *pf*
Philips Great Pianists of the 20th Century 456 706-2PM2 (two discs: 157 minutes: ADD). Released in association with Steinway & Sons.
Albéniz Iberia, Book 1. **Bach** Chromatic Fantasia and Fugue in D minor, BWV903. **Balakirev** Islamey. **Brahms** Variations on a Theme by Paganini, Op. 35. Piano Concerto No. 1 in D minor, Op. 15 (**Concertgebouw Orchestra / Bernard Haitink**). **Liszt** Rhapsodie espagnole, S254. Harmonies poétiques et réligieuses, S173 – No. 3, Bénédiction de Dieu dans la solitude. Années de pèlerinage – Troisième année, S163 – Les jeux d'eau à la Villa d'Este. Etudes d'exécution transcendante, S139 – Chasse-neige.

It will come as a big surprise to many admirers of Claudio Arrau, a thoughtful philosopher of the keyboard, to hear the first item on this issue. You could hardly imagine a more dazzling virtuoso display in Balakirev's spectacular showpiece, *Islamey*. It was recorded for Polydor in the late 1920s, when Arrau was in his mid-twenties, and the panache is irresistible. Not only are the brilliant outer sections breathtaking in the clarity of the scampering triplets, with the heaviest textures made clear – helped by a full-toned transfer – the tonal resonance and the velvety warmth of *legato* in the sensuous melodic writing of the central section are equally distinctive. That item alone is enough to make this a compelling issue, and the other items on the first of the two discs amplify that spectacular start, presenting Arrau in his earlier years as a dazzling virtuoso, evidently uninhibited in the recording studio. That is so, whether in the Bach *Chromatic Fantasia* (aptly improvisatory in tone and again with textures crystal-clear); in Liszt (the *Rhapsodie espagnole* given astonishing lightness and clarity in this 1936 performance) and Albéniz (with the mystery and keen originality of the piano-writing heightened).

Both the Bach and the Albéniz date from the mid-1940s, and one imagines the Philips compilers may have wondered how to cap all these free and intense studio performances. Overall, the present set does tend to confirm the impression that over the years Arrau grew increasingly self-conscious in the recording studio, not exactly inhibited but less able to indulge in flights of spontaneous imagination, as he had done earlier. The three Liszt performances which complete the programme on the first disc, recorded between 1969 and 1976, are among the finest he made for Philips, with the cello-like resonances of *Bénédiction* reminding one of Arrau's playing in the central section of *Islamey* and the shimmering at the start of 'Chasse-neige', the twelfth *Transcendental Study*, made magical in an impressionistic way. There is much to enjoy too in Arrau's 1974 reading of Brahms's *Paganini* Variations, when the relatively broad speeds never sound slack or lack tension. Rather the Brahmsian textures are clarified, and rhythms pointed the more persuasively, particularly in the flights of fantasy in the Second Book. In the performance of the 1969 version of the First Brahms Concerto with Haitink and the Concertgebouw, the first two movements are rather heavy-going, not helped by an expressive style which tends towards rallentandos in what are already broad basic speeds. The finale is sharper, clean and unrushed, strong and dramatic, yet it is a pity that in the single representation of Arrau in this wide-ranging series, this second of the two discs is devoted completely to Brahms, instead of developing the imaginative pattern of the first.

Emil Gilels *pf*
ᵇ**New Philharmonia Orchestra / Lorin Maazel.**
Philips Great Pianists of the 20th Century 456 796-2PM2 (two discs: 159 minutes: ADD). Released in association with Steinway & Sons. Recorded 1935-77.
Bach (arr. Siloti) Prelude in E minor, BWV855. **Liszt** Fantasia on two themes from Mozart's 'Le nozze di Figaro', S697 (arr. Busoni). Hungarian Rhapsody in E flat major, S244 No. 9, 'Carnival in Pest'. Rhapsodie espagnole, S254. Valse oubliée in F sharp major, S215 No. 1. **Medtner** Forgotten Melodies, Op. 38 – No. 1, Sonata reminiscenza. **Prokofiev** Piano Sonatas – No. 3 in A minor, Op. 28; No. 8 in B flat major, Op. 84. Visions fugitives, Op. 22 – No. 1, Largamente; No. 3, Allegretto; No. 5, Molto giocoso; No. 7, Pittoresco; No. 8, Commodo; No. 10, Ridicolosamente; No. 11, Con vivacità; No. 17, Poetico. The Love for Three Oranges, Op. 33a –

March (arr. *pf*). **Stravinsky** (arr. and expanded Gilels) Three Movements from 'Petrushka'.
Tchaikovsky (rev. Siloti) Piano Concerto No. 2 in G major, Op. 44.

'Indispensable ... definitive': one hesitates anxiously over what should be taboo words in this business. Yet the cooler substitutes – 'highly desirable ... exemplary' – scarcely do justice to playing of this order. Ideally finished it certainly isn't. The *Petrushka* Movements sound as technically challenging as they are, and the climax to 'The Shrovetide Fair' is frankly messy. Strain also surfaces in the acrobatic codas to the outer movements of Prokofiev's Eighth Sonata, and it's a similar story in the Liszt *Rhapsodies*, where cartloads of wrong notes accompany the concluding perorations. And yet, what fabulous colours and idiomatic textures Gilels conjures in 'Petrushka's Cell', and what daring rewrites in 'The Shrovetide Fair', with beefed-up opening flourishes, an unscheduled guest appearance by the Peasant with the Bear, and an effective if alarming short-cut thence to the last page. Then what hypnotic floating he conveys in the first movement of the Prokofiev, what soul-baring intensity and will power in the toccata-like accumulations, what hypnotically subdued timing and what a compelling sense of spiritual loneliness in the lyrical plateaux. And what orchestral richness he offers, what exhilarating abandon, in the Liszt pieces.

Add to all that Medtner's *Sonata reminiscenza*, whose moments of searing passion set in relief by overall restraint bring you closer to the heart of this composer than any other performance. Add eight of Prokofiev's *Visions fugitives* and his Third Sonata, all coloured and paced to the manner born, plus a fantastic whirl through Liszt's first *Valse oubliée*. Then consider that the greatest performance of all is that of the Tchaikovsky Second Concerto: ennobled, made structurally coherent, and accompanied with an irresistible mixture of fire and elegance. In short, if you want two discs to illustrate the finest of Gilels's playing and a peak of the entire Russian piano tradition, you can confidently turn to these. Newcomers or sceptics should perhaps be warned that this is not a recital for the faint-hearted, nor indeed for anyone allergic to the percussive side of the instrument. The *Rhapsodie espagnole* is arguably more armour-plated than majestic, and in the 'March' from *The Love for Three Oranges* Gilels seems determined to push the piano through the floor. The quality of some of the earlier recordings is at times a little muffled or a little acidic. In compensation we have 159 minutes of simply spellbinding piano playing.

Julius Katchen *pf*
Philips Great Pianists of the 20th Century 456 856-2PM2 (two discs: 157 minutes: ADD).
Released in association with Steinway & Sons. Recorded 1949-62.   Ⓜ
Balakirev Islamey. **Brahms** Piano Sonata No. 3 in F minor, Op. 5. Variations on an original theme in D, Op. 21 No. 1. Hungarian Dances. **Chopin** Ballade No. 3 in A flat major, Op. 47. Fantasie in F minor, Op. 49. **Franck** Prélude, choral et fugue. **Liszt** Hungarian Rhapsody No. 12 in C sharp minor, S244. **Mendelssohn** Prelude and Fugue in E minor/E, Op. 35. Introduction and rondo capriccioso, Op. 14. **Rorem** Piano Sonata No. 2.

The booklet-essay claims that Katchen's 1949 Brahms F minor Sonata was the first ever piano LP. You are likely to be totally bowled over by it now. The slow movement's combination of beguiling sound, airborne phrasing and symphonic paragraphing are a revelation, as are the waves of passion which engulf the finale. In fact Katchen plays each of the five movements as to the manner born, calling to mind Schumann's eulogy: 'We heard the most genial playing, which made an orchestra out of the piano. There were sonatas, more like disguised symphonies ...'. You begin to wonder if this colossal performance will spoil the rest of the programme. It all has immense character, but apart from the Brahms at the end nothing quite reaches the same heights. Katchen certainly makes a good case for Ned Rorem's Sonata, a pastiche-Gallic affair which in less temperamental and skilful hands would almost certainly sound merely insipid. The Mendelssohn *Prelude and Fugue* eventually tips over into Wagnerian hyperbole, while the *Introduction and rondo capriccioso* is treated enjoyably as a pretext for flash-fingered display, as is, more justifiably, the Liszt *Rhapsody*.

Not many pianists would dare to deliver *Islamey* with such delirious abandon, and the central section is fabulously atmospheric. Whether the last few pages come off depends on personal tolerance levels, however; at these tempos they're inevitably something of a smash and grab affair. The Franck *Prélude* is unfolded patiently and with marvellously natural rhetorical presence and the two Chopin pieces have the feeling of one-off, showstopping encores designed to bring the house down, rather than considered interpretations for repeated listening. In these instances the recording quality must be partly to blame, because the Brahms Variations sound immediately warmer and less concerned with effect. They are all the better for Katchen's letting the climaxes grow organically rather than screaming them out. And the *Hungarian Dances* are pure joy: Brahms without the beard, with a spring in his step and a twinkle in his eye. Katchen played music on his own terms rather than the composer's. He was a big enough artist to get away with that most of the time, and when the temperamental affinity was particularly strong, as with early Brahms, the results were well-nigh incomparable.

Wilhelm Kempff *pf*
Philips Great Pianists of the 20th Century mono 456 862-2PM2 (two discs: 153 minutes: ADD).
Released in association with Steinway & Sons. Recorded 1950-56. Ⓜ Ⓗ
Brahms Ballades, Op. 10. Piano Pieces – Op. 76; Op. 116-19. **Schumann** Arabeske in C major,
Op. 18. Kreisleriana, Op. 16.

Many of Kempff's recordings, made in stereo, have been regularly reissued, but the mono
recordings of Brahms and Schumann, like so many from that mono LP era, have been seriously
neglected. Yet in many ways these were the high points of Kempff's work in the recording studio.
They are masterly, notable for their utmost concentration and sense of spontaneity, the magnetic,
improvisatory quality in the playing. The transfers are superb, full and firm, bringing out the
resonance and warmth of Kempff's piano sound, often giving the illusion of full stereo. Indeed,
comparing this recording of the four *Ballades*, Op. 10 with the stereo one which Kempff made later
in 1972 for DG (available on a nine-disc set), the Decca mono sound is preferable, and the
interpretations here are more keenly concentrated, with a greater sense of repose at speeds generally
a shade broader. The beauty of Kempff's playing, his ability to produce a singing *legato*, while
using the pedal lightly, plainly stems from Kempff's early training as an organist. So it is that even
the densest passages in the Brahms pieces, involving much octave doubling, have a rare
transparency, with the melodic line always brought out, as in the middle section of the *Capriccio*,
Op. 116 No. 3.

The seven *Fantasies* of Op. 116 mark a high point in their range of expression and the way that
Kempff builds them as a sequence, three *Capriccios* and four *Intermezzo*s. With his incisive
articulation Kempff is as strong and positive as anyone, while finding extra clarity, and using the
subtlest dynamic shading. And though his style is flexible in an improvisatory way, it is fascinating
to find that he is much less inclined than other pianists to use agogic hesitations, preferring not to
disturb his seamless melodic lines. The Schumann performances have similar qualities, with the
Arabeske flowing easily, totally charming. *Kreisleriana* dates from a little later, 1956, again songful
and flowing, with the fifth section sparkling and full of fantasy and the sixth, *Sehr langsam*, as rapt
as you will ever hear it.

Sviatoslav Richter *pf*
Philips Great Pianists of the 20th Century 456 946-2PM2 (two discs: 149 minutes: ADD).
Released in association with Steinway & Sons. Recorded live in 1958. Ⓜ Ⓗ
Chopin Etude in E major, Op. 10 No. 3. **Liszt** Valses oubliées, S215 – No. 1; No. 2. Etudes
d'exécution transcendante, S139 – No. 5, Feux follets; No. 11, Harmonies du soir. **Mussorgsky**
Pictures at an Exhibition. **Rachmaninov** Prelude in G sharp minor, Op. 32 No. 12. **Prokofiev**
Piano Sonatas – No. 6 in A major, Op. 82; No. 7 in B flat major, Op. 83; No. 8 in B flat, Op. 84.
Schubert Moment musical No. 1 in C major, D780. Impromptus, D899 – No. 2 in E flat major;
No. 4 in A flat major.

Even at the height of his powers Richter could be an erratic player, but on this occasion the force
was with him from first note until last. Not only did the recital help to spread the Richter 'legend'
in the months leading up to his much-hyped London and New York débuts in 1960, his Mussorgsky
Pictures made a decisive contribution to the rehabilitation of that piece as a staple of the piano
repertoire. Here is virtuosity entirely at the service of the music, defying anyone to say a word
against Mussorgsky's pianistic imagination or to want to hear Ravel's orchestral make-over ever
again. The rest of the recital displays Richter's view of the romantic repertoire at its first mature
flowering, after a period of occasionally experimental overstatement and before its (also only
occasional) rigidification. His Schubert, Chopin and Liszt share a common core of determined
resistance to buffeting emotions. Yet on the surface his Schubert is as beautiful and refined as
anyone's (no controversial tempos either); the possibly disconcerting intensity of his Chopin is built
strictly around the composer's expression markings; and as all collectors of recorded piano music
already know, his Liszt *Feux follets* remains a benchmark performance to this day. It is impossible
to say for sure if the Prokofiev sonatas presented here are the absolute best available, though one
suspects they are. He was in at the birth, or nearly so, of all three pieces, and his identification with
their expressive worlds is complete. Defiance and unstoppable momentum are at the heart of the
matter, and virtuosity of the highest order is pressed into the service of those core values. It is
doubtful whether anyone has taken the *Scherzo* of the Sixth Sonata more convincingly at this
tempo (the fast end of *allegretto*), for instance, or found more wide-ranging yet integrated drama
in all three movements of the Eighth. You could certainly wish for more refined recording quality
on the first disc, though the Prokofiev sonatas are well enough recorded, especially the Eighth.
Overall it's difficult to imagine a truer encapsulation of the Richter phenomenon. If by any chance
you have missed these recordings in past incarnations you now have an opportunity not to be
passed up.

Piano Recital
Aleksandar Serdar pf
EMI Debut CDZ5 72821-2 (74 minutes: DDD). Recorded 1997. Ⓑ
Bach Partita in D minor, BWV1004 – Chaconne. **Brahms** Waltzes, Op. 39. **Chopin** Andante spianato and Grande Polonaise in E flat major, Op. 22. **Galuppi** Piano Sonata No. 5 in C major. **Mendelssohn** Variations serieuses in D minor, Op. 54.

This disc from EMI's Debut series presents a richly varied recital with playing of consistently high quality. It has been superbly recorded in the Abbey Road studios, giving this Belgrade-born pianist every opportunity to show his talent to best effect. Serdar gives a diverse and hugely enjoyable programme; he is clearly a thoughtful musician with imagination and personality. His Galuppi Sonata No. 5 (which used to be a favourite of Michelangeli's) is exquisitely moulded, balancing tonal refinement with wonderful freshness and spirit. The same qualities of beauty and elegance abound in Chopin's *Andante spianato and Grande Polonaise*: there are many more crisp and muscular performances of the *Polonaise* on record, but few so concerned with colour, nuance and melodic shape. Maybe this piece should set the pulse racing a little more, but it is good to hear it treated so lovingly, rather than rushed off its feet merely to prove a pianist's virtuoso credentials. Less convincing is Serdar's Mendelssohn: while his sharp reflexes in the *Variations serieuses* are impressive, it needs more warmth of tone and, towards the end, a more heroic sweep and greater expressive intensity. The Brahms *Waltzes* begin belligerently, but he goes on to delight and tease with his range of expressive resource. Busoni's pianistic amplification of Bach's great D minor *Chaconne* – a much maligned, but still much performed, transcription – sits slightly uncomfortably at the end of the recital (the shift of expressive weight following the Brahms *Waltzes* jolts at first). Serdar's individual imagination is still in evidence, but some passages lack poise and grandeur.

Piano Transcriptions
Arcadi Volodos pf
Sony Classical SK62691 (61 minutes: DDD). Recorded 1996. ⒻⓈⒺ
Horowitz Variations on a Theme from Bizet's 'Carmen'. **Rachmaninov** (arr. Volodos) Morning, Op. 4 No. 2. Melody, Op. 21 No. 9. **Liszt** Hungarian Rhapsody No. 2 in C sharp minor, S244 (arr. Horowitz). Litanei, S562 No. 1. Schwanengesang, S560 – No. 3, Aufenthalt; No. 10, Liebesbotschaft. **Rimsky-Korsakov** (arr. Cziffra) The tale of Tsar Saltan – Flight of the bumble-bee. **Prokofiev** Pieces from Cinderella – Gavotte, Op. 95 No. 2; Oriental dance, Op. 97 No. 6; Grand waltz, Op. 107 No. 1. **Tchaikovsky** (arr. Feinberg) Symphony No. 6 in B minor, Op. 74, 'Pathétique' – Allegro molto vivace. **Bach** (arr. Feinberg) Trio Sonata No. 5 in C major, BWV529 – Largo. **Volodos** Concert Paraphrase on Mozart's 'Turkish March'.

Arcadi Volodos, Russian-born but Spanish-based, here declares himself both as elegant lyricist and spectacular virtuoso; his playing is as tactful as it is audacious, the work, surely, of a romantic pianist for our times. His tributes to Horowitz (the ultimate Russian virtuoso icon) and Cziffra (the *ne plus ultra* of pianistic necromancy) are as coolly masterful as they are personally engaging and are wholly devoid of wilfulness or undue idiosyncrasy. Those anxious for Horowitz's splintering treble and thundering bass or for Cziffra's manic explosions and accelerations will listen in vain. Mercifully, Volodos remains his own man, tempering some heart-stopping octaves and *glissandos* at the close of Feinberg's transcription of the *Scherzo* from Tchaikovsky's *Pathétique* Symphony with a touch of nonchalance, and in Feinberg's other arrangement, guiding Bach gently but firmly into the nineteenth century. Volodos is no less beguiling in his own Rachmaninov song transcriptions; here is that dreamed-of vocal 'line', luscious *cantabile* and aristocratic rather than ostentatious voicing and texturing. Last but far from least his elaboration of Mozart's 'Turkish March' seasons the most decadent and epicurean taste with a teasing wit and insouciance. Sony's sound is superlative and this delectable recital makes one long for more substantial as well as glittering fare from a pianist who, as his producer puts it, 'never loosens the reins of his guiding intellect'.

Piano Works
Arturo Benedetti Michelangeli pf
Testament mono SBT2088 (two discs: 130 minutes: ADD).
Includes a half-hour rehearsal sequence. Recorded live in 1957. ⒻⒽ
Chopin Fantasie in F minor, Op. 49. Ballade No. 1 in G minor, Op. 23. Waltz in E flat major, Op. posth. **Debussy** Images – Reflets dans l'eau; Hommage à Rameau; Cloches à travers les feuilles; Et la lune descend sur le temple qui fût. **Schumann** Carnaval, Op. 9. Faschingsschwank aus Wien, Op. 26. **Mompou** Cançons i danses No. 6 – Canción.

Readers who are familiar with Michelangeli's 1971 DG recording of Debussy's *Images* will be astonished at this highly mobile 1957 concert performance of 'Cloches à travers les feuilles', which is almost a full minute faster than its stereo successor; or 'Reflets dans l'eau', which glides across the water's surface with such swiftness and ease that the more considered DG alternative – glorious though it is – sounds studied by comparison. 'Hommage à Rameau' is shaped with the utmost finesse and 'Et la lune descend sur le temple qui fût' coloured by exquisitely graded nuances. The performance of Schumann's *Carnaval* is a choice gallery of aural sculpture, whether in the minutely calculated responses of 'Pierrot', the teasing rubato of 'Coquette', the energy and attack of 'Papillons', the effortless flow of 'Chopin' or the ecstatic lingerings in 'Aveu'. Michelangeli's 'Eusebius' is tender but unsentimental, whereas his 'Florestan' has enough 'reflective' ingredients to suggest that the two characters are closer in spirit than we often think. *Faschingsschwank aus Wien* contrasts muscular assertiveness (the opening *Allegro*) with the most amazing control (in the 'Romanze'), while the 'Intermezzo' promotes a virtually orchestral range of dynamics. Michelangeli's Chopin has a rare nobility, the *Fantasie* especially which, at a rather faster tempo than usual, holds together as a narrative entity. Then there is the imposing First *Ballade* and the encores – a sunny posthumous E flat *Waltz* (a regular extra on Michelangeli's concert programmes) and Mompou's sad but tender 'Canción'. This disc leaves you humbled by, and grateful for, some wonderful piano playing. Michelangeli's art is both rare and elusive, his expressive vocabulary finely distilled and unlikely to impress those who listen only for technical mastery. It's therefore ironic that those who criticize Michelangeli for 'coldness' or 'aloofness' are often the very commentators who are so dazzled by his virtuosity that they cannot hear beyond it. Testament's transfers are superb.

Piano Recital
Maurizio Pollini *pf*
DG The Originals 447 431-2GOR (68 minutes: ADD). Recorded 1971-76. Ⓜ
Prokofiev Piano Sonata No. 7 in B flat major, Op. 83. **Boulez** Piano Sonata No. 2.
Stravinsky Petrushka – three movements. **Webern** Piano Variations, Op. 27.

Perfection needs to be pursued so that you can forget about it. Pollini's *Petrushka* movements are almost inhumanly accurate and fast; but what comes across is an exhilarating sense of abandon, plus an extraordinary cumulative excitement. The Prokofiev Seventh Sonata remains a benchmark recording not only for the athleticism of its outer movements but for the epic remorselessness of the central *Andante*. The Webern Variations are a magical fusion of intellectual passion and poetry, and the Boulez Sonata vividly reminds us why the European avant-garde was such a powerful force in the 1950s. These recordings are a monument to what it is possible for two hands to achieve on one musical instrument. The 'original-image bit-processing' has given a bit more brilliance and presence, just as claimed, and another definite gain is the retention of atmosphere between movements.

The Rachmaninov Piano
Mikhail Pletnev *pf*
DG 459 634-2GH (74 minutes: DDD). Recorded 1998. Ⓕ
Beethoven Piano Sonata No. 26 in E flat, Op. 81*a*, 'Les adieux'. **Chopin** Andante spianato and Grande Polonaise in E flat, Op. 22. **Mendelssohn** Andante cantabile and Presto agitato in B major. Rondo capriccioso in E, Op. 14. **Rachmaninov** Etudes-tableaux – Op. 33: No. 6 in E flat minor; No. 8 in G minor; No. 9 in C sharp minor; E flat minor, Op. 39 No. 5. Variations on a theme of Corelli, Op. 42.

Gimmickry? Not a bit of it. This is a genuinely illuminating and thought-provoking issue. More than that, it's immensely enjoyable. The freedoms and avoidances of convention which Pletnev often likes to allow himself here sound consistently inspired and true to the spirit of the music. The instrument is Rachmaninov's pre-war American Steinway. What you hear is a well-regulated tone, a little more uneven between the registers and a little thinner overall than its modern counterpart, but never measly or tinny, with the exception of the high treble, which sometimes gives an impression similar to excessive use of the soft pedal. Some of the glittering passagework in the Chopin does becomes rather glaring, especially when pushed beyond *mezzo-forte*. On the whole though, even this is easy to adapt to, because in Pletnev's hands the texture is so rich in nuance, his own eloquence apparently released from all inhibitions. There's also a significant gain in transparency. Indeed if anyone wanted to claim that this kind of instrument has all the advantages of the 'early' piano with none of the drawbacks it would be hard to disagree. Whether it would stand up to the demands of having to project to the back of a full-size concert hall is debatable, but heard in DG's close yet well-ventilated recording, it sounds marvellous. Rarely will you hear as involving an account of the Rachmaninov *Corelli* Variations, and only Richter has surpassed Pletnev in the *Etudes-tableaux*. Nor is it only Rachmaninov's own opulent textures which are thrillingly clarified. The *Les adieux* Sonata is wonderfully free, both in rubato and voicing, and never so at the expense of the longer lines of the structure. Pletnev's Mendelssohn is breathtakingly poetic and, in the *Rondo capriccioso*, stunningly articulate, every single phrase subtle yet unselfconscious. All in all, this is one of the very finest achievements in Pletnev's already imposing discography.

Russian Piano Works
Boris Berezovsky *pf*
Teldec 4509-96516-2 (61 minutes: DDD). Recorded 1994. Ⓕ
Mussorgsky (arr. Tchernov): A Night on the Bare Mountain. **Rachmaninov** Etudes-tableaux,
Op. 39 – No. 3 in F sharp minor; No. 4 in B minor; No. 7 in C minor; No. 9 in D major. **Liadov**
Preludes – C major, Op. 39 No. 4; F sharp minor, Op. 40 No. 2; D flat major, Op. 57 No. 1.
Medtner Four Fairy Tales, Op. 34 – No. 2 in E minor; No. 3 in A minor. Fairy Tale in B flat minor,
Op. 20 No. 1. Fairy Tale in D minor, Op. 51 No. 1. Romantic Sketches for the Young, Op. 65 –
Book 2: Tale. **Balakirev** Islamey.

In this most imaginative programme Boris Berezovsky displays a formidable technique and, for the
greater part, the sort of emotional commitment that is second nature to the greatest Russian
pianists. His selection from the Op. 39 *Etudes* confirms that he is among Rachmaninov's most
powerful and eloquent interpreters. In No. 3 in F sharp minor Berezovsky's romantic freedom and
richness of expression are several removes from other, more conventional, approaches. His rubato is
pained and ecstatic and the music seems to move across an immense emotional and dynamic
spectrum within its brief but intricate space. What drama he achieves too, in the great funeral elegy
of No. 7, complementing a hair-raising advance to the dissonant and audacious climax with a rare
finesse in the central triple *piano* and *legatissimo* reminder of the Russian liturgy. And it is this
finesse which makes every bar of the Liadov *Preludes* memorable, whether in the ultra-Russian
memory of Chopin in No. 1, or the octave storms of No. 3 (where the parallel with Scriabin's
Etude, Op. 8 No. 9 is remarkably close). Medtner's dark-hued *Fairy Tales*, too, find a potent and
ideal interpreter both in malignant antics (the 'Wood goblin', Op. 34 No. 3) and subtle and elusive
attributes (the *Romantic Sketch*: the perfect encore to keep an audience guessing). The recital is
framed by two towering feats of virtuoso pianism. Mussorgsky's *Night on the Bare Mountain*,
arranged by Konstantin Tchernov, is a pulverizing experience – *allegro feroce*, indeed! And
Balakirev's *Islamey* is tossed off at breakneck speed, its sadistic, madcap difficulties resolved like so
much child's play. In its stunningly imperious way this performance is unrivalled. The recordings are
close and airless.

Segovia – Canciones populares
Elliot Fisk *gtr*
MusicMasters 67174-2 (76 minutes: DDD). Recorded 1996. Ⓕ
De Narvaez La canción del Emperador. **C.P.E. Bach** March, H1. Keyboard Sonata in B minor,
H73 – Siciliana. **Haydn** String Quartet in G major, Op. 76 No. 1 – Minuet. **Chopin** Prelude in
A major, Op. 29 No. 7. **Schumann** Romanze. **Brahms** Waltz in B flat major, Op. 39 No. 8.
Ponce Preludio, Balletto and Giga – Preludio. **Mussorgsky** Pictures at an Exhibition – The old
castle. **Franck** L' Organiste, Volume 1 – Andantino poco allegretto. **Debussy** Préludes, Book 1 –
La fille aux cheveux de lin. **Scriabin** Prelude in E flat minor, Op. 16 No. 4 (all arr. Segovia).
Tansman Segovia. **Segovia** Canciónes populares de distintos paises. Estudio sin luz.
La macarena. Prelude No. 14 in B minor. Estudio in E major. **Roussel** Segovia, Op. 29. **Milhaud**
Segoviana, Op. 366. **Castelnuovo-Tedesco** Tonadilla, sur le nom de Andrés Segovia, Op. 170
No. 5.

Very many guitarists have paid tribute to Segovia's evangelistic work on behalf of the guitar in the
twentieth century – his artistry, his establishing of a repertory that looked both backwards and
forwards, his long concert career and, in some cases, his personal help. None has done so more
faithfully and with greater affection than Elliot Fisk. Fisk wisely makes no attempt to ape the style
and sounds of Segovia's performances – they were touched by genius but, as has been said of
Landowska's, 'we don't do it that way now'. Time has in all respects moved on. Fisk has recorded
many of the pieces that were arranged by or written for Segovia, and he does it in his own way –
with a pulse that is firmer than Segovia's often was, and with moments of tonal sweetness that
recall but do not mimic those of the maestro. Segovia wrote many charming and beautifully crafted
vignettes, some of which Fisk has recorded (three of them for the first time), and has included 16 of
Segovia's arrangements of folk-songs from various countries. The relationship between Segovia and
Fisk was one of mutual respect and affection, and this magnificent recording pays due tribute to it.

Solomon in Berlin Piano works.
Solomon *pf*
APR mono APR7030 (two discs: 92 minutes: ADD). Recorded live in 1956. Ⓜ Ⓗ
Bach Concerto in the Italian style, BWV971. **Beethoven** Piano Sonatas – No. 3 in C major, Op. 2
No. 3; No. 14 in C sharp minor, Op. 27 No. 2, 'Moonlight'. **Chopin** Fantasie in F minor, Op. 49.
Nocturne in B flat minor, Op. 9 No. 1. Scherzo No. 2 in B flat minor, Op. 31. **Brahms** Intermezzos
– E major, Op. 116 No. 4; E flat minor, Op. 118 No. 6. Rhapsody in B minor, Op. 79 No. 1.

This invaluable issue brings together on two short CDs recitals given by Solomon in 1956 for Berlin Radio. This was the time of Solomon's greatest success when, as Bryan Crimp puts it in his excellent notes, he had acquired a Midas touch, at long last reaping the rewards his artistry deserved. The recordings are clean but airless, yet they do little to dim one's sense of Solomon's quality, his masterly but unobtrusive virtuosity, his unsullied honesty and musicianship. How typical is his robust, pacy opening *Allegro* in the Bach, how impeccable his unfolding of the central *Andante*; a truly seamless aria in such hands. His rhythmic zest in the finale, too, is hard to resist. In Beethoven Solomon is, not surprisingly, no less remarkable. By 1956 he had modified his celebrated slow tempo for the first movement of Op. 27 No. 2, yet the playing remains sculpted and marmoreal, a statement mixing abstraction and elegy and wholly devoid of impressionism or 'moonlit' overtones. Solomon's Brahms is no less lucid and classic, though his B minor *Rhapsody* has a truly *agitato* sweep and propulsion. Here Solomon's poise and *sang-froid* are only just on the right side of detachment. The same might be said of his Chopin *Fantasie*. Solomon was hardly a pianist to wear his heart on his sleeve, and although there have been other, more richly idiosyncratic *Fantasies* on record, there are few more masterly or refined. Finally, criticism falls silent when you listen to Solomon in the B flat minor *Nocturne*, where his magically 'contained' eloquence re-creates a pearl beyond price. Here, heart and mind work in faultless harmony and alliance.

Symphony
Wayne Marshall *org*
Virgin Classics VC5 45320-2 (72 minutes: DDD). Recorded on the Marcussen organ of
Bridgewater Hall, Manchester in 1997.   Ⓕ
Dupré Symphony No. 2 in C sharp minor, Op. 26. Evocation, Op. 37 – Allegro deciso.
Hakim Vexilla Regis prodeunt. **Roger-Ducasse** Pastorale in F major. **Widor** Symphony No. 6
in C minor, Op. 42 No. 2.

Although you may be torn between open-mouthed admiration for the sheer technical bravado of the playing and horror at Wayne Marshall's breathtaking speeds, the former sentiment will win the day. He plays at speeds beyond the ability of any normal human being. The first movement of Widor's Sixth Symphony is marked *Allegro*, a word musical dictionaries translate as 'lively'. There are plenty of markings implying a faster speed. Yet it just cannot be possible to play faster than this. Listening amazed at such incredibly athletic finger- and foot-work you won't know whether to laugh or cry. Surely Widor could never have expected his works to sound quite like this – yet if he wanted his music to amaze and excite he surely can have no cause for complaint here. For while Marshall's stunning virtuosity is certainly the main feature of this performance, he is also an astute musician who successfully treads that fine line between mere exhibitionism and musical respectability. Perhaps highest praise must go to the mighty Manchester Marcussen; certainly no Cavaillé-Coll could have supported playing of this agility with such clarity. Marshall displays the organ mostly in hefty, full-throated combinations of stops; even the tranquil opening of the lovely Roger-Ducasse *Pastorale* only gives passing glimpses of some of the gentler stops. Sadly, a somewhat violently waving swell pedal and a rather unfortunate piece of tuning mar the character of the lone reed stop featured in the fourth movement of the Widor. Yet this is a stunning recording of a magnificent organ and there is no denying that few organ discs on the market present quite such brilliant playing.

Tchaikovsky and his Friends
Margaret Fingerhut *pf*
Chandos CHAN9218 (78 minutes: DDD). Recorded 1992.   Ⓕ
Arensky Intermezzo in F minor, Op. 36 No. 12. Le ruisseau dans la forêt. Romance, Op. 53
No. 5. **Glazunov** Etudes, Op. 31 – No. 2 in C minor; No. 3 in E minor. Prelude in D major,
Op. 25 No. 1. **Liadov** Two Bagatelles, Op. 17. Prelude in B minor, Op. 11 No. 1. Prelude in
F sharp minor, Op. 39 No. 4. **Rachmaninov** Canon in E minor. Morceaux de fantaisie, Op. 3 –
No. 1, Elégie in E flat minor; No. 3, Mélodie in E major; No. 4, Policinelle in F sharp minor.
Taneyev Scherzo in E flat minor. Andante semplice. **Tchaikovsky** Humoresque in E minor,
Op. 10 No. 2. Nocturne in C sharp minor, Op. 19 No. 4. Chant sans paroles in A minor, Op. 40
No. 7. Dumka, Op. 59.

The title is a reasonable one, for the younger five composers here were Tchaikovsky's musical friends as well as being known to him and greatly admiring of him. The Russian salon piano piece, owing a good deal to song and therefore to French example, was an immensely popular genre in Moscow and St Petersburg circles, and Tchaikovsky set examples both good and risky. The lively pieces, such as his wonderfully catchy Humoresque, not only put Russian folk idioms into currency, but could seize the sharpest of twentieth-century Russian ears, Stravinsky's, and go into *The Fairy's Kiss* with his own rhythmic bounce. The tender ones could veer in the direction of sentimentality, and sometimes lurch over the margins of good taste. A good variety is represented here. Margaret

Fingerhut has chosen intelligently. She has not spared herself, for there are one or two occasions where her technique is fully stretched. However, she has a real understanding of the genre, and can knock off the rapid fancy (such as Taneyev's *Scherzo*) and the sudden, almost manic burst of energy (uncharacteristically in the indolent Liadov's F sharp minor Prelude), as well as the dreamy meditation (Liadov's first Op. 17 Bagatelle, 'La douleur' or Tchaikovsky's own Nocturne or Rachmaninov's *Mélodie*) and a genre piece such as Arensky's pretty little picture of a brook running through a forest. Her greatest talent is for a flexibility of phrasing that always sings. These are in the best sense sympathetic performances, and should give pleasure.

Virtuoso Piano Transcriptions
Earl Wild *pf*
Sony Classical SK62036 (67 minutes: DDD). Recorded 1995.   Ⓕ
Saint-Saëns (trans. Wild) Le rouet d'Omphale in A major, Op. 31. **Handel** Keyboard Suite No. 5 in E minor, HWV430 – Adagio and Variations, 'The Harmonious Blacksmith'. **Chopin** (trans. Wild) Piano Concerto No. 2 in F minor, Op. 21 – Largo. **Rachmaninov** (trans. Wild) These summer nights, Op. 12 No. 5. **Pabst** Paraphrase on 'Sleeping Beauty' (Tchaikovsky). **Wild** Improvisation on 'Après un rêve' (Fauré). Hommage à Poulenc. Reminiscences of 'Snow White and the Seven Dwarfs' (Churchill). **Mozart** (trans. Backhaus) Don Giovanni – Deh! vieni alla finestra. **Tchaikovsky** (trans. Wild) At the ball, Op. 38 No. 3. Swan Lake – Dance of the Swans. **Tausig** Man lebt nur einmal. **Kreisler** (trans. Rachmaninov) Liebeslied.

Wild resurrects some of his old favourites (Rachmaninov's *These summer nights* and the Kreisler/Rachmaninov *Liebeslied*, for example) but for the most part provides new and delectable offerings. Take the Wild *Hommage à Poulenc* for example, where the Sarabande from Bach's First *Partita* is held in a relentlessly 'blue' spotlight, enveloped in luscious night-club harmony; a naughty but affectionate tilt at 'the old wig' and also at all purists and Beckmessers. His arrangement of Saint-Saëns's *Le rouet d'Omphale*, deriving in style from the Wagner-Liszt Spinning Chorus from *Der fliegende Holländer*, is dazzlingly resourceful and Handel's *Harmonious Blacksmith* takes on a new lease of life, decked out with mischievous but stylish additions. The decadent commentary on the Rachmaninov song ends with comic abruptness while Tchaikovsky's *At the ball* concludes with a flight nimble enough to show how lightly Wild has worn his years. Lovers of easy sentiment will enjoy the effusive *Reminiscences of 'Snow White'* though admirers of Fauré's chaste voluptuousness will react to Wild's way with *Après un rêve* with more than a raised eyebrow. The Dance of the Swans from *Swan Lake* is as ear-tickling as ever and so, all in all, the instantly recognizable sheen and sparkle of this recital reflect a great pianist's tireless relish and delight in all things pianistic and seductive. The recordings are superb.

Arcadi Volodos at Carnegie Hall
Arcadi Volodos *pf*
Sony Classical SK60893 (72 minutes: DDD). Recorded live in 1998.   Ⓕ Ⓔ
Liszt (arr. Horowitz) Hungarian Rhapsody No. 15 in A minor, S244, 'Rákóczy'. A Midsummer Night's Dream – Wedding March, S410. **Rachmaninov** Fragment in A flat major. Etudes-tableaux – No. 8 in D minor, Op. 39; C minor, Op. posth. **Schumann** Bunte Blätter, Op. 99. **Scriabin** Piano Sonata No. 10 in C, Op. 70. Enigma, Op. 52 No. 2. Caresse dansée, Op. 57 No. 2. Prelude in B, Op. 2 No. 2.

Taken live from his Carnegie Hall début recital at the age of 26, this recital confirms a daunting legend. Volodos is unquestionably among the world's master pianists, a virtuoso for whom even the most fiercely applied difficulties simply do not exist. At the same time everything is given with an unfaltering sense of equilibrium; as fast as you marvel at one thing it is immediately counterpointed by another. His technique in, say, the Liszt *Rhapsody* and *Wedding March* Variations (the first of two encores) is stupendous but never at the expense of musical quality. His sonority can be as delicate as it is thunderous and full-blooded. His accuracy and taste are impeccable so that instead of celebrating something self-serving or rip-roaring you find yourself conscious of higher virtues, of rhythm that can be magically free or held in a vice-like grip, as well as an unequalled fluency and aplomb. In Scriabin's Tenth Sonata he is faithful to the composer's obsessive and opalescent vision at every point, more than equal to even the most decadent and esoteric directions. Volodos's Rachmaninov, in his brief but gloriously enterprising selection, is played with the same magical sense of flux and clarity, and never more so than in the D minor *Etude-tableau* with its yearning and disconsolate double-note flow or in the C minor, posthumously published *Etude-tableau*. Yet if one had to choose just one item from this recital for a desert island, it would have to be Schumann's *Bunte Blätter*, an audacious gathering with a graphic shift from the lighter to the darker side of romanticism (Nos. 1-8 and 9-14 respectively). Sony's sound triumphs over difficult circumstances and if a teasing touch of enigma remains, both in performance and choice of repertoire, with an artist of this calibre you can hardly say that the golden age of pianism is dead.

Choral

Advent at St Paul's
St Paul's Cathedral Choir / John Scott [c]org with [b]Andrew Lucas org
Hyperion CDA66994 (71 minutes: DDD). Texts and translations included. Recorded 1997. Ⓕ
Anonymous Laudes Regiae. Angelus ad Virginem (arr. Willcocks)[b]. O come, O come, Emmanuel
(arr. Carter)[b]. Rejoice in the Lord alway. **Palestrina** Matins Responsory. Vesper Responsory.
Handl Ecce concipies[c]. **Peerson** Blow out the trumpet[b]. **R. Lloyd** Drop down, ye heavens[b].
Byrd Laetentur coeli. **Wilby** Echo Carol[b]. **Weelkes** Hosanna to the Son of David. **Britten**
A Hymn of St Columba[b]. **Gibbons** This is the record of John[b]. **Rutter** Hymn to the Creator of
Light. **Bruckner** Virga Jesse floruit. **Parsons** Ave Maria. **A. Carter** Toccata on Veni Emmanuel[c].

As in the seasonal calendar a single window opens first, so in this Advent recital a solo voice sings
in the distance; and by the end, all windows alight, the great Cathedral is filled with the organ's
fortissimo from deepest pedal sub-bass to brightest trumpet and topmost piccolo. The programme
begins with some plainsong dating back to the first millennium of the era. The end, more plainsong
but not so plain now, has *O come, O come, Emmanuel* decked in twentieth-century garb,
audaciously arranged, then to become the subject of an organ toccata with sufficient energy to
propel the hymn, the Cathedral and all into the new age. In between comes a satisfying alternation
of ancient and modern. Particularly splendid is Martin Peerson's *Blow out the trumpet*, an anthem
strong in rhythm and colour. Robert Parsons's five-part *Ave Maria* is also a joy. The modern works
include an interesting, deeply felt piece by John Rutter, *Hymn to the Creator of Light*, its first
section less ingratiating (but not therefore less good) than is his more characteristic style and,
followed by an angular refulgence of praise, preparing for a lovely effect as a chorale-melody is
introduced and sung quietly in octaves amid an affectionate interweave of gentle polyphony. The
famous choir is on top form. Britten's *Hymn of St Columba* is especially well performed, probably
making the strongest impression of all. Andrew Lucas is the remorselessly exercised organist in this,
and John Scott takes over for the Toccata: both do excellent work.

Agnus Dei I
New College Choir, Oxford; [a]Capricorn / Edward Higginbottom.
Erato 0630-14634-4; (73 minutes: DDD). Texts and translations included. Recorded 1996. Ⓕ
Barber Agnus Dei, Op. 11. **Fauré** Cantique de Jean Racine, Op. 11 (arr. Rutter)[a]. Requiem,
Op. 48 – In paradisum[a]. **Palestrina** Missa Papae Marcelli – Kyrie. **Mozart** Ave verum corpus,
K618[a]. **Bach** Cantata No. 147, Herz und Mund und Tat und Leben – Jesu, bleibet meine Freude[a].
Rachmaninov Vespers, Op. 37 – No. 6, Ave Maria. **Elgar** (arr. Cameron) Variations on an
original theme, 'Enigma'. Op. 36 – Lux aeterna. **Górecki** Totus tuus, Op. 60.
Mendelssohn Hear my prayer. Tavener: The Lamb. **Allegri** Miserere mei.

It is becoming almost a statutory reward or 'treat' for a hardworking choir of established repute
that they should take time off from psalms and canticles, polyphonic motets and (dread event)
specially commissioned anthems, so as to indulge themselves and their listeners in a programme of
the kind we have here. The Allegri, Bach, Fauré and Mendelssohn are clear favourite. When we
realize that Barber's *Agnus Dei* is an arrangement of his famous *Adagio* and that Elgar's *Lux
aeterna* is 'Nimrod' with a halo, then those must be added too. One by one the remaining
compositions join the charts, leaving only poor old Palestrina, whose *Missa Papae Marcelli* is
nevertheless the first, and quite probably the only, work of his that comes very readily to memory
by name. There is, one supposes, just a chance that so much familiar loveliness will prove too rich a
feast – many readers might not object to the omission of (say) one section of the *Miserere* or
practically the whole of Górecki's *Totus tuus* – but in general the selection has been uncommonly
well made and skilfully designed so that one item leads naturally to the next. The performances are
delightful, with the single exception of 'Jesu, bleibet meine Freude' ('Jesu, joy of man's desiring')
where each of the choir's minims has its swell and *diminuendo* so that they bounce along before us
like so many faintly ridiculous balloons. Thomas Herford is the excellent soloist in *Hear my prayer*
and a capital exponent of the high C in the *Allegri*. In his admirable insert-notes, Edward
Higginbottom writes that the programme 'begins with something rather unusual', the arrangement
of Barber's *Adagio*; actually, there are many other recordings of that currently available though the
Elgar is a rarity. What is unusual, and common to both, is the quality of choral sound: also the
warmth of the acoustic, not usually associated with New College Chapel but here it is ideal.

Agnus Dei II
New College Choir, Oxford; [a]Capricorn / Edward Higginbottom.
Erato 3984-21659-2 (66 minutes: DDD). Recorded 1997. Ⓕ Ⓔ

Albinoni Adagio in G minor[a]. **Bizet** Agnus Dei. **Schubert** Psalm 23, D706 (all arr. Cameron)[a].
Brahms Geistliches Lied, Op. 30[a]. **Fauré** Ave verum, Op. 65 No. 1 (both arr. Higginbottom)[a].
Requiem, Op. 48[a] – Pie Jesu; Libera me. **Martin** Mass for Double Choir – Agnus Dei. **Byrd**
Ave verum corpus. **Lotti** Crucifixus a 8. **Monteverdi** Selva morale e spirituale – Beatus vir[a].
Bruckner Christus factus est[a]. **Purcell** Hear my prayer, O Lord, Z15. **Bach** St John Passion,
BWV245 – Ruht wohl.

A wise man said you should not swim in the same river twice, and somebody is bound to add that it
wouldn't be the same river anyway. 'Agnus Dei I' was an immediate winner when it was first
released. The camel's prospects with regard to the needle's eye are rosy compared to the likelihood
of a genuinely good choral record getting into the charts; but that one made it. 'Agnus Dei II', with
a similar programme, was marginally less successful. On the first disc it was Barber's *Adagio* that
won so many hearers and hearts; this time the famous *Adagio* ascribed to Tomaso Albinoni,
courtesy of Remo Giazotti, and set here by John Cameron to a text, in Latin, from the New
Testament, is deserving of equal success. The disc's subtitle is 'music to soothe the soul', which
tends to prefer the sweet melancholy of a nostalgic *adagio* to the brisk *allegro* of a bracing
Brandenburg, even though this would be much better for it. The programme certainly has its quota
of soothers, but they are taken at rather faster speeds than usual. Lotti's *Crucifixus*, Schubert's 23rd
Psalm and Martin's *Agnus Dei* from the Mass for Double Choir are examples, and all of them
benefit, especially in this context. The choir itself has long been one of the best in its normal
repertoire of church music, and these excursions have emboldened it in coloration and expressive
scope. Purcell's *Hear my prayer*, for instance, is sung with exceptional intensity. Some of the
arrangements may be questionable. Albinoni is fair game, but Brahms's lovely Op. 30 forfeits the
spiritual quietness of church when deprived of its organ accompaniment, and Schubert is not really
in need of strings and harp. It remains a delightful disc, and not to be dismissed by 'serious'
musicians on account of its wider appeal.

Carols from Ampleforth
Ampleforth Schola Cantorum / Ian Little with **Simon Wright** *org*
Ampleforth Compact Discs AARCD1 (58 minutes: DDD).   Ⓕ
Traditional O come, all ye faithful. Once in Royal David's city. Unto us is born a son.
The Sussex Carol. God rest you merry, gentlemen. Hark! the herald angels sing (all arr. Willcocks).
Personent hodie (arr. Holst). Good King Wenceslas (arr. Jacques). Adam lay y-bounden
(arr. Warlock). Angel tidings (arr. Rutter). Past three a clock. Ding dong! merrily on high (both
arr. Wood). It came upon a midnight clear. Come with torches. Silent Night (all arr. Little). Still, still,
still (arr. Ledger). The Infant King (arr. Pettman). The First Nowell (arr. Stainer/Willcocks).
H.C. Stewart On this day earth shall ring. **M. Praetorius** A great and mighty wonder.
Mathias Sir Christemas.

Here is a programme of carols as traditional as turkey and plum pudding, and as wholesome. You
don't have to groan at the approach of *Have yourself a merry little Christmas* or any other feeble
compromise with the changing times; there's not even a bleat from John Tavener and William
Blake's unprofitably questioned little lamb. Musically, the programme is in the first place a triumph
for Anon, and then for Sir David Willcocks whose arrangements are rich in seasonable splendour
and knowledge of how to get the best out of choir and organ. Other arrangers have done good
work too, including the Choir's Director, Ian Little, who provides inspired embellishments in the
last verse of *It came upon a midnight clear* but may just possibly have gone a little over the top
towards the end of *Silent Night*. He has also trained a splendid choir. Forthright tone from the
trebles, ample tone from the men, combine to live up to the name of their foundation. The organist,
Simon Wright, does an excellent job, varying the might of his invincible reeds and implacable
pedals with a scattering of two-foot spangle-dust, light and bright as a Christmas-tree fairy. The
building itself is orally spacious, the harmonies of *Ding dong! merrily on high* engaging in merry
argument with their echo. There will doubtless be homes in which a playing of this disc will
constitute the Christmas Day reveille, and if the rest of the day goes as well they can count
themselves lucky.

Credo
[a]**Paul Nicholson** *counterten* [b]**Richard Eteson**, [c]**Edward Saklatvala** *cantors*
King's College Choir, Cambridge / Stephen Cleobury.
EMI CDC5 56439-2 (64 minutes: DDD). Texts and translations included. Recorded 1997.   Ⓕ Ⓢ
Rachmaninov Vespers, Op. 37[a] – Bless the Lord, O my soul; Blessed is the man. Liturgy of
St John Chrysostom, Op. 31 – Cherubic Hymn; The Lord's Prayer. **Penderecki** The Cherubic
Hymn. Agnus Dei. **Stravinsky** Ave Maria. Credo. **Panufnik** Song to the Virgin Mary.
Plainchant Stetit angelus (Offertory antiphon); Credo I[b]; Ave Maria (Offertory antiphon); Alleluia;
Tota pulchra es, Maria (Alleluia with verse); Missa pro defunctis – Agnus Dei[bc]; Pater noster[b].

The logic of this programme, juxtaposing two very different responses to religious texts, is not entirely apparent. The twentieth-century works are not directly influenced by the plainchant of the Western Catholic church yet neither are they all rooted in the Eastern Orthodox tradition. It is the second (1949) version of Stravinsky's *Credo* that is performed here – setting the Catholic rather than the Orthodox text – while both Panufnik and Penderecki were practising Catholics. Indeed only Rachmaninov's gorgeous pieces give us the genuinely Orthodox view – and that from a man who was not himself a staunch follower of the faith. Frankly, though, with music as indescribably beautiful as this and performances which are of almost breathtaking artistry, who needs logic in programming? The climax of Penderecki's *Cherubic Hymn* is measured to absolute perfection, every last ounce of passion squeezed from the long-drawn-out build-up to this shattering moment: the chanted *Pater noster* has that timeless quality which seems to come from another world – enhanced, as is everything on this disc, by a deliciously atmospheric recording. If there is a niggling reservation it is in the lack of real bass resonance, especially in the Rachmaninov. By the very nature of its make-up an English collegiate choir will never possess men's voices with the kind of maturity you would hear in a Russian Orthodox choir. But with such committed, sensitive and musically perceptive singing, we have here one of the very finest discs to have come from King's during Stephen Cleobury's tenure as Director.

English Choral Works
Netherlands Chamber Choir / John Alldis with [a]**Manja Smits** *hp*
Globe GLO5170 (59 minutes: DDD). Texts included. Recorded 1996.   Ⓕ
Vaughan Williams Three Shakespeare Songs. **Howells** Requiem. **Holst** Choral Hymns from the Rig Veda – Group 3, H99[a]. **Britten** Five Flower Songs, Op. 47. **Bedford** The Golden Wine is Drunk.

This superb Dutch group under their permanent guest conductor, John Alldis, offers high-class choral singing. The magical start of 'Full fathom five' (the first of Vaughan Williams's *Three Shakespeare Songs* from 1951) immediately proclaims an exceptional degree of perception from all involved. These artists give a no less sympathetic rendering of Howells's Requiem, that haunting soul mate and precursor to *Hymnus Paradisi*. Holst's third group of *Rig Veda* hymns receive luminously beautiful treatment from the Netherlands choir with harpist Manja Smits. The collection concludes with David Bedford's *The Golden Wine is Drunk* (1974), a 13-minute setting of Ernest Dowson for two eight-part choirs, whose textural imagination, melismatic beauty and liberating dissonance cast quite a spell, especially in a performance as hypnotically controlled and utterly dedicated as here. Recorded sound is admirable.

German Baroque Cantatas
Andreas Scholl *counterten*
Concerto di Viole (Brian Franklin, Friederike Heumann, Brigitte Gasser, Arno Jochem de la Rosée); **Basle Consort** (Pablo Valetti, Stephanie Pfister *vns* Karl Ernst Schröder *lte* Markus Märkl *hpd/org*).
Harmonia Mundi HMC90 1651 (72 minutes: DDD). Texts and translations included. Recorded 1997.   ⒻⒺ
Albertini Sonata quarto in C minor. **J. Christoph Bach** Ach, das ich Wassers g'nug hätte. **Buxtehude** Fried- und Freudenreiche Hinfahrt, BuxWV76 – Muss der Tod denn auch entbinden (Klag-Lied). Jubilate Domino, omnis terra, BuxWV64. **Erlebach** Wer sich dem Himmel übergeben. **Legrenzi** Libro quarto di sonate, La cetra' – Sonata quinta. **Rovetta** Salve mi Jesu. **Tunder** Ach, Herr lass deine lieben Engelein. **Schütz** Kleiner geistlichen Concerten, SWV306-37 – Was hast du verwirket, SWV307; O Jesu, nomen dulcem, SWV308. Symphoniae sacrae, SWV341-67 – Herzlich lieb hab ich dich, o Herr, SWV348.

Expressively versatile though Scholl unquestionably can be, it is perhaps in the sphere of elegy and plaint that his art can be heard to strongest advantage. Two pieces of outstanding merit fall into this category and are sung here with tonal beauty, stylistic assurance and expressive *puissance*. One of them is Johann Christoph Bach's lament *Ach, das ich Wassers g'nug hätte*. This member of the family worked during the second half of the seventeenth century and was greatly admired by J. S. Bach, who described him as 'profound'. The lament, in *da capo* form, is scored for countertenor, violin, three violas da gamba, cello and organ. The other is the much better-known strophic 'Klag-Lied' from the longer *Fried- und Freudenreiche Hinfahrt* by Buxtehude, written in memory of his father who had died early in 1674. Scholl does great justice to each of these intimate pieces, attending as much to the spirit and utterance of the texts as to the sorrowful and at times searing inflexions of the music.

These performances alone would be sufficient enticement to acquire the disc but, happily, there is much else in the programme to touch our sensibilities. Schütz is well represented with three tenderly expressive pieces, two of them from the *Kleiner geistlichen Concerten* and a third from the *Symphoniae sacrae* (1647); and Franz Tunder by a declamatory and rhythmically graceful setting of a verse of the hymn *Herzlich lieb hab ich dir, o Herr*. This piece is one of two whose composers have been wrongly exchanged on the track listing: the other is *Salve mi Jesu* which, though preserved in a Tunder manuscript, is probably the work of the Venetian, Giovanni Rovetta. Sensibly, the order of events is punctuated by two works for instrumental ensemble, one of them by Ignazio Albertini, the other by Legrenzi whose position in the history of recording seems still to be that of occasional stand-in. He deserves better, and doubtless will come into his own one day. The playing of the two groups, Concerto di Viole and the Basle Consort, is accomplished and refined, both in ensemble and tuning, providing sensitive support in the vocal pieces and affecting insights to the instrumental ones. Despite the fanciful (if ingenious) packaging, which is brittle, inconvenient and impractical, this is strongly recommended.

Great Cathedral Anthems, Volume 8.
Choir of St Mary's Cathedral, Edinburgh / Timothy Byram-Wigfield with
[a]Peter Backhouse *org*
Priory PRCD557 (64 minutes: DDD). Recorded 1996.   Ⓕ
Harwood O how glorious is the Kingdom[a]. **Byrd** Christe, qui lux es et dies. O Lord, make thy servant Elizabeth our Queen. **Taverner** Quemadmodum desiderat cervus. **Gibbons** O clap your hands. **Lotti** Crucifixus a 8. **Stanford** Three Motets, Op. 38. **Ley** Prayer of King Charles I. **Brahms** Ein deutsches Requiem, Op. 45 – Wie lieblich sind deine Wohnungen (sung in English)[a]. **Howells** Salve regina. **Walton** The Twelve[a].

If there are some to whom the choir of Edinburgh's Episcopal Cathedral are introducing themselves in this recital, they are likely to be impressed and want to hear more. This is a choir that can sustain long phrases (fine ones in the marvellous motet by Taverner), lengthy and concentrated works too (as with Walton's *The twelve*), finding plentiful resources of energy in matters of attack and rhythm. The trebles (14 plus four girls) are bright-toned and sing some formidably challenging music with well-founded confidence. The choir also possess useful soloists, most notably the baritone who so effectively opens *The twelve*. The organist proves his merit from the start with an exciting performance of the virtuosic solo which introduces *O how glorious is the Kingdom*, and skilfully manages the accompaniment (not as easy as it may sound) to 'How lovely are Thy dwellings'. It is an enterprising programme, finding room for cherished old acquaintances such as Charles I's evening prayer in its graceful setting by Henry Ley. The acoustic is helpful, neither dry nor excessively reverberant, and the balance between choir and organ is judiciously established.

Hail, Gladdening Light
Cambridge Singers / John Rutter.
Collegium COLCD113 (72 minutes: DDD). Texts and translations included.   Ⓕ
Anonymous Rejoice in the Lord. **Purcell** Remember not, Lord, our offences, Z50. **J. Amner** Come, let's rejoice. **Tomkins** When David heard. **Bairstow** I sat down under his shadow. **J. Goss** These are they that follow the lamb. **Taverner** Christe Jesu, pastor bone. **Philips** O beatum et sacrosanctum diem. **Howells** Nunc dimittis. **Vaughan Williams** O vos omnes. **Dering** Factum est silentium. **Stanford** Justorum animae, Op. 38 No. 1. **C. Wood** Hail, gladdening light. **Tavener** A hymn to the mother of God. Hymn for the dormition of the mother of God. **Elgar** They are at rest. **Walton** A litany. **Morley** Nolo mortem peccatoris. **Tallis** O nata lux. **Rutter** Loving shepherd of Thy sheep. **R. Stone** The Lord's Prayer. **J. Sheppard** In manus tuas. **W.H. Harris** Bring us, O Lord God.

This has the subtitle 'Music of the English Church' and it is arranged under four main headings: anthems and introits (these count as one), Latin motets, settings of hymns and other poetry, and prayer-settings. Each of them is well represented in a programme that varies delightfully in period and style, and in performances which are remarkably consistent in quality. Some of the items will come as discoveries to most listeners: for example, the anthem *Come, let's rejoice*, a splendid, madrigal-like piece written by John Amner, organist from 1610 to 1641 at Ely Cathedral where these recordings were made. Others are equally impressive in their present performance: a deep quietness attends the opening of Richard Dering's *Factum est silentium*, which ends with rhythmic Alleluias set dancing with subdued excitement. Among the hymn-settings is one by a 16-year-old called William Walton. Included in the prayers is the choirmaster's own setting, characteristically made for pleasure, of *Loving shepherd of Thy sheep*. All are unaccompanied, and thus very exactly test the choir's blend of voices, its precision, articulation and feeling for rhythm. In all respects it does exceptionally well; the tone is fresh, the attack unanimous, the expression clear and sensitive, the rhythm on its toes. These are young and gifted singers, formed with disciplined enthusiasm into a choir with a distinctive style – and, incidentally, recorded with admirable results by a family firm which operates from a studio built at the bottom of the garden.

Hear my Prayer
[a]Jeremy Budd *treb*
St Paul's Cathedral Choir / John Scott with [b]Andrew Lucas *org*
Hyperion CDA66439 (76 minutes: DDD). Texts and translations included. Recorded 1990.　　Ⓕ
Allegri Miserere mei (with **Nicholas Thompson** *treb* **Wilfred Swansborough** *counterten*
Timothy Jones *bass*)[a]. **B. Rose** Feast Song for St Cecilia (**Simon Hill** *counterten*
Alan Green *ten*)[a]. **Brahms** Ein deutsches Requiem – Ich hab' nun Traurigkeit (sung in English)[ab].
Britten Festival Te Deum, Op. 32[ab]. **Harvey** Come, Holy Ghost (**Andrew Burden** *ten*
Nigel Beaven *bass*)[a]. **Mendelssohn** Hear my prayer[ab]. **Stanford** Evening Canticles in G major
(Jones)[ab]. **Tavener** I will lift up mine eyes. **Wise** The ways of Zion do mourn
(**Charles Gibbs** *bass*)[ab].

The special distinction of this disc is the work of the treble soloist, Jeremy Budd. He sings in a
programme which is very much the choirboy's equivalent of an operatic soprano's 'Casta diva' and
more of that sort (come to think of it, Master Budd could probably have sung a splendid 'Casta
diva' into the bargain). As it is, he crowns the Allegri *Miserere* with its five top Cs, spot-on, each of
them (rather like Melba singing 'Amor' at the end of Act 1 in *La bohème* five times over). He
commands the breath, the long line and the purity of tone necessary for the solo in Brahms's
Requiem and copes with the difficult modern idiom of Jonathan Harvey's *Come, Holy Ghost* with an
apparent ease that to an older generation may well seem uncanny. Other modern works are included.
John Tavener's *I will lift up mine eyes*, written for St Paul's in 1990, has its characteristic compound
of richness and austerity; and in this, the words penetrate the mist of echoes more successfully than
do those of the *Feast Song for St Cecilia*, written by Gregory Rose and set to some very beautiful
music by his father Bernard. It is good, as ever, to hear Stanford's Evening Service in G, with its
almost Fauré-like accompaniment finely played by the excellent Andrew Lucas; and for a morning
canticle there is Britten's *Te Deum* with its effective build-up to 'Lord God of Sabaoth' and its faint
pre-echo of *The Turn of the Screw* at 'O Lord, save Thy people'. There is also a melancholy anthem
by Michael Wise, whose fate it was to be knocked on the head and killed by the watchman to whom
he was cheeky one night in 1687.

Magnificat and Nunc Dimittis, Volume 4.
Portsmouth Cathedral Choir / Adrian Lucas with **David Thorne** *org*
Priory PRCD527 (79 minutes: DDD). Texts included. Recorded 1995.　　Ⓕ
Brewer Evening Service in E flat major. **Andrews** Evening Service in G major.
Howells Evening Service in E major. Evening Service in B minor. **Lassus** Magnificat quarto toni.
Victoria Nunc dimittis. **Stanford** Evening Service in C major, Op. 115. **Weelkes** Evening
Service for Trebles – Magnificat; Nunc dimittis. **Darke** Evening Service in F major.
R. Shephard Salisbury Service. **Bairstow** Evening Service in D major.

One good thing after another; it almost surprises that a succession of *Mags* and *Nuncs* can be so
varied, satisfying and enjoyable. The programmes in this excellent series allow for a fair variety of
styles and centuries, but in this instance a particularly generous share of the credit must go to the
performances. Forthright and invigorating, they give rise to a distinct suspicion that the whole
business may be a pleasure: that the choristers have some rhythm in their bones and at certain
points might even have a smile on their faces. It is there right from the start, with Brewer in E flat
(and how undeservedly stodgy that can sound in performance) bright with energy and encouraging
a conviction that there genuinely is something in which to rejoice. This extends to Lassus, Victoria
and Weelkes, where, instead of the more usual formal reading of notes, there is a common effort of
understanding and imagination, lifting the notes off the page and sometimes, with a little judicious
semi-*staccato*, setting them a-dance. Nor is there any lack of sensitive shading or of repose in the
right places – a fine feeling for mood in the lovely and little-known B minor setting of Howells, for
example. A splendid recital, with a fine choice of repertoire, and consistently admirable playing by
the organist.

Magnificat and Nunc dimittis, Volume 7.
Hereford Cathedral Choir / Roy Massey with [a]Huw Williams *org*
Priory PRCD535 (68 minutes: DDD). Texts included. Recorded 1995.　　Ⓕ
Sumsion Evening Service in D major[a]. **Darke** Evening Service in A minor. **Lloyd** Hereford
Service[a]. **Davies** Evening Service in G major (Festal)[a]. **Vann** Hereford Service[a]. **Dyson** Evening
Service in F major[a]. **Harwood** Evening Service in A flat major[a]. **Shephard** Hereford Service[a].
Stanford Services in F major, Op. 36 – Evening Service[a].

We follow these reliable generations of church musicians (which is what most of them are, the
presence of Walton and Tippett being exceptions), and recall that composing was a part-time

occupation, almost a luxury, in the daily round that normally comprised taking choir practice and playing the organ, giving lessons and conducting the choral society. The variety of the settings here is a striking feature – Harold Darke's for unaccompanied choir, Dyson's quietness. Almost invariably the individual finds something of his own to add – for example, Richard Lloyd reintroducing 'My soul doth magnify' at the end of his *Magnificat*. Hearing again the well-known favourites (Sumsion in D major, Harwood in A flat), one appreciates exactly why they have so established themselves, just as in Stanford in F major (not among his most familiar settings) we see the hand of the master. We also watch 'modernity' cautiously advancing – in Stanley Vann's fine Hereford Service, for instance. Hereford Cathedral Choir is admirable throughout, and benefit from the clear recorded sound.

Magnificat and Nunc dimittis, Volume 14.
Ely Cathedral Choir / Paul Trepte with David Price *org*
Priory PRCD592 (71 minutes: DDD). Recorded 1996.   Ⓕ
Bairstow Evening Service in G major. **Blow** Evening Service in G major. **Bullock** Evening Service in D major. **Child** Evening Service in E minor. **Cruft** Collegium Regale. **Greene** Evening Service in C major. **Orr** Short Service. **Rose** Evening Service in C minor. **Wills** Evening Service on Plainsong tones. **C. Wood** Evening Service in G major.

All of the items here are worthy of the series, and each has its distinctive flavour. Ernest Bullock's *Magnificat*, which opens the recital, is a good example of Anglican unpredictability. Gentle and lyrical in mood and manner, it develops with what seems to be an almost rhapsodic freedom, the organ part moving with a fluent independence, and as intimate as a piano accompaniment. Bernard Rose, in his Service for trebles, approaches the canticle in similar mood but with entirely different results, making much of the resonance of boys' voices in thirds, and giving full rein to his invention in his writing for the organ. Robin Orr is another who puts much of his more creatively adventurous self into the organ part, and his settings are not made for comfort: the first *Gloria* for instance strikes an awed note, with its rather severe minor tonality. Adrian Cruft, most modern of these composers, in both date and style, writes boldly, with skill in the deployment of the voices in his men-only settings, which, the notes tell us, were originally for accompaniment by wind instruments as an alternative to accompaniment by the organ. From the seventeenth century there are masterly settings by John Blow and William Child; from the eighteenth, Maurice Greene; nothing from the nineteenth (unless it be said that Bullock, Wills, Wood and Bairstow were all children of the nineteenth). With fine work by the organist, David Price, and with the choir showing itself a confident, spirited master of its business, the performances are to be relished.

Missa Salisburgensis
Musica Antiqua Köln / Reinhard Goebel *vn*
Gabrieli Consort and Players / Paul McCreesh.
Archiv Produktion 457 611-2AH (72 minutes: DDD). Texts and translations included.
Recorded 1997.   ⒻⓅ
Augustiner Ein schöner Aufzug. **Biber** Missa Salisburgensis. Plaudite tympana. Sonatae tam aris quam aulis servientes – V in E minor; XII in C major. Sonata Sancti Polycarpi. **Riedl** Ein langer und schöner Aufzug.

Paul McCreesh ventures here into Central Europe for the distinctive mid-baroque splendour encapsulated in Biber's large-scale choral works. He is joined by Reinhard Goebel in a recording of a Mass once thought to have been written by Orazio Benevoli a generation earlier and now considered to be either Biber's own work or possibly that of his predecessor as Court Kapellmeister, Andreas Hofer. The reason why either composer would wish to 'claim' or demur from such authorship in the political fray of imminent court appointments is explained speculatively by Goebel in his note. At the risk of sounding glib, it matters little; the spirit of this enterprise is about re-celebrating a historically significant occasion, adorned in a gargantuan musical edifice, to mark the 1,100th anniversary, in 1682, of the founding by St Rupert of the Archbishopric of Salzburg. By all accounts, this festival at the great abbey of St Peter's was as richly symbolic an occasion as the powerful Archdiocese of Salzburg could possibly have conceived, reflecting its perceived place as the uniquely privileged 'interlocutor' between Roman and Venetian Christian traditions. The event took years to plan, incurring a cost to the taxpayer which makes Millennium Dome dissenters seem curmudgeonly in the extreme.

On its own terms, the 53-part *Missa Salisburgensis* is a work whose remarkable opulence and gigantic scale cannot fail to impress. Even by baroque standards, the dimensions are considerable: among six main 'groups' which form the architectural acoustic in a grand antiphonal scheme are two main choruses, each divided up into eight soloists and tutti choruses, with strings attached, so to speak. This large but conventional palette is coloured by an *à la mode* French wind ensemble of oboes and recorders (who memorably irradiate 'the Lord and giver of life' in the *Credo*) and reinforced by cornetts, trombones, eight ceremonial court trumpeters in two choirs, drums, five organs and two solo clarinos. The latter pair are used as delicate obbligati trumpets, lending a shining incandescence in a further 'aspect' to this ritual pageantry. Throughout the work, there is a felicitous contrast of intimate, solo passages juxtaposed with an endlessly metamorphosed profusion of instruments and voices proclaiming in dynamic spatial perspectives. The thrilling sound of the Gabrieli Consort and Players (of which Musica Antiqua Köln make up the numbers) captures the raw power and dignified regal rhetoric which lie at the heart of the Salzburg aesthetic, revealed in much of the music of Biber and his contemporaries. There can, however, be no escaping the fairly unyielding and bombastic homogeneity of a work whose melodic and harmonic fabric is distinctly limited (some smaller-scale sections apart, such as the shimmering *Agnus*), essentially to cope with a super-resonant cathedral acoustic whose galleries of musicians relied on a dialogue of straightforward gestures; this is brought into sharp perspective by invigoratingly performed string sonatas, taken from Biber's *Sonatae tam aris* collection (1676), whose subtle expressive properties are doubtless intended to re-charge our batteries for each new onslaught. It would be invidious to pick out individuals in such a tightly-knit team but McCreesh's guild of trumpeters is awe-inspiring. The recording is brilliantly engineered.

Miserere and other choral works
Trinity College Choir, Cambridge / Richard Marlow.
Conifer Classics CDCF219 (79 minutes: DDD). Recorded 1993. Ⓕ
Parry I was glad. Jerusalem. **Schubert** Deutsche Messe, D872 – Sanctus. Ave Maria, D839.
Barber Agnus Dei, Op. 11. **Burgon** Nunc dimittis. **Bach** Cantata No. 129, Gelobet sei der Herr, mein Gott – Dem wir das Heilig itzt (sung in English). **Allegri** Miserere. **Mendelssohn** Hear my prayer. **Gardiner** Evening Hymn. **Walford Davies** God be in my head. **Berlioz** L'Enfance du Christ – Shepherds' Farewell. **Franck** Panis angelicus. **Purcell** Hear my prayer, O Lord, Z15.
C. Wood Hail, gladdening light. **Mozart** Ave verum corpus in D, K618. **Gounod** Ave Maria.
Vaughan Williams The Old Hundredth Psalm Tunes. O taste and see.

The choir is at its absolute best here in Barber's arrangement of his famous *Adagio for Strings* as an *Agnus Dei* for unaccompanied voices. In texture and balance, as in the precision of attack and chording, it is really superb. *Jerusalem* is phrased with breadth and care for sense. Breadth, too, distinguishes the performance of *I was glad*, the choir's fine sustaining power serving it well. It is expert in making the most of its resources, so that the quiet 'O pray for the peace of Jerusalem', like the solo choir in the Allegri *Miserere*, makes doubly effective the rich sonority to come. All the solo work is good, with a remarkably authentic treble tone supplied by Andrea Cockerton in Mendelssohn's *Hear my prayer*. Purcell's *Hear my prayer* is probably the gem of the whole programme, which is broadly popular in character, a generous mix of periods and styles, with the choir's own style helping to impose a unity and always guaranteeing performances that will be careful in preparation and scrupulous in beauty of tone.

Officium
Jan Garbarek *sax*
The Hilliard Ensemble (David James *counterten* Rogers Covey-Crump, John Potter *tens* Gordon Jones *bar*).
ECM New Series 445 369-2 (78 minutes: DDD). Latin texts included. Recorded 1993.
Also includes Plainchant, Notre Dame polyphony and motets by Dufay, de la Rue and Morales –
with saxophone. Ⓕ

The play between ancient chant and structured jazz-style improvisation creates a sort of spiritual time warp where past and present happily co-exist on the basis of shared musical goals. For no matter how one views so-called crossover (such a silly term), or the relative lack of wisdom in sticking to rigid musical boundaries, the evidence remains conclusive: 'Officium' successfully transcends any limitations imposed by time and style. If you have any doubts, then play either the opening or closing tracks, both of which find Jan Garbarek (a master of apposite extemporization) easing around Christóbal de Morales's polyphonic 'Pace mihi domine' (from the *Officium defunctorum*) as if it were his own creation. The effect is enchanting and when, eight tracks later or earlier, according to whether you're in 'forward' or 'reverse' mode), the same piece is presented *sans* Garbarek's saxophone, we somehow miss the commentary. If the probable success of this album prompts certain jazz fans and early music specialists to commiserate over their invaded territories, or cynics to align Garbarek and the Hilliards with Górecki and the Monks, then take heart: we're still listening to Respighi's ancient masters, Stravinsky's 'Pergolesi', Tchaikovsky's Mozart and Loussier's Bach, not to mention Ellington's Tchaikovsky. Stylistic cross-pollination makes for a healthy creative environment, and this CD is one of its happiest symptoms. Recordings, documentation and presentation are exemplary.

Once as I Remember …

John Anderson *ob/cor anglais* Ian Watson *org*
Monteverdi Choir; instrumental ensemble / Sir John Eliot Gardiner.
Philips 462 050-2PH (73 minutes: DDD). Texts and translations included. Recorded 1998. Ⓕ Ⓔ
Traditional Gabriel's Message (arr. Bateman). Past three a clock. There is no rose of such virtue.
This Endris Night. The Cradle (arr. Shaw). El rorro. Once as I remember. The King of all Kings.
Cowper Gloria in Excelsis Deo. **Anonymous** Ave Maria gracia plena. Angelus ad Virginem
(arr. Hughes/Grainger). Jolly Shepherd. **Palestrina** Alma redemptoris mater. **G. Bassano** Hodie
Christus natus est. **Sweelinck** Hodie Christus natus est (arr. Wood). **M. Praetorius** Es ist ein
Ros' entsprungen. Psallite unigenito. **L. Bárdos** Ave maris stella. **Howells** A spotless rose. **Byrd**
Gradualia, Vol 2: Nativity of our Lord Jesus Christ – O magnum misterium. Lullaby, my sweet little
baby. **Schütz** Ach Herr, du Schöpfer aller Ding, SWV450 (arr. Vaughan Williams). Entre le Boeuf.
Guillaume, prends ton tambourin. **Dering** Quad videstes pastores. **Tavener** The Lamb.
J. Walther Joseph lieber, Joseph mein. **Gardner** Entry of the Three Kings (arr. Sharp).
R. Armstrong Ring Out ye Crystal Spheres. **Weelkes** Gloria in excelsis Deo.

If you wouldn't normally dream of buying a record for Christmas, well, you'll just have to make an
exception. Its subtitle is "The story of Christmas in readings and music based on the Springhead
Christmas Play". Springhead in Fontmell Magna, Dorset, is the family home in which the Gardiners
celebrated every Christmas with a play. People from the farm and the village took part, and it was a
great occasion for the children. Sir John, once (as he says) 'a somewhat grumpy angel', recalls the
staging and rehearsals, some of the individuals involved and the performances themselves: 'Even
now I cannot hear the opening *Gloria* by Robert Cowper without sensing the complete darkness of
the stage up to the moment when the two Angels with lighted tapers parted the curtains to light the
candles set in the old painted cart-wheels'. Hence no doubt the title proper, 'Once as I Remember'.
But fear not, this is no licensed nostalgic indulgence: the words form the opening line of a
sixteenth-century carol, and the programme justifies itself perfectly well on its own merits
irrespective of family history.

Between Prologue and Epilogue (or the *Glorias* of Robert Cowper and Thomas Weelkes) comes a
sequence, mainly of carols and motets, assembled so as to illustrate the Christmas story in seven
phases: 'The Appearance of the Angels to the Shepherds', for instance, begins with a fine richness
of choir and brass, followed by a round, then Sweelinck's unashamedly tuneful *Hodie* and the crisp,
anticipatory excitement of *Past three a clock*. The next section, 'The Birth', corresponds to a
symphonic slow movement or the 'Et incarnatus' section of the Creed. Carols from many lands,
including Mexico, have found their way to Dorset, and, though most of the music is old, some, such
as the one by Sir John's near-namesake John Gardner, post-date his own childhood participations.
The performances are excellent throughout, singers and players all having the feel of the thing
within them. The acoustic of the church at Salle in Norfolk is ideal, and Nicholas Parker's
production is both imaginative and unobtrusive.

Prometheus

[a]Ingrid Ade-Jesemann, [a]Monika Bair-Ivenz *sops* [a]Susanne Otto *contr* [a]Peter Hall *ten*
[a]Ulrike Krumbiegel, [a]Mathias Schadock *spkrs* [a]Michael Hasel *bass fl* [a]Manfred Preis *bass cl*
[a]Christhard Gössling *euph/tuba* [b]Martha Argerich *pf* [b]Berlin Singakademie;
[a]Freiburg Soloists Choir; Berlin Philharmonic Orchestra / Claudio Abbado.
Sony Classical SK53978 (75 minutes: DDD). Texts and translations included.
Recorded live in 1993. Ⓕ Ⓔ
Beethoven Der Geschöpfe des Prometheus – excerpts. **Liszt** Prometheus, S99.
Scriabin Prometheus, 'Le poème du feu', Op. 60[b]. **Nono** Promoteo – suite[a].

Prometheus's theft of fire from Zeus and the cruelty of his punishment are all but absent from
Beethoven's ballet. Even Melpomene's outburst of violence sounds disarmingly Schubertian, while
the ensuing dances and finale are among the most diverting in the whole of Beethoven's orchestral
output. It would be difficult to imagine a more beautifully shaped performance than Abbado's,
where relative tensions are artfully judged, instrumental solos given with real style and the whole is
captured in a warm, luminous recording. Liszt's glowering outburst – one of his most daring
symphonic poems – is more an informed commentary than a genuine 'performance': lean, sinewy
and consistent, yes, but too cool-headed by far. The disc's real *tour de force*, both sonically and
musically, is Scriabin's Promethean effusion, his *Poem of fire*. Abbado serves as master of
ceremonies, Argerich as a crazed high priestess, her delirious, delicate and unpredictable solo
weaving through the orchestra like a bubbling stream of consciousness. That is how it *should* sound
– overwrought, overpowering, utterly unhinged and yet calculated even to the smallest detail. The
stylistic leap from Scriabin's tantalizing chromatics to Nono's non-gravitational soundscape – with
its solo voices, synthesized sounds and woodwind-blown choruses – is tantamount to leaving the

earth's orbit, and one's earthly body with it. Here we meet Prometheus head-on, lynched on an aural anxiety-loop where vague distortions are as many ripples on a sickly sea of sound. In short, this is a hugely stimulating production.

Sermons and Devotions
The King's Singers (David Hurley, Nigel Short *countertens* Robert Chilcott *ten* Bruce Russell, Philip Lawson *bars* Stephen Connolly *bass*).
RCA Red Seal 09026 68255-2 (69 minutes: DDD). Texts and translations included.
Recorded 1995. Ⓕ
Górecki Totus tuus, Op. 60. **Tormis** The Bishop and the Pagan. **Stravinsky** Pater noster. Ave Maria. **Poole** Wymondham Chants. **Tavener** Funeral Ikos. The Lamb. **Bennett** Sermons and Devotions.

Richard Rodney Bennett is probably better acquainted with The King's Singers' sound than anyone else. It's telling, then, that of the three works on this disc written specially for them, Bennett's is the only one which relies solely on their conventional singing ability. *Sermons and Devotions* uses an austere, unequivocally modern idiom, yet sung with such consummate artistry and pure vocal skills as it is here it all becomes remarkably accessible. Veljo Tormis's contribution to their repertoire sets pagan fifths and peasantish gruntings against quasi-medieval chants – all rather blatant and unsubtle but utterly captivating none the less – while Geoffrey Poole's *Wymondham Chants* employs yet more pseudo-medieval music, with high-pitched chattering vocalizations in the kind of aural spectacular which The King's Singers have made their own. *Totus tuus* has, over the decade of its existence, become something of a choral classic. Its rich, eight-part harmonies have a singularly warming effect. So it comes as something of a surprise to hear it not only reduced to six parts with a single male voice on each but sung by a group who are more usually associated with light-hearted, humorous music. Yet after the initial shock, the singers' sublime musicianship wins the day and in the end Górecki's masterpiece loses none of its intensity and maybe has even gained an extra dimension. As, indeed, is the case of equally outstanding and emotionally charged accounts of music by Stravinsky and Tavener. It all serves to remind us that The King's Singers, shorn of their usual vocal acrobatics, are still a musical group of the very highest order.

Spanish Baroque, Volume 1.
Al Ayre Español / Eduardo López Banzo.
Deutsche Harmonia Mundi 05472 77325-2 (70 minutes: DDD). Ⓕ Ⓟ
Texts and translations included. Recorded 1994.
Anonymous Canción a dos tiples. Two Pasacalles. **Literes** Ah del rustico pastor.
C. Galán Al espejo que retrata. Humano ardor. **J. de Torres** Más no puedo ser. Al clamor.
F. Valls En un noble, sagrado firmamento. **F. de Iribarren** Quién nos dira de una flor. Viendo que Jil, hizo raya.

López Banzo could well be set to achieve for the Spanish baroque what William Christie and Les Arts Florissants have done for French music of the seventeenth and eighteenth centuries. There are many parallels between English and Spanish musical cultures in the baroque: French and Italian stylistic and structural elements are incorporated into a musical language that is nevertheless as clearly Spanish as the Purcell idiom is English. The melodiousness characteristic of the Spanish repertory and its distinctive rhythmic patterns are immediately apparent. The *villancicos* and *cantadas* by Torres, Literes, Iribarren and Valls are all sectional works that alternate recitative and arias in the manner of the Italian cantata, but they also introduce minuets, elegant slow movements, lively refrains and even Spanish dances of popular origin such as the *jácara*. Indeed, the disc ends with one of those characteristically foot-tapping pieces (performed in cathedrals and chapels on such joyous feasts as Christmas) by Iribarren who was chapelmaster at Malaga Cathedral. The performances are very fine. The instrumentalists seem to be completely at home with the style and point up the idiomatic syncopations with just the right degree of emphasis. Under the secure direction of López Banzo, they generally serve the music extremely well. The singers are Spanish which is probably essential, at least at this stage in our knowledge of the repertory. They, too, are consistently excellent. The soprano Marta Almajano's voice is agile and well focused with a hint of that dark, enriching quality – like velvet-clad steel – that seems to characterize the Spanish voice (think of Victoria de los Angeles or even Plácido Domingo). She is, as the music demands, expressive or virtuoso, lyrical or brilliant, and in everything she has a superb sense of line.

The Spirite of Musicke
Suzie Le Blanc *sop* **Les Voix Humaines** (Susie Napper, Margaret Little *vas da gamba*).
ATMA ACD22136 (63 minutes: DDD). Texts included. Recorded 1997. Ⓕ

Coprario Songs of Mourning – 'Tis now dead night; To the World. **A. Ferrabosco II** Like hermit poore. So Beautie on the waters stood (all arr. Little/Napper). **Hume** Captaine Humes Poeticall Musicke – What greater grief; Sweet ayre; Cease leaden slumber. The First Part of Ayres – Touch me sweetly; The Spirite of Musicke. **Jenkins** Suite in A minor. **C. Simpson** Divisions on a Ground – F major; G major.

Over the years they have been playing together as Les Voix Humaines, the bass viol players Susie Napper and Margaret Little have developed a command of their repertory and a rapport that few other ensembles have approached. They express themselves very clearly as individuals but play together with perfect precision. In Tobias Hume's flirtatious *Touch me sweetly* they banter playfully, their control of articulation and dynamics superb; so too in Hume's evocation of a bandora by two bass viols in *The Spirite of Musicke*. To Simpson's divisions for two bass viols they bring a depth of expression not often heard, but they seem especially in their element in John Jenkins's sublimely crafted Suite in A minor. Not content with the existing music for their instruments, they have taken inspiration from Hume, who composed the deeply affecting *Cease leaden slumber* and *What greater grief* for voice and two bass viols, and arranged the lute accompaniment of songs by the Jacobean violists Giovanni Coprario and Alfonso Ferrabosco II for two viols. The result is most often ravishing – the viol has after all been called a 'bowed lute' – although the melancholic simplicity of the vocal line of Coprario's *'Tis now dead night* is overpowered by busy viols. Elsewhere, in Coprario's *To the World* and Ferrabosco's *So Beautie on the waters stood*, their arrangements are more successful. They are joined on this recording by Suzie Le Blanc whose clear, bell-like upper register, excellent diction and formidable breath control suit the music ideally. She seems completely at one with the texts and their settings, investing just the right emotional weight to her readings. The viol players rely perhaps too much for this repertory on a swelled bow stroke which can add too much colour to a delicate accompaniment or unsteady a dance. All in all, though this is an appealing recording which you will want to listen to again and again.

Twentieth-Century Choral Music
[a]Andrew Angus *bass* [b]John Keys *org*
Vasari Singers / Jeremy Backhouse.
EMI Eminence CD-EMX2251 (74 minutes: DDD). Texts and translations included.
Recorded 1995.   Ⓜ
Pärt Summa. The Beatitudes[b]. Seven Magnificat Antiphons. **Tavener** The Lamb. Funeral Ikos. A Hymn to the Mother of God. Hymn for the Dormition of the Mother of God. Magnificat and Nunc dimittis. **Ridout** Litany[a]. **Górecki** Totus tuus, Op. 60.

It is not immediately obvious from listening to this disc where Pärt finishes and Tavener or Górecki takes over, so similar are their musical language and idiom. That is not to say that these works lack individuality or originality. Each in its own right is an expression of unarguably sincere emotion and immense musical beauty, and it is these two facets which are most immediately apparent from these lovingly nurtured performances. The sound is pure, the soprano line often floating ethereally above immaculately measured harmonies, Andrew Angus's delivery of the Priest's words in Alan Ridout's *Litany* achieving an ideal mix of dispassionate intoning and operatic fervour, and the overall choral tone so perfectly blended and exquisitely balanced that it quite takes the breath away. The Vasari Singers bring something distinctive to the programme, and certainly no lover of these composers' music should be without their hypnotic performance of Pärt's *Beatitudes* with its continual alternation of two unrelated chords and ending with a shattering organ postlude – marvellously played by John Keys.

Vespers at the Oratorio dei Girolamini
Emanuela Galli, Roberta Andalò, Roberta Invernizzi *sops* Daniela del Monaco *contr*
Giuseppe de Vittorio, Rosario Totaro *tens* Giuseppe Naviglio *bar*
Coro Mysterium Vocis; Cappella de'Turchini / Antonio Florio.
Opus 111 OPS30 210 (75 minutes: DDD). Texts and translations included. Recorded 1998.   ⒻⒺ
Provenzale Dixit Dominus. Confitebor. Beatus vir. Exulta, jubila. Laudate pueri. Magnus secundum nomen suum. Magnificat. Lauda Jerusalem. **Caresana** Vanitas vanitatum. Iste confessor. **Giamberti** Similabo eum viro sapienti. **F. Rossi** Sinfonia a 5. **Tricarico** Accipite jucunditatem. **Anonymous** Plainchant Antiphons and Responses.

Those who have collected any of the other volumes (this one is the fifth) of this enterprising series of Neapolitan baroque music will relish the unabashed and inimitable vocabulary of these forgotten composers; declamatory vocal concerto, operatic theatricality, as well as earthy allusions to vernacular dance and other distilled and aurally transmitted traditions – cocking a snook at the forbidding gaze of Vesuvius – leaven themselves with purely sacred traditions with delectable ease. Antonio Florio's exotic-sounding group, Cappella de'Turchini (Turchini means turquoise, which was the colour of the tunics of one of Naples's leading conservatories at the time) are just the fillip for those who need constantly reminding that the musical world revolved more around seventeenth-century Naples than it did the majority of centres that patronized the great composers. Neapolitans may not have enjoyed being lorded over by the Spanish but musically it often makes for a fascinating musical cocktail, and judging by Francesco Provenzale's Vespers, such a historical juxtaposition of styles contributes directly to the resourceful realization of strong texts and responsive musical imagery. This is a speculative reconstruction of a Vespers service for the Order of Girolamo, *c*1670, and much of the music displays impressive and inventive craftsmanship. With the majority of the music by Provenzale, Naples's most celebrated composer of the period, there is still an equally invigorating and spontaneous colouring of text. In the case of the *Beatus vir*, a solo soprano conveys this distinctly fulsome text with chromatic melodic inflexions as if they were still wet on the page. Such movements give us the most penetrating view of the composer's expressive powers as Provenzale is forced to plan for over a quarter-of-an-hour, a long time in the stop-start, fashion-conscious mid-baroque. Here, and in the refined *Dixit Dominus* and *Confitebor*, the Cappella de'Turchini is more concerned with conveying originality and characterization than the finer points of ensemble and intonation. If that sounds a little backhanded, there are enough reasons to feel that declaiming text, by the glorious exploitation of open-throated Latin larynxes, is justifiably the ultimate priority. Even if some of the voices don't bear the closest scrutiny, this is musicianship that communicates where it matters.

Opera and song recitals

American Anthem – from Ragtime to Art Song
Nathan Gunn *bar* Kevin Murphy *pf*
EMI Debut CDZ5 73160-2 (68 minutes: DDD). Recorded 1998.   Ⓑ
Barber Songs, Op. 13 – No. 3, Sure on this shining night; No. 4, Nocturne. **Bolcom** Cabaret Songs – Over the piano; Fur (Murray the Furrier); Song of Black Max. **Copland** Old American Songs, Set 1 – Long time ago. Old American Songs, Set 2 – At the river. **Gorney** Americana – Brother, Can You Spare a Dime? **Hoiby** The lamb. **Ives** General William Booth Enters into Heaven. Slugging a vampire. Two little flowers. **Musto** Recuerdo. **Niles** The lass from the Low Countree. **Rorem** Early in the morning. The lordly Hudson. **Scheer** Lean Away (arr. Thomas). American Anthem. At Howard Hanks' House. Holding each other (all arr. Musiker). **Traditional** I wonder as I wander (arr. Niles/Horton). Shenandoah (arr. Musiker).

Nathan Gunn is a protégé of the Met in New York and this is an exceptional début. As the title of the collection implies, there is a wide range of styles united simply through being American music and Gunn wanted to illustrate the rich diversity of his inheritance. He has plenty of classics at his disposal. Of the three by Ives, *Slugging a vampire* is swashbuckling; *General William Booth* is delivered with complete confidence; and *Two little flowers* is suitably charming. Copland's arrangements of *Long time ago* and *At the river* are dead right and particularly moving in Gunn's smooth and steady delivery. The two Barber songs show the same effortless command. When Gunn moves towards the vernacular he chooses three hilarious character sketches from William Bolcom's *Cabaret Songs*, which are done with perfect rhythmic control in partnership with Kevin Murphy at the piano. In the traditional tunes and the real pop songs by Scheer they are just as effective as a team. Gunn's flexible, lyrical baritone often resembles Thomas Hampson and he brings the same intelligence to a wide range of Americana. Well recorded, if slightly harsh at times, but negligible notes and you are referred to the EMI web site for the texts. But a real discovery.

Victoria de los Angeles
Victoria de los Angeles *sop* with various artists.
EMI mono/stereo CMS5 66937-2 (four discs: 301 minutes: ADD/DDD). Texts and translations included. Recorded 1950-92.   Ⓜ
Songs of Spain – traditional and early; medieval; renaissance; baroque. Medieval and renaissance songs of Andalusia. Renaissance songs. Nineteenth- and twentieth-century arrangements and art songs by Barrera/Calleja, Falla, Granados, Guridi, Halffter, Lorca, Mompou, Montsalvatge, Nin, Rodrigo, Toldrá, Vals and Valverde. Opera arias – Goyescas, La Tempricana (Giménez) and La vida breve.

Nothing could be more appropriate in celebrating Victoria de los Angeles's 75th birthday than this extensive conspectus of her recordings of Spanish song over 40 years. It's hardly possible in a brief review to do justice to such an astonishing achievement on the part of the Spanish soprano; indeed had she sung nothing else her place in recorded history would be assured. We begin with her 1950 set of traditional songs arranged by Graciano Tarragó, evocative of an era and a style preserved amazingly in various collections. The singer here is not as outgoing or communicative as she was soon to become, perhaps a shade intimidated by this early encounter with the microphone. There is a certain sameness to her approach, but the voice of the young artist, so refulgent, is a delight in itself. The renaissance and baroque pieces that fill the rest of the first disc are another matter. Not only is the music more accessible but de los Angeles performs it with a winning charm. The second disc is devoted entirely to medieval and renaissance songs recorded in 1960 and 1967 with the Ars Musicae de Barcelona (an early band of authenticists), gleaned from two LPs, the one devoted to songs of Andalusia, including several haunting Sephardic songs, the other to renaissance pieces of a more advanced kind including several expressing deep feelings by Juan Vásquez, among which 'Duélente di mi, Señora' is particularly appealing.

The last two discs bring us to nineteenth- and twentieth-century arrangements of traditional material and original compositions. Among the former, Lorca's set, *Canciones populares españolas*, is absolutely irresistible both in themselves and as performed by the unflagging Victoria in 1970. These imaginative re-creations, full of sentiment, verve and fun, release every aspect of the singer's genius – eager, forward tone, vital enunciation of the texts and unfettered joy in the mere act of communication. The remainder of the songs on this CD, all of which featured frequently in the soprano's recitals, maintain this high standard, including Mompou's touching 'Damunt de tu, només les flors', Montsalvatge's lullaby for a black baby, with which she always bewitched her audiences, and Rodrigo's 'De los álamos vengo' (which, incidentally, appears in its unadorned form earlier in the set). Then what was perhaps de los Angeles's signature-tune, Valverde's 'Clavelitos', not the early 78rpm version but the 1960 stereo remake, and don't miss Victoria accompanying herself in Granados's 'Adios, Granada', a sure-fire encore at most of her recitals.

The final CD includes her unrivalled recordings of Granados's *Tonadillas*, and his *Tres majas dolorosa*, suffering love epitomized in music and interpretation, as it is in Salud's arias from Falla's *La vida breve*. Then, dating from a live recital at Hunter College, NY, in 1971 with her close contemporary Alicia de Larrocha at the piano, we have Granados's *Canciones amatorias*, another favourite item of the singer's, and her dark-grained, intense account of Falla's *Seven Spanish Popular Songs*, with exuberant, subtly shaped support from Larrocha. Catching the bird on the wing, as it were, adds a further dimension of immediacy to our appreciation of this much loved artist. And we leave her at the end of that recital and this engrossing set, tapping our feet as she sings a Zapateado from a zarzuela, the vocal patter delivered with stunning verve, about a tarantula (a metaphor for a young lover) that has stung the precocious singer. Lionel Salter provides the predictably well-informed and amusing notes, but it is a pity he was not allowed space to describe in more detail the wide variety of material. Andrew Walter's transfers are impeccably done.

Janet Baker Song Recital.
Dame Janet Baker *mez* Gerald Moore *pf*
EMI CDM5 65009-2 (75 minutes: ADD). Texts and translations included. Recorded 1967-69. Ⓜ
Fauré Automne, Op. 18 No. 3. Prison, Op. 83 No. 1. Soir, Op. 83 No. 2. Fleur jetée, Op. 39 No. 2. En sourdine, Op. 58 No. 2. Notre amour, Op. 23 No. 2. Mai, Op. 1 No. 2. La chanson du pêcheur, Op. 4 No. 1. Clair de lune, Op. 46 No. 2. **Schubert** Am Grabe Anselmos, D504. Abendstern, D806. Die Vögel, D691. Die Götter Griechenlands, D677. Gondelfahrer, D808. Auflösung, D807. **R. Strauss** Morgen, Op. 27 No. 4. Befreit, Op. 39 No. 4. **Stanford** La Belle Dame sans merci. **Parry** Proud Maisie. O mistres mine. **Busch** Rest. **Warlock** Pretty ring-time. **Vaughan Williams** Linden Lea. **Gurney**: The fields are full. **Britten** Corpus Christi carol. **Ireland** The Salley Gardens. **Quilter** Love's philosophy, Op. 3 No. 1.

This CD is a timely reminder, a generous one too, of Baker in her prime. At the peak of her career at the end of the 1960s, the tone is at its most beautiful, the singing as secure as it is intelligent. One realizes anew that here is one of the great singers of the century and one comfortable in so many idioms. It may be that some native singers of Fauré and Schubert capture the soul of these songs more unerringly, but few actually sing them so glowingly, so intensely. The typical Schubertian sadness brings out the very best in her. Nobody has sung *Am Grabe Anselmos* with so much sincere and deep feeling, nor have the lamenting echoes of *Die Götter Griechenlands* ever sounded more haunting. Technically the performances are also without fault. In her own language, Dame Janet is at home in every sense. The gems here are the Stanford ballad, the tensions of the tale sustained throughout by both artists, the tender sorrow of Britten's *Corpus Christi*, the fervent outpouring of Quilter's *Love's philosophy*. Everywhere Moore is at one with his partner, always supportive, perceptive, with that soft and inimitable touch of his. The recordings, for their dates, are exemplary in balance and presence.

Olaf Bär Lieder by German Opera Composers.
Olaf Bär *bar* **Helmut Deutsch** *pf*
EMI CDC5 55393-2 (67 minutes: DDD). Texts and translations included. Recorded 1994.   Ⓕ
Kreutzer Frühlingsglaube. Die Post. Die Kapelle, Op. 64 No. 1. Nachtreise. Entschluss, Op. 64
No. 2. Nähe des Geliebten. **Nicolai** Scarco d'affanni. Herbstlied, Op. 37. Il mistero, Op. 24 No. 2.
Goetz Lieder, Op. 12 – No. 1, Geheimnis; No. 2, Schliesse mir die Augen beide; No. 3,
Wandervöglein. Lieder, Op. 19 – No. 1, Ein Frühlingstraum; No. 2, Der Frühling kommt!; No. 3,
Wandrers Nachtlied, 'Der du von dem Himmel bist'. **Humperdinck** Romanze. Blauveilchen.
Entsagung. Oft sinn ich hin und wieder. Das Lied von Glück. Sonntagsruhe. **Marschner**
Rheinromanzen, Op. 128 – No. 1, Die sieben Freier. Gesänge und Balladen, Op. 160 – No. 1, Der
König von Thule; No. 2, Die Rache. Das Flämmchen auf der Heide, Op. 80 No. 12. Die Monduhr,
Op. 102 No. 2. Das Lied von alten König, Op. 82 No. 2. Der betrogene Teufel, Op. 87 No. 1.

For all but the most knowledgeable in Lieder this will be a real and fascinating voyage of discovery.
Each of the composers represented is known, if at all, by one or two operas, but all wrote liberally
as song composers. Kreutzer's setting of *Die Post*, written before Schubert's, is worthy to stand
beside it. *Die Kapelle* is even better, a funeral piece in the minor of much more than passing interest
in its acute setting of an Uhland text, changes of key worthy of Schubert and intense repeats of the
single word 'Hirtenknabe'. The three songs by Nicolai are pleasing but slight. Goetz, who died all
too young, was admired by Brahms and one can hear why in the very Brahmsian *Schliesse mir die
Augen beide*, a setting of an admirable poem by Ludwig Sturm. Goethe's other Lieder here are not
so remarkable. Humperdinck also proves something of a disappointment except in the Wagnerian
Sonntagsruhe. The remainder do not evince sufficiently individual personality. Marschner is quite
another matter. Each song here is at least to be spoken of in the same breath as those by his
contemporary, Loewe, whom he much resembles in style. *Die sieben Freier* is another of those
Lorelei-inspired poems so beloved of the German romantics. This one deserves to stand alongside
the best. Even better is the Gothic horror of both *Die Rache*, with its ostinato imitation of
hoofbeats, and *Die Monduhr*, imbued throughout with a constantly varied motif in thirds. Perhaps
these pieces aren't so unexpected from the composer of *Der Vampyr*. *Der betrogene Teufel* is a nice
essay in the ribald, which is delivered by Bär in an appropriately biting timbre. But then throughout
he is back on his most convincing form, relishing every word and note and singing with restored
freedom. Deutsch proves a worthy partner and the recording is forward and well balanced.

Cecilia Bartoli Arie Antiche.
Cecilia Bartoli *mez* **György Fischer** *pf*
Decca 436 267-2DH (66 minutes: DDD). Texts and translations included. Recorded 1990-91.   Ⓕ
A. Scarlatti Già il sole dal Gange. Son tutta duolo. Se Florindo è fedele. O cessate di piagarmi.
Spesso vibra per suo gioco. **Giordani** Caro mio ben. **Lotti** Pur dicesti, o bocca bella. **Cesti**
Intorno all'idol mio. **Paisiello** Nel cor più non mi sento. Il mio ben quando verrà. Chi vuol la
zingarella. **Anonymous** O leggiadri occhi belli. **Marcello** Quella fiamma che m'accende.
Caldara Selve amiche. Sebben, crudele. **Caccini** Tu ch'hai le penne, amore. Amarilli. **Parisotti**
Se tu m'ami. **Cavalli** Delizie contente. **Vivaldi** Sposa son disprezzata. **Carissimi** Vittoria, vittoria!

With Scarlatti and Vivaldi among the composers, these *arie antiche* are not necessarily very old.
Italian singers have long been accustomed to lumping together all songs earlier than Mozart (or
perhaps Haydn) under this heading, piously including them at the start of a recital so as to establish
a classical tone and give them time to try out their voices before entering on the more strenuous and
popular part of their programme. Bartoli here devotes a whole disc to them, as things delightful in
themselves, varied in mood and style, and calling in turn on almost all the essential arts of a good
singer. No one can come away with a feeling of having been short-changed at the end of this. Her
voice is ideal, both silken and chaste, finely controlled, cleanly produced. With a simple, direct song
such as the famous *Caro mio ben* she will never fuss or show off; with Vivaldi's *Sposa son
disprezzata* she exploits the most deliciously languishing tone and sometimes one more frankly
passionate and 'operatic'. Most of the items are gems, and to all of them György Fischer brings the
touch of the expert jeweller, knowing exactly how best to set off the beauties of voice and melody.

Cecilia Bartoli Chant d'amour.
Cecilia Bartoli *mez* **Myung-Whun Chung** *pf*
Decca 452 667-2DH (68 minutes: DDD). Texts and translations included. Recorded 1996.   Ⓕ🅴
Bizet Chant d'amour. Ouvre ton coeur. Adieus de l'hôtesse arabe. Tarantelle. La Coccinelle.
Delibes Les filles de Cadix. **Viardot-Garcia** Hai luli!. Havanaise. Les filles de Cadix.
Berlioz Tristia, Op. 18 – La mort d'Ophélie. Zaïde, Op. 19 No. 1. **Ravel** Chants populaires –
Chanson française; Chanson espagnole; Chanson italienne; Chanson hébraïque. Vocalise en
forme de Habanera. Deux mélodies hébraïques. Tripatos.

Cecilia Bartoli goes from strength to strength. Taking on the French repertory in this delightful disc, she also gives us some great rarities. The opening Bizet group includes two of his best-known songs, *Ouvre ton coeur* and *Adieux de l'hôtesse arabe*. In the first, one perhaps might ask for more of a smile in the voice. Predictably, in the pessimistic Hugo poem about the Arab girl bidding farewell to the handsome traveller, Bartoli relishes the muezzin-like vocalise on 'Hélas, adieu, souviens-toi'. This is one of the best performances of this mini-drama since Conchita Supervia's orchestral-accompanied version. In this, and the succeeding *Tarantelle*, 'tra-la-la's and froth, one is prompted to wonder if there will one day be a Bartoli *Carmen. La Coccinelle* ('The ladybird') is a little salon gem, with a fast waltz motif. Bartoli uses a croaky little voice to act out the Ladybird. This song alone is worth the price of the CD.

Delibes's *Les filles de Cadix*, all trills and sunshine, is contrasted with an equally demanding setting of the same poem by Pauline Viardot. *Hai luli!* with words by Xavier de Maistre is a sad second-cousin to the Willow Song from Rossini's *Otello. Havanaise* is a real curiosity: the first and last stanzas, sung in Spanish, frame a middle section in French which breaks into a Rossinian flight of coloratura before returning to the swaying movements of the dance. Evenings *chez* Viardot must have been enlivened considerably by such songs. The narration of Ophelia's death, words by Ernest Legouvé, vaguely based on Shakespeare, ends with a wordless melody which Bartoli sings in a hushed, beautiful tone. In *Zaïde* she plays the castanets with skill; if this song is less interesting than the evocations of Spain by Bizet, Delibes and Viardot, that's Berlioz's fault, not Bartoli's. In the concluding Ravel group, an interesting contrast can be made between Viardot's *Havanaise* of the 1840s and Ravel's *Habanera* of 1907. In the four popular songs, Bartoli is especially effective in the Hebrew number as well as the two other *Mélodies hébraïques*, 'Kaddish' and 'L'énigme éternelle'. All these Ravel songs have often been recorded, so one cannot help wishing that Bartoli and Chung had stayed with the nineteenth-century French salon repertory to uncover more rarities. Still, this is one of the most satisfying recitals by one of the great singers of our time. First-rate recording and sensitive accompaniment throughout.

Cecilia Bartoli – Live in Italy
Cecilia Bartoli *mez* Jean-Yves Thibaudet *pf*
Sonatori de la Gioiosa Marca.
Decca 455 981-2DH (77 minutes: DDD). Texts and translations included.
Recorded live in 1998.   Ⓕ Ⓔ
Bellini Malinconia, ninfa gentile. Ma rendi pur contento. **Berlioz** Zaïde, Op. 19 No. 1. **Bizet** Carmen – Près des remparts de Séville. **Caccini** Nuove musiche e nuova maniera di scriverle – Al fonte al prato; Tu ch'hai le penne. Amarilli mia bella. **Donizetti** La conocchia. Me voglio fa'na casa. **T. Giordani** Caro mio ben. **Handel** Il trionfo del Tempo e del Disinganno – Lascia la spina. **Montsalvatge** Canto negro. **Mozart** Oiseaux, si tous les ans, K307/K284d. Le nozze di Figaro – Voi che sapete. **Rossini** Mi lagnerò tacendo, Book 1 – No. 2 in D major; No. 3 in D minor, 'Sorzico'; No. 4 in E major, 'Il risentimento'. L'orpheline du Tyrola. Zelmira – Riedi al soglio. Canzonetta spagnuola. **Schubert** La pastorella al Prato, D528. **Viardot** Havanaise. Hai luli!. **Vivaldi** Griselda – Agitata da due venti.

Bartoli's voice is still in lovely, almost unflawed condition. With the assurance of a practised technique that she has made completely her own she is free to discover more in the music she sings and to realize the expressive resources open to her. If one wishes to take stock of her growth as an artist, the second item in her programme, Caccini's *Amarilli*, affords an opportunity. She recorded it first in 1990 with piano accompaniment by György Fischer in a touching performance, beautiful as sound and sensitive in mood (available on Decca). But the mood was set, and she was singing a song written and remembered. In the newer recording she is living and seemingly inventing it. Thus the development of feeling at 'Credilo pur' brings a fresh impulse, a more urgent appeal, and the repetitions of the beloved name acquire a musing, improvisatory quality. All of this (and much more of its kind) is sheer enrichment.

Nevertheless, if the vocal equivalent of a selective weedkiller could be employed, it might make short work of two other fast-growing products of this fair field. One, the persistent aspirating of runs, is probably too deep-rooted by now; the other, more insidious, is of comparatively recent cultivation, a breathy winsomeness, an exhalation of pretty pathos or girlish wide-eyed intimacy. If this were reserved for occasional use it might be acceptable and effective, but in the present recital it is habitual. As for the technique used in passagework such as abounds in the Vivaldi aria, it does facilitate rapid movement and helps to ensure clear articulation. Everything is heightened in these performances – the rich depth of contralto tone, languor and vivacity in the Viardot songs, the panache of the Berlioz, and smouldering promise and fiery fulfilment of Rossini's *Canzonetta spagnuola*. The variety of accompaniments is another attraction, all delightfully played. With the live atmosphere of the concert hall and the sense of freedom around the voice, this is surely the most faithful and revealing of all Bartoli's records to date.

Cecilia Bartoli An Italian Songbook.
Cecilia Bartoli *mez* **James Levine** *pf*
Decca 455 513-2DH (67 minutes: DDD). Texts and translations included. Recorded 1996.　　Ⓕ🅱
Rossini Péchés de vieillesse: Book 3 – L'esule; Book 11 – A ma belle mère; Aragonese. La passeggiata. Mi lagnerò tacendo – Boléro. Soirées musicales – La danza. **Bellini** Vaga luna che inargenti. L'abbandono. Malinconia, ninfa gentile. Il fervido desiderio. Torna, vezzosa Fillide. Vanne, o rosa fortunata. Dolente imagine di figlia mia. La farfalleta. Per pietà, bell'idol mio. **Donizetti** Il barcaiolo. Ah, rammenta, o bella Irene. Amore e morte. La conocchia. Me voglio fa'na casa.

The transforming power of imagination is rarely shown so clearly. On record and in recital these songs and their like have so often appeared as tepid little exercises, cautious investigations of the voice, the acoustic, the audience. But now, behold, they burgeon. Life abundant lies within the vocal line, and even the silly old accompaniments sound well. Such is the effect of the Bartoli-Levine combination. From the very first bars it feels that something special among Bartoli's many fine recordings have come into being here with these two distinguished artists in association. These are thoughtful, passionate and colourful performances, which outshine all previous versions of the more familiar songs. Among the less familiar items, Bellini's *Torna, vezzosa Fillide* may come as the most engaging discovery. Rossini's miniature Requiem for his mother-in-law seems not to be a joke, whereas the *Aragonese* (a setting in the style of Aragon of *Mi lagnerò tacendo*) surely must be. There might have been something to say here and now about intrusive 'h's and that other intrusion, a breathy quality sometimes cultivated in the interests of expression or intimacy, but they are not gross or prohibitive features of the singing here, and the lovely voice and lively art make ample amends.

Cecilia Bartoli Italian Songs.
Cecilia Bartoli *mez* **András Schiff** *pf*
Decca 440 297-2DH (68 minutes: DDD). Texts and translations included. Recorded 1992.　　Ⓕ🅱
Beethoven La Partenza, WoO124. Four Ariettas, Op. 82. In questa tomba oscura, WoO133. **Mozart** Ridente la calma, K152/K210a. **Schubert** Didone abbandonata, D510. Im Haine, D738. An die Leier, D737. La Pastorella al Prato, D528. Vier Canzonen, D688. Pensa, che questo istante, D76. Willkommen und Abschied, D767. **Haydn** Arianna a Naxos, HobXXVIb/2.

It is good to be reminded of these composers' responses to the Italian muse in this particularly well-cast recital. Central Europe, in the person of András Schiff, meets Italy, in Cecilia Bartoli, to delightful, often revelatory effect. The simple form and undemanding vocal line of Beethoven's little *La Partenza* makes for a truthfulness of expression which Bartoli's clear, light-filled enunciation recreates to the full. With her warm breath gently supporting the voice's lively, supple inflexion, she reveals Beethoven's own skill in word-setting both here and in two fascinatingly contrasted settings of 'L'amante impaziente' in the *Ariettas*, Op. 82. Schubert's ten *Canzone* selected here show a wide range of treatment, from the compressed lyric drama of Dido's lament 'Vedi quanto adoro', in which Bartoli's lives intensely from second to second, to the honeyed Goldoni *pastorella* and the thrumming, pulsating serenade of 'Guarda, che bianca luna', D688 No. 2. A gently, fragrantly shaped Mozart *Ridente la calma*, and a Haydn *Arianna a Naxos* of movingly immediate and youthful response complete this unexpectedly and unusually satisfying recital.

Bel Canto Opera Arias.
Marcelo Alvarez *ten*
ᵃChorus and Orchestra of Welsh National Opera / **Carlo Rizzi**.
Sony Classical SK60721 (66 minutes: DDD). Texts and translations included. Recorded 1998.　　Ⓕ
Bellini I Puritani – Son salvo … A una fonte ... Son già lontani (with **Ying Huang** *sop*). **Donizetti** L'elisir d'amore – Una furtiva lagrima. Il duca d'Alba – Inosservato, penetrava ... Angelo casto e bel. La favorita – Favorita del re! ... Spirto gentil. Lucia di Lammermoor – Tombe degl'avi miei ... Fra poco a me ricovero. Linda di Chamounix – Se tanto in ira agli uomini. **Verdi** Rigoletto – Questa o quella; Ella mi fu rapita! ... Parmi veder le lagrime ... Scorrendo uniti remota ... Possente amor mi chiamaᵃ; La donna è mobile. La traviata – Lunge da lei ... De' miei bollenti spiriti ... O mio rimorso!

Fêted at La Scala, Covent Garden and the Vienna State Opera among other houses, Marcelo Alvarez explains just why in arias from various roles he has sung in those theatres. His voice has a typically Spanish timbre analogous to that of the young Carreras, dark-grained and plaintive, the ideal instrument for his chosen parts in Bellini, mid-period Verdi and above all Donizetti. As Nemorino, Marcello, Edgardo, Fernando and especially Carlo (the part – in *Linda di Chamounix* – in which he made his début at La Scala), he evinces the line, the shaping of phrase and the intelligent accentuation of the text essential for a tenor in the *ottocento* repertory. The way he shapes Carlo's gentle aria 'Se tanto in ira agli uomini' and Fernando's 'Spirto gentil' is so fine and sensitive that he need fear few comparisons from singers of the past except that the highest notes are not always as easily produced as they might be, and ideally one would like more shading of tone in Nemorino's much-recorded piece. He again shows his artistry by giving us the opening scene from *I Puritani* complete, singing the lovely cantilena, 'A una fonte', in an ingratiating manner, the phrasing and breath control exemplary. As for Verdi, Alvarez gives us a generous tranche of the Duke of Mantua's role right at the start, an ebullient, elegant rake this, never vulgar or macho. Alfredo's expression of eternal love for his Violetta and the subsequent cabaletta have the spontaneous, youthful ardour that is the exact opposite of routine: with the words very forward the model here is surely Pavarotti, though Alvarez's voice is probably a size smaller. Rizzi and his Welsh forces provide well-honed support and the recording gives Alvarez real presence.

Black Roses
Solveig Kringelborn sop **Malcolm Martineau** pf
Virgin Classics VC5 45273-2 (55 minutes: DDD). Texts and translations included.
Recorded 1996.   Ⓕ
Grieg Six Songs, Op. 25. **Nielsen** Six Songs, FS18. **Rangström** The Girl under the New Moon.
Pan. The Only Moment. Melody. Prayer to the Night. Villemo. **Sibelius** Six Songs, Op. 36.

The Grieg and Sibelius sets are decently represented on CD, particularly the obvious songs like 'A swan' and 'Black Roses', after which the whole disc is named. All the Rangström songs have been recorded at one time or another, though not all are currently available, and two of the six Nielsen, FS18 set are not easily come by. But any addition to the *romans* repertoire (the *romans* incidentally, is the Scandinavian equivalent of the German Lied or the French *mélodie*) is welcome and one with as much charm as this, doubly so. Kringelborn opens with the Rangström group – and with the haunting Runeberg setting, 'The Only Moment' – and characterizes all of them with real sensitivity. On home territory and Grieg, Kringelborn is very persuasive though the Sibelius set is not uniformly successful. She could have made more of the ending of 'But my bird is long in homing'. 'Black Roses' comes off very well indeed. So, for the most part, do the Nielsen songs, except 'Lake of memory', where Kringelborn sounds a shade tentative – and slightly under the note. Summing up, if there are any reservations, it is that Kringelborn tends to set greater store by a smooth *legato* and beauty of sound than dramatic character. Mind you, she has beauty of sound to set store by, and a pleasing vocal personality and there is so much that gives delight. Malcolm Martineau's accompanying throughout is admirable. He is wonderfully supportive and responsive to every change of mood, and the recording is absolutely first-class.

Barbara Bonney American Songs.
Barbara Bonney sop [a]**Sato Knudsen** vc **André Previn** pf
Decca 455 511-2DH (76 minutes: DDD). Texts included. Recorded 1996.   Ⓕ Ⓢ
Previn Sallie Chisum remembers Billy the Kid. Vocalise[a]. **Copland** 12 Poems of Emily Dickinson.
Argento Six Elizabethan Songs. **Barber** Ten Hermit Songs, Op. 29.

Barbara Bonney is allegedly related to Billy the Kid. Allegedly. She herself is convinced, or rather was convinced, when she first saw the pictures. The resemblance to her own father was 'terrifying': the big searching eyes, the ears that stick out – the look. And then an American friend in London gave her a copy of *The Collected Works of Billy the Kid*, and that's where André Previn came in. *Sallie Chisum remembers Billy the Kid* – the spur of this all-American programme – takes its cues from Wild West history – or is that mythology? Sallie Chisum was a prostitute who went to bed with both Billy and Pat Garrett, and her words are starry-eyed. Previn sets them as she will have remembered them, touches of sweet sentiment in the voice played off against the dusty and gritty realities of the keyboard. There's more than a hint of the bar-room piano in that. And then up soars the voice recalling the 'flower in his lapel' and the fragrance of it lends a touch of naïvety. The Argento was a shrewd choice, not just on account of its rarity value (this is the world première recording), but because Bonney and Previn both have ties with England which adds something to our perception of the cycle's Anglo/American cross-breeding. Both are brilliantly articulate and quick of reflex, the mix of ancient and modern, the ornate and the reflective – indeed the somnambulant – is beautifully judged.

The Copland and Barber sets are splendid, too. In Copland's Emily Dickinson, Bonney of course has the wholesome, homespun qualities – the pure and simple gifts – this music demands. We know how raptly she will sustain 'Heart, we will forget him!', and she does. There is ecstasy and truth in this voice. But she can be feisty, too, deploying a determined and surprisingly resilient low register for 'There came a wind like a bugle' and the awesome plunge to 'East of eternity' in 'Sleep is supposed to be'. And where Dickinson is the playful child – as in 'Why do they shut me out of Heaven?' and 'Going to Heaven!' – there is a knowing coyness. In all this, Previn's contribution, his partnership, is invaluable. Listen to him sign off 'Going to Heaven!' Not so much the exclamation mark, more the wink. And listen to him, too, lending weight and masculinity to the bolder illuminations of Barber's *Hermit Songs*. His resoluteness undoubtedly helps Bonney darken and intensify her response to these songs. 'The Monk and his Cat' sounds all the more cosy and incongruous in consequence. We may have each other, it seems to say, but in the end we have only ourselves. To that end, the closing song – 'The Desire for Hermitage' – is marvellous. A very real sense of isolation permeates the final stanza. Bonney and Previn may be two, but for the time being they are one.

Maria Callas Rarities.
Maria Callas *sop*
[a]Paris Conservatoire Orchestra / Nicola Rescigno; [b]Maggio Musicale Fiorentino Orchestra / Tullio Serafin; [c]Rome RAI Orchestra / Alfredo Simonetto; [d]Philharmonia Orchestra / Antonio Tonini; [e]Paris Opera Orchestra / Georges Prêtre.
EMI CDC7 54437-2 (78 minutes: ADD). Texts and translations included.
Items marked [c] recorded live in 1954.   (F) **H**
Beethoven Ah! perfido, Op. 65[a]. **Mozart** Don Giovanni – Non mi dir[b] (recorded 1953). Die Entführung aus dem Serail – Martern aller Arten[c] (sung in Italian). **Weber** Oberon – Ozean du Ungeheuer![d] (English. rec. 1962). **Rossini** Armida – D'amore al dolce impero[c]. **Donizetti** Lucrezia Borgia – Tranquillo ei posa ... Com'è bello![d] (rec. 1961). **Verdi** Don Carlos – O don fatale[d] (rec. 1961). I vespri siciliani – Arrigo! ah, parli[d] (rec. 1960). Il trovatore – Vanne ... lasciami ... D'amor sull'ali rosee[a]. I Lombardi – Te, Vergin santa[a]. (both rec. 1964-65). Aida – Pur' ti riveggo ... Fuggiam gli ardor[e] (with Franco Corelli *ten* rec. 1964).

'Rarity' is one of those tricky words which, being really only quantitative, seems to imply something about quality as well. So the reader may well look doubtfully at the title: the 'Callas Rarities' may indeed be rarities for the best of reasons, that of inferiority to versions and recordings that are less rare. In this instance, though, they are genuinely well worth having. For example, here is the Nile Duet from *Aida* with Franco Corelli, sole survivor of a projected album of duets to be recorded in 1964. Corelli provides the vocal thrills, sometimes even responding in kind to the dramatic intensity which characterizes Callas's performance from the start. Her voice is sometimes raw, and the soft B flat on 'fuggiam' only just arrives and stays put. But always there is something distinctive: here it is the nostalgia, 'Là tra foreste' being sung as a wistful, private vision of the homeland. Then there are the two incredibly brilliant solos from a concert at San Remo in 1954 ('Martern aller Arten' and 'D'amore al dolce impero'); also previously unpublished versions, not alternative 'takes' but different performances, products of a different session. Usually one can see why they were not issued at the time, but here it is easier to see why they deserve to see the light of this later day.

Cecilia & Bryn – Duets
Cecilia Bartoli *mez* Bryn Terfel *bass-bar*
Orchestra dell'Accademia di Santa Cecilia / Myung-Whun Chung.
Decca 458 928-2DH (54 minutes: DDD). Texts and translations included. Recorded 1998.   (F) **E**
Donizetti L'elisir d'amore – Come sen va contento! ... Quanto amore! Ed io spietata!
Mozart Le nozze di Figaro – Cinque dieci; Cosa stai misurando; Se a caso madama; Or bene, ascolta, e taci ... Se vuol balare signor Contino; Signor ... la vostra sposa ... Crudel! perchè finora; Un moto di gioia, K579. Così fan tutte – Passeggiamo anche noi ... Il core vi dono. Don Giovanni – Alfin siam liberati ... Là ci darem la mano. Die Zauberflöte – Pa-Pa-Pa-Papagena. **Rossini** Il barbiere di Siviglia – Ebben, signor Figaro? ... Dunque io son? L'italiana in Algeri – Ai capricci della sorte.

Splendidly well-matched duettists, Bartoli and Terfel (or are we on Christian-name terms even in review?) are as vivid a pair of vocal comedians-and-charmers as any in the business. The fatal thing would be if they tried to outdo each other, but, to all aural appearances, they do not: they spark naturally and nicely, and gain accordingly, both as individuals and as an act. They are also instinctively good at making records. Recitative can be light and quick-witted – listeners are following the libretto and don't need points underlined or played for laughs. Don Giovanni can whisper sweet nothings in Zerlina's ear, Adina can suggest a subtle compound of feelings in a shading of tone. Both singers know that their voice-faces must never go blank, the unseen movements inert, and in the Papagena-Papageno duet (for instance) the interplay is as clear to the mind's eye as any stage-action would be in the theatre. Sometimes there is a hair's-breadth misjudgement (in *Il barbiere* Rosina's 'Un biglietto?' should surely be all surprise and wonderment, and the 'Eccola quà' a businesswoman's *fait accompli*), but generally all goes well, the point being that there is nothing 'general' about it (when Figaro, in the other opera, starts on his room-measurements in the very opening moments of the disc he is actually counting, we 'see' him and know that this is what for the moment is on his mind). Of the singing as such, it is good to be able to report Terfel on graceful form and Bartoli in fine voice. There is much to be enjoyed in this recital, finely recorded and with stylish accompaniment under Myung-Whun Chung.

Tracey Chadwell's Song Book
Tracey Chadwell sop [a]Pamela Lidiard pf [b]John Turner recs
British Music Society BMS420/1CD (two discs: 141 minutes: ADD). Texts included.
Recorded 1988-94.
(F)
Maconchy Sun, Moon and Stars[a]. Three Songs[a]. **Lefanu** I am Bread[a]. A Penny for a Song[a].
Whitehead Awa Herea[a]. **Cresswell** Words for Music[a]. **Lumsdaine** A Norfolk Songbook[b].
Lilburn Three Songs[a]. **Farquhar** Six Songs of Women[a]. **Joubert** The Turning Wheel, Op. 95[a].
R. R. Bennett A Garland for Marjory Fleming[a].

Tracey Chadwell, a soprano of exceptional gifts and intelligence, died in her mid-thirties early in 1996 after a long and courageous battle with leukaemia. Nicola Lefanu, who contributes an affectionate note to this anthology of recordings from the BBC archives, was at her last concert, three weeks before her death, and says that 'she looked and sounded ravishing'. She always did, and apart from its value as a memorial to a much loved and deeply missed artist and as a collection of fine songs (many of them written for her), this pair of discs could stand as a model to other singers in the expert management of a voice, in fearless vocal resource and joyful adventurousness in choice of repertory. She had admirable taste: there is no music here that needs special pleading, and her advocacy of all of it is compelling. Most of it is unfamiliar, much of it not recorded before, so it is probably helpful to single out a few particular pleasures that you might care to sample: Lefanu's haunting, intimate and subtle *I am Bread* easily sustaining its seven-minute duration, not least because of Chadwell's care over line and florid detail; the elegant talent of David Farquhar, making a simple but memorable thing of Sir Philip Sidney's 'My true love hath my heart and I have his'; the strong drama and toughly strong melody of Gillian Whitehead's *Awa Herea*, using texts in Maori and English, and making huge demands of the singer's technique as well as her imagination; Richard Rodney Bennett's beautiful settings of the poems of a child who died at eight years old (Chadwell's tender line in 'Sweet Isabell' is deeply moving here); the big, striking gestures of John Joubert's fine short cycle. She brings a wonderfully pure tone and limpid line to Elizabeth Maconchy's Thomas Traherne settings. She was an adorable singer. Pamela Lidiard, her regular accompanist, is an ideally sensitive partner and the recordings are excellent.

Régine Crespin Vocal Recital.
Régine Crespin sop [b]John Wustman pf
[a]Suisse Romande Orchestra / Ernest Ansermet.
Decca Legends 460 973-2DM (68 minutes: ADD). Texts and translations included.
Recorded 1963-67.
(F) **RR**
Berlioz Les nuits d'été. **Ravel** Shéhérazade[a]. **Debussy** Trois chansons de Bilitis[b].
Poulenc Banalités[b] – Chansons d'Orkenise; Hôtel. La courte paille[b] – Le carafon; La reine de coeur. Chansons villageoises[b] – Les gars qui vont à la fête. Deux poèmes de Louis Aragon[b].

Some recordings withstand the test of time and become acknowledged classics. This is one of them. Régine Crespin's voluptuous tone, her naturally accented French and her feeling for the inner meaning of the songs in the Berlioz and Ravel cycles are everywhere evident. Better than most single interpreters of the Berlioz, she manages to fulfil the demands of the very different songs, always alive to verbal nuances. In the Ravel, she is gorgeously sensuous, not to say sensual, with the right timbre for Ravel's enigmatic writing. The Debussy and Poulenc songs on this disc enhance its worth. Crespin offers an extremely evocative, perfumed account of the Debussy pieces and is ideally suited to her choice of Poulenc, of which her interpretation of 'Hôtel' is a classic. Ansermet and his orchestra, though not quite note perfect, are – like the singer – right in timbre and colour for both these rewarding cycles. The sound is reasonable given the age of the recording.

Renée Fleming The Beautiful Voice.
Renée Fleming sop
English Chamber Orchestra / Jeffrey Tate.
Decca 458 858-2DH (70 minutes: DDD). Texts and translations included. Recorded 1997.
(F)
Charpentier Louise – Depuis le jour. **Gounod** Faust – O Dieu! que de bijoux! ... Ah! je ris.
Massenet Manon – Obéissons quand leur voix appelle. **Dvořák** Songs my mother taught me, B104 No. 4. **Flotow** Martha – 'Tis the last rose of summer. **Puccini** La rondine – Chi il bel sogno di Doretta. **Korngold** Die tote Stadt – Glück, das mir verblieb. **Orff** Carmina Burana – In trutina.
R. Strauss Morgen, Op. 27 No. 4. **Rachmaninov** (arr. Braden) Vocalise, Op. 34 No. 14.
J. Strauss II Die Fledermaus – Klänge der Heimat. **Lehár** Die lustige Witwe – Es lebt eine Vilja.
Cano Luna – Epilogo. **Canteloube** Chants d'Auvergne – Baïlêro.

Sweet tooth, prepare for action. What does Lamb say in his *Chapter on Ears*? Something about piling honey upon sugar and sugar upon honey. The programme capitulates in stages. It begins well, sharpening the palate with Marguerite's Jewel Song after Louise's erotic musings. Soon we are swaying dreamily with the 'Viljalied' and then reclining in the drowsy sunshine and languid trickle of Canteloube's 'Baïlèro'. Louise, in this performance, cares for words and feelings as well as tone, Marguerite relishes her new role of 'coquette', and Manon plays lovingly with the consciousness of her own beauty. Throughout, the singing provides pleasures that are *not* simply those of 'the beautiful voice', as the title has it. Occasionally, it is true, one wishes for a more athletic style (the creamy Caballé-Te Kanawa associations spiced with a dash of Ninon Vallin perhaps). But this *is* 'the beautiful voice', no doubt about that, exercised with skill and heard in what will appeal widely as a programme of captivatingly beautiful music. Jeffrey Tate provides lively support.

Renée Fleming Great Opera Scenes.
Renée Fleming *sop* [a]Larissa Diadkova *mez* [b]Jonathan Summers *bar*
London Symphony Orchestra / Sir Georg Solti.
Decca 455 760-2DH (72 minutes: DDD). Texts and translations included. Recorded 1996. Ⓕ 🅴
Mozart Le nozze di Figaro – Porgi, amor; E Susanna non vien! ... Dove sono.
Tchaikovsky Eugene Onegin – Letter scene[a]. **Dvořák** Rusalka – O silver moon. **Verdi** Otello –
Era più calmo? ... Mia madre aveva ... Piangea cantando ... Ave Maria[a]. **Britten** Peter Grimes –
Embroidery in childhood[b]. **R. Strauss** Daphne – Ich komme, grünende Brüder.

Here's a singer who has reached complete maturity as an artist, revelling in her vocal and interpretative powers. To the warm and vibrant voice is added an imagination that places Fleming in the first rank among today's lyric sopranos. The eclectic, ambitious choice of programme allows us to hear every aspect of her art. She is exactly the impulsive Tatyana, the girl's unreasoned ardour pouring out here in a stream of richly varied tone and feeling. Desdemona's Willow song is full of foreboding, also full of lovely singing, the repeated 'Cantiamo' voiced with precision of tone and timing, notes fined away with the utmost sensitivity. Ellen Orford's Embroidery aria is sung beautifully, the high B flat and A flat on 'Now' taken perfectly *pianissimo* after the *forte* A. These scenes benefit enormously from being placed in context, allowing Fleming to fit into the relevant situation. Diadkova is an idiomatic, responsive Filipyevna, and she makes the most of Emilia's few phrases. Summers is a wise and experienced Balstrode. All in all, Fleming lays claim here to Te Kanawa territory, and proves a worthy successor. More than Dame Kiri, she identifies with each character and moulds her voice to the woman in question. For Sir Georg this is obviously a labour of love, nowhere more so than in the postlude to *Daphne*, most sensuously done; he and the LSO provide worthy support for their superb soloist. The recording is faultless, capturing voice and orchestra in ideal balance.

Lesley Garrett A Soprano Inspired.
Lesley Garrett *sop*
[a]chorus; Britten Sinfonia / Ivor Bolton.
Conifer Classics 75605 51329-2 (73 minutes: DDD). Recorded 1997. Ⓕ
Mozart Exsultate, jubilate, K165/K158*a* – Alleluia. Vesperae solennes de confessore in C major,
K339– Laudate Dominum. Mass No. 18 in C minor, 'Great Mass' – Laudamus te. **Caccini**
(arr. Ingham) Ave Maria. **Malotte** The Lord's Prayer. **Brahe** Bless this house. **Verdi** La forza del
destino – La Vergine degli angeli[a]. **Vivaldi** Nulla in mundo pax, RV630 – Nulla in mundo pax.
R. Strauss Zueignung, Op. 10 No. 1. **Handel** Messiah – I know that my Redeemer liveth.
Schubert Ave Maria, D839. **Tippett** Five Negro Spirituals – By and By[a]. **Rodgers** The Sound of
Music – Climb ev'ry mountain[a]. **Fauré** Requiem, Op. 48 – Pie Jesu. **Franck** Panis angelicus.
S. Adams The Holy City. **Humperdinck** Hänsel und Gretel – Abends will ich schlafen gehn (sung
in English). **d'Hardelot** Because. **Mascagni** Cavalleria rusticana – Regina coeli ... Inneggiamo, il
Signor.

Lesley Garrett is such a 'conviction' singer. She has always caught the imagination by the way she sings every word as if she meant it – as here in *The Holy City*, turning dross almost into gold. The programme for this CD is typically eclectic, drawn from the baroque to the Broadway musical. She sings Vivaldi, Handel (a nicely decorated 'I know that my Redeemer liveth') and Mozart (the 'Laudamus te' from the C minor Mass and a joyous 'Alleluia' at the start) with straightforward vigour. In her opera selection, she phrases Leonora's Prayer from *Forza* with a fine feeling for Verdian line, follows the somewhat dubious tradition started by Elisabeth Schumann of singing the 'Abendgesang' from *Hänsel und Gretel* with herself, and gives the Easter Hymn, though she couldn't undertake Santuzza on stage, with the passion appropriate to its context. Of the two Lieder, an open-hearted *Zueignung* is preferable to a rather sentimental *Ave Maria*. The 'Pie Jesu' from Fauré's Requiem and Franck's *Panis angelicus*, both sung with the simple sincerity that is Garrett's hallmark, confirm that she has lost little or none of that fresh, forward, no-nonsense sound that is so appealing to her large audience. The unexpected choice of the Tippett item and the revival of d'Hardelot's *Because*, delivered with the security of technique that marks all these readings, is welcome. It is hard to resist her glorious account of 'Climb ev'ry mountain'. Ivor Bolton switches easily between idioms, though is obviously most at home in the baroque. The recording is brightly lit but not offensively so.

Lesley Garrett Soprano in Red.
Lesley Garrett *sop*
ªCrouch End Festival Chorus; Royal Philharmonic Concert Orchestra / James Holmes.
Silva Screen Classics SILKTVCD1 (60 minutes: DDD). All items sung in English. Recorded 1995. *Gramophone* Award Winner 1996.   Ⓕ
Romberg The New Moon – Softly, as in a morning sunrise; Lover, come back to me.
J. Strauss II (arr. Benatzky) Casanova – Nuns' Chorus and Laura's Songª. **Offenbach** La belle Hélène – On me nomme Hélène la Blonde. Orphée aux enfers – J'ai vu le Dieu Bacchusª; Ce bal est originalª. **Novello** Perchance to dream – We'll gather lilacs. The Dancing Years – Waltz of my heart. **Lehár** Zigeunerliebe – Hör' ich Cymbalklänge. Friederike – Warum hast du mich wachgeküsst? Die lustige Witwe – Es lebt eine Vilja, ein Waldmägdeleinª. **Coward** Bitter Sweet – If love were all. **Chabrier** L'étoile – O petite étoile; Je suis Lazuli!. **Heuberger** Der Opernball – Im chambre séparée. **Sullivan** The Contrabandista – Only the night wind sighs alone.

Lesley Garrett has won herself a huge following of those who respond to her straightforward, unaffected vocalizing, to the clarity and brightness of her voice and its ringing top notes. What also appeals about Garrett's recordings is the attention paid to less familiar material and the quest for authenticity of period style. Both facets are fully evident in this collection of operetta numbers from Paris, Vienna, Berlin, London and New York, ranging in time from classical Offenbach through to Coward, Novello and Romberg. The eager entreaties of Laura's Song from *Casanova*, the bright expressiveness of 'If love were all' and the sheer joyfulness of 'Waltz of my heart' (complete with piano contribution) are highlights. Especially gratifying, though, are the rarities. In the pedlar Lazuli's two numbers from Chabrier's *L'étoile*, Garrett's clarity of diction shows off Jeremy Sams's lyrics to fine effect and she should certainly win over the Sullivan faction with the first ever recording of an engaging little number from the pre-Gilbert operetta *The Contrabandista*. The aria from *La belle Hélène* is performed to Michael Frayn's text for the ENO adaptation of the work as *La belle Vivette*, while in Novello's 'We'll gather lilacs' double tracking permits Garrett to duet with herself. Ensemble and momentum go curiously adrift at the choral entries in Offenbach's 'Hymn to Bacchus', but this detracts only a little from another delightful Garrett collection.

German Romantic Opera Arias
Ben Heppner *ten*
North German Radio Symphony Orchestra / Donald Runnicles.
RCA Red Seal 09026 63239-2 (70 minutes: DDD). Texts and translations included. Recorded 1998.   Ⓕ Ⓔ
Beethoven Fidelio – Gott! Welch Dunkel hier! … In des Lebens. (with **Bavarian Radio Symphony Orchestra / Sir Colin Davis**). **Korngold** Die tote Stadt – O Freund, ich werde sie nicht wiedersehen. **Wagner** Rienzi – Allmächt'ger Vater. Die fliegende Holländer – Willst jenes Tag's; Tristan und Isolde – Dünkt dich das? Siegfried – Selige Ode auf sonniger Höh'! Götterdämmerung – Brünnhilde, heilige Braut! Parsifal – Nur eine Waffe taugt. **Weber** Der Freischütz – Nein! länger trag'ich nicht die Qualen … Durch die Wälder. Euryanthe – Wehen mir Lüfte Ruh.

Ben Heppner must be counted among the most consistent of tenors in this kind of repertory this century, the only drawback to this excellent recital being the nonsensical chronological order chosen by RCA. How could it place Wagner (his items themselves out of chronology) before Beethoven and Weber and then suddenly follow Weber with Korngold? All of which cannot detract from the beauty, reliability and musicality of every item in this pot-pourri of German opera. Particularly welcome is Heppner's singing of Tristan's, Siegfried's and Parsifal's music: with his secure technique and sturdy frame these roles have surely found their ideal interpreter for the first decade of the coming century. Much as you might dislike bleeding chunks and the way they end in mid-air, such firmly sung and intelligently phrased readings justify the practice on this occasion. Heppner would also be an ideal interpreter, on this evidence, of Max and Adolar in the Weber operas, the lyrical and dramatic nicely held in balance. In the items, other than the Beethoven, Heppner is admirably partnered by Donald Runnicles, who always makes us aware of the context and, by dint of forward movement and the maintenance of line, avoids the pseudo-profundity of much Wagner conducting these days. The recording is in all respects exemplary.

Angela Gheorghiu My World.
Angela Gheorghiu *sop* Malcolm Martineau *pf*
Decca 458 360-2DH (75 minutes: DDD). Texts and translations included. Recorded 1997. Ⓕ Ⓔ
J. Martini Plaisir d'amour. **Parisotti** Se tu m'ami, C xxii, 68. **Respighi** Nebbie.
Leoncavallo Mattinata. **Falla** El paño moruno. **Montsalvatge** Canto negro. **Satie** Je te veux.
Delibes Les filles de Cadix. **Poulenc** Les chemins de l'amour. **Grieg** Solveig's Song.
Schumann Myrthen, Op. 25 – No. 1, Widmung; No. 24, Du bist wie eine Blume. **Schubert**
Ständchen, D957 No. 4. **R. Strauss** Zueignung, Op. 10 No. 1. **Brediceanu** Mult mă'ntreabă
inima. **Mezzetti** Cântec se sirenă. **Cavadia** Umbra. **Dvořák** Songs my mother taught me, B104
No. 4. **Liszt** Oh! quand je dors, S282. **Hadjidakis** Pai efiye to treno. **Traditional** (arr. Behar):
Durme, kerido hijico. **Sup** Guriwoon Guemgang San. **Mitake** Kawa no Nagare no yô ni.
Ovalle Azulão. **Brodszky** Be my love.

This eclectic programme makes a welcome change from recorded recitals devoted to one composer,
one genre. Gheorghiu avers, in a disarmingly frank note, that she thrives on change, loves to be in
different countries and experience different idioms so she 'wanted to create a unique recital
programme that would reflect all these aspects of my interests'. She certainly has done that: her
generous choice boxes the compass from classical through German, Spanish, Italian and French
song to ethnic pieces. She also points out that many of the items exploit the warm qualities of her
lower voice: the haunting pieces, semi-popular, from the far east, for instance; even more the Greek
popular song. Still better, not surprisingly, are the three songs from her native Romania, especially
the seductive Siren's song and the glorious *Umbra*, a late-nineteenth-century romance. Then there's
Ovalle's insinuating *Azulão*, chosen apparently at the suggestion of Martineau, the singer's creative
partner, and sung in that soft-grained manner peculiar to Gheorghiu. She ends with a bravura
account of the Lanza favourite *Be my love*, the slight accent in the English almost an advantage.
Similarly her indeterminate German makes her three Lieder sound unidiomatic, but each of these
love-songs is given with such conviction that the customary criteria for judgement can for once be
set aside. Her French is much better; in any case the erotic charge of the Satie and Poulenc pieces is
amply felt. There's much else to commend: the elegiac quality in Respighi's infinitely sad *Nebbie*
contrasting with the earthy high spirits of Montsalvatge's *Canto negro* and the Delibes song, and
the wistful touch in the famous Dvořák. With an admirably faithful recording as a bonus, this
ought to be a runaway success.

Angela Gheorghiu Opera Arias.
Angela Gheorghiu *sop*
Orchestra and ᵃChorus of Teatro Regio, Turin / John Mauceri.
Decca 452 417-2DH (57 minutes: DDD). Texts and translations included. Recorded 1995. Ⓕ
Verdi Falstaff – Ninfe! Elfi! Silfi!; Sul fil d'un soffio etesioᵃ. **Massenet** Chérubin – Aubade: Vive
amour qui rêve, embrase et fuitᵃ. Hérodiade – Celui dont la parole … Il est doux, il est bon.
Catalani La Wally – Ebben? Ne andrò lontana. **Bellini** I Capuleti e i Montecchi – Eccomi in lieta
vesta … Oh! quante volte. **Puccini** La bohème – Sì. Mi chiamano Mimì; Donde lieta uscì.
Boito Mefistofele – L'altra notte. **Gounod** Faust – O Dieu! que de bijoux! … Ah! je ris.
Donizetti Don Pasquale – Quel guardo il cavaliere … So anch'io la virtù magica.
Grigoriu Valurile Dunării – Muzica.

Here is a recital that begins in enchantment and ends in something a little less. If any two items are
individually responsible they are the arias from *Mefistofele* and *La Wally*. Perhaps Gheorghiu is
telling us to refine our ideas of these things: that the chesty Italian manner of Burzio and Muzio,
Callas and Scotto, should have 'gone out' with the actresses of the silent screen. Even so, what she
gives us in its place is surely incomplete. So it is that the most satisfying performances here are those
of a less overtly passionate nature. That does not include the Jewel song from *Faust*, where the
rather lazy tempo and lack of excitement in the style fail to catch the passionate impulses of
laughter, coquettishness, desire and even vanity in this naturally modest and simple girl. Massenet's
Salomé and Bellini's Giulietta are better suited; the Aubade from *Chérubin* is delightful; and we are
back to the beginning with Nannetta in Windsor Forest which is utter enchantment. The voice of
course is a feast in itself, the loveliest lyric soprano heard since Dame Kiri first came to us in the
1970s. The reticence, which can be a limitation, has its positive side, and repeatedly one has to
admire the way in which fullness of volume and emotion is held in reserve for effective use at a
climax.

Angela Gheorghiu and Roberto Alagna Opera Arias and Duets.
ᵃAngela Gheorghiu *sop* ᵇRoberto Alagna *ten*
Orchestra of the Royal Opera House, Covent Garden / Richard Armstrong.
EMI CDC5 56117-2 (61 minutes: DDD). Texts and translations included. Recorded 1995. Ⓕ Ⓔ

Mascagni L'amico Fritz – Suzel, buon di ... Tutto tace[ab]. **Massenet** Manon – Je suis seul! ... Ah! fuyez, douce image[b]; Toi! Vous! ... N'est-ce plus ma main[ab]. **Donizetti** Anna Bolena – Al dolce guidami[a]. Don Pasquale – Tornami a dir[ab]. **Offenbach** La belle Hélène – Au mont Ida[b]. **Bernstein** West Side Story – Only You ... Tonight, it all began tonight[ab]. **Gounod** Faust – Il se fait tard! ... O nuit d'amour[ab]. **G. Charpentier** Louise – Depuis le jour[a]. **Berlioz** Les troyens – Nuit d'ivresse![ab]. **Puccini** La bohème – O soave fanciulla[ab].

Ideally matched, the two young lyric artists of our day who have most taken the hearts and hopes of public and critics sing here in a programme that is both aptly and imaginatively selected. It ranges quite widely over the French and Italian repertoires, always combining instant satisfaction with a wish for more. The Cherry duet from *L'amico Fritz* comes first, and the voices have just the right freshness for it, the soprano warm-toned, the tenor elegant and cleanly defined; the style too is charming, natural and mutually responsive. Then with the excerpts from *Manon* they are not only well suited but show already a real dramatic impulse in their duet, again with its developments so well felt and understood. The Garden scene works unusual magic. The solos provide welcome opportunities: Gheorghiu, delightful in 'Depuis le jour', is even more so in the aria from *Anna Bolena*, exquisitely phrased and shaded as though it were the slow movement of a sonata by Mozart. 'Ah! fuyez, douce image' opens with the softness associated from long ago with Smirnov and Muratore; Alagna never forgets what he is singing about, is thrilling on his high B flats and finely controlled in the concluding *diminuendo*. His Mount Ida song from *La belle Hélène* has panache and humour, a deliciously promising *pianissimo* start to the last verse and a good robust C thrown in before he finishes. And then, inspiration on somebody's part, there is *West Side Story*. 'Tonight' has never been better sung, and it also brings us to the other element in this recital – the playing of the Covent Garden orchestra under Richard Armstrong. In this, they make us realize afresh how distinctively flavoured (in harmony and orchestration) is Bernstein's marvellous score: the duet is intensely moving, yet the rhythm is kept strong and there is no sugar-coating or melting into slush. Repeatedly, in Gounod and Bernstein as in Mascagni and Puccini, one reacts with an 'I'd never noticed that before' or simply a smile or sigh of pleasure in the sound.

Jill Gomez Cabaret Classics.
Jill Gomez *sop* John Constable *pf*
Unicorn-Kanchana DKPCD9055 (57 minutes: DDD). Texts and translations included.   Ⓕ
Weill Marie Galante – Les filles de Bordeaux; Le grand Lustucru; Le Roi d'Aquitaine; J'attends un navire. Lady in the Dark – My Ship. Street Scene – Lonely house. Knickerbocker Holiday – It never was you. **Zemlinsky** Songs, Op. 27 – Harlem Tänzerin; Elend; Afrikanischer Tanz. **Schoenberg** Arie aus dem Spiegel von Arcadien. Gigerlette. Der genügsame Liebhaber. Mahnung. **Satie** La diva de l'Empire. Allons-y, Chochotte. Je te veux.

Schoenberg writing cabaret songs with a popular touch? Yes, and quite catchy ones too, as can be heard particularly in *Gigerlette* – prompting the intriguing speculation of what might have been had he not concentrated on *Gurrelieder*. On the other hand, his *Der genügsame Liebhaber* and Zemlinsky's three songs would have been most unlikely to go down well with cabaret audiences, however intellectual. At the other end of the spectrum are Satie's café-concert songs (the sentimental waltz *Je te veux* is languidly attractive) and the Weill items, which were not written for cabaret but are drawn from a 1934 Paris play and post-war Broadway musicals. That all these songs do not require a gin-sodden voice or raucous delivery is demonstrated with the utmost artistry by Jill Gomez, in turn seductive, pathetic, sly, sweet, swaggering, passionate, salacious – or simply singing beautifully. Her performance of Weill's *Lonely house* remains hauntingly in the mind.

Great Operatic Arias, Volume 2.
Diana Montague *mez* Mary Plazas *sop* Bruce Ford *ten*
Philharmonia Orchestra / David Parry.
Chandos Opera in English Series CHAN3010 (76 minutes: DDD). English texts included.   Ⓕ Ⓔ
Recorded 1997.
Berlioz La damnation de Faust, Op. 24 – D'amour l'ardente flamme. **Delibes** Lakmé – Viens Mallika; Dôme épais le jasmin ... Sous le dôme épais (Flower duet). **Donizetti** La favorite – Fia dunque vero? ... O mio Fernando. **Gluck** Orfeo ed Euridice – Che farò senza Euridice?. **Gounod** Faust – Faites-lui mes aveux. **Offenbach** La périchole – O mon cher amant, je te jure; Ah! quel dîner je viens de faire!; Tu n'es pas beau, tu n'es pas riche. **Rossini** Le comte Ory – A la faveur de cette nuit obscure. **Saint-Saëns** Samson et Dalila – Printemps qui commence; Amour! viens aider ma faiblesse!; Mon coeur s'ouvre à ta voix. **A. Thomas** Mignon – Connais-tu le pays?; Me voici dans son boudoir.

Montague, our leading interpreter of what the French call the *Falcon* repertory (after a singer of this special character), has been far too little celebrated, at least on disc, so this superbly executed programme of French opera arias, with one exception, sung in the vernacular with impeccable diction and full of dramatic import, must be reckoned the jewel so far in the Chandos Opera in English series. Above all it is Montague's distinctive timbre, sense of the correct style and complete identification with each character in turn that makes the recital so thrilling, exciting and pleasing at once to the ear and the senses. An account of Orfeo's 'What is life?' that equals if not surpasses Ferrier's, a Delilah to die for, each of her arias given a different character as required, a Marguérite (Berlioz's) who yearns with the best on disc (Montague's low tones here so eloquent, the climax given all its due before the intense reprise), a Mignon who is suitably mysterious ('Have you heard of the land?' so full of longing for a lost ideal with a marvellous lift at the words 'my home') and a Donizetti Léonore who 'speaks' so tenderly of her love for her Fernando, with a cabaletta, including repeat, to show off the singer's forceful attack. All these emotional states are contained within a line and tone that respect vocal verities. It is good to be reminded of her lighter touch not only as Siebel and Frédéric, but also Isolier, a part she sang to critical approval at Glyndebourne in 1997: the trio from *Comte Ory* is graced by Bruce Ford's elegant Ory and Plazas as the Countess Adèle. Plazas also partners Montague in a nicely flowing account of *that* duet from *Lakmé*. Finally we have Montague the witty comedienne in three deliciously articulated numbers of *Périchole* – a nice smile in the tone for 'I adore you, you wretch'. Parry and the Philharmonia provide euphonious, Francophile accompaniments and, where needed, as in the Gluck and Berlioz, true passion. The recording keeps a nice balance between voice and orchestra. This is undoubtedly a triumph for Diana Montague.

Jerry Hadley Vienna.
Jerry Hadley *ten*
Munich Radio Orchestra / Richard Bonynge.
RCA Red Seal 09026 68258-2 (61 minutes: DDD). Texts and translations included. Ⓕ 🅔
Recorded 1995.
Eysler Bruder Straubinger – Küssen ist keine Sünd. Der lachende Ehemann – Weinlied.
Fall Die Rose von Stambul – Ein Walzer muss es sein; O Rose von Stambul. **Kálmán** Die Csárdásfürstin – Tanzen möcht'ich; Ganz ohne Weiber geht die Chose nicht. **Lehár** Friederike – O Mädchen, mein Mädchen. Das Land des Lächelns – Immer nur lächeln; Von Apfelblüten einen Kranz; Dein ist mein ganzes Herz. Paganini – Gern hab'ich die Frau'n geküsst. Schön ist die Welt – Schön ist die Welt. Der Zarewitsch – Wolgalied. **Tauber** Der singende Traum – Du bist die Welt für mich.

Jerry Hadley's self-professed love of Viennese operetta shines through this fine collection, which winningly mixes the obvious tenor hits of twentieth-century Viennese operetta with some less obvious items. The obvious, of course, include the Franz Lehár songs that became associated with Richard Tauber. Hadley delivers these in less dramatic form than Tauber, but with no less compelling lyricism and with some typically Tauberian *pianissimo*. The less obvious items include yet another 'Tauber-Lied' in one that Tauber himself composed for his 1934 operetta, *Der singende Traum*. We are also treated to a couple of waltz numbers by the wickedly underrated Leo Fall; even rarer, and thus perhaps most welcome of all, are the charming numbers by Edmund Eysler, composer of homely Viennese operettas neglected since the days when they provided rewarding material for the likes of Julius Patzak. Beautifully recorded, this really is a model Viennese operetta recital.

Thomas Hampson German Opera Arias.
Thomas Hampson *bar*
ᵃPestalozzi Gymnasium Children's Choir; Munich Radio Orchestra / Fabio Luisi.
EMI CDC5 55233-2 (79 minutes: DDD). Texts and translations included. Recorded 1994. Ⓕ
Korngold Die tote Stadt – Mein Sehnen, mein Wähnen. **Lortzing** Zar und Zimmermann – Verraten! ... Die Macht des Zepters. Der Wildschütz – Wie freundlich strahlt ... Heiterkeit und Fröhlichkeit. **Marschner** Hans Heiling – An jenem Tag. Der Vampyr – Ha! Noch einen ganzen Tag. **Weber** Euryanthe – Wo berg' ich mich? ... So weih' ich mich den Rachgewalten. **Spohr** Faust – Der Hölle selbst will ich...Liebe ist die zarte Blüthe. **Kreutzer** Das Nachtlager in Granada – Die Nacht ist schön. **Schreker** Der ferne Klang – In einem Lande ein bleicher König. **Humperdinck** Die Königskinder – Verdorben! Gestorben!ᵃ. **Wagner** Tannhäuser – Wie Todesahnung ... O du mein holder Abendstern. Die Walküre – Winterstürme wichen dem Wonnemond.

In addition to being a singer of outstanding gifts and versatility, Hampson is also scholarly in his approach. He himself, with Jens Mete Fischer, contributes an essay on 'the baritone in German opera', making it clear that he is aware of the tradition in which he sings. It is not surprising, then, that voices from the past should come to mind and stay there quite contentedly during the course of this recital. Schlusnus (in *Hans Heiling*), Hüsch (in *Königskinder*), Janssen (*Tannhäuser*), and for just one phrase ('sie bringet Wünsche mancher Art mir dar' in *Der Wildschütz*) Fischer-Dieskau: a formidable array, and assuredly not assembled in order to bar the young American from entry to their ranks. His voice is uncommonly beautiful, he is scrupulous in his musicianship, and like the best Germans he knows the value of the Italian connection. If there is a limitation to his success in the chosen programme, it is simply the price that often has to be paid by a singer whose voice is an unmixed pleasure to the ear. For the villain of *Euryanthe* and the maniac of *Der Vampyr*, his voice-character is simply too good: goodness, not villainy, is its element. At times, too, there is need for more depth and body in the lower range (Spohr's Faust and Schreker's Count in *Der ferne Klang* are examples). Otherwise the singing is delightful, the *Zar und Zimmermann*, *Tannhäuser* and *Die tote Stadt* solos especially. In including Siegmund's 'Winterstürme' from *Die Walküre*, Hampson was probably providing a talking-point as much as anything, and it is certainly interesting to hear how he will occasionally 'tenorize' while usually keeping to his normal baritone production, perhaps giving his admirers a moment's concern as he opens the voice for the F of 'vereint' in the last phrase. The programme itself contains several rarities. The imaginative use of the solo violin in *Das Nachtlager in Granada* and the rich orchestration of *Der ferne Klang* are additional pleasures in a recital that is well accompanied, well recorded and informatively presented.

Thomas Hampson To the Soul – Songs to the Poetry of Walt Whitman.
Thomas Hampson *bar* Craig Rutenberg *pf*
EMI CDM5 55028-2 (67 minutes: DDD). Texts included. Recorded 1993-94.
Also includes readings by Thomas Hampson of 'One's self I sing', 'The mystic trumpeter',
'I hear it was charged against me' and 'Song of myself'. Ⓜ
Rorem As Adam early in the morning. Look down fair moon. Sometimes with one I love. That shadow, my likeness. **Bridge** The last invocation, H136. **Stanford** To the soul, Op. 97 No. 4. **Vaughan Williams** Poems by Walt Whitman – No. 2, A clear midnight; No. 3, Joy, shipmate, joy!. **Strassburg** Prayer of Columbus. **Bacon** One thought ever at the fire. **Dalmas** As I watch'd the ploughman ploughing. **Hindemith** Memories of Lincoln – Sing on there in the Swamp. **Naginski** Look down fair moon. **Neidlinger** Memories of Lincoln. **H.T. Burleigh** Ethiopia saluting the colours. **Weill** Dirge for Two Veterans. **Ives** Walt Whitman. **G. Busby** Behold this swarthy face. **E.R. Warren** We two. **Urquhart** Among the multitude, 1980. **Tilson Thomas** We two boys together clinging. **Bernstein** Songfest – To what you said.

For a song recital to be devoted to settings of a single poet he must preferably be capable of inspiring music of widely differing types. This splendidly planned collection certainly demonstrates that to be true of Whitman: apparently Hampson has traced no fewer than 400 Whitman settings for voice and piano, and all his choices are at least interesting; some are real discoveries. Henry Thacker Burleigh was the first African-American to receive professional training as a composer (Dvořák was Burleigh's first teacher), and his use of jazzy syncopation (in 1915!) and Ives-like quotation of Civil War melodies in *Ethiopia saluting the colours* is vividly original. Elsewhere Stanford demonstrates that Whitman is accessible to Brahmsian gravity and eloquence while Ernst Bacon, with moving simplicity, sets three lines on human brotherhood to a melody like a chapel hymn. Kurt Weill effectively treats the *Dirge for Two Veterans* in his Broadway manner and in 'Sing on there in the Swamp' Hindemith beautifully evokes the falling star of *Memories of Lincoln* with two coolly shining chords that generate a lyrical counterpoint to the vocal line. Ned Rorem, surely the most consistently fine contemporary composer of concert songs, is represented by four, all characteristically subtle and refined. There is not a weak song here; the performances throughout are exceptionally fine, intimately and subtly expressive but opening out nobly to expressions of passionate idealism. Hampson's readings are just that: they are pleasingly unhistrionic, not in the least bit acted, but they effectively frame the songs with his obvious commitment to Whitman. A most enterprising, absorbing and magnificently sung recital.

Heroes
Andreas Scholl *counterten*
Orchestra of the Age of Enlightenment / Sir Roger Norrington.
Decca 466 196-2OH (58 minutes: DDD). Texts and translations included. Recorded 1998. Ⓟ Ⓔ
Gluck Orfeo ed Euridice – Che farò senza Euridice. Telemaco – Ah non turbi.
Handel Serse – Fronde tenere … Ombra mai fù. Semele – Where'er you walk. Saul – O Lord, whose mercies; Such haughty beauties. Rodelinda – Con rauco mormorio; Vivi tiranno!. Giulio Cesare – Dall' ondoso periglio … Aure deh, per pietà. **Hasse** Artaserse – Palido il sole. **Mozart** Ascanio in Alba – Al mio ben. Mitridate, Re di Ponto – Venga pur, minacci.

Heroes indeed! This is some of the finest heroic singing around, and in a countertenor voice – often supposed to be weakly or effeminate. There is heroism here in both love and war. Andreas Scholl's countertenor is formidable in every sense and transmits sturdy, masculine emotion just as forcefully as the softer sorts called for in, for example, what are probably the two most famous of the arias here: 'Ombra mai fù' ('Handel's Largo'), which opens the recital, and 'Che farò' from *Orfeo*. The first of these discloses a wonderfully ample, creamy voice, beautifully even and controlled, capable of a poignantly soft top F and firm in profile in the lower register; the latter elicits an outpouring, a passionate one, of lovely tone, with a line of the chastity and purity that exactly captures Gluck's vision of his semi-divine hero. In 'Where'er you walk' – a tenor piece, transposed – he seems tonally more constrained, yet it is an uncommonly smooth and flowing performance. Of the other Handel items, particular mention should be made of the *Saul* aria 'O Lord, whose mercies', one of the loveliest Handel ever wrote, sung with great intensity of tone; the *Rodelinda* arias, one of them full of rapid *fioritura*, riskily but faultlessly delivered, and a peaceful one about a murmuring stream which, if perhaps taken rather quickly, nevertheless is a fine, serene piece of singing. The Hasse item is strong and impassioned, giving scope to Scholl's full bottom register; and of the two Mozart arias the one from *Mitridate* is a noble, powerful statement of defiance, done strongly and directly. Norrington provides generally sympathetic accompaniments. This is quite an exceptional recital in which one of today's most beautiful and imaginatively used voices is heard at its finest.

Dmitri Hvorostovsky Songs and Dances of Death.
Dmitri Hvorostovsky *bar*
Kirov Theatre Orchestra / Valery Gergiev.
Philips 438 872-2PH (62 minutes: DDD). Texts and translations included. Recorded 1993.　Ⓕ
Rimsky-Korsakov Sadko – The paragon of cities; Beautiful city! Kashchey the Immortal – In this, night's darkest hour. Snow Maiden (second version) – Under the warm blue sea. The Tsar's Bride – Still the beauty haunts my mind. **Borodin** Prince Igor – No sleep, no rest. **Rubinstein** The Demon – Do not weep, my child; On the airy ocean; I am he whom you called. Nero – Vindex's Epithalamium: I sing to you, Hymen divine! **Rachmaninov** Aleko – Aleko's cavatina.
Mussorgsky Songs and Dances of Death.

In the scenes from Rubinstein's *The Demon* Hvorostovsky, superbly supported by Valery Gergiev and his Kirov orchestra recorded in their own theatre, has done nothing better than his impersonation of the devil; in the scenes from the third he projects the gloating demon to the life. This is splendid stuff. So is Vindex's rollicking Epithalamium from the same composer's *Nero*, sung with wonderful breadth and confidence. Then he changes character again to bring before us the emotional torment of Rachmaninov's *Aleko* as he recalls the love Zemfira once had for him. The best of the Rimsky items as regards music and interpretation are Nizgir's aria from the *Snow Maiden* and Gryaznoy's musing on past triumphs in the field of love from *The Tsar's Bride*. Here Hvorostovsky varies his tone more successfully than in the other Rimsky items. Mussorgsky's *Songs and Dances of Death* really need an imposing bass rather than a lyric baritone to make their true mark, yet these are more than acceptable performances, immeasurably helped by the excellent recording. This is a fascinating disc.

I Want Magic
Renée Fleming *sop*
Metropolitan Opera Orchestra, New York / James Levine.
Decca 460 567-2DH (58 minutes: DDD). Texts and translations included. Recorded 1998.　ⒻⒺ
Barber Vanessa – He has come … Do not utter a word, Anatol. **Bernstein** Candide – Glitter and be gay. **Floyd** Susannah – Ain't it a pretty night; The trees on the mountains. **Gershwin** Porgy and Bess – Summertime; My man's gone now. **Herrmann** Wuthering Heights – I have dreamt. **Menotti** The Medium – Monica's Waltz. **D. Moore** The Ballad of Baby Doe – The Letter Song. **Previn** A Streetcar Named Desire – I want magic!. **Stravinsky** The Rake's Progress – No word from Tom … I go to him.

This survey of operas old and new reinforces the feeling that the current generation of star singers in the USA is making an effort to explore home-grown repertory. Fleming's voice is sumptuous, her lower register especially sounds so warmly resonant that it is reminiscent of Leontyne Price in her glory days. Fleming shows herself equal to every mood; only at the end of 'Glitter and be gay' is there a false moment when she rather overdoes the brittle laughter. What beautiful tunes there are here, including the waltz song from *The Medium* and 'Ain't it a pretty night' from *Susannah*. This was recorded before Fleming took part in the world première of André Previn's *A Streetcar Named Desire* in San Francisco and her programme ends with a sneak preview of that. 'I want magic!' is Blanche's philosophy of life, justifying her constant flights of fancy; since Previn and his librettist, Philip Littell, pulled off the challenge of adapting this play for opera, the last years of the twentieth century found a new demented prima donna role. Among the other items, Fleming makes the extract from *Wuthering Heights* sound positively Mahleresque, and Anne's great aria from *The Rake's Progress* – 'officially' an American opera, Stravinsky, Auden and Kallman at least all being resident there when it was written – suits her surprisingly well. (It's another role she has sung on stage.) James Levine and the Metropolitan Opera Orchestra provide idiomatic accompaniment. If Fleming can stay the course, she's surely destined to be one of the greats.

Kalinka
Dmitri Hvorostovsky *bar*
St Petersburg Chamber Choir / Nikolai Korniev.
Philips 456 399-2PH (57 minutes: DDD). Texts and translations included. Recorded 1996. Ⓕ
Kalinka. Barinya. Ah! Do you hear, my dearest friend? On the little mountain. Round Dance.
Why have you misted over, clear sunset? I met you. The Little Willow. How was I, a tender young
maiden? Rhyming Song. Ah, you field. As never the white birch tree. The noise of the town cannot
be heard. In the dark forest. Already the fog has descended. Ah, shady spot. Birch-broom. I set
off alone down the road.

These Russian folk-songs are all arrangements, by different hands, some hands as distinguished
as those of Rimsky-Korsakov and Shostakovich. Mostly they are for solo voice with a chorus
sometimes participating in the narrative or verbal sketch, sometimes humming, sometimes bearing
the burden of the song (in the sense of the refrain as well as the weight). There is not, however,
much attempt to imitate a folk manner. The arrangements are sometimes light and barely
intervene, as with Shostakovich's, especially in some of the rapidly pattering numbers. Others
are slow and suffused with melancholy, richly harmonized in a manner that would surprise any
peasant but can, at best, make a beautiful new composition altogether. Among them is Paul Reade's
version of *Ivushka*, or *The Little Willow*, sung with soaring intensity by Hvorostovsky over
warmly shifting harmonies from the chorus. Some arrangements are quite elaborate, not always
as effectively as this. It is a striking collection, with most of the songs rather closer to original
composition than to what we normally think of as arrangement. The recording does justice
not only to the admirable Hvorostovsky but to the choir's nimble sopranos and to basses
who can move around the area below the bass stave without effort. An unusual, enjoyable
anthology.

Vesselina Kasarova A Portrait.
Vesselina Kasarova *mez*
[a]Bavarian Radio Chorus; Munich Radio Orchestra / Friedrich Haider.
RCA Red Seal 09026 68522-2 (64 minutes: DDD). Texts and translations included.
Recorded 1996. Ⓕ Ⓔ
Handel Rinaldo – Or la tromba in suon festante. **Gluck** Orfeo ed Euridice – Che farò senza
Euridice?. **Mozart** Le nozze di Figaro – Voi che sapete. Don Giovanni – Batti, batti, o bel Masetto.
Rossini La Cenerentola – Nacqui all'affano[a] (with **Isolde Mitternacht-Geissendörfer** *sop*
Barbara Müller *contr* **Dankwart Siegele** *ten* **Tim Hennis** *bass*). Il barbiere di Siviglia – Una voce
poco fa. L'Italiana in Algeri – Pronti abbiamo e ferri e mani … Amici in ogni evento … Pensa alla
patria[a]. **Donizetti** Anna Bolena – Sposa a Percy … Per questa fiamma indomita … Ah! pensate
che rivolti[a] (**Andreas Schulist** *ten* **Leonid Savitzky** *bass*). La favorita – Fia dunque vero … O mio
Fernando!. **Bellini** I Capuleti e i Montecchi – Se Romeo t'uccise un figlio … La tremenda ultrice
spada[a] (**Schulist; Savitzky**).

This is the stuff of legends: it is difficult to imagine a début opera recital that could give so much
pleasure. The vibrant richness of Kasarova's tone allied to her totally uninhibited manner before the
microphone allow her to bring to astonishing life each of the characters portrayed within. She
begins as she continues, with tremendous panache as Rinaldo invokes trumpets to great deeds and
Kasarova proves the warrior-lover to the life, Handel's complex coloratura used as an engine to
express youthful fire. Then immediately she becomes the tender, lamenting Orpheus, real grieving in
the plush, well-controlled tone. The two Mozart pieces disclose different timbres in the voice –
bright and palpitating as befits Cherubino, soft-grained and sensuous as suits Zerlina. Kasarova is a
fabulous Rossinian. In the three pieces here she combines vitality, verbal acuity and dispatch of
fioriture. It's wonderful how she starts in mild, forgiving manner, caressing the start of 'Non più
mesta', then lets fly in viscerally exciting manner for the roulades.

Even the well-trodden path of 'Una voce' sounds newly-minted as you seem to hear Rosina's
varied thoughts passing through her mind, the text freshly inflected. As Isabella inspires her
followers in 'Pensa alla patria', one notes the subtle accents on 'il tenero amor' and 'Caro, ti
parli in petto', evincing all Isabella's inner feelings for her beloved Lindoro. Then it's off on
another invigorating display at 'Fra pochi istanti'. From here Kasarova moves on to so-called
bel canto territory. With 'O mio Fernando!' it's again the judgement of tonal colour, here
sensual, heartstopping, while Jane Seymour's resistance to Henry VIII (weakly impersonated here)
shows yet another 'face', dignified and noble. But in both Leonora's and Romeo's cabaletta,
'La tremenda ultrice spada', a little less might mean so much more: there is too much emphasis,
too many breaths. But that is part of the style of a singer who is making no concessions to the
studio, rather living out every moment of the given dramas, admirably supported by Haider
and his orchestra.

Lamenti
[a]**Anne Sofie von Otter** *mez* [b]**Franz-Josef Selig** *bass* [c]**Jakob Lindberg** *theorbo*
[d]**Musica Antiqua Köln / Reinhard Goebel** [e]*vn*
Archiv Produktion 457 617-2AH (60 minutes: DDD). Texts and translations included.
Recorded 1997.
Bertali Lamento della Regina d'Inghilterra[abd]. **Legrenzi** Il ballo del Gran Duca, Op. 16 –
Corrente nona[de]. **Monteverdi** Madrigals, Book 7 – Con che soavità[ade]. Lamento d'Arianna[ac].
Piccinini Ciaccona[c]. **Purcell** Incassum, Lesbia, rogas, Z383[ad]. O Solitude! my sweetest choice,
Z406[ac]. **Vivaldi** Cessate, omai cessate, RV684[ad].

Anne Sofie von Otter adds to her laurels with this issue, which belies any doom and gloom
suggested by its title with singing of an intensity of expression, subtlety of nuance and rich palette
of vocal colour that leave one full of admiration. Whether lamenting a stony-hearted lover (*Cessate,
omai cessate*) or a faithless one (in *Arianna*, all that remains of a lost Monteverdi opera), a queen of
Arcadia (*Incassum, Lesbia, rogas*) or the husband of an English queen (presumably Charles I, in
view of the frenzied cries for revenge), von Otter fills every word with vivid meaning while still
preserving the musical line. Vengeance is also the passionate response of the lover in the Vivaldi
cantata (no stranger to the record catalogue), superbly performed here, with full-blooded
instrumental backing by Musica Antiqua Köln. At the opposite end of the emotional spectrum,
another highlight of the disc is Purcell's sad, touching *Incassum, Lesbia*. His *O Solitude!* is built on
a ground bass, as of course is the little piece for solo theorbo by Piccinini, as well as the Legrenzi
Corrente – neither of which, in fact, suggests lamenting. The most varied instrumentation occurs in
Monteverdi's sectional *Con che soavità*, with its changeable tempos and ornamental vocal line. The
contribution by an admirable bass, Franz-Josef Selig, in two brief but exceptionally low-lying
narrations in the Bertali (a work largely in recitative, but with interludes for three violas) should not
be overlooked. Altogether an outstanding disc.

Sergei Larin Russian Arias, Volume 1.
Sergei Larin *ten*
[a]**Ambrosian Opera Chorus; Philharmonia Orchestra / Gennadi Rozhdestvensky.**
Chandos CHAN9603 (75 minutes: DDD). Texts and translations included.
Tchaikovsky Eugene Onegin – I love you, Olga; Monsieur Triquet, favour us with a coupleta;
Faint echo of my youth. Mazeppa – In bloody battle, on the field of honour ... Here days passed
by in happy succession. Cherevichki – Does your heart, maiden, not hear. The Queen of Spades –
I do not know her name; Forgive me, loveliest of creatures; What is our life? A game!.
Rimsky-Korsakov May Night – Hey there! Boys!; How calm, how cool it is here. Sadko –
Song of the Indian guest. **Rachmaninov** Boris Godunov – One last story. **Dargomïzhsky**
Rusalka – Some unknown power. **Glinka** Ruslan and Lyudmila – There is a desert country.
Borodin Prince Igor – Daylight is fading.

Since he has started making recital discs with Chandos Sergei Larin has come into focus as a
recording artist much more clearly than when his name tended to get lost among many others in the
cast-list of Russian operas. His art has certainly deepened now, with more fully expressive
delineation of phrases and, perhaps with Rozhdestvensky to help, a more complete responsiveness
to mood and structure. But perhaps he has outgrown Lensky, the impetuous, ill-fated young poet in
Eugene Onegin. The love-song in Act 1 hasn't the youthful ardour and impulse, and the great aria of
the Duel scene is a fine piece of singing rather than the elegiac and then impassioned utterance of
doomed youth. Larin now is much closer (vocally) to Hermann in *The Queen of Spades* than to
Lenski, and the fire burns bright in Hermann's 'What is our life?' The programme is full of plums:
there's the Hindu Guest with his famous song, Vladimir of *Prince Igor* with that lovely nocturnal
invocation, and Levko with his lullaby in *May Night*. Less expected presences are Monsieur Triquet
from *Eugene Onegin* and Pimen, the old monk in *Boris Godunov*. At first one thinks that that must
be a crazy misprint; but no, it is a setting by Rachmaninov, an imaginatively orchestrated piece of
student-work. The orchestra here make a notable contribution to the recital's success, and it is a
further sign of grace that the chorus are brought in for the Cossacks' 'Go get the Mayor' spree in
May Night.

Jennifer Larmore My Native Land.
Jennifer Larmore *mez* **Antoine Palloc** *pf*
Teldec 0630-16069-2 (75 minutes: DDD). Selected texts included. Recorded 1996.
Heggie He's gone away. The leather-winged bat. Barb'ry Allen. To say before going to sleep.
White in the moon. **Copland** Old American Songs, Set 2 – The little horses; Zion's walls; At the
river; Ching-a-ring. **J. Duke** In the fields. Twentieth century. Heart! We will forget him!.
Barber Bessie Bobtail, Op. 2 No. 3. Songs, Op. 10 – No. 1, Rain has fallen; No. 2, Sleep now;

No. 3, I hear an army. Sure on this shining night, Op. 13 No. 3. **Hoiby** Winter Song. A letter. **Hundley** The astronomers. **Aborn** 'Tis Winter now. Shall I compare thee to a Summer's day. Make me an instrument of Thy peace. **Niles** Black is the color of my true love's hair. Fee Simple. **Abramson** Soldier, Soldier. **Naginski** Richard Cory. **Ives** My native land. The things our fathers loved. Memories.

Jennifer Larmore has chosen this programme with care: it feels like a personal choice, sung with personal concern. Whether it's recast traditional, homegrown original or something altogether loftier, she seems to know where it's coming from. American song is nothing if not outspoken and this is a full, ripe, outspoken voice. *Black is the color of my true love's hair* gives you the measure of it – a handsome song, handsomely recast, the low-lying phrases of its glorious melody just as dark as dark can be. Occasionally the characterization slips into the Bryn Terfel school of the overstated. But then again you wouldn't want to be without the broadness of her Southern Belle in Robert Abramson's setting of *Soldier, Soldier*. For the rest, the unfamilar are among the richest pickings. The directness of Jake Heggie's setting of the traditional text *He's gone away* is at once disarming. It's impossible to date and yet there is something longstanding and venerable about it. Four other Heggie songs are offered, and in each case it's amazing how he assumes the identity of his texts. Lee Hoiby's work is most appealing, not least his impassioned Wilfred Owen setting, *Winter Song* and Emily Dickinson's *A letter* which is as shy, sly and wry as its deliciously knowing text. But ultimately, there is Samuel Barber. His two James Joyce settings, *I hear an army* and *Rain has fallen* are stunning, the former vivid, vehement, the latter defined by an inconsolable and very particular melancholy, culminating in a furious piano cadenza that says more about frustration and despair than even Joyce's text. Antoine Palloc plays it here with an awareness and strength of purpose that mark out his contributions throughout the disc. And, of course, there is *Sure on this shining night* – as fine a song about wonder and the infinite as any. James Agee's text is one of nine reproduced in the beautifully illustrated booklet. It is a pity all the texts have not been included. Good as Larmore's diction is, they are needed.

Dame Felicity Lott My Garden.
Dame Felicity Lott *sop* Graham Johnson *pf*
Hyperion CDA66937 (65 minutes: DDD). Texts and translations included. Recorded 1996.   Ⓕ
Schumann Mein Garten, Op. 77 No. 2. Jasminenstrauch, Op. 27 No. 4. Herzeleid, Op. 107 No. 1. Die Blume der Ergebung, Op. 83 No. 2. Erstes Grün, Op. 35 No. 4. Volksliedchen, Op. 51 No. 2. **Wolf** Mörike Lieder – Er ist's; Im Frühling; Der Gärtner. Eichendorff Lieder – Nachtzauber. Goethe Lieder – Frühling übers Jahr; Anakreons Grab. **Franck** Le mariage des roses. **Chausson** Le temps des lilas. **Fauré** Green, Op. 58 No. 3. Les roses d'Ispahan, Op. 39 No. 4. **Chabrier** Lied. Toutes les fleurs. **Stanford** From the red rose. **Haydn Wood** Roses of Picardy. **Musto** Triolet. The Rose Family. **Barab** One Perfect Rose. **Berners** Red Roses and Red Noses.
Stanley & Allen Cabbages, Cabeans and Carrots.

The green-fingered accompanist has cultivated another fine display. Graham Johnson's garden of song is a splendid place for finding not only the usual hardy annuals from Germany, but also rare flowerings of the repertoire from France, England and the United States. The first half of this disc is devoted to Schumann and Wolf in about equal measure. There are some unusual items among the Schumann, such as the opening 'Mein Garten' and Ophelia's 'Herzeleid'; for the Wolf selection, Johnson extends the frontiers of his garden rather drastically, so as to take in the green hill of 'Im Frühling' and the graveyard of 'Anakreons Grab'. No doubt he wanted to include a few major songs, but it is in these that Dame Felicity is most likely to be found wanting. Compared with the best rival performances, neither 'Im Frühling' nor 'Nachtzauber' reveals its hidden depths though her warm and affectionate singing of 'Anakreons Grab' is on a higher level. The lighter Wolf songs, by contrast, are nicely turned. Once into the French and English half, there is no looking back, not least because the singer is twice as communicative in these languages as she is in German. The opening line of Chausson's *Le temps des lilas* is as idiomatic as one could wish, floating elegantly and sensuously over the long opening sentence and knowing just where to place the crucial change in vocal colour. The English-language group finds her lavishing a sensuality on Stanford's music that would probably have made the composer blush. There are two fine pithy songs by the American John Musto and another sarcastic one by Seymour Barab; then, in another rapid change of costume, she reappears in Eliza Doolittle's rags to end the disc with a delightfully upper-class fake Cockney rendering of *Cabbages, Cabeans and Carrots*. In the best Graham Johnson style, the disc is instructive and fun at the same time.

Dame Felicity Lott and Ann Murray On Wings of Song – Songs and Duets.
[a]Dame Felicity Lott *sop* [b]Ann Murray *mez* Graham Johnson *pf*
EMI CDC7 54411-2 (76 minutes: DDD). Texts and translations included. Recorded 1991.   Ⓕ
Purcell (arr. Britten) Come ye sons of art, away, Z323 – Sound the trumpet[ab]. The Indian Queen –

I attempt from love's sickness[b]. Lost is my quiet for ever, Z502[ab]. King Arthur – Fairest isle[a]. What can we poor females do, Z518[ab]. **Mendelssohn** Wasserfahrt[ab]. Duets, Op. 63[ab] – No. 5, Volkslied; No. 6, Maiglöckchen und die Blümelein. Auf Flügeln des Gesanges, Op. 34 No. 2[b]. Neue Liebe, Op. 19a No. 4[ab]. Abendlied[ab]. **Rossini** Soirées musicales – No. 1, La promessa[a]; No. 10, La pesca[ab]. Péchés de vieillesse, Book 1 – Anzoletta co passa la regata[b]. Duetto buffo di due gatti[ab]. **Gounod** La siesta[ab]. **Delibes** Les trois oiseaux[ab]. **Massenet** Rêvons, c'est l'heure[ab]. Joie![ab]. **Paladilhe** Au bord de l'eau[ab]. **Aubert** Cache-cache[ab]. **Balfe** Trust her not[ab]. **Sullivan** Coming home[ab]. **Quilter** It was a lover and his lass, Op. 23 No. 3[ab]. **Britten** Mother comfort[ab]. Underneath the abject willow[ab].

These expert duettists (fellow contributors to the Songmakers's Almanac and Marschallin and Octavian in many a *Rosenkavalier*) have already one highly successfully disc ('Sweet Power of Song' – reviewed further on) to their joint credit, and now achieve what often proves the more difficult task of providing an equally good sequel. But of course this is not really a double-act but a trio, and Graham Johnson is, as ever, more than accompanist. When he arranges a programme, delight follows as sure as night follows day. Here the delight lies partly in discovery (for instance, there is a charmer of Gounod's, in Spanish style, the voices in dreamy thirds, the ending softly delicate). Then there is the range of mood, from Purcell's assured, outward-going 'Sound the trumpet' at the start to the desolation that burrows within Britten's haunting *Mother comfort* near the end. Solos are deftly chosen to bring out the best in each singer, as in the clean style and unostentatious manner of Felicity Lott's 'Fairest isle' and Ann Murray's finely phrased, evenly sustained *Auf Flügeln des Gesanges*. Then there are the charming oddities: Sullivan's 'Coming home' turns out to be a duet from *Cox and Box* (but with different words), and 'Rossini's' cat-duet is now attributed to that singularly unpredictable minor genius, Robert Pearsall. The recording is exemplary.

Opera Duets
Angela Gheorghiu *sop* **Roberto Alagna** *ten*
London Voices; Berlin Philharmonic Orchestra / Claudio Abbado.
EMI CDC5 56656-2 (70 minutes: DDD). Texts and translations included. Recorded 1998. (F) E
Otello – Già nella notte densa; Venga la morte!. Aida – La fatale pietra; Morir si pura e bella;
O terra addio (with **Sara Mingardo** *mez*). Il trovatore – Miserere … Ah, che la morte ognora.
Simon Boccanegra – Cielo di stelle orbato; Vieni a mirar la cerula. I vespri siciliani – Pensando a me!. I Lombardi alla prima crociata – Oh belle, a questa misera; All'armi!. La traviata – Libiamo, ne'lieti calici. Rigoletto – Ah! veglia, o donna; Signor nè principe; T'amo! T'amo; E il sol dell'anima; Addio, addio (**Mingardo; Brian Parsons, Rodney Gibson** *tens*). Don Carlo – E dessa! … Un detto, un sol; Vago sogno m'arrise; Ma lassù ci vedremo. I masnadieri – Qual mare, qual terra; Qui nel bosco?; Lassù risplendere.

This long, fascinating, highly ambitious recital, nothing less than a conspectus of Verdi's soprano-tenor duets, is executed with distinction on all sides. Gheorghiu deserves particular plaudits. It seems that nothing in Verdi (and indeed in much else) is beyond her capabilities. Her singing here, especially as Gilda, Aida and Desdemona, is so exquisite, the tone so warm and limpid, the phrasing so shapely as surely to melt any heart. Take, for example, Gilda's touching exchanges with Giovanna, herself sung by the superb mezzo, Sara Mingardo (also heard as a grieving Amneris, the whole of Aida's solo beginning 'Presago il core', with the soprano's warm lower register coming into play, and that ultimate test, Desdemona's poised 'Amen'. Throughout, musically and interpretatively, she cannot be faulted. Neither she nor her husband is backward in coming forward with less hackneyed pieces, those from the early operas – try the section starting 'Ma un'iri di pace' in the *Masnadieri* duet, the two voices in ideal blend, phrases and tone sweetly shaded with the following cabaletta all light eagerness on both sides. Then there's plangent singing on both sides in the sad little piece from *Vespri*, though it's a pity they did not attempt this in the original French. Here and throughout Alagna is his customary self, assured (a few over-pressed high notes, some unwritten, apart), impassioned, thoughtful and accurate in his phraseology, nowhere more so than in the parts he is unlikely as yet to take on stage – Radames and Otello. Even more important in so many passages, Alagna finds the right *mezzo-piano*, where heavier tenors have to sing *forte*, notably in the closing phrases where Otello wafts his love of Desdemona on to the night air – a moment of sheer magic. Abbado and the BPO are at their peak of achievement and the recording catches these voices in their full glory, making this a most desirable issue, possibly the best the pair has yet made.

Anne Sofie von Otter Wings in the night – Swedish Songs.
Anne Sofie von Otter *mez* **Bengt Forsberg** *pf*
DG 449 189-2GH (74 minutes: DDD). Texts and translations included. Recorded 1995. (F) E
Peterson-Berger Nothing is like the time of waiting. Swedish folk ballads, Op. 5 – No. 1, When I go myself in the dark forest; No. 3, Like Stars in the Heavens. Three Marit's Songs, Op. 12. Böljeby Waltz. Return. Aspåkers Polka. **Sigurd von Koch** Exotic Songs – No. 1, In the

month of Tjaitra; No. 3, Of lotus scent and moonlight. The wild swans – spring night's rain; Mankind's lot; The wild swans. **Stenhammar** Songs and Moods, Op. 26 – No. 1, The Wanderer; No. 4, Miss Blonde and Miss Brunette; No. 5, A ship sails; No. 9, Coastal song. Songs, Op. 37 – No. 1, Jutta comes to the Volkungs; No. 2, In the maple's shade. **Rangström** Poems by Bo Bergman – No. 1, Wings in the night; No. 3, Melody. The Dark Flower – No. 2, Prayer to the night; No. 4, Farewell. Pan. Old Swedish. **Alfvén** Songs, Op. 28 – No. 3, I kiss your hand; No. 6, The forest sleeps. **Sjögren** Lieder from Wolff's 'Tannhäuser', Op. 12 – No. 4, Hab'ein Röslein dir gebrochen; No. 6, Ich möchte schweben. Du schaust, mich an mit stummen Fragen.

If von Otter's and Forsberg's intention in compiling this recital was to provide an introduction to the riches of Swedish song so compelling that purchasers of it will hunger for more, they have succeeded. There are very few songs here that could not be programmed without apology or fear of comparison alongside the best German Lieder of the same period (the 40 years between 1884 and 1924). They contain considerable variety of mood and musical style, and the recital has been cleverly programmed to demonstrate in particular the range and the development of the two finest song composers here, Wilhelm Peterson-Berger and Wilhelm Stenhammar. Both were greatly gifted melodists, Peterson-Berger holding to an almost folk-like vein of simple lyricism, while Stenhammar reached further and touched darker moods, and the other composers here are by no means cast into the shade by these two masters. The performances are superb, quiet shadings of colour and subtle phrasings under immaculate control, a mere thread of voice often used to draw you into the heart of a song quite magically. Forsberg is an ideally imaginative and positive partner. You will probably find yourself playing several of these songs over and over again (for von Otter's exquisite little flourish of coloratura at the end of von Koch's *Of lotus scent*, for example, or for her delightful touch of humour and affection describing little chicks 'who can hardly walk' stumbling into the first warm sun of summer in the first of Peterson-Berger's *Marit's Songs*).

Sir Peter Pears The Land of Lost Content.
Sir Peter Pears *ten* [a]**Benjamin Britten,** [b]**Alan Bush,** [c]**Viola Tunnard** *pf*
Belart 461 550-2 (69 minutes: ADD). Recorded 1963-64.　　　　　　　　　Ⓑ
Ireland The Land of Lost Content[a]. The trellis[a]. **Bridge** 'Tis but a week, H146[a]. Goldenhair, H165[a]. When you are old and gray, H142[a]. So perverse, H61[a]. Journey's End, H167[a]. **Tippett** Songs for Ariel[a]. **A. Bush** Voices of the Prophets, Op. 41[b]. **Delius** To Daffodils[c]. **Moeran** The merry month of May[c]. **Dieren** Dream pedlary[c]. Take, o take those lips away[c]. **Warlock** Piggesnie[c]. Along the stream[c]. **Grainger** Bold William Taylor, BFMS43[c]. **Busch** The echoing Green[c]. The shepherd[c]. If thou wilt ease thine heart[c]. Come, o come, my life's delight[c].

Though Ireland's settings of Housman come first and give the disc its title, the group by Frank Bridge is stronger and more immediately impressive, with his particularly lovely setting of Yeats's *When you are old and gray and full of sleep* and the jaunty, catchy *So perverse*. The cycle by Alan Bush, *Voices of the Prophets*, gives the recital a firm centre, with its strongly committed treatment of politically correct passages from Isaiah, Milton, Blake and Peter Blackman. Warlock's *Piggesnie* is a delightful encore-song, Grainger's *Bold William Taylor* another, the one having Pears charmingly managing each verse in a single breath, the other a fine example of his vividness in narrative and dialogue. Three excellent pianists accompany him.

Leontyne Price A Program of Song.
Leontyne Price *sop* David Garvey *pf*
RCA Living Stereo 09026 61499-2 (40 minutes: ADD). Texts and translations included.
Recorded 1959.　　　　　　　　　　　　　　　　　　　　　　　　Ⓜ
Fauré Clair de lune, Op. 46 No. 2. Notre amour, Op. 23 No. 2. Au cimetière, Op. 51 No. 2. Au bord de l'eau, Op. 8 No. 1. Mandoline, Op. 58 No. 1. **Poulenc** Main dominée par le coeur. Miroirs brûlants. Ce doux petit visage. **R. Strauss** Allerseelen, Op. 10 No. 8. Schlagende Herzen, Op. 29 No. 2. Freundliche Vision, Op. 48 No. 1. Wie sollten wir geheim, Op. 19 No. 4.
Wolf Mörike Lieder – Der Gärtner; Lebe wohl. Lieder für eine Frauen-stimme – Morgentau. Spanisches Liederbuch – Geh' Geliebter, geh' jetz.

There can be few recordings which so vividly resemble the sound of singer and pianist performing live in one's own home. This forward, warts-and-all 1959 RCA recording has a disconcerting immediacy, but it's not just the recorded sound which creates this sense of close intimacy. Leontyne Price sings with a captivating directness which belongs more to a domestic setting than the concert hall – or even the opera house, for it was here that her reputation was made, becoming revered as one of the foremost Verdi sopranos. Her recorded legacy encompasses major roles from Mozart through Berlioz and Puccini to Gershwin and Samuel Barber, but this CD is special. This was her recording début made in the Town Hall, New York City, and shows her in repertoire with which she has not generally been associated. Yet she sings it with an intuition and sensitivity which would be the envy of singers whose lifetimes' work has been in Lieder and *chanson*. The French and German accents have an unmistakable American twang, but it's not the words which matter so much as the sense of involvement she brings to each and every one of these beautiful and memorable songs. A CD of great historic and artistic value.

Dame Margaret Price The Romantic Lied.
Dame Margaret Price *sop* **Graham Johnson** *pf*
Forlane UCD16728 (71 minutes: DDD). Texts and translations included. Recorded 1993.   Ⓕ
Wolf Mörike Lieder – Er ist's; Begegnung; Der Gärtner; In der Frühe; Lebe wohl; Heimweh; Gesang Weylas; Bei einer Trauung. **Cornelius** Trauer und Trost, Op. 3. **Liszt** Freudvoll und leidvoll, S280. Über allen Gipfeln ist Ruh, S306. Mignons Lied, S275. Der du von dem Himmel bist, S279. **Wagner** Wesendonk Lieder.

Price and Johnson have done it again. He has chosen a programme for her that exactly suits her talents and style, and she (with his inestimable help) has executed it with commitment and understanding. The programme in itself is fascinating, comparing and contrasting composers of roughly the same generation and period. The cross-fertilization of musical ideas is apparent, yet each emerges as an artist with something highly individual to say. Wolf isn't a composer with whom Price has been very much associated until now, but in a group of the Mörike settings, she proves herself at one with the poems and their music, catching in particular the restless ardour of *Begegnung*, the timeless mystery of *Gesang Weylas*, and the peculiarly Wolfian charm of the lighter pieces. Liszt is even more to her liking. She and Johnson choose the later, longer version of *Freudvoll und leidvoll* and make a grand romantic statement of it that is just right. The interpretation of the *Wesendonk Lieder* is the crowning glory of this wonderful recital. A virtually faultless reading, speeds (no unwanted lingering), phrasing, line and tone ideally adapted to the words and music. Johnson places the piano part in perfect relationship with the voice, helped by the exemplary recording of both.

La Promessa
Sumi Jo *sop* **Vincenzo Scalera** *pf*
Erato 3984-23300-2 (68 minutes: DDD). Texts and translations included. Recorded 1997.   Ⓕ
G. Giordani Caro mio ben. **Sarti** Giulio Sabino – Lungi dal caro ben (arr. Parenti).
Bellini Malinconia, ninfa gentile. **D. Scarlatti** Qual farfalletta amante. **Verdi** Ad una stella.
Handel Rinaldo – Lascia ch'io pianga. **Bellini** Per pietà, bell'idol mio. **Gluck** Paride ed Elena – IO del mio dolce ardor. **Rosa** Star vicino. **A. Scarlatti** Se Florindo è fedele. **Tosti** Non t'amo più!.
Cesti Intorno all'idol mio. **Rossini** Soirées musicales – La promessa. **Benedict** La capinera.
Donaudy O del mio amato ben. Vaghissima sembianza. **Handel** Giulio Cesare – V'adoro, pupille.
Mozart Ridente la calma, K152/K210a. **Caldara** Alma del core. **Paisiello** L'amor contrastato – Nel cor più non mi sento.

Here is one of the most delightful singers of our time heard in a programme that extends her repertoire on record and, being apt and congenial in itself, brings a double refreshment. There is a delicious coolness about the Korean soprano's singing: an eighteenth-century elegance. And not the slightest coldness about it; simply a humanity and a civilization where the heart is not worn on the sleeve. Interestingly, this is so even in the songs which often excite a more overtly passionate style of performance, Tosti's *Non t'amo più!* and the two by Stefano Donaudy. Similarly, such light-hearted nineteenth-century pieces as Rossini's 'La promessa' and Benedict's *La capinera* carry their gaiety with poise and refinement. It is partly that they benefit from the company of Handel and Mozart; partly that the clear voice and graceful style bring out the classicism in which their composers were educated rather than the thicker romanticism to which their age was tending. Voice and style here are as one, and the opening *Caro mio ben* is a fine example of both. The tone remains unequivocally that of a high lyric soprano but now with a mature and reassuring warmth in the lower notes. The phrases are beautifully sustained and are shaded with respect for the unity of line. The quickening pace of the middle section is well judged, as is the modestly decorated 'tanto rigor' leading back to the principal melody. Sumi Jo is responsive to the urgency of Bellini's *Malinconia* and the lightness of Domenico Scarlatti's *Farfalletta*. Vincenzo Scalera accompanies tastefully, and recorded sound is fine.

Samuel Ramey Ev'ry time we say goodbye – American Songs.
Samuel Ramey *bar* **Warren Jones** *pf*
Sony Classical SK68339 (71 minutes: DDD). Texts included. Recorded live in 1995.   Ⓕ
Barber Hermit Songs, Op. 29 – No. 6, Sea-snatch. I hear an army, Op. 10 No. 3. Sure on this shining night, Op. 13 No. 3. Bessie Bobtail, Op. 2 No. 3. **Foster** If you've only got a moustache. Gentle Annie. Don't bet your money at the Shanghai. **Griffes** Evening song. An old song re-sung.

The lament of Ian the Proud. Song of the dagger. **Gershwin** Nice work if you can get it. They all laughed. Embraceable you. Just another rhumba. **Bowles** They cannot stop death. Blue Mountain Ballads. **Porter** Blow, Gabriel, blow. Begin the Beguine. Ev'ry time we say goodbye. The tale of the oyster.

The opening Barber group kicks off with the short 'Sea-snatch' (one of the *Hermit Songs*, composed for soprano); this, like the James Agee setting, *Sure on this shining night*, is sung by Cheryl Studer on the complete Barber songs set (see review under Barber; refer to the Index), where Thomas Hampson sings the baritone songs. Ramey's darker-hued voice lends a more wintry feel to the James Joyce poem, *I hear an army* as well as to the sad story of mad *Bessie Bobtail*. It's quite a leap to the three Stephen Foster ballads. *If you've only got a moustache* must have brought a touch of vaudeville into the parlours of pre-Civil War America. This, and the rather nasty cock-fighting song, *Don't bet your money at the Shanghai*, frame a more typical Foster song, *Gentle Annie*, a near cousin to the more celebrated *Jeannie*. Charles Griffes's songs have been recorded by Hampson, but he stuck to his settings of German poetry. Ramey here climaxes with the bloodthirsty *Song of the dagger*, projecting such lines as 'My tears and thy blood shall flow together' with all the operatic fervour at his command. The groups of show tunes by Gershwin and Porter come either side of the five Paul Bowles songs. Of these the rarest is *They cannot stop death* to a text by Joe Massey. In the four *Blue Mountain Ballads* (words by Tennessee Williams) Ramey sounds quite straight. In the Gershwin group, 'Embraceable you' sounds very surprising so low down; when Ramey sings 'you alone bring out the gipsy in me' the effect is very different from what one imagines was achieved by Ginger Rogers when she first sang this in *Girl Crazy*. His version of 'Just another rhumba' is notable for the agility he manages in the fast-moving refrain, prompting a built-in encore with the final verse. 'The tale of the oyster', written by Porter for *Fifty Million Frenchmen*, was dropped after the opening, considered too *risqué*. Ramey does it with charm and diction that would have pleased the composer. Warren Jones provides a few words to help 'Blow, Gabriel, blow' get going. This is a serious, and at the same time amusing, ride around a century of American song.

Russian Opera Arias, Volume 2.
Sergei Alexashkin *bass*
Ambrosian Opera Chorus; Philharmonia Orchestra / Gennadi Rozhdestvensky.
Chandos CHAN9629 (74 minutes: DDD). Texts and translations included. Recorded 1997.　　Ⓕ
Rimsky-Korsakov Sadko – O fearful crags (Song of the Viking Guest). The Tsar's Bride – Sleep has overcome her. Mozart and Salieri – Everyone says there's no justice; No, I can't oppose my fate; You will sleep for a long time, Mozart! **Borodin** Prince Igor – I hate a dreary life; No sleep, no rest; How goes it Prince? **Mussorgsky** Boris Godunov – Once in the town of Kazan. **Rachmaninov** Aleko – By the magical power of the singing; The entire encampment sleeps. **Tchaikovsky** Mazeppa – So this is my reward. Eugene Onegin – Everyone knows love on earth.

Over this recital shines the steady light of Osip Petrov, the great artist who with the première of Glinka's *Life for the Tsar* in 1836 initiated a tradition of bass singing that was to colour the whole of Russian opera. It includes, as this admirably selected programme shows, a grave solemnity of voice, but also a baritonal elegance and a wide range of colour, a manner tragic, ruminative or seductive, together with the ferocious humour we encounter in Mussorgsky's Varlaam (another of Petrov's creations). The characteristics touch on much lying deep in Russia's life, and the line has included Stravinsky's father, Feodor, Mikhail Koryakin, Feodor Chaliapin and many others. Sergei Alexashkin is a worthy inheritor of it and this recital arouses hopes for more than just glimpses of some great roles. Alexashkin has the range to give subtle contrast to different roles in the same opera: the gloomy regret of Prince Igor's aria and also the brighter manliness which the Khan Konchak brings to their exchanges, the exhausted sorrowfulness of Rachmaninov's Old Gipsy and the more youthful acquaintance with the identical betrayal now encountered by Aleko. There is the dignity but also the coldness and the sudden glint of paranoia which possesses Salieri as he faces what he conceives to be his artistic duty in murdering Mozart, yet the jollity only just this side of the maudlin in Mussorgsky's Varlaam and Borodin's Galitsky. Much depends on subtle modifications of tone, still more on his ability to phrase with due care for meaning, whether in the free-ranging recitative of Salieri or, in Gremin's declaration of his devotion to Tatyana, the soaring melodic response to the warmth of the sun that has lit his life. Rozhdestvensky and the Philharmonia is a superb companion in these ventures into a great repertory; and Chandos backs it well with full texts and translations.

Leonie Rysanek Opera Arias.
Leonie Rysanek *sop* ^cJon Vickers *ten* ^dHarold Steinberg *bass*
orchestra / Arturo Basile; ^bOrchestra of the Metropolitan Opera, New York / Erich Leinsdorf; ^cRome Opera Orchestra / Tullio Serafin.
RCA Classics 74321 37719-2 (78 minutes: ADD). Recorded 1958-60.　　Ⓜ Ⓗ

Verdi La forza del destino – Pace, pace, mio Dio!ª. Aidaª – Ritorna vincitor; O patria mia. Macbeth – Nel di della vittoria ... Vieni t'affrettabd; La luce langueb. Otello – Già nella notte densac; Mia madre aveva ... Piangea cantandoª; Ave Mariaª. Un ballo in maschera – Ma dall'arido stelo divulsa; Morrò, ma prima in grazia (recorded 1958). **Puccini** Tosca – Vissi d'arteª. Turandot – In questa reggiaª. **Giordano** Andrea Chénier – La mamma mortaª. **Mascagni** Cavalleria rusticana – Voi lo sapeteª.

In 1996 Rysanek made her emotional farewell to the opera house (as Klytemnestra in *Elektra*) at the Salzburg Festival after virtually 50 years on stage, a remarkable if not unique record. Though she has been long recognized as an exceptional interpreter of Leonore and of many roles in the operas of Wagner and Richard Strauss, her extraordinary skills in the Italian *spinto* repertory have not been so fully recognized, at least in Britain. In all the wide-ranging arias she chooses she proves herself one of the most exciting and exacting interpreters of the respective roles on disc. She provided a kind of ideal marriage between the styles of her coevals, Callas, Tebaldi and Leontyne Price, with the interpretative insights of the one, the vocal opulence of the others, confirmed in her *Aida* solos. In every piece she has thought herself into the heart of the role and in every case she substantially obeys what is written in the score as regards phrasing and dynamics, most notably perhaps in 'O patria mia' and 'In questa reggia'. Tosca was one of her few Covent Garden roles and 'Vissi d'arte' shows her as the sensual heroine of Puccini's opera *par excellence*. The *Otello* love duet with Vickers comes from the admired complete set, a wonderfully balanced, eloquent rendering on both sides, Rysanek here as elsewhere providing ravishing *piano* singing to recall that of Milanov. The *Macbeth* items come from the complete RCA set and prove why the diva caused such a stir when she replaced Callas in the part at the Met in 1959. On the recital items Basile is a vital accompanist. The recordings sound much more vivid than on LP, marred by only fleeting moments showing tape degradation. No lover of Italianate singing at its best should be without this invaluable issue.

Elisabeth Schwarzkopf – The Unpublished EMI Recordings (1946-52)
Dame Elisabeth Schwarzkopf *sop* with various artists.
Testament mono SBT2172 (two discs: 134 minutes: ADD). Texts and translations included.
Recorded 1946-52.   Ⓕ
Opera arias – La bohème, La traviata and Die Zauberflöte (sung in English); songs and sacred works by Bach, Gounod, T. Arne, Morley, Mozart, Schubert, R. Strauss and Wolf.

Good heavens!, I hear you cry, what need for more Schwarzkopf when there's already a heap of her recordings available, including performances of much of the same repertory. Well, there's a very good reason why Testament – and Schwarzkopf herself, after some persuasion – thought this unissued material worth unearthing from the copious EMI archive where Testament continues to find new treasure. It may be heretical in the record world to say so, but Walter Legge had an Achilles' heel: he demanded perfection and it was just occasionally bought at the expense of spontaneity. In the case of the commercial recordings included here, he thought his wife could perform the pieces better on a later occasion, but now we may judge that these earlier interpretations have that much more eager freshness than the previously published versions. That's particularly so in the case of Bach's *Jauchzet Gott* and Mozart's *Exsultate, jubilate*. With Schwarzkopf in pristine, youthful voice, her production at its easiest, her breath long, both works shine forth as joyful things to hear – tone, line, runs, all in perfect accord. The remainder of the first CD, bar the final track, is a conspectus of the work the soprano was doing at the time, in the late 1940s, at Covent Garden where she was for a while a member of the resident company. Her Violetta, in English, and her Mimì, in Italian, both show her care over the words, which are inflected with heartfelt meaning in both cases. But the gem here is Schwarzkopf's own private recording of all Pamina's role sung at home in English to piano accompaniment in order that she might learn the role properly in the vernacular. So here we have an invaluable souvenir of a quite beautifully sung performance of 51 years ago. Schwarzkopf introduces this delightful oddity herself, a further bonus for posterity. The very last item on this CD brings a discovery of a very different kind. Legge apparently thought the Bach-Gounod *Ave Maria* wasn't musically worthy of the partnership, so the performance was never issued. How wrong he was: it turns out to be one of those occasions when a great artist can convert dross into gold.

On the second disc we have another addition to the singer's recorded legacy in a charming account of Morley's *It was a lover and his lass*. For the rest, it's all discarded takes of Lieder issued in later performances. None is as compelling as the 1948 *Gretchen am Spinnrade*, a performance of concentrated feeling urgently executed, and an irresistible account of *Der Musensohn* is preferable to issued versions because of its uninhibited verve. Two versions of Wolf's *Storchenbotschaft* are included; the first from 1948 the simpler, more natural, the second from 1951 a shade over-elaborated, not quite avoiding the song's insufferable coyness. Of the remaining Wolf songs, all recorded in 1951, three songs demand mention: *Bedeckt mich mit Blumen*, always a favourite with the singer, for its dreamy eroticism ideally adumbrated and sung with just the vibrancy called for, a reading of *Im Frühling*, filled with spring's yearning, and *Wiegenlied im Sommer*, in which Schwarzkopf's soothing, tender tones would persuade any child to untroubled sleep (as would Schubert's lullaby earlier on the disc). Throughout, Gerald Moore is the soprano's ever-faithful and supportive partner, and EMI's clear, clean recording adds to profound pleasure in an issue lovingly performed and lovingly prepared, with evocative photos and full texts and translations.

Mitsuko Shirai Songs with Viola.
Mitsuko Shirai *mez* **Tabea Zimmermann** *va* **Hartmut Höll** *pf*
Capriccio 10 462 (66 minutes: DDD). Texts and translations included. Recorded 1993-94.　　　Ⓕ
R. Strauss Stiller Gang, Op. 31 No. 4. **Brahms** Zwei Lieder, Op. 91. **A. Busch** Nun die Schatten dunkeln. Wonne der Wehmut. Aus den Himmelsaugen. **Loeffler** Quatre poèmes, Op. 5. **Dargomïzhsky** Elegy, 'She is coming'. **Marx** Durch Einsamkeiten. **Reutter** Fünf antike Oden, Op. 57. **Gounod** Evening song.

Voice and viola, we think, form a soothing combination: the sound of the words suggests as much, and memories of Brahms's Op. 91 (which is what we are likely to think of first and probably last) confirm it. The Brahms songs come second in this present programme, and on either side are compositions by Richard Strauss and Adolf Busch that are very much in keeping, the mood generally peaceful, the style essentially lyrical. Then come the *Quatre poèmes* of Charles Martin Loeffler (1861-1935). These, like the songs by Busch and, later, Hermann Reutter, are recorded now for the first time and they form a welcome addition to the small catalogue of Loeffler's works on record. In this programme, they, together with Reutter's 'Sappho', provide a contrast, a more bracing and varied use of the combination: a relief from the soothing. Mitsuko Shirai, now mezzo-soprano, sings with almost consistently firm and beautiful tone. She lightens the voice skilfully, as in Brahms's 'Gestillte Sehnsucht', and produces some beautifully sustained singing, as in the third of the Loeffler *Poèmes*, 'Le son du cor'. There is also an assured authority in this deeper voice with no less of the familiar charm. With fine playing by Tabea Zimmermann, especially in the Reutter cycle where the instrument is most imaginatively exploited, and with Hartmut Höll as sensitive as ever, this is a desirable disc.

Song Recital
Dame Janet Baker *mez* [f]**Dietrich Fischer-Dieskau** *bar* [e]**Cecil Aronowitz** *va*
[cf]**Daniel Barenboim** *pf*
[a]**New Philharmonia Orchestra / Sir John Barbirolli;**
[b]**London Symphony Orchestra / André Previn** [de]*pf*
EMI CZS5 68667-2 (two discs: 134 minutes: ADD). Recorded 1967-77.　　　Ⓜ
Ravel Shéhérazade[a]. **Chausson** Poème de l'amour et de la mer, Op. 19[b]. **Duparc** Phidylé[b]. La vie antérieure[b]. Le manoir de Rosemonde[b]. Au pays où se fait la guerre[b]. L'invitation au voyage[b]. **Schumann** Frauenliebe und -leben, Op. 42[c]. **Brahms** Vier ernste Gesänge, Op. 121[d]. Lieder, Op. 91[e]. Four Duets, Op. 28[f].

There comes a time in each great singer's career when they are at the peak of their form: artistry, voice, confidence, everything is at the maximum. Where Dame Janet Baker is concerned, that happy coincidence was in the years from 1967 to 1971. On the opera stage, her Dido in *Les troyens*, her Lucretia, Octavian, Dorabella and finally Diana in *Calisto* showed us her range of dramatic and comic skills. On the concert platform, working with Barbirolli, Szell, Giulini, Boult, Boulez and Barenboim, everything she did seemed well-nigh perfect. This two-CD selection from her EMI recordings opens with her famous performance of Ravel's *Shéhérazade* under Barbirolli, recorded in 1967. Of the song-cycles they recorded, this is perhaps the least regarded – Baker's voice never had quite the sensuous quality one is hoping for in this piece; but the security, the joy in the sound of her voice as she sings of Asia, and the right pace, all add up to a very fine recording. What is missing can be noted in the final line, about the beautiful boy walking past, with his feminine movements. One waits for a hint of irony, a slight smile of regret in the voice, but it isn't there. Baker was not given to innuendo; her humour was more robust. The succeeding Chausson *Poème de l'amour et de la mer* and then the group of songs by Duparc, recorded nearly ten years later, show up a marked deterioration in her voice. Where once all had been steady, there is a beat that becomes intrusive, a sense of strain on some of the high notes, even here and there a slight worry over the pitch. *Le manoir de Rosemonde* is the best performance, the high drama bringing out the best in her.

The performance of Schumann's *Frauenliebe und -leben* dates from 1975. Although at the time many people thought this outshone if not eclipsed Baker's earlier, justly famous Saga disc, this is debatable. The sound is certainly better on EMI and in the mid-1960s she had the ability to convey both the hushed, girlish quality of the earlier songs and the mature, and then even tragic, tones for the last three. The extra verbal clarity of this later performance does not make up for the slight sense of strain. There are no reservations whatsoever about the Brahms songs, with Previn. The extra darkness in Baker's voice by 1977 makes these the highlight of the whole selection. In the *Vier ernste Gesänge*, and then the two Op. 91 songs with piano and viola, Baker, Previn and Cecil Aronowitz achieve the perfect balance. As an encore we get four Brahms duets with Dietrich Fischer-Dieskau. Everything Dame Janet recorded is worth hearing, and this pair of discs gives an unusual cross-section of her repertory. There are no texts or translations, nor even synopses of the songs. Since these mid-price reissues are presumably aimed at the widest possible audience, all we can ask is 'Why not?'. As with every great Lieder singer, 50 per cent of Baker's art resides in her enunciation of the text; to be denied the chance to follow the words is infuriating.

Sumi Jo at Carnegie Hall
Sumi Jo *sop*
Orchestra of St Luke's / Richard Bonynge.
Erato 3984-21630-2 (64 minutes: DDD). Recorded live in 1996. Ⓕ
Mozart Vorre spiegarvi, oh Dio, K418. **Adam** Le toréador – Ah, vous dirai-je, maman. **Bellini**
I Puritani – Son vergin vezzosa; Qui la voce ... Vien, diletto. **Offenbach** Les contes d'Hoffmann –
Les oiseaux dans la charmille. **Bishop** Lo, here the gentle lark. **Benedict** The Gipsy and the Bird.
Bernstein Candide – Glitter and be gay. **Kim** I shall live in the Blue Mountains. **Cho** Seonguja.
J. Strauss II Die Fledermaus – Mein Herr Marquis (arr. Rauber). **Herbert** Naughty Marietta –
Italian Street Song. **Hong** Springtime of home.

This sounds like a good night out at Carnegie Hall, and not one whose memory is spoilt when heard again, transferred to disc. Apart from a little wear on the upper register at a *forte*, the voice remains pure, firm and lovely, its tone rather fuller than when we first knew it, the technique secure, its accomplishments impressively displayed. Expressiveness is perhaps not a prime requisite here, and indeed one might wish for a programme that did require a little more than a pretty smile shaded off now and again into a pretty pathos; but all goes well and the audience's evident enthusiasm is well justified. The only item which doesn't really succeed is Adam's variations on the nursery tune, *Ah, vous dirai-je, maman*, usually thought of simply as a display piece. The air is a wistful little thing, sung by a girl feeling the first torments of love and finding consolation in the tender, softly rocking melody of a song. That feeling is absent in Sumi Jo's technically admirable performance. Happily, in the very next item, 'Qui la voce' from *I Puritani*, Sumi Jo's singing has just the right degree of emotion for a concert performance, with Bonynge and his players responding sensitively to the quickening of pulse and its sad relaxation. This and the Polonaise, sung later in the programme, find the singer at her delightful best, as does the Mozart with which the recital so enchantingly opens. The three songs said to be of Korean origin sound thoroughly western, and application to the booklet-notes gains no further enlightenment. Still, this is not the kind of occasion for queries and complaints. Here is a delectable singer amidst an appreciative public, and we are fortunate to have the opportunity of sharing their enjoyment.

Sumi Jo Virtuoso Arias.
Sumi Jo *sop*
ᵃMonte-Carlo Philharmonic Orchestra / Paolo Olmi;
ᵇParis Orchestral Ensemble / Armin Jordan.
Erato 4509-97239-2 (74 minutes: DDD). Texts included. Recorded 1994. Ⓕ
Rossini Il barbiere di Siviglia – Una voce poco fa ... Io son docileᵃ. **Bellini** La sonnambula –
Ah! non credea mirarti ... Ah! non giungeᵃ. **Delibes** Lakmé – Ou va la jeune indoue ... Là-bas
dans la forêt plus sombreᵃ. **Verdi** Rigoletto – Gualtier Maldè ... Caro nomeᵃ. **Meyerbeer**
Dinorah – Ombre légèreᵃ. **Donizetti** Lucia di Lammermoor – Mad sceneᵃ. **R. Strauss** Ariadne
auf Naxos – Noch glaub' ich dem einen ganz ... So war es mit Pagliazzo ... Als ein Gott kam
jeder gegangenᵃ. **Bernstein** Candide – Glitter and be gayᵃ. **Mozart** Die Zauberflöte – Der
Hölle Racheᵇ. **Yoon** (arr. Constant) Barley Fieldᵃ.

Many listeners, well disposed towards most kinds of vocal recital, still tend to approach a new 'coloratura' programme with misgivings – all of which would seem to be obviated here. The emotional range of the music goes well beyond mere prettiness, whether of girlish glee or wilting pathos. The florid passages (commonly tagged 'display') are assumed by the singer to have an expressive purpose, which she then seeks out and fulfils. Her tone is bright but not piercing, her style clean but not cold; she understands perfectly well that, though these arias are famous for their high notes, far more of the singer's time is spent in the middle register, where a scrawny or breathy tone and flawed *legato* will not be excused on account of a few brilliances *in alt*. Intelligence is clearly at work from the start, in the enunciation of the words. 'Una voce poco fa qui nel cuor mi risuono': the 'qui' ('here') is the 'gesture-word', the one that makes it actual and individual. 'La vincerò' is determined, but not doubly-underlined or given that arch, over-confident touch which may gain a point but, in doing so, forfeits likeableness. In *La sonnambula* sympathy is actually *strengthened* by the cleaning-up of all those downward portamentos that have threatened to become inseparable from the music since Callas and Sutherland introduced them. Similarly, the Mad scene from *Lucia di Lammermoor* is enacted as a genuinely dramatic piece but with a fresh realization, rather than from a mind loaded with memories of those illustrious predecessors. The only way in which Jo appears at a disadvantage is in the relative hardness of some high notes. Zerbinetta's aria, for instance, is a shade uncomfortable (clearly written with more of the German *Kopfstimme* in mind), while the Korean song, *Barley Field*, is entirely lovely in sound and does not rise above an A flat.

Dame Joan Sutherland The Art of the Prima Donna.
Dame Joan Sutherland *sop*
ªChorus and Orchestra of the Royal Opera House,
Covent Garden / Francesco Molinari-Pradelli.
Decca The Classic Sound 452 298-2DCS2 (two discs: 109 minutes: ADD).
Texts and translations included. Recorded 1960.   Ⓜ
Opera Arias – Artaxerxes, Die Entführung aus dem Serail, Faust, Hamlet, Les Huguenots, Lakmé, Normaª, Otello, I Puritani, Rigolettoª, Roméo et Juliette, Samson, Semiramideª, La sonnambula and La traviata.

The occasion of Dame Joan Sutherland's seventieth birthday in November 1996 prompted Decca to reissue numerous opera sets from the 1960s. The two-disc recital, 'The Art of the Prima Donna' has hardly ever been out of the catalogue since 1960 – now it's remastered for Classic Sound. There cannot be many admirers who haven't already got this, so for newcomers to Sutherland on disc one can only say – listen and wonder. Her voice, even throughout its range right up to the high E, always keeping its natural quality, is heard at its early fullness. Perhaps the best tracks of all are the first two on the first disc, 'The soldier tir'd' from *Artaxerxes* and 'Let the bright seraphim' from *Samson*, but every track is beautiful. 'Casta Diva' – her earliest attempt at it – is certainly her most limpid recording of this prayer, 'Bel raggio' from *Semiramide* has sparkling decorations, quite different from the ones she sang on the complete recording six years later, and the whole thing ends with the Jewel Song from *Faust*. It was a big voice and sounded at its best in larger theatres; listening to 'O beau pays' from *Les Huguenots*, one can see Sutherland in one's mind's eye, in pale blue silk, as Marguerite de Valois at the Royal Albert Hall in 1968. It is difficult to imagine anyone, coming to it for the first time, being disappointed.

Dame Kiri Te Kanawa German Opera Arias.
Dame Kiri Te Kanawa *sop*
Philharmonia Orchestra / Julius Rudel.
EMI CDC5 56417-2 (57 minutes: DDD). Texts and translations included. Recorded 1996.   Ⓕ
Weber Der Freischütz – Wie nahte mir der Schlummer ... Leise, leise, fromme Weise; Und ob die Wolke. **Mozart** Die Zauberflöte – Ach, ich fühl's. **Wagner** Tannhäuser – Dich teure Halle; Allmächt'ge Jungfrau. Die Meistersinger von Nürnberg – O Sachs! Mein Freund!. Die Walküre – Du bist der Lenz. **R. Strauss** Daphne – Ich komme ... Ich komme, grünende Brüder. Ariadne auf Naxos – Es gibt ein Reich. Die Aegyptische Helena – Zweite Brautnacht!.
Korngold Die tote Stadt – Glück, das mir verblieb.

This makes such a lovely beginning that one is doubly loath to report occasional disappointment. The arias from *Der Freischütz* are sung in the fine Lemnitz tradition of gently rounded tone, beautifully sustained phrases and unspoilt line. In the cavatina the mood is serenely set, and the quickened impulse of the middle section is sensitively reflected. The great solo in Act 2 has a delightful freshness of response: when she exclaims about the brightness of the stars it is as though she has just this minute looked up and noticed them. The 'grand tune' from the Overture, so awkwardly written for the voice, is clearly articulated without smudges or intrusive changes of register. Pamina's aria, too, is sung with all due beauty of voice and expression, the unaccompanied falling notes at the end touchingly lonesome and disconsolate. It may not be until the fifth track, Elisabeth's greeting in *Tannhäuser*, that Time 'that takes survey of all the world' has to be acknowledged. This most lovely voice retains a good deal of its quality but it is not untouched. The vibrations are not as tight, the upper notes not as pure and the middle register has not acquired power and fullness to compensate. This is the most important factor in determining the success of much that follows. Sieglinde's 'Du bist der Lenz' wants power and colour in just that part of the voice where they are least available. In *Daphne* and *Die Aegyptische Helena* one is too often aware of a tinkle on the surface of notes which a few years earlier would have been glorious to hear. Even in Marietta's song from *Die tote Stadt* the expectation of full-bodied sound freely released is thwarted as she opts instead for a more delicate style and produces this rather small, rather undernourished tone with a dreamy, inward expression in place of the rapt exultancy we remember from Lotte Lehmann. The orchestral playing provides pleasure throughout, especially in the lengthy passage in *Daphne* before the wordless voice is heard from off-stage. Recorded sound is fine.

Bryn Terfel Opera Arias.
Bryn Terfel *bass-bar*
Orchestra of the Metropolitan Opera, New York / James Levine.
DG 445 866-2GH (71 minutes: DDD). Texts and translations included. Recorded 1994-95. ⒻⒺ
Mozart Le nozze di Figaro – Non più andrai. Don Giovanni – Madamina, il catalogo è questo; Deh! vieni alla finestra. Così fan tutte – Rivolgete a lui lo sguardo. Die Zauberflöte – Der Vogelfänger bin ich ja. **Wagner** Tannhäuser – Wie Todesahnung … O du mein holder Abendstern. Der fliegende Holländer – Die Frist ist um. **Offenbach** Les contes d'Hoffmann – Allez! … Pour te livrer combat … Scintille, diamant. **Gounod** Faust – Vous qui faîtes l'endormie. **Borodin** Prince Igor – No sleep, no rest. **Donizetti** Don Pasquale – Bella siccome un angelo. **Rossini** La Cenerentola – Miei rampolli femminini. **Verdi** Macbeth – Perfidi! All'angelo caontra me v'unite! … Pietà, rispetto, amore. Falstaff – Ehi! paggio! … L'Onore! Ladri!.

In a careless moment we might describe Bryn Terfel as a very physical singer, and it would be true up to a point. His physical presence is much in evidence when he sings, or for that matter when he talks or just breathes. Having seen him 'in the flesh', one seems to see him while hearing the sound of his voice on records. But the crowning distinction of Terfel's art (granted the voice, the technique and, the general musicianship) is its intelligence. As with words, so with characters: each is a specific, sharp-minded creation, and none is a stereotype. This Leporello exhibits his master's catalogue with pride; it is the book of life and not to be taken lightly. This Don Magnifico recounts his dream in all good faith (he doesn't *know* that he's a complete idiot, and doesn't deliberately set himself up to sound like one). No less impressive, as an aspect of intelligence, is the linguistic command, and still more so the use he makes of it: the sheer mental concentration of his Dutchman carries intense conviction and an ever-specific understanding. In short, a magnificent recital with fine recorded sound fine.

Three Rossini Tenors
Nelly Miricioiu *sop* Paul Austin Kelly, Bruce Ford, William Matteuzzi *tens*
Geoffrey Mitchell Choir; Philharmonia Orchestra,
Academy of St Martin in the Fields / David Parry.
Opera Rara ORR204 (70 minutes: DDD). Texts and translations included. Recorded 1996. Ⓕ
Rossini La donna del lago – Alla ragion deh rieda; Qual pena in me. Otello – No, no temer, serena; Non m'inganno, al mio rivale; Ah! vieni, nel tuo sangue … Ahimè fermate … Che fiero punto è questo. Ricciardo e Zoraide – Donala a questo core. Armida – Come l'aurette placide; In quale aspetto imbelle.

'Only *three*?' Rossini might have remarked. During the years 1815-22 which this recital so thrillingly celebrates, Rossini had four, possibly five, world-class tenors at his disposal. Still, it is a good marketing ploy, with Opera Rara's three tenors turning in bravura performances in repertoire which *the* three tenors have only occasionally flirted with. It says much for Rossini's guile, and the guile of the programming, that one comes away from this recital, not bored or sated, but thrilled and satisfied. Amusingly, there is no actual trio for tenors until the last track, the astonishingly beautiful scene in *Armida* where Carlo and Ubaldo hold the adamantine shield up to Rinaldo's gaze and, in so doing, confront him with an image of his own baseness. Rossini's leading heroic tenor was Andrea Nozzari. Bruce Ford sings the Nozzari roles here, with Paul Austin Kelly and William Matteuzzi taking turn and turn about with the more purely brilliant roles (Uberto, Rodrigo, Ricciardo) Rossini wrote for the celebrated *tenore contraltino* in the Naples company, Giovanni David. All three acquit themselves superbly. (Rarely, if ever, has Matteuzzi, on record, sounded quite as sweet-toned as here.) To have Nelly Miricioiu on hand to sing Elena and Desdemona is an added bonus. David Parry and the Philharmonia Orchestra give performances of great dash and beauty. The recording places the orchestra rather obviously to the rear of the singers, but that is no bad thing. Slightly more distracting is the fact that the Rossini tenor is clearly a difficult creature for the microphone to decipher and absorb, particularly *en masse*. Thus, while Matteuzzi and Kelly are allowed to coo into the microphones like a pair of sucking doves, Bruce Ford is cast more in the role of the blackguard outsider, never quite as well forward, the sound never quite as 'clean'. The insert-notes are altogether excellent.

Dawn Upshaw Goethe Lieder.
Dawn Upshaw *sop* Richard Goode *pf*
Nonesuch 7559-79317-2 (53 minutes: DDD). Texts and translations included.
Recorded 1993. ⒻⒺ

Schubert Rastlose Liebe, D138. Gretchen am Spinnrade, D118. Mignons Gesang, D877 No. 4. Suleika I, D720. Versunken, D715. Wanderers Nachtlied II, D768. Ganymed, D544. An den Mond, D296. **Schumann** Liebeslied, Op. 51 No. 5. Nachtlied, Op. 96 No. 1. Lieder und Gesänge aus Wilhelm Meister, Op. 98a – No. 1, Mignon; No. 5, Heiss mich nicht reden; No. 7, Singet nicht in Trauertönen. **Wolf** Blumengruss. Die Bekehrte. Die Spröde. Frühling übers Jahr. **Mozart** Das Veilchen, K476.

Upshaw and Goode are a musical marriage made in heaven, each a highly individual, probing and sincere artist prepared to challenge received views on a song. Thus their *Gretchen am Spinnrade* in this programme of all-Goethe settings is an outburst of a desperate and infinitely perturbed woman breaking conventional bonds. To emphasize the point Upshaw leans into the first syllable of 'nimmer' at each repetition with added feeling and times the climax of the great song at the word 'Kuss' in an overwhelming way, only such a similarly involving (although very different) interpreter as Lotte Lehmann could. Goode's playing simply underlines and reinforces the singer's intense utterance. The Schumann settings are filled with just as much spontaneous emotion and direct imagination. The pair make as strong a case as is possible for Schumann's setting of Mignon's *Kennst du das Land* being superior even to Wolf's, the repeated 'Kennst du das wohl?' carrying an extraordinary charge. The singer's voice is also ideally fitted for Wolf's teasingly sensual *Die Spröde* and *Die Bekehrte* and the pair bring the lightest touch to *Blumengruss*. Finally they give Mozart's *Das Veilchen* a deeper meaning than almost any interpreters from the past. An ideally balanced, forward yet spacious recording enhances the pleasure to be derived from this deeply satisfying disc.

Dawn Upshaw I wish it so.
Dawn Upshaw *sop*
orchestra / Eric Stern.
Nonesuch 7559-79345-2 (45 minutes: DDD). Texts included. Recorded 1993.
Gramophone Award winner 1995. Ⓕ
Blitzstein Juno – I wish it so. No for an Answer – In the clear. Reuben, Reuben – Never get lost. **Sondheim** Anyone Can Whistle – There won't be trumpets. Saturday Night – What more do I need? The Girls of Summer – The Girls of Summer. Merrily We Roll Along – Like it was. Evening Primrose – Take me to the world. **Weill** One Touch of Venus – That's him. Lady in the Dark – The saga of Jenny; My ship. Lost in the Stars – Stay well. **Bernstein** West Side Story – I feel pretty. Candide – Glitter and be gay. The Madwoman of Central Park West – My new friends.

Bernstein, Blitzstein, Sondheim and Weill are a good quartet to explore in a recital and Dawn Upshaw's clear soprano is well suited to nearly all these songs. The Blitzstein numbers will only be familiar to specialists. 'I wish it so' from Blitzstein's adaptation of O'Casey's *Juno* seems to herald the mood of the whole disc, songs of longing, some optimistic, some resigned. 'In the clear' is one of the songs from *No for an Answer*, Blitzstein's follow-up to *The Cradle Will Rock*; it was first given in 1940, the same week that saw the first night of Weill's *Lady in the Dark*. In the Blitzstein, Eric Stern's arrangement with a solo cello part played by Matthias Niegele turns the song into a melancholy lullaby. This and a brilliant performance of 'Glitter and be gay' from *Candide* show off Dawn Upshaw's impressive range – from the coloratura of the Bernstein to mezzo-ish moodiness for the Blitzstein. Of the Weill songs, 'Stay well' from *Lost in the Stars* is especially successful, and 'That's him' from *One Touch of Venus* is playful. The two numbers from *Lady in the Dark* are given the most extensive overhaul, the melody of 'The saga of Jenny' such as it is disappears beneath Larry Wilcox's rearrangement and although Upshaw sings 'My ship' quite beautifully, again Daniel Troob has made an arrangement that pulls it about rather. All in all, this is a very attractive foray into the Broadway territory.

Historic vocal

Victoria de los Angeles
Victoria de los Angeles *sop* with various artists.
Testament mono SBT1087 (75 minutes: ADD). Recorded 1942-53. ⒻⒽ
Songs and Arias by Brahms, Falla, Fusté, Granados, Guridi, Handel, Nin, Respighi, Schumann, Toldrá, Turina, Valverde and Vives.

The two Respighi songs are magical performances – *Stornellatrice*, with the golden voice at its richest and *E se un giorno tornasse*, a study in subtle shading of tone, a dialogue between a mother and her dying, jilted daughter. For those two brief items alone, superbly transferred, this collection is an essential for all admirers of this singer, but there is so much more. Having Handel's 'O had I Jubal's lyre' in German rather than English may be odd, but the performance sparkles and among the Lieder it is good to have not just 'Der Nussbaum' – the Schumann song which was always special to her – but two previously unpublished, 'Widmung' from the Myrthe songs and 'Ich grolle nicht' from *Dichterliebe*. Through the whole collection the superb transfers capture the full-throated glory of los Angeles's voice at the beginning of her career. The 1942 recordings of two Hungarian folk-songs, previously unpublished, may be rough and limited – made when the singer was only 18 – but they amply demonstrate that already the voice was fully developed in its beauty. No fewer than 18 of the 27 items are of Spanish songs, and though in one or two instances los Angeles was destined to make even more idiomatic readings later with a Spanish accompanist, these ones with Gerald Moore as her partner have a freshness and brilliance that has rarely been matched in this repertory. In particular it is good to have her first recording of the encore number which she made her own, *Clavelitos*.

Dame Isobel Baillie and Kathleen Ferrier To Music.
[a]Dame Isobel Baillie *sop* [b]Kathleen Ferrier *contr* Gerald Moore *pf*
APR mono APR5544 (69 minutes: ADD). Recorded 1941-45. All items sung in English.   Ⓜ Ⓗ
Songs, Arias and Duets by [a]Arne, [ab]Brahms, [b]Elgar, [b]Gluck, [b]Greene, [a]Grieg, [b]Handel,
[ab]Mendelssohn, [ab]Purcell, [a]Schubert and [a]Scott.

This is a delightful disc, with a happily chosen programme and well-matched contributions from both singers. Even so, it has to be admitted that the first thought concerns date. The piano arrangements of Purcell duets and Handel arias are definitely of the period; nothing could be more remote from the modern style which was even then coming into vogue. But 'dated' in a much better way is the quality of the singing itself. Would you today find the runs in Purcell and Handel sung with at once such clear articulation and such smoothness? Dame Isobel is sometimes a little pipey but for the most part charming. Ferrier is royal. The transfers are excellent.

Lucrezia Bori
Lucrezia Bori *sop* with various artists.
Romophone mono 81017-2 (two discs: 147 minutes: ADD). Recorded 1925-37.   Ⓕ Ⓗ
Opera Arias – Acis y Galatea, Amantes chasqueaos, L'amour mouillé, La bohème, Les contes d'Hoffmann, Don Giovanni, Don Quijote de la mancha, Louise, Madama Butterfly, Manon, Mignon, Le nozze di Figaro, La rondine, Il segreto di Susanna, La traviata and La vida breve; songs by Arditi, Falla, Glazunov, Goetz, Götze, Joves, Nin, Pagans, Pestalozzi, Rumbold, Schumann, J. Strauss II, A. G. Thomas and Valverde.

Until Romophone brought out the complete run of her Victor recordings, Bori looked like becoming the forgotten prima donna. Volume 1 was welcomed in *Gramophone* as reintroducing 'one of the most adorable and fascinating of singers on records', and its successor now follows her from the heyday of her career to the time of her last recordings, some 18 months after her official retirement at the age of 50. The originals were often issued on noisy shellac, and at 78rpm most played above the correct pitch. In these conditions the voice could sound thin, and the 'image' (if that overused word were permitted) suffered accordingly. The repertoire of songs may not have helped: perhaps in its time *Ciribiribin* and so forth were welcomed as a form of 'crossover', but even now, at this distance in time, from behind the sweetly tweet-a-tweeting singer, Groucho has only to lift an eyebrow or Harpo to turn down his nether lip, and the bird-song takes a perilously farcical flight. Fortunately we are just sufficiently far away to detach the records from impediments of this kind. The complete edition, which the two volumes comprise, returns the singer to us as new. Among the recordings said to be previously unpublished, best are two songs by Nin, dating from the singer's last session, at the end of 1937. There are also some alternative takes (all good), and the two 1925 duets with McCormack. A great pleasure lies in the discovery (or maybe confirmation) that the 1937 recordings show only slight deterioration of voice and have such vividness of character. Best remain well-known things such as Mimì's narrative, Musetta's waltz-song (sung as though it were Mimì's also), the *Mignon* solos and some of the Spanish songs such as the *Malagueña* by Don Pagans. The most commonplace, trivial or exasperatingly 'pretty' banalities endear themselves if they provide an additional opportunity to hear this exquisite, highly individual, totally lovable artist.

Emma Calvé The Complete 1902 G&T, 1920 Pathé and 'Mapleson Cylinder' Recordings.
Emma Calvé, Cécille Merguillier *sops* with various artists.
Marston mono 52013-2 (two discs: 139 minutes: ADD). Recorded 1902-20.   Ⓕ Ⓗ
Opera arias – Amadis de Gaulle, Carmen, Cavalleria rusticana, Les contes d'Hoffmann, Le domino noir, Faust, Galathée, Hamlet, Manon, Mignon, Mireille, Norma, Le nozze di Figaro,

Le pardon de Ploëmel, La perle du Brésil, La périchole, Philémon et Baucis, Pré aux clercs, Roméo et Juliette, Sapho and La vivandière; songs by Beethoven, Bland, De Lara, Foster, Gounod, Hahn, Key, Massenet, Thomas and Traditional.

In the alphabetical index of great singers, Calvé follows Callas, and the sequence is suggestive. Both were actress-singers who brought revelations of opera-as-theatre to the audiences of their time; both acted with the voice (as contemporary accounts of Calvé tell and as we know to be so with Callas); and both were strong personalities among the most famous women in the world. One sad and striking difference is that Callas's recordings testify amply to this, while Calvé's are inadequate in repertoire as well as technical conditions to do her justice. Yet much is caught, right from those extraordinary cylinders made at performances in the Metropolitan in 1902 where, among all that is lost, her high-notes can be heard ringing out well into the house above the orchestra, with a tone sufficiently distinctive for us to associate it with the studio recordings made later that same year. They in turn are reinforced by the amazingly vivid series made for Pathé in 1920, by which year the singer was in her early sixties. The quality of copies used and results obtained is fine. There is a second singer here and her presence adds greatly to its attractions. Cécile Merguillier recorded for Pathé and Edison in 1904 and 1905 when virtually in retirement though only in her early forties, and still singing with fresh voice, assured technique and captivating style. A light soprano, she was singing Philine in *Mignon* (an energetic performance of the Polonaise is among her records) in 1887, the night the old Opéra-Comique burnt down. Her solos from *Mireille* and *Philémon et Baucis* are especially delightful, and as far as can be ascertained, this is the first time a full sequence of her records has been collected on disc. The issue is finely presented, with informative notes.

Caruso in Opera, Volume 2.
Enrico Caruso *ten* with various artists.
Nimbus Prima Voce mono NI7866 (79 minutes: ADD). Recorded 1905-20.   Ⓜ Ⓗ
Arias – L'Africaine, Andrea Chenier, La bohème (Leoncavallo and Puccini), Carmen, Cavalleria rusticana, Don Pasquale, Eugene Onegin, La favorita, Les Huguenots, Macbeth, Martha, Nero, La reine de Saba, Rigoletto, Tosca and Il trovatore.

The 1906 recording of 'M'appari' from *Martha* comes first, and it introduces an aspect of Caruso's singing that rarely finds a place in the critical commentaries: his subtlety. Partly, it's rhythmic. The move-on and pull-back seems such an instinctive process that we hardly notice it (though no doubt a modern conductor would – and check it immediately). It makes all the difference to the emotional life of the piece, the feeling of involvement and spontaneous development. Then there is the phrasing, marvellously achieved at the melody's reprise. The play of louder and softer tones, too, has every delicacy of fine graduation; and just as masterly is the more technical (though still expressive) covering and (rare) opening of notes at the *passaggio*. An edition of the score which brought out all these features of Caruso's singing would be a densely annotated document. It would, even so, be a simplification, for accompanying all this is the dramatic and musical feeling, which defies analysis – and, of course, the voice. That voice! You may feel you know all these records and hardly need to play them, yet there is scarcely an occasion when the beauty of it does not thrill with a sensation both old and new (the first 'Ah!' is one of recognition, the second of fresh wonder). So it is with nearly all of the items here: all, in fact, save the *Eugene Onegin* aria, which remains external, and the late *L'Africaine* recording with its saddening evidence of deterioration. The transfers are excellent.

Boris Christoff
Boris Christoff *bass* with various artists.
EMI Références mono CDH5 65500-2 (80 minutes: ADD). Recorded 1949-55.   Ⓜ Ⓗ
Opera Arias – Don Carlo, Don Giovanni, Ernani, La forza del destino, Iphigénie en Aulide, Mefistofele, Nabucco, Norma, Simon Boccanegra, La sonnambula and I vespri siciliani.

The grieving king, the patriarchal priest, the smirking demon: these are all expected presences in Christoff's gallery of vivid characters, and one might well extend the list mentally by a dozen or so more before thinking of Leporello. Christoff sang very little Mozart but the Catalogue aria in *Don Giovanni* featured in his concert programmes. It is a marvellous performance, and alone provides a very good reason for buying this disc. Almost as unlooked for may be the Count's aria in *La sonnambula*, sung with affection and a nearly perfect *legato*. Warmth of tone perhaps is wanting, in both that and the 'Infelice' (*Ernani*), but there is certainly no lack of emotional warmth in the fine solos from *I vespri siciliani* and *Simon Boccanegra*. Philip's great aria in *Don Carlo* ends with a too overt and prolonged tearfulness (avoided in later versions) but this recording is still among the supremely impressive mementos of its era. It comes from one of Christoff's first sessions in the studios, and is strikingly natural and lifelike, as are all the 78s heard here. In the 1955 recordings one is more aware of the microphone: for example, in his most authoritative vein, Christoff is splendidly represented by the Gluck aria (*Iphigénie en Aulide*) made in 1951, whereas the same magnificence is present in the excerpts from *Nabucco* (1955) but just slightly diminished by seeming to be made larger than life. When all is over, however, the first item demands a replay: that Catalogue song of Leporello's. John Hughes's admirable notes concede that the performance 'may lack the necessary touch of humour' – but it surely does not! Gaiety, rhythm, even a chuckle, a swelling grandeur in the portrayal of the 'maiestosa', a daintiness in 'la piccina': it is all there, and with it a certain suavity of style, and, rarer still, the elegant phrases of 'Nella bionda' sung with scrupulous *legato*. This disc goes into the 'Essential Christoff Collection' forthwith.

Giuseppe Di Stefano
Giuseppe Di Stefano *ten* with various artists.
Testament mono SBT1096 (79 minutes: ADD). Recorded 1944-56.   Ⓕ H
Opera Arias – L'amico Fritz, L'Arlesiana, L'elisir d'amore, La fanciulla del West, La forza del destino, Gianni Schicchi, Manon, Mignon, Tosca and Turandot; songs by Bixio, Tagliaferri; Sicilian folk-songs.

Very moving it is to hear this voice again in its absolute prime. It is hardly possible to hear those Swiss recordings of 1944, with piano, and be untouched by the thought, as well as the sound, of this 22-year-old, singing his heart out, with so much voice and, already, with so much art. The 'Una furtiva lagrima' is perhaps not the fully polished article, but what Forster called the Italian 'instinct for beauty' is there, with lovely shading and phrasing. It is good to have the two Bixio songs (*Se vuoi goder la vita* and *Mamma*), previously unpublished, heartfelt, open-throated performances in the national tradition that used to get mocked and is now so missed. Indeed, thinking of that sequence of recordings, one could well wish this disc had given priority to reproducing them all: there is an amazingly good 'Pourquoi me réveiller?', for instance, and (till the end) a beautifully restrained *Musica proibita*. Still, what we have here fulfils exactly the promise of the label's name: it is a testament, and a testament of youth. The later operatic recordings, from 1955, find the tenor with some signs of wear and with a recklessly open way of taking his high As and B flats, but there is real passion, and imagination with it. In the latest recording, a commonplace song called *Passione* from 1956, one almost looks up at the speakers to see the face there: it seems so very clear and lifelike. Some of the sound (recording or transfer) seems overbright – the second *Manon* solo is a prime example – but it is always vivid and compelling. In the booklet-listing a translation of the song-titles would have been welcome. It would also have been useful if Peter Hutchinson's notes had related the excerpts to Di Stefano's career (did he for instance ever sing Dick Johnson, Rinuccio and Calaf on stage?).

Geraldine Farrar in French Opera
Geraldine Farrar *sop* with various artists.
Nimbus Prima Voce mono NI7872 (79 minutes: ADD). Recorded 1908-21.   Ⓜ H
Opera Arias and Duets – Carmen, Les contes d'Hoffmann, Manon, Mignon, Roméo et Juliette and Thaïs.

This is a lovely addition to the Prima Voce series. Farrar's Carmen appears as a model of effectiveness within the restraints of good musical and dramatic behaviour. The 'Séguedille' is sheer enchantment (irresistible promise in that breathed 'je l'aimerai' and the dreamily provocative reprise of 'Près des remparts'), while in the 'Chanson bohème' we catch the energy of her personality as well as the carrying power of her by no means robust lyric soprano. These are all cherishable records, of the kind that on some pleasant desultory evening with the gramophone one will feel a prompting to take down from the shelves. Seasoned collectors should not necessarily assume that they already have everything on the disc: there is, for instance, the unpublished 'Je veux vivre' (*Roméo et Juliette*) from 1911, a performance of surprising delicacy and charm. The Prelude to Act 4 is there, too, in a recording from 1921 said to be by the orchestra of La Scala conducted by Toscanini, one of those legendary sessions which put him off the gramophone for a decade. If he had heard the results as cleanly defined as they are here, he might have thought again.

Amelita Galli-Curci Opera Arias and Songs.
Amelita Galli-Curci *sop* with various artists.
Conifer Happy Days mono CDHD201 (70 minutes: ADD). Recorded 1917-29.   Ⓜ H
Arias from Don Pasquale, The Golden Cockerel, Lucia di Lammermoor, Rigoletto, Semiramide, La sonnambula, La traviata and Il trovatore; songs by Bishop, A. Scarlatti and Yradier.

Amelita Galli-Curci Opera Arias and Songs.
Amelita Galli-Curci *sop* with various artists.
Romophone mono 81003-2 (two discs: 159 minutes: ADD). Recorded 1916-20.   Ⓕ H

Arias from Il barbiere di Siviglia, Dinorah, Don Pasquale, Lakmé, Lucia di Lammermoor, Manon
Lescaut (Auber), Martha, Le nozze di Figaro, I Puritani, Rigoletto, Roméo et Juliette,
La sonnambula and La traviata; songs by Alvarez, Benedict, Bishop, Buzzi-Peccia, David, Delibes,
Giordani, Grieg, Massenet, Proch, Samuels and Seppilli.

These two issues complement each other very happily, the Romophone going up to 1920, the
Conifer concentrating on later recordings, with an overlap of only three items. In *Gramophone* in
1923 the Editor wrote: 'One of the most solid grounds I have for facing the coming of old age with
equanimity is the reasonable hope that I shall spend it listening to as many records of *la diva*
Galli-Curci's voice as there are of Caruso's'. The purity of her voice was certainly a delight; it was
at that time firm and even throughout its wide compass; and her fluency in scalework, precision in
staccato, and ability to swell and diminish on a long-held high note were exceptional. She was an
artist who could phrase and nuance exquisitely and who, within the boundaries of a more or less
pretty joy and sadness, could be quite poignantly expressive. In the years of her greatest fame and
success, roughly the decade from 1916 to 1926, her operatic repertoire was the standard one for the
'coloratura' soprano, and it is well represented by her records. What they also have, making them
treasurable beyond anything that such a summary might suggest, is a personal flavour, a caress, a
way of making words sound like water purling gently on a summer's afternoon, a dreaminess that
can awaken to fun and affection though she could also flatten rather sadly in pitch. For
completeness and also for the fine quality of the transfers many will want the Romophone. The
Conifer selection is certainly a good one, including rarities such as the Scarlatti cantata (*Solitudini
amene, apriche collinetti*), 'Bel raggio' and 'Ah, non giunge'. On the whole, the early records have
been transferred on this CD more enjoyably than the electricals.

Beniamino Gigli The Complete HMV Recordings 1918-32.
Beniamino Gigli *ten* with various artists.
Romophone mono 82011-2 (two discs: 139 minutes: ADD). Recorded 1918-19 and 1931-2. Ⓜ Ⓗ
Opera arias and duets – L'amico Fritz, La bohème, Cavalleria rusticana, Faust, La favorita, Fedora,
La Gioconda, Iris, Lodoletta, Mefistofele, Les pêcheurs de perles, Stabat mater (Rossini), Tosca;
songs by Cannio, de Curtis, Niedermeyer, Schubert, Sullivan and Tosti.

The first of these two CDs enshrines the golden youth of Gigli, and therefore some of the most
beautiful tenor sounds ever committed to disc. Listen to the three extracts from *La Gioconda* – the
Act 1 encounter with Barnaba, 'Cielo e mar' and the love duet with Laura made at the first sessions
in Milan in 1918 – and imagine yourself with the audiences when the singer had one of his earliest
successes as Enzo; also enjoy the honeyed, mellifluous timbre, the homogeneous tone, the fluid
delivery, the enthusiastic attack that must have enthralled Gigli's contemporaries. The ease and
naturalness of the sound still have the power to amaze the ear, as they do in such a dreamy, sweet
account of 'Apri la tua finestra' from Mascagni's *Iris*. Then in 'Spirto gentil' (*La favorita*), the
subtle, suave way Gigli moves into the reprise has surely never been equalled, let alone surpassed.
Pieces that he repeated later – the arias of Cavaradossi and *Faust*, the Act 1 duet from *La bohème*,
for instance – are here done with fewer of the maddening if endearing traits that informed the later
recordings. Faust was not yet in his repertory, but the aria and even more the Garden Duet with the
estimable Maria Zamboni are filled with the kind of immediate, open-hearted passion that is the
hallmark of all Gigli's records. A pity he has such an acid-toned partner in the Cherry Duet from
L'amico Fritz because he is perfectly suited by the role of the shy Korbus.

Six tracks into the second disc we are carried forward 12 years to 1931, when Gigli returned to
HMV from his fruitful spell with Victor, chronicled on Romophone. This is the fully-fledged Gigli
with which collectors will be most familiar, the voice more mature, the style a deal coarsened. Yet
who can resist Tosti's *Addio* or Sullivan's *The Lost Chord* (conducted by Barbirolli), both sung in
delightfully accented English, or even his outrageously self-indulgent account of the Dream from
Manon, in Italian? The 1931 coupling of the arias from *Faust* and *La bohème* must have been Gigli's
best-selling operatic 78s: both pieces are sung in score pitch, the tenor's high C now firmly in place.
Neither reading is a model of style, but both are emotionally overwhelming, the boyish charm, use
of *portamento* and verbal detailing of his Rodolfo especially winning. In a famous account of the
Cavalleria duet, he is partnered by an impassioned Giannini: both artists exhibit an authentic *spinto*
style now severely in jeopardy. At the end come a wonderfully forthright account of 'Cujus animam'
from Rossini's *Stabat mater* (though he abjures the high D flat) and two soulful Neapolitan songs
by de Curtis, perfect Gigli territory. The transfers of the electrics are faultless; the sound of the
acoustics, poor recordings in themselves, is less amenable.

Great Singers at the Maryinsky Theatre Opera Arias with various accompaniments.
Nimbus Prima Voce mono NI7865 (78 minutes: ADD). Notes and some synopses included.
Recorded 1908-13. Ⓜ Ⓗ

Sopranos – **Olimpia Boronat** (Les Huguenots), **Eugenia Bronskaya** (Hamlet, A Life for the Tsar), **Elena Katulskaya** (Mireille, Thaïs), **Maria Kovalenko** (The Queen of Spades), **Lydia Lipkowska** (The Snow Maiden), **Antonina Nezhdanova** (Fra Diavolo, Lakmé, La traviata, Die Zauberflöte). *Mezzo-soprano* – **Evgenia Popello-Davidova** (Lakmé). *Contralto* – **Evgenia Zbrueva** (The Queen of Spades). *Tenors* – **David Juzhin** (La Gioconda), **Andrei Labinsky** (Halka), **Dmitri Smirnov** (Mefistofele, La traviata), **Leonid Sobinov** (The Demon), **Eugene Vitting** (The Queen of Spades). *Baritone* – **Mikhail Karakash** (The Queen of Spades). *Basses* – **Vladimir Kastorsky** (Eugene Onegin), **Lev Sibiriakov** (Judith, Thaïs, Requiem – Verdi).

Here is a superb collection, 'courtesy [we are told] of the Director of Staff of the St Petersburg State Museum of Theatre and Music'. All of the originals are rare, and some must be practically unique. Among the soprano solos, particularly exciting is Boronat's account of the Queen's cabaletta in *Les Huguenots*, queenly indeed as far as the letter of the score is concerned but brilliant in technique and often exquisite in shading. Nezhdanova in both *Lakmé* excerpts (the Bell song and now even more famous 'flower' duet) sings with lovely purity and easy command. Lipkowska's *Snow Maiden* is an utter charmer, and also delightfully youthful in tone is Katulskaya's Mireille. Of the tenors, Labinsky's *Halka* solo has exemplary evenness of line, as has the baritone Karakash in Yeletsky's aria. Kastorsky's Gremin and Sibiriakov's admonition of the Israelites in *Judith* are among the finest of all; and how skilfully Sibiriakov subdues his mighty bass in the *Thaïs* duet with Katulskaya. The original copies used are all in pristine condition.

Greatest Voices of Bolshoi Opera Arias. Various artists.
Melodiya mono/stereo 74321 39505-2 (two discs: 149 minutes: ADD). Recorded 1910-80.   Ⓜ ⓗ
Sopranos – **Valeria Barsova** (Snow Maiden), **Xenia Derzhinskaya** (The Queen of Spades), **Vera Firssova** (Christmas Eve), **Tamara Milash-kina** (The Enchantress), **Antonina Nezhdanova** (A Life for the Tsar), **Bella Rudenko** (Lakmé), **Natalia Spieller** (Iolanta), **Galina Vishnevskaya** (La forza del destino). *Mezzo-sopranos* – **Irina Arkhipova** (Samson et Dalila), **Elena Obraztsova** (Boris Godunov), **Nadezhda Obukhova** (Prince Igor). *Tenors* – **Zurab Andzhaparidze** (The Queen of Spades), **Vladimir Atlantov** (Prince Igor), **Ivan Kozlovsky** (Boris Godunov, Snow Maiden), **Sergei Lemeshev** (Eugene Onegin, Sadko), **Georgi Nelepp** (Askold's Grave), **Leonid Sobinov** (Lohengrin). *Baritones* – **Pavel Lisitsian** (The Queen of Spades), **Yuri Mazurok** (Mazeppa), **Grigori Pirogov** (Askold's Grave). *Basses* – **Feodor Chaliapin** (Don Quichotte), **Maxim Mikhailov** (Prince Igor), **Evgeny Nesterenko** (A Life for the Tsar), **Ivan Petrov** (Iolanta), **Alexander Pirogov** (Prince Igor), **Mark Reizen** (Boris Godunov).

Here's richness. From Glinka onwards, standards were set for Russian singing which we can, for the great nineteenth-century artists, only deduce from their music but which we may fairly suppose founded the great tradition we can hear upheld on record for much of the twentieth. What did Osip Petrov, the bass who dominated Russian opera for half a century from 1826, really sound like? Probably less like Chaliapin – though the great dramatic bass is represented here in lyrical vein by his beautiful performance of Don Quichotte's death scene in 1927 (Massenet) – than his namesake Ivan Petrov as King René (1952), or than the powerful Maxim Mikhailov, superb in Khan Konchak's aria (1953), or than the cultivated Mark Reizen, whose début was as Pimen in 1921, singing wonderfully here in 1951 and who made his final appearance as Gremin in 1985, on his ninetieth birthday, to a devoted Bolshoi cast and audience. Alexander Pirogov's fine delivery of Galitsky's aria (1951) and Evgeny Nesterenko's of Susanin's farewell (1979) seem but younger branches of this great oak planted by Petrov.

The tenor tradition lies closer to French style than to anything more intrinsically Russian, let alone Italian. Here is the superlative Leonid Sobinov, in fine voice as Lohengrin (1910); but why not some of his Lensky, who here goes to the elegant Sergei Lemeshev (1953)? Here too is Ivan Kozlovsky, unforgettable as the Simpleton in *Boris* in 1927 and still in full command as Tsar Berendey in 1957. On the other hand, the powerful Slavonic line of dominating mezzos and contraltos has made a mark upon opera that has at times led to tradition becoming something of a prison. Nadezhda Obukhova exhibits some of these risks in the very strength of her singing of Konchakovna (1941); however, here are Elena Obraztsova (part of Marina's aria in 1968) and Irina Arkhipova (Dalila's 'Mon coeur' in 1980) showing how rich and diverse it can be.

The sopranos are the most varied group. Some exhibit the powerful vibrato which has been such a cause of complaint in the West, though Valeria Barsova (1951) shows how it can be lightly and expressively applied to the Snow Maiden. Bella Rudenko's chirpy coloratura sparkles in Lakmé's Bell Song (1967). Antonina Nezhdanova exhibits a warmer, stronger manner in Antonida's Romance (1914) that suggests her as a mother figure to Galina Vishnevskaya, at the height of her powers as Verdi's *Forza* Leonora in 1959. Much more could be mentioned, and Grigori Pirogov's remarkable baritone as the Unknown in *Askold's Grave* (1910) should certainly not be overlooked. The transfers are fine.

Hans Hotter – Opera Monologues, 1957-62
Hans Hotter *bass-bar* Dorothea Siebert *sop* Lorenz Fehenberger *ten*
Bavarian Radio Chorus and Symphony Orchestra / Meinhard von Zallinger,
Rudolf Alberth, Eugen Jochum.
Orfeo d'Or C501991B (67 minutes: ADD). Recorded 1957-62. All items sung in German. Ⓜ Ⓗ
Mussorgsky Boris Godunov – I have attained the highest power; Your Majesty, I make
obeisance; Farewell, my son, I am dying. **Rossini** Il barbiere di Siviglia – La calunnia è un
venticello. **R. Strauss** Die schweigsame Frau – Wie schön ist doch die Musik. **Verdi** Don Carlo –
Ella giammai m'amò. **Wagner** Der fliegende Holländer – Die Frist ist um. Die Meistersinger von
Nürnberg – Was duftet doch der Flieder; Wahn! Wahn! Uberall Wahn!

Too many young collectors today know Hotter only as a Wagnerian (then usually in the Solti *Ring*
where he was past his best) and/or as a fine interpreter of Lieder. In fact he was also renowned in
Austria and Germany in other repertory, and even as an accomplished comedian, singing his roles,
as was then the custom, in the vernacular. These tracks, drawn from Bavarian Radio archives, tell us
something of that other Hotter. In *Don Carlos*, he sang both King Philip and, more often, the
Grand Inquisitor. He gives us a haunted yet commanding Philip, sung in a commendable *legato*.
His amusing Don Basilio – the Slander Aria – couldn't be a greater contrast. A video exists showing
Hotter's giant, scheming, faintly ridiculous prelate, commanding the scene, as he commands the aria
here. He is equally in character in Sir Morosus's monologue – the old man at last contented and at
peace. But the revelation here is Hotter's Boris. He sang the role on stage just once, at Hamburg in
1937, but 20 years later Bavarian Radio mounted a studio production of Mussorgsky's opera under
Jochum with Hotter in the title-role. In both Act 2 monologues, the scene with Shuisky (the subtle,
wily Fehenberger) and Boris's death, Hotter presents a frightened, superstitious yet still
authoritative and curiously sympathetic Tsar. All are sung with a wealth of inner meaning and
fidelity to dynamic marks while avoiding histrionics that are not in the notes. Here, at the peak of
his powers, Hotter is superb as he is in his 1960 account of the Dutchman's monologue, a
benchmark reading. Equally setting standards for others to emulate are his versions of Sachs's
monologues, so refined and thoughtful. As in all Hotter's performances, it is the interior meaning
conveyed through a deep understanding of the text, allied to warmth and beauty of the voice, that
remains so telling; here is the singing-actor *par excellence*.

Maria Ivogün Opera Arias and Songs.
Maria Ivogün *sop* [a]Michael Raucheisen *pf*
[b]orchestra; [c]Berlin State Opera Orchestra / Leo Blech.
Nimbus Prima Voce NI7832 (78 minutes: ADD). Ⓜ Ⓗ
Bishop Lo, here the gentle lark[b]. **Handel** L'allegro, il penseroso ed il moderato, HWV55 – Sweet
bird[b] (recorded 1925). **Donizetti** Don Pasquale – Ah! un foco insolito[b] (rec. 1924). Lucia di
Lammermoor – Ardon gl'incensi[b] (rec. 1917). **Rossini** Il barbiere di Siviglia – Una voce poco fa[b]
(rec. 1925). **Verdi** La traviata – E strano ... Ah, fors'è lui ... Sempre libera[b] (sung in German,
rec. 1916). **Chopin** Nocturne in E flat major, Op. 9 No. 2[b] (arr. *sop/orch.*). **Meyerbeer** Les
Huguenots – Une dame noble et sage[b] (German). **Nicolai** Die lustigen Weiber von Windsor – Nun
eilt herbei[b] (all rec. 1917). **Schubert** Ständchen (Horch! Horch! die Lerch), D899[b]. Winterreise,
D911 – Die Post[b]. **J. Strauss II** Frühlingsstimmen, Op. 410[b] (rec. 1924). G'schichten aus dem
Wienerwald, Op. 325[b]. An die schönen, blauen Donau, Op. 314[c]. Die Fledermaus – Klänge der
Heimat[c]. **Kreisler** Liebesfreud[b]. **Anonymous** O du liebs Angeli[a]. Z'Lauterbach han i'mein
Strumpf verlor'n[a]. Gsätzli. Maria auf dem Berge[a].

Somewhere or other, after much searching of the memory, ransacking of the catalogues and
phoning around among connoisseurs, it might be possible to discover a more delightful example of
the coloratura's art than that of Maria Ivogün as displayed in her recording of Kreisler's
Liebesfreud, made in 1924: if so, one such does not spring to mind now. With the most pure and
delicate of tones, nothing shrill or piercing about them, she sings way above a normal mortal's
reach, ease and accuracy in the purely technical feats going along with a lilt and feeling for the
idiomatic give-and-take of waltz rhythm that are a joy musically. Turn to Handel, with the solo
from *Il penseroso*, and the same art is put to lovely use in a different idiom. Her *Traviata* aria has
warmth and spontaneity; her Frau Fluth in *Die lustigen Weiber von Windsor* is a woman of charm
and energy; and the 1934 recording of the Czardas in *Die Fledermaus* shines as bright in spirit as in
clarity of timbre. From the same period comes the set of four songs, Swiss and German, that show
most touchingly her command of the art to be simple. This is an admirable introduction to a most
lovely singer, and it represents the Prima Voce series at its best.

Hilde Konetzni
Preiser mono 90078 (74 minutes: AAD). Recorded 1937-50. Ⓟ Ⓗ

Opera Arias – The Bartered Bride, Don Giovanni, Fidelio, Der Freischütz, Madama Butterfly, Der Rosenkavalier, Tannhäuser and Tosca; songs by R. Strauss.
Hilde Konetzni *sop* with various artists.

Look no further than this disc to hear a near ideal tone and technique. A lovely singer suggesting the very essence of natural, sincere, open-faced interpretation, Hilde Konetzni, leading soprano at the Vienna State Opera from the late 1930s to the early 1950s, projects the varying emotions of Leonore, Agathe, Elisabeth, Butterfly (albeit in German) and Mařenka (again in German) with an eager sincerity that at once silences criticism and puts her in the class of her coevals in similar repertory – the Marias Reining and Müller and Tiana Lemnitz (what a wealth of talent to draw on!). None of these attempted Leonore, and Konetzni's 'Abscheulicher!' is a totally convincing interpretation – and marvellously sung. Here is the vulnerable, heroic wife to the life, pouring out her feelings in steady, even, unfettered tones, negotiating the awkward intervals and the difficult tessitura as if they were no problem at all. That performance comes from the series of Telefunken discs that Konetzni made in 1937, with the admirable support of Schmidt-Isserstedt as conductor. They include versions of Agathe's 'Wie nahte mir der Schlummer' and Elisabeth's arias that would be hard to better, so radiant and unencumbered is the delivery. Konetzni must also have been a touching Butterfly: her version of Cio-Cio-San's entrance and the Flower duet with Marie Luise Schilp as a warm Suzuki touch the heart. The mind is dazzled by the exquisite refinement evinced at the end of 'Vissi d'arte' – or rather 'Nur der Schönheit' as it is here. Ten years later Konetzni made a few treasured 78s for Columbia with Karajan at the helm. Her account of Mařenka's 'Endlich allein' from *The Bartered Bride* shows no diminution of the singer's skills, only a deepening of the tone that also allowed her to convey all the Marschallin's sadness in that character's Act 1 Monologue. Also included here are four Richard Strauss songs made with the composer at the piano, in 1943. They are a trifle disappointing: in terms of colour and inflexion they are penny-plain. Nevertheless, do get this disc if you want to hear some truly wonderfully sung readings.

Erich Kunz
Erich Kunz *bar* with various artists.
Testament mono SBT1059 (79 minutes: ADD). Recorded 1947-53.   ⓕ Ⓗ
Opera Arias – Don Giovanni, Der lustige Krieg, Eine Nacht in Venedig, Le nozze di Figaro, Der Vogelhändler, Der Waffenschmied, Der Wildschütz, Zar und Zimmermann, Die Zauberflöte and Der Zigeunerbaron; Viennese songs by various composers.

Here is Kunz in his absolute prime, moving his agreeable voice around Figaro's, Leporello's and Papageno's music with the confidence derived from experience in the roles in Vienna, but without the slightest sense of routine. It should not be forgotten that he was one of the first German-speaking singers to learn his Da Ponte roles in Italian: his diction and accent in them, as we find here, are virtually perfect. Under Karajan, in Figaro's 'Non più andrai' he is disciplined by a fast tempo, while Ackermann is more yielding in Leporello's 'Madamina'. Karajan also conducts the Giovanni/Zerlina duet (with the incomparable Seefried). It is a wonderful souvenir of two artists, their voices blending ideally, who sang so often together in that notable ensemble in Vienna. Kunz was also loved in his home city for his assumption of *buffo* parts in Lortzing's operas, and he brings to their arias, again with Ackermann in sympathetic support, a rich vein of comic characterization without ever resorting to caricature – Kunz was, above all, a sensitive musician. The second half of this issue is devoted to operetta items and Viennese songs. In the former it may be complained that he was often adopting, and transposing down, music written originally for a tenor: four songs from *Ein Nacht in Venedig*, in the Korngold rescension, rather suffer in that respect, yet Kunz's wholly idiomatic approach almost makes us forget the anomaly. In what are mostly Heurigen songs, he is absolutely in his element; only his older, tenor colleague, Julius Patzak was his peer in these. The accompanying Schrammel Ensemble are wholly authentic. Try, if you can, *Da draussen in der Wachau*, so beguiling in tone and style, and you will not be able to resist the rest.

Legendary Baritones Opera Arias and Songs with various accompaniments.
Nimbus Prima Voce mono NI7867 (77 minutes: ADD).Recorded 1905-41.   Ⓜ Ⓗ
Lucien Fugère (Le jongleur de Notre Dame); **Victor Maurel** (Tosti: Au temps du grand roi); **Antonio Magini-Coletti** (Falstaff); **Mattia Battistini** (La traviata); **Mario Ancona** (Un ballo in maschera); **Maurice Renaud** (Le roi de Lahore); **Eugenio Giraldoni** (Otello); **Riccardo Stracciari** (Tosca); **Giuseppe de Luca** (Ernani); **Titta Ruffo** (Falstaff); **Pasquale Amato** (I due Foscari); **Joseph Schwarz** (Tannhäuser); **Heinrich Schlusnus** (Hans Heiling); **Renato Zanelli** (Zazà); **Carlo Galeffi** (Rigoletto); **John Charles Thomas** (Andrea Chenier); **Lawrence Tibbett** (Il barbiere di Siviglia); **Gerhard Hüsch** (Der Wildschütz); **Igor Gorin** (Attila).

Prizes for all here, except possibly John Charles Thomas. *Andrea Chenier* is not the subtlest of operas, and 'Nemico della patria' does not call for the fine nuance of a Fischer-Dieskau, but it does want more than the mouthing of words and *tutta forza* for the notes. The voice is magnificent, but in this 'legendary' company we look also for taste. And in its various guises we find it: in the 80-year-old Fugère with his immaculate definition and unmawkish tenderness; in Maurel with a charm of old-world manners in his courtly song to Madame la Marquise; Magini-Coletti with his humorous but gentlemanly Falstaff; Battistini wearing his elegant paternal suit, and Ancona bestowing upon the outraged husband the dignity of more-in-sorrow-than-in-anger. After that comes Maurice Renaud, about whom one might raise a complaint concerning emotional expression achieved at the expense of the vocal line; yet there is stylistic refinement too, and a richly imaginative care for the Massenet aria, phrase by phrase. With Stracciari one might wonder about the voice production, so free one moment, throat-laden in another; then there is Amato with his rapid vibrancy, Galeffi with his weakness for the emotional quiver. Yet all are artists, and their work will repay study. The Germans are a distinguished trio too, and the Russian-born Igor Gorin is superb in his *Attila* aria. Ruffo, rich in vocal colours, de Luca gracious in the exercise of traditional virtues ... But there it is: a prize-giving here would have something for (almost) everybody, including those responsible for the transfers and booklet, for the choice of singers and their matching up with arias.

Lotte Lehmann

Songs – Balogh, Beethoven, Brahms, Cimara, Franz, Gounod, Grechaninov, Hahn, Jensen, Marx, Mozart, Pfitzner, Sadero, Schubert, Schumann, Sjöberg, Wolf and Worth.
Lotte Lehmann *sop* with various artists.
Romophone mono 81013-2 (two discs: 157 minutes: ADD). Recorded 1935-40.　　　Ⓕ🄷

Lotte Lehmann was at the height of her powers as a song interpreter in the late 1930s: the bloom of youth is still in the tone, now enhanced by the experience of many years of stage interpretation. Thus, her characters *in extremis* become something of a talisman of suffering women. Her impassioned Gretchen in Schubert's great song is sister to, and inhabits the same world as, Lehmann's Leonore and Sieglinde. The searing intensity of 'Was hör ich alte Laute?' in Schumann's *Alte Laute* goes through you, becomes etched in the mind, just as do certain phrases in her operatic portrayals. Yet while the passions are felt on a large scale throughout these songs, the intimate mould of Lieder singing is never breached. The readings are generous and free, never dull, careful or limited, or by another token overladen with detailed word-painting in the Schwarzkopf manner. Unlike many of her contemporaries Lehmann ranged wide in her choice of repertory. She digs out Jensen's *Lehn' diene Wang' an meine Wange* and makes you believe that this little sentimental song is a masterpiece. However, it is for the Schubert (including 12 songs from *Winterreise*, so immediate in effect, no holds barred), Schumann, Brahms and Wolf, that the myriad admirers of this artist will want these two lavishly filled CDs. The transfers are clean and clear, but at times impart a slight glare to Lehmann's tone. This offering is an essential addition to the Lehmann discography.

Giovanni Martinelli – Complete Acoustic Recordings, 1912-24.

Giovanni Martinelli *ten* with various artists.
Romophone mono 82012-2 (three discs: 208 minutes: ADD). Recorded 1912-24.　　　Ⓕ🄷
Arias and Duets – L'Africaine, Aida, Un ballo in maschera, La bohème, Carmen, Cavalleria rusticana, Don Pasquale, Ernani, Eugene Onegin, Faust, La Gioconda, Guillaume Tell, Iris, La Juive, Lucia di Lammermoor, Madama Butterfly, Manon Lescaut, Martha, Pagliacci, Rigoletto, Tosca, La traviata, Il trovatore, Werther and Zazà; songs by Bizet, Castaldo, Leoncavallo, Mascagni, Roxas and Tosti.

As John Steane points out in his predictably perceptive notes to this reissue of all Martinelli's recordings by the acoustic process, he has always – and still – divides opinion, the believers admiring his distinctive voice and style, his amazing breath control, the disbelievers reviling his (to them) dry and strained tone. His acoustic recordings often serve to confirm the view of the detractors, his voice sounding drier and more nasal than is the case with the electrics, which suddenly reveal, like a picture cleaned, the strength of his tone and the power of its projection. So where titles here were remade after 1925, in every case the later versions to the pre-electrics are preferable, not least the items from *Trovatore*, but there is so much material not later repeated and so important to understanding Martinelli that this is a 'must' for collectors, especially in such faultless transfers.

Many tracks chronicle roles Martinelli essayed during the early part of his long career at the Metropolitan, when Caruso was still alive. The long list of Puccini arias, Edisons of 1912 and Victors of 1913-14, and two versions of 'Cielo e mar' reveal the tenor's peculiar gifts of keenly etched line, long breath and classic definition of the text. Then, among the Verdi items, we gain an intimation of what his Riccardo and Ernani must have been like on stage, the former's Barcarolle a model of Verdian style where the singing is concerned but a shade stiff in expression, the latter's aria evincing the fire and straightforward honesty of Martinelli's Verdi singing. The famous souvenirs of his Don José to Farrar's Carmen, wonderfully vivid on both sides, take us to the heart of a real performance, with the tenor almost too noble in feeling. Other notable partnerships are remembered in the *Aida* duets with Ponselle (in even finer voice than on the electric remake) and the *Butterfly* love duet with Alda, Martinelli's *legato* ideal in all cases. Arias from *L'Africaine*, *Don Pasquale*, *Lucia di Lammermoor*, *Onegin* and *Zazà* are interesting but not perhaps essential Martinelli. The main reason, however, for acquiring these three CDs is the irreplaceable recordings from *Guillaume Tell* – aria, duet with Journet, trio with de Luca and Mardones (including an unpublished take). Nobody before or since has conveyed Arnold's patriotic fervour with Martinelli's *élan*, or sustained the high-lying phrases with such technical control. And who, Caruso apart, has sung Eleazar's arias (both previously unpublished) with such dignity and feeling? And don't overlook, with de Luca, the gentle avowal of friendship from *Don Carlo*, notable for its unforced entwining of the two voices. No, by the end of three CDs, the disbelievers are surely put to flight.

Giovanni Martinelli Opera Arias and Duets.
Giovanni Martinelli *ten*
[a]Metropolitan Opera Chorus and Orchestra / Giulio Setti, [b]Josef Pasternack,
[c]Rosario Bourdon.
Preiser Lebendige Vergangenheit mono 89062 (68 minutes: AAD). Recorded 1926-27.   Ⓕ Ⓗ
Verdi Rigoletto – La donna è mobile. Il trovatore – Quale d'armi fragor ... Di quella pira[a] (with **Grace Anthony** *sop*). La forza del destino – Oh, tu che in seno; Invano Alvaro ... Le minacciei fieri accenti (**Giuseppe de Luca** *bar*). Aida – Se quel guerrier io fossi ... Celeste Aida[b]; Nume, custode e vindici (**Ezio Pinza** *bass*). **Giordano** Andrea Chenier – Un dì all'azzurro spazio[b]; Come un bel di di maggio[c]. Fedora[b] – Amor ti vieta; Mia madre, la mia vecchia madre. **Mascagni** Cavalleria rusticana[c] – O Lola; Mamma, quel vino è generoso. **Leoncavallo** Pagliacci – Recitar! ... Vesti la giubba[c]; Per la morte! smettiamo ... No, Pagliaccio non son[a] (**Grace Anthony**). Zazà – E un riso gentil[c]. **Puccini** La bohème – Che gelida manina[b]. Tosca – E lucevan le stelle[b].

Here is one of the most fascinating of singers. He can also be one of the most thrilling, his voice having at its best a beauty unlike any other, his art noble in breadth of phrase and concentration of tone. It also has to be said that his records hardly make easy or restful listening, but what at first may even repel soon becomes compulsive, the intensity of expression and individuality of timbre impressing themselves upon the memory with extraordinary vividness. Martinelli's career was centred on the Metropolitan, New York, where he sang first at the height of the Caruso era, inheriting Caruso's more dramatic roles in 1921. This selection makes an unrepresentative start with 'La donna è mobile', but the excerpts from *Il trovatore* and *La forza del destino* have the very essence of the man, masterly in his shaping and shading of recitative, or in the long curves of his melodic line and the tension of his utterance. There are also superb performances of solos from *Andrea Chénier* and *Pagliacci*, the involvement of his 'No, Pagliaccio non son' unequalled before or since. These are recordings from 1926 and 1927, the period in which his vocal and artistic qualities were probably best matched. The transfers are fine apart from the song from Leoncavallo's *Zazà* which plays below pitch.

John McCormack
John McCormack *ten* with various artists.
Romophone mono 82006-2 (two discs: 155 minutes: ADD). Recorded 1910-11.   Ⓕ Ⓗ
Opera and Operetta Arias – Il barbiere di Siviglia, Barry of Ballymore, La bohème, Carmen, L'elisir d'amore, Faust, La fille du régiment, La Gioconda, In a Persian garden, Lakmé, Lucia di Lammermoor, Naughty Marietta, Les pêcheurs de perles, Rigoletto and La traviata; songs by Balfe, Barker, Blumenthal, Cherry, Claribel, Crouch, MacMurrough, Marshall, Parelli, Rossini and Traditional.

You think, at the start of this journey through the recordings of two years, that here is McCormack at his absolute best, in the first of the *Lucia di Lammermoor* solos; but no, for the second one ('Tu che a Dio spiegasti l'ali'), made two months later, is better still, a perfection of lyrical singing, the music lying ideally within his voice as it was at that time, and with the heart and imagination more evidently involved. A little later comes 'Una furtiva lagrima', where the modulation into D flat major ('m'ama') brings surely some of the most beautiful, most unflawed tenor singing ever recorded. This album, from 1910 and 1911, presents him in finest voice. He was only 25 at the outset: in the first flush of his operatic success and already the partner of Melba (heard with him in the *Rigoletto* Quartet and *Faust* Trio) and Tetrazzini. His favourite baritone partner was Mario Sammarco, who turns up as a blustery Figaro to his elegant Almaviva, retiring to a more discreet distance behind the recording horn in the duet from *Les pêcheurs de perles* (the deservedly rare version included here along with the more familiar ten inch). They also join in the *gondolieri*-like harmonies of Rossini's *Li marinari* (splendid high Bs from McCormack) and give each other a run for their money in a full-bodied, exciting account of the duet from *La Gioconda*. McCormack, it is true, had still to develop eloquence as a singer of songs, but his eventual mastery is clearly foretold in the old Irish song, *She is far from the land*, a haunting and heartfelt piece of tender nostalgia. The transfers are excellent.

Claudia Muzio

Claudia Muzio *sop* with various artists.
Romophone mono 81010-2 (two discs: 140 minutes: ADD). Recorded 1917-25. Ⓕ Ⓗ
Opera Arias – Aida, Un ballo in maschera, La bohème, Carmen, Cavalleria rusticana, Les contes d'Hoffmann, Ernani, La forza del destino, Gianni Schicchi, La Gioconda, Guillaume Tell, Louise, Madama Butterfly, Madame Sans-Gêne, Manon, Manon Lescaut, Mefistofele, Mignon, Otello, Pagliacci, Il segreto di Susanna, Suor Angelica, Tosca, La traviata, Il trovatore, I vespri siciliani and La Wally; songs by Braga, Burleigh, Buzzi-Peccia, Delibes, Donaudy, Giordano, Mascheroni, Olivieri, Roxas and Sanderson.

Romophone has put us in its debt by issuing the 1917-25 Pathés and adding four unpublished and fascinating Edison titles. Inevitably there is some overlapping with the first set (reviewed further on) but it is surprising how many titles were not remade by the soprano. Here we have, on the first disc, an impassioned and nicely shaded 'Suicidio!' in a reading that is amazingly accomplished when you realize Muzio was just 28 at the time. 'O patria mia' and 'Un bel dì', neither repeated by her, adumbrate the sheer beauty of the voice of the young *spinto*: strength is there, but also refinement and feeling, although the technical command, as often with this singer, isn't always faultless. Above all, we catch an echo over the years of what Muzio must have been like: deeply affecting, in these roles, confirming contemporary comment. The songs are, as ever with this singer, irresistible. Buzzi-Peccia's *Baciarmi* is poised sensuously on a skein of gossamer tone. In another song, Burleigh's *Jean*, we can delight in Muzio's excellent and clear English and also in the better sound. Then come the four 'new' Edisons, which include Donaudy's *O del mio amato ben*, later repeated in 1935 for Columbia: the performance here is just as plangent. Even more tenderly accented is a little-known and unattributed song, *Torna amore*, and the even more evocative traditional *Mon jardin*.

Claudia Muzio

Claudia Muzio *sop* with various artists.
Romophone mono 81015-2 (two discs: 155 minutes: ADD). Recorded 1934-35.
Opera Arias and Duets – Adriana Lecouvreur, Andrea Chénier, L'Arlesiana, La bohème, Cavalleria rusticana, Cecilia, La forza del destino, Mefistofele, Norma, Otello, La sonnambula, Tosca, La traviata and Il trovatore; songs by Buzzi-Peccia, Debussy, Delibes, Donaudy, Parisotti, Refice and Reger. Also contains part of Tosca, Act 1, recorded live in 1932. Ⓕ Ⓗ

This set completes Romophone's comprehensive survey of all Muzio's records, masterminded by Ward Marston. Since their first release, Muzio's Columbias of 1934-5 have always been her most accessible discs, but they have never, even on previous CD reissues, sounded so present and clear as they do here. This most eloquent of divas seems to be in the room with us and the music in hand is delivered with such sincere passion, such total conviction that tears are brought to the eyes. All those anonymous-sounding sopranos with their dull recitals today should sit down and listen to the individuality Muzio brings to every track here. Not for a moment can one be anything but enthralled by these readings. Since there is not enough material to fill two CDs, Romophone have added a substantial extract from Act 1 of a 1932 San Francisco *Tosca*, primitively recorded and so far known only to a few Muzio fanatics. However, as a whole this is an essential issue for anyone wanting to know about the art of one of the century's most lovable and vital interpreters.

Claudia Muzio

Claudia Muzio *sop* with various artists.
Romophone mono 81005-2 (two discs: 153 minutes: ADD). Recorded 1911-25. Ⓕ Ⓗ
Opera Arias and Songs – Adriana Lecouvreur, L'Africaine, L'amico Fritz, Andrea Chénier, Bianca e Fernando, La bohème, Carmen, Les contes d'Hoffmann, Eugene Onegin, La forza del destino, Hérodiade, I Lombardi, Loreley, Madame Sans-Gêne, Mefistofele, Pagliacci, Paride e Elena, Rinaldo, Salvator Rosa, La traviata, Il trovatore, I vespri siciliani, La Wally and Zazà; songs by Bachelet, Buzzi-Peccia, Chopin, Guagni-Benvenuti, Herbert, Mascheroni, Monahan, Pergolesi, Rossini and Sodero.

The crackles and surface noise that usually afflict Edison reproduction have all but been eliminated, so that we can hear Muzio's voice in its absolute prime without, as it were, the effort of listening through a sea of interference. The sheer beauty of the soprano's voice and her wonderful intensity of expression can now be experienced with astonishing immediacy. All the Muzio gifts, including that of refined, exquisite phrasing combined with that peculiarly heart-rending intensity that was hers alone, are heard in that enchanting song by Bachelet, *Chère nuit* (first disc, track 8). If your dealer will let you hear that, even if you are sceptical about singers of the past, you are sure to make off home with this set, eager to hear the rest. A feast of captivating interpretations from one of the century's three or four greatest singing-actresses.

The Incomparable Heddle Nash
Heddle Nash *ten* with various artists.
London Philharmonic Orchestra / Sir Thomas Beecham.
Dutton Laboratories mono CDLX7012 (69 minutes: ADD). Recorded 1929-35.　　　Ⓜ Ⓗ
Puccini La bohème – Act 4ª.
Lisa Perli *sop* Mimì; **Heddle Nash** *ten* Rodolfo; **Stella Andreva** *sop* Musetta;
John Brownlee *bar* Marcello; **Robert Alva** *bass* Schaunard; **Robert Easton** *bass* Colline;
Opera Arias and Duets – Il barbiere di Siviglia, Così fan tutte, Don Giovanni, Die Fledermaus,
La jolie fille de Perth and Rigoletto.

When he made this recording of Act 4 of *La bohème* in 1935 Nash was at the height of his powers and sings a spontaneous, quite Italianate Rodolfo. Perli makes a simple, heartfelt Mimì. The rest of the cast falls far short of the principals, but Beecham is at his most alert, and sensitive too. Nash's Mozart is most elegantly represented by the well-nigh faultless versions of Ottavio's arias, made at the time of his sensational Covent Garden début in 1929 in *Don Giovanni*. The phrasing is refined, the breath long, the big run in 'Il mio tesoro' encompassed in a single span. The Duke of Mantua's three arias tell us just why this was one of Nash's favourite roles early in his career. He makes the most of the execrable translation by singing it with total conviction, and his lyric tenor rings out with just the right *élan*, matched by subtle colourings. The Serenade from *La jolie fille de Perth* is justly renowned because it displays to perfection the elegiac, minstrel-like quality of Nash's tone and his impassioned delivery – and yet he is said to have had a cold on the day it was made! The transfers (including the solo items) are superior to any previous issues, bringing the voices into one's room without let or hindrance.

Adelina Patti Opera Arias and Songs.
Adelina Patti *sop* with various artists.
Nimbus Prima Voce mono NI7840/1 (two discs: 120 minutes: ADD). Recorded 1902-28.　　Ⓜ Ⓗ
Mario Ancona, Mattia Battistini, Emma Calvé, Fernando De Lucia, Edouard de Reszke,
Emma Eames, Lucien Fugère, Wilhelm Hesch, Lilli Lehmann, Félia Litvinne, Francesco Marconi,
Victor Maurel, Dame Nellie Melba, Lillian Nordica, Adelina Patti, Pol Plançon, Maurice Renaud,
Sir Charles Santley, Marcella Sembrich, Francesco Tamagno and Francesco Viñas.

This is a 'historical' issue for straightforward enjoyment. Although the originals were made in the very earliest years of recording, they are reproduced here with a vividness that calls for very little in the way of 'creative listening', making allowances and so forth. It starts in party mood with the first Falstaff of all, Victor Maurel, singing to a bunch of cronies in the studio of 1907 the 'Quand'ero paggio' which he sang at La Scala in the première of 1893. They cheer and call for an encore, which he gives them, then again (and best of all) this time in French. The record has been transferred many times to LP and CD, but never has it been so easy for the listener to 'see' it and feel part of it. The magnificent bass Pol Plançon follows with King Philip's solo from *Don Carlos*, beautifully even in production and deeply absorbed in the character and his emotions. The hauntingly pure, well-rounded soprano of Emma Eames in Tosti's *Dopo* (a real passion there despite its restraint), and then the miraculously spry and elegant 80-year-old Lucien Fugère lead to the first of the Patti records: the one her husband thought unladylike and asked to be withdrawn from the catalogue, *La calesera*, and the most joyous she ever made. Tamagno, Melba, Nordica, Renaud: they are all here, and on thrillingly good form. The copies of these rarities have been selected with great care, and, while other transfers have, technically, got more 'off' the record, none has captured the beauty of the voices more convincingly.

Ezio Pinza
Opera Arias – Aida, Attila, La bohème, Le caïd, Don Carlo, Don Giovanni, Faust, La Juive,
Lucia di Lammermoor, Mignon, Norma, I Puritani, Robert le diable, Il trovatore, I vespri siciliani and
Die Zauberflöte.
Ezio Pinza *bass* with various artists.
Nimbus Prima Voce mono NI7875 (73 minutes: ADD). Recorded 1923-30.　　Ⓜ Ⓗ

There can surely be few dissenting voices where the quality of Pinza's singing is concerned. Play a record of his to a hardened old collector or a green newcomer and they will undoubtedly join in praising his golden, vibrant tone, seamless *legato*, the evenness of his vocal emission through a couple of octaves. It has been said that he seldom sings below *forte*: that is wholly negated here by a performance of the lullaby from Thomas's *Mignon*, sung almost entirely *mezza voce*, a lulling and soft-grained song that would send any child into blissful slumber. Another French item, the famous Tambour-major air from Thomas's lesser-known *Le caïd*, not only confirms Pinza's excellence in French enunciation, but also shows quite another side of his personality: jocular, a smile in the tone, exuberance in the delivery. The RCA Victors of Italian opera are well known, yet one marvels anew at the easy command of Pinza's Oroveso, Procida, King Philip and Ramphis, the character of each nicely etched in, even in extract. To complement these there is his grave Sarastro, his warmly sighing Colline. All the phrases where other basses either exaggerate or lose focus in reaching a high or low note are done quite effortlessly. His Giovanni suggests a formidable personality, and we end with him in the distinguished company of Rethberg and Gigli for their glorious account of the *Attila* trio. All the electrics are transferred carefully from RCA Victors in good condition. Where the six 1923-24 HMV acoustics are concerned you hear Nimbus's much-discussed additional resonance, room or otherwise, come into play. It is an acceptable procedure if you understand that you are not hearing exactly what the original sound is like. The most persuasive title here is 'Cinta di fiori' from *I Puritani*, where the *cantabile* rolls out with fabulous ease.

Rosa Raisa The Complete Recordings, 1917-26.
Rosa Raisa *sop* with various artists.
Marston mono 53001-2 (three discs: 227 minutes: ADD). Recorded 1917-26. Ⓜ Ⓗ
Opera arias and duets – L'Africaine, Aida, Andrea Chénier, Cavalleria rusticana, Don Giovanni, Ernani, La forza del destino, La Gioconda, Madama Butterfly, Mefistofele, Norma, Otello, Tosca, Il trovatore and I vespri siciliani; songs by Tchaikovsky and Yradier.

'I would listen to them, and then break them into pieces' wrote Raisa in 1962, explaining why she possessed none of her own records. It is a pity she could not have heard them in these fine transfers and reproduced on modern equipment. Her objection was that they failed to show the volume of her voice, and that is very probably true. The impression they give is that of an ample lyric soprano with a dramatic style rather than a full dramatic voice. What they preserve is a sound of exceptional beauty and in several instances singing of equally exceptional skill. Outstanding is the single previously unpublished item, the cabaletta 'Ah! bello a me ritorna' from *Norma*, recorded for Brunswick in 1929. A superb demonstration of vocal mastery, it seems totally unaware of difficulties. The semiquaver passagework, the bold intervals, the matching of rhythmic energy with lyric grace, all are mastered with apparent ease. It is of course sad to think that this is all that remains of a Norma often reported as having been the finest of all in this century, at any rate up to Callas's time.

There are many other lovely things here. Raisa's chequered career as a recording artist began with the aria from *Andrea Chénier*, 'La mamma morta', on Pathé in 1917, and this was also the subject of her last recording, in 1933. Despite the difference in tempo (the later version being more expansive), they are very alike in style and affectionate in feeling. Similarly with the six (no less) versions of 'Voi lo sapete'. Her 'Un bel di' is unexpectedly touching and intimate, the manner delicate and girlish, till the 'per non morir', when the girl becomes woman. The duets with her baritone husband, Giacomo Rimini, include one (clear-voiced and dramatic against a scrunchy background) from *Il trovatore* on a Vitaphone soundtrack. Then the third disc ends with an interview, not especially illuminating but nice to have, given in 1962 and in lively style, a year before her death. Raisa was one of the great singers of her time, and among them perhaps the most outstanding example of neglect by the major record companies. The Marston catalogue is significantly enriched by this release.

Elisabeth Rethberg
Elisabeth Rethberg *sop* with various artists.
Romophone mono 81012-2 (two discs: 158 minutes: ADD). Recorded 1924-29. Ⓕ Ⓗ
Opera Arias – Aida, Andrea Chenier, La bohème, Der Freischütz, Lohengrin, Madama Butterfly, Le nozze di Figaro, Otello, Serse, Sosarme, Tannhäuser, Tosca and Die Zauberflöte; songs by Bishop, Braga, Cadman, Densmore, Flies, Gounod, Grieg, Griffes, Hildach, Jensen, Korschat, Lassen, Loewe, Massenet, Mendelssohn, Rubinstein, Schubert, Schumann, Taubert and Tchaikovsky.

They're very collectable, these Romophone complete editions. Up they go on the shelves, and you know that there is another small but quite important area in the history of singing on records properly covered, ready for reference at any time, and reference that will be a pleasure because the standard of transfer is so reliable. In this instance it is the Rethberg Brunswicks: records which capture the voice in its lovely prime. Purely as a singer, Rethberg was surely the most gifted and accomplished lyric soprano of her age. The essential gift was a voice of exquisite quality, and her upbringing contributed to the purity of intonation and a feeling for musical style. Her production was even and fluent; on all these records there is scarcely a note or a phrase that is not delightful purely as singing. Some of the later records show it also as a voice capable of considerable expansion in volume. In Aida's 'O patria mia' Rethberg is celestial, ample in volume, sensitive in feeling, phrasing beautifully, taking the C softly and in a broad single sweep. Equally lovely is her Mimi, and then in the *Andrea Chenier* aria there is such an unpressed beauty of utterance that it almost becomes a different composition. A previously unpublished delight is a blissful performance of Eugen Hildach's *Der Spielmann*, and among the less familiar songs is a charmer by Carl Taubert, *Es steht ein Baum in jenem Tal*.

Elisabeth Rethberg
Elisabeth Rethberg *sop* with various artists.
Preiser Lebendige Vergangenheit mono 89051 (71 minutes: AAD). Recorded 1920-25.   ⒻⒽ
Opera Arias and Duets – L'Africaine, Andrea Chenier, The Bartered Bride, La bohème, Carmen, Madama Butterfly, Le nozze di Figaro, Tosca, Die Zauberflöte and Der Zigeunerbaron;
songs by Bizet, Mozart, Pataky and R. Strauss.

Elisabeth Rethberg died in 1976, when little notice was taken of the passing of a singer once voted the world's most perfect. The year 1994 was the centenary of her birth, so this fine selection of her early recordings was well timed.The earliest catch her at the charming age of 26 (the voice settled, but still that of a young woman), and the last of them, made in 1925, find her just into her thirties, mature in timbre, feeling and artistry. It is doubtful whether a judicious listener would at any point cry 'Ah, it's an Aida voice!', but Aida was the part for which she became most famous. In Countess Almaviva's first aria, her *legato* is the next thing to perfection; in Pamina's 'Ach, ich fühl's' the head tones are beautifully in place, the portamentos finely judged, emotion always implicit in the singing. The duets with Richard Tauber include the music of Micaëla and Don José sung with unrivalled grace and intimacy, Rethberg shading off the end of her solo most elegantly, Tauber softening in his so as to welcome and not overwhelm the soprano's entry. The songs are equally delightful.

Elisabeth Rethberg
Elisabeth Rethberg *sop* with various artists.
Romophone mono 81014-2 (two discs: 155 minutes: ADD). Recorded 1927-34.   ⒻⒽ
Opera Arias and Ensembles – L'Africaine, Aida, Attila, Un ballo in maschera, Boccaccio, Carmen, Cavalleria rusticana, Don Giovanni, Faust, Die Fledermaus, Der fliegende Holländer, Lohengrin, I Lombardi, Madama Butterfly, Die Meistersinger von Nürnberg, Le nozze di Figaro, Otello, Il rè pastore, Tannhäuser and Der Zigeunerbaron; songs by Brahms, Mendelssohn and Wolf.

To the older collector of vocal recordings it is to be feared that not many of these records will come as new. Attention can be directed, however, to the last three. These were made in 1932 in the Bell Telephone Laboratories as part of an experiment in improved recording methods. They were recorded at 33rpm, and they achieved startling results. The quality of the voice is captured to perfection, but most impressive is the freedom of emission, no longer confined within the studio but able to ring and expand, the contrasts of loud and soft tones being effective and often as exquisite as they would have been in the flesh. Most revealing is Elisabeth's Greeting from *Tannhäuser*, sung with piano accompaniment but with a dramatic conviction and enthusiasm far more vivid than that of the earlier orchestral version. Other new items are unpublished takes of the two Verdi trios with Gigli and Pinza, differing slightly in balance, but very little in style. The six electric Parlophones include the tender Micaëla's aria and the solo from *L'Africaine* with its haunting unaccompanied introduction. Supreme among the Victors is the second *Un ballo in maschera* aria, the *Meistersinger* duet with Schorr running it close. It is also good to have the complete Nile scene from *Aida*, with Lauri-Volpi in his prime, de Luca a bit past his. Transfers are of the usual high standard, and with the first volume, this is clearly the primary source of a comprehensive Rethberg collection on disc.

Bidù Sayão
Bidu Sayão *sop* with various artists.
Opera Arias – Faust, Manon and Roméo et Juliette; songs by Braga, Debussy, Duparc, Hahn, Koechlin, Moret, Ravel and Villa-Lobos.
Sony Classical Masterworks Heritage mono MHK62355 (73 minutes: ADD).   ⒻⒽ
Recorded 1941-50.

Beauty, charm, exquisite voice, brilliant technique, personality, Bidù Sayão had them all. This recital opens with her most famous recording, *Bachianas Brasileiras* No. 5 by Villa-Lobos, with the composer conducting. She recognized the opportunity for her particular soprano in the violin part that Villa-Lobos had written for this work and persuaded him to adapt it for soprano. Their famous recording was achieved in just one experimental take. In that her voice is used in a purely instrumental way, when she enters on the next track as Gounod's Juliette, one is struck by the presence the use of words adds to the voice. In the Jewel song from *Faust* she conveys a sense of joyous laughter to the 'Ah' in 'Ah, je ris de me voir belle', without any sense of vulgarity, or playing to the (armchair) gallery. Massenet's *Manon* was the role of her Met début in 1937 and again her vocal acting immediately sketches in Manon's playful character in the Act 1 aria about the 'premier Voyage'. How can a voice suggest a pout? One would have to ask Brigitte Bardot, but Sayão can do it, when she starts to sing about the 'couvent' she's being sent to. Sayão's voice had none of the acid nasal quality of the typical French light soprano, so she can manage to do all sorts of little things with the language without making it sound harsh. Sayão studied with Jean de Reszke; she is the youngest of his pupils on disc, and perhaps the only one still around today, at least the only one who had a great career. The presentation is superb: there are splendid photographs and reproductions of the original LP sleeves.

Bidù Sayão
Bidù Sayão *sop* with various artists.
Sony Classical Masterworks Heritage mono MHK63221 (73 minutes: ADD). Recorded 1941-50. Ⓜ
Opera Arias – La bohème, Don Giovanni, Gianni Schicchi, Madama Butterfly, Le nozze di Figaro, Pagliacci, La sonnambula and La traviata. La damoiselle élue (Debussy).

Charm is an elusive thing Singers guilty of laying it on too thick might listen to Sayão and try to hear what she does, and just as important, what she doesn't do. Take the contrast between Violetta and Mimì. In the Act 1 aria from *La traviata*, there is no smile in the voice. It's all beautiful, limpid singing, but when she reaches that crucial 'Follie!' recitative, there is no joy in the cries of 'gioir!' but, as is surely correct, desperation. Then comes Mimì and the tone is at once warmer, full of the reticent hopefulness that is typical of the personality; when she gets to the climactic 'Ma quando ven lo sgelo' she really lets it all glow. Strange that these two Parisian coughers are so often bracketed together – in fact their basic characters are quite different and in the subtlest way Sayão shows how a singer can differentiate without resorting to any distortion or method-acting tricks. The revelation in this recital was Sayão's Cherubino. Lord Harewood in his notes says that she probably never sang it on the stage, but she makes of the two overfamiliar arias something totally delicious and new. Her Susanna was well known and one of her favourite parts (with Pinza as her Figaro), but although she has no difficulty in singing the Countess's aria, somehow one knows that the part isn't quite right for her. Both the Zerlina arias are done with just the right mixture of coquetry and toughness. Sayão sang Debussy's *La damoiselle élue* in New York with Toscanini, the year before her Met début in 1937. This recording, made in 1947 with Ormandy and the Philadelphia Orchestra, is a remarkable instance of her ability to invest words and vocal line with character. In a recent interview, Sayão related how much she had wanted to sing Madam Butterfly but, although she felt she could have acted it, the orchestration was too heavy for her voice, and so she never dared take on the role. Her recording of 'Un bel dì' shows how she would have tackled it. Surprisingly, she did sing Nedda in *Pagliacci*, in her final season at San Francisco and she must have made an unusually sympathetic impression. With its companion volume this CD restores much of Sayão's recorded legacy to the catalogue. She is one of the most consistently fascinating singers of this era at the Met, in the two decades surrounding the Second World War. The booklet, as with all these beautifully produced Masterworks reissues, has colour reproductions of early record sleeves and nostalgic photographs, including two of Sayão modelling a hat fashioned from a copy of her first LP.

Aksel Schiøtz The Complete Recordings 1933-46, Volume 1.
Aksel Schiøtz *ten* with various artists.
Danacord mono DACOCD451 (75 minutes: ADD). Recorded 1933-46. Ⓕ Ⓗ
Opera and Oratorio Arias – Così fan tutte, Die Entführung aus dem Serail, Eugene Onegin, Don Giovanni, Faust and Die Zauberflöte; Acis and Galatea, Christmas Oratorio, Messiah, St Matthew Passion, Die Schöpfung and Solomon; songs by Dowland and Was mich auf dieser Welt betrübt (Buxtehude).

Schiøtz's singing was always the very epitome of silvery elegance. His attributes in Handel, Haydn and Mozart are amply confirmed in this, the first disc of Danacord's comprehensive ten-disc survey of all his recorded output. Sadly his career was cut short by a brain tumour in 1946, but for the ten years of his prime, he was rightly fêted for his beautiful singing and masterly sense of style. Long before period-instrument performances were current, Schiøtz and Wöldike were seeking an authentic style of performing Handel and Bach as exemplified here in the poised, unaffected account of the opening solos from *Messiah*, and arias from the *St Matthew Passion* and *Christmas Oratorio*. 'Frohe Hirten' from the latter and the lovely aria by Buxtehude sound even better now that they have been released from the scratch on the originals, the transfers expertly done by EMI's Andrew Walter. Also in the oratorio field the aria from *Die Schöpfung* demonstrates perfectly the singer's delicately etched line and pure tone. There are few more fine-grained versions of Tamino's 'Portrait' aria, Ottavio's arias nor of Pedrillo's Serenade, but 'Un aur'amorosa' suffers from an uncomfortably fast speed. Schiøtz is also among the most elegiac of Lenskys in that character's lament (slightly cut), the most sweet-toned of Fausts, the top C taken in the head as is the case with other tenors of his ilk. It seems hardly to matter that these pieces are sung in Danish. The Dowland, like the Handel, is given authentically, though a guitar rather than a lute is used for the accompaniments. As a bonus there are rehearsal performances of Acis's 'Love sounds the alarm', minus *da capo*, and 'Sacred raptures' from *Solomon*, the former impeccable, the latter showing an unaccustomed fallibility in the runs. The booklet is full of interesting photos and articles.

Aksel Schiøtz The Complete Recordings, 1933-46, Volume 2.
Aksel Schiøtz *ten* ᵃGerald Moore,ᵇᶜFolmer Jensen *pf*
Danacord mono DACOCD452 (75 minutes: ADD). Texts and translations included.　　Ⓕ🅷
Schubert Die schöne Müllerin, D795ᵃ. **Grieg** Melodies of the Heart, Op. 5ᵇ – No. 1, Two brown eyes; No. 3, I love but thee. Songs, Op. 33 – No. 2, Last Springᵇ; No. 9, At Rondaneᶜ. Songs and Ballads, Op. 9 – No. 4, Outward Boundᶜ.

Aksel Schiøtz The Complete Recordings, 1933-46, Volume 3.
Aksel Schiøtz *ten* with various artists.
Danacord mono DACOCD453 (69 minutes: ADD). Texts and translations included.　　Ⓕ🅷
Schumann Dichterliebe, Op. 48ᵃ. **Brahms** Die Mainacht, Op. 43 No. 2. Sonntag, Op. 47 No. 3. Ständchen, Op. 106 No. 1. **Grieg** Songs, Op. 49 – No. 3, Kind greetings, fair ladies; No. 6, Spring showers. The Poet's farewell, Op. 18 No. 3. **Bellman** Fredman's Epistles – Dearest brothers, sisters and friends; Old age is with me; Sit down around the spring here. Fredman's Songs – Hear bells give out a frightful boom; So tipsy we are taking leave; Joachim lived in Babylon. **Buxtehude** Aperite mihi portas justitiae, BuxWV7.

The years 1945-46 were particularly fruitful ones for Schiøtz in relation to recording. With Walter Legge's eager support the Danish tenor could at last come to London to resume his recording career with *Die schöne Müllerin*, which takes up the lion's share of Vol. 2. The Danacord transfer of this sensitive reading is now the one to go for: not only is the sound marginally superior to Preiser's earlier transfer but added to it are five wonderful readings of Grieg songs, these actually recorded for the composer's centenary in 1943. In particular the popular *I love but thee* and the gloriously ardent *Last Spring* find in Schiøtz an ideal interpreter, a singer whose style so effortlessly and unassumingly goes to the heart of the matter. He is just as convincing in the three lesser-known songs by Grieg in Vol. 3, devoted to six months of recording activity at the start of 1946. Yet another facet of his art is revealed in the Bellman songs, aptly recorded in Sweden, Schiøtz disclosing his sense of humour in the bawdy songs of the eighteenth-century, pleasure-loving Bellman. In *So tipsy we are taking leave*, he captures to perfection the devil-may-care, bawdy mood and in all these attractive pieces finds a willing partner in Ulrik Neumann's guitar. But this third volume is most valuable for giving us Schiøtz's marvellous *Dichterliebe*, perhaps his finest achievement of all on disc. Then come three Brahms songs, never issued on 78s, that are also near ideal, especially the delicately floated line of *Die Mainacht*. Gerald Moore, as ever, fits his playing intuitively to the singer he's partnering. Then, after the Grieg and Bellman, comes more evidence of the tenor's and Wöldike's championship of Buxtehude, then a neglected figure, which again benefits from Schiøtz's innate sense of the right style for the music in hand. It also allows us to hear a pleasing mezzo (Elsa Sigfuss) and bass (Holger Nørgaard). Andrew Walter's remastering of all this disparate material at Abbey Road is faultless.

Aksel Schiøtz The Complete Recordings, 1933-46, Volume 4.
Aksel Schiøtz *ten* with various artists.
Danacord mono DACOCD454 (72 minutes: ADD). Texts and translations included.　　Ⓕ🅷
Schubert Die schöne Müllerin, D795 – No. 1, Das Wandern; No. 6, Der Neugierige; No. 7, Ungeduld; No. 8, Morgengruss; No. 10, Tränenregen; No. 11, Mein; No. 15, Eifersucht und Stolz; No. 17, Die böse Farbe; No. 19, Der Müller und der Bach; No. 20, Des Baches Wiegenlied. **Mozart** Per pietà, non ricercate, K420. **Weyse** Angel of Light, go in splendour. In distant steeples. The Sleeping-Draught – Fair lady, open your window. **Hartmann** Tell me, star of night, Op. 63. Little Christine – Sverkel's romance. **Lange-Müller** Once upon a time – Serenade; Midsummer Song. **Riisager** Mother Denmark. **Schubert/Berté** Das Dreimäderlhaus – excerpts.

'Hidden Treasure' is the appropriate subtitle for this volume of the complete Schiøtz recordings. It begins with the ten songs from what ought to have been a complete *Schöne Müllerin*, two songs recorded in London in 1939, eight with Hermann D. Koppel, who took over from Moore, in

Denmark in 1939-40. The cycle was never finished, because – it seems – Koppel as a Jew had to flee his country when the Nazis occupied it. Schiøtz's voice, when he was 33, was even fresher, his reading even more spontaneous in suggesting the vulnerable youth's love and its loss, most poignant in an account of 'Der Müller und der Bach' that surpasses in forlorn expression other famed tenor interpreters such as Patzak, Pears, Schreier and Bostridge but the whole sequence is a pleasure to hear for the plangency of Schiøtz's singing. There follows part of the Mozart aria *Per pietà* that the tenor sang as test for EMI in 1938, interesting as a rarity but not special. By contrast all the Danish items are desirable, among them the two Hartmann offerings: *Tell me, star of night*, a haunting song, is given ideal voicing by Schiøtz as is 'Sverkel's romance' from a romantic work, *Little Christine*, based on an Andersen fable.

The two items by Lange-Müller, written as incidental music for a play called *Once upon a time*, are even better, in particular the magical 'Midsummer Song'. The note-writer tells how wonderful was Schiøtz's singing of this item in an open-air performance in 1941. His recordings had made Schiøtz famous and he also appeared the same year playing the role of Schubert in *Lilac Time* of which we hear an amusing pot-pourri (a photo in the booklet shows him in the part). That Schiøtz was not averse to popular items is confirmed by Riisager's *Mother Denmark*, which he brought to London for that first session in May 1939. It is a song written for a *diseuse* about the delights of the homeland and Schiøtz delivers it with the intimacy it calls for. Again, the transfers are faultless and this example of Anglo-Danish co-operation is highly recommendable.

Tito Schipa

Tito Schipa *ten* with various artists.
Preiser Lebendige Vergangenheit mono 89160 (77 minutes: AAD). Recorded 1925-28.　　Ⓕ 🄷
Opera Arias – L'Arlesiana, Il barbiere di Siviglia, La bohème, Don Giovanni, Don Pasquale, L'elisir d'amore, La favolita, Lakmé, Luisa Miller, Manon, Martha, Pagliacci, Rigoletto, La traviata and Werther.

The Master. And yes: he surely is, and never more so than in the recordings of this period. Schipa was then at the height of his fame and fortune, the voice approaching the end of its very best days (a thrill and a freshness which began to diminish in the early 1930s) and with the art having developed just about as far as it would go. Lovely examples are: 'Sogno soave' (*Don Pasquale*), 'Questa o quella' and 'E il sol dell'anima' (*Rigoletto*), the *Traviata* duets, the *Lakmé* and *Werther* solos, Harlequin's Serenade (*Pagliacci*), 'E la solita storia' (*L'Arlesiana*) and the finale of *La bohème* with the exquisite Bori. But if 'The Master', then one whose mastery was exercised within severe limitations. Today's tenors in the repertoire cultivate an extensive upper range, whereas Schipa sings here nothing above a B flat, transposing 'La donna è mobile', and even lowering 'M'appari' so that the B flat becomes an A. His modern successors attempt and often attain a brilliance of bravura which can make Schipa sound tame and cautious (his 'Ecco ridente' is fine but lacks the brilliance of true virtuosity, and his 'Il mio tesoro' is essentially a bit of artful dodging). There are other limitations too, but these are enough for the present: and enough remains to place him among the unforgettables and irreplaceables. Any of the recommendations mentioned will show why, and there is the added, vital and elusive quality of voice-personality. This collection comprises a complete run of Schipa's operatic records made electrically for the Victor company. Transfers are faithful, with the sound well defined. Among all the many CDs currently devoted to him this would be a very suitable first choice.

Irmgard Seefried

Irmgard Seefried *sop* with various artists.
Testament mono SBT1026 (74 minutes: ADD). Recorded 1946-53.　　Ⓕ 🄷
Lieder by Brahms, Flies, Mozart, Schubert and Wolf.

Another 'must' for anyone who loves Seefried. In these wonderfully immediate and faithful transfers of performances made between 1946 and 1953 in Vienna and London, Seefried is heard at the peak of her powers, when her voice was at its freshest and easiest. In the Mozart whether the mood is happy, reflective or tragic, Seefried goes unerringly to the core of the matter. Here we have the archness of *Die kleine Spinnerin*, the naughty exuberance of *Warnung*, the deep emotion of *Abendempfindung* and *Unglückliche Liebe*. We are offered five Schubert songs, including an unsurpassed *Auf dem Wasser zu singen*, so airy and natural; a pure, elevated *Du bist die Ruh* and a poised, ravishing *Nacht und Träume*. The lullabies of Flies, Schubert and Brahms are all vintage Seefried. The Wolf items are a real treasure trove: a sorrowful, plangent account of *Das verlassene Mägdelein* (perhaps the most compelling interpretation of all here; unutterably moving), an enchanting, spontaneous *Elfenlied* (with Gerald Moore marvellously delicate here). For the most part, Moore is in attendance to complete one's pleasure in an irresistible and generously filled disc.

Singers of Imperial Russia, Volumes 1-4.
35 singers with various accompaniments.
Pearl mono GEMMCDS9997/9, GEMMCDS9001/3, GEMMCDS9004/6 and GEMMCDS9007/9
(four three-disc sets, oas: 207, 209, 222 and 221 minutes: AAD).
Gramophone Award Winner 1993.   Ⓜ Ⓗ

GEMMCDS9997/9: recorded 1900-11: *Soprano* – Medea Mei-Figner. *Tenors* – **Ivan Ershov,
Nikolai Figner** and **Leonid Sobinov**. *Baritone* – **Ioakim Tartakov**. *Basses* – **Adamo Didur** and
Vasili Sharonov. GEMMCDS9001/03: 1901-11: *Sopranos* – **Natalia Ermolenko-Juzhina** and
Maria Michailova. *Mezzo-soprano* – **Antonina Panina**. *Tenors* – **David Juzhin, Andrei Labinsky**
and **Gavril Morskoi**. *Baritones* – **Oskar Kamionsky** and **Polikarp Orlov**. *Basses* – **Dmitri
Bukhtoyarov, Vladimir Kastorsky, Vasili Sharonov** and **Lev Sibiriakov**. GEMMCDS9004/06:
1901-24: *Sopranos* – **Irena Bohuss, Anna El-Tour, Janina Korolewicz-Wayda, Maria
Kuznetsova, Lydia Lipkowska** and **Nadezhda Zabela-Vrubel**. *Contralto* – **Evgenia Zbrueva**.
Tenors – **Dmitri Smirnov** and **Eugene Witting**. *Bass* – **K.E. Kaidanov**. GEMMCDS9007/09:
1901-14: *Sopranos* – **Maria Michailova** and **Antonia Nezhdanova**. *Mezzo-soprano* – **Galina
Nikitina**. *Contralto* – **Evgenia Zbrueva**. *Tenors* – **Alexandr Alexandrovich, Alexandr
Bogdanovich, Alexandr Davidov, Andrei Labinsky** and **Eugene Witting**. *Baritone* – **Nikolai
Shevelev**. *Basses* – **Vladimir Kastorsky** and **Lev Sibiriakov**.

This is the equivalent of one of those exhibitions for which queues form long and deep and daily
outside the Tate Gallery or the Royal Academy: in fact, if a similar exhibition of paintings,
furniture and porcelain from the Tsar's palaces were mounted in London it would surely be a sell-
out. Quite simply, there has never been a published collection to match this, both in the quality of
the items and in its extensiveness. Of the singers of Imperial Russia, the world came to know
Chaliapin, who eclipsed the rest. He is not among the artists presented here, but we have, among the
basses, two who at least for vocal splendour are his equal: Adamo Didur, the Pole who was New
York's first Boris Godunov (preceding Chaliapin there), and Lev Sibiriakov, another giant of a man
with a magnificently produced voice to match. The tenors include Smirnov and Sobinov, a kind of
collector's Tweedledum and Tweedledee, though in fact very unalike indeed. New to most listeners
will be Ivan Ershov, heard in Siegfried's Forging Song from St Petersburg, 1903, with piano and
anvil accompaniment: an astonishing voice and most accomplished in technique. Evgenia Zbrueva
the contralto, sopranos Nezhdanova, Ermolenko-Jushina, Mei-Figner and the superbly recorded
Korolewicz-Wayda are also plentifully represented. Most amazing of all, perhaps, is the vividness of
sound. These are some of the world's rarest recordings and they are almost all in pristine condition.

Stars of English Oratorio, Volume 1.
Opera and oratorio arias with various orchestras and conductors.
Dutton Laboratories mono CDLX7025 (77 minutes: ADD). Recorded 1928-49.   Ⓜ
Sopranos – **Florence Austral** (The Golden Legend, Rossini Stabat mater), **Dame Isobel Baillie**
(The Creation, Judas Maccabaeus, The Kingdom, Solomon), **Gwen Catley** (Joshua).
Contralto – **Kathleen Ferrier** (Elijah). *Tenor* – **Webster Booth** (The Creation), **Heddle Nash**
(Judas Maccabaeus, Messiah). *Basses* – **Sir Keith Falkner** (Paulus), **Oscar Natzke** (Samson).

Heddle Nash's 1945 *Messiah* recordings were made in Kingsway Hall: the acoustical wonders of
that legendary venue can be heard so clearly on Mike Dutton's transfers that the disc sounds as if it
were new-minted. As Lyndon Jenkins comments in his note, this was the first recording with a
soloist made by Legge's newly formed Philharmonia, as yet only the Philharmonia Chamber
Orchestra. Just as fine are Nash's two *Judas Maccabaeus* solos made a year or so later. Dame Isobel
Baillie, so often beside Nash at oratorio performances, is hardly less impressive, heard in four items,
her Handel singing as clear and pure as Emma Kirkby's; but most welcome back in circulation, as
Jenkins suggests, is Baillie's unsurpassed account of 'The sun goeth down' from Elgar's *The
Kingdom*, Sargent on the podium. In Handel's 'Oh! had I Jubal's lyre', Catley matches Baillie in
pure, unfettered singing: a lovely performance. Finally, in Handel, comes Natzke in a version of
'Honour and Arms'. Other classics refurbished by Dutton include Ferrier's involving account of the
contralto's *Elijah* arias, Falkner's highly sympathetic solo from Mendelssohn's *Paulus*, and Austral's
sensational 'Inflammatus' from Rossini's *Stabat mater*, Barbirolli conducting. Its coupling, the solo
from Sullivan's *The Golden Legend*, a fine piece, is much less familiar in transfers and thus doubly
welcome. These, like everything here, sound as though they were recorded yesterday.

Stars of English Opera, Volume 1.
Opera Arias with various orchestras and conductors.
Dutton Laboratories mono CDLX7018 (75 minutes: ADD). All items sung in English.   Ⓜ Ⓗ
Recorded 1938-49.

Sopranos – **Gwen Catley** (Rigoletto), **Joan Cross** (Così fan tutte), **Dame Joan Hammond** (Gianni Schicchi, Tosca); *Mezzos* – **Janet Howe** (Samson et Dalila), **Gladys Ripley** (Don Carlo), **Marjorie Thomas** (Alcina); *Tenors* – **Webster Booth** (Esmeralda), **James Johnston** (The Bartered Bride), **David Lloyd** (Don Giovanni, Die Zauberflöte), **Heddle Nash** (La favorita, Les pêcheurs de perles); *Baritones* – **John Hargreaves** (Rigoletto), **Redvers Llewellyn** (Falstaff), **Dennis Noble** (Il barbiere di Siviglia); *Bass* – **Oscar Natzke** (Die lustigen Weiber von Windsor).

The discs chosen come from that fruitful period in British singing in the years before, during and just after the Second World War, when Columbia and HMV were busy recording a crop of native singers performing so eloquently in their native tongue. The group of tenors alone is a distinguished one, headed by Heddle Nash, whose dreamy, poised *mezza voce* is heard to perfection in Nadir's Romance from *Les pêcheurs de perles*, one of his most beguiling records. His ardent, refined singing of 'Spirit so fair' from *La favorita,* made during the same 1944 Liverpool session, is equally desirable. So is James Johnston's account of Jeník's aria from *The Bartered Bride*. Most welcome of all are Don Ottavio's second aria and Tamino's Portrait solo as sung by David Lloyd, whose forthright, mellifluous tone and persuasive performances offer Mozart singing of the highest calibre. Joan Cross's account of Fiordiligi's Act 2 aria, is another fine piece of Mozart singing – and isn't that Dennis Brain playing the horn solos? Marjorie Thomas's refined art is recalled in her pure Handelian *legato* while Llewellyn offers character but a rather attenuated tone in Ford's aria, Hargreaves much feeling but stilted diction as Rigoletto. If these two baritones were limited in appeal, Noble was one of great distinction regarding tone, line and diction. His 1939 HMV 'I'm the factotum' launches this disc in the most engaging way. Transfers, as usual from this source, are exemplary, surface noise wholly eliminated, voices clean and forward.

Stars of English Opera, Volume 2.
Opera Arias and Ensembles with various orchestras and conductors.
Dutton Laboratories mono CDLX7020 (77 minutes: ADD). Recorded 1928-49. All items except those marked ᵃ sung in English.　　　　Ⓜ Ⓗ
Sopranos – **Gwen Catley** (Don Giovanni, Die Zauberflöte), **Joan Cross** (Sadko, Il trovatore), **Noel Eadie** (Rigoletto), **Dame Joan Hammond** (Oberon), **Victoria Sladen** (Tosca), **Dame Eva Turner** (Turandotᵃ); *Mezzo* – **Edith Coates** (Carmen, Rigoletto); *Contralto* – **Kathleen Ferrier** (Orfeo ed Euridice, Rodelinda); *Tenors* – **Webster Booth** (Rigoletto, Il trovatore), **Richard Lewis** (Manonᵃ, Les pêcheurs de perles); *Baritones* – **Heddle Nash** (Carmen); **John Hargreaves** (Prince Igor), **Dennis Noble** (Don Giovanni, Le nozze di Figaro, Die Zauberflöte); *Bass* – **Arnold Matters** (Rigoletto).

These transfers are revelatory. The old favourites leap out of the speakers with amazing presence, beginning with Eva Turner's famous 'In questa reggia', the 1928 version, which has never sounded quite as thrilling. Nor has Joan Hammond, heard in her vivid account of Rezia's scena, ever seemed quite as lifelike or Joan Cross's clean, clear singing been transferred so faithfully as here in the *Miserere*. Praise too for the intelligent reclamation of several neglected, worthwhile items. Cross's account of the Indian Guest's Song from *Sadko*, strictly a tenor piece, catches her plangent tones at their most compelling. On another rare Decca 78, Richard Lewis's smooth, youthfully mellifluous tone is ideal for Des Grieux's Dream Song and Nadir's Romance, although emotionally he sounds a shade detached, especially when compared with Nash's impassioned account of another French aria, José's Flower Song, also distinguished by Nash's typically memorable use of the vernacular. Another piece of singing worthy of revival is John Hargreaves's heartfelt account of Prince Igor's homesick aria, surely the baritone's most desirable recording. Noble as a nimble Figaro and Papageno, Catley as a fiery Queen of Night, Coates as a haughty Carmen, Sladen as an affecting Tosca, and of course Ferrier in her best-selling 'What is life?', show the strengths of British singing in the 1940s. The version of the *Rigoletto* Quartet headed by Booth's too-polite Duke might have been replaced by an earlier, Columbia version led by an exuberant Nash (with Noble as Rigoletto).

Stars of English Opera, Volume 3.
Opera Arias and Ensembles with various orchestras and conductors.
Dutton Laboratories mono CDLX7024 (77 minutes: ADD). Recorded 1927-50.　　　　Ⓜ
Sopranos – **Dame Isobel Baillie** (Alessandro), **Joyce Gartside** (Simon Boccanegra), **Dame Joan Hammond** (Faust), **Dora Labbette** (La bohème), **Miriam Licette** (Le nozze di Figaro), **Dame Maggie Teyte** (The Maid of Orleans);
Contraltos – **Kathleen Ferrier** (Orfeo ed Euridice), **Jean Watson** (Un ballo in maschera);
Tenors – **Gerald Davies** (La bohème), **Tano Ferendinos** (L'Arlesiana, Werther), **James Johnston** (Simon Boccanegra), **Heddle Nash** (L'elisir d'amore, Faust);
Baritones – **Arnold Matters** (Simon Boccanegra), **Frederick Sharp** (Simon Boccanegra);
Basses – **Norman Allin** (La reine de Saba), **Owen Brannigan** (Faust), **Howell Glynne** (Simon Boccanegra).

Norman Allin is perhaps the most striking revelation: sturdy and firm as a rock but by no means as hard-hearted, individual and memorable, but no joke, and (making a quick mental survey) nothing to be found quite like him today. Somewhat like him a generation after was Howell Glynne, who is heard here in Fiesco's aria from *Simon Boccanegra*, one of the best of the old Sadlers Wells singers and later a very good Baron Ochs at Covent Garden. It is good also to hear Jean Watson: Canadian-born, she came to us after the war and sang a stunning Azucena. Her Ulrica solo is scrupulous but not very dramatic. 'Scrupulous' is the word for all these, including the Melboid sopranos, Licette, (Labbette) Perli and Teyte. If there is a disappointment it is with Arnold Matters's dull-toned Boccanegra, balanced, however, by the pleasure of hearing Joyce Gartside and James Johnston as the lovers. And shedding her light over all is Kathleen Ferrier, whose test-pressing of 'What is life?' suggests not so much a star of the British opera as a nearly full moon in the international firmament. It is a delightful collection, the sound vivid and compelling as ever.

Elsie Suddaby
Elsie Suddaby *sop* with various artists.
Amphion mono PHICD134 (80 minutes: ADD). Recorded 1924-52. Ⓜ H
Songs and Arias by M. Arne, T. Arne, Bach, Besly, Carey, Denza, Ford, German, Handel, Haydn, Jackson, MacCunn, Mendelssohn, Morley, Mozart, Purcell, Schubert, Somervell, Stanford and Warlock.

Elsie Suddaby (1893-1980) was a close contemporary of Isobel Baillie and Dora Labbette and in many ways she evinces the strongest personality of the three, and has a distinctive timbre very much her own. That can be heard in the first item, Michael Arne's *The lass with the delicate air*, a piece she virtually appropriated as her signature tune. She sings it with such variety of tone and, yes, such delicacy of accent, that one capitulates at once to so graceful an artist. In Dido's Lament, the singular quality of being able, simply and naturally, to move the listener is there: adding appoggiaturas to the recitative and discreetly employing *portamento* in the Lament itself she goes to the heart of the matter. There is also the joyfully affirmative side of her art, shown in a fresh account of 'Rejoice greatly' from *Messiah* and 'Endless pleasure', as Semele wallows in her conquest of Jupiter. Better still is a version of 'Let the bright Seraphim' (*Samson*) that rings the rafters with its zealous delivery. Runs in all these Handel pieces are keenly accomplished though not quite with Baillie's assurance. These HMV recordings catch Suddaby in her prime, when she was in her thirties, yet on a Decca ten-inch of 1941 of Thomas Arne's *Where the bee sucks* and Morley's *It was a lover and his lass*, there is no diminution of her powers, and even the Warlock songs and Mozart's *Agnus Dei*, when Suddaby was in her late fifties, find the tone almost as fresh as ever and wholly free of wobble. The CD is a generous offering, the transfers are mostly well done and the booklet is obviously a labour of love.

Richard Tauber
Richard Tauber *ten* with various artists.
Preiser Lebendige Vergangenheit mono 89219 (two discs: 143 minutes: AAD).
Recorded 1919-26. Ⓕ H
Opera Arias and Duets – Aida, Il barbiere di Siviglia, The Bartered Bride, La bohème, Carmen, Don Giovanni, Eugene Onegin, Der Evangelimann, La forza del destino, Fra Diavolo, I gioielli della Madonna, Der Kuhreigen, Madama Butterfly, Martha, Mignon, Der Rosenkavalier, Tosca, Die tote Stadt, La traviata, Il trovatore, Die Walküre and Die Zauberflöte.

Richard Tauber Das Deutsche Volkslied.
Richard Tauber *ten* with various artists.
Claremont mono CDGSE78-50-64 (67 minutes: ADD). Recorded 1924-39. Ⓜ H
Opera Arias – Don Giovanni and Die tote Stadt; songs by Heymann and R. Strauss.

These two issues present a neatly complementary view of Tauber's career. The Preiser set gives us a picture of the young tenor in his days almost exclusively as an opera artist in German-speaking lands singing his repertory in the vernacular. It evinces the golden, sappy, honeyed tone of Tauber in his prime. The style at this stage is wholly disciplined but already we hear that outgoing, spontaneous exuberance that was soon to bring him world-wide fame in operetta. Few if any tenors have sung Mozart quite so beautifully as Tauber at this point in his career: the 1922 Bildnis aria is a model of its kind, preferable to his later version, and an object-lesson in phrasing for any aspiring tenor. His interpretations of Lensky's aria, the famous piece from *Der Evangelimann*, José's Flower Song, Jenik's aria (a glorious 1919 version) and Wilhelm Meister's farewell to Mignon show the plangent, almost melancholic timbre with which Tauber could invest such repertory. Then for pure singing his readings of the Italian Tenor's aria, Siegmund's Spring Song, Alfredo's aria and Pinkerton's outpouring of remorse are hard to beat. Add to this the many duets he never repeated in electric versions and you have a most desirable issue. In the company of regular colleagues of that time, such as Rethberg, Bettendorf, Sabine Kalter and, best of all perhaps, Lotte Lehmann (*Die tote Stadt* duets), his contributions reveal his generosity of both voice and manner. This is free-ranging, rich-hued singing marred only by most of the music being sung in the 'wrong' language. There are a few downward transpositions in the solos, but that was common practice at the time. Otherwise there's little to criticize here in the performances and none in the excellent transfers. The more intimate side of Tauber's art comes in the series of *Volkslieder* he recorded for Parlophone in 1926, nicely transferred by Claremont. Here one admires the very personal way in which he caresses these charmingly unassuming pieces. Four Strauss songs from 1932 sessions follow, notable for the passion in the tone. What a pity the CD wasn't completed with more Lieder rather than operatic items already available in numerous transfers, including the less-than-satisfactory Ottavio arias of 1939. But at the end there's a gem: 'Kennst du das kleine Haus am Michigansee?' where Tauber lavishes on a trifle all the magic of his incredible technique and heady tone, including those *pianissimos* conjured from nowhere. The transfers are excellent.

Luisa Tetrazzini

Luisa Tetrazzini *sop* with various artists.
Romophone mono 81025-2 (two discs: 150 minutes: ADD). Recorded 1904-20.   Ⓕ Ⓗ
Opera Arias – Un ballo in maschera, Il barbiere di Siviglia, Carmen, Dinorah, La forza del destino, Las hijas del Zebedeo, Lakmé, Linda di Chamounix, Lucia di Lammermoor, Mignon, La perle du Brésil, Rigoletto, Roméo et Juliette, Rosalinda, La sonnambula, La traviata, Il trovatore, I vespri siciliani and Die Zauberflöte; songs by Benedict, Brahms, Cowen, De Koven, Eckert, Gilbert, Grieg, Moore, Pergolesi, Proch and Venzano.

Though Tetrazzini was one of the most prized and assiduously collected of recording artists in her time, her career on record was not really very satisfactory. As was true of several others she repeated the same items in several versions, whereas, especially in those days of such restricted recording-time, an extension to the repertoire would have been so much more welcome. The repertoire itself relied heavily on the familiar *chevaux de bataille*, the Mad scenes, Bell song, Shadow song and so forth, and often when something out of the way comes along, either, like the 'Pastorale' from Veracini's *Rosalinda*, it is not well suited, or, as with Proch's vapid variations, it was not worth doing in the first place. There must also have been difficulties in successfully catching a voice which combined such brilliance and power with what could all too often emerge on record as a colourless and even infantile quality. Of the Victors reproduced here the best and most essential Tetrazzini is the 1911 'Ah, non giunge' (*La sonnambula*). The cabaletta, 'Di tale amor', following 'Tacea la notte' (*Il trovatore*) is also a joy. The *Lucia di Lammermoor* sextet and *Rigoletto* quartet with Caruso, Amato and others are also prime attractions, fine performances in many (not all) ways and remarkably clear and lifelike as recorded sound. The five Zonophones are interesting collector's pieces, not the write-off they are sometimes said to be, but a mixed pleasure, with Tetrazzini cheerfully distributing pearls while her brother-in-law, Cleofonte Campanini, administers a remorselessly clonking piano accompaniment.

Maggie Teyte

Dame Maggie Teyte *sop* **Gerald Moore** *pf* with various artists.
EMI Références mono CHS5 65198-2 (two discs: 157 minutes: ADD). Recorded 1940-48.   Ⓜ Ⓗ
Songs by Berlioz, Chausson, Debussy, Duparc, Fauré, Hahn, Massenet and Ravel.

'Je rapporte une rare émotion', the line from 'Le martin-pêcheur', one of Ravel's *Histoires naturelles*, as Dame Maggie sings it, seems to signal the mood into which one is cast, listening to these famous recordings. The opening songs on the first CD, 'Le spectre de la rose' and 'Absence' from Berlioz's *Les nuits d'été* reveal at once all her positive virtues. The firmness of tone, the beauty of her high soft notes – like clear mountain spring water – which is not to say that there is anything watery about her interpretations; then the surprising sensuality of much of her phrasing and pronunciation. She excelled above all in the *mélodie*, but her voice had none of the acid shrillness associated with French sopranos. Teyte's diction was excellent, but is not what one thinks of now as idiomatic French. 'On ne chante pas comme on parle' she used to insist, and what one can hear is the Parisian fashion in the 1900s for affecting a slight English accent. That this came naturally to her must have added to her allure for audiences of the time. (Proust mentions her in his letters.) All the songs by Chausson are very fine. In *Le colibri* she demonstrates the richness of her low notes, and although the sound in *Poème de l'amour et de la mer* is somewhat restricted, this, too, is heady stuff. Chausson's *Chanson perpétuelle*, in which she is accompanied by Gerald Moore and the Blech String Quartet, has never been reissued before. This is one of Teyte's greatest records: the weight of sadness she brings to the poem by Charles Cros, with its tragic 'Il est devenu mon amant', is reason enough to buy this compilation. The Duparc songs are superbly dramatic – Teyte wrote that 'the deeper shades of pastel' were not enough for song recitals and that a singer needed to use as much power and expression as for opera. Her deep understanding of Ravel's *Shéhérazade* makes hers a fascinating version, even if at first those brought up on later, more expansive recordings may find it a little cool. All the items on the second CD are accompanied by Gerald Moore. In her autobiography she lamented the passing of 'the lost art of the musicale'. What she meant was the chance of intimate contact between artist and audience in a drawing-room – something she achieves immediately in the opening *Elégie* of Massenet. Then flow 13 songs by Fauré; *Soir* was a special favourite of Dame Maggie's – she had once sung it with Fauré as her accompanist – 'Bravo, ma petite!' he exclaimed afterwards. There is not a single piece on this set that does not merit attention, and each song reveals something of Teyte's art. There are no texts or translations.

Maggie Teyte
Dame Maggie Teyte *sop* with various artists.
Pearl mono GEMMCD9134 (74 minutes: ADD). Recorded 1936-41.   Ⓜ Ⓗ
Chansons by Berlioz, Debussy, Duparc and Fauré.

There was some sort of magic in the air at the EMI Abbey Road Studios in London on March 12th and 13th, 1936. Maggie Teyte, just short of her forty-eighth birthday, and Alfred Cortot, both of whom had been well acquainted with Claude Debussy, recorded 14 of his *mélodies*. This is no studio-bound recital but a performance, the passion and beauty of tone matched stroke for stroke by pianist and singer. These records, and the later ones Teyte made with Gerald Moore, are among the jewels of Debussy singing and playing. No one with an interest in French song should hesitate to acquire them, for they provide a lesson, not just in pronunciation of the French language (though like her contemporary and supposed rival, Mary Garden, Teyte sang with a pronounced English accent – something which entranced the French in the *belle époque*, when all things English were *à la mode*). The beauty of Teyte's tone, the freshness and girlish quality of her high notes – something which never deserted her, and she continued to sing for another 20 years – are constantly astonishing. So is the passion she puts into phrases such as 'Qu'il était bleu, le ciel, et grand l'espoir!' in 'Colloque sentimental' from the second book of *Fêtes galantes*, or the dark-hued 'Il me dit: "Les satyres sont morts," in 'Le tombeau des Naïdes' from *Chansons de Bilitis*. Those who already have some of the other reissues of Teyte's Debussy recordings will find that this Pearl disc has a rather higher surface noise, perhaps the price one has to pay for getting the voice more forward. One wonders why Pearl have called the disc 'Chansons', the correct term for these settings is *Mélodies* – or there is the good old English word 'song'.

Tosti ritorna Songs of Tosti and other Great Song Composers.
Anna Case, Enriqueta Basavilbaso de Catelin, Salomea Kruszelnicka, Maria Labia, Elizabeth Parkina *sops* Ninì Frascani *mez* Giuseppe Anselmi, Gösta Björling, Charles Dalmorès, Stefan Islandi, Fernando de Lucia, Angelo Minghetti, Augusto Scampini *tens* Giuseppe Ballantoni, Richard Bonelli, Ferruccio Corradetti, Cesare Formichi, Oscar Kamionsky, Antonio Magini-Coletti, Umberto Urbano *bars* Jean François Delmas, Andrey Labinsky, Juste Nivette *basses* with various artists.
The Record Collector mono TRC12 (75 minutes: ADD). Recorded 1903-42.   Ⓜ Ⓗ

Many of the singers on this disc are likely to be new to many of our readers; and all of the originals are rarities. Sir Paolo himself is the composer of no more than five of the 23 songs represented here. The others include several, such as Renato Brogi, Vincenzo Valente and Franco Vittadini, on whom it is good to have a biographical note. Not all are of Tosti's vintage or nationality; for instance, the programme begins with Sir Henry Bishop (*My pretty Jane*) and has room for Eric Coates (*I heard you singing*). A folk-song variously described as Ukrainian and Polish brings the recital to a jolly conclusion with, as the editor Larry Lustig says, 'a rattling good tune', its four or five verses giving ample opportunity for familiarization – and time to reflect that it would be nice to know what it is all about. Musically, the songs are probably very slight, yet most have a charm which good singing will enhance, and good singing abounds. A few personal favourites: Gösta Björling (Jussi's slightly younger brother) sings the Eric Coates song most touchingly; Anna Case (New York's first Sophie in *Der Rosenkavalier*) brings a lovely voice and a real *legato* to the once-famous song by Bishop; Maria Labia exercises a fascinating art in a beguiling song of Tosti's called *Seconda Mattinata*; and Cesare Formichi, presented to London in 1924 as the world's loudest baritone, coaxes the shy little *Obstination* with persuasive delicacy. The transfers are splendid, and a richly informative booklet accompanies the issue. It does not fail to mention, and neither must we, that the disc is produced by *The Record Collector* magazine, a publication brave, unique and invaluable to anyone with a keen interest in singers on record.

A Portrait of Norman Walker
Norman Walker *bass* with various artists.
Dutton Laboratories mono CDLX7021 (71 minutes: ADD). Recorded 1928-54.   Ⓜ Ⓗ

Opera and Oratorio Arias – Acis and Galatea, The Children of Don, The Creation, The Dream of Gerontius, Dylan, Die Entführung aus dem Serail, Faust, Judas Maccabaeus, Messiah, La morte d'Orfeo, La quattro stagioni (B. Marcello), Die Zauberflöte; songs by Capel, Haynes, Lane Wilson, Purcell and Storace.

Norman Walker was one of our leading basses for some 17 years from 1937 when he sang as the Commendatore and the Speaker at Glyndebourne and King Mark (with Dame Eva Turner as Isolde) at Covent Garden. From then on he balanced his career nicely between the stage and the concert hall. After the war, he shared the role of Collatinus with Brannigan in the early performances of *The Rape of Lucretia* at Glyndebourne and was principal bass for six years with the Covent Garden company from 1948. At the same time he appeared up and down the country in countless oratorio performances, a much-loved soloist. This welcome reissue opens resplendently with Walker singing Handel and Haydn in the classic manner: steady, burnished tone, every run in its place and diction exemplary. Then comes Walker's unsurpassed account of the Angel of the Agony's solo from *Gerontius*, so urgent, so sympathetic, here allowed to run on to let us hear Heddle Nash sing 'I go before my judge' so movingly. Of Walker's opera repertory we hear a student account of 'O Isis und Osiris', which gives some evidence of what was to follow, and a test made in 1944 for Walter Legge of Osmin's aria, which suggests he might have been a good interpreter of that role. The extracts indicate Walker's dramatic prowess (though his Italian is far from idiomatic) – as does his brief contribution to the closing trio from *Faust*, with Joan Cross a suitably distraught Marguérite. More valuable than these, however, because they display so unerringly Walker's gifts as a conviction-singer, are the four British songs made at one session in 1952 with Gerald Moore. They are exemplified in the bass's confident tone, unobtrusive word-painting and subtle use of rubato. Indeed the singer, in these faultless transfers, seems in the room with us. Malcolm Walker provides a warm, personal cameo of his father in his notes.

Early music

Plainchant

Gregorian Chant The complete 1930 HMV Recordings.
Solesmes Abbey Choir / Dom Joseph Gajard.
Pearl mono GEMMCDS9152 (two discs: 96 minutes: ADD). Recorded 1930.   Ⓜ Ⓗ

When Solesmes produced their album of 12 records of Gregorian chant, it was a historic moment. They were making the first major contribution to the documentation of an art having its roots well back in the first millennium, an art underlying much of the subsequent development of Western music. The remarkable unity and flow of the chant was surely due to the fact that they were all singing this music day in, day out, and an occasional *portamento*, or lack of ensemble was a normal, understandable part of the package. This is a sound of youthful vigour, with all the hallmarks of the familiar Solesmes style already there, well in place: the soaring phrases with their softened peaks and quiet final syllables; the firm enunciation of first syllables; the lifted accents on short notes; the quaint interpretation of the salicus; but over it all, its own special, innate quality, which combines unmistakable spirituality with robust everyday living. That quality, and a certain quiet confidence, are present in this singing to a degree rarely attained by any other monastic choir. The remastering, naturally, has not succeeded in eliminating all the needle hiss. One hardly notices this, by the way, such is the selective power of the human ear! This collection is really Everyman's basic anthology of Gregorian chant. It ranges from well-known hymns and pieces of the Ordinary, through gems from the Temporale and the Common of Saints, to some of the greatest masterpieces of the repertoire, including the Good Friday responsory *Tenebrae factae sunt* and the splendid first mode offertory *Jubilate Deo* for the second Sunday after Epiphany. It also contains some items one rarely hears nowadays, such as the powerfully moving *Media vita* – 'In the midst of life we are in death'.

Gregorian Chant
Lay Clerks of Canterbury Cathedral Choir / David Flood.
Metronome METCD1003 (74 minutes: DDD). Texts and translations included. Recorded 1994.   Ⓕ
Mass for the Feast of St Thomas of Canterbury. The Office of Matins for St Thomas of Canterbury. St Dunstan's Kyrie.

A recording of music for the Feast of St Thomas à Becket by the Lay Clerks of Canterbury Cathedral is a delightful idea. The music for this feast in the Salisbury rite is rich and memorable, particularly that for the Offices. In this case the selection from Matins includes five magnificent responsories and two antiphons, as well as the hymn *Martyr Dei* and the Invitatory, *Assunt Thomas Martyris*. This last item is particularly valuable, since though the Invitatory has generally not found much favour in recordings and concerts (either as chant or set polyphonically), the cumulative effect of the form is extraordinary. This anthology also includes the Mass for the Feast of St Thomas (in which the Sequence, *Solemne canticum*, is especially impressive) and the *Kyrie, Rex Splendens*, attributed to St Dunstan. The singing is restrained and sober and somewhat lacking in colour. The problem seems to be that there is little response to the words on the part of the singers: the chant somehow does not sound 'organic', as though it were sung liturgically. This is a difficult problem to solve, but there is no doubt that the quality of the singing itself is very high. Certainly no one with an interest in Western chant should hesitate to buy this very worthwhile recording.

Chants of the Church of Rome
Ensemble Organum / Marcel Pérès *bar*
Harmonia Mundi HMC90 1604 (79 minutes: DDD). Texts and translations included. Ⓕ
Vespers for Easter Sunday. Recorded 1996.

Most scholars agree that a link exists between the Old Roman repertoire and the so-called Gregorian. The latter became official in Carolingian times, leading to the invention of Western notation. The main problem regarding this link is the absence of notated sources of Old Roman chant before the twelfth to thirteenth centuries. These reconstructed Vespers are an attempt to demonstrate not only the magnificent service of Easter Vespers as sung in St John of the Lateran in the twelfth century, but also a whole repertoire and performance style, carried through from at least six centuries previously. Marcel Pérès defends his theory that as late as the twelfth century and beyond, the style of performance in a Roman basilica would have been similar to that practised today in Eastern rite Christianity. Indeed, many of the earliest neume shapes we strive to interpret spring to life in the light of such a style. This performance is exhilarating, even convincing. An outline of the famous Gregorian *Alleluia*, *Pascha nostrum*, for example, which we sing today from sources dating from the late ninth and early tenth centuries, can be detected – and this is exciting – in the Old Roman tradition as presented here, buried beneath countless repetitions of typical phrases and a proliferation of ornament, elements that serve to build up a cumulative impression of strength. They are pruned away in the (presumed later) Gregorian revision, which is terser, more structured melodically, more coherent, according to a later understanding of modality. An important and fascinating disc.

Melchite Sacred Chant
Sister Marie Keyrouz *sop*
L'Ensemble de la Paix.
Harmonia Mundi HMC90 1497 (63 minutes: DDD). Recorded 1993. Ⓕ
Hymns to the Blessed Virgin.

With very little hint of nasality or of singing from the throat, Sister Marie Keyrouz accomplishes the most florid ululations with the greatest of ease, the voice continuously and impressively set in relief by a reverberant acoustic and a drone bass provided by a small choir of male voices. The area touched on by this extremely rare repertory is a fascinating one, not much illuminated by the brief, at times almost impenetrable notes provided. The Melchite churches of the Near East in the fourth and fifth centuries AD were those that remained, in a period of frequent schism, faithful to Byzantium ('Melchite' derives from a Syriac word meaning 'Emperor'). The liturgy of these churches was very influential: many of the most famous hymns of the Orthodox church, for example, were composed in the sixth century by Romanos the Melodist in Syriac style; like Sister Marie, Romanos was born in what is now the Lebanon. So some of these melodies, if authentic, may be part of a repertory more ancient than any other surviving Christian chant. For the earlier part of their history, of course, they would have had to rely on oral transmission for their survival. How far they were changed in that process, how far they were affected by an Islamic tradition growing up around them and by translation of their texts from Greek and Syriac into Arabic, only a specialist could say; certainly the notes accompanying this collection do not. This would be only a quibble were not three of the longer chants attributed to Sister Marie herself, described either as 'in improvised style' or as 'written improvisation'; one of these is a setting of part of Romanos's most celebrated text, the Akathistos. The main difference between these and most of those whose origin is unattributed is their greater virtuosity: in them Sister Marie uses a wider vocal range, a rather more dramatic, declamatory utterance and still more florid melismata. It makes fascinating listening: a border territory between Christian and Islamic chant, at times revealing a modal simplicity beneath the flexible ornament, at others well-nigh hiding it in ecstatic wailings.

A Star in the East Medieval Hungarian Christmas Music.
Anonymous 4 (Ruth Cunningham, Marsha Genensky, Susan Hellauer, Johanna Rose *sngrs*).
Harmonia Mundi HMU90 7139 (68 minutes: ADD). Texts and translations included. Ⓕ 🇪

This disc is a selection of liturgical and paraliturgical Christmas pieces, taken from medieval Hungarian sources. Most are monophonic, but there is a modest sprinkling of simple polyphonic pieces for two, three and four voices. The charm of the performance lies in its unpretentious, almost childlike simplicity – suggested, maybe, by the delightful extracts from the Christmas story as quoted in the notes. The classic liturgical pieces, which include the Introit *Dum medium silentium*, the splendid Gradual *Speciosa forma*, and others, are heard in a version which tends to use the pentatonic scale, thus avoiding both B natural and B flat. The sung readings are impressive with their polyphonic settings. The rich Genealogy (*Liber generationis*) with its beautifully constructed melody are most enjoyable. Some of the vernacular pieces, as well as the Latin song for New Year's Day, have a regular ternary rhythm. The Hungarian *Te Deum* offers an interesting alternative for the concluding verses: it simply transposes the original theme up a fourth. The booklet is a marvel.

Edda – Myths from medieval Iceland
Sequentia (Barbara Thornton, Lena Susanne Norin *vocs* Elizabeth Gaver *vn*
Benjamin Bagby *voc/lyre*).
Deutsche Harmonia Mundi 05472 77381-2 (77 minutes: DDD). Recorded 1996. Ⓕ 🇪
Baldur's Dreams. The End of the Gods. Havamal – Odin's Rune-verses. In Memory of Baldur.
The Song of Fire and Ice. The Song of the Mill. The Tale of Thrym. Völuspa I-III, 'The Prophecy of the Sybil'.

Sequentia has amazed and delighted even native Icelanders with the curiosity, imagination and dedication with which it has been bringing to life some of the island's earliest music. The Cologne-based Sequentia, specialists in the northern European oral song tradition, have worked painstakingly on Iceland's great store of *rímur* – the medieval sung poetry, possibly related to the early *chanson de geste*, and whose strains can still be detected in children's playground songs in Reykjavík today. Sequentia has applied its research into the performance of *rímur* to re-creating sung texts from the *Elder* or *Poetic Edda*. Of course we have no way of knowing how this music really did sound; but listening to Benjamin Bagby and his colleagues, you will find yourself compelled by the vigour, eloquence and integrity of their own re-created authenticity. Isolation has at least ensured that living Icelandic offers pretty good indications for the pronunciation of Old Norse – and Bagby has listened with a keen ear. The late Barbara Thornton's copper-bright soprano is heard alone and with her colleagues in three 'panels' from the apocalyptic *Prophecy of the Sybil*, 'Völuspá'. They form the real set-pieces of this recital. In between, spirited fiddle pieces are played by Elizabeth Gaver; Bagby gives a virtuoso 14-minute performance of *The Tale of Thrym* (he who stole the hammer from Thor); and the voices entwine in the haunting *In Memory of Baldur*, the dreams of young Baldur, most beautiful of all the gods. It's a wonderful disc.

El canto espiritual judeoespañol
Alia Musica / Miguel Sánchez *voc*
Harmonia Mundi HMI98 7015 (62 minutes: DDD). Texts and translations included. Ⓕ
Anonymous (arr. Sánchez) Albinu malkenu. Yede rašim. Nostalgia y alabanza de Jerusalén.
`Et ša'aré rašón. Yirú `enenu. Los siete hijos de Hana. Hodú l'Adonay. Yašen al teradam.
El mélej. Noche de aljad. Ki ešmerá šabat. La fragua del estudio. Dodí yarad leganó.
La ketubá de la ley.

This is a recital of sacred music, liturgical and paraliturgical, from the Judeo-Spanish or Sephardic tradition, where ancient Jewish psalmody and cantillation have assimilated many of the musical characteristics and compositional techniques of Muslim Spain and the Ottoman empire. One doesn't listen for long before hearing the augmented second, the typical ornamentation, the voice-production with its Middle Eastern flavour, the interplay of free rhythm, Arabic metrical, and also what Solange Corbin has described as 'rythme unaire'. Then there are all those characteristic Turkish instruments: kanun, 'ud, ney, kaval and kamanya, each with its own delightfully unusual timbre. Alia Musica is an ensemble of eight singers and players, all male with one exception, three of them being both players and singers. The leader, Miguel Sánchez, sings his solos with remarkable ease and flexibility. The contralto, Albina Cuadrado, has a powerful, yet tender voice, well suited to her highly elaborate lament for the seven sons of Hannah, sung in 'ladino' (Jewish-Spanish); and also to the Sabbath evening *Noche de aljad* intercessions. One striking example of the interplay of styles is the twelfth-century Hebrew poem by Yehudá aben Abbas, `Et ša'aré rašón, with its abundant ornamentation in the dramatic slow-beat solo cantillation, contrasting with a measured chorus with drone, and a vigorously animated rhythmic finale. This is a splendid achievement.

Jerusalem: Vision of Peace
Gothic Voices / Christopher Page.
Hyperion CDA67039 (73 minutes: DDD). Texts and translations included. Recorded 1998.   Ⓕ
Anonymous Plainchant – Te Deum; Mass of Easter Day in Jerusalem: Gradual, Hec dies quam
fecit Dominus; Alleluia, Pascha nostrum; Gospel. Luto carens et latere. Jerusalem! grant damage
me fais. Jerusalem accipitur. O levis aurula!. Hac in die Gedeonis. In salvatoris/Ce fu en tres douz
tens/In veritate. Veri vitis germine. Luget Rachel iterum. Invocantes Dominum/Deus, qui venerunt.
Congaudet hodie celestis curia. **Guiot de Dijon** Chanterai por mon coraige.
Huon de St Quentin Jerusalem se plaint et li pais. **Hildegard of Bingen** O Jerusalem
aure civitas.

This disc explores numerous aspects of the Crusades. The stirring three-part conductus *Luto carens*
suggests a parallel between the crossing of the Red Sea and the journey undertaken by the Christian
armies marching towards the Holy Land. Rachel weeping for her children, *Luget Rachel*, may refer
to the fall of Jerusalem in 1187. Other aspects include the emotions of those left behind; chants and
prayers for victories as well as losses; devotion to the Blessed Virgin, often chosen as patron of the
military Orders, and, not surprisingly, a certain anti-Semitism. Broadly speaking, we hear three
styles of performance. The polyphonic pieces, alert and rhythmic, have that delightfully rough-
edged vocal quality the men singers exploit to perfection. If one slid a page of parchment between
finger and thumb, theirs would undoubtedly be the hairy side. By contrast, Catherine King's would
be the smooth. Her quiet, subtle phrasing graces her three solo pieces, including Hildegard's
O Jerusalem. The third style is the men's quaint, peculiarly un-French singing of the chant: a
Rogations antiphon, *Invocantes Dominum* for times of war, from the thirteenth-century Worcester
MS F160 (or an identical source). Incidentally, the *Alleluia* cue should have led into the full version.
Then a *Te Deum* (also from F160), sung triumphantly to the joyful accompaniment of bells; and the
Easter *Hec dies*, *Alleluia* and *Gospel* from an exciting find, a twelfth-century Sacramentary from the
Holy Sepulchre itself. The whole programme is a truly fascinating compilation.

Dame de Flors Ecole Notre-Dame de Paris.
Discantus (Anne Guidet, Claire Jéquier, Lucie Jolivet, Brigitte Le Baron, Anne Quentin,
Catherine Schroeder, Catherine Sergent) / **Brigitte Lesne.**
Opus 111 OPS30-175 (59 minutes: DDD). Texts and translations included. Recorded 1996.   Ⓕ

One is struck by the overwhelming majority of pieces in honour of the Virgin Mary in the extant
sources of the School of Notre-Dame. Indeed, the rich and many-faceted devotion to Our Lady,
which characterized the Middle Ages and reached its peak in the twelfth and thirteenth centuries,
was itself paralleled by the secular devotion to the ideal Lady of chivalry sung by troubadour and
trouvère alike. Such devotion may well have contributed in no small measure to the development of
the art of music, in particular of the *ars antiqua* with its musical forms: organum, conductus and
motet. This is a gentle, unaffected programme of such pieces, some of them of almost childlike
simplicity, others of ingenious complexity. The theme that unites them is Mary, seen as Star,
Fountain, Maidservant, but above all, as Lady of Flowers, herself the mystical Flower watered by
celestial dew, Rose, Lily, Blossom without a thorn. Discantus present her with imagination and
sensitivity. An all-female ensemble of eight singers – might that not be a recipe for a bland
'sameness' in an hour-long Marian programme? However, Discantus achieve an amazing degree of
variety by the simplest of means: by opposing vocal registers, by alternating solo and tutti, by
varying the tempos and by delicate phrasing. The mood of each piece is carefully studied. Despite
one slight imperfection of pitch, the listener's ear is absolutely captivated by the sheer beauty and
purity of the music.

Mystery of Notre Dame
[a]**Orlando Consort** (Robert Harre-Jones *counterten* Charles Daniels, Angus Smith *tens*
Donald Greig *bar*) with [b]**Simon Berridge** *ten* **Westminster Cathedral Choir.**
Archiv Produktion 453 487-2AH (76 minutes: DDD). Texts and translations included.
Recorded 1996.   Ⓕ Ⓔ
Léonin[a] Et valde mane una sabbatorum; Alleluya – Assumpta est Maria; Alleluya – Video celos
apertos. **Pérotin**[b] Sederunt principes. **School of Pérotin**[a] Cristus resurgens – Dicant nunc;
Benedicta – Virgo, Dei genitrix. **Plainchant** Pascha nostrum immolatus; Victimae paschali laudes;
Beata es, virgo Maria; Eternim sederunt principes; Video celos apertos.

Anyone who has followed the work of the Orlando Consort has been waiting for them to record
Notre Dame music ever since they were formed ten years ago. As we may expect from their earlier
records, they use here the best and newest editions, namely the grand new set currently being

produced by L'Oiseau-Lyre. As we may also expect, they present the music with remarkable lyricism and sweetness. In the two-voice organa of the *Magnus liber*, generally thought the work of Léonin, they sing with such refined intonation that the music is irresistible. For the three-voice organa of the 'School of Pérotin' they magnificently succeed in the most important task, which is to make the lilting triple rhythms fluid, whereas they can so easily sound joggy and meaningless. But their finest achievement is in what must count as the grandest and most difficult piece in this entire repertory, the enormous four-voice *Sederunt principes* of Pérotin. The work is quite exceptionally minimalist in its restraint, its gentle onward flow, its almost obsessive concentration on a very small number of chords, its glorious canvases generated from so little material. Here the suave approach of the Orlandos brings the very best results, and it makes the recording required listening for anybody who loves this music. The intervening monophonic sections, and the separate chants, are performed by men and boys from the Westminster Cathedral Choir in an extreme equalist manner – that is, not just giving every note absolutely equal length but also making each note equally important. They actively resist any temptation to make the melodies flow or take on any subjective shape. Some listeners may find this extreme position fascinating, though it is not easy to understand how anybody could gain any aesthetic satisfaction from it. But the wonders of the CD are such that these are easily skipped in favour of the glorious singing of the Orlando in the polyphony.

Campus Stellae Twelfth-Century Pilgrims' Songs.
Discantus / Brigitte Lesne.
Opus 111 OPS30-102 (69 minutes: DDD). Recorded 1994.　　　　　　　　　Ⓕ
Tropes of 'Benedicamus domino' – Ad superni regis decus; Dies ista celebris; Congaudeant catholici; Dies ista gaudium; Gregis pastor; Mira dies oritur. Conductus motets – Plebs domini; Flore vernans gratie. Prosae – Alleluia ... Gratulemur et letemur; Res est admirabilis; Quam dilecta tabernacula; Clemens servulorum gemitus tuorum. Versi – Uterus hodie virginis floruit; Lilium floruit. Kyrie tropes – Rex immense; Cunctipotens genitor Deus. Judicii signum.

All-female ensembles have hitherto been rather thin on the ground, but following on from Anonymous 4 and the high-voice section of Sequentia, here is Discantus, a ten-member group of sopranos and contraltos, dedicated to breathing new life into the performance of sacred monody and early polyphony. This is an attractive and varied selection of pieces illustrating different aspects of twelfth-century French music, the main sources being two manuscripts from the school of St Martial de Limoges and the *Codex Calixtinus*, or *Liber Sancti Jacobi*, compiled in Burgundy, but relating to the famous pilgrimage to the shrine of St James of Compostela. The work which remains in the memory, after listening with delight to the whole of this absorbing programme, is undoubtedly a piece (from a rather later source) based on the Sibylline Oracles, *Judicii signum*, with its ominous, low-voiced announcement of the Last Judgement. Indeed, the alternation from piece to piece of high and low voices, of solo and choir, of monody and polyphony is adroitly and effectively managed throughout the recital, so that the musical interest of a well-balanced and well-planned programme is sustained. Brigitte Lesne and her singers have learnt how to make repercussion sound discreetly convincing. The cadential ornamentation, sometimes involving a kind of double polyphonic shake, might perhaps have gained from being allowed a little more panache. The vocal timbre is clear and fresh and the whole performance moves along with cheerful confidence.

The Pilgrimage to Santiago
New London Consort / Philip Pickett.
L'Oiseau-Lyre 433 148-2OH2 (two discs: 126 minutes: DDD).
Texts and translations included.　　　　　　　　　　　　　　　　　ⒻⓅⓈ
Including Cantigas de Santa María (coll./comp. Alfonso el Sabio), the seven Cantigas de Amigo by Martin Codax; other medieval vocal and instrumental works from the Codices Las Huelgas and Calixtinus.

In recent years a far higher standard of performance together with more rigorous scholarship has come to be expected from those who choose to perform this kind of repertoire. Philip Pickett has been in the forefront of this impressive rise in confidence (as much about what is not known as is definitely known) as this two-disc set amply demonstrates. What may perhaps be surprising to some is the quality of the music itself. The *Cantigas* remain some of the most enticing melodies ever written, and the New London Consort do them full justice with an array of instrumentalists and singers who are, however, used with discretion. Similarly the moving *Cantigas de Amigo* of Martin Codax are beautifully sung with a restraint that pays expressive dividends. The polyphonic music from the Las Huelgas and Calixtinus manuscripts completes, with a flourish, the survey tied together by the Santiago label. If there is early polyphony that sounds fresher than the four-part *Belial vocatur*, for example, it has yet to be recorded. In addition to polyphonic works of various genres, Pickett has also chosen to record the four *planctus* settings from the Las Huelgas Codex: moving in themselves, they are valuable pieces also for their historical associations.

Vox Iberica I Sons of Thunder.
Sequentia / Benjamin Bagby, Barbara Thornton.
Deutsche Harmonia Mundi RD77199 (74 minutes: DDD). Texts and translations included.
Recorded 1989. Ⓕ
Codex Calixtinus Ad superni regis decus. Alleluia: Vocavit Ihesus Iacobum. Annua gaudia, Iacobe debita. Benedicamus Domino. Congaudeant catholici. Cum vidissent autem. Cunctipotens genitor deus. Dum pater familias. Dum esset. Exultet celi curia. Gratulantes celebremus festum. Huic Iacobo. Iacobe sancte tuum repettio. Iacobi virginei. In hac die laudes cum gaudio. Jocundetur et letetur. Misit Herodes. Nostra phalans. O adiutor. Regi perhennis glorie. Rex immense, pater pie. Vox nostra resonet.

Vox Iberica II
Sequentia / Benjamin Bagby, Barbara Thornton.
Deutsche Harmonia Mundi 05472-77238-2 (75 minutes: DDD). Texts and translations included.
Recorded 1989. Ⓕ
Codex Las Huelgas Audi, pontus. Ave Maria, gracia plena. Benedicamus Domino cum cantico. Benedicamus: Hic est enim precursor. Benedicamus virgini matri. Casta catholica. Catholicorum concio. Ex illustri. Fa fa mi fa/ut re mi ut. In hoc festo gratissimo. Maria, virgo virginum. Mater patris et filia. Mundi dolens de iactura. O gloriosa Dei genitrix. O, plangant nostri prelati. O plena gracia. Psallat chorus in novo carmina. Qui nos fecit ex nichilo. Resurgentis Domini. Salve regina glorie. Stabat iuxta Christi crucem. Verbum patris hodie.
Virgo sidus aureum. Four Planctus – Plange Castella misera; Quis dabit meo aquam; Rex obiit et labitur Castelle gloria; O monialis concio Burgensis.

Vox Iberica III Cantigas de Santa Maria.
Sequentia / Benjamin Bagby, Barbara Thornton.
Deutsche Harmonia Mundi 05472-77173-2 (78 minutes: DDD). Texts and translations included.
Recorded 1989. Ⓕ
Alfonso el Sabio Por nos, Virgen Madre. Como o nome da Virgen. Sobelos fondos do mar. Nenbre-sse-e, Madre de. Dized', ai trobadores. Maldito seja quen non loara. Quantos me creveren loaran. Quen bõa dona querrá. Pero que seja a gente. Santa Maria, strela do dia. Pois que Deus quis da Virgen. Macar poucos cantares acabei e con son. En todo logar á poder. **Riquier** Humils, forfaitz, repres e penedens. **Anonymous Thirteenth Century** Kharajas – Que faray, mamma?; Meu sidi Ibrahim; Gar si yes devina; Gardi vos ay yermanellas.

These three generously-filled discs provide a fascinating insight into Spain between the twelfth and fourteenth centuries. The country's history and culture as encompassed in the texts and music of the three repertoires recorded is brought to life by Sequentia with all the immediacy of an illuminated miniature in a mediaeval manuscript. The music comes from three famous Spanish mediaeval manuscripts – the Las Huelgas manuscript, the Codex Calixtinus, and the collection of Cantigas de Santa María compiled at the court of King Alfonso 'El Sabio' of Castile. What strikes one immediately is the freshness and imagination of virtually every piece here recorded. Sequentia's performances are commensurate with these qualities – listen, for example, to the magical textures of the women's choir singing *Sobelos fondos do mar* from the Cantigas collection, or the robust, steely harmony projected by the men in the organa from the Calixtinus manuscript. Surely one of the most remarkable pieces of the Middle Ages is the enormous *Virgo sidus aureum*, a prosa *'de Sancta Maria'* lasting over 14 minutes, whose text is a radiant mystical contemplation of the Mother of God. Liturgico-poetic parallels for it may well be sought in the East rather than the West – the Greek *Akathist* hymn from several centuries earlier, for example. It must be said that the poetic quality of all three of these collections is so high that the music could hardly fail to be of the same level of inspiration. This astonishing piece is given a splendid, coherent rendition (no easy task with a monophonic work of this length) by two soloists, female choir and symphonia, and one only has to listen to it after one of the rather shorter three-part conductus, such as *Mundi dolens de iactura*, or one of the powerful *organa* for St James, the 'Son of Thunder', from the Calixtinus collection, to gain some idea of the impact and the extent of the variety to be found on these discs. The Cantigas collection convincingly conveys the accomplishments of the court of the king who 'while he was pondering the heavens and looking at the stars…lost the earth and his kingdom', and places the Cantiga repertory in the context not only of the troubadours (in particular Guirault Riquier) but also the Mozarabic *kharjas* (or *jarchas*), whose music has been reconstructed, with some success, by Bagby. This testament to the richness of musical life in medieval Spain should not be missed.

Love's Illusion Motets from the Montpellier Codex.
Anonymous 4 (Ruth Cunningham, Marsha Genensky, Susan Hellauer, Johanna Rose *sngrs*). Harmonia Mundi HMU90 7109 (64 minutes: DDD). Texts and translations included.
Recorded 1992-93. Ⓕ

One could easily imagine that a programme such as this, of 29 thirteenth-century motets, all composed around the same theme of *fin amours* and all sung unaccompanied by an all-female vocal ensemble, might end by becoming wearisome on the ear. Anonymous 4 have proved conclusively in this recording that this need not be so, that, in any case, there is already an infinite variety of mood and style among the songs and that it is possible further to vary them in performance, using no other means than the voices themselves. The directness of the group's approach is always refreshing: their tone is unaffected, their pitch secure. The songs are presented with simplicity in a clear acoustic. There is a total absence of any improvised doodling on reconstructed medieval instruments, which is rather a relief. One gets a sense of quiet satisfaction and enjoyment from the singers themselves, also the feeling that the singers are trying to teach us something about the music, the mechanics of the motet and how it works, almost as if they were demonstrating to a class of music students. They sometimes go out of their way to sing a single part and then to repeat it with another part added, and then finally to give us a polished rendering of the whole motet, complete with all its parts. Occasionally they add a drone – once with a doubling at the fifth above.

The Spirits of England and France, Volume 1.
Gothic Voices / Christopher Page; [a]Pavlo Beznosiuk *medieval fiddle*
Hyperion CDA66739 (63 minutes: DDD). Texts and translations included. Recorded 1994. (F)
The fourteenth and fifteenth centuries **Anonymous** Quant la douce jouvencelle. En cest mois de May. Laus detur multipharia. Credo. La uitime estampie real[a]. **J. Cooke** Gloria.
da Perugia Belle sans per. **Machaut** Ay mi! dame de valour. **Pykini** Plaisance, or tost.
The twelfth and thirteenth centuries **Anonymous** Deduc, Syon, uberrimas. Je ne puis/Par un matin/Le premier jor/Iustus. Beata nobis gaudia. Virgo plena gratie/Virgo plena gratie/Virgo. Crucifigat omnes. Flos in monte cernitur. In Rama sonat gemitus. Ave Maria. La septime estampie real[a]. La quarte estampie real[a]. **Pérotin** (attrib.) Presul nostri temporis.

From the beautifully swift and unsentimental reading of the opening song, *Quant la douce jouvencelle*, through to the magically perfumed close with what Page calls the 'irredeemably English style' of *Ave Maria*, each piece has its own musical excellence. In the works of around 1400 it is usually Rogers Covey-Crump who leads the singing, with a skilled and nuanced grasp of the style that seems to grow with each recording: long may his career continue. For the earlier works the spoils are divided between Paul Agnew, Julian Podger, Andrew Tusa and Leigh Nixon, all tenors with spirit and individuality. Finally, as an innovation in Gothic Voices recordings, Pavlo Beznosiuk plays three *estampes* on the medieval fiddle, without percussion and without any embellishment or deviation from the notes of their single surviving manuscript. While not everybody will be happy about this literal attitude to the problem of early instrumental music, Beznosiuk's playing is so rhythmically alive and so irresistible as to justify the approach. Once again, then, a superb recording from Gothic Voices; one that raises questions, that stimulates, that charms.

Worcester Fragments English Sacred Music of the Late Middle Ages.
Orlando Consort (Robert Harre-Jones *counterten* Charles Daniels, Angus Smith *tens* Donald Grieg *bar*).
Amon Ra CD-SAR59 (58 minutes: DDD). Texts and translations included. Recorded 1992. (F)

In this recording the Orlando Consort provides the listener with the chance to gain an overall impression of how music developed in England during the thirteenth and early fourteenth centuries – a development distinguished by its intriguing variety, creativity and undoubted beauty, its peculiar sweetness being marked by the constant harmonic use of the interval of a third. The Orlando Consort manage to achieve a balance between the type of buzzing vocal timbre, believed to have been that of the Middle Ages with its roughness of approach, and their own good solid modern standards of professional musicianship. The Consort also attempt to reproduce what scholars now believe to have been the way in which ecclesiastical Latin was pronounced in medieval England.

Music for the Lion-Hearted King
Gothic Voices / Christopher Page.
Hyperion CDA66336 (60 minutes: DDD). Texts and translations included. (F)
Anonymous Twelfth Century Mundus vergens. Novus miles sequitur. Sol sub nube latuit. Hac in anni ianua. Anglia, planctus itera. Etras auri reditur. Vetus abit littera. In occasu sideris. Purgator criminum. Pange melos lacrimosum. Ver pacis apperit. Latex silice. **Gace Brulé** A la doucour de la bele seson. **Blondel de Nesle** L'amours dont sui espris. Ma joie me semont.
Gui IV, 'Li chastelain de Couci' Li nouviaz tanz.

Christopher Page has a remarkable gift for creating enthralling programmes of early music bound together by a brilliantly-chosen central theme, or appellation. This collection is no less distinguished and every bit as fascinating, musically and historically. Whether or not Richard himself ever actually listened to any of these pieces is beside the point: they are all representative of the period of his lifetime and are gathered together here in his name for the 800th anniversary of his coronation (1189). Two types of twelfth-century vocal music are represented: the *conductus* – which can be written for one, two, three or even four voices and the *chanson*, or noble, courtly love song. The singers cannot be applauded too highly for performances marked by an extraordinary insight into how this music should be tackled, that is, with a fair degree of restraint as well as know-how, given the sort of audience it might have had in Richard's day: the royal court or the household of some high-ranking ecclesiastical figure.

Le Jeu d'Amour The Game of Love in Medieval France.
Anne Azéma *sop/spkr* Noël Bisson, Catherine Jousselin, Ellen Santaniello *sngrs*
Shira Kammen *rebec/vielle/hp* Margriet Tindemans *vielle/cittern/hp* Robert Mealy *vielle/hp*
John Fleagle *ten/bagpipes/hp* Jesse Lepkoff *rec/fl*
Erato 0630-17072-2 (60 minutes: DDD). Texts and translations included. Recorded 1996.   Ⓕ Ⓟ
Moniot d'Arras Ce fu en mai, au dous tens gai. **Thibault de Champagne** Amour me fait commencier. **Jehannot de l'Escurel** Bien se lace. **Adam de la Halle** Je muir d'amourete.
Guillaume d'Amiens Je mais ne serai saous. Prendés i garde. **Guillaume le Vinier**
Pastourelle: Valuru, valuraine. **Muset** En mai, quant li rossignolet. **Anonymous** L'on dit qu'amors est dolce chose. Lai del Kievrefuel. Caroles on 'La verte olive' – La jus desous la verte olive; C'est desoz l'olive; C'est la jus par dessous l'olive. Prennés i garde. Margot, Margot grief sunt li mau d'amer. Trois serors sor rive mer. En un vergier. Tuit cil qui sunt enamourat.
Jean de Flagy Et tous les gens. **Guillaume de Dole** Main à main.

This recital of courtly songs and dances is drawn from the repertoire of the trouvères of Northern France, with named composers such as Colin Muset, Thibault de Champagne and Adam de la Halle, but also a host of other musicians of whom we can only catch glimpses through their music. Anne Azéma is herself responsible for the research, the selection, the transcriptions and their interpretation. She is also the prime performer, singing and declaiming with her customary verve and spirited delivery. Her pronunciation of the courtly French in the spoken items is quite delightful and her vocal timbre, with its lively edge, is always appealing. She sings of the courtly game of love, with its rules and sophistication, but also of the more unruly pastoral delights of May Day celebrations, the 'caroles' and 'rondels'. One of the most stunning pieces is the fully developed *Lai del Kievrefuel* – the *Lay of the Honeysuckle*, traditionally the love-song composed by Tristan for Isolde and so-called because no plant in the woodland is sweeter or more fragrant. It begins with a long instrumental introduction, followed by fiery, passionate singing and one section comes across as hoarse semi-speech. Instruments – fiddles, rebec, flute, recorder, harp – play a large part, both independently, as introductions or interludes, and as discreet accompaniments, to complement the voice. But there are also a number of unaccompanied songs, and this variety is refreshing. The sound quality is excellent. Delightfully entertaining and instructive.

Chansons de Trouvères
Paul Hillier *voc* Andrew Lawrence-King *psaltery/hp/org*
Harmonia Mundi HMU90 7184 (70 minutes: DDD). Texts and translations included.
Recorded 1996.   Ⓕ
Thibault de Champagne Aussi conme unicorne sui. Deus est ensi conme li pellicanz. Chançon ferai, que talenz m'en est pris. **Gace Brulé** Les oxelés de mon païx. A la douçor de la bele seson. **Moniot d'Arras** Ce fu en mai. **Colin Muset** En mai, quant li rossignolez.
Anonymous Volez vous que je vous chant. Quant voi la flor nouvele.

The repertoire of *trouvère* songs is one 'we are only now beginning to explore' writes Margaret Switten. Here we have an enlightened and well-chosen selection, sensitively presented and delightfully sung by Paul Hillier with insight and feeling. The main object of the poets' attention is *fin'amor*, but other themes, including the return of spring (*Volez vous que je vous chant* and *En mai, quant li rossignolez*), make their joyful appearance, and there is one piece in a completely different vein, a serious piece of religious polemics: *Deus est ensi conme li pellicanz*. The melodies, simple and stanzaic, are of great beauty. Outstanding in this respect is Gace Brulé's *A la douçor de la bele seson*. Many are modal (Dorian) and a few share a well-known opening phrase with a Gregorian *melodie-type* that Andrew Lawrence-King has made much use of in his accompaniments. His own contribution is momentous: if the manner in which these songs were originally performed still remains a mystery for the singer, it is even more of an enigma for the accompanist. But Andrew Lawrence-King has taken the word *trouvère* to heart: he is a true 'finder'. His empathy with text, music and singer is total: he 'invents' with a sure touch, and it is not going too far to say it is a touch of genius.

The Courts of Love Music from the time of Eleanor of Aquitaine.
Sinfonye (Mara Kiek *voc* Andrew Lawrence-King *medieval hp* Jim Denley *perc*) / Stevie Wishart.
Hyperion CDA66367 (64 minutes: DDD). Texts and translations included. Ⓕ🅿
Gui d'Ussel Si be'm partetz, mala domna, de vos. **Raimbaut de Vaqeiras** Calenda maya
(vocal and instrumental versions). **Anonymous Twelfth Century** L'on qui dit q'amors est dolce
chose. **Bernart de Ventadorn** Ara'm conseillatz seignor. Conartz, ara sai au be. Quan vei la
lauzeta mover. **Cadenet** S'anc fuy belha ni prezada (vocal and instrumental versions). **Giraut de
Bornelh** S'ie'us queir conseil, bel' amig' Alamanda. **Gace Brulé** Quant je voi la noif remise.
Quant voi le tens bel et cler. Quant flours et glais et verdues s'esloigne. Quant li tens reverdoie.

This recital consists of songs and instrumental pieces dating from the end of the twelfth century
and derived from the 'courts of love' of Aquitaine, Champagne, Flanders and elsewhere. These
courts, created around aristocratic figures such as Marie of Champagne and Eleanor of Aquitaine,
were essentially a charade of the medieval law courts, to which lovers could bring their complaints.
Thus the texts of the songs are concerned with the dilemmas of infidelity, betrayal and unrequited
love. All that survives of this music is melodies for singing: these have been sensitively arranged by
Stevie Wishart for a small selection of medieval instruments, including the symphony, a sort of
hurdy-gurdy, medieval fiddles, lutes and percussion. All the players of Sinfonye are both expert
and relaxed, projecting the music with great character. Six of the pieces are sung by Mara Kiek
with considerable feeling: her unusual voice production and tone help to give a sense of 'distance'
to the performances, and throughout strike a suitably plaintive note. Hyperion's recording catches
all the vocal and instrumental inflexions with great fidelity and a most natural sense of balance.
All in all, a fascinating glimpse of music and manners from a remote if influential corner of
medieval civilization.

L'Unicorne Medieval French Songs.
Anne Azéma *sop* Jesse Lepkoff *fl* Cheryl Ann Fulton *hp* Shira Kammen *vielle/rebec/hp*
Erato 4509-94830-2 (57 minutes: DDD). Texts and translations included. Recorded 1993. Ⓕ🅿
Philippe de Thaon Serena en mer hante. Monosceros. **Anonymous** En mai au douz tens
nouvel. Ensement com la panthere. Au renouvel. Bele Doette. **Marie de France** Issi avint qu'un
cers. D'un gupil. La danse de gupil. **Thibault de Champagne** Aussi come unicorne sui.
Gauthier de Coincy Le Cycle de Sainte Leochade. **Moniot de Paris** Je chevauchoie l'autrier.

Anne Azéma always seems to bring a breath of fresh air to whatever she does, whether reading or
singing. Here she is singing of springtime and love, of beasts and miracles, of a woman's grief but
also of her joy. The melodies, often unforgettable in their simplicity, are interpreted with tenderness
and quiet understanding. Many are ravishingly beautiful, in particular those describing the panther
and the unicorn and also several of the songs from the *Cycle de Sainte Leocadie* in Gauthier de
Coincy's *Miracles of Our Lady*. One of the finest songs in the programme is the thirteenth-century
Bele Doette, a saga of grief experienced by a noble lady on hearing the news of her beloved's
untimely death during the jousting. Azéma's control of the slow rhythm and deepening emotion is
total, and she matches this with perfection, as the story unfolds, in her singing of the short sad
refrain that ends each strophe. The occasional instrumental interludes, for example *D'un gupil* ('The
fox's dance') or *Au renouvel* provide graceful linkage between songs and readings; the
accompaniments are generally discreet and understated, though the flute comes into its own in one
song – *En mai au douz tens nouvel* – with its charming imitations of birdsong.

The Play of Daniel
Douglas Nasrawi *ten* Daniel; **Jeremy Birchall** *bass* Habacuc;
Harry van der Kamp *bass* King Baltassar; **Ian Honeyman** *ten* King Darius;
Barbara Borden *sop* Queen; **Caitríona O'Leary** *voc* Child;
The Harp Consort / Andrew Lawrence-King *hp/psaltery/org*
Deutsche Harmonia Mundi 05472 77395-2 (78 minutes: DDD). Notes, text and translation
included. Ⓕ

Andrew Lawrence-King has assembled a thoughtful and attractive rendering of *The Play of Daniel*.
The rhythmic interpretation of the unmeasured pitches is sensitively varied. A single pitch-standard
is retained throughout – which seems to be the best approach, though there are plenty of good
reasons for thinking otherwise. And, most important of all, the drama works well because careful
and original thought has been given to the meaning of the words: as one example among many,
Daniel's final speech is prefaced with a grand organ introduction that actively frames it as a
prophecy well apart from the story. In fact the entire flow of the closing scenes is particularly
effectively caught. Douglas Nasrawi is an excellent Daniel, managing to encompass the wide range
of musical styles in the role without losing the strong character; and he gives a wonderfully

expressive reading of the great lament as Daniel enters the lions' den. Ian Honeyman may well be the first Darius on record to portray him fully as a thoroughly nice but weak man: somehow the music invites a bolder approach at the moment when Darius usurps Belshazzar, but plainly the present interpretation works better. Harry van der Kamp is a splendidly strong Belshazzar; and all the smaller roles are well characterized. Alongside this is a superbly skilled instrumental ensemble. There is a reasonable case for thinking instruments are unnecessary in *Daniel* and impede the musical flow; but here their performances are so good and so well judged that most listeners will welcome their contribution. There are many different ways of doing *The Play of Daniel*, but this one is thoroughly viable throughout.

Canticum Canticorum The sacred symbol of love in the medieval musical tradition.
Ensemble Cantilena Antiqua / Stefano Albarello *counterten*
Symphonia SY95135 (72 minutes: DDD).   Ⓕ

This intriguing collection of music on the Song of Solomon includes not only twelfth- and thirteenth-century Western monody and polyphony, but also Hebrew, Sephardic and Maronite melodies. The performances blend voices and instruments in a manner much favoured by Italian ensembles today; there is some fine singing, that of the countertenor Stefano Albarello being particularly striking. Text and documentation are intelligently and stylishly presented.

The Spirits of England and France, Volume 2 – Songs of the Trouvères.
Gothic Voices / Christopher Page *medieval lte* with **Robert White** *bagpipes*
Nick Bicat *perc* **Pavlo Beznosiuk** *fiddle*
Hyperion CDA66773 (62 minutes: DDD). Texts and translations included. Recorded 1994.   Ⓕ
Richart de Semilli Je chevauchai. **Gace Brulé** Desconfortez, plains de dolor. Quant define fueille et flor. De bien amer grant joie atent. Cil qui d'amours. **Gontier de Soignies** Dolerousement commence. **Guibert Kaukesel** Un chant novel. Fins cuers enamourés. **Gautier de Dargies** La doce pensee. **Adam de la Halle** Assenés chi, Grievilier. **Ernoul li Vielle** Por conforter mon corage. **Audefroi le Bastart** Au novel tens pascor. **Anonymous** Domna pos vos ay chausida. Quant voi la fleur nouvele. Amors m'art con fuoc am flamma. Trois Estampies.

This is a disc devoted to monophonic song and one of startling power and originality. Essentially it explores two repertories: the serious *grand chant*, particularly in the work of Gace Brulé, whose four songs here are presented with tremendous conviction and in wonderfully spacious readings; and the lighter dance songs, where Page often includes instruments, played with robust good humour. As regards the rhythmic approach, this is neatly varied to match the needs of particular songs: sometimes an equalist interpretation, sometimes syllabic, and sometimes in strict metre roughly derived from the principles of modal rhythm. That seems a thoroughly judicious and musical solution, and it gives the disc considerable variety of pace. Margaret Philpot shows her astonishing stylistic range in the five songs she sings, from Richart de Semilli's jovial *Je chevauchai* via Gace Brulé's wonderful *De bien amer* and concluding with *Au novel tens pascor*, the late *chanson de toile* by Audefroi le Bastart. Emma Kirkby makes a welcome return to Gothic Voices with two glorious performances: her success in later music has been so great over the last few years that it has been too easy to forget quite how expressive she can be in early monophony, especially with Page's rattling folk-style lute playing in *Domna pos vos ay chausida*. Beyond these it is particularly good that the disc includes a *descort* – that fascinating but undervalued genre – and a *jeu-parti*. Once again Gothic Voices have produced a record that sets new standards.

The Marriage of Heaven and Hell Thirteenth-Century French Motets and Songs.
Gothic Voices / Christopher Page.
Hyperion CDA66423 (46 minutes: DDD). Texts and translations included.   Ⓕ
Anonymous Je ne chant pas. Talens m'est pris. Trois sereurs/Trois sereurs/Trois sereurs. Plus bele que flors/Quant revient/L'autrier jouer. Par un martinet/Hé, sire!/Hé, bergier! De la virge Katerine/Quant froidure/Agmina milicie. Ave parens/Ad gratie. Super te Jerusalem/Sed fulsit virginitas. A vous douce debonnaire. Mout souvent/Mout ai esté en doulour. Quant voi l'aloete/Dieux! je ne m'en partiré ja. En non Dieu/Quant voi la rose. Je m'en vois/Tels a mout. Festa januaria. **Blondel de Nesle** En tous tans que vente bise. **Colin Muset** Trop volontiers chanteroie. **Bernart de Ventadorn** Can vei la lauzeta mover. **Gautier de Dargies** Autre que je ne seuill fas.

The reasons for the dazzling success of Gothic Voices both in the recording studio and in the concert hall are once again evident in this collection. It is both an entertaining and well-planned recital and, if one chooses to take it that way, reading Christopher Page's insert-notes while listening, a detailed lecture-recital. The music, all French and dating from the thirteenth century, is that seemingly impenetrable repertoire of polytextual motets, unexpectedly compared and contrasted with monophonic trouvère songs. The comparison is illuminating, and the performances of both genres of music are up to Gothic Voices' usual high standards: intonation is perfect, textures are finely balanced, the performances are always conceived just as much melodically as harmonically, and the greatest respect is always paid to the words (even when there are three texts at the same time, as is often the case here!). The clever juxtaposition of the trouvère Bernart de Ventadorn's *Can vei la lauzeta mover* with the triple-texted motet *Quant voi l'aloete/Dieux! je ne m'en partiré ja/NEUMA* encapsulates the thinking behind this recording: a compelling musical experience and a provocative intellectual one.

The Study of Love French Songs and Motets of the Fourteenth Century.
Gothic Voices / Christopher Page.
Hyperion CDA66619 (60 minutes: DDD). Texts and translations included. Recorded 1992.　　Ⓕ
Machaut Dame, je suis cilz/Fins cuer. Trop plus/Biauté paree/Je ne suis. Tres bonne et belle. Se mesdisans. Dame, je vueil endurer. **Pycard** Gloria. **Solage** Le basile. **Anonymous** Pour vous servir. Puis que l'aloe ne fine. Jour a jour la vie. Combien que j'aye (two versions). Marticius qui fu. Renouveler me feïst. Fist on dame. Il me convient guerpir. Le ior. En la maison Dedalus. La grant biaute. En esperent. Ay las! quant je pans.

The title of the disc speaks of the ways in which the discourses of love (and 'love') in the late Middle Ages are partly, perhaps largely, derived from books – the Bible, classical poetry and myths, the earlier medieval literary tradition – rather than some expression of unmediated personal feeling. But music was a powerful means for the late medieval artist to attempt to transcend the bookish intertextualities of the literary texts. Rarely have Gothic Voices, both as individuals and as a group, sounded more alive and present. The accord of vowel colour between the singers in some of the fully texted pieces is marvellous, a feature pointed up the more by juxtaposition with those works in which Page continues his experiments with lower-voice vocalization. Where some slight untidiness creeps in, the impression often (though not invariably) given is the positive one of risk being happily taken in the recording sessions, the very absence of which has so often been the downfall of lesser groups (and not just in medieval music). A wonderful addition to the catalogue, and the recorded sound is superlative.

Lancaster and Valois French and English Music, 1350-1420.
Gothic Voices / Christopher Page *lte*
Hyperion CDA66588 (59 minutes: DDD). Texts and translations included. Recorded 1991.　　Ⓕ
Machaut Donnez, signeurs. Quand je ne voy ma dame. Riches d'amour et mendians. Pas de tor en thies pais. **Solage** Tres gentil cuer. **Cesaris** Se vous scaviez, ma tres douce maistresse. Mon seul voloir/Certes m'amour. **Cordier** Ce jur de l'an. **Pycard** Credo. **Sturgeon** Salve mater domini/Salve templum domini. **Fonteyns** Regali ex progenie. **Anonymous** Puis qu'autrement ne puis avoir. Soit tart, tempre, main ou soir. Le ior. Avrai je ja de ma dame confort? Sanctus. Je vueil vivre au plaisir d'amours.

This is the tenth recording to come from Christopher Page's Gothic Voices and, the considerable success of their previous recordings notwithstanding, this is perhaps their best yet. In the space of 11 years, Page and his group have reinvented performance practice in medieval and fifteenth century music, as powerful and popularizing an influence as David Munrow and his Early Music Consort of London in the 1970s. 'Lancaster and Valois' takes its name from the chosen repertoire: French secular songs of the late fourteenth and early fifteenth centuries juxtaposed with sacred English pieces from around 1400. Much thought has been given to the ordering of the pieces and the grouping of the voices, resulting in the greatest possible diversity. In *Tres gentil cuer* by Solage, Page sets an ideally lilting tempo, with the text finely enunciated by Margaret Philpot, the tenors (in this instance Charles Daniels and Leigh Nixon) adding definition but never threatening to engulf. This is followed by a *Credo* by the English composer Pycard, the longest and most stately piece on the disc, exploiting the richer timbres of tenors and baritones. With excellent sound and entertaining and scholarly notes by Christopher Page (the like of which also regularly inform his spoken interjections in concerts), this is an irresistible disc.

Italian sacred simple polyphony of the Middle Ages and after
Acantus
Gimell 462 516-2PH (58 minutes: DDD). Recorded 1997.　　ⒻⒺ
Adoramus te Christe. Adoramus te Domine. Alleluia. Benedictus. Credo apostolorum. Cum autem venissem. De profundis. Gaude flore. O crux fructus. O Virgineta bella. Quasi cedrus. Qui nos fecit ex nichilo. Salva sponsa Dei. Salve, sancte Pater. Salve Virgo rubens rosa. Sanctus. Sicut pratum. Vergene madre pia. Verzene benedeta.

For those expert in medieval music, this disc offers a relatively unknown repertory hardly ever recorded; for music lovers who just want a new musical experience, it's here in trumps; and for those who are not particularly musical it offers a vivid, ethnic-sounding experience with that taste of earthy spirituality that seems to go down well almost anywhere these days. There are some very odd things about the packaging, quite apart from the meaningless cleavage that adorns the cover. The only title for the disc seems to be the name of the group, Acantus, which includes Alessandra Fiori, Gloria Moretti, Stefano Pilati and Marco Ferrari, people who have been doing excellent work for years but who have never quite managed to find an ensemble or a record company that remains intact. As the first 'guest' group ever to be issued by Gimell (of The Tallis Scholars fame), it's a confidence-inspiring choice. Another odd feature is that there is only the most indirect indication of what is recorded here, essentially just a list of titles (as given in the heading above) without mentioning that some pieces are from the thirteenth century, some from the fifteenth, one from the nineteenth and one from the contemporary folk tradition. Hints of that information appear in the Italian version of the insert-notes, rather less in the digest of it provided in other languages. This repertory of semi-popular sacred music – known to scholars as 'cantus planus binatim', 'primitive polyphony' (in the days when such language was allowable), 'polifonia semplice' and 'folk polyphony' – contains many glorious pieces, and Acantus gives a massively convincing account of them.

Balades a III chans
Ferrara Ensemble / Crawford Young.
Arcana A32 (59 minutes: DDD). Texts and translations included. Recorded 1994. Ⓕ Ⓟ
Trebor Helas pitié envers moy dort si fort. Si Alexandre et Hector fussent en vie.
Cordier Tout par compas suy composés. **Matteo da Perugia** Rondeau-refrain. Pres du soloil deduissant s'esbanoye. **Antonius de Civitate** Io vegio per stasone. **Grimace** Se Zephirus, Phebus et leur lignie. **Anonymous** Adieu vous di, tres doulce compaynie. Lamech Judith et Rachel de plourer. Le mont Aon de Thrace.

The *ballade*, that noblest form (in every sense) of fourteenth century secular music, was meant to honour the dukes and counts who did so much to foster the fine arts while war, famine and plague raged round them. Their musical protégés were by all accounts a slightly surreal bunch, dedicated seekers-out of weirdness, addicted to the bottle – possibly even to hashish. Small wonder that so much of their music seems hopelessly capricious on the page. Crawford Young's special achievement is to demonstrate what many enthusiasts of *Ars subtilior* have felt all along. In performance, that wilful strangeness can suddenly come across with astonishing naturalness: all it takes is the right singers, and here they are. Or perhaps that last sentence should read: 'here she is'. It is no slight on the other members of the Ferrara Ensemble to say that the mezzo-soprano, Lena Susanne Norin, steals the show. Her singing can only be described as luscious. True, the quality of these performances is partly a matter of direction. Tempo is of the first importance because it determines the specific gravity of the dissonances. Pitched too slow, the phrases are weighed down by them; too fast, and the dissonances are trivialized. Beyond that, however, the sensitivity to these details is down to Norin herself. This fierce-looking music, once tamed, becomes almost unbelievably sensuous. The tone of the accompanying string instruments is perfectly judged, the sound-recording outstanding – warm and glowing. The presentation of *ballades* is a tricky business: to perform all three stanzas can take well over ten minutes. In the past, singers have tended to confine themselves to just one or two stanzas. That has the advantage of fitting more music into a recital, but aesthetically it makes about as much sense as trimming the tail of a peacock. Young gives all three stanzas of the poem wherever possible, and in so doing he restores the *ballade*'s length, weight, complexity, in a word, the *heroic* intent that is the form's very *raison d'être*. A glorious recital.

Il Solazzo
The Newberry Consort / Mary Springfels.
Harmonia Mundi HMU90 7038 (62 minutes: DDD). Texts and translation included.
Recorded 1990. Ⓕ Ⓟ Ⓔ
Anonymous Fourteenth Century Italian La Badessa. Bel fiore danza. Nova stella. Cominciamento di gioia. Trotto. Principe di virtu. **Jacopo da Bologna** Non al suo amante. **Landini** La bionda treccia. Dolcie signorie. Donna, s'i, t'o fallito. El gran disio. **Ciconia** O rosa bella. Ligiadra donna. **Zacharo de Teramo** Rosetta. Un fior gentil. **Bartolino da Padova** Alba columba.

If medieval Italian music pales somewhat in comparison to the glories of opera from the nineteenth century onwards, there are still riches to be discovered in this collection of *trecento* vocal and instrumental works. The Chicago-based ensemble, The Newberry Consort, use a mere five performers to provide over an hour of entertainment. This was the era of writers such as Dante, Petrarch, Boccaccio, but also of Simone Prodenzani – the author of a cycle of sonnets entitled

Il Solazzo, many of which were later set to music. Whilst some of the *Solazzo* texts are presented here in musical form (the scurrilous *La Badessa* is one), Italian ballata from leading composers of the time are also represented – Ciconia's *O rosa bella* and Landini's *La bionda treccia*, for example. The vocal numbers are all taken by mezzo Judith Malafronte and countertenor Drew Minter who clear the hurdles of tricky pronunciation and flamboyantly complex vocal lines to give a thoroughly communicative performance of this wonderful music. Mary Springfels provides elegant and musical direction as well as that essential ingredient to a disc such as this – the informative booklet. If the prospect of an hour of early Italian song sounds daunting, fear not, for the instrumental dances on the disc (especially the anonymous *Cominciamento di gioia*) are played with a vitality that will make you want to jump up and join in! Explorers of the riches from Italian times long gone by need have no qualms when sampling from this lively, superbly performed disc.

En doulz chastel de Pavie Songs from the Visconti court around 1400.
Ferrara Ensemble (Lena Susanne Norin *contr* Eric Mentzel *ten* Stephen Grant *bar*
Randall Cook *va d'arco* Marion Fourquier *hp* Crawford Young *gtr*)
Harmonia Mundi HMC90 5241 (61 minutes: DDD). Texts and translations included.
Recorded 1997. Ⓕ
Anonymous Istanpitta Isabella. Chanconeta tedesca (two versions). Constantia. **Ciconia** La fiamma del to amor. Le ray au soleyl. Sus une fontayne. **Philippus de Caserta** En remirant. De ma doulour. En attendant souffrir. **Senleches** La harpe de mélodie.

This disc focuses on one of *Ars subtilior*'s most influential figures, Philippus de Caserta, three of whose songs are quoted in Johannes Ciconia's virelai, *Sus une fontayne* in an unusually comprehensive form of homage. All four works appear here, along with two canonic pieces by Ciconia and the admirable Jacob de Senleches. The latter deserves a disc all to himself, but here at least we have his incomparable *La harpe de mélodie*, one of *Ars subtilior*'s most perfect creations. Caserta's pieces are dense and labyrinthine, but once again the Ferrara Ensemble triumphs over all but the most intractable intricacies: only *En remirant* remains elusive. Several instrumental items are included to round off the disc and refresh the ear, incidentally giving violist, Randall Cook (an admirable accompanist) his place in the sun. The recorded sound is excellent.

Red Iris Instrumental music from fourteenth-century Italy.
Istampite – Trotto; Tre Fontane; Principio di virtu; La manfredina and la rotta;
Chominciamento di gioa; Palamento; Two Salterellos; Belicha.
Sinfonye (Jim Denley, Pedro Estevan *perc*) / **Stevie Wishart** *medieval fiddle/hurdy-gurdy/dir*
Glossa GCD920701 (53 minutes: DDD). Interactive CD. Recorded 1996. ⒻⓅ

Many people have recorded the fourteenth-century instrumental dances that appear only in a single manuscript now in London. Apart from some pieces apparently for keyboard, they are almost the only known early works for a solo melody instrument. The nine pieces (out of a total of 15) presented here offer no repertorial novelty. What is new is the way Stevie Wishart plays them. She views the shorter pieces as dances, to be performed with percussion accompaniment. This is common enough, though they are done extremely well, with Jim Denley and Pedro Estevan producing a stunning range of sounds from their various percussion instruments. But the longer ones are treated as elaborate and weaving instrumental solos, without any accompaniment. Stevie Wishart plays them on the vielle and, in one case, on the hurdy-gurdy, never rushing, never tempted to gloss over the many unexpected details in the lines. This kind of approach seems extremely productive: it stresses the sheer quality and inventiveness of the melodies, and it perhaps aligns them with their true historical context, the repertory of long monophonic *lais* from the fourteenth century. That in its turn somehow makes the pieces considerably more than virtuoso showpieces. But it says much for the power of Stevie Wishart's playing that she keeps the music constantly interesting (one of the pieces lasts over ten minutes) and is invariably persuasive. The disc comes with a CD-ROM track that portrays, among other things, frescoes of the time, the instruments and the manuscript. But even without that this is a superbly convincing performance, recorded with a nice full sound and giving relatively familiar music an added intellectual depth.

Anonymous Vigil in Kiev.
Russian Patriarchate Choir / Anatoly Grindenko.
Opus 111 OPS30-223 (78 minutes: DDD). Texts and translations included. Recorded 1997. Ⓕ

Here is a revelatory exploration of unknown Russian riches, here monastic polyphony. This is a repertory that contains more or less familiar versions of harmonized chants and often some spectacularly startling variants: notable are the Deacon's *Priidite* (invitatory, monophonic), the elaborate fourfold response 'Tebe Gospodi' in the insistent litany, and the astonishing chromatic 'slips' in the *Canticle of Simeon*, the *Megalynarion* and in the *Trisagion* at the end of the *Great Doxology*. Another item worthy of note is the Vespers prayer in which the bass is given the lion's share, especially at cadences, while the upper voices move smoothly from chord to chord. Full texts are provided, though there are one or two oddities in the English translation. The singing is sublime. There can be few choirs in the world who are able to combine such richness of sound with such prayerful attention to text, always perfectly declaimed.

The Spirits of England and France, Volume 3.
Gothic Voices / Christopher Page.
Hyperion CDA66783 (67 minutes: DDD). Texts and translations included. Recorded 1995.　　Ⓕ
Anonymous Abide, I hope it be the best. Exultavit cor in Domino. **Binchois** Qui veut mesdire si mesdie. Amoureux suy et me vient toute joye. Adieu mon amoureuse joye. Ay douloureux disant helas. Magnificat secundi toni. Se la belle n'a le voloir. **Bittering** En Katerina solennia/Virginalis concio/Sponsus amat sponsum. **Cardot** Pour une fois et pour toute. **Dunstable** Beata Dei genitrix. **Fontaine** J'ayme bien celui. **Johannes de Lymburga** Descendi in ortum meum. **Legrant** Se liesse. **Machaut** Il m'est avis qu'il n'est. **Power** Gloria. **Velut** Lassies ester vostres chans de liesse. Un petit oyselet chantant.

Gothic Voices continue their long-term exploration of early English and French polyphony with an offering devoted to the work of Binchois and his musical forebears of both 'nationalities'. Consistent with the ensemble's usual approach to this repertoire, voices and instruments are not mixed; instead, Christopher Page is joined by the lutenists Christopher Wilson and Shirley Rumsey in energetic renderings of several of the songs: light, and delightful, relief. The songs of Binchois are relatively late territory for Gothic Voices. It has been 12 years or so – in 'The Castle of Fair Welcome' (on Hyperion) – since they covered this repertoire in any depth (who can forget the chilly pathos of *Dueil angoisseus*?), and comparison with the present disc is instructive. Over the years there have been more, and deeper, men's voices; the hard-edged, polished chrome patina has perhaps mellowed and burnished with time. Perhaps, too, the almost obsessive concern with clarity and intonation has been allowed to ease a little, in favour of a heightened sensitivity to the affective projection of both text and music. Perhaps, but only just. The hard edge creeps back in when the programme strays from Binchois back on to earlier repertoire, such as Power's marvellous five-voice *Gloria* – here portrayed as an exercise in risk-taking for composer and singers alike. Its brashness, though glorious to listen to, leads to an inevitable query, for there seem to be not one but two programmes here. Binchois's songs, characterized by their restraint and understatement, seem uneasy in the company of so many of his exuberant contemporaries and immediate predecessors (and the not-so-immediate – what is Machaut doing here?). The singers do their utmost to reflect the difference in tone, but that only makes the discrepancy more telling. This is a pity, for the Binchois pieces are finely pitched, and deserved to have more space to themselves – more space also for the singers to acclimatize themselves to Binchois's languorous melancholy. Page knows a show-stopper when he hears one, and the haunted *Ay, douloureux*, clocking in at nearly nine minutes, stands out from other items in the collection like a hothouse plant. That is not meant to belittle the rest, but to suggest that, as a programme, this particular collection is perhaps not as well rounded as so many of its predecessors: the sum of its parts. And yet there is so much that is deeply moving and magical that anything less than a warm recommendation would be positively Scrooge-like.

The Spirits of England and France, Volume 4.
ªShirley Rumsey, ªChristopher Wilson *ltes* Gothic Voices / Christopher Page ª*lte*.
Hyperion CDA66857 (66 minutes: DDD). Texts and translations included. Recorded 1996.　　Ⓕ 🅴
Anonymous Missa Caput (ed. Curtis). The story of the Salve regina. Salve regina. Jesu for thy mercyª. Clangat tuba. Alma redemptoris mater. Old Hall Manuscript – Agnus Dei. **Smert** Jesu fili Deia. **Traditional** Make we merryª. Nowell, nowell, nowell.

This recording (going by the title 'The Spirits of England and France, Volume 4') breaks new ground for Gothic Voices in terms of repertory. For the first time, the group tackles a large-scale, multi-movement work. One could hardly imagine a more appropriate Mass for their début in the genre than the anonymous English *Caput* cycle. Composed c1440 and long thought to be by Dufay, it lays fair claim to being the single most influential work of the fifteenth century. Its most innovative technical features were widely copied by continental composers, but on this recording we can at last begin to appreciate what all the fuss was about: few on the continent at the time were capable of writing music of such breathtaking confidence. One can feel the impact, the delighted surprise of contemporary listeners on hearing that very first burst of four-note writing in the *Kyrie*. In that respect, it is sobering to think that the identity of this supremely influential composer may forever remain a mystery. That phrase 'breathtaking confidence' aptly describes Gothic Voices, who are on the top of their form. Initially one could hardly fail to be surprised by the briskness of this performance, but there is little sign of hurry even in the most demandingly athletic places. Although the declamation of the text is kept fairly low-key, the sense of phrase and line, of the notes taking their place amid a kaleidoscope of changing sounds, is all beautifully judged. And with intonation and ensemble of this consistency, it is possible to revel in sheer sonority. What else? The accompanying items, consisting mostly of carols, make for lighter listening and a nicely balanced programme. This, then, is a disc that grows in stature with each hearing. Anyone who might be put off by the 'anonymous' listing can rest assured that this is music of the very highest order. The recording is unobtrusively impressive.

The Spirits of England and France, Volume 5.
Gothic Voices / Christopher Page.
Hyperion CDA66919 (65 minutes: DDD). Texts and translations included. Recorded 1996.　　Ⓕ
Anonymous Missa, 'Veterem hominem'. Jesu, fili virginis. Doleo super te. Gaude Maria virgo. Deus creator omnium. Jesu salvator. A solis ortus. Salvator mundi. Christe, qui lux es. To many a well. Sancta Maria virgo. Mater ora filium. Ave maris stella. Pange lingua. **Dunstable** Beata mater.

As in their previous recordings, Gothic Voices' peculiar brand of extrovert dynamism puts a new spin on the performance of fifteenth-century Mass music; more than just a Mass, what we have here is a glimpse (one might say) into the very mind of a medieval composer. Music as contemplation, certainly, but active, not passive; music in which each single voice conveys weight, number, proportion. Thus, the recurring head-motif at the beginning of each movement of the *Veterem hominem* Mass cycle is experienced not so much as a structural device as a manifestation of divine immutability. In a similar spirit, the same tempos are retained in all the movements; this has not been attempted very often, but far from being unrelenting, the result suits both pieces very well. If Page and friends let rip in the Mass and in the carols (delivered with exhilarating brashness), they deliberately adopt a more placid, even 'mainstream' approach for some of the smaller Marian pieces. As to the chants that intersperse the polyphony, they certainly provide contrast; but can it be that the fifteenth-century singers who polished off their polyphony with such gusto, took their 'daily bread' of plainsong with so little salt?

Armes, Amours Songs of the Fourteenth and Fifteenth Centuries.
Alla Francesca (Emmanuel Bonnardot, Raphaël Boulay, Pierre Hamon, Marco Horvat, Brigitte Lesne); **Alta** (Michèle Vandenbroucque, Pierre Boragno, Gilles Rapin).
Opus 111 OPS30-221 (56 minutes: DDD). Texts and translations included. Recorded 1997.　　ⒻⒺ
Anonymous Ho, ho, ho. Man, assay. Or sus vous dormes trop. Helas, Olivier Basselin. Ecce quod natura. Bel fiore. **Andrieu** Armes, amours/O flour des flours. **Binchois** Tant plus ayme. Busnois Est-il merchy. **Ghiselin** La spagna. **Grimace** A l'arme, a l'arme. **Joye** Ce qu'on fait a quatimini. **Morton** Il sera/L'ome armé (two versions). N'aray je jamais mieulx. **Paumann** Mit ganczem Willen.

This disc is an impressive vindication of the marriage of voices and instruments in secular music of this period. The case for all-vocal performance, very prevalent among English groups, has perhaps been greeted more cautiously elsewhere; but rarely has instrumental participation been so positively espoused. In any case, the performance of the songs by wind-bands alone is well attested, and Alta manages brilliantly on its own: those war-horses, *Or sus* and *A l'arme, a l'arme* are as exciting as if they had been sung. Oddly enough, it is the vocal selections that are more of a mixed bag: certain songs seem somehow under-interpreted, like Morton's *N'aray je jamais mieulx*, whose poignant melancholy is belied by a disconcertingly brisk tempo. And what of Busnois's *Est-il merchy*, here shorn of the repeats prescribed by the rondeau form? Ironically, this abridged version is admirable for its subtle handling of the tactus, and an impressive fluidity of exchange between the three singers: coming from musicians of this calibre, the formal solecism is all the more disconcerting. Yet in songs like *Ho, ho, ho, Ce qu'on fait a quatimini* and *Helas, Olivier Basselin* we find the group at its inventive and sure-footed best once again. And it certainly deserves credit for its adroit blend of well-known pieces with lesser-known finds. A few strange moments, then, but many more marvellous ones.

The Art of the Netherlands
Early Music Consort of London / David Munrow.
Virgin Classics Veritas VED5 61334-2 (two discs: 132 minutes: ADD).
Texts and translations included. Recorded 1975.　　Ⓜ
Josquin Desprez Scaramella va alla guerra. Allégez moy, doulce plaisant brunette. Allégez moy, doulce plaisant brunette (anonymous arrangement for two lutes). El grillo è buon cantore. De profundis clamavi a 5. Benedicta es, caelorum regina. Credo 'De tous biens playne'. Guillaume se va chauffer. Adieu mes amours. Adieu mes amours (sixteenth-century anonymous arrangement

for organ). Inviolata, integra et casta es, Maria. **Isaac** Donna di dentro dalla tua casa. Missa 'La bassadanza'. **Hayne Van Ghizeghem** De tous biens plaine. De tous biens plaine (arr. Josquin). **A. Agricola** De tous biens plaine (two versions). Fortuna desparata. **Brumel** Du tout plongiet/Fors seulement. Missa 'Et ecce terrae motus'. **Ghiselin** Ghy syt die wertste boven al. **Barbireau** Een wrolick wesen. **Hofhaimer** Ein fröhlich wesen. **Obrecht** Ein fröhlich wesen. Haec Deum caeli. Laudemus nunc Dominum. **Ockeghem** Prenez sur moi vostre exemple. Ma bouche rit. Intemerata Dei mater. **Busnois** Fortuna disperata. **Anonymous** Fortuna desperata. Mijn morken gaf mij een jonck wijff. **Tinctoris** Missa sine nomine. **La Rue** Missa 'Ave sanctissima Maria'. Ave sanctissima Maria. **Compère** O bone Jesu. **Mouton** Nesciens mater virgo virum.

This is arguably Munrow's most consistent and most polished collection, devoted to the sacred and secular polyphony of the mid- to late-fifteenth century. These recordings remain marvellously fresh and vital – even in the case of pieces that have since had more polished or more clearly recorded interpretations. That is especially true of the sacred music, recorded entirely vocally and (in most cases) one to a part. It would be a challenge to name a more tempestuous reading of Brumel's 'Earthquake Mass', a more sombre, self-absorbed *Intemerata Dei mater* (this is still the only recording at super-low pitch), or more luminously clear canons (in *Ave sanctissima Maria* and *Nesciens mater*). In the recordings of secular music, the passage of time is rather more obvious. But idiosyncratic though it may now appear, the choice of instruments always combines flair and verve. In the songs, tempos are rather more languorous than one is now used to, but Munrow's finest inspirations still strike very deep. The phrase 'essential listening' is often used (perhaps too often), but it surely applies to 'The Art of the Netherlands'. A word of warning: the contents of the three original LPs are not reproduced exactly. The entire instrumental portion, some 20 minutes of music, is cut. This is one of the most influential recordings of early music ever made.

Passion
Orlando Consort (Robert Harre Jones *counterten* Charles Daniels, Angus Smith *tens* Donald Greig, Robert Macdonald *basses*).
Metronome METCD1015 (62 minutes: DDD). Texts and translations included. Recorded 1996. Ⓕ
Tinctoris Lamentationes Jeremie. **Dufay** Victimae paschali laudes. Vexilla regis prodeunt.
Josquin Desprez Victimae paschali laudes. **Isaac** Easter Mass Proper. **Compère** Crux triumphans. **Obrecht** Salve crux.

This is an attractive programme of Holy Week and Easter pieces, some by unlikely composers such as Tinctoris, the fifteenth-century musical theorist. It is centred around Isaac's four-part *Easter Mass*, with its polytextual structure. Isaac sets all the pieces of the Proper, with the exception of the Offertory, and he interweaves three popular Easter tunes. The end product is a wonderfully joyful and festive Mass, the nearest modern equivalent that comes to mind being Honegger's Christmas cantata with its carol sequence. Isaac's Mass is flanked by Tinctoris's moving *Lamentation*, two settings of the *Victimae paschali laudes*, and three fine pieces honouring the Cross. The Orlando Consort do full justice to this splendid programme. Their reedy vocal quality has come to be accepted as that of the late medieval and early renaissance period. The singing is superb, the individual parts easily identifiable yet marvellously blended. Listeners may be slightly foxed by the pronunciation of the Latin, particularly by the nasal French vowels. Much care has gone into this search for authenticity.

Beauté Parfaite The Autumn of the Middle Ages.
Alla Francesca.
Opus 111 OPS30-173 (68 minutes: DDD). Texts and translations included. Recorded 1996. Ⓕ
Anonymous Pour vous servir. Or sus, mon cuer, vers ma dame t'encline. Tousjours servir je veuil. Tant qu'en mon cuer/Sur l'erbette. Or sus, vous dormes trop. Cheulz qui volent retourner. La belle et la gente rose. Quant la douce jouvencelle. Instrumental Piece.
Anthonello de Caserta Beauté parfaite. **Binchois** Adieu, jusques je vous revoye. Ay douloureux disant helas. **Dufay** J'ay mis mon cuer. Je vous pri/Ma tres douce amie/Tant que mon argent. **Fontaine** Pastourelle en un vergier. **Grenon** La plus belle. **Legrant** Entre vous, nouviaux mariés. **Libert** Se je me plains. **Paullet** J'aim. Qui?. **Raulin de Vaux** Savés pour quoy suy sy gay. **Solage** Fumeux fume par fumee. **Vaillant** Par maintes foys.

This is probably the most rounded and successfully varied anthology of late-fourteenth- and early-fifteenth-century songs available. There have been several fine recordings of secular music from this period – a relief to those who feel that this area has suffered relative neglect in comparison to sacred genres. This collection spans a range of styles – from Solage at his weirdest (the famous *Fumeux fume*, sung here at a very slow tempo that is surprisingly effective) to Binchois at his most melancholy (*Ay douloureux*) and Dufay in his sprightly, May Day mode – and includes a number of light pastoral or genre pieces, jocose or slightly scurrilous: *Pastourelle en un vergier* is an example of the ballade form at its liveliest and most direct. As a cross-section of expressive registers and attitudes, it is a very astute and intelligent piece of programming. Equally impressive is the variety of interpretative approaches, and the polish with which each is carried off. There is great discrimination in the use of instruments. The astonishing artistry of the flautist and recorder player, Pierre Hamon is notable (*Par maintes foys*), but the individual singers are also given greater chance to shine individually and (most importantly) the two agendas no longer compete with each other. This is the place to mention Brigitte Lesne, whose distinctive but perfectly controlled vibrato is a singing-lesson in itself; and the scarcely less individual timbre of Emmanuel Bonnardot, restrained yet intense. Both are heard in *Adieu, jusques je vous revoye*. Even as straightforward a piece as *Pastourelle en un vergier* is fastidiously shaped, yet without the least bit of fuss. This awareness of the importance of detail is evident in the treatment of the texts. In all cases, they are responded to imaginatively, with a clear understanding of the intention, and the structural integrity of the poetic form (both literary and musical) is respected. Thus, it is easier to engage with the music on the many levels present both between and within pieces. Yet nearly every piece is approached in a different way: no mean feat with 22 works on offer. The disc closes with the magical *Je vous pri*, on paper a slight enough piece, but here deeply intelligent and compellingly expressive – adjectives that apply to these interpretations as well.

Missa Alleluia Music at the Burgundian Court.
Capilla Flamenca.
Eufoda CDEUF1232 (60 minutes: DDD).   Ⓕ
Works include **La Rue** Missa Alleluia. **Obrecht** Salve regina. **Josquin Desprez** Huc me sydereo.

Here is classically full-throated, rich Flemish singing. The motets are hardly new to the catalogue, but these readings more than hold their own. Worth noting is the use of choirboys, notably in Obrecht's six-voice *Salve regina*, and Josquin's *Huc me sydereo*, here in its six-voice version. But the centrepiece here is unquestionably the Mass by Pierre de la Rue. The singing is mostly very stylish, with a sound image to wallow in. Strongly recommended.

The Voice in the Garden Spanish Songs and Motets, 1480-1550.
Gothic Voices / Christopher Page with **Christopher Wilson** *vihuela* **Andrew Lawrence-King** *hp*
Hyperion CDA66653 (52 minutes: DDD). Texts and translations included. Recorded 1993.   ⒻⓅⒺ
Encina Mi libertad en sosiego. Los sospiros no sosiegan. **Peñalosa** Por las sierras de Madrid. Ne reminiscaris, Domine. Precor te, Domine. Sancta Maria. **Mena** Yo creo que n'os dió Dios. La bella malmaridada. **Enrique** Mi querer tanto vos quiere. **Anonymous** Pase el agoa, ma Julieta. Harto de tanta porfía. Dindirín, dindirín. Ave, Virgo, gratia plena. Dentro en el vergel. Entra Mayo y sale Abril. Instrumental works – **Narváez** Fantasía II tono; Fantasía III tono. Paseávase el rey moro. **Fernández Palero** Paseávase el rey moro. **Milán** Fantasías 10, 12 and 18. **Segni** Tiento. **Anonymous** A la villa voy.

As usual with Gothic Voices, there is a mixture of all-vocal and solo-instrument performances, never the twain meeting and a mixture of what used to be called sacred and secular: motets by Peñalosa sit cheek by jowl with love songs and instrumental fantasies, giving an unusual and intriguing picture of the repertory. In general the record has all the qualities that make anything by Gothic Voices a required purchase for collections that aim at serious coverage of early centuries; and the resourceful selection of music makes it an important contribution to the understanding of Spanish culture. A note of special praise for Christopher Wilson's performances of the vihuela solos which have a control and eloquence that are truly impressive. Andrew Lawrence-King characteristically throws new light on some of this repertory with his immaculate range of colours and textures on the harp.

Canciones, Romances and Sonetos
La Columbina Ensemble (Mariá Cristina Kiehr *sop* Claudio Cavina *counterten* Josep Benet *ten* Josep Cabré *bass*).
Accent ACC95111D (56 minutes: DDD). Texts and translations included. Recorded 1995.   Ⓕ
Encina Triste España sin ventura! Antonilla es desposada. Tan buen ganadico. Mi libertad en sosiego. Pues que tú, Reina del cielo. Cucú, cucú, cucú. **Vásquez** A, hermosa, abrime cara de rosa. Con qué la lavaré. Torna, Mingo, a namorarte. Si no os uviera mirado. En la fuente del rosel. Soledad tengo de tí. Buscad buen amor. O dulce contemplación. De los álamos vengo. **Guerrero** Niño Dios, d'amor herido. Prado verde y florido. Huyd, huyd. Si tu penas no pruevo. Todo quanto pudo dar. **Romero** A quién contaré mis quejas. En Belén están mis amores. Como suele el blanco zisne. Soberana María. Las voces del fuego.

In this survey of Spanish song in the sixteenth- and seventeenth-centuries the pieces chosen admirably reflect the consistency of idiom and quality during the period. Distinctive to the repertory is the blend of popular and *culto* elements, in both text and music. Madrigalian elements gradually infiltrate the simple, homophonic idiom cultivated by Encina and are thoroughly mastered by Juan Vásquez, the genius of Spanish song of the first half of the sixteenth-century, and subsequently by Francisco Guerrero. All these developments are further consolidated by Romero, a near contemporary of Monteverdi, the two- and three-part songs selected here reflecting the sixteenth-century continuum that dominates the early Spanish baroque. Apart from some *stile concitato* effects in the battle-cry refrains to *En Belén están mis amores* and *Las voces del fuego*, these technically highly accomplished but effective pieces are still predominantly in the renaissance polyphonic idiom. None of the songs is more than about four minutes long, and most last around two, so that La Colombina's carefully chosen groupings of works by the same composer help to make a larger structure, and they very successfully juxtapose the more familiar (Guerrero's *Prado verde y florido* or Vásquez's *De los álamos vengo*) with the less well known while giving a good insight into the range of the repertory. Their interpretations are always expressive and sensitive to the imagery of the text, and the blend and accuracy of ensemble are exemplary. These are utterly convincing performances without any need whatsoever for the 'orchestrated' approach so familiar from, say, Hespèrion XX. Here the madrigalian writing so apparent within Spanish forms such as the *villancico*, *romance* and *soneto* finally comes into its own for about the first time on CD.

El Cançoner del Duc de Calabria
La Capella Reial de Catalunya / Jordi Savall.
Auvidis Astrée E8582 (68 minutes: DDD). Texts and translations included. Recorded 1995. Ⓕ Ⓔ
Almodar Ah, Pelayo que desmayo! **Morales** Si n'os hubiera mirado. **Carceres** Soleta so jo ací. **Flecha** Que farem del pobre Joan! Teresica hermana. **Anonymous** Ay luna que reluzes. Dizen a mi que los amores he. Gózate, Virgen sagrada. Si de vos mi bien. Un niño nos es nacido. Con qué la lavaré. Ojos garços ha la niña. Si la noche haze escura (attrib. F. Guerrero). Estas noches à tan largas. Vella, de vós som amorós (attrib. M. Flechaa). Yo me soy la morenica. Falai, meus olhos.

This is vintage Capella Reial. The singing and playing are superb (as always), and the repertory – melodious and dancey by turn – of the Cançoner del Duc de Calabria is right up its alley. Amazingly, this is the first commercial recording dedicated to this songbook from the Valencian court of the Duke of Calabria – surprising because of the accessibility and quality of the music. Several items from the book have become well known (notably the ubiquitous *Riu, riu, chiu*, which, thankfully, is not included here), but up till now it has been difficult to gain an appreciation of the collection as a whole. Published in Venice in 1556, it records an earlier repertory, dating from the first decade of the sixteenth-century through the 1530s and, possibly, 1540s. The Valencian court was one of the major cultural centres of the Iberian peninsula at this period, and the court culture was heavily influenced by the latest humanistic trends from Italy. In musical terms, the repertory of the *Cançoner* reflects this mix of imported and indigenous elements; most of the songs conform to the fixed-form *villancico* of the later fifteenth-century, but within the essential refrain-and-verse structure much of the writing reveals a more madrigalian idiom. Indeed, popular-style refrains are often succeeded by madrigalian verses, and Capella Reial reinforce this through the scoring adopted; popular songs and refrains attract full-blown 'orchestrations' (the tutti ensemble of viols, winds, plucked instruments and percussion so characteristic of the Capellaensemble), or at least varied combinations of instruments, while the more imitative sections blend voices, viols and harp or vihuela. The songs are well chosen and nicely varied in poetic content and interpretation; it is particularly good to have the relatively few Catalan items from the songbook, which when sung by Jordi Savall's excellent team of native singers, are lent a distinctly dark flavour – thanks to the covered vowel sounds of the language. This is an outstanding disc which brings to light another unjustly neglected corner of the repertory in performances that reveal Capella Reial at its very best.

Canciones y Ensaladas
Ensemble Clément Janequin / Dominique Visse *counterten*
Harmonia Mundi HMC90 1627 (58 minutes: DDD). Texts and translations included. Recorded 1997. Ⓕ Ⓟ Ⓔ
Brudieu En los mon pus sou dotada del set goigs. **Flecha** La bomba. La guerra. **Mudarra** Fantasias – primer tono; quarto tono; quinto tono. **Valderrábano** Contrapunto sobre el tenor del conde claros. **Vásquez** Ojos morenos. Que yo, mi madre, yo. Mi mal de causa es. Gentil senora mia. Cavallero, queraysme dexar. Agora que sé de amor. El que sin ti bivir, ya no querrìa. Lágrimas de mi consuelo.

It is a real pleasure to hear some more of Vásquez's excellent songs on disc: usually it is the *villancicos* in popular vein that are featured, but here we have some of the more serious, madrigalian pieces. Try *Lágrimas de mi consuelo*, one of his most extended settings in which he comes closest to the motet style of the period, and savour those mournful suspensions. Mostly the songs are considerably shorter, lasting only two or three minutes, but Vásquez is a masterful songster and perfectly encapsulates the mood of each text. Brudieu's strophic setting, in Catalan, of the Seven Joys of the Virgin calls for sustained singing, around which the instrumentalists here weave increasingly elaborate extemporized divisions. All the songs, and also the *ensaladas*, are performed with one voice to a part and slightly varying combinations of organ, viol and plucked strings (lute, vihuela, guitar). Each member of the Ensemble Clément Janequin is closely miked, but the overall blend is superb, and the rich, translucent sonority achieved is utterly compelling. What distinguishes this CD above all is the liveliness of the musical response to the words that are being sung: the pronunciation is not 100 per cent consistent, but every word is crystal-clear and the level of vocal energy and focus is always spot on, all of which is especially noticeable in the *ensaladas*. Here the interpretation is just right: theatrical and colourful, often funny, but never camp or ludicrously over the top, all this stemming from Visse's own instinctive and secure sense of the theatrical. Even if Flecha had not considered this plausible combination of voices and instruments when he composed the *ensaladas*, surely he would have appreciated these versions of *La bomba* and *La guerra* for their sensitivity to the texts and the real flair at the heart of the performance.

Al alva venid Spanish Secular Music of the Fifteenth- and Sixteenth-Centuries.
La Romanesca (Marta Almajano *sop* Paolo Pandolfo *va da gamba* Juan Carlos de Mulder *vihuela/gtr* Pedro Estevan *perc*) / **José Miguel Moreno** (*vihuela*).
Glossa GCD920203 (60 minutes: DDD). Texts and translations included. Recorded 1995. Ⓟ🄴
Anonymous Al alva venid. L'amor, dona, ch'io te porto. Rodrigo Martines. A los maitines era. Nina y vina. **Narváez** Paseavase el rey moro. Lós Seys libros del delphin – Diferencias de Guardame las vacas. **Encina** Más vale trocar. Si abrá en este baldrés! Qu'es de ti, desconsolado? Hoy comamos y bevamos. **D. Ortiz** Trattado de glosas – Recercarda segunda sobre el passamezzo moderno; Recercada tercera para viola de gamba sola; Recercada quarta sobre la folia; Recercada quinta sobre el passamezzo antiguo; Recercada settima sobre la Romanesca. **Pisador** Libro de música – En la fuente del rosel; La manana de Sant Juan.
Vásquez Orphenica lyra – De los álamos vengo; Con qué la lavaré; Glosa sobre Tan que vivray; De Antequera sale el moro. **Mudarra** Tres libros de musica – Si me llaman a mi; Ysabel, perdiste la tu faxa; Guárdame las vacas.

Many of these pieces – songs and vihuela music from sixteenth-century Spain – have been recorded at least once, if not dozens of times before, but this CD takes pride of place in this repertory. La Romanesca performs with true *fantasía* but without any of the mannerisms – the excesses and the understatements – of many of its predecessors and rivals: it seem to hit it just right. It has mostly selected songs with a strong popular flavour – precisely those songs that have attracted most attention because they are simply so attractive – but their realizations are restrained in terms of instrumental accompaniment (plucked strings, viol and a smattering of percussion), but full of musical vitality – in other words, the emphasis is, justly, on the music and not the 'orchestrated' arrangement of it. The players, led by José Miguel Moreno, are brilliant, and the singer, Marta Almajano shines in this repertory. She brings out perfectly the lyricism inherent in the popular-inspired court song tradition – take, for example, Vásquez's lovely *De los álamos vengo*: these songs demand an elusive blend of sophistication and simplicity. The instrumentalists make the most of the virtuoso element already making itself felt in the works of the vihuelists and Ortiz's *recercadas*. It's good to have a 'straight' version of Encina's *Más vale trocar*, which is often treated in an upbeat manner at odds with the text. The same applies to Vásquez's *Con qué la lavaré* although this is, arguably, just a touch too slow. Overall, and above all, it is purely a pleasurable experience to listen to this disc. Take it with you wherever you go, and especially to that desert island.

Spain and the New World
The Hilliard Ensemble (David James, Ashley Stafford *countertens* Rogers Covey-Crump, John Potter, Mark Padmore *tens* Gordon Jones *bar*).
Virgin Classics Veritas VED5 61394-2 (two discs: 126 minutes: DDD).
Texts and translations included. Recorded 1990-91. Ⓑ
Mondéjar Ave rex noster. **Peñalosa** Inter vestibulum et altare. Magnificat quarti toni.
Anonymous Tierra içelos se quexavan. Di, por que mueres en cruz. Dindirin, dindirin. Si la noche haze escura. **Rivafrecha** Vox dilecti mei. **Escobar** Clamabat autem mulier. Pásame por Dios barquero. Salve regina. **Alba** Stabat mater. **Encina** Triste España sin ventura!. Cucú, cucú, cucú. Hoy comamos y be bamos. Mas vale trocar. **Franco** In ilhuicac cihuapille (attrib.). Memento mei, Deus. Dios itlazo nantzine (attrib.). **Lienas** Salve regina. **Morales** Pater noster. Parce mihi, Domine. Magnificat a 6. **Lobo** O quam suavis est, Domine. **Guerrero** Ave Virgo sanctissima. **Padilla** Transfige, dulcissime Domine. **Luchas** A la caça, sus, a caça. **Urreda** Nunca fué pena ma yor. **Millán** O dulce y triste memoria. **Alonso** La tricotea.

Originally released in late-1991, this two-CD set was The Hilliard Ensemble's contribution to the Columbus commemorations of the following year. It was also their first recording after Paul Hillier's departure from the group. In keeping with the Columbus theme, the collection includes music composed both in the Old World and in the New. Unsurprisingly, the languages used are Latin for the sacred music and Spanish for the secular – but in addition there are two small pieces in Nahuatl, the tongue of the Aztecs. With well over two hours of music, there is time for The Hilliard to dwell on many composers and genres, most of whom have but a small representation on disc. Spanish polyphony has a marked tendency to asperity in its treatment of dissonance, and generally eschews the more complex forms of polyphony adopted by Franco-Flemish composers: that makes for sobriety in its sacred music, and directness in the secular. This is best heard in the music of Encina and Peñalosa in the early-sixteenth-century; the closest Spain comes to a home-grown exponent of the international style is Morales, one of whose splendid *Magnificat*s stands out as a high point in the collection. All in all it is clear that The Hilliard Ensemble is more at ease with sacred music than with secular pieces. Those in the latter category come across either as forced, or as insufficiently defined – humour is an elusive attribute. The collection as a whole, however, is a distinctive one, and offers a convincing picture of a country whose polyphonic tradition has often passed for a poor relation of the mainstream continental idiom.

The Old Hall Manuscript
The Hilliard Ensemble (David James, Ashley Stafford *countertens* Rogers Covey-Crump, John Potter, Mark Padmore *tens* Gordon Jones *bar* Paul Hillier *bass*).
Virgin Classics Veritas VER5 61393-2 (65 minutes: DDD). Texts and translations included. Recorded 1990. Ⓜ

The Old Hall Manuscript is the principal source for the school of composers from which Leonel Power and John Dunstable sprang (though many of the composers in this quintessentially English source have French-sounding names). The Hilliard's Old Hall recital is very even-handed in its representation both of composers and styles (though Power, as far and away the best-represented composer in the source, gets more than most). As the only disc of its kind it warrants a strong recommendation, even though the performances occasionally lack the dynamic quality so abundantly present on other Hilliard recordings. The acoustic may have something to do with it: here it is so reverberant that details are all too often drowned out, and in a few places there are displeasing flashes of 'countertenor glare' (e.g. the *Credo* by Pennard). In the more demanding selections one has the inexplicable impression that the ensemble has somehow failed to click, and there is occasionally a hint of strain (as in *Gloria* by Pycard). Yet, there are moments of great beauty: the three-voice, descant-based *Pia mater* comes to mind, or the two pieces by Forest, perhaps one of the younger composers in the manuscript. As an album to be dipped into, rather than taken at one sitting, this disc is eminently recommendable.

French Chansons
The Scholars of London.
Naxos 8 550880 (60 minutes: DDD). Texts and translations included. Recorded 1993. Ⓢ
Arcadelt En ce mois délicieux; Margot, labourez les vignes; De temps que j'estois amoureux; Sa grand beauté. **Bertrand** De nuit, le bien. **Clemens Non Papa** Prière devant le repas; Action des Graces. **Costeley** Arrête un peu mon coeur. **Gombert** Aime qui vouldra; Quand je suis aupres. **Janequin** Le chant des oiseaux. Or vien ça, vien, m'amye. **Josquin Desprez** Faulte d'argent. Mille regretz. **Lassus** Beau le cristal. Bon jour mon coeur. Un jeune moine. La nuict froide et sombre. Si je suis brun. **Le Jeune** Ce n'est que fiel. **Passereau** Il est bel et bon. **Sandrin** Je ne le croy. **Sermisy** Tant que vivray en eage florissant. Venez, regrets. La, la Maistre Pierre. **Tabourot** Belle qui tiens ma vie. **Vassal** Vray Dieu.

Listening to this carefully crafted selection, one is struck by the flexibility of a style that accommodates so many distinctive temperaments – the verve of Janequin, the suavity of Sermisy, the gravity of Gombert. It is a democratic genre in the truest sense, appealing to the great (Josquin and Lassus) while permitting lesser figures to shine as well. The term 'democratic' also describes the *chanson*'s appeal, then as now: here are some of the most beguiling tunes of any period. To call these performances unobtrusive is to do them no injustice. The Scholars of London capture the wistful elegance of the courtlier pieces – for example, Le Jeune's *Ce n'est que fiel*. In some of the more scurrilous songs (such as Josquin's *Faulte d'argent*) there is a Gallic rambunctiousness but at times the tempos are a shade too brisk for comfort, and the choice of pitch-standard in Janequin's famous *Chant des oiseaux* (sung here in its through-composed version) sets a strain on the singers' accustomed agility. But such details merely affect the odd piece. This is a disc that gives great pleasure: like ephemera trapped in amber, the music in this collection bears modest yet touching testimony to a period that produced much 'great' music. Its smaller creations are no less admirable.

Late Renaissance-Early Baroque

16th-17th centuries

All the King's Horses

I Fagiolini; Concordia / Mark Levy *viol*
Metronome METCD1013 (67 minutes: DDD). Texts and translations included.   Ⓕ
Anonymous Basses danses: Par fin despit; La volunté. **Bransle gay** Mari je songerois. Der Hundt. Saltarello el francosin. **Arcadelt** O felic'occhi miei. **Cara** Mentre io vo per questi boschi. **Certon** La, la, la, je ne l'ose dire. **Finck** In Gottes Namen faren wir. **Isaac** J'ay pris amours. **Janequin** Frère Thibault. Le chant des oyseaulx. **Othmayr** Der Winter kalt. Ich weiss mir ein Maidlein. **Patavino** Dillà da l'aqua. **Rore** Or che'l ciel e la terra. **Ruffo** La gamba. El travagliato. **Sandrin** Puisque vivre en servitude. La volunté. **Senfl** Ach Elslein. Sich hat ein' neue Sach' aufdraht. Ich weiss nit. Wiewohl viel Herter Orden sind. **Sermisy** Au pres de vous.

We travel here to France, Germany and Italy, and the results are most appealing: these spirited performances articulate both text and music in a clear and attractive manner. In the French repertory I Fagiolini successfully takes up the challenge of emulating the Ensemble Clément Janequin's masterful approach to text-projection, and its softer sound and slightly more relaxed approach (try *Frère Thibault*) will please those who find the French ensemble too rough. Even in such a well-known piece as *Le chant des oyseaulx* it finds new, delightful inflexions. The German selections are rather less well known (or at any rate less often recorded) than the French, but just as convincingly dispatched: the pieces by Senfl, Othmayr and Isaac are well worth discovering. Isaac's arrangement of *J'ay pris amours* (performed here by Concordia) reminds us just how much of a virtuoso contrapuntalist he was. The disc aims to represent the sheer diversity of early sixteenth-century secular music: diversity of mood and content, and of possible relations between voices and instruments. This anthological ambition is the set's most conspicuous success, and carries the disc forward even when individual items or details appear to miss the mark (the concluding madrigal by Rore is too slow, and more generally the Italian selection is the least satisfying of the three). The sound-recording, immediate and close, is well up to Metronome's usual standard, and the booklet is well laid-out and presented.

Live in Oxford

The Tallis Scholars / Peter Phillips.
Gimell 454 998-2PH (71 minutes: DDD). Texts and translations included. Recorded live in 1996. Ⓕ
Byrd Cantiones, quae ab argumento sacrae vocantur – Tribue, Domine. **Josquin Desprez** Absalon fili mi. Gaude Virgo, Mater Christi. **W. Mundy** Adolescentulus sum ego. Vox patris caelestis. **Obrecht** Salve regina. **Tallis** O sacrum convivium. **Taverner** Gaude plurimum.

Silver – The Best of The Tallis Scholars

The Tallis Scholars / Peter Phillips.
Gimell 454 990-2PM2 (two discs: 156 minutes: DDD). Recorded 1980-95.   Ⓜ
Allegri Miserere mei. **Victoria** Ave Maria, gratia plena. **Palestrina** Sicut lilium inter spinas I. **Josquin Desprez** Praeter rerum seriem. **Clemens Non Papa** Pater peccavi. Ego flos campi. **Isaac** Tota pulchra es. **Rore** Descendi in ortum meum. **Lassus** Salve regina mater. Alma redemptoris mater. Ave regina caelorum. **Brumel** Missa, 'Et ecce terrae motus' – Gloria. **Sheppard** Media vita. **Tallis** In manus tuas. O nata lux de lumine. Audivi vocem de caelo. **R. White** Exaudiat te Dominus. **Cornysh** Ah, Robin. Salve regina. **Byrd** Mass for Five Voices.

These recordings mark 25 years from the first concert that Peter Phillips directed, including three singers who are still associated with The Tallis Scholars. Their first record came out in 1976 so there may be more celebrations in 2001. But there is already much to celebrate. They have surely contributed more than any other group to making renaissance choral music with mixed voices a commercial reality. Phillips writes: 'All the music sung here benefits from clarity, both in the singing and the surrounding building'; and that ideal has perhaps been the main factor in their astonishing success. Other factors are the consistently flawless balance and the extraordinary musical flexibility of their best singers. There are listeners who have become tired of what can seem their perfection-above-all-else approach. So this is perhaps a moment to remember that we are exceptionally lucky to have The Tallis Scholars, as well as the other ensembles that have arisen from their lead. There are other ways of doing the music, but enormous quantities of renaissance polyphony have been recorded in the last quarter century by English groups in performances of a stunningly high musical quality. It is highly likely that future listeners will look back on this as a golden age, largely fuelled by The Tallis Scholars.

Both anthologies cover the most significant of their repertory, English and mainland-continental from about 1480 to the end of the sixteenth-century. The 'Live in Oxford' disc suffers from a few tentative entries (though no audience noise, which is slightly puzzling: what is meant by 'live'?), but is consistently exciting, from the glorious opening six-voice *Salve regina* of Obrecht to the wonderful 18-minute *Vox patris caelestis* of William Mundy. The two-disc retrospective opens with its famous 1980 recording of the Allegri *Miserere* and includes many favourites from its output, among them the *Gloria* from their beautifully clear and muscular reading of the Brumel *Et ecce terrae motus* Mass and the whole of their 1984 recording of Byrd's five-voice Mass. Plenty to celebrate then; and plenty to look forward to in the future.

Exultate Deo Masterpieces of Sacred Polyphony.
[a]**Alexander Semprini**, [a]**Francis Faux**, [a]**Raymond Winterflood** *trebs* [a]**Adrian Peacock** *bass*
Westminster Cathedral Choir / James O'Donnell with [b]**Joseph Cullen** *org*
Hyperion CDA66850 (72 minutes: DDD). Texts and translations included. Recorded 1995. Ⓕ
Palestrina Exsultate Deo. Sicut cervus desi-derat. **Byrd** Ave verum corpus. Civitas sancti tui.
Haec dies. **Parsons** Ave Maria. **Viadana** Exultate justi[b]. **Tallis** Salvator mundi, salva nos I.
O nata lux de lumine. In manus tuas. **Philips** Ascendit Deus. Ave verum corpus Christi.
Allegri Miserere mei[a]. **G. Gabrieli** Jubilate Deo I[b]. **Lotti** Crucifixus[b]. **Tye** Omnes gentes,
plaudite. **Victoria** O quam gloriosum. **Monteverdi** Cantate Domino[b].

This anthology lives up to its billing: even those with only a nodding acquaintance with renaissance polyphony will probably have heard a fair proportion of these pieces. Most of them are mainstays, not just of the Catholic liturgical repertory, but of most major Anglican choral establishments. The selection of pieces here is wide-ranging and varied. More importantly, where pieces are especially famous, the standard of performance gives the competition a fair run for its money. There *is* the thrill in Allegri's *Miserere* of a boy treble (here, Alexander Semprini) hitting that high C – and no quibbles about the phrasing of the adjoining notes, either. The choir as a whole sound very well focused, and the unanimity of the trebles is admirable (though at times a slightly more veiled tone might have better suited the text). Where required, it sounds very bright and forward (at the end of Tye's *Omnes gentes*, for example), despite a recording that could have been a bit withdrawn with a more timid choir.

Utopia Triumphans
Huelgas Ensemble / Paul van Nevel.
Sony Classical Vivarte SK66261 (53 minutes: DDD). Texts and translations included.
Recorded 1994. Ⓕ
Tallis Spem in alium. **Porta** Missa Ducalis – Sanctus; Agnus Dei. **Josquin Desprez** (attrib.)
Qui habitat in adjutorio Altissimi. **Ockeghem** (attrib.) Deo gratias. **Manchicourt** Laudate
Dominum. **G. Gabrieli** Symphoniae sacrae – Exaudi me Domine. **Striggio** Ecce beatam lucem.

Paul van Nevel describes this disc as a gallery of the renaissance's utopian visions, the musical counterparts of the seemingly miraculous discoveries and inventions that marked the period. Certainly these pieces stake out new realms of musical space, culminating in the two rival compositions for 40 voices by Striggio and Tallis. The most unexpected discovery here is the Mass by Costanzo Porta for a maximum of 14 voices. Porta (d.1601) was one of the last composers outside the Iberian peninsula to write in the purest Palestrinian idiom. The style is familiar enough, but the sheer opulence of the sound cannot fail to impress: one would like to have had more of it. By contrast, the 36-voice *Deo gratias* and the 24-voice *Qui habitat* (attributed to Ockeghem and Josquin respectively) are far less convincing. Both attributions have been called into question: the *Deo gratias* has no more than 18 voices sounding at any given time – could a composer of Ockeghem's reach have contented himself with such a sleight of hand? It seems unlikely. On a more positive note, the inclusion of Gabrieli's 16-voice motet brings a welcome hint of mannerism to this otherwise classical programme, and brings out the best in van Nevel's characteristic quirkiness. The Huelgas Ensemble are no strangers to such polyphonic behemoths. Their usual trademarks are in evidence here – a very Flemish depth and throatiness of timbre, captured in a warm acoustic – and if one disregards the odd fluffs, the balance between overall effect and attention to detail is finely judged. Even in the Tallis, where there is fierce competition, the Huelgas more than holds its own. One may prefer The Tallis Scholars for its more balanced casting, but this *Spem* presents the familiar work in the unfamiliar context of a distinctly un-English sound.

A Venetian Coronation, 1595
Gabrieli [a]**Consort and Players / Paul McCreesh.**
Virgin Classics Veritas VC7 59006-2 (71 minutes: DDD). Texts and translations included.
Gramophone Award Winner 1990. ⒻⓅ
G. Gabrieli Intonazioni – ottavo tono; terzo e quarto toni; quinto tono alla quarta bassa
(**James O'Donnell** *org*). Canzonas – XIII a 12; XVI a 15; IX a 10. Sonata VI a 8 pian e forte.
Deus qui beatum Marcum a 10[a]. Omnes gentes a 16[a]. **A. Gabrieli** Intonazioni – primo tono
(**O'Donnell**); settimo tono (**Timothy Roberts** *org*). Mass Movements[a] – Kyrie a 5-12;

Gloria a 16; Sanctus a 12; Benedictus a 12. O sacrum convivium a 5ª. Benedictus Dominus Deus sabbaoth (arr. Roberts) (**O'Donnell, Roberts** *orgs*). **Bendinelli** Sonata CCC-XXXIII. Sarasinetta. **M. Thomsen** Toccata I.

The coronation of a new Doge of Venice was always a special occasion, and never more so than when Marino Grimani (1532-1605) was elected to that office. We do not know what music was played then, but the whole ceremony is notionally and credibly reconstructed in this recording by Paul McCreesh and his cohorts. The recording was made in Brinkburn Priory, a church whose acoustic (aided by some deft manipulation of the recording controls) is spacious enough to evoke that of the Basilica of St Mark, the site of the original event. Space *per se* is vital to the music of the Gabrielis, who excelled in using it by placing instrumental and vocal groups in different parts of the building – which thereby became an integral part of the music. A fine selection of music that *could* have been played then is enhanced by the opening tolling of a bell, a *crescendo* marking the leisurely approach of the ducal procession, and the impression of architectural space created by changing stereo focus. It would be difficult to speak too highly of the performances, supplemented by first-class annotation, in this memorable recording. A trip to Venice would cost a lot more than this disc but, though you could visit the real St Mark's, it would not buy you this superb musical experience.

The Feast of San Rocco, Venice, 1608
ªLa Capella Ducale; Cologne Musica Fiata / **Roland Wilson** with **Christoph Lehmann** *org*
Sony Classical S2K66254 (two discs: 126 minutes: DDD). Texts and translations included.
Recorded 1994.
G. Gabrieli Toccata. Symphoniae sacrae, liber secundus – Benedictus es, Dominusª; Cantate Dominoª; In ecclesiisª; Jubilate Deoª; Misericordia tua Domine. Canzoni et Sonate – Canzon V, a 7; Canzon X, a 8; Canzon XVII, a 12; Sonata XIX, a 15; Sonata per tre violini. Dulcis Jesu patris imagoª. Sacrae symphoniae – Canzon primi toni, a 10; Canzon in echo duodecimi toni, a 12. Buccinate in neomenia tuba a 19. Timor et tremorª. Toccata primi toni. Magnificatª. **Grandi** Motets, Book 2 – Cantemus Dominoª; Heu mihiª. O quam tu pulchra esª. Motets with sinfonie – Salvum me fac, Deusª. **Monteverdi** Salve, O Reginaª. **Cima** Concerti ecclesiastici – Sonata per il violino, cornetto e violone; Sonata per il violino e violone. **Barbarino** Motets, Book 1, 'Il Primo libro de motetti' – O sacrum conviviumª. **Castaldi** Capricci a 2 stromenti – Capriccio detto svegliatoioª.

Wilson's starting-point is the famous description of the festivities that took place on the patronal feast-day in the Scuola di San Rocco, the most luxurious of the six Venetian *scuole grandi*, written by the English eccentric and traveller Thomas Coryate. Frustratingly, although Coryate provides a well-observed and detailed account of the various instrumental and vocal groupings used, the names of neither performers nor composers are revealed. To this extent 'The Feast of San Rocco' is something of a fiction; nevertheless, it is an intelligent one, a thoughtful and well-researched attempt to put flesh and blood on the bare bones of Coryate's anecdote. Three main repertories are drawn upon: Gabrieli's large-scale motets; canzonas and other purely instrumental works also mostly by him; and smaller-scale solo motets mostly by Alessandro Grandi. The latter are especially welcome. Evidence of Monteverdi's influence is everywhere in his music, but that doesn't detract from its freshness and charm. There are darker moments, too, as in the extraordinary four-voice dialogue *Heu mihi*, an essay in the affective, chromatic manner.

More typical of Grandi's work is the exquisite *O quam tu pulchra es*, an atmospherically erotic text from the Song of Songs, delivered here with urgent rhetorical force by David Cordier and underpinned by the lightest of continuo accompaniments. And one of the most virtuosic of all Grandi's motets, *Salvum me fac, Deus*, with its range of more than two octaves, is expertly negotiated by Harry van der Kamp in an engaged yet controlled performance. As regards the interpretation of the larger-scale festive pieces, Wilson has adopted the Praetorius approach to the thorny problem of instrumentation and voice distribution. Just occasionally the solo voices are overwhelmed by the instrumental forces, in the sense that vocal strain is evident and the words disappear; both *Buccinate in neomenia tuba* and *Dulcis Jesu patris imago* suffer from such moments. But at its best, as with *In ecclesiis*, this recording is as compelling as any comparative version on offer.

Lo Sposalizio The Wedding of Venice to the Sea.
The King's Consort Choir; The King's Consort / Robert King.
Hyperion CDA67048 (two discs: 89 minutes: DDD). Texts and translations included.
Anonymous Fanfares – Rotta; Imperiale prima; Imperiale seconda. Sursum corda. Variazoni sopra 'La Ciaccona'. **A. Gabrieli** Vieni, vieni Himeneo. Cantiam de Dio. **Canzona** La Battaglia. Intonationi – Primo tono; Settimo tono. Gloria a 16. **G. Gabrieli** Lieto godea sedendo.

Udite, chiari et generosi figli. Kyrie a 12. Sanctus a 12. Sonata XX. **Guami** Canzona XXIV.
Gussago Canzon XIX, 'La Leona'. **Kapsberger** Kapsberger. **Massaino** Canzon per otto
tromboni. **Monteverdi** Christe, adoramus te. **Piccinini** Variazoni sopra 'La Folia'. **Viadana**
Canzona, 'La Veneziana'.

This mouth-watering celebration of Venice is devised with considerable expertise in ritual,
contextual aspects and the imaginative allocation of music to, in this particular instance, the
processions and journey across the lagoon and the subsequent solemn Mass held in San Nicolò.
Robert King explains in the note, with his inimitable enthusiasm and clarity, how, from the
eleventh-century, mariners congregated annually to ask for St Nicholas's protection. The festival
became, over the centuries, an important social event in the calendar as the symbolic 'fertility rite':
the marriage between Venice and her blessed Adriatic, prayerfully celebrated on Ascension Day. The
central act was when the Doge would toss a gold ring into the sea from his resplendently ornate
galley (rowed by 400 hapless slaves). He would them move amongst the flotilla, with glorious music
wafting over the calm ripples of the lagoon, his progress punctuated by various stop-offs for
blessings and further ceremonial. The musical journey across to the Lido is principally a secular
exercise and we are treated to some delectable madrigals by both Gabrielis. Although some listeners
may find the ensemble a touch undernourished in the first madrigal, *Vieni, vieni Himeneo*, it soon
transpires that sweetness and balance are the essential ingredients for King; the result in the
exquisite instrumental numbers is a sensitivity to matching timbre which is an unusual delight both
in the Guami *Canzona XXIV a 8* and the imploring counterpoint that acts as a foil to the fencing in
Andrea Gabrieli's *Battaglia*. Indeed, what shines through with great dignity is the sense of an
unfolding procession with a seemingly effortless choreography, the musical highlight of which is
Giovanni Gabrieli's eight-part madrigal *Lieto godea sedendo*, set here with two falsettists and
strings, portraying 'the disturbance of spring' in all its poignant and fleeting glory. The intimate and
affectionate duetting of James Bowman and Robin Blaze, so beautifully rendered here, is something
of a landmark as the inimitable mentor shares the reins with the pick of the younger generation of
countertenors.

The depth of quality and the control within individual voices of the vocal consort is a match for
anyone in the effervescent and magisterial 16-part Gabrieli piece *Udite, chiari et generosi*, though the
acoustic of St Jude's, Hampstead – and the pragmatic recording techniques required for such an
undertaking – demand that tutti work is clearly defined and that a strong interpretative angle is
projected. This is where the Gabrieli Mass movements for San Nicolò, which constitute the second
disc, are far more successfully realized than in *Cantiam de Dio*: this is the only multi-voiced work
where the performance appears prosaic compared with the poised elegance that informs the vocal
and instrumental dialogue of the *Kyrie* and *Sanctus a 12*. This is a small gripe in an otherwise
exceptional recorded event. Running through the veins of nearly all the pieces are the ingredients of
commitment, immediacy and spontaneous musicianship which allow one to view this ravishing
music on its own terms, rather than losing sight of it – as can happen too easily – with endless
speculative reconstruction for its own sake. The documentation is outstanding. A very fine
achievement all round.

Venetian Vespers
Gabrieli Consort and Players / Paul McCreesh with [a]Timothy Roberts *org*
Archiv Produktion 437 552-2AH2 (two discs: 96 minutes: DDD). Texts and translations included.
Recorded 1990. *Gramophone* Award Winner 1993 ⓟⓅ
Sacristy bell. **Gabrieli** (ed. Roberts) Intonazione[a]. Versicle and response: Deus in adiutorium;
Domine ad adiuvandum. **Rigatti** Dixit Dominus. **Grandi** O intemerata. Antiphon: Beata es Maria.
Monteverdi Laudate pueri. **Banchieri** Suonata prima[a]. Antiphon: Beatam me dicent.
Monteverdi Laetatus sum. **Finetti** O Maria, quae rapis corda hominum. Antiphon: Haec est
quae nescavit. **Rigatti** Nisi Dominus. **Banchieri** Dialogo secondo[a]. Antiphon: Ante thronum.
Cavalli Lauda Jerusalem. **Grandi** O quam tu pulchra es. **Anonymous** Praeambulum[a]. Chapter:
Ecce virgo. **Monteverdi** Deus qui mundum crimine iacentem. Versicle and response. Ave maria;
Dominus tecum. Antiphon. Spiritus Sanctus. **Rigatti** Magnificat. **Marini** Sonata con tre violini in
eco. Collect: Dominus vobiscum – Deus, qui de beatae Mariae. Dismissal: Dominus vobiscum –
Benedicamus Domino. **Monteverdi** Laudate Dominum. **Fasolo** (ed. Roberts) Intonazione –
excerpts[a]. **Rigatti** Salve regina.

Paul McCreesh's sense of adventure made quite an impact with his reconstruction of Doge
Grimani's Coronation in 1595. This follow-up recording takes as its starting point a Vespers service
'as it might have been celebrated in St Mark's, Venice 1643', and it is no less striking a speculation.
McCreesh is wisely not attempting to re-create a historical event but to provide a rejuvenating
context for some more wonderful Venetian church music. There can be little doubt that listening to
psalm settings within a liturgical framework illuminates the theatricality and significance of the
works in a unique way, barely possible in an ordinary format where one work simply follows

another. Yet the quality of the music is what really counts and this is where McCreesh deserves the greatest praise. He has skilfully blended a range of diverse concerted works with equally innovative and expressive solo motets, each one offset by ornate organ interludes and home-spun plainchant. Monteverdi is well represented, as one would expect, but by introducing resident composers (who were regularly employed by the great basilica) a strong Venetian sensibility prevails in all these works despite the many contrasting styles of the new baroque age. The little-known Rigatti is arguably the sensation of this release with his highly dramatic and richly extravagant sonorities. The settings of *Dixit Dominus* and *Magnificat* are almost operatic at times though they maintain the spatial elements inspired by St Mark's. The Gabrieli Consort and Players is a group with an extraordinary homogeneity of sound and focused energy: Monteverdi's *Laetatus sum* is one of the many examples where it reaches new heights in early seventeenth-century performance. The solo performances are deliciously executed too, particularly those involving the falsettists. This two-disc set is an achievement of the highest order.

The Triumph of Maximilian – Songs and Instrumental Music from Sixteenth-Century Germany
Musica Antiqua of London / Philip Thorby with John Potter *ten*
Signum Records SIGCD004 (69 minutes: DDD). Recorded 1993.   Ⓕ
Anonymous Elslein. **Aich** Ein frolyk wesen. Elslein à 3. Der Hundt. **Barbireau** Ein frolyk wesen.
Busnois Fortuna disperata. **Dietrich** Elslein à 3. **Finck** Ich stünd an einem Morgen.
Ghiselin Ein frolyk wesen. **Isaac** Fortuna disperata. Der Hundt. Ich stünd an einem Morgen.
Josquin Desprez Fortuna à 3. Missa pange lingua – Pleni sunt coeli (Quis seperabit).
Othmayr Entlaubet ist der Walde. **Rhau** Elslein à 2. Ich stünd an einem Morgen. **Senfl** Es taget vor dem Walde. Es taget à 4. Es taget: Elslein à 4. Exemplum. Es taget. Entlaubet ist der Walde à 4. Entlaubet ist der Walde. Ich stünd an einem Morgen à 3. Ich stünd an einem Morgen à 5. Ich stünd an einem Morgen à 4. Ich stünd an einem Morgen ... Es taget ... Kein Adler. Paciencia muss ich han. Quattour. Will niemand singen. **Senfl/Gerle** Elslein à 4. **Stolzer** Entlaubet ist der Waldea.

Ludwig Senfl has not yet received the recognition that he deserves; and as this issue demonstrates, he is one of the most fascinating composers of the early sixteenth-century. He combines an astonishing contrapuntal skill with a range of moods and formal control that make his German song settings among the finest of their century. One reason why he is little heard is that the music is hard to sing: for most of it you need a tenor with an extreme lightness of touch. But in John Potter they seem to have the perfect singer, perhaps the best ever heard in this repertory. He floats the lines with effortless grace and with an uncannily sensitive projection of the texts. Just listen to his control in the longest and most serious song on the disc, Senfl's *Paciencia muss ich han*. But he is also superbly supported by the viols and recorders of Musica Antiqua of London. Its playing, too, is apparently effortless. Some listeners may feel that the recorders are occasionally allowed to run too fast, giving less than full measure to the real substance of the music; but the playing is undeniably wonderful, and superbly recorded. For the viol playing, no praise is too high: they do everything with a pleasingly light touch and always with a real sensitivity to the music. There is another reason why we hear less Senfl than we should: that his best work needs to be understood within the broader context of the German *Tenorlied* repertory. To cope with this, the disc puts Senfl alongside settings of the same material by other composers of the time. This works nicely enough here, but it would have been so good to be able to hear more of Senfl's own work, given the quality of these performances.

Sacred Choral Works
aVienna Hofburgkapelle Schola;
bConcerto Palatino; Gradus ad Parnassum / Konrad Junghänel.
Deutsche Harmonia Mundi 05472 77326-2 (74 minutes: DDD). Texts and translations included.
Recorded 1994.   ⒻⓅ
Biber Missa allelujaab. **Schmelzer** Vesperae sollennesab. Sonata per Chiesa et Camera. Sacro-Profanus Concentus Musicus – Sonata XII. **Palestrina** Coelestis urbs Jerusalem. **Froberger** Fantasia II in A minor. **Anonymous** Gregorian Chant for the Dedication of a Church – Mass Propersa. Gregorian Chant for Vespersa.

What this record achieves above all else is to confirm the suspicion that Austrian choral music of the seventeenth-century is not confined to a couple of Requiem settings by Biber and a few other works of little or no musical interest. The spatial and textural intricacy of Biber's 36-part setting of the Mass is a wonder in itself and the product of a composer who 'worked' the galleries of Salzburg Cathedral to his advantage. A degree of this multi-antiphonal style is Venetian in flavour but only superficially; the quicker harmonic rhythm and sophisticated groupings, as well as other colourful central European quirks, reveal a composer whose manipulation of singers and instrumentalists has more to offer than abstract sonic resplendence; Biber is admirably sensitive to the text he is setting. The performances are equally sensitive. Junghänel never allows his singers or players to overblow as can be the temptation with polychoral repertoire. Obtaining the right balance between wafting, majestic sonorities and clearly defined solo contributions takes direction of a high order and one is left in no doubt that Biber's detailed but solemn score is being taken with the utmost seriousness. There are a few moments where articulation is under-explored and the strings can sound a little too diffident. Schmelzer's *Vespers* are finely constructed, too, with an imaginative range of scorings which Junghänel and his musicians execute with tenderness and great nobility throughout. A fine and illuminating release.

Music from Renaissance Portugal
Cambridge Taverner Choir / Owen Rees.
Herald HAVPCD155 (69 minutes: DDD). Texts and translations included. Recorded 1992. Ⓕ **E**
P. de Cristo Magnificat. Ave Maria. Sanctissimi quinque mar tires. De profundis. Lachrimans sitivit anima mea. Ave Regina caelorum. **D. Lôbo** Missa pro defunctis. **Anonymous** Si pie Domine. **A. Fernandez** Libera me Domine. Alma redemptoris mater. **Carreira** Stabat mater.

This is one of those rare examples of scholarship and musicianship combining to result in performances that are both impressive and immediately attractive to the listener in excellent music, totally neglected until now. There is a wonderful glow about this recording that reflects the skilful engineering on the part of Herald as well as the imagination of the sonority on Rees's part. The striking feature of his approach is the emphasis on the meaning of the words. This choir sings of the Day of Judgement or the rejoicing due to the Virgin as if it really means it: Rees is not afraid to shape phrases, to use dynamics, to vary the intensity of the sound in the service of the words which, though even more familiar to the monks and chapel singers who originally performed these pieces at the monastery of Santa Cruz in Colmbra, would have had an immediacy and a reality for them that it is hard to recapture today. How graphic those texts, in fact, are, and how well this choir brings them to life.

Alla Venetiana
Paul O'Dette *lte*
Harmonia Mundi HMU90 7215 (73 minutes: DDD). Recorded 1997. Ⓕ
Anonymous Laudate Dio. **Capirola** Spagna seconda. Non ti spiaqua l'ascoltar. Padoana belissima. Ricercar I, II, V and XIII. Tientalora. La Villanella. **Cara** O mia cieca de dura sorte. **Dalza** Calata ala Spagnola. Pavana alla ferrarese. Pavana alla venetiana. Piva I-III. Recercar. Recercar dietro. Saltarello. **Ghizeghem** De tous bien playne (arr. O'Dette). De tu biens plaene (arr. Capirola). **Josquin Desprez** Adieu mes amours. Et in terra pax. Qui tolis pechata mondi. **Martini** Malor mi bat. **Pesenti** Che farala, che dirala. **Spinacino** Recercare I and II.

When lutenists began to use the fingers of their right hands to pluck the strings, the instrument made a quantum leap forward. Three- and four-part counterpoint was suddenly on the agenda and the expanded range of the repertory made the lute popular even in Italian court circles. O'Dette focuses on two of the earliest printed books of tablature by Spinacino (1507), Dalza (1508), and the handwritten book of music by Capirola (*c*1520). Whoever it was who wrote the last of these, his student 'Vidal' or Capriola himself, touchingly showed his human fallibility; in a book written with much tender loving care and lavishly adorned with paintings, he had to insert the missing 'a' in 'Pado(a)na' with a caret! The selected items cover the basic genres of *tastar de corde, recercare*, dances and intabulations of vocal music by non-lutenist composers. In the last of these a lutenist demonstrated his skill in adapting and embellishing the original, as O'Dette does in his own intabulation of van Ghizegem's *De tous bien playne*. What comes through clearly is the joyous freshness of this music and the quickly acquired ingenuity in bringing more complex counterpoint to the fingerboard, as though the right-hand fingers had uncorked a bottle and released an inspirational genie. O'Dette has many talents and an unusual ability to bring this music to life is one of them; another is shown in his superb annotation. It is a disc to lift the spirits and the recording is appropriately first-class.

Italian Harpsichord Works, 1550-1700
Rinaldo Alessandrini *hpd*
Opus 111 OPS30-118 (77 minutes: DDD). Recorded 1994. Ⓕ **P**
A. Valente Tenore del passo e mezzo. **Facoli** Pass'e mezzo moderno.
Giovanni de Maque Due Gagliarde. Seconde Stravaganze. **A. Mayone** Partite sopra 'Fidele'.
Trabaci Partite sopra 'Rugiero'. **Picchi** Balli – Ballo ongaro; Ballo alla polacha; Ballo ditto il Picchi. **Buono** Sonata quinta. **Frescobaldi** Toccata. **Lambardi** Gagliarda. Partite sopra 'Fidele'.
Merula Capriccio cromatico. Toccata del secondo tono. **M. Rossi** Toccata settima.

Salvatore Toccata prima. Canzon Francese terza. Due Correnti. **B. Storace** Toccata e Canzon.
B. Strozzi Corrente terza. **Stradella** Toccata. **A. Scarlatti** Toccata per il cembalo.

Rinaldo Alessandrini has made a special study of sixteenth- and seventeenth-century Italian music, and here presents (with the co-operation of the West German Radio) two dozen pieces that illustrate changes of style there between 1576 (the year of Antonio Valente's pioneering harpsichord collection) and around 1700, and, to some extent, differences between the more austere northern school and the more extrovert southern one. It may perhaps not be generally realized that the keyboard virtuosity demanded by our own brilliant John Bull is matched by his Italian contemporaries: Alessandrini's rhythmically vital, stylish and engaged performances leave us in no doubt of that. He gives us a well-chosen range of forms. There are variations on the *passamezzo* ground, in the minor mode and in the major variant ('moderno') – both examples here of considerable elaboration: and there are other variations (*partite*) on the harmonic bass variously known as 'Ruggiero' or 'Fedele'. Dance forms are represented by two examples of the *gagliarda* (both chordal in treatment), two of the *corrente* (that by Salvatore full of chromaticisms), and 'exotic' dances from Poland and Hungary. Of particular interest in several items is their composers' fascination with chromaticism (which produces some curious intonation in the unidentified tuning system of the 1678 Italian harpsichord used here): a *stravaganza* by de Macque (who was Flemish by birth but spent his life in Naples, where he taught Mayone and Trabaci) contains several bold surprises; a Merula *capriccio*, a contrapuntal Salvatore *canzona*, a Buono 'sonata' and a Rossi *toccata* with a truly astonishing ending likewise feature chromaticism. The seven in this programme – mostly rhapsodic and improvisatory-sounding – include a splendid example by Frescobaldi and a sombrely declamatory one by Merula; but the eventual falling-off of this keyboard style is signalled by Stradella' toccata, which is too reliant on formulas.

Romanesca Italian Harpsichord Works.
Sophie Yates *hpd*
Chandos Chaconne CHAN0601 (64 minutes: DDD). Recorded 1996.   Ⓕ Ⓟ
Picchi Toccata. Intavolatura di Balli d'Arpicordo – Ballo ongaro; Ballo alla polacha; Todesca;
Ballo ditto il Picchi. **Macque** Seconde stravaganze. **Frescobaldi** Partite – XIV, sopra l'aria della
Romanesca; VI, sopra l'aria di Follia; Cento Partite, sopra Passacagli. Toccata in A minor.
Rossi Toccata settima. **Gesualdo** Canzon francese del Principe. **Valente** Tenore del passo
e mezzo con sei mutanze. **Merulo** Susanne un jour.

Fleetness of finger, on which these early Italians set much store, is a requisite for performing this repertoire; and in this Sophie Yates is eminently accomplished. Another requisite is to convey a sense that the music is being improvised on the spur of the moment. This is especially so in toccatas but it also applies to some extent in the outwardly stricter form of *partite* or variations, the commonest structural basis for keyboard music of the time. Yates provides a firm framework for Frescobaldi's variations on the *Follia* ground bass, but while neatly pointing its rhythmic quirks allows herself greater freedom in the set on the *Romanesca*; and she clearly relishes the harmonic twists in the variations on *Passacagli*. Valente's variations on the *Passamezzo antico* are different in kind, more overtly dance-like and lively, with a strongly marked rhythmic accompaniment. There are two *canzone* – keyboard versions of songs – here: a highly elaborate working by Merulo of Lasso's famous *Susanne un jour,* and an extraordinary piece by Gesualdo which contains some weird and wonderful chromatic trills. The most developed of the toccatas here is that by Frescobaldi, which inserts a formal contrapuntal section into its otherwise free style. Not the least of the pleasures on this disc is Yates's vigorous playing of four tuneful dances by Frescobaldi's contemporary, Picchi, of whom little more is known other than that he was an organist in Venice: how this dazzling Toccata of his found its way into the Fitzwilliam Virginal Book is a minor mystery.

Consonanze stravaganti Neapolitan music for organ, harpsichord and chromatic harpsichord.
Christopher Stembridge *hpd/org*
Ars Musici AM1207-2 (68 minutes: DDD).   Ⓕ Ⓟ

This magnificent recital charts a relatively unexplored corner of Italian music, played on rare and beautiful Italian instruments (including exotic plucked keyboards with 'split' chromatic keys). The opening *Capriccio* by Giovanni de Macque is alone worth the price of admission. Christopher Stembridge draws more than other interpreters from this weird and wonderful repertory.

English Folksongs and Lute Songs
Andreas Scholl *counterten* **Andreas Martin** *lte*
Harmonia Mundi HMC90 1603 (69 minutes: DDD). Texts included. Recorded 1996.   Ⓕ Ⓔ
Dowland The First Booke of Songs or Ayres – Can she excuse my wrongs?; All ye, whom love
or fortune. The Second Booke of Songs or Ayres – I saw my Lady weepe; Flow my teares fall from

your springs; Sorrow sorrow stay, lend true repentant tears. The Third and Last Booke of Songs or Ayres – Behold a wonder heere; Me, me and none but me; Say, loue, if euer thou did'st find. The Lady Russell's pavan. Go from my window. **Campion** I care not for these ladies. My love hath vow'd. My sweetest Lesbia. **Traditional** The three ravens. O waly, waly. I will give my love an apple. Barbara Allen. Lord Rendall. **Anonymous** King Henry. Kemp's jig. Go from my window.

'Interval' is not a word that has ever been inserted into a song recital on CD, but it would be quite a good idea if it were. In this instance the stopping-point hardly needs to be marked, as it is so natural and obvious; and that is one of the many attractions of this well-designed programme. A group of songs by Dowland, followed by a piece for lute, makes a substantial first section; then come two folk-songs, another couple by 'Anon.' and a lively, well-contrasted selection of songs by Campion. The second half starts with more Dowland, a satisfyingly representative sequence constituting the heart of the programme, with more folk-songs to conclude. The mixture is a charming one and delightfully well ordered. The performances are equally pleasing. Perhaps it is inevitable that an English listener should still think of Alfred Deller in this repertoire, but here the name comes to mind also because of a distinct similarity of timbre. At the resonant centre of Andreas Scholl's voice is a passage of lower middle notes (perhaps D to G) where the vibrancy is strong and rich in a way very comparable to Deller's. Stylistically, on the other hand, Scholl has developed an art that is quite independent of his great original: his manner is more forthright, less responsive to the spiritual intensity of *Sorrow sorrow stay*, though still capable of introducing that 'poisoned' intonation which Deller and his successors would bring to *All ye, whom love or fortune hath betrayed*. As regards balance, the lute is placed as the accompanying instrument rather than as one of an equal, intimate partnership; still, all is clear, and the lute solos are played with fine technical skill and sensitive feeling for the essential rhythmic flexibility.

Earth, Water, Air and Fire A new look at John Dowland and friends.
The Consort of Musicke (Evelyn Tubb *sop* Lucy Ballard *contr* Andrew King *ten*
Simon Grant *bass*) / **Anthony Rooley** *lte*
ASV Gaudeamus CDGAU187 (71 minutes: DDD). Texts included. Recorded 1998. Ⓕ
Dowland The First Book of Songs or Ayres – Sleepe wayward thoughts; Would my conceit; Come againe, sweet loue doth now enuite. The Second Booke of Songs or Ayres – Sorrow sorrow stay; Wofull heart with griefe opressed; Toss not my soule. A Pilgrimes Solace – Goe nightly cares the enemy to rest; From silent night; Thou mighty God. In darknesse let mee dwell. Shall I strive. **Locke** Psyche – Break, distracted heart. **Morley** Canzonets, or Little Short Songs to Three Voyces – Deep lamenting, grief betraying. The First Booke of Canzonets to Two Voyces – Leave now, mine eyes lamenting. **Sermisy** Las, je m'y plains. **Tomkins** O let me live for true love. **Weelkes** Madrigals to Three, Four, Five and Six Voyces – Cease sorrowes now.

This is a fascinating recording, not least because one may very well be inclined to take against it from the start or even before. Its eye-catching title is not helpful: either too superficially or too profoundly relevant, and if the latter then requiring a more convincing justification than is given in Anthony Rooley's short and barely adequate introductory note. And then the first sounds of the first track: Dowland's *Come againe* has its first phrase sung in a low octave in a two-part arrangement (by whom?) till the other voices enter. They slow down and speed up, ending with a further *accelerando* ('by sighs and tears more hot than are thy shafts') and a defiant isolation of the last word ('while she for triumph – laughs!'). There is always something irritating about performances which draw attention to themselves *as* performances, and a lot of that may be found in this recital. The isolated 'laughs' makes its point (the monstrosity of it, the comic indignity, that after all this palaver – 'I sit, I weep, I faint, I die' – what does she do? 'Laughs'!). Then into more serious matters, as in *Would my conceit*; and this carefully studied text, so deliberately punctuated and insistently inflected, does yield rewards, while in Tomkins's *O let me live* the play of languishingly poignant harmonies against the light movement of the 'fa la's goes well beyond what one might have thought of as merely the conventions of madrigal. In *Shall I strive*, there is a thoughtful, and actual, working-through of a dilemma. In the final item, *Thou mighty God*, a first reaction, noting the difference in timing (7'44" to this group's previous recording's 3'50", on L'Oiseau-Lyre), may well be to think 'Well, they've surely overdone it this time'. But just you listen.

The dark is my delight
Brian Asawa *counterten* David Tayler *lte*
RCA Red Seal 09026 68818-2 (74 minutes: DDD). Texts included. Recorded 1997. Ⓕ
Anonymous This merry pleasant spring. There were three ravens. The dark is my delight. Willow Song. Miserere my Maker. Where the bee sucks. O death, rock me asleep. **Campion** How hath Flora robb'd her bower. Ayres – Come let us sound with melodie the praises; Turne backe you wanton flier. Author of light, revive my dying spright. Oft have I sigh'd for him that heares me not. **Dowland** The First Book of Songs or Ayres – Can she excuse my wrongs with vertues cloake;

Now, O now I needs must part; Go, Cristall teares; Come againe, sweet loue doth now enuite; His goulden locks time hath to siluer turnd; Awaie with these selfe louing lads. The Second Booke of Songs or Ayres – Flow my teares fall from your springs; Sorrow sorrow stay, lend true repentant teares; A Sheperd in a shade his plaining made. The Third and Last Book of Songs or Aires – Time stands still; It was a time when silly Bees could speake.

The singing here is most distinctive at a clear, forthright *forte*, most pleasing at a gentle *piano*. The impression is of a bright voice, unusually high-toned, quite unlike (say) Deller and Bowman. The programme is most welcome. Campion's melodic grace after Dowland's more complex utterance earns its place, and both find a happy follow-up in the mixed anonymous group. Asawa's mellower tones give pleasure in *Time stands still* and *Go, Cristall teares*. He measures up to many of the challenges in *Sorrow sorrow stay* and is sensitive to the modulations in Campion's *Oft have I sigh'd*. In the first of the 'popular' songs, *This merry pleasant Spring*, he introduces an admirable trill. David Tayler accompanies tastefully. It is regrettable that the recording is marred by little bumps and bulges and that the voice and lute have an unequal share in the balance.

Alfred Deller Songs and Airs – Anonymous, Bedyngham, Campion, Ciconia, Dowland, R. Joynson, Morley, Purcell, Rosseter and J. Wilson.
Alfred Deller *counterten* with various artists.
EMI Références mono CDH5 65501-2 (77 minutes: ADD). Recorded 1949-54. ⓂⒽ

All but two of the pieces here are by English composers of the late sixteenth- and seventeenth-centuries; the odd ones out are Johannes Ciconia's *O rosa bella* and John Bedyngham's setting of the same text, which belong to the fourteenth- and fifteenth-centuries, respectively. Curiously, some of these recordings reveal Deller on rather less than top form. Dowland's *Slow my tears*, for instance, is marred by a persistent huskiness while certain others display a marked expressive restraint. But, almost needless to say, there is also plenty of vintage Deller here, in which category Morley's Shakespeare settings, *It was a lover and a lass* and *O Mistress mine*, certainly belong. Comparably affecting are Robert Johnson's *Full fathom five* and the celebrated anonymous setting of Desdemona's *Sing, willow, willow, willow*. Most touching of all, though, is the anonymous *Caleno custure me!* from *Henry V*, which Deller sings with exquisite sensibility. That and the popular *Greensleeves* would be quite sufficient on their own to make you go at once in search of this disc. Sadly, the Purcell songs seem rather dated, not so much for Deller's singing of them as for the archaic sound of the harpsichord, the tuning, and the playing of them, sometimes technically insecure and often with quaintly realized continuo lines. Notwithstanding these reservations, the anthology is a precious one, with moments of real magic. The transfers to CD have been remastered skilfully with virtually no background noise at all.

Elizabethan Consort Music
Hespèrion XX / Jordi Savall *va da gamba*
Alia Vox AV9804 (66 minutes: DDD). Recorded 1997. ⒻⒺ
Anonymous In Nomine a 5. Desperada. Gallyard I-III. Allemande. Ronda. La represa I and II. Allemana d'amor. Dance I and II. Pavana I and II. Brandeberges. **Alberti** Pavin of Albarti. Gallyard. **Daman** Di sei soprani. **W. Mundy** O mater mundi. **Parsons** In Nomines a 7 – IV; V. The Songe called Trumpetts. **Strogers** In Nomines – III a 5; IV a 6. **Taverner** Quemadmodum. **R. White** In Nomine V. **Woodcock** Browning my dere. In Nomines a 5 – II; III.

It is unusual to commit the contents of a rare manuscript collection to CD. This is what Jordi Savall and Hespèrion XX have done in this recording of Elizabethan consort music. The manuscript, from the 1570s and 1580s, containing dances, transcriptions of chansons and motets and fantasies, was intended for performance at court by the Queen's musicians, we are reliably informed by Peter Holman; it now resides in the British Library. These performances are highly sonorous and imaginatively realized. Savall orchestrates the repeats of the dances and chansons, usually beginning with a drum, a solo treble viol or lute and then building up the layers of sound with each restatement. Here, more than in any of their previous recordings, the tambour and tambourines are used to great effect, not merely to mark the beat, but, as in the anonymous Allemande in track 7 or the *Brandeberges*, to presage the mood of the piece. The manuscript contains a fascinating array of pieces: numerous *In Nomines* which climax in the astonishingly rich seven-part settings by Robert Parsons contrast with transcriptions of bawdy chansons, the evergreen *Browning my dere*, an ethereal fantasy by William Daman for six treble viols (surely a collectors' item), William Mundy's eponymous *O mater mundi* (intended as a pun?) and the sublimity of John Taverner's *Quemadmodum*. And, as listeners will discover, there is more. This is music fit for a courtly Sunday Elizabethan banquet, with a bit of dancing thrown in, should you wish to entertain in that style. For some tastes, the slower pieces may be performed rather too seamlessly and the balance between solo instrument – such as the lute in the first and second tracks or the treble viol in track 21 – and the rest of the ensemble does not always seem natural. The recording does offer a wonderful glimpse of the variety of music enjoyed at the court of Elizabeth I; it is a one-off and should be treasured as such.

A High-Priz'd Noise Violin Music for Charles I.
Parley of Instruments Renaissance Violin Band / Peter Holman.
Hyperion CDA66806 (67 minutes: DDD). Recorded 1995. Ⓕ🅿
R. Johnson II The Prince's Alman and Coranto. Air in G minor. The Temporiser a 4. The Witty Wanton. Fantasia in G minor. **A. Ferrabosco II** Pavan and Alman. **Webster** Four Consort pieces. **Nau** Suite in F major. Ballet in F major. Pavan and Galliard in D minor. **Notari** Variations on the 'Ruggiero'. **W. Lawes** Alman in D major 'for the Violins of Two Trebles'. Airs for consort.

This recording is less concerned with musical monuments, such as Lawes's large consorts, than in rejuvenating a repertoire which might have accompanied the King's recreation, or been the actual means for it. Most of the works are written in dance forms, though we can be reasonably certain that the majority would not have been conceived for accompanying dance. The violin's specific association with active dance music – except of a more base and popular kind – goes only so far, as the seventeenth-century progresses. Of the courtly violin bands it is the more expansive one in the Presence Chamber (performing for public rather than private space at court) which has the most instantly appealing repertory – the opening set of works by Robert Johnson and the wonderful *Pavan and Alman* by Alphonso Ferrabosco II; the latter composition, although timeless in its exquisite part-writing, is given new life with a period violin band. Both pieces gleam with an engaging transparency, a compelling sound for those who have yet to hear this ensemble. The *Pavan* is magically forthcoming in its gracious lines with just a hint of melancholy, a poignant fragility which gives way to the noble rapture of the *Alman*. The Parley's 14-strong group of four violins, six violas and four bass violins is marshalled with a degree of characterization that gleefully extricates this music from dusty library shelves. A high-priz'd noise indeed, with further insights into our rich instrumental heritage, performed here with fragrance and deep affection.

The Masque of Oberon reconstructed by Peter Holman and Peter Downley.
Musicians of the Globe / Philip Pickett.
Philips 446 217-2PH (50 minutes: DDD). Texts and translations included. Recorded 1994. Ⓕ
Music by Augustine and Jerome Bassano, Ferrabosco II, Holborne, Holman, Johnson, Lübeck, Nelham and Thomsen.

Shakespeare's Musick
Musicians of the Globe / Philip Pickett.
Philips 446 687-2PH (68 minutes: DDD). Texts included. Recorded 1995. Ⓕ
Music by Byrd, Dowland, Farnaby, Johnson, Jones, Morley and Wilson.

That the 'house musicians' to the Globe Theatre should be such an eminent band of specialists in sixteenth- and seventeenth-century performance is tantalizing in itself to theatre-goers. Of still greater musical significance are the projects which Philip Pickett, Artistic Director of the Musicians of the Globe, has put together for an exciting series of recordings for Philips. 'The Masque of Oberon' is an ominous début, judging by its spirited instrumental playing and fragrant vocal contributions; this is a skilfully concocted 'reconstruction' by Peter Holman. The occasion celebrated here is New Year's Day, 1611, where Ben Jonson's *Masque of Prince Henries* was performed at the Banqueting House. The Prince Henry in question is, of course, James I's eldest son whose young life ended only a year later. This Masque is anything but prescient of approaching sadness, rather an excuse for an uplifting and eclectic celebration of dance. Although we know that Alphonso Ferrabosco II and Robert Johnson – both court musicians – wrote music for *Oberon*, most of the music has had to be patiently stitched together from contemporary sources. A curmudgeon would point out that there is no evidence that the majority of songs and dances were heard on this particular occasion.

Such a view, however, limits the imaginative process of reaching beyond the fragmentary nature of masque sources and rediscovering something of the distinctive features of a celebrated indigenous genre. Through fine performances (Paul Agnew, amongst the soloists, stands out) and a thoroughly satisfying choice of instrumental music for the revels, Pickett and Holman have contributed something especially valuable to English recorded music. The Musicians of the Globe's second programme, 'Shakespeare's Musick', is equally adventurous. Few original song settings survive though it is hard to imagine that a good proportion of dance music in 'neutral' sources would not have had theatrical connections. This is a sensitively devised programme with artistic merit well beyond its contextual *modus operandi*, and one which alerts us to the elusive and multi-faceted role of music in and around contemporary Shakespearean theatre.

Celestiall Witchcraft The Private Music of Henry and Charles, Princes of Wales.
Fretwork with **Mark Padmore** *ten* **Paul Nicholson** *org* **Nigel North** *lte* **William Carter** *theorbo*
Virgin Classics Veritas VC5 45346-2 (72 minutes: DDD). Texts included. Recorded 1998. Ⓕ Ⓔ
Coprario Chi può miravi. When pale famine. Fortune and Glory. **Gibbons** Fantasias a 3 'for the
great double bass' – No. 2; No. 3. Fantasias a 6 – No. 5; No. 6. **A. Ferrabosco II** So beauty on
the waters stood. Pavan. In Nomine a 6. So breake off this last lamenting kisse. **W. Lawes**
Consort Sett a 5 in A minor. Pavin and Almain. Fantazia and Serabrand. **Mico** Parte Seconda.
Monteverdi Madrigals, Book 3 – O come è gran martire (arr. Lawes). Là tra'l sangue (arr. Mico).

The title of this recording comes, appropriately, from Thomas Campion's *Elegie upon the untimely
death of Prince Henry*: 'his carriage was full of celestiall witchcraft, winning all to admiration and
love personall.' Henry's musical taste was equally so and listeners to this CD are implicitly asked to
consider whether, had he lived to become king instead of Charles, the course of English musical
history (not to say non-musical history) might have been quite different. Coprario's two airs – one
mourning the death of Henry, the other comforting Charles – must have provided the initial
inspiration for the CD. Happily, Henry's music tutor, Alfonso Ferrabosco II, figures prominently
here: two airs from his 1609 collection, sublimely sung and accompanied on the lute; a wistful
pavan in three parts, delicately played with cadences that end with a whisper; and an *In Nomine*
'through all parts' of great subtlety. Thomas Lupo's polished six-part fantasia that opens the
recording – offering a further example of the sort of music Henry is known to have enjoyed –
Fretwork's performance doesn't disappoint: it captures the rhetoric of the beginning, bringing
crystal clarity to the syncopations of the middle section while articulating the musical architecture.
William Lawes is the composer most closely associated with the young Charles I and his music is
represented on this disc by a fantasia, three dances (a mournful Pavin followed by a wittily played
Almain and a danceable Saraband), an affecting transcription he made of a Monteverdi madrigal,
and one of the Royal Consorts in the richer, six-part version calling for two theorbos. The two
Gibbons *Fantasias for the great double bass* allow William Hunt to shine on his wonderfully
resonant larger viol. Fretwork produces polished, sophisticated performances complemented by
those of Padmore and North, offering delightfully bewitching entertainment fit for a king.

Johnny, Cock thy Beaver

[a]**John Potter** *sngr* [b]**Richard Campbell** *viol/bandora/gtr* [c]**David Miller** *lte/theorbo/gtr/cittern*
The Dufay Collective.
Chandos New Direction CHAN9446 (74 minutes: DDD). Texts and translations included.
Recorded 1995. Ⓕ
Playford The English Dancing Master: Part 1 – Halfe Hannikin; Goddesses. Part 2 – Aye me;
Saturday night and Sunday morn; Pauls Wharfe. Appendix – The Indian Queen; On the cold
ground; Of noble race was Shinkin; A Morisco; Jamaica; The Waits; Ham House; Pell Mell;
Kettledrum; Johnny, Cock thy Beaver. **Dowland** Settings of Ballads and Other Popular Tunes –
My Lord Willoughby's Welcome Home, P66a[c]. **T. Simpson** Ricercar, 'Bonny Sweet Robin'[bc].
Divisions[bc]. **Farnaby** Mal Sims. Muscadin. A Maske. The Old Spagnioletta. **T. Ravenscroft**
There were three ravens[abc]. New oysters. Jolly Shepherd[a]. A wooing song of a Yeoman of Kents
Sonne[ab]. Come follow me[a]. Of all the birds that I ever see[a]. **Anonymous** Daphne[ac]. Fortune my
foe[bc]. Bonny Sweet Robin. Jamaica[abc]. The Clothiers Song[abc].

This kaleidoscopic programme gives an overview of popular music in Jacobean and Carolean
England. It defines two levels of popularity – with the upper-middle classes and with the common
people. The former centres mainly on the material of domestic music-making, the modest songs
they would have sung, and the instrumental solo or consort music with which, in the absence of
radio or television, the household might have entertained themselves (and maybe guests) in their
leisure time. Amateurs and professionals may have rubbed shoulders in the more virtuoso consort
music. The latter, the common people's music, embraces 'dance tunes and ballads sold and learnt on
the street or in the tavern'. To the efforts of the unschooled man in the street were added those of
municipal waits and itinerant players. The album's title, that of the last song, refers to the cap-
raising of buskers when approaching potential 'clients'. The Dufay Collective have assembled a rich
and varied collection of 25 items, played and sung with patent enthusiasm and considerable skill;
the bowed-string sound sometimes has rough edges and a few notes are not quite centred, which,
even if not regarded as a touch of 'authenticity', does not diminish the pleasure given by this
splendid disc. The variety of the music and of the sounds made possible by the battery of instruments
used, prevents the ear from settling into any kind of rut. This disc, then, is a gust of refreshing air.

His Majesty's Harper
Andrew Lawrence-King *hp*
Deutsche Harmonia Mundi 05472 77504-2 (65 minutes: DDD). Recorded 1998. Ⓕ

Anonymous Scott's Lament. **Byrd** Alman in G major. La coranto. Fantasia. A gigg. Praeludium to Ye Fancie Fantasia. Rowland (arr. Dowland). **Dowland** Awake, sweet loue, thou art return'd. Can she excuse. A fancy. Farwell. Fine knacks for Ladies. Frogg galliard. Go Cristall teares. Mrs Winter's Jump. My dear Adieu, my sweet love farewell. My Lady Hunsdons Puffe. My thoughts are wingd with hopes. Pavana lacrima. Robin. Semper Dowland Semper Dolens. Suzanna Galliard. Tarleton's Jigge. Tarletones Riserrectione. **le Flelle** The Queens Maske. **Macdermott** Allmane. Cormacke. Mr Cormake Allman. Schoc.a.torum Cormacke.

Andrew Lawrence-King's resourceful plundering of the harpsichord and lute books in search of an elusive early harp repertoire takes him here to music from seventeenth-century England. With some of the best instrumental music of the time on offer, much of it displaying that irresistible folk-like charm and melancholy peculiar to English melody, he cannot go far wrong. Here, making delightful appearances, are Dowland's *Pavana lacrima* and *Semper Dowland Semper Dolens*, some of his shorter catchy dance-songs, and more dances and contrapuntal pieces by Byrd. All transfer to the harp superbly in Lawrence-King's hands, which once again manage to find in his instrument the subtleties of the lute together with the power and agility of the harpsichord. More importantly, it is hard to imagine this music being played with a greater or more honest expressiveness. Most of the pieces here are played on a gut-string Italian triple harp – gentle and mellow of tone but powerful and macho when it needs to be – but there are also some intriguing contributions from the brass-strung Irish *cláirseach*, which Lawrence-King uses in the anonymous *Scott's Lament* and four pieces by Cormack Macdermott, harpist at the court of James I. It is an instrument which, if you have not come across it before, is almost certain to confound your expectations with its rippling, metallic, almost oriental sound. This is a thoroughly enjoyable disc, the kind which touches you with its sound alone; the music seems as if it could have been intended for the harp all along, a simple effectiveness which makes it all the more strange that so little real harp music from this time survives.

La Folia, 1490-1701
Jordi Savall *va da gamba/viol* **Rolf Lislevand** *gtr/theorbo/vilhuela* **Michael Behringer** *org/hpd*
Arianna Savall *triple hp* **Bruno Cocset** *vc* **Pedro Estevan** *perc*
Adela Gonzalez-Campa *castanets*
Alia Vox AV9805 (55 minutes: DDD). Recorded 1998.   Ⓕ
Anonymous Folia: Rodrigo Martínez. **Cabezón** Folia: Para quien crié cabellos.
Corelli Violin Sonata in D minor, Op. 5 No. 12, 'La folia'. **Enzina** Folia: Hoy comamos y bebamos. **Marais** Deuxième Livre de Pièces de viole – Couplets de folies.
Martín y Coll Diferencias sobre las folias. **Ortiz** Ricercadas sobre la Folia – IV; VIII.

This release on Jordi Savall's own Alia Vox label charts two centuries of musical madness in the shape of the *folia* (which can mean anything from 'wild amusement' to 'insanity'). The earliest references to the *folia* are to a Portuguese dance of popular origin that by the end of the fifteenth-century had become still more popular in court circles. Its distinctively minimalist harmonic patterns, but on only four different chords, make it a perfect vehicle for instrumental jam sessions in the renaissance and it is this improvisatory tradition that is explored by Savall and his team. Virtuosity is a *sine qua non* in the *folia* business and Savall, of course, is an established virtuoso. Allied to this, is his ability to make the music seem as spontaneous and full of fantasy as the improvisatory practice from which the endless chameleon-like variations by Corelli and Marais sprang. These works are well known to all *aficionados* of baroque music; less familiar is the set of *diferencias* by the Spanish composer Antonio Martín y Coll, although he is almost equally inventive. Here Savall chooses to emphasize the Iberian origin of the *folia*, with an accompaniment of triple harp, baroque guitar and castanets which he describes as being 'in keeping with the characteristic Iberian sound of the period.' Such a sound world may well have more to do with late twentieth-century preconceptions than historical fact and the castanets seem lost and uncertain in these elaborate, sophisticated variations. Savall's re-creations of the early *folia* (the group of pieces by Enzina, Cabezón and Ortiz) are much freer still; indeed, his version of *Rodrigo Martínez*, a dance-song from the *Cancionero Musical de Palacio*, is almost outrageously exuberant in its percussionization. Still, Savall's attempt to trace an important improvisatory tradition is fascinating and it is a tribute to his musical imagination that the ear never tires of those four chords in almost an hour's music. Some listeners may, however, find his improvised humming along as he plays more intrusive than endearingly eccentric, so be warned!

Grand Tour Music from Sixteenth- and Seventeenth-Century Italy, Spain and Germany.
His Majestys Sagbutts and Cornetts (Jeremy West *cornett* David Staff *cornett/tpt*
Susan Addison, Peter Bassano, Paul Nieman, Stephen Saunders *sackbuts*
Timothy Roberts *org/hpd*
Hyperion CDA66847 (69 minutes: DDD). Recorded 1993-95.   Ⓕ

Buonamente Sonata a 6. Canzona a 6. **Marini** Sinfonia grave: La Zorzi. Sonata a quattro. Sonata a 6. **Merula** Chiacona. **Macque** Seconde Stravaganze. **Bassano** Vestiva i colli. **Castello** Sonate concertate in still moderno – Sonata duodecima. **Peñalosa** O Domina sanctissima. **Correa de Arauxo** Tiento de segundo tono. **Ximénez** (arr. Roberts) Batalla de octavo tono. **Anonymous** (arr. Roberts) Canciones de clarines. **Weckmann** Toccata III. **Schein** Padoana in D minor. **Vierdanck** Sonata, 'Als ich einmal Lust bekam'. Sonata a 4. **Scheidt** Canzona super Cantionem Gallicam. Galliard battaglia a 5.

HMSC reads like an arcane government department but over the years this distinguished group has become deservedly recognized by its acronym for being consistently approachable. This skilfully constructed 'tour' of European consort activity in the sixteenth- and seventeenth-centuries is a case in point: whilst 14 largely unknown composers, performed on primitive instruments, can appear a mite unpromising for all but the *cognoscenti*, one only has to experience the variety of timbre, articulation and expressive nuance to realize that HMSC is, first and foremost, a group of fine and imaginative chamber musicians. As Italy, the first port of call, reveals, in the right hands these instruments can resonate nobly with palpably rich textures in sonatas by the likes of Buonamente, tickle and tease in the modern monodic world of Marini, and dart about with easy and virtuosic precision in Bassano's sophisticated *Vestiva i colli*. Here and elsewhere the cornettists Jeremy West and David Staff exhibit a lucid and collected understanding of what makes good musical sense. Such a lead is deftly followed by the sackbuts – Susan Addison's in particular – whose lyrical side is heard to great effect in the Castello (the recorded sound differs from neighbouring numbers, a consequence, no doubt, of sessions spread out over two years). It is the easy dialogue of the ensemble, elasticity of phrasing and the capacity to shape the lines with colour and interest which repeatedly captivates; the Spanish selection contains an anonymous *Canciones* where Staff's natural trumpet gives an added spice to proceedings. The only misgiving is that the perspective of the ensemble is often a touch too sweet and refined in an idiom which would have needed a more rasping and redoubtable demeanour to be heard outside – where a good deal of this music would have been performed. Much of the success of HMSC is down to Timothy Roberts's sensitive arrangements, both preconceived and spontaneously at the keyboard; his realizations are always a joy, not to mention his solos which break up a well-paced programme.

A Solo
Paolo Pandolfo *viol/va da gamba*
Glossa GCD920403 (77 minutes: DDD). Recorded 1997.   ⓇⒺ
Anonymous Aria della Monicha (arr. Pandolfo). **Abel** Arpeggiata. Adagio. Allegro.
Bach Solo Cello Suite No. 4 in E flat major BWV1010. **Corkine** The Punckes delight. Come live with me. **Hume** Captaine Humes Musicall Humors – A Pavane. **Machy** Prélude. **Marais** Pièces de viole – Les voix humaines; Le badinage. **Ortiz** Trattado de glosas – Pass'emezzo antico; Pass'emezzo moderno. **Pandolfo** A Solo. **Sainte-Colombe le fils** Aire en rondeau. **Sumarte** Daphne. Whoope doe me no harm.

Seventy-seven minutes of music for unaccompanied viola da gamba? Well yes, and every second of it is a pleasure in the company of one of the most brilliant and, on this evidence, poetic of the instrument's current exponents. Using three different instruments (unfortunately, we are not told which ones in which pieces) Paolo Pandolfo takes us on a well-planned journey through gamba-playing Europe, starting with Italy and proceeding through early seventeenth-century England, mid-baroque France, eighteenth-century Germany and the brink of the classical style, and finally back to Italy for a composition of his own. Throughout, not a single accompanying instrument is heard, a feat Pandolfo makes light of by the simple expedient of dispensing with continuo parts where they exist (for instance in the Marais) and by exploiting to the full the gamba's ability to play chords. Surely few listeners will be prepared, however, for the variety of rich sonorities and colourings to be encountered in this recital, or for Pandolfo's expressive versatility; the Italian pieces are virtuosic and vigorous (Pandolfo's own variations on the song tune, *La Monicha* being especially eloquent), the French ones refined and deeply personal, and the bold transcription of Bach's Fourth Solo Cello Suite, though it loses out in cleanness to cello performances, full of strength and energy. Most striking of all, however, is the English group: the soldier-musician, Tobias Hume has never sounded so touching as in the spread pizzicatos which open his Pavan, while Richard Sumarte's *Daphne* has a hauntingly wistful folk quality which comes as an almost eerie surprise. Pandolfo has put a lot of himself into this recording, not least in his own piece, which carries a touching personal dedication. The result is a beautiful and moving recital.

Sit Fast, Volume 1.
Michael Chance *counterten* **Paul Agnew** *ten* **Fretwork** (Wendy Gillespie, Richard Campbell, Williams Hunt, Julia Hodgson, Susanna Pell, Richard Boothby *viols*).
Virgin Classics VC5 45217-2 (76 minutes: DDD). Texts included. Recorded 1996.   ⓇⓅ

B. Guy Buzz. **Isaac** O decus ecclesiae. **Ruders** Second Set of Changes. **Tan Dun** A Sinking Love. **Tye** Sit fast. **Bainbridge** Henry's Mobile. **Beamish** in dreaming. **A. Ferrabosco I** Hexachord fantasy. **Sculthorpe** Djilile. **Ockeghem** Ut heremita solus. **Bryars** In nomine. **Costello** Put away forbidden playthings.

Early Music
Kronos Quartet (David Harrington, John Sherba *vns* Hank Dutt *va* Joan Jeanrenaud *vc*); [a]Marja Mutru *harmonium* [b]David Lamb *bagpipes* [c]Wu Man *dzhong ruan/da ruan* [d]Olov Johansson *nyckelharpa* [e]Judith Sherman *drum* [f]Huun-Huur Tu (Kaigal-ool Khovalyg *vocs/igil* Anatoly Kuular *vocs/byzaanchi* Kongar-ool Ondar *vocs/toschpuluur*). Nonesuch 7559-79457-2 (69 minutes: DDD). Recorded 1993-97. Ⓕ Ⓔ
Machaut Kyries I-III[a] (arr. Kronos). **Tye** Rachell's weepinge. Farewell my good one forever. **D. Lamb** Långdans efter Byfåns Mats[b]. **Dowland** Lachrimae Antiquae[c]. **Pärt** Psalom. **Partch** Two Studies on Ancient Greek Scales (arr. Johnson). **Body** Long-Ge. **Cage** Totem Ancestor (arr. Salzman). Quodlibet. **Kassia** Using the apostate tyrant as his tool (arr. Touliatos). **Hardin** Synchrony No. 2[e]. **Pérotin** Viderunt omnes (arr. Kronos). **Purcell** Fantasia in B flat major, Z736. **Hildegard of Bingen** O virtus sapientae (arr. Pfau). **Schnittke** Collected songs where every verse is filled with grief (arr. Kronos). **Traditional** Brudmarsch frå Osta[d] (arr. Marin). Uleg-Khem[f] (arr. Mackey). *Bells*: Tolling of the knell (St Peter's of Solesmes).

Guy and Ruders are united with six others in Fretwork's programme, which alternates the old with the new and introduces, along the way, such moreish miniatures as Peter Sculthorpe's hypnotic *Djilile* (Whistling-duck on a bilabong) – which swaps Purcellian cadences for an Aboriginal prompting – and Sally Beamish's highly imaginative *in dreaming*, based on words from Act 3 of Shakespeare's *The Tempest*. Gavin Bryars conjures the expected homogeneity for his 9'25" *In nomine* (after Purcell's six-part composition of the same name and the longest piece on the disc); Tan Dun breathes fire into the words of T'ang Dynasty poet, Li Po; Simon Bainbridge hints at (though never reveals) a fragment of one of Purcell's *fantazias* and Elvis Costello has countertenor Michael Chance sing us out with a text that 'laments the interrupted access to the musical possibilities of the music of Purcell's time'. Clever stuff, all of it; quietly compelling too, even occasionally abrasive. 'Sit Fast' approximates a garlanded bridge across the centuries; it is superbly engineered and surely strong enough to sustain repeated journeys.

While Fretwork take Henry Purcell as their starting point, Kronos's 'Early Music' is subtitled *Lachrimae Antiquae* (after John Dowland) and is scarcely less absorbing. The Kronos Quartet adapt their playing style to suit whichever period is to hand – or at least that appears to be the general rule. Pérotin's multi-paragraph *Viderunt omnes* is delivered without vibrato and with the kind of phrasal emphases that any conscientious early music vocal group might employ, but Hildegard of Bingen's *O virtus sapientae* – which is an even earlier piece than the Pérotin – shimmers to expressive vibrato and great warmth of tone. The chordal clashes in Guillaume de Machaut (which serve throughout the disc as a sort of ritornello) emerge out of Cage, converge with Swedish folk music or transport us to one of Purcell's greatest *fantazias* (No. 2), while Christopher Tye prefaces Schnittke's searingly intense *Collected songs where every verse is filled with grief* and Schnittke himself fades to silence and the eventual *Tolling of the knell* The sequence is its own story, and the story itself will vary according to each listener's individual sensibilities or imagination. Both discs balance profundity and daring with a touch of flippancy, always with style and interpretative finesse but never merely for the sake of novelty.

The Passion of Reason
Sour Cream (Frans Brüggen, Walter van Hauwe *fls* Kees Boeke *fls/va da gamba*) with Isabel Alvarez *voc* Toyohiko Satoh *lte*
Glossa GCD921102 (two discs: 115 minutes: DDD). All arrangements by Sour Cream. Recorded 1994. Ⓜ
Anonymous Three Kyries. **Bach** Goldberg Variations, BWV988 – Four Canons. Musikalisches Opfer, BWV1079 – Canon 4 (arr. Boeke); Canon 5. **Bedyngham** Salva Jesu. **Boeke** Eclipse. **Brumel** Tandernack. **Cornysh** Fa la sol. Catholicon. **Fayrfax** That was my woe. **Giles** Salvator mundi. **Isaac** Fortuna disperata. La morra. Si dormiero. **Janequin** L'alouette. **Machaut** Hoquetus David. Ma fin est mon commencement. Sans cuer m'en vois. **Newark** The farther I go, the more behind. **T. Preston** Upon La Mi Re. O lux beata trinitas. **Solage** Fumeux fume par fumee. **Trebor** En seumeillant. **Tye** Sit fast. **Walter** Canon.

While not wishing in any way to mislead readers, we should start by saying, unequivocally, that 'the less said about this release, the better'. Both the 'passion' and the 'reason' are in the listening, which is unalloyed pleasure from start to finish, opening with Machaut (the players edge on to our consciousness from the far distance) and closing among the fading cadences of Bach's *Canon per augmentationem*. What emerges in between is a fastidious sequence of delights, some slow, others dance-like and with telling contrasts throughout, both in tone and harmony. Early music melds with distant bird-song for a sweet and edifying diversion, ranging across two discs and surveying a generous host of ancient miniatures, from a busy Canon by Johann Walter to Janequin's lively *L'alouette*; from Solage and the ubiquitous 'anon' to Robert Fayrfax and the fourteenth-century composer, Trebor. There are 28 tracks in all, with 16 named composers represented.

Sour Cream finds flautists Frans Brüggen, Kees Boeke and Walter van Hauwe, with lutenist Toyohiko Satoh, mixing and matching where 'reason and passion' blend, a concept that Boeke explains with the help of pertinent printed quotations from Roman and Greek philosophers and various music theorists of the period. But the theory is optional: what matters most is the music itself, whether sombre and austere as in Solage's *Fumeux fume par fumee* (with added viola da gamba) or hypnotically formulaic as in Thomas Preston's achingly beautiful (and decidedly pre-minimalist) *Upon La Mi Re*. Fayrfax's *That was my woe* and Newark's *The farther I go* summon sweet singing by Isabel Alvarez and the final sequence opens to Boeke's own Bachian *Eclipse*, conceived – like everything else on the disc – in terms of order, symmetry and spirit. Both recordings and presentation are models of their kind.

Manufacturers and Distributors

Entries are listed as follows: **Manufacturer** or **Label** – UK Distributor

Accent One for You
Albany Priory
Alia Vox Select
Altarus Kingdom
Amon Ra (Saydisc) Harmonia Mundi
Amphion Recordings Priory
Ampleforth Complete Record Co.
Analekta Koch International
APR Harmonia Mundi
Arabesque Complete Record Co.
Arcana Discovery Records
Archiv Produktion Universal
Argo Universal
Arion Discovery Records
Arte Nova Classics BMG UK
Arts Music Complete Record Co.
ASV Select
Athene Priory
Atma Harmonia Mundi
Auvidis Harmonia Mundi
Avid Masters Avid Records/BMG UK
BBC Music Legends New Note
Beecham Trust Sir Thomas Beecham Trust
Belart Universal
Berlin Classics Complete Record Co.
Beulah Priory
Biddulph Complete Record Co.
BIS Select
Black Box Complete Record Co.
Bridge Koch International
British Music Society Priory/British Music Society
Cala Complete Record Co.
Calig Priory
Calliope Harmonia Mundi
Capriccio Target
Caprice Complete Record Co.
Carlton Classics Hallmark
CBS TEN
CdM Russian Season (Le Chant du Monde) Harmonia Mundi
Celestial Harmonies Discord Distribution
Chandos Chandos
Channel Classics Koch International
Chesky Direct Distribution
Claremont Complete Record Co.
Clarinet Classics Select
Classic fM BMG UK
Classics for Pleasure EMI
Claves Discovery Records
Collegium Select
Collins Classics Complete Record Co.
Conifer Classics BMG UK
CPO Select
CRD Complete Record Co.
Cyprès Discovery Records
Dabringhaus und Grimm (MDG) Chandos
Danacord Discovery Records
Dante One for You
Da Capo (Marco Polo) Select

Decca Universal
dell'Arte Symposium Records
Delos Nimbus
Denon Complete Record Co.
Deutsche Harmonia Mundi BMG UK
DG Universal
Dorian Nimbus
Dutton Laboratories Complete Record Co.
Dynamic Priory
ECM New Series New Note
Edition Abseits DI Music
Elan Discovery Records
Elektra Nonesuch TEN
EMI Eminence EMI
EMI EMI
L'Empreinte Digitale Harmonia Mundi
Erato TEN
Etcetera Koch International
Eufoda One for You
Everest Complete Record Co.
Finlandia TEN
Forlane Harmonia Mundi
Gimell Universal
Globe Koch International
Glossa Harmonia Mundi
Guild Priory
Hänssler Classic Select
Harmonia Mundi Harmonia Mundi
Herald Complete Record Co.
HMV Classics HMV UK
Hungaroton Red Hedgehog
Hyperion Select
IMP Classics Hallmark
IMP Masters Hallmark
Jecklin Vanderbeek and Imrie
Koch International Classics Koch International
Koch Schwann Koch International
Kontrapunkt Discovery Records
Linn Records RMG Distribution
L'Oiseau-Lyre Universal
Lyrita Nimbus
Marco Polo Select
Marston Complete Record Co.
Mediaphon Seaford Music
Melodiya BMG UK
Mercury Universal
Meridian Nimbus
Metier Priory
Metronome Complete Record Co.
Music and Arts Harmonia Mundi
MusicMasters Nimbus
Naim Audio Koch International
Naxos Select
New Albion Harmonia Mundi
New World Harmonia Mundi
Nightingale Classics Koch International
Nimbus Nimbus
NMC Complete Record Co.
Nonesuch TEN

Olympia Priory
Ondine Complete Record Co.
Opera Rara Select
Opus 111 Select
Orfeo Chandos
Ottavo One for You
Panton Koch International
Pavane Kingdom
Pearl (Pavilion) Harmonia Mundi
Philips Universal
Pianissimo Pianissimo
Pierre Verany Discovery Records
Point Music Universal
Praga Harmonia Mundi
Preiser Harmonia Mundi
Priory Priory
RCA BMG UK
The Record Collector The Record Collector
Reference Recordings Vivante London
REM TradeLink Music Distribution
Revelation Records TEN
Ricercar Discovery Records
Romophone Harmonia Mundi
Royal Opera House Records BMG UK
Russian Disc Koch International
Signum Records Priory

Silva Screen Koch International
Simax Chandos
Somm Recordings Priory
Sony Classical TEN
SoundCircus SoundCircus
Sterling Priory
Stradivarius Priory
Supraphon Koch International
Symphonia Discovery Records
Tahra Records Priory
Telarc BMG Conifer
Teldec Warner Classics
TER Classics Koch International
Testament Complete Record Co.
Thorofon Kingdom Distribution
Tring International Priory
Unicorn-Kanchana Harmonia Mundi
Vanguard Classics Complete Record Co.
Virgin Classics EMI
Wergo Harmonia Mundi
Winter & Winter Harmonia Mundi

For additional information on Manufacturers and Distributors, refer to the Label Distribution Directory published in *Gramophone*

Record Company Names and Addresses

Unless otherwise indicated all the Companies listed below are based in the UK; addresses for Record Companies from outside the UK are given, where available (telephone and fax numbers should be prefixed with the appropriate international dialing code)

Accent Records Eikstraat 31, 1673 Beert, *BELGIUM*
Telephone 32 2 356 1878 Fax 32 2 360 2718

Albany Records PO Box 12, Carnforth, Lancashire LA5 9PD
Telephone 01524 735873 Fax 01524 736448

Alia Vox Travessera de Gràcia 18, 2N, 08021 Barcelona, *SPAIN*
Telephone 34 93 580 6194 Fax 34 93 5800 5606

Altarus Records *UK* Easton Dene, Bailbrook Lane, Bath BA1 7AA
Telephone 01225 852323 Fax 01225 852523
USA 31 Conant Road, Ridgefield, CT 06877
Telephone 1 203 438 8342

Amphion Recordings Norton Lodge, 109 Beverley Road, Norton-on-Derwent, Malton, North Yorkshire YO17 9PH
Telephone 01653 698372

Analekta 364 Rue Guy, Montreal, Quebec H3J 1S6, *CANADA*
Telephone 1 514 939 0559 Fax 1 514 939 0232

Appian Publications and Recordings (APR) PO Box 1, Wark, Hexham, Northumberland NE48 3EW
Telephone 01434 220627 Fax 01434 220628

Arabesque Recordings 32 West 39th Street, 11th Floor, New York, NY 10018, *USA*
Telephone 1 212 730 5000 Fax 1 212 730 8316

Arcana 7 Rue de Valmy, 44000 Nantes, *FRANCE*
Telephone 33 2 5188 2337 Fax 33 2 5188 2339

Archiv Produktion 22 St Peter's Square, London W6 9NW
Telephone 0181-910 5000 Fax 0181-910 3132

Argo 22 St Peter's Square, London W6 9NW
Telephone 0181-910 5000 Fax 0181-910 3132

Disques Arion 36, Avenue Hoche, 75008 Paris, *FRANCE*
Telephone 33 1 4563 7670 Fax 33 1 4563 7954

Ars Musici Freiburger Musik Forum GmbH, Schwarzwaldstraße 298a, Schloßpark Ebnet, 79117 Freiburg, *GERMANY*
Telephone 49 761 62205 Fax 49 761 62229

Arte Nova Bedford House, 69-79 Fulham High Street, London SW6 3JW
Telephone 0171-384 7500 Fax 0171-384 7922

Arts Music 2 Jersey Road, Poole, Dorset BH12 4LQ
Telephone 49 8122 972740 Fax 49 8122 972721

ASV 1 Lochaline Street, London W6 9SJ
Telephone 0181-741 2807 Fax 0181-741 8477

Athene (D&J Recording) 7 Felden Street, London SW6 5AE
Telephone 0171-736 9485 Fax 0171-371 7087

Disques Atma 835A Rue Querbes, Bureau 310B, Outremont, Québec H2V 3X1, *CANADA*
Telephone 1 514 270 9444 Fax 1 514 270 1427

Auvidis/Naïve 9 Rue Victor Massé, 75009 Paris, *FRANCE*
Telephone 33 1 5602 2000 Fax 33 1 5602 2020

Avid Records Unit 2, Boeing Way, Brent Road, Southall, Middlesex UB2 5LD
Telephone 0181-893 5767 Fax 0181-893 5955

Sir Thomas Beecham Trust The West Wing, Denton House, Denton, Harleston, Norfolk IP20 0AA. Telephone 01986 788780

Belart 22 St Peter's Square, London W6 9NW
Telephone 0181-910 5000 Fax 0181-910 3132

Berlin Classics Edel Records, Wichmannstraße 4, 22607 Hamburg, *GERMANY*
Telephone 49 40 890 85-611 Fax 49 40 890 85-605

Biddulph Recordings 34 St George Street, London W1R 0ND
Telephone 0171-408 2458 Fax 0171-495 6501

Grammofon AB BIS Bragevägen 2, 18264 Djursholm, *SWEDEN*
Telephone 46 8 755 4100 Fax 46 8 755 7676

Black Box 93-95 Wigmore Street, London W1H 9AA
Telephone 0171-935 1046 Fax 0171-935 5833

BMG Conifer UK Bedford House, 69-79 Fulham High Street, London SW6 3JW
Telephone 0171-384 7500 Fax 0171-384 7922

BMG UK 24 Crystal Drive, Warley, West Midlands B66 1Q
Telephone 0121-543 4000 Fax 0121-543 4399

Bridge Records GPO Box 1864, New York, NY 10116, *USA*
Telephone 1 914 654 9270 Fax 1 914 636 1383

British Music Society 7 Tudor Gardens, Upminster, Essex RM14 3DE
Telephone 01708 224795

Cala Records 17 Shakespeare Gardens, London N2 9LJ
Telephone 0181-883 7306 Fax 0181-365 3388

Calig Musik und Video Steinerne Furt 68-72, Augsburg 86167, *GERMANY*
Telephone 49 821 7004 787 Fax 49 821 7004 785

Calliope 14 Rue de la Justice, BP 40 433, 60204 Compiègne Cedex, *FRANCE*
Telephone 33 3 4423 2765 Fax 33 3 4486 8278

Capriccio Delta Music, Sailerbachstraße 16, 83115 Neubeuern, *GERMANY*
Telephone 49 8035 1047 Fax 49 8035 1049

Caprice Records Nybrokajen 11, 111 48 Stockholm, *SWEDEN*
Telephone 46 8 407 1600 Fax 46 8 407 1648

CBS Records *see* SONY MUSIC ENTERTAINMENT

Celestial Harmonies PO Box 30122, Tucson, Arizona 85751, *USA*
Telephone 1 520 326 4400 Fax 1 520 326 3333

Chandos Records Chandos House, Commerce Way, Colchester, Essex CO2 8HQ **Telephone** 01206 225200 **Fax** 01206 225201

Channel Classics Records Waaldijk 76, 4171 CG Herwijnen, *THE NETHERLANDS* **Telephone** 31 418 581800 **Fax** 31 418 581782

Le Chant du Monde 31 Rue Vandrezanne, 75013 Paris, *FRANCE* **Telephone** 33 1 5380 0222 **Fax** 33 1 5380 0225

Chesky Records 355 West 52nd Street, 6th Floor, New York, NY 10019-6239, *USA* **Telephone** 1 212 586 7799 **Fax** 1 212 262 0814

Claremont GSE Claremont Records, PO Box 250, Newlands 7725, *SOUTH AFRICA* **Telephone** 27 21 686 6915 **Fax** 27 21 686 6043

Clarinet Classics 77 St Albans Avenue, London E6 4HH **Telephone/Fax** 0181-472 2057

Classic fM Bedford House, 69-79 Fulham High Street, London SW6 3JW **Telephone** 0171-384 7500 **Fax** 0171-384 7922

Classics for Pleasure EMI House, Brook Green, London W6 7EF **Telephone** 0171-605 5000 **Fax** 0171-605 5050

Claves Records Trüelweg 14, 3600 Thun, *SWITZERLAND* **Telephone** 41 33 223 1637 **Fax** 41 33 222 8003

Collegium Records PO Box 172, Whittlesford, Cambridge CB2 4QZ **Telephone** 01223 832474 **Fax** 01223 836723

Collins Classics Windsong International, Electron House, Cray Avenue, St Mary Cray, Orpington, Kent BR56 3RJ **Telephone** 01689 899062 **Fax** 01689 899030

The Complete Record Co. 22 Prescott Place, London SW4 6BT **Telephone** 0171-498 9666 **Fax** 0171-498 1828

Conifer Classics Bedford House, 69-79 Fulham High Street, London SW6 3JW **Telephone** 0171-384 7500 **Fax** 0171-384 7922

Continuum 20 Lochiel Road, Remuera, Auckland 5, *NEW ZEALAND* **Telephone/Fax** 64 9 520 7499

CPO Lübeckerstraße 9, 49124 Georgsmarienhütte, *GERMANY* **Telephone** 49 5401 851-0 **Fax** 49 5401 851-299

CRD PO Box 26, Stanmore, Middlesex HA7 4XB **Telephone** 0181-958 7695 **Fax** 0181-958 1415

Cyprès 8 Rue Gachard, 1050 Bruxelles, *BELGIUM* **Telephone** 32 2 647 4714 **Fax** 32 2 648 0449

Dabringhaus und Grimm (MDG) Bachstraße 35, 32756 Detmold, *GERMANY* **Telephone** 49 5231 93890 **Fax** 49 5231 26186

Da Capo (Marco Polo) Christianshavns Torv 2, 3, 1410 Copenhagen K, *DENMARK* **Telephone** 45 32 960 602 **Fax** 45 35 962 602

Danacord Records Nørregade 22, 1165 Copenhagen, *DENMARK* **Telephone** 45 33 151 716 **Fax** 45 33 12 1514

Dante 7 Rue Gaudray, 92170 Vanves, *FRANCE* **Telephone** 33 1 4638 3022 **Fax** 33 1 4638 3703

Decca Classics 22 St Peter's Square, London W6 9NW **Telephone** 0181-910 5000 **Fax** 0181-810 3132

dell'Arte Records PO Box 26, Hampton, Middlesex TW12 2NL **Telephone** 0181-979 2479

Delos International Hollywood and Vine Plaza, 1645 North Vine Street, Suite 340, Hollywood, California CA 90028, *USA* **Telephone** 1 213 962 2626 **Fax** 1 213 962 2636

Denon/Nippon Columbia 14-14, Akasaka 4-Chome, Minatu-Ku, Tokyo 107-11, *JAPAN* **Telephone** 81 3 3584 8271 **Fax** 81 3 3584 8135

Deutsche Grammophon 22 St Peter's Square, London W6 9NW **Telephone** 0181-910 5000 **Fax** 0181-810 3132

Deutsche Harmonia Mundi BMG Classics Music, Kastenbauerstraße 2, 81677 München, *GERMANY* **Telephone** 49 89 4136-0 **Fax** 49 89 4136-160

DI Music 1st & 2nd Floors, 7 High Street, Cheadle, Cheshire SK8 1AX **Telephone** 0161-491 6655 **Fax** 0161-491 6688

Direct Distribution 50 Stroud Green Road, London N4 3EF **Telephone** 0171-281 3465 **Fax** 0171-281 5671

Discord Distribution PO Box 50, Tunbridge Wells, Kent TN3 9ZP **Telephone** 01892 863888 **Fax** 01892 863808

Discovery Records The Old Church Mission Room, King's Corner, Pewsey, Wiltshire SN9 5BS **Telephone** 01672 563931 **Fax** 01672 563934

Dorian Recordings 8 Brunswick Road, Troy, NY 12180, *USA* **Telephone** 1 518 274 5475 **Fax** 1 518 274 4276

Dutton Laboratories PO Box 576, Harrow, Middlesex HA3 6YW **Telephone** 0181-421 1117 **Fax** 0181-421 2998

Dynamic Via Mura delle Chiappe 39, 16136 Genoa, *ITALY* **Telephone** 39 10 27 22884 **Fax** 39 10 2139 37

ECM Postfach 600331, 81203 München, *GERMANY* **Telephone** 49 89 851048 **Fax** 49 89 854 5652

Editions Abseits Kannegießer, Maillard & Wuthenow GbR, Erkelenzdamm 63, 10999 Berlin, *GERMANY* **Telephone/Fax** 49 30 6140 3640

Elan PO Box 101, Riverdale, Maryland 20738, *USA* **Telephone** 1 301 864 0499 **Fax** 1 301 209 8573

EMI Records Customer Services Dept, 64 Baker Street, London W1M 1DJ **Telephone** 0171-467 2000 **Fax** 0171-467 2243

EMI Sales & Distribution Centre, Hermes Close, Tachbrook Park, Leamington Spa, Warwickshire CV34 6RP **Telephone** 01926 888888 **Fax** 0181-479 5922

L'Empreinte Digitale Domaine de la Garde, 13510 Eguilles, *FRANCE* **Telephone** 33 4 4233 3322 **Fax** 33 4 4233 3324

Erato *FRANCE* 50 Rue des Tournelles, 75003 Paris. **Telephone** 33 1 4027 7000 **Fax** 33 1 4804 9543; *UK* The Warner Building, 28 Kensington Church Street, London W8 4EP **Telephone** 0171-938 0167 **Fax** 0171-938 3986

Record Company Names and Addresses

Etcetera Maygreen House, Maynards Green. Heathfield, East Sussex TN21 0DD
Telephone 01435 811511 **Fax** 01435 811518

Finlandia The Warner Building, 28 Kensington Church Street, London W8 4EP
Telephone 0171-938 0167 **Fax** 0171-938 3986

Forlane 15 Rue de l'Ancienne Mairie, 92100 Boulogne Billancourt, *FRANCE*
Telephone 33 1 4825 0217 **Fax** 33 1 4603 2547

Gimell Records 22 St Peter's Square, London W6 9NW
Telephone 0181 910 5000 **Fax** 0181 910 3132

Globe Tapuit 4, 1902 KP Castricum, *THE NETHERLANDS*
Telephone 31 2518 55584 **Fax** 31 2516 59511

Glossa Timoteo Paradós 31, 28200 San Lorenzo de El Escorial, *SPAIN*
Telephone 34 1 896 1480 **Fax** 34 1 896 1961

Guild Music *UK* PO Box 1425, Piermont House, 33-35 Pier Road, St Helier, Jersey JE4 8QZ. *SWITZERLAND* Wiesholzerstraße 42b, 8262 Ramsen
Telephone 41 52 743 1600 **Fax** 41 52 743 1553

Hallmark Music and Entertainment 25-26 Ivor Place, London NW1 6HR
Telephone 0171-616 8100 **Fax** 0171-616 8158

Hänssler Classic Max-Eyth-Straße 41, 71088 Holzgerlingen, *GERMANY*
Telephone 49 7031 7414-0 **Fax** 49 7031 7414-209

Harmonia Mundi: *UK* 19-21 Nile Street, London N1 7LL. **Telephone** 0171-253 0865 **Fax** 0171-253 3237; *FRANCE* Mas de Vert, 13200 Arles **Telephone** 33 4 9049 9049 **Fax** 33 4 9049 9614; *USA* 2037 Granville Avenue, Los Angeles, CA 90025-6103.
Telephone 1 310 478 1311 **Fax** 1 310 996 1389

Herald Audiovisual Publications The Studio, 29 Alfred Road, Farnham, Surrey GU9 8ND
Telephone 01252 725349 **Fax** 01252 735567

HMV UK 4th Floor, Film House, 142 Wardour Street, London W1V 4LN
Telephone 0171-432 2050 **Fax** 0171-534 8103

Hungaroton Fotex Plaza, 1126 Budapest XII, *HUNGARY*
Telephone 36 1 201 5390 **Fax** 36 1 202 3794

Hyperion Records PO Box 25, Eltham, London SE9 1AX
Telephone 0181-294 1166 **Fax** 0181-294 1161

Jecklin and Co Rämistraße 42, 8024 Zürich, *SWITZERLAND*
Telephone 41 1 261 7733 **Fax** 41 1 251 4102

Kingdom Distribution Clarendon House, Shenley Road, Borehamwood, Hertfordshire WD6 1AG
Telephone 0181-207 7006 **Fax** 0181-207 5460

Koch International: *UK* Charlotte House, 87 Little Ealing Lane, London W5 4EH **Telephone** 0181-832 1800 **Fax** 0181-832 1808; *USA* 2 Tri-Harbor Court, Port Washington, New York, 11050-4617
Telephone 1 516 484 1000 **Fax** 516 484 4746

Koch Schwann Lochhamerstraße 9, 82152 München-Martinsried, *GERMANY*
Telephone 49 89 857 95-0 **Fax** 49 89 857 95100

Kontrapunkt PO Box 35, Slottsalleen 16, 2930 Klampenborg, *DENMARK*
Telephone 45 3964 4244 **Fax** 45 31 3964 5044

Linn Records 257 Drakemire Drive, Castlemilk, Glasgow G45 9SZ
Telephone 0141-303 5189 **Fax** 0141-631 1485

L'Oiseau-Lyre 22 St Peter's Square, London W6 9NW
Telephone 0181-910 5000 **Fax** 0181-910 3132

Lyrita 99 Green Lane, Burnham, Slough, Bucks SL1 8EG **Telephone** 01628 604208

Marston 412 N. Chester Road, Swarthmore, PA 19081, *USA*
Telephone 1 610 690 1703 **Fax** 1 610 328 6355

Mercury 22 St Peter's Square, London W6 9NW
Telephone 0181-910 5000 **Fax** 0181-910 3132

Meridian Records PO Box 317, Eltham, London SE9 4SF
Telephone 0181-857 3213 **Fax** 0181-857 0731

Metier Sound and Vision PO Box 270, Preston, Lancashire PR2 3LZ
Telephone 01772 866178

Metronome Productions Carrick Business Centre, Beacon House, Commercial Road, Penryn TR10 8AR
Telephone 01326 377738 **Fax** 01326 378643

Music and Arts Programs of America PO Box 771, Berkeley, California CA 94701, *USA*
Telephone 1 510 525 4583 **Fax** 1 510 524 2111

MusicMasters 1710 Highway 35, Ocean, NJ 07712-9885, *USA*
Telephone 1 908 531 3375 **Fax** 1 908 531 1505

Naim Audio Southampton Road, Salisbury, Wiltshire SP1 2LN
Telephone 01722 33226 **Fax** 01722 412034

New Albion Records 584 Castro Street, Suite 515, San Francisco, CA 94114, *USA*
Telephone 1 415 621 5757 **Fax** 1 415621 4711

New Note Electron House, Cray Avenue, St Mary Cray, Orpington, Kent BR5 3RJ
Telephone 016898 77884 **Fax** 016898 77891

New World Records 701 Seventh Avenue, 7th Floor, New York, NY 10036, *USA*
Telephone 1 212 302 0460 **Fax** 1 212 944 1922

Nightingale Classics Nussdorferstraße 38, 1090 Wien, *AUSTRIA*
Telephone 43 1 310 4017 **Fax** 43 1 310 4967

Nimbus Records Wyastone Leys, Monmouth, Gwent NP5 3SR
Telephone 01600 890682 **Fax** 01600 890779

NMC Francis House, Francis Street, London SW1P 1DE **Telephone/Fax** 0171-828 3432

Nonesuch: *USA* 75 Rockefeller Plaza, New York NY 10019 **Telephone** 1 212 484 7200; *UK* The Warner Building, 28 Kensington Church Street, London W8 4EP
Telephone 0171-938 0167 **Fax** 0171-938 3986

Olympia Compact Discs The Courtyard, Evelyn Road, London W4 5JL
Telephone 0181-995 8080 **Fax** 0181-995 8012

Ondine Fredrikinkatu 77 A 2, 00100 Helsinki, *FINLAND*
Telephone 358 9 4342 210 **Fax** 358 9 493 956

One for You 39 Lemur Drive, Cambridge CB1 4XZ **Telephone** 01223 504620 **Fax** 01223 413360

Opera Rara 134-146 Curtain Road, London EC2A 3AR
Telephone 0171-613 2858 Fax 0171-613 2261

Opus 111 37 Rue Blomet, 75015 Paris, *FRANCE*
Telephone 33 1 4567 3344 Fax 33 1 4567 3388

Orfeo International Music Augustenstraße 79, 80333 München, *GERMANY*
Telephone 49 89 5421 36-0 Fax 49 89 5421 36-21

Ottavo Recordings Westeinde 10, 2512HD Den Haag, *THE NETHERLANDS*
Telephone 31 70 346 9494 Fax 31 70 346 9684

Panton Palackého 1, 11299 Praha 1, *CZECH REPUBLIC*
Telephone 420 2 962 45441 Fax 420 2 24946920

Pavane Records 17 Rue Ravenstein, 1000 Bruxelles, *BELGIUM*
Telephone 32 2 513 0965 Fax 32 2 514 2194

Pavilion Records Sparrows Green, Wadhurst, East Sussex TN5 6SJ
Telephone 01892 783591 Fax 01892 784156

Philips Classics 22 St Peter's Square, London W6 9NW
Telephone 0181-910 5000 Fax 0181-910 3132

Pianissimo Ridgeway Road, Pyrford, Woking, Surrey GU22 8PR Telephone 01932 345371

Pinnacle Electron House, Cray Avenue, St Mary Cray, Orpington, Kent BR5 3RJ
Telephone 016898 70622 Fax 01698 78269

Point Music 22 St Peter's Square, London W6 9NW
Telephone 0181-910 5000 Fax 0181-910 3132

Praga 31 Rue Vandrezanne, 75013 Paris, *FRANCE*
Telephone 33 1 5380 0222 Fax 33 1 5380 0225

Preiser Fischerstiege 9/4, 1010 Wien, *AUSTRIA*
Telephone 43 1 553 6228-0 Fax 43 1 553 4405

Priory Records Unit 9b, Upper Wingbury Courtyard, Wingrave, Nr. Aylesbury, Bucks HP22 4L.
Telephone 01296 682255 Fax 01296 682275

RCA Bedford House, 69-79 Fulham High Street, London SW6 3JW
Telephone 0171-384 7500 Fax 0171-384 7922

The Record Collector 111 Longshots Close, Broomsfield, Chelmsford, Essex CM1 7DU
Telephone 01245 441661 Fax 01245 443642

Red Hedgehog Music PO Box 25, Shepshed, Loughborough, Leicestershire LE12 9ZB
Telephone 01509 829301 Fax 01509 829302

Reference Recordings Box 77225X, San Francisco, California, CA 94107, *USA*
Telephone 1 650 355 1892 Fax 1 650 355 1949

Ricercar Disques Burnaumont 73, 6890 Anloy-Libin, *BELGIUM*
Telephone 32 61 656144 Fax 32 61 656246

RMG Distribution 43-51 Wembley Hill Road, Wembley, Middlesex HA9 8AU
Telephone 0181-903 0360 Fax 0181-782 4706

Romophone PO Box 49, Teignmouth, Devon TQ14 8YS
Telephone/Fax 01626 777195

Royal Opera House Records *see* BMG Conifer

Russian Disc 577 Brown Brook Road, Southbury, CT 06488, *USA*
Telephone 1 203 264 4073 Fax 1 203 264 4185

Saydisc Chipping Manor, The Chipping, Wotton-under-Edge, Gloucestershire GL12 7AD
Telephone 01453 845036 Fax 01453 521056

Seaford Music 24 Pevensey Road, Eastbourne, East Sussex BN21 3HP
Telephone 01323 732553 Fax 01323 417455

Select Music and Video Distributors 34a Holmethorpe Avenue, Holmethorpe Estate, Redhill, Surrey RH1 2NN
Telephone 01737 760020 Fax 01737 766316

Signum Records 10 Kensington Hall Garden, Beaumont Avenue, London W14 9LS
Telephone/Fax 0171-386 1877

Silva Screen 3 Prowse Place, London NW1 9PH
Telephone 0171-428 5500 Fax 0171-482 2385

Simax Skippergt. 28, 0154 Oslo, *NORWAY*
Telephone 47 2233 0309 Fax 47 2241 2041

Somm Recordings 13 Riversdale Road, Thames Ditton, Surrey KT7 0QL
Telephone 0181-398 1586 Fax 0181-339 0981

Sony Music Entertainment 10 Great Marlborough Street, London W1V 2LP
Telephone 0171-911 8200 Fax 0171-911 8600

SoundCircus PO Box 354, Reading RG1 5TX.
Telephone 0118-931 2580 Fax 0118-931 2582

Sterling Grammofonskivor Jungfrugatan. 26, 114 44 Stockholm, *SWEDEN*
Telephone 46 8 667 1177 Fax 46 8 661 7318

Stradivarius Via G Fantoli 7, 20138 Milano, *ITALY*
Telephone 39 2 55400 332 Fax 39 2 55400 385

Supraphon Palackého 1, 11299 Praha 1, *CZECH REPUBLIC*
Telephone 420 2 962 45441 Fax 420 2 24946920

Symposium Records 36 Paul's Lane, Overstrand, Cromer, North Norfolk NR27 0PF Telephone/Fax 01263 579715

Tahra 1 Allée Georges Bizet, 95870 Bezons, *FRANCE*
Telephone 33 1 3961 2690 Fax 33 1 3961 1908

Target Records 222 Cray Avenue, Orpington, Kent BR5 3PZ
Telephone 01689 888888 Fax 01689 888800

Telarc International 23307 Commerce Park Road, Cleveland, Ohio OH 44122, *USA*
Telephone 1 216 464 2313 Fax 1 216 464 4108

Teldec Classics The Warner Building, 28 Kensington Church Street, London W8 4EP
Telephone 0171-938 0167 Fax 0171-938 3986

TEN – The Entertainment Network Rabans Lane, Aylesbury, Buckinghamshire HP19 3RT
Telephone 01296 426151 Fax 01296 481009

TER Classics 107 Kentish Town Road, London NW1 8PD
Telephone 0171-485 9593 Fax 0171-485 2282

Testament 14 Tootswood Road, Bromley, Kent BR2 0PD
Telephone 0181-464 5947 Fax 0181-464 5352

Thorofon Records Eichhornweg 11, 30900 edemark/Hannover, *GERMANY*
Telephone 49 5130 79360 Fax 49 5130 79829

Record Company Names and Addresses

TradeLink Music Distribution St Thomas Place, Ely, Cambridgeshire CB7 4GG
Telephone 01353 646500 Fax 01353 646501

Unicorn-Kanchana Records PO Box 339, London W8 7TJ
Telephone 0171-727 3881 Fax 0171-243 1701

Universal Classics and Jazz
22 St Peter's Square, London W6 9NW
Telephone 0181-910 5000 Fax 0181-910 3132

Universal Manufacturing and Logistics
Chippenham Drive, Kingston, Milton Keynes MK10 0AN
Telephone 0181-910 1500 Fax 01908 452600

Vanderbeek and Imrie 15 Marvig, Lochs, Isle of Lewis PA86 9QP
Telephone/Fax 01851 880216

Vanguard Classics PO Box 227, 1200 AE Hilversum, *THE NETHERLANDS*
Telephone 31 35 689 8899 Fax 31 35 689 8897

Disques Pierre Verany 36, Avenue Hoche, 75008 Paris, *FRANCE*
Telephone 33 1 4563 7670 Fax 33 1 4563 7954

Vivante London Unit 4, 60 High Street, Hampton Wick, Surrey KT1 4DB
Telephone 0181-977 6600 Fax 0181-977 4445

Virgin Classics 64 Baker Street, London W1M 1DJ
Telephone 0171-467 2000 Fax 0171-467 2243

Warner Classics (UK) The Warner Building, 28 Kensington Church Street, London W8 4EP
Telephone 0171-938 0167 Fax 0171-938 3986

Wergo Postfach 3640, 55026 Mainz, *GERMANY*
Telephone 49 6131 246896 Fax 49 6131 246216

Winter and Winter Osterwaldstraße 10, Haus 19, 80805 München, *GERMANY*
Telephone 49 89 3610 1050 Fax 49 89 3610 1055

Index to Reviews

Index to Reviews

Index to Reviews

Index to Reviews

Index to Reviews

Index to Reviews

Index to Reviews

Index to Reviews

Index to Reviews

Handl, Jacob

Hanson, Howard

Hardelot, Guy d'

Hardin, Louis

Harris, Roy

Harris, Sir William

Index to Reviews

Index to Reviews

Index to Reviews

Index to Reviews

Index to Reviews

Index to Reviews

Index to Reviews

Index to Reviews

Index to Reviews

Index to Reviews

Index to Reviews

Index to Reviews

Index to Reviews

Index to Reviews

Index to Reviews

Index to Reviews

Index to Reviews

Index to Reviews